THE

NEWBURY

HOUSE

DICTIONARY

OF

AMERICAN

ENGLISH

AN ESSENTIAL REFERENCE FOR LEARNERS

OF AMERICAN ENGLISH AND CULTURE

Heinle & Heinle Publishers
20 Park Plaza
Boston, MA 02116 USA

International Thomson Publishing
Berkshire House 168–173
High Holborn
London WC1V7AA
England

Thomas Nelson Australia
102 Dodds Street
South Melbourne, 3205
Victoria, Australia

Nelson Canada
1120 Birchmont Road
Scarborough, Ontario
Canada M1K5G4

International Thomson Publishing GmbH
Königwinterer Straße 418
53227 Bonn
Germany

International Thomson Publishing Japan
Hirakawacho-cho Kyowa
Building, 3F
2-2-1 Hirakawacho-cho
Chiyoda-ku, 102 Tokyo
Japan

International Thomson Publishing Asia
Block 211, Henderson Road #08-03
Henderson Industrial Park
Singapore 0315

International Thomson Editores
Campos Eliseos 385, Piso 7
Col. Polanco
11560 Mexico D.F.,
Mexico

The publication of **The Newbury House Dictionary of American English**, was directed by the members of the Newbury House Publishing Team at Heinle & Heinle:

Chief Editor:	Philip M. Rideout
Editorial Director:	Erik Gundersen
Managing Developmental Editor:	Amy Lawler
Market Development Director:	John F. McHugh
Production Services Coordinator:	Kristin Thalheimer

Also participating in the publication were:

Director of Production:	Elizabeth Holthaus
Publisher:	Stanley J. Galek
Associate Editors:	Caroline Boyle, Karen Hazar
Senior Assistant Editor:	Ken Pratt
Manufacturing Coordinator:	Mary Beth Hennebury
Senior Pronunciation Editor:	Sharon Goldstein
Pronunciation Editor:	Rima McKinzey
Pronunciation Proofreader:	Rebecca Dauer
Interior Design:	Remo Cosentino
Compositors:	Datapage Technologies, Inc. Laura Ferry Sullivan
Cover Designer:	Kim Wedlake
Illustrator:	Gary Undercuffler
Map Illustrator:	Charles Martin

With editorial assistance from: Nicole Daniel, Anne Edmondson, Jacqueline Georges, Tim Lemire, Victoria Levin, Donald Pharr, Angela Schoenherr, Peter Wilson, Susan Winer Slavin, Paula Woolley, Katherine Wroth

For Asian bilingual and other special Asian editions, contact:

Amy Lee, President
Creative Transaction Corporation
17 Stepping Stone Lane
Greenwich, CT 06830
USA

Heinle & Heinle Publishers is a division of International Thomson Publishing, Inc.

Manufactured in the United States of America.

ISBN 0-8384-5532-8

10 9 8 7 6 5 4 3 2 1

CONTENTS

ACKNOWLEDGMENTS

The Chief Editor and the Newbury House Team would like to thank the following individuals who offered their years of teaching expertise and thoughtful insight and suggestions to the careful development of the manuscript. Their enthusiastic support of this project shown in attending focus groups, editing portions of the manuscript, and field-testing the material in the classroom, is much appreciated.

CONTENT EDITORS
- Linda Butler
- Mary Jane Curry
  University of Massachusetts, Boston
- Marisa Garman
- Joann Kozyrev
  Ohio University
- Robin Longshaw
  Brown University
- Melanie May
- Steve Murray
- Lois Poulin
  Mount Ida College, Massachusetts
- Laura Rideout
- Caroline Schwarzwalder
  North Shore Community College, Massachusetts
- Jane Selden
  LaGuardia Community College, City University of New York
- Paula Woolley

BUSINESS EDITOR
- Laurie Winfield
  Department of Education, State of Texas

TECHNOLOGY EDITOR
- Deborah Healey
  Oregon State University

USAGE NOTES EDITORS
- Eleanor Jones
  American Language Institute, Lisbon, Portugal
- Linda Lee
- Helen Solorzano
  Northeastern University

CONSULTANTS
- Linda Abe
  Indiana University
- Jean Bernard-Johnston
  Western New England College, Massachusetts
- Bob Betts
  University of California, Irvine Extension
- Stacey Hagen
  Edmonds Community College, Washington
- Deborah Healey
  Oregon State University
- Mark Landa
  University of Minnesota
- Martha Grace Low
  University of Oregon

- Maidy Giber Kiji
  Konan Women's University, Japan
- Bruce Mitchell
  EF International, Massachusetts
- Meg Morris
  Lee Community Center,
  Massachusetts
- Meredith Pike-Baky
  University of California, Berkeley
- Karen Price
  Graduate School of Education,
  Harvard University

- Carole Thurston
  Northern Virginia Community College
- Marjorie Vai
  The New School for Social Research,
  New York
- Sarah Zovich
  LaGuardia Community College,
  City University of New York

CONTRIBUTORS

- Anne Albarelli-Siegfried
  North Harris College, Texas
- Chris Antonellis
  Boston University
- Louise Beyer
  Middlesex Community College,
  New Jersey
- Merilee Brand
  Bickford Adult ESL Centre
  Ontario, Canada
- Suzannah Bray
  Glendale Community College,
  California
- Milada Broukal
  Glendale Community College,
  California
- Dorothy Burak
  University of California, San Diego
- Metta Callahan
  The New School for Social Research,
  New York
- Berry Chi
  Union County College, New Jersey
- Effie Cochran
  Papatzikov Baruch College,
  City University of New York
- Sue Dicker
  Hostos Community College,
  City University of New York
- John DiFiore
  Union County College, New Jersey

- Olga Drapanos
  ELS Language Centers, Boston
- John Dumicich
  New York University
- Ardis Flenniken
  California State University, Northridge
- Kathleen Flynn
  Glendale Community College,
  California
- Helen Kalkstein Fragiadakis
  Contra Costa College, California
- Marjorie Friedman
  ELS Language Centers, St. Petersburg
- Hyacinth Gaudart
  Universiti Malaya, Kuala Lumpur
- Linda Griffith
  Glendale Community College,
  California
- Patty Heiser
  University of Washington
- Kathy Hitchcox
  International English Institute,
  California
- Elliot Judd
  University of Illinois, Chicago
- Grazyna Kenda
  Technical Career Institute, New York
- Victoria Kimbrough
  The New School for Social Research,
  New York

- Suzanne Koons
  West Valley College, California
- Alice Lawson
  Rice University, Texas
- Candace Matthews
  The George Washington University
- Kevin McClure
  ELS Language Centers, San Francisco
- J.V. McKenzie
  California State University, Northridge
- Martha McNamara
  University of Akron, Ohio
- Maureen McNerney
  York University, Ontario, Canada
- Loretta Meaker
  Peel Board of Education, Ontario, Canada
- Jane Merivale
  Centennial College, Ontario, Canada
- Lise Minovitz
  Indiana State University
- Betsy Morgan
  Eastern Michigan University
- Dale Myers
  University of Tennessee
- John Myers
  Coast Language Academy, Oregon
- Jill Neely
  Merritt College, California
- Linda Pelc
  *LaGuardia Community College
  City University of New York*
- Margene Petersen
  ELS Language Centers, Philadelphia
- Eva Ramirez
  Laney College, California
- Alison Rice
  *Hunter College
  City University of New York*
- Eric Rosenbaum
  *Bronx Community College,
  City University of New York*
- Janine Rudnick
  El Paso Community College
- Tim Rushing
  University of Akron, Ohio

- Howard Sage
  New York University
- Brett Sherman
  Pace University, New York
- Lorraine C. Smith
  *Queens College,
  City University of New York*
- M.E. Sokolik
  University of California, Berkeley
- Anne Sokolsky
  Golden Gate University, California
- Robert Stein
  *Bronx Community College
  City University of New York*
- Robby Steinberg
  *Harvard University
  Division of Continuing Education*
- Deborah Stewart
  *La Guardia Community College,
  City University of New York*
- Jerome Su
  Bookman Books, Taipei, Taiwan
- Sandra Taverner
  Sheridan College, Ontario, Canada
- Maria Thomas-Růzíc
  University of Colorado, Boulder
- Andrea Tobias
  *SHOWA Women's Institute,
  Massachusetts*
- Nancy Tulare
  School for TESOL, Washington
- Connie Vernon
  University of Evansville, Indiana
- Linda Vinay
  Fisher College, Massachusetts
- Susan Weil
  *City College,
  City University of New York*
- Jennifer Wharton
  EF International, Boston
- Hoda Zaki
  *Camden Community College,
  New Jersey*
- Ladislav Zgusta
  *University of Illinois,
  Champaign-Urbana*

FOREWORD

What is a learner's dictionary?

The Newbury House Dictionary of American English is the first learner's dictionary developed from an American English vocabulary base. Under the guidance of an experienced lexicographer, ESL and EFL teachers used that vocabulary to write the dictionary, putting themselves into the minds of their students and anticipating students' language needs based on many years of teaching experience. The definitions are composed in an easy-to-understand, limited vocabulary, while the sample sentences are designed to show how the words and expressions are actually used. The work is teacher-generated and student-oriented to ensure both the appropriate level of definitions and the illustrative value of sample sentences.

Why should you use a learner's dictionary?

A learner's dictionary is easier to use than a collegiate or any other monolingual dictionary because it contains:

- straightforward definitions and sample sentences for each entry
- American cultural references, such as *green card* and *Little League*
- up-to-date business and technology terms such as *CEO* and *laptop*
- a wealth of expressions, including idioms and phrasal verbs that Americans really use, such as *easy as pie, sit up and take notice,* and *look up*
- contemporary, up-to-date vocabulary, like *junk mail, on-line, HMO,* and *virtual reality*
- "Challenge synonyms," which expand the vocabulary base of advanced students, such as *juicy → succulent*
- pronunciations presented in a slightly modified version of the International Phonetic Alphabet (IPA) for ease of access
- numerous usage notes explaining shades of meaning, cultural references and important grammatical information
- helpful appendixes containing maps, irregular verbs, lists of states, and other useful information to introduce students to the wide world of reference materials

The first truly American learner's dictionary...
look us up!

The vocabulary base comprises more than 40,000 headwords and related words, ranging from words and phrases essential for an intermediate learner to those that the educated speaker would need in order to read literature or serious periodicals, or to write in a business or academic style. Subthemes of useful business, technological, contemporary, and American cultural terminology are included to enrich the standard vocabulary. The dictionary will serve students throughout their lives as English speakers.

Many minds and hearts contributed to the fulfillment of this work as noted in the acknowledgments with deepest gratitude from both the chief editor and the publisher.

Philip M. Rideout
Chief Editor

H I J K L M

GUIDE TO THE DICTIONARY

G

I. Notes on Spelling

1. The English alphabet

The English alphabet has 26 letters arranged in the following order:

> Capital or uppercase letters:
> A B C D E F G H I J K L M N O P Q R S T U V W X Y Z
> Lowercase letters:
> a b c d e f g h i j k l m n o p q r s t u v w x y z

The word list in the dictionary is arranged in alphabetical order.
Words are divided into syllables by black dots:

> **judge** /ʤʌʒ/ *n.* a public official, in charge of a court of law
> **judge•ship** /'ʤʌʒ ʃɪp/ *n.* the position or job of a judge in the
> public legal system
> **judg•ment** or **judge•ment** /'ʤʌʒmənt/ *n.* **1** a decision (ver-
> dict, ruling) in a court of law

The preferred spelling is given first, then the alternative spelling if one
exists:

> **judg•ment** or **judge•ment**

2. Irregular verbs are shown when the spelling of a verb changes in
different tenses.

Most verbs add **-ed** for the past tense and for the past participle, **-ing** for the present participle and **-s** for the third-person singular. For example:

> **jump, jumped, jumping, jumps**
> The children **jump** rope every day.
> They **jumped** rope for four hours yesterday.
> They have **jumped** rope many times.
> They are **jumping** rope right now.
> My daughter **jumps** rope after school every day.

Whenever a form of the verb does not follow this pattern, the irregular spelling is shown:

> **nab** /næb/ *v.infrml.***nabbed, nabbing, nabs** to seize s.o., esp. a criminal, (*syn.*) to capture: *The police nabbed the thief after he robbed the bank.*

> **nar•rate** /'nær,eɪt, næ'reɪt/ *v.* **rated, -rating, -rates** to tell a story in writing or speech: *He narrated a television show on the history of Mexico. -n.* [C;U] **narration** /næ'reɪʃən/; **narrator** /'nær,eɪtər, næ'reɪ-, 'nærə-/.

We have also included the ending **-es** where necessary to show where it must be added in the third person singular if a verb ends in **sh, ch, s, x,** or **z.** For example:

> wash, washes

3. Irregular plurals of nouns

Usually the plural of a noun is formed by adding an **s** at the end of the word. However, if the noun ends in **sh, ch, s, x, z, -es** must be added. We have provided this plural form: **-es** after the part of speech.

> **blue•fish** /'blu,fɪʃ/ *n.* **-fish** or **-fishes** a large blue-colored fish with sweet, good-tasting meat: *Bluefish are found in the Atlantic and Indian oceans.*

If the noun ends in a **y** preceded by a consonant, the **y** must be changed to an **i** and **es** added. For example:

> **cit•y** /'sɪti/ n. **-ies** 1 an area with many thousands of people living and working close together, (*syn.*) a metropolis: *Many tourists visit the city of London.*

The forms of these and other irregular nouns such as **child, children** or **knife, knives** are also shown.

4. Adjectives

In English, when we want to express the idea of a greater or stronger quality, the comparative and superlative forms are used. These forms are usually made by adding **-er** or **-est** to the end of short adjectives. The spelling of these forms changes if the adjectives are of one syllable, or if they are of two syllables and the second syllable ends in a **y** preceded by a consonant. These spelling changes are shown after the part of speech:

> **hot** /hat/ *adj.* **hotter, hottest** 1 having a high degree of heat, burning: *The water is very, very hot.* 2 warm, sultry, (*syn.*) torrid: *The weather is hot today.*

Other adjectives of two syllables and all adjectives of three or more syllables do not change their spelling in the comparative and superlative. For example:

> honest, more honest, most honest
> beautiful, more beautiful, most beautiful

These forms are not included as part of the entry.

A few adjectives have irregular comparative and superlative forms. These are included as part of the entry.

> **good** /gʊd/ *adj.* **better** /'bɛtər/, **best** /bɛst/ 1 (in general) having a pleasing quality, great, pleasurable: *She had a good time on her vacation.||That singer is very good.||You look good; I like your new hair style.*

II. Notes on Pronunciation

1. Symbols

The symbols used in the dictionary are based on the International Phonetic Alphabet, adapted for American English.

Note that the sounds /ʌ/ and /ə/ are phonetically very similar or identical in American English, but /ə/ occurs only in unstressed syllables. Similarly, /ər/ occurs only in unstressed positions, while the equivalent sound /ɜr/ occurs in stressed position.

2. American English and the choice of pronunciations

The pronunciations shown are those used by speakers of the most common American English dialects. There is no single "best" pronunciation in American English, and often a word has more than one pronunciation. Not all dialects or pronunciations of a word are shown—only the most common ones. For example, many Americans pronounce the **wh** in words like **what** and **when** with the sound /hw/. This dictionary shows only /w/, the more common pronunciation. Speakers of some dialects do not generally make a distinction between the sounds /ɑ/ and /ɔ/ (except before the sound /r/). These speakers use /ɑ/ in many words where this dictionary shows /ɔ/, such as **cost** or **bought**; to save space, only /ɔ/ has been shown. As another example, many Americans add a sound like /ə/ between a vowel and /r/ in the same syllable, as in **here** or **care**, pronouncing these as /hɪər/ and /kɛər/; this is a predictable variation and is not generally shown in the dictionary.

3. Entries with more than one pronunciation

When more than one pronunciation is shown, sometimes only the part of the word that is different is shown. A hyphen is used to replace the part of the word that stays the same, as in **abdomen** /ˈæbdəmən, æbˈdoʊ-/.

4. Entries with no pronunciation shown

a. Compound words

Some entries are compounds, formed from two separate words that are combined to form a new word. The pronunciation of a compound that is written with a space or hyphen between the parts is not generally given if the words that form it are entered in the dictionary. For example, the pronunciation of **junk food** or **air-condition** can be found by looking up the individual words **junk** and **food** or **air** and **condition** elsewhere in the dictionary. Compounds, especially compounds used as nouns,

typically have primary stress on the first element and secondary st.
on the second: **junk food** /'ʒʌŋk,fud/, **hot dog** /'hɑt,dɔg/, **post office**
/'poust,ɔfɪs/, **swimming pool** /'swɪmɪŋ,pul/.

b. Inflected words

Pronunciations are not shown for regular inflected forms that follow the
normal rules for pronunciation. According to these rules:

The verb endings **-ed/-d** are pronounced as:

- /t/ after the voiceless consonants /p, k, f, θ, s, ʃ, ʧ/, as in
  cooked /kʊkt/, laughed /læft/, or pushed /pʊʃt/;

- /d/ after vowels or the voiced consonants /b, g, v, ð, z, ʒ, m, n, ŋ,
  l, r/, as in **stayed** /steɪd/, **robbed** /rɑbd/, **saved** /seɪvd/, or **called**
  /kɔld/;

- /ɪd/ after the sounds /t, d/, as in **started** /'stɑrtɪd/ or **needed**
  /'nidɪd/. The same pronunciation rules apply to noun possessives
  ending in **'s** or **s'**, as in **student's** /'studnts/, **teacher's** or **teachers'**
  /'tiʃərz/, and **class's** or **classes'** /'klæsɪz/.

The ending **-s** and **-es** (for nouns and verbs) are pronounced as:

- /s/ after the voiceless consonants /p, t, k, f, θ/, as in **cups** /kʌps/,
  sleeps /slips/, **laughs** /læfs/, or **month** /mʌnθs/;

- /z/ after a vowel or the voiced consonants /b, d, g, v, ð, m, n, l, r/,
  as in **plays** /pleɪdz/, **dogs** /dæɔgz/, **gloves** /glʌvz/, **gives** /gɪvz/;
  sings /sɪŋz/, or **cars** /kɑrz/;

- /ɪz/ after the consonants /s, z, ʃ, ʒ, ʃ, ʒ/, as in **buses** /'bʌsɪz/;
  wishes /'wɪʃɪz/, **reaches** /'riʧɪz/, or **pages** /'peɪʒɪz/.

For compound words where one part of the compound is an inflected
form, such as **air conditioned**, the pronunciation is not shown.

c. Derived words

Words that appear in bold type at the end of an entry are words that are
derived from the main entry word. If the pronunciation follows the same
pattern as the entry word, with a common suffix added, then no separate
pronunciation is shown. If there is a shift in stress or other change in
pronunciation, then the pronunciation of the derived word is shown
directly after it.

5. Strong forms and weak forms

Some common words in English have both a strong form, used when the word is emphasized or in a stressed position, and a weak form, used when the word is not stressed. For example, the word **can** is stressed, and has its strong form, at the end of a sentence like "Yes, I can" /kæn/. It has its weak form /kən/ in a sentence such as "When can I see you?". Both strong and weak forms are shown for words that have them; the choice of pronunciation depends on the context in which the word occurs.

6. Syllables without a vowel sound

The sounds /n/ and /l/ can form syllables by themselves, as in the word **garden** /ˈgɑrdn/ or **little** /ˈlɪtl/. Syllabic /n/ and /l/ are shown in the dictionary pronunciations especially in words where they follow a /d/ or /t/ sound, where it is most important to use a syllabic consonant. In many other words, a syllabic consonant can be used but is not specifically shown in this dictionary; in these cases it does not matter whether you pronounce the word with a syllabic consonant or with a short vowel before the final consonant. For example, **table** can be pronounced as either /ˈteɪbəl/ or /ˈteɪbl/; only the first pronunciation is shown. Note that these words often drop the /ə/ sound entirely when certain endings are added: **whistle** /ˈwɪsəl/, **whistling** /ˈwɪslɪŋ/, **whistler** /ˈwɪslər/.

7. American /t/

One special feature of American English involves the pronunciation of /t/. When /t/ occurs after a vowel or /r/ and before an unstressed vowel or a syllabic /l/, it usually sounds like a quick /d/ in American English. The word **latter**, then, sounds the same as **ladder**. Some other examples of words that have this sound include **city**, **water**, **party**, and **little**. This sound, called a "flap" or "tap," can also occur between words, as in **forget it**, where the **t** in **forget** is followed by the word **it**, even though **forget** pronounced by itself does not have a flap. This sound is considered predictable and is not represented by a special symbol in this dictionary.

8. Foreign words

The pronunciations for foreign words are provided as American pronunciations of these words. In a few cases, a common pronunciation for a foreign word in English may include a sound that does not normally occur in English. The symbols used for these sounds are the /x/ shown for the velar fricative in one pronunciation of **Chanukah** /ˈxɑnəkə/ and the symbol /~/, used to show a nasalized vowel, as in the word **denouement** /ˌdeɪnuˈmɑ̃/.

See page Appendix 12 for a handy guide to the pronunciation symbols used in this dictionary.

III. Notes on Entries

1. Headword

This is the word or phrase being defined, set in boldface at the beginning of the entry.

2. Meanings are given in simple English that is easy to understand. Words and expressions often have more than one meaning, and each meaning begins with a number (1, 2, 3, and so on) as shown below.

> ► **sen•ior** /'sɪnyər/ *n.* **1** *abbr.* **Sr.:** the father of a son with exactly the
> ► same name: *John Page Borden, Sr. is the father and John Page Borden, Jr. is the son.* **2** s.o. higher than another in rank or longer in length of service: *She is senior to the others in the company because she has worked here the longest.* **3** an older person: *His sister is eight years his senior.* **4** in the USA, s.o. in the last (usu. fourth) year of high school or college: *Mr. Yamamoto's son is a senior in high school about to graduate.*

3. Sample sentences and phrases

Samples are provided to aid the reader in understanding the word's meaning(s) and to show how the word can be used in every day speech or writing. Two sample sentences are sometimes given for a definition when shades of meaning need to be shown. They are separated by the symbol: ||.

> **ter•rif•ic** /tə'rɪfɪk/ *adj.* **1** *fig.* wonderful, superior: *He did a terrif-*
> ► *ic job in remodeling the kitchen.||Congratulations on your new job! That's terrific!* **2** powerful, tremendous: *The storm had terrific winds of 100 MPH (160 km).* **3** very bad, awful:
> ► *We are having terrific difficulty with our telephone system.*

4. Special vocabulary

New words dance onto the stage of American English with great regularity, inspired by all domains of life. For example, the world of technology has produced **cyberspace** and **virtual reality**, the business world has been **downsizing** and **outsourcing**, and contemporary culture has given us **Generation X** and **grunge**. Meanwhile, terms such as **Perestroika** and **Glasnost** have moved permanently offstage into the archives of history.

The Newbury House Dictionary of American English includes a careful selection of those new words still on stage and likely to remain so for readers of periodicals, recent literature, and for participants in American cultural life. These words are generously sprinkled throughout the dictionary, both as specific entries and in the context of the many sample sentences provided.

American and contemporary cultural references, business and technology terms are the three chief areas under which special vocabulary items have been included in this dictionary. Following is a brief overview of the ways in which vocabulary from these special areas has been included.

a. Business terminology

Business terms are presented in various ways. Words used in daily living are given and defined, such as **money, money order, cash, credit card, paycheck**, and **bills**. Then, "second-level" terms are included that apply both to daily living and to basic business, such as **contract, savings account, CD (certificate of deposit), deed**, and so on. On a more specific level, everyday words used in business are included on a controlled basis so as not to be too technical, for example, **account executive, capital gain, profit sharing**, and **TQM**.

> **ac•count ex•e•cu•tive** *n.* a person who takes care of a customer's account, a sales representative: *The account executive from our insurance company called this morning to ask about our policy.*

b. Technological terms

In that the computer is common both in society at large and in many schools and households, useful computer terms like **PC, laptop, download, Internet**, and **World Wide Web** are defined without becoming too technical. The surge in medical machines and techniques also provides a rich field of vocabulary terms like **MRI** and **microsurgery**. Finally, terms in everyday use that touch on the world of technology, like **VCR, CD (compact disc)**, and **cable TV**, abound in the dictionary.

> **In•ter•net** /'intər,nɛt/ *n.* [U] a huge computer network of electronic mail and information, used by millions of people and organizations all over the world: *On my business trip, I used the Internet to receive a note from my boss and send a birthday message to my daughter.*

c. American and contemporary cultural vocabulary

There is an ever-changing nature to the language that we hear in everyday conversation and read in newspapers and magazines. Some words go in and out of style very quickly, while others have staying power. In developing *The Newbury House Dictionary of American English,* we have strived to include those terms and expressions that are likely to become a permanent part of our vocabulary such as **Generation X, glass ceiling, fanny pack**, and **HMO.**

> **fanny pack** *n.* a small bag worn around the waist for carrying money, keys, etc.: *When Pedro rides his bike, he puts his money and some crackers in a fanny pack.*

In addition, we have included numerous American cultural terms that students of English are likely to be curious about, such as **ATM, delicatessen, drive-in, FBI, Fourth of July, Super Bowl**, and **World Series**.

IV. Grammar Notes

1. Parts of speech are given as abbreviations, such as *n.* for noun, *v.* for verb, etc. Some words change their meaning when they are used as more than one part of speech. These definitions start on a new line, starting with the abbreviation of the new part of speech.

> **week•ly** /'wikli/ *adj.* happening once a week or every week: *This is a weekly newspaper.*
> —*adv.* once a week or every week: *She visits her grandmother weekly.*
> —*n.* [C] a magazine or newspaper that appears once a week: *The village newspaper is a weekly; I buy it every Thursday.*

Not all headwords that are used as more than one part of speech are listed separately. A headword can have two parts of speech listed directly after it when the weight of the word does not warrant a separate entry for the less common form. In this way, the student is given an indication that the word has another part of speech, but its meaning can be derived from the definition treated fully. For example:

> **jaunt** /dʒɔnt/ *n.v.* a short trip for pleasure: *I took a <n.> jaunt to the Carribean to relax for a few days.*

2. Derived Words

Words that are part of the same word family as the headword are often placed at the end of the entry. If the word is pronounced differently from the headword, its pronunciation is provided.

mir•a•cle /'mɪrɪkəl/ *n.* an event that cannot be explained by the laws of nature: *All the passengers in a sinking boat drowned except one who was saved by a miracle.* *-adj.* **miraculous** /mɪ'rækyələs/; *-adv.* **miraculously.**

3. Labels

Labels are sometimes placed after the parts of speech to give additional information about a word. For example, the labels *infrml.* and *fig.* mean that the word or expression is used informally and the meaning is figurative, for example:

red cent *n.infrml.fig.* a very small amount of money, s.t. worthless: *That old car is not worth a red cent.*

See the inside back cover to find the abbreviations for all parts of speech as well as other important abbreviations and terms used in the dictionary.

4. Countable and uncountable nouns and noun phrases

In English, most nouns are either countable or uncountable. Some nouns are countable in some contexts and uncountable in others. Uncountable nouns do not have a plural.

If a noun is countable, you can count it with numbers, as in **three cups**, or **two ideas**. If it is uncountable, you cannot count on it with numbers. It has only a singular form—it has no plural. For example, **luggage** and **literature** are uncountable.

I bought some **furniture.** (Uncountable)
I bought two **chairs.** (Countable)

If a noun is *always* countable, like **pencil**, the label indicating it is countable, [C], is not provided in this dictionary. If a noun is always uncountable, like **humankind**, it is marked with the label [U] after the other labels and before the definition.

Some words, such as **people**, can either be countable *or* uncountable, depending on how they are used. These nouns are often labeled [C;U]. However, if one definition of a noun is countable and another is uncountable, each definition is labeled with the appropriate label, as the word **oak**:

> **oak** /oʊk/ *n.* **1** [C] tall hardwood tree that grows small nuts called acorns: *The park has many oaks in it.* **2** [U] the wood of oak trees: *Bookshelves made of oak last for many years.*

5. "Challenge" synonyms are words with meanings similar to the headword but often at a more advanced level. These are included to help interested readers and advanced-level learners improve their vocabulary. Here is an example with the headword, showing the challenge synonym:

> **false** /fɔls/ *adj.* **falser, falsest** **3** not real, made to deceive, (*syns.*) artificial, fake: *She wears false eyelashes.*

6. Expressions are defined after the main meanings; they are formed mainly with nouns, adjectives and verbs. Verb expressions include verbs with prepositions, phrasal verbs, idioms, and other expressions. Here is an example of an expression:

> **jump** /dʒʌmp/ *v.* **1** to push one's feet against the ground to go into the air, (*syns.*) to leap, spring: *The basketball player jumped up to catch the ball.*||*The dog jumped over the wall.*
> **9** *infrml.* **to jump down s.o.'s throat**: to answer s.o. angrily before he or she has finished speaking

7. Phrasal verbs are formed when a verb is combined with a preposition or an adverb. They can cause problems for learners of English because the meanings of phrasal verbs are often very different from the separate meanings of the words that are combined to form them. For example:

> **3** *phrasal v.insep.* **to own up to s.t.**: to confess, admit to s.t.: *The little boy finally owned up to the fact that he ate all the cookies.*

Phrasal verbs can be transitive or intransitive, that is, they can take a direct object or not. When they are transitive, there are two possible locations of the object. The first is between the verb and the adverb or preposition. When the object can be located in this position, the phrasal verb is called "separable." In this dictionary, this type of phrasal verb is labeled *phrasal v.sep.*

The second possible position for the object is after the adverb or preposition. Phrasal verbs that follow this pattern are called "inseparable" because the adverb or preposition must remain right next to the verb to hold its special meaning. In this dictionary, inseparable phrasal verbs are labeled *phrasal v.insep.* If the phrasal verb is inseparable, the definition is followed by one sample sentence showing the object in the correct position:

> **19** *phrasal v.insep.* **to look into s.t.:** to try to find the truth about s.t., (*syn.*) to investigate: *The police looked into the crime and solved it.*

When phrasal verbs can be followed by the object in either position, they are labeled *phrasal v.sep.* and you will see a sample sentence for each position. Usually, the first sample sentence will contain a noun or noun phrase as the object; the second sample sentence usually shows the object in pronoun form:

> **9.** *phrasal v.sep.* **to leave s.o. or s.t. behind** to fail to bring or take, usually by accident: *I can't believe I left my reading glasses!*||*I left them behind.*

Some phrasal verbs that have multiple meanings, often depending on whether the object is a person or a thing. Phrasal verbs may also change their meaning depending on whether the form is separable or inseparable. This dictionary contains complete definitions and sample sentences for all of the meanings that a phrasal verb may have.

8. Cross references

Cross references are placed at the end of entries after the word *See:* and direct the user to look at another entry for additional information:

> **vac•cine** /væk'sin/ *n.* [C;U] a medication taken to protect against many diseases, such as measles, cholera, etc.: *She takes a vaccine against influenza every fall. See:* serum.

9. Usage Notes

A wide range of USAGE NOTES are included at the end of selected entries. Some of them guide the reader as to the proper use of a word, while others contain important cultural information:

glass ceiling *n.fig.* an upper level or point that is difficult for s.o., usu. a woman, to pass because of discrimination: *She hit the glass ceiling in her company after she became a manager, and could not rise any higher.*

USAGE NOTE: While 45 percent of middle managers in the USA are women, only 5 percent are senior managers. One reason it is difficult for women to rise above the *glass ceiling* is because these senior-level jobs have been traditionally held by men. As more and more women enter the workforce, these patterns of discrimination will change more rapidly.

V. Related Publications

The Newbury House Dictionary of American English is one of several key reference tools for learners. Related publications include:

1. *The Newbury House Dictionary of American English*—Hardcover edition. This version of the dictionary is preserved within a durable cover that will withstand years of wear and tear.

2. *The Newbury House Adult Learner's Dictionary.* Containing roughly 15,000 entries and 2000 illustrations, this dictionary is designed chiefly with the needs of adult education students in mind. Simpler definitions and larger print contribute to its ease-of-use.

3. *The Newbury House Dictionary Activity Guide.* Designed to accompany *The Newbury House Dictionary of American English*, this companion worktext encourages students and instructors to work with the dictionary to incorporate communicative vocabulary-building activities into classroom learning. Thematically focused activities on topics like the law and international cuisine set a context within which students practice useful dictionary skills like skimming, scanning, and guessing meaning from context.

Please take a look at some sample activities from *The Newbury House Dictionary Activity Guide* on the next two pages.

Sample from the Activity Guide

12 IT'S THE LAW

DICTIONARY SKILLS: FINDING SYNONYMS • IDENTIFYING WORD FORMS

1. FINDING SYNONYMS

You can use your dictionary to find a synonym for each boldfaced word below. Write the synonym on the blank line.

a. Today there are about 800,000 **attorneys** in the United States. That's roughly one _____ for every 300 people.

b. Between 1985 and 1995, the number of **paralegals** in the US grew from 76,000 to about 140,000. In the future, the number of _____ _____ will probably continue to grow.

c. Today Americans are spending about $90 billion on **litigation** and insurance. Most of the money spent on _____ goes to lawyers.

d. In 1972, the US government temporarily outlawed **capital punishment**. Today 35 of the 50 states have the _____

2. DICTIONARY SEARCH

Your dictionary has all the information you need to complete the sentences in this activity. Each answer should fit in the appropriate space in the crossword puzzle.

ACROSS

2. A juvenile delinquent is a young person who has done something
_____.

4. The plural form of the word "jury" is _____.

7. The judiciary is one branch of the U.S. _____.

9. What part of speech is the word "jurisprudence"?

10. The past tense form of the verb "sue" is _____.

11. A synonym for the word "judgment" is _____.

13. Both lawyers and _____ are called jurists.

DOWN

1. In the US, a man and a woman can get _____ by a justice of the peace.

3. A synonym for the word "lawyer" is _____.

5. Is the word "juror" a countable noun or an uncountable noun? (If it's a countable noun, it has a plural form.)

6. Is the plaintiff in a court case a person or an object?

8. A jury is usually made up of _____ people.

12. How many different meanings does the word "jury" have?

GUIDE TO PRONUNCIATION SYMBOLS

Vowels

Symbol	Key Word	Pronunciation
/ɑ/	hot	/hɑt/
	far	/fɑr/
/æ/	cat	/kæt/
/aɪ/	fine	/faɪn/
/aʊ/	house	/haʊs/
/ɛ/	bed	/bɛd/
/eɪ/	name	/neɪm/
/i/	need	/nid/
/ɪ/	sit	/sɪt/
/oʊ/	go	/goʊ/
/ʊ/	book	/bʊk/
/u/	boot	/but/
/ɔ/	dog	/dɔg/
	four	/fɔr/
/ɔɪ/	toy	/tɔɪ/
/ʌ/	cup	/kʌp/
/ɜr/	bird	/bɜrd/
/ə/	about	/ə'baʊt/
	after	/'æftər/
/ð/	they	/ðeɪ/
/θ/	think	/θɪŋk/
/ʃ/	shoe	/ʃu/
/ʒ/	vision	/'vɪʒən/

Consonants

Symbol	Key Word	Pronunciation
/b/	boy	/bɔɪ/
/d/	day	/deɪ/
/dʒ/	just	/dʒʌst/
/f/	face	/feɪs/
/g/	get	/gɛt/
/h/	hat	/hæt/
/k/	car	/kɑr/
/l/	light	/laɪt/
/m/	my	/maɪ/
/n/	nine	/naɪn/
/ŋ/	sing	/sɪŋ/
/p/	pen	/pɛn/
/r/	right	/raɪt/
/s/	see	/si/
/t/	tea	/ti/
/tʃ/	cheap	/tʃip/
/v/	vote	/voʊt/
/w/	west	/wɛst/
/y/	yes	/yɛs/
/z/	zoo	/zu/

Stress

/'/ city /'sɪti/
used before a syllable to show primary (main) stress

/ˌ/ dictionary /'dɪkʃəˌnɛri/
used before a syllable to show secondary stress

A, a

A, a /eɪ/ *n.* **A's, a's** or **As, as, 1** the first letter of the English alphabet **2** the highest grade: *I got an A on my history exam.*

a /ə; *strong form* eɪ/ or **an** *indef. article* **1** used before a noun or noun phrase to show one person or thing: *A man stopped me to ask what time it was.* **2** used before terms that show a general number, amount, or quantity (a few, a lot, etc.): *A lot of people went to the concert.||That item costs $10 a pound (a dozen, a ton, etc.). See:* **an, USAGE NOTE, apiece.**

A-1 /ˈeɪˈwʌn/ or **A Num·ber One** *adj.* the best, excellent: *That movie (restaurant, person, etc.) is A Number One.*

aard·vark /ˈɑrd,vɑrk/ *n.* a small, strong African animal with long ears and a long nose (or snout): *The aardvark digs for insects with its long snout.*

a·back /əˈbæk/ *adv.* **taken aback: 1** surprised, startled: *He was taken aback when she ran suddenly into the room.* **2** unpleasantly surprised, offended, *(syn.)* shocked: *I was taken aback by his rudeness.*

ab·a·cus /ˈæbəkəs/ *n.* **-es** a device made of beads and rods used for counting: *The abacus has been used for solving arithmetic problems for thousands of years.*

a·ban·don /əˈbændən/ *v.* **1** to stop, *(syn.)* to discontinue: *We abandoned the project because it was too expensive.* **2** to leave s.o. or s.t., *(syn.)* to desert: *The people abandoned the village before the soldiers came.* —*n.* [U] wildness, *(syn.)* recklessness: *The guests danced at the party with abandon.* -*n.* [U] **abandonment.**

a·ban·doned /əˈbændənd/ *adj.* **1** left behind, *(syn.)* forsaken: *The abandoned puppies were hungry.* **2** empty, *(syn.)* deserted: *Abandoned houses look sad.*

a·base /əˈbeɪs/ *v.frml.* **abased, abasing, abases 1** to cause oneself or s.o. else to feel bad or ashamed: *She won't abase herself by listening to his criticism.* **2** to lower in rank, office, or respect: *The lazy soldier was abased by an officer.* -*n.* **abasement.**

a·bashed /əˈbæʃt/ *adj.frml.* ashamed or embarrassed: *The student was abashed at failing the exam.* -*v.* **abash.**

a·bate /əˈbeɪt/ *v.* **abated, abating, abates 1** to lessen, decrease: *The pain in my shoulder abated after a day.* **2** (in law) to lower, reduce: *The town abated taxes on new businesses.* -*n.* **abatement.**

ab·bey /ˈæbi/ *n.* a place where monks or nuns live, *(syns.)* a monastery, convent: *We visited an old abbey near Westminster.*

ab·bot /ˈæbət/ *n.* the male head of the monks in an abbey

ab·bre·vi·ate /əˈbriviˌeɪt/ *v.* **-ated, -ating, -ates** to shorten, esp. a word: *This dictionary abbreviates the word "noun" by using "n." -n.* **abbreviation** /ə,briviˈeɪʃən/.

ABC /ˌeɪbiˈsi/ *n.* **ABC's 1** the alphabet: *A child in school must learn his/her ABC's.* **2** *fig.* the basics of an activity: *In business, you have to learn the ABC's of profit and loss.* **3 as easy as ABC:** s.t. simple, not difficult: *"No problem! Those instructions are as easy as ABC."*

ab·di·cate /ˈæbdɪˌkeɪt/ *v.* **-cated, -cating, -cates** to give up s.t., to step down as from a high office: *The king abdicated his throne and left the country. -n.*[C;U] **abdication** /,æbdɪˈkeɪʃn/.

ab·do·men /ˈæbdəmən, æbˈdoʊ-/ *n.* the belly, stomach area: *My abdomen hurts. -adj.* **abdominal** /æbˈdɑmənəl/.

ab·duct /æbˈdʌkt, əb-/ *v.* to take away by force, *(syn.)* to kidnap: *A stranger abducted the child outside a store. -n.*[C;U] **abduction.**

a·bed /əˈbɛd/ *adv.frml.* old usage in bed: *My grandfather's abed with the flu.*

ab·er·ra·tion /,æbəˈreɪʃən/ *n.* an unusual happening, *(syn.)* a deviation: *The fact that he is late for our meeting is an aberration; he's normally on time.*

a·bet /əˈbɛt/ *v.frml.* **abetted, abetting, abets** to help, encourage: *That man was jailed because he aided and abetted a friend who robbed a bank.*

a·bey·ance /ə'beɪəns/ *n.frml.* [U] **to hold in abeyance:** delay, (*syn.*) suspension: *A decision is being held in abeyance until more information is available.*

ab·hor /əb'hɔr, æb-/ *v.frml.* **-horred, -horring, -hors** to hate, (*syn.*) to detest: *She abhors bad table manners.* **-n.** [U] **abhorrence** /əb'hɔrəns, -'har-/.

ab·hor·rent /əb'hɔrənt, -'har-/ *adj.* hateful, (*syn.*) detestable: *His cruelty to animals is abhorrent.*

a·bide /ə'baɪd/ *v.* **abided, abiding, abides** **1** to suffer, stay in, (*syn.*) to endure: *I can't abide the hot weather.* **2 to abide by:** to comply with, to agree to s.t.: *I will abide by the judge's decision.* **-n.** [U] **abidance.**

a·bid·ing /ə'baɪdɪŋ/ *adj.* enduring, lasting: *I have an abiding desire to become a teacher.*

a·bil·i·ty /ə'bɪləti/ *n.* **-ties** **1** [U] skill, (*syn.*) competence: *She has great ability at playing the piano.* **2** [C] power to do s.t., (*syn.*) capacity: *He has many abilities, but he doesn't always use them.*

ab·ject /'æb,dʒɛkt/ *adj.* **1** in the worst condition, miserable, (*syn.*) wretched: *In a slum, people live in abject poverty.* **2** not worthy of respect: *He is an abject liar.*

a·blaze /ə'bleɪz/ *adj.frml.* **1** on fire, burning: *The building is ablaze.* **2** *fig.* highly motivated, filled with strong emotion: *My heart is ablaze with love for you.*

a·ble /'eɪbəl/ *adj.* **1** skilled, competent: *She is a very able teacher.* **2** having the power to do s.t., (*syn.*) capable: *After the surgery, he was able to walk again.* **3** free to do s.t., ready: *I am able to leave now; let's go.*
—n.pl. people who can move around and care for themselves: *My grandparents are still among the able at the home for old people. See:* ready.

a·bly /'eɪbli/ *adv.* in a skilled manner, (*syn.*) competently: *He fixed my car very ably.*

ab·nor·mal /æb'nɔrməl/ *adj.* not normal, unusual: *The high temperatures are abnormal for this time of year.* **-adv.** **abnormally.**

ab·nor·mal·i·ty /,æbnɔr'mæləti/ *n.* **-ties** an unusual mental or physical condition: *It is an abnormality to have six toes on one foot.*

a·board /ə'bɔrd/ *prep.* on a ship, train, airplane, or other vehicle: *The train conductor says "All aboard" before the train leaves the station.*

a·bode /ə'boʊd/ *n. frml.* a place where one lives, (*syn.*) a residence: *The phone book lists his abode as 370 West 58th Street.*

a·bol·ish /ə'balɪʃ/ *v.* to end s.t., (*syn.*) to cancel: *The government abolished the tax on food.*

ab·o·li·tion /,æbə'lɪʃən/ *n.* [U] the stopping of s.t. by law, (*syn.*) prohibition: *The abolition of slavery in the USA occurred in the 19th cen-*

tury. **-n.** [U] (act) **abolitionism;** (person) **abolitionist.**

a·bom·i·na·ble /ə'bamənəbəl/ *adj.frml.* hateful, disgusting: *Her cruel treatment of others is abominable.* **-adv.** **abominably.**

a·bom·i·na·tion /ə,bamə'neɪʃən/ *n.frml.* s.t. that causes disgust or hatred: *The murder of those children was an abomination.*

ab·o·rig·i·ne /,æbə'rɪdʒəni/ *n.* a person whose ancestors were the original people living in a place, a native: *The aborigines of Australia have lived there for thousands of years.* **-adj.** **aboriginal.**

a·bort /ə'bɔrt/ *v.* **1** to end a pregnancy before the normal time of birth: *The doctor aborted the baby to save the mother's life.* **2** *fig.* to stop an action before its end: *The general aborted the attack and ordered his soldiers back to their camp.* **-n.**[C;U] **abortion** /ə'bɔrʃən/.

a·bor·tive /ə'bɔrtɪv/ *adj.* failed, unsuccessful: *The politician made an abortive attempt at running for mayor and failed.*

a·bound /ə'baʊnd/ *v.* to exist in great numbers, (*syns.*) to teem, be abundant: *Deer and rabbits abound in this forest.*

a·bout /ə'baʊt/ *prep.* **1** related to, (*syn.*) concerning: *The meeting was about a new product.* **2** occupied with, doing: *He goes about his business every day.*
—adv. **1** around, (*syn.*) approximately: *About 20 people attended the meeting.* **2** almost: *Are you about done with that project?* **3** ready to: *I'm just about to go out the door.* **4 How about:** asking s.o. if they would like s.t.: *How about a movie (dinner, drink, etc.) tonight?* **5 not about to:** showing strong disagreement: *I am not about to drive in a bad snowstorm.* **6 to come about:** to change direction to the reverse: *The ship came about and headed for home.*

a·bout-face *n.frml.* **1** (in the military) an order to soldiers to change direction to the reverse: *On command, the soldiers did an about-face.* **2** *fig.* a complete change (of attitude, opinion, etc.): *He did an about-face and became pleasant when his angry behavior hurt his business.*

a·bove /'ə'bʌv/ *prep.* **1** higher than: *The sky above 10,000 feet is clear for flying.||She raised her hands above her head.* **2** more or greater than: *We have only a few products priced above $100.* **3 above all:** most important: *Above all, we must do more business this year.* **4 above and beyond:** in addition to, most importantly: *Above and beyond everything else that's wrong with her, she has an angry attitude.* **5 above s.o.'s head:** too difficult for s.o. to understand: *Fixing computers is above my head!* **6 to be above it all:** to be too important to deal with daily problems: *The President doesn't have to cook his meals or clean the White House; he's above it all.* **7 to**

be above s.t.: to be too honest or moral to do s.t. wrong: *He would never tell your secrets; he is above that.*
—*adv.* **1** overhead, (*syn.*) aloft: *The clouds above are dark.* **2** upstairs: *A family lives on the floor above.*
—*n.frml.* [U] an earlier part of a document: *The above states that the contract lasts for one year.*

a·bove·board /ə'bʌv,bɔrd/ *adj.* honest: *He is an honest businessperson; he is aboveboard with everyone.*

ab·ra·sion /ə'breɪʒən / *n.* **1** [U] wear caused by rubbing: *Constant abrasion from shoes wore down the wooden floor.* **2** [C] a small wound where skin has been rubbed off, (*syn.*) a scrape: *Her knees were covered with abrasions after she fell on the sidewalk.*

ab·ra·sive /ə'breɪsɪv/ *n.* **1** s.t. that is rough to the touch and can cause wear and tear: *Concrete is an abrasive.* **2** a substance that causes a small amount of abrasion in order to clean (smooth, polish, grind, etc.): *Use an abrasive, such as a strong soap with sand in it, to clean the kitchen sink.*
—*adj.fig.* rough, making people feel bad, (*syn.*) irritating: *His abrasive manner makes people want to stay away from him. -adv.* **abrasively.**

a·breast /ə'brɛst/ *adv.* **1** aware of what is happening in the world or in an area of work or study, (*syns.*) current, up-to-date: *She keeps abreast of what is happening by reading newspapers.* **2** side-by-side, together: *Students walk into school two abreast.*

a·bridge /ə'brɪdʒ/ *v.* **abridged, abridging, abridges** to shorten, remove parts, esp. from a written work: Reader's Digest *abridges long books so that people can read them quickly. -n.* [C] **abridgment.**

a·bridged /ə'brɪdʒd/ *adj.* shortened: *I read an abridged version of the report.*

a·broad /ə'brɔd/ *adv.* **1** out of the country, (*syn.*) overseas: *Our company ships goods abroad.* **2** far and wide: *The wind carried the seeds abroad.* **3** *old usage* outside one's house, (*syn.*) outdoors: *He was finally able to walk abroad, after being ill in his house for so long.*

a·brupt /ə'brʌpt/ *adj.* **1** quick and unfriendly, rude: *He talks to everyone in an abrupt manner.* **2** sudden, happening by surprise: *The bus came to an abrupt halt. -adv.* **abruptly;** *-n.* **abruptness.**

ab·scess /'æb,sɛs/ *n.* **-es** an infected sore or wound filled with a white liquid: *He has an abscess on his mouth.*
—*v.* to form an abscess

ab·scond /əb'skɑnd, æb-/ *v.frml.* to leave quickly to avoid being caught: *The thief absconded with the jewels.*

ab·sence /'æbsəns/ *n.* **1** [C] a situation of not being present: *His absence from work was because of his illness.* **2** [U] a lack of s.t.: *An absence of sleep left her tired.* **3 a leave of absence:** an approved time of being absent: *She took a three-month leave of absence from her job to have a baby.*

ab·sent /'æbsənt/ *adj.* not present: *The student is absent from class. -n.* **absentee** /,æbsən'ti/.

ab·sen·tee·ism /,æbsən'ti,ɪzəm/ *n.* [U] **1** a condition of people being absent: *The rate of absenteeism at that school is very high.* **2** being absent from work or school without a good reason: *That worker was fired because of her high rate of absenteeism; she missed ten days of work in one month.*

ab·sent-mind·ed /,æbsənt'maɪndɪd/ *adj.* not remembering things, forgetful: *He's so absent-minded that he often forgets where he put his car keys. -adv.* **absent-mindedly.**

ab·so·lute /'æbsə,lut, ,æbsə'lut/ *n.* s.t. that does not change, such as a rule (law, requirement): *You must be at work from 9:00 A.M. to 5:00 P.M.; that is an absolute.*
—*adj.* **1** complete, without question, total: *The king has absolute authority over the kingdom.* **2** certain, definite: *She told you the absolute truth. -adv.* **absolutely** /,æbsə'lutli, 'æbsə,lut-/; *-n.* [U] **absolutism.**

ab·so·lu·tion /,æbsə'luʃən/ *n.* [U] the formal removal of guilt (sin, crime, etc.), forgiveness: *In some religions, a priest can give absolution to s.o. who has done s.t. wrong.*

ab·solve /əb'zalv, -'salv/ *v.* **-solved, -solving, -solves** **1** to free of responsibility or guilt: *A judge absolved a woman of punishment for killing a man because she was protecting herself.* **2** (in religion) to forgive, (*syn.*) to pardon: *After praying for forgiveness, he was absolved of sin.*

ab·sorb /əb'sɔrb, -'zɔrb/ *v.* **1** to soak up, take in: *The sponge absorbed water from the sink.* **2** to accept a loss (expense, punishment): *Sending the wrong refrigerator is our mistake, so we'll absorb the cost of sending the right one.* **3** *fig.* to learn and remember: *She absorbs new ideas very quickly.* **4** to concentrate completely, (*syn.*) to immerse oneself: *He is absorbed in his work.*

ab·sorb·ent /əb'sɔrbənt, -'zɔr-/ *adj.* able to absorb liquids: *That paper towel is very absorbent.*

ab·stain /əb'steɪn/ *v.* **1** not to allow oneself to do s.t., (*syn.*) to refrain from: *He abstains from drinking alcohol (eating meat, smoking, etc.).* **2** (in politics) not to vote: *Two senators ab-*

A

stained on the vote on the new law to raise taxes.

ab·sten·tion /əb'stɛnʃən/ *n.* not voting: *The vote was 10 in favor of the plan, one against it, and two abstentions.*

ab·sti·nence /'æbstənəns/ *n.* [U] **1** refusal to use s.t., such as alcohol or cigarettes: *He must have total abstinence from drinking because of his heart problem.* **2** refusal to have sex: *The Catholic Church demands abstinence of its priests.* *-adj.* **abstinent.**

ab·stract (1) /æb'strækt, 'æb,strækt/ *adj.* **1** related to ideas, feelings, etc. (not concrete things): *"Beauty" and "truth" are abstract ideas.* **2** unclear, vague: *He has abstract ideas about what to do, but no specific thoughts.* *-adv.* **abstractly.**

ab·stract (2) /æb'strækt/ *v.* to shorten, (*syn.*) to summarize: *I abstracted the main ideas of his two-page report into one page.*
—*n.* /'æb,strækt/ a summary: *I then read the abstract at the meeting.*

ab·strac·tion /æb'strækʃən, əb-/ *n.* a vague, general idea not related to concrete things: *"Love" and "faith" are abstractions.*

ab·struse /əb'strus, æb-/ *adj.frml.* difficult to understand, unclear: *That writer's ideas are abstruse.* *-adv.* **abstrusely.**

ab·surd /əb'sɜrd, -'zɜrd/ *adj.* foolish, stupid: *He made some absurd comments about taxes being too low.*

a·bun·dance /ə'bʌndəns/ *n.* [U] **1** many of s.t., plenty: *Flowers grow in abundance in our garden.* **2** wealth, (*syn.*) affluence: *North America is a land of abundance.*

a·bun·dant /ə'bʌndənt/ *adj.* plentiful, (*syn.*) profuse: *Food is in abundant supply in this country.* *-adv.* **abundantly.**

a·buse /ə'byuz/ *v.* **abused, abusing, abuses** **1** to hurt badly, either physically or emotionally: *The man abused his wife by yelling at her often.* **2** to take unfair advantage of, (*syn.*) to exploit: *He abuses his job by coming to work late and leaving early.* **3** to give hard use to s.t., to misuse: *He abused his car by not changing the oil, and now it needs major repairs.*
—*n.* /ə'byus/ **1** [U] cruel treatment, (*syn.*) neglect: *The boy was beaten and starved; he was a victim of abuse.* **2** [C;U] misuse, such as cheating or stealing: *There were several abuses of the honor system at the military academy last year.* **3** [U] vulgar language or criticism: *He made a mistake, and the boss shouted abuse at him.*

a·bu·sive /ə'byusɪv/ *adj.* **1** using vulgar language or criticism: *Two cars collided and the drivers shouted abusive language at each other.* **2** unfair, (*syn.*) exploitative: *He's abusive of his parents by borrowing money from them and not repaying it.* *-adv.* **abusively.**

a·but /ə'bʌt/ *v.frml.* to touch on one side, border on: *In New York City, buildings abut each other and there's no open space between them.* *-n.* **abutment.**

a·buzz /ə'bʌz/ *adj.* full of talk (noise, buzzing sound, etc.): *The office is abuzz with the latest news.*

a·bys·mal /ə'bɪzməl/ *adj.frml.* **1** too deep to be measured **2** *fig.* terrible, awful: *That movie was an abysmal failure.* *-adv.* **abysmally.**

a·byss /ə'bɪs/ *n.* **-es** **1** *frml.* a dark bottomless crack, (*syn.*) a chasm: *The earthquake opened up a huge abyss.* **2** *fig.* too deep to be measured: *That event happened so long ago that it has been buried in the abyss of time.*

AC /,eɪ'si/ **1** *abbr. of* alternating current: *Household electricity in the USA is AC.* **2** *abbr. for* air conditioner: *Will you turn on the AC?*

ac·a·dem·ia /,ækə'dimiə/ *n. frml.* [U] the world of students and teachers, esp. colleges and universities: *She entered the world of academia as an assistant professor.* *-n.* **academe** /'ækə,dim, ,ækə'dim/.

ac·a·dem·ic /,ækə'dɛmɪk/ *adj.* related to studying and learning: *His academic work is excellent.*
—*n.* a professor: *He is an academic at the university.* *-adv.* **academically;** *-n.* [C] **academician** /,ækədə'mɪʃən/.

a·cad·e·my /ə'kædəmi/ *n.* **1** a private school or college: *My daughter attends the police (military, naval, etc.) academy.* **2** higher education

ac·cede /æk'sid, ɪk-/ *v.frml.* **-ceded, -ceding, -cedes** to agree, (*syn.*) to acquiesce: *Her father finally acceded to her demands to move into an apartment of her own.*

ac·cel·er·ate /ɪk'sɛlə,reɪt/ *v.* **-ated, -ating, -ates** to speed up, move faster: *The automobile accelerated to a speed of 100 miles (160 km) per hour.* *-n.* [U] **acceleration** /ɪk,sɛlə'reɪʃən/.

ac·cel·er·a·tor /ɪk'sɛlə,reɪtər/ *n.* a device, usu. a floor pedal in a vehicle, that increases the speed of an engine: *I stepped on the accelerator to increase my car's speed and pass another car.*

ac·cent /'æk,sɛnt/ *n.* **1** a particular sound in speech typical of a country or region: *He speaks English with a Spanish accent.* **2** a mark on a word to show how it is pronounced: *The accent is on the "i" in "sí" for "yes" in Spanish.* **3** a mark on part of a word to show where stress is put as it is spoken: *In the word "accent" there is a heavier accent on the first part of the word.*
—*v.* /'æk,sɛnt, æk'sɛnt/ **1** to show the importance of, (*syn.*) to emphasize: *The teacher accented her desire for quiet in the classroom by raising her voice.* **2** to decorate, (*syn.*) to complement: *Her hat was accented with flowers.*

ac·cen·tu·ate /ɪk'sɛnʧu,eɪt, æk-/ v. -ated, -ating, -ates to show the importance of s.t., (syn.) to emphasize: *The Mayor's speech accentuated the need to get rid of poverty and disease.*

ac·cept /ɪk'sɛpt/ v. **1** to take willingly: *He accepted my apology for being late.* **2** to say "yes," that you will do s.t.: *Are you going to accept his invitation to the party?* **3** to approve: *They accepted the new girl as a member of their group of friends.* **4** to become used to s.t. that one cannot change: *He finally accepted his wife's death (defeat in the election, etc.).* **5 to accept with open arms:** to welcome, (syn.) to embrace: *Her boyfriend's parents accepted her with open arms when they met her.*

ac·cept·a·ble /ɪk'sɛptəbəl/ adj. **1** satisfactory: *We received an acceptable price for our house.* **2** all right to do, (syn.) permissible: *Wearing a shirt without a tie is acceptable dress for dinner here.* -adv. **acceptably.**

ac·cep·tance /ɪk'sɛptəns/ n. **1** favor, approval: *His work received acceptance by his peers.* **2** the act of accepting: *She received an acceptance for admission to college.*

ac·cept·ed /ɪk'sɛptɪd/ adj. agreed upon, (syn.) standard: *Calling the doctor's office is the accepted way of making an appointment.*

ac·cess /'æk,sɛs/ v. to get into s.t., enter: *He accessed the computer program by typing in the correct access code.*
—n. [U] **1** entrance, permission to use: *I got access to the library by showing my identity card.* **2** a way or means of reaching or entering a place: *The only access to the island is by boat or plane.*
—adj. related to entering: *This is your access code for the computer.‖Please use the access road behind the building.*

ac·ces·si·ble /ɪk'sɛsəbəl/ adj. **1** able to be entered or reached: *The opera house is accessible by bus, subway, or car.* **2** easy to get to, (syn.) approachable: *He is an important man, but always accessible to his workers.* -n. [U] **accessibility** /ɪk,sɛsə'bɪləti/.

ac·ces·so·ry /ɪk'sɛsəri/ n. -ries **1** s.t. that adds to or enhances an item: *Accessories to cars, like a stereo or telephone, make them more useful and enjoyable.* **2** small items of clothing, such as jewelry, shoes, belts, pocketbooks, and ties: *She bought a new suit, then shopped for accessories, including shoes and a purse to go with it.* **3** a person who helps a criminal or takes part in a crime: *The police charged him with being an accessory to a robbery.*

ac·ci·dent /'æksədənt, -,dɛnt/ n. s.t. harmful or unpleasant that happens by surprise, (syn.) mishap: *He had an accident on the way to work: he fell and broke an ankle.*

ac·ci·den·tal /,æksə'dɛntl/ adj. by chance, (syn.) unforeseen: *I didn't know she was on my plane; our meeting was accidental.* -adv. **accidentally.**

ac·ci·dent-prone adj. likely to have accidents: *She is always hurting herself by falling; she's accident-prone.*

ac·claim /ə'kleɪm/ n.frml. [U] public congratulations, praise: *The athlete received great acclaim for winning a medal in the Olympics.*
—v.frml. to give congratulations, praise: *She was acclaimed as the greatest writer of her generation.* -n. [U] **acclamation** /,æklə'meɪʃən/.

ac·cli·mate /'æklə,meɪt/ v. -mated, -mating, -mates to become used to a climate or place, (syn.) to adapt: *We acclimated ourselves to the hot weather in Florida.* -n. **acclimation** /,æklə'meɪʃən/; -v. **acclimatize** /ə'klaɪmə,taɪz/.

ac·co·lade /'ækə,leɪd, ,ækə'leɪd/ n.frml. praise, (syn.) encomium: *The student was given accolades for his high grades.*

ac·com·mo·date /ə'kamə,deɪt/ v. -dated, -dating, -dates **1** to have enough space: *That hotel room accommodates four people.* **2** to make an extra effort to do what s.o. asks: *The company accommodated the customer's wish and sent the delivery overnight.*

ac·com·mo·dat·ing /ə'kamə,deɪtɪŋ/ adj. helpful, cooperative: *The hotel staff is very accommodating with its guests.* -adv. **accommodatingly.**

ac·com·mo·da·tion /ə,kamə'deɪʃən/ n. [C;U] **1** pl. rooms and other parts (restaurants, swimming pool, etc.), esp. in a hotel; lodgings: *The accommodations at that hotel are first class.* **2** arrangements made for s.o.: *We had to make special accommodations for food because our friend is a vegetarian.*

ac·com·pa·ni·ment /ə'kʌmpənimənt, ə'kʌmpni-/ n. [U] **1** s.t. that goes along with s.t. else **2** music played to go with a soloist (another musician, singer, dancer, etc.): *The singer's accompaniment was piano music.*

ac·com·pa·nist / ə'kʌmpənɪst, ə'kʌmpnɪst/ n. a musician who plays for others, such as a soloist: *The singer's accompanist was a piano player.*

ac·com·pa·ny /ə'kʌmpəni, ə'kʌmpni/ v.frml. -nied, -nying, -nied **1** to go with s.o. else, (syn.) to escort: *I accompanied my friends to the party.* **2** to play music in support of a singer or musician

ac·com·plice /ə'kamplɪs/ n. a partner in crime: *The police caught the thief and his accomplice, who was driving the car.*

ac·com·plish /ə'kamplɪʃ/ v. **1** to finish, complete: *We accomplished the job in an hour.* **2**

to achieve, do important things: *She has accomplished much in her short career.*

ac·com·plished /ə'kɑmplɪʃt/ *adj.* **1** finished, done: *The task was accomplished in an hour.* **2** skilled, experienced, and honored: *She is an accomplished musician who has won many prizes.*

ac·com·plish·ment /ə'kɑmplɪʃmənt/ *n.* a difficult task done well, success, (*syn.*) an achievement: *Climbing that high mountain was an accomplishment for the hikers.*

ac·cord /ə'kɔrd/ *n.frml.* **1** [C] agreement: *Two countries reached an accord and avoided war.*||*The politicians acted in accord with the President.*
—*v.frml.* to give, grant, (*syn.*) to bestow: *Our host accorded us a warm welcome.*

ac·cord·ance /ə'kɔrdns/ *n.frml.* [U] agreement, (*syn.*) harmony: *The teams played the game in accordance with the rules.*

ac·cord·ing·ly /ə'kɔrdɪŋli/ *adv.* in agreement with what is already known or expected, therefore, (*syn.*) consequently: *Accordingly, now that you have completed your classes, the school will give you a diploma.*

ac·cord·ing to *prep.* **1** in accordance with, in agreement with: *According to the law, you must pay a small fine.* **2** as stated by, by the authority of: *According to John, Sue was home at 8:00 p.m.*.||*According to the teacher, all homework must be handed in on time.*

USAGE NOTE: "According to" is not used with "me."

ac·cor·di·on /ə'kɔrdiən/ *n.* a musical instrument played with the hands by forcing air out through holes that are opened and closed with the fingers: *My father plays country music on the accordion.*

accordion

ac·cost /ə'kɔst, ə'kɑst/ *v.frml.* to come up to a stranger and speak: *A man accosted a woman on the street, asking her for her name and phone number.*

ac·count /ə'kaʊnt/ *n.* **1** money kept in a bank for present or future use: *I have a checking* (or) *savings account at Metropolitan Bank.* **2** a line of credit given by a business: *I have an account at the big department store.* **3** a description, narrative: *The police wrote an account of the accident.* **4 on account:** to be extended a line of credit by a business, to make a partial payment: *I paid some money on account, but still owe more at that clothing shop.* **5 on account of:** because of: *On account of bad weather, the picnic was cancelled.* **6 on no account:** never, in no way: *On no account will I let you go to that wild party.* **7 on one's own**

account: on one's own responsibility or (*syn.*) behalf: *I didn't go to visit my sick aunt out of kindness; I went on my own account.* **8** *fig.* **to give a good account of oneself:** to perform well: *He played tennis against more experienced players, but he still gave a good account of himself.* **9 to hold s.o. to account** or **call s.o. to account:** to hold s.o. responsible: *He must pay the fine or the police will hold him* (or) *call him to account.* **10 to take into account:** to consider with other matters in a decision: *The judge took into account that the young man had never been in trouble before and let him go free.*
—*v.* to explain: *He accounted for the missing items as lost but found them later. See:* no account.

ac·count·a·ble /ə'kaʊntəbəl/ *adj.* **1** responsible: *He is accountable for the missing money.* **2 to be held accountable:** to be obligated to answer for s.t. or s.o.: *He will be held accountable for any missing money.*

ac·count·a·bil·i·ty /ə,kaʊntə'bɪləti/ *n.* [U] responsibility: *The accountability for the project's success is hers.*

ac·count·ant /ə'kaʊntnt/ *n.* a person who keeps records and provides information about a company's or person's money: *She is an accountant who works for our company.*|| *My accountant prepares my tax returns every year.* **-n. accounting.**

ac·count ba·lance *n.* the amount of money in a bank account (checking, savings, etc.) at any time: *Our checking account balance is $486.42.*

ac·count ex·e·cu·tive *n.* a person who takes care of a customer's account, a sales representative: *The account executive from our insurance company called this morning to ask about our policy.*

ac·cred·it /ə'krɛdɪt/ *v.* **1** to approve, for meeting a set standard: *A committee of professors accredits colleges and universities in the USA.* **2** to give s.o. credit for having or doing s.t.: *She is accredited with writing that poem.*

ac·cred·i·ta·tion /ə,krɛdə'teɪʃən/ *n.* [C;U] approval, (*syn.*) endorsement: *Our school received accreditation from the state education department.*

ac·cred·i·ted /ə'krɛdətɪd/ *adj.* approved, (*syn.*) endorsed by an authority: *That school is accredited to receive government funds for its students' financial aid.*

ac·crue /ə'kru/ *v.* **-crued, -cruing, -crues 1** to grow slowly, (*syn.*) to accumulate: *Interest accrues to my savings account monthly.* **2** to include in a business's financial accounts an expected earning or expense that has not yet been paid. **-n. accrual.**

ac·cu·mu·late /əˈkyumyəˌleɪt/ *v.* **-lated, -lating, -lates** to add up, increase: *Interest accumulates in my savings account month by month.*

ac·cu·mu·la·tion /əˌkyumyəˈleɪʃən/ *n.* [U] an increase, adding up: *His accumulation of wealth amazes his friends.*

ac·cu·ra·cy /ˈækyərəsi/ *n.* [U] **1** *s.t.* that is correct and true, (*syns.*) exactness, precision: *He is a professional, and the accuracy of what he says is not to be questioned.* **2** the ability to hit a target: *Her accuracy with the gun surprised everyone.*

ac·cu·rate /ˈækyərɪt/ *adj.* **1** exact, correct: *The numbers in the report are accurate.* **2** able to hit a target, having good aim: *She is extremely accurate with a bow and arrow, hitting the bull's-eye every time.* **-adv.** **accurately.**

ac·cu·sa·tion /ˌækyəˈzeɪʃən/ *n.* a charge of crime or wrongdoing, (*syn.*) an indictment: *The judge read accusations of theft to the criminal.*

ac·cuse /əˈkyuz/ *v.* **-cused, -cusing, -cuses** to charge *s.o.* with wrongdoing, to blame: *The police accused him of theft.* **-adj.** **accusatory** /əˈkyuzəˌtɔri/; **-adv.** **accusingly; -n.** **accuser.**

ac·cused /əˈkyuzd/ *n.* a person charged with crime or wrongdoing: *The accused sat in the courtroom with her lawyer.*
—*adj.* charged, blamed: *The accused murderer's trial is set for next week.*

ac·cus·tom /əˈkʌstəm/ *v.* to become used to *s.t.*, (*syn.*) to adapt: *I will accustom myself to studying hard at the university.*

ac·cus·tomed /əˈkʌstəmd/ *adj.* used to, (*syn.*) adapted to: *I am accustomed to the cold in Alaska.*

ace /eɪs/ *n.* **1** in the USA a playing card marked with a letter "A" for "Ace": *In card games, the ace is often the card with the highest value.* **2** an expert, esp. the pilot of a fighter plane: *He was a flying ace during World War II.* **3** **ace in the hole** (or) **up one's sleeve** : a secret advantage: *The exam was supposed to be very difficult, but she had an ace up her sleeve; she had seen a copy of the questions before the exam.*

ace

—*v.* **aced, acing, aces 1** (in tennis) to make the first hit so that one's opponent cannot return the ball: *My opponent aced me three times during the match.* **2** *infrml.fig.* to do *s.t.* very well, (*syn.*) to excel: *He aced his exam with a score of 98.*

a·cer·bic /əˈsɜrbɪk/ *adj.frml.* **1** harsh, (*syn.*) biting: *The critic wrote an acerbic review of the play.* **2** sour or bitter: *Lemon has an acerbic taste.* **-adv.** **acerbically.**

ache /eɪk/ *n.* a dull, lasting pain: *I have an ache in my leg from walking too much.‖ a toothache, headache, etc.*
—*v.* **ached, aching, aches 1** to feel a dull pain, hurt: *My back aches every morning.* **2** *fig.* to desire, (*syn.*) to yearn for: *I am aching to go on vacation.*

a·chieve /əˈtʃiv/ *v.* **achieved, achieving, achieves** to reach, gain, (*syn.*) to acquire (success, happiness, one's goals, etc.): *The movie star achieved success and wealth.‖ He has achieved his goals in life by having a good job and raising a family.*

a·chieve·ment /əˈtʃivmənt/ *n.* success, (*syn.*) accomplishment: *He had many achievements in his career.*

a·chiev·er /əˈtʃivər/ *n.* [C] a person who accomplishes things, a doer: *She was a high achiever in college, always getting the best grades in her class.*

A·chill·es' heel /əˈkɪliz'hil/ *n. fig.* (from Greek mythology) a person's major weakness: *He can't stand pressure; that is his Achilles' heel.*

a·chy /ˈeɪki/ *adj.* having a dull pain: *My body feels achy all over today, so I think I'll stay in bed.*

a·cid /ˈæsɪd/ *n.* **1** [C] (in chemistry) a substance or liquid that has a sour taste, makes blue litmus paper turn red, or can react with a base to make salt: *Acids are widely used in industry.* **2** *infrml.* [U] *slang* for the dangerous illegal drug LSD: *When he took acid, he could see, hear, and feel things that weren't really there.*
—*adj.* **1** having a sour, acid taste: *Vinegar has a strong acid taste.* **2** harsh, (*syn.*) biting: *She made some acid comments about the poor quality of his writing.* **-adj.** **acidic** /əˈsɪdɪk/; **-n.** [U] **acidity** / əˈsɪdəti/.

a·cid test *n.frml.* **1** *fig.* a test of the real worth or value of *s.t.*: *The agreement to buy the house is signed, but the acid test is whether the buyer can make the first big payment on it.* **2** a test for the quality of gold

ac·knowl·edge / ɪkˈnɑlɪdʒ/ *v.* **-ledged, -ledging, -ledges 1** to respond, notify: *I acknowledged his offer by sending him a letter saying I had received it.* **2** to admit, (*syn.*) to concede: *He acknowledges the fact that he is wrong.*

ac·knowl·edged /ɪkˈnɑlɪdʒd/ *adj.* recognized: *She is the acknowledged leader in her field of chemistry.*

ac·knowl·edg·ment /ɪkˈnɑlɪdʒmənt/ *n.* answer, response: *I received an acknowledgment of my order in the mail.*

ac·me /ˈækmi/ *n.* the highest point of achievement, success, etc.: *She reached the acme of perfection as an artist.*

ac·ne /ˈækni/ *n.* [U] a skin condition of red spots (pimples), esp. on the face, common among teenagers: *The doctor cured the boy's acne with a special cream.*

a·corn /ˈeɪˌkɔrn/ *n.* the nut of the oak tree: *"Mighty oaks from little acorns grow."*

a·cous·tic /əˈkustɪk/ or **acoustical** *adj.* relating to a musical instrument whose sound is not electronically changed: *She plays an acoustic guitar. -adv.* **acoustically.**

a·cous·tics /əˈkustɪks/ *n.pl.* **1** *used with a sing. verb* the scientific study of sound: *Acoustics is an interesting field for engineers.* **2** the effect of sound: *The acoustics in the lecture hall are poor.*

ac·quaint /əˈkweɪnt/ *v.* **1** to learn about (usu. a place), *(syn.)* to familiarize: *I acquainted myself with my new neighborhood.* **2** to know s.o., but not well: *We met several times and are acquainted.*

ac·quain·tance /əˈkweɪntns/ *n.* a person whom one knows, but not well: *We are acquaintances and talk now and then.*

ac·quaint·ed /əˈkweɪntɪd/ *adj.* **1** familiar with (a person): *We are acquainted with each other, but are not friends.* **2** familiar with, informed about (a subject): *I am acquainted with the neighborhood (mathematics, the matter, etc.).*

ac·qui·esce /ˌækwiˈɛs/ *v.frml.* **-esced, -escing, -esces** to agree to s.t. but usu. not willingly, *(syn.)* to yield: *He acquiesced to her demands for money. -n.* [U] **acquiescence.**

ac·quire /əˈkwaɪr/ *v.* **-quired, -quiring, -quires 1** to buy, purchase: *She acquired property in the town.* **2** to build up, *(syn.)* to accumulate: *Over time, he acquired much wealth.* **3** to gain, *(syn.)* to obtain: *She acquired a knowledge of Spanish while living in Latin America.*

ac·qui·red im·mune de·fic·ien·cy syn·drome (AIDS) /eɪdz/ *n.* a disease of the immune system caused by the HIV virus: *The acquired immune deficiency syndrome is called AIDS in English and SIDA in Spanish and French.*

ac·qui·si·tion /ˌækwəˈzɪʃən/ *n.* **1** [C] the purchase, the process of getting ownership of s.t.: *My parents' latest acquisitions are a dishwasher and a new car.* **2** (in business) a business or part of a business taken over or bought by another company: *The software company's acquisition of Acme Company will help it compete in the hardware market.* **3** [U] building up of skill, knowledge, etc., *(syn.)* attainment: *The acquisition of the knowledge of medicine takes years of study.*

ac·qui·si·tive /əˈkwɪsətɪv/ *adj.* **1** wanting to own things: *She has an acquisitive nature and collects everything of value.* **2** greedy, *(syn.)*

avaricious: *Some politicians are acquisitive of power. -n.* [U] **acquisitiveness.**

ac·quit /əˈkwɪt/ *v.* **-quitted, -quitting, -quits 1** (in law) to clear s.o. of a crime, *(syn.)* to exonerate: *The jury acquitted a man accused of theft.* **2** *frml.* to perform or behave esp. well: *She lost the game to a better tennis player but acquitted herself very well.*

ac·quit·tal /əˈkwɪtl/ *n.* (in law) the clearing of charges or accusations against s.o., *(syn.)* exoneration: *His acquittal of all charges was a big victory for him.*

a·cre /ˈeɪkər/ *n.* a square piece of land measuring 69.57 yards (63.57 m.) on each side: *The farmer owns 150 acres of land.*

ac·rid /ˈækrɪd/ *adj.* irritating to the senses, harsh: *Acrid smoke from the fire burned my throat and eyes.*

ac·ri·mo·ni·ous /ˌækrəˈmoʊniəs/ *adj.* angry, *(syn.)* bitter feelings: *The issue of raising taxes causes acrimonious arguments. -adv.* **acrimoniously** *-n.* [U] **acrimony** /ˈækrəˌmoʊni/.

ac·ro·bat /ˈækrəˌbæt/ *n.* a person who performs gymnastic movements, usu. in the air: *Three acrobats swung high above the circus floor. -adj.* **acrobatic** /ˌækrəˈbætɪk/.

ac·ro·bat·ics /ˌækrəˈbætɪks/ *n.pl. used with a sing. verb* jumping, running, flying through the air, walking on wires, etc., in dangerous ways: *A family of acrobats performs acrobatics in the circus.*

ac·ro·nym /ˈækrəˌnɪm/ *n.* a word formed from the first letters or parts of other words: *"SCUBA" is an acronym for "self-contained underwater breathing apparatus."*

a·cross /əˈkrɔs/ *prep.* in a motion on or over s.t.: *We walked across the bridge.*
—*adv.* from one side to the other: *We swam across the lake to get to the island.*
—*v.* **1** *infrml.* **to come across as:** to make people think about one in a certain way, *(syn.)* to create an impression: *He comes across as an honest guy.* **2** *phrasal v. insep.* **to come across:** to encounter or find by chance: *I came across a pen that I had lost last week.*

a·cross-the-board *adj.* complete, including a whole group of things or people: *The company gave an across-the-board salary increase of 5 percent.*

a·cryl·ic /əˈkrɪlɪk/ *n.adj.* [U] a type of plastic: *Acrylic windows break less often than glass windows.*

act /ækt/ *v.* **1** to take action, do s.t.: *The boss acted right away on my suggestion.* **2** to behave, to show, esp. an emotion: *He acts as though he is pleased.* **3** to perform a role: *He acted in a Shakespeare play.* **4** to work, to function, *(syn.)* to operate: *That medicine acts fast to relieve pain.*

—*n.* **1** an event, happening: *Attacking another nation is an act of war.* **2** a part of a play: *We especially enjoyed the third act of the play.* **3** (in acting) a routine: *He is a comedian with a funny act.* **4** *infrml.* **to get one's act together:** to organize oneself and do s.t. useful: *Tomorrow there will be an important meeting, so I'd better get my act together and prepare for it.* **5 to put on an act:** to make believe, pretend, (*syn.*) to feign: *He put on an act of being sick so he could leave work early.* **6** *phrasal v. sep.* **to act out s.t.:** to perform, cary out: *We acted out a story in English class.‖We acted it out.* **7** *phrasal v.* **to act up: a.** to behave badly, inappropriately: *The children acted up in class and broke a chair.* **b.** to function badly: *If your car is acting up again, take it back to the garage.*

act·ing /ˈæktɪŋ/ *n.* [U] performing in plays or movies: *She chose acting as a career.*

ac·tion /ˈækʃən/ *n.* **1** [U] happenings, movement: *We watched the action of the football game on TV.* **2** [C] the effect or force of s.t. on s.t. else: *The action of the waves hitting the beach made the sand wash away.* **3 to take action:** to bring s.o. to court, (*syn.*) to sue: *The company took action against an employee who stole a computer.*

ac·ti·vate /ˈæktə,veɪt/ *v.* **-vated, -vating, -vates** to put in motion, start: *She activated the machine by pressing a button. -n.* [U] **activation** /ˌæktəˈveɪʃən/.

ac·tive /ˈæktɪv/ *adj.* **1** busy, (*syn.*) involved in: *She is active in politics.* **2** up and about, moving: *He was sick but is active again. -adv.* **actively.**

ac·tiv·ist /ˈæktəvɪst/ *n.* a person who works at changing s.t., esp. in politics: *She is a political activist who works on lowering taxes. -n.* [U] **activism.**

ac·tiv·i·ty /ækˈtɪvəti/ *n.* **-ties 1** [U] the state of being active, (*syn.*) movement: *There isn't much activity on the roads after midnight.* **2** [C] a planned event: *The activities at the school include sports and dances.* **3** [U] rapid movement: *People were running everywhere; there was a lot of activity.*

ac·tor /ˈæktər/ *n.* a person who acts in plays or movies: *My friend is an actor in the movies.*

ac·tress /ˈæktrɪs/ *n.* **-es** a female actor

ac·tu·al / ˈæktʃuəl/ *adj.* real, exact: *Our actual expenses for food and clothes for last year were much lower than we thought.*

ac·tu·al·i·ty /ˌæktʃuˈæləti/ *n.* [U] fact, (*syn.*) reality: *In actuality, our costs are higher than we thought.*

ac·tu·al·ize /ˈæktʃuə,laɪz/ *v.* to put into action, (*syn.*) to realize: *The government actualized its plan to stop crime. -n.* [U] **actualization** /ˌæktʃuələˈzeɪʃən/.

ac·tu·al·ly /ˈæktʃuəli, ˈækʃəli/ *adv.* **1** in truth or in fact, (*syn.*) really: *Actually, that student needs to study more to pass the exams.‖The Liberal Party actually has the power in that country.* **2** as surprising as it may seem, contrary to appearances: *He seems so quiet, but actually he likes to talk.*

a·cu·men / əˈkyumən, ˈækyəmən/ *n.frml.* [U] the ability to see opportunities and dangers, (*syn.*) insight: *She handles her business with much acumen.*

ac·u·punc·ture /ˈækyə,pʌŋktʃər/ *n.* [U] a part of Chinese medicine that treats diseases and pain by putting needles into the body: *I thought acupuncture would hurt, but I couldn't even feel the needles.*

a·cute /əˈkyut/ *adj.* great, (*syn.*) severe: *An acute lack of food brought hunger to the people. -adv.* **acutely.**

A.D. /ˈeɪˈdi/ *abbr. of* anno Domini; (Latin for) the year of Jesus Christ's birth: *The Spanish tried to invade England in 1588 A.D.* See: B.C.

ad /æd/ *n.infrml.* short for advertisement

ad·age /ˈædɪdʒ/ *n.* a saying that contains truths or helpful information: *There is an adage that says: "When threatened, it is better to run away and live to fight another day."*

ad·a·mant /ˈædəmənt/ *adj.* not willing to change one's opinion, stubborn, (*syn.*) unbending: *She is adamant about not seeing her old boyfriend anymore. -adv.* **adamantly.**

Ad·am's ap·ple /ˈædəmz,æpəl/ *n.* the bump in the front of the throat, usu. seen in men: *His Adam's apple moves up and down when he swallows.*

a·dapt /əˈdæpt/ *v.* to change to function in a new way, to adjust: *She adapted herself* (or) *adapted quickly to her new job. -n.*[C;U] **adaptation** /ˌædəpˈteɪʃən, ˌædæp-/.

a·dapt·a·ble /əˈdæptəbəl/ *adj.* **1** capable of being changed and used for s.t. else: *The movie producers think that book is adaptable because it's full of adventures; it should make a good movie.* **2** capable of handling changes, flexible: *The child is very adaptable; she will be happy in her new house and school.*

a·dapt·er /əˈdæptər/ *n.* **1** s.o. or s.t. that adapts **2** a device that allows s.t. to be used in a new way: *My computer uses an adapter to change the type of electrical current that it runs on.*

add / æd/ *v.* **1** to combine two or more numbers into a total: *The cashier added up the bill.* **2** to increase the size or amount of s.t.: *We added a room to our house.* **3 to add insult to injury:** to be insulted as well as harmed: *A guy hit my car while it was parked, and to add insult to injury he yelled at me.* **4** *phrasal v. insep.* **to add up:** to make sense, seem true: *What he says does not add up.*

ad·den·dum /ə'dɛndəm/ *n.* **-da** (Latin for) a piece of writing that is added to a larger one, such as at the end of a contract or book: *The lawyer wrote an addendum to the contract that says how much money she will be paid.*

ad·dict /'ædɪkt/ *n.* **1** a person physically or emotionally dependent on a substance, such as a drug: *He is a heroin addict.* **2** *infrml.fig.* a fan, (*syn.*) a devotee: *He is a golf addict; he plays every day.*
—*v.* /ə'dɪkt/ (of a substance) to make s.o. dependent: *Heroin addicts many people.* *-n.*[C;U] **addiction** /ə'dɪkʃən/; *-adj.* **addictive** /ə'dɪk-tɪv/. *See:* drug, narcotic.

ad·di·tion /ə'dɪʃən/ *n.* **1** [U] the arithmetic process of adding things or numbers: *the addition of 2 + 2 = 4* **2** [C] s.t. more, an extension: *We built a one-room addition to our house.* *-adj.* **additional** /ə'dɪʃənl/; *-adv.* **additionally.**

ad·di·tive /'ædətɪv/ *n.* s.t. added, esp. to food or medicine: *Food companies put vitamin additives in breakfast cereals.*

ad·dress /ə'drɛs, 'æˌdrɛs/ *n.* **-es 1** the specific location (street number, city, state, etc.) of a person, business, or institution: *My business address is 2 Wall St., New York, NY 10002.* **2** a speech: *She gave an address to the United Nations.*
—*v.* /ə'drɛs/ **1** to write an address: *Our secretary addressed the envelopes before mailing them.* **2** to speak to: *He addressed a large group of doctors.*

ad·dress·ee /ˌædrɛ'si, əˌdrɛ'si/ *n.* a person, business, etc. to whom s.t. is addressed: *The addressee of that letter no longer lives here.*

a·dept / ə'dɛpt/ *adj.* skillful, clever: *She is adept at playing the guitar (swimming, solving problems, etc.). -adv.* **adeptly;** *-n.* [U] **adeptness.**

ad·e·quate /'ædəkwɪt/ *adj.* **1** enough, (*syn.*) sufficient: *He makes an adequate salary, enough to pay his bills.* **2** not bad, but not very good, (*syn.*) minimal: *Her work is only adequate; I'm not impressed. -n.* [U] **adequacy** /'ædəkwəsi/; *-adv.* **adequately.**

ad·here /əd'hɪr/ *v.* **-hered, -hering, -heres 1** to hold, stick to a surface: *That glue does not adhere to the wall.* **2** to obey, pay attention to: *Car drivers must adhere to the rules of driving or be punished. -n.* **adhesion** /əd'hiʒən/.

ad·her·ence /əd'hɪrəns/ *n.frml.* [U] **1** attention to laws, rules, etc., (*syn.*) obedience: *He pays strict adherence to the rules in his work.* **2** ability to hold, such as glue, (*syn.*) adhesion: *The glue does not have enough adherence to stick to the surface of the wall.*

ad·her·ent /əd'hɪrənt/ *n.frml.* a believer, member: *She is an adherent of Christianity (Judaism, Islam, etc.).*

ad·he·sive /əd'hisɪv/ *adj.* able to stick or join s.t. to s.t. else: *I used adhesive tape to stick a note on the door.*
—*n.* a substance that sticks: *Glue is an adhesive.*

ad hoc /ˌæd'hak, -'hoʊk/ *adj.* (Latin for) put together for a purpose, temporary: *The teacher created an ad hoc committee of five students to discuss the textbook.*

ad·ja·cent /ə'dʒeɪsənt/ *adj.* next to, (*syn.*) neighboring: *We live in the house adjacent to the church.*

ad·jec·tive /'ædʒɪktɪv/ *n.* a word that describes a noun: *In the sentence "The boy made a large sandwich," the word "large" is an adjective. -adj.* **adjectival** /ˌædʒɪk'taɪvəl/.

ad·join /ə'dʒɔɪn/ *v.frml.* to be next to, (*syn.*) to abut: *The bathroom adjoins the bedroom.*

ad·journ /ə'dʒɜrn/ *v.* to stop a meeting for a while, (*syn.*) to recess: *The judge adjourned the trial so people could go to lunch. -n.*[C;U] **adjournment.**

ad·junct /'æˌdʒʌŋkt/ *n.* an addition or attachment that is often not essential: *That small building is an adjunct to the main library.*
—*adj.* attached to, connected: *She is an adjunct professor at the law school; she's a lawyer and teaches one class a year.*

ad·just /ə'dʒʌst/ *v.* **1** to feel comfortable, (*syn.*) to acclimate: *I adjusted to the increased work load when my coworker went on vacation.* **2** to change, (*syn.*) to modify: *I adjusted the air conditioner to stay cool.* **3** to fix, repair: *The mechanic adjusted the engine to make it work better. -n.* **adjustable.**

ad·just·ment /ə'dʒʌstmənt/ *n.* **1** [U] a change in feeling or behavior, (*syn.*) an adaptation: *I made the adjustment to life in the big city when I moved to Chicago.* **2** [C] a small change, (*syn.*) a modification: *The store made an adjustment to the price of meat by lowering it.*

ad lib /ˌæd'lɪb/ *v.n.adj.infrml.* to speak, sing, or act without a script, saying whatever words come into one's mind: *When the actor forgot her lines, she <v.> ad libbed her part.*

ad·min·is·ter /əd'mɪnəstər/ *v.* **1** to give, (*syns.*) to dispense, mete out: *The doctor administered medicine to the patient.* **2** to manage, supervise: *She administered the committee meeting to make sure that everything worked smoothly. -v.* **administrate** / əd'mɪnəˌstreɪt/.

ad·min·is·tra·tion /ədˌmɪnə'streɪʃən/ *n.* **1** [C] in the USA, the executive branch of the federal government, esp. the President: *The administration in Washington is usually criticized by the newspapers and TV.* **2** [U] control of the business, management: *The administration of a company requires hard work.*

ad·min·is·tra·tive /əd'mɪnə,streɪtɪv, -strə-/ *adj.* managing, controlling the business of: *The administrative work in the company is done by four men and women.* -*adv.* **administratively.**

ad·min·is·tra·tor /əd'mɪnə,streɪtər/ *n.* a person who supervises or manages: *She is an administrator in the Department of Health.*

ad·mi·ra·ble /'ædmərəbəl/ *adj.* worthy of approval or respect: *The way she manages her company is admirable.* -*adv.* **admirably.**

ad·mi·ral /'ædmərəl/ *n.* the highest rank of naval officers: *He is an admiral in the US Navy.*

ad·mi·ra·tion /,ædmə'reɪʃən/ *n.* [U] an attitude of approval or respect, (*syn.*) awe: *I have great admiration for the way he plays football.*

ad·mire /əd'maɪr/ *v.* **-mired, -miring, -mires** **1** to respect, approve of: *I admire how well she speaks English.* **2** to like, be pleased by s.t.: *He admires her good looks.*

ad·mir·er /əd'maɪrər/ *n.* a person who thinks highly of another: *He is an admirer of her fine writing.*

ad·mis·si·ble /əd'mɪsəbəl/ *adj.* **1** (in law) according to rules, acceptable: *The judge ruled that what the witness to the crime said is admissible, in the court.* **2** allowable, following standards of good behavior: *His jokes were admissible but not really proper.*

ad·mis·sion /əd'mɪʃən/ *n.* **1** [U] entrance fee, the right to enter a place: *Admission to the concert was $10 per person.* **2** [U] acceptance at a university or school: *She was offered admission to the local university.* **3** [C] revealing s.t. held secret, confession: *He made an admission that he had stolen a candy bar. See:* admittance.

ad·mit /əd'mɪt/ *v.* **-mitted, -mitting, -mits** **1** to confess, reveal s.t. held secret: *He admitted that he had made a mistake.* **2** to allow to enter, pass through: *We were admitted to the party by the hostess herself.* **3 to admit to s.t.:** to accept responsibility: *She admitted to stealing the money.*

ad·mit·tance /əd'mɪtns/ *n.frml.* [U] entrance, (*syn.*) admission: *Admittance to the movie is only half price on Mondays. See:* admission.

ad·mit·ted·ly /əd'mɪtɪdli/ *adv.* clearly, obviously: *Admittedly, I made a mistake, and I'm sorry.*

ad·mon·ish /əd'mɑnɪʃ/ *v.frml.* **1** to warn, (*syn.*) to caution: *The boy's mother admonished him to be careful crossing streets.* **2** to criticize, (*syn.*) to scold: *When he behaves badly, she admonishes him.* -*n.frml.*[C;U] **admonition** /,ædmə'nɪʃən/.

a·do /ə'du/ *n.* [U] bother, delay, (*syn.*) fuss: *A speaker said to the audience, "And now, without further ado, here's our special guest!"*

a·do·be /ə'doubi/ *n.* [U] **1** a building material made of clay and straw hardened in the sunlight **2** a style of houses and other buildings common in the American Southwest: *We lived in New Mexico in a house made of adobe.*

ad·o·les·cence /,ædl'ɛsəns/ *n.* [U] the teenage years between puberty and adulthood: *During her adolescence, she argued a lot with her parents.*

ad·o·les·cent /,ædl'ɛsənt/ *n.adj.* a teenager, esp. ages 13-17: *The person you are looking for is an <n.> adolescent (or) an <adj.> adolescent boy of 15.*

a·dopt /ə'dɑpt/ *v.* **1** to take legal responsibility for acting as parents to a child: *We adopted two children whose parents were killed in an accident.* **2** (in law) to make into a law, (*syn.*) to enact: *The legislature adopted a law to stop the sale of guns.* **3** to copy, (*syn.*) to imitate: *The boy adopts the same way of talking that his father has.*

a·dop·tion /ə'dɑpʃən/ *n.* [C;U] **1** (in law) taking legal responsibility for parenting: *The process of adoption can be lengthy.* **2 to put s.o. up for adoption:** to offer a child or an animal for others to adopt: *The young mother put her child up for adoption.*

a·dop·tive /ə'dɑptɪv/ *adj.* (in law) related to adoption as parent or child: *The girl's adoptive parents take good care of her.*

a·dor·a·ble /ə'dɔrəbəl/ *adj.* lovable, cute, (*syn.*) darling: *That little girl is just adorable!* -*adv.* **adorably.**

ad·o·ra·tion /,ædə'reɪʃən/ *n.* [U] **1** religious worship, (*syn.*) veneration: *Adoration of God is an act of religious faith.* **2** *frml.* love, (*syn.*) infatuation: *She was so beautiful that she was an object of adoration by many men.*

a·dore /ə'dɔr/ *v.* **adored, adoring, adores** **1** to worship as a god or God, to love deeply: *He simply adores his wife.* **2** *fig.* to like very much, (*syn.*) to relish: *I just adore roses!*

a·dorn /ə'dɔrn/ *v.frml.* **1** to make beautiful, to decorate: *She adorned the dinner table with flowers.* **2** *fig.* to enliven, (*syn.*) to ornament: *Many interesting people adorned the party.* -*n.*[C;U] **adornment.**

ad·ren·a·line /ə'drɛnəlɪn/ *n.* [U] a natural chemical produced by the body because of danger or anger that makes one ready to fight or run away: *That was some argument; your adrenaline was really flowing!*

a·drift /ə'drɪft/ *adj.* **1** *frml.* without power and floating helplessly: *The motor on our boat died, leaving us adrift in a calm sea.* **2** *fig.* without purpose, confused: *The young man seems adrift in life, unsure of what to do.*

a·droit /ə'drɔɪt/ *adj.frml.* skillful, clever: *She is adroit at getting people to do what she wants.* -*adv.* **adroitly.**

A

ad·u·la·tion /ˌædʒə'leɪʃən/ n.frml. [U] extreme praise, worship: *The actor enjoyed the adulation of his audience.* -v. adulate / 'ædʒə,leɪt/.

a·dult /ə'dʌlt, 'æ,dʌlt/ n. a person or animal who has finished growing physically and mentally: *At 21 years of age, he is now an adult.* —adj. **1** able to make one's own decisions, mature: *Her adult behavior made her parents feel she was ready to rent her own apartment.* **2** showing or using sex, violence, and dirty language: *That nightclub features adult entertainment, such as nude dancing.* -n. [U] **adulthood** / ə'dʌlt,hʊd/.

a·dul·ter·ate /ə'dʌltə,reɪt/ v. -rated, -rating, -rates to mix with harmful or unwanted substances: *The orange juice was adulterated with insect poison.* -n. [U] **adulteration** /ə,dʌltə'reɪʃən/.

a·dul·ter·y /ə'dʌltəri, -tri/ n. [U] sex between a married person and s.o. other than his or her spouse: *He committed adultery and his wife left him.* -n. **adulterer; (female) adulteress** /ə'dʌltərɪs, -trɪs/; -adj. **adulterous.**

ad·vance /əd'væns/ n. **1** an improvement, (syn.) a breakthrough: *New advances in medicine improve the quality of health care.* **2** a forward movement: *Troops made an advance into enemy territory.* **3** an attempt at sexual contact, a pass: *The young man made advances to the woman by asking if he could buy her a drink.* **4** a payment made to a writer before his or her book is published —v. **-vanced, -vancing, -vances 1** to move forward: *The hikers advanced up the mountain.* **2** to improve, progress: *Medical science advances by finding new treatments and medicines.* **3** to make an early payment: *My company advanced me a week's salary when I had to pay for emergency car repair.*

ad·vanced /əd'vænst/ adj. difficult, complex: *He took advanced courses in mathematics.*

ad·vance·ment / əd'vænsmənt/ n. [U] **1** success, getting ahead, esp. in a career, promotion: *His job advancement was rapid, with three promotions in five years.* **2** [C;U] progress, improvement: *The advancement of medicine is based on discovering new medicines and techniques.*

ad·van·tage /əd'væntɪdʒ/ n. **1** [U] having greater ability or strength than s.o. else, (syn.) superiority: *The greater experience of our company gives us an advantage over our competitors.* **2** [C] a good feature, benefit: *The house is new and near a good school: It has many advantages.* **3** **to have all the advantages in life:** to have the best, (syn.) to be privileged: *She had all of the advantages in life, such as wealthy parents and fine schools.* **4 to have an** or **the advantage:** to be in a better position: *Our product is cheaper than the others, so we have an advantage.* **5 to take advan-**

tage of: a. to use an opportunity: *I will take advantage of my business trip to Paris to see the beautiful sights.* **b.** to cheat s.o., (syn.) to exploit: *The salesperson took advantage of me by charging me too much.*

ad·van·ta·geous /ˌædvən'teɪdʒəs, -væn-/ adj. good to do, (syn.) beneficial: *I found it advantageous to combine a business trip with a vacation.* -adv. **advantageously.**

ad·vent /'æd,vɛnt/ n.frml. [U] beginning, (syn.) outset: *Since the advent of modern science, many wonderful discoveries have been made.*

ad·ven·ture /əd'vɛntʃər/ n. an exciting time (incident, event), (syn.) an exploit: *Our camping trip turned into an adventure when we became lost and had to be rescued.*

ad·ven·tur·er /əd'vɛntʃərər/ n. a person who looks for adventure: *Most mountain climbers are adventurers, for they often must face danger.*

ad·ven·tur·ous /əd'vɛntʃərəs/ adj. **1** daring, bold: *She is an adventurous young woman who rode across the country alone on a motorcycle.* **2** exciting, (syn.) stimulating: *She had an adventurous time.* -adv. **adventurously.**

ad·verb /'æd,vɜrb/ n. a word that modifies a verb, adjective, or another adverb: *The word "truly" in the sentence "I can truly say I like her" is an adverb.* -adj. **adverbial** /æd'vɜrbiəl/.

ad·ver·sar·i·al /ˌædvər'sɛriəl/ adj. against s.o., opposing: *The two leaders are in adversarial positions over how to handle the problem.*

ad·ver·sar·y /'ædvər,sɛri, -və-/ n. -ries an opponent, (syn.) a foe: *Two politicians (boxers, teams, etc.) are adversaries in the election.*

ad·verse /æd'vɜrs, 'æd,vɜrs/ adj. **1** angry, (syn.) hostile: *The politician has suffered adverse criticism in the newspapers.* **2** difficult, unfavorable: *He lost all of his money and now lives in adverse circumstances as a poor man.* -adv. **adversely.**

ad·ver·si·ty /æd'vɜrsəti/ n. -ties **1** [C] bad luck, (syn.) misfortune: *She has suffered much adversity in her life.* **2** [U] a difficult situation (poverty, illness, etc.): *She lives in adversity as a result of losing her job.*

ad·ver·tise /'ædvər,taɪz/ v. -tised, -tising, -tises **1** to sell, (syn.) to promote a product or service: *Our company advertises on television and in newspapers.* **2** fig. to announce, make known publicly: *He advertised the fact that he is getting promoted.*

ad·ver·tise·ment /ˌædvər'taɪzmənt, əd'vɜrtɪz-, əd'vɜrtɪs-/ n. a notice of a product or service: *We place advertisements about our products in the newspapers every week.* See: commercial, USAGE NOTE.

ad·ver·tis·ing /'ædvər,taɪzɪŋ/ n. [U] the field of making print, radio, or TV descriptions to

ad·vice /əd'vaɪs/ n. [U] 1 opinion(s) given to
promote products and services: *My friend who
works in advertising makes TV commercials.*
—*adj.* related to advertising: *She is an advertising manager at a big company.*

ad·vice /əd'vaɪs/ n. [U] 1 opinion(s) given to
s.o. about what to do, (*syn.*) guidance: *She took
my advice and did not drop out of school.* 2
direction, warning: *On the advice of her doctor, she no longer smokes cigarettes.*

ad·vis·a·ble /əd'vaɪzəbəl/ adj. strongly suggested for good reasons, recommended: *It is
advisable that you do your homework.*

ad·vise /əd'vaɪz/ v. **-vised, -vising, -vises** 1 to
give s.o. an opinion about what to do, (*syn.*) to
counsel: *My teacher advised me to go to college.* 2 to caution, warn: *His doctor advises
him not to take his medicine with alcohol.*

ad·vised /əd'vaɪzd/ adj. informed, notified:
Please be advised that your rent is due.

ad·vi·sor or **ad·vi·ser** /əd'vaɪzər/ n. a person
who gives opinions to s.o. on what to do, (*syn.*)
a counselor: *My college advisor said I should
take courses in mathematics.*

ad·vi·sor·y /əd'vaɪzəri/ adj. helping by giving
opinions, (*syn.*) guiding: *The personnel manager has an advisory role with company employees.*

ad·vo·cate /'ædvəkɪt/ n. 1 a worker for a
cause, a supporter: *He is an advocate of
human rights.* 2 an attorney, lawyer: *She is an
advocate for the poor.*
—*v.* /'ædvə,keɪt/ **-cated, -cating, -cates** to propose or support an idea: *She advocates lower
taxes.* -n. **advocacy** /'ædvəkəsi/.

ae·gis /'idʒɪs/ n. control, (*syn.*) sponsorship:
*That school is operated under the aegis of a
religious group.*

aer·i·al /'ɛriəl/ adj. taking place in the air: *The
airplane did aerial tricks such as flying upside-down.* -n. **aerialist.**

aer·o·bic /ɛ'roubɪk/ adj. of hard exercise, such
as running or swimming, that conditions the
heart and lungs: *He does an aerobic workout
for 30 minutes four times per week.*

aer·o·bics /ɛ'roubɪks/ n.pl. a type of dance exercise to music: *She does aerobics for 45 minutes every morning.*

USAGE NOTE: *Aerobics* or *aerobic exercise* became popular in the USA in the 1970s, and is
now a major industry. There are special shoes,
clothes, equipment, classes, and videos for
every taste and physical condition.

aer·o·dy·nam·ic /,ɛroudaɪ'næmɪk/ adj. 1 of
the science of air flowing against and over objects 2 having the ability to move (through the
air) smoothly: *Automobiles with good aerody-
namic designs save fuel.* -adv. **aerodynami-
cally;** -n. **aerodynamics.**

aer·o·space /'ɛrou,speɪs/ n. 1 the air surrounding the earth 2 the earth's atmosphere
and outer space
—*adj.* related to flight in outer space: *The
country's aerospace program has made much
progress.*

aes·thet·ic /ɛs'θɛtɪk, ɪs-/ adj. related to understanding and liking beauty and art: *As an
artist, she has a well-developed aesthetic
sense.* -adv. **aesthetically;** -n. [U] **aestheti-
cism** /ɛs'θɛtə,sɪzəm, ɪs-/.

aes·thet·ics /'ɛs'θɛtɪks, ɪs-/ n.pl. used with a
sing. verb 1 the study or philosophy of beauty
and art: *I took a course in aesthetics last semester.* 2 a sense of beauty: *The carpenters
just want to build the house and not worry
about its aesthetics.*

a·far /ə'far/ adv.frml. a long way away: *We had
visitors who came from afar.*

af·fa·ble /'æfəbəl/ adj.frml. friendly, (*syn.*) approachable: *He is an affable man, always willing to stop and talk.* -adv. **affably.**

af·fair /ə'fɛr/ n. 1 a business matter: *Our company lost money in that affair.* 2 a social gathering, such as a party or wedding: *I have to go
to a social affair this evening.* 3 a relationship, usu. sexual in nature, between two people who are not married to each other: *The two
had a brief affair, then did not see each other
again.* 4 **man or woman of affairs:** a businessperson: *He's always going to meetings;
he's a man of affairs.*

af·fect /ə'fɛkt/ v. 1 to change, (*syn.*) to influence: *Very hot weather affects how people feel
and act.* 2 to touch one's emotions, move s.o.:
He was deeply affected by his mother's death.
3 to behave in a fake way, pretend: *She affects
a French accent, but she doesn't speak French.*

USAGE NOTE: The verb "*affect*" means to have
an influence or cause a change. The noun "*effect*" means the result of this change:*The flood
affected the town. The effects were homelessness and disease. See: effect.*

af·fec·ta·tion /,æfɛk'teɪʃən/ n. [C;U] false behavior, (*syn.*) pretension: *He speaks with a
British accent, but that is just an affectation
because he's not British.*

af·fec·tion /ə'fɛkʃən/ n. [U] 1 a feeling close
to love, warmth for s.o.: *He feels affection for
his grandchildren.* 2 tender actions, such as
hugging and kind words: *The child needs his
mother's affection.*

af·fec·tion·ate /ə'fɛkʃənɪt/ adj. loving, warm:
*She is an affectionate child and loves to be
hugged and kissed.* -adv. **affectionately.**

af·fi·da·vit /,æfə'deɪvɪt/ n. a written statement
that a person swears is true before a notary
public or other official: *I gave an affidavit to
the judge about the accident I witnessed.*

A

af·fil·i·ate /ə'fɪliɪt/ n. a business or person associated with another business or person: *Our New York company has an affiliate in Los Angeles.*
—v. /ə'fɪli,eɪt/ **-ted, -ting, -tes** to join with, become part of: *We became affiliated with this company last year.*

af·fil·i·a·tion /ə,fɪli'eɪʃən/ n. [C;U] an association, relationship: *There is no affiliation between our organization and theirs, even though our names are similar.*

af·fin·i·ty /ə'fɪnəti/ n.frml. **-ties** **1** [C] a liking, attraction to: *He has an affinity for fine food.* **2** [C;U] a likeness, similarity: *You can see the affinity in appearance between mother and daughter.*

af·firm /ə'fɜrm/ v. to repeat s.t. as being true, to confirm: *He affirmed his plan to make payments on time.* -n.[C;U] **affirmation** /,æfər'meɪʃən/.

af·firm·a·tive /ə'fɜrmətɪv/ adj. positive, saying "yes": *He replied in the affirmative to my question.* -adv. **affirmatively.**

af·firm·a·tive action n. [U] employment practices that look for and encourage minorities, women, and the handicapped to apply for jobs: *Our company has an affirmative action program to avoid discrimination in hiring.*

af·fix /ə'fɪks/ v.frml. **-ed, -fixing, -fixes** to put on, attach: *He affixed the sign to the wall.*

af·flict /ə'flɪkt/ v.frml. to cause pain, make suffer: *Disease and poverty afflict many people.* -n.[C;U] **affliction** / ə'flɪkʃən/.

af·flu·ence /'æfluəns/ n. [U] wealth, (syn.) prosperity: *There is a lot of affluence in this part of the state because it has many businesses.*

af·flu·ent /'æfluənt/ adj. wealthy, (syn.) prosperous: *He is an affluent man.*
—n.pl. prosperous people: *The affluent are located mainly in towns near big cities.* -adv. **affluently.**

af·ford /ə'fɔrd/ v. **1** to be able to pay for s.t. without difficulty: *We can't afford that expensive car.* **2** to risk: *He can't afford to travel alone for fear of being kidnapped.* **3** frml.to provide, give: *The tall building affords a beautiful view of the ocean.*

af·ford·a·ble /ə'fɔrdəbəl/ adj. capable of being paid for without difficulty, not too expensive: *There are few affordable apartments in big cities.*

af·front /ə'frʌnt/ n.frml. an insult, (syn.) an outrage: *His refusal to see me was an affront.*
—v. frml. to insult, (syn.) to offend: *I was affronted by his actions.*

a·field /ə'fild/ adv. away, esp. from a familiar area: *Once he starts talking, he will go far afield from his original topic.*

a·fire /ə'faɪr/ adj. on fire, burning, (syn.) ablaze: *The house is afire!*

a·flame /ə'fleɪm/ adj. **1** ablaze, in flames: *The curtains are aflame!* **2** fig. full of emotion, (syn.) impassioned: *Her heart is aflame with love for him.*

a·float /ə'flout/ adj. on or above the water: *The boat is afloat.*
—adv. fig. not in bad trouble, surviving: *His business is having difficulty, but it is staying afloat.*

a·foot /ə'fʊt/ adj.adv. **1** on foot **2** fig. happening, esp. s.t. dishonest, negative, or strange: *There's s.t. afoot here, but I don't know what it is.*

a·fore·men·tioned /ə'fɔr,mɛnʃənd/ adj.frml. stated before, said earlier in writing or speech: *The aforementioned person was at the scene of the accident.*

a·fraid /ə'freɪd/ adj. **1** fearful, (syn.) apprehensive: *The child is afraid of dogs.* **2** feeling sorry, not wanting to tell s.o. s.t.: *I'm afraid that I have bad news for you.*

a·fresh /ə'frɛʃ/ adv. from the beginning, (syn.) anew: *I wrote a letter that I didn't like, so I started afresh on a new one.*

Af·ri·can-American /'æfrɪkən/ n.adj. an American of African descent: *He is an <n.> African-American (or) <adj.> is African American.* See: Black.

USAGE NOTE: Compare *African-American* and *Black.* In the USA, the terms African-American and Black are both used to identify Americans of African descent. Some people prefer to use the term African-American, others prefer the term Black.

Af·ro /'æfrou/prefix. adj. related to Africa: *Afro-American culture is widespread in the USA.*
—n. a type of round, fluffy hairstyle: *Afros were popular in the 1960s.*

Af·ro-A·mer·i·can n.adj. old usage an American of African descent: *She is an <n.> Afro-American (or) <adj.> is Afro-American.* See: African-American.

af·ter /'æftər/ prep. **1** in back of, behind: *I told my dog to stay home, but he followed after me.* **2** in search of, toward: *A police officer chased after the criminal.* **3** later in time: *We had dinner after the movie.*
—conj. later than: *She arrived at the party after I did.*
—adv. **after all** or **after all is said and done:** all things considered: *He should do well at college, after all; he is a very smart boy.*

af·ter·ef·fect /'æftərɪ,fɛkt/ n. a problem directly resulting from an experience: *He was at a party all night and felt the aftereffects, a headache and a stomach ache, the next day.*

af·ter·life /'æftər,laɪf/ n. [U] life after death: *People of many religions believe in an afterlife.*

af·ter·math /'æftər,mæθ/ n. [U] the usu. bad result, or (syn.) consequence, of s.t.: *In the aftermath of the hurricane, many people's homes were destroyed.*

af·ter·noon /,æftər'nun/ n. the time between noon and evening: *At school, we play sports in the afternoon.*

af·ter·thought /'æftər,θɔt/ n. idea(s) that s.o. thinks of after an event: *After he wrote the report, he had several afterthoughts that were too late to put in it.*

af·ter·ward /'æftərwərd/ or **afterwards** adv. after an event, (syn.) subsequently: *We went for a walk, and afterward we ate lunch.*

a·gain /ə'gɛn/ adv. **1** another time, once more: *Oh, it's raining again!* **2 again and again:** repeatedly, frequently: *I've told you again and again not to spend so much money!*

a·gainst /ə'gɛnst/ prep. **1** touching, next to, near: *The bookshelves are against the wall.* **2** in strong contact with: *Hurricane winds hit against the buildings.* **3** in opposition to, feeling negative toward: *The people voted against that new tax.* **4** subtracted from: *I wrote two checks against my bank account.* **5 as against:** in comparison to: *I like my new car, as against the old one which did not run well.*

age /eɪdʒ/ n. **1** [C;U] how many years s.o. has lived: *The boy is 15 years of age.* **2** [U] a time period in life: *Middle age starts after 40.||That lady died of old age, not disease.* **3** [C] a historical time period: *The ancient Greeks spoke of a Golden Age.*
—v. **1** to grow older: *He is 60 years old but has aged well.* **2** to ripen, mature: *Wine ages in barrels before it is put into bottles.*

a·gen·cy /'eɪdʒənsi/ n. **-cies 1** a part of government: *The Environmental Protection Agency tries to stop pollution.* **2** a type of business that helps people do s.t., (syn.) a bureau: *She found a job through an employment agency.*

a·gen·da /ə'dʒɛndə/ n. **1** a list of topics to be talked about: *The three-day meeting of scientists covered a long agenda.* **2** a calendar or date book.

a·gent /'eɪdʒənt/ n. **1** a person who does business for others, representative: *A travel agent makes airline and hotel reservations.||She is a literary agent who represents authors.* **2** a spy or special government employee: *He is an FBI agent.* **3** a person or thing that causes an effect: *People use chemical agents to clean things.*

age of con·sent n. the legal age at which a person may agree to have sex: *The age of consent in this state is 18.*

ag·gra·vate / 'ægrə,veɪt/ v. **-vated, -vating, -vates 1** to irritate, annoy: *He aggravates me by complaining all the time.* **2** to worsen, (syn.) to exacerbate: *I hurt my foot, then aggravated it by trying to walk too soon.* -n. **aggravation.** *See:* anger, v., USAGE NOTE(S).

ag·gre·gate /'ægrəgɪt/ n.[C;U] /'ægrə,geɪt/ adj.v. **-gated, -gating, -gates 1** s.t. made of separate parts: *The population of Los Angeles is an aggregate of people from nearly all the world's countries.* **2 in the aggregate:** with all things considered: *In the aggregate, I am happy with my life at this moment.* -n. [U] **aggregation** /,ægrə'geɪʃən/.

ag·gres·sion /ə'grɛʃən/ n. [U] unfriendly or harmful action against s.o.: *He committed an act of aggression by walking up to the man and hitting him.* -n. **aggressor** /ə'grɛsər/.

ag·gres·sive /ə'grɛsɪv/ adj. **1** unfriendly, (syn.) hostile: *That dog always barks at strangers; he's very aggressive.* **2** competitive, (syn.) assertive: *Our company has several aggressive salespeople.* -adv. **aggressively;** -n. **aggressiveness.**

ag·grieved /ə'grivd/ adj. wronged, esp. in a moral or legal way, mistreated: *She is the aggrieved person whose fiancé did not show up for their wedding.*

a·ghast /ə'gæst/ adj. shocked, esp. with one's mouth open in surprise, (syn.) horrified: *He was aghast when he learned that all his retirement money was lost.*

a·ging /'eɪdʒɪŋ/ n. **1** the process of growing old: *His aging does not permit him to work anymore.* **2** the process of growing mature or ripe: *Wine growers put wine in a cellar for aging.*

a·gile /'ædʒəl, 'æ,dʒaɪl/ adj. quick and skillful in moving, (syn.) nimble: *She is such an agile dancer!* -adv. **agilely;** -n. [U] **agility.**

ag·i·tate /'ædʒə,teɪt/ v. **-tated, -tating, -tates 1** to argue or fight for a cause, (syn.) to incite: *He is a politician who agitates constantly for change.* **2** to irritate, disturb: *She was agitated because her train was an hour late.* -n. [U] (act) **agitation** / ,ædʒə'teɪʃən/; [C] (person) **agitator** / 'ædʒə,teɪtər/.

a·glit·ter /ə'glɪtər/ adj. shining brightly, (syn.) sparkling: *At night, the New York City skyline is aglitter with lights in tall buildings.*

a·glow /ə'glou/ adj. **1** frml. giving off (light, warmth), (syn.) radiating: *The wood stove is aglow with heat.* **2** fig. happy, (syn.) delighted: *He is aglow with the feeling of success.*

ag·nos·tic /æg'nɑstɪk, əg-/ n.adj. s.o. who believes God may exist but is unknowable: *He was an <n.> agnostic until he was cured of cancer; then he became very religious.* -n. [U] **agnosticism** / æg'nɑstə,sɪzəm, əg-/.

a·go /ə'goʊ/ *adv.* in the past, (*syn.*) previously: *We met for the first time five years ago.*

ag·o·nize /'ægə,naɪz/ *v.* **-nized, -nizing, -nizes** **1** to suffer great pain: *He broke his leg and agonized for hours before s.o. found him.* **2** to suffer mental or emotional pain about s.t.: *She agonized for days over whether to take a job in another city.*

ag·o·ni·zing /'ægə,naɪzɪŋ/ *n.* [U] *adj.* the suffering of physical pain or indecision: *He did a lot of <n.> agonizing before deciding to quit his job; it was an <adj.> agonizing decision for him.* *-adv.* **agonizingly.**

ag·o·ny /'ægəni/ *n.* [C;U] **-nies** great pain: *She burned herself on the stove and was in agony.*

a·grar·i·an /ə'grɛriən/ *adj.frml.* related to farming and farmland: *People are leaving an agrarian way of life to go to the city. -n.* [U] **agrarianism.**

a·gree /ə'gri/ *v.* **agreed, agreeing, agrees** **1** to have the same idea or opinion, (*syn.*) to concur: *He agreed with what I said.* **2** to approve, esp. after disagreeing, (*syn.*) to consent: *He agreed to buy the more expensive watch.*

a·gree·a·ble /ə'griəbəl/ *adj.* **1** willing, (*syn.*) amenable: *The buyer is agreeable to paying the price that we asked.* **2** friendly, (*syn.*) congenial: *He is an agreeable man who always wants to make people happy. -adv.* **agreeably.**

a·greed /ə'grid/ *adj.* **1** accepted, approved: *Are you willing to pay that price? Yes, agreed.* **2** acceptable to everyone involved, (*syn.*) in accord: *I will pay the agreed-upon price.*

a·gree·ment /ə'grimənt/ *n.* **1** [C] a decision between two or more people, an understanding: *We have an agreement not to talk about certain things.* **2** [C] a written arrangement, contract: *We reached an agreement and signed it yesterday.* **3 to be in agreement:** sharing the same view or opinion

ag·ri·cul·ture /'ægrɪ,kʌltʃər/ *n.* [U] the science of growing food: *Agriculture is a big business in North America. -adj.* **agricultural** /,ægrɪ'kʌltʃərəl/.

a·ground /ə'graʊnd/ *adv.adj.* stuck on or in sand, soil, rocks, etc.: *Our ship ran <adv.> aground on some rocks in the fog; it was <adj.> aground for several hours.*

ah /ɑ/ *exclam.* expression of surprise, disgust, pain, understanding, pleasure, etc.: (disgust) *Ah! This is a waste of time!*||(pleasure) *Ahhhhh! The taste of a cold beer on a hot day is great!*

a·head /ə'hɛd/ *adv.* **1** forward: *The traffic is bad, but I am moving ahead slowly.* **2** in the distance: *There is a car accident ahead causing this traffic jam.* **3** to a better position: *She works very hard to get ahead in life.*
—*prep.* **ahead of:** in front of: *He stepped ahead of everyone else in line.*

a·hoy /ə'hɔɪ/ *exclam.* (among sailors) a greeting, upon sighting another ship

aid /eɪd/ *v.* to help financially or physically, (*syn.*) to assist: *I aided my friend by giving him some money.*
—*n.* **1** [U] help, assistance: *The Red Cross gives aid in the form of both money and material goods to those in need of it.* **2** [C] s.t. useful, such as tools or other equipment: *A computer is an aid in writing.*||*She doesn't hear well and wears a hearing aid.*

aide or **aid** /eɪd/ *n.* a helper, assistant: *She is a nurse's aide.*

AIDS /eɪdz/ *abbr. for* acquired immune deficiency syndrome

USAGE NOTE: People with *AIDS* die because their bodies can't fight the illnesses they develop. As there is no cure for AIDS, private and government organizations are trying to teach the public how to stop the disease from spreading. Many community groups help feed and care for people living with AIDS. *See:* HIV.

ail /eɪl/ *v.* **1** to be sick, (*syn.*) to suffer illness: *The patient is ailing from his fever.* **2** to be bothered by s.t., to be annoyed: *I wonder what's ailing him today; he's so irritable.*

ail·ment /'eɪlmənt/ *n.* an illness, esp. a lasting condition: *His ailments include a mild heart condition and arthritis.*

aim /eɪm/ *v.* **1** to direct s.t., such as a gun or ball, at a certain point: *He aimed the basketball at the net and shot the ball.* **2** *fig.* to direct one's words or actions toward a person or group: *The boss's comments were aimed at you.* **3** to plan to do s.t.: *She aims to go to college.*

aim·less·ly /'eɪmlɪsli/ *adv.* **1** without purpose: *She talked aimlessly, because she disliked silence.* **2** without direction: *He walked around aimlessly trying to find a way out of the woods.*||*He went (fig.) aimlessly through life. -adj.* **aimless.**

ain't /eɪnt/ *infrml.slang contr. of* is not or are not: *I (we, they, he, etc.) ain't ready to leave yet.*

USAGE NOTE: *Ain't* is common in some dialects of English: *She ain't here yet.*||*I ain't seen her.* Most people avoid using it in school or business situations.

air /ɛr/ *n.* [U] **1** the gases that surround the earth and which we breathe: *The air in the countryside is cleaner than the air of the city.* **2** the actions or appearance, (*syn.*) the manner: *She has the air of a lady.* **3** *n.pl.* false behavior, (*syn.*) affectations: *He sometimes puts on airs pretending that he's rich, when he is not.* **4 in the air:** a general feeling, scent: *Spring is*

in the air. **5 on** or **off the air:** to start or stop showing or playing on TV or radio: *My favorite radio station goes on the air at 5:00 A.M. and goes off the air at 1:00 P.M.* **6 to be full of hot air:** to speak foolishness, nonsense: *He doesn't know what he's talking about; he's full of hot air.* **7 to take the air:** to go for a walk: *It's hot in here; I think I'll take the air.* **8 to walk on air:** to be very happy, *(syn.)* elated: *When she heard about her acceptance to college, she was walking on air for days.* **9 up in the air:** undecided, *(syn.)* uncertain: *We planned on leaving tomorrow, but our plans are up in the air because I feel sick.*
—*v.* **1** to put out in the air, esp. to dry or freshen: *He hung his clothes in the yard to air.* **2** to speak about: *He aired his feelings about love and marriage.* **3** to show or play on television or radio, *(syn.)* to broadcast: *Channel 7 aired a show about lions in Africa. See:* airs.

air·borne /'ɛr,bɔrn/ *adj.* moving in the air: *Our plane has lifted off the runway and is now airborne.*

air-con·di·tion *v.* to cool the air with an air conditioner; to install an air-conditioning system: *We air-conditioned our house to stay cool during the hot summer. -n.*(machine) **air conditioner.**

air con·di·tion·ing *n.* [U] a machine or a system used to cool air in buildings

air·craft /'ɛr,kræft/ *n.* **-craft** an airplane, glider, or other flight vehicle: *The Air Force maintains many kinds of aircraft.*

air·craft car·ri·er *n.* a large ship that acts as a military airport at sea: *The aircraft carrier has 5,000 workers and 50 airplanes.*

aircraft carrier

air·fare /'ɛr,fɛr/ *n.* the cost of an airline ticket

air·field /'ɛr,fild/ *n.* an area from which airplanes take off and land, usu. smaller than an airport and without buildings

air force *n.* the part of a nation's military force that flies planes: *The air force flies planes around the country's border.*

air·ing /'ɛrɪŋ/ *n.* [C;U] public discussion: *Politicians gave the matter of a new health care plan an airing on television.*

air·lift /'ɛr,lɪft/ *n.* a system that delivers goods or people by airplane: *The government ordered an airlift of medical and food supplies to the disaster area because the roads were destroyed.*

air·line /'ɛr,laɪn/ *n.* a business that carries passengers and cargo by airplane: *Airlines compete with each other for passengers.*

air·li·ner /'ɛr,laɪnər/ *n.* an airplane made especially to carry passengers, baggage, and light cargo

air·mail /'ɛr,meɪl/ *n.* [U] *adj.* letters, packages, etc. shipped by air: *A letter sent <n.> airmail will get to Europe quickly.*

air·plane /'ɛrpleɪn/ *n.* a machine for flying passengers or goods: *The airplane allows people to travel large distances quickly.*

air·port /'ɛrpɔrt/ *n.* a place where planes take off and land with buildings for passengers and cargo

air raid *n.* an attack by military airplanes dropping bombs and shooting at a ground target

airs /'ɛrz/ *n.pl. See:* air, *n.,* 3.

air·space /'ɛr,speɪs/ *n.* the sky above a country: *The nation reported that a foreign aircraft was in its airspace.*

air·strip /'ɛr,strɪp/ *n.* a small path or field for planes to take off and land: *We flew over the jungle to an airstrip near a river.*

air·tight /'ɛr,taɪt/ *adj.* **1** not allowing air to enter or leave s.t., sealed: *The fish is packed in airtight cans.* **2** *fig.* completely believable, able to be proved: *The police officer has an airtight case against the criminal.*

air·time /'ɛr,taɪm/ *n.* [U] **1** the amount of time a pilot spends flying in the air: *Student pilots must put in a lot of airtime before getting licensed.* **2** the amount of time that a radio or TV show is on the air: *The government hearings on crime used a lot of airtime on TV.*

air·waves /'ɛr,weɪvz/ *n.pl.* all radio and television signals as a group: *News that the war had ended was sent out over the airwaves.*

air·y /'ɛri/ *adj.* **-ier, -iest** open, *(syn.)* breezy: *All the windows were open, giving the house an airy feeling. -adv.* **airily** /'ɛrəli/.

aisle /aɪl/ *n.* a long open path between rows of seats: *We walked down the aisle to our seats in the theater.*

a·jar /ə'dʒar/ *adj.* slightly open: *The door was ajar, so the cat was able to come in.*

a·kin /ə'kɪn/ *adj.* like, similar to: *He writes romantic adventure stories akin to those of earlier writers.*

à la carte /,alə'kart, ,ælə-/ *adj.adv.* (French for) ordering each dish separately instead of a complete meal: *I ordered roast chicken and a vegetable à la carte, but no salad or dessert.*

à la mode /,alə'moʊd, ,ælə-/ *adj.* served with ice cream: *I love apple pie à la mode.*

a·larm /ə'larm/ *n.* **1** [C] a warning device, such as a bell, siren, or buzzer: *A prisoner set off an alarm as she tried to escape.* **2** [C] a warning call or signal: *A guard shouted an alarm as he saw the prisoner running away.* **3** [U] shock, fear: *The other guards saw the escape with alarm.*

A

—*v.* to warn, signal danger: *The escape of the dangerous prisoner alarmed people who lived in the area.*

a·larm clock *n.* a clock that can be set to give a signal at a later time: *I set the alarm clock to wake me up at 7:00 A.M.*

a·larm·ist /ə'lɑrmɪst/ *n.* a person who gives others false or misleading alarms: *She always talks about the worst that can happen; she's an alarmist.*

a·las /ə'læs/ *frml. exclam. of* sadness, regret, or disappointment: *Alas, my love, I must leave now.*

al·ba·tross /'ælbə,trɔs, -,trɑs/ *n.* **-es 1** a large seabird **2** *fig.* a problem, s.t. stopping progress: *The man cannot read, which is an albatross around his neck.*

al·be·it /ɔl'biət, æl-/ *conj.frml.* even though, despite: *Albeit difficult, the job is getting done.*

al·bin·o /æl'baɪnoʊ/ *n.* **-nos** a person or animal without skin pigment: *That albino horse has a white coat and blue eyes.*

al·bum /'ælbəm/ *n.* **1** a book with blank pages for holding photographs, newspaper articles, and other things: *We have a photo album full of family pictures.* **2** a collection of musical pieces: *The singer recorded an album of her most popular songs.*

al·che·mist /'ælkəmɪst/ *n.* a scientist of the Middle Ages who tried to change other metals into gold *-n.* [U] **alchemy.**

al·co·hol /'ælkə,hɔl, -,hɑl-/ *n.* [U] **1** a colorless liquid that can be made naturally from grains or fruits: *Alcohol burns easily and can be used as a fuel.* **2** the many beverages made from grains and fruits, such as wine, vodka, and gin: *You should not drink alcohol and then drive.*

al·co·hol·ic /,ælkə'hɔlɪk, -'hɑ-/ *adj.* related to alcohol: *The alcoholic content of some beers and wines is as high as 12-13 percent.*
—*n.* a person who has great difficulty not drinking alcohol because he or she suffers from the disease of alcoholism: *He is a recovering alcoholic; he used to drink a lot of alcohol, but now he never drinks. -n.* [U] **alcoholism** /'ælkə,hɔ,lɪzəm, -,hɑ-/.

al·cove /'æl,koʊv/ *n.* a small, partly enclosed area that opens off a room: *We eat breakfast at a table in an alcove in our kitchen.*

al·der·man /'ɔldərmən/ *n.* **-men** /-mən/ a low-level government official, esp. an elected member of a city council: *My brother won an election as alderman for our area in Wyoming. -n.* **alderwoman.**

ale /eɪl/ *n.* [C;U] an alcoholic beverage similar to beer but with a higher alcohol content: *I sometimes enjoy a pint of ale.*

a·lert /ə'lɜrt/ *adj.* **1** aware, *(syn.)* attentive: *The guard stayed alert to watch for anything un-* usual. **2** bright, intelligent: *Their son is an alert little boy.*

al·gae /'ælʤi/ *n.pl.* simple tiny plants that live in water: *The green covering on top of the water in that pond is algae. -n.sing.* **alga** /'ælgə/.

al·ge·bra /'ælʤəbrə/ *n.* [U] a branch of mathematics using signs and symbols to represent unknown numbers in a problem. *The letter x represents 4 in the algebra problem* $x + 3 = 7$. *-adj.* **algebraic** /,ælʤə'breɪɪk/; *-adv.* **algebraically.**

al·go·rithm /'ælgə,rɪðəm/ *n.* (in computers) a set of instructions to do s.t. specific: *Common computer languages, such as BASIC or FORTRAN, use algorithms to perform their functions.*

a·li·as /'eɪliəs, 'eɪlyəs/ *n.adv.* **-es** a name used to hide one's identity, esp. by criminals, a false name, *(syn.)* a pseudonym: *His real name is John Smith, but he lives under an alias, Johann Schmidt.*

al·i·bi /'ælə,baɪ/ *n.* (in law) proof that a person was not near a crime scene and therefore could not have committed the crime: *The police think that he committed the crime, but he has a good alibi proving he was out of town at the time.*

a·li·en /'eɪliən, 'eɪlyən/ *n.* a stranger, *(syn.)* a foreigner: *He is an alien in this country; he is here on a student visa.*
—*adj.* **1** belonging to another country, *(syn.)* foreign: *Alien goods are brought into this country illegally.* **2** from another planet, *(syn.)* extraterrestrial **3** different, not typical: *Cheating is alien to his nature.*

al·ien·ate /'eɪliə,neɪt, 'eɪlyə-/ *v.* **-nated, -nating, -nates 1** to make an enemy of s.o., *(syn.)* to estrange: *He alienated most of his friends by drinking too much.* **2** to make one feel that one does not belong, to separate: *Many people feel alienated in new places. -n.* [U] **alienation** /,eɪliə'neɪʃən, ,eɪlyə-/.

a·light /ə'laɪt/ *v.* **alighted** or **alit** /ə'lɪt/, **alighting, alights** to land, descend upon: *A bird flew through the air and then alit on the telephone wire.*

a·lign /ə'laɪn/ *v.* **1** to place one or more objects in line with another: *The worker aligned the chairs in straight rows in the meeting hall.* **2** to join, *(syn.)* to affiliate: *Two small political parties aligned themselves so that together they would have more power. -n.*[C;U] **alignment.**

a·like /ə'laɪk/ *adj.* similar, *(syn.)* comparable: *The two dresses look alike in shape, length, and color.*

a·li·mo·ny /'ælə,moʊni/ *n.* [U] regular payments a person makes to his or her former spouse: *He paid alimony to his former wife until she married again.*

a·live /ə'laɪv/ *adj.* **1** living, functioning: *After the accident, he was barely alive.* **2** *fig.* energetic, full of life: *The football stadium is alive with excitement.*

all /ɔl/ *adj.* **1** of a total: *All the students (adults, citizens, etc.) came to the meeting.* **2** regarding the most of s.t.: *In all honesty, I hate my job.* **3 all in:** to be exhausted, totally fatigued: *The runner finished the race but afterwards he was all in.*
—*n.* **1 all or nothing:** unless s.t. is done, all will be lost: *We either put more money in the business or close it; it's all or nothing.* **2** *adv.* **all the same:** no difference: *It's all the same to me if he leaves or stays.* **3** *infrml.fig.* **and all that** or **and all that jazz:** et cetera, and all else: *We moved our furniture, books, refrigerator, and all that jazz to a new apartment.* **4 on all fours: a.** (people) on both hands and knees: *He got down on all fours to look for the pin that he had dropped.* **b.** (animals) on all four legs: *Dogs and cats walk on all fours.* **5 the be all and end all:** (usu. ironic) a total solution, ultimate happiness: *My boss has bought a new computer system, which he sees as the be all and end all of his problems.* **6 to give one's all:** to give one's total energy (effort, commitment): *She gave her all to finish the job on time.*
—*pron.* **1** everyone, everything: *My friends and I attended a party and all had a good time.* **2 all but:** most, all except: *All but a few people ran toward the speaker.*
—*adv.* **1** totally, completely: *Jack was upset because he came late and the beer was all gone.* **2** for a given time period: *It rained all night (day, week, etc.).* **3 all along:** at the same time, for the whole time s.t. else was happening: *He knew all along that he was dying of cancer, but he stayed cheerful.* **4 all at once:** suddenly, abruptly: *The crowd was quiet; then all at once it began to applaud.* **5** *infrml.fig.* **all fired up:** excited, (*syn.*) eager: *The audience is all fired up by what the speaker has said.* **6 all in all:** considering everything: *It rained for a while, but all in all we had a good time at the picnic.* **7 all in good time:** eventually: *Don't worry; that problem will be taken care of all in good time.* **8** *adv.* **all of a sudden:** abruptly, by total surprise: *We were driving in the country when all of a sudden a deer ran across the road.* **9** *n.* **all out:** with total effort, (*syn.*) completely dedicated: *We have to go all out to finish the job on time.* **10 all over: a.** everywhere, covered completely: *The dog knocked over the dish, and water spilled all over.* **b.** finished, (*syn.*) terminated: *Our relationship is finished; it's all over between us.* **11** *n.* **all right: a.** well, healthy: *I feel all right today.* **b.** OK, yes: *Would you like to join us? All right.* **c.** satis-

factorily: *The motor in the car works all right.* **d.** *exclam.infrml.* wonderful, great: *The football team scored, and a fan shouted, "All right!"* **12** *infrml.fig.vulg.* **all the way:** (to have) sex: *The couple hugged and kissed, but she refused to go all the way.* **13** *adv.* **all things considered:** taking everything into account: *We made a profit this year, so all things considered, we did well.* **14 all told:** *adv.* in total, in sum: *All told, five thousand people were at the concert.* **15 at all:** (used with a negative) totally: *I don't like the way that you are behaving at all, so stop it!*

all-A·mer·i·can *adj.* **1** of an honor given to the best college athletes in the USA: *He is an all-American football player from Notre Dame.* **2** a person who has all the best American qualities: *She is an all-American girl.*
—*n.* a male athlete awarded such an honor: *He is an all-American from Notre Dame.*

all-a·round *adj.* complete, total: *He is an all-around athlete who can play many sports very well. See:* well-rounded.

al·lay /ə'leɪ/ *v.frml.* to calm, to make (fears, doubts, etc.) less strong: *The leader allayed the fears of his followers by telling them success was near.*

al·lege /ə'lɛdʒ/ *v.* **-leged, -leging, -leges** to claim but not yet prove that s.o. has committed a crime: *The police allege that man stole the car, but they must go to court to prove it.* -*n.* **allegation** /,ælə'geɪʃən/.

al·le·giance /ə'lidʒəns/ *n.* [C;U] loyalty, strong feeling for a country, leader, political cause: *Schoolchildren say the Pledge of Allegiance to the US flag every morning.*

al·le·go·ry /'ælə,gɔri/ *n.* [C;U] **-ries** a story, poem, or play in which the people, things, and events have a second meaning, usu. religious or moral -*adj.* **allegorical** /,ælə'gɔrɪkəl/; -*adv.* **allegorically.** *See:* fable.

al·ler·gic /ə'lɜrdʒɪk / *adj.* very sensitive to some plants, chemicals, dust, or foods: *When I go near plants that I'm allergic to, I start sneezing.*

al·ler·gy /'ælərdʒi/ *n.* **-gies** an unusually high sensitivity to substances such as certain plants, chemicals, foods, animals, or dust: *She has an allergy to cats that makes her sneeze.*

al·le·vi·ate /ə'livi,eɪt/ *v.frml.* **-ated, -ating, -ates** to make less difficult (painful, etc.), (*syn.*) to relieve: *The medicine alleviated the pain.* -*n.* [U] **alleviation.**

al·ley /'æli/ *n.* **-leys 1** a path between or behind buildings: *We walked down an alley and entered the building from the back door.* **2** *infrml.fig.* **to be up one's alley:** (to have) a job or activity that one likes very much: *Using*

A

computers is right up my alley; I love them! See: blind alley.

al·li·ance /ə'laɪəns/ n. [C;U] a group of countries (political parties, people, etc.) joined for a purpose: *The two nations formed an alliance to make peace between them.* See: ally.

al·lied /ə'laɪd, 'ælaɪd/ adj. united, joined for a purpose

al·li·ga·tor /'ælə,geɪtər/ n. a large animal (reptile) of the crocodile family, but with a shorter, broader head: *Both alligators and crocodiles have long bodies and tails, short legs, and strong jaws with sharp teeth.*

alligator

all-in·clu·sive adj. complete, including everything: *The price of the vacation tour is all-inclusive (of hotel, meals, and transportation).*

al·li·ter·a·tion /ə,lɪtə'reɪʃən/ n. [U] the repetition of the same sound, usu. at the beginning of words: *The sentence, "Happy Harry hates to hurry" uses alliteration. -adj.* **alliterative** /ə'lɪtərətɪv, -,reɪtɪv/.

al·lo·cate /'ælə,keɪt/ v. **-cated, -cating, -cates** to plan to use an amount of money for a specific purpose, (syn.) to allot: *The city government allocated money for schools and the police in this year's budget. -n.* [U] **allocation** /,ælə'keɪʃən/.

al·lot /ə'lɑt/ v. **-lotted, -lotting, -lots** to allocate, plan on a sum of money for a specific use: *I allotted money from my household budget for a new car. -n.* **allotment.**

al·low /ə'laʊ/ v. **1** to let, permit: *We allowed our son to use the family car.* **2** to agree reluctantly, (syn.) to concede: *The witness allowed that he had not told the complete truth. -adj.* **allowable.**

al·low·ance /ə'laʊəns/ n. **1** money for everyday expenses: *We give our son a weekly allowance.* **2** (in business) money set aside to cover a loss or debt: *We set aside an allowance for bad debts this year.* **3 to make allowances for:** to forgive s.o.'s weaknesses: *She made a few mistakes playing the violin, but you should make allowances for her since she's only been playing for a year.*

al·loy /'ælɔɪ/ n. **-loys** a mixture of metals: *Bronze is an alloy of copper and tin.*

all-pur·pose adj. with many uses: *Swiss Army knives are all-purpose instruments, with a knife, screwdriver, saw, scissors, and other tools.*

all-star adj. among the best players in sports or the best entertainers (movie stars, singers, etc.): *The all-star football game will be played this weekend.*

all-time adj. **1** for all time, forever: *The band is playing my all-time favorite song.* **2** the best, worst, highest, etc. so far: *The temperature was at an all-time low last night; it has never been that cold before.*

al·lude /ə'lud/ v.frml. **-luded, -luding, -ludes** to talk or write about s.t. indirectly, (syn.) to intimate: *The politician alluded to the idea that she might not run for office again.*

al·lure /ə'lʊr/ v.frml. **-lured, -luring, -lures** to attract with s.t. desirable, (syn.) to tempt: *He was allured by the hope of making a lot of money easily.*
—n. [U] attractiveness: *She is a woman with great allure.*

al·lu·sion /ə'luʒən/ n. talking or writing about s.o. or s.t. indirectly: *He made an allusion to his wife without saying her name.*

al·ly /'ælaɪ, ə'laɪ/ n. **-lies** a partner, friend: *The USA and Great Britain were allies in World War II.*
—v. /ə'laɪ, 'ælaɪ/ **-lies** to combine, unite: *Several political parties allied with each other against higher taxes.* See: alliance.

al·ma ma·ter /,ælmə'mɑtər, ,ɑl-/ n. **1** (Latin for) the university, college, or high school where one studied: *My alma mater is Williams College.* **2** the school song

al·ma·nac /'ɔlmə,næk/ n. a book giving the days of the year, holidays, and the times, tides, and phases of the moon: *The Old Farmer's Almanac is a favorite publication of many people, esp. for its weather forecasts.*

al·migh·ty /ɔl'maɪti/ adj.infrml.fig. great, (syn.) extreme: *He is always in an almighty hurry to go somewhere.*
—n. **All Mighty** /ɔl'maɪti/God, the Supreme Deity: *He prays to the All Mighty everyday.*

al·mond /'ɑmənd, 'æ-/ n. **1** a nut tree first grown in Mediterranean countries **2** the nut itself: *In California, I ate fresh almonds right off the tree!*
—adj. a light brown color: *He wore an almond sweater.*

al·most /'ɔlmoust, ɔl'moust/ adv. **1** nearly, not quite: *I have almost finished my homework.* **2** just short of being correct: *The pants almost fit, but they are too tight.*

alms /ɑmz/ n.pl.frml. money, food, etc. given to poor people: *The Bible speaks of giving alms to the poor.*

a·loft /ə'lɔft/ adv. **1** in flight, in the air: *All the planes are aloft.* **2** up in a ship's sails: *Sailors go aloft on a ship to set the sails.*

a·lone /ə'loun/ adv. **1** by oneself, without anyone else: *He is not married and lives alone.* **2** by itself, only: *The cost of the hotel alone is very high; meals and air travel cost extra.* **3 to go it alone:** to act or work by oneself: *She had a business partner, but she's going it alone now.* **4 to leave s.o.** or **s.t. alone:** not to disturb or bother s.o. or s.t.: *Leave me alone; I don't feel well.* **5 to leave** or **let well enough alone:** to avoid more action on s.t.: *My car works all right, so I left well enough alone and did not try to make it work better.*

a·long /ə'lɔŋ/ *prep.* **1** by the side of: *Cars are parked along the sides of the street.* **2** in the route or path of: *Trucks are moving along the highway at high speed.*
—*adv.* **1** forward, into the future: *I have to move along now; see you later.* **2** with another person: *Joe brought his girlfriend along to the party.* **3 to be along:** to arrive: *He's left his house; he'll be along soon.* **4** *phrasal v. insep.* **to come** or **go along for the ride:** to go with s.o. for the fun of it: *She had to take a business trip to Chicago, so she asked her husband if he would like to come along for the ride.* **5** *phrasal v. insep.* **to· get along: a.** to leave: *I have to get along now; see you later.* **b.** to be friendly with, to be on good terms with: *My boss and I get along just fine together.* **6** *phrasal v. insep.* **to go along with: a.** to go with s.o.: *I'll go along with you to do some shopping.* **b.** to agree with, support: *He goes along with my idea of starting a new business.* **c.** to agree reluctantly, (*syn.*) to acquiesce: *I didn't want to argue, so I went along with his idea.*

a·long·side /ə,lɔŋ'saɪd/ *prep.adv.* beside, close to: *Another boat pulled alongside <adv.> ours. The boat is now alongside <prep.> our boat.*

a·loof /ə'luf/ *adj.* **1** distant, not willing to participate: *The President should remain aloof from everyday politics, but often does not.* **2** emotionally distant, (*syn.*) snobbish: *She acts aloof toward people because she is very shy.*

a·loud /ə'laʊd/ *adv.* out loud, spoken: *The student read her poem aloud in class.*

al·pha /'ælfə/ *n.* the first letter of the Greek alphabet *See:* omega.

al·pha·bet /'ælfə,bɛt/ *n.* **1** the letters in a language: *The English alphabet has 26 letters.* **2** *fig.* **alphabet soup:** a mixture of many different things: *The population of North America is an alphabet soup of people from Argentina to Zimbabwe.*

al·pha·be·ti·cal /,ælfə'bɛtɪkəl/ *adj.* in order of the alphabet (from A to Z): *He put the words in the list in alphabetical order.* -*adv.* **alphabetically; -***v.* **alphabetize** /'ælfəbə,taɪz/.

al·pine /'æl,paɪn/ *adj.* of or relating to high mountains, like the Swiss Alps: *We stayed in an alpine cabin for a week.*

al·read·y /ɔl'rɛdi/ *adv.* earlier, (*syn.*) previously: *The planning has already been done, so we can begin work.*

al·right /ɔl'raɪt/ *adv.infrml.* all right, OK

al·so /'ɔlsoʊ/ *adv.* in addition, too: *We bought a new sofa and also a new coffee table.*

al·tar /'ɔltər/ *n.* a raised flat surface like a table, where religious ceremonies are performed: *The priest said a prayer at the altar.*

al·ter /'ɔltər/ *v.* **1** to change, (*syn.*) to falsify: *A student altered the grade on his paper to make it seem higher than it actually was.* **2** to make small changes, (*syn.*) to modify: *The tailor altered the waistband on my pants because it was too tight.* -*adj.* **alterable.**

al·ter·a·tion /,ɔltə'reɪʃən/ *n.* [C;U] **1** a small change, (*syn.*) a modification: *The dress didn't fit, so I took it to the tailor for alterations.* **2** s.t. changed falsely, (*syn.*) a deception: *The alteration of the amount of money on the check was obvious.*

al·ter·ca·tion /,ɔltər'keɪʃən/ *n.frml.* a struggle, such as a fight; a heated argument: *Two men had an altercation about who should get the parking space.*

al·ter e·go /,ɔltər'igoʊ/ *n.* **-egos 1** another side of one's personality: *Although she is usually relaxed, her alter ego sometimes gets the best of her and she becomes anxious and tense.* **2** a companion, esp. one similar in personality and looks: *John seems to have Ed, his alter ego, with him wherever he goes. See:* ego.

al·ter·nate /'ɔltərnɪt/ *n.adj.* another, s.t. different: *If that business does not make what we want, we can always find an <n> alternate one that does.*
—*v.* /'ɔltər,neɪt/ **-nated, -nating, -nates** to move or switch back and forth: *We alternate living between Florida in the winter and Maine in the summer.* -*n.* **alternation** /,ɔltər'neɪʃən/.

al·ter·nat·ing cur·rent *See:* AC,**1.**

al·ter·na·tive /ɔl'tɜrnətɪv/ *n.* another choice (way, means, etc.): *We can take a boat to Florida or, as an alternative, we can fly.*
—*adj.* different: *An alternative way would be to travel by railroad.* -*adv.* **alternatively.** *See:* lifestyle, USAGE NOTE.

al·though /ɔl'ðoʊ/ *conj.* even though: *Although he is heavy, he can still run fast.*

al·ti·tude /'æltə,tud/ *n.* distance above sea level: *Our airplane is flying at an altitude of 35,000 feet (10,660 meters).*

al·to /'æltoʊ/ *n.* a low, female singing voice: *She sings alto in the chorus.*
—*adj.* having an alto musical range: *He plays an alto saxophone.*

al·to·geth·er /,ɔltə'gɛðər, 'ɔltə,gɛðər/ *adv.* **1** completely, totally: *He is altogether wrong in what he says.* **2** in total, counting all: *Altogether, 200 people attended the conference* **3** everything considered, on the whole: *Altogether, the conference went well.*

A

al·tru·is·tic /ˌæltruˈɪstɪk/ *adj.* giving without thinking of oneself, (*syn.*) charitable: *That rich woman is altruistic; she pays the expenses for poor students to go to college.* -*adv.* **altruistically;** -*n.* [U] **altruism** /ˈæltruˌɪzəm/.

a·lu·mi·num /əˈlumənəm/ *n.* [U] a lightweight, silver gray metal with many uses: *Beer and soda cans are made of aluminum.*

a·lum·na /əˈlʌmnə/ *n.* **-nae** /-ni/ a female graduate of an educational institution: *She is an alumna of Yale University.*

a·lum·nus /əˈlʌmnəs/ *n.* **-ni** /-ˌnaɪ/ a male graduate of an educational institution: *He is an alumnus of Harvard University.*

al·ways /ˈɔlweɪz, -wɪz/ *adv.* **1** forever: *I will be with you always.* **2** whenever, anytime: *If you don't like that sweater, you can always wear another one.* **3** regularly, every time: *We always go to the mountains for our vacation.*

Alz·heim·er's disease /ˈɔlzˌhaɪmərz,/ *n.* a disease of the nervous system whose symptoms are early senility and memory loss

USAGE NOTE: Finding a cure for *Alzheimer's disease* becomes more important as America's population ages. Victims of the disease may be in good physical health and as young as 40 or 50, but they often feel confused, forget things, and don't recognize family members.

am /m, əm; *strong form* æm/ *v.* first person singular present tense form of the verb *to be: I am ready to go now.*

USAGE NOTE: "*Am*" often contracts to "'m" after "I": *I'm ready to go now.*

AM /ˌeɪˈɛm/ *abbr. for* amplitude modulation, *n.* a type of radio and television sound signal, AM radio (as opposed to FM): *AM radio uses amplitude modulation of its signal. See:* frequency modulation. *See:* ante meridiem.

A.M. /ˌeɪˈɛm/ *abbr. for* ante meridiem, the time between 12:00 midnight and 11:59 in the morning: *My meeting was at 9:00 A.M. today.*

a·mal·ga·mate /əˈmælɡəˌmeɪt/ *v.frml.* **-mated, -mating, -mates** to combine, unite: *Two labor unions amalgamated into one large one.* -*n.*[C;U] **amalgamation** /əˌmælɡəˈmeɪʃən/.

a·mass /əˈmæs/ *v.* **-es** to put together, (*syn.*) to accumulate: *Over the years, she amassed a fortune making cosmetics.*

am·a·teur /ˈæmətʃər, -ˌtʃʊr, -ˌtɜr/ *n.adj.* a person who does activities, such as sports, for pleasure and without pay: *He is an <n.> amateur at golf, but he loves the game; he is an <adj> amateur golfer.* -*n.* [U] **amateurism.**

am·a·teur·ish /ˌæməˈtʃʊrɪʃ, -ˈfɜr-,-ˈtɜr-/ *adj.* unprofessional, poorly done: *His artwork is amateurish and not good enough to sell.*

a·maze /əˈmeɪz/ *v.* **amazed, amazing, amazes** **1** to surprise or favorably impress: *She plays tennis so well that she amazes me!* **2** to shock: *His singing was so bad that it amazed me.* -*n.* [U] **amazement;** -*adv.* **amazingly.**

am·bas·sa·dor /æmˈbæsədər, -ˌdɔr/ *n.* the highest level official who represents a government in a foreign capital city: *The United States ambassador to France works in Paris.* -*n.* **ambassadorship;** -*adj.* **ambassadorial** /æmˌbæsəˈdɔriəl/.

am·ber /ˈæmbər/ *n.* [U] a hard, clear substance of yellow or light brown color used in making jewelry: *She is wearing a pin made of amber.* —*adj.* the color of amber

am·bi·ance or **am·bi·ence** /ˈæmbiəns, ˈɑm-biəns/ *n.* [U] atmosphere, the appearance and feeling of a place: *The ambiance in that hotel is one of warmth and charm.* -*adj.* **ambient** /ˈæmbiənt/.

am·bi·dex·trous /ˌæmbɪˈdɛkstrəs/ *adj.* capable of doing things equally well with either hand: *He's ambidextrous and can write with either hand.*

am·big·u·ous /æmˈbɪɡyuəs/ *adj.* confusing, able to be understood in different ways: *He is ambiguous when he says he loves her but does not want to marry her.* -*adv.* **ambiguously;** -*n.*[C;U] **ambiguity** /ˌæmbəˈɡyuəti/.

am·bi·tion /æmˈbɪʃən/ *n.* **1** [U] desire to succeed, (*syn.*) drive: *He has ambition and works hard to get a salary increase.* **2** [C] a goal, objective: *Her ambition is to become a chef.*

am·bi·tious /æmˈbɪʃəs/ *adj.* wanting success, (*syn.*) driven: *He is very ambitious and wants to make more money.* -*adv.* **ambitiously;** -*n.* **ambitiousness.**

am·biv·a·lent /æmˈbɪvələnt/ *adj.frml.* uncertain, (*syn.*) ambiguous: *Although she loves the man, she is ambivalent about marrying him because she's not sure he's right for her.* -*n.* [U] **ambivalence;** -*adv.* **ambivalently.**

am·ble /ˈæmbəl/ *v.* **-bled, -bling, -bles** to walk in a slow, easy manner, (*syn.*) to stroll: *The two old men ambled along toward the lake. See:* walk, USAGE NOTE.

am·bu·lance /ˈæmbyələns/ *n.* a vehicle used to bring sick or injured people to a hospital: *An ambulance came to the car accident in two minutes.*

am·bu·la·to·ry /ˈæmbyələˌtɔri/ *adj.frml.* walking or capable of walking: *Her parents are very old but are still ambulatory.*

am·bush /ˈæmˌbʊʃ/ *n.* **-es** an attack made from a hidden position: *A soldier hid in a tree and set an ambush for any enemy soldiers passing below.*
—*v.* **-ed, -ing, -es** to attack from a hidden position: *The mugger ambushed them from behind.*

a·me·ba /ə'mibə/ *n*. var. of amoeba **-bas** or **-bae** *-adj*. **amebic.**

a·me·lio·rate /ə'milyə,reɪt/ *v.frml*. **-rated, -rating, -rates** to lessen the difficulty of s.t., improve: *The government ameliorated the lives of the poor by giving them food. -n*. [U] **amelioration** /ə,milyə'reɪʃən/.

A·men /,eɪ'mɛn, ,ɑ-/ *exclam*. (in religion) an expression of approval: *After saying a prayer, she said "Amen."*

a·mend /ə'mɛnd/ *v*. to change (especially a rule or law), *(syn.)* to modify: *The politicians amended the law to provide more money. -adj*. **amendable.** *See:* amends.

a·mend·ment /ə'mɛndmənt/ *n*. a change, *(syn.)* a modification: *It is difficult to make amendments to the US Constitution.*

a·mends /ə'mɛndz/ *n.pl*. **1** an apology or gift to pay back for s.t. wrong that one has done: *No amends could take away the pain of the insult.* **2 to make amends:** to do s.t. to pay back for s.t. wrong that one has done: *I apologized to my friend to make amends for criticizing him too much.*

a·men·i·ty /ə'mɛnəti/ *n.frml.pl*. **-ties** **1** a pleasant, polite introduction, esp. at the beginning of a social gathering: *The host of the party began with the usual amenities of introducing himself and his guests.* **2** s.t. that adds to people's comfort, convenience, and pleasure (such as a restaurant, a swimming pool, air-conditioning): *The only amenity at that hotel is a swimming pool.*

A·mer·i·can /ə'mɛrɪkən/ *n*. a person native to North, Central, or South America: *She is a Latin American.*
—*adj*. related to the Americas: *The Central American beaches are very beautiful.*

A·mer·i·ca·na /ə,mɛrɪ'kanə, -'kænə/ *n*. objects, stories, etc., typical of the USA, its history, and its people: *The covered bridges of New England are examples of Americana.*

A·mer·i·can dream *n.sing*. in USA, success, measured by having one's own house and automobile, a good education and job, as well as the promise of an even better life for one's children: *As immigrants, they achieved the American dream when their daughter became a doctor.*

USAGE NOTE: Making the *American dream* come true was easier in the days when many people worked at the same job all their lives. Today having a job doesn't guarantee lifelong income, health care, and a comfortable retirement. People must work hard just to live as well as their parents did.

A·mer·i·can·ism /ə'mɛrɪkə,nɪzəm/ *n*. a saying or expression found only in American

English: *The expression of surprise "Well, I'll be darned!" is an Americanism.*

A·mer·i·can·ize /ə'mɛrɪkə,naɪz/ *v*. to become similar to people in the USA in appearance or character: *She no longer wears robes but wears dress suits and even wears jeans on the weekend. She's been Americanized.*

A·mer·i·cas /ə'mɛrɪkəz/ *n.pl*. North, Central, and South America: *Representatives from the Americas met in Mexico City for a conference.*

am·e·thyst /'æməθɪst/ *n*. a violet or purple semiprecious stone often used in jewelry: *The amethyst was set in a pretty gold ring.*

a·mi·a·ble /'eɪmiəbəl/ *adj*. friendly, cheerful: *The owner of this candy store is always amiable to her young customers. -n*. [U] **amiability** /,eɪmiə'bɪləti/; *-adv*. **amiably.**

am·i·ca·ble /'æmɪkəbəl/ *adj*. friendly, esp. in resolving a disagreement: *We had an argument, but eventually reached an amicable agreement. -adv*. **amicably.**

a·mid /ə'mɪd/ *prep*. amidst, among, in the middle of: *Amid all her other troubles, she now has a bad back.*

a·min·o a·cid /ə'minou/ *n*. a chemical that forms into chains of protein: *Amino acids are necessary to life.*

a·miss /ə'mɪs/ *adj*. wrong, not in order: *We were worried that s.t. was amiss when we came home and found our apartment door open.*

am·mo /'æmou/ *n. infrml*. [U] *short for* ammunition

am·mo·nia /ə'mounyə/ *n*. [U] a strong-smelling gas that, when mixed with water, is used as a cleanser: *He used ammonia to wash the bathroom floor.*

am·mu·ni·tion /,æmyə'nɪʃən/ *n*. [U] objects that can be fired from a gun or made to explode, such as bullets, cannon shells, hand grenades, etc.

am·ne·sia /æm'niʒə/ *n*. [U] loss of memory, usually from shock or injury: *The accident victim has amnesia and can't remember her name. -n*. **amnesiac** /æm'niʒi,æk, -zi-/.

am·nes·ty /'æmnəsti/ *n.[C;U]* **-ties** a pardon for a crime, esp. for political prisoners: *The government granted amnesty to all protestors.*

a·moe·ba /ə'mibə/ *n*. [C] **-bas** or **-bae** a tiny one-celled animal, microorganism: *Amoebas do not stay one shape, but change shape as they move. -adj*. **amoebic.**

a·mong /ə'mʌŋ/ or **amongst** *prep*. **1** included within, in the midst of: *Among her many friends, John is her favorite.* **2** with each other, between: *In our family, we do not argue among ourselves.*

a·mor·al /eɪ'mɔrəl, -'mɑr-/ *adj*. **1** having no idea of or interest in what is right or wrong: *He has an amoral view of life in which anything* he wants to do is all right. **2** neither moral nor immoral

am·o·rous /'æmərəs/ adj. **1** feeling love and affection for s.o.: *He is feeling amorous toward his new girlfriend.* **2** of sexual love: *She rejected his amorous advances.* -adv. **amorously;** -n. **amorousness.**

a·mor·phous /ə'mɔrfəs/ adj.frml. **1** shapeless, without clear form **2** fig. general, (syn.) vague: *An amoeba is amorphous, changing from one shape into another.*

am·or·tize /'æmər,taɪz/ v. to repay a loan in monthly payments: *We amortized our $30,000 loan into $300 per month for several years.*

a·mount /ə'maʊnt/ n. a total, sum: *The amount of the bill is $100.*
—v. **1** to total, to add up: *The bill amounts to $20.* **2 to amount to s.t.:** to succeed, (syn.) to flourish: *I hope that my son amounts to s.t. when he grows up.*

am·per·age /'æmpərɪdʒ, -,pɪr-/ n. [U] the strength of an electrical current -abbr. **amp.**

am·per·sand /'æmpər,sænd/ n. the sign (&), meaning "and": *Many people use the ampersand in note taking and informal letter writing.*

am·phet·a·mine /æm'fɛtə,min, -mɪn/ n. [C] a type of drug that causes increased activity: *Amphetamines are used in diet pills and for Parkinson's disease, yet they are also abused by drug addicts.*

am·phib·i·an /æm'fɪbiən/ n. **1** a type of animal that can live both in water and on land, such as frogs, toads, and newts **2** an airplane that can land and take off on water or land; a vehicle that can go across land and in water: *The military uses amphibians for landing troops on beaches.* -adj. **amphibious.**

am·phi·the·a·ter /'æmfə,θiətər/ n. a theater or arena with a central stage or playing field with rows of seats rising above it: *The Coliseum in Rome is a famous amphitheater.*

am·ple /'æmpəl/ adj. more than enough, plenty: *We have an ample supply of food in the house to feed our guests.* -adv. **amply** /'æmpli/.

am·pli·fi·ca·tion /,æmpləfə'keɪʃən/ n.[C;U] **1** an increase in sound level: *The amplification of the sound on the stereo was too high.* **2** more information about s.t., an explanation: *The teacher gave an amplification of her thoughts to the class.* -v. **amplify** /'æmplə,faɪ/, **-fies.**

am·pli·fi·er /'æmplə,faɪər/ n. a device that increases an electronic signal, esp. the level of sound: *The amplifier in my stereo is very powerful.*

am·pli·tude /'æmplə,tud/ n. [U] **1** the size of a radio wave See: AM. **2** frml. size, space: *The football stadium has seating space of great amplitude.*

am·pu·tate /'æmpyə,teɪt/ v. to cut off surgically: *The doctor amputated the patient's leg*

because it was too infected to cure. -n. [C;U] **amputation** /,æmpyə'teɪʃən/.

am·pu·tee /,æmpyə'ti/ n. a person with arm(s) or leg(s) removed

a·muck /ə'mʌk/ or **a·mok** /ə'mʌk, ə'mɑk/ adv. **to run amuck:** doing damage in an angry, violent way, (syn.) (to be) on a rampage: *The elephant escaped and ran amuck, destroying the village.*

am·u·let /'æmyəlɪt/ n. a charm or object worn around the neck to prevent evil or harm: *He wore an amulet of tigers' teeth around his neck.*

a·muse /ə'myuz/ v. **1** to please, delight: *Our friend's jokes amused us all evening.* **2** to hold the attention of s.o., (syn.) to engross: *The little girl amuses herself for hours by playing with her toys.*

a·muse·ment /ə'myuzmənt/ n. **1** [U] pleasure, delight: *When our friend starts to tell jokes, our amusement doesn't stop.* **2** [C;U] entertainment, fun: *For amusement, we go to the movies once a week.*
—adj. related to pleasure and entertainment: *The amusement park has camel and elephant rides.*

a·mus·ing /ə'myuzɪŋ/ adj. causing laughter or pleasure: *We found the new movie very amusing.*

an /ən; *strong form* æn/ indef. article one, some: *I have an idea for a good vacation; let's go to the mountains.*

USAGE NOTE: Use *an* before vowel sounds: *an apple*||*an expensive gift.* Use *a* before consonant sounds: *a door*||*a good book.* Note that the sound of the following word, not its spelling, determines whether to use *a* or *an: an umbrella* but *a unit; an hour* (h is silent) but *a historical novel* (h is sounded); *a YMCA* but *an RV .*

a·nach·ro·nism /ə'nækrə,nɪzəm/ n. s.t. out of its time and place, (syn.) a throwback to another era: *It is almost an anachronism to use a typewriter these days, since computers are used everywhere.* -adj. **anachronistic** /ə,nækrə'nɪstɪk/; -adv. **anachronistically.**

a·nal /'eɪnl/ adj. related to the anus

an·al·ge·sic /,ænl'dʒizɪk, -sɪk/ n.adj. a pain-relieving drug that allows one to stay awake while it works: *Aspirin is an <n.> analgesic.*

a·nal·o·gous /ə'næləgəs/ adj.frml. similar, nearly the same: *This summer is analogous to last summer, which was also hot and rainy.*

a·nal·o·gy /ə'nælədʒi/ n.pl. **-gies** a situation or story similar to another that helps one to understand: *An analogy works like this: As a reservoir stores water, the mind stores knowledge.*

a·nal·y·sis /ə'næləsɪs/ n. **-ses** /-,siz/ **1** work done to find facts and solutions to problems, a study: *We did an analysis of the problem and* *proposed solutions to it.* **2** a written report of that study

an·a·lyst /'ænəlɪst/ *n.* a person who studies and gives information about analyses: *She is an economic analyst for the government.*

an·a·lyt·ic /ˌænl'ɪtɪk/ or **an·a·lyt·i·cal** /ˌænl'ɪtɪkəl/ *adj.* having the ability to understand problems, (*syn.*) insightful: *She has an analytical mind and can solve problems easily.* -*adv.* **analytically.**

an·a·lyze /'ænl,aɪz/ *v.* **-lyzed, -lyzing, -lyzes** to examine s.t. to understand what it is and means, to study: *A scientist analyzed data from a study of cancer patients.*

an·ar·chism /'ænər,kɪzəm/ *n.* [U] a political belief that there should be no government -*n.* **anarchist.**

an·ar·chy /'ænɑrki/ *n.* [U] a condition without governmental control, laws, military, etc.: *The nation experienced anarchy after the revolution.*

a·nath·e·ma /ə'næθəmə/ *n.* [U] **1** a curse by a religious authority **2** s.t. that is hated: *The thought of changing to another religion is anathema to many people.*

a·nat·o·my /ə'nætəmi/ *n.* **-mies 1** [U] the study of the structure of living things and their parts, such as bones, nerves, etc. **2** [C] *usu. sing.* the structure of a living thing: *Is the anatomy of a frog similar to that of a toad?* -*adj.* **anatomical** /ˌænə'tamɪkəl/ -*adv.* **anatomically.**

an·ces·tor /'æn,sɛstər/ *n.* the persons from whom one is descended (great-grandmother, father, etc.): *She can name her ancestors all the way back to sixteenth-century England.* -*adj.* **ancestral** /æn'sɛstrəl/.

an·ces·try /'æn,sɛstri/ *n.* [U] one's descent, heritage, (*syn.*) lineage: *My grandfather came from Italy, so I am of Italian ancestry.*

an·chor /'æŋkər/ *n.* **1** a heavy metal device used to keep boats from moving: *Sailors put the ship's anchor into the water.* **2** s.t. that gives stability, to set or fasten s.t.: *She tied rocks to the kite strings to serve as anchors on a windy day.* **3** *fig.* something that gives emotional or mental support: *He moved around the country often, but his family was an anchor for him.*
—*v.* **1** to use an anchor, (*syn.*) to moor: *They anchored their ship in the harbor.* **2** to coordinate and comment on a news show in which several reporters are participating: *She anchors the 6:00 news.*

anchor

an·chor·age /'æŋkərɪdʒ/ *n.* a place where boats can be anchored, (*syn.*) a mooring: *We*

used the mouth of a river as an anchorage, and we went on land.

an·chor·man /'æŋkər,mæn/ *n.* **-men** /-,mɛn/ a man who reports news and coordinates and comments on the reports in a news show: *Stanley Stunning is the anchorman on the television news program.* -*n.* **anchorwoman.**

an·cho·vy /'æntʃouvi/ *n.* [C] **-vies** a small fish that is often salted: *I like anchovies in my salad and on pizza.*

an·cient /'eɪntʃənt/ *adj.* **1** very old, usu. dating from more than 5,000 years ago to the fall of the Roman Empire in 476 A.D.: *In school, we studied the ancient Greek and Roman civilizations.* **2** *infrml.* old, uninteresting: *I used to date him, but that's ancient history now.*

an·cil·lar·y /'ænsə,lɛri/ *adj.frml.* subordinate: *The poor economic situation was an ancillary cause of the war.*

and /ənd, ən; *strong form* ænd/ *conj.* **1** in addition, plus: *She likes to fish and to play tennis.* **2** added to, plus: *20 and 20 equals 40.* **3** then, thereafter: *She stopped at the store and bought some groceries.*

an·ec·dot·al /ˌænɪk'doutl/ *adj.* related to or based on stories, reports, or observations: *His manner of speaking is anecdotal; he tells lots of little stories.*

an·ec·dote /'ænɪk,dout/ *n.* a short story, esp. about one's own experiences: *The sailor tells amusing anecdotes about his travels around the world.*

a·ne·mi·a /ə'nimiə/ *n.* [U] a medical condition of not having enough oxygen-carrying red cells in one's blood: *Anemia can be caused by not eating the right foods.* -*adj.* **anemic.**

an·es·the·sia /ˌænəs'θiʒə/ *n.* [U] the loss of sensation or feeling in the body, esp. as produced by a drug: *The patient was under anesthesia during the operation.* -*n.* [U] **anesthesiology** /ˌænəs,θizi'alədʒi/.

an·es·thet·ic /ˌænəs'θetɪk/ *n.* [C;U] a substance (often a gas) used by doctors to prevent a patient from feeling pain: *The patient was given an anesthetic before surgery.*

an·es·the·tist /ə'nɛsθətɪst/ *n.* a person trained to administer anesthetic: *Before the surgeon began the operation, the anesthetist gave the patient a shot to numb the patient's leg.* -*v.* **anesthetize** /ə'nɛsθə,taɪz/.

a·new /ə'nu/ *adv.* over again, (*syn.*) afresh: *His report had incorrect numbers, so he began anew and did them correctly.*

an·gel /'eɪndʒəl/ *n.* **1** a spiritual being, esp. a messenger of God: *Angels of many kinds are found in the Bible.* **2** *fig.* a term of affection for a person who is well-behaved, beautiful, or as kind as an angel: *That child is so well-behaved; what an angel!* **3** *fig.* a financial supporter, esp. of a musical or theater production:

The elaborate staging for the play was made possible by the many angels of the theatre troupe. *-adj.* **angelic** /æn'dʒɛlɪk/; *-adv.* **angelically.**

an·ger /'æŋgər/ *n.* [U] a strong feeling often with a show of hate about what s.o. or s.t. is doing to you, (*syn.*) rage: *After their argument, he expressed his anger by punching the other man in the face. See:* aggravate.
—*v.* to enrage, infuriate: *Her constant criticism finally angered me.*

an·gle /'æŋgəl/ *n.* **1** the figure formed by two or more straight lines coming together at one point: *A 90 degree angle has one line that is straight up which meets with another line that is level with the floor.* **2** *infrml.fig.* **to have an angle on s.t.:** to hold an opinion or (*syn.*) perspective on s.t.: *What's your angle on this problem?* **3** *infrml.fig.* **to have an angle:** to have an improper method for gaining personal profit or advantage: *That guy has an angle in everything he does.*
—*v.* **-gled, -gling, -gles 1** to be shaped like an angle: *One road angles off to the left while the other continues in a straight line* **2** to fish: *As his favorite sport, he angles in the summer. See:* angling.

an·gling /'æŋglɪŋ/ *n.* [U] sport fishing: *My friend likes to go angling in the spring. -n.* **angler.**

An·glo /'æŋgloʊ/ *n.* **-glos** a white-skinned North American not of Hispanic or French heritage: *Anglos have opened businesses throughout Latin America. See:* white.
—*prefix* **Anglo-** related to the British: *An Anglo-American economic conference will take place in London next month.*

An·glo·phile /'æŋglə,faɪl/ *n.* a person who likes and admires England and English people or things: *As an Anglophile, he collects memorabilia of the British Royal Family and travels often to England.*

An·glo·phone /'æŋglə,foʊn/ *n.* a native speaker of English, whether British, North American, Australian, or New Zealander: *As an Anglophone in Japan, his English language skills were widely sought.*

An·glo-Sax·on /,æŋgloʊ'sæksən/ *n.adj.* a person of English heritage or one of the Germanic peoples (the Angles, Saxons, and Jutes) that invaded England in the fifth and sixth centuries: *"Beowulf," probably written in the eighth century, is the best known piece of <adj.> Anglo-Saxon literature.*

an·gry /'æŋgri/ *adj.* **-grier, -griest** feeling anger: *His wallet was stolen, and he is very angry about it. -adv.* **angrily** /'æŋgrəli/.

USAGE NOTE: One becomes *annoyed* or *irritated* before one becomes *angry.* If one is very angry, one may be described as being *infuri-*ated or *enraged.*

angst /ɑŋkst/ *n.frml.* [U] (German for) great anxiety, often accompanied by depression: *Her angst about the future drove her to seek counseling.*

an·guish /'æŋgwɪʃ/ *n.* [U] painful sadness: *She felt anguish when her 15-year-old dog died.*
—*v.* **1** to suffer painful sadness: *She anguished over the death of her dog.* **2** to be unable to decide on s.t., which makes one feel pain: *She anguished for days over whether or not she should try to keep the dog alive.*

an·gu·lar /'æŋgyələr/ *adj.* having angles: *The roofs of the houses are not flat; they are angular. -n.* [U;C] **angularity** /,æŋgyə'lærəti/.

an·i·mal /'ænəməl/ *n.* **1** any creature, living or dead, that is not a plant or human: *Horses are animals.* **2** *infrml.* a person of very bad habits or behavior: *He's angry all the time, eats with his fingers, and is dirty; he's an animal!*

an·i·mate /'ænə,meɪt/ *v.frml.* **-mated, -mating, -mates 1** to enliven, make s.o. or s.t. full of life and fun: *He is so lively that he animated the party last evening.* **2** to draw, design, or produce (e.g., a cartoon) in a manner that creates motion: *Walt Disney animated characters including Mickey Mouse and Snow White. -n.* **animator** /'ænə,meɪtər/; *-adj.* **animated;** *-adv.* **animatedly.**
—*adj.frml.* /'ænəmɪt/ alive, living: *Creatures or things that have life are animate.*

an·i·ma·tion /,ænə'meɪʃən/ *n.* **1** [U;C] the process of giving life, spirit, motion, or activity: *Through animation, the newspaper comic strip became a popular cartoon on television.* **2** *frml.* [U] having life, liveliness: *The animation of the figures in the toy store window was very cleverly done.*

an·i·mos·i·ty /,ænə'masəti/ *n.* [U;C] **-ties** hostility, hatred: *The two men have a mutual animosity for each other.*

an·kle /'æŋkəl/ *n.* the joint connecting the foot and lower leg: *She tripped on the sidewalk and twisted her ankle.*

an·nals /'ænlz/ *n.pl.frml.* a written record or collection of historical events, discoveries, etc., on a certain subject: *He was the greatest player in the annals of football.*

an·nex /'æ,nɛks, 'ænɪks/ *n.* **-es 1** an addition to an existing building **2** a separate building of smaller size near a main building: *Our rooms were in the annex close to the main hotel.*
—*v.* **-es** to take possession of another country: *Germany annexed Austria just before World War II. -n.* **annexation** /,ænɛk'seɪʃən/.

an·ni·hi·late /ə'naɪə,leɪt/ *v.* **-lated, -lating, -lates** to eradicate by force, destroy totally: *The army annihilated the enemy soldiers; all were killed. -n.* [C] **annihilation** /ə'naɪə'leɪʃən/; **annihilator.**

an·ni·ver·sa·ry /ˌænə'vɜrsəri/ *n.* **-ries** the date one year (and in following years) after the date on which an event took place: *Our first wedding anniversary was last Tuesday.*

an·no Dom·i·ni /ˌænou'dɑməni, -ˌnaɪ/ *adv.frml.* See: A.D.

an·no·tate /'ænəˌteɪt/ *v.* **-tated, -tating, -tates** to write notes on s.t.: *The businesswoman annotated the report with her comments and suggestions.* *-n.* [C;U] **annotation** /ˌænə'teɪʃən/.

an·nounce /ə'nauns/ *v.* **-nounced, -nouncing, -nounces** **1** to make public, declare: *The parents announced the wedding of their daughter in the newspaper.* **2** to act as an announcer: *He announces the Giants' football games, commenting on and explaining the players' movements.* *-n.* **announcement** /ə'naunsmənt/.

an·nounc·er /ə'naunsər/ *n.* a person who tells what will happen or what is happening in an event, e.g., a parade, a sports event, etc.: *He is the television announcer for football games.*

an·noy /ə'nɔɪ/ *v.* to cause mild anger, (*syn.*) to irritate: *The constant noise from the street traffic annoyed me.* See: angry, USAGE NOTE.

an·noy·ance /ə'nɔɪəns/ *n.* [C;U] an irritation, bother: *His constant complaining is an annoyance.*

an·nu·al /'ænyuəl/ *adj.* occurring every year: *The annual rainfall in this area is light.*
—n. a yearly publication of important events, etc., from the past year: *The annual of the Graphic Artist Society presents beautiful pictures and designs. -adv.* **annually.**

an·nu·i·ty /ə'nuəti/ *n.* **-ties** an investment (often in the form of an insurance policy) that provides fixed payments for a lifetime or other specified amount of time: *The businessman bought an annuity for his daughter that pays her a monthly income for life.*

an·nul /ə'nʌl/ *v.* **-nulled, -nulling, -nuls** to declare s.t. nonexistent, state legally s.t. never existed or happened: *The couple had their marriage annulled. -n.* **annulment.**

a·noint /ə'nɔɪnt/ *v.* to pour oil or an oily substance on s.o. as in a religious ceremony, (*syn.*) to sanctify: *The bishop anointed the priest's head with holy oil.*

a·nom·a·ly /ə'nɑməli/ *n.frml.* **-lies** a departure from the normal, a mystery: *The flying machine was unlike any craft the engineers had ever seen; it was an anomaly. -adj.* **anomalous** /ə'nɑmələs/.

a·non·y·mous /ə'nɑnəməs/ *adj.* not being named, unknown: *An anonymous person called the police and identified the thief. -adv.* **anonymously** *-n.* [U] **anonymity** /ˌænə'nɪməti/.

an·o·rex·i·a /ˌænə'rɛksiə/ *n.* [U] the inability to eat, resulting in low body weight and possible death: *Her weight loss and eating habits*

led the doctor to suspect she suffered from anorexia. *-adj.* **anorectic** /ˌænə'rɛktɪk/; *-adj.n.* **anorexic.**

an·oth·er /ə'nʌðər/ *pron.* **1** a different person (animal, thing): *She no longer loves him; she loves another.* **2** an additional thing (person, animal, etc.): *He ate one hamburger, then ordered another.*
—adj. different, (*syn.*) alternative: *She loves another man now.*

an·swer /'ænsər/ *n.* a spoken or written response, reply: *I received an answer to my letter yesterday.*
—v. **1** to respond, reply: *The company answered that it is interested in my offer.* **2** *phrasal v.* **to answer back:** to reply impolitely: *When the teacher told the student to be quiet, he answered back, "No!"* **3** *phrasal v.* **to answer for:** to be held responsible for: *The criminal will have to answer for his crimes by going to jail.* **4** *phrasal v.* **to answer to:** to work for, be judged by: *I do not have to answer to you, you're not my boss.*

an·swer·a·ble /'ænsərəbəl/ *adj.* responsible for, (*syn.*) liable: *He is answerable to society for his crimes.*

ant /ænt/ *n.* an insect with a narrow waist, two bent antennae, and biting jaws, noted for living in colonies and for working hard: *Having left their food uncovered while they played softball, the picnickers returned to find the ants eating it.*

ant·ac·id /ænt'æsɪd/ *n.adj.* a pill or liquid used to stop an acid, burning feeling: *He took an <n.> antacid (or) <adj.> antacid tablet for his upset stomach.*

an·tag·o·nism /æn'tægəˌnɪzəm/ *n.* [C;U] the state of acting against s.o. or s.t., (*syn.*) hostility: *Our neighbor's antagonism toward us is obvious; he is always throwing things in our yard. -n.* **antagonist;** *-adj.* **antagonistic;** *-adv.* **antagonistically.**

an·tag·o·nize /æn'tægəˌnaɪz/ *v.* **-nized, -nizing, -nizes** to cause others to feel angry, (*syn.*) to offend: *He antagonizes his neighbors by playing his stereo loudly, day and night.*

an·te /'ænti/ *n.* [C;U] **1** (in card games) money or chips put into a pot that the winner takes: *We played poker with a $1 ante.* **2** *infrml.fig.* **to up the ante:** to raise the cost of s.t.: *We made an offer to buy a house for $100,000, but the owner upped the ante to $125,000.*
—v. **-ted** or **-teed, -teing, -tes** **1** (in cards) to put money in a pot **2** *infrml.fig.* **to ante up:** to pay for s.t.: *You owe me $10, so ante up.*

an·te·ced·ent /ˌæntə'sidnt/ *adj.frml.* **1** that which comes before, (*syn.*) the preceding: *The antecedent noise and smoke were signs that the volcano might explode.*
—n. **1** (in grammar) the word, phrase, or clause to which a pronoun refers: *"Scientist" is*

A

the antecedent of "he" in the sentence: *The scientist became famous because he discovered a vaccine.* **2** *pl.* **antecedents:** ancestors, forbears: *Her antecedents came from England.*

an·te·date /'ænti,deɪt/ *v.* **-dated, -dating, -dates** to occur earlier, predate: *The discovery of Africa antedated that of America.*

an·te·lope /'æntl,oʊp/ *n.* any of various fast, hoofed, four-legged animals with horns: *Most antelopes are found in Africa, but some are found in Asia.*

an·te me·rid·i·em /'æntimə'rɪdiəm/ *See:* AM.

antelope

an·ten·na /æn'tɛnə/ *n.* **-nas 1** a rod, wire, dish, etc., used to receive or send electronic signals: *The antenna for my car radio is a fine wire in the windshield.* **2** *pl.* **-nae** /-ni/ a thread-like feeler on the heads of some animals: *An ant has two antennae on its head.*

an·te·ri·or /æn'tɪriər/ *adj.frml.* located in front: *The head of an insect is located on the anterior part of its body.*

an·them /'ænθəm/ *n.* **1** a song of devotion or admiration: *The national anthem is sung before every baseball game.* **2** a religious song of praise, written for different types of voices

ant·hill /'ænt,hɪl/ *n.* a pile of earth made by ants as their house: *Some anthills found in Africa are five feet high.*

an·thol·o·gy /æn'θɑlədʒi/ *n.* **-gies** a collection of writings by one or many writers: *She received an anthology of the works of 20th century American poets as a gift for her birthday.* *-v.* **anthologize** /æn'θɑlə,dʒaɪz/.

an·thrax /'æn,θræks/ *n.* [U] a disease, often deadly, of warm-blooded animals, esp. cattle and sheep: *Countries take strong action against anthrax spreading among their sheep and cattle.*

an·thro·pol·o·gy /,ænθrə'pɑlədʒi/ *n.* [U] the study of humans and their cultures: *In their anthropology course, the students learned about the Mayan civilization.* *-n.* **anthropologist;** *-adj.* **anthropological** /,ænθrəpə'lɑdʒɪkəl/; *-adv.* **anthropologically.**

an·ti- /'ænti, -tɪ, -,taɪ/ *prefix* against, (*syn.*) contra: *She is anti-smoking.*

an·ti·a·bor·tion /,æntiə'bɔrʃən, ,æntaɪ-/ *adj.* opposed to the practice of terminating a pregnancy: *The anti-abortion group provided information on alternatives to abortions. See:* abort, 1.

an·ti·au·thor·i·tar·i·an /,æntiə,θɔrə'tɛriən, -,θɑr-, ,æntaɪ-/ *adj.* against authority: *He has an anti-authoritarian attitude toward his boss.*

an·ti·bi·ot·ic /,æntibaɪ'ɑtɪk, ,æntaɪ-/ *n.* a type of medicine made from tiny microorganisms that are effective in fighting off other disease-causing microorganisms: *Penicillin and tetracycline are widely used antibiotics.* || *I took an antibiotic for my ear infection.*

an·ti·bod·y /'ænti,bɑdi/ *n. pl.* **-bodies** a type of substance produced by the body against disease-causing germs: *A mother's milk passes antibodies on to her baby.*

An·ti·christ /'ænti,kraɪst/ *n.* **1** (in the Christian religion) the term used for the enemy who is against Christ and all Christians in the last days before the Second Coming of Christ **2 antichrist** an evil enemy: *During the war, the media portrayed the leader of the enemies as a type of antichrist.*

an·tic·i·pate /æn'tɪsə,peɪt/ *v.* **-pated, -pating, -pates 1** to await, expect: *I anticipate that the weather will improve soon.* **2** to believe s.t. will happen in the future, (*syn.*) to envision: *I anticipate that the economy will improve next year.* *-n.* [U] **anticipation** /æn,tɪsə'peɪʃən/.

an·ti·cli·max /,ænti'klaɪ,mæks/ *n.* **-es** a disappointing, uneventful result: *Having seen the champion skate so well in the past, her poor performance was an anticlimax.* *-adj.* **anticlimactic** /,æntiklaɪ'mæktɪk/.

an·tics /'æntɪks/ *n.pl.* foolish acts, (*syn.*) clowning: *The little boy danced on his chair, and the teacher punished him for his antics.* *-adj.* **antic.**

an·ti·dote /'ænti,doʊt/ *n.* (in medicine) a substance that stops the action of a poison or other harmful substance: *The doctor prescribed an antidote for the poison the boy had swallowed.*

an·ti·freeze /'ænti,friz/ *n.* [U] a liquid used in engine radiators to lower their freezing point: *Because he forgot to put antifreeze in his car radiator, his car wouldn't start in the subzero weather.*

an·ti·his·ta·mine /,ænti'hɪstə,min, -mɪn/ *n.* a type of medicine used to reduce the symptoms of allergies and colds: *I took an antihistamine to relieve my hay fever.*

an·ti·pas·to /,ænti'pɑstoʊ/ *n.[C;U]* **-ti** /-ti/ or **-tos** Italian-style snacks used to start a meal: *Antipasto often includes sausage, cheese, and olives with bread.*

an·tip·a·thy /æn'tɪpəθi/ *n.frml.* **-thies** [C;U] a strong feeling ranging from dislike to hatred: *The antipathy that exists between the two men has lasted for years.* *-adj.* **antipathetic** /,æntɪpə'θɛtɪk, æn,tɪpə-/.

an·ti·per·spi·rant /,ænti'pɛrspərənt/ *n.* a substance put under the arms to stop sweating and odor: *When his antiperspirant failed to keep his underarms dry, he switched to another one.*

USAGE NOTE: Compare *antiperspirant* and *deodorant.* An antiperspirant stops a person from sweating, but a deodorant stops sweat from smelling bad. Americans spend millions of dollars on soaps, deodorants, and antiperspirants, and take daily baths or showers to remove natural body odor (B.O.).

an·ti·quar·i·an /ˌæntɪˈkwɛriən/ *n.adj.* a person who has to do with or deals in antiques or other old, rare objects: *The antiquarians of Paris have their showrooms along the river Seine.*

an·ti·quat·ed /ˈæntɪˌkweɪtɪd/ *adj.* old, having been replaced by s.t. more advanced, (*syn.*) obsolete: *Our typewriter is not as efficient as a computer system, so it is antiquated. -v.* **antiquate.**

an·tique /ænˈtik/ *n.adj.* an object that has particular value because of its age: *The clock in the hallway is an <n.> antique* (or) *an <adj.> antique clock.*

an·tiq·ui·ty /ænˈtɪkwəti/ *n.* **-ties** **1** the time of ancient societies: *In antiquity, Greek and Roman civilizations lasted for many hundreds of years.* **2** ancient objects, such as statues and vases: *The museum has many antiquities from ancient Egypt.*

an·ti·Sem·ite /ˌæntiˈsɛmaɪt/ *n.* a person who is hostile toward or discriminates against Jews: *Hitler was an anti-Semite. -adj.* **anti-Semitic** /ˌæntisəˈmɪtɪk, ˌæntaɪ-/; *-n.* [U] **anti-Semitism** /ˌæntiˈsɛməˌtɪzəm, ˌæntaɪ-/.

an·ti·sep·tic /ˌæntəˈsɛptɪk/ *n.adj.* a chemical, such as iodine or hydrogen peroxide, that stops harmful bacteria from causing disease: *I put <n.> antiseptic on the cut on my hand. -adv.* **antiseptically.**

an·ti·so·cial /ˌæntiˈsouʃəl, ˌæntaɪ-/ *adj.* **1** preferring to be alone, (*syns.*) unfriendly, withdrawn: *He seldom goes out and never goes to parties; he's antisocial.* **2** causing trouble in society: *Riots and crime are antisocial.*

an·tith·e·sis /ænˈtɪθəsɪs/ *n.frml.* **-ses** /-ˌsiz/ the opposite of s.t.: *Good is the antithesis of evil. -adj.* **antithetical** /ˌæntəˈθɛtɪkəl/.

an·ti·trust /ˌæntiˈtrʌst, ˌæntaɪ-/ *adj.* preventing one company from taking over all the sales of a certain good or service in an effort to control the price: *The USA's antitrust laws have helped keep telephone rates down. See:* monopoly.

ant·ler /ˈæntlər/ *n.* a branched horn grown in pairs on the heads of male deer, elk, etc.: *We saw a deer with large antlers.*

an·to·nym /ˈæntəˌnɪm/ *n.* a word that means the opposite of another word: *"Happy" is an antonym of "sad."*

a·nus /ˈeɪnəs/ *n.* **-es** the opening in the lower colon between the human buttocks: *Human waste is discharged through the anus.*

an·vil /ˈænvəl/ *n.* an iron or steel platform on which hot metal is hammered into desired shapes: *A blacksmith hammers horseshoes into shape on an anvil.*

anx·i·e·ty /æŋˈzaɪəti/ *n.* [C;U] **-ties** worry, nervous fear with or without reason about what will happen in the future: *As the man waited to learn the extent of his wife's injuries, his anxiety rose.*

anx·ious /ˈæŋkʃəs/ *adj.* **1** wanting to do s.t., (*syn.*) impatient: *The student was anxious to finish the final examination.* **2** worried, nervously fearful: *The examination was very difficult, and he was anxious that he may have failed it. -adv.* **anxiously.**

an·y /ˈɛni/ *pron.* **1** some, an amount of s.t.: *My friend asked me for some money, but I didn't have any with me.* **2** all, a total amount: *I told him that later he could have any I have at home.* **3** each person or thing in a group: *Among our friends, any could see I was poor.* —*adj.* **1** some: *I don't have any money.* **2** all: *I'm going fishing, and I will give you any fish that I catch.* **3** each of a group: *Any student could pass that test; it was easy.* —*adv.* at all: *I was ill yesterday and don't feel any better today. See:* at, (at any rate), **13.**.

an·y·bod·y /ˈɛniˌbɑdi, -ˌbʌdi/ *pron.* anyone: *Anybody can say what they think.*

an·y·how /ˈɛniˌhaʊ/ *adv.* **1** in any way, by whatever means: *He can pay for the purchase anyhow he wants.* **2** *slang* no matter, whatever (indicating unimportance): *Anyhow, I don't care as long as he pays.*

an·y·more /ˌɛniˈmɔr/ *adv.* **1** now, any longer: *They moved away; they don't live here any longer.* **2** from now on, (*syn.*) henceforth: *I have done enough for today; I won't work anymore.*

an·y·place /ˈɛniˌpleɪs/ *adv.* anywhere, somewhere: *You can sit anyplace you would like.*

an·y·thing /ˈɛniˌθɪŋ/ *n.* [U] *pron.* **1** any object, occurrence, or matter: *I would give anything to be beautiful.* **2 anything but:** except, not that: *I will eat anything but broccoli.* **3 anything goes:** all behavior, even improper or illegal, is permitted: *When they have a party and start drinking, anything goes!* **4 anything like:** similar to: *She looks old in that picture; it doesn't look anything like her!*

an·y·time /ˈɛniˌtaɪm/ *adv.* whenever, at any time: *We can leave anytime you are ready.*

an·y·way /ˈɛniˌweɪ/ *adv.* **1** either, in addition (to strengthen a decision): *It's OK that we can't go for a walk because I didn't feel like going anyway.* **2** and so (to continue a discussion): *Anyway, to make a long story short, we finally found out what the problem was.*

an·y·where /ˈɛniˌwɛr/ *adv.* **1** at any place, wherever: *You can sit (walk, go, etc.) anywhere you want.* **2 to not get anywhere:** to get nowhere, to achieve nothing: *We have had*

A

meeting after meeting, but we haven't gotten anywhere in reaching an agreement.

A-OK /'eɪoʊ'keɪ/*exclam.* all right, yes: *Shall we leave now? A-OK, let's go!*
—adj. great, terrific: *How are you? I'm A-OK.*

a·or·ta /eɪ'ɔrtə/ *n.* the main blood artery coming from the left side of the heart: *Blood flows from the aorta throughout the body.*

a·pace /ə'peɪs/ *adv.* **1** at a fast pace, (*syn.*) quickly **2** according to a schedule: *Our work on the project proceeds apace.*

a·part /ə'pɑrt/ *adj.* not together, separated: *When my parents are apart, they telephone each other every day.*
—adv. in parts or pieces: *The mechanic took the engine apart.*

a·part·heid /ə'pɑr,teɪt, -,taɪt/ *n.* [U] racial separation of people by government policy: *In the Republic of South Africa, the policy of apartheid has officially been stopped.*

USAGE NOTE: Compare *apartheid* and *segregation*. The term apartheid comes from South Africa, where it is no longer officially practiced, but some forms of apartheid may still exist in other countries.

a·part·ment /ə'pɑrtmənt/ *n.* a room or set of rooms designed as living space in a building or house: *We have a two-bedroom apartment in a building containing 100 apartments.*

ap·a·thet·ic /,æpə'θɛtɪk/ *adj.* not interested, (*syn.*) indifferent: *The voters are apathetic about the candidates running for office.* *-adv.* **apathetically.**

ap·a·thy /'æpəθi/ *n.* [U] indifference, lack of interest: *The apathy of voters was shown by the low number of votes cast.*

ape /eɪp/ *n.* a gorilla, monkey, or other similar animal: *The apes in the zoo are a popular attraction.*
—adv.infrml.slang **1 to go ape:** to become very angry: *When I gave him the bad news, he went ape and started yelling at me.* **2** to be enthusiastic about s.t.: *She got a new bicycle for her birthday, and she went ape over it.* See: apish.

ape

a·pe·ri·tif /ə,pɛrə'tif/ *n.* an alcoholic beverage taken before a meal: *Sherry is a typical aperitif.*

ap·er·ture /'æpərtʃər/ *n.* a hole or other opening: *The aperture controls the amount of light allowed in a camera.*

a·pex /'eɪ,pɛks/ *n.* **-es** the top, (*syn.*) the pinnacle: *The climber reached the mountain's apex.*

aph·o·rism /'æfə,rɪzəm/ *n.* a short saying containing a truth: *"The great die young" is an aphorism.*

aph·ro·dis·i·ac /,æfrə'dizi,æk, -'dɪ-/ *n.* a substance thought to cause sexual excitement: *In many parts of the world, alcohol is drunk as an aphrodisiac.*

a·pi·ar·y /'eɪpi,ɛri/ *n.* **-aries** a place where honeybees are kept: *The beekeeper has an apiary of 10 beehives from which he collects honey.*

a·piece /ə'pis/ *adv.* per piece, each: *Those tennis balls cost $1 apiece.*

a·plen·ty /ə'plɛnti/ *adv.frml.* in great amount, much or many: *In this lake, there are fish aplenty.*

a·plomb /ə'plam, ə'plʌm/ *n.* [U] calm, esp. in a difficult situation, (*syn.*) composure: *People yelled at the speaker, but she never lost her aplomb.*

a·poc·a·lypse /ə'pakəlɪps/ *n.* the end of the world: *The earthquake was so terrible that many thought that the apocalypse had come.*
—adj. **apocalyptic** /ə,pakə'lɪptɪk/ *See:* Armageddon.

a·po·lit·i·cal /,eɪpə'lɪtɪkəl/ *adj.* not done for political reasons, nonpartisan: *When the country is threatened, politicians become apolitical and agree with each other to defend it.*

a·pol·o·gize /ə'palə,dʒaɪz/ *v.* **-gized, -gizing, -gizes** to express regret for doing s.t. wrong and usu. to ask forgiveness: *The young man apologized to the woman for spilling coffee on her dress.* *-adj.* **apologetic** /ə,palə'dʒɛtɪk/; *-adv.* **apologetically.**

a·pol·o·gy /ə'palədʒi/ *n.* **-gies** an expression of regret for doing s.t. wrong: *The woman accepted his apology for spilling coffee on her dress.*

ap·o·plec·tic /,æpə'plɛktɪk/ *adj.* **1** appearing to faint, become unconscious: *When he heard the bad news, he became apoplectic.* **2** *fig.* very angry, furious *-n.* [U] **apoplexy** /'æpə,plɛksi/. *See:* stroke.

a·pos·tle /ə'pasəl/ *n.* **1** a follower and missionary: *Christ had 12 apostles who spread the word of Christianity.* **2** a leader of a new cause: *She is an apostle for working parents' rights.* *-adj.* **apostolic** /,æpə'stalɪk/.

a·pos·tro·phe /ə'pastrəfi/ *n.* the punctuation mark ('): *An apostrophe is used in contractions ("isn't," "doesn't") and in possessives ("that man's wife").*

a·poth·e·car·y /ə'paθə,kɛri/ *n.frml.* **-caries 1** a place where one can buy medicine, (*syns.*) a pharmacy, drugstore: *The patient had his prescription filled at the apothecary.* **2** a person who mixes the medicine in such a store: *The apothecary carefully counted out the prescribed number of pills.*

ap·pall /ə'pɔl/ *v.* to shock, deeply offend: *The murder of the child appalled everyone in the* *city.* -*adj.* **appalling;** -*adv.* **appallingly.**

ap·pa·rat·us /ˌæpə'rætəs, -'reɪ-/ *n.*[C;U] -**uses** or -**us** a device or group of devices (machines, tools, wires, etc.) designed to perform a certain task: *With their sophisticated apparatus the scientists were able to determine the epicenter of the earthquake. See:* device, appliance.

ap·par·el /ə'pærəl, -'pɛr-/ *n.* [U] a general term for clothing, such as suits or dresses: *XYZ Company is a manufacturer of ladies' apparel.*

ap·par·ent /ə'pærənt, -'pɛr-/ *adj.* obvious, clear: *He's very unhappy, and it is apparent that he wants to leave now.* -*adv.* **apparently.**

ap·pa·ri·tion /ˌæpə'rɪʃən/ *n.frml.* a spirit of the dead appearing to s.o., a ghost: *The old man says that he saw an apparition in that cave.*

ap·peal /ə'pil/ *v.* **1** to attract, please s.o.: *The idea of spending two weeks on vacation appeals to me.* **2** to ask for, plead for help: *The Red Cross appealed for money to help people after the hurricane.* **3** (in law) to bring a decision by a lower court to a higher court for review: *He was found guilty but appealed the decision to a higher court.*
—*n.* **1** [U] attractiveness, a pleasing aspect or quality: *A winter vacation holds a lot of appeal for me.* **2** [C] a plea, request: *The Red Cross made an appeal for money and clothing.* **3** [U;C] (in law) a request for higher court review: *The decision in the case is now on appeal in a higher court.*

ap·pear /ə'pɪr/ *v.* **1** to become visible: *The sun suddenly appeared from behind a big cloud.* **2** to seem, to be likely: *It appears the weather will be nice.*

ap·pear·ance /ə'pɪrəns/ *n.* **1** [C] the arrival, the coming into public view: *The singer's appearance on the stage caused everyone to applaud.* **2** [U] how one looks and dresses: *The woman has such a nice appearance.* **3** **to make an appearance:** to show oneself: *The movie star made a brief appearance at the party and then left.*

ap·pease /ə'piz/ *v.* -**peased, -peasing, -peases** **1** to make s.o. feel better about being wronged, (*syn.*) to placate: *The man appeased his wife's anger about forgetting her birthday by taking her out to dinner.* **2** to surrender or to make concessions: *The small, weak country appeased its strong neighbor by giving up part of its land.* -*n.* [U] **appeasement.**

ap·pel·late /ə'pɛlɪt/ *adj.* (in law) able to review and change a decision of a lower court: *The attorneys submitted their briefs to the appellate court.*

ap·pend /ə'pɛnd/ *v.* to add on, (*syn.*) to affix: *The lawyer appended two more pages to the contract.*

ap·pend·age /ə'pɛndɪdʒ/ *n.* an extension of s.t.: *Fingers and toes are appendages of the hand and foot.*

ap·pen·dec·to·my /ˌæpən'dɛktəmi/ *n.* -**mies** the surgical removal of the human appendix: *Our daughter had an appendectomy at the hospital.*

ap·pen·di·ci·tis /əˌpɛndə'saɪtɪs/ *n.* [U] infection of the appendix causing swelling and pain: *Our daughter was suffering from appendicitis.*

ap·pen·dix /ə'pɛndɪks/ *n.* -**dixes** or -**dices** /-də, siz/ **1** a bodily organ located on the right side of the abdomen: *The appendix is apparently a useless organ that when infected can cause serious illness.* **2** s.t. added on, esp. to the end of a book: *The geography textbook has an appendix in which all the countries of the world and their capitol cities are listed.*

ap·pe·tite /'æpə,taɪt/ *n.* [C;U] desire and capacity for food, drink, or pleasure: *Our son is a football player and has a big appetite for steak.*

ap·pe·tiz·er /'æpə,taɪzər/ *n.* a small amount of food served before the main meal: *We served some crackers and cheese as an appetizer. See:* hors d'oeuvre.

ap·pe·tiz·ing /'æpə,taɪzɪŋ/ *adj.* stimulating or appealing to the appetite: *The roast beef is very appetizing.*

ap·plaud /ə'plɔd/ *v.* **1** to clap one's hands in approval: *The audience applauded the orchestra's performance.* **2** *fig.* to express admiration: *The boss applauded my efforts by praising my work.*

ap·plause /ə'plɔz/ *n.* [U] hand clapping in approval of a performance: *The speaker was shocked at the lack of applause from the audience.*

ap·ple /'æpəl/ *n.* **1** a round fruit with red, green, or yellow skin and a sweet, juicy flesh: *I ate an apple for dessert.* **2** *infrml.fig.* **the apple of one's eye:** one's most loved person: *His two-year-old daughter is the apple of his eye.* **3** **the Big Apple:** New York City: *People visit the Big Apple from all over the world.*

apple

USAGE NOTE: Popular nicknames for other American cities include: Beantown (Boston), the Windy City (Chicago), the Big Easy (New Orleans), and Tinsel Town (Hollywood).

ap·ple·sauce /'æpəl,sɔs/ *n.* [U] apples crushed and cooked into a soft and pulpy state: *Before they get teeth, babies enjoy eating applesauce.*

ap·pli·ance /ə'plaɪəns/ *n.* a device used for a specific function, usu. electrical and used in the home: *Major appliances include stoves, re-frigerators, washing machines, and dishwashers.*

ap·pli·ca·ble /'æplɪkəbəl, ə'plɪkə-/ *adj.* **1** belonging to, for the purpose of: *This payment is applicable to my rent.* **2** having meaning, significance: *His earlier comments were not applicable to our later discussion. See:* apply, **4.**

ap·pli·cant /'æplɪkənt/ *n.* a person seeking a specific job: *We have 10 applicants for the position of secretary.*

ap·pli·ca·tion /ˌæplɪ'keɪʃən/ *n.* **1** [C] a document or blank form for writing down information for a specific purpose, such as requesting a job or a loan: *I filled out an application for a job at the factory.* **2** [C] a use in s.t.: *Mathematics has applications in science.* **3** [C;U] the act of putting s.t. on: *An application of paint improved the appearance of the house.*

ap·pli·ca·tor /'æplɪˌkeɪtər/ *n.* a tool, such as a sponge or stick, used to apply things: *I used an applicator to put glue on the paper.*

ap·plied /ə'plaɪd/ *adj.* put to practical use, esp. in one's work: *She studied applied science at college and is a computer programmer now. See:* theoretical.

ap·pli·qué /ˌæplɪ'keɪ/ *n.* a decoration made from cloth, then cut out and fastened to a larger piece of cloth: *I put an appliqué of the moon and stars on my T-shirt.*

ap·ply /ə'plaɪ/ *v.* **-plies 1** to request or seek admission or assistance: *I applied for a visa to travel abroad.* **2** to put on, or upon: *The nurse applied a bandage to the wound.* **3** to credit, enter into account: *The bookkeeper applied a payment to a debt.* **4** to be meaningful to, to be relevant to: *His answer does not apply to the test question.*

ap·point /ə'pɔɪnt/ *v.* to choose s.o. for a position, (*syn.*) to designate: *The President appointed scientists to a committee on the environment.*

ap·point·ee /ˌəpɔɪn'ti/ *n.* a person appointed to a position: *The scientist is the President's new appointee to the committee on the environment.*

ap·point·ment /ə'pɔɪntmənt/ *n.* **1** [C] a time, place, and date to see s.o.: *I have a doctor's appointment tomorrow.* **2** [C;U] the act of giving s.o. a job or position: *The appointment of the new judge by the governor took place last week.*

ap·por·tion /ə'pɔrʃən/ *v.* to divide s.t., (*syn.*) to allocate: *The federal government apportioned money among the states.* -n. [U] **apportionment.**

ap·prais·al /ə'preɪzəl/ *n.* [C;U] an estimate of value of s.t., usu. made by an expert: *The insurance company required a written appraisal before it would insure the jewels.*

ap·praise /ə'preɪz/ *v.* **-praised, -praising, -praises** to estimate the value of property: *He appraised the necklace at $100,000.* -n. **appraiser.**

ap·pre·cia·ble /ə'priʃəbəl/ *adj.* **1** capable of being estimated or perceived: *I can find no appreciable differences in the witnesses' descriptions of the accident; they seem the same.* **2** capable of increasing (in value): *We bought an appreciable piece of property.* -adv. **appreciably.**

ap·pre·ci·ate /ə'priʃiˌeɪt/ *v.* **-ated, -ating, -ates 1** to be thankful for: *The elderly lady appreciated help in getting on the bus.* **2** to understand the value or importance of s.t., (*syn.*) to esteem: *He appreciates modern art.* **3** to sympathize with, have a feeling for: *I can appreciate how sad you are because of your dog's death.* **4** to increase in value: *The value of our company's stock has appreciated greatly.*

ap·pre·ci·a·tion /əˌpriʃi'eɪʃən/ *n.* [U] **1** gratitude, thankfulness: *The man showed his appreciation to the waiter by leaving him a big tip.* **2** esteem for the beauty or complexity of s.t.: *She has an appreciation of painting and sculpture.* **3** understanding, (*syn.*) sympathy: *He has an appreciation for how difficult it is to write well.* **4** increase in the value of s.t.

ap·pre·cia·tive /ə'priʃətɪv, -ʃiə-/ *adj.* **1** thankful, grateful: *He is appreciative of the gift.* **2** understanding a reason for s.t., (*syn.*) sympathetic: *I am appreciative of the fact that you were late because you were delayed in traffic.* -adv. **appreciatively.**

ap·pre·hend /ˌæprɪ'hɛnd/ *v.frml.* **1** to capture, arrest: *The police apprehended the criminal.* **2** to understand, to grasp the meaning of: *She apprehended the complicated law very quickly.* -adj. **apprehensible** /ˌæprɪ'hɛnsəbəl/.

ap·pre·hen·sion /ˌæprɪ'hɛnʃən/ *n.* [U;C] worry, fear: *The parents were filled with apprehension about letting their 19-year-old daughter drive across country alone.* -adj. **apprehensive** /ˌæprɪ'hɛnsɪv/.

ap·pren·tice /ə'prɛntɪs/ *n.* one who is learning a skill or trade from an expert (usu. a master craftsman or artist): *My son is an apprentice in a furniture maker's workshop.*

ap·pren·tice·ship /ə'prɛntiˌʃɪp, -tɪsˌʃɪp/ *n.* a period of time, often three to four years, spent working with a master craftsman or expert artist to learn a skill or trade: *That great artist served an apprenticeship before becoming well-known.*

ap·prise /ə'praɪz/ *v.frml.* **-prised, -prising, -prises** to inform: *I apprised my boss of my reasons for leaving my job.*

ap·proach /ə'prouʧ/ *n.* **-es 1** a course of action, a way of handling a situation: *She took a quiet, friendly approach in dealing with her daughter about the problem.* **2** means of ac-

cess: *The pilot made a slow, gradual approach to the airport runway.*
—*v.* **-es** **1** to near, move toward: *As I approached the house, I noticed that the door was open.* **2** to begin to handle a situation or work on s.t.: *I approached the problem of reducing costs by making a list of them.*

ap·proach·a·ble /ə'proʊtʃəbəl/ *adj.* friendly, willing to talk, (syn.) accessible: *Even though she is famous, she is still quite approachable.*

ap·pro·ba·tion /ˌæprə'beɪʃən/ *n.frml.* [U] formal approval: *The committee of professors gave approbation of my application to go to graduate school.*

ap·pro·pri·ate /ə'proʊpriɪt/ *adj.* correct, suitable: *That school is excellent, so she made the appropriate choice in going there.*
—*v.* /ə'proʊpri,eɪt/ **-ated, -ating, -ates** **1** to allocate, make (money) available: *The government appropriated funds for the construction of a park.* **2** to take by force of law, confiscate: *The state appropriated the farmer's land to build a highway on it.* -*n.* [C;U] **appropriation** /ə,proʊpri'eɪʃən/.

ap·prov·al /ə'pruvəl/ *n.* [U] **1** permission, consent: *The owner gave his approval for a salary increase for all employees.* **2** admiration, praise: *The violinist's performance met with the approval of the audience.*

ap·prove /ə'pruv/ *v.* **-proved, -proving, -proves** **1** to consent, permit: *The consulate approved my request for a travel visa.* **2** to admire, praise: *His mother approves of his new girlfriend's family.* -*adv.* **approvingly.**

ap·prox·i·mate /ə'prɑksəmɪt/ *adj.* estimated, not exact: *The builder gave an approximate cost for the roof repairs.*
—*v.* /ə'prɑksə,meɪt/ **-mated, -mating, -mates** to estimate, guess: *The mechanic approximated the cost of a new engine for my car.* -*adv.* **approximately;** -*n.* [U;C] **approximation** /ə,prɑksə'meɪʃən/.

ap·ri·cot /'æprɪ,kɑt, 'eɪ-/ *n.* a small, peach-like fruit: *I like apricots for dessert.*

A·pril /'eɪprəl/ *n.* the fourth month of the year, the month between March and May: *April has 30 days.*

A·pril Fools' Day *n.* the first day of April, celebrated in some countries by people playing tricks on each other: *A person called me to say that I had won a million dollars, and then he said, "April Fool!"*

a·pron /'eɪprən/ *n.* **1** a covering, usu. made of a piece of cotton cloth, worn over the front of one's body to keep one's clothes clean while cooking or cleaning: *The cook was preparing spaghetti sauce and his apron was covered with tomato juice.* **2** *n.pl.fig.* **apron strings:** usu. used with "tied" to indicate s.o. is totally controlled and protected: *The young man is* still tied to his mother's apron strings and won't do a thing without consulting her.

ap·ro·pos /ˌæprə'poʊ/ *prep.* about, regarding, concerning: *Apropos your request for money, I agree to loan it to you.*
—*adj.* relevant: *I felt that her comments were apropos.*

apt /æpt/ *adj.* **1** appropriate, suitable for a situation: *The speaker made apt remarks when answering questions from the audience.* **2** intelligent, capable: *She is a very apt student and learns quickly.* **3** likely to do s.t., (syn.) liable: *She is apt to make mistakes if you pressure her too much.* -*adv.* **aptly;** -*n.* [U] **aptness.**

ap·ti·tude /'æptə,tud/ *n.* [C;U] capacity for, to be good at doing s.t.: *That student has an aptitude for mathematics.*

ap·ti·tude test *n.* a test to determine the type of work and activities a person may be successful at or to determine a person's potential for learning: *My brother took an aptitude test that showed that he is well suited to photography.*

aqu·a /'ɑkwə, 'æ-/ *adj.* a light bluish green color: *The ocean was a lovely shade of aqua.*

aqu·a·ma·rine /ˌɑkwəmə'rin, ˌæ-/ *n.* a jewel colored light blue to darkish blue: *My wife wears a gold ring with a large aquamarine in it.*

a·quar·i·um /ə'kwɛriəm/ *n.* **-iums** or **-ia** /-iə/ a glass tank of varying sizes used to house fish and other water creatures: *The Boston Aquarium has many tanks of fish.*

a·quat·ic /ə'kwætɪk, ə'kwɑ-/ *adj.* related to water: *Aquatic sports include swimming, diving, and boating.*

aq·ue·duct /'ækwə,dʌkt/ *n.* a waterway made of stone blocks: *Many aqueducts from ancient Roman times still stand today near the Mediterranean Sea.*

Ar·a·bic /'ærəbɪk/ *n.* [U] the major language of the Arab world: *Millions of people speak Arabic.*

ar·a·ble /'ærəbəl/ *adj.* fit for plowing: *Farmers must have arable land in order to grow crops.*

ar·bi·ter /'ɑrbətər/ *n.* s.o. with the power to decide, a judge; an arbitrator: *The court named an arbiter to decide the disagreement between the factory's workers and owners.*

ar·bi·trar·y /'ɑrbə,trɛri/ *adj.* unwilling to use reason or listen to others, (syn.) dogmatic: *He made an arbitrary decision to sell the house without asking his wife.* -*adv.* **arbitrarily** /ˌɑrbə'trɛrəli/.

ar·bi·trate /'ɑrbə,treɪt/ *v.* **-trated, -trating, -trates** to help others reach a decision, (syn.) to referee: *The judge arbitrated a disagreement between workers and management.*

A

ar·bi·tra·tion /ˌarbəˈtreɪʃən/ n. [U] the process of solving disagreements with the help of an impartial person or group: *The wage disagreement is under arbitration.*

ar·bi·tra·tor /ˈarbəˌtreɪtər/ n. [C] a mediator, judge: *The lawyer acts as an arbitrator in labor disagreements.*

ar·bor /ˈarbər/ n. a shaded place in a garden, often made by climbing vines or branches that have grown together or by latticework that has become covered with climbing vines or roses: *The rose arbor was beautiful when the roses were in bloom.*

ar·bo·re·tum /ˌarbəˈritəm/ n. **-tums** or **-ta** /-tə/ a garden for the scientific study and public showing of trees and usu. other plants: *The city has an arboretum that is nice to walk through on a sunny day.*

arc /ark/ n.v. **1** a curved path, such as of electricity between two metal rods: *An <n.> arc of electricity <v.> arced between the two points.* **2** (in geometry) a section of a curve: *The diagram showed an <n.> arc between the two points.*

ar·cade /arˈkeɪd/ n. a building or passageway with many shops or amusements in it: *We go to the amusement arcade on Saturdays to play the electronic games.*

arch /artʃ/ n. **arches** **1** (in architecture) a curved structure of stone or metal, usu. rounded or pointed in the middle: *The arches inside a big church are marvelous to see.* **2** the middle portion of the underside of the foot, usu. raised: *The poor man has fallen arches; that is, flat feet.*
—v. to curve in the shape of an arch: *The dancer arched her back off the floor and jumped to her feet.*

ar·chae·ol·o·gy /ˌarkiˈaləʤi/ n. [U] the study of human life and civilizations through items of the past such as buried houses, statues, pots, etc.: *I took a course in archaeology before we traveled to Egypt.* **-adj. archaeological** /ˌarkiəˈlaʤɪkəl/; **-adv. archaeologically; -n. archeologist** /ˌarkiˈaləʤɪst/.

ar·cha·ic /arˈkeɪɪk/ adj. old and useless, (syn.) antiquated: *The company does some things in archaic ways, such as not using computers for bookkeeping.*

arch·di·o·cese /ˌartʃˈdaɪəsɪs, -ˌsis, -ˌsiz/ n. (in Christianity) the head office of a group of churches: *The archdiocese is headed by an archbishop.*

arched /artʃt/ adj. curved in the shape of an arch: *The arched windows inside the church are beautiful.*

ar·che·ol·ogy /ˌarkiˈaləʤi/ var. of archaeology

arch·er /ˈartʃər/ n. a person who shoots arrows, (syn.) a bowman: *In the 12th century warfare was often carried out by archers.*

arch·er·y /ˈartʃəri/ n. [U] the sport of using a bow to shoot arrows at targets: *I took a class in archery and learned to hit the bull's-eye.*

ar·che·type /ˈarkɪˌtaɪp/ n. the most typical of a group: *Old Mr. Higginbotham is the archetype of the elderly British gentleman.*

ar·chi·pel·a·go /ˌarkəˈpɛləˌgoʊ/ n. **-gos** or **-goes** a string of islands in a sea: *Indonesia is a nation of archipelagos.*

ar·chi·tect /ˈarkəˌtɛkt/ n. a trained professional who designs buildings and is often in charge of their construction: *My friend is an architect who designs school buildings.*

ar·chi·tec·ture /ˈarkəˌtɛktʃər/ n. **1** [U] the art and science of designing buildings and other structures: *She studied architecture and art history at the university.* **2** a style of design and construction: *The architecture of New York City is mostly tall buildings.* **-adj. architectural** /ˌarkəˈtɛktʃərəl/; **-adv. architecturally.**

ar·chives /ˈarˌkaɪvz/ n.pl. a place or collection of records and books of historical interest: *The emperor's decrees and letters were in the national archives.* **-n. archivist** /ˈarkəvɪst, -ˌkaɪ-/.

arch·way /ˈartʃˌweɪ/ n. the passage under an arch or group of arches: *We walked under the archway and into the palace.*

arc·tic /ˈarktɪk, ˈartɪk/ adj. very cold or related to the Arctic: *An arctic wind blew during the snow storm.*

ar·dent /ˈardnt/ adj. full of devotion, passionate loyalty: *She is a beautiful woman and has many ardent admirers.* **-adv. ardently.**

ar·dor /ˈardər/ n. [U] passion, extreme devotion: *He is full of ardor for her.*

ar·du·ous /ˈarʤuəs/ adj. difficult, tiring: *The refugees made an arduous journey through the mountains.* **-adv. arduously.**

are /ər; *strong form* ar/ v. present pl. of to be

ar·e·a /ˈɛriə/ n. **1** [C] a place, location: *The picnic area is near the parking lot.* ||*The New York area has high rents.* **2** [C] part of a room or a building: *My kitchen has a dining area.*||*My apartment building has a storage area in the basement.* **3** [C] one's field of knowledge or expertise: *Sales is not my area; I'm in accounting.* **4** [C;U] the size of a flat surface measured by multiplying the length by the width: *What's the area of your garden?*

ar·e·a code n. [C] in USA and Canada, the first three numbers of a telephone number, used in making a long-distance call: *My telephone number in Michigan is 555-6543, area code 313.*

a·re·na /əˈrinə/ n. a large building for the presentation of sports and other events, such as concerts: *The sports arena has basketball games and rock concerts.*

A

ar·gu·a·ble /'argyuəbəl/ *adj.* capable or worthy of being argued, doubted: *That fellow has opinions about everything, but what he says is arguable.*

ar·gue /'argyu/ *v.* **-gued, -guing, -gues 1** to disagree, contest what s.o. says in a formal, logical way: *The two lawyers argued their case in court.* **2** to fight with words, *(syn.)* to wrangle: *His mother and father argue with each other all the time.* *-adj.* **arguably.**

ar·gu·ment /'argyəmənt/ *n.* **1** a difference of opinion, disagreement: *There are at least two sides to every argument.* **2** a verbal fight, *(syn.)* a wrangle: *Every discussion with him turns into an argument.*

ar·gu·men·ta·tive /,argyə'mɛntətɪv/ *adj.* liking to argue, combative: *He is very argumentative.*

a·ri·a /'ariə/ *n.* a song for a single voice in an opera: *The audience applauded after the soprano sang the aria so beautifully.*

ar·id /'ærɪd, 'ɛr-/ *adj.* very dry, *(syn.)* parched: *The Sahara Desert is arid.*

a·rise /ə'raɪz/ *v.frml.* **arose** /ə'rouz/**, arisen** /ə'rɪzən/**, arising, arises 1** to get out of bed, awaken: *He arose at noon.* **2** to occur, happen: *Trouble arises when people have no food.*

ar·is·toc·ra·cy /,ærə'stakrəsi/ *n.* **-cies 1** a group of people named as nobles by the king or queen in a country: *Much of the aristocracy was killed during the French Revolution.* **2** the upper class: *Doctors and lawyers are often considered the aristocracy in our city.*

a·ris·to·crat /ə'rɪstə,kræt/ *n.* a noble, member of the aristocracy: *The countess is an aristocrat from an old family.* *-adj.* **aristocratic** /ə,rɪstə'krætɪk/**.**

a·rith·me·tic /ə'rɪθmə,tɪk/ *n.* [U] the branch of mathematics dealing with addition, subtraction, multiplication, and division: *All that most businesspeople need to know of mathematics is arithmetic.*

ark /ark/ *n.* a large, ancient ship: *Ancient Egyptians sailed in arks.*

arm /arm/ *n.* **1** one of two parts of the upper human body that extends from the shoulder to the hand: *The mother wrapped her arms around her child.* **2** the sleeve of a shirt, blouse, jacket, dress, etc., designed to cover the human arm: *Is the shirt long enough in the arms?* **3** the part of a chair or sofa designed to support the human arm: *The arms of the chair were too high.* **4** any of the long, usu. narrow parts of a machine: *The arm of the turntable is broken so we can't listen to the old records on the stereo.*

—v. **1** to provide weapons to s.o.: *The military arms its soldiers with modern weapons.* **2** to prepare for war: *The citizens armed themselves against their enemies.*

ar·ma·da /ar'madə/ *n.* a large fleet of warships: *An armada of ships sailed across the Atlantic Ocean in World War II.*

ar·ma·dil·lo /,armə'dɪlou/ *n.* **-los** an animal that digs for food and shelter in the ground and has tough skin made of hard plates: *The armadillo is found in the American South and in Central America.*

armadillo

Ar·ma·ged·don /,armə'gɛdn/ *n.fig.* the final great battle that would destroy the world: *For many years, people thought that Armageddon would happen between the USA and Russia. See:* apocalypse.

ar·ma·ment /'arməmənt/ *n.* **1** military weapons and supplies: *The unit had insufficient armament with which to do battle.* **2** *pl.* **armaments:** the weaponry owned or sold by a nation: *A small number of nations provide the world with armaments.*

arm·band /arm,bænd/ *n.* a piece of cloth worn around an arm, usu. black and worn to symbolize the death of s.o. or s.t.: *He wore a black armband when his mother died.*

arm·chair /'arm,ʧɛr/ *n.* a chair with armrests: *The armchair in the living room is very comfortable.*

armed /armd/ *adj.* equipped with a weapon: *The criminal is armed and dangerous.*

armed forces *n.pl.* the military of a nation: *The armed forces in the USA are the army, navy, air force, and marines.*

ar·mi·stice /'arməstɪs/ *n.* a military truce, a temporary agreement to stop military fighting: *The two nations signed an armistice.*

ar·mor /'armər/ *n.* [U] a protective covering worn by a soldier or on a piece of military equipment; military tanks and other vehicles equipped with protective plates: *The general sent his armor to meet the enemy.* *-v.* **armor;** *-n.* **armorer.**

ar·mor·y /'arməri/ *n.* **-ies** a large building for keeping military equipment: *An armory often serves as a military headquarters.*

arm·pit /'arm,pɪt/ *n.* the hollow under the arm where it joins the shoulder: *He applies deodorant to his armpits after he showers.*

arms /armz/ *n.pl.* weapons of war, such as rifles and cannons: *Countries sell arms to other countries for defense and war.*

arm-twist·ing *n.fig.* [U] pressuring or persuading s.o. to do s.t., *(syn.)* coercion: *After much arm-twisting, the parents agreed to install a second phone line in the house for their children.*

ar·my /'armi/ *n.* **-mies 1** a military land force of soldiers and tanks: *The army gathered on*

A

the border to invade its neighbor. **2** a great number (of people, ants, etc.): *An army of helpers arrived to clean up after the hurricane.*

a·ro·ma /ə'roumə/ *n.* a pleasant smell, esp. of cooking: *The aroma of coffee filled the air.*

ar·o·mat·ic /ˌærə'mætɪk/ *adj.* having an aroma, pleasant smell: *The pipe tobacco that he smokes is aromatic.*

arose /ə'rouz/ *past tense of* to arise

a·round /ə'raʊnd/ *prep.* **1** in a circular motion: *The teacher told the student to turn around in his seat and stop bothering the student behind him.* || *The crowd gathered around the movie star.* **2** *infrml.* approximately, about: *I'll meet you at the restaurant around noon.||Meals there cost around $20 per person.*
—*adv.* about: *We visited the shopping center and simply looked around.*

a·round-the-clock *adv.* non-stop, going for 24 hours: *They worked around-the-clock to finish the project on time.*

a·rouse /ə'raʊz/ *v.* **aroused, arousing, arouses** **1** to awaken s.o.: *I was aroused by traffic noises at 6:00 A.M.* **2** to excite: *The leader aroused the people to fight. -n.* [U] **arousal.**

ar·raign /ə'reɪn/ *v.* (in law) to force s.o. to appear before a court to answer a legal complaint: *The young man was arraigned in criminal court for theft. -n.* [C;U] **arraignment.**

ar·range /ə'reɪndʒ/ *v.* **-ranged, -ranging, -ranges** **1** to make specific plans, *(syn.)* to schedule: *I arranged the airline reservations for my trip.* **2** to put in order, *(syn.)* to organize: *The manager arranged the papers on her desk and then began work.* **3** to change a musical composition: *The composer arranged the song, which was originally written for the piano, for the orchestra.* **4** to come to an agreement: *The lawyers arranged a purchase agreement between the two businesses.* **5** to put s.t. in a pleasing way: *He arranged the flowers in a vase.*

ar·range·ment /ə'reɪndʒmənt/ *n.* **1** [C;U] agreement, understanding: *By arrangement with our neighbor, our lawn will be mowed once a week while we are away.* **2** [C] something made by putting things together: *The flower arrangements at the wedding were beautiful.* **3** [C] an adaptation, changed piece of music: *The guitarist wrote a new arrangement of the old song.* **4 to make arrangements for s.t.:** to schedule, prepare, such as hotel and airline reservations: *I have made all the arrangements for our summer vacation.*

ar·ray /ə'reɪ/ *n.* [C;U] a grouping, a way that things are put in order: *An array of TV antennas stands on the roof.*
—*v.* to form into a group: *The military arrayed its soldiers against the enemy. -n.* [U] **arrayal.**

ar·rears /ə'rɪrz/ *n.pl.* **1** overdue payments, such as rent or car payments not made on time **2 in arrears:** *The payments on that car loan are in arrears* (or) *are in arrears by three months. -n.* [U] **arrearage** /ə'rɪrɪdʒ/.

ar·rest /ə'rɛst/ *n.* **1** the seizure or holding of a person, usu. by police, for breaking the law: *She was placed under arrest after robbing the grocery store.* **2** [C;U] a stopping or delay: *Strong medicine brought an arrest to the spread of his cancer.*
—*v.* **1** to seize or hold s.o. by legal authority: *The policeman arrested the thief and took him to jail.* **2** to stop, delay: *A bandage arrested the flow of blood.* **3** to seize the attention of s.o.: *The beautiful sunset arrested our attention, and we stopped to watch it.*

ar·riv·al /ə'raɪvəl/ *n.* **1** [C;U] the coming to a place, appearance: *The arrival of my airline flight will be at gate 10.* **2** [C] a person who has recently reached a new destination: *That student is a new arrival on campus.*

ar·rive /ə'raɪv/ *v.* **-rived, -riving, -rives** **1** to reach a place or destination: *We arrived in town yesterday.* **2** *fig.* to reach financial or social success: *After years of hard work, she has finally arrived.*

ar·ro·gance /'ærəgəns/ *n.* [U] self-importance usu. offensive to others, *(syn.)* haughtiness: *The arrogance of that man annoys everyone.*

ar·ro·gant /'ærəgənt/ *adj.* self-important, *(syn.)* haughty: *Ever since he met the Queen, he's been quite arrogant. -adv.* **arrogantly.**

ar·row /'ærou/ *n.* **1** a long thin piece of wood, metal, or plastic with a point at one end and feathers at the other: *People shoot arrows at targets. See:* archery. **2** a sign or symbol shaped like an arrow to show direction: *An arrow pointed to the building's exit.*

ar·se·nal /'ɑrsənl, 'ɑrsnəl/ *n.* a storehouse of weapons and explosives: *The military maintains arsenals all over the country.*

ar·se·nic /'ɑrsənɪk, 'ɑrsnɪk/ *n.* [U] *adj.* a type of deadly poison: *Workers put out meat containing arsenic in order to kill the rats in the warehouse.*

ar·son /'ɑrsən/ *n.* [U] the deliberate setting of fires by s.o.: *The store burned down, and the police suspected arson. -n.* **arsonist.**

art /ɑrt/ *n.* **1** [U] making or expressing of that which is beautiful: painting, sculpture, architecture, music, literature, drama, dance, etc.: *That museum has a great collection of art.* **2** [U] the skill to do s.t. well: *She knows the art of making good conversation with people.*
—*n.pl.* **1 the arts:** dance, music, painting, sculpture, poetry, plays, and other writings **2 the liberal arts:** literature, music, languages, etc., as distinguished from the sciences: *He was a liberal arts major in college.*

ar·ter·y /ˈɑrtəri/ *n.* **-teries** **1** one of several large blood vessels going from the heart: *One of the patient's heart arteries is blocked.* **2** a highway: *The main arteries out of the city are filled with holiday traffic.* *-adj.* **arterial.**

art·ful /ˈɑrtfəl/ *adj.* **1** showing skill and ability: *The new ballet is an artful combination of traditional ballet and modern dance.* **2** skilled in gaining one's purpose, esp. through cunning means: *The thief was artful in hiding his loot before he was questioned.*

art gal·ler·y *n.* a place, esp. a showroom, to display works of art, such as paintings, sculpture, etc.: *The artist had a showing of her works in a well-known art gallery.*

ar·thri·tis /ɑrˈθraɪtɪs/ *n.* [U] inflammation of one or many joints such as in the hands, hips, and knees, resulting in pain: *My mother has arthritis in her knees and hips.* *-adj. -n.* **arthritic.**

ar·ti·choke /ˈɑrtəˌtʃoʊk/ *n.* a small green plant with leaves, whose flower head is cooked and eaten as a vegetable: *The growing of artichokes is a big business in California.*

artichoke

ar·ti·cle /ˈɑrtɪkəl/ *n.* **1** a thing, object: *Articles of clothing are kept in the dresser.* **2** a short written piece, such as a newspaper story: *I read a magazine article on a new type of medicine.* **3** a part of a longer piece of writing, such as a contract or constitution: *Article I of the contract names the buyer and the seller of the property.* **4** (in grammar) any of a set of adjectives used to limit a noun: *The English definite article is "the"; the English indefinite articles are "a" and "an".*

ar·tic·u·late /ɑrˈtɪkyəˌleɪt/ *v.* **-lated, -lating, -lates** **1** to express s.t. in clear and effective language: *The leader articulated the needs of his group for better housing.* **2** to speak distinctly: *People cannot understand what he says because he does not articulate his words.* *-adv.* **articulately;** *-n.* [U] **articulation** /ɑrˌtɪkyəˈleɪʃən/.
—*adj.* /ɑrˈtɪkyəlɪt/ able to express oneself in clear, effective language; good with words

ar·ti·fact /ˈɑrtəˌfækt/ *n.* an object used by humans a very long time ago: *Archaeologists dig for artifacts, such as old pots and bones of ancient peoples.*

ar·ti·fice /ˈɑrtəfɪs/ *n.frml.* **1** a trick: *Through artifice the magician created the illusion that he had sawed his assistant in half.* **2** a clever device or plan: *The general's artifice enabled him to surprise the enemy.*

ar·ti·fi·cial /ˌɑrtəˈfɪʃəl/ *adj.* **1** made by man, not made from natural things, (*syn.*) synthetic: *The chef always used real vanilla made from* vanilla beans rather than artificial vanilla flavoring. **2** insincere: *His artificial attempts at saying he is sorry don't fool anyone.* *-n.* [U] **artificiality** /ˌɑrtəˌfɪʃiˈæləti/; *-adv.* **artificially.**

ar·ti·fi·cial limb *n.* an arm, hand, leg, or foot made to replace the living one, (*syn.*) a prosthesis: *He lost his leg in an accident and wears an artificial limb.*

ar·til·ler·y /ɑrˈtɪləri/ *n.* [U] large, powerful guns, (*syn.*) cannonry: *The artillery fired its shells against the enemy.*

ar·ti·san /ˈɑrtəzən/ *n.* a craftsman, one skilled in a trade, such as bricklaying, painting houses, etc.: *The man is an artisan in a woodworking shop.*

art·ist /ˈɑrtɪst/ *n.* a person who creates art, such as a painter or musician: *The singer is a recording artist with Passion Records.*

ar·tis·tic /ɑrˈtɪstɪk/ *adj.* **1** related to art or artists: *Picasso's painting* Guernica *is an artistic impression of war's horrors.* **2** having ability in art or sensitivity to it: *She loves to decorate and has an artistic sense of colors.* *-adv.* **artistically.**

art·ist·ry /ˈɑrtəstri/ *n.* [U] artistic expression: *The violinist displayed her artistry in an exciting performance.*

art·sy or **art·y** /ˈɑrti/ *adj.infrml.* **-ier, -iest** wearing clothes or behaving in a way intended to be like an artist: *She wears very arty clothes and likes to be around actors.*

art·work /ˈɑrtˌwɜrk/ *n.* [U] pieces of art, such as paintings and sculpture: *The artwork in the museum is displayed with just the right lighting.*

as /əz; *strong form* æz/ *adv.* **1** to the same amount, just as much as s.o. or s.t. else: *He is just as willing to discuss the problem as you are.* **2** for example, for instance: *We enjoy playing sports, such as golf and tennis.*
—*conj.* **1** to the same extent (degree, amount): *She is as intelligent as she is pretty.* **2** because: *He fell asleep on the sofa, as he was so tired.* **3** in the same way: *Walk as fast as I am walking.*
—*pron.* that, which, or who, used after *such* or *same*: *He thinks the same as I do.*
—*prep.* **1** in the role of: *He works as a business consultant.* **2** in the same way: *We agree as a group on how to handle the matter.* **3 as far as it goes:** to a limited extent, not enough: *That report is acceptable as far as it goes, but it leaves out important ideas.* **4 as for:** with regard to: *As for raising salaries, we should discuss that next week.* **5 as if:** in such a way that it would seem to be true (or not true); as though: *(true) He is acting as if he's tired.* ‖*(untrue) He's spending money as if he were a millionaire.* **6 as is:** in its present condition, unchanged: *I offered my car for sale as is, without any repairs.* **7 as it were:** as if it is so,

A

when it isn't: *This so-called antique, as it were, is a fake.* **8** *infrml.fig.* **as long as your arm:** extensive, very lengthy: *She has a shopping list as long as your arm.* **9 as such:** the way it is, in its present state or condition: *The plan is big and as such requires a lot of money to make it succeed.* **10 as though:** apparently, as if: *He acts as though he owns this company, but he doesn't.* **11 such as:** for example, for instance: *I need some supplies, such as pencils, a notebook, and a ruler.*

ASAP or **asap** *abbr. for* as soon as possible: *She completed the work asap.*

as·bes·tos /æs'bestəs, æz-/ *n.* [U] a fibrous, fire-resistant material used in building materials (it is believed to cause cancer): *Asbestos was used to cover pipes in old buildings.*

as·cend /ə'send/ *v.* **1** to rise, climb: *The airplane ascended into the sky.* **2** to attain, gain a more important position: *The prince ascended the throne after the king died.*

as·cen·dan·cy /ə'sendənsi/ *n.frml.* [U] domination: *The superpower's ascendancy in world trade was the topic of much debate among the world's struggling nations.*

as·cen·dant /ə'sendənt/ *adj.* **1** rising, climbing: *The sun is ascendant in the eastern sky.* **2** *frml.* in control, superior: *The young woman is in an ascendant position in the company.* -*n.* **ascendance.**

as·cen·sion /ə'senʃən/ *n.* [U] the elevating of s.o. to s.t.: ascent: *The politician's ascension to power was slow but sure.*

as·cent /ə'sent/ *n.* [U;C] climb, upward path: *His ascent up the mountain was slow and difficult.*

as·cer·tain /ˌæsər'teɪn/ *v.frml.* to determine, find out (facts, a situation, etc.): *The lawyer ascertained the facts about the accident.* -*adj.* -*adv.* **ascertainable** -*n.* [U] **ascertainment.**

as·cet·ic /ə'setɪk/ *adj.* severe in self-denial, (*syn.*) austere: *Ascetic practices include eating little, not drinking any alcoholic beverages, and living very simply.*
—*n.* a person who leads a life of severe self-discipline, esp. for religious reasons -*adv.* **ascetically.**

as·cribe /ə'skraɪb/ *v.frml.* -**cribed,** -**cribing,** -**cribes** to give s.t. as a reason for, (*syn.*) to attribute: *The politician ascribed the failing economy to high taxes.*

a·sex·u·al /eɪ'sekʃuəl/ *adj.* nonsexual, having no sex: *Some bacteria are asexual and multiply by cell division.* -*adv.* **asexually.**

ash /æʃ/ *n.* **ashes** **1** [U;C] the powdery substance left after s.t. has burned: *He dropped his cigarette ash in the ashtray.* **2** [U] a type of hardwood tree: *Baseball bats are made from ash.*

a·shamed /ə'ʃeɪmd/ *adj.* feeling guilt, (*syn.*) chagrined: *He failed the test and was ashamed of himself.*

ash·en /'æʃən/ *adj.* pale, having a white, sickly look: *His illness made his face ashen for several weeks.*

a·shore /ə'ʃɔr/ *adv.* on shore: *After arriving in port, the ship's passengers went ashore to see the sights.*

ash·tray /'æʃˌtreɪ/ *n.* a type of dish for tobacco ashes: *I put my cigarette out in the ashtray.*

A·sian /'eɪʒən/ *adj.* related to Asia: *Products of Asian manufacture are sold worldwide.*
—*n.* a person from Asia: *She is an Asian from India.*

USAGE NOTE: Compare *Asian* and *Oriental.* In the USA, most people use Asian to refer to people, places, or things from countries such as Japan, Korea, and Indonesia on the continent of Asia: *There are ten Asian students in my class.*||*Several million Asians live in Los Angeles.* Oriental is more commonly used to describe rugs and art: *My mother has a blue Oriental rug in her living room.*

A·si·at·ic /ˌeɪʒi'ætɪk/ *adj.* related to the Asian continent, Asian: *The boat sank in Asiatic waters.*

a·side /ə'saɪd/ *adv.* to one side, away: *He put his newspaper aside and watched TV.*
—*adv.phr.* **aside from:** except for: *Aside from the chilly weather, our vacation was fun.*
—*n.* a comment made off the main point, (*syn.*) a digression: *We are talking about costs, but, as an aside, the product quality is excellent.*

as·i·nine /'æsəˌnaɪn/ *adj.* stupid, completely foolish: *His ideas about politics are asinine.*

ask /æsk/ *v.* **1** to question, (*syn.*) to inquire: *I asked my friend how she felt.* **2 to ask for it** or **for trouble:** to do s.t. that is sure to get one in trouble: *By not paying her bills, she asked for it; I'm taking her to court!* **3** *fig.* **to ask for the moon:** to ask for too much: *When the vice president demanded double his present salary, he was asking for the moon.*

USAGE NOTE: "*To ask*" is the most common verb used to request information or an answer from s.o. "*To inquire*" is more formal and often used in writing. "*To question s.o.*" implies doubt, such as in: *The police questioned a man about the theft.*

a·skance /ə'skæns/ *adv.frml.* with disapproval, distrust, or suspicion: *My father thinks I'm too young and looks askance at my drinking beer.*

a·skew /ə'skyu/ *adj.frml.* crooked, out of position: *That picture on the wall is askew and needs straightening.*

a·sleep /ə'slip/ *adj.* **1** sleeping, dozing: *The baby is asleep now.* **2** *infrml.fig.* **asleep on the job** or **asleep at the switch:** lazy, not aware, not active: *He never catches any mistakes; he's always asleep on the job.*

asp /æsp/ *n.* a small, poisonous snake of Africa and Asia: *In ancient times, people committed suicide by having an asp bite them near the heart.*

as·par·a·gus /ə'spærəgəs/ *n.* [C;U] **-gus** a green plant with long stems that are cooked and eaten

as·pect /'æ,spɛkt/ *n.frml.* **1** [C] a feature, part of s.t.: *What aspect of the show did you like the best--the dancing or the music?* **2** [U;C] point of view, consideration: *From the cost aspect, the product is not expensive.*

as·per·sion /ə'spɜrʒən/ *n.frml.* a remark that says s.t. bad about s.o., *(syn.)* a slur: *He hates his competitor and casts aspersions on him constantly.*

as·phalt /'æs,fɔlt/ *n.* [U] a black coal-based substance used for covering roads or roofs: *Our driveway is made of asphalt.*
—*v.* to coat with this substance: *The new road was asphalted.*

as·phyx·i·ate /æs'fɪksi,eɪt, əs-/ *v.* **-ated, -ating, -ates** to kill by cutting off s.o.'s supply of air, *(syn.)* to suffocate: *The mine roof fell in, and a miner was asphyxiated.* -*n.* [U] **asphyxiation** /æs,fɪksi'eɪʃən, əs-/.

as·pic /'æspɪk/ *n.* [U] a clear firm jelly made from fish, beef, or other gravy in which food is usu. placed: *We enjoy eating chicken in aspic in the summer.*

as·pir·ant /'æspərənt, ə'spaɪrənt/ *n.* [C] one who has a strong desire to advance or gain a higher position: *All the aspirants for the directorship had superb qualifications.*

as·pi·ra·tion /,æspə'reɪʃən/ *n.frml.* a strong desire, a great ambition: *She has aspirations to be company president some day.*

as·pire /ə'spaɪr/ *v.frml.* **-pired, -piring, -pires** to desire strongly, hope to do or to be: *He aspires to be a great actor someday.*

as·pi·rin /'æsprɪn, -pərɪn/ *n.* [C;U] **-rin** or **-rins** a painkiller (salicylic acid) in tablet form: *I had a headache and took two aspirin(s) for it.*

ass /'æs/ *n.* **asses 1** a donkey: *The ass is often used as a pack animal in remote mountain terrains.* **2** *vulg.slang* the buttocks **3** *infrml.fig.* **to make an ass of oneself:** to behave stupidly: *When he drinks too much, he makes an ass of himself.*

USAGE NOTE: To describe a part of the body, *ass* is a vulgar term and should not be used in polite company. In American English, the terms *posterior* and *buttocks* are used in for-

mal speech and writing: *The firefighter was badly burned on his legs and buttocks. Bottom* is an informal term used around friends and acquaintances: *My mother spanked my bottom when I hit my baby brother.*

as·sail /ə'seɪl/ *v.frml.* **1** to attack physically, storm: *Soldiers assailed the enemy.* **2** to criticize or attack verbally: *The two politicians assailed each other with insults.*

as·sail·ant /ə'seɪlənt/ *n.* a person who attacks s.o.: *The police caught the victim's assailant.*

as·sas·sin /ə'sæsən/ *n.* a person who kills another, usu. for a reward or political reasons: *He is a hired assassin for a radical political group.*

as·sas·si·nate /ə'sæsə,neɪt/ *v.* **-nated, -nating, -nates** to murder s.o. in a planned way: *President Kennedy was assassinated in 1963.* -*n.* [C;U] **assassination** /ə,sæsə'neɪʃən/.

as·sault /ə'sɔlt/ *v.* to strike with force, *(syn.)* to attack: *A thief assaulted me with a club.*
—*n.* **1** [C;U] a violent attack, physically or verbally: *The knights' assault on the castle was successful.* **2** [U] **assault and battery:** (in law) an attack (assault) in which physical harm is done to s.o. (battery): *A police officer caught the fleeing man and arrested him for assault and battery.*

as·sem·blage /ə'sɛmblɪdʒ/ *n.* **1** [U] putting parts of s.t. together, *(syn.)* construction: *The assemblage of the motor parts took several hours.* **2** [C] *frml.* a grouping of people: *The assemblage of important people at the political gathering was impressive.*

as·sem·ble /ə'sɛmbəl/ *v.* **-bled, -bling, -bles 1** to put together, make: *The workers in that factory assemble trucks.* **2** to gather, come together: *The crowd assembled in the meeting hall.*

as·sem·bler /ə'sɛmblər/ *n.* a worker who puts together parts of an item being manufactured: *She works as an assembler in a factory that manufactures computers.*

as·sem·bly /ə'sɛmbli/ *n.* **-blies 1** [U] putting parts of s.t. together: *The assembly of a rifle by a soldier can be done in seconds.* **2** [C] a grouping of people, gathering: *The assembly of students takes place in the auditorium.*

as·sem·bly·man /ə'sɛmblimən/ *n.* **-men** /-mən/ a member of a local or state legislature: *The assemblyman from our district has an office near city hall.* -*n.* **assemblywoman** /ə'sɛmbli,wʊmən/ **-women** /-,wɪmən/.

as·sent /ə'sɛnt/ *v.frml.* to agree to, to approve: *The father assented to his daughter's marriage.*
—*n.* [U] affirmative response, permission

as·sert /ə'sɜrt/ *v.* **1** to claim, say s.t. is true: *The lawyer asserts that his client is not guilty.*

2 to put oneself forth forcefully, become aggressive: *She asserted herself on the job and won a promotion.*

as·ser·tion /ə'sɜrʃən/ *n.* **1** [C] a claim, statement s.t. is true: *The lawyer made an assertion that his client was not guilty.* **2** [U] the aggressive use of s.t.: *The President's assertion of his power to stop the fighting succeeded.*

as·ser·tive /ə'sɜrtɪv/ *adj.* bold, confident, aggressive: *His assertive nature helped him attain his goals.* *-adv.* **assertively**; *-n.* [U] **assertiveness.**

as·sess /ə'sɛs/ *v.* **-es** **1** to evaluate, analyze: *I assessed how much it would cost to build a new house.* **2** to place a value on s.t., esp. as a basis for taxation: *Our house is assessed at $50,000.* *-n.* [C] **assessor** /ə'sɛsər/.

as·sess·ment /ə'sɛsmənt/ *n.* [C;U] **1** an evaluation, analysis: *The planner made an assessment of what should be done next.* **2** a valuation, estimate of worth as a basis for taxation: *We have a low assessment on our property.*

as·set /'æsɛt/ *n.* **1** an advantage, an important person, thing, or quality: *She is very talented and is a real asset to our company.* **2 assets:** (in accounting) items of value to a person, business, or institution: *The company assets include a building, equipment, and cash.*

as·sid·u·ous /ə'sɪdʒuəs/ *adj.frml.* hard-working, (*syn.*) diligent: *Being very assiduous, he completed the report well before the deadline.* *-adv.* **assiduously** *-n.* [U] **assiduousness.**

as·sign /ə'saɪn/ *v.* **1** to give a job or tasks to s.o. to do, (*syn.*) to designate: *My boss assigned me the task of finding new offices to rent.* **2** to transfer, sign over property, rights, or interests: *I assigned the ownership (rights, deed, etc.) of the property to my son.* *—n.* (in law) a person, business, etc., to whom one transfers rights and other assets, (*syn.*) assignee: *The contract that I signed transfers ownership of the property to my heirs and assigns.*

as·sign·a·ble /ə'saɪnəbəl/ *adj.* capable of being given or sold to another: *My house mortgage is assignable, meaning that my bank can assign it to another owner if I sell it.* *-n.* [U] **assignability** /ə,saɪnə'bɪləti/.

as·sign·ment /ə'saɪnmənt/ *n.* **1** a task, duty, or other obligation given to s.o.: *His manager gave him the assignment of planning the sales meeting.* **2** (in law) the transfer, signing over of rights, etc., to another: *The assignment of the property deed will take place tomorrow.*

as·sim·i·late /ə'sɪmə,leɪt/ *v.frml.* **-lated, -lating, -lates** **1** to eat and absorb food, (*syn.*) to digest: *People assimilate nutrients from food.* **2** to take in, absorb into the mind: *The student assimilates knowledge rapidly.* **3** to become part of a nation's culture, acculturated: *The*

children of the immigrants easily assimilated into American culture. *-n.* [C;U] **assimilation** /ə,sɪmə'leɪʃən/.

as·sist /ə'sɪst/ *v.* to aid, help s.o. do s.t.: *My friend assisted me in moving to a new apartment.*
—n. in sports, esp. baseball and ice hockey, the official credit given for helping a teammate (by throwing the ball or passing the puck) to score: *His teammate was given an assist when he scored the winning goal.*

as·sis·tance /ə'sɪstəns/ *n.* [U] **1** aid, help in doing s.t.: *My friend's assistance in helping me to move was much appreciated.* **2 public assistance:** welfare; money or food given by the government to the homeless and other people in need of financial aid, such as the elderly or people living in an area struck by a disaster: *He lost his job and is now living on public assistance.*

as·sis·tant /ə'sɪstənt/ *n.* a person who helps another at work: *Her assistant types letters and answers the telephone.*

as·so·ci·ate /ə'soʊʃiɪt, -si-/ *n.* a coworker or a person with whom one works as a partner: *My associates and I work for the city government.*
—v. /ə'soʊʃi,eɪt, -si-/ **-ated, -ating, -ates** **1** to work, socialize, or mingle with: *We associate with our neighbors at church.* **2** to connect in the mind, (*syn.*) to correlate: *I associate his bad behavior with his difficult childhood.*

as·so·ci·ate de·gree *n.* in USA, a rank earned after a set two-year course at a college or university. *See:* B.A., USAGE NOTE.

USAGE NOTE: Compare B.A. (*bachelor's degree*) and A.A. (*associate degree*). People who aren't prepared to study at a university may earn an A.A. at a junior or community college. They may then transfer their credits to a four-year college or university. An A.A. is also given for completion of two-year vocational courses in such fields as accounting, business administration, and restaurant management.

as·so·ci·a·tion /ə,soʊsi'eɪʃən, -ʃi-/ *n.* **1** [C] a group with common interests, (*syn.*) an alliance: *Our company belongs to the National Association of Manufacturers.* **2** [U] relationship, affiliation: *We work in association with our neighbors to improve the community.* **3** [C] a connection, (*syn.*) a correlation: *Experts have found an association between poverty and crime.*

as·sort·ed /ə'sɔrtɪd/ *adj.* of different kinds, mixed: *The bowl contains assorted hard candies.* *-v.* **assort.**

as·sort·ment /ə'sɔrtmənt/ *n.* a group of things of different kinds, a mixture: *That store sells an assortment of shoes, boots, and sneakers.*

as·suage /ə'sweɪdʒ/ v.frml. **-suaged, -suaging, -suages** to calm: *The king assuaged the fears of his nobles about a war.*

as·sum·a·ble /ə'suməbəl/ adj. capable of being taken on by another: *We have an assumable mortgage, so any qualified buyer can assume it.*

as·sume /ə'sum/ v. **-sumed, -suming, -sumes 1** to believe s.t. is true without knowing, (syn.) to conjecture: *I assume that the moving van will be here this morning.* **2** to presume, take for granted: *He assumed that we would give money, so he put our names on the givers' list.* **3** to take on responsibility: *The winner of the election assumed the office of senator.*

as·sum·ing /ə'sumɪŋ/ conj. thinking that s.t. will happen or has happened, or is a certain way, (syn.) supposing: *Assuming that he arrives on time, we can start our meeting soon.*

as·sump·tion /ə'sʌmpʃən/ n. **1** [C] a belief that s.t. will happen, (syn.) a supposition: *It is only an assumption on my part that what he says is true.* **2** [U] acceptance, a taking on of responsibility: *His assumption of the duties of mayor takes place in January.* **3 based on the assumption that:** based on the belief that: *Based on the assumption that she does want to marry him, we can go ahead with the wedding plans.*

as·sur·ance /ə'ʃurəns/ n. a guarantee, pledge: *I give you my assurance that I shall pay you on time.*

as·sure /ə'ʃur/ v. **-sured, -suring, -sures** to promise that s.t. is so, (syn.) to guarantee: *I assure you that I'm telling you the truth.*

as·sured /ə'ʃurd/ adj. guaranteed, made certain: *The policy offers an assured income of $800 per month upon retirement.* -adv. **assuredly** /ə'ʃurɪdli/.

as·ter /'æstər/ n. a flower with a round center button and white, pink, or purple petals: *We grow asters in our garden.*

as·ter·isk /'æstərɪsk/ n. the symbol (*); the asterisk is often used in writing to show that there is a comment at the bottom of the page or that something has been omitted

a·stern /ə'stɜrn/ adv. of the back part of a boat: *The captain has gone astern.*

as·ter·oid /'æstə,rɔɪd/ n. any of thousands of usu. irregularly shaped heavenly bodies: *Ceres is the largest asteroid in our solar system.*

asth·ma /'æzmə/ n. [U] a chronic medical condition which causes difficulty in breathing: *My friend suffers from asthma and must use an inhaler to relieve her breathing difficulties.* -n. adj. **asthmatic** /æz'mætɪk/.

as·ton·ish /ə'stanɪʃ/ v. to greatly amaze, to surprise overwhelmingly: *I am astonished at how beautifully that little girl dances.*

as·ton·ish·ment /ə'stanɪʃmənt/ n. [U] great amazement, surprise: *The crowd reacted with astonishment when the speaker suddenly dropped dead.*

as·tound /ə'staund/ v. to amaze, astonish: *I was astounded at how high the repair bill was.*

a·stray /ə'streɪ/ adv. **1** in a wrong (evil, bad) way: *The boy is leading his younger brother astray by teaching him bad habits.* **2 to go astray:** to fall into bad or evil ways: *His younger brother has gone astray and become a thief.*

a·stride /ə'straɪd/ prep.adv. mounted on or over s.t. with one's legs on either side: *The rider is astride her horse.* -adv. **astride.**

as·trin·gent /ə'strɪndʒənt/ n.adj. a substance, esp. a liquid, capable of shrinking body tissues, such as the skin: *These <n.> astringents are used to freshen and tighten facial skin.*

as·trol·o·gy /ə'stralədʒi/ n. [U] a system of belief in the influence of heavenly bodies (stars, planets, sun, moon) upon human affairs and events: *Millions of people believe in astrology and read their horoscope daily.* -n. **astrologer** ;-adj. **astrological** /,æstrə'ladʒɪkəl/; -adv. **astrologically.**

as·tro·naut /'æstrə,nɔt/ n. a person who flies into outer space: *The astronauts trained for years in how to navigate their spacecraft.*

astronaut

as·tron·o·mer /ə'stranəmər/ n. a scientist who studies heavenly bodies and outer space: *Many astronomers work at night, looking at the stars.*

as·tro·nom·i·cal /,æstrə'namɪkəl/ adj. **1** related to astronomy: *The institute's budget for astronomical research was cut back as the institute refocused its research on the earth's environment.* **2** fig. huge, extremely high: *The cost of the new government program is astronomical; it's billions of dollars!* -adv. **astronomically.**

as·tron·o·my /ə'stranəmi/ n. [U] the science of outer space, of heavenly bodies, and related phenomena: *I took a course in astronomy in college because I was interested in the planets.*

As·tro·turf /'æstrou,tɜrf/ n.TM [U] tough, man-made ground covering used instead of grass: *The playing fields of many sports stadiums are covered with Astroturf.*

as·tute /ə'stut/ adj. intelligent, keen in judgment: *She is an astute investor in the stock market and always knows which stocks to avoid.* -adv. **astutely.**

a·sun·der /ə'sʌndər/ adv.frml. torn or broken into parts or pieces: *The bomb blew the building asunder.*

A

a·sy·lum /ə'saɪləm/ *n.* **1** [U] a safe place, a refuge from harm: *The refugee sought asylum in the Swiss embassy.* **2** [C] a type of hospital, esp. for people with mental illness: *He became insane and was sent to an asylum.*

a·sym·met·ri·cal /,eɪsə'mɛtrɪkəl/ *adj.* not of equal size or similar shape: *That rabbit has one ear missing, and it looks asymmetrical.* *-adv.* **asymmetrically.**

at /ət; *strong form* æt/ *prep.* **1** toward, in the direction of: *I looked at her and smiled.* **2** during, while: *He works at night.* **3** located in, in the position of: *The important information is at the bottom of the page.* **4** in the location of: *She is at her office.* **5** related to time: *He leaves at five o'clock.* **6** doing, engaged in: *She is hard at work on a project.* **7** in the condition of: *The country is at peace now.* **8** in the manner of: *The horse ran off at a gallop.* **9** in a superlative description: *at most, at least, at best, at worst,* etc.: *At least you can tell me what's going on here!* **10 at all:** most definitely not: *I don't like what he says at all.* **11 at all costs:** whatever is necessary: *The company must increase its sales at all costs.* **12 at a loss: a.** *frml.* at a price less than original cost: *I had to sell my house at a loss of $5,000.* **b.** *fig.* not knowing what to do: *I am at a loss as to how to solve the problem.* **13 at any rate:** anyhow, whatever the situation is: *We lost some of our business in Chicago; at any rate, we made up for it with increases in California.*

ate /eɪt/ *v. simple past tense of* to eat: *This morning, I ate eggs for breakfast.*

a·the·ism /'eɪθi,ɪzəm/ *n.* [U] a belief that God does not exist: *She was raised as a Protestant, but as an adult she realized she believed in atheism.*

a·the·ist /'eɪθiɪst/ *n.* a person who does not believe in the existence of God: *She is an atheist, but believes in people.* *-adj.* **atheistic** /,eɪθi'ɪstɪk/.

ath·lete /'æθ,lit/ *n.* a person who is trained in or has a natural talent for exercises and sports: *His son was an outstanding athlete who played several team sports.*

ath·lete's foot *n.* [U] a type of skin disease that causes cracking and itching in the skin between the toes, (*syn.*) tinea pedis: *The doctor suggested he use a certain cream to alleviate the itching caused by his athelete's foot.*

ath·let·ic /æθ'lɛtɪk/ *adj.* **1** related to sports: *She entered many athletic competitions just for fun.* **2** having ability in sports: *Despite her advanced years, she is very athletic.* *-adv.* **athletically.**

ath·let·ics /æθ'lɛtɪks/ *n.pl.* sports in general: *He was good in athletics in high school, where he played baseball and football.*

ath·let·ic sup·port·er *n.* a garment worn to support and protect the male genital area, (*syn.*) jockstrap: *He puts on an athletic supporter before he goes running.*

At·lan·tic /ət'læntɪk, æt-/ *n.adj.* the ocean located between Europe and Africa on one side and North and South America on the other: *The <n.> Atlantic (or) <adj.> Atlantic Ocean was first crossed by the Scandinavians 1,000 years ago.*

at·las /'ætləs/ *n.* **-es** **1** a collection of maps in book form: *We have a world atlas that has maps of every country on earth.* **2 Atlas: a.** (from Greek mythology) a Titan who was forced by Zeus to support the heavens on his shoulders **b.** a strong man: *He can lift hundreds of pounds; he's an Atlas.*

ATM *abbr. for* automated teller machine

USAGE NOTE: ATMs are found in business districts and shopping malls of all American cities. People use them to get cash from their bank accounts and, in many places, to pay for gas, groceries, and other things.

at·mos·phere /'ætməs,fɪr/ *n.* [U;C] **1** the air space above the earth: *The atmosphere is becoming more polluted each day.* **2** the special tone or mood of a particular place or created by a place or thing: *A reading room in a library has a quiet atmosphere.* *-adj.* **atmospheric** /,ætmə'sfɪrɪk, -'fer-/.

at·om /'ætəm/ *n.* the smallest unit of matter, a nucleus surrounded by protons and electrons: *Atoms form into molecules that make up matter.*

at·om bomb *n.* a bomb of great destructive force powered by the splitting of atoms: *Dropping atom bombs on Japan brought the end of World War II.*

a·tom·ic /ə'tɑmɪk/ *adj.* **1** of or relating to an atom: *He studied atomic reactions in his physics course.* **2** of or using nuclear energy: *The atomic submarine was on patrol in the Pacific Ocean.*

a·tom·ic bomb *n. See:* atom bomb.

a·tom·ic en·er·gy *n.* [U] energy made from splitting atoms in a nuclear reactor, usu. for electricity: *Atomic energy is a major source of electrical power for many nations.*

a·tone /ə'toʊn/ *v.* **atoned, atoning, atones** to ask for forgiveness, esp. for sin, and to do good works to pay for it: *The man atoned for his bad behavior by working for a charity.* *-n.* [U] **atonement.**

a·tri·um /'eɪtriəm/ *n.* **atria** /'eɪtriə/ or **atriums** in modern buildings, an area often on the ground floor, with a high ceiling that has a skylight: *The atrium in our building is open to the public for sitting and eating.*

a·tro·cious /ə'troʊʃəs/ adj. **1** very cruel: *The military committed atrocious acts of violence in shooting women and children.* **2** disgusting, sickening: *His manners are atrocious.* -adv. **atrociously** -n. **atrocity** /ə'trɑsəti/ -ties.

at·ro·phy /'ætrəfi/ v. **-phied, -phying, -phies** to harden, grow small and useless: *From lack of exercise, the muscles in his legs atrophied.*

at·tach /ə'tæʧ/ v. **-es 1** to put s.t. on, (*syn.*) to affix: *I attached a note to my report with a paper clip.* **2** to affiliate with, associate with: *That official is attached to the government's treasury.* **3** to be in love with, emotionally dependent upon: *They are a loving couple and are quite attached to each other.* **4** to assign, attribute: *I attach no importance to what he says.*

at·ta·ché /,ætæ'ʃeɪ, ,ætə-/ n. an embassy official responsible for reporting information in a specific area: *My brother is the economics attaché at the British embassy.*

at·ta·ché case n. a case with a handle for carrying work-related papers, (*syn.*) a briefcase: *My attaché case is made of leather.*

at·tach·ment /ə'tæʧmənt/ n. **1** [C] an accessory, s.t. added on: *A vacuum cleaner has various attachments, such as a narrow nozzle and a brush.* **2** [U] the process of joining, putting s.t. together: *The attachment of parts of the child's crib took a long time.* **3** [C] an emotional bond, love: *His attachment to his dog was very strong.*

at·tack /ə'tæk/ v. **1** to assault, strike: *The criminal attacked his victim with a club.* **2** to find fault with, (*syn.*) to assail: *The critics attacked the writer's latest book as weak.* **3** to make a serious effort to do s.t., to undertake: *Relief organizations attacked the problem of hunger by seeking to increase the food supply.*
—n. **1** [C;U] the use of violent force, an assault: *The military attack began at dawn.* **2** [C] criticism, faultfinding: *The critic's attack on the novel was sharp.* **3** [C] a serious undertaking, particular approach: *The scientist made an attack on solving a difficult problem by running a simulation on his computer.*

at·tack·er /ə'tækər/ n. a person or group, such as a military unit or gang, that assaults: *The victim's attacker was caught by the police.*

at·tain /ə'teɪn/ v. to achieve, reach: *The salesperson attained her sales goal for the month.* -adj. **attainable;** -n. [U] **attainment.**

at·tempt /ə'tɛmpt/ v. to try, strive for: *He attempted to pass the examination and succeeded.*
—n. an effort, endeavor: *She made an attempt to telephone, but no one was home.*

at·tend /ə'tɛnd/ v. **1** to be present at: *I attended the wedding at the church.* **2** to take care of,

see to: *One secretary attends to all of the paperwork in my office.*

at·ten·dance /ə'tɛndəns/ n. [U] **1** presence: *My attendance at my brother's wedding was required.* **2** to take attendance: to check on people's presence: *Every morning the teacher takes attendance to determine who is absent.*

at·ten·dant /ə'tɛndənt/ n. a person who performs a service, esp by waiting on others: *The attendant in the washroom hands out towels and brushes off people's clothes.*
—adj.frml. accompanying or in connection with: *The politician negotiated the peace settlement and its attendant problems.*

at·ten·tion /ə'tɛnʃən/ n. [U] **1** looking and listening, (*syn.*) concentration: *His attention to his work was constantly interrupted by the ringing telephone.* **2** work, care: *Sick people need attention from doctors and nurses.* **3** a military command to stand in a still, straight way: *The sergeant ordered the troops to stand at attention.*

at·ten·tive /ə'tɛntɪv/ adj. **1** paying attention, (*syn.*) alert: *Students should be attentive in class.* **2** concerned, considerate: *As his parents age, he becomes more attentive to their needs.* -adv. **attentively.**

at·ten·u·ate /ə'tɛnyu,eɪt/ v.frml. **-ated, -ating, -ates** to dilute, thin, weaken: *The two people argued so much that their friendship was attenuated.*

at·test /ə'tɛst/ v. to swear s.t. is true, certify: *I attest to the fact that that is my signature on the contract.*

at·tic /'ætɪk/ n. a space, often used as storage, under the roof of a house: *We put trunks and old books in our attic.*

at·tire /ə'taɪr/ n.frml. [U] clothing, dress: *We wear formal attire when we attend the opera.*

at·ti·tude /'ætə,tud/ n. feeling about or toward s.o. or s.t.: *She has a good attitude toward work; she's always cheerful.*

at·tor·ney /ə'tɜrni/ n. a legal counselor, lawyer: *The attorneys for the company were present in court today.*

at·tor·ney gen·er·al n. **attorneys general** the chief lawyer for a nation or state: *Citizens were so upset by an investment scandal that they wrote to the state attorney general about it.*

at·tract /ə'trækt/ v. to draw interest, (*syn.*) to appeal to: *San Francisco attracts millions of tourists each year.*

at·trac·tion /ə'trækʃən/ n. **1** [U] appeal: *Because she is afraid of heights, the long trip by airplane had little attraction for her.* **2** [U;C] a popular place, entertainment: *Niagara Falls is a major attraction for people visiting the United States.* **3** [U;C] the ability and quality in a person to attract, (*syn.*) charm: *His* *winning smile and easy manner were attractions that drew the public to him.*

at·trac·tive /əˈtræktɪv/ *adj.* **1** appealing, interesting: *I have an offer of a new job at an attractive salary.* **2** causing interest, (*syn.*) charming: *She is a very attractive woman with many admirers.* -*adv.* **attractively.**

at·trib·ut·a·ble /əˈtrɪbyutəbəl, -byə-/ *adj.* be the reason for, assignable to: *Her success is attributable to her intelligence and hard work.*

at·trib·ute /ˈætrə,byut/ *n.* a characteristic, quality of a person or thing: *He is a handsome man with many other good attributes.*
—*v.* /əˈtrɪbyut, -byət/ **-uted, -uting** to credit, be the reason for: *I attribute his success to his talent and hard work.* -*adj.* **attributable** /əˈtrɪbyutəbəl, -byə-/; -*n.* [U] **attribution** /ˌætrəˈbyuʃən/.

at·tri·tion /əˈtrɪʃən/ *n.* [U] a slow lessening in number or strength through resignation, retirement, or death: *Through attrition, the police department went from 40 members to 23 members in one year.*

at·tuned /əˈtund/ *adj.* aware and sensitive to s.o. or s.t.: *The husband and wife are attuned to each other's needs.||The reporter is attuned to what is going on in the city.* -*v.* **attune.**

a·twit·ter /əˈtwitər/ *adj.* chirping rapidly like a bird or chattering nervously: *The guests arrived late and were all atwitter about a bad car accident they had seen.*

a·typ·i·cal /eɪˈtɪpɪkəl/ *adj.* not typical, unusual: *He is always on time; it is atypical of him to be late.* -*adv.* **atypically.**

au·burn /ˈɔbərn/ *adj.* -*n.* reddish brown to brown in color: *The color of her hair is <adj.> auburn.*

auc·tion /ˈɔkʃən/ *n.* a public sale of property in which items are sold to the person who bids the highest: *When the old woman died, her son held an auction of her furniture.*
—*v.* to sell property by auction: *Her family auctioned off her jewels.*

auc·tion·eer /ˌɔkʃəˈnɪr/ *n.* a person who runs an auction: *Some auctioneers repeat buyers' offers very rapidly.*

au·da·cious /ɔˈdeɪʃəs/ *adj.* **1** bold, adventurous, (*syn.*) brave: *The buyer was audacious in his attempt to take over another company.* **2** offensive, brazen: *The boy was audacious in yelling at his father.*

au·dac·i·ty /ɔˈdæsəti/ *n.* [U] brazenness, insolence: *The son had the audacity to demand that his mother resign so that he could take over the company.*

au·di·ble /ˈɔdəbəl/ *adj.* capable of being heard: *The music and laughter were audible from the street outside the nightclub.* -*adv.* **audibly** -*n.* [U] **audibility** /ˌɔdəˈbɪləti/.

au·di·ence /ˈɔdiəns/ *n.* **1** the people who gather to listen to and watch an event: *The audience at the rock concert was very enthusiastic.* **2** a group of customers who are likely to buy a particular book or other printed matter: *The audience for her textbook is university students.*

au·di·o /ˈɔdi,ou/ *n.* [U] *adj.* **1** of or relating to sound, the transmission and production of recorded sound: *The audio portion of the broadcast was not good.* **2** short for audio equipment: *The <n.> audio is broken on that TV.*

au·di·o·lin·gual /ˌɔdiouˈlɪŋgwəl/ *adj.* related to a method of learning a language that stresses intensive listening and speaking: *My French teacher uses the audio-lingual approach to teaching.*

au·di·o·vis·u·al /ˌɔdiouˈvɪʒuəl/ *adj.* related to the educational use of a variety of teaching aids, such as charts, films, television, overhead transparencies, and other forms of nonwritten instruction: *During the 1940s, audiovisual education was introduced.*

au·di·o·vis·u·als /ˌɔdiouˈvɪʒuəlz/ *n.pl.* materials, such as charts, films, and television programs, that combine sound and visual images: *We made our own audiovisuals for use in our company training program.*

au·dit /ˈɔdɪt/ *n.* an official examination by an accountant or accounting firm of an individual's or company's financial records: *An accountant did a year-end audit of our financial records.*
—*v.* to officially examine the financial records of a person or company: *The accounting firm audited the company every year.*

USAGE NOTE: *"Internal audit"* means a company is having its own financial records examined. An audit conducted by an outside organization is called an *"independent audit,"* and an audit by the US Internal Revenue Service (IRS) is called a *tax audit.*

au·di·tion /ɔˈdɪʃən/ *v.* (in the theater) to try out for a role: *Fifty actresses auditioned for the lead in the new play.*
—*n.* a performance as a tryout: *The dancer's audition for the ballet company went well.*

au·di·tor /ˈɔdətər/ *n.* an accountant or public official who does auditing: *The auditors from the accounting firm began looking at our books.*

au·di·to·ri·um /ˌɔdəˈtɔriəm/ *n.* a large room with seats and often a stage for delivering lectures and usu. entertainment: *Our class was called to the auditorium to hear a speech on job opportunities.*

au·di·to·ry /ˈɔdəˌtɔri/ *adj.* related to hearing and sound: *The auditory canal in my left ear is blocked.*

aug·ment /ɔgˈmɛnt/ *v.* to increase, add to: *We augmented the advertising budget in order to increase sales.* *-n.* [U] **augmentation** /ˌɔgmɛnˈteɪʃən/; *-adj.* **augmentative** /ɔgˈmɛntətɪv/.

au gra·tin /ouˈgratn, -ˈgræ-, ɔ-/ *adj.* (French for) covered with melted cheese and bread crumbs: *I had potatoes au gratin with fish for dinner.*

au·gur /ˈɔgər/ *v.frml.* to predict: *All signs augur well for success in the future.* *-n.* **augury** /ˈɔgyəri/ **-ries.**

au·gust /ɔˈgʌst/ *adj.frml.* illustrious, renowned: *A young professor was invited to dinner with the august group of scientists.*

Au·gust /ˈɔgəst/ *n.* the eighth month of the year, between July and September: *We go on vacation in the mountains in August to escape the heat.*

aunt /ænt, ɑnt/ *n.* one's father's or mother's sister, or one's uncle's wife: *My aunt Betty, who is my mother's sister, visits us every Thanksgiving.*

aunt·ie /ˈænti, ˈɑn-/ *n.infrml.* aunt.

au pair /ouˈpɛr/ *n.* (French for) a young person who goes to live with a family (usu. in a foreign country) to care for the family's children in return for room, board, and usu. an opportunity to learn the family's language: *Jane was an au pair for a year in Germany. See:* nanny, USAGE NOTE.

au·ra /ˈɔrə/ *n.* an effect or feeling that is given off or surrounds a thing or person: *He has an aura of wealth, with his fine clothes and expensive car.*

au·ral /ˈɔrəl/ *adj.* related to hearing and the ear: *He has an aural disorder, so you need to speak clearly.* *-adv.* **aurally.**

aus·pic·es /ˈɔspəsɪz -ˌsiz/ *n.pl.* with the support, (*syn.*) patronage: *The concert is presented free under the auspices of the city government.*

aus·pi·cious /ɔˈspɪʃəs/ *adj.* favorable, good: *This party is an auspicious occasion to announce the marriage plans of my daughter.* *-adv.* **auspiciously.**

aus·tere /ɔˈstɪr/ *adj.* **1** (a person) cold and self-disciplined: *The chairman has an austere appearance in his black suit.* **2** (a place) with no human warmth or comfort: *The desert is an austere place, hot by day and cold by night.* *-adv.* **austerely;** *-n.* [C;U] **austerity** /ɔˈstɛrəti/.

au·then·tic /ɔˈθɛntɪk/ *adj.* genuine, real: *That dealer in precious coins sells only authentic ones, not fakes.* *-adv.* **authentically.**

au·then·ti·cate /ɔˈθɛntɪˌkeɪt/ *v.* **-cated, -cating, -cates** to prove s.t. is genuine, (*syn.*) to substantiate: *Experts authenticated the painting as a Picasso.* *-n.* [U] **authentication** /ɔˌθɛntɪˈkeɪʃən/.

au·then·tic·i·ty /ˌɔθɛnˈtɪsəti, ˌɔθən-/ *n.* [U] the genuineness, validity of s.t.: *The authenticity of the painting as one of Picasso's was proven by an expert.*

au·thor /ˈɔθər/ *n.* a person who writes a work (book, article, poem, etc.): *Cervantes is one of the most famous authors in the Spanish language.*

au·thor·i·tar·i·an /əˌθɔrəˈtɛriən, əˌθɑr-/ *adj.* demanding or requiring others to do exactly what you tell them to do without questioning that it is right or wrong: *The authoritarian government has been in power for many years.* *—n.* a person who demands that others do exactly what he or she says without questioning if the orders are right or wrong: *The Commanding General was an authoritarian.*

au·thor·i·ta·tive /əˈθɔrəˌteɪtɪv, əˈθɑr-/ *adj.* the most reliable, (*syn.*) definitive: *Dr. Harry Gray wrote the authoritative book on chemistry.* *-adv.* **authoritatively.**

au·thor·i·ty /əˈθɔrəti, əˈθɑr-/ *n.* **1** [U] power, control: *The company's owner granted each manager authority to spend up to $10,000 on travel and entertainment.* **2** [C] **-ties** expert, master: *Professor Smith is an authority on chemistry.* **3 authorities** *pl.* people in charge, specifically government: *Government authorities arrested a swindler.* **4 to be in authority:** to be in charge: *Teachers are in authority in the classroom.* **5 to have the authority:** to have permission (the power, right, etc.): *Managers have the authority to use money from their budgets.*

au·thor·i·za·tion /ˌɔθərəˈzeɪʃən/ *n.* [U;C] the granting of permission (authority, the right, etc.): *The company gave authorization to all managers to spend money as they wished.*

au·thor·ize /ˈɔθəˌraɪz/ *v.* **-ized, -izing, -izes** to grant permission (authority, the right, etc.): *Congress authorizes the government to tax the people.*

au·thor·ship /ˈɔθərˌʃɪp/ *n.* [U] the source of a piece of writing: *The authorship of some of Shakespeare's works is still being questioned.*

au·to /ˈɔtou/ *n.* **-tos** short for automobile, a four-wheel passenger vehicle: *Too many autos are on the highways.* *—adj.infrml.* short for automatic: *The pilot put the airplane on auto control after takeoff.*

au·to·bi·og·ra·phy /ˌɔtəbaɪˈɑgrəfi, ˌoutou-/ *n.* **-phies** the story of a person's life written by that person: *The famous film star wrote her autobiography.* *-adj.* **autobiographical** /ˌɔtəˌbaɪəˈgræfɪkəl, ˌoutou-/; *-adv.* **autobiographically.**

A

au·toc·ra·cy /ɔ'tɑkrəsi/ n.[C;U] -**cies** an extremely strict government run by one person, despotism: *Before the revolution, the government of the country was an autocracy.*

au·to·crat /'ɔtə,kræt/ n. s.o. who rules alone with unlimited power, (*syns.*) a despot, dictator: *Louis XIV (1638-1715) was an autocrat who ruled France by himself.* -*adj.* **autocratic** /,ɔtəkrætɪk/.

au·to·graph /'ɔtə,græf/ n. one's signature given to an admirer: *The boy asked a famous baseball player for his autograph.*
—*v.* to write one's signature on s.t.: *The player autographed the boy's baseball.*

au·to·mak·er /'ɔtou,meɪkər/ n. a manufacturer of automobiles: *American automakers face strong competition from both Japan and Europe.*

au·to·mate /'ɔtə,meɪt/ v. -**mated, -mating, -mates** to use machinery to do jobs once done by hand: *We automated our order department with computers.*

au·to·mat·ed tell·er ma·chine n.abbr. ATM [C] a computerized bank machine for obtaining cash, seeing one's account balances, and making deposits: *Automated teller machines are very convenient, especially on weekends.*

au·to·mat·ic /,ɔtə'mætɪk/ adj. self-operating, working by itself: *Once he turns on his computer, the appearance of the main menu is automatic.*
—*n.* an automatic weapon (pistol, rifle, machine gun): *Once I pull the trigger, my automatic fires all nine bullets.* -*adv.* **automatically.**

au·to·ma·tion /,ɔtə'meɪʃən/ n. [U] the use of machines, esp. computers, to do the work once done by people: *Automation has taken over the car industry, causing some people to lose their jobs.*

au·to·mo·bile /,ɔtəmə'bil, 'ɔtəmə,bil/ n. a four-wheeled motor vehicle used to transport people from place to place: *The invention of the automobile has resulted in great personal freedom to go places.*

au·to·mo·tive /,ɔtə'moutɪv/ adj. related to the automobile: *Many automotive parts are made overseas now.*

au·ton·o·mous /ɔ'tɑnəməs/ adj. independent, self-governing: *Each of the 50 US states has an autonomous government that runs that state.* -*adv.* **autonomously;** -*n.* [U] **autonomy.**

au·top·sy /'ɔ,tɑpsi/ n. -**sies** a medical examination of a dead human body to determine what caused death: *The autopsy revealed that the man died of poisoning.*

au·to·work·er /'ɔtou,wɜrkər/ n. an employee in the automobile industry: *The autoworkers went on strike for higher wages.*

au·tumn /'ɔtəm/ n. [U;C] the season between summer and winter, (*syn.*) the fall: *Maple trees turn bright red and yellow in the autumn.* -*adj.* **autumnal** /ɔ'tʌmnəl/.

aux·il·ia·ry /ɔg'zɪlyəri, -'zɪləri/ adj. kept for use in case another fails, (*syn.*) standby: *An auxiliary electricity generator is kept in working condition in case the main power unit fails.*
—*n.pl.* -**ries** a reserve unit: *The police auxiliary works evenings and weekends to help the regular police force.*

a·vail /ə'veɪl/ n. [U] benefit, advantage, use, good purpose: *The old man's heart stopped, and a doctor tried to save him to no avail.*
—*v.frml.* **to avail oneself of:** to take advantage of, use: *While working in Paris, I availed myself of the opportunity to visit the museums.*

a·vail·a·ble /ə'veɪləbəl/ adj. **1** free, uncommitted: *I am available tomorrow to see you.* **2** in good supply, (*syn.*) obtainable: *Office supplies are available at many stores in the city.* -*n.* [U] **availability** /ə,veɪlə'bɪləti/.

av·a·lanche /'ævə,lænʃ/ n. **1** a sudden breaking away of snow, rocks, or mud down a hill or mountain: *Several skiers were buried in the avalanche.* **2** *fig.* a response from a great number of people: *An avalanche of protest came from those opposed to a tax increase.*

a·vant-garde /,ɑvɑnt'gɑrd, æ-/ n.adj. [U] pathbreakers, people in the forefront (of art, fashion, literature, social thought, product development, etc.): *The <n.> avant-garde in fashion this summer are wearing short skirts.*

av·a·rice /'ævərɪs/ n. [U] extreme desire for money, (*syn.*) greed: *The avarice of the country's dictator had no end.*

av·a·ri·cious /,ævə'rɪʃəs/ adj. desiring money, (*syn.*) greedy: *The avaricious politician used his position to become rich.* -*adv.* **avariciously.**

a·venge /ə'vɛndʒ/ v. **avenged, avenging, avenges** to seek revenge, repay s.o. for a wrong: *He avenged his brother's murder by sending the murderer to jail.*

av·e·nue /'ævə,nyu, -,nu/ n. a wide street, often a main street and one lined with trees: *People love to walk down the avenues of Paris. See:* street, USAGE NOTE.

av·er·age /'ævrɪdʒ 'ævərɪdʒ/ n. the number found by adding all items in a group, such as test scores, and then dividing the total by the number of items: *The average of the sum of 10, 16, and 4 is 10; that is, 10 plus 16 plus 4 equals 30, and 30 divided by 3 is 10.*

—*adj.* ordinary, common, neither very good nor very bad: *He's not exceptional; he's just an average child.*

—*v.* **-aged, -aging, -ages** to take an average: *We bought 10 of those fasteners over the past year, and the price averaged $1.43 per item.*

av·er·age Joe /dʒoʊ/ *n.infrml.* an ordinary guy, the common man: *The average Joe doesn't care about international politics.*

a·verse /ə'vɜrs/ *adj.frml.* against, disinclined: *I am averse to spending much money.*

a·ver·sion /ə'vɜrʒən/ *n.frml.* **1** [C;U] dislike, disinclination: *I have an aversion to traveling during the heat of August.* **2** [C] repugnance, revulsion: *She has an aversion to eating cow liver; it makes her ill.*

a·vert /ə'vɜrt/ *v.frml.* to avoid, prevent from happening: *We averted a loss in the stock market by selling our shares early, before the stock fell.*

a·vi·a·tion /ˌeɪvi'eɪʃən/ *n.* [U] the manufacture and use of aircraft, esp. airplanes: *My friend has a career in aviation; he is a pilot.*

a·vi·a·tor /'eɪvi.eɪtər/ *n.* a person working aboard an airplane, esp. in the military: *My grandfather was an aviator during the war.*

av·id /'ævɪd/ *adj.* keenly dedicated, enthusiastic: *My sister is an avid golfer; she golfs every weekend.* **-adv.** **avidly.**

av·o·ca·do /ˌævə'kɑdoʊ, ˌɑ-/ *n.* **-dos** a pear-shaped tropical fruit with a green interior: *I love California avocados stuffed with shrimp.*

av·o·ca·tion /ˌævə'keɪʃən/ *n.* a hobby: *Her avocation is reading about history.*

a·void /ə'vɔɪd/ *v.* **1** to stay away from, (*syn.*) to bypass: *She avoids walking on dark streets at night.* **2** to elude, evade: *The thief avoided capture by the police.* **3** to not do s.t., abstain from doing: *We avoid eating fattening foods.* **-adj.** **avoidable** **-adv.** **avoidably.**

a·void·ance /ə'vɔɪdns/ *n.* [U] **1** the act of bypassing s.t., going around s.t.: *The avoidance of dangerous areas is a good idea.* **2** an evasion, escape: *The criminal's avoidance of arrest mystifies the police.* **3** not using s.t., abstention from s.t.: *His avoidance of cigarettes and alcohol has made him healthier.*

a·vow /ə'vaʊ/ *v.frml.* to say openly and clearly, (*syn.*) to declare: *He is an avowed atheist.* **-n.** [C;U] **avowal.**

a·wait /ə'weɪt/ *v.* to wait for s.t., to anticipate: *I am awaiting an answer to my application for admission to law school.*

a·wake /ə'weɪk/ *v.* **awoke,** /əwoʊk/ or **awoken, awaking, awakes** **1** to get someone up from sleep: *The mother awoke the baby from its afternoon nap so it would sleep through the night.* **2** to wake up, to come out

of a sleeping state: *I awoke to find I was late for work.*

a·wake /ə'weɪk/ *adj.* to be alert, not sleeping: *The baby is awake now and wants to eat.*

a·wak·en /ə'weɪkən/ *v.* **1** to cause to wake up: *I awakened her early so she would be sure to get her train.* **2** to realize, become aware of: *The athlete finally awakened to the fact that he was growing too old to compete.* **3** to arouse, make others feel s.t.: *The invasion by a foreign army awakened patriotism in people's hearts.*

a·ward /ə'wɔrd/ *v.* **1** to give a prize (honor, praise, etc.) to s.o.: *The school principal awarded a prize in history to the best student.* **2** to give, grant: *A buyer awarded a contract to the supplier.*

—*n.* a prize (honor, praise, etc.) given to s.o. for outstanding performance: *The teacher gave her best student an award.*

a·ware /ə'wɛr/ *adj.* **1** conscious of, alert to: *He is out of the coma, but he can't speak. He is aware of people around him, though.* **2** knowledgeable about, understanding of: *A newspaper reporter must be aware of current events.* **-n.** [U] **awareness.**

a·wash /ə'wɑʃ, ə'wɔʃ/ *adj.* flooded with, covered with: *After the flood, the ground floors of houses were awash with water and mud.*

a·way /ə'weɪ/ *adv.* **1** somewhere else, afar: *When no one answered the doorbell, the stranger went away.* **2** absent, not present: *I was away on vacation for two weeks.*

awe /ɔ/ *n.* [U] a feeling of great admiration or respect: *The boy was in awe of the famous football player and couldn't believe he was going to meet him.*

—*v.* **awed, awing, awes** to create a feeling of awe or admiration: *The player awed the boy.*

awe·some /'ɔsəm/ *adj.* creating awe, worthy of great admiration: *The size of the cathedrals in France is awesome.*

aw·ful /'ɔfəl/ *adj.* **1** bad, dreadful: *We've been having awful weather lately.* **2** offensive, repugnant: *What an awful odor is coming from that dump!*

aw·ful·ly /'ɔfli, 'ɔfəli/ *adv.* **1** badly, dreadfully: *He lost his job, his wife left him, and his son had a bad accident; things have been going awfully for him.* **2** very, exceptionally: *I must hurry; I'm awfully late for work!*

a·while /ə'waɪl/ *adv.* for a short time, briefly: *I'll stay awhile; then I must leave.*

awk·ward /'ɔkwərd/ *adj.* **1** ungainly, clumsy: *He runs with an awkward gait.* **2** embarrassing, disconcerting: *The speaker experienced an awkward moment when people interrupted him.* **-adv.** **awkwardly; -n.** [U] **awkwardness.**

A

awn·ing /'ɔnɪŋ/ *n.* a sunshade usu. hung outside at an angle to shield a window from the sun's rays: *Stores in our area have awnings that they use on sunny days.*

awning

awoke /ə'woʊk/ *past tense of* awake.

AWOL /'eɪ,wɔl *or pronounced as the letters/ adj. adv. abbr. for* absent without leave: *The soldier was <adj.> AWOL over the weekend.||The soldier had gone <adv.> AWOL over the weekend.*

a·wry /ə'raɪ/ *adv.* wrong, (*syn.*) astray: *Our flight has been cancelled, and our trip has gone awry.*

ax or **axe** /æks/ *n.* axes /'æksɪz/ **1** a cutting tool with a sharp metal head on a long wooden handle: *He chopped the tree down with an ax.* **2** *infrml.fig.* **to get the ax:** to be fired or eliminated from employment: *Thursday afternoon, he got the ax.* **3** *infrml.fig.* **to give the ax:** to fire or eliminate: *Her boss gave her the ax.* **4** *infrml.fig.* **to have an ax to grind:** to have a selfish, often hidden, reason to do s.t.: *He has an ax to grind when he complains about the company; he really just wants more money.*
—*v.* **axed, axing, axes 1** to cut with an ax: *The warrior was axed to death.* **2** *infrml.fig.* to

eliminate or dismiss: *The corporation axed 200 employees all at one time.*

ax·i·om /'æksiəm/ *n.* an obvious truth, a saying: *"All that glitters is not gold" is an axiom.* —*adj.* **axiomatic.**

ax·is /'æksɪs/ *n.* axes /'æk,siz/ **1** a straight line on which points are marked: *I drew a horizontal and a vertical axis on a sheet of paper.* **2** a straight line around which an object turns: *The earth rotates on its axis.*

axis

ax·le /'æksəl/ *n.* a metal pole on which wheels turn: *My car's rear axle needs grease.*

a·ya·tol·lah /,aɪə'toʊlə/ *n.* a male Shiite Muslim religious leader: *The ayatollahs believe in basic Muslim teachings.*

a·zal·ea /ə'zeɪlyə/ *n.* a green shrub with brightly colored flowers: *The azaleas burst into blossom in the springtime.*

Az·tec /'æztɛk/ *n.* a member of a central Mexican people who declined after the Spanish conquest, starting in 1519: *The Aztecs are noted for their advanced civilization.* —*adj.* related to the Aztecs: *Aztec pyramids hold many wonders of their civilization.*

az·ure /'æʒər/ *adj.* a bright blue: *She wore a dress of azure.*

B,b

B, b /bi/ **B's, b's** or **Bs, bs** **1** the second letter of the English alphabet **2** the academic grade below an A, which is the highest: *She received a B on her exam.* **3** second in a list or series: *I would like you to a) clean your room, b) do your homework, and c) go to bed.*

B.A. /ˌbiˈeɪ/ *abbr. for* Bachelor of Arts degree, (*syn.*) baccalaureate degree: *He received his B.A. in June. See :* associate degree, USAGE NOTE.

USAGE NOTE: A *B.A.*, like a *B.S.* (Bachelor of Science) is often called a *bachelor's degree* and is given after one finishes four years of college. Two-year colleges give *associate's degrees (A.A.);* graduate programs award *master's degrees (M.A., M.S.,* etc.), and *doctorates (PhDs)* or professional degrees (*M.D., J.D.,* etc.) *After getting my B.A. in English, I went to graduate school and got my M.A. in teaching.*

bab·ble /ˈbæbəl/ *n.v.* **-bled, -bling, -bles 1** to talk without making sense: *The baby can't really talk yet; she just babbles.* **2** to speak a long time about nothing important, (*syn.*) to chatter: *He babbled on and on about the weather. -n. adj.* **babbling.** *See:* jabber.

babe /beɪb/ *n.* **1** *frml.* a baby: *He held a young babe in his arms.* **2** a person as innocent or unknowledgeable as a baby: *He had no idea that they were cheating him; he was just a babe* (or) *a babe in the woods.* **3** *infrml.pej.* an attractive young woman: *Who is that babe I saw you with last night?*

ba·boon /bæˈbun/ *n.* a large monkey that lives in Africa and southeast Asia: *Baboons have sharp teeth and powerful jaws.*

ba·by /ˈbeɪbi/ *n.* **-bies 1** a child younger than two, an infant: *His wife had a baby.* **2** a very young animal: *Look at the young kangaroo; he is still a baby.* **3** *infrml.fig.* the youngest person in a group, esp. a family: *She is the baby of the family.* **4** *infrml.* a favorite, important project or special interest: *That old car is his baby; he works on it all the time.*

—*v.* **-bied, -bying, -bies** to treat like a baby: *This plant is very delicate; you have to baby it.*

—*adj.* **babyish.**

ba·by·sit /ˈbeɪbiˌsɪt/ *v.* **-sat, -sitting, -sits** *infrml.* to watch a child while the parents are away: *She babysits her friends' daughter. -n.* **babysitter.** *See:* nanny, USAGE NOTE.

bac·ca·lau·re·ate /ˌbækəˈlɔriət/ *n. See:* B.A.

bach·e·lor /ˈbætʃlər, ˈbætʃələr/ *n.* an unmarried man: *He was a bachelor for years, then finally married.*

back /bæk/ *n.* **1** the side of the human body opposite the stomach and chest: *I hurt my back when I lifted a heavy box.* **2** the top of an animal, from the neck to the tail: *Cowboys ride on horseback.*‖*The cat put her back up and hissed.* **3** backbone, spine: *She broke her back.* **4** the rear part of s.t., opposite the front: *The back of the house needs to be painted.* **5 behind s.o.'s back:** to do or say s.t. without s.o.'s knowledge: *They are nice to her when she is with them, but they say mean things about her behind her back.* **6 to break one's back:** to work very hard: *Workers broke their backs to get all the orders out on time.* **7** *infrml.* **to get off s.o.'s back:** to stop criticizing or annoying s.o.: *I repaid the money that I owed my friend so he would get off my back.* **8 to get** (or) **put one's back up:** to become (or) make angry or offended: *Comments about losing his hair always get his back up.* **9 to have one's back to the wall:** to have a bad problem, usu. with no solution: *He can't find a job and has his back to the wall without any money.* **10 in back of:** behind, at the back of: *The garage is in back of the house.* **11 on one's back: a.** to be sick and have to stay in bed: *She's been on her back for a week with the flu.* **b.** bothering, annoying s.o. **12 to turn one's back on: a.** to refuse to help s.o. in trouble: *How can you just turn your back on those poor children?* **b.** to show anger, rejection, or (*syn.*) disdain: *When he married a woman that his parents disapproved of, they turned their backs on him and never spoke to him again.*

—*adv.* **1** in the direction from which one came: *A tree fell across the road and we had to drive back home.*‖*Put things back where you* *found them!* **2 back and forth:** from one side to another, (*syn.*) to and fro: *The tree moved back and forth in the wind.*

—*v.* **1** to support s.o., esp. by giving money: *Some rich people backed a politician running for mayor. See:* backer. **2** *phrasal v.* **to back away:** to move away from a position, (*syn.*) to retreat: *He backed away slowly from the snake.* **3** *phrasal v.* **to back down:** to stop one's demands, (*syn.*) to retreat: *She demanded a bigger salary, but she backed down when her boss said, "No."* **4** *phrasal v.* **to back off:** to move backwards, draw away: *The dog barked at the man, and the man backed off.* **5** *phrasal v.* **to back out: a.** to go backwards: *She backed the car out of the garage.* **b.** to withdraw, (*syn.*) to cancel: *He backed out of the business agreement.* **6** *phrasal v. sep.* **to back s.o. or s.t. up: a.** s.o.: to support, help: *Two police officers backed up another one who was arresting a criminal.* ‖*They backed him up.* **b.** s.t.: to copy computer records: *She backed up her day's work on the computer.* ‖*She backed it up.* **c.** s.o. or s.t.: to go backwards: *The driver backed up his car and stopped.* ‖*He backed it up.*

back·bite /'bæk,baɪt/ *v.infrml.* **-bit** /-,bɪt,/ **-bitten** /-,bɪtn,/ **-biting, -bites** to criticize people cruelly, esp. when they are not present: *The backbiting that goes on in that company is awful.*

back·bone /'bæk,boʊn/ *n.* **1** *lit.* the spine **2** *fig.* the moral strength to do the right thing, (*syn.*) character: *He has a lot of backbone; he always tells the truth.* **3** *fig.* the main support: *Good citizens are the backbone of society.*

back·break·ing /'bæk,breɪkɪŋ/ *adj.infrml. fig.* taking great effort: *Picking vegetables by hand in the hot sun is backbreaking.* **-n.** **backbreaker.**

back burner *n.infrml. fig.* inactive status: *The company put its plans for a new building on the back burner until business gets better.*

back·drop /'bæk,drɑp/ *n.* **1** (in the theater) the scenery at the back of the stage: *The backdrop for that play is the scenery of a forest.* **2** *fig.* the general events during which s.t. else, such as a person's life, happens: *Her childhood happened against the backdrop of a war.*

back·er /'bækər/ *n.* a supporter, esp. s.o. who gives money: *That politician has many wealthy backers. See:* back.

back·fire /'bæk,faɪr/ *v.* **-fired, -firing, -fires** **1** to go off, explode (backwards): *He was injured when his gun backfired during target pratice.* **2** *fig.* to produce an undesired result: *Her plan to steal her friend's boyfriend backfired; he married her friend, and the couple never spoke to her again.*

back·gam·mon /'bæk,gæmən/ *n.* a game played by two people using dice to move pieces on a board: *Many people play backgammon for money.*

back·ground /'bæk,graʊnd/ *n.* **1** s.t. behind s.t. else, (*syn.*) a backdrop: *The hunter waited in the background of the trees for deer to pass by.* **2** a person's family, education, and experience: *What is your background? I was educated at Harvard and have 10 years' business experience. See;* foreground.

back·hand /'bæk,hænd/ *v.n.* (in tennis, hockey, etc) to hit a ball with the back of the hand pointed in the direction of the hit: *The tennis player hit a <n.> backhand to her opponent.*

back·hand·ed /'bæk,hændɪd/ *adj.* **1** (in sports) hit with a backhand **2** not said directly: *She paid me a backhanded compliment by telling me I was not as fat as I used to be.*

back·ing /'bækɪŋ/ *n.* [U] support, esp. giving money: *She started her own business and got backing from a bank.*

back·lash /'bæk,læʃ/ *n.* **-es** a strong action against s.t., (*syn.*) a reaction: *There was a backlash of anger when the university closed the library on Sundays.*

back·log /'bæk,lɔg,-,lɑg/ *n.* unfinished work or unfilled orders: *The factory has a 30-day backlog of orders to fill.*

back order *v.n.* [C;U] to place an order for s.t. that is not available at the moment: *Having no desks in his warehouse, the store owner <v.> back ordered two for me.*‖*He put the desks on <n.> back order.*

back·pack /'bæk,pæk/ *n.* a type of sack carried on the back with two shoulder straps and often with a metal frame, (*syn.*) a knapsack: *Backpacks are used to carry things like books, clothes, or food.*

backpack

—*v.* to hike, go walking in the country wearing a backpack: *We backpacked for two weeks in the mountains.* **-n.** **backpacker; backpacking.**

back·pedal /'bæk,pɛdl/ *v.* **1** to try to pedal backwards **2** *fig.* to take back s.t. one said, (*syn.*) to retract: *She started to call him a mean person and backpedaled and said he was strict.*

back·room /'bæk'rum/ *adj.* hidden, often dishonest (acts): *Political decisions in that big city are backroom.*

back·scratch·ing /'bæk,skrætʃɪŋ/ *n.infrml. fig.* [U] doing a favor for s.o. and getting s.t. good in return: *I'll buy your product if you give my son a job; that's backscratching.*

back·seat /'bæk'sit/ *n.* **1** *lit.* the rear seat of a car or bus **2** *infrml.* **a backseat driver:** s.o. who constantly tells a car's driver what to do: *Most people are irritated by backseat drivers.*

3 *infrml.* **to take a backseat to:** to be less important than s.o. or s.t. else: *The younger brother takes a backseat in that family to his older brother, a baseball star.*

back·side /'bæk,saɪd/ *n.infrml.* the buttocks: *She fell down and hurt her backside.*

USAGE NOTE: The part of the body upon which a person sits is called the *buttocks;* backside is a polite synonym.

back·stab·ber /'bæk,stæbər/ *n.infrml. fig.* a person who seems friendly but says bad things about people, *(syn.)* a malicious gossiper: *Paul is a horrible backstabber; George told him secrets, and then Paul used them to get George in trouble.*

back·stage /'bæk'steɪʤ/ *n.adv.* the area behind the stage in a theater: *After the performance, I went <adv.> backstage to meet the actors.*

back·talk /'bæk,tɔk/ *n.* [U] rude replies to a question, *(syn.)* sass: *I asked you five times for the reports and all you do is give me a lot of backtalk!*

back taxes *n.* overdue taxes: *It took him two years to pay his back taxes of $20,000 to the government.*

back·track /'bæk,træk/ *v.* **1** to return along the same path: *The hunter got lost in the snow and had to backtrack home.* **2** to reverse or take back what one has said: *When the politician realized that her new policy angered the voters, she backtracked, saying that it was only one approach to the problem.*

back·up /'bæk,ʌp/ *n.* **1** support, such as having more people help to do a job: *A police officer saw a robbery happening and called for backup (more officers).* **2** a copy of computer work: *The computer operator has a back-up of her work on a diskette.*
—*adj.* more information, esp. proving s.t. is true: *The report had back-up information attached to it.*

back·ward or **back·wards** /'bækwərdz/ *adv.* **1** in the direction opposite to the one in which one is moving: *She looked backwards over her shoulders.* **2** in the opposite or wrong order: *He got the instructions backwards.* **3** *infrml.* **backwards and forwards:** to the back, then to the front: *He moved the car backwards and forwards trying to get into the parking space.* **4 to know something backwards and forwards:** to memorize or know s.t. perfectly: *She knew the material for her presentation backwards and forwards.*
—*adj.* not modern, primitive: *They live in a backward part of the country.*

back·woods /'bæk,wʊdz/ *n.pl.* used with a *sing. v.* forest land far from any village or town: *Not many people live in the backwoods.*

back·yard /'bæk'yɑrd/ *n.* the land behind and belonging to a house: *We have a flower garden in our backyard.*

ba·con /'beɪkən/ *n.* [U] **1** salted, smoked meat from a pig's side: *Bacon with eggs and toast is good for breakfast.* **2 to bring home the bacon:** to earn a living: *For 40 years, he brought home the bacon with a weekly paycheck.*

bac·te·ri·a /bæk'tɪriə/ *n.pl., sing.* **-terium** /-'tɪriəm/ tiny living things, microorganisms: *Many bacteria cause diseases.* -*adj.* **bacterial.** *See:* virus.

bad /bæd/ *adj.* **worse** /wɜrs/ **worst** /wɜrst/ **1** evil, *(syn.)* criminal: *He lies and steals and does many other bad things.* **2** poorly behaved, *(syn.)* naughty: *She was bad, so her mother punished her.* **3** not of good condition or quality, *(syn.)* poor: *He has some bad teeth.* **4** incorrect, wrong: *The letter was returned because the address is bad.* **5** not good to eat or drink, *(syn.)* spoiled: *The milk has gone bad; it is sour.* **6** with a feeling of guilt, *(syn.)* shame: *I feel bad about the nasty things I said to you.* **7** with a feeling of sympathy, *(syn.)* compassion: *I feel bad that you are sick.* **8** s.t. extreme, severe, esp. very sick: *She has a bad sore throat (toothache, cold, etc.).* **9** *slang* very good, *(syns.)* excellent, wonderful: *Oh man, can that guy dance; he's bad!* **10 bad at:** not to do s.t. well: *She is bad at spelling words.* **11 bad news: a.** *lit.* information about s.t. disappointing: *He learned the bad news that he failed the exam.* **b.** *slang* an annoying or troublemaking person: *She never pays back the money she owes; she's bad news!* **12 It's too bad:** to feel sorry, *(syn.)* to regret: *It's too bad that you have to leave now.* **13** *infrml.* **not (so) bad:** fair, alright: *That movie wasn't so bad.* -*n.* [U] **badness.**

badge /bæʤ/ *n.* **1** a sign or mark worn to show honor or membership, position, etc. in a group: *The military officer wore a badge showing his rank.* **2** a name tag, such as a plastic plate with one's name on it: *He pinned his name badge on his shirt.*

badg·er /'bæʤər/ *n.lit.* an animal that digs and lives in the ground: *Badgers have a wide, furry body, short legs, and long front claws.*
—*v.fig.* to tell or criticize s.o. about s.t. repeatedly, *(syn.)* to pester: *Her boss badgered her to do the sales report early.*

bad·lands /'bæd,lændz/ *n.pl.* (in USA) areas where few plants grow and it is difficult to live: *The badlands of North Dakota stretch to the Rocky Mountains.*

bad·ly /'bædli/ *adv.* **worse** /wɜrs/ **worst** /wɜrst/ **1** in a bad way, not well: *He sings badly.* **2** not well, doing poorly, such as with one's health, money, or life: *She is very sick and doing* *badly.* **3** very much, a lot: *He badly wants to be healthy again.*

bad·min·ton /'bæd,mɪntn/ *n.* [U] a court game like tennis in which one hits a small object across a high net: *Badminton can be played by two or four people.*

bad·mouth /'bæd,maʊθ/ *v.slang* to say bad things about s.o., (*syn.*) to slander: *After he divorced her, she badmouthed him to everyone.*

baf·fle /'bæfəl/ *v.* **-fled, -fling, -fles** not to understand s.t. at all, to confuse completely: *His disappearance baffled the police. -n.* [U] **bafflement;** *-adj.* **baffling.**

bag /bæg/ *n.* **1** a sack, a container made of paper, plastic, cloth, etc.: *I carried the groceries home in a shopping bag.* **2** *pej.slang* disagreeable old woman **3** *slang* **my bag:** an interest, favorite pastime, (*syn.*) a hobby: *I really like to play the guitar; it's my bag!* **4 in the bag:** *infrml.fig.* **a.** certain, sure: *That business deal is in the bag.* **b.** drunk, intoxicated: *After drinking five beers, Amy was in the bag.* **5 to let the cat out of the bag:** to reveal a secret by mistake
—v. **bagged, bagging, bags 1 to bag groceries:** to put food purchases in bags **2 to bag game:** to kill animals by hunting **3 his pants bag:** to hang loosely *See:* bag lady; mixed bag.

ba·gel /'beɪgəl/ *n.* a round piece of thick bread with a hole in its middle: *I had a toasted bagel and tea for breakfast.*

bag·gage /'bægɪdʒ/ *n.* [U] bags, suitcases, etc. used to carry clothing and other goods while traveling, (*syn.*) luggage: *I carried my baggage onto the train.*

bag·gy /'bægi/ *adj.* **-gier, -giest** loose fitting (clothes): *His pants are so baggy that they are nearly falling off.*

bag lady *n.slang* a homeless woman who lives on the street: *A bag lady carries her belongings in shopping bags.*

USAGE NOTE: It is considered rude to call s.o. a *bag lady;* a more polite term is *homeless person.*

bag·pipes /'bæg,paɪps/ *n.pl.* a musical instrument that makes sounds by forcing air from a bag out through pipes: *Bagpipes are common in Scotland.*

bail (1) /beɪl/ *n.* [U] **1** money left with a court of law when a person awaiting trail is released from jail: *If s.o. released on bail does not show up for trial, the bail is lost.* **2 to post bail for s.o.:** to provide the money or credit used for bail: *He posted $5,000 bail for his brother's release from jail.*
—v. **1** *phrasal v. sep.* **to bail s.o. out:** to help s.o. out of a bad situation, esp. jail: *The protesters were taken to jail; he bailed out several of them.* ‖ *He bailed them out.* **2** *phrasal v.* **to**

bail out: a. to escape from a plane that is about to crash: *Airmen bailed out of an airplane by parachute.* **b.** to leave quickly for fear of harm: *The company was in such bad condition that many employees bailed out.*

bail (2) *v.* to scoop water out of a boat: *As the water began to seep into the canoe, we had to bail it out with buckets.*

bail·i·wick /'baɪlɪ,wɪk/ *n.* **1** a person's area of authority, importance, etc. **2 not to invade s.o.'s bailiwick:** *I don't want to invade the accountant's bailiwick by giving you advice on money matters.*

bait /beɪt/ *n.sing.* [U] animal food used to catch animals and fish, (*syn.*) a lure: *A fisherman used chopped fish as bait on his hooks.*
—v. **1** to use bait: *He baited his fishhooks.* **2** to anger s.o., (*syn.*) to torment: *A soldier baited a captured enemy by laughing at him.*

bake /beɪk/ *n.v.* **baked, baking, bakes** to cook in an oven usu. slowly, for a long time: *The baker <v.> bakes fresh bread every morning. See:* clambake.

bak·er /'beɪkər/ *n.* **1** a person who bakes bread, cakes, etc. for sales: *Our supermarket has a butcher, a florist, and a baker who bakes wonderful cakes.* **2 baker's dozen:** thirteen of s.t.: *I bought a baker's dozen of bread rolls.*

bak·er·y /'beɪkəri, 'beɪkri/ *n.* **-ies** a business where bread, cakes, etc. are baked and offered for sale: *I bought an apple pie at the bakery.*

bal·ance /'bæləns/ *n.sing.* [U] **1** the ability to stand, walk, etc. without falling down, (*syn.*) equilibrium: *She lost her balance and fell down.* **2** to keep in equal strength, weight, etc.: *When his mother died, he tried to keep his emotions in balance.*
—v. **-anced, -ancing, -ances 1** to keep s.t. from falling: *For fun, he balanced a ball on his nose.* **2 to balance the books (in accounting):** to make sure that the financial records of a business are accurate: *Every month the company balances the books. See:* to hang in the balance.

balance of power *n.* a condition where one country or group within a country is not stronger than the other: *In the USA, there is a balance of power between the Congress and the President.*

balance of payments or **trade** *n.* the amount of money that a country owes to other countries for buying their goods, less the amounts owed by those countries: *The USA has had a negative balance of payments with other countries by importing more than it exports.*

balance sheet *n.* statement of what a company owns, or assets (property, products, cash, etc.), and owes, or liabilities (loans, debts, etc.): *The accountant prepared the company's* *balance sheet for the year. See:* P/L, profit and loss statement.

bal·co·ny /ˈbælkəni/ *n.* **-nies 1** a platform, such as a porch, built on the outside of a building: *That hotel has balconies where people can sit outside their rooms.* **2** rows of seats upstairs in a theater or hall

bald /bɔld/ or **bald-headed** /ˈbɔld,hɛdɪd/ *adj.* **1** with little or no hair on the head: *His bald head shines in the light.* **2** plain, undecorated: *the bald truth -n.* [U] **baldness.**

bald eagle *n.* a large, dark brown bird with a white head: *The bald eagle is a symbol of the USA.*

bald-faced /ˈbɔld,feɪst/ *adj. fig.* obvious; shameless, *(syn.)* brazen: *He told a bald-faced lie.*

bale /beɪl/ *n.* a large bunch of s.t. tied together, esp. cotton, hay, cloth, etc.: *The farmer put bales of hay into his barn.*

bale·ful /ˈbeɪlfəl/ *adj.frml.* showing evil desire, esp. to harm s.o., *(syns.)* sinister, ominous: *The criminal gave a man a baleful look before hitting him. -adv.* **balefully.**

balk /bɔk/ *n.v.* to stop, be unwilling to continue: *He <v.> balked at the high price of the car and refused to buy it.*||*The horse <v.> balked at jumping the fence.*

ball (1) /bɔl/ *n.* **1** a formal dance party: *Men and women put on their best clothes to go to a ball.* **2** *infrml.* **to have a ball:** to enjoy oneself, have a happy party: *We all got together last night and had a ball!*

ball (2) *n.* **1** a round object used in games: *The football player kicked the ball.* **2** the way a ball is thrown: *The pitcher threw a fastball (curveball, screwball, etc.).* **3** a rounded part of the body: *She stood on the balls of her feet so she could see over the wall.* **4** s.t. shaped into a ball: *She made a sweater from balls of yarn.* **5** *infrml.* **a ball of fire:** full of energy: *John did that job so fast that he's a ball of fire!* **6** *infrml.* **the ball is in s.o.'s court:** (from tennis) a situation where s.o. else must act: *I offered to buy the house, so now the ball is in the owner's court as she must decide about my offer.* **7** *infrml.* **on the ball:** (a person) intelligent, knowledgeable, and hard-working: *Mary did the job fast and accurately—she's really on the ball.* **8** *infrml.* **whole ball of wax:** the complete, usu. difficult situation: *When you have children you take on the whole ball of wax, the good and the bad.* **9** *infrml.* **to get, start,** or **keep the ball rolling:** to start and keep s.t. going: *To get the ball rolling, let's make a list of food that we need to buy for the party.* **10 to play ball: a.** *frml.* to play baseball, football, etc. **b.** *infrml.fig.* to cooperate with s.o.: *The police told the drug dealer that they would get him a shorter jail sentence if he*

would play ball and tell them who his bosses were.

bal·lad /ˈbæləd/ *n.frml.* a poem or song that tells a story with simple words and a group of words, called a refrain, repeated after each stanza

bal·last /ˈbæləst/ *n.* [U] weights kept in the bottom parts of ships

bal·le·ri·na /ˌbæləˈrinə/ *n.* a female ballet dancer: *Ballerinas dance on their toes.*

bal·let /bælˈeɪ, ˈbæleɪ/ *n.* [C;U] a type of dancing with formal movements, usu. to classical music: *We went to see the ballet (or) we went to the ballet last evening. -n.* **ballet dancer.**

ball game *n.* **1** *lit.* sporting event, such as baseball or football **2** *fig.infrml.* situation: *With a new product coming on the market, it is a new ball game (a new competitive situation).*

bal·lis·tics /bəˈlɪstɪks/ *n.* the study of the flight of objects, such as bullets, that fly or are thrown through the air: *Ballistics is a necessary science for the military. -adj.* **ballistic;** *-n.* **ballistic missile.**

bal·loon /bəˈlun/ *n.* **1** a small bag of thin rubber filled with a gas: *Children have fun with balloons at birthday parties.* **2** a large bag of soft material filled with gas so it can float through the air: *We went on a balloon ride for my birthday. -n.* **balloonist.**

bal·lot /ˈbælət/ *n.* **1** a piece of paper used in secret voting, sometimes with a list of candidates: *People vote for politicians by marking their ballots.* **2** the system of secret voting *-n.* **ballot box.**

ball·park /ˈbɔl,park/ *n.* **1** baseball stadium, a place where ball games are played **2** *infrml.fig.* **ballpark figure:** a guess, estimate: *I don't need the exact cost of the computer, just a ballpark figure.* **3** *infrml.fig.* **in the ballpark:** s.t. in a general area or range, s.t. likely to be expected or acceptable: *To pay one million dollars for that office building is in the ballpark.*

ball·point pen /ˈbɔl,pɔɪnt/ *n.* a writing instrument with a ball-shaped tip

ball·room /ˈbɔl,rum/ *n.* a large hall for dances —*adj.* a type of close dancing in which partners move together with set steps to the music: *The waltz and the fox-trot are favorite ballroom dances.*

balm /bam/ *n.frml.* **1** [C;U] a cream that stops pain or heals the skin: *He put a soothing balm on his cut.* **2** [C] *fig.* s.t. that makes one feel better: *A good vacation is a balm for bad nerves.*

balm·y /ˈbami/ *adj.* **-ier, -iest 1** (of weather) pleasant, mild, and breezy **2** *infrml.fig.* crazy, *(syn.)* highly eccentric: *He is under so much pressure that he's become balmy.*

ba·lo·ney or **bo·lo·ney** or **bo·lo·gna** /bə'louni, -nə/ *n.* [U] **1** a type of sausage: *She sliced sausage baloney for sandwiches.* **2** *infrml.fig.* nonsense: *What she says is baloney, and her husband is full of baloney, too.*

bal·sa /'bɔlsə/ *n.* [C;U] a light tropical wood: *Model airplanes are made of balsa wood.*

bal·sam /'bɔlsəm/ *n.* [U] a substance from the balsam fir tree: *Balsam is used in making cough medicine and perfumes.*

bam·boo /bæm'bu/ *n.* [U] a tall plant of the grass family used in construction and furniture: *Bamboo is lightweight, hollow, and strong.*

bam·boo·zle /bæm'buzəl/ *v.infrml.* **-zled, -zling, -zles** to cheat, (*syn.*) to swindle: *I was bamboozled when I bought that bad used car.*

ban /bæn/ *n.* a stop, block: *The government put a ban on the sale of that drug.*
—*v.* **banned, banning, bans** to block, (*syn.*) to forbid: *They banned pornography in that city.*

ba·nal /bə'næl, 'beɪnl, bə'nɑl/ *adj.* not interesting, boring: *Life is banal in the town; all people do is eat, sleep, and watch television. -n.* [U] **banality** /bə'næləti/.

ba·nan·a /bə'nænə/ *n.* **1** a long, yellow-skinned (when ripe) fruit with soft edible insides **2** *infrml.* **top banana:** highest person, such as in a company: *She is the top banana in her business.*
—*adv.infrml.* **to go bananas:** to act crazy or angry: *When he heard the bad news, he went bananas and started yelling at everyone.*

band /bænd/ *n.* **1** a group of s.t.: *There was a great musical band at the party.||A band of thieves has been robbing the neighborhood.* **2** a strip of material (rope, tape, cloth): *A worker tied metal bands around a box.* **3** in radio, a range of wavelengths **4** a ring: *He wore a gold wedding band.*
—*v.* **1** to group together: *The workers banded together to stop the sale of the company.* **2** to tie together: *He banded the box before mailing it.*

ban·dage /'bændɪdʒ/ *n.* a fabric covering for a wound or injury: *A nurse put a bandage over the cut.*
—*v.* **-daged, -daging, -dages** to cover or tie up a wound with bandages: *She bandaged the cut.*

Band-Aid /'bænd,eɪd/ *n.TM* **1** a small, self-adhesive bandage: *He put a Band-Aid over a cut on his finger.* **2** *infrml.fig.* a small solution to a big problem: *The government passed new laws against drug dealers, but that is only a Band-Aid solution that won't work.*

ban·dan·a /bæn'dænə/ *n.* a large, colorful handkerchief: *That cowboy wears a red bandana around his neck to keep out the dust.*

ban·dit /'bændɪt/ *n.* an armed thief, esp. one who attacks travelers on the road: *A group of bandits stole a truck on the highway.*

band·stand /'bænd,stænd/ *n.* a platform on which a musical band plays, usu. outdoors: *A small orchestra played on the bandstand in the park.*

band·wag·on /'bænd,wægən/ *n.* **1** a decorated truck with a flat open back on which a musical band can play **2** *infrml.fig.* **to jump on the bandwagon:** a popular idea or cause, esp. political: *When a cause like reducing taxes becomes popular, politicians jump on the bandwagon to support it.*

ban·dy /'bændi/ *v.* **-died, -dying, -dies 1** to talk back and forth informally; to argue, disagree: *They bandied several ideas about.* **2** to talk about s.o. unfavorably, (*syn.*) to gossip: *His arrest was bandied about in his neighborhood.*
—*adj.* curved outward at the knees, (*syn.*) bowed: *The cowboy had bandy legs.*

bane /beɪn/ *n.* **1** *frml.* one's ruin or death: *Alcoholism was his bane.* **2 the bane of one's existence:** one's worst problem: *A bad, aching back is the bane of her existence.*

bang /bæŋ/ *n.* **1** a loud noise: *The gunshot made a loud bang.* **2** a hard blow, bump: *The cars crashed into each other with a bang!* **3** *infrml.fig.* enjoyment, delight: *The kids got a bang out of going to the circus.* **4 to go over with a bang:** accepted with enthusiasm: *His speech about workers' rights went over with a bang at the workers' meeting.*
—*v.* **1** to make a loud noise or hit: *The door banged shut.* **2** to hurt, (*syn.*) to injure: *She fell and banged her knees.* **3** *phrasal v.* **to bang away: a:** to ask questions without stopping, (*syn.*) to interrogate: *The police banged away at the prisoner, but he wouldn't tell them anything.* **b:** to work hard at s.t.: *When I went by his office he was still banging away at the project.* **4** *phrasal v. sep.* **to bang s.t. up:** to damage, injure s.t.: *When she fell, she banged up her leg.* || *She banged it up.*
—*adj.infrml.* exactly, directly: *She called me bang in the middle of dinner.*

ban·gle /'bæŋgəl/ *n.* a metal band worn on the wrist as jewelry, a stiff bracelet: *He bought her silver bangles for her birthday.*

bangs /bæŋz/ *n.pl.* hair combed over the forehead: *She has long brown hair and bangs.*

bang-up /'bæŋʌp/ *adj.infrml.* very good, excellent: *She did a bang-up job on her report.*

ban·ish /'bænɪʃ/ *v.frml.* **-ishes** to send s.o. away (usu. from a country): *The king banished the murderer from the land. -n.* [U] **banishment.** *See:* exile.

ban·is·ter /'bænəstər/ *n.* a railing next to stairs for people to hold onto: *Children like to slide down a banister.*

ban·jo /'bændʒoʊ/ *n.* **-jos** or **-joes** a musical instrument with strings: *A banjo is played like a guitar in country-western music.*

bank (1) /bæŋk/ *n.* **1** a place to put one's money for safekeeping that also makes loans: *Both individuals and businesses put their money in banks.* **2** a bank building: *I have to go to the bank.* **3** a place where things are stored: *People give blood to blood banks.* **4 to break the bank:** to win a lot of money: *The gambler broke the bank at the casino.*
—*v.* **1** to put or keep money in a bank: *She banks at the Liberty Bank on the corner.* **2** *phrasal v. insep.* **to bank on s.o. or s.t.:** to trust, (*syn.*) to rely on: *You can bank on him to do what he promises. See:* deposit; withdraw.

bank (2) *n.* **1** the land at the edge of a river, lake, etc.: *We walked along the river bank. See:* shore. **2** a group or mass: *A bank of clouds darkened the sky.* **3** the sideways leaning of an aircraft during a turn: *The airplane made a bank to the left.*
—*v.* to lean sideways, (*syn.*) to tilt: *The airplane banked to the right.*

bank account *n.* an amount of money in a bank that one adds to or subtracts from: *She has two bank accounts: a savings account and a checking account.*

bank·book /'bæŋk,bʊk/ *n.* a record of the activities of a bank account: *I have a bank book for my savings account. See:* checkbook, passbook.

bank·er /'bæŋkər/ *n.* an officer or manager of a bank

bank·ing /'bæŋkɪŋ/ *n.* [U] the business of a bank: *She entered banking right after college and is now a vice president.*

bank·roll /'bæŋk,roʊl/ *n.* a sum of money, esp. cash to deposit in a bank
—*v.* to finance s.t., make money available for a purpose: *A rich lady bankrolled a new business that a friend wanted to start.*

bank·rupt /'bæŋkrəpt/ *v.adj.* without money or credit, unable to pay one's bills: *That company is <adj.> bankrupt.||The managers <v.> bankrupted the company by buying too much equipment.*

bank·rupt·cy /'bæŋkrəptsi, -rəpsi/ *n.* **-cies** [C;U] **1** the legal state of being without money or credit, unable to pay bills **2 to declare** or **file for bankruptcy:** to file formal statements of bankruptcy with a legal court: *The company declared bankruptcy.*

ban·ner /'bænər/ *n.* a large flag or piece of cloth or plastic with writing on it used for decoration or business: *The company banner is displayed at meetings.*
—*adj.* excellent, successful: *Sales were up 40 percent; it was a banner year.*

ban·quet /'bæŋkwɪt/ *n.* a formal dinner with many people, often for a purpose: *The wedding banquet seated 200 people.*

ban·ter /'bæntər/ *n.* [U] lively, light conversation
—*v.* to talk in a lively way: *The couple bantered with each other at the party.*

bap·tism /'bæptɪzəm/ *n.* [C;U] **1** a religious ceremony in which a person is covered with or touched by water to join a church and considered cleansed of sin: *The baby's baptism will be next Sunday.* **2** *fig.* **baptism by fire:** s.t. that tests one's abilities, courage, etc., esp. in war: *The new soldiers went through a baptism of fire when they were ambushed. -adj.* **baptismal** /bæp'tɪzməl/; *-v.* **baptize** /bæp'taɪz, 'bæp,taɪz/.

bar /bɑr/ **(1)** *n.* a public place where liquor is served, (*syns.*) a pub, a nightclub: *Can you tell me where the bar is in this hotel?*

USAGE NOTE: A *bar* is the counter where liquor is served inside a *barroom* but is also a general term for any business that serves alcohol; a *pub* often also serves light food, such as sandwiches; a *tavern* usually offers food and sometimes bedrooms for travelers; a *nightclub* (or club) offers live music or other entertainment. A *snack bar* does not serve alcohol, only food.

bar (2) *n.* **1** a flat, hard piece of metal longer than it is wide: *That bank keeps bars of gold in its safe.* **2** any material shaped like a bar: *She loves to eat candy bars.* **3** an obstacle, barrier: *The prisoner was behind bars (in jail).*
—*v.* **barred, barring, bars 1** to lock with a bar: *I barred the door.* **2** to block s.o. or s.t.: *Police barred entrance to the building.*
—*prep.* except: *The whole office staff was invited to the wedding, bar none.*

bar (3) *n.* the professional organization of lawyers: *The law student was admitted to the Bar and became a lawyer after passing the bar exam.*

barb /bɑrb/ *n.* **1** a sharp point that sticks out from the main point on an arrow, fishhook, etc. **2** *fig.* sharp criticism: *The irritated teacher shot barbs at the lazy student.*

bar·bar·i·an /bɑr'bɛriən/ *n.* a crude, uncivilized person *-n.* [C] **barbarism** /'bɑrbərɪzəm/ [C;U] **barbarity;** *-adv.* **barbarically.**

bar·bar·ic /bɑr'bærɪk, -'bɛr-/ *adj.* wild, uncivilized, (*syn.*) barbarous: *Some people think capital punishment is barbaric.*

bar·be·cue /'bɑrbɪ,kyu/ *v.* **-cued, -cuing, -cues** to cook meat and other food on a metal grill over an open fire, usu. outside: *We're going to barbecue chicken tonight. See:* grill.
—*n.* **1** a party where food is grilled or barbecued: *On July 4, we ate hamburgers and hot dogs at a family barbecue.* **2** a type of grilled,

spicy food originally from the South (Georgia, Texas, etc.): *My boyfriend and I love to eat barbecue; he likes spicy chicken and I like ribs. See:* charcoal, BBQ, cookout.

USAGE NOTE: *Barbecuing* is an informal American style of cooking in warm weather. It consists of covering meat such as chicken or pork with a barbecue sauce and cooking it on a metal grill over burning wood chips or charcoal. *Grilling* is a way to cook foods without sauce, such as hamburgers, hotdogs, and vegetables. When you are invited to a barbecue, any of these foods may be served.

---

barbed wire /barbd/ *n.* [U] a wire with sharp points on it used as a fence: *Farmers use barbed wire to keep cattle and sheep in their pastures.*

bar·bell /'bar,bɛl/ *n.* a metal bar with weights at each end: *People exercise with barbells to strengthen their muscles.*

bar·ber /'barbər/ *n.* a person who cuts the hair of and shaves men, a hairdresser: *He goes to the barber every two weeks.*
—*v.* to cut hair -*n.* **barber shop.**

bar·bi·tu·rate /bar'bɪtʃərɪt, -,reɪt/ *n.* a drug that calms, a sedative: *Her doctor gave her a barbiturate to help her sleep*

bard /bard/ *n.frml.* a poet: *Shakespeare is known as the Bard of Avon. -adj.* **bardic.**

bare /bɛr/ *adj.* **1** uncovered, nude: *The baby lies in bed as bare as the day he was born.* **2** plain, simple, without extras: *Just give me the bare facts; I can find out the details later.*||*She earns enough money only to buy the bare necessities.*
—*v.* **bared, baring, bares** to show, (*syn.*) to expose: *I don't usually tell my secrets, but I bared my soul to her.*||*He took off his shirt and bared his chest. -n.* [U] **bareness.**

bare·bones /'bɛr'bounz/ *adj.infrml.fig.* with the basics, (*syn.*) essentials only: *The company is a barebones operation with a small staff, old furniture, and two telephones.*

bare·foot /'bɛr,fut/ *adj.adv.* without shoes: *Holding hands, the couple walked <adv.> barefoot on the beach.*

bare·head·ed /'bɛr,hɛdɪd/ *adj.* without a hat: *She went bareheaded in the sun and got burned.*

bare·ly /'bɛrli/ *adv.* **1** almost not at all, just, hardly: *I hurt my foot and can barely walk.* **2** in a bare way: *The concert was barely attended.* **3 barely (do s.t.), let alone (do s.t. else):** just able to do s.t. and unable to do s.t. more difficult: *I can barely speak Spanish, let alone write a business letter in it.*

barf /barf/ *v. slang* to vomit: *He drank so much beer that he barfed all night.*

bar·fly /'bar,flaɪ/ *n.infrml.* **-flies** .s.o. who spends a lot of time in bars, a heavy drinker *See:* lounge lizard.

bar·gain /'bargɪn/ *n.* **1** a good, low price for s.t., (*syn.*) a deal: *I got a bargain when I bought that suit for half price.* **2** an agreement: *If you agree to sell me the car for $10,000, you and I have a bargain.* **3 to drive a hard bargain:** to negotiate well: *You drive a hard bargain; I'll give you the radio free with the car.* **4 into the bargain:** as well, in addition
—*v.* **1** to ask for a lower price, (*syns.*) to barter, to haggle: *In some cultures it is common for buyers and sellers to bargain.* **2** *phrasal v.* **to bargain for:** to expect: *Her stay in the hospital cost her $30,000, which was a lot more than she bargained for.*||*I invited him to visit and he stayed for three weeks, which was longer than I had bargained for.*
—*adj.* very inexpensive: *The goods were for sale at a bargain price.*

bargaining chip *n.* item to be offered or taken away in a negotiation: *The threat of a strike is a strong bargaining chip that a union brings to a negotiation with management.*

barge /bardʒ/ *n.* a long, low boat that carries heavy loads: *The load of wheat was carried up river by a barge.*
—*v.* **barged, barging, barges** **1** to move heavily **2** *phrasal v. insep.* **to barge in** or **into s.t.:** to interrupt often and rudely: *He barged into our conversation and took over.*

bar·hop /'bar,hap/ *v.slang* **-hopped, -hopping, -hops** to drink in one bar after another: *After work on Friday we barhopped all over town.*

bar·i·tone /'bærɪ,toun/ *n.* a male singer with a voice lower than tenor but higher than bass

bark (1) /bark/ *v.n.* [U] the covering of a tree or woody plant: *The <n.> bark of a birch tree is white and black.*

bark (2) *n.* [C] **1** a sound a dog makes: *The dog barked at the neighbors.* **2** *fig.*to not be as dangerous as one seems: *He yells but never hurts anyone: his bark is worse than his bite.*
—*v.* **1** to make sounds like a dog **2** *fig.* to shout: *The boss barks orders at everyone.* **3 to bark up the wrong tree:** to complain to the wrong person

bar·ley /'barli/ *n.* [U] a grain used for food and drink: *I had some mushroom barley soup for lunch.*

barn /barn/ *n.* a building for storing crops and keeping animals and their food: *We keep horses, sheep, and chickens in the barn.*

bar·na·cle /'barnəkəl/ *n.* a small shellfish that grows on rocks and ships' bottoms: *Barnacles slow down a ship.*

barn·storm /'barn,stɔrm/ *v.* to give many political speeches in different places: *The politician barnstormed through the western part of the state.*

barn·yard /'bɑrn,yard/ *n.* an area fenced off beside a barn for animals: *Barnyards are often muddy in the springtime.*

ba·rom·e·ter /bə'rɑmɪtər/ *n.* an instrument that measures air pressure: *A barometer shows possible changes in the weather.* -*adj.* **barometric** /,bærə'mɛtrɪk/

bar·on /'bærən/ *n.* **1** the lowest ranking nobleman: *A baron's wife is a baroness.* **2** *fig.* a powerful businessperson, (*syn.*) a magnate: *He is a newspaper baron.* -*adj.* **baronial** /'bə'rouniəl/.

bar·racks /'bærəks/ *n.pl.* building where soldiers live

bar·ra·cu·da /bærə'kudə/ *n.* a fish with sharp teeth of warm (tropical) oceans that attacks meanly: *Swimmers get out of the water quickly when they see barracudas.*

bar·rage /bə'rɑʒ/ *n.v.* **-raged, -raging, -rages 1** many weapons shot at the same time: *Soldiers fired a <n.> barrage of machine guns at the enemy.* **2** *fig.* a heavy fast response: *The politician's remarks caused a <n.> barrage of criticism.*

bar·rel /'bærəl/ *n.* **1** a large, round container made of metal or wood: *Oil is sold by the barrel.* **2** the amount that a barrel holds, usu. between 117 and 159 liters (31 to 42 gallons) **3** a cylinder, esp. the straight, hollow tube of a gun: *The barrel of a gun guides the bullet.* **4** *infrml.fig.* **to have s.o. over a barrel:** to give s.o. no choice: *The government had the man over a barrel by demanding that he sell his land for little money or they would take it for nothing.*
—*adj.* big like a barrel: *Many well-fed workers are barrel-chested.*
—*phrasal v.* **to barrel along:** to drive fast: *He barrels along in his car at 80 mph on the highway.*

bar·ren /'bærən/ *adj.* **1** having no life, no animals, plants or people: *Some deserts are barren, with no life.* **2** not able to have children: *Because of an illness, she is barren.* **3** lacking s.t., such as interest or creativity. -*n.* **barrenness.** *See:* fertile.

bar·ri·cade /'bæri,keɪd/ *n.* a barrier that stops people from passing: *Firefighters put up barricades so traffic could not drive by the burning house.*
—*v.* **-caded, -cading, -cades** to block entrance with a barricade: *A criminal barricaded himself in a house.*

bar·ri·er /'bæriər/ *n.* s.t. that blocks the way, (*syn.*) an obstacle: *A tree fell across the road and made a barrier to traffic.||Being a woman has not been a barrier to her success.*

bar·ring /'bɑrɪŋ/ *prep.* unless, except: *Barring bad weather (if it doesn't rain), we will have a picnic tomorrow.||Barring the boss, we all went out for drinks on Friday.*

bar·room /'bɑr,rum/ *n.* a business where alcohol is served: *In the USA, you must be 21 years old to enter many barrooms.*

bar·ri·o /'bɑriou, 'bær-/ *n.* **-os** a mainly Spanish-speaking neighborhood in a USA city: *There are many barrios in Los Angeles and Miami.*

bar·ten·der /'bɑr,tɛndər/ *n.* a person who makes and serves alcoholic drinks as a job: *She is a bartender at a popular restaurant.*

bar·ter /'bɑrtər/ *v.n.* [U] the exchange of materials for other goods, not money: *Years ago, hunters <v.> bartered furs for guns.*

base /beɪs/ *n.* **1** the lower part of s.t., foundation: *That vase is on a wooden base.* **2** the point where a part of s.t. is connected to the whole: *The boxer hit the base of his opponent's neck.* **3** s.t. (a fact, an assumption, etc.) from which a start is made: *We will begin with your salary as a base and give you a 5 percent increase.* **4** the main place where one works or lives, (*syn.*) headquarters: *They use their apartment in New York as a home base from which they travel frequently.* **5** (in chemistry) a bitter-tasting substance that turns litmus paper blue **6** a military camp, building, airport, etc.: *The Air Force planes flew back to their base.* **7** (in baseball) one of four squares touched by runners **8** *infrml.* **to get to first base: a.** to start: *He tried to get a new job but did not get to first base.* **b.** *slang* to kiss **9** *infrml.* **off base:** wrong: *She is off base in her ideas about what is wrong with the economy.* **10** *infrml.* **to touch all the bases:** (from baseball) to address all major points: *He touched all the bases in his talk about the new product.*
—*phrasal v. insep.* **based, basing, bases: to base s.t. on s.t.:** to use as a reason for doing s.t.: *She based her decision to marry him on love, not money.*
—*adj.* **baser, basest: 1** basic, (*syn.*) fundamental: *These are the base figures for the house's value.* **2** low, (*syn.*) undesirable: *That man operates from base desires: sex, drugs, and greed.* -*adv.* **basely;** -*n.* [U] **baseness.**

base·ball /'beɪs,bɔl/ *n.* **1** a hard ball approx. the size of an adult's fist **2** a game played on a field by nine

baseball

players on each team who hit the ball with a bat and run around four bases to score: *Baseball is considered America's favorite sport. See:* Hall of Fame, USAGE NOTE.

USAGE NOTE: The game of *baseball* is called *America's pastime,* meaning the favorite sport of the country. The game is played with a small, hard ball and a bat, with two teams of nine players each, on a large field. Professional baseball has Major League and Minor League teams; many children play in Little League baseball.

base·ment /'beɪsmənt/ *n.* rooms under a house or building, (*syn.*) a cellar: *They keep old furniture in their basement.*

bash /bæʃ/ *n.slang* **bashes** a lively and usu. expensive party or celebration: *For her 50th birthday, her husband threw a bash for 100 friends.*
—*v.* **bashed, bashing, bashes 1** to hit with a heavy instrument, (*syn.*) to smash: *Firefighters bashed in the door of the burning house with an ax.* **2** *fig.infrml.* to criticize: *The newspapers and TV bashed the politician daily.* *-n.* **bashing.**

bash·ful /'bæʃfəl/ *adj.* afraid to talk to people, shy, timid: *He was too bashful to ask her for a date.* *-n.* [U] **bashfulness;** *-adv.* **bashfully.**

ba·sic /'beɪsɪk/ *adj.* **1** having the simple facts or ideas about s.t., (*syn.*) elementary: *He has a basic understanding of the problem.* **2** (in chemistry) having to do with a base *-adv.* **basically.**

ba·sics /'beɪsɪks/ *n.pl.* the necessary parts, fundamentals of s.t.: *She is just starting the job, so she has to learn the basics first.*

ba·sil /'beɪzəl, -səl, 'bæzəl/ *n.* an herb with a sweet smell like mint, used in cooking: *Pesto is a sauce made from basil.*

ba·sil·i·ca /bə'sɪlɪkə/ *n.* a type of church or public building in an oblong shape

ba·sin /'beɪsɪn/ *n.* **1** a hollow pan (for liquids): *He put water in the basin to wash his hands.* **2** a sink, a bathroom washbasin **3** a low, bowl-shaped, valley: *The land in that basin is good for growing crops.*

ba·sis /'beɪsɪs/ *n.* **bases** /'beɪˌsiz/ **1** the main reason(s) for s.t., foundation: *What is the basis of your opinion?* **2 on the basis of s.t.:** based on: *On the basis of his research, he says that the earth is round.*

bask /bæsk/ *v.* to sit and enjoy heat, sun, or s.t. enjoyable: *Birds and animals sit on the rocks and bask in the sun.‖She basked in the admiration of her colleagues.*

bas·ket /'bæskɪt/ *n.* **1** an open, light-weight container made of straw, reeds, or strips of wood: *He bought a basket of fruit.‖She put dirty clothes in a laundry basket.* **2** a hoop, usu. metal, with an open-ended net (used in basketball). *See:* wastebasket.

bas·ket·ball /'bæskɪtˌbɔl/ *n.* a game played by two teams of five players each who throw a large ball through a basket to score points

basket case *n.slang* s.o. who is very tired and can't function: *After her mother died, she was a basket case for a month.*

bass (1) /bæs/ *n.pl.* **bass** or **basses** an edible freshwater or marine fish

basketball

bass (2) /bes, beɪs/ *n.* **basses 1** a singing voice below baritone **2** the lower section of written music: *the bass clef* **3** an instrument that plays very low notes: *bass drum, bass fiddle, bass guitar*

bas·soon /bə'sun, bæ-/ *n.* a musical instrument of the woodwind variety

bas·tard /'bæstərd/ *n.* **1** a child whose parents are not married, (*syn.*) an illegitimate child **2** *vulg.* a nasty, difficult person *-v.* **bastardize;** *-adj.* **bastardized.**

baste /beɪst/ *v.* **basted, basting, bastes 1** to pour cooking juices over s.t.: *I basted the chicken roasting in the oven.* **2** to sew with long, loose, temporary stitches: *You can baste the pants until you have time to hem them correctly.*

bas·tion /'bæstʃən/ *n.* **1** part of a fortress that stands out **2** a fortress or other defense, esp. one near an enemy **3** *fig.* a source of strength: *He was a bastion of support to his wife while her father was dying.*

bat (1) /bæt/ *n.* **1** a flying animal active at night that looks like a rat with wings: *Bats eat insects and fruit!* **2** *pej.slang* an irritable old woman: *She is so rude; what an old bat!* **3** *infrml.* **as blind as a bat:** unable to see well **4** *infrml.* **like a bat out of hell:** fast, very quickly: *When the dog barked at him, he ran like a bat out of hell.* *See:* bats; batty; belfry.

bat

bat (2) *n.* **1** a thick, wooden stick, (*syns.*) a cudgel, a club: *He beat his victim with a bat.* **2** a long, rounded piece of metal or wood used to strike a baseball: *A baseball bat has a handle at one end.* **3 (right) off the bat:** (from baseball) at this moment, now: *Right off the bat, I don't know how much it costs.*
—*v.* **batted, batting, bats 1** to use a bat to hit a baseball: *He batted first in the game.* **2** to open and close the eyelids quickly: *She batted her eyes when dust got in them.* **3 at bat:** (in baseball) taking one's turn at hitting the ball: *Which team is at bat?* **4** *phrasal v. sep.* **to bat s.t. around:** to discuss, talk back and forth:

Before they left, they batted around what they were going to say to the tax auditor. **5** *infrml.* **to go to bat for s.o.:** to help s.o.: *When she needed help with the tax authorities, her friend went to bat for her by going to see them with her.* **6** *infrml.* **without batting an eyelid:** not caring that s.t. is shocking or painful, unconcerned: *Without batting an eyelid, he said she owed $50,000 and that he would put her in jail unless she paid it now.*

batch /bætʃ/ *n.* **batches 1** a group of persons or things, (*syn.*) a set: *He made a batch of cookies.* **2** an amount of s.t. made at one time: *Computers can work on a number of jobs in a batch.*

bat·ed /'beɪtɪd/ *adj.* **with bated breath:** anxious, hardly breathing from fear: *She waited with bated breath to learn if she passed the exam.*

bath /bæθ/ *n.* **baths** /bæðz, bæθs/ **1** a washing, esp. all of one's body at one time: *I took a hot bath last night. See:* bathe. **2** a tub in which to wash oneself: *The faucet in the bath is dripping.* **3** *infrml.* **to take a bath:** to lose a lot of money: *When the stock market crashed, he took a bath.* **4 baths:** a building for bathing or swimming

bathe /beɪð/ *v.* **bathed, bathing, bathes 1** to wash, clean oneself: *He bathes daily in the bathtub.* **2** to swim: *The family likes to bathe in the ocean. -n.* **bather.**

bath·ing suit /'beɪðɪŋ/ *n.* clothing worn to go swimming, (*syn.*) a swimsuit: *She wears a bikini bathing suit at the beach.*

bath·robe /'bæθ,roʊb/ *n.* a long, loose-fitting piece of clothing to wear at home: *After a bath, I put on my bathrobe and slippers.*

bath·room /'bæθ,rum/ *n.* restroom, room with a bath and toilet: *"Excuse me, I have to go to the bathroom."*

USAGE NOTE: In the USA, *bathroom* usu. means a room with a toilet and bathtub or shower in a house, but *restroom* refers to a toilet facility in a public building. *See:* ladies' room; men's room; powder room.

bath·tub /'bæθ,tʌb/ *n.* a large basin for bathing: *I tested the water and got into the bathtub.*

ba·ton /bə'tɑn/ *n.* **1** a short, thin piece of wood: *The leader of the orchestra moves a baton so that the players can see the rhythm.* **2** a long, round club, stick, (*syn.*) a club: *The police took out their batons to frighten the rioters, but they didn't hit anyone.*

bats /bæts/ *adj.slang* **to go bats:** to get upset or go crazy: *That poor guy went bats when he heard the bad news. See:* bat (1); batty.

bat·tal·ion /bə'tælyən/ *n.* **1** a unit of 500-1000 soldiers **2** *fig.* a large group of people: *The*

politician brought a battalion of supporters to the demonstration.

bat·ter (1) /'bætər/ *n.* a mixture of foods to be cooked, such as flour, sugar, butter, and milk, mixed together: *He put the cake batter in the oven to bake.*

bat·ter (2) (in baseball) the person who hits the ball: *The batter swung at the pitch and missed.*
—v. to hit s.o. repeatedly: *A man battered his girlfriend, and she called the police.*

bat·ter·y /'bætəri/ *n.* **-ies 1** a storage container for electricity: *I put two batteries in my flashlight.* **2** a military unit with mounted guns **3** a group of things used or put together, (*syn.*) an array: *Students take a battery of tests.* **4** a beating **5 to recharge one's batteries:** to rest, feel strong again: *Tired, she took a three-week vacation to recharge her batteries. See:* assault and battery.

bat·tle /'bætl/ *n.* **1** a fight between enemy soldiers (airplanes, warships, etc.) **2** *fig.* a struggle: *Our company is fighting a legal battle.*
—v. **-tled, -tling, -tles 1** to fight: *Two armies battled for days.* **2** to struggle: *She has been battling cancer for years.*

bat·tle·field /'bætl,fild/ *n.* **1** a place where battles are fought **2** *fig.* a place where people are always arguing: *Arguments between employees turned the company into a battlefield.*

bat·tle·ground /'bætl,graʊnd/ *n.* battlefield

bat·tle·ship /'bætl,ʃɪp/ *n.* a large warship with long guns: *A battleship can shoot its guns over 20 miles (32 km).*

bat·ty /'bæti/ *adj.infrml.* **-tier, -tiest** crazy, (*syn.*) insane: *She's quite batty; she talks to people who don't exist.*

bau·ble /'bɔbəl/ *n.* a piece of cheap jewelry or decoration: *Earrings and necklaces made of plastic are baubles.*

bawd·y /'bɔdi/ *adj.* **-ier, -iest** funny in a crude, indecent way, esp. about sex: *They saw a bawdy movie. -n.* [U] **bawdiness.**

bawl /bɔl/ *v.infrml.* **1** to cry loudly: *The baby bawled for her milk.* **2** *phrasal v. sep.* **to bawl s.o. out:** to scold, yell at s.o.: *His boss bawled the manager out for his accounting mistake.||He bawled him out.*

bay /beɪ/ *n.* **1** a large body of water around which the land bends: *Ships are anchored in the bay.* **2** a curved area set into or coming out of a wall, (*syn.*) an alcove: *There was a small couch and table in the bay.||a bay window* **3** a section set off from the other parts of a building, (*syn.*) a wing **4** a long, high sound a dog makes: *The sound of the dog's baying filled the air.* **5** a reddish brown color, esp. of a horse: *She rode a handsome bay mare.* **6** a tree with shiny, thick leaves used in cooking **7 to bring to bay:** to put s.o. in a situation from which there is no escape: *The dogs brought the fox to bay.*

bay·ou /'baɪu, 'baɪoʊ/ *n.* a stream that moves slowly through a swamp: *There are many bayous in Louisiana.*

ba·zaar /bə'zɑr/ *n.* **1** a group of outdoor shops: *People shop for food in a bazaar.* **2** a fair, usu. for charity, where things are sold in booths: *Our church had a bazaar last weekend.*

BBQ /'bɑrbɪ,kyu/ *n.abbr.* for barbecue.

B.C. /'bi'si/ *abbr.* Before Christ, the years before the birth of Christ in the Christian calendar: *The great Roman Emperor Augustus was born in 63 B.C. See: A.D.*

be (1) /bi/ *v.* used as an *auxiliary verb, a helping verb,* or with another verb: *I am* (helping verb) *shopping* (main verb) *for a new coat.* The tenses of *to be* are:

Present Tense

Singular	Plural
I am	*We are*
You are	*You are*
He/she/it is	*They are*

Present Participle: *being*
Past Tense

Singular	Plural
I was	*We were*
You were	*You were*
He/she/it was	*They were*

Past Participle: *been*
Negative Contractions:
Present Tense

He/she/it isn't	*You/they aren't*

Past Tense

He/she/it wasn't	*You/they weren't*

1 used with present participles (*-ing* forms) of other verbs: *I am/was shopping for a new coat.*‖*Are you/Were you going with me?*‖*They are/were waiting for us at the store.* **2** used with a past participle (often *-ed* forms) of other verbs: *I am/was stuck in traffic.*‖*You are/were invited to the party.*‖*They are/were dressed for work.* **3** used with infinitives (*to* + verb form) to indicate **a.** the future: *We are to go on vacation in July.* **b.** intention: *We are to be married next month.* **c.** duty, obligation: *She is to be in class at 9 a.m.*

be (2) *v.* **1** used as a connecting verb to show s.o. or s.t. is the same as the subject of the sentence: *George Washington* (subject) *was* (linking verb) *the first President* (the same as Washington) *of the USA.* **2** to show membership in a group: *She is a police officer.*‖*They are teachers.* **3** to show a characteristic: *The sky is blue.*‖*His face is red.* **4** to show position and location: *Moscow is in Russia.*‖*The rug is on the floor.*

be (3) *v.* to exist: *"I think, therefore I am."*

be (4) *v.* imperative of to be: **1 be good:** behave well: *Be good, or you will be punished.* **2 be my guest:** take s.t.: *Be my guest and help yourself to the potato chips.* **3 be well:** stay healthy

be (5) *prefix* used with a noun or verb as in to become (friends with s.o.): *He befriended the boy and taught him to swim.*

beach /bitʃ/ *n.* **beaches** a sandy area by a lake or ocean: *We went to the beach yesterday.*
—*v.* **1** to pull or push a boat onto a beach. **2 to get beached:** to be left, stranded: *the whales got beached on the shore.*

beach ball *n.* a large, round ball: *People play with a beach ball by throwing it to each other.*

beach·comb·er /'bitʃ,koʊmər/ *n.* **1** a person who looks for pretty things on a beach: *The beachcomber looks for seashells.* **2** a person who sells things he or she finds on the beach

bea·con /'bikən/ *n.* a strong guiding light usu. on a tall tower: *Tall buildings near airports have red beacons to warn airplanes away at night.*

bead /bid/ *n.* **1** a small round piece of material with a hole for stringing: *Her necklace is made of red glass beads.* **2** a small amount of liquid: *Beads of sweat fell from the tennis player's face.*
—*v.* to form into beads: *The sweat beaded up and fell into his eyes.*

bead·y /'bidi/ *adj.* **-ier, -iest** (of the eyes) shiny, sharp, angry: *The criminal gave the policeman a beady look and ran away.*

bea·gle /'bigəl/ *n.* a type of short hunting dog usu. with three colors of hair

beak /bik/ *n.* the nose and mouth of a bird, turtle, etc.: *Some birds have long beaks.*

beak·er /'bikər/ *n.* **1** a clear, glass container for liquids: *Chemistry students use beakers to measure materials in laboratories.* **2** *frml.* a drinking glass

beam /bim/ *n.* **1** a long, thick piece of metal or wood used to make buildings, bridges, etc.: *Steel beams are put together to make the insides of buildings.* **2** a ray of light: *Beams of light came from the car's headlights.* **3** the width of s.t.: *Big ships have wide beams.* **4** *infrml.* **on** (or) **off the beam:** correct or incorrect: *He is off the beam when he says that teaching is an easy job.*
—*v.* **1** to shine **2** *fig.* to smile widely: *She beamed with happiness.* **3** to send a signal, (*syn.*) to broadcast: *Radio stations beam their programs to listeners.*

bean /bin/ *n.* **1** an edible seed of many plants: *I like to eat lima beans and black beans.* **2** *infrml.fig.* the head **3** *infrml.* **a hill of beans:** a small, unimportant amount: *That wet, sandy land isn't worth a hill of beans.* **4** *infrml.* **full of beans:** full of energy, very active: *Those*

kids run all day; they're full of beans. **5** *infrml.* **to spill the beans:** to tell a secret by mistake: *He spilled the beans when he told her about her surprise party.*
—*v.infrml.fig.* to hit s.o. on the head: *A boy beaned his friend with a baseball.*

bear (1) /bɛr/ *n.* **bears** or **bear** **1** a large animal with thick fur and sharp teeth: *Grizzly bears are big and often aggressive.* **2** *infrml.fig.* an irritable person, (*syn.*) a grouch: *When he's under pressure, he acts like a bear.* **3** a person who thinks s.t. bad will happen, (*syn.*) a pessimist: *A*

bear

bear is s.o. who thinks the stock market will go down. See: bearish; bear market.

bear (2) *v.* **bore,** /bɔr/ **bearing, bears** **1** to support, carry (s.t. heavy, burden): *Steel beams bear the weight of buildings.* **2** *fig.* to suffer, feel bad: *He cannot bear the pain of a toothache.* **3** to produce, (*syn.*) to yield: *Cherry trees bear cherries.* **4** to give birth to: *After having five daughters, she hoped to bear a son.* **5** to go in a certain direction: *Go to the corner, then bear right and you will find the grocery store.* **6** to relate to, have meaning: *The old man's poor health bears on how long he will live.* **7 to bear a resemblance to:** to look like s.o. else **8** *phrasal v.* **to bear down:** **a.** to apply pressure: *She bore down with her pen to write clearly.* **b.** to work hard, apply oneself: *He always bears down and studies hard to make good grades.* **9** *phrasal v. insep.* **to bear down on s.o. or s.t.:** **a.** to punish: *His enemies challenged him, so now he will bear down on them.* **b.** to rush toward: *The speeding car bore down on the dog and almost hit it.* **10 to bear in mind:** to remember: *Bear in mind that she was only 10 years old when she committed the crime.* **11 to bear no relation:** not to be relevant, important to s.t. **12** *phrasal v. sep.* **to bear s.t. out:** to support, prove correct: *Other people bear out that what she says is true.||They bear it out.* **13** *phrasal v. insep.* **to bear up under s.t:** to deal with s.t. without complaining, tolerate: *He bears up well under pressure.* **14** *phrasal v. insep.* **to bear with s.o. or s.t.:** **a:** s.o.: to wait: *Please bear with me for a moment while I finish writing this sentence.* **b:** s.t.: to suffer, (*syn.*) to tolerate: *Bear with the heavy workload for a while until it gets better.*

bear·a·ble /ˈbɛrəbəl/ *adj.* able to be withstood, endurable, (*syn.*) tolerable: *The hot weather is uncomfortable but bearable.* *-adv.* **bearably.** *See:* unbearable.

beard /bɪrd/ *n.* hair on the face, (*syn.*) whiskers: *My father has always worn a beard and moustache.* *-adj.* **bearded.** *See:* side-burns.

bear·er /ˈbɛrər/ *n.* a carrier, person who brings s.t.: *Paul was the bearer of bad news.*

bear·ing /ˈbɛrɪŋ/ *n.* [U] **1** importance to s.t. else, (*syn.*) influence: *Good weather has a bearing on farmers' growing good crops.* **2** a direction on a compass: *That ship is on a southerly bearing.* **3** the way one holds one's body: *Dancers have a graceful bearing.*

bear market *n.* a financial market in which the value of stocks and bonds goes down: *Investors usually lose money in a bear market.*

beast /bist/ *n.* **1** *frml.* an animal: *Donkeys are beasts of burden that carry heavy loads.* **2** *fig.* an evil, badly behaved person, esp. a man: *That beast (of a man) punched the guard and robbed the bank.* *-adv.* **beastly.**

beat /bit/ *v.* **beat, beating, beats** **1** to hit again and again, (*syn.*) to strike: *A man beat another man with a club.* **2** to mix or blend: *She beat the eggs with a spoon.* **3** to move regularly: *The bird beat its wings as it flew away.* **4** to defeat an opponent: *Our team beat the other team again.* **5** to get around the rules: *He beat the system by getting unemployment payments while he was still working.* **6** to throb, (*syn.*) to pulse: *He could hear the beating of his heart as he ran.* **7** to cause s.t. to make a sound by striking it: *She beat a rhythm on the drum.* **8** to flatten by hitting again and again: *They had beaten a trail from the house to the lake.* **9** *infrml.* **to beat it:** leave quickly: *You're not wanted here—beat it!* **10** *infrml.* **it beats me:** not to know: *What is the answer? It beats me!* **11** *infrml.* **to beat a dead horse:** to do or say s.t. that will not succeed, a useless effort: *She's beating a dead horse when she talks about opening foreign offices because no one listens to her.* **12** *phrasal v. sep.* **to beat s.o. or s.t. back:** to stop or make go backwards: *Our competitors took sales away from us, but we beat them back with an improved product.* **13** *infrml.* **to beat the bushes:** to search: *Salespeople beat the bushes for sales by visiting many customers.* **14** *phrasal v. sep.* **to beat s.t. down:** to convince s.o. to lower a price: *We beat down the price of the car to $6,000.||We beat it down.* **15** *infrml.* **to beat one's brains out:** to try very hard: *She beat her brains out trying to solve the math problem.* **16** *infrml.* **to beat s.o. to it** or **the punch:** to do s.t. first: *I beat my competitor to the punch by selling a new product first.* **17** *infrml.* **to beat s.t. out of s.o.:** to cheat: *The drug dealer beat his boss out of some profits and then was murdered.* **18** *phrasal v. sep.* **to beat s.o. up:** to hurt badly: *When I was little, the other kids used to beat up my brother and me.||They beat us up.* **19 off the beaten path** or **track:** where few people go: *We went off the beaten path to a small island for our vacation.*

—*n.* tempo, rhythm of music: *The beat of the music makes me want to dance.*

—*adj.infrml.fig.* tired: *I am really beat from working hard all week.*

beat·er /'bitər/ *n.* **1** a tool or machine used to mix and soften food: *I used an egg beater to whip some cream.* **2** one who beats: *That woman is a child beater.*

beat·ing /'bitɪŋ/ *n.* **1** the act of hitting repeatedly **2 to take a beating: a.** to be hit or punched badly **b.** *fig.* to lose a lot of money: *I really took a beating because I had to sell my house for much less than I paid for it.*

beau·ti·cian /byu'tɪʃən/ *n.* a person who cuts hair, gives manicures, etc.: *A beautician put on the bride's makeup before the wedding.*

beau·ti·ful /'byutəfəl/ *adj.* pleasing to the senses or the mind: *The mountains are beautiful in the summer. See:* handsome, USAGE NOTE.

beau·ti·fy /'byutə,faɪ/ *v.* **-fied, -fying, -fies** to make s.t. pretty: *She beautified her garden by planting flowers.*

beau·ty /'byuti/ *n.* [C;U] **-ties 1** s.t. pleasing to the senses or the mind: *People see beauty in paintings.* **2** an advantage: *The beauty of leaving early is that we avoid traffic.*

beauty parlor or **shop** a business for hairdressing, manicures, etc., a salon: *She goes to the beauty parlor to have her hair cut.*

bea·ver /'bivər/ *n.* **1** an animal that looks like a large rat with a long flat tail: *Beavers build dams by cutting down trees with their sharp teeth.* **2** *infrml.* **eager beaver:** a hard worker: *He is an eager beaver who does every job with enthusiasm.*

beaver

be·bop /'bi,bɑp/ or **bop** /'bɑp/ *n.slang* a style of jazz music

be·cause /bɪ'kɔz, -'kʌz/ *conj.* for the reason that, as: *I cannot go to work today because I am sick.*

—*prep.* **because of:** by reason of: *I worked late because of a deadline.*

beck and call /bɛk/ *n.* ready to obey: *The servant was at the beck and call of his master.*

beck·on /'bɛkən/ *v.* to motion or call someone to come to you: *The teacher beckoned the student to her desk.*

be·come /bɪ'kʌm/ *v.* **-came,** /-'keɪm/ **-coming, -comes 1** to grow, come to be: *She wants to become a doctor.* **2** to make s.o. look good, (*syn.*) to flatter: *The new hairstyle really becomes you.* **3** *phrasal v.* **to become of:** to happen to: *What has become of John?*

be·com·ing /bɪ'kʌmɪŋ/ *adj.* pleasing, attractive to the eye: *That new dress is very becoming on you.*

bed /bɛd/ *n.* **1** a piece of furniture for sleeping: *I have a single bed in my bedroom.* **2** a platform for other things: *That house is built on a bed of cement.* **3** formations of the earth: *The bottom of the ocean is called the seabed.* **4** a small area of land used for growing s.t.: *Keep the dog out of the flower bed.* **5** *infrml.* **a bed of roses:** a good, easy situation in life: *Working in a coal mine is no bed of roses.* **6** *infrml.* **to get up on the wrong side of the bed:** to be irritable, angry: *She got up on the wrong side of the bed and was irritable all day.* **7 to make a bed:** to put on or make neat the sheets, blankets, etc. of a bed: *I make the bed every morning by smoothing the sheets and putting on the bedspread.* **8 to put to bed:** to take a child to its bed **9 to take to one's bed:** to go to bed, esp. when sick: *He had a terrible headache and took to his bed to rest.*

—*v.* **bedded, bedding, beds** *phrasal v.* **to bed down:** to find or make a place to sleep for the night: *Campers bed down in sleeping bags on the ground after they put up their tent.*

bed and breakfast *n.adj.* a private home that rents rooms to guests and serves breakfast: *We stayed at a <n.> bed and breakfast last night. See:* room and board.

USAGE NOTE: A *bed and breakfast* (or *B & B*) is a private home that offers guests a bedroom, bathroom, and a full breakfast. B & Bs are usually located in the countryside. An *inn* is a small *hotel,* also often in the country. A hotel is usually larger than an inn, and may be located in the city or country. A *motel* is a small, usually one-storey hotel along a highway where guests can park their cars in front of their rooms.

bed·bug /'bɛd,bʌg/ *n.* a tiny insect that sucks blood and lives in beds, (*syn.*) bed louse: *The bite of a bedbug really itches!*

bed·clothes /'bɛd,klouz, -,klouðz/ *n.pl.* sheets, blankets, pillows, etc. used to cover beds: *I changed the bedclothes after I had slept in them for a week.*

bed·ding /'bɛdɪŋ/ *n.* [U] **1** material that animals sleep on: *A horse's bedding can be chips of wood.* **2** bedclothes: *I put some fresh bedding on the bed.*

be·deck /bɪ'dɛk/ *v.frml.* to decorate, (*syn.*) to adorn: *The walls were bedecked with flags and the tables with flowers.*

be·dev·il /bɪ'dɛvəl/ *v.* to annoy s.o. a lot, (*syn.*) to distress: *She is bedeviled by a bad back that hurts often. -n.* [U] **bedevilment.**

bed·fel·low /'bɛd,fɛlou/ *n.* **1** a person who shares a bed with s.o. else **2** *fig.* a partner, associate: *Business makes bedfellows of people who would not usually work with each other.*

bed·lam /ˈbɛdləm/ n. [U] a wild place full of noise and chaos, (syn.) a madhouse: *With three children, our house is bedlam sometimes.*

bed·pan /ˈbɛd,pæn/ n. a shallow pan used as a toilet by people who cannot get out of bed: *A nurse took the bedpan away to empty it.*

be·drag·gled /bɪˈdrægəld/ adj. messy, bad-looking from wrinkled clothes, etc.: *He walked in the rain without an umbrella and looked bedraggled.* -v. **bedraggle.**

bed·rid·den /ˈbɛd,rɪdn/ adj. staying in bed because of illness or weakness

bed·rock /ˈbɛd,rɑk/ n. [U] **1** solid rock under the earth: *That building is built on bedrock.* **2** a firm foundation **3** the very bottom of s.t.

bed·roll /ˈbɛd,roʊl/ n. a thick, soft piece of material used as a bed, esp. in camping

bed·room /ˈbɛd,rum/ n. a room for sleeping: *The house has two bedrooms.*

bed·side /ˈbɛd,saɪd/ n. the area near or to the side of a bed: *The family came to the old man's bedside.*

bed·spread /ˈbɛd,sprɛd/ n. a covering, usu. decorative, put over the bedding

bed·time /ˈbɛd,taɪm/ n. [C;U] the time to go to sleep: *The parents told the babysitter that 9:00 p.m. is bedtime for the children.*

bee /bi/ n. **1** an insect with wings that stings and makes honey **2 to have a bee in one's bonnet:** always to be talking about a single idea, an obsession: *She has a bee in her bonnet; she is always talking about the dangers of illegal drugs. See:* busy bee.

beech /bitʃ/ n. [C;U] **beeches** a tree with edible nuts and a smooth gray trunk

bee

beef /bif/ n. [U] **1** the meat of cattle: *We had roast beef for dinner.* **2** fig.slang **a beef:** a complaint: *He always has a beef about something.*
—phrasal v. sep. **to beef s.t. up:** to strengthen, add more: *Fearing war, the country beefed up its defenses.||It beefed them up.*

beef·y /ˈbifi/ adj.slang **-ier, -iest** muscular, strong, sometimes fat: *Football players are big, beefy guys.*

bee·hive /ˈbi,haɪv/ n. **1** a home for bees: *I stuck my hand in the beehive and was stung three times!* **2** fig. a very busy place: *The office was a beehive of activity. See:* hive.

bee·line /ˈbi,laɪn/ n. a path directly to s.t., esp. walked quickly: *The boy makes a beeline for home after school every day*

been /bɪn/ past part of to be

beep /bip/ n.v.infrml. the sound of a car horn or electronic device: *He <v.> beeped his horn,*

then heard a <n.> beep from his electronic beeper.

beep·er /ˈbipər/ n. an electronic device that beeps to tell you to call s.o., (syn.) a pager: *He wears a beeper on his belt when he is away from his office.*

beer /bɪr/ n. [C;U] **1** a bitter alcoholic drink usu. made from grain: *She had a sandwich and a beer for lunch.* **2** a drink made from a plant or root: *ginger beer, root beer*
—adj.infrml. **1 beer belly:** a big stomach, (syn.) a paunch: *That guy has a beer belly.* **2 beer joint:** a bar

bees·wax /ˈbiz,wæks/ n. [U] wax made by bees to hold honey in their hive, used in candles, furniture polish, etc.

beet /bit/ or **beet root** // n. **1** a plant with a thick red root eaten as a vegetable **2 sugar beet:** a variety of beet from whose white root sugar is made

bee·tle /ˈbitl/ n. a hard-shelled, winged insect: *Beetles crawl slowly on the ground.*

be·fall /bɪˈfɔl/ v.frml. **-fell,** /-ˈfɛl/, **-falling, -falls** to have s.t. bad happen: *A car accident befell him.*

be·fit /bɪˈfɪt/ v.frml. **-fitted, -fitting, -fits** to be suitable and correct: *As befits a wedding, the bride wore a white dress.* -adj. **befitting.**

be·fore /bɪˈfɔr/ prep. in front of: *He stood before me.*
—adv. **1** earlier than: *It is 10 minutes before 12 o'clock.* **2** ahead of: *The child ran before her classmates.*
—conj. **1** ahead of in time: *I hope he quits his job before it makes him crazy.* **2** rather than, instead of

be·fore·hand /bɪˈfɔr,hænd/ adv. before s.t. happens, earlier: *We had decided to make airline reservations beforehand.*

be·friend /bɪˈfrɛnd/ v. to become friends with s.o.: *The man befriended the boy and showed him how to play chess.*

beg /bɛg/ v. **begged, begging, begs** **1** to ask for s.t., usu. money, on the street: *A poor woman begged for coins.* **2** to ask strongly, (syn.) to plead: *He begged her to stay with him, but she left anyhow.* **3** frml. **to beg the question: a.** to know the answer to a question: *"He has found a job hasn't he?" "The fact that he leaves at the same time every morning dressed for work begs the question."* **b.** to try not to answer the question. (syn.) to evade: *When his mother asked him if he had finished his homework, the student begged the question by saying it was difficult.* **4** frml. **to beg to differ:** to disagree politely: *I beg to differ with you, but it was not sunny last Thursday.* **5** phrasal v. **to beg off:** to make excuses and not do s.t. one has agreed to: *He* *agreed to work on Saturday, then begged off at the last moment.*

be·gan /bɪ'gæn/ *past part. of* begin

be·get /bɪ'gɛt/ *v.frml.* **-got** /-'gɑt/, **-getting, -gets 1** to produce: *The mother begets a child.* **2** to cause to happen: *War begets more war.*

beg·gar /'bɛgər/ *n.* **1** a person who asks for money, (*syn.*,) a panhandler: *The beggar stopped me on the street and asked for change.* **2** *infrml.* **beggars can't be choosers:** not to be too particular in an emergency: *I ate the sandwich she made even though I hate ham, because beggars can't be choosers. -adj.* **beggarly.**

be·gin /bɪ'gɪn/ *v.* **-gan** /-gæn/, **-ginning, -gins 1** to start, (*syn.*) to commence: *We began our trip on August 1.* **2 to begin with:** first of all, to start

be·gin·ner /bɪ'gɪnər/ *n.* **1** s.o. starting, (*syn.*) a novice: *He is a beginner at golf.* **2** *infrml.* **beginner's luck:** success the first time one does s.t.: *She had beginner's luck by playing golf well her first time.*

be·gin·ning /bɪ'gɪnɪŋ/ *n.* [C;U] a start, (*syn.*) the commencement: *At the beginning, our business grew slowly.*

be·go·nia /bɪ'gounyə/ *n.* a garden plant with small, pretty flowers

be·grudge /bɪ'grʌdʒ/ *v.* **-grudged, -grudging, -grudges** to envy, not want s.o. else to have or do s.t.: *I begrudge him his wealth because he did not earn it. See:* grudge.

be·guile /bɪ'gaɪl/ *v.* **-guiled, -guiling, -guiles 1** to cheat, (*syn.*) to delude: *She was beguiled by the man and lost all her money to him.* **2** to charm: *She is so beautiful that she beguiles every man she meets.*

be·gun /bɪ'gʌn/ *past part. of* begin

be·half /bɪ'hæf/ *n.* **1 on behalf of:** as the representative of: *As her lawyer, I act on behalf of Mrs. Jones by going to court.* **2 in behalf of:** for the benefit of: *The couple gave to charity in behalf of disabled children.*

be·have /bɪ'heɪv/ *v.* **-haved, -having, -haves 1** to act in a certain way: *As a manager, she behaves with competence.* **2** to act well: *Children, behave yourselves! See:* misbehave.

be·hav·ior /bɪ'heɪvyər/ *n.* [U] a way of acting: *She refused to work closely with anyone and was fired for bad behavior*

be·head /bɪ'hɛd/ *v.frml.* to cut s.o.'s head off, (*syn.*) to decapitate: *The traitor was beheaded at the king's order.*

be·hest /bɪ'hɛst/ *n.frml.* command, order: *At the behest of the captain, the soldiers began to march.*

be·hind /bɪ'haɪnd/ *adv.* **1** last, in back of: *Runners must run fast or be left behind by the others.* **2** in a time, place, or condition that has passed: *The landlady was behind the times.* **3**

late in doing s.t.: *He was behind on his rent.‖The doctor is running behind today.*
—*prep.* **1** at the back of: *She sat behind me.* **2** below in rank, grade, etc.: *She was behind her peers at school.* **3** *infrml.fig.* **behind the eight ball:** in a bad situation: *When they could not pay their taxes, they were behind the eight ball because the government fined them more money.*
—*n.infrml.* part of the body on which one sits, (*syn.*) the buttocks: *She fell on her behind.*

be·hold /bɪ'hould/ *v.frml.* **-held** /-hɛld/, **-holding, -holds** to see, look at: *Behold how beautiful the sunset looks! -n.* **beholder.**

be·hold·en /bɪ'houldən/ *adj.* owing, obligated to s.o.: *I feel beholden to my friend because he loaned me money.*

be·hoove /bɪ'huv/ *v.frml.* **-hooved, -hooving, -hooves** to be required by duty: *It behooves students to study.*

beige /beɪʒ/ *adj.* a light-brown or tan color: *His beige sweater did not look good with his orange pants.*

be·ing /'biɪŋ/ *n. pres. part. of* be **1** in existence: *The United States of America came into being with the signing of the Declaration of Independence.* **2** a living thing: *Every being on earth depends on the environment.* **3** one's basic nature: *He loves painting with his whole being.*
—*adj.* **for the time being:** for the present, meanwhile: *They are looking for a house, but for the time being they are staying in a hotel.*

be·la·bor /bɪ'leɪbər/ *v.frml.* to work or talk too long, repeat a point too often: *She belabored how angry she felt until no one listened anymore.*

be·lat·ed /bɪ'leɪtɪd/ *adj.* too late, after s.t. has happened: *His birthday was last week, but I sent him a belated birthday card today. -adv.* **belatedly.**

be·lea·guer /bɪ'ligər/ *v.* **1** to make many demands on s.o., (*syn.*) to harass: *a man beleaguered by debts* **2** to surround with soldiers

belch /bɛltʃ/ *v.* **belches 1** to have gas come out of the mouth, (*syn.*) to burp: *He belches after every meal.* **2** to throw forcefully: *The car's tail pipe belched black smoke. -n.* **belch.**

bel·fry /'bɛlfri/ *n.* **-fries 1** bell tower: *The belfry is in the top of the church.* **2** *infrml.fig.* **to have bats in one's belfry:** to be foolish or crazy: *The man walks around the streets barefoot in all weather; they say he has bats in his belfry.*

be·lie /bɪ'laɪ/ *v.* **-lied, -lying, -lies** to give a wrong idea: *His soft words belied a hard heart.*

be·lief /bɪ'lif/ *n.* [C;U] **1** an idea, condition, or way of behaving that one thinks is true, (*syn.*) a conviction: *She has the belief that he loves her.* **2** trust: *She has belief in her daughter's* good judgment. **3** a religious principle or moral standard: *She is a woman with strong religious beliefs.* **4 beyond belief:** untrue, incredible

be·liev·a·ble /bɪ'livəbəl/ *adj.* capable of being thought true: *His description of the crime was believable.* *-adv.* **believably.**

be·lieve /bɪ'liv/ *v.* **-lieved, -lieving, -lieves 1** to be convinced of s.t., know or feel that an idea, situation, or way of behaving is true: *She believed her son when he said he didn't start the fight.* **2** to think, (*syn.*) to expect: *I believe he is coming on Friday.* **3** *phrasal v. insep.* **to believe in s.o. or s.t.: a. s.o.:** to support, trust in s.o.: *His mother believes in him and knows he would never hurt anyone.* **b. s.t.:** to have faith, hold as a principle: *Do you believe in God?*‖*She doesn't believe in lying.* **4 to make believe:** to pretend: *The boys make believe they are cowboys.*

be·liev·er /bɪ'livər/ *n.* **1** s.o. who has an idea or principle: *He is a believer in working hard for a living.* **2** a follower, a supporter of s.o. or s.t., esp. in religion: *She is a believer in the principles of Judaism.*

be·lit·tle /bɪ'lɪtl/ *v.* **-tled, -tling, -tles** to make s.t. seem small or not important, (*syn.*) to disparage: *The father belittled his son's good grades in school.*

bell /bɛl/ *n.* **1** a hollow metal object that makes pleasant sounds when hit: *The mail carrier rang the doorbell.* **2** *infrml.* **to ring a bell:** to recognize, cause to remember: *You mentioned his name, but it doesn't ring a bell as to who he is.*

bell-bot·toms /'bɛl,batəmz/ *n.pl.* a style of pants popular in the 60's and 70's that widen near the ankles

bell·boy /'bɛl,bɔɪ/ *n.* a person, usu. male, who carries luggage to hotel guests' rooms

belle /bɛl/ *n.* a pretty and popular woman: *She was the belle of the ball (dance) last night.*

bell·hop /'bɛl,hap/ *n.* See: bellboy.

bel·li·cose /'bɛlɪ,kous/ *adj.frml.* angry, ready to fight: *That nation is bellicose, always threatening to go to war. -n.frml.* [U] **bellicosity** /,bɛlɪ'kasəti/.

bel·lig·er·ent /bə'lɪdʒərənt/ *adj.* angry, ready to fight: *His belligerent attitude made it difficult to work with him. -n.* [U] **belligerence.**

bel·low /'bɛlou/ *v.n.* to shout or make noise loudly: *The teacher <v.> bellowed orders at the students.*

bel·lows /'bɛlouz/ *n.pl.* used with a sing.v. a tool used to blow air on a fire to make it bigger: *I pumped the bellows to heat up the fire.*

bel·ly /'bɛli/ *n.infrml.* **-lies 1** the abdomen, stomach: *I lay on my belly all day at the beach and sunburned my back.* **2** a curved part of s.t. **3** *infrml.* **fire in one's belly:** a strong desire to

succeed: *He has fire in his belly because he wants badly to succeed.* **4** *infrml.fig.* **to go belly up:** to fail: *That business had so many debts that it went belly up. See:* beer belly.

bel·ly·ache /'bɛli,eɪk/ *n.infrml.* stomach pains: *I have a bellyache from eating too much.*
—v.fig. **-ached, -aching, -aches** to complain, (*syn.*) to whine: *Every time you listen to her she is bellyaching.*

belly button *n.infrml.* the navel, stomach area

bel·ly·ful /'bɛli,fʊl/ *n.infrml.* **1** a stomach full of s.t. **2** *fig.* too much: *He was working 18 hours a day before he finally had a bellyful and quit his job.*

be·long /bɪ'lɔŋ/ *v.* **1** to be the property of, be owned by: *That car (house, guitar, etc.) belongs to me.* **2** to go together naturally, (*syn.*) to suit: *That couple belongs together; they really get along well.* **3** to be a member of a group: *He belongs to the health club.* **4** to be part of s.t., connected: *That part belongs to the engine.*

be·long·ings /bɪ'lɔŋɪŋz/ *n.pl.* personal property, such as clothes, etc.: *He packed his belongings in a suitcase and left.*

be·lov·ed /bɪ'lʌvɪd, -'lʌvd/ *adj.* (s.o. who is) highly loved: *a beloved daughter*

be·low /bɪ'lou/ *prep.* **1** lower than, under: *The foot is below the knee.*‖*The gold ore was located below the earth's surface.* **2** on a later page or part of s.t.: *See page 17 below for more information.*
—adv. to the lower part of s.t.: *I went down below into the cellar.*

belt /bɛlt/ *n.* **1** a piece of leather, plastic, etc. worn around the waist: *Belts are used to hold up pants.* **2** an endless strap used as part of a machine: *The conveyor belt took the packages to the loading platform.* **3** an area of land with special qualities: *Most wheat grown in the USA is from the Grain Belt.* **4 to hit below the belt:** to attack unfairly: *Criticizing her accent is hitting below the belt; she speaks perfect English.* **5 to tighten one's belt:** to economize, spend less money: *When my father lost his job, we all had to tighten our belts.*
—v.slang to strike, hit: *If he says one more word, I'll belt him in the mouth.*

be·moan /bɪ'moun/ *v.frml.* to feel sad about s.t., regret: *She bemoans the fact that she did not finish high school.*

be·mused /bɪ'myuzd/ *adj.* a little annoyed and a little amused: *The teacher was bemused by the fact that no one in the class could answer her question. -adv.* **bemusedly** /bɪ'myuzɪdli/.

bench /bɛntʃ/ *n.* **benches 1** a long seat, often made of wood: *People sit on benches in the park.* **2** judicial authority: *The lawyers went to the bench for a conference with the judge.*

B

—*v.* **benched, benching, benches** to order s.o. to stop playing or working, (*syn.*) to inactivate: *He made so many mistakes in the game that the coach benched him.*

bench·mark /'bɛnʧ,mɑrk/ *n.* **1** a point from which distances are measured **2** *fig.* a level or standard of excellence or achievement: *The company's first million dollars in sales was a benchmark.* *See:* milestone.

bend /bɛnd/ *n.* **1** a turn, curve: *I followed the bend in the road.* **2** *pl.* **a.** pains after coming up from deep water too quickly **b.** *infrml.fig.* exhausted, unable to work: *He started up a new company by himself and now has the bends.* **3** *infrml.* **to bend over backwards:** to try very hard to please s.o., (*syn.*) to accommodate: *The director of personnel bends over backwards to help each new employee.* *See:* bent.

—*v.* **bent** /bɛnt,/ **bending, bends 1** to turn, make st curved: *I bent a stick and broke it in two* **2** to lean over at the waist: *She bent over and picked up a piece of paper.*

be·neath /bɪ'niθ/ *prep.* **1** below, under: *Solid rock lies beneath the earth.* **2** not worthy of s.o., (*syn.*) undignified: *He used to be a corporate manager, so he thinks driving a taxi is beneath him.*

—*adv.* below: *The dog was sleeping beneath the front porch.*

ben·e·dic·tion /,bɛnə'dɪkʃən/ *n.* a request for divine favor, (*syn.*) a blessing: *The priest gave the benediction on Sunday morning.*

ben·e·fac·tor /'bɛnə,fæktər/ *n.* a person who helps s.o. or s.t., esp. by giving money: *A rich woman was a benefactor to a young artist.* -*n.* [U] **benefaction** /,bɛnə'fækʃən/; -*adj.* **beneficent** /bə'nɛfəsənt/.

ben·e·fi·cial /,bɛnə'fɪʃəl/ *adj.* good, advantageous: *The vacation was beneficial to his health.* -*adv.* **beneficially.**

ben·e·fi·ci·ar·y /,bɛnə'fɪʃəri, -'fɪʃi,ɛri/ *n.* -**ries** s.o. who receives s.t. good, (*syn.*) a recipient, esp. from s.o. who dies: *His wife was the beneficiary of his will and got all his money when he died.*||*I am the beneficiary of his kindness.*

ben·e·fit /'bɛnə,fɪt/ *n.* **1** gain, positive result: *She received a benefit for her good work, which was a large raise.* **2** social event to raise money for charity: *The fire department organized a benefit to raise money for poor children.* **3** **to give s.o. the benefit of the doubt:** not to judge s.o. too quickly: *It looks as though she made a bad mistake, but let's give her the benefit of the doubt, until we talk with her.*

—*v.* -**fited, -fiting, -fits** to gain from s.t.: *The company benefited from selling a new product.* *See:* fringe benefits.

be·nev·o·lence /,bə'nɛvələns/ *n.* [U] an act of generosity and kindness: *As an act of benevo-lence, she helped her unemployed son pay his rent* -*adj.* **benevolent;** -*adv.* **benevolently.**

be·nign /bɪ'naɪn/ *adj.* **1** harmless, gentle: *Though he talks in a rough manner, his actions are benign.* **2** not having cancer: *The doctor took out a benign tumor.* -*adv.* **benignly.** *See:* malign.

bent (1) /bɛnt/ *adj.* **1** crooked, not straight: *That piece of metal is bent.* **2 bent on s.t.:** set on doing s,t., determined, often wrongly: *He seems bent on hurting himself by lifting heavy things.* **3** *infrml.* **bent out of shape:** very angry: *I didn't want to upset her, but she got all bent out of shape anyhow.*

bent (2) *n.* an ability or skill: *He has a natural bent for playing musical instruments.*

be·queath /bɪ'kwiθ, -'kwið/ *v.* to give by a will after death, leave: *The man bequeathed his house to his children.* -*n.* **bequeathal.**

be·quest /bɪ'kwɛst/ *n.* a benefit from a will, (*syn.*) a legacy: *He left his house as a bequest to his wife.*

be·rate /bɪ'reɪt/ *v.frml.* -**rated, -rating, -rates** to criticize s.o. severely, (*syns.*) to scold, rebuke.

be·reave /bɪ'riv/ *v.* -**reaved** or **-reft** /-'rɛft/, **-reaving, -reaves** to experience the death of a loved one: *She was bereaved when her husband died.* -*n.* [U] **bereavement.**

be·reft /bɪ'rɛft/ *adj.* without (s.o. or s.t.), lacking: *The room is bereft of any furniture.*

be·ret /bə'reɪ/ *n.* a round, soft woolen cap common in France: *He wears a beret in cold weather.*

ber·ry /'bɛri/ *n.* -**ries** a small fruit: *I baked muffins with berries in them.*

ber·serk /bər'sɜrk, -'zɜrk/ *adj.* crazy, insanely violent: *When his son was killed, the man went berserk.*

berth /bɜrθ/ *n.* **1** a place near a dock where a ship can stay: *The ship needed fuel, so it spent an extra night in its berth before leaving.* **2** a bed on a ship or train: *The berth was so narrow that I was afraid of falling out in the middle of the night.* **3 to give a wide berth to:** to stay away from: *You should give a wide berth to illegal drugs.*

—*v.* (a ship) to move close to a dock and tie up: *Our ship berthed, and we went ashore.*

be·seech /bɪ'siʧ/ *v.frml.* -**seeched** or **-sought** /-'sɔt/ **-seeching, -seeches** to ask strongly, (*syn.*) to beg: *The woman beseeched the thief not to steal her purse.*

be·set /bɪ'sɛt/ *v.frml.* -**set, -setting, -sets** to attack from all directions, annoy

be·side /bɪ'saɪd/ *prep.* **1** next to: *He sat down beside her.* **2** apart from, other than: *The fact that you like your old car is beside the point; it is so old that it does not work.* **3** compared with: *Beside me, she seems tall.* **4** *infrml.* **be-**

side oneself: upset or excited: *After she left him, he was beside himself with unhappiness.* —*adv.prep.* **besides:** also, in addition to: *Besides talking to him, she wrote him a letter.*

be·siege /bɪ'siʤ/ *v.* **-sieged, -sieging, -sieges** to attack from all sides: *An army besieged the fortress for days. See:* seige.

be·smirch /bɪ'smɜrtʃ/ *v.frml.* to ruin, make dirty, (*syn.*) to soil: *The scandal besmirched his reputation.*

be·sot·ted /bɪ'sɑtɪd/ *adj.frml.* foolish or drunk from alcohol, drugs, power, love, etc.: *He was besotted with his girlfriend.*

best (1) /bɛst/ *adj. superlative of* good **1** of the highest quality or ability: *He buys the best clothes.‖She is the best student in the class.* **the best part:** most: *I've been out of town for the best part of a week.* —*n.* **1** the highest quality: *He buys only the best in clothes.* **2 at best:** the most one can expect: *At best, you will get only a small increase in salary.* **3 to do one's best:** to try for the most in effort and excellence: *She always does her best.* **4 to give it one's best shot:** to make one's best effort: *We need the job done by tomorrow, so give it your best shot.* **5 to give one's best (regards** or **wishes):** to offer the warmest of wishes for s.o.: *Please give him my best when you see him.* **6 to look one's best:** to have the nicest possible appearance: *He likes to look his best at all times.* **7 to make the best of:** to look for the high points in a situation: *It rained a lot during our vacation, but we made the best of it.* —*v.* to do better than s.o., esp. to win: *Our team bested the other team, 6 to 0.*

best (2) *adv. superlative of* well **1** in the most positive way: *I feel best in cool weather.* **2 had best:** ought or have to do s.t.: *We had best go home now; it's starting to rain.*

bes·tial /'bɛstʃəl, 'bis-/ *adj.* **1** like an animal: *He is bestial; he runs around without any clothes on.* **2** *fig.* inhuman, cruel, (*syn.*) brutal: *The killing of the little girl was a bestial act.* -*n.* [U] **bestiality** /,bɛstʃi'æləti, ,bis-/.

best man *n.* the witness and attendant for the groom in a marriage ceremony: *The best man carries the wedding rings for the groom. See:* maid of honor.

be·stow /bɪ'stou/ *v.frml.* to give s.t. formally: *The President bestowed a medal on a soldier.* -*n.* [C;U] **bestowal.**

best-sell·er /'bɛst'sɛlər/ *n.* a book or recording (music, comedy, etc.) that sells many copies: *Her novel about life in Canada was a best-seller.*

bet /bɛt/ *n.* **1** an agreement that the person in the wrong must give the other s.t., such as a sum of money, etc., (*syn.*) a wager: *People place bets on sporting events.* **2** the terms of a

bet: *The bet is that our team will score 20 points more than yours.* **3** the item or sum of money risked in a bet: *The bet is $25.* **4** *infrml.* **best bet:** best way, opportunity to succeed: *Your best bet is to finish school, then look for a job.* **5 to make a bet:** to wager: *She made a bet on the horse race and won.* —*v.* **betted, betting, bets 1** *infrml.fig.* to say s.t. as in a bet, (*syn.*) to predict: *I bet it's going to rain.* **2** *infrml.fig.* to know s.t. is true or sure: *You can bet your bottom dollar (or) your boots that the sun will come up each morning.* **3** *infrml.* **you bet:** of course, certainly: *You bet I'd like to go to the play!*

be·tray /bɪ'treɪ/ *v.* **1** to be disloyal to one's country, (*syn.*) to commit treason: *The spy betrayed his country by selling its military secrets to an enemy country.* **2** to harm people who count on your loyalty: *The soldier betrayed his friends by telling the enemy where they were hiding.‖The wife betrayed her husband by sleeping with her neighbor.* **3** to show s.t., usu. without meaning to, (*syn.*) to reveal: *She tried to look calm, but her weak voice betrayed her fear.‖His white hair betrays his age.* **4 to betray a confidence:** to tell the secrets of others: *He betrayed her confidence by talking about her secrets to his friends.* -*n.* [C;U] **betrayal, betrayer.**

be·troth·al /bɪ'trouðəl, -'trɔθ-/ *n.* [U] a promise to marry, (*syn.*) an engagement: *The couple announced their betrothal after dating for five years.* -*v.* **betroth;** -*adj.* **betrothed.**

bet·ter (1) /'bɛtər/ *adj.* comparative of good higher quality, skill, achievement, etc.: *The USA is building better cars today than it used to.‖He is a better runner than I am.* —*adv.* **1** *comparative of* well: *My mother was sick, but she's feeling better now.* **2 had better:** ought to, should: *I had better be going now; it's late.‖The company is going to lay off 3,200 workers? You had better believe it; it was just announced.* **3 to go s.o. one better:** to add to s.t. or do it better: *That joke is funny, but I'll go you one better; listen to this one.* —*n.* **1 to get the better of s.o.:** to be defeated by s.t. or s.o.: *The heat got the better of her, and she fainted.* **2** *infrml.* **one's better half:** one's mate, spouse: *My better half is working late tonight.* **3** *pl.frml.* **one's betters:** people with more money, education, higher social standing, etc.: *He is rude to his betters, and they don't like it.* —*v.* to improve: *She has bettered herself by getting a good education.*

better or **bettor (2)** *n.* a person who bets, (*syn.*) a gambler

bet·ter·ment /'bɛtərmənt/ *n.frml.* improvement: *The government helps the poor for the betterment of society.*

be·tween /bɪ'twin/ *prep.* **1** in the space separating two things: *The cat was between the wall and the fence.||Airplanes fly people between New York and Washington every half hour.* **2** connected to, esp. in being in love: *They seem to be in love, but there is nothing between them.* **3** *infrml.* **between you and me:** to show that s.t. is a secret: *Between you and me, I know that John loves Mary.*

USAGE NOTE: between: In American English, many people say, "Between you and I" which is incorrect. "Between you and me" is correct.

bev·el /'bɛvəl/ *v.* to cut an edge so it is curved or sloped: *He used a file to make a bevel in the picture frame.*
—*n.* a rounded or sloped edge -*adj.* **beveled.**

bev·er·age /'bɛvrɪdʒ, 'bɛvərɪdʒ/ *n.frml.* a drink, usu. not water: *Restaurants and hotels serve hot and cold beverages.*

be·wail /bɪ'weɪl/ *v.frml.* to express great sadness, (*syn.*) to lament: *He bewailed the death of his wife. See:* bemoan.

be·ware /bɪ'wɛr/ *v.* to be careful about s.t., aware of danger: *"Beware of the dog" means that a dog might attack you.*

be·wil·der /bɪ'wɪldər/ *v.* to confuse greatly: *He was fired without warning and is completely bewildered about the reason. -n.* [U] **bewilderment.**

be·witch /bɪ'wɪtʃ/ *v.* **-ches** to charm, (*syn.*) to captivate: *She is so charming that men are bewitched by her. -adj.* **bewitching.**

be·yond /bɪ'yand/ *prep.* **1** on the other side of: *The campground is beyond the next field.* **2** to a greater amount or degree: *She is educated beyond everyone in her family.* **3** too difficult for: *Understanding mathematics is beyond him.* **4** further in time than, later: *Looking beyond this year, I see a good future.* **5** besides, in addition: *I don't know anything about him beyond what I've told you.*

bi /baɪ/ *short for* bisexual

bi·an·nu·al /baɪ'ænyuəl/ *adj.* happening twice a year, semiannual

bi·as /'baɪəs/ *n.* **-es 1** a general tendency: *She has a bias against wasting money.* **2** prejudice: *He has a bias against people who wear glasses.* **3 on the bias:** (of clothing) on a slant, angled
—*adj.* **biased:** inclined: *He is biased against spending (glasses, the plan, etc.).*

bib /bɪb/ *n.* a cloth with strings to tie around the neck: *Babies wear bibs when they eat.*

bi·ble /'baɪbəl/ *n.* **1** (*cap.*) the holy writings of Christianity and Judaism, (*syn.*) the Scriptures: *She reads the Bible every day.* **2** a book or writings that cover a field expertly: *That professor wrote the bible on European history. -adj.* **biblical** /'bɪblɪkəl/.

bib·li·og·ra·phy /ˌbɪbli'ɑgrəfi/ *n.* **-phies** a list of sources of information (author, title, publisher, date) often used as references in formal writing

bi·cam·er·al /baɪ'kæmərəl/ *adj.* (in government) referring to a legislative system that has two groups or houses of lawmakers

bi·cen·ten·ni·al /ˌbaɪsɛn'tɛniəl/ *n.adj.* a 200-year anniversary: *The USA's <adj.> bicentennial celebration of independence from Britain was in 1976.*

bi·cep /'baɪˌsɛp/ *n.* the upper-arm muscle: *The boy lifts weights to strengthen his biceps and shoulders.*

bick·er /'bɪkər/ *v.infrml.* to argue about little things, (*syn.*) to quarrel: *The couple bickers often about which roads to drive on to get places.*

bi·cy·cle /'baɪsɪkəl/ *n.* a two-wheeled vehicle moved by pedaling: *I bought a new bicycle.*
—*v.* **-cled, -cling, -cles** to travel by bicycle: *The students bicycled through Europe last summer. -n.* [U] **bicycling;** [C] **bicyclist.**

bid /bɪd/ *v.frml.* **bid, bidding, bids 1** to ask or command: *She bid the child stand still.* **2** to make a monetary offer: *We bid to sell at $10 per pound.*
—*n.* **1** an offer to sell s.t. at a certain price: *Our company made a bid to sell coffee beans at $10 per pound.* **2** an attempt, try: *She bid for the job opening, but did not get the job.*

bid·ding /'bɪdɪŋ/ *n.* [U] **1** offers to buy or sell things: *The bidding at auctions can go very fast.* **2** instructions: *I did my wife's bidding and changed the baby's diapers.*

bide /baɪd/ *v.* **bided, biding, bides to bide one's time:** to wait until the right time to do s.t.: *He is biding his time until he feels ready to ask her to marry him.*

bi·en·ni·al /baɪ'ɛniəl/ *n.adj.* happening every two years: *There is a <adj.> biennial art exhibition in Venice. -adv.* **biennially.**

bi·fo·cals /'baɪˌfoukəlz/ *n.pl.* eyeglasses with two sets of lenses, one for seeing close and the other for distance: *When I reached age 45, I needed bifocals to read. -adj.* **bifocal.**

big /bɪg/ *adj.* **bigger, biggest 1** large in size, shape, etc.: *She has big feet.* **2** important: *Our company has a big meeting next month.* **3 a big fish in a small pond:** an important, powerful person out of place: *Working in the regional county office, she is a big fish in a small pond.* **4** *infrml.* **big on s.t.:** enthusiastic: *He is very big on baseball and goes to a game twice a week.* **5** *infrml.* **bigger fish to fry:** more important things to do: *The company president has bigger fish to fry and can't be bothered by the problems of a little employee like me.* **6 big of (s.o.):** generous: *It's big of you to drive me home so late at night.*

—*n.infrml.* **Mr. Big:** important person: *He is Mister Big in that company.*

big·a·my /'bɪgəmi/ *n.* [U] being married to two people at the same time: *Bigamy is illegal in the USA -n.* **bigamist;** *-adj.* **bigamous.**

Big Apple *n.infrml.fig.* New York City: *Tourists visit the Big Apple from all over the world. See:* USAGE NOTE: apple.

Big Brother *n.* a dictator, *(syn.)* an oppressive state: *People who live in countries with cruel leaders often feel that Big Brother is watching them.*

big cheese *n. fig.slang* an important person: *She is the big cheese in that bank.*

big deal *n.infrml.* **1** an important person or situation: *She is a big deal in her company.||He is angry all the time and makes a big deal out of every little thing.* **2** an unimportant situation: *"The queen is visiting town." "Big deal; I'm not interested."*

big·gie /'bɪgi/ *n.infrml.* an important person or situation: *When the US government buys computers, that order is a biggie.*

big-heart·ed /'bɪg,hɑrtɪd/ *adj.* generous, warm, and friendly, *(syn.)* compassionate: *She is always doing s.t. good for s.o.; she's big-hearted.*

big leagues *n.infrml.* (from baseball) highest level of competition, major leagues: *He worked in a small town, then moved to New York and hit the big leagues.*

big·mouth /'bɪg,maʊθ/ *n.slang* s.o. who talks or says things too soon: *That guy is a big mouth. See:* loudmouth.

big name *adj.n.* famous person or reputation: *That musician works for <adj.> big-name bands.||The young scientist made a <n.> big name for herself in the computer industry.*

big·ot /'bɪgət/ *n.* s.o. who has strong, unreasonable opinions or beliefs about others' race, religion, etc: *He is a bigot who hates everyone not just like him. -n.* **bigotry.** *See:* prejudiced.

big shot *n.slang* a person who acts important or arrogant: *He's just an office manager, but he acts like a big shot.*

big talk *n.infrml.* untrue talk about important things: *Buying his wife a new car and a second home is just big talk.*

big thing *n.* **1** great concern about small matters, *(syn.)* a fuss: *She made such a big thing about plans for her trip.* **2** a style that doesn't last, *(syn.)* a fad: *The big thing now is wearing red ties and socks. See:* big deal.

big-ticket item *n.* s.t. that costs a lot of money: *A new car is a big-ticket item*

big-time *adj.infrml.* important: *She is a big-time politician in the national government.*
—*n.* **in the big time:** at the top level of business, sports, etc: *He began by playing guitar for fun and is now in the big time.*

big top *n.infrml.* a circus: *The main tent of a circus is called the "big top."*

big wheel *n.infrml.fig.* an important, powerful person: *She is a big wheel in government.*

big·wig /'bɪg,wɪg/ *n.infrml.* an important, powerful person: *He's a bigwig in that bank.*

bike /baɪk/ *n.v.* **biked, biking, bikes** *infrml.* bicycle or motorcycle: *I ride my <n.> bike to work every day. -n.* **biker.**

bi·ki·ni /bɪ'kini/ *n.* a small two-piece swimsuit for women or one-piece swimsuit for men
—*adj.* small underpants: *Some men wear boxer shorts for underwear, others wear bikini briefs.*

bi·lat·er·al /baɪ'lætərəl/ *adj.frml.* with or involving two sides equally: *The officials of two countries held bilateral talks. -adv.* **bilaterally.** *See:* unilateral.

bile /baɪl/ *n.* [U] **1** a liquid from the liver that helps digest food: *Bile breaks down fats.* **2** *frml.* anger, *(syn.)* bitterness: *She is unhappy and filled with bile. -adj.* **bilious** /'bɪlyəs/.

bilge /bɪldʒ/ *n.* **1** dirty water at the bottom of a ship **2** *fig.* nonsense or foolish talk or writing

bi·lin·gual /baɪ'lɪŋgwəl/ *adj.* **1** able to communicate well in two languages: *She is bilingual in English and Chinese.* **2** written or spoken in two languages: *Bilingual instructions are included in every page of the manual.*

bilk /bɪlk/ *v.* to trick s.o. for money, to cheat: *He bilked the old lady out of her life savings.*

bill (1) /bɪl/ *n.* **1** a printed piece of paper that lists item(s) and their price(s), *(syn.)* an invoice: *Our company sends out its bills each month.* **2** (in USA) paper money: *She paid with a $100 bill.* **3** (in government) a new law or plan that legislators vote to accept or reject: *Congress worked on an anticrime bill.* **4** a poster, *(syn.)* an advertisement: *Bills are posted on the walls of the subway station.* **5 to fill the bill:** to meet, satisfy a need: *The new air conditioner really fills the bill in hot weather.* **6** *infrml.* **to foot the bill:** to pay for s.t.: *We want to paint our house, but we can't foot the bill.*
—*v.* to send invoices: *The company bills its customers at the beginning of every month. See:* billing.

bill (2) *n.* a bird's beak: *That bird has a long yellow bill.*

bill·board /'bɪl,bɔrd/ *n.* a large, flat board for advertisements, usu. by the side of the road: *That billboard near the highway is advertising a motel.*

bill·fold /'bɪl,foʊld/ *n.* a small case with pockets for carrying money, etc., a wallet: *She took out her billfold and paid for lunch.*

bil·liards /'bɪlyərdz/ *n.* [U] a game played with balls and (cue) sticks on a table: *In bil-*

liards, players hit the balls off other balls and the inner cushions of the table.

bill·ing /ˈbɪlɪŋ/ n. [U] **1** sending out bills, (syn.) invoicing **2** pl. the amount of business that a company does in a month or year

bil·lion /ˈbɪlyən/ n.adj. (in USA) 1,000,000,000: *That company sells a <adj.> billion dollars of shoes a year.* -adj. **billionth.**

bil·lion·aire /ˈbɪlyə,nɛr, ,bɪlyəˈnɛr/ n. a person who has a billion dollars or property of that worth

Bill of Rights n. (in USA) rights given by law, such as freedom of speech, freedom to meet publicly, etc.: *The Bill of Rights is part of the Constitution.*

bill of sale n. a piece of paper showing the change of ownership of property: *When I bought my new car, the dealer gave me a bill of sale.*

bil·low /ˈbɪloʊ/ v. to fill with air and become larger: *The sails on the boat billowed in the wind.*
—n. a wave or gust (of water, smoke, etc.) -adj. **billowy.**

bil·ly club /ˈbɪli/ n. a short, thick stick used to hit people, used by police officers: *The police officer hit the criminal with her billy club.*

billy goat n. a male goat

bim·bo /ˈbɪmboʊ/ n.pej.slang **-bos** or **-boes** a person seen as stupid and mostly interested in sex, usu. a woman with a bad reputation: *Her neighbors called her a bimbo because she went out with many different men.*

bi·month·ly /baɪˈmʌnθli/ n.adj.adv. every two months (approx. 60 days): *They publish a <adj.> bimonthly magazine.*

bin /bɪn/ n. a large, open container: *That store keeps nails and screws in bins.*

bi·na·ry /ˈbaɪnəri, -,nɛri/ adj. **1** having two parts, double **2** using the numbers 0 and 1: *Some computers use 0 and 1 as a binary system.*

bind /baɪnd/ v. **bound** /ˈbaʊnd,/ **binding, binds 1** to wrap with bandages: *Doctors bind wounds.* **2** to tie, esp. with string: *She bound the package.* **3** to stick together: *Milk and eggs bind the flour in the cake batter.* **4** to make s.o. obey: *His duty to his parents binds him to live near them.*
—n.infrml. **in a bind:** in difficulty: *He is in a bind for cash because he lost his wallet.*

bind·er /ˈbaɪndər/ n. **1** a firm removable cover for documents: *A three-ring binder has rings inside that open and close to hold papers.* **2** a machine or person that binds books **3** a sum of money given to hold property for a time period at a fixed price

bind·ing /ˈbaɪndɪŋ/ n. [C;U] **1** the cover on a book or document: *My textbook has a cloth binding.* **2** material put on the edge of s.t. to strengthen or decorate it
—adj. permanent, unbreakable: *A marriage agreement is considered binding for life.*

binge /bɪndʒ/ v. **binged, binging, binges** to eat, drink, or do too much of s.t., esp. to consume alcohol or food, gamble, have sex: *He binged and ate a whole chocolate cake by himself.*
—n. the act of binging, (syn.) a spree: *She went on a shopping binge and bought 10 pairs of shoes.*

bin·go /ˈbɪŋgoʊ/ n. [U] a gambling game in which players cover the numbers printed on their cards as s.o. calls out the numbers: *When he had five numbers in a row, the player shouted "Bingo!" and won a prize.*

bin·oc·u·lars /bəˈnɑkyələrz, baɪ-/ n.pl. glasses that make distant objects seem closer and larger: *The biologist looked through her binoculars to see birds far off. See:* telescope.

bi·o·chem·is·try /,baɪoʊˈkɛmɪstri/ n. [U] the science of the chemistry of living things

binoculars

bi·o·de·grad·a·ble /,baɪoʊdəˈgreɪdəbəl/ adj. capable of breaking down to be absorbed by nature, esp. without harming it: *Those paper plates are biodegradable. See:* recycle.

USAGE NOTE: *Biodegradable* means that the material in s.t. can break down naturally and be absorbed by the earth. *Recyclable* means that the materials in a product, such as paper, plastic, glass, aluminum, etc., can be *recycled*. Recycled means that the materials in a product have been processed to be used again.

bi·o·feed·back /,baɪoʊˈfid,bæk/ n. [U] a way of controlling the mind to lower the blood pressure and heartbeat

bi·og·ra·phy /baɪˈɑgrəfi/ n. [C;U] **-phies** the history of a person's life: *He read a biography of a baseball hero.* -n. **biographer;** -adj. **biographical** /,baɪəˈgræfɪkəl/ -adv. **biographically.** *See:* autobiography, fiction, USAGE NOTE.

bi·ol·o·gy /baɪˈɑlədʒi/ n. [U] the science and study of life: *In the biology class students looked at leaves under a microscope.* -adj. **biological** /,baɪəˈlɑdʒɪkəl;/ -adv. **biologically;** -n. **biologist.**

bi·on·ic /baɪˈɑnɪk/ adj. using mechanical and/or electrical devices to increase a person's power

bi·op·sy /ˈbaɪ,ɑpsi/ n. **-sies** a piece of the body cut out and examined for disease: *The doctor* took a biopsy of a lump in her neck to test it for cancer.

bi·par·ti·san /baɪ'partɪzən, -sən/ adj.frml. involving two political parties: *The new law was passed with bipartisan support.*

bi·par·tite /baɪ'partaɪt/ adj.frml. in two parts or sides: *The two countries made a bipartite agreement.*

bi·ped /'baɪˌpɛd/ n. s.t. that has two feet: *Humans are bipeds.* -adj. **bipedal** /baɪ'pɛdl./ *See:* quadruped.

bi·plane /'baɪˌpleɪn/ n. an airplane with two sets of wings: *A biplane can go up and down easily with its four wings*

birch /bɜrtʃ/ n. **-es** a northern tree with smooth white bark: *Beautiful birches line the country road.*

bird /bɜrd/ n. **1** an animal with feathers, wings, and a beak: *Most birds can fly.* **2** infrml. an airplane **3 a bird's-eye view:** a sight from a high place: *On the hilltop, we had a bird's-eye view of the valley below.* **4 a bird in the hand is worth two in the bush:** s.t. of small value is worth more than s.t. that is unsure **5** infrml. **the birds and the bees:** sex: *The father told his son about the birds and the bees.* **6 early bird:** s.o. who gets up or goes somewhere early. **7** infrml. **for the birds:** no good, inferior: *That film was so boring; it's for the birds.* **8 to kill two birds with one stone:** to do two things with one effort: *I had a business appointment in the city, then met my friend for lunch, so I killed two birds with one stone.*

bird·brain /'bɜrdˌbreɪn/ n.slang a stupid person: *That birdbrain delivered the wrong box again.* -adj. **birdbrained.**

bird dog n. a dog used for hunting birds —v.fig. to watch s.t. very closely: *The owner bird dogs every customer who comes into her store.*

bird·seed /'bɜrdˌsid/ n. grain and other seeds used to feed birds: *In the winter, I put birdseed in the bird feeder outside my window.*

birth /bɜrθ/ n. [C;U] **1 a.** the time and act when a baby comes out of its mother or an egg: *The time of her birth was 3:00.‖Our cat gave birth to three kittens.* **b.** to cause or produce s.t.: *The woman's courageous actions gave birth to a movement for freedom among her people.* **2** fig. the beginning of s.t.: *Astronomers watched the birth of a star.* **3** one's origin or ancestry (parents, grandparents, etc.): *He is German by birth, but is now a citizen of Venezuela.*

birth certificate n. legal document stating when and where one was born

birth control n. [U] a method, such as a condom or medication that prevents children,

(syn.) contraception: *She uses birth control regularly.*

birth·day /'bɜrθˌdeɪ/ n. **1** the date when one was born: *She bought me a present for my birthday.* **2** infrml. **birthday suit:** the naked body: *Little children ran on the beach in their birthday suits.*

birth·mark /'bɜrθˌmark/ n. a spot on the body that one is born with: *He has a birthmark, a red spot on his cheek.*

birth·place /'bɜrθˌpleɪs/ n. where one was born: *Her birthplace is San Francisco, but she lives in New Orleans.*

birth·rate /'bɜrθˌreɪt/ n. the number of births for each 100, 1000, or 100,000 people in an area (country, city, region, etc.) in a time period: *The birth rate is going up in this country.*

bis·cuit /'bɪskɪt/ n. small airy bread, (syn.) a scone: *He had biscuits and gravy for breakfast.*

bi·sect /'baɪˌsɛkt, baɪ'sɛkt/ v. to cut, cross, or divide into two equal parts: *That road bisects a farm.* -n. **bisection.**

bi·sex·u·al /baɪ'sɛkʃuəl/ n.adj. **1** attracted to both sexes: *She is a <n.> bisexual who dates men and women.* **2** having the qualities of both sexes -n. [U] **bisexuality** /baɪˌsɛkʃu'æləti/. *See:* heterosexual; homosexual.

bish·op /'bɪʃəp/ n. **1** a high-ranking official in some Christian religions: *A bishop supervises many priests or ministers.* **2** a piece in the game of chess that can only move in a diagonal direction -n. **bishopric.**

bi·son /'baɪsən/ n. **bison** or **bisons** a large four-footed animal with a shaggy coat and short, curved horns, like the buffalo: *Thousands of bison once lived on the North American plains.*

bisque /bɪsk/ n. a thick, rich soup made with cream: *I had lobster bisque for lunch.*

bis·tro /'bɪstrou, bi-/ n. **-tros** (French for) a small bar, nightclub, or restaurant that serves food and drinks

bit /bɪt/ n. **1** a small amount of s.t.: *She brushed a bit of dirt off of her pants.* **2** a little, some: *I am having a bit of trouble (bad luck, difficulty, etc.) with my car.* **3** little-by-little: *He is building a house bit-by-bit.* **4** one's part, contribution to a cause: *Do your bit for your political party by working hard during the election.* **5** in computers, a unit of information in a language that has two units: *Eight bits is equal to one byte.* **6** a bar (on a bridle) that goes into a horse's mouth to control it: *He pulled on the reins, and the bit put pressure on the horse's mouth, causing it to stop.* **7** a small piece: *The bowl broke into many bits.* **8** a grooved, pointed metal part of a tool: *I lost one of the bits for my drill. See:* two-bit.

B

bitch /bɪtʃ/ *n.* **bitches** **1** a female dog **2** *fig.vulg.pej.* a difficult woman: *She is always angry and mean; she's a real bitch.* **3** *vulg.* a difficult job to do: *The computer lost a lot of information; what a bitch to redo it all!*
—*v. vulg.* **bitched, bitching, bitches** to complain: *Some employees bitch all the time; there's no way to stop their complaining.*

bitch·y /ˈbɪtʃi/ *adj.vulg.* **-ier, -iest** difficult, complaining: *Every so often, he gets very bitchy and unpleasant to be around.* *-adv.* **bitchily.**

bite /baɪt/ *v.* **bit** /bɪt,/ **biting, bites 1** to cut, put teeth into: *Some dogs will bite you.* **2** *infrml.fig.* to cause pain, hurt: *The increase in my rent payments is beginning to bite.* **3** *phrasal v. sep.* **to bite s.t. back:** to hold in, control: *She bit back words of anger at her boss.*‖*She bit them back.* **4** *infrml.* **to bite off more than one can chew:** to try to do s.t. that is too difficult: *That course in physics was too hard for him; he bit off more than he could chew.* **5** **to bite s.o.'s head off:** to speak in anger, rudely: *When I asked her to move, she bit my head off.* **6** *infrml.* **to bite the bullet:** to do an unpleasant job: *We have to bite the bullet and fire 20 percent of our workers.* **7** *infrml.* **to bite the dust:** to die: *We must cut expenses or the company will bite the dust.* **8** *infrml.* **to bite the hand that feeds one:** to anger or harm a person who gives you s.t. good: *She argues with her boss so often that she bites the hand that feeds her.*
—*n.* **1** an act of biting: *The cat's bite hurt my hand.* **2** a small amount of food: *I had a bite to eat for breakfast.* **3** a painful event: *a tax bite, the bite of a cold wind* *-n.* **biter.** *See:* **bark** (2).

bit·ing /ˈbaɪtɪŋ/ *adj.* causing pain, bitter: *I feel the biting cold wind on my face.*

bit·ter /ˈbɪtər/ *adj.* **1** having a sharp, acid taste: *That black tea has a bitter taste.* **2** giving pain, hurtful: *It was a bitter cold winter.* **3** angry, hateful: *The two friends became bitter enemies.* *-adv.* **bitterly;** *-n.* [U] **bitterness.**

bit·ter·sweet /ˈbɪtərˌswit/ *adj.* **1** having a mixture of good and sad feelings: *She had bittersweet thoughts about moving to a new city.* **2** a type of chocolate that has little sugar
—*n.* a plant, climbing vine with orange and yellow berries

bi·week·ly /baɪˈwikli/ *n.adj.* every two weeks (14 days): *They publish a <adj.> biweekly newspaper. See:* bimonthly.

bi·zarre /bɪˈzar/ *adj.* very strange, (*syns.*) odd, weird: *She died under bizarre circumstances—no one knows how.* *-adv.* **bizarrely.**

blab /blæb/ *v.* **blabbed, blabbing, blabs** to tell a secrets to everyone: *His secretary blabbed his secret love affairs to the office.*

blab·ber·mouth /ˈblæbərˌmauθ/ *n.infrml.* **-mouths** /-ˌmauðz, -ˌmauθs/ a person who gossips and/or tells secrets about others

black /blæk/ *n.* **1** the darkest color: *She is dressed in black.* **2** a person of African descent: *North American blacks sometimes prefer to be called African-Americans.* **3** **black and white: a.** *infrml.* in writing: *He put his offer in black and white.* **b.** *infrml.fig.* very clear: *Most situations in life are not black and white, but gray.* **4** *infrml.* **in the black:** to be profitable: *Our company is operating in the black this year.*
—*adj.* **1** very dark, like the color of coal: *She wore a black dress today.* **2** bad, evil: *She was in a black mood after losing an afternoon's work on the computer.* **3** **black-and-blue:** having dark colors from bruises on the skin: *Her arm was black and blue from falling on the ice.* *-n.* [U] **blackness.**
—*v.* **1** *phrasal v.* **to black out:** to faint, lose consciousness: *He blacked out when he got hit by a car.* **2** *phrasal v. sep.* **to black s.t. out: a.** to cover so no light can get in or out **b.** to block or control communication: *Many dictatorships black out all radio and TV communication.*

USAGE NOTE: The term *black* is used to designate people whose ancestors were Africans; in North America many blacks prefer to be called *African-Americans* or *people of color.*

black·ball /ˈblækˌbɔl/ *v.* not to allow s.o. to become a member or to do s.t.: *A club member blackballed a man from joining the club. See:* blacklist.

black·belt /ˈblækˌbɛlt/ *n.* **1** the rank of expert, such as in martial arts **2** a person holding that rank **3** the black belt worn as the symbol of rank

black·ber·ry /ˈblækˌbɛri/ *n.* **-ries** a sweet berry, black in color when ripe: *blackberry jam*

black·bird /ˈblækˌbɜrd/ *n.* any of various small North American birds, the male of which has black feathers: *Female blackbirds have brownish feathers.*

black·board /ˈblækˌbɔrd/ *n.* a flat surface to write on in classrooms, a chalkboard: *The teacher wrote on the blackboard with white chalk.*

black·en /ˈblækən/ *v.* **1** to make s.t. become black: *Cooking the meat for too long blackened it.* **2** to make others think badly of s.o., (*syn.*) to slander: *She blackened his reputation by telling lies about him.*

black eye *n.* **1** an eye discolored black and blue from an injury **2** *infrml.fig.* a bad reputation: *The scandal gave the politician a black eye among the voters.*

black·head /'blæk,bɛd/ *n.* a small, black spot on the skin, like a pimple: *As a teenager, he had blackheads on his face.*

black hole *n.* **1** a body in outer space whose gravity draws everything into it including light **2** *fig.* a hopeless, bad situation: *After she made a bad mistake, her career fell into a black hole.*

black·jack /'blæk,dʒæk/ *n.* **1** a small club or stick: *A thief hit me over the head with a blackjack.* **2** a card game, often played in gambling, also called 21: *The goal in blackjack is to get the sum of the cards to reach 21 without going over it.*

black·list /'blæk,lɪst/ *v.n.* to put people's names on a list to stop them from doing certain activities, going places, or receiving benefits: *In the 1950s, movie companies <v.> blacklisted some actors they thought were communists. See:* blackball.

black magic *n.* [U] a religious practice that tries to harm others, *(syn.)* witchcraft: *He used black magic to make his enemies get sick.*

black·mail /'blæk,meɪl/ *v.n.* [U] to demand actions or money by threatening to tell a harmful secret about s.o., *(syn.)* to extort: *She had sex with a married man and then <v.> blackmailed him by saying that she would tell his wife. -n.* **blackmailer.**

black market *n.adj.* the illegal economy, not approved by a government: *They buy radios on the <n.> black market.*

black·out /'blæk,aʊt/ *n.v.* **1** controlled darkness, turning off electricity: *The city used blackouts to hide from nighttime enemy bombings.* **2** an electrical power failure: *The city had a blackout when one of the main power generators was hit by lightning.*

black·smith /'blæk,smɪθ/ *n.* a skilled worker who makes and fixes things of iron: *A blacksmith can make horseshoes.*

black·top /'blæk,tɑp/ *n.* a thick black substance made from coal used to cover roads

black widow *n.* a spider of which the female is highly poisonous: *Black widow spiders are found in the Americas.*

blad·der /'blædər/ *n.* **1** a small bag of skin that holds and forces out urine from the body: *My bladder is so small that I constantly have to go to the bathroom.* **2** a small sack of rubber, leather, etc. that holds liquids or gas

blade /bleɪd/ *n.* narrow, flat piece of s.t.: *The blades of an airplane propeller turn very fast.ǁa blade of grass*

blah /blɑ/ or **blah, blah** *n.infrml.* **1** ordinary talk, *(syn.)* chatter: *The people sitting in the park go blah, blah for hours.* **2** *pl.* tiredness, *(syn.)* fatigue: *The hot summer weather gives me the blahs.*

blame /bleɪm/ *v.* **blamed, blaming, blames** to say s.o. is responsible for s.t. bad, *(syn.)* to accuse: *I blame him for the accident.*
—*n.* [U] **1** a charge, accusation of wrongdoing: *I put the blame on him for causing the accident.* **2 to take the blame:** (be forced to) accept guilt: *Others were responsible too, but he took the blame for it. -adj.* **blameless; -adv. blamelessly.**

blanch /blæntʃ/ *v.* **-ched, -ching, -ches** **1** to become pale with shock: *She blanched when she saw the dead man.* **2** to boil vegetables quickly: *He blanched the broccoli for five minutes.* **3** to make s.t. colorless: *blanched almonds*

bland /blænd/ *adj.* **1** having little taste, *(syn.)* mild: *Some foods, like white rice, taste bland.* **2** mild, boring, *(syn.)* nondescript: *He has a very bland personality. -n.* [U] **blandness; -adv. blandly.**

blank (1) /blæŋk/ *adj.* **1** clear, without writing or markings: *I wrote a letter on a blank piece of paper.ǁI wrote my name in a blank space on the form.* **2** without expression, interest, or understanding **3** *infrml.* **to give s.o. a blank check:** to allow s.o. to spend an unlimited amount of money: *I gave my son a blank check to pay for his college expenses.* **4 to draw a blank:** to be unable to remember: *She drew a blank when she tried to remember my name. -adv.* **blankly; -n.** [U] **blankness.**
—*v.* (in sports) to keep an opponent from scoring: *Our team blanked our opponent, 14 to 0.*

blank (2) or **blank cartridge** *n.* a cartridge with gun powder but no bullet: *In the movies, cowboys shoot blanks.*

blan·ket /'blæŋkɪt/ *n.* **1** a warm bed covering: *To keep warm, she has two blankets on her bed.* **2** *fig.* any type of covering: *A blanket of snow covered the ground.* **3** including everyone or everything, all cases **4** *infrml.* **a wet blanket:** a person who spoils the fun of others: *He's such a wet blanket—he always wants to leave when the fun is just beginning.*
—*v.* to cover completely: *A heavy rain blanketed the fields with water.*

blare /blɛr/ *v.* **blared, blaring, blares,** to make a horn sound loudly: *Car horns blared in the traffic jam.*

bla·sé /blɑ'zeɪ/ *adj.* (French for) not caring, without emotion, *(syn.)* indifferent: *She is blasé about her new job; she doesn't love it, she doesn't hate it.*

blas·phe·my /'blæsfəmi/ *n.* [C;U] **-mies** saying disrespectful things about God, religion, or anything sacred: *Long ago, people were killed for blasphemy. -adv.* **blasphemously; -v. blaspheme** /blæs'fim, 'blæs,fim/; *-adj.* **blasphemous**

blast /blæst/ v. **1** to explode: *A bomb blasted a hole in the road.* **2** *infrml.fig.* to criticize harshly: *My mother blasted me for staying out late.* **3** *phrasal v.* **to blast off:** to leave the ground forcefully: *The rocket blasted off the launch pad. See:* blast-off.
—n. **1** an explosion: *You could hear that blast for miles.* **2** a strong movement of air, (*syn.*) a gust **3** *infrml.* **to have a blast:** to have a great time: *We had a blast at the beach with our friends.*

blast-off n. (of a rocket) leaving the ground

bla·tant /'bleɪtnt/ adj. obvious, going against one's sense of honesty (truth, reason), (*syn.*) shameless: *That report is full of blatant lies.* -adv. **blatantly.**

blaze (1) /bleɪz/ v. **blazed, blazing, blazes 1** to burn strongly: *A fire blazed in the fireplace.* **2** to burn out of control: *When the firefighters arrived, the house was blazing.* **3** to shine brightly: *Lights blazed in every window.* **4** *fig.* to be filled with a strong emotion (anger, love, etc.): *My heart blazes with love for you.*
—n. **1** a big fire: *The blaze lasted for three hours.* **2** a very bright, intense light: *They played baseball at night under the blaze of spotlights.* **3** a bright display: *The fall leaves were a blaze of colors.* **4 what the blazes:** expressing anger, frustration: *What the blazes is taking him so long to get here!*

blaze (2) n. **1** a white or light-colored mark on an animal's face **2** a mark made on a tree by slicing off a piece of bark: *He put a blaze on each of the trees as he passed so that he could find his way back to the camp site.*
—v. **blazed, blazing, blazes to blaze a trail:** to create or mark a path: *The hikers blazed a trail through the forest.*

blaz·er /'bleɪzər/ n. a type of jacket that does not match the pants worn, esp. by men: *He wore a blue blazer to the party.*

blazer

bleach /blitʃ/ v.n. [U] **-es** a strong liquid chemical used to whiten clothes: *Those pants were so dirty that he put some* <n.> *bleach in the washing machine with them.||The sun* <v.> *bleached the curtains hanging out to dry.*

bleak /blik/ adj. **1** cold, gray, and unfriendly: *On a cold, rainy day the beach area looks bleak.* **2** with little or no hope: *He has no job and his future is bleak.* -n. [U] **bleakness;** -adv. **bleakly.**

blear·y /'blɪri/ adj. **-ier, -iest** unable to see well, unclear: *When she wakes up in the morn-*

ing, her eyes are bleary. -adv. **blearily.**

bleed /blid/ v. **bled** /blɛd,/ **bleeding, bleeds 1** to lose blood: *She cut her hand and it is bleeding.* **2** *fig.* to suffer or feel pain at another's suffering: *My heart bleeds for those people in a civil war.* **3** to take out or let out sap, juice, etc., (*syn.*) to ooze: *That plant has been damaged; it is bleeding sap.* **4** (of colors) to run together: *My red shirt bled onto my white socks in the washer; now my socks are pink.* **5** to show through: *They didn't put enough new paint on the wall, and the old color is bleeding through.*

bleed·ing /'blidɪŋ/ n. [U] **1** the flowing of blood: *The doctor stopped the bleeding with a bandage.* **2** *fig.* **bleeding heart:** a person who cares deeply about the poor and oppressed of society

bleep /blip/ v.n. **1** to make a quick, sharp, usu. electronic sound **2** to block out another sound: *On the TV show, dirty words* <v.> *were bleeped out by a technician.*

blem·ish /'blɛmɪʃ/ v.n. **-ishes 1** a spot or mark (pimple, scar, etc.): *That pretty woman has a blemish on her cheek.* **2** a bad reputation: *That report was so poor it will certainly leave a blemish on his record.* -adj. **blemished.**

blend /blɛnd/ v.n. **1** to mix together: *I blended milk and butter into the flour.* **2** to fit well: *She blends in well with other students in her class.*

blend·er /'blɛndər/ n. a small kitchen machine used to cut and mix foods together: *I mixed eggs and milk in the blender.*

bless /blɛs/ v. **blessed, blessing, blesses 1** to make holy, esp. by asking God: *The priest blessed the people in church.* **2** to be lucky, fortunate: *She was blessed with a healthy long life.*

bless·ing /'blɛsɪŋ/ n. [C;U] **1** an act of making s.t. holy: *She asked for God's blessing for her new baby.* **2** a good event (situation or condition): *It is a blessing to have good health.* **3** approval: *I have my teacher's blessing to do a special project.* **4 a blessing in disguise:** a hidden, unexpected benefit: *After he was fired, he found a better job, so his firing was a blessing in disguise.*

blew /blu/ v. past of blow

blight /blaɪt/ n.v. [U] **1** a disease of plants that makes them turn brown and die: *The* <n.> *blight left no leaves on the trees.* **2** a bad condition: *Houses in many cities suffer from urban* <n.> *blight.*

blimp /blɪmp/ n. a long, rounded aircraft filled

blimp

with gas: *In the USA, blimps with advertising on their sides fly over outdoor sports events.*

blind (1) /blaɪnd/ *adj.* **1** unable to see because of injured or diseased eyes **2** unwilling to recognize a problem: *Most people in that company are blind to its real problems.* **3** out of control: *blind passion, anger, love, drunkeness* **4** *fig.* **a blind alley:** the wrong direction: *We spent days working on a solution but it led us up a blind alley.* **5** *infrml.* **to rob s.o. blind:** to steal in large amounts: *After the accountant left the company, they learned that she had robbed them blind.* **6 to turn a blind eye to:** to avoid seeing s.t. wrong, *(syn.)* to overlook: *She turns a blind eye to her children's faults.*
—*v.* **1** to make s.o. lose sight: *An injury blinded him for life.* **2** to make s.o. unable to see for a short time: *The bright sun blinded me for a moment.* **3** *fig.* to confuse s.o. by emotion: *Her love for him blinded her to his inconsiderate actions.* *-n.* [U] **blindness;** *-adv.* **blindly.** *See:* disabled, USAGE NOTE.

blind (2) a covering for a window, such as a venetian blind: *She closes the blinds when the sun shines in.*

blind date *n.fig.* an arranged meeting with s.o. one has not met: *I went out on a blind date with a friend of my sister.*

blind·ers /blaɪndərz/ *n.pl.* coverings placed next to the eyes of horses so they can only look straight ahead

blind·fold /blaɪnd,foʊld/ *n.* a piece of cloth tied over the eyes so a person cannot see
—*v.* to put a blindfold on s.o.: *The thief blindfolded his victim.*

blind spot *n.* **1** an area where one cannot see: *Most cars have blind spots so one has to be careful when passing other cars.* **2** being unreasonable, unwilling to see or do s.t.: *The owner has a blind spot about paying people; he pays them poorly and many leave the company.*

blink /blɪŋk/ *v.n.* **1** to open and close the eyelids rapidly: *If you don't blink, your eyes will dry out.* **2** to go on and off quickly: *The car blinked its lights to signal me.*

blink·er /blɪŋkər/ *n.* a light that goes on and off as a warning, such as a directional signal on a car

blip /blɪp/ *n.* a short electronic signal (sound, picture, etc.): *An airplane makes a blip on a radar screen. See:* bleep.

bliss /blɪs/ *n.* [U] **1** extreme happiness: *After they got married, they lived in bliss.* **2** a state of extreme religious joy, *(syn.)* ecstasy: *She knelt, praying, in a state of bliss.*
—*phrasal v. slang* **blissed, blissing, blisses to bliss out:** to become drunk or high and not able to think: *Too much beer and marijuana blissed him out. -adj.* **blissful;** *-adv.*

blissfully.

blis·ter /blɪstər/ *n.* **1** (in medicine) a pocket under the skin filled with liquid: *A burn caused blisters on her hand.* **2** a swelling on a painted surface, etc.

blithe /blaɪð, blaɪθ/ *adj.* **1** happy, not worried **2** not concerned, casual: *He made some blithe remarks about the coming hurricane. -adv.* **blithely.**

blith·er·ing /blɪðərɪŋ/ *adj.* nonsensical: *Don't be a blithering idiot!*

blitz /blɪts/ *n.* **blitzes 1** a rapid attack using great power: *The bomber <n.> blitz flattened the city.* **2** *fig.* a lot of advertising: *Before an election, politicians often do a media <n.> blitz to get lots of coverage.*

bliz·zard /blɪzərd/ *n.* a severe snowstorm

bloat·ed /bloʊtɪd/ *adj.* too big as from eating too much food, *(syn.)* swollen: *After a big meal, his stomach felt bloated.*

blob /blɑb/ *n.* **1** a soft, shapeless drop or mass: *A blob of butter fell onto the table.* **2** a small amount: *a blob of ink, a blob of mashed potatoes* **3** *pej.slang* a fat, lazy person

bloc /blɑk/ *n.* a group of nations or politicians acting together in a cause: *The liberal bloc voted for the tax increase.*

block (1) /blɑk/ *n.* **1** hard substances shaped like a block: *She carved a statue out of the block of ice.* **2** a cube-shaped piece of plastic (wood, metal, etc.) used as a toy: *Children play with blocks.* **3** (in real estate) land with buildings on it between two streets: *I walk ten blocks to work each morning.* **4** a group of s.t. taken as a whole: *He bought a block of 100,000 shares of IBM stock this morning.* **5** *infrml.* **a chip off the old block:** to act or look like one's parent: *He's interested in politics, just like his father—he's really a chip off the old block.*

block (2) *n.* s.t. that prevents flow or movement, *(syn.)* stoppage: *An accident caused a block in traffic.*
—*v.* **1** to prevent s.t. from happening: *Congress blocked the President's new plan.* **2** to stand in the way, *(syn.)* to obstruct: *A big tree fell and blocked the road.* **3** *phrasal v. sep.* **to block s.t. out: a.** to erase from one's mind: *He blocked out his wife's death.||He blocked it out.* **b.** to plan: *She blocked out her future plans.||She blocked them out.* **4** *phrasal v. sep.* **to block s.t. up:** to have a stoppage: *The coffee grounds blocked up the sink.||They blocked it up.*

block·ade /blɑˈkeɪd/ *v.n.* **-aded, -ading, -ades** to close off an area to stop supplies (food, weapons, etc.) and communication: *Warships <v.> blockaded the seaport.*

block·age /blɑkɪdʒ/ *n.* [C;U] s.t. that prevents flow or movement, *(syn.)* an obstruction: *That* *man had a blockage in a blood vessel and almost had a heart attack.*

block·bust·er /'blɑk,bʌstər/ *n.fig.* a big surprise or great success: *That new movie is a blockbuster.*

block·head /'blɑk,hɛd/ *n.infrml.* stupid person: *That blockhead delivered the wrong box!*

blond /blɑnd/ *adj.n.* having light, yellowish hair: *That man has <adj.> blond hair.*

blonde /blɑnd/ *n.* a woman with blond hair *See:* brunette, redhead.

blood /blʌd/ *n.* [U] **1** the red liquid pumped by the heart through the body: *Blood carries food to and takes waste away from the cells in our bodies.* **2** relatives, (*syn.*) kin: *She is my father's sister, so we are related by blood.* **3** national or racial family origins: *He is of Scandinavian blood.* **4** interests or temperament: *She gets angry easily; she has very hot blood.* **5 bad blood:** long-lasting anger or hatred: *The couple's divorce was very bitter; there is a lot of bad blood between them.* **6 blood is thicker than water:** family ties are stronger than other ties (business, friendship, etc.) **7 in cold blood:** deliberately and without emotion: *He walked up to the man and shot him in cold blood.* **8 new blood:** new people with lots of energy: *The company's owners are old and tired; the company needs some new blood.* **9 out for blood:** wanting to kill or harm s.o.: *When her daughter was murdered, she was out for blood to find the killer.* **10 to have s.o.'s blood on one's head** or **hands:** to be responsible for s.o.'s injury or death: *She sent the boy on a dangerous job, and he was killed; his blood is on her hands.* **11 to make one's blood boil:** to make one angry or bitter: *His cruelty to animals makes my blood boil.* **12 to make one's blood run cold:** to fill one with fright and horror: *The terrible screams made our blood run cold.*

blood·bath /'blʌd,bæθ/ *n.* the murder of many people at one time, (*syn.*) massacre: *Soldiers killed the people of that village in a bloodbath.*

blood·hound /'blʌd,haʊnd/ *n.* **1** a large dog with the ability to follow a person's or animal's smell: *The police used a bloodhound to find the lost girl.* **2** *fig.* s.o. who pursues without giving up: *That detective is a bloodhound; he always catches the criminal.*

blood·less /'blʌdlɪs/ *adj.* without blood or injury; *The 1974 revolution in Portugal was bloodless; nobody died.* -*adv.* **bloodlessly.**

blood pressure *n.* [U] measurement of the force with which blood moves through the body: *High blood pressure can cause heart attacks.*

blood·shed /'blʌd,ʃɛd/ *n.* [U] acts of killing and injury: *Soldiers shot the villagers, causing much bloodshed.*

blood·shot /'blʌd,ʃɑt/ *adj.* having a red look in the eyes: *After staying up all night, her eyes were bloodshot.*

blood·stain /'blʌd,steɪn/ *n.* a spot of blood: *Bloodstains on his shirt showed where he was knifed.* -*adj.* **bloodstained.**

blood·stream /'blʌd,strim/ *n.* the flow of blood through the vessels: *Her bloodstream was blocked in her right leg.*

blood·thirst·y /'blʌd,θɜrsti/ *adj.* liking or wanting to kill others: *While laughing, the bloodthirsty soldiers murdered their enemies.*

blood type *n.* one of four classes of blood a person can have: *His blood is type A; hers is B.*

blood vessel *n.* a small tube (artery, vein, capillary) that carries blood through the body: *A blood vessel to his heart became blocked and caused a heart attack.*

blood·y /'blʌdi/ *adj.* -**ier, -iest** covered with blood: *After a fight, his face was bloody.*

bloom /blum/ *v.* (of plants) to flower: *Our apple tree bloomed last week.*
—*n.* a flower in bloom *See:* blossom.

bloop·er /'blupər/ *n.* a mistake: *The announcer on the radio made a blooper by saying "good morning" instead of "good evening."*

blos·som /'blɑsəm/ *n.* a flower as it opens: *The blossoms on the apple tree appeared last week. See:* bloom.
—*v.* **1** to flower: *The roses blossomed last week.* **2** *fig.*to develop into s.t. very good: *She blossomed into a top student in school.*

blot /blɑt/ *n.* **1** a spot that makes s.t. dirty or stained, (*syn.*) a blotch: *an ink blot* **2** *fig.* a shameful event: *The crime he committed is a blot on his record.*
—*v.* **blotted, blotting, blots 1** to soak up a liquid: *She blotted water off the table with a towel.* **2** *phrasal v. sep.* **to blot s.t. out:** to prevent from seeing, cover up: *The fog blotted out our view of the road. See:* blotter.

blotch /blɑtʃ/ *n.* -**es** a spot, such as an ugly stain: *He has a blotch of ink on his shirt.* -*n.* [U] **blotchiness**

blotch·y /'blɑtʃi/ *adj.* -**ier, -iest 1** having spots, badly stained **2** discolored: *Her skin is blotchy, with lots of red spots.*

blot·ter /'blɑtər/ *n.* a soft, flat sheet of thick paper that soaks up liquid and protects a surface: *A blotter on his desk protects it from spills and scratches.*

blouse /blaʊs/ *n.frml.* a woman's shirt: *She wears white silk blouses.*

blow (1) /bloʊ/ *v.* **blew** /blu,/ **blowing, blows 1** to force air in a current, such as through pipes or the mouth: *She blew out the candles on her cake.* **2** to move (air) through space: *The wind blew hard during the storm.* **3** to sound a horn or whistle: *I had to blow the horn to warn another car.* **4** to make s.t. stop working: *Using the electric heater with the TV on blew a fuse.* **5** *slang* to spend or lose a lot of money: *He blew $10,000 by gambling on horse races.* **6** *phrasal v. sep.* **to blow s.o. away: a.** to affect intensely: *His performance blew away the audience.||It blew them away.* **b.** to kill by shooting: *The criminals blew away their enemy.||They blew him away.* **7** *phrasal v. insep.* **to blow by s.o.** or **s.t.:** to get ahead of: *The car blew by us at high speed.* **8** *infrml.* **to blow hot and cold:** to be for then against s.t., (*syn.*) to waver: *One day, he says he wants a new job, and then he doesn't; he blows hot and cold about it.* **9** *phrasal v. slang* **to blow in:** to arrive unexpectedly: *She blew in from Los Angeles last night.* **10** *infrml.* **to blow it:** to make a mistake: *I ordered the wrong item; I'm sorry, I blew it.* **11** *phrasal v. sep.* **to blow s.o.** or **s.t. off: a.** *s.o. slang* to ignore: *She blew off her parents and did what she wanted to.||She blew them off.* **b.** *s.t. slang* to decide not to attend s.t.: *We blew off our lunch meeting.||We blew it off.* **12** *infrml.* **to blow off steam:** to say what annoys you, release emotions: *Her work irritated her so much that she blew off steam by yelling.* **13** *slang* **to blow one's mind:** to be shocked by s.o.'s actions: *It blows my mind that you can spend so much money on shoes.* **14** **to blow one's own horn:** to speak well of oneself: *She blew her own horn about getting an A+ on the exam.* **15** *infrml.* **to blow one's top** or **stack:** to become angry: *He blew his top when his wallet was stolen.* **16** *phrasal v. sep.* **to blow s.t. out: a.** to put out by blowing, (*syn.*) to extinguish: *The boy blew out the candles on his cake.||He blew them out.* **b.** to explode violently: *We blew out a tire on the highway.||We blew it out.* **c.** to (cause to) stop working: *The electrical storm blew out the computers.||It blew them out.* **17** *phrasal v.* **to blow over:** to become unimportant after a while: *Scandals usually blow over in a few months.* **18** *infrml.* **to blow the whistle on s.o.:** to tell the authorities (police, business managers) about s.o.'s wrongdoing: *Workers at the store stole so much that one of the employees blew the whistle on the others.* **19** *phrasal v. sep.* **to blow s.t. up: a.** to explode: *Soldiers blew up the bridge.* **b.** *fig.* to become very angry: *He's so irritable that he blows up at any little mistake.* **c.** to make s.t. larger by filling it with air, (*syn.*) to inflate: *She blew up balloons for the party.* **d.** to make bigger: *He blew up some photographs.*

blow (2) *n.* **1** a hard hit as with a fist or hammer: *He died from a blow on the head by a club.* **2** a shock, upset: *The sudden death of her husband was a severe blow to her.* **3** *pl.* **to come to blows:** to fight **4 low blow:** an unfair

act: *It was a low blow when one player said another had cheated when she had not.*
—*adj.* **blow-by-blow:** detail-by-detail: *He gave a blow-by-blow description of the accident.*

blow-dry /'blou,draɪ/ *v.* **-dried, -drying, -dries** to dry hair with a hand-held machine that blows hot air *-n.* **blow-dry; blow-drier.**

blow·hard /'blou,hɑrd/ *n.pej.infrml.* a person who talks for a long time, but says little, (*syn.*) a windbag: *That blowhard never stops talking.*

blow·out /'blou,aut/ *n.* a tire that becomes flat while a vehicle is moving: *She had a blowout on the highway.*
—*adj.n.* a huge discount sale: *Some stores have a <adj.> blowout sale twice a year.*

blow·torch /'blou,tɔrtʃ/ *n.* **-torches** a hand-held tool that sends out a flame: *He melted the metal with a blowtorch.*

blow·up /'blou,ʌp/ *n.* **1** a large photo: *They have a blowup of their baby on their living-room wall.* **2** an explosion of anger: *When the company lost money, there was a big blowup between the owner and some employees.*

blub·ber /'blʌbər/ *n.* [U] **1** thick fat on ocean animals: *whale blubber* **2** fat on a person: *He can hardly squeeze all that blubber into his clothes.*
—*v.* to cry, (*syn.*) to sob: *She blubbered when her pet dog died.*

blud·geon /'blʌdʒən/ *n.* a short, thick club used to hit people, (*syn.*) a truncheon
—*v.* to hit with a bludgeon: *The man was bludgeoned to death.*

blue /blu/ *adj.* **1** having the color of: *My car is blue.||Blue and yellow make green.* **2** sad, (*syn.*) depressed: *She is blue (or) feels blue today.* **3** **once in a blue moon:** almost never: *He visits once in a blue moon; we almost never see him.*
—*n.* **1** the sky: *The bird flew off into the blue.* **2** the sea: *She threw her wedding ring over the side of the ship and watched it sink into the blue.* **3** *infrml.* **out of the blue:** suddenly, unexpectedly: *Out of the blue, I got a phone call from a friend I hadn't seen in years.* -*adj.* **bluish.** *See:* **blues.**

blue·bell /'blu,bɛl/ *n.* a plant with blue flowers shaped like bells

blue·ber·ry /'blu,bɛri/ *n.* **-ries 1** a bush that produces small, dark berries **2** the berries themselves: *Blueberries taste delicious with cream and sugar.*

blue·bird /'blu,bɜrd/ *n.* **1** a small North American bird with blue feathers **2** *fig.* symbol of happiness

blue blood *n.fig.* a person from the upper classes, (*syn.*) an aristocrat: *She is a blue blood from the French aristocracy.*

blue bonnet *n.* a plant with small flowers, found in the Texas region

blue cheese *n.* a rich, sharp, thick white cheese with blue areas: *Would you like blue cheese or Italian dressing on your salad?*

blue chip *adj.fig.* high quality: *Companies that have performed well for a very long time are called blue chip companies.*

blue-collar *adj.* of people who work with their hands in jobs that require some training, working-class: *Most blue-collar workers in the USA do not belong to unions. See:* white-collar.

USAGE NOTE: *Blue collar* refers to people who work at manual jobs; traditionally such laborers have belonged to the *working class*. Blue collar therefore is also used symbolically to refer to the working class. *White collar* workers generally work in office jobs and form the middle or upper-middle classes of North American society.

blue·fish /'blu,fɪʃ/ *n.* **-fish** or **-fishes** a large blue-colored fish with sweet, good-tasting meat: *Bluefish are found in the Atlantic and Indian Oceans.*

blue·grass /'blu,græs/ *n.* [U] **1** a type of grass found in the southern USA, esp. Kentucky **2** a type of country music: *Bluegrass is lively music played on violins, guitars, and banjos.*

blue jay *n.* a bird with blue and gray feathers, common in North America: *Bluejays are noisy birds.*

blue jeans *n.* blue pants made of a thick cloth, usu. cotton: *People wear blue jeans all over the world. See:* jeans.

blue laws *n.pl.* laws that make certain activities, such as working or selling alcoholic beverages on Sundays illegal

blue·print /'blu,prɪnt/ *n.* **1** a detailed drawing of s.t. to show how to make it, (*syn.*) a pattern: *Workers read blueprints to see how to construct a building.* **2** *fig.* a plan: *Our company has a blueprint for its future.*

blues /bluz/ *n.pl.* **1** sadness, depression: *He has the blues because his girlfriend left him.* **2** slow jazz music about sad feelings: *Blues music is popular in New Orleans and Memphis.* **3** **to sing the blues:** to complain about s.t.: *She flunked a course and is singing the blues. See:* blue 2.

blue streak *n.fig.* a stream of words: *Once he gets started, he'll talk a blue streak for hours.*

bluff (1) /blʌf/ *v.* **1** to pretend so that one gets s.t.: *I think that he is bluffing about quitting his job so he will get a salary increase.* **2** *phrasal v. insep.* **to bluff s.o. into s.t.:** to deceive s.o. so he or she will do what one wants
—*n.* **1** [C;U] make-believe, (*syn.*) pretense: *His tough talk is a bluff.* **2** **to call s.o.'s bluff:** to challenge s.o. to carry out his or her threats

bluff (2) *n.* [C] a cliff: *She stood on the bluff and looked at the sea.*
—*adj.* having a crude, blunt manner: *His bluff manner puts people off, but he is very kind.*

blun·der /'blʌndər/ *n.* a mistake, esp. a bad or stupid one: *He made a blunder by calling his boss by the wrong name.*
—*v.* **1** to make a mistake: *She blundered into the wrong room in the middle of the class period.* **2** to move as if one is blind: *She blundered through the dark house.*

blunt /blʌnt/ *adj.* **1** direct in, (*syn.*) frank: *She is blunt because she tells people exactly what she thinks.* **2** not sharp, (*syn.*) dull: *a knife with a blunt edge*
—*v.* to reduce the effect of s.t.: *His heavy drinking blunted his chances for success.* -*n.* [U] **bluntness.**

blur /blɜr/ *v.* **blurred, blurring, blurs** to make s.o. unable to see clearly, (*syns.*) to cloud, obscure: *Her terrible headache blurred her eyesight.||Fog blurred our view of the hills.*
—*n.* s.t. unclear: *Time has gone so quickly; this summer was just a blur.*

blurb /blɜrb/ *n.* a brief piece of writing: *The famous writer wrote a blurb about the new author to put on the book jacket.*

blurt /blɜrt/ *phrasal v.* **to blurt out:** to speak suddenly: *He blurted out the truth, that he committed the crime.*

blush /blʌʃ/ *v.n.* **-es** to become red in the face from nervousness or shame: *Some boys <v.> blush when a pretty girl smiles at them.*
—*n.* **1** a reddened face **2** red makeup put on the cheeks, (*syn.*) rouge

B mov·ie /'bi,muvi/ *n.* a poorly made film, usu. older and cheaply produced: *Ronald Reagan starred in many B movies.*

B.O. /'bi'oʊ/ *abbr. for* body odor

bo·a /'boʊə/ *n.* **1** a long, powerful snake: *Boa constrictors wrap themselves around animals and crush them.* **2** a long scarf of feathers or fabric: *a feather boa*

boar /bɔr/ *n.* **1** a wild male pig **2** a male farm pig that can father young

board /bɔrd/ *n.* **1** [C] a thin, flat piece of wood: *Workers nail boards together to build a house.* **2** [C] a group of people that oversees a business or institution: *the company's board of directors, the school board* **3** [C] a flat piece of material: *a blackboard, a bulletin board* **4** [U] meals: *The cost of room and board at college is high.* **5** **above board:** totally honest and open in one's interactions **6** **across the board:** in general, including everyone **7** **to go by the boards:** to let an opportunity disappear without acting on it: *He had several chances to go to college, but he let them go by the boards. See:* down the drain. **8** **on board: a.** on a ship, airplane, train, etc.: *There are 150 passengers*

B

on board this jet. **b.** included: *We have a new employee on board.*
—*v.* **1** to cover with boards: *During the storm, we boarded up the house's windows.* **2** to enter a ship, train, etc.: *Sailors boarded their ship.* **3** to pay to live somewhere (not one's home): *He boards at a friend's house.*

board·er /'bɔrdər/ *n.* a person who pays to live in another person's house: *She has three boarders in her large house. See:* tenant.

board·ing·house /'bɔrdɪŋ,haus/*pl.* **-houses** /-,hauzɪz/ *n.* a private house where people rent rooms to live: *She runs a boardinghouse where eight students live.*

boarding school *n.* a school where students live and study

board·walk /'bɔrd,wɔk/ *n.* a path made of wooden boards: *The boardwalk is built above the sand next to the ocean. See:* promenade..

√**boast** /boust/ *v.n.* [C] **1** *pej.* to praise oneself, *(syn.)* to brag: *He <v.> boasted about how strong he is.* **2** to be proud of s.t.: *He boasted about his three grandchildren. -adj.* **boastful; -adv. boastfully; -n.** [U] **boasting.**

boat /bout/ *n.* **1** an open vessel smaller than a ship that sails on water, *(syn.)* a craft: *We watched the boats sail by.||We went fishing on the river in a rowboat.* **2** *fig.* **in the same boat:** in the same situation or condition: *When it started to rain at the picnic, we were all in the same boat; we all got wet. See:* rock the boat .

bob /bab/ *v.* **bobbed, bobbing, bobs 1** to move up and down on water: *The little boat bobbed on the waves* **2** *phrasal v.* **to bob up:** to appear suddenly: *A good opportunity to buy a car just bobbed up.*

bob·bin /'babɪn/ *n.* a small roller that holds thread in a sewing machine

bob·by pin /'babi/ *n.* a small metal clip with tight ends used to hold things: *Bobby pins are used to hold your hair off your face. See:* safety pin.

bob·cat /'bab,kæt/ *n.* a wild cat with light brown spotted fur and a short tail, native to North America

bob·sled /'bab,sled/ *n.v.* **-sledded, -sledding, -sleds** a small vehicle with blades that is shaped like a boat that goes down an ice-covered race course: *Bobsledding is a Winter Olympic sport.*

bod·ice /'badɪs/ *n.* **1** the front of a woman's dress that is buttoned **2** a laced vest

bod·il·y /'badəli/ *adj.* of the body: *no bodily harm*
—*adv.* the whole body: *I'll move you bodily if I have to.*

bod·y /'badi/ *n.* **-ies 1** the physical form usu. of a human or animal, not including the mind or soul: *The old man's body is healthy, but his mind is weak.* **2** a dead person: *They buried the body in the graveyard.* **3** the main part of s.t.: *The body of the newspaper article is quite long.* **4** an object in the sky: *The stars and moon are heavenly bodies.* **5** a large amount: *body of water* **6 body and soul:** one's whole being: *I love that woman with all my body and soul.* **7 to keep body and soul together:** to survive: *That elderly woman is so poor that it's all she can do to keep body and soul together.*

body building *n.* [U] the sport of lifting weights and eating special foods to strengthen the body

bod·y·guard /'badi,gard/ *n.* a person whose job is to keep another person safe: *That famous movie star has a big bodyguard. See:* life-guard.

body odor *n.* [C;U] the unpleasant smell of sweat: *Athletes create strong body odor as they exercise. See:* BO.

body shop *n.* an auto repair business: *My car had a dent in it, so I took it to a body shop to get it fixed.*

bod·y·work /'badi,wɜrk/ *n.* [U] repairs on the body of a car, truck, etc: *I took my car to the garage for bodywork.*

bog /bag, bɔg/ *n.* a wet, muddy area that is difficult to cross, *(syns.)* a swamp, a quagmire
—*v.* **bogged, bogging, bogs 1** to sink into a bog **2 bogged down:** to have too much work, *(syn.)* to be overburdened: *She is bogged down in a big project.*

bog·ey·man /'bugi,mæn, 'bou-, 'bu-/ *n.* **-men** *See:* boogieman.

bog·gle /'bagəl/ *v.* **-gled, -gling, -gles** to be difficult to understand, to confuse: *The U.S. government's debt is so huge that it boggles the mind.*

bo·gus /'bougəs/ *adj.* false, *(syn.)* counterfeit: *That $20 bill is bogus.*

bo·he·mi·an /bou'himiən/ *n.adj.* [C;U] an artist or musician and the unconventional lifestyle connected to them: *Greenwich Village in New York is a <adj.> bohemian place.*

boil /bɔɪl/ *v.* **1** to heat a liquid until it reaches the temperature of 212°F or 100°C: *I boiled the water to cook the eggs.* **2** to cook: *I boiled the vegetables.* **3** *phrasal v.* **to boil away:** to boil s.t. until it has disappeared: *The milk boiled away and ruined the sauce.* **4** *phrasal v. insep.* **to boil down:** to reduce s.t. to its basics: *It boils down to the fact that I was injured and it wasn't my fault.* **5** *phrasal v.* **to boil over:** to spread or spill over: *Unhappiness with the government boiled over from the cities into the rest of the country.* **6** *phrasal v.* **to boil up:** to get to a dangerous level: *Frustration is boiling up in the workers who lost their jobs.* **7 to make one's blood boil:** to make s.o. very

angry: *Every time my brother takes s.t. of mine without asking me he makes my blood boil.*
—*n.* **1** [U] liquid when boiling: *I heated the water to a boil.* **2** [C] a painful inflammation of the skin: *I have a boil on my back.* **3 to bring to a boil:** to heat liquid until it bubbles: *I brought the water to a boil and dropped the vegetables in.*

boil·er /'bɔɪlər/ *n.* a tank for heating water: *Our boiler is in the cellar.*

boil·er·mak·er /'bɔɪlər,meɪkər/ *n.* **1** a technician who fixes boilers **2** *slang* a beer with whiskey: *He drinks boilermakers after work.*

boil·er·plate /'bɔɪlər,pleɪt/ *n.fig.* standard legal language used in many contracts: *The contract (lease) to rent the apartment was just boilerplate with a few blank lines to fill in one's name, date, and the rent.*

boiling mad *adj.* to be very angry, (*syn.*) enraged: *She was boiling mad when her briefcase was stolen.*

boiling point *n.* **1** the temperature at which a liquid boils: *The boiling point of water is 212° Fahrenheit and 100° Celsius.* **2** *fig.* the time when s.t. violent happens: *Her temper reached the boiling point and she started screaming.*

bois·ter·ous /'bɔɪstərəs/ *adj.* noisy and playful, (*syn.*) rowdy: *Children in the classroom became boisterous.* -*adv.* **boisterously;** -*n.* [U] **boisterousness.**

bold /boʊld/ *adj.* **1** courageous, willing to take risks, (*syn.*) daring, adventuresome: *Business leaders like to think of bold plans.* **2** *pej.* rude, too direct **3** strong and clear (in art, buildings, ideas): *a building with bold lines* -*adv.* **boldly;** -*n.* [U] **boldness.**

bold·face /'boʊld,feɪs/ *n.adj.* heavy black print

bol·lix /'balɪks/ *v.* to mess up, confuse: *The sales clerk bollixed my order and gave me the wrong things.*

bo·lo·gna /bə'loʊni, -nə/ *n.var. of* baloney

bo·lo·ney /bə'loʊni/ *n.var. of* baloney

bol·ster /'boʊlstər/ *v.* to strengthen, improve, (*syn.*) to enhance: *By going to graduate school at night, the young manager bolstered her reputation.*
—*n.* a long, narrow pillow: *She held up her neck with a bolster while she read in bed.*

bolt (1) /boʊlt/ *n.* **1** a metal bar used to lock doors, windows, etc.: *I shut the bolt on the bathroom door.* **2** a thin, grooved piece of metal that twists into a circle (a nut) to hold things together: *The parts of the car are held on by strong bolts.* See: nuts and bolts.

bolt (2) *n.* **1** a roll of cloth fabric: *A tailor made a suit from a bolt of wool.* **2** a flash of lightning, (*syn.*) a streak: *A bolt of lightning hit the tree.*
—*v.* **1** to close or lock with a bolt **2** to run away suddenly: *He felt sick and bolted to the*

bathroom.||*The horse bolted from the barn.* **3** to eat quickly: *I bolted my dinner.*

bomb /bam/ *n.* **1** an explosive device: *A bomb blew up a building.* **2** *infrml.* a failure: *The play was a bomb; everyone left at intermission.*
—*v.* **1** to drop bombs: *Airplanes bombed the city.* **2** to damage or destroy with a bomb: *Terrorists bombed the mayor's office.* **3** *infrml.fig.* to fail: *She bombed on her driver's test.* **4** *slang* **bombed:** to get drunk: *He got bombed last night at a party.*

bom·bard /bam'baard/ *v.* **1** to hit with explosive shells (from big guns, artillery, etc.): *Cannons bombarded enemy lines.* **2** *fig.* to criticize heavily: *The TV and newspapers bombarded the politicians with criticism.* -*n.* [C;U] **bombardment.**

bom·bast /'bam,bæst/ *n.* speech or writing that sounds very important -*adj.* **bombastic** /bam'bæstɪk/**.**

bom·ber /'bamər/ *n.* **1** a person who bombs **2** a military airplane used for bombing: *Bombers flew low over the city.*

bomb·shell /'bam,ʃɛl/ *n.* **1** a big explosion **2** *fig.* a sudden shock: *Their mother's death was a bombshell.* **3** *fig.vulg.* a sexy woman: *That movie star was known as the "Blonde Bombshell."*

bo·na fide /'boʊnə,faɪd, banə-/ *adj.* (Latin for) real, honest, (*syn.*) genuine: *That painting is a bona fide original, not a fake.*

bo·nan·za /bə'nænzə/ *n.* sudden riches: *Oil was discovered under her property, which was a bonanza. See:* gold mine.

bon·bon /'ban,ban/ *n.* a candy with chocolate on the outside and nuts or sweet filling inside

bond /band/ *n.* **1** a relationship of trust (cooperation, friendship, love), connection: *There is a strong bond between the two sisters.* **2** (in chemistry, physics) the forces that hold matter together: *a chemical bond* **3** a certificate of debt: *Companies sell bonds to raise money.*
—*v.* **1** to become friends, esp. to trust, like, or love s.o.: *People often bond when they face danger together.* **2** to insure against loss: *Companies bond employees who handle money against their stealing it.* -*adj.* **bondable.** *See:* bind.

bond·age /'bandɪdʒ/ *n.* [U] **1** lack of freedom, (*syn.*) slavery: *Slaves are in bondage to their masters.* **2** being physically tied up or restrained

bone /boʊn/ *n.* **1** a hard, white part that makes up the frame of the body, the skeleton: *Our bones give us our shape.* **2 a bone of contention:** a point of disagreement, problem: *His low salary is a bone of contention with his boss.* **3 a bone to pick:** a complaint, problem: *He told his boss that he has a bone to pick with her about his low salary.* **4 to make no bones about s.t.:** to speak directly, complain: *He*

made no bones about feeling that his salary is too low. **5 to the bone:** to the minimum, *(syn.)* to the core: *With the drop in sales, the company cut the number of employees to the bone.||chilled to the bone*
—*v.* **boned, boning, bones** **1** to remove bones: *She boned the chicken before cooking it.* **2** *phrasal v. insep.* **to bone up on s.t.:** to study, review: *He is boning up on chemistry for his exam tomorrow.* -*adj.* **boneless.**

bone-dry /'boʊn'draɪ/ *adj.* very dry, *(syn.)* arid: *The desert is bone-dry, with no water at all.*

bone·head /'boʊn,hɛd/ *n.slang* a stupid person: *That bonehead put the wrong address on the envelope!*

bon·fire /'bɑn,faɪr/ *n.* a large fire made outside for pleasure: *We built a bonfire to celebrate Independence Day.*

bon·go /'bɑŋgoʊ/ *n.* **-goes** or **-gos** a type of drum, often in pairs: *Bongos are played with the hands.*

bon·kers /'bɑŋkərz/ *adj.infrml.* crazy, confused, and upset: *The boss is so nervous that he drives everyone bonkers.*

bon·net /'bɑnɪt/ *n.* **1** a soft hat that ties under the chin: *The baby's bonnet keeps the sun out of her eyes. See:* bee. **2** *Brit.* the hood of a car

bo·nus /'boʊnəs/ *n.* **-nuses** **1** a payment, usu. in addition to regular pay: *Our company pays everyone a bonus at the end of the year.* **2** something unexpected but positive: *I didn't think anyone would remember my birthday, so when all my friends sent cards it was a real bonus.*

bon·y or **boney** /'boʊni/ *adj.* **-ier, -iest** **1** having many bones: *That fish is bony and difficult to eat.* **2** very thin, showing bones: *He eats so little that he is bony.*

boo (1) /bu/ *n.v.* **booed, booing, boos** a sound of disapproval: *The football player heard <n.> boos from the audience when he made a bad play.||They <v.> booed him.*

boo (2) *n.* a sound made to frighten or surprise s.o.: *When she walked up behind him and shouted "Boo!," he jumped.*

boob /bub/ *n.slang* **1** a stupid person **2** a woman's breast

boo·bie /'bubi/ *n.slang var. of* booby

boob tube *n.slang* television: *I watched the baseball game on the boob tube.*

boo·by /'bubi/ *n.infrml.* **-bies 1** a stupid person **2 booby hatch:** an insane asylum: *He lost control of his life and ended up in the booby hatch.* **3 booby prize:** a funny prize given to s.o. who finishes last in a competition

booby trap *n.v.* **trapped, trapping, traps** a hidden device or situation meant to harm or kill s.o.: *A soldier was killed when a <n.> booby trap exploded in his face.*

boog·ie /'bugi/ *n.v.slang* **-ied, -ying, -ies** dance, have a good time: *We're going to <v.> boogie tonight!*

boog·ie·man /'bugi,mæn, 'boʊ-, 'bu-/ *n.infrml.* **-men** /-,mɛn/ a frightening, evil, imaginary man: *At night, the little boy is afraid that the boogieman is hiding under his bed.*

book /bʊk/ *n.* **1** pages of words kept together with a paper or hard cover: *We read two books for our English class.* **2** things put together in book form: *a book of stamps* **3 by the book:** strictly by the rules: *That police officer goes by the book; when she sees s.o. doing s.t. wrong, she arrests the person.* **4 to keep the books:** to record money going in and out of a business: *The accountant keeps the company books.* **5 to throw the book at s.o.:** to punish severely: *The judge threw the book at the killer and gave her 100 years in jail.* **6 to write the book on s.t.:** to be an expert: *Katharine Hepburn wrote the book on acting.*
—*v.* **1** to save a seat, room, *(syn.)* to reserve: *I booked an airline flight and a room at a hotel.* **2** to charge with a crime: *The police booked her for shoplifting.*

book·case /'bʊk,keɪs/ *n.* shelves with sides and usu. a back: *My bookcase holds almost 100 books.*

book·end /'bʊk,ɛnd/ *n.* one of a pair of objects used to hold up a row of books: *Bookends on my desk keep my dictionary and reference books standing up.*

book·ie /'bʊki/ *n. slang short for* bookmaker

book·ing /'bʊkɪŋ/ *n.* [C;U] a place saved for s.o., *(syn.)* a reservation (hotel, flight, etc.): *That passenger ship already has 1,000 bookings for its next trip. See:* book.

book·ish /'bʊkɪʃ/ *adj.* liking books, intellectual, *(syn.)* studious: *He's a bookish guy who prefers reading to playing sports. See:* egg head.

book·keep·er /'bʊk,kipər/ *n.* a person who maintains the accounts of a business, accountant: *A bookkeeper notes money received and paid in the company's books.* -*n.* [U] **bookkeeping.**

book·let /'bʊklɪt/ *n.* a small book with a paper cover, *(syn.)* a pamphlet: *That company's booklet describes its products.*

book·mak·er /'bʊk,meɪkər/ *n.* (in gambling) a person who takes illegal bets, *(syn.)* a bookie: *Bookmakers take bets on horse races, ball games, etc.*

book·mark /'bʊk,mɑrk/ *n.* a small item placed between pages of a book to remind one where one stopped reading

book·rack /'bʊk,ræk/ *n.* shelves, usu. of metal, for displaying books: *That bookstore has bookracks along its walls.*

B

book·store /'bʊk,stɔr/ n. a shop that sells books: *That bookstore on the corner carries lots of books.*

book·worm /'bʊk,wɜrm/ n. **1** fig. a person who reads books or studies most of the time: *After she learned to read, she became a bookworm.* **2** insects that destroy books by eating the paste in the books' binding

boom (1) /bum/ v. **1** to make a deep, loud noise: *Cannons boom when they shoot.* **2** to grow rapidly, (syn.) to prosper (an economy, industry): *Our business is booming this year.*
—n. **1** a deep, loud noise: *Fireworks make a loud boom when they explode.* **2** a time of rapid growth in business, (syn.) prosperity: *There was a boom in the oil industry.* **3 boom or bust:** to do well, then poorly: *The oil business is boom or bust: good one year, bad the next.*

boom (2) n. a long horizontal pole that holds the bottom of a sail on a boat

boo·mer·ang /'bumə,ræŋ/ n. a flat, curved piece of wood used as a weapon that will return to the thrower if thrown correctly
—v.fig. to produce the opposite result from what one wanted: *Her criticism of her boss boomeranged when she was fired.*

boon /bun/ n. s.t. good, an important help: *Having a good library at the school is a boon for the students.*

boon·docks /'bun,daks/ n.pl.infrml. usu. pej. a simple, country area far from city life, (syn.) the sticks: *They live in the boondocks far in the north.*

boon·dog·gle /'bun,dagəl/ n.infrml. time wasted on unimportant work, esp. a trip paid for by a company or the government: *He went on a boondoggle to South America.* See: junket.

boon·ies /'buniz/ n.pl. infrml. short for boondocks

boor /bʊr/ n. a crude, unpleasant person: *He's an insensitive boor.* -adj. **boorish** -adv. **boorishly.**

boost /bust/ v.n. **1** to lift or push up, (syn.) to raise: *The mother <v.> boosted her child into a high chair.* **2** to improve one's emotions: *He was feeling sad, so his friends <v.> boosted his spirits by giving him a party.*

boost·er /'bustər/ n. **1** a supporter, (syn.) enthusiast: *She is a booster of the local girls' club.* **2** the part of a rocket that contains fuel and an engine to send it into space **3** a later, additional dose of a vaccine that one has already received

boot /but/ n. **1** a strong shoe with a tall top: *Cowboys wear leather boots.* **2** Brit. the trunk of a car **3 to boot:** in addition, also: *They fired him and gave him a bad reference to boot.* **4** infrml.fig. **to bet one's boots:** to know s.t. as certain, a sure thing: *You can bet your boots that I'm going to watch the championship basketball game!* **5 to lick s.o.'s boots:** to flatter or be too polite to s.o. so he or she will do what one wants
—v.infrml. **1** to hit with the foot, kick: *The football player booted the ball.* **2 to boot up:** to start a computer program: *We had to boot up the computer again after the electricity came back on.*

boot camp n. a place soldiers go for training: *Boot camp can be a difficult experience for soldiers.*

booth /buθ/ n. **1** a small closet-like place with a door: *She went into a telephone booth to make a phone call.* **2** in a market, a table that displays products: *That booth sells handmade jewelry.* **3** the space for such a display: *Our company rented a booth at the big conference hall.* **4** in a restaurant, unmovable cushioned benches on both sides of a table

boo·tie or **bootee** /'buti/ n. a small shoe for babies

boot·leg /'but,lɛg/ adj.v. **-legged, -legging, -legs** to make and sell illegal goods, esp. liquor: *That man sells <adj.> bootleg whiskey.* -n. **bootlegger.**

boot·straps /'but,stræps/ n.pl. **1** ties or laces on a boot **2** fig. **by one's (own) bootstraps:** by one's own hard work: *She started with no money and pulled herself up by her bootstraps to run her own company.*

boo·ty /'buti/ n. **1** [U] valuable things stolen, esp. in war, (syn.) loot: *Pirates took booty from ships they captured.* **2** slang the buttocks

booze /buz/ n.slang [U] alcoholic beverages: *He went out to buy some booze.*
—v. slang **boozed, boozing, boozes** to drink alcoholic beverages -n. **boozer;** -adj. **boozy.**

bop (1) /bap/ n.slang [U] short for bebop, a style of jazz music
—v.infrml. **bopped, bopping, bops** **1** to dance: *We went to a party and bopped all night.* **2** phrasal v. **to bop around:** to go here and there, from one place to another

bop (2) v.n.infrml. to strike, hit: *That guy got nasty with me, so I <v.> bopped him.*

bor·del·lo /bɔr'dɛloʊ/ **-los** n. a place where one pays to have sex, (syns.) a brothel, a house of prostitution: *Bordellos are illegal in most parts of the USA.*

bor·der /'bɔrdər/ n. **1** the edge of s.t.: *The border of that rug is torn.* **2** the legal line separating two states or countries, (syn.) a boundary: *We crossed the Mexican border into the USA.*
—v. **1** to make a line: *Trees border the road on both sides.* **2** phrasal v. insep. **to border on/upon s.t.:** to seem like s.t., (syn.) to resemble: *His behavior borders on being crazy.*

bor·der·line /'bɔrdər,laɪn/ *adj.* on the edge of, almost: *He's borderline crazy.*

bore (1) /bɔr/ *adj.v.* **bored, boring, bores 1** to make s.o. feel tired, (*syn.*) to weary: *That movie about the war <v.> bored me.* **2 bored stiff** or **to tears:** extremely bored: *The old man is alone all the time and is bored to tears.*
—*n.* **1** a dull, tiresome event **2** a dull person: *He talks all the time and is such a bore.* -*n.* [U] **boredom.**

bore (2) *v.* **1** to cut a hole in s.t., (*syn.*) to drill: *Workers bore a hole in the ground for an oil well.* **2** *phrasal v. insep.* **to bore into s.t.:** to examine, (*syn.*) to analyze: *The accountant bored into the company's books and found out the facts.*
—*n.* the size of the hole in a gun barrel or pipe, (*syn.*) gauge

bor·ing /'bɔrɪŋ/ *adj.* uninteresting, (*syn.*) dull: *He is so boring; he never says anything interesting but talks a lot.*

born /bɔrn/ *past part. of* to bear **1** given life: *The child was born on December 25.* **2** *fig.* **born out of:** forced to do s.t.: *The cost-cutting plan was born of the need (necessity, requirement) to lower expenses.*
—*adj.* **1** having a natural ability to do s.t.: *She is a born athlete.* **2 born and bred:** raised from childhood: *He is a born and bred New Yorker. See:* silver spoon.

borne /bɔrn/ *past part of* to bear

bor·ough /'bɜrou, 'bʌr-/ *n.* a political division and geographical area of a city: *Manhattan is one of the five boroughs of New York City.*

bor·row /'barou, 'bɔr-/ *v.* **1** to receive a loan of s.t. with the promise to return it: *She borrowed $2,000 from the bank.* **2** to copy or take words, ideas, etc.: *English has borrowed many words from French.*
—*adj.* **on borrowed time:** time that one did not expect to have: *Several years ago the doctor told her she would die from cancer in a few months; two years later, she is still alive and is living on borrowed time. -n.* **borrower.**

bor·row·ing(s) /'barouɪŋ(z), 'bɔr-/ *n.* (in business) loans, usu. of money: *The company's borrowings must be repaid to the bank.*

bos·om /'buzəm/ *n.* **1** the human chest, esp. the breasts: *She held her infant child to her bosom.* **2** *fig.* **bosom buddy** or **friend:** very close friend: *Those guys have been bosom buddies since childhood.*

boss /bɔs/ *n.* **bosses 1** the person in charge of others, (*syns.*) supervisor, manager, owner: *She is the boss at that publishing company.* **2** *pej.* a politician who controls a political organization or party: *Whatever the party boss wants gets done immediately.*
—*v.* to give orders: *She bosses everyone around.*

boss·y /'bɔsi/ *adj. pej.* **-ier, -iest** telling others what to do in a self-important way, (*syn.*) domineering: *He is bossy with everybody.* -*n.* [U] **bossiness.**

bo·ta·ny /'batni/ *n.* [U] the study of plant life -*adj.* **botanical** /'bə'tænəkəl/; -*adv.* **botanically;** -*n.* **botanist.**

botch /batʃ/ *v.* **botched, botching, botches** to do s.t. badly: *The printer botched the job with spots on every page; he really botched it up.*

both /bouθ/ *adj.* of two things or people: *Both friends arrived at the same time.||They had both traveled on the same plane.||He held her with both arms.*

both·er /'baðər/ *v.* **1** to give unwanted attention, (*syns.*) to pester, annoy: *She told him to stop bothering her.* **2** to hurt, pain, (*syn.*) to trouble: *My back (liver, throat, etc.) is bothering me today.* **3** to do nothing, (*syn.*) to disregard: *The company president does not bother with small details.*
—*n.* [U] an annoyance, (*syn.*) an irritation: *For him, details are a bother.* -*adj.* **bothersome.**

bot·tle /'batl/ *n.* **1** a round container for liquids: *I bought a bottle of wine.* **2** *infrml.* **to hit the bottle:** to drink alcohol: *He hit the bottle when he got laid off from work.*
—*v.* **-tled, -tling, -tles 1** to put into bottles: *That company bottles soft drinks.* **2 to bottle up:** to hold emotions inside oneself

bot·tle·neck /'batl,nɛk/ *n.* **1** a narrow part of a road, passageway, etc.: *The four-lane road narrows into a bottleneck as you get near the city.* **2** *fig.* a place where an activity slows or stops: *An accident on the road caused a bottleneck in traffic.*

bot·tom /'batəm/ *n.* **1** the lowest part of s.t.: *There is mud on the bottom of the lake.* **2** the lowest point s.t. reaches: *The price of oil hit bottom last week.* **3** *infrml.* the buttocks, (*syn.*) the behind: *She fell on her bottom.* **4 (at) the bottom:** the cause, source of s.t. **5 bottom of the barrel:** the worst: *Drug addicts and drunks are seen as the bottom of the barrel in society.* **6 Bottoms up!:** a drinking toast: *She poured wine for everyone and said, "Bottoms up!"* **7 from the bottom of my heart:** most sincerely: *I tell you that I love you from the bottom of my heart.* **8 to get to the bottom of s.t.:** to learn the truth about s.t.: *I don't know how my window was broken, but I will get to the bottom of this mystery.*
—*v.* **1** to reach the lowest level: *A submarine bottomed on the ocean floor.* **2** *phrasal v.* **to bottom out:** to reach the lowest point then begin to rise: *The economy bottomed out in the spring.*

bot·tom·less /'batəmlɪs/ *adj.* **1** without a bottom, extremely deep: *the bottomless ocean* **2 a bottomless pit: a.** an opening in the earth that has no visible bottom, (*syn.*) an abyss **b.**

fig. a very difficult problem: *The government's debt is a bottomless pit.*

bottom line *n.* **1** the line on a company's accounting statement that shows profit or loss: *She cut $500,000 from the company's expenses, which went right to the bottom line.* **2** *fig.* the important, (*syn.*) crucial, point: *The bottom line is that we have to increase our sales or take a cut in pay.*

bot·u·lism /ˈbɑtʃə,lɪzəm/ *n.* [U] bad food poisoning caused by bacteria in some meat and vegetables

bough /baʊ/ *n.* a large tree branch: *A bough of the pine tree broke and fell to the ground.*

bought /bɔt/ *adj.* paid for, (*syn.*) purchased: *That crooked politician is a bought man; he takes bribes.*

boul·der /ˈboʊldər/ *n.* a large rock: *A boulder came down the mountain and crushed the car.*

boul·e·vard /ˈbʊlə,vɑrd/ *n.* a wide major street in a city, often with trees lining it *See:* street.

bounce /baʊns/ *v.* **bounced, bouncing, bounces** **1** to spring off a surface, (*syn.*) to rebound: *A ball bounces off the sidewalk.* **2** to move up and down: *The mother bounced her little boy on her knee.* **3** *slang* to have a check returned to the owner of a bank account for lack of money: *My rent check bounced because I'd forgotten to deposit my paycheck in my account.* **4** to force s.o. to leave, (*syn.*) to expel: *She was bounced out of the bar for her wild actions.*
—*n.* **1** a spring, (*syn.*) a rebound **2** liveliness, energy: *She walks with a bounce in her step.* -*adj.* **bouncy;** -*adv.* **bouncily;** -*n.* [U] **bounciness.**

bounc·er /ˈbaʊnsər/ *n.* a strong person who makes people leave bars if they behave badly: *A bouncer threw a drunk out on the street.*

bound (1) /baʊnd/ *n.* **1** a jump, (*syn.*) a leap: *The dog jumped over the fence in one bound.* **2** a bounce: *The ball hit the ground with a bound.* **3** *pl.* limits **4 out of bounds: a.** the sides and limits of a sports field: *The football player kicked the ball out of bounds.* **b.** *fig.* s.t. impolite, bad behavior: *Her nasty remarks to her husband were out of bounds.*
—*v.* **1** to jump, leap: *The dog bounded over the fence.* **2** to spring off a surface after hitting it, (*syn.*) to bounce: *The ball bounded against the wall. See:* to grow by leaps and bounds.

bound (2) *adj.* **1** tied up, fastened: *Her hands were bound with rope.* **2** going to, headed toward: *I am bound for home* (or) *homeward bound.* **3** required to do s.t., (*syn.*) obligated: *He was bound by the contract to make monthly payments on the car.* **4** certain, (*syn.*) destined: *That person was bound to fail (succeed, die, live, etc.).* **5** held back as if tied up: *The bird's broken wing has left it bound to the earth* (or) *earth-bound (home-bound, etc.).* **6 bound and**

determined: strongly planning to do s.t.: *She was bound and determined to finish high school.* **7 bounded by:** bordered by, contained within: *The field is bounded by a high fence.* **8 bound up with: a.** blocked: *That pipe was bound up with old leaves and mud.* **b.** *fig.* dependent on, related to: *Our buying the car is bound up with whether we can get a loan from the bank.*

bound·a·ry /ˈbaʊndri, -dəri/ *n.* **-ries 1** a legal line dividing two places, (*syn.*) a border: *The boundary between the two towns (countries, cities) is shown by a line on the map.* **2** a limit of s.t.: *Some things are beyond the boundaries of human understanding.* **3** in sports, the limit of the court, field, etc.: *A ball must be within the boundary, not "out of bounds," to be played.*

bound·less /ˈbaʊndlɪs/ *adj.* **1** unlimited: *She is a worker with boundless energy.* **2** without limits, (*syn.*) endless: *The boundless universe is waiting to be explored.* -*adv.* **boundlessly.**

boun·ti·ful /ˈbaʊntəfəl/ or **boun·te·ous** /ˈbaʊntiəs/ *adj.* much of s.t., (*syn.*) abundant: *The harvest of wheat and corn was bountiful this year.*

boun·ty /ˈbaʊnti/ *n.* **-ties 1** [C] a price or reward paid to kill or capture s.o. or s.t.: *There were too many raccoons in the town, so the government paid a $25 bounty for each animal killed.* **2** [U] plenty, a generous amount: *The bounty of wheat and cattle from the farms is great.*

bou·quet /boʊˈkeɪ, bu-/ *n.* **1** a bunch of flowers: *He sent her a beautiful bouquet of roses.* **2** a smell, (*syn.*) a scent: *The wine has a fine bouquet.*

bour·bon /ˈbɜrbən/ *n.* [C;U] an American whiskey

bour·geois /bʊrˈʒwɑ, ˈbʊrʒwɑ/ *adj.* (French for) **1** middle-class **2** *pej.* interested only in money and material things: *That man is very bourgeois, only thinking about money.* -*n.* [U] **bourgeoisie** /ˌbʊrʒwɑˈzi/.

bout /baʊt/ *n.* **1** (in boxing) a fighting match: *The boxer fought a 12-round bout.* **2** *fig.* a short, difficult time, esp. with illness: *Every winter, I have a bout of the flu.*

bou·tique /buˈtik/ *n.* a small, usu. fashionable, shop: *He owns a women's clothes boutique.*

bo·vine /ˈboʊ,vaɪn, -vɪn/ *adj.frml.* relating to cows and other cattle

bow (1) /boʊ/ *n.* **1** a piece of ribbon (thin cloth) tied into loops: *I tied the package with a bright red bow.* **2** a curved piece of wood (metal, etc.) and a string used to shoot arrows: *He hunts deer with bow and arrows.*

bow (2) /baʊ/ *n.* **1** the front part of a ship: *The bow moves through the water.* **2** a formal gesture of bending at the waist: *The singer came*

on stage and took a bow in front of the audience. See: curtsy.
—*v.* **1** to bend at the waist: *She bowed to the audience.* **2** *phrasal v. insep.* **to bow down:** to be weak and obedient, *(syn.)* to be servile: *When he asks for s.t., he expects you to bow down and do it immediately.* **3** *phrasal v.* **to bow out:** not to participate, *(syn.)* to withdraw: *She decided to bow out of the real estate deal.*

bow·el /ˈbaʊəl, baʊl/ *n.* **1** the tubes from the stomach where wastes are prepared to go out of the body, *(syn.)* lower intestine **2 bowel movement:** an expelling of solid waste from the body
—*pl.fig.* in the deepest inner places: *The coal mines go into the bowels of the earth.*

bowl /boʊl/ *n.* a dish with upward curved sides: *I'd like a bowl of soup, please.*
—*v.* **1** to roll a ball on a flat surface (bowling alley, green): *We bowl every Thursday night.* **2** *phrasal v.* **to bowl over:** to surprise: *He was bowled over by the good news. -n.* **bowler.**

bow·leg·ged /ˈboʊˌlɛgɪd, -lɛgd/ *adj.* having legs that curve outward: *Some cowboys are bowlegged from riding horses.*

bowl·ing /ˈboʊlɪŋ/ *n.* the game of rolling a ball on a flat surface: *When I go bowling with my friends, I always try to get the highest score.*

bow tie /ˈboʊˌtaɪ/ *n.* a short necktie for men fastened into a bow: *He wears bow ties with stripes.*

box (1) /bɑks/ *n.* **boxes** **1** a square or rectangular container made of wood or cardboard, *(syns.)* a case, a carton: *I put my books in a box and closed it.* **2** the amount in a box: *The family ate a box of cereal (candy, etc.).* **3** a small, closed-in seating area in a theater, stadium, etc.: *The box seats at the basketball game were the best seats in the stadium.*
—*v.* **boxed, boxing, boxes 1** to put in a box, *(syn.)* to encase: *I boxed my books and sent them home from college.* **2** *phrasal v. sep.* **to box s.o. or s.t. in: a.** to be unable to get out of a bad situation: *She signed a bad contract; it boxed in all of her time.||It boxed her in.* **b.** to have too little space, *(syn.)* cramp: *The small office boxes in the workers.||It boxes them in.* **3** *phrasal v. sep.* **to box s.o. or s.t. off:** to put in an enclosed space: *We decided to box off the play area.||We boxed it off.*

box (2) *v.* to fight with fists: *Two men boxed each other.*

box·car /ˈbɑksˌkɑr/ *n.* a large container shaped like a box used on railroads, *(syn.)* freight car: *Boxcars carry heavy loads of coal, wheat, and metals over long distances.*

box·er /ˈbɑksər/ *n.* **1** a person who fights with his fists: *Boxers try to knock each other down and out.* **2** a medium-sized dog with short golden-brown fur

boxer shorts *n.pl.* men's underwear with loose legs: *Boxer shorts are longer and looser than briefs.*

box·ing /ˈbɑksɪŋ/ *n.* [U] the sport of fist-fighting: *Boxing is a rough sport in which one boxer tries to knock the other out in a boxing match.*

box number *n.* an address, in a post office: *She sent a letter to Mr. John Smith, Post Office Box Number 20, Radio City Station, New York, NY 10019.*

box office *n.* a place that sells tickets to entertainment and sports events, *(syn.)* ticket office: *We bought our movie tickets at the box office.*

box spring *n.* a base with hard sides and metal coils that goes under a softer mattress

boy /bɔɪ/ *n.* **1** a young human male: *When he was a boy, he loved sports.* **2** a son, esp. young
—*exclam.* of delight, surprise, or disgust: *Boy! This hot weather is too much for me! -n.* [C;U] **boyhood; -***adj.* **boyish.**

boy·cott /ˈbɔɪˌkɑt/ *n.v.* a refusal for political reasons to buy certain products or do business with a certain store or company: *Protesters <v.> boycotted grapes and lettuce because of the bad treatment of the farm workers.*

boy·friend /ˈbɔɪˌfrɛnd/ *n.* male friend or companion, usu. romantic: *Her boyfriend brings her flowers. See:* girlfriend.

USAGE NOTE: A *boyfriend* can describe a man of any age who has a romantic friendship with s.o. *Girlfriend* can describe both a romantic friend and a *platonic* (nonromantic) friend who is female.

Boy Scouts *n.pl. used with a sing. v.* an international organization for boys, 11 or older, to develop character and outdoor skills *See:* Brownies; Cub Scouts; Girl Scouts.

bo·zo /ˈboʊzoʊ/ *n.infrml.* **-zos** a fool: *She dislikes her boss and tells everyone he is a bozo.*

bra /brɑ/ *n. short for* brassiere

brace /breɪs/ *n.* **1** a support, such as a heavy wooden beam, for part of a building, tunnel roof, etc. **2** a piece of medical equipment used as support: *She wears a brace on her bad knee.* **3** *pl.* wires made of metal or strong plastic used to straighten teeth
—*v.* **braced, bracing, braces 1** to put up a support: *Workers braced the falling roof with metal poles.* **2** to prepare oneself to be strong: *Sailors braced themselves before hitting a big wave.*

brace·let /ˈbreɪslɪt/ *n.* jewelry worn around the wrist or arm: *She wears gold bracelets.*

brac·ing /ˈbreɪsɪŋ/ *adj.* a feeling of freshness, *(syn.)* invigorating: *The cold air of autumn is bracing.*

B

brack·et /'brækɪt/ n. **1** a metal or wooden support used to hold things, such as wall shelves **2** a pair of marks [ ] used to set off words: *[This sentence is in brackets.]* **3** a level or range in which people (salaries, taxes, etc.) fit: *That doctor's salary is in the top tax bracket.*
—v. **1** to support s.t., such as a shelf, with brackets **2** to mark words with brackets **3** to place people or things in the same group, *(syn.)* to categorize: *The wealthiest people are bracketed to pay the highest taxes.*

brack·ish /'brækɪʃ/ adj. of a mixture of fresh and salt water: *The water from a river becomes brackish when it meets the sea.* -n. [U] **brackishness.**

brag /bræg/ v. **bragged, bragging, brags** to praise one's own successes, *(syn.)* to boast: *He brags about his own strength and good looks.*

brag·gart /'brægərt/ n. a person who brags

braid /breɪd/ v. to put pieces of hair (rope, grass, etc.) around each other, and between each other, *(syn.)* to weave: *She braids her hair every morning.*
—n. a length of woven hair, rope, etc., *(syn.)* a plait: *She wears her hair in a braid.‖She has gold braid on her uniform.*

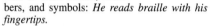

braid

braille /breɪl/ n. [U] a system of reading and writing for the blind that uses raised dots to show letters, numbers, and symbols: *He reads braille with his fingertips.*

brain /breɪn/ n. **1** the organ in the head used for thinking and feeling: *Humans have large brains.* **2** fig. intelligence: *She is so bright; she's a real brain.‖He has a lot of brains.* **3** infrml. **on the brain:** in one's mind **4** infrml. **to pick s.o.'s brain:** to find out what s.o. knows or thinks: *I picked my friend's brain about a good place to go on vacation.* **5 to wrack one's brain:** to think very hard: *I wracked my brain, trying to remember her telephone number.*
—v. infrml.fig. to hit s.o. hard on the head: *A branch fell off the tree and brained the child below.* See: brainy.

brain·child /'breɪn,tʃaɪld/ n.fig. an important project or idea of a person: *That new product is the owner's brainchild.*

brain·less /'breɪnlɪs/ adj.fig. stupid: *Walking on thin ice on a lake is a brainless thing to do.* -adv. **brainlessly.**

brain·storm /'breɪn,stɔrm/ v. to think of as many ideas as possible without criticizing them: *Every month, we brainstorm ideas for new products.*
—n. a good idea that comes to s.o.'s suddenly: *I just had a brainstorm about what to make for dinner.*

brain trust n. a group of experts (usu. serving a politician): *The President has a brain trust of professors to help him with the economy.*

brain·wash /'breɪn,wɑʃ, -,wɔʃ/ v. to make s.o. think and act as one wants, *(syn.)* to indoctrinate: *Prisoners of war are often brainwashed by their enemy.*

brain·y /'breɪni/ adj. **-ier, -iest** very intelligent: *She is brainy; she is first in her class.* **-n, braininess.** See: brain.

braise /breɪz/ v. **braised, braising, braises** to cook the outside of s.t. fast over high heat, then slowly in liquid: *We braised then ate the beef and potatoes for dinner; they were delicious.*

brake /breɪk/ n. **1** a device that stops a wheel from turning: *I stepped on the brakes and slowed the car down.* **2** fig. **to put the brakes on:** to stop: *The public put the brakes on using coins instead of paper money.*
—v. **braked, braking, brakes** to put on the brakes: *I braked suddenly and the car stopped.*

bram·ble /'bræmbəl/ n. a type of bush with thorns: *Raspberries and blackberries grow on brambles.*

bran /bræn/ n. [U] the outer covering of grains such as wheat, rye, etc.: *This bread is made of flour with the bran still on it.*

branch /bræntʃ/ n. **branches 1** a tree limb: *A bird is standing on a branch of a tree.* **2** fig.a smaller office of a company or institution: *Our New York company has a branch (branch office) in San Francisco.*
—v. **branched, branching, branches 1** to divide into two or more directions, *(syn.)* to fork: *The river branches into two smaller rivers south of here.‖The river branches (off) south of here.* **2** phrasal v. **to branch out:** to go in new directions: *Our company branched out from making shoes to making suits as well.*

brand /brænd/ n. **1** the commercial name of a product made: *Ivory™ is a brand of soap known nationwide.* **2** a mark put on animals to identify their owner
—v. to call s.o. a name, *(syn.)* to label: *The man branded her a liar.*

bran·dish /'brændɪʃ/ v.frml. **-dished, -dishing, -dishes** to wave s.t. in the air, to threaten with a weapon: *A woman brandished a knife at a police officer.*

brand name n. a product often of excellent quality that costs more because it is heavily advertised: *Bayer Aspirin™ is a pain reliever with a brand name.* See: generic, name brand.

brand-new /'bræn'nu, 'brænd-/ adj. new and never used before: *That is a brand-new television, not secondhand.*

bran·dy /'brændi/ n. **-dies** [C;U] an alcoholic beverage made from boiled (distilled) wine or fruit juice: *She likes apricot brandy.*

brash /bræʃ/ adj. **1** pej. rude, (syn.) pushy **2** hasty, foolish: *It was very brash to run out into the street without looking.* -adv. **brashly;** -n. [U] **brashness.**

brass /bræs/ n. [U] **1** a hard bright metal made from zinc and copper **2** decorations and railings made of brass: *A worker polished the brass in the restaurant.* **3** musical horns (trumpet, French horn, etc.): *He plays in the brass section of a jazz band.* **4** top officials: *The military brass (or) brass hats (generals, admirals, etc.) arrived in Washington.* **5** too much self-confidence, (syn.) gall: *That young man has the brass to suggest that he run the company.* **6 (to get down to) brass tacks:** to talk about specific points of business: *We stopped talking about the weather and got down to the brass tacks about specific items on the contract. See:* brassy.

bras·siere /brə'zir/ n.frml. a garment that supports a woman's breasts *See:* bra.

brass knuckles n.pl. a bar of metal that fits around the fingers, used to hurt s.o.: *A criminal broke the man's jaw with brass knuckles.*

brass·y /'bræsi/ adj. **-ier, -iest 1** like brass in color **2** like the sound of brass instruments **3** (a person) loud and pushy: *New Yorkers have a stereotype as being loud and brassy, but I find them to be very friendly.*

brat /'bræt/ n.pej. a spoiled, badly behaved child: *Her children act like brats; they won't obey anyone.* -adj. **bratty.**

bra·va·do /brə'vadou/ n. [U] unnecessary bravery, (syn.) false courage: *He is full of bravado about how he will climb that tall mountain someday.*

brave /breIv/ adj. unafraid of danger, (syn.) courageous: *Firefighters are brave in saving people from burning buildings.*
—n. a native American warrior -adv. **bravely;** -n. [U] **bravery** /'breIvəri, 'breIvri/.

bra·vo /'bravou, brɑ'vou/ exclam. of approval and admiration: *After the singer performed, the audience shouted, "Bravo!"*

brawl /brɔl/ n.v. a noisy fistfight: *Two men were in a barroom <n.> brawl.* -n. **brawler.**

brawn·y /'brɔni/ adj. **-ier, -iest** having strength, strong muscles: *Two brawny men lifted the heavy furniture.* -n. [U] **brawn.**

bray /breI/ v.n. a loud sound of a donkey: *The donkey <v.> brayed and would not move.*

bra·zen /'breIzən/ adj. shocking and annoying, (syn.) cheeky: *What a brazen man! He got ahead of everyone in line for the bus.* -adv. **brazenly.**

bra·zier /'breIʒər/ n. a metal pan that holds hot coals: *He poured hot coals out of the brazier to start a fire.*

breach /britʃ/ v. **breaches 1** to do s.t. wrong, (syn.) to violate a contract: *She breached her* loan contract by not making payments. **2** to make a large hole in s.t.: *Workers breached a wall by driving a tank through it.*
—n. **-es 1** an act of not doing s.t. formally agreed on, (syn.) a violation: *He sued the company for breach of contract when it did not finish the work he had paid for.* **2** a large hole: *The pounding waves made a breach in the sea wall.* **3** an interruption or breaking off of a good relationship: *Their friendship developed a breach when she found out that he had lied to her.*

bread /brɛd/ n. [U] **1** a food made of baked flour (from grain such as wheat or rye), water or milk, and yeast: *I baked a loaf of bread.* **2** food in general, the basics: *They work hard just to put bread on the table.* **3** money and the things needed to live, (syn.) livelihood: *She earns her bread and butter.* **4** fig.slang money: *Hey, man, can you give me some bread?*
—adj. **bread and butter issue** or **matter:** basic concerns: *The workers talked about bread and butter issues, like a wage increase and vacation time.*
—v. to cover with bread crumbs, flour, etc. for cooking: *The cook breaded the fish and fried it. See:* breadwinner; butter.

bread·bas·ket /'brɛd,bæskIt/ n.fig. the region where a lot of food is produced, (syn.) the heartland: *The Middle West is the breadbasket of the USA.*

bread·board /'brɛd,bɔrd/ n. a flat piece of wood or plastic on which bread is sliced

bread·line /'brɛd,laIn/ n. a line of poor people waiting to be given food

breadth /brɛdθ/ n. **1** [C] the size of s.t. from side to side, (syn.) width **2** [C;U] fig. an area of knowledge, character, etc.: *The professor has great breadth of knowledge. See:* length.

bread·win·ner /'brɛd,wInər/ n.fig. a person who works to support others: *She is a breadwinner who supports two children.*

break /breIk/ n. **1** the act or result of breaking, (syns.) a crack, a fracture: *He has a break in his leg from an accident.* **2** a change from s.t. usual: *Going out to dinner is a nice break from cooking.* **3** a stop or interruption of s.t. constant: *The light went out because of a break in the supply of electricity.||There was a break in the hot weather yesterday.* **4** an escape from prison: *There was a break at the city jail last night; two prisoners escaped.* **5** a beginning to appear, (syn.) an emergence: *The break of day started activity at the camp as people woke up.* **6** a quick, downward move, (syn.) a sharp decline: *There was a break in the stock market (prices) today.* **7 the breaks:** bad luck: *I lost my wallet! Well, I guess that's the breaks.* **8 to get a break:** to have good or bad luck: *The factory fired 300 workers; they got a bad* break. But I got a break (or) they gave me a break; I still have my job. **9** infrml. **to give s.o. a break: a.** to stop annoying s.o.: Give me a break; stop criticizing me. **b.** a lower price, (syn.) a discount: She gave me a break on the price, $20 off. **c.** to not punish s.o.: I'll give you a break this time, but if you steal again, I'll call the police. **10 to take a break:** to relax for a short time: We worked hard all morning, then took a break.

—v. **broke** /broʊk/ , **breaking, breaks 1 a.** to turn into pieces: The dish broke when it hit the floor. **b.** to crack, (syn.) to fracture: She broke the vase, so there's a crack in it now. **2** to damage s.t. so that it doesn't work: The refrigerator broke because it was so old. **3** to fall apart, (syn.) to collapse: The dam finally broke and the waters flooded the land. **4** to push through, (syn.) to pierce: The child's tooth broke through the skin.‖These flowers are the first to break through the ground each spring. **5 a.** to stop constant activity: Bad storms break the flow of electricity to buildings.‖The cold weather broke. **b.** to pause to relax: Let's break for lunch now. **6** to disobey the law: She broke the law by stealing that money. **7** to destroy s.o.'s spirit: His biggest customer did not pay him and that broke him financially and emotionally. **8** infrml. **break a leg!** to wish s.o. good luck. **9 to break a habit:** to stop s.t.: He finally broke the habit; he stopped smoking cigarettes. **10** phrasal v. **to break away:** to escape: The child broke away from his mother's hand and ran out of the yard. **11 to break cover:** to come out of a hiding place: The hunters broke cover when ducks flew overhead. **12** phrasal v. sep. **to break s.t. or s.o. down: a.** to stop working, (syn.) to malfunction: This old car breaks down all the time. **b.** to lose control of one's feelings: When his mother died, he broke down and cried. **c.** to separate s.t. into small steps or pieces: The cookbook breaks down how to cook the meal.‖It breaks the process down. **13** phrasal v. **to break in: a.** to enter a building by force, (syn.) to burglarize: A thief broke in and stole my TV. **b.** to interrupt: She broke in on the conversation. **14** phrasal v. sep. **to break s.o. or s.t. in: a.** s.o.: to become able to do s.t.: It took me a month to get used to my new job; my boss helped by breaking in all the new employees.‖She broke us in. **b.** s.t.: to make s.t. more comfortable: I have to break in my new shoes; they hurt me.‖I have to break them in. **15** phrasal v. sep. **to break s.t. off: a.** to snap off: That tree branch broke off and fell. **b.** to stop doing s.t., (syn.) to cease: That man and woman broke off their relationship.‖They broke it off. **16** phrasal v. **to break out: a.** to develop a disease, esp. a rash: The child broke out with red spots (the measles, etc.). **b.** to escape: The prisoner broke out of jail. **17 to**

break right (or) **badly:** to have events go a certain way: If things break right for her, she will get a new job this month.‖If things break badly for her at work, she will lose her job. **18** phrasal v. insep. **to break through s.t.: a.** to force through: Firefighters broke through the door to the house. **b.** to make a scientific discovery **19** phrasal v. **to break up: a.** to laugh or cry: His girlfriend made funny faces, and he broke up (laughing). **b.** to separate: Their marriage broke up after a year. **20** phrasal v. insep. **to break with s.o.** or **s.t.:** to stop being in agreement with, conforming to: It was a very unusual wedding; the couple broke with tradition. **21 to go broke:** to lose all of one's money: He went broke without even a penny. See: broke.

break·a·ble /ˈbreɪkəbəl/ adj. fragile: Those glass lamps are breakable, so pack them carefully.

break·down /ˈbreɪkˌdaʊn/ n. **1** a stopping, ceasing to work, (syn.) a malfunction: The truck had a breakdown on the highway. **2** a collapse: She had a nervous breakdown.‖He worked so hard that he had a complete physical breakdown. **3** the separation of s.t. into parts to explain it, (syns.) an outline, a summary: I made a breakdown of this 200-page report.

break·er /ˈbreɪkər/ n. **1** a large wave that comes close to or on a beach **2** a device that stops the flow of electricity, water, etc.: An electrical circuit breaker blew out in the storm.

break even (in business) to make neither a profit nor a loss -adj. **break-even.**

break·fast /ˈbrɛkfəst/ n. [C;U] v. the morning meal: We ate bacon and eggs for <n.> breakfast.

break·in /ˈbreɪkˌɪn/ n. a forced entry into a building (house, store, etc.): During a break-in in our apartment, the TV was stolen. -v. **break in.**

break·ing point /ˈbreɪkɪŋ/ n. the time when s.o. or s.t. will change or fall apart, a crisis: Her nerves are at the breaking point.

break·neck /ˈbreɪkˌnɛk/ adj. too fast, dangerous, (syn.) risky: The car was going at breakneck speed.

break·through /ˈbreɪkˌθru/ n. **1** the act, result, or place of pushing past s.t. that blocks one's way: We finally had a breakthrough in negotiations with management. **2** an advance: The discovery of penicillin was an important breakthrough in stopping many diseases.

break·up /ˈbreɪkˌʌp/ n. **1** a coming apart, (syn.) a split: In the spring, you can hear the breakup of ice on the lake. **2** a separation, (syn.) a dissolution: That man and woman had a breakup of their relationship.

break·wa·ter /'breɪk,wɔtər, -wɑ-/ n. a wall of rocks, cement, or earth used to stop waves: *A breakwater crosses part of the harbor.*

breast /brɛst/ n. **1** one of a pair of glands on a woman's chest: *The baby drank milk from her mother's breast.* **2** the front part of the body, between the neck and the stomach: *The baby slept next to her father's breast.* **3** the front part of an animal: *She cooked a chicken breast.* **4 to make a clean breast:** to confess wrongdoing: *He made a clean breast of things by telling the police he had robbed the store.*

breast·bone /'brɛst,boʊn/ n. the flat chest bone attached to the ribs

breast-feed /'brɛst,fid/ v. **-fed** /-,fɛd/, **-feeding, -feeds** to give milk to a baby from a woman's breasts: *She breast-feeds her baby several times a day.* -n. [U] **breastfeeding.**

breast·stroke /'brɛst,stroʊk/ n. a way of swimming like a frog, pulling the arms to the side then backwards: *The breaststroke and freestyle are Olympic swimming races.*

breath /brɛθ/ n. **1** a taking in of air, (syn.) an inhalation: *She opened her mouth and took a deep breath.* **2** the air taken in or let out while breathing: *His breath smelled like coffee.* **3** a small amount: *A breath of perfume came from the flowers.||Add just a breath of mint to the ice cream.* **4 a breath of fresh air:** a new person who brings energy or a new viewpoint to a situation **5 to catch one's breath:** to try to breathe normally: *He stopped and tried to catch his breath.* **6 out of breath:** needing air: *He ran so fast that he is out of breath.* **7 to take one's breath away:** to be made unable to speak from surprise, love, etc.: *The sunset took my breath away; it was so beautiful.* **8 under one's breath:** in a whisper, (syn.) muttering: *She criticizes her boss under her breath, but not directly.*

breathe /brið/ v. **breathed, breathing, breathes 1** to take air into and out of the lungs, (syn.) to inhale and exhale: *She breathes deeply and slowly while she sleeps.* **2** to live: *"Does he breathe?" she asked, looking at the injured man.* **3** to speak softly, (syns.) to whisper, to murmur: *She breathed a few words of love into her daughter's ear.* **4** to rest, relax: *Take some time to breathe before you begin your next paper.* **5 to breathe down s.o.'s neck:** to put pressure on s.o. to do s.t. **6 to breathe easy or freely:** to stop worrying: *The doctor says that you don't have cancer, so you can breathe easy now.*
—n. **breathing room** (or) **space:** time to work or live normally: *The due date on the project has been moved to next month, so we have some breathing room to finish it.*

breath·er /'briðər/ n.slang a break: *We have worked for two hours; let's take a breather.*

breath·less /'brɛθlɪs/ adj. out of breath from running, hurrying, etc.

breath·tak·ing /'brɛθ,teɪkɪŋ/ adj. so beautiful one cannot breathe for a moment: *The view from the mountaintop was breathtaking.* -adv. **breathtakingly.**

breech·es /'brɪtʃɪz/ n.pl. or **britches** a knee-length style of pants usu. made of strong material: *She wears breeches for horseback riding.*

breed /brid/ n. a specific type of animal with characteristics passed down from generation to generation: *A French poodle is a breed of dog.*
—v. **bred** /brɛd/, **breeding, breeds 1** to have babies, (syn.) to procreate: *Animals breed in the springtime.* **2** to be the source of, (syn.) to engender: *Familiarity breeds contempt (a lack of respect).* **3** to raise animals for fun or profit: *That woman breeds dogs professionally.* -n. **breeder.**

breed·ing /'bridɪŋ/ n. [U] good social conduct, manners: *She is so polite; she has such good breeding.*

breeding ground n. **1** a place where animals raise their young: *That park is a breeding ground for birds.* **2** fig. a place where ideas are born and behavior is formed: *Universities are breeding grounds for new theories.||Caring communities are breeding grounds for good citizenship.*

breeze /briz/ n. **1** a light wind: *The breeze felt good on a hot day.* **2** fig. an easy task: *That exam was a breeze.*
—v. **breezed, breezing, breezes** fig.to move quickly and easily: *She breezed by me without saying a word.*

breez·y /'brizi/ adj. **-ier, -iest 1** windy, (syn.) gusty: *breezy weather* **2** fig.(said of people) light: *He has a breezy manner; nothing bothers him.* -adv. **breezily;** -n. [U] **breeziness.**

breth·ren /'brɛðrən/ n.frml. people who belong to the same group, including women and children: *The brethren gathered in the church.*

brev·i·ty /'brɛvəti/ n. [U] shortness, esp. of speech or writing: *She says what she wants to with brevity. See:* brief.

brew /bru/ v. **1** to make a beverage by boiling, mixing, or soaking solids, such as tea leaves or coffee beans: *I brewed a pot of coffee in the coffeemaker.* **2** to make beer **3** fig. to plan s.t. bad: *The crowd began to get loud and angry; trouble was brewing.*
—n. **1** a mixture, esp. a heated one **2** fig. a bad combination: *a witch's brew* **3** slang a beer: *Let's go to the bar and have a few brews.* -n. **brewer.**

brew·er·y /'bruəri/ n. **-ies** a place where beer is made (brewed): *That brewery brews light beer.*

bri·ar or **brier** /'braɪər/ n. [C;U] **1** a plant with needles **2** a wood from the root of the briar: *Fine pipes for smoking tobacco are made from briar.*

bribe /braɪb/ n. money or actions given illegally for s.t.: *She gave the official a bribe so she could get a driver's license in another state.*
—v. **bribed, bribing, bribes** to give or take (money, goods, etc.), to have s.o. act dishonestly or illegally: *She bribed the official. -n.* [U] **bribery.**

bric-a-brac /'brɪkə,bræk/ n. used with a sing. or pl.v. small decorative items: *The bric-a-brac on her table includes little vases and china animals.*

brick /brɪk/ n. [C;U] **1** a block of hard clay used as building material: *Apartment buildings are made of thousands of bricks.* **2** s.t. shaped like a brick: *a brick of cheese* **3 a ton of bricks:** with a lot of force or anger: *That old tree fell on my car and crushed it like a ton of bricks.* **4 to run into** or **beat one's head against a brick wall:** to be stopped: *She ran into a brick wall when officials would not give her permission to leave the country.*
—phrasal v. sep. **to brick s.t. up:** to fill in, block up with bricks: *Workers bricked up the windows in that old house.*

brick·lay·er /'brɪk,leɪər/ n. a worker who puts down bricks: *Bricklayers build walls. -n.* [U] **bricklaying.**

brid·al /'braɪdl/ adj. of a bride or wedding: *She wore a pretty bridal gown.*

bride /braɪd/ n. a woman who is getting married, a female marriage partner: *She became a bride at age 24.*

bride·groom /'braɪd,grum/ or
groom n. a man who is getting married: *The bridegroom waited for his bride in the church.*

brides·maid /'braɪdz,meɪd/ n. the bride's unmarried attendant: *There were six bridesmaids at the wedding. See:* best man; maid of honor.

bridge (1) /brɪdʒ/ n. **1** a structure that crosses rivers, roads, etc., (syn.) a span: *Trains go across a bridge over the river.* **2** fig. a connection between people and/or ideas: *Public officials built a bridge of understanding between the rich and the poor.* **3** the round top of the nose between the eyes **4** a partial denture, false tooth **5** the part of a ship where the officers stand to give orders **6 to burn one's bridges:** to destroy relationships, make enemies: *The manager left her old company without making anyone angry there, so as not to burn her bridges.*
—v. **bridged, bridging, bridges 1** to build a bridge: *Workers bridged the river with a new span.* **2 to bridge the gap:** to fill in a missing part: *My parents loaned me money to bridge the gap between my new and my old job. See:* to cross that bridge.

bridge (2) n. a card game played with two teams of two players

bri·dle /'braɪdl/ n. leather straps on a horse's head to control it
—v. **-dled, -dling, -dles 1** to put a bridle on a horse **2** fig. to refuse to cooperate, (syn.) to balk: *She bridled at the idea of spending so much money. See:* unbridled.

brief /brif/ adj. **1** short, to the point: *The manager made a brief statement to open the meeting.* **2 in brief:** in summary
—v. to inform: *The generals briefed the President on the military situation. -n.* **briefing.**
—n. a legal document: *Our lawyer filed a brief with the court. -adv.* **briefly.** See: debrief.

brief·case /'brif,keɪs/ n. a soft, flat piece of luggage for holding books and papers: *She put her laptop computer and papers in her briefcase.*

briefs /brifs/ n.pl. short, tight-fitting underwear used by both men and women *See:* boxer shorts; panties.

brig /brɪg/ n. a military prison: *The navy sailor was put in the brig for stealing.*

bri·gade /brɪ,geɪd/ n. **1** a group of soldiers, smaller than a division and larger than a regiment **2** a group organized for a purpose: *a fire brigade, a workers' brigade*

bright /braɪt/ adj. **1** having a strong shine or glow: *The sun is so bright that it hurts my eyes.* **2** having strong colors, (syns.) vivid, radiant: *She wears bright red dresses.* **3** intelligent: *He has a bright mind.* **4** promising: *With an accounting degree, she has a bright future.* **5 the bright side:** the positive part of a situation *-adv.* **brightly;** *-n.* [U] **brightness.**

bright·en /'braɪtn/ v. **1** to become lighter (or) clearer: *The clouds left and the sky brightened.* **2** to become cheerful, happy: *His face brightened with a smile.*

bright-eyed /'braɪt,aɪd/ adj.fig. **1** quick and eager: *He is a bright-eyed child.* **2 bright-eyed and bushy-tailed:** quick of mind and eager to work: *Companies like workers who are bright-eyed and bushy-tailed.*

bril·liant /'brɪlyənt/ adj. **1** having a very bright surface, (syn.) sparkling: *Diamonds are brilliant.* **2** extremely intelligent: *She has a brilliant mind.* **3** perfect: *The violinist gave a brilliant performance.* **4** extremely successful, (syns.) magnificent, illustrious: *She has a brilliant future as a musician. -n.* [U] **brilliance;** *-adv.* **brilliantly.**

brim /brɪm/ n. **1** the top of a glass, pot, jar, etc.: *She filled the glass full to the brim.* **2** the bottom outer edge of a hat: *His hat has a wide brim.*

—*v.* **brimmed, brimming, brims** **1** to be full to the top: *The baskets were brimming with wheat and potatoes.* **2** *phrasal v.* **to brim over:** to be full of happiness, excitement, etc.: *He's brimming over with stories about his recent trip.* -*adj.* **brimful.**

brine /braɪn/ *n.* [U] **1** a mixture of salt, water: *Pickles are soaked in brine.* **2** the ocean: *He fell off the ship, into the brine.* -*adj.* **briny.**

bring /brɪŋ/ *v.* **brought** /brɔt/, **bringing, brings** **1** to carry s.t.: *I bring an umbrella with me in case it rains.* **2** to go with s.o., (*syn.*) to escort: *She brought a friend to the party.* **3** to cause to happen, (*syn.*) to initiate: *He brought the conversation to a close (the water to a boil, grief to his parents).* **4** to sell for: *That house will bring $100,000.* **5** *phrasal v. sep.* **to bring s.t. about:** to make happen, (*syn.*) to achieve: *She brought about a major change in the way her company designs its products.*‖*She brought it about.* **6** *phrasal v. sep.* **to bring s.o. around** or **over:** to influence s.o.'s actions or opinions, (*syn.*) to persuade: *I'm sure we can bring the committee members around to our point of view.*‖*We can bring them around.* **7** *phrasal v. sep.* **to bring s.o.** or **s.t. back: a. s.t.:** to return s.t. to a store: *She brought back the broken clock to the store.*‖ *She brought it back.* **b. s.t.:** to remember: *An old photograph brought back pleasant memories.* **c. s.o.** or **s.t.:** to make s.o. or s.t. as it was, (*syn.*) to restore: *A doctor brought back the old man from his illness.*‖*She brought him back.* **8 to bring charges against:** to accuse s.o. of wrongdoing: *The police brought charges of theft against the criminal.* **9** *phrasal v. sep.* **to bring s.o.** or **s.t. down: a. s.o.:** to ruin s.o.'s career, reputation, etc.: *The scandal brought down the President.*‖*It brought him down.* **b. s.o.:** to depress, sadden: *The death of her cat brought down my roommate.*‖*It brought her down.* **c. s.t.:** to bring great applause from an audience: *The singer's wonderful performance brought down the house.*‖*She brought it down.* **d. s.t.:** to kill, destroy: *The hunter's shot brought down the deer.*‖*He brought it down.* **10** *phrasal v. sep.* **to bring s.t. forth:** *frml.* to cause to happen, (*syn.*) to elicit: *The violinist's brilliant performance brought forth loud applause.*‖*It brought it forth.* **11** *phrasal v. sep.* **to bring s.t. forward:** to propose, suggest: *She brought forward the idea to hire temporary workers.*‖*She brought it forward.* **12** *phrasal v. sep.* **to bring s.o.** or **s.t. in: a. s.o.:** to arrest: *The FBI agents brought in three suspects.*‖*They brought them in.* **b. s.t.:** to earn money: *Her job brings in $800 a week.*‖*It brings it in.* **c. s.t.:** to give a decision in a court of law: *The jury brought in a verdict of guilty.*‖*They brought it in.* **13** *phrasal v. insep.* **to bring s.t. into s.t.:** to cause to happen: *Her*

hard work brought a new company into being. **14** *phrasal v. sep.* **to bring s.t. off:** to succeed: *He failed twice; then he finally brought off the deal.*‖*He brought it off.* **15** *phrasal v. insep.* **to bring s.t. on** or **upon s.o.:** to cause s.t., usu. negative, to happen: *After smoking cigarettes for 40 years, he brought lung cancer on himself.* **16** *phrasal v. sep.* **to bring s.t. on:** to cause to happen: *The winter brings on cold weather.*‖*It brings it on.* **17** *phrasal v. sep.* **to bring s.t. out: a.** to take outside: *I brought out the trash.*‖*I brought it out.* **b.** to improve, (*syn.*) to enhance: *Adding salt brings out the flavor in some foods.*‖*It brings it out.* **c.** to show a hidden quality, (*syn.*) to reveal: *She was a good student in high school, but going to college brought out the best in her.* **18** *phrasal v. insep.* **to bring s.o. through s.t.:** to survive s.t.: *His faith in God brought him through his problems.* **19** *phrasal v. sep.* **to bring s.o. to** or **around:** to regain consciousness: *He fell down unconscious and a nurse brought him to.* **20** *phrasal v. sep.* **to bring s.o.** or **s.t. up: a. s.o.:** to raise s.o.: *Her aunt brought up my neighbor.*‖*She brought her up.* **b. s.t.:** to introduce a topic to discuss: *He brought up the question of his raise with his boss.*‖*He brought it up.* **21** *phrasal v. sep.* **to bring s.o.** or **s.t. up short:** to cause to stop quickly: *Hearing my name called when I was on vacation in Madrid brought me up short.*

brink /brɪŋk/ *n.* **1** the top edge of a steep incline, such as a cliff: *She looked over the brink at the water below.* **2** **on the brink of disaster:** a point after which s.t. terrible may happen: *The economy is in such bad shape that it is on the brink of disaster.*

brink·man·ship /ˈbrɪŋkmənˌʃɪp/ *n.* the art of threatening one's opponent to gain an advantage: *The Cold War was full of Russian and American brinkmanship about using nuclear weapons.*

brisk /brɪsk/ *adj.* **1** rapid and energetic: *We took a brisk walk around the block.* **2** sharp and cool, (*syn.*) invigorating: *A brisk wind blew through our hair.* -*n.* [U] **briskness;** -*adv.* **briskly.**

bris·ket /ˈbrɪskɪt/ *n.* meat cut from the chest of an animal: *brisket of beef*

bris·tle /ˈbrɪsəl/ *n.* [C;U] short, stiff hair: *Some brushes are made from pigs' bristles.*

—*v.* **-tled, -tling, -tles** (of hair) to stand up from anger: *The dog bristled at the sight of the cat.*

britch·es /ˈbrɪtʃɪz/ *n.infrml.* **1** pants made of strong material, (*syn.*) breeches **2 too big for one's britches:** acting too important, (*syn.*) arrogant: *That young man is too big for his britches; he thinks he's smarter than he is in business.*

British thermal unit *n. abbr.* BTU a unit of measurement for heat: *The ability of air conditioners to cool is measured in BTUs.*

brit·tle /'brɪtl/ *adj.* hard and easy to break, (*syn.*) fragile: *The bones of elderly people become brittle and easily broken.* *-n.* [U] **brittleness.**

broach /broʊʧ/ *v.* **broaches** to introduce a topic of conversation: *My manager broached the subject of when I planned to retire.* *See:* brooch.

broad /brɔd/ *adj.* **1** big from side to side; wide: *The avenues of big cities are often broad.* **2** covering a large amount, many topics, etc., (*syn.*) large in scope: *That professor has a broad knowledge of history.*
—*n.pej.slang* a woman *-adv.* **broadly.**

broad·cast /'brɔd,kæst/ *v.* **-cast** or **-casted, -casting, -casts** **1** to send over the air (radio, TV): *Some radio and TV stations broadcast programs 24 hours a day.* **2** to make widely known: *She broadcasted her marriage plans to all her friends.*
—*n.* an act of broadcasting, (*syn.*) a transmission: *I heard the good news on the TV broadcast.* *-n.* **broadcaster.**

broad·en /'brɔdn/ *v.* to make s.t. wider or larger: *Workers broadened the road.||She broadened her knowledge of accounting by taking more courses.* *See:* narrow.

broad-mind·ed /'brɔd,maɪndɪd/ *adj.* open to different ideas, (*syn.*) tolerant: *She is broad-minded and accepts the customs, traditions, habits, etc. of all the people she meets.* *-n.* [U] **broad-mindedness.** *See:* narrow-minded.

broad·side /'brɔd,saɪd/ *adv.* from (or) against the side: *The car hit the bus broadside*
—*n.* an angry verbal or written attack: *He jumped up and began a broadside against the government.*

broc·co·li /'brɑkəli/ *n.* [U] a vegetable with thick green flowers and stems: *He eats boiled broccoli with cheese on it.*

bro·chure /broʊ'ʃʊr/ *n.* a small, short, printed booklet describing a company's products or services: *The travel*
broccoli
agency mails out brochures about trips to wonderful places.

brogue /broʊg/ *n.* **1** an accent, esp. Irish: *The man from Dublin speaks with a brogue.* **2** a thick, low shoe

broil /brɔɪl/ *v.* to cook (meat, fish) with direct heat, (*syn.*) to grill in an oven: *She broiled a steak over a charcoal fire.*

broil·er /'brɔɪlər/ *n.* **1** the part of an oven that has a direct source or heat: *He put the steak under the broiler.* **2** a medium-sized chicken: *We cooked a broiler for dinner.* **3** *fig.* a very* hot day

broke /broʊk/ *past tense of* break
—*adj.infrml.* **1** without money: *I am broke(or) stone cold broke.||That company went broke last month.* **2 to go for broke:** to risk all to accomplish s.t., try very hard: *She started a new business and she went for broke by investing all of her money in it.* *See:* broken.

bro·ken /'broʊkən/ *adj.* **1** s.t. that is cracked, smashed, or is not working: *The coffeepot has broken into pieces.||His arm is broken.* **2** not kept, (*syn.*) violated: *He reminded her of her broken promise.* **3** extremely sad, crushed in spirit: *She has a broken heart.* **4** (of a language) imperfect: *When I lived in Costa Rica, my Spanish was not good; I spoke broken Spanish.*

bro·ken-down *adj.* not working, (*syn.*) in disrepair: *My car is a broken-down mess; the wheel fell off.*

bro·ken-heart·ed /'broʊkən'hɑrtɪd/ *adj.* extremely sad, (*syn.*) crushed: *He was broken-hearted when his wife died.* *-adv.* **brokenheartedly.**

brok·er /'broʊkər/ *n.v.* a person who matches buyers and sellers, (*syn.*) an agent: *She works as a real estate broker (a stockbroker, cattle broker, etc.).*

bro·ker·age /'broʊkərɪʤ/ *n.* the business of a broker: *He runs a coffee brokerage in the city.*

bro·mide /'broʊ,maɪd/ *n.* a boring saying that is used too often, (*syn.*) a platitude: *"Have a nice day" is a bromide.*

bron·chi·tis /brɑŋ'kaɪtɪs, brɑn-/ *n.* a disease of the bronchial tubes that go from the windpipe to the lungs

bron·co /'brɑŋkoʊ/ *n.* **-cos** a wild horse of the USA's western region *See:* mustang.

bronze /brɑnz/ *n.* [U] a gray to reddish-brown metal made of tin and copper: *a bronze statue*
—*v.* **bronzed, bronzing, bronzes** **1** to make or cover with bronze **2** *frml.fig.* to suntan: *She was bronzed by the sun.*

brooch /broʊʧ, bruʧ/ *n.* **-es** a pin that is worn near the neck

brood /brud/ *n.* **1** a group of young, esp. of birds: *There is a brood of chickens in the barn.* **2** *fig.* children: *A husband and wife took their brood to the circus.*
—*v.* **1** to sit on eggs (a hen) **2** to think deeply and worry: *He brooded over whether or not to quit his job.*

brook /brʊk/ *n.* a small stream: *A brook runs in front of their house in the country.*
—*v.frml.* to agree to, (*syn.*) to tolerate: *She would brook no delay in the repairs to her car.*

broom /brum/ *n.* a cleaning tool made of long, stiff bristles attached to a handle: *He used a broom to sweep the floor.*

broth /brɔθ/ *n.* [C;U] a clear soup made from vegetables, fish, or meat: *On a cold day, he likes to eat a bowl of beef broth for lunch.*

broth·el /'brɑθəl, -ðəl/ *n.* a place where sex is bought, (*syns.*) a bordello, a house of prostitution: *In some countries, brothels are legal.*

broth·er /'brʌðər/ *n.* **1** the male of two or more children of the same parents: *My brother, Richard, lives in New York.* **2** a male member of a religious order but not a priest, (*syn.*) a monk: *Most of the brothers are working in the fields.* **4** *slang* (in USA) a close male friend -*n.* [U] **brotherliness;** -*adj.* **brotherly.**

broth·er·hood /'brʌðər,hʊd/ *n.* **1** [U] the state of being a brother **2** [C;U] a group with a common interest: *the brotherhood of street cleaners*

broth·er-in-law /'brʌðərɪn,lɔ/ *n.* **brothers-in-law** a brother of one's husband or wife or the husband of one's sister: *My brother-in-law Ken married my sister Maria in 1996.*

brow /braʊ/ *n.* the front upper area of the head between the eyes and hairline, (*syn.*) the forehead: *He has wrinkles in his brow from worry.*

brow·beat /'braʊ,bit/ *v.* **-beat, -beating, -beats** to demand s.t. from s.o. again and again, (*syn.*) to nag: *The husband browbeats his wife about not working late every night.*

brown /braʊn/ *n.* [C;U] the color that is a mixture of red, yellow, and black: *Chocolate and dirt are both brown.*
—*v.* make s.t. look brown: *He browned the potatoes in a pan.*

brown·bag /'braʊn,bæg/ *v.* **-bagged, -bagging, -bags** to bring one's lunch to work (in a paper bag): *That man is a millionaire, but he still brownbags his lunch every day.* -*n.* **brown bagger.**

brown·ie /'braʊni/ *n.* **1** a small, flat piece of chocolate cake: *American children love brownies and cookies with milk.* **2 Brownies** an organization for young girls, ages 6-10, which they join before the Girl Scouts

Brownie points *n.pl.infrml.* approval of s.o. in authority (boss, teacher, etc.) by doing something to please him or her: *He finished the report early to get some Brownie points with his boss.*

brown·stone /'braʊn,stoʊn/ *n.* **1** a reddish-brown rock used in building **2** a house made of that rock: *New York City has many brownstones.*

browse /braʊz/ *v.* **browsed, browsing, browses 1** to look over in a slow, relaxed way: *She browsed through some books in the library.* **2** to feed on (grass, leaves, etc.), (*syn.*) to graze

bruise /bruz/ *n.* **1** a discoloration of the skin made by a blow that does not break the surface of the skin, (*syn.*) a contusion: *He fell on the*

sidewalk and got a bruise on his arm. **2** a similar mark on plants, fruit, etc.: *This banana has a bruise on it.*
—*v.* **bruised, bruising, bruises 1** to make bruises: *He bruised his knee.* **2** *fig.* to hurt s.o.'s feelings: *Her boss yelled at her and bruised her feelings.*

bruis·er /'bruzər/ *n.slang* a strong man: *Some football players are bruisers.*

brunch /brʌntʃ/ *n.* [C;U] **brunches** (*a combination of* breakfast *and* lunch) a meal in the late morning: *We had brunch on Sunday morning at 11:00 a.m.*

bru·net(te) /bru'nɛt/ *n.* a person with dark hair *See:* blonde, redhead.

brunt /brʌnt/ *n.* the main part of s.t., usu. unpleasant: *The sales manager took the brunt of the criticism for low sales.*

brush /brʌʃ/ *n.* **brushes 1** a tool made of bristles (of nylon, wire, hair, etc.) on a hard back: *Brushes can be used to clean, polish, smooth, or paint.* **2** a light touch in passing
—*v.* **brushed, brushing, brushes 1** to use a brush: *She brushed her teeth with a toothbrush.* **2** to touch or bump s.o. lightly while passing: *Her coat brushed me as she ran past.* **3** *phrasal v. sep.* **to brush s.o.** or **s.t. away** or **aside:** to ignore, esp. problems: *She brushed aside our concerns.||She brushed them aside.* **4** *phrasal v. sep.* **to brush s.o. off:** to reject: *He brushed off his boss at the company picnic.||He brushed her off.* **5** *phrasal v. sep.* **to brush s.t. up (on):** to improve one's knowledge of s.t., review: *He needs to brush up on his math before taking the exam.||He needs to brush it up.*

brush-off *n.* a refusal without an explanation, (*syn.*) an abrupt rejection: *She gave him the brush-off.*

brusque or **brusk** /brʌsk/ *adj.* rude, (*syn.*) abrupt: *She has a brusque manner with everyone she works with.*

Brus·sels sprouts /'brʌsəlz/ *n.pl.* small green vegetables similar to cabbage

bru·tal /'brutl/ *adj.* **1** violent without feeling, cruel: *It was a brutal murder.* **2** difficult to bear, (*syn.*) harsh: *Last winter was so cold that it was brutal.* -*n.* [U] **brutality** /bru'tæləti/; -*v.* **brutalize** /'brutl,aɪz/; -*adv.* **brutally.**

brute /brut/ *n.* **1** a large animal, (*syn.*) a beast **2** a violent person who does not care about hurting others: *That brute knocked down an old lady.*
—*adj.* involving strength, not intelligence: *He used brute force to knock down the door.* -*adj.* **brutish;** -*adv.* **brutishly.**

B.S. /'bi'ɛs/ *abbr. for* a Bachelor of Science degree, a type of four-year college degree: *She graduated with a B.S. in physics.*

BTU /'biti'yu/ *abbr. of* British thermal unit

bub·ble /'bʌbəl/ *n.* a small ball of gas, esp. air, covered with a liquid: *Bubbles in soft drinks don't last long.*
—*v.* **-bled, -bling, -bles 1** to make bubbles: *Boiling water bubbles.* **2 to blow bubbles:** to make bubbles for fun: *Children blow bubbles with soapy water.* **3** *phrasal v.* **to bubble over:** to be cheerful or enthusiastic: *She bubbles over with enthusiasm. See:* bubbly.

bubble gum *n.* [U] a chewing gum that can make bubbles: *People blow bubbles with bubble gum.*

bub·ble·head /'bʌbəl,hɛd/ *n.slang* stupid person

bub·bly /'bʌbli/ *adj.* **-blier, -bliest 1** having bubbles: *Soda pop, beer, and champagne are all bubbly.* **2** *fig.* cheerful, (*syn.*) enthusiastic: *She has a bubbly personality.*
—*n.infrml.fig.* champagne: *Can I pour you some bubbly?*

buck (1) /bʌk/ *n.* the adult male of some animals, esp. a deer: *A hunter shot a buck. See:* doe.
—*v.* **1** to jump forward and up violently: *A wild horse bucked and threw its rider off its back.* **2** to disagree, resist doing s.t.: *She bucks making changes in her way of doing things.* **3** to work very hard: *She is bucking for a salary raise.*

buck (2) 1 *infrml.fig.* a US dollar: *I need ten bucks to go to the movie tonight.* **2** *infrml.* **to pass the buck:** to avoid responsibility or put blame on s.t. else: *Any time he makes a mistake, he passes the buck.*

buck·et /'bʌkɪt/ *n.* **1** a round container with an open top, (*syn.*) a pail: *He filled a bucket with water.* **2 in buckets:** a lot (of rain) **3** *infrml.* **to kick the bucket:** to die

buck·le /'bʌkəl/ *n.* a metal fastener, esp. for a belt
—*v.* **-led, -ling, -les 1** to close a buckle: *I buckled the seat belt in the car.* **2** to bend, (*syns.*) to give way, yield: *A wooden beam in the tunnel buckled, then fell.*‖*The thief finally buckled under pressure from the police and told them where to find the stolen car.* **3** *phrasal v. infrml.* **to buckle down:** to start to work hard: *As the deadline got closer, we really buckled down on the project. See:* unbuckle.

buck·toothed /'bʌk,tuθt/ *adj.* having teeth that stick out over the lower lip

bud /bʌd/ *n.* [C;U] **1** a young, not fully grown leaf or flower **2** *infrml.short for* buddy
—*v.* **budded, budding, buds** to grow buds: *Trees and flowers bud in the springtime.*

bud·dy /'bʌdi/ *n.* **-dies** a friend, (*syn.*) a pal: *My buddies and I go fishing every Saturday.*

budge /bʌʤ/ *v.* **budged, budging, budges** to move a little, give way: *This door is stuck; it won't budge.*

budg·et /'bʌʤɪt/ *n.* **1** a plan of expected income and expenses over time (one year, five years, etc.): *Our company does a budget every year.* **2** an amount of money set aside for a purpose: *We try not to spend more than is in our food budget.*
—*v.* to make financial predictions: *We budget how much money we expect to make and to spend.* -*adj.* **budgetary.**

buff /bʌf/ *v.* to rub s.t. to make it shiny, (*syn.*) to polish: *I buffed my shoes with a cloth.*
—*n.* **1** s.o. who enjoys and knows a lot about a subject: *Ask her anything about movies; she's a big film buff.* **2** a shine: *I gave my shoes a buff.* **3** a soft, thick, pale-yellow leather made from the skin of buffalo, oxen, or elk **4** *infrml.* **in the buff:** without any clothes, (*syn.*) nude: *She likes to sunbathe in the buff.*
—*adj.* a brownish-yellow color: *He wore a buff jacket.*

buf·fa·lo /'bʌfəloʊ/ *n.* **-los, -loes** or **-lo 1** a large, four-legged, hoofed animal: *In Asia, farmers use water buffalos to pull plows.* **2** the North American bison

buffalo

—*v. fig.infrml.* to confuse or frighten, (*syn.*) to intimidate: *He was buffaloed by the problem for weeks.*

buff·er /'bʌfər/ *n.v.* **1** s.o. or s.t. (a layer, an area, etc.) that softens or stops a blow, (*syn.*) a cushion: *The mountains are a <n.> buffer against the storms from the sea.* **2** a tool used to shine: *a fingernail <n.> buffer*
—*adj.* **buffered:** a chemical that stops (neutralizes) the effect of an acid or a base: *Buffered aspirin is supposed to avoid damage to the stomach.*

buf·fet (1) /bə'feɪ, bʊ-/ *adj.n.* **1** food put on a table for people to serve themselves: *We had a <adj.> buffet lunch.* **2** a table for this purpose, (*syn.*) a sideboard: *Please put the dessert on the <n.> buffet.*

buf·fet (2) /'bʌfɪt/ *v.* to strike with force repeatedly: *The seacoast was buffeted by high winds and rain from the storm.*

buf·foon /bə'fun/ *n.* a loud and foolish person

bug /bʌg/ *n.* **1** an insect: *There are bugs in that dirty kitchen.* **2** *infrml.fig.* a tiny organism that causes diseases, (*syn.*) a germ: *I'm sick; I've caught a flu bug.* **3** *fig.* a hidden listening device: *The spy hid a bug in the lamp.* **4** *fig.* a fault in an electrical or mechanical device or system: *My computer program has a bug in it; every time I type the letter n, it goes to the bottom of the page.* **5** *infrml.fig.* an interest, fad: *the travel bug*
—*v.* **bugged, bugging, bugs 1** *infrml.* to annoy: *His boss keeps bugging him to work*

faster. **2** *fig.* to use a listening device, *(syn.)* to eavesdrop: *Police bugged the criminal's telephone.* **3** *phrasal v.* **to bug off:** to leave, go away: *Bug off! You annoy me!* **4** *phrasal v.* **to bug out:** to leave quickly: *As the police arrived, the thief bugged out.* **5** *infrml.* **a bug in s.o.'s ear:** a suggestion

bug·gy /ˈbʌgi/ *n.* **-gies** a horse-drawn carriage —*adj.* **-ier, -iest 1** full of insects: *The garden at sunset is buggy.* **2** *fig.* very worried, crazy: *She is driving herself buggy about preparing for the exam.*

bu·gle /ˈbyugəl/ *n.v.* **-gled, -gling, -gles** type of musical horn without keys: *A soldier plays a <n.> bugle at military funerals. -n.* [C] **bugler;** [U] **bugling.**

build /bɪld/ *v.* **built** /bɪlt/ , **building, builds 1** to make s.t. from parts, materials, etc., *(syns.)* to construct, to erect: *Workers built a house (car, airplane, etc.).* **2** to base on, *(syn.)* to establish: *Theories should be built on facts.* **3** to create: *He built an industrial empire.* **4** *phrasal v. sep.* **to build s.t. up: a.** to add to over time: *She built up a successful business.||She built it up.* **b.** to improve an image or reputation through advertising or publicity: *The local newspapers really built up the state fair this year.||They built it up.* **c.** to add buildings: *Developers have built up this area in recent years.||They've built it up.* —*n.* the shape of a person's body, *(syn.)* a physique: *He has a strong (fat, short, weak, etc.) build. See:* body building.

build·er /ˈbɪldər/ *n.* a company or person who builds (buildings, houses, organizations): *He is a big builder of houses in this area. See:* contractor; developer.

build·ing /ˈbɪldɪŋ/ *n.* **1** [C] a permanent structure, such as a house or office building: *She owns some office buildings in this area.* **2** [U] the business of making buildings **3** [U] growth: *The building of a country (business, career) can take many years.*

build·up or **build-up** /ˈbɪld,ʌp/ *n.* **1** growth, *(syn.)* an increase: *There was a heavy buildup of dust in our house when we came back from vacation.* **2** improving an image or reputation through advertising, *(syn.)* a publicity campaign: *The British rock stars got a big build-up before their tour.*

built-in *adj.* constructed into or onto a wall, not movable

built-up *adj.* crowded with buildings: *We live in a built-up part of the city.*

bulb /bʌlb/ *n.* **1** the round root of some plants: *a tulip bulb* **2** the glass in an electric light, of this shape: *The bulb in that lamp has burned out. -adj.* **bulbous.**

bulge /bʌldʒ/ *n.v.* **bulged, bulging, bulges** to swell or stick out, *(syn.)* to protrude: *Her stomach <v.> bulged because she was pregnant.*

bulk /bʌlk/ *n.* [U] **1** large size: *Big animals, such as elephants and whales, have huge bulk.* **2** the most of s.t., *(syn.)* the majority: *The bulk of the students passed the exam.* —*adj.* **a bulk shipment:** a large quantity: *The bulk shipment was 500 boxes of shoes.*

bulk·y /ˈbʌlki/ *adj.* **-ier, -iest** large and difficult to handle, *(syn.)* unwieldy: *A mattress is bulky for one person to carry.*

bull /bʊl/ *n.* **1** the male of cattle that can produce young: *A bull is feeding in a field.* **2** the male of some other animal types: *a bull elephant* **3** *vulg.slang* nonsense: *What he says is a lot of bull.* **4** a person who believes that the stock market will go up, *(syn.)* an optimist **5** **like a bull in a china shop:** a careless person in a delicate situation, *(syns.)* clumsy, tactless: *He makes big mistakes; he's like a bull in a china shop.* **6** **to take the bull by the horns:** to face a difficult or dangerous situation boldly: *She took the bull by the horns and told her family that she had lost her job.*

bull·dog /ˈbʊl,dɔg, -dɑg/ *n.v.* a dog with big jaws and short legs: *<n.> Bulldogs don't let go easily when they bite.*

bull·doz·er /ˈbʊl,douzər/ *n.* a large, powerful machine with a shovel and a blade in front: *Bulldozers move earth for the building of roads, buildings, etc. -v.* **bulldoze.**

bul·let /ˈbʊlɪt/ *n.* **1** a round, usu. pointed piece of metal (lead or steel) shot out of a gun: *A bullet hit the man in the leg.* **2** the metal casing used to hold the bullet, *(syn.)* the cartridge: *That pistol holds nine bullets. See:* bite the bullet.

bul·le·tin /ˈbʊlətn/ *n.* **1** a short public announcement (on television, radio, etc.): *A TV news bulletin said there is a big earthquake in California.* **2** a small periodical publication, *(syn.)* a newsletter: *The college bulletin lists all of the classes offered this semester.*

bulletin board *n.* a board on a wall where notices, information, etc., are displayed: *I saw our class schedule on the school bulletin board.*

bul·let·proof /ˈbʊlɪt,pruf/ *adj.* capable of stopping bullets: *The police wear bulletproof vests.*

bullet train *n.* a very fast passenger train: *Bullet trains run in Japan and France.*

bull·fight /ˈbʊl,faɪt/ *n.* a fight between a bull and a man (matador) as sport in an arena: *In a bullfight, the matador tries to kill the bull with a sword. -n.* [C] **bullfighter,** [U] **bullfighting.** *See:* bullring.

bull·frog /ˈbʊl,frɔg, -,frɑg/ *n.* a large male frog

bull·head·ed /'bʊl,hɛdɪd/ *adj.* determined to have one's way, (*syn.*) stubborn: *He won't co-operate; he's bullheaded.*

bul·lion /'bʊlyən/ *n.* [C;U] bars of precious metals (gold, silver, platinum): *The bank keeps bullion locked in its cellars. See:* ingot.

bull·ish /'bʊlɪʃ/ *adj.fig.* believing s.t. will succeed, (*syn.*) optimistic: *She is bullish on the stock market now. See:* bull; bear.

bull·ring /'bʊl,rɪŋ/ *n.* a flat area surrounded by rows of seats, (*syn.*) an arena: *A bullring is a dangerous place.*

bull's-eye /'bʊlz,aɪ/ *n.* **1** the center of a circular target: *People shot arrows at the bull's-eye.* **2 to hit the bull's-eye:** to produce an excellent idea, point, or job: *Her solution to the problem hit the bull's-eye.*

bul·ly /'bʊli/ *n.* **-lies** a person who forces others to do things by using fear or strength: *That big boy is a bully in the schoolyard.*
—*v.* **-lied, -lying, -lies** to force others to do things: *He bullies smaller boys into giving him money and food.*

bul·wark /'bʊlwərk/ *n.* **1** a wall or high pile of earth, etc. used for defense, (*syn.*) rampart **2** *fig.* s.t. that protects: *The law is a bulwark for a person's freedoms.*

bum /bʌm/ *n.* **1** *pej.* a person who asks for money, food, etc., (*syns.*) beggar, homeless person **2** *pej.* a bad person: *He drinks and does not take care of his family; he's a bum.* **3** *vulg.* the buttocks
—*adj.* **1** *infrml.* bad, no good: *Those cheap shoes are of bum quality.* **2** *infrml.* **a bum rap:** an unfair accusation: *She was accused of stealing, but got a bum rap because she didn't do it.* **3** *infrml.* **bummed out:** disappointed: *She was bummed out when I said, "I don't have any cigarettes."*
—*v.* **bummed, bumming, bums 1** to ask for s.t. without repaying it: *Can I bum a cigarette from you?* **2** *phrasal v.* **to bum around:** to wander from place to place: *He bummed around the country for the summer. See:* bummer.

bum·ble /'bʌmbəl/ *v.* **-bled, -bling, -bles** to do s.t. in a stupid, clumsy way, (*syn.*) to blunder -*n.* [C] **bumbler,** [U] **bumbling.**

bum·ble·bee /'bʌmbəl,bi/ *n.* a large, flying insect that makes honey: *Bumblebees fly from flower to flower.*

bum·mer /'bʌmər/ *n. slang* a bad or disappointing experience: *She complains so much that talking with her is a bummer.*

bump /bʌmp/ *n.* **1** a rounded piece of s.t. (earth, skin, etc.): *There is a bump on my arm where a mosquito bit me.* **2** the feeling of a bump, (*syn.*) a jolt: *Bumps in the road make driving uncomfortable.*
—*v.* **1** *phrasal v.* **to hit with force:** *I bumped my leg on the table.* **2** *phrasal v.* insep. **to**

bump into s.o.: to meet by accident: *Two friends bumped into each other on the street.*

bump·er /'bʌmpər/ *n.* a bar on the back or front of a vehicle to protect it: *The car bumper hit the wall.*
—*adj.* **bumper-to-bumper:** crowded and close together: *Bumper-to-bumper traffic made us all late.*

bumper sticker *n.* a strip of paper with a message on it put on a car bumper: *The bumper sticker on my car says "I'd rather be sailing than working."*

bump·kin /'bʌmpkɪn/ *n.* a simple person from the country

bump·y /'bʌmpi/ *adj.* **-ier, -iest 1** covered with bumps, having an uneven surface: *The dirt road was very bumpy.* **2** moving suddenly up and down, (*syns.*) rough, jerky: *The airplane flight was bumpy.*

bun /bʌn/ *n.* **1** a small, roundish bread: *I had an egg on a bun for breakfast.* **2** hair coiled into a round shape, usu. at the back of the head **3** *fig.vulg.* a buttock *See:* muffin.

bunch /bʌntʃ/ *n.pl.* **bunches 1** a group of s.t. growing or put together: *She bought a bunch of bananas and a bunch of carrots at the store.* **2** *infrml.fig.* a large amount of s.t.: *That dress cost a bunch.‖They bought a bunch of things at the store.*
—*v.* to crowd together: *People bunched together* (or) *up in the crowded bus.*

bun·dle /'bʌndl/ *n.* **1** things close together usu. tied or fastened: *I put a bundle of clothes in the washing machine.* **2** *fig.* a lot of money: *A new car costs a bundle.*
—*v.* **-dled, -dling, -dles 1** to put together, to wrap up: *She bundled dirty clothes in a bag.* **2** *phrasal v.* **to bundle up:** to dress warmly: *Bundle up; it's cold outside!*

bung /bʌŋ/ *n.* a short, round piece of wood (cork, rubber) put in a hole in a jug or barrel: *A worker closed a beer barrel with a bung.* -*n.* **bunghole** /'bʌŋ,houl/.

bun·ga·low /'bʌŋgə,lou/ *n.* a small house on one level, (*syn.*) a cottage: *We have a bungalow by the sea.*

bun·gle /'bʌŋgəl/ *n.v.* **-gled, -gling, -gles** to do s.t. badly, (*syn.*) to botch: *He <v.> bungled a report; it had many mistakes.* -*n.* **bungler.**

bun·ion /'bʌnyən/ *n.* a painful swelling of the big toe: *A foot doctor operated on her bunions.*

bunk /bʌŋk/ *n.* **1** [C] a narrow bed, often placed one above the other: *Soldiers sleep in bunks.* **2** [U] nonsense: *What he says is bunk!*
—*v.* to sleep at s.o.'s house as a guest: *Don't go to a hotel; bunk with us in our guest room. See:* bunkhouse.

bun·ker /'bʌŋkər/ *n.* a room, usu. underground, with thick walls: *When the enemy came near, the soldiers ran into their bunker.*

bunk·house /'bʌŋk,haus/ *n.* a simple building with beds for workers, cowboys, etc

bun·kum /'bʌŋkəm/ *n.infrml.* nonsense, esp. by politicians: *The mayor's plan to bring new jobs to the city was pure bunkum.*

bun·ny /'bʌni/ *n.infrml.* **-nies 1** a baby rabbit, small rabbit: *She petted the bunnies in the children's zoo.* **2** *infrml.fig.pej.* an active, attractive young woman: *She is a ski bunny in winter and a beach bunny in summer.*

bunt·ing /'bʌntɪŋ/ *n.* decorations made of cloth or paper: *Bunting hangs on the stage where the politicians are speaking.*

buoy /'bui, bɔi/ *n.* **1** a marker floating in the water used to warn of danger or mark a passageway (channel): *Don't swim out beyond the red buoy.* **2** a device made from material that floats, used to keep a person from sinking, *(syn.)* a life preserver: *She threw the drowning man a buoy.*
—*v.* **1** to lift up, to keep afloat in the water **2** *fig.* to make s.o. feel good: *The good news buoyed his spirits.*

buoy·ant /'bɔiənt/ *adj.* **1** able to float: *Fallen trees are buoyant in water.* **2** *fig.* cheerful, happy: *She has a buoyant personality.* *-n.* **buoyancy;** *-adv.* **buoyantly.**

bur·den /'bɜrdn/ *n.* **1** a heavy weight: *Elephants can carry heavy burdens, such as tree logs.* **2** *fig.* a worry, trouble: *Having cancer is a burden on both body and mind.* **3** *fig.* a responsibility: *She has the burden of running a business.* **4 burden of proof:** the responsibility of s.o. to prove s.t.: *He has paid his phone bill, but he must show his canceled check because the burden of proof is on him.*
—*v.* **1** to weigh down: *He was burdened with two big suitcases.* **2** *fig.* to worry, trouble: *She is burdened by money troubles and she burdens others with them.* *-adj.* **burdensome** /'bɜrdnsəm/.

bu·reau /'byurou/ *n.* **bureaus** or **bureaux 1** a piece of furniture with drawers, a dresser: *She keeps her towels and sheets in a bureau.* **2** a government agency: *the Federal Bureau of Investigation* **3** a business with a purpose: *travel bureau*

bu·reau·cra·cy /byu'rakrəsi/ *n.* **-cies** a group of government or business departments with complex rules and slow decision making: *Her application for citizenship has not gotten through the bureaucracy.*

bu·reau·crat /'byurə,kræt/ *n.* **1** an employee of a bureaucracy **2** *pej.* a slow person without imagination: *He is a nice guy, but he thinks like a bureaucrat.* *-adj.* **bureaucratic** /,byurə'krætɪk/; *-adv.* **bureaucratically.**

bur·geon /'bɜrdʒən/ *v.frml.* to grow quickly, *(syn.)* to mushroom: *Our company's business is burgeoning now.*

burg·er /'bɜrgər/ *n.infrml.* short for hamburger

bur·glar /'bɜrglər/ *n.* a thief who illegaly enters a building to steal: *A burglar broke the door lock and stole my TV.* *-v.* **burglarize** /'bɜrglə,raiz/; *-n.* [C;U] **burglary.**

bur·i·al /'beriəl/ *n.* putting a dead person in a grave, *(syn.)* interment *See:* bury; cremate.

bur·lap /'bɜr,læp/ *n.* [U] a rough cloth used to make bags for holding coffee beans, onions, etc.

bur·lesque /bər'lɛsk/ *n.* a type of theater comedy that makes fun of people and events

bur·ly /'bɜrli/ *adj.* **-lier, -liest** (of men) with strong muscles, *(syn.)* tough

burn /'bɜrn/ *v.* **burned** or **burnt** /'bɜrnt/, **burning, burns 1** to be on fire: *The house is burning.* **2** to hurt with fire: *The fire burned her hand.* **3** to spoil with fire: *He burned the meat.* **4** to produce light: *Street lights burn all night.* **5** *phrasal v. sep.* **to burn s.t. down:** to destroy by fire: *Vandals burned down the house.*||*They burned it down.* **6** *phrasal v. insep.* **to burn s.t. into s.t.:** to put permanently into consciousness: *The look on his face is burned into my mind.* **7** *phrasal v. sep.* **to burn s.o.** or **s.t. out: a.** *s.o.:* to be unable to work anymore, usu. from exhaustion: *Her hard work burned out the doctor.*||*It burned her out.* **b.** *s.t.:* to stop burning: *The fire finally burned itself out.* **c.** *s.t.:* to stop working: *That light bulb has burned out.* **8** *phrasal v. sep.* **to burn s.o.** or **s.t. up: a.** *infrml.fig.* to be very angry: *The theft of his car burned up my cousin.*||*It burned him up.* **b.** to be destroyed: *The fire burned up all her furniture.* **9** *infrml.* **to be** or **get burned:** to have a loss: *She paid a lot of money for a painting that turned out to be fake; she got burned.*
—*n.* an injury or wound caused by fire or sunlight: *She suffered a burn on her hand. See:* bridge; sunburn.

burn·er /'bɜrnər/ *n.* **1** the part of a stove, heater, furnace, etc. that creates a flame: *There is a pot boiling on the front burner.* **2 on the back burner:** stopped, delayed, *(syn.)* on hold: *The owner put plans for building a new factory on the back burner until the company's sales improve.*

burn·ing /'bɜrnɪŋ/ *n.* [C;U] an act of burning, *(syn.)* combustion: *the burning of candles in a church*
—*adj.* **1** on fire: *The burning house (forest, building, etc.) attracted a large crowd.* **2** *fig.* having a strong wish: *She has a burning desire to succeed in business.* **3** *fig.* causing arguments or worry: *High taxes are a burning issue.*

burn·ish /'bɜrnɪʃ/ *v.* **-es** to polish: *He burnished the metal on his rifle.*

B

B

burn·out /'bɜrn,aʊt/ n. **1** [C] the failure of a machine, esp. because of heat from too much friction: *Don't run the engine without oil, or you'll have a burnout.* **2** [U] extreme fatigue: *Many students have burnout after taking exams.* **3** [C] a person who is burned out

burnt /bɜrnt/ adj. about s.t. that is burned: *He made a burnt offering to God.*

burp /bɜrp/ n.v. gas coming from the stomach through the mouth, (syn.) a belch: *The man <v.> burped after eating lunch.*

burr (1) /bɜr/ n. to roll one's r's when speaking: *She speaks with a Scottish burr.*
—v. to make a buzzing sound

burr (2) n. **1** a rough or sharp edge on metal: *If one is not careful when cutting, drilling, or molding metal, the edges will have burrs.* **2** a seed ball with sharp needles found on some plants: *Our dog came home with burrs in his coat.*

bur·ro /'bɜroʊ, 'bʊr-, 'bʌr-/ n. -ros a donkey: *Even small burros can carry heavy loads.*

bur·row /'bɜroʊ, 'bʌr-/ n. a hole in the ground where animals live, (syn.) a den: *Rabbits live in burrows.*
—v. to dig into the ground: *Some animals burrow with their paws.*

bur·sar /'bɜrsər, -,sɑr/ n. the person in charge of finances, esp. at a college: *I paid my tuition at the bursar's office.*

bur·si·tis /bər'saɪtɪs/ n. a painful condition of the joints: *He has bursitis in his shoulder.*

burst /bɜrst/ n. **1** a sudden outpouring: *There was a burst of laughter from the audience.||A cloud burst got us wet on our way home.* **2** a fast action: *She ran by me in a burst of speed.*
—v. **burst, bursting, bursts 1** to break open suddenly, esp. because of inside pressure, (syn.) to explode: *A pipe burst, shooting water into the air.* **2 to burst at the seams:** to overflow: *Her suitcase is so full that it is bursting at the seams.* **3** phrasal v. insep. **to burst in on s.o.** or **s.t.:** to interrupt, esp. noisily: *The children burst in on our conversation.* **4** phrasal v. insep. **to burst into** or **onto s.t.: a.** to enter or come to notice, suddenly and forcefully:|| *The young actor burst onto the Hollywood scene.* **b.** to suddenly express s.t., such as an emotion:|| *She burst into laughter.* **5** phrasal v. **to burst out:** to begin doing s.t. suddenly: *She burst out laughing when I told her a funny joke.*

bur·y /'bɛri/ v. **-ied, -ying, -ies 1** to put a dead person in a grave, (syn.) to inter: *He buried his father yesterday.* **2** to hide, esp. in the ground: *A dog buried a bone.* **3** fig.not to tell s.t., (syns.) to cover up, to conceal: *They buried the scientist's discoveries because they didn't want to believe them.||She buried a secret deep inside herself.* **4** to sink into, (syn.) to imbed: *The dog buried its teeth in the steak.* **5** fig. to

give one's full attention, (syn.) to immerse: *She buried herself in her reading.* **6** fig. to forgive: *The business partners buried their differences and shook hands.*

bus /bʌs/ n. **buses** or **busses** a large, often public vehicle used to carry passengers: *He takes the bus to work every day.*
—v. **bused** or **bussed, busing** or **bussing, buses** or **busses** to travel by bus: *Schoolchildren are bused from their home to school and back. See:* busing.

bus·boy /'bʌs,bɔɪ/ n. a person who takes away dishes in a restaurant: *First I worked as a busboy, and then I became a waiter.*

bush /bʊʃ/ n. **bushes 1** a plant shorter than a tree, usu. with branches and leaves, (syns.) shrub, hedge: *I cut the rose bushes in the front yard.* **2** [U] **the bush:** land far from towns and cities, (syn.) wilderness, esp. in Africa and Australia **3** pl. an area of land with many shrubs: *Birds hide in the bushes.* **4 to beat around the bush:** to talk about s.t. without getting to the point, (syn.) to hint: *Say what you have to say and stop beating around the bush.*

bushed /bʊʃt/ adj. very tired, (syn.) worn out: *I worked fourteen hours today; I'm bushed.*

bush·el /'bʊʃəl/ n. **1** a unit of dry measure equal to 2,150.42 cubic inches (35.24 liters) in the USA **2** an amount equal to a bushel or a large basket: *She bought a bushel of corn.*

bush-league adj. **1** (from baseball) teams that are worse than top professional ones **2** weak, (syns.) inferior, second-rate: *He runs a bush-league business.*

bush·whack /'bʊʃ,wæk/ v. to make a path through bushes and trees -n. **bushwhacker;** [U] **bushwhacking.**

bush·y /'bʊʃi/ adj. **-ier, -iest 1** covered with bushes: *The path went down a bushy hillside.* **2** thick: *He has a bushy moustache.* -n. [U] **bushiness.**

busi·ness /'bɪznɪs/ n. **-es 1** [U] activities of people buying and selling goods and services: *Business is good in today's economy.* **2** [C] an organization of people, buildings, and products or services, (syn.) a commercial enterprise: *The businesses on Main Street include a supermarket, a candy store, and a dry cleaners.* **3** [C;U] a type of work, (syn.) an occupation: *She is in the furniture (real estate, fashion, etc.) business.* **4** sing. activities necessary for daily living, such as shopping, eating, working, and paying bills: *People attend to* (or) *go about the business of daily living.* **5** [U] the amount of money coming into a business, (syn.) sales volume: *Our business is increasing (going down, etc.).* **6** [U] one's own interest or responsibility, (syn.) a duty: *It is parents' business to care for their children.* **7** [U] matter, event, (syn.) affair: *That murder last month was a strange business.* **8 funny** or **monkey**

business: s.t. illegal or dishonest: *That house has strange people coming and going; I think there is funny business there.* **9 to get down to business:** to start talking about business: *After talking about the weather, we got down to business about the contract details.* **10 to mean business:** to be serious, (*syn.*) to be earnest: *They really mean business. If you don't pay them by next week, they're going to take you to court.* **11 to mind one's own business:** not to interfere in the lives of others: *You mind your own business and stay out of mine!* **12 no business:** no right (to do s.t.): *You have no business reading my mail!* **13 none of your business:** not of concern to you **14 to take care of business:** to discuss business before pleasure: *We met at his office to take care of business, then went for a pleasant lunch.*

business card *n.* a small paper with a person's name, business address, and telephone number, etc.: *Business cards are often given to customers so that they remember you.*

busi·ness·like /'bɪznɪs,laɪk/ *adj.* working carefully and seriously: *The owner is very businesslike and never talks about the weather or her weekend activities.*

busi·ness·man /'bɪznɪs,mæn/ *n.* **-men** /-,mɛn/ a man who does business: *Businessmen travel all over the world.*

USAGE NOTE: *Businessperson* is used to discuss both men and women in business.

business suit *n.* a man's or woman's suit that is often dark-colored and well-made: *That lawyer always wears a business suit to court.*

busi·ness·wom·an /'bɪznɪs,wʊmən/ *n.* **-women** /-,wɪmən/ a woman who does business: *Businesswomen can earn high salaries in Los Angeles.*

bus·ing /'bʌsɪŋ/ *n.* (in USA) transporting public school students by bus to schools in other neighborhoods for racial integration of white with nonwhite students

bus stop *n.* a specific place usu. marked with a sign where buses let off and pick up passengers

bust (1) /bʌst/ *v.slang* for broken **1** not to work or run: *My TV is busted.* **2** *infrml.* to arrest: *That drug user was busted by the police.* **3** (in the military) to lower s.o. in rank **4 to go bust:** to become bankrupt: *That company went bust last month.*

—*n.slang* **1** a failure, (*syn.*) a flop: *That party was a bust—no fun.* **2** *infrml.* an arrest: *There was a drug bust downtown last night.* **3** a bad fall in an economy with a lot of unemployment

bust (2) *n.* **1** a statue of the head and upper part of the chest and shoulders: *There are busts of famous writers in the library.* **2** a woman's chest area, (*syn.*) bosom: *The dressmaker mea-*

sured her bust and waist to make the wedding dress. *-adj.* **busty.**

bust·er /'bʌstər/ *n.* **1** a person who stops s.t.: *He is a crime buster.* **2** a form of address to men, usu. impolite: *Hey, buster, what do you think you're doing?*

bus·tle /'bʌsəl/ *v.* **-tled, -tling, -tles** to hurry, do s.t. with energy: *At mealtime, that restaurant bustles with activity.*

—*n.* a frame, pad, or bunch of material used to make a skirt stick out: *Women rarely wear bustles today*

bus·y /'bɪzi/ *adj.* **-ier, -iest 1** active, working: *I'm busy writing a report now, but I can talk to you later.* **2** on the telephone, (*syn.*) engaged: *Her line is busy now. See:* busy signal. **3 busy as a bee:** working hard and fast: *He is as busy as a bee cooking dinner in the kitchen.*

—*v.* **-ied, -ying, -ies** to occupy oneself: *She busied herself with housework to keep her mind off her problems. -adv.* **busily.**

bus·y bee /'bɪzi'bi/ *n.infrml. fig.* a very active, energetic person: *She has five projects going at once; what a busy bee!*

bus·y·bod·y /'bɪzi,badi, -,bʌdi/ *n.pej.* **-ies** a person too interested in other people's lives: *He is always asking others what they are doing; what a busybody! See:* gossip.

bus·y·work /'bɪzi,wɜrk/ *n.* [U] easy work that takes a lot of time: *Folding invoices and putting them in envelopes is busywork.*

but /bət; *strong form* bʌt/ *conj.* **1** in contrast, on the other hand: *She is pretty, but he is ugly.* **2** except for, save: *No one but John saw the accident happen.* **3** except that: *We wanted to buy that house, but the price was too high.* **4** instead of the expected, (*syn.*) however: *It rained all day, but we still had a good time.* **5** without the result that, (*syn.*) unless: *It never rains but it pours.* **6** that (after a negative): *I don't doubt but you're telling the truth.* **7** other than: *She has no goal but to win the tennis match.*

—*prep.* with the exception of, (*syn.*) save: *I want nothing but the truth from you.*

—*adv.* **1** *frml.* only: *If you had but told her in time.* **2** only, (*syn.*) merely: *She's but a baby.*

—*n.* **no ifs, ands, or buts:** no excuses or exceptions: *Let's get the job done now with no ifs, ands, or buts.*

butch·er /'bʊtʃər/ *n.* **1** a person or business that cuts and sells meat: *I went to the butcher to buy a chicken.* **2** *fig.* a violent killer, (*syn.*) a mass murderer: *He's killed 24 people; that man is a butcher!*

—*v.* **1** to kill animals and cut their meat **2** to kill violently **3** *infrml.* to do s.t. badly: *A person with a bad singing voice can butcher even the most beautiful music. -n.* [U] **butchery.**

but·ler /'bʌtlər/ *n.* the main male servant in a household: *The butler poured the wine.*

B

butt (1) /bʌt/ v. **1** to hit or push with the head or an animal's horns: *Two goats butted each other.* **2** *phrasal v. insep.* **to butt in (on s.t.):** to interrupt: *He butted in on my conversation with my friend.*

—n. a blow with the head or horns

butt (2) n. **1** the unsmoked end of a cigarette or cigar: *She threw the cigarette butt into the ashtray.* **2** the thicker or larger end of s.t.: *a rifle butt* **3** a person or thing that other people make fun of: *He was the butt of their jokes.* **4** *vulg.slang* the buttocks: *That guy's got a big butt. See:* rear end, buttocks.

butte /byut/ n. a hill with a flat top and steep sides: *Buttes are found in the USA's Southwest.*

but·ter /'bʌtər/ n. [U] a yellowish fat made from milk or cream and used in cooking: *I spread some butter on my bread.*

—v. **1** to put butter: *She buttered her toast.* **2** *phrasal v. sep.* **to butter s.o. up:** to get s.o.'s help by being nice, *(syn.)* to flatter: *The boss butters up his assistant after she has worked late by buying her theater tickets.||He butters her up.* **3** *fig.* **to know which side one's bread is buttered on:** to know who and what is good for one's best interests: *He knows which side his bread is buttered on, so he is nice to his boss.*

but·ter·ball /'bʌtər,bɔl/ n.pej. a fat person: *He's a butterball from eating too much ice cream.*

but·ter·cup /'bʌtər,kʌp/ n. a wild plant with yellow flowers

but·ter·fin·gers /'bʌtər,fɪŋgərz/ n.pl. s.o. who cannot hold on to things, *(syn.)* clumsy person: *He is always dropping things on the floor; he's a butterfingers.*

but·ter·fly /'bʌtər,flaɪ/ n. **-flies 1** an insect with a narrow body and four wings: *There are many types of butterflies, most of which are very pretty and colorful.* **2** *pl.fig.* nervousness, often causing an unsettled feeling in the stomach, *(syn.)* the jitters: *Before she sings to an audience, she gets butterflies in her stomach.*

butterfly

but·ter·milk /'bʌtər,mɪlk/ n. the thick, sour milk left over after butterfat has been removed from whole milk

but·ter·scotch /'bʌtər,skɑʧ/ adj.n. [U] a candy of melted butter and brown sugar: *I like <adj.> butterscotch sauce on vanilla ice cream.*

but·tocks /'bʌtəks/ n.pl. the part of the body where one sits, the behind, *(syn.)* the posterior *See:* bottom; butt; rear end.

but·ton /'bʌtn/ n. **1** a small round fastener for

holding clothing together: *A button on his shirt fell off.* **2** a part like a button on a machine **3** a pin or badge with a message: *The candidate gave out campaign buttons.*

—adv. **right on the button:** accurately, exactly right: *She hit the answers to the exam questions right on the button; she got all of them correct.*

—v. **1** to fasten a button: *He buttoned his shirt.* **2** *phrasal v. sep.* **to button s.t. up: a.** to fasten with buttons: *He buttoned up his shirt. ||He buttoned it up.* **b.** to finish s.t.: *Let's button up the business deal by signing the contract.||Let's button it up.*

button-down or **buttoned-down** n. a shirt with buttoned collars: *He wears button-downs.* —adj.fig. upper-class conservative: *That company is very buttoned-down and old fashioned.*

but·ton·hole /'bʌtn,houl/ n. an opening on fabric for a button

—v.fig. **-holed, -holing, -holes** to prevent s.o. from leaving by talking to them: *I was walking down the hallway, and my boss buttonholed me.*

but·tress /'bʌtrɪs/ n. **-tresses** a structure that supports a wall or building

—v. to support as with a buttress: *Workers buttressed the weak wall with steel beams.*

bux·om /'bʌksəm/ adj. large-chested: *Marilyn Monroe was a buxom blonde.*

buy /baɪ/ n. **1** s.t. that one buys, a purchase **2** *infrml.* s.t. bought at a low price, *(syn.)* a bargain: *That house (car, TV, etc.) is a great buy.*

—v. **bought** /bɔt/, **buying, buys 1** to pay for s.t., *(syn.)* to purchase: *I buy a newspaper every morning.* **2** *fig.* to agree, *(syn.)* to believe: *John says to Paul: "I think the economy is in trouble." Paul says, "I'll buy that."* **3** to pay s.o. to do s.t. illegal or dishonest, *(syn.)* to bribe: *The criminal was let go free because his friends bought the judge.* **4** *phrasal v. insep.* **to buy in** or **into s.t.:** to be convinced s.t. is good or true: *I bought into his plan to start a restaurant; I liked the opportunity, so I bought in.* **5** *phrasal v. sep.* **to buy s.o. off:** to pay s.o. not to talk or complain: *He buys off his children with expensive toys because he never spends any time with them.||He buys them off.* **6** *phrasal v. sep.* **to buy s.o. out:** to purchase another's share of s.t. so that one owns all or most of it: *She bought out her partners' shares in the business.||She bought them out.* **7** *phrasal v. sep.* **to buy s.t. up:** to purchase all that is available: *She bought up all the shrimp in the store for her party.|| She bought it up.*

buy·er /'baɪər/ n. **1** a person who buys s.t., *(syn.)* a purchaser: *I have a meeting with the buyer of my house.* **2** a person whose job is to purchase items for a business, *(syn.)* a purchasing agent: *She is a women's shoes buyer for a department store.* **3 a buyer's market:** a market condition of low prices: *If you're buying a house, you would rather have a buyer's market than a seller's market. See:* seller's market.

buy·out /'baɪ,aʊt/ *n.v.* the purchase of a controlling interest in a business

buzz /bʌz/ *n.* **buzzes 1** a low sound of zzz's, like that made by a fly: *The buzz of the bee around me was annoying.* **2** constant, quiet, but excited talking: *The buzz in the audience quieted as the curtain on the stage went up.* **3** *infrml.* a telephone call: *Give me a buzz tomorrow.* **4** *infrml.* a pleasant feeling as from drinking alcoholic beverages: *She drank a couple of glasses of wine and got a buzz.*
—*v.* **buzzed, buzzing, buzzes 1** to make a low humming sound: *Bees buzz as they fly.* **2** to be full of energy: *That office buzzes with activity.* **3** to talk constantly in a quiet, excited tone: *The audience buzzed with the news that the star of the play was ill.* **4** to fly low over: *Airplanes buzzed the parade.* **5** *phrasal v.* **buzz off:** (used in rude requests) to go away: *I was shocked when he told me to buzz off. -n.* [C] **buzzer;** [U] **buzzing.**

buz·zard /'bʌzərd/ *n.* **1** a large bird that eats dead meat, *(syn.)* a vulture: *Buzzards gathered around the dead deer.* **2** *fig.pej.* an old man, usu. irritable: *That old buzzard complains about everything.*

buzz·word /'bʌz,wɜrd/ *n.* popular words from a particular field or industry that people use to impress others: *People use buzzwords from the business and computer worlds, like "bottom line," "input," and "output."*

by /baɪ/ *prep.* **1** next to: *The chair is by the door.* **2** through the action of s.t.: *She was hit by a car.*‖*The letter was brought by a messenger.* **3** across or past: *The bird flew by the window.*‖*The highway runs by the town.* **4** not later than: *You must wake up by 8 o'clock.* **5** during: *They traveled by night.* **6** according to: *He's five minutes late by my watch.* **7** in the authority or presence of: *If you hurt her, by God, I'll kill you!* **8** for, *(syn.)* in behalf of: *She's done well by her children.* **9** in the amount, extent, or degree of: *He takes pills by the dozen.*‖*That star in the sky is brighter by far.* **10** adding one direction of measurement to another: *The room is 8' by 10', meaning that*

it is eight feet long and ten feet wide.
—*adv.* **1 by and by:** after a short period of time, *(syn.)* after a while: *He's not ready yet, but he'll be here by and by.* **2 by and large:** looking at the whole situation, *(syns.)* on the whole, overall: *He made a few mistakes, but by and large he did a good job.* **3 by the by:** by the way, *(syn.)* incidentally: *By the by, have you seen her today?* **4** *infrml.* **by the seat of one's pants:** casually, thoughtlessly: *He runs the company by the seat of his pants.* **5 by the way:** introducing a new topic of conversation *See:* large.

bye-bye /'baɪ,baɪ, baɪ'baɪ, bə'baɪ/ *interj.* good-bye, so long: *Bye-bye, I'll see you tomorrow.*

by·gone /'baɪ,gɔn, -,gɑn/ *adj.* **1** in the past, long ago: *In bygone years* (or) *days, people traveled by horse or paddle boats.* **2 to let bygones be bygones:** to not blame s.o. about past injuries anymore: *We used to argue all the time, but now we have let bygones be bygones and are friends.*

by·law /'baɪ,lɔ/ *n.* a law for special purposes in a business or other organization (not a national or state law): *The bylaws of our business say that we can sell only furniture.*

by·pass /'baɪ,pæs/ *n.* **-passes 1** a temporary road around a road being repaired **2** a blood vessel going around a blocked vessel in the heart: *He had a bypass* (or) *bypass surgery.*
—*v.* **1** to find a way around: *The problem is so difficult that we must find a way to bypass it.* **2** to go around, avoid

by-product *n.* **1** a product created while making another product: *Molasses is a by-product of making sugar from sugar cane.* **2** s.t. that happens as a result of s.t. else: *His red face is a by-product of his being angry all the time.*

by·stand·er /'baɪ,stændər/ *n.* s.o. near but not participating in s.t., *(syn.)* an onlooker: *My brother was an innocent bystander when he saw a robbery happening across the street.*

byte /baɪt/ *n.* a unit of measurement for computer data, equal to eight bits: *One character (such as the letter "a") takes up one byte of space.*

by·way /'baɪ,weɪ/ *n.* a smaller, unimportant path or road: *We traveled on the highways and byways of eastern Canada.*

C, c

C, c /si/ *n.* **C's, c's,** or **Cs, cs** **1** the third letter of the English alphabet **2** a school grade below B and above D: *She got a C on her exam.* **3 C:** the Roman numeral for 100

cab /kæb/ *n.* **1** a car that carries passengers for a fare (price), (*syn.*) a taxicab: *Let's take a cab to the office.* **2** a closed-in section where the driver sits in a large vehicle or piece of machinery: *Trucks, train engines, bulldozers, etc., have cabs.*

cab·a·ret /ˌkæbə'reɪ/ *n.* **1** [C] a type of nightclub where people eat and drink during a performance: *We went to a cabaret last night.* **2** [U] a type of music and dance entertainment

cab·bage /'kæbɪdʒ/ *n.* [C;U] a large, round, green or purple leafy vegetable similar to lettuce, eaten cooked or raw: *Coleslaw is a kind of salad made of finely chopped cabbage and mayonnaise.*

cab·by or **cab·bie** /'kæbi/ *n.infrml.* **-bies** a person who drives a taxicab, (*syn.*) a cabdriver: *Cabbies know the city streets well.*

cab·driv·er /'kæbˌdraɪvər/ *n.* a person who drives a taxicab: *Cabdrivers work long hours in some cities.*

cab·in /'kæbɪn/ *n.* **1** a small, usu. inexpensive, simply built house: *We own a cabin in the mountains.* **2** a room for sleeping on a ship: *We had a pleasant cabin on the cruise ship.* **3** an enclosed section of a boat or plane: *The passengers and crew (pilot, copilot, etc.) are in the cabin.*

cabin cruiser *n.* a boat with a cabin or cabins for sleeping: *They sailed down the coast in their cabin cruiser.*

cab·i·net /'kæbənɪt, 'kæbnɪt/ *n.* **1** a piece of furniture with shelves and doors used to store dishes, food, supplies, etc.: *We keep dishes and canned food in the cabinets over the kitchen sink.* **2** a group of high-level government officials who give advice to the nation's leader, such as to the President of the USA: *The Secretary of State, Secretary of Education, and Secretary of Transportation are all members of the President's cabinet.*

cabin fever *n.* [U] a feeling of restlessness and a desire to be outdoors: *By the end of winter, many people suffer from cabin fever.*

ca·ble /'keɪbəl/ *n.* **1** [C;U] strong, thick rope, usu. made of many wires twisted together: *Steel cables support that bridge.* **2** [C;U] a covered bundle of wires that carries electronic messages **3** [C] a message sent by underwater cable: *I received a cable from London this morning.* **4** [U] a type of television service: *Do you get cable? See:* cable television.
—*v.* **-bled, -bling, -bles** to send a message electronically: *The newspaper reporter cabled a story to his newspaper.*

cable car *n.* a type of trolley car pulled by a cable up and down hills as it carries passengers: *San Francisco is famous for its cable cars.*

cable car

ca·ble·cast /'keɪbəlˌkæst/ *v.* **-cast, -casting, -casts** to send TV broadcasts by cable television: *That TV station cablecasts news events.*

cable television or **TV** *n.* [U] a type of television service that sends its programs to customers who pay for the service: *The TV pictures sent by cable television are very clear.*

ca·boose /kə'bus/ *n.* the last car on a freight train

cab·stand /'kæbˌstænd/ *n.* a place where taxis wait for passengers: *There is a cabstand in front of our hotel.*

ca·ca·o /kə'kaʊ/ *n.* [C;U] **-os** a tree of Latin America that bears seeds (beans) from which chocolate and cocoa are made: *Cacao beans are made into fine soaps, medical products, and chocolate.*

cache /kæʃ/ *n.* **1** a hidden storage place, esp. for valuable items: *She kept the jewelry in a cache under the stairs.* **2** an amount of valuable things (jewels, money, guns, etc.) hidden away: *She had a cache of gold hidden in the wall.*

ca·chet /kæ'ʃeɪ/ *n.* **1** [C] a seal on an official letter or document **2** [U] a special quality, a mark of distinction: *That fine jewelry store has a certain cachet; many wealthy people buy jewelry there.*

cack·le /'kækəl/ *n.v.* **-led, -ling, -les 1** to make a sound like that of a hen: *The hen <v.> cackled after she laid an egg.* **2** a loud, high-pitched laugh: *The old witch whispered, then let out a <n.> cackle.*

cac·tus /'kæktəs/ *n.* **-ti** /-,taɪ/ or **-tuses** a green desert plant with sharp needles: *There are many cactuses in the deserts of Mexico.*

cactus

cad /kæd/ *n.frml.* a man with bad manners, *(syn.)* an ungentlemanly fellow: *That cad knocked over the old woman, and never even looked back!*

ca·dav·er /kə'dævər/ *n.frml.* a dead human body, *(syn.)* a corpse: *Medical students study cadavers at medical school.*

ca·dence /'keɪdns/ *n.* a balanced rhythm and flow (of poetry, voice, dance, etc.): *That poetry has a pleasing cadence.*

ca·det /kə'dɛt/ *n.* a student in military school: *Cadets must wear military uniforms to class.*

cad·re /'kædri, -,dreɪ, 'kɑ-/ *n.* a group of trained personnel who manage and teach others: *A cadre of military officers trains new soldiers.*

Cae·sar /'sizər/ *n.* **1** the title given to many Roman emperors: *Augustus was the first Roman emperor to use the title "Caesar."* **2** *infrml.* a self-important man who demands that others do what he says: *The owner behaves like a little Caesar with his employees.*

cae·sar·e·an /sɪ'zɛriən/ or **caesarian section** *n. See:* cesarean.

ca·fe or **ca·fé** /kæ'feɪ, kə-/ *n.* **1** a restaurant that serves simple food and drinks: *We went to a cafe for coffee.* **2** a restaurant that serves alcoholic drinks, and sometimes provides entertainment, *(syns.)* a bar, nightclub

USAGE NOTE: *Café* is one of several words used to describe kinds of *restaurants*. Cafés and coffee shops usually serve drinks such as coffee, tea, and soda, but cafés serve simple meals, and coffee shops usually serve dessert foods. A *coffee house* is like a café or coffee shop except that people at coffee houses often share or listen to poetry or music while they drink and eat. *Cafeterias* and *diners* are inexpensive restaurants that serve complete hot meals. At a cafeteria, customers walk along a line of food, choose their food, and pay at the end of the line. Diners are informal restaurants that serve homestyle food, and are often open from the early morning until late at night.

caf·e·te·ri·a /,kæfə'tɪriə/ *n.* a restaurant where customers serve themselves: *Our college has a big cafeteria. See:* café, USAGE NOTE.

caf·feine /kæ'fin, 'kæ,fin/ *n.* [U] an ingredient in coffee and tea that energizes the heart and breathing, *(syn.)* a stimulant: *The caffeine in coffee makes me nervous. See:* decaffeinated.

cage /keɪdʒ/ *n.* an area enclosed with metal bars to keep animals from escaping: *At the zoo, you can see many animals in cages.*
—*v.* **caged, caging, cages 1** to close an animal in a cage: *Birds are caged to keep them from flying away.* **2** *infrml.fig.* **to rattle s.o.'s cage:** to startle s.o. into action or a change in behavior: *I'm going to rattle his cage about that problem and get him to fix it.*

ca·gey or **ca·gy** /'keɪdʒi/ *adj.* **-gier, -giest** not willing to tell others what one is thinking or doing, *(syns.)* secretive, coy: *She won't say yes or no; she is being cagey.* -*adj.* **cagily;** -*n.* **caginess.**

ca·hoots /kə'huts/ *n.pl.infrml.* **in cahoots (with):** working or acting together, often secretly on s.t. dishonest: *The two men are in cahoots to cheat on taxes.*

ca·jole /kə'dʒoul/ *v.* **-joled, -joling, -joles** to persuade s.o. gently, usu. with humor and charm: *Her boyfriend cajoled her into giving him a kiss.*

cake /keɪk/ *n.* **1** [C;U] a sweet baked food made of a mixture of flour, eggs, milk, sugar, etc.: *He ate some chocolate cake.* **2** [C] s.t. shaped like a cake: *She bought a cake of soap.* **3** [C] a flat, round baked or fried portion of batter (potatoes, chopped fish, etc.): *We had pancakes (fishcakes, etc.) for dinner.* **4 a piece of cake:** s.t. that is simple to do, an easy task: *That job is so easy; it's a piece of cake!* **5 to have one's cake and eat it too:** to want to keep s.t., like money, but also want to spend or use it: *He wants to save money, but he buys fancy cars and expensive clothes; he wants to have his cake and eat it, too.*
—*v.* **caked, caking, cakes** to put s.t. on in large amounts or layers that harden: *Mud (was) caked on the farmer's boots.*

ca·lam·i·ty /kə'læməti/ *n.frml.* [C;U] **-ties** a major disaster, *(syn.)* a catastrophe: *An earthquake that kills people is a calamity.*

cal·ci·um /'kælsiəm/ *n.* [U] a white, metallic mineral that is found in bones, shells, and milk: *People need calcium to have strong bones.*

cal·cu·late /'kælkyə,leɪt/ *v.* **-lated, -lating, -lates 1** to do math (to add, subtract, etc.), *(syns.)* to figure s.t. (cost, price, equation, problem), to compute: *The businesswoman calculated the cost of producing a car.* **2** to estimate: *Her sales manager calculates the number of cars that must be sold each year.*

cal·cu·lat·ed /'kælkyə,leɪtɪd/ *adj.* carefully

planned: *The politician made a calculated attempt to persuade the voters to accept more taxes.*

cal·cu·lat·ing /'kælkyə,leɪtɪŋ/ *adj.* coldly and carefully arranging things or manipulating people for one's own selfish purposes, *(syn.)* manipulative: *She is a calculating woman, always trying to get other people to do what she wants.*

cal·cu·la·tion /,kælkyə'leɪʃən/ *n.* [C;U] **1** an act of doing math: *Scientists use computers to help them make their calculations.* **2** careful planning, often for selfish purposes

cal·cu·la·tor /'kælkyə,leɪtər/ *n.* a small electronic device for doing math: *Calculators let you do calculations fast and accurately.*

cal·cu·lus /'kælkyələs/ *n.* [U] a type of advanced mathematics

cal·en·dar /'kæləndər/ *n.* a chart of the days and months of a year or years: *She writes the names and times of her meetings on her appointment calendar.*

calf /kæf/ *n.* **calves** /kævz/ **1** a baby cow or bull: *The young of some large animals, such as the cow and hippopotamus, are called "calves."* **2** the back part of the lower leg: *He is a ballet dancer and has big calf muscles.*

cal·i·ber /'kæləbər/ *n.* [C;U] **1** the measurement of the size of the hole in the barrel of a pistol, rifle, etc.: *She has a .25 caliber pistol.* **2** [C;U] the size of a bullet **3** *fig.sing.* [U] the quality of s.t.: *He is a lawyer of high caliber.*

cal·i·brate /'kælə,breɪt/ *v.* **-brated, -brating, -brates 1** to check, adjust, or measure s.t. exactly: *The worker calibrated a cutting tool.* **2** to determine the quality (caliber) of s.t. -*n.* **calibrator; calibration** /,kælə'breɪʃən/.

cal·i·co /'kælɪ,kou/ *n.* [U] *adj.* rough cotton cloth usu. printed with bright designs: *She wore a red and white <adj.> calico dress.*

cal·is·then·ics /,kælɪs'θɛnɪks/ *n.pl.* exercises done to strengthen the body: *Push-ups and sit-ups are forms of calisthenics.*

call /kɔl/ *n.* **1** a shout: *He gave a call to his friend across the street.* **2** a telephone conversation: *I will give you a call at home tonight.* **3** a short visit: *I made a call at my aunt's house before going home.* **4** a sound made by animals: *Bird calls filled the air.* **5 a close call:** **a.** almost an accident, injury, or death: *That car almost hit me; that was a close call!* **b.** (in sports) a difficult decision for a referee: *It was difficult to see who got to the base first; it was a close call.* **6 to be on call:** ready to work if needed: *Firefighters are always on call to respond to any emergency.*

—*v.* **1** to shout or say s.t. loudly: *She called her friend's name.* **2** to cry out: *A swimmer in difficulty called out for help.* **3** to ask s.o. to come to you, *(syn.)* to summon: *The mother called her children inside the house.* **4** to order

to appear, *(syn.)* to summon: *He was called before a court of law.* **5** to telephone: *I called you yesterday.* **6** to name s.o. or s.t.: *We live in a town called San Marcos.* **7 to be called on the carpet:** to be held responsible and harshly corrected for s.t.: *A worker made a bad mistake and was called on the carpet for it.* **8** *phrasal v. insep.* **to call for:** to need, *(syn.)* to require: *This situation calls for immediate action.* **9 to call into question:** to question the value or authenticity of s.t.: *His honesty was called into question.* **10 to call it a day:** to stop doing s.t.: *We've been working for ten hours and we're tired; let's call it a day.* **11** *phrasal v. insep.* **to call on** or **upon s.o.:** **a.** to visit s.o.: *We called on our new neighbors.* **b.** *frml.* to request that s.o. do s.t.: *The governor called on state residents to conserve water.* **12** *phrasal v. sep.* **to call s.o.** or **s.t. back:** **a.** s.o.: to ask to come back: *The director called back two actors.*||*She called them back.* **b.** s.o.: to return a telephone call: *I called you back, but there was no answer.* **c.** s.t.: to ask that s.t. be returned for repairs: *The car manufacturer called back some cars to fix the brakes.* **13** *phrasal v. sep.* **to call s.o.** or **s.t. in:** **a.** to telephone into a place (office, home, etc.): *During your trip, please call in once a day.* **b.** s.o.: to ask s.o. for help: *They called in an expert.*||*They called her in.* **c.** s.t.: to ask for the return of s.t.: *Our company called in the orders from last week.* **14** *phrasal v. sep.* **to call s.o. out:** to (officially) request s.o.'s assistance: *The President called out the National Guard to help stop the flooding.*||*He called them out.* **15 to call s.o.'s bluff:** to challenge s.o. to prove s.t. or carry out a threat (when you think the person is faking): *I called his bluff when he pretended to have a winning hand (in cards).* **16** *phrasal v. sep.* **to call s.o. up: a.** to telephone s.o.: *I called up the police for help.*||*I called them up.* **b.** to tell to come for military duty, *(syn.)* to draft: *He was called up for duty last week.* **17** *phrasal v. sep.* **to call s.t. down:** to ask a higher power to do s.t., *(syn.)* to invoke: *The preacher called down the power of God.*||*He called it down.* **18** *phrasal v. sep.* **to call s.t. forth:** to bring into being or action, *(syn.)* to evoke: *The music called forth memories of my childhood.* **19** *phrasal v. sep.* **to call s.t. off: a.** to order away, *(syn.)* to restrain: *The owner called off his dog when it barked at the child.* **b.** to stop or put off, *(syns.)* to cancel, postpone: *We called off the picnic when it began to rain.* **20 to call the shots:** to have the power to say what will be done: *The owner calls all the shots in that company.* **21 to call to account:** to demand that s.o. explain and be responsible for his or her actions: *He stole money and the owner called him to account and had him arrested.* **22 to call to mind:** to cause to remember, *(syn.)* to remind of: *The sight of my old house called to mind my childhood days.*

call·back /'kɔl,bæk/ *n.* a return telephone call or return visit: *You left 10 phone messages yesterday. How many callbacks have you received today?*

call·er /'kɔlər / *n.* **1** a person who telephones another person: *The caller on the phone is from your bank.* **2** a visitor: *Come downstairs, you have a caller.*

call girl *n.* a woman who is paid to have sex, *(syn.)* a prostitute

cal·lig·ra·phy /kə'lɪgrəfi/ *n.* [U] the art of fine, elegant handwriting

call·ing /'kɔlɪŋ/ *n.* **1** one's life's work (or) great desire: *Buddhist ministry is his calling in life.* **2 to go calling:** to go visit s.o.: *We went calling on our friends.*

calling card *n. See:* business card, cash card.

cal·lous /'kæləs/ *adj.* not caring about others, *(syns.)* unfeeling, insensitive: *She has a callous attitude toward the suffering of others.* *-adv.* **callously;** *-n.* **callousness.**

cal·low /'kælou/ *adj.frml.* young and inexperienced, *(syn.)* immature: *He is a callow 20-year-old man who behaves like a 12-year-old boy.*

cal·lus /'kæləs/ *n.v.* **-luses** a hard place on the skin, esp. on the hands and feet: *I have <n.> calluses on my hands from working in the garden.*

calm /kɑm/ *adj.* **1** peaceful, *(syn.)* composed: *I feel calm now that my exams are over.* **2** almost or totally motionless, *(syn.)* tranquil: *The ocean is calm today; it looks like a mirror.*
—*n.* **1** *sing.* [U] peace, *(syn.)* tranquillity: *At night, a calm settled over the battlefield.* **2 the calm before the storm:** a time of quiet before s.t. bad happens
—*v.* to make quiet, peaceful: *She calmed her nerves with a cup of tea.* *-adv.* **calmly;** *-n.* [U] **calmness.**

ca·lor·ic /kə'lɔrɪk, -'lar-/ *adj.* **1** related to heat and calories **2** fattening: *Red meat and chocolate cake are highly caloric; both are fattening.*

cal·o·rie /'kæləri/ *n.* **1** a unit used to measure the amount of heat in s.t. **2** a unit used to measure the amount of energy produced by food: *Potatoes with gravy and butter have a lot of calories.* **3 calorie conscious:** being careful not to eat fattening foods: *She's trying to lose weight; she's very calorie conscious.*

calve /kæv/ *v.* **calved, calving, calves** to give birth to a calf: *The cow calved today.*

calves /kævz/ *n.pl. of* calf

ca·lyp·so /kə'lɪpsou/ *n.* **-sos** or **-soes** a type of lively music originally from the Caribbean (Trinidad): *I love dancing to calypso music.*

ca·ma·ra·de·rie /,kɑmə'radəri, -'ræ-, ,kæ-/ *n.* [U] a good feeling of togetherness, friendship

cam·cord·er /'kæm,kɔrdər/ *n.* a hand-held TV camera and recorder whose tapes can be played on a videocassette recorder (VCR): *We used our camcorder to tape our vacation.*

came /keɪm/ *v. past tense of* come

cam·el /'kæməl/ *n.* a large, four-legged animal with a long neck and hump(s) on its back: *Camels can live in the desert without water for a long time.*

ca·mel·lia /kə'milyə/ *n.* a plant with large white flowers: *She wore a camellia in her hair.*

cam·e·o /'kæmi,ou/ *n.* **-os 1** a piece of jewelry made of a picture cut from a gemstone: *She wears a cameo on her blouse.* **2** a brief appearance by a famous person in a movie or play: *Alfred Hitchcock made cameo appearances in several of the movies he directed.*

cam·er·a /'kæmrə, 'kæmərə/ *n.* a device used to take pictures, such as photographs, movies, or pictures for TV: *She used her camera to take pictures on her vacation.*

cam·er·a·man /'kæmrə,mæn, -mən, 'kæmərə/ or **camerawoman** /-,wumən/*n.* **-men** /-,mɛn, -mən/ or **-women** /-,wɪmən/ a person who uses a camera professionally: *In the TV studio, the cameraman stands behind the camera.*

cam·ou·flage /'kæmə,flɑʒ, -,flɑdʒ/ *n.* [C;U] a way of hiding s.t. by making it look like its surroundings: *Soldiers put camouflage over a big gun to hide it from the enemy.*
—*v.* **-flaged, -flaging, -flages** to cover s.t. to hide it, *(syn.)* to conceal: *Soldiers camouflaged themselves to blend in with the jungle by wearing green uniforms.*

camp /kæmp/ *n.* **1** a place outdoors where people live in tents: *Lisa and Rumi set up camp in the woods.* **2** a cabin in the countryside: *Her parents have a camp by a lake in Canada.* **3** an organized program set in cabins or other simple living shelters (tents, huts): *The children were looking forward to summer camp.* **4** a group of people that support a particular cause, idea, or movement: *That whole camp is sure to vote for him.*
—*v.* **1** to set up a camp and sleep outdoors: *People camp (or) camp out in the woods in the summer.* **2 to go camping:** *They like to go camping.*
—*adj.* related to an obviously fake manner or style: *Movies that are camp are meant to be funny.* — **campy.**

cam·paign /kæm'peɪn/ *n.v.* an organized effort by people to reach a goal: *A politician runs a political <n.> campaign to get elected to office.*

camp·er /'kæmpər/ *n.* **1** a person who goes camping: *Campers enjoy the outdoors.* **2** a vehicle used for camping trips that usu. includes a place to sleep

camp·ground /'kæmp,graʊnd/ n. a place or area for camping: *The campground is located in the woods.*

cam·pus /'kæmpəs/ n. [C;U] the land and buildings of a college, university, or some business headquarters: *I study on campus in the college library.*

can (1) /kæn; *weak form* kən/ aux. v. **1** able to do s.t. with one's body: *She can run fast.* **2** to have skills of the mind: *He can speak English and Spanish.* **3** to have the right or power to do s.t.: *We can vote.* **4** to have or not have permission: *You can* (or) *cannot go to the movies tonight.* **5 can do:** to be very willing, (syns.) enthusiastic, cooperative: *"I need this report by tomorrow."—"Can do! I will have it for you by noon."||She has a <adj.> can-do attitude.* See: auxiliary verb.

USAGE NOTE: Compare *can* and *may. Can* is used to talk about the ability to do something: *The little boy can tie his own shoes now.* May is used to talk about permission: *You may sit down now.||May I go to the bathroom?* Some people use *can* to ask for permission as in *"Mom, can I go to the movies?"* but *May I go to the movies?* is more formal English.

can (2) /kæn/ n. **1** a metal container, usu. with flat ends and rounded sides, sealed without air to keep foods and drinks fresh and pure: *I opened a can of beans (soup, peaches, etc.).* **2** *vulg.slang* a toilet, bathroom: *I'm going to the can.* **3** *slang* the buttocks, part of the body where one sits: *While running he tripped and fell on his can.* **4** *slang* jail, prison: *She was caught stealing and ended up in the can.* **5 to open a can of worms:** to deal with a difficult problem requiring much time and trouble: *When our company decided to fight the government about taxes, it opened a can of worms that took three years to settle.*

—v. **1** to put s.t. in a can: *Big companies can foods and drinks, like beans and beer.* **2** *fam.* to fire s.o., (syn.) to sack s.o.: *He was late for work too often and got canned.*

ca·nal /kə'næl/ n. **1** a waterway, often dug by workers, for boats to carry goods and passengers: *The Erie Canal connects the Great Lakes with New York Harbor.* **2** (in medicine) a tube in the body that holds or carries fluid: *the ear canal*

ca·nar·y /kə'nɛri/ n. **-ies** a small, usu. yellow bird that sings: *People keep pet canaries in cages.*

can·cel /'kænsəl/ v. **1** to stop s.t. previously agreed on or planned, (syns.) to call off, to nullify: *I canceled my airline (hotel, dinner) reservations.* **2** to mark a check as paid: *A can-*

celed check is proof that it was paid. **3** *phrasal v. sep.* **to cancel s.t. out:** to make two things equal in strength, importance, etc., (syns.) to neutralize, to counterbalance: *The team got a new player and canceled out their rivals' advantage.||They canceled it out.*

can·cel·la·tion /,kænsə'leɪʃən/ n. [C;U] stopping s.t. previously agreed on: *The restaurant had some cancellations of reservations because of bad weather.||The doctor had a cancellation, so she can see you today.*

can·cer /'kænsər/ n. **1** [C;U] a disease that causes lumps (tumors) to grow in the body and which may be fatal: *Smoking causes lung cancer.* **2** [C]*fig.* a dangerous, quickly spreading condition: *The use of illegal drugs is a cancer on society.*

can·did /'kændɪd/ adj. **1** saying what one thinks even if it is unpleasant, (syns.) frank, forthright: *The owner was candid with her employees about the financial problems the company was having.* **2** natural, not practiced or posed: *The photographer took some candid shots of the wedding.* **3** not favoring one side or view over another, (syns.) unbiased, impartial: *The judge will give a candid opinion.* -adv. **candidly.** See: candor.

can·di·date /'kændə,deɪt, -dɪt/ n. **1** a person running for a political office: *She and two other politicians are candidates for mayor.* **2** a person or thing ready for s.t.: *He is a candidate for a job promotion.* -n. **candidacy** /'kændədəsi/.

can·dle /'kændl/ n. **1** a round, usu. long piece of wax with a wick (piece of string) that is burned for light: *The candles lit the dining room with a soft glow.* **2 not to hold a candle to s.o.:** not to compare favorably with s.o.: *A man named Pele was the greatest soccer player ever; no one can hold a candle to him.* **3 to burn the candle at both ends:** to tire oneself out with too much work or play: *She stays up late partying and gets up early for class; she's burning the candle at both ends.*

can·dle·stick /'kændl,stɪk/ n. a holder for a candle: *Candlesticks are often made of metal, like brass, silver, or gold.*

can·do /'kæn'du/ adj.infrml. enthusiastic, willing: *She has a can-do attitude.*

can·dor /'kændər/ n. [U] saying what one thinks even if it is unpleasant, (syn.) frankness: *The manager spoke of the company's mistakes with great candor.* See: candid, **1.**

can·dy /'kændi/ n. [C;U] **-dies** sweet food made with sugar and often with chocolate, nuts, or fruits: *I ate some chocolate candy.*

—v. **-died, -dying, -dies** to cook or cover with sugar: *He candied the plums for Christmas.*

cane /keɪn/ n. **1** a stick made of wood or metal used to help a person walk: *The old man walks with the aid of a cane.* **2** any of a variety of

plants with thin, woody, usu. flexible and hollow stems: *Bamboo and rattan are types of cane.* **3** dried pieces of these plants used to weave baskets and chairs: *The furniture on our porch is made of cane.* **4** a tall green plant used to make sugar, molasses, and rum: *Workers cut the cane and crush it to get the juice out to make sugar.*
—*v.* **caned, caning, canes** to beat s.o. with a cane: *Some countries cane criminals as punishment.*

ca·nine /'keɪ,naɪn/ *n.adj.* **1** one of two long, sharp teeth: *People have two <n.> canines* (or) *<adj.> canine teeth in their mouth.* **2** *frml.* a dog: *All <n.> canines in the city of San Diego must have a license.*

can·is·ter /'kænəstər/ *n.* a metal or plastic container for dry goods: *There is a canister of flour (coffee, bubble bath, etc.) on the shelf.*

can·ker or **canker sore** /'kæŋkər/ *n.* [C;U] a sore inside the mouth: *She put some medicine on a canker to stop it from hurting.*

can·na·bis /'kænəbɪs/ *n.frml.* [U] hemp, the plant dried and smoked as a drug (marijuana): *Cannabis grows wild in many places. See:* joint.

canned /kænd/ *adj. & past part. of* can (2) **1** sealed in a can: *I bought some <adj.> canned fruit, <adj.> canned beans, etc.* **2** *slang* fired from a job: *She got <v.> canned yesterday.* **3** *fig.* prepared beforehand, not real: *That TV program uses <adj.> canned laughter recorded from other shows.*

can·ner·y /'kænəri/ *n.* **-ies** a business where food is prepared and put in cans: *a fish cannery*

can·ni·bal /'kænəbəl/ *n.* a person who eats other people: *Cannibals captured a man and ate him. -n.* [U] **cannibalism.**

can·ni·bal·ize /'kænəbə,laɪz/ *v.* **-ized, -izing, -izes** **1** for humans to eat humans **2** *fig.* to destroy s.t. for use in s.t. else: *The sales of the company's new product cannibalized the sales of their old product.*

can·non /'kænən/ *n.* **-nons** or **-non** a large gun, usu. mounted or attached to wheels, used to fire shells long distances: *A ship fired its cannons against soldiers on land.*

cannon

can·non·ball /'kænən,bɔl/ *n.* a heavy metal ball fired from a cannon

can·not /'kæ,nɑt, kə'nɑt, kæ-/ *v.* negative of can (1) **1** to be unable to do s.t.: *I cannot play the piano.* **2** to not have permission: *Her boss told her that she cannot take the day off from work. See:* can't.

can·ny /'kæni/ *adj.* **-nier, -niest** careful and intelligent, esp with money, (*syn.*) shrewd: *She has a canny sense for finding bargains.*

ca·noe /kə'nu/ *n.v.* **-noed, -noing, -noes** a light, narrow type of boat: *Native Americans used <n.> canoes to travel on rivers. See:* kayak.

can·on /'kænən/ *n.frml.* **1** a law or body of laws, esp. in a religion: *Priests obey religious canons.* **2** a basic standard of behavior: *His bad behavior violates the canons of good conduct. -adj.* **canonical** /kə'nɑnɪkəl/.

can·on·ize /'kænə,naɪz/ *v.* **-ized, -izing, -izes** to declare a dead person to be a saint

can·o·py /'kænəpi/ *n.* **-pies** a cloth covering usu. held up by poles: *The canopy over the bed is made of red cloth. -adj.* **canopied** /'kænəpid/.

cant /kænt/ *n.* [U] **1** words and talk special to a field of work: *They speak in the cant of computer experts.* **2** meaningless, insincere talk, (*syns.*) trite phrases, clichés: *The politician's speech didn't contain anything important; it was just cant.*

can't /kænt/ *v. contr. of* cannot: *I can't speak French. See:* cannot.

can·ta·loupe /'kæntl,oʊp/ *n.* [C;U] a round melon with rough skin and sweet, light-orange insides: *Cantaloupe tastes good for dessert on a hot day.*

can·tan·ker·ous /kæn'tæŋkərəs/ *adj.* bad-tempered, always wanting to argue, (*syn.*) grumpy: *The cantankerous old man won't pay his rent.*

can·teen /kæn'tin/ *n.* **1** a container for liquid: *When we take a long walk, we carry water in our canteens.* **2** a military store or snack bar: *Soldiers buy sandwiches and cigarettes in the canteen.* **3** an area for relaxing and eating in an institution, such as a school: *We had lunch in the canteen.*

can·ter /'kæntər/ *n.v.* the smooth run of a horse, faster than a trot, slower than a gallop: *Horses <v.> cantered around the show ring.*

can·vas /'kænvəs/ *n.* **-vases** **1** [U] a thick, rough cloth used for ships' sails, tents, and coverings: *The canvas in sails is so strong that it lasts for years.* **2** [C;U] cloth stretched over a wooden frame for painting pictures: *She paints with oil on canvas.* **3** [C] a painting itself: *She has many canvases for sale.*

can·vass /'kænvəs/ *v.* **-vassed,-vassing, -vasses** **1** to ask people their opinions about other people and products, (*syn.*) to conduct a poll: *Workers <v.> canvassed 1,000 people by telephone to get their opinion of the President's performance.* **2** to go around asking people for their votes: *Politicians <v.> canvass voters for their votes. -n.* **canvasser;** [U] **canvassing.** *See:* opinion poll.

can·yon /'kænyən/ *n.* a long, deep crack in the earth's surface, (*syn.*) a gorge: *The Colorado River flows through the Grand Canyon.*

C

cap /kæp/ n. **1** a removable top to a bottle, jar, etc.: *Please put the cap back on the medicine bottle.* **2** a soft hat, often with a visor: *She wears a baseball cap when she runs.* **3** a soft hat with no visor: *a nurse's cap, a soldier's cap* **4** a limit on s.t.: *The government put a cap on its spending.*
—v. **capped, capping, caps 1** to cover with a cap: *Workers capped an oil well to prevent oil from spilling.* **2** to add s.t. special at the end of (one's career, a special occasion, etc.): *The businesswoman capped her career by starting another successful company just before she retired.*

ca·pa·bil·i·ty /ˌkeɪpəˈbɪləti/ n. [C;U] **-ties** the ability or power to do s.t., (syn.) competence: *He has the capability to speak four languages.*

ca·pa·ble /ˈkeɪpəbəl/ adj. having the ability or power to do s.t., or things in general, well: *She is a very capable doctor.* -adv. **capably.**

ca·pac·i·ty /kəˈpæsəti/ n. **-ties 1** sing. [U] the ability to contain, hold, or absorb: *That restaurant has a 100-seat capacity.* **2** sing. [U] the greatest amount that s.t. can contain, (syn.) the maximum volume: *There is no more room in the bottle; it is filled to capacity.* **3** [C;U] the ability to do s.t.: *He has the capacity to work long hours.* **4** [C;U] the power to learn and remember knowledge, (syn.) mental ability: *She has a great capacity for learning.* **5** [C] the power that goes with a certain position or role: *She signs the company checks in her capacity as owner.* **6** [U] the best or maximum amount of production: *That factory is working at capacity.*

cape (1) /keɪp/ n. a loose, sleeveless outer garment hanging from the shoulders, (syn.) a cloak: *She wears a thick woolen cape in winter.*

cape (2) n. an area of land stretching out into the sea: *Cape Cod, Massachusetts, is a popular vacation area.*

ca·per (1) /ˈkeɪpər/ v. to jump joyfully in the air: *The children capered about on the beach.*
—n. **1** a wild, foolish act, (syn.) a reckless adventure: *The young man's capers eventually got him into trouble.* **2** a type of flower bud which is often pickled: *She added ground capers to the dish.*

caper (2) n. a criminal act: *The thief's next caper was a bank robbery.*

cap·il·lar·y /ˈkæpəˌlɛri/ n. **-ies** (in medicine) a tiny blood vessel: *Capillaries feed blood to the smallest parts of the body.*

cap·i·tal (1) /ˈkæpətl/ n. the official place where a state, provincial, or national government is located: *Washington, DC is the capital of the USA.*

USAGE NOTE: In the USA, the building(s) where a state's or the country's elected officials meet is called the "capitol," spelled with an "o".

capital (2) n. [U] **1** wealth, such as money, land, buildings, etc., owned by a person, business, or institution (church, government) **2** the net worth of a business: *The capital of a business is the value of its assets (cash, buildings, land, etc.) after liabilities (money owed, etc.) are subtracted.* **3** money put into a business by its owners or outside stockholders: *Businesses use capital to buy new equipment and new inventory.* See: working capital.

capital (3) n.adj. a letter written in tall form, (syn.) upper-case: *This sentence begins with a <n> capital (or) a <adj.> capital T.*

capital asset n. property owned by a business: *Land, offices, warehouses, factories, equipment, and furniture are capital assets.*

capital gain n. the increase in value of an asset above its purchase price: *When the price of a stock goes up above the cost you paid for it, that is a capital gain.*

cap·i·tal·ism /ˈkæpətlˌɪzəm/ n. [U] an economic system based on private ownership, competition, and a free market: *After the Soviet Union broke up, the government there began to move from communism toward capitalism.* -adj. **capitalistic** /ˌkæpətlˈɪstɪk/. See: communism; socialism.

cap·i·tal·ist /ˈkæpətlɪst/ n. a wealthy person, esp. one who loans money to businesses for interest payments, (syn.) an investor

cap·i·tal·i·za·tion /ˌkæpətləˈzeɪʃən/ n. [U] the value of the stock shares in a company: *The capitalization of that company is $10 million.*

cap·i·tal·ize /ˈkæpətlˌaɪz/ v. **-ized, -izing, -izes 1** to provide a business with capital (money): *A company capitalized at $10 million.* **2** phrasal v. insep. **to capitalize on s.t.:** to take advantage of an opportunity: *She started a successful store, then capitalized on its success by opening more of them in other cities.* **3** to make a letter upper case: *Don't forget to capitalize the first letter of an English sentence.*

capital punishment n. [U] the option to put to death criminals who commit very serious crimes, (syn.) the death penalty: *Some states in the USA allow capital punishment; others do not.*

USAGE NOTE: Each state in the USA makes its own laws about punishing criminals for certain crimes. Therefore, some states allow *capital punishment* and other states do not. Capital punishment is a social issue that is very important in the United States right now: *She believes in capital punishment, so she voted for a senator who believes in capital punishment.*

cap·i·tol /'kæpətl/ n. **1** the building in which the governing body of a state meets: *Elected representatives discussed new laws in the capitol.* **2 the Capitol:** the building where the Congress of the USA meets in Washington, DC See: USAGE NOTE at capital, (1).

ca·pit·u·late /kə'pɪʧə,leɪt/ v.frml. **-lated, -lating, -lates 1** to surrender on agreed terms: *The owners capitulated to the workers' demands by giving them a 5% pay increase.* **2** to give up, stop resisting, (syn.) to acquiesce: *She finally capitulated and agreed to go to the party.* -n. [C;U] **capitulation** /kə,pɪʧə'leɪʃən/.

cap·let /'kæplɪt/ n. a smooth, hard capsule containing medicine: *I take two caplets of aspirin when I have a headache.* See: tablet.

ca·po /'kɑpou, 'kæ-/ n. slang **-pos** a captain in the Mafia: *A capo gives orders to soldiers in the Mafia.*

ca·pon /'keɪ,pɑn, -pən/ n. a male chicken with its sex organs removed: *Fat capons are good to eat.*

ca·price /kə'pris/ n.frml. [C;U] **1** a foolish change of behavior, usu. without a good reason **2** a sudden desire to do s.t., (syn.) a whim: *They went on an unplanned trip to the mountains as a caprice last weekend.*

ca·pri·cious /kə'prɪʃəs, -'pri-/ adj.frml. **1** doing s.t. unexpected, (syns.) undependable, unreliable: *He changes his mind in a capricious manner.* **2** changing frequently: *The weather has been capricious this winter; one day it is cold and rainy, the next day it is hot and sunny.* -adv. **capriciously.**

cap·puc·ci·no /,kæpə'ʧinou, ka-/ n. frothy, Italian-style coffee drink: *I love cappuccino with pastries for breakfast.*

cap·size /'kæp,saɪz, kæp'saɪz/ v. **-sized, -sizing, -sizes** to tip over: *The ship capsized and sank in the storm.*

cap·sule /'kæpsəl/ n. **1** a dose of medicine contained inside a soft, clear, usu. rounded coating: *Capsules dissolve in your stomach, releasing the medicine.* **2** the part of a vehicle that usu. contains people and/or special equipment for air or space flight: *a space capsule* —adj. small, short, or brief: *She gave a capsule summary of the long report.*

cap·tain /'kæptən/ n.v. **1** the top officer in command of a ship: *The <n.> captain went on board his ship.* **2** in the USA, a military officer rank in the army, air force, or marines, below major and above first lieutenant; in the navy, below rear admiral and above commander **3** general head of a group or team: *The captain of the football team encouraged the players.*

cap·tion /'kæpʃən/ n.v. an explanation written above, below, or beside a picture: *Newspapers*

have *<n.>* captions that name the people in the pictures.

cap·ti·vate /'kæptə,veɪt/ v.frml. **-vated, -vating, -vates** to capture the admiration or love of s.o., (syn.) to charm: *Her beauty and intelligence have captivated many men.* -adj. **captivating;** -n. **captivation** /,kæptə'veɪʃən/.

cap·tive /'kæptɪv/ n.adj. s.o. taken and held by force against their will, (syn.) a prisoner: *Soldiers put an enemy <n.> captive in prison.*||fig. *The rock star had a <adj.> captive audience.*

cap·tiv·i·ty /kæp'tɪvəti/ n. [U] a condition of holding s.o. or s.t. by force against their will, (syns.) confinement, imprisonment: *The zoo holds animals like lions and tigers in captivity.*

cap·tor /'kæptər/ n. s.o., such as a police officer or a soldier, who captures another: *His captors were enemy soldiers.*

cap·ture /'kæpʧər/ v. **-tured, -turing, -tures 1** to take s.o. or s.t. by force: *The police captured a criminal.* **2** to hold the attention of: *The thought of going to the moon captured her imagination.* **3** to preserve information: *Cameras capture special memories.* —n. [U] an act of capturing s.o. or s.t.: *The capture of the criminal involved a fight.*

car /kar/ n. **1** an automobile: *I drive my car to work every day.* **2** a vehicle that runs on tracks or wires: *a railroad car, a subway car, a cable car, an elevator car*

car·a·mel /'kærəməl, -,mɛl, 'karməl/ n. [C;U] **1** a candy made with sugar, butter, and milk or cream: *Caramel candy is smooth, rich, and chewy.* **2** burnt sugar used as a flavoring in cooking

car·at /'kærət/ n. a measurement of the weight of precious stones (diamonds, rubies, etc.) or gold equal to 200 milligrams: *Her diamond is five carats.* See: karat.

car·a·van /'kærə,væn/ n. a group of people making a trip together: *A caravan of merchants and their camels crossed the desert.*

car·bo·hy·drate /,karbou'haɪ,dreɪt, -ba-/ n. any of a group of nutrients, such as sugar and starch, that provide the body with energy: *Grains and fruits are high in carbohydrates.*

car·bon /'karbən/ n. [U] the chemical element found in coal, graphite, and diamonds: *The black lead in pencils is made of soft carbon.*

car·bon·at·ed /'karbə,neɪtəd/ adj. containing carbon dioxide gas bubbles: *Soft drinks, like Coca-Cola™, are carbonated.* See: fizz.

carbon copy n. **-ies 1** a duplicate copy of s.t. made with carbon paper: *He made carbon copies of the report.* **2** s.t. that looks just like s.t. else, (syn.) an imitation: *His style of playing tennis is a carbon copy of his teacher's.* See: carbon paper; photocopy.

carbon di·ox·ide /daɪˈɑk,saɪd/ n. [U] a gas with no color, taste, or smell, formed when people and animals exhale and used in fire extinguishers and carbonated drinks: *About 1% of the air around the earth is made up of carbon dioxide.*

carbon mon·ox·ide /məˈnɑk,saɪd/ n. an extremely poisonous gas with no color, taste, or smell, and occurring esp. in the exhaust from gasoline engines: *Breathing too much carbon monoxide can kill a person in a few minutes.*

carbon paper n. [U] a paper covered on one side with dry ink and put between pieces of paper to make duplicate copies of written documents: *Before photocopy machines, carbon paper was used to make copies.*

car·bu·re·tor /ˈkɑrbə,reɪtər/ n. a device on an engine that mixes fuel and air so the engine can burn it: *When the carburetor is not working, a car won't run.*

car·cass /ˈkɑrkəs/ n. **-casses** the body of a dead animal: *Lions fed on the carcass of a zebra.*

card /kɑrd/ n. **1** a piece of stiff paper or plastic used for many purposes, such as a credit card, business card, greeting card, or postcard **2** a playing card: *There are 52 cards in a deck.* **3** *fig.* a person who makes others laugh: *He is always joking; he's a card.* **4** a piece of lined paper for keeping score in a game or sport: *At the end of play, the golfer handed in her card.* **5 to lay one's cards on the table:** to say what one thinks, (*syns.*) to reveal all, be frank: *After many meetings, she finally laid her cards on the table and offered me the job.*
—*v. slang* **to be carded:** to be asked to prove that one is old enough to drink, usu. at a bar: *If you're carded at a bar, you must show an I.D. card such as a driver's license to prove your age.*

card·board /ˈkɑrd,bɔrd/ n.adj. [U] flat, stiff, thick paper: *The gift arrived in a <adj.> cardboard box.*

car·di·ac /ˈkɑrdi,æk/ adj. related to the heart

cardiac arrest n. [C;U] heart failure, (*syn.*) a heart attack: *The man died of cardiac arrest.*

car·di·gan /ˈkɑrdɪgən/ n. a type of long-sleeved sweater that buttons up the front: *He wears a wool cardigan in winter.*

car·di·nal /ˈkɑrdnəl/ n. **1** a Roman Catholic clergyman ranking below the Pope: *Cardinals from all over the world meet in Rome.* **2** a red songbird common in North America
—*adj.* **1** related to numbers used in counting: *Some cardinal numbers are 1, 2, 3, and 200.* **2** of great importance: *This is a matter of cardinal importance. See:* ordinal.

car·di·ol·o·gy /,kɑrdiˈɑləʤi/ n. [U] medical treatment or study of the heart and its disease

care /kɛr/ v. **cared, caring, cares 1** to feel concern about the well-being of others: *She cares about everyone; she is interested in and concerned about people.*‖*He doesn't care about anyone but himself.* **2** to be concerned about s.t., (*syn.*) to worry: *She cares about the quality of her work.*‖*I really want to buy that car; I don't care if it costs too much!* **3 not to care for:** to like or love: (love) *I don't care for her.*‖(like) *He doesn't care for carrots or beans.* **4** *phrasal v. insep.* **to care for s.o.** or **s.t.:** to look after s.o.'s health, (*syn.*) to nurse: *When she was sick, he cared for her day and night.* **5 to not care less:** to not care at all: *He is such a bad manager; I could not care less if he leaves the company.*
—*n.* **1** [U] concern for others, (*syn.*) kindness: *He shows care for every one of his children.* **2** [U] supervision of s.o.'s health or well-being: *The nurses and doctors took good care of me in the hospital.* **3** [U] close attention, (*syn.*) carefulness: *She did her school report with great care.* **4** concern not to damage, (*syn.*) gentleness: *You should handle those dishes with care.* **5 to take care: a.** to be careful: *Take care not to break any glasses.* **b.** to stay safe and well: *I will talk to you again tomorrow; take care (of yourself).* **6 to take care of:** to do, handle, or solve: *I'll take care of the problem myself. -adj.* **caring.**

ca·reen /kəˈrin/ v. to go fast and usu. out of control: *The car careened down the hill and hit a wall.*

ca·reer /kəˈrɪr/ n. a life's work, esp. in business or in a profession: *She has a career in teaching high school English.*

care·free /ˈkɛr,fri/ adj. without worry or cares: *He always seems happy; he has a carefree attitude.*

care·ful /ˈkɛrfəl/ adj. **1** being aware of danger, (*syn.*) cautious: *Be careful when you cross the street.* **2** attentive to detail, (*syn.*) meticulous: *He was very careful to say exactly what he meant in his report.* **3** good with money: *She is very careful; she never goes out to restaurants for dinner, and always takes the bus instead of a taxi. -adv.* **carefully;** *-n.* [U] **carefulness.**

care·less /ˈkɛrlɪs/ adj. **1** inattentive to danger, (*syn.*) reckless: *She is careless when she drives a car.* **2** inattentive to detail, (*syn.*) sloppy: *That report is full of mistakes; he did a careless job on it.* **3** thoughtless, (*syn.*) inconsiderate: *That was careless of you to make a joke about cancer, since her mother died of cancer. -adv.* **carelessly;** *-n.* **carelessness.**

ca·ress /kəˈrɛs/ n. **-resses** a gentle touch or pat, showing affection: *She gave the baby a caress on the cheek.*

—*v.* **-ressed, -ressing, -resses** to rub lightly or pat tenderly: *He caressed her shoulders with his hands.*

USAGE NOTE: Compare *caress, massage,* and *rub,* which are all ways of touching people. A *caress* is a soft touch to show s.o. that he or she is liked or loved. A *massage* is a firm squeezing of muscles, often used to make painful muscles feel better: *The athlete massaged her sore leg.* Rub is a way of touching in which the hand is moved back and forth firmly and regularly: *The child rubbed her eyes because she was tired.||The cat rubbed against his legs.*

---

care·taker /'kɛr,teɪkər/ *n.* **1** a person who takes care of a piece of property, (*syn.*) a custodian: *Large houses often have a caretaker who does the gardening and repairs.* **2** a person who does a job temporarily until s.o. permanent takes over

care·worn /'kɛr,wɔrn/ *adj.* tired from worry, or showing signs of worry and tiredness, (*syn.*) haggard: *He is careworn from all the trouble in his life.*

car·fare /'kar,fɛr/ *n.* money to pay for rides on subways, buses, taxis, etc.: *Make sure you take enough money for carfare.*

car·go /'kargoʊ/ *n.* **-goes** or **-gos** [C;U] goods usu. in large amounts, (*syn.*) freight: *Cargo is carried on ships, airplanes, and trucks.*

car·i·bou /'kærə,bu/ *n.* **-bou** or **-bous** a large reindeer of North America

car·i·ca·ture /'kærɪkətʃər, -,ʃʊr/ *n.v.* [C;U] **-tured, -turing, -tures 1** a drawing or imitation of s.o. or s.t. that exaggerates distinctive features, either as a joke or to point out faults: *Cartoonists in the USA like to draw* <*n.*> *caricatures of the Presidents.* **2** an imitation so poor that it is laughable: *She tries to dress and act like that movie star, but the result is so funny it's a* <*n.*> *caricature.*

car·load /'kar,loʊd/ *n.* a full load of cargo on a truck or train: *That truck is carrying a carload of coal.*

car·nage /'karnɪdʒ/ *n.* [U] **1** the killing of many people or animals, (*syn.*) a massacre **2** the dead bodies of a massacre: *The carnage after the battle was horrifying.*

car·nal /'karnəl/ *adj.frml.* related to bodily or worldly desires, esp. related to sex, (*syn.*) sensual: *To have carnal knowledge of s.o. means to have had sex with that person.*

car·na·tion /kar'neɪʃən/ *n.* a sweet-smelling, long-stemmed flower with white, red, yellow, or pink blossoms: *He wore a red carnation in the buttonhole of his suit.*

car·ni·val /'karnəvəl/ *n.* **1** a celebration with singing, dancing, and usu. a parade, (*syn.*) a festival: *The carnival in Rio in Brazil is world-famous.* **2** a group of entertainers, including

salespeople and amusement rides, that goes from place to place: *The carnival is coming to town next week. See:* festival.

car·ni·vore /'karnə,vɔr/ *n.* animal that eats meat to live: *Lions are carnivores who like to eat zebras.* **-adj. carnivorous** /kar'nɪvərəs/**.**

car·ol /'kærəl/ *n.v.* **-oled** or **-olled, -oling** or **-olling, -ols** a song of joy and praise, esp. for Christmas: *We sang* <*n.*> *carols in church.*

ca·rouse /kə'raʊz/ *n.v.* **-roused, -rousing, -rouses** to have a good time, esp. to drink heavily: *They* <*v.*> *caroused all night, going from one bar to another.* **-n. carouser.**

ca·rou·sel /,kærə'sɛl/ *n. See:* merry-go-round.

carp (1) /karp/ *v.* to criticize and complain all the time: *That man carps about everything.*

carp *n.* **carps** [C;U] a large fish that lives in lakes and rivers

car·pal /'karpəl/ *adj.* (in medicine) related to the wrist: *She has a carpal injury and moves her wrist with difficulty.*

car·pen·ter /'karpəntər/ *n.v.* a person who earns a living by making and building things with wood: *A team of 12* <*n.*> *carpenters built that house.* **-n.** [U] **carpentry** /'karpəntri/**.**

car·pet /'karpɪt/ *n.* [C;U] a floor covering of woven fabric or other material, (*syn.*) a rug: *The carpet needs cleaning; someone dropped food on it.*
—*v.* to cover with or as if with a carpet: *The field was carpeted with flowers.*

car·pool *n.v.* a travel arrangement to and from work (school, etc.) in which the riders share a car and travel expenses: *My high-school son* <*v.*> *car-pools to school with two of his friends.*

car·rel /'kærəl/ *n.* a desk in a library used for quiet, individual study: *I am studying at a carrel on the third floor of the library.*

car·riage /'kærɪdʒ/ *n.* **1** [C] a wooden, four-wheeled vehicle: *Long ago, people traveled in horse-drawn carriages.* **2** [C] a four-wheeled vehicle for a baby, pushed by s.o. on foot: *He put the baby in her carriage and took her for a walk.* **3** [U] the manner of carrying one's head and body, (*syns.*) posture, bearing: *She is very graceful; she has excellent carriage.* **4** [C] a part of a machine that moves another part: *The carriage in my old typewriter holds the roller that moves the paper.* **5** [U] old usage the cost of carrying, (*syn.*) the transport charge: *Carriage for that item will be $12.*

car·ri·er /'kæriər/ *n.* **1** a means of transportation, esp. by truck, airline, or railroad: *We used a trucking company as the carrier to ship our products.* **2** a person or animal that is not ill from a disease, but gives it to others: *Some mosquitoes are carriers of malaria.* **3** a warship that carries aircraft, (*syn.*) an aircraft carrier: *A dozen fighter jets took off from the air-craft carrier.*

car·ri·on /'kæriən/ *n.* [U] the flesh and bones of a dead animal that is unfit for human food: *After the lion ate the zebra, birds fed on the carrion.*

car·rot /'kærət/ *n.* **1** [C;U] a plant whose orange-colored root is eaten as a vegetable **2** *fig.* a reward offered, often falsely, to get s.o. to do s.t.: *The director waved a carrot in front of the young actress by telling her that they would make her famous.*

car·ry /'kæri/ *v.* **-ried, -rying, -ries 1** to hold and move s.o. or s.t. from one place to another, (*syn.*) to convey: *The bus carries people to work. ||The diplomat carried a letter from the President to the Prime Minister.* **2** to bear weight, esp. a heavy load, (*syns.*) to support: *Those thick wires carry the weight of that bridge.* **3** to have or keep with one: *She always carries her purse.* **4** to bring with it, (*syns.*) to involve, imply: *Management always listens to her; her opinions carry a lot of weight with them.* **5** to include a guarantee or penalty: *That car carries a five-year warranty.||The parking ticket carries a $50 fine.* **6** to bear the responsibility of: *He is very ill and has little money; he carries a heavy load on his shoulders.* **7** to convince, esp. to win votes: *The President carried the South (the state, the election).* **8** to hold and move the head, shoulders, and body in a certain way: *She carries herself with dignity.* **9 to become** or **get carried away:** to do too much of s.t. and lose control of oneself: *He got carried away and talked for hours.* **10** *phrasal v. sep.* **to carry s.o.** or **s.t. through: a. s.o.:** to help s.o. to do s.t. despite trouble, illness, etc.: *Her friends and family carried her through her breakdown.* **b. s.t.:** See: carry s.t. out, **b. 11** *phrasal v. sep.* **to carry s.t. forward** or **over: a.** to move ahead: *We carried our plans forward and started the new project.* **b.** (in accounting) to move money into a later time period **12** *phrasal v. sep.* **to carry s.t. off: a.** to take away: *The thief carried off the TV.||He carried it off.* **b.** to succeed: *Despite the bad weather, we still carried off the family picnic.* **13** *phrasal v. sep.* **to carry s.t. on: a. s.t.:** to bring s.t. on: *She carried her bag on the airplane.* **b. s.t.:** to continue an activity despite an interruption or change: *Ms. Valdez told her assistant, Mr. Khan, to carry on while she was away.* **c.** (with s.o.): to conduct a love affair: *They have carried on an affair for years.* **d.** to flirt: *Ed and Nora carry on during coffee breaks.* **e.** to behave badly: *As soon as their parents left, the children began to carry on.* **14** *phrasal v. sep.* **to carry s.t. out: a.** to remove s.t.: *He carried his groceries out of the supermarket.* **b.** to do s.t. completely, (*syn.*) to ful-

fill: *She carried out her plans to get a divorce.||She carried them out.*
—*n.* the distance traveled by a voice, ball, bullet, etc.

car·ry-on /'kæri,an, -,ɔn/ *adj.* describing a bag that is carried on an airplane, bus, etc., instead of being stored in the luggage compartment: *I took two small bags as carry-on luggage on my plane trip.*

car·ry-out /'kæri,aut/ *n.* [U] a restaurant meal that is packaged and carried out to eat at home, (*syns.*) take-out: *That Chinese restaurant does a lot of carryout business.*

car·ry-over /'kæri,ouvər/ *n.* (in accounting) money that is transferred to a later time period: *That debt is a carryover from last year.*

cart /kart/ *n.* a small, light vehicle: *Shopping carts are pushed by hand.*
—*v.* **1** to carry s.t. by hand, cart, truck, etc.: *Trucks carted garbage to the dump.* **2** to carry s.t. heavy in a rough or awkward manner: *I had to cart my luggage from one end of the airport to the other.*

carte blanche /'kart'blanʃ, -'blɑnʃ/ *n.* [U] (French for) freedom to do whatever needs to be done, esp. with authority and money: *Her company gave her carte blanche to start a new project; she has carte blanche to spend whatever she needs to spend.*

car·tel /kar'tɛl/ *n.* a group of companies working together to control prices and markets: *The oil cartel controls the prices of crude oil.*

car·ti·lage /'kartlɪdʒ/ *n.* [C;U] a tough but flexible substance found in parts of the body: *Parts of our ears and nose are made of cartilage.*

car·tog·ra·phy /kar'tagrəfi/ *n.* [U] the art and science of making maps: *He learned cartography at the university.* -*n.* **cartographer.**

car·ton /'kartn/ *n.* a container made of stiff, usu. thick paper or cardboard: *I bought a carton of milk.*

car·toon /kar'tun/ *n.v.* **1** a picture or group of pictures, often with words, drawn to make people laugh: *I like to look at the <n.> cartoons in the morning newspaper.* **2** a short usu. funny film containing animated characters. -*n.* **cartoonist.**

car·tridge /'kartrɪdʒ/ *n.* **1** a bullet with gun powder inside a round, metal case: *She loaded the cartridges into the gun.* **2** a small, removable container in a larger device: *I changed the ink cartridge in my ballpoint pen. ||The film for some cameras comes in a cartridge.*

cart·wheel /'kart,wil/ *n.* **1** a jump in which one puts one's hands on the ground and one's legs in the air and turns sideways in a circle, moving like a wheel: *Many children learn to do cartwheels in gym class.* **2 to turn cartwheels:** to feel delighted, joyful: *When he heard the good news, he turned cartwheels.*

carve /karv/ v. **carved, carving, carves 1** to cut (meat, vegetables) into pieces: *She carved the turkey at the table.* **2** to shape s.t. by cutting it with artistry and exactness, *(syn.)* to sculpt: *She carves jewelry out of precious stones.* **3** to cut designs, letters, etc., into the surface of s.t.: *He carved his name on the tree.* **4** *phrasal v. sep.* **to carve s.t. up:** to divide s.t., esp. in order to favor oneself: *After their father died, the children carved up the family business.||They carved it up. -n.* **carver.**

carv·ing /'karvɪŋ/ n. [C;U] an art object that has been carved: *There is a wood carving of a man's head on my table.*

car wash n. **washes** a business where cars are washed, polished, etc.: *We took our car to the car wash to have it cleaned and waxed.*

cas·cade /kæ'skeɪd/ v. **-caded, -cading, -cades** to fall fast and steeply: *After a rainfall, water cascades down from the mountains.*
—n. a steep waterfall, often one in a series of waterfalls

case (1) /keɪs/ n. **1** [C] a protective cover for other things: *a suitcase, cigarette case, a bookcase* **2** [C] a container holding a certain number of cans, bottles, etc.: *I bought a case of canned beans (beer, shampoo, baby food).* **3** [C;U] the size of letters in writing: *This "S" is in upper case and this "s" is in lower case.*
—v. **cased, casing, cases 1** to put or wrap s.t. in a case **2** *slang* **to case the joint:** to carefully examine a place (store, house) that one intends to rob: *He cased the joint before he robbed it.*

case (2) n. **1** an example, particular event, or condition: *The accident was simply a case of being in the wrong place at the wrong time.||She had a case of the flu last month.* **2** a situation or set of <u>circumstances</u>: *The student said he could explain why his paper was so late, and was told to state his case briefly.* **3** convincing arguments or proof, (in law) a good cause or reason for an action: *His lawyer told him that he had a good legal case.* **4** a situation (such as a crime) investigated by the police or other officials: *The police are investigating the case.* **5** a client of a doctor, social worker, lawyer, etc.: *The psychiatrist had several difficult cases this week.* **6 in any case:** no matter what happens: *Bring your umbrella in any case; it might rain, or it might not.* **7 in case** (or) **in case of:** should s.t. happen: *In case of fire, call the fire department.* **8 in no case:** under no circumstances: *In no case should you open a door that feels hot during a fire.* **9 in that case:** if that situation occurs: *Oh, your mother is coming to dinner with us? In that case, I won't go since she and I fight a lot.* **10 just in case:** to be sure: *Just in case we need extra money on vacation, I'll put some more in my bag.* **11** *infrml.* **to be** or **get on s.o.'s case:**

to criticize s.o. frequently: *My report is late and my boss is on my case (about it).*

case study n. **-ies** a study in detail of a person or event for its educational value, esp. in business and medicine: *A case study of the family showed that they all had too much fat in their diet.*

case·work /'keɪs,wɜrk/ n. [U] (in social work) working to solve the problems of a specific person (case): *Casework with the elderly man involved helping him with his health and rent. -n.* **caseworker.**

cash /kæʃ/ n. [U] **1** paper currency, such as dollar bills, and metal coins used in making daily purchases: *I am going to the bank to get some cash.||Will you pay in cash or by credit card? |||I will pay cash.* **2** (in business) money in a company's bank account(s) that can be used to pay bills
—v. **cashes 1** to exchange a check for currency: *I cashed a $100 check at the bank.* **2** *phrasal v. insep.* **to cash in (on s.t.):** to make a lot of money: *He bought some houses at low prices and waited for their value to go up; then he cashed in.* **3 to cash in one's chips:** to stop investing or gambling: *She bought stocks for 10 years, then cashed in her chips.*

cash bar n. a bar where drinks are paid for by each person rather than being for free, usu. at a big party: *Our company paid for the dinner, but we had a cash bar before the meal.*

cash card n. a plastic identity card permitting its owner to cash checks at a bank or to take out funds from automated teller machines,*(syn.)* ATM card: *I showed my cash card to the bank teller and got some money.*

USAGE NOTE: Most banks now give customers a *cash card* to use at *ATMs (automated teller machines)*, which are available in most places in the USA. Some cash cards can be used internationally and, sometimes, the same card can be used as a cash card, *credit card* and *phone* or *calling card*. Each card has a *PIN (personal identification number)* that allows the user to use the card: *I put my cash card into the ATM, entered my PIN and took $20 from my bank account.*

cash cow n. a highly profitable business or product: *Ivory Soap™ sells all over the world and is a cash cow for its manufacturer.*

cash·ew /'kæʃu, kæ'ʃu/ n. **1** a tree of the tropical Americas that produces curved edible nuts **2** the nut itself: *Cashews taste delicious.*

cash flow n. [U] the amount of money coming into a person's, a business's, or an institution's account(s), minus the amount of money being spent: *The cash flow in our company is good because we take in much more money than we spend.*

cash·ier /kæ'ʃɪr/ n. a person responsible for accepting payment from customers in a store, restaurant, etc.: *The cashiers at the supermarket ring up sales, take your money, and give you change. See:* teller.

cash·mere /'kæʒ‚mɪr, 'kæʃ-/ n.adj. [U] **1** wool from a type of goat found in Kashmir and Tibet **2** the cloth made from this wool: <adj.> *Cashmere sweaters are soft and expensive.*

cash on delivery or **C.O.D.** adv. with payment made by the buyer upon receiving the purchase: *I ordered a pair of shoes and paid $50, cash on delivery, to the mailman.*

cas·ing /'keɪsɪŋ/ n. a covering around s.t.: *The electric wires in the wall have a protective metal casing around them.*

ca·si·no /kə'sinoʊ/ n. **-nos** a large hall, esp. for gambling: *The casinos in Las Vegas are as big as football fields.*

USAGE NOTE: Each state in the USA makes its own laws about *gambling,* so in some places casinos are legal and in other places they are not. The most famous cities with *casinos* are *Las Vegas, Nevada,* and *Atlantic City, New Jersey.*

---

cask /kæsk/ n. a type of barrel, esp. made of wood: *Wine casks sit in rows in the wine cellar.*

cas·ket /'kæskɪt/ n. a box-shaped container for burying the dead, (syn.) a coffin: *Six men carried the casket into the church.*

cas·se·role /'kæsə‚roʊl/ n. **1** [C] a deep dish for baking and serving mixed foods **2** [C;U] the food contents of a casserole: *We had a casserole of pasta and cheese.*

cas·sette /kə'sɛt/ n. a container (cartridge) with photographic tape or sound tape used to record or play back sights or sounds: *I put a cassette in the tape player and listened to some jazz.* -n. **cassette player.**

cast (1) /kæst/ n. the group of actors and actresses in a play or movie or the characters in a novel: *The cast of characters in the movie included some big stars.*
—v. **cast, casting, casts** to choose actors and actresses for a play, etc.: *The director cast a famous actress in the leading role.*

cast (2) v. **cast, casting, casts 1** to throw s.t. (a net, line, rope): *A fisherman cast a net into the water.* **2** to throw s.t. down violently: *A hurricane cast trees to the ground.* **3** to look at: *He cast his eyes downward toward the floor.* **4** to pour metal into a mold: *to cast iron (steel, bronze)* **5 to cast a** or **one's ballot:** to vote: *She cast her ballot in the election.* **6** phrasal v. sep. **to cast s.t. aside:** to throw s.t. away as useless or no longer needed: *A worker cast aside a broken part.||He cast it aside.* **7** phrasal v. sep. **to cast s.o. away:** to leave s.o. behind, as in a shipwreck: *The crew cast away the captain on*

a Pacific island.||They cast him away. **8** phrasal v. sep. **to cast s.t. off: a.** to undo the ropes or chains holding a boat and start moving, (syn.) to get underway: *The boat is about to cast off.* **b.** to throw s.t. away, such as clothes: *She cast off her clothes and dove into the lake.* **9** phrasal v. sep. **to cast s.o. out:** to send s.o. away, usu. by force: *They cast the thief out of the village.* **10 to cast one's lot with s.o.:** to join s.o., esp. in a risky situation: *A young politician cast her lot with the small liberal party and lost the election. See:* castoff.
—n. **1** a throw, esp. of a fishline or net: *That was a good cast.* **2** (in medicine) a hard covering made from a pastelike substance, used to keep a broken bone still while it heals: *The doctor put a cast on the football player's broken leg* **3** a mold: *A worker poured metal into a cast to make an auto part.*

cas·ta·nets /‚kæstə'nɛts/ n.pl. a musical instrument made of a pair of ivory or hardwood shells, held in one hand by a cord or ribbon over the thumb: *The Spanish dancer clicked her castanets in rhythm to the music.*

cast·a·way /'kæstə‚weɪ/ n. a person from a wrecked ship, forced to live in a strange land: *The castaways swam ashore to a deserted, tropical island.*

caste /kæst/ n. [C;U] a social class of people, membership in which is passed from parents to children: *She belongs to the highest caste in India, the Brahmins.*

cast·er or **cas·tor** /'kæstər/ n. **1** a small wheel that can roll in any direction: *Casters are placed on the bottom of heavy objects, like furniture, so that they can be moved more easily.* **2** a small bottle with a hole in the top to allow olive oil, sugar, salt, etc. to be poured from it

cas·ti·gate /'kæstɪ‚geɪt/ v.frml. **-gated, -gating, -gates** to criticize severely, (syn.) to rebuke: *A judge castigated a vicious criminal and sent him to jail.* -n. [U] **castigation** /‚kæstɪ'geɪʃən/.

cast·ing /'kæstɪŋ/ n. **1** [C] s.t. shaped in a mold: *Workers poured metal in a mold and made castings of little statues.* **2** [U] the selection of actors for a play, film, etc.: *She is in charge of casting for the new film.*

cast iron n. [U] a hard metal often used in making heavy cooking pots and pans
—adj. **cast-iron 1** not to be changed, (syn.) rigid: *This is a cast-iron rule.* **2** a **cast-iron stomach:** the ability to eat almost anything without trouble: *He eats hot, spicy food every day; he must have a cast-iron stomach.*

cas·tle /'kæsəl/ n. **1** a large building or group of buildings with thick walls and other defenses against attack: *Europe has many old castles.* **2** fig. a place of peace, privacy, and comfort: *"A man's home is his castle."* **3** a playing piece in chess, shaped like the tower on a castle

cast·off /'kæ,stɔf/ *n.adj.* anything cast aside as useless or unwanted: *She wears <adj.> castoff clothes unwanted by others.*

cas·tor oil /'kæstər/ *n.* [U] a thick oil made from seeds of the castor tree, used to reduce friction (lubricate) or to help empty the bowels: *He took a teaspoon of castor oil to help clean out his digestive system.*

cas·trate /'kæ,streɪt/ *v.* **-trated, -trating, -trates** to remove the sex organs, esp. of a male: *Animal doctors castrate male horses.* *-n.* [C;U] **castration** /kæ'streɪʃən/.

ca·su·al /'kæʒuəl/ *adj.* **1** informal: *In the summer, people dress in casual clothes, like T-shirts and shorts.* **2** not very serious, relaxed, *(syn.)* slang laid back: *He has a casual attitude toward his work.* *-adv.* **casually;** *-n.* [U] **casualness.**

ca·su·al·ty /'kæʒuəlti, 'kæʒəl-/ *n.* **-ties** a person hurt or killed in an accident, a war, or by epidemic disease, esp. a soldier, sailor, etc. wounded, captured, or killed in battle: *We won the battle, but had several hundred casualties.*

cat /kæt/ *n.* **1** a general term for a group of four-legged, furry animals with sharp teeth and claws: *Cats include lions, tigers, leopards, house cats, etc.* **2** a small cat with soft fur, *(syn.)* a house cat: *People love having cats as pets.* **3 the cat's meow:** the very best: *They love their new house; they think it's the cat's meow.* **4 to let the cat out of the bag:** to reveal a secret, usu. by mistake: *He let the cat out of the bag when he accidentally told his wife about her surprise birthday party.* **5 to rain cats and dogs:** to rain very heavily: *I wouldn't go out right now; it's raining cats and dogs.*

cat·a·clys·mic /,kætə'klɪzmɪk/ *adj.frml.* relating to a violent event, such as an earthquake, flood, or revolution, *(syn.)* catastrophic: *The huge fire was a cataclysmic event that destroyed the town.* *-n.* **cataclysm** /'kætə,klɪzəm/.

cat·a·combs /'kætə,koumz/ *n.pl.* underground passages for burying the dead: *The ancient catacombs under Rome are a tourist attraction.*

cat·a·log or **cat·a·logue** /'kætl,ɔg, -,ɑg/ *n.* a booklet containing information about products, school courses, etc.: *Businesses mail out catalogs of their products to customers.*
—v. **-loged** or **-logued, -loging** or **-loguing, -logs** or **-logues** to list items in or make a catalog: *He cataloged the books in his library.*

cat·a·lyst /'kætəlɪst/ *n.* **1** a chemical that changes or speeds up a reaction between other chemicals **2** a person, idea, or event that creates important changes: *The invention of the*

telephone was a great catalyst in improving communications.

cat·a·ma·ran /,kætəmə'ræn, 'kætəmə,ræn/ *n.* a type of boat with two hulls on either side of the sail(s): *Catamarans move fast through the water.*

cat·a·pult /'kætə,pʌlt, -,pʊlt/ *n.* long ago, a machine used in war to shoot big rocks against an enemy
—v. to throw or propel suddenly and with great force or speed: *Her role in the movie catapulted her to fame.*

cat·a·ract /'kætə,rækt/ *n.* **1** a disease of the eye that clouds its lens and causes blindness if not treated **2** the cloudy spots caused by the disease: *He had his cataracts operated on and can see now.* **3** a huge waterfall, or a downpour like a waterfall: *The melting snow caused water to come rushing down the mountain in cataracts.*

ca·tas·tro·phe /kə'tæstrəfi/ *n.* **1** a great disaster: *Strong earthquakes are catastrophes that kill thousands of people.* **2** a great defeat, failure: *The company lost its biggest customer and that was a catastrophe for its future.* *-adj.* **catastrophic** /,kætə'strɑfɪk/.

cat·bird /'kæt,bərd/ *n.* **1** a gray North American songbird **2 the catbird's seat:** to have choices that are very desirable: *She sits in the catbird's seat because she has two excellent job offers.*

cat·call /'kæt,kɔl/ *n.v.* a whistle or shout of disapproval or insult: *The audience disliked the performance and made <n.> catcalls at the singer.*

catch /kætʃ/ *n.* **catches 1** an act of taking hold of s.t. in motion, *(syns.)* a grasp, snatch: *One player threw the ball and the other made a good catch.* **2** a fastener: *I opened the catch on a door.* **3** a hidden difficulty or unpleasant requirement: *There is a catch in that contract where you have to pay all the money now, but wait six months for delivery of the product.* **4** s.t. that has been caught: *The catch of the day is bluefish.* **5 a good catch: a.** s.o. who is very desirable to marry: *He married a beautiful, rich woman; she was a good catch.* **b.** the prevention of a mistake: *She found and corrected a big mistake in an order before it was shipped; it was a good catch.* **6 to play catch:** to throw a ball back and forth between people: *The children are playing catch in the playground.*
—v. **caught** /kɔt/, **catching, catches 1** to grasp s.t. in motion: *Here, catch the ball.* **2** to close the distance between you and s.o. else, *(syn.)* to overtake: *A runner caught up with the others and passed them.* **3** to get somewhere on time: *Hurry, we've got a plane to catch!* **4** to stop and hold, *(syns.)* to seize, capture: *The police catch criminals every day.* **5** to trap: *We*

caught the skunk by putting food in a cage. **6** to hook on s.t., *(syn.)* to snag: *The sleeve of his coat caught on the door handle.* **7** to fasten, *(syn.)* to latch: *Did the lock catch?* **8** to get a sickness, *(syn.)* to contract an illness or disease: *I catch a cold every winter.* **9** to take in (to see, hear, etc.), understand, and remember: *Did you catch everything he said?* **10** to come upon s.o. suddenly or unexpectedly: *I caught her just as she was leaving the office.* **11** to discover: *He caught a mistake in his report and corrected it.* **12** *fig.* **not** or **never to catch s.o. (doing s.t.):** to never see s.o. doing s.t. because one dislikes and avoids it: *I hate carrots (TV, big cities, etc.); you won't catch me eating them (watching it, visiting there, etc.).* **13 to catch hold:** to grab s.t. suddenly: *The boat rolled, but he caught hold of the rail.* **14 to catch it** or **catch hell:** to be punished: *You are always late; you are going to catch it* (or) *catch hell from the boss!* **15** *phrasal v.* **to catch on: a.** to understand, *(syn.)* to comprehend: *She is a bright student; she catches on to new things quickly.* **b.** to become popular: *That new product (actor, film, etc.) has really caught on.* **16 to catch one's breath: a.** to begin to breathe normally: *The runner stopped and caught her breath.* **b.** *fig.* to rest: *I've been doing so many things that I haven't had time to catch my breath.* **17 to catch s.o. in the act:** to capture s.o. as he or she commits the crime: *The police caught the thief in the act of robbing the bank.* **18 to catch s.o. off guard:** to surprise s.o. when he or she is distracted or relaxed: *The thief stole her pocketbook while she was looking in a store window; he caught her off guard.* **19 to play catch-up:** to try to complete late work or catch up to a competitor: *He is out of the office so often that he has to play catch-up on his paperwork all the time.*

catch-as-catch-can *n.adj.* doing s.t. by whatever way is possible: *We ran out of paper for the photocopier; it was catch-as-catch-can, so we used company stationery instead.*

catch·ing /'kætʃɪŋ/ *adj.* likely to go from one person to another, as a disease, *(syn.)* contagious: *I have the flu and it's catching, so stay away from me.*||*Her enthusiasm is catching.*

catch phrase *n.* a saying, idea, etc. in popular use: *"You know" is a catch phrase in this sentence: "New York is an exciting place, you know." See:* catchword; buzzword.

Catch-22 /'kætʃ,twɛni'tu, -,twɛnti-/ *n.adj.* a problem for which the only possible solution is another problem: *The manager told her she couldn't get a job unless she had experience. How was she going to get experience if she couldn't get a job? It was a Catch-22.*

catch·word /'kætʃ,wɜrd/ *n.* a word or phrase expressing a shallow thought, *(syns.)* a cliché, slogan: *The man did not know how to manage*

a company; all that he offered was catchwords, like "Time is money." See: catch phrase; buzzword.

catch·y /'kætʃi/ *adj.* **-ier, -iest** lively and pleasant: *She played a catchy song on the piano.*

cat·e·chism /'kætə,kɪzəm/ *n.* a question and answer book used to teach the basic ideas of a religion: *She read the catechism in church.*

cat·e·gor·i·cal /,kætə'gɔrɪkəl, -'gɑr-/ *adj.* with complete certainty, *(syns.)* absolute, unequivocal: *He made a categorical statement that he did not commit the crime.*

cat·e·go·rize /'kætəgə,raɪz/ *v.* **-rized, -rizing, -rizes** to place (things, ideas, etc.) into categories: *Would you categorize the company's problems as financial?* *-n.* **categorization** /,kætəgərə'zeɪʃən/.

cat·e·go·ry /'kætə,gɔri/ *n.* **-ries** a group or type of thing (idea, problem, etc.): *I place him in the category of being a troublemaker.*

ca·ter /'keɪtər/ *v.* **1** to provide food and beverages as a business for parties: *The Good Food Company catered our high school graduation party with a chicken dinner and ice cream.* **2** *phrasal v. insep.* **to cater to s.o.** or **s.t.:** to satisfy s.o.'s special needs and desires: *He caters to his wife by buying her flowers and jewels.* *-n.* **caterer.**

cat·er·pil·lar /'kætə,pɪlər, -tər-/ *n.* a small, usu. fuzzy worm-like creature with many legs: *A caterpillar turns into a butterfly or moth at a later stage in its life. See:* larva.

cat·fish /'kæt,fɪʃ/ *n.* [C;U] **-fish** a scaleless, edible freshwater fish with whisker-like feelers around the mouth: *I had broiled catfish for lunch.*

ca·the·dral /kə'θidrəl/ *n.* the main church in the area (called a "diocese") that a bishop is responsible for: *St. Patrick's Cathedral stands tall and gray on New York's Fifth Avenue.*

cath·o·lic /'kæθlɪk, 'kæθə-/ *adj.frml.* **1** broad in scope: *Her interests are catholic in nature, as she travels all over the world.* **2** universal, widespread

Cath·o·lic /'kæθlɪk, 'kæθə-/ *n.adj.* of or belonging to the Roman Catholic Church, one of the branches of the Christian religion: *She is* <adj.> *Catholic* (or) *a* <n.> *Catholic.* *-n.* [U] **Catholicism** /kə'θɑlə,sɪzəm/.

cat·nap /'kæt,næp/ *n.v.* **-napped, -napping, -naps** a short, light sleep: *I take a 20-minute* <n.> *catnap in the afternoon.*

cat·nip /'kæt,nɪp/ *n.* [U] a type of intoxicating herb containing an oil that some cats love to rub their noses against

cat·sup /'kɛtʃəp, 'kæ-, 'kætsəp/ *n.var.* [U] *of* ketchup

cat·tle /'kætl/ *n.pl.* cows, bulls, and oxen as a group: *Cattle are raised for meat, milk, and leather.*

cat·ty /ˈkæti/ *adj.* **-tier, -tiest** saying bad things about s.o., (*syn.*) spiteful: *She made catty remarks about how much weight I've gained.*

cat·ty-cor·nered /ˈkæti,kɔrnərd/ *adv.adj.* at an angle, in a diagonal position: *The car skidded in the snow and got stuck <adv.> catty-cornered in the street.*

cat·walk /ˈkæt,wɔk/ *n.* **1** a narrow walkway like those on the sides of a bridge: *Workers stood on the catwalk and painted the bridge.* **2** the platform where models walk at a fashion show, (*syn.*) the runway: *The models walked down the catwalk in very fashionable dresses.*

Cau·ca·sian /kɔˈkeɪʒən/ *n.adj.* a white person: *The criminal was a male <n.> Caucasian.*

cau·cus /ˈkɔkəs/ *n.v.* **-cused, -cusing, -cuses** a meeting of a special group of people, closed to all others, for policy making, esp. in politics: *The political party's <n.> caucus met to decide what issues they would concentrate on.*

caught /kɔt/ *v.* past tense & past part. *of* catch *phrasal v.* **to be caught up: a.** to have all one's work done: *I am caught up on all my studying.* **b.** to be trapped in s.t.: *He was caught up in the scandal (lawsuit, bad situation).* **c.** to want to do only one thing, (*syns.*) to be absorbed, engrossed: *She was so caught up in the project that she worked night and day on it.*

cau·li·flow·er /ˈkɔli,flaʊər, ˈkɑ-/ *n.* [C;U] a plant in the cabbage family whose white, densely flowered head is eaten as a vegetable: *Boiled cauliflower tastes good with melted cheese on it.*

cauliflower

caulk /kɔk/ *v.n.* [U] to put a type of cement in cracks: *The plumber <v.> caulked the sides of the bathtub to keep water from going into the wall.*

caus·al /ˈkɔzəl/ *adj.* related to or being a cause or reason for s.t.: *Icy roads are a causal factor in auto accidents.*

cause /kɔz/ *n.* **1** [C;U] a reason why s.t. happens: *The cause of fire was a broken electric wire.* **2** an effort concentrated on a goal, (*syns.*) a movement, crusade: *She works for a political cause against higher taxes.*
—*v.* **caused, causing, causes** to make s.t. happen: *His carelessness caused the car accident.*

cause·way /ˈkɔz,weɪ/ *n.* an elevated road or walkway: *Many cars travel on the causeways over the wetlands outside of New Orleans.*

caus·tic /ˈkɔstɪk/ *adj.* **1** able to burn, wear away, or dissolve things, (*syn.*) corrosive: *Lye is a caustic substance.* **2** humorous in a cruel way, (*syns.*) biting, sarcastic: *She makes caustic remarks about the people she works with.*

cau·ter·ize /ˈkɔtə,raɪz/ *v.* **-ized, -izing, -izes** to close a wound by burning it shut: *The doctor cauterized a mole on my nose because it was bleeding a lot.*

cau·tion /ˈkɔʃən/ *n.* **1** [U] concern about not making a mistake: *He uses caution when he puts money into the stock market.* **2** [C;U] warning about danger: *A big sign blocking the road says, "Caution! Danger Ahead."*
—*v.* **1** to warn s.o. about s.t. *The street sign cautions people to be careful when crossing the street.* **2** to criticize, usu. gently: *The father cautioned his son about using dirty language.* -*adj.* **cautionary** /ˈkɔʃə,nɛri/.

cau·tious /ˈkɔʃəs/ *adj.* **1** careful: *He has a cautious attitude about spending money.* **2** concerned about danger, (*syn.*) wary: *She is very cautious when she goes out alone at night.* -*adv.* **cautiously.**

cav·al·cade /ˈkævəl,keɪd, ,kævəlˈkeɪd/ *n.* a line of cars, horses, or carriages, (*syn.*) a procession: *A cavalcade of black, expensive cars and police on motorcycles took the President to the airport.*

cav·a·lier /,kævəˈlɪr/ *n.* **1** an armed man on horseback, (*syn.*) a knight **2** a stylish and well-mannered gentleman
—*adj.* **1** not caring, (*syn.*) arrogant: *He has a cavalier attitude toward people he doesn't know.* **2** free and easy, (*syns.*) nonchalant, off-hand: *This is a serious problem; stop treating it in such a cavalier manner.*

cav·al·ry /ˈkævəlri/ *n.* [U] **1** soldiers trained to fight on horseback **2** a military unit with armored vehicles that can move fast: *The cavalry attacked the enemy with lightning speed.*

cave /keɪv/ *n.* a hole in the ground, usu. with an opening in the side of a hill or mountain: *People lived in caves long ago.*
—*v.* **caved, caving, caves** *phrasal v.* **to cave in: a.** to fall in, (*syn.*) to collapse: *The tunnel caved in on the workers.* **b.** to stop resisting, (*syns.*) to surrender, give in: *After arguing a lot, he finally caved in to her demands for money.*

cave·man /ˈkeɪv,mæn/ *n.* **-men** /-,mɛn/ old usage humans as they first lived long ago: *Cavemen lived thousands of years ago and hunted wild animals.*

cav·ern /ˈkævərn/ *n.* a large cave: *We stood in the cavern and shined a flashlight on its high ceiling.*

cav·i·ar /ˈkævi,ɑr/ *n.* [U] the eggs of various fish, esp. the sturgeon: *Caviar tastes salty and costs a lot.*

cav·i·ty /ˈkævəti/ *n.* **-ties 1** a hole or hollow place: *The explosion left a cavity in the ground.‖Your intestines are in your abdominal cavity.* **2** a hole caused by decay in a tooth: *I went to the dentist to have two cavities filled.*

ca·vort /kə'vɔrt/ *v.frml.* to run and jump in a happy way, (*syn.*) to frolic: *At the end of the school year, children cavorted on their way home.*

caw /kɔ/ *v.n.* to make a loud, harsh birdcall: *Black crows <v.> cawed as the sun rose.*

cay·enne /kaɪ'ɛn, keɪ-/ *n.* a hot-tasting seasoning for food, (*syn.*) red pepper

cc /'si'si/ *n. abbr. for* **1** carbon copy: *I sent a memo to my boss with a cc to our lawyer.* **2** cubic centimeter

---

USAGE NOTE: This abbreviation is often put at the end of a business letter to let the receiver of a letter know who else received a copy of the letter: *I see that you sent a cc of this letter to my boss, so she should already know about our meeting.*

CD /,si'di/ *n.abbr. for* **1** certificate of deposit **2** compact disc: *I bought two new CDs today, one with classical music and the other with rock. See:* certificate of deposit.

CD-ROM /,si,di'rɑm/ *n.abbr. for* Compact Disc - Read Only Memory,(in computers) a disk that holds up to 600K of information, but the information usu. cannot be changed

cease /sis/ *v.frml.* **ceased, ceasing, ceases** to stop an action: *The government ordered the company to cease selling the bad medicine. See:* cessation.

cease-fire *n.* a stop to shooting in a war, (*syn.*) the cessation of military hostilities: *The two countries agreed to a cease-fire while they discuss a peace plan.*

cease·less /'sislɪs/ *adj.* without stopping, continuous: *The ceaseless noise from the city streets makes sleeping difficult. -adv.* **ceaselessly.**

ce·dar /'sidər/ *n.* [C;U] a type of tree with green needles and a reddish good-smelling wood: *We have a chest of drawers made of cedar.*

cede /sid/ *v.* **ceded, ceding, cedes 1** to give, (*syns.*) to surrender, yield by necessity: *After losing the war, the country ceded land to the winner.* **2** to leave to s.o., esp. in a will: *He ceded the property to his nephew.*

ceil·ing /'silɪŋ/ *n.* **1** the top part of a room: *The ceilings in our house are covered with white plaster.* **2** an upper limit: *The congress put a ceiling on government spending.*

cel·e·brate /'sɛlə,breɪt/ *v.* **-brated, -brating, -brates 1** to do something special (like having a party) to mark an occasion: *I celebrated my birthday with friends in a restaurant.* **2** to honor: *Many people celebrate Christmas by going to church. -n.* [C;U] **celebration** /,sɛlə'breɪʃən/.

ce·leb·ri·ty /sə'lɛbrəti/ *n.* **-ties** a famous, living person: *Popular movie stars are celebrities, recognized wherever they go.*

cel·er·y /'sɛləri, 'sɛlri/ *n.* [U] a pale green plant whose crunchy, juicy stalks are eaten as a vegetable: *Celery makes a crunching noise when you eat it raw.*

ce·les·tial /sə'lɛstʃəl/ *adj.* **1** of the sky or heavens: *Celestial navigation uses the positions of the stars to chart the course of ships and airplanes.* **2** of, or seeming to be of, heaven, (*syns.*) heavenly, divine: *The angels in her paintings have a celestial beauty.*

cel·i·ba·cy /'sɛləbəsi/ *n.* [U] the condition of not having sex, (*syn.*) sexual abstinence: *In Roman Catholicism, priests and nuns take a vow of celibacy. -adj.* **celibate** /'sɛləbɪt/.

cell /sɛl/ *n.* **1** the basic unit of living things: *Our bodies are made up of cells.* **2** a small room locked from the outside: *The police put the thief in a prison cell.* **3** a small room for one person in a religious institution: *The monk had only a small bed in his cell.* **4** a unit for making or storing electricity: *Some cells change chemical energy into electrical energy.*

cel·lar /'sɛlər/ *n.* the space below ground level under a building: *We keep canned food and some old furniture in the cellar of our house.*

cel·list /'tʃɛlɪst/ *n.* a musician who plays the cello: *Pablo Casals was perhaps the greatest cellist of the twentieth century.*

cell·mate /'sɛl,meɪt/ *n.* a person sharing a prison cell with another: *The two cellmates planned an escape.*

cel·lo /'tʃɛloʊ/ *n.* **-los** a stringed musical instrument held between the knees and played with a bow: *The cello produces lower sounds than the viola, and higher sounds than the double bass.*

cello

cel·lo·phane /'sɛlə,feɪn/ *n.* [U] a clear, thin, flexible wrapping material that keeps moisture in: *Meat is wrapped in cellophane, so shoppers can see the quality of the meat.*

cel·lu·lar /'sɛlyələr/ *adj.* of the cell: *Doctors must study the cellular structure of a disease in order to cure it.*

cel·lu·loid /'sɛlyə,lɔɪd/ *n.adj.* [U] photographic film made from natural substances: *Old movies were made on <adj.> celluloid film.*

cel·lu·lose /'sɛlyə,lous/ *n.adj.* [U] a basic substance in nearly all plant cells: *<n.> Cellulose* *is important in the manufacture of paper and explosives.*

Cel·si·us /ˈsɛlsɪəs/ *n.* a system of measuring temperature that places the boiling point of water (at ground pressure) at 100 degrees, and the freezing point at 0 degrees, *(syn.)* centigrade: *Many parts of the world use Celsius in measuring temperature. See:* Fahrenheit.

ce·ment /sɪˈmɛnt/ *n.* [U] **1** a building material that can be poured or spread when mixed with water, then hardens like rock: *That sidewalk is made of cement.* **2** a soft substance that holds things together when it hardens, *(syn.)* glue: *rubber cement*
—*v.* **1** to cover with cement: *They're cementing the sidewalk today.* **2** to make s.t. firm, *(syn.)* to bind (a relationship): *The couple cemented their friendship.*

cem·e·ter·y /ˈsɛmə,tɛri/ *n.* **-ies** a burial place for the dead, *(syn.)* a graveyard: *His parents are buried in a cemetery near the center of town.*

cen·sor /ˈsɛnsər/ *v.* **1** to remove parts of printed or filmed materials that are considered offensive: *School (government, church, etc.) officials disapproved of certain parts of the book and censored it.* **2** to stop publication, *(syn.)* to ban s.t.: *Some governments censor books that point out faults in the government.*
—*n.* a person, committee, or institution that censors: *A government censor removed parts of the book.* -*n.* [U] **censorship.**

cen·sure /ˈsɛnʃər/ *v.n.* **-sured, -suring, -sures** to disapprove of s.o. officially, *(syn.)* to rebuke: *The Congress <v.> censured one of its members for bad behavior.*

cen·sus /ˈsɛnsəs/ *n.* **-suses** a count of the people in a country by the government: *The census is taken in the USA every ten years.*

cent /sɛnt/ *n.* **1** 1/100 of a dollar, *(syn.)* a penny: *That pen costs just 20 cents to make.* **2** *fig.* **two cents' worth:** advice given without being asked: *I know that you have made up your mind, but I'd like to put in my two cents' worth.*

cen·ten·a·ry /sɛnˈtɛnəri, ˈsɛntə,nɛri/ *n.adj.* **-ries** a 100th anniversary, *(syn.)* a centennial: *The company celebrated the <n.> centenary of its founding.*

cen·ten·ni·al /sɛnˈtɛniəl/ *n.adj.* a year that is 100 years after the date that s.t. happened or began, a 100th anniversary: *The town celebrated its <n.> centennial with a parade and fireworks. See:* bicentennial.

cen·ter /ˈsɛntər/ *n.* **1** a point that is equally far from all the points on the outer limits of s.t., *(syn.)* the middle: *the center of the earth (of a target, of a crowd)* **2** the main location of some activity, *(syn.)* the headquarters:

Hollywood is the center for American filmmaking. **3** a position in politics between extremes, *(syn.)* a moderate **4** (in sports) a player that occupies a middle position: *He's the center on that football team.*
—*v.* **1** to put s.t. in a central position: *She centered the picture on the wall.* **2** to concentrate or focus around a point: *Their argument centered around money issues.*

cen·ter·piece /ˈsɛntər,pis/ *n.* **1** a decoration placed in the center of a table: *The centerpiece was a bowl of flowers.* **2** *fig.* the most important feature of s.t.: *Cutting taxes was the centerpiece of the politician's campaign.*

cen·ti·grade /ˈsɛntə,greɪd/ *n. See:* Celsius.

cen·ti·me·ter /ˈsɛntə,mitər/ *n.* a unit of length in the metric system equal to 1/100 of a meter: *One centimeter is .3937 inch long.* *abbr.* **cm.**

cen·ti·pede /ˈsɛntə,pid/ *n.* a worm-like creature with many body segments, each of which has a pair of legs: *Centipedes crawl along the ground.*

cen·tral /ˈsɛntrəl/ *adj.* **1** in, at, near, or forming the center: *That store has a central location in the town square.* **2** main, most basic or important: *The Prime Minister is the central figure (or) central force in the government.* -*adv.* **centrally.**

central air conditioning *n.* a system using a central machine to produce cool air that is spread evenly throughout a building: *The central air conditioning in our house cools upstairs and downstairs.*

central heating *n.* [U] a furnace to produce heat that is spread evenly throughout a building by pipes: *Central heating makes our house comfortable in winter.*

cen·tral·ize /ˈsɛntrə,laɪz/ *v.* **-ized, -izing, -izes 1** to move to a central location: *Brazil centralized its government offices from different areas into the city of Brasil* concentrate in one place, esp. power: *The power in that company was centralized; now all the important decisions are made by its president.* -*n.* [U] **centralization** /,sɛntrələˈzeɪʃən/.

cen·tri·fuge /ˈsɛntrə,fyuʒ/ *n.v.* **-fuged, -fuging, -fuges** a machine that separates materials with different densities by spinning them at high speed: *The outward spinning (centrifugal) force of a <n.> centrifuge can also be used to create an effect similar to gravity.* -*adj.* **centrifugal** /sɛnˈtrɪfyəgəl, -fə-/.

cen·tu·ri·on /sɛnˈturiən/ *n.* an army officer of ancient Rome: *A centurion commanded a company of about 100 soldiers.*

cen·tu·ry /ˈsɛnʧəri/ *n.* **-ries 1** a time period of 100 years **2** one of the 100-year time periods before or after the birth of Christ: *Many*

C

scientific discoveries were made during the twentieth century (1901-2000). See: A.D.; B.C..

CEO /ˌsiˌi'ou/ *n. abbr. for* Chief Executive Officer

ce·ram·ic /sə'ræmɪk/ *adj.* of or related to a hard, baked material usu. made of clay, used in industry and art: *Square ceramic tiles cover the bathroom walls.*

ce·ram·ics /sə'ræmɪks/ *n.* **1** [U] the art of making vases, pots, and other things out of clay: *Ceramics is difficult to learn but fun to do.* **2** *used with a pl.v.* the objects themselves (vases, pots, etc.): *Ceramics are on sale at the store.*

ce·re·al /'sɪriəl/ *n.adj.* [C;U] grain, like wheat and oats, or food made of it: *Many people in the USA eat <n.> cereal for breakfast, esp. cold cereal. See:* scrambled egg, USAGE NOTE.

ce·re·bral /sə'ribrəl, 'sɛrə-/ *adj.* **1** (in medicine) of the brain or cerebrum: *The cerebral cortex covers the two parts of the cerebrum.* **2** very intelligent, (*syn.*) intellectual: *Our physics professor is a very cerebral woman.*

ce·re·brum /sə'ribrəm, 'sɛrə-/ *n.* **-brums** or **-bra** /-brə/ the large, front part of the brain that is involved in thinking and other conscious processes

cer·e·mo·ni·al /ˌsɛrə'mouniəl/ *adj.* involving or used in a ceremony, (*syns.*) formal, ritualistic: *The new mayor's swearing into office was a ceremonial occasion attended by many officials.*

cer·e·mo·ny /'sɛrəˌmouni/ *n.* **-nies** [C;U] a formal event usu. with rituals (customary words and actions done many times before): *The priest performed a marriage ceremony.* *-adj.* **ceremonious** /ˌsɛrə'mouniəs/.

cer·tain /'sɜrtn/ *adj.* **1** definite, without doubt: *She has so much talent that she is certain to be a success.* **2** sure to happen, (*syn.*) irreversible: *If he jumps off the bridge, he goes to a certain death.* **3** not specific, but real: *She has a certain charm about her.* **4** one who is not named, but is usu. known: *A certain person has been stealing cookies from the kitchen.* **5** some, a limited amount: *There is a certain amount of truth to what he says.* **6 of a certain age:** roughly 45-70 years old: *He is a man of a certain age who has a lot of experience.* **7 to make certain:** to make sure: *I made certain that I had my keys with me before I left the house.*

cer·tain·ly /'sɜrtnli/ *adv.* **1** of course, yes: *"Will you help me with my homework?"—"Certainly, I will."* **2** for sure, definitely: *It is so cold outside that you will certainly freeze unless you wear a heavy coat.*

cer·tain·ty /'sɜrtnti/ *n.* **-ties** [C;U] s.t. that is certain, (*syn.*) a certitude: *With the bad weather, it is a certainty that the planes will not fly.*

cer·tif·i·cate /sər'tɪfɪkɪt/ *n.* a formal document that states, under oath, a fact, qualification, or promise: *I showed my birth certificate when I applied for a passport.*

certificate of deposit or **CD** *n.* an official document from a bank that shows how much money you gave them, the amount of interest they pay you, and the period of time that they will keep the money: *I have most of my savings in certificates of deposit* (or) *CD's at Citibank.*

cer·ti·fi·ca·tion /ˌsɜrtəfɪ'keɪʃən/ *n.* [C;U] formal recognition, usu. with a printed license, of having met requirements to perform a function: *He has his certification as a math teacher.*

certified check *n.* a check stamped (certified) by your bank, showing that funds have been set aside in your account to guarantee its payment: *I went to the bank and got a certified check for partial payment on a new car.*

certified mail *n.* [U] in the USA, mail that is signed for by the person who receives it, using a green postcard attached to the piece of mail (letter, package) that is then returned to the sender to show that the mail was delivered: *I sent an important check payment to my bank by certified mail.*

certified public accountant or **CPA** *n.* in the USA, an accountant who has passed examinations required by the state licensing officials: *A CPA does the accounting for a business, and also prepares tax returns.*

cer·ti·fy /'sɜrtəˌfaɪ/ *v.* **-fied, -fying, -fies** **1** to state formally that s.t. is true, esp. in writing: *The witness signed a document certifying that what she had said about the accident was true.* **2** to provide an official document about s.o.'s or s.t.'s qualifications and rights: *The State of New York certified that the secretarial school is allowed to do business in the state.* **3** to certify mail, to send mail in a special package that must be signed for by the person receiving it *-adj.* **certifiable** /'sɜrtəˌfaɪəbəl, ˌsɜrtə'faɪ/.

cer·ti·tude /'sɜrtəˌtud/ *n.frml.* [U] the state of knowing that s.t. is sure or true, (*syn.*) certainty: *I can say with certitude that the man has died.*

cer·vix /'sɜrvɪks/ *n.* **-vices** /-vəˌsiz/ or **-vixes** **1** the neck **2** the neck-shaped outer opening of the uterus, the female reproductive organ: *During childbirth, a woman's cervix widens so the baby can pass through it. -adj.* **cervical** /'sɜrvɪkəl/.

ce·sar·e·an /sɪ'zɛriən/ or **cesarean section** *n.* a surgical operation in which a baby is delivered by cutting open the mother's stomach and uterus: *The doctor delivered the baby girl by cesarean.*

ces·sa·tion /sɛ'seɪʃən/ *n.frml.* [C;U] a stop to an activity, a halting: *The cessation of war between the two countries brought peace.*

cess·pool /'sɛs,pul/ *n.* a covered hole in the ground to receive human waste (urine, feces, etc.): *The cesspool is located behind the farmhouse.*

CFO /,si,ɛf'ou/ *n.abbr. for* Chief Financial Officer

chafe /ʃeɪf/ *v.* **chafed, chafing, chafes 1** to rub together so as to irritate: *My shoes are too tight; they're chafing my feet.* **2** to irritate, annoy, (*syn.*) to vex: *The slow traffic chafed her as she hurried to work.*

chaff /ʃæf/ *n.* [U] **1** the outer covering of a seed of grain (wheat, oats, etc.) separated from the edible insides **2 to separate the wheat from the chaff:** to separate unwanted, useless things (chaff) from useful ones (wheat): *The manager separated the wheat from the chaff by dropping unpopular products and selling only the good ones.*

cha·grin /ʃə'grɪn/ *n.v.* [U] extreme embarrassment or disappointment: *He made a bad mistake, much to his <n.> chagrin.*

chain /ʃeɪn/ *n.* **1** a flexible line of (usu. metal) rings or loops locked inside each other: *The dog pulled on its chain but could not get loose.‖She wore a pretty silver chain around her neck.* **2** a series of related things or events: *The king's murder started a chain of events that led to a war.* **3** a group of stores, restaurants, etc., owned by the same person or company: *That restaurant is part of a large chain; you can find it in cities all over the country.*
—*v.* to limit with or as if with a chain: *The owner chained her dog to a fence.‖The accountant was chained to her desk during tax season.*

chain reaction *n.* **1** a chemical or physical action that creates other actions **2** a series of events in which one event causes the next: *The revolution in that country set off a chain reaction of other revolutions in neighboring countries.*

chain saw *n.* a saw driven by a motor: *Lumberjacks use chain saws to cut down trees.*

chain saw

chain smoker *n.* a person who smokes one cigarette after another: *Chain smokers often don't live long.*

chain store *n.* a store owned by a person or company that has others by the same name in many locations: *Chain stores buy products in large amounts to offer cheaper prices.*

chair /ʃɛr/ *n.* **1** a piece of furniture with a back,

for one person to sit on: *We bought some new chairs for the apartment.* **2** an of-fice or seat of authority and importance
—*v.* to be in charge of a meeting, committee, or school department: *We would like you to chair this committee.*

chair·per·son /'ʃɛr,pɜrsən/ *n.* **-persons** a male or female head of a meeting, committee, or school faculty: *She is the chairperson of the history department at the University of South Florida.* *-n.* **chairman** /'ʃɛr,mən/**; chairmanship; chairwoman** /'ʃɛr,wumən/**.**

chaise longue /'ʃeɪz'lɔŋ, -'laundʒ/ or **chaise lounge** /'ʃeɪz' laundʒ, 'ʃeɪs-/ *n.* a type of chair with a long flat part to support the legs

chaise longue

cha·let /ʃæ'leɪ, 'ʃæleɪ/ *n.* **1** (French for) a Swiss mountain cabin: *The sheep herder left his chalet early each morning.* **2** a country house with a sharply sloping roof: *They have a chalet in the woods near a lake.*

chal·ice /'ʃælɪs/ *n.* **1** a type of drinking cup with a stem that spreads into a base, (*syn.*) goblet: *Chalices are often made of gold or silver with jewels.* **2** (in Christianity) the cup used to hold the wine for Holy Communion: *The priest raised a golden chalice from the altar.*

chalk /ʃɔk/ *n.* **1** [U] a soft, white type of rock made from ancient seashells and used to make lime **2** [U] a stick (of chalk) used for writing and marking: *The teacher writes on the blackboard with chalk.*
—*v.* **1** *phrasal v.* **to chalk s.t. up:** to earn, (*syn.*) to score: *She chalked up a lot of points with her manager when she saved a failing project.* **2 to chalk up s.t. to experience:** to learn from one's mistakes: *He failed in his new store; but his friends told him to chalk it up to experience and try s.t. different.* *-adj.* **chalky.**

chalk·board /'ʃɔk,bɔrd/ *n.* a blackboard used to write on with chalk: *In the USA, many classrooms have a chalkboard.*

chal·lenge /'ʃæləndʒ/ *v.* **-lenged, -lenging, -lenges 1** to ask or dare s.o. to play a game or sport: *I challenged her to a game of tennis.* **2** to test one's abilities: *The difficult courses at school challenged his ability to make good grades.* **3** to question, (*syns.*) to confront, dispute: *The police challenged the suspect's story.*
—*n.* **1** an invitation to play a game or sport: *I accepted her challenge to a tennis match.* **2** a difficult job: *She found her new sales job to be quite a challenge. -n.* **challenger.**

cham·ber /'ʃeɪmbər/ *n.* **1** *often pl.* **cham-**

bers a judge's private room: *Two lawyers talked with the judge in her chambers.* **2** a hall where politicians hold formal meetings: *the legislative chambers of Congress* **3** an opening in the barrel of a gun, or in the body of a person or animal: *He put the bullets into the gun's chamber.||The heart has four chambers.* **4** *old usage* a room: *a bedchamber*

cham·ber·maid /ˈʧeɪmbər,meɪd/ *n.* a cleaning woman, esp. in a hotel: *The chambermaids in the hotel clean the rooms and make the beds.*

chamber of commerce *n.* an association to which businesses belong in a town, city, or region: *Business people talk about increasing their business at chamber of commerce meetings.*

cha·me·leon /kəˈmilyən/ *n.* **1** a small lizard that can change its skin color to match the color of the things around it: *The chameleon changed to green while sitting on green leaves.* **2** a person who adopts the behaviors of others around him or her: *He's a real chameleon; when he's with liberal friends he says he's a liberal, but when he's with conservative friends, he tells them he's conservative.*

cham·ois /ˈʃæmi/ *n.* **chamois** /ˈʃæmiz/ **1** a goat-like animal living in the mountains of Europe **2** a soft leather made from the skin of a chamois: *He used a chamois to clean his car.*

champ /ʧæmp/ *v.* **to champ at the bit: a.** to chew hard and nervously: *Horses champed at the bit before the race.* **b.** *fig.* to be impatient and eager to do s.t.: *She is champing at the bit to get started on her new job.*

—*n.infrml. short for* champion: *Joe Louis was boxing champ of the world for many years.*

cham·pagne /ʃæmˈpeɪn/ *n.* [U] a type of wine with bubbles in it: *People drink champagne to celebrate New Year's Eve.*

cham·pi·on /ˈʧæmpiən/ *n.* the winner of a final contest: *She is the national champion in tennis.*

—*v.* to support eagerly: *He championed the civil rights movement in the 1960s.*

cham·pi·on·ship /ˈʧæmpiən,ʃɪp/ *n.* the last in a series of contests, the winner of which will be champion: *He won the championship in golf.*

chance /ʧæns/ *n.* **1** [U] the way some things happen for no obvious reason, by accident, etc., *(syn.)* luck: *When she arrived late for her train, chance was on her side; the train was running late and had not yet left.* **2** [C;U] the possibility of s.t. happening, *(syn.)* probability: *There is a good chance that it will snow tomorrow.* **3** [C] an opportunity: *I had the chance to go to San Francisco on vacation.* **4 as chance would have it:** luck was (or) was

not helping me: *As chance would have it, my old girlfriend and my new girlfriend live in the same apartment building.* **5 by chance:** accidentally: *We met by chance at the library.* **6** [U] **games of chance:** games of luck: *Some people like to play games of chance, such as cards, dice, and slot machines.* **7 on the (off) chance that:** on the possibility that: *On the chance that he was going to the store, I asked him to buy toothpaste.* **8** [C] **to take a chance:** to take a risk: *She took a chance by crossing the busy street against the traffic light, but was not hurt.*

—*v.* **chanced, chancing, chances** **1** to happen accidentally: *I chanced to run into her at the library.* **2 to chance it:** to risk s.t.: *I know that snow has made the roads very bad, but I am going to chance it and try to drive anyway.*
-*adj.* **chancy.**

chan·cel·lor /ˈʧænslər, -sələr/ *n.* **1** the president of some American universities **2** a high government official: *The Chancellor of Germany runs the government.*

chan·de·lier /ˌʃændəˈlɪr/ *n.* a fancy, decorative holder hung from a ceiling with metal branches for lights or candles: *The shiny glass leaves on the chandelier sparkle in the light.*

chandelier

change /ʧeɪnʤ/ *v.* **changed, changing, changes** **1** to become s.t. different, *(syn.)* to transform: *I changed my life by going back to college because doing so helped me get a better job.* **2** to make s.t. different, *(syn.)* to alter: *The painter changed the color from red to green.* **3** to exchange, *(syn.)* to switch: *The two people changed places with each other.* **4** to convert money: **a.** to give or receive an equal amount of money for bills or coins that are smaller: *"Can you change (or) make change for a $20 bill?"—"Yes, I have two $10's."* **b.** to give one country's money for an amount of another's: *I changed my dollars into French francs at the bank.* **5 to change (clothes):** to put on different clothes: *I went home and changed from jeans to a suit.||We are having over-night guests; we need to change the bed linen and the tablecloth.||After work, I changed into my jeans.* **6 to change hands:** to have a new owner: *That store on the corner has changed hands often.* **7 to change one's mind:** to think differently: *I changed my mind and stayed home instead of going out.*

—*n.* **1** [C;U] s.t. different, *(syn.)* a transformation: *There was a change in the weather* *from sun to rain (change of government, administration).* **2** [C] an exchange, *(syn.)* a switch: *He removed one painting and replaced it with another, but no one noticed the change.* **3** [U] coins: *I have a pocket full of change; can you give me dollar bills for these quarters?* **4 small change:** a small, *(syn.)* insignificant amount: *The cost of operating that expensive car is small change compared with its purchase price. -n.* **changer.**

change·a·ble /'ʧeɪnʤəbəl/ *adj.* becoming different, *(syn.)* variable: *The weather is very changeable in the springtime.*

change of life *n. See:* menopause.

change·o·ver /'ʧeɪn,ʤoʊvər/ *n.* a change (from one group of people, procedures, machinery to another): *The company bought a new telephone system and the changeover from the old one to the new took two months.*

chan·nel /'ʧænl/ *n.* **1** a television station's place on the dial and its broadcasts of news, sports, etc.: *We watch the news on Channel 2 every evening.* **2** a waterway: *The English Channel separates England from France.* **3** a pathway of communications: *Our government opened a channel of communications with the top officials of a foreign government.*

chant /'ʧænt/ *n.v.* **1** a short, simple song, often religious in nature **2** a short saying, *(syn.)* a slogan: *"No more war! No more war!" is a war protesters' <n.> chant.*

Cha·nu·kah /'hɑnəkə, 'xɑ-/ *n. var.* of Hanukkah

cha·os /'keɪ,ɑs/ *n.* [U] extreme, usu. violent disorder, *(syn.)* mass confusion: *After the earthquake, the area was in chaos: no electricity, roads blocked, injured people everywhere. -adj.* **chaotic** /keɪ'ɑtɪk/.

chap /ʧæp/ *n.infrml. Brit.* a man or boy, *(syn.)* fellow: *He's a good chap.*

—*v.* **chapped, chapping, chaps** to dry and crack, such as the skin on lips or hands: *In the winter my lips get chapped from the cold.*

chap·el /'ʧæpəl/ *n.* a small church: *At that school, students go to chapel every evening.*

chap·er·on or **chap·er·one** /'ʃæpə,roʊn/ *n.v.* **-oned, -oning, -ons** or **-ones** an older person who accompanies young unmarried people to make sure that they behave properly: *My father is a <n.> chaperone at the school dance tonight.*

chap·lain /'ʧæplɪn/ *n.* a member of the clergy, esp. in a college or military post: *The college chaplain led the church service on Sunday.*

chaps /ʧæps, ʃæps/ *n.pl.* leather coverings worn over a cowboy's trousers: *Cowboys wear chaps to protect their legs against scratches and bruises.*

chap·ter /'ʧæptər/ *n.* **1** a section of a book: *I read Chapter 11 of my history book.* **2** *fig.* a

time period: *Finding a new job opens a new chapter in one's life.* **3** a local branch of a large organization: *She is president of her chapter of the Daughters of the American Revolution.*

char /ʧɑr/ *v.* **charred, charring, chars** to blacken by burning, *(syn.)* to scorch: *The fire in the house charred the walls and furniture.*

char·ac·ter /'kærɪktər/ *n.* **1** [U] the combination of qualities or features that make one person, place, or thing different from others: *the character of a neighborhood* **2** [U] the general tendency of a person's behavior: *He is a man of good (bad, strong, etc.) character.* **3** [U] honesty, moral strength, *(syn.)* integrity: *She has a lot of character; I admire her.* **4** [C] *infrml.* one whose behavior is very strange or funny, *(syn.)* an eccentric: *He's quite a character; you never know what to expect from him.* **5** [C] a single letter or mark used in writing: *"Letter" is a word with six characters.‖Chinese characters* **6** [C] a person in a novel, play, or film: *I didn't like the main character in that book.* **7** [U] **in** or **out of character:** like or unlike a person's usual behavior: *It was out of character for her to be so rude. See:* cast (1).

char·ac·ter·is·tic /,kærɪktə'rɪstɪk/ *adj.* typical: *It is characteristic of him to say positive things.*

—*n.* a special quality, *(syn.)* a trait: *The ideal person for the job has these characteristics: ten years' experience and an advanced degree -adv.* **characteristically.**

char·ac·ter·ize /'kærɪktə,raɪz/ *v.* **-ized, -izing, -izes** **1** to describe the character of: *Right now, the situation can be characterized as excellent.* **2** to be a special quality or typical feature of: *writing that is characterized by its clarity -n.* [C;U] **characterization** /,kærɪktərə'zeɪʃən/.

cha·rade /ʃə'reɪd/ *n.* **1** a faked situation, *(syn.)* a pretense: *The couple pretended to be happy, but it was just a charade.* **2** *pl.* **charades** used with a *sing. v.* a game in which players try to guess a word described only with the face and gestures (in pantomime)

char·coal /'ʧɑr,koʊl/ *n.adj.* **1** [U] a black form of carbon made by partially burning wood in an airless container: *<n.> Charcoal can be used as a fuel, a filter, a gas absorbent, etc.* **2** [C;U] a pencil or crayon made from charcoal, or a drawing done with such a pencil: *He did a drawing of a house in <n.> charcoal.* **3** dark gray: *She wore <adj.> charcoal pants.*

charge /ʧɑrʤ/ *n.* **1** [C] price: *What is the charge for a night in that hotel?* **2** [C] a purchase made on credit: *Will you pay cash or will this be a charge?* **3** [C] a fast move forward, *(syn.)* a surge: *The soldiers made a charge up the hill.* **4** [C;U] **a.** an ability in some substances to cause electrical events: *There are* *two types of electrical charges, negative and positive.* **b.** a measure of the amount of this ability in s.t.: *The charge in my car battery is low.* **5** [C] a statement of blame against s.o., (*syn.*) an accusation: *a charge against s.o. in a court of law*||*The charge of drunk driving, if one is found guilty, carries a large fine.* **6** [C] s.o. put in another's care: *The baby-sitter took her two young charges to the park.* **7** [C] *frml.* a responsibility, (*syn.*) a mission: *As sales manager, my charge is to hire 20 new sales representatives.* **8** *sing.infrml.* excitement: *She gets a charge out of cliff diving.* **9 to be in charge (of):** to be in control or command (of): *I'm leaving you in charge while I'm gone.*||*She's in charge of the new project.*

—*v.* **charged, charging, charges 1** to put a price on: *They're charging $25 for these jeans.* **2** to purchase on credit: *I charged a new pair of shoes on my credit card.* **3** to ask for payment from: *The store is charging her for the glass that she broke.* **4** to give s.o. a responsibility: *She charged him with watching the children while she was gone.* **5** to blame s.o. for s.t., (*syn.*) to accuse: *She was charged with drunk driving.* **6** to rush forward, (*syn.*) to surge: *Soldiers charged at the enemy.* **7** to put the ability to produce electricity back into s.t., (*syn.*) to energize: *to charge a dead battery* **8** *phrasal v. sep.* **to charge s.o.** or **s.t. up: a.** to make s.o. enthusiastic, to excite: *The football coach charged up the team to win the game.* **b.** to fill with electricity: *The garage charged up my dead battery.*

charge·a·ble /'tʃɑrdʒəbəl/ *adj.* **1** (of an expense) capable of being charged: *The cost of business travel is an expense chargeable to the company.* **2** (in law) able or likely to bring punishment: *Theft is a chargeable crime punishable by time in prison.*

charge account *n.* the right and privilege to buy things from a business and pay for them later: *I opened a charge account at the department store.*

charge card *n.* a type of credit card that must be paid completely each month: *American Express offers a charge card. See:* credit card.

char·i·ot /'tʃæriət/ *n.* in ancient times, a two-wheeled vehicle drawn by horse(s): *Roman soldiers rode chariots into battle* -*n.* **charioteer** /ˌtʃæriə'tɪr/.

cha·ris·ma /kə'rɪzmə/ *n.* [U] the attractiveness of a person for others; charm and appeal: *That popular movie star has charisma.* -*adj.* **charismatic** /ˌkærɪz'mætɪk/; -*adv.* **charismatically.**

char·i·ta·ble /'tʃærətəbəl/ *adj.* **1** giving help or money to those who need it, (*syn.*) generous: *He puts a great deal of his time and money into helping needy children; he is a very charitable man.* **2** of or for charity: *Charitable organizations help the poor.* **3** not judging, (*syn.*) for-

giving: *He was charitable in his gentle criticism of the man.* -*adv.* **charitably.**

char·i·ty /'tʃærəti/ *n.* -**ities 1** [C] an organization that helps poor people: *People give money to charities to help the homeless.* **2** [U] an act or condition of giving without thinking of being paid back: *He believes in charity and gives generously.* **3** [U] the act of stopping oneself from judging others, (*syn.*) forgiveness: *She showed a lot of charity by not saying anything bad about the woman who stole her husband.*

char·la·tan /'ʃɑrlətən/ *n.pej.* a person who tricks others, esp. one who claims to have special knowledge, (*syns.*) a quack, fake: *Charlatans trick people out of their money.*

char·ley horse /'tʃɑrli,hɔrs/ *n.infrml.* a cramp or stiffness in a muscle, esp. in the leg, from injury or too much exercise

charm /tʃɑrm/ *n.* **1** [C;U] the ability to please, attractiveness: *She is a woman with a great deal of charm.* **2** [C] s.t. worn because it is thought to be magical: *He wore a charm to protect himself from evil spirits.* **3** [C] a little ornament (figure, etc.) hanging on a bracelet: *The silver charms on her bracelet jingle when she moves her arm.* **4** [C] a set of actions or words thought to produce a magical effect, (*syn.*) a spell: *The witch cast a charm on the prince to make him fall in love.* **5 to work like a charm:** (of a plan, idea, etc.) to be very successful or effective

—*v.* to please s.o. with warmth and pleasantness: *He charms everyone he meets.* -*n.* **charmer.**

charm·ing /'tʃɑrmɪŋ/ *adj.* pleasing, attractive, delightful: *We vacationed in a charming little village.*||*a charming man*

chart /tʃɑrt/ *n.* **1** a map, esp. one of the oceans **2** a display of information in the form of a diagram, graph, etc.: *The accountant made a chart comparing the company's sales over the last five years.*

—*v.* **1** to record information on a chart: *He charted their progress on a graph.* **2 to chart a course:** to plan the way to go: *The ship's captain charted a course to China.*

char·ter /'tʃɑrtər/ *n.* **1** a document from a government or other authority giving rights to others to do certain things: *The United Nation's charter states its activities and powers.* **2** (the hiring or leasing of) a plane, boat, or other vehicle for special use: *a fishing charter*

—*v.* **1** to officially give power to (a corporation, organization, etc.) **2** to purchase seats as a group for special trips on airplanes, buses, trains, etc.: *Our church group chartered a plane to go to Jerusalem for the holidays.*

charter flight *n.* an airplane rented or hired for a special trip and not part of a regular airline:

We took a charter flight from San Francisco to Tokyo.

charter member *n.* one of the first members of an organization, club, etc.: *In the 1950s, people became charter members of the American Express charge card.*

char·y /ˈtʃɛri, ˈtʃæri/ *adj.frml.* **-ier, -iest** worried about danger, (*syn.*) cautious: *She is chary about losing money in the stock market.* -*n.* [U] **chariness.**

chase /tʃeɪs/ *v.* **chased, chasing, chases 1** to hurry quickly after s.o. or s.t. to catch them, (*syn.*) to pursue: *The police chased (after) the thief and caught her.* **2 to chase around** or **in and out:** to run, hurry: *She was distracted by the students chasing around.* **3** *phrasal v. sep.* **to chase s.o.** or **s.t. away** or **off:** to frighten or force away: *The farmer used a rifle to chase off trespassers.||He chased them off.*
—*n.* **1** an act of chasing: *The movie began with a police chase through the streets of San Francisco.* **2 the chase: a.** hunting animals as a sport: *He loves the chase.* **b.** the animal being hunted: *Hunters followed the chase deep into the forest.* **3** *phrasal v. sep.* **to give chase:** to chase after: *A criminal robbed a bank and the police gave chase.*

chas·er /ˈtʃeɪsər/ *n.* a milder drink taken after a strong one: *She drank a chaser of water after a whiskey.*

chasm /ˈkæzəm/ *n.* **1** any deep break in the earth, (*syn.*) a rift: *The Grand Canyon is a long, deep chasm.* **2** *fig.* a big difference of opinion or belief between people or nations: *There is a great chasm between those two systems of government.*

chas·sis /ˈtʃæsi, ˈtʃæ-/ *n.* **chassis** /ˈtʃæsiz, ˈtʃæ-/ the rectangular frame on which a vehicle's body rests: *The chassis of that car is made of steel.*

chaste /tʃeɪst/ *adj.* not having had sexual intercourse, (*syn.*) virginal: *That couple was chaste until their marriage.* -*adv.* **chastely.**

cha·sten /ˈtʃeɪsən/ *v.frml.* to punish so as to improve: *His loss of a lot of money in real estate chastened him.*

chas·tise /tʃæsˈtaɪz, ˈtʃæsˌtaɪz/ *v.frml.* **-tised, -tising, -tises 1** to punish, as by beating **2** to criticize severely: *The newspaper chastised the politician for bad behavior.* -*n.*[C;U] **chastisement.**

chas·ti·ty /ˈtʃæstəti/ *n.* [U] **1** the condition of not having sexual intercourse **2** the practice of avoiding sexual activity: *Members of some religious orders take vows of chastity.*

chat /tʃæt/ *n.* casual, friendly talk: *My friend and I have a little chat every day.*
—*v.* **chatted, chatting, chats** to talk informally: *We chatted on the phone this morning.*

chat·ty /ˈtʃæti/ *adj.* **-tier, -tiest 1** inclined to talk in a friendly, informal way, (*syn.*) talkative: *I sat next to a very chatty man on the plane.* **2** having the informal style of a conversation: *She wrote me a long, chatty letter, full of news about the family.*

cha·teau /ʃæˈtoʊ/ *n.* **-teaus** or **-teaux** /-ˈoʊz, -ˈtoʊ/ **1** a French castle **2** a large French country house, (*syn.*) a manor: *They grow wine grapes around their chateau.*

chat·ter /ˈtʃætər/ *n.* [U] **1** informal conversation about unimportant matters: *The teacher told her students to stop their chatter.* **2** rapid sounds made by some animals: *The chatter of monkeys filled the zoo.* **3** the sound of teeth clicking from shivering in the cold or from fear
—*v.* **1** to talk rapidly about unimportant matters, (*syn.*) to jabber: *At the party, people chattered about the weather and movies.* **2** to click the teeth from shivering in the cold or from fear: *The winter weather makes my teeth chatter.*

chat·ter·box /ˈtʃætərˌbɑks/ *n.infrml.* **-boxes** a person who talks much about little: *She is such a chatterbox that no one else can speak when she talks.*

chauf·feur /ˈʃoʊfər, ʃoʊˈfɜr/ *n.v.* a person whose job is driving others in a vehicle: *Their chauffeur drove the rich couple to the opera.*

chau·vin·ist /ˈʃoʊvənɪst/ *n.* a person who believes their sex (male or female) or nation is superior to others': *He regards women as weak; he is a male chauvinist.* -*n.* [U] **chauvinism;** -*adj.* **chauvinistic** /ˌʃoʊvəˈnɪstɪk/.

cheap /tʃip/ *adj.* **1** costing very little, (*syn.*) inexpensive: *The hotel room was cheap, so we could afford to stay an extra night.* **2** of poor quality, (*syn.*) shoddy: *The clothes from that store are cheap; they fall apart.* **3** not generous with money, (*syn.*) stingy: *Everything that he buys has to be a bargain; he's really cheap.* **4** *infrml.fig.* **a cheap shot:** an unfair, hurtful criticism: *One politician called his opponent's wife an alcoholic; that was a cheap shot.* -*adv.* **cheap, cheaply;** -*n.* **cheapness.** *See:* **cheapskate.**

cheap·en /ˈtʃipən/ *v.* to lower the quality of s.t.: *The manufacturer used lower quality cloth in the dresses and cheapened them.*

cheap·skate /ˈtʃipˌskeɪt/ *n.infrml.* a person who is not generous with money, (*syn.*) a miser: *He is such a cheapskate that he refuses to tip waiters.*

cheat /tʃit/ *v.n.* **1** to do s.t. dishonest for gain, (*syn.*) to deceive: *She <v.> cheated on her examinations; she is a <n.> cheat.* **2** to take from (s.o.) unfairly, (*syn.*) to swindle: *That store <v.> cheated me out of $10 on that sweater by charging me too much.* -*n.* **cheater.**

check /tʃɛk/ n. **1** [C] a piece of printed paper used as an order to a bank to pay s.o. the amount of money one writes on it, (syn.) a bank draft: *Every month, I write checks to pay my bills.*‖*I pay them by check.* **2** [C] a type of ticket, such as for storing things: *I lost my luggage claim check.* **3** [C] the bill in a restaurant or bar: *The waiter handed me the lunch check.* **4** [C] a mark as with a pen or pencil, usu. (√), (syns.) a checkmark, Brit. a tick: *I put a check by each item on my grocery list as I took it from the shelf.* **5** [C] an examination to see that s.t. is correct or in good condition: *I added up some figures, then asked my coworker to give my answer a check (for accuracy).* **6** [C;U] **a.** a pattern of small squares **b.** material with such a pattern on it: *Her dress was a black and white check.* **7** a stop, (syn.) restraint: *She was eating too much and now keeps her eating in check. See:* checking account; checks and balances.
—v. **1** to test to see if s.t. is correct: *I checked my report for any errors.* **2** to ask about: *Oh, I was just checking to see how you are feeling.*‖*I checked for messages at the office.* **3** to give for safekeeping: *She checked her coat in the restaurant coatroom.* **4** to put a checkmark beside s.t.: *I checked (off) each item on the list.* **5** to agree: *The printed list of items checks with what we received.* **6** to stop, hold back, (syn.) to restrain: *She was about to speak but checked herself and waited.* **7** phrasal v. insep. **to check in** or **into s.t.:** to register at a hotel, motel, airport, etc.: *The tourist checked into the hotel.*‖*She checked in this morning.* **8** phrasal v. insep. **to check into s.t.:** to find out if s.t. is true, (syn.) to investigate s.t.: *The company checked into the worker's background before hiring him.*‖*They checked into it.* **9** phrasal v. insep. **to check on s.o.** or **s.t.:** to look at or investigate briefly: *I checked on my facts before going to the meeting.* **10** phrasal v. insep. **to check out: a.** to pay the bill and leave a hotel: *He checked out (of his hotel) in the morning.* **b.** to be found to be true: *The police said the man's story checked out; he really was in the hospital at the time of the murder.* **11** phrasal v. sep.infrml. **to check out s.o.** or **s.t.: a.** to look at s.o. or s.t.: *Have you checked out the new teacher?*‖*Check her out.* **b.** sep. to ask many questions so as to investigate s.t. thoroughly: *The police checked out the man's story with witnesses before they would let him go.*‖*They checked it out.* **c.** sep. (of library books, tapes, etc.) to borrow: *I checked out two novels from the library.*‖*I checked them out.* **12** phrasal v. insep. **to check up on s.o.** or **s.t.:** to examine, usu. with suspicion: *When the owner saw that items were missing from the store shelves, he checked up on them and found*

that they had been stolen. -n. **checker.** *See:* check-in; checkout.

check·book /'tʃɛk,bʊk/ n. a folder containing checks: *When I write checks to pay my bills, I keep a list of those checks in my checkbook.*

check·ered /'tʃɛkərd/ adj. **1** divided into squares **2** marked by both good and bad luck or behavior: *He has a checkered past, including time in prison, but is a good citizen now.*

check·ers /'tʃɛkərz/ n.pl. used with a sing.v. a game played by two people, each with 12 small, round black or red pieces (checkers) moved on a board divided into squares of two different colors: *Checkers is easy to learn and fun to play.* -n. **checkerboard** /'tʃɛkər,bɔrd/.

check-in n.adj. a registration area or counter, as in a hotel or airport: *The hotel <n.> check-in is in the lobby.*

check·ing /'tʃɛkɪŋ/ n. [U] the service provided by a bank to accept or pay checks: *That bank does not offer checking; it is a savings bank only.*

checking account n. an account at a bank against which checks can be written: *I opened a checking account with a $500 deposit. See:* savings account.

check·list /'tʃɛk,lɪst/ n. a list of items reviewed by checking them off: *Students in computer repair use a checklist to be sure that they have all of their equipment.*

check·mate /'tʃɛk,meɪt/ n. a winning move in the game of chess: *When players win, they say "Checkmate."*
—v. **-mated, -mating, -mates 1** to make a winning move in chess **2** fig. to totally block and ruin s.o.'s plans, (syn.) to defeat

check·out /'tʃɛk,aʊt/ n.adj. [C;U] **1** an area for making payment before leaving a hotel or store: *The <n.> checkout (or) <adj.> checkout counter is near the front door.* **2** an examination of a machine before operating it: *The repairer did a <n.> checkout of the copier before leaving.*

check·point /'tʃɛk,pɔɪnt/ n. an area for examining identity cards: *The military in that country maintains checkpoints at all border crossings.*

checks and balances n.pl. a system in which one group limits the power of another: *In the USA, the Congress, the Supreme Court, and the Executive Branch limit each other's power in a system of checks and balances.*

check·up /'tʃɛk,ʌp/ n. a medical examination of a person by a doctor: *I am going to my doctor for a checkup.*

ched·dar or **Ched·dar** /'tʃɛdər/ n. [U] a firm, white to orange-colored cheese: *Cheddar can taste mild or very sharp.*

USAGE NOTE: Other kinds of cheese popular in the USA are American, Swiss, provolone, brie, monterey jack, parmesan, mozzarella, and colby.

cheek (1) /tʃik/ *n.* **1** either side of the face, from below eye level to the chin: *The little boy has rosy cheeks in the winter.* **2** either round part of the buttocks

cheek (2) *n.* [U] bold behavior that takes advantage of others, (*syns.*) gall, nerve: *She has a lot of cheek going ahead of everyone else in line.* -*n.* [U] **cheekiness;** -*adj.* **cheeky.**

cheek·bone /ˈtʃik,boʊn/ *n.* the bone below and beside each eye: *She put some makeup on her cheekbones.*

cheer /tʃɪr/ *v.* **1** to shout with delight, admiration, or support: *The crowd cheered when their team scored.‖They cheered their team on to victory.* **2** *phrasal v. sep.* **to cheer up (s.o.): a.** *insep.* to become happier: *He cheered up when he heard the good news.* **b.** *sep.* to make s.o. feel happier: *Her visit to the hospital cheered up the patients.‖It cheered them up.*
—*n.* **1** [C] a shout of delight, approval, or support: *The crowd gave a cheer for their team.* **2** [U] a feeling of warmth and good spirits among people: *There is a feeling of good cheer during the holidays.* **3** *n.pl.* **cheers** a toast to good health: *They lifted their drinks and said "Cheers" to each other.*

cheer·ful /ˈtʃɪrfəl/ *adj.* **1** happy, pleasant: *She whistled a cheerful tune.* **2** believing the future will be good, (*syn.*) optimistic: *She has a cheerful attitude toward life.* -*adv.* **cheerfully;** -*n.* [U] **cheerfulness.**

cheer·lead·er /ˈtʃɪr,lidər/ *n.* **1** one who leads a crowd in cheering for a sports team **2** *fig.* a leader who strongly encourages others: *The company president is the cheerleader for her employees.*

cheer·y /ˈtʃɪri/ *adj.* **-ier, -iest** showing joy or good spirits: *She's always cheery on her birthday.*

cheese /tʃiz/ *n.* **1** [U] a solid or soft food made from the thickest part of milk: *She likes Cheddar cheese.* **2** *infrml.fig.* **a big cheese:** an important person: *That man is a big cheese at Empire Bank.*

cheese·burg·er /ˈtʃiz,bɜrgər/ *n.* a hamburger with melted cheese on top, served on a roll: *I'll have a cheeseburger with fries, please.*

cheese·cake /ˈtʃiz,keɪk/ *n.* **1** [C;U] a cake made from cream cheese or cottage cheese, eggs, sugar, etc.: *I ordered chocolate cheesecake for dessert.* **2** [U] *fig.* a picture of a woman wearing very little clothing

cheese·cloth /ˈtʃiz,klɔθ/ *n.* [C;U] a cotton cloth with spaces between the threads, often used to pour foods and liquids through to catch unwanted pieces

cheet·ah /ˈtʃitə/ *n.* a large, fast African cat with spotted fur: *Cheetahs are among the fastest animals in the world.*

chef /ʃɛf/ *n.* a cook, esp. the head cook in a restaurant: *The chef changes items on the menu each day.*

chef's salad *n.* a salad made with lettuce and pieces of ham and cheese

chem·i·cal /ˈkɛmɪkəl/ *adj.* **1** having to do with chemistry: *She is studying chemical engineering.* **2** having to do with chemicals: *There was a chemical fire at a warehouse last night.‖"Chemical abuse" refers to the use of illegal drugs and too much alcohol.*
—*n.* a substance made from or used in a chemical process: *Many household cleaners contain dangerous chemicals.* -*adv.* **chemically.**

chem·is·try /ˈkɛməstri/ *n.* [U] **1** the science of matter, how it is structured, and how it combines and changes: *She took a course in chemistry in college.* **2** *fig.* **a.** the quality of personal relationships: *There is good chemistry between the teacher and her students.* **b.** sexual attraction: *She says he's a nice guy, but there's just no chemistry between them.* -*n.* **chemist.**

che·mo·ther·a·py /ˌkimoʊˈθɛrəpi/ *n.* [U] strong chemical medications given esp. as a treatment for cancer

cher·ish /ˈtʃɛrɪʃ/ *v.* **-ishes 1** to love most dearly: *She cherishes her children and does everything for them.* **2** to hold dear in one's mind: *He cherishes the idea of retiring to Florida someday.*

cher·ry /ˈtʃɛri/ *n.* **-ries** a small, round, usu. dark-red fruit that grows on a tree: *Ripe cherries taste sweet.*

cher·ub /ˈtʃɛrəb/ *n.* **-ubs** or **-ubim** /-ə,bɪm/ a small, imaginary child with rosy cheeks: *In old paintings, cherubs are seen floating like angels in the sky.* -*adj.* **cherubic** /tʃəˈrubɪk/.

chess /tʃɛs/ *n.* [U] a board game for two players, each starting with 16 pieces (chessmen) that are moved across a board divided into squares (chessboard) in an attempt to capture the other player's pieces: *You have won the game of chess when your opponent has nowhere to safely move his king.* See: checkmate.

chest /tʃɛst/ *n.* **1** the front of the human body above the stomach area **2** a strong box used for storage or shipping goods **3** a small cabinet, usu. hanging on a wall: *There's some aspirin in the medicine chest in the bathroom.* **4 to get s.t. off one's chest:** to say what is troubling you: *He was upset about his low salary and got that off his chest by telling his boss about it.*

chest·nut /ˈʧɛs.nʌt, -nət/ n. a tree and its brown nut: *Many people like to roast chestnuts and eat them.*
—adj. deep reddish-brown: *chestnut hair*||*a chestnut horse*

chest·y /ˈʧɛsti/ adj. **-ier, -iest** having a large chest

chew /ʧu/ v. **1** to move the lower jaw to grind (food) with the teeth: *She chewed on a piece of meat.* **2** phrasal v. sep. **to chew s.o. out:** to criticize s.o. severely: *She chewed out her assistant when he forgot to send an important package.*||*She chewed him out.* **3** phrasal v. sep. **to chew s.t. over:** to spend time thinking about s.t.: *Let's chew over this idea.*||*Let's chew it over.* **4** phrasal v. sep. **to chew s.t. up: a.** to destroy by chewing: *My dog chewed up my shoe and ruined it.*||*He chewed it up.* **b.** fig. to waste, (syn.) to squander: *That project chewed up too much time and money before it was finally finished.* **5** infrml. **to chew the fat:** to talk in a friendly way, (syn.) to chat: *Two friends chewed the fat about football.*
—n. [U] a piece of tobacco chewed in the mouth: *It is very rude to spit chew on the sidewalk.* -n. **chewer,** [U] **chewiness;** -adj. **chewy.**

chew·ing gum n. [U] a soft, sweet substance made for chewing: *She put a stick of chewing gum in her mouth.*

chic /ʃik/ adj.n. [U] having an attractive, stylish look: *Her little black dress and pretty hat made her look <adj.> chic.* -n. [U] **chicness.**

chi·ca·ner·y /ʃɪˈkeɪnəri/ n.frml. [U] trickery or deceit, usu. illegal: *A politician accused his opponent of using chicanery to win the election.*

Chi·ca·no /ʧɪˈkɑnoʊ/ n.adj. **-nos** a person of Mexican descent living in the USA: *Many <n.> Chicanos live in southern California. -n. adj.* (woman) **Chicana** /ʧɪˈkɑnə/.

chi·chi /ˈʃi,ʃi/ adj. fashionable, often in a showy way: *People going to that fancy party wore chichi clothes.*

chick /ʧɪk/ n. **1** a baby bird, esp. a baby chicken **2** slang a young woman: *She is a cool chick!*

chick·a·dee /ˈʧɪkə,di/ n. a small North American bird, esp. a light gray bird with a black cap: *The name of the chickadee sounds like its call.*

chick·en /ˈʧɪkən/ n. **1** [C] a farm bird raised for its eggs and meat: *The chickens pecked at their food.* **2** [C;U] its meat: *We had fried chicken for dinner.* **3** [U] infrml.fig. a person without courage, (syn.) a coward: *I asked him to go skiing with me, but he's a chicken; he's afraid he might get hurt.* **4 to count one's chickens before they hatch:** to rely on s.t. that may not happen: *She spent a lot of money before she knew whether her bank loan was approved; she counted her chickens before they hatched.*

—phrasal v. slang **to chicken out:** to agree to do s.t., then not do it because of fear: *He said he would go skiing, but he chickened out at the last minute. See:* chick, **1** ; hen; rooster.

chicken feed n. [U] **1** grain (corn, soybeans, etc.) given to chickens to eat **2** fig. a small, unimportant amount of money: *The cost of the computer equipment is chicken feed in comparison with the salaries of the people needed to run it.*

chicken pox n. [U] a mild disease, mainly of children, with fever and itchy, red, pus-filled spots (a rash) on the skin: *Our little girl had the chicken pox for 10 days.*

chic·o·ry /ˈʧɪkəri/ n. [U] **1** a plant with blue flowers and leaves that are used in making salads **2** its dried and roasted root, used in making tea or coffee: *Chicory in that coffee gives it a special flavor.*

chide /ʧaɪd/ v.frml. **chided** or **chid** /ʧɪd/, **chiding, chides** to criticize s.o. to improve their behavior, (syn.) to reprimand: *The mother chided her son about the necessity of washing his hands before eating.*

chief /ʧif/ n. the top person in an organization: *He is the fire chief.*
—adj. most important: *What is that country's chief export?*

Chief Executive n. the President of the USA

Chief Executive Officer n. the top person in a business: *The Chief Executive Officer runs the company day-to-day. -abbr.* **CEO.**

Chief Financial Officer n. the top financial person in a business: *The Chief Financial Officer deals with banks to get loans for the company. -abbr.* **CFO.**

Chief Justice n. the top judge: *The Chief Justice of the Supreme Court hands down the court's decisions.*

chief·ly /ˈʧifli/ adv. **1** most importantly, especially: *We are chiefly concerned for your safety.* **2** mostly but not completely: *This fruit drink is chiefly made from apple juice.*

chief·tain /ˈʧiftən/ n. the head of a tribe or tribal nations, a chief: *Chieftains met to discuss peace among their tribes.*

chif·fon /ʃɪˈfɑn/ n. [U] a light cloth made of thin silk or rayon: *That pretty scarf is made of chiffon.*

child /ʧaɪld/ n. **children** /ˈʧɪldrən/ **1** a very young person, who is no longer a baby but not yet an adolescent **2** a son or daughter: *The couple has three children, all married and in their thirties now.* **3** a person with a bad temper or little experience: *When the company's owner does not get what he wants, he behaves like a child.* **4** frml. **with child:** pregnant: *She is with child now.*

child·bear·ing /ˈʧaɪldˌbɛrɪŋ/ adj. (of women) capable of having children: *At 38, she is still of childbearing age.*
—*n.* [U] an act of giving birth to a child

child·birth /ˈʧaɪldˌbɜrθ/ n. [U] the act of giving birth: *Childbirth was difficult with her first baby.*

child·hood /ˈʧaɪldˌhʊd/ n. [C;U] the period from birth to about age 13: *She had a happy childhood.*

child·ish /ˈʧaɪldɪʃ/ adj. unreasonable, failing to be adult, (syn.) immature: *Oh, don't be so childish! Take your medicine! -adv.* **childishly;** *-n.* [U] **childishness.**

child·less /ˈʧaɪldlɪs/ adj. not having had a child: *Theirs is a childless marriage.*

child·like /ˈʧaɪldˌlaɪk/ adj. looking or acting like a child: *She looked up at him with large, childlike eyes.*

child·proof /ˈʧaɪldˌpruf/ adj. unable to be opened by a child: *Her medicine bottles are childproof, so her kids cannot poison themselves accidentally.*

chil·dren /ˈʧɪldrən/ n.pl. of child

child's play n.fig. [U] s.t. easy to do: *Fixing that door handle is not difficult; in fact, it is child's play.*

chil·i /ˈʧɪli/ n. -ies or **chili pepper 1** any of a variety of peppers with a hot, spicy taste, used fresh or dried in cooking **2** a dish made with beans in a hot, spicy sauce made with chili powder. *See:* chili con carne.

chili con carne /ˈʧɪlikɑnˈkɑrni, -kən-/ n. a dish of bits of meat and often beans in a hot, spicy sauce made with chili peppers or chili powder

chill /ʧɪl/ n. **1** a cold temperature, but not freezing: *In the morning, there is a chill in the air.* **2** a cold feeling: *She shivered suddenly, and said she just got a chill.*
—*v.* to cool: *He chilled the wine in the refrigerator.*

chill·y /ˈʧɪli/ adj. -ier, -iest **1** a little cold: *We have chilly weather in the early winter.* **2** unfriendly: *She doesn't like him and gave him a chilly hello. -n.* [U] **chilliness.**

chime /ʧaɪm/ n. **1** a set of bells, each of which makes a different note when struck **2** an electronic device that produces a bell-like sound: *I heard the chime of the doorbell.*
—*v.* **chimed, chiming, chimes 1** to make the sound of chimes: *Our doorbells chime.* **2** phrasal v. **to chime in:** to suddenly join a conversation, (syn.) to interrupt: *The husband and wife were arguing when one of their children chimed in that it was time to leave.*

chim·ney /ˈʧɪmni/ n. -neys the large metal pipe or hollow brick structure for passing smoke from a fire or furnace into the open air:

The chimneys of that factory rise high into the air.
—*n.* **chimney sweep.**

chim·pan·zee /ˌʧɪmpænˈzi/ n. a type of African ape with long arms: *Chimpanzees are intelligent animals.*

chin /ʧɪn/ n. **1** the front of the lower jaw beneath the lips **2 to do chin-ups:** to exercise by pulling oneself up on a bar until one's chin is just above it **3 to keep one's chin up:** to keep one's courage: *Keep your chin up; you will do well on the exam.* **4 to take it on the chin:** to suffer a bad loss: *He took it on the chin when he lost all his savings in the stock market crash.*

chi·na /ˈʧaɪnə/ n. [U] **1** fine dishes, cups, plates, and bowls: *We use our best china only for Sunday dinner.* **2** the white clay used in making fine china

Chi·na·town /ˈʧaɪnəˌtaʊn/ n. a neighborhood or area in a city (not in China) populated mainly by Chinese: *We had dinner in a restaurant in Chinatown.*

chin·chil·la /ʧɪnˈʧɪlə/ n. a small South American animal like a squirrel, or its soft valuable fur: *a chinchilla coat*

chink /ʧɪŋk/ n. **1** a narrow opening, like a crack, (syn.) fissure: *Light came through a chink in the wooden wall.* **2** a short metallic sound

chi·nos /ˈʧinoʊz/ n.pl. pants made of a soft, long-wearing cotton cloth: *He wears chinos to school every day.*

chintz /ʧɪnts/ n. [U] cotton cloth printed with bright patterns: *Those red and yellow curtains are made of chintz.*

chintz·y /ˈʧɪntsi/ adj.infrml. cheap and bright: *Do not buy that chintzy dress; you can see right through it.*

chip /ʧɪp/ n. **1** a piece of wood, paint, etc. knocked or fallen off s.t.: *Chips of paint fell on the floor from the old wall.* **2** a crisp, usu. salty slice of fried food: *a bag of potato chips* **3** a round piece of plastic used for money in gambling: *She counted her chips before placing her bet.* **4** short for microchip, the part of an electronic device that controls it: *A computer chip allows the computer to store and process information.* **5 a chip off the old block:** s.o. who is very much like one of his or her parents **6 to have a chip on one's shoulder:** to be bitter or resentful and become angry easily: *He has a chip on his shoulder and will argue about the littlest thing.*
—*v.* **chipped, chipping, chips 1** to break or cut off a small piece or small bits: *I've chipped a tooth.||The hunter chipped pieces of wood off a branch to use in a fire.* **2** phrasal v. insep. **to chip away at s.t.:** to reduce s.t. slowly: *She chipped away at the man's authority until he*

had none left. **3** *phrasal v.* **to chip in:** to put in one's share of money: *We all chipped in and bought the boss a birthday present.*

chip·munk /'tʃɪp,mʌŋk/ *n.* a small squirrel-like animal with brown fur and black stripes on its back: *Chipmunks like to eat seeds and nuts.*

chip·per /'tʃɪpər/ *adj.infrml.* happy and full of energy, (*syn.*) cheerful: *My uncle is 80 years old and still as chipper and active as ever.*

chi·ro·prac·tor /'kaɪrə,præktər/ *n.* a licensed professional who lines up people's bones, esp. the spine, with pressure of the hands: *Chiropractors try to free people of back pain.* **-n. chiropractic** /,kaɪrə'præktɪk, 'kaɪrə,præk-/.

chirp /tʃɜrp/ *n.v.* a high, short, sharp sound: *Birds <v.> chirped in the early morning.*

chis·el /'tʃɪzəl/ *n.* a metal tool with a V-shaped point for cutting wood or stone: *Sculptors use chisels to carve statues.*
—*v.* **1** to carve with a chisel: *A worker chiseled stones to fit together to make a wall.* **2** *phrasal v. insep.* **to chisel s.o. out of s.t.:** to cheat or trick s.o. and take their money: *That man chiseled me out of $100.* **-n. chiseler.**

chit /tʃɪt/ *n.* **1** a note signed for money owed for food and drink in a restaurant or bar **2** a printed piece of paper used as a substitute for money: *That government paid its soldiers in chits, not real cash.*

chit·chat /'tʃɪt,tʃæt/ *n.v.* **-chatted, -chatting, -chats** [U] friendly conversation about unimportant matters: *Entering the house, we could hear the <n.> chitchat at the party.*

chiv·al·rous /'ʃɪvəlrəs/ *adj.frml.* **1** having good manners, esp. toward women, (*syn.*) gallant: *That chivalrous gentleman helped the elderly lady across the street and into a taxi.* **2** related to the rules of good behavior among male nobility (knights) in the Middle Ages **-n.** [U] **chivalry.**

chive /tʃaɪv/ *n.* a small, onion-like plant with long, thin, green leaves used to flavor food: *I put chives in my salad for flavor.*

chlo·ri·nat·ed /'klɔrə,neɪtɪd/ *adj.* treated with chlorine to kill germs: *Our drinking water is chlorinated.* **-v. chlorinate.**

chlo·rine /'klɔr,in/ *n.* [U] a yellowish, poisonous gas used to kill germs, in industry, etc. —*adj.* containing chlorine: *I used chlorine bleach to whiten my laundry.*

chlo·ro·form /'klɔrə,fɔrm/ *n.v.* [U] a colorless, heavy liquid chemical: *<n.> Chloroform can be used in refrigeration, pressured cans, and as an anesthetic.*

chlo·ro·phyll /'klɔrə,fɪl/ *n.* [U] the green substance in plants

chock /tʃak/ *n.v.* a thick piece of wood or metal used to block s.t. from moving: *She put a chock under the rear tire while she changed a flat in the front.*

chock·full /'tʃak'fʊl/ *adj.infrml.* full to overflowing, (*syn.*) crammed: *The football stadium is chockfull of people.*

choc·o·late /'tʃɔklɪt, 'tʃak-/ *n.* **1** [U] a light to dark brown candy, powder, or syrup made from roasted cacao beans: *He sent a box of chocolates to his sweetheart.* **2 hot chocolate:** a drink made from sweet chocolate powder and hot milk
—*adj.* a reddish brown: *He wore a chocolate-colored sweater.*

choice /tʃɔɪs/ *n.* **1** [C;U] the power or right to choose: *The choice is yours; tell us what you decide.* **2** [C] a variety of things from which to choose: *The college offers a wide choice of courses.* **3** [C] s.o. or s.t. chosen: *His first choice for a vacation would be Disney World.*
—*adj.* **choicer, choicest 1** special, very desirable: *They bought a choice piece of property near the water.* **2** being a high grade of meat below prime meat: *choice steak See:* choose.

choir /'kwaɪər/ *n.* a group of singers: *Our neighbors sing in the church choir.*

choke /tʃoʊk/ *v.* **choked, choking, chokes 1** to stop breathing because of a block in the air passage in the throat: *He choked on a piece of meat that stuck in his throat.* **2** to cut off s.o.'s air supply by squeezing the neck, (*syn.*) to strangle: *The murderer choked his victim to death.* **3** to be unable to speak, esp. because of sadness: *She choked on her tears at her mother's burial.* **4** *infrml.* to become so nervous under pressure as to fail: *In the final game, the tennis player choked* (or) *choked up and lost by repeatedly missing the ball.* **5** *phrasal v. sep.* **to choke s.t. back:** to control anger, etc.: *He choked back his anger.‖He choked it back.*

chol·er·a /'kalərə/ *n.* [U] a serious, often deadly disease of the stomach and intestines found mainly in tropical countries: *Those poor people caught cholera from bad drinking water.*

cho·les·ter·ol /kə'lɛstə,rɔl, -,roʊl/ *n.* [U] a slippery white crystal-like substance found in the body, including the blood and the brain: *Too much cholesterol can block the blood vessels and cause a heart attack.*

choose /tʃuz/ *v.* **chose** /tʃoʊz/ or **chosen** /'tʃoʊzən/, **choosing, chooses 1** to pick (one or more) out of a greater number, to make a choice, (*syn.*) to select: *I had to choose between two job offers.* **2** to decide: *I chose to go to the movies alone.*

choos·y /'tʃuzi/ *adj.* **-ier, -iest** selecting only what one wants, and often difficult to please, (*syn.*) finicky: *He is very choosy about what he eats.*

chop /tʃap/ *v.* **chopped, chopping, chops 1** to cut with hard, sharp blows: *She chops wood for*

the fire with an ax. **2** to cut into small pieces: *She chopped carrots and onions with a knife.*
—*n.* **1** a sharp blow: *the chop of an ax, a karate chop* **2** a cut of meat, usu. on a bone: *She had lamb (pork, veal) chops for dinner.* **3** *slang* the lower part of the face, (*syn.*) the jaw: *He punched the man right in the chops.*

chop·per /ˈtʃɑpər/ *n.* **1** a sharp metal tool for cutting **2** *slang* a helicopter: *The army uses choppers to carry soldiers by air.*

chop·py /ˈtʃɑpi/ *adj.* **-pier, -piest 1** (said of oceans and lakes) having waves, esp. high ones: *We had a rough boat ride on a choppy sea* **2** not smooth, (*syn.*) jerky: *choppy movements‖choppy speech* -*adv.* **choppily;** -*n.* [U] **choppiness.**

chop·sticks /ˈtʃɑpˌstɪks/ *n.pl.* two thin sticks of wood, ivory, etc., used to take hold of food and put it in the mouth: *Chopsticks are commonly used in China and Japan.*

chop suey /ˈtʃɑpˈsui/ *n.* [U] a dish of chicken or beef cooked with bean sprouts and sauce: *I eat chop suey with a bowl of rice.*

cho·ral /ˈkɔrəl/ *adj.* having to do with a chorus or choir (singing group): *She sings in a church choral group.*

chord /kɔrd/ *n.* **1** (in music) three or more musical notes played together **2** *fig.* a feeling: *The sound of her voice on the telephone struck a chord (of love) with him.* **3** a straight line connecting two points on a circle or curve

chore /tʃɔr/ *n.* a boring but necessary act: *I have to do the chores at home, like taking out the garbage and washing the dishes.*

cho·re·og·ra·phy /ˌkɔriˈɑgrəfi/ *n.* [U] the art of arranging dance steps for dancers to perform: *The choreography of that ballet was done by a famous <n.> choreographer.* -*v.* **choreograph** /ˈkɔriəˌgræf/; -*n.* **choreographer.**

chor·tle /ˈtʃɔrtl/ *v.n.* **-tled, -tling, -tles** to laugh softly with delight: *I <v.> chortled at his funny joke.*

cho·rus /ˈkɔrəs/ *n.v.* **-ruses 1** a usu. large group of singers, (*syn.*) a choir: *My daughter sings in the high-school chorus.* **2** a piece of music for a chorus **3** a part of a song that is repeated after each verse, (*syn.*) refrain: *The audience joined the folksinger in singing the chorus.* **4** a group of people who sing and dance together, esp. in a musical comedy: *She started her career as a chorus girl on Broadway.* **5** words spoken by a group at the same time: *Everyone complained all at once about the new taxes; there was a chorus of protest.*

chose /tʃouz/ *v.* past tense of choose

cho·sen /ˈtʃouzən/ *v.* past part. of choose

chow /tʃaʊ/ *n. slang* food—*phrasal v. slang* **to chow down:** to eat: *It's lunch time and I'm going to chow down.*

chow·der /ˈtʃaʊdər/ *n.* [U] a thick soup, usu. made with some type of fish, milk, and vegetable: *She ordered a bowl of fish (corn, clam) chowder.*

chris·ten /ˈkrɪsən/ *v.* **1** (in some churches) to make s.o., usu. a child, a Christian and/or give them a first name in a church ceremony, (*syn.*) to baptize: *The minister christened our son and we named him Joseph.* **2** to formally name and launch a new ship -*n.* [C;U] **christening.**

Chris·tian /ˈkrɪstʃən/ *adj.* **1** related to Jesus Christ and his religious teachings **2** of Christianity, its churches, beliefs, etc.
—*n.* a believer in Christianity: *He became a Christian at age 17.*

Christ·mas /ˈkrɪsməs/ or **Christmas Day** *n.* **1** (in Christianity) Christ's birthday, celebrated on December 25th: *She spends Christmas (Day) with her family.* **2** Christmas Day and the days just before and after it: *They're going skiing for a week at Christmas (time).*

Christmas Eve *n.* the time from evening to 12 midnight on December 24th: *Many Christians go to church on Christmas Eve.*

Christmas tree *n.* a natural or artificial pine tree decorated with lights and colorful ornaments: *Many American Christians put up Christmas trees in their houses in December.*

chrome /kroʊm/ *n.v.* [U] **chromed, chroming, chromes 1** a shiny, hard, steel-gray metal, (*syn.*) chromium: *<n.> Chrome is used to make stainless steel.* **2** a shiny coating of chromium on metal: *The bumpers on that car are made of steel covered with <n.> chrome.* -*adj.* **chrome-plated.**

chro·mi·um /ˈkroʊmiəm/ *n.* [U] a basic metal that is shiny, hard, and gray: *Chromium has many uses, including to harden steel and as a shiny coating over metal.*

chro·mo·some /ˈkroʊməˌsoʊm/ *n.* the part of a plant or animal's cells that contains the characteristics that are passed on from parent to offspring: *Chromosomes look like tiny threads and contain the DNA in each cell.*

chron·ic /ˈkrɑnɪk/ *adj.* **1** long lasting, (*syn.*) persistent: *She has had chronic pain in her back for years.* **2** failing to change, (*syn.*) habitual: *He is a chronic troublemaker.* -*adv.* **chronically.**

chron·i·cle /ˈkrɑnɪkəl/ *n.* a written and/or photographic record of events as they happen
—*v.* **-cled, -cling, -cles** to record (historical events): *Newspapers and television chronicle world events each day.*

chron·o·log·i·cal /ˌkrɑnəˈlɑdʒɪkəl/ *adj.* of the order of events as they happen over time, (*syn.*) sequential: *A television reporter gave a*

C

chronological description of the football game. **-adv. chronologically.**

chro·nol·o·gy /krə'nɑlədʒi/ *n.* **-gies** a list or description of events in the order in which they happen: *That history book gives a chronology of battles in World War II.*

chry·san·the·mum /krɪ'sænθəməm/ *n.* a plant with large, showy flowers in late summer and fall: *They planted many different colors of chrysanthemums in their garden.*

chub·by /'ʧʌbi/ *adj.* **-bier, -biest** fat, (*syn.*) plump: *Many babies are chubby.*

chuck /ʧʌk/ *v.infrml.* **1** to throw: *I chucked the ball to him.* **2** to gently pat in an upward motion: *He chucked the baby under the chin.* **3** *phrasal v. sep.* **to chuck s.o.** or **s.t. out: a. s.o.:** to force to leave: *They chucked out the protestor.‖They chucked him out.* **b. s.t.:** to throw out, (*syn.*) to discard: *She chucked out some old shoes.*
—n.infrml. **1** [C] a gentle pat in an upward motion: *He gave the baby a chuck under the chin.* **2** [C] a throw **3** [C] a holder for a tool **4** [U] a cut of beef from the neck and shoulder **5** [U] *infrml.* (in Western USA) food

chuck·le /'ʧʌkəl/ *v.n.* **-led, -ling, -les** to laugh softly: *He does not laugh out loud; he only <v.> chuckles.*

chug /ʧʌg/ *v.n.* **chugged, chugging, chugs 1** to make short, explosive sounds, like an engine working hard **2** to move while making these sounds: *The train <v.> chugged through the mountains.* **3** *infrml.* to drink rapidly, causing the throat to make chugging sounds as one swallows: *He felt ill after <v.> chugging a beer.*

chum /ʧʌm/ *n.* a good friend, esp. among boys *— chummed, chumming, chums phrasal v. insep.* **to chum around together** or **with:** to go places with one's chums: *Those boys chum around with each other after school.*

chum·my /'ʧʌmi/ *adj.* **-mier, -miest** friendly: *They are very chummy (with each other).*

chump /ʧʌmp/ *n. slang* s.o. easily tricked by others, (*syn.*) a fool: *He was a chump to believe those lies.*

chunk /ʧʌŋk/ *n.* a thick piece: *He cut off a chunk of meat from the roast turkey.* **-adj. chunky.**

church /'ʧɜrʧ/ *n.* **churches 1** a building for worship, esp. a Christian one: *I go to church every Sunday.* **2** *sing.* [U] **the church:** the whole of a Christian institution including all its churches, members, and beliefs: *the Catholic church‖the Protestant church*

USAGE NOTE: Jews go to worship in a synagogue or *schul,* and Muslims go to a mosque.

church·yard /'ʧɜrʧ,yard/ *n.* the area around a church: *Part of a churchyard is often used as a cemetery.*

churl·ish /'ʧɜrlɪʃ/ *adj.frml.* rude, unpleasant, (*syn.*) surly: *His churlish behavior annoys everyone.* **-adv. churlishly; -n.** [U] **churlishness.**

churn /ʧɜrn/ *v.* **1** to beat cream or milk until it becomes butter **2** to mix and move violently: *Water churns under a waterfall.* **3** *phrasal v. sep.* **to churn s.t. out:** to produce in large amounts: *That newspaper reporter churns out many stories each week.‖He churns them out.*
—n. a device used to churn cream or milk into butter: *a butter churn*

chute /ʃut/ *n.* an open slide with sides, (*syn.*) an inclined trough: *In some apartment buildings, people throw waste down a garbage chute.*

chutz·pah /'hʊtspə, 'xʊt-/ *n.* [U] *infrml.* boldness without shame, (*syn.*) brazenness: *He had the chutzpah to ask for a raise after working here one week!*

CIA /,si,aɪ'eɪ/*abbr.* for Central Intelligence Agency, a branch of the US government that secretly gathers information about other countries: *The CIA has its agents in nearly every country of the world.*

ci·der /'saɪdər/ *n.* [U] **1** juice squeezed from fruit, esp. apples **2 hard cider:** an alcoholic beverage made from apple cider

ci·gar /sɪ'gɑr/ *n.* a round, wrapped roll of tobacco leaves made for smoking: *Some cigars are very expensive.*

cig·a·rette /,sɪgə'rɛt, 'sɪgə,rɛt/ *n.* a round roll of finely cut tobacco wrapped in paper for smoking: *She lit a cigarette.*

cinch /sɪnʧ/ *n.* **cinches 1** [C] a type of belt usu. made of thick leather: *The cinch on a saddle holds it tight on the horse.* **2** *sing.infrml.* an easy task: *Passing that driver's test was a cinch.* **3** *sing.infrml.* s.t. certain to happen: *It's a cinch that our team will win the tournament.*
—v. **cinches 1** to tighten a belt **2** *infrml.* to make secure or certain: *We offered to pay what they asked and cinched the deal right there.*

Cin·co de Ma·yo /'sɪŋkoʊdeɪ'mayoʊ, -ðeɪ-/ *n.* May 5, a celebration of the defeat of the French military in Mexico in 1862: *Mexicans and Mexican-Americans celebrate Cinco de Mayo.*

cin·der /'sɪndər/ *n.* a piece of burned substance (coal, wood) not completely burned to ashes: *He cleaned out cinders of coal from the stove.*

cinder block *n.* a large gray block made of concrete and cinders, used in building: *The walls of that factory are made of cinder blocks.*

Cin·der·el·la /,sɪndə'rɛlə/ *n.* **1** a poor girl who marries a prince in a famous fairy tale **2** a girl or woman who succeeds after a period of difficulty: *Hers is a real Cinderella story: she came* *from a small farm town and later married the richest man in New York.*

cin·e·ma /ˈsɪnəmə/ *n.* **the cinema:** the industry of making movies: *He is an actor in the cinema in Hollywood.*

cin·e·ma·tog·ra·pher /ˌsɪnəməˈtɑgrəfər/ *n.* a person who operates the camera in making a movie

cin·na·mon /ˈsɪnəmən/ *n.* [U] a brown spice from Asia: *The baker put cinnamon on the doughnuts.*

ci·pher /ˈsaɪfər/ *n.* **1** [C] the number zero **2** [U] a secret code for written messages: *The spy sent the information in cipher.* **3** [C] *pej.* a person who is not good for much of anything

cir·ca /ˈsɜrkə/ *prep.frml.* (used with dates) about, (*syn.*) approximately: *The war ended circa 1917* (or) *c. 1917. -abbr.* **c.**

cir·cle /ˈsɜrkəl/ *n.* **1** a closed curved line whose every point is equally far from the center: *The teacher drew a circle on the blackboard.* **2** a group of people with a shared interest: *a circle of friends||political circles* **3** a seating area in a theater above the main floor **4 to go in** or **around in circles:** to be confused and make no progress: *I have been going around in circles all day trying to solve that problem.* **5 to come full circle:** to return to the starting point: *The company started out as a small one, grew large, then had to cut back sharply; it has come full circle.*
—*v.* **-cled, -cling, -cles** **1** to draw a circle around: *The student circled the answers on the test.* **2** to go around: *The soldiers circled around their enemy to avoid them.*

cir·cuit /ˈsɜrkɪt/ *n.* **1** a closed path for an electrical current: *electrical circuits* **2** a route with regular stops: *That truck driver makes a circuit of the stores in this area.*

cir·cu·i·tous /sərˈkyuətəs/ *adj.* taking a long, indirect course, (*syn.*) roundabout: *We took a circuitous route to avoid driving through the center of the city.*

cir·cu·lar /ˈsɜrkyələr/ *adj.* **1** having a round shape or design: *The dancers made circular movements.* **2** marked by reasoning in a circle: *His circular argument persuaded no one.* **3** *infrml.* **the circular file:** a wastebasket: *I threw that letter in the circular file.*
—*n.* a printed advertising piece: *A boy handed out circulars on sales items for the local grocery store. -v.* **circularize.**

cir·cu·late /ˈsɜrkyə,leɪt/ *v.* **-lated, -lating, -lates** **1** to pass around: *I circulated the report to everyone on the committee.* **2** to flow: *Blood circulates in the body.* **3** to move around: *The hostess circulated among her guests at the party. -adj.* **circulatory** /ˈsɜrkyələ,tɔri/.

cir·cu·la·tion /ˌsɜrkyəˈleɪʃən/ *n.* **1** [U] the motion of s.t. about a circular path **2** [C;U] the motion of the blood as it is pumped through the body by the heart: *For an old man, he has good circulation.* **3** [C] the number of copies of a newspaper, magazine, etc., sold at one time: *The circulation of the Sunday newspaper is over one million.*

cir·cum·cise /ˈsɜrkəm,saɪz/ *v.* **-cised, -cising, -cises** to cut the tip of the skin off the human male sex organ (penis) or cut the clitoris of the female: *The doctor circumcised the baby boy shortly after birth. -n.* [C;U] **circumcision** /ˌsɜrkəmˈsɪʒən, ˈsɜrkəm,sɪ-/.

cir·cum·fer·ence /sərˈkʌmfrəns, -fərəns/ *n.* **1** the distance around a circle **2** the distance around the outer boundary of s.t. round or circular: *The circumference of the earth is over 40,000 km (nearly 25,000 miles).*

cir·cum·stance /ˈsɜrkəm,stæns/ *n.* **1** a condition (fact, situation, etc.) that affects s.t. else: *Ice on the roads and a bad storm are circumstances that lead to car accidents.* **2 in difficult circumstances:** in trouble, such as with money: *He is in difficult circumstances because he has no job.* **3 under no circumstances:** never, in no way: *The mother told her daughter that under no circumstances is she to go out alone at night.* **4 under the circumstances:** because the situation requires it: *His father was having his eyes operated on; so under the circumstances, the son stayed with him until he could see. -adj.* **circumstantial** /ˌsɜrkəmˈstænʃəl/.

cir·cum·stan·tial evidence *n.* [U] indirect evidence about a crime that no one actually saw happen: *Police found the man's knife at the murder scene, but that was only circumstantial evidence.*

cir·cum·vent /ˌsɜrkəmˈvɛnt/ *v.frml.* **1** to find a way around, avoid: *The company was going bankrupt and the owner circumvented the problem by getting a bank loan.* **2** to go around s.t., esp. by dishonest means: *to circumvent the law -n.* [U] **circumvention.**

cir·cus /ˈsɜrkəs/ *n.* **-cuses** **1** a traveling show of performers (clowns, acrobats) and trained animals **2** *fig.* a busy, often funny situation: *With 25 children at the birthday party, the house was a circus.*

cir·rho·sis /səˈroʊsɪs/ *n.* [U] a disease of the liver that finally causes it to fail: *He died of cirrhosis of the liver.*

cis·tern /ˈsɪstərn/ *n.* a container or tank for holding water: *A cistern in the village catches and holds rainwater.*

cit·a·del /ˈsɪtədəl, -,dɛl/ *n.* a military fortress in or near a city: *A citadel overlooks the old city.*

ci·ta·tion /saɪˈteɪʃən/ *n.* **1** an order to appear in court to answer charges, (*syn.*) a summons **2** praise for doing s.t. good, (*syn.*) a commendation: *The police officer received a citation for saving a man's life.* **3** *frml.* a mention or quotation of s.o. else's words

cite /saɪt/ *v.* **cited, citing, cites 1** to issue a citation (legal summons): *A policeman cited her for illegal parking (drunk driving, speeding, etc.).* **2** to honor s.o. officially: *A policewoman was cited for bravery.* **3** to mention or quote as an example or authority: *In his report, the scientist cited the work of other researchers.*

cit·i·fy /ˈsɪtɪˌfaɪ/ *v.* **-fied, -fying, -fies** to make s.o. behave like city people with fine clothes and interests in city entertainments

cit·i·zen /ˈsɪtəzən, -sən/ *n.* **1** a legal member of a country, state, or city: *She is a US citizen.* **2** a non-military person: *ordinary citizens -n.* **citizenry.**

citizens band *n.* in the USA, radio frequencies available to ordinary citizens to communicate with each other: *Truck drivers often talk with each other on their CB radios. -abbr.* **CB.**

cit·i·zen·ship /ˈsɪtəzənˌʃɪp, -sən-/ *n.* [U] the legal status of belonging to a country, usu. including the right to vote: *I had to wait five years, but I now have my US citizenship.*

cit·ric acid /ˈsɪtrɪk/ *n.* [U] the acid found in citrus juice

cit·rus /ˈsɪtrəs/ *n.* [U] **-ruses 1** a general term for trees bearing citrus fruits **2** the fruits themselves, such as oranges, lemons, and grapefruit: *Lots of citrus is grown in Florida and California.*

cit·y /ˈsɪti/ *n.* **-ies 1** an area with many thousands of people living and working close together, (*syn.*) a metropolis: *Many tourists visit the city of London.* **2 the city:** the part of a city where people work and shop, usu. its center: *I live in a suburb and commute to the city every day.* **3** *infrml.fig.* **fat city:** an excellent, secure life with money: *He has a high-paying job; he's sitting in fat city.* **4 the big city:** city life with entertainment, restaurants, and bright lights: *She is a city girl; she likes (the life of) the big city.*

city hall *n.* **1** [C] a building where a city's government is located **2** [C;U] a center of power that will force you to do or not do s.t.: *You can't fight city hall (and win); I tried for years to build a garage next to my house, but they wouldn't let me do it.*

city slicker *n.infrml.* s.o. who is used to the comforts of the city, and is not used to country life: *City slickers go everywhere in the country during vacation.*

civ·ic /ˈsɪvɪk/ *adj.* of a city, citizenship, or a citizen: *It is your civic duty to vote.*

civ·ics /ˈsɪvɪks/ *n.* [U] a branch of political science that deals with the rights and responsibilities of citizens: *She took a course in civics at her high school.*

civ·il /ˈsɪvəl/ *adj.* **1** of citizens in general, not religious or military: *A judge married the couple in a civil ceremony at City Hall.* **2** (in law) of a citizen's rights and responsibilities: *Civil courts deal with cases like divorce and business disagreements, not criminal matters.* **3** polite, esp. without being friendly, (*syn.*) courteous: *to behave in a civil manner -adv.* **civilly; -n.** **civility** /səˈvɪləti/.

civil disobedience *n.* [U] peaceful noncooperation with governmental policy and laws, as a way of saying that you disagree with them: *As an act of civil disobedience, protesters blocked traffic to the capitol.*

ci·vil·ian /səˈvɪlyən/ *n.adj.* s.o. who is not a member of the military or police forces, an ordinary citizen: *He has left the army; he's a <n.> civilian again.*

civ·i·li·za·tion /ˌsɪvələˈzeɪʃən/ *n.* [C;U] a high level of government, laws, written language, art, music, etc., within a society or culture: *Ancient Greek civilization had important effects on Roman culture.*

civ·i·lize /ˈsɪvəˌlaɪz/ *v.* **-lized, -lizing, -lizes 1** to improve the behavior or manners of, (*syns.*) to refine, polish: *A good education civilizes people.* **2** to bring from a lower level of human social organization to a higher one

civil law *n.* [U] the body of law dealing with the rights of individual citizens (not criminal law)

civil rights *n.pl.* in the USA, the rights of each citizen guaranteed by the US Constitution, such as the rights to vote and not be discriminated against because of race, ethnic background, etc.: *The political movement for civil rights was strongest during the 1950s and 1960s. See:* non-violent, USAGE NOTE.

civil service *n.* [C;U] government employees and the governmental work that they do: *The civil service does not include the law-making, military, or judicial parts of government. See:* bureaucracy. **-n. civil servant.**

civil war *n.* **1** a war between groups in a country **2 the Civil War:** in the USA, the war between the North and South: *The Civil War lasted from 1861 to 1865.*

clack /klæk/ *v.n.* to make a sharp, loud sound: *A worker <v.> clacked two wooden boards together to knock the dust off them.*

clad /klæd/ *adj.* **1** *litr.* clothed: *He was clad only in his underwear.* **2** *suffix* covered with s.t.: *a copperclad frying pan See:* ironclad.

claim /kleɪm/ *v.* **1** to state s.t. as being true, esp. when there is some doubt, (*syn.*) to maintain: *She claims that she has a college degree.*

2 to take possession of as a right: *After the airplane landed, I claimed my luggage.* See: claim check.
—*n.* **1** a right to s.t.: *He has a claim on part of the money left by his dead father.* **2** a demand for s.t. that one has a right to: *He filed an insurance claim after his car was stolen.* **3** a statement that s.t. is true: *The police don't believe her claim that she knows who the thief is.* **4** *infrml.* **a claim to fame:** s.t. important about a person or place: *His claim to fame is that he played professional football years ago.* -*n.* **claimant** /'kleɪmənt/.

claim check or **ticket** *n.* a paper ticket or plastic chip with the same numbers on both parts, one attached to an item, the other held by the owner: *I showed my claim check at the airport luggage area and claimed my bags.*

clair·voy·ant /klɛr'vɔɪənt/ *adj.n.* able to tell what will happen in the future: *She was <adj.> clairvoyant when she said that she would later marry the man that she had just met.* -*n.* **clairvoyance.**

clam /klæm/ *n.* **1** a sea creature with two hard shells: *In New England, many people eat fried clams.* **2** *slang* a US dollar: *That shirt cost me 50 clams.*
—*v.* **clammed, clamming, clams** **1** to dig for clams **2** *phrasal v.* **to clam up:** to shut one's mouth and not speak: *When I asked him where he had heard the news, he clammed up.*

clam·bake /'klæm,beɪk/ *n.* a party where clams, lobster, corn, etc., are baked and served, usu. on a beach: *We celebrated the end of summer with a big clambake by the sea.*

clam·ber /'klæmbər/ *v.* to climb with difficulty: *The baby clambered onto the sofa.*

clam·my /'klæmi/ *adj.* **-mier, -miest** **1** moist, damp: *clammy weather* **2** unpleasantly wet: *He has a clammy handshake.*

clam·or /'klæmər/ *v.* to make loud, noisy demands or protests: *Outside the factory, the protesters clamored for higher pay.*
—*n.* a loud protest: *They created quite a clamor.*

clamp /klæmp/ *n.* a tool used to hold things tightly: *I used a clamp to hold the board still while I sawed it in half.*
—*v.* **1** to put a clamp on s.t.: *She clamped the two pieces of wood together while the glue dried.* **2** *phrasal v. insep.* **to clamp down on s.t.:** to stop s.t., esp. by use of authority or force: *The police clamped down on crime.* -*n.* **clampdown** /'klæmp,daʊn/.

clan /klæn/ *n.* a large group of relatives or families, usu. with the same ancestor: *The Highlanders of Scotland have many clans.*

clan·des·tine /klæn'dɛstɪn/ *adj.* done in secret, (*syn.*) covert: *The government carries on clandestine activities, like spying.* -*adv.* **clandestinely.**

clang /klæŋ/ *v.n.* to make a loud sound of metal hitting metal: *The heavy prison door <v.> clanged shut.*

clang·or /'klæŋər, 'klæŋgər/ *n.* a loud or continuing clanging sound: *The clangor coming from the street woke me early in the morning.*

clank /klæŋk/ *v.n.* to make a loud, dull sound of metal hitting s.t. hard, not as loud as a clang: *A hammer <v.> clanked as it dropped on the floor.*

clan·nish /'klænɪʃ/ *adj.* loyal to family members and usu. showing dislike of strangers: *That family is very clannish and distrustful of outsiders.* -*n.* [U] **clannishness.**

clap /klæp/ *v.* **clapped, clapping, claps** to strike the hands together in approval, (*syn.*) to applaud: *The audience clapped after the concert.* **2** to slap with the open hand in a friendly way: *I clapped him on the back and said, "Congratulations!"* **3** *infrml.* to put or send quickly: *The police clapped the thief in jail.*
—*n.* **1** a very loud noise: *I heard a clap of thunder in the distance.* **2** the sound of hands being struck together: *There was not a single clap from the audience.* **3** a friendly slap

clap·board /'klæbərd, 'klæp,bɔrd/ *n.* [C;U] a long, narrow board whose thicker bottom partly covers the one below it: *Clapboards are used to cover the outside of houses.*

clap·per /'klæpər/ *n.* the piece of metal with a ball-shaped end found inside a bell: *The clapper struck and made the bell ring.*

clar·i·fy /'klærə,faɪ/ *v.* **-fied, -fying, -fies** **1** to make clear, (*syn.*) to explain: *The student was confused and the teacher clarified the idea.* **2** (of liquids) to make pure

clar·i·fi·ca·tion /,klærəfə'keɪʃən/ *n.* [C;U] an explanation or correction: *Government officials often issue clarifications of their earlier statements.*

clar·i·net /,klærə'nɛt/ *n.* a usu. wooden musical instrument shaped like a long, narrow black tube with a bell-shaped end

clar·i·on /'klæriən/ *n.adj.* a loud, high, clear sound, usu. made by a trumpet or bugle, calling people to action: *(fig.) A politician sounded the <adj.> clarion call to reform the government.*

clar·i·ty /'klærəti/ *n.* [U] **1** clearness of ideas, writing, or situations: *She speaks with great clarity on difficult matters.* **2** clearness or purity of physical things: *the clarity of a diamond, the clarity (purity) of water*

clash /klæʃ/ *v.n.* **clashes** **1** to hit together violently, (*syn.*) to strike: *the <n.> clash of armies in battle* **2** to argue heatedly, (*syn.*) to quarrel: *The man and wife <v.> clashed over spending too much money.* **3** to not look good with: *That bright red tie <v.> clashes with his green suit.*

clasp /klæsp/ *n.* **1** a fastener made of two parts that lock together: *She fastened the clasp on her necklace.* **2** a firm hold of the hands
—*v.* **1** to hold tightly: *He clasped his hands together and prayed.* **2** to lock together with a clasp: *She clasped her necklace.*

class /klæs/ *n.* **classes 1** [C;U] a level in society based on money, education, and family standing, *(syn.)* socioeconomic group: *There are four social classes in the USA, namely the upper class, middle class, working class, and lower class.* **2** [C] a group whose members have at least one similarity, *(syn.)* category: *A motorcycle belongs to a different class of vehicle from cars and trucks.* **3** [C] **a.** a meeting between teacher and students for educational purposes: *My English class meets at 10:00 A.M.* **b.** the students in such a meeting: *The class listened and took notes.* **4** [C] a group of students who will finish school in the same year: *He graduated with the class of 1995.* **5 in a class by itself:** much better than everything else of its kind **6** *slang* **to have class:** to show high quality in appearance and manners: *She always looks great and knows the right thing to say; she has a lot of class. See:* classy.

class action suit *n.* a lawsuit brought against s.o. or s.t. by a group of people with the same complaint: *When the chemical plant blew up and killed thousands of people, a lawyer brought a class action suit against it.*

class-conscious *adj.* aware of what part of society one belongs to: *He's so class-conscious that he feels too good to associate with some people, and he worries that he isn't good enough for others.*

clas·sic /ˈklæsɪk/ *n.* **1** an object regarded as an example of the best of s.t.: *That 1950 Mercedes is a classic.* **2** a musical or literary work (novel, play, etc.) that has been regarded as important for a long time: *The novel* The Adventures of Huckleberry Finn *by Mark Twain is a classic of American literature.* **3** *pl.* **classics:** the literature of ancient Greece, and of Rome: *Homer's* Odyssey *is considered a classic.*
—*adj.* **1** among the best of its kind: *He collects classic cars.* **2** of the highest order: *a classic novel* **3** typical of its kind: *a classic example*

clas·si·cal /ˈklæsɪkəl/ *adj.* **1** proven and accepted: *classical methods of raising children* **2** related to 18th-century European music: *Beethoven and Mozart were classical composers.* **3** related to the literature, art, architecture, etc., of ancient Greece and Rome: *classical literature* -*adv.* **classically;** -*n.* **classicism** /ˈklæsəˌsɪzəm,/, **classicist.**

clas·si·fi·ca·tion /ˌklæsəfəˈkeɪʃən/ *n.* [C;U] a category, esp. one used for formal purposes by government or science: *The classification of steel is as a metal.*

classified ad *n.* a brief advertisement printed in a special section of a newspaper or magazine with others of the same kind, offering or asking for goods or services, jobs, etc.

clas·si·fy /ˈklæsəˌfaɪ/ *v.* **-fied, -fying, -fies 1** to put (things, ideas, etc.) in groups with similar characteristics, *(syn.)* to categorize: *The biologist classified that big plant as a flower, not a tree.* **2** to mark as secret: *Governments classify military plans, so only a few know about them.*

class·mate /ˈklæsˌmeɪt/ *n.* a student with whom one attends school: *She was one of my classmates in high school.*

class·room /ˈklæsˌrum/ *n.* a room where students are taught by a teacher: *My classroom is on the fourth floor.*

class·y /ˈklæsi/ *adj. slang* **-ier, -iest** among the best in appearance or behavior, *(syn.)* elegant: *They live in a very classy neighborhood.*

clat·ter /ˈklætər/ *n.sing.v.* a loud sound of hard things hitting other hard things: *I heard the <n.> clatter of horses' hoofs on the street.*

clause /klɔz/ *n.* **1** a part in a document that requires s.t. to be agreed on and/or done, *(syn.)* a stipulation: *The rent clause in my apartment lease says I must pay on the first day of each month.* **2** one part, with its own subject and verb, of a complex or compound sentence: *There are two clauses in this sentence, and they are divided by a comma.*

claus·tro·pho·bi·a /ˌklɔstrəˈfoubiə/ *n.* [U] a fear of small, closed-in places: *She gets claustrophobia in elevators and closets.* -*adj.* **claustrophobic.**

clav·i·cle /ˈklævɪkəl/ *n.* the collarbone: *He fell and broke his clavicle.*

claw /klɔ/ *n.* **1** one of the sharp nails on an animal's paw or toe: *a bear claw, a lion's claws* **2** the pincers of certain sea animals, used to catch and hold things: *a lobster claw*
—*v.* **1** to scratch or strike with claws: *My cat clawed me on the hand.* **2** *fig.* **to claw one's way:** to work very hard, *(syn.)* to struggle: *He clawed and fought his way to the top and lost many friends in the process.*

clay /kleɪ/ *n.adj.* **1** a type of fine-grained material from the ground that can be shaped when wet, and will hold the shape when dried or baked: *She likes to make dishes out of <n.> clay.* **2 to have feet of clay:** to have bad characteristics while seeming to be perfect: *That politician seemed so fine, yet his personal life was a mess; he has feet of clay.*

clean /klin/ *adj.* **1** free of dirt, dust, or soil: *I just finished the wash, so now I have clean*

clothes.||*Please get me a clean piece of paper to write on.* **2** *slang* free of bad habits or guilt: *She stopped taking drugs and is now clean.* **3** *slang* **to come clean:** to confess the truth: *The thief came clean and admitted that he stole the watch.*
—*v.* **1** to free from dirt, such as by wiping or washing: *She cleaned her eyeglasses with a handkerchief.* **2** to put in proper order: *The boy cleaned his room by putting his toys and clothes back where they belong.* **3** *phrasal v. sep.* **to clean s.o.** or **s.t. out: a. s.o.:** to leave s.o. without any money: *His friends won all his money playing cards; they really cleaned him out.* **b. s.t.:** to remove dirt or objects from s.t.: *After seven years, we finally cleaned out our closets in our apartment.* **c. s.o.** or **s.t.:** to steal everything from: *The robbers cleaned out the store.||They cleaned it out.* **4** *phrasal v. sep.* **to clean (s.o.** or **s.t.) up: a. s.o.** or **s.t.:** to make a place or oneself cleaner: *After the party, I cleaned up (the glasses, ashtrays, etc.).||I cleaned them up.* **b.** to make a lot of money: *She invested in good stocks and really cleaned up.* **5** *slang* **to clean up one's act:** to get free of bad habits: *He was on drugs, but finally cleaned up his act.*
—*adv.infrml.* completely: *I didn't buy bread because I clean forgot.*

clean-cut *adj.* (said of men and boys) with shaved face, well-cut short hair, and neat clothes

clean·er /ˈklinər/ *n.* **1** a substance, like strong soap, used to clean surfaces, (*syn.*) a cleanser **2** a person who cleans (offices, houses, etc.) **3** a cleaning business for clothes, (*syn.*) a dry cleaner: *I took my suit to the cleaner (or) cleaners to be cleaned and pressed.* **4** *fig.infrml.* **to take s.o. to the cleaners:** to charge s.o. too much money or cheat s.o.: *My car broke down, and the garage that fixed it took me to the cleaners.*

clean·ing /ˈklinɪŋ/ *n.* [U] **1** the ordinary household and office work of making bathrooms and kitchens clean, vacuuming rugs, etc.: *That couple shares the cooking and the cleaning.* **2** clothes taken to the cleaner: *She picked up her cleaning on the way home from work. See:* cleaner, **3.**

cleanse /klɛnz/ *v.* **cleansed, cleansing, cleanses** **1** to remove dirt from: *The nurse cleansed a bloody cut in the patient's hand.* **2** to make pure and free from guilt: *She asked God to forgive her sins and cleanse her soul.*

cleans·er /ˈklɛnzər/ *n.* [C;U] a substance, like strong soap, used to clean surfaces: *I used a strong cleanser to clean the bathroom.*

clean-up /ˈkliˌnʌp/ *n.* the cleaning of any mess and/or putting things back in their proper places: *For the cleanup after the party, we washed the glasses and vacuumed the rugs.*

clear /klɪr/ *adj.* **1** easy to understand, (*syn.*) lucid: *clear writing, clear instructions* **2** easy to see through, (*syn.*) transparent: *clear glass||clear water* **3** having no rain or snow and few clouds: *clear weather* **4** free of objects that block the way: *The road is now clear after the storm.* **5** **to make it clear** or **oneself clear:** to state strongly so that there is no misunderstanding: *He made it quite clear what he wanted.*
—*adv.* **1** free from s.t.: *She finally got clear of legal difficulties.* **2** *infrml.* completely: *He hit the baseball clear out of the park.*
—*v.* **1** to remove things that block the way: *Workers cleared fallen trees from the road.||They cleared the road.* **2** to get approval for or from: *He cleared the project with his boss.||She cleared customs at the airport.* **3** to gain as a profit: *We cleared $15,000 on the sale of our house.* **4** *phrasal v. sep.* **to clear s.t. away:** to remove: *A waiter cleared away dirty dishes from the table.||He cleared them away.* **5** *phrasal v.* **to clear off:** to leave a place, usu. quickly: *When they heard the police car coming, they decided to clear off.* **6** *phrasal v. sep.* **to clear s.t. out:** to clean out: *She cleared out her desk drawers.||She cleared them out.* **7** *phrasal v. insep.* **to clear out (of some place):** to leave suddenly: *When a fire started, people cleared out (of the building) quickly.||They cleared out of there.* **8** *phrasal v. (sep.)* **to clear (s.t.) up: a.** to become free of bad weather: *The sky is clearing up and the sun is coming out.* **b.** *sep.* to clarify or explain s.t.: *She cleared up the misunderstanding.||She cleared it up.* **c.** *sep.* to finish, put in order, (*syn.*) to tidy: *He decided to clear up his desk before going on vacation.||He cleared it up.*
—*n.* **to be in the clear:** to be free of danger or blame: *The judge said that she is not guilty, and she is now in the clear. -n.* [U] **clearness.**

clear·ance /ˈklɪrəns/ *n.* [C;U] **1** a statement that s.t. will be allowed, (*syns.*) approval, permission: *The airport gave the airplane clearance to land.* **2** enough space, (*syn.*) headroom: *There was enough clearance for the big truck to go under the bridge.*

clear-cut *adj.* definite, without question: *The criminal's guilt was clear-cut because two people saw him steal.*

clear-head·ed /ˈklɪrˌhɛdɪd/ *adj.* having a clear mind: *He was out all night drinking and is not clear-headed.*

clear·ing /ˈklɪrɪŋ/ *n.* an open space, as in the woods: *There is a cabin in a clearing in the forest.*

clear·ing·house /ˈklɪrɪŋˌhaʊs/ *n.* **-houses** /-ˌhaʊzɪz/ an office in which checks, accounts, or information are processed: *Banks maintain clearinghouses to settle checks drawn between them.*

clear·ly /ˈklɪrli/ *adv.* **1** without being blocked or blurred: *After I hit my head, I could not see clearly.* **2** it is obvious that: *Clearly, she must improve her grades in school.*

cleat /klit/ *n.* a short, pointed piece of metal or plastic, (*syn.*) spike: *Baseball and golf shoes have cleats to keep the player from slipping.*

cleav·age /ˈklivɪdʒ/ *n.* [C] a separation: *a cleavage in a rock* **2** [C;U] the space between a woman's breasts: *When women wear low cut dresses, they show cleavage.*

cleave /kliv/ *v.* **cleaved** or **cleft** /klɛft/ or **clove** **cloven** /ˈkloʊvən/, **cleaving, cleaves** to divide into two parts by or as if by cutting forcefully: *The boat cleaved the water as it sped across the lake.*

cleav·er /ˈklivər/ *n.* a heavy, hand-held cutting tool: *A butcher uses a meat cleaver to cut meat.*

clef /klɛf/ *n.* a symbol put on a set of lines of music (a staff) to show what pitch the lines and spaces represent

cleft /klɛft/ *adj.n.* & past tense and past part. of cleave: split, divided: *Children born with a <adj.> cleft palate can be operated on successfully.*

clem·en·cy /ˈklɛmənsi/ *n.* [U] **1** a show of forgiveness, esp. to a criminal: *The governor gave clemency to the murderer and stopped the order for his death.* **2** mildness, esp. of weather: *The clemency of the winter surprised us.* *-adj.* **clement.**

clench /klɛntʃ/ *v.* **clenches** to force together, grip tightly: *She clenched her fists and teeth in anger.*

cler·gy /ˈklɜrdʒi/ *n.pl.* the group of ministers, priests, rabbis, mullahs, etc., as a whole: *The government asks advice from members of the clergy.*

cler·gy·man /ˈklɜrdʒimən/ *n.* **-men** /-mən/ a minister, priest, rabbi, mullah, or other religious leader: *The clergyman blessed the church members.*

cler·gy·wo·man /ˈklɜrdʒi,wʊmən/ **-women** /-,wɪmən/ a woman who is a member of the clergy

cler·ic /ˈklɛrɪk/ *n.* a member of the clergy

cler·i·cal /ˈklɛrɪkəl/ *adj.* **1** of basic office work, such as answering the telephone, writing down orders, etc.: *He is a clerical worker with a clerical job.* **2** of the clergy: *a clerical collar*

clerk /klɜrk/ *n.* **1** a person who keeps records, accounts, etc., in an office **2** a salesperson in a store: *My friend is a (sales)clerk in the store's shirt department.*

—*v.* to work or serve as a clerk

clev·er /ˈklɛvər/ *adj.* **1** intelligent and quick at understanding: *She is a clever student.* **2** skillful, esp. in solving problems, (*syn.*) ingenious: *He solves computer problems that no one else*

can; *he has clever ideas.* *-adv.* **cleverly;** *-n.* **cleverness.**

cli·ché /kliˈʃeɪ/ *n.pej.* a saying or idea used too often to be meaningful: *Her report is full of clichés, and contains no useful ideas.* *-adj.* **clichéd.**

click /klɪk/ *n.* a light, snapping sound: *the click of a camera shutter*

—*v.* **1** to make a clicking sound: *The key clicked as it turned in the lock.* **2** to move s.t. that makes a click: *He clicked the light switch on.* **3** *phrasal v. insep.* **to click with s.o.:** to get along well with or be a success with s.o.: *The young couple clicked with each other the first time that they met.*||*The product (idea, solution, etc.) clicked with customers and became popular.*

cli·ent /ˈklaɪənt/ *n.* a customer of s.o. who provides a professional service, such as a lawyer, tailor, hairdresser, etc.: *He likes to take his clients to lunch. See:* customer, USAGE NOTE.

cli·en·tele /,klaɪənˈtɛl, ,kliən-/ *n.* a group of customers: *That expensive store has a rich clientele.*

cliff /klɪf/ *n.* a high rock formation with a steep drop: *She stood on the cliff and looked down at the ocean below.*

cliff·hang·er /ˈklɪf,hæŋər/ *n.* a situation or story where the result is not known until the last moment: *That basketball game was a real cliffhanger, won by one point in the last second of play.*

cli·mac·tic /klaɪˈmæktɪk/ *adj.* producing a climax: *The graduation ceremony was a climactic moment after four years of hard work.*

cli·mate /ˈklaɪmɪt/ *n.* [C;U] **1** the type of weather that a place or region has: *Places can have cold, warm, or hot climates.* **2** a general condition: *The business climate is very good (bad, uncertain, etc.) now.*

cli·mat·ic /klaɪˈmætɪk/ *adj.* of a climate: *The climatic conditions in California are warm and sunny, with a rainy season in the north.*

cli·max /ˈklaɪ,mæks/ *n.* **-maxes** **1** [C] the most exciting or intense point in a series of events: *The game came to a climax with our team winning in the last second of play.* **2** [C;U] the most intense moment of pleasure during sexual activity, (*syn.*) an orgasm

—*v.* **-maxes** to reach the most exciting moment: *The game climaxed with a winning score in its final seconds.*

climb /klaɪm/ *v.* **1** to move upward: *The airplane took off and climbed above* (or) *climbed up above the clouds.*||*Prices climbed higher on the stock exchange.* **2** to rise slowly and steadily in power, rank, etc.: *He climbed from selling newspapers on the street to owning several newspaper companies.* **3** to slant up: *The ground climbed steadily toward the mountains.* **4** *phrasal v. insep.* **to climb down:** to go down,

esp. using the hands and feet, (*syn.*) to descend: *The painter climbed down the ladder to the ground.* **5 to climb out on a limb:** to put oneself in a position where one can easily be criticized or harmed: *He climbed out on a limb when he told his boss that she could fire him if he did not make a sales increase.*
—*n.* an upward movement on land or into the air, (*syn.*) an ascent: *Our group made the climb up the mountain.*

climb·er /'klaɪmər/ *n.* **1** a person who climbs: *a mountain climber* **2** a plant or animal that climbs **3 social climber:** a person who tries to move into a higher social class, such as by marrying s.o. with money

clinch /klɪntʃ/ *v.n.* **clinches 1** (in boxing) to fasten the arms around each other: *Two boxers punched, then <v.> clinched.* **2** *fig.* to finish an agreement finally and definitely: *Her boss congratulated her on <v.> clinching the deal.*

cling /klɪŋ/ *v.* **clung** /klʌŋ/**, clinging, clings 1** to hold closely, tightly: *The baby clings to her mother.* **2** to refuse to release or let go: *The sick woman clung to the idea that she would be well again.*

clin·ic /'klɪnɪk/ *n.* **1** a medical building: *In that health clinic, doctors treat patients who go back home afterwards.* **2** a group of doctors in the same field **3** a meeting for educational purposes: *I'm going to a clinic on money management next week.*

clin·i·cal /'klɪnɪkəl/ *adj.* **1** related to a clinic **2** involving direct examination of s.o. or s.t.: *The doctor made a clinical evaluation of the sick man.* **3** done scientifically, usu. without emotion, analytical: *a clinical approach* -*adv.* **clinically;** -*n.* **clinician** /klɪ'nɪʃən/.

clink /klɪŋk/ *v.n.* to make a short, light, high sound: *The glasses <v.> clinked together as the waiter picked them up.*

clip /klɪp/ *n.* a device that holds things together, a fastener: *a paper clip, a hair clip* **2** *infrml.* speed, pace: *He ran past me at a good clip.* **3** a short part of a film: *Before the showing of the movie, we saw clips from other films.*
—*v.* **clipped, clipping, clips 1** to fasten with a clip: *I clipped my papers together with a paper clip.* **2** to cut with short strokes: *The hairdresser clipped her hair with scissors.* **3** *infrml.* to hit with a short, sharp blow: *That car clipped our bumper as it sped by.*

clip·board /'klɪp,bɔrd/ *n.* a flat board with a clip at the top to hold papers

clip·pers /'klɪpərz/ *n.pl.* a cutting tool in many shapes and sizes: *Barbers use electric clippers to cut people's hair.*

clip·ping /'klɪpɪŋ/ *n.* an article cut out of a newspaper, magazine, etc.: *My friend showed me a clipping about her school.*

clique /klik, klɪk/ *n.* a group of people who keep others out: *A clique runs the local school district and they all vote for each other.* -*adj.* **cliquish.**

clit·o·ris /'klɪtərɪs/ *n.* **-rises** a small place on a woman's outer sexual organ where she can experience sexual pleasure

cloak /kloʊk/ *n.* **1** [C] a loose-fitting outer garment that hangs from the shoulders: *Cloaks are open in the front.* **2** *sing.fig.* s.t. that hides or covers: *The thieves worked under a cloak of darkness.*
—*v.* to hide or keep secret, (*syn.*) to conceal: *How the woman disappeared is cloaked in mystery.*

cloak-and-dagger *adj.* mysterious and full of adventure, esp. spying: *He writes cloak-and-dagger stories about spies.*

cloak·room /'kloʊk,rum/ *n.* a room in a public place where coats and other articles are left for a short time: *I checked my hat in the cloakroom.*

clob·ber /'klɑbər/ *v.* **1** *slang* to strike with s.t. heavy: *A thief clobbered his victim with a club.* **2** *slang* to defeat decisively: *Our basketball team clobbered the other team 112 to 70.*

clock /klɑk/ *n.* **1** an instrument for showing the time (that is not a wrist or pocket watch): *an alarm clock, a wall clock* **2 around the clock:** all day and night without stopping: *Rescue workers worked around the clock to help victims of the earthquake.* **3 to punch the clock:** to record the time, usu. on a card, when one starts and stops work: *Workers at that factory punch the clock when they arrive and leave.* **4 to race the clock:** to work against a deadline: *Workers raced the clock to finish the job by five o'clock.* **5** *infrml.pej.* **to watch the clock:** to have little interest in one's work: *He watches the clock and leaves with work not done.*
—*v.* **1** to measure time: *Officials clocked the races at the Olympics.* **2 to clock in/out:** to record the time that one starts and stops work *See:* o'clock.

clock·wise /'klɑk,waɪz/ *adv.* in the direction that the hands of a clock move: *Starting at 12, looking at the clock, the hands move clockwise to the right. See:* counter-clockwise.

clock·work /'klɑk,wɜrk/ *n.* [U] **1 like clockwork:** smoothly, according to plan: *The whole operation went like clockwork.* **2** the insides of a clock, its mechanism: *The clockwork needs oil.*

clod /klɑd/ *n.* **1** a lump of earth: *The horse kicked a clod of earth into the air.* **2** *fig.* a clumsy, stupid person, lacking good manners: *He may be a great football player, but he behaves like a clod.*

C

clog /klɑg, klɔg/ *n.* **1** a blockage: *a clog in a water pipe* **2** a type of shoe, usu. with a thick wooden bottom
—*v.* **clogged, clogging, clogs** to block: *My nose is all clogged up from a cold.*

clois·ter /ˈklɔɪstər/ *n.* **1** a covered walkway along the wall of a building, one side of which is open to a garden or courtyard **2** a place, esp. a monastery or convent, for religious peace and prayer
—*v.* to put in a place away from the ordinary world: *While writing her book, she cloistered herself in a small cabin in the woods.*

clone /kloʊn/ *v.n.* **cloned, cloning, clones** **1** to make a duplicate copy of a living thing **2** *fig.* to make a copy of s.t., (*syn.*) to imitate: *Many cars look like <n.> clones of each other because their makers <v.> cloned their competitors' designs.* *See:* knockoff.

clop /klɑp/ *n.v.* **clopped, clopping, clops** a loud, dull click like the sound made by a horse's hoofs: *I can hear the <n.> clop of horses on the street below.*

close (1) /kloʊs/ *adj.* **closer, closest** **1** with little space between, nearby: *Her chair is close to the wall.* **2** near in time: *It's close to 5:00.* **3** very friendly, (*syn.*) intimate: *They are a close family with a few close friends.* **4** with air that is not fresh and is usu. too warm, (*syn.*) stuffy: *It is very close in this room; let's open a window.* **5** with strict control: *The doctor put her patient under close observation.* **6 a close call: a.** s.t. that is difficult to judge: *The two runners crossed the finish line together, so who won was a close call (or) too close to call.* **b.** a narrow escape from danger or death: *The speeding taxi nearly hit him; that was a close call.* (or) *a close shave. -adv.* **closely;** *-n.* **closeness.**

close (2) /kloʊz/ *v.* **closed, closing, closes** **1** to shut or cause to shut: *The store closes at 6:00 on Saturdays.||I closed the window (door, curtains, etc.).* **2** to come or bring to an end, (*syns.*) to terminate, conclude: *The movie closed with a love scene.||The police closed the case on the robbery after the thief went to prison.* **3** *phrasal v. sep.* **to close s.t. down:** to cease operations, to stop from doing business: *The government closed the factory down because of safety violations.||They closed it down.* **4** *phrasal v. insep.* **to close in s.t.:** to surround and enclose: *The farmer closed in his property with a fence.* **5** *phrasal v. insep.* **to close in (on s.o.):** to come close to trapping or capturing: *The police are closing in on the criminal.* **6** *phrasal v. sep.* **to close s.t. out: a.** to sell off goods at low prices: *The store closed out its winter clothes with a big close-out sale.||It closed them out.* **b.** to finish an accounting period: *The accountants closed out the books for the month (quarter, year).* **7**

phrasal v. sep. **to close s.t. up: a.** to lock a business temporarily: *The store owner closed up (his store) for the night.||He closed it up.* **b.** to stop doing business permanently: *Business was so bad that the owners closed up and sold the store.* **8** *phrasal v. insep.* **to close with s.o.:** to reach a business agreement: *We expect to close with them soon on the sale of the house.*
—*n.* the end: *The meeting came to a close.*

closed-circuit television *n.* [U] TV broadcasts sent out over wires, instead of through the air: *That big university holds some of its classes over closed-circuit television.*

closed shop *n.* a business where only union members can work: *Only a small part of the US workforce is in closed shops.*

close-fit·ting /ˈkloʊsˈfɪtɪŋ/ *adj.* fitting tightly around the body: *Professional bicycle riders wear close-fitting clothes.*

close-knit /ˈkloʊsˈnɪt/ *adj.* **1** (of cloth) with the threads very close together **2** (of people) bound together, trusting and helping each other: *That family is close-knit, and they help each other when trouble strikes.*

close-mouthed /ˈkloʊsˈmaʊðd, -ˈmaʊθt/ *adj.* saying little, (*syn.*) secretive: *He is close-mouthed about his past.*

close-out /ˈkloʊˌzaʊt/ *n.adj.* a special sale of reduced prices to sell the last pieces of some product: *The store had a <n.> close-out of summer dresses as the fall fashions arrived.*

close quarters /kloʊs/ *n.pl.* **1** a very close, face-to-face position: *Soldiers fought at close quarters with knives.* **2** crowded conditions: *Sailors live in close quarters on submarines.*

close shave /kloʊs/ *n.fig.* a close call *See:* close (1), **6.**

clos·et /ˈklɑzɪt/ *n.* **1** a small room for storing clothes, towels, sheets, etc.: *We keep our coats and umbrellas in the closet by the front door.* **2 to come out of the closet:** to make known s.t. that was secret, esp. one's homosexuality: *When he was 20, Julio came out of the closet by telling his family that he was gay. See:* gay.

close-up /ˈkloʊˌsʌp/ *n.* **1** a picture taken close to the subject: *The photographer took a close-up of the woman's face.* **2** a detailed look at s.t.

clo·sure /ˈkloʊʒər/ *n.* [C;U] *frml.* a finish of s.t., (*syn.*) a conclusion: *We achieved closure on an agreement after months of talks.*

clot /klɑt/ *v.n.* **clotted, clotting, clots** to form a semifirm mass of s.t., esp. blood: *The blood <v.> clotted in the cut.*

cloth /klɔθ/ *n.* [C;U] **cloths** /klɔðz, klɔθs/ material woven from synthetic (nylon, rayon) or natural (cotton, wool) threads: *That suit is made of woolen cloth.*

clothe /kloʊð/ *v.* **clothed** or **clad** /klæd/, **clothing, clothes** to provide with clothing: *Parents feed and clothe their children.*

clothes /klouz/ *n.pl.* coverings for a person's body, (*syns.*) garments, apparel: *She likes to wear expensive clothes.*

clothes·line /'klouz,laɪn/ *n.* a line or rope on which washed clothes are hung out to dry: *The wash is hung on the clothesline in the backyard.*

clothes·pin /'klouz,pɪn/ *n.* a pin used to fasten clothes to a line to dry them

cloth·ing /'klouðɪŋ/ *n.* [U] clothes in general, (*syn.*) attire: *Food and clothing are basic necessities.*

cloud /klaud/ *n.* **1** a mass of water droplets in the sky: *The sky is full of gray clouds today.* **2** a mass of smoke, fog, or dust: *A dust cloud followed the galloping horses.* **3** many rapidly moving things close together: *A cloud of bees came out of the hive.* **4** *fig.* s.t. causing sadness, gloom: *Each year, on the date that her son died, a cloud of sadness hangs over her.* **5 to be on cloud nine:** to be very happy: *They are in love and are on cloud nine.* **6 to have one's head in the clouds:** to be a dreamer, (*syn.*) to be idealistic: *He has his head in the clouds because he is always dreaming of becoming famous.* **7 under a cloud:** under suspicion, out of favor: *After he was caught in a lie, he worked under a cloud (of suspicion) because no one trusted him.*

—*v.* **1** to become covered with clouds: *The sky is clouding up now.* **2** to make s.t. difficult to see or understand: *Mud has clouded the water.‖The new plan is clouded with difficult problems.*

cloud·burst /'klaud,bɜrst/ *n.* a sudden, hard rainfall

cloud·y /'klaudi/ *adj.* **-ier, -iest 1** covered with clouds: *The weather is cloudy today.* **2** unclear: *The mud in the water made it cloudy.‖It is not clear who is right; the issue is still cloudy.*

clout /klaut/ *n.* **1** [C] a heavy blow: *He gave him a clout on the head.* **2** [U] *fig.* power and influence: *As a rich woman in a small town, she has a lot of clout with the mayor.*

—*v.* to strike with a heavy blow

clove /klouv/ *n.* [C;U] **1** the brown, dried flower bud of a tropical tree, used as a spice **2** a section of a bulb of a plant, esp. garlic: *a clove of garlic*

clo·ver /'klouvər/ *n.* [C;U] **1** a small green plant, usu. with three heart-shaped leaves **2** *infrml.* **in clover:** living a comfortable, easy life: *His uncle died and left him a lot of money, and now he is in clover.*

clo·ver·leaf /'klouvər,lif/ *n.* **-leafs** or **-leaves** /-,livz/ a connected set of roads that allow vehicles to circle on and off of a main highway, (*syn.*) an interchange: *Cars go on the cloverleaf to go in a different direction.*

cloverleaf

clown /klaun/ *n.* a performer in colorful clothes who makes people laugh by doing funny things: *She liked the circus clown with the big red shoes and the red nose.*

—*v.* **1** to act like a clown: *Don't mind him; he's just clowning.* **2** *phrasal v.* **to clown around: a.** to amuse others: *He likes to clown around by putting on a funny hat and dancing.* **b.** to act stupidly or foolishly: *Stop clowning around and get to work! -adj.* **clownish;** *-adv.* **clownishly;** *-n.* [U] **clownishness.**

cloy·ing /'klɔɪɪŋ/ *adj.* causing sickness or distaste from too much sweetness or pleasure: *She saw five movies in five nights, and she found the experience was cloying.‖a cloying dessert -v.* **cloy.**

club /klʌb/ *n.* **1** a group of people who meet because of a common interest: *He belongs to a book club that reads and discusses one book each month.* **2** a social gathering place where people pay for sport, food, etc.: *a tennis club* **3** a long, round, thick stick used to hit people: *Police officers carry billy clubs.* **4** (in golf) a stick with a specially shaped head for hitting the ball **5** in the USA, a playing card with black cloverleafs on it

—*v.* **clubbed, clubbing, clubs** to strike with a club: *Police clubbed the rioters.*

club·house /'klʌb,haus/ *n.* **-houses** /-,hauzɪz/ a building where players of a sport gather: *a golf clubhouse*

club sandwich *n.* **-wiches** a thick sandwich made with three pieces of bread

club soda *n.* [C;U] soda water, clear water with bubbles

cluck /klʌk/ *v.n.* **1** to make a sound like a chicken: *Chickens <v.> clucked in the hen house.* **2** (of people) to make a sound of disapproval: *She <v.> clucked her tongue as she watched the couple arguing loudly.*

clue /klu/ *n.* **1** a thing or fact that helps provide an answer to a question, (*syn.*) evidence: *Police look for clues at the scene of a crime, like the criminal's gun or fingerprints.* **2** in-

frml. **not to have a clue:** not to understand at all: *Why did she do it? I don't have a clue.*

—*v.* **clued, cluing, clues** *phrasal v. insep.* **to clue s.o. in on s.t.:** to tell s.o. what is happening, usu. s.t. that is important and not well known: *My friend clued me in on a job opportunity.* -*adj.* **clueless.**

clump /klʌmp/ *n.* **1** a group or mass, (*syn.*) a cluster: *a clump of bushes (trees, flowers)* **2** the dull sound of s.t. heavy falling onto a hard surface: *We could hear the clump of boots on the street.*

—*v.* **1** to make a dull, heavy sound, esp. when walking, (*syn.*) to thud: *The tired man clumped up the stairs.* **2** to group together in a clump: *The child's toys are clumped together in a box.*

clum·sy /ˈklʌmzi/ *adj.* **-sier, -siest** not able to do things in careful way, (*syn.*) awkward: *He is so clumsy that he is always bumping into people.* -*adv.* **clumsily;** -*n.* [U] **clumsiness.**

clung /klʌŋ/ *v. past tense & past part. of* cling

clunk /klʌŋk / *v.n.* to make a dull, heavy sound, (*syn.*) to thump: *He dropped a hammer, and it <v.> clunked on the floor.*

clus·ter /ˈklʌstər/ *n.* a tight grouping of s.t.: *a cluster of grapes‖a star cluster*

—*v.* to bring or come into a tight grouping: *The children clustered around the teacher.*

clutch /klʌtʃ/ *v.* **clutches** **1** to grasp tightly with the hand(s): *She clutched her pocketbook as she walked.* **2** to reach for s.t. quickly and desperately, (*syn.*) to snatch: *The man in the water clutched at a rope to save himself.*

—*n.* **clutches** **1** the grip of a hand **2** a handful of s.t.: *a clutch of flowers* **3** a device for shifting gears: *the clutch in a car* **4 s.o.'s clutches:** the control or possession of s.o., esp. s.o. evil: *We can't let this information fall into the clutches of the enemy.* **5 in the clutch:** in an important situation where what you do means winning or losing: *Our basketball star came through in the clutch by scoring the winning basket in the last seconds of the game.*

clut·ter /ˈklʌtər/ *n.* [C;U] a mess: *There is a clutter of papers on his desk.*

—*v.* **1** to mess up: *People have cluttered the street with papers and cans.* **2** to confuse: *Her mind is cluttered with bad ideas.*

c/o /ˈkərˌʌv/ *abbr.for* (in) care of (used in an address so that s.o. will pass it on to the right person): *You can write to Mr. Jones in care of his company. Address the letter: Mr. John Jones, c/o XYZ Company, 123 Main St., Anywhere, USA.*

co- /koʊ/ *prefix* together with, joint: *coauthor, cochairman*

coach /koʊtʃ/ *n.* **coaches** **1** a person who leads, teaches, and trains people in sports or in acting, singing, etc.: *a football coach‖a voice coach* **2** *Brit.* a railroad passenger car or bus

—*v.* **coaches** to lead, train, and teach others in sports, singing, etc.: *He coaches a baseball team.*

co·ag·u·late /koʊˈægyəˌleɪt/ *v.* **-lated, -lating, -lates** to change from liquid to firm or hard form: *Blood coagulates and closes a cut.* -*n.* [U] **coagulation** /koʊˌægyəˈleɪʃən/.

coal /koʊl/ *n.* [C;U] **1** a mineral made of carbon, black or dark brown, dug from the ground and burned for heat, that also provides gas for burning: *That stove burns coal, not wood.* **2 to carry coals to Newcastle:** to do s.t. unnecessary or unwanted by providing s.t. that there is already a lot of (A great deal of coal can already be found in Newcastle.): *I took her a bunch of flowers when I went to visit, but then I saw her beautiful gardens and realized that I'd carried coals to Newcastle.* **3 to rake** or **haul s.o. over the coals:** to criticize s.o. severely: *The worker made a mistake, and his boss raked him over the coals.*

co·a·lesce /ˌkoʊəˈlɛs/ *v.frml.* **-lesced, -lescing, -lesces** to come together and form a whole: *Our plans for a long trip finally coalesced when we mapped out exactly where to go.* -*n.* [U] **coalescence.**

co·a·li·tion /ˌkoʊəˈlɪʃən/ *n.* two or more groups who get together for a common purpose: *Three political parties formed a coalition against higher taxes.*

coarse /kɔrs/ *adj.* **coarser, coarsest** **1** of poor quality: *The poor woman could only afford coarse clothing.* **2** rough, not smooth: *That sweater is made of coarse wool.* **3** made of large particles: *coarse sand* **4** lacking good manners, (*syns.*) crude, rude: *He is a coarse man who uses dirty language.* -*v.* **coarsen** /ˈkɔrsən/.

coast /koʊst/ *n.* **1** land near the ocean: *the coast of Panama* **2** *infrml.* **the coast is clear:** there is no danger of being seen or stopped: *When the guard fell asleep, the coast was clear and we escaped.*

—*v.* **1** to move without power: *The sled coasted down the hill.* **2** to work without pressure: *He worked day and night for a year, then coasted for several months.* -*adj.* **coastal.**

coast·er /ˈkoʊstər/ *n.* a small, round, flat piece of metal, paper, etc., put under a glass containing a drink: *I put my beer glass on a coaster to prevent the wet glass from marking the tabletop.*

Coast Guard *n.* a type of navy responsible for guarding a country's coast(s) from invasion, helping people in trouble on water, and enforcing laws at sea: *The Coast Guard helicopter saved a man whose boat had sunk.*

coast·line /ˈkoʊstˌlaɪn/ *n.* the land along an ocean: *The Maine coastline is beautiful on a sunny day.*

coat /koʊt/ *n.* **1** an outer garment: *She is wearing a fur coat.* **2** a covering spread over a surface: *A worker put a coat of paint on the walls.* —*v.* to cover with s.t.: *The furniture was coated with dust.*

coax /koʊks/ *v.* **coaxes** to try patiently to ask s.o. to do s.t., (*syn.*) to persuade: *The mother coaxed her child to take some bad-tasting medicine.*

cob /kɑb/ *n.* **1** an ear of corn without any corn left on it, a corncob: *After the meal, I threw the cobs in the garbage.* **2** a male swan

co·balt /'koʊ,bɔlt/ *n.* [U] a hard but easily breakable metal combined with others for industrial purposes, or used in blue dyes —*adj.* bright blue: *Her shoes are cobalt blue.*

cob·ble /'kɑbəl/ *v.* **-bled, -bling, -bles 1** to make or fix shoes and boots **2** *phrasal v. sep.* **to cobble s.t. together:** to put together in a crude way: *He cobbled together a living by working three part-time jobs.||He cobbled it together. -n.* **cobbler.**

cob·ble·stone /'kɑbəl,stoʊn/ *n.* a stone shaped like a small loaf of bread and used to cover streets: *Most of the cobblestone streets are covered over with tar now.*

COBOL /'koʊ,bɔl/ *n.abbr.for* Common Business Oriented Language, a language used to write programs for computers: *He programs in COBOL at work.*

co·bra /'koʊbrə/ *n.* a highly poisonous snake of Asia and Africa: *A bite from a cobra can kill in minutes.*

cob·web /'kɑb,wɛb/ *n.* a net of thin, sticky threads made by spiders to catch food: *She cleaned away the dust and cobwebs in the old house.*

co·ca /'koʊkə/ *n.* [U] the shrub and leaves from which cocaine is made: *Coca is grown in many places high in the mountains.*

Co·ca-Co·la /,koʊkə'koʊlə/ *n.* [C;U] ™ a soft drink, dark and bubbly, usu. with caffeine for energy: *Coca-Cola is probably the world's best-known product.*

co·caine /koʊ'keɪn, 'koʊ,keɪn/ *n.* [U] the drug made from coca leaves: *Cocaine is used by doctors as a painkiller but mainly by people as an illegal drug.*

cock /kɑk/ *n.* **1** a male chicken, (*syn.*) a rooster **2** *infrml.* **a cock-and-bull story:** a false story or excuse: *He has never repaid the money that he owes me because he always has some cock-and-bull story about having to pay medical expenses.* —*v.* **1** to pull back a gun's hammer before shooting: *She cocked the pistol.* **2** *infrml.* **to go off half-cocked:** to do things without thinking, (*syn.*) to be impulsive: *He goes off half-cocked when he is in a panic and often does foolish things.*

cock·er spaniel /'kɑkər/ *n.* a type of small dog with long ears and long, soft fur

cock·eyed /'kɑk,aɪd/ *adj.fig.* **1** hopelessly wrong, foolish: *He has a lot of cockeyed ideas.* **2** crooked: *The photos on that page are cockeyed, and some are even upside down.*

cock·pit /'kɑk,pɪt/ *n.* **1** a sunken area for cockfighting **2** the front area of an airplane where the pilot sits and flies it: *The pilot climbed into the cockpit.*

cock·roach /'kɑk,roʊtʃ/ *n.* **-roaches** a type of brown, flat-bodied insect found esp. in dark wet places and houses that are not properly cleaned: *We kill cockroaches with traps and an insecticide.*

cock·tail /'kɑk,teɪl/ *n.* **1** an alcoholic drink made by mixing several liquors: *She likes to have a cocktail before dinner.* **2** a type of food presentation: *A shrimp cocktail has several shrimp in a glass with sauce.*

cock·y /'kɑki/ *adj.* **-ier, -iest** feeling very sure of one's importance and abilities, (*syn.*) arrogant: *The young boxer won his first fight; now he's cocky. -n.* [U] **cockiness.**

co·coa /'koʊkoʊ/ *n.* [U] **1** chocolate powder made from crushed cacao: *The cake recipe called for 2/3 cup of cocoa.* **2** a hot chocolate-flavored drink, (*syn.*) hot chocolate: *She had some cocoa for breakfast.*

co·co·nut /'koʊkə,nʌt/ *n.* [C;U] the large nut of the palm tree: *The juice inside coconuts is called coconut milk.*

co·coon /kə'kun/ *n.* a silk-like protective covering of some insects when young: *The butterfly came out of its cocoon.*

cod /kɑd/ or **cod·fish** /'kɑd,fɪʃ/ *n.* [C;U] **cod** or **cods** a fish found in the North Atlantic Ocean: *For hundreds of years, the cod was an important food for North Americans.*

C.O.D. or **COD** /,sioʊ'di/ *n. abbr.for* cash on delivery, meaning that one pays the person who delivers the goods for the goods, and for the cost of sending them: *I paid for the shoes C.O.D.*

cod·dle /'kɑdl/ *v.* **-dled, -dling, -dles** to treat in a loving and (too) protective way, to baby: *He accused his wife of coddling their son.*

code /koʊd/ *n.* **1** [C;U] a way of hiding the true meaning of communications from all except those people who have the keys to understand it: *Spies use secret codes.* **2** [C] a written set of rules of behavior: *That school has a dress code requiring boys to wear shirts and ties, no jeans.* **3** [C] a formal group of principles or laws: *a code of ethics for doctors||the legal code in a country* —*v.* **coded, coding, codes** to put s.t. into code, (*syn.*) to encode: *A spy coded a message.*

co·deine /'koʊ,din/ *n.* [U] a drug and painkiller made from opium

co·ed /ˌkoʊˈɛd, ˈkoʊˌɛd/ *adj. short for* coeducational: of a school or college open to both male and female students: *That high school is coed.* —*n. old usage* a female student in a college or university open to both male and female students

USAGE NOTE: Most schools and universities in the United States are *coed*, but there are some single sex schools and universities. These are usually private schools and they are referred to as boy's schools and men's colleges or girl's schools and women's colleges.

co·ed·u·ca·tion·al /ˌkoʊɛdʒəˈkeɪʃənəl/ *adj.* referring to the education of both male and female students in the same school or college: *My son and daughter both go to coeducational colleges.* -*n.* [U] **coeducation.**

co·e·qual /koʊˈikwəl/ *n.adj.* a person who is equal to another (in importance, rank, authority, etc.): *Heads of governments regard themselves as <n.pl.> coequals in discussing agreements between their countries.*

co·erce /koʊˈɜrs/ *v.* **-erced, -ercing, -erces** to make s.o. do s.t. against their will by force or threats, (*syn.*) to compel: *The son coerced his elderly mother into selling her house.* -*n.* [U] **coercion** /koʊˈɜrʃən, -ʒən/; -*adj.* **coercive** /koʊˈɜrsɪv/.

co·ex·ist /ˌkoʊɪgˈzɪst/ *v.* **1** to exist at the same time or place **2** to live peacefully with a person (or people) with whom one has differences in opinion, religious beliefs, lifestyle, political policy, etc.: *We hope that someday all people can coexist.* -*n.* **coexistence.**

cof·fee /ˈkɔfi, ˈkɑ-/ *n.* **1** [C;U] a dark brown, energy-giving drink made by brewing the ground-up beans (seeds) of a tropical tree, usu. served hot: *She drinks coffee for breakfast each morning.* **2** [U] the beans themselves, often ground up into a powder

cof·fee·house /ˈkɔfiˌhaʊs, ˈkɑ-/ *n.* **-houses** /-ˌhaʊzɪz/ a type of restaurant for serving and drinking coffee *See:* café, USAGE NOTE.

coffee shop *n.* a type of restaurant for serving coffee and usu. inexpensive food. *See:* café.

coffee table *n.* a long, low table often set in front of a sofa: *After dinner, we drank coffee and put the cups on the coffee table.*

cof·fer /ˈkɔfər, ˈkɑ-/ *n.frml.* **1** a type of box that can be locked to keep coins, jewels, etc.: *The treasure was locked away in coffers.* **2** *fig.* the money available to a government or business: *The government's coffers are empty, and it must raise taxes.*

cof·fin /ˈkɔfɪn, ˈkɑ-/ *n.* a box-like container in which a dead person is put for burial: *Workmen lowered the dead man's coffin into a grave.*

cog /kɑg, kɔg/ *n.* **1** one of many teeth on a wheel that fit into teeth on another wheel and

turn it: *I have an old-fashioned wristwatch where cogs inside turn its hands.* **2** *infrml.* **a cog in a wheel:** s.o. with a low-level job in a large organization

co·gent /ˈkoʊdʒənt/ *adj.* well presented and creating belief in s.t., (*syn.*) convincing: *My lawyer's statement to the judge was so cogent that the judge dismissed the complaint against me. n.* [U] **cogency;** *adv.* **cogently.**

cog·i·tate /ˈkɑdʒəˌteɪt/ *v.frml.* **-tated, -tating, -tates** to think, (*syn.*) to reflect: *The professor cogitated about a difficult problem.* -*n.* [U] **cogitation** /ˌkɑdʒəˈteɪʃən/.

co·gnac /ˈkoʊnˌyæk, ˈkɑn-/ *n.* brandy, esp. from France: *She had a glass of cognac after dinner.*

cog·ni·tion /kɑgˈnɪʃən/ *n.* [U] the process of thinking or perceiving -*adj.* **cognitive** /ˈkɑgnətɪv/.

cog·ni·zant /ˈkɑgnəzənt/ *adj.frml.* having knowledge, aware: *He is cognizant of the fact that he must pay back the money he borrowed.* -*n.* [U] **cognizance.**

co·hab·it /koʊˈhæbɪt/ *v.* to live together as partners or husband and wife, although unmarried: *That couple has cohabited for many years.* -*n.* [U] **cohabitation** /koʊˌhæbəˈteɪʃən/.

co·her·ent /koʊˈhɪrənt, -ˈhɛr-/ *adj.* **1** clear, logical: *His plan is a coherent presentation of each step that we need to take.* **2** awake and clear-headed: *After the accident, the driver was hurt but coherent.* -*v.* **cohere;** -*n.* [U] **coherence.**

coif·fure /kwɑˈfyʊr/ *n.frml.* a hairstyle: *She always wears the same coiffure.*

coil /kɔɪl/ *n.* s.t. wrapped in a circle or spiral: *a coil of wire\a spring shaped in a coil* —*v.* to wind or wrap into a circle: *A workman coiled the garden hose. See:* spiral.

coin /kɔɪn/ *n.* a piece of metal money, usu. small, round, and flat: *She has some old silver coins.* —*v.* **1** to make coins **2 to coin a phrase:** to invent a special way of describing s.t. **3 on the other** or **the flip side of the coin:** considering the opposite side of the same situation: *That artist is difficult to work with, but on other side of the coin, his art is beautiful.* -*n.* **coinage** /ˈkɔɪnɪdʒ/.

co·in·cide /ˌkoʊɪnˈsaɪd/ *v.* **-cided, -ciding, -cides 1** to happen at the same time: *My trip to New York coincided with Thanksgiving, so I had a big turkey dinner there.* **2** to agree: *Two different people saw the accident, and their stories coincide about what happened.*

co·in·ci·dence /koʊˈɪnsədəns, -ˌdɛns/ *n.* [C;U] the happening of two or more events at the same time by chance: *By coincidence, she met an old friend on the street whom she had* *not seen in years.* -*adj.* **coincidental** /koʊˌɪn-sə'dɛntl/; -*adv.* **coincidentally.**

coke /koʊk/ *n.* [U] **1** coal with the gases removed: *Coke is used as fuel, and in making steel.* **2** *slang* cocaine: *He's been snorting coke.*

Coke /koʊk/ *n.* [C;U] *TM short for* the soft drink, Coca-Cola: *People drink Coke everywhere in the world.*

co·la or **kola** /'koʊlə/ *n.* [C;U] **1** a tropical tree and its seeds that produce caffeine used to make soft drinks, like Coca-Cola, Pepsi, etc. **2** a drink made with cola: *He drank cola with lunch.*

COLA /'koʊlə/ *n.abbr. for* cost of living adjustment: an increase in wages and pensions usually given each year

col·an·der /'kɑləndər, 'kʌl-/ *n.* a type of bowl with many small holes, used to let water fall through when rinsing fruit, vegetables, pasta, etc.: *I washed some lettuce and put it in the colander to drain.*

cold /koʊld/ *adj.* **1** having a low temperature: *Many people do not like cold weather.* **2** feeling uncomfortable because of a lack of warmth, feeling chilled **3** lacking warmth, not friendly: *He has a cold personality in his dealings with people.* **4** *infrml.* **out cold:** unconscious: *The boxer lay on the floor, out cold.* **5** **to get cold feet:** to agree to do s.t., then not do it, because of fear or nervousness: *He agreed to marry her, then got cold feet and left her.* **6** **to give s.o. the cold shoulder:** to avoid s.o., (*syn.*) to snub s.o.: *She left her boyfriend and now gives him the cold shoulder every time they happen to be near each other.* **7 to have s.t. (down) cold:** to know s.t. perfectly: *The actor had his part down cold.* **8 to leave s.o. cold:** to fail to interest or impress s.o.
—*n.* **1** [C] an illness, usu. with a blocked runny nose, fever, and general achiness, also called the common cold: *He [U] has a bad cold.* **2** [C] **to catch cold** or **a cold:** to get this illness: *She caught cold yesterday.* **3** [U] **the cold:** a condition of low temperature: *I don't like the cold.* **4 to be out** or **to get left out in the cold:** to be left with nothing: *When the owner closed his company, the employees got left out in the cold with no jobs.* -*adv.* **coldly;** -*n.* [U] **coldness.**

cold-blood·ed /'koʊld'blʌdɪd, 'koʊl-/ *adj.* **1** having a body temperature that varies with the outside temperature: *Snakes and insects are cold-blooded animals.* **2** *pej.* having no feeling or emotion: *a cold-blooded murder‖a killing in cold blood*

cold cream *n.* [C;U] a creamy beauty product for cleaning and softening the skin: *She used some cold cream to take makeup off her face.*

cold cuts *n.pl.* cold slices of meat, such as balogna, salami, or beef: *She put some cold cuts on the table for the family to make sandwiches.*

cold front *n.* a wave of cold air moving into a region: *New York experienced a cold front moving down from Canada.*

cold-heart·ed /'koʊld'hɑrtɪd/ *adj.* having no feeling for the needs of others, (*syn.*) insensitive: *He is a cold-hearted businessman who shows no kindness to others.*

cold sore *n.* a sore on or near the lips produced by a virus

cold turkey *n.adv. fig.slang* **to quit** or **go cold turkey:** to stop a bad habit (cigarettes, drugs, alcohol) suddenly and completely: *I smoked cigarettes for 20 years; then one day I quit cold turkey.*

cold war *n.* a competition between great nations, such as in building powerful weapons, that does not go into real fighting: *The cold war between the USA and the Soviet Union began after World War II.*

cole·slaw /'koʊlˌslɔ/ *n.* [U] raw cut cabbage in a mayonnaise dressing

col·ic /'kɑlɪk/ *n.* [U] an illness of severe pain in the stomach area, esp. suffered by babies -*adj.* **colicky.**

col·i·se·um /ˌkɑlə'siəm/ *n.* a large round or oval building with seats that rise gradually away from the open area in the center, used for holding sports events or other exhibitions: *We saw a basketball game at the coliseum last night.*

col·lab·o·rate /kə'læbəˌreɪt/ *v.* **-rated, -rating, -rates 1** to work with s.o.: *Two writers collaborated in writing a textbook.* **2** to help an enemy, (*syn.*) to commit treason: *The army officer collaborated with the enemy, giving them information about the army's plans.* -*n.* [U] **collaboration** /kəˌlæbə'reɪʃən/; **collaborator;** -*adj.* **collaborative** /kə'læbəˌreɪtɪv, -bərətɪv/.

col·lage /kə'lɑʒ/ *n.* [C;U] pieces of paper, cloth, and photos glued on a flat surface to make a picture: *The artist made a collage that showed pictures of her family.*

col·lapse /kə'læps/ *n.* [C;U] **1** a falling into ruin, (*syn.*) a caving in: *Heavy rainfall caused the collapse of the roof.* **2** a loss of strength: *She worked so hard that she suffered a collapse.*
—*v.* **-lapsed, -lapsing, -lapses 1** to fall into ruin: *The stock market collapsed, and many people lost a lot of money.* **2** to lose strength and fall down: *The runner collapsed at the finish line.* **3** to fold up s.t. so it needs less space: *to collapse an umbrella* -*adj.* **collapsible.**

col·lar /'kɑlər/ *n.* **1** the material around the neck of a shirt, coat, etc. **2** a round leather or

C

cloth strap or chain: *He puts a collar on his dog before walking it.* **3** *slang* an arrest by police
—*v.* **1** to place a collar on: *to collar a dog* **2** *slang* to suddenly stop or arrest s.o.: *She collared the boy, who was running wildly around the house.*

col·lar·bone /'kɑlər,boʊn/ *n.* a bone on each side of the lower neck running to the top of the shoulder, (*syn.*) the clavicle: *He fell and broke his right collarbone.*

col·late /kə'leɪt, 'koʊ,leɪt, 'kɑ-/ *v.* **-lated, -lating, -lates** to place papers in correct order: *The photocopy machine collated the report as it printed it.* **-n. collator.**

col·lat·er·al /kə'lætərəl/ *n.* [U] money or property signed over to a bank to insure that a loan will be repaid, (*syn.*) loan security: *I took out a loan at the bank and gave them my savings passbook as collateral.*
—*adj.* related to s.t. but not the main point: *a collateral issue*

col·lat·er·al·ize /kə'lætərə,laɪz/ *v.* **-ized, -izing, -izes** to provide collateral for: *She collateralized a car loan by signing over ownership of it to the bank.*

col·league /'kɑ,lig/ *n.* a person with whom one works, esp. in a profession: *My colleagues in the office (university, club, etc.) agree to the proposal.*

col·lect /kə'lɛkt/ *v.* **1** to come or bring together as a group, (*syn.*) to assemble: *The teacher collected the homework.*||*A crowd collected in front of the burning building.* **2** to get and keep things as a hobby: *He collects stamps.* **3** to ask for and receive money: *Businesses have workers who collect payments from their customers.* **4** to get back control of: *to collect one's thoughts (emotions, oneself)* **5 to call collect:** to telephone s.o. who pays the cost: *The student called her mother collect from college.*

col·lect·i·ble /kə'lɛktəbəl/ *n.adj.* **1** s.t. that is worth being collected: *Paintings and stamps are among many <n.pl.> collectibles.* **2** money owed that can be collected: *That debt is not <adj.> collectible, as the company is out of business.*

col·lec·tion /kə'lɛkʃən/ *n.* **1** [C] a group of similar objects brought together by s.o. as a hobby or by a museum: *I have a coin collection.*||*That museum has a collection of Chinese paintings.* **2** [C;U] a request for payment of money owed a business **3** [C;U] the act of collecting money, or the money given, for some good cause: *a church collection See:* collection agency.

collection agency *n.* **-cies** a business that collects money owed other businesses who are unable to collect it themselves: *Some of our customers refuse to pay, so we gave their names to a collection agency.*

col·lec·tive /kə'lɛktɪv/ *n.* an organization where people and businesses group together to help each other: *The farm collective stores their grain in a big warehouse that they bought together.*
—*adj.* of a group: *the people's collective concern about high taxes, poverty, etc.*

collective bargaining *n.* [U] negotiations between representatives of workers and management over wages, working conditions, and extra benefits: *Collective bargaining started between officials of the workers' union and management.*

col·lec·tor /kə'lɛktər/ *n.* a person, business, or museum that collects objects or money: *The Internal Revenue Service in the USA is a collector of taxes.*

col·lege /'kɑlɪdʒ/ *n.* [C;U] **1** in the USA, an institution of higher or professional education: *a four-year college, a community college* **2 to go to college:** to enter and attend a college or university: *I plan to go to college next year.* -*adj.* **collegiate** /kə'lidʒɪt/. *See:* university.

college degree *n.* in the USA, a diploma from a university or four-year college: *She has a college degree in chemistry.*

col·lide /kə'laɪd/ *v.* **-lided, -liding, -lides** to hit against s.t. with force, to crash: *Two cars collided on the street.* ||*They collided with each other.*

col·lie /'kɑli/ *n.* a medium-sized dog with a thin, pointed nose and long, light-brown, black, and white fur: *Some farmers use collies to control sheep.*

col·li·sion /kə'lɪʒən/ *n.* [C;U] **1** a crashing together: *Two cars were involved in a collision.* **2 to be on a collision course: a.** to be headed toward crashing together: *two cars on a collision course* **b.** to be headed for an argument or other conflict: *The two politicians are on a collision course over raising taxes.*

col·lo·cate /'kɑlə,keɪt/ *v.frml.* **-cated, -cating, -cates** (of two words) to be used together regularly, to sound correct together: *The word "heavy" collocates with "rain," but "weighty" does not; we say "a heavy rain," not "a weighty rain." -n.* [U] **collocation** /,kɑlə'keɪʃən/.

col·lo·qui·al /kə'loʊkwiəl/ *adj.* typical of informal spoken or written language: *Talk among friends uses colloquial language. -n.* **colloquialism;** *-adv.* **colloquially.**

col·lo·qui·um /kə'loʊkwiəm/ *n.* **-quiums** or **-quia** /-kwiə/ a meeting, such as among professors, to exchange ideas: *The chemistry department held a colloquium on new developments.*

col·lu·sion /kə'luʒən/ *n.* [U] a secret agreement to cheat or steal, (*syn.*) a conspiracy to defraud: *Two employees were in collusion to* *steal money from the company.* -v. **collude** /kə'lud/.

co·logne /kə'loʊn/ *n.* [C;U] a type of perfume: *He puts cologne on his face after he shaves.*

co·lon /'koʊlən/ *n.* **1** the lower intestine: *He had cancer of the colon.* **2** the punctuation mark (:): *Colons are used in this dictionary to introduce the sample sentence.*

colo·nel /'kɜrnəl/ *n.* a military rank below general and above lieutenant colonel: *In the USA, there are colonels in the army, air force, and marines, but not in the navy.*

co·lo·ni·al /kə'loʊniəl/ *adj.* **1** related to colonies (nations governed by other nations): *Colonial America was controlled mainly by the Spanish, French, and British.* **2 Colonial:** related to the 13 original American colonies **3** in the style, esp. of buildings, common during the time that people lived in colonies in America: *They live in a four-bedroom colonial house.*
—*n.* a person living in a colony -*n.* [U] **colonialism.**

col·o·ni·za·tion /ˌkɑlənə'zeɪʃən/ *n.* [U] the process of gaining control of another country or land, esp. by sending groups of people, who are still governed by their home countries, to live there: *The colonization of the Americas by the Spanish took many years.*

col·o·nize /'kɑlə,naɪz/ *v.* -**nized, -nizing, -nizes** **1** to send people to live in another area of land or country, while still governing them from the home country: *The Spanish, British, and French colonized the Americas.* **2** to go live in a colony

col·o·ny /'kɑləni/ *n.* -**nies** a group of people who have moved to another area of land, but are still governed by their home country **2** a region, country, or land of colonization, esp. one controlled by a foreign power: *the (former) French colonies of North Africa* **3** a group of people with similar backgrounds or interests living in one area: *That seaside resort is an artists' colony.* -*n.* (a person) **colonist.**

col·or /'kʌlər/ *n.* **1** [C;U] a shade, hue, or tint: *Red, yellow, and blue are colors.* **2** [C;U] paint, ink, pastel, chalk, etc., used to create color: *She paints with watercolors.* **3** [U] skin color as related to race: *Some people are discriminated against because of their color.* **4** [U] the look of one's skin, esp. the face, that shows one's health: *That little boy is almost well again; he's getting his color back.* **5** [U] liveliness, brightness: *Your decorations certainly add color to the room.* **6 to show one's true colors:** to show what one is really like: *He seems pleasant but shows his true colors by becoming angry when he does not get what he wants.* **7 with flying colors:** very well: *She passed the exam with flying colors, a perfect score.*

—*v.* **1** to apply color to: *The child colored the picture yellow and red.* **2** to give a special effect to, influence: *A bad car accident has colored his attitude, and he is very cautious while driving now.* **3** to present in an unfair or untrue way: *She colors her group's reports so that it sounds as if she does all the work.* **4** to have one's face, esp. the cheeks, turn red, (*syn.*) to blush: *She colored with embarrassment as she realized her mistake. See:* colored.

col·or·blind /'kʌlər,blaɪnd/ *adj.* **1** not able to see the difference between some or all colors: *He could not fly for the air force because he was colorblind.* **2** not concerned by s.o.'s skin color and race, (*syn.*) unprejudiced: *Most people like to think of themselves as colorblind.* -*n.* [U] **colorblindness.**

col·ored /'kʌlərd/ *adj.* **1** having color: *The invitations can be printed on white or colored paper.* **2** containing incorrect information, (*syns.*) slanted, biased: *This report is colored, because the authors put in only the information that they agreed with.*

col·or·ful /'kʌlərfəl/ *adj.* **1** having bright colors: *She wore a colorful dress with red and orange flowers on it.* **2** full of interesting behavior or activity: *She is a colorful person who is a pilot, explorer, and writer.*

col·or·ing /'kʌlərɪŋ/ *n.* **1** [U] the color of the skin, esp. of the face, indicating good or poor health **2** [C;U] a substance added to s.t. such as food to give it a color

co·los·sal /kə'lɑsəl/ *adj.* huge, (*syn.*) immense: *Some of the tall buildings in that city are colossal.*

colt /koʊlt/ *n.* a young male horse: *The mare gave birth to a colt. See:* filly.

col·umn /'kɑləm/ *n.* **1** in some buildings, a tall, thick beam used as support or decoration, (*syn.*) a pillar: *Those stone columns hold up the roof.* **2** a row, esp. a vertical one: *He added up a column of numbers.‖A column of ants crawled through the yard.* **3** an article in a newspaper or magazine written regularly by a writer (called a *columnist*): *She writes a weekly column about politics for* The New York Times.

co·ma /'koʊmə/ *n.* a medical condition like a long, deep, sleep, (*syn.*) unconsciousness caused by disease or injury: *He injured his head in a fall and fell into a coma for a month.* -*adj.* **comatose** /'koʊmə,toʊs, 'kɑ-/.

comb /koʊm/ *n.* a flat piece of plastic (wood, metal) with teeth used to neaten the hair
—*v.* **1** to pass a comb through the hair or s.t. else, such as wool from a sheep: *I washed my face and combed my hair.* **2** to search thoroughly: *The police combed our neighborhood for a thief who was hiding.*

com·bat /'kɑm,bæt/ *n*. [C;U] a violent struggle: *Soldiers shoot at each other in combat.*
—*v*. /kəm'bæt, 'kɑm,bæt/ **-bated** or **-batted, -bating** or **-batting, -bats** to fight against: *Police combat crime.* *-n.* **combatant** /kəm'bætnt/.

com·bat·ive /kəm'bætɪv/ *adj*. eager to fight or argue, (*syn*.) pugnacious: *The young boys were combative; they argued about everything with everyone.* *-n.* [U] **combativeness.**

com·bi·na·tion /,kɑmbə'neɪʃən/ *n*. two or more things, ideas, or events put together: *Chicken soup is a combination of pieces of chicken, vegetables, and water.*

com·bine (1) /kəm'baɪn/ *v*. **-bined, -bining, -bines** to join together: *Rain and freezing temperatures combine to make snow.*‖*The child combined dirt and water to make mud cakes.*

com·bine (2) /'kɑm,baɪn/ *n*. **1** a big machine on wheels used to harvest crops: *A farmer ran his combine over the wheat field.* **2** a group of people or businesses

com·bus·ti·ble /kəm'bʌstəbəl/ *adj*. capable of burning: *Wood and coal are combustible substances.*

com·bus·tion /kəm'bʌstʃən/ *n*. [U] the act or process of burning

come /kʌm/ *v*. **came** /keɪm/, **come, coming, comes** **1** to move toward the speaker or a certain place: *Come here and look at this!*‖*He came to my party.* **2** to arrive: *The train comes at 9:09.*‖*Labor and management finally came to an agreement.* **3** to be located in a certain position: *Five comes before six.*‖*That law comes under article 3 on page 10.* **4** to reach: *The coat comes down to my knees.*‖*That typist does not come up to our standards of accuracy.* **5** to be available: *Ice cream comes in many flavors.*‖*Do those shoes come in my size?* **6** to result in: *All my work came to nothing when it burned up in the office fire.* **7** to become: *My shoelaces have come untied.*‖*A button on my jacket came loose and fell off.* **8** to have importance, to rank: *For him, his job always comes first.*‖*His family comes before anything else.* **9** to begin: *I hope you will come to like your new school.* **10 Come on: a.** an expression of encouragement: *Come on, you can do it!* **b.** an expression of skepticism: *Oh come on, you don't really believe that!* **c.** an expression of impatience: *Come on, we're going to miss the train!* **11 Come off it:** an expression of annoyance: *Oh, come off it! Stop talking that nonsense!* **12** *infrml*. **How come:** why: *How come you got a salary increase and I didn't?* **13 in the days (weeks, months, etc.) to come:** in the future: *In the years to come, I hope to stay healthy.* **14** *phrasal v*. **to come about: a.** to happen: *How did the accident come about?* **b.** to turn around: *The ship came about and headed home.* **15** *phrasal v. insep.*

to come across (s.t.): a. *infrml*.to make an impression: *He comes across badly in meetings, but he is really just shy.* **b.** *s.t.*: to do or give what is wanted: *He finally came across with the money.* **c.** *s.t.*: to find, discover: *In cleaning out a desk, I came across (or) came upon some $100 bills.* **16** *phrasal v*. **to come along:** to progress: *How is your mother coming along after her operation?* **17 to come and go:** to come into and go out of fashion quickly: *Wide neckties, then thin ones; they come and go.* **18** *phrasal v*. **to come apart:** to fall into pieces: *That car is so old that it is coming apart.* **19** *phrasal v*. **to come around: a.** to visit: *She came around to my place at eight o'clock.* **b.** to come back to consciousness, (*syn*.) to come to: *He came around a few hours after the surgery.* **c.** to agree after a time of disagreement: *She will come around to our way of thinking.* **20** *phrasal v. insep.* **to come at s.o.** or *s.t.*: to approach in a threatening way, to attack: *The dog came at me with its teeth bared.* **21** *phrasal v*. **to come back: a.** to return to one's memory: *I can't remember his name at the moment, but it'll come back to me.* **b.** to return to a good level of success: *The singer was unpopular for many years; then he came back as a big success. See:* comeback. **22** *phrasal v. insep.* **to come between s.o.** or *s.t.*: to divide or cause trouble between people, or between a person and a thing: *They were a happy couple until money problems came between them.* **23** *phrasal v. insep.* **to come by (s.t.): a.** to visit: *Come by my office when you have time to talk.* **b.** *s.t.*: to get, (*syn*.) to acquire: *How did you come by that new car (information, idea, etc.)?* **24 to come down in life** or **in the world:** to make less money and live less well than before **25** *phrasal v. insep.* **to come down on s.o.** or *s.t.*: to punish: *The attorney general has promised to come down hard on fraud.* **26** *phrasal v. insep.* **to come down to s.t.:** to result in, be reduced to: *Her concerns come down to worries about losing money.* **27** *phrasal v. insep.* **to come down with s.t.:** to get an illness, to contract a disease: *I came down with a cold yesterday.* **28** *phrasal v*. **to come forward:** to present or offer oneself: *He came forward and told the police that he saw the crime happen.* **29** *phrasal v. insep.* **to come from s.t.: a.** to be a native or resident of: *He comes from London (Texas, Japan, etc.).* **b.** to be produced by: *Honey comes from bees.* **30** *phrasal v. insep.* **to come in (on s.t.):** to begin to participate in, to join: *Another company came in on the project, and a third company may come in and join us as well.* **31** *phrasal v. insep.* **to come into s.t.:** to inherit: *When her rich uncle died, she came into a lot of money.* **32** *phrasal v. insep.* **to come of s.t.:** to be the result of: *What do you think will come of your investigation?* **33** *phrasal v*. **to come**

off: to happen, esp. to succeed: *The big party we gave came off well; everyone liked it. See:* come, **11. 34** *phrasal v. insep.* **to come on to s.o.:** to make sexual advances to s.o.: *While we were having dinner at the restaurant, he kept coming on to me.* **35** *phrasal v.* **to come out:** **a.** to state one's beliefs: *The politician came out in favor of (for, against, etc.) lower taxes.* **b.** to become known: *When the truth about his past came out, everyone was shocked.* **c.** to appear: *The sun will come out tomorrow at 6:15 A.M.* **d.** to be presented to society at a dance: *The young lady came out at the December ball.* **e.** to announce one's homosexuality: *He came out to his parents after college.* **36** *phrasal v. insep.* **to come over (s.o.):** **a.** *My friend came over (to my house) to play cards.* **b.** s.o.: to become clear to, be understood by: *It suddenly came over me that I had forgotten my keys.* **37 to come s.o.'s way:** to happen for s.o. (after a long wait): *After ten years of being alone, love finally came my way.* **38** *phrasal v.* **to come through:** to do what is needed or expected, esp. after a wait: *My citizenship papers finally came through.* **39** *phrasal v. insep.* **to come to (s.o.):** **a.** to come back to consciousness, *(syn.)* to come around: *She fainted, then slowly came to.* **b.** s.o.: to return to s.o.'s memory: *His name? Wait a minute and it will come to me.* **40** *phrasal v.* **to come up: a.** to come to s.o.'s attention, be spoken of: *The topic of money came up in our conversation.* **b.** to approach: *A man came up (to me) on the street and asked for money.* **41** *phrasal v. insep.* **to come up against s.t.:** to meet or face difficulty or trouble: *She came up against a stone wall when she asked her boss for a raise; he just said, "No."* **42** *phrasal v. insep.* **to come up with s.t.:** to think of, invent, discover: *She came up with a good solution to the problem.* **43** *phrasal v. insep.* **to come upon s.t.:** to find, *(syn.)* to come across: *A man on a bicycle came upon a dead body by the road.*

come·back /'kʌm,bæk/ *n.* **1** a return to the top level of success: *That singer retired at 35, then made a comeback at 50 with a new hit song.* **2** a quick, funny reply, *(syn.)* a retort: *People tease her a lot, but she always has a comeback.*

co·me·di·an /kə'midiən/ *n.* **1** a man or woman /kə,midi'ɛn/ who says and often does funny things for a living: *The comedian made the audience laugh.* **2** a person who does or tries to do funny things: *Juan is always joking around; he's quite the comedian.*

come·down /'kʌm,daʊn/ *n.* a lowering of one's standard of living: *It was a big comedown for him when he had to sell his house and move into a tiny apartment.*

com·e·dy /'kɑmədi/ *n.* [C;U] **-dies 1** a funny movie, play, piece of writing, etc.: *That movie I saw was a really good comedy.* **2** s.t. so wrong as to become very amusing: *He did everything wrong; it was a comedy of errors.*

come-hith·er /,kʌm'hɪðər/ *adj.* inviting s.o. to come over, esp. by a sexy look: *She gave the handsome guy a come-hither look.*

come·ly /'kʌmli/ *adj.frml.* **-lier, -liest** good-looking, *(syns.)* pretty, handsome: *She is a comely child.*

come-on /'kʌm,ɑn, -,ɔn/ *n. slang* **1** s.t. offered to get s.o. to do s.t.: *The offer of a free clock by that store was just a come-on to get you to buy an expensive TV.* **2** a sexual invitation: *She flirts and laughs with him; she is giving him a big come-on.*

com·et /'kɑmɪt/ *n.* a fast-moving heavenly body with a solid head surrounded by a glowing cloud of gases that circles the sun: *As a comet gets closer to the sun, a long, glowing tail of gas forms behind it.*

come·up·pance /,kʌ'mʌpəns/ *n.* [C;U] well-deserved punishment: *That man has been cheating people for years; he got his comeuppance when s.o. finally caught him and had him arrested.*

com·fort /'kʌmfərt/ *n.* **1** a peaceful feeling of freedom from pain or worry: *People like to live in comfort.* **2** kind and gentle care: *Nurses give comfort to sick people.* **3** s.o. or s.t. that gives comfort: *She is a comfort to her parents in their old age.‖It is a comfort to know that our son will be well taken care of while we're out of town.* **4** s.t. that makes life easier or more comfortable: *Today, we enjoy many comforts that people did not have in the past (cars, air conditioning, microwave ovens, etc.).*

—*v.* to soothe s.o. in pain or worry: *Mothers comfort their sick children.*

com·fort·a·ble /'kʌmftəbəl, -tər-, 'kʌm-fərtəbəl/ *adj.* **1** relaxed and restful: *I sat on the big, soft sofa and made myself comfortable.* **2** s.t. that provides comfort: *The big, soft sofa is very comfortable.* **3** enough to be satisfied and happy: *She earns a comfortable living.‖The front runner has a comfortable lead.* **4** feeling s.t. is all right, *(syn.)* content: *She is comfortable with the idea of moving to a new city.* **-adv. comfortably.**

com·fy /'kʌmfi/ *adj.infrml.* **-fier, -fiest** short for comfortable: *She took off her shoes and made herself comfy.‖This is a comfy chair.*

com·ic /'kɑmɪk/ *n.* a comedian: *We watched a comic on TV.*

—*adj.* funny, *(syn.)* amusing: *a comic opera*

com·i·cal /'kɑmɪkəl/ *adj.* **1** funny, *(syn.)* amusing: *Everyone laughed at her comical remarks.* **2** stupid, but amusing, *(syn.)* ludicrous: *It was comical watching the thief with* *the stolen wallet trying to tell the police that he'd found it.*

comic book *n.* a book of comic strips (color drawings that tell a story): *Children love to read about the adventures of their favorite superheroes in comic books.*

com·ics /'kɑmɪks/ *n.pl.* picture stories of fun and adventure in newspapers: *He reads the comics every morning.*

comic strip *n.* a picture story, amusing or adventurous, by one artist: *The comic strips are in the back of my newspaper.*

com·ing /'kʌmɪŋ/ *n.* **1** *sing.*a formal arrival, *(syn.)* advent: *We look forward to the coming of peace after five years of war.* **2 to have it coming: a.** to deserve a reward: *She works so hard that she deserves a vacation; she has it coming to her.* **b.** to deserve punishment: *He robbed a store and is going to jail; he has it coming to him.*
—*adj.* **1** arriving next: *I am leaving on a trip this coming Sunday.* **2 up and coming:** seeming likely to be successful: *She is an up and coming young lawyer.*

com·ma /'kɑmə/ *n.* the punctuation sign (,): *The comma is used to separate parts of a sentence.*

com·mand /kə'mænd/ *n.* **1** [C] an instruction on what to do, *(syns.)* an order, a mandate: *An army officer gave a command to the soldiers to shoot at the enemy.* **2** [U] the act of using one's authority over a person, group, etc.: *The officer is in command, and the soldiers must obey on (his) command.* **3** [C] a group of officers in charge of the military: *the army's high command* **4** [C;U] one's skill or ability to do s.t. well: *She has a good command of English.* **5** [C] a signal containing instructions given to a machine or device: *She typed a command into the computer (alarm system, VCR, etc.).*
—*v.* **1** (in the military) to have control over a person or group: *The general commands the Third Army.* **2** *frml.* to demand with authority that s.o. do s.t.: *He commanded the dog to leave the house.* **3** to be skilled at or able to use s.t.: *She commands a broad knowledge of history.* **4** to be worth s.t.: *That car is so well built that it commands a very high price.‖She has accomplished many things, and commands a great deal of respect.*

com·man·dant /'kɑmən,dɑnt, -,dænt/ *n.* the chief military officer of a fort or military post

com·man·deer /,kɑmən'dɪr/ *v.* to take s.t. suddenly without permission or payment, esp. by police or military authority: *The police officer commandeered a taxi cab to chase the bank robbers.*

com·mand·er /kə'mændər/ *n.* a person in charge, esp. of military personnel or police: *In the USA, the President is the commander in chief of all military forces.*

com·mand·ing /kə'mændɪŋ/ *adj.* **1** in command, *(syn.)* in charge: *The officer responsible for directing you is your commanding officer.* **2** looking important and powerful, *(syn.)* impressive: *The President is a man with a commanding presence (appearance).* **3** in a position of control, *(syn.)* dominating: *Our team has a commanding lead of 50 to 10.*

com·mand·ment /kə'mændmənt, -'mæn-/ *n.* **1** an order, *(syn.)* a mandate **2** any of the Ten Commandments in the Bible: *God gave Moses the Ten Commandments.*

com·man·do /kə'mændoʊ/ *n.* **-dos** or **-does** a highly trained soldier used to make quick, deadly attacks against an enemy: *Commandos swam ashore and captured an enemy general as he slept.*

com·mem·o·rate /kə'mɛmə,reɪt/ *v.* **-rated, -rating, -rates** to celebrate the memory of s.o. or some event: *In the USA, they commemorate Independence Day on July 4th. -n.* [U] **commemoration** /kə,mɛmə'reɪʃən/; *-adj.* **commemorative** /kə'mɛmərətɪv, -'mɛmrə-/.

com·mence /kə'mɛns/ *v.frml.* **-menced, -mencing, -mences** to begin: *Our company commenced business on January 2 last year.*

com·mence·ment /kə'mɛnsmənt/ *n.frml.* **1** [C;U] a beginning: *a commencement of political negotiations* **2** [C] graduation ceremonies at a school or college: *Parents attended the commencement of their sons and daughters from high school.*

com·mend /kə'mɛnd/ *v.* **1** to praise: *The teacher commended the students for doing well on the exam.* **2** to say that s.o. or s.t. is worthy and good, *(syn.)* to recommend: *She commended the hotel in her letter to me.* **3** to place in s.o. else's care: *The minister commended the dead man's spirit to heaven. -adj.* **commendable;** *-n.* **commendation** /,kɑmən'deɪʃən/.

com·ment /'kɑ,mɛnt/ *n.* a remark, opinion (often criticism): *The teacher wrote a comment on the student's paper about how good it was.*
—*v.* to express an opinion about s.t., *(syn.)* to remark: *The boss commented on how poorly the work had been done.*

com·men·tar·y /'kɑmən,tɛri/ *n.* [C;U] **-ies** a written or spoken opinion about s.t., explaining and/or criticizing it: *A TV sports announcer gave the commentary on the football game, explaining what the players were doing, and how well they were doing it. -v.* **commentate** /'kɑmən,teɪt/.

com·men·ta·tor /'kɑmən,teɪtər/ *n.* a person, esp. on TV or radio, who explains and/or criticizes events

com·merce /'kɑmərs/ *n.* [U] business in general in the buying and selling of goods and services within a country, and with other countries: *Commerce between the USA and Asia is good.*

com·mer·cial /kəˈmɜrʃəl/ *adj.* related to business: *He is a Chinese businessman with commercial interests in both China and New York.||There are only businesses, no homes, in this area; it is a commercial district.*
—*n.* a radio or television advertisement: *Television programs are often interrupted by commercials.*

USAGE NOTE: Compare *commercial* and *advertisement. Commercials* are a kind of advertising on TV or radio. *Advertisements* in newspapers, magazines, billboards, and on the *World Wide Web* are not called *commercials.*

---

commercial bank *n.* in the USA, a bank offering checking and savings accounts, mortgages for both individuals and businesses: *There is a commercial bank, like Citibank, on nearly every corner in New York City.*

com·mer·cial·ize /kəˈmɜrʃə,laɪz/ *v.* **-ized, -izing, -izes 1** to change s.t. so that making money is its main goal: *This used to be a quiet beach that few people knew about, but it's been commercialized, and is now covered with hotels.* **2** to cheapen the quality of s.t. for larger profits: *A large company commercialized that wonderful mustard to make more money from its good name.*

com·mis·er·ate /kəˈmɪzə,reɪt/ *v.frml.* **-ated, -ating, -ates** to share feelings of sadness with s.o., *(syn.)* to sympathize with s.o.: *When my friend's mother died, I commiserated with her.*
-*n.* [C;U] **commiseration** /kə,mɪzəˈreɪʃən/.

com·mis·sion /kəˈmɪʃən/ *n.* **1** [C] an amount of money paid, esp. to a sales representative, for making sales of products and services: *Our company pays the salespeople a 10-percent commission.* **2** [U] a doing, a committing, *(syn.)* perpetration: *The commission of the crime was quick.* **3** [C] **a.** authorization (permission) to do a certain duty or task: *I have a commission to paint a picture of the mayor.* **b.** the document giving s.o. this permission: *I have the commission to organize a new committee for the president.* **c.** the task so given: *What is your commission?* **4** [C] a group of people authorized, usu. by a government, to do s.t.: *The town council created a commission to protect its historical landmarks.* **5** [C] a formal document of acceptance as an officer into the military: *She received her commission as a lieutenant in the navy today.*
—*v.* **1** to set up a group of people as a commission: *They commissioned a group of engineers to study the problem.* **2** to accept a person as an officer in the military **3** to ask formally for s.t. to be done: *to commission a painting or study See:* commitment USAGE NOTE.

commissioned officer *n.* an officer in the military with the rank of lieutenant, captain, colonel, or general

com·mis·sion·er /kəˈmɪʃənər/ *n.* **1** an official in charge of a government department or an athletic association: *The police commissioner of York||the baseball commissioner* **2** a member of a commission

com·mit /kəˈmɪt/ *v.* **-mitted, -mitting, -mits 1** to do s.t.: *He committed a crime.* **2** to give money for a purpose: *to commit funds to a project* **3** **to commit oneself:** to promise to do s.t., *(syn.)* to dedicate oneself: *The priest committed himself to a life of poverty.* **4** to obligate or bind by a promise: *My aunt feels committed to go to my wedding, but she does not want to.*

com·mit·ment /kəˈmɪtmənt/ *n.* **1** [C] a promise: *The mayor made a commitment to speak at the celebration.* **2** [C] a decision: *The company made a commitment to spend a million dollars on advertising.* **3** [C;U] deep loyalty to a person or cause, *(syns.)* dedication, devotion: *That husband and wife have a strong commitment to each other.* **4** **to honor** or **meet one's commitment(s):** to do what one promises to do, *(syn.)* to fulfill one's obligations: *She honors her commitments.*

USAGE NOTE: When a crime has been committed, one speaks of the commission of a crime; *commitment* is not used in this sense.

---

com·mit·tee /kəˈmɪti/ *n.* a group of people organized for a purpose: *The company has a committee to handle complaints from employees.*

com·mod·i·ty /kəˈmɑdəti/ *n.* **-ties** a general word for items or substances for sale, like grains and metals: *Some important commodities are wheat and corn, or silver and gold.*

com·mo·dore /ˈkɑmə,dɔr/ *n.* a former navy rank above captain and below rear admiral: *The commodore was in charge of a group of ships.*

com·mon /ˈkɑmən/ *adj.* **1** happening or appearing often, *(syn.)* frequent: *Car accidents are a common occurrence.||"Smith" is a very common name.* **2** ordinary, having no special position or quality: *The common people go to work and raise families.* **3** shared by two or more people or things: *They became friends because of their common interest in bird watching.||The two countries share a common border.* **4** related to the people in general, involving the whole community: *During the war, people made sacrifices for the common good.* **5** **common ground:** what people agree on, esp. when they disagree about other things: *They disagreed on many issues, but found some common ground in their concern for* *poor children.* **6** *pej.* rude and unpolished in looks, manners, or speech, (*syn.*) vulgar: *She is very common; she needs to be taught some manners.*

—*n.* **to have s.t. in common:** to share the same interests, experiences, or qualities: *I hardly ever talk to my brother; we just don't have anything in common. -adv.* **commonly.**

common knowledge *n.* what most people know: *It is common knowledge that the national debt is huge.*

common law *n.* [U] unwritten law based on customs and previous court judgments, rather than laws passed by Parliament or Congress: *British common law was developed over hundreds of years and brought to North America in the 17th century.*

Common Market *n.* a group of European countries that cooperate with each other in trade: *The Common Market was a step toward the European Union.*

com·mon·place /ˈkɑmən,pleɪs/ *adj.* frequent or usual: *Car accidents are commonplace in the city.*

common property *n.* [U] property belonging to both husband and wife: *For their divorce, the couple agreed to divide common property on a 50-50 basis.*

common sense *n.* [U] the understanding of s.t. from thinking intelligently and from everyday experience, (*syn.*) good judgment: *He knows about the harmful effects of smoking cigarettes, so it is common sense to stop.*

common stock *n.* [U] shares of a company that have a claim on that company's assets after all other debts are paid: *The New York Stock Exchange trades the common stock of thousands of companies.*

com·mon·wealth /ˈkɑmən,wɛlθ/ *n.* **1** a state or a nation governed by the people for the common good (commonwealth), (*syn.*) republic: *Virginia and Massachusetts are commonwealths, as is the nation of Australia.* **2 the Commonwealth:** the free association of former British colonies and dominions: *Canada, India, and Kenya are all members of the Commonwealth.*

com·mo·tion /kəˈmoʊʃən/ *n.* [C;U] a disturbing confusion: *Two men made a commotion by yelling at each other in the theater.*

com·mu·nal /kəˈmyunəl, ˈkɑmyə-/ *adj.* for a community, (*syn.*) public: *Parks are communal property for all the people to enjoy.*

com·mune /kəˈmyun/ *v.* **-muned, -muning, -munes** to feel as one with s.t., to communicate: *to commune with God*‖*She goes to the country to commune with nature. See:* communion.

—*n.* /ˈkɑ,myun/ **1** a group of people and property organized for their common purpose: *a religious commune* **2** (in France, Italy, Spain)

the smallest political area with a mayor and council

com·mu·ni·ca·ble /kəˈmyunɪkəbəl/ *adj.* capable of being communicated or given to others: *The common cold and the plague are communicable diseases.*

com·mu·ni·cate /kəˈmyunɪ,keɪt/ *v.* **-cated, -cating, -cates 1** to give information to others: *People communicate with each other by spoken or written language or by gestures.* **2** to understand one another: *My boss and I communicate well with each other.* **3** to contact others: *People can communicate by telephone easily.*

com·mu·ni·ca·tion /kə,myunɪˈkeɪʃən/ *n.* **1** [U] an act of passing on information, feelings, etc.: *the communication of the news on TV* **2** [C] the message itself: *That communication is clear.* **3** [U] understanding: *There is no communication in this company; no one knows what is going on.*

com·mu·ni·ca·tive /kəˈmyunɪkətɪv, -,keɪtɪv/ *adj.* **1** willing and able to communicate: *She is communicative about how she feels.* **2** about the ability to communicate: *one's communicative skills, like speaking and writing*

com·mun·ion /kəˈmyunyən/ *n.* **1** [U] a feeling of oneness: *I feel a sense of communion with my cousin; we both love nature.* **2** [C] a religious grouping, (*syn.*) a denomination **3 Holy Communion:** the Christian religious act (church rite) of taking wine and bread as a sign of one's faith in Christ and God, (*syn.*) the Eucharist: *He takes Holy Communion every Sunday.* **-n. communicant** /kəˈmyunɪkənt/**.**

com·mu·ni·qué /kəˈmyunɪ,keɪ, -,myunɪˈkeɪ/ *n.* an official communication, (*syn.*) bulletin: *The government issued a communiqué giving the military officers their instructions.*

com·mu·nism also **Com·mu·nism** /ˈkɑmyə,nɪzəm/ *n.* [U] a political system in which all businesses and other property are owned by the government for the use and good of the people: *Communism took hold in Europe and Asia after World War II. -n. adj.* **Communist.**

com·mu·ni·ty /kəˈmyunəti/ *n.* **-ties 1** the people as a group in a town, city, or other area: *The community is concerned about crime.* **2** people forming a group in a racial, religious, occupational, etc., way: *The Dominican community in New York City is very large.* **3 to have community spirit:** to think about and work for the good of a community: *The children in that neighborhood pick up the garbage in the park every weekend; they have a lot of community spirit.*

community college *n.* in the USA, a two-year college, (*syn.*) junior college: *She is studying at a community college.*

com·mute /kə'myut/ *v.* **-muted, -muting, -mutes 1** to travel to and from one's work or school regularly: *He commutes between his house in the country and his office in the city every day.* **2** to make punishment less severe: *The official commuted the criminal's sentence from death to life in prison.*
—*n.* a regular trip, usu. between home and workplace: *He has a long commute to work from home.* -*n.* **commutation** /ˌkɑmyə'teɪʃən/.

com·mut·er /kə'myutər/ *n.* a person who travels regularly, esp. between home and the workplace: *At five o'clock, commuters leave their offices and rush to buses and trains.*

com·pact /kəm'pækt, 'kɑm,pækt/ *adj.* small compared with others, taking up little space: *That compact suitcase is easy to carry.* **2** close together, (*syn.*) dense: *The equipment in that case is packed in a compact way.*
—*n.* /'kɑm,pækt/ a small case used to hold women's face powder and a mirror
—*v.* /kəm'pækt/ to pack or pound tightly: *to compact garbage*
—*adv.* compactly: *It fits compactly behind the door for storage.* -*n.* [U] **compactness;** (machine) **compactor** /kəm'pæktər, 'kɑm,pæk-/.

com·pact disc /'kɑm,pækt/ or **CD** *n.* a disc used to record music, other sounds, images, and other information that is read by a laser: *We use compact discs to play music on our stereo.*

com·pan·ion /kəm'pænyən/ *n.* **1** a person who goes with another person: *a traveling companion‖a working companion‖John was her companion at the party.* **2** a thing that goes with another to form a pair: *a companion volume (book)* -*adj.* **companionable.**

com·pan·ion·ship /kəm'pænyən,ʃɪp/ *n.* [U] a condition of being together with s.o., (*syn.*) friendship: *She has a pet dog for companionship.*

com·pa·ny /'kʌmpəni, 'kʌmpni/ *n.* **-nies 1** [U] visitors, guests, often to a home: *We had company over for dinner.* **2** [C] a business: *She owns a company that makes fancy clothes.* **3** [U] companionship: *He likes her company.* **4** [C] a military unit: *a company of 50 soldiers* **5 to keep company:** to go with, associate with: *He keeps bad company with rough guys.* **6 to keep s.o. company:** to go with s.o. for companionship: *He kept her company while she went to the doctor.* **7 to part company:** to no longer spend one's time with s.o.: *She and her boyfriend had an argument and parted company.*

com·pa·ra·ble /'kɑmpərəbəl/ *adj.* **1** similar to: *The two cars are comparable in appearance.* **2** equal to in value: *They are also comparable to each other in price.*

com·par·a·tive /kəm'pærətɪv/ *adj.* **1** as compared with s.t. else, whether that thing is men-

tioned or not, (*syn.*) relative: *The comparative worth of a car is much greater than that of an old bicycle.* **2** being the form of an adjective or adverb that compares one thing with another: *"Taller" (not "tall" or "tallest") is the comparative form of "tall."* **3** comparing things in order to study them: *I'm taking a course in comparative literature.* -*adv.* **comparatively.**

com·pare /kəm'pɛr/ *v.* **-pared, -paring, -pares 1** to look for similarities and differences between two or more things, ideas, people, etc.: *The company's sales this year are excellent compared to* (or) *compared with last year's.* **2 to compare apples and oranges:** to attempt to compare things that are not at all alike: *Comparing s.o. who uses heroin to s.o. who smokes cigarettes is like comparing apples and oranges.* **3** *phrasal v. insep.* **to compare with s.o.** or **s.t.:** to be worth a comparison: *His cooking is good, but it can't compare with mine.*

com·par·i·son /kəm'pærəsən/ *n.* [C;U] an analysis of similarities and differences between things, ideas, people, etc.: *The student made a comparison between what people do at Christmastime in her country and what people do in the USA.*

com·part·ment /kəm'pɑrtmənt/ *n.* an enclosed space within s.t. larger, often with a cover or door: *Some trains have sleeping compartments.*

com·part·men·tal·ize /kəm,pɑrt'mɛntl,aɪz, ,kɑmpɑrt-/ *v.* **-ized, -izing, -izes** to put s.t. or s.o. into a category: *Students are compartmentalized into separate classes for beginning, intermediate, and advanced speakers of English.*

com·pass /'kʌmpəs/ *n.* **-passes 1** a device to determine direction (north, south, east, west, etc.): *Sailors use a compass to know in which direction their ship is headed.* **2 to box the compass:** to cover all possible points: *When that professor discusses a topic in class, she boxes the compass by covering everything.*

com·pas·sion /kəm'pæʃən/ *n.* [U] sympathy for s.o., esp. in doing s.t. kind for him or her: *She suffered cold, starvation, and the death of her family during the war, so she has great compassion for other people who suffer, too.* -*adj.* **compassionate** /kəm'pæʃənɪt/.

com·pat·i·ble /kəm'pætəbəl/ *adj.* capable of working or living well together, (*syn.*) harmonious: *That husband and wife are very compatible; they'll never get divorced.‖Those computer programs are compatible with each other; they can run at the same time.* -*n.* **compatibility** /kəm,pætə'bɪləti/.

com·pel /kəm'pɛl/ *v.* **-pelled, -pelling, -pels** to force s.o. to do s.t.: *His illness compelled him to stay in bed.*

com·pen·sate /'kampən,seɪt/ v. **-sated, -sating, -sates** **1** to pay s.o.: *That company compensates its employees well.||The insurance company compensated the man for his injuries.* **2** to overcome a weakness with a strength: *He is not intelligent, but he compensates for that with his warmth and charm.* -adj. **compensatory** /kəm'pɛnsə,tɔri/.

com·pen·sa·tion /,kampən'seɪʃən/ n. **1** sing. [U] payment in money: *Her compensation from the company is $50,000 per year.* **2** [U] payment in satisfaction: *That teacher is not paid much, but he gets compensation from his love of teaching.*

com·pete /kəm'pit/ v. **-peted, -peting, -petes** to participate in a contest, (syn.) to vie: *Our basketball team competed against another team and won.*

com·pe·tent /'kampətənt/ adj. having the ability to do s.t. well, having good or excellent skills: *She is competent in accounting.||He is a competent manager.* -n. **competence;** -adv. **competently.**

com·pe·ti·tion /,kampə'tɪʃən/ n. [C;U] **1** an organized event in which people try to do a specific activity better than everyone else: *She is an excellent runner, and she enters every competition that she can.* **2** [U] **the competition:** the people, as a group, that one is trying to do better than, esp. in business: *The competition in the computer field is made up of hundreds of companies.*

com·pet·i·tive /kəm'pɛtətɪv/ adj. **1** s.o. who likes to compete: *He is very competitive in football; he likes to win.* **2** . s.t. that is as good or better than s.t. else, esp. worthy of purchase: *Our company's soap products are competitive with other companies'.* -n. [U] **competitiveness.**

com·pet·i·tor /kəm'pɛtətər/ n. **1** a person or team that participates in sports: *The Olympic Games attract competitors from all over the world.* **2** a product or company that competes with others for the same customers: *He's losing business to his competitors.*

com·pile /kəm'paɪl/ v. **-piled, -piling, -piles** to put s.t. together item by item: *She compiled a list of things to take on vacation.* -n. [C;U] **compilation** /,kampə'leɪʃən/.

com·pil·er /kəm'paɪlər/ n. **1** a central computer program that translates other programs into usable ones **2** a person who compiles: *She is a compiler of dictionaries.*

com·pla·cent /kəm'pleɪsənt/ adj. **1** quiet, satisfied: *He likes his job and has a complacent attitude toward life.* **2** feeling superior and not worried, (syn.) smug: *He remained complacent even though the lawyer threatened to sue him.* -n. [U] **complacency;** -adv. **complacently.**

com·plain /kəm'pleɪn/ v. **1** to express dissatisfaction, such as with pain or s.t. that is wrong:

She complains that her back hurts. **2** to annoy others with complaints, (syn.) to whine or gripe: *He is always complaining about the weather or the government.* -n. **complainer.**

com·plaint /kəm'pleɪnt/ n. **1** an expression of unhappiness or irritation about s.t.: *I went to the doctor with a complaint about my bad back.* **2** criticism: *That customer has a complaint about a bad product.*

com·ple·ment /'kampləmənt/ n. a useful, appropriate addition to s.t.: *The new lamps are a beautiful complement to the living room.*

—v. /'kamplə,mɛnt/ to be an appropriate addition that makes s.t. more effective or complete: *The delicate sauce perfectly complemented the fish.* -adj. **complementary** /,kamplə'mɛntri, -təri/. See: compliment.

com·plete /kəm'plit/ adj. **1** finished, done: *Repair of the bridge is now complete.* **2** whole, having all its parts: *He has a complete collection of Elvis Presley records.*

—v. **-pleted, -pleting, -pletes** to finish s.t.: *He completed the report yesterday.*

com·ple·tion /kəm'pliʃən/ n. [U] the finishing of s.t., its end: *The completion of the work is scheduled for next week.*

com·plex /kəm'plɛks, 'kam,plɛks/ adj. **1** having many parts or details that make s.t. hard to understand or deal with, (syn.) complicated: *Finding a cure for cancer involves complex scientific research.* **2** having many related parts: *That powerful computer has complex wiring inside.*

—n. /'kam,plɛks/ **-plexes** **1** a group of buildings and parking lots: *That shopping complex has five restaurants, ten stores, and a day care center.||My apartment complex contains 20 separate units.* **2** a psychological problem, a constant concern with s.t.: *He has a complex about cleanliness, and he washes his hands 20 times a day.*

com·plex·ion /kəm'plɛkʃən/ n. **1** the appearance and condition of the skin of the face: *She has a good (clear, bad, reddish, etc.) complexion.* **2** fig. the appearance or condition of a situation: *Bad weather put a different complexion on our picnic plans; we didn't go.*

com·plex·i·ty /kəm'plɛksəti/ n. **-ties** a situation or condition with many difficult parts to it: *He prefers the simplicity of checkers to the complexity of chess.*

com·pli·ance /kəm'plaɪəns/ n. [U] cooperation with a requirement (law, wish): *When you pay your taxes according to the rules, you are in compliance with the tax regulations.* -adj. **compliant.**

com·pli·cate /'kamplə,keɪt/ v. **-cated, -cating, -cates** to make more difficult, more complex: *He complicated our agreement by asking for many more changes before he would sign it.*

com·pli·ca·tion /ˌkɑmpləˈkeɪʃən/ *n.* difficulty, problem: *A serious complication came up during the operation; her heart stopped beating.*

com·plic·i·ty /kəmˈplɪsəti/ *n.* [U] participation in s.t. bad: *The police suspect him of complicity in several recent crimes.* *-adj.* **complicit.**

com·pli·ment /ˈkɑmpləmənt/ *n.* **1** an expression of praise, admiration, or congratulations: **to pay s.o. compliments:** *People paid her compliments on her pretty dress.* **2 with one's compliments** or **compliments of the house:** s.t. given free as a courtesy or repayment: *The restaurant owner gave me a glass of wine with her compliments for being a good customer.* —*v.* /ˈkɑmpləˌment/ to express praise, admiration, etc., to s.o.: *She complimented the nine-year-old boy on his good manners.*

com·pli·men·ta·ry /ˌkɑmpləˈmentri, -təri/ *adj.* **1** expressing praise, (*syn.*) admiring: *She made complimentary remarks to the restaurant owner about the good food.* **2** free, without charge: *The owner gave her a complimentary glass of wine.*

com·ply /kəmˈplaɪ/ *v.frml.* **-plied, -plying, -plies** to cooperate with a requirement (law, wish): *Her husband complied with her wishes that he stop drinking.||Our company complies with governmental regulations on paying taxes every three months.*

com·po·nent /kəmˈpoʊnənt/ *n.* a part of a whole of s.t.: *Tires, the engine, the body, and the seats are components of a car.*

com·port·ment /kəmˈpɔrtmənt/ *n.* [U] *frml.* behavior, manners *-v.* **comport.**

com·pose /kəmˈpoʊz/ *v.* **-posed, -posing, -poses 1** *frml.* to put together with care, esp. writing: *She composed a letter to her lawyer.* **2** to create art: *to compose music or poetry* **3** to calm oneself: *He cried at his wife's funeral, but was able to compose himself after a few minutes.*

com·pos·er /kəmˈpoʊzər/ *n.* a person who writes music: *The music of great composers, like Beethoven and Mozart, is played around the world.*

com·pos·ite /kəmˈpɑzɪt/ *adj.* grouping together different pieces or elements to form a whole: *Police talked to witnesses and came up with a composite picture of how the accident happened.*

com·po·si·tion /ˌkɑmpəˈzɪʃən/ *n.* **1** [C;U] the writing of s.t.: *She began composition of a letter to her mother.* **2** [U] the artistic creation of music, poetry, literature **3** [C] a written report, esp. an essay: *A student wrote a composition for her English class.* **4** [C;U] how s.t. is put together, (*syn.*) its makeup: *That medicine is a composition of three different drugs.*

com·post /ˈkɑmˌpoʊst/ *n.* [U] *v.* decayed grass, leaves, or manure, etc., usu. used for fertilizer: *I put <n.> compost in the garden to make the flowers grow.*

com·po·sure /kəmˈpoʊʒər/ *n.* [U] control of one's emotions: *She lost her composure and cried at her mother's funeral.*

com·pound /ˈkɑmˌpaʊnd/ *n.* **1** s.t. made by combining two or more parts or elements: *Water is a chemical compound made from hydrogen and oxygen.* **2** an area with a fence around it: *The soldiers live inside a military compound.* —*v.* /kəmˈpaʊnd, ˈkɑmˌpaʊnd/ **1** to make s.t. more difficult, (*syn.*) to complicate: *Our car broke down, and heavy rain compounded our problem of getting help.* **2** to add s.t. on top of s.t. else, (*syn.*) to accumulate: *Interest compounds monthly in my savings account.* —*adj.* /ˈkɑmˌpaʊnd/ made up of two or more parts: *The compound word "bookstore" is formed from the words "book" and "store."*

com·pre·hend /ˌkɑmprɪˈhend/ *v.* to get the meaning of s.t., (*syn.*) to understand: *That student comprehends that he must improve his work, or fail the course.*

com·pre·hen·si·ble /ˌkɑmprɪˈhensəbəl/ *adj.* capable of being understood, (*syns.*) clear, intelligible: *Her writing is quite comprehensible.*

com·pre·hen·sion /ˌkɑmprɪˈhenʃən/ *n.* [U] **1** an event of understanding **2** the ability to get the meaning of s.t.: *His comprehension of what is said in class is good.*

com·pre·hen·sive /ˌkɑmprɪˈhensɪv/ *adj.* that which includes everything, (*syns.*) all encompassing, total: *Our company has a comprehensive health plan that covers expenses for doctors, hospital, medicine, and dental care.*

com·press /kəmˈpres/ *v.* **-presses** to press together, (*syn.*) to compact: *That big garbage truck compresses cartons and tin cans until they are flat.* —*n.* /ˈkɑmˌpres/ **-presses** a soft pad used to cover a wound, soothe a headache, etc: *She put a cold compress on her aching head.*

com·pres·sion /kəmˈpreʃən/ *n.* [U] a pressing together: *The compression of gases in the earth can cause a volcano.*

com·prise /kəmˈpraɪz/ *v.* **-prised, -prising, -prises** to include, contain: *Our company's product line comprises 2,500 different items.*

com·pro·mise /ˈkɑmprəˌmaɪz/ *n.* [C;U] an agreement reached where each side gets some, but not all, of what it wants, while the other side also gets some, but not all, of what it wants: *My boss and I reached a compromise on my salary increase where I get what I asked for, but I have to wait six months for it.* —*v.* **-mised, -mising, -mises 1** to reach a compromise: *We compromised, so I get the in-*

crease I asked for, but I have to wait for it. **2** to put s.o. in a position of harm or difficulty

comp time /kɑmp/ *n.* [U] *abbr.for* compensatory time: time off earned by an employee who has worked overtime or on holidays: *I have enough comp time to take several days off next week.*

USAGE NOTE: Some companies do not pay salaried workers for extra time they work on holidays or long days. These companies may give *comp time* instead. So the workers can take a day off at some other time and still receive their normal salary.

comp·trol·ler /kən'troulər/ *n.* the chief accountant in a business: *Comptrollers usually work for the treasurer in a company. See:* controller.

com·pul·sion /kəm'pʌlʃən/ *n.* [C;U] a need to do s.t. that cannot be stopped, *(syn.)* an obsession: *He has a compulsion to smoke cigarettes.*

com·pul·sive /kəm'pʌlsɪv/ *adj.* needing to do s.t. and not being able to stop : *She has a compulsive need to talk a lot.*

com·pul·so·ry /kəm'pʌlsəri/ *adj.* related to s.t. that must be done, *(syn.)* required: *It is compulsory for children to attend school until the age of 16 in the USA.*

com·punc·tion /kəm'pʌŋkʃən/ *n.* [C;U] a sense of feeling bad (guilty) about s.t.: *He has no compunctions about lying; he does it all the time.*

com·pute /kəm'pyut/ *v.* **-puted, -puting, -putes** to do arithmetic or other calculations: *He computed the cost of building a new house.* -*n.* [C;U] **computation** /ˌkɑmpyu'teɪʃən/.

com·put·er /kəm'pyutər/ *n.* an electronic device that stores and allows changes in information through the use of instructions (programs) to do various types of tasks, like word processing and accounting: *She uses her computer to write her books. See:* PC.

com·put·er·ize /kəm'pyutəˌraɪz/ *v.* **-ized, -izing, -izes** **1** to equip a business (or person) with computers: *The owner computerized his business; now, all of the accounting is done automatically.* **2** to put information into a computer: *We did our accounting by hand for years, then we computerized it.*

computer language *n.* a set of instructions that tells the computer what to do with information

com·rade /'kɑm,ræd/ *n.* **1** a soldier or worker in one's group: *During the war, he fought with his comrades.* **2** a form of address in groups such as Communist societies: *Good morning, comrade.* -*n.* [U] **comradeship.**

con (1) /kɑn/ *n.* a reason against s.t.: *We talked over the pros (for) and cons (against) of buying a new house.*

con (2) *n.slang* **1** an arrangement that cheats s.o., *(syn.)* a swindle: *That real estate deal was a real con; the land for sale was under water.* **2** a person in prison, *short for (syn.)* a convict **3 a con artist:** a swindler
—*v.* **conned, conning, cons** to fool s.o. and take their money, *(syn.)* to swindle s.o.: *That guy conned me into buying a used car that was no good.*

con·cave /kɑn'keɪv/ *adj.* curving inward: *The inside of those eyeglasses is concave. See:* convex.

con·ceal /kən'sil/ *v.* **1** to hide s.t.: *The thief concealed a pistol under his coat.* **2** to keep s.t. secret, esp. to trick s.o.: *The owners of the company concealed last year's financial losses from the new buyer.* -*n.* [U] **concealment.**

con·cede /kən'sid/ *v.* **-ceded, -ceding, -cedes** **1** to admit that s.t. is true: *The person who caused the accident finally conceded to the police that he had done it.* **2** to give over as s.t. justly deserved, *(syn.)* to yield as a right: *to concede victory to an opponent*

con·ceit /kən'sit/ *n.* [U] too high an opinion of oneself, *(syn.)* vanity: *His conceit about being so intelligent annoys everyone.*

con·ceit·ed /kən'sitɪd/ *adj.* too high an opinion of oneself, *(syn.)* vain: *He is so conceited that he acts like he's a movie star.*

con·ceiv·able /kən'sivəbəl/ *adj.* possible, believable, *(syn.)* imaginable: *My grandmother left her glasses somewhere in the house; we have looked for them in every conceivable place, but have not found them.* -*adv.* **conceivably.**

con·ceive /kən'siv/ *v.* **-ceived, -ceiving, -ceives** **1** to think of s.t.: *I can't conceive of why he did such a stupid thing!* **2** *frml.*to become pregnant: *She conceived and had a son.*

con·cen·trate /'kɑnsən,treɪt/ *v.* **-trated, -trating, -trates** **1** to think hard about s.t., *(syn.)* to focus one's attention: *During exams, students concentrate hard on answering the questions.* **2** to reduce the amount of s.t. and increase its strength, *(syn.)* to condense: *Orange juice that is concentrated can be stored in the freezer.*
—*n.* [C;U] a condensed form of s.t.: *a chemical concentrate*

con·cen·tra·tion /ˌkɑnsən'treɪʃən/ *n.* **1** [U] total attention to s.t.: *He studies his textbook with complete concentration.* **2** [C] a close grouping of s.t.: *There is a concentration of five Japanese restaurants on 14th Street.*

concentration camp *n.* a type of prison camp where captured soldiers or ordinary people thought to be enemies of the state are kept: *Millions of people died in Nazi concentration camps.*

con·cen·tric /kən'sɛntrɪk/ *adj.* having the same center.

con·cept /'kɑn,sɛpt/ *n.* a general idea that usu. includes other related ideas: *Democracy is a concept that includes, among other things, the ideas of individual freedom and the right to vote.* *-adj.* **conceptual** /kən'sɛptʃuəl/; *-v.* **conceptualize.**

con·cep·tion /kən'sɛpʃən/ *n.* **1** [C;U] the creation of life: *The conception of a baby happens when a man's sperm fertilizes a woman's egg.* **2** [U] a beginning: *At the conception of this project, our company had five employees; now, three years later, the company has 20 employees.* **3** [C;U] an idea, (*syn.*) an understanding: *Most people have no conception of how difficult it is to write a book.*

con·cern /kən'sɜrn/ *n.* **1** [C;U] care, attention: *He shows constant concern about how his mother is feeling.* **2** [U] worry: *When she was sick, he regarded her condition with great concern.* **3 a going concern:** a business that is successful: *He opened a business last year, and it is now a going concern.* **4 no concern:** *When you want to tell s.o. to mind their own business, you can say, "That is no concern of yours."*
—v. **1** to be about: *This letter concerns payment for my new TV.* **2 a.** to deal with, care about, or worry about: *He is concerned about his mother's sickness.* **b. to concern oneself:** *She concerns herself with her business and nothing else.*

con·cern·ing /kən'sɜrnɪŋ/ *prep.* about, with regard to: *I am writing concerning my order for shoes, which has not arrived yet.*

con·cert /'kɑnsərt/ *n.* **1** a musical event: *I went to a rock concert last night.* **2 in concert (with):** together with: *Two countries acted in concert (or) in concert with each other to stop a war.*

con·cert·ed /kən'sɜrtɪd/ *adj.* strong, (*syn.*) intense: *He made a concerted effort to finish the job on time.*

con·cer·to /kən'tʃɛrtou/ *n.* **-tos** or **-ti** /-ti/ a piece of classical music, shorter than a symphony, with a soloist and orchestra: *We listened to a wonderful violin concerto.*

con·ces·sion /kən'sɛʃən/ *n.* **1** [C;U] (a surrender to) a special demand by s.o.: *To sell our house, we made a concession to the buyer by agreeing to put on a new roof.* **2** [C] a right to do business, esp. on government land or other area (sea): *She owns the restaurant concession that sells food in the public park.*

con·cierge /kɔ'syɛrʒ, kɑnsi'ɛrʒ/ *n.* a person in a hotel who sits in the lobby and helps guests with problems or answers questions: *The concierge at the hotel suggested a wonderful Korean restaurant.*

con·cil·i·ate /kən'sɪli,eɪt/ *v.* **-ated, -ating, -ates** to win back the good feelings of s.o., (*syns.*) to soothe, placate: *The owner concili-* ated the anger of her employees at having to work longer hours by giving them wage increases. *-n.* [U] **conciliation** /kən,sɪli'eɪʃən/.

con·cil·i·a·to·ry /kən'sɪliə,tɔri/ *adj.* seeking to please, esp. to stop s.o.'s anger: *After arguing with her, he made conciliatory remarks about how much he loves her.*

con·cise /kən'saɪs/ *adj.* said in few words with much meaning, (*syn.*) succinct: *The speaker made a concise statement of his ideas.* *-adv.* **concisely;** *-n.* [U] **conciseness.**

con·clave /'kɑn,kleɪv/ *n.* a meeting held in secret: *Generals held a conclave to plan a surprise attack.*

con·clude /kən'klud/ *v.* **-cluded, -cluding, -cludes** **1** to bring to an end, (*syn.*) to finish: *The concert concluded with an exciting song.* **2** to form an opinion: *After not getting a salary increase, I concluded that I must find a new job.* **3 to reach** or **come to a conclusion:** to come to an agreement: *The agreement was concluded and signed in 1945.*

con·clu·sion /kən'kluʒən/ *n.* **1** the end of s.t., the finish: *At the conclusion of the show, everyone clapped their hands.* **2** an opinion, a judgment: *The police reached* (or) *came to the conclusion that the murder was done by a friend of the dead man.*

con·clu·sive /kən'klusɪv/ *adj.* without doubt, (*syn.*) convincing: *The police have conclusive proof about who stole the money.*

con·coct /kən'kɑkt/ *v.* **1** to mix together, usu. in a strange way: *He concocted a drink made from five different liquors.* **2** to invent a story or excuse that is not true: *He concocted a story about why his homework wasn't done. -n.* **concoction.**

con·cor·dance /kən'kɔrdns/ *n.frml.* **1** an agreement: *The two countries signed a concordance on trade.* **2** an alphabetical list of important words and their meanings *-n.* [U] **concord** /'kɑn,kɔrd/.

con·course /'kɑn,kɔrs/ *n.* an open place or building hall where people can gather or walk through: *The concourse in the railroad station leads to the trains and the street.*

con·crete /kɑn'krit, 'kɑn,krit/ *n.* [U] a building material made of cement and small rocks: *Workers poured concrete to build the bridge.*
—adj. **1** dealing with facts and certainties: *The police have concrete evidence (proof, facts) about who committed the crime.* **2** about real, specific things and situations, not general ideas: *She gave some concrete examples of how to put their new knowledge to use.* **3** made of concrete: *This is a concrete sidewalk.*

con·cur /kən'kɜr/ *v.frml.* **-curred, -curring, -curs** **1** to have the same opinion, (*syn.*) to agree: *Two doctors concurred that the man needs a heart operation.* **2** to happen at the

same time: *Jonah's wedding anniversary concurs with his parents' anniversary. -n.* [C;U]
concurrence /kən'kɜrənt,=ˈkʌr-/; **-adj. concurrent.**

con·cus·sion /kən'kʌʃən/ *n.* **1** a violent shock: *A bomb was dropped nearby, and the concussion knocked us off our feet.* **2** an injury to the head and brain: *He got a concussion while playing football.*

con·demn /kən'dɛm/ *v.* **1** to find legally guilty or unfit: *The judge condemned the criminal to life in prison.‖He condemned the old house as unfit to live in.* **2** to express disapproval of s.o. or s.t. strongly: *The wife condemned her husband for drinking too much. -n.* [C;U] **condemnation** /ˌkandəm'neɪʃən, -dɛm-/.

con·den·sa·tion /ˌkandɛn'seɪʃən, -dən-/ *n.* **1** [C;U] a piece of writing made shorter, (*syn.*) an abridgment: *This 10-page summary is a condensation of a 100-page report.* **2** [U] liquid formed from a gas: *In cold weather, condensation forms on the kitchen window.*

con·dense /kən'dɛns/ *v.* **-densed, -densing, -denses** **1** to shorten: *The writer condensed his letter from six pages to two pages.* **2** to make thicker, esp. by removing water **3** to form liquid from a gas: *Moisture condensed (out of the air) on the window. -n.* **condenser.**

con·de·scend /ˌkandɪ'sɛnd/ *v.* **1** to act toward others in a self-important manner, (*syn.*) to patronize: *She owns a big hotel and condescends to the workers who dislike working for her.* **2** to agree to do s.t. that one thinks is below one's importance or rank: *The queen condescended to speak to the peasant. -n.* [U] **condescension** /ˌkandɪ'sɛnʃən/.

con·des·cend·ing /ˌkandɪ'sɛndɪŋ/ *adj.* having a self-important manner toward others, (*syns.*) disdainful, patronizing: *He has a condescending attitude toward everyone.*

con·di·ment /'kandəmənt/ *n.* seasoning for food: *Condiments, like mustard and soy sauce, add flavor to food.*

con·di·tion /kən'dɪʃən/ *n.* **1** [U] the state of s.t. (good, bad, weak, strong): *The condition of his health is excellent.‖The condition of that machinery is bad.* **2** [C] a disease, medical problem: *My grandmother has a heart condition.* **3** [C] a requirement: *Our book contract has two special conditions in it: we must pay $10,000 in advance, and we must renew the contract annually.* **4** [C] external factors: *My living conditions were terrible at my old apartment building; I had no running water or heat for two months.* **5 on the condition that:** provided that: *Yes, we will renew the contract next year on the condition that we make money on the deal.*
—v. to shape the attitudes or behavior of: *We conditioned our children to not watch TV during the week.*

con·di·tion·al /kən'dɪʃənəl/ *adj.* dependent upon, requiring that (s.t. be done): *Our purchase of the house is conditional on our making the first payment on it by tomorrow.*

con·di·tion·er /kən'dɪʃənər/ *n.* [C;U] a cream for the hair that makes it easier to comb: *He puts conditioner on his long hair every time he washes it.*

con·do /'kandou/ *n.* **-dos** *short for* condominium

con·do·lence /kən'douləns/ *n.* [C;U] expression of sympathy upon s.o.'s death: *I wish to express my condolences on your father's death.*

con·dom /'kandəm/ *n.* a covering for the male sex organ worn during intercourse to prevent disease or pregnancy, (*syns.*) prophylactic, rubber: *Wearing a condom reduces the chances of a woman becoming pregnant. See:* contraceptive.

USAGE NOTE: *Condoms* are used to help stop *sexually transmitted diseases (STDs)* such as *HIV, herpes,* or *syphilis* from spreading from one person to another. For this reason, it is common for one sexual partner to ask the other to wear a condom. *Condoms* for both males and females are available.

con·do·min·i·um /ˌkandə'mɪniəm/ *n.* housing, usu in an apartment building, in which each apartment is privately owned: *She owns a two-bedroom condominium in that building. See:* co-op, cooperative.

con·done /kən'doun/ *v.* **-doned, -doning, -dones** to accept, but not approve of s.t., esp. s.o.'s bad behavior: *The boss condoned her lateness to work because of her family problems.*

con·dor /'kandər, -ˌdər/ *n.* a very large bird of the western Americas: *Most condors live high in the mountains of South America.*

con·du·cive /kən'dusɪv/ *adj.* helping to produce: *Exercise is conducive to good health*

con·duct /'kan,dʌkt/ *n.* [U] **1** behavior, (*syn.*) comportment: *Good conduct is expected of students in school.* **2** the process of doing s.t.: *the conduct of diplomacy‖the conduct of business*
—v. /kən'dʌkt/ **1** to behave: *The students conducted themselves well in class today.* **2** to do s.t.: *That store conducts business from 9:00 A.M. to 7:00 P.M.* **3** to direct an orchestra, band, etc.: *He conducts the London Philharmonic Orchestra.*

con·duc·tor /kən'dʌktər/ *n.* **1** a person who sells and checks tickets on a train, bus, etc. **2** a person who directs an orchestra: *The conductor told the musicians how he wanted the music to be played.*

cone /koun/ *n.* an object pointed at one end and then becoming wider at the other end: *An ice-*

cream cone is wide at the top and pointed at the bottom.

con·fec·tion /kən'fɛkʃən/ *n.frml.* s.t. sweet: *Candy is a confection.* -*n.* **confectionery** /kən'fɛkʃə,nɛri/.

con·fed·er·a·cy /kən'fɛdərəsi/ *n.* -**cies** **1** a union of people or states **2 the Confederacy:** in the USA, the 11 southern states that separated from the United States in 1860 and 1861: *The Civil War began with the Confederacy against the North.*

con·fed·er·ate /kən'fɛdərɪt/ *n.* **1** a person or state that joins in a confederacy **2** a partner in crime or a plot, (*syn.*) accomplice: *His confederate is a tall man with red hair and a mustache; that's all they know about him.*

con·fed·er·a·tion /kən,fɛdə'reɪʃən/ *n.* an organization of people, states, etc., united in a common purpose: *A confederation of workers formed a labor union.*

con·fer /kən'fɜr/ *v.frml.* -**ferred, -ferring, -fers** **1** to talk to, discuss s.t. in a formal way: *The judge conferred with the two lawyers.* **2** to give an honor to s.o., (*syn.*) to bestow: *The queen conferred a knighthood on the man in honor of his brave deeds.*

con·fer·ence /'kɑnfrəns, -fərəns/ *n.* **1** [C] a professional meeting, convention, usu. at a big hotel: *Members of every profession, from architects to zoologists, go to conferences to learn about the newest ideas and equipment in their field.* **2** [C;U] a private business meeting among people: *Mr. Smith cannot talk to you now; he is in a conference with his boss.*

conference call *n.* a telephone call made between three or more people: *We organized a conference call among employees in New York, Chicago, and Denver.*

con·fess /kən'fɛs/ *v.* -**fesses** to admit s.t., esp. guilt for s.t. bad: *The criminal confessed his guilt in committing the robbery.*

con·fes·sion /kən'fɛʃən/ *n.* **1** [C;U] the admission of guilt: *The criminal gave (or) made a confession of guilt.* **2** [U] the religious act of confessing sin: *Catholics go to confession as part of their religion.*

con·fet·ti /kən'fɛti/ *n.* [U] little bits of brightly colored paper: *Guests threw confetti as the newlyweds left the church.*

con·fi·dant /'kɑnfə,dɑnt, -,dænt/ *n.* a special friend one can talk to about secret and personal matters: *The President's lawyer is also a friend and confidant.*

con·fide /kən'faɪd/ *v.* -**fided, -fiding, -fides** to tell secrets to s.o.: *Throughout his lifetime, the owner confided only in his wife.*

con·fi·dence /'kɑnfədəns/ *n.* **1** [U] belief in one's abilities, self-esteem: *That salesman has a lot of confidence in his ability to sell to difficult customers.* **2** [C;U] a secret, esp. one told

to another person that one trusts: *I told my friend in confidence (as a secret) how much money I have in the bank.||He kept that confidence (a secret) and told no one. See:* betray.

confidence man *n.* **men** a person who cheats others out of their money, (*syns.*) a con man, a swindler: *A confidence man swindled the old lady out of her savings. See:* con man.

con·fi·dent /'kɑnfədənt/ *adj.* with strong belief in one's ability or that s.t. will definitely happen: *She behaves in a confident manner.||He is confident that next year's sales will be excellent.*

con·fi·den·tial /,kɑnfə'dɛnʃəl/ *adj.* intended for only a few people to know, almost secret: *The doctor keeps his patients' health records confidential; only his nurse and the patient can see them.* -*n.* [U] **confidentiality** /,kɑnfə,dɛnʃi'æləti/; -*adv.* **confidentially.**

con·fig·u·ra·tion /kən,fɪgyə'reɪʃən/ *n.* an arrangement of things, usu. related to each other: *With the furniture in this configuration, we have much more space.* -*v.* **configure** /kən'fɪgyər/.

con·fine /kən'faɪn/ *v.* -**fined, -fining, -fines** **1** to keep within certain limits, (*syn.*) to restrict: *You should stop making jokes and confine your attention to what the teacher is saying.||The police confined the criminal to a jail cell.* —*n.* /'kɑn,faɪn/ **confines** *pl.* the limit(s) of s.t.: *The criminals must stay within the confines of the prison.*

con·fine·ment /kən'faɪnmənt/ *n.* [U] the state of being kept within certain limits: *When a prisoner is kept in solitary confinement, he or she is the only one in a prison cell.*

con·firm /kən'fɜrm/ *v.* **1** to make sure s.t. is right by checking it again, (*syn.*) to verify: *I made my airline reservations last month, and I called the airline to confirm them today.* **2** to make s.t. certain that was only suspected before: *The police came to our house and confirmed my worst fears that my son was injured in a car accident.||The rumor that the President is resigning is not confirmed.* **3** to make s.t. legal: *The Senate confirmed the judge as the new member of the Supreme Court.* **4 a confirmed bachelor:** a man who never intends to get married

con·fir·ma·tion /,kɑnfər'meɪʃən/ *n.* [C;U] **1** written or spoken proof that s.t. is done, (*syn.*) verification (of an order, reservation, fact, etc.): *The store sent me written confirmation of my order for a new sofa.* **2** an act of making s.t. legal or formally accepted: *the confirmation by the Senate of a judge to the Supreme Court||the confirmation of a rumor as true*

con·fis·cate /'kɑnfə,skeɪt/ *v.* -**cated, -cating, -cates** to legally take s.t. away without getting permission from the owner, (*syn.*) to seize: *The* *police confiscated the criminal's pistol.* -*n.*[C;U] **confiscation** /ˌkɑnfəˈskeɪʃən/.

con·fla·gra·tion /ˌkɑnfləˈgreɪʃən/ *n.frml.* a large, destructive fire: *The conflagration destroyed the entire town.*

con·flict /ˈkɑnˌflɪkt/ *n.* **1** [C;U] a difference, disagreement: *There is a conflict between what you are saying and what the contract says.* **2** [C] an argument: *The two men had a conflict over who would run the company.* **3** [C;U] a war: *The Persian Gulf War was an armed conflict between Iraq and a group of other nations.* —*v.* /kənˈflɪkt/ to differ, disagree: *What the contract says and what you say conflict.*

conflict of interest *n.* **conflicts of interest** one activity that conflicts with another, thereby questioning the person's ability to act honestly: *He's a government official who sets controls for the auto industry, so his owning stock in that industry represents a conflict of interest.*

con·flu·ence /ˈkɑnfluəns/ *n.* [C;U] the place where two or more streams of water flow together: *Pittsburgh built Three River Stadium near the confluence of three rivers.*

con·form /kənˈfɔrm/ *v.* **1** to obey legal requirements: *Our company conforms to government regulations on worker safety.* **2** to act in the same way as others do: *Many of those students walk, talk, and dress alike; they conform to each other rather than picking an individual style.* -*n.* [U] **conformity.**

con·form·ist /kənˈfɔrmɪst/ *n.* a person who acts in the same way that most others do: *She is a conformist who dresses and talks like all of her friends in school.*

con·found /kənˈfaʊnd/ *v.* to make a person or group confused and worried as to why they are wrong: *The great football player's critics said that his career was over, but he confounded them by playing an exciting game.*

con·front /kənˈfrʌnt/ *v.* **1** to demand that s.o. explain s.t. wrong: *The owner confronted the employee with the stolen supplies found in his desk.* **2** to deal boldly with s.t. difficult or dangerous: *I confronted the problem of losing my job by working hard to find another one.||The letter carrier confronted the growling dog and made it move away.* -*n.* [C;U] **confrontation** /ˌkɑnfrənˈteɪʃən/.

con·fuse /kənˈfyuz/ *v.* **-fused, -fusing, -fuses** **1** to mix things up: *He sent the wrong reports because he confused them with other ones.* **2** to mix up mentally so that one cannot understand or think clearly: *The teacher's question confused him.*

con·fu·sion /kənˈfyuʒən/ *n.* [U] **1** a mixed-up situation: *We went to the wrong classroom, so there was confusion as to which room was the correct one.* **2** disorder, (*syns.*) commotion, panic: *When the bomb went off in the center of*

Paris, there was confusion everywhere. -*adj.* **confused; confusing.**

con·geal /kənˈdʒil/ *v.* to become solid, harden: *When water freezes, it congeals into ice.*

con·ge·nial /kənˈdʒinyəl/ *adj.* friendly, warm: *She's very congenial, always smiling and saying nice things.*

con·ges·tion /kənˈdʒestʃən/ *n.* [U] **1** a condition of overcrowding: *Traffic congestion caused us to be late.* **2** a condition of overfilling: *I have congestion in my nose and chest from a cold.* -*v.* **congest.**

con·glom·er·ate /kənˈglɑmərɪt/ *n.* a large corporation, usu. with many different kinds of businesses: *That conglomerate has some companies that make clothing, some that make candy, and others that make cigarettes.*

con·grat·u·late /kənˈgrætʃəˌleɪt, -ˈgrædʒə-/ *v.* **-lated, -lating, -lates** to praise for s.t. well done or important: *I would like to congratulate you on your promotion to manager.*

con·grat·u·la·tions /kənˌgrætʃəˈleɪʃənz, -ˌgrædʒə-/ *n.pl.* an expression of praise or pleasure for s.t. well done or important: *Congratulations on the new baby!* -*adj.* **congratulatory** /kənˈgrætʃələˌtɔri,-ˈgrædʒə-/.

con·gre·gate /ˈkɑŋgrɪˌgeɪt/ *v.* **-gated, -gating, -gates** to gather together: *People congregated to watch the house burn.*

con·gre·ga·tion /ˌkɑŋgrɪˈgeɪʃən/ *n.* a group of people, esp. those at a church service: *The minister spoke to the congregation.*

con·gress /ˈkɑŋgrɪs/ *n.* **-gresses** **1** in the USA, a governing group made up of the elected members of the House of Representatives and the Senate: *Congress passes laws that must be obeyed by the people.* **2** a group of people chosen to represent organizations: *The Congress on Racial Equality reported that very few African-Americans are presidents of companies in the USA.* -*adj.* **congressional** /kənˈgreʃənəl/; -*n.* **congressman** /ˈkɑŋgrɪsmən/; **congresswoman.**

con·gru·ent /ˈkɑŋgruənt, kənˈgruənt/ *adj.* **1** (in math) having a similar size and shape: *congruent triangles* **2** *frml.* agreeing with: *Martin and I have the same philosophy on life; we share congruent beliefs.* -*adj.* **congruous** /ˈkɑŋgruəs/.

con·ic /ˈkɑnɪk/ *adj.n.* (s.t.) cone-shaped: *An ice-cream cone is* <*adj.*> *conic.* -*adj.* **conical.**

con·i·fer /ˈkɑnəfər/ *n.* a general term for trees, such as pines and firs, that bear seeds on cones

con·jec·ture /kənˈdʒektʃər/ *n.* [C;U] *v.* **-tured, -turing, -tures** the forming of an opinion or conclusion without having enough evidence, (*syns.*) guesswork, speculation: *The police have few real facts about the crime, so all they have is conjecture about who did it.*

con·ju·gal /ˈkɑndʒəgəl/ *adj.frml.* related to marriage: *conjugal happiness*

con·ju·gate /ˈkɑndʒə,geɪt/ *v.* **-gated, -gating, -gates** to give the forms of a verb: *I conjugated "to be" as "I am, you are, he/she/it is."* **-n.** [C;U] **conjugation** /,kɑndʒə'geɪʃən/.

con·junc·tion /kən'dʒʌŋkʃən/ *n.* **1** a type of word that joins other words, phrases, etc.: *"And," "but," and "whereas" are conjunctions.* **2 in conjunction with:** together with: *We are working in conjunction with a builder in planning our new house.*

con·jure /ˈkɑndʒər/ *v.* **-jured, -juring, -jures 1** to do magic tricks **2 to conjure up:** to imagine: *I have never met your girlfriend, but from your stories I can conjure up a picture of her.* **-n. conjurer.**

con man *n.infrml.* **men** short for confidence man

con·nect /kə'nɛkt/ *v.* **1** to attach, join together: *I connected the TV antenna to the TV.* **2** to plug into an electrical supply: *Then, I connected the TV to an outlet. See:* to disconnect. **3** to reach s.o. by telephone: *After waiting 10 minutes, I was connected with my boss.* **4** (transportation) to join for another part of a trip: *The bus line connects with the trains at the railroad station.||I fly from New York to Chicago, and then connect on another flight to San Francisco.* **5** to make an association with: *The police connected that man to the robbery.* **6** *infrml.* to make s.o. understand: *We talked and talked, then I finally connected with the guy; he now understands that I want my money back.*

con·nect·ed /kə'nɛktɪd/ *adj.* **1** related, linked: *There were several unanswered questions connected with the accident.||The two events were not connected.* **2 well-connected:** knowing many important people: *She is well-connected with officials in the government.*

con·nec·tion /kə'nɛkʃən/ *n.* **1** [C;U] an attachment, a joining together: *I fixed the loose connection between the TV antenna and the TV.* **2** [C] a wire or line that joins two telephones or other modes of communication: *I telephoned my office from my car phone, but we had a bad connection, and I couldn't hear what they were saying.* **3** [C] a change to another vehicle or mode of transportation: *She got off the bus and made her connection with the train.* **4** [C] a relationship (between people, actions, ideas): *(people) She has connections with officials in the government. ||(actions) The police found a clear connection between that man and the murder.* **-adj. connective.**

con·niv·ance /kə'naɪvəns/ *n.* [U] secret cooperation with s.o.: *The soldier's connivance with the enemy caused many deaths.* **-v. connive; -n. conniver.**

con·nois·seur /,kɑnə'sɜr, -'sʊr/ *n.* a person with much knowledge of fine things: *He is a connoisseur of fine wines (art, rare books, etc.).*

con·no·ta·tion /,kɑnə'teɪʃən/ *n.* the meaning(s) that a word can have beyond its basic one: *The color red has connotations of warmth and passion.* **-v. connote** /kə'noʊt/.

con·quer /ˈkɑŋkər/ *v.* **1** to fight and take control, (syn.) to vanquish: *A huge army conquered that country.* **2** to overcome (fears, illness, bad habits): *She conquered her fear of heights; now she works on the 28th floor of that building.* **-n. conqueror.**

con·quest /ˈkɑn,kwɛst/ *n.* **1** [U] a military victory: *the Roman conquest of Gaul (early France)* **2** [C] the winning of s.o.'s love: *He is so charming that he has made many conquests; many women have fallen in love with him.*

con·science /ˈkɑnʃəns/ *n.* [C;U] one's sense of right and wrong, esp. feelings of guilt: *After he stole the money, he had a guilty conscience and returned it.*

con·sci·en·tious /,kɑnʃi'ɛnʃəs/ *adj.* careful about doing things one is supposed to do and doing them well, (syns.) thorough, painstaking: *She does all her work in a conscientious manner.* **-adv. conscientiously; -n.** [U] **conscientiousness.**

con·scious /ˈkɑnʃəs/ *adj.* **1** awake: *The boxer was knocked out, but he was conscious again after one minute.* **2** knowing or noticing s.t., (syn.) aware: *The salesman is conscious of the fact that he must increase sales.||He felt very conscious of his foreign accent.* **3** with deliberate intention: *She made a conscious effort to do her homework nightly.* **-adv. consciously.**

con·scious·ness /ˈkɑnʃəsnɪs/ *n.adj.* [U] **1** the state of being awake: *The boxer regained <n.>consciousness after a minute.* **2** awareness: *Minority groups in the USA have <adj.>consciousness-raising events to make others aware of their concerns and problems.*

con·se·crate /ˈkɑnsə,kreɪt/ *v.* **-crated, -crating, -crates 1** to make or announce that s.t. is holy: *The ground in the church's cemetery is consecrated.* **2** to set aside for a special purpose: *The priest consecrated his life to religion.* **-n.**[C;U] **consecration** /,kɑnsə'kreɪʃən/.

con·sec·u·tive /kən'sɛkyətɪv/ *adj.* following one after the other in regular order: *She had a pain in her stomach for three consecutive days—Monday, Tuesday, and Wednesday.*

con·sen·sus /kən'sɛnsəs/ *n.* agreement reached among members of a group: *The three owners of the company reached a consensus that they must sell it.*

con·sent /kən'sɛnt/ *v.* **1** to agree to s.t.: *She consented to marry John.* **2** to approve, (syn.)

to sanction: *Her father consented to her marrying John.*
—*n.* [U] **1** agreement: *She gave John her consent.* **2** approval, (*syn.*) sanction: *John asked for her father's consent. See:* age of consent.

con·se·quence /'kɑnsə,kwɛns, -kwəns/ *n.* **1** [C] the result of doing s.t.: *He drank heavily and died as a consequence.* **2** [U] importance: *World War II was an event of great consequence in human history.* **3 to pay the consequences of:** to suffer for: *Henry paid the consequences of his drinking by dying at the age of 45.* -*adj.* **consequent; consequential** /,kɑnsə'kwɛnʃəl/.

con·se·quent·ly /'kɑnsə,kwɛntli, -kwənt-/ *adv.* following as a result: *She lost a lot of weight and consequently feels better.*

con·ser·va·tion /,kɑnsər'veɪʃən/ *n.* [U] **1** keeping s.t. from getting into bad condition, (*syn.*) preservation, esp. of nature: *Conservation of forests by law keeps them looking beautiful.* **2** protecting s.t. from becoming weak: *conservation of one's energy, wealth, etc. See:* conserve.

con·ser·va·tive /kən'sɜrvətɪv/ *adj.* **1** having a political view toward keeping old and often proven ways of doing things: *In the USA, Republicans are the conservative party.* **2** slow to change, cautious **3** not too much or too high: *She is conservative in her spending.||He made a conservative estimate of the costs.* **4** not showy, restrained in manner and dress: *Tomiko is a banker who wears a conservative business suit to work.*
—*n.* a person who is a conservative -*adv.* **conservatively.** *See:* Republican, USAGE NOTE.

con·ser·va·tor /kən'sɜrvətər, -,tɔr/ *n.* a person appointed to administer a trust or to settle a dead person's estate: *The old man's daughter is the conservator of his estate.*

con·ser·va·to·ry /kən'sɜrvə,tɔri/ *n.* **-ries 1** a school for music: *She studied the piano at a conservatory.* **2** a glass greenhouse structure, usu. attached to a house: *On summer evenings they dined in the conservatory.*

con·serve /kən'sɜrv/ *v.* **-served, -serving, -serves 1** to save: *In winter, some people conserve energy by lowering the heat at night.* **2** to keep from becoming weak, less, or bad: *The sick man conserves his strength by resting in bed.*

con·sid·er /kən'sɪdər/ *v.* **1** to think about s.t.: *I will consider your offer and tell you my decision tomorrow.* **2** to debate: *Congress considered the new tax and voted it down.* **3** to have an opinion about s.t.: *He considers this to be the best book on the subject.* **4 all things considered:** in view of everything: *All things considered, our old car is no good, so we should buy a new one now. See:* considering.

con·sid·er·a·ble /kən'sɪdərəbəl/ *adj.* much, a lot: *That family owns a considerable amount of land.* -*adv.* **considerably.**

con·sid·er·ate /kən'sɪdərɪt/ *adj.* sensitive to the feelings and comfort of others: *He is always considerate of others; he is kind and sympathetic.* -*adv.* **considerately.**

con·sid·er·a·tion /kən,sɪdə'reɪʃən/ *n.* **1** [U] careful thought: *The buyer gave the offer careful consideration and said, "Yes."* **2** [U] careful attention to the feelings and wishes of others: *After my mother's death, many people showed consideration for my sadness.* **3 to take into consideration:** to treat s.o. or s.t. specially, (*syn.*) to make allowances for: *We must take the rainy weather into consideration and allow more time to travel to the airport.* **4 to take s.t. under consideration:** to think about seriously: *I asked my boss for a raise, and she said she will take the matter under consideration.* **5 in consideration of:** because of, in view of: *In consideration of my good work, she gave me a raise.* **6 for (a) consideration:** payment of money: *The lawyer said that he would handle the company's legal problem for a consideration, that is, $500 an hour.*

con·sid·er·ing /kən'sɪdərɪŋ/ *prep.* in view of, (*syn.*) having evaluated s.t.: *Considering the large amount of work involved, the study should take a year to complete.||Considering how sick he is, he should go to the doctor.*

con·sign·ment /kən'saɪnmənt/ *n.* [U] the act of leaving in care of, usu. for sale: *Our company shipped 12 chairs on consignment to a store; the store will pay us after the chairs are sold.* -*v.* **consign.**

con·sist /kən'sɪst/ *v.* to be made up of, (*syn.*) to be composed of: *The problem consists of two parts.*

con·sis·ten·cy /kən'sɪstənsi/ *n.* **-cies 1** [C;U] the degree of thickness, softness, etc., of s.t.: *The consistency of a steak is firm and thick.* **2** [U] the condition of doing things in the same way: *The consistency of the teacher's making the students work hard helps them learn a lot.*

con·sis·tent /kən'sɪstənt/ *adj.* **1** in accord with: *His description of the accident is consistent with what the police reported.* **2** repeated in the same way: *His high performance is consistent day after day.* -*adv.* **consistently.**

con·so·la·tion /,kɑnsə'leɪʃən/ *n.* [C;U] comfort from a loss: *Her car was wrecked, but she received consolation from the fact that the insurance company paid for a new one.* **2** [C] a prize awarded to a loser: *He lost the final tennis match, but received a prize of $100 as consolation.*

con·sole (1) /kən'soʊl/ *v.* **-soled, -soling, -soles 1** to comfort s.o. in grief or disappointment: *He held his mother in his arms and con-*

soled her on the death of her sister.‖*You made a bad mistake, but be consoled by the fact that you did not lose your job. -adj.* **consolable.**

con·sole (2) /'kɑn,soʊl/ *n.* **1** a cabinet standing on the floor that holds a TV, stereo, etc. **2** a panel that holds the controls of equipment: *I turned one of the knobs on my car's console to turn the radio up. See:* dashboard.

con·sol·i·date /kən'sɑlə,deɪt/ *v.* **-dated, -dating, -dates** to group together to reduce in number: *I had so many bank accounts at different banks that I consolidated them all into one. -n.* [C;U] **consolidation** /kən,sɑlə'deɪʃən/.

con·som·mé /,kɑnsə'meɪ, 'kɑnsə,meɪ/ *n.* [C;U] a clear soup made from meat and/or vegetables: *I heated up some chicken consommé for lunch.*

con·so·nance /'kɑnsənəns/ *n.* [U] **1** harmony **2** *frml.* **in consonance with:** in agreement with: *In consonance with your request for more information, I am enclosing a copy of our catalog.*

con·so·nant /'kɑnsənənt/ *n.* any letter of the alphabet that is not a vowel: *The letters "b," "c," "d," "f," etc., are consonants.*
—*adj.frml.* in agreement, (*syn.*) consistent

con·sort /'kɑn,sɔrt/ *n.* the wife or husband of a king or queen: *Prince Philip is Queen Elizabeth II's consort.*
—*v.frml.* /kən'sɔrt/ to associate with: *She consorts with bad people.*

con·sor·ti·um /kən'sɔrʃiəm, -ti-/ *n.* **-tia** /-ʃiə, -tiə/ a group of companies, schools, or other organizations joined in a common purpose: *A consortium of oil companies agreed to cooperate in finding oil in Siberia.*

con·spic·u·ous /kən'spɪkyuəs/ *adj.* evident, noticeable, often causing negative comments or suspicion: *Everyone at the wedding was well-dressed, but she was conspicuous in jeans and a cowboy hat. -adv.* **conspicuously.**

con·spir·a·cy /kən'spɪrəsi/ *n.* [C;U] **-cies** a secret plan to do s.t. (harm, fraud, revolt): *The generals joined in a conspiracy to overthrow their country's dictator.*

con·spire /kən'spaɪr/ *v.* **-spired, -spiring, -spires** **1** to join in a plan to harm, defraud, or revolt: *The generals conspired to take over the government.* **2** to work together, (*syn.*) to combine for an effect: *He made a fortune in real estate, then events conspired against him as the market crashed and he lost everything.* -*n.* **conspirator** /kən'spɪrətər/; -*adj.* **conspiratorial** /kən,spɪrə'tɔriəl/.

con·sta·ble /'kɑnstəbəl/ *n.* a police officer, esp. in a small town: *The constable arrested a driver for speeding.*

con·stan·cy /'kɑnstənsi/ *n.frml.* [U] loyalty to a person or purpose, (*syn.*) faithfulness: *The*

constancy of that couple's love for each other is admirable.

con·stant /'kɑnstənt/ *adj.* **1** happening all the time, continuous: *I can't sleep because of the constant noise of the cars and trucks on the street.* **2** unchanging: *For 15 years, I have had a constant problem with a bad back.* **3** *frml.* faithful: *He is constant in his love for her.*
—*n.* a quantity or quality that does not change: *In Rhode Island, the speed limit is a constant at 55 miles per hour. -adv.* **constantly.**

con·stel·la·tion /,kɑnstə'leɪʃən/ *n.* a grouping of stars that looks like an animal or other thing: *The Big Dipper and Little Dipper are constellations that we see in the sky at night.*

con·ster·na·tion /,kɑnstər'neɪʃən/ *n.* [U] surprise, confusion, and often anger: *We were full of consternation when the speaker failed to appear at our celebration.*

con·sti·pa·tion /,kɑnstə'peɪʃən/ *n.* [U] difficulty in moving waste from one's bowels: *He suffers from constipation because he eats too much bread and meat, but he doesn't eat fruit.* -*v.* **constipate** /'kɑnstə,peɪt/; -*adj.* **constipated.**

con·stit·u·en·cy /kən'stɪtʃuənsi/ *n.* **-cies** **1** a group of people who are loyal to a politician **2** the voters in a politician's area, district, or state: *The Senator sent a newsletter to her constituency about what she had accomplished.* -*n. adj.* **constituent.**

con·sti·tute /'kɑnstə,tut/ *v.frml.* **-tuted, -tuting, -tutes** **1** to make up, compose: *Crime and illegal drugs constitute the city's major problems.* **2** (legal) to give lawful form to: *The mayor constituted a committee to study the city's problems.*

con·sti·tu·tion /,kɑnstə'tuʃən/ *n.* **1** the principles and rules, set forth in a written document, governing a country: *The American constitution guarantees that the people have certain rights.* **2** one's body and its strength: *He has a strong constitution and is seldom sick. -adj.* **constitutional.**

con·strain /kən'streɪn/ *v.* to limit, control: *A law constrains the government from spending more money than it takes in.*

con·straint /kən'streɪnt/ *n.* [C;U] s.t. that holds back or controls, (*syn.*) a limitation: *That manager works under a lot of constraints because he cannot do anything without the owner's approval.*

con·strict /kən'strɪkt/ *v.* to narrow, make smaller: *Cholesterol constricts his blood vessels.* -*n.* [C;U] **constriction;** -*adj.* **constrictive.**

con·struct /kən'strʌkt/ *v.* to build, to put together piece by piece: *Builders construct buildings.*‖*Managers construct plans for businesses. -n.* **constructor.** *See:* contractor.

C

con·struc·tion /kən'strʌkʃən/ *n.* **1** [U] the act(s) of building s.t.: *That house has been under construction for two months now.* **2** [U] the way in which s.t. is built: *The finest materials are being used, so the house will be of solid construction.*

con·struc·tive /kən'strʌktɪv/ *adj.* **1** useful: *The office manager has a lot of constructive ideas for solving problems.* **2** helpful, positive: *She always has a constructive attitude; whenever I have a problem, she helps me find a solution.*

con·strue /kən'stru/ *v.* **-strued, -struing, -strues** to understand s.t. in a certain way, *(syn.)* to interpret it: *He construed my joke as a serious comment, not as a funny comment. See:* misconstrue.

con·sul /'kansəl/ *n.* an official who represents his or her country's citizens and trade in a foreign city and is the head of a consulate: *The Brazilian consul in San Francisco likes his assignment. -adj.* **consular** /'kansələr/. *See:* ambassador.

con·sul·ate /'kansəlɪt/ *n.* the offices (and sometimes living quarters) of a consul: *Most countries have consulates in New York to help their citizens and to increase tourism and business.*

con·sult /kən'sʌlt/ *v.* **1** to ask or seek the opinion of s.o.: *The President consults with top officials.* **2** to act as a consultant: *My husband consults for many major corporations.* **3** to look s.t. up, esp. in a reference book: *I consulted the telephone directory for his phone number.*

con·sul·tant /kən'sʌltnt/ *n.* a person who provides advice for pay: *The professor acts as a consultant to the government.*

con·sul·ta·tion /ˌkansəl'teɪʃən/ *n.frml.* [C;U] **1** the act of consulting with s.o.: *Doctors have consultations with their patients.* **2** a private talk with s.o.: *Mr. Jones is in consultation and cannot be disturbed.*

con·sume /kən'sum/ *v.* **-sumed, -suming, -sumes** **1** to eat and drink: *That big guy consumed six bottles of beer and three hamburgers. See:* eat. **2** to use up, *(syns.)* to spend, deplete: *Her work consumes most of her time and energy.* **3** to destroy: *Fire consumed the building.* **4 to be consumed:** to be controlled by strong emotion, *(syn.)* to be obsessed: *He is consumed by his hatred of others.*

con·sum·er /kən'sumər/ *n.* the ordinary person who buys and uses goods and services: *Companies do research on what the consumer thinks about their products.*
—*adj.* related to the consumer: *Advertising reports are referred to as "research in consumer preference."*

consumer credit *n.* [U] the funds (money) made available to the public by banks and businesses through credit cards and delayed payments to finance the purchase of consumer goods (TV's, cars, etc.): *Last year, the amount of consumer credit that was not paid was $50 billion.*

consumer goods *n.pl.* articles necessary for daily living, such as food, clothes, and everyday things: *The market for consumer goods is huge, but so is the competition. See:* capital goods.

consumer price index *n.* the average cost, published monthly, of a group of consumer goods, such as bread, milk, chicken, etc, in comparison to their past cost: *The consumer price index keeps going up as a result of inflation. See:* cost of living index.

con·sum·mate /'kansə,meɪt/ *v.* **-mated, -mating, -mates** **1** to finish, *(syn.)* to bring to a conclusion: *We consummated an agreement after a year of negotiation.* **2** *frml.* to have sex after a marriage ceremony: *José and Antonia consummated their marriage at a beautiful hotel in Miami.*
—*adj.* /'kansəmɪt, kən'sʌmɪt/ perfect: *consummate happiness -n.* [C;U] **consummation** /ˌkansə'meɪʃən/.

con·sump·tion /kən'sʌmpʃən/ *n.* [U] the process of consuming (eating, drinking, using things): *The consumption of alcohol in that country is high.*

con·tact /'kan,tækt/ *n.* **1** [U] touch: *My clothes come in contact with my skin.* **2** [C] a person one knows, esp. who can get s.t. done: *She has contacts with top officials in the government.* **3** [C] an electrical point: *The contact on the car battery is broken.* **4** communication with s.o.: *He made contact by telephone with his friend.*
—*v.* to communicate with, to get in touch with: *He contacted his friend by telephone. -adj.* **contactable.**

contact lens or **contact lenses** *n.* a small, round lens put directly on top of the cornea of the eye to improve one's eyesight: *I put my contacts in every morning and take them out at night.*

con·ta·gious /kən'teɪdʒəs/ *adj.* (a disease) capable of being given to others through physical contact or by air, *(syn.)* infectious: *The common cold is a contagious disease. -n.* [U] **contagion.**

con·tain /kən'teɪn/ *v.* **1** to hold within a container: *That can contains peanuts.‖The story contains a lot of action.* **2** to hold back, stop: *The students could not contain their laughter in class.*

con·tain·er /kən'teɪnər/ *n.* an object for holding things, such as a can, carton, box, or bottle: *I went to the store to buy a container of milk.*

con·tam·i·nate /kən'tæmə,neɪt/ *v.* **-nated, -nating, -nates** to make unclean, impure, unfit for use or consumption: *The drinking water was contaminated with gasoline.* -*n.* [U] **contamination** /kən,tæmə'neɪʃən/.

con·tem·plate /'kɑntəm,pleɪt/ *v.frml.* **-plated, -plating, -plates 1** to think about s.t. seriously: *The manager contemplated the results of the report for hours.* **2** to look forward to, (*syn.*) to anticipate: *She contemplates a good future in business after her graduation from college.* -*n.* [U] **contemplation** /,kɑntəm'pleɪʃən/; -*adj.* **contemplative** /kən'templətɪv, 'kɑntəm,pleɪtɪv/.

con·tem·po·ra·ne·ous /kən,tempə'reɪniəs/ *adj.frml.* occurring at the same time as s.t. else: *Two scientists at the university worked on separate but contemporaneous experiments.*

con·tem·po·rar·y /kən'tempə,reri/ *adj.* of today, (*syn.*) modern: *We like contemporary furniture in our apartment.*
—*n.* **-ies** another person of the same age or sharing the same time period: *George was a contemporary of mine at my old job; we both worked there in the 1980s.*

con·tempt /kən'tempt/ *n.* [U] a low opinion of s.o., (*syn.*) scorn: *She has contempt for anyone who is not as intelligent as she is.* -*adj.* **contemptuous** /kən'temptʃuəs/.

con·tempt·i·ble /kən'temptəbəl/ *adj.* worthy of contempt: *He is so cowardly that he behaves in a contemptible manner.*

con·tend /kən'tend/ *v.* **1** to state formally that s.t. is true, (*syn.*) to assert: *The lawyer contends that the criminal is guilty.* **2** to fight, (*syn.*) to struggle: *The two armies contended for possession of the fort.‖Young doctors have to contend with long hours and hard work.* -*n.* **contender.**

con·tent (1) /'kɑn,tent/ *n.* **1** *usu. pl.* things contained inside s.t.: *A customs official examined the contents of my suitcase.* **2** [U] the ideas or meanings expressed in a speech or piece of writing, (*syns.*) subject matter, substance: *The teacher returned his paper and said the content was not very interesting.* **3 (table of) contents:** a listing of the topics in a book, report, etc.: *She looked it up in the table of contents.* **4** [C, *usu. used in the sing.*] the amount of s.t. in a certain substance: *The fat content of this cheese is very high.*

con·tent (2) /kən'tent/ *adj.* satisfied, pleased: *He is content with his life.*
—*v.* to be satisfied, pleased: *He contents himself with a small house and a regular salary.*
—*n.* [U] satisfaction: *Go on vacation and rest to your heart's content.* See: happy.

con·ten·tion /kən'tenʃən/ *n.* **1** argument, controversy: *There is some contention over who should get the award.* **2** competition, esp. for s.t. important: *Our team is in contention to win the championship.* **3** a point that one is trying

to prove: *It is my contention that these new taxes will only hurt the city.*

con·ten·tious /kən'tenʃəs/ *adj.frml.* ready to disagree, (*syn.*) argumentative: *He is a contentious man, always arguing with everyone.*

con·tent·ment /kən'tentmənt/ *n.* [U] a feeling of satisfaction, happiness: *He gets great contentment from gardening.*

con·test /'kɑn,test/ *n.* **1** a competition: *The teacher organized a spelling contest in her English class.* **2** a struggle or fight
—*v.* /kən'test/ **1** to fight for: *The two armies contested every inch of ground.* **2** to disagree formally, (*syn.*) to dispute: *to contest a dead person's will in court*

con·tes·tant /kən'testənt/ *n.* a competitor in a competition: *She is the youngest contestant in the piano competition.*

con·text /'kɑn,tekst/ *n.* the information surrounding a word or phrase that determines exactly how it was meant: *Repeating a statement out of context can change its meaning.*

con·tig·u·ous /kən'tɪgyuəs/ *adj.frml.* touching, having a common boundary: *In the USA, 48 of the 50 states are contiguous.*

con·ti·nent (1) /'kɑntənənt/ *n.* one of the seven great land masses in the world: *People travel to the European Continent from all over the world.* -*adj.* **continental** /,kɑntə'nentl/.

continent (2) *adj.* **1** able to control one's urination and bowel movement: *Babies wear diapers because they are not yet continent.* **2** using self-restraint, esp. by not having sex, (*syns.*) abstinent, chaste: *Those priests stay continent.*

con·tin·gen·cy /kən'tɪndʒənsi/ *n.* **-cies** a surprise event, esp. one causing difficulty: *A fire in our warehouse was a contingency that we had not expected.*

con·tin·gent /kən'tɪndʒənt/ *adj.frml.* **1** likely but not certain to happen, (*syn.*) possible: *After days of heavy rain, we were on guard for contingent flooding.* **2** depending upon s.t., (*syn.*) conditional: *We will buy this house contingent on selling our current home.*
—*n.* a group: *a contingent of soldiers*

con·tin·u·al /kən'tɪnyuəl/ *adj.* **1** occurring again and again: *That dog's barking is a continual annoyance.* **2** never stopping, (*syn.*) incessant: *The continual ticking of the grandfather clock could be heard throughout the house.* See: continuous. -*adv.* **continually.**

con·tin·u·ance /kən'tɪnyuəns/ *n.* **1** the continuing of s.t.: *The continuance of business at our company depends on our getting a bank loan.* **2** (legal) the postponement of s.t. (a hearing, trial date, etc.) until a later date: *The company lawyer asked the judge for a continuance of a month on the trial so he could locate his most important witness.*

con·tin·u·a·tion /kən,tɪnyu'eɪʃən/ n. **1** [U] unbroken activity: *Continuation of business was not interrupted by the bad storm.* **2** [C] the continuing of s.t., esp. after a pause: *Part 2 of the movie on TV was a continuation of Part 1.*

con·tin·ue /kən'tɪnyu/ v. **-ued, -uing, -ues 1** to carry on for a period of time: *The storm continued for three days.* **2** to proceed after a pause: *The movie on TV continued after the commercial break.*

continuing education or **continuing ed.** /ɛd/ n. **1** courses taken in new topics or advances: *Doctors take continuing education on new advances in medicine.* **2** education taken, esp. by adults, on a part-time basis, (syn.) adult education: *That college offers continuing education courses in foreign languages, accounting, etc.*

con·ti·nu·i·ty /,kɑntə'nuəti/ n. [U] the fact or quality of continuing without change over a period of time, esp. in a way that makes sense, (syns.) logical sequence, coherence: *People in the State Department change so often that there is no continuity in how the USA treats foreign nations.*

con·tin·u·ous /kən'tɪnyuəs/ adj. continuing without pause: *Our homes and offices need a continuous supply of electricity.* -adv. **continuously.**

con·tort /kən'tɔrt/ v. to twist the body in an unnatural manner -n. **contortion.**

con·tour /'kɑn,tʊr/ n. the shape, esp. curves of s.t.: *The contours of cars are smooth, but those of trucks are mostly square.*

con·tra·band /'kɑntrə,bænd/ n. [U] adj. goods that are brought illegally into a country or state: *Those American cigarettes secretly trucked into Canada without payment of the import tax are <n.> contraband.*

con·tra·cep·tion /,kɑntrə'sɛpʃən/ n. [U] the use of any method that prevents a woman from becoming pregnant, (syn.) birth control: *That couple practices contraception by using a condom.*

con·tra·cep·tive /,kɑntrə'sɛptɪv/ n.adj. a device or drug such as a condom, diaphragm, or pill used to prevent pregnancy (making babies): *She takes the pill, which is an oral <n.> contraceptive.*

con·tract (1) /'kɑn,trækt/ n. an agreement, usu. written and signed by those making it: *I signed a contract for the purchase of a new car.*
—v. **1** to make a written agreement: *I contracted for delivery of a new car.* **2 to contract out:** to have work done for a business outside that business: *They contract out their accounting to an outside accounting firm.* See: to outsource.

con·tract (2) /kən'trækt/ v. **1** to become smaller: *When you bend your arms, your mus-*cles contract. **2** frml. to develop or catch a disease: *He contracted tuberculosis.*

con·trac·tion /kən'trækʃən/ n. **1** a shortened word or words, as in "can't" for "cannot" and "I'm" for "I am": *Contractions are common in spoken English.* **2** a pain, often muscular, esp. starting the birth of a baby, (syn.) spasm: *Elaine is having contractions every two minutes.* **3** [U] the act of contracting, as a muscle

con·trac·tor /'kɑn,træktər/ n. a business or person who agrees to do s.t. under contract, esp. a builder: *He is a contractor who builds small houses.*

con·trac·tu·al /kən'træktʃuəl/ adj. related to a contract: *Our business has a contractual agreement with a company to provide us with office supplies.*

con·tra·dict /,kɑntrə'dɪkt/ v. **1** to tell s.o. what he or she says isn't true, (syn.) to dispute: *They contradict each other all the time: when he says, "It's white," she says, "It's black."* **2** to be different, (syn.) to disagree: *The police report about the crime contradicts what a witness says about it.* -n. [C;U] **contradiction;** -adj. **contradictory** /,kɑntrə'dɪktəri/.

con·tral·to /kən'træltoʊ/ n. **-tos** adj. the lowest level of a woman's voice, below soprano, (syn.) alto: *She is a <n.> contralto in the singing group.*

con·trap·tion /kən'træpʃən/ n. a device put together in a strange or awkward way: *He made a fan to cool himself out of a car battery tied to some old wires; it was quite a contraption, but it worked well.*

con·trar·y /'kɑn,trɛri/ adj. **1** different from, opposite: *He holds an opinion contrary to mine.* **2** /'kɑn,trɛri, kən'trɛri/ difficult, uncooperative: *She has a contrary attitude and disagrees with everything that you say.*
—n. **on the contrary:** the opposite of what has been said: *"You hate jazz." "On the contrary, I love it."* -n. (person) **contrarian** /kən'trɛriən/; [U] (attitude) **contrariness.**

con·trast /'kɑn,træst/ n. **1** [C] a difference in color or meaning: *The photograph has good contrast between the blue lake and green hills.||There is a big contrast between what that man says and what he does.* **2** [U] a comparison between two objects, etc., which shows a difference: *Her work shows the contrast between the artist's early and late works.*
—v. /kən'træst, 'kɑn,træst/ to differ in color or meaning: *The blue and gold colors in the painting contrast beautifully with each other.*

con·tra·vene /,kɑntrə'vin/ v.frml. **-vened, -vening, -venes** to cancel or violate: *The general contravened the captain's order to attack.* -n. [C;U] **contravention** /,kɑntrə'vɛnʃən/.

con·trib·ute /kən'trɪbyut, -yət/ v. **-uted, -uting, -utes 1** to give, (syn.) to donate (money, one's time, etc.): *She contributes* *money to her church.* **2** to participate positively in s.t.: *Everyone on the team contributed to winning the game.* -*n.* **contributor.**

con·tri·bu·tion /ˌkɑntrəˈbyuʃən/ *n.* [C;U] **1** a giving of money, one's time, etc., (*syn.*) donation: *That rich man makes big contributions to charity.* **2** positive or helpful participation: *She made an important contribution to the company's success.*

con·trib·u·to·ry /kənˈtrɪbyəˌtɔri/ *adj.* **1** involving or requiring a contribution: *Our company has a contributory health plan where each employee must pay 20 percent of the cost.* **2** helping to make s.t. happen: *Bad weather was a contributory factor in the accident.*

con·trite /kənˈtraɪt, ˈkɑnˌtraɪt/ *adj.frml.* feeling sorry for having done s.t. hurtful or bad: *The boy was contrite after he broke the lamp.* -*adv.* **contritely;** -*n.* [U] **contrition** /kənˈtrɪʃən/.

con·trive /kənˈtraɪv/ *v.* -**trived, -triving, -trives** **1** to plan or act with evil intent: *He contrived a plan to cheat people out of their money.* **2** to make s.t. up that is not true: *Then, he contrived excuses for why the money had disappeared.* **3** to manage to do s.t., often by cleverness or scheming: *She somehow contrived to get tickets to the Academy Awards.*

con·trol /kənˈtroʊl/ *n.* **1** [U] the power and authority to decide or tell others what to do: *The owner has control over* (or) *of the company.* **2** [C] a device used to guide a vehicle or aircraft: *The pilot is at the controls of the airplane.* **3** **in control: a.** in charge: *She is in control of the company.* **b.** managing one's behavior: *She gets upset, but keeps her anger in* (or) *under control.* **4 out of control: a.** behaving badly: *The airplane went out of control and crashed.*‖*When he gets angry, he gets out of control.* **b.** not in one's authority or power: *After that package is put on a truck, when it is delivered is out of my control.* **5 (to get, have, or keep) under control:** to manage s.t. properly: *The pilot kept the plane under control during the storm.* **6 to take control:** to put oneself in power or authority: *The military took control of the government.*
—*v.* **-trolled, -trolling, -trols** **1** to have power or authority: *Mr. Shin controls the company, but he cannot control his anger.* **2** to guide s.t.: *The pilot controls the airplane from the cockpit.* -*adj.* **controllable.**

con·trol·ler /kənˈtroʊlər/ *n.* **1** the chief accountant in a business *See:* comptroller. **2** a person who directs or controls s.t.: *He works as an air-traffic controller.*

control tower *n.* the building in an airport where air traffic is routed in and out of the airport: *The people who work in a control tower pay close attention to where each airplane is located.*

con·tro·ver·sial /ˌkɑntrəˈvɛrʃəl/ *adj.* causing disagreement: *Religion and politics are very personal and controversial subjects.*

con·tro·ver·sy /ˈkɑntrəˌvɛrsi/ *n.* [C;U] **-sies** public disagreement, usu. involving strong opinions and an important subject: *There is a lot of controversy about the effect on children of violence on television.* -*v.* **controvert** /ˈkɑntrəˌvɜrt, ˌkɑntrəˈvɜrt/.

con·va·les·cence /ˌkɑnvəˈlɛsəns/ *n.* [C, *usu.* used in the sing.; U] a time of rest to recover from an illness, (*syn.*) recuperation: *After his heart attack, he went through a long convalescence at home.* -*v.* **convalesce;** -*adj. n.* **convalescent.**

con·vec·tion /kənˈvɛkʃən/ *adj.n.* [U] the transfer of heat in the air or in a liquid: *My new <adj.> convection oven cooks food much faster than my old one because it has a fan that circulates the heat.*

con·vene /kənˈvin/ *v.frml.* **-vened, -vening, -venes** to call (or) gather together for a meeting: *The manager convened the committee members at 9:00 A.M.* ‖*The committee members convened for a meeting at 9:00 A.M.*

con·ven·ience /kənˈvinyəns/ *n.* **1** [U] a situation suitable to one's time or needs: *She has the convenience of being able to walk to work.* **2 at your convenience:** at a time and place suitable to you: *We can meet at your convenience any time next week.* **3** [C] s.t. useful that helps make life more comfortable, such as a household appliance: *The apartment has a microwave oven, a dishwasher, and other modern conveniences. See:* inconvenience.

convenience store *n.* a store that stays open late into the evening for the convenience of its customers: *That convenience store sells beer and cigarettes as well as basic groceries, like bread and milk.*

con·ven·ient /kənˈvinyənt/ *adj.* **1** acceptable and suitable to one's time or needs: *Is it convenient that I meet you in your office at noon today?* **2** easy and comfortable to do or get to: *We live in a neighborhood that is convenient to the stores and subway. See:* inconvenient. -*adv.* **conveniently**

con·vent /ˈkɑnˌvɛnt, -vənt/ *n.* **1** a group of unmarried religious women (nuns) who live and often work together: *She belongs to the Convent of the Sacred Heart.* **2** the building(s) where nuns live and often work

con·ven·tion /kənˈvɛnʃən/ *n.* **1** [C] a gathering of people of similar interests who listen to speakers: *We always go to the yearly convention of English teachers at a big hotel.* **2** [C;U] rule of behavior, a standard custom: *Guests observe the conventions at parties by always speaking first with the person(s) giving the party.* **3** [C] a formal agreement among countries: *Countries agreed in the Geneva*

C

Conventions on how prisoners of war should be treated.

con·ven·tion·al /kən'vɛnʃənəl/ *adj.* based on or conforming to accepted ways of doing things, (*syn.*) traditional: *People give conventional greetings to each other, like, "Hi, how are you?"*
—*adv.* **conventionally.**

con·verge /kən'vɜrdʒ/ *v.* **-verged, -verging, -verges** to meet at a common point: *On hot days, people converge on the beach to cool off.* *-adj.* **convergent.**

con·ver·sant /kən'vɜrsənt/ *adj.frml.* to be familiar with s.t.: *He is very conversant with computers and can answer any questions you may have.*

con·ver·sa·tion /,kɑnvər'seɪʃən/ *n.* [C;U] **1** a talk: *I had a conversation about the party with my friend.* **2 to make conversation:** to talk to be friendly and polite: *While waiting at the bus stop, I made conversation with a stranger about the weather.* *-adj.* **conversational.**

con·verse /kən'vɜrs/ *v.frml.* **-versed, -versing, -verses** to talk: *Two officials conversed about their government's interests.*

con·ver·sion /kən'vɜrʒən, -ʃən/ *n.* [C;U] a change from one condition or status to another: *The conversion of that hotel to an apartment building required a lot of construction work.‖They were upset by their son's conversion to another religion.*

con·vert /kən'vɜrt/ *v.* to change the condition or status of s.t.: *The owner converted the hotel into an apartment building.‖He wants to convert to Catholicism.*
—*n.* /'kɑn,vɜrt/ a person who changes status, esp. religions: *He is a convert to Buddhism.*

con·vert·i·ble /kən'vɜrtəbəl/ *adj.* capable of being changed from one form to another: *That bond is convertible into common stock.*
—*n.* a car that has a top that can be rolled or folded down

con·vex /,kɑn'vɛks, kən-/ *adj.* curved outward: *The outside surfaces of my eyeglasses are convex, and the insides are concave.*

con·vey /kən'veɪ/ *v.frml.* **1** to carry from one place to another: *A messenger conveyed a message from the king to his nobles.* **2** (legal) to transfer: *to convey ownership of property from one person to another* *-n.* [C] **conveyance.**

con·vict /kən'vɪkt/ *v.* to find s.o. guilty of a crime in a court of law: *He was convicted of murder.*
—*n.* /'kɑn,vɪkt/ a person sentenced to jail for a crime, (*syn.*) a prisoner: *The police are searching the area for an escaped convict.*

con·vic·tion /kən'vɪkʃən/ *n.* **1** [C] the act of finding s.o. guilty in a court of law for committing a crime: *He received a murder conviction from the jury.* **2** [C;U] a strong belief: *She*

has strong convictions about being honest and working hard.

con·vince /kən'vɪns/ *v.* **-vinced, -vincing, -vinces** to cause s.o. to believe s.t. is worth doing or true, (*syn.*) to persuade: *The young man convinced the beautiful woman to marry him.‖He convinced her that he loves her.*

con·viv·i·al /kən'vɪviəl/ *adj.frml.* friendly, cheerful: *During the holidays, people are in a convivial mood.*

con·vo·ca·tion /,kɑnvə'keɪʃən/ *n.* [C] a formal calling together: *The priest spoke at a convocation of church members, opening with a prayer.* *-v.frml.* **convoke** /kən'voʊk/.

con·vo·lut·ed /'kɑnvə,lutɪd/ *adj.* **1** twisted in form, (*syns.*) coiled, like a snake **2** difficult to understand, complex: *That lawyer presented a convoluted argument to the judge, who rejected it.* *-n.* [C] **convolution** /,kɑnvə'luʃən/.

con·voy /'kɑn,vɔɪ/ *n.* an organized group or formation, esp. of ships or trucks: *When we drove from San Diego to Phoenix, we passed a convoy of trucks on the highway.*

con·vul·sion /kən'vʌlʃən/ *n.*, usu. used in the *pl.* a violent movement of the body, (*syn.*) a spasm: *He began to choke and went into convulsions.* *-v.* **convulse** /kən'vʌls/; *-adj.* **convulsive.**

coo /ku/ *n.* a soft sound made by pigeons and doves
—*v.* **1** to make such a sound **2** *fig.* to talk in a soft, breathy way, usu. about love: *The man and woman cooed about their love for each other.*

cook /kʊk/ *v.* to prepare food either cold or by heating it in various ways (frying, boiling, etc.): *She cooks dinner for us every evening.* **2** *infrml.* **to cook s.o.'s goose:** to ruin s.o.: *First, he lost a lot of money in the stock market, and then when his house burned down, that really cooked his goose.* **3** *phrasal v. sep.* **to cook s.t. up:** to cheat, (*syn.*) to scheme: *That man is so tricky that he's cooking up a plan to give us trouble.‖He's cooking it up.* **4** *slang* **to cook the books:** to enter false numbers in a company's accounting records: *The owner cooked the books to give the impression that the company has made no profit.*
—*n.* a person who prepares and cooks food: *My mother is a terrific cook!*

cook·book /'kʊk,bʊk/ *n.* a book of recipes for preparing food to eat: *I looked in the cookbook for a recipe for apple pie.*

cook·ie /'kʊki/ *n.* a small, flat, sweet, often crisp cake: *I like chocolate-chip cookies.*

cook·ing /'kʊkɪŋ/ *n.* the art and practice of preparing and cooking food: *She studied cooking in Paris.*

cook·out /'kʊkaʊt/ *n.* a meal prepared and eaten outside with a group of people, often including hamburgers, hot dogs, and potato salad: *On Labor Day, we have a cookout for friends and family in our back yard; we grill hamburgers and hot dogs, and then eat watermelon for dessert. See:* barbecue.

—*v.* **to cook out:** to prepare a meal outside: *If the weather is good tonight, we can cook out on the back porch. See:* barbecue, USAGE NOTES.

cool /kul/ *adj.* **1** neither warm nor very cold, but more cold than hot: *San Francisco has a cool climate.* **2** calm, composed: *My boss never gets nervous or upset; she has a cool manner.* **3** not friendly: *He made a cool reply to a question.* **4** *slang* excellent, admirable: *He's a cool guy!*
—*n.* **1** one's calm, (*syn.*) composure **2 to keep one's cool:** to stay calm, (*syn.*) to remain unruffled: *The house was on fire, but the mother kept her cool and led her kids to safety.*
—*v.* **1** to lose or take away heat, (*syn.*) to chill: *The beer is cooling in the refrigerator.* **2** to become unfriendly, distant: *Relations between the two countries cooled.* **3** *slang* **Cool it:** to stop or calm down: *Cool it! Stop shouting for a second while I explain!* **4** *phrasal v.* **to cool down** or **off: a.** to stop sweating: *Let's go for a swim and cool off.* **b.** to calm down: *Two men in a bar argued, and the bartender told them to go outside and cool off. See:* coolheaded.

USAGE NOTE: Americans of all ages understand the word *cool* when it means very good. Sometimes people use cool to respond to good news: *"I bought a new album of music by your favorite band." "Cool!"* Cool also describes a thing: *He was wearing a really cool T-shirt.* Cool can also refer to a person's behavior: *My dad was really cool when I wrecked the car. Instead of yelling at me, he hugged me and said he was glad I was safe.*

---

cool·er /'kulər/ *n.* a container with ice for cooling food and beverages: *The beer is in the cooler.*

cool-head·ed /'kul'hɛdɪd/ *adj.* calm and able to think or work under pressure: *She works in a hospital emergency room, but she always stays cool-headed.*

coop /kup/ *n.* **1** a small house for chickens and small animals: *Seven chickens live in the chicken coop on my farm.* **2** a small uncomfortable place **3** *fig.* **to fly the coop:** to leave hurriedly or escape—*phrasal v. sep.* **to coop s.o.** or **s.t. up:** to enclose or limit s.o. or s.t., to feel uncomfortable in a small place: *The bad snowstorm had us cooped up in a small apartment for three days.*

co-op /'kou,ap/ *n.adj.* short for cooperative: *She owns a <n.> co-op (or) a <adj.> co-op apartment.*

co·op·er·ate /kou'apə,reɪt/ *v.* **-ated, -ating, -ates** to agree to help s.o. toward a common goal, (*syn.*) to collaborate: *The two workers cooperated with each other to fix the broken pipe.*

co·op·er·a·tion /kou,apə'reɪʃən/ *n.* [U] the act of working with s.o. toward a common goal: *It takes cooperation between employees to make a business run well.*

co·op·er·a·tive /kou'aprətɪv, -'apərə-/ *adj.* willing to do what is needed or being asked: *He has a cooperative attitude.*
—*n.* **1** an apartment building owned by the people who live there: *She owns a two-bedroom cooperative. See:* co-op. **2** a business owned jointly with others: *I have five cousins in Wisconsin who have formed a farm cooperative; their five small farms are now one big farm.*

co-opt /kou'apt, 'kou,apt/ *v.* **1** to take control of s.t. from s.o. else: *The president gradually co-opted the power of the vice president.* **2** to put s.o. on a committee without electing that person, (*syn.*) to appoint s.o.

co·or·di·nate /kou'ɔrdneɪt/ *v.* **-nated, -nating, -nates 1** to bring together various people and activities for a common purpose: *She coordinated a research project by telling each scientist what to do and sharing the results with all of them.* **2** to harmonize: *We coordinated the colors of wall paint and furniture in our living room.*
—*n.* /kou'ɔrdnɪt/ a point of location on a map or graph: *The teacher asked us to find the coordinates of Iceland on a map.* -*n.* **coordinator.**

co·or·di·na·tion /kou,ɔrdn'eɪʃən/ *n.* [U] **1** the act of making arrangements for a purpose: *The coordination of that project is done by the teacher.* **2** harmony of various elements **3** the ability to move the body well, basic athletic ability: *Baseball players need to have good coordination; their eyes, arms, and legs need to work together.*

coot /kut/ *n.* **1** a gray ducklike waterbird of North America and Europe **2** *pej.* a foolish, stupid, or senile person, esp. a man: *That old coot forgets where he lives.*

coo·tie /'kuti/ *n.slang* a blood-sucking insect, a louse: *Don't put his hat on your head because it will give you cooties.*

cop /kap/ *n.slang* a police officer: *After he hit me, I called the cops to come get him.*
—*v.slang* **copped, copping, cops 1** to steal s.t. **2** *phrasal v.* **to cop out:** to agree to do s.t., then not do it: *He promised to help us with the work, but didn't show up, so he copped out on us. See:* cop-out.
—*v.* **to cop a plea:** (in law) to plead guilty to a lesser charge to be free of a more severe one:

He copped a plea, so the judge let him off with a small fine.

co·pa·cet·ic /ˌkoʊpə'sɛtɪk/ *adj.slang* excellent, in good shape: *"How are things going? Great! Everything is copacetic."*

cope /koʊp/ *v.* **coped, coping, copes** to face difficulties and try to overcome them: *He coped with the pain of cancer and finally got well again.*

cop·i·er /'kɑpiər/ *n.* a machine used to make copies of s.t., a photocopier: *The copier in our office gets heavy use. See:* Xerox.

co·pi·lot /'koʊˌpaɪlət/ *n.* the second pilot on an airplane

co·pi·ous /'koʊpiəs/ *adj.frml.* many, much, (*syn.*) abundant: *She took copious notes of the professor's lecture.*

cop-out /'kɑpˌaʊt/ *n.slang* a weak excuse: *What a cop-out! He promised to help us in the office, but then he called in sick. See:* to cop out.

cop·per /'kɑpər/ *n.* [U] **1** a brownish red metal and basic chemical element: *The pipes in that building are made of copper.* **2** *slang* a police officer *See:* cop.
—*adj.* related to or made of copper: *a copper mine\\a copper kettle*

cop·per·head /'kɑpərˌhɛd/ *n.* a brown poisonous snake of North America

cop·ter /'kɑptər/ *n. short for* helicopter

cop·u·late /'kɑpyəˌleɪt/ *v.frml.* **-lated, -lating, -lates** to perform sexual intercourse: *Animals copulate during their mating seasons.* -*n.* [U] **copulation** /ˌkɑpyə'leɪʃən/.

cop·y /'kɑpi/ *n.* **-ies 1** [C] a duplicate of s.t., esp. a photocopy: *I made three copies of my report on the copy machine.* **2** [C] an imitation of s.t., esp. a fake: *What a mistake! That museum paid $1,000,000 for a copy of a painting by Monet; the museum thought that the painting was an original.* **3** one of a number of identical books, magazines, newspapers, etc.: *This book has sold over 50,000 copies.* **4** [U] material to be printed: *She sent her copy to the editor. See:* cc, USAGE NOTE.
—*v.* **-ied, -ying, -ies 1** to duplicate s.t.: *I copied into my notebook what the teacher said.* **2** to imitate s.t.: *The art student copied a great painting for practice.* **3** to steal someone else's written work, (*syn.*) to plagiarize: *The student copied part of his paper from a textbook and did not credit the author.* **4 to copy down:** to write down: *Students copy down what professors say and write in class.*

cop·y·right /'kɑpiˌraɪt/ *n.* [C;U] **1** ownership of written or visual material (books, music, paintings) by authors, composers, and painters **2** an act of registering the copyright: *Publishers register their copyrights with the US Library of Congress in Washington, D.C.*

—*v.* to register a copyright under protection of the copyright laws

co·quette /koʊ'kɛt/ *n.* a girl or woman who teases men with sexual talk and facial expressions: *That coquette makes eyes at men.*

cor·al /'kɔrəl, 'kɑr-/ *n.* [U] a type of brightly colored stone made of tiny sea animals, used in making jewelry: *My sister has a coral necklace.*
—*adj.* having a reddish-pink color

cord /kɔrd/ *n.v.* **1** [C;U] strong string or rope: *I tied the package with some <n.> cord.* **2** a pile of wood measuring 4 x 4 x 8 feet: *She bought a <n.> cord of wood for use in her fireplace.*

cor·dial /'kɔrdʒəl/ *adj.* warm, friendly: *Everyone at the party was cordial to each other.*
—*n.* an alcoholic drink, such as fruit brandy or sweet sherry: *We had a cordial before dinner.* -*n.* [U] **cordiality** /ˌkɔrdʒi'æləti, kɔr'dʒæ-/; -*adj.* **cordially.**

cord·less /'kɔrdlɪs/ *adj.* being a device powered by batteries: *When I talk on my cordless telephone, I can walk around my house.*

cor·don /'kɔrdn/ *n.* a line of police, soldiers, etc., placed around an area as protection: *There was a cordon of police between the protestors and the museum entrance.*
—*phrasal v. sep.* **to cordon s.t. off:** to enclose an area: *The soldiers cordoned off the military base.\\They cordoned it off.*

cor·du·roy /'kɔrdəˌrɔɪ/ *n.adj.* [U] strong, thick cloth with soft raised lines, used to make pants, jackets, and suits: *Those <adj.> corduroy pants will last for years.*

core /kɔr/ *n.* **1** the hard center of some fruits, containing the seeds: *an apple core* **2** the center of anything: *a computer's memory core* **3** the most important part of s.t.: *At the core of the problem is the fact that the company needs a bank loan to grow.* **4 rotten to the core:** totally corrupt, bad: *He lies, steals, and is rotten to the core.*
—*v.* **cored, coring, cores** to remove a core: *I cored some apples to make an apple pie.*

cork /kɔrk/ *n.v.* a bottle stopper: *The waiter pulled the <n.> cork out of the wine bottle.*

cork·screw /'kɔrkˌskru/ *n.* a device with a twisting metal piece that ends in a point, used to pull a cork out of a bottle

cor·mo·rant /'kɔrmərənt, -ˌrænt/ *n.* a large black seabird with a long neck: *Fishermen can train cormorants to catch fish for them.*

corn (1) /kɔrn/ *n.* in the USA, a tall green plant with large, yellow seeds on long ears, fed to cattle or eaten cooked by people

corn (2) *n.* a hard growth mainly on top of the toe(s): *Corns can hurt when you walk.*

corn·ball /'kɔrnˌbɔl/ *adj.infrml.* intended to be funny, but instead seeming unsophisticated or boring, (*syn.*) corny: *Many New Yorkers dislike cornball humor.*

corn·bread /'kɔrn,brɛd/ *n.* a type of sweet cake made of ground corn (cornmeal): *He likes cornbread and coffee for breakfast.*

cor·ne·a /'kɔrniə/ *n.* the outer covering lens of the eye: *She had an operation on her corneas and can see better now.*

cor·ner /'kɔrnər/ *n.* the area where two streets, walls, etc., meet: *I will meet you on the corner of Main St. and 3rd Ave. at noon.*
—*v.* to force s.o. or s.t. into a position from which escape is impossible: *The police chased a criminal down a narrow street and cornered him so he could not escape.*

cor·ner·stone /'kɔrnər,stoun/ *n.* **1** a stone placed in the corner of a building with its date of completion **2** *fig.* the centerpiece or foundation of s.t.: *The cornerstone of the President's plan is a tax cut for everyone.*

cor·net /kɔr'nɛt/ *n.* a type of trumpet: *The famous jazzman Dizzy Gillespie played the cornet.*

corn·flakes /'kɔrn,fleɪks/ *n.pl.* breakfast cereal made from corn cooked into dry flakes: *He eats cornflakes with milk and sugar every morning.*

cor·nice /'kɔrnɪs/ *n.* the decorative top of a building or wall: *The cornices in my room are made of carved wood.*

corn·meal /'kɔrn,mil/ *n.adj.* [U] coarsely ground corn: *I had a yellow <adj.> cornmeal muffin and some coffee for breakfast.*

corn·row /'kɔrn,rou/ *n.* a narrow braid of hair
—*v.* to arrange the hair in rows of narrow braids close to the head: *Many Jamaicans cornrow their hair.*

corn·stalk /'kɔrn,stɔk/ *n.* the long narrow (stem) part of a corn plant: *Farmers cut down cornstalks to feed cattle.*

corn·starch /'kɔrn,stɑrtʃ/ *n.* [U] a white, tasteless powder made from corn and used in cooking: *She put some cornstarch in the gravy to make it thicker.*

cor·nu·co·pi·a /,kɔrnə'koupiə/ *n.* **1** a horn-shaped basket flowing over with good things to eat, used as a symbol for good times, prosperity **2** a large supply, (*syn.*) abundance: *American farmers grow a cornucopia of food for people.*

corn·y /'kɔrni/ *adj.* **-ier, -iest** too obvious, old-fashioned, or unsophisticated to be effective, esp. relating to jokes that are meant to be funny but are not: *He tells corny jokes and bores everyone.*

cor·ol·lar·y /'kɔrə,lɛri, 'kɑr-/ *n.* **-ies** an expected result or outcome of s.t.: *Disease is a corollary of poverty.*

cor·o·nar·y /'kɔrə,nɛri, 'kɑr-/ *adj.* related to arteries and veins of the heart: *a blocked coronary artery*
—*n.* **-ies** a heart attack, (*syn.*) a coronary thrombosis: *He was taking the train home from work and had a coronary.*

cor·o·na·tion /,kɔrə'neɪʃən, ,kɑr-/ *n.* the ceremony of crowning a king or queen: *When Princess Elizabeth became Queen Elizabeth II, England celebrated her coronation.*

cor·o·ner /'kɔrənər, 'kɑr-/ *n.* the city or town official who investigates suspicious deaths for possible murder

cor·po·ral (1) /'kɔrpərəl, -prəl/ *adj.frml.* related to the body, not the spirit: *In the USA it is against the law to use corporal punishment in schools.*

corporal (2) *n.* an officer in the US Army or Marine Corps ranking below a sergeant

cor·po·rate /'kɔrprɪt, -pərɪt/ *adj.* related to a business, esp. one that is incorporated: *The owner opened a corporate checking account at the bank.*

cor·po·ra·tion /,kɔrpə'reɪʃən/ *n.* a business with a legal status (incorporated) where the assets and debts belong to shareholders who are not responsible for them beyond the value of their stock: *When a corporation becomes bankrupt, its stock is of no value anymore.*

corps /kɔr/ *n.* [C] **corps** /kɔrz/ an organized and usu. highly trained group: *The Marine Corps is trained to fight.*‖*A fife and drum corps makes music. See:* esprit de corps.

corpse /kɔrps/ *n.* a lifeless human body (as opposed to a carcass of an animal), (*syn.*) a cadaver: *The murder victim's corpse lay in the street.*

cor·pu·lent /'kɔrpyələnt/ *adj.frml.* fat, very overweight: *He weighs 350 lbs; he is so corpulent that he can hardly walk. -n.* [U] **corpulence.**

cor·pus /'kɔrpəs/ *n. frml.* [C] **-pora** /-pərə/ or **-puses** a body of written work: *There is a large corpus of literature on medicine.*

cor·pus·cle /'kɔrpəsəl,-,pʌ-/ *n.* [C] a red or white blood cell: *White corpuscles in the blood kill germs.*

cor·ral /kə'ræl/ *n.* an area with a fence around it to keep horses, cattle, etc., inside: *Cowboys leave their horses in the corral after work.*

cor·rect /kə'rɛkt/ *v.* **1** to make s.t. accurate: *The teacher corrected the student's spelling mistake.* **2** to change s.o.'s or one's own behavior to the right way: *He was lazy and irresponsible, but two weeks in army camp corrected his behavior.*
—*adj.* **1** accurate: *The student gave the correct answer to the question.* **2** honest, proper: *She found the man's wallet and returned it to him because that is the correct thing to do.*

-*adj.* **corrective;** -*adv.* **correctly;** -*n.* **correctness.**

cor·rec·tion /kəˈrɛkʃən/ *n.* **1** a change made to correct a mistake: *I spelled that word incorrectly, but have made the correction now.* **2** an adjustment: *The ship made a correction in its course.||The stock market made a correction by dropping 100 points.*

cor·re·late /ˈkɔrəˌleɪt, ˈkɑr-/ *v.* **-lated, -lating, -lates** to show or see how one thing relates meaningfully to another: *We can correlate the increase in profits to the increase in our sales.*

cor·re·la·tion /ˌkɔrəˈleɪʃən, ˌkɑr-/ *n.* a meaningful connection between things: *There is a direct correlation between an increase in sales volume and an increase in profits.*

cor·re·spond /ˌkɔrəˈspand, ˌkɑr-/ *v.* to write to s.o.: *I correspond regularly with a friend in Seoul.* **2** to agree, match: *The article in the newspaper does not correspond to what the politician actually said.*

cor·re·spon·dence /ˌkɔrəˈspandəns, ˌkɑr-/ *n.* **1** [U] letters or E-mail sent between people: *She answers the correspondence from her customers every day.* **2** [C] an agreement, matching: *There is a correspondence between spending less money and being able to save more.*

cor·re·spon·dent /ˌkɔrəˈspandənt, kɑr-/ *n.* **1** a reporter for a publication or TV: *The news report was made by the TV's correspondent in Rio de Janeiro.* **2** a business that cooperates with another located elsewhere: *The Bank of New York has a correspondent in Tokyo.* **3** a person to whom you write letters: *My correspondent in Chicago is named Talani Smith.* —*adj.* related to s.t., corresponding: *An increase in the amount of time that you study brings a correspondent* (or) *corresponding improvement in your grades.*

cor·ri·dor /ˈkɔrədər, -ˌdɔr, ˈkɑr-/ *n.* a hallway: *That corridor leads to the classrooms.*

cor·rob·o·rate /kəˈrabəˌreɪt/ *v.frml.* **-rated, -rating, -rates** to indicate s.t. that another person said is true: *A witness to the robbery corroborated the victim's description of what happened.* -*n.* [U] **corroboration** /kəˌrabəˈreɪʃən/.

cor·ro·sive /kəˈrousɪv/ *adj.* **1** wearing away by chemical action: *The corrosive effect of air pollution on great buildings and statues eventually turns them to powder.* **2** *fig.* having a negative attitude, (*syn.*) abrasive -*v.* **corrode** /kəˈroud/; -*n.* [U] **corrosion** /kəˈrouʒən/.

cor·ru·gat·ed /ˈkɔrəˌgeɪtɪd, ˈkɑr-/ *adj.* having a wavy surface: *Corrugated boxes are stronger than others.*

cor·rupt /kəˈrʌpt/ *adj.* dishonest: *That official is corrupt because he takes bribes.* —*v.* **1** to make dishonest: *He corrupts everyone around him.* **2** to change s.t. to a bad state

or wrong purpose, (*syn.*) to pervert: *The French are very concerned that their language is being corrupted by the use of foreign words.* -*adj.* **corruptible;** -*n.* [U] **corruption.**

cor·sage /kɔrˈsaʒ, -ˈsadʒ/ *n.* a flower or small group of flowers worn by a woman on special occasions

cor·set /ˈkɔrsɪt/ *n.v.* an old-fashioned, tight-fitting undergarment, worn esp. by women, to shape and support the hips and stomach: *She wears a <n.> corset every day.*

co·sign /ˈkouˌsaɪn/ *v.* to add one's signature to, and guarantee one's responsibility for, a contract, loan, or check signed by s.o. else: *My daughter wanted to buy a car, so I cosigned her bank loan to guarantee that I would repay the loan if she could not.* -*n.* **cosigner.**

cos·met·ic /kazˈmɛtɪk/ *n.* a beauty preparation, like makeup, lipstick, and skin cream, used on the body, esp. on the face: *She likes European brands of cosmetics.* —*adj.* **1** meant to hide s.t., (*syn.*) superficial: *The wooden house was rotting, but the owner gave it a cosmetic coat of paint in order to sell it.* **2** related to improving one's appearance: *He had cosmetic surgery done to straighten his nose.*

cos·me·tol·o·gy /ˌkazməˈtaladʒi/ *n.* [U] the art and science of beauty care, including hair dressing, manicuring, and skin care

cos·mic /ˈkazmɪk/ *adj.* throughout the universe (cosmos), universal: *An exploding star is a cosmic event.*

cos·mo·naut /ˈkazməˌnɔt/ *n.* an astronaut, esp. a Russian: *Russian cosmonauts were the first people in space.*

cos·mo·pol·i·tan /ˌkazməˈpulətn/ *adj.* from or of many parts of the world, (*syn.*) international: *Hong Kong is a cosmopolitan city with people from all over the world.* —*n.* [C] a sophisticated person who is comfortable anywhere: *She is a cosmopolitan who speaks seven languages and has apartments in several foreign cities.*

cos·mos /ˈkazməs, -ˌmous/ *n.* **the cosmos** all space, stars, planets, etc., (*syn.*) the universe: *Astronomers study the cosmos.*

cost /kɔst/ *n.* **1** the price of s.t.: *What is the cost of a loaf of bread in Vancouver?* **2** *usu. used in the sing.* the sacrifice of time, effort, or hurt of s.t.: *That terrible war was won at a cost of 50 million lives.* **3 at all costs:** regardless of the money or sacrifice involved: *We must rescue those lost sailors at all costs.* —*v.* **cost, costing, costs 1** to have as its price: *That car costs $30,000.* **2** to cause a loss: *That car accident cost five lives.* **3** to figure out a group of costs to find a total cost or price of s.t.

co·star /ˈkouˌstar/ *n.v.* **-starred, -starring, -stars** a star in a movie, play, or concert who is of equal importance to another star: *Meryl*

Streep <v.> costarred with Clint Eastwood in "The Bridges of Madison County."

cost-benefit analysis *n.phr.* the cost of goods or services in comparison to the money and/or good will they bring to a business: *We did a cost-benefit analysis on building new offices compared with refurnishing our old ones, and decided to build new ones.*

cost-effective *adj.* worth its cost (goods and services): *We found that building a new building was more cost-effective than fixing up the old one.*

cost·ly /ˈkɔstli/ *adj.* **-lier, -liest 1** expensive: *Their dinner was costly but delicious.* **2** hurtful in time, effort, money, or pain: *That was a costly mistake.* *-n.* [U] **costliness.**

cost of living *n.* the cost of necessities of life, such as food, housing, clothes, transportation, etc.: *The cost of living in cities like New York, Paris, and Tokyo is very high.*

cost-of-living adjustment *n.* an increase in wages or retirement payments based on the increase in the cost of living: *I got a 4% COLA in my salary this year.* *-abbr.* **COLA** /ˈkoʊlə/

cost-of-living index *n.* (in USA) a measurement by the government each year of the cost-of-living: *The cost-of-living index went up 5% this year.*

cos·tume /ˈkɑs,tum/ *n.v.* **-tumed, -tuming, -tumes** a style of clothes worn esp. by an actor or for entertainment: *We went to a Halloween party where everyone wore historical <n.> costumes.*

cot /kɑt/ *n.* a simple bed that usu. can be folded up and moved easily: *I took a cot out of the closet for my friend to sleep on.*

cot

cot·tage /ˈkɑtɪdʒ/ *n.* a small, simple house usu. in the country: *She lives in a cottage by the lake.*

cottage cheese *n.* [U] a soft, white cheese made of sour milk: *He had cottage cheese and fruit for lunch.*

cottage industry *n.* **-tries** work that can be done at home, such as typing, knitting, etc.: *Making clay pots is a cottage industry in that small town.*

cot·ton /ˈkɑtn/ *n.* [U] **1** a plant whose seeds are covered with soft, white fiber that is made into thread and cloth **2** cloth made from this fiber: *His shirts are made of cotton.* *—phrasal v. insep.* **to cotton to s.o. or s.t.:** to like s.o. or s.t.: *Cowboys cotton to cowgirls.*

cot·ton-pick·ing /ˈkɑtn,pɪkən, -,pɪkɪŋ/ *adj.infrml.* no good, unwanted: *Keep your cotton-picking hands off my money!*

cot·ton·tail /ˈkɑtn,teɪl/ *n.* a rabbit with a short white tail: *Cottontails live in the western USA.*

cot·ton·wood /ˈkɑtn,wʊd/ *n.* a tree with white cotton-like seeds: *Cottonwoods grow by rivers and streams.*

couch /kaʊtʃ/ *n.* **couches** a piece of furniture for sitting or lying on, a sofa: *The couch in our living room is soft and comfortable.* *—v.frml.* **couches** to say s.t. in a certain way, express: *She couched her complaint in a pleasant way.*

couch

cou·gar /ˈkugər/ *n.* a large cat found in mountains of western North, Central, and South America: *Cougars attack sheep and cows.*

cough /kɔf/ *v.* **1** to push air out of the throat suddenly with a sharp sound **2** *phrasal v. sep.* **to cough s.t. up:** *infrml.* to produce s.t. unwillingly: *He had to cough up the money to pay the fine or go to jail.*||*He coughed it up.* *—n.* a pushing of air from the throat because of irritation or sickness: *She has a bad cough from a cold.*

could /kʊd; *weak form* kəd/ *auxiliary v. & past tense of* can **1** used to indicate that s.t. is possible: *The volume was on high so everyone could hear the radio program.* **2** used to make a suggestion or give permission: *You could go to the movie, if you want to.* **3** used to make a request: *Could you pass me the salt and pepper, please? See:* can; may; would.

coun·cil /ˈkaʊnsəl/ *n.* a group of officials or advisors, esp. to a politician: *The city council advises the mayor on what to do.* *-n.* **councilor** /ˈkaʊnslər, -sələr/**.**

coun·sel /ˈkaʊnsəl/ *n.* [U] **1** advice, usu. given by an expert) **2** a lawyer *—v.* (usu. of an expert) to give advice: *My lawyer counseled me not to start a lawsuit over my car accident.*

coun·sel·or or **counsellor** /ˈkaʊnslər, -sələr/ *n.* **1** an advisor: *The school counselor and I talked about which courses I should take.* **2** a lawyer **3** s.o. who takes care of children at a summer camp

count (1) /kaʊnt/ *v.* [C] **1** to add up, calculate: *I counted my suits one by one.* **2** to say numbers in order: *to count to three* **3** to consider, think of: *I count her as one of my best friends.* **4** to be of importance, to matter: *Having money counts because you can't do much without it.* **5** *phrasal v.* **to count down:** to call out numbers from larger to smaller: *He counted down the number of seconds: "...5, 4, 3, 2, 1, blastoff!," until the rocket went up into the sky. See:* countdown. **6** *phrasal v. sep.* **to count s.o. in:** to include: *That concert sounds like fun, so count me in.* **7** *phrasal v.* **to count off:** to

count out loud by groups of one or more: *The students counted off by three to form groups of three people.* **8** *phrasal v. insep.* **to count on** or **upon s.o. or s.t.:** to be sure of, rely on: *You can count on her to do a good job.* **9** *phrasal v.* **to count s.o. or s.t. out: a.** *sep.* **s.o.:** to not participate, exclude: *You can count me out because that deal is too risky.* **b.** *sep.* **s.o.:** (a referee) counting a boxer as knocked out **c.** *insep.* **s.t.:** to call numbers out loud *See:* to count off. **d.** *insep.* **st:** to name amounts of money while giving the money to s.o.: *The bank teller took my $200.00 check and counted out four $50.00 bills.* **e.** to declare that a boxer has lost if he does not get up from the floor before the referee finishes counting to ten **10** *phrasal v. sep.* **to count s.t. up:** to add, calculate: *I counted up all of the employees in the office.║I counted them up.* **11 to stand up and be counted:** to support s.t. strongly: *It is time for everyone to vote, so stand up and be counted!*
—*n.* [C] **1** a total, a sum: *I made a count of all the sweaters I have: 12 to be exact.* **2** a legal charge against s.o.: *She was guilty on all counts.* **3 to keep count:** to note, keep track of: *I must keep count of how many students are in class today.* **4 to lose count:** to not know the exact number: *She's lost count of how many grandchildren she has.* -*adj.* **countable.**

count (2) *n.* a European nobleman ranked above a baron: *The count lives in a large castle.*

count·down /ˈkaʊntˌdaʊn/ *n.* **1** a counting of numbers from higher to lower: *The countdown for a space rocket goes, "... 5, 4, 3, 2, 1, Blastoff!"* **2** the time period and actions just before an important event: *The countdown for the election next Tuesday begins as politicians go on TV for the last time.*

coun·te·nance /ˈkaʊntənəns/ *n.frml.* **1** the face and its expression: *a soldier with an angry countenance* **2** approval
—*v.frml.* **-nanced, -nancing, -nances** to give approval of s.t.: *I will not countenance your stealing that money!*

coun·ter (1) /ˈkaʊntər/ *n.* **1** a flat, table-like surface: *The waiter put my hamburger and cola on the counter in front of me.* **2 over the counter:** referring to s.t. that can be sold without a doctor's prescription: *Aspirin and cold medicine are sold over the counter.* **3 under the counter:** sold or done secretly and often illegally

coun·ter (2) *adv.* **counter to:** against, opposite to: *She acted counter to my wishes by spending the rent money on books.*
—*v.* to react to s.t. or oppose it, (*syn.*) to retaliate: *Senator Jones criticized his opponent, Ms. Smith, who countered with criticism of Jones.*

—*prefix* **1** in response to: *counterattack* **2** similar to: *counterpart* **3** in the opposite direction: *counterclockwise*

count·er (3) *n.* **1** a person who counts **2** a machine used for counting: *A man stands at the door of the disco holding a counter and counts the people who go in.*

coun·ter·act /ˌkaʊntərˈækt/ *v.* to stop or neutralize s.t., esp. with an opposite force: *The doctor counteracted the poison by giving the patient medicine (an antidote).* -*n.*[C;U] **counteraction.**

coun·ter·at·tack /ˈkaʊntərəˌtæk/ *v.n.* to attack an attacker: *When the enemy attacked our army, our soldiers <v.> counterattacked with cannon fire.*

coun·ter·bal·ance /ˈkaʊntərˌbæləns/ *n.* **1** a weight equal to another, (*syn.*) counterweight **2** *fig.* an action, force, or influence equal to another
—*v.* /ˌkaʊntərˈbæləns, ˈkaʊntərˌbæl-/ **-anced, -ancing, -ances** to give a counterbalance: *The President, Congress, and Supreme Court counterbalance each other in sharing the power of the U.S. government.*

coun·ter·claim /ˈkaʊntərˌkleɪm/ *n.v.* an accusation or charge made against s.o. who has made an accusation: *Our company says that a customer owes us money, but that customer makes the <n.> counterclaim that we owe them money. See:* to countersue.

coun·ter·clock·wise /ˌkaʊntərˈklɑkˌwaɪz/ *adv.adj.* moving in the direction opposite to which the hands of a clock move: *I turn my key <adv.> counterclockwise to open my door.*

coun·ter·cul·ture /ˈkaʊntərˌkʌltʃər/ *n.* people who are against the traditional values and lifestyles of most people: *The counterculture of the 1960s rejected the North American desire for money and property. See:* bohemian; hippie.

coun·ter·feit /ˈkaʊntərˌfɪt/ *adj.* fake, false, esp. referring to a copy of s.t., such as money or a work of art: *Counterfeit money in fake $20 bills was found in stores all over the city.*
—*v.* to copy s.t. to deceive: *Criminals counterfeited the $20 bills by printing them secretly* -*n.* **counterfeiter.** *See:* forge.

coun·ter·in·tel·li·gence /ˌkaʊntərɪnˈtɛlədʒəns/ *n.* [U]

coun·ter·move /ˈkaʊntərˌmuv/ *n.v.* **-moved, moving, -moves** a move made to match or defeat an opponent's move: *An unfriendly company tried to buy our company, but our boss made a <n.> countermove by finding a friendly buyer.*

coun·ter·of·fer /ˈkaʊntərˌɔfər, -ˌɑfər/ *n.v.* a different offer made as a response to s.o. else's offer: *I offered to sell my house for $100,000 and the buyer made a <n.> counteroffer of $90,000. See:* counterproposal.

coun·ter·part /'kaʊntər,pɑrt/ *n.* a person or thing that is like another or does the same type of job: *The owner talked with her counterpart, the owner of another company.*

coun·ter·pro·duc·tive /,kaʊntərprə'dʌktɪv/ *adj.* not useful, damaging: *Correcting every mistake students make can be counterproductive by making them nervous.*

coun·ter·pro·pos·al /'kaʊntərprə,poʊzəl/ *n.* a different plan, offer, idea, etc, made in response to one made earlier: *My company offered to buy another company, but they made a counterproposal that we buy some of their products, not their whole company*

coun·ter·sign /'kaʊntər,saɪn/ *v.n.* **1** to sign s.t. again, esp. a check to show that the signature is real: *I signed the check on the front, then with a bank official watching me, I <v.> countersigned it on the back.* **2** to sign a contract, will, etc. signed by s.o. else: *I signed a contract to buy the apartment and the seller <v.> countersigned it.* -*n.* **countersignature** /,kaʊntər'sɪgnətʃər/.

coun·ter·spy /'kaʊntər,spaɪ/ *n.* -**spies** a spy who tries to find and to work against enemy spies.

coun·ter·sue /'kaʊntər,su/ *v.* -**sued, -suing, -sues** (in law) to sue so who has sued (you) first: *An employee sued us for firing him and our company countersued him for stealing our secrets.* -*n.* **countersuit** /'kaʊntər,sut/.

count·ess /'kaʊntɪs/ *n.* -**esses** a noblewoman ranked above a baroness

count·less /'kaʊntlɪs/ *adj.* too many to be counted, without number: *The mother told the child countless times to stop sucking his thumb.*

coun·tri·fied /'kʌntrə,faɪd/ *adj.* **1** (land) looking like areas outside cities with fields, woods, usu. farms **2** (people) simple, (*syn.*) unsophisticated: *He has a countrified look with jeans, boots, and a cowboy hat.*

coun·try /'kʌntri/ *n.* -**tries 1** [C] a nation: *the country of Canada* **2** [C] a rural area outside cities and towns: *We drive to the country to relax.* **3** [U] land suitable for a particular purpose: *farm country*
—*adj.* typical of the country, esp. in being simple, rough, or old fashioned: *country furniture*

coun·try·man /'kʌntrimən/ *n.* -**men** /-mən/ a citizen of the same nation: *When I traveled to South America, I met some of my countrymen from New York at the hotel.* -*n.* **country·woman** /'kʌntri,wʊmən/.

country music or **country and western** *n.* [U] a type of popular music based on folk music of the southern and western USA: *Country music is played usually with guitars, a fiddle, and drums.*

USAGE NOTE: Although *country music* was first popular in the southern and western parts of the USA, it is now popular throughout the country. Country dancing, in which people dance to country music, is also becoming more popular. One well-known country dance is the *Texas two-step.*

coun·try·side /'kʌntri,saɪd/ *n.* [U] the land outside a city or town with trees, farms, and few houses: *The countryside near our city is full of hills and farms.*

coun·ty /'kaʊnti/ *n.* -**ties** *adj.* (in USA) a smaller political and geographical area within states: <*adj.*> *County governments are often responsible for some of a state's highways.*

coup /ku/ *n.* **coups** /kuz/ **1** taking control suddenly of a government, (*syn.*) a coup d'état **2** a big, unexpected success: *When the movie star decided to make a film with a small new company, it was a coup for them.*

coup d'é·tat /,kudeɪ'tɑ/ *n.* **coups d'état** /,kudeɪ'tɑ, -'tɑz/ taking control suddenly of a government by force

cou·ple /'kʌpəl/ *n.* **1** two people (usu. of the opposite sex) who are married, living together, or on a date: *Jane and Tom are a couple that love to go dancing.* **2** several, usu. two or three: *Can you lend me a couple of dollars? Yes, for a couple of days. See:* pair.
—*v.* -**pled, -pling, -ples 1** to put or link together: *to couple railroad cars* **2** (said of animals) to have sex, (*syn.*) to mate

cou·pon /'ku,pɑn, 'kyu-/ *n.* **1** a piece of paper that offers a payment, service, or reduction in the price of goods, esp. food: *to clip coupons from the newspaper‖He gives coupons to the supermarket cashier who takes money off the price of the food.* **2** an order form to write in one's name, address, credit card number, etc., (*syn.*) order blank: *to fill in the coupon and mail it to buy a pair of shoes, See:* rebate.

cour·age /'kɜrɪdʒ/ *n.* [U] bravery, the strength of mind and/or body to face and overcome danger and difficulties: *The police officer showed great courage by jumping into the cold lake to save a drowning boy.* -*adj.* **courageous** /kə'reɪdʒəs/; -*adv.* **courageously.**

cou·ri·er /'kɜriər, 'kʊr-, 'kʌr-/ *n.* a messenger, esp. one on important business: *The jeweler sent a courier to pick up the diamonds.*

course /kɔrs/ *n.* **1** a series of lessons in a subject, usu. at a school: *I took a college course in English literature.* **2** an area for sports events: *a race course, a golf course* **3** a planned route: *That ship headed for China is on course/off course.* **4** a period of time: *In the course of events (time, progress), we finally learned the truth about the crime.* **5 as a matter of course:** routinely: *As a matter of course, the*

judge told the jury to listen equally to both sides. **6 course of action:** a way of doing s.t.: *Our company faces a lawsuit, so what course of action will we take, to pay the money or fight it in court?* **7 in due course:** eventually, finally: *In due course, we decided to fight the lawsuit in court.* **8 of course:** naturally, clearly: *Of course I'll come to your wedding.*
—*v.frml.* **coursed, coursing, courses** to travel or run fast: *Water courses over a waterfall.*

court (1) /kɔrt/ *n.* **1** [C;U] a government building with rooms (courtrooms) where a judge and often a jury hear complaints: *civil court, superior court, Supreme Court‖The murder trial took place in a court of law.* **2** [C, usu. sing.; U] the people attending a trial: *The judge asked the court to be silent.* **3 to go** (or) **take s.o. to court:** to make a legal, written complaint against s.o., *(syn.)* to sue: *When the company would not pay the money it owed us, we went to court to get it.*

court (2) *n.* **1** an area marked off for sports: *We played on a tennis (volleyball, handball, etc.) court. See:* course. **2** the place where a king or queen lives or meets with others: *the royal court at Versailles*

court (3) *v.* **1** to seek the favor or good will of s.o. **2** *old usage* to seek the love of s.o., esp. used of a man who wants a woman to marry him: *He courted her for two years before she agreed to marry him.* **3** to act in a way that makes s.t. likely to happen: *You are courting disaster with your wild behavior. See:* courtship.

cour·te·ous /'kɜrtiəs/ *adj.* having good manners, polite: *The taxi driver is very courteous to his customers.* -*adv.* **courteously.**

cour·te·sy /'kɜrtəsi/ *n.* [U] -**sies 1** good manners, politeness: *The telephone operator treats all callers with courtesy.* **2 to do s.o. a courtesy:** to do s.o. a favor: *Please do me the courtesy of calling my office to say I'll be late.*

court·house /'kɔrt,haus/ *n.* -**houses** /-'hauzɪz/ the building in which courts of law and other legal activities are located: *I went to the courthouse to get a copy of my birth certificate.*

cour·ti·er /'kɔrtiər/ *n.* a person who is often present at the court of a king or queen

court·ly /'kɔrtli/ *adj.* polite, dignified

court-mar·tial /'kɔrt,marʃəl/ *n.* **courts-martial** or **court-martials** [C;U] *v.* **1** a military court to judge those who may have broken military law **2** a trial in a military court **3** to try someone in a military court: *That soldier received a* <*n.*> *court-martial for stealing and was put in jail.They* <*v.*> *court-martialed him.*

court·room /'kɔrt,rum/ *n.* the room in which a court of law meets: *The judge sits at the back of the courtroom behind a high desk.*

court·ship /'kɔrt,ʃɪp/ *n.* [C;U] a period of getting to know s.o. you are planning to marry as

the relationship develops, formal dating: *The couple had a two year courtship before marrying.*

court·yard /'kɔrt,yard/ *n.* an enclosed outdoor area next to a house or building: *Cars drove into the courtyard to let people out at the building's front door. See:* patio.

cous·in /'kʌzən/ *n.* a child of an aunt or uncle: *My cousins live in Florida.*

couth /kuθ/ *n.adj.* (often used in the negative) good manners and good taste in clothes and actions: *That rude young man has no* <*n.*> *couth. See:* uncouth.

cove /kouv/ *n.* a small bay, a sheltered area in the coastline of a sea, lake, or river: *Our boat waited in the safety of a cove for the storm to pass.*

cov·en /'kʌvən/ *n.* a group of witches: *She is the head of a coven.*

cov·e·nant /'kʌvənənt/ *n.* **1** (in law) a contract, formal written agreement **2** a part of a formal agreement: *We sued that company for breaking three of the covenants in our contract.* **3** (in religion) God's agreement with the human race or an agreement among members of a congregation

cov·er /'kʌvər/ *n.* **1** [C] a removable top of s.t., a lid: *a cover for a jar (pot, frying pan)* **2** [C] a layer of cloth or other material: *The bed covers have a pretty flower design.* **3** [C] the strong outer part of a book, magazine **4** [U] concealment: *The soldiers moved out under the cover of darkness.* **5** a false appearance or secret use: *That business acts as a cover for criminals to hide illegal money.* **6** shelter or safety: *When it started to rain, I ran for (or) took cover under a tree.‖The soldiers took cover in a cave when the enemy started shooting.* **7 under separate cover:** in a separate package: *This letter confirms your order for shoes; they will be sent under separate cover.*
—*v.* **1** to put s.t. on or over s.t. else: *She covered the table with a cloth.‖The old paint on the wall is covered with wallpaper.* **2** to include: *That big farm covers five square miles (8 km).‖The teacher covered the lesson on adjectives yesterday.* **3** to report on an event: *That newspaper reporter covered the story about the fire.* **4** to travel a distance: *We covered 30 miles (48 km) on bicycles yesterday.* **5** to be enough money to pay for s.t.: *This $400 will cover the cost of a new coat.* **6** to point a gun so that s.o. cannot run away: *One police officer covered the criminal while the other put handcuffs on her.* **7** (in sports) to guard, defend: *The basketball player covered his opponent.* **8** to act in place of s.o. else, *(syn.)* to substitute: *When my teacher was sick, another one covered for her.* **9** *fig.* **to cover oneself:** to protect oneself from criticism or loss: *He covered himself by putting in writing that if the books were*

damaged when he received them, he didn't have to pay for them. **10 to cover one's tracks:** to hide one's participation: *The criminal wore a mask and left nothing at the scene of his crimes; he covered his tracks well.* **11 to cover the ground:** to treat s.t. thoroughly: *We had a good discussion that really covered the ground on all topics.* **12** *phrasal v. sep.* **to cover s.t. up:** to hide s.t., keep others from knowing about it: *The company covered up the scandal about stealing money.*‖*They covered it up.* **13** *phrasal v. insep.* **to cover up for s.o.:** to hide s.t. in order to protect s.o. else from punishment: *He covered up for me when I forgot to mail the report.*

cov·er·age /'kʌvərɪdʒ, 'kʌvrɪdʒ/ *n.* [U] **1** reporting by TV, newspapers, or other media: *When important politicians speak, there is a lot of coverage in the press and on television.* **2** insurance: *My policy gives coverage against fire and theft.*

cov·er·ing /'kʌvərɪŋ, 'kʌvrɪŋ/ *n.* s.t. put on or over s.t. else: *Bushes and grass make a ground covering.*

cover letter *n.* a letter sent to explain s.t.: *I sent a cover letter with my résumé to apply for a job.*

co·vert /'kouvərt, 'kʌ-, kou'vɜrt/ *adj.* secret, *(syn.)* concealed: *Spies had a covert plan to steal secrets.*

cov·er-up /'kʌvər,ʌp/ *n.* an act of hiding s.t. bad, *(syn.)* concealment (of the truth): *Officials managed a cover-up of scandal.*

cov·et /'kʌvɪt/ *v.* to want s.t. with great desire and envy: *She covets her neighbor's big house and fancy car.* *-adj.* **covetous** /'kʌvətəs/**;** *-n.* [U] **covetousness.**

cow (1) /kaʊ/ *n.* the adult female of cattle and some other large animals: *Farmers get up early to milk the cows.*‖*a cow elephant See:* calf; heifer.

cow (2) *v.* to make others afraid and obedient, *(syn.)* to intimidate: *The substitute teacher cowed the students into behaving well.*

cow·ard /'kaʊərd/ *n.* a person without courage: *She was a coward when she ran out of the burning house and left her children to die.* *-adj.* **cowardly.**

cow·ard·ice /'kaʊərdɪs/ *n.* [U] lack of courage, the shameful behavior of a coward: *When the boat turned over, the man showed cowardice by saving himself while leaving his wife to drown.*

cow·boy /'kaʊ,bɔɪ/ *n.* **1** a man who works on a cattle ranch or rodeo, taking care of the cattle **2** *fig.slang* a person who drives too fast and usu. recklessly: *The cowboy driving that subway train scared the passengers. See:* cowgirl.

cow·er /'kaʊər/ *v.* to move back in fear and submission, *(syn.)* to cringe: *The little boy cowered in fear when his father yelled at him.*

cow·girl /'kaʊ,gɜrl/ *n.* a woman who works on a cattle ranch or rodeo, taking care of cattle *See:* cowboy.

cow·hide /'kaʊ,haɪd/ *n.adj.* the thick, strong leather made from the skin of a cow: *He wears boots made of <n.> cowhide.*

cowl /kaʊl/ *n.* **1** a long, loose robe with a hood, as worn by a monk **2** the hood itself: *The monk pulled the cowl over his head as it started to rain.* **3** (on women's clothes) a neckline style with loose folds of material

co·work·er /'kou,wɜrkər/ *n.* a person with whom one works, *(syns.)* colleague, fellow worker: *My coworkers and I went out for a beer after work.*

cow·slip /'kaʊ,slɪp/ *n.* a wild plant with small, sweet-smelling yellow flowers: *Cowslips flower in the springtime.*

cox·swain /'kɑksən, -,sweɪn/ *n.* a person who steers a rowboat in races: *After winning the race, the crew threw the coxswain in the water to celebrate.*

coy /kɔɪ/ *adj.* pretending to be shy, evasive esp. in a playful, mocking manner: *She likes him, but is coy about telling him so.* *-adv.* **coyly;** *-n.* [U] **coyness.**

coy·o·te /kaɪ'outi, 'kaɪ,out/ *n.* **-tes** or **-te** a kind of wolf similar to a medium-sized dog found mainly in western North and Central America: *Coyotes often hunt rats and mice at night.*

coyote

co·zy /'kouzi/ *adj.* **-zier, -ziest 1** warm, friendly, and comfortable: *We had dinner at a cozy restaurant with a fireplace.* **2** involving a close relationship, esp. a dishonest one

—*phrasal v. insep.* **-zied, -zying, -zies to cozy up to s.o.:** to try to become friendly with s.o.: *The politician cozied up to some rich people so they would give him money.*

CPA /,sipi'eɪ/ *abbr. for* certified public accountant: *My CPA did my federal income tax return.*

crab /kræb/ *n.* **1** a shellfish with a flat shell, four pairs of legs, and two claws **2** [U] the meat of crabs: *We ate crab (or) crab meat.* **3** *infrml.fig.* a difficult, irritable person: *That man is such a crab, angry all the time.*

—*v.* **crabbed, crabbing, crabs 1** to fish for crabs **2** *infrml.fig.* to complain *-adj.* **crabby.**

crack /kræk/ *n.* **1** a line of separation in a material, a split: *That drinking glass has a crack*

in it.‖ *a wall with cracks* **2** a small amount of space: *He opened the window a crack.* **3** a break in a surface, *(syns.)* fracture, fissure: *After the earthquake, the ground had wide cracks running through it.* **4** a sudden, very loud noise: *the crack of a whip* **5** a funny and/or critical remark *See:* wisecrack. **6** *slang* a strong, highly addictive form of cocaine: *He smokes crack.* **7 to fall between the cracks:** to become lost or ignored: *She had a great idea for a new product; but no one would listen to her, so it fell between the cracks.*
—*v.* **1** to break without coming apart: *A small stone hit the window and cracked it.* **2** *phrasal v. insep.* **to crack down on s.o. or s.t.:** to take strong actions to stop s.t., to discipline severely: *The government cracked down on drug dealers by putting them in jail.*‖*It cracked down on them. See:* crackdown. **3** *phrasal v. sep.* **to crack s.t. open:** to break apart with force: *He cracked open the coconut with a knife.*‖*He cracked it open.* **4** *phrasal v. sep.* **to crack s.o. or s.t. up: a. s.o.:** to have a nervous breakdown: *She was under so much pressure at work that she cracked up.* **b. s.o.:** (used negatively) not to be as good as one's reputation: *That singer is not all that she is cracked up to be.* **c.** *sep.* **s.o.:** to break out into laughter: *That comedian is so funny that he cracks up his audiences every time.*‖*He cracks them up.* **d.** to ruin, wreck: *He cracked up his car by hitting a tree.* **5 to get cracking:** to begin work with energy: *We know what we have to do, so let's get cracking!*
—*adj.* excellent; expert: *a crack shot with a rifle*

crack·down /ˈkræk͵daʊn/ *n.* strong actions taken to stop s.t., severe discipline: *The government began a crackdown on crime by hiring more police.*

crack·er /ˈkrækər/ *n.* **1** a small, thin piece of unsweetened baked dough: *She likes to eat cheese on crackers.* **2** *pej.* a poor, white person of the southern USA

crack·er·jack /ˈkrækər͵dʒæk/ *adj.n.* having excellent ability, the best: *He is a <adj.> crackerjack mechanic.*

crack·le /ˈkrækəl/ *v.n.* **-led, -ling, -les** *usu.* used in the sing. a sound like that of small things breaking, snapping: *The oil <v.> crackles in the hot frying pan.*

crack·pot /ˈkræk͵pɑt/ *n.* a person with strange ideas or behavior, *(syn.)* an eccentric: *That crackpot thinks he will lead a world revolution.*

crack·up /ˈkræk͵ʌp/ *n.* **1** a bad accident with a vehicle: *She had a crackup in her car on the highway.* **2** a nervous breakdown: *He has so many problems that he finally had a crackup last month.*

cra·dle /ˈkreɪdl/ *n.* **1** a baby's bed, esp. one that moves back and forth on rockers **2** the place where s.t. begins, origin: *Ancient Greece was the cradle of western civilization.* **3**

cradle

from the cradle to the grave: from birth to death
—*v.* **-dled, -dling, -dles** to hold gently: *She cradled the baby in her arms.*

craft /kræft/ *n.* **1** a skilled trade: *the craft of carpentry* **2** skill in making things by hand: *the craft of basketweaving, the craft of making pottery See:* arts and crafts. **3** a boat, airplane, or space vehicle: *water craft, aircraft, spacecraft* **4** skill in tricking people *See:* crafty.
—*v.* to make s.t with skill: *He crafts fine furniture by hand.* *-n.* **craftsman** /ˈkræftsmən/; [U] **craftsmanship.**

craft·y /ˈkræfti/ *adj.* **-ier, -iest** good at tricking people: *The criminal was crafty and hid his crimes well. -adv.* **craftily;** *-n.* [U] **craftiness.**

crag /kræg/ *n.* a high, steep rock formation: *He stands on a crag and looks out to sea.*

crag·gy /ˈkrægi/ *adj.* **-gier, -giest** **1** rocky, steep **2** rough, rugged: *He has a craggy face. -n.* [U] **cragginess.**

cram /kræm/ *v.* **crammed, cramming, crams** **1** to force s.t. into a small space, stuff: *She crammed clothes into her suitcase.*‖*He crammed food into his mouth.* **2** to study quickly and hard: *He crammed all night for the exam the next day.*
—*adj.* **a cram course:** a course that teaches or reviews a lot of material quickly in preparation for a test: *She took a one-week cram course for a real estate license.*

cramp /kræmp/ *n.* **1** a painful tightening of a muscle, *(syn.)* a spasm: *After running, he got a cramp in his leg.* **2 to have cramps:** to have pains in the stomach or abdomen
—*v.* **1** to have muscle spasms: *His leg muscles cramped up.* **2 to cramp s.o.'s style:** to prevent s.o. from doing s.t. freely

cramped /kræmpt/ *adj.* small and uncomfortable: *She lives in a cramped little apartment.*

cran·ber·ry /ˈkræn͵bɛri/ *n.* **-ries** a small, sour red berry grown in wet land esp. in New England, or the plant it grows on: *Cranberries* *are cooked and made into a kind of jelly that is served with turkey on Thanksgiving.*

crane /kreɪn/ *n.* **1** a large waterbird with long legs and neck **2** a large machine used to lift heavy loads

—*v.* **craned, craning, cranes** to lift one's head and stretch one's neck like a crane: *People craned their necks to see the accident scene as they passed by.*

crane

cra·ni·um /'kreɪniəm/ *n.* **-niums** or **-nia** /-niə/ the bones of the head around the brain: *He has an injury to the cranium.* -*adj.* **cranial.**

crank /kræŋk/ *n.* **1** a metal rod used for starting an engine or lifting heavy objects **2** *fig.* an eccentric, a person who complains all the time

—*v.* **1** to use a crank: *He cranked the engine to get it started.* **2** *phrasal v. sep.* **to crank s.t. out:** to produce quickly, manufacture a lot of: *She cranked out cakes for the party.* ||*She cranked them out.*

—*adj.* **a crank call:** an anonymous telephone call made to bother or scare s.o.

crank·y /'kræŋki/ *adj.* **-ier, -iest** angry and complaining, irritable: *That child is cranky and needs to sleep.*

cran·ny /'kræni/ *n.* **-nies** an opening or crack in a wall *See:* nooks and crannies.

crap /kræp/ *n.vulg.slang* **1** useless nonsense: *What he says is a lot of crap.* **2** useless or poorly made things, (*syn.*) junk **3** excrement, feces -*v.* **crapped, crapping, craps** to defecate; -*adj.* **crappy.**

crash /kræʃ/ *n.* **crashes 1** a violent hit against s.t., usu. with damage, an accident, (*syn.*) a smashup: *a car crash, a plane crash* **2** the loud, violent sound of a crash: *Cars hit together with a loud crash.* **3** a failure or collapse, esp. an economic ruin: *the stock market crash of 1929*

—*v.* **crashes 1** to smash against s.t. violently: *The bus went out of control and crashed against cars and telephone poles.* **2** to fail or collapse: *The computer crashed and all its data was lost.* **3** *fig.* to enter a party, concert, etc. without an invitation or ticket *See:* gate crasher.

—*adj.* using speed and concentrated effort to get quick results: *He took a crash course in Spanish before a vacation to Mexico.*

crash-land *v.* to land an airplane in an emergency: *The airplane's engines failed and the*

pilot crash-landed it (or) made a crash landing. -*n.* **crash landing.**

crass /kræs/ *adj.* **1** stupid and insensitive, (*syn.*) coarse: *He was drunk and made crass remarks about a woman being too fat.* **2** obvious, outrageous, or deceitful: *She made a crass attempt to sell me a coat that was too big for me.* -*adv.* **crassly;** -*n.* **crassness.**

crate /kreɪt/ *n.* **1** a box made of wood used to ship things: *That store has crates of oranges and tomatoes.* **2** *slang* an old car, (*syn.*) a jalopy

—*v.* **crated, crating, crates** to put in crates: *Farmers crated lettuce and apples to ship to stores.*

cra·ter /'kreɪtər/ *n.* a large hole in the ground: *the crater of a volcano*||*A meteor hit the earth and made a huge crater.*

cra·vat /krə'væt/ *n.frml.* a colorful cloth worn as a necktie, (*syn.*) ascot: *He wears silk cravats.*

crater

crave /kreɪv/ *v.* **craved, craving, craves** to desire greatly or uncontrollably: *She craves chocolate.*||*He craves to be loved.* -*n.* **craving.**

craw /krɔ/ *n.* **1** the stomach of some animals **2** an area above the stomach of some birds where food is stored

craw·fish /'krɔ,fɪʃ/ *n.* **-fish** or **-fishes** *var. of* crayfish

crawl /krɔl/ *v.* **1** to move slowly and close to the ground, (*syn.*) to creep: *Ants and spiders crawl along the ground.*||*Babies crawl on their hands and knees.* **2** to be covered with s.t.: *The ground was crawling with ants.* **3** *fig.* to ask for forgiveness, (*syn.*) to grovel: *He made his girlfriend angry, but he crawled back to her.*

—*n.* **1** a slow movement: *Traffic is moving at a crawl today.* **2 the crawl:** the fastest swimming stroke which uses the arms lifted over the head and kicks the feet

cray·fish /'kreɪ,fɪʃ/ *n.* **-fish** or **-fishes** a small, lobster-like animal with a hard shell, or its meat: *Crayfish live in fresh water streams and lakes.*

cray·on /'kreɪ,ɑn, -ən/ *n.v.* a stick made of colored wax used for drawing: *Children love to draw with colored <n.> crayons.*

craze /kreɪz/ *n.* a popular style that passes soon, (*syn.*) fad: *Wearing black shoes with thick soles was the craze this year.*

—*v.* **crazed, crazing, crazes** to become insane, crazy: *Fighting in the jungle crazed many soldiers.*

crazed /kreɪzd/ *adj.* crazy, insane: *A crazed man killed the child.*

cra·zy /ˈkreɪzi/ *adj.* **-zier, -ziest 1** sick in the mind, insane: *The crazy man talked to himself all the time.* **2** making no sense, foolish: *He is crazy if he thinks that he is going to make $1 million next year.* **3** wildly enthusiastic: *When she saw that new car, she went crazy over it.*||*John is crazy about Jane.* **4 like crazy:** actively, hard: *She ran like crazy to catch the bus.* -*adv.* **crazily;** [U] -*n.* **craziness.**

creak /krik/ *n.* the sound of s.t. that cannot move freely, (*syn.*) a squeak
—*v.* to make a creaking sound: *That old wooden floor creaks when we walk on it.*

creak·y /ˈkriki/ *adj.* **-ier, -iest 1** making creaking noises: *a creaky door* **2** feeling old and full of aches: *After playing football, I feel creaky today.*

cream /krim/ *n.* **1** [U] the fatty part of milk that goes to its surface: *Butter is made from cream.* **2** [U] the yellowish-white color of cream: *a cream-colored shirt* **3** [C;U] a thick, smooth substance used in cosmetics and medicine: *She put cold cream on her face.* **4** *fig.* **the cream of the crop:** the best among people: *That college admits only the cream of the crop of high school students.*
—*v.* **1** to blend or mix, usu. with cream: *He creamed the spinach and carrots.* **2** *slang* to defeat or harm badly: *Our basketball team got creamed 110 to 70.*

cream cheese *n.* a soft, white, smooth cheese made of milk and cream: *She put cream cheese on her toast.*

cream·er·y /ˈkriməri/ *n.* **-ries** a business that makes cheese and butter and processes milk and cream: *That farmer runs a creamery. See:* dairy.

cream puff *n.* **1** a pastry filled with whipped cream: *I ate a cream puff covered with chocolate.* **2** *fig.* a weak person unable to play rough sports or take punishment, (*syn.*) a pansy

cream·y /ˈkrimi/ *adj.* **-ier, -iest 1** (food) smooth and thick like cream: *I like a creamy salad dressing.* **2** (appearance) light colored and smooth like cream: *She has a creamy complexion.*

crease /kris/ *n.v.* **creased, creasing, creases** a fold in cloth or paper, (*syn.*) a wrinkle: *The cleaners put a <n.> crease in my pants with an iron.*

cre·ate /kriˈeɪt/ *v.* **-ated, ating, ates 1** to give life to: *Parents create their children.* **2** to make s.t. in a special way, usu. with skill or artistry: *That company created a new product.*||*That artist created great paintings.* **3 to create a scene:** to do s.t. bad or rude in front of others: *He created a scene at the party by drinking too much and falling down.*

cre·a·tion /kriˈeɪʃən/ *n.* **1** [U] the beginning of existence of s.t.: *the creation of the universe* **2 the Creation:** (in religion) the creating by God of the world **3** [C] the making of s.t. often using special skill or artistry: *That statue of Venus is a great artistic creation.*

cre·a·tive /kriˈeɪtɪv/ *adj.* **1** showing artistic skill and imagination: *That artist has the creative ability to paint beautiful pictures.* **2** having the ability to think well and solve problems, clever: *a creative solution to a problem* -*adv.* **creatively;** -*n.* [U] **creativity** /ˌkrieɪˈtɪvəti/.

cre·a·tor /kriˈeɪtər/ *n.* **1** a person who creates s.t.: *He was the creator of television many years ago.* **2 the Creator:** God

crea·ture /ˈkritʃər/ *n.* **1** a living being: *The creatures on earth include humans and animals.*

cre·dence /ˈkridns/ *n.frml.* [U] **1** belief **2 to give (or) lend credence to:** to support a belief: *The bank records give (or) lend credence to his story that he borrowed the money and did not steal it.*

cre·den·tials /krɪˈdɛnʃəlz/ *n.pl.* **1** identity papers: *That government inspector carries his credentials with him to show who he is.* **2** papers (diplomas, awards, references of good employment) that show one's accomplishments: *She has excellent credentials for the job.*

cred·i·bil·i·ty /ˌkrɛdəˈbɪləti/ *n.* [U] the quality of making other people trust you and feel confident that you will do what you say: *She treats her workers well and she has credibility with them.*

cred·i·ble /ˈkrɛdəbəl/ *adj.* believable: *That student told the teacher a credible story that she missed classes because she was sick.*

cred·it (1) /ˈkrɛdɪt/ *n.* [U] **1** a cause for admiration, honor, praise, etc.: *Her many awards are a credit to her skill.* **2 to give credit:** to give admiration for s.t. well done or for a person's good qualities: (well done) *I give the teacher credit (or) I give credit to the teacher for explaining things so clearly.*||(*good quality*) *I give him credit for looking so healthy.* **3 to take credit for s.t.:** to accept admiration or feel pleasure for s.t. well done: *The teacher takes credit for her students' doing well on the exams.*
—*v.* **to credit s.o. for (or) with s.t.:** to express admiration for s.t. well done, etc.: *People in the burning building credit the fire fighters for (or) with saving their lives.*||*The teacher credits the discovery to the entire class.* -*adj.* **creditable.**

credit (2) *n.* **1** [U] the ability to buy now and pay later: *Our company has credit with other companies, so we buy now and pay them in 30 days.* **2** [U] an act of buying now and paying

later: *I bought this new suit on credit.* **3** [U] an amount of money available to draw on at a store, at a company, or on a credit card: *The credit limit on my Visa credit card is $7,000.* **4** [U] an amount paid on an account: *When I paid my Visa bill, they put a $300 credit on my account.* **5** [C] a unit of a course at a school, college, etc.: *I earned three credits in my English course this semester.* **6** *pl.* **credits** a list of people who made a movie, etc.: *The movie star's name was first in the credits.*
—*v.* (in accounting) to add a sum to s.o.'s account: *When I sent a $300 check, Visa credited my account for that amount.*

credit card *n.* a small, flat plastic card that allows a person to buy goods and services on credit: *I used my credit card to pay for dinner. See:* charge card, cash card, **USAGE NOTE.**

credit line *n.* an amount of money available at a bank or on a credit card for a person or business to use when needed and repay with interest: *Our company has a $1 million credit line at Commercial Bank.*

credit limit *n.* a limit on the amount of money available on credit: *The credit limit on my Visa card is $7,000.*

credit memo or **credit slip** *n.* **-os** a document that shows the amount of credit one has with a business: *I returned a pair of shoes and the store gave me a credit memo for future purchases.*

cred·i·tor /'krɛdɪtər/ *n.* a person, bank, or business that gives credit: *My creditors are Visa credit card and my bank for a car loan. See:* debtor.

credit rating *n.* the amount of credit that can be given to a person or business without too much risk: *That company has a good credit rating because it pays all its bills on time.*

cre·do /'kridoʊ, 'kreɪ-/ *n.* **-dos 1** system of beliefs **2** a statement of one's beliefs, *(syn.)* motto: *Our company's credo is: "Quality Products—Customer Education—Service."*

cred·u·lous /'krɛdʒələs/ *adj.frml.* believing too quickly or easily in s.t., *(syn.)* naive: *She was credulous when she listened to the salesman and bought the car for too much money.* -*n.* [U] **credulity** /krɛ'duləti/.

creed /krid/ *n.frml.* **1** a formal statement of one's religious beliefs: *The church published its creed about belief in God.* **2** a system of beliefs, principles, etc.

creek /krik, krɪk/ *n.* **1** a small stream: *We went fishing in the creek.* **2** *fig.* **to be up the creek (without a paddle):** to be in a difficult situation: *When he lost his job and could not pay his bills, he was up the creek without a paddle.*

creep /krip/ *v.* **crept** /krɛpt/, **creeping, creeps 1** to move slowly and quietly, usu. with care or fear: *The husband came home very late and he crept by his wife so he would not wake her up.* **2** to move slowly: *Cars creep through a traffic jam.* **3** to move or grow close to the ground —*adj.* growing close to the ground: *creeping plants*
—*n.* **1** a slow movement **2** a person with offensive usu. sneaky behavior, a jerk: *That creep has been following me from the train station.* **3 to give s.o. the creeps:** to cause a feeling of disgust: *That man is so dirty that he gives me the creeps.*

creep·er /'kripər/ *n.* **1** a plant that grows and spreads along the ground or over walls, a trailer **2** an animal, such as an insect, that moves along with its body close to the ground: *Spiders are creepers.*

creep·y /'kripi/ *adj.* **-ier, -iest** causing fear and disgust, scary: *a creepy movie full of horror scenes||He is a creepy guy with an evil look.*

cre·mate /'krimeɪt, krɪ'meɪt/ *v.* **-mated, -mating, -mates** to burn a dead body to ashes for burial: *My father wanted to be cremated after his death.* -*n.*[C;U] **cremation** /krɪ'meɪʃən/.

cre·ma·to·ri·um /ˌkrimə'tɔriəm/ *n.* **-riums** or **-ria** a building or furnace in which dead bodies are cremated

Cre·ole /'krioʊl/ *n.* **1** [C;U] a person descended from the Spanish, French, or Portuguese settlers of the West Indies and Louisiana **2** often **creole:** a language that has developed from a mixture of two languages and has become the native language of people in a place: *She speaks Haitian Creole.*
—*adj.* often **creole:** related to Creole culture: *Creole cooking uses tomatoes, onions, peppers and spicy sauces.*

crepe /kreɪp, krɛp/ *n.* [C] a thin fabric with a wrinkled surface

crepe paper *n.* paper with a wrinkled surface that comes in strips and is used for decoration: *They hung colored balloons and crepe paper for the party.*

crept /krɛpt/ *v. past tense and past part. of* creep

cre·scen·do /krə'ʃɛndoʊ/ *n.* **dos 1** a gradual increase in loudness in a piece of music **2** a high-energy ending: *Our talks ended with a crescendo of agreement and friendliness.*

cres·cent /'krɛsənt/ *adj.* shaped like part of a circle: *A full moon changes to a crescent moon.*
—*n.* a crescent-shaped area or object: *a parking crescent in front of a building*

cress /krɛs/ *n.* [U] a plant of the mustard family with strong flavor: *I put cress in my lettuce salad.* See: watercress.

crest /krɛst/ *n.* **1** the top of s.t.: *the crest of a hill, the crest of a wave* **2** feathers that stick up from the top of a bird's head or a soldier's helmet **3** a shield with the special markings of one's ancestors: *the family crest*
—*v.* to reach the top of s.t.: *After the heavy rain, the river crested at 20 feet, then went down to 10 feet.*

crest·fall·en /'krɛst,fɔlən/ *adj.* sad, disappointed: *When she failed her exams, she was crestfallen.*

cre·tin /'kritn/ *n.* **1** a person who is deformed and mentally retarded because of a thyroid disease **2** *fig.* a person who is stupid or offensive, an idiot: *That cretin stole my car!*

cre·vasse /krə'væs/ *n.* a deep crack, esp. in ice or a snow-covered mountain: *The mountain climbers fell into a crevasse.*

crev·ice /'krɛvɪs/ *n.* a narrow crack in rock: *Water dripped from a crevice in the cave.*

crew /kru/ *n.* **1** the workers (often except the officers) on a ship, airplane, train, space vehicle, etc.: *the captain and crew on a cruise ship* **2** a group of workers: *the stage crew in a theater* **3** rowers on a racing boat
—*v.* to work as a sailor: *to crew for s.o.*

crew cut *n.* a haircut with the hair cut very short: *He wears a crew cut.*

crib (1) /krɪb/ *n.* **1** a baby's bed with high sides: *The baby cannot fall out of her crib.* **2** a holder for animal feed

crib

crib (2) *v.* **cribbed, cribbing, cribs** to copy answers or information from s.o. else or from a crib sheet

crib sheet *n.* a copy of answers or information used to cheat on an examination: *He hides a crib sheet up his sleeve so he can crib on his exams.*

crick /krɪk/ *n.* a pain or muscle cramp: *I have a crick in my neck this morning.*

crick·et /'krɪkɪt/ *n.* **1** a small, dark brown insect that makes a high-pitched noise: *I can hear the crickets chirp at night.* **2** an outdoor ball game popular in the British Commonwealth

cri·er /'kraɪər/ *n. old usage* an official who makes public announcements by speaking in a loud voice

crime /kraɪm/ *n.* **1** [C] a serious, illegal act: *the crime of murder* **2** [C] serious illegal acts in general: *The police fight crime, murder, theft, and drug dealing.* **3** [C] a bad situation that should not happen, s.t. shameful: *It is a crime that such a nice man has so much trouble in his life.* See: misdemeanor.

crim·i·nal /'krɪmənəl/ *n.* a person who commits a serious crime, like theft or murder, (*syn.*) a felon
—*adj.* related to crime: *Robbery is a criminal act.*

crim·i·nol·o·gy /,krɪmə'nɑlədʒi/ *n.* [U] the study of crime and criminals

crimp /krɪmp/ *v.* to press or shape into small, regular folds, (*syn.*) to pleat
—*n.* **1** a small, regular fold **2** *fig.* **to put a crimp in s.t.:** to make s.t. difficult, (*syn.*) to hinder: *He had to work late, and that put a crimp in his dinner plans.*

crim·son /'krɪmzən/ *adj.* a deep, dark red: *Red roses have crimson flowers.*

cringe /krɪndʒ/ *v.* **cringed, cringing, cringes** to show distress in one's face and move back in fear, (*syn.*) to cower: *She cringed when the dirty man touched her.*

crin·kle /'krɪŋkəl/ *v.n.* **-kled, -kling, -kles** to form into folds or thin lines: *The leaves of the plant <v.> crinkled up because it needed water.*

crip·ple /'krɪpəl/ *n.* a person or animal unable to walk or use limbs normally: *The taxi driver had a bad car accident and now he is a cripple.*
—*v.* **-pled, -pling, -ples** **1** to injure so that one cannot walk or use one's limbs normally, (*syn.*) to disable: *He was crippled during the war.* **2** *fig.* to hurt or weaken s.t. so that it cannot function normally: *The city was crippled by the big snowstorm. -adj.* **crippled.** See: handicapped.

cri·sis /'kraɪsɪs/ *n.* **-ses** /-,siz/ **1** an emergency: *The hurricane caused a crisis without houses or food for people.*

crisis management *n.adj.* a method of handling a crisis by taking quick and organized action: *When the earthquake hit San Francisco, the city's <adj.> crisis management team took immediate action with firefighters putting out fires, the police directing traffic, etc.*

crisp /krɪsp/ *adj.* **1** having a fresh, firm feel: *crisp lettuce||crisp, new $1 bills* **2** cool, refreshing: *crisp sea air* **3** done in a quick, sure way: *The student gave a clear, crisp answer to the teacher's question. -adv.* **crisply;** *-n.* [U] **crispness;** *-adj.* **crispy.**

criss·cross /'krɪs,krɔs/ *v.n.* **-crosses** to make lines that cross each other: *Roads and highways <v.> crisscross the country.*

cri·te·ri·on /kraɪ'tɪriən/ *n.* **-ria** /-riə/ , **-rions** a rule used to judge s.t., standard of measurement: *Our company must make a 10% profit; that is the criterion of success that we use.*

crit·ic /'krɪtɪk/ *n.* **1** a person who reviews and gives opinions about art, music, film, etc.: *She is the movie critic for our local newspaper.* **2** a person who criticizes s.t. or s.o.: *That critic of government policies was put in jail.*

crit·i·cal /'krɪtɪkəl/ *adj.* **1** pointing out faults, (*syns.*) derogatory, disparaging: *The teacher wrote critical remarks on my paper about mistakes that I made.* **2** very important: *It is critical that you study for the exam or you will fail it.* **3** dangerous, urgent: *Her illness is at the critical stage where she may die.* **4** analytical: *That reviewer published his critical comments on art in the newspaper.* -*adv.* **critically.**

crit·i·cism /'krɪtə,sɪzəm/ *n.* [C;U] **1** evaluation, esp. as a profession, of the good and bad points of art, music, film, etc.: *He takes a class on film criticism.* **2** the pointing out of bad points about s.o. or s.t.: *The teacher's criticism was very helpful.*

crit·i·cize /'krɪtə,saɪz/ *v.* **-cized, -cizing, -cizes** **1** to evaluate art, music, theater, etc. as a profession: *The newspaper's theater critic criticized the new play as dull.* **2** to point out faults in s.o. or s.t.: *The teacher criticized the student's poor spelling.*

cri·tique /krɪ'tik/ *n.v.* **-tiqued, -tiquing, -tiques** a formal evaluation of s.t. (a book, plan, proposal, s.o.'s work, etc.): *I wrote a <n.> critique of a book for my English class.*

crit·ter /'krɪtər/ *n.slang* (used humorously) an insect or animal, (*syn.*) a creature: *That old house has critters in it, mostly mice and cockroaches.*

croak /kroʊk/ *n.* a deep sound such as that made by a frog
—*v.* **1** to make such a sound: *Frogs croaked in the pond.* **2** *fig.slang* to die: *The old man was sick and finally croaked yesterday.*

cro·chet /kroʊ'ʃeɪ/ *v.* **-cheted** /-'ʃeɪd/ **, -cheting** /-'ʃeɪɪŋ/ **, -chets** /'ʃeɪz/ *n.* [U] to make sweaters, scarves, etc. with a hooked needle and thread: *She <v.> crocheted a tablecloth. See:* knit.

crock /krɑk/ *n.* **1** a pot or jar made of clay **2** *fig.vulg.* nonsense: *What that guy says is a crock!*

crocked /krɑkt/ *adj.slang* drunk: *He got crocked again last night.*

crock·er·y /'krɑkəri/ *n.* [U] dishes, pots, jars, etc. made of clay

croc·o·dile /'krɑkə,daɪl/ *n.* **1** a very long, thin reptile with hard skin and a long mouth with sharp teeth **2** *fig.* **crocodile tears:** pretended sadness or regret: *He fired one employee after another and each time cried crocodile tears about having to do it. See:* alligator.

cro·cus /'kroʊkəs/ *n.* **-cuses** a small plant with purple, white, or yellow flowers: *The crocuses are the first flowers to bloom in the spring.*

crois·sant /krə'sɑnt, krwɑ-/ *n.* a light, flaky pastry shaped in a crescent

cro·ny /'kroʊni/ *n.* **-nies** (often used negatively) a good friend in business or government to exchange favors with: *The mayor always gives city business to one of his cronies. -n.* **cronyism.**

crook (1) /krʊk/ *n.* a criminal, esp. a thief, cheat, or swindler: *There are crooks everywhere ready to cheat you.*

crook (2) *n.v.* a bend or turn: *She carried her books in the <n.> crook of her arm.*

crook·ed /'krʊkɪd/ *adj.* **1** bent, not straight: *a crooked stick (nose, path, piece of wire, etc.)* **2** criminal, dishonest: *a crooked businessman||a crooked deal*

croon /krun/ *v.n.* to sing softly: *Frank Sinatra <v.> crooned about love. -n.* **crooner.**

crop /krɑp/ *n.* **1** a planting and harvest of grain, vegetables, or fruit: *Farmers had a good crop of rice this year.* **2** *fig.* a group of things or people: *Our school had a good crop of freshman students this fall.* **3** a short haircut **4** a short whip used in riding horses
—*v.* **cropped, cropping, crops 1** to chew the tops off plants: *Sheep cropped the grass in the pasture.* **2** to cut hair short **3** *phrasal v.* **to crop up:** to appear unexpectedly: *Some problems cropped up in our new computer system, but we fixed them.*

cro·quet /kroʊ'keɪ/ *n.* [U] a game played on short grass where one hits a ball through wickets (metal arches) with a mallet (long hammer): *Croquet is fun to play on a summer's day.*

cross /krɔs/ *n.* **crosses 1** a vertical wooden pole with a horizontal piece of wood running across it near the top, on which people were killed in ancient times **2** **the Cross:** (in Christianity) the cross on which Jesus Christ was killed (crucified) **3** a representation of the Cross as jewelry or a medal **4** a sign made like a + or an X **5** such a sign written as a signature by people **6** such a sign made as a gesture by Christians in religious devotion **7** a mix of two different things, (*syn.*) hybrid: *That dog is a cross between a collie and a Great Dane.* **8** **to have a heavy cross to bear:** to have many problems, worries: *She has a bad heart and her husband is an alcoholic; so she has a heavy cross to bear.*
—*adj.* **1** horizontal: *a cross bar used in building* **2** angry, (*syn.*) bad-tempered: *She is very cross today; she complains about everything.* -*n.* [U] **crossness.**
—*v.* **crosses 1** to go over or across s.t., (*syn.*) to traverse: *I crossed the street to catch the bus.* **2** to pass while going in opposite directions: *Our letters crossed in the mail.* **3** to oppose, to anger s.o.: *He crossed his friend by not paying back the money that he owed him.*

See: to double-cross. **4 to cross one's fingers:** to wish for good luck: *I have my fingers crossed that I pass the exam today.* **5 to cross one's heart:** to promise, swear s.t. is true: *I cross my heart that I will not tell anyone your secret.* **6** *phrasal v. sep.* **to cross s.o. or s.t. off:** to remove, draw a line through: *I make a list of things to do, then cross off the ones that are done.||I cross them off.* **7 to cross one's mind:** to be a brief thought: *The thought never crossed my mind to tell anyone about your secret.* **8 to cross oneself (or) to make the sign of the cross:** to touch the head, heart, and shoulders with the hand: *In the church, worshipers make the sign of the cross before approaching the altar.* **9** *phrasal v. sep.* **to cross s.t. out:** to draw a line through: *Please cross out the spelling mistakes.||Cross them out.* **10** *phrasal v. insep.* **to cross over s.t.: a.** to go across s.t.: *I crossed over the bridge.* **b.** to vote for the candidate of a different political party from one's own: *In the last election, many Democrats crossed over and voted for a Republican President. See:* crossover. **11** *phrasal v. sep.* **to cross that bridge when one comes to it:** to deal with a problem later: *I know that we will need to buy a new computer, but not for six months; so let's cross that bridge when we come to it.* **12** *phrasal v. sep.* **to cross s.o. up:** to prevent s.o. from doing s.t.: *I crossed up my friend by promising her that she could use my car, but I forgot and she missed her job interview.||I crossed her up.* **13 to cross swords:** to argue with s.o.: *Two politicians crossed swords about raising taxes.*

cross·beam /'krɔs,bim/ *n.* a strong piece of metal or wood resting on two support beams used in making buildings: *Floors are built on crossbeams.*

cross·bow /'krɔs,bou/ *n.* a bow-like weapon used long ago that shoots arrows

cross·breed /'krɔs,brid/ *n.v.* **-bred** /,brɛd/, **-breeding**, **-breeds** a combination of two types of plants or animals, (*syn.*) a hybrid: *A farmer made a <n.> crossbreed between an orange and a grapefruit; she <v.> crossbred them.*

cross·check /'krɔs,tʃɛk, -'tʃɛk/ *v.n.* to check one thing against another for accuracy: *I <v.> crosschecked the list of goods delivered with the list of what I ordered.*

cross·country *adj.* across the land, esp. referring to a sport: *We like to go cross-country skiing in the winter.*

USAGE NOTE: When Americans talk about driving, flying, biking, or traveling *cross-country,* they mean traveling from one coast to the other. *My parents drove cross-country last fall and went swimming first in the Pacific Ocean, then in the Atlantic Ocean.*

cross-examine *v.* **-ined, -ining, -ines** (in law) to ask a witness questions about what she or he has said in a court of law: *My lawyer cross-examined the witness to the accident to show that she did not actually see it happen.* *-n.* [C;U] **cross-examination.**

cross-eyed *adj.* having one or both eyes pointed toward the nose: *She has a cross-eyed cat.*

cross·fire /'krɔs,faɪər/ *n.* [U] shooting (such as by soldiers, police, or criminals) that comes from two sides and crosses the same point: *The soldiers were caught in the crossfire from enemy soldiers shooting from buildings on opposite sides of the square.*

cross·ing /'krɔsɪŋ/ *n.* **1** a place where a street, river, etc. can be crossed, (*syn.*) an intersection: *The river crossing is about a mile south of here.||The school crossing is on the next corner.* **2** a trip, usu. across the ocean

cross-leg·ged /'krɔs,lɛgɪd, -,lɛgd/ *adj.* with one leg placed over the other: *She sat cross-legged on the floor.*

cross·o·ver /'krɔs,ouvər/ *adj.* **1** (a vote) changed from one political party's candidate to another: *There was a big crossover vote by Republicans voting for the Democratic candidate for Senate.* **2** moved from one group or category to another: *Her country and western song was a crossover hit in rock music, too.*

cross-purposes *n.pl.* **at cross-purposes:** doing or saying s.t. that conflicts with or involves misunderstanding of what s.o. else is doing or saying: *working at cross-purposes||talking at cross-purposes*

cross-reference *v.n.* **-enced, -encing, -ences** to tell s.o. about related information in another part of a book, file, index, etc.: *The English textbook <v.> cross-references nouns and verbs to the section on grammar.* *-v.* **cross-refer.**

cross·road /'krɔs,roud/ *n.* or **crossroads** *n.pl.* used with a sing. v. **1** the place where one road crosses another road **2** *fig.* a time of decision about what to do next: *At age 65, she is at a crossroads about whether to retire or keep on working.*

cross section *n.* a part or sample that is typical of a larger group or body: *The mayor asked a cross section of business owners and workers for their opinions on the city's transportation system.||The biology teacher showed us a cross section of a tree.* *—v.* **cross-section.**

cross·walk /'krɔs,wɔk/ *n.* a place on a street marked with lines for people to cross while vehicles stop: *School children are told to cross the street only at the crosswalks.*

cross·word   puzzle /'krɔs,wɜrd/ *n.* a printed word game with numbered squares to be filled in with answers from numbered clues: *Crossword puzzles are fun to do if you like words.*

crossword puzzle

crotch /krɑʧ/ *n.* **crotches** **1** the area at the top of the human legs, (*syn.*) genital area **2** the place where two branches of a tree meet: *Birds built their nest in the crotch of a tree.*

crotch·et·y /'krɑʧəti/ *adj.* irritable, complaining, (*syn.*) crabby: *That crotchety man will not listen to anyone.*

crouch /krauʧ/ *v.n.* **crouches** to bend down at the knees: *The grandfather <v.> crouched down to talk to his small granddaughter.*

crow /kroʊ/ *n.* **1** a large black bird with a loud cry **2** the cry made by a rooster **3** **to eat crow:** to have to admit that one was wrong
—*v.* **1** to make the sound of a rooster: *The rooster crows every morning at sunrise.* **2** *fig.* to brag or boast about s.t.: *She is crowing about how beautiful her new baby is.*

crow·bar /'kroʊ,bar/ *n.v.* **-barred, -barring, -bars** a thick, heavy metal bar used to open things: *A worker pushed a <n.> crowbar into the stuck door and forced it open.*

crowd /kraʊd/ *n.* **1** a large group of people close together, (*syn.*) a throng: *the crowd at the football game‖Some people push their way through the crowd.* **2** a group of friends, similar people: *That crowd takes illegal drugs!* **3** **to gather a crowd:** to attract many people: *That movie star gathers a crowd wherever she goes.*
—*v.* **1** to form into a crowd: *The people crowded into the theater.* **2** to pressure s.o.: *She likes her freedom and her boyfriend crowded her so much that she left him.‖Don't crowd me! I'll make up my mind when I'm ready!*

crowd·ed /'kraʊdɪd/ *adj.* full of people (*syn.*) packed: *That subway train is so crowded no one else can get on.*

crown /kraʊn/ *n.* **1** a decoration for the head usu. made of gold and jewels to show high position:

crown

The queen of England wears her crown for special ceremonies. **2** *usu. used in the sing.* the title held by the winner or top player in a sport: *He wears the boxing crown.* **3** the top back part of the head or a hat
—*v.* **1** to place a crown on s.o.'s head: *The high priest crowned the new king.* **2** to declare s.o. a winner: *She was crowned Miss Universe in a beauty contest.* **3** *slang* to hit s.o. on the head **4** **crowning achievement:** the best after many other good actions: *Winning the Nobel Prize was the crowning achievement of her brilliant scientific career.*

crown jewels *n.pl.* the jewels of a king or queen: *The queen wears some of the crown jewels on special occasions.*

crown prince or **crown princess** *n.* the child of a king or queen who is legal heir to the throne: *The crown princess is in training for becoming queen one day. See:* heir apparent.

CRT /,siar'ti/ *abbr. of See:* cathode-ray tube.

cru·cial /'kruʃəl/ *adj.* extremely important, (*syns.*) critical, decisive: *It is of crucial importance that we sign that contract for our future success. -adv.* **crucially.**

cru·ci·ble /'krusəbəl/ *n.* [C] **1** (in chemistry) a pot in which metals are melted **2** *fig.* a situation where strong action changes things: *The political scandal became public in the crucible of people searching for the truth.*

cru·ci·fix /'krusə,fɪks/ **-fixes** *n.* a cross with the image of Christ on it: *She wears a crucifix on a chain around her neck.*

cru·ci·fix·ion /,krusə'fɪkʃən/ *n.* [C;U] **1** an act of killing by nailing or tying s.o. to a cross: *In ancient times, officials killed criminals by crucifixion.* **2** **the Crucifixion:** the killing of Christ on the Cross

cru·ci·fy /'krusə,faɪ/ *v.* **-fied, -fying, -fies 1** to nail or tie s.o. to a cross as punishment **2** *fig.* to punish s.o. severely

crud /krʌd/ *n.slang* dirt, filth: *His clothes are covered with crud from working on his car. -adj.* **cruddy.**

crude /krud/ *adj.* **cruder, crudest 1** rough, unfinished: *He lives in a cabin with crude chairs and a table made of unpainted wood.* **2** ill-mannered, offensive: *crude behavior -adv.* **crudely;** *-n.* [C;U] **crudity** /'krudəti/; [U] **crudeness.**

cru·el /'kruəl, krul/ *adj.* **1** willing to cause others mental or physical pain, mean, (*syn.*) vicious: *She makes cruel remarks about her husband being too fat.* **2** painful, very difficult: *Cancer is a cruel disease because of the suffering it causes. See:* kind (2), 3.

cru·el·ty /'kruəlti, 'krul-/ *n.* **-ties** an act of causing others mental or physical pain: *His cruelty to his dog by beating and not feeding it is sad.*

cru·et /ˈkruɪt/ *n.* a small glass bottle of oil, vinegar, etc: *I poured oil and vinegar from cruets onto my salad.*

cruise /kruz/ *n.* a pleasure trip on a boat or ship: *We took a cruise in the Caribbean.*

—*v.* **cruised, cruising, cruises** **1** to sail on a boat or ship in a pleasant, comfortable manner: *We cruised down the coast in our sailboat.* **2** to move in a vehicle or airplane at its best, fast, comfortable speed: *Jet planes cruise at 600 miles (960 km) per hour.* **3** *infrml.* to walk or drive around, usu. looking for a sexual partner

cruis·er /ˈkruzər/ *n.* **1** (in USA) a police car: *A cruiser came right after the accident.* **2** a fast powerful warship

cruise ship *n.* a large ship that offers entertainment to its passengers: *The cruise ship had music, dancing, sports, and good food.*

crumb /krʌm/ *n.* **1** a small piece of dry bread, cake, or other baked foods: *She feeds bread crumbs to the pigeons.* **2** *fig.* a small amount of s.t., (*syn.*) a bit: *The article contained only a few crumbs of real information.* **3** *slang* an unimportant, offensive person: *That crumb borrowed my radio and then disappeared.*

crum·ble /ˈkrʌmbəl/ *v.* **-bled, -bling, -bles** **1** to fall into pieces, esp. from age: *Over many years, that old church crumbled into ruins.* **2** **that's the way the cookie crumbles:** bad things do happen: *I lost my job, then had a car accident; oh, well, that's the way the cookie crumbles. -adj.* **crumbly.**

crum·my /ˈkrʌmi/ *or* **crumby** *adj.slang* **-mier, -miest** **1** no good, cheap: *Those shoes are crummy; they fell apart in three weeks.* **2** acting in a bad way (unfair, cheating, etc.): *The shoe store refused to give me my money back, which was a crummy thing to do.*

crum·ple /ˈkrʌmpəl/ *v.* **-pled, -pling, -ples** to crush or press, usu. by hand: *The teacher crumpled (or) crumpled up a piece of paper into a ball and threw it away.*

crunch /krʌnʧ/ *n.* **crunches** **1** a sound like teeth biting an apple: *You hear the crunch when she bites into a raw carrot.* **2** a difficult, high-pressure situation or a tight deadline: *Two employees did not come to work today, so we are in a crunch to do their work, too.*

—*v.* **crunches** to make a crunching sound: *Her teeth crunched into the apple. -adj.* **crunchy.**

cru·sade /kruˈseɪd/ *n.v.* **-saded, -sading, -sades** **1** an organized effort to reach an idealistic goal: *a <n.> crusade for world peace‖He <v.> crusades for peace by marching in front of the United Nations building.* **2** *pl.* **the Crusades:** religious wars made by European Christians against Muslims in the eastern Mediterranean in the 11th to 13th centuries: *The <n.> Crusades began in 1096 and lasted for hundreds of years.*

crush /krʌʃ/ *v.* **crushes** **1** to push, press hard: *She crushed a piece of paper in her hand.* **2** to smash violently: *The roof fell in and crushed the people in the building.* **3** to make s.o. feel very bad, (*syn.*) to devastate: *When her business failed, she was crushed.‖When his wife left him, he was crushed.* **4** to defeat badly: *Our basketball team crushed the other team with a score of 110 to 75.*

—*n.* **crushes** **1** a moving crowd of people: *the crush in the subway of people going to work* **2** a brief love, (*syn.*) an infatuation: *He has a crush on the girl next door.*

crust /krʌst/ *n.* **1** a hard covering: *the earth's crust* **2** a firm outer layer (of food): *a pie crust* ‖ *Bread crust is brown and often crunchy.* **3** **the upper crust:** the top class in a society

crus·ta·cean /krʌˈsteɪʃən/ *n.* an animal with a hard outer shell, such as a lobster, shrimp, or crayfish: *Most crustaceans live in the water.*

crust·y /ˈkrʌsti/ *adj.* **-ier, -iest** **1** having a hard crust: *crusty bread* **2** *fig.* irritable, or rude: *No one can talk to that crusty old man.*

crutch /krʌʧ/ *n.* **crutches** **1** a support made of metal or wood to put under the arm of injured or handicapped people to help them walk: *He broke his foot and is on <n.pl.> crutches now.* **2** *fig.*(used negatively) s.t. used for support: *He drinks alcohol as a <n.> crutch to face life.*

crux /krʌks/ *n. usu. used in the sing.* the central point, main issue: *The crux of the matter is he must find a job to pay his rent.*

cry /kraɪ/ *n.* **cries** **1** a loud sound made by living things: *a cry of pain, a cry for help* **2** a normal sound made by some animals and birds: *the cry of a bird* **3** an act or period of tears running from the eyes from strong emotion: *She had a good cry when the heroine died at the end of the movie.* **4** **a far cry:** very different, far from: *His life as a dishwasher here is a far cry from his job as a doctor in his own country.*

—*v.* **cried, crying, cries** **1** to make a loud sound from the mouth in pain or fear: *The swimmer cried out for help.* **2** to have tears running from the eyes because of sadness, pain, or strong emotion, (*syn.*) to weep: *He cried when his mother died.‖fig.He cried his eyes out.* **3** **For crying out loud:** an expression of annoyance: *For crying out loud, will you stop complaining!* **4** **to cry for joy:** to weep from happiness: *When her lost son was found, the mother cried for joy.* **5** *phrasal v.* **to cry out against s.t.:** *Voters are crying out against new taxes.* **6** *phrasal v. insep.* **to cry out for s.o. or s.t.:** to demand, need: *That problem is crying out to be solved. See:* milk.

cry·ba·by /ˈkraɪˌbeɪbi/ *n.* **-bies** *fig.* a person who complains frequently without good reason, (*syn.*) a wimp: *He is such a crybaby that every time he catches cold, he thinks he is going to die.*

cry·ing /'kraɪɪŋ/ *adj.* bad, needing attention: *It's a crying shame they don't fix those stairs.*

crypt /krɪpt/ *n.* an underground room of a church, a chamber used for burying the dead, (*syn.*) a vault: *The family has a crypt where 10 of its ancestors are buried.*

cryp·tic /'krɪptɪk/ *adj.* brief with hidden meaning: *The criminal left a cryptic message as to where the dead body can be found.* -*adv.* **cryptically.**

crys·tal /'krɪstəl/ *n.* **1** [U] clear, high quality glass: *Those fine wine glasses are made of crystal.* **2** [U] a clear mineral **3** [C] a small regular shape of some substance: *ice crystals* —*adj.* **1** made of crystal: *crystal glasses* **2** *fig.* **crystal clear: a.** very clear, (*syn.*) transparent: *The water is crystal clear; we can see the ocean bottom.* **b.** clear, obvious: *It is crystal clear what we must do.* **3 a crystal ball:** s.t. that tells the future, as a fortuneteller's ball: *I wish I had a crystal ball to tell me how our actions will work out.*

crys·tal·lize /'krɪstə,laɪz/ *v.* -**lized, -lizing, -lizes 1** to form into a crystal: *Cold rain crystallized into snow.* **2** *fig.* to come together clearly, (*syn.*) to jell: *After weeks of work, our plan for a vacation trip crystallized.* -*n.* [U] **crystallization.**

cub /kʌb/ *n.adj.* **1** the young of some wild animals (bear, wolf, fox, etc.): *Lion <n.> cubs depend on their mother to feed them.* **2** a beginner: *a <adj.> cub reporter for a newspaper*

cube /kyub/ *n.* **1** a square object with four sides, a top and a bottom: *an ice cube* —*v.* **cubed, cubing, cubes 1** to cut into cubes: *The cook cubed a piece of cheese to put on a salad.* **2** to multiply a number by itself twice: *Two cubed is 2 x 2 x 2 = 8, or 2³.* -*adj.* **cubic.**

cube

cu·bi·cle /'kyubɪkəl/ *n.* a small area with walls on three sides for work or study: *She studies in a cubicle in the school library.* See: carrel.

Cub Scouts *n.pl.* a division of the Boy Scouts for boys ages eight through ten: *He joined the Cub Scouts because he likes to go camping.* See: Brownies.

cuck·old /'kʌkəld/ *n.v.* a man whose wife has had sexual relations with another man: *He was <v.> cuckolded by his best friend.*

cuck·oo /'ku,ku, 'kʊ-/ *n.* -**oos 1** a gray bird whose call sounds like "cuckoo" **2** *slang* a crazy person —*adj. slang* **1** crazy, foolish **2 to go cuckoo (or) drive s.o. cuckoo:** to become or to make s.o. insane: *The noise on the street is so loud that it is driving me cuckoo.*

cu·cum·ber /'kyu,kʌmbər/ *n.* **1** a long, round fruit with green skin and crisp white flesh, or the plant it grows on: *Cucumbers are used to make pickles or are cut in slices for salads.* **2 as cool as a cucumber:** calm, composed: *Her boss was yelling at her, but she was as cool as a cucumber.*

cud·dle /'kʌdl/ *v.n.* -**dled, -dling, -dles** to hold tenderly and close, to hug gently: *The mother <v.> cuddled her baby in her arms.* -*adj.* **cuddly.**

cue (1) /kyu/ *n.* **1** a sign or signal, esp. one used to start an action: *The film director pointed at the actors as a cue for them to start acting.* **2** *phrasal v. sep.* **on cue:** when given a signal: *The actors started acting on cue from the director.||They acted on his cue.* **3 to take one's cue: a.** to begin on a signal **b.** to follow s.o.'s actions: *I didn't know where to go so I took my cue from the people leaving the elevator.* —*v.* **cued, cuing, cues 1** to give s.o. a sign or signal to do s.t. **2** *phrasal v. sep.* **to cue s.o. in:** to inform s.o.: *I was late for the meeting and my friend cued me in on what was already said.*

cue (2) *n.* a long, rounded, smooth wooden stick with a leather tip used in playing pool or billiards

cue (3) *n.v.* **cued, cuing, cues** a line of people, (*syn.*) a queue

cuff /kʌf/ *n.* **1** an upward fold at the bottom of a pair of pants **2** the bottom part of a long sleeve: *I unbuttoned my shirt cuffs.* **3** *pl.* **cuffs** handcuffs **4** *infrml.* a blow with the open hand, a slap **5 off the cuff:** without planning: *She gave a speech off the cuff.* —*v.* **1** to make cuffs on shirts or trousers **2** to put handcuffs on s.o.: *A police officer captured a thief and cuffed him.* **3** *slang* to hit s.o. with the open hand, to slap: *The mother cat cuffed her kittens to keep them together.*

cuff links *n.pl.* jewelry used to hold shirt cuffs together: *He wears gold cuff links.*

cuff link

cui·sine /kwɪ'zin/ *n.* [U] **1** the art and science of cooking **2** a style of cooking: *He likes French cuisine and his wife enjoys Mexican cuisine.*

cul-de-sac /'kʌldə,sæk, 'kʊl-/ *n.* **cul-de-sacs** or **culs-de-sac** a dead-end street or path

cu·li·nar·y /'kyulə,nɛri, 'kʌlə,nɛri,/ *adj.* related to the kitchen and cooking: *She is studying culinary arts, like baking fine cakes, in school.*

cull /kʌl/ *v.* to remove unwanted things from those that are wanted, (*syn.*) to glean: *Farmers cull herds of cattle by killing sick cows and leaving the healthy ones.*

cul·mi·nate /'kʌlmə,neɪt/ *v.* -**nated, -nating,**

-nates 1 to reach the highest point of an activity **2** to result in: *All our hard work culminated in a good year for our business.* *-n.* [C] **culmination** /ˌkʌlməˈneɪʃən/.

cul·pa·ble /ˈkʌlpəbəl/ *adj.frml.* guilty, esp. of committing a crime, (*syn.*) blameworthy: *The judge found the man culpable and put him on trial.* *-n.* [U] **culpability.**

cul·prit /ˈkʌlprɪt/ *n.* a person guilty of doing wrong, esp. committing a crime: *The police put the culprit in jail.*

cult /kʌlt/ *n.adj.* a religious group considered extreme or false: *The members of that <n.> cult do anything their leader says.* **2** extreme devotion to a person or idea: *That rock musician has a <adj.> cult following.* See: religion; sect.

cul·ti·vate /ˈkʌltəˌveɪt/ *v.* **-vated, -vating, -vates 1** to prepare the land to grow food crops, trees, and flowers; to plow, plant seed, water, and fertilize the land: *From ancient times, people have cultivated crops, like wheat, for food.* **2** to study and develop a fine understanding, such as of art, music, books, etc.: *She has cultivated her knowledge of art.* **3** to develop friendships with people: *He cultivates important people.*
—*adj.* *She is a cultivated woman.*

cul·ti·va·tion /ˌkʌltəˈveɪʃən/ *n.* **1** preparation of land, such as plowing, planting seed, etc. to grow crops **2** growth in understanding fine things (art, music, books, etc.) **3** fine manners and tastes

cul·tu·ral /ˈkʌltʃərəl/ *adj.* related to culture and its activities: *In New York City, there are many cultural events, such as the ballet, concerts, and plays.* *-adv.* **culturally.**

cul·ture /ˈkʌltʃər/ *n.* [C;U] **1** the ideas, activities (art, foods, businesses), and ways of behaving that are special to a country, people, or region: *In North American culture, men do not kiss men when meeting each other. They shake hands.* **2** [U] the achievements of a people or nation in art, music, literature, etc.: *The Chinese have had a high culture for thousands of years.‖She is a person of culture and refinement.* **3** [C] (in medicine) a small piece of material from the body tested for a disease: *The doctor took a culture from my sore throat to see if I have a strep throat.*
—*v.* **-tured, -turing, -tures** to grow (in a laboratory, hothouse): *to culture bacteria in a medical laboratory*

cul·tured /ˈkʌltʃərd/ *adj.* **1** having knowledge of art, music, books, etc.: *He is a cultured man who knows a lot about music and dance.* **2** grown with the help of people: *Cultured pearls are grown by putting grains of sand in oysters.*

cum·ber·some /ˈkʌmbərsəm/ *adj.* **1** heavy and difficult to handle, (*syns.*) awkward, bulky: *That new TV is in a big, cumbersome box.*

cu·mu·la·tive /ˈkyumyələtɪv, -ˌleɪ-/ *adj.* adding amounts gradually over time: *The cumulative effects of drinking too much alcohol finally killed him.‖Seven percent cumulative interest on $100 = $7 in the first year and $7.49 in the second.*

cun·ning /ˈkʌnɪŋ/ *n.* [U] careful deception, (*syns.*) slyness, shrewdness: *A spy used cunning to find out secrets.*
—*adj.* cute, lovable, (*syn.*) precious: *a cunning little girl*

cup /kʌp/ *n.* **1** a small, round, open container, usu. with a handle, for drinking liquids: *She drinks coffee from a cup.* **2** a measure of 8 fluid ounces or 16 tablespoons: *The recipe called for a cup of flour.* **3** a prize for winning a sports competition, (*syn.*) a trophy **4** either side of a brassiere **5 one's cup of tea:** (often used negatively) a favorite thing: *Driving in a bad snowstorm is not my cup of tea.* **6 to be in one's cups:** to be drunk
—*v.* **cupped, cupping, cups** to form one's hands into a cup: *The farmer cupped his hands to drink water from the stream.*

cup

cup·board /ˈkʌbərd/ *n.* a piece of furniture or a closet with shelves and doors, esp. for dishes and canned food: *I put the cans of beans in the cupboard.*

cup·ful /ˈkʌpˌfʊl/ *n.* **-fuls** the amount of s.t. held in a cup: *She put two cupfuls of milk in the cake batter.*

cu·pid·i·ty /kyuˈpɪdəti/ *n.* [U] *frml.* greed, a strong desire for money and property: *Her cupidity for owning cars, houses, and bank accounts is well known.*

cur /kɜr/ *n.* *old usage* a bad-tempered, often ugly dog, (*syn.*) a mongrel: *That cur tried to bite me!*

cur·a·ble /ˈkyʊrəbəl/ *adj.* capable of being cured: *Tuberculosis is a curable disease.*

cu·rate /ˈkyʊrɪt/ *n.* (in religion) a clergyman or clergywoman who helps run a parish: *The curate helped the minister prepare for Sunday services.*

cu·ra·tor /ˈkyʊrˌeɪtər, kyuˈreɪtər/ *n.* the person in charge of a museum, library, or a collection within it: *The curator of paintings put on an exhibition of some of them.*

curb /kɜrb/ *n.* **1** the edge and border area of a sidewalk, (*syn.*) a curbstone: *Two boys sat on the curb and watched the cars go by.* **2** a check, s.t. (an idea, law, order) that stops or

slows an activity, (*syn.*) a restraint: *She put a curb on her spending.*
—*v.* to restrain or restrict: *I went on a diet and curbed my appetite for food and drink.*

curb·stone /'kɜrb,stoʊn/ *n.* the curb, border area of a sidewalk: *Years ago, curbstones were long narrow pieces of stones laid next to each other. See:* curb.

curd /kɜrd/ *n.* [C;U] a soft lump made when milk turns sour: *Curds are used to make cheese.*

cur·dle /'kɜrdl/ *v.* **-dled, -dling, -dles** to thicken, turn into curds: *The sour milk curdled.*

cure /kyʊr/ *v.* **cured, curing, cures 1** to make s.o. healthy by using medicines and treatments, to heal: *A doctor cures sick people.* **2** to solve problems or bad conditions: *The government cured poverty by giving jobs to poor people.* **3** to preserve food by cooking, salting, etc. it so it will last a long time: *He cured fish by smoking them over a fire.*
—*n.* **1** the healing of a disease: *a cure for cancer* **2** a solution to a problem or bad condition: *a cure for poverty*

cur·few /'kɜrfyu/ *n.* a period of time when people may not go outdoors usu. imposed by the government: *Some cities enforce a 10 P.M. curfew for teenagers.*

cu·ri·o /'kyʊri,oʊ/ *n.* **-os** a small, unusual decoration: *That store in Paris sells curios of the Eiffel Tower.*

cu·ri·os·i·ty /,kyʊri'ɑsəti/ *n.* **-ties 1** [U] interest in knowing about things: *He has a natural curiosity about how machines work.* **2** [U] asking too much about s.t., (*syn.*) inquisitiveness: *The old man shows curiosity about everything his neighbors are doing.* **3** [C] s.t. unusual, strange, or worthy of interest: *That huge, old house is a curiosity for all who pass by it.* **4 curiosity killed the cat:** being too curious can be dangerous: *When you walk in the woods, stay away from those dangerous caves; remember, curiosity killed the cat!*

cu·ri·ous /'kyʊriəs/ *adj.* **1** interested in knowing about things: *I am curious; where did you buy that beautiful dress?* **2** too interested in the lives of others, (*syn.*) nosy: *She is always curious about what her neighbors are doing.* **3** strange, unusual, (*syn.*) puzzling: *His curious behavior has many people worried. -adv.* **curiously.**

curl /kɜrl/ *n.* **1** hair formed into a spiral: *Her hair is full of pretty curls.* **2** s.t. formed like a coil: *a curl of ribbon‖a curl of smoke*
—*v.* **1** to form hair into curls: *The hairdresser curled her hair.* **2** *phrasal v. insep.* **to curl around s.t.:** to wrap around s.t., (*syn.*) to coil: *That plant curls around the tree branch.* **3** *phrasal v.* **to curl up: a.** to fold up: *She curls up (her legs) in bed and reads a book.* **b.** to

dry up, (*syn.*) to wither: *Without water, the plant curled up and died.*

curl·y /'kɜrli/ *adj.* **-ier, -iest** having curls: *The little boy has curly hair. -n.* [U] **curliness.**

cur·rant /'kɜrənt, 'kʌr-/ *n.* **1** a small, dark type of raisin (dried grape), used esp. in baking **2** a small black, red, or white berry, or the bush it grows on: *I like jam made of black currants on bread.*

cur·ren·cy /'kɜrənsi, 'kʌr-/ *n.* **-cies 1** [C;U] the money used to pay for goods and services in a country: *The currency in the USA is made up of dollar bills and coins.* **2** [U] *frml.* wide acceptance, (*syn.*) relevance: *Socialist ideas have little currency in the USA.*

cur·rent /'kɜrənt, 'kʌr-/ *n.* **1** a flow of s.t., such as electricity or water: *The current in the river is slow.* **2** a way of doing things, (*syn.*) tendency: *the currents of change in countries*
—*adj.* **1** belonging to present time, (*syn.*) contemporary: *The current situation is peaceful.* **2** knowing what has happened, (*syn.*) up-to-date: *She reads the newspaper to stay current with what is happening in the world.* **3** having all one's bills paid: *All our bills are current and we owe no one anything.*

cur·rent·ly /'kɜrəntli, 'kʌr-/ *adv.* at this time, now: *We are currently fixing up our old house.*

cur·ric·u·lum /kə'rɪkyələm/ *n.* **-la, /-lə/** or **lums** the courses offered at an educational institution (school, college, etc.): *The curriculum at that college is heavy on science and engineering.*

curriculum vi·tae /'vi,taɪ, 'vaɪ,ti/ *n.frml. usu. used in the sing.* a résumé of one's personal information (name, address, telephone number, education, etc.) and work history: *In the business world, you send in your résumé for a job opening and in the world of education, you send a curriculum vitae. See:* c.v.

cur·ry (1) /'kɜri, 'kʌri/ *n.* **-ries** [C;U] a mixture of hot spices in powder form, originally from India, used to prepare a dish of meat, vegetables, etc.: *chicken curry*

curry (2) *v.* **-ried, -rying, -ries 1** to rub esp. a horse with a currycomb **2 to curry favor:** to seek approval and benefits from s.o.: *He curries favor with his boss by bringing him coffee.*

curse /kɜrs/ *n.* **1** a request or prayer to God, the Devil, etc., for harm to be done to s.o.: *That evil man put a curse on his neighbor.* **2** s.t. that causes harm: *Those flies are a curse in the kitchen.* **3** dirty word(s), swear word(s)
—*v.* **cursed, cursing, curses 1** to put a curse on s.o. **2** to speak or write swear words: *That guy curses all the time! See:* cuss. **3 to be cursed with (or) by:** to have bad luck: *She is cursed with a bad back that hurts her all the time.*

C

cur·so·ry /'kɜrsəri/ *adj.* quick, without paying attention, (*syn.*) superficial: *She gave the newspaper a cursory look, then put it down.*

curt /kɜrt/ *adj.* rude and short (in manner), (*syn.*) abrupt: *He asked his boss a question, but got a curt reply, "I have no time for you now!"* *-adv.* **curtly.**

cur·tail /kər'teɪl/ *v.* to cut back, (*syns.*) to diminish, shorten: *After his heart attack, he curtailed all his activities and worked only a few hours a day.*

cur·tain /'kɜrtn/ *n.* **1** a cloth covering usu. hanging in front of a window or theater stage: *We have a plastic shower curtain to keep water in the bathtub.* **2** *pl.infrml.slang:* **curtains:** death: *He drives his car much too fast and someday it will be curtains for him.* —*v.* to hang curtains: *She curtained every window of her house with lace curtains.*

curt·sy or **courtsey** /'kɜrtsi/ *n.v.* **-sied, -sying, -sies** (done by women) bending the knees and nodding of the head made as a sign of respect for important people: *Women <v.> curtsied as the queen shook their hands.*

cur·va·ceous /kər'veɪʃəs/ *adj.frml.* curvy, shapely: *That young woman has a curvaceous figure.*

cur·va·ture /'kɜrvətʃər, -,tʃʊr/ *n.* a curved line or surface: *From outer space you can see the curvature of the earth's surface.*

curve /kɜrv/ *n.* **1** a line or surface that bends without angles: *There is a curve in the road ahead.* **2** (from baseball) **to throw s.o. a curve (ball):** to surprise, deceive s.o.: *He threw me a curve ball by telling me the meeting was at three when it was at two and I missed it.* —*v.* to bend in a curved line: *The highway curves to the left about a mile from here.* *-adj.* **curvy.**

cush·ion /'kuʃən/ *n.* **1** a type of soft pillow: *The cushions on the sofa are covered with silk.* **2** *fig. s.t.* extra, a margin of safety, (*syn.*) a reserve: *We keep an extra $3,000 in our checking account as a cushion for emergencies.* —*v.* to soften the force or harm of s.t.: *Her company fired her, but cushioned the blow by paying her for six months while she looks for another job.*

cush·y /'kuʃi/ *adj.* **-ier, -iest** easy, comfortable, and not demanding: *He has a cushy job working for his father.*

cusp /kʌsp/ *n.* a point: *The cusp of his tooth is broken.*

cuss /kʌs/ *v.infrml.* **cusses** to curse, speak, or write dirty words, (*syn.*) to swear: *That woman cusses like a truck driver.* —*n.* **cusses** *infrml.*: an odd or unpleasant person or animal: *That man is an old cuss.* *-n.* **cussword** /'kʌs,wɜrd/.

cus·tard /'kʌstərd/ *n.* [U] a soft, yellowish dessert made of baked milk, eggs, sugar, and flavorings: *I like a sweet custard for dessert.*

cus·to·di·an /kʌ'stoʊdiən/ *n.* **1** a person who cleans and makes repairs in a building, janitor **2** a person, bank, etc. that keeps valuables safe for s.o. else: *That bank is the custodian of the woman's stock certificates and savings.* *-adj.* **custodial.**

cus·to·dy /'kʌstədi/ *n.* [U] **1** safekeeping, protection: *After the parents divorced, the mother got custody of the children.* **2** being held under arrest by the police: **into (and) in custody:** *The police found the criminal and took him into custody; he is in custody in jail now.*

cus·tom /'kʌstəm/ *n.* **1** [C;U] a habitual way of behaving that is special to a person, people, region, or nation: *It is his custom to smoke a cigar after dinner.||It is British custom to drink tea at four o'clock each afternoon.* **2** *n.pl.* **customs** taxes on goods brought into a country, (*syn.*) duties: *I paid the customs on some wine and perfume from France.* **3** *n.pl.* **customs** used with a sing.v. the branch of government and its workers who keep track of the goods brought into a country: *I had to go through customs when I came to this country.*

cus·tom·ar·y /'kʌstə,mɛri/ *adj.* expected and traditional way to behave: *It is customary to thank the people who invite you to their party.*

custom-built *adj.* made the way s.o. wants it, made to one's specifications: *Their house is custom-built with a large kitchen.*

cus·tom·er /'kʌstəmər/ *n.* a person or business that buys from another person or business, (*syns.*) client, purchaser: *Our company treats its customers well with fast service and good products.*

USAGE NOTE: Businesses have *customers.* Providers of services, such as lawyers have *clients.* Doctors, dentists, etc. have *patients.* A person who stays at a hotel or motel is a *guest.* Business people and companies that sell to others are called *vendors* or *suppliers.*

cus·tom·ize /'kʌstə,maɪz/ *v.* **-ized, -izing, -izes** to make s.t. to the way s.o. wants, often by hand: *That company customizes kitchens by making cabinets just the way you want them.* See: custom-built; custom-made.

custom-made *adj.* made the way s.o. wants it: *She wears custom-made suits that she has made by a tailor.*

cus·toms /'kʌstəmz/ *n.pl.* See: custom (**2**), (**3**).

cut /kʌt/ *n.* **1** a wound caused by a knife or other sharp edge: *I have a cut on my finger.* **2** a hole or opening made by s.t. sharp (knife, saw, scissors): *He made cuts in the fabric for buttonholes.* **3** a reduction in the amount of s.t.: *He was given a cut in salary.* **4** *infrml.* a part or share of s.t.: *The salespeople here get a 10% cut of the price of everything.* **5** a piece that is cut from a whole, esp. a particular part of an animal body used for meat: *I bought an inexpensive cut of beef for making stew.* **6** a style: *the cut of a dress* **7 a cut above (or) below:** s.t. better (or) worse than s.t. else: *Our product is a cut above our competitor's in quality.* **8 to survive the cut:** to keep one's job while others lose theirs: *Our company has laid off many employees but I have survived the cut and still have my job.* **9** slang **to take a cut at:** to make an attempt at doing s.t.: *He took a cut at solving the problem.*

—*v.* **cut, cutting, cuts 1** to open with a knife by accident, *(syn.)* to wound: *She cut her finger with a knife.* **2** to slice into bits: *She cut the carrots and potatoes into small pieces.* **3** to divide into pieces or parts, *(syn.)* to partition: *She cut the apple pie into six pieces.*||*The three thieves cut the stolen money three ways among them.* **4** to reduce the strength or quality of s.t., *(syn.)* to dilute: *They cut the whiskey with water.* **5** to remove completely: *He cut (or) cut out meat from his diet. (He no longer eats meat.)*||*That company cut 100 employees from its staff.* **6** to stop or interrupt s.t.: *A storm cut off the electricity.* **7** to prevent people from going, *(syn.)* to isolate: *The fallen bridge cut people off from the other side of the river.* **8** to remove the top half of a deck of cards and put it on the bottom: *I cut the cards (pack, deck).* **9 cut!:** to stop an action esp. filming s.t.: *The film scene was going badly, so the director yelled, "Cut!"* **10 to cut a check, tape, or compact disk:** *infrml.* to prepare or record: *Our company cuts paychecks every two weeks.*||*That singer cut a new CD of her latest songs.* **11** *phrasal v. insep.* **to cut across s.t.: a.** to take a shorter way (shortcut) to go somewhere: *The farmer cut across his field to go home instead of the longer way by the road.* **b.** to affect many different things: *The damage caused by the use of drugs cuts across all social classes.* **c.** (a line) to go across, *(syn.)* to bisect **12** *slang* **to cut a deal:** to discuss and sign a contract: *We met for lunch yesterday and cut a deal on leasing 100 new cars.* **13** *phrasal v. sep.* **to cut s.o. or s.t. apart:** to put into pieces with a knife, *(syn.)* to dismember: *The cook cut apart the chicken by cutting off the legs and wings.*||*She cut it apart.* **14** *phrasal v. insep.* **to cut back (or) cut back on s.t.: a.** to reduce s.t.: *Our company cut back the number of employees from 100 to 75.*||*The owner cut back on the size of salary increases.* **b.** to turn back: *The thief ran from the police, then cut back toward his hiding place.* **15 to cut both ways:** to do s.t. that has a two-sided, double effect: *When you get angry at people, it cuts both ways because they get angry at you, too.* **16 to cut class:** not to go to classes at a

school or college: *That student has cut so many of his classes that he will not graduate.* **17 to cut corners:** to do s.t. the easiest and/or cheapest way, usu. with a bad result: *The city cut corners on building that new road and now it is falling apart.* **18** *phrasal v. sep.* **to cut s.t. down: a.** to reduce the amount of s.t., *(syn.)* to lessen: *She cut down on the number of cigarettes that she smokes from 30 to 10 a day.* **b.** to chop down, *(syn.)* to fell: *He cut down a tree for firewood.* **c.** to kill: *The man was cut down by gunfire.* **19** *phrasal v. insep.* **to cut in on s.o. or s.t.: a.** to interrupt: *While we were talking, a stranger cut in and asked directions.* **b.** to ask a woman to dance while she is dancing with s.o. else **20** *phrasal v. insep.* **to cut into s.t.:** to reduce the amount of s.t.: *Losses cut into profits.* **21** *infrml.* **to cut it:** to perform to a required standard, succeed: *She works two jobs and she can cut it at both of them.* **22 Cut it out!:** to stop annoying (or) bad behavior: *I told you to stop playing that radio so loudly. Cut it out!* **23 to cut loose: a.** to free oneself: *The magician was tied up with ropes but he was able to cut himself loose.* **b.** to perform in an excellent, unusual way: *He was an ordinary football player, but he cut loose today and won the game.* **24** *phrasal v. sep.* **to cut s.o. or s.t. off: a.** s.o or s.t.: to eliminate from contact, *(syn.)* to estrange, disinherit: *His conservative family cut off the young poet.*||*They cut him off.* **b.** s.t.: to remove *(syns.)* to amputate, sever: *A doctor cut off the man's diseased foot.* **25 to cut off one's nose to spite one's face:** to harm oneself: *She wants people to like her, but she cuts her nose off to spite her face by being difficult with them.* **26 to cut one's losses:** to stop losses and get out of a losing situation: *I bought a stock at $10 a share and it went down to $8 where I sold it to cut my losses; it is now $3 a share.* **27 to cut one's teeth on:** to learn s.t. useful, to start a career: *She cut her teeth on selling the company's products, then became a manager.* **28** *phrasal v. sep.* **to cut s.t. out: a.** to remove: *The doctor cut out the woman's appendix.* **b.** *infrml.* to stop doing s.t.: *I cut out smoking cigarettes.* ||*I cut it out.* **29 cut out for:** to be right for (or) suited to: *He is cut out for sports because he is fast and strong.* **30** *phrasal v. sep.* **to cut s.o. or s.t. short: a.** to stop s.o. from talking, esp. rudely: *His wife tried to talk to him about a problem, but he cut her short and left the room.* **b.** to stop s.t. before the planned time: *When my mother became very ill, I cut short my vacation to be with her.* ||*I cut it short.* **31 to cut s.o. down to size:** to make people understand that they are not as important as they think they are: *A worker started telling the boss what to do, so she told him to stop and that cut him down to size.* **32 to cut s.t. too fine:** to make s.t. too difficult, esp. unimportant details: *She argued over small points in the contract and I told her that she cut the matter too fine, so we can't agree.* **33** *phrasal v. insep.* **to cut through** *s.t.:* **a.** to go through by force, (*syns.*) to hack, slash: *The firefighter cut through the door with an axe and saved the child.* **b.** to make a difficult matter easy, (*syn.*) to facilitate: *The politician cut through the governmental delays and got the problem solved quickly.* **34** *infrml.* **to cut to the bone:** to take strong measures to stop spending money: *The company is having money problems and has cut all expenses to the bone.* **35** *phrasal v. insep.* **to cut s.o. or s.t. up:** **a.** to slice into pieces: *He cut up the paper into little pieces.* **b.** to injure by cutting: *He fell through the window and cut himself up with pieces of glass.* **c.** to behave playfully: *She loves to cut up by making funny faces with her friends. See:* mustard.

cut-and-dried *adj.* **1** done earlier and not going to be changed **2** without surprises, routine: *The yearly meeting of that company is cut-and-dried because they elect the same people to run it each year.*

cut·back /ˈkʌtˌbæk/ *n.* a reduction in *s.t.*: *Business is not good, so the company made a cutback in workers from 50 to 25.*

cute /kyut/ *adj.* **cuter, cutest** **1** pleasing to look at, (*syns.*) adorable, darling: *a cute baby* **2** attempting to deceive *s.o.*, (*syns.*) shrewd, clever: *She was being cute with the boss trying to get a raise.* *-adv.* **cutely;** *-n.* [U] **cuteness.**

cu·ti·cle /ˈkyutɪkəl/ *n.* a hard layer of skin at the bottom of a fingernail or toenail

cut·ler·y /ˈkʌtləri/ *n.* [U] knives, forks, and spoons: *We keep the cutlery in a kitchen cabinet.*

cut·let /ˈkʌtlɪt/ *n.* a small slice of meat: *I had veal cutlets for dinner. See:* chop *n.* **2.**

cut·off /ˈkʌtˌɔf/ *n.* an interruption or stopping of *s.t.*: *After the accident, there was a cutoff of electricity to the train tracks.*
—*adj.* related to a limit or deadline when *s.t.* must stop: *The cutoff date for the talks to finish is tomorrow.*

cut-rate *adj.* **1** sold at a lower price **2** of poor quality, cheap: *Those cut-rate shoes will fall apart quickly.*

cut·ter /ˈkʌtər/ *n.* **1** a person or tool that cuts things **2** a small, fast boat with one large sail

cut·throat /ˈkʌtˌθroʊt/ *n.* a murderer: *That mean man is a cutthroat.*
—*adj.* very competitive, (*syns.*) vicious, dog-eat-dog: *That chemistry course is cutthroat; none of the students will help each other.*

cut·ting /ˈkʌtɪŋ/ *adj.* **1** sharp, painful: *a cold, cutting wind* **2** meant to hurt *s.o.'s* feelings, (*syn.*) sarcastic: *He made cutting comments about his wife's being too fat.*

—*n.* [C] **1** editing, taking out pieces of film: *An editor does the cutting of film to shorten a movie.* **2** a piece of a plant used to grow a new plant: *She gave me a cutting of her plant that I liked.*

c.v. /sivi/ *abbr. for* curriculum vitae

cy·a·nide /ˈsaɪəˌnaɪd/ *n.* [U] a white, poisonous chemical. *Cyanide is used to kill insects.*

cy·ber·space /ˈsaɪbərˌspeɪs/ *n.* the world (space) of communications, information, and entertainment created by the use of computers: *She turns on her computer and travels in cyberspace by sending messages to friends around the world. See:* virtual reality.

cy·cle /ˈsaɪkəl/ *n.* **1** an event or activity that changes from time to time from one characteristic to another and then back to the first one: *We have weather cycles of good rainfall, then dry weather, then rain again.‖a business cycle* **2** a bicycle or motorcycle
—*v.* **-cled, -cling, -cles** **1** to go through a cycle (weather, business) **2** to ride on a bicycle or motorcycle: *He cycles to work on his motorcycle.* *-adj.* **cyclical** /ˈsaɪklɪkəl, ˈsɪk-/; **cyclic.**

cy·clist /ˈsaɪklɪst/ *n.* a person who rides a bicycle or motorcycle: *Cyclists pedal around the park.*

cy·clone /ˈsaɪˌkloʊn/ *n.* a violent windstorm: *A cyclone tore up trees and houses. See:* tornado.

cyl·in·der /ˈsɪləndər/ *n.* **1** a shape or object with a flat, circular top and bottom and straight sides **2** a usu. hollow metal object with this shape, esp. a mechanical part: *One of the cylinders in my car engine does not work.* *-adj.* **cylindrical** /səˈlɪndrɪkəl/.

cym·bal /ˈsɪmbəl/ *n.* one of a pair of thin, round, metal plates used in music by hitting them together

cyn·ic /ˈsɪnɪk/ *n.* a negative person, *s.o.* who thinks others do things only for money and pleasure: *She is a cynic about politics and politicians.* *-n.* [U] **cynicism** /ˈsɪnəˌsɪzəm/.

cyn·i·cal /ˈsɪnɪkəl/ *adj.* having the negative attitude of a cynic, (*syns.*) mocking, sneering: *The manager has a cynical attitude toward everyone.* *-adv.* **cynically.**

cy·press /ˈsaɪprəs/ *n.* **-presses** a tall tree (evergreen) with small dark needles instead of leaves: *Cypresses grow in places with warm climates, like Florida and Louisiana.*

cyst /sɪst/ *n.* a growth that contains liquid: *He has a harmless cyst in his mouth.*

czar or **tsar** /zɑr/ *n.* **1** a Russian emperor **2** a manager with a lot of power: *The government's drug czar can use workers from all government departments to work for him.*

cza·ri·na /zɑˈrinə/ *n.* a Russian empress

D, d

D, d /di/ **D's, d's,** or **Ds, ds 1** the fourth letter of the English alphabet **2** the symbol the Romans used for 500 *See:* Roman numeral.

'd *contr.* **1** would: *He said he'd eat with us.* **2** had: *He said he'd already eaten.* **3** did: *Where'd he eat?*

D.A. /ˌdiˈeɪ/ *abbrev.* for district attorney: *Dave Deakin is the D.A. in our county.*

dab /dæb/ *n.* a small amount of s.t.: *I put a dab of butter on my bread.*
—*v.* **dabbed, dabbing, dabs 1** to apply a small amount of s.t.: *She dabbed paint on a canvas (antiseptic on a cut, makeup on her nose, etc.).* **2** to touch with quick strokes: *He dabbed at the spot on his tie with a napkin. -n.* **dabber.**

dab·ble /ˈdæbəl/ *v.* **-bled, -bling, -bles 1** to do or engage in an activity in a casual manner, to play at: *She dabbles in painting as a hobby.* **2** to invest money in small amounts: *They dabble in the stock market (in real estate, in art, etc.). -n.* **dabbler.**

dachs·hund /ˈdɑks,hʊnt, ˈdɑksənt/ *n.* a small dog, usu. brown or black, with a long body and very short legs

Dac·ron /ˈdeɪ,krɑn, ˈdæ-/ *n.TM* [U] artificial fiber used widely in the manufacture of clothes: *These shirts don't have to be ironed because they are made of Dacron.*

dad /dæd/ *n.infrml. short* for daddy, one's father: *Dad, can I have some money? See:* daddy.

dad·dy /ˈdædi/ *n.infrml.* **-dies** one's father, a word usu. used in the Southern USA or by small children: *My daddy works for the government. See:* dad; granddaddy; sugar daddy.

daf·fo·dil /ˈdæfə,dɪl/ *n.* a yellow flower: *Daffodils are among the first flowers to bloom in the spring.*

daf·fy /ˈdæfi/ *adj.infrml.* **-fier, -fiest 1** strange, *(syns.)* ec-

daffodil

centric, zany: *That comedian sometimes acts a bit daffy.* **2** foolish: *Buying an old car like that was a daffy thing to do!*

dag·ger /ˈdægər/ *n.* a short knife used as a weapon in the past: *Long ago, pirates carried daggers.*

da·guerre·o·type /dəˈgɛrə,taɪp/ *n.* an early form of photography co-invented by Jacques Daguerre: *Some families have daguerreotypes in picture albums from the mid-1800s.*

dahl·ia /ˈdɑlyə, ˈdæl-/ *n.* a brightly colored flower native to Central America: *Dahlias make beautiful table decorations.*

dai·ly /ˈdeɪli/ *adv.* each day: *I take a walk daily.*
—*adj.* related to a day: *Do you read a daily newspaper?*

dain·ty /ˈdeɪnti/ *adj.* **-tier, -tiest 1** small and finely made, *(syn.)* delicate: *They drank tea in dainty cups.* **2** small and beautiful: *The little girl wore a dainty dress. -adv.* **daintily.**

dai·qui·ri /ˈdækəri, ˈdaɪ-/ *n.* a rum drink made with lime and ice: *Daiquiris are popular drinks in hot weather.*

dair·y /ˈdɛri/ *n.* **-ies 1** a building in which cows are kept and milked: *Cows are milked at the dairy each morning.* **2** a business that produces milk, cheese, butter, etc.
—*v.* to engage in the dairy business *-n.* [U] **dairying.**

dairy farm *n.* a farm for raising and keeping milk cows: *He runs a dairy farm in Illinois.*

da·is /ˈdeɪəs, ˈdaɪ-/ *n.* **-ises** a platform, usu. with chairs, a long table, and a podium for

dais

speakers (at a banquet, lecture, etc.): *There are 20 people sitting on the dais, but only the guest of honor will speak.*

dai·sy /ˈdeɪzi/ *n.* **-sies** a flower with a flat wheel of long, thin white or yellow petals:

Daisies grow wild in many places.

dale /deɪl/ *n.frml.* **1** a valley **2** *fig.* **up hill and down dale:** in many directions: *He had me running up hill and down dale, looking for his lost wallet.*

dal·li·ance /ˈdælians/ *n.* a love relationship, usu. a brief and casual one: *Their dalliance lasted only a month.*

dal·ly /ˈdæli/ *v.* **-lied, -lying, -lies** **1** to toy with an idea: *He dallied with the idea of becoming an actor.* **2** to waste time, (*syn.*) to dillydally: *She dallied in the stores instead of going back to work.* **3** to undertake a casual love affair *See:* dalliance.

dal·ma·tian /dælˈmeɪʃən/ *n.* a white dog with black spots often kept as a pet by firefighters

dam /dæm/ *v.* **dammed, damming, dams** to build a barrier across a river to stop or limit its flow, often to produce electrical power: *Governments often dam large rivers to generate electrical power.*
—*n.* the barrier itself: *Beavers build dams with logs and sticks.*

dam·age /ˈdæmɪdʒ/ *v.* **-aged, -aging, -ages** **1** to hurt, injure (s.o.'s property, business, reputation, etc.): *They damaged the car badly in the crash.* **2** to ruin: *The hurricane damaged the entire island.*
—*n.* **1** harm, injury: *How much damage did the storm do?* **2 to sue for damages** or **to seek damages:** (in law) to ask in court for compensation: *That newspaper hurt our business with its story, so we are suing it for damages.* -*adj.* **damaging.**

dame /deɪm/ *n.* **1** in England, a title given to a lady: *Dame Margot is Margot Fonteyn, the great ballerina.* **2** a title assumed by the wife of a knight: *Dame Elizabeth, wife of Sir John Winters* **3** *slang* a woman

damn /dæm/ *v.* **1** to condemn to hell: *Christians believe the Lord damns sinners.* **2** to curse with bad luck: *Bad weather has damned farmers' chances for good crops this year.*
—*n.exclam.* **1** a strong expression of anger: *Damn! I hurt my finger!* **2** *slang* **to not give a damn:** to not care: *I don't give a damn what you say!* -*adj.* **damning.**

dam·na·ble /ˈdæmnəbəl/ *adj.* shameful, deserving strong blame: *Killing that child was a damnable act.*

dam·na·tion /dæmˈneɪʃən/ *n.* [U] condemning to hell or to a bad fate: *They believe he will suffer damnation for his sins.*

damned /dæmd/ *adj.* **1** cursed, condemned: *That woman is damned with endless bad luck.* **2** *slang* trouble-causing: *Get that damned dog out of here!* **3** *slang* **I'll be damned!:** a phrase indicating surprise or disbelief

damp /dæmp/ *adj.* a little wet, (*syn.*) moist: *He wiped the tables with a damp cloth.* -*n.* [U] **dampness.**

damp·en /ˈdæmpən/ *v.* **1** to wet, (*syn.*) to moisten: *to dampen a cloth with water* **2 to dampen s.o.'s spirits:** to sadden, (*syn.*) discourage: *The bad news dampened our spirits.*

damp·er /ˈdæmpər/ *n.* **1** a flat, movable metal plate used to block or open the flow of air, as in a chimney: *When the fire is cool, close the damper in the chimney.* **2 to put a damper on s.t.:** to block, discourage: *Their child is sick, and that puts a damper on their vacation plans.*

dam·sel /ˈdæmzəl/ *n.litr.* **damsel in distress** a girl or young woman in trouble: *The hero in an old silent movie always saves the damsel in distress.*

dance /dæns/ *v.* **danced, dancing, dances** to move the body rhythmically, usu. in tune with music: *I danced for joy on hearing the good news.*
—*n.* **1** an act of dancing: *He did a little dance of joy.* **2** the art of dance: *She teaches dance.* **3** a dance lasting the length of one piece of music: *Please save the next dance for me.*

danc·ing /ˈdænsɪŋ/ *n.* [U] dance as recreation: *Dancing is my favorite nighttime activity.*

dan·de·li·on /ˈdændəlaɪən/ *n.* a weed with a yellow blossom and green leaves that can be eaten: *I want to remove all the dandelions from my lawn.*

dan·der /ˈdændər/ *n.* [U] **1** loose, dry skin on cats, dogs, and horses **2 to get s.o.'s dander up:** to become angry: *Losing money gets his dander up.*

dan·druff /ˈdændrəf/ *n.* [U] dry skin that flakes from the scalp: *Every winter he has a problem with dandruff in his hair.*

dan·dy /ˈdændi/ *n.* **-dies** a man who dresses in extravagantly fine clothes: *That man is quite a dandy; he always wears expensive new clothes.*
—*adj.infrml.* excellent, wonderful (often used ironically to mean awful, bad): *That's just dandy! The baby broke a vase!* -*adj.* **dandified** /ˈdændəˌfaɪd/; -*v.* **dandify.**

dan·ger /ˈdeɪndʒər/ *n.* **1** [U] a harmful situation, (*syn.*) peril: *Driving too fast puts people in danger.* **2** [C;U] risk, hazard: *There is danger in borrowing too much money.*

dan·ger·ous /ˈdeɪndʒərəs/ *adj.* **1** harmful, (*syn.*) perilous: *Smoking is dangerous to your health.* **2** risky, hazardous: *It can be dangerous to gamble in Las Vegas.* -*adv.* **dangerously.**

dan·gle /ˈdæŋgəl/ *v.* **-gled, -gling, -gles** **1** to hang down, swing freely: *She likes earrings that dangle.* **2 to dangle s.t.** (money or another attraction) **in front of s.o.:** to tempt, (*syn.*) to entice: *The saleswoman dangled a 5,000-mile warranty in front of them to get them to buy the car.* -*adj.* **dangling.**

dan·ish /'deɪnɪʃ/ *n.sing. or pl.* a type of pastry made of sweet dough baked with a sugary topping and filled with cheese or fruit: *I'll have a danish and coffee, please.*

dank /dæŋk/ *adj.* **-er, -est** unpleasantly damp and cool: *They went downstairs into the dank cellar.* -*n.* **dankness.**

dap·per /'dæpər/ *adj.* (said of men) dressed with style, (*syn.*) natty: *I enjoyed watching the dapper gentlemen strolling down the avenue.*

dap·pled /'dæpəld/ *adj.* spotted, covered with spots: *He rode a white horse dappled with gray.‖We sat in the dappled shade under the trees.*

dare /dɛr/ *n.* a challenge to do s.t. that is dangerous or difficult, a bet: *He walked along the top of a fence on a dare.*
—*v.* **dared, daring, dares** **1** to challenge, bet s.o.: *His friend dared him to do it.* **2** to have enough courage, nerve: *His mother said, "Don't you dare do that again!"*

dare·dev·il /'dɛr,dɛvəl/ *n.* s.o. who risks harm or death in performing difficult acts, (*syn.*) a stunt person: *The daredevil rode his motorcycle over 15 parked cars.*
—*adj.* daring, courageous: *The firefighter made a daredevil attempt to save the boy from the fire.*

dar·ing /'dɛrɪŋ/ *adj.n.* [U] courageous, risky: *The policewoman made a <adj.> daring leap from one building to another.*

dark /dɑrk/ *adj.* **-er, -est** **1** without light, unlit: *a dark cave* **2** shadowy, with little light: *a dark movie theater* **3** not light in color: *He wore a dark blue suit.‖She has dark eyes.* **4** without hope, (*syn.*) pessimistic: *He takes a dark view of life.*
—*n.* **1** nighttime, darkness: *Don't try to work in the dark.* **2** **in the dark:** in ignorance, unknowing: *I didn't know that the owners were selling the business; they kept me in the dark about it.*

Dark Ages *n.pl.* in Europe, the period between the fall of the Roman Empire (in the 5th century A.D.) and the 10th century A.D.: *During the Dark Ages, most people had little education, money, or property.*

dark horse *n.adj.fig.* a person who is not well-known and then becomes a possible winner, esp. in an election: *The Senator from Oregon was a <n.> dark horse* (or) *a <adj.> dark-horse candidate who nearly won the Presidential election.*

dark·en /'dɑrkən/ *v.* **1** to lose light: *Each day darkens into night.* **2** to make (draw, paint)

dark in color: *The artist darkened the sea in her painting.* **3** to show anger, pain: *His eyes darkened at the news of the war.*

dark·ness /'dɑrknɪs/ *n.* [U] **1** nighttime, a condition without light: *We enjoyed sitting outdoors in the darkness of night.* **2** ignorance, unfamiliarity: *They grew up in the darkness of ignorance and poverty.*

dark·room /'dɑrk,rum/ *n.* a room for developing film: *A photographer works in a darkroom.*

dar·ling /'dɑrlɪŋ/ *adj.* **1** adorable, sweet: *a darling little girl* **2** adored, beloved: *my darling son*
—*n.* **1** a loved one, (*syn.*) a sweetheart: *His wife is his darling.* **2** a favorite, pet: *Their youngest son is the darling of the family.*

darn /dɑrn/ *v.* to mend, to sew repairs in worn or torn cloth: *You should darn those socks.*
—*n.v.exclam.* a mild expression of anger or dismay: *<n.> Darn! I burned the toast!‖<v.> Darn it! I forgot my keys!*

dart /dɑrt/ *v.* to move quickly: *A child darted out in front of the car.*
—*n.* **1** [C] a small object with a sharp point to be thrown, blown, or shot: *Some people blow poison darts to kill animals for food.* **2** **darts:** [U] a game of throwing darts at a target: *Darts is his favorite game. See:* dartboard.

d a r t · b o a r d /'dɑrt,bɔrd/ *n.* a circular board used as a target for the game of darts

dartboard

dash /dæʃ/ *v.* **-es** **1** to run quickly over a short distance, (*syn.*) to sprint: *I dashed into the house to get out of the rain.* **2** to leave quickly: *I have to dash now; see you later!* **3** to throw down with violence, smash: *The storm at sea dashed many boats against the rocks.* **4** **to dash off: a.** to leave hurriedly: *Sorry, but I have to dash off now.* **b.** to write s.t. hurriedly: *I dashed off a letter to my mother to tell her when I would arrive.*
—*n.* **dashes** **1** a short, rapid run, (*syn.*) a sprint: *Let's make a dash across the street while there's no traffic.* **2** an athletic event: *He runs the 100-meter dash.* **3** a short, horizontal line used for punctuation in writing or printing: (-) *or* (—) **4** a small amount of s.t.: *Put a dash of pepper in the soup.* **5** **the dash:** the dashboard of a car *See:* dashboard. **6** **to make a dash for it:** to move fast to try to avoid danger or discomfort: *The soldiers were nearly surrounded, and they made a dash for it through enemy lines*

dash·board /'dæʃ,bɔrd/ n. in a vehicle, the front panel covered with instruments: *On the dashboard of a car, you can see the gas gauge, the mileage, etc.*

dashboard

dash·ing /'dæʃɪŋ/ adj. stylish, dynamic: *a dashing young man*

da·ta /'deɪtə, 'dætə/ n.pl. used often with a sing. v. [U] raw or organized information: *Scientists gather data, then study it for its meaning.* ||*Computers process data to create information.*

da·ta·base /'deɪtə,beɪs, 'dæ-/ n. information on a general topic stored in a computer system, (syn.) a data bank: *When I go to the bank, the teller checks the customer database for information about my account.*

data entry n. -tries the preparing and typing of information into a computer: *Our data entry department has 10 operators who input data.*

data processing n. [U] the encoding (preparation), inputting (typing), and retrieval (printing out) of data by computer: *The data processing department of a bank processes the information about accounts.*

date (1) /deɪt/ n. 1 a particular day, month, or year: *The date of their marriage was June 24, 1996.*||*The date on the building was 1910.* 2 a social appointment, usu. of a couple: *The boy and girl went on their first date last night.* 3 the person with whom one has a social appointment: *She introduced her date to everyone at the party.* 4 **blind date:** a date with s.o. that one has never met before: *They met for the first time on a blind date.*
—v. **dated, dating, dates** 1 to show a date: *The letter was dated May 1, 1895.* 2 to go out on dates with: *She dates several young men.* 3 to age and so become useless: *After several years, a reference book begins to date.*

date (2) n. the fruit of a date palm tree: *I like to eat dates.*

dat·ed /'deɪtɪd/ adj. 1 marked with a date: *The letter was dated June 10, 1997.* 2 old and so no longer valid, (syn.) obsolete: *Information that is dated is not useful.*

daub /dɔb/ v.n. to coat or apply (grease, paint, cement, etc.), usu. quickly, on a surface: *He daubed some grease on the door hinge.*

daugh·ter /'dɔtər/ n. a female child: *They are married and have two daughters. See:* son.

daugh·ter-in-law /'dɔtərɪn,lɔ/ n. **daughters-in-law** the wife of one's son: *She became our daughter-in-law last year.*

daunt /dɔnt/ v. to make afraid, discourage, (syn.) to intimidate: *The thought of starting a business daunted him, but he decided to try it.* -adj. **daunting.**

daunt·less /'dɔntlɪs/ adj. courageous and unstoppable: *She was dauntless in fighting cancer.*

daw·dle /'dɔdl/ v. **-dled, -dling, -dles** to delay, waste time: *I dawdled over a cup of coffee instead of working.* -n. **dawdler.**

dawn /dɔn/ n. [C;U] 1 sunrise: *We see the light of dawn in the east.* 2 fig. a beginning: *She is studying the dawn of civilization in ancient Egypt.*
—v. 1 (used with "the sun") to come up: *The sun is dawning over the land.* 2 fig. **to dawn on:** to become clear to: *It dawned on him that he was safe at last.* -n. [U] **dawning.**

day /deɪ/ n. 1 the time period between sunrise and sunset: *Most people work during the day and sleep at night.* 2 the 24-hour period from midnight to midnight: *There are seven days in a week.* 3 **not to give s.o. the time of day:** to treat s.o. with no respect: *She won't give him the time of day because she doesn't like him.* 4 **to call it a day:** to stop working: *We've done enough, so let's call it a day.* 5 infml. **to make s.o.'s day:** to make s.o. very happy: *Receiving your letter really made my day.*
—adv. 1 **day in and day out:** all the time, in a steady, dedicated way: *He works hard day in and day out.* 2 **days:** during the day: *She works days and her husband works nights.* 3 **(just) the other day:** one day recently: *I saw that movie (just) the other day.* 4 **these days:** now (but not in the past): *These days many students have personal computers.*

day·break /'deɪ,breɪk/ n. [U] dawn, sunrise: *They left on their trip at daybreak.*

day care n. [U] a service of caring for preschool-aged children while the parents work: *She drops her child off at day care on her way to work.*

day care center n. a school-like place where parents pay to have small children cared for while the parents work: *He takes his child to the day care center each morning.*

day·dream /'deɪ,drim/ n. thoughts that are pleasant but not real, (syn.) a fantasy: *The boy has daydreams about being a baseball star.*
—v. to allow the mind to think pleasantly, (syn.) to fantasize: *I daydream about winning the lottery.* -n. **daydreamer.**

Day-Glo /'deɪ,gloʊ/ n.TM bright fabrics, plastics, and other materials that glow in a striking way: *The boy's Day-Glo pink T-shirt shocked his parents.*

day·light /'deɪ,laɪt/ n. [U] 1 the light from the sun during the day: *She opened the curtains to let the daylight in.* 2 **to see (day)light at the end of the tunnel:** to see the end of a long process (difficult job, task, etc.): *We have* worked for months to solve that problem, and now we are happy to see (day)light at the end of the tunnel.

daylight saving time *n.* the period when clocks are set one hour forward in April and one hour backward in October to increase useful daylight hours for work and play: *We go on daylight saving time next Sunday, so remember to set your clock back one hour.*

USAGE NOTE: People use the saying, "Spring forward, fall back" to remember when to set their clocks an hour forward in the spring or backward in the fall. Arizona is the only state that does not change its clocks for *daylight saving time.*

day·time /'deɪ,taɪm/ *n.sing.* [U] the daylight hours: *During the daytime, I play golf and at nighttime, I work in a restaurant.*

day-to-day *adj.* related to the daily routine of usual living and business affairs: *My partner takes care of the day-to-day operations of the company.*

daze /deɪz/ *v.* **dazed, dazing, dazes** to make semiconscious, *(syn.)* to stun: *A blow on the head dazed him.*
—*n.* **in a daze:** unable to think clearly (after a shock, a blow, etc.): *She was in a daze after learning the bad news.*

daz·zle /'dæzəl/ *v.* **-zled, -zling, -zles 1** to blind with bright light: *The sunlight dazzles me.* **2** to amaze, *(syns.)* to awe, astound: *The Olympic athletes dazzled the audience.*
—*n.sing.* the quality of creating a bright light or amazing effect: *The dazzle of her smile left him unable to speak. -adj.* **dazzling.**

DC /'di,si/ *abbr. for* direct current *See:* AC.

D.C. /'di'si/ *n.* **1** *abbr. for* District of Columbia, location of U.S. capital city of Washington **2** *infrml. short for* Washington, D.C.: *He's planning a trip to D.C.*

DDT /'didi'ti/ *n.* [U] a strong chemical used to kill insects in order to increase crops: *The use of DDT is against the law in many places because it is dangerous to the environment.*

D-Day /'di,deɪ/ *n.* **1** the invasion of France on June 6, 1944, by the Allied forces in World War II **2** *fig.* a day when a decisive event is going to happen, esp. a major battle: *Today is D-Day because the unions must come to an agreement with management or the business will be closed.*

dea·con /'dikən/ *n.* a person who assists the minister or pastor in some Christian churches: *He has the honor to be a deacon in the local Baptist Church. -n.* **deaconess.**

de·ac·ti·vate /di'æktə,veɪt/ *v.* **-vated, -vating, -vates** to take out of active service: *They deactivated that military unit and sent the soldiers home. -n.* **deactivation.**

dead /dɛd/ *adj.* **1** lifeless, no longer living: *The old man is dead; he died yesterday.* **2** not working, without power: *The batteries in this flashlight are dead.* **3** *infrml.* lacking activity, lifeless: *That small town is dead on Saturday nights.* **4 dead (and buried):** not important anymore: *Don't waste time discussing it; that issue is dead and buried.* **5** *infrml.* **dead (tired)** or **dead on one's feet:** very tired **6 dead to the world:** in a deep sleep
—*n.pl.* **the dead:** people who have died: *We bury the dead in cemeteries.*
—*adv.* **1** directly in the middle of: *He hit the target dead center.*||*There's s.t. standing in the road dead ahead.* **2** *slang* exactly: *You're dead right about that.* **3 wouldn't be caught dead:** would never agree to doing s.t. horrible: *He hates to dance so much that he wouldn't be caught dead on a dance floor.*

dead·beat /'dɛd,bit/ *n.adj.slang* a person or business that does not pay their bills: *I loaned him some money last month and that <n.> deadbeat has not paid me back.*||*<adj.> "Deadbeat dads" are fathers who leave their families and don't support their children.*

dead duck *n.slang* a person who is sure to be punished: *If I drive without a driver's license and the police catch me, I'll be a dead duck.*

dead·en /'dɛdn/ *v.* **1** to make less, reduce: *I take aspirin to deaden the pain of a headache.* **2** to make less noisy: *We put soundproofing in the walls to deaden the noise from the road outside.*

dead end *n.adj.* **1** a road without an exit: *We live on a <n.> dead end* (or) *<adj.> dead-end street.* **2** a situation that leads nowhere: *We tried all sorts of solutions to that problem, and they all came to a dead end.*

dead·eye /'dɛd,aɪ/ *n.* an expert shot: *She's a deadeye who hits her target every time.*

dead heat *n.* [C;U] a tie among competitors in an athletic event: *The two horses finished the race in a dead heat.*

dead·line /'dɛd,laɪn/ *n.* a time or date by which s.t. must be finished: *The deadline for the project is two o'clock tomorrow.*

dead·lock /'dɛd,lak/ *n.* total disagreement between parties in a negotiation, *(syn.)* an impasse: *The management and the workers have reached a deadlock in contract talks.*
—*v.* to bring to or arrive at a deadlock: *The owners and the union have deadlocked over the pay increase.*

dead·ly /'dɛdli/ *adj.* **-lier, -liest 1** so dangerous as to cause death: *deadly weapons, deadly poison* **2** *fig.* destructive, terrible: *His deadly remark about her work made her want to quit her job.* **3** *slang* very boring: *It was a deadly lecture.*

dead·pan /'dɛd,pæn/ *adj.n.v.* showing an expressionless face while saying s.t. funny or shocking: *He is famous for his <adj.> deadpan humor.*

dead weight *n.* **1** a heavy, motionless weight: *A load of bricks is all dead weight.* **2** *fig.* a difficult, hopeless situation: *Thoughts of the coming exam were a dead weight on her mind.*

dead·wood /'dɛd,wʊd/ *n.* [U] **1** dead trees, fallen tree branches: *There is a lot of deadwood in that forest.* **2** *fig.* employees who no longer perform well or who do little: *The company has too much deadwood on its staff.*

deaf /dɛf/ *adj.* **-er, -est 1** unable to hear: *He is deaf in one ear.* **2 to turn a deaf ear:** to pay no attention, (*syn.*) ignore: *The boy wants a new car, but his mother turns a deaf ear to his wishes. See:* disabled, USAGE NOTE.

deaf·en /'dɛfən/ *v.* to cause an inability to hear, esp. for a short time: *I was deafened by the noise of the train passing by.* -*adj.* **deafening.**

deal /dil/ *v.* **dealt** /dɛlt/, **dealing, deals 1** to give, esp. cards to players of a card game: *First, deal each player five cards.* **2** *phrasal v. insep.* **to deal in s.t.:** to buy s.t. from producers and sell it to customers: *This business deals in furniture (toys, watches, etc.).* **3** *frml.* **to deal s.o. a blow:** to hit hard: *Life dealt her a blow when her son died.* **4** *infrml.* **to deal s.o. in:** to include or involve s.o.: *You can deal me in; your plan sounds like a great opportunity.* **5** *infrml.* **to deal s.o. out:** to exclude, to keep out: *Deal him out; he's not interested in the project.* **6** *phrasal v. insep.* **to deal with s.o.** or **s.t.: a.** to interact with s.o. or s.t., esp. in business: *Have you ever dealt with this company before?* **b.** to treat, to manage: *Her job is dealing with customer complaints.* **c.** to concern, to be about: *This book deals with tax laws.*
—*n.* **1** an agreement, trade, or transaction, esp. in business: *We have made a deal to buy that building.* **2** *infrml.* a good transaction, (*syn.*) a bargain: *You paid only $5 for this? Wow, what a deal!* **3** a turn to give out the playing cards in a game: *Give me the cards; it's my deal.* **4** *infrml.* **a big deal:** s.t. important: *Don't worry about that; it's no big deal.* **5 a good** or **great deal (of):** a lot: *He has a great deal of money (experience, free time, etc.).||The price was a good deal higher than I expected. See:* wheel and deal.

deal·er /'dilər/ *n.* **1** a person who deals cards: *She's a dealer in a casino in Las Vegas.* **2** a businessperson who buys from producers and sells to customers: *a car dealer, a drug dealer*

deal·er·ship /'dilərʃɪp/ *n.* the business of a dealer, esp. the store or other place where the products are shown and sold: *I bought my car at a dealership on Main Street.*

deal·ings /'dilɪŋz/ *n.pl.* discussions and transactions, esp. in business: *I have had some deal-ings with those people (ABC Company, that governmental agency, etc.), and they have been very helpful. See:* wheel and deal.

dealt /dɛlt/ *v. past part. of* deal

dean /din/ *n.* **1** an academic administrator: *He is the Dean of Students at a small college.* **2** a well-known, senior authority in a field or area of study: *She is called the dean of architecture in the USA.*

dean's list *n.* a listing of students who have earned high grades: *She made the dean's list in her first year at the university.*

dear /dɪr/ *adj.* **-er, -est 1** loved, cared for: *She's a dear friend.* **2 dear to:** important to: *He's an old friend and very dear to me.* **3** *Brit.* expensive, costly
—*n.* **1** a sweet, good person: *You brought me flowers? What a dear you are!* **2 my dear:** an expression of affection and caring for s.o.: *Angela, my dear, how are you?*
—*exclam.* **Oh, dear!** or **Dear me!:** expressions of surprise or dismay: *Oh, dear! What a sad situation.*
—*salutation* a polite word to greet s.o. in a letter: *Dear Mr. Lee, I am writing this letter to ask for your help.*

Dear John letter /'dɪr'dʒɑn/ *n.* a letter from a girlfriend or wife ending the relationship: *My girlfriend wrote me a Dear John letter and moved to Argentina.*

dear·ly /'dɪrli/ *adv.* **1** with strong (good) feeling: *I dearly hope you will succeed.* **2 to pay dearly:** to pay a high price (in money, time, trouble, etc.): *I paid dearly for not checking the map; we were lost for two hours.*

dearth /dɜrθ/ *n.sing.* little or none of s.t.: *The dearth of information made it hard for me to write my report.*

death /dɛθ/ *n.* **1** [C;U] the end of life: *His death came in his sleep.* **2** [C] an occurrence of death: *There were two deaths in that accident.* **3** *sing.* end, destruction: *In 1989 we saw the death of communism in East Germany.* **4 a matter of life or death:** a serious emergency: *He's having a heart attack! Call an ambulance; it's a matter of life or death!* **5 to catch one's death of cold:** to become very sick: *Dress warmly, or you will catch your death of cold!* **6 to death:** very, extremely: *I was worried to death when you didn't come home.*

death·bed /'dɛθ,bɛd/ *n.* the last stage before death: *The old lady lay on her deathbed for a week before dying.*

death·blow /'dɛθ,bloʊ/ *n.* **1** a hard hit that causes death: *The deathblow came from a rock that hit him on the head.* **2** *fig.* the final act that makes s.t. end: *They had several problems, but the bank's refusal of more credit was the death-blow to the business.*

death penalty *n.* **-ties** the punishment of death for a crime: *He was given the death penalty for killing a police officer.*

death rate *n.* the number of people who die in a nation or other area in relation to its total population, usu. measured on a yearly basis: *The US death rate from cancer increased last year.*

death·trap /'dɛθ,træp/ *n.* **1** a very dangerous situation: *Terrorists set a deathtrap for the President.* **2** an unsafe building or part of one: *People still live in that old building but it is a deathtrap. See:* firetrap.

death·watch /'dɛθ,wɑʧ/ *n.* **-watches** the act of waiting (usu. near the bedside) as a person is dying: *When news spread that the rock star was dying, fans held a deathwatch outside the hospital.*

death wish *n.* **wishes** a desire to die or to do dangerous things, risking death: *He keeps trying to commit suicide; he has a death wish.*

de·ba·cle /də'bɑkəl, -'bæk-/ *n.* **1** a sudden, terrible event, destruction: *The country was beaten in a two-week war; it was a total debacle.* **2** a complete failure: *The new automobile was laughed at by the public; it is a debacle for the company.*

de·bark /di'bɑrk/ *v.frml.* to leave a ship, (*syn.*) to disembark: *The passengers debarked at noon. -n.* [U] **debarkation** /,dibɑr'keɪʃən/.

de·base /di'beɪs/ *v.* **-based, -basing, -bases** **1** to lower in value: *Our government debased our money by printing too much of it.* **2** to lower the quality of: *The manufacturer debased their products by using cheaper materials in them.* **3** to lower the opinion of other people: *She debased the reputation of the company when she accused them of dishonesty. -n.* [U] **debasement.**

de·bat·a·ble /dɪ'beɪtəbəl/ *adj.* open to debate, questionable, (*syn.*) doubtful: *His innocence of the crime is debatable.*

de·bate /dɪ'beɪt/ *v.* **-bated, -bating, -bates** **1** to argue, present differing views on a question: *The two political parties debated the merits of the bill before voting it into law.* **2** to consider, discuss, (*syn.*) to deliberate: *She debated with herself about going to college.*
—*n.* **1** a formal argument: *The two presidential candidates agreed to hold a debate on TV.*‖*US high schools often have <adj.> debating teams.* **2** an argument, discussion: *There was a debate during the committee meeting about the new budget.*

de·bauch /dɪ'bɔʧ/ *v.frml.* **-es** to have a bad influence on the morals and usually the health of s.o., (*syn.*) to corrupt: *Drugs debauch the youth of this nation.*

de·bauch·er·y /dɪ'bɔʧəri/ *n.* [U] too much participation in physical pleasures: *That rock star led a life of debauchery.*

de·bil·i·tate /dɪ'bɪlə,teɪt/ *v.* **-tated, -tating, -tates** to weaken, esp. by disease or neglect: *His health is debilitated from not getting enough good food. -adj.* **debilitating;** *-n.* [U] **debilitation** /dɪ,bɪlə'teɪʃən/.

de·bil·i·ty /dɪ'bɪləti/ *n.* [C;U] **-ties** a weakness, (*syn.*) a frailty: *He suffers from the debility of old age.*

deb·it /'dɛbɪt/ *v.* to enter an amount of money owed on a personal or business account: *When the XYZ Co. bought fuel oil, the oil company debited XYZ's account for the cost.*
—*n.* **1** a debt charged against s.o.'s account: *The XYZ Co. has a debit of $1200.* **2 debit side:** negative side: *On the debit side, they are asking too much for their company; but on the plus side, it has excellent products.*

deb·o·nair /,dɛbə'nɛr/ *adj.* well-dressed and cheerful (usu. a man), (*syn.*) dapper: *He's a debonair gentleman! -adv.* **debonairly.**

de·brief /di'brif/ *v.* to ask and usually record what s.o. knows about a particular event or subject: *They debriefed the spy when she returned from her mission. -n.*[C;U] **debriefing.**

de·bris /də'bri, deɪ-, -'deɪ,bri/ *n.* [U] ruins, remains of s.t. broken, (*syn.*) refuse: *Old newspapers, dead leaves, and tin cans formed the debris in the park.*

debt /dɛt/ *n.* **1** a sum of money owed to another: *He owes a debt of $50 to a friend.* **2** an obligation: *I owe a debt of gratitude to you for helping me.* **3 in debt:** owing money **4 out of debt:** having paid money owed

debt·or /'dɛtər/ *n.* a person, business, or government that owes money: *The debtors of the bank had trouble making payments. See:* creditor.

de·bug /di'bʌg/ *v.* **-bugged, -bugging, -bugs** to find and correct errors, esp. in a computer program: *I've debugged the program and now it runs well. -n.* [U] **debugging.**

de·bunk /di'bʌŋk/ *v.* to show the falseness of s.t.: *He wants to debunk the story of ghosts being in that old house. -n.* [C;U] **debunking.**

de·but /deɪ'byu, 'deɪbyu/ *v.* to appear for the first time, esp. a play, film, or artist: *The actress debuted on Broadway last year.*
—*n.* a first appearance: *The debut of the play was a great success.*

deb·u·tante /'dɛbyu,tɑnt/ *n.* a young woman who was presented to upper-class society at a special ball or party: *She was a debutante early this year.*

dec·ade /'dɛkeɪd/ *n.* a period of 10 years: *the decade of the 1990s*‖*The development of the park took a decade to complete.*

dec·a·dence /'dɛkədəns/ *n.* [U] **1** a low level of moral behavior: *Decadence among the leadership was widespread.* **2** a period of lowering or worsening standards, *(syn.)* the decline, decay: *Their immoral behavior led to the decadence of the Empire itself.* -*n.* [U] **decadency.**

dec·a·dent /'dɛkədənt/ *adj.* **1** showing decadence, *(syns.)* degenerate, dissolute: *The decadent lifestyle of the leaders led to a revolution by their people.* **2** weakened, in decline: *As the nation became decadent, its power and influence lessened.* -*adv.* **decadently.**

de·caf·fein·ate /di'kæfə,neɪt/ *v.* **-nated, -nating, -nates** to remove or lessen the caffeine, esp. in coffee: *He drinks decaffeinated coffee in the evening.*

decaf /'di,kæf/ *n.* [U] decaffeinated coffee: *Would you like regular coffee or decaf?*

de·cal /'di,kæl/ *n.* a picture or design usu. on plastic and stuck to s.t. as a decoration or permit: *The decal on my car window is my parking permit.*

de·can·ter /di'kæntər/ *n.* a fancy container often of clear crystal used to hold wine or other alcohol: *The host poured a fine sherry from the decanter.* -*v.* **decant.**

de·cap·i·tate /di'kæpə,teɪt/ *v.* **-tated, -tating, -tates** to cut the head off: *The guillotine decapitated the French King Louis XVI.*

de·cath·lon /di'kæθlən, -,lɑn/ *n.* a track-and-field competition of 10 events with the highest combined score determining the winner: *The Olympic Decathlon is a very difficult event.*

de·cay /di'keɪ/ *v.* **1** to rot, *(syn.)* to decompose: *Fallen leaves and trees decay into the ground over time.* **2** to fall into ruin or poor condition: *The Roman Empire slowly decayed and lost its power.*
—*n.* [U] **1** rot or breakdown of a substance: *Tooth decay can result from poor care of your teeth.* **2** ruin: *That old house is in complete decay.* **3** lowering of standards of behavior, *(syns.)* decline, decadence: *The moral decay of the leadership destroyed the nation.*

de·ceased /di'sist/ *v.* past part. of decease
—*adj.* dead
—*n.* **the deceased:** the dead person(s): *The body of the deceased was removed from his home.*

de·ceit /di'sit/ *n.* [U] dishonesty, trickery, *(syn.)* deception: *The salesman disappeared before people learned of his deceit.*

de·ceit·ful /di'sitfəl/ *adj.* dishonest, *(syn.)* deceptive: *She used deceitful promises of big profits to attract the investors she cheated.* -*adv.* **deceitfully.**

de·ceive /di'siv/ *v.* **-ceived, -ceiving, -ceives** to fool, *(syn.)* to mislead: *He deceived me when he said he loved me, because he really doesn't.*

de·cel·er·ate /di'sɛlə,reɪt/ *v.* **-rate, -rating, -rates** to slow down, move more slowly: *The train decelerated as it approached a station.* -*n.* [C;U] **deceleration** /di,sɛlə'reɪʃən/.

De·cem·ber /di'sɛmbər/ *n.* the 12th and last month of the year: *Christmas comes on December 25.*

de·cen·cy /'disənsi/ *n.* [U] **1** respectful concern for doing the right thing, *(syn.)* propriety: *As a matter of common decency, you should tell him the truth.* **2 to have the decency to do s.t.:** to be polite enough to do s.t.: *When he could not attend the wedding, he had the decency to call and apologize.*

de·cent /'disənt/ *adj.* **1** proper, correct (behavior, attitude): *To help the poor is the decent thing to do.* **2** well-behaved and kind: *a decent human being* **3** properly clothed: *Wait outside until I put some clothes on; I'm not decent.* **4** *infrml.* good enough: *It's not a great job, but the pay is decent.* -*adv.* **decently.**

de·cen·tral·ize /di'sɛntrə,laɪz/ *v.* **-ized, -izing, -izes** to move from one large center of activity, authority, etc., out into several smaller centers: *The large corporation decentralized its manufacturing operations into five regional facilities.* -*n.* [U] **decentralization** /di,sɛntrəlɪ'zeɪʃən/.

de·cep·tion /di'sɛpʃən/ *n.* **1** [C;U] s.t. that causes s.o. to believe what is not true: *She spread false information as a deception to mislead investors.* **2** [U] trickery, *(syn.)* betrayal: *His deception of the people who trusted him was a shock to them all.*

de·cep·tive /di'sɛptɪv/ *adj.* causing s.o. to believe what is not true, *(syn.)* misleading: *She made deceptive remarks about the property to persuade us to buy it.* -*adv.* **deceptively;** -*n.* **deceptiveness.**

dec·i·bel /'dɛsəbəl, -,bɛl/ *n.* a unit of measurement of sound levels: *A sound level of 90 decibels is extremely loud.*

de·cide /di'saɪd/ *v.* **-cided, -ciding, -cides 1** to reach a conclusion (opinion, choice, plan, etc.), to make up one's mind: *We've decided to go on vacation August 1.* **2** to determine, to bring to a certain end: *One point decided the football game.*

de·cid·ed /di'saɪdɪd/ *adj.* **1** definite, clearly seen: *The medicine made a decided difference in the patient's health.* **2** without hesitation or doubt: *She has a decided manner of giving her opinion.* -*adv.* **decidedly.**

de·cid·ing /di'saɪdɪŋ/ *adj.* decisive, key: *The deciding factor (reason, vote) in his keeping the job was the big increase in pay.*

de·cid·u·ous /di'sɪdʒuəs/ *adj.* related to shedding or falling off: *Maples, oaks, and elms are deciduous trees, as their leaves fall off in the autumn.*

dec·i·mal /'dɛsəməl/ *n.* a fraction expressed in tens to the right of a dot: .1=1/10, .01=1/100, .001=1/1000
—*adj.* related to decimals: *a decimal fraction*

decimal point *n.* a dot placed to the left of a decimal: *In .23, the dot to the left of the 2 is a decimal point.*

USAGE NOTE: The number *.23* is read as *"point two three."*

dec·i·mate /'dɛsə,meɪt/ *v.* **-mated, -mating, -mates** to destroy much of s.t. (a population, army): *Smallpox decimated half of the army.* -*n.* **decimation** /,dɛsə'meɪʃən/.

de·ci·pher /dɪ'saɪfər/ *v.* to puzzle out, figure out the meaning of s.t., esp. a code: *In the military, he deciphered messages written in numbers.||His handwriting is so bad that I can't decipher his note.*

de·ci·sion /dɪ'sɪʒən/ *n.* **1** a choice made, conclusion: *She made a decision to go on vacation.* **2** a determination: *The jury has come to the decision that the accused man is not guilty.* **3** the ability to make judgments and act on them: *She was a poor leader because she lacked decision.*

decision maker *n.* a person who has the power to make decisions: *The decision makers in government have great influence on policy.*

de·ci·sive /dɪ'saɪsɪv/ *adj.* **1** showing a clear result, unquestionable: *The team had a decisive victory by winning 20 to 2.* **2** determining, with great influence: *a decisive factor (event, battle, vote) that changed public opinion.* **3** bold, able to make decisions quickly and follow them firmly: *a decisive leader* -*adv.* **decisively.**

deck /dɛk/ *n.* **1** the various horizontal levels of a ship: *the main deck, quarter deck* **2** a pack of playing cards: *A deck has 52 cards.* **3** a wooden platform attached to a house: *Let's have lunch out on the deck.* **4 a double** or **triple-**

deck

decker: s.t. with two or three layers or levels: *a double-decker sandwich ||We live on the top floor of a triple-decker (house).* **5 on deck:** ready and waiting for one's turn to do s.t.
—*adj.slang* **decked out:** decorated, dressed especially well
—*v.* **1** to decorate: *We decked the room with balloons for the party.* **2** *slang* to knock s.o. down, usu. with a punch: *The boxer decked his opponent in the third round.*

de·claim /dɪ'kleɪm/ *v.frml.* to speak loudly and often critically about: *The Senator declaimed his opposition.* -*n.* **declamation** /,dɛklə'meɪʃən/.

dec·la·ra·tion /,dɛklə'reɪʃən/ *n.* **1** a serious oral or written statement: *He made a quiet declaration of his love for her.* **2** an important statement, esp. a formal written one: *the Declaration of Independence, a declaration of war* **3** a written statement to Customs of taxable goods **4** (in law) a statement of complaint by s.o. bringing a case to court

de·clar·a·tive /dɪ'klærətɪv/ *adj.* related to making a statement: *"Today is July 10" is a declarative sentence.*

de·clare /dɪ'klɛr/ *v.* **-clared, -claring, -clares** **1** to state s.t., usu. formally: *She declared her love to him in a letter.* **2** to state publicly and officially, (*syns.*) to proclaim, decree: *The President declared May 1 a national holiday.* **3** to make a declaration of taxable goods: *At the airport, the customs officer asked if I had anything to declare.*

dé·clas·sé /,deɪklɑ'seɪ/ *adj.* related to the lower class and unfashionable: *That restaurant has become déclassé; we wouldn't be seen there.*

de·clas·si·fy /di'klæsə,faɪ/ *v.* **-fied, -fying, -fies** to remove the classification, esp. from secret documents: *The government declassified the papers, so they are available to the public.||They are now <adj.> declassified.*

de·cline /dɪ'klaɪn/ *v.* **-clined, -clining, -clines** **1** to refuse, usu. politely: *He declined our invitation to dinner.* **2** to move downward: *Prices (the markets for goods, wages, etc.) have declined to record lows.* **3** to weaken, (*syn.*) to deteriorate: *My grandfather's health (strength, mind, etc.) is declining.* **4** to descend, to slope downward: *From the hilltop, I walked down a path that declined toward a lake.*
—*n.* **1** a lowering (of prices, markets, temperature, etc.): *The decline in the stock market scared investors.* **2** a weakening, (*syn.*) deterioration: *The old woman's health is in decline.* **3** a downward slope: *The steep decline of the road down the mountain made me nervous.* **4** a refusal, usu. polite, of an offer

de·code /di'koʊd/ *v.* **-coded, -coding, -codes** **1** to translate a message from code into plain language: *The spy decoded the secret message and read it.* **2** to figure out a mystery, (*syn.*) to decipher: *Scientists are trying to decode the structure of human genes.*

dé·colle·tage /,deɪkɔl'tɑʒ/ *n.* a low neckline of a woman's dress: *The décolletage on that evening gown is too revealing.*

de·col·o·nize /di'kɑlə,naɪz/ *v.* **-nized, -nizing, -nizes** to remove a nation's colonial status, to permit (a colony) self-government:

Several African nations were decolonized by European powers after World War II. -n. [U] **decolonization** /di,kɑlənə'zeɪʃən/.

de·com·pose /,dikəm'pouz/ v. **-posed, -posing, -poses** to rot, decay: *Over time, dead leaves (bodies, plants, etc.) decompose into the ground.* -n. [U] **decomposition** /di,kɑmpə'zɪʃən/.

de·com·press /,dikəm'prɛs/ v. to lessen pressure so it returns to normal: *Deep-sea divers decompress by returning to the surface of the water slowly.* -n.[C;U] **decompression.**

de·con·ges·tant /,dikən'dʒɛstənt/ n. a medication used to lessen nasal congestion: *I use a decongestant to clear my nose when I have a cold or allergy.* -v. **decongest.**

de·con·tam·i·na·tion /,dikən,tæmə'neɪʃən/ n. the process of removing contaminants (poisons, radiation, germs, etc.) from s.t.: *After being exposed to radiation, the workers had to go through decontamination.* -v. **decontaminate.**

de·con·trol /,dikən'troul/ v.n. **-trolled, -trolling, -trols** to remove (governmental) controls: *The minister of finance <v.> decontrolled prices.*

décor /deɪ'kɔr/ n. [C;U] the style of a room, house, etc.: *Their office has a modern décor.*

dec·o·rate /'dɛkə,reɪt/ v. **-rated, -rating, -rates 1** to beautify, make festive: *We decorated our house for the holidays.* **2** to present a mark or medal of merit to s.o.: *They decorated the soldier for his bravery.* -n. [U] **decorating; decorator.**

dec·o·ra·tion /,dɛkə'reɪʃən/ n. **1** [C;U] s.t. added to create a beautiful effect: *The decoration on the picture frame consists of pretty flowers on gold paint.||We had balloons and colored paper decorations for the party.* **2** [C] a mark or medal of merit: *The soldier wore many decorations.*

dec·o·ra·tive /'dɛkərətɪv, 'dɛkrə-/ adj. **1** making more beautiful and attractive: *The balloons, bright-colored hats, and streamers for the party are very decorative.* **2** related to the style of a room, house, etc.: *The decorative plan for the building is conservative.* -adv. **decoratively.**

de·co·rum /də'kɔrəm/ n. [U] proper behavior: *Children are instructed to be quiet in order to maintain decorum in church.* -adj. **decorous** /'dɛkərəs/.

de·coy /'di,kɔɪ/ v.n. to mislead or deceive s.o. (with a fake model or other attraction): *The hunter set out duck <n.> decoys meant to <v.> decoy live ducks into flying near to be shot.*

de·crease /dɪ'kris/ v. **-creased, -creasing, -creases 1** to grow smaller in number: *The population (prices, sales, rainfall, etc.) de-*

creased last year. **2** to lessen in strength or intensity: *Light decreases at sunset.*
—n. **1** a reduction of an amount: *a decrease in temperature (salary, prices, economic activity, etc.)* **2** a lessening in strength or intensity: *a decrease in light (interest, popularity, etc.)* **3 to be on the decrease:** in the process of decreasing: *The crime rate is on the decrease compared with last month.*

de·cree /dɪ'kri/ n. an order given by an authority: *We were shocked by the governmental decree banning all public meetings.*
—v. **-creed, -creeing, -crees** to give out a decree: *The dictator decreed that no one could leave the country.*

de·crep·it /dɪ'krɛpɪt/ adj. **1** (person) very weak, usu. from bad health or old age: *His illness has made him decrepit.* **2** (structure) in terrible condition, run-down, (syn.) delapidated: *a house in a decrepit state* -n. [U] **decrepitude** /dɪ'krɛpɪ,tud/.

de·crim·i·na·lize /di'krimənə,laɪz/ v. **-lized, -lizing, -lizes** to make s.t. no longer illegal or criminal: *Some states have decriminalized the use of marijuana.*

de·cry /dɪ'kraɪ/ v.frml. **-cried, -crying, -cries** to condemn or criticize publicly: *He is a rebel who decries society as it is.*

ded·i·cate /'dɛdə,keɪt/ v. **-cated, -cating, -cates 1** to give completely: *She dedicated herself to her career (to religion, to her children, etc.).* **2** to formally open in honor of s.o.: *The park is dedicated to a poet named Walt Whitman.* **3** to put aside, give for a special purpose: *We must dedicate funds to house the poor.*

ded·i·cat·ed /'dɛdə,keɪtɪd/ adj. **1** given completely to s.o. or s.t., (syn.) devoted: *She is a dedicated athlete who practices every day.* **2** (in computers) used only for one purpose: *The modem is on a dedicated phone line, so you can't use the phone to make a call.*

ded·i·ca·tion /,dɛdə'keɪʃən/ n. **1** [U] personal devotion, commitment to s.t.: *That doctor has great dedication to her work.* **2** [C] a formal ceremony to open a building, etc.: *The mayor will attend the dedication of the new park.*

de·duce /dɪ'dus/ v. **-duced, -ducing, -duces** to reach a conclusion by reasoning from the general to the specific: *My friend becomes quiet when his girlfriend is angry with him; today he is quiet and so I deduce she is angry.*

de·duct /dɪ'dʌkt/ v. to take away, subtract: *They offered a discount: they said they would deduct 20 percent from the retail price.*

de·duct·i·ble /dɪ'dʌktəbəl/ adj. capable of being deducted: *Interest charges on a mortgage are deductible from your income tax payments.*
—n. (in insurance) the amount a person must pay before their insurance company makes a

payment: *The damage done to my car cost $5,000 to fix, so with the $500 deductible, the insurance paid $4,500 and I paid $500.*

de·duc·tion /dɪ'dʌkʃən/ *n.* **1** an amount taken away, a subtraction: *Can I get a tax deduction if I give money to The Cancer Fund?* **2** a conclusion deduced: *I think we will find that your deduction is correct.*

de·duc·tive /dɪ'dʌktɪv/ *adj.* based on deduction (reasoning): *He used deductive reasoning to reach his conclusion.*

deed /did/ *n.* **1** the official paper showing ownership of real estate: *This is a photocopy of the deed to my house and land.* **2** *frml.* an act done by s.o.: *The man was hated for his evil deeds.*
—*v.* to transfer property by a deed: *She deeded her land to her daughter.*

deem /dim/ *v.frml.* to consider, believe: *Do you deem him an honest man?*

deep /dip/ *adj.* **-er, -est 1** going far below or back from the surface of s.t.: *a deep river, a deep hole, a deep closet* **2** serious, intense, (*syn.*) profound: *in deep thought, in deep trouble, a deep sleep* **3** hidden, mysterious: *a deep secret* **4** difficult to understand: *a deep thinker* **5** (of sound) low, (*syn.*) resonant: *a radio announcer with a deep voice, a deep note from a cello* **6** (of color) rich and dark: *the deep green of the forest* **7 in deep water:** in trouble **8** *infrml.* **to go off the deep end:** to become crazy, act careless of danger: *He was very successful until he began drinking and went off the deep end.* -*adv.* **deeply.** *See:* deep-rooted; deep-seated.
—*adv.* **1** below the surface of s.t.: *The water here is only two feet deep.* **2** far down or in: *They live deep in the jungle.||We talked deep into the night.* **3 to dig deep: a.** to pay or give a lot of money: *The mother dug deep to help her son start a business.* **b.** to investigate, examine very carefully: *The police are digging deep into this case to solve it.* **4 to run deep:** to be intense, go to great depth (feelings, ties, etc.): *The love of opera runs deep in Italy.*
—*n.* **the deep:** the deep part of an ocean: *The ship was lost in the deep and never found.*

deep·en /'dipən/ *v.* **1** to make deeper: *We deepened the hole by digging more.* **2** to become deeper: *A boy's voice deepens as he grows older.* **3** to extend, make larger: *The student deepened her knowledge of mathematics.*

Deep·freeze /'dip,friz/ *n.TM* **1** a type of refrigerator in which food is frozen and stored **2 to go into a Deepfreeze** or **deep freeze:** to be stopped and left waiting, become frozen and ineffective: *The boss stopped the project, and it went into a deep freeze.*

deep-fry *v.* **-fried, -frying, -fries** to fry food, such as chicken or fish, in hot oil: *I deep-fried some potatoes to make French fries.*

deep-rooted *adj.* **1** with deep roots: *Oak trees are deep-rooted.* **2** *fig.* strongly fixed in place: *She has deep-rooted loyalties to her family (nation, land, etc.).*

deep-sea *adj.* related to the deeper or deepest parts of an ocean or sea: *He goes deep-sea fishing (diving, exploring, etc.) in the Caribbean.*

deep-seated *adj.fig.* deep-rooted: *Deep-seated loyalties (customs, practices, etc.) change very slowly.*

deep-six *v.slang* to dispose of, throw in the waste basket: *You should deep-six that silly letter of complaint (stupid idea, expensive proposal, etc.).*

deer /dɪr/ *n.* **deer** a hoofed, four-footed mammal, usu. with antlers: *There are many deer in the woods behind our house.*

deer·skin /'dɪr,skɪn/ *n.* soft leather made from the hide (or skin) of a deer: *The Indian woman made deerskin clothes.*

de·es·ca·late /di'ɛskə,leɪt/ *v.* **-lated, -lating, -lates** to lower the intensity of: *Government officials tried to deescalate tensions between the two nations.*

de·es·ca·la·tion /di,ɛskə'leɪʃən/ *n.* [C;U] a lowering of intensity: *The deescalation of the war made peace talks possible.*

de·face /di'feɪs/ *v.* **-faced, -facing, -faces** to damage the appearance of: *The protesters defaced the government building with spray paint.* -*n.* **defacement.**

de fac·to /dɪ'fæktoʊ/ *adj.* true or real, but not recognized or spoken of: *Everyone knows that the General, not the President, is the de facto leader of that government.*

def·a·ma·tion /,dɛfə'meɪʃən/ *n.frml.* [U] hurting the reputation of s.o. with lies: *When a newspaper accused him of cheating on his taxes, the businessman took the paper to court for defamation of character.* -*adj.* **defamatory** /dɪ'fæmə,tɔri/; -*v.* **defame** /dɪ'feɪm/.

de·fault /dɪ'fɔlt/ *v.* **1** to fail to pay an obligation on time: *He defaulted on the loan by missing three payments.* **2** to fail to perform: *They defaulted on our contract when they didn't deliver the materials promised.*
—*n.* /'di,fɔlt/ [C;U] **1** an act of defaulting: *The unpaid loan is now in default.* **2 to win by default:** to win because the opposing team or player can't or won't compete

de·feat /dɪ'fit/ *v.* **1** to beat, win a victory over: *They defeated the enemy after a long war.* **2** to make fail, (*syn.*) to thwart: *Taking work with you defeats the purpose of a vacation.*
—*n.* **1** a victory over: *They celebrated their defeat of the enemy.* **2** a failure, loss: *We suffered many small defeats before our business finally succeeded.*

D

de·feat·ism /dɪ'fit,ɪsəm/ n. [U] an attitude of feeling unable to progress in life: *She has had so many disappointments that she has an attitude of defeatism.* -n.adj. **defeatist.**

def·e·cate /'dɛfə,keɪt/ v.frml. **-cated, -cating, -cates** to move the bowels: *The hospital patient defecated into the toilet.*

de·fect (1) /dɪ'fɛkt/ v. to leave a country, group, political party, etc., to go to another: *He defected to the enemy.* -n.[C;U] **defection; defector.**

defect (2) /'difɛkt, dɪ'fɛkt/ n. an imperfection, (syn.) a flaw: *Don't buy that tie; there's a defect in the material.*

de·fec·tive /dɪ'fɛktɪv/ adj. imperfect, (syn.) flawed: *A defective part stopped the machine from working.*

de·fend /dɪ'fɛnd/ v. **1** to protect against attack: *The army defended the city.* **2** (in law) to protect the rights of s.o. accused of a crime: *You'll need a lawyer to defend you in court.* **3** to explain, argue in support of: *to defend one's views (opinion, position, etc.)*

de·fen·dant /dɪ'fɛndənt/ n. a person or group (business, organization, etc.) accused of wrongdoing and called into court: *The defendant in this trial is accused of stealing a car.* See: plaintiff.

de·fense /dɪ'fɛns also 'di,fɛns/ n. **1** [C] a protection against attack: *This soccer team has a strong defense.* **2** [C] (in law) the protection of a defendant: *The lawyer presented an effective defense of her client.* **3** [C;U] an explanation, an argument to support a position, a choice, etc.

de·fense·less /dɪ'fɛnslɪs/ adj. without a defense, unprotected: *Soldiers were killed and so were defenseless civilians.*

defense mechanism n. a response, either instinctive or learned, to protect oneself against danger: *She immediately tells you that you are wrong as a defense mechanism to give her time to think.*

de·fens·i·ble /dɪ'fɛnsəbəl/ adj. **1** capable of being defended: *The military has a good defensible position behind high walls to protect the city.* **2** deserving defense, (syn.) justifiable: *Is there any defensible argument for the bad thing he did?*

de·fen·sive /dɪ'fɛnsɪv/ adj. **1** good for defense: *defensive weapons, defensive players on a team* **2** protective of oneself (from criticism): *She's so defensive that it's hard to discuss her ideas with her.* -adv. **defensively.**

—n. **on the defensive:** ready to protect oneself against criticism

de·fer /dɪ'fɜr/ v.frml. **-ferred, -ferring, -fers 1** to delay, move to a later time, (syn.) to postpone: *We wish to defer our decision for a week.* **2 to defer to:** to give preference to or accept

the opinion (wishes, advice, etc.) of another person over one's own: *I defer to your judgment.||He defers to his wife in matters involving the children.* -n.[C;U] **deferral.** See: deference.

def·er·ence /'dɛfərəns, 'dɛfrəns/ n. [U] respect for another's preferences, polite concern: *She showed deference to the wishes of her parents in planning her wedding.*

def·er·en·tial /,dɛfə'rɛnʃəl/ adj. respectful, considerate: *He has a deferential attitude toward important visitors.* -adv. **deferentially.**

de·fer·ment /dɪ'fɜrmənt/ n. [C;U] a delay, (syn.) a postponement: *The lawyer got a deferment of the trial to a later date.||I have a deferment from military service while I am a student.*

de·ferred /dɪ'fɜrd/ adj. delayed, (syn.) postponed: *The meeting (decision, party, etc.) has been deferred until tomorrow.*

de·fi·ance /dɪ'faɪəns/ n. [U] **1** open refusal to obey (an authority), (syn.) rebelliousness: *The people marched in the streets in defiance of the new military government.* **2** an attitude showing lack of fear or respect: *His defiance toward the boss cost him his job.* -adj. **defiant;** -adv. **defiantly.**

de·fi·cien·cy /dɪ'fɪʃənsi/ n. **-cies 1** [C;U] a lack, an amount that is not enough: *The child grew poorly because of a vitamin deficiency in her diet.* **2** [C] a failing, substandard quality: *to have a deficiency in the quality of work*

de·fi·cient /dɪ'fɪʃənt/ adj. **1** not enough, (syn.) insufficient: *Her diet is deficient in protein.* **2** of poor quality, substandard: *They fired him because his work was deficient.* -adv. **deficiently.**

def·i·cit /'dɛfəsɪt/ n. a lack of money created by spending more than one's income: *Our business did poorly last year; we must reduce our deficit this year!* See: surplus.

deficit financing n. [U] a government practice of borrowing money to cover the deficit: *Deficit financing pushes up interest rates.*

deficit spending n. [U] a government practice of spending more money than it takes in and so creating a deficit: *Deficit spending stimulates the economy, then creates inflation.*

de·file /dɪ'faɪl/ v.frml. **-filed, -filing, -files 1** to make unclean and so unusable (s.t. that is sacred): *Someone used paint to defile the church (synagogue, monument, etc.).* **2** to destroy in the opinion of others: *They have tried to defile her reputation.*

de·file·ment /dɪ'faɪlmənt/ n. a narrow rocky place through which soldiers pass in a line

de·fine /dɪ'faɪn/ v. **-fined, -fining, -fines 1** to explain the meaning of: *Dictionaries define words.* **2** to describe exactly, (syn.) to specify: *Please define the terms of the agreement.* **3** to show the shape of: *Can you define the limits of the property on this map?*‖*She defined her eyes with make-up.*

def·i·nite /'dɛfənɪt/ *adj.* **1** sure, without doubt: *Do you have a definite date for their arrival?* **2** clear, easy to see: *a definite improvement in his health* **3** clearly explained, precise: *definite wording for a contract*

def·i·nite·ly /'dɛfənɪtli/ *adv.* clearly, without doubt: *He is definitely right (the best, going out, etc.).*

def·i·ni·tion /,dɛfə'nɪʃən/ *n.* **1** [C] an exact explanation: *The teacher gave definitions of the new words.* **2** [U] clearness of an image (picture, photo, etc.): *a small TV screen with poor definition*

de·fin·i·tive /dɪ'fɪnətɪv/ *adj.* **1** clear and leaving no further question: *I received a definitive answer to my question.* **2** complete and without equal: *She has written the definitive book on modern poetry.* -*adv.* **definitively.**

de·flate /dɪ'fleɪt/ *v.* **-flated, -flating, -flates 1** to let the air out of s.t.: *Someone deflated the tires of our car, we're stuck!* **2** to lose air or gas: *The balloon deflated and went flat.* **3** *fig.* to cause a loss of self-confidence or sureness: *Any criticism quickly deflates him.* **4** to lower the prices of goods and services: *The economic recession has deflated prices.*

de·fla·tion /dɪ'fleɪʃən/ *n.* [C;U] a drop in prices of goods and services: *We have seen a sharp deflation in the price of oil. See:* disinflation.

de·fla·tor /dɪ'fleɪtər/ *n.* s.t. that causes a deflation: *The end of fighting in the Middle East is a deflator of oil prices.*

de·flect /dɪ'flɛkt/ *v.* **1** to turn away, redirect: *He deflects criticism from himself by blaming others.* **2** to change direction: *A bullet deflected off the wall and hit the table.* -*n.* [C;U] **deflection.**

de·fog·ger /di'fagər/ *n.* an electronic heating device, as in a car, that clears mist, frost, and ice from a window: *Turn on the rear window defogger.*

de·fo·li·ant /di'fouliant/ *n.* a chemical that causes trees and other plants to drop their leaves: *Planes dusted trees with a defoliant to destroy hiding places for the enemy.* -*v.* **defoliate.**

de·for·est /di'fɔrɪst, -'far-/ *v.* to remove the trees from an area as by fire, flood, logging, etc.: *Loggers deforested a valley by cutting its trees.* -*n.* [U] **deforestation** /,di,fɔrɪ'steɪʃən, -,far-/.

de·form /dɪ'fɔrm/ *v.* to force s.t. out its normal shape or appearance: *An earthquake deformed steel beams in a bridge.*‖*The child was born* <*adj.*> *deformed because of a gen-*

etic problem. -*n.* [U] **deformation** /,difɔr'meɪʃən,,dɛfər-/.

de·for·mi·ty /dɪ'fɔrməti/ *n.* **-ties** s.t. not normal in a person's appearance, such as a harelip or missing fingers caused by a birth defect, accident, etc.: *The baby suffers two deformities from birth defects.*

de·fraud /dɪ'frɔd/ *v.* to steal money by trickery or deceit, (*syn.*) to swindle: *He defrauded the government by cheating on his taxes.*

de·fray /dɪ'freɪ/ *v.* to arrange to pay the costs of s.t.: *He defrayed the costs of a new car by taking a second job.*

de·frock /di'frak/ *v.* to remove the right of a clergyman (lawyer, doctor, etc.) to work at his or her profession: *A Catholic priest was defrocked because he married.*

de·frost /dɪ'frɔst/ *v.* to cause frost and ice to melt, such as from a freezer or frozen food: *You can defrost a frozen cake by putting it in a microwave oven.*

de·frost·er /dɪ'frɔstər/ *n.* a blower system used to clear mist, frost, or ice from windows of a car or other vehicle: *Turn on the defroster to clear the windshield.*

deft /dɛft/ *adj.* **-er, -est** skillful and quick: *What a deft typist you are!* -*adv.* **deftly;** -*n.* [U] **deftness.**

de·funct /di'fʌŋkt/ *adj.* no longer functioning or living: *That company is now defunct; it closed last month.*

de·fuse /dɪ'fyuz/ *v.* **-fused, -fusing, -fuses 1** to remove the fuse from: *They defused the bomb, so it couldn't explode.* **2** *fig.* to reduce the danger of: *to defuse the threat of a riot (conflict, war, scandal, etc.) by calming the people involved*

de·fy /dɪ'faɪ/ *v.* **-fied, -fying, -fies 1** to oppose openly, refuse to obey: *The union defied management and went on strike.* **2** *fig.* to resist: *The lock defied all my efforts to open it.* **3** to dare or challenge s.o. to do s.t. thought impossible: *I defy you to find anything wrong with this plan.*

de·gen·er·ate (1) /dɪ'dʒɛnəˌreɪt/ *v.* **-ated, -ating, -ates 1** to fall into a worse condition, (*syn.*) to deteriorate: *The business has degenerated into a confused mess.* **2** to fall to a lower standard of moral behavior: *people who degenerate into drug addiction and crime*

de·gen·er·ate (2) /dɪ'dʒɛnərɪt/ *adj.* **1** fallen to a low condition, (*syn.*) deteriorated: *The professor argued that we have become a degenerate society.* **2** fallen to low standards in morals or character: *He's an alcoholic leading a degenerate life.*
—*n.* a person who acts in ways unacceptable to society: *They are a group of degenerates; they use drugs, steal cars, and rob people.* -*n.* [U] **degeneracy.**

de·gen·er·a·tion /dɪˌdʒɛnəˈreɪʃən/ *n.* [U] the process of falling to a lower condition or standard: *They left New York because of the degeneration in the quality of city life.*

de·grad·a·ble /dɪˈɡreɪdəbəl/ *adj.* capable of being decomposed or broken down: *This garbage is degradable into compost for the garden.*

de·grade /dɪˈɡreɪd/ *v.* **-graded, -grading, -grades** **1** to lower in the opinion of others or in self-respect: *Don't degrade yourself by accepting such a poor job offer.* **2** to lower the quality or worth of s.t.: *They degraded the value of the house by letting it fall into ruin.* **3** to break down and lose effectiveness: *Medicine (chemicals, materials, etc.) can degrade over time.* *-n.* [U] **degradation** /ˌdɛɡrəˈdeɪʃən/.

de·grad·ing /dɪˈɡreɪdɪŋ/ *adj.* causing shame, (*syn.*) humiliating: *The new soldiers suffered degrading comments about their abilities.*

de·gree /dəˈɡri/ *n.* **1** [C] a unit of measurement, such as for temperature, angles, or geographical direction and location: *Water freezes at 32 degrees Fahrenheit (32 F).*||*The corner of a square is a 90 degree angle.* **2** [U] amount or intensity: *a high degree of intelligence (skill, respect for s.o., etc.)* **3** [C] a diploma from a college or university: *She has a degree in chemistry.* **4** [U] measurement of the seriousness of s.t.: *second-degree burns, first-degree murder* **5 by degrees:** little by little, (*syn.*) gradually **6 to give s.o. the third degree:** to question sharply, (*syn.*) to interrogate: *The young man had a car accident and his father gave him the third degree as to what happened.*

de·hu·man·i·za·tion /diˌhyumənəˈzeɪʃən/ *n.* [U] a removal of civilized human qualities, (*syn.*) a degradation: *The dehumanization of work can turn people into machines.* *-v.* **dehumanize.**

de·hu·mid·i·fy /ˌdihyuˈmɪdəˌfaɪ/ *v.* **-fied, -fying, -fies** to remove water from the air: *An air conditioner cools and dehumidifies the air.* *-n.* **dehumidifier.**

de·hy·drate /diˈhaɪˌdreɪt/ *v.* **-drated, -drating, -drates** to remove moisture: *Too much heat dehydrates the body.*

de·hy·dra·tion /ˌdihaɪˈdreɪʃən/ *n.* [U] a lack of water, esp. in the body: *Long distance runners often suffer from dehydration.*

de·ice /diˈaɪs/ *v.* **-iced, -icing, -ices** to remove ice: *It's important to de-ice a freezer (airplane wings, windshield).* *-n.* **de-icer.**

de·i·fy /ˈdiəˌfaɪ/ *v.frml.* **-fied, -fying, -fies** to make into a god: *The Roman Senate deified Emperors after death.* *-n.* [U] **deification** /ˌdiəfəˈkeɪʃən/.

deign /deɪn/ *v.* to lower oneself to do s.t. considered below one's status or dignity, (*syn.*) to condescend: *He deigned to visit his poor relatives.*

de·ism /ˈdiˌɪzəm/ *n.* [U] the belief in a god who created the physical universe but since then has had no more influence over it or life: *Christians do not believe in deism.*

de·i·ty /ˈdiɪti/ *n.* **-ties** **1** a god or goddess: *Jupiter was the most powerful of the Roman deities.* **2 Supreme Deity:** God: *Many people believe in a Supreme Deity.* *-adj.* **deistic** /diˈɪstɪk/.

dé·jà vu /ˈdeɪʒɑˈvu/ *n.* the feeling that one is repeating an experience even though it is actually happening for the first time: *When I entered the house, I had a strong sense of déjà vu, but I had never been there before.*

de·ject·ed /dɪˈdʒɛktɪd/ *adj.* sad, in low spirits: *A man with a dejected look sat waiting for a bus.* *-adv.* **dejectedly.**

de·jec·tion /dɪˈdʒɛkʃən/ *n.* [U] a feeling of sadness or tiredness, as from overwork or failure: *We could see the dejection on the faces of the losing players of the baseball team.* *-v.* **deject.**

de·lay /dɪˈleɪ/ *v.* **1** to slow or stop for a time: *We must delay our decision for a day.* **2** to cause to be late: *Her late arrival delayed the start of the meeting.* **3** to move to a later time, (*syn.*) to postpone: *They have delayed the court hearing until next month.*
—*n.* **1** a time that s.t. is slowed or stopped: *a brief delay in finishing the job, a long delay in traffic* **2** a stopping or slowing of s.t.: *This delay puts us behind schedule.* **3** (in law) a postponement, (*syn.*) a stay: *The lawyers asked for a delay in the trial date.*

de·lec·ta·ble /dəˈlɛktəbəl/ *adj.* tasty, delicious: *What a delectable meal!*

del·e·gate (1) /ˈdɛləˌɡɪt/ *n.* a representative (of a government, political party, etc.) with the power to speak, act, or vote: *Many nations send delegates to the United Nations.*

del·e·gate (2) /ˈdɛləˌɡeɪt/ *v.* **-gated, -gating, -gates** to give (power or authority to s.o. to act in one's place): *The president delegates authority to his vice-presidents.* *-n.* [U] **delegacy** /ˈdɛləɡəsi/.

del·e·ga·tion /ˌdɛləˈɡeɪʃən/ *n.* **1** [C] a group of official representatives: *He is a member of the Brazilian delegation to the United Nations.* **2** [U] the act of giving (power or authority to s.o. to act in one's place): *Her delegation of so much authority to her assistant upset her business partners.*

de·lete /dɪˈlit/ *v.* **-leted, -leting, -letes** to take out, (*syns.*) to eliminate, erase: *By mistake, the secretary deleted a paragraph from the letter he was typing.*

del·e·te·ri·ous /ˌdɛləˈtɪriəs/ *adj.frml.* harmful, unhealthy: *Smoking cigarettes can be deleterious to your health.*

de·le·tion /dɪ'liʃən/ *n.* [C;U] erasing or taking out of a word or words: *I have made deletions in the document.*

del·i /'dɛli/ *n.infrml. short for* delicatessen: *I'm going to the deli for some cheese.*

de·lib·er·ate (1) /də'lɪbərɪt,-'lɪbrɪt/ *adj.* **1** done on purpose, (*syn.*) intentional: *That was no accident; it was deliberate!* **2** slow and careful: *She is a very serious woman and acts in a deliberate manner.*

de·lib·er·ate (2) /də'lɪbə,reɪt/ *v.* **-ated, -ating, -ates** to discuss, debate: *The Legislature is deliberating whether to pass that law.* *-adv.* **deliberately.**

de·lib·er·a·tion /də,lɪbə'reɪʃən/ *n.* [C;U] an act of discussing or debating: *The Senate began its deliberations yesterday.*

de·lib·er·a·tive /də'lɪbərətɪv, -ə,reɪtɪv/ *adj.* characterized by deliberation: *The United Nations is a deliberative body.*

del·i·ca·cy /'dɛləkəsi/ *n.* **-cies** **1** [C] special food that tastes great and is hard to get: *Caviar is a delicacy.* **2** [U] careful, sensitive attention not to upset or offend: *Diplomats must treat difficult matters with delicacy.*

del·i·cate /'dɛləkɪt/ *adj.* **1** easily broken or hurt: *This teacup is made of delicate china.* **2** made in a fine, sensitive manner, (*syn.*) dainty: *These china plates have a lovely, delicate flower pattern.* **3** needing sensitive treatment: *He is upset at failing the course, so talking to him about it is a delicate matter.* *-adv.* **delicately.**

del·i·ca·tes·sen /,dɛləkə'tɛsən/ *n.* a food market and sandwich shop featuring high quality cooked meats and other fine foods, such as cheeses, condiments, and pastries: *Many people like to go to a delicatessen for lunch. See:* deli.

USAGE NOTE: The type of food sold in a *delicatessen* depends on the store's location in the USA. A New York deli traditionally sells Reuben sandwiches, made from rye bread, corned beef, swiss cheese, and sauerkraut (pickled cabbage). A deli in California may sell California Rolls, a Japanese-style dish made of rice, avocado, and crab meat rolled in a piece of seaweed.

---

de·li·cious /də'lɪʃəs/ *adj.* **1** good-tasting, (*syn.*) tasty: *Thank you for the delicious meal.* **2** pleasing or exciting, (*syn.*) titillating: *a delicious rumor* *-adv.* **deliciously.**

de·light /dɪ'laɪt/ *v.* **1** to make happy, bring joy to, (*syn.*) to thrill: *Their beautiful gift delighted her.* **2** *phrasal v. insep.* **to delight in s.t.:** to enjoy greatly: *She delights in telling funny stories.*
—n. **1** [C;U] happiness, pleasure: *He finds delight in giving to others.* **2** [C] s.t. that gives pleasure, joy: *The child is so loving and sweet that she's a delight.*

de·light·ed /dɪ'laɪtɪd/ *adj.* very happy, pleased: *I am delighted to accept your invitation to dinner.*

de·light·ful /dɪ'laɪtfəl/ *adj.* **1** very enjoyable, thrilling: *We had a delightful time at your party.* **2** very pleasing: *He has a delightful personality.* *-adv.* **delightfully.**

de·lim·it /dɪ'lɪmɪt/ *v.* to set the limits or boundaries of s.t.: *Company policy delimits a supervisor's spending authority to $1,000 and no more.*

de·lin·e·ate /dɪ'lɪni,eɪt/ *v.frml.* **-ated, -ating, -ates** **1** to describe, usu. in specific detail: *You must delineate exactly what you want in a contract.* **2** to show by drawing, (*syn.*) to depict: *The buyer delineated the kind of house she wants on a sheet of paper.*

de·lin·quen·cy /dɪ'lɪŋkwənsi/ *n.* [U] lawbreaking, esp. by young people: *Juvenile delinquency means antisocial actions and crimes by children and teenagers.*

de·lin·quent /dɪ'lɪŋkwənt/ *adj.* late in paying a bill: *The company has too many delinquent customers.*
—n. a lawbreaker, esp. a youth: *Juvenile delinquents can be sent to a special school by the courts.* *-adv.* **delinquently.**

de·li·ri·ous /dɪ'lɪriəs/ *adj.* **1** suffering from confusion and wild imaginings: *She was delirious from a high fever.* **2** wildly excited, (*syn.*) ecstatic: *delirious with joy* *-adv.* **deliriously.**

de·li·ri·um /dɪ'lɪriəm/ *n.* **1** a state of confusion and wild imaginings, usu. from fever: *The patient was very sick and in a delirium.* **2** great excitement, (*syn.*) ecstasy: *in a delirium over wonderful news*

delirium trem·ens /'trimənz, 'trɛm-/ or **D.T.'s** /'di'tiz/ *n.pl.* a delirium caused by drinking too much alcohol: *Alcoholics with delirium tremens should go to the hospital.*

de·liv·er /də'lɪvər/ *v.* **1** to take goods to a place of business, a home, etc.: *Trucks deliver food to supermarkets.* **2** to give, pass on: *to deliver a speech, deliver a message* **3** to help (a baby) to be born: *Which doctor delivered your baby?* **4** *infrml.fig.* to produce good results: *I'd call her a great salesperson because she really delivers!* **5** *frml.* **to deliver from:** to free, save from (danger) **6** **to deliver on one's promises:** to do what one has promised: *The voters were angry that the man they elected failed to deliver on his promises.*

de·liv·er·ance /də'lɪvərəns, -'lɪvrəns/ *n.frml.* [U] **1** saving from danger, (*syn.*) liberation: *We hope for deliverance from the enemy.* **2** (in religion) salvation: *Many Christians pray to Jesus for deliverance.* *-n.* **deliverer.**

de·liv·er·y /də'lıvəri, -'lıvri/ *n.* **-ies 1** [C;U] the taking of goods to a place of business, a home, etc.: *This company promises fast delivery.* **2** [C;U] giving or passing on s.t., (*syn.*) transmittal: *delivery of a message* **3** [C] the act of giving birth: *She had a difficult delivery, but the baby is fine.*

dell /dɛl/ *n.* a small valley with grass and trees: *There is a farmer in the dell with his cows.*

del·ta /'dɛltə/ *n.* a flat low area shaped like a triangle (Δ) made by a river entering a sea: *The Mississippi delta and the delta of the Nile are huge areas.*

de·lude /dɪ'lud/ *v.* **-luded, -luding, -ludes** to fool or mislead, esp. oneself: *He deluded himself into thinking that he is an important man.*

del·uge /'dɛlyudʒ/ *n.* **1** a heavy rain, usu. brief and sudden: *The deluge caused flooding.* **2** *fig.* a great outpouring: *a deluge of praise for a great achievement*
—*v.fig.* **-luged, -luging, -luges** to come down on in a heavy outpouring, (*syn.*) to inundate: *Reporters deluged the President with questions.*

de·lu·sion /dɪ'luʒən/ *n.* an unrealistic thought or expectation, (*syn.*) self-deception: *That poor woman has delusions of fame and fortune.*

de·luxe /dɪ'lʌks/ *adj.* representing the finest quality, (*syn.*) luxurious: *They had deluxe rooms in an expensive hotel.*

delve /dɛlv/ *v.* **delved, delving, delves** to look deeply into, examine: *Good students delve into a subject to understand it thoroughly.*

dem·a·gogue /'dɛmə,gɔg, -,gag/ *n.* a political leader who gets power by exciting the people's emotions, esp. fears and prejudices: *Hitler was a demagogue.* -*adj.* **demagogic** /,dɛmə'gadʒık, -'gag-/.

dem·a·gogu·er·y /,dɛmə'gɔgəri, -'gag-/ *n.* [U] acting like a demagogue: *Watch out for politicians who engage in demagoguery.*

de·mand /də'mænd/ *v.* **1** to ask for very strongly, (*syn.*) to command: *They demand payment today.* **2** to require, have a strong need for: *This problem demands immediate attention.*
—*n.* **1** a command, claim: *This is our second demand for payment.* **2 in demand:** much wanted: *After two successful films, that actor is in great demand in Hollywood.* **3 to make demands on:** to have strong need of, make claims on: *Small children make great demands on parents' time and energy.*

de·mand·ing /də'mændıŋ/ *adj.* **1** requiring high performance, (*syn.*) exacting: *My boss is very demanding of others.* **2** requiring great effort, (*syn.*) arduous: *Climbing a mountain is a demanding task.*

demand-pull inflation *n.* [U] price inflation caused by demand that is greater than supply: *Demand-pull inflation causes prices to rise.*

de·mar·ca·tion /,dimar'keıʃən/ *n.* [U] a line of separation drawn to show a boundary or limit: *A line of demarcation has been drawn between the two countries.* -*v.* **demarcate** /dɪ'mar,keıt, 'dimar-/.

de·mean /də'min/ *v.frml.* to treat in a way that hurts one's pride or dignity, (*syn.*) to humiliate: *The soldiers demeaned their prisoners by giving them dirty jobs to do.* -*adj.* **demeaning.**

de·mean·or /də'minər/ *n.frml.* manner, way of behaving: *I like his gentlemanly demeanor.*

de·ment·ed /də'mɛntɪd/ *adj.* insane, crazy: *Don't listen to her advice because she's talking like a demented person.*

de·mer·it /də'mɛrɪt/ *n.* a bad mark against a person's record: *The sergeant gave a soldier 10 demerits for not cleaning his rifle properly.*

de·mil·i·ta·rize /di'mılətə,raɪz/ *v.* **-rized, -rizing, -rizes** to remove the military from an area: *The two nations at war agreed to demilitarize a zone between them.*

de·mise /dɪ'maɪz/ *n.frml.* [U] **1** death: *He met his demise in an accident.* **2** end, (*syn.*) ruin: *The demise of the business left 100 workers without jobs.*
—*v.* **-mised, -mising, -mises** to die

de·mis·sion /dɪ'mıʃən/ *n.* a resignation from a position: *The Prime Minister accepted the demission of the Minister of Justice.* -*v.* **demit.**

dem·i·tasse /'dɛmi,tas/ *n.* (French for) a small cup: *I had a demitasse of coffee after dinner.*

dem·o /'dɛmoʊ/ *n.* short for demonstration: *Our sales people do demos of our new equipment for customers.*

de·mo·bil·ize /di'moʊbə,laɪz/ *v.* **-lized, -lizing, -lizes** to return members of the military to civilian life: *After the war, the army was demobilized and the soldiers came home.* -*n.* [C;U] **demobilization** /di,moʊbələ'zeıʃən/.

de·moc·ra·cy /dɪ'makrəsi/ *n.* [C;U] a government based on a written constitution and laws made by representatives elected by the people: *Democracy guards and respects the rights of the individual.* -*v.* **democratize** /dɪ'makrə,taɪz/.

Dem·o·crat /'dɛmə,kræt/ *n.* in the USA, a member of the Democratic Party: *She has voted Democrat all her life. See:* Republican.

dem·o·crat·ic /,dɛmə'krætɪk/ *adj.* **1** related to a democracy and democratic ideas **2** treating people as equals: *Even though she comes from a very rich family, she treats others in a democratic manner.* -*adv.* **democratically.**

Democratic Party *n.* in the USA, a political party begun in 1828 and often considered liberal: *In 1994, the Democratic Party lost control of the House of Representatives.*

D

The two main political parties in the USA are the *Democratic Party* and the *Republican Party.* Democrats are more liberal than Republicans and generally believe in greater government involvement in social issues. The symbol of the Democratic Party is the donkey.

dem·o·graph·ics /,dɛmə'græfɪks/ *n.pl.* demographic information about groups of people used esp. in politics and marketing: *The demographics of New York show a great variety of people.*

de·mog·ra·phy /dɪ'mɑgrəfi/ *n.* [U] the study of characteristics of large groups of people (local, regional, or national), analyzing size, growth, age, sex, income, etc.: *Experts in demography advise politicians and advertisers.* *-adj.* **demographic** /,dɛmə'græfɪk/; *-adv.* **demographically.**

de·mol·ish /də'mɑlɪʃ/ *v.* **1** to pull down, (*syn.*) to raze: *A wrecking team demolished the old building.* **2** to destroy: *They demolished the enemy.* *-n.*[C;U] **demolition** /,dɛmə'lɪtʃən/.

de·mon /'dimən/ *n.* **1** an imaginary evil creature, a devil: *demons in a nightmare* **2** *infrml.fig.* a person known for very special abilities: *That runner is a speed demon.* *-adj.* **demonic** /dɪ'mɑnɪk/.

de·mon·stra·ble /də'mɑnstrəbəl/ *adj.* able to be shown or demonstrated: *Our company's product has demonstrable advantages over theirs.* *-adv.* **demonstrably.**

de·mon·strate /'dɛmən,streɪt/ *v.* **-strated, -strating, -strates 1** to show (how s.t. works, its advantages, etc.): *I'll demonstrate for you how our new computer works.* **2** to march in protest: *Students demonstrated in the streets outside the Capitol.*

dem·on·stra·tion /,dɛmən'streɪʃən/ *n.* **1** [C;U] a display or explanation of s.t.: *Workers watched an engineer give a demonstration of a new machine.* **2** [C] a public show of opinion, esp. a protest: *A demonstration against the war was held in front of the embassy.* **3** [C;U] a show of feeling: *a demonstration of good will, affection, trust*

Political *demonstrations* against the US government are legal under the First Amendment of the Constitution, which gives Americans freedom of speech and the right to assemble and peacefully protest government policies.

de·mon·stra·tive /də'mɑnstrətɪv/ *adj.* **1** showing feelings openly, esp. affection: *She's quiet and reserved, not a demonstrative person.* **2** showing, (*syns.*) indicative of, suggestive of: *Their written offer of a job is demonstrative of their very real interest.*

dem·on·stra·tor /'dɛmən,streɪtər/ *n.* **1** a protester: *Demonstrators carried signs as they marched and shouted.* **2** a person who explains s.t.: *a demonstrator of a new product* **3** a product used as an example: *a demonstrator model of a new car*

de·mor·al·ize /di'mɔrə,laɪz, -'mɑr-/ *v.* **-ized, -izing, -izes** to lower the spirits or morale of s.o., (*syn.*) to discourage: *Poor leadership demoralized the workers.*

de·mote /dɪ'moʊt/ *v.* **-moted, -moting, -motes** to lower in position or rank: *The editor was angry when the general manager demoted her to assistant editor.*

de·mo·tion /dɪ'moʊʃən/ *n.* [C;U] a lowering in position or rank: *He was given a demotion because of his poor performance on the job.*

de·mur /dɪ'mɜr/ *v.frml.* **-murred, -murring, -murs** to object, speak against: *She demurred when asked to take a salary cut.*

demure /dɪ'myʊr/ *adj.* quiet, modest: *The demure young man waited to be asked to dance.* *-adv.* **demurely.**

de·mys·ti·fy /di'mɪstə,faɪ/ *v.* **-fied, -fying, -fies** to make s.t. clear, to remove the mystery from: *We must demystify science by improving people's understanding of it.*

den /dɛn/ *n.* **1** the home of certain animals: *a bear's (lion's, fox's) den* **2** a room for relaxation and study: *Our family watches TV in the den.*

de·na·tion·al·ize /di'næʃənə,laɪz/ *v.* **-ized, izing, izes** to sell to private businesses, to remove government ownership: *France and England denationalized much of their industry.*

de·ni·a·ble /dɪ'naɪəbəl/ *adj.* capable or worthy of denial: *All the accusations made in court against the defendant were deniable.* *-adv.* **deniably.**

de·ni·al /dɪ'naɪəl/ *n.* **1** [C] a statement saying that s.t. is not true: *The Senator issued a denial of the story connecting her to organized crime.* **2** [C] refusal, rejection: *I was angry at his denial of my request for a day off.* **3** [C;U] refusal to accept s.t. as true: *Her denial of her heart condition keeps her from getting the medical care she needs for it.*

den·i·grate /'dɛnə,greɪt/ *v.* **-grated, -grating, grates** to speak against the value, importance, character, or quality of, (*syns.*) to disparage, belittle: *Some players denigrated the abilities of the other team.*

den·im /'dɛnəm/ *n.adj.* [U] a strong fabric made of cotton and used in jeans: *The cowboy wore a denim jacket and jeans.*

den·i·zen /'dɛnəzən/ *n.* s.o. or s.t. living in a particular place: *A bear is a denizen of the forest.*

de·nom·i·na·tion /də,namə'neɪʃən/ *n.* **1** a religious group with its own set of beliefs within a larger religion: *Within Christianity, there are many denominations, such as Roman Catholics, Protestants, and the Eastern Orthodox Church.* **2** an amount (of money): *The bank robbers got only bills in small denominations, such as fives and tens.* -*v.* **denominate;** -*adj.* **denominational.**

de·nom·i·na·tor /dɪ'namə,neɪtər/ *n.* **1** the number below the line in a fraction: *In gallon, the denominator 4 shows that the gallon is divided in fourths or quarters.* **2 (lowest) common denominator:** an indicator of a quality shared by all the members of a group: *Although my sisters and brothers are always fighting, they have one common denominator: they all belong to the same political party.*

de·note /dɪ'noʊt/ *v.* **-noted, -noting, -notes** to show clearly, signify: *The high quality of her writing denotes clear thinking.*

dé·noue·ment /,deɪnu'maN/ *n.* the final moment after a climax in action, as in a play or opera: *In the death scene, the dénouement is the moment of death.*

de·nounce /dɪ'naʊns/ *v.* **-nounced, -nouncing, -nounces** to speak strongly against, condemn: *The Presidential candidate denounced his opponent as a liar.* -*n.* [U] **denouncement.**

dense /dɛns/ *adj.* **denser, densest 1 1** stupid: *He's too dense to understand our plan.* **2** crowded together: *a dense forest, dense traffic* -*adv.* **densely.**

den·si·ty /'dɛnsɪti/ *n.* [C;U] **-ties** a degree of concentration: *The population density in Tokyo is very high.*

dent /dɛnt/ *n.* **1** a hollow or depression made by a blow or impact: *The accident left a dent in my car door.* **2** *infrml.fig.* **to make a dent in:** to progress a little: *We finally made a dent in our competitor's market, and we have 5 percent more market share now.*
—*v.* to make a dent in s.t.: *Another car hit mine and dented the back fender.*

den·tal /'dɛntl/ *adj.* related to teeth and dentistry: *She runs a dental office (practice, clinic, etc.).*

den·tist /'dɛntɪst/ *n.* a person qualified in dentistry: *The dentist examined my teeth.*

den·tist·ry /'dɛntɪstri/ *n.* [U] the branch of medicine specializing in care and treatment of the teeth and gums: *He practices dentistry in Chicago.*

den·ture /'dɛntʃər/ *n.* false teeth, an artificial dental plate: *She wears a denture in her lower jaw.*
—*n. pl.* **dentures:** a complete set of false teeth: *My seventy-year-old father has dentures.*

de·nude /dɪ'nud/ *v.* **-nuded, -nuding, -nudes** to remove the covering from s.t.: *The hurricane denuded the trees of their leaves.*

de·nun·ci·a·tion /dɪ,nʌnsi'eɪʃən/ *n.* [C;U] strong statement against, condemnation (usu. in public): *The government issued a denunciation of the terrorist group.*

de·ny /dɪ'naɪ/ *v.* **-nied, -nying, -nies 1** to say s.t. is not true, (*syn.*) to disavow: *The defendant denied the accusations made against her in court.* **2** to refuse, reject: *They denied their son permission to go.*

de·o·dor·ant /di'oʊdərənt/ *n.* [C;U] a substance that contains a perfume to hid unpleasant smells, esp. of the human body: *I wish he would use an underarm deodorant!*
—*adj.* related to deodorants: *a deodorant product. See:* antiperspirant, USAGE NOTE.

de·o·dor·ize /di'oʊdə,raɪz/ *v.* **-ized, -izing, -izes** to cover the odor of s.t., to use a disinfectant that removes a bad smell: *The cleaning woman deodorized the bathroom with Lysol™.*

de·part /dɪ'part/ *v.* **1** to leave, begin a trip: *The plane to Paris will depart at 3:00.* **2 to depart from:** to move away from: *The secretive author departed from his custom of privacy when he agreed to give an interview.* **3** to die: *The old woman departed in her sleep last night.*
—*n.* **the departed:** a dead person: *The departed will be buried tomorrow.*

de·part·ment /dɪ'partmənt/ *n.* **1** a division (of a business, college, organization, etc.) with a specific function: *He works for a newspaper in the art (editorial, advertising, etc.) department.* **2** a branch of government: *the Department of Defense* -*adj.* **departmental** /,dipart'mɛntl/; -*adv.* **departmentally.**

de·part·men·tal·ize /,dipart'mɛntl,aɪz/ *v.* **-ized, -izing, -izes** to organize into departments: *They departmentalized the military into the Department of the Army, the Department of the Navy, etc.*

department store *n.* a store that carries a wide variety of goods, such as clothes, furniture, dishes, etc.: *Macy's in New York City is a famous department store.*

de·par·ture /dɪ'partʃər/ *n.* **1** [C;U] an act of departing, a leaving: *My departure for Los Angeles is at 8:00 A.M. tomorrow.* **2** [C] a different way from the usual way of doing s.t., (*syn.*) a deviation: *We were surprised by their departure from their normal practice.*

de·pend /dɪ'pɛnd/ *v.* **1** to rely on, trust: *I depend on you to be on time.* **2** to need (for support): *Her family depends upon her salary from that job.* **3** to vary with, be controlled by: *Tomorrow's picnic depends on our having good weather.*

de·pend·a·ble /dɪ'pɛndəbəl/ *adj.* responsible, reliable, trustworthy: *A good friend must be dependable.* -*adv.* **dependably.**

de·pend·ence /dɪ'pɛndəns/ n. **1** sing. [U] reliance, a need for support: *The son has a dependence on his parents for money.* **2** [C;U] addiction: *She has a dependence on alcohol.*

de·pend·en·cy /dɪ'pɛndənsi/ n. **-cies 1** [C;U] a strong need for, an addiction: *He has a dependency on drugs.* **2** [C] a nation or territory dependent on another power: *The island of Guam is a dependency of the United States.*

de·pend·ent /dɪ'pɛndənt/ adj. **1** in need of support from, reliant upon: *A dog is dependent upon its owner for food.* **2** controlled by, varying with: *Our bonuses are dependent on good profits.*
—n. a person who depends on another for food, clothes, housing, etc.: *He has three dependents, his wife and two children.*

de·per·son·a·lize /di'pɜrsənə,laɪz/ v. **-ized, -izing, -izes 1** to make impersonal, (syn.) to dehumanize: *The use of computers can depersonalize service by treating people as mere numbers.* **2** to change the focus of a situation from a person to the issue: *We must depersonalize this discussion and focus on the problem, not on who is to blame.*

de·pict /dɪ'pɪkt/ v.frml. **1** to paint, draw: *The artist depicted a landscape in bright colors.* **2** to describe, (syn.) to portray: *Her letters depict the situation as wonderful.* -n.[C;U] **depiction** /dɪ'pɪkʃən/.

de·pil·a·to·ry /də'pɪlə,tɔri/ n. **-ries** a product that removes hair: *She uses a depilatory to remove unwanted body hair.*

de·plane /di'pleɪn/ v. **-planed, -planing, -planes** to leave an airplane: *We deplaned in Chicago and then drove to Milwaukee.*

de·plete /dɪ'plit/ v. **-pleted, -pleting, -pletes** to reduce by using much of: *That country has depleted its natural resources completely.* -n. [U] **depletion** /dɪ'pliʃən/.

de·plor·a·ble /dɪ'plɔrəbəl/ adj. **1** very bad, (syn.) distressing: *Poor people live in deplorable conditions.* **2** worthy of strong criticism or condemnation: *the deplorable actions of a dictator* -adv. **deplorably.**

de·plore /dɪ'plɔr/ v. **-plored, -ploring, -plores 1** to feel or express sadness or regret over: *Every citizen must deplore the poor housing conditions in the city.* **2** to strongly disapprove of, condemn: *The newspaper printed an editorial deploring police brutality.*

de·ploy /dɪ'plɔɪ/ v. to spread out for use, esp. for military action: *The general deployed his forces along the battlefront.* -n.[C;U] **deployment.**

de·po·lit·i·cize /,dipə'lɪtə,saɪz/ v. **-cized, -cizing, -cizes** to remove the politics from a situation: *The President depoliticized poverty issues and has all parties working together on solving their causes.*

de·pop·u·late /di'pɑpyə,leɪt/ v. **-lated, -lating, -lates** to remove the population from an area, usu. by a disaster: *A long period without rain depopulated the region.* -n. [U] **depopulation** /di,pɑpyə'leɪʃən/.

de·port /dɪ'pɔrt/ v. to force s.o., usu. a foreigner or criminal, to leave a country, esp. by taking away his or her citizenship: *The government deported the spy.* -adj. **deportable** /dɪ'pɔrtəbəl/.

de·por·ta·tion /,dipɔr'teɪʃən/ n. [C;U] forced removal of s.o. from a country by law: *Prison officials took her to the airport for deportation.*

de·port·ee /,dipɔr'ti/ n. a person who is deported: *Deportees must find a country prepared to take them.*

de·port·ment /dɪ'pɔrtmənt/ n.frml. [U] conduct, behavior: *His deportment in college was excellent; he worked hard and never got into trouble.*

de·pose /di'pouz/ v. **-posed, -posing, -poses 1** to remove s.o. from power, such as a dictator, king, or other powerful person: *The army deposed the dictator.* **2** (in law) to take a deposition, usu. oral testimony put in writing by a stenographer, to discover facts from a person in a lawsuit before a court trial: *A lawyer deposed a witness in her office.*

de·pos·it /dɪ'pɑsɪt/ v. **1** to place s.t. valuable, such as money, in a bank or brokerage account: *I deposit my paycheck in the bank.* **2** to place valuables for safekeeping: *to deposit jewelry in a safe, to deposit your children with a baby sitter* **3** to come down, settle: *Sediment deposits slowly on the ocean bottom.*
—n. **1** the act of placing money in an account: *I made a deposit at the bank this morning.* **2** a partial payment to hold goods or property until the buyer makes complete payment: *to make (or) leave a deposit on a new TV set* **3** s.t. deposited through a natural process: *deposits of sand at the mouth of a river*

dep·o·si·tion /,dɛpə'zɪʃən/ n. **1** (in law) statements sworn to be true that are recorded before a trial: *I gave a deposition to the court because I was excused from testifying at the trial.* **2** a deposing (from power)

de·pos·i·to·ry /dɪ'pɑzə,tɔri/ n. **-ies 1** a place of safekeeping, (syn.) a repository: *Stock certificates are kept in a depository at the brokerage house.* **2** a vault-like container for safekeeping, such as those found outside banks: *A store employee puts the day's receipts in the bank depository at night.*

de·pot /'dipou, 'dɛ-/ n. **1** a bus or train station: *Meet me at the bus depot.* **2** a place to store goods, a warehouse: *Military supplies are stored at the depot.*

de·praved /dɪ'preɪvd/ *adj.* of low moral character: *That depraved man abused children.*

de·prav·i·ty /dɪ'prævəti/ *n.* [U] moral corruption, (*syn.*) degeneracy: *After he lost his job, he fell slowly into a life of drugs and depravity.*

dep·re·cate /'dɛprə,keɪt/ *v.* **-cated, -cating, -cates 1** to express disapproval of: *She doesn't like to hear her parents deprecate her husband.* **2** to speak of s.t. as if it is of little value, (*syn.*) to belittle: *She is a modest person, so she responds to praise with self-deprecating remarks.* *-adj.* **deprecatory** /'dɛprəkə,tɔri/.

de·pre·cia·ble /də'priʃəbəl/ *adj.* capable of being reduced in value, esp. for tax deduction purposes: *They were wise to invest in depreciable real estate*

de·pre·ci·ate /dɪ'priʃi,eɪt/ *v.* **-ated, -ating, -ates 1** to go down in value: *This house has depreciated since we bought it.* **2** to take a deduction from taxes for the loss over time in value of property and equipment: *Our accountant advised us to depreciate the office building at 3 percent a year.* **3** to speak of as not valuable or important, (*syns.*) to disparage, belittle: *The boss depreciated the abilities of a worker.*

de·pre·ci·a·tion /dɪ,priʃi'eɪʃən/ *n.* [U] reduction in value, esp. for tax purposes: *How do you calculate the rate of depreciation for taxes?*

dep·re·da·tion /,dɛprə'deɪʃən/ *n.frml.* [C;U] robbing and destruction: *World leaders protested the depredations of the invading army on the civilian population.*

de·press /dɪ'prɛs/ *v.* **1** to sadden, dismay: *The loss of his job depressed him.* **2** to press down: *To stop, you must depress this button (lever, computer key, etc.).* **3** to make less active, weaken: *Uncertainty about the coming Presidential election depressed the stock market.* *-adj.* **depressing;** *-adv.* **depressingly.**

de·pres·sant /dɪ'prɛsənt/ *n.* s.t. that depresses (the mind, spirit, bodily systems): *Too much alcohol acts as a depressant, esp. on the heart and nerves.* *-adj.* **depressive.**

de·pressed /dɪ'prɛst/ *adj.* **1** saddened, in low spirits: *I feel depressed in bad weather.* **2** suffering from little business activity and high unemployment: *a depressed region in the state*

de·pres·sion /dɪ'prɛʃən/ *n.* **1** a feeling of temporary sadness: *She's in a depression over the death of her husband.* **2** a mental illness: *The doctor is treating him for depression.* **3** a long period of economic slowdown and much unemployment: *the Great Depression of the 1930's* **4** a great decline in business activity

de·pres·sor /dɪ'prɛsər/ *n.* a tool for pressing down: *Doctors use tongue depressors to examine your throat.*

dep·ri·va·tion /,dɛprə'veɪʃən/ *n.* [C;U] a condition of want and need: *The people of that country live in a state of deprivation without freedom or enough food.*

de·prive /də'praɪv/ *v.* **-prived, -priving, -prives 1** to take s.t. away from, (*syn.*) to dispossess: *The military dictatorship deprived people of their freedom (rights, peace of mind, etc.).* **2** to keep s.t. from, (*syn.*) to deny: *Her illness deprived her of a chance to go to college.*

de·prived /də'praɪvd/ *adj.* prevented from having basic rights or necessities: *He is away from home and feels deprived of his loved ones.*

depth /dɛpθ/ *n.* **1** a distance below a surface: *The swimmer went down to a depth of five meters.* **2** a large amount: *I respect her depth of knowledge (understanding, feeling, etc.).* **3** a distance on a horizontal flat surface: *a building lot with a depth of 100 feet* **4 in depth:** carefully and completely, in detail: *The accountant studied the company's financial position in depth.* **5 out of one's depth** or **beyond one's depth:** beyond one's understanding: *I am out of my depth when it comes to understanding higher mathematics.*

dep·u·tize /'dɛpyə,taɪz/ *v.* **-tized, -tizing, -tizes** to give power to an assistant to act in one's place: *A sheriff can deputize ordinary citizens to find and arrest a criminal.* *-n.* [U] **deputation** /,dɛpyə'teɪʃən/.

dep·u·ty /'dɛpyəti/ *n.* **-ties** a person, usu. in a police function, given power to act as an official: *The deputy sheriff arrested a thief.*

de·rail /di'reɪl/ *v.* to go off the track: *The train derailed after it hit a tree.* *-n.* [C;U] **derailment.**

de·ranged /di'reɪndʒd/ *adj.* **1** crazy, insane: *Traffic was stopped by a deranged man shouting at the sky.* **2** in disorder, confused: *deranged papers spread across the floor* *-n.* [U] **derangement.**

der·by /'dɜrbi/ *n.* **-bies 1** a race: *That horse won the Kentucky Derby.* **2** a type of man's hat: *He wears a black derby.*

de·reg·u·late /di'rɛgyə,leɪt/ *v.* **-lated, -lating, -lates** to take away governmental rules and limits on, (*syn.*) to decontrol: *The government deregulated the airlines and allowed them to compete with each other on price and routes.* *-n.* [U] **deregulation.**

der·e·lict /'dɛrə,lɪkt/ *n.* **1** a person without a home or means of self-support, (*syn.*) a vagrant: *Derelicts often beg on the streets.* **2** property left and not cared for, esp. a ship: *A storm drove that derelict onto the beach.*

USAGE NOTE: *"Derelict"* is an insensitive word to use when talking about people who don't have a home. Many people prefer *"a homeless person."*

der·e·lic·tion /ˌdɛrə'lɪkʃən/ [U] *n.* failure to take proper care, esp. of one's duty or work: *The soldier went to prison for dereliction of duty.*

de·ride /dɪ'raɪd/ *v.frml.* **-rided, -riding, -rides** to make fun of, to speak of as foolish, *(syn.)* to ridicule: *That newspaper columnist derides the mayor whenever she can.*

de ri·gueur /ˌdəri'gɜr/ *adj.* (French for) required of everyone who wishes to be considered fashionable: *Red ties (this style of shoes, earrings like those, etc.) are de rigueur now.*

de·ri·sion /də'rɪʒən/ *n.* [U] speech or actions showing s.o. or s.t. is considered foolish, *(syns.)* ridicule, belittling: *His idea was greeted with derision; people laughed at him.*

de·ri·sive /də'raɪsɪv, -zɪv, -'rɪs-, 'rɪz-/ *adj.* showing derision, *(syns.)* mocking, belittling: *That controversial artist has suffered many derisive comments about her paintings.* -*adv.* **derisively.**

de·riv·a·tive /də'rɪvətɪv/ *n.* s.t. that comes from s.t. else: *The English word "derelict" is a derivative of the Latin "derelictus."*
—*adj.* copying s.t. else (instead of showing new ideas): *That poet doesn't interest me; his poems are too derivative.*

de·rive /də'raɪv/ *v.* **-rived, -riving, -rives 1** to get, *(syn.)* to obtain: *She derives her income from freelance work.* **2** to come from, *(syn.)* to originate: *The word "apple" derives from the Old English word "aeppel." -n.* **derivation** /ˌdɛrə've ɪʃən/.

der·ma·tol·o·gy /ˌdɜrmə'tɑlədʒi/ *n.* [U] the branch of medicine dealing with disorders and diseases of the skin: *She studied dermatology to treat acne and rashes. -n.* **dermatologist.**

der·o·gate /'dɛrə,geɪt/ *v.frml.* **-gated, -gating, -gates** to lessen, take away from: *His bad behavior derogates from his reputation. -n.* [U] **derogation.**

de·rog·a·to·ry /də'rɑgə,tɔri/ *adj.* showing lack of respect, *(syns.)* critical, disparaging: *The two candidates for mayor criticized each other's ideas, but without making derogatory remarks.*

der·ri·ère /ˌdɛri'ɛr/ *n.infrml.* (French for) the buttocks: *He slipped and fell on his derrière.*

de·scend /dɪ'sɛnd/ *v.* **1** to go down: *He descended the stairs.||A plane descends in preparation for landing.* **2** to slope downward: *This road descends to the river.* **3 to descend from:** to be a descendant of: *She says she's descended from the first English settlers in America.* **4** *fig.* **to descend on:** to arrive suddenly, as in an attack: *The opera star's fans descended on him, begging for autographs.* **5 to descend to:** to lower oneself to unacceptable

behavior: *The couple descended to arguing over even the smallest expense.*

de·scen·dant /dɪ'sɛndənt/ *n.* s.o. born into a certain family line: *She is a descendant of our first President.*

de·scen·dent /dɪ'sɛndənt/ *adj.* moving downwards: *He threw the baseball low with a descendent curve.*

de·scent /dɪ'sɛnt/ *n.* **1** a move downward: *The airplane made a long descent before landing.* **2** family origin: *She is of Chilean descent.*

de·scribe /dɪ'skraɪb/ *v.* **-scribed, -scribing, -scribes 1** to explain: *The teacher described how to do the experiment.* **2** to tell what s.t. looks like, to report: *The reporter described the event as it was happening.*

des·crip·tion /dɪ'skrɪpʃən/ *n.* **1** an explanation: *His book gives a description of how a house is built.* **2** a report, *(syn.)* a narrative: *You can hear a description of the ball game on the radio.*

de·scrip·tive /dɪ'skrɪptɪv/ *adj.* giving an explanation of s.t. (people, events, places, etc.): *The book is full of descriptive passages about life in Russia. -adv.* **descriptively.**

des·e·crate /'dɛsə,kreɪt/ *v.* **-crated, -crating, -crates** to damage or misuse (s.t. considered sacred), *(syn.)* to defile: *The invading army desecrated this holy place when they camped here. -n.*[C;U] **desecration** /ˌdɛsə'kreɪʃən/.

de·seg·re·ga·tion /diˌsɛgrə'geɪʃən/ *n.* the ending by law of racial segregation or separation of races, esp. in public places: *Desegregation of the school system brought black and white students into the same public schools.*

de·sen·si·tize /di'sɛnsə,taɪz/ *v.* **-tized, -tizing, -tizes** to lessen or remove the sensitivity: *Does watching violence on TV desensitize people to violence so that it disturbs them less? -n.* [U] **desensitization** /diˌsɛnsətɪ'zeɪʃən/.

des·ert (1) /'dɛzərt/ *n.* a dry region with little or no rain resulting in large areas of sand and rock with few plants or animals: *The Sahara Desert is in Africa.*

desert (2) /dɪ'zɜrt/ *v.* to leave forever, *(syn.)* to abandon: *He deserted his wife, so she divorced him.||A soldier deserted from the army; he is a <n.> deserter.*
—*n.pl.* **one's just deserts:** a deserved (or earned) punishment: *He stole and was put in jail; he got his just deserts.*

de·ser·tion /dɪ'zɜrʃən/ *n.* **1** [C;U] an abandonment, esp. of one person by another: *The father's desertion of the family left them with no support.* **2** [C;U] leaving military service without permission: *During a war, there are often desertions from the losing army.*

D

de·serve /dɪ'zɜrv/ v. **-served, -serving, -serves** to merit, be worthy of, (syn.) to warrant: *A good worker deserves good pay.*

de·serv·ing /dɪ'zɜrvɪŋ/ adj. **1** worthy, meriting: *A job well done is deserving of praise.* **2** worthy of special consideration: *She's a deserving young woman and should be given a college scholarship.*

des·ic·cant /'dɛsəkənt/ n. [U] a substance that absorbs moisture: *My stereo was shipped with little bags of desiccant to keep it dry.*

de·sign /dɪ'zaɪn/ n. **1** style, form, (syn.) motif: *Their house was built in a modern design.* **2** a picture or layout (sketch, blueprint, etc.) to show how s.t. will be made: *Here is the design (or layout design) for our next magazine cover.* **3** the art of making designs: *She studies fashion design.* **4** a pattern that decorates: *I like the design on his tie.* **5** a mental plan: *a grand design for a new social order* **6 to have designs on:** to make secret plans for getting s.t. or s.o.: *I think he has designs on her job, so she should be careful of him.*
—v. **1** to draw sketches or plans for: *They've designed a new airplane.* **2** to form mental plans for: *We must design a better advertising campaign.* **3** to intend for a certain goal or purpose: *a movie designed to appeal to teenagers*

des·ig·nate /'dɛzɪg,neɪt/ v. **-nated, -nating, -nates 1** to appoint: *An official designated his aide to represent him at the conference.‖His aide became his <n.> designee.* **2** to mark or point out, indicate: *Some cars on the train are designated as no smoking areas. -n.* [U] **designation** /,dɛzɪg'neɪʃən/.

de·sign·er /dɪ'zaɪnər/ n. a person who creates and draws plans for things, usu. beautiful objects: *She is a great designer of women's clothes (book covers, home interiors, etc.).*

de·sign·ing /dɪ'zaɪnɪŋ/ adj. tending to make secret plans, (syn.) calculating: *He is a designing individual, always trying to figure out how he can get others to do his work for him.*

de·sir·able /dɪ'zaɪrəbəl/ adj. **1** worthwhile, valuable: *They own a desirable piece of property by the sea.* **2** attractive, appealing: *She is a beautiful and intelligent woman; any man would think she is desirable. -adv.* **desirably; -n.** [U] **desirability** /dɪ'zaɪrə'bɪləti/.

de·sire /dɪ'zaɪr/ v.frml. **-sired, -siring, -sires 1** to wish, want: *The President desires that we leave tomorrow.* **2** to want very strongly: *She desires to succeed in business, no matter the cost.*
—n. **1** a wish, want: *She expressed a desire to go on vacation.* **2** a strong wish, (syn.) craving: *The refugees were filled with the desire to see their homeland again.* **3** a strong sexual want, (syn.) lust: *The sight of him filled her with desire.*

de·sir·ous /dɪ'zaɪrəs/ adj.frml. wanting, longing for: *The President is desirous of your presence at dinner this Tuesday.*

de·sist /dɪ'sɪst/ v.frml. to stop doing s.t., discontinue: *The court has ordered him to desist from bothering his neighbor.*

desk /dɛsk/ n. a piece of furniture like a table, usu. with drawers and used to write on: *She reads, writes, thinks, and works at her desk every day.*

desk·top computer or **desk·top** /'dɛsk,tɑp/ n. a computer small enough to fit on top of a desk: *We have three desktop computers (or) three desktops in our office.*

USAGE NOTE: A smaller, portable computer is called a *laptop,* because it fits on top of a person's lap.

des·o·late /'dɛsəlɪt, 'dɛz-/ adj. **1** empty of people, (syn.) barren: *After the terrible fire, we looked out over the desolate landscape.* **2** depressed, lonely and sad: *The death of his wife left him desolate. -adv.* **desolately.**
—v. /'dɛsə,leɪt/ **-lated, -lating, -lates 1** to cause great destruction of, (syn.) to ravage: *War has desolated the city of Beirut.* **2** to depress, deeply sadden: *Her death desolated him. -n.* [U] **desolation.**

de·spair /dɪ'spɛr/ n. [U] sadness without hope of relief: *When she learned that she had cancer, she fell into the depths of despair.*
—v. to completely lose hope: *His family despaired for him when he was lost at sea.*

des·patch /dɪ'spætʃ/ v. *See:* dispatch.

des·per·a·do /,dɛspə'rɑdoʊ/ n. **-does** or **-dos** a desperate, dangerous criminal: *Tourists were afraid to travel outside the city for fear of attacks by desperadoes on lonely roads.*

des·per·ate /'dɛspərɪt, -prɪt/ adj. **1** in immediate, very strong need: *The refugees are desperate for food (money, help, etc.).* **2** wild and dangerous: *a desperate criminal willing to kill anyone so anyone. -adv.* **desperately; -n.** **desperation** /,dɛspə'reɪʃən/.

des·pi·ca·ble /'dɛspɪkəbəl, də'spɪk-/ adj. shamefully bad, (syns.) contemptible, vile: *He was drunk and his behavior at the party was despicable. -adv.* **despicably.**

de·spise /də'spaɪz/ v. **-spised, -spising, -spises** to hate, detest: *The two teenage gangs despised each other.*

de·spite /dɪ'spaɪt/ prep. even though, in spite of: *Despite the fact that she is short, she is an excellent basketball player.*

de·spon·dent /də'spɑndənt/ adj. sad and without hope, (syn.) melancholy: *He is despondent over his inability to find a job. -adv.* **despondently.**

des·pot /'dɛspət/ n. a dictator, tyrant: *The king was a despot and his people lived in terror of* him. *-adj.* **despotic** /dɪ'spɑtɪk/**; -***n.* [U] **despotism.**

des·sert /dɪ'zɜrt/ *n.* the last course in a meal, usu. a sweet dish, such as cake, fruit, etc.: *We had apple pie and coffee for dessert.*

de·sta·bi·lize /di'steɪbə,laɪz/ *v.* **-lized, -lizing, -lizes** to upset the stability of and make open to a change of political leadership: *Revolutionaries destabilize a government by forcing leaders to resign.* *-n.* [U] **destabilization** /di,steɪbəlɪ'zeɪʃən/.

des·ti·na·tion /,dɛstə'neɪʃən/ *n.* the place where s.o. is going or s.t. is being sent: *The destination of our trip is San Francisco.*

des·tined /'dɛstɪnd/ *adj.* intended by fortune or heavenly forces, fated: *She was destined to be a great singer (failure, writer, etc.) from childhood.*

des·ti·ny /'dɛstəni/ *n.* **-nies 1** [U] the influence of uncontrollable forces on the course of life and its events, fate: *It was destiny, not an accident, that brought the two lovers together.* **2** [C] the future, final result: *The destiny of the planet depends on how humans control themselves.*

des·ti·tute /'dɛstɪ,tut/ *adj.* without money or hope of having any, *(syn.)* penniless: *With no inheritance, he left his family destitute.* *-n.* [U] **destitution.**

de·stroy /dɪ'strɔɪ/ *v.* **1** to pull or break down, *(syn.)* to demolish: *The storm destroyed every house on the coast.* **2** to ruin, put an end to: *to destroy one's reputation, hopes, chances*

de·stroy·er /dɪ'strɔɪər/ *n.* **1** a heavily armed warship: *Destroyers fought in the Atlantic in World War II.* **2** s.o. or s.t. that destroys: *Disease is a destroyer of lives.*

de·struct /dɪ'strʌkt/ *v.* to fall apart usu. by force, such as an explosion: *A bomb destructs when it explodes.*‖*A missile that is off course self-destructs.*

de·struc·ti·ble /dɪ'strʌktəbəl/ *adj.* capable of being destroyed: *The army wanted vehicles that were not easily destructible.*

de·struc·tion /dɪ'strʌkʃən/ *n.* [U] **1** terrible and complete ruin, *(syn.)* devastation: *A hurricane causes great destruction to buildings and trees.* **2** the act of pulling or breaking down, *(syn.)* demolition: *The destruction of the old building will take two weeks.*

de·struc·tive /dɪ'strʌktɪv/ *adj.* causing great damage, *(syns.)* ruinous, devastating: *Hurricanes bring the destructive force of high winds.*‖*A destructive drug habit ruined her career.* *-adv.* **destructively.**

des·ul·to·ry /'dɛsəl,tɔri/ *adj.* aimless in moving from one thing to another without completion: *She works in a desultory way and completes nothing.*

de·tach /dɪ'tætʃ/ *v.* **-taches 1** to remove, separate, disconnect: *We need a carpenter to detach this bookshelf from the wall.* **2** to move away, distance: *The Board of Directors tried to detach themselves from the company president and his illegal actions.*

de·tached /dɪ'tætʃt/ *adj.* **1** removed from, distant: *The company president is detached from the day-to-day operations of the business.* **2** free from emotional involvement, *(syn.)* aloof: *Through all the arguments among other committee members, she kept a detached attitude.*

de·tach·ment /dɪ'tætʃmənt/ *n.* **1** [U] emotional distance, *(syn.)* aloofness: *Her attitude of detachment toward the problem hides the real concern that she feels.* **2** [U] an act of removal, separation, disconnection: *The detachment of cables from the computer will take an hour.*

de·tail /'di,teɪl, dɪ'teɪl/ *n.* **1** a small point, *(syn.)* a particular: *There is one detail in the plan (contract, agreement, etc.) that is unclear to me.* **2** a small item of little or no importance: *Forget the details for now so we can focus on the overall plan.* **3** small, fine parts (of a work of art): *This painting is rich with detail.* **4 in detail:** with specifics: *She explained the problem in detail to the store manager.*
—*v.* **1** to describe fully, with all the fine points: *The letter detailed the company's requirements for a new product.* **2** to choose s.o. to do a job, esp. in the military: *They have detailed a squad of soldiers to guard the prisoner.*

de·tain /dɪ'teɪn/ *v.* **1** to keep waiting, delay: *I am late because I was detained in traffic.* **2** to hold at a police station: *The police detained a man for questioning in the crime.* *-n.* [U] **detainment.**

de·tect /dɪ'tɛkt/ *v.* **1** to uncover, find: *They detected a problem in the computer program and fixed it.* **2** to notice, observe: *I detect a sense of frustration among my employees.*

de·tec·tion /dɪ'tɛkʃən/ *n.* **1** [U] a discovery: *The city worker won praise for his detection of a break in a water pipe.* **2** [U] close watching, *(syn.)* surveillance: *The store has a detection system for security.*

de·tec·tive /dɪ'tɛktɪv/ *n.* a police officer whose work is getting information about crimes: *a police detective* ‖ *I will do some <adj.> detective work to find out what is happening.*

de·tec·tor /dɪ'tɛktər/ *n.* a device used to locate the presence of s.t.: *Metal detectors are used in airports to find guns.*

dé·tente /deɪ'tɑnt/ *n.* [C;U] a period of calm between hostile nations when problems can be discussed: *The USA and Soviet Union reached détente, and the arms race is over.*

de·ten·tion /dɪ'tɛnʃən/ n. [U] **1** holding or keeping from moving freely or going away: *The man was held in detention by immigration authorities until his citizenship was known.* **2** jail: *a prisoner held in detention* or *in a house of detention*

de·ter /dɪ'tɜr/ v. **-terred, -terring, -ters** to stop or prevent from acting: *A woman deterred a criminal from attacking her by yelling for the police.*

de·ter·gent /dɪ'tɜrdʒənt/ n. [C;U] a strong synthetic soap made to remove dirt and stains caused by grease, tea, blood, etc.: *This laundry detergent can remove grass stains from clothes.*

de·te·ri·o·rate /dɪ'tɪriə,reɪt/ v. **-rated, -rating, -rates** to fall into bad condition, become weak: *The old man's health has deteriorated. -n.* [U] **deterioration.**

de·ter·mi·nant /dɪ'tɜrmənənt/ n.adj. s.t. that influences or decides, an important consideration: *The salary that a new job offers is the* <n.> *determinant* (or) *the* <adj.> *determinant factor in my changing jobs.*

de·ter·mi·nate /dɪ'tɜrmənɪt/ adj.frml. precisely limited, counted, or defined: *They have a determinate amount of money to invest.*

de·ter·mi·na·tion /dɪ,tɜrmə'neɪʃən/ n. **1** [U] strong will, (*syn.*) resoluteness: *She has great determination to succeed.* **2** [C] a finding, conclusion: *The detective made a determination as to the cause of the car accident; he found that the brakes had failed.*

de·ter·mine /dɪ'tɜrmɪn/ v. **-mined, -mining, -mines 1** to conclude, decide, (*syn.*) to ascertain: *The judge determined that the defendant was guilty.* **2** to influence or control: *The weather will determine if we have the party outdoors or not. -n.* **determiner.**

de·ter·mined /dɪ'tɜrmɪnd/ adj. of strong will, (*syn.*) resolute: *The workers are determined to finish the job on time.*

de·ter·rence /dɪ'tɜrəns, -'tʌr-/ n. [U] prevention, usu. by frightening with force: *By threatening a nuclear attack, they achieved their goal, the deterrence of an invasion.*

de·ter·rent /dɪ'tɜrənt, -'tʌr-/ n. s.t. that prevents (an attack, a crime, etc.): *Police serve as a deterrent to crime.||a nuclear deterrent*

de·test /dɪ'tɛst/ v. to hate, (*syn.*) to loathe: *The two political rivals detest each other. -n.frml.* [U] **detestation** /,ditɛs'teɪʃən/.

de·test·a·ble /dɪ'tɛstəbəl/ adj. deserving hatred, (*syns.*) odious, repulsive: *He deserves life in prison for his detestable act.*

dethrone /dɪ'θroʊn/ v. **-throned, -throning, -thrones** to remove from power, depose: *The palace guard dethroned the emperor. -n.* **dethronement.**

det·o·nate /'dɛtn,eɪt/ v. **-nated, -nating, -nates** to explode or cause to explode: *The bomb detonated.||They detonated a bomb.*

det·o·na·tion /,dɛtn'eɪʃən/ n. [C;U] an explosion: *The detonation of the bomb blew the house up.*

det·o·na·tor /'dɛtn,eɪtər/ n. s.t. used to detonate an explosive: *Police bomb squads know how to remove the detonator from a bomb so that it will not explode.*

de·tour /'di,tʊr/ n. **1** a temporary road opened while the main road is under repair: *Signs directed traffic to a detour.* **2** a move away from the direct or planned way to go: *On the way home, she made a detour to the store for milk.* —*v.* to make a detour: *Let's detour around the downtown traffic.*

de·tox /'ditɑks/ n.v.adj.infrml.short for detoxification (from drug use): *The patient is in* <n.> *detox now in a* <adj.> *detox facility; he* <v.> *detoxes each time he overdoses.*

de·tox·i·fi·ca·tion /di,tɑksəfə'keɪʃən, ,ditɑk-/ n. [U] **1** the cleaning out of drugs from a drug user's body: *Drug addicts go to that clinic for detoxification.* **2** the removal of poisons: *the detoxification of an area that was used as a dump -v.* **detoxify.**

de·tract /dɪ'trækt/ v. to take s.t. good from, lower the value of s.o. or s.t.: *Her heavy makeup detracts from her good looks. -n.* **detraction.**

de·tract·or /dɪ'træktər/ n. s.o. who speaks against (s.o. or s.t.), a critic: *His detractors say that he is handsome but not smart.*

det·ri·ment /'dɛtrəmənt/ n. **1** [C] s.t. that causes damage or loss: *Being unable to write well is a detriment to professional success.* **2** [C;U] harm, injury: *She failed to eat and sleep enough, to the detriment of her health. -adj.* **detrimental** /,dɛtrə'mɛntl/.

de·tri·tus /dɪ'traɪtɪs/ n.frml. [U] **1** debris: *The road was blocked by the detritus from a rock slide.* **2** remains, waste: *the detritus found in an archaeological dig*

deuce /dus/ n. **1** a playing card with the number two: *I have a pair of deuces in my hand.* **2** on dice, the surfaces with two spots **3** *exclam.infrml.* **the deuce:** expression used to show anger or frustration: *What the deuce are you doing to my car?!*

de·val·u·ate /di'vælyu,eɪt/ v. **-ated, -ating, -ates** to lower the value of money: *The French government has devalued the franc by 10 percent. -n.*[C;U] **devaluation.**

de·val·ue /di'vælyu/ *See:* devaluate.

dev·as·tate /'dɛvə,steɪt/ v. **-tated, -tating, -tates 1** to destroy completely, lay waste to: *A storm devastated the island.* **2** to crush emotionally (spiritually, financially, etc.): *Her fa-*

ther's sudden death devastated her.||It was a <adj.> devastating loss.

dev·as·ta·tion /ˌdɛvəˈsteɪʃən/ n. [U] complete, widespread ruin: *War and famine bring devastation to a country.*

de·vel·op /dəˈvɛləp/ v. **1** to happen, occur, (*syn.*) to transpire: *Before making any plans, let's see what develops when the storm hits (business increases, etc.).* **2** to change a place by building: *They're going to develop this open land into a shopping center.* **3** to process: *to develop photographic film* **4 to develop from/into:** to grow, progress, (*syn.*) to evolve: *A girl develops into a woman.||This giant corporation developed from a small business.* **5 to develop on:** to make larger or fuller: *The professor gave a short overview of his thoughts and then developed on them at length.*

de·vel·op·er /dəˈvɛləpər/ n. **1** a person or company that develops land: *She's a real estate developer.* **2** the chemicals used to develop photographic film: *to put film in the developer*

de·vel·op·ing /dəˈvɛləpɪŋ/ adj. **1** in process, moving towards completion or maturity: *We must keep close watch on the developing situation (storm, opposition, etc.).* **2** economically weak, but growing: *A developing nation often wants trade with superpowers.* —n. [U] film processing: *The developing of the film will take two days.*

de·vel·op·ment /dəˈvɛləpmənt/ n. [U] **1** growth, progress: *We are responsible for the development of our children's bodies (our students' minds, the country's economy, etc.).* **2** [C] an important event or occurrence: *the latest development in computer technology||TV news reports of further developments in a murder case* **3** [U] making larger or fuller, (*syn.*) the amplification: *the development of an idea* **4** [C] a housing or business complex of buildings, roads, etc.: *They live in a new development (or) housing development.* **5** [U] **under development:** in the process of being analyzed or created: *A new computer is under development in the laboratory.*

de·vi·ant /ˈdiviənt/ n.adj. a person who deviates from socially accepted standards of behavior: *As a pornographer, he is a <n.> deviant.|| sexually <adj.> deviant behavior* -n. **deviance;** -adv. **deviantly.**

de·vi·ate /ˈdiviˌeɪt/ v. **-ated, -ating, -ates 1** to act in a socially unacceptable way: *He deviated from society by becoming a drug addict.* **2** to vary from the rule or standard: *He deviated from his normal good habits by becoming drunk once.*

de·vi·a·tion /ˌdiviˈeɪʃən/ n. **1** [C;U] a move away from or a difference (from what is expected): *The storm caused a deviation from the plane's*

planned route.||The girl's friendliness is a deviation from her parents' shyness.* **2** [C] an antisocial act: *Drug-taking is a deviation from accepted norms.* **3** (in statistics) the difference between a number and the mean of the set it is in

de·vice /dɪˈvaɪs/ n. **1** an electrical or mechanical machine: *The computer is an electronic device.* **2** a tool or implement: *An electric can opener is also a device.* **3** a trick or secret means to an end: *His outbursts of anger are just a device to move everyone's attention from his guilt.* **4 to leave to one's own devices:** to leave s.o. alone without help or interference

dev·il /ˈdɛvəl/ n. **1** (in Judaism and Christianity) Satan, the most powerful of evil spirits and enemy of God: *The Devil rules in Hell.* **2** a person who has caused mischief or trouble, esp. a boy: *That little devil has eaten all the cookies again!* **3 between the devil and the deep blue sea:** in an impossible situation: *She may be killed if she tells what she saw, but she'll go to prison if she doesn't, so she's between the devil and the deep blue sea.* **4 like the devil:** with great energy: *work like the devil to finish on time* **5 to give the devil his due:** to admit s.t. good about s.o. who is disliked: *I must give the devil his due and say that my opponent did an excellent job.* **6 exclam. the devil:** expression of annoyance: *Where the devil did I put my reading glasses?* **7 the devil to pay:** serious trouble as a result: *If the company is late with this shipment, we'll have (or) there'll be the devil to pay.* **8 the devil you know is better than the devil you don't:** it is better to stay with a known difficulty than to risk a possibly worse one: *The workers dislike their manager but they don't want a new one, because the devil you know is better than the devil you don't.* -n. [U] **deviltry.**

devil's advocate n. **1** a person who tests an idea (plan, argument, etc.) by asking critical questions of another person to uncover possible weaknesses in it **2 to play the devil's advocate:** to act as a friendly critic: *When I proposed an expensive project, a coworker played the devil's advocate to show what could go wrong with it.*

dev·il·ish /ˈdɛvəlɪʃ/ adj. **1** evil, like the devil: *She is a devilish enemy.* **2** *fig.* complex and risky: *We have a devilish problem in disposing of nuclear waste.*

dev·il·ish·ly /ˈdɛvəlɪʃli/ adv. in a very frustrating way: *I had a devilishly difficult problem to solve.*

de·vi·ous /ˈdiviəs/ adj. not direct or honest, (*syns.*) underhanded, deceitful: *Their accountant used devious methods to cheat them out of a lot of money. But his <n.> deviousness was discovered.* -adv. **deviously.**

de·vise /də'vaɪz/ v. **-vised, -vising, -vises** **1** to create, develop: *She has devised a plan for company expansion.* **2** to invent (s.t. clever), dream up: *to devise a scheme to get rich quick* **3** (in law) to transfer or give property in a will: *When he died, he devised his house to his daughter.*

de·void /dɪ'vɔɪd/ adj. empty, lacking: *Her writing is clear, but her ideas are devoid of substance.*

de·volve /dɪ'vɑlv/ v. **-volved, -volving, -volves** frml. to pass or be passed: *These responsibilities will devolve on the next President.* -n. [U] **devolution** /,dɪvə'luʃən, ,dɛvə-/.

de·vote /dɪ'vout/ v. **-voted, -voting, -votes** **1** to give, (syn.) to dedicate: *He devotes a great deal of time (money, effort, etc.) to his garden (church, politics, etc.).* **2** to use for a special purpose: *to devote an area to housing for the poor*

de·vot·ed /dɪ'voutɪd/ adj. **1** attentive, loving: *They are a devoted couple.* **2** dedicated, showing great care: *This doctor is devoted to her work.* -adv. **devotedly.**

de·vo·tee /,dɛvə'ti, -'teɪ/ n.frml. s.o. who greatly admires s.t.: *She is a devotee of the opera.*

de·vo·tion /dɪ'vouʃən/ n. [U] **1** dedication, loyalty: *The soldier won praise for his devotion to duty.* **2** loving attention: *She is full of devotion to her family.*

de·vo·tion·al /dɪ'vouʃənəl/ adj. religious: *The priest reads only devotional literature.*

de·vour /dɪ'vaur/ v. **1** to eat quickly and completely: *The lions devoured a zebra in a short time.* **2** to use up, usu. in a wasteful manner: *The heavy spending of the dictator devoured the country's resources.*

de·vout /dɪ'vaut/ adj. **1** deeply religious: *She is a devout Catholic (Baptist, Jew, Muslim, etc.).* **2** serious, deeply felt: *a devout wish to help the poor* -adv. **devoutly;** -n. [U] **devoutness.**

dew /du/ n. [U] drops of water, esp. on grass and other plants, that come from the night air: *You'll wet your shoes walking through the morning dew.*

dex·ter·i·ty /dɛk'stɛrəti/ n. [U] skill or ability, esp. with the hands: *She plays the guitar with great dexterity.*

dex·ter·ous /'dɛkstərəs, -strəs/ or **dex·trous** /'dɛkstrəs/ adj. skillful or clever, esp. with the hands: *His fingers are very dexterous in carving figures out of wood.* -adv. **dexterously.**

dex·trose /'dɛk,strous/ n. [U] a form of glucose (plant sugar) contained esp. in fruits and used in making candies, jams, and other foods: *Dextrose is a good source of energy for humans.*

di·a·be·tes /,daɪə'bitɪs, -tiz/ n. [U] a disease involving a body's inability to absorb sugar properly: *She has had diabetes since childhood but controls it with insulin.*

di·a·bet·ic /,daɪə'bɛtɪk/ n.adj. a person with diabetes: *He is a <n.> diabetic.*||*She had a <adj.> diabetic reaction but is okay now.*

di·a·bol·ic /,daɪə'bɑlɪk/ adj. evil, devilish: *He has a diabolic mind, always making evil plans.* -adj. **diabolical;** -adv. **diabolically.**

di·ag·nose /'daɪəg,nous, ,daɪəg'nous/ v. **-nosed, -nosing, -noses** to discover or identify (as disease, sickness): *Doctors diagnose illnesses.*

di·ag·no·sis /,daɪəg'nousɪs/ n. **-ses** /-siz/ a finding, conclusion: *The doctor has made a diagnosis of the illness as diabetes.*

di·ag·nos·tic /,daɪəg'nɑstɪk/ n.adj. an analysis made to find the cause of an illness or the source of a problem: *The medical laboratory ran a diagnostic analysis* (or) *a complete diagnostic on the patient.*

di·ag·o·nal /daɪ'ægənəl/ n.adj. **1** a line connecting two opposite corners of a four-sided figure, such as a square **2** a straight line that slants or slopes: *Don't cross the street in a <adj.> diagonal line.* -v. **diagonalize;** -adv. **diagonally.**

di·a·gram /'daɪə,græm/ n.v. **-grammed, -gramming, -grams** a drawing with markings to show how s.t. is put together or works: *The engineer drew a diagram of a telephone circuit (a machine, ventilation system, etc.).* ||*He <v.> diagrammed it.* -adj. **diagrammatical** /,daɪəgrə'mætɪkəl/.

di·al /'daɪəl/ n. a surface, usu. round, divided into markings with meaning: *the dial of a watch (telephone, radio, water meter, etc.)* —v. to make a call (usu. using a rotary telephone): *If you want to phone long distance, dial the Operator.* See: dial tone.

di·a·lect /'daɪə,lɛkt/ n. a regional variety of language differing from other varieties in pronunciation, grammar, or word usage: *The characters in the movie spoke in a Scottish dialect that was strange to the American audience.*

di·a·lec·tic /,daɪə'lɛktɪk/ n.adj. a method of argument for discovering the truth of ideas: *He is a student of <n.> dialectics* (or) *of Marxian <adj.> dialectic materialism.*

di·a·log or **di·a·logue** /'daɪə,lɔg, -,lɑg/ n.v. **-logged, -logging, -logs** **1** conversation between people in a book, play, etc.: *You should read this story; the dialogue is very funny.* **2** discussion, esp. of differing ideas and opinions: *When the fighting is stopped, a dialogue between the two countries can begin. Their representatives can <v.> dialog about the problems.*

dial tone *n.* a humming sound made when a telephone receiver is picked up: *There's no dial tone, so I guess the phone isn't working.*

di·al·y·sis /daɪˈæləsɪs/ *n.* [U] a process used to clean the blood: *A patient with kidney disease undergoes dialysis on a dialysis machine.*

di·am·e·ter /daɪˈæmətər/ *n.* the width of a circle, measured by a straight line through its center from side to side: *She drew a circle two inches in diameter.*

di·a·met·ri·cal·ly /ˌdaɪəˈmɛtrɪkli/ *adv.* directly (opposite or opposed): *She is diametrically opposed to everything he says.*

di·a·mond /ˈdaɪəmənd, ˈdaɪmənd/ *n.adj.* **1** [C;U] the hardest gemstone, made of colorless carbon and very valuable: *What a beautiful diamond ring!* **2** [C] a figure with four straight sides and pointed at the top, bottom, and sides **3** [C] a playing card with one or more red diamonds: *the six (king, ace, etc.) of diamonds* **4** [C] a baseball playing field

di·a·per /ˈdaɪəpər, ˈdaɪpər/ *n.* a soft thick cloth (or thick paper with a plastic covering) used to cover the area between the legs, esp. for babies: *Parents can put cloth diapers or disposable diapers on their babies.*

di·aph·a·nous /daɪˈæfənəs/ *adj.* **1** light and see-through fabric: *The movie star wore a diaphanous gown.* **2** not strong or long-lasting: *diaphanous dreams of riches and fame*

di·a·phragm /ˈdaɪəˌfræm/ *n.* **1** the muscle separating the chest and lungs from the stomach: *Do deep breathing to exercise your diaphragm.* **2** a small device worn inside a woman to prevent pregnancy: *She went to a doctor to get fitted for a diaphragm.*

di·a·rist /ˈdaɪərɪst/ *n.* a person who keeps a diary, esp. an author who publishes diaries: *Samuel Pepys is a famous English diarist.*

di·ar·rhe·a /ˌdaɪəˈriə/ *n.* [U] a disorder in which bowel movements are too watery and too frequent: *He ate too much unripe fruit and has diarrhea now.*

di·a·ry /ˈdaɪəri/ *n.* **-ries** a personal record written about one's daily activities and feelings or with accounts of important events: *She has kept a diary since she was a child.*

di·a·tribe /ˈdaɪəˌtraɪb/ *n.* very strong criticism, an attack with words: *The politician launched into a diatribe against the government policy.*

dibs /dɪbz/ *n.slang* a right to have (s.t.): *I have dibs on that last piece of cake.*

dice /daɪs/ *n.pl. of* die **1** small cubes with a set of one to six dots on each side and rolled in games of chance: *With one roll of the dice, he won $50.* **2** *infrml.* **no dice:** an expression meaning "no" (strongly): *I wanted to go to the movies, but my father said, "No dice!"*

dic·ey /ˈdaɪsi/ *adj.infrml.* uncertain, risky: *His chances of living after the accident are dicey.*

di·chot·o·my /daɪˈkatəmi/ *n.frml.* **-mies** a division into two parts, esp. opposing ones: *We have a dichotomy of opinion about what to do: I want to go and he wants to stay.*

dick·er /ˈdɪkər/ *v.* to argue about the price of s.t., *(syns.)* to haggle, bargain: *The woman dickered with the salesman over the price of a camera.||Their <n.> dickering took 20 minutes.*

dic·tate /ˈdɪkˌteɪt/ *v.* **-tated, -tating, -tates** **1** to speak s.t. to be recorded or written down exactly by s.o.: *He dictated a letter to his secretary.* **2** to command, say what s.o. must do: *The winner of a war can dictate to the loser the terms for peace.*
—*n.* a demand, absolute requirement: *He accepts the dictates of his job and works the long hours required by it.*

dic·ta·tion /dɪkˈteɪʃən/ *n.* [U] a communication (letter, memorandum, etc.) spoken so that it can be written down: *The manager gave dictation to her secretary for an hour.*

dic·ta·tor /ˈdɪkˌteɪtər/ *n.* a ruler with total power, *(syns.)* a despot, tyrant: *The leader of that country is a dictator and no one dares to speak against him.*

dic·ta·to·ri·al /ˌdɪktəˈtɔriəl/ *adj.* using power like a dictator, *(syns.)* domineering, high-handed: *The owner has a dictatorial way of dealing with people.* **-adv. dictatorially.**

dic·ta·tor·ship /dɪkˈteɪtərˌʃɪp, ˈdɪkteɪ-/ *n.* a form of government with complete power in the hands of one person: *The dictatorship in that country has lasted for 30 years.*

dic·tion /ˈdɪkʃən/ *n.* [U] the ability of a person to pronounce words clearly: *Actors must have excellent diction so that the audience can hear them.*

dic·tion·ar·y /ˈdɪkʃəˌnɛri/ *n.* **-ies** a book or computer program listing words in alphabetical order with their meanings: *For a definition of that word, consult the dictionary.*

dic·tum /ˈdɪktəm/ *n.* **dicta** /ˈdɪktə/ a command, an order that must be obeyed: *Tyrants issue <n.pl.> dicta that limit their people's rights and freedoms.*

did /dɪd/ *v.* **1** past tense of do: *I did all my work yesterday.* **2** past auxiliary verb: *Did she go home?*

did·n't /ˈdɪdnt/ *short for* did not

did·dle /ˈdɪdl/ *v.infrml.* **-dled, -dling, -dles** **1** to waste time: *He diddled for days trying to fix the motor, but couldn't.* **2** to cheat, get s.t. from s.o. by tricking them: *The repairman diddled me out of $50 but didn't fix my car.*

die (1) /daɪ/ *v.* **died, dying, dies** **1** to stop living, *(syn.)* to perish: *He died of a heart attack.* **2** to stop working (said of an object): *My car died on the way to work.* **3** *infrml.* **to be dying to/for:** to want very much: *I'm dying to see*

D

your new baby!\|\|*She was dying for an ice cream soda.* **4** *phrasal v.* **to die away:** to gradually become weaker and disappear, (*syn.*) to diminish: *The wind died away after dark.* **5** *phrasal v.* **to die down:** to calm down, lose force, (*syn.*) to abate: *Public protests over new taxes have died down.* **6 to die for: a.** to give one's life for: *He died for his country in the last war.* **b.** *fig.* to enjoy very much: *I love pizza; it's to die for!* **7 to die hard:** to stop or disappear only under great force: *Old habits, like smoking cigarettes, die hard.* **8** *phrasal v.* **to die out:** to pass out of existence: *Dinosaurs died out millions of years ago.* **9** *phrasal v.* **to die off:** to die one after another: *The five sisters grew old and died off one by one.* **10** *fig.* **to die laughing:** to laugh very hard **11** *fig.* **to die a thousand deaths:** to feel great fear and anxiety: *She's dying a thousand deaths waiting for her final exam results.* **12 to one's dying day:** with strong lifelong commitment: *She's a liberal and will be one to her dying day.* See: do (2),. 19 to do or die; live or die

die (2) *n.* **1** a device for making things by cutting or stamping (metal, plastic, etc.) or by pressing or pouring material into it: *A die is used to make pennies with President Lincoln's image on them.* **2** *sing.* of dice

die·hard /'daɪ,hɑrd/ *n.* a person who does not change old habits (ideas, ways) easily, despite pressure to change: *He's a diehard who always votes Conservative even though the party keeps losing.*

die·sel /'disəl, -zəl/ *n.* a vehicle with a diesel engine: *That truck is a diesel.*

di·et /'daɪɪt/ *n.* **1** one's regular foods: *The boy lives on a diet of junk food.* **2** a weight loss program: *I have to go on a diet to lose 15 pounds.*\|\|*My friend <v.> diets all the time.* **3** a formal law-making assembly, a congress

di·e·tar·y /'daɪə,tɛri/ *adj.* related to diet: *People with diabetes must follow certain dietary rules, like not eating sugar.*

di·e·ti·cian /,daɪə'tɪʃən/ *n.* a person who specializes in planning food combinations for healthy meals: *Most hospitals employ a dietician to prescribe meals for the patients.*

dif·fer /'dɪfər/ *v.* **1** to vary, to be different from: *Our new product differs from the earlier model in many ways.* **2** to hold a different opinion, disagree: *The second doctor differed with the first on the reason for the patient's condition.* **3** *frml.* **to beg to differ:** to disagree: *Oh, my good friend, I beg to differ with you on that point.*

dif·fer·ence /'dɪfərəns, 'dɪfrəns/ *n.* **1** a way of being different, (*syn.*) a dissimilarity: *What is the difference between the new model and the old one?* **2** the amount by which two numbers differ: *The difference between 7 and 9 is 2.* **3 a difference of opinion:** a disagreement, argu-

ment: *He quit his job after a difference of opinion with his boss.* **4 it makes no difference:** it doesn't matter, it's not important **5 to have their (our) differences:** to have arguments or an unfriendly relationship: *She and her sister have had their differences, but now they're close.* **6 to make a difference:** to bring a change (for the better): *She received an increase in pay and it has made a big difference in her attitude.*

dif·fer·ent /'dɪfərənt, 'dɪfrənt/ *adj.* **1** unlike, not the same: *The new and old models are very different from each other.* **2** varied, several: *This model comes in different colors; which one would you like?* **3** strange, unusual: *I agree that he's different, but I like him.* -*adv.* **differently.**

dif·fer·en·tial /,dɪfə'rɛnʃəl/ *n.adj.* **1** the amount of a difference, esp. in comparisons of money (pay, cost of living, rates of interest, etc.): *We must consider the differential in the cost of living between New York and New Orleans.* **2** the mathematics of variations: *differential calculus* **3 differential rate:** a difference in rates of pay to workers: *The company pays a differential rate in wages, more for employees in New York than in Alabama.*

dif·fer·en·ti·ate /,dɪfə'rɛnʃi,eɪt/ *v.* **-ated, -ating, -ates** **1** to describe or show differences: *The speaker differentiated between a partnership and a corporation as types of business ownership.* **2** to see, or (*syn.*) to discern, differences: *These two plans seem the same; I can't differentiate between them.* **3** to make (develop, manufacture, etc.) differences: *We have differentiated our product from the competition by its higher quality.*

dif·fi·cult /'dɪfɪ,kʌlt/ *adj.* **1** hard, requiring effort (mental or physical): *We have a difficult problem to solve (job to do, race to run, etc.).* **2** causing trouble or worry: *She's having a difficult time finding a job.* **3** unwilling to agree or cooperate: *a difficult person to work with, a difficult child*

dif·fi·cul·ty /'dɪfɪ,kʌlti/ *n.* **1** [C;U] s.t. requiring effort or time: *I had difficulty understanding the directions.* **2** [C] s.t. that creates problems, (*syn.*) an obstacle: *There's one difficulty in the plan you propose, and that is it costs too much.* **3** [C;U] trouble: *in difficulty with the law, in financial difficulties*

dif·fi·dent /'dɪfədənt/ *adj.* showing little self-confidence, shy about giving one's ideas: *He is a diffident student; he never speaks in class.* -*n.* **diffidence;** -*adv.* **diffidently.**

dif·frac·tion /dɪ'frækʃən/ *n.* [U] the changing of light waves: *We studied the diffraction of light through various openings.*

dif·fuse /dɪ'fyuz/ *v.* **-fused, -fusing, -fuses** to spread, or cause to spread, (*syn.*) to scatter: *The*

sunlight was diffused in the darkness of the room.
—*adj.* /dɪ'fyus/ **1** spread out widely or thinly: *Don't read in such diffuse light.* **2** using too many words so that the ideas are not clear: *a diffuse paper, speech, etc.* -*n.* [U] **diffusion** /dɪ'fyuʒən/.

dig /dɪg/ *v.* **dug** /dʌg/, **digging, digs 1** to make (a hole or opening) by taking away earth: *They used heavy equipment to dig a hole for the building foundation (a tunnel through a mountain, etc.).* **2** to break up or turn over earth: *She's digging in the garden.* **3** *slang* **a.** to like: *Hey, man, I dig this music!* **b.** to understand: *So that's the plan, do you dig?* **4 to dig deep:** to give money generously: *When they asked me to give to the fund for hungry children, I dug deep.* **5 to dig for: a.** to look for by digging: *to dig for gold, oil, coal, etc.* **b.** to look for (information), (*syn.*) to investigate: *A newspaper reporter digs for the facts.* **6** *phrasal v.* **to dig in: a.** to begin eating or working with great energy: *Lunch is ready, so dig in!* **b.** to fix oneself in a certain position: *The soldiers dug themselves in for battle.* **7** *phrasal v. insep.* **to dig (s.t.) into s.o.** or **s.t.:** push s.t. into: *A woman dug her elbow into my side.* **8** *phrasal v.* **to dig (s.o.** or **s.t.) out: a.** to escape by digging: *The coal miners dug out of the fallen tunnel to safety.* **b.** to find out (by looking for information): *Reporters try to dig out the truth.*
—*n.* **1** a place where archaeologists dig: *They're on a dig in Egypt.* See: diggings. **2** *infrml.* s.t. said that is both funny and critical, (*syn.*) a gibe: *She got in a few digs at her husband as she told us the funny story of their vacation trip.*

di·gest /'daɪ,dʒɛst/ *n.* a collection of articles in short form: *Here is a digest of today's news.*||*Do you know the magazine called the* Reader's Digest?
—*v.* /daɪ'dʒɛst/ **1** to process in the stomach: *Meat digests slowly.*||*He can't digest milk.* **2** to think over and come to understand: *He received the report, but wanted to digest it slowly before commenting on it.* -*adj.* **digestible.**

di·ges·tion /daɪ'dʒɛstʃən, dɪ-/ *n.* [U] the process of breaking down food in the body: *She has good digestion; she can eat anything!* -*adj.* **digestive.**

dig·ger /'dɪgər/ *n.* **1** a person who digs: *He found work as a grave digger.* **2** a machine, esp. a backhoe, used to dig: *The construction team uses a digger.*

diggings /'dɪgɪŋz/ *n.pl.* a dig; a place where digging occurs: *We visited archaeological diggings near the pyramid.*

dig·it /'dɪdʒɪt/ *n.* **1** one of the Arabic numerals from 0 to 9: *The sum 1,234 is a four-digit num-*

ber. **2** *frml.* a finger or toe: *The hand has five digits.* -*adj.* **digital.**

dig·i·tal clock or **watch** *n.* an electronic clock or watch showing numbers: *A digital clock shows the time as numbers in a row, like 10:20.*

dig·i·tal·is /,dɪdʒə'tælɪs/ *n.* [U] a strong heart stimulant made from the plant foxglove: *Doctors prescribe digitalis for people with heart trouble.*

digital recording *n.* the recording of sound, esp. music, by a series of numbers (digits) producing clarity close to the original sound: *Digital recording does not get worse in quality as copies are made.*

digitize /'dɪdʒɪ,taɪz/ *v.* **-tized, -tizing, -tizes** to put into digital form: *Some thermometers show a digitized reading of a temperature.*

dig·ni·fied /'dɪgnə,faɪd/ *adj.* with a formal, serious, and calm manner: *The students at the graduation listened in dignified silence to the college president.*

dig·ni·fy /'dɪgnə,faɪ/ *v.* **-fied, -fying, -fies** to give dignity, honor, or prestige to: *The presence of the ambassador dignified the party (occasion, reception).*

dig·ni·tar·y /'dɪgnə,tɛri/ *n.* **-ies** an important person, esp. a high official: *The dignitaries from the foreign ministries dined with the President.*

dig·ni·ty /'dɪgnɪti/ *n.* [U] self-respect, a calm and formal manner: *My doctor is a woman of great dignity.*

di·gress /daɪ'grɛs/ *v.* to move away from the main point in speaking or writing: *The speaker talked about modern art, then digressed into a discussion of a painter from 500 years ago.*

di·gres·sion /daɪ'grɛʃən/ *n.* [C;U] a move away from the main topic: *The writer made a digression from discussing politics to discussing rock music.* -*adj.* **digressive.**

digs /dɪgz/ *n.pl.slang* short for diggings, or one's place of living (room, apartment, etc.): *I'm going back to my digs to change clothes.*

dike /daɪk/ *n.* s.t. built to hold back sea water, a river, etc.: *We visited the dikes of Holland.*

di·lap·i·dat·ed /də'læpɪ,deɪtɪd/ *adj.* falling apart, in disrepair: *Those poor people live in a di-*

dike

lapidated house with holes in the roof and broken windows. -*v.* **dilapidate.**

di·late /'daɪ,leɪt, daɪ'leɪt, dɪ-/ *v.* **-lated, -lating, -lates** to make larger, widen: *When there is less light, the pupils in our eyes dilate.* -*n.* [U] **dilation; dilator.**

dil·a·to·ry /'dɪlə,tɔri/ *adj.frml.* slow in doing s.t.: *The company has no patience for employees with dilatory work habits.*

di·lem·ma /də'lɛmə/ *n.* a difficult choice between two (usu. undesirable) alternatives, (*syn.*) a quandary: *She was in a dilemma over staying in her tiny apartment or taking the time and trouble to move.*

dil·et·tante /'dɪlə,tɑnt/ *n.* a man or woman with some understanding of and a taste for the arts and fine things: *His occasional trips to the opera show he is a dilettante in the arts.* -*adj.* **dilettantish;** -*n.* **dilettantism.**

dil·i·gence /'dɪlədʒəns/ *n.* [U] continuous effort and dedication, esp. to one's work, (*syn.*) perseverance: *She works with diligence because she loves her work.*

dil·i·gent /'dɪlədʒənt/ *adj.* hard-working, (*syns.*) persevering, dedicated: *He raised his grades by being a very diligent student.* -*adv.* **diligently.**

dil·ly-dal·ly /'dɪli,dæli/ *v.* **-lied, lying, -lies** to waste time, (*syn.*) to dawdle: *My children try to dilly-dally before going to bed.* **2** to delay, (*syn.*) to procrastinate: *She dilly-dallied for weeks before deciding.*

di·lute /daɪ'lut, dɪ-/ *v.* **-luted, -luting, -lutes 1** to weaken by adding s.t.: *My tea was too strong, so I diluted it with more water.* **2** to reduce the value of: *The corporation issued more stock and diluted the shareholders' equity.*

di·lu·tion /daɪ'luʃən, dɪ-/ *n.* [U] **1** the weakening of the force of a liquid: *Follow the instructions for the dilution of the acid with water.* **2** a reduction in value: *Stockholders protested the dilution of their equity in the corporation.*

dim /dɪm/ *v.* **dimmed, dimming, dims 1** to lower the force of, esp. a light: *The driver dimmed the headlights.* **2** to make less possible: *Rebellion dims the chances for peace.* —*adj.* **1** (of light) weak: *Don't work in dim light.* **2** not very possible, (*syn.*) unlikely: *His chances of recovery (from illness) are dim.* -*adv.* **dimly.**

dim sum /'dɪm'sʌm/ *n.* a Chinese meal made up of small portions of steamed foods, such as dumplings: *I often eat dim sum at a Chinese restaurant near my office.*

dime /daɪm/ *n.* **1** in USA, a 10-cent coin: *Ten dimes equal one dollar.* **2 to not be worth a dime:** to have very little value: *The house burned down and isn't worth a dime now.*

di·men·sion /də'mɛnʃən, daɪ-/ *n.* **1** [C] a measurement of s.t. in one direction: *The dimensions of a room (package, building lot, etc.) are its length, width, and depth (or height).* **2** [C;U] size: *a problem of great dimension.*

di·min·ish /də'mɪnɪʃ/ *v.* **1** to lessen in force: *The need to take action has diminished.* **2** to lessen in number: *The supply of oil has dimin-*

ished. **3** to lessen in quality: *The company's reputation for quality has diminished; it has a <adj.> diminished reputation.*

diminishing returns *n.pl.* an economic idea that, after a certain point, continued investment brings smaller profits: *Our investment and sales have tripled, but our profits have stayed the same; we have reached the point of diminishing returns.*

dim·i·nu·tion /,dɪmɪ'nuʃən/ *n.frml.* [C;U] a lessening, reduction: *The company is experiencing a diminution in productivity.*

di·min·u·tive /dɪ'mɪnyətɪv/ *adj.* **1** *frml.* very small: *a diminutive child* **2** a form of a word used to show small size, affection, or informality: *A diminutive for "Robert" is "Bobby."*

dim·mer /'dɪmər/ *n.* a device used to lower the intensity of light: *We have dimmers on our living room lights; we dim the lights when we watch TV.*

dim·ple /'dɪmpəl/ *n.* a little dent or hollow in the skin, esp. of the face: *She has lovely dimples when she smiles.*

dim·wit /'dɪmwɪt/ *n.infrml.* a stupid person: *That dimwit sent the wrong form!*

din /dɪn/ *n.* [U] *v.* a loud, annoying, persistent noise: *There was a terrible din made by the crowd waiting for the rock concert.*

dine /daɪn/ *v.frml.* **dined, dining, dines 1** to eat a meal, esp. a special or formal one: *They dined at a fancy restaurant.* **2 to dine on:** to eat (a particular food): *We dined on lobster at the Ritz Hotel.*

diner /'daɪnər/ *n.* **1** a person who dines: *There are few diners in the restaurant tonight.* **2** a type of restaurant with low prices, fast service, and simple food: *Truck drivers stop to eat at diners on the highway.*

di·nette /daɪ'nɛt/ *n.* **1** a small informal dining area: *We usually eat in the dinette in the kitchen.* **2 a dinette (set):** table and chairs used in a dinette: *Come see our new dinette (set).*

ding /dɪŋ/ *n.v.* a sharp metallic ringing sound: *The <n.> ding of the bell at the hotel's front desk brought s.o. to serve the people waiting there.*

ding-a-ling /'dɪŋə,lɪŋ/ *n.* **1** the sound of a small bell: *Did you hear that ding-a-ling?* **2** *infrml.* a stupid person: *Sometimes he acts like a ding-a-ling.*

ding-dong /'dɪŋ,dɔŋ, -dɑŋ/ *n.* the sound of a bell: *The doorbell went ding-dong when I rang it.*

ding·bat /'dɪŋ,bæt/ *n.* **1** a small symbol used esp. to decorate chapter openings in books **2** *slang* a stupid person

din·ghy /'dɪŋi/ *n.* **-ghies** a small rowboat often carried on a larger boat: *The captain uses the dinghy to go from the ship in to the shore.*

din·gy /'dɪnʤi/ **-gier, -giest** *adj.* gray and dirty-looking: *He could find only a dingy room in an old rundown hotel.*

din·ing /'daɪnɪŋ/ *adj.* related to eating: *We ate in the dining room (a dining car on a train, etc.).*

din·ky /'dɪŋki/ *adj.slang* **-kier, -kiest** foolishly small: *My clothes won't fit in this dinky little suitcase.*

din·ner /'dɪnər/ *n.* the main meal of the day (in USA, usu. in the evening): *We go out to dinner one evening a week. See:* supper.

di·no·saur /'daɪnə,sɔr/ *n.* **1** any of a variety of small to huge reptiles that lived millions of years ago: *Tyrannosaurus Rex was a large, meat-eating dinosaur.* **2** *infrml.* s.o. who stubbornly keeps to old ways and ideas: *He is an old dinosaur; he won't touch a computer.*

dinosaur

dint /dɪnt/ *n.* [U] **1** force, effort **2 by dint of:** by means of: *By dint of hard work, she rose in her profession.*

di·o·cese /'daɪəsɪs, -,sis, -,siz/ *n.* an area or the churches under the care of a (Catholic or Protestant) bishop: *The dioceses of New York raised money to help refugees. -adj.* **diocesan** /daɪˈɑsəsən/.

di·ode /'daɪoʊd/ *n.* a semiconductor device used in electronic circuits: *There are many diodes in a transistor radio.*

di·o·rama /,daɪəˈræmə, -ˈrɑmə/ *n.* a small to life-size model of some event or scene: *The museum displayed a diorama of the battle fought in this town.*

di·ox·in /daɪˈɑksɪn/ *n.* [U] a cancer-causing chemical: *We must clean up the dioxin found in chemical waste dumps.*

dip /dɪp/ *n.* **1** a small drop: *There has been a dip in the price of sugar.* **2** a short swim: *We took (or) went for a dip in the ocean.* **3** a creamy mixture for dipping chips, crackers, vegetables, etc.: *Try this delicious dip!* **4** *slang* a jerk, a stupid person
—*v.* **dipped, dipping, dips 1** to go down a little: *The price of oil dipped today by $1.00 a barrel.* **2** to put (s.t.) into a liquid for a moment: *The artist dipped his brush in the paint.* **3** *phrasal v. insep.* **to dip into s.t.:** to use some of: *She dipped into her savings to buy him a present.*

diph·the·ria /dɪfˈθɪriə, dɪp-/ *n.* [U] a serious contagious disease affecting the throat and breathing: *Diphtheria has almost disappeared in the USA.*

diph·thong /'dɪf,θɔŋ, -θɑŋ, 'dɪp-/ *n.* a unified sound made from two vowel sounds: *The "æw" in "cow" is a diphthong.*

di·plo·ma /dɪˈploʊmə/ *n.* an academic certificate, an official paper stating that s.o. has passed a course of study: *He has a high school (trade school, college, etc.) diploma.*

di·plo·mac·y /dɪˈploʊməsi/ *n.* [U] **1** skill in handling personal, business, and governmental relationships, (*syn.*) tact: *You must use diplomacy in convincing s.o. to do a difficult job.* **2** the formal conduct of relations between countries: *Officials in the U.S. Department of State practice the art of diplomacy with foreign nations.*

dip·lo·mat /'dɪplə,mæt/ *n.* **1** a person who acts as a diplomatic representative of a nation: *Diplomats from many countries met in Geneva for a conference on world peace.* **2** a person who acts with care and sensitivity towards others: *She is a diplomat with all her friends and business contacts.*

dip·lo·mat·ic /,dɪpləˈmætɪk/ *adj.* **1** related to diplomacy: *a diplomatic service (mission, channel, corps, etc.)* **2** showing skill at handling people sensitively: *She gave a diplomatic response to a hostile question and brought calm to the situation. -adv.* **diplomatically.**

diplomatic corps *n.* an organized group of diplomats and other governmental employees responsible for managing relations with other countries: *The diplomatic corps of the USA has its central office in Washington, D.C.*

diplomatic immunity *n.* [C;U] protection given to foreign diplomats by a government so they cannot be arrested for certain crimes: *Under diplomatic immunity, the diplomat could tear up tickets he received for parking violations.*

dip·per /'dɪpər/ *n.* **1** a large spoon that looks like a cup or small bowl with a long handle: *I used a dipper to drink water from a barrel.* **2** **the Big Dipper, the Little Dipper:** constellations of stars in the shape of cups (in Ursa Major and Ursa Minor)

dip·py /'dɪpi/ *adj.slang* **-pier, -piest** crazy, silly: *She often acts a little dippy.*

dip·so·ma·ni·ac /,dɪpsəˈmeɪni,æk/ *n.* a person who can't stop drinking alcohol after he or she begins: *He is a dipsomaniac (or) a <slang> dipso; once he starts drinking, he doesn't stop until he passes out. -n.* **dipsomania.**

dip·stick /'dɪp,stɪk/ *n.* **1** a long metal rod put into a liquid to measure its level: *I used the dipstick to check how much oil there was in my car's engine.* **2** *slang* a jerk, a stupid person: *Don't be such a dipstick!*

dip·tych /'dɪp,tɪk/ *n.* a painting in two panels, often hinged together: *A beautiful diptych hangs behind the altar in that church.*

dire /daɪr/ *adj.* grave, very serious: *His business is bankrupt and he is in dire trouble.*

di·rect /dəˈrɛkt, daɪ-/ v. **1** to guide, control: *The police officer directed traffic.* **2** to manage and guide in the arts: *She directed a film (orchestra, play).* **3** to lead, manage: *Chief Executive Officers direct the affairs of large corporations.* **4** to order, command: *An officer directed the soldiers to attack.* **5** to focus, turn: *We directed our attention to the speaker.* **6** to point, aim: *A computer directs a missile to its target.* **7** to send, route: *The government directs aid to a disaster zone.*
—*adj.* **1** straight, without interruptions: *We have little time, so we must go the most direct route.* **2** open and honest: *She liked his direct answers to her questions.* **3** without anyone or anything coming between: *direct sunlight, a direct result, direct knowledge of an event*

direct action *n.* an act, like a labor strike, work slowdown, or sabotage, meant for such goals as wage and benefit increases: *The union took direct action and called a strike.*

direct current *n.* [U] electrical current that flows in only one direction: *Direct current is used in Europe. See:* AC; DC.

direct flight *n.* a flight with one or more stops on its way, but no change of plane: *She took a direct flight from New York to Denver with a short stop in Chicago. See:* non-stop flight.

direct mail *n.* [U] advertising, political literature, requests for donations, etc., mailed to many people: *Their company has had great success in selling their products by direct mail.*

di·rec·tion /dəˈrɛkʃən, daɪ-/ n. **1** [C] a route, line of movement geographically: *We walked (flew, ran, drove) in a northerly direction.* **2** [C;U] leadership, guidance toward goals: *The new manager gave direction to the company's efforts.* **3** [U] artistic management and control: *The orchestra is under the direction of Sir George Smith.* **4** [U] an approach, a line of thought, or action: *What direction would you like to take in solving this problem?* **5** *n.pl.* **directions: a.** instructions (how to do s.t.), guidance: *The teacher gave me directions for the experiment.* **b.** instructions (how to go somewhere): *We followed the policeman's directions and got to the museum.* **6 sense of direction:** the ability to sense where one is and which way to go: *Because of her good sense of direction, she got us there even without a map.*

di·rec·tion·al /dəˈrɛkʃənəl, daɪ-/ adj. **1** showing direction: *Drivers use the directional signals to show that they are going to make a right or left turn.* **2** coming from or going to a geographical point: *The airplane was helped by a directional signal from the airport.*

di·rec·tive /dəˈrɛktɪv, daɪ-/ n.frml. an order, command: *An administrator (military commander, government agency, etc.) issues direc-*

tives to personnel to do s.t. or to follow certain rules.

di·rect·ly /dəˈrɛktli, daɪ-/ adv. **1** in a direct manner: *Go directly to school and do not stop on the way.* **2** openly and honestly, (syn.) candidly: *He answers questions directly and without hesitation.*

direct object *n.* usu. a noun or pronoun acted on by a verb: *The word "ball" in the sentence "The boy hit the ball" is a direct object.*

di·rec·tor /dəˈrɛktər/ n. **1** the manager, head: *She is the director of personnel (operations, the computer department, etc.).* **2** artistic manager and guide: *a film director, the director of the Metropolitan Opera* **3** a member of the Board of Directors of a corporation

di·rec·tor·ate /dəˈrɛktərɪt, daɪ-/ n.frml. a board of directors, a group that governs or controls an organization, corporation, or institution: *That decision will be made by the directorate of the United Nations.*

di·rec·tor·ship /dəˈrɛktərˌʃɪp, daɪ-/ n. the position of director: *His directorship ends next year.*

di·rec·to·ry /dəˈrɛktəri, daɪ-/ n. **-ries** a listing of items, such as names, addresses, businesses, etc., usu. in alphabetical order: *You can find my phone number in a telephone directory.*

dirge /dɜrdʒ/ n. slow, sad music to honor the dead: *A band played a funeral dirge at the service for the dead President.*

dir·i·gi·ble /ˈdɪrɪdʒəbəl, dəˈrɪdʒəbəl/ n. an airship filled with a lighter-than-air gas, (syn.) a blimp: *A pilot flies a dirigible from a cockpit attached under it.*

dirt /dɜrt/ n. [U] **1** loose soil, earth: *I planted flowers in the dirt.* **2** s.t. unclean: *What's that dirt on your shirt?* **3** information about bad behavior, esp. about sex, (syn.) gossip: *I can't believe they print that dirt in the newspaper.*

dirt-bike a motorbike made for use off roads: *They rode their dirt bikes up the mountain trail.*

dirt-cheap *adj.* very inexpensive: *I think I will buy that rug; it is dirt-cheap.*

dirty /ˈdɜrti/ adj. **-ier, -iest 1** unclean, (syn.) soiled: *The girl came home from the playground wearing a dirty shirt.* **2** dishonest, (syns.) underhanded, devious: *Your hiding his book when he needed it was a dirty trick to play on him.* **3** impolite and offensive: *dirty jokes, dirty language*
—*adv. phr.* **to play dirty:** to play unfairly, without respect for rules: *The opposing team played dirty, but the referee didn't see it.*
—*v.* **-tied, -tying, -ties** to make or become dirty: *She dirtied her hands in the garden.*

dirty linen or **laundry** *n.fig.* [U] private personal or family matters, esp. embarrassing problems: *We do not discuss our family troubles with strangers; we do not wash* (or) *air our dirty linen in public.*

dirty old man *n.infrml.* **men** a man, esp. an old one, with too strong an interest in sex: *He is 80 years old and chases young women; he's a dirty old man.*

dirty pool *n.slang fig.* [U] dishonest, tricky acts intended to harm: *The company promised him a raise, then fired him with no notice; that was dirty pool.*

dirty tricks *n.pl.* dishonest or tricky practices, esp. in politics: *The campaign manager put out false information about the opposing candidate; he played dirty tricks on him.*

dirty word *n.* a curse word, bad language: *I don't like it when she uses dirty words in the presence of my children.*

dirty work *n.* [U] **1** work that causes the hands and clothes to get dirty: *Being a mechanic is dirty work.* **2** *fig.* work that is esp. disagreeable (unpleasant or demeaning): *The manager decided to fire 50 people, so now I have to do the dirty work of telling them.*

dis·a·bil·i·ty /ˌdɪsəˈbɪləti/ *n.* **-ties** **1** s.t. that takes away a normal ability, esp. as a result of a birth defect, accident, or disease: *She lost her hearing as a child, but she has led a happy, successful life despite that disability.* **2** short for disability insurance payments: *After he broke his foot, he couldn't work, and his family lived on disability for six months.*

dis·a·ble /dɪsˈeɪbəl/ *v.* **-bled, -bling, -bles** to make (esp. a person) unable to do s.t. anymore: *The accident disabled her so she lost the use of her legs.*

dis·a·bled /dɪsˈeɪbəld/ *adj.* **1** having a (mental or physical) disability: *He is disabled and uses a wheelchair.* **2** not working, damaged: *We saw a disabled vehicle on the side of the road.*

USAGE NOTE: In the USA, laws give *disabled* people the same rights as nondisabled people. Schools, employers, businesses, and government agencies must offer special services to people with disabilities, such as Braille books for *blind* people, sign-language translators for *deaf* people, and ramps to enter buildings for people in wheelchairs. The US government also offers a monthly disability payment to people who can't work because of disability.

dis·a·buse /ˌdɪsəˈbyuz/ *v.* **-bused, -busing, -buses** to correct s.o.'s wrong idea or illusion: *He thinks that he can say whatever he wants, but I will disabuse him of that idea.*

dis·ac·cord /ˌdɪsəˈkɔrd/ *n.* [U] *v.frml.* disagreement, lack of harmony: *There was a long argument because of the disaccord among committee members.*

dis·ac·cus·tom /ˌdɪsəˈkʌstəm/ *v.frml.* to stop a habit or custom: *She disaccustomed herself to smoking gradually; she finally stopped.*

dis·ad·van·tage /ˌdɪsədˈvæntɪdʒ/ *n.* **1** s.t. that hurts or gets in the way (of success), (*syn.*) a drawback: *The high cost of living is a disadvantage to living in a big city.* **2 at a disadvantage:** in a bad position: *The team was at a disadvantage because their star player was sick.*

dis·ad·van·taged /ˌdɪsədˈvæntɪdʒd/ *adj.* without the normal benefits of society, esp. because of poverty or racial prejudice: *He comes from a disadvantaged family and had to quit school at 16 to get a full-time job.*
—*n.* **the disadvantaged:** poor people: *The disadvantaged are helped by government programs.*

dis·ad·van·ta·geous /ˌdɪsædvənˈteɪdʒɪs, dɪsˌæd-/ *adj.* related to a disadvantage or drawback, (*syn.*) detrimental: *A bad storm has started, so it is disadvantageous for us to travel.* *-adv.* **disadvantageously.**

dis·af·fect·ed /ˌdɪsəˈfɛktɪd/ *adj.* **1** no longer satisfied, content, or loyal: *She has become disaffected by her work (situation, pay, etc.).* **2** feeling set apart, (*syn.*) alienated: *He is disaffected from his coworkers because of their unfriendliness.*

dis·a·gree /ˌdɪsəˈgri/ *v.* **-greed, -greeing, -grees** **1** to differ, hold a different opinion: *I disagree with what you say.* **2** to show different opinions: *They never disagree in public.* **3** to make sick, upset: *That meal disagreed with me; I feel ill.*

dis·a·gree·a·ble /ˌdɪsəˈgriəbəl/ *adj.* **1** unfriendly (uncooperative, difficult to deal with): *She is so disagreeable that no one will work with her.* **2** unpleasant: *a disagreeable job to do -adv.* **disagreeably.**

dis·a·gree·ment /ˌdɪsəˈgrimənt/ *n.* **1** a difference of opinion: *We are in disagreement about what to do.* **2** an argument, conflict: *They had a violent disagreement over money.* **3** a difference, a failure to be the same, (*syn.*) a disparity: *There is a disagreement between the two descriptions of what happened.*

dis·al·low /ˌdɪsəˈlaʊ/ *v.* to refuse to accept, reject: *The controller for the company disallowed my travel expenses, so I had to pay them myself.*

dis·ap·pear /ˌdɪsəˈpɪr/ *v.* **1** to go out of sight, (*syn.*) to vanish: *The little dog was just here, then he disappeared.* **2** to pass out of existence: *Dinosaurs disappeared from the earth long ago.*

dis·ap·pear·ance /ˌdɪsəˈpɪrəns/ *n.* [C;U] an act of disappearing: *The disappearance of the necklace is still a mystery.*

dis·ap·point /,dɪsə'pɔɪnt/ v. **1** to sadden s.o. by failing to meet their expectations or hopes: *I was disappointed when she cancelled our date.* **2** to keep s.t. from happening, (*syns.*) to frustrate, block: *Our hopes for a picnic were disappointed by the rain storm.* -*adj.* **disappointing.**

dis·ap·point·ment /,dɪsə'pɔɪntmənt/ n. **1** [C;U] sadness over the loss of s.t. expected or hoped for, (*syn.*) disillusionment: *He suffered disappointment when she refused to marry him.* **2** [C] s.t. that disappoints: *It was a disappointment when rain prevented the family picnic.*

dis·ap·pro·ba·tion /dɪs'æprə'beɪʃən/ n.*frml.* strong moral disapproval, (*syn.*) condemnation: *After he got out of prison, the criminal had to leave town because of the disapprobation of the community.*

dis·ap·prov·al /,dɪsə'pruvəl/ n. [U] **1** bad opinion, objection: *The teacher showed her disapproval by making the class stay after school.* **2** criticism, condemnation, rejection: *widespread disapproval of the government's programs* **3** refusal, rejection: *His request for a larger office met with disapproval.*

dis·ap·prove /,dɪsə'pruv/ v. **-proved, -proving, -proves** **1** have a bad opinion of: *Her father disapproved of her behavior.* **2** to express a bad opinion of, criticize, (*syn.*) to condemn: *The public disapproves of that government program.* **3** to refuse to accept, reject: *The agency disapproved his request for money.*

dis·arm /dɪs'ɑrm/ v. **1** to take away weapons: *The policeman disarmed the criminal by taking away his gun.* **2** to lay down or destroy arms (weapons, armed forces, etc.) voluntarily, esp. by treaty: *The two nations agreed to disarm.* **3** to drive away (s.o.'s) anger or distrust: *She disarmed her opponent with her friendly manner.*

dis·ar·ma·ment /dɪs'ɑrməmənt/ n. [U] the process of reducing or destroying weapons and armed forces: *The two nations began negotiations on disarmament.*

dis·arm·ing /dɪs'ɑrmɪŋ/ n. [U] an act of removing weapons: *the disarming of the criminal by the police*
—*adj.* charming, tending to make s.o. less angry or distrustful: *I was very angry when his car hit mine, but he apologized so nicely that I found it disarming.*

dis·ar·range /,dɪsə'reɪndʒ/ v. **-ranged, -ranging, -ranges** to disorder, disorganize: *A thief broke into the house and disarranged the furniture while looking for valuables.*

dis·ar·ray /,dɪsə'reɪ/ n.*frml.* [U] disorder, disorganization: *Her hair and clothes were in disarray after she fell.*

dis·as·sem·ble /,dɪsə'sɛmbəl/ v. **-bled, -bling, -bles** to take apart: *I had to disassemble the bookshelves in order to move them.*

dis·as·so·ci·ate /,dɪsə'souʃi,eɪt, -si,eɪt/ v. **-ated, -ating, -ates** to separate, esp. oneself: *He disassociated himself from a group of bad people (a dishonest act, an organization, etc.).* -*n.* [U] **disassociation.**

dis·as·ter /dɪ'zæstər/ n. **1** a sudden great act of destruction and loss, (*syns.*) a catastrophe, calamity: *The earthquake created a disaster.* **2** *fig.* a total failure: *The party was a disaster; the food was bad and the band was lousy.*

disaster area or **zone** n. an area of destruction, usu. created by a natural force such as an earthquake or violent storm: *After the earthquake, the government declared the city a disaster area and flew in supplies.*

dis·as·trous /dɪ'zæstrəs/ adj. **1** related to a disaster, (*syn.*) catastrophic: *The island was in a disastrous situation because of the hurricane.* **2** *fig.* related to a total failure: *The results of the election were disastrous for the Republican Party.* -*adv.* **disastrously.**

dis·a·vow /,dɪsə'vaʊ/ v. **1** to deny, (*syn.*) to disclaim: *She disavowed any knowledge of the crime.* **2** to reject, refuse: *He disavows any further connection with what we now know is a criminal organization.* -*n.* **disavowal.**

dis·band /dɪs'bænd/ v. to separate, dissolve: *The group (army, meeting, etc.) disbanded and everyone went home.* -*n.* **disbanding.**

dis·bar /dɪs'bɑr/ v. **-barred, -barring, -bars** to officially force (a lawyer) out of the legal profession: *The state bar association disbarred that lawyer for dishonest uses of his clients' money.* -*n.* [U] **disbarment.**

dis·be·lief /,dɪsbə'lif/ n. a refusal or unwillingness to believe: *When the nuclear disaster was first announced, the public received the news with shock and disbelief.*

disbelieve /,dɪsbə'liv/ v. **-lieved, -lieving, -lieves** to doubt or refuse to believe: *She disbelieves what he says because he often lies.*

dis·bur·sal /,dɪs'bɜrsəl/ n.*frml.* a payment: *The business makes monthly disbursals to its creditors.* -*n.* [U] **disbursement.**

dis·burse /dɪs'bɜrs/ v.*frml.* **-bursed, -bursing, -burses** to give out, (*syn.*) to dispense: *The federal government disburses tax money to the states.* -*n.* **disburser.**

disc /dɪsk/ var. of disk, a thin flat circular plate: *Her collection includes old phonograph records and compact discs.*

dis·card /dɪ'skɑrd/ v. to throw away, dispose of as useless: *We must discard this trash (those old ideas, etc.).*

dis·cern /dɪ'sɜrn/ v.*frml.* **1** to see (differences between), (*syn.*) to differentiate: *He discerned major differences between the two job offers.*

2 to see and understand: *He discerned the importance of those differences.* **3** to see, spot: *to discern a ship in the distance -n.* [U] **discernment.**

dis·cern·ing /dɪ'sɜrnɪŋ/ *adj.* intelligent, *(syn.)* perceptive: *She has a discerning mind and quickly understood how to solve our problem.*

dis·charge /dɪs'tʃɑrdʒ/ *v.* **-charged, -charging, -charges 1** to ask or allow (s.o.) to go: *Management discharged 100 workers.||The navy discharged the sailor.* **2** to fulfill, perform (a responsibility): *Management discharged its obligation by reducing the workforce.* **3** to fire, explode (guns, cannons, bombs, etc.): *A rifle discharged by accident.* **4** to let or send out (s.t. from within): *The cut discharged blood.||The volcano (chimney, fire) discharged smoke.* **5** *frml.* to pay (s.t. owed): *I must discharge my debt to him.*
—*n.* /'dɪs,tʃɑrdʒ/ **1** [U] a fulfillment of responsibility: *She completed the discharge of her obligations under the contract.* **2** [C] a release from military service: *The sailor received his discharge and went home.* **3** [C;U] a firing of a weapon, explosion: *the discharge of a gun* **4** [C;U] s.t. that is let out or sent out: *the discharge of pollution from a factory*

dis·ci·ple /dɪ'saɪpəl/ *n.* a student of a teacher or school of thought who spreads their teachings: *She is a disciple of the British school of economics.*

dis·ci·pli·nar·i·an /,dɪsəplə'nɛriən/ *n.* a person who believes in and demands obedience to rules: *The teacher is a strict disciplinarian in his classroom.*

dis·ci·pli·nar·y /'dɪsəplə,nɛri/ *adj.* characterized by punishment: *The university administration took disciplinary action against the students on strike.*

dis·ci·pline /'dɪsə,plɪn/ *n.* **1** [U] obedience to rules of good behavior and order: *The students were quiet because their teacher insisted on discipline in the classroom.* **2** [U] control of the mind and body: *College students need self-discipline to succeed in their studies.* **3** [C] a field of study: *In which discipline does that teacher work? She teaches mathematics.*
—*v.* **-plined, -plining, -plines 1** to punish for breaking the rules: *The student disrupted the class, so the teacher disciplined him by giving him extra work to do.* **2** to train to control the mind and body: *He disciplined himself to keep to a demanding work schedule.*

dis·ci·plined /'dɪsə,plɪnd/ *adj.* showing control resulting from training of mind and body: *The military training school produced highly disciplined soldiers.*

disc jockey *n. See:* disk jockey.

dis·claim /dɪs'kleɪm/ *v.* **1** to deny, *(syn.)* to disavow: *She disclaimed any knowledge of the missing money.* **2** (in law) to give up a right or

to deny an obligation: *The defendant disclaimed his right to trial by jury and chose instead trial before a judge.*

dis·claim·er /dɪs'kleɪmər/ *n.* **1** a statement that s.t. is not true: *The man accused of murder issued a disclaimer of any knowledge about the crime.* **2** (in law) the giving up of a right, esp. to sue: *Before the operation, the doctor's patient signed a disclaimer of any right to sue.* **3** a denial of legal responsibility: *The doctor's disclaimer gave her legal protection against a suit by a patient.*

disclose /dɪs'klouz/ *v.* **-closed, -closing, -closes** to tell or show, esp. that which was kept hidden or secret, *(syn.)* to divulge: *He disclosed new information on the project (his secrets, his innermost feelings, etc.).*

dis·clo·sure /dɪs'klouʒər/ *n.* [C;U] the telling of s.t. that was secret: *The disclosure in the newspapers of a scandal involving the Senator ruined her career.*

dis·co /'dɪskou/ *n.* short for discotheque, a dance hall with recorded popular music: *We like to go to a disco on Saturday nights.*

dis·col·or /dɪs'kʌlər/ *v.* to change (to a worse) color, *(syn.)* to stain: *Smoking has discolored my teeth. -n.* [U] **discoloration** /dɪs,kʌlə'reɪʃən/.

dis·com·bob·u·late /,dɪskəm'bɑbyə,leɪt/ *v.infrml.* **-lated, -lating, -lates** to confuse, upset, *(syn.)* to disorient: *The noise discombobulates him so that he can't think.*

dis·com·fit /dɪs'kʌmfɪt/ *v.frml.* **-fitted, -fitting, -fits** to distress, upset: *The king was discomfitted by the loss of the battle. -n.* **discomfiture.**

dis·com·fort /dɪs'kʌmfərt/ *n.* [U] (mental or physical) pain that is not serious: *The patient suffered discomfort in her legs.||He felt some discomfort about asking his boss for a raise in pay.*
—*v.* to make uncomfortable, upset: *The bad news discomforted her.*

dis·con·cert /,dɪskən'sɜrt/ *v.* to cause to feel doubt and nervousness, disturb: *I was disconcerted by the sight of a strange man at my door. -adj.* **disconcerting.**

dis·con·nect /,dɪskə'nɛkt/ *v.* to break a connection, *(syn.)* to detach: *Disconnect the wires from the machine before you try to fix it.*

dis·con·nect·ed /,dɪskə'nɛktɪd/ *adj.* **1** removed, detached: *The machine doesn't work because of a disconnected wire.* **2** having lost contact during a telephone call: *We were disconnected during our conversation.* **3** (of ideas) unclear because of poor connections between parts, *(syn.)* incoherent: *a disconnected story (set of remarks, presentation, etc.) -n.*[C;U] **disconnection.**

dis·con·so·late /dɪs'kɑnsəlɪt/ *adj.frml.* hopelessly sad, (*syn.*) melancholy: *She was disconsolate over the death of her dog.* *-adv.* **disconsolately.**

dis·con·tent /ˌdɪskən'tɛnt/ *n.* [U] dissatisfaction, unhappiness: *She suffers discontent with her life and wants a major change.* *adj.* **discontent** or **discontented**: *dissatisfied, unhappy: He is discontented (or) discontent with his small pay increase.* *-v.* **discontent.**

dis·con·tin·ue /ˌdɪskən'tɪnyu/ *v.* **-ued, -uing, -ues** **1** to stop, end: *The company has discontinued manufacturing that item.* **2** to stop for a period of time, interrupt: *to discontinue peace talks for a week* *-n.* [U] **discontinuation.**

dis·con·ti·nu·i·ty /ˌdɪskɑntə'nuəti/ *n.* **-ties** **1** [C;U] a lack of continuity or logical order: *I was confused by the discontinuity in his argument.* **2** [C;U] interruption, break: *Mechanical problems caused discontinuities in the production process.*

dis·con·tin·u·ous /ˌdɪskən'tɪnyuəs/ *adj.* not continuous, interrupted: *A discontinuous supply of steel caused a slowdown in automobile production.* *-adv.* **discontinuously.**

dis·cord /'dɪs,kɔrd/ *n.* **1** [U] disagreement, conflict: *A meeting full of discord left everyone with headaches.* **2** [C;U] an unpleasant combination of notes or sounds: *The children trying out musical instruments produced a terrible discord.*

dis·cord·ant /dɪs'kɔrdnt/ *adj.* **1** full of conflict and disagreement: *A discordant meeting ended without agreement.* **2** harsh-sounding, disagreeable in sound: *They live in a discordant household full of arguing.*

dis·co·theque /'dɪskə,tɛk/ *n. See:* disco.

dis·count /'dɪs,kaʊnt/ *n.* an amount subtracted from a price: *The discount on this item is 10 percent off the retail price.*
—*v.* **1** to reduce a price by an amount: *The store discounted the item by 10 percent.* **2** to doubt, not accept completely as true: *You have to discount what he says, because he exaggerates often.*

discount rate *n.* the interest rate charged by the US Federal Reserve Bank to other banks: *The discount rate has a big effect on interest rates in general.*

discount store *n.* a store that offers discounts on all or most merchandise in order to attract many customers: *This chain of discount stores has sales every week.*

dis·cour·age /dɪ'skɜrɪdʒ, -'skʌr-/ *v.* **-raged, -raging, -rages** **1** to take away one's confidence or hope, (*syn.*) to dishearten: *Poor grades on her exams discouraged her.* **2** to advise against, try to prevent: *I discouraged him from staying in college any longer.* *-n.* **discouragement;** *-adj.* **discouraging.**

dis·cour·aged /dɪ'skɜrɪdʒd, -skʌr-/ *adj.* feeling a loss of confidence or hope, (*syn.*) disheartened: *He felt discouraged after receiving bad grades.*

dis·course /'dɪs,kɔrs/ *n.frml.* [C;U] spoken or written (formal) communication: *College students become familiar with academic discourse.*

dis·cour·te·ous /dɪs'kɜrtiəs/ *adj.* impolite, rude: *I spoke to the manager after a salesperson was quite discourteous to me.* *-adv.* **discourteously.**

dis·cour·te·sy /dɪs'kɜrtəsi/ *n.* [C;U] impoliteness, rudeness: *The discourtesy of the taxi driver made me angry.*

dis·cov·er /dɪ'skʌvər/ *v.* **1** to learn, find out: *When she got to her door, she discovered she had lost her key.* **2** to find, see, or learn of (s.t. no one knew before): *Galileo discovered the planet Jupiter.* **3** to invent: *Scientists in England discovered penicillin.*

dis·cov·er·y /dɪ'skʌvəri/ *n.* **-ries** **1** the finding of s.t. new: *Since the discovery of penicillin, millions of lives have been saved with it.* **2** s.t. that is discovered or learned: *His discoveries in physics made him famous.*

dis·cred·it /dɪs'krɛdɪt/ *v.* **1** to show that s.t. is of little or no truth or value: *Scientists have discredited many popular beliefs, like the belief the world was flat.* **2** to cause a loss of trust or belief (in s.o.): *After the scandal, the Minister was <adj.> discredited and resigned from the government.*

dis·creet /dɪ'skrit/ *adj.* **1** careful not to tell embarrassing or secret information: *People tell her their secrets and she is very discreet; she never speaks about them.* **2** (in general behavior) polite, modest: *He never shouts or does anything wild; he's discreet.* *-adv.* **discreetly.**

dis·crep·an·cy /dɪ'skrɛpənsi/ *n.* **-cies** a disagreement between what s.t. should be and what it appears to be: *The published price is $100, but the check is made out for $90; there is a discrepancy there.* *-adj.* **discrepant.**

dis·crete /dɪ'skrit/ *adj.* separate, apart, having a distinct identity or existence: *That company is a discrete entity from the others, which are all owned by the parent company.* *-adv.* **discretely.**

dis·cre·tion /dɪ'skrɛʃən/ *n.* [U] **1** the quality of being discreet, (*syns.*) prudence, caution: *Lawyers and doctors must act with discretion and not speak about their clients.* **2 at (s.o.'s) discretion:** as (s.o.) chooses or decides: *Use the money at your own discretion.*

dis·cre·tion·ar·y /dɪ'skrɛʃə,nɛri/ *adj.* allowing to the responsible use of one's own judgment: *A discretionary account is one where the owner allows a stockbroker to make and act on decisions to trade.*

dis·crim·i·nate /dɪ'skrɪmə,neɪt/ v. **-nated, -nating, -nates 1** to see the differences (between): *The expert discriminated between two periods of art.* **2 to discriminate (against):** to treat (s.o.) unfairly, esp. because of prejudice based on race, sex, religion, etc.: *Some whites discriminate against blacks.*

dis·crim·i·nat·ing /dɪ'skrɪmə,neɪtɪŋ/ adj. having good taste or judgment, (*syns.*) discerning, refined: *She dresses beautifully and is a woman of discriminating tastes.*

dis·crim·i·na·tion /dɪ,skrɪmə'neɪʃən/ n. [U] **1** unfair treatment, esp. because of race, sex, religion, etc.: *There is much racial discrimination in the world.* **2** the ability to appreciate small differences, (*syns.*) discernment, refinement: *He is a man of discrimination in his tastes.*

dis·crim·i·na·tor /dɪ'skrɪmə,neɪtər/ n. a person who treats others unfairly: *That employer is a discriminator against women; he pays them less than men.*

dis·crim·i·na·to·ry /dɪ'skrɪmənə,tɔri/ adj. resulting in unfair treatment (due to prejudice): *That business was taken to court for discriminatory practices against minorities in its hiring.*

dis·cur·sive /dɪ'skɜrsɪv/ adj. (of a person or s.t. written) passing with many words from one subject to another: *Her writing is discursive but thorough.* -adv. **discursively.**

dis·cus /'dɪskəs/ n. **-cuses** a heavy plate thrown in an athletic competition: *The discus is hurled as far as possible by a discus thrower as a sport.*

dis·cuss /dɪ'skʌs/ v. **-es** to talk about, examine: *Please discuss the problem with the other employees.*

dis·cus·sion /dɪ'skʌʃən/ n. **1** [C;U] a talk, serious conversation: *We had a discussion about solving the problem.* **2** a formal conference: *They are holding a discussion in Geneva about international banking.* **3 under discussion:** being talked about: *A new contract is now under discussion.*

dis·dain /dɪs'deɪn/ n. [U] the feeling that s.o. or s.t. deserves no attention or respect, (*syn.*) contempt: *I left my job because my boss treated the workers with disdain.*
—v. **1** to refuse because of disdain: *He disdained going to the office party.* **2** to consider or treat with disdain: *He disdains his coworkers and avoids speaking to them.*

dis·dain·ful /dɪs'deɪnfəl/ adj. showing no respect, (*syn.*) contemptuous: *The oldest students sometimes have a disdainful attitude toward the newly arrived students.* -adv. **disdainfully.**

dis·ease /dɪ'ziz/ n. [C;U] **1** a sickness or serious disorder that is inherited or caused by in-

fection or bad living conditions: *Disease destroys many lives in poor parts of the world.* **2** *fig.* an abnormal social condition: *The love of money can spread like a disease.*

dis·eased /dɪ'zizd/ adj. sick, suffering from disease: *The refugee camps were filled with hungry and diseased people.*

dis·em·bark /,dɪsəm'bɑrk/ v. to leave a ship or airplane after a voyage: *They disembarked in Amsterdam after crossing the Atlantic Ocean.* -n. [U] **disembarkation** /dɪs,embɑr'keɪʃən/.

dis·em·bod·y /,dɪsɪm'bɑdi/ v. **-died, -dying, -dies** to free the human soul or spirit from the body: *Many people believe that at the moment of death, a person's soul becomes disembodied.*

dis·em·bow·el /,dɪsɪm'bauəl/ v. to cut the bowels out: *The hunter disemboweled the deer that she had killed.*

dis·en·chant·ed /,dɪsən'tʃæntɪd/ adj. no longer believing in (s.t. that was valued), (*syn.*) disillusioned: *Her boss made her promises but didn't keep them; now she is disenchanted with him.* -n. [U] **disenchantment.**

dis·en·fran·chise /,dɪsən'fræntʃaɪz/ v. **-chised, -chising, -chises** to take away s.o.'s rights, esp. the right to vote: *The white majority disenfranchised the black minority by creating a poll tax they could not pay, so they could not vote.* -n. [U] **disenfranchisement.**

dis·en·gage /,dɪsɛn'geɪdʒ/ v. **-gaged, -gaging, -gages 1** to take apart: *The technician disengaged the wiring from a large device.* **2 to disengage the gears (on a vehicle's transmission):** to shift a clutch: *Be sure to disengage the gears when you park the car.* **3** to stop fighting and move apart: *The two armies disengaged.*

dis·en·tan·gle /,dɪsɛn'tæŋgəl/ v. **-gled, -gling, -gles 1** to clear away knots from and make straight: *The hairdresser disentangled the woman's hair.* **2** *fig.* to free from confusion, (*syn.*) to extricate: *The bookkeeper disentangled the records and cleared up mistakes.*

dis·e·qui·lib·ri·um /dɪs,ikwə'lɪbriəm, -,ɛkwə-/ n. [U] lack of balance, instability: *This chemical solution (government, financial situation, etc.) is in disequilibrium.*

dis·es·tab·lish /,dɪsə'stæblɪʃ/ v. to remove s.t. from an official position: *The new government disestablished the church (as the official church of the state).*

dis·fa·vor /dɪs'feɪvər/ n. [U] *frml.* disapproval, dislike: *The politician (representative, businessman, etc.) is in disfavor with his colleagues for acting against their wishes.*
—v. *frml.* to disapprove of, dislike: *Some businesspeople disfavor that approach to marketing.*

dis·fig·ure /dɪsˈfɪgyər/ v. **-ured, -uring, -ures** to spoil or hurt the appearance of: *In the car accident, she hit the windshield and it disfigured her face.* -n. [U] **disfigurement.**

dis·gorge /dɪsˈgɔrdʒ/ v. **-gorged, -gorging, -gorges** 1 to throw out from the throat: *A mother bird disgorged food for her young.* 2 to pour or put out forcefully: *A volcano disgorges smoke and dust.*

dis·grace /dɪsˈgreɪs/ n. 1 [U] dishonor, a state of rejection (for an offense): *He suffered disgrace for stealing.* 2 [C;U] a cause of shame or dishonor: *She's a disgrace to her family.* 3 **in disgrace:** in a state of dishonor, public rejection: *The official left office in disgrace.*
—v. to dishonor, bring shame to: *The official disgraced himself (his family name, his country, etc.) by his dishonesty.*

dis·grace·ful /dɪsˈgreɪsfəl/ adj. 1 shameful, shocking: *Her parents were angered and embarrassed by her disgraceful behavior.* 2 dishonorable, (syn.) ignominious: *The idea of winning-at-any-cost led to disgraceful actions by some competitors.* -adv. **disgracefully.**

dis·grun·tled /dɪsˈgrʌntld/ adj. discontented and dissatisfied: *He is disgruntled about not receiving an increase in pay.*

dis·guise /dɪsˈgaɪz/ v. **-guised, -guising, -guises** 1 to change one's appearance to fool others: *The secret agent disguised his identity (or) disguised himself to look like a farmer.* 2 to hide, cover up: *She disguised her evil intentions by pretending to be friendly.*
—n. 1 a change of appearance made to hide one's true identity: *The robber wore a ski mask as a disguise.* 2 s.t. that hides the truth, (syn.) a ruse: *His friendly manner was just a disguise for his brutal intentions.*

dis·gust /dɪsˈgʌst/ v. to cause feelings of strong dislike, (syns.) to offend, revolt: *Garbage on the streets disgusts everyone.*
—n. [U] a feeling of strong dislike: *The terrible smell filled me with disgust.*

dis·gust·ed /dɪsˈgʌstɪd/ adj. 1 feeling strong dislike and impatience, (syn.) offended: *She is disgusted with dirty politics.* 2 sickened, (syn.) nauseated: *The neighbors are disgusted by the smell from his pigs.* -adv. **disgustedly.**

dis·gust·ing /dɪsˈgʌstɪŋ/ adj. 1 causing strong dislike and impatience, (syn.) offensive: *The politicians can't solve anything; it's disgusting!* 2 sickening, (syn.) nauseating: *That garbage in the streets is disgusting.*

dish /dɪʃ/ n. **dishes** 1 any of a variety of plates, bowls, and platters used to serve and hold food: *Please put the dishes on the table for dinner.* 2 an amount of food: *a dish of ice cream* 3 a type of cooked food: *She made his favorite dish for dinner.* 4 slang an attractive woman: *His girlfriend is a dish!* 5 **to do** or **wash the**

dishes: to wash dirty dishes, plates, etc.: *I'll do the dishes tonight, since you cooked.*
—v. 1 phrasal v. sep. **to dish s.t. out:** to give, hand out, (syn.) to distribute: *I'll dish out the soup to everyone.*||*I'll dish it out.* 2 phrasal v. sep. **to dish s.t. up: a.** to put (food) into dishes, (syn.) to serve: *The chef dished up the macaroni and cheese.*||*He dished it up.* **b.** slang to give or present (as fact): *What excuse did he dish up this time?*

dis·har·mo·ny /dɪsˈhɑrməni/ n. [C;U] **-nies** lack of agreement, (syns.) discord, friction: *There is constant disharmony among members of that family; they're always arguing.*

dish·cloth /ˈdɪʃˌklɔθ/ n. a cloth used to wash dishes, dishrag: *Leave the dishcloth to dry on the sink.*

dis·heart·en /dɪsˈhɑrtn/ v. to take away the will to continue, discourage: *A lack of cooperation disheartened him in his effort to find a solution to the problem.*

di·shev·el /dɪˈʃɛvəl/ v. to disorder, (syn.) to muss: *The wind disheveled her hair.*

di·shev·eled /dɪˈʃɛvəld/ adj. to have one's appearance (hair, clothes, etc.) in disorder: *After falling down, he was all disheveled.*

dis·hon·est /dɪsˈɑnɪst/ adj. not honest, untruthful, (syn.) deceitful: *That company is dishonest; it cheats on its taxes.* -adv. **dishonestly.**

dis·hon·es·ty /dɪsˈɑnɪsti/ n. [U] the failure or refusal to be honest or truthful, (syn.) deceit: *The liar is guilty of dishonesty in what he says and does.*

dis·hon·or /dɪsˈɑnər/ v.frml. 1 to cause a loss of honor, bring shame to, (syn.) to disgrace: *The scandal dishonored him in polite society.* 2 to insult, treat without respect: *Burning a nation's flag dishonors its citizens.*
—n. [U] 1 disgrace, public shame: *She brought dishonor on her family by defecting to the enemy.* 2 an insult, lack of respect: *to show dishonor to a nation by burning its flag*

dis·hon·or·a·ble /dɪsˈɑnərəbəl/ adj. disgraceful, shameful, offensive to moral standards: *His stealing money that was entrusted to him was dishonorable.* -adv. **dishonorably.**

dish·pan /ˈdɪʃˌpæn/ n. a pan for washing dishes: *I soaked the dishes in the dishpan, then washed them.*

dish·rag /ˈdɪʃˌræg/ n. See: dishcloth.

dish·tow·el /ˈdɪʃˌtaʊəl/ n. a cloth towel used to dry dishes after washing: *Pass me the dishtowel, so I can dry the dishes.*

dish·ware /ˈdɪʃˌwɛr/ n. [U] dishes in general (plates, bowls, cups, etc.): *We store the dishware in a kitchen cabinet.*

dish·wash·er /ˈdɪʃˌwɑʃər, -ˌwɔ-/ n. 1 a machine used to wash dishes: *Our dishwasher uses a lot of water.* 2 a person whose job is washing dishes: *He's a dishwasher in a Chinese restaurant.*

dish·wa·ter /'dɪʃ,wɔtər, -,wɑt-/ *n.* [U] **1** the water in which dishes were washed: *I poured the dishwater out of the dishpan.* **2** s.t. unpleasant or undesirable, esp. to the taste: *This soup tastes like dishwater.*

dis·il·lu·sion /,dɪsɪ'luʒən/ *v.* to take away (s.o.'s) pleasant belief or faith: *He did not keep his promises and that fact disillusioned her.* -*n.*[C;U] **disillusionment.**

dis·il·lu·sion·ed /,dɪsɪ'luʒənd/ *adj.* unhappy from a loss of belief or faith: *He doesn't vote anymore because he's disillusioned with politics.*

dis·in·clined /,dɪsɪn'klaɪnd/ *adj.* unwilling, reluctant: *She is disinclined to accept the job offer because the pay is too low.*

dis·in·fect /,dɪsɪn'fɛkt/ *v.* to clean by killing germs or bacteria: *He disinfected the bathroom with a germicide.*

dis·in·fec·tant /,dɪsɪn'fɛktənt/ *n.* [C;U] a germ killer: *Hospitals use strong disinfectants to keep the rooms clean.*

dis·in·fla·tion /,dɪsɪn'fleɪʃən/ *n.* [U] a slowing of the increase in prices of goods and services (as contrasted with deflation, which is a drop in prices): *We are in a period of disinflation during this recession.*

dis·in·for·ma·tion /dɪs,ɪnfər'meɪʃən/ *n.* [U] false information spread on purpose, esp. by a government to confuse an enemy: *The military spread disinformation that it was going to attack from the south, when it really planned to attack from the west.*

dis·in·gen·u·ous /,dɪsɪn'dʒɛnyuəs/ *adj.* not open and honest, insincere: *She is disingenuous when she says that she loves him; she doesn't.* -*adv.* **disingenuously.**

dis·in·her·it /,dɪsɪn'hɛrɪt/ *v.* to take away rights of inheritance, remove (s.o.) from one's will so that person gets nothing when one dies: *The old man disinherited his son after years of disagreements and arguments.*

dis·in·te·grate /dɪ'sɪntə,greɪt/ *v.* **-grated, -grating, -grates** to break into small pieces, fall apart: *The papers were so old that they disintegrated when touched.*

dis·in·te·gra·tion /dɪ,sɪntə'greɪʃən/ *n.* [U] a breakdown into small pieces: *Autumn leaves begin a process of disintegration after they fall.*

dis·in·ter /,dɪsɪn'tɜr/ *v.* **-terred, -terring, -ters** to dig up (a body that was buried): *A gravedigger disinterred a body by court order.*

dis·in·ter·est /dɪs'ɪntərɪst, -'ɪntrɪst/ *n.* [U] freedom from self-interest or bias, (*syn.*) impartiality: *Her disinterest in the case means that she can judge it fairly.*

dis·in·ter·est·ed /dɪs'ɪntrəstɪd, -'ɪntə,rɛstɪd/ *adj.* not influenced by the chance of personal gain: *We need a disinterested person to decide what is fair.* -*adv.* **disinterestedly.**

dis·in·vest·ment /,dɪsɪn'vɛstmənt/ *n.* [U] a reduction of capital investment by selling off assets or by not investing further: *A recession is often a period of disinvestment when companies sell assets.*

dis·joint·ed /dɪs'dʒɔɪntɪd/ *adj.fig.* not well connected, awkward: *Feeling confused and embarrassed, he made a disjointed speech (argument, presentation).* -*adv.* **disjointedly.**

dis·junc·tion /dɪs'dʒʌŋkʃən/ *n.* a condition of being disjointed: *A disjunction in computer logic caused the problem.* -*adj.* **disjunctive.**

disk /dɪsk/ *n.* **1** *var. of* disc, a thin flat circular plate: *A computer disk is for data storage and retrieval. See:* diskette. **2** a pad between two bones in the spine: *A slipped disk is causing the pain in her back.*

disk drive *n.* the place (in a computer or compact disc player) where the disk is inserted

disk jockey or **DJ** /'di,dʒeɪ/ *n.* a person who plays recorded music on the radio or in a disco: *Some disk jockeys on the radio talk and tell jokes between songs.*

disk·ette /dɪs'kɛt/ *n.* (in computers) a portable, plastic plate on which computer data is stored and read magnetically: *We use both five- and three-inch diskettes in our computer systems.*

dis·like /dɪs'laɪk/ *v.* **-liked, -liking, -likes** to not like or enjoy: *He dislikes pickles, so he never eats them.*
—*n.* a feeling of not liking: *She has a dislike for fruits and vegetables.*

dis·lo·cate /dɪs'loukeɪt, 'dɪslou,keɪt/ *v.* **-cated, -cating, -cates** to move s.t. out of its normal place: *The skier fell and dislocated a shoulder.*

dis·lo·ca·tion /,dɪslou'keɪʃən/ *n.* [C;U] the movement of s.t. from its normal place: *He suffered a dislocation of his knee in an accident.*

dis·lodge /dɪs'lɑdʒ/ *v.* **-lodged, -lodging, -lodges** to force s.o. or s.t. from its present place: *They tried to dislodge the enemy from its position (a rock from a cliff, a bureaucrat from his job, etc.).*

dis·loy·al /dɪs'lɔɪəl/ *adj.* unfaithful, not loyal: *Giving away secrets is disloyal to one's friends (company, boss, country, etc.).* -*adv.* **disloyally.**

dis·loy·al·ty /dɪs'lɔɪəlti/ *n.* [U] unfaithfulness, lack of loyalty: *Her disloyalty to her friend ended their friendship.*

dis·mal /'dɪzməl/ *adj.* causing sadness or depression, (*syns.*) dreary, gloomy: *Dismal* *weather (rain and fog) brought everyone's spirits down.* -adv. **dismally.**

dis·man·tle /dɪsˈmæntl/ v. **-tled, -tling, -tles** to take apart, break down into pieces: *A mechanic dismantled the engine to replace one part.*

dis·may /dɪsˈmeɪ/ v. to shock and discourage, (syn.) to dishearten: *The loss of his job dismayed him.*

dis·mem·ber /dɪsˈmɛmbər/ v. to cut off the arms and legs (of a human or animal): *The mad killer dismembered his victim with an axe.* -n. [U] **dismemberment.**

dis·miss /dɪsˈmɪs/ v. **1** to send away: *The teacher dismissed the students at the end of class.* **2** [C;U] frml. to end s.o.'s employment: *The company dismissed the employees.* **3** [U] to ignore as unimportant, (syn.) to brush off: *She dismissed the accusation (proposal, idea, etc.) as not worth thinking about.*

dis·miss·al /dɪsˈmɪsəl/ n. **1** [U] end of the school day: *Dismissal is at 3:00 P.M.* **2** frml. [C;U] the end of (s.o.'s) employment: *His dismissal took place yesterday.* **3** [U] rejection as unimportant: *His dismissal of her idea angered her.*

dis·mount /dɪsˈmaʊnt/ v.n. to get off s.t., such as a horse or motorcycle: *The horseman <v.> dismounted and walked to the stable.||It was a graceful <n.> dismount.*

dis·o·be·di·ence /ˌdɪsəˈbidiəns/ n. [U] refusal to follow an order or rule: *Disobedience of orders is a serious offense in the military.* -adj. **disobedient;** -adv. **disobediently.**

dis·o·bey /ˌdɪsəˈbeɪ/ v. to refuse to follow an order, not to do what one is told: *The girl disobeyed her mother and broke the rule.*

dis·or·der /dɪsˈɔrdər/ n. **1** [U] a state of rebellion and confusion: *Mass demonstrations threw the nation into disorder.* **2** [U] lack of order, a mess: *a room in a state of disorder* **3** [C] a sickness or disturbance (of the mind or body): *a stomach disorder*
—v.frml. to disturb, throw into disorder: *The experience disordered her mind.*

dis·or·dered /dɪsˈɔrdərd/ adj. **1** lacking order, messy: *We couldn't understand her disordered presentation.* **2** physically or mentally ill

dis·or·der·ly /dɪsˈɔrdərli/ adj. **1** using violence in public, (syn.) rowdy: *The protesters became disorderly and were arrested.* **2** disorganized, messy: *His disorderly manner of leading a meeting causes confusion.*

disorderly conduct n. [U] (in law) behavior in public that disturbs the peace: *He became drunk and noisy, so the police arrested him for disorderly conduct.*

dis·or·gan·ize /dɪsˈɔrgəˌnaɪz/ v. **-ized, -izing, -izes** to confuse, put out of proper order: *The late airline flight disorganized her plans.*

dis·or·gan·ized /dɪsˈɔrgəˌnaɪzd/ adj. confused, not in order: *She is so disorganized that she can never find anything.*

dis·o·ri·ent /dɪsˈɔriˌɛnt/ v. to confuse, esp. as to where one is and what to do: *A fall disoriented him for a few minutes.*

dis·own /dɪsˈoʊn/ v. **1** to reject all connection with, (syn.) to disinherit: *The woman disowned her two children.* **2** frml. to refuse to accept, deny: *He disowned any responsibility for making a mistake.*

dis·par·age /dɪˈspærɪdʒ/ v. **-aged, -aging, -ages** to speak of (s.o. or s.t.) as having little value or importance, (syn.) to belittle: *He called his opponent a fool and disparaged his abilities.* -n. [U] **disparagement.**

dis·par·ag·ing /dɪˈspærɪdʒɪŋ/ adj. making (s.o. or s.t.) seem of little value or importance, (syns.) belittling, deprecating: *She is too polite to ever make disparaging remarks about another person.*

dis·pa·rate /ˈdɪspərɪt, dɪˈspærɪt/ adj. different, unconnected: *He had no speech prepared, so he only made disparate remarks.*

dis·par·i·ty /dɪˈspærəti/ n. **-ties** a difference or inequality: *There is a disparity between what he says and what he does (between their ages, between their salaries, etc.).*

dis·pas·sion /dɪsˈpæʃən/ n. [U] neutrality, disinterest without emotion: *A judge must consider matters objectively, with dispassion.*

dis·pas·sion·ate /dɪsˈpæʃənɪt/ adj. neutral, calm and fair: *The judge takes a dispassionate attitude toward matters before her.* -adv. **dispassionately.**

dis·patch or **des·patch** /dɪˈspætʃ/ v. **-es 1** to send (s.o. or s.t.): *The Ministry dispatched a message (representative, car, etc.).* **2** frml. to kill quickly: *The injured horse was suffering, so we dispatched it with a shot to the head.*
—n. [also ˈdɪsˌpætʃ] **-es 1** a message or report sent with speed: *An officer brought the general the dispatches from the battlefront.* **2 with dispatch:** with efficiency: *He performs his duties with dispatch by quickly doing what his boss asks.*

dis·patch·er /dɪˈspætʃər/ n. a person who sends and keeps track of people, vehicles, messages, etc.: *She works as a taxi dispatcher, using a radio to tell the taxis where to go.*

dis·pel /dɪˈspɛl/ v. to cause to go away, (syn.) to dissipate: *The wind dispels a fog.||He dispelled her fears by telling her he was faithful to her.*

dis·pen·sa·ble /dɪˈspɛnsəbəl/ adj. **1** not necessary, (syn.) expendable: *We have too much luggage now; let's leave anything that's dispensable at home.* **2** capable of being given out: *dispensable drugs, dispensable candy (from a vending machine)*

dis·pen·sa·ry /dɪˈspɛnsəri/ n. **-ries** a place from which medical supplies are given out: *I went to the hospital dispensary for some bandages.*

dis·pen·sa·tion /ˌdɪspənˈseɪʃən, -pɛn-/ n. [C;U] a right or permit given as an exception to a rule, law, or custom: *The town gave the school a dispensation to allow school buses to park in the no-parking zone.*

dis·pense /dɪˈspɛns/ v. **-pensed, -pensing, -penses** **1** to distribute, give out: *The Red Cross dispensed medical supplies to the refugees.* **2** to administer, deal out: *The judicial system dispenses justice to the people.* **3** *phrasal v. insep.* **to dispense with s.o.** or **s.t.:** to do or manage without, (*syn.*) to eliminate: *The participants in the meeting dispensed with the usual formalities and started negotiating immediately.*

dis·pen·ser /dɪˈspɛnsər/ n. a device used to give out s.t.: *There's a soap dispenser next to the sink.*

dis·per·sal /dɪsˈpɜrsəl/ n. [C;U] **1** giving out, distribution: *She is responsible for the dispersal of funds to each department in the company.* **2** a breaking up and sending or going away: *Police began the dispersal of the crowd around the scene of the accident.*

dis·perse /dɪsˈpɜrs/ v. **-persed, -persing, -perses** **1** to give out, dispense: *The federal government disperses funds to the states.* **2** to break up and send or go away, (*syn.*) to scatter: *The crowd dispersed after the demonstration.*

dis·per·sion /dɪsˈpɜrʒən, -ʃən/ n. **1** [U] flow or movement, esp. in a scientific sense: *The experiment showed the dispersion of particles in a liquid.* **2** [C;U] a breaking up, scattering in different directions: *the dispersion of light into its spectrum of colors* **3** [U] a spread over an area: *He studied the dispersion of plants throughout that region.*

dis·pir·it·ed /dɪˈspɪrɪtɪd/ adj.frml. discouraged, disheartened: *She feels dispirited by the loss of her job.*

dis·place /dɪsˈpleɪs/ v. **-placed, -placing, -places** **1** to remove, take the place of: *The younger executive displaced his boss as department head.* **2** to make a refugee: *The war displaced her and her whole family.* -adj. **displaced;** -n. [U] **displacement**

dis·play /dɪsˈpleɪ/ v. **1** to place in a position to be seen, to show: *The store displays merchandise in glass cases.* **2** to allow to be seen: *He displayed his bad temper by shouting at me.* —n. [C;U] **1** a presentation, showing: *What a beautiful display of clothing in that store window!* **2** a demonstration: *The child's display of bad temper surprised his teacher.*

dis·please /dɪsˈpliz/ v. **-pleased, -pleasing, -pleases** frml. to cause displeasure, (*syns.*) to offend, annoy: *Her little boy's lack of good manners displeased her.*

dis·pleas·ure /dɪsˈplɛʒər/ n. [U] annoyance, irritation: *She showed her displeasure at his bad manners by frowning at him.*

dis·pos·a·ble /dɪˈspoʊzəbəl/ adj. **1** capable of being thrown away after use: *Paper napkins are disposable.* **2 disposable income:** money one is free to spend after taxes are taken out

dis·pos·al /dɪˈspoʊzəl/ n. **1** [U] the throwing away or dumping of: *the disposal of trash* **2 at (s.o.'s) disposal:** available for (s.o's) use: *I was at her disposal whenever she needed my advice.* **3** [C] **garbage disposal:** a small machine attached under a kitchen sink for cutting up food waste as it passes through

dis·pose /dɪˈspoʊz/ v. **-posed, -posing, -poses** **1** to make, be ready for s.t.: *The police were disposed to enter the criminal's house.* **2** *phrasal v. insep.* **to dispose of:** **a.** to throw away, put in a trash container: *After your picnic, please dispose of the trash (garbage, litter, etc.).* **b.** to deal with s.t. and bring to a conclusion: *At the meeting, the committee quickly disposed of the first matter on the agenda.*

dis·posed /dɪˈspoʊzd/ adj.frml. **1** willing: *I think the President is disposed to listen to our idea.* **2 disposed toward:** friendly toward, favoring: *The people in both countries were well disposed toward the peace plan.*

dis·pos·sess /ˌdɪspəˈzɛs/ v.frml. **-es** to force out of a home or land by legal action or by wrongful act: *The court dispossessed the family from their house for not paying their taxes.*

dis·pro·por·tion /ˌdɪsprəˈpɔrʃən/ n. [U] s.t. that is too large or small in relation to s.t. else, (*syn.*) an imbalance: *The price that he wants is in disproportion to the property's value.* -adj. **disproportional.**

dis·pro·por·tion·ate /ˌdɪsprəˈpɔrʃənət/ adj. too large or small compared to s.t. else: *The size of the mirror is disproportionate to that of the dresser, so we should get a smaller one.* -adv. **disproportionately.**

dis·prove /dɪsˈpruv/ v. **-proved, -proving, -proves** to prove that s.t. is untrue (*syn.*) to refute: *The lawyer disproved her opponent's claim, so her client went free.*

dis·put·a·ble /dɪˈspyutəbəl/ adj. questionable, doubtful: *What he says is disputable; I don't believe it.*

dis·pute /dɪˈspyut/ n. **1** an argument, quarrel: *The couple had a dispute over money.* **2** a lawsuit, court case: *The two landowners have a dispute over water rights.||These two <n.> disputants will meet in court.*

—v. **-puted, -puting, -putes** **1** to argue against, quarrel over: *One person disputes what the other says.* **2** to question the truth of:

The two people disputed each other's claims in court.

dis·qual·i·fi·ca·tion /dɪs,kwɑləfə'keɪʃən/ *n.* [C;U] a forcing out of a person or group, such as a sports team, from participation: *When the soccer team suffered a disqualification for breaking the rules, they couldn't play for the rest of the season.*

dis·qual·i·fy /dɪs'kwɑləfaɪ/ *v.* **-fied, -fying, -fies** to take away the right to participate: *The referee disqualified the player after tests showed he had used drugs.*

dis·qui·et /dɪs'kwaɪɪt/ *v.frml.* to make uneasy or anxious: *City life <v.> disquieted the poet, so she returned to the countryside.* *-adj.* **disquieting.**

dis·re·gard /,dɪsrɪ'gɑrd/ *v.* to pay no attention to, (*syn.*) to ignore: *Please disregard my last letter, as I now have new information for you.* —*n.* [U] lack of attention to or care for: *He has complete disregard for the needs of others.*

dis·re·pair /,dɪsrə'pɛr/ *n.* [U] a condition of being broken down and needing to be fixed: *The house has fallen into disrepair with broken windows and a leaky roof.*

dis·rep·u·table /dɪs'rɛpyətəbəl/ *adj.* having a bad reputation, not to be trusted: *She advised us not to do business with that disreputable company.* *-adv.* **disreputably.**

dis·re·pute /,dɪsrə'pyut/ *n.* [U] disgrace, bad reputation: *Dishonest dealings have brought that company into a state of disrepute.||The owner is considered to be dishonest, and he is in disrepute.*

dis·re·spect /,dɪsrə'spɛkt/ *n.* [U] lack of respect, (*syn.*) rudeness: *The customer treated the waiter with disrespect by shouting at him.* *-adj.* **disrespectful;** *-adv.* **disrespectfully.**

dis·robe /dɪs'roub/ *v.* **-robed, -robing, -robes** *frml.* to remove clothing, undress: *The patient disrobed in the doctor's examination room.*

dis·rupt /dɪs'rʌpt/ *v.* **1** to interrupt, cause a break in the flow of: *The storm disrupted our telephone service, so we could not make phone calls for two days.* **2** to cause a disorder in, upset: *A protester disrupted a meeting of the Board of Directors by shouting slogans.* *-n.*[C;U] **disruption.**

dis·rup·tive /dɪs'rʌptɪv/ *adj.* upsetting, disturbing: *The angry young man has a disruptive influence on the work of others.* *-adv.* **disruptively.**

dis·sat·is·fac·tion /dɪs,sætɪs'fækʃən/ *n.* [U] lack of satisfaction, discontent: *There is much dissatisfaction with the low salaries at our company.*

dis·sat·is·fac·to·ry /dɪs,sætɪs'fæktəri/ *adj.frml.* not good enough, unsatisfactory: *Since the student's performance is dissatisfac-*

tory, she received low grades. *-adv.* **dissatisfactorily.**

dis·sat·is·fy /dɪs'sætɪs,faɪ/ *v.* **-fied, -fying, -fies** to displease, discontent: *The violin performance dissatisfied the critical audience.* *-adj.* **dissatisfied; dissatisfying.**

dis·sect /dɪ'sɛkt, daɪ-/ *v.* **1** to cut apart for analysis: *The biology student dissected a frog in the laboratory.* **2** *fig.* to examine s.t. piece by piece with great care: *The lawyer dissected the story told by the witness.* *-n.*[C;U] **dissection.**

dis·sem·ble /dɪ'sɛmbəl/ *v.* **-bled, -bling, -bles** *frml.* to hide the truth, pretend: *He dissembled about his past employment history.*

dis·sem·i·nate /dɪ'sɛmə,neɪt/ *v.* **-nated, -nating, -nates** *frml.* to make known, (*syn.*) to promulgate: *The newspapers disseminate information to the public.* *-n.* [U] **dissemination.**

dis·sen·sion /dɪ'sɛnʃən/ *n.* [C;U] a difference of opinion, esp. resulting in argument: *There was a great deal of noisy dissension among the arguing committee members.*

dis·sent /dɪ'sɛnt/ *v.* **1** to have or give a different opinion: *One member of the Supreme Court dissented from the majority opinion.||She wrote a <adj.> dissenting opinion.* **2** to speak in protest, esp. politically: *Students dissented against the government.* —*n.* [U] opposition, disagreement: *The people rose in dissent over food shortages.* *-n.* **dissenter.**

dis·ser·ta·tion /,dɪsər'teɪʃən/ *n.* a long formal treatment of a subject, esp. one written for a higher university degree: *After years of writing it, her doctoral dissertation was accepted and she received her Ph.D.*

dis·ser·vice /dɪ'sɛrvɪs/ *n.sing.* an action that creates a problem for s.o.: *That company did me a great disservice when they made a mistake that hurt my credit rating.*

dis·si·dence /'dɪsədəns/ *n.* [U] disagreement, opposition: *He started a campaign of political dissidence.*

dis·si·dent /'dɪsədənt/ *n.* one who dissents: *Political dissidents are often put in jail in that country.*

dis·sim·i·lar /dɪs'sɪmələr/ *adj.* different, unlike in some way: *The girls are identical twins, but dissimilar in that one likes sports and the other does not.*

dis·sim·i·lar·i·ty /dɪ,sɪmə'lærəti/ *n.* **-ties** a difference: *The two products are much alike, but they do have dissimilarities.*

dis·si·pate /'dɪsə,peɪt/ *v.* **-pated, -pating, -pates 1** to disappear or to lessen in intensity, (*syn.*) to disperse: *The fog slowly dissipated in the morning sunlight.* **2** to spend or use up carelessly, (*syn.*) to squander: *The dictator dissipated the riches of his country.*

dis·si·pat·ed /ˈdɪsəˌpeɪtɪd/ *adj.* foolish and careless in living only for pleasure: *Her dissipated lifestyle has destroyed her health.* -*n.* **dissipation** /ˌdɪsəˈpeɪʃən/.

dis·so·ci·ate /dɪˈsoʊʃiˌeɪt, -si-/ *v.* **-ated, -ating, -ates** *frml.* to separate, set apart: *The candidate tried to dissociate himself in the minds of the voters from the past failures of his party.* -*n.* [U] **dissociation.**

dis·sol·u·ble /dɪˈsɑlyəbəl/ *adj.* capable of being dissolved: *Aspirin is dissoluble in water.*

dis·so·lute /ˈdɪsəlut/ *adj.* lacking good character and morals, (*syn.*) immoral: *He is dissolute; he cheats on his taxes every year.* -*adv.* **dissolutely.**

dis·so·lu·tion /ˌdɪsəˈluʃən/ *n.* **1** a breaking down into parts or pieces, (*syn.*) disintegration: *Sadly, we watched the dissolution of the government (the team's spirit, the patient's courage, etc.).* **2** [C;U] a formal breaking of an association, group, or contract: *the dissolution of a marriage* **3** [U] immoral behavior, (*syn.*) degeneracy: *Drinking and using drugs, she fell into dissolution.*

dis·solve /dɪˈzɑlv/ *v.* **-solved, -solving, -solves 1** to put s.t., like sugar or powder, into a liquid and make it seem to disappear: *The powder dissolved in water.* **2** to end (an association, group, or contract): *to dissolve a marriage (a formal meeting, business, etc.)* **3** *fig.* to break down emotionally: *He dissolved into tears at the news.*

dis·so·nance /ˈdɪsənəns/ *n.frml.* [U] **1** discord, harsh sound: *I dislike the dissonance in serious modern music.* **2** conflict, lack of agreement: *They ended their marriage because of the dissonance in their relationship.* -*adj.* **dissonant.**

dis·suade /dɪˈsweɪd/ *v.* **-suaded, -suading, -suades** *frml.* to persuade s.o. not to do s.t., (*syn.*) to deter: *My father dissuaded me from taking a job in another city.* -*n.* [U] **dissuasion.**

dis·tance /ˈdɪstəns/ *n.* [C;U] **1** amount of space between two points: *What is the distance between the earth and the moon* (or) *the distance from the earth to the moon?‖The distance between Boston and New York is 250 miles (400 km.).* **2** *sing.* an unfriendly relation, (*syn.*) an aloofness: *There is a distance now between those two friends.* **3 in the distance:** far away: *We saw dark clouds in the distance.* **4 to keep one's distance: a.** to stay away because of safety: *When I'm out walking, I keep my distance from strange dogs.* **b.** to be unfriendly, aloof: *Since our argument, she's kept her distance from me and never even says hello.*

—*v.* **-tanced, -tancing, -tances** to put or keep at a distance: *After he became rich, he distanced himself from old friends.*

dis·tant /ˈdɪstənt/ *adj.* **1** far away: *She's studying the distant stars (the distant past, her distant relatives, etc.).* **2** not friendly, cold: *She used to have a close relationship with her sister, but now they are distant toward each other.* -*adv.* **distantly.**

dis·taste /dɪsˈteɪst/ *n.sing.* [U] a dislike: *He has a distaste for red meat (opera, arguing, etc.).*

dis·taste·ful /dɪsˈteɪstfəl/ *adj.* unpleasant, causing dislike: *I find his loud voice in public to be distasteful.* -*adv.* **distastefully.**

dis·tem·per /dɪsˈtempər/ *n.* [U] a viral disease, esp. suffered by dogs: *Our dog had distemper, but is OK now.*

dis·tend /dɪˈstend/ *v.frml.* to grow large because of pressure inside: *The starving children had <adj.> distended stomachs.* -*n.* [U] **distention.**

dis·till /dɪˈstɪl/ *v.* **1** to make (a liquid) into gas by boiling it and then collecting the condensation, esp. to make alcohol: *Whisky is distilled from grain.* **2** to reduce s.t. to its central or most important quality: *The student distilled the general ideas of the course into a few pages of notes.* -*n.* [C;U] **distillation.**

dis·til·late /ˈdɪstəˌleɪt, -lɪt/ *n.* the product of distillation: *Vodka is a distillate of wheat, corn, or potatoes.*

dis·till·er·y /dɪˈstɪləri/ *n.* **-ies** a business or factory where drinking alcohol, esp. whiskey, is distilled: *They own a whiskey distillery in Scotland.* -*n.* **distiller.**

dis·tinct /dɪˈstɪŋkt/ *adj.* **1** clear, easy to see: *Medical care has made a distinct improvement in his health.* **2** separate, different: *Those two types of birds are quite distinct (from each other).* -*adv.* **distinctly.**

dis·tinc·tion /dɪˈstɪŋkʃən/ *n.* **1** [C;U] a clear difference: *The history teacher made* (or) *drew a distinction between the customs of the past and present.* **2** [U] excellence: *She achieved distinction in the field of history.* **3** *sing.* s.t. that sets s.o. apart, esp. an honor: *She had the distinction of graduating first in her class.*

dis·tinc·tive /dɪˈstɪŋktɪv/ *adj.* different from others, special: *Spices give that dish its distinctive flavor.* -*adv.* **distinctively.**

dis·tin·guish /dɪˈstɪŋwɪʃ/ *v.* **-es 1** to see or understand differences, (*syn.*) to discriminate: *That child cannot distinguish between right and wrong!* **2** to show as different, set apart: *What distinguishes our company from our competitors is our excellent record of customer satisfaction.* **3 to distinguish oneself:** to gain notice, honor, or respect: *He distinguished himself as a leading writer of books.*

D

dis·tin·guished /dɪˈstɪŋgwɪʃt/ *adj.* famous for excellent achievement: *She is a distinguished novelist.*

dis·tort /dɪˈstɔrt/ *v.* **1** to twist, bend out of shape: *Anger distorted his face.* **2** to change so as to make false, (*syn.*) to misrepresent: *He distorts the truth.*

dis·tor·tion /dɪˈstɔrʃən/ *n.* [C;U] a change that makes (s.t.) false, (*syn.*) a misrepresentation: *The story she told was a distortion of the truth.*

dis·tract /dɪˈstrækt/ *v.* to pull (s.o.'s) attention away: *Noise distracts him, so he can't study for exams.*

dis·tract·ed /dɪˈstræktɪd/ *adj.* **1** having one's attention pulled away: *Distracted from her reading by a noise outside, she ran to the window.* **2** very upset or troubled: *The distracted father ran looking for his lost child.* -*adv.* **distractedly.**

dis·trac·tion /dɪˈstrækʃən/ *n.* **1** s.t. that interrupts, a disturbance: *Noise is a distraction when I'm trying to study.* **2** entertainment, pleasing places and events: *He goes to London on business, but finds many pleasant distractions there as well.*

dis·traught /dɪˈstrɔt/ *adj.* very upset, extremely troubled: *She was distraught by the death of her aunt.*

dis·tress /dɪˈstrɛs/ *n.* -**es** [U] **1** emotional pain or suffering: *We could see her distress over the death of her aunt.* **2** difficulty, danger: *That ship is in distress; it is sinking.*
—*v.* to cause emotional pain: *Her aunt's death distressed her deeply.*

dis·trib·ute /dɪˈstrɪbyut/ *v.* -**uted, -uting, -utes** **1** to give out or deal out: *The government distributes free food to the poor.* **2** to spread out, place at separate points: *The population in the desert is distributed over a wide area.*

dis·trib·ut·ing /dɪˈstrɪbyətɪŋ/ *n.* [U] the business and occupation of a distributor, esp. of goods: *He is in distributing; he distributes office supplies.*

dis·tri·bu·tion /ˌdɪstrɪˈbyuʃən/ *n.* **1** [U] a giving or dealing out (of s.t.): *The Red Cross was responsible for the distribution of medical supplies.* **2** [C;U] a supplying of (s.t.), a shipment: *the distribution of goods from a factory* **3** [C;U] spread, placement (over an area): *War brought change in the distribution of population over the country.* -*adj.* **distributive** /dɪˈstrɪbyətɪv/.

dis·trib·u·tor /dɪˈstrɪbyətər/ *n.* **1** a person or business that distributes goods, usu. at wholesale prices: *She is a distributor of cosmetics to stores locally.‖She has her own* <*n.*> *distributorship.* **2** a small device that passes electric current to the spark plugs in an engine

dis·trict /ˈdɪstrɪkt/ *n.* **1** an area of special character: *Wall Street is in the financial district of New York.* **2** an area officially marked for a purpose: *a postal district, a political district*
—*v.* to divide into districts: *The legislature districts the state, and each district elects a representative.*

district attorney *n. abbr.* **D.A.** /ˈdiˈeɪ/ the prosecuting lawyer for a political district or group of districts: *Chicago's district attorney works to send criminals to jail.*

district court *n.* a Federal court in the USA, usu. with power over a wide area: *The case is being tried before a jury in the District Court for the Southern District of New York.*

dis·trust /dɪsˈtrʌst/ *v. sing.* [U] to lack trust in, doubt the honesty, intentions, or ability of: *The two nations (people, relatives, etc.) have distrusted each other for years.*
—*n.sing.* doubt, lack of trust: *Enemies have a distrust for each other.*

dis·trust·ful /dɪsˈtrʌstfəl/ *adj.* doubtful, suspicious: *The two business partners are now distrustful of each other.* -*adv.* **distrustfully.**

dis·turb /dɪˈstɜrb/ *v.* **1** to interrupt: *Bad dreams disturbed her sleep.* **2** to worry, upset: *The bad news disturbed him.*

dis·tur·bance /dɪˈstɜrbəns/ *n.* [C;U] **1** a break in the peace or quiet: *I heard a disturbance in the hallway outside my apartment; two people were arguing.* **2** an interruption: *a disturbance in telephone service*

dis·turbed /dɪˈstɜrbd/ *adj.* **1** worried, upset: *She is disturbed about her mother's poor health.* **2** mentally ill or not normal: *He is emotionally disturbed and needs a doctor's care.*

dis·u·nite /ˌdɪsyuˈnaɪt/ *v.* -**nited, -niting, -nites** **1** to move apart: *The two political parties broke their coalition and disunited.* **2** to break apart: *The country became disunited and fell into a state of disorder and lawlessness.* -*n.* [U] **disunion** /dɪsˈyunyən/.

dis·u·ni·ty /dɪsˈyunɪti/ *n.* [U] lack of agreement or organization, (*syn.*) discord: *The leaders do not agree, so there is disunity in their political party.*

dis·use /dɪsˈyus/ *n.* [U] **1** lack of use: *His leg muscles are weak from disuse.* **2 to fall into disuse:** to gradually stop being used: *I never hear that word anymore, so I guess it has fallen into disuse.*

ditch /dɪtʃ/ *n.* -**es** a long narrow hole dug in the earth, esp. to hold or carry water: *I fell into the ditch that runs by the side of the road.*
—*v.* **1** *infrml.fig.* to throw away quickly: *The thieves ditched the stolen goods, so the police won't find them.* **2** *slang* to suddenly break a relationship with: *She ditched her boyfriend for another man.*

dith·er /'dɪðər/ v. to hesitate in a confused way, delay: *The manager dithered over the decision for days.*
—n.sing. a state of confusion and nervousness: *He is always in a dither about s.t.; he should try to calm down.*

dit·to /'dɪtoʊ/ n. **-tos** *exclam.* **1** [U] an expression of agreement: *"He thinks she's a terrific worker!"—"Ditto!" (meaning that I do, too)* **2** the symbol (") placed under a word (phrase, another symbol, etc.) to indicate that it repeats itself

dit·ty /'dɪti/ n. **-ties** a short song: *We sang little ditties last night.*

di·u·ret·ic /,daɪə'rɛtɪk/ n.adj. a chemical that reduces the water content of the blood and causes an increase in urine: *He uses a diuretic to control his blood pressure.*

di·ur·nal /daɪ'ɜrnəl/ adj.frml. daily: *Sunlight affects the diurnal rhythms of life.* -adv. **diurnally.**

di·va /'divə/ n. a female opera star: *She was a famous diva for many years.*

di·van /dɪ'væn/ n. a sofa: *We sit on the divan and watch television at night.*

dive /daɪv/ v. **dove** /doʊv/, or **dived, diving, dives 1** to jump (into the water) head first: *The swimmer dove into the pool.* **2** to go down sharply: *The plane (submarine, stock market) dove suddenly.* **3** *infrml.* **to dive into:** to begin with energy: *She dives into her work early each morning.*
—n. **1** a headfirst jump into the water: *She made a graceful dive.* **2** a fast downward movement: *a dive in the stock market* **3** *slang* a cheap, not respectable nightclub **4 to take a dive:** (in boxing) to pretend to be knocked out: *The boxer was paid to take a dive.*

div·er /'daɪvər/ n. a person who goes down into deep water or jumps from an airplane: *He is a deep-sea diver* (or) *skydiver.*

di·verge /dɪ'vɜrdʒ, daɪ-/ v. **-verged, -verging, -verges** to separate and go in different directions, esp. in conflict: *The nation was united, then political opinion diverged and several political parties were formed.* -n. **divergence.**

di·ver·gent /dɪ'vɜrdʒənt, daɪ-/ adj. moving apart and differing: *She and I hold divergent opinions.*

di·verse /dɪ'vɜrs, daɪ-/ adj. varied, different from each other: *New York City has a diverse population, including many Asians, African Americans, and Puerto Ricans.*

di·ver·si·fi·ca·tion /dɪ'vɜrsɪfɪ'keɪʃən, daɪ-/ n. [U] a spreading of assets among different investments to lessen the risk by remaining in one or a few: *Many businesses follow a program of diversification to reduce the chance of a big loss.*

di·ver·si·fy /dɪ'vɜrsə,faɪ, daɪ-/ v. **-fied, -fying, -fies 1** to make or become varied: *The college biology department has diversified by adding new courses in biotechnology.* **2** to enter new types of businesses *See:* diversification.

di·ver·sion /dɪ'vɜrʒən, daɪ-/ n. **1** a break from normal activity (esp. work), entertainment: *While on business in Chicago, I went to a football game as a diversion.* **2** an action designed to distract and trick s.o.: *Two men pretended to fight as a diversion while their friend stole wallets from people watching them.*

di·ver·si·ty /dɪ'vɜrsɪti, daɪ-/ n. [U] **-ties 1** variety: *Diversity in one's diet—such as eating vegetables, fruit, fish, and grains—is important for good health.* **2** [U] differences among people in race, ethnic group, religion, etc.: *the diversity of the American people* **3** [C] **a diversity of opinion:** disagreement: *There is a diversity of opinion about what to do.*

di·vert /dɪ'vɜrt, daɪ-/ v. **1** to distract, cause to turn away: *A loud noise diverted everyone's attention from their work.* **2** to direct away, esp. from an intended purpose: *The bookkeeper diverted company funds to his own bank account.* **3** *frml.* to amuse, entertain: *She diverted the child with a game.*

di·vest /dɪ'vɛst, daɪ-/ n. **1** *frml.* to take away (rights or property): *He was divested of all parental rights by the court.* **2 to divest oneself of (assets, investments, etc.):** to sell off: *The corporation divested itself of real-estate holdings.* **3** *frml.* to undress: *The knight divested himself of his armor.*

di·ves·ti·ture /dɪ'vɛstɪtʃər, daɪ-/ n. [U] an instance of selling off an asset: *They advised the divestiture of real-estate holdings.*

di·vide /dɪ'vaɪd/ v. **-vided, -viding, -vides 1** to separate (s.t. into shares): *Divide the candy between the two children.* **2** to separate (into parts), break up: *They have divided the first floor into five rooms.||The huge corporation divided into smaller companies.* **3** to break up, cause to disagree: *Arguments over politics divided the two brothers.* **4** to figure how many times one number contains another: *4 divided by 2 is 2.*
—n. mountains that divide watersheds: *The Rocky Mountains form the Great Divide in North America.*

div·i·dend /'dɪvɪ,dɛnd/ n. **1** money paid to stockholders in a company as a share of company profits: *The board of directors of this company declares a quarterly dividend, then sends out checks.* **2** *infrml.* a benefit or advantage, usu. surprising: *He went there just for a vacation, so meeting his true love was an unexpected dividend.* **3** a number to be divided: *In dividing 20 by 5, the number 20 is the dividend and 5 is the divisor.*

D

di·vid·er /dɪ'vaɪdər/ n. anything used as a separator, esp. as to divide a room into two parts: *The carpenter built a divider to make two rooms out of one.*

di·vine /dɪ'vaɪn/ adj. **1** heavenly, related to a godly force: *Do you believe in a divine power that controls all life?* **2** *fig.* excellent, wonderful: *We attended a divine party last night.* -adv. **divinely.**

—v. -**vined, -vining, -vines 1** to guess, know by intuition: *The wise man divined the truth.* **2** to find (water underground) with a divining rod

—n. *frml.* a Christian minister or priest

divine right n. [U] the belief that a king's right to rule came from God: *The Bourbon kings ruled France by divine right.*

div·ing /'daɪvɪŋ/ n. [U] various (under)water sports: *My friend has gone scuba diving in the Caribbean Sea.*

diving board n. a flat, flexible board used for the fun or sport of springing into water: *Swimmers run onto the diving board and jump into the pool.*

diving suit n. a tough, flexible covering with equipment for breathing used for work and exploration: *The deep-sea diver put on his diving suit.*

diving board

di·vin·ing rod /dɪ'vaɪnɪŋ/ n. a forked stick used to find underground water: *Some people have special talent for finding water with a divining rod.*

di·vin·i·ty /dɪ'vɪnɪti/ n. -**ties 1** a god **2 the Divinity:** God: *Many people pray to the Divinity.*

—adj. related to religion: *She is a divinity student.*

di·vis·i·ble /dɪ'vɪzəbəl/ adj. capable of being divided: *All even numbers, such as four and eight, are divisible by two.*

di·vi·sion /dɪ'vɪʒən/ n. **1** [C] a separation, breaking up (into parts, shares, etc.): *We need to agree on a fair division of labor.* **2** [C] a unit within a larger organization: *The marketing division is the largest unit in this company.* **3** [U] the mathematical operation of dividing one number by another: *An example of division is "4 divided by 2 equals 2."* **4** a large military unit: *an army division of 30,000 men* **5** a separation, esp. through disagreement: *There is a division in the union membership over accepting the new contract.*

di·vi·sive /dɪ'vaɪsɪv/ adj. causing disagreement and division between people: *He spreads false information and is a divisive force among the workers.*

di·vi·sor /dɪ'vaɪzər/ n. a number by which another one is divided: *In 4 divided by 2, the number 2 is the divisor and 4 is the dividend.*

di·vorce /dɪ'vɔrs/ n. [C;U] a legal ending of a marriage: *She sued her husband for divorce.*

—v. -**vorced, -vorcing, -vorces 1** to end a marriage by law: *He divorced his wife.* **2** to separate: *She believes in divorcing her personal life from her life as a businessperson.*

di·vor·cé /dɪ,vɔr'seɪ, -'si/ n. a divorced man: *He became a divorcé last year.*

di·vor·cée /dɪ,vɔr'seɪ, -'si/ n. a divorced woman: *She is a divorcée now.*

di·vulge /dɪ'vʌldʒ/ v. -**vulged, -vulging, -vulges** to tell (s.t. that was secret), (syn.) to disclose: *He divulged his feelings to his closest friend.*

div·vy up /'dɪvi'ʌp/ v. -**vied, -vying, -vies** *infrml.* to divide into shares: *The partners divvied up the profits from the sale.*

Dix·ie /'dɪksi/ n. *infrml.* the southern part of the USA, esp. the Confederate States: *I want to leave New York and go home to Dixie.*

Dix·ie·land jazz /'dɪksi,lænd/ n. [U] a type of jazz with a fast beat: *Dixieland jazz is played all over the country.*

diz·zi·ness /'dɪzinɪs/ n. [U] lightheadedness, a feeling of losing consciousness and balance: *Her high fever caused dizziness and she fell.*

diz·zy /'dɪzi/ adj. -**zier, -ziest 1** lightheaded, faint: *He felt dizzy from the heat (turning in circles, looking down from the top of the building).* **2** *infrml.fig.* foolish, silly: *She changes her mind constantly; she's just a dizzy person.*

diz·zy·ing /'dɪziɪŋ/ adj. highly exciting: *I went on a roller coaster ride and it was a dizzying experience.*

DJ /'di,dʒeɪ/ n. See: disk jockey.

DNA /'diɛn'eɪ/ abbr. of deoxyribonucleic acid, which carries genetic information in the cells of each living thing: *The discovery of DNA won the Nobel Prize for Watson and Crick.*

do /du/ **(1)** aux. verb (**do, does, did** or their negatives **don't, doesn't, didn't) 1** (used to form simple present or past tense questions): *Do they speak English?||Where did he go?||Don't you like this music?* **2** (used so as not to repeat words): *He likes jazz and I do too.||She works in Miami and so does her brother.||I didn't call her and he didn't either.* **3** (used for emphasis, to give another verb more force): *He really does need a haircut.||But I did tell you the truth!*

do (2) v. **did** /dɪd/ **or done** /dʌn/ **or doing, does** /dʌz/ **1** to perform (an action): *The doctors will do everything they can for her.||What should we do?* **2** to perform (a job): *He's doing* the laundry (some painting, the dishes, etc.). **3** to complete (a job): *I did my homework (the cleaning up, what the boss wanted, etc.).* **4** to work at (for a living): *What do you do (for a living)?||He does accounting.* **5** to get along, progress, (*syn.*) to fare: *The patient is doing poorly today.||She has done well as a lawyer (dentist, store owner, etc.).* **6** to be enough, (*syn.*) to suffice: *A small piece of cake will do for me, thanks.* **7** to act or behave: *Do as your teacher tells you.* **8** to produce or act (in a play): *Our college theater group did Othello.* **9** to cover (a distance): *He can do 100 miles (160 km) a day on his bicycle.* **10** to arrange or put in order: *do one's hair, make-up, etc.* **11** *slang* **to do a number on s.o.:** to treat very badly (by cheating, criticizing, beating, etc.): *He came out of the boss's office looking pale and shaken, so the boss must have really done a number on him.* **12** *phrasal v. insep.* **to do away with s.o.** or **s.t.: a.** (s.o.): to kill, murder: *The dictator did away with anyone who opposed him.* **b.** (s.t.): to bring to an end, get rid of: *The new department head plans to do away with weekly meetings.* **13** *phrasal v. insep.* **to do by s.o.:** to treat, deal with: *That company does very well by its customers.* **14** *phrasal v. insep.* **to do for (s.o.** or **s.t.): a.** s.o.: to care for s.o.: *His grandfather is paralyzed, so a nurse does for him.* **b.** s.t.: to be sufficient, acceptable for: *This shirt is old, but it'll do fine for working in the garden today.* **15** *phrasal v. insep.slang* **to do in: a.** to make very tired, (*syn.*) to exhaust: *Shopping all day always does me in.* **b.** to hurt or kill: *She drank too much and that finally did her in.* **16** *slang* **to do one's (own) thing: a.** to do as one pleases: *At the shopping center, we each went off and did our own thing for an hour before we met for lunch.* **b.** to perform s.t. one is good at: *He's a great dancer, so I love to watch him do his thing.* **17** *fig.* **to do or die:** to make a great final effort: *At this point, it's do or die, because either we finish on time or we lose the contract.* **18** *phrasal v. insep.* **to do (s.o.) out of s.t.:** to take away by cheating or (*syn.*) swindling: *When they divided the profits, they did him out of his fair share.* **19** *phrasal v. sep.* **to do s.t. over: a.** to do again, redo (s.t. done badly): *His teacher asked him to do over the problems she had marked.||He did them over.* **b.** to redecorate, redo: *The new vice president had her office done over in blue and white.* **20** *slang* **to do time:** to have to spend time in prison: *He did time for robbing a bank.* **21** *phrasal v. sep.* **to do s.o.** or **s.t. up:** to make more beautiful, decorate: *I want to do up the house for Christmas.||I want to do it up.* **22** *phrasal v. insep.* **to do with s.o.** or **s.t.: a.** to use: *I can do with my money as I please.* **b.** (with **oneself**): to keep busy doing: *The kids don't know what to do with themselves on rainy days.* **23** *phrasal v. insep.* **to do without s.o.** or **s.t.:** to manage or survive without (s.o. or s.t. wanted or needed): *She spends all her money on her sons and does without new clothes.* **24** **to have to do with: a.** to be about, (*syn.*) to concern: *This letter from a customer has to do with the prices of our products.* **b.** to have a connection with: *His influence had nothing (something, a lot, etc.) to do with my getting the job.* **25** *infrml.* **to make do:** to manage (with s.t. that is not enough or not perfect): *I had no umbrella when it rained, so I made do by putting a newspaper over my head. See:* done. **26** *infrml.* **could do with:** want or need: *You look like you could do with a good night's sleep.* **27** *infrml.* **How are you doing?:** How are you? **28** *frml.* **How do you do?:** polite response when so is introduced **29 That will do: a.** Stop!: *That will do, children! No more fighting!* **b.** an expression used to dismiss so: *That will do, thank you; you may go now.*

do (3) *n.* **1** *infrml.* a party: *We're having a big do at our house Saturday night.* **2 do's and don'ts:** rules for behavior: *It takes time to learn the do's and don'ts in a new workplace (culture, classroom, etc.).*

do·a·ble /'duəbəl/ *adj.* possible, capable of being done: *Building a dam across that river will take a great effort, but it is doable.*

doc·ile /'dɑsəl, -ˌaɪl/ *adj.* easy to teach, lead, or command: *Some teachers prefer docile students, but others prefer students with creative minds.* **-n.** [U] **docility** /dɑ'sɪləti/.

dock /dɑk/ *n.* **1** a type of wharf or pier where boats or ships stop for (un)loading or repairs: *We got on our boat at the dock.* **2** the place where a prisoner stays in court: *The accused man stood in the dock.*

—*v.* **1** to approach and then tie a boat to a dock: *We carefully docked our boat.* **2** to attach a space vehicle to another one: *The two spacecraft docked over Africa.||The <n.> docking in space was successful.* **3** to take away money from, usu. as punishment or to force repayment of a debt: *The company docked his pay because he was late to work.*

dock

dock·et /'dɑkɪt/ *n.* a listing (of people, court cases to be called up): *Our case was the third one on the court docket.*

dock·work·er /'dɑk,wɜrkər/ *n.* a person who works on the docks, esp. at loading and unloading ships' cargo: *The dock workers will go on strike tomorrow.*

dock·yard /'dak,yard/ *n.* a business concerned with selling, repairing, and storing boats: *We plan to have our boat stored at the dockyard for the winter.*

doc·tor /'daktər/ *n.* **1** a physician: *I visited the doctor yesterday for a medical examination.* **2** a person with an advanced university degree: *The English professor's name is Dr. Smith.* See: PhD.
—*v.* **1** *infrml.* to treat medically: *Who doctors the players on the team?* **2** to change, esp. to make false, (*syn.*) to tamper with: *The job of the observers was to stop anyone from doctoring the results of the election.*

doc·tor·ate /'daktərɪt/ *n.* an advanced university degree: *She has a doctorate in physics.*

doc·tri·naire /,daktrə'nɛr/ *adj.* keeping stubbornly to a way of thinking (doctrine, idea, etc.), without caring about practical matters: *He is a conservative (liberal, radical, etc.) and quite doctrinaire in his opinions.*

doc·trine /'daktrɪn/ *n.* a statement of beliefs or principles made to guide human behavior or relations between countries: *The Monroe Doctrine of 1823 says that no foreign power may create a colony on the American continents.*

doc·u·ment /'dakyəmənt/ *n.* **1** a paper, such as a formal letter, contract, record, etc.: *The official documents showing who owns land are kept in the courthouse.* **2** a letter, report, etc., created on a computer: *Documents can be stored on diskettes or on the computer's hard drive.*
—*v.* to provide written evidence: *The police documented their case with accounts of the accident by people who saw it.*

doc·u·men·ta·ry /,dakyə'mɛntəri/ *n.* **-ries** a film or television program based on facts and historical records: *We saw a television documentary on the Civil War.*
—*adj.* related to documents: *The police have documentary evidence.*

doc·u·men·ta·tion /,dakyəmɛn'teɪʃən/ *n.* [U] **1** evidence (written documents, tape recordings, photographs, etc.) to prove s.t. is true: *We have documentation in the form of canceled checks to show that we paid the bill.* **2** a record, usu. written, of a business meeting, agreement, or transaction **3** (in computers) a written description of a computer program, made to help s.o. using the program

dod·der /'dadər/ *v.* to move in a shaky way as from old age: *The <adj.> doddering old man almost fell on the stairs.*

dodge /dadʒ/ *v.* **dodged, dodging, dodges 1** to move quickly out of the way: *The boxer dodged the punch.* **2** to avoid (a responsibility): *Politicians dodge hard questions from reporters.*

—*n.infrml.* a trick, (*syn.*) a deception: *That telephone call was an offer for a free vacation, but it was just a dodge to sell me s.t.* -*n.* **dodger.**

dodg·y /'dadʒi/ *adj.Brit.* **-ier, -iest** risky, dangerous: *Hiking in those mountains could be dodgy; be careful!*

do·do /'doʊdoʊ/ *n.* **-does** or **-dos 1** a flightless bird that no longer exists **2** *infrml.fig.* a stupid person: *He's so stupid; he's a dodo.* **3 dead as a dodo bird:** clearly finished, no longer possible: *That building is as dead as a dodo* (or) *dodo bird!*

doe /doʊ/ *n.* **1** a female deer: *Does give birth to fawns.* **2 doe-eyed:** with large beautiful brown eyes: *She is a lovely doe-eyed girl.*

do·er /'duər/ *n.infrml.* s.o. who takes action rather than just talking: *She is a doer; she gets things done.*

does /dʌz/ third person sing., pres. tense of do: *He does carpentry for a living.*

does·n't /'dʌzənt/ *aux. verb, contr.* of does not: *She doesn't like spinach.*

doff /daf, dɔf/ *v.* to take off: *The man doffed his hat to the woman.*

dog /dɔg, dag/ *n.* **1** any of a variety of four-legged meat-eating animals usu. kept as pets or to work (for farmers, police, etc.): *Americans have a saying, "A dog is man's best friend."* **2** *infrml.* a guy: *He won Lotto? What a lucky dog he is!* **3** *infrml.pej.* s.o. who is not good-looking **4 dog days of summer:** very hot summer weather: *August usually brings the dog days of summer.* **5** *infrml.* **to go to the dogs:** to get into bad condition: *No one has taken care of the grass or equipment at our local playground, so it's gone to the dogs.* **6** *fig.* **to let sleeping dogs lie:** to leave things as they are, so as not to start up trouble: *I know we should get her to do more of the work, but I'd rather let sleeping dogs lie.* **7** *infrml.* **top dog:** the winner or person with most power: *In the competition among the salespeople, she came out as top dog.* See: underdog. **8** *fig.* **to teach an old dog new tricks:** to get s.o. to change old ways and habits: *I've tried to show him how much easier his job would be with a computer, but you can't teach an old dog new tricks.* **9** *infrml.* **to work like a dog:** to work hard without rest: *We worked like dogs to finish the job on time.*
—*v.* **dogged, dogging, dogs** to follow closely, (*syn.*) to pursue: *Her new friend dogs her footsteps wherever she goes.*

dog-ear *v.* to turn down the corner of a page in a book: *My favorite paperback books have lots of <adj.> dog-eared pages.*

dog-eat-dog *adj.* fiercely competitive, trying to win with no care for what is fair: *It's a dog-eat-dog world in the printing business now.*

dog·fight /'dɔg,faɪt, 'dag-/ n. **1** a loud, hard fight between dogs: *The owners stopped a dogfight.* **2** *fig.* a fight in the air between warplanes: *In World War II, there were dogfights between German and American aircraft.*

dog·ged /'dɔgɪd, 'dag-/ adj. not giving up easily, (*syns.*) determined, tenacious: *She finished a difficult job because of her dogged devotion to it.* -adv. **doggedly.**

dog·ger·el /'dɔgərəl, 'dag-/ n. [U] bad poetry, usu. with awkward rhymes: *He writes doggerel, not real poetry.*

dog·gie bag or **dog·gy bag** /'dɔgi, 'dagi/ n. a bag to hold and carry away leftover food from a meal at a restaurant: *I couldn't eat all of my meal, so I asked the waiter for a doggie bag.*

dog·gone /'dɔg'gɔn, -'gɑn, 'dag-/ exclam.of annoyance or surprise: *Doggone! I've lost my pen* (or) *my doggone pen!*

dog·house /'dɔg,haʊs, 'dag-/ n. **1** a small house, usu. in a backyard, used for a dog **2** *fig.* **in the doghouse:** to be treated with dislike, usu. because one has done s.t. wrong: *He forgot his wife's birthday and now he's in the doghouse.*

dog·ma /'dɔgmə, 'dag-/ n. [C;U] a statement of belief (principle, custom, etc.) made by an authority that people are supposed to accept without question: *Church dogma has remained unchanged for many, many years.*

dog·mat·ic /dɔg'mætɪk, dag-/ adj. insisting on one's own belief as the only truth, opinionated: *She is dogmatic about there being only one way to win an election.* -adv. **dogmatically; -n.** [U] **dogmatism; dogmatist.**

do·good·er or **do-gooder** /'du,gʊdər/ n. a person who works for the good of others in society but is unrealistic: *She's a do-gooder who thinks she can change the world by doing volunteer work among the poor.*

dog·wood /'dɔg,wʊd, 'dag-/ n. a tree with pink or white flowers: *The dogwoods are lovely in the spring.*

doi·ly /'dɔɪli/ n. **-lies** a small, round, or rectangular pretty cloth: *There is a lace doily under the flower vase on the dinner table.*

do·ings /'duɪŋz/ n.pl. parties and other social events: *There are a lot of doings at school graduation time.*

do-it-yourself adj. requiring planning and work with one's own hands, rather than having s.t. done for you: *Many Americans like do-it-yourself projects, from putting together furniture to repairing their own cars.*

Dol·by System /'doʊlbi/ n. TM a noise filter system that improves recorded sound: *That movie theater has a Dolby System so the audience enjoys better sound quality.*

dol·ce vi·ta /'doʊltʃeɪ'vitɑ/ n.sing. (Italian for) a carefree, pleasure-filled lifestyle: *He dreams about living la dolce vita on the French Riviera.*

dol·drums /'doʊldrəmz/ n.pl. used with a sing. v. **1** an area of the ocean with little or no wind **2** infrml. **in the doldrums:** in low spirits: *Her career is going nowhere and she's feeling depressed; she's in the doldrums.*

dole /doʊl/ v. **doled, doling, doles** to give in small amounts (money, food, clothes): *The boy's mother doles out an allowance to him.* —n. Brit. **on the dole:** receiving money from the government because of being out of work: *He lost his job and now he's on the dole.*

dole·ful /'doʊlfəl/ adj. sad: *She has a doleful expression on her face.* -adv. **dolefully.**

doll /dɑl/ n. **1** a child's toy that looks like a small person or baby: *Many little girls play with dolls.* **2** infrml.fig. a pretty girl or woman: *Your baby is very pretty; she's a doll!*

dol·lar /'dɑlər/ n. **1** the unit of money of the USA, Canada, and Australia: *The price of oil is given in US dollars.* **2 dollars and cents:** thought of only in terms of money: *Her choice of a career was simply a matter of dollars and cents, not one of personal desires.* **3 the almighty dollar: a.** (symbol of) a love of money: *He'll do anything for the almighty dollar.* **b.** (symbol of) financial strength: *Governments try to lower its value, but the almighty dollar stays strong!*

dollar diplomacy n. [U] the use of US foreign aid and other economic support to influence world events: *The USA often uses dollar diplomacy with foreign nations to persuade them to take certain actions.*

dollar sign n. the symbol ($) used to mean the US dollar: *I bought that coat for $100.*

dol·lop /'dɑləp/ n.infrml. a small mass of s.t., such as from a serving spoon: *My father put a dollop of mashed potato on my plate.*

dol·ly /'dɑli/ n. **-lies 1** (used by or with children) a doll: *Do you like to play with your dolly?* **2** a platform on wheels for moving heavy things: *The delivery man wheeled the sofa into the house on a dolly.*

dol·phin /'dɑlfɪn, 'dɔl-/ n. an intelligent ocean mammal that can swim at great speed: *Dolphins are a delight to watch as they perform in an aquarium.*

dolt /doʊlt/ n.infrml. a stupid person: *That guy is a dolt!*

do·main /doʊ'meɪn/ n. **1** a land area controlled by s.o.: *The lion (king, principal, etc.) looks out over his domain.* **2** an area of responsibility or knowledge: *Deciding on accounting procedures is (in) the comptroller's domain.*

dome /doʊm/ *n.* a rounded roof: *The dome on the capitol building in Boston is painted gold.*

do·mes·tic /dəˈmɛstɪk/ *adj.* **1** related to one's home life: *The couple has a happy domestic life.* **2** related to national concerns (not foreign relations): *The President excels at domestic matters.* *-adv.* **domestically.**
—*n.* a person employed as a household servant: *She works as a domestic for a rich family.* *-n.* [U] **domesticity** /ˌdoʊmɛsˈtɪsɪti/.

do·mes·ti·cate /dəˈmɛstɪˌkeɪt/ *v.* to tame (an animal that was wild), esp. for human use or life in a household: *Cats and dogs are <adj.> domesticated animals.*

dom·i·cile /ˈdɑməˌsaɪl, ˈdoʊ-/ *n.frml.* the place where s.o. lives: *He has a house in the country, but his legal domicile is in the city.*

dom·i·nant /ˈdɑmənənt/ *adj.* **1** having greater power, commanding: *She is dominant in her relationship with her younger brother.* **2** holding the most important position or greatest influence: *Football, basketball, and baseball are the dominant sports in the USA.* *-n.* **dominance.**

dom·i·nate /ˈdɑmɪˌneɪt/ *v.* **-nated, -nating, -nates** **1** to have the most important place or greatest influence in: *She is the greatest opera singer in the world; she dominates the field.* **2** to have or use power or command over: *He dominates his company with an iron hand.* *-n.* **domination.**

dom·i·neer /ˌdɑməˈnɪr/ *v.* [U] to force to obey, (*syn.*) to tyrannize: *She is a <adj.> domineering mother whose children are afraid of her.*

do·min·ion /dəˈmɪnyən/ *n.* [U] **1** the right to rule or control: *The King holds dominion over the people of his nation.* **2** [C] a self-governing country within the British Commonwealth: *The Queen pays visits to the Dominions.*

dom·i·no /ˈdɑməˌnoʊ/ *n.* **-noes** or **-nos** a black rectangular game piece with one to six white dots on each half of one surface: *We like to play dominoes during a quiet evening.*

domino

domino effect *n.* a series of events like the fall of one domino causing others to fall after it in a chain reaction: *The closing of a large manufacturing plant led to a domino effect, causing the closure of other businesses dependent on it.*

domino theory *n.* (in politics) the idea that the fall of one government to Communism would cause the fall of others: *The domino theory held that if South Vietnam fell to the Communists, then the rest of Southeast Asia would soon follow.*

don /dɑn/ *v.frml.* **donned, donning, dons** to put on, dress: *She donned a beautiful dress and went to the opera.*

Don Juan /dɑnˈwɑn/ *n.* a great lover, a womanizer: *He loves the ladies; he's a Don Juan.*

do·nate /ˈdoʊneɪt/ *v.* **-nated, -nating, -nates** to give without charge: *She donated blood when the Red Cross held a blood drive.*

do·na·tion /doʊˈneɪʃən/ *n.* a gift, (*syn.*) a contribution: *The company makes donations of its products and also gives money for poor families.*

done /dʌn/ *adj.v.* *past part. of* do **1** finished, completed: *The task is done.* **2** cooked: *My steak is too well done.* **3 done for:** ruined, dying: *He's been shot; he's done for.* **4 done to a turn:** perfectly cooked **5 it isn't done:** it is not socially acceptable: *You can't ask them to invite you; it just isn't done.* **6 (over and) done with:** completely finished: *Don't keep thinking about the game we lost; it's over and done with.*

don·key /ˈdɑŋki, ˈdʌŋ-, ˈdɔŋ-/ *n.* a type of horse, a long-eared animal, also called an ass: *Donkeys are used for transportation and for carrying loads.*

don·or /ˈdoʊnər/ *n.* a person who gives s.t. without charge: *Blood donors visit the hospital to donate (or) give blood.*

do-nothing *adj.* not active or effective: *At work she talks and reads the newspaper; she's a do-nothing employee.*

don't /doʊnt/ *aux. v.,contr. of* do not: *Don't forget to call!*

do·nut /ˈdoʊˌnʌt/ *n. See:* doughnut.

doo·dad /ˈduˌdæd/ *n.infrml.* a small thing of any kind: *He pins little doodads on his hat as souvenirs.*

doo·dle /ˈdudl/ *n.* a casual drawing: *Her school notebook is covered with doodles that look like flowers.*
—*v.* **-dled, -dling, -dles** to draw casually, often while doing s.t. else: *He doodles while he talks on the telephone.*

doo·hick·ey /ˈduˌhɪki/ *n.infrml.* a small thing of any kind, esp. one whose name is forgotten or not known: *My stereo has a doohickey on it that lets me change stations fast.*

doom /dum/ *v.* to send to an unhappy, inescapable end (failure, ruin, destruction, etc.), (*syn.*) to condemn: *Heavy rains and floods doomed the corn harvest to failure.*
—*n.* [C;U] a terrible fate, an unhappy end, esp. death: *A sense of doom to come spread across the land at the start of war.*

doom·say·er /ˈdumˌseɪər/ *n.* a person who expects and often speaks about future troubles and misfortune: *The doomsayers predict that the economy will get worse.*

dooms·day /ˈdumz,deɪ/ n. **1** the end of the world: *According to the Bible, God judges all humans on Doomsday.* **2** a time when an important bad event occurs: *When notice of the plant closing appeared, it was doomsday for the employees.* **3** *infrml.* **till doomsday:** forever: *The memory of that terrible day will be with me till doomsday.*

door /dɔr/ n. **1** a movable panel to permit entrance to or exit from a building, room, vehicle, etc.: *I opened the refrigerator door and took out the milk.* **2 (a number of) doors away/up/down:** (a number of) houses away: *My sister lives in the blue house just three doors down the street.* **3 door-to-door:** from house to house: *Children sometimes sell candy door-to-door to raise money for their school.* **4 next door:** in the next house or apartment: *We have wonderful neighbors next door.* **5 to answer the door:** to go to open the door when s.o. knocks or rings the doorbell **6** *fig.* **to open** or **close the door to:** to make possible or impossible (progress, advances, etc.): *The new trade agreement opens the door to better relations between the two nations.* **7** *infrml.* **to show s.o. the door:** to tell s.o. to leave: *If that troublemaker comes here again, show him the door.* **8 to show s.o. to the door:** to go to the door with a guest who is leaving: *Thank you for coming; let me show you to the door.*

door·bell /ˈdɔr,bɛl/ n. a bell rung to show s.o. is at a door: *I rang the (door)bell and waited for s.o. to come to the door.*

door·knob /ˈdɔr,nɑb/ n. a round handle used to open and close a door: *I turned the doorknob and entered the room.*

door·man /ˈdɔr,mæn/ n. **-men** /-,mɛn/ an apartment-building employee usu. in uniform who opens doors and announces visitors: *The doorman in our building helps me with packages and calls taxis for me.*

door·mat /ˈdɔr,mæt/ n. **1** a small rug placed before a door to catch dirt: *We have "Welcome" written on our doormat.* **2** *infrml.fig.* s.o. who lets himself or herself be treated badly: *When other children hit you or call you names, don't be such a doormat; tell them to stop.*

door·step /ˈdɔr,stɛp/ n. **1** the top step of a staircase, esp. to a house **2** *infrml.fig.* **to arrive on one's doorstep:** to enter one's life unexpectedly, esp. as a new responsibility: *I wasn't looking for a new job; it simply arrived on my doorstep when I was talking to a friend about my skills, and she told me about a great job at her company.*

door·way /ˈdɔr,weɪ/ n. the opening through a door: *The doorway is blocked by a guard.*

dope /doʊp/ n. **1** [U] an illegal drug (cocaine, heroin, marijuana, etc.): *He takes dope; in fact he's on dope now.* **2** [C] *infrml.fig.* a fool, a

stupid person: *I was a dope to forget my luggage at the airport.* **3** *slang* information: *So what's the dope on this new guy?*
—v. **doped, doping, dopes 1** to give drugs to: *His friends doped him by putting dope in his drink.* **2 to be doped** or **doped up:** to be under the influence of narcotics: *She just had surgery and she's doped up from the anesthetic.*

dop·ey /ˈdoʊpi/ adj.infrml. **-ier, -iest 1** half asleep from the influence of drugs: *She is feeling dopey after her surgery.* **2** foolish: *He forgot his luggage; that was a dopey thing to do!*

dorm /dɔrm/ n. short for dormitory

dor·mant /ˈdɔrmənt/ adj. inactive: *In winter, the plants are dormant; then they come to life again in the spring.*

dor·mi·to·ry /ˈdɔrmɪ,tɔri/ or **dorm** /dɔrm/ n. **-ties** a college or university building where students live: *The dormitories can be noisy places to live because many students play loud music.*

dor·sal /ˈdɔrsəl/ adj. related to the back: *We were terrified to see the dorsal fin of a shark coming through the water.*

dos·age /ˈdoʊsɪdʒ/ n. the giving of medicine in doses: *The doctor decided on the dosage for the patient and counted out the pills for the dose. See:* dose, 1.

dose /doʊs/ n. **1** an amount (of medicine): *The doctor prescribed a large dose of 20 pills for the infection* **2** an amount (of s.t. bad) that one receives: *an accidental dose of radiation, a dose of hard luck*

dos·si·er /ˈdɑsi,eɪ, ˈdɔ-/ n. a file containing written information: *Interpol keeps dossiers on well-known criminals.*

dot /dɑt/ n. **1** a small point, mark: *the dot over an "i"* **2** a round figure, either large or small, in a pattern: *She wore a blouse with large polka dots on it.*
—v. **dotted, dotting, dots 1** to mark with a dot or dots: *The writer dotted an "i."*‖*Small towns dot the map in farm country.* **2 to dot the i's and cross the t's:** to finish the details: *We have the general agreement; now it is time to dot the i's and cross the t's.* **3** *infrml.* **on the dot:** exactly on time: *He arrived at 9:00 on the dot.*

dot·age /ˈdoʊtɪdʒ/ n. [U] time of weakness of mind and body because of old age: *The senile woman is in her dotage.*

dote /doʊt/ v. **doted, doting, dotes** to pay too much loving attention to s.o., (syn.) to fawn: *The grandfather doted on his grandson.*

dou·ble /ˈdʌbəl/ v. **-bled, -bling, -bles 1** to make or become two times as much: *She doubled her investment in a year.*‖*In summer the demand for electricity doubles because of air conditioners.* **2** *phrasal v. insep.* **to double as:** to serve in two ways: *She doubles as the*

company's lawyer and tax advisor. **3** *phrasal v.* **to double back:** to turn back in the direction one came from: *The escaped prisoner led police toward the airport, but then doubled back into the city.* **4** *phrasal v. insep.* **to double for:** to look like s.o. else and take their place: *A stand-in is s.o. who looks like an actor in a movie and doubles for him or her at times during the filming.* **5** *phrasal v.* **to double over (in laughter or pain):** to bend over helplessly: *He doubled over with laughter at the joke.* **6** *phrasal v.* **to double up: a.** to share a room with s.o.: *When he went to New York on business, he doubled up at the hotel with another salesman from the company.* **b.** *See:* double over. **7 to see double:** to see two things where there is only one, to have double vision: *She was hit on the head and saw double for a few moments*
—*n.* **1** s.o. who looks like s.o. else: *Without his glasses, he's a double for the President, don't you think?* **2** a hotel room for two people: *We reserved a double at the hotel.* **3** in baseball, a two-base hit **4 doubles:** a game (such as tennis) with two teams of two players each **5 on the double:** very quickly: *The sergeant ordered the soldiers to hurry out on the double.*
—*adj.* **1** two times as much: *I'd like a double order of mashed potatoes.* **2** made for two people: *a double bed, a double room* **3** having two parts: *a double door, a double-barreled shotgun, a word with a double meaning*

double agent *n.* a person who is employed as a spy for one government but in reality works for another: *The head of the secret service was discovered to be a double agent working for the enemy.*

double bass /beɪs/ *n.* **bass** or **basses** a musical instrument, the largest in the violin family: *She plays the double bass with the Chicago Symphony Orchestra.*

double-breasted *adj.* (of a suit or jacket) with one side of the front covering a row of buttons and fastening to a second row of buttons: *The executive wears double-breasted suits.*

double-check *v.* to look carefully at s.t. twice for correctness: *I double-checked the numbers and found no mistakes.*

double chin *n.* a layer of fat from the chin to the throat: *The fat man loves to eat and has a double chin to prove it.*

double-cross *v.infrml.* to betray by agreeing to do s.t. but then not doing it, esp. to cause s.o. harm: *The criminal's partner agreed not to talk to the police, then she did talk; she double-crossed her partner.*

double-dealing *v.* [U] a dishonest act, cheating: *The buyer made a good salary at his com-*

pany, but was taking secret payments from suppliers; he was double-dealing.

double-decker *adj.n.* having two similar layers: *A <adj.> double-decker bus has two levels for passengers.||My house is a <n.> double-decker; I live on the first floor and rent out the second-floor apartment.*

double-digit *adj.* characterized by a number between 10 and 99: *Our company has had a double-digit sales increase this year; it is up 20 percent.*

double-dip *v.* **-dipped, -dipping, -dips** to receive a pension from a company or the government as a retired employee, but continue to work for it and earn more money from it in another position: *The retired military officer works for a civilian branch now as a consultant, so he's double-dipping.* -*n.* **double-dipper.**

double entendre /ˈdʌbəlanˈtandrə/ *n.* (French for) a word or phrase with a double meaning: *His question "Are you free?" sounded to her like a double entendre; she wasn't sure if he was just asking if she had some free time or really asking if she was free to start a relationship with him.*

double entry *n.* **entries** related to double entry bookkeeping: *Our bookkeeper does double entries for each purchase and sale, so that each is entered both as a debit and as a credit.*

double indemnity *n.* [U] an agreement in an insurance policy to pay double if the holder dies accidentally: *I have a double indemnity clause in my life insurance policy.*

double jeopardy *n.* [U] (in law) putting s.o. on trial twice for the same crime: *It is illegal in the USA to put a person in double jeopardy.*

double-jointed *adj.* having joints that allow fingers, arms, or legs to move with unusual flexibility: *She is double-jointed; she can wrap a leg around the back of her neck.*

double negative *n.* the use of two negatives in speaking or writing: *"I don't have no money" contains a double negative.*

USAGE NOTE: Use of the *double negative* is considered incorrect in English.

double-park *v.* to park a vehicle in the street beside another one already parked at the curb: *He double-parked his car, and the police gave him a parking ticket.*

double-space *v.* **-spaced, -spacing, -spaces** to leave two spaces between lines: *The professor expects all student papers to be typed and <adj.> double-spaced.*

double standard *n.* a set of principles or a moral rule used in one case but not in another: *The government will not allow trade with some* *countries because of human rights violations, but it allows trade with others who also violate those rights; that policy is a double standard.*

double talk *n.* [U] talk that seems serious but means nothing, usu. to fool s.o.: *She says that she doesn't have any money, but will pay me soon; all I get is double talk from her.*

doubt /daʊt/ *v.* **1** to be unsure but tend not to believe: *I doubt that interest rates will come down soon.* **2** to question the truth of, disbelieve: *I doubt the newspaper reports.*
—*n.* **1** uncertainty, lack of sureness: *Our doubts about the weather made us cancel the picnic.* **2** disbelief, distrust: *There's a lot of doubt that he's telling the truth.* **3 beyond** or **without (a) doubt:** certainly, without question: *He is without a doubt the best-looking man I've ever seen!* **4 to have one's doubts:** to be doubtful: *I have my doubts about the health of the economy.*

doubt·ful /ˈdaʊtfəl/ *adj.* **1** questionable, causing doubt: *The accuracy of that information is doubtful.* **2** hesitant, distrustful, (*syn.*) skeptical: *She is still doubtful about investing her money with them.*

doubt·ing Thomas /ˈdaʊtɪŋˈtɑməs/ *n.* s.o. who doubts until he or she sees proof: *No one can convince him of anything; he's a doubting Thomas.*

doubt·less /ˈdaʊtlɪs/ *adj.* without doubt, certainly: *She will doubtless keep her promise.* -*adv.* **doubtlessly.**

douche /duʃ/ *v.* **douched, douching, douches** to clean with a spray of liquid: *The nurse douched the surgical wound.*
—*n.* a liquid used by women for personal cleaning: *Women can buy douches at the drugstore.*

dough /doʊ/ *n.* [C;U] **1** a mixture of flour, liquid(s), and other ingredients to be baked: *A baker makes dough for pie crusts (bread, pizza, etc.).* **2** *slang* money, wealth: *He's a guy with a lot of dough.*

dough·nut or **do·nut** /ˈdoʊˌnʌt/ *n.* a small O-shaped cake deep-fried in oil: *This morning we went out for coffee and doughnuts.*

dough·y /ˈdoʊi/ *adj.* **-ier, -iest** like dough, thick and pasty: *The bread was not baked enough; it tasted doughy.*

dour /dʊr, daʊr/ *adj.* unsmiling, (*syns.*) gloomy, sullen: *A man with a dour look on his face lives alone in that house.* -*adv.* **dourly.**

douse /daʊs/ *v.* **doused, dousing, douses 1** to throw water on: *The firemen doused the fire and it went out.* **2** *frml.* to put out (a light or fire): *Please douse the lights.*

dove (1) /dʌv/ *n.* a bird similar to a small pigeon that coos (makes a soft call) and is a sym-

bol of peace and harmony: *The white dove is a symbol of the international peace movement.*

dove (2) /doʊv/ *v. past tense of* dive

dove·tail /ˈdʌvˌteɪl/ *v.* to fit together closely: *The joints of wood in that cabinet dovetail nicely.*

dove

dow·a·ger /ˈdaʊədʒər/ *n.frml.* an older woman usu. with property: *Her husband died and now she is a dowager living in a great big house.*

dow·dy /ˈdaʊdi/ *adj.* **-dier, -diest** poorly dressed in old-fashioned clothes: *Why does that girl wear such dowdy clothes?*

dow·el /ˈdaʊəl/ *n.* a pin or peg usu. of wood: *The cabinet is held together with dowels instead of screws.*

Dow-Jones average /ˈdaʊˈdʒoʊnz/ *n.* a number based on the stock prices of 30 big US companies to show how the New York stock market is performing: *The newscaster said that the Dow-Jones average closed at a new high today.*

down (1) /daʊn/ *adv.* **1** to or toward a lower place or level: *I slipped and fell down.* **2** to a lower level of sound or activity: *Please turn down the TV.||Settle down and go to sleep, children.* **3** in or toward the south: *She goes down to Florida for the winter.* **4** as part payment at the time of buying: *They're selling cars for $199 a month and no money down!*
—*prep.* **1** toward a lower level of: *He went down the stairs.* **2** at a distance along: *The post office is down the street (from here).*
—*adj.* **1** *fig.* in low spirits, depressed: *She's feeling down, so let's try to cheer her up.* **2** lower in amount, reduced: *Sales are down, and the company is in trouble.* **3** (of computers) not working: *Without power, our computer network has been down all day.* **4** completed: *The students are almost finished with their exams, with three down and one to go.* **5 down and out:** with no money or hope: *His alcoholism has left him down and out.* **6 down but not out:** in serious trouble but still with a chance of success: *Our team is behind by two goals, but fighting back hard; we're down but not out.* **7 down in the mouth:** sad, (*syn.*) discouraged: *You're looking down in the mouth; what's wrong?* **8** *infrml.* **to be down on:** to dislike, disapprove of, be impatient with: *Lately she's been down on city life (her job, her old friends, etc.).* **9 to be down to:** left with only (*s.t.* small): *He lost his job and he's down to his last dollar.* **10 to be down with:** sick with: *The boss is at home, down with the flu.*

D

—*v.* **1** to put or bring down: *The hunter downed the deer with one shot.* **2** to drink quickly and completely: *In the morning he downs a glass of juice and runs off to school.*

down (2) *n.* [U] small, soft feathers of a bird: *Some winter jackets are filled with goose down. -adj.* **downy.**

down·cast /'daʊnˌkæst/ *adj.* **1** pointing downward: *with downcast eyes* **2** sad, low in spirits: *The downcast look on her face told me that she had failed the test.*

down·er /'daʊnər/ *n.slang* **1** a tranquilizing drug that slows down the mind, heart, etc.: *He takes downers to relax.* **2** a depressing experience: *That movie about the war was a downer.*

down·fall /'daʊnˌfɔl/ *n.* s.t. that causes a fall from power or a high position: *Her downfall was making too many promises she couldn't keep. -adj.* **downfallen.**

down·grade /'daʊnˌgreɪd/ *v.* **-graded, -grading, -grades** to lower in status (quality, rank, importance): *When it was clear that the patient would live, the hospital downgraded his status from critical to serious.*

down·heart·ed /'daʊn'hɑrtɪd/ *adj.* feeling sad, (*syn.*) discouraged: *After failing the exam, she felt downhearted.*

down·hill /'daʊn'hɪl/ *adv.* **1** in a downward direction: *We walked downhill toward the river.* **2 it's all downhill from here:** from this point, it will all be easier: *We have finished the biggest repairs to our house, so it's all downhill from here.* **3 to go downhill:** to become worse, (*syn.*) to degenerate: *The quality of service is going downhill.*

down-home *adj.* informal, friendly: *She is a big star but still has a down-home personality.*

down·load /'daʊnˌloʊd/ *v.* (in computers) to get computer files on a network or with a modem from a server

down payment *n.* a part payment at the time of buying s.t.: *We made a down payment on the refrigerator and agreed to monthly payments on the rest.*

down·play /'daʊnˌpleɪ/ *v.* to speak of or treat as less important or serious: *To keep us from worrying, he downplayed the dangers of his job.*

down·pour /'daʊnˌpɔr/ *n.* a sudden heavy rain, a cloudburst: *We were caught in a downpour and ran for cover under a tree.*

down·range /'daʊnˈreɪndʒ/ *adv.* located in a gunnery area: *The target is located 500 yards downrange.*

down·right /'daʊnˌraɪt/ *adj.infrml.* completely, wholly: *That idea is downright stupid!*

down·scale *v.* **-scaled, -scaling, -scales** (in business) to lower the quality of products or services: *In order to attract more customers,* the expensive department store decided to downscale.

down·size /'daʊnˌsaɪz/ *v.* **-sized, -sizing, -sizes** to make smaller, esp. a work force or business: *The management downsized (the work force) from 2,700 to 400 employees.*

Down's syndrome /daʊnz/ *n.* a birth defect characterized by lowered intelligence, shortened roundness of body and facial features: *That child with Down's syndrome has a loving relationship with his parents.*

down·stairs /'daʊn'stɛrz/ *adv.* in the direction of or located on floors below: *I walked downstairs to answer the doorbell.*

down·state /'daʊn'steɪt/ *adj.adv.* to or in the southern part of a state: *I moved <adv.> downstate last year; I now live in a <adj.> downstate location.*

down·stream /'daʊn'strim/ *adv.* in the direction of the water's flow, away from a stream's source: *The town is located five miles downstream from here.*

down·swing /'daʊnˌswɪŋ/ *n.* a downward curve, esp. of prices or economic activity: *There was a temporary downswing in stock prices last month.*

down·time /'daʊnˌtaɪm/ *n.* [U] the amount of productive time lost because a person, machine, or activity is forced to be inactive: *Her computer is not reliable, so she has a lot of downtime while it is being repaired.*

down-to-earth *adj.* practical, realistic (in a friendly, informal way): *The banker gives down-to-earth advice to his clients.*

down·town *adj.* /'daʊn'taʊn/ *adv.* /ˌdaʊn'taʊn/ to or in the business center of a city: *Our business moved <adv.> downtown last year; we have an excellent <adj.> downtown location.*

down·trend /'daʊnˌtrɛnd/ *n.* a movement downward seen over time in prices or activity: *The price of copper (stocks, bonds, silver, etc.) is on a downtrend.*

down·trod·den /'daʊnˌtrɑdn/ *adj.* treated badly by people in power, (*syn.*) oppressed: *She dreams of returning home to help the downtrodden people of her country.*
—*n.* [U] **the downtrodden:** oppressed people in general: *The downtrodden of the world must not be forgotten.*

down·turn /'daʊnˌtɜrn/ *n.* the beginning of a downward movement in prices or activity: *There was a downturn in interest rates this week.*

down under *adv.n.infrml.* (in or to) Australia or New Zealand: *He left London and sailed <adv.> down under to breed kangaroos.*

down·ward /'daʊnwərd/ *adv.* toward a lower place: *Prices moved downward.*

down·wind /'daʊn'wɪnd/ *adv.* in the direction that the wind is blowing: *The wind carried the* *smell of the hunter downwind to the deer, who then ran away.*

dow·ry /ˈdaʊri/ *n.* **-ries** in some cultures, money or other valuables brought to a marriage by a woman: *The bride's father could provide only a small dowry.*

dowse /daʊs/ *v. var. of* douse

doy·enne /dɔɪˈɛn, dwɑˈyɛn/ *n.* the oldest leading woman, esp. in a social group: *She is the doyenne of Washington society.* *-n.*(man) **doyen.**

doze /doʊz/ *v.* **dozed, dozing, dozes** to sleep lightly for a short time: *At home, he dozes (off) after dinner for an hour.*

doz·en /ˈdʌzən/ *n.* **1** a group of 12: *I bought a dozen eggs (apples, doughnuts, etc.).* **2 a baker's dozen:** a group of 13

Dr. /ˈdɑktər/ *abbr. of* doctor

drab /dræb/ *adj.* **drabber, drabbest 1** dull brown or gray green: *People in the army often wear olive drab uniforms.* **2** dull in color, uninteresting: *She doesn't like bright colors, so she wears drab clothes.* **3** gloomy, depressing: *He lives in a drab city neighborhood.*

dra·co·ni·an /drəˈkoʊniən/ *adj.* extremely severe or harsh: *The invading army used draconian measures to control the people: they cut off the hands and feet of anyone who opposed them.*

draft /dræft/ *n.* **1** one version of s.t. written: *the first draft of a letter, the final draft of a report* **2** a system of requiring people by law to serve in the military, *(syn.)* conscription: *The army relies on volunteers now, not on the draft.* **3** air currents that chill the body: *This room has a cold draft in it.*
—v. **1** to write a version of s.t.: *I drafted a letter and showed it to my lawyer.* **2** to draw the plans for s.t.: *The architect drafted the blueprints for the building.* **3** to require military service of s.o.: *The government drafted him into the army; he is a <n.> draftee now.*
—adj. (of beer) poured from a barrel or keg: *I'd like a <adj.> draft beer* (or) *a <n.> draft, please.* **2** used for pulling heavy loads: *draft horses -n.* [U] **drafting.**

drafts·man /ˈdræftsmən/ *n.* **-men** /-mən/ a person who draws such things as blueprints: *She works as a draftsman for an architectural firm.*

draft·y /ˈdræfti/ *adj.* **-ier, -iest** with unwanted cool air currents: *Please close the window; this room is too drafty for me!*

drag /dræg/ *v.* **dragged, dragging, drags 1** to pull with difficulty s.t. or s.o. that resists: *I dragged the sofa across the room.‖His wife drags him to the store to buy clothes.* **2** to search or sweep the bottom (of a lake, river, etc.): *They dragged the river for the sunken car.* **3** *phrasal v.* **to drag on:** to continue for

too long: *The meeting dragged on for two hours.* **4 to drag one's feet** or **heels:** to act slowly and unwillingly: *The manager is dragging her heels on announcing the layoffs because she doesn't want to face the workers' anger.* **5** *phrasal v. sep.* **to drag s.t. out:** to make s.t. last too long: *Everyone grew impatient when he dragged out the story with unnecessary details.‖He dragged it out.* **6** *phrasal v. sep.* **to drag s.t. out of s.o.:** to force s.o. to tell s.t.: *She didn't want to talk about the accident, but I dragged the story out of her.*
—n.sing. **1** [U] *infrml.* s.t. that is boring or disliked, a chore: *She hates to shop, so shopping is a drag for her.* **2** [C] s.t. or s.o. that holds s.o. back from advancing or progressing, a burden: *He refused to marry, thinking that a wife would only be a drag on his career.* **3** [C] *slang* a taking in of breath on a cigarette: *Let me have a drag on your cigarette, OK?* **4** *slang* a street or road: *You'll find a lot of stores on the main drag in our town.* **5** *infrml.* **in drag:** (of a man) wearing women's clothes:

drag·net /ˈdrægˌnɛt/ *n.* **1** police checkpoints combined with searches to catch a criminal: *After the murder, the police set up a dragnet to catch the criminal.* **2** a fishnet used by trawlers

drag·on /ˈdrægən/ *n.* **1** a large fierce, imaginary reptile usu. able to fly and breathe fire: *Children's stories sometimes tell of fire-breathing dragons.* **2** s.o. who frightens people by being fierce and severe: *When she's angry, she is a dragon.*

drag queen *n.slang* a male homosexual who wears women's clothes

drag race *n.* a car race from a standstill with the winner being the first one across the finish line: *We went to the drag strip and watched some exciting drag races.*

drain /dreɪn/ *v.* **1** (of a liquid) to pass or flow out: *The water drained slowly out of the sink.* **2** to remove (liquid from s.t.): *The mechanic drained the oil from the engine.* **3** *fig.* (to cause) to pass or flow out, leaving s.o. weakened: *With illness, her strength drained away.‖The constant disagreement between the two men drained all their energy.*
—n. **1** a pipe that carries away liquid waste: *With all the rain, the drains in the streets have overflowed.* **2** s.t. that uses up strength, energy, or resources: *Emergency repairs to my car have been a drain on my bank account.* **3** *infrml.fig.* **to go down the drain:** to be wasted or lost: *We worked for months on that project, and when it was stopped, all that time and effort went down the drain. -adj.* **draining.**

drain·age /ˈdreɪnɪdʒ/ *n.* [U] **1** the system of draining away water, esp. rainfall, from an area: *Our back yard is flooded by heavy rain* *because the drainage is poor.* **2** s.t. that is drained: *drainage from a wound*

drain·pipe /'dreɪn,paɪp/ *n.* a pipe used to carry off waste water and other liquids: *The drainpipe under the sink is leaking and needs repair.*

dram /dræm/ *n.* **1** a small amount of liquid: *I like a dram of whiskey before dinner.* **2** a unit of weight: *There are 16 drams in an ounce.*

dra·ma /'dræmə, 'drɑ-/ *n.* **1** [C] a play, esp. a serious one, for acting on a stage: *Our theater group is producing a drama by Shakespeare.* **2** [U] the writing and performance of plays: *She's studying drama.* **3** [U] an event that excites strong emotion: *Watching the drama of firemen battling the huge fire made many onlookers cry.*

dra·mat·ic /drə'mætɪk/ *adj.* **1** related to drama: *He has written dramatic works for the stage.* **2** related to a high emotional point: *a dramatic scene in a play* **3** making a big impression, *(syn.)* striking: *She wore an amazing dress for a dramatic entrance into the theater.* -*adv.* **dramatically.**

dra·mat·ics /drə'mætɪks/ *n.* [U] **1** the art and practice of presenting plays: *Students who are interested in dramatics can take theater department courses.* **2** behavior or speech that is exaggerated: *Don't pay any attention to his dramatics; he's not really as sick as he says.*

dram·a·tist /'dræmətɪst, 'drɑ-/ *n.* s.o. who writes plays, *(syn.)* a playwright: *Shakespeare was a brilliant dramatist.*

dram·a·ti·za·tion /,dræmətɪ'zeɪʃən, ,drɑ-/ *n.* [C;U] a theatrical presentation (on film, radio, television, etc.) of a real-life situation: *The play is a dramatization of her family's difficult move from Europe to Argentina.*

dram·a·tize /'dræmə,taɪz, 'drɑ-/ *v.* **-tized, -tizing, -tizes** **1** to present as a play: *Their adventures in Africa will be dramatized in a TV series.* **2** to describe in a startling way, exaggerate to impress others: *He dramatizes events as important when they really are not.*

drank /dræŋk/ *v.* past tense of drink

drape /dreɪp/ *n.* **1** the flow of cloth: *The drape of her long dress is beautiful.* **2** *n.pl.infrml.* **drapes:** draperies, curtains: *In the morning we open the window drapes to let the sunlight in.* —*v.* **draped, draping, drapes** to hang s.t. loosely: *He draped his coat over the back of a chair.*

drap·er·y /'dreɪpəri/ *n.* **-ies** [C;U] **1** cloth arranged in loose folds: *The drapery made a beautiful effect behind the display in the store window.* **2** *n.pl.* **draperies:** long heavy curtains: *We have red velvet draperies over the windows in the living room.*

dras·tic /'dræstɪk/ *adj.* sudden, extreme, and severe: *We must take drastic steps to stop the disease.* -*adv.* **drastically.**

drat /dræt/ *exclam.of* annoyance: *Oh, drat, I dropped an egg!*

draw /drɔ/ *v.* **drew** /dru/ or **drawn** /drɔn/, **drawing, draws** **1** to make a picture: *The artist drew a pencil sketch of a boat.* **2** to take out, remove: *He drew a gun from his pocket (a playing card from the deck, $50 from his account, etc.).* **3** to take out (a liquid), *(syn.)* to extract: *The nurse drew blood from the patient for testing.* **4** to take in (air): *He drew a deep breath and announced he was getting married.||The fire died because the chimney drew poorly.* **5** to pull closer: *The woman drew her husband to her for a kiss.* **6** to move steadily: *I was surprised when the police car drew alongside my car.* **7** to attract: *The sidewalk musician drew a crowd to hear him play his violin.* **8 to draw a blank:** to not find or remember s.t.: *I tried to remember her name but drew a blank.* **9 to draw and quarter: a.** to tie s.o.'s hands and feet to four horses that pull the person apart and then cut him or her into four pieces **b.** *fig.* to punish severely: *I am so mad at that man that I'll have him drawn and quartered!* **10** *phrasal v. insep.* **to draw away (from s.o.** or **s.t.): a.** to move back, usu. quickly, *(syn.)* to recoil: *She drew away from the fire.* **b.** to gradually move ahead: *One runner drew away from the rest and went on to win the race.* **11** *phrasal v.* **to draw back: a.** to move back to avoid: *The boy drew back in fear of the snake.* **b.** to refuse to complete or fulfill: *At the last minute, the union drew back from signing the contract.* **12 to draw blood:** to wound with a weapon or with severe criticism: *She spoke so harshly to the boy that she finally drew blood: he cried.* **13** *phrasal v.* **to draw down:** to reduce or use up: *The company is drawing down the money in its checking account.* **14** *phrasal v. insep.* **to draw even with s.o.** or **s.t.:** to move up to the same level or place: *The runner in second place drew even with the leader and then passed her.* **15 to draw fire:** to do s.t. that brings criticism on oneself: *His proposal to close the school drew fire from the community.* **16** *phrasal v. sep.* **to draw near: a.** to move toward: *The frightened girl drew near her mother.||Her mother drew the little girl near.* **b.** to come close (in time), approach: *The deadline for paying taxes is drawing near.* **17 to draw one's own conclusions:** to decide for oneself from the facts given: *He arrives late, leaves early, and his work is full of mistakes, so draw your own conclusions about his future at this job.* **18 to draw s.o. a picture:** to explain in clear detail (usu. said with impatience): *The company is nearly bankrupt, so do I have to draw you a picture about our future there?* **19** *phrasal v. insep.* **to draw on (s.t.):** to use s.t. as a resource, *(syn.)* to rely on s.t.: *She drew on her knowledge of American history to write the*

novel. **20** *phrasal v. sep.* **to draw s.o. out:** to get s.o. to talk by encouraging them: *He's very shy and never speaks about himself, so I was surprised at how well she drew him out.* **21 to draw straws:** to choose s.o. to do s.t. by pulling out straws (matchsticks, slips of paper, etc.), with the person who chooses the longest or shortest one getting the job: *Let's draw straws to see who will have to give the boss the bad news.* **22 to draw the line:** to fix a limit on what one is willing to do: *I'll help her organize her term paper, but there I draw the line; I won't write it for her.* **23** *phrasal v. sep.* **to draw up: a.** to prepare (s.t. written): *The lawyer drew up a contract for the sale of the property.||She drew it up.* **b.** (of a vehicle) to arrive and stop: *A taxi drew up in front of the hotel.* **24** *phrasal v. insep.* **to draw upon s.t.:** to make use of: *The artist drew upon childhood memories in creating his paintings.*
—*n.* **1** a tie in a competition: *The game ended in a draw, with a score of 12 to 12.* **2** the removal of a playing card from a deck: *It was my draw, so I took a card from the deck.* **3** s.t. that attracts customers: *There are four good films at that theater, but the horror movie is the biggest draw.* **4 quick on the draw:** fast with a gun, or quick-witted: *You'll see how intelligent she is when you talk with her: she's really quick on the draw.* **5 the luck of the draw:** a bad or good result determined by chance: *My brother inherited our father's height, while I ended up being short like Mom; it's just the luck of the draw.*

draw·back /'drɔ,bæk/ *n.* s.t. that can create a problem, (*syns.*) a disadvantage, a minus: *The house is far from public transportation, which is a drawback since I don't own a car.*

draw·bridge /'drɔ,brɪdʒ/ *n.* a bridge over a waterway that can be lifted to allow tall ships to pass under it: *We had to stop our car while the drawbridge was being lifted.*

draw·er /drɔr/ *n.* a box-like compartment that slides in and out of a piece of furniture: *The letters are in the top drawer of that desk (filing cabinet, bureau, etc.).*

draw·ers /drɔrz/ *n.pl.infrml.* (men's) underpants: *I can't go to the door; I'm in my drawers!*

draw·ing /'drɔɪŋ/ *n.* **1** a sketch: *The artist did a drawing in pencil of a house.* **2** a random selection to choose a winner: *After the dinner, there was a drawing of names from a barrel to choose winners of prizes.*

drawing board *n.* **1** a flat surface made of wood or other material used to draw sketches, blueprints, etc.: *The designer has a portable drawing board that he works on.* **2 (to go) back to the drawing board:** to remake one's plans after a failed attempt: *The customer re-*

jected our proposal, so it's back to the drawing board to try again.

drawing card *n.* a special attraction that brings an audience to an event: *She is a well-known singer, so her name is a big drawing card.*

drawl /drɔl/ *v.n.* to speak in a slow manner, lengthening words: *He <v.> drawls when he speaks; he speaks with a southern <n.> drawl.*

drawn /drɔn/ *past part. of* draw
—*adj.* looking very tired or worried, (*syn.*) haggard: *She stayed up all night and looked drawn in the morning.*

dread /drɛd/ *v.* to fear (some future event or experience): *I always dread going to the dentist to have a tooth pulled.*
—*n.* [U] a strong fear (of s.t. that is coming in the future): *She is full of dread about moving to a strange city.*

dread·ful /'drɛdfəl/ *adj.* **1** frightening, terrible: *We had a dreadful time driving on the icy roads.* **2** offensive, disgusting: *He is so rude; he's a dreadful man!* -*adv.* **dreadfully.**

dream /drim/ *v.* **dreamed** or **dreamt** /drɛmt/ **1** to experience fantasies while asleep: *I dreamed last night that I was on an ocean voyage.* **2** to imagine and hope for: *She dreams of* (or) *about owning her own business.* **3** to think of, consider: *He would not dream of disappointing his mother.* **4** *phrasal v. sep.* **to dream s.t. away:** to spend time in dreaming: *We dreamed away the afternoon, watching the clouds.||We dreamed it away.* **5** *phrasal v. insep.* **to dream up:** to invent or imagine: *Who dreamed up that crazy idea?*
—*n.* **1** a fantasy experienced while asleep: *The child has bad dreams.* **2** s.t. hoped for, (*syn.*) an aspiration: *She has a dream about being an engineer.* **3** a beautiful person or thing: *They're building their dream house. See:* American Dream; daydream.

dream·boat /'drim,bout/ *n.fig.* a very desirable person: *That pretty woman is his dreamboat.*

dream·er /'drimər/ *n.* a person with unrealistic plans or ideas: *I think he's just a dreamer and will never produce any of the inventions he describes.*

dream·land /'drim,lænd/ *n.fig.* a state of sleep: *Little children go off to dreamland each night.*

dream·y /'drimi/ *adj.* **-ier, -iest** **1** soft and pleasant as in a good dream: *That tropical island has a dreamy atmosphere.* **2** tending to daydream: *Her teacher calls her a dreamy child.*

drear·y /'drɪri/ *adj.* **-ier, -iest** dark and sad, (*syn.*) gloomy: *That old house has such a dreary look.*

dredge /drɛdʒ/ *n.v.* **dredged, dredging, dredges** **1** a large machine or type of ship used to dig up sand, mud, and debris from a harbor, river, etc.: *The <n.> dredge is working in the harbor; it has <v.> dredged sand to increase the depth so ships can pass.* **2** *phrasal v. sep.* **to dredge up s.t.:** to uncover information about the past: *The politician dredged up old scandals to make his opponent look bad.||He dredged them up.*

dregs /drɛgz/ *n.pl.* **1** unwanted material in the bottom of a container of liquid, (*syn.*) sediment: *No one drinks the dregs in a bottle of old wine.* **2** *fig.* s.t. or s.o. undesirable: *Some people think of homeless people on city streets as the dregs of society.*

drench /drɛntʃ/ *v.* **-es** to make completely wet, (*syns.*) to soak, saturate: *The heavy rain drenched our clothes.* **-n. drenching.**

dress /drɛs/ *v.* **-es** **1** to put clothes on, get dressed: *I dressed quickly.||She dresses her twin boys in matching clothes.* **2** to choose and wear clothes: *He always dresses informally.* **3** to clean, treat, and bandage: *The nurse dressed the wound.* **4** to prepare for eating or cooking: *dress a salad, dress a turkey* **5** *phrasal v. sep.* **to dress s.o. down:** to criticize, usu. severely: *The boss dressed down the worker for making a mistake.* **6** **to dress in one's Sunday best:** to put on one's best clothes: *When they go to see their grandfather, they dress in their Sunday best.*
—*n.* **-es** **1** [C] an article of girl's or woman's clothing **2** [U] a style of clothes: *Soldiers parade in military dress.*
—*adj.* **1** (of clothing) formal: *a dress shirt, a dress suit, a dress uniform* **2** *phrasal v.* **to dress up: a.** to put on special, more formal clothes: *She dressed up in her nicest outfit to attend the wedding.* **b.** (usu. of children) to put on adult clothes or costumes for fun: *Little children love dressing up* (or) *playing dress-up.* **c.** to make s.t. prettier or more interesting: *dress up the room, dress up one's story*

dress code *n.* requirements as to how one must dress: *The school dress code requires white blouses and plaid skirts for all girls.*

USAGE NOTE: *Dress codes* in public schools in the USA are not usually very strict. Children can wear any style of clothing, but are not allowed to wear T-shirts with sexual messages, revealing clothing, or clothing associated with gangs. Many private schools, especially religious and military schools, have much stricter dress codes that make children wear uniforms to school.

dress rehearsal *n.* the final practice before a performance: *Actors wear their full costumes and make-up for a dress rehearsal.*

dress·er /'drɛsər/ *n.* **1** a large piece of bedroom furniture for storing clothes: *I keep underwear and sweaters in my dresser.* **2** a person judged on his or her style of dressing: *He is a sharp dresser.*

dresser

dress·ing /'drɛsɪŋ/ *n.* [C] **1** a bandage: *The nurse put a dressing on the wound.* **2** [C;U] sauce for salad: *That restaurant bottles their "house" (own special) salad dressing.* **3** [U] stuffing cooked in chicken, fish, etc.: *dressing for a Thanksgiving turkey*

dressing room *n.* a room or an area for dressing: *The movie star is in her dressing room.*

dress·mak·er /'drɛs,meɪkər/ *n.* a person who makes dresses: *He is a dressmaker to celebrities.*

dress·y /'drɛsi/ *adj.* **-ier, -iest** formal, stylish: *The opening night at the opera is always a dressy occasion.*

drew /dru/ *v. past tense of* draw

drib·ble /'drɪbəl/ *v.* **-bled, -bling, -bles 1** to pour out in small amounts: *The baby dribbled milk from its mouth.* **2** to bounce (a basketball): *The basketball player dribbled the ball down the court.*

dribs and drabs /'drɪbzən'dræbz/ *n.* small, irregular amounts: *The agency gives out news by dribs and drabs, now and then.*

dri·er /'draɪər/ *adj. comparative of* dry
—*n. See:* dryer.

drift /drɪft/ *v.* **1** to float, carried by wind or water currents: *An empty boat drifts with the current.* **2 to catch** or **get the drift:** to understand the meaning in a discussion or other communication: *After a few minutes, I caught the drift of what the speaker was saying.*
—*n.* **1** [C;U] a floating movement: *A high wind is causing a drift in the airplane's course.* **2** [C] snow or sand blown into a pile by the wind: *We had to dig the car out of the snow drift.*

drift·er /'drɪftər/ *n.* a person who moves from place to place without regular work or goals in life: *I hope she doesn't fall in love with that drifter; he'll never hold a good job or stay in one place.*

drift·wood /'drɪft,wʊd/ *n.* [U] logs and other pieces of wood afloat in a body of water: *Boaters must be careful not to hit driftwood in the lake.*

drill /drɪl/ *n.* **1** [C] a tool with a long, sharp metal shaft that turns to bore holes: *a carpenter's drill, a dentist's drill* **2** [C;U] a repetitive practice exercise: *School children do arithmetic drills.*

—*v.* **1** to bore (holes) with a drill: *A carpenter drills holes for screws with an electric drill.* **2** to perform practice exercises: *Soldiers drill with their rifles.* **3 to drill s.t. into s.o.:** to force s.o. to learn s.t. by constant repetition: *The coach drilled into his players the importance of a strong defense.*

drink /drɪŋk/ *n.* **1** an amount of liquid for drinking: *I need a drink of water.* **2** an alcoholic beverage: *She's had too many drinks.*
—*v.* **drank** /dræŋk/ or **drunk** /drʌŋk/, **drinking, drinks 1** to swallow a liquid: *He drinks water with his meals.* **2** to drink alcoholic beverages: *It's dangerous to drink and drive.* **3** *phrasal v. sep.* **to drink s.t. in:** to take s.t. in through the senses: *She drank in all of her grandmother's stories.‖She drank them in.* **4** *phrasal v. insep.* **to drink to s.o.** or **s.t.:** to wish success, good luck, etc. to s.o. or s.t.: *We drank to their new business.*

drink·a·ble /'drɪŋkəbəl/ *adj.* OK to drink, (*syn.*) potable: *Is this drinkable water?*

drink·er /'drɪŋkər/ *n.* a person who drinks alcoholic beverages, usu. too much: *She's a heavy drinker.*

drip /drɪp/ *n.* **1** a series of small drops of liquid or one of these drops: *The kitchen faucet has a drip.* **2** *infrml.fig.* a weak and annoying person, a jerk: *That guy is a drip.*
—*v.* **dripped, dripping, drips** to pour in drips: *The faucet has dripped water for a week now.*
—*adj.* **dripping wet:** completely wet, (*syn.*) saturated: *The dog got soaked in the rain and is dripping wet.*

drip-dry *adj.v.* **-dried, -drying, -dries** wash-and-wear, wearable without ironing: *I washed my <adj.> drip-dry shirt and hung it to dry.*

drive /draɪv/ *v.* **drove** /droʊv/ or **driven** /'drɪvən/**, driving, drives 1** to control and steer (a vehicle): *She's 16 and learning to drive the family car.* **2** to travel or take s.o. in a vehicle: *We drove across the country on vacation.‖He's driving her home.* **3** to force in some direction: *The increase in prices has driven away customers.‖The carpenter drove a nail into the wood with a hammer.* **4** to force into some (bad) state: *His complaints drive me crazy (to drink, out of my mind, etc.).* **5** to cause forcefully, (*syn.*) to compel: *Her parents have driven her to study hard.* **6** to herd: *Cowboys on horseback drove the cattle to market.* **7** *phrasal v. insep.* **to drive at s.t.:** to mean s.t. without openly saying it, (*syn.*) to imply: *I don't understand what you're driving at (when you say that).* **8** *phrasal v. sep.* **drive s.t. home:** to make a point, message, etc. well understood, state forcefully: *The doctor drove home the importance of good nutrition.‖He drove his point home.* **9** *phrasal v. sep.* **to drive s.o.** or **s.t. off: a. s.o.:** to force

away: *The army drove off the attackers.‖It drove them off.* **b. s.t.:** to leave in a vehicle: *They drove off in a hurry.‖They drove the car off.* **10 to drive a hard bargain:** to settle an agreement without giving up anything: *Union members were nervous about the coming contract talks, knowing that management would drive a hard bargain.*
—*n.* **1** [C] a trip in a vehicle: *We went for (or) took a drive into the mountains.* **2** [C] a road or driveway: *a scenic drive* **3** [U] high energy, force of mind and spirit: *He works very hard; he has a lot of drive.‖He's a <adj.> hard-driving man.* **4** [C] a strong instinctive need or urge: *the sex drive* **5** [C] a strong, organized group effort to gain s.t.: *The Red Cross held a blood drive.* **6** [C;U] the means for turning power from an engine into movement: *a car with four-wheeled drive* **7** a herding of animals: *a cattle drive* **8** the part of a computer where a disk goes: *the disk drive*

drive-in *n.* an outdoor movie theater: *We used to go to the drive-in on Saturday nights in the summer.*

driv·el /'drɪvəl/ *n.* [U] nonsense, stupid talk: *What he says is drivel; don't believe him.*

driv·en /'drɪvən/ *v. past part. of* drive
—*adj.* **1** acting on a strong need or desire, (*syn.*) obsessed: *She works seven days a week; she is a driven woman.* **2** *suffix* influenced or dominated by: *The computer business (economy, society, etc.) is innovation-driven (price-driven, cost-driven, etc.).*

driv·er /'draɪvər/ *n.* **1** the person in control of a vehicle: *The driver of the car sits behind the steering wheel.* **2 in the driver's seat:** having the power of decision: *She decides what will be done; she is in the driver's seat.*

drive-up window *n.* a service area of a restaurant, bank, etc., for customers who remain in their cars: *We drove up to the drive-up window at the fast-food restaurant and ordered a meal.*

drive·way /'draɪv,weɪ/ *n.* a paved or unpaved roadway leading to a garage or house: *We parked the car in the driveway and walked into the house.*

driv·ing /'draɪvɪŋ/ *adj.* **1** striking with force: *I can hear the driving rain against the window.* **2** forceful, energetic: *Her driving personality sometimes overpowers people.*

driz·zle /'drɪzəl/ *n.* a light rain: *There is a fine drizzle this morning.*
—*v.* **-zled, -zling, -zles** to rain lightly: *It drizzled all day.*

droll /droʊl/ *adj.* **-er, -est** funny in a mild, odd way: *He makes droll remarks that always make me laugh.* -*n.* **drollery.**

drone /droʊn/ *n.* **1** a low humming sound: *We could hear the drone of a distant plane.* **2** a male honeybee who mates with the queen bee: *Drones gather no honey and do no work.*

—*v.* **droned, droning, drones** to make a sound like a low hum: *The speaker seemed to drone on endlessly.*

drool /drul/ *v.* **1** to let saliva pass from the mouth: *The dog drooled when he smelled his dinner.* **2** *fig.* to show great desire: *That lady drools over the idea of vacationing in Europe.*
—*n.* [U] liquid in the mouth, (*syns.*) saliva, spittle: *The baby has drool on his chin.*

droop /drup/ *v.* to lean over or hang down with tiredness or weakness: *The flowers drooped from lack of water.*
—*n.* a hanging down, (*syn.*) a sag: *The droop of her shoulders told me that her spirits were low.*

drop /drɑp/ *v.* **dropped, dropping, drops** **1** to fall: *Apples drop from trees.* **2** to let fall by mistake: *She dropped her purse on the floor.* **3** to cause to fall: *The plane dropped bombs.* **4** to suddenly stop and leave unfinished: *I dropped what I was doing and ran to help.||This conversation is getting too personal, so please drop it.* **5** *phrasal v. insep.* **to drop by** or **drop in (on s.o.):** to make an informal visit without an appointment: *Drop by whenever you can.* **6** *phrasal v. insep.* **to drop (or) fall behind s.o.** or **s.t.:** to move ahead more slowly than others are moving: *His teacher says he has dropped behind in the class.* **7** *phrasal v.* **to drop out:** to leave or stop taking part in: *She dropped out of the race because of an injury. See:* dropout. **8** *phrasal v.* **to drop off: a.** *infrml.* to fall asleep: *I dropped off on the sofa while watching TV.* **b.** to lessen, decrease: *Sales have dropped off sharply. See:* drop-off, *n.*. **9** *phrasal v. sep* **to drop s.o.** or **s.t. off: a. s.o.:** to take s.o. to a place in a vehicle: *The bus dropped off its passengers in front of the library.||It dropped them off.* **b. s.t.:** to deliver: *We dropped off their order at noon.||We dropped it off.* **10** *infrml.* **to drop s.o. a line:** to write s.o. a note: *I usually drop her a line on her birthday.* **11 to drop dead:** to die suddenly (often used in insults): *He's trying to threaten me, but he can just drop dead.* **12** *fig.* **to drop the ball:** to make a mistake: *He was supposed to set up a meeting, but he dropped the ball and now it's too late.*
—*n.* **1** a very small amount of liquid: *I put a drop of medicine in my eye.* **2** a fall or a sharp movement down: *There was a 20-degree drop in the temperature last night.* **3** a distance down: *There's a 12-foot drop from that window.* **4** a delivery of supplies by parachute: *The plane made a food drop to the refugee camp.* **5** a small candy: *A lemon cough drop eased my sore throat.* **6** *fig.* **(only) a drop in the bucket:** a small unimportant amount: *We*

have saved $1000, but that's only a drop in the bucket because we need $50,000.

drop-in *adj.* without an appointment: *She hurt her hand and went to a drop-in clinic for medical attention.*

drop-let /'drɑplɪt/ *n.* a small drop: *I felt a few droplets of rain on my shoulder.*

drop-off *n.* a sharp descent: *That mountain road is dangerous because of the steep drop-off.*
—*adj.* related to a place where s.t. is left for further transport: *The school is a drop-off point for donations of clothing for refugees.*

drop-out /'drɑp,aʊt/ *n.* a student who leaves school without graduating: *He is a high school (college, trade school) dropout.*

drought /draʊt/ *n.* a time of little or no rainfall: *The farming region is experiencing a two-year drought.*

drove /droʊv/ *v. past tense of* drive
—*n.pl.* **in droves:** in large crowds: *The people lined up in droves to buy tickets to the concert.*

drown /draʊn/ *v.* **1** to die by breathing in water or other liquid: *The swimmer drowned in the lake.* **2** *fig.* to be overpowered or overwhelmed (with work, strong feelings, disorder, etc.): *That company is drowning in debt.* **3 to drown one's sorrows:** to drink alcohol in order to forget one's problems: *She went out to a bar to drown her sorrows.* **4** *phrasal v. sep.* **to drown s.o.** or **s.t. out:** to cover (a sound) by making a louder one: *We turned up the volume on the TV to drown out the sound of the neighbors' arguing.||We drowned it out.*

drown-ing /'draʊnɪŋ/ *n.* [C;U] an act of death by breathing in water or other liquid: *The drowning took place in the swimming pool.*

drowse /draʊz/ *v.* **drowsed, drowsing, drowses** to sleep lightly, (*syn.*) to doze: *The old man is drowsing in his chair.*

drows-y /'draʊzi/ *adj.* **-ier, -iest** feeling the need for sleep, (*syn.*) sleepy: *I'm feeling drowsy, so I'm going to bed.*

drudge /drʌdʒ/ *n.* a person who performs boring, low-level work: *She is a drudge in a large accounting firm.*
—*v.* **drudged, drudging, drudges** to work very hard at boring work: *He drudges away at clerical work all day long.*

drudg-er-y /'drʌdʒəri/ *n.* **-ies** [U] boring, low-level work: *I fasten screws on an assembly line and the work is pure drudgery.*

drug /drʌg/ *n.* **1** a medication: *The doctor gave the patient a new drug.* **2** a narcotic, esp. an illegal one: *Cocaine is a hard drug.* **3 on drugs:** addicted to, or under the influence of, drugs: *She is on drugs for the pain.*
—*v.* **drugged, drugging, drugs** to place under the influence of a drug: *The kidnapper drugged*

his victim to keep her quiet.||*He kept her <adj.> drugged (up).*

drug dealer *n.* a person who buys and sells illegal narcotics: *He is a major drug dealer in North America.*

drug·gist /'drʌgɪst/ *n.* the owner of a drugstore or the pharmacist at a drugstore: *I'm going to ask the pharmacist for her advice about that new medicine.*

drug pusher *n.infrml.* a person who sells illegal drugs, usu. in small amounts: *Police have arrested drug pushers near the school.*

drug·store /'drʌg,stɔr/ *n.* in the USA, a store with a registered pharmacy to sell medicine prescribed by doctors, as well as health and beauty supplies: *She went to the drugstore to fill a prescription and buy some cosmetics.*

drum /drʌm/ *n.* **1** a musical instrument made of a round, hollow vessel with a skin stretched tightly over one or both ends to be struck with a drumstick or by hand: *My brother plays the drums in a band.* **2** a large drum-shaped container: *an oil drum*
—*v.* **drummed, drumming, drums 1** to play the drums: *He drummed loudly.* **2** to create a rhythmic sound: *When she's thinking, she drums her fingers on her desk.* **3** *phrasal v.* **to drum s.t. into s.o.:** to put an idea, etc. into s.o.'s mind by repetition, practice, etc.: *My mother drummed good manners into all her children.* **4** *phrasal v. sep.* **to drum s.t. up:** to get or increase (sales, interest, support, etc.): *We need to drum up some new clients; let's increase advertising.*||*We need to drum them up.*

drum·beat /'drʌm,bit/ *n.* the rhythmic sound of a drum: *The band is playing with a fast drumbeat.*

drum·mer /'drʌmər/ *n.* **1** a person who plays the drums: *the drummer in a band* **2** *infrml.fig.* a sales representative, esp. a traveling salesman: *He is a drummer with a furniture manufacturer.*

drunk /drʌŋk/ *v. past part. of* drink
—*adj.* **-er, -est** under the influence of alcohol, (*syn.*) to be inebriated: *She has had too much to drink; in fact, she's drunk.*
—*n.* a person addicted to alcohol: *He's never sober; he's a drunk. -n.* **drunkard.**

drunk·en /'drʌŋkən/ *adj.* related to drinking too much alcohol: *Our neighbors had a drunken party last night. -adv.* **drunkenly.**

druth·ers /'drʌðərz/ *n.pl.infrml.* **1** preferences **2** **to have one's druthers:** to be free to choose: *If I had my druthers, I'd be at the beach and not at work.*

dry /draɪ/ *adj.* **drier, driest 1** without water or moisture: *I have dry skin in the winter.* **2** amusing but expressed in a serious manner: *You have a dry sense of humor; I never know when you're serious or joking.* **3** where alco-

holic drinks are not permitted, esp. in public places: *In a dry town, stores can't sell alcohol.* **4** (of wine) not sweet or fruity: *dry champagne*
—*v.* **dried, drying, dries 1** to remove moisture from s.t.: *Dry the dishes with a dish towel.* **2** to preserve by drying, (*syn.*) to cure: *Fishermen dry fish in order to eat them at a later time without refrigeration.* **3** *phrasal v. sep.* **to dry (s.o.) out:** (to cause s.o.) to stop drinking alcohol: *He decided to try to dry out his roommates.*||*He tried to dry them out.*

dry-clean *v.* to clean clothes, curtains, etc. by passing a cleaning fluid through them: *The <n.> dry cleaner dry-cleans men's and women's suits without shrinking them.*

dry dock *n.* [C;U] **1** a shipyard where boats can be stored out of the water: *Each autumn, I put my boat in dry dock.* **2** an enclosed area on land in which a boat can be repaired: *My boat is in dry dock now for repairs.*

dry·er /'draɪər/ *n.* any of several electrical devices used to dry (hair, clothes, etc.): *Handheld blow dryers are popular for drying hair.*

dry goods *n.pl.* fabrics, clothing, bedding, and other textile articles: *In the USA, most dry goods stores have been replaced by department stores.*

dry ice *n.* [U] ice made from solid carbon dioxide: *We caught some fish and packed them in dry ice for transport.*

dry measure *n.* [C;U] a system of measurement by volume, not weight, used esp. for vegetables, fruits, and grains: *The USA uses pints, quarts, pecks, and bushels as volumes of dry measure.*

dry·ness /'draɪnɪs/ *n.* [U] a condition without moisture: *The dryness of the soil in this area is a problem for farmers.*

dry rot *n.* [U] a disease that destroys wood: *Dry rot turned the wooden roof beams to powder, and the roof fell in.*

dry run *n.* **1** an experimental test or rehearsal: *We first drove the truck over difficult ground without a load as a dry run.* **2** a military exercise without live ammunition: *The soldiers did a dry run with their new rifles.*

D.T.'s /'di'tiz/ *n. abbr. of* delirium tremens

du·al /'duəl/ *adj.* double, having two parts: *He uses his van for a dual purpose, namely for business and personal use. -n.* [U] **duality** /du'ælɪti/.

dub /dʌb/ *v.* **dubbed, dubbing, dubs 1** to replace the original spoken language of (a film): *The voices in that English film were dubbed into French (Spanish, Chinese, etc.).* **2** to copy a recording, usu. from the original: *The studio dubbed the soundtrack of the film and sold it as a tape.* **3** to name, describe as: *The 1950's were dubbed as the "Age of Anxiety."*

du·bi·ous /'dubiəs/ adj. **1** causing doubt about its value or truth: *She gave a dubious excuse for her absence from class.* **2** having doubts, (syns.) suspicious, skeptical: *I am dubious about what he says. -adv.* **dubiously.**

duch·ess /'dʌʧɪs/ n. **-es** a woman holding a high hereditary rank, or the wife or widow of a duke: *She is the Duchess of Kent.*

duck /dʌk/ n. **1** any of a variety of water birds with short, plump bodies, rounded beaks, and webbed feet: *There are mallard ducks nesting in the pond nearby.* **2 lame duck:** in the USA, a political official soon to leave office: *If he is not re-elected in November, the President will be a lame duck and have little influence during the rest of his term.*
—v. **1** to lower (one's head or body) quickly to avoid being hit by s.t.: *The tall man ducked his head to avoid a low tree branch.* **2** *phrasal v. insep.* **to duck out of s.t.:** to leave hurriedly and unnoticed: *She ducked out the back door before the meeting began.* **3** *phrasal v. insep.* **to duck s.o.:** *infrml.* to avoid contact with s.o.: *I keep trying to make an appointment to see him, but he has been ducking me.*

duck·ling /'dʌklɪŋ/ n. a baby duck: *The ducklings are swimming close to their mother.*

duct /dʌkt/ n. **1** a tube in living things: *Tears pass through tear ducts near the eyes.* **2** in buildings, a tube or passage, esp. for air: *a ventilation duct in the ceiling*

duc·tile /'dʌktəl, -,taɪl/ adj.frml. (of metal) capable of being easily shaped, (syn.) malleable: *Lead and silver are ductile metals.*

dud /dʌd/ n. **1** a bomb or bullet that fails to explode **2** *infrml.fig.* a failure, disappointment: *That lousy play we saw last night was a dud. See:* duds.

dude /dud/ n.infrml. **1** a person from the city not tough enough for cowboy life: *The dudes from New York can't ride horses all day.* **2** *slang* a man, guy: *Ask that dude over there what time it is.*

dude ranch n. **-es** a vacation resort like a ranch where city people can experience an outdoor life, esp. horseback riding: *Every summer, we spend two weeks on a dude ranch in Wyoming.*

duds /dʌdz/ n.pl. *slang* clothes: *I'm going home to change my duds.*

due /du/ adj. **1** required to be finished, submitted, paid, etc. (at the stated time): *The report is due next week.‖The rent is due tomorrow.* **2** expected, scheduled: *The plane is due to arrive at 4:00.* **3 due to:** because of, as a result of: *Her good grades are due to her hard work.* **4** *frml.* **in due time** or **course:** at the proper time: *The boss said to be patient, and I'll get a raise in due time.*
—n. [U] **to give s.o. their due:** to give s.o. what he or she deserves: *I thought he would*

make a mess of it, but to give him his due, he did a good job. *See:* dues.
—adv. **due north (south, east, etc.):** exactly (in the direction given): *We'll fly due west from here.*

du·el /'duəl/ n. **1** in the past, a fight with swords or guns between two men over a question of honor: *The nobleman who had been insulted challenged the other to a duel.* **2** *fig.* a competition or fight between two rivals: *The two companies are fighting a duel to dominate the market.*
—v. **1** to fight a duel: *The noblemen will duel at dawn.* **2** *fig.*to compete, fight: *The companies dueled over market share.*

due process n. [U] (in law) the full use by an individual or institution of the legal system, including the right to a fair hearing and trial: *The right to appeal the decision of a lower court is part of (the) due process (of law).*

dues /duz/ n.pl. **1** the cost of membership in some organizations: *Doctors, lawyers, and teachers pay yearly dues to their professional associations.* **2 to pay one's dues:** to suffer before achieving success and respect: *She paid her dues by singing in smoky nightclubs in small towns before becoming a big star.*

du·et /du'ɛt/ n. music sung by two voices or played by two performers: *The sopranos sang a duet in the opera.*

duff /dʌf/ n. *slang* the buttocks, rear end: *He finally got off his duff and finished the job.*

duf·fel bag /'dʌfəl/ n. a large, heavy cloth bag used for luggage: *Soldiers and athletes use duffel bags to carry their clothes and belongings.*

dug /dʌg/ v. past tense and part. of dig

dug·out /'dʌg,aʊt/ n. **1** a type of canoe made from a log with the passenger area dug or burned out: *Indians fish from dugouts in the lake.* **2** a shelter dug in the ground: *Soldiers crowded into the dugout.* **3** (in baseball) a team's shelter at the side of the field

duke /duk/ n. a man with a high hereditary rank below a prince: *The Duke of Kent waved to the people outside the palace.*

dukes /duks/ n.pl. *slang* the fists, in boxing: *One angry man said to another, "Put up your dukes and defend yourself!"*
—v.slang **to duke it out:** to fight: *The two boys duked it out on the playground.*

dul·cet /'dʌlsɪt/ adj.frml. soft, musical: *Poets write of ladies who speak in dulcet tones.*

dull /dʌl/ adj. **-er, -est 1** not shiny or bright: *I need to polish that dull table top.* **2** not sharp: *a dull knife, a dull pain* **3** boring, tiresome: *That movie (lecture, party, etc.) was very dull.* **4** unintelligent, slow-witted: *He has a dull mind; it takes him a long time to learn new things.*

—*v.* to make less bright or sharp: *Does watching too much TV dull the mind? -n.* **dullard.**

du·ly /'duli/ *adv. frml.* in the correct way, properly: *The prisoner was duly advised of her rights by the arresting police officer.*

dumb /dʌm/ *adj.* **-er, -est** **1** incapable of speaking **2** stupid: *He's too dumb to succeed.*

dumb·bell /'dʌm,bɛl/ *n.* **1** a metal weight used to exercise the muscles **2** *fig.* a stupid person: *That person can't do anything right; what a dumbbell!*

dum-dum /'dʌmdʌm/ *adj. slang* a stupid person, (*syn.*) a dumbbell: *He does stupid things; he's a dum-dum.*

dumb·found /'dʌm,faʊnd/ *v.* to confuse or shock and make speechless, (*syn.*) to bewilder: *She dumbfounds people with her outrageous opinions.*

dumb·struck /'dʌm,strʌk/ *adj.* made speechless: *I am dumbstruck by the crazy things that he says sometimes.*

dumb·wait·er /'dʌm,weɪtər/ *n.* a small elevator for carrying food between a kitchen and a higher floor: *The cook puts food on the dumbwaiter and sends it to the upstairs dining room.*

dum·my /'dʌmi/ *n.* **-mies** **1** a model of a person: *a ventriloquist's dummy, a dressmaker's dummy* **2** *fig.* a stupid person, often used in a friendly way: *That's not the right answer, you dummy!*

dump /dʌmp/ *n.* **1** a place where trash is put: *We put our garbage out by the street for a truck to pick up and take to the town dump.* **2** *fig.* a dirty, messy place: *This apartment (room, house) is a dump!* **3** output of computer data: *I did a dump of our inventory records.* **4** *fig.* **down in the dumps:** sad, depressed: *He failed his exam and is down in the dumps about it.*

—*v.* **1** to drop or unload suddenly or carelessly: *The truck dumped a load of sand in the road.* **2** *infrml.fig.* to suddenly end a personal relationship with: *She dumped her boyfriend for another guy.* **3** to sell (goods) in large quantity at a low price to reduce an oversupply or to win a greater share of the market from competitors: *That company is dumping their products there, trying to secure a place in that market.*

dump truck *n.* a truck that drops its cargo by lifting its rear bed up: *The dump truck poured gravel onto the street.*

dump·ling /'dʌmplɪŋ/ *n.* **1** a ball of mashed food, cooked with soup or served with dessert: *We had chicken dumplings for dinner last night.* **2** *fig.* a term of affection, esp. for a well-fed person: *I'm crazy about my daughter; she's my little dumpling!*

dump·ster /'dʌmpstər/ *n.* a very large container for trash: *We throw our trash into the dumpster behind our apartment building.*

dump·y /'dʌmpi/ *adj.* **-ier, -iest** *infrml.* messy and in poor condition: *What a dumpy place!* **2** (of a person) short and fat: *She has a dumpy figure.*

dunce /dʌns/ *n.* a stupid person: *He's such a dunce, with no brains at all!*

dunce cap *n.* a tall pointed hat that shows the wearer is stupid: *Many years ago, a bad student would have to wear a dunce cap and sit in the corner.*

dune /dun/ *n.* a small hill of sand: *The sand dunes on the desert are formed by the wind.*

dune buggy *n.* **-gies** a car designed to travel on sand: *She loves racing her dune buggy on the beach.*

dung /dʌŋ/ *n.* animal manure, (*syn.*) excrement: *Farmers and gardeners use cow dung to enrich the soil for vegetables.*

dun·ga·rees /,dʌŋgə'riz/ *n.pl.* a type of blue jeans: *Before the 1960's, people wore dungarees.*

dun·geon /'dʌnʤən/ *n.* a prison or cell in the cellar, esp. of a castle: *The king had prisoners thrown into a dungeon for displeasing him.*

dunk /dʌŋk/ *v.* **1** to dip into a liquid: *I like to dunk a doughnut in my coffee.* **2** (in basketball) to drop the ball through the hoop from above: *She's not very tall, but she can jump high enough to dunk the ball.*

—*n.fig.* a swim: *I go for a dunk in hot weather.*

du·o /'duoʊ/ *n.* **duos** a pair of people, usu. musicians: *She and her husband are a singing duo in nightclubs.*

du·o·de·num /,duə'dinəm, du'ɑdnəm/ *n.* the first 10 inches of the small intestine below the stomach: *Liver and pancreatic juices mix with food in the duodenum. -adj.* **duodenal.**

dupe /dup/ *v.* **dupped, duping, dupes** to trick and cheat: *The dishonest bookkeeper duped his victim by making her trust him, then stealing her money.*

—*n.* a person who is tricked: *She was a dupe.*

du·plex /'duplɛks/ *n.* **-es** an apartment or house that has two living quarters: *Our house is a duplex, and we rent the other half to some students.*

—*adj.* having two sections of living quarters: *A duplex apartment has rooms on two floors with an inside connecting staircase.*

du·pli·cate /'duplɪkɪt/ *n.* an exact copy: *I'll make a duplicate of his letter and send it to you.*

—*v.* /'duplɪˌkeɪt/ **-cated, -cating, -cates** **1** to make an exact copy: *I duplicated that letter for him.* **2** to repeat: *I duplicated the original experiment, and it worked. -adj.* **duplicative.** *See:* photocopy.

du·pli·ca·tion /ˌduplɪ'keɪʃən/ n. [C;U] **1** a copy of an original: *The vase is a duplication of a very expensive original.* **2** a repetition: *Her work is an unnecessary duplication of my effort.*

du·plic·i·ty /du'plɪsɪti/ n.frml. [U] actions disguised as friendly, but designed to trick s.o., (syns.) deceit, double-dealing: *He acted with duplicity when he asked for my help only to use my information against me.* -adj. **duplicitous.**

du·ra·ble /'durəbəl/ adj. long-wearing, sturdy: *The soles on those shoes have lasted a year; they are quite durable.* -n.pl. **durables.** See: durable goods;. -n. [U] **durability** /ˌdurə'bɪləti/.

durable goods n.pl. items, such as automobiles and kitchen appliances, that last a long time: *The market for durable goods (or) durables is very, very big.*

du·ra·tion /dʊ'reɪʃən/ n. [U] **1** the time that s.t. continues or exists: *We hope that the business recession (illness, rainy season, etc.) will be of short duration.* **2 for the duration:** for as long as s.t. lasts: *He entered the military at the start of the war and stayed for the duration.*

du·ress /dʊ'rɛs/ n.frml. [U] force or threats used to get s.o.'s cooperation: *She signed a loan agreement with high interest payments under duress.*

dur·ing /'dʊrɪŋ/ prep. **1** for all the time of: *We took shelter in a store during the rainstorm.* **2** at some point (in a period of time): *I hope to see him during the next few days.*

dusk /dʌsk/ n. [U] the period between sunset and night: *It's hard to see at dusk, so I drive carefully.*

dusk·y /'dʌski/ adj. **-ier, -iest** shadowy, rather dark: *Even on sunny days, this room is dusky.*

dust /dʌst/ n. [U] **1** fine dry particles like powder: *There's dust on the bookshelves.* **2 to turn to dust:** to end as nothing, to be ruined: *All of his dreams have turned to dust.*
—v. **1** to remove dust: *I dusted my bookshelves.* **2** to cover with a light coat of s.t.: *The baker dusted the cake with powdered sugar.*

dust·er /'dʌstər/ n. a cloth or brush used to dust s.t.: *I use a feather duster to dust my bookshelves.*

dust jacket or **dust cover**
—n. a paper cover for a hard-cover book that protects and decorates it: *The author's photo is on the dust jacket.*

dust·pan /'dʌst,pæn/ n. a flat pan used when sweeping to pick up dust and refuse: *I emptied the dustpan into a garbage pail.*

dust·y /'dʌsti/ adj. **-ier, -iest** covered with dust: *My clothes are dusty from cleaning my apartment.*

Dutch /dʌtʃ/ n. [U] adj. **to go Dutch:** to go out together socially with each person paying his or her own way: *Whenever they have a date, they always go Dutch.*

du·ti·ful /'dutɪfəl/ adj. devoted to fulfilling one's responsibilities, (syn.) diligent: *He is a dutiful son to his parents.* -adv. **dutifully.**

du·ty /ˌduti/ n. **-ties 1** [C;U] responsibility, obligation: *Her duty is to see that the business runs well.* **2** [U] special service: *jury duty, military duty* **3** [C;U] a tax, esp. on imported goods See: duty-free. **4 on** or **off duty:** working or not working (in a position of responsibility): *A police officer usually wears a uniform when on duty.*

duty-free adj. not requiring payment of duty fees: *Perfume, if bought at the airport for an international flight, is duty-free.*

dwarf /dwɔrf/ n. **dwarfs** or **dwarves** /dwɔrvz/ a small person with dwarfism: *"Snow White and the Seven Dwarfs" is a classic movie.*
—v. to make s.t. seem small by comparison: *The World Trade Center dwarfs even the tall buildings around it.*

dwarf·ism /'dwɔr,fɪzəm/ n. [U] smallness in size in humans due to abnormal development before birth: *Not all short people suffer from dwarfism.*

dwell /dwɛl/ v. **dwelt** /dwɛlt/ or **dwelled, dwelling, dwells 1** frml. to live, (syn.) to reside: *The princess dwells in a castle.* **2 to dwell on:** to continue thinking or speaking about: *The professor dwelt on the topic too long.*

dwell·ing /'dwɛlɪŋ/ n.litr. a place where people live: *She lives in an old dwelling on the edge of town.*

dwelt /dwɛlt/ v. past tense & past part. of dwell

dwin·dle /'dwɪndl/ v. **-dled, -dling, -dles** to lessen in number or intensity: *By the end of the boring football game, the crowd had dwindled to a few fans.*

dye /daɪ/ n. [C;U] a solution used to color cloth or hair: *He used a blue dye to color the curtains.*
—v. **dyed, dyeing, dyes** to color with dye: *She dyes her hair red.* -n. [U] **dyestuff.**

dyed-in-the-wool adj. **1** dyed before being made into cloth **2** fig. completely, deeply: *He is a dyed-in-the-wool-conservative.*

dy·ing /'daɪɪŋ/ v. pres. part. of die

dyke /daɪk/ n. pej. a lesbian

dy·nam·ic /daɪ'næmɪk/ adj. energetic, very active: *She is a dynamic executive and will bring lots of energy and ideas to our company.* -adv. **dynamically.**

dy·nam·ics /daɪ'næmɪks/ n.pl. **1** the study of force and motion **2** the factors that shape a personal relationship: *Their love and devotion are the key dynamics in their marriage.*

dy·nam·ism /'daɪnə,mɪzəm/ n. [U] (in a person) high energy and activity: *He is full of dynamism, on the go all day long.*

dy·na·mite /'daɪnə,maɪt/ n. [U] an explosive: *a stick of dynamite*
—*adj. infrml. fig.* wonderful, excellent: *She is a dynamite rock star.*
—*v.* **-mited, -miting, -mites** to blow up with dynamite: *They dynamited the bridge and completely destroyed it.*

dy·na·mo /'daɪnə,moʊ/ n. **-mos 1** an electrical generator **2** *infrml.fig.* a forceful and very energetic person: *He teaches gymnastics and is a dynamo at work.*

dy·nas·ty /'daɪnəsti/ n. **-ties** a series of family members who hold power in politics or business: *The Kennedys have a dynasty in American politics.*

dys·en·ter·y /'dɪsən,tɛri/ n. [U] any of several intestinal infections marked by diarrhea, cramps, and weakness: *I suffered from dysentery when traveling because I drank unclean water.*

dys·func·tion /dɪs'fʌŋkʃən/ n. [U] imperfect or abnormal functioning (of a system, a body part, etc.): *The doctor is treating her for a dysfunction of the kidneys. -adj.* **dysfunctional.**

USAGE NOTE: A *dysfunctional family* is a family with serious emotional problems. The problems are often caused by alcoholism, drug abuse, or violence in the family.

dys·lex·i·a /dɪs'lɛksia/ n. [U] a reading difficulty: *He has a learning disability called dyslexia. -adj.* **dyslexic.**

dys·pep·sia /dɪs'pɛpsia/ n. [U] indigestion: *She suffered from dyspepsia and had trouble digesting her food. -n. adj.* **dyspeptic.**

D

E,e

E, e /i/ *n.* **E's, e's** or **Es, es** the fifth letter of the English alphabet

each /itʃ/ *adv.* for one, per piece: *Those toys cost $1.00 each.*
—*adj.* every: *Each toy is a different color.*
—*pron.* every one: *Each of the toys has a different shape. See:* each other, every, all.

USAGE NOTE: Always use a singular verb with *each* because it refers to one of a group of things or people: *Each of the students has to meet with the teacher.||Each of the cars is blue.*

---

each other *pron.* an expression showing that each one in a pair or group (of people, animals, or things) does s.t. to the other one(s): *The two friends smiled at each other.||The puppies all chased each other.*

ea·ger /'igər/ *adj.* full of desire or interest, (*syn.*) enthusiastic: *We are eager to go on our vacation.* -*adv.* **eagerly;** -*n.* **eagerness.**

eager beaver *n.infrml.* an enthusiastic person, esp. a hard worker who wants a better job, salary, and life: *She works 12-hour days; she is a real eager beaver.*

ea·gle /'igəl/ *n.* **1** a large strong bird that kills smaller animals for food and can be found in the wilderness areas of North America and elsewhere: *The symbol of the USA is the bald eagle.* **2** (in golf) two strokes less than par on any hole

eagle

eagle-eyed *adj.* having excellent eyesight: *That hunter is eagle-eyed; he can see animals a mile away.*

ear /ɪr/ *n.* **1** one of the two organs for hearing and balance, located on either side of the head: *Rabbits have big ears.* **2 ear of corn:** corn on the cob, the part of the corn plant that holds the kernels of corn together: *At American barbecues, people eat hamburgers, hot dogs, and ears of corn with butter.* **3 to be all ears:** to be eager to hear news or gossip: *My friend was all ears when I told her about my new boyfriend.*

4 to go in one ear and out the other: for s.o.'s words or instructions to be heard but ignored or disregarded: *She tells her children what to do, but it goes in one ear and out the other.* **5 to have a good** or **tin ear:** to have good or poor ability to understand sounds: *He has a good ear for music.* **6 to have an ear to the ground:** to be aware of what is going on: *He knows all the latest news; he always has his ear to the ground.* **7 to lend an ear:** to listen carefully to s.o. **8 to play by ear:** to play (an instrument) without following written music **9 to play it by ear:** to react as events happen without planning: *We can't plan for this meeting, so let's just go and play it by ear.* **10 to turn a deaf ear:** not to listen: *When I tell him to stop drinking, he turns a deaf ear to me.* **11** *infrml.* **up to one's ears:** having too much work or trouble: *She's up to her ears in work.*

ear·ache /'ɪr,eɪk/ *n.* a pain inside the ear

ear·drum /'ɪr,drʌm/ *n.* the part inside the ear that moves so that one can hear sound

ear·ful /'ɪrfʊl/ *n.sing.* **to get** or **be an earful:** to hear complaints, criticism, or gossip: *The boss was angry with me; I really got an earful when she criticized me.*

earl /ɜrl/ *n.* a British rank of nobility: *the Earl of Somerset*

ear·lobe /'ɪr,loʊb/ *n.* the soft lower part of the outer ear where some people hang earrings

ear·ly /'ɜrli/ *adv.* **-lier, -liest 1** at the beginning: *early in the morning||early in the program* **2** before the expected time: *The plane landed 15 minutes early.*
—*adj.* **-ier, -iest 1** happening before the expected time: *I was early for my appointment.* **2** happening toward the beginning of a period of time: *Early morning is a good time to exercise.* **3** happening far back in time: *Early civilizations discovered fire.*

early bird *n.fig.* **1** s.o. who gets up early or arrives early: *She is at work before the others; she's an early bird.* **2 The early bird catches the worm.:** the person who is early is usu. rewarded and has an advantage over other people

ear·mark /'ɪr,mɑrk/ n.fig. the sign of s.o.'s work or quality: *That music has the earmark of excellence on it.*
—v.fig. to set aside or reserve for a special purpose: *The city has earmarked funds for street repairs.*

ear·muffs /'ɪr,mʌfs/ n.pl. coverings placed over the ears to keep them warm in cold weather: *He wears earmuffs in winter. See:* hat, scarf.

earmuffs

earn /ɜrn/ v. **1** to get (money) by working: *She earns her living as a doctor.* **2** to get s.t. one deserves as the result of action or effort, (syn.) to merit: *She earned highest honors at school.* **3** to produce, esp. on an investment: *His savings account earns 8 percent interest per year. See:* salary, invest.

ear·nest /'ɜrnɪst/ adj. **1** eager to do right, (syn.) sincere: *She is earnest in her desire to help the poor.* **2 in earnest:** seriously, intensively: *They began to work in earnest when the boss arrived.* -adv. **earnestly;** -n. **earnestness.**

earn·ings /'ɜrnɪŋz/ n.pl. wages, salary, or income from work or investments: *Our earnings are taxed at the rate of 30 percent.*

ear·phone /'ɪr,foʊn/ n. a device placed over or in the ear to provide sound: *I use earphones to listen to tapes on my Sony Walkman™.*

ear·plug /'ɪr,plʌg/ n. a small object placed in the ears to keep out water or sound: *She wears earplugs when she swims.*

ear·ring /'ɪrɪŋ/ n. jewelry worn on or hanging from the earlobe: *She wore silver earrings along with a silver necklace.*

ear·shot /'ɪr,ʃɑt/ n. [U] the normal distance at which a human can hear sounds: *I called to him, but he could not hear me because he was out of earshot.*

ear·split·ting /'ɪr,splɪtɪŋ/ adj. extremely loud, so loud as to cause pain: *The rock music was earsplitting and gave me a headache.*

earth /ɜrθ/ n.sing. **1 Earth** or **earth:** the planet we live on: *Earth is the third planet from the sun.* **2** the land masses surrounded by oceans: *Plants grow in the oceans and on the earth of our planet.* **3** [U] soil, the surface layer: *The workers dug a hole in the earth.* **4 down to earth:** honest and simple in personality and behavior: *She is really down to earth; she says what she thinks.* **5** exclam. **Why (What, Who, How, etc.) on earth?:** Why (what, who, how), of all possible choices: *Why on earth did you say a stupid thing like that!‖What on earth were you thinking?*

USAGE NOTE: In formal writing, esp. in astronomy or geology, *Earth* is often spelled with a

capital *E* to note that it is the planet Earth.

earth·bound /'ɜrθ,baʊnd/ adj. restricted to stay on earth: *The ostrich is an earthbound bird that cannot fly at all.*

earth·en /'ɜrθən/ adj. made of earth or clay: *She makes earthen jars in her pottery class.*

earth·ling /'ɜrθlɪŋ/ n. s.o. who lives on the planet Earth: *Earthlings are trying to explore outer space.*

earth·ly /'ɜrθli/ adj. **1** related to everyday concerns on Earth, not heavenly: *Most people worry about earthly concerns such as earning a living.* **2** (used in questions and negative statements) possible: *It does no earthly good to complain! See:* heavenly.

earth·quake /'ɜrθ,kweɪk/ n. sudden, violent movements of the earth's surface: *The western area of North America suffers from earthquakes.*

earth·shak·ing /'ɜrθ,ʃeɪkɪŋ/ adj.fig. extremely important (often used in the negative): *The President did not say anything earthshaking at his news conference.*

earth·worm /'ɜrθ,wɜrm/ n. See: worm.

earth·y /'ɜrθi/ adj. **-ier, -iest** vulgar in language and behavior, crude: *The comedian uses earthy jokes in his act.* -n. [U] **earthiness.**

ease /iz/ n. [U] **1** a lack of difficulty: *She climbed the mountain with ease.* **2** lack of worry, comfort: *He is rich and lives a life of ease.* **3 ill at ease:** uncomfortable or worried: *The student felt ill at ease when he gave his report to the class.*
—v. **eased, easing, eases 1** to move gently and slowly: *He eased into a comfortable bed and fell asleep.* **2** to make or become less difficult or severe: *Her son's phone call eased her worry.* **3** phrasal v. infrml. **to ease up** or **off:** to do s.t. with less effort: *She decided to ease up on her studies for a while; instead of taking five courses this semester, she will take three.* -adj. **easeful.**

ea·sel /'izəl/ n. a stand with three long legs and a narrow shelf in front used to hold a display or an artist's canvas

eas·i·ly /'izəli/ adv. without difficulty, effortlessly: *She can fix that motor easily.*

east /ist/ n.sing. **1** the direction straight ahead when facing a sunrise: *The sun rises in the east.* **2** the eastern part of the world or a country **3 the East:** in the USA, usu. the east coast: *New York is in the East.* **4 back East:** in the USA, how people on the west coast refer to the east coast: *My brother lives back East in Providence, Rhode Island.*
—adv. moving toward the east: *We are heading (sailing, flying, etc.) east.*
—adj. **1** located in the east: *The east side of Manhattan has some very fancy apartments.* **2**

coming from the east: *I feel the chill of that east wind off the ocean.*

Eas·ter /'istər/ *n.* the Christian religious holiday celebrating Jesus Christ's return to life: *Christians go to church on Easter.*

east·er·ly /'istərli/ *adj.adv.* from or to the east: *<adj.> Easterly winds blow from the east.*

east·ern /'istərn/ *adj.* located in the east: *Denver, Colorado, is on the eastern side of the Rocky Mountains.*

east·ern·er /'istərnər/ *n.* a person from an eastern area: *He is an easterner from Boston.*

Eastern Hemisphere *n.* the half of the earth that includes Europe, Africa, Asia, and Australia

Eastern Standard Time *n.abbr.* **EST** [U] used in the part of the world that is in the fifth time zone to the west of Greenwich, England: *Miami, New York, and the rest of eastern North America are on Eastern Standard Time.||The President's speech will be televised at 7:00 P.M. EST.*

East Indies *n.* a name once used for India, Indonesia, and much of Southeast Asia: *Fifteenth-century explorers were looking for new trade routes to the East Indies.*

east·ward /'istwərd/ *adj.adv.* toward the east: *We are driving in an <adj.> eastward direction.*

eas·y /'izi/ *adj.* **-ier, -iest 1** simple to do: *Fixing the lock was easy.* **2** relaxed, smooth: *She is very pleasant; she has an easy manner.* **3** pleasant, calm: *He has an easy life with few worries.* **4** *infrml.* **as easy as pie:** very easy to do: *The test was as easy as pie.* **5 easier said than done:** easy to talk about but hard to do: *To climb a mountain is easier said than done.* **6 easy money:** money made with little effort: *I made easy money on that job; I just sat around reading all day.* **7** *infrml.* **easy on the eye:** pleasant to look at: *The view from the mountain was easy on the eye and so relaxing.* **8** *infrml.* **on easy street:** financially secure and content: *He has been on easy street since he won the lottery.* -*n.* [U] **easiness;** -*adv.* **easily.** —*adv.* **1 to go easy on: a.** to be less strict or be gentle with: *The judge went easy on the teenagers because they had never been in trouble before.* **b.** to use less of: *Go easy on the salt; it's not good for you.* **2 to take it easy:** to relax: *After work, I watch TV and take it easy.*

easy chair *n.* a soft, comfortable chair meant for relaxation: *He reads in his easy chair by the fireplace.*

easy·go·ing /'izi,gouɪŋ/ *adj.* relaxed, unhurried: *Nothing annoys him; he is easygoing.*

easy mark *n.infrml.* a person who can be easily stolen from (manipulated, cheated, etc.): *Thieves look for easy marks to steal from.*

eat /it/ *v.* **ate** /eɪt/, **eaten** /'itn/, **eating, eats 1** to take (food) into the mouth, chew, and swallow: *He eats anything put in front of him.* **2** to have a meal: *Let's go out to eat.* **3** *fig.* to annoy, irritate: *He's angry; I wonder what's eating him?* **4** *phrasal v. insep.* **to eat away at** or **into s.t.:** to corrode, waste away: *The metal is eaten away by rust.* **5 to eat crow** or **eat dirt** or **eat humble pie** or **eat one's hat** or **eat one's words:** to be forced to admit defeat or being wrong: *Now that they've proved him wrong, he's eating crow (his words, etc.).* **6 to eat high off the hog:** to dine or live very well: *They are going out to dinner nearly every night; they are eating high off the hog.* **7 to eat like a bird** or **like a horse:** to eat very little or a lot **8 to eat one's heart out:** to have strong and painful desires or regret: *When his wife left him, he ate his heart out.* **9 to eat oneself up with s.t.:** to be overcome with a negative feeling, such as jealousy, desire, guilt, etc.: *He feels responsible for his son's death and is eating himself up with guilt.* **10** *phrasal v.* **to eat out:** to dine in a restaurant: *He is a bachelor and eats out frequently.* **11 to eat out of s.o.'s hand:** to be controlled or influenced by s.o.: *She has the group eating out of her hands; they agree with everything she says.* **12 to eat s.o. alive:** to destroy in some way: *He didn't know how to do the job and was eaten alive by his boss when he made mistakes.* **13 to eat s.o. out of house and home:** to eat all the food in the house: *When our cousin came to visit, he was so hungry that he ate us out of house and home.* **14** *infrml.slang* **to eat s.t. up:** to delight in s.t.: *When his girlfriend praises him, he just eats it up.* **15 to have one's cake and eat it too:** to spend s.t. or use it up, but also try to keep it: *She wants to save money but also have expensive cars, vacations, and parties; she wants to have her cake and eat it, too.*

eat·a·ble /'itəbəl/ *adj.infrml.* clean and good enough to be eaten: *The food at that restaurant is eatable but not very good. See:* edible.

eat·en /'itn/ *v. past part. of* eat

eau de co·logne /'oudəkə'loun/ *n.* [U] a diluted form of perfume: *She wears eau de cologne since it is not as strong as perfume.*

eaves /ivz/ *n.pl.* the overhang of a roof: *Birds make their nests under the eaves and along the drainpipe.*

eaves·drop /'ivz,drɑp/ *v.* **-dropped, -dropping, -drops** to listen secretly to other people's conversation: *He liked to eavesdrop on his neighbors' conversations.* -*n.* **eavesdropper.** *See:* overhear, USAGE NOTE.

ebb /ɛb/ *n.* [U] **1** a flowing away, esp. the ocean's water moving away from the shore: *The tide is on the ebb now.* **2 ebb tide:** the period when the tide flows out

—*v.* to flow away, decline, (*syn.*) to recede: *The tide ebbed early this morning.||The old man's strength ebbed as his illness got worse.*

eb·o·ny /'ɛbəni/ *n.* [U] a black Asian hardwood: *The dark keys on the piano were made of ebony.*
—*adj.* a dark, lustrous black

e·bul·lient /ɪ'bʊlyənt, ɪ'bʌl-/ *adj.frml.* lively, (*syn.*) exuberant: *She has an ebullient personality, always very happy and smiling.* -*n.* **ebullience.**

ec·cen·tric /ɪk'sɛntrɪk, ɛk-/ *adj.* odd, unusual: *The students are amused by the professor's eccentric habit of pulling his hair while he talks.*
—*n.* an eccentric person: *He is the neighborhood eccentric.* -*adv.* **eccentrically;** -*n.* **eccentricity** /ˌɛksɛn'trɪsəti/.

ec·cle·si·as·tic /ɪˌklizi'æstɪk/ *n.adj.* a priest or minister: *He is a strict <n.> ecclesiastic who closely follows tradition.*

ec·cle·si·as·ti·cal /ɪˌklizi'æstɪkəl/ *adj.* related to church matters: *ecclesiastical laws, music, architecture, etc.*

ECG /'isi'ʤi/ or **EKG** /'ikeɪ'ʤi/ *n.abbr. of* electrocardiogram

ech·e·lon /'ɛʃəˌlɑn/ *n.* a level of authority, power, or importance within a type of organization: *That news reporter interviews people in the highest echelons of government.*

ech·o /'ɛkoʊ/ *n.* **-oes** the repetition of a sound caused by its bouncing off a hard surface: *The echoes of our voices in the caves were scary.*
—*v.* **-oed, -oing, -oes** **1** to be repeated as an echo: *Our shouts echoed in the canyon.* **2** to repeat s.t. that s.o. else has said: *That official's assistant echoes all his opinions.* **3** to show the influence of, to imitate: *Some modern paintings echo the work of primitive artists.*

é·clair /eɪ'klɛr/ *n.* a long pastry filled with cream and covered with chocolate: *I had a cup of coffee and a chocolate éclair for dessert.*

ec·lec·tic /ɪ'klɛktɪk/ *adj.* choosing from a variety of sources or styles: *She has eclectic tastes in collecting art.* -*n.* [U] **eclecticism.**

e·clipse /ɪ'klɪps/ *n.* the partial or complete blocking out of one object when another passes in front: *We saw a partial eclipse of the sun by the moon.*
—*v.* **eclipsed, eclipsing, eclipses** **1** to cause an eclipse: *The moon eclipsed the sun.* **2** to fade, diminish: *His reputation slowly eclipsed with age.* **3** to be much better than, (*syns.*) to surpass, outshine: *Great runners of the past have been eclipsed by today's top runners.*

e·col·o·gy /ɪ'kɑləʤi/ *n.* [U] the study of the natural connections among plants, animals, people, and the environment: *An understanding of ecology is central to keeping our planet safe from destruction.* -*n.* **ecologist;** -*adj.* **ecological** /ˌɛkə'lɑʤəkəl, ˌikə-/.

ec·o·nom·ic /ˌɛkə'nɑmɪk, ˌikə-/ *adj.* related to economics: *Investors watch the rate of economic growth closely.*

ec·o·nom·i·cal /ˌɛkə'nɑməkəl, ˌikə-/ *adj.* getting good value for money spent, (*syn.*) thrifty: *That car burns so much gasoline that it is not economical to own it.* -*adv.* **economically.**

ec·o·nom·ics /ˌɛkə'nɑmɪks, ˌikə-/ *n.* [U] *used with a sing.v.* the study of how society uses resources, such as money, labor, raw materials, and factories: *Economics is at the center of most governmental concerns.*

e·con·o·mist /ɪ'kɑnəmɪst/ *n.* a person who specializes in economics: *She is an economist who works for the government.*

e·con·o·mize /ɪ'kɑnəˌmaɪz/ *v.* **-mized, -mizing, -mizes** to spend less than before: *He lost his job, so he has to economize by not buying expensive things.*

e·con·o·my /ɪ'kɑnəmi/ **-mies** *n.* [C;U] **1** the economic conditions on a worldwide, national, or regional scale: *The national economy is strong now.* **2** careful use of time, money, resources, etc.: *The design of the offices emphasizes economy of space.*
—*adj.* with a lower price: *economy class airfares||large economy-size cereal boxes*

ec·o·sys·tem /'ɛkoʊˌsɪstəm, 'ikoʊ-/ *n.* an ecological unit in nature: *A swamp and its plants, animals, and water supply form an ecosystem.*

ec·sta·sy /'ɛkstəsi/ *n.* [U] great delight, (*syn.*) rapture: *When she agreed to marry him, he went into a state of ecstasy.* -*adj.* **ecstatic** /ɛk'stætɪk/; -*adv.* **ecstatically.**

ec·u·men·i·cal /ˌɛkyə'mɛnəkəl/ *adj.* concerning the unity of Christianity throughout the world: *The ecumenical movement is strongly supported by the Pope.* -*n.* **ecumenicalism.**

ec·ze·ma /'ɛksəmə, 'ɛgzə-, ɪg'zi-/ *n.* [U] a skin condition with itching and redness, most often caused by an allergic reaction to s.t.: *She wore gloves to cover her hands because she had a bad case of eczema.*

ed·dy /'ɛdi/ *n.v.* **-died, -dying, -dies** a turning or swirling, esp. of water, into a pool that hardly moves: *The river formed <n.pl.> eddies near its banks.*

edge /ɛʤ/ *n.* **1** the border where two surfaces meet: *He looked over the edge of the cliff.* **2** a sharp, thin side of a blade or cutting tool: *She tested the edge of the knife blade.* **3** *fig.sing.* a small advantage: *That horse can run fast; it has an edge over the others in the race.* **4** **on the edge:** in a dangerous state: *He's a race car driver who likes living on the edge.* **5** **to be on edge:** to feel nervous or apprehensive: *The candidates are on edge waiting for the test results.*
—*v.* **edged, edging, edges** **1** to move slowly and carefully: *He edged toward the door, then*

ran for help. **2** to put a border or edge on: *She edged the garden with tiny pink flowers.*

edg·ing /'ɛdʒɪŋ/ *n.* [U] a border: *The edging around the curtain is made of lace.*

edge·wise /'ɛdʒ,waɪz/ *adv.* **1** with the edge forward or first, toward the edge: *I kept the door open by pushing a book under it edgewise.* **2 to get a word in edgewise:** to get a chance to speak when s.o. else is speaking nonstop: *On the phone, my friend talks so much I can hardly get a word in edgewise.*

edg·y /'ɛdʒi/ *adj.* **-ier, -iest** nervous, *(syn.)* fidgety: *She is edgy about her examination results.*

ed·i·ble /'ɛdəbəl/ *adj.* can be eaten, eatable: *The fruit of that tree is not edible.*
—*n.pl.* food: *There are edibles in the refrigerator; help yourselves!*

e·dict /'idɪkt/ *n.* a formal order given with the force of law, a command: *A dictatorial government issues edicts on every aspect of life.*

ed·i·fi·ca·tion /,ɛdəfə'keɪʃən/ *n.frml.* [U] improvement of one's understanding, enlightenment: *For my edification, the teacher explained the idea.* -*v.* **edify** /'ɛdə,faɪ/.

ed·i·fice /'ɛdəfɪs/ *n.frml.* a large, impressive building: *Politicians like to build large edifices to honor one another.*

ed·it /'ɛdɪt/ *v.* **1** to correct and clarify written or recorded works: *A copy editor edits the manuscripts of books.* **2** *phrasal v. sep.* **to edit s.t. out:** to remove or delete s.t.: *The filmmaker edited out some of the violent scenes in the movie.‖He edited them out.*

e·di·tion /ə'dɪʃən/ *n.* a specific printing of a book or periodical: *the evening edition of the daily newspaper‖a new edition of a textbook*

ed·i·tor /'ɛdɪtər/ *n.* **1** a person in charge of publishing a periodical, a newscast, or a book series: *She is an editor at The Washington Post.* **2** a person who corrects, clarifies, and shapes written and recorded works: *He is the editor of a series of dictionaries.* -*n.* **editor-in-chief.**

ed·i·to·ri·al /,ɛdɪ'tɔriəl/ *adj.* about editing: *The intern works in the editorial department of a publisher.*
—*n.* a written opinion published in a newspaper or magazine or broadcast on radio or television: *An editorial on the economy was printed in today's newspaper.* -*adv.* **editorially.**

USAGE NOTE: Most American newspapers have *editorial pages* where people can express their personal opinions and agree or disagree with items in the newspaper. There are usually three types of writing in the *editorial pages: editorials,* essays written by the editors of the newspaper; *op-ed pieces,* essays written by people who know about a topic; and *letters to the editor,* letters from newspaper readers.

ed·i·to·ri·al·ize /,ɛdɪ'tɔriə,laɪz/ *v.* **-ized, -izing, -izes** to give one's opinion on a topic, not just the facts or news about it: *That journalist can't tell a simple story without editorializing.*

ed·u·cate /'ɛdʒə,keɪt/ *v.* **-cated, -cating, -cates** to give s.o. knowledge through schooling, *(syn.)* to instruct: *He was educated in the public schools of Chicago.* -*n.* **educator;** -*adj.* **educable** /'ɛdʒəkəbəl/.

ed·u·cat·ed /'ɛdʒə,keɪtɪd/ *adj.* **1** literate, having education, esp. the basic abilities to read, write, and do math: *She went to school through the tenth grade and considered herself educated.* **2** having knowledge and powers of reasoning based on a good education: *She has gone to the finest universities and is an educated person.*

ed·u·ca·tion /,ɛdʒə'keɪʃən/ *n.* **1** [C;U] basic instruction or training in schools: *The public schools in our neighborhood offer a good education.* **2** [U] the institutions for teaching and learning: *He's in education; he works as a physics teacher.* **3** [U] the field of learning to teach, *(syn.)* pedagogy: *She is majoring in education at the teacher's college.* -*adj.* **educational;** -*adv.* **educationally.**

eel /il/ *n.* **1** a snake-like saltwater or freshwater fish: *Many people like to eat eels.* **2 slippery as an eel:** tricky, deceitful: *That guy is as slippery as an eel; don't trust him.*

ee·rie or **ee·ry** /'ɪri/ *adj.* **-rier, -riest** strange and frightening, *(syn.)* weird: *That old house is an eerie place at night.* -*adv.* **eerily;** -*n.* **eeriness.**

ef·face /ɪ'feɪs/ *v.* **-faced, -facing, -faces** **1** to erase, *(syn.)* to eradicate, obliterate: *The worker effaced the writing on the wall by painting over it.* **2 to efface oneself:** to act so as not to attract attention or praise: *That talented young man is too quick to efface himself; he's too self-effacing.* See: **deface.**

ef·fect /ɪ'fɛkt/ *n.* **1** a result, *(syn.)* a consequence: *One effect of being poor is not having enough food for your family.* **2** an influence, *(syn.)* an impact: *Lowering taxes had a strong effect on the taxpayers, who definitely liked it!* **3** *pl.* one's belongings: *The retiree removed her personal effects from her office before leaving.* **4 in effect: a.** active, *(syn.)* operative: *The new law is in effect as of today.* **b.** in reality, *(syn.)* actually: *This law is, in effect, an increase in taxes.* **5 to take effect:** to begin to be active: *The new law takes effect today at 9:00 A.M.*
—*v.* to cause, esp. by law: *The governor effected many changes to improve the tax situation.* See: **affect, USAGE NOTE.**

ef·fec·tive /ɪ'fɛktɪv/ *adj.* **1** having the result that one wants, *(syn.)* productive: *The medication is quite effective; it relieves pain quickly.* **2** in use, current, *(syn.)* in operation: *The law* *was effective on January 1. -adv.* **effectively;** *-n.* [U] **effectiveness.**

ef·fec·tu·al /ɪˈfɛktʃuəl/ *adj.* producing the desired effect: *The President was effectual in getting people to vote for his re-election. -adv.* **effectually.**

ef·fem·i·nate /ɪˈfɛmənɪt/ *adj.pej.* showing behavior thought to be more typical of women than of men *-n.* [U] **effeminacy.**

ef·fer·ves·cent /ˌɛfərˈvɛsənt/ *adj.* **1** bubbly, sparkling with tiny bubbles: *Champagne is effervescent.* **2** *fig.* cheerful, laughing, high-spirited: *That lady has an effervescent personality. -v.* **effervesce;** *-n.* [U] **effervescence;** *-adv.* **effervescently.**

ef·fete /ɪˈfit/ *adj.frml.* weak, self-absorbed, and decadent: *The young writer's book was too effete to interest readers.*

ef·fi·ca·cious /ˌɛfəˈkeɪʃəs/ *adj.frml.* effective, practical: *The improvements in the way we work proved efficacious. -adv.* **efficaciously;** *-n.* [U] **efficacy** /ˈɛfəkəsi/.

ef·fi·cien·cy /əˈfɪʃənsi/ *n.* **-cies** good productivity or performance: *Management praised the workers for their efficiency.*

ef·fi·cient /əˈfɪʃənt/ *adj.* productive, economical: *She performs her job well and quickly; she is very efficient. -adv.* **efficiently.**

ef·fi·gy /ˈɛfədʒi/ *n.* **-gies** a representation, such as a crude dummy, of a person hated by others: *The demonstrators hanged an effigy of the politician outside the embassy.*

ef·fort /ˈɛfərt/ *n.* [C;U] **1** physical or mental work, *(syn.)* exertion: *The workers made a great effort to finish the building on time.* **2** an attempt, a try, *(syn.)* an endeavor: *Most students made an effort to improve their test scores.*

ef·fort·less /ˈɛfərtlɪs/ *adj.* easy, not difficult: *She skis beautifully; she makes it look effortless. -adv.* **effortlessly;** *-n.* **effortlessness.**

ef·fron·ter·y /ɪˈfrʌntəri/ *n.frml.* [U] rudeness, *(syns.)* audacity, gall: *That idiot had the effrontery to push ahead of everyone else waiting in line. See:* affront.

ef·fu·sive /ɪˈfyusɪv/ *adj.* with too much feeling, *(syn.)* gushy: *The critic was effusive in his praise of the movie. -adv.* **effusively;** *-n.* **effusiveness.**

e.g. /ˈiˈdʒi/ *abbr. for* exempli gratia, (Latin for) for example: *Our university offers strong programs in the sciences, e.g., chemistry, biology, and physics.*

e·gal·i·tar·i·an /ɪˌgælɪˈtɛriən/ *n.adj.* a believer in equal economic opportunity and equal legal and political rights for all people: *He is an <n.> egalitarian, not an elitist. -n.* [U] **egalitarianism.**

egg /ɛg/ *n.* **1** a round or oval-shaped shell in which a baby bird, reptile, or insect grows: *Chickens lay eggs, as do other birds.* **2 a bad egg:** a bad or dishonest person: *Don't trust your new friend; she is really a bad egg.* **3 to have egg on one's face:** to make a fool of oneself: *Our team was completely unprepared to answer questions at the meeting; when it was over, we had egg on our faces.* **4 to lay an egg:** to fail miserably: *The audience did not laugh at the comedian; he laid an egg.* **5 to put** or **have all of your eggs in one basket:** to risk all that one has in one investment or situation: *We were warned not to invest all our money in one stock so we wouldn't have all of our eggs in one basket.*

eggs

—phrasal v. sep. **to egg s.o. on:** to strongly encourage s.o. to do s.t.: *The crowd egged on the wrestlers to be more violent.‖They egged them on.*

egg·head /ˈɛgˌhɛd/ *n.infrml.fig.pej.* a person who thinks about intellectual ideas most of the time: *Her mind is in another world; she is an egghead who spends hours studying everyday. See:* bookish.

egg·nog /ˈɛgˌnɑg, -ˌnɔg/ *n.* [U] a traditional drink usu. made with light cream, eggs, sugar, liquor, and nutmeg: *We serve eggnog at Christmastime.*

egg·plant /ˈɛgˌplænt/ *n.* [C;U] a plant with edible fruit shaped like a pear, usu. with purple skin

egg roll *n.* a small shell of egg-based dough stuffed with chopped vegetables and often with bits of meat, then deep-fried: *We order egg rolls as an appetizer at Chinese restaurants.*

egg·shell /ˈɛgˌʃɛl/ *n.* **1** the hard outer covering of an egg **2 to walk on eggshells:** to behave with extreme caution: *Everyone is afraid of him; they walk on eggshells when he's around.* *—n.adj.* off-white or pale yellow: *The apartment walls are painted in an <adj.> eggshell white.*

e·go /ˈigoʊ/ *n.* **egos 1** one's feeling about one's self: *The awards he received for his talent as a painter strengthened his ego.* **2** a feeling of self-importance: *He has a big ego; he thinks he's important.*

e·go·cen·tric /ˌigoʊˈsɛntrɪk/ *adj.* self-centered, selfish: *She doesn't consider the feelings of other people; she's an egocentric person.*

e·go·ism /ˈigoʊˌɪzəm/ *n.* **1** the belief that morality is based on self-interest **2** too much concern with one's own interest or importance: *His egoism made him think only about his own needs.*

e·go·ma·ni·ac /ˌigoʊˈmeɪniˌæk/ *n.* a person who is completely self-centered: *An egomaniac thinks only he or she is a great human being. -n.* [U] **egomania.**

e·go·tism /ˈigəˌtɪzəm/ *n.* [U] self-importance, self-centered behavior, such as boastfulness or conceit: *Her egotism offends many; she's always talking about herself. -n.* **egoist** /ˈigoʊɪst/; *-adj.* **egoistical** /ˌigəˈtɪstəkəl/; *-adv.* **egotistically.**

ego trip *n.slang* self-centered speech or behavior that adds to *f* one's sense of importance: *He's on an ego trip because he won the scholarship to study in London for two years.*

e·gre·gious /ɪˈgridʒəs/ *adj.frml.* extremely bad, outrageous: *Our supervisor unfortunately made an egregious mistake in the report and it had to be rewritten. -adv.* **egregiously.**

e·gret /ˈigrɪt/ *n.* a tall waterbird with white feathers: *Egrets increased in numbers in the USA in the 1950s after being hunted nearly to extinction.*

ei·der·down /ˈaɪdərˌdaʊn/ *n. See:* down, *n.*

eight /eɪt/ *adj.n.* the cardinal number 8: *An octopus has <adj.> eight legs.‖She wanted children and now has <n.> eight.*

eight ball *n.* **1** the black ball with an eight on it in the game of pool: *You must hit the eight ball last in order to win.* **2 behind the eight ball:** blocked or having bad luck: *With no job, he is stuck behind the eight ball and can't do anything to help himself.*

eight ball

eight·een /eɪˈtin/ *adj.n.* the cardinal number 18: *She is <adj.> eighteen years old.‖They have <n.> eighteen on their team.*

USAGE NOTE: At age 18, Americans are allowed to vote in state and federal elections and can join or be drafted into the military forces

eight·eenth /eɪˈtinθ/ *adj.n.* the ordinal number 18: *She is the <adj.> eighteenth (or) 18th person in line.‖She is <n.> eighteenth.*

eighth /eɪtθ, eɪθ/ *adj.n.* the ordinal number 8: *She is the <adj.> eighth (or) 8th child in the family.‖He is the <n.> eighth (or) 8th in line.*

eight·i·eth /ˈeɪtiəθ/ *adj.n.* the ordinal number 80: *his <adj.> eightieth (or) 80th birthday*

eight·y /ˈeɪti/ *adj.n.* **-ies** the cardinal number 80: *She is <adj.> eighty years old.*

ei·ther /ˈiðər, ˈaɪðər/ *adj.* **1** one or the other: *We can follow either route to go there.* **2** one and the other, each: *Wildflowers bloomed on either side of the road.* **3 an either-or situation:** a situation with only two opposite choices: *It's an either-or situation; that is, we both go or neither of us goes.*
—*pron.* one or the other: *I'll take tea or coffee; either is fine.*
—*conj.* **either. . . or** used to introduce two or more possibilities: *Either we vacation this month or not at all.*
—*adv.* (used with a negative) also, likewise: *He doesn't smoke and she doesn't either.*

e·jac·u·late /ɪˈdʒækyəˌleɪt/ *v.* **-lated, -lating, -lates 1** to throw out semen from the penis with sudden force: *When they have sex men ejaculate.* **2** *frml.* to speak or cry out suddenly *-n.*[C;U] **ejaculation.**

e·ject /ɪˈdʒɛkt/ *v.* **1** to go out rapidly and with force: *The pilot ejected from the falling airplane.* **2** to throw out or force out: *A troublemaker was ejected from the theater. -n.*[C;U] **ejection.**

eke /ik/ *v.* **eked, eking, ekes** to manage to make enough money to survive (usu. used with "a living"): *He eked out a living by selling newspapers on the street.*

EKG /ˈikeɪˈdʒi/ *n.abbr.* of electrocardiogram

el /ɛl/ *n.* short for elevated railway: *In Chicago, many people ride the el to work.*

e·lab·o·rate /ɪˈlæbəˌreɪt/ *v.* **-rated, -rating, -rates** to give more detail, explain: *The manager elaborated on the plan to expand the business.*
—*adj.* /ɪˈlæbərɪt, ɪˈlæbrɪt/ complex, detailed: *It was an elaborate plan involving many steps. -adv.* **elaborately;** *-n.* [U] **elaboration.**

é·lan /eɪˈlɑn/ *n.* [U] (French for) liveliness and enthusiasm, (*syn.*) flair: *My lab partner does everything with élan; he wears nice clothes and eats at great restaurants. See:* esprit de corps.

e·lapse /ɪˈlæps/ *v.n.* **elapsed, elapsing, elapses** to go by, pass: *Three years have <v.> elapsed since I saw my friends in Boston; that is a long time. See:* lapse.

e·las·tic /ɪˈlæstɪk/ *adj.* **1** capable of being stretched, (*syns.*) flexible, pliant: *These rubber gloves are elastic and will fit any size hand.* **2 elastic price:** demand varies up or down with price: *A market with elastic prices appears if the demand for goods goes down when the price is raised and vice versa.*
—*n.* [C;U] a flexible fabric that can be stretched, or s.t. made of this fabric: *These pants have an elastic sewn into the waist. -v.* **elasticize;** *-n.* [U] **elasticity** /ɪˌlæsˈtɪsəti, ˌilæs-/.

elastic band or **elastic** *n.* a rubber band! *I put an elastic (band) around the package to hold it together.*

e·late /ɪˈleɪt/ *v.* **elated, elating, elates** to make happy, delight: *The good news elated him.* *-adj.* **elated.**

e·la·tion /ɪˈleɪʃən/ *n.* [U] delight, happiness: *How happy she looks; you can see the elation in her face.*

el·bow /ˈɛlboʊ/ *n.v.* **1** the middle joint in the arm between the wrist and shoulder **2** the back point of that joint: *He hurt his <n.> elbow playing tennis.* **3 to elbow** or **give s.o. the elbow:** to push with an elbow: *He was in a hurry, and he <v.> elbowed people aside as he made his way through the crowd.*

elbow grease *n.infrml.fig.* [U] hard work, esp. by scrubbing and cleaning: *The floor was filthy, but with some elbow grease, I made it shine.*

elbow room *n.* [U] enough space to work or act freely: *Our little apartment is too small; we need a place with some elbow room.*

eld·er /ˈɛldər/ *adj.n.* older than another person: *Hans is the <adj.> elder brother* (or) *the <n.> elder of the two brothers.*

—n.pl. **the village elders:** the older people in positions of respect and usu. power in a community: *The town mayor is one of the village elders.*

eld·er·ly /ˈɛldərli/ *adj.* old, aged: *My aunt is elderly; she is 88 years old now. See:* old.

—n.pl. **the elderly:** old people: *The elderly are taken care of by their children in most parts of the world.*

eld·est /ˈɛldɪst/ *adj.* oldest: *She is the eldest child in the family.*

e·lect /ɪˈlɛkt/ *v.* **1** to select by voting: *The people elected her to the Senate.* **2** *frml.* to choose, decide: *The student elected to attend a university in Germany.*

—n. **the elect:** the chosen people, the elite: *She is among the elect, chosen to attend the national conference.*

—adj. suffix **-elect:** chosen but not yet in office: *the president-elect*

e·lec·tion /ɪˈlɛkʃən/ *n.* [C] **1** an event when people vote for or against s.o. or s.t.: *The Presidential election is held every four years in the USA.* **2** [U] *frml.* choice, decision: *His election to attend Harvard, not Yale, was a difficult decision.*

USAGE NOTE: Election day in the USA is the first Tuesday following the first Monday in November. This is when important state and federal elections are held.

e·lec·tion·eer /ɪˈlɛkʃəˈnɪr/ *v.* to try to get votes; to act as a candidate: *The candidates for office electioneered for a month before election day.*

e·lec·tive /ɪˈlɛktɪv/ *adj.* **1** filled or decided by election: *The mayor's office is an elective one.* **2** having power to elect: *an elective assembly* **3** *n.adj.* (a course) not required in school or college: *The course on current films is an <n.> elective.*

e·lec·tor·al /ɪˈlɛktərəl/ *adj.* related to elections: *The electoral system in the USA is part of the democracy.* *-n.* **elector.**

Electoral College *n.* in the USA, a group of electors chosen in each state to elect the President and Vice President: *The Electoral College meets to cast its votes.*

USAGE NOTE: In a presidential election in the USA, people do not vote directly for the President and Vice President. Instead, people vote for *presidential electors,* who form the *electoral college.* The electors vote for the President. This system is different from all other elections in the USA.

e·lec·tor·ate /ɪˈlɛktərɪt/ *n.* those citizens who can vote: *The electorate voted the Democrats into office.*

e·lec·tric /ɪˈlɛktrɪk/ *adj.* **1** related to electricity: *an electric charge (current, power plant, etc.)* **2** powered by electricity: *electric lights (guitars, stoves, etc.)* **3** *fig.* charged with emotion, exciting: *The atmosphere at the sports stadium was electric with excitement.*

e·lec·tri·cal /ɪˈlɛktrəkəl/ *adj.* related to electricity: *electrical engineering* *-adv.* **electrically.**

electric chair *n.* a chair giving a powerful electric charge used to put murderers to death: *He went to the electric chair because he killed an entire family. See:* USAGE NOTE *at* capital punishment *and* death penalty.

electric eye *n.* a device that sends out an invisible electric beam that, when broken, sets off an alarm or opens a door

e·lec·tri·cian /ɪˌlɛkˈtrɪʃən, ˌilɛk-/ *n.* a person trained in putting in and repairing electrical wiring and devices: *She is an electrician who works for the telephone company.*

e·lec·tric·i·ty /ɪˌlɛkˈtrɪsəti, ˌilɛk-/ *n.* [U] **1** flow of energy used as a power source: *Before moving into the new house, we had the electricity turned on.* **2** *fig.* intense excitement: *There was electricity in the air at the big rock concert.*

e·lec·tri·fy /ɪˈlɛktrəˌfaɪ/ *v.* **-fied, -fying, -fies** **1** to provide with electricity: *The government electrified farm areas in the USA in the 1930s.* **2** to excite: *The singer electrified her audience.* *-n.* [U] **electrification;** *-adj.* **electrifying.**

e·lec·tro·car·di·o·gram /ɪˌlɛktrəˈkɑrdiə-/ˌgræm/ *n*. a graph made by an electrocardiograph showing a patient's pattern of heartbeats and used by doctors to detect heart disease: *An electrocardiogram is also called an EKG, ECG, or cardiogram.*

e·lec·tro·car·di·o·graph /ɪˌlɛktrəˈkɑrdiə ˌgræf/ *n*. a device used to track heart activity

e·lec·tro·cute /ɪˈlɛktrəˌkyut/ *v*. **-cuted, -cuting, -cutes** to kill with a powerful charge of electricity: *The fallen power line electrocuted and killed the workers when they touched it by mistake. -n.* [C;U] **electrocution** /ɪˌlɛktrə ˈkyuʃən/.

e·lec·trode /ɪˈlɛkˌtroud/ *n*. the points at which a current enters or leaves an electrical device: *The nurses put electrodes on the patient to test his heartbeat.*

e·lec·trol·y·sis /ɪlɛkˈtrɑləsɪs/ *n*. [U] a method of permanently removing hair roots by applying electricity to them: *She had hair removed from her face by electrolysis.*

e·lec·tron /ɪˈlɛkˌtrɑn/ *n*. a part of the atom with a negative charge: *Electrons are parts outside the nucleus of an atom.*

e·lec·tron·ic /ɪlɛkˈtrɑnɪk, ˌilɛk-/ *adj*. **1** related to electronics: *TVs and radios are electronic devices.* **2** related to a flow of electrons *-adv.* **electronically.**

e·lec·tron·ics /ɪlɛkˈtrɑnɪks, ˌilɛk-/ *n*. [U] *used with a sing.v.* **1** the science that deals with electrons: *With the study of electronics, the company continues to improve the quality of their products.* **2** the use of electrons in products like televisions and musical equipment: *the electronics industry*

electronic banking *n*. [U] the deposit, withdrawal, and transfer of money done with computerized machines: *You can get your money 24 hours a day with electronic banking. See:* ATM.

electronic mail or **E-mail** /ˈiˌmeɪl/ *n*. [U] messages sent and received electronically by computers over telephone lines or computer networks and shown on computer screens: *Our sales force uses electronic mail to send in orders. See:* E-mail, Internet, World Wide Web, information superhighway.

USAGE NOTE: *Electronic mail* is a rapidly growing form of communication using the computer. It is popular because messages, documents and computer programs can be sent anywhere in the world in a few seconds.

electronic music *n*. [U] sounds produced electronically, such as by an electric guitar

electron microscope *n*. a microscope using electrons to produce enlarged images of objects: *The Biology Department has an electron microscope.*

e·lec·tro·plate /ɪˈlɛktrəˌpleɪt/ *v*. **-plated, -plating, -plates** to coat with a layer of metal: *That steel plate is electroplated with copper. -n.* [U] **electroplating.**

el·e·gant /ˈɛləgənt/ *adj*. **1** stylish in appearance, graceful, (*syn.*) refined: *The living room of the model apartment has elegant furniture.* **2** refined in behavior: *She has elegant manners. -n.* [U] **elegance; -adv.** **elegantly.**

el·e·gy /ˈɛlədʒi/ *n*. **-gies** a poem or song full of sadness for the dead, (*syn.*) a lament: *The choir sang elegies for the dead man at the funeral service.*

el·e·ment /ˈɛləmənt/ *n*. **1** a part, aspect: *The most negative element of the project is its high cost.* **2** a particular group of people: *He belongs to a bad element in this city.* **3** any of more than one hundred basic chemical substances: *The elements hydrogen and oxygen combine to form water.* **4** *pl.* **the elements** aspects of weather (wind, temperature, storms, etc.): *People live in houses as protection against the elements.* **5 to be in** or **out of one's element:** to be in or away from one's familiar and comfortable role or area of expertise: *The farmer was out of her element in the big city.*

el·e·men·tal /ˌɛləˈmɛntl/ *adj*. basic, (*syn.*) fundamental: *The wheel is an elemental part of any vehicle.*

el·e·men·ta·ry /ˌɛləˈmɛntəri, -tri/ *adj*. **1** simple, basic: *She is studying elementary mathematics.* **2** beginning: *We are still in the elementary stage of making our decision.*

elementary school *n*. in USA, the lower grades of schooling, (*syns.*) grammar school, grade school: *He has two young children in elementary school; one is in the first grade and the other is in sixth grade. See:* grade school.

el·e·phant /ˈɛləfənt/ *n*. the largest earthbound mammal, with four legs, usu. gray skin, a trunk, and long tusks *-adj.* **elephantine.** *See:* white elephant.

el·e·vate /ˈɛləˌveɪt/ *v*. **-vated, -vating, -vates** **1** to raise: *The machine elevated the heavy load off the ground.* **2** to promote, raise in rank: *The company president elevated two employees to the position of vice president. -adj.* **elevated.**

elevated train or **railway** *n*. in the USA, a subway system that runs on tracks elevated above the street on a bridge-like structure; sometimes called "the elevated": *The elevated railway runs across the city.*

elevated train

el·e·va·tion /ˌɛləˈveɪʃən/ *n.* **1** [C] a place or height above sea level: *Mountain goats live in the higher elevations above the valley.* **2** [C] an upward angle: *The line is drawn at an elevation of 45 degrees.* **3** [U] *frml.* a move up in rank, a promotion: *His elevation to company secretary pleased him.* **4** [C] a drawing of one side of a building

el·e·va·tor /ˈɛləˌveɪtər/ *n.* a box-like car used to carry people and freight between floors in a building: *We took the elevator to the tenth floor.*

e·lev·en /ɪˈlɛvən/ *adj.n.* the cardinal number 11: *She is <adj.> eleven years old.||There were <n.> eleven of us at the meeting.*

e·lev·enth /ɪˈlɛvənθ/ *adj.n.* the ordinal number 11: *She is the <adj.> eleventh person in line.||She is the <n.> eleventh or the 11th.*

eleventh hour *n.fig.* the last possible moment for acting before difficulty or disaster: *Labor and management reached an agreement at the eleventh hour and avoided a nationwide strike.*

elf /ɛlf/ *n.* **elves** /ɛlvz/ a small, mischievous imaginary person in folktales -*adj.* **elfish.** *See:* leprechaun.

elf·in /ˈɛlfɪn/ *adj.* small and mischievous like an elf, elfish: *The little boy had an elfin smile.*

e·lic·it /ɪˈlɪsɪt/ *v.frml.* to get, bring out: *Her letter of complaint elicited a quick response from the company.*

el·i·gi·ble /ˈɛlɪdʒəbəl/ *adj.* **1** having the right to do or be chosen for s.t., qualified: *He graduated from high school with good grades, so he is eligible to enroll in the state college.* **2** not married and with good qualities for marriage: *He is unmarried and has a good job, so he is an eligible bachelor.* -*n.* [U] **eligibility** /ˈɛlɪdʒəˈbɪləty/.

e·lim·i·nate /ɪˈlɪməˌneɪt/ *v.* **-nated, -nating, -nates** **1** to remove from consideration, to exclude: *The losing team was eliminated from further competition.* **2** to remove or get rid of, (*syn.*) to abolish: *The government eliminated the unpopular new tax.* -*n.* [U] **elimination.**

e·lite /ɪˈlit, eɪˈlit/ *n.* the leaders and professionals in the highest levels of a society: *The ruling elite in that country is made up of political leaders and heads of large corporations.*

e·lit·ist /ɪˈlitɪst, eɪˈli-/ *adj.* related to the belief that an elite group in society should be recognized as superior: *She has an elitist attitude that government should be run only by college graduates.* -*n.* [U] **elitism.**

e·lix·ir /ɪˈlɪksər/ *n.* **1** [C;U] an imaginary medicine with the power to cure all ills **2** *fig.* s.t. that makes s.o. feel strong: *A two-week vacation was an elixir for him; he returned full of energy.*

elk /ɛlk/ *n.* **elk** a large member of the deer family: *Those elk are over six feet (two meters) tall at the shoulder.*

el·lipse /əˈlɪps/ *n.* a symmetrical oval: *The path of the earth around the sun is an ellipse.* -*adj.* **elliptical.**

elm /ɛlm/ *n.* a tall, leafy shade tree: *The elms of New England are dying from Dutch elm disease.*

el·o·cu·tion /ˌɛləˈkyuʃən/ *n.frml.* [U] the study and practice of public speaking: *As a young man, he took lessons in elocution.* -*n.* **elocutionist.** *See:* speech.

e·lon·gate /ɪˈlɔŋˌgeɪt/ *v.* **-gated, -gating, -gates** to make longer, stretch: *The mirror was curved so that it elongated my image, making me look tall and thin.* -*n.* [C;U] **elongation** /ˌɪlɔŋˈgeɪʃən, ˌilɔŋ-/.

e·lope /ɪˈloup/ *v.* **eloped, eloping, elopes** to marry secretly and simply without the permission or presence of one's parents: *The couple eloped to Las Vegas because they did not want a fancy church wedding.* -*n.* [C;U] **elopement.**

el·o·quence /ˈɛləkwɪns/ *n.* clear and persuasive speech or writing: *The senator often speaks with eloquence before the Senate.* -*adj.* **eloquent;** -*adv.* **eloquently.**

else /ɛls/ *adj.* **1** other, different: *I did not do that; someone else did.* **2** more, additional: *I haven't finished shopping yet; I have s.t. else to buy.*
—*adv.* **1** in a different time, way, or location: *When else can I leave?||How else can I travel?||Where else can I go?* **2 or else: a.** or suffer bad results: *You do what I say, or else!* **b.** used to introduce an undesirable possibility: *We have to leave now or else we'll be late.*

else·where /ˈɛlsˌwɛr/ *adv.* in some other place: *She doesn't live here; she must live elsewhere.*

e·lu·ci·date /ɪˈlusəˌdeɪt/ *v.frml.* **-dated, -dating, -dates** to explain and make clear: *The professor elucidated the main topics of the course.* -*n.* [U] **elucidation.**

e·lude /ɪˈlud/ *v.* **eluded, eluding, eludes** **1** to escape capture by: *The criminal eluded the police by hiding in the woods.* **2** to escape s.o.'s efforts to remember or understand: *I knew her name, but it eludes me now.* -*adj.* **elusive** /ɪˈlusɪv/; -*adv.* **elusively.**

elves /ɛlvz/ *n.pl.* of elf

e·ma·ci·ate /ɪˈmeɪʃiˌeɪt/ *v.* **-ated, -ating, -ates** to make very thin and weak, esp. through lack of food: *The captured soldier had not eaten in two weeks and became emaciated.* -*n.* [U] **emaciation.**

E-mail or **e-mail** /ˈiˌmeɪl/ *n.v.* [U] *short for* electronic mail: *I placed a book order by <n.> e-mail.|| I <v.> e-mailed my order to the company.* *See:* Internet, World Wide Web, information superhighway.

em·a·nate /ˈɛməˌneɪt/ *v.frml.* **-nated, -nating, -nates** to come from: *The sounds emanated from a room down the hall. -n.* [U] **emanation.**

e·man·ci·pate /ɪˈmænsəˌpeɪt/ *v.* **-pated, -pating, -pates** to free from slavery, liberate: *The Civil War emancipated the slaves in the USA.*

e·man·ci·pa·tion /ɪˌmænsəˈpeɪʃən/ *n.* [C;U] a freeing, *(syn.)* a liberation: *The emancipation of slaves was announced in President Abraham Lincoln's Emancipation Proclamation in 1863.*

e·mas·cu·late /ɪˈmæskyəˌleɪt/ *v.* **-lated, -lating, -lates 1** to remove a male's sexual organs, *(syn.)* to castrate **2** *fig.* to weaken: *Politicians emasculated the new law by making the penalties too light to stop criminals. -n.*[C;U] **emasculation.** *See:* geld.

em·balm /ɛmˈbɑm/ *v.* to preserve a dead body with chemicals: *He embalmed the body so it wouldn't decay. -n.* **embalmer;** [C;U] **embalmment.**

em·bank·ment /ɛmˈbæŋkmənt/ *n.* a mound of earth or rocks built to support the sides of a roadway or to hold back flood waters: *The rising water in the river will not flow over the embankment.*

em·bar·go /ɛmˈbɑrgoʊ/ *n.v.* **-goed, -going, -goes** a restriction or total ban on trade with another nation: *The USA placed an <n.> embargo on all imports from and exports to that country.‖The United Nations voted to <v.> embargo that country.*

em·bark /ɛmˈbɑrk/ *v.* **1** to go onboard a ship or airplane: *We embarked on the cruise ship in the Caribbean.* **2** to begin a journey, venture, or new activity: *She quit her job and embarked on a new venture, her own business. -n.* [C;U] **embarkation** /ˌɛmbɑrˈkeɪʃən/.

em·bar·rass /ɛmˈbærəs, ɪm-/ *v.* to cause s.o. to feel self-conscious or ashamed, *(syn.)* to humiliate: *Her boyfriend embarrassed her by teasing her about her new hairstyle in front of others. -adj.* **embarrassing.**

em·bar·rass·ment /ɛmˈbærəsmənt, ɪm-/ *n.* [C;U] **1** a feeling of shame, discomfort, or self-consciousness: *His face turned red with embarrassment.* **2** *s.t.* or *s.o.* that embarrasses: *The child's bad behavior made her an embarrassment to her parents.*

em·bas·sy /ˈɛmbəsi/ *n.* **-sies** the offices of a country's ambassador and staff in a foreign country: *I visited the US Embassy in Paris.*

em·bat·tled /ɛmˈbætld/ *adj.* in a fight with one's enemies or critics, *(syn.)* besieged: *The embattled Prime Minister finally resigned.*

em·bed /ɛmˈbɛd, ɪm-/ *v.* **-bedded, -bedding, -beds** to put into another substance: *The gardener embedded stones in the earth around each tree. See:* implant.

em·bel·lish /ɛmˈbɛlɪʃ/ *v.* **1** to add decorations or details to, to make more beautiful: *The artist embellished the design by adding flowers to it.* **2** to add to (a story, a report, etc.), to exaggerate: *The witness embellished the truth with her own opinions. -n.* [C;U] **embellishment.**

em·ber /ˈɛmbər/ *n.* a glowing piece (coal, wood) remaining after a fire: *The embers of the fire glowed red in the dark.*

em·bez·zle /ɛmˈbɛzəl/ *v.* **-zled, -zling, -zles** to steal money one is trusted to care for: *He embezzled company funds to pay for his vacation in Europe. -n.* [U] **embezzlement; embezzler.**

em·bit·ter /ɛmˈbɪtər/ *v.* to make s.o. feel bitter, hostile, angry: *He was embittered by his company's refusal to pay his health insurance. -n.* [U] **embitterment.**

em·bla·zon /ɛmˈbleɪzən/ *v.* to display in a bold manner: *The company name is emblazoned in big letters on their office building.*

em·blem /ˈɛmbləm/ *n.* a sign or symbol for decoration or for a purpose: *Her shirt has the company emblem on it. -adj.* **emblematic.**

em·bod·i·ment /ɛmˈbɑdimənt, ɪm-/ *n.* [U] *s.t.* that represents the best, worst, or most typical of *s.t.* else: *The devil is the embodiment of evil.*

em·bod·y /ɛmˈbɑdi/ *v.* **-ied, -ying, -ies** to express, symbolize: *The Statue of Liberty embodies the hope of a better life for all.*

em·bold·en /ɛmˈboʊldən/ *v.* to make bold, encourage: *His early success emboldened him to take even greater risks.*

em·bo·lism /ˈɛmbəˌlɪzəm/ *n.* a block in a blood vessel: *Her heart attack was caused by an embolism.*

em·boss /ɛmˈbɔs/ *v.* to decorate with a raised pattern: *Her writing paper is embossed with her name in gold.*

em·brace /ɛmˈbreɪs, ɪm-/ *v.* **-braced, -bracing, -braces 1** to hold in one's arms as a sign of love or affection: *He embraced his wife when she came home from work.* **2** to accept an idea: *He embraced religion late in life.* *—n.* a hug: *She gave her son a warm embrace.*

em·broi·der /ɛmˈbrɔɪdər, ɪm-/ *v.* **1** to decorate with fine needlework: *She embroiders handkerchiefs.* **2** *fig.* to exaggerate with fanciful ideas: *She often embroiders the truth. -n.* [U] **embroidery.**

em·broil /ɛmˈbrɔɪl/ *v.* to involve in a complicated situation, *(syn.)* to entangle: *He became embroiled in a scandal that lasted for months.*

em·bry·o /ˈɛmbriˌoʊ/ *n.* **-os** a fertilized egg, the early stage of growth before birth: *The chicken embryo is growing inside the eggshell. -n.* [U] **embryology** /ˌɛmbriˈɑlədʒi/.

em·bry·on·ic /ˌɛmbriˈɑnɪk/ *adj.frml.* **1** related to the embryo **2** *fig.* early, beginning: *Our new business is in its embryonic stages of development.*

em·cee /ɛm'si/ *n.v.* **-ceed, -ceeing, -cees** *short for* master of ceremonies, the host of an event, esp. on a radio or television program: *He <v.> emceed the television game show for years; he was its <n.> emcee.*

e·mend /ɪ'mɛnd/ *v.* to make improvements, esp. corrections, to a written document, (*syn.*) to revise: *We emended the contract before signing it.* *-n.* [U] **emendation** /ˌɪmɛn'deɪʃən, ˌimɛn-/.

em·er·ald /'ɛmərəld, 'ɛmrəld/ *n.adj.* a precious, green gemstone: *She wore a ring of diamonds and <n.pl.> emeralds.*

e·merge /ɪ'mɜrdʒ/ *v.* **emerged, emerging, emerges 1** to appear: *The hunter emerged from the forest and walked toward us.* **2** to become known or important: *She emerged as the winner among those who tried out for the part in the play.* *-n.* [U] **emergence.**

e·mer·gen·cy /ɪ'mɜrdʒənsi/ *n.* **-cies** a crisis, disaster: *Call the police; this is an emergency!* *—adj.* related to an emergency: *emergency exit*

emergency room or **ER** *n.* part of a hospital that takes care of sick or injured people who need immediate attention: *The woman hurt in the accident was taken to the emergency room in an ambulance.*

e·mer·gent /ɪ'mɜrdʒənt/ *adj.* new to come out or become noticeable: *The personal digital assistant (PDA) is one of many products from emergent technologies.*

e·mer·i·tus /ɪ'mɛrətəs/ or **e·mer·i·ta** /ɪ'mɛrɪtə/ *adj.* retired with honors: *He is a professor emeritus from Princeton University; his wife is a professor emerita from Yale.*

em·er·y board /'ɛməri/ *n.* a cardboard nail file coated with fine hard emery powder: *A manicurist uses an emery board to file down long fingernails.*

e·met·ic /ɪ'mɛtɪk/ *n.adj.* a substance that causes vomiting: *The child ate poison, so the doctor gave her an <n.> emetic to bring it up.*

em·i·grant /'ɛməgrənt/ *n.* a person who leaves their country to live in another: *My assistant is an emigrant from Romania.* *-n.* **émigré** /'ɛmə,greɪ/. *See:* immigrant.

USAGE NOTE: Compare *emigrant* and *immigrant.* A person who goes to live permanently in another country becomes both an emigrant and an immigrant. This person is an emigrant *from* the homeland left behind and an immigrant *to* the new country.

em·i·grate /'ɛmə,greɪt/ *v.* **-grated, -grating, -grates** to leave one's country to live in another *-n.*[C;U] **emigration.**

em·i·nent /'ɛmənənt/ *adj.* widely recognized as important, (*syn.*) distinguished: *She is emi-* nent in the field of linguistics. *-n.* [U] **eminence;** *-adv.* **eminently.**

eminent domain *n.* [U] the right of the government to take and pay for private property for better use by the public: *The town took most of our land by eminent domain to build a high school.*

e·mir or **e·meer** /ɪ'mɪr, eɪ'mɪr/ *n.* a prince or governor usu. in Islamic countries: *the Emir of Kuwait -n.* **emirate.**

em·is·sar·y /'ɛmə,sɛri/ *n.* **-ies** a representative on a special mission, esp. from one government to another government: *The President sent his personal emissary to the Middle East to talk to the leaders there.*

e·mis·sion /ɪ'mɪʃən/ *n.* [C;U] s.t. that is sent out, (*syn.*) a discharge: *Automobiles and trucks produce emissions that pollute the air.*

e·mit /ɪ'mɪt/ *v.* **emitted, emitting, emits 1** to send out, transmit (radio waves, radiation, sound, etc.): *The siren emitted a warning sound.* **2** *frml.* to let out (a cry, yell, sound, etc.): *The victim emitted a scream.*

Em·my /'ɛmi/ *n.* a small statue awarded for excellence in American television broadcasting: *The ABC Evening News won an Emmy this year. See:* Oscar, USAGE NOTE.

e·mol·lient /ɪ'malyənt/ *n.* a substance used to soften or heal the skin: *dishwashing liquid with emollients*

e·mote /ɪ'moʊt/ *v.frml.* **-ted, -ting, -tes** to express emotion in a theatrical or exaggerated way: *The grandmother emoted when she talked about the wonderful time of her youth.* *-adj.* **emotive.**

e·mo·tion /ɪ'moʊʃən/ *n.* [C;U] **1** a feeling, such as love, hate, happiness, or sorrow: *He felt mixed emotions when he thought of her.* **2 to deal with one's emotions:** to control oneself: *He struggled to deal with his emotions when his wife died.*

e·mo·tion·al /ɪ'moʊʃənəl/ *adj.* **1** related to feelings: *Her emotional health is good; she's happy.* **2** full of strong feelings, excited with emotion: *When he disagrees with you, he becomes quite emotional. -n.* [U] **emotionalism;** *-adv.* **emotionally.**

em·pa·thize /'ɛmpə,θaɪz/ *v.* **-thized, -thizing, -thizes** to understand another's feelings (attitudes, reasons, etc.): *He's fearful about his illness, and I empathize with him; it's scary when you're that ill.* *-adj.* **empathetic** /ˌɛmpə'θɛtɪk/.

em·pa·thy /'ɛmpəθi/ *n.sing.* [U] the ability to share or understand another person's feelings (attitudes, reasons, etc.): *I have empathy for you in your fear about speaking in a group.*

em·per·or /'ɛmpərər/ *n.* the male ruler of an empire: *The ancient Roman Empire was ruled by emperors.*

E

em·pha·sis /'ɛmfəsɪs/ n. **-ses** /-ˌsiz/ special importance placed on s.t.: *She put great emphasis on beginning work immediately.*

em·pha·size /'ɛmfəˌsaɪz/ v. **-sized, -sizing, -sizes** to place importance on, (syn.) to stress: *The manager emphasized the need to reduce expenses.*

em·phat·ic /ɛm'fætɪk/ adj. stressed to the point of leaving no doubt, clear: *Her explanation was detailed; she was emphatic about the need to cut expenses.* -adv. **emphatically.**

em·phy·se·ma /ˌɛmfə'simə, -'zi-/ n. [U] a lung disease causing extreme difficulty in breathing: *He got emphysema from smoking cigarettes.*

em·pire /'ɛmˌpaɪr/ n. **1** a group of nations ruled by a central government and usu. an emperor: *the ancient Roman Empire* **2** fig. a very large business operation: *The new organization has created a publishing empire.*

em·pir·i·cal /ɛm'pɪrəkəl/ adj. based on knowledge or experience of the real world, observable: *The paintings on cave walls are empirical proof that people were on Earth many thousands of years ago.* -n. [U] **empiricism;** -adv. **empirically.**

em·ploy /ɛm'plɔɪ, ɪm-/ v. **1** to provide paid work to people: *That company employs 1,000 workers.* **2** to use, (syn.) to utilize: *The company employs computers to keep track of expenses.*

em·ploy·a·ble /ɛm'plɔɪəbəl/ adj. **1** ready and able to be employed: *She has computer skills and a positive outlook; she's employable.* **2** frml. usable, workable: *That computer is employable for accounting purposes.* -n. **employability.**

em·ploy·ee /ɛm'plɔɪi, ˌɛmplɔɪ'i/ n. s.o. who works for a person, business, or government: *She is an employee of this company.*

em·ploy·er /ɛm'plɔɪər, ɪm-/ n. a person, business, or government that employs people: *My employer is United Chemical.*

em·ploy·ment /ɛm'plɔɪmənt, ɪm-/ n. [U] **1** a job paying a salary or wages: *He is out of work and looking for employment.* **2** frml. use: *The employment of force will lead to greater violence.*

em·po·ri·um /ɛm'pɔriəm/ n. **-riums** or **-ria** /-riə/ **1** a center of trade: *Chicago was a livestock emporium.* **2** old usage a large store with different types of goods, a department store **3** a shopping mall: *We bought some shoes and some CD's, and then had lunch at the emporium.*

em·pow·er /ɛm'paʊər/ v. to give power to, (syn.) to authorize: *The judge empowered the police to search the house for stolen goods.* -n. **empowerment.**

em·press /'ɛmprɪs/ n. **-presses 1** the wife of an emperor: *Napoleon's Empress Josephine* **2** the female ruler of an empire

emp·ty /'ɛmpti/ adj. **-tier, -tiest 1** without contents, having nothing or no one inside: *There is nothing in the box; it is empty.||There is no one in the room; it is empty.* **2** fig. having no meaning, purpose, or emotion: *He felt empty after his family left him.*
—v. **-tied, -tying, -ties 1** to remove the contents of: *I emptied the drawer by taking my clothes out of it.* **2** to become empty: *The movie theater emptied after the film ended.* -n. **emptiness.**

empty-handed adj. with nothing, without result: *He tried to make a sale but came up empty-handed.*

empty-headed adj. lacking in good sense or knowledge, (syn.) vacuous: *Some people never have anything to say; they seem empty-headed.*

empty nest syndrome n. feelings of loneliness and uselessness experienced by parents after their children move away from home: *Their youngest son has gone away to college, and they're suffering from empty nest syndrome.*

em·u·late /'ɛmyəˌleɪt/ v.frml. **-lated, -lating, -lates** to try to speak, act, or write like, (syn.) to imitate: *The boy tried to emulate the famous baseball player.* -n. [U] **emulation; emulator.**

e·mul·sion /ɪ'mʌlʃən/ n. [C;U] **1** a combination of liquids that do not mix well together: *an emulsion of oil and water* **2** a coating on photographic film that forms a picture when exposed to light -v. **emulsify** /ɪ'mʌlsəˌfaɪ/.

en·a·ble /ɛn'eɪbəl/ v. **-bled, -bling, -bles** to make possible for, (syn.) to empower: *Their earnings enabled them to retire early.* -adj. **enabling.**

en·act /ɛn'ækt/ v. to make or pass (a law), to legislate: *The Congress enacted a new law.* -n. **enactment.**

e·nam·el /ɪ'næməl/ n. [U] **1** a hard, shiny substance used for decoration and as a coating: *The sink is covered in white enamel.* **2** the outer covering of teeth: *The enamel protects the inside part of the tooth.*
—v. to coat with enamel

en·am·ored /ɪ'næmərd/ adj. filled with love for: *He is enamored of the beautiful girl next door.*

en·camp /ɛn'kæmp/ v. to set up camp: *The soldiers encamped near the river.* -n. **encampment.**

en·cap·su·late /ɛn'kæpsəˌleɪt/ v. **-lated, -lating, -lates 1** to enclose in capsule form: *The manufacturer encapsulates the medicine in jelly capsules.* **2** to summarize, make brief: *The speaker encapsulated his main thoughts first, then gave details.* -n. [U] **encapsulation.**

en·case /ɛnˈkeɪs/ v. -cased, -casing, -cases to cover with protective material: *The worker encased the pipe in a layer of cement.* -n. [U] **encasement.**

en·chant /ɛnˈʧænt/ v. **1** to charm, delight: *That lovely beach enchants everyone who sees it.* **2** to use magic to control: *The witch enchanted the forest animals to do as she told them.* -n. **enchanter;** [U] **enchantment;** -adj. **enchanting;** -adv. **enchantingly.**

en·chi·la·da /ˌɛnʧəˈlɑdə/ n. a tortilla (thin cornmeal bread) usu. baked around a combination of meat, cheese, and other ingredients and topped with sauce: *You can get great enchiladas at the Mexican restaurant around the corner.*

USAGE NOTE: Other popular Mexican-American dishes are *burritos* (meat, rice and beans rolled in large tortillas), *tacos* (meat and beans rolled in small tortillas), *nachos* (fried tortilla chips covered with cheese and toppings), and fried tortilla chips dipped in *guacamole* (avocado sauce) or *salsa* (tomato and chili pepper sauce).

en·cir·cle /ɛnˈsɜrkəl/ v. -cled, -cling, -cles to make a circle around, surround: *The soldiers encircled the enemy camp.* -n. [U] **encirclement.**

en·clave /ˈɛnˌkleɪv, ˈɑn-/ n. a small area controlled by people who differ in culture, social status, ethnic background, etc., from those in the surrounding area: *Chinatown is an enclave in New York City.||an enclave of the rich. See:* ghetto.

en·close /ɛnˈkloʊz/ v. -closed, -closing, -closes **1** to place within, put inside: *I enclosed a check in the envelope with my rent bill.* **2** to shut in, close in: *The animals were enclosed by a fence.*

en·clo·sure /ɛnˈkloʊʒər/ n. **1** an area with a fence or other barrier around it: *During the day, the cattle are kept in an enclosure next to the barn.* **2** s.t. put in an envelope with a letter: *The report is an enclosure with the letter explaining it.*

en·code /ɛnˈkoʊd/ v. -coded, -coding, -codes **1** to change written material into secret symbols: *During World War II, he encoded secret messages sent to the allies.* **2** to put s.t. into a computer language: *She encoded the material so the computer could read it.* -n. **encoder.**

en·com·pass /ɛnˈkʌmpəs/ v. **1** to include: *My history course encompasses the 19th and 20th centuries.* **2** frml. to encircle, surround: *The wall encompasses the entire college campus.*

en·core /ˈɑnˌkɔr/exclam. Again! More!: *The violinist played so beautifully that the audience shouted, "Encore!"*

—n. an addition to a performance to please the audience: *She then played an encore.*

USAGE NOTE: It is common in the USA for the audience to clap at the end of a performance until the musicians return to play another piece of music as an *encore.* Audiences may also give a *standing ovation,* when everyone stands and claps loudly. In rock concerts, audience members often hold up lit cigarette lighters or stamp loudly on the floor to encourage an encore.

en·coun·ter /ɛnˈkaʊntər/ v. **1** to meet by chance, run into: *We encountered some strangers on the road.* **2** to come face-to-face with, (syn.) to confront: *Our army encountered the enemy at the river and fought them.*
—n. a meeting, usu. unplanned: *She had an encounter with a drunk on the subway.*

en·cour·age /ɛnˈkɜrəʤ, -ˈkʌr-/ v. -aged, -aging, -ages to give strength or hope to s.o., (syn.) to urge: *She encouraged her son to go to college.* -n. [U] **encouragement;** -adj. **encouraging.**

en·croach /ɛnˈkroʊʧ/ v. to go beyond proper limits, (syns.) to intrude, trespass: *Soldiers from the neighboring nation crossed our border and encroached upon our territory.* -n. [C;U] **encroachment.**

en·crust /ɛnˈkrʌst/ v. to cover with a hard layer (a crust): *His boots were encrusted with dried mud.* -n. [C;U] **encrustation** /ˌɛnkrʌsˈteɪʃən/.

en·cum·ber /ɛnˈkʌmbər/ v. to burden so as to make action difficult, handicap, (syn.) to hinder: *Too much debt encumbers her business.* -n. **encumbrance.**

en·cy·clo·pe·di·a /ɛnˌsaɪkləˈpidiə/ n. a group of informative articles on general and specific topics that comes in book form or on CD-ROM (usu. arranged in alphabetical order): *I like the Microsoft Encarta™ multimedia encyclopedia because it has great pictures and video clips for many subjects.* -adj. **encyclopedic;** -n. **encyclopedist.**

end /ɛnd/ n. **1** the last part of s.t., (syn.) the extremity: *the end of a stick (wire, street, etc.)* **2** the last part in time, the finish, (syns.) the termination, conclusion: *the end of a story (a class, a year, etc.)* **3** a serious conclusion, such as destruction or death: *the end of all hope (one's marriage, a life, etc.)* **4** frml. a goal, purpose: *The company wanted to improve its image, so to that end, it hired a popular athlete to appear in its advertisements.* **5 at s.o.'s end:** in s.o.'s area of responsibility: *Have there been any problems at your end of the project?* **6 at the end of one's rope:** totally blocked and frustrated: *He has tried everything to stop smoking, but he cannot do it, and now he is at the end of his rope.* **7 (at) the end of the line:**

(at) the final point of an activity or relationship where there can be no more progress: *We argue all the time, so this is the end of the line. Goodbye!* **8 end to end:** with the ends of objects touching each other: *We put two tables end to end to make one long table.* **9** *infrml.* **no end of:** a lot of: *The boy caused no end of trouble for his parents.* **10 on end: a.** placed on an extremity, upright: *A worker stood the table on end so that he could paint its underside.* **b.** (of time) for a long time without stopping: *She waited for days on end before his letter finally arrived.* **11 to bring to an end:** to conclude, terminate: *The manager brought the meeting to an end.* **12** *infrml.* **to go off the deep end:** to do s.t. that is very foolish or risky: *He bought a boat he cannot afford; he went off the deep end!* **13 to hold up** or **keep up one's end:** to do what one agreed to do: *You promised to pay half the cost, so give me a check and hold up your end of the bargain.* **14 to make ends meet:** to get enough money to pay for necessities and survive financially: *I make just enough money to make ends meet, to pay the rent and buy food.* **15 to put an end to:** to stop (usu. s.t. that is annoying): *I put an end to her complaints by simply telling her to stop!*
—*v.* **1** to make stop, bring to an end, (*syn.*) to terminate: *We ended our conversation with a promise to see each other again.* **2** to come to a stop, finish: *The sandy beach ends two miles north of here.* **3** *phrasal v. insep.* **to end in s.t.:** to result in: *The meeting ended in a confrontation.* **4 to end it all** or **to put an end to it all:** to kill oneself, commit suicide: *He had cancer and decided to end it all by shooting himself.* **5** *phrasal v.* **to end up:** to come finally to a particular place or position: *She ended up owning the company where she had gotten her first job. See:* dead end.

en·dan·ger /ɛn'deɪndʒər/ *v.* to place in danger, (*syn.*) to jeopardize: *They went boating on the ocean in stormy weather and endangered their lives.* -*n.* **endangerment.**

endangered species *n.* used with a sing. or pl.v. a plant or animal whose population is so low that it is in danger of extinction: *We give money to the wildlife fund to protect endangered species.*

en·dear /ɛn'dɪr/ *v.* to create a liking or affection for (esp. oneself): *She is so warm and generous that she endears herself to everyone.* -*adj.* **endearing;** -*n.*[C;U] **endearment.**

en·deav·or /ɛn'dɛvər/ *v.frml.* to try, to attempt: *He endeavors to do his best work all the time.*
—*n.* **1** *frml.*an effort, attempt: *Despite his best endeavors, the company failed.* **2** a project, affair, (*syn.*) a venture: *She has many business endeavors; she is a partner in three businesses.*

en·dem·ic /ɛn'dɛmɪk/ *adj.frml.* often found within a particular area or group of people: *Ill health is endemic to the poor.*

end·ing /'ɛndɪŋ/ *n.* [C;U] the end, the finish: *The ending of the novel (relationship, story, etc.) was quite sad.*

en·dive /'ɛn,daɪv, 'ɑn,dɪv/ *n.* a plant with crisp, whitish leaves used in salads

end·less /'ɛndlɪs/ *adj.* **1** without limits, (*syn.*) infinite: *Seen through a telescope at night, the universe appears endless.* **2** without stopping, continuous: *The traffic on the highway makes an endless noise.* -*adv.* **endlessly.**

en·dorse /ɛn'dɔrs/ *v.* **-dorsed, -dorsing, -dorses 1** to sign one's name on the back of a check or note: *He endorsed his paycheck and deposited it in his bank.* **2** to approve an idea, act, or product: *Famous athletes endorse sports equipment and other products.* -*n.* [C;U] **endorsement.**

en·dow /ɛn'daʊ/ *v.* **1** to give money or property for the support of (a school, organization, etc.): *Graduates endow their colleges with funds to support their operation.* **2** to give a good quality or ability: *Her parents endowed their daughter with high intelligence.* -*n.* [C;U] **endowment.**

en·dur·ance /ɛn'dʊrəns, ɪn-/ *n.* [U] the ability to function (work, run, swim, etc.) properly over a long period of time, (*syn.*) stamina: *Olympic athletes have great endurance.*

en·dure /ɛn'dʊr, ɪn-/ *v.* **-dured, -during, -dures 1** to last, survive: *Great art endures for centuries.* **2** to bear, tolerate: *Athletes endure pain to win races.* -*adj.* **endurable; enduring.**

end·ways /'ɛnd,weɪz/ or **end·wise** /'ɛnd'waɪz/ *adv.* **1** standing up, upright: *We turned the sofa endways so it would fit through the door.* **2** with the end first

en·e·ma /'ɛnəmə/ *n.* liquid put into the rectum to clear out feces: *The nurse gave the patient an enema before the operation.*

en·e·my /'ɛnəmi/ *n.* **-mies** a person, military, or nation that intends harm to another: *During the Civil War in the USA, the Northern and Southern states were enemies.*

en·er·get·ic /,ɛnər'dʒɛtɪk/ *adj.* having energy, active, vigorous: *She is a very energetic woman with many interests.* -*adv.* **energetically.**

en·er·gize /'ɛnər,dʒaɪz/ *v.* **-gized, -gizing, -gizes 1** to fill with energy, (*syn.*) to motivate: *The sales manager energized her sales force with enthusiasm.* **2** to provide power to: *The battery energized the motor and made it run.* -*n.* **energizer.** *See:* enervate.

en·er·gy /'ɛnərdʒi/ *n.* [U] **1** the power to do work: *Energy to run machines sometimes comes from electricity.* **2** the capacity or power to be active (work, play): *He is full of energy and is active all the time.*

en·er·vate /'ɛnər,veɪt/ *v.frml.* **-vated, -vating, -vates** to drain of energy, weaken: *The hot weather enervates me; I don't move around very much and am tired all the time. See:* energize.

en·fee·ble /ɛn'fibəl/ *v.* **-bled, -bling, -bles** to weaken, make feeble: *His long illness enfeebled him.*

en·fold /ɛn'foʊld/ *v.frml.* to wrap, encircle: *The mother tenderly enfolded the child in her arms.*

en·force /ɛn'fɔrs, ɪn-/ *v.* **-forced, -forcing, -forces** to make people obey (laws, rules, etc.): *The police enforce the law by arresting lawbreakers. -adj.* **enforceable;** *-n.* [U] **enforcement; enforcer.**

en·fran·chise /ɛn'fræn,tʃaɪz/ *v.* **-chised, -chising, -chises** to provide with a right, esp. to vote: *The voting rights bill enfranchises thousands who could not vote before. -n.* [U] **enfranchisement.**

en·gage /ɛn'geɪdʒ, ɪn-/ *v.frml.* **-gaged, -gaging, -gages 1** to make things fit and move together, *(syn.)* to interlock: *The driver engaged the car's gears.* **2** to employ, hire: *The company engaged 50 new workers.* **3** to be involved, participate: *She didn't want to engage in conversation.* **4** to get and hold the attention of: *The professor engaged his students in discussion.*

en·gaged /ɛn'geɪdʒd, ɪn-/ *adj.* **1** having a formal agreement to get married: *The engaged couple plan to get married in the spring.* **2** busy, occupied: *My boss is engaged right now, but she should be free in an hour.*

en·gage·ment /ɛn'geɪdʒmənt, ɪn-/ *n.* **1** an agreement to marry: *We announced our engagement last week.* **2** a meeting, appointment: *I have an engagement this evening.* **3** a battle: *The two armies fought an engagement.*

engagement ring *n.* a gold or platinum ring with a diamond given to a woman by a man to show their agreement to marry

en·gag·ing /ɛn'geɪdʒɪŋ/ *adj.* charming, captivating: *She has an engaging personality. -adv.* **engagingly.**

en·gen·der /ɛn'dʒɛndər/ *v.frml.* to produce, bring into being: *Poverty often engenders disease.*

en·gine /'ɛndʒɪn/ *n.* **1** a machine that produces force and motion: *The engine in my car drives the wheels to make it move.* **2** a machine that pulls a train, a locomotive

en·gi·neer /,ɛndʒə'nɪr/ *n.* **1** a person highly trained in science and mathematics who plans the making of machines (mechanical engineer, electrical engineer), roads and bridges (civil engineer), etc.: *She is an electrical engineer who works for a computer company.* **2** the person who drives a train: *The engineer slowed the train as it neared the station.*
—*v.* **1** to plan the making of s.t. by using the skills of engineering: *He engineered a tiny computer.* **2** to put together in a skillful or forceful way, manage: *My boss engineered the purchase of another company.*

en·gi·neer·ing /,ɛndʒə'nɪrɪŋ/ *n.* [U] **1** the profession of an engineer: *She studies automotive engineering.* **2** the scientific planning of a machine, road, bridge, etc.

Eng·lish /'ɪŋglɪʃ/ *n.adj.* [U] **1** the people of England: *The <n.> English are proud of their history.* **2** the English language: *Kristin speaks <n.> English, German, and Mandarin.* **3** related to the English: *<adj.> English woolens, an <n.> Englishman, an <n.> Englishwoman*

USAGE NOTE: Because *English* is used around the world as a language of international communication, today many more people speak English as a second or foreign language than people who speak English as a first or native language.

English muffin *n.* a round yeasty bread usu. cut and toasted in halves: *For breakfast, I had eggs and an English muffin.*

en·gorge /ɛn'gɔrdʒ/ *v.* **-gorged, -gorging, -gorges** to fill to the limit, swell: *His wound was engorged with blood.*

en·grave /ɛn'greɪv, ɪn-/ *v.* **-graved, -graving, -graves** to cut or carve words, pictures, or designs in metal, stone, etc.: *She engraved a winter scene on a copper plate for printing. -n.* **engraver;** [C;U] **engraving.**

en·gross /ɛn'groʊs/ *v.* to keep one's attention completely, *(syn.)* to captivate: *He engrossed himself in his writing for many months. -adj.* **engrossed; engrossing.**

en·gulf /ɛn'gʌlf/ *v.* to enclose and swallow up, overwhelm: *The flood waters engulfed the town.*

en·hance /ɛn'hæns/ *v.* **-hanced, -hancing, -hances** to improve, add to: *She enhanced the value of her house by painting it.*

e·nig·ma /ɪ'nɪgmə/ *n.* a mystery, puzzle: *No one knows what happened to the airplane; its disappearance is an enigma. -adj.* **enigmatic;** *-adv.* **enigmatically.**

en·join /ɛn'dʒɔɪn/ *v.frml.* to stop, prevent: *The court enjoined the prosecution from convicting an innocent man.*

en·joy /ɛn'dʒɔɪ, ɪn-/ *v.* **1** to get pleasure from, to like: *He enjoys music.* **2** *frml.* to have, esp. s.t. that is good: *She enjoys good health; she is very healthy.* **3 to enjoy oneself:** to have fun: *We enjoyed ourselves at their wedding. -n.* **enjoyment.**

en·joy·able /ɛn'dʒɔɪəbəl, ɪn-/ adj. pleasurable, pleasant: *We had an enjoyable time at the picnic.*

en·large /ɛn'lɑrdʒ/ v. **-larged, -larging, -larges** **1** to make larger, expand the size of: *We enlarged our house by adding two new rooms.* **2** (in photography) to make a picture bigger *-n.* [C;U] **enlargement; enlarger.**

en·light·en /ɛn'laɪtn/ v. to make (s.o.) understand for the first time: *The instructor enlightened his students on how to use adjectives in English. -adj.* **enlightened; enlightening.**

en·light·en·ment /ɛn'laɪtnmənt/ n. [U] **1** an explanation: *The professor provided enlightenment on the subject.* **2 the Enlightenment:** a movement in 18th-century Europe that emphasized scientific and rational thought, also known as the Age of Reason

en·list /ɛn'lɪst, ɪn-/ v. **1** to join the military voluntarily: *I enlisted in the army when I was 18.* **2** to ask for and receive (support, assistance, etc.): *He enlisted the help of his friends in moving his furniture. -n.* [C;U] **enlistment.**

en·liv·en /ɛn'laɪvən/ v. to make lively, brighten up: *Her funny stories enlivened the party.*

en masse /ɑn'mæs/ adv. as a group, in a mass of people or things: *The crowd moved en masse from Amy's house to the city square.*

en·mesh /ɛn'mɛʃ/ v. to catch as in a net: *The politician became enmeshed in a scandal.*

en·mi·ty /'ɛnmɪti/ n.frml. [U] hatred, (syn.) animosity: *There is enmity between those two men; they once had a fight.*

e·nor·mi·ty /ɪ'nɔrməti/ n. [U] great evil, (syn.) wickedness: *People were appalled by the enormity of the crime; many people were hurt and killed.*

e·nor·mous /ɪ'nɔrməs/ adj. extremely big, huge, (syn.) immense: *The Sears Tower in Chicago is enormous; it's more than 100 stories tall! -n.* **enormousness;** *-adv.* **enormously.**

e·nough /ɪ'nʌf/ adj. as much or as many as needed, (syns.) sufficient, adequate: *We have enough money to pay the bills.‖Do we have enough books to go around* (or) *enough books for everyone?*
—*adv.* to the amount or degree necessary, (syns.) adequately, sufficiently: *She plays the piano well enough.*
—*n.* [U] an adequate amount, a sufficiency: *The basketball game was boring; we saw enough and went home.* —*exclam.* Stop!: *Enough! I don't want to hear anymore!*

en·quire /ɛn'kwaɪr/ v. **-quired, -quiring, -quires** var. of inquire

en·qui·ry /ɛn'kwaɪri, 'ɛnkwəri/ n. **-ries** var. of inquiry

en·rage /ɛn'reɪdʒ/ v. **-raged, -raging, -rages** to make very angry, (syns.) to infuriate, incense: *The lies said about him enraged him. See:* angry, USAGE NOTE.

en·rap·ture /ɛn'ræptʃər/ v. **-tured, -turing, -tures** to fill with delight, (syn.) to enthrall: *The beautiful music enraptured her; what lovely sounds! See:* rapture, ecstasy.

en·rich /ɛn'rɪtʃ/ v. **1** to make rich or richer: *The growth of industry enriched the small town.* **2** to add good things to: *The farmer enriched the soil with fertilizer. -adj.* **enriching;** *-n.* [U] **enrichment.**

en·roll /ɛn'roʊl/ v. to join officially: *I enrolled in college this autumn; I will graduate in four years. -n.* **enrollee** /ˌɛnroʊl'i/.

en·roll·ment /ɛn'roʊlmənt/ n. **1** [U] an act of joining, as in a school or class: *My enrollment in the fall classes took two hours.* **2** [C] the number of students enrolled in a class or school: *My English course has an enrollment of 200 students.*

en route /ɑn'rut, ɛn/ adj.adv. on the way, traveling: *He is <adj.> en route to a meeting in London.*

en·sconce /ɛn'skɑns/ v. **-sconced, -sconcing, -sconces** to place (esp. oneself) in a comfortable, secure position: *She has ensconced herself in front of the TV for the evening.*

en·sem·ble /ɑn'sɑmbəl/ n. **1** a musical group: *a singing ensemble* **2** frml. a set of matching clothes: *The model is wearing an attractive ensemble—a suit with matching shoes and belt.*

en·shrine /ɛn'ʃraɪn/ v. **-shrined, -shrining, -shrines** to keep so as to honor the memory of (a person, event, or god): *The remains of Napoleon Bonaparte are enshrined in Paris.*

en·shroud /ɛn'ʃraʊd/ v. to cover with s.t. dark or sad: *Gray clouds enshrouded the city. See:* shroud, envelop.

en·sign /'ɛnsən/ n. **1** the lowest-ranking naval officer: *She is an ensign, soon to be made a lieutenant.* **2** a national flag, emblem, or insignia

en·snare /ɛn'snɛr/ v. **-snared, -snaring, -snares** **1** to catch as in a net, trap, or snare: *The hunter ensnared a rabbit.* **2** to trap in difficult circumstances, (syn.) to entrap: *The criminal ensnared his victims in a scheme to steal their money.*

en·sue /ɛn'su/ v. **-sued, -suing, -sues** to result after an event, happen in sequence: *As a result of heavy rain, bad flooding ensued.*

en·sure /ɛn'ʃʊr/ v. **-sured, -suring, -sures** to make sure: *He ensured that all the doors were locked before he left his apartment.‖Your passport ensures your entry into your home country. See:* insure.

en·tail /ɛn'teɪl/ v. to make necessary, require: *The loss of your wallet entails getting all new documents.*

en·tan·gle /ɛn'tæŋgəl/ v. **-gled, -gling, -gles 1** to cause to mix in with and be caught by s.t. else: *The comb became entangled in her hair.* **2** *fig.* to involve others in a difficult situation or problem, (*syn.*) to enmesh: *She entangled her friends in foolish schemes to get rich.* -n. [C;U] **entanglement.**

en·ter /'ɛntər/ v. **1** to go into: *I entered the classroom.* **2** to begin, engage in: *She will enter college in the autumn.* **3** to write down, record: *The command on the computer screen told me to enter my name, so I typed it in.* **4** *phrasal v. insep.* **to enter into s.t.:** to contract for, cooperate with: *Our company entered into an agreement with a foreign government.*

en·ter·prise /'ɛntər,praɪz/ n. **1** [U] an act that requires courage, hard work, and intelligence, esp. in business: *Her business has prospered because of her enterprise.* **2** [C] a business, company, esp. a new one: *His enterprise is located in the financial district.* -adj. **enterprising.**

en·ter·tain /,ɛntər'teɪn/ v. **1** to amuse, provide entertainment to: *She is a singer who entertains at a local nightclub.* **2** to give parties (dinners, cookouts, etc.): *That couple often entertains on weekends.* **3** to have in mind, consider: *He refused to entertain my suggestion.* -n. **entertainment.**

en·ter·tain·er /,ɛntər'teɪnər/ n. a person who entertains professionally: *The singer, Frank Sinatra, is a well-known entertainer.*

en·ter·tain·ing /,ɛntər'teɪnɪŋ/ adj. amusing, delightful: *I enjoyed the movie that we saw last night; it was very entertaining.* -adv. **entertainingly.**

en·thrall /ɛn'θrɔl/ v. to hold s.o.'s attention completely, (*syns.*) to captivate, spellbind: *The dancer enthralls her audiences with the beauty of her movements.*

en·thuse /ɛn'θuz/ v.infrml. **-thused, -thusing, -thuses** to fill with enthusiasm, excite: *The thought of going to Europe enthused her greatly.*

en·thu·si·asm /ɛn'θuzi,æzəm/ n. [U] **1** eagerness, (*syn.*) zeal: *He loves his job; he works with enthusiasm every day.* **2** strong interest, general good feeling: *You can see the enthusiasm of the employees of that company.*

en·thu·si·ast /ɛn'θuzi,æst/ n. a person full of eagerness for s.t. or s.o.: *He is a skiing enthusiast; in the winter, he skis every weekend.*

en·thu·si·as·tic /ɛn,θuzi'æstɪk/ adj. eager, excited: *She is enthusiastic about beginning her new job.* -adv. **enthusiastically.**

en·tice /ɛn'taɪs/ v. **-ticed, -ticing, -tices** to attract or persuade: *He enticed her into marrying him with promises of a house, car, and money.* -n. [C;U] **enticement;** -adj. **enticing.**

en·tire /ɛn'taɪr/ adj. complete, whole: *Of course he is our landlord; he owns the entire building.* -adv. **entirely.**

en·tire·ty /ɛn'taɪrti, -'taɪrə-/ n. [U] all of s.t., the whole: *He painted the building in its entirety.*

en·ti·tle /ɛn'taɪtl/ v. **-tled, -tling, -tles 1** to allow, authorize: *That pass entitles you to enter the concert for free.* **2** to call, name: *That book is entitled* Gone with the Wind.

en·ti·tle·ment /ɛn'taɪtlmənt/ n. [C;U] **1** legal authorization: *She has an entitlement to one half of her husband's property.* **2** a right, esp. for governmental aid: *The man has entitlements to Social Security and medical care.*

en·ti·ty /'ɛntəti/ n. **-ties** a group viewed as a whole: *All the buildings in this area are for sale as a single entity.*

en·tomb /ɛn'tum/ v.frml. to bury in a tomb: *The dead queen is entombed near the palace.* -n. [C;U] **entombment.**

en·to·mol·o·gy /,ɛntə'malədʒi/ n. the study of insects: *He's a professor of entomology; spiders are his specialty.* -n. **entomologist.**

en·tou·rage /,antə'raʒ/ n. a group of people who follow s.o. important, (*syn.*) a retinue: *The movie star has an entourage of employees and admirers.*

en·trails /'ɛn,treɪlz/ n.pl. the insides (intestines, liver, heart, kidney), esp. of an animal: *Smaller animals feed on the entrails of zebras killed by lions.*

en·trance /'ɛntrəns/ n. **1** a door, gate, or other opening allowing one to enter: *We walked through the entrance to the museum.* **2** the area around an entrance: *We had waited for a friend at the entrance.* **3** an act of entering: *He has formally announced his entrance into the race for President.* **4 to make an entrance:** to appear, often in a dramatic fashion: *The princess waited for all the other guests to arrive, then made an entrance in a beautiful gown.*
—v. /ɛn'træns/ v. **-tranced, -trancing, -trances** to hold s.o.'s attention and give delight, (*syn.*) to enchant: *Her beauty and intelligence entranced him.* -adj. **entrancing.**

en·trant /'ɛntrənt/ n. a person who enters a competition: *She was one of 50 entrants in the race.*

en·trap /ɛn'træp/ v. **-trapped, -trapping, -traps 1** to attract into difficulty or trick into harm: *A criminal entrapped an elderly man in a bad investment and stole his money.* **2** to catch as in a trap: *Workers were entrapped when the roof fell in on them.* -n. [C;U] **entrapment.**

en·treat /ɛn'trit/ v.frml. to ask very seriously, to plead: *The sick man entreated the doctor to ease his pain.* -n. [C;U] **entreaty.**

en·trée /'ɑntreɪ/ n. **1** in USA, the main part of the meal at dinner or lunch: *We started with soup and had steak as the entrée.* **2** special permission to enter a place: *My friend is the secretary to the president of that company, so I have an entrée there.*

en·trench /ɛn'trɛntʃ/ v. to put in a firm and protected position: *The owner's son entrenched himself in a job given him by his father.* -n. [U] **entrenchment.**

en·tre·pre·neur /,ɑntrəprə'nɜr, -'nʊr/ n. a person who starts a business with an idea, makes it grow, and takes the risk of failure: *She was an entrepreneur who built a company around a new type of beauty product.*

en·tre·pre·neur·i·al spirit /,ɑntrəprə'nɜriəl, -'nʊr-/ n. [U] a positive attitude toward risking time and money on new business ideas or on better ways of doing business

en·trust /ɛn'trʌst/ v. to give for safekeeping, place in trust: *Airline passengers entrust their safety to the pilot.*

en·try /'ɛntri/ n. **-tries 1** an act of entering: *Many people opposed the entry of the USA into the war.* **2** a record of a transaction or event, such as a birth: *The clerk made an entry of the sale in the company books.* **3** a word and its definition in a dictionary: *College dictionaries have about 200,000 entries.* **4 entry-level:** (of a job) in the lowest category *See:* data entry.

USAGE NOTE: Jobs that require the least experience are called *entry-level positions.* Many people begin their careers at entry-level positions and work their way *up the ladder,* or advance into high-level positions. *She began at the entry level as a clerk and worked her way up the ladder to become president of the company.*

en·try·way /'ɛntri,weɪ/ n. a place or way to go in, an access: *There is only one entryway to the building.*

en·twine /ɛn'twaɪn/ v. **-twined, -twining, -twines** to wrap around: *A climbing plant has entwined itself around that tree.*

e·nu·mer·ate /ɪ'numə,reɪt/ v. **-ated, -ating, -ates** to count off, list: *She enumerated five things that she liked about the new apartment.* -n. [C;U] **enumeration.**

e·nun·ci·ate /ɪ'nʌnsi,eɪt/ v. **-ated, -ating, -ates 1** to speak clearly: *He enunciated his words so I could understand him.* **2** to express, state: *The buyer enunciated her conditions for buying the house.* -n. [U] **enunciation.**

en·ure /ɪn'yʊr/ v. **-ured, -uring, -ures** *var. of* inure

en·vel·op /ɛn'vɛləp/ v. to surround, enclose, cover completely: *Fog enveloped the airport.* -n. [U] **envelopment.** *See:* enshroud.

en·ve·lope /'ɛnvə,loʊp, 'ɑn-/ n. **1** a paper cover for letters (documents, computer disks, products, etc.): *We put our bills in envelopes to mail to our customers.* **2 to push the envelope:** to extend the limits of human achievement in an area: *Test pilots push the envelope by setting faster speed records.*

en·vi·a·ble /'ɛnviəbəl/ adj. very desirable, worthy of envy, admiration: *She is in the enviable position of having two excellent job offers.*

en·vi·ous /'ɛnviəs/ adj. wanting to have what s.o. else has: *He is envious of my new car and wants one like it.* -adv. **enviously.** *See:* envy; jealousy.

en·vi·ron·ment /ɛn'vaɪrənmɛnt, -'vaɪərn-/ n. **1** [C;U] the air, land, water, and surroundings that people, plants, and animals live in: *The environment in big cities is usually polluted.* **2** [C] a set of social conditions that affect people, an atmosphere: *That child is growing up in a bad environment.* -adj. **environmental;** -adv. **environmentally.**

en·vi·ron·men·tal·ist /ɛn,vaɪrən'mɛntlɪst, -'vaɪərn-/ n. a person devoted to or employed in environmental concerns: *She is an environmentalist working for the Pure Water Coalition.* -n. **environmentalism.**

en·vi·rons /ɛn'vaɪrənz, -'vaɪərnz/ n.pl.frml. a local area, neighborhood: *She is living somewhere in the environs of Miami.*

en·vis·age /ɛn'vɪzɪdʒ/ v. **-aged, -aging, -ages** *See:* envision.

en·vi·sion /ɛn'vɪʒən/ v. to have in mind, (syns.) to envisage, foresee: *What kind of career do you envision for yourself?*

en·voy /'ɛn,vɔɪ, 'ɑn-/ n. a messenger, esp. a diplomatic representative of a government: *The President sent a special envoy to the trade talks.*

en·vy /'ɛnvi/ v. **-vied, -vying, -vies** to want the same things s.o. else has: *He has a wonderful job (wife, house, life, etc.); I envy him.*
—n. **1** [U] a desire to have what belongs to another: *She is full of envy of her friend's good looks.* *See:* jealous. **2 the envy of s.o.:** s.o. or s.t. envied by others: *The boy's new bicycle was* (or) *made him the envy of all his friends.*

en·zyme /'ɛn,zaɪm/ n. a natural chemical in living cells that helps make them work: *Enzymes in the mouth help digest food.*

e·on /'i,ɑn, 'iən/ n. **1** an extremely long period of time, thousands or millions of years: *The layers of rock on the ocean floor took eons to develop.* **2 in eons:** in a long time: *Where have you been? I haven't seen you in eons.*

ep·au·let /'ɛpə,lɛt, ,ɛpə'lɛt/ n. a shoulder ornament, worn esp. on dress military uniforms

e·phem·er·al /ɪ'fɛmərəl/ adj.frml. of little importance and lasting only a short time: *He had* *an ephemeral career as a professional ski racer: -n.pl.* **ephemera.**

ep·ic /ˈɛpɪk/ *n.adj.* a poem, story, or adventure of heroic proportions: *The journey of the Jews from Egypt was an <n.> epic (or) an <adj.> epic event.*

ep·i·cen·ter /ˈɛpəˌsɛntər/ *n.* the exact center of an important event, esp. a violent one: *The epicenter of the earthquake that shook Los Angeles was 50 miles away.*

ep·i·cure /ˈɛpɪˌkyʊr/ *n.* s.o. who greatly enjoys fine food and drink, esp. wines *-adj.* **epicurean.**

ep·i·dem·ic /ˌɛpəˈdɛmɪk/ *n.adj.* a disease that spreads quickly among many people: *There are <n.pl.> epidemics of influenza nearly every winter.*

ep·i·der·mis /ˌɛpəˈdɜrmɪs/ *n.* **-mises** the outer layer of the skin

ep·i·gram /ˈɛpəˌgræm/ *n.* a brief, wise saying, often in poetic form: *"It is better to have loved and lost than never to have loved at all" is an epigram. -adj.* **epigrammatic** /ˌɛpəgrə-ˈmætɪk/.

ep·i·lep·sy /ˈɛpəˌlɛpsi/ *n.* [U] a disorder of the nervous system with uncontrolled movements and sometimes loss of consciousness: *Julius Caesar suffered from epilepsy.*

ep·i·lep·tic /ˌɛpəˈlɛptɪk/ *n.adj.* a person who has epilepsy: *He is an <n.> epileptic; he suffers from <adj.> epileptic seizures.*

ep·i·logue /ˈɛpəˌlɔg, -ˌlɒg/ *n.* an addition at the end of a literary work or play, usu. about what has happened or will happen afterward: *The book is about a terrible disease, and the author added an epilogue about recent research into a cure.*

ep·i·sode /ˈɛpəˌsoʊd/ *n.* one in a series of events: *I watched an episode of a soap opera on television. -adj.* **episodic** /ˌɛpəˈsɑdɪk/.

e·pis·tle /əˈpɪsəl/ *n.frml.* a letter, *(syn.)* a missive: *The Christian Bible includes the epistles of the apostles.*

ep·i·taph /ˈɛpəˌtæf/ *n.* an inscription on a gravestone about the dead person: *His epitaph reads "John Smith, Born 1930—Died 1993."* See: *in memorium.*

ep·i·thet /ˈɛpəˌθɛt/ *n.frml.* a word of phrase used to describe s.o., often negatively or offensively: *The enemies hurled epithets at each other.*

e·pit·o·me /əˈpɪtəmi/ *n.* the ultimate of s.t., usu. the best but can be used to mean the worst: *She sings beautifully; she's the epitome of what a singer should be.||Her singing is terrible; she's the epitome of what a singer should not be. -v.* **epitomize.**

e plu·ri·bus u·num /iˈplʊrəbəsˈyunəm/ *adv. phr.* Latin for "out of many, one"; used as the

motto of the USA to express the ideal of unity among the many peoples living in the country

ep·och /ˈɛpək/ *n.* a period in geologic time or in history with a special character: *The end of the nuclear arms race began a new epoch of peace and cooperation. -adj.* **epochal.**

ep·ox·y /ɪˈpɑksi/ *n.* **-ies** a very strong glue: *I glued the handle back on the teacup with epoxy.*

eq·ua·ble /ˈɛkwəbəl/ *adj.* calm, even-tempered: *His equable manner makes him a good boss. -n.* **equability;** *-adv.* **equably.**

e·qual /ˈikwəl/ *n.* the same, an equivalent (in amount, size, appearance, power, etc.): *Those two managers are equals; both are vice presidents of the company.*

—adj. **1** being the same, equivalent, alike: *The two tables are of equal length (importance, height, etc.).* **2 to be equal to:** (of a person) to be strong or skilled enough for: *It's a big responsibility to take on, so I hope she's equal to the task.*

—v. **1** to be the same as, match, *(syn.)* to correspond to: *The two horses equal each other in speed.* **2** to result in (from adding, multiplying, etc.): *Two plus two equals four. -adv.* **equally.**

e·qual·i·ty /ɪˈkwɑləti/ *n.* [U] a condition of being equal (in importance, rank, power, etc.): *Some countries are working toward economic equality.*

e·qual·ize /ˈikwəˌlaɪz/ *v.* **-ized, -izing, -izes** to make equal (in weight, appearance, size, power, etc.): *One boxer equalized his weight with his opponent's weight by losing ten pounds. -n.* **equalizer.**

Equal Rights Amendment *n.sing. abbr.* **ERA** in USA, a proposed amendment to the Constitution guaranteeing equal treatment under the law to men and women

equal sign *n.* [U] the symbol (=) that means terms on either side of it are equivalent: $2 + 2 = 4$.

e·qua·nim·i·ty /ˌikwəˈnɪməti, ˌɛk-/ *n.frml.* [U] peace of mind, calmness: *to have equanimity of mind*

e·quate /ɪˈkweɪt/ *v.* **equated, equating, equates** to compare two things in importance (meaning, value, etc.), *(syn.)* to liken: *He equates wealth with success in life.*

e·qua·tion /ɪˈkweɪʒən/ *n.* a mathematical statement that two amounts are equal: *The following is a simple equation:* $2 + 2 = 4$.

e·qua·tor /ɪˈkweɪtər/ *n.* a theoretical line around the middle of the earth that is equal in distance from the North and South Poles: *The nations located on or near the equator have very hot climates. -adj.* **equatorial** /ˌikwə-ˈtɔriəl, ˌɛk-/.

e·ques·tri·an /ɪˈkwɛstriən/ *n.adj.* a person who rides horses: *She is an <n.> equestrian, and she competes in <adj.> equestrian events.*

e·qui·dis·tant /ˌikwəˈdɪstənt, ˈɛk-/ *adj.* located halfway between two points: *New York City is about equidistant from Boston and Washington, D.C. -adv.* **equidistantly.**

e·qui·lat·er·al /ˌikwəˈlætərəl/ *adj.* having sides of the same length: *The four sides of a square are equilateral.*

e·qui·lib·ri·um /ˌikwəˈlɪbriəm, ˈɛk-/ *n.* [U] one's sense of balance: *She lost her equilibrium and fell down.*

e·quine /ˈiˌkwaɪn, ˈɛk-/ *adj.* related to horses

e·qui·nox /ˈikwəˌnɑks, ˈɛk-/ *n.* **-es** the two days each year (around March 21 and September 22) when day and night are of equal length

e·quip /ɪˈkwɪp/ *v.* **equipped, equipping, equips** to provide with equipment, to outfit: *Our office is equipped with two powerful computers.*

e·quip·ment /ɪˈkwɪpmənt/ *n.* [U] useful items needed for a purpose (work, sports, etc.): *I have sports equipment that includes golf clubs, tennis rackets, and ice skates.*

eq·uit·a·ble /ˈɛkwɪtəbəl/ *adj.* reasonable to everyone concerned, fair: *We made an equitable arrangement; the two of us will split the profits in half. -adv.* **equitably.**

eq·ui·ty /ˈɛkwəti/ *n.* [U] **1** fairness, justice **2** (in business, esp. real estate) the difference between the value of s.t. and the money owed against it: *My equity in my brokerage account is $15,000 because I have $20,000 in stock but owe $5,000 as a loan.*

e·quiv·a·lent /ɪˈkwɪvələnt/ *adj.* equal, the same: *The two computers are equivalent in speed.*
—*n.* [U] s.t. that is the same: *What is the equivalent of one US dollar in Japanese yen? -n.* **equivalence.**

e·quiv·o·cal /ɪˈkwɪvəkəl/ *adj.* **1** undecided, uncertain: *He still remains equivocal about going ahead with the project.* **2** ambiguous, unclear: *I asked him yesterday, and his answer was equivocal: "Maybe we will; maybe we won't." -v.* **equivocate.**

ER *n.abbr.* of emergency room

e·ra /ˈɪrə, ˈɛrə/ *n.* a time period with a general character: *The Eisenhower era in the USA was one of peace and prosperity.*

ERA /ˈiɑrˈeɪ/ *n.abbr. for* Equal Rights Amendment

e·rad·i·cate /ɪˈrædəˌkeɪt/ *v.* **-cated, -cating, -cates** to destroy completely, (*syn.*) to eliminate: *Modern medicine has eradicated some diseases. -n.* [U] **eradication.**

e·rase /ɪˈreɪs/ *v.* **erased, erasing, erases 1** to clean off: *The teacher erased the blackboard.* **2** to remove completely, (*syn.*) to eradicate: *I*

erased the music on the audiotape before recording on the tape again.

e·ras·er /ɪˈreɪsər/ *n.* a stub or small block of rubber or felt used to erase pencil, chalk, or other marks: *I like to use pencils with erasers on top. -n.* **erasure** /ɪˈreɪʃər/.

e·rect /ɪˈrɛkt/ *adj.* standing up, straight: *She is elderly, but she stands erect.*
—*v.* **1** to raise into position: *Workmen erected a ladder against the building.* **2** to build, construct: *A construction company erected a building across the street. -n.* [C;U] **erection;** -*adv.* **erectly.**

er·go·nom·ics /ˌɜrgəˈnɑmɪks/ *n.* [U] the study of the best way to design machines for human comfort, convenience, and business efficiency: *She is an expert in computer ergonomics.*

e·rode /ɪˈroʊd/ *v.* **eroded, eroding, erodes 1** to wear away, wash away: *Rain and wind eroded the topsoil from the farmland.* **2** to become worn away: *The beach has eroded since the hurricane.* **3** to weaken, lessen: *People demanded rights and eroded the king's power.*

e·rog·e·nous /ɪˈrɑdʒənəs/ *adj.* sexually excitable: *The sex organs are among the erogenous zones of the body.*

e·ro·sion /ɪˈroʊʒən/ *n.* [U] **1** a wearing away, (*syn.*) a deterioration: *Erosion has washed away the earth from the hill.* **2** a weakening, lessening: *The Presidency has suffered a steady erosion of power taken by the legislature.*

e·rot·ic /ɪˈrɑtɪk/ *adj.* about sexual desire: *That store has a large section of erotic literature.* -*n.pl.* **erotica;** -*n.* [U] **eroticism** /ɪˈrɑtəˌsɪzəm/; -*adv.* **erotically.** *See:* sexual, sensual, sensuous.

err /ɜr, ɛr/ *v.frml.* to make a mistake, (*syn.*) to blunder: *He erred when he added the numbers incorrectly.*

er·rand /ˈɛrənd/ *n.* a short trip made for a specific purpose: *I have to deposit money in the bank, pick up a package, and run* (or) *do some other errands.*

er·rant /ˈɛrənt/ *adj.frml.* **1** old usage looking for adventure **2** in the wrong direction, (*syn.*) off course: *While golfing, he hit an errant shot into the woods.*

er·ra·ta /ɪˈrɑtə/ *n.pl.* errors, mistakes, usu. in printed material: *We corrected the errata in the book before the new printing.*

er·rat·ic /ɪˈrætɪk/ *adj.* not working or performing consistently, irregular: *Her heartbeat is erratic; it misses beats. -adv.* **erratically.**

er·ro·ne·ous /ɪˈroʊniəs/ *adj.* incorrect, wrong: *He has the erroneous idea that I'm going to lend him money; I'm not. -adv.* **erroneously.**

er·ror /ˈɛrər/ *n.* **1** [C] a mistake, an inaccuracy: *He made an error in arithmetic.* **2** *frml.* [U] **in error:** mistaken: *She was in error when she* thought the meeting was today; it's tomorrow. **3** *frml.* **the error of one's ways:** the wrong in one's behavior or lifestyle: *The young man was always in trouble until he saw the error of his ways and made changes in his life.*

er·satz /'ɛr,zɑts, ɛr'zɑts/ *adj.frml.* substitute, artificial: *That leather on the sofa is ersatz, not genuine. See:* fake.

erst·while /'ɜrst,waɪl/ *adj.frml.* former: *He is her erstwhile boyfriend; she doesn't talk to him now.*

er·u·dite /'ɛryə,daɪt, 'ɛrə-/ *adj.* learned, scholarly: *an erudite professor* -*adv.* **eruditely;** -*n.* [U] **erudition** /, ɛryə'dɪʃən, ,ɛrə-/.

e·rupt /ɪ'rʌpt/ *v.* to explode: *A volcano erupts.||The audience erupted with laughter.* -*n.* [C;U] **eruption.**

es·ca·late /'ɛskə,leɪt/ *v.* -**lated, -lating, -lates** (of prices, wages, or conflicts) to raise in level: *The minor disagreement between the two countries escalated into war.* -*n.* [U] **escalation.**

es·ca·la·tor /'ɛskə,leɪtər/ *n.* **1** a moving conveyor belt of steps: *The escalators in the department store run to all six floors.* **2** an increase made on some agreed-upon basis: *The wage contract has an escalator of a 5 percent wage increase on July 1.*

escalator

es·ca·pade /'ɛskə,peɪd/ *n.* an adventure, esp. an illegal or dangerous one: *Their last escapade got them a weekend in jail.*

es·cape /ɪ'skeɪp/ *v.* -**caped, -caping, -capes 1** to get away (from prison or another place of confinement), *(syn.)* to break out: *The lion escaped from its cage.* **2** to get free temporarily: *We escaped to an island in the Pacific for our vacation.* **3** to manage to stay free of, to avoid: *He escaped military service because of his bad eyesight.* **4** to resist one's efforts to remember: *Her name escapes me at the moment.* —*n.* **1** an act of escaping, *(syn.)* a breakout: *The criminal made an escape from prison.* **2** a temporary break from cares or worries: *They enjoyed an escape from the city at their country house.* -*n.* **escapee.**

escape clause *n.* a part of a contract stating conditions that would free a person, company, etc., from it: *The actor insisted on an escape clause releasing him if filming were not begun by June 1.*

es·cap·ist /ɪ'skeɪpɪst/ *n.adj.* s.o. who escapes boring or unpleasant realities of life through fantasy or entertainment: *She prefers <adj.> escapist romances for reading at the beach.* -*n.* [U] **escapism.**

es·car·got /,ɛskɑr'goʊ/ *n.* an edible snail: *I had escargots as an appetizer at the French restaurant.*

es·ca·role /'ɛskə,roʊl/ *n.* [U] a leafy green vegetable with frilled edges: *Escarole tastes good in salads.*

es·chew /ɛs'tʃu/ *v.frml.* to avoid, *(syn.)* to shun: *He eschews arguments; he is quite a shy person.*

es·cort /ɪ'skɔrt, 'ɛs,kɔrt/ *v.* to guide, lead: *I escorted my guest to my office.* —*n.* /'ɛs,kɔrt/ s.o. who goes with another as a guide, guard, or companion: *The Prime Minister's car has a police escort.*

es·crow /'ɛskroʊ/ *n.* **1** money or property kept by s.o. until after two other persons, companies, etc., meet the conditions of an agreement between them: *The lawyer held the escrow until the sale was complete.* **2 in escrow:** in trust: *The money was placed in escrow.*

Es·ki·mo /'ɛskə,moʊ/ *n.adj.* -**mos** one of the people native to Alaska and northern Canada, an Inuit: *She is an <n.> Eskimo from Alaska.*

e·soph·a·gus /ɪ'sɑfəgəs/ *n.* -**gi** the tube running from the mouth to the stomach: *Food passes down the esophagus to the stomach.*

es·o·ter·ic /,ɛsə'tɛrɪk/ *adj.* rare, specialized: *That branch of mathematics is so esoteric that few study it.* -*adv.* **esoterically.**

ESP /'iɛs'pi/ *abbr. for* extrasensory perception

es·pe·cial·ly /ɪ'spɛʃəli/ *adv.* **1** just (for a special purpose), *(syn.)* exclusively: *I bought this present especially for you.* **2** to a very great degree, *(syns.)* extraordinarily, uncommonly: *He is especially fond of Swiss cheese.*

es·pi·o·nage /'ɛspiə,nɑʒ/ *n.* [U] an act of spying: *The official was put in jail for espionage.*

es·pouse /ɛ'spaʊz/ *v.* -**poused, -pousing, -pouses 1** to believe in and support: *She espouses the view that the state should own all businesses.* **2** to speak in favor of, *(syns.)* to advocate, promote: *He espouses socialism to all who will listen.* -*n.* [U] **espousal.**

es·pres·so /ɛ'sprɛsoʊ/ *n.adj.* [U] a strong coffee: *I like an <n.> espresso after dinner.*

es·prit de corps /ɛ'spridə'kɔr/ *n.* [U] group enthusiasm, *(syn.)* camaraderie: *The ballet group has esprit de corps. See:* élan.

Esq. /'ɛs,kwaɪr/ *abbr. for* Esquire, used in the USA after a lawyer's name in writing: *The memo to the lawyer was addressed "To: John Smith, Esq."*

es·say /'ɛseɪ/ *n.* a short, written work on a topic presented as the author's opinion: *I wrote an essay on Shakespeare for my English class.* -*n.* **essayist.** *See:* fiction, USAGE NOTE.

E

—*v.frml.* /ɛ'seɪ/ to attempt, try

es·sence /'ɛsəns/ *n.* **1** [U] the central point (issue, idea, etc.) of a subject, its substance: *The essence of the matter is that the two people really love each other.* **2** [C;U] a pure substance made by crushing or boiling s.t., (*syns.*) a concentrate, an extract: *The liquid from crushed rose petals is the essence that we want to use.*

es·sen·tial /ɪ'sɛnʃəl/ *adj.* **1** central, major: *The essential point is we must do what the contract says.* **2** necessary, required: *It is essential that you deliver the message this morning.* -*adv.* **essentially.**

—*n.pl.* **the essentials:** the things necessary to s.t.: *The essentials of life are food, shelter, and clothing.*

es·tab·lish /ɪ'stæblɪʃ/ *v.* **1** to found, create: *The English established a colony in Africa.* **2** to build in a secure, solid way: *Over a period of years, she established a reputation as a fine lawyer.* **3** to prove, (*syn.*) to substantiate: *The tourist established her identity by showing her passport.*

es·tab·lish·ment /ɪ'stæblɪʃmənt/ *n.* **1** [U] the creation or founding of s.t.: *The establishment of a new business takes many years.* **2** [C] a place of business: *He runs a clothing establishment in Boston.* **3** [U] **the Establishment:** the people with the power, influence, and money to control a society: *Government officials and business leaders are part of the Establishment.*

es·tate /ə'steɪt/ *n.* **1** a large house with much land **2** the wealth (money, property) left by a dead person: *His estate was worth a million dollars.*

es·teem /ə'stim/ *n.* [U] honor, respect, admiration: *These students hold their English professor in high esteem.*

—*v.frml.* to honor, admire

es·thet·ic /ɛs'θɛtɪk/ *adj.* related to art and beauty: *She has a strong esthetic sense of color and texture.*

—*n.* **1** a principle of art and beauty: *Harmony is an esthetic in music.* **2** *pl. used with a sing. v.* a branch of philosophy dealing with the nature of art and beauty: *He took a course in esthetics at the university.* -*adv.* **esthetically.**

es·ti·ma·ble /'ɛstəməbəl/ *adj.* valuable, worthy of respect: *She has an estimable reputation for choosing wise investments.*

es·ti·mate /'ɛstə,meɪt/ *v.* **-mated, -mating, -mates 1** to make a judgment about (the price of s.t.), (*syn.*) to appraise: *The dealer estimated the value of my painting at $1,000.* **2** to figure the amount or extent of, (*syn.*) to calculate: *I estimated that the trip would take about two hours.*

—*n.* /'ɛstəmɪt/ a calculation or approximation of the value of s.t.: *The mechanic gave me a*

rough estimate of two or three hundred dollars for the repairs to my car.

es·ti·ma·tion /,ɛstə'meɪʃən/ *n.* [U] evaluation of worth, (*syn.*) appraisal: *In my estimation, she is a good administrator.*

es·trange /ɪ'streɪndʒ/ *v.* **-tranged, -tranging, -tranges** to make unfriendly and distant, (*syn.*) to alienate: *He estranges people by his odd behavior.* -*n.* [U] **estrangement.**

es·tranged /ɪ'streɪndʒd/ *adj.* (of a married person) separated: *His estranged wife won't speak to him anymore.*

es·tro·gen /'ɛstrədʒən/ *n.* [U] a body chemical that regulates the production of eggs and determines other female characteristics

es·tu·ar·y /'ɛstʃu,ɛri/ *n.* **-ies** the place where a river meets the sea; the saltwater part of such a river: *We sailed our boat down the estuary to the sea.*

et al. /ɛt'æl, 'ɑl/ *n.pl.abbr. for* et alia, (Latin for) and others: *I sent a letter to everyone concerned, the chairperson, et al.*

etc. /ɛt'sɛtərə, 'sɛtrə/ *adv.abbr. for* et cetera, (Latin for) and other similar things, and so on: *I told him all about the table that I need: the color, the width, the height, etc.*

et cet·er·a /ɛt'sɛtərə, 'sɛtrə/ *adv.* See: etc.

USAGE NOTE: The term *et cetera* is used in this full-length form in speaking but not in writing. Its abbreviation, *etc.,* is used in writing.

---

etch /ɛtʃ/ *v.* **etched, etching, etches 1** to cut lines in wood, metal, stone, or other hard substance, by using acid: *The artist etched flowers in metal.* **2** *fig.* to leave a clear impression: *Her beauty was etched deeply in his memory.* -*n.* [C;U] **etching.**

e·ter·nal /ɪ'tɜrnəl/ *adj.* lasting forever, timeless: *People of many religions believe that God is eternal.* -*adv.* **eternally.**

e·ter·ni·ty /ɪ'tɜrnəti/ *n.sing.* [U] **1** a time period without end: *A billion years is an eternity.* **2** life after death, immortality: *Many people wonder about eternity.* **3** *fig.* a boring time that seems endless: *That play was so dull that it lasted an eternity.*

e·ther /'iθər/ *n.* [U] **1** an anesthetic (pain reliever) and agent with wide industrial uses, made from a distillation of ethyl alcohol and sulfuric acid: *The doctor anesthetized the patient with ether.* **2** the highest atmosphere of the earth: *The balloon flies to the upper ether.*

e·the·re·al /ɪ'θɪriəl/ *adj.* **1** delicate, light in weight: *The ethereal ballet dancer seemed to float across the stage.* **2** not real, distant: *He has vague, ethereal thoughts (ambitions, dreams, etc.).* -*adv.* **ethereally.**

eth·ic /'ɛθɪk/ *n.* **1** moral or correct behavior: *The priest spoke about the ethic: "Love your neighbor as yourself."* **2** *pl.* a system of moral or correct conduct, moral principles: *Her ethics in business are excellent.*

eth·i·cal /ˈɛθɪkəl/ *adj.* related to moral or correct behavior: *He found a woman's purse and did the ethical thing; he returned it to her.* *-adv.* **ethically.**

eth·nic /ˈɛθnɪk/ *adj.* related to group characteristics, such as race, country of origin, religion, or culture: *The ethnic make-up of the USA is incredibly varied.* *-n.* [C;U] **ethnicity** /ɛθˈnɪsəti/.

eth·no·cen·tric /ˌɛθnouˈsɛntrɪk/ *adj.* related to belief in the superiority of one's own people and culture: *The experience of living in another culture made him rethink his ethnocentric ideas.* *-n.* [U] **ethnocentrism;** *-adv.* **ethnocentrically.**

eth·nol·o·gy /ɛθˈnɑlədʒi/ *n.* [U] the study of human cultures *See:* anthropology.

et·i·quette /ˈɛtəkɪt/ *n.* [U] the correct and expected way to behave, *(syn.)* manners: *Proper etiquette requires a bride to write thank-you notes for wedding gifts.*

et·y·mol·o·gist /ˌɛtəˈmɑlədʒɪst/ *n.* an expert in the origin and history of words: *She is an etymologist as well as an English professor.* *-n.* [U] **etymology.**

eu·ca·lyp·tus /ˌyukəˈlɪptəs/ *n.* **-tuses** or **-ti** /-ˌtaɪ/ [C;U] a tall tree originally from Australia that provides wood, oil, and gum

eu·lo·gy /ˈyulədʒi/ *n.frml.* **-gies** a speech or piece of writing full of praise for s.o. (usu. a dead person): *The Vice President gave the eulogy at the general's funeral.* *-v.* **eulogize.**

eu·nuch /ˈyunək/ *n.* a human male whose sex organs have been removed

eu·phe·mism /ˈyufəˌmɪzəm/ *n.* [C;U] a mild (indirect, poetic, etc.) word or description used to replace a strong, hurtful, or offensive one: *"Pass away" is a euphemism for the word "die."* *-adj.* **euphemistic;** *-adv.* **euphemistically.**

eu·pho·ri·a /yuˈfɔriə/ *n.* [U] great delight, happy excitement: *He was full of euphoria when he heard the good news.* *-adj.* **euphoric;** *-adv.* **euphorically.**

eu·re·ka /yuˈrikə/ *interj.* an expression of delight, esp. for a discovery: *Eureka! I've found the answer!*

Eu·rope /ˈyʊrəp/ *n.* the world's sixth largest continent: *Spain, Germany, and Greece are countries in Europe.*

Eu·ro·pe·an /ˌyʊrəˈpiən/ *n.* a native of Europe: *He is a European.*

—*adj.* **1** related to Europe: *Many Americans admire European culture.* **2 European plan:** a hotel room rate that does not include meals

European Union *n.abbr.* **EU** formerly the European Community or EC, a group of countries in Europe working to create a stronger

world market for European goods and services.

eu·tha·na·sia /ˌyuθəˈneɪʒə/ *n.* [U] the killing of a person who is suffering from an incurable illness, *(syn.)* mercy killing

e·vac·u·ate /ɪˈvækyuˌeɪt/ *v.* **-ated, -ating, -ates** **1** to leave or take people away from (because of danger), *(syn.)* to vacate: *The people evacuated the town because of the flood.*||*Soldiers helped evacuate the town.* **2** to empty, drain: *The patient evacuated his bowels.* *-n.*[C;U] **evacuation; evacuee** /ɪˌvækyuˈi/.

e·vade /ɪˈveɪd/ *v.* **evaded, evading, evades** **1** to avoid (s.t. that one should do), *(syn.)* to dodge: *She evaded answering the reporter's question by changing the subject.* **2** to escape, *(syn.)* to elude: *The criminal evaded the police by hiding.*

e·val·u·ate /ɪˈvælyuˌeɪt/ *v.* **-ated, -ating, -ates** **1** to study and make a judgment about: *The committee evaluated the reports and reached a conclusion.* **2** to estimate worth, determine the value of s.t.: *The buyer evaluated the property and offered $200,000 for it.*

e·val·u·a·tion /ɪˌvælyuˈeɪʃən/ *n.* [C;U] **1** an analysis, study: *An accountant did an evaluation of the company's financial health.* **2** estimate of worth (ability, value, etc.): *My boss did an evaluation of my job performance.*

e·van·gel·i·cal /ˌivænˈdʒɛləkəl, ˌɛvən-/ *adj.* related to the preaching of a religious faith, esp. Christianity: *Evangelical ministers become very enthusiastic in their sermons.* *-n.* [U] **evangelism** /ɪˈvændʒəˌlɪzəm/, **evangelist.**

e·vap·o·rate /ɪˈvæpəˌreɪt/ *v.* **-rated, -rating, -rates** **1** to change from a liquid into a vapor: *Water evaporates from lakes and oceans.* **2** *fig.* to disappear, vanish: *Without a job, her savings evaporated.* *-n.* [U] **evaporation.**

e·va·sion /ɪˈveɪʒən/ *n.* **1** [C;U] a statement or action that avoids what should be said or done: *tax evasion*||*an evasion of the truth* **2** [U] escape, avoidance: *The criminal's evasion of the police lasted for days.*

e·va·sive /ɪˈveɪsɪv/ *adj.* **1** not direct, clear, or frank, *(syn.)* ambiguous: *He's always evasive and seldom gives a clear answer.* **2** designed to deceive or elude: *An enemy airplane appeared, and we took evasive action to get away from it.* *-n.* **evasiveness;** *-adv.* **evasively.**

eve /iv/ *n.sing.* **1** the evening before an event, esp. a holiday: *We celebrated on New Year's Eve.* **2** a period just before an event: *In 1917, Russia was on the eve of revolution.*

e·ven /ˈivən/ *adj.* **1** the same in measurement (distance, height, etc.), equal: *The pieces of wood are even in length.*||*The two children are of even height.* **2** the same (in place, score, etc.) in a contest, tied: *The two runners were*

E

even at the finish line. **3** smooth, level: *The table has an even finish, with no bumps.* **4** (of numbers) exactly divisible by 2: *The numbers 2, 4, and 6 are even; 1, 3, and 5 are odd numbers.* **5** *fig.* on equal terms after repayment of a debt: *Here's the $20 that I owe you; now we're even.* **6** *fig.* on equal terms after repayment of some hurt or insult: *One man insulted the other, and the other insulted him back; then they were even.* **7 to break even:** to neither win nor lose: *We finally broke even on the deal, as we got back the amount we invested in it.* **8 to get even:** to (try to) punish s.o. for some hurt or insult: *When the outlaw shot my brother, I vowed to get even.* **9 to get** or **give s.o. an even break:** to treat s.o. fairly and honestly: *With the new employment law, minorities will finally get an even break in being hired.* —*adv.* **1** more, to a greater extent: *He makes things even better (worse, harder, etc.) than they were by acting the way he does.* **2** so little as: *She left him without even a word of explanation.||She didn't even call her mother on Mother's Day.* **3** used to give force to a comparison: *Even a child would have known what to do (so that adult should have known).* **4 even if:** no matter if, although: *He says he'll finish the job even if it kills him!* **5 even so:** nonetheless, despite that: *I know you are tired, but even so, you have to go to school.* —*v.* **1** to make equal, the same (height, length, etc., or smooth, flat, etc.): *I'll even the surface of this table by sanding it down.* **2** *phrasal v. sep.* **to even s.t. out:** to come into balance or stability: *He had some bad luck; then he evened out his business, and he's doing well now.||He evened it out.* **3 to even the odds:** to put competitors on a more equal basis: *Their team has beaten ours every year, but we have a new star player now, and that will even the odds.* **4** *phrasal v. sep.* **to even up: a.** to become equal: *Our team evened up the score in the last half of the game.||We evened it up.* **b.** to make the same: *I evened up the length of those pieces of wood.||I evened them up.* -*adv.* **evenly;** -*n.* **evenness.**

e·ven·hand·ed /ˌivənˈhændɪd/ *adj.* treating people justly, fair: *The judge is evenhanded; she treats the poor and the rich with equal justice.* -*adv.* **evenhandedly.**

eve·ning /ˈivnɪŋ/ *n.* [C;U] the period generally between 6:00 P.M. and midnight: *We went to a movie yesterday evening.*
—*adv.* **evenings** usually or regularly in the evening: *Evenings, we sit at home and watch television.*

e·vent /ɪˈvɛnt/ *n.* **1** a happening, esp. an important one, (*syn.*) an incident: *The events that led to the war were complex and numerous.* **2** a competition, contest: *I entered the 10K run, an event in which I specialize.* **3** an entertain-

ment, gathering: *The showing of Impressionist paintings at the museum is quite an event.*

e·vent·ful /ɪˈvɛntfəl/ *adj.* **1** full of important happenings: *The evening was quite eventful, full of pleasant surprises.* **2** historic, (*syn.*) momentous: *The political meetings were eventful because of the agreements signed during them.* -*adv.* **eventfully.**

e·ven-tem·pered /ˈivənˌtɛmpərd/ *adj.* not easily angered, calm: *Our family dog is very even-tempered, even if the children hurt her.*

e·ven·tu·al /ɪˈvɛntʃuəl/ *adj.* happening later, (*syn.*) ultimate: *The tennis match was long, but he was the eventual winner.* -*adv.* **eventually.**

e·ven·tu·al·i·ty /ɪˌvɛntʃuˈæləti/ *n.* **-ties** a possible happening, situation, or result: *In the eventuality that you are able to get tickets, would you buy one for me, too?*

ev·er /ˈɛvər/ *adv.* **1** at any time: *Is he ever on time?||Don't ever do that again!||It was the best movie I've ever seen.* **2** always, at all times: *The instructor is ever patient with her students.* **3** (used to add force to a question): *Where ever have you been all this time? ||Who ever would do such a crazy thing?*
— *prefix* **ever-** always: *the ever-popular chocolate chip cookie*

ev·er·glade /ˈɛvərˌgleɪd/ *n.* a flat, swampy area full of marsh grass and waterways: *The Everglades in south Florida are famous for their beautiful pink birds called flamingos.*

ev·er·green /ˈɛvərˌgrin/ *n.adj.* a conifer tree with needles as leaves that stay green all year: *The pine on our lawn is an <n.> evergreen; it's an <adj.> evergreen tree.*

ev·er·last·ing /ˌɛvərˈlæstɪŋ/ *adj.* **1** timeless, (*syn.*) eternal: *I love the everlasting beauty of nature.* **2** *fig.* boring without end, (*syn.*) tedious: *No one can stand his everlasting stories.*

ev·er·more /ˌɛvərˈmɔr/ *adv.frml.* from now on, forever: *You should be thankful now and evermore for what he did for you. See:* forever.

eve·ry /ˈɛvri/ *adj.* **1** each: *Every driver must have a license.* **2** once in each (period of time): *You must take your medicine every two hours.* **3 every bit as:** just as, equally: *She is every bit as worried as you are.* **4 every man for himself:** caring for one's own safety without regard for others: *The ship is sinking! It's every man for himself!* **5 every now and then** or **every so often:** once in a while, occasionally: *She stops by to see me every now and then.* **6 every other:** choosing one of each two in a sequence: *The mayor serves a two-year term, so elections are held every other November.* **7 every Tom, Dick, and Harry:** all ordinary people: *Every Tom, Dick, and Harry wears jeans now.* **8 every which way:** mixed up, out of order: *No one can find anything on his desk because he leaves his papers and files every which way.*

eve·ry·bod·y /ˈɛvriˌbɑdi, -ˌbʌ-/ *pron.* everyone, all persons: *Everybody who wants to go fishing, should let me know.*

eve·ry·day /ˈɛvriˌdeɪ/ *adj.* ordinary, common, routine: *She takes care of everyday decisions for her boss.*

eve·ry·one /ˈɛvriˌwʌn/ *pron.* everybody, all persons: *Everyone must eat in order to live.*

eve·ry·thing /ˈɛvriˌθɪŋ/ *pron.* **1** all things: *Everything in the kitchen was destroyed by the fire.* **2** all that is important in life: *Her health is everything to her.*

eve·ry·where /ˈɛvriˌwɛr/ *adv.* in all places: *I lost my keys and looked everywhere for them.*

e·vict /iˈvɪkt/ *v.* to force out of a property by threat, law, or physical force: *They did not pay the rent on their apartment for three months, so the landlord evicted them.* -*n.* [C;U] **eviction.**

ev·i·dence /ˈɛvədəns/ *n.* **1** [U] words or objects that support the truth of s.t., proof: *The lawyer presented the murder weapon as evidence in court.* **2 in evidence:** present and easily seen: *There were reporters in evidence at the scene of the crime.*
—*v.frml.* **-denced, -dencing, -dences** to show, demonstrate: *The murder suspect evidenced surprise upon seeing the weapon in court.* -*adj.* **evidential** /ˌɛvəˈdɛnʃəl/.

ev·i·dent /ˈɛvədənt/ *adj.* plain, clear, obvious: *It is evident that he is guilty; his fingerprints were found at the crime scene.*

ev·i·dent·ly /ˌɛvəˈdɛntli, ˈɛvədənt-/ *adv.* as it appears, seemingly, (*syn.*) apparently: *Evidently, he likes music so much that he's taking piano lessons.*

e·vil /ˈivəl/ *adj.* extremely bad, wicked, (*syn.*) malevolent: *He tries to hurt people; he's evil.* -*adv.* **evilly.**
—*n.* [C;U] extremely bad behavior, wickedness, corruption, (*syn.*) malevolence: *The world is full of both good and evil.*

e·vil-mind·ed /ˈivəlˌmaɪndɪd/ *adj.* thinking of how to harm people, (*syn.*) malicious: *Criminals scheme to hurt people; they are evil-minded.*

e·vis·cer·ate /iˈvɪsəˌreɪt/ *v.* **-ated, -ating, -ates** to cut the insides out of, to gut: *The hunter eviscerated the dead deer.* -*n.* **evisceration.**

e·voke /ɪˈvouk/ *v.* **evoked, evoking, evokes** to bring out a feeling, response, (*syn.*) to elicit: *The poetry evoked a feeling of love in the reader.* -*adj.* **evocative** /ɪˈvɑkətɪv/.

ev·o·lu·tion /ˌɛvəˈluʃən, ˌivə-/ *n.* [U] the development of living things (cultures, ideas, etc.): *The evolution of the computer was rapid.* -*adj.* **evolutionary.**

e·volve /iˈvɑlv/ *v.* **evolved, evolving, evolves** to develop, change: *Agriculture evolved slowly over thousands of years.*

ewe /yu/ *n.* a mature female sheep: *The ewes have a full coat of wool now.*

ex /ɛks/ *n.* **exes 1** the letter *x* **2** *slang* short for ex-wife or ex-husband, one's former spouse: *My ex and I are still friends.*
—*prefix* **ex-** former: *She is ex-treasurer of the company, now retired.*

ex·ac·er·bate /ɪgˈzæsərˌbeɪt/ *v.* **-bated, -bating, -bates** to make worse, (*syn.*) to aggravate: *I hurt my foot, and walking on it exacerbated the pain.*

ex·act /ɪgˈzækt/ *adj.* accurate, precise: *He gave me the exact cost (measurements, requirements, etc.) of the item.*
—*v.frml.* to demand and get, (*syn.*) to extract: *The law exacts severe penalties for not paying one's taxes.* -*n.* **exactness;** [U] **exactitude.**

ex·act·ly /ɪgˈzæktli/ *adv.* **1** accurately, precisely: *The job must be done exactly as she wants it done.*||*The race is exactly ten kilometers long.* **2** *exclam.* Right! I agree!: *Exactly! You've said just what I was thinking.*

ex·ag·ger·ate /ɪgˈzædʒəˌreɪt/ *v.* **-ated, -ating, -ates** to say s.t. is better, worse, more important, etc., than it really is, (*syn.*) to overstate: *He said he caught a fish as long as his arm, but I think he was exaggerating.* -*n.* [U] **exaggeration.**

ex·alt /ɪgˈzɔlt/ *v.* to praise highly, honor: *The nobles exalted the king by telling him how wonderful he was.* -*n.* [U] **exaltation** /ˌɛgzɔlˈteɪʃən, ˌɛksəl-/. *See:* exult.

ex·am /ɪgˈzæm/ *n.short for* examination (*syn.*) test: *I have to take a science exam (driver's license exam, medical exam, etc.) tomorrow.*

ex·am·i·na·tion /ɪgˌzæməˈneɪʃən/ *n.* **1** [C] a test of one's knowledge: *I took an examination in English yesterday.* **2** [C;U] an inspection and analysis: *The doctor gave me a physical examination. See:* test, USAGE NOTE.

ex·am·ine /ɪgˈzæmən/ *v.* **-ined, -ining, -ines 1** to look at closely, (*syn.*) to scrutinize: *The mechanic examined the motor for defects.*||*The doctor examined a patient.* **2** to question (s.o.) to test their knowledge or to get information: *Lawyers examine witnesses in court.*

ex·am·in·er /ɪgˈzæmənər/ *n.* **1** a person who gives spoken or written examinations to others: *She is an examiner for the state government.* **2** an inspector: *He is an insurance examiner and visits damaged property.*

ex·am·ple /ɪgˈzæmpəl/ *n.* **1** a sample, case, or instance illustrating s.t.: *The sales representative showed an example of her new product.* **2 for example:** as a model of the kind of person or thing I mean: *He wants a luxury car, a Mercedes, for example.* **3 to make an exam-**

ple of s.o.: to punish s.o. in order to make others behave correctly: *The boy talked in class, and the teacher made an example of him by making him stand in the corner.* **4 to set an example** or **a good example:** to behave in the way others should: *She is an excellent worker; she sets an example for others in her company.*

ex·as·per·ate /ɪgˈzæspəˌreɪt/ v. **-ated, -ating, -ates** to anger and frustrate: *Time after time, he refused to cooperate; he exasperated me completely.* **-n.** [U] **exasperation;** **-adj.** **exasperating.**

ex·ca·vate /ˈɛkskəˌveɪt/ v. **-ated, -ating, -ates** **1** to remove the earth from an area: *The workers excavated the earth to make a foundation for the building.* **2** to uncover by digging: *Archeologists excavated ancient ruins in Egypt.* **-n.** [C;U] **excavation.**

ex·ca·va·tor /ˈɛskəˌveɪtər/ n. a machine used to dig holes in the earth: *A bulldozer is one kind of excavator.*

ex·ceed /ɪkˈsid/ v. **1** to be more than (what is expected): *Sales of the new product exceeded our estimates.* **2** to do or say more than (what is needed, allowed, etc.): *The manager exceeded the bounds of her authority by spending too much money.*

ex·ceed·ing·ly /ɪkˈsidɪŋli/ adv. very, extremely: *We had an exceedingly good (bad, boring, etc.) time at the party.*

ex·cel /ɪkˈsɛl/ v. **-celled, -celling, -cels** **1** to do very well: *She excels at swimming (solving problems, singing, etc.).* **2** to perform much better than others: *He excels in running; he's the fastest on the team.*

ex·cel·lent /ˈɛksələnt/ adj. very high in quality, (syns.) outstanding, superior: *The violinist gave an excellent performance; everyone applauded loudly.* **-n.** [U] **excellence;** **-adv.** **excellently.**

ex·cept /ɪkˈsɛpt/ prep. excluding: *Everyone was invited except me.*
—conj. but: *I would lend you the money except that I don't have any.‖We would have had a picnic except for the rain.*
—v. to exclude, leave out, omit: *The army called men to serve, but they excepted men with wives and children.*

ex·cep·tion /ɪkˈsɛpʃən/ n. [C] **1** s.t. unusual, (syn.) an oddity: *He is usually on time; his lateness today is an exception.* **2** [C;U] s.o. or s.t. that is left out, (syns.) an omission, an exclusion: *Everyone is here with the exception of one person.* **3 an exception to the rule:** s.o. or s.t. that is different from what is expected: *Most basketball players are very tall, but he's an exception to the rule; he's short.* **4 to make an exception (to the rule):** to depart from the usual practice: *No one is allowed to enter without written permission, but we'll make an ex-*

ception and let you go in. **5 to take exception to s.t.:** to disagree with s.t.

ex·cep·tion·al /ɪkˈsɛpʃənəl/ adj. unusual and excellent, (syns.) outstanding, admirable: *The pianist gave an exceptional performance; it was great! -adv.* **exceptionally.**

ex·cerpt /ˈɛkˌsɜrpt/ n. a part quoted from a larger written or spoken work: *The newspaper gave a short excerpt from the speech.*
—v. to quote such a part: *The paper excerpted parts of her speech.*

ex·cess /ɪkˈsɛs, ˈɛkˌsɛs/ n. **1** an amount that is more than what is needed or wanted: *We have an excess of paperwork under the present system.* **2** [C;U] an act of doing too much of s.t.: *He spends too much money; his excesses put him into debt.* **3 in excess of:** more than: *Trucks weighing in excess of five tons cannot use this bridge.* **4 to be given to excess:** to tend to do too much without considering the risks, to be reckless: *She is given to excess; she goes on shopping binges she can't afford.* **5 to excess:** too much: *They drink to excess.*

ex·ces·sive /ɪkˈsɛsɪv/ adj. too much, beyond acceptable limits: *Their drinking is excessive; they are drunk every night. -adv.* **excessively.**

ex·change /ɪksˈtʃeɪndʒ/ n. **1** [C] a place where transactions are made: *At the stock exchange, securities are bought and sold.* **2** [C;U] a trade, transaction: *I gave him $50 for his power saw, and the exchange was made at his house.‖I gave him $50 in exchange for his saw.* **3** [C] a giving and receiving of words, ideas, etc., in speaking or writing: *There was an exchange of opinion between the speakers.*
—v. **-changed, -changing, -changes** **1** to give and receive (one thing in place of another), to trade: *People exchange money for goods in stores.* **2** to return (s.t.) to a store and get another in its place: *She went back to the store and exchanged the shirt because her husband didn't like the color.* **3** to communicate: *We exchanged ideas during the meeting.*

exchange rate n. the price at which one country's money may be traded for another's: *For years, the exchange rate for the Danish crown was seven crowns to one US dollar.*

exchange student n. a student from another country or college who exchanges places with another student: *That woman from Spain is now an exchange student at California State University, Northridge.*

ex·cise /ɪkˈsaɪz/ v.frml. **-cised, -cising, -cises** to remove, usu. by cutting: *The doctor excised the man's appendix with a scalpel. -n.* [C;U] **excision.**

ex·cise tax /ˈɛkˌsaɪz/ n. taxes in USA, a fee or tax on certain products or licenses: *Governments place excise taxes on tobacco and liquor.*

ex·cit·able /ɪk'saɪtəbəl/ *adj.* easily excited, *(syns.)* temperamental, emotional: *He is very excitable; he gets angry very quickly.*

ex·cite /ɪk'saɪt/ *v.* **-cited, -citing, -cites 1** to cause s.o. to feel delight, *(syns.)* to exhilarate, thrill: *The band played louder and excited the audience.* **2** to cause s.o. to act, *(syns.)* to inspire, arouse: *The politician's speech to the crowd excited them into a frenzy.* *-adj.* **exciting;** *-n.* [U] **excitation** /ˌɛksaɪ'teɪʃən/.

ex·cit·ed /ɪk'saɪtɪd/ *adj.* **1** filled with a strong pleasant feeling, *(syns.)* enthusiastic, eager: *She is excited about going on vacation.* **2** thrilled, delighted: *She was excited by the surprise party.* *-adv.* **excitedly.**

ex·cite·ment /ɪk'saɪtmənt/ *n.* [U] a strong, pleasant feeling *(syn.)* exhilaration: *The children felt great excitement on the rollercoaster ride.*

ex·claim /ɪks'kleɪm/ *v.frml.* to cry out, shout: *"I'm insulted!" he exclaimed.* *-n.* **exclamation** /ˌɛksklə'meɪʃən/ *-adj.* **exclamatory** /ɪk'sklæmə,tɔri/.

exclamation point *n.* a punctuation symbol (!) used for emphasis or forceful expression (anger, surprise, delight, etc.): *Ouch! I hit my finger with the hammer!*

ex·clude /ɛk'sklud/ *v.* **-cluded, -cluding, -cludes 1** not to include, to leave out, *(syn.)* to omit: *I put all but one ingredient into the soup; I excluded the hot peppers.* **2** to keep out, *(syns.)* to prohibit, ban: *The restaurant excludes anyone who is not properly dressed from entering.* *-n.* [U] **exclusion.**

ex·clu·sive /ɪk'sklusɪv/ *adj.* **1** limited to people with a lot of money and high social position, *(syns.)* restricted, prestigious: *an exclusive club‖an exclusive neighborhood* **2** belonging to one person, company, or contract: *Our company has the exclusive rights to distribute that product.* **3 exclusive of:** not including or considering
—n.fig. a sole right: *We have an exclusive on that product; no one else can sell it.* *-adv.* **exclusively;** *-n.* [U] **exclusivity** /ˌɛksklu'sɪvəti/.

ex·com·mu·ni·cate /ˌɛkskə'myunə,keɪt/ *v.* **-cated, -cating, -cates** to prohibit from receiving the holy blessings, esp. in the Roman Catholic Church: *When the divorced man remarried, he was excommunicated.* *-n.* [C;U] **excommunication.**

ex·cre·ment /'ɛkskrəmənt/ *n.frml.* [U] solid waste matter from the body, feces: *Excrement is flushed away in toilets.*

ex·crete /ɪk'skrit/ *v.frml.* **-creted, -creting, -cretes 1** to eliminate waste, esp. feces **2** to send out, esp. waste products: *Sweat is excreted through pores in the skin.* *-n.* [C;U] **excretion.**

ex·cru·ci·at·ing /ɪk'skruʃi,eɪtɪŋ/ *adj.* extremely painful, *(syn.)* agonizing: *I have an excruciating stomachache (headache, back pain, etc.).* *-adv.* **excruciatingly.**

ex·cur·sion /ɪk'skɜrʒən/ *n.* a trip, esp. a short one for pleasure: *We took an excursion to Alaska on a cruise ship.*

ex·cuse /ɪk'skyuz/ *v.* **-cused, -cusing, -cuses 1** to pardon, forgive: *She excused him for being late.* **2** to allow to leave, *(syn.)* to dismiss: *The teacher excused the students, and they left class.* **3** to give acceptable reasons for a wrong; *(syn.)* to justify: *His being sick excused his absence from work.* **4 Excuse me:** an expression used to get s.o.'s attention, esp. a stranger's, or to apologize for a small offense: *Excuse me, is this seat free?‖Oh, excuse me! I stepped on your toe!* **5 to excuse oneself:** to leave a group of people politely: *I excused myself from the dinner table to make a phone call.*
—n. /ɪk'skyus/ [C;U] **1** a reason given to explain a wrong or an offense: *He had a good excuse for not doing his report; his father had died.* **2 a poor excuse for:** an inferior substitute for: *What a poor excuse for a report; a child could have written a better one!* **3 to make excuses:** to give reasons (usu. untrue or unacceptable ones) for not doing s.t. expected: *She made excuses about being sick and not being able to pay her bills.*

ex·ec /ɪg'zɛk/ *n.infrml.short* for executive: *After the meeting, the execs all went out to lunch.*

ex·e·cra·ble /'ɛksəkrəbəl/ *adj.frml.* very bad, *(syn.)* abominable: *He made an execrable decision and was fired for it.*

ex·e·cute /'ɛksə,kyut/ *v.* **-cuted, -cuting, -cutes 1** to put to death, kill, esp. by government or military: *Soldiers executed the traitor by shooting him.* **2** to perform, carry out: *A computer executes the commands given to it.* **3** to make s.t. legal, esp. by signing it: *We executed the contract by signing it yesterday.*

ex·e·cu·tion /ˌɛksə'kyuʃən/ *n.* **1** [C;U] the act of putting s.o. to death: *The execution of the murderer will take place tomorrow.* **2** [U] the performance or carrying out, such as of a contract or order: *The execution of the plan will take weeks. See:* capital punishment.

ex·e·cu·tion·er /ˌɛksə'kyuʃənər/ *n.* a person who puts another to death

ex·ec·u·tive /ɪg'zɛkyətɪv/ *n.* a manager or administrator in a company or institution who has the power to spend money, hire, and fire employees, etc.: *She is an executive with a bank.*
—adj. **1** related to the responsibilities of an executive: *As a bank officer, she has the executive authority to approve loans.* **2** in USA, related to the President, his or her powers, cab-

inet, and staff: *the Executive branch of government*

executive officer *n.* **1** a business executive in charge of day-to-day business: *The executive officer in our company has all department heads reporting to her.* **2** a military officer second in command

executive secretary *n.* **-ies** a secretary with superior skills who works for an executive and often does important projects: *My executive secretary writes all my letters and places purchase orders for the company. See:* administrative assistant.

ex·ec·u·tor /ɪg'zɛkyətər/ *n.* a person appointed in the will of a dead person or by a court to carry out the wishes expressed in the will: *The son is the executor of his father's estate.*

ex·em·pla·ry /ɪg'zɛmpləri/ *adj.* outstanding, worthy of imitation: *The young girl's playing at the piano recital was exemplary.*

ex·em·pli·fy /ɪg'zɛmplə,faɪ/ *v.* **-fied, -fying, -fies** to serve as an example, illustrate: *Her willingness to accept more responsibility exemplifies her desire to succeed.* **-n. exemplification.**

ex·empt /ɪg'zɛmpt/ *v.adj.* to exclude or free from a duty, restriction, etc.: *The court <v.> exempted me from jury duty because I'm a minister.||My being a minister made me <adj.> exempt.*

ex·emp·tion /ɪg'zɛmpʃən/ *n.* [C;U] **1** freedom from a duty, requirement, or restriction: *He received an exemption from military duty because he is disabled.* **2** s.t. that frees a person from owing tax money: *You can claim these expenses as exemptions when you file your income taxes.*

ex·er·cise /'ɛksər,saɪz/ *v.* **-cised, -cising, -cises** **1** to do physical activities to strengthen the body: *I exercise by lifting weights and jogging.* **2** *frml.* to use (one's rights, power, etc.): *In a democracy, the people can exercise their right to vote.* —*n.* **1** [C;U] physical movements to train and strengthen the body: *Every morning, I do sit-ups and other exercises.||He doesn't get much exercise.* **2** [C] a question or task for mental training: *The teacher gives the students exercises in math.* **3** *sing.* [U] a use of power: *She stopped smoking cigarettes by an exercise of willpower.* **4 an exercise in futility:** a useless activity: *He tries to lose weight but puts it back on again; his dieting is an exercise in futility.*

ex·ert /ɪg'zɜrt/ *v.* **1** to act with power, force, influence, etc.: *The manager exerted her authority and demanded better performance from her employees.* **2 to exert oneself:** to try hard, esp. physically: *He exerted himself to get good grades* (or) *to reach the top of the mountain.*

ex·er·tion /ɪg'zɜrʃən/ *n.* **1** [U] physical work: *Walking up stairs requires exertion.* **2** [C;U] a use or an act of power, influence, force, etc.: *The exertion of authority is to tell others what to do.*

ex·hale /ɛks'heɪl, 'ɛks,heɪl/ *v.* **-haled, -haling, -hales** to let out air from the lungs: *The doctor told me to exhale as she listened to my heartbeat.* **-n.**[C;U] **exhalation** /,ɛkshəleɪʃən/.

ex·haust /ɪg'zɔst/ *v.* **1** to use completely, run out of, (*syn.*) to deplete: *We have exhausted our supply of pencils and must order more.* **2** to treat thoroughly: *We exhausted one topic of discussion and started another.* **3** to make very tired, (*syn.*) to wear s.o. out: *Waking up several times a night to feed her baby exhausted the new mother.* —*n.* discharge in the form of smoke, steam, etc.: *Exhaust from a car's engine escapes through the tailpipe.*

ex·haust·ed /ɪg'zɔstɪd/ *adj. & v.past part.* extremely tired: *After the long race, the runners felt exhausted.*

ex·haust·ing /ɪg'zɔstɪŋ/ *adj.* very tiring: *I've had an exhausting day, so I'm going to bed.*

ex·haus·tion /ɪg'zɔstʃən/ *n.* [U] complete tiredness, fatigue: *She worked all night and is suffering from exhaustion.*

ex·haus·tive /ɪg'zɔstɪv/ *adj.* complete, thorough: *A committee made an exhaustive study of the labor problem and gave recommendations.* **-adv. exhaustively.**

ex·hib·it /ɪg'zɪbɪt/ *v.* **1** to show, display: *A museum exhibits paintings for people to see.* **2** *frml.* to demonstrate, perform: *She exhibited great patience by not becoming angry with the noisy child.* —*n.* a display: *We visited an art exhibit at the museum.* **-n. exhibitor.**

ex·hi·bi·tion /,ɛksə'bɪʃən, ,ɛgzə-/ *n.* **1** a display (of art, products, etc.): *I enjoyed the art exhibition at the museum.* **2 to make an exhibition of oneself:** to behave in a way that causes embarrassment: *He drank too much and made an exhibition of himself at the wedding.*

ex·hi·bi·tion·ist /,ɛksə'bɪʃənɪst, ,ɛgzə-/ *n.* a person who behaves or dresses in an unusual way to get attention: *He dresses in bright pink clothes to shock people; he's an exhibitionist.* **-n.** [U] **exhibitionism.**

ex·hil·a·rate /ɪg'zɪlə,reɪt/ *v.* **-rated, -rating, -rates** to make s.o. feel strong and happy, (*syns.*) to invigorate, enliven: *The cold autumn air exhilarates me.* **-adj. exhilarating; -n.** [U] **exhilaration.**

ex·hort /ɪg'zɔrt/ *v.frml.* to urge with strong argument: *The politician exhorted the people to vote for her.* **-n.**[C;U] **exhortation** /,ɛgzɔr'teɪʃən, ,ɛksɔr-/.

ex·hume /ɪg'zum, ɪk'sum/ v. **-humed, -hum-ing, -humes** to remove s.t., usu. a dead body, from its burial place -n. [C;U] **exhumation** /ˌɛgzu'meɪʃən, ˌɛksu-/.

ex·i·gen·cy /'ɛksədʒənsi, ɪg'zɪ-/ n. **-cies** an urgent need, emergency -adj. **exigent.**

ex·ile /'ɛg,zaɪl, 'ɛk,saɪl/ v. **-iled, -iling, -iles** to force s.o. out of his or her home country, (syn.) to deport: *The government exiled him because of his radical politics.*
—n. **1** a forced absence from one's country: *Napoleon died in exile in 1821.* **2** s.o. who has been exiled, (syns.) a deportee, a refugee: *She fled her country and became an exile in Canada.*

ex·ist /ɪg'zɪst/ v. **1** to be present physically or emotionally: *Poverty and hatred exist all over the world.* **2** to live with difficulty, (syn.) to subsist: *Poor people exist on very little money.* -adj. **existing.**

ex·is·tence /ɪg'zɪstəns/ n. **1** [U] the presence of s.t. in the real world: *The company has been in existence for 20 years.* **2** *sing.* a type of life: *People in the mountains lead a simple existence.* -adj. **existent.**

ex·it /'ɛgzɪt, 'ɛksɪt/ v. to leave, depart: *We exited the building through a side door.*
—n. a door or passageway leading outside: *A movie theater has exits on three sides.*

exit poll n. a survey asking voters as they leave the polling places which candidates and propositions they voted for: *The exit polls done by the television stations indicate that the President will be reelected.*

ex·o·dus /'ɛksədəs/ n. **-es 1** a departure or withdrawal of large numbers of people: *The Exodus of the Jews from Egypt was a slow and dangerous journey.* **2** *sing.* a hurried escape by many people: *When the people in the town learned their water was poisoned, there was a mass exodus from the area.*

ex·on·er·ate /ɪg'zɑnəˌreɪt/ v. **-ated, -ating, -ates** to clear a person from guilt, (syn.) to absolve: *He was charged with fraud, but the trial exonerated him.* -n. [U] **exoneration.**

ex·or·bi·tant /ɪg'zɔrbɪtnt/ adj. much too high, (syns.) excessive, outrageous: *During the lettuce shortage, many stores charged exorbitant prices for it.* -n. [U] **exorbitance.**

ex·or·cise /'ɛksɔrˌsaɪz, -sər-/ v. **-cised, -cising, -cises** to remove evil from s.o.: *The priest exorcised the devil from the young woman.* -n. [U] **exorcism; exorcist.**

ex·ot·ic /ɪg'zɑtɪk/ adj. unusual and attractive, esp. from other countries: *The exotic plants from the tropics are especially beautiful.*

ex·pand /ɪk'spænd/ v. **1** to grow larger, (syns.) to enlarge, swell: *The balloon expanded, then exploded.* **2** to increase, or make larger (in size, number, etc.): *The company expanded its*

sales force from 10 to 20 representatives. **3** phrasal v. insep. **to expand on** or **upon s.t.:** to explain or add details to, (syn.) to elaborate: *The speaker made a brief introduction, then expanded upon her subject.* -adj. **expanded.**

ex·panse /ɪk'spæns/ n. a large, wide open area: *We left the mountains and entered the vast expanse of farmland.*

ex·pan·sion /ɪk'spænʃən/ n. [C;U] an enlargement, increase: *The company is hiring more people and is going through an expansion.* -adj. **expansionary; expansionist.**

ex·pan·sive /ɪk'spænsɪv/ adj. friendly and generous: *The father was in an expansive mood and gave presents to all of his children.* -adv. **expansively.**

ex·pa·tri·ate /ɛks'peɪtriət/ n. **1** a person from one country who lives in another country **2** a person who gives up (renounces) his or her country: *A group of expatriates from the USA live in Paris.*

ex·pect /ɪk'spɛkt/ v. **1** to think (s.t. will happen or s.o. will come): *I expect him (to arrive) very soon.* **2** to want and believe (that s.o. will do s.t.): *The mother told her little boy that she expected him to behave in school.* **3 to be expecting (a baby):** to be pregnant: *She is expecting a baby in May.*

ex·pec·tant /ɪk'spɛktənt/ pregnant: *She is six months pregnant; she's an expectant mother.* -n. [U] **expectancy.**

ex·pec·ta·tion /ˌɛkspɛk'teɪʃən/ n. [C;U] **1** hope, desire: *He has expectations that he will make a lot of money.* **2 to live** or **come up to s.o.'s expectations:** to be as good as s.o. expected: *He tries hard to live up to his parents' expectations.*

ex·pe·di·ent /ɪk'spidiənt/ adj. **1** effective in quickly solving an urgent problem: *My car broke down, so I rented one; it was the expedient thing to do so I could attend the meeting.* **2** based on one's interest rather than on what is right or just: *The politician made an expedient decision to vote for the tax cut.* -adv. **expediently;** -n.[C;U] **expediency.**

ex·pe·dite /'ɛkspəˌdaɪt/ v. **-dited, -diting, -dites** to do s.t. faster than usual, to process rapidly: *The company expedited the shipment by sending it overnight by air.* -n. **expediter.**

ex·pe·di·tion /ˌɛkspə'dɪʃən/ adj. a journey usu. made by a group organized and equipped for a special purpose: *Admiral Byrd made an expedition to reach the North Pole.* -adj. **expeditionary.**

ex·pe·di·tious /ˌɛkspə'dɪʃəs/ adj.frml. done quickly and well: *The airline handled my luggage in an expeditious manner; I got it back quickly.* -adv. **expeditiously.**

ex·pel /ɪk'spɛl/ v. **-pelled, -pelling, -pels 1** to send away for a reason, (syns.) to dismiss, eject: *The principal expelled the troublemaking student from school.* **2** *frml.* to force out, (*syns.*) to emit, discharge: *The volcano expels smoke.*

ex·pend /ɪk'spɛnd/ *v.* to spend or use (resources such as money, time, energy, etc.): *The company expends funds on purchases each week.||She expended a great deal of effort to learn French.*

ex·pend·able /ɪk'spɛndəbəl/ *adj.* not need-ed, (*syn.*) dispensable: *When traveling, things that seem necessary at home may become expendable.*

ex·pen·di·ture /ɪk'spɛndətʃər/ *n.* [C;U] the spending or using (of resources such as money, time, energy, etc.): *The company has made several big expenditures on new equipment.||The expenditure of so much time on that project was worthwhile; it's a success.*

ex·pense /ɪk'spɛns/ *n.* **1** [U] a cost, price: *he expense of moving from one house to another is high.* **2** [C] s.t. that must be paid, (*syns.*) a disbursement, expenditure: *The company expenses are increasing.* **3 at s.o.'s expense:** with harm, suffering, or financial cost to s.o.: *He got the praise at her expense because she did most of the work.* **4 at the expense of:** causing a loss to: *He succeeded in business at the expense of his personal life.*

expense account *n.* a budget to pay for s.o.'s business expenses, such as travel and entertainment: *Advertising executives have large expense accounts they use for travel and taking clients to dinner.*

ex·pen·sive /ɪk'spɛnsɪv/ *adj.* costly, high-priced: *He gives expensive gifts to his family at Christmastime.* -*adv.* **expensively.**

ex·pe·ri·ence /ɪk'spɪriəns/ *n.* **1** [U] an event, a happening: *Our visit to Alaska was a pleasant experience.* **2** [U] understanding gained through doing s.t.: *She has years of experience in teaching.*
—*v.* **-enced, -encing, -ences** to feel or know by personal involvement in: *She has experienced difficulties (satisfaction, success, etc.) in her new job.*

ex·pe·ri·enced /ɪk'spɪriənst/ *adj.* having background in an area: *She is an experienced secretary.*

ex·per·i·ment /ɪk'spɛrəmənt, -ˌmɛnt/ *n.* **1** a test done to see if s.t. works or happens: *We do experiments in chemistry class each week.* **2** a test project undertaken to see whether more of s.t. should be done: *We marketed the product in five cities as an experiment to see if we should market it nationwide.*
—*v.* **1** to test: *We experimented with magnetism in the physics laboratory.* **2** to try s.t.: *The company experimented with different sales techniques.* -*n.* [U] **experimentalism;** [U] **experimentation.**

ex·per·i·men·tal /ɪkˌspɛrə'mɛntl/ *adj.* related to experiments: *Our company opened office in London on an experimental basis, then closed it after low sales.* -*adv.* **experimentally.**

ex·pert /'ɛkˌspɜrt/ *n.* a master at s.t., authority: *She is an expert with computers.*
—*adj.* very knowledgeable or skilled, highly competent: *He is an expert shot with a pistol.* -*adv.* **expertly;** -*n.* [U] **expertness.**

ex·per·tise /ˌɛkspər'tiz/ *n.* [U] a special skill in doing s.t.: *He has expertise in computer programming.*

ex·pi·ra·tion /ˌɛkspə'reɪʃən/ *n.* [U] a date at which s.t. is no longer valid: *The expiration of my passport (driver's license, credit card, etc.) meant I had to get a new one.*

ex·pire /ɪk'spaɪr/ *v.* **-pired, -piring, -pires** to cease to be valid, (*syn.*) to lapse: *My driver's license expires in June.*

ex·plain /ɪk'spleɪn/ *v.* **1** to give information about, make clear, (*syn.*) to explicate: *The instructor explained the causes of the French Revolution.* **2** to give reasons for: *He explained why he was late.*

ex·pla·na·tion /ˌɛksplə'neɪʃən/ *n.* information given to help s.o. understand: *The computer salesperson gave an explanation of how to use that computer.* -*adj.* **explanatory** /ɪk'splænəˌtɔri/.

ex·ple·tive /'ɛksplətɪv/ *n.frml.* an obscene word or remark, usu. made in anger: *That film is full of expletives.*

ex·pli·ca·ble /'ɛksplɪkəbəl, ɪk'splɪ-/ *adj.* capable of being explained: *That situation is explicable if you understand the motives of the people involved.*

ex·pli·cate /'ɛkspləˌkeɪt/ *v.frml.* **-cated, -cating, -cates** to explain, make clear: *The instructor explicated the theory of relativity.* -*n.* [C;U] **explication.**

ex·plic·it /ɪk'splɪsɪt/ *adj.* **1** precise, clear: *he gave explicit directions on how to get to the train station.* **2** giving every detail openly: *That film has explicit sex scenes in it.* -*adv.* **explicitly;** -*n.* [U] **explicitness.**

ex·plode /ɪk'sploʊd/ *v.* **-ploded, -ploding, -plodes** **1** to blow apart with force, (*syn.*) to burst: *A bomb exploded on the battlefield.||Terrorists exploded a bomb.* **2** *fig.* to express sudden violent anger: *He exploded when told the bad news.*

ex·ploit /ɪk'splɔɪt/ *v.* **1** to use or develop to a good purpose: *The country exploits its natural resources in coal and timber.* **2** to treat unfairly, take advantage of: *He exploited workers by paying them very little.*
—*n.* an adventure, feat: *Her exploits as a safari guide are legendary.* -*adj.* **exploitive;** -*n.* [U] **exploitation** /ˌɛksplɔɪ'teɪʃən/.

ex·plo·ra·tion /ˌɛksplə'reɪʃən/ n. **1** [C] a journey of discovery, a search: *the exploration of space (the moon, the oceans)* **2** [C;U] an examination, study: *We began an exploration of ideas for new products.* -adj. **exploratory** /ɪk'splɔrə,tɔri/.

ex·plore /ɪk'splɔr/ v. **-plored, -ploring, -plores 1** to travel into in order to learn about, (syn.) to scout: *The children went to xplore the playground.* **2** to investigate, study: *Scientists explore theories of the beginning of the universe.* -n. **explorer.**

ex·plo·sion /ɪk'sploʊʒən/ n. **1** [C;U] a blowing apart with force, (syn.) a blast: *A bomb plosion damaged the building.* **2** [C] a sudden large increase: *There has been an explosion of growth in the computer industry.* **3** an expression of violent anger: *An explosion came from the crowd of angry people.*

ex·plo·sive /ɪk'sploʊsɪv/ n. a substance, such as dynamite, used to make explosions: *Soldiers used explosives to blow up a bridge.* —adj. related to an explosion: *A hurricane tore apart houses with explosive force.* -adv. **explosively.**

ex·po /'ɛkspoʊ/ n.short for exposition, a public show

ex·po·nent /ɪk'spoʊnənt/ n. **1** a person who believes in s.t., (syns.) an advocate, proponent: *She is an exponent of vegetarianism.* **2** (in math) a number or symbol above and beside another indicating a mathematical operation: *In 10^2, the 2 is an exponent meaning to square the 10.* -adj. **exponential** /ˌɛkspə'nɛnʃəl/; -adv. **exponentially.**

ex·port /ɪk'spɔrt/ v. to ship from one country to another, to market in foreign countries: *Canada exports wheat and lumber in great quantities.* —n. /'ɛk,spɔrt/ [C;U] an act of exporting or the item that is exported: *Wheat is a big export for Canada.* -n. **exporter.**

ex·por·ta·tion /ˌɛkspɔr'teɪʃən/ n. [U] an act of exporting: *The exportation of goods employs many workers in the seacoast cities.*

ex·pose /ɪk'spoʊz/ v. **-posed, -posing, -poses 1** to make known, reveal: *A politician exposed a plot to overthrow the government.* **2** to leave unprotected: *By swimming alone, he exposed himself to danger.* **3** to bare, uncover: *By taking off his shirt, he exposed the hair on his chest.* **4** to allow light to reach (photographic film)

ex·po·sé /ˌɛkspoʊ'zeɪ/ n. a disclosure that makes public a scandal: *The newspaper ranan exposé on corruption at City Hall.*

ex·po·si·tion /ˌɛkspə'zɪʃən/ n. **1** [C] a show where manufacturers display their products: *We attended a computer exposition* (or) *expo at the Trade Center.* **2** [C;U] a written work of

explanation, an essay: *She wrote an exposition of her views on politics.*

ex·pos·i·to·ry /ɪk'spazə,tɔri/ adj. serving to explain, explanatory: *The students are taking a course in expository writing.*

ex post facto /'ɛkspoʊst'fæktoʊ/ adv.adj.phr. (Latin for) after the fact: *He should have stated his views first, rather than <adv.> ex post facto, when it was too late.*

ex·po·sure /ɪk'spoʊʒər/ n. **1** [C;U] being nprotected, esp. from cold weather: *The lost mountain climbers suffered from exposure.* **2** [U] risk of loss: *We limit our exposure by investing only one quarter of the money.* **3** [C] a section of photographic film: *That roll of film contains 36 exposures.* **4** [C] a position or view in relation to a direction on he compass (north, south, east, or west): *The living room has a southern exposure.*

ex·pound /ɪk'spaʊnd/ v.frml. to comment or talk, usu. at length: *The professor expounded on the events leading up to the revolution.*

ex·press /ɪk'sprɛs/ v. **-pressed, -pressing, -presses 1** to speak about, declare: *She expressed her worries about money to her friend.* **2** infrml. to send s.t. the fastest way: *I expressed the package overnight.* **3 to express oneself:** to demonstrate one's ability to communicate: *She expresses herself well in French.* —adj. **1** nonstop, rapid: *an express train* **2** definite, clearly stated: *His express wish is that you go with him to the house.*

ex·pres·sion /ɪk'sprɛʃən/ n. **1** [C] the look n one's face: *You should have seen his expression when we gave him a surprise party.* **2** [C;U] a sign, demonstration: *He sent her roses as an expression of his love.* **3** [C] group of words, a statement, (syn.) an idiom: *When you tell s.o. to "break a leg," it is just an expression meaning "good luck."*

ex·pres·sive /ɪk'sprɛsɪv/ adj. showing obvious emotion: *His gestures (speech, laughter, etc.) were very expressive of the happiness he felt.* -adv. **expressively.**

ex·press·ly /ɪk'sprɛsli/ adv. with one clear purpose, (syn.) explicitly: *He sent flowers expressly for you* (or) *expressly to please you.*

ex·press·way /ɪk'sprɛs,weɪ/ n. a superhighway usu. with six to eight lanes and few roads leading to it: *The expressway takes you into Boston quickly and avoids all those back streets.*

ex·pro·pri·ate /ɛks'proʊpri,eɪt/ v.frml. **-ated, -ating, -ates** to take s.o.'s property by law, decree, or theft: *The state expropriated the criminal's property as payment of a fine.* -n.[C;U] **expropriation.**

ex·pul·sion /ɪk'spʌlʃən/ n. [C;U] **1** a sending out by force, (syn.) an ejection: *The expul-*

sion of dust from the volcano was visible from miles away. **2** a sending away for a reason, dismissal: *The child's bad behavior resulted in her expulsion from school.*

ex·punge /ɪk'spʌndʒ/ *v.frml.* **-punged, -punging, -punges** to erase, remove: *His offense was expunged from the prison records because of his good behavior.*

ex·pur·gate /'ɛkspər,geɪt/ *v.frml.* **-gated, -gating, -gates** to remove unwanted writing, esp. offensive words or errors: *The author complained because the editor expurgated certain words from her manuscript.* -n. [U] **expurgation.**

ex·qui·site /ɪk'skwɪzɪt, 'ɛkskwɪ-/ *adj.* **1** delicate, finely made: *The detail on the watch face is exquisite.* **2** perfect, outstanding: *Her singing of the opera was exquisite.* -adv. **exquisitely.**

ext. *n.short for* (telephone) extension

ex·tant /'ɛkstənt, ɛk'stænt/ *adj.* still existing, used of s.t. that is rare: *The few extant copies of the Gutenberg Bible are in museums.*

ex·tem·po·ra·ne·ous /ɪk,stɛmpə'reɪniəs/ *adj.* not written down, unrehearsed: *The politician made some extemporaneous remarks before his formal speech.* -adv. **extemporaneously;** -v. **extemporize.**

ex·tend /ɪk'stɛnd/ *v.* **1** to make longer in space or time; to stretch out: *I extended the antenna on my radio to its full length.‖We're extending our vacation from two to three weeks.* **2** to continue in space or time, to reach: *The roof extends a foot beyond the wall of the house.‖The President's term extends until January.* **3** *frml.* to offer or give: *extend an invitation (a helping hand, a word of advice, etc.)* -adj. **extended; extendible.**

extended family *n.* an entire family including many generations and relatives who may live in other households: *Our entire extended family will be here for Thanksgiving dinner. See:* nuclear family.

ex·ten·sion /ɪk'stɛnʃən/ *n.* **1** [C;U] more time: *The businessman asked the bank for an extension on his bank loan.* **2** [C] an addition to a building: *We added an extension for an extra bedroom onto our house.* **3** [C] any one of many connected telephone lines: *Call the company's main number, 555-2000, and ask for my office extension, 245 (said "extension 2-4-5").*

ex·ten·sive /ɪk'stɛnsɪv/ *adj.* great in amount or area, considerable: *She has extensive knowledge of Chinese history.‖He owns extensive property.* -adv. **extensively.**

ex·tent /ɪk'stɛnt/ *n.sing.* [U] an amount, degree: *Inflation has slowed to a great (small, certain, etc.) extent.*

ex·ten·u·at·ing /ɪk'stɛnyu,eɪtɪŋ/ *adj.* making (wrongdoing) seem less serious by providing an excuse: *The judge did not send the man to jail; there were extenuating circumstances since the man had never broken the law before.* -n.[C;U] **extenuation.**

ex·te·ri·or /ɪk'stɪriər/ *n.* **1** the outside of s.t., surface: *The exterior of the house needs painting.* **2** appearance, looks: *He has a rough exterior, but inside, he has a heart of gold.* —adj. outside: *The exterior walls of the building are made of glass and steel.*

ex·ter·mi·nate /ɪk'stɜrmə,neɪt/ *v.* **-nated, -nating, -nates** to kill all (of a group or type of people or other living things), (*syn.*) to eradicate: *Some people exterminate garden insects by spraying poison on the plants.* -n. [U] **extermination.**

ex·ter·mi·na·tor /ɪk'stɜrmə,neɪtər/ *n.* a person or business that exterminates: *An exterminator comes to our building every week to kill insects and rodents.*

ex·ter·nal /ɪk'stɜrnəl/ *adj.* **1** outside, exterior: *The external surface of the airplane is very smooth and shiny.* **2** coming from the outside: *Children's experiences in school are affected by many external influences.* -adv. **externally;** -n. **externality** /,ɛkstər'næləti/.

ex·tinct /ɪk'stɪŋkt/ *adj.* no longer in existence, esp. a kind of plant or animal: *The passenger pigeon is an extinct species.* -n. [U] **extinction.**

ex·tin·guish /ɪk'stɪŋgwɪʃ/ *v.* to stop, put out: *Firefighters extinguished a fire.*

ex·tin·guish·er /ɪk'stɪŋgwɪʃər/ *n.short for* a fire extinguisher, a device that shoots out liquid to stop a fire

extinguisher

ex·tol /ɪk'stoʊl/ *v.* **-tolled, -tolling, -tols** to praise, (*syn.*) to laud: *The speaker extolled the accomplishments of the political candidate.*

ex·tort /ɪk'stɔrt/ *v.* to force payment of (money) by threatening s.o., (*syn.*) to coerce: *Gang members extorted money from store owners by threatening to burn their stores.* -n. [U] **extortion; extortionist.**

ex·tor·tion·ate /ɪk'stɔrʃənɪt/ *adj.* much too high in price, excessive: *The rent she is demanding is extortionate!*

ex·tra /'ɛkstrə/ *adj.* **1** more than the usual, additional, further: *That store charges an extra amount for home delivery.* **2** spare, duplicate: *We keep extra light bulbs in the closet.* **3** more than needed, (*syn.*) superfluous: *After the party was over, we had extra food.*

—*adv.* very, exceptionally: *That knife is extra sharp.*

—*n.* **1** *pl.* an addition, an add-on: *The basic service costs $100, plus 20 percent for the extras.* **2** a spare, a duplicate: *I used almost all the nails and left the extras in a box.* **3** an actor hired for a small role in a film: *The movie director hired 1,000 extras for the battle scene.*

ex·tract /ɪkˈstrækt/ *v.* **1** to remove, pull out (s.t. firmly fixed): *The dentist extracted a bad tooth.* **2** to get by using force or coercion: *The police extracted a confession from the criminal.*
—*n.* /ˈɛkˌstrækt/ **1** [C;U] a concentration or essence of a food or other substance: *I use vanilla extract in baking cakes.* **2** [C] an excerpt from a written work: *She used an extract from a novel in her term paper.*

ex·trac·tion /ɪkˈstrækʃən/ *n.* [C;U] removal of a tooth: *The dentist did the extraction quickly.*

ex·tra·cur·ric·u·lar /ˌɛkstrəkəˈrɪkyələr/ *adj.* outside (or) after school: *His extracurricular activities include playing football and singing in the choir.*

USAGE NOTE: *Extracurricular activities* are strongly encouraged for high school and college students in the USA because they help students develop many different skills and abilities. Common activities are playing sports, writing for a school newspaper, join-ing a science or language club, playing in a band, or running for student government.

---

ex·tra·dite /ˈɛkstrəˌdaɪt/ *v.* **-dited, -diting, -dites** (in law) to transfer a prisoner from one legal jurisdiction to another: *The State of New York extradited a prisoner from Florida back to New York.* **-adj. extraditable; -n.** [U] **extradition** /ˌɛkstrəˈdɪʃən/.

ex·tra·mar·i·tal /ˌɛkstrəˈmærətl/ *adj.* outside of marriage: *He had an extramarital affair with a woman he met at work.*

ex·tra·ne·ous /ɪkˈstreɪniəs/ *adj.* unneeded, (*syn.*) superfluous: *The report contained extraneous information of no use to anyone.* **-adv. extraneously.**

ex·traor·di·nar·y /ɪkˈstrɔrdnˌɛri, ˌɛkstrəˈɔr-/ *adj.* **1** outstanding, wonderful: *The violinist gave an extraordinary performance.* **2** unusual, uncommon: *She is a woman of extraordinary strength (ability, intelligence, etc.).* **-adv. extraordinarily.**

ex·trap·o·late /ɪkˈstræpəˌleɪt/ *v.frml.* **-lated, -lating, -lates** to infer a meaning or result from a few facts: *That product has sold five units a month for six months, so I extrap-*

olate *60 units for the year's sales.* **-n.** [C;U] **extrapolation.**

ex·tra·sen·so·ry perception /ˌɛkstrəˈsɛn-səri/ *n.abbr.* **ESP** [U] the ability to sense information or events beyond the normal senses of seeing, hearing, etc.: *She has extrasensory perception (or) ESP and knows when s.o. is thinking about her.*

ex·tra·ter·res·tri·al /ˌɛkstrətəˈrɛstriəl/ *adj.* related to outer space: *Scientists search for extraterrestrial life.*

ex·trav·a·gance /ɪkˈstrævəgəns/ *n.* **1** [C;U] wastefulness, esp. of money: *He is known for his extravagance when shopping for sports equipment.* **2** [C;U] a too-expensive item or act: *That family cannot afford any extravagances; they're not rich.*

ex·trav·a·gant /ɪkˈstrævəgənt/ *adj.* **1** too generous or expensive: *She gives extravagant gifts to her family for their birthdays.* **2** unreasonable, excessive: *He made an extravagant demand on his employer by asking for a huge raise.* **-adv. extravagantly.**

ex·trav·a·gan·za /ɪkˌstrævəˈgænzə/ *n.* a spectacular event: *The carnival was a three-day extravaganza of parades, dancing, and eating.*

ex·treme /ɪkˈstrim/ *adj.* **1** the farthest away, outermost: *You will find our house at the extreme end of the road.* **2** (of ideas) far from what is generally accepted, (*syns.*) radical, fanatical: *She holds extreme political views.* **3** the greatest possible, (*syns.*) drastic, severe: *The government took extreme measures to put down the rebellion.*
—*n.* **1** an extreme degree or amount: *The climate there is mild, without extremes of heat or cold.* **2 to go to** or **be driven to extremes:** to act in an exaggerated way: *He was driven to extremes by financial pressures, and in the end he killed himself.*

ex·treme·ly /ɪkˈstrimli/ *adv.* very: *That movie was extremely funny (violent, sad, etc.).*

ex·trem·ism /ɪkˈstrimˌɪzəm/ *n.* [U] extreme radicalism in thought or action, (*syn.*) fanaticism: *The group's policies are based on religious extremism.* **-n. extremist.**

ex·trem·i·ty /ɪkˈstrɛməti/ *n.* **1** the far end of something: *the extremities of the earth* **2** *pl.* the feet and hands: *The man was so cold that he lost feeling in his extremities.*

ex·tri·cate /ˈɛkstrɪˌkeɪt/ *v.frml.* **-cated, -cating, -cates** to free: *She extricated herself from financial difficulty by working two jobs.* **-n.** [U] **extrication.**

ex·trin·sic /ɪkˈstrɪnsɪk, -zɪk/ *adj.* external, outside of: *What he says is extrinsic to the main idea.* **-adv. extrinsically. See:** intrinsic.

ex·tro·vert /'ɛkstrə,vɜrt/ *n.* a person who likes others and social activities: *She is a real extrovert, a cheerleader and president of her class. -n.* [U] **extroversion.** *See:* introvert.

ex·tro·vert·ed /'ɛkstrə,vɜrtɪd/ *adj.* liking other people and outside events, sociable, *(syn.)* outgoing: *She is very extroverted, always talking with friends. See:* introvert.

ex·u·ber·ant /ɪg'zubərənt/ *adj.* high-spirited, enthusiastic: *She is exuberant about her new job offer. -n.* [U] **exuberance;** *-adv.* **exuberantly.**

ex·ude /ɪg'zud/ *v.* **-uded, -uding, -udes** **1** to send out (a liquid) slowly, *(syn.)* to ooze: *As the weight lifter trained with heavier weights, moisture slowly exuded from his skin.* **2** *fig.* to show in one's face and behavior, *(syn.)* to display: *She exuded happiness (confidence, pride, etc.).*

ex·ult /ɪg'zʌlt/ *v.frml.* to feel great happiness, rejoice: *The people exulted when their country won the war. -adj.* **exultant;** *-n.* [U] **exultation** /,ɛgzəl'teɪʃən, ,ɛksəl-/.

eye /aɪ/ *n.* **1** the organ of sight: *She has beautiful brown eyes.* **2** the center of s.t.: *the eye of a hurricane* **3** the hole in a needle **4 an eye for an eye:** hurting s.o. in the same way they hurt s.o. else: *That kid broke my brother's nose, so I broke that kid's nose; it's an eye for an eye!* **5 in the eyes of:** in the opinion of, according to: *I think you did the right thing, but in the eyes of the law, it was wrong.* **6** *infrml.* **My eye!** or **In a pig's eye!:** I don't believe it; I disagree. **7 to catch s.o.'s eye:** to get s.o.'s attention: *I tried to catch the waiter's eye.* **8** *infrml.* **to give s.o. the eye** or **to make eyes at:** to show admiration, to flirt: *As soon as she walked into the room, he started giving her the eye.* **9 to have an eye for:** to be a good judge of (esp. s.t. requiring a sense of beauty): *She has an eye for color, and her house and clothes are very attractive.* **10 to keep an eye on s.o. or s.t.:** to watch in a protective way: *When we went away on vacation, I asked the neighbors to keep an eye on our house.* **11** *infrml.* **to keep an eye on the ball:** to pay close attention to what one is doing so as not to make mistakes: *He makes mistakes in his work; he needs to keep his eye on the ball.* **12 to keep an eye out for:** to watch for, *(syn.)* to be on the lookout for: *We need a new sofa, so I'm keeping an eye out for a good sale on furniture.* **13** *infrml.* **to keep one's eyes open** or **peeled:** to watch carefully: *We're going into a dangerous neighborhood, so keep your eyes peeled.* **14 to only**

have eyes for: to be interested only in (a person): *Lots of men are attracted to her, but she only has eyes for her husband.* **15 to see eye to eye (with s.o.):** to agree: *We see eye to eye on the matter, so let's sign a contract.* **16 with an eye to:** with a plan in mind to: *He's buying land with an eye to building a house on it someday.* **17 with one's eyes open:** knowing the risks of s.t.: *It's a difficult job, but she went into it with her eyes open, so she has no right to complain now.*
—*v.* **eyed, eyeing** or **eying, eyes** to look at, esp. with interest or suspicion: *The old man eyed his new neighbor with distrust.*

eye·ball /'aɪ,bɔl/ *n.* the entire ball-shaped eye: *The eyeball is a delicate organ.*
—*v.slang* to look at closely, examine: *What you are telling me about the place is interesting, but I want to go there and eyeball it for myself.*

eye·brow /'aɪ,braʊ/ *n.* **1** the line of hair over the eye **2 eyebrow pencil:** a cosmetic pencil: *She uses an eyebrow pencil to color her eyebrows.*

eye-catching *adj.* interesting and attractive: *That's an eye-catching tie you're wearing.*

eye contact *n.* [U] a look directly at the eyes of another person: *They are angry at each other and do not make eye contact when they meet or talk.*

USAGE NOTE: In American culture, a person who does not use *eye contact* might be considered rude or dishonest. On the other hand, someone who *looks you in the eye* is believed to be honest and truthful.

eyed /aɪd/ *adj.suffix* having eyes as described (bright-eyed, one-eyed, etc.): *He is brown-eyed. See:* cross-eyed.

eye·ful /'aɪfʊl/ *n.sing.* a startling view: *Two men had a fistfight right in front of us; we really had an eyeful.*

eye·glass·es /'aɪglæsɪz/ *n.pl.* a pair of lenses in a frame used for better sight: *She wears eyeglasses for reading.*

eye·lash /'aɪ,læʃ/ *n.* **-lashes** a hair from the row of hairs on the eyelids: *She wears false eyelashes that are long and black.*

eye·let /'aɪlɪt/ *n.* a round opening usu. in clothing: *He wears shoes with eyelets for the laces.*

eye·lid /'aɪ,lɪd/ *n.* the folds of skin over the eyeballs: *She carefully applied make-up to her eyelids.*

eye·lin·er /'aɪ,laɪnər/ *n.* [U] a cosmetic used to draw a line around the eye: *She uses black eyeliner in pencil form.*

eye-opener *n.* s.t. that surprises or shocks: *The scandal at the bank was an eye-opener.*

eye shadow *n.* [U] cosmetics used mainly on the upper eyelid to highlight the eyes: *She uses blue eye shadow.*

eye·sight /'aɪ,saɪt/ *n.* [U] ability to see, (*syn.*) vision: *He lost his eyesight in an accident.*

eye·sore /'aɪ,sɔr/ *n.* an unpleasant sight, esp. a building in ruins: *That burned-out house is the* eyesore of the neighborhood.

eye·tooth /'aɪ,tuθ/ *n.* **-teeth** /-,tiθ/ **1** one of two long, sharp teeth located beside the four upper front teeth **2 to give one's eyeteeth for s.t.:** to desire greatly: *I'd give my eyeteeth for a vacation in Paris.*

eye·wit·ness /,aɪ'wɪtnɪs/ *n.* **-nesses** a person who saw an event happen, esp. a crime: *The two eyewitnesses to the theft testified in court.*

E

F,f

F, f, /ɛf/ *n.* **F's, f's** or **Fs, fs** **1** the sixth letter of the English alphabet **2** *abbr.* a failing grade: *He was shocked when he received an F on the exam. See:* Fahrenheit.

fa·ble /ˈfeɪbəl/ *n.* a story or poem, usu. with animals acting out a moral truth: *The students discussed the meaning of the fable.*

fab·ric /ˈfæbrɪk/ *n.* **1** [C;U] cloth material: *The sofa is covered with a soft cotton fabric.* **2** *fig.* [U] the composition, substance of s.t.: *The fabric of our society has been torn by crime and a bad economy.*

fab·ri·cate /ˈfæbrɪˌkeɪt/ *v.frml.* **-cated, -cating, -cates** **1** to put together or make s.t., (*syn.*) to manufacture: *The furniture was fabricated from pieces of old wood.* **2** to lie, (*syn.*) to falsify: *The witness's statement to the police was fabricated.*

fab·ri·ca·tion /ˌfæbrɪˈkeɪʃən/ *n.* [U] **1** the act of making s.t., (*syn.*) manufacture: *The fabrication of auto parts is a worldwide industry now.* **2** a lie, (*syn.*) falsehood: *The child's story is a complete fabrication.*

fab·u·lous /ˈfæbyələs/ *adj.* great, wonderful: *We had a fabulous time on our vacation!*

fa·cade /fəˈsad/ *n.* **1** the front or outer covering of a building: *The facade of that building is made of wood.* **2** a false appearance, (*syn.*) veneer: *He puts on a facade of being a rich man, but he is not.*

face /feɪs/ *n.* **1** the front of a being's head: *That young woman has a pretty face.* **2** the front part of a structure: *The face of that building (cliff, mountain, etc.) is gray and flat.* **3 on the face of it:** on the surface: *On the face of it, his offer seems genuine, but does he have the money to pay?* **4 to keep a straight face:** to hold oneself back from smiling or laughing when s.t. is funny: *When he tried to explain why he was late, she couldn't keep a straight face.* **5 to lose face:** to lose status or the respect of others: *When the man went to jail for stealing, he lost face among his family members.* **6 to make a face:** to express dislike or disapproval by the expression on one's face: *My son makes a face when I tell him to eat his vegetables.* **7 to save face:** to keep one's dignity in an embarrassing situation: *Instead of firing him, the company let him quit to save face.* **8 to show one's face:** to appear somewhere when in difficulty or embarrassment: *After failing his exams at college, he didn't dare show his face at home.* **9 to s.o.'s face:** directly to s.o.: *She could never tell him to his face that his jokes aren't funny.*

—*v.* **faced, facing, faces** **1** to present a front to s.o. or s.t.: *I sat in the first row and faced the teacher.‖The building that we work in faces a park.* **2** to meet with courage, (*syn.*) to confront: *I decided finally to stand up and face my enemy.* **3** *phrasal v. sep.* **to face down:** to meet an enemy with courage, (*syn.*) to intimidate: *The king faced down his enemies on the battlefield.‖He faced them down.* **4 to face facts** or **to face the fact:** to understand a bad situation and do s.t. about it: *We have to face the fact that the business is losing money.* **5** *phrasal v.* **to face off:** to get into position prior to a fight or athletic event: *The two boxers faced off before the fight started.* **6** *infrml.* **to face the music:** to step forward and accept punishment: *The business is losing so much money that we must face the music and close it.* **7** *phrasal v. insep.* **to face up to s.t.** or **face up to the fact(s):** to accept a bad situation and be willing to suffer the consequences: *We have to face up to the fact that he's not doing the job and fire him.*

face cloth *n.* a small towel used to wash one's face, (*syn.*) washcloth: *I wash my face with a face cloth every morning.*

face-lift *n.* cosmetic surgery used to regain a youthful appearance: *At age 60 the actor had a face-lift that made him look much younger.*

face mask *n.* a covering used to protect the face in sports or to hide one's identity: *She couldn't describe the thief because he had worn a face mask.*

face-saving *n.* [U] an action designed to keep one's self-respect in an embarrassing situation: *Face-saving is an important part of many Asian and other cultures.*

—*adj.* keeping one's self-respect: *The government allowed the man to resign as a face-saving measure; he didn't have to go to prison.*

fac·et /ˈfæsɪt/ *n.* **1** one of many small, flat surfaces cut in a stone or jewel: *A jeweler cuts facets in a rough diamond.* **2** *fig.* a part, (*syn.*) aspect: *The problem that we face now has many legal and financial facets.*

fa·ce·tious /fəˈsiʃəs/ *adj.frml.* humorous in a way that can be rude or disrespectful: *Many people at the party were offended by his facetious comments.* -*adv.* **facetiously**; -*n.* [U] **facetiousness.**

face value *n.frml.* **1** [U] the truthfulness of s.t. as it appears on the surface: *I accept what he says at face value because he is an honest man.* **2** [C] the value written on a stock or bond versus its market value: *The face value of the bond is $1,000, but its market value is only $900.*

fa·cial /ˈfeɪʃəl/ *adj.* related to the face: *Her facial expression changed to happiness when she heard the good news.*
—*n.* a treatment of the face's skin: *She went to a beauty salon to have a facial.*

fac·ile /ˈfæsəl/ *adj.* **1** done easily, (*syn.*) skillful: *The dancer's facile movements were beautiful to watch.* **2** smooth but untruthful: *He has a facile tongue when he explains his mistakes.*

fa·cil·i·tate /fəˈsɪləˌteɪt/ *v.* **-tated, -tating, -tates** to help, (*syn.*) to expedite: *The tourist office sent us a guide who facilitated our travel through Japan.*

fa·cil·i·ty /fəˈsɪləti/ *n.* **-ties** **1** [C] service(s), including the physical area, provided by an organization: *The sports facility at that club includes tennis courts, a golf course, and a swimming pool.* **2** [U] ease, (*syn.*) expertise: *The facility with which she explains difficult topics is amazing.*

fac·ing /ˈfeɪsɪŋ/ *n.* outside covering, (*syn.*) facade: *The facing on that building is made of stone.*

fac·sim·i·le /fækˈsɪməli/ *n.* **1** an exact copy, (*syn.*) duplicate: *That print is a facsimile of the original painting.* **2** an electronic transmission of printed materials via telephone wires: *I sent my letter by facsimile to Mexico City this morning. See:* fax.

fact /fækt/ *n.* **1** a reality (as opposed to an opinion), such as an event, date, physical object, or number: *The facts are that sales are up by 10%, but profits are down by 5%.* **2 the facts of life** or **a fact of life: a.** a usually unpleasant reality that one must accept: *Having to work for a living is a fact of life for most people.* **b.** *fig.* information about sex: *She knew it was time to explain the facts of life to her daughter.* **3 to get the facts:** to find out accurate information about s.t.: *The detective*

questioned the victim and witnesses to get the facts about the accident.

fact-finding *adj.n.* related to finding out accurate information about s.t.: *The President sent a diplomat on a <adj.> fact-finding mission to the disaster area.‖He finished his <n.> fact-finding in two days.*

fac·tion /ˈfækʃən/ *n.* a group of people within a larger group, (*syn.*) bloc: *One faction within the Liberal Party wants a tax freeze.*

fac·tor /ˈfæktər/ *n.* **1** a fact to be considered: *The high cost of labor is an important factor in the price of steel.* **2** a number by which a larger number can be divided: *Two and four are factors of eight.* **3** a person or an organization doing business for another: *His relatives work as factors in the clothing industry.*
—*v.* to consider, include in one's reasoning: *We factored in all of the company's needs and decided to locate the office in Florida.*

fac·to·ry /ˈfæktəri, -tri/ *n.* **-ries** a building or group of buildings where goods are produced, (*syn.*) manufacturing plant: *The furniture factory has five buildings with a fence around them.*

fac·tu·al /ˈfæktʃuəl/ *adj.* true, based on facts: *A reporter checked out the story and found it to be factual.*

fac·ul·ty /ˈfækəlti/ *n.* **-ties** **1** an ability, esp. of the mind: *She has the faculty to express herself well.* **2** *pl.* mental powers: *The old man has lost his faculties and cannot take care of himself.* **3** used with a sing. or pl.v. the teaching staff at a school or college: *That university has an excellent faculty.*

fad /fæd/ *n.* a fashion that lasts a short time: *The current fad among young people is to wear baseball caps.*

fad·dish /ˈfædɪʃ/ *adj.* related to a fashion that lasts a short time: *Some students dress in a faddish manner.*

fade /feɪd/ *v.* **faded, fading, fades** **1** to lose the original color, grow pale: *The wallpaper has faded from red to pale pink.* **2** to disappear gradually: *The horseman passed by me and faded into the distance.* **3** to appear or disappear gradually, esp. in films and television
—*n.v.* **1 fade-in:** a gradual appearance, esp. in films and television: *The camera operator did a <n.> fade-in of the next scene.* **2 fade-out:** a gradual disappearance: *The camera operator did a <n.> fade-out of a scene in a house; she <v.> faded out to pick up action occurring outdoors.*

fag /fæg/ *n.* **1** *pej.slang* a male homosexual **2** *slang* a cigarette: *Can you give me a fag?*

USAGE NOTE: Many people consider the terms *fag* and *faggot* offensive. *Gay* is the preferred alternate term for homosexual.

fag·got /'fægət/ n. pej.slang a male homosexual

Fahr·en·heit /'færən,haɪt, 'fɛr-/ adj. a system of measuring temperature in which water freezes at 32° and boils at 212°: *The temperature is 90 degrees Fahrenheit this afternoon; it's really hot! See:* Centigrade, Celsius.

fail /feɪl/ v. **1** to not succeed: *He failed his test in math.* **2** to not operate when needed: *The brakes failed on his automobile when he tried to stop.* **3** to break: *A wire failed on a bridge and fell over the roadway.* **4** to lose strength and ability: *The old man is failing rapidly and may die soon.*

fail·ing /'feɪlɪŋ/ n. a fault, (syn.) shortcoming: *The student's failing is that he does not study enough.*

fail-safe adj. served by a device or action that saves s.t. from major or total failure: *As a fail-safe action, my computer automatically copies my work every two minutes, so almost nothing can be lost.*

fail·ure /'feɪlyər/ n. **1** [C] a person who fails: *He cannot keep a job, so he feels he is a failure in life.* **2** [C] an activity or project that does not succeed: *That new play was a failure on Broadway.* **3** [C] a breakdown, (syn.) a malfunction: *A failure in the electrical system caused the lights to go out.* **4** [C;U] neglect, not caring about one's responsibilities: *Her failure to act in time caused the company to suffer a big loss.*

faint /feɪnt/ v. to fall unconscious, (syn.) to pass out: *The summer sun was so strong that she fainted.*
—adj. **1** unclear, weak: *The image on the photograph is too faint to see what it is.||The radio signal is too faint to be heard clearly.* **2** dizzy, weak: *I feel faint from the heat.*

faint-heart·ed /'feɪnt'hɑrtɪd/ adj. lacking courage, fearful, (syn.) cowardly: *He was too faint-hearted to climb the mountain with the others.*

fair /fɛr/ adj. **1** just, (syn.) equitable: *The judge's decision was fair to both sides.* **2** light-haired and light-skinned: *Both she and her brother are fair.* **3** bright, sunny: *We are having fair weather this week, so we will be able to work in our garden.* **4** neither good nor bad, (syn.) average: *The student's grades were just fair this semester.* **5** (in baseball) inside the foul line: *The baseball player hit a fair ball to right field.* **6 a fair deal:** an arrangement or purchase satisfactory to both sides: *The couple felt they had gotten a fair deal on their new house.* **7 a fair shake:** just treatment: *He's an honest man and will give you a fair shake in his dealings with you.* **8 to be fair game:** to be in danger of being taken advantage of: *If you are careless and leave your purse open in public, you are fair game for a thief.*
—n. an event at which goods are shown and sold: *One of our pigs won first prize at the county fair.||There is a famous book fair in Frankfurt, Germany, every year.*
—adv. **1 fair and square:** justly and honestly: *I won the race fair and square.* **2 to play fair:** to play a game and behave generally by the rules: *That team uses dirty tricks to win; they don't play fair.*

fair·ground /'fɛr,graʊnd/ n. usu. used in pl. a large outdoor area, usu. with barns, to display farm animals and amusements: *The fairgrounds have a place for animals on one side and some rides for children on the other.*

fair-haired /'fɛr,hɛrd/ adj.frml. **1** with blond hair **2 fair-haired boy:** a favored boy or man: *In his class, he is the teacher's fair-haired boy.*

fair·ly /'fɛrli/ adv. **1** justly, (syn.) impartially: *The boss acts fairly toward all her employees.* **2** moderately, not extremely: *He should arrive here fairly soon. See:* kind of, USAGE NOTE.

fair-mind·ed /'fɛr,maɪndɪd/ adj. without showing favor to anyone, (syn.) just, impartial: *After hearing his decision, everyone agreed that the judge had been fair-minded.*

fair·ness /'fɛrnɪs/ n. [U] **1** lightness of complexion and hair: *The fairness of her skin prevents her from staying in the sun too long.* **2** justness, (syn.) impartiality: *The fairness of the judge's decision was admired by all.*

fair play n. [U] behaving according to commonly accepted rules of fairness: *In the interest of fair play, you should hear both sides of the story.*

fair trade agree·ment n. an agreement between a manufacturer and its distributors that its products will be sold at or above an agreed-upon price: *Fair trade agreements prevent one store from selling a product at a much lower price than another.*

fair·way /'fɛr,weɪ/ n. an area of carefully cut grass between tee and green: *The golfer hit the golfball in a perfect line, straight down the fairway.*

fair-weath·er adj. **1** related to good weather conditions: *I wear a cap, sweater, and jeans as fair-weather clothing on our sailboat.* **2** fig. referring to people who are one's friends only in good times: *After I lost my job and became ill, my fair-weather friends disappeared.*

fair·y /'fɛri/ n. -ies **1** a small, imaginary creature with magical powers: *When children lose their baby teeth, the tooth fairy puts money under their pillows.* **2** fig.pej. a male homosexual

USAGE NOTE: Many people consider this term offensive. *Gay* is the preferred alternate term for homosexual.

fair·y·land /ˈfɛriˌlænd/ n. an imaginary place where fairies live: *The little girl dreamed that she traveled to fairyland.*

fairy tale n. **1** a children's story with magical creatures and interesting adventures: *Parents read fairy tales to their children before bedtime.* **2** fig. a polite term for an untrue story: *His adventures in Alaska are fairy tales; he's never been there.*

fait ac·com·pli /ˈfeɪtəˌkɑmˈpli, -tɑ-, ˈfɛ-/ n.sing.frml. (French for) a completed action that cannot be changed: *Your daughter's marriage to that fellow whom you dislike is a fait accompli, so accept it.*

faith /feɪθ/ n. **1** [U] belief in a favorable result with no factual proof, (syn.) conviction: *I have faith that my surgery will turn out well.* **2** [C] a specific religion, (syn.) denomination: *He belongs to the Jewish faith.* **3 to have faith in:** to believe in s.t., esp. in God: *My husband has faith in God.* **4 to keep the faith: a.** to remain devoted to one's religion: *He goes to church each Sunday to keep the faith.* **b.** to remain devoted to one's efforts or goals: *Whenever my work becomes too difficult, I tell myself to keep the faith.*

faith·ful /ˈfeɪθfəl/ adj. **1** devoted to a religion: *Churchgoers are faithful to their religious beliefs.* **2** loyal to one's spouse by not having a sexual relationship with s.o. else: *He has always been faithful to his wife.* **3** factual, accurate: *Her book was a faithful account of the years she spent in jail as a political prisoner.* -adv. **faithfully.**

faith·less /ˈfeɪθlɪs/ adj. immoral, disloyal: *The wife rejected her faithless husband.*

fa·ji·tas /fəˈhitəz, fɑ-/ n.pl. a dish created in Texas and influenced by Mexican-style food, usu. with grilled meat or chicken placed inside a thin bread called a "tortilla": *When I eat at Mexican restaurants, I always order fajitas.* See: tortilla; Tex-Mex.

fake /feɪk/ n. **1** a copy, imitation: *That painting is a fake.* **2** person claiming to be s.o. or s.t. he or she is not, (syns.) impostor, phony: *That guy pretends to be a cop, but he's a fake.* —v. **faked, faking, fakes 1** to make or write s.t. in order to deceive, (syn.) to forge: *He faked his wife's signature on a check.* **2 to fake it:** to do s.t. without preparation, out of necessity, (syns.) to improvise, to wing it: *She was called upon suddenly to make a speech, so she had to fake it.*

fal·con /ˈfælkən, ˈfɔl-/ n. a bird that can be trained to hunt small animals: *He spent the summer training the falcon.* -n. [C] **falconer;** [U] **falconry** /ˈfælkənri, ˈfɔl-/.

fall /fɔl/ n. **1** a sudden move to the ground from a standing position, (syn.) a tumble: *He took a bad fall and broke his ankle.* **2** a severe loss of

status or power: *The political leader had a fall from power.* **3** a decline, loss of value: *The housing market experienced a fall in prices.* **4** the season between summer and winter, (syn.) autumn: *In the fall, the leaves change to bright colors.* **5 to be headed for a fall:** to be on a dangerous path to ruin: *We knew he was headed for a fall when the boss kept calling him into his office.* See: rainfall; snowfall; waterfall.

—v. **fell** /fɛl/, **fallen** /ˈfɔlən/, **falling, falls 1** to move suddenly to the ground from a standing position, (syn.) to tumble: *She fell and hurt her head.‖He fell over the low table.* **2** to come down from a higher place: *Some dishes fell off the table and broke.‖He fell into the pool (out of the window, down the stairs etc.).* **3** fig. to suffer a severe loss of status or power: *The government fell and was replaced by another.* **4** to decline: *The price of oil fell sharply.* **5** to pass into a new state or condition: *He fell asleep while watching TV.‖She fell ill for a month.‖He fell into alcoholism and was rejected by his friends.* **6 to fall all over oneself:** to try hard, be eager: *When he first got the job, he fell all over himself trying to please his new boss.* **7 to fall all over s.o.:** to flatter s.o. in an attempt to please: *He falls all over his girlfriend every time he sees her.* **8** phrasal v. **to fall back:** to retreat, withdraw: *The enemy forces fell back under the counterattack.* **9** phrasal v. insep. **to fall back on s.o. or s.t.:** to depend on in case of need: *When she lost her job, she fell back on piano playing for money.* **10** phrasal v. insep. **to fall behind s.o. or in/on s.t.:** not to keep pace: *One marcher fell behind the others.‖The woman fell behind in her rent payments.* **11 to fall by the wayside:** to disappear, no longer be of interest: *He had big plans about starting a new business, but they fell by the wayside.* **12 to fall down on the job:** to fail to perform in a satisfactory way: *He fell down on the job and did not complete his assignment on time.* **13 to fall flat:** to fail, meet disapproval: *The new play fell flat and closed in a week.* **14 to fall flat on one's face: a.** infrml. fig. to move completely to the ground from a standing position: *He was ice skating and fell flat on his face.* **b.** fig. to fail completely: *She tried acting in New York but fell flat on her face.* **15** phrasal v. insep. **to fall for s.o.: a.** to fall in love with: *She was so charming that he fell for her right away.* **b.** to be deceived by a trick: *He told the teacher he hadn't done the assignment because he was sick, and she fell for it.* **16 to fall from favor** or **grace:** to be no longer favored by s.o.: *The count fell from favor with the queen, and she sent him away.* **17** phrasal v. **to fall in:** (military) to join in a military formation: *The sergeant ordered the troops to fall in.* **18 to fall in battle:** to be killed or wounded: *The* *soldier fell in battle.* **19 to fall in line:** to co-operate with others after being unwilling to do so: *The Senator first refused to cooperate, but she fell in line after meeting with the President.* **20 to fall in love:** to suddenly form deep feelings of affection for s.o. or s.t.: *He fell in love with her the first time that he met her.‖She fell in love with California on a trip there.* **21** *phrasal v. insep.* **to fall in with s.o.:** to join a group of people, esp. with troublemakers: *In high school, he fell in with the wrong crowd and ended up in jail.* **22 to fall into (debt, trouble, difficulty, etc.):** to suffer problems by poor management or bad luck: *When her business failed, she fell into debt.* **23** *phrasal v.* **to fall into s.t.:** to experience good fortune by pure luck: *He made a small fortune on a business deal that he just fell into on information from a friend.* **24** *phrasal v.* **to fall off:** to decline, decrease: *Business has fallen off lately.* **25** *phrasal v. insep.* **to fall on/upon:** to attack suddenly: *The robber fell on him and stole his money.* **26** *phrasal v. insep.* **fall out (with s.o.):** to have an argument (with s.o.): *They were best friends for years before they fell out over a business decision.* **27 to fall prey to:** to be hurt by s.o. or s.t.: *While traveling, he fell prey to some dishonest people who took his money.* **28 to fall short:** to be lacking, *(syn.)* inadequate: *The trip fell short of our expectations and was not much fun.* **29** *phrasal v.* **to fall through:** to fail to happen: *The deal that we made fell through at the last minute.* **30** *phrasal v. insep.* **to fall to s.o. or s.t.: a.** to begin to do s.t. energetically: *When he sat down at the table, he fell to eating like a starving man.* **b.** *frml.* to be conquered by: *The city fell to the invading army.* **31** *phrasal v. insep.* **to fall under s.o. or s.t.:** to be classified as: *The matter fell under the authority of the lower court.*

fal·la·cious /fəˈleɪʃəs/ *adj.frml.* **1** false, deceitful: *The witness made several fallacious statements to the police officer.* **2** incorrect, *(syn.)* erroneous: *Some facts in the newspaper article were fallacious and later corrected.*

fal·la·cy /ˈfæləsi/ *n.* **-cies** a false belief, *(syns.)* misconception, misinterpretation: *It is a fallacy that everyone is equal before the law because people with money hire expensive lawyers to keep them out of jail.*

fall·en /ˈfɔlən/ *past part. of* fall

fall guy *n.infrml.* s.o. chosen to take the blame for the wrongdoing of others, *(syn.)* a dupe: *My boss made a big mistake, but I was the fall guy so they fired me!*

fal·li·ble /ˈfæləbəl/ *adj.* capable of making errors, imperfect: *All humans are fallible.*

falling-out *n.* a disagreement between people resulting in an end to their friendship: *The two*

men had a falling-out over a woman and didn't speak to each other for many years.

fall·off /ˈfɔlˌɔf/ *n.* a slow period of activity, *(syn.)* a decline: *Our business had a falloff in sales in April and May.*

fal·lo·pi·an tube /fəˈloʊpiən/ *n.* one of two tubes connecting the uterus with the ovaries: *The woman had a blocked fallopian tube.*

fall·out /ˈfɔlˌaʊt/ *n.* [U] **1** radioactive particles falling slowly to earth after a nuclear explosion or accident: *The fallout from the nuclear power plant accident traveled 800 miles over Europe.* **2** unplanned side effects: *Raising taxes produced negative fallout for the politicians responsible.*

fal·low /ˈfæloʊ/ *adj.* **1** referring to farmland that is plowed but not planted with crops: **to lie fallow:** *The farmer lets some of his land lie fallow each year.* **2** *fig.* unproductive, *(syn.)* dormant: *The new product design is just lying fallow until there is money to produce it.*

false /fɔls/ *adj.* **falser, falsest 1** incorrect, untrue: *The test consisted of questions that had to be answered as either true or false.* **2** disloyal, unfaithful: *She pretended to be my friend, but her friendship was false.* **3** not real, made to deceive, *(syns.)* artificial, fake: *She wears false eyelashes.* **-n.** [U] **falsity.**

false alarm *n.* an alarm sounded without the existence of a real emergency: *False alarms anger firefighters, who have to respond to them.*

false bottom *n.* a section in a container, such as luggage, where things can be hidden: *The box of oranges had a false bottom where stolen art objects were hidden.*

false-heart·ed /ˈfɔlsˌhɑrtɪd/ *adj.* deceitful, disloyal: *He was a false-hearted man who only pretended to love her.*

false·hood /ˈfɔlsˌhʊd/ *n.frml.* a lie, untruth: *The boy's father punished him for telling a falsehood.*

false pretense *n.* an action meant to deceive, *(syns.)* deceit, duplicity: *He borrowed money from friends under the false pretense of needing to buy food, and then he spent it on a party.‖He borrowed the money under false pretenses.*

fal·set·to /fɔlˈsetoʊ/ *n.* [C;U] **-tos** an artificially high singing voice: *The male quartet has a style of singing in falsetto.*

fals·ie /ˈfɔlsi/ *n.slang* a padded bra: *She wears falsies to improve her figure.*

fal·si·fi·ca·tion /ˌfɔlsəfəˈkeɪʃən/ *n.* an act of falsifying: *The falsification of the documents was proved in a court of law.*

fal·si·fy /ˈfɔlsəˌfaɪ/ *v.* **-fied, -fying, -fies 1** to make s.t. false by changing it, *(syns.)* to doctor, tamper with: *The teacher falsified the student's records to protect himself.* **2** to present in a false way, lie about: *He falsified his past in order to get the job.*

fal·ter /ˈfɔltər/ v. **1** to walk, speak, or move in an unsteady way: *The old man started to falter as he climbed the steps.* **2** to become weak, decline: *The economy faltered last year but has now started to improve.* -adj. **faltering.**

fame /feɪm/ n. [U] the state of being well-known and talked about, (syn.) renown: *Charles Darwin won fame throughout the world because of his theories.*

fa·mil·ial /fəˈmɪlyəl/ adj.frml. related to the family: *The couple's familial responsibilities are considerable because they have ten children.*

fa·mil·iar /fəˈmɪlyər/ adj. **1** knowing about, (syn.) acquainted: *I'm familiar with that neighborhood because I lived there for many years.* **2** more friendly than is proper, (syns.) forward, overbearing: *When he tried to kiss her, she told him that he was getting too familiar.* **3 a familiar face:** s.o. that one knows: *After being alone in a strange city for two weeks, he was happy to see a familiar face.* -adv. **familiarly.**

fa·mil·i·ar·i·ty /fə,mɪliˈærəti, -,mɪlˈyær-/ n. [U] knowledge of s.t.: *My familiarity with the French language was helpful during my trip to France last year.*

fa·mil·iar·ize /fəˈmɪlyə,raɪz/ v. **-ized, -izing, -izes** to learn about, to become acquainted with: *I familiarized myself with a map of the city before visiting Boston.*

fam·i·ly /ˈfæməli, ˈfæmli/ n. **-lies 1** one's closest relatives, usu. parents, children, brothers, and sisters: *His family consists of his mother, a sister in Florida, and himself.* **2** a group of people related by blood or marriage: *Most of my family lives on the West Coast, but I have some cousins in Chicago.* **3** a group of related plants or animals: *A wolf is a member of the dog family.* **4** a group of similar things: *That company produces a family of household products.*

family name n. **1** one's last name: *His family name is Cruz.* **2** a symbol of one's position in society: *When he went to jail, he shamed the family name.*

family planning n. [U] the use of birth control methods to limit the number of children one has: *One can learn about family planning by reading books or by visiting social service clinics.*

family tree n. a drawing that shows the relationship of a large number of family members: *The couple has their family tree hanging on a wall in their living room.*

fam·ine /ˈfæmɪn/ n. [C;U] a serious lack of food: *Famine is sometimes caused by a long period without rainfall.*

fam·ished /ˈfæmɪʃt/ adj. very hungry, (syn.) starved: *I am famished; I haven't eaten all day!*

fa·mous /ˈfeɪməs/ adj. **1** very well-known, (syns.) renowned, celebrated: *She is a famous Hollywood actress.* **2** well-known in a bad way, (syn.) notorious: *Her husband is famous for his bad manners.* -adv. **famously.** See: infamous, USAGE NOTE.

fan /fæn/ n. **1** an admirer: *When the rock star appeared on stage, her fans went wild.* **2** a handheld or mechanical device that creates a current of air in order to cool: *In the summer, we turn on the fan to keep cool.*
—v. **fanned, fanning, fans 1** to move air with a fan: *I fanned the flames in the fireplace.* **2** to spread out: *The villagers fanned out across the countryside in search of the lost child.*

fa·nat·ic /fəˈnætɪk/ n. a person who shows excessive enthusiasm for s.t., (syns.) a zealot, extremist: *He is a political fanatic who is in favor of violent revolution.*

fa·nat·i·cal /fəˈnætɪkəl/ adj. showing excessive enthusiasm for s.t., (syns.) extremist, radical: *She is fanatical in her political beliefs.||He is a vegetarian and fanatical about eating things such as brown rice.*

fa·nat·i·cism /fəˈnætə,sɪzəm/ n. [U] excessive enthusiasm for s.t.: *The political leader's increasing fanaticism has caused him to lose many of his followers.*

fan·ci·er /ˈfænsiər/ n. a person with a strong interest in s.t., such as a certain type of plant or animal: *She is a cat fancier and has three cats of her own.*

fan·ci·ful /ˈfænsɪfəl/ adj. imaginative rather than real, (syns.) whimsical, playful: *She has some fanciful ideas about becoming a movie star someday.||The artist was famous for his fanciful drawings.*

fan·cy /ˈfænsi/ adj. **-cier, -ciest 1** not plain or simple, (syns.) elegant, elaborate: *They wear fancy clothes and live in a fancy neighborhood.* **2** of superior quality, special, (syn.) choice: *He enjoys eating and buys fancy foods at gourmet shops.*
—v. **-cied, -cying, -cies 1** to desire, find pleasing: *I fancy eating out tonight.* **2** to imagine, fantasize about: *He fancies himself a great storyteller.*
—n. **-cies** a desire for s.t.: *I have a fancy for some lobster for dinner.*

fancy-free adj. See: footloose.

fan·fare /ˈfæn,fɛr/ n. [C;U] a loud, showy introduction to an event, such as the sound of trumpets: *The national political convention was opened with a fanfare of marching bands and cheering crowds.*

fang /fæŋ/ n. a long, sharp, pointed tooth, such as those of lions and wolves: *Some snakes* *have long fangs that inject poison into the animals they kill.* -*adj.* **fanged.**

fan letter *n.* a letter expressing admiration: *Movie stars often receive fan letters.*

fan mail *n.* [U] letters sent by admirers to famous people: *Rock stars receive tons of fan mail.*

fan·ny /ˈfæni/ *n.slang* **-nies** the part of the body on which a person sits: *I slipped while roller skating and fell on my fanny.*

fanny pack *n.* a small bag worn around the waist for carrying money, keys, etc.: *When Pedro rides his bike, he puts his money and some crackers in his fanny pack.*

fanny pack

fan·ta·size /ˈfæntəˌsaɪz/ *v.* **-sized, -sizing, -sizes** to have imaginary desires and experiences: *She fantasizes that she is a famous singer.*

fan·tas·tic /fænˈtæstɪk/ *adj.* **1** *infrml.* wonderful, (*syn.*) fabulous: *We had a fantastic time on our vacation in the Rocky Mountains.* **2** imaginative, strange, and unreal: *The movie was filled with fantastic, strange-looking animals.* -*adv.* **fantastically.**

fan·ta·sy /ˈfæntəsi, -zi/ *n.* **-sies 1** a product of the imagination, (*syns.*) daydream, illusion: *He has fantasies about dating a beautiful movie star.* **2** the product of a creative imagination: *This science fiction writer has created wonderful space fantasies.*

far /fɑr/ *adv.* **farther** /ˈfɑrðər/ or **further** /ˈfɜrðər/, **farthest** /ˈfɑrðɪst/ or **furthest** /ˈfɜrðɪst/ **1** to a great distance: *We had to walk far to get to the nearest gas station.* **2** to a great extent: *The effects of the disaster will last far into the future.* **3** to a greater extent, much: *He failed the test but promises to do far better next time.* **4** to a certain distance or extent (usu. used in questions): *How far away is the nearest subway station?* **5 as far as: a.** to a specific point in space: *From the hill, we could see as far as the nearest village.* **b.** to the extent that: *As far as I know, the trains are running on time.* **6 by far:** greatly, very much: *He is by far the best football player in the league.* **7 far and away:** without any doubt, (*syns.*) absolutely, unequivocally: *She is far and away the best teacher on campus.* **8 far and wide:** everywhere, all over the place: *He looked far and wide for his lost wallet.* **9 far be it for me to say:** I cannot say because I have the same or worse fault: *Far be it for me to say that you should get married; I've been divorced twice.* **10 far from:** not at all: *We are far from happy with the results of the election.* **11 far from it:** definitely not, not the way it is: *I don't want to go on vacation; far from it, I need to look for a new*

job. **12 far off: a.** in the distant future: *The date of our departure is not far off.* **b.** incorrect: *He is not far off when he says that the economy is improving.* **13 on the far right/left:** (in politics) holding extreme views: *Some politicians on the far right are becoming more powerful in that country.* **14 so far, so good:** everything has been fine until now: *I was worried that my math course was going to be difficult, but so far, so good.* **15 to go far:** to succeed: *She is a hard worker and will go far in her profession.*

—*adj.* **1** distant: *Flying to China is a far journey.* **2 a far cry:** very different, a long way from: *That textbook is a far cry from being readable; no one can understand it.*

far·a·way /ˈfɑrəˌweɪ/ *adj.* very far, (*syn.*) remote: *On his vacations, he likes to go to faraway places.*

farce /fɑrs/ *n.* **1** (in the theater) a type of humorous play filled with ridiculous situations: *I thought the farce was funny, but my friend found it silly.* **2** [C] a ridiculous situation or event: *That man's presentation was a farce; he was not prepared at all.* -*adj.* **farcical.**

fare /fɛr/ *n.* **1** [C] the cost of a ride, such as on a bus, train, or boat: *You pay the fare when you get on the bus.* **2** [C] a passenger: *The bus has 20 fares on it.* **3** [U] *frml.* food and drink: *That restaurant has excellent fare.*

—*v.* **fared, faring, fares** to result in s.t. good or bad, (*syn.*) to make out: *He fared well on his trip because he did some good business.*

Far East *n.* the countries of eastern Asia: *I travel on business to the Far East once a year.*

fare·well /ˌfɛrˈwɛl/ *interj.old usage* good-bye (for a long time or forever): *The retiree said farewell to his co-workers and moved to Florida.*

—*adj.* relating to a person's departure: *We had a farewell party* or *dinner for him before he left.*

far-fetched /ˈfɑrˈfɛtʃt/ *adj.* not likely to happen, (*syns.*) improbable, ridiculous: *He has some far-fetched ideas about building a huge company in only a year's time.*

far-flung /ˈfɑrˈflʌŋ/ *adj.* covering a wide area: *Her travels have taken her to the most far-flung countries of the world.*

farm /fɑrm/ *n.* a piece of land for raising crops and animals, usu. with a farmhouse, barn(s), and equipment: *As a boy, I lived on a farm in Maine.*

—*v.* to raise crops and animals: *Her family has farmed their land for a hundred years.*

farm·er /ˈfɑrmər/ *n.* a person who farms: *The farmer drove to the city each week to sell his fruits and vegetables.*

farm·ing /'farmɪŋ/ n. [U] the business and practice of raising crops and animals: *That man has been in farming all of his life.*

farm·land /'farm,lænd/ n. [U] land used in farming: *The farmland in Iowa is so rich that it is called "black gold."*

farm·yard /'farm,yard/ n. the area around farm buildings often fenced off to contain animals: *The farmer keeps some sheep in one section of his farmyard.*

far-off adj. distant, faraway: *He dreams of visiting far-off lands.*

far-out adj.slang very strange, incredible, (syns.) outlandish, mind-boggling: *He has some far-out ideas on how to save the world.* See: groovy, USAGE NOTE.

far-reaching adj. having a strong effect or influence: *The head of state proposed some far-reaching changes in government.*

far-sighted adj. **1** able to see clearly only at a distance: *He is far-sighted, so he needs glasses for reading.* **2** fig. able to plan effectively for the future: *The political leader has far-sighted programs to benefit the country's future.*

far·ther /'farðər/ adj. comp. of far: more distant: *He moved farther away from the table and stood up.*

far·thest /'farðɪst/ adj. superlative of far: *Of all our friends, the Nelson family lives farthest away.*

fas·ci·nate /'fæsə,neɪt/ v. -nated, -nating, -nates **1** to interest greatly, hold the attention of s.o., (syn.) to engross: *The customs and traditions of other cultures often fascinate people.* **2** to strongly attract: *She fascinates friends with her intelligence and charm.*

fas·ci·nat·ing /'fæsə,neɪtɪŋ/ adj. **1** very interesting, (syns.) absorbing, engrossing: *I find the study of history fascinating.* **2** attractive, (syns.) charming, captivating: *She met a fascinating man at the party.* -adv. **fascinatingly.**

fas·ci·na·tion /,fæsə'neɪʃən/ n. [U] **1** s.t. that powerfully holds one's attention: *I have a fascination for books on history.* **2** strong attraction, (syn.) captivation: *She creates a fascination in every man she meets.*

fas·cism /'fæ,ʃɪzəm/ n. [U] a political system in which one party, run by a person with great power, has total control over industry, banking, and the military: *She authored a book on the rise of fascism in Europe in the 1930s.*

fas·cist /'fæʃɪst/ n.adj. a follower of fascism: *The <adj.> fascist governments in Europe fell as a result of World War II.*

fash·ion /'fæʃən/ n. **1** [C; U] any style of dress popular for a period of time: *It used to be the fashion for women to wear gloves when they went out.* **2** sing. a manner, way: *The children formed a line in an orderly fashion.* **3 in fashion** or **out of fashion:** popular or unpopular at a particular time: *Although the writer died over fifty years ago, his ideas are still in fashion.*

—v. to design and make: *He fashioned a walking stick out of a piece of wood.*

USAGE NOTE: New York is the center of the USA's *fashion* industry. Hollywood has a big influence on popular styles, too, because the clothes worn in music videos, movies, and TV shows are seen by millions of people.

fash·ion·a·ble /'fæʃənəbəl, 'fæʃnə-/ adj. in the latest style, (syns.) stylish, trendy: *Her clothes are very fashionable.* -adv. **fashionably.**

fashion plate n.fig. a person who dresses in the latest style: *He is a fashion plate, always dressed like a model.*

fast /fæst/ adv. **1** rapidly, quickly: *That athlete can run fast.* **2** faster than normal speed: *My watch is running five minutes fast.* **3** deeply, (syn.) soundly: *The baby is fast asleep now.* **4** firmly, tightly: *That door won't open; it is stuck fast.* **5 to live life hard and fast:** to enjoy bad habits: *He lives life hard and fast: drinking, smoking, and partying every night.*

—adj. **1** rapid, quick: *We took a fast train from New York to Boston.* **2** done quickly: *He finished the job in half an hour, which was fast work!* **3** loyal, faithful: *The two men have been fast friends for years.* **4** (of colors in fabric) firmly fixed, permanent: *The colors in that sweater are fast, so they won't run when it's washed.* **5** acting freely in sexual relationships: *He is fast and likes fast women.* **6 hard and fast rule:** a strict rule: *There is a hard and fast rule that no one may enter the library without showing an identification card.* **7 on the fast track:** making rapid advancement in one's career: *She is the youngest manager in the company and on the fast track to a top executive position.* **8 to live in the fast lane:** to live one's life with high intensity: *He lives life in the fast lane with a high-pressure Wall Street job and a fast-paced night life.* **9 to make a fast buck:** to make some money rapidly, often in a dishonest way: *The owner made a fast buck by selling his business before it failed.* **10 to make fast work of:** to complete a task quickly and usu. with great skill: *The winning team made fast work of their opponents by beating them 6-0.*

—v. to eat and drink little or nothing: *From time to time, I fast for a day to lose weight.*

—n. a period of fasting: *The religious leader went on a fast for a week to protest the war in his country.*

fas·ten /'fæsən/ v. **1** to attach, (syn.) to affix: *He fastened pictures on the wall with hooks.* **2** to close (button, tie, etc.): *She fastened the buttons on her blouse.* **3** fig. to direct one's eyes or attention to: *The student fastened his attention on the teacher.* -n. **fastener.**

fas·ten·ing /ˈfæsənɪŋ, ˈfæsnɪŋ/ n. [C;U] s.t. that joins together two things: *The fastening on the window is broken.*

fast food n. food prepared in advance, kept warm or covered until ordered, and served rapidly as one pays for it: *I eat fast food every day at lunch.*

USAGE NOTE: An American invention, *fast food* is now sold in countries all over the world at restaurants such as McDonald's, Burger King, Pizza Hut, and Wendy's.

fas·tid·i·ous /fæˈstɪdiəs, fə-/ adj. **1** very careful, paying (too) close attention to details, *(syn.)* meticulous: *Our English teacher is fastidious about our spelling.* **2** hard to please, *(syn.)* fussy: *He is so fastidious about cleanliness that he always wipes his glass before drinking even though it's clean.*

fat /fæt/ adj. **fatter, fattest** **1** overweight, heavy: *She exercises every day to avoid getting fat.* **2** thick: *The thief began to follow the man with the fat wallet.* **3 a fat check:** a check for a large amount of money: *I received a nice fat check in the mail this morning.* **4 fat chance:** (used ironically) no chance at all: *I told my friend that I'm going to win the lottery this week, and he said, "Fat chance!"* See: overweight, USAGE NOTE.
—n. **1** the layer of flesh under the skin: *He has a lot of fat around his middle.* **2** a soft solid or liquid oily substance found in animals or plant seeds: *Some beef has a lot of fat in it.* **3** this substance specially prepared for use in cooking: *There's a lot of butter in the cream sauce, so it's high in fat.* **4 to live off the fat of the land:** to live well without having to work: *That man has no intention of looking for a job; he's just going to live off the fat of the land as long as he can.*

fa·tal /ˈfeɪtl/ adj. **1** causing death, *(syns.)* lethal, deadly: *The poor man had a fatal heart attack.* **2** disastrous, tragic, *(syn.)* ruinous: *She made the fatal mistake of returning to her country just as the war began.* -adv. **fatally.**

fa·tal·is·tic /ˌfeɪtlˈɪstɪk/ adj. related to the belief that everything that happens is determined in advance and cannot be changed by human effort: *He has a fatalistic attitude about life and is never happy.* -n. [U] **fatalism** /ˈfeɪtlˌɪzəm/.

fa·tal·i·ty /feɪˈtæləti, fə-/ n. **-ties** a death resulting from accident, disease, natural disaster, or war: *On long holiday weekends there is always a rise in the number of fatalities due to auto accidents.*

fate /feɪt/ n. **1** [U] a force or power believed to determine in advance everything that happens: *Fate brought the two leaders together so that*

they might bring peace to the world. **2** [C] a tragic end, *(syn.)* doom: *It was while mountain climbing in Nepal that he fell and met his fate.* **3 as fate would have it:** as a result of good or bad luck: *As fate would have it, our flight was canceled because of a snowstorm and we missed an important meeting.*

fat·ed /ˈfeɪtɪd/ adj. determined by fate, *(syn.)* destined: *The ill-fated airliner crashed in heavy fog, and there were no survivors.*

fate·ful /ˈfeɪtfəl/ adj. determined by fate, important, usu. involving harm or death: *The fateful moment arrived when the two great armies met in battle for the last time.*

fat·head /ˈfætˌhɛd/ n.infrml. a stupid person: *He's such a fathead; he won't listen to anybody.* -adj. **fatheaded;** -n. [U] **fatheadedness.**

fa·ther /ˈfɑðər/ n. **1** one's male parent: *His father lived to be 90 years old.* **2 Father: a.** God: *Oh Father, please listen to my prayer.* **b.** the form of address for a Catholic or Anglican priest: *Father Tomkins conducted the service.* **3** a person who starts s.t. new, *(syns.)* originator, founder: *He was the father of modern medicine.*
—v. **1** to cause a woman to become pregnant and give birth to a child: *He fathered two children.* **2** to start s.t. new, *(syns.)* to originate, found: *The leaders fathered a new nation.* -n. [U] **fatherhood** /ˈfɑðərˌhʊd/.

father figure n. a man to whom others look for advice and support: *Since the death of the boy's father, his uncle has acted as a father figure.*

fa·ther-in-law /ˈfɑðərɪnˌlɔ/ n. **fathers-in-law** the father of either one's husband or one's wife: *He and his father-in-law often have disagreements.*

fa·ther·land /ˈfɑðərˌlænd/ n. the country of one's birth.

USAGE NOTE: It is more common to use "motherland."

fa·ther·ly /ˈfɑðərli/ adj. having the ideal characteristics of a father: *That teacher has a fatherly attitude towards his students, and they often seek his advice.*

Fa·ther's Day n. a day honoring fathers, held on the third Sunday in June: *We celebrated Father's Day by bringing Dad breakfast in bed.*

fath·om /ˈfæðəm/ n. a measurement of six feet of water depth: *A sailor measured the water depth at five fathoms.*
—v. to understand after deep thought, *(syn.)* to comprehend: *I cannot fathom why he would leave such a good job.* See: unfathomable.

fa·tigue /fəˈtig/ n. **1** [U] great tiredness, *(syn.)* exhaustion: *He is suffering from fatigue and* *wants to go to bed early.* **2** *pl.* military clothes: *Soldiers wear fatigues.*

—*v.* **-tigued, -tiguing, -tigues** to make tired, (*syn.*) to exhaust: *The child has so much energy that she fatigues her mother.*

fat·ten /'fætn/ *v.* **1** to make fat, esp. farm animals used for food: *The farmer started to fatten the turkey in preparation for the Thanksgiving Day meal.* **2** to grow fat: *That baby has really started to fatten up.*

fat·ty /'fæti/ *adj.* **-tier, -tiest** containing a lot of fat: *I didn't buy the meat because it was too fatty.*

fat·u·ous /'fætʃuəs/ *adj.* stupid without appearing to know it: *Everybody is always laughing behind his back at his fatuous statements.* -*adv.* **fatuously.**

fau·cet /'fɔsɪt/ *n.* a device through which the flow of water or other liquids is controlled, (*syns.*) a tap, spigot: *The plumber said that I needed to buy a new faucet.*

fault /fɔlt/ *n.* **1** an imperfection, (*syns.*) a flaw, defect: *There is a fault in the computer system.* **2** a weak point in s.o.'s character, (*syns.*) a shortcoming, foible: *He has some faults, such as sometimes talking too much.* **3** blame, responsibility (for a mistake): *Nobody knew who was at fault for the train accident.* **4** a large crack in the surface of the earth: *The San Andreas fault lies near San Francisco, where the fault line runs north and south.* **5 to a fault:** more than is necessary: *That man is careful in his business dealings to a fault.* **6 to find fault with:** to criticize usu. too often, (*syn.*) to carp about: *He complained that his boss was always finding fault with her work.*

—*v.* to criticize, blame: *I fault him for not delivering the product on time.* -*adj.* **faultless;** -*adv.* **faultlessly.**

fault·y /'fɔlti/ *adj.* **-ier, -iest 1** not working properly, (*syn.*) defective: *The fire was caused by faulty electrical wiring.* **2** incorrect, (*syn.*) flawed: *Faulty thinking on his part caused the mistake.*

faun /fɔn/ *n.* an ancient Roman god of the woods and fields that was half-man, half-goat: *The fauns liked to play tricks on people.*

fau·na /'fɔnə/ *n.frml.* [C;U] **-nas** or **-nae** /-ni, -naɪ/ the animals in a specific place or time period: *She spent a year studying the fauna of the Amazon.*

USAGE NOTE: "Fauna" is often used in the phrase "flora (plants) and fauna." *See:* flora.

faux pas /ˌfouˈpɑ/ *n.frml.* **faux pas** /ˌfouˈpɑz/ a socially awkward mistake: *He made a faux pas when he called his new boss by the wrong name.*

fa·vor /'feɪvər/ *v.* **1** to prefer, (*syn.*) to opt for: *I favor leaving today instead of tomorrow.* **2**

to give preference to s.o., often unfairly: *The mother favors her youngest daughter among all her children.* **3** to look like, (*syn.*) to resemble: *Our daughter favors her mother's side of the family.*

—*n.* **1** a helpful act, (*syn.*) a good turn: *He did me a favor by helping me get a loan.* **2** a little gift, usu. given out at parties: *The children's table was covered with party favors, such as funny hats and candies.* **3** *pl.* **favors** intimate affections of a woman: *He longs for her favors.* **4 in favor** or **out of favor with s.o.:** (not) having the approval of s.o.: *That union leader is currently out of favor with the mayor.* **5 in favor of:** on the side of, in support of: *The hospital workers voted in favor of the new contract.* **6** *frml.* **to be looked upon with favor:** to be approved of or supported: *The nobleman's request for land was looked upon with favor by the king.* **7 to seek favor with:** to attempt to gain the approval of s.o.: *The new employee seeks favor with the boss by working late every night.*

fa·vor·a·ble /'feɪvərəbəl, 'feɪvrə-/ *adj.* **1** approving, positive: *I received a favorable report from the doctor.* **2** pleasing: *The first day of class, the instructor made a favorable impression on the students.* **3** advantageous, (*syn.*) conducive: *We have favorable weather for our sailing trip now.*

fa·vor·a·bly /'feɪvərəbli, 'feɪvrə-/ *adv.* **1** approvingly, positively: *The bank looks favorably on your request for a loan.* **2** in an advantageous way, (*syn.*) beneficially: *I hope that your job interview turns out favorably for you.*

fa·vored /'feɪvərd/ *adj.* preferred over others: *Tea is favored over coffee in England.‖The youngest is the favored child in that family.*

fa·vor·ite /'feɪvərɪt, 'feɪvrɪt/ *adj.* most preferred: *Mozart is his favorite composer.*

—*n.* **1** most preferred, chosen one: *The father's older son is his favorite.* **2** the most likely to win: *Last year's winner is the favorite in this year's race.* **3 favorite son:** a politician preferred as a presidential candidate by his own state: *As a candidate, he was the favorite son from Missouri.*

fa·vor·it·ism /'feɪvərəˌtɪzəm, 'feɪvrə-/ *n.* [U] preferential treatment, esp. when it is unfair: *The owner of the company is guilty of favoritism in promoting her son because he is not qualified for the job.*

fawn /fɔn/ *n.* a young deer: *Fawns are born in the springtime.*

—*v.* to seek s.o.'s favor through flattery and false humility, (*syn.*) to grovel: *He's always fawning over his rich uncle.*

fax /fæks/ *n.* **faxes 1** a document sent electronically through telephone lines: *I sent a fax of my letter (order, illustration, etc.) to our*

Hong Kong office. **2** a machine used to send an electronic document, a fax machine
—*v.* **faxed, faxing, faxes** to send a fax: *I faxed it this morning. See:* facsimile.

faze /feɪz/ *v.* **fazed, fazing, fazes** to disturb, worry, (*syn.*) to disconcert: *The bad news did not faze him at all.*

FBI /ˌɛfbiˈaɪ/ *n.abbr. for* Federal Bureau of Investigation in USA, the government agency that investigates crimes in which a national law has been broken: *The FBI discovered that the man was selling military secrets to a foreign government.*

USAGE NOTE: People usu. refer to government agencies such as the *FBI* (Federal Bureau of Investigation) by their initials because their names are so long. Others are the FDA (Food and Drug Administration), EPA (Environmental Protection Agency), and IRS (Internal Revenue Service).

FDA /ˌɛfdiˈeɪ/ *n. abbr. See:* Food and Drug Administration.

fear /fɪr/ *n.* **1** [C;U] a strong feeling of fright about danger (harm, trouble, etc.): *The hunter was filled with fear when he saw the bear running toward him.* **2** [C] worry or anxiety that s.t. bad will happen: *He has a fear that the economy will become worse.* **3** [C] a specific cause of fright or anxiety: *She has had a fear of dogs ever since she was bitten as a child.*
—*v.* **1** to feel a strong fright: *He fears snakes.* **2** to view with anxiety: *She fears that her children might be harmed on their way to school.*

fear·ful /ˈfɪrfəl/ *adj.* **1** feeling afraid: *He was fearful when he saw the elephant approaching him.* **2** anxious, worried, (*syn.*) apprehensive: *She is fearful of losing her job. -n.* [U] **fearfulness;** *-adv.* **fearfully.**

fear·less /ˈfɪrlɪs/ *adj.* without fear, (*syns.*) courageous, bold: *Even though her fight for women's rights is unpopular, she is fearless in continuing it. -adv.* **fearlessly;** *-n.* [U] **fearlessness.**

fea·si·ble /ˈfizəbəl/ *adj.* **1** workable, possible: *Your work plan is feasible, so we can build the bridge immediately.* **2** suitable, acceptable: *There is no feasible alternative. -adv.* **feasibly;** *-n.* [U] **feasibility** /ˌfizəˈbɪləti/.

feast /fist/ *n.* a large, rich meal, (*syn.*) a banquet: *Every Thanksgiving, my whole family gets together and has a feast.*
—*v.* **1** to have a feast: *We feasted on turkey, sweet potatoes, and corn bread.* **2 to feast one's eyes on s.t.:** to look at s.t. with admiration: *Jane, feast your eyes on those diamonds in the store window.*

feat /fit/ *n.* an impressive act, showing strength, courage, or unusual ability, (*syn.*) an exploit: *The soldier's feats of courage in battle were*

extraordinary.||*Passing that exam without studying was a real feat!*

feath·er /ˈfɛðər/ *n.* **1** one of the many soft, thin growths that cover a bird's body: *The feathers of the local pigeons are gray.* **2 a feather in one's cap:** an honor for others to admire: *His graduating first in his class is a feather in his cap.*

feather

3 birds of a feather flock together: people with similar backgrounds and interests spend time with each other: *I thought he was a good guy until I saw him with those troublemakers; as people say, birds of a feather flock together.* **4 as light as a feather:** very light: *The moving fmen lifted the heavy sofa as if it were as light as a feather.* **5 to ruffle s.o.'s feathers:** to annoy, disturb: *Her mother-in-law's negative comments about her cooking really ruffle her feathers.*
—*v.* **to feather one's nest:** to profit by using s.o. else's money: *We were shocked to discover that our local Congressman had been feathering his nest for years.*

feath·er·bed·ding /ˈfɛðərˌbɛdɪŋ/ *n.* [U] under a labor union rule, the hiring of more workers than are actually needed: *The owner of the newspaper blamed featherbedding for the price increase.*

feath·er·brain /ˈfɛðərˌbreɪn/ *n.* a stupid person, (*syn.*) birdbrain: *She is such a featherbrain that she doesn't know what day it is.*

feath·er·head /ˈfɛðərˌhɛd/ *n.* a stupid person, (*syn.*) dunce: *What a featherhead!*

feath·er·weight /ˈfɛðərˌweɪt/ *n.* **1** a boxer who weighs 118 to 127 pounds **2** *fig.* a person of limited ability and importance, (*syn.*) lightweight: *Sally's boss is such a featherweight; nobody listens to him.*

feath·er·y /ˈfɛðəri/ *adj.* **1** covered with feathers: *Some men's hats have feathery headbands.* **2** light and soft: *That plant has feathery leaves.*

fea·ture /ˈfitʃər/ *n.* **1** an important part or characteristic of a product or service: *The salesman described to us the car's many features.* **2** *pl.* **features** the mouth, chin, nose, eyes, etc. of the human face: *That model has beautiful features.* **3** an important article in a newspaper or magazine: *There was a feature in the local newspaper about the high cost of housing.* **4** a full-length movie: *We saw a feature about a plane crash in the Amazon jungle.*

USAGE NOTE: One can also say "feature film" or "feature-length film" or "movie."

—*v.* **-tured, -turing, -tures** to advertise as important, (*syns.*) to highlight, promote: *The department store featured lamps and rugs in its annual sale.*

feb·rile /'fɛbraɪl, -brəl, 'fi-/ *adj.frml.* **1** having a fever, (*syn.*) feverish: *The patient is febrile.* **2** *fig.* very active, (*syns.*) feverish, hectic: *The pace of business here is febrile.*

Feb·ru·ar·y /'fɛbyuˌɛri, 'fɛbru-/ *n.* the second month of the year, between January and March: *In February, everyone in New York is sick of the winter and wants a vacation in the sun.*

fe·ces /'fisiz/ *n.pl.* solid waste sent out from the bowels, (*syn.*) excrement: *A laboratory tested the feces for blood.* -*adj.* **fecal** /'fikəl/.

feck·less /'fɛklɪs/ *adj.* ineffective, irresponsible: *The father was angry at his son's feckless performance in college.* -*adv.* **fecklessly.**

fe·cund /'fikənd, 'fɛ-/ *adj.frml.* productive, (*syn.*) fertile: *The soil in this area is fecund.* -*n.* [U] **fecundity** /fɪ'kʌndəti/.

fed /fɛd/ *adj.* past tense & past part. *of* feed **1** provided with food: *You can see from his big stomach that he is well fed.* **2 fed up:** annoyed or angry about a bad situation that has existed for a long time, (*syns.*) frustrated, disgusted: *I am completely fed up with all of the false promises and delays.*

Fed /fɛd/ *n.* **1** *short for* the Federal Reserve System: *The Fed lowered interest rates again.* **2** *short for* a federal agent: *The feds are investigating that labor union.* See: Federal Reserve System.

fed·er·al /'fɛdərəl/ *adj.* (in USA) related to the national government: *The federal court system is large and spread out over the nation.* -*adv.* **federally.**

Federal Bureau of Investigation *n.* See: FBI.

fed·er·al·ism /'fɛdərəˌlɪzəm/ *n.* [U] a political system in which power is divided between a central government that has control over foreign affairs, defense, etc., and state governments that decide local issues: *Federalism is based on the concept of a strong federal government having superiority over the states.* -*n.adj.* **federalist.**

Federal Reserve System *n.* (in USA) 12 federal banks and their branches that control the nation's banking system: *The Federal Reserve System was founded by law in 1913.*

USAGE NOTE: *Federal Reserve* banks lend money to commercial banks, which then make loans to businesses and individual customers.

fed·er·ate /'fɛdəˌreɪt/ *v.* -**ated, -ating, -ates** to unite as in a group of states or unions: *The states federated but left defense and foreign policy to the central government.*

fed·er·a·tion /ˌfɛdə'reɪʃən/ *n.* a union of organizations or states: *A federation of teachers' unions is working hard to improve the educational system.*

fee /fi/ *n.* a charge, cost, (*syn.*) payment: *We pay all sorts of fees: a parking fee, a license fee for driving a car, a registration fee, tuition fees, lawyers' fees, and doctors' fees.*

fee·ble /'fibəl/ *adj.* weak, without power or energy: *The elderly lady has become feeble and unable to care for herself.||His feeble attempts at solving the problem are worthless.* -*adv.* **feebly.**

fee·ble-mind·ed /'fibəlˌmaɪndɪd/ *adj.* **1** having below-normal intelligence: *The poor man has been feeble-minded since birth.* **2** mentally weak because of old age, (*syn.*) senile: *We knew the old woman was becoming feeble-minded when she started getting lost in her own neighborhood.*

feed /fid/ *n.* **1** [U] grain or other food supplied to animals: *Each morning the farmer gives the cows their feed.* **2** [U] *infrml.* a meal, esp. a large one: *We've worked hard all day, so let's go have a good feed.* **3** [C] material supplied to a machine **4** [C] the device used to supply material to the machine: *The feed on the printer is broken.* **5** [U] **chicken feed:** a small amount of money (said with strong disapproval): *He's crazy to think we will work on Sundays for chicken feed.*
—*v.* **fed** /fɛd/, **feeding, feeds** **1** to provide with food: *She gets up early every morning to feed her baby.||The farmer feeds his cows.* **2** to take in as food: *Big fish feed on smaller fish.* **3** *fig.* to supply with s.t., such as information or material: *The accounting department feeds information to the other departments in the company.||A worker feeds wood into the machine.* **4 to spoon feed:** to inform s.o. in little steps as one feeds a baby with a spoon: *Whenever he has a computer problem, I have to spoon feed him the solution.* See: bite (the hand that feeds).

feed·back /'fidˌbæk/ *n.* [U] **1** the return of some computer output into input in order to control a process: *The feedback in the order process function updates inventory levels.* **2** the response to one's ideas (proposals, actions, etc.) in the form of approval, disapproval, suggestions, etc.: *The radio station decided to cancel the show after receiving negative feedback from its listeners.*

feed·bag /'fidˌbæg/ *n.* **1** a bag containing food placed over a horse's nose: *Our horse is eating oats from a feedbag.* **2** *infrml.* **to tie on the feedbag:** to have a meal: *Let's tie on the feedbag before doing any more work.*

feed·er /'fidər/ *n.* **1** a device that supplies food: *We have a bird feeder in our backyard.* **2** a device used to feed material into a machine: *The feeder on the printer isn't working properly.*
—*adj.* a local transportation service (airline, railroad, etc.) that leads into a national one:

The feeder airlines in Texas connect to the major airlines in Dallas-Fort Worth.

feed·ing /'fidɪŋ/ *n.* [C;U] a meal, when referring to babies and animals: *The baby is ready for her midnight feeding.*
—*adj.* related to a meal: *It is feeding time for the cats.*

feel /fil/ *v.* **felt** /fɛlt/, **feeling, feels 1** to experience a sensation (warmth, cold, pain, hunger, etc.): *I feel a little cold.* **2** to touch in order to find or learn s.t.: *He felt around in his pocket for the key.*||*The doctor could feel that the bone was broken.* **3** to experience a condition: *The patient feels better today.*||*She felt ill yesterday.* **4** to experience an emotion (to feel afraid, angry, happy, etc.): *She felt nervous on her wedding day.* **5** to produce a certain sensation: *Mountain air feels cool and fresh.* **6** to experience a need or desire: *After a few days in Mexico, he felt the need to improve his Spanish.* **7** to have an opinion: *He feels that smoking is bad for his health, so he quit.* **8 to feel for s.o.:** to have sympathy for: *I really felt for Tom when his wife died.* **9 to feel free:** to be invited to do s.t.: *My host told me, "Feel free to help yourself to coffee or tea."*||*A businessman wrote me a letter saying "Feel free to contact me with any questions that you have."* **10 to feel like:** to have a desire for s.t.: *I feel like having some ice cream.* **11 to feel like a million dollars:** to feel unusually well: *Having passed all of my examinations, I feel like a million dollars.* **12 to feel one's way: a.** to move ahead without being able to see, using one's sense of touch: *I felt my way down the stairs.* **b.** to act with great care, usu. because of a lack of knowledge or experience: *The first year our store was open, we were still feeling our way.* **13** *phrasal v. sep.* **to feel (s.o.) out:** to try to get information, esp. from s.o., in an indirect way: *I felt out his intentions in asking me for help.*||*I felt them out.* **14** *phrasal v. slang* **to feel s.o. up:** to excite s.o. sexually by touching: *He felt her up in the back seat of his car.* **15** *phrasal v.* **to feel up to s.t.:** to be ready to do s.t. difficult or unpleasant: *He feels up to cleaning out the garage today.*||*She is still not well and doesn't feel up to going out.*
—*n.* **1** a touch: *I gave the paint a feel to see if it was still wet.* **2** an understanding, a special skill: *My daughter does well in math; she seems to have a real feel for numbers.* **3** the sensation produced by s.t.: *The feel of fine leather is smooth and soft.* **4 to get the feel of s.t.:** to become accustomed to: *She drove around to get the feel of the new car.*

feel·er /'filɚ/ *n.* **1** *fig.* a suggestion, polite question to determine s.o.'s interest: *My friend is sending out feelers to see if other companies have a job opening for him.* **2** *lit.* a long, hair-

like part of some animals used for feeling: *Insects have feelers on their heads.*

feel·ing /'filɪŋ/ *n.* **1** [U] physical sensation, recognition of touch: *His hands are so cold that he has lost feeling in them.* **2** [C] an emotion: *The mother has a strong feeling of love for her family.* **3** [C] a belief that s.t. is true: *I have a feeling that he's an excellent teacher.* **4** *pl.* one's general sensitivity: *Her strong criticism hurt her daughter's feelings.*

fee-splitting *n.* [U] a practice, usu. among lawyers and physicians, of sending clients to other members of their profession and then dividing the fees: *I stopped going to that doctor when I discovered that he practiced fee-splitting.*

feet /fit/ *n.pl. of* foot

feign /feɪn/ *v.* to pretend, to fake: *He feigned illness so he would not have to work.*

feint /feɪnt/ *v.* to make an action designed to distract or deceive an opponent: *The fighter feinted with his left hand and then hit his opponent with his right hand instead.*

feist·y /'faɪsti/ *adj.* **-ier, -iest** full of energy, tending to argue: *She's a feisty child who isn't afraid of anyone.*

fe·lic·i·ta·tions /fə,lɪsə'teɪʃənz/ *n.pl.frml.* congratulations: *Felicitations on your promotion!*

fe·lic·i·tous /fə'lɪsətəs/ *adj.frml.* appropriate in an agreeable way: *The speaker made a number of felicitous remarks that pleased his audience.* -*adv.* **felicitously.**

fe·lic·i·ty /fə'lɪsəti/ *n.frml.* [U] happiness: *The children brought much felicity into their parents' lives.*

fe·line /'fi,laɪn/ *adj.* related to cats: *The feline world includes lions, tigers, panthers, jaguars, and house cats.*

fell (1) /fɛl/ *past tense of* fall

fell (2) *v.* to cut s.t. down: *They felled two trees near the river.*

fel·low /'fɛloʊ/ *n.* **1** *infrml.* a man or boy: *Charles is a friendly fellow.* **2** *frml.* (at a university) a person who receives an award of money and a position for advanced study: *She is a fellow at Yale University.*
—*adj.* referring to people with whom one has something in common: *He lunches with some of his fellow workers (students, scientists, etc.) each day.*

fellow man *n.* **men** other humans, (*syns.*) mankind, humankind: *She shares the same everyday problems as her fellow man.*

fel·low·ship /'fɛloʊ,ʃɪp, -lə-/ *n.* **1** [C] a group of people joined together by common interests: *We belong to a Christian fellowship and meet once a week.* **2** [U] the feeling of friendship gained through shared interests: *After graduating from the university, she missed the warmth*

and good fellowship of her college roommates.
3 [C] (at a university) an award of money and a position for advanced study: *My professor is away on a fellowship to Oxford.*

fel·on /'fɛlən/ *n.* (in law) a person guilty of a major crime, such as murder or rape: *The company didn't want to hire him when they found out he had served time in prison as a felon.*

fel·o·ny /'fɛləni/ *n.* **-nies** *adj.* a major crime, such as murder or rape: *He was sentenced to jail for committing two <n.> felonies* (or) *sentenced on two <adj.> felony counts. -adj.* **felonious** /fə'louniəs/.

felt (1) /fɛlt/ *past tense & past part. of* feel

felt (2) *n.* [U] *adj.* a fabric made by pressing together wool and other materials: *His hat is made of <n.> felt.*

fe·male /'fi,meɪl/ *adj.n.* a human or animal of the sex that can produce young: *Male and <adj.> female students live in separate housing.‖In the past, <n.> females were not permitted to join that club.*

USAGE NOTE: Many people avoid the use of "female" as a noun for a person and use "woman" instead.

---

fem·i·nine /'fɛmənɪn/ *adj.* **1** having characteristics traditionally considered typical of women, such as warmth and softness: *The dress she wore to the party made her look very feminine.* **2** (in grammar) referring to a certain class of words: *The word for "house" is feminine in Spanish. -adv.* **femininely.**

fem·i·nin·i·ty /,fɛmə'nɪnəti/ *n.* [U] the characteristics traditionally considered typical of women: *She does not believe that working as a police officer has caused her to lose her femininity.*

fem·i·nism /'fɛmə,nɪzəm/ *n.* [U] the belief that women should have the same rights, opportunities, and treatment as men: *Feminism is a strong movement in the USA.*

fem·i·nist /'fɛmənɪst/ *n.adj.* a person who believes that women should have the same rights, opportunities, and treatment as men: *Both she and her husband are active <n.> feminists.‖They are active in the <adj.> feminist movement.*

femme fa·tale /,fɛmfə'tæl, -'tɑl, ,fæm-/ *n.* (French for) a woman who is very attractive and can easily seduce men: *She is a femme fatale; men always fall in love with her.*

fe·mur /'fimər/ *n.* **femurs** or **femora** /'fɛmərə/ the bone in the leg that is above the knee: *The skier broke his femur. -adj.* **femoral** /'fɛmərəl/.

fence /fɛns/ *n.* **1** a structure made of various materials, such as wood or wire, designed to prevent people or animals from entering or leaving an area: *The fence around the factory is ten feet tall.* **2** *slang* a person who sells

stolen property for thieves: *He is a fence for stolen jewelry.* **3 on the fence** or **straddling the fence:** undecided: *She was on the fence about buying a new car.*
—*v.* **fenced, fencing, fences 1** to put a fence around an area: *We fenced the property around the lake.* **2** *slang* to sell stolen property: *He fenced famous artwork before he was arrested.* **3** to fight with a sword as a sport: *He liked to fence for exercise.* **4** *fig.* to argue with s.o.: *The two of you should stop fencing and try to work together.* **5 to fence in:** to limit s.o.'s freedom: *My boss fenced me in so much that I couldn't do my job.*

fence sitter *n.fig.* a person who will not commit to either side of an issue: *That politician is a fence sitter on the subject of raising taxes.*

fenc·ing /'fɛnsɪŋ/ *n.* [U] **1** a fence or fences: *Workers put up fencing around the house in one day.* **2** fighting with swords as a sport: *Many students enjoy fencing as a university sport.*

fend /fɛnd/ *v.* **1** to defend oneself: *He fended off the blows of his attacker.* **2** to take care of oneself without anybody's help: *When her parents died, she had to fend for herself.*

fend·er /'fɛndər/ *n.* the outer covering above the tire of a car: *The right front fender on my car needs to be repaired.*

fen·nel /'fɛnl/ *n.* [U] a tall plant with feathery green leaves whose seeds can be used as a seasoning: *The cook flavored the soup with some fennel.*

fens /fɛnz/ *n.pl.* a low wet area of land: *Fens are not good areas to walk in after it rains.*

fe·ral /'fɪrəl, 'fɛr-/ *adj.frml.* wild, in the natural state: *After living in the woods for many years, the dog had become feral.‖We admired the feral beauty of the rain forest.*

fer·ment /fər'mɛnt/ *v.* to mix together substances, esp. natural sugars and grains, which turn into alcohol: *A winemaker ferments grapes into wine.*
—*n.* /'fɜr,mɛnt/ [U] excitement, unrest, *(syn.)* agitation: *The sudden death of the political leader created ferment among his followers.*

fer·men·ta·tion /,fɜrmən'teɪʃən, -mɛn-/ *n.* [U] the changing of substances through the action of certain chemical processes: *Grain changes into alcohol through fermentation.*

fern /fɜrn/ *n.* a type of flowerless green plant with feathery leaves: *The ferns in her garden grow in the cool area under the trees.*

fe·ro·cious /fə'rouʃəs/ *adj.* violently cruel, *(syns.)* fierce, savage: *The ferocious attack of the hungry lions left three zebras dead. -adv.* **ferociously.**

fe·roc·i·ty /fə'rasəti/ *n.* [U] violent cruelty, *(syns.)* fierceness, savagery: *The storm (wild animal, soldier, etc.) attacked with ferocity.*

fer·ret /'fɛrɪt/ *n.* a small, dark brown, furry animal that can be kept as a pet and used to hunt rats and rabbits: *I had a pet ferret when I was a child.*

—*v.* **to ferret out:** to search and find s.o. or s.t., (*syns.*) to uncover, reveal: *The detective ferreted out the truth by questioning many people.*

Fer·ris wheel /'fɛrɪs/ *n.* an amusement park ride consisting of a large wheel with chairs rising to the top as the wheel goes around: *The children enjoyed themselves on the Ferris wheel.*

Ferris wheel

USAGE NOTE: The *Ferris wheel* and the *carousel* (a revolving platform on which people ride painted wooden horses) are traditional rides at amusement parks and state fairs. Much more exciting is the *roller coaster,* a train of small, open cars traveling on tracks that rise and fall dramatically and sometimes make 360 degree turns in the air.

---

fer·rous /'fɛrəs/ *adj.* containing iron: *Steel is a ferrous metal.*

fer·ry /'fɛri/ *n.* **-ries** a type of boat used to transport passengers and goods between two or more locations that are close to each other: *You can take a ferry to the Statue of Liberty from lower Manhattan.* -*n.* **ferryman** /'fɛrimən/.

—*v.* **-ried, -rying, -ries** to transport people and goods a short distance: *The boat ferried the soldiers from the ships to the island.*

fer·ry·boat /'fɛri,boʊt/ *n.* a boat used to ferry passengers on short trips: *The ferryboat leaves every hour.*

fer·tile /'fɜrtl/ *adj.* **1** able to produce offspring or new plants, productive: *The farmland in Iowa is very fertile.||The doctor performed some tests to see if she was fertile.* **2** filled with new ideas, (*syn.*) inventive, creative: *The author of that children's book has a fertile imagination.*

fer·til·i·ty /fər'tɪləti/ *n.* [U] **1** the ability to produce offspring or new plants: *The fertility of the desert soil is poor.* **2** *fig.* the ability to produce new ideas, (*syn.*) creativity: *The fertility of his mind is impressive.*

fer·til·i·za·tion /,fɜrtələ'zeɪʃən/ *n.* [U] **1** the union of egg and sperm that starts the development of new life: *The fertilization of many plants is done by bees.* **2** the adding of a chemical or natural substance to soil to make plants grow well: *Fertilization of the soil is done in the fall before snow falls. See:* sperm; ovum.

fer·til·ize /'fɜrtl,aɪz/ *v.* **-ized, -izing, -izes 1** to add fertilizer: *Most farmers fertilize their*

farmland with chemicals. **2** to start the development of new life: *Male fish fertilize the eggs of female fish.*

fer·til·iz·er /'fɜrtl,aɪzər/ *n.* [C;U] a chemical or natural substance used to make the soil richer and increase the productivity of plants: *That farmer uses natural fertilizer from his cows.*

fer·vent /'fɜrvənt/ *adj.* intense, (*syn.*) impassioned: *Fervent cries for help came by radio from the disaster area.* -*adv.* **fervently.**

fer·vid /'fɜrvɪd/ *adj.frml.* having intense beliefs or feelings, (*syn.*) impassioned: *The political leader gave a fervid speech calling for the government to end the war.* -*adv.* **fervidly** -*n.* **fervor** /'fɜrvər/.

fes·ter /'fɛstər/ *v.* **1** (of a wound) to become irritated, infected: *The soldier's wound festered in the jungle heat.* **2** (of bad feelings) to become worse over time: *The people's anger toward the dictatorship festered for many years.* -*adj.* **festering.**

fes·ti·val /'fɛstəvəl/ *n.* **1** a public celebration or feast, usu. of some special occasion: *On Norwegian independence day, the Norwegians in my town hold a festival with singing and dancing.* **2** a series of events, such as films, plays, or concerts, occurring for a limited period of time: *The New York Film Festival takes place every spring.*

fes·tive /'fɛstɪv/ *adj.* joyful, with feasting and good spirits: *Our birthday parties each year are festive occasions with food, wine, and friends.*

fes·tiv·i·ty /fɛ'stɪvəti/ *n.* **-ties 1** the joyful celebration of a special occasion: *There is a great festivity at Christmas time.* **2** *pl.* ways of celebrating a special occasion: *Every New Year's Eve the festivities include a big dinner and dancing.*

fe·ta /'fɛtə/ *n.adj.* [U] white cheese made from the milk of a goat or sheep: *My daughter loves* <*n.*>*feta* (or) <*adj.*>*feta cheese in salads.*

fe·tal po·si·tion /'fitl/ *n.* having the knees bent up toward the head like a fetus, often when lying on one's side: *He was asleep in the fetal position.*

fetch /fɛtʃ/ *v.* **fetches 1** to get s.t. and bring it back: *If I throw a stick in the air, my dog will fetch it.* **2** to be worth: *That painting will fetch $100,000 on the market.*

fetch·ing /'fɛtʃɪŋ/ *adj.* attractive: *She looked fetching in her new dress.*

fete /feɪt, fɛt/ *n.* a big party, usu. held outside

fet·id /'fɛtɪd, 'fi-/ *adj.* having a very bad smell, (*syns.*) stinking, foul: *The polluted lake has a fetid smell.*

fet·ish /'fɛtɪʃ/ *n.* **-ishes 1** an object believed to have magical power, (*syn.*) a talisman: *The tribal leader wore a rabbit's foot around his neck as a fetish.* **2** s.t. to which one devotes an excessive amount of care and attention: *She has* *a fetish about neatness and cleans her apartment every day.* **3 to make a fetish of:** to devote an excessive amount of care and attention to s.t.: *He makes a fetish of always being on time to meetings.*

fet·ter /'fɛtər/ n. a chain put on the ankle of a prisoner: *The ship's captain put the prisoner in fetters.*
—v. **1** to chain **2** *fig.* to restrict s.o.'s freedom of action: *He felt fettered by his having to care for a family.*

fe·tus /'fitəs/ n. **-tuses** the developed embryo in humans and other mammals: *The pregnant woman went to the doctor to make sure that the fetus was healthy. –adj.* **fetal** /'fitl/.

feud /fyud/ n. a long-lasting dispute, hatred (between persons, families, groups, etc.): *The feud between the families has gone on for almost seventy years.*
—v. to have a feud: *The two countries have been feuding over that island for years.*

feu·dal /'fyudl/ adj. related to the feudal era or system: *The feudal lords of Europe had to serve their king in times of war.*

feu·dal·ism /'fyudl,ɪzəm/ n. [U] a political and social system in which a king and the people of the upper classes owned the land and people of the lower classes worked it: *Feudalism existed in Europe from the ninth century to the fifteenth century.*

fe·ver /'fivər/ n. **1** higher than normal body temperature, usu. due to infection: *I have a fever and a terrible headache.* **2** a state of nervous excitement: *There is a fever for freedom in many countries. See:* headache, USAGE NOTE.

fe·ver·ish /'fivərɪʃ/ adj. **1** having a fever: *The baby has been feverish for several days.* **2** fast, excited, (*syn.*) vigorous: *There was a lot of feverish activity before the opening of the new store. -adv.* **feverishly.**

fe·ver pitch *n.fig.* high intensity, (*syn.*) fervor: *The enthusiasm of the crowd reached a fever pitch before the appearance of the star performer.*

few /fyu/ adj.n. [U] **1** (with "a") a small number: *Those plastic rings cost only <adj.> a few cents to make.‖Most students come on time, but <n.> a few are always late.* **2** (without "a") not many, not enough: *Few people registered for the course, so the college canceled it.* **3 few and far between:** rare: *Shoppers are few and far between today because of the bad weather.* **4 quite a few:** a satisfactory number: *She has received quite a few job offers.* **5** *infrml.* **to have a few:** to have too many alcoholic drinks: *He has had a few.*

USAGE NOTE: Compare: "He has a few friends" with "he has few close friends." We use "a" before "few" if we want to say that he has at least some friends, though not many. We omit "a" if we want to stress that he has almost no close friends.

fez /fɛz/ n. **fezzes** or **fezes** a round felt hat with a flat top, usu. dark red: *The fez was a popular hat for men in the Mediterranean region at one time.*

fi·an·cé /,fian'seɪ, fi'ɑn,seɪ/ n. a woman's future husband: *Her fiancé is Brazilian.*

fi·an·cée /,fian'seɪ, fi'ɑn,seɪ/ n. a man's future wife: *His fiancée works as a lawyer.*

fi·as·co /fi'æskou/ n. **-cos** or **-coes** a complete and usu. embarrassing failure: *Her attempt to run for Senator was a fiasco.*

fi·at /'fi,æt, -,ɑt, -ət/ n.frml. [C;U] an order, (*syns.*) a dictate, decree: *He runs his company by fiat, never discussing his decisions with anyone.*

fib /fɪb/ v. **fibbed, fibbing, fibs** to tell a harmless lie: *The student fibbed when she said she was late to class because of an accident; actually, she overslept.*
—n. a harmless lie, (*syn.*) a white lie: *She told the teacher a fib.* **-n.** **fibber.**

fi·ber /'faɪbər/ n. **1** [C;U] threads from a natural (plant or animal) or synthetic source used for making cloth or rope: *The fiber from the hemp plant makes good rope.* **2** [U] the material made from these threads: *cotton, wool, nylon, silk fiber* **3** [U] the part of a plant taken in as food that cannot be absorbed by the body: *Doctors say you should eat food that is high in fiber.* **4** [U] character: *She is a woman of strong moral fiber.*

fi·ber·board /'faɪbər,bord/ n. [U] building material made of plant fibers pressed into flat sheets: *The inside walls of the house are lined with fiberboard.*

fi·ber·glass /'faɪbər,glæs/ n.TM [U] a material made from glass fibers, with many commercial uses: *Boats are sometimes made of fiberglass.*

fi·brous /'faɪbrəs/ adj. having fiber: *Sugar cane plants are fibrous.*

fib·u·la /'fɪbyələ/ n. **-lae** /-,li/ or **-las** the smaller of two bones in the lower leg: *A skier broke the fibula in her right leg.*

fiche /fiʃ/ n.abbr. of microfiche.

fick·le /'fɪkəl/ adj. changeable, (*syn.*) flighty: *She is young and fickle, liking one boy this week and a different one next week.*

fic·tion /'fɪkʃən/ n. [U] **1** a type of literature based upon the author's imagination as opposed to true stories: *The author's new novel is a fine work of fiction.* **2** s.t. unreal, a lie, (*syn.*) falsehood: *What that man says about his past is pure fiction.*

USAGE NOTE: *Novels* and *short stories* are

works of *fiction*. The class of nonfiction includes *essays, biographies,* and *history books.*

fic·tion·al /ˈfɪkʃənəl/ *adj.* **1** related to fiction, works of the imagination: *Most of her fictional work consists of short stories.* **2** untrue, false: *A suspect gave a purely fictional account of his activities at the time of the crime.*

fic·ti·tious /fɪkˈtɪʃəs/ *adj.* false, *(syn.)* imaginary: *The criminal used a fictitious name. -adv.* **fictitiously.**

fid·dle /ˈfɪdl/ *n.* **1** a violin used for folk or popular music: *My friend plays the fiddle in a country band.* **2 to play second fiddle:** to be the less important person in a situation or activity: *She was tired of always playing second fiddle to her talented older sister.*
—*v.* **-dled, -dling, -dles 1** to play the fiddle: *She fiddles in that band.* **2** to change s.t. in order to deceive: *Some investors fiddled with the price of the stock to make money.* **3** to move s.t. around a little with one's fingers, *(syn.)* to tinker: *He fiddled with the wires and got the radio to work again.* **4** to waste time on useless activities: *He fiddled around with going to college, and then dropped that to become a mechanic.*

fid·dle·sticks /ˈfɪdlˌstɪks/ *interj.old usage* a polite expression of displeasure at s.t.: *Oh, fiddlesticks, I dropped an egg on the floor!*

fi·del·i·ty /fɪˈdɛləti/ *n.* [U] **1** faithfulness, devotion to duty: *His fidelity to his wife is very strong.* **2** the quality of a copy as compared to the original: *The fidelity of that recording of the concert is excellent.*

fidg·et /ˈfɪdʒɪt/ *v.* to move one's body, esp. the hands, in a nervous fashion: *He fidgeted by tapping his desk with his fingers.*

fidg·et·y /ˈfɪdʒɪti/ *adj.* showing nervousness, *(syn.)* restless: *The boy becomes fidgety if he has to sit still for even a few minutes.*

Fi·do /ˈfaɪdoʊ/ *n.* a dog's name: *In many American stories the dog's name is Fido.*

fi·du·ci·ar·y /fɪˈduʃiˌɛri, -ʃəri/ *n.* a person or business that controls property or money for s.o. else: *As the widow's fiduciary, he was responsible for the sale of her late husband's company.*

field /fild/ *n.* **1** an area of land used for a specific purpose: *a field of corn‖an oil field‖a baseball (football, soccer) field* **2** an area of activity, interest, or study: *He works in the field of international law.‖His daughter has always been interested in the field of medicine.*
—*v.* **1** to answer questions: *The politician fielded questions from reporters.* **2** (in baseball) to catch a ball: *The pitcher fielded the ball.*

field day *n.* **1** a day of festivities, esp. including outdoor contests such as footraces: *We have a field day every Fourth of July.* **2 to**

have a field day: to have a good time: *The reporters had a field day when they discovered the Senator's secret love affair.*

field·stone /ˈfildˌstoʊn/ *n.* any of the large rocks found in fields: *Farmers make stone walls from fieldstones.*

field-test *v.n.* to test s.t., such as a product or military weapon, under actual conditions: *The automaker <v.> field-tested the new car on rough roads.‖The <n.> field-test was successful.*

field trip *n.* a trip taken outside the classroom, laboratory, or office for the purpose of study: *The students went on a field trip to study the ocean.*

field·work /ˈfildˌwɜrk/ *n.* [U] work done on location: *A social worker does fieldwork by visiting clients at their houses.*

fiend /find/ *n.* **1** an evil person, *(syns.)* monster, demon: *The man who committed those terrible crimes is a fiend.* **2** a person with a very strong interest in s.t., *(syn.)* fanatic: *He is a football fiend.*

fiend·ish /ˈfindɪʃ/ *adj.* evil, cruel, *(syn.)* monstrous: *She takes fiendish delight in hurting people. -adv.* **fiendishly.**

fierce /fɪrs/ *adj.* **fiercer, fiercest 1** cruelly violent, *(syn.)* ferocious: *Fierce animals, such as the lion and bear, are very frightening when they attack.* **2** powerful, intense: *A fierce storm struck the coastline.‖The government ran into fierce opposition to its proposal. -adv.* **fiercely;** *-n.* [U] **fierceness.**

fi·er·y /ˈfaɪəri, ˈfaɪri/ *adj.* **-ier, -iest 1** full of flames: *The building became a fiery trap for the firefighters.* **2** passionate: *The Senator gave a fiery speech against his opponent.*

fi·es·ta /fiˈɛstə/ *n.* a public celebration frequently of a religious nature in Latin countries, with food, music, and dancing: *During the fiesta, there was dancing in the street every day.*

fife /faɪf/ *n.* a musical instrument similiar to a small flute: *He played the fife in the military parade.*

fif·teen /ˌfɪfˈtin/ *adj.n.* the cardinal number 15: *The wine is <adj.> fifteen years old.‖<n.> Fifteen of those books are mine.*

fif·teenth /ˌfɪfˈtinθ/ *adj.n.* the ordinal number 15: *Luiza's office is on the <adj.> fifteenth floor.*

fifth /fɪfθ/ *adj.n.* **1** the ordinal number 5: *She is the <adj.> fifth child in the family* (or) *the <n.> fifth.* **2** a liquid measure of one fifth of a gallon: *He bought a <n.> fifth of Scotch for the celebration.*

Fifth Amendment *n.* **1** (in law) from the Fifth Amendment to the U.S. Constitution, which says that a person accused of a crime is permitted to remain silent **2 to take** or **plead the Fifth (Amendment):** To refuse to incriminate oneself: *In court, she took the Fifth; she did not respond to the lawyer's questions.*

USAGE NOTE: Many famous criminals have taken the *Fifth Amendment*, so people think that almost anyone who does must be guilty. It is common to hear the phrase used as a joke: *"Did you borrow my red sweater?" "I'll have to take the Fifth on that."*

---

fifth wheel *n.fig.* an unwanted person: *He was invited out by two couples, but he refused, saying that he would feel like a fifth wheel.*

fif·ti·eth /ˈfɪftiɪθ/ *adj.n.* the ordinal number 50: *We celebrated his <adj> fiftieth birthday.*

fif·ty /ˈfɪfti/ *adj.n.* **-ties 1** the cardinal number 50: *She gave me <adj> fifty dollars to add to my <n.> fifty.* **2 fifty-fifty:** an equal share or chance: *The plan has a <adj> fifty-fifty chance of succeeding.‖My business partner and I divide the profits <adv.> fifty-fifty.*

fig /fɪg/ *n.* **1** a soft, sweet fruit with many small seeds: *Figs grow in the Mediterranean region.* **2 fig leaf:** a leaf used in art to cover male and female sex organs

fig. *abbr. for* **1** figurative, not real **2** figure, as in a picture in a book: *See fig. 4 on page 237.*

fight /faɪt/ *v.* **fought** /fɔt/, **fighting, fights 1** to argue, quarrel: *That couple fights continually over* (or) *about money.* **2** to make a great effort to get s.t.: *Political parties fight each other for votes.‖Women fought for the right to vote.* **3** to make a great effort to stop s.t.: *That organization was formed to fight racism.* **4** to use physical force: *The two children fought each other with sticks.‖As a soldier, he fought bravely for his country.* **5 to fight a losing battle:** to fight with no chance of winning: *She fought a losing battle against drug addiction.* **6** *phrasal v.* **to fight back: a.** to defend oneself: *When the company accused her of stealing, she fought back by hiring a lawyer.* **b.** to hold back: *She fought back her tears.* **7** *phrasal v.* **to fight it out:** to argue or struggle until the matter is resolved: *The two managers can fight it out until one agrees with the other.* **8 to fight like a tiger: a.** to use strong physical force: *During the attack, the father fought like a tiger to save his son.* **b.** to make a very strong effort: *She fought like a tiger to keep her job.* **9** *phrasal v.* **to fight on:** to continue fighting in spite of obstacles: *The soldier's companions were all killed, but he fought on alone.*
—*n.* **1** an argument, quarrel: *Two friends had a fight over money.* **2** a struggle for or against s.t., (*syn.*) a contest: *The politicians had a fight over legislation.* **3** a physical struggle, (*syn.*) a battle: *The two teenagers had a knife fight.* **4** a boxing match: *The championship fight took place in Manila.* **5 to put up a fight:** to strug-

gle mentally or physically: *After discovering she had cancer, she put up a fight, but died six months later.* **6 a fight to the finish:** to fight until one side can fight no longer: *Neither fighter would give up: it was a fight to the finish.*

fight·er /ˈfaɪtər/ *n.* **1** a person who fights as a sport, (*syn.*) boxer: *He has been a fighter for many years.* **2** a courageous person: *She was severely hurt in an accident, but she is a fighter and is fully recovered now.* **3** aircraft used to fight other aircraft: *The fighters circled over the enemy lines.*

fight·ing /ˈfaɪtɪŋ/ *n.* [U] **1** an act of battle: *The fighting on the border lasted for days.*

fighting chance *n.* a possibility to succeed with great effort: *Our team is way behind in the score but still has a fighting chance to win.*

fig·ment /ˈfɪgmənt/ *n.* fantasy: *He says he saw some people from Mars, but that was a figment of his imagination.*

fig·u·ra·tive /ˈfɪgyərətɪv/ *adj.* related to a word or phrase that expresses meaning in a colorful way, usu. through comparison, (*syn.*) metaphorical: *When you call a timid, fearful person a mouse, you are using figurative language.* -*adv.* **figuratively.**

fig·ure /ˈfɪgyər/ *n.* **1** a number, sum: *The cost figure for that project is a million dollars.* **2** a person's shape: *That actor has a good figure.* **3** the form of a person: *In the moonlight, we could see two figures in the distance.* **4** an important person: *Martin Luther King, Jr. is a famous historical figure.* **5** a drawing in a book: *The figure on page 63 shows how a car engine works.*
—*v.* **-ured, -uring, -ures 1** to believe, predict: *I figure that the seller wants a better price than my first offer.* **2** to be a part of: *He figures largely in her dreams for the future.* **3 That figures!:** to be expected, logical: *That figures! He's always late.* **4** *phrasal v.* **to figure in:** to add in, include: *I figured in an extra 5% in the budget for possible additional costs.* **5** *phrasal v.* **to figure on:** to plan, expect: *You can figure on spending $800 for the plane fare.* **6** *phrasal v. infrml.* **to figure out:** to solve, understand: *The student figured out the solution to the math problem.*

fig·ure·head /ˈfɪgyərˌhɛd/ *n.* a leader without power: *The president is only a figurehead: the prime minister has the real power.*

figure of speech *n.* a word or phrase that expresses meaning in a colorful way, usu. through comparison: *A typical figure of speech is "They danced until the cows came home," which means they danced for a very long time.*

figure skating *n.* [U] the sport of ice skating in various patterns (or figures): *People love to go figure skating on frozen lakes.* -*n.* **figure skater.**

fig·u·rine /ˌfɪgyəˈrin/ n. a small statue of a person or animal: *She collects figurines of horses.*

fil·a·ment /ˈfɪləmənt/ n. the thin metal thread of a light bulb: *The light bulb has gone out because the filament is broken.*

filch /fɪltʃ/ v. **filches** to steal s.t. of little value, (syns.) to pinch, swipe: *He constantly filched pencils, paper, and tape from the supply room.*

file (1) /faɪl/ n. a piece of hard metal with a rough edge used to smooth objects: *She uses a nail file to shape her fingernails.*
—v. to make an object smooth with a file: *The worker filed the rough spots off a piece of wood.*

file (2) n. **1** a folder, box, cabinet, space on a computer disk, etc. used for holding information: *The personnel office keeps a file on each employee.* **2 on file:** existing in a file: *The interviewer promised to keep my job application on file.*
—v. **filed, filing, files** to place s.t. in a file: *I file the daily reports in that cabinet.*

file (3) n. [U] a line of people or objects: *The children walked in single file.*
—v. **filed, filing, files** to move in a line: *Many people filed into the office to pick up an application.*

file clerk n. a person employed to get files for use and then put them back: *Computers have replaced file clerks in some businesses.*

fi·let /fɪˈleɪ, ˈfɪleɪ/ n.v. var. of fillet

file name n. the name of a computer file: *The file name for that report is "Work.1A."*

fi·let mi·gnon /fɪˈleɪmɪnˈyan, -minˈyoʊn, ˈfɪleɪ-/ n. [C;U] a high-quality cut of beef: *Filet mignon is very expensive.*

fil·i·al /ˈfɪliəl/ adj.frml. relating to relationships of children to parents: *Their eldest son has a filial responsibility to care for his parents.*

fil·i·bus·ter /ˈfɪləˌbʌstər/ n.v. an action by a lawmaker designed to delay passage of a bill: *The senators <v.> filibustered for two days by making long speeches.||Every effort was made to prevent the <n.> filibuster.*

USAGE NOTE: A legislator may *filibuster* as long as he or she can stay awake. Legislators have done silly things such as reading the phone book aloud and reciting poetry from memory just to delay a vote.

fil·i·gree /ˈfɪləˌgri/ n. detailed ornamentation, usu. of gold or silver: *The picture has filigree on its frame.*

fill /fɪl/ v. **1** to use all available space: *Children filled the hole with sand.||The church was filled with people.* **2** to pour liquid or pack a substance into a container: *A machine fills cartons with milk.||A waiter filled my glass with water.* **3** to cause s.o. to experience intense emotion: *The child fills her mother's heart with joy.* **4** to

supply what is needed: *A clerk fills orders for a product.||A pharmacist fills a prescription.* **5** phrasal v. infrml. **to fill 'er up** or **fill it up:** to fill a gasoline tank in a car or truck: *I told the gas station attendant to fill 'er up for our trip.* **6** phrasal v. **to fill in: a.** to replace s.o. temporarily: *The boss was ill, so his assistant filled in for him at the meeting.* **b.** to complete, supply information as on a form: *I filled in the blanks on a job application.* **7** phrasal v. **to fill out: a.** to complete: *I filled out a form to apply for a driver's license.* **b.** to mature, become full-bodied **8** phrasal v. **to fill s.o. in on:** to give s.o. information, (syns.) to inform about, apprise: *He missed the meeting, so I filled him in on all the details.* **9 to fill s.o.'s shoes:** to replace s.o., esp. a highly successful person: *The office manager does such a good job that no one will be able to fill her shoes when she leaves.*
—n. [U] **1** loose earth used to build up low-lying land, (syn.) landfill: *A construction company put fill into the low, wet land so they could build on it.* **2 to eat** or **drink one's fill:** to eat or drink to one's capacity: *After work, he drank his fill of beer and went home.* **3 to have had one's fill of s.o. or s.t.:** to be dissatisfied, (syn.) to be fed up: *I have had my fill of bad weather and am going to Florida for a vacation.*

fill·er /ˈfɪlər/ n. material or food added to s.t. to increase the amount: *The cook added bread to the meatballs as filler.*

fil·let or **filet** /fɪˈleɪ, ˈfɪleɪ/ n. a boneless piece of fish or meat: *Fillet of sole is my favorite fish recipe.*
—v. **filleted** or **fileted, filleting** or **fileting, fillets** or **filets** **1** to cut into thin pieces: *The cook filleted the steak into thin slices.* **2** to remove bones: *I filleted the fish before cooking.*

fill-in n. a substitute: *The TV show's host was ill, so a comedian acted as a fill-in for him.*

fill·ing /ˈfɪlɪŋ/ n. **1** a usu. soft food put inside a cake, candy, or sandwich: *Those chocolate candies have a creamy filling.* **2** a substance used to fill a cavity in a tooth: *The dentist replaced two fillings I had lost.*
—adj. (of food) making one feel full: *Spaghetti is very filling.*

filling station n.infrml. a gas station: *We stopped the car at a filling station to buy some gasoline.*

USAGE NOTE: At a *full-service filling station* an attendant puts gas in your car and will, if asked, clean the windshield, check the oil, and put air in the tires. A *selfservice* station may have no attendant, so you must pump the gas and do any other tasks yourself.

fil·ly /'fɪli/ *n.* **-lies** a young, female horse: *There was a special race for fillies.*

film /fɪlm/ *n.* **1** a thin coating: *I washed away a film of grease on the frying pan.* **2** material used in photography: *A tourist bought some film for his camera.* **3** a movie, motion picture: *The movie theatres on Broadway show the latest films.*
—*v.* **1** to cover with a coating of film **2** to make a movie: *The cameraman filmed a scene for a motion picture.*

film·ing /'fɪlmɪŋ/ *n.* [U] the act of making movies (TV shows, etc.): *The filming of the motion picture took place in Kenya.*

film·mak·er /'fɪlm,meɪkər/ *n.* a person or studio that makes movies: *Orson Welles was a great filmmaker.*

film·y /'fɪlmi/ *adj.* **-ier, -iest 1** covered with a film: *The water at the beach was filmy with oil from passing ships.* **2** very thin and light: *The curtains were made of a filmy material.*

fil·ter /'fɪltər/ *n.* a device to trap unwanted matter as liquids and gases pass through it: *I use a filter in my coffee machine.*
—*v.* **1** to pass through a filter: *We filter our drinking water.* **2** to move gradually: *The audience slowly filtered into the concert hall.* **3** *phrasal v.* **to filter out:** to remove through a filter: *The fisherman filtered out the small fish with the net.* -*adj.* **filterable.**

filth /fɪlθ/ *n.* [U] **1** an excessive amount of dirt: *The city streets were filled with filth.* **2** *fig.* offensive books, pictures, and films, usu. related to sex, (*syns.*) obscenity, smut: *That magazine contains filth.* **3** *fig.* indecent or immoral behavior, (*syns.*) vice, depravity: *The police vice squad fights filth in that area of town.*

filth·y /'fɪlθi/ *adj.* **-ier, -iest 1** covered with filth, disgustingly dirty: *The beggar's clothes are filthy.* **2** *fig.* offensive, usu. in a sexual way, (*syns.*) obscene, smutty: *That store sells filthy magazines.* **3** *fig.* immoral, indecent, (*syns.*) depraved, vice-ridden: *People do filthy things in that place.* **4 filthy rich:** very rich: *Her family is filthy rich.* -*n.* [U] **filthiness.**

fil·trate /'fɪl,treɪt/ *v.* **-trated, -trating, -trates** to filter s.t.: *This machine filtrates the water.*
—*n.* the substance that is filtered: *The filtrate is an improved product.* -*n.* **filtration** /fɪl'treɪʃən/.

fin /fɪn/ *n.* **1** the flat wing-like part of a fish that it uses for movement and balance: *One of the fish's fins got caught in a net.* **2** a guidance device (for aircraft): *The pilot checked the tail fins on his plane.*

fi·na·gle /fə'neɪgəl/ *v.infrml.* **-gled, -gling, -gles** to achieve one's goal through trickery and deception: *He finagled his way into an exclusive club by lying about his past.* -*n.* **finagler.**

fi·nal /'faɪnl/ *n.* **1** the last contest in a series (often *pl.* finals): *The world tennis final will be played tomorrow.* **2** end of term examination: *I have my chemistry final tomorrow.*
—*adj.* **1** last: *I sat in the final row of the airplane.* **2** unchangeable, (*syn.*) absolute: *The judge's decision is final.* -*adv.* **finally.**

fi·nal·e /fɪ'næli, -'nɑ-/ *n.* the last part of a musical piece, performance, or public event: *The orchestra played some marching music as the grand finale.*

fi·nal·ist /'faɪnəlɪst/ *n.* a participant in the last contest of a series of competitions: *She was a finalist in the tennis tournament but lost to the champion.*

fi·nal·i·ty /faɪ'næləti, fɪ-/ *n.* [U] a condition of definiteness about s.t.: *Coming from the chairman himself, the company's announcement about closing the factory had an air of finality about it.*

fi·nal·ize /'faɪnl,aɪz/ *v.* **-ized, -izing, -izes** to finish, complete in a definite fashion: *We finalized the details of our contract and signed it.*

fi·nal·ly /'faɪnəli/ *adv.* in the end, at last: *He finally arrived after driving for ten hours.*

fi·nance /fə'næns, 'faɪ,næns/ *n.* **1** [U] the science and art of raising and managing large sums of private and public money: *My friend works in finance at an international bank.* **2** *pl.* **finances** the money that an individual, company, or institution has: *He has difficulty managing his finances and is always in debt.*
—*v.* **-nanced, -nancing, -nances** to provide money: *His bank just financed a large construction project in India.||She is financing her child's college education.*

finance charge *n.* the interest charge on a loan, plus any fees: *The finance charge on the loan is 10%, plus a $50 application fee.*

fi·nan·cial /fə'nænʃəl, faɪ-/ *adj.* related to finance: *She was always careful with her money in order to have financial security when she retired.* -*adv.* **financially.**

financial institution *n.* a bank or company that handles money for business and individuals: *Financial institutions in the USA are regulated by the government.*

financial markets *n.pl.* the bond markets, stock markets, commodities markets, etc. that accept money and turn it into equity instruments: *The financial markets suffered in the recession.*

financial statement *n.* a report showing profit and loss for a business or institution: *We received the financial statement of the company that is for sale.*

financial year *n.* *See:* fiscal year.

fi·nan·cier /,fɪnən'sɪr, fə,næn-, ,faɪnæn-/ *n.* a person who provides money for a business: *A* *well-known financier arranged for the funding of the new hotel.*

fi·nan·cing /fə'nænsɪŋ, 'faɪˌnæn-/ *n.* [U] money and credit needed by businesses and individuals: *Financing for the company comes from individual investors.*

finch /fɪntʃ/ *n.* **finches** a type of small bird, such as canaries, sparrows, and house finches: *Finches generally feed on seeds.*

find /faɪnd/ *v.* **found** /faʊnd/, **finding, finds** **1** to discover by chance: *I found $10 on the sidewalk.* **2** to learn from experience: *She finds that she can lose weight just by eating less.* **3** to discover after searching: *He found a new job (apartment, school, etc.).*‖*Politicians found money in the budget to increase help to the poor.* **4** to reach an objective: *The arrow found its target.*‖*I was lost but finally found my way back to the hotel.* **5** to meet: *We found our friends waiting for us at the restaurant.* **6** to express a reaction to s.o. or s.t.: *She found the museum fascinating.* **7 to find for** or **against s.o.:** (in law) to decide that s.o. is guilty or not guilty: *The jury found for the defendant* (or) *found the defendant not guilty.* **8 to find it in one's heart:** to search deeply within oneself for kind feelings: *He could not find it in his heart to forgive her.* **9 to find it (odd, unusual, unlikely, etc.) that:** to make an observation that s.t. is strange: *I find it odd that my friend hasn't called recently; I hope he's not ill.* **10 to find oneself:** to discover one's true abilities and be at peace with oneself: *She is doing well as a lawyer and has finally found herself.* **11 to find one's way clear to do s.t.:** to agree to do s.t. unlikely or difficult: *After much discussion, the bank found its way clear to give me a loan.* **12** *phrasal v. sep.* **to find s.o. out:** to discover s.o. is guilty of a wrongdoing, (*syn.*) to unmask: *He was stealing from the company, but the manager found him out.* **13** *phrasal v. sep.* **to find s.t. out:** to learn, (*syn.*) to uncover: *I just found out that the payment is due tomorrow.*‖*I found it out.* **14 to find the use of:** to be able to use again, esp. an arm, leg, or sense: *He was hurt but gradually found the use of his injured legs.*
—*n.* a valuable discovery: *The deep sea treasure was an exciting find.*‖*The new secretary in my office is a real find.*

find·er /'faɪndər/ *n.* a device used to determine position: *The military uses a range finder to determine the distance of a target from a weapon.*

find·er's fee *n.* a sum of money paid to s.o. for performing a service, such as finding a job or apartment: *A company in Hong Kong paid a finder's fee to an agent in New York for finding new customers.*

find·ing /'faɪndɪŋ/ *n.* a decision made after an investigation: *The finding of the Senate com-*

mittee is that the program should not be continued.

fine /faɪn/ *n.* money paid as punishment for wrongdoing: *He paid a fine for parking illegally.*
—*v.* **fined, fining, fines** to order payment for wrongdoing: *The court fined the company for dumping garbage illegally.*
—*adj.* **finer, finest** **1** excellent, (*syn.*) advantageous: *Now is a fine time to buy property.* **2** of superior quality: *That store sells fine jewelry.*‖*She has fine taste in furnishings (clothes, music, restaurants, etc.).*‖*She is a person of fine character.* **3** deeply felt (senses, perception), (*syns.*) keen, heightened: *He has a fine sense of hearing (smell, touch, etc.).* **4** sharp, pointed: *That knife has a fine edge on its blade* (or) *a fine point on its tip.* **5** composed of thin threads or very small pieces: *That scarf is made of a fine silk.* **6** well, healthy: *I feel fine today.* **7 the fine print:** a contract's small print which could alter the meaning of a document as a whole: *They did not read the fine print in the written agreement and lost all their money.*
—*adv.infrml.* **1** well: *You did fine on your exam.* **2** in small pieces, finely: *Chop the nuts fine.* -*n.* [U] **fineness.**

fine arts *n.pl.* the arts of painting, drawing, music, dance, literature, drama, and architecture: *She has a degree in fine arts from Columbia University.*

fine·ly /'faɪnli/ *adv.* **1** well and delicately: *The plates were finely painted.* **2** in small pieces: *Chop the nuts finely.*

fin·er·y /'faɪnəri/ *n.frml.* [U] elegant, expensive clothes: *Men and women dressed in their finery for the concert.*

fin·esse /fɪ'nɛs/ *n.* [U] fine skill, smoothness, (*syn.*) deftness: *The chef makes elegant desserts with great finesse.*‖*The owner handles complaints with finesse.*

fine-tooth(ed) comb /'faɪnˌtuθ(t)/ *n.fig.* **to go over with a fine-tooth(ed) comb:** to examine carefully and closely: *She went over the contract with a fine-toothed comb and asked many questions before signing it.*

fin·ger /'fɪŋgər/ *n.* **1** one of the movable parts of the hand, (*syn.*) digit: *A hand has four fingers and a thumb* (or) *five fingers.* **2** *infrml.fig.* **a finger in the pie:** to be involved, have influence: *The sales manager is in charge of the project, but his boss has his finger in the pie.* **3 to give s.o. the finger:** (a vulgar act) to show a strong dislike for s.o. by displaying the middle finger: *When he passed the car in front of him, the driver gave him the finger.* **4** *fig.* **to keep one's fingers crossed:** to wish strongly for s.t.: *I hope it doesn't rain tomorrow; let's keep our fingers crossed.* **5 to not lift a finger:** to make no effort to help: *She made all the preparations* *for the party; her husband didn't lift a finger.* **6** *fig.* **to put one's finger on s.t.:** to identify, say exactly what s.t. is: *There's something strange about that man, but I can't put my finger on it.* **7 to slip through one's fingers:** to miss or lose an opportunity: *She had a chance to get a promotion, but she let it slip through her fingers.*

—*v.* **1** to touch or rub with the fingers: *The buyer fingered the cloth to check the quality.* **2** *fig.* to choose: *The president of the company fingered his assistant to run the new project.*

fin·ger·nail /ˈfɪŋgərˌneɪl/ *n.* the hard covering at the end of each finger: *She puts red polish on her fingernails.*

fin·ger·print /ˈfɪŋgərˌprɪnt/ *n.v.* the fine pattern made by a person's fingertips when covered with ink and pressed against paper: *The police <v.> fingerprint suspects and keep these <n.> fingerprints for their records.*

fin·ger printing *n.* the process of getting fingerprints: *The finger printing of the suspect took place at the police station.*

fin·ger·tip /ˈfɪŋgərˌtɪp/ *n.* **1** the end of the human finger including the nail and flesh on the bottom: *The fingertip has many nerve endings that are very useful in the sense of touch.* **2** *fig.* **to have s.t. at one's fingertips:** to have instantly available: *With the aid of a computer, I have all the information I need at my fingertips.*

fin·ick·y /ˈfɪnɪki/ *adj.* difficult to please, unpredictable, (*syns.*) fussy, persnickety: *Children can sometimes be finicky eaters.*

fin·is /ˈfɪnɪs, fɪˈni/ *n.* the end: *The last page in the book says "Finis."*

fin·ish /ˈfɪnɪʃ/ *v.* **-ishes 1** to complete, accomplish: *I finished my assignment in three hours.* **2** to coat the surface of s.t.: *The carpenter finished the table with furniture oil.*

—*n.* **-ishes 1** the end, termination of an activity or event: *We were present at the finish of the race.* **2** a covering or surface: *That table has a smooth and shiny finish.*

fin·ished /ˈfɪnɪʃt/ *adj.* no longer able to function, (*syn.*) ruined: *She's finished as a politician.*||*The business is out of money; it's finished.*

finishing school *n.* a two-year school for young rich women as preparation for taking their place in society: *She went to finishing school in New England and then returned to Michigan to marry.*

fin·ish line *n.* the line that marks the end of a race: *Our horse crossed the finish line far ahead of the others.*

fi·nite /ˈfaɪnaɪt/ *adj.* limited in number (quantity, availability), countable: *The company has finite resources that must be divided among a limited number of projects.*

fink /fɪŋk/ *n.infrml.* s.o. who tells about the wrongdoing of others, (*syn.*) informer: *That fink told the teacher that s.o. cheated on the exam.*

—*v.infrml.* to inform on s.o.: *He finked on his friends.*

fiord /fyɔrd, fiˈɔrd/ *n. var. of* fjord

fir /fɜr/ *n.* a type of tall pine tree with thin pointed leaves found in cool climates: *Firs are often used as Christmas trees.*

fire /faɪr/ *n.* **1** [C] the process of burning, which produces heat and light: *The fire in the stove is hot enough to cook now.* **2** [C] flames, (*syn.*) a blaze: *We sat around the fire to keep warm.*||*The restaurant was closed because of a fire.* **3** [U]*fig.* passion, intensity: *His speeches are full of fire.* **4 on fire:** burning, in flames, (*syn.*) ablaze: *The house next door is on fire.* **5 on the fire:** to be cooking: *The hamburgers are on the fire and will be ready soon.* **6 to be under fire: a.** to be under attack: *The soldiers on the bridge are under fire from enemy aircraft.* **b.** *fig.* to suffer criticism: *The politician is under fire from his conservative opponents.* **7 to catch (on) fire: a.** to start to burn, (*syns.*) to ignite, become ablaze: *If you're not careful, the rug will catch fire.* **b.** *fig.* to become popular, widely accepted: *After her great speech, the politician's election campaign caught fire with the people.* **8 to fight fire with fire:** to use the same methods as s.o. else: *He complains to the boss about us, so we'll fight fire with fire and complain to the boss about him.* **9 to have fire in one's eye:** to be angry: *I know she's determined to do what she wants; I can see the fire in her eyes.* **10 to have fire in the belly:** to have a strong desire for advancement, (*syn.*) to be ambitious: *He has a real fire in his belly; he is so determined to succeed.* **11 to set a fire under s.o.:** to pressure s.o. to do s.t., (*syn.*) to prod: *He has been delaying action for months; I'm going to set a fire under him to start the project.* **12 to set fire to** or **to set on fire:** to start s.t. burning, (*syns.*) to torch, set ablaze: *She accidentally set the bed on fire (or) set fire to the bed with a cigarette.* **13** *fig.* **to set the world on fire:** to enjoy great success (usu. used negatively): *She did not set the world on fire at college, but she did make some good grades.*

—*v.* **fired, firing, fires 1** to shoot a weapon: *The soldier fired his rifle (missile, cannon, etc.) at the enemy.* **2** to start a fire, (*syn.*) to ignite **3** *fig.* to talk or shout at s.o. with intensity: *The detective fired questions at the suspect.* **4** to dismiss from employment, (*syn.*) to terminate: *The boss fired two workers.* **5** to excite, (*syn.*) to inspire: *That speaker fires the imagination of his listeners.* **6** *infrml.fig.* **to be fired up:** to be enthusiastic, highly motivated: *He is fired up about his new job and wants to* *get started.* **7** *phrasal v. insep.* **to fire away at s.o. or s.t.: a.** to shoot at s.o. with full force: *The officer gave the signal, and the soldiers fired away at the enemy.* **b.** *infrml.fig.* (you) go ahead: *I'm listening to your idea; fire away!* **8** *phrasal v. sep.* **fire s.t. off:** to speak or write quickly: *She fired off three letters in ten minutes.‖She fired them off.* See: quit, USAGE NOTE.

fire alarm *n.* a device that makes a loud sound to warn people of a fire: *Everyone left the building when the fire alarm went off.* See: smoke detector.

fire·arm /'faɪr,ɑrm/ *n.* any of a variety of guns (pistols, rifles, machine guns, etc.): *In order to use a firearm, you have to have a permit.*

fire·ball /'faɪr,bɔl/ *n.* **1** any round mass on fire: *Fireballs of burning grass rolled down the hill from the fire above.* **2** *fig.* a very energetic person: *That woman is a fireball of energy; she's always full of good ideas.*

fire·bomb /'faɪr,bɑm/ *n.v.* a bomb that spreads fire: *The airplanes <v.> firebombed the city.*

fire·brand /'faɪr,brænd/ *n.fig.* a person very involved in a political cause: *He was a firebrand in the civil rights movement.*

fire·bug /'faɪr,bʌg/ *n.slang* a person who maliciously sets fires, *(syn.)* arsonist: *The store fires were set by a firebug.*

fire·crack·er /'faɪr,krækər/ *n.* a light, often colorful explosive intended for celebration: *Some people like to set off firecrackers on Independence Day. See:* fireworks.

fire department *n.* the organization responsible for putting out unwanted fires in a city or town: *The fire department put out a blaze in the building next door to my house.*

fire drill *n.* a procedure in which all people leave a building as practice for a real fire: *The schools in our town have fire drills every month.*

fire-eater *n.* **1** an entertainer who creates the illusion of swallowing fire: *At the circus the children especially enjoyed the fire-eater.* **2** *fig.* an angry person who likes to argue: *People avoid him; he's a fire-eater when the subject is politics.*

fire engine *n.* a truck with equipment used to put out fires: *A fire engine with six firefighters arrived and put out the grass fire.*

fire escape *n.* a series of platforms and ladders attached outside a building to let its occupants climb down and escape a fire: *We can reach the fire escape by going out our living-room window. See:* fire exit; fire stairs.

fire extinguisher *n.* a container containing chemicals under pressure that are shot through a hose to put out fires: *We keep a fire extinguisher in the kitchen.*

fire·fight·er /'faɪr,faɪtər/ *n.* a person employed to put out fires: *The firefighter went into the burning building to save the child.*

fire·fly /'faɪr,flaɪ/ *n.* **-flies** a flying insect that sends out a light that can be seen at night: *We enjoy watching fireflies flashing their lights in the early evening.*

fire·house /'faɪr,haʊs/ *n.* a building where fire engines and equipment are kept, often with living space for firefighters, *(syn.)* fire station: *The new firehouse in this town holds three fire engines and ten firefighters.*

fire hydrant *n.* an upright metal container holding a pipe connected to an underground water supply, *(syn.)* fireplug: *Firefighters connected their hoses to the fire hydrant and sprayed water on the blaze.*

fire·man /'faɪrmən/ *n.* **-men** /-mən/ *var. of* firefighter

USAGE NOTE: Many people find the term *fireman* sexist and prefer *firefighter.*

fire·place /'faɪr,pleɪs/ *n.* a space built into the wall of a building, made of brick or stone, in which fires are set, *(syn.)* hearth: *Our family sits around the fireplace on cold winter nights.*

fire·plug /'faɪr,plʌg/ *n. See:* fire hydrant.

fire·pow·er /'faɪr,paʊər/ *n.* the amount of weapons that a military unit can put into action: *With its many fighter planes and guns, an aircraft carrier has enormous firepower.*

fire·proof /'faɪr,pruf/ *adj.v.* (to make) incapable of being harmed by fire: *That building is <adj.> fireproof because the builders <v.> fireproofed it with steel doors, cement floors, and brick walls.*

fire sale *n.* **1** a sale at very reduced prices of goods damaged in a fire **2** *fig.* any sale at very reduced prices: *We bought some new dishes at a fire sale.*

fire·side /'faɪr,saɪd/ *n.adj.* the area near or beside a fire, esp. a fireplace: *I'll never forget those <adj.> fireside talks we used to have on cold winter nights.*

fire station *n. See:* firehouse.

fire·trap /'faɪr,træp/ *n.* a building that is dangerous during a fire because it burns easily or has few exits: *That old theater is a firetrap and should be closed down.*

fire wall *n.* a wall designed to stop or slow the progress of a fire: *That ship has fire walls between its sections.*

fire·wa·ter /'faɪr,wɔtər, -,wɑ-/ *n.infrml.old usage* [U] an alcoholic drink, such as cheap whiskey: *The cowboy said to the bartender, "Give me some more of that firewater!"*

fire·wood /'faɪr,wʊd/ *n.* [U] wood used to start a fire or to keep it burning: *They cut down the trees for firewood.*

fire·works /ˈfaɪrˌwɜrks/ n.pl. light, colorful explosives used for celebrations: *The Independence Day fireworks are beautiful to see in the night sky. See:* firecracker.

fir·ing line n. a practice area or a battle line from which weapons are fired: *Fresh troops moved up to the firing line to help the others.* **2 on the firing line:** (of a person) in the position of having to defend against criticism: *As the head of the company, he's always on the firing line.*

fir·ing squad n. a small unit of soldiers who shoot to kill a prisoner on command: *The firing squad consisted of five young soldiers commanded by a lieutenant.*

firm /fɜrm/ adj. **1** quite solid, (syn.) taut: *His muscles are firm from exercise.*||*The mattress is firm.* **2** fixed, definite: *Her decision is firm and will not be changed.*||*The price on that item is firm.* **3** strong, stable: *That house is built on a firm foundation.*||*She gave him a firm handshake.* **4** determined to be obeyed, (syn.) unyielding: *The boy's mother was firm with him about not crossing the street alone.* **5 to be on firm ground:** to know one's facts: *My manager is on firm ground when she describes the costs of production.*
—*phrasal v.* **to firm up:** to become stable, solid: *Food prices finally stopped falling and firmed up.*
—*n.* a business of professionals: *He belongs to a law firm* (or) *an accounting firm.*
—*adv.* **to hold** or **remain firm:** to remain steady, dedicated: *She holds firm to* (or) *remains firm in her religious beliefs.* *-adv.* **firmly** *-n.* [U] **firmness.**

fir·ma·ment /ˈfɜrməmənt/ n.frml. [U] the sky, (syn.) the heavens: *He raised his eyes to the firmament and prayed for forgiveness.*

first /fɜrst/ adj. **1** located as number one in a series: *She is the first person in line.* **2 at first glance:** viewed quickly, on the surface, (syn.) superficially: *At first glance, the jewels looked real.* **3 first thing:** at the beginning of a time period: *I will do it first thing in the morning.* **4 first things first:** The most important or necessary things must be done before any others: *First things first, you must earn the money to pay for the trip before you go.* **5 in first place:** the winner, the best: *I thought my baseball team was in first place, but it turned out we finished second.* **6 in the first place:** to be considered before other matters (often used to express frustration): *In the first place, I don't understand what you are talking about, so how can I make a decision?*
—*pron.* **1** number one in a series: *She was the first to hear the news.* **2 at first:** in the beginning in comparison to later events: *At first, I thought he was lying, but I later learned that he was telling the truth.* **3 first come, first**

served: those who arrive first are attended to first, and later arrivals wait: *First come, first served is how the free clothing is given out at the church.*
—*adv.* **1** occurring before any other action, person, or thing: *He cleaned the floors first before doing the windows.*||*The horse I picked finished first in the race.*||*This meeting will cover three issues: First, we shall discuss last year's sales; second, this year's new products; third, strategies for selling our product line.* **2** *fig.* **first, last, and always:** forever: *First, last, and always, she is the best dancer of our time.*

USAGE NOTE: Some prefer to use "firstly, secondly, thirdly," etc. Either is correct.

first aid n. [U] emergency medical treatment given before the injured person receives whatever further treatment may be necessary: *When the worker received a bad cut on his hand, a co-worker administered first aid and then took him to the hospital.*

first base n. [U] **1** (in baseball) the base that must be reached first by the runner: *The player hit the ball and ran to first base.* **2** *fig.* **to get to first base: a.** to successfully complete the first step of a plan of action: *He tried to sell that company a new health plan but could not get to first base with them.* **b.** *fig.* to kiss s.o. on a romantic date: *Carlos got to first base last night with Laura.*

first-born n. [U] adj. a couple's first child: *He was their <n.> first-born* or *their <adj.> first-born child.*

first-class adj. referring to the best quality, usu. of service: *They stayed at a first-class hotel.*
—*adv.* by rapid mail: *I will send the letter first-class.*

first cousin n. the son or daughter of one's aunt or uncle: *Two of my first cousins live in Chicago.*

first edition n. the first printing of a book: *I have a first edition of* Gone with the Wind *signed by the author.*

first floor n. the entry-level floor of a house or building: *Our office is on the first floor.*

USAGE NOTE: In the USA, the first floor is usually at sidewalk or ground level.

first-generation adj. being the first children of immigrants to be born in the new country: *My parents came from Italy to America, and I was born in America; I am a first-generation American.*

first·hand /ˈfɜrstˈhænd/ adj. direct, based on direct experience and knowledge of s.t.: *She has worked with computers for years and has firsthand knowledge of how they work.*

F

first lady or **First Lady** *n.* **-dies** the wife of a leader of a country: *The first lady gave a speech about the drug problem.*

USAGE NOTE: As the wife of the President, the *First Lady* of the USA serves as the official hostess of the White House. She also accompanies her husband on state visits, campaigns for his reelection, and usu. devotes attention to a social issue such as literacy, drug abuse, or child welfare.

first·ly /'fɜrstli/ *adv.* occurring before all others: *Firstly, I would like to welcome you; secondly, let's discuss some serious matters.*

first mate *n.* a ship's officer second in rank to the captain: *The captain gave an order to the first mate.*

first name *n.* the name given one at birth, as opposed to one's family name: *His first name is Thomas, but I can't remember his last name.* —*adj.* **first-name basis:** referring to a friendly, informal relationship: *The owner and I are on a first-name basis.*

first offender or **first-time offender** *n.* a person who has broken the law for the first time: *The judge let the man go without punishment because he was a first offender.*

first person *n.* [U] **1** (in grammar) the form of a pronoun or verb that refers to the speaker(s): *For the verb "to be," "I am" is the singular form of the person and "we are" is the plural form.* **2** a style of storytelling in which the narrator is a participant in the story: *The novel, told in the first person, began, "My father died before I was born."*

first-rate *adj.* excellent, among the best: *She is a first-rate lawyer; all the well-known criminals want her to represent them.*

first-string *adj.* referring to athletes on a team who play regularly as opposed to second-string players who act as substitutes: *Martin Marvelous is the first-string quarterback for our football team.*

first-time *adj.* occurring for the first time: *She is a first-time lottery winner and hopes to win again.*

First World *n.* [U] the industrialized and wealthy countries of the world: *Representatives of the First World held an economic conference in Paris. See:* Third World.

First World War *n.* World War I: *Germany and Italy were on opposing sides in the First World War.*

fis·cal /'fɪskəl/ *adj.* **1** related to taxation and spending of government money: *The country's fiscal policy is to lower taxes and increase spending in order to stimulate the economy.* **2** **fiscal year:** related to a 12-month period of business activity: *Our company's fiscal year is*

the calendar year, January 1 to December 31. -*adv.* **fiscally.**

fish /fɪʃ/ *n.* **fish** or **fishes** [C;U] **1** an animal usu. with scales that lives in water and uses gills to breathe: *I love to eat fish that I catch in the ocean.* **2** *fig.* **a big fish in a small pond:** an important, usu. powerful person in a work or social setting where there is little competition: *The well-known professor chose to stay at the small college rather than teach at a large university because he wanted to be a big fish in a small pond.* **3 a cold fish:** a person who does not show warmth or affection: *That man is such a cold fish; he never smiles!* **4 to be** or **feel like a fish out of water:** to feel awkward, in the wrong place: *I felt like a fish out of water at that fancy restaurant since I usually eat at fast-food places.* **5 to be neither fish nor fowl:** not to fit into a clear category, confusing: *The owners decided to make the newspaper less serious, but now it is neither fish nor fowl because it limits its serious articles and still has too few of the lighter ones.* **6 to drink like a fish:** to drink large amounts of alcohol: *He used to hate beer, but now he drinks like a fish.* **7 to have other fish to fry:** to have more important things to do: *I cannot spend any more time on that project; I have other fish to fry.*

—*v.* **fishes 1** to try to catch fish: *When I was little, my uncle used to fish with me.* **2** *fig.* to search for s.t. with the hand, (*syns.*) to grope, fumble around: *She fished in her bag for a pen.* **3** *fig.* to search, inquire (often indirectly): *The detective fished for information by asking neighbors if they had seen the crime.* **4 to fish for compliments:** to ask questions to invite praise: *The girl asked her boyfriend if he liked her hair and her dress; she was fishing for compliments.* **5 to fish or cut bait:** to make a definite decision: *He has been deciding whether or not to buy my car for a month now; he has to fish or cut bait because I need to sell it.* **6** *phrasal v. sep.* **to fish s.o. or s.t. out:** to pull out: *Two women fished a little boy out of the water.||They fished him out.*

fish and chips *n.* fried pieces of fish served with French fries: *Every Friday, he enjoys fish and chips for lunch.*

fish·bowl /'fɪʃ,boʊl/ *n.* **1** a bowl in which pet fish are kept: *There are two goldfish in the fishbowl.* **2** *fig.* a place with little or no privacy: *The President lives in a fishbowl; he has no privacy.*

fish·cake /'fɪʃ,keɪk/ *n.* a fried mixture of ground fish and potato, often with light spices: *We're having fishcakes for lunch.*

fish·er·man /'fɪʃərmən/ *n.* **-men** /-mən/ **1** a person who enjoys fishing for sport **2** a person who earns his living by fishing: *The fisherman takes his boat out to sea early in the morning.*

USAGE NOTE: To avoid sexism, many people use "fisher" or "angler."

fish·er·y /'fɪʃəri/ n. **-ies 1** an area where fish are caught: *The boats were headed towards the fisheries off the East Coast.* **2** the business of catching, processing, and selling fish: *The fisheries in our state are now owned by one group.* **3** a place where fish are raised: *That fishery sells to expensive restaurants in the city.*

fish·hook /'fɪʃ,hʊk/ n. a curved piece of thin metal with a sharp, pointed end designed to catch fish by the mouth: *I put a worm on the end of the fishhook.*

fish·ing /'fɪʃɪŋ/ n. [U] **1** the sport of fishing: *We like to go fishing during our vacation.* **2** the business of catching and selling fish: *Fishing can be a difficult way to make a living.*

fishing rod n. a long, metal stick, fitted with cord or plastic line and used to catch fish: *We use a very strong fishing rod to go deep-sea fishing.*

fish·mon·ger /'fɪʃ,mɑŋgər, -,mʌŋ-/ n. a person who sells fish: *My mother is a fishmonger at the outdoor market in Seattle.*

fish·net /'fɪʃ,nɛt/ n. an open fabric of nylon, wire, or other material designed to capture fish: *Some fishnets are so huge that they catch every creature in their path.*

fish·pond /'fɪʃ,pɑnd/ n. a body of water smaller than a lake in which fish are kept: *There's a fishpond in the park.*

fish·stick /'fɪʃstɪk/ n. finger-sized processed pieces of fresh or frozen fish: *We have fishsticks for dinner once a week.*

fish story n. **-ries** a story that is hard to believe, (syn.) a tall tale: *He wears a cowboy hat and tells fish stories about his former career as a movie actor.*

fish·tail /'fɪʃ,teɪl/ v. to move back and forth: *Our airplane fishtailed as we landed in a strong wind.*

fish·y /'fɪʃi/ adj. **-ier, -iest 1** having an odor of fish: *The garbage has a fishy smell that is making me sick.* **2** fig. strange, possibly dishonest, (syn.) suspicious: *Strangers keep going in and out of that house; there is s.t. fishy going on there.*

fis·sion /'fɪʃən/ n. [U] the splitting of an atom, producing a release of energy: *Nuclear fission releases a powerful explosion of energy.*

fis·sure /'fɪʃər/ n. a split, crack, (syns.) crevice, cleavage: *Water has gotten into fissures in the rock.*

fist /fɪst/ n. the closed hand, esp. when used for striking: *He hit the table with his fist to get everyone's attention.*

fist·fight /'fɪst,faɪt/ n. a fight in which fists are used: *An argument between two men outside a disco soon turned into a fistfight.*

fist·ful /'fɪst,fʊl/ n. a handful: *The child grabbed a fistful of cookies and ran outside.*

fist·i·cuffs /'fɪstɪ,kʌfs/ n. (frequently used humorously) a fistfight: *The fight between the two children began as an argument and ended in fisticuffs.*

fit /fɪt/ v. **fitted,** or **fit, fitting, fits 1** to be the right size and shape: *These shoes fit well; I'll buy them.*‖*The key fits into the lock.* **2** to be suitable for a specific purpose: *That telephone system fits our needs.* **3** fig. **if the shoe fits, wear it:** if the description of s.o. is true, then it has to be accepted: *My friend said, "My girlfriend just told me that I lived like a pig." I said, "Well, if the shoe fits, wear it; your apartment is a complete mess."* **4 to fit like a glove:** to fit closely and comfortably, almost perfectly: *These shoes fit like a glove.* **5 to fit the bill:** to satisfy, provide just what is needed: *The new paint job really fits the bill in brightening up the house.*
—n. **1** [C] a sudden strong display of anger, (syn.) a temper tantrum: *He nearly had a fit when he got a parking ticket.* **2** [U] the suitability of s.t.'s size and shape to its purpose: *That suit looks good on you; it has a nice fit.* **3** [C] a sudden attack of a disease: *a coughing fit* **4 to give s.o. fits:** to worry, (syn.) to exasperate: *He gives me fits because he never does what he is supposed to do.*
—adj. **fitter, fittest 1** in good physical condition, healthy: *He looks fit after his vacation.* **2** suitable, proper: *Because of his dishonesty, he isn't fit to be mayor.* **3 fit as a fiddle:** to be healthy, in good condition: *I've been jogging a lot lately, and I feel as fit as a fiddle!* **4 fit to be tied:** very frustrated, (syn.) exasperated: *When she heard that her son had crashed the car again, she was fit to be tied.*

fit·ful /'fɪtfəl/ adj. irregular, disturbed: *I slept badly; I had a fitful night.* **-adv. fitfully.**

fit·ness /'fɪtnɪs/ n. [U] **1** a person's physical condition: *As part of her desire for fitness, she jogs two miles every day.* **2** suitability: *His poor performance as assistant manager made us question his fitness for the position of manager.*

fit·ting /'fɪtɪŋ/ n. the act of trying on clothing in order to get the proper size: *The costume designer asked the actor to come in for a fitting this week.*
—adj. suitable, (syn.) proper: *It was a fitting end to the story.*

five /faɪv/ adj.n. the cardinal number 5: *He gave me <adj.> five dollars.*‖<n.> *Five of the children lived on the same street.*

five-and-dime n.adj. See: five-and-ten.

five-and-ten *n.adj.* a general store selling inexpensive household items: *We did some shopping at the <n> five-and-ten* (or) *at the <adj.> five-and-ten store.*

fix /fɪks/ *v.* **fixes 1** to repair: *I had the brakes on my car fixed.* **2** to correct, to adjust: *He fixed the mistakes in the report, so it is correct now.* **3** *fig.* (of a competition) to arrange in advance who will win, (*syn.*) to rig: *The horse race had been fixed.* **4** to prepare: *He fixed dinner for his wife.* **5** *fig.* to give an animal a medical operation that prevents it from producing young, (*syn.*) to neuter: *He didn't want his cat to have any more kittens, so he had her fixed.*
—*n.* **fixes 1** difficulty, a troublesome situation: *He used his credit card too freely and has gotten himself into a fix with high payments.* **2** *slang* an amount of narcotic: *The drug addict started to shake because he needed a fix so badly.*

fix·ate /'fɪkˌseɪt/ *v.* **-ated, -ating, -ates 1** to focus one's attention intensely on s.t.: *As she looked at jewelry in the window, she fixated on a beautiful ring.* **2** to spend an excessive amount of time thinking about s.o. or s.t., (*syn.*) to obsess: *The young girl fixated on the handsome movie star as the man of her dreams.*

fix·a·tion /fɪk'seɪʃən/ *n.* s.o. or s.t. one cannot stop thinking about, an obsession: *He has a fixation on one of his professors.*

fix·a·tive /'fɪksətɪv/ *n.* **1** a substance used to hold two things together: *People who wear false teeth use a fixative to hold them in place.* **2** a substance used to make s.t. permanent: *The artist uses a fixative on her drawings to preserve them.*

fixed /fɪkst/ *adj.* **1** firmly in place: *The computer is locked in a fixed position, so it can't be moved.* **2** definite, stable: *That product is sold at a fixed price with no discounts.* **3** not able to be changed, (*syns.*) unyielding, insistent: *She has fixed ideas on how to cook.*

fix·ture /'fɪkstʃər, 'fɪkʃtʃər/ *n.* **1** internal parts of a building, such as faucets, sinks, or bathtub: *We are planning to replace the bathroom fixtures next year.* **2** *fig.* a person or thing connected to a place for a long time and unlikely to leave it: *Mr. Kim is a fixture at the company; he's worked there for over thirty years.*

fizz /fɪz/ *v.* **fizzes** to bubble: *Champagne fizzes when it is poured into a glass.*

fiz·zle /'fɪzəl/ *v.* **-zled, -zling, -zles 1** to fizz **2** *fig.* to fail in a disappointing way, (*syn.*) to peter out: *Her interest in going back to college fizzled.‖The new movie fizzled after it received bad reviews.*

fjord /fyɔrd, fi'ɔrd/ *n.* a narrow body of sea water between tall cliffs: *The fjords in Norway are a famous tourist attraction.*

flab /flæb/ *n.* loose, fatty flesh: *That man has flab around his waistline.*

flab·ber·gast /'flæbərˌgæst/ *v.* to shock into disbelief: *The news that he had won a million dollars flabbergasted him.*

flab·by /'flæbi/ *adj.* **-bier, -biest** having loose, fatty flesh: *He is flabby from eating too much chocolate.*

flac·cid /'flæksɪd, 'flæsɪd/ *adj.* flabby: *He is flaccid from lack of exercise.*

flack /flæk/ *n.v.* a person employed to manage public relations for s.o., a press agent: *John is a <n.> flack* (or) *he <v.> flacks for a local politician. See:* flak.

flag /flæg/ *n.* **1** a piece of fabric, usu. with a design, used as a symbol: *The flags of many countries fly near the United Nations building.* **2 to fly the flag: a.** to display a flag in support of one's country: *On Independence Day, we fly the flag in front of our house.* **b.** *fig.* to indicate one's participation in a group gathering: *We attended the trade show this year just to fly the flag.*
—*v.* **flagged, flagging, flags 1** to slow down, become weak, (*syn.*) to falter: *My interest in poetry began to flag after I studied it for four years.* **2** *phrasal v.* **to flag down:** to make s.t. (usu. a vehicle) stop by waving: *I flagged down a cab to take me to the airport.*

flag·el·late /'flædʒəˌleɪt/ *v.* **-lated, -lating, -lates 1** *frml.* to whip, esp. as religious punishment or for sexual pleasure **2** to move like a whip: *The hair-like parts of some microorganisms flagellate to produce motion. -n.* [U] **flagellation** /ˌflædʒə'leɪʃən/.

flag·ging /'flægɪŋ/ *adj.* becoming less, (*syn.*) faltering: *The bicyclist's energy is flagging as he struggles up a hill.*

flag·on /'flægən/ *n.* **1** a large bottle for wine or other liquids: *People bought wine by the flagon and filled smaller bottles from it.* **2** a serving container with handle and lid: *The host poured wine from a flagon.*

flag·pole /'flægˌpoʊl/ *n.* a tall pole from which flags are hung: *The flagpole in the center of town flies the country's flag every day.*

flag·rant /'fleɪgrənt/ *adj.* openly bad, (*syns.*) blatant, brazen: *A trucker dumped toxic waste in a lake in flagrant violation of the law. -n.* [U] **flagrancy; -adv. flagrantly.**

flag·ship /'flægˌʃɪp/ *n.* **1** (in military) the ship of a group's commander displaying his flag **2** the major unit of a group: *The New York Times newspaper is the flagship of a large publishing company.*

flag·stone /'flægˌstoʊn/ *n.* a flat section of stone used to make paths, patios, or floors: *The flagstones in our patio are gray and black.*

flag·wav·ing /'flægˌweɪvɪŋ/ *n.* [U] **1** the waving of flags **2** *fig.* an excessive display of strong loyalty or patriotism: *The President's speech included a great deal of flagwaving.*

flail /fleɪl/ *n.* a machine used to separate the seed or grain from the rest of the plant
—*v.* **1** to use a flail **2** to whip, *(syn.)* to flog: *A cruel owner flailed the dog for disobedience.* **3** to move the arms or legs in an uncontrolled way: *A skater slipped, and his arms flailed around as he tried to regain his balance.*

flair /flɛr/ *n.* [U] **1** a special talent, *(syn.)* knack: *He has a flair for speaking well.* **2** good taste, style: *She dresses with flair.*

flak /flæk/ *n.* [U] **1** guns fired against aircraft **2** the explosions from such a gun's shells **3** *infrml.* strong criticism: *My boss is always giving me flak about coming to work late.*

flake /fleɪk/ *n.* **1** a small piece of s.t., light in weight with a rough or smooth surface: *Americans love breakfast cereals in the form of flakes.* **2** *slang* a strange, crazy, or unpredictable person: *My math professor is a flake; he always forgets to give us homework. See:* snowflake.
—*v.* **flaked, flaking, flakes** **1** to fall off in flakes: *The paint on the wall is flaking.* **2** *phrasal v. slang* **to flake out:** to be forgetful or behave in an unusual way: *She told me she would help me, but she flaked out and went to the movies instead.*

flak·y /ˈfleɪki/ *adj.* **-ier, -iest** **1** in the form of flakes: *The wall paint is flaky and is peeling off.* **2** *slang* strange, crazy, or unpredictable: *He's a flaky guy.*

flam·bé /flɑmˈbeɪ/ *adj.* referring to main dishes and desserts that are set on fire briefly before serving: *My favorite flambé dish is crepes suzettes.*

flam·boy·ant /flæmˈbɔɪənt/ *adj.* showy, colorful, *(syns.)* dashing, bold: *The rock star acts and dresses in a flamboyant manner. -n.* [U] **flamboyance** *-adv.* **flamboyantly.**

flame /fleɪm/ *n.* **1** a hot, bright light produced by burning: *The flames from the fireplace give off a warm glow.* **2** *fig.* **old flame:** a past boyfriend or girlfriend: *She met an old flame at a party.* **3** **to go down in flames:** to end in a disastrous, abrupt manner: *His new play went down in flames after only a week.* **4** **to go up in flames:** to burn completely: *The fire spread quickly, and the house went up in flames.*
—*v.* **flamed, flaming, flames** **1** to produce a flame: *The campfire flamed brightly when we added wood.* **2** (in computers) to attack s.o. by sending an electronic message on the Internet: *She flamed me on the Internet yesterday.*

USAGE NOTE: To give the impression of shouting at a person you're *flaming,* you can type your message in all capital letters. For example: AND DON'T ASK ME AGAIN!

fla·men·co /fləˈmɛŋkou/ *n.* **-cos** or **-coes** a spirited Spanish dance with foot stamping, handclapping, and castanets: *That dancer performs the flamenco at a local nightclub.*

flame-proof /ˈfleɪmˌpruf/ *adj.* completely resistant to fire: *The high-quality steel used to make that door is flameproof. See:* fireproof.

flame-re·tard·ant /ˈfleɪmriˌtɑrdnt/ *adj.* resistant to fire by not burning quickly: *The materials used in some rugs (clothing, curtains, etc.) are treated with a flame-retardant chemical.*

flame-throw·er /ˈfleɪmˌθrouər/ *n.* a weapon that shoots fire: *Soldiers fired flamethrowers into the enemy camp to force the enemy out.*

flam·ing /ˈfleɪmɪŋ/ *adj.* **1** in flames, burning: *We could see the flaming ruins of the house for hours after the fire was under control.* **2** very bright: *Her flaming red dress caught everyone's attention.*

fla·min·go /fləˈmɪŋgou/ *n.* **-gos** or **-goes** a tall, long-legged, bright pink water bird associated with Florida: *Flamingos are colorful, attractive birds.*

flam·ma·ble /ˈflæməbəl/ *adj.* capable of catching fire: *That company keeps flammable liquids in a special fireproof area. -n.* [U] **flammability** /ˌflæməˈbɪləti/.

flan /flæn, flɑn/ *n.* [U] **1** a baked dessert made with milk, eggs, and sugar **2** a pastry filled with custard, cheese, or fruit: *We had flan for dessert with our coffee.*

flange /flændʒ/ *n.* an extended edge on various construction materials: *The flange on the metal wheel kept it on the track.*

flank /flæŋk/ *n.* **1** the side area of a human's or animal's body between the ribs and hip **2** the outer sides or ends of a military formation: *The enemy went around our right flank.*
—*v.* **1** to be on one or both sides of s.o. or s.t.: *Two police officers flanked the prisoner on either side.* **2** to go around the side of a military formation: *Our soldiers flanked the enemy on their right. -n.* **flanker.**

flan·nel /ˈflænl/ *n.* [U] *adj.* a soft wool or cotton fabric: *He wears gray <adj.> flannel suits.*

flap /flæp/ *v.* **flapped, flapping, flaps** to move up and down, or sideways: *Birds flap their wings.*
—*n.* **1** an up-and-down or side-to-side motion: *The bird took off with a flap of its wings.* **2** a piece of material used as a covering: *The flaps on my jacket pockets keep things from falling out.* **3** *infrml.fig.* a dispute, minor scandal, *(syn.)* controversy: *Every year, there is a flap in Washington over salary increases for government employees.*

flap·jack /ˈflæpˌdʒæk/ *n.* a pancake: *He likes to eat flapjacks for breakfast.*

flap·per /ˈflæpər/ *n.infrml.* in the 1920s, a woman who didn't follow traditional standards of behavior: *In her youth, she was a flap-per and went out dancing every night.*

flare /flɛr/ *n.* a flame-producing chemical device used to light up an area: *The police put flares around the scene of the car accident.*
—*v.* **flared, flaring, flares 1** to burst forth with intense light: *The fire flared when gasoline was poured on it.* **2** *fig.* to show sudden anger or to rebel: *The argument grew heated, and tempers suddenly flared.*

flare-up *n.* **1** a sudden burst of light **2** a rapid, intense build-up such as of light, anger, rebellion, or disease: *I had a flare-up of my back problem yesterday.*

flash /flæʃ/ *n.* **-es 1** a sudden burst of light: *That flash of lightning startled us.* **2** (in photography) a device for adding light: *The flash on my camera needs batteries.* **3** *fig.* a burst of mental activity: *Suddenly, she had a flash of insight.* **4** *fig.* **a flash in the pan:** a success that happens only once: *Her first film won many awards, but it turned out to be only a flash in the pan.* **5** *fig.* **in a flash:** very quickly: *I'll be back in a flash.*
—*v.* **-es 1** to burst forth suddenly, esp. light or fire: *Lightning flashed in the distance.* **2** to display very briefly: *The gambler flashed a roll of $100 bills.* **3** to move rapidly: *The race cars flashed by us.*

flash·back /ˈflæʃˌbæk/ *n.* (in literature and film) a movement in time from the present to the past: *Film directors and novelists use flash-backs to explain earlier events.*

flash·bulb /ˈflæʃˌbʌlb/ *n.* a bulb that gives off a brief, intense light used for photography: *As soon as the president walked into the room, many flashbulbs went off.*

flash card *n.* a small card with writing on both sides, used for memorizing information: *Those flash cards have a question on one side and the answer on the other.*

flash·er /ˈflæʃər/ *n.* **1** a light that goes on and off repeatedly: *Road workers place flashers near holes to warn drivers to avoid them.* **2** *infrml.fig.* a man who briefly displays his sexual parts to strangers: *The police arrested the flasher; he was wearing a raincoat but no other clothes.*

flash·light /ˈflæʃˌlaɪt/ *n.* a hand-held light operated by batteries: *When the lights went out, we used a flashlight to find the exit.*

flash point *n.* **1** the lowest temperature at which a substance produces fire **2** *fig.* the moment at which a situation becomes serious, usu. resulting in violence: *Events reached the flash point in the conflict, and both sides decided to go to war.*

flash·y /ˈflæʃi/ *adj.* **-ier, -iest** showy, (*syn.*) ostentatious: *He wears flashy clothes and drives an expensive sports car.*

flask /flæsk/ *n.* a small container used for a variety of liquids: *Her companion carries a flask of brandy in his pocket.*

flat /flæt/ *adj.* **flatter, flattest 1** level, even: *The farmland near the river is very flat.* **2** lying full length: *He is flat on his back with the flu.* **3** *fig.* uninteresting: *This dinner party has gone flat.* **4** *fig.* (business activity) the same as the previous period: *Sales are flat this month; there has been no increase over last month's sales.* **5** referring to a drink that has lost its bubbles: *The beer is flat.* **6 a flat tire** or **a flat:** a tire that has lost air: *During our trip across the country, we had a flat (or) a flat tire.* **7 as flat as a pancake:** very flat: *The desert in Arizona is as flat as a pancake.*
—*adv.* **1** completely, firmly: *When I asked him for a favor, he turned me down flat.* **2** (of time) exactly: *He ran the race in six minutes flat.* **3 to fall flat:** to fail totally: *The comedian's jokes fell flat; no one laughed.* **4 flat out:** at top speed: *We drove flat out for hours just to arrive in New York on time.* -*adv.* **flatly;** -*n.* [U] **flatness.**

flat·car /ˈflætˌkar/ *n.* a railroad car with a flat bottom, no roof, and usu. no sides: *Cars and trucks are transported by rail on flatcars.*

flat-chest·ed /ˈflætˌtʃɛstɪd/ *adj.* with small breasts: *The sweater is too big for her because she's flat-chested.*

flat-foot·ed /ˈflætˌfʊtɪd/ *adj.* with fallen arches of the feet: *He is flat-footed and must wear special shoes.*

flat·land /ˈflætˌlænd/ *n.* [C;U] level land without hills or valleys: *The farmland in this area is flatland with a few streams.*

flat·ten /ˈflætn/ *v.* to make horizontal: *The cook flattens the ground beef into hamburgers.*

flat·ter /ˈflætər/ *v.* **1** to compliment s.o. usu. in order to win favor: *He flatters his boss by telling her how intelligent she is.* **2** to increase one's feeling of self-importance: *He was flattered when she told him that he looked young for his age.* -*n.* **flatterer.**

flat·ter·y /ˈflætəri/ *n.* [U] praise or compliments that are excessive or insincere: *She was never fooled by his flattery.*

flat·top /ˈflætˌtap/ *n.* something with a flat surface: *The barber cut the marine's hair in a flat-top.*

flat·u·lence /ˈflætʃələns/ *n.* [U] **1** gas sent out from the bowels **2** *fig.* speech filled with unnecessary words and showy language: *The professor was famous for his flatulence.* -*adj.* **flatulent.**

flat·ware /ˈflætˌwɛr/ *n.* [U] tools for eating, such as knives, spoons, and forks, (*syn.*) silverware: *The flatware in that restaurant is rather elegant, but the plates are plastic!*

flaunt /flɔnt/ v. to display in a showy way: *She flaunts her wealth by driving big cars and wearing expensive jewelry.*

fla·vor /'fleɪvər/ n. **1** a specific taste: *That steak has an excellent flavor.* **2** *fig.* a quality, impression: *The furniture and artwork give that room the flavor of Spain.*
—v. to add a specific taste to s.t.: *She flavored the sauce with salt, pepper, and garlic.*

fla·vor·ful /'fleɪvərfəl/ adj. tasty, (syn.) savory: *The sauce on the fish is quite flavorful.*

fla·vor·ing /'fleɪvərɪŋ/ n. any ingredient added to food to give it a specific taste: *The company added vanilla flavoring to its ice cream.*

flaw /flɔ/ n. s.t. that is not perfect, a fault, imperfection: *She noticed that there was a flaw in the diamond.*

flawed /flɔd/ adj. **1** faulty, (syn.) defective: *He presented a flawed argument.* **2** imperfect, (syn.) blemished: *The decoration on those dinner plates is flawed.*

flaw·less /'flɔlɪs/ adj. perfect: *The actor gave a flawless performance.* -adv. **flawlessly.**

flax /flæks/ n. [U] **1** a plant with blue flowers, grown for its stem, from which linen is made **2** the fibers of this plant, used for making linen cloth

flax·en /'flæksən/ adj. **1** woven from the flax plant **2** light yellow, blond: *The poet spoke of women with flaxen hair.*

flay /fleɪ/ v. **1** to pull the skin off: *The company flays lambs to make lambskin gloves.* **2** to criticize strongly: *The critics flayed Mr. Stark's writing.*

flea /fli/ n. a very small jumping insect that feeds on blood: *His dog has fleas.*

flea·bag hotel /'fli,bæg/ n. a cheap hotel, (syn.) flophouse: *He is a poor man who lives in a fleabag hotel.*

flea market n. an informal outdoor marketplace where goods are sold at low prices: *The flea market in our area sells used clothing and furniture.*

fleck /flɛk/ n. a very small spot or piece of s.t.: *I wiped flecks of dust off the mirror.*
—v. to mark with very small spots or pieces of s.t.: *A carpenter flecked the coffee table with paint to give it an antique look.*

fledg·ling /'flɛdʒlɪŋ/ n. **1** a young bird ready to fly **2** *fig.* a beginner, (syn.) neophyte: *He just joined the company and is the fledgling of our sales staff.*

flee /fli/ v. **fled** /flɛd/, **fleeing, flees** to run away, escape: *After criticizing certain government leaders, the writer had to flee the country or go to prison.*

fleece /flis/ n. [U] the coat of wool of an animal, such as a sheep: *The coat's lining was made of fleece.*

—v. **fleeced, fleecing, fleeces** **1** to cut the woolly coat from an animal **2** *fig.* to rob or cheat s.o., (syn.) to swindle: *A clever thief fleeced an old man out of his savings.*

fleet /flit/ n. **1** all the ships in a navy or a group of ships: *Honolulu is a major port for the U.S. naval fleet.* **2** a number of airplanes, trucks, or cars grouped together: *American Airlines has a large fleet of planes.*
—adj.frml. fast, quick: *The runner is fleet of foot.*

fleet·ing /'flitɪŋ/ adj. passing quickly: *I saw a shooting star for a fleeting moment.* -adv. **fleetingly.**

flesh /flɛʃ/ n. [U] **1** the skin and the soft substance beneath it: *The doctor cut into the flesh to remove the bullet.* **2** the body as opposed to the mind or spirit: *He enjoys pleasures of the flesh, such as food and sex.* **3** the soft inside of a fruit or vegetable: *He bit into the sweet flesh of the ripe mango.* **4 flesh and blood: a.** the human body: *Those soldiers are made of flesh and blood; be careful with their lives.* **b.** one's closest relatives (parents, brothers, sisters, children): *I must help those children, for they are my own flesh and blood.* **5 in the flesh:** the actual person, (syn.) in person: *She was very excited about finally seeing the famous movie actor in the flesh.* **6** *fig.* **to press the flesh:** to meet voters and shake their hands: *The politician felt the need to press the flesh, so he spent Saturday meeting many people.*
—v. **to flesh out:** to add details, fill out: *She wrote a brief report and then fleshed it out later with details.*

flesh·y /'flɛʃi/ adj. **-ier, -iest** **1** related to flesh: *A bullet entered the fleshy part of his leg.* **2** having a lot of flesh, fat: *He is a tall, fleshy man who eats a lot and never exercises.*

flew /flu/ v. past tense of fly

flex /flɛks/ v. **flexes** **1** to stretch or bend one's limbs: *She flexed her legs and yawned as she woke up.* **2 to flex one's muscles: a.** to show one's muscles as a show of strength: *He flexed his upper arm muscles to show how strong he is.* **b.** *fig.* To perform an act to show one's power or authority: *The manager flexed her muscles when she eliminated her employees' coffee break.*

flexible /'flɛksəbəl/ adj. **1** capable of bending easily: *Rubber and plastic are flexible materials.* **2** *fig.* able to change easily in response to the situation, (syns.) cooperative, accommodating: *She is flexible and always open to new ideas.* -n. [U] **flexibility** /,flɛksə'bɪləti/.

flex·time /'flɛks,taɪm/ n. [U] a system in which employees can choose their work schedule, as long as they work the required number of hours: *I was very pleased when our company went on flextime; now I work 6:00* *a.m. to 2:00 p.m. so that I can be with my children after school.*

flib·ber·ti·gib·bet /'flɪbərti‚dʒɪbɪt/ *n.infrml.* a silly, talkative person: *Everyone thought of her as a flibbertigibbet; no one took her ideas seriously.*

flick /flɪk/ *n.* **1** a quick movement of a finger or wrist: *He removed the piece of dust from the chair with a flick of his finger.* **2** *infrml.* a movie: *Did you catch that 1930s flick on TV last night?* **3 to go to the flicks:** to see a movie: *I went to the flicks last weekend.*
—*v.* to leaf through s.t.: *She flicked through a photo album of her vacation.*

flick·er /'flɪkər/ *n.* an unsteady movement of a light: *The candle burned with a flicker in the wind.*
—*v.* to shine unsteadily, (*syn.*) to glimmer: *The flames of the campfire flickered in the night.*

fli·er or **flyer** /'flaɪər/ *n.* **1** [C;U] a person who travels on an airplane: *Frequent fliers receive free flights from airlines.* **2** a pilot: *He is a flier in the Air Force.* **3** a small printed notice that gives information or advertises s.t.

flight /flaɪt/ *n.* **1** [C;U] the act of traveling through the air: *The flight of birds seems very elegant.* **2** [C] a trip by air: *Our flight from Chicago to Seattle was pleasant.* **3** [C;U] escape, (*syn.*) exodus: *The television news program showed the flight of families from the war.* **4** [C] a set of stairs, (*syn.*) a staircase: *The women's dress department is up one flight.* **5 in flight: a.** to run away, esp. to escape punishment: *The escaped prisoner is in flight from the law.* **b.** to be in the air: *We arrived late at the airport; our plane was already in flight.* **6 to take flight: a.** to fly: *Birds take flight in the morning to look for food.* **b.** *fig.* to go far beyond the ordinary: *Poets can make one's spirit (imagination, thoughts, etc.) take flight.*

flight attendant *n.* a person who serves passengers on a plane: *The flight attendants served dinner on our flight from Los Angeles to Dallas. See:* stewardess.

flight-test *v.* to test an airplane's performance in the air: *The pilot flight-tested a new airplane at high speed.*

flight·y /'flaɪti/ *adj.* **-ier, -iest** unsteady (usu. of behavior), (*syns.*) unpredictable, impulsive: *My cousin is flighty; she has a different job every month.*

flim·flam /'flɪm‚flæm/ *v.infrml.* **-flammed, -flamming, -flams** to trick, deceive, (*syns.*) to swindle, bamboozle: *The politician flimflammed the public into voting for him by promising not to raise taxes, but he did raise them once in office.*
—*n.infrml.* trickery, nonsense: *What he says is just flimflam.*

flim·sy /'flɪmzi/ *adj.* **-sier, -siest 1** poorly made, thin: *The jacket is made of flimsy cloth.* **2** not strong, (*syns.*) unstable, rickety: *That house was constructed with flimsy materials.* **3** *fig.* weak, (*syn.*) feeble: *Erika gave a flimsy excuse for being late.* -*n.* [U] **flimsiness.**

flinch /flɪntʃ/ *v.* **flinches** to move back suddenly without thinking, such as from a threat of being hit: *The boy flinched when the ball flew by his face.*
—*n.* a sudden backward movement: *He reacted with a flinch.*

fling /flɪŋ/ *v.* **flung,** /flʌŋ/ **flinging, flings** to throw, toss forcefully: *When he is angry, he flings his jacket off.*
—*n.* **1** a forceful throw: *He gave the ball a fling toward his friend.* **2** *infrml.* **to have a fling: a.** a brief, intense time of enjoyment: *She had a one-week fling in New York going to nightclubs and discos every night before returning to Iowa.* **b.** a brief romantic relationship: *She was angry with her husband after discovering he had had a fling with her best friend.*

flint /flɪnt/ *n.* [U] a hard gray stone, used to make fire -*adj.* **flinty.**

flint·lock /'flɪnt‚lɑk/ *n.* an old-fashioned rifle that uses flint to light the gunpowder: *Flintlocks were used long ago by soldiers in the American Revolutionary War.*

flip /flɪp/ *v.* **flipped, flipping, flips 1** to turn end over end: *He flipped a coin into the air.* **2** to throw lightly and quickly: *He flipped the ball to me.* **3** to turn over suddenly: *The truck flipped over on its side on the icy road.* **4** *infrml.fig.* to explode in anger, lose self-control: *He flipped when the teacher told him that he had failed the exam.* **5** *infrml.fig.* to react with intense pleasure or delight: *She flipped when she learned that she had won the prize.* **6 to flip a coin:** to decide a matter by each person choosing one side of a coin, tossing the coin in the air, and seeing how it lands: *We flipped a coin to decide who would pay for dinner.* **7 to flip one's wig:** to become very angry: *If you wreck your mother's car she'll flip her wig.* **8 to flip out: a.** to become insane **b.** to be astounded: *He flipped out when he won the lottery* **9** *phrasal v. insep.* **to flip through s.t.:** to turn the pages quickly: *She flipped through the magazine.*
—*n.* a quick throw: *He gave the ball a flip.*
—*adj.infrml.* **to be flip:** to be disrespectful: *I tried to talk to her, but she was flip with me.*

flip chart *n.* a display used by turning one large page over the

flip chart

other: *The president used a flip chart with diagrams to illustrate her ideas.*

flip-flop /ˈflɪpˌflɑp/ v. **-flopped, -flopping, -flops** to announce one decision now, but a different one later: *The politician flip-flopped on taxation: first she was for the new tax, then against it.*

—n. **1** an act of flip-flopping: *She did a flip-flop on the tax issue.* **2** an open summer shoe usu. made of rubber: *I wore my flip-flops to the beach so that I could walk in the water.*

flip-flops

flip·pant /ˈflɪpənt/ adj. not showing proper respect, (syn.) impertinent: *He made flippant remarks when I tried to discuss the problem.* -n. [U] **flippancy;** -adv. **flippantly.**

flip·per /ˈflɪpər/ n. **1** a wide flat limb on certain sea animals, used for swimming: *Dolphins have front flippers.* **2** a large flat rubber attachment for the foot to help in swimming: *The scuba diver put on his flippers before jumping in the sea.*

flip side n.infrml. the other or opposite side of s.t.: *The flip side of accepting this new job is I have to move away from my family.*

flirt /flɜrt/ v. **1** to smile and talk with s.o. in a way that invites romantic interest: *He flirts with every woman he meets.* **2** to treat s.t. serious in a light manner: *He flirted with disaster when he bet a lot of money at the horseraces.*

—n. a person who flirts: *Her brother is still a real flirt even though he's married.*

flir·ta·tion /flərˈteɪʃən/ n. [C;U] **1** an act of flirting **2** a brief, usu. unimportant love affair: *Their love affair was just a harmless flirtation.*

flir·ta·tious /flərˈteɪʃəs/ adj. related to behavior that invites romantic interest: *She is flirtatious at parties.* -adv. **flirtatiously.**

flirt·y /ˈflɜrti/ adj. **-ier, -iest** var. of flirtatious.

flit /flɪt/ v. **flitted, flitting, flits** to move quickly, (syn.) to dart: *Some birds flit from flower to flower.*

float /floʊt/ v. **1** to rest or move on the top of water or other liquid: *Logs floated downstream on the river.* **2** to rest or move in the air: *A balloon floats by us.* **3** fig. to move lightly and gracefully: *The dancer floats through the air.* **4 to float s.o. a loan:** to lend s.o. money: *When I had no money last week, my friend floated me a loan of $100.*

—n. **1** an object resting on the surface of the water that holds a fishline or net: *The fisherman left early in the morning to set up his floats.* **2** a flat, unmovable structure in a lake or pond: *People sun themselves on a float near the beach.* **3** a colorful display mounted on wheels in a parade: *Clowns wave from a float in the Easter parade.* **4** (in banking) the period of time between when a check is issued and when it is credited: *The float for checks within the city is three days.*

float·ing /ˈfloʊtɪŋ/ adj. **1** capable of riding on top of water, (syn.) buoyant: *He is the floating accountant for three offices.* **2** moving from place to place: *We will buy a floating raft to use at the beach this summer.*

flock /flɑk/ n. **1** a group of certain animals, such as sheep, goats, chickens, and geese: *A flock of sheep came down from the mountain.* **2** fig. a group of many people: *A flock of people crowded into the hall.*

—v. to gather or crowd together, (syn.) to congregate: *Thousands of people flocked to see the famous religious leader.*

flog /flɑg, flɔg/ v. **flogged, flogging, flogs 1** to hit with a whip or stick, usu. as punishment: *A guard flogged a prisoner.* **2** infrml.fig. to sell s.t. aggressively: *I hate that store because the salespeople flog their products as soon as I walk in the door.* -n. [C;U] **flogging.**

flood /flʌd/ v. **1** to cover dry land with water, to overflow: *The river ran over its banks and flooded the town.* **2** fig. to provide too much of s.t.: *Several large manufacturers flooded the market with cheap goods.*

—n. **1** covering of dry land with water, an overflow: *The flood caused great damage.* **2** fig. a large amount: *The mayor received a flood of complaints from voters.*

flood·gate /ˈflʌdˌgeɪt/ n. a barrier, like a dam, allowing the level of water behind it to be raised or lowered: *Workers opened the floodgates so that the spring rains could pass through.*

flood·light /ˈflʌdˌlaɪt/ n.v. **-lit** /-ˌlɪt/ or **-lighted, -lighting, -lights** a type of powerful light used at night to light the outside of buildings or ground areas for security purposes: *We use <n.> floodlights when we play baseball at night.* -adj. **floodlit.**

floor /flɔr/ n. **1** the bottom surface area inside a building: *The floor in her apartment is made of wood.* **2** a level of a building, (syn.) story: *That skyscraper has 50 floors.* **3** a bottom limit placed on a price: *The government placed a floor on the price of milk.* **4** fig. **to have the floor:** to have the opportunity to speak at a public meeting: *Right now Susan has the floor; please don't interrupt her.*

—v.infrml.fig. to shock s.o. so that he or she cannot speak: *He was floored by all the good news.*

floor·ing /ˈflɔrɪŋ/ n. [U] **1** the bottom surface of a room or other area of a building: *The wood flooring needs to be replaced.* **2** a covering on floors: *The flooring is made of cement covered with industrial carpeting.*

floor plan *n.* an architectural drawing showing the size and location of walls, doors, and windows of a building or a specific space within a building: *We took a floor plan of our new apartment with us when we went to buy furniture.*

floor sam·ple *n.* a piece of furniture or other item put on display for customers: *The furniture store encourages you to sit on the floor samples to see how comfortable they are.*

floor show *n.* nightclub entertainment, such as singers, dancers, and comedians: *We had dinner and stayed for the floor show.*

floo·zy /'fluzi/ *n.infrml.* **-zies** a woman with loose morals, esp. one who is a prostitute: *She dresses like a floozy.*

flop /flɑp/ *v.* **flopped, flopping, flops** **1** to move awkwardly, (*syn.*) to thrash about: *A fish flopped about on the beach.* **2** to drop heavily, (*syn.*) to collapse: *He was so tired that he flopped on the sofa and fell asleep.* **3** *fig.* to fail: *The new play flopped and was closed promptly.*
—*n.fig.* a failure: *The play was a flop.*

flop·house /'flɑp,haʊs/ *n.infrml.* **-houses** /-,haʊzɪz/ a cheap hotel: *Arriving in town with very little money, he was forced to stay in a flophouse.*

flop·py /'flɑpi/ *adj.* **-pier, -piest** **1** loose and usu. oversized: *She wears floppy hats, and her dog has big, floppy ears.* **2** easily bent, very flexible: *We use floppy disks in our computer.*
—*n.* **-pies** a computer diskette. *See:* floppy disk.

floppy disk or **diskette** *n.* a square piece of plastic used to store computer information: *His computer has two openings for 3.5-inch floppy diskettes.*

flo·ra /'flɔrə/ *n.frml.* [C;U] **-ras** or **-rae** /-ri, -raɪ/ the plants in a specific place or time period: *The flora in this part of the desert consists mainly of cactus plants. See:* fauna.

flo·ral /'flɔrəl/ *adj.* related to flowers: *The restaurant has two beautiful floral arrangements in the dining room.*

flor·id /'flɔrɪd, 'flar-/ *adj.* **1** having a reddish color: *He has a florid complexion from working outdoors in the cold.* **2** *fig.* very or too detailed, (*syn.*) flowery: *His novel is filled with florid descriptions of the Amazon rain forest.*
—*adv.* **floridly.**

flo·rist /'flɔrɪst, 'flar-/ *n.* a person who owns or runs a flower shop: *The florist sent flowers for Mother's Day.*

floss /flɔs, flas/ *n.* [U] soft thread used to clean teeth: *I bought some dental floss at the drugstore.*
—*v.* **flosses** to use dental floss: *He flosses twice daily.*

flo·ta·tion /floʊ'teɪʃən/ *n.* [U] the condition of floating

flo·til·la /floʊ'tɪlə/ *n.* a group of ships: *A flotilla of war ships moved slowly up the coast of India.*

flot·sam /'flatsəm/ *n.* [U] the floating remains of a sunken ship and its cargo: *We found an old boot among the flotsam. See:* jetsam.

flounce /flaʊns/ *v.* **flounced, flouncing, flounces** to walk or dance with showy movements: *She flounced down the sidewalk in a tight dress.*

floun·der /'flaʊndər/ *v.* **1** to move about awkwardly and usu. with difficulty: *He cannot swim, so he floundered even in the shallow water.* **2** to be unsure about what to say or do: *When we asked him about his past, he floundered for a moment and then answered.*
—*n.* [C;U] a common type of flatfish: *In New England many people eat flounder.*

flour /'flaʊər/ *n.* [U] finely ground grain: *We use wheat flour to bake bread.*

flour·ish /'flɜrɪʃ, 'flʌrɪʃ/ *n.* **-ishes** a showy movement: *The conductor ended the symphony with a great flourish of her baton.*
—*v.* **-ishes** **1** to become rich, grow strong: *People have flourished in America for centuries.||Many plants flourish in warm humid climates.* **2** to wave s.t. in a showy way: *The soldier flourished his sword.*

flout /flaʊt/ *v.* to openly oppose, (*syns.*) to defy, scoff at: *She flouted nineteenth century standards of behavior by living with a man and not marrying him.*

flow /floʊ/ *v.* to move smoothly, (*syn.*) to stream: *The river flows gently to the sea.*
—*n.* [U] a steady movement: *The flow of the water from the pipe is slow.*

flow chart *n.* a drawing showing steps in a process: *We drew a flow chart of our banking procedures.*

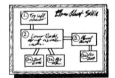

flow chart

flow·er /'flaʊər/ *n.* **1** the colorful part of a plant or the plant itself: *We planted flowers—roses and tulips—in the garden.* **2** *frml.* **in the flower of youth:** young and attractive: *The photograph, taken on their wedding day, showed them in the flower of youth.*
—*v.* **1** to produce flowers, (*syn.*) to blossom: *The plant flowered overnight.* **2** to fully develop, to flourish: *At the Academy of Art my son flowered as a painter.*

flow·er·y /'flaʊəri, 'flaʊri/ *adj.* **1** having flowers: *She wears flowery dresses.* **2** showy, (*syn.*) elaborate: *After receiving the award, she gave a flowery acceptance speech.*

flown /floʊn/ *past part.* of fly

flu /flu/ *n.* [U] *short for* influenza: *He is sick with the flu.*

flub /flʌb/ *v.* **flubbed, flubbing, flubs** to make a mistake: *The football player flubbed the ball as it was passed to him; he dropped it.*

fluc·tu·ate /'flʌktʃu,eɪt/ *v.* **-ted, -ting, -tes** to change, move up and down: *During this past week, temperatures have fluctuated 50 degrees. -n.* [C;U] **fluctuation** /,flʌktʃu'eɪʃən/.

flue /flu/ *n.* the opening in a chimney: *Smoke from the fireplace goes up the flue.*

flu·en·cy /'fluənsi/ *n.* [U] the ability to easily speak and write a language: *She improved her fluency in both French and Mandarin by taking extra classes.*

flu·ent /'fluənt/ *adj.* able to easily speak or write a language: *She speaks fluent Japanese. -adv.* **fluently.**

fluff /flʌf/ *n.* [U] **1** a soft loose particle on the surface of fabric **2** the soft airiness of s.t., esp. pillows: *The fluff in the pillow makes it very comfortable.*
—*v.* **1** to pat so as to make s.t. soft and full of air: *She fluffed the pillows on the sofa.* **2** to make a mistake, esp. to forget memorized lines, (*syn.*) to botch: *The actor became nervous and fluffed his lines.*

fluff·y /'flʌfi/ *adj.* **-ier, -iest** soft and airy: *The pillows are fluffy.||The new snow is fluffy.*

flu·id /'fluɪd/ *n.* [C;U] a liquid: *The mechanic put fluid in the brake system.*
—*adj.* smooth, graceful: *The dancer's fluid movements were a pleasure to watch. -n.* [U] **fluidity** /flu'ɪdəti/.

fluke /fluk/ *n.* **1** [C] a lucky surprise: *That football player never scores, but today he did; what a fluke!* **2** [C;U] a commonly eaten type of flatfish, such as flounder *-adj.* **fluky.**

flum·mox /'flʌməks/ *v.* **-moxes** to confuse, (*syn.*) to baffle: *The test was so difficult that she was flummoxed by it.*

flung /flʌŋ/ *v. past tense and past part. of* fling

flunk /flʌŋk/ *v.* **1** to not pass, to fail: *He flunked a test in history.* **2** *phrasal v.* **to flunk out:** to be dismissed from school for poor performance: *He flunked out of college in his first year.*

flun·ky /'flʌŋki/ *n.* **-kies** a person who performs tasks for another person, (*syns.*) factotum, gofer: *The politician arrived at the meeting with several flunkies.*

fluo·res·cent /flɔ'rɛsənt, flu-/ *adj.* bright and glowing: *There is a fluorescent pink sign in the window that reads "RESTAURANT." -n.* [U] **fluorescence.**

fluo·ride /'flɔr,aɪd, 'flur-/ *n.* [U] a combination of fluorine and another chemical element: *Manufacturers add fluoride to toothpaste to reduce cavities.*

fluo·ro·car·bon /,flɔrou'karbən, ,flur-/ *n.* a combination of chemicals containing carbon and fluorine: *Fluorocarbons are widely used in spray cans and in the making of plastics.*

USAGE NOTE: *Fluorocarbons* are bad for the earth's atmosphere. Many products in spray containers, such as insecticides, deodorants, and hairsprays, are now made without them.

flur·ry /'flɜri, 'flʌri/ *n.* **-ries 1** a rush of activity: *A flurry of buying took place in the stock market today.* **2** a strong rush of wind **3** a light snowfall: *A snow flurry left a thin layer of snow on the ground.*
—*v.* **-ried, -rying, -ries** to briefly intensify: *The wind flurried and then died down.*

flush /flʌʃ/ *v.* **flushes 1** to wash with water, (*syn.*) to rinse away: *A doctor will flush the man's injured eye.||A child flushed the toilet.* **2** to become red in the face, (*syn.*) to blush: *His face flushed after working in the heat.*
—*n.* **flushes 1** an act of washing with a rush of water: *John gave the toilet a flush.* **2** reddening of the face, a blush: *After she has been dancing, her face has a light flush.* **3** (in poker) a hand of cards all of the same suit: *One player has a flush of five hearts.*
—*adj.* **1** fitting tightly against s.t.: *The bookcases are flush with the wall.* **2** proud and excited: *He won the championship and is flush with success.*

flus·ter /'flʌstər/ *v.* to upset s.o. so that he or she behaves awkwardly, (*syn.*) to unnerve: *The teacher's question flustered the little boy.*

flute /flut/ *n.* a long, tube-shaped musical instrument made of metal with holes along the side

flut·ist /'flutɪst/ *n.* a person who plays the flute: *He's a flutist with the symphony orchestra.*

flut·ter /'flʌtər/ *v.* **1** to wave very quickly and lightly: *The flag fluttered in the wind.* **2** to shake: *Her heart fluttered with excitement.* **3** to move wings up and down rapidly: *You could hear birds' wings flutter in the tree.*
—*n.* rapid movement: *I could also hear the flutter (or) the fluttering in that tree. -adj.* **fluttery.**

flux /flʌks/ *n.* [U] **1** a flow **2 to be in flux** or **to be in a state of flux:** to be always changing: *Because our son is sick, our vacation plans are in flux.*

fly /flaɪ/ *v.* **flew** /flu/, **flown** /floun/, **flying, flies 1** to move through the air: *Birds fly north in the spring.* **2** to guide an aircraft: *He flies planes for Swissair.* **3** *fig.* to move quickly, hurry: *He was late and flew out the door to his next appointment.* **4** *phrasal v. insep.* **to fly at s.o.:** to attack physically or verbally: *She didn't like what he said and flew at him in anger.*

F

5 to fly blind: a. *fig.* to fly (an aircraft) without being able to see where one is going: *The pilot was flying blind in the fog.* **b.** *fig.* to act without proper information: *With no one to guide her, she was flying blind when she opened her business.* **6** *fig.* **to fly by the seat of one's pants:** to act by guessing rather than by specific rules or behavior: *He flies by the seat of his pants when he makes decisions.* **7 to fly in the face of:** to be in direct opposition to, (*syns.*) to contradict, defy: *Her lifestyle is odd and flies in the face of socially acceptable behavior.* **8** *fig.* **to fly into a rage** or **off the handle:** to explode in anger: *When he doesn't get what he wants, he flies into a rage* (or) *off the handle.* **9** *fig.* **to fly the coop:** to leave hurriedly, escape: *When the police arrived at the scene, the criminal had already flown the coop.*

—*n.pl.* **flies 1** a small, usu. two-winged insect: *A fly landed on the table.* **2** an opening in pants held together by a zipper or buttons: *He zipped up the fly on his jeans.* **3** *fig.* **a fly in the ointment:** a single negative factor that destroys a good situation: *Everything was agreed on; then his refusal to cooperate became a fly in the ointment.* **4** *fig.* **to be a fly on the wall:** to be an unseen observer: *When the managers are deciding who will get a raise, I would like to be a fly on the wall at their meeting.* **5** *fig.* **to be on the fly:** to be in a hurry: *I'm on the fly and can't talk to you now.*

fly·by /'flaɪ,baɪ/ *n.* **-bys** the path of an aircraft or spacecraft past a specific location: *The Voyager spacecraft did a flyby of Mars to take pictures of its surface.*

fly-by-night *adj.* a person or situation of uncertain honesty: *His business is a fly-by-night operation.*

fly·er /'flaɪər/ *n.var. of* flier

fly·ing /'flaɪɪŋ/ *n.* [U] guiding an aircraft or being a passenger on one: *He likes flying as a hobby.*||*She has a fear of flying and prefers to take trains.*
—*adj.* **1** moving through the air: *She took a flying jump and landed on top of the wall.* **2** *fig.* **with flying colors:** very successfully: *She passed her exams with flying colors.*

fly·ing sau·cer *n.* a spacecraft from another world: *People frequently report seeing flying saucers.*

flying start *n.* an excellent beginning: *She made excellent grades at college her first semester and is off to a flying start.*

fly·swat·ter /'flaɪ,swɑtər/ *n.* a device with a long handle attached to a flat piece of flexible material, used for killing flies

FM /,ɛf'ɛm/ *n. short for* frequency modulation: *My FM radio plays wonderful music.*

foal /foʊl/ *n.* a newborn horse

—*v.* to give birth to a foal: *The mare foaled in the springtime.*

foam /foʊm/ *n.* a liquid substance full of air bubbles acting as a covering: *Ocean waves are covered with white foam.*
—*v.* to form into a foam: *Shaving cream foams when it comes out of the can.*

foam rub·ber *n.* [U] rubber filled with small pockets of air: *There is foam rubber inside the chair to make it comfortable.*

foam·y /'foʊmi/ *adj.* **-ier, -iest** having a bubbly covering, (*syn.*) frothy: *That beer is foamy.*

fo·cal /'foʊkəl/ *adj.* related to focus: *The focal length is 6 1/2 feet between your face and the camera lens.*

focal point *n.* **1** a point at which an object is in focus in a lens system **2** s.t. on which attention is focused: *Democracy in that country is the focal point of political discussion.*

fo·cus /'foʊkəs/ *n.* **-cuses** or **-ci** /-,saɪ, -,kaɪ/ **1** an adjustment (of the eye, camera lens, microscope, etc.) to a clear picture: *I adjusted the focus of the camera to 6 feet.* **2** an object of attention: *The focus of the news report was the state of the economy.*
—*v.* **-cuses 1** to adjust in order to get a clear picture: *A scientist focused her microscope on the bacterium.* **2** to center one's attention on: *The Senator's speech focused on health care reform.* **3 to be in** or **out of focus:** to have a clear or unclear picture: *We couldn't see their faces because the photograph was out of focus.*

fod·der /'fɑdər/ *n.* [U] food for farm animals: *The farmer grows corn as fodder for his cattle.*

foe /foʊ/ *n.* s.o. who is against you, (*syns.*) enemy, opponent: *The conservative party is a foe of higher taxes.*

fog /fɔg, fɑg/ *n.* [U] **1** a heavy gray vapor near the ground that makes it difficult to see: *The heavy morning fog made driving difficult.* **2** *fig.* **to be in a fog:** to be unable to think clearly: *She is so tired from studying that she is in a fog.*
—*v.* **fogged, fogging, fogs 1** to cover or become covered with a gray vapor: *The roads are fogged tonight; it will be difficult to drive.*||*The front window is fogged up, so the driver can't see well.* **2** *fig.* to cause confusion: *Heavy drink fogged his mind.* **3 to be fogged in:** to be unable to travel because of fog: *The airport in Chicago is fogged in, so no flights are leaving.*

fog·bound /'fɔg,baʊnd, 'fɑg-/ *adj.* prevented from traveling because of fog: *The plane is fogbound at the airport; we will leave tomorrow.*

fog·gy /'fɔgi, 'fɑ-/ *adj.* **-gier, -giest 1** covered with fog, full of fog: *The weather is foggy tonight.* **2** *fig.* unclear, incomplete (one's memory, understanding, etc.): *His memory of the accident is foggy.* **3 to not have the foggi-**

est (idea): to have no understanding, information, etc. about s.t.: *I don't have the foggiest idea what you are trying to say.*

fog·horn /ˈfɔgˌhɔrn, ˈfɑg-/ *n.* a powerful air horn used to warn ships away from land or dangerous waters during foggy weather: *The foghorn on Long Island can be heard from many miles away.*

fo·gy or **fogey** /ˈfoʊgi/ *n.* **-gies** or **-geys** a person with old-fashioned ideas who won't change: *He acts like an old fogy; he doesn't use his electric heat because he still thinks a house should be heated by a fireplace.*

USAGE NOTE: "Fogy" usually appears with the word "old": "old fogy."

foi·ble /ˈfɔɪbəl/ *n.* a minor weak point in a person's character, *(syn.)* shortcoming: *One of her foibles is being disorganized, but she's very intelligent.*

foil /fɔɪl/ *v.* to prevent the success of s.t. or s.o.: *Her plan to steal money from the company was foiled by a co-worker.*
—*n.* **1** [U] a very thin sheet of metal used to wrap or line things: *The cook wrapped the chicken in foil.* **2** [C] a thin sword with a softened point to prevent injury **3** *pl.* **foils** fighting with these swords for sport, *(syn.)* fencing: *We practice foils each day in the gym.* **4** [C] a person or an object used to show contrast: *The princess kept an ugly servant woman as a foil to emphasize her own beauty.*

foist /fɔɪst/ *v.* to force s.t. on s.o.: *My brother and sister-in-law went away for the weekend and foisted their children on me.*

fold /foʊld/ *v.* **1** to turn one part of s.t. over another part: *I folded a piece of paper in half.* **2** to push movable parts of s.t. together: *We folded the chairs together and set them against the wall.* **3** to bend inward until against the body: *The man folded his arms on his chest.* **4** *infrml.fig.* to quit, stop completely: *She played tennis so badly yesterday that she folded and went home.* **5** *infrml.* (of a business) to fail: *Sorry. We can't eat at that restaurant; it folded last year.*
—*n.* **1** one part of s.t. folded over another part: *The folds in that napkin give it an elegant shape.* **2** a group of sheep: *The shepherd watches over his fold.* **3** *fig.* the members of a church: *A pastor greets his fold in church.* **4** **to return to the fold:** to return to one's earlier family, church, friends, home, beliefs, etc.: *After serving as a Republican mayor for many years, he decided to return to the fold and become a Democrat again.*

fold·er /ˈfoʊldər/ *n.* a container for documents, made of a folded piece of heavy paper: *The folder contained information on the company's investments.*

fo·li·age /ˈfoʊliɪdʒ/ *n.* [U] leaves of plants and trees: *The foliage in the jungle is very thick.*

fo·li·o /ˈfoʊliˌoʊ/ *n.* **1** a sheet of large paper folded in two: *Expensive books are often published in folios.* **2** a page number: *The folios in that book are on the bottom center of each page.*

folk /foʊk/ *n.* **folks** or **folk 1** *used with pl. v.* ordinary people: *The common folk are mostly farmers in this part of the country.* **2** *used with pl. v.* a certain group of people: *His family are country folk; hers are city folk.* **3** *pl.infrml.* **folks** parents: *Her folks live in New England.* **4** *pl.infrml.* **folks** used when speaking directly to friends, guests: *You folks come in and sit down and make yourselves comfortable.*

folk dance *n.* a traditional dance of a people, country, or region: *The jig is a folk dance typical of Ireland.*

folk·lore /ˈfoʊkˌlɔr/ *n.* [U] the traditional customs, beliefs, stories, etc. of a people, country, or region: *People are fascinated by Native American folklore.* -*adj.* **folkloric** /ˈfoʊkˌlɔrɪk/ -*n.* [C] **folklorist.**

folk music *n.* [U] the traditional music of a people, country, or region, passed down through generations: *Folk music became popular again in the 1950s.*

USAGE NOTE: Singers of American *folk music* are usu. accompanied by a guitar. Joan Baez and the group Peter, Paul, and Mary are well-known folk musicians.

folks /foʊks/ *n.pl.* See: folk.

folk singer *n.* a person who sings folk songs: *The favorite instrument of the folk singer is the guitar.*
—*n.* **folk song.**

folk·sy /ˈfoʊksi/ *adj.* **-sier, -siest** friendly, informal: *That restaurant has a folksy atmosphere; the people are warm and friendly.*

folk·tale /ˈfoʊkˌteɪl/ *n.* a well-known story, often by an unknown author, passed down through earlier generations: *Folktales make good bedtime stories for children.*

fol·li·cle /ˈfɑlɪkəl/ *n.* a very small hole from which a hair grows: *There are thousands of hair follicles on top of your head.*

fol·low /ˈfɑloʊ/ *v.* **1** to go after s.o. or s.t., to chase, pursue: *A dog followed its owner down the street.* **2** to go along a path, road, trail, etc.: *We followed the dirt road until we reached the lake.* **3** to happen after another event: *Rain followed the dark clouds and lightning.* **4** to replace (or come after) s.o. or s.t.: *A younger professor followed the department chairperson in that position.* **5** *fig.* to understand, *(syn.)* to comprehend: *I follow what you are saying.* **6** to obey, cooperate with: *Most members of the political party followed the orders*

F

of their leader. **7** to pay attention to: *She follows the news closely.* **8 as follows:** to introduce a particular order of actions or list of items: *Her qualifications are as follows: an excellent education, previous experience in the field, an excellent performance record.* **9 so it follows that:** it is logical that, (*syns.*) hence, therefore: *The company has no cash, so it follows that it must borrow money or go out of business.* **10** *fig.* **to follow in s.o.'s footsteps or tracks:** to do the same as the person before you: *She followed in her mother's footsteps and became a musician.* **11 to follow one's intuition:** to act on feeling, rather than according to facts and reason: *He wasn't sure what to do, so he decided to follow his intuition.* **12 to follow one's nose:** to go in the direction in which you are pointed: *The bookstore is located straight ahead, so just follow your nose.* **13 to follow suit:** to do the same as another person: *He asked for a raise, and soon other employees followed suit.* **14 to follow the crowd:** to do the same as everyone else: *She has an unusual style of dressing; she doesn't follow the crowd.* **15** *phrasal v. sep.* **to follow s.t. through: a.** (as in golf, tennis, and baseball) to continue an arm movement after a ball is hit: *She has a good golf swing; she follows through nicely.* **b.** *fig.* to complete a task once it is begun: *He always follows through on projects he begins.||He follows them through.* **16** *phrasal v. sep.* **to follow s.t. up:** to take additional steps to further a previous action: *You start with sales visits, and then you should follow up with telephone calls.||You should follow them up.*

fol·low·er /'faləʊər/ *n.* person who follows a leader, (*syn.*) a supporter: *The religious leader and his followers entered the temple.*

fol·low·ing /'faləʊɪŋ/ *adj.* next, (*syn.*) succeeding: *She then moved to Mexico the following year.||Write down the following address: 123 Center Street.*
—*n.* **1** a group of admirers or followers: *The writer has a following among college students.* **2** people or items (in a list): *Bring one of the following as identification: a passport, birth certificate, or a driver's license.*
—*prep.* after: *Following the graduation ceremony, there was a party.*

follow-through *n.* [U] **1** (as in golf, tennis, and baseball) the arm movement that continues after a ball is hit: *She plays tennis well and has a good follow-through.* **2** step(s) to completion: *He has creative ideas, but is weak on the follow-through.*

fol·low-up *n.adj.* additional action, steps to be taken to finish s.t.: *I gave my customer some ideas and have to do a* <*n.*> *follow-up* (or) <*adj.*> *follow-up call to find out what she thinks about them.*

fol·ly /'fali/ *n.* [C;U] **-lies** foolishness, a thoughtless act, (*syn.*) recklessness: *Buying such an expensive car on your small salary was pure folly.*

fo·ment /foʊˈmɛnt, ˈfoʊˌmɛnt/ *v.frml.* to cause trouble (unrest, unhappiness, etc.), (*syns.*) to stir up, agitate: *The political leader fomented rebellion against the government.*

fond /fand/ *adj.* **1** having warm feelings toward s.o. or s.t.: *She is fond of children.||He has fond memories of his childhood.* **2** having a liking, preference for: *He is fond of food and drink.*

fon·dle /'fandl/ *v.* **-led, -ling, -les** to touch tenderly, gently: *The mother fondled her baby in her arms.*

fond·ly /'fandli/ *adv.* **1** in a friendly, loving way: *He fondly placed his children's photograph on his desk.* **2** in a hopeful way, sometimes without good reason: *I fondly hoped that my brother would lend me his new car.*

fond·ness /'fandnɪs/ *n.* [U] **1** a warm feeling: *He has a fondness for his nephew and helps him with loans.* **2** a liking, preference: *She has a fondness for silk blouses.*

fon·due /fanˈdu/ *n.* [C;U] cheese or chocolate melted in a heated pot: *We dipped pieces of bread in the cheese fondue.*

font /fant/ *n.* **1** a style of print: *We changed the font to make the report easier to read.* **2** *frml.fig.* a source: *He is a font of wisdom (knowledge, information, etc.).*

food /fud/ *n.* [C;U] **1** s.t. to eat, nourishment: *She likes to eat spicy food.* **2 food for thought:** ideas to think about: *The speaker gave us much food for thought about the future of planet Earth.*

Food and Drug Administration *n. abbr.* **FDA** in the USA, the government agency that checks the safety of food, medicine, and medical procedures: *The FDA has recently approved a new drug for the treatment of AIDS.*

food poi·son·ing *n.* [U] a stomach illness caused by eating contaminated food: *A traveler got food poisoning from eating bad shellfish.*

food proc·es·sor *n.* a machine that cuts and mixes food: *My father uses a food processor to make soup.*

food stamps *n.pl.* in USA, tickets provided by the government and used to buy food by people of low income: *She pays for her food at the local supermarket with food stamps.*

food·stuff /'fudˌstʌf/ *n.* any substance used as food: *Flour, milk, and butter are several basic foodstuffs.*

fool /ful/ *v.* **1** to deceive, trick: *He fooled her into paying a large sum of money for the fake necklace.* **2** to surprise, do s.t. unexpected: *I thought that the exam would be difficult, but it fooled me—it was easy.* **3** to pretend, (*syn.*) to

feign: *He appeared to be angry but said he was only fooling.* **4** *phrasal v. insep.* **to fool around with s.o. or s.t.: a.** to play with, (*syn.*) to mess around with: *On weekends he fools around with old cars for fun.* **b.** to be unfaithful in marriage: *Everyone but his wife knows that he fools around.* **c.** to joke, have fun: *Stop fooling around and do some work.* **5** *phrasal v. infrml.* **to fool with:** to handle s.t. dangerous: *Guns are dangerous; don't fool with them.*
—*n.* **1** a person with poor judgment: *He is a fool who gambles his money away.* **2** a person who makes a silly mistake: *I was a fool to buy that used car; it's no good.*

fool·har·dy /'ful,hɑrdi/ *adj.* risky, (*syns.*) reckless, rash: *He was foolhardy to try to drive his car through a snowstorm.* -*n.* [U] **foolhardiness.**

fool·ish /'fulɪʃ/ *adj.* **1** showing poor judgment, (*syns.*) imprudent, unwise: *She was foolish to spend all her savings on an expensive vacation.* **2** stupid, risky, (*syn.*) reckless: *He does foolish things like climbing trees and not being able to get down again.* -*adv.* **foolishly** -*n.* [U] **foolishness.**

fool·proof /'ful,pruf/ *adj.* **1** easily understood, not capable of going wrong: *The computer comes with foolproof instructions on how to use it.* **2** safe, not capable of being misused: *The bank uses a foolproof security system.*

fool's gold *n.* [U] **1** a mineral that looks like gold **2** *fig.* s.t. that looks valuable but is not: *The stock of that company turned out to be fool's gold and a total loss.*

fool's par·a·dise *n.* a state of happiness based on an illusion: *She's living in a fool's paradise if she thinks her job is secure.*

foot /fʊt/ *n.* **feet** /fit/ **1** the body part attached to the lower leg and used for walking: *My right foot hurts.* **2** a length of measurement equal to 12 inches (approx. 26 cm.): *That table is seven feet* (or) *7' long.* **3** the lowest part: *He stood at the foot of the stair (foot of the mountain, hill, etc.).* **4 on foot:** by walking: *We took a train to the town and went the rest of the way on foot.* **5 to get a foot in the door:** a get a chance on the first job opportunity of a career: *He wanted to be an actor, but nobody would hire him; he couldn't get his foot in the door.* **6 to get cold feet:** to become too nervous to act: *She was about to ask her boss for a raise but then got cold feet.* **7 to get to one's feet:** to stand up: *She got to her feet and made a speech.* **8 to have one foot in the grave:** to be old and sickly, near death: *I didn't realize your father was so ill; he looks like he has one foot in the grave.* **9 to put one's best foot forward:** to make one's best effort: *He put his best foot forward and took his guests to the fanciest restaurant in town.* **10 to put one's**

foot down: to insist on s.t., demand obedience: *When her son was getting poor grades in school, she put her foot down and made him study every night.* **11 to put one's foot in one's mouth:** to say the wrong thing, usu. by mistake: *He put his foot in his mouth by calling his mother-in-law by the wrong name.* **12 to sit at s.o.'s feet:** to admire and learn from s.o.: *He was a great teacher, and the students used to sit at his feet. See:* inch.
—*v.* **to foot the bill:** to pay the cost of s.t.: *I footed the bill for my daughter's wedding. See:* feet of clay.

foot·age /'fʊtɪdʒ/ *n.* [U] **1** a measurement, esp. of property in feet: *There is enough footage behind the house to plant a garden.* **2** a length of film (movie, videotape, etc.): *The television news program showed footage of the plane crash.*

foot·ball /'fʊt,bɔl/ *n.* **1** [U] in USA, a sport played by two 11-person teams with the object of carrying or passing the ball over the opponent's goal line: *My friends and I watch football on TV on weekends.* **2** [U] (non-USA) soccer: *Football is an international sport followed by millions of fans.* **3** [C] the ball used in either sport

foot-dragging *n.* [U] deliberate slowness in doing s.t., delaying: *He applied for a travel visa long ago, but because of foot-dragging the consulate has not approved it yet.*

foot·hill /'fʊt,hɪl/ *n. usu. pl.* a hill below a mountain: *They traveled through the foothills of the Rocky Mountains.*

foot·hold /'fʊt,hould/ *n.* **1** a firm position for one or both feet: *The climber lost his foothold and fell down the mountain.* **2** *fig.* a small, but firm position in a situation as a means for progressing further: *Our company's success in Taiwan gave us a foothold in the Asian market.*

foot·ing /'fʊtɪŋ/ *n.* [U] **1** the firmness (or lack of it) of the ground under one's feet: *She lost her footing on the icy steps.* **2** the solidity of a position: *Our business in Asia is now on a firm footing.*

foot·lights /'fʊt,laɪts/ *n.pl.* lights in the floor at the front of a stage: *The footlights went down and the curtain went up as the play began.*

foot·lock·er /'fʊt,lɑkər/ *n.* a box, usu. made of metal, used for clothing and other belongings: *The soldier keeps a footlocker at the end of his bed.*

foot·loose /'fʊt,lus/ *adj. usu. in the phrase* **footloose and fancy-free:** without responsibilities and free to travel: *After military service, he was footloose and fancy-free, so he toured Europe.*

foot·note /'fʊt,nout/ *n.* an explanation or some added information placed at the bottom of a page of a text: *The footnote explained where the author had found this information.*

—*v.* **-noted, -noting, -notes** to place in a text a number or letter that refers to a corresponding number or letter on a footnote: *She footnoted her text throughout.*

foot·path /'fʊt,pæθ/ *n.* a narrow path for walking: *We walked down a footpath from the house to the garden.*

foot·print /'fʊt,prɪnt/ *n.* the mark left by a bare foot or shoe on a surface, such as dirt, sand, or a floor: *We followed the footprints in the garden.*

foot·race /'fʊt,reɪs/ *n.* a running or speedwalking competition, esp. of an informal nature: *My friend and I had a footrace from our car to the beach.*

foot·sie /'fʊtsi/ *n.* **to play footsie:** to secretly touch s.o.'s legs or feet under a table in a flirting way

foot·sore /'fʊt,sɔr/ *adj.* pained in the feet: *I was footsore from walking around Paris all day.*

foot·step /'fʊt,stɛp/ *n.* **1** the sound of feet moving on a surface: *We could hear footsteps in the hallway.* **2** *fig.* the length of a step: *The shop that we want to visit is a few footsteps away from our hotel.*

foot·wear /'fʊt,wɛr/ *n.* [U] shoes and boots, etc.: *This shoe store has a large selection of footwear for both men and women.*

foot·work /'fʊt,wɜrk/ *n.* [U] **1** movement of the feet, esp. in dancing and sports: *He is an ice skater and practices his footwork every morning.* **2** *fig.* work done in preparation for s.t.: *Wayne did a lot of footwork before the president's visit.*

fop /fɑp/ *n.* a man who is very or too interested in clothes, (*syn.*) a dandy: *He is a fop and wears a new suit almost every day.* -*adj.* **foppish.**

for /fər; *strong form* fɔr/ *prep.* **1** with the purpose of: *I am cutting some wood for fire.‖She needs glasses for reading.* **2** in exchange, instead of: *I'll give you twenty dollars for that watch.* **3** in relation to: *The child is tall for his age.‖Exercise is good for you.* **4** because of: *San Francisco is famous for its fog.* **5** in the interest of, to the benefit of: *Mr. Chen speaks for all of us.‖I baked a cake for you.* **6** in favor of: *The Senator is for raising taxes.* **7** as long as (used to express time): *She has lived in Miami for five years.* **8** as far as (used to express distance, length): *We walked for many miles.* **9** in the direction of, as a destination: *Our plane is headed for Taipei.* **10 for nothing: a.** with no payment in return: *I did some work for a friend for nothing.* **b.** with no gain, uselessly: *My computer failed, so I did a lot of work today for nothing.*

—*conj.* for the reason that, because: *The government provided food, for the people were hungry.*

for·age /'fɔrɪdʒ, 'fɑr-/ *v.* **-aged, -aging, -ages** (esp. of animals) to search for food: *The deer foraged for food beneath the snow.*

for·ay /'fɔr,eɪ, 'fɑr-/ *n.v.* an attack with the purpose of taking away food, animals, and weapons: *Armed rebels made a <n.> foray on the town at dawn.‖They <v.> forayed for horses and guns.*

for·bear /fɔr'bɛr/ *v.frml.* **-bore** /-'bɔr/, **-borne** /-'bɔrn/, **-bearing, -bears** to hold back, be patient: *Although she was very angry, she forbore from taking any action.* /'fɔr,bɛr/ *See:* forebear.

for·bear·ance /fɔr'bɛrəns/ *n.* [U] self-control, patience: *He is a politician who is often attacked for his views, but he always acts with forbearance.*

for·bid /fər'bɪd, fɔr-/ *v.* **-bade** /-'bæd, -'beɪd/ **-bidden** /-'bɪdn/, **-bidding, -bids** to not permit, (*syns.*) to prohibit, ban: *The law forbids selling alcohol to anyone under the age of twenty-one.*

for·bid·ding /fər'bɪdɪŋ, fɔr-/ *adj.* uninviting, possibly dangerous, (*syns.*) intimidating, daunting: *The old house had a forbidding appearance, and we were afraid to enter.*

force /fɔrs/ *n.* **1** [U] a source or instrument of power or energy: *The force of the wind knocked over a tree.* **2** [U] the use of power to make s.o. do s.t., (*syn.*) compulsion: *The police took the suspect to jail by force.* **3** [C] a military, police, or other unit organized to use physical power: *New York City has a large police force.* **4** [C] political power, influence: *The Congresswoman is a force for reform in the government.* **5** [U] persuasiveness, power of mind or personality: *The force of his argument (logic, reasoning, etc.) is convincing.* **6 force of habit:** repetition of s.t. done out of habit, without thinking: *He smokes cigarettes by (or) from force of habit.* **7 in force:** (in law) to be in effect, active: *The law that says one cannot smoke in public buildings is in force (or) is no longer in force.*

—*v.* **forced, forcing, forces 1** to use power or energy: *Strong winds forced boats onto the beaches.* **2** to use power to make s.o. do s.t., (*syn.*) to compel: *The police forced a confession from a suspect.* **3** to use physical strength to open s.t.: *The police forced open the door and entered the apartment.* **4** to push beyond normal limits: *The singer forced his voice and now has a sore throat.*

forced /fɔrst/ *adj.* **1** unconvincing, (*syn.*) artificial: *His arguments sound forced.* **2** s.t. done out of necessity: *The plane had to make a forced landing because of the storm.*

force-feed *v.* **-fed, -feeding, -feeds** to force food into an animal or person: *Farmers force-feed ducks to make them fat and tasty.*

force field *n.* a field of energy: *The spacecraft produces a force field that protects it against enemy attack.*

force·ful /'fɔrsfəl/ *adj.* **1** using force, strength: *The police used forceful methods to get the suspect to confess to the crime.* **2** powerful, effective: *That woman has a forceful personality.* *-adv.* **forcefully** *-n.* [U] **forcefulness.**

force ma·jeure /'fɔrsmɑ'ʒɜr/ *n.* (French for) an act of God, referring to damage to goods by flood, fire, accident, etc.: *According to the agreement, the company is not responsible for force majeure.*

for·ceps /'fɔr,sɛps, -səps/ *n.pl.* (in medicine) an instrument used to hold firmly and pull, such as one occasionally used in childbirth: *Sometimes doctors use forceps when a baby has difficulty being born.*

forc·i·ble /'fɔrsəbəl/ *adj.* referring to the use of force: *The broken lock on the door showed that there had been forcible entry.* *-adv.* **forcibly.**

ford /fɔrd/ *n.* **1** a shallow crossing place in a river or stream: *The ford in the river is a mile away.* **2** *TM* **Ford:** the name of an automobile manufacturer: *We drive a Ford.*
—*v.* to cross the shallow part of a river or stream: *The soldiers forded the river with little difficulty.*

fore /fɔr/ *n.* **1** the front **2** the public's attention: *Portable telephones have come to the fore in recent years.*

fore and aft /'fɔrən'æft/ *adv.* regarding the front and back (of a boat): *The sailors searched fore and aft for the missing boxes.*

fore·arm /'fɔr,ɑrm/ *n.* the part of the arm between the wrist and elbow: *She exercises a lot and has big, strong forearms.*

fore·bear or **for·bear** /'fɔr,bɛr/ *n.frml.* ancestor: *His forebears came to America from Japan. See:* forbear.

fore·bod·ing /fɔr'boudɪŋ/ *n.* a fear that s.t. bad is going to happen: *He thought of the sea voyage ahead with foreboding.* *-v.* **forebode.**

fore·cast /'fɔr,kæst/ *n.* a statement about what one thinks will happen in the future, (*syn.*) a prediction: *According to the weather forecast, it's going to snow tonight.*
—*v.* **-cast, -casted, -casting, -casts** to try to say what will happen in the future: *The President's advisers forecast that the economy will improve this year.*

fore·close /fɔr'klouz/ *v.* **-closed, -closing, -closes 1** to stop s.t. before it happens, (*syn.*) to preclude: *His death forecloses the possibility of changing his will.* **2** (in real estate) to take possession of a property by court order for nonpayment of a mortgage: *The bank foreclosed on his house -n.*[C;U] **foreclosure** /fɔr'klouʒər/.

fore·fa·ther /'fɔr,fɑðər/ *n.* ancestor (usu. *pl.*): *Our forefathers founded a great democracy.*

fore·fin·ger /'fɔr,fɪŋgər/ *n.* the first finger beside the thumb, (*syn.*) index finger: *The tips of each forefinger contain very sensitive nerves.*

fore·front /'fɔr,frʌnt/ *n.* [U] the most advanced part, (*syn.*) vanguard: *She is in the forefront of scientific research on cancer.*

fore·go /fɔr'gou/ *v. See:* forgo.

fore·go·ing /fɔr'gouɪŋ, 'fɔr,gouɪŋ/ *adj.* referring to what has just come before, (*syn.*) preceding: *The foregoing information is accurate as of this date.*

fore·ground /'fɔr,graund/ *n.* [U] the part of a picture or photograph that seems closest to the viewer: *In the foreground of the photo we can see a young couple sitting on a bench.*

fore·head /'fɔrɪd, -,hɛd, 'far-/ *n.* the part of the face above the eyebrows

for·eign /'fɔrɪn, 'far-/ *adj.* **1** (from) outside one's own country: *This country imports a great variety of foreign goods.* **2** *fig.* not typical of s.o. or s.t., (*syn.*) uncharacteristic: *Being late is foreign to him; he is usually on time.*

for·eign·er /'fɔrənər, 'far-/ *n.* s.o. from outside one's own country: *Many foreigners from Europe and Asia enjoy visiting Disneyland in California.*

foreign exchange *n.* **1** payments made between foreign governments, countries, and businesses **2** the process of changing the type of money used in one country into that of another's **3** the system for this: *The value of the dollar has gone down on the foreign exchange.*

foreign policy *n.* **-cies** the set of beliefs guiding a government's relations with other countries: *Many people disagree with the President's recent foreign policy decisions.*

for·eign serv·ice *n.* [U] the government department representing the interests of the nation in foreign countries: *She began her career in the foreign service working at the American Embassy in Tokyo.*

fore·knowl·edge /'fɔr,nɑlɪʤ, fɔr'nɑlɪʤ/ *n.* [U] knowledge about s.t. before it happens: *He made the trip into the jungle with the foreknowledge that the area was dangerous.*

fore·man /'fɔrmən/ *n.* **-men** /-mən/ a boss of a group of workers: *He is a foreman in that factory.*

fore·most /'fɔr,moust/ *adj.* **1** most important, best: *She is the world's foremost authority on tropical diseases.* **2** first, most urgent: *Finishing that project is foremost in my mind.*

fo·ren·sic /fə'rɛnsɪk, -zɪk/ *adj.* **1** related to using scientific, medical methods to get information about a crime: *He has a degree in forensic medicine.* **2** related to public debate

fore·play /'fɔr,pleɪ/ *n.* [U] activities such as kissing and touching that come before sexual intercourse: *Always in a hurry, he never engaged in foreplay when he made love to his wife.*

fore·quar·ters /'fɔr,kwɔrtərz, -,kɔr-/ *n.pl.* the chest, shoulders, and legs of an animal: *The forequarters of that racehorse are well-developed.*

fore·run·ner /'fɔr,rʌnər/ *n.* **1** *fig.* ancestor, (*syn.*) predecessor: *The wolf was a forerunner of the dog.* **2** *fig.* a first step that leads to better things: *The invention of the transistor was the forerunner of great advances in electronics, such as the development of better computers.* **3** *lit.* a person who goes before another to announce him or her: *The king sent his forerunner ahead to the next town.*

fore·see /fɔr'si/ *v.* **-saw** /-'sɔ/, **-seen** /-'sin/, **-seeing, -sees** to have knowledge of future events, (*syns.*) to predict, foretell: *She foresaw the troubles ahead and took steps to avoid them. -adj.* **foreseeable.**

fore·shad·ow /fɔr'ʃædoʊ/ *v.* to be a sign of future events, (*syn.*) to portend: *The failure of that bank foreshadowed a general financial crisis.*

fore·short·en·ing /fɔr'ʃɔrtnɪŋ/ *n.* [U] (in drawing or painting) the technique of making a figure short to show depth and distance: *Ancient Greek artists discovered foreshortening. -v.* **foreshorten.**

fore·sight /'fɔr,saɪt/ *n.* [U] the ability to be prepared for future events, (*syn.*) prudence: *She had the foresight to pack some warm clothes as they were needed for her summer trip.*

fore·skin /'fɔr,skɪn/ *n.* the piece of skin over the end of a penis: *The foreskin is sometimes removed soon after birth in a process called circumcision.*

for·est /'fɔrɪst, 'fɑr-/ *n.* [C;U] **1** a large area with many trees: *In some national parks, the forest continues for miles and miles.* **2 to not see the forest for the trees:** to see only details and not understand their larger meaning: *The owner of the company couldn't see the forest for the trees; he was so busy dealing with the daily problems of running the factory that he didn't realize that the business was headed towards failure.*
—*v.* to plant trees, cover with trees: *Workers forested the land to improve the soil.*

fore·stall /fɔr'stɔl/ *v.* to prevent an unwanted event by taking action before it happens: *She forestalled the closing of her company by getting a loan from the bank.*

for·est·er /'fɔrəstər, 'fɑr-/ *n.* a person who works in forestry: *He is a forester for the National Parks Service.*

for·est·land /'fɔrɪst,lænd, 'fɑr-/ *n.* [C;U] land covered with trees: *The farmer has forestland behind his fields.*

for·est·ry /'fɔrəstri, 'fɑr-/ *n.* [U] the scientific field of forest management: *Her son went to Yale University to study forestry.*

fore·taste /'fɔr,teɪst/ *n.* an advance experience of s.t.: *Those beautiful days in March are a foretaste of spring.*

fore·tell /fɔr'tɛl/ *v.* **-told** /-'toʊld/, **-telling, -tells** to know and tell about future events, (*syn.*) to predict: *The religious leader foretold the arrival of an age of peace.*

fore·thought /'fɔr,θɔt/ *n.* [U] the ability to prepare for future events, (*syn.*) prescience: *Although it was sunny in the morning, he had the forethought to take an umbrella.*

for·ev·er /fə'rɛvər, fɔ-/ *adv.* **1** always, for an unlimited time, (*syn.*) eternally: *Our love will last forever.* **2** continually, constantly, (*syn.*) perpetually: *The little boy is forever asking questions.*

for·ev·er·more /fə,rɛvər'mɔr, fɔ-/ *adv.frml.* always, for an unlimited time, (*syn.*) eternally: *A stranger saved her life, and she is thankful to him forevermore.*

fore·warn /fɔr'wɔrn/ *v.* to warn in advance, (*syn.*) to caution: *The guide forewarned tourists about dangers in the jungle.*

fore·word /'fɔrwərd, -,wɜrd/ *n.* an introductory statement in a book: *The author wrote a foreword to be used as the first page of her book.*

for·feit /'fɔrfɪt/ *v.n.* to give up s.t. because of a failure to perform according to the rules, agreement, etc.: *When he failed to appear, the tennis player <v.> forfeited the match to his opponent.||The tennis match was won by <n.> forfeit.*

for·fei·ture /'fɔrfətʃər/ *n.* [C;U] the act of giving up s.t. because of a failure to perform according to the rules, agreement, etc.: *When he failed to repay the loan, the bank repossessed his car as forfeiture.*

forge /fɔrdʒ/ *n.* **1** a machine or apparatus used for melting and shaping metals **2** a place where such equipment is used
—*v.* **forged, forging, forges 1** to falsify, produce a fake copy of s.t.: *She forged her husband's signature on the check.||An artist forged a painting.* **2** to set up: *The two countries have recently forged a new trade agreement.* **3** to melt, soften, and shape metals: *A metalworker used a hammer to forge a sword from heated steel.* **4 to forge ahead:** to proceed with strength or speed despite problems or difficulties: *Despite problems, she forged ahead with her plans to have her own business. See:* forging.

forg·er /'fɔrdʒər/ *n.* a person who fakes s.t., such as money, a signature, or piece of art: *The $100 bills were made by a forger.*

for·ger·y /ˈfɔrdʒəri/ *n.* **-es 1** [C] a false copy of s.t. made and offered as real, a fake: *The painting, which sold for $500,000, turned out to be a forgery; it was only really worth $10,000.* **2** [U] an act of forgery: *He was put in jail for forgery; he had been printing false bank notes.*

for·get /fərˈgɛt/ *v.* **-got** /-ˈgɑt/, **-gotten** /-ˈgɑtn/, **-getting, -gets 1** to not remember, drop from memory without intending to: *I've forgotten how to play the piano.*‖*I forgot my keys (my purse, a ten o'clock appointment, etc.)!* **2** to stop thinking about s.t.: *You should forget about going to Europe on vacation; it costs too much.* **3** *fig.* **to forget oneself:** to lose one's self-control: *He generally follows a strict diet, but forgets himself when he goes out to eat.*

for·get·ful /fərˈgɛtfəl/ *adj.* often not remembering things, (*syn.*) absent-minded: *He is forgetful and leaves behind umbrellas or even his briefcase.* -*adv.* **forgetfully;** -*n.* [U] **forgetfulness.**

forget-me-not *n.* a small plant with blue flowers

forg·ing /ˈfɔrdʒɪŋ/ *n.* [U] the science and craft of melting and shaping metals: *Forging is an ancient craft dating back to 4,000 B.C. in Egypt and Asia.*

for·give /fərˈgɪv/ *v.* **-gave** /-ˈgeɪv/, **-given** /-ˈgɪvən/, **-giving, -gives 1** to pardon, excuse: *He forgot his wife's birthday, but she forgave him.* **2** to free s.o. from repaying a loan: *She still owed $1,000 to her father, but he forgave the debt.*

for·give·ness /fərˈgɪvnɪs/ *n.* [U] freeing from guilt or obligation, pardon: *He told a lie but later asked his friend for forgiveness.*

for·go /fɔrˈgoʊ/ *v.* **-went** /-ˈwɛnt/, **-gone** /-ˈgɔn, -ˈgɑn/, **-going, -goes** to do without, (*syn.*) to abstain from: *Let's forgo dessert; I'm full.*

fork /fɔrk/ *v.* **1** to divide into two parts at a certain point, (*syn.*) to branch: *The road forks about a mile from here.* **2** *phrasal v. sep.slang* **to fork s.t. over:** to give to s.o. or s.t.: *I want you to fork over the money that you owe me.*‖*Fork it over now!*
—*n.* **1** a division into two parts, (*syn.*) branching: *To get to the town, turn left at the fork in the road.* **2** an instrument for eating, with a handle and at least two long points: *The dinner table is set with knives, forks, and spoons.*

forked /fɔrkt/ *adj.* divided into two parts at a certain point, (*syn.*) branched: *The trunk of that tree is forked near its base.*

fork·lift /ˈfɔrkˌlɪft/ *n.* a vehicle with two long narrow pieces of steel in front used to lift and carry heavy loads: *The forklift*

forklift

carried the boxes from the truck to the factory.

for·lorn /fɔrˈlɔrn, fər-/ *adj.frml.* sad and alone without hope, (*syns.*) wretched, miserable: *Victims of the earthquake sat forlorn outside their ruined homes.* -*adv.* **forlornly.**

form /fɔrm/ *v.* **1** to shape, make an object: *She formed a dish from clay.* **2** to become the shape of: *The children formed a circle.* **3** to arrange s.t., put it together: *The manager formed a committee to study the project.* **4** to produce, cause to happen: *I haven't yet formed an opinion about this.* **5** to come into existence: *Ice forms on the river in the winter.* **6** to make up, (*syn.*) to constitute: *Good eating habits form the basis of a healthy diet.*
—*n.* **1** [C] the shape of s.t.: *The human form can be quite graceful.* **2** [C] a type, kind: *People live under different forms of government, such as democracies or dictatorships.* **3** [C] a printed paper with spaces to be filled in: *When you apply for a visa, you must fill out some forms.* **4** [U] a way of doing s.t.: *The political leader responded to the criticism in the form of a letter to the newspaper.* **5** [C] an empty container used for creating shapes, (*syn.*) a mold: *A company made a form to produce a new toy.* **6** *fig.* [U] correct and proper behavior: *Good form requires you to attend the funeral.* **7 in good (bad, great, etc.) form:** the quality of a performance, such as in athletics, music, or acting: *The singer is in good form tonight.*

for·mal /ˈfɔrməl/ *adj.* **1** according to rules, laws, customs, etc.: *I received a formal invitation to the wedding today.* **2** very or too proper: *He's a difficult person to get to know because he's always so formal.* **3** official, (*syn.*) ceremonial: *A formal meeting between the President and the Prime Minister will take place today.* **4** elegant, typical of official occasions: *They wore formal clothes to the dinner party.* **5** (of written or spoken language) used in serious writing, such as literature, or in official situations rather than in common speech: *Formal words in this dictionary are marked "frml."*
—*n.* a dance where one wears elegant clothes: *Many high school students go to a formal at the end of the school year.* -*adv.* **formally.**

form·al·de·hyde /fɔrˈmældəˌhaɪd, fər-/ *n.* [U] an unpleasant-smelling gas with many industrial uses: *Formaldehyde is used in making plastics and fertilizers.*

for·mal·ism /ˈfɔrməˌlɪzəm/ *n.* [U] strict observance of forms of conduct, style, procedure, etc.: *In his lecture the professor discussed the formalism of the artist's early work.*

for·mal·i·ty /fɔrˈmæləti, fər-/ *n.* [C;U] **-ties 1** customary behavior, observances, procedures (usu. **to observe the formalities):** *We must observe the formalities and introduce ourselves*

F

to the other guests at the party. **2** the meaningless observance of a rule or custom: *All visitors must sign in at the front desk as a formality.*

for·mal·ize /ˈfɔrməˌlaɪz/ v. **-ized, -izing, -izes** to make s.t. definite and official: *We formalized the business deal with a written agreement.* -n. [U] **formalization** /ˌfɔrmələˈzeɪʃən/.

for·mat /ˈfɔrˌmæt/ n. **1** the visual style of a publication: *That magazine's new format makes it easier to read.* **2** any general arrangement of s.t.: *The format of the lesson was a short lecture followed by a discussion.*

—v. **-matted, -matting, -mats** to design or arrange s.t.: *The designer formatted the pages of a magazine.*

for·ma·tion /fɔrˈmeɪʃən/ n. **1** [U] a bringing together, creation: *The formation of a committee on health issues took several days.* **2** [C;U] a group of people or things arranged a certain way: *Soldiers marched by in military formation.*

form·a·tive /ˈfɔrmətɪv/ adj. in the process of growing or being shaped or organized: *Children must have good nutrition during their formative years.*

for·mer /ˈfɔrmər/ adj. **1** previous, past: *He is a former employee of this company.* **2** referring to the first thing or person named in a pair

—n. the first thing or person named in a pair: *We eat lots of fish and chicken, but we prefer the former* (meaning "the fish"). See: latter.

for·mer·ly /ˈfɔrmərli/ adv. in the past, some time ago, (syn.) previously: *She was formerly president of that organization.*

form·fit·ting /ˈfɔrmˌfɪtɪŋ/ adj. fitting close to the body: *Those biking shorts are made of formfitting material.*

For·mi·ca /fɔrˈmaɪkə/ n.TM a hard plastic used as surface material, such as on tables and countertops: *Formica provides good protection against burns and stains.*

for·mi·da·ble /ˈfɔrmədəbəl, fɔrˈmɪdə-/ adj. strong, difficult to defeat, (syn.) daunting: *The people of that country must overcome formidable obstacles to win their freedom.* -adv. **formidably.**

form·less /ˈfɔrmlɪs/ adj. without form, shapeless: *That report is a formless collection of facts; it needs to be rewritten.* -adv. **formlessly** -n. [U] **formlessness.**

form letter n. a general letter from a company or organization sent to many people, usu. to sell a product or ask for money: *We receive form letters all the time from companies trying to sell their merchandise.*

for·mu·la /ˈfɔrmyələ/ n. **-las** or **-lae** /-ˌli, -ˌlaɪ/ **1** (in math) a rule expressed in symbols **2** (in chemistry) a group of symbols representing a chemical **3** a fixed combination of ingredients:

Each manufacturer of cough syrup has its own formula. **4 a formula for (success, defeat, etc.):** a combination of factors leading to a result: *Lee Iaccoca wrote a book about his formula for success at Chrysler Motors.* -adj. **formulaic** /ˌfɔrmyəˈleɪɪk/.

for·mu·late /ˈfɔrmyəˌleɪt/ v. **-lated, -lating, -lates 1** to create, combine: *The manager formulated a marketing plan for the year.* **2** to state in a clear way: *She formulated her ideas about solving the drug problem.* **3** to prepare, blend: *The chemist formulated various ingredients into an effective cold medication.*

for·mu·la·tion /ˌfɔrmyəˈleɪʃən/ n. [U] careful preparation, creation of s.t.: *The formulation of a new environmental policy required months of study.*

for·ni·ca·tion /ˌfɔrnɪˈkeɪʃən/ n.frml. [U] an act of sexual intercourse between two unmarried persons: *Religious warnings against fornication are not often obeyed.* -v. **fornicate** /ˈfɔrnɪˌkeɪt/.

for·sake /fɔrˈseɪk, fər-/ v.frml. **-sook** /-ˈsʊk/, **-saken** /-ˈseɪkən/, **-saking, -sakes** to leave, give up, (syns.) to abandon, desert: *He forsook his homeland and emigrated to a new country.*

for·swear /fɔrˈswɛr/ v.frml. **-swore** /-ˈswɔr/, **-sworn** /-ˈswɔrn/, **-swearing, -swears 1** to give up s.t., (syn.) to renounce: *The partner sold his half of the company and forswore any further interest in the business.* **2** to not tell the truth in a court of law: *The judge determined that the witness's testimony was forsworn and rejected it.*

for·syth·i·a /fərˈsɪθiə, fɔr-/ n. [C;U] a bush that produces bright yellow flowers: *Forsythias bloom early in the spring.*

fort /fɔrt/ n. **1** a group of buildings surrounded by high walls and used for military purposes: *Enemy soldiers attacked the fort.* **2** fig. **to hold (down) the fort:** to handle another person's responsibilities for a short time: *The store manager asked her assistant to hold the fort while she was away.*

forte /fɔrt, ˈfɔrˌteɪ/ n. a skill, s.t. that a person does well: *His forte is money management; hers is sales.*

forth /fɔrθ/ adv. **1** frml. forward, ahead: *Explorers went forth to discover a new world.* **2 and so forth:** and other similar things, (syns.) et cetera, and so on: *She complained that the city was dirty, dangerous, expensive, crowded, and so forth.* **3 back and forth:** between two points: *She flies back and forth between Chicago and Los Angeles for her work.* **4 to come forth:** to present oneself: *Several witnesses came forth to give a description of the criminal.*

forth·com·ing /ˌfɔrθˈkʌmɪŋ, ˈfɔrθˌkʌmɪŋ/ adj.frml. **1** arriving in the future, due to be delivered: *More information will be forthcoming* *shortly.* **2** helpful, (*syn.*) cooperative: *The neighbors were forthcoming in helping us settle in our new house.* **3** *usu.* used in the negative willing to provide information: *She was not forthcoming about the source of her sudden wealth.*

forth·right /'fɔrθ,raɪt/ *adj.* honest, open, (*syn.*) frank: *The politician was forthright in stating his views on the issues.* -*n.* [U] **forthrightness.**

for·ti·eth /'fɔrtiiθ/ *adj.n.* the ordinal number 40: *He celebrated his <adj.> fortieth birthday with a party* (or) *the birthday was his <n.> fortieth.*

for·ti·fi·ca·tion /,fɔrtəfə'keɪʃən/ *n.* **1** [U] an act of strengthening a military position or fort: *Fortification of the town went ahead quickly.* **2** [C] *usu.* plural the walls and other structures of a military position: *The fortifications were ten feet thick.*

for·ti·fy /'fɔrtə,faɪ/ *v.* **-fied, -fying, -fies 1** to strengthen with fortifications: *Workers fortified the castle by building an outer wall.* **2** to strengthen oneself, usu. with food or drink: *He fortified himself with a glass of whisky before going out in the cold weather.*

for·ti·tude /'fɔrtə,tud/ *n.* [U] courage in the face of difficulties: *He showed fortitude in his battle against cancer.*

fort·night /'fɔrt,naɪt/ *n.frml.* a period of two weeks: *He issued a report on his activities each fortnight.*

FOR·TRAN /'fɔr,træn/ *n.* a computer programming language used mainly for scientific purposes: *She needed to learn FORTRAN for her research.*

for·tress /'fɔrtrɪs/ *n.* **-tresses** a building, group of buildings, or town well-protected against attack: *Soldiers attacked the fortress high on a hill. See:* fort.

for·tu·i·tous /fɔr'tuətəs/ *adj.frml.* **1** by chance, accidental: *Meeting my mother at the train station was completely fortuitous.* **2** lucky, fortunate: *By fortuitous circumstances, we were able to take a bus after our car had broken down.* -*adv.* **fortuitously.**

for·tu·nate /'fɔrtʃənɪt/ *adj.* lucky at a particular time: *We were fortunate to escape the accident without injury.* **2** lucky in general, (*syn.*) blessed: *We are fortunate to have money and good health.*

fortunately /'fɔrtʃənɪtli/ *adv.* luckily: *Fortunately, I found my passport.*

for·tune /'fɔrtʃən/ *n.* **1** [C] wealth, riches: *He made a fortune in the oil business.* **2** [U] chance, (good or bad) luck, (*syn.*) fate: *Then he had the bad fortune to fall ill.*

fortune cookie *n.* a cookie containing a small piece of paper that gives advice or tells one's future: *Chinese restaurants offer fortune cookies as dessert.*

fortune teller *n.* a person who tells one's future: *The fortune teller said that I would live to be a hundred.*

for·ty /'fɔrti/ *n.* **-ties** the cardinal number 40 —*adj.* forty of s.t.: *He is forty years old.*

forty-five *n.* a powerful handgun that shoots .45 caliber bullets: *He was shot dead with a forty-five.*

fo·rum /'fɔrəm/ *n.* **1** a square in ancient Rome where public business was conducted: *The forums were busy places.* **2** a place for the open exchange of ideas, opinions, and information: *This radio talk show is a forum for political discussions.*

for·ward /'fɔrwərd/ or **forwards** /'fɔrwərdz/ *adv.* ahead (in space or time): *We are moving forwards with our plans to open a new store.||Walk three steps forward and turn left.* —*adj.* **1** front: *Our cabin is in the forward section of the ship.* **2** bold, (*syn.*) brazen: *The little boy is forward in asking for favors even from strangers.* **3 forwarding address:** a new address to which mail should be sent: *She moved without leaving a forwarding address.* —*v.* to send ahead to s.o.'s address; ship to another: *While we are away in the summer, our neighbor forwards our mail to us.* -*n.* [U] **forwardness.**

for·ward·er /'fɔrwərdər/ *n.* a business that ships goods to a new destination: *Our company uses a freight forwarder for overseas shipments.*

fos·sil /'fɑsəl/ *n.* **1** the remains of ancient animal or plant life preserved in rock: *We know about dinosaurs from the fossils that they left behind.* **2** *fig.pej.* an old person with old-fashioned ideas: *He's the fossil in the English department that nobody listens to; he hasn't had a new idea since 1963.*

fossil fuel *n.* fuel, such as coal and oil, produced by the change of ancient plant and animal life into carbon: *Fossil fuels produce substantial air pollution.*

fos·sil·ize /'fɑsə,laɪz/ *v.* **-ized, -izing, -izes 1** to turn into a fossil: *The remains of dinosaurs have fossilized in rock.* **2** *fig.* to become fixed, rigid: *As he became older, his political ideas fossilized.*

fos·ter /'fɔstər, 'fɑs-/ *v.* to help to develop, (*syns.*) to encourage, nurture: *Her trainer fostered her career as a champion skater.* —*adj.* related to a system in which adults receive money from the government to take care of children who are not their own: *That woman cares for three foster children.*

fought /fɔt/ *v. past tense & past part. of* fight

foul /faʊl/ *v.* **1** to dirty, often with mud, bodily waste, etc.: *The farmer fell in the mud and fouled his clothes.* **2** (of rope, string, etc.) to get twisted together and not be able to work:

The two little boys fouled the lines of their fishing rods. **3** to make an improper move in certain sports: *A basketball player fouled an opponent.* **4** *phrasal v. sep.* **to foul s.t. up:** to make a mistake, often one causing serious problems: *The repairman attached the wrong wires and fouled up our telephone system.||He fouled it up.*
—*adj.* **1** very dirty, (*syn.*) filthy: *His clothes were foul with mud.* **2** rude, offensive, (*syns.*) vulgar, obscene: *When she gets angry, she sometimes uses foul language.* **3** bad-smelling, (*syn.*) rank: *His muddy clothes smelled foul.* **4** very unpleasant, (*syn.*) mean: *She's been in a foul mood all day.*
—*n.* **1** an improper move in certain sports: *The basketball player committed a foul.* **2** (in baseball) a ball hit outside the foul lines: *The batter hit a foul.* -*adv.* **foully;** -*n.* [U] **foulness.**

foul play *n.* [U] a criminal act, esp. murder: *A man was found dead; I think that he was a victim of foul play.*

foul-up *n.infrml.* a mistake often resulting in a serious problem: *The foul-up in the computer system will take several weeks to fix.*

found (1) /faʊnd/ *v.* to start and support s.t., usu. a building or organization: *My grandmother founded this company.*

found (2) *v.* past tense & past part. *of* find

foun·da·tion /faʊnˈdeɪʃən/ *n.* **1** [C] a base on which a physical structure is built: *The foundation for our house is made of cement.* **2** [C] the basis on which an institution or system of beliefs is founded: *The right to vote is one of the foundations of a democracy.* **3** [U] the creation of s.t., such as an institution, (*syn.*) establishment: *She contributed money towards the foundation of a new library.* **4** [C] an organization, usu. nonprofit, that provides money for projects in education, politics, science, and the arts: *The Ford Foundation supports many educational projects.*

found·er (1) /ˈfaʊndər/ *n.* a creator of s.t.: *The founder of that college was a wealthy businessman.*

found·er (2) /ˈfaʊndər/ *v.* **1** to fill up with water and sink: *The ship foundered in the violent storm.* **2** *fig.* to fall apart, fail: *Without popular support, the President's plan for health care reform foundered.* **3** to trip or fall from great tiredness: *The horse ran until it foundered.*

founding father *n.* **1** a person who sets up or originates s.t.: *He is the founding father of that law firm.* **2 Founding Fathers:** in the USA, the people who created the country's political system, esp. a signer of the Declaration of Independence: *The Founding Fathers met at the Constitutional Convention in 1787.*

found·ling /ˈfaʊndlɪŋ/ *n.* a child left by his or her mother, usu. in a public place, for others to find and take care of: *He was a foundling who was left on the doorstep of a church.*

found·ry /ˈfaʊndri/ *n.* **-ries** a workshop or factory in which metal is melted and shaped: *Machine parts can be made in foundries.*

foun·tain /ˈfaʊntn/ *n.* **1** an ornamental structure that sends water into the air for display: *The water fountain in the square attracts tourists each summer.* **2** a device usu. found in public buildings that provides water for drinking: *There's a water fountain outside the restrooms.* **3** *fig.* an active source of information, ideas, etc.: *The librarian is a fountain of knowledge about the community. See:* font.

foun·tain·head /ˈfaʊntn,hɛd/ *n.* source of a river or stream, (*syn.*) wellspring: *The fountainhead of that river lies deep in the jungle.*

fountain pen *n.* a pen that contains an ink container or is filled from an ink bottle: *She always uses a fountain pen for her personal letters.*

four /fɔr/ *adj.n.* the cardinal number 4: *The child had <adj.> four toys.*

four·fold /ˈfɔr,foʊld, -ˈfoʊld/ *adj.* four times s.t.: *The sale of that product has had a fourfold increase in the last ten years.*

four-foot·ed /ˈfɔrˈfʊtɪd/ or **four-legged** /ˈfɔrˈlɛgɪd/ *adj.* describing animals with four feet: *Horses and dogs are four-footed animals.*

4-H Club /ˈfɔrˈeɪtʃ/ *n.* a farm youth club set up by the U.S. Department of Agriculture: the H's stand for head, heart, hands, and health: *The 4-H Club helps young people learn about modern farming.*

four-leaf clover *n.* a small green plant with four leaves, seen as a symbol of good luck: *It's difficult to find a four-leaf clover.*

four-letter word *n.* any of several rude, offensive words in general typically containing four letters: *He uses four-letter words constantly.*

401(k) plan /ˈfɔr,oʊ,wʌnˈkeɪ/ *n.* (in USA) a savings plan offered by some companies and institutions in which an untaxed portion of an employee's salary is invested and not used until retirement: *Many employees take advantage of our company's 401(k) plan.*

four·post·er /ˈfɔrˈpoʊstər/ *n.adj.* a bed whose frame has four tall posts for curtains: *The couple bought a <adj.> four-poster made of wood.*

four·score /ˈfɔrˈskɔr/ *adj.old usage* 80 (4 times 20): *Lincoln began his Gettysburg Address with "Fourscore and seven years ago. . . . "*

four·some /ˈfɔrsəm/ *n.* a group of four people: *Golfers play in foursomes.*

four·square /ˈfɔrˈskwɛr/ *adj.* **1** *frml.* having four equal sides **2** *fig.* direct, honest, (*syn.*) forthright: *In dealing with him, you will find him foursquare and dependable.*

four·teen /,fɔr'tin/ *n.adj.* the cardinal number 14: *The meal cost <adj.> 14 dollars.||Only <n.> fourteen (of the passengers) survived the plane crash.*

four·teenth /,fɔr'tinθ/ *adj.n.* the ordinal number 14th: *He is the <adj.> fourteenth person on the list* (or) *he is <n.> fourteenth.*

fourth /fɔrθ/ *adj.n.* the ordinal number 4th: *She is the <adj.> fourth child in the family* (or) *she is the <n.> fourth.*

fourth dimension *n.* (in physics) time in addition to the three dimensions of height, width, and depth: *Science fiction writers sometimes explore the fourth dimension.*

fourth estate *n.* newspapers and magazine journalists: *The fourth estate has great influence on public opinion.*

Fourth of July *n.* (in USA) Independence Day: *The Fourth of July is a day of great celebration across the United States.*

four-wheel *adj.* related to vehicles in which all four wheels have power: *Vehicles with four-wheel drive are used in mountainous areas.*

fowl /foʊl/ *n.* **fowls** or **fowl** birds such as chickens, ducks, and geese: *Hunters shoot fowl in the autumn.*

fox /fɑks/ *n.* **foxes** or **fox** **1** [C] a variety of small dog-like animal with a thick furry tail, considered to be clever: *In the UK, people hunt foxes (or fox) on horseback.* **2** [U] the fur of a fox: *Women often wore coats made of red fox in the 1940s.* **3** *fig.* [C] a clever, tricky person: *In business matters, he is a smart fox.*
—*v.* **foxes** to gain s.t. through cleverness and trickery, to confuse others, *(syn.)* to outwit: *In business, he foxed his competition. See:* out-fox.

fox

fox·hole /'fɑks,hoʊl/ *n.* a hole dug in the ground where soldiers stay for protection against enemy gunfire: *It is necessary for a foxhole to be deep so it can protect a soldier.*

fox·hound /'fɑks,haʊnd/ *n.* a large, short-haired hunting dog: *Foxhounds were used originally to hunt foxes or rabbits.*

foxtrot /'fɑks,trɑt/ *n.v.* a ballroom dance with quick steps: *The <n.> foxtrot was a popular dance in the 1940s.*

fox·y /'fɑksi/ *adj.* **-ier, -iest 1** clever, tricky: *He is a foxy old man.* **2** *infrml.* sexy, attractive, *(syn.)* alluring: *His girlfriend is a foxy lady.*

USAGE NOTE: The term *foxy* as in, *"She looks very foxy tonight,"* is rude or offensive to many people.

foy·er /'fɔɪər, 'fɔɪ,eɪ/ *n.* an entrance room of a house, apartment, or public building: *I met my guest in the foyer of our office building.*

fra·cas /'freɪkəs, 'fræ-/ *n.* **-cases** a noisy fight, *(syn.)* commotion: *Two men started a fracas in a barroom.*

frac·tion /'frækʃən/ *n.* **1** a portion of s.t.: *A large fraction of the workforce is employed.* **2** a small portion of s.t.: *She spoke so quickly that I understood only a fraction of what she said.* **3** a portion less than a whole number, expressed in symbols: *The fraction one-half can also be expressed as .5 or 1/2. -adj.* **fractional; -adv. fractionally.**

frac·tious /'frækʃəs/ *adj.* **1** easily upset, *(syns.)* petulant, cranky **2** unwilling to obey rules, *(syns.)* rebellious, unruly: *That little boy is a fractious child. -adv.* **fractiously; -n.** [U] **fractiousness.**

frac·ture /'fræktʃər/ *v.* **-tured, -turing, -tures** to break, crack: *She fractured her leg while skiing.*
—*n.* a break, crack: *They found a small fracture in the wing of the plane.*

frag·ile /'frædʒəl, -,dʒaɪl/ *adj.* easily broken, delicate: *That dish is fragile, so be careful. -n.* [U] **fragility** /frə'dʒɪləti/.

frag·ment /'frægmənt/ *n.* **1** a bit or piece of s.t.: *The clay pot had broken into fragments long ago.*
—*v.* /'fræg,mɛnt, fræg'mɛnt/ to break, divide into bits and pieces: *His eyeglasses fragmented as they hit the ground.*

frag·men·tar·y /'frægmən,teri/ *adj.* partial, incomplete: *The witness could give only a fragmentary description of the accident.*

frag·men·ta·tion /,frægmən'teɪʃən, -mɛn-/ *n.* [U] the process of breaking into pieces: *The fragmentation of political parties makes governing difficult.*

fra·grance /'freɪgrəns/ *n.* **1** [U] pleasant smell, *(syn.)* bouquet: *The fragrance of roses filled the air.* **2** [C] perfume: *She uses an expensive fragrance.*

fra·grant /'freɪgrənt/ *adj.* pleasant smelling, perfumed: *Freshly cut grass has a fragrant smell. -adv.* **fragrantly.**

frail /freɪl/ *adj.* physically weak: *His mother has grown old and frail.*

frail·ty /'freɪlti, 'freɪəl-/ *n.* **-ties 1** [U] the condition of being physically weak: *Her frailty prevents her from going out to shop.* **2** [C] human moral weakness, *(syn.)* fallibility: *Jealousy and selfishness are common human frailties.*

frame /freɪm/ *n.* **1** a border placed around s.t.: *She put the photo in a plastic frame.||The window frames need painting.* **2** a supporting structure on which s.t. is built: *The frame of the sailboat was constructed in two weeks.* **3**

the human body: *He is a man with a large frame.* **4** *pl.* the part of a pair of eyeglasses into which the lenses are set: *Her reading glasses have red frames.* **5** the section of a roll of film that develops into a picture: *Several frames didn't come out clearly.* **6 frame of mind:** one's mental attitude at a specific time: *She's ill, but in a good frame of mind today.* **7 frame of reference:** the knowledge and beliefs that affect one's understanding of new information: *The philosophy professor's introductory lecture gave us a frame of reference for our first assigned readings.*
—*v.* **framed, framing, frames 1** to place a frame around s.t.: *She framed the painting and hung it in the living room.* **2** to put together, (*syn.*) to devise: *She framed her response in the form of a question.* **3** *fig.* to arrange the proof of a crime so that an innocent person appears guilty: *The accused murderer said that he was framed by his brother.*

frame-up *n.infrml.* the arrangement of proof of a crime so that an innocent person appears guilty: *The thief put some stolen jewels in my pocket as a frame-up to save himself.*

frame-work /'freɪm,wɜrk/ *n.* **1** a structure used to support other things: *The framework of that house is made of wood.* **2** *fig.* an organization of ideas: *The framework for our project is described in this 10-page proposal.*

fram-ing /'freɪmɪŋ/ *n.* [U] a frame: *The framing around that painting is made of metal.*

franc /fræŋk/ *n.* unit of money used in France, Switzerland, Belgium, Ivory Coast, Senegal, Rwanda, and other countries

fran-chise /'fræn,tʃaɪz/ *n.* a legal agreement giving an individual or company the right to sell another company's goods or services: *He bought a McDonald's franchise.*

fran-chi-see /,fræntʃaɪ'zi/ *n.* the person or business who buys a franchise: *My friend is a franchisee of a fast-food restaurant.*

fran-chis-er /'fræn,tʃaɪzər/ *n.* the company that sells franchises: *McDonald's is the franchiser of hundreds of fast-food restaurants.*

frank (1) /fræŋk/ *adj.* open, direct, unafraid to express the truth, (*syn.*) candid: *The rock star was frank about his drug problem.* -*n.* [U] **frankness.**

frank (2) *n.* *See:* frankfurter.

frank-furt-er /'fræŋkfərtər, -fətər/ *n.* a meat mixture usu. made with beef or pork in the shape of a tube; a hot dog: *Hamburgers and frankfurters are two popular American foods.*

frank-in-cense /'fræŋkɪn,sɛns/ *n.* [U] a substance found in certain trees and used to make incense and perfume: *Frankincense has been used in religious ceremonies since ancient times.*

frank-ly /'fræŋkli/ *adv.* **1** with openness and honesty, (*syn.*) candidly: *The official spoke frankly about the region's problems.* **2** stated directly and honestly but not necessarily politely: *Frankly, he thinks that your ideas are completely wrong.*

fran-tic /'fræntɪk/ *adj.* **1** very rushed, (*syn.*) frenzied: *Rescuers made a frantic effort to save the drowning man.* **2** almost crazy with fear (grief, anxiety, etc.): *The mother was frantic after she lost her child.* -*adv.* **frantically.**

frat /fræt/ *n.infrml.* a college fraternity

fra-ter-nal /frə'tɜrnl/ *adj.* **1** related to the relationship between brothers, like a brother: *He belongs to a fraternal order of firemen.* **2 fraternal twins:** non-identical twins -*adv.* **fraternally.**

fra-ter-ni-ty /frə'tɜrnəti/ *n.adj.* **-ties 1** in U.S. colleges, a social organization for male students, usu. sharing the same housing: *That student belongs to a <n.> fraternity and lives at the <adj.> fraternity house.* **2** *fig.* any general grouping of people with common interests or characteristics: *He belongs to the fraternity of educated men. See:* sorority.

USAGE NOTE: The names of college *fraternities* are often two or three Greek letters, such as Sigma Chi or Delta Tau Delta. Fraternities often have secret expressions, handshakes, and celebrations.

---

frat-er-nize /'frætər,naɪz/ *v.* **-nized, -nizing, -nizes** to be friendly with people from a different, sometimes opposing group: *He was arrested during the war for fraternizing with the enemy.*

frat-ri-cide /'frætrə,saɪd/ *n.* [U] the murder of one's brother: *In the Bible, Cain committed fratricide by killing his brother, Abel.*

fraud /frɔd/ *n.* **1** [U] deceit with the purpose of gaining another's money or property: *The company offered property for sale in Arizona, but it was a fraud; the property didn't exist.* **2** [C] s.o. or s.t. that is not what he, she, or it appears to be: *He said he was an Italian prince, but he was a fraud.*

fraud-u-lent /'frɔdʒələnt/ *adj.* dishonest, false, (*syn.*) deceitful: *The company made fraudulent statements in its television commercials for its shampoo.* -*n.* [U] **fraudulence** -*adv.* **fraudulently.**

fraught /frɔt/ *adj.frml.* full of, filled: *That plan is fraught with difficulties.*

fray /freɪ/ *v.* **1** to cause a small piece of cloth to become thin from rubbing: *The cuffs on his shirt (raincoat, pants, etc.) have frayed.* **2** *fig.* to irritate, annoy: *The constant noise has frayed her nerves.*

—*n.* [U] a fight that can be either physical or verbal, a battle: *Two men started to fight, and others jumped into the fray.*

fraz·zle /ˈfræzəl/ *v.* **-zled, -zling, -zles** *n.* to make very tired, upset, or nervous: *The summer heat <v.> frazzled her* (or) *she is in a <n.> frazzle from the heat.*

freak /frik/ *n.* **1** a person or animal with an abnormal shape: *The animal was a freak, born with two heads.* **2** *infrml.* a person with a very strong interest in s.t.: *She's an exercise freak and goes to the gym every day.*
—*adj.* strange, as in a very unusual happening: *In New York, there was a freak snowstorm last year in June.*
—*phrasal v. infrml.* **to freak out:** to lose self-control, become crazy, esp. as a result of taking drugs: *When a stranger insulted him in a bar, he freaked out and started screaming.*

freck·le /ˈfrɛkəl/ *n.v.* **-led, -ling, -les,** a small light brown spot on the skin, often from being in the sun: *She develops <n.> freckles in the summer.* *-adj.* **freckled; freckle-faced** /ˈfrɛkəl,feɪst/.

free /fri/ *adj.* **freer, freest 1** not under the control of another person or institution: *After twenty years in prison, he was a free man.* **2** without political, religious, or economic restrictions: *We live in a free country.* **3** completely without: *The property is free of any debt.‖The river is not yet free of pollution.* **4** without payment: *Admission to the concert is free.* **5** not in use, (*syn.*) available: *The telephone (hotel room, bathroom, etc.) is free now.* **6** not busy: *Are you free to talk now, or should I come back later?* **7** generous: *She is free with help and advice for those who need it.* **8** giving or spending (too) easily, careless: *She is free with her money when she has it.* **9 free and clear:** without financial obligations, such as debt: *The property is free and clear for you to buy.* **10 free and easy:** relaxed, without worries: *Your father is feeling free and easy today, so you can ask him for money.* **11 free hand:** complete control over s.t.: *The couple gave the architect a free hand in designing their new house.* **12 to have free rein:** to have the power to take any action one wishes: *The owner has given her free rein to reorganize the company.*
—*v.* **freed, freeing, frees 1** to let go, release from s.t. unpleasant, (*syn.*) to liberate: *The jailer freed the prisoner.‖Winning the lottery freed him of financial worries forever.* **2** to clear away, remove an obstacle: *The workers freed the road of the fallen trees.* **3 to free s.o.'s mind:** *The mother learned that her lost son was safe, and that freed her mind of fear.* **4** *phrasal v. sep.* **to free s.o. or s.t. up:** to make available: *The state government freed up funds to build housing for the poor.‖It freed them up.*

—*adv.* **1** moving around without restrictions: *The children can run free in the park.* **2 for free:** without payment: *You can visit the museum for free on Tuesdays.* **3 to set free:** to let go, release, (*syn.*) to liberate: *The judge set the prisoner free.‖We opened the cage and set the bird free.* *-adv.* **freely.**

free agent *n.* a person without ties to any company or institution: *The baseball team's owner made their star a free agent.*

free associate *v.* **-ated, -ating, -ates** (in psychiatry) to say all the things that come to mind on a given topic: *The therapist encouraged the client to free-associate on all the things he remembered about his mother.*

free·bie or **freebee** /ˈfribi/ *n.infrml.* a gift, s.t. free: *My friend gave me a concert ticket and other freebies.*

free·dom /ˈfridəm/ *n.* **1** [U] the condition of being free, having the power to act and speak without restrictions: *The boy has the freedom to go where he wants to go.* **2** [C] a set of legal rights protected by the government, such as freedom of speech or religion: *Our various freedoms are the foundation of our nation.* **3** [U] release from prison or slavery: *The jury found the suspect not guilty, and the judge gave him his freedom.* **4** [U] protection against, release from s.t.: *The medication gave him freedom from pain.* **5** [U] ability to move s.t.: *His leg was broken, but he gradually regained freedom of movement.*

free en·ter·prise *n.* [U] an economic system in which individuals and companies conduct business with minimal government control: *<n.> Free enterprise encourages competition between businesses.*

free fall *n.* **1** a rapid downward movement, (*syns.*) a plunge, dive: *The skydiver went into a long free fall before opening his parachute.‖During the stock market panic, prices went into a free fall for several days.*

free-floating *adj.* (in finance) responding to natural market forces without government interference: *The exchange rates between currencies are free-floating as they change hourly.*

free-for-all /ˈfrifə,rɔl/ *n.* **1** a noisy fight involving a group of people, (*syn.*) a melee: *A fight started between two men at a football game and then turned into a free-for-all.* **2** a disorganized discussion: *The town meeting became a free-for-all, with everyone talking at once.*

free-form *adj.* done without restrictions, loose and informal: *The meeting turned into a free-form discussion.*

free·hand /ˈfri,hænd/ *adj.adv.* (of drawing) by hand, without the aid of mechanical devices: *The artist did a <adj.> freehand drawing of* the building (or) *drew the building <adv.>* *freehand.*

free·lance /'fri,læns/ *v.* **-lanced, -lancing, -lances** to work as an independent, self-employed person who performs jobs usu. for a variety of companies: *She is a writer who freelances for several health magazines.* *—adj.* related to freelancing: *He is a freelance artist (journalist, photographer, etc.).* *-n.* **free·lancer.** *See:* moonlight.

free·liv·ing *adj.* always seeking pleasure, (*syn.*) hedonistic: *He is a free-living guy who enjoys nightclubs, good food, and long vacations.*

free·load /'fri,loʊd/ *v.infrml.* to accept the food, money, and housing offered by others without repayment: *He's been freeloading off his sister for years. -n.* **freeloader.**

free lunch *n.fig.* **There is no such thing as a free lunch:** a saying that means one always has to pay for s.t. of value.

free market *n.adj.* an economic market, both domestic and international, that is allowed to compete freely without government restriction: *<n.> Free markets allow the most efficient manufacturer to succeed.||We live in a <adj.> free market economy.*

free port *n.* a ship's port or a section of an airport where goods are sold tax-free: *The ship stops at free ports in the Caribbean so that passengers can buy perfume, watches, and other luxury items.*

free ride *n.fig.* a service or favor done for s.o. without payment: *The sales manager's wife goes to conferences with him at company expense; she gets a free ride.*

free speech or **freedom of speech** *n.* [U] the right to speak or write what one wishes without government interference: *The right of free speech is one of this country's most treasured freedoms.*

free·stand·ing /'fri'stændɪŋ/ *adj.* standing without attachment to a wall or supporting device, unattached: *There are several freestanding bookshelves in the living room.*

free·style /'fri,staɪl/ *n.adj.* **1** (in gymnastics or skating competitions) the participant's choice of moves **2** (in swimming) the swimmer's choice of a stroke: *She does the crawl in the <n.> freestyle or <adj.> the freestyle competition.*

free·think·er /'fri'θɪŋkər/ *n.* a person who develops his or her own beliefs independently of accepted beliefs and tradition: *He is a freethinker who has many exciting ideas about educational reform. -adj.n.* [U] **freethinking.**

free trade *n.adj.* the movement of trade between countries with few government restrictions, such as import duties: *<n.> Free trade among nations results in increased competi-*

tion and lower prices.||*The United States signed a <adj.> free trade agreement with Mexico in 1994.*

free·way /'fri,weɪ/ *n.* a wide road for high-speed travel: *Los Angeles is famous for its many freeways. See:* expressway; highway.

free·wheel·ing /'fri'wilɪŋ/ *adj.fig.* acting boldly, without concern for rules or proper behavior: *His freewheeling style of doing business caused him to lose many customers. -v.* **freewheel;** *-n.* **freewheeler.**

free will *n.* [U] the power to make one's own choices: *He joined the Army of his own free will.*

freeze /friz/ *v.* **froze** /froʊz/, **frozen** /'froʊzən/, **freezing, freezes 1** to change into a solid state due to low temperature: *The water in the pond freezes in winter.* **2** to have the temperature drop below the freezing point: *It's going to freeze tonight.* **3** to preserve food by keeping it very cold: *We froze the soup we made yesterday.* **4** to stop and stand completely still: *A man pointed a gun at me and told me, "Freeze or I'll shoot!"* **5** to stop the movement of s.t.: *The Senator wants to freeze government spending.||The bank froze my account for two days, so I couldn't use it.* **6** *phrasal v. sep.* **to freeze s.o. or s.t. out:** to prevent from participating, (*syn.*) to exclude: *He froze out his competition by lowering his prices.||He froze them out.* **7** *phrasal v.* **to freeze over:** to solidify into ice: *The surface of the pond froze over last night.* **8** *phrasal v.* **to freeze up: a.** to be unable to move or function because of ice: *We had no water last night because the pipes froze up.* **b.** to be unable to perform because of nervousness: *As soon as she saw the large audience, she froze up and couldn't make her speech.* *—n.* a condition of freezing by low temperature: *The freeze last night destroyed the farmer's tomatoes.* **2** an action that stops movement: *The company put a freeze on salaries; nobody is going to get a raise.*

freeze-dry *v.* **-dried, -drying, -dries** to preserve s.t. (food, coffee, etc.) by freezing it and then removing its water: *Coffee makers freeze-dry beans to make instant coffee. -adj.* **freeze-dried.**

freez·er /'frizər/ *n.* a compartment or a separate unit in a refrigerator designed to freeze food and to keep it frozen: *We put some steaks in the freezer for future use.*

freez·ing /'frizɪŋ/ *adj.* very cold: *It's freezing outside; put on your winter coat.*

freezing point *n.* the point at which water freezes: *The freezing point is 32 degrees Fahrenheit or 0 degrees Celsius.*

free zone *n.* a tax-free area in a city or port: *Goods can be brought into a free zone in San Juan, Puerto Rico, and then shipped to many* *countries in Latin America.*

freight /freɪt/ *n.* [U] transported goods, (*syn.*) cargo: *A truck brought a load of freight to the warehouse.*
—*v.* to ship, transport: *We freighted the goods to the warehouse by truck.*

freight·age /'freɪtɪdʒ/ *n.* [U] **1** a technical term for transportation of freight in general **2** the cost of freight: *The freightage for those goods was minimal because they went by ship and not by air.*

freight car *n.* a railroad car designed to carry freight: *For years, freight cars were painted brown.*

freight·er /'freɪtər/ *n.* a ship designed to carry freight: *The freighter carries a few passengers in addition to its cargo.*

freight train *n.* a train with one or more powerful engines pulling a large number of freight cars: *Some freight trains have so many freight cars that they are a mile long.*

French dress·ing /frɛntʃ/ *n.* [C;U] (in USA) **1** vinegar and oil mixed together, often with herbs for salads **2** a pinkish, creamy salad dressing: *French dressing tastes delicious on a fresh salad.*

French fries *n.pl.* strips of potatoes deep-fried in fat: *Americans love hamburgers with French fries.*

French kiss *n.* **kisses** a kiss where one partner's tongue enters the other's mouth: *He gave her a French kiss.*

fre·net·ic /frə'nɛtɪk/ *adj.* very rushed, nervously excited, (*syn.*) frenzied: *The activity backstage before the show was frenetic. -adv.* **frenetically.**

fren·zied /'frɛnzid/ *adj.* very rushed, panicked, (*syns.*) frantic, frenetic: *The boy's friends made a frenzied attempt to save him from drowning. -adv.* **frenziedly.**

fren·zy /'frɛnzi/ *n.* **-zies** [C;U] **1** a state of panic, causing a wild display of emotion, (*syn.*) hysteria: *When she learned of her son's death, she went into a frenzy, tearing at her hair and screaming.* **2** very great excitement: *When the singer finally appeared on stage, the crowd was in a frenzy.*

fre·quen·cy /'frikwənsi/ *n.* **-cies 1** [U] the rate at which s.t. happens, occurs: *The buses stop here with regular frequency.* **2** [U] s.t. that happens often: *The article discussed the reasons for the frequency of violent crime in urban areas.* **3** [C] the number given to a transmission wave, esp. of a radio station: *The various frequencies on the radio are crowded together in large areas such as New York.*

fre·quent /'frikwənt/ *adj.* often: *Car theft is a frequent occurrence in this area.*
—*v.* to visit, (*syn.*) to patronize: *He frequents the local restaurants often. -adv.* **frequently.**

fres·co /'frɛskoʊ/ *n.* **-coes** or **-cos** a wall painting: *The frescoes in these churches are magnificent.*

fresh /frɛʃ/ *adj.* **1** recently picked, (prepared, produced, etc.), not canned or frozen: *We enjoy fresh vegetables and fruit, straight from the garden: fresh orange juice, fresh fish, fresh bread.* **2** bright, new: *The house has a fresh coat of paint.* **3** different, exciting, original, (*syn.*) innovative: *New people with fresh ideas joined the company.* **4** pleasantly cool, (*syn.*) refreshing: *A fresh breeze feels wonderful on a hot day.* **5** rude, (*syn.*) impudent: *The little boy was fresh to the teacher.* **6** having recently arrived from: *She's fresh out of college and looking for work. -adv.* **freshly; -n. freshness.**

fresh·en /'frɛʃən/ *v.* **1** to make or become fresher: *I'll freshen your drink with more soda and ice cubes.* **2** *phrasal v. sep.* **to freshen s.o. or s.t. up:** to make s.o. or s.t. feel or look better by washing, cleaning, etc.: *She freshened up the room with some flowers.||She freshened it up.*

fresh·man /'frɛʃmən/ *n.* **-men** /-mən/ *adj.* a student in the first year of high school or college: *She is a <n.> freshman at the University of Notre Dame; she lives in the <adj.> freshman dormitory.*

USAGE NOTE: First-year high school and college students are called *freshmen;* second year students are *sophomores;* third year students are *juniors*; and fourth year students are *seniors.*

---

fresh·wa·ter /'frɛʃ,wɔtər, -,wɑ-/ *adj.* of inland water, such as lakes, rivers, and ponds: *Trout and bass are two types of freshwater fish.*

fret /frɛt/ *v.* **fretted, fretting, frets** to worry, express anxiety: *She fretted when her children came home late from school.*

fret·ful /'frɛtfəl/ *adj.* complaining and irritable: *The baby was fretful because he didn't sleep. -adv.* **fretfully.**

Freud·i·an /'frɔɪdiən/ *n.* a therapist who is a follower of Sigmund Freud's theory of psychoanalysis: *He is a strict Freudian.*
—*adj.* **1** related to the psychoanalytic theories of Sigmund Freud **2 Freudian slip:** a word or phrase, said accidentally, that reveals a feeling the speaker is unaware of: *The husband made a Freudian slip by calling his wife by his mother's name.*

fri·a·ble /'fraɪəbəl/ *adj.frml.* breaking apart easily: *The pages of the old book are yellowed and friable.*

fri·ar /'fraɪər/ *n.* a male member of a usu. Roman Catholic religious order: *He is a Dominican friar.*

fric·as·see /ˌfrɪkəˈsi/ *n*. meat or chicken cut into pieces and cooked slowly in its own juices: *We like to eat chicken fricassee.*

fric·tion /ˈfrɪkʃən/ *n*. **1** [U] resistance that results when two surfaces are rubbed together, (*syn.*) abrasion: *When you rub your hands together rapidly, the friction produces heat.* **2** [C;U] conflict, (*syn.*) strife: *The friction between the two secretaries created tension in the office.*

Fri·day /ˈfraɪdeɪ, -di/ *n*. **1** the fifth day of the week between Thursday and Saturday in the weekly calendar **2 Thank God it's Friday!:** An expression that people who are tired of working use to express relief that the weekend is near.

fridge /frɪdʒ/ *n.infrml.short for* refrigerator: *I put the milk and meat in the fridge.*

fried /fraɪd/ *past tense & past part. of* fry —*adj.infrml.fig.* drunk, (*syn.*) inebriated: *He got really fried at the party last night.*

friend /frɛnd/ *n*. **1** a person whom one likes and trusts, (*syn.*) a pal: *She's a good (=close) friend of mine.||Anna and Paul are just friends (=not lovers).* **2** a person who supports one's cause or group: *The Senator, who is from an agricultural state, is a friend of the farmer.* **2** a person who gives money to support an institution, such as a college, museum, or hospital, (*syns.*) benefactor, donor: *The new chemistry lab was paid for by friends of the college.* **3 to make friends with s.o.:** to form a relationship with s.o. one likes and trusts: *She made friends with some of her co-workers.* -*adj.* **friendless;** -*n.* [C;U] **friendship.**

friend·ly /ˈfrɛndli/ *adj.* **-lier, -liest 1** helpful, pleasant, agreeable: *She has a friendly manner with customers.||This bar has a friendly atmosphere.* **2** referring to a relationship of mutual fondness and trust: *He is friendly with his supervisor; they often go out to lunch together.* **3 friendly fire:** a situation in which soldiers are accidentally killed or wounded by other soldiers from their own side: *She discovered that her brother was killed by friendly fire.* -*n.* [U] **friendliness.**

fries /fraɪz/ *n.pl.infrml.* French fries: *A hamburger and fries are my favorite meal.*

frieze /friz/ *n*. architectural wall ornamentation consisting of a band of designs: *The living room has a frieze of flower designs carved in wood.*

frig /frɪg/ *v.slang* an expression showing strong displeasure with s.t., (*syn.*) to hell with it!: *Frig it! I'm not going to work on Saturday even if my boss threatens to fire me! See:* frigging.

USAGE NOTE: Many people find this term offensive.

frig·ate /ˈfrɪgɪt/ *n*. a fast warship: *The British navy was famous for the power and speed of its frigates.*

frig·ging /ˈfrɪgɪŋ/ *adj.slang* terrible, (*syn.*) damnable: *What a frigging mess he's made of things!*

fright /fraɪt/ *n*. [C;U] sudden fear, shock: *A tree fell on the house and gave him a fright.*

fright·en /ˈfraɪtn/ *v*. to cause fear, shock: *Strange sounds in the night frightened the child.*

fright·ened /ˈfraɪtnd/ *adj.* afraid: *The child is frightened of dogs.*

fright·en·ing /ˈfraɪtnɪŋ/ *adj.* causing fear: *The horror movie was very frightening.* -*adv.* **frighteningly.**

fright·ful /ˈfraɪtfəl/ *adj.* **1** causing fear, shocking: *The boat trip in the storm was frightful.* **2** offensive, terrible: *His behavior at the wedding party was frightful.* -*adv.* **frightfully.**

frig·id /ˈfrɪdʒɪd/ *adj.* **1** freezing, very cold: *Dress warmly; it's frigid out there.* **2** unfriendly, distant: *The atmosphere at the meeting was frigid.* **3** sexually unresponsive, cold: *He is a frigid man.* -*adv.* **frigidly;** -*n.* [U] **frigidity** /frɪˈdʒɪdəti/.

frill /frɪl/ *n*. **1** an ornamental border on a piece of clothing: *She wore a dress with frills on the sleeves.* **2 no frills:** basic, without extras or luxuries: *The airline offered a flight with no frills: food service, drinks, or movies.* -*adj.* **frilly.**

fringe /frɪndʒ/ *n*. **1** [C;U] the border of a piece of clothing, rug, tablecloth, etc., made of hanging threads or other material: *His jacket had fringes on the arms.* **2** [C] the outer edge or limit of s.t.: *The building is located on the fringes of the city.||The criminal lives on the fringes of society.* **3 to be on the fringe:** to have very odd behavior, be mentally ill: *He's on the fringe; he just sits alone in his room all day with the lights off.* **4 the lunatic fringe:** a group of people who want to completely change or destroy society: *A member of the lunatic fringe planted bombs on the subway.*
—*adj.* minor, very unlike most of the other members of a particular group: *She is a member of a liberal fringe group within the Republican Party.*
—*v.* **fringed, fringing, fringes** to add, be a border: *Trees fringe the park.*

fringe benefit *n*. a valuable service or privilege provided to an employee by an employer in addition to salary, such as medical, dental and life insurance, or a retirement plan: *The fringe benefits at that company are excellent.*

frip·per·y /ˈfrɪpəri/ *n.frml.* [U] very showy clothes: *The men and women arrived at the party in their frippery.*

Fris·bee /'frɪzbi/ *n.TM*
1 a flat round disk
made usu. of plastic,
tossed back and forth
between players **2** the
game of Frisbee: *We
played Frisbee at the beach.*

Frisbee

frisk /frɪsk/ *v.* **1** *infrml.* to search a person for
hidden weapons: *The police frisked the sus-
pect for a knife or pistol.* **2** to run in a playful
manner, (*syn.*) to gambol: *The kittens frisked
about on the kitchen floor.*

frisk·y /'frɪski/ *adj.* **-ier, -iest** lively, playful:
My cat feels frisky this morning. **-adv. friskily.**

frit·ter /'frɪtər/ *phrasal v.* **to fritter away
(time, money, opportunity):** to waste, spend
unwisely: *He fritters away his money on silly
things.*

fri·vol·i·ty /frɪ'vɑləti/ *n.* **-ties** [C;U] light
hearted fun, high spirits: *The atmosphere of
frivolity grew as friends told jokes.*

friv·o·lous /'frɪvələs/ *adj.* **1** unimportant, unnecessary: *She spends money on frivolous
things.* **2** silly, stupid: *He often makes frivolous comments.* **-adv. frivolously; -n.** [U] **friv-
olousness.**

frizz /frɪz/ *v.* **frizzes** (of hair) to become very
curly: *Her hair frizzes* (or) *frizzes up in the
rain.* **-adj. frizzy.**

fro /frou/ *adv.frml.* usu. *in the phrase* **to and
fro:** first in one direction and then back again,
(*syn.*) back and forth: *In the park, there were
children running to and fro.*

frock /frɑk/ *n.* **1** a long robe, usu. of heavy material with a hood, worn by monks: *The monk's
frock is made of brown woolen cloth.* **2** *old
usage* a woman's dress: *She was dressed in a
blue cotton frock.* See: defrock.

frog /frɔg, frag/ *n.* **1** a small usu. green or
brown animal with a large mouth and long,
powerful legs: *The children like to catch frogs
at the pond.* **2** *fig.* difficulty in speaking
caused by a sore throat: *I can't speak clearly
because I have a frog in my throat.*

frol·ic /'frɑlɪk/ *v.* **-icked, -icking, -ics** to play
about happily: *Children went on a picnic and
frolicked in a field.*
—*n.* a happy, carefree time: *They had a frolic
in the country.*

from /frəm; *strong form* frʌm, fram/ *prep.* **1**
showing a starting location, source: *She moved
from Los Angeles to Chicago.*‖*This beer is imported from Mexico.*‖*The letter is from my sister.* **2** showing a beginning point in time: *We
worked on the project from May to July.*‖*I'll
meet with you again a week from Friday*
(=showing a future time).‖*The two of them
have been friends from that day on* (=since that
day). **3** showing origin, material s.t. is made
of: *Coffee comes from beans.*‖*Those gloves are*

made from leather. **4** showing distance: *Those
boats are two miles from the shore.*‖*Boston is
250 miles from New York.* **5** showing a range,
esp. of sizes and numbers: *That type of fish
measures from three to six feet in length.* **6**
showing a reason or cause: *His death from
heart failure was shocking news.* **7** showing
difference: *I don't know one type of computer
from another.* **8** showing separation: *He removed his hand from her arm.*

frond /frand/ *n.* leaf of a fern plant or palm tree

front /frʌnt/ *n.* **1** [C] the forward area or side
of s.t.: *The front of the store has a toy display.*‖*To enter the building, you have to go
around to the front.* **2** [U] outward appearance, (*syn.*) demeanor: *He is a funny, relaxed
man, but always puts on a serious front for
strangers.* **3** [C] in war, the area where there
is fighting: *The general sent fresh troops to the
front.* **4** [U] a political movement with popular support: *They started a reform movement
called the Popular Front.* **5** [U] a strip of land
bordering on a body of water: *The restaurant
is located on the beach front.* **6** [C] a person,
organization, business, etc. acting as a cover
for an illegal activity: *That store is a front for
an illegal gambling operation.* **7** [C] a mass of
air of the same temperature: *A warm* or *cold
front will arrive in our area tomorrow.* **8 false
front:** to appear to be what one is not: *He
gives the impression of wealth, but that is a
false front.* **9 to put on a brave front:** to act
bravely when one is actually fearful: *The soldier put on a brave front as he went into battle.*
—*adj.* **1** forward: *The front windows of our
house overlook the park.*‖*The front row of
seats in the theater is full.* **2 in front:** ahead of
all others, first: *The fastest runner is very far
in front.*‖*In the race for governor, the
Republican candidate is in front.* **3 in front
of: a.** directly ahead of: *In the class photo,
Maria is sitting in front of Tony.*‖*There are
some trees in front of the building.* **b.** facing:
He stood in front of the mirror. **c.** in the presence of: *Don't talk about that in front of the
children.*

front·age /'frʌntɪdʒ/ *n.* **1** the forward part of a
building or piece of land: *The frontage of the
factory is on a main street.* **2** the amount of
land in front of a building: *The factory has a
50 foot (15.15 m) frontage from the front entrance to the street.* **3** the width of that
frontage: *The frontage is 300 feet (95m) wide.*

fron·tal /'frʌntəl/ *adj.* toward or from the front:
*The enemy made a frontal attack on our
troops.* **-adv. frontally.**

fron·tier /frʌn'tɪr/ *n.* **1** the outer edge of land
exploration: *The American West was still a
frontier a century ago.* **2** unknown area of a

field of knowledge: *She is a biochemist who works on the frontiers of biology.* **3** the border between two countries: *There have been reports of fighting on the frontier.*

fron·tiers·man /frʌn'tɪrzmən/ *n.* **-men** /-mən/ a man living on a frontier: *He is a frontiersman who lives alone in a cabin in the woods.*

fron·tis·piece /'frʌntɪs,pis/ *n.* an illustrated page at the beginning of a book: *The frontispiece has a picture of the Queen and a dedication to her.*

front man *n.* **-men** a person who acts for another individual or for a group, often to hide the other's identity: *The lawyer is a front man for big investors.*

front money or **up-front money** *n.* [U] money provided by investors to start a business: *A wealthy friend provided the front money for his new restaurant.*

front office *n.* (in business) office where the most important decisions are made: *Orders came from the front office to change accounting procedures.*

front-runner *n.* in a competition, the person who is in the lead: *A Democrat is the front-runner in the race for governor.*

frosh /frɑʃ/ *n.pl.infrml.* college or university freshmen: *The frosh have arrived at the university and are at the dorm.*

frost /frɔst/ *n.* **1** [U] white icy covering on a surface formed when water vapor in the air freezes: *There was frost on my window this morning.* **2** [C;U] weather condition when the temperature drops below freezing: *An early frost destroyed much of the orange crop.*
—*v.* **1** to form frost: *The car windows have frosted over in the autumn air.* **2** to apply a sugary covering to a cake: *After frosting the cake, we put it in the refrigerator.*

frost·bite /'frɔst,baɪt/ *n.* [U] a condition of frozen flesh, with blood circulation having stopped: *A mountain climber suffered frostbite in his toes.* *-adj.* **frostbitten** /'frɔst,bɪtn/.

frost·ing /'frɔstɪŋ/ *n.* [C;U] **1** a sugary covering, such as on cakes: *That cake has delicious chocolate frosting.* **2 frosting on the cake:** s.t. especially pleasing in a pleasant situation: *I found a new job, but the frosting on the cake is that I get six weeks' vacation in the first year.*

frost·y /'frɔsti/ *adj.* **-ier, -iest 1** related to cold weather: *It is frosty out today.* **2** covered with frost: *The kitchen windows are frosty this morning.* **3** cool, distant in manner: *She was very frosty to him when they met.* *-adv.* **frostily;** *-n.* [U] **frostiness.**

froth /frɔθ/ *n.* [U] **1** a coating of white bubbles, (*syn.*) foam: *Froth on the waves contrasts with the ocean's blue color.* **2** unimportant, empty talk: *Political speeches contain a lot of froth.*

—*v.* /frɔθ, frɔð/ to produce froth: *The dog growled and frothed at the mouth.* *-adj.* **frothy.**

frou-frou /'fru,fru/ *n.infrml.* unnecessary ornamentation, showiness, esp. of clothing: *She always dresses with a lot of frou-frou.*

frown /fraʊn/ *n.* a look of disapproval (doubt, annoyance, etc.) made by pulling the eyebrows downward and tightening the mouth: *He had a frown on his face after being unfairly criticized.*
—*v.* **1** to have a frown on one's face: *She frowned when she heard the bad news.* **2** *phrasal v.* **to frown on:** to disapprove of: *The teacher frowns on talking in the classroom.*

froze /froʊz/ *past tense of* freeze

fro·zen /'froʊzən/ *adj. & past part. of* freeze

fruc·tose /'frʌk,toʊs, 'frʊk-/ *n.* [U] a natural sugar found in fruit and honey: *Fructose gives you quick energy.*

fru·gal /'frugəl/ *adj.* **1** careful about spending money or wasting things, (*syn.*) thrifty: *Having been frugal all their lives, they can now live on their savings.* **2** small and costing little: *We had a frugal meal.* *-adv.* **frugally;** *-n.* [U] **frugality** /fru'gæləti/.

fruit /frut/ *n.* **1** the part of a plant that contains the seed, esp. when used as food: *Apples, pears, and oranges are some common types of fruit.‖You should eat at least three servings of fruit a day.* **2** *often pl.* result, product: *The fruits of his labors resulted in a large fortune.* **3** *pej. slang* a male homosexual **4 to bear fruit:** to produce s.t.: *Years of research finally bore fruit with the development of a new drug for treating cancer.*

fruit·cake /'frut,keɪk/ *n.* [C;U] **1** a heavy, rich cake made with chopped nuts and candied fruit: *We have fruitcake only at Christmas time.* **2** *infrml.* a crazy person: *That old lady is a fruitcake.*

fruit cup *n.* a serving of mixed fruit cut into small pieces: *We had fruit cup for dessert.*

fruit fly *n.* **flies** a type of tiny fly that feeds on and lays its eggs in fruit: *Fruit flies are an annoyance in households where fruit is left in the open.*

fruit·ful /'frutfəl/ *adj.* productive, profitable: *Representatives from the hospital and labor union had a fruitful discussion concerning the new contract.* *-adv.* **fruitfully** *-n.* [U] **fruitfulness.**

fru·i·tion /fru'ɪʃən/ *n.* [U] production of favorable results: *After months of hard work, our efforts finally came to fruition with the development of a new and exciting product.*

fruit·less /'frutlɪs/ *adj.* without benefit, useless: *After several fruitless attempts to start his own business, he went to work for his father.* *-n.* [U] **fruitlessness** *-adv.* **fruitlessly.**

fruit·y /ˈfruti/ *adj.* **-ier, -iest** having the sweet taste of a fruit: *That drink has a fruity taste.*

frump /frʌmp/ *n.pej.* a woman who wears plain, unstylish clothes and has a generally sloppy appearance: *She's such a frump; it's hard to believe she used to be a fashion model.* **-adj. frumpy.**

frus·trate /ˈfrʌˌstreɪt/ *v.* **-trated, -trating, -trates 1** to prevent s.o. from doing s.t., (*syn.*) to thwart: *Their attempts to climb the mountain were frustrated by winter storms.‖Her husband frustrated all her attempts to be happy.* **2** to have the feeling (of irritation, disappointment, anger, etc.) that results from this: *She felt frustrated when she didn't get a promotion after all her hard work.‖It was frustrating to work for such a demanding boss.*

frus·tra·tion /frʌˈstreɪʃən/ *n.* **1** [C;U] the feeling (of irritation, disappointment, anger) that results when one is prevented from doing s.t. one wants to do: *She suffered frustration in trying to find happiness.* **2** [U] interference, obstruction: *He found only frustration in searching for a new job.*

fry /fraɪ/ *v.* **fried, frying, fries 1** to cook in a fatty substance, such as butter or vegetable oil: *He fried eggs in a frying pan.* **2** *infrml.* to feel very hot: *We really fried at the beach today.* **3** *slang* to die, esp. in the electric chair: *He's going to fry for that murder.*

fry·er /ˈfraɪər/ *n.* **1** a deep pan used to fry foods: *We cooked some chicken in the fryer.* **2** a chicken for frying: *She bought a fryer for dinner.*

frying pan *n.* **1** a shallow pan with a handle used for frying food: *She used the frying pan to cook some onions and potatoes.* **2 out of the frying pan and into the**

frying pan

fire: from one difficult situation to an even worse one: *First he lost his job, and then he was called into court for nonpayment of debts; he really went out of the frying pan and into the fire.*

fuch·sia /ˈfyuʃə/ *n.* **1** [C] a garden plant that produces usu. pink, purplish-red, or red hanging flowers **2** [U] a purplish-red color

fud·dy-dud·dy /ˈfʌdiˌdʌdi/ *n.pej.* **-dies** a dull person with old-fashioned ideas: *He's an old fuddy-duddy who does nothing but complain.*

fudge /fʌdʒ/ *n.* [U] a rich sweet made of sugar, butter, and milk, usu. with chocolate: *We had chocolate fudge with coffee for dessert.*
—*v.* **fudged, fudging, fudges** to respond in an indirect way, falsify, usu. to avoid blame: *The Senator fudged when the reporter asked him why he had broken his campaign promise to cut taxes.*

fu·el /ˈfyuəl, fyul/ *n.* [C;U] a substance, such as coal, oil, or gasoline, that when burned releases heat to provide energy and power: *Gasoline is the fuel used in most motor vehicles.*
—*v.* **1** to provide with fuel, fill with fuel: *The plane is being fueled right now.* **2** *fig.* to provide energy, (*syn.*) to intensify: *Her desire to help the poor was fueled by her strong religious beliefs.* **-n.** [U] **fueling.**

fuel cell *n.* a device that provides continuous electricity: *The fuel cells in the space vehicle lasted the entire flight.*

fu·gi·tive /ˈfyudʒətɪv/ *n.* a person who is running away, (*syn.*) an escapee: *The prisoner escaped from prison and is now a fugitive.*

fugue /fyug/ *n.* a musical form in which a basic melody is repeated and developed in different ways: *Bach's fugues are a delight to hear.*

füh·rer /ˈfyʊrər/ *n.* (German for) leader: *The Führer was the title of Adolf Hitler.*

ful·crum /ˈfʊlkrəm, ˈfʌl-/ *n.* **-crums** or **-cra** /-krə/ **1** a point on which a lever is supported **2** *fig.* a person, organization, or object used to apply power and get results: *He is considered the fulcrum in the company and the reason for its success.*

ful·fill /fʊlˈfɪl/ *v.* **1** to perform, complete: *He fulfilled his obligations by making loan payments on time.* **2** to satisfy, (*syn.*) to accomplish: *She fulfilled her dreams of becoming an actress.*

ful·fill·ment /fʊlˈfɪlmənt/ *n.* [U] **1** performance or completion of s.t.: *The fulfillment of obligations under the contract will take two years.* **2** a feeling of satisfaction, success: *She found great fulfillment in her acting career.*

full /fʊl/ *adj.* **1** filled to the limit: *That bottle won't hold any more water; it's full.‖I'm not going to order dessert; I'm full.* **2** containing a large number amount of s.t., filled with: *The report is full of errors.‖That meat is full of fat.* **3** complete: *We've already spent a full week on this project.‖I need to get a full night's sleep.* **4** to the maximum: *The ship traveled at full speed.* **5** having as its most important characteristic: *That argument is full of nonsense.‖His speech was full of hope about the future.* **6 to go full blast:** to do s.t. with the most possible energy (speed, dedication, etc.): *My co-workers and I worked full blast for a week to finish the plan.* **7 to be full of baloney (it, beans,** *slang* **bull, crap, etc.):** to be all wrong: *He's full of it; he doesn't know what he's talking about.* **8 to be full of oneself:** to have too high an opinion of one's abilities: *He's so full of himself that no one can stand him.*
—*adv.* **1** forcefully, completely, (*syn.*) squarely: *A bullet hit the soldier full in the*

chest. **2 full well:** with certainty: *He knows full well that it's his turn to cook dinner tonight.* **3 in full:** with the complete amount: *I've repaid the loan in full.*

full-blood·ed /'fʊl,blʌdɪd/ *adj.* having a single ethnic ancestry: *The writer is a full-blooded Comanche Indian.*

full-blown /'fʊl'bloʊn/ *adj.* complete with everything, in the final stage of development: *The storm turned into a full-blown hurricane.||He has full-blown AIDS.*

full-bod·ied /'fʊl,bɑdid/ *adj.* rich with flavor: *That red wine has a full-bodied taste.*

full dress *n.* [U] *adj.* formal dress for formal and ceremonial occasions: *The officers were in <n.> full dress (or in <adj.> full-dress uniforms) for the party at the embassy.*

full house *n.* a theater that is full: *The musical played to full houses every night.*

full-length *adj.* **1** complete, of the appropriate length: *This is her first full-length novel (film, play, etc.).* **2** floor-length, from head to toe: *She wore an elegant full-length dress to the dance.*

full moon *n.* the moon when fully lit by the sun so that it appears completely round: *Some believe that the full moon makes people do strange things.*

full plate *n.fig.* a full workload, too much to do: *The manager has a full plate and cannot take on any additional responsibilities.*

full-scale *adj.* **1** (of a drawing or other representation) of the actual size of the original object: *The sales representative showed us a full-scale drawing of the new product.* **2** with the most power or force possible: *The generals were planning a full-scale invasion of the neighboring country.*

full stop *n.* **1** a complete stop: *Your car must come to a full stop at the red light.* **2** a period at the end of a sentence

full-tilt *adv.infrml.* at maximum speed, as fast as one can go: *The schoolboy was hungry, so he ran home full-tilt.*

full-time *adj.adv.* 35-40 hours a week: *He works <adv.> full-time (or he is a <adj.> full-time employee) during the day and goes to school at night. See:* part-time.

ful·ly /'fʊli/ *adv.* completely: *I didn't fully understand your question.*

ful·mi·nate /'fʌlmə,neɪt, 'fʊl-/ *v.* **-nated, -nating, -nates** to criticize strongly and at length: *The politician fulminated against corruption.* *-n.* [U] **fulmination** /,fʌlmə'neɪʃən, ,fʊl-/.

ful·some /'fʊlsəm/ *adj.frml.* excessive, insincere, or offensively flattering: *His fulsome comments about her dress annoyed her.*

Fu Man·chu mustache /'fuːmæn'tʃu/ *n.* a style of mustache that hangs down on either side of

the mouth: *He looks very mysterious with his dark glasses and Fu Manchu mustache.*

fum·ble /'fʌmbəl/ *v.* **-bled, -bling, -bles 1** to struggle with s.t., handle in an awkward fashion: *She fumbled with the keys as she tried to open the front door.* **2** to drop, lose control of: *The baseball player fumbled the ball.*
—*n.* a drop, loss of control: *He made a fumble.* *-n.* **fumbler;** [U] **fumbling.**

fume /fyum/ *v.* **fumed, fuming, fumes 1** to give off gas, smoke, or strong odors: *Clouds of black smoke fumed from the burning building.* **2** *fig.* to feel and/or show great anger: *When s.o. insulted her, she fumed and walked out of the room.*
—*n. usu. pl.* **fumes** the gas, smoke, or odor given off usu. from a chemical: *The gas fumes from the broken stove were very strong.*

fu·mi·gate /'fyumə,geɪt/ *v.* **-gate, -gating, -gates** to destroy (disease, insects, etc.) with chemicals: *Workers fumigated the house to kill cockroaches. -n.* **fumigator;** [U] **fumigation** /,fyumə'geɪʃən/.

fun /fʌn/ *n.* [U] **1** pleasurable activity, enjoyment: *We had fun at the picnic.* **2** a source of pleasure: *She's a lot of fun at parties.||Going to the dentist is no fun.* **3 for the fun of it:** to do s.t. for pure enjoyment, without a serious purpose: *When we went on the picnic, we decided to have some footraces just for the fun of it.* **4 fun and games:** pure pleasure: *Life is not just fun and games, but a lot of work and some grief.* **5 to make fun of s.o. or s.t.:** to laugh at s.o. or s.t. in an unkind way: *He often makes fun of his sister by imitating her.*
—*adj.infrml.* giving pleasure or enjoyment: *Waterskiing is a fun sport.*

func·tion /'fʌŋkʃən/ *v.* **1** to perform a task, serve as: *She functions as both administrator and teacher.* **2** to work (well, poorly, etc.): *The new computer has been functioning well.*
—*n.* **1** purpose, use: *The computer has a number of important functions.* **2** a formal social occasion: *They attended a function at the museum last night.*

func·tion·al /'fʌŋkʃənəl/ *adj.* **1** useful, practical: *The furniture is not fancy, just functional.* **2** capable of working, (*syn.*) operative: *The elevator was out of order, but is functional now.* *-adv.* **functionally.**

func·tion·ar·y /'fʌŋkʃə,nɛri/ *n.* **-ies** a person with an official position but not a lot of power, esp. in a large organization: *The President visited Europe and brought functionaries along.*

fund /fʌnd/ *n.* **1** a sum of money for a specific purpose: *The company pension fund is well-managed.||I'm short of funds at the moment; I can't buy that new car.* **2** a large amount of s.t.: *We were impressed by his fund of knowledge about foreign trade.*

—*v.* to provide money for a purpose: *The school lunch program is funded by the government.*

fun·da·men·tal /ˌfʌndəˈmɛntəl/ *adj.* **1** basic, primary: *Honesty is a fundamental principle in dealing with others.* **2** essential, necessary: *Food, shelter, and clothing are fundamental needs.*
—*n.* **1** a basic, primary principle (matter, concept): *Openness to new ideas is a fundamental in business.* **2** an essential, necessity: *Having work is a fundamental in life.*

fun·da·men·tal·ism /ˌfʌndəˈmɛntəˌlɪzəm/ *n.* (in religion) an insistence on a traditional interpretation of basic religious documents, such as the Bible, and strict obedience to their teachings and laws: *Fundamentalism has had a rebirth in many parts of the world.* -*n.adj.* **fundamentalist.**

fund rais·er *n.* **1** a person who collects money for public, charitable, or political purposes: *She is an excellent fund raiser for her political party.* **2** a party held to raise funds for public, charitable, or political purposes: *We attended the fund raiser held at the governor's mansion.* -*n.* [U] **fund-raising.**

fu·ner·al /ˈfyunərəl/ *n.* the ceremony that accompanies the burial or burning of a dead person: *His aunt's funeral will be held tomorrow.*

fu·ner·al home or **fu·ner·al par·lor** *n.* a house or building where a body is usu. prepared for burial and where people view the body for the last time

fu·ne·re·al /fyuˈnɪriəl/ *adj.* serious, sad like a funeral: *The day before the company closed, the atmosphere in the office was funereal.*

fun·gi·ble /ˈfʌndʒəbəl/ *adj.frml.* (in business) exchangeable (goods, merchandise): *The goods were damaged in shipment, but the manufacturer says they are fungible.*

fun·gi·cide /ˈfʌndʒəˌsaɪd, ˈfʌŋgə-/ *n.* a substance that kills a fungus: *Farmers sometimes use fungicides on their crops.*

fun·gus /ˈfʌŋgəs/ *n.* **fungi** /ˈfʌnˌdʒaɪ, ˈfʌŋˌgaɪ/ or **funguses** an organism that feeds on living or dead plants or animals and cannot survive apart from them: *Mushrooms are a type of fungus.* -*adj.* **fungal** /ˈfʌŋgəl/.

fun house *n.* a building at an amusement park where one walks through a series of rooms with strange noises and frightening man-made creatures that move: *Children like to visit the fun house because it's so scary.*

fu·nic·u·lar /fyuˈnɪkyələr, fə-/ *n.* a small railroad used to travel up and down hills and mountains: *The funicular takes tourists up the mountain.*

funk /fʌŋk/ *n.* [U] **1 in a funk:** feeling sad and low, (*syn.*) depressed: *She's been in a funk since she found out she didn't get a promotion.* **2** a type of popular music with a heavy beat and strong emotional effect that has elements of jazz, blues, and soul music

funk·y /ˈfʌŋki/ *adj.* **-ier, -iest 1** referring to a fashionable style with an often boldly original, unusual look: *It's a funky restaurant with very interesting art on the walls.* **2** referring to funk music: *They were playing some funky music at the party last night.* **3** *infrml.* having an unpleasant odor, (*syn.*) smelly: *These sneakers smell really funky.*

fun·nel /ˈfʌnl/ *n.* a utensil with a wide opening on top leading into a narrow bottom and used to control the flow of a liquid: *She used a funnel to pour water from a pitcher into a bottle.*
—*v.* to use a funnel or to control as if with a funnel: *The bank funnels loans into small businesses.*‖*Small streams funnel water into the river.*

fun·nies /ˈfʌniz/ *n.pl.* a section of some newspapers containing a number of humorous hand-drawn picture stories, often with a familiar set of characters, (*syn.*) funny pages: *Sometimes I turn to the funnies first before reading the serious news.*

fun·ny /ˈfʌni/ *adj.* **-nier, -niest 1** humorous, comical: *Her story was so funny that we couldn't stop laughing.*‖*She's a funny person.* **2** odd, strange, (*syn.*) suspicious: *Something funny is going on in that house next door.* **3** a little sick: *I started to feel funny about an hour after I ate lunch.* **4** referring to a coincidence, s.t. interesting: *Funny that you should mention that, I was thinking about doing the same thing myself.* -*n.* [U] **funniness.**

funny bone *n.infrml.* a sensitive spot in the elbow: *Ouch! I hit my funny bone against the door!*

fun·ny·man /ˈfʌniˌmæn/ *n.* **-men** /-ˌmɛn/ a comedian: *We saw a funnyman at the show.*

fur /fɜr/ *n.adj.* **1** [U] the hairy coat of an animal: *The cat's fur is soft and shiny.* **2** [C] clothing made from this: *She always wears her* <*n.*> *fur* (or) <*adj.*> *fur coat on cold winter days.* **3 to see** or **watch the fur fly:** to see a heated argument: *While we were waiting on the long line to buy tickets, one person tried to get ahead of another; you should have seen the fur fly.*

fur·bish /ˈfɜrbɪʃ/ *v.frml.* **-bishes** to put s.t. into better condition, make s.t. look brighter or fresher: *She furbished the house before trying to sell it. See:* refurbish.

fu·ri·ous /ˈfyuriəs/ *adj.* **1** very angry, (*syns.*) enraged, infuriated: *He is furious over the theft of his wallet.* **2** very rushed, intensive, (*syns.*) frantic, all out: *Rescuers made a furious attempt to save the trapped child.* -*adv.* **furiously.**

furl /fɜrl/ v. to roll up: *Two soldiers furled the flag. See:* unfurl.

fur·long /'fɜr,lɔŋ/ n. 220 yards: *A furlong is an old unit of linear measurement today used mainly in horse racing.*

fur·lough /'fɜrloʊ/ n. (in the military) a vacation: *Some soldiers went on furlough for two weeks.*
—v. to put on vacation, esp. to dismiss with the possibility of being recalled: *The Navy furloughed him and never called him back to active duty.*

fur·nace /'fɜrnɪs/ n. a heavy container for burning fuel esp. to provide heat: *That old house has a coal furnace.*

fur·nish /'fɜrnɪʃ/ v. **-nishes 1** to provide, give s.t.: *The travel agency furnished me with the information that I needed for my trip.* **2** to provide with furniture, lamps, curtains, etc.: *She furnished the apartment with modern furniture.*

fur·nish·ings /'fɜrnɪʃɪŋz/ n.pl. **1** furniture, curtains, rugs, and other objects for homes and offices: *The furnishings in that house are quite elegant.* **2** clothing

fur·ni·ture /'fɜrnɪtʃər/ n. [U] articles such as tables, chairs, beds, sofas, and other objects for homes and offices: *The house is filled with antique furniture.*

fu·ror /'fyʊrɔr, -ər/ n. an angry disturbance, (syn.) uproar: *The government's attempt to raise taxes created a furor across the country.*

fur·row /'fɜroʊ, 'fʌroʊ/ n. **1** the line cut into a layer of soil by a plow **2** a deep line in the skin of the face: *He has furrows in his forehead from worry.||He has a <adj.> furrowed brow.*
—v. to plow or make furrows: *The plow furrowed the garden.*

fur·ry /'fɜri/ adj. **-rier, -riest 1** having a coat of fur: *Furry animals grow long coats in winter.* **2** having a soft fur-like covering: *The child received a furry toy rabbit for her birthday.*

fur·ther /'fɜrðər/ adv. **1** more, additionally: *We can discuss the plan further tomorrow.* **2** comp. of far more ahead, more distant: *I can't walk any further.||He is further away from his goals than ever before.*
—adj. more, additional: *Have you received any further news about the accident?*
—v. to help move forward, progress: *He is taking business courses to further his career.*

USAGE NOTE: "Further" (and "furthest") may be used instead of "farther" (and "farthest") to express physical distances, as in " He has moved his business farther (or) further from town." However, you cannot substitute "farther" for "further" to express abstract meanings, as in "After further consideration, he rejected the plan."

fur·ther·ance /'fɜrðərəns/ n.frml. [U] continuation, advancement: *In furtherance of meeting sales objectives, we are increasing our advertising budget.*

fur·ther·more /'fɜrðər,mɔr/ adv. in addition, also, (syn.) moreover: *You have arrived late to the office every day this week; furthermore, your work has been unsatisfactory.*

fur·ther·most /'fɜrðər,moʊst/ adj. most distant, farthest away: *Hurting anyone is furthermost from his mind.*

fur·thest /'fɜrðɪst/ adj. superlative of far: most distant, farthest away: *Lowering salaries is the furthest option in the company's plan.||Pluto is the furthest planet from the sun. See:* further.

fur·tive /'fɜrtɪv/ adj. hidden from public view, secret, and possibly deceitful: *The teacher was suspicious of the student's furtive behavior during the exam.||He gave her a furtive smile.*
-adv. **furtively** -n. [U] **furtiveness.**

fu·ry /'fyʊri/ n. violent anger, (syn.) rage: *The storm attacked the coast with the fury of a hurricane.*

fuse /fyuz/ n. **1** a safety device designed to break if an excessive amount of electricity passes through it: *The air conditioner caused a fuse to blow.* **2** a flammable string or other device used to set off an explosive: *The miner lit the fuse that set off the dynamite.* **3 to blow a fuse: a.** to cause a fuse to break: *When we had the electric heater and the microwave on at the same time, we blew a fuse.* **b.** fig. to become angry suddenly, (syn.) to lose one's temper: *He blew a fuse when his flight was canceled.* **4 to have a short fuse:** short-tempered, to become angry quickly: *You have to be careful with him, because he has a short fuse.*
—v. **fused, fusing, fuses** to melt together, become one: *A worker fused together two hot metals into an alloy.*

fuse box n. **-boxes** a box set into the wall of a house, apartment, or other building that contains the structure's fuses: *The fuse box is in the basement. See:* circuit breaker.

fu·se·lage /'fyusə,lɑdʒ, -lɪdʒ/ n. the main body of an aircraft: *The passenger section of an airplane is contained within the fuselage.*

fu·sil·lade /'fyusə,lɑd, -,leɪd/ n. a burst of shots from weapons: *The gangster was killed in a fusillade of gunshots.*

fu·sion /'fyuʒən/ n. [C;U] the fusing or melting together of such things as metals, ideas, or cultures: *The fusion of ideas results from trade between nations. See:* nuclear fusion.

fuss /fʌs/ n. [U] **1** a show of great concern over s.t. unimportant: *What a fuss over such a small mistake!* **2 to make a fuss:** to show great annoyance, complain noisily about s.t. unimportant: *He makes a fuss if his breakfast eggs aren't cooked right.* **3** phrasal v. **to make a fuss over (or) fuss over s.o.:** to pay a lot of at-

tention to, (*syn.*) to dote on: *Every time her son comes to dinner, his mother makes a fuss over* (or) *fusses over him.*
—*v.* **-fusses** to act anxious, to handle s.t. nervously: *Stop fussing with your hair; it's time to go.*

fuss·budget /ˈfʌsˌbʌdʒɪt/ *n. See:* fusspot.

fuss·pot /ˈfʌsˌpɑt/ *n.infrml.* a person who is never satisfied with anything: *She is a fusspot and is constantly complaining.*

fuss·y /ˈfʌsi/ *adj.* **-ier, -iest 1** critical, difficult to please, (*syn.*) picky: *He is so fussy about what he eats that nothing pleases him.* **2** very careful, selective, (*syns.*) particular, choosy: *She is quite fussy about her clothes and shops only in the most elegant stores. -adv.* **fussily; -***n.* [U] **fussiness.**

fu·tile /ˈfyutl, ˈfyuˌtaɪl/ *adj.* useless, unsuccessful: *He made a second and futile attempt to pass the examination. -adv.* **futilely.**

fu·til·i·ty /fyuˈtɪləti/ *n.* [U] **1** hopelessness, uselessness, (*syn.*) pointlessness: *She finally saw the futility of trying to save her marriage.* **2 an exercise in futility:** a useless act: *Searching*

for peace in that part of the world is an exercise in futility.

fu·ture /ˈfyutʃər/ *n.* **1** [U] the state of life and events ahead, things to come: *No one knows what will happen in the future.* **2** [C] one's life ahead in time, esp. a career: *She is planning for a future in medicine.* **3** [U] the possibility of success: *He has no future with this company.*
—*adj.* related to the future: *Future relations between the two countries should improve.||She introduced him as her future husband.*

fu·tur·is·tic /ˌfyutʃəˈrɪstɪk/ *adj.* very modern, advanced

fuzz /fʌz/ *n.* [U] **1** a layer of short, soft hair or threads: *The baby's hair is fuzz.||A peach has fuzz on it.* **2** *slang* used with "the": the police: *The fuzz picked up his friend for selling drugs.*

fuzz·y /ˈfʌzi/ *adj.* **-ier, -iest 1** covered with short soft hair or threads: *The surface of that cloth feels fuzzy.* **2** unclear, (*syn.*) blurry: *The image in that picture is fuzzy. -adj.* **fuzzily; -***n.* [U] **fuzziness.**

FYI /ˈɛfwaɪˈaɪ/ *abbr. of* For Your Information: *FYI, today's meeting will be at 10:00, not 9:30.*

F

G, g

G, g /dʒi/ *n.* **G's, g's** or **Gs, gs** the seventh letter of the English alphabet

gab /gæb/ *v.* **gabbed, gabbing, gabs** to talk informally, (*syn.*) to chat: *Students like to gab while they eat lunch.*

gab·ar·dine or **gab•er•dine** /ˈgæbər,din, ˌgæbarˈdin/ *n.* cloth usu. of finely woven material: *I have worn my wool gabardine coat for many years.*

gab·by /ˈgæbi/ *adj.* **-bier, -biest** talkative, (*syn.*) chatty: *My friend is gabby; he loves to talk.*

ga·ble /ˈgeɪbəl/ *n.* the triangular section of a house formed under a pointed roof: *Gables make a house look elegant.*
—*adj.* **gabled:** *That house has a gabled roof.*

gable

gad·fly /ˈgæd,flaɪ/ *n.* **-flies 1** a type of fly that sucks blood from animals **2** *fig.* a person who offers many critical, but also helpful comments and questions: *He is a political gadfly always asks difficult questions that make politicians think hard.*

gadg·et /ˈgædʒɪt/ *n.* any small or unusual and useful object (an electronic device, machine, tool, etc.), (*syn.*) *infrml.* a gismo: *She has many electronic gadgets in her house, from computers to an electric toothbrush.*

gadg·et·ry /ˈgædʒɪtri/ *n.* a group of small or unusual and useful objects: *The engineer has a house full of gadgetry.*

gaff /gæf/ *n.v.* a pole with a hook on one end: *A fisherman stuck a <n.> gaff in a fish's gill and hauled it aboard his boat.*

gaffe /gæf/ *n.* an embarrassing social mistake, (*syn.*) a faux pas: *A guest made a gaffe at the wedding; he called the bride by the wrong name.*

gag /gæg/ *v.* **gagged, gagging, gags 1** to choke for a moment, (*syn.*) to retch: *The child gagged on the strong medicine.* **2** to put s.t. into the

mouth to stop s.o. from speaking: *The robber gagged his victim with a towel.* **3** *fig.* to stop s.o. from speaking freely: *The police gagged people who did not agree with the president.*
—*n.* **1** tape or other material that covers, or is put into, the mouth: *The burglar covered the man's mouth with a gag made of tape.* **2** *infrml.* a joke, (*syn.*) a prank: *A friend told some funny gags at lunch today.*

ga·ga /ˈgɑ,gɑ/ *adj.pej.* **1** slightly crazy, (*syns.*) insane, senile: *He is so old that he has gone gaga.* **2 to go gaga over:** to be very excited about, (*syn.*) to be infatuated with: *From the moment they met, he was gaga over her.*

gage /geɪdʒ/ *n. See:* gauge.

gag·gle /ˈgægəl/ *n.* a number of geese together, (*syn.*) a flock of geese: *A gaggle of Canadian geese swam in the lake.*

gag order *n.* (in law) a court decision not permitting discussion and reporting of a court case: *In the trial of a well-known criminal, the judge issued a gag order to stop reporters from writing about the story.*

gag rule *n.* an order that stops discussion for a limited time: *The Senate made a gag rule; for two days lawmakers could not talk about a new tax proposal.*

gai·e·ty /ˈgeɪəti/ *n.* [U] high spirits, (*syn.*) merriment: *The laughter and gaiety at the party made everyone feel good.*

gain /geɪn/ *v.* **1** to obtain, acquire: *Students gain useful knowledge by taking a computer course.* **2** to make money, (*syn.*) to profit: *An investor gains by buying stocks that go up in value.* **3** to come closer to s.o. or s.t.: *The runner gained on her opponent and finally won the race.* **4** to go up, (*syns.*) to increase, advance: *Prices gained yesterday on the stock exchange.* **5 nothing to gain:** no benefit from doing s.t.: *You have nothing to gain by becoming angry; anger will not solve the problem.* **6 to gain ground: a.** *frml.* to move ahead, (*syn.*) to advance: *The soldiers gained ground by pushing the enemy back.* **b.** *fig.* to move closer to s.o. or s.t. in a spirit of competition: *To gain* *ground on his opponent, the politician promised to cut taxes.*

—*n.* **1** a profit: *A banker made a big gain on his investment.* **2** an increase, advance: *The discovery of a new kind of star was a gain for science.||Stocks made a gain in today's trading.* **3 one man's gain is another man's loss:** one person benefits from the loss of another person: *When two people bet money against each other, one man's gain is another man's loss.*

gain·ful /ˈgeɪnfəl/ *adj.* related to earning a living, (*syn.*) profitable: *My friend found gainful employment in another city.* -*adv.* **gainfully.**

gains /geɪnz/ *n.pl.* **1** winnings: *When she won money in the lottery, the woman took her gains and bought a new car.* **2 ill-gotten gains:** money made illegally or by clever practices: *The dishonest banker used his ill-gotten gains to buy a vacation house.*

gait /geɪt/ *n.* the way a person (or horse) walks (runs, gallops, etc.): *He walks with a slow, uneven gait because of a bad leg.*

gal /gæl/ *n.old usage* (used in a friendly context) a girl or woman: *She's a wonderful gal; everyone loves to talk with her.*

ga·la /ˈgeɪlə, ˈgæ-, ˈgɑ-/ *n.* a special public event (social, artistic, sporting, etc.) usu. with famous people: *Opera stars from all over the world sang at the gala last night.*

gal·ax·y /ˈgæləksi/ *n.* **-ies** a large system of stars: *Our galaxy is called the Milky Way.* -*adj.* **galactic** /gəˈlæktɪk/.

gale /geɪl/ *n.adj.* **1** a strong wind (of approx. 60 miles per hour): *The gale knocked over trees in our area.* **2 gale-force winds:** *The gale-force winds knocked down the old tree in the garden.*

gall /gɔl/ *n.* **1** a liquid produced by the liver, (*syn.*) bile **2** *fig.* rudeness, (*syns.*) nerve, cheek: *After nearly knocking me down, she had the gall to demand an apology.*

—*v.* to annoy, (*syn.*) to humiliate: *It galled me when my best friend stopped speaking to me.*

gal·lant /ˈgælənt/ *adj.* **1** (of a man) polite to women, considerate, (*syn.*) *frml.* chivalrous: *Women like him because he is gallant; he always asks them what they want to do.* **2** brave: *The man's gallant act saved my life.* -*adv.* **gallantly.**

gal·lant·ry /ˈgæləntri/ *n.* **-ries** **1** politeness toward women **2** bravery, courage: *The soldier was honored for gallantry in battle.*

gall·blad·der /ˈgɔlˌblædər/ *n.* an organ attached to the liver that stores and sends out bile: *The gallbladder helps the body digest fat.*

gal·ler·y /ˈgæləri, ˈgælri/ *n.* **-ies** **1** a room or building used to display or sell art, usu. smaller than a museum: *He saw many art galleries in the Soho area of New York City.* **2** a

raised section of a theater or public hall where people watch a performance or event: *Visitors sat in the gallery to watch the Senate debate.*

gal·ley /ˈgæli/ *n.* **1** the kitchen of a ship: *The cook serves excellent meals from a small galley.* **2** a sailing ship in former times, rowed by many men: *Galleys sailed the seas in ancient times.*

gal·li·vant /ˈgæləˌvænt, ˌgæləˈvænt/ *v.infrml.* (used humorously) to look for fun by going from one place to another: *On Saturday nights, he likes to go gallivanting around to different bars.*

gal·lon /ˈgælən/ *n.* in the USA, a liquid measurement equal to four quarts of 32 ounces each: *Yesterday, I bought five gallons of juice for the party.*

G

USAGE NOTE: A *gallon* is equal to 3.8 liters: Gasoline, paint, wine and other liquids are commonly sold in gallons: *My car is old, but gets about 20 miles to the gallon.* A *quart* equals one-fourth of a gallon or .95 liters: *We need eggs, bread, and a quart of milk.*

gal·lop /ˈgæləp/ *n.* the fastest run of four-legged animals, esp. horses: *The horse raced to the rescue at full gallop.*

—*v.* (usu. of horses) to run at a gallop: *Race horses gallop around the race track.*

gal·lows /ˈgælouz/ *n.* **-lows** a raised, wooden structure used to hang criminals: *A murderer was sent to the gallows to die.*

gall·stone /ˈgɔlˌstoun/ *n.* a hard stone formed in the gallbladder: *The sick man is in pain from gallstones.*

ga·lore /gəˈlɔr/ *adj.* plenty of s.t., (*syn.*) in abundance: *There are flowers galore in the garden every spring.*

USAGE NOTE: *Galore* is placed after the word that it modifies.

ga·losh·es /gəˈlɑʃɪz, ˈglɑ-/ *n.pl.* rubber overshoes that protect ordinary shoes from the rain or snow: *He wears galoshes when it rains.*

gal·va·nize /ˈgælvəˌnaɪz/ *v.* **-nized, -nizing, -nizes** **1** to cover metal (usu. iron or steel) with zinc **2** *fig.* to stimulate, make s.o. act: *The politician's ideas galvanized the opposition against him.*

gam·bit /ˈgæmbɪt/ *n.* **1** an opening move in a chess game where one piece is given up to gain a more important piece later **2** a statement or an action designed to gain an advantage over s.o., (*syn.*) a ploy: *The businessman's gambit is to say that his investment will double in value.*

gam·ble /ˈgæmbəl/ *n.* **1** the playing of games of chance, (*syn.*) bet: *He took a gamble when he put his money on a horse.* **2** a risk: *She took*

a gamble that it would not rain when she decided to go camping in cloudy weather.
—*v.* **-bled, -bling, -bles 1** to play games of chance: *He gambles on the stock market.* **2** to take a risk: *She gambled that he would fall in love with her.* **3** *phrasal v. sep.* **to gamble s.t. away:** to lose money in games of chance or by taking bad risks: *He gambled away all his money on dog races.*‖*He gambled it away.*

gam·bler /'gæmblər/ *n.* **1** a person who plays games of chance **2** a risk-taker: *She is a gambler; she buys the stock of companies in financial trouble.*

USAGE NOTE: Because many *gamblers* can't control their desire to bet, gambling is considered a serious disease, like alcoholism. An organization called Gamblers Anonymous (a twelve-step program like Alcoholics Anonymous) helps gamblers break the habit and rebuild their lives.

gam·bling /'gæmblɪŋ/ *n.* **1** betting of money in games of chance, (*syn.*) wagering: *His wife put a stop to his gambling.* **2** risk-taking: *She likes gambling in real estate. See:* casino.

gam·bol /'gæmbəl/ *v.n.* to run and jump in a playful way, (*syn.*) to cavort: *The sheep* <*v.*> *gamboled happily in the field.*

game /geɪm/ *n.* **1** an activity or sport, often with rules, that people play: *A favorite children's game is hide-and-seek.* **2 Games** *pl.* athletic events: *The Summer Olympic Games take place every four years.* **3** wild animals, birds, and fishes captured or killed for sport: *The hunters captured deer and other wild game.* **4 to be fair game:** to be a person or institution that may with reason be criticized or attacked: *Politicians are fair game for criticism from reporters.* **5 to give the game away:** to reveal information by accident: *The chocolate around the little boy's mouth gives the game away; he ate all the chocolate cookies.* **6** *fig.* **to play games:** to try to get people to do what one wants by changing decisions, tricks, etc.: *At first, he said that he would sell at that price and now he's playing games to see if he can get more money from us.* **7 to play the game:** to act or play according to the rules: *She didn't like the company's methods of doing business, but she played the game because she needed the job.*
—*adj.* **1** related to hunting animals: *Game animals like deer and ducks are hunted for food.* **2 to be game:** to be ready and willing to do s.t. new, unusual, or difficult: *I wanted to climb a tall mountain nearby, and my grandmother said she was game to do it, too.*

game·keep·er /'geɪm,kipər/ *n.* an employee who watches over wild game animals and protects them from danger: *The gamekeeper on*

the African preserve worries about hunters shooting the elephants there.

game plan *n.* **1** a number of steps and goals planned by a team in a sporting event: *The football team's game plan is to control the ball as much as possible.* **2** *fig.* a plan of action, esp. in business: *Our game plan is to make a low first offer and then to increase it until we have an agreement.*

game show *n.* a television program featuring a game for prizes: *Her friend won a new car on the game show.*

games·man·ship /'geɪmzmən,ʃɪp/ *n.* the method of winning a game (in business, life, etc.) by disturbing the other players, but without breaking the rules: *It is gamesmanship to make a loud noise when the other player is trying to play. See:* sportsmanship.

gam·ing /'geɪmɪŋ/ *n. See:* gambling.

gam·ma ray /'gæmə/ *n.* high energy radiation often from nuclear sources: *Gamma rays can come from the waste of nuclear power plants.*

gam·ut /'gæmət/ *n.* **1** a range of things, (*syn.*) spectrum **2 to run the gamut:** to have examples of a wide range of possibilities: *The many colors in her dress run the gamut of the rainbow from red to yellow to blue.*

gam·y /'geɪmi/ *adj.* **-ier, -iest** tasting or smelling like wild animals killed for food: *That bear meat has a gamy taste.*

gan·der /'gændər/ *n.* **1** a male goose **2** *infrml.* a quick look: *This new magazine may interest you; give it a gander.*

gang /gæŋ/ *n.* **1** a group of (young) people (usu. used in a negative way) joined together for support and protection: *She joined a street gang when she was 12 years old.* **2** a group of criminals **3** a group of friends: *Where is the gang going on Friday night?*
—*v.* **1** to join together and act against s.o. or s.t.: *The boys ganged together to take control of their neighborhood.* **2** to group things together: *We ganged the order forms and worked on them all at one time.* -*n.* **gangland** /'gæŋ,lænd, -lənd/.

gang·bus·ter /'gæŋ,bʌstər/ *n.* **1** *infrml.* an officer of the law **2** *fig.* **like gangbusters:** with force, vigor: *Our sales have started off the new year like gangbusters.*

gan·gling /'gæŋglɪŋ/ *adj.* tall, thin, and awkward: *He is tall with gangling arms.*

gang·plank /'gæŋ,plæŋk/ *n.* a wooden or metal board that is used as a bridge between a ship and the land: *The sailors walked up the gangplank to get on their ship.*

gan·grene /'gæŋ,grin, gæŋ'grin/ *n.* death of tissue in the body usu. requiring surgical removal: *Gangrene developed in the boy's fingers from the cold.* -*adj.* **gangrenous** /'gæŋgrənəs/.

gang·ster /'gæŋstər/ *n.* a member of an orga-nized group of criminals: *The police arrested three gangsters after the shooting in Las Vegas yesterday.*

gang·way /'gæŋ,weɪ/ *n.* **1** a passageway in a ship: *Passengers walked a gangway to their cabins.* **2** a gangplank

gan·try /'gæntri/ *n.* **-tries** a tall metal structure used to support and service space rockets or support a crane that moves heavy loads: *A crane operator moved the gantry to unload the ship's cargo.*

gap /gæp/ *n.* **1** an empty space between two things: *He has a gap between his two front teeth.* **2** an unfilled period of time: *After a gap of five years, she returned to school to finish her college degree.* **3** a pass between moun-tains: *The climbers walked through the gap in the mountains to the next valley.* **4 to bridge the gap: a.** to fill an empty moment: *He bridged the gap in the conversation by offer-ing some drinks.* **b.** to fill an empty place: *The teacher bridged the gaps in the textbook with her own lectures.*

gape /geɪp/ *v.* **gaped, gaping, gapes 1** to look at s.o. or s.t. with the mouth open, usu. in sur-prise: *The children gaped at the big elephant in the zoo.* **2** to open wide or come apart: *After the earthquake, holes in the walls of the house gaped open. -adj.* **gaping.**

ga·rage /gə'raʒ, -'radʒ/ *n.* **1** a building where a vehicle is kept: *I keep my car in the garage next to my house.* **2** a place where cars can be repaired
—*v.* **-raged, -raging, -rages** to park in a garage: *We garaged our car for the winter.*

garage sale *n.* a sale of used household items (old lamps, tables, etc.) inside and near a per-son's garage: *When my parents moved to a smaller house, they held a garage sale one weekend.*

USAGE NOTE: Also known as yard sales, rum-mage sales, tag sales or sidewalk sales, *garage sales* are popular in both cities and suburbs. Homeowners may post signs around their neighborhood to advertise a sale. People who live in apartments usu. just put things out on the sidewalk and wait for passersby: *I need some bookshelves. Let's drive around the uni-versity area and look for a garage sale.*

garb /gɑrb/ *n.frml.* type of clothing, *(syn.)* at-tire: *The soldiers paraded in their military garb (uniforms).*

gar·bage /'gɑrbɪdʒ/ *n.* **1** things you do not want any more, *(syns.)* trash, refuse: *I put the garbage from last night's party in the trash can this morning.* **2** ideas and opinions that are considered stupid or worthless, *(syns.)* non-sense, foolishness: *What he says is just*

garbage! **3 garbage can:** a container that you put trash into, usu. in the kitchen **4 to take out** or **put out the garbage:** to remove trash from a household: *I take out the garbage every day.*

gar·bled /'gɑrbəld/ *adj.* mixed up, confused (words, message, thoughts, etc.): *I couldn't read the garbled message on my computer screen. -v.* **garble.**

gar·den /'gɑrdn/ *n.* an area of land used to grow flowers and vegetables: *We have a small flower garden behind our house.*
—*v.* to work in a garden *-n.* **gardener; gar-dening.**

gar·de·nia /gɑr'dinyə/ *n.* a plant with large white or yellow flowers: *Gardenias are pretty flowers.*

garden-variety *adj.* ordinary, common: *It's just your ordinary garden-variety mystery novel, nothing special.*

gar·gan·tu·an /gɑr'gæntʃuən/ *adj.* very big, huge, *(syn.)* colossal: *The statues of past pres-idents were gargantuan in size.*

gar·gle /'gɑrgəl/ *v.* **-gled, -gling, -gles** to soothe and clean the throat and mouth: *Each morning, he gargles with mouthwash. -n.* **gar-gling.**

gar·goyle /'gɑr,gɔɪl/ *n.* an ugly animal made of stone used as a decoration on many old European buildings: *The gargoyles on the Cathedral of Notre Dame in Paris are famous.*

gar·ish /'gærɪʃ, 'gɛr-/ *adj.* showy, *(syn.)* osten-tatious: *The chairs and rugs in that apartment are garish: red, orange, and purple.*

gar·land /'gɑrlənd/ *n.* a circle of flowers usu. worn in the hair: *The little girl wore a garland on her birthday.*

gar·lic /'gɑrlɪk/ *n.* a member of the onion fam-ily used as seasoning in food: *We put garlic in our spaghetti sauce. -adj.* **garlicky.**

gar·ment /'gɑrmənt/ *n.adj.* a general term for an article of clothing: *That company makes* <n.> *garments, mainly dresses, and is located in the* <adj.> *garment district in New York City. See:* apparel.

garment bag *n.* a thin luggage bag with a zipper used to carry suits and dresses: *She carries a gar-ment bag right on the air-plane when she travels.*

gar·ner /'gɑrnər/ *v.frml.* to collect or store (informa-tion, knowledge, wealth), *(syn.)* to amass *-n.* **gar-nering.**

garment bag

gar·net /'gɑrnɪt/ *n.* a red stone used in jewelry: *My new ring has three garnets in it.*

gar·nish /'gɑrnɪʃ/ *n.* a food decoration: *Restaurants often use parsley and lemon as a garnish for fish.*

G

—*v.* (in law) to take part of a person's wages/salary in repayment of a debt

gar·ret /'gærɪt/ *n.* a small room at the top of a house: *The author lived in a garret while writing his book.*

gar·ri·son /'gærəsən/ *n.* **1** a group of soldiers who guard a town or building **2** a camp or post where soldiers live: *The garrison consisted of 50 soldiers to protect the town.*
—*v.* to provide a place with soldiers and supplies: *The government garrisoned the fort with a company of soldiers.*

gar·ru·lous /'gærələs, 'gæryə-/ *adj.frml.* talking too much, talkative, (*syn.*) loquacious: *The crowd grew garrulous before the speaker arrived.* -*adv.* **garrulously.**

gar·ter /'gɑrtər/ *n.* **1** an elastic band worn around the leg to hold up socks or stockings: *His socks were too big, so he wore garters to keep them up.* **2** a decorative band worn usu. around the upper leg: *The nightclub dancers wore pink garters.*

gas /gæs/ *n.* **gases** [C;U] **1** any air-like substance, which usu. cannot be seen, that is not a liquid or solid: *Oxygen is a gas that exists in large quantities in the air.* **2** a substance used for cooking and heating: *She turned on the gas* (or) *gas stove to boil some water.* **3** *infrml.short for* gasoline: *I stopped the car for gas at the local gas station.* **4** *infrml.* wind from the stomach or intestine: *Eating onions gives me gas.* **5** a substance (e.g., nitrous oxide) given to you by a dentist or doctor to prevent pain, (*syn.*) an anesthetic: *The dentist gave me gas before he pulled out my tooth.* **6** *infrml.* a very funny thing: *The new comedy show is a real gas.* **7 to run out of gas: a.** to have no more gasoline: *Our car ran out of gas on the highway.* **b.** *fig.* to become very tired, unable to continue: *I worked very late last night; then I ran out of gas and went to bed.*
—*v.* **gassed, gassing, gases 1** to kill or injure with poisonous gas: *The army gassed the village with mustard gas and killed many people.* **2** *phrasal v. sep.* **to gas s.t. up:** to fill s.t. with gasoline: *I'm going to gas up the car for our long trip.||I'm going to gas it up.*

gas·bag /'gæs,bæg/ *n.slang* s.o. who talks very much, (*syn.*) a windbag: *He talks all the time; he's a gasbag.*

gas·e·ous /'gæsiəs, 'gæʃəs/ *adj.* in the form of gas: *Gaseous clouds are released from the factory into the atmosphere every day.*

gas-guzzler *n.infrml.* a car that uses a lot of gasoline: *That car is an old gas-guzzler; it gets only 10 miles to the gallon.*

USAGE NOTE: The big, American cars of the "60s and 70s" were *gas-guzzlers*, but today people buy cars that are more compact, energy-efficient, and economical.

gash /gæʃ/ *n.v.* **gashes** a long, deep cut, (*syn.*) a slash: *The boy fell and <v.> gashed his cheek.*

gas·ket /'gæskɪt/ *n.* **1** a soft, flat piece of material placed between two surfaces (usu. metal), so that liquids and gases cannot come out: *That engine was so old that the gaskets needed replacing.* **2 to blow a gasket** *infrml.fig.* to become very angry, explode with anger: *When a salesclerk was rude, the customer blew a gasket and complained to his manager.*

gas·light /'gæs,laɪt/ *n.* **1** light from burning gas **2** an old-fashioned lamp that uses gas: *Gaslights were used on streets and in houses before electricity replaced them.*

gas main *n.* a pipe carrying gas under the streets

gas·o·hol /'gæsə,hɔl, -,hɑl/ *n.* a fuel made from a mixture of gasoline and alcohol: *Some vehicles can use gasohol instead of gasoline.*

gas·o·line /,gæsə'lin, 'gæsə,lin/ *n.* a liquid produced from petroleum, used as an engine fuel. *See:* gas **3.**

gasp /gæsp/ *v.n.* **1** to breathe in quickly, usu. from surprise or shock: *I heard a <n.> gasp from the crowd when the speaker made the surprising announcement.* **2** to take short quick breaths usu. with difficulty: *She <v.> gasped for air after she finished the marathon.*

gas station *n.* a place that sells gasoline and repairs vehicles: *I stopped at the gas station to fill up the tank.*

gas·sy /'gæsi/ *adj.* **-sier, -siest** full of gas, esp. bubbles in liquids: *The soda was very gassy; it had a lot of bubbles.*

gas·tric /'gæstrɪk/ *adj.* related to the stomach and the system that breaks down food in the stomach: *He has a gastric ulcer.*

gas·tron·o·my /gæ'strɑnəmi/ *n.* [U] the art and study of fine food and drink: *My father is an expert in French gastronomy.* -*adj.* **gastronomic** /,gæstrə'nɑmɪk/.

gas·works /'gæs,wɜrks/ *n.pl.* a place that provides gas to the public for use in the home: *The gasworks is located outside of the city.*

gate /geɪt/ *n.* **1** a moveable barrier that closes an open space in a wall, fence, city, etc.: *A gate in the fence opens into a flower garden.* **2** an entrance or exit, usu. at an airport: *My flight to Paris is leaving from gate number four.* **3** the total number of people who attend a concert or sports game, or the total amount of money paid by them **4** *suffix* **-gate:** a political scandal often named for the place it is connected with: *Watergate, Irangate*

gate·crash·er /'geɪt,kræʃər/ *n.* a person who enters a private social event, usu. a party, without an invitation or ticket: *There were about 20* gatecrashers at my party; it was terrible. I'd never met any of them before.

gate·keep·er /'geɪt,kipər/ *n.* a person who is in charge of opening and closing a gate to control who enters: *The gatekeeper at the rich family's estate keeps strangers away.*

gate·post /'geɪt,poʊst/ *n.* a wooden or metal post on which a gate is hung: *The gatepost in front of the house has a lamp on it.*

gate·way /'geɪt,weɪ/ *n.* **1** a passage where there is a gate **2** *fig.*a way of reaching s.t., usu. better opportunities: *A good education can be the gateway to a good job.* **3** a machine that connects two networks and passes information between them

gath·er /'gæðər/ *v.* **1** to bring together, collect: *He gathered his clothes together and packed them in the suitcase.* **2** to meet, (*syn.*) to assemble: *Townspeople gathered in the town hall to talk about the new school.* **3** to understand, (*syn.*) to conclude: *I gather from what I hear that your business is doing well.* **4** (in sewing) to pull together material into small folds: *She wore a <adj.> gathered skirt.* **5** to bring in, pick, (*syn.*) to harvest: *Farmers gather their corn when it is ready.‖We gathered flowers by the river.* **6 to gather steam** or **momentum:** to become quicker, speed up: *Our sales of the new product are gathering steam* (or) *momentum with new increases every month.*

gath·er·ing /'gæðərɪŋ/ *n.* **1** a group of people: *A gathering of fans formed near the movie star's hotel.* **2** a meeting, social function: *We had a social gathering at the church last night.*

Ga·tor·ade /'geɪtə,reɪd/ *n.TM* a flavored drink made to replace chemicals in the body (water, sugar, potassium, etc.) lost through exercise: *After a fast game of tennis in the summer, I drink Gatorade.*

gauche /goʊʃ/ *adj.* **1** uncomfortable in social situations, (*syns.*) clumsy, awkward: *He's gauche; he doesn't know how to behave at formal meetings.* **2** doing or saying the wrong things, (*syns.*) tactless, insensitive: *She made several gauche remarks about how fat I've become.*

gaud·y /'gɔdi/ *adj.* **-ier, -iest** too brightly colored, (*syn.*) ostentatious: *At the Mardi Gras carnival, dancers were wearing gaudy costumes in the parade.* *-adv.* **gaudily;** *-n.* [U] **gaudiness.**

gauge or **gage** /geɪdʒ/ *n.* **1** an object for measuring size, fuel, pressure, etc.: *The gauge showed that the steam temperature is normal.* **2** a standard of measurement: *As a gauge of our success, we want sales volume to increase each month.*
—*v.* **gauged, gauging, gauges 1** to measure, (*syn.*) to evaluate: *We gauge our progress by*

increasing company profits. **2 to gauge s.o.'s reaction:** to find out how s.o. feels about s.t., (*syns.*) to assess, determine: *I told him just a little about the problem to gauge his reaction.*

gaunt /gɔnt/ *adj.* thin and unhealthy, (*syns.*) emaciated, haggard: *The prisoners were gaunt after many years in prison.* *-n.* [U] **gauntness.**

gaunt·let /'gɔntlɪt/ *n.* **1** a metal glove worn by soldiers in former times **2** a long, heavy glove that protects the hand, usu. worn for sports or industry **3 to pick up** or **take up the gauntlet:** to accept s.o.'s invitation to fight or disagree: *I picked up the gauntlet when she challenged my new health care plan.* **4 to run the gauntlet:** to be open to, suffer an unpleasant or violent experience: *After making an expensive mistake, the manager must run the gauntlet of questions from his superiors.* **5 to throw down the gauntlet:** to invite s.o. to fight or disagree with you: *The Democrat threw down the gauntlet to the Republican over her new health care plan.*

gauze /gɔz/ *n.* a very thin, light material with very small holes, usu. used as a covering in medicine or as a curtain: *The doctor covered the cut with a piece of gauze.*

gave /geɪv/ *past tense of* give

gav·el /'gævəl/ *n.* a small wooden hammer used by officials to get attention or to bring order to a gathering: *The judge banged the gavel to bring silence to the court.*

gawk /gɔk/ *v.* to look at s.o. or s.t. with the mouth open, usu. in a stupid or rude way: *The crowd gawked at the man with blue hair.*

gawk·y /'gɔki/ *adj.* **-ier, -iest** awkward, uncomfortable in the way one moves, (*syn.*) ungainly: *The boy from the country looked gawky in the big city.*

gay /geɪ/ *adj.* **1** relating to the lives and concerns of homosexual people: *There are large communities of gay people in New York and San Francisco.‖My friends Amy, Sally, and Michael volunteer at the Miami Lesbian and Gay Center.* **2** *old usage:* merry, happy: *Everyone at the party is having a gay time.*
—*n.* a person who is homosexual, usu. a man: *American gays have formed a political organization called the Human Rights Campaign. See:* lesbian, homosexual, bisexual.

USAGE NOTE: The term *gay* applies to both male and female homosexuals, but many gay women prefer the term *lesbian: She is active in the Gay and Lesbian Alliance.* The term *queer* is pej.

gaze /geɪz/ *v.n.* **gazed, gazing, gazes 1** to look steadily at s.o. or s.t. for a long time, usu. without giving it much attention: *The students <v.> gazed out of the window because their class was boring.* **2** to look steadily at s.o. or s.t., usu. with pleasure or admiration: *She gazed at her beautiful new diamond ring.*

ga·ze·bo /gə'zibou, -'zeɪ-/ *n.* **-bos** a small building, usu. in a pleasant place, away from a main building: *The lady has a gazebo in her garden where she reads in the summer.*

gazebo

ga·zelle /gə'zɛl/ *n.* **-zelles** or **-zelle** an animal like a small deer: *Most gazelles are found in African plains.*

ga·zette /gə'zɛt/ *n.* a newspaper or periodical: *The* Police Gazette *is published once a week.*

gaz·pa·cho /gə'spatʃou, ga-/ *n.* [U] a cold soup made from tomato, onion, cucumber, and pepper: *Gazpacho is a favorite soup in the summer.*

gear /gɪr/ *n.* **1** a flat, round piece of metal with teeth around the edge that turns other gears in machinery: *The gears in my old clock need repair.* **2** one of several speeds in a vehicle: *I put the car into high gear and drove away.* **3** equipment, usu. connected with sports: *The climber gathered up his gear and headed toward the mountain.*
—*v.* **1** to provide with gear, equip **2** *phrasal v. insep.* **to gear s.t. to:** to make s.t. suitable: *Educational programs should be geared to the ages of children who watch them.* **3** *phrasal v. insep.* **to gear up for s.t.:** to get ready for s.t., (*syn.*) to prepare: *We're all geared up for our trip.*

gear·shift /'gɪr,ʃɪft/ *n.* a handle used to change from one gear to another: *The gearshift in a car is located on the floor to the driver's right.*

GED /ˌdʒii'di/ *n.abbr. for* General Equivalency Diploma: *A GED is similar to a high school diploma (in the USA).*

USAGE NOTE: The *GED* is needed for many jobs. Night school and television courses that lead to the GED make it possible for working people to complete a high school education.

gee /dʒi/*exclam.* an expression of wonder or surprise: *Gee, I didn't know that you found a new job!*

geese /gɪs/ *n.pl.* of goose: *One goose, two geese*

gee whiz /'dʒi'wɪz/*exclam.* a mild expression of surprise (dismay, annoyance): *Oh, gee whiz, my computer isn't working right again!*

gee·zer /'gizər/ *n.infrml.pej.* an old man: *That old geezer is always in the coffee shop.*

USAGE NOTE: It is better not to use *geezer* to describe a difficult old man, because this word is impolite. *Elderly man* is the term of respect: *An elderly man gave us directions to the park.* It is also polite to refer to old people as *elderly folks* or *senior citizens.*

gei·sha /'geɪʃə, 'gi-/ *n.* a type of Japanese waitress who also sings and dances: *The traditional tea ceremony was performed by five elegantly dressed geishas.*

gel /dʒɛl/ *n.* a soft, clear substance between a liquid and a solid state, such as jelly: *She uses gel in her hair to keep the style in place.*
—*v.* **gelled, gelling, gels** **1** to form into a gel **2** to come together, (*syn.*) to coalesce: *All our work finally gelled into an excellent new product. See:* jell.

gel·a·tin /'dʒɛlətn/ *n.* **1** a clear substance made from boiled animal bones that has no taste, usu. used to make jellies, medicines, and glue: *Gelatin has many food and industrial uses.* **2** Jello™ or other gelatins used for desserts: *The salad contained pieces of orange-flavored gelatin.* *-adj.* **gelatinous** /dʒə'lætnəs/.

geld /gɛld/ *v.* to remove the testicles (male sexual organs), usu. of animals, (*syn.*) to castrate

geld·ing /'gɛldɪŋ/ *n.* a castrated male horse: *That gelding has won many competitions.*

gem /dʒɛm/ *n.* **1** a jewel or precious stone, usu. cut into a shape: *The rich lady keeps her gems, mostly diamonds and rubies, in the bank.* **2** *fig.* a thing or person that is esp. pleasing or valuable: *The baby is a real gem; he never cries.*

gem·stone /'dʒɛm,stoun/ *n.* a jewel or precious stone, usu. before it is cut into a shape: *South America exports many gemstones, such as diamonds and emeralds.*

gen·der /'dʒɛndər/ *n.* **1** the grouping of words into masculine, feminine, or neuter classes: *The gender of "la maison" is feminine.* **2** The classification of male and female living things: *Most companies do not discriminate based on race, age, gender, or sexual orientation. See:* sex.

gene /dʒin/ *n.* the basic part of a living cell that contains characteristics of one's parents: *You have good genes from your parents, so you should live a long time.*

ge·ne·al·o·gy /ˌdʒini'alədʒi, -'æ
lə-/ *n.* **-gies** the names and history of one's family: *My uncle is the expert in our family's genealogy. -n.* **genealogist;** *-adj.* **genealogical** /ˌdʒiniə'ladʒɪkəl/.

gen·er·a /'dʒɛnərə/ *n.pl.* of genus

gen·er·al (1) /'dʒɛnərəl, 'dʒɛnrəl/ *adj.* **1** overall, (*syn.*) prevalent: *The general feeling among her friends is that she is a kind person.* **2 in general:** overall, all things considered: *In general, the economy is doing well now. -n.* **generality** /ˌdʒɛnə'ræləti/. *See:* generalization.

general (2) *n.* a military officer (US Army, US Air Force, US Marines) belonging to the highest level: *Generals in the army have great responsibility.*

general anesthetic *n.* a substance that stops the feeling of pain throughout the whole body: *The patient was given a general anesthetic for major surgery on his stomach.*

General Assembly *n.* **1** the main group of members of the United Nations: *The General Assembly met to hear the Russian President speak.* **2** the law-making group in some US states

general election *n.* an election (as opposed to a primary) in which citizens choose members of local, state, and national governments: *The general election for Congress is held in November every other year.*

gen·er·al·ist /ˈdʒɛnərəlɪst/ *n.* a person who has knowledge and ability in many areas: *She is a generalist in management.*

gen·er·al·i·za·tion /ˌdʒɛnərələˈzeɪʃən, ˈdʒɛnrə-/ *n.* a general statement about s.t. without reference to details or important differences, *(syn.)* generality: *Politicians are famous for making speeches full of generalizations.*

gen·er·al·ize /ˈdʒɛnərəˌlaɪz, ˈdʒɛnrə-/ *v.* **-ized, -izing, -izes** to make general statements without reference to details, important differences, etc.: *He generalizes when he speaks and leaves out important details.*

gen·er·al·ly /ˈdʒɛnərəli, ˈdʒɛnrə-/ *adv.* **1** usually: *We generally take the bus to work.* **2** by most people: *The bad news was generally accepted well, but some people were unhappy.* **3** without referring to details, in general: *Generally speaking, the weather has been mild this winter.*

general partner *n.* one of two or more partners in a company who are responsible for any financial problems in that company: *The general partners in that law firm make a lot of money.*

general practitioner or **GP** *n.* a doctor of general medicine, a nonspecialist: *Our family doctor is a general practitioner.*

gen·er·ate /ˈdʒɛnəˌreɪt/ *v.* **-ated, -ating, -ates** **1** to produce, create: *The local power station generates electricity.* **2** to make happen, to produce, *(syn.)* to initiate: *The sales force has generated a big sales increase.*

gen·er·a·tion /ˌdʒɛnəˈreɪʃən/ *n.* **1** the making of s.t., *(syn.)* production: *The generation of electricity is done with nuclear power.* **2** any of the different age levels in a family, such as grandparents, children, and grandchildren **3** a group of people of approximately the same age: *The older generation is always complaining about the younger generation.*

generation gap *n.* the differences in interests and ideas between older and younger people

Generation X /ɛks/ *n.* in the USA, the people born during the 1960s and early 1970s: *Many members of Generation X have a college education but are not hopeful about the future.*

USAGE NOTE: You may abbreviate *Generation X* to *Gen X* and refer to its members as *Generation Xers* or *Gen Xers*. Members of *Generation X* grew up watching the American dream on television, but have found the real world quite different. They are discouraged by the difficulty of finding jobs, the state of the national economy, world politics, and the environment.

gen·er·a·tor /ˈdʒɛnəˌreɪtər/ *n.* a machine used to produce electricity: *The hospital has two emergency generators in case of a power cut.*

ge·ner·ic /dʒəˈnɛrɪk/ *adj.* **1** shared by a group of things: *The generic term for bananas, apples, oranges, etc. is "fruit."* **2** referring to a basic product that does not have a trademark: *We buy generic cola if possible because it is cheaper than Coca-Cola™.* -adv. **generically.**

gen·er·os·i·ty /ˌdʒɛnəˈrɑsəti/ *n.* [U] **1** readiness to give, giving: *Her generosity in support of the arts allowed the museum to buy many new paintings.* **2** big-heartedness, a forgiving nature: *His generosity toward those people who attacked him is wonderful.*

gen·er·ous /ˈdʒɛnərəs/ *adj.* **1** ready to give, giving: *My brother is very generous; he gave me $20,000 to buy a new car.* **2** given freely, plentiful, *(syn.)* ample: *The cook gave us generous portions of food.* **3** not unkind, forgiving, *(syn.)* magnanimous: *He was generous to his enemies and released them from prison.* -adv. **generously.**

gen·e·sis /ˈdʒɛnəsɪs/ *n.frml.* **-ses** /-ˌsiz/ **1** a beginning, origin: *Many people disagree about the genesis of life.* **2 Genesis:** the first book of the Old Testament

ge·net·ic /dʒəˈnɛtɪk/ *adj.* related to genes or genetics -adv. **genetically.**

genetic code *n.* the organization of genes that controls the development of living things: *His heart problems are a result of his genetic code his father also had heart problems.*

ge·net·ics /dʒəˈnɛtɪks/ *n.pl. used with a sing.v.* the scientific study of the passing of physical characteristics from parents to children -n. **geneticist** /dʒəˈnɛtəsɪst/.

Ge·ne·va Convention /dʒəˈnivə/ *n.* a set of rules followed by some countries about the treatment of people hurt or taken prisoner during war: *Most nations follow the Geneva Convention in wartime.*

gen·ial /ˈdʒinyəl, ˈdʒiniəl/ *adj.* **1** friendly and warm, *(syn.)* cordial: *When the couple gives a* *party, they are always genial hosts.* **2** (of weather) warm and mild, good for plants to grow: *Florida has a genial climate.* -*n.* **geniality** /,dʒini'æləti/; -*adv.* **genially.**

gen·i·ta·lia /,dʒenə'teɪlyə/ *n.pl.* genitals

gen·i·tals /'dʒenətlz/ *n.pl.* the external sexual organs: *The doctor examined the boy's genitals for infection.*

gen·ius /'dʒinyəs/ *n.* **-iuses 1** a person of great intelligence and ability: *Albert Einstein was a genius in physics.* **2** a special ability: *I have a genius for learning languages; I can speak 10 languages fluently.*

gen·o·cide /'dʒenə,saɪd/ *n.* the systematic killing of a population, such as a country, race, or local group: *Genocide still takes place in many parts of the world.*

gen·re /'ʒɑnrə/ *n.* a specific type of literature, art, or music grouped according to a style or subject: *Comedy and horror movies are different genres.*

gent /dʒent/ *n.infrml.* short for gentleman

gen·teel /dʒen'til/ *adj.* characterized by being very polite: *She is a genteel lady of fine breeding.* -*n.* **gentility** /dʒen'tɪləti/.

gen·tile /'dʒen,taɪl/ *n.* a person who is not Jewish (esp. a Christian or Muslim)

gen·tle /'dʒentl/ *adj.* **-tler, -tlest 1** kind, soft, not rough: *The mother is very gentle with her newborn baby.* **2** well-behaved, (*syn.*) docile: *My dog is very gentle; he would never bite.* **3** light, slow: *A gentle breeze comes from the ocean.* **4 gentle slope:** a slanted area that is not steep: *It was easy to go up the gentle slope on our bicycles.* -*n.* **gentleness;** -*adv.* **gently.**

gen·tle·man /'dʒentlmən/ *n.* **-men** /-mən/ **1** a polite and honorable man: *He is a real gentleman; he always helps me carry the heavy bags to my car.* **2** a man who does not have to work for a living, usu. of a high social position: *He is a gentleman who inherited all his money and land from his family.* **3** *n.pl.* used as a form of address: *"Gentlemen, thank you for coming this evening."*

gentleman's agreement *n.* a spoken, unwritten agreement made between people who trust each other: *We have a gentleman's agreement to share expenses for a summer house with five others.*

gen·tri·fi·ca·tion /'dʒentrəfɪ'keɪʃən/ *n.* the process of changing a poor (housing) area into a middle-class area by people with money who move there and make the area too expensive for poorer people to live in: *Gentrification is taking place in parts of Harlem, New York, and rent prices are going up quickly.* -*v.* **gentrify** /'dʒentrə,faɪ/.

gen·try /'dʒentri/ *n.* people of a high social position and with lots of money: *Many of the gen-*

try from Newport, Rhode Island, live in very large, famous houses.

gen·u·flect /'dʒenyə,flɛkt/ *v.frml.* to bend the knee in respect, (*syn.*) to kneel: *The people in the church genuflected in prayer.*

gen·u·ine /'dʒenyuɪn/ *adj.* **1** true, real, (*syns.*) authentic, bona fide: *That old vase is a genuine antique.*||*We are genuine Egyptian food in Cairo.* **2** honest, (*syn.*) sincere: *Her sadness over the death of her cat is genuine; she cried all night.* -*adv.* **genuinely;** -*n.* **genuineness.**

ge·nus /'dʒinəs/ *n.* **genera** /'dʒenərə/ (in biology) a type of classification: *Humans belong to the genus Homo.*

ge·og·ra·phy /dʒi'agrəfi/ *n.* **1** the scientific study of the earth's surface, features, climate, people, etc.: *I bought a new atlas for my geography class.* **2** the way parts of a place are positioned within it, (*syn.*) layout: *I can't meet you inside the mall because I don't know the geography of the place, and I might get lost.* -*adj.* **geographic** /,dʒiə'græfɪk/.

ge·ol·o·gy /dʒi'alədʒi/ *n.* the scientific study of the earth through its rocks, soil, etc.: *In geology we studied the rocks and deserts of California.* -*n.* **geologist;** -*adj.* **geologic** /,dʒiə'ladʒɪk/.

ge·o·met·ric /,dʒiə'mɛtrɪk/ *adj.* with regular shapes and lines: *The mosque's walls are decorated with geometric designs.*

ge·om·e·try /dʒi'amətri/ *n.* the study in mathematics of lines, angles, shapes, etc.: *It is important to study geometry if you want to be an architect.*

ge·o·phys·ics /,dʒiou'fɪzɪks/ *n.pl.* used with a *sing.v.* the study in geology that uses physics to examine the movements and activities of the earth

ge·o·pol·i·tics /,dʒiou'palətɪks/ *n.pl.* used with a *sing.v.* the study of how geography affects the politics of a country

ge·o·ther·mal /,dʒiou'θərməl/ *adj.* related to heat found deep inside the earth: *The geysers in Yellowstone National Park are geothermal because of hot water coming from inside the earth. See:* geyser.

ge·ra·ni·um /dʒə'reɪniəm/ *n.* a garden plant with attractive red, pink, or white flowers: *His mother grows geraniums in window boxes.*

ger·i·at·rics /,dʒeri'ætrɪks, ,dʒɪr-/ *n.pl.* used with a *sing. v.* the branch of medicine that specializes in illnesses and cures of elderly people: *Many doctors in Florida specialize in geriatrics because so many elderly people live there.* -*adj.* **geriatric.**

germ /dʒərm/ *n.* **1** a very small living thing or organism that can cause illnesses or disease: *She washes her hands with soap before cooking to kill any germs.* **2** a very small living thing or organism from which another may* grow: *Apple seeds have a germ from which apple trees grow.* **3** *fig.* the beginning or seed of s.t., such as an idea, that may grow: *The technician has the germ of an idea for a new computer program.*

ger·mane /dʒərˈmeɪn/ *adj.* connected in an important way, (*syns.*) pertinent, relevant: *My new hairstyle is not germane to this discussion about politics.*

Ger·man shepherd /ˈdʒɜrmən/ *n.* a type of strong, large dog with a blackish-brown coat: *The German shepherd is often used as a police dog.*

ger·mi·cide /ˈdʒɜrməˌsaɪd/ *n.* a substance used to kill germs: *We use a germicide to clean the bathroom.*

ger·mi·nate /ˈdʒɜrməˌneɪt/ *v.* **-nated, -nating, -nates** **1** (in biology) to make s.t. begin growing from a seed, (*syn.*) to sprout: *In the springtime, plants germinate.* **2** *fig.* to begin developing, growing: *The early success of television germinated into a multi-billion dollar industry.* *-n.* **germination** /ˌdʒɜrməˈneɪʃən/.

ger·on·tol·o·gy /ˌdʒerənˈtalədʒi/ *n.* the scientific study of elderly people: *Boston City Hospital does a lot of research in gerontology.*

ger·ry·man·der /ˈdʒeriˌmændər/ *v.* to redraw the lines of a political district to give one political party an advantage over another *-n.* **gerrymandering.**

ges·ta·tion /dʒeˈsteɪʃən/ *n.* **1** the time a baby or young animal is carried in the mother's body before birth, pregnancy: *Baby elephants have a long gestation period; it is 23 months before they are born.* **2** **gestation period:** the period of time in which an idea (plan, project, etc.) develops: *The concept for a new product went through a long gestation period of testing before it reached the market.* *-v.* **gestate** /ˈdʒeˌsteɪt/.

ges·tic·u·late /dʒeˈstɪkyəˌleɪt/ *v.frml.* **-lated, -lating, -lates** to make movements with your arms and hands, usu. when talking, (*syn.*) to gesture: *The speaker gesticulated to stress the importance of the point.* *-n.* **gesticulation** /dʒeˌstɪkyəˈleɪʃən/.

ges·ture /ˈdʒestʃər, ˈdʒeʃtʃər/ *n.* **1** a body movement to show s.t. (a feeling, an idea, etc.): *She made a gesture to the right with her hand to show the direction of the park.* **2** s.t. you do or say to show your feelings: *We gave some money to the hospital as a gesture of support.* —*v.* **-tured, -turing, -tures** to make a movement with your hand or head to show s.t.: *He gestured to me to sit down.*

Ge·sund·heit /gəˈzʊntˌhaɪt/ *n.exclam.* (German for) health; Bless you! (said to s.o. after he or she sneezes to wish them good health): *My friend sneezed, and I said, "Gesundheit!" and she said, "Thank you."*

get /gɛt/ *v.* **got** /gat/, **gotten** /ˈgatn/ or **got, getting, gets** **1** to receive, obtain: *I got a telephone call (message, letter, etc.).* **2** to go for, acquire: *She went to get some food at the supermarket.* **3** to become: *The weather is getting warmer.* **4** to go, move, or arrive: *When you get home, please call me.* **5** to cause s.o. or s.t. to do s.t.: *I got the taxi driver to help me carry my bags up the stairs.* **6** to put into a situation or state: *We got eight people in my car.* **7** to make ready, prepare (meal): *She's getting lunch ready now.* **8** *infrml.* to understand: *She doesn't get it when I tell her she can't stay out late.* **9** to have s.t. done: *I got my hair cut.* **10** to experience s.t.: *She got her car stolen last night.‖We got a thrill seeing the movie stars in Hollywood.* **11** to catch an illness: *He's gotten the flu.* **12** to manage, be allowed to: *When I was younger, I got to go to the movies alone.* **13** to irritate, annoy: *His behavior really gets to me sometimes.* **14** to affect s.o., usu. to delight s.o.: *The beauty of the mountains really gets to me.* **15** to hit: *The bullet got him in the leg.* **16** to receive as a punishment: *They got four months in prison for the robbery.* **17 to get going/cracking:** to begin work on s.t.: *Let's get going on the new contract* **18 to get nowhere/somewhere:** to see no results/progress: *I am getting nowhere with this math homework; I don't understand anything.‖After my friend explained it to me, I really got somewhere and understood it.* **19** *phrasal v.* **to get about:** *See:* to get around. **20** *phrasal v. sep* **to get s.t. across:** to cause s.t to be understood: *The speaker was able to get her point across to the audience.* **21** *phrasal v.* **to get ahead:** to succeed, improve oneself: *She got a good job and is getting ahead in life.* **22** *phrasal v.* **to get along: a.** to leave, depart: *I must get along now; I'll talk to you later.* **b.** *insep.* to have a friendly relationship with: *My coworkers and I get along well together.* **23** *phrasal v.* **to get around: a.** to circulate, spread: *The rumor has gotten around that you are leaving.* **b.** *insep.* **s.o. or s.t.:** to find a way to do s.t.in spite of a problem: *You can get around your parking problem by using my permit.* **24** *phrasal v. insep.* **to get (a)round to s.t.:** to find the time to do s.t., usu. after a delay: *I finally got around to replying to your letter; I am sorry it took so long.* **25** *phrasal v. insep.* **to get at s.o. or s.t.: a.** to reach s.t.: *The book is on the top shelf and I can't get at it.* **b.** to try to say, explain s.t.: *It is often difficult to understand what politicians are getting at.* **26** *phrasal v. insep.* **to get away (from s.o. or s.t.): a.** to escape: *The criminal got away from the police.* **b.** to go on vacation: *I got away for a week in the Caribbean.* **27** *phrasal v. insep.* **to get away with s.t.:** to escape punishment for doing s.t. bad: *That driver got away with speeding because the police didn't see him.* **28**

G

phrasal v. **to get back: a.** to return: *She got back from vacation last week.* **b.** to reply, respond: *I will get back to you with an answer tomorrow.* **29** *phrasal v. insep.* **to get back at s.o.:** to hurt s.o. who has hurt you: *He hurt her feelings, so she got back at him by not speaking to him for a week.* **30** *phrasal v. insep.* **to get behind: a.** s.o. or s.t.: to support, help succeed: *Many people got behind the politician and helped her win the election.* **b. in s.t.:** to be late with, one's work, payments, etc.: *He got behind in his rent payments and had to leave the apartment.* **31** *phrasal v.* **to get by: a.** to have enough room to pass s.o. or s.t.: *I'll move my chair so that you can get by.* **b.** to have just enough of s.t. to manage: *My grandmother gets by on her social security check.* **32** *phrasal v. sep.* **to get s.o. or s.t. down: a.** s.o.: to make one feel unhappy, to depress: *Her work is really boring and it is starting to get her down.* **b. s.t.:** to write down, to record: *He spoke too quickly; I couldn't get the number down.* **33** *phrasal v. insep.* **to get down to s.t.:** to begin doing s.t., usu. seriously: *After talking about the job in general, we got down to the specifics, such as the salary.* **34** *phrasal v. insep.* **to get in s.t.: a.** to enter: *We got in the house by the back door.‖She got in her car.* **b.** to arrive: *I got in at 9:00 A.M.‖The bus gets in at 4 o'clock.* **c.** (in politics) to be elected: *A Republican mayor got in at the last election.* **35** *phrasal v. insep.* **to get in on s.t.:** to join in, participate: *Our company got in on buying a building with another company.* **36** *phrasal v. insep.* **to get into s.t.: a.** to enter (a vehicle): *She got into her car.* **b.** to put oneself or s.o. else into a certain situation, usu. bad: *The children are always getting into trouble.‖He has gotten himself into debt with the bank.* **c.** to become used to s.t.: *I can't get into this new style of music.* **37** *phrasal v. insep.* **to get off s.t.: a.** to leave (a vehicle): *They got off the bus/train/plane.* **b.** to step down from: *He got off the horse/bicycle/roof.* **c.** to (cause to) escape punishment: *The lawyer got me off and I didn't go to prison.* **38** *phrasal v. insep.* **to get off with s.t.:** to escape serious punishment: *The robber got off with only one year in prison.* **39** *phrasal v. insep.* **to get on s.t.: a.** to enter (a vehicle): *She got on the bus/train/plane.* **b.** to step up and sit on: *He got on the horse/bicycle.* **c.** to leave, depart: *I must get on now; I'll talk to you later.* **d.** to become more advanced in time, age, etc.: *My grandfather is getting on in years now.‖It's getting on; we should leave soon.* **40** *phrasal v. insep.* **to get onto s.t.: a.** to enter (a vehicle): *She got onto the bus/train/airplane.* **b.** to begin talking about a particular topic: *Suddenly, she got onto the topic of new software for her computer.* **41** *phrasal v. insep.* **to get on with s.t. or s.o.: a. s.t.:** to start doing or continue with s.t., often

after interruption: *Stop watching television and get on with your homework!* **b. s.o.:** to have a friendly relationship with: *How do you get on with your boss?* **42** *phrasal v.* **to get out: a.** to leave: *He will get out at 4 P.M., when his classes are finished.* **b. sep. s.t.:** to remove: *This new soap gets chocolate stains out.* **c.** to become known (as of news), *(syn.)* to leak out: *The news of his secret marriage has gotten out.* **d. sep. s.t.:** to produce: *Our company got the new product out before our competitors.* **43** *phrasal v. insep.* **to get out of s.t.: a.** to escape from: *The prisoner got out of jail by hiding in a truck.* **b.** to escape from the responsibility or obligation for s.t.: *I got out of washing the car by saying I had work to do.* **c.** to receive a benefit from s.t.: *I didn't get anything out of that computer course I took.* **d.** to obtain or learn s.t. by force: *She finally got the truth out of her son.* **44** *phrasal v.* **to get over (s.o. or s.t.): a. insep.** to return to a normal state after a bad experience or illness, *(syn.)* to overcome: *She still hasn't gotten over her mother's death.* **b. insep. can't get over:** to be very surprised: *I can't get over how quickly he recovered after the accident.* **c. sep. with:** to come to the end of s.t.: *Hurry up! Let's get this trial over with!* **d. sep.** to make s.t. clear or understood: *The professor got her ideas over to the students.* **45** *phrasal v. insep* **to get through: a. to s.o.:** to make contact, reach: *I was finally able to get through to my friend on the telephone.* **b. to s.o. to:** cause s.o. to understand: *The doctor finally got through to him that smoking was dangerous for his health.* **c. with s.t.:** to finish: *After I got through with my work, I went to bed.* **d. sep. s.t.:** to come through a difficult situation or experience: *My sister helped me get through the difficult days after our mother's death.* **46** *phrasal v.* **to get together:** to meet, *(syn.)* to socialize: *Let's get together for lunch next week.* **47** *phrasal v.* **to get up: a.** to awaken, arise: *I get up at 6 A.M. every morning.‖She got up from her seat and left the room.* **b. to s.t.:** to reach a certain point: *I got up to page 200 in the textbook.* **48** *phrasal v. insep.* **to get with s.t.:** to become aware, alert, to show an interst in s.t.: *Get with the program and do your work!* **49 to have got:** *See:* have.

get·a·way /'getə,weɪ/ *n.* **1** an escape: *The thief made his getaway in a stolen car.* **2** a vacation: *A week in the mountains is a great getaway.*

get-together *n.* an informal meeting for fun, a gathering: *After work, some of us had a get-together at a friend's apartment.*

get-up /'get,ʌp/ *n.infrml.* an unusual set of clothes: *He wore a strange cowboy get-up for work yesterday.*

gey·ser /ˈgaɪzər/ *n.* a natural hot spring that sends water into the air from time to time: *Many tourists come to photograph the geysers in the state park.*

geyser

ghast·ly /ˈgæstli/ *adj.* **-lier, -liest 1** very bad, terrible: *a ghastly dinner* **2** causing horror or shock: *We saw a ghastly accident on the highway.* **3** very pale, sickly: *Right after the operation, he looked ghastly, but he is okay now.*

gher·kin /ˈgɜrkɪn/ *n.* a small green cucumber, usu. pickled in vinegar *See:* pickle.

ghet·to /ˈgɛtou/ *n.* **-tos** an area in a city where many people of a particular nationality, race, or religion live, usu. a poor area: *There are many types of ghettos in New York City.*

ghost /goust/ *n.* **1** the spirit of a dead person, (*syn.*) an apparition: *People say ghosts haunt that old house.* **2 a ghost of a chance:** to have no chance, or a very small chance, of success: *The other runners are too fast; he doesn't have a ghost of a chance of winning the race.* **3 a ghost of s.t.:** a very small or slight amount of s.t.: *After her illness, she was a ghost of her former self.*||*a ghost of a smile*

ghost·ly /ˈgoustli/ *adj.* **-lier, -liest** with a strange light or shape like a ghost: *The ghostly lights in that empty old house frightened children at night.*

ghost town *n.* a town that is now empty because people no longer live there: *The Old West has many ghost towns.*

ghost·write /ˈgoust,raɪt/ *v.* **-wrote** /-ˈrout/, **-written** /-,rɪtn/, **writing, writes** to write s.t. (article, books, speech) for s.o. and not accept any personal credit for it: *He ghostwrites books for famous people.* -*n.* **ghostwriter.**

ghoul /gul/ *n.* a bad or evil spirit: *That old horror movie has ghouls living in a castle.* -*adj.* **ghoulish.**

GI /,dʒiˈaɪ/ **1** *abbr. See:* government issue. **2 GI's** or **GIs** a soldier in the US Army: *My father was a GI in World War II.*

gi·ant /ˈdʒaɪənt/ *n.* **1** a person, animal, plant, or object much larger than normal: *This tomato plant is a giant.* **2** (in fairy stories) an imaginary person who is very big and strong **3** *fig.* a very big company: *IBM is a giant in the computer industry.*
—*adj.* much larger than normal: *The giant redwood trees in California are very beautiful.*

gib·ber·ish /ˈdʒɪbərɪʃ/ *n.* words without meaning, (*syn.*) nonsense: *He is speaking gibberish.*

gibe /dʒaɪb/ *n.* a remark that makes fun of s.o., or points out s.o.'s faults: *The speaker made gibes at his political opponent's statement. See:* jibe.

gib·lets /ˈdʒɪblɪts/ *n.pl.* the liver, heart, etc. of a turkey, chicken, or other bird: *My mother makes soup from chicken giblets.*

gid·dy /ˈgɪdi/ *adj.* **-dier, -diest 1** lightheaded, a little dizzy: *The summer heat makes me feel giddy.* **2** lightheaded from enjoyment, lighthearted: *We had some giddy moments at the party.* -*adv.* **giddily;** -*n.* **giddiness.**

gift /gɪft/ *n.* **1** s.t. given freely to another, a present: *My father gave me a watch as a birthday gift.* **2** a special natural ability: *She has a gift for languages; she can speak 10 different languages.*

gift·ed /ˈgɪftɪd/ *adj.* having special natural ability: *She is a gifted violinist.*

gig /gɪg/ *n.* **1** *infrml.* a performance by musicians or comedians: *The group had a gig last night at a local club.* **2** *short for* gigabyte

gig·a·byte /ˈgɪgə,baɪt, ˈdʒɪ-/ *n.adj.* (in computers) one billion bytes or approx. 1,000 megabytes: *I saw a computer with a <adj.> two-gigabyte hard drive last night.*

gi·gan·tic /dʒaɪˈgæntɪk/ *adj.* very large, huge: *Elephants are gigantic creatures.*

gig·gle /ˈgɪgəl/ *v.n.* **-gled, -gling, -gles** to laugh in a silly, uncontrolled way, usu. when nervous, amused, or embarrassed, (*syn.*) to titter: *The schoolchildren <v.> giggled when the famous football player walked into their classroom.*

gig·o·lo /ˈdʒɪgə,lou, ˈʒɪ-/ *n.* **-los** a man whom a woman pays for romantic companionship

gild /gɪld/ *v.* **gilded** or **gilt** /gɪlt/, **gilding, gilds** to cover with gold: *He gilded the picture frame.*

gill (1) /gɪl/ *n.* an organ on the sides of a fish through which the fish breathes

gill (2) /dʒɪl/ *n.* one quarter of a pint of liquid measure

gilt-edged /ˈgɪlt,ɛdʒd/ *adj.* **1** with a border of gold **2** *fig.* of the highest quality **3 gilt-edged stocks** or **securities:** stocks or securities sold by the government for people to invest in for a fixed time at a fixed interest rate; therefore considered very safe

gim·let /ˈgɪmlɪt/ *n.* a small tool for making holes in wood

gim·mick /ˈgɪmɪk/ *n.* **1** a clever or unusual method or object used to attract attention: *The sales assistant gave me a free shopping bag as a sales gimmick when I entered the store.* **2** s.t. used to trick s.o. into believing s.t. and/or buying it -*n.* **gimmickry** /ˈgɪmɪkri/; -*adj.* **gimmicky.**

gin /dʒɪn/ *n.* **1** a strong, clear alcoholic beverage made from grain and berries: *Gin and tonic is a popular before-dinner drink.* **2** a machine used to separate seeds from cotton fiber

gin·ger /'ʤɪnʤər/ n. the root of a plant from Asia used in cooking for a hot, spicy flavor: *I like slices of ginger with Japanese food.*
—adj. n. a bright orange-brown color: *She has <adj.> ginger hair.*

ginger ale n. a carbonated soft drink flavored with ginger: *A glass of cool ginger ale is refreshing on a hot day.*

gin·ger·bread /'ʤɪnʤər,brɛd/ n.adj. a cake or cookie flavored with molasses and ginger: *My mother makes <adj.> gingerbread cookies in the shape of little people.*

gin·ger·ly /'ʤɪnʤərli/ adv. in a careful and controlled way: *She picked up the expensive glass vase gingerly.||He gingerly walked around the snakes.*

gin·ger·snap /'ʤɪnʤər,snæp/ n. a flat, dry gingerbread cookie

ging·ham /'gɪŋəm/ n.adj. a cotton or linen material, usu. woven in checks: *Diane made a yellow and white gingham dress.*

gin·gi·vi·tis /,ʤɪnʤə'vaɪtɪs/ n. (in dentistry) a disease of the gums

gin rummy n. a card game for two or more people: *We like to play gin rummy with friends once a week.*

gip·sy /'ʤɪpsi/ n. -sies See: gypsy.

gi·raffe /ʤə'ræf/ n. an African animal with long legs, a very long neck, and a spotted coat: *Giraffes eat leaves located high in trees.*

giraffe

gird /gɜrd/ v.frml. **girded** or **girt** /gɜrt/, **girding**, **girds** 1 to put on a belt, strap, etc. 2 to get ready for a difficult task: *Soldiers girded themselves for battle.*

gird·er /'gɜrdər/ n. a horizontal or vertical metal or wooden beam used in building: *The steel girders support the roof of the new building.*

gird·le /'gɜrdl/ n. an elastic piece of women's underwear that fits very tightly around the hips and stomach to change her shape. See: corset.
—v. -led, -ling, -les to go around, (syn.) to encircle: *The equator girdles the globe.*

girl /gɜrl/ n. 1 a female child 2 a daughter: *They have two boys and a girl.* -adj. **girlish.**

girl·friend /'gɜrl,frɛnd/ n. 1 a female friend: *His wife goes bowling with her girlfriends once a week.* 2 a male's female friend with whom he has a romantic relationship: *He bought his girlfriend a gold watch.*

USAGE NOTE: Women may use *girlfriend* to refer to any female friend, but when men use the term, it usu. indicates a romantic relationship: *Bill said his girlfriend made him a sweater.* The term *boyfriend* always indicates a romantic relationship: *Mary's new boyfriend is very good-looking.*

Girl Scout n. a member of the Girl Scouts, an international organization that trains girls in character building and healthy activities: *His daughter joined the Girl Scouts and loves to go camping.*

girth /gɜrθ/ n. 1 the measurement around the body of s.t.: *He is a man of large girth.* 2 a (leather) band put around a horse's stomach to keep the saddle in place: *The cowboy tightened the saddle girth before riding off.*

gis·mo or **gizmo** /'gɪzmoʊ/ n.infrml. -mos a small object used for a particular purpose, usu. whose correct name is not known, (syn.) a gadget: *He has a gismo on his computer that stores extra memory.*

gist /ʤɪst/ n. the general idea (of a discussion, situation, writing, etc.): *The speaker gave many details and examples, but the gist of her presentation was that the economy will get better soon.*

give /gɪv/ v. **gave** /geɪv/, **given** /'gɪvən/, **giving, gives** 1 to hand over, pass to s.o., esp. as a gift: *I gave my friend a birthday present.||Please give me a pencil.* 2 to produce, provide: *Good food gives you energy.* 3 to cause to have: *He gave his wife the flu.||She gave him a good idea.* 4 to make or do s.t.: *I will give you a phone call tomorrow.||The children gave a shout of surprise when they saw their presents.* 5 to permit, allow (often of time): *You should give yourself an hour to drive to the meeting.||My teacher gave me another chance to do the homework correctly.* 6 to be worth, pay: *That savings account gives a good return of seven percent a year.* 7 to perform: *Musicians give concerts.* 8 to bend, loosen: *These shoes are so tight that they won't give.* 9 to look upon, have a view of: *The front of our house gives onto the park.* 10 **not to give a darn** (a hoot, two cents, vulg. **a damn,** etc.): not to care about s.t at all: *I don't give a darn what you say; I won't go!||She doesn't give a hoot about that idea.* 11 phrasal v. sep. **to give (s.o. or s.t.) away: a.** s.o.: to present a woman to her husband at a wedding: *The mother and father both gave away the bride.||They gave her away.* **b.** s.t.: to offer s.t. freely, to make a gift of: *They are giving away prizes at the new store.||They are giving them away.* **c.** s.o. or s.t.: to reveal a secret, usu. unintentionally: *The children said they didn't eat the cake, but the chocolate around their mouths gave them away.||It gave them away.* 12 **to give away the store:** to pay too much for s.t.: *He wanted to buy his competitor's business so badly that he gave away the store to get*

it. **13** *phrasal v. sep.* **to give s.t. back s.t.:** to return s.t.: *The labor union gave back last year's wage increase in order to keep their jobs.‖They gave it back.* **14** *phrasal v. insep.* **to give in (to s.o. or s.t.):** to surrender, *(syn.)* to yield: *The little boy cried so much that his mother finally gave in to him and bought some candy.* **15** *phrasal v. insep.* **to give off s.t.:** to send out (a smell, heat, light, etc.): *She gives off a smell of roses.‖She gives it off.* **16 to give one's life for/to: a.** to die for a cause: *The soldier gave his life for his country.* **b.** to spend one's life doing s.t., to dedicate oneself to s.t.: *The priest gave his life to the service of God.* **17 give or take:** more or less, approximately: *Boston is 250 miles (400 km) from New York City, give or take a few miles.* **18** *phrasal v. sep.* **to give (s.t.) out: a.** *s.t.:* to hand out: *Our volunteer group gives out free food to the homeless.‖We give it out.* **b.** to come to an end, *(syn.)* to wear out: *The air conditioner gave out, so we bought a new one.* **c.** *See:* to give off . **19 to give rise to:** to cause to happen: *Electricity gave rise to the electronic age of computers, TVs, and telephones.* **20** *infrml.* **to give s.o. a hard time:** to make things difficult for s.o.: *She gave the police officer a hard time by not answering any questions.* **21** *phrasal v. sep* **to give s.o. or s.t. up: a.** to stop doing s.t.: *I gave up smoking last year.‖I gave it up.* **b.** to surrender: *After weeks of fighting, the rebels gave up the fortress.‖They gave it up.* **22** *phrasal v. insep.* **to give up on s.o. or s.t.:** to stop hoping or wishing for s.o. or s.t. to arrive, happen, etc.: *We gave up on the missing mountain climber after he had been missing for 13 days.* **23** *phrasal v. insep.* **to give way: a.** to fall down, collapse: *The ceiling in the tunnel gave way and killed a worker.* **b. to s.o.:** to let others pass, *(syn.)* to yield: *Before I drive onto the highway, I give way to the cars already on the highway, so that they don't hit me.* **c. to s.t.:** to let s.t. through, esp. emotions: *When the baby saw the candy, her cries gave way to smiles.*
—*n.* willingness or ability to bend or yield: *These shoes are too tight; there is no give in them.‖Both negotiators are firm; there is no give in their positions. See:* tumble; what for.

give-and-take *n.* a willingness of people on both sides to listen to each other and to accept (some of) the other's wishes or opinions, *(syn.)* a compromise: *There must be give-and-take from both countries if this war is to end.*

give·a·way /ˈgɪvəˌweɪ/ *n.* **1** a sign or s.t. that shows the truth of a situation, usu. that s.o. is trying to hide: *The shoes under the curtain were a giveaway that the man was hiding there.* **2** s.t. given away, usu. for free: *Our company provides small product samples as giveaways to customers.*

giv·en (1) /ˈgɪvən/ *adj.* **1** particular, referring to a specific time or place, usu. decided in advance: *She finished her job on the given day.* **2** if permitted: *Given the chance, I'd leave my job and travel the world.* **3 any given:** one or another, referring to no particular time, situation, object, etc.: *They might arrive at any given time.* **4 to be given to doing s.t.:** to have s.t. as a habit: *He's given to going to the movies on Saturday night.*

given (2) *prep.* considering, taking into account: *Given my experience in this area and my excellent qualifications, I'm sure they will give me the job.*

given name *n.* first name(s): *The given names of Mr. and Mrs. Smith's daughters are Jane and Nicole.*

giz·mo /ˈgɪzmoʊ/ *-n.* **-mos** *See:* gismo.

giz·zard /ˈgɪzərd/ *n.* the second stomach of a bird, where food is broken up

gla·cial /ˈgleɪʃəl/ *adj.* **1** related to ice or glaciers: *A glacial mass is moving slowly down to the sea.* **2** cold, silent: *The man made her angry and she looked at him with a glacial stare.*

gla·cier /ˈgleɪʃər/ *n.* a large mass of ice that moves slowly, usu. down a mountain: *Glaciers are similar to slow-moving rivers of ice.* *-v.* **glaciate.**

glad /glæd/ *adj.* **gladder, gladdest** pleased, happy: *I am glad that you had a good time at the party. See:* happy, USAGE NOTE.

glad·den /ˈglædn/ *v.* to please, make happy: *It gladdened her to be home after traveling for so long.*

glade /gleɪd/ *n.frml.* an open space in the woods or forest, *(syn.)* a clearing

glad hand *n.* a warm (and often insincere) handshake: *The candidate for governor gave everyone a glad hand.* *-v.* **glad-hand.**

glad·i·a·tor /ˈglædiˌeɪtər/ *n.* (in ancient Rome) a man (usu. a slave or prisoner) who fought with other men or animals for show: *Gladiators fought before large crowds in ancient Rome.*

glad·i·o·la /ˌglædiˈoʊlə/ *n.* **-li** /-ˌlaɪ, -ˌli/ a garden plant with orchid-like flowers growing out of a single long, vertical stalk: *We keep gladioli in a vase in the living room.*

glad·ly /ˈglædli/ *adv.* with enthusiasm, *(syns.)* willingly, eagerly: *I'll gladly help you with your French homework; I studied French for many years.*

glam·or·ize or **glamourize** /ˈglæməˌraɪz/ *v.* **-ized, -izing, -izes** to make s.t. (look) more attractive than it really is: *Newspapers glamorize the lives of movie stars.*

glam·or·ous or **glamourous** /ˈglæmərəs/ *adj.* having an atmosphere of elegance and class: *Marilyn Monroe was a glamorous movie star.* *-adv.* **glamorously.**

glam·our or **glamor** /'glæmər/ *n.* an atmosphere of elegance, beauty, and usu. excitement: *The glamour of Hollywood is known worldwide.*

glance /glæns/ *v.* **glanced, glancing, glances 1** to take a quick short look at s.t.: *I glanced at the newspaper in the elevator this morning.* **2** *phrasal v. insep.* **to glance off s.t.:** to hit s.t. and then bounce away immediately: *The bullet glanced off the wall and broke the window.*
—*v.* **1** a quick short look at s.t.: *She took a quick glance at her watch.* **2 at a glance:** at once, with one look: *I could tell at a glance that the numbers were wrong.* **3 at first glance:** at first, initially: *At first glance I thought I had lost an important file, but then I found it in my desk drawer.*

gland /glænd/ *n.* one of the many small organs in the body that sends out substances to change body chemistry: *The sweat glands produce perspiration.* *-adj.* **glandular** /'glændʒələr/.

glare /glɛr/ *n.* **1** a strong, blinding, reflected light: *The sun's glare on the car's windshield made driving difficult.* **2** a look of anger or hatred, a harsh stare
—*v.* **glared, glaring, glares 1** to shine with a strong, blinding light: *The sun glared off the metal.* **2** to look hard at s.o. with anger or hatred: *The woman glared at the man after he shouted rudely at her.*

glar·ing /'glɛrɪŋ/ *adj.* **1** very bright, shiny: *I put on my sunglasses because of the glaring lights.* **2** (of a color) too bright: *He wore a glaring green tie with a red shirt.* **3** very clear, noticeable: *She made a glaring mistake in her calculations.* *-adv.* **glaringly.**

glass /glæs/ *n.* **glasses 1** [U] a hard transparent material used in windows (buildings, ornaments, objects, etc.): *Be careful with that vase; it is made of glass.* **2** [U] objects that are made of glass; glassware: *She collects antique glass.* **3** [C] a drinking container made of glass: *I had toast and two glasses of milk for breakfast.* **4** *pl.* **glasses:** two pieces of glass or plastic in a frame that one wears in front of the eyes to see better, eyeglasses, (*syn.*) spectacles: *She wears glasses* (or) *eyeglasses for reading.* **5 people who live in glass houses should not throw stones:** people who are not perfect should not say bad things about other people

glass blowing *n.* the art of forming glass into bottles, glasses, ornaments, etc., by blowing through a tube into a ball of hot liquid glass: *Glass blowing is a famous industry in Italy.*

glass ceiling *n.fig.* an upper level or point that is difficult for s.o., usu. a woman, to pass because of discrimination: *She hit the glass ceiling in her company after she became a manager, and could not rise any higher.*

USAGE NOTE: While 45% of middle managers in the USA are women, only 5 percent are senior managers. One reason it is difficult for women to rise above the *glass ceiling* is because these senior level jobs have traditionally been held by men. As more and more women enter the workforce, these patterns of discrimination will begin to change more rapidly.

glass·ful /'glæs,fʊl/ *n.* the volume contained in a glass: *The child had a glassful of milk at lunch.*

glass·ware /'glæs,wɛr/ *n.* [U] *used with a sing.v.* household objects, such as drinking glasses and ornaments, made of glass: *She has glassware made of fine crystal.*

glass·y-eyed /'glæsi,aɪd/ *adj.* with eyes showing signs of dullness, tiredness, or illness: *After the accident she was glassy-eyed from shock.*

glau·co·ma /'glau'koʊmə, glɔ-/ *n.* [U] an eye disease that can end in loss of sight if left untreated: *Medication helped reduce the pressure on her eyes due to glaucoma.*

glaze /gleɪz/ *v.* **glazed, glazing, glazes 1** to cover or fit with glass: *We glazed the windows with new glass.* **2** to put a thin (usu. shiny) cover over s.t.: *I glazed the donut with sugar.*|| *After making the ceramic plate, he glazed it to protect it.* **3 to glaze over** (of eyes): to look uninterested, dreamy, usu. when tired or bored: *The audience was so bored that you could see their eyes glaze over.*
—*n.* a thin, shiny cover on s.t. (ceramics, food, etc.) *-n.* **glazing.**

gla·zier /'gleɪʒər/ *n.* a worker who fits and repairs windows and doors made of glass or plastic: *The store window was broken, so the owner called a glazier to repair it.*

gleam /glim/ *v.* to shine brightly: *Diamonds gleam.*
—*n.* **1** a bright light **2** *fig.* a sudden light in a person's face or eyes that shows a strong feeling for s.t.: *You could see the gleam in the writer's eye as he thought of an idea for a new book. See:* glimmer.

glean /glin/ *v.* to collect (usu. with difficulty) in small amounts: *Reporters gleaned information by conducting numerous interviews.*

glee /gli/ *n.* a feeling of delight, joy: *He jumped up and down with glee when he won the prize.* *-adj.* **gleeful** /'glifəl/.

glee club *n.* a chorus of singers: *The glee club practices every Thursday night.*

glib /glɪb/ *adj.* **glibber, glibbest 1** able to talk easily and well with little thought or preparation: *a glib salesperson* **2** spoken quickly and easily without thought, usu. not true: *He gave the police officer a glib excuse for not stopping at the red light.* *-adv.* **glibly;** *-n.* **glibness.**

glide /glaɪd/ *v.* **glided, gliding, glides 1** to fly through the air without power: *Birds and kites glide in the air.* **2** to move easily and quickly over a surface: *Skaters glided across the ice.*
—*n.* a smooth motion or movement: *The airplane reached a high altitude, then went into a glide.*

glid·er /'glaɪdər/ *n.* a type of airplane that rides air currents without an engine

glider

glim·mer /'glɪmər/ *n.* **1** a weak, unsteady light: *The glimmer of candlelight made the restaurant romantic.* **2** *fig.* a small, weak sign of an idea (fact, information, etc.): *I don't have a glimmer of an idea as to what is wrong with that machine.*
—*v.* to give out a weak, unsteady light: *Moonlight glimmered through the clouds.* -*adj.* **glimmering.**

glimpse /glɪmps/ *n.* **1** a short look at s.t., often not very clear **2 to catch a glimpse of s.t.:** to see briefly: *I only caught a glimpse of the thief before he ran away.*
—*v.* **glimpsed, glimpsing, glimpses** to see s.t. quickly, often not very well: *I glimpsed the house through the trees. See:* glance.

glint /glɪnt/ *v.* to produce or reflect small flashes of light: *The diamond glinted in the sunlight.*
—*n.* **1** a small flash of light **2** *fig.* **(to have) a glint in one's eye:** (of eyes) to shine showing a particular feeling: *There was an angry glint in his eye when he saw the report wasn't finished.*

glis·ten /'glɪsən/ *v.* to shine, usu. as if from wetness: *After he stopped crying, his eyes glistened.*

glitch /glɪtʃ/ *n.infrml.* **glitches** a small (technical) problem: *A glitch in the computer is stopping the printer from working.*

glit·ter /'glɪtər/ *v.* **1** to shine brightly with flashes of light, (*syn.*) to sparkle: *Her jewels glittered.* **2 all that glitters is not gold:** everything that looks or seems attractive is not always attractive in reality: *You can be rich and still be unhappy because all that glitters is not gold.*
—*n.* sparkle, (*syns.*) glamour, showiness: *The glitter of Hollywood attracts tourists.* -*adj.* **glittering.**

glitz /glɪts/ *n.* a show of fancy clothes, cars, glamour, etc. (usu. used in a negative way), (*syn.*) ostentation: *Some actors dislike the glitz of Hollywood; they choose to live in San Francisco, New York, or another city.* -*adj.* **glitzy.**

gloat /gloʊt/ *v.* to take or show great pleasure in oneself: *The young boxer gloated over his defeat of the champion.* -*n.* **gloating.**

glob /glɑb/ *n.infrml.* **1** a portion of s.t. soft, often a thick liquid, with a round or undefined shape, (*syn.*) a blob: *Globs of oil washed up on the beach from passing ships.‖a glob of lotion* **2** *short for* globule

glob·al /'gloʊbəl/ *adj.* relating to all the world, worldwide: *We have a global economy today.* -*adv.* **globally.**

glob·al·i·za·tion /gloʊbələ'zeɪʃən/ *n.* the spread of s.t. worldwide: *The globalization of illegal drug use has taken only several decades.* -*v.* **globalize** /'gloʊbə,laɪz/.

globe /gloʊb/ *n.* **1** the earth, world: *Airplanes circle the globe in hours these days.* **2** a circular shell with a map of the world on it: *The students used a globe to measure the distance between two cities.*

globe·trot·ter /'gloʊb,trɑtər/ *n.* a person who travels overseas frequently: *The Secretary of State is a globetrotter who visits foreign countries constantly.*

glob·ule /'glɑbyul/ *n.* a very small drop of liquid or melted solid: *Globules of water fell from the umbrella to the floor.* -*adj.* **globular** /'glɑbyələr/.

gloom /glum/ *n.* **1** a feeling or atmosphere of sadness or depression: *After the child's death, the house was full of gloom.* **2** darkness

gloom·y /'glumi/ *adj.* **-ier, -iest 1** sad, depressed: *After the death, the family felt gloomy.* **2** dark: *After the light went out, the house looked gloomy.* **3** with little hope, (*syns.*) depressing, pessimistic: *With the recession, the economic outlook is gloomy.*

glop /glɑp/ *n.slang* a thick liquid mass of s.t.: *The cook put a glop of mashed potato on the plate.*

glo·ri·fy /'glɔrə,faɪ/ *v.* **-fied, -fying, -fies 1** to give honor, fame, and admiration: *Poets glorified the Roman emperors in their poems.* **2** to make s.t. or s.o. seem more important than is true: *His castle is just a glorified old stone house.* -*n.* **glorification** /,glɔrəfə'keɪʃən/.

glo·ri·ous /'glɔriəs/ *adj.* **1** full of great honor and fame, (*syn.*) illustrious: *The Roman Empire had a glorious history.* **2** wonderful: *We went for a picnic because it was a glorious day.* -*adv.* **gloriously.**

glo·ry /'glɔri/ *n.* **-ries 1** [U] great honor, fame, and admiration: *The candidate accepted the glory of winning the Presidency.* **2** *pl.* **glories** great beauty, special attraction: *The Empire State building is one of New York City's glories.*
—*v.* **-ried, -rying, -ries to glory in:** to enjoy the feeling of s.t., (*syn.*) to revel in: *The writer gloried in the public's admiration.*

gloss /glɑs, glɔs/ *n.* **glosses 1** a shiny appearance: *I put a gloss on the table by waxing it.* **2** an explanation of a word or idea: *A dictionary is full of glosses.*

G

—*v.* **glossed, glossing, glosses 1** to put a shiny coating on s.t. **2 to gloss over:** to hide the truth, make s.t. seem acceptable by not giving all of the important information: *In his job interview, he glossed over the fact that he had been in prison for five years, and they gave him the job.*

glos·sa·ry /'glɑsəri, 'glɔ-/ *n.* **-ries** an alphabetical list of terms and their definitions: *A glossary at the end of the book gives explanations of foreign words.*

gloss·y /'glɔsi, 'glɑ-/ *adj.* **-ier, -iest** smooth and shiny: *I washed and polished my car and now the metal is glossy.*

—*n.* **-ies** a photograph on shiny paper: *I had several glossies made of my favorite photo.*

glove /glʌv/ *n.* **1** a covering for the hand with a separate part for each finger and thumb: *In the winter, she wears leather gloves.* **2 to go hand in glove:** to be closely related to s.t.: *How well a person lives goes hand in glove with a good job that pays well.* **3 to fit like a glove:** to fit perfectly: *She wears body suits that fit like a glove.*

glove compartment *n.* a small box in front of the passenger's seat in a car that holds small items and has a door that opens and closes: *We store maps in the glove compartment.*

glow /gloʊ/ *n.* **1** a reflection of light and heat: *The warm glow of a fire in the fireplace on a cold night gives comfort.* **2** a slightly reddish color to the skin, usu. in the face: *After her vacation, she has a glow of good health.*

—*v.* to give off light, usu. without a flame: *The cigarette glowed in the dark.*

glow·er /'glaʊər/ *v.n.* to look at s.t. angrily: *The teacher <v.> glowered at the students who arrived late for class.* *-adj.* **glowering.**

glow·ing /'gloʊɪŋ/ *adj.* showing enthusiasm for s.t.: *We loved our visit to Boston, and we gave a glowing report of the city to all our friends.*

glow·worm /'gloʊ,wɜrm/ *n.* an insect that gives off light in the dark

glu·cose /'glu,koʊs/ *n.* **1** a type of natural sugar found in plants and animals: *Glucose is the main source of energy for your body cells.* **2** a sugar mixture used in baking

glue /glu/ *n.* a sticky liquid or solid that joins things together, (*syn.*) an adhesive: *I use glue to stick pictures on paper.*

—*v.* **glued, gluing, glues 1** to join things together with glue: *I glued the pictures to a piece of paper.* **2** *fig.* to watch s.t. with all your attention for a long period: *The children stay glued (or) glue themselves to the television set.*

glum /glʌm/ *adj.* **glummer, glummest** sad, unhappy: *She failed the exam and was glum for several days.*

glut /glʌt/ *n.* a supply of more goods on a market than is necessary, (*syn.*) an excess: *There is a glut of office space available now as many buildings are empty.*

—*v.* **glutted, glutting, gluts 1** to supply too much of s.t. **2** *frml.* to overeat, (*syn.*) to gorge: *Lions glutted on a newly killed zebra.*

glu·ten /'glutn/ *n.* a substance found in wheat and corn, used as gluc and as flour

glut·ton /'glʌtn/ *n.* **1** a person or animal that eats too much, (*syns.*) *slang* a pig, hog: *That man is a glutton; he eats three portions of everything.* **2** *fig.* **a glutton for s.t.:** a person who is always ready for more of s.t. difficult or unpleasant: *She is a glutton for hard work; she works every weekend. -n.* **gluttony.**

glyc·er·ine or **glyc·er·in** /'glɪsərɪn/ *n.* a thick, sweet liquid with no color used to make soap, medicine, explosives, and some foods

GMAT /,ʤiemeɪ'ti/ *n.abbr.* for Graduate Management Admissions Test, a test students must pass for admission to graduate-level business colleges

gnarled /nɑrld/ *adj.* twisted with a rough surface: *Old trees have gnarled branches.*

gnash /næʃ/ *v.* **gnashes** to rub s.t. (usu. one's teeth) together, usu. with noise to show anger, worry, or pain: *The man was so angry that he gnashed his teeth. -n.* **gnashing.**

gnat /næt/ *n.* a small fly that bites: *There are many gnats in the woods in early summer.*

gnaw /nɔ/ *v.* **1** to keep biting at s.t. over a period of time: *Rats gnaw through cartons to get at food inside.* **2** to cause worry or pain: *My money problems are gnawing (away) at me. -n. adj.* **gnawing.**

gnome /noʊm/ *n.* (in stories) a short person, usu. a man, living under the ground

GNP /,ʤien'pi/ *n.abbr. of* gross national product

go /goʊ/ *v.* **went** /wɛnt/, **gone** /gɔn, gɑn/, **going, goes 1** to move to a place: *I go to my office every morning.‖She goes to London twice a year.* **2** to leave a place: *I have to go (or) to be going now, but I'll see you later.* **3** to move somewhere to do s.t.: *She likes to go swimming (shopping, driving, jogging, etc.).* **4** to operate, run: *The engine is still going; shut it off.* **5** to change from one condition to another, become: *He went crazy.‖The value of the dollar is going down.* **6** to extend, reach to: *This highway goes to Washington.‖The Mississippi goes from Minnesota to Louisiana.* **7** to stop, break, or collapse: *The motor went and won't restart.* **8** to perform, be: *Business (life, my job, etc.) is going well.‖How are things going?* **9** to belong to, be placed with: *This cap goes on that bottle.‖Empty bottles go in this box for recycling.* **10** to look good with, match: *That blue tie and green suit don't go to-*

gether. **11** to result in: *Our meeting went well today.* **12** to continue, remain in the same state: *That hole in the roof went unnoticed until the rain came through it.* **13** to circulate, spread: *The flu goes from person to person.* **14** to be awarded: *First prize in the math competition went to my sister.* **15** to throw out: *These old curtains must go!* **16** to die: *The old man went last night.* **17** to start s.t.: *"When I say 'go,' you can begin the exam."* **18** to have specific words or a melody: *How does the tune for this children's song go?* **19 anything goes:** anything is possible or acceptable (often referring to behavior that is usu. restricted): *You can wear jeans or shorts to school; at this school anything goes.* **20 to be going to do s.t.:** (shows the future, what is planned or determined): *It's going to snow tomorrow.‖They're going to get married next year.* **21 Go, man, go!:** *exclam.infrml.* showing that one likes s.t., giving encouragement, said esp. to a musician: *Hey, he can really play that guitar, "Go, man, go!"* **22 to go: a.** to remain (of time): *I have four days to go before my vacation ends.* **b.** to take out (of food) for eating at home: *I got some Chinese food to go and ate it at home.* **23 that (just) goes to show:** that proves: *He didn't do his homework again; that just goes to show (you) how lazy he really is.* **24** *phrasal v.* **to go about: a.** to move or spread from place to place: *A rumor went about that he had lost all his money.* **b. with:** *See:* to go around (c). **c. s.t.:** to work at s.t.: *I talked with my friends for a while, then I went about my business.* **25** *phrasal v. insep.* **to go after s.o. or s.t.:** to try (hard) to obtain, chase: *The police went after the thief.* **26** *phrasal v. insep.* **to go against s.t.: a.** to place against: *That bookshelf goes against the wall.* **b.** to disagree, (*syn.*) to oppose: *She went against her mother's wishes by staying out late.* **27** *phrasal v. insep.* **to go ahead: a. of:** to go before, (*syn.*) to precede: *My father went ahead of us and made hotel reservations before we arrived.* **b. with:** to begin or continue to do s.t., (*syn.*) to proceed: *We went ahead with our plans for a vacation.* **28** *phrasal v.* **to go along:** to do s.t. at the same time as one is doing s.t. else: *She tried to calculate the total as she went along.* **29** *phrasal v. insep.* **to go along with s.o. or s.t.: a.** to accompany: *I will go along with you to the bus stop.* **b.** to agree with: *I go along with what you are saying.* **30 to go and do s.t.:** to do s.t. (said in surprise or shock, often showing disapproval): *She went and bought two new gold watches!* **31** *phrasal v. insep.* **to go around: a.** *See:* to go about (a). **b. s.o. or s.t.:** to avoid s.o. or s.t.: *We avoided the city traffic by going around it.* **c. with:** to spend time with, socialize: *I go around with my friends from college on weekends* **d.** to be enough of s.t.: *There aren't enough computers*

to go around in the class; the students are sharing. **32** *phrasal v. insep.* **to go at s.o. or s.t.: a.** to attack with words or physically: *The senator really went at the journalist when he asked her another personal question.* **b.** to work hard: *He went at it until he had finished his math homework.* **33** *phrasal v.* **to go away:** to leave, depart: *My son went away to college this year.* **34** *phrasal v. insep.* **to go back:** to return: *He went back home after the game.* **35** *phrasal v. insep.* **to go back on s.t.:** to break one's promise (agreement, deal, etc.): *He promised to pay back my money, but he went back on his word and didn't pay.* **36** *phrasal v. insep.* **to go by s.t.: a.** to pass by: *We went by our favorite restaurant but it was too crowded.* **b.** to be directed or guided by s.t., to follow: *You can't go by what he says; he lies sometimes.* **37** *phrasal v.* **to go down: a.** to go lower, descend: *I went down the stairs and out the door.‖House prices are going down.* **b.** to stop working or functioning: *The air-conditioning in our office went down and it became very hot.* **c.** to sink: *The boat went down after it was hit.* **d.** *slang* to happen: *There is a police raid going down at that club tonight.* **e.** to be received (of a reaction): *My proposal for the new L.A. office went down very well/badly.* **38** *phrasal v.* **to go far:** to succeed: *He is very smart and will go far in life.* **39** *phrasal v. insep.* **to go for s.o. or s.t.: a.** to do s.t., fetch s.t.: *I went for a driver's license test this morning.* **b.** *See:* to go at (a). **c.** *infrml.* to like, adore: *He really goes for blonde women.* **d.** to be sold for: *That antique vase went for $15,000.* **e.** *See:* to go after. **40** *phrasal v. insep.* **to go in s.t.:** to enter: *The swimmer went in the water.* **41** *phrasal v. insep.* **to go in for s.t.: a.** to enter a competition: *She went in for the college tennis tournament.* **b.** to do s.t. often, esp. for pleasure: *She doesn't go in for cooking; she usually eats in restaurants.* **42** *phrasal v. insep.* **to go into s.t.: a.** to enter (a place): *She went into town.* **b.** to enter a profession: *He went into the law.* **c.** to look at closely: *I went into the contract in detail before signing it.* **43** *phrasal v.* **to go off: a.** to leave, depart: *My friend went off and left me alone.* **b.** to shut off, go out (said of mechanical devices): *The lights went off.* **c.** to explode: *A bomb went off in the post office.* **d.** *insep.* **s.t.:** to lose interest in s.t. or s.o.: *I went off cigarettes last week.‖I went off the idea of a picnic when it began to rain.* **44** *phrasal v. insep.* **to go off with s.o. or s.t.:** to leave with s.o. or s.t., usu. without permission: *He went off with the keys to my new car.‖She went off with another woman's husband.* **45** *phrasal v. insep.* **to go on: a.** to happen: *What's going on in that meeting?* **b.** to continue (a trip, journey): *After visiting Paris, we went on to Berlin.‖She will go on working,* *even after her car accident.* **c.** to turn on, begin working (said of mechanical devices): *The alarm went on when he left the house.* **d.** to talk too much: *He went on and on about their wonderful trip.* **e.** to have useful information (facts, evidence): *The police could not solve the crime because they have nothing to go on.* **f.** to pass (said of time): *As life goes on, I find money more important.* **46** *phrasal v.* **to go out: a.** to stop working or operating: *The power went out because of the storm.||The fire went out in the rain.* **b.** to leave one's home or office: *Miss Jones has gone out to lunch.* **c.** to leave one's home in order to have fun: *That evening, she and a friend went out (to a movie, play, dinner, dance, etc.).* **d.** to spend time with s.o., (syn.) to date: *They went out for two years before getting married.* **e.** no longer to be fashionable: *Wide neckties went out in the 70s.* **47** *phrasal v. insep.* **to go out for s.t.:** to try out in hope of being chosen as a player or member of a team, society, etc.: *He went out for the college football team.* **48** *phrasal v. insep.* **to go over: a. s.t.:** to climb or jump over s.t.: *The horse went over a fence.* **b.** to visit: *I went over to my friend's house.* **c. s.t.:** to look at s.t. carefully: *I went over the contract, then signed it.* **d.** *See:* to go down (e). **e. to:** to change one's preference for s.t. (e.g., a political party, football team, etc.): *She's gone over to the Democrats.* **49** *phrasal v. insep* **to go through s.o. or s.t.: a.** to pass through: *The needle goes through the cloth easily.* **b.** to be processed, approved: *Laws go through the Congress to the President.* **c.** to experience, usu. s.t. painful, (syn.) to endure: *He went through a difficult time after his wife died.* **d.** *See:* to go over (c). **50** *phrasal v. insep.* **to go through with s.t.:** to finish s.t. (a difficult event or situation): *She was nervous about getting married, but finally she went through with the marriage ceremony.* **51** *phrasal v. insep.* **to go to s.t.:** to cause oneself to experience s.t.: *My new company went to a lot of trouble to make me feel welcome.* **52** *phrasal v.* **to go together: a.** to be suitable, match: *Those blue shoes and that blue skirt go well together.* **b.** to have a personal relationship: *That man and woman have been going together with each other for a year now.* **53 to go too far:** to do s.t. unacceptable (not good manners): *He went too far when he asked to borrow his boss's new car.* **54** *phrasal v.* **to go under:** to fail, go bankrupt: *The corporation went under last year.* **55** *phrasal v.* **to go up:** to rise, (syn.) to ascend: *The economy is going up at the moment.* **56** *phrasal v. insep.* **to go with s.t.:** to be suitable, match: *Those blue shoes go well with your blue dress.* **57 to go without saying:** to be obvious, evident: *The President is visiting and it*

goes without saying that everyone wishes to see him. **58 to have s.t. going: a.** to have good business or other exciting opportuni-ties: *I met the company owner, and we really have something going with that new product.* **b.** to have a love affair: *He has something going with her.* **59 to have to go:** to need to go to the toilet: *I have to go badly, where's the men's room?* **60 to tell s.o. where to go:** to tell s.o. to go or leave: *He annoyed her, so she told him where to go.* **61 what goes around, comes around:** when you do wrong to s.o., the wrong will come back to hurt you: *When he was the boss, he was mean to everyone. Now that he's out of work, no one will hire him. What goes around, comes around.*

—*n.* **goes 1** a try, attempt at s.t.: *I couldn't solve the problem, so I asked my friend to have a go at it.* **2 to be on the go:** to be very busy: *I've been on the go all week and am very tired.* **3 to have a go situation:** to be free to proceed: *Our new budget is approved, so we have a go situation in hiring more people.* **4 to have get-up-and-go:** to be energetic, vigor-ous: *She is very athletic; she has a lot of get-up-and-go.* **5 to make a go of (things, it, etc.):** to succeed: *She started a new company and is making a go of it.*

goad /goʊd/ *v.* to cause s.o. to do s.t. by mak-ing him or her angry with words or actions, (syn.) to incite: *The woman goaded her hus-band into getting a job by calling him "lazy."*
—*n.* a pointed stick used for making animals go forward

go-ahead *n.* permission to do s.t., (syn.) ap-proval: *The manager gave the go-ahead to buy new computers.*

goal /goʊl/ *n.* **1** a score in some sports, such as soccer or hockey: *The player scored two goals during the last game.* **2** the place used for scoring points: *In both soccer and hockey, the goal is a metal frame with a net.* **3** an ob-jective, purpose: *Our goal is to increase com-pany sales by 10 percent this year.*

goal·ie /ˈgoʊli/ *n.infrml.* a goalkeeper

goal·keep·er /ˈgoʊlˌkipər/ *n.* a player who stands in the goal and tries to stop the other team from scoring, (syn.) goaltender: *Our goalkeeper stopped 20 of the other team's shots today, and we won the game.*

goal post *n.* one of two upright pieces of wood or metal used to mark the scoring area: *The football player kicked the ball between the goal posts for a score.*

goal·tend·er /ˈgoʊlˌtɛndər/ *n. See:* goalkeeper.

go-around *n.* **1** an argument: *My boss and I had a big go-round today; I got angry and then I quit.* **2** *See:* run-around.

goat /goʊt/ *n.* **1** a small four-legged animal, re-lated to a sheep, that has horns and a rough coat and gives milk: *Many wild goats live in the mountains.* **2** an unpleasant old man, esp. one who is active sexually, (*syn.*) a lecher **3** *fig.* **to get s.o.'s goat:** to make s.o. angry, (*syn.*) to annoy, provoke: *He really gets my goat; he never stops talking.*

goat·ee /gouˈti/ *n.* a small beard on the point of the chin: *He doesn't like long beards; he just has a goatee. See:* sideburns, USAGE NOTE.

gob /gɑb/ *n.infrml.* **1** a small amount or lump of s.t.: *The server put a gob of mashed potato on my plate.* **2** *pl.***gobs** a lot of s.t.: *She has gobs of money.*
—*v.* **gobbed, gobbing, gobs** to place in gobs: *He gobbed the potato onto my plate.*

gob·ble (1) /ˈgɑbəl/ *v.infrml.* **-bled, -bling, -bles** to eat quickly and noisily: *He was so hungry that he gobbled his food up.*

gobble (2) *v.n.* to make the noise that a turkey makes

gob·ble·dy·gook /ˈgɑbəldiˌgʊk/ *n.infrml.* language used by specialists that is difficult to understand and usu. has no important meaning: *The company report was mostly gobbledygook; it didn't give any useful information.*

gob·bler /ˈgɑblər/ *n.* a male turkey

go-between *n.* a person who carries information or messages between two or more people or groups who cannot meet, (*syn.*) an intermediary: *The diplomat acts as a go-between between his government and foreign repre-sentatives.*

gob·let /ˈgɑblɪt/ *n.* a drinking container (usu. for wine) made of glass or metal with a long stem and often decorated: *She serves wine in silver goblets.*

gob·lin /ˈgɑblɪn/ *n.* (in stories) a small, ugly person or spirit who does bad things to people

go-cart *n.* a small toy wagon that children pull or push: *The boy pulled his little sister in a go-cart.*

god /gɑd/ *n.* **1 God:** the Supreme Being, Creator in many religions (Christianity, Islam, Judaism) **2** any of a number of beings or spirits worshipped in various cultures: *Mars was the ancient Roman god of war.* **3 God forbid (that):** to hope that s.t. will not happen: *God forbid that he lose his job again.* **4 God knows:** *infrml.* it is difficult or impossible to say: *God knows what time she will finally come home.* **5 God willing:** if all goes well: *He is going to have major surgery today, and, God willing, we'll visit him tomorrow.* **6 to play God:** to think you have power to do anything you want: *She's the boss and thinks that she can play God with her worker's lives.*

god-awful *adj.infrml.* terrible, (*syn.*) dreadful: *The traffic was so bad that we had a god-awful time getting here.*

god·child /ˈgɑdˌʧaɪld/ **-children** /-ˌʧɪldrən/ *n.* the child (**godson** or **goddaughter**) of s.o. else for whom one promises to take responsibility if the natural parents die: *My best friend's daughter is my godchild.*

god·daugh·ter /ˈgɑdˌdɔtər/ *n. See:* godchild.

god·dess /ˈgɑdɪs/ *n.* **-desses 1** a female god **2** a beautiful woman: *Marilyn Monroe was a goddess among film stars.*

god·fa·ther /ˈgɑdˌfɑðər/ *n.* **1** *See:* godparent. **2** *fig.* the head or leader of a criminal organization, esp. in the Mafia

god·for·sak·en /ˈgɑdfərˌseɪkən/ *adj.* (of a place) far from civilization with very little of interest or attraction, usu. depressing, (*syn.*) desolate, bleak: *The travelers rode their horses for weeks through the godforsaken land before arriving at the farm.*

god·less /ˈgɑdlɪs/ *adj.frml.* without religion, (*syn.*) pagan: *Athiests don't believe in a supreme being; they believe in a godless world.*

god·like /ˈgɑdˌlaɪk/ *adj.* looking like a god: *The statue was huge and represented the dictator as godlike.*

god·ly /ˈgɑdli/ *adj.* **-lier, -liest** believing in God, very religious, (*syn.*) devout

god·moth·er /ˈgɑdˌmʌðər/ *n. See:* godparent.

god·par·ent /ˈgɑdˌpɛrənt, -ˌpær-/ *n.* a person (**godfather** or **godmother**) who promises to take responsibility for s.o. else's child if the child's parents die: *My godparents are my mother's best friend and her husband.*

god·send /ˈgɑdˌsɛnd/ *n.* unexpected help often needed in an emergency: *Fresh water and food sent quickly to earthquake victims was a godsend.*

god·son /ˈgɑdˌsʌn/ *n. See:* godchild.

God·speed /ˌgɑdˈspid/ *n.frml.old usage* good luck, usu. when one is leaving on a journey: *I wish you Godspeed in your journey into the jungle.*

go·fer /ˈgoufər/ *n.infrml.* a person or employee who carries things and messages for other people: *He does some paperwork and acts also as the company gofer.*

go-get·ter /ˈgouˌgɛtər, -ˌgɛ-/ *n.infrml.* an energetic person who is determined to be successful: *As the company's best salesperson, he's a real go-getter.*

gog·gle /ˈgɑgəl/ *v.infrml.* **-gled, -gling, -gles** to look at s.t. with one's eyes wide open, usu. in surprise: *The children goggled at the man's blue hair.*

gog·gles /ˈgɑgəlz/ *n.pl.* plastic glasses that protect the eyes: *In the laboratory, she wears goggles to protect her eyes from chemicals.*

go-go /ˈgoʊˌgoʊ/ *adj.infrml.* related to discotheques or the music or dancing performed at discotheques: *She is a go-go dancer at a local disco.*

goggles

go·ing /ˈgoʊɪŋ/ *adj.* **1** related to the rate or fee charged at that moment: *The going rate for a lawyer is $150 an hour.* **2 a going concern:** a successful, profitable business: *He started his business three years ago and now it's a going concern.* **3 going on:** almost approaching: *My mother is 50 years old, going on 51.*
—*n.* **1** the act of leaving, departure: *His going means we need to find a new salesperson.* **2** the condition of the ground, the road, etc. for walking, driving, etc.: *When it rains, the going is hard on this old road.* **3 while the going's good:** while it is still possible: *The storm is coming closer; let's leave now while the going's good.*

going-over *n.* **goings-over** complete examination: *The doctor gave me a good going-over and found nothing wrong.*

goings-on *n.pl.* happenings, events, often used negatively: *Some people were selling drugs on our street and the neighbors reported those goings-on to the police.*

gold /goʊld/ *n.* **1** a precious yellow metal used for jewelry, coins, etc.: *Her bracelet and rings are made of gold.* **2** s.t. of great value: *The land in Minnesota is so rich that the farmers call it "black gold."* **3 to have a heart of gold:** to be a kind and generous person: *She gives the impression of being tough, but she has a heart of gold.* **4 worth one's** or **its weight in gold:** of great value: *She is an incredibly good worker; she's worth her weight in gold. See:* glitter.
—*adj.* made of or related to gold

gold digger *n.infrml.* a person, esp. a woman, who tries to attract rich people, usu. men, to get money and presents from them: *She is a gold digger who goes out with men just for their money.*

gold·en /ˈgoʊldən/ *adj.* **1** yellow, gold colored: *The sunset turned from a golden yellow to orange.* **2** made of gold or gold leaf: *That picture has a golden frame.* **3** very valuable, excellent: *She was accepted by Harvard University; she has a golden opportunity to receive an excellent education.* **4** senior, late middle age: *The couple spent their golden years living in a mountain village.*

golden oldie *n.infrml.* a song, movie, or idea remaining popular for many years:

Bing Crosby's "White Christmas" is a golden oldie.

gold·en·rod /ˈgoʊldənˌrɑd/ *n.* a plant with small yellow flowers: *In late August I love to see the goldenrod blooming along the sides of the roads.*

Golden Rule *n.* a rule that you should treat others as you would like to be treated yourself: *Some people try to live by the Golden Rule.*

gold·fish /ˈgoʊldˌfɪʃ/ *n.* **-fish** or **-fishes** small tropical, usu. yellow-orange, fish kept in a bowl or tank by people: *Her hobby is collecting goldfish.*

goldfish bowl *n.* **1** a bowl in which goldfish are kept **2** *fig.* a small place without privacy: *My office is like a goldfish bowl; people can see everything I do.*

gold leaf *n.* a very thin layer of gold: *That picture frame is covered with gold leaf.*

gold mine *n.* **1** a place, usu. underground, from which gold is taken **2** *fig.* a business or activity that is very successful: *That business of his is a gold mine.*

gold-plated *adj.* covered with gold **-n. gold plating.**

gold rush *n.* a sudden rush of people into a newly discovered gold mining area: *The California gold rush of 1849 made some people millionaires. See:* prospector, USAGE NOTE.

gold·smith *n.* a person who makes jewelry, etc. out of gold: *A goldsmith made my wife a gold ring.*

golf /gɑlf, gɔlf/ *n.* a game in which people try to hit a small hard ball with a special stick (a club) into a small hole over a large outdoor course: *I like to play golf on weekends.* **-n. golfer.**

golf club *n.* **1** one of 14 standard sticks used to hit a golf ball: *I carry my golf clubs in a leather bag.* **2** a social club organized for playing golf: *I belong to a local golf club.*

golf course *n.* the outdoor area where golf is played, with nine or 18 holes: *The local golf course is public, so anyone can play.*

gol·ly /ˈgɑli/ *exclam.* an expression of surprise

go·nad /ˈgoʊˌnæd/ *n.* a sexual organ that produces sperm or eggs

gon·do·la /ˈgɑndələ/ *n.* **1** a long narrow boat with a flat bottom used on canals in Venice **2** the passenger cabin of a suspended cable of a cable car or airship: *We took the gondola to the top of the mountain and then skied down.* **-n. gondolier** /ˌgɑndəˈlɪr/.

gondola

gone /gɔn, gan/ *past part. of* go
—*adj.infrml.* in love with, (*syn.*), infatuated: *He's gone on the girl next door.*

gon·er /ˈgɔnər, ˈga-/ *n.infrml.* a person or thing that will die soon or be in a hopeless situation: *He is very sick—he' a goner.*

gong /gɔŋ, gaŋ/ *n.* a large, flat, round musical instrument made of metal: *A slave hit the gong to announce the king's entrance.*

gon·or·rhe·a /ˌganəˈriə/ *n.* a sexually transmitted disease: *Gonorrhea can be treated with an antibiotic medication.*

goo /gu/ *n.infrml.* **1** a thick, sticky substance: *The baby dropped his food and now there's goo on the floor.* **2** a sound made by a baby

goo·ber /ˈgubər/ *n.infrml.* a peanut: *Farmers grow goobers near Atlanta, Georgia.*

good /gʊd/ *adj.* **better** /ˈbɛtər/, **best** /bɛst/ **1** (in general) having a pleasing quality, great, pleasurable: *She had a good time on her vacation.‖That singer is very good.‖You look good; I like your new hair style.* **2** having a satisfactory, right quality: *Housing prices are good in this area.‖The senator has a new education policy that will be good for college students.* **3** of a high quality or standard: *She speaks very good Japanese.* **4** having the talent to do s.t. well, (*syns.*) skillful, adept: *He's good at (playing) the piano.‖I am no good at numbers; I always need help with my taxes.* **5** kind: *She's very good with children; they all love her.* **6** beneficial to one's health or character: *Milk and cheese are good for your bones and teeth.‖Too much television is not good for children.* **7** useful or suitable for s.t. specific: *This software program is good for financial documents.‖This sauce is very good with pasta.* **8** well-behaved: *Her son is very good; he never fights with other children.* **9** fresh, not spoiled: *The bread from yesterday is still good.* **10** genuine, authentic: *That coin is good, not a fake.* **11** behaving in a moral way, (*syn.*) virtuous: *She is a good woman.* **12** able to be used legally, (*syn.*) valid: *Her driver's license is good for five years.* **13** *infrml.* **a good deal:** a sizeable amount of s.t.: *There was a good deal of anger when the employees lost their jobs.* **14 all in good time:** when s.t. is ready, unhurried: *You will learn the answer all in good time.* **15 as good as:** almost, practically: *I washed those old curtains and now they look as good as new.* **16 as good as done (finished, taken care of):** s.t. that will be done quickly: *We will start immediately; you can consider the job as good as done.* **17 for good:** forever: *He is gone for good and won't be back.* **18 good and ready:** expressing firmness about acting only when one wants to: *I'll answer your question when I'm good and ready.* **19 good enough:** adequate, satisfactory: *That dress is simple but good enough just to wear*

around the house. **20 no good:** useless, worthless: *It's no good turning the computer on; the system is down.* **21 that's a good one:** usu. about a joke or funny situation: *That's a good one! That joke is very funny!*
—*n.* **1** not evil, that which is considered good: *In many movies, good always beats evil.‖There is some good in him; don't send him to jail.* **2** s.t. that is beneficial: *Her long summer vacation did her good.‖The government works for the good of the people.* **3 for your own good:** in one's own best interest (said to s.o. who should do s.t. difficult for their own benefit): *You should stay away from those troublemakers for your own good.* **4 It's no good:** it's useless, there is no point in doing s.t.: *It's no good trying to run; the police will catch you.* **5 to come to no good:** to develop into a bad situation or person: *He runs around with bad people and he will come to no good someday.* **6 to do good:** to benefit others, perform a kindness: *The church does good by helping the poor.*
—*exclam.* **1** wonderful, excellent: *Good! The rain has stopped.* **2 Good for you:** congratulations: *Good for you; I'm really happy that you won the tournament!*
—*adv.* **1 to make good:** to succeed: *She made good in a banking career.* **2** to make up for s.t.: *The printer made a mistake on my order, but they made good on their mistake by giving me a discount. See:* do-gooder, hard goods, soft goods.

USAGE NOTE: *Good* should not be used as an adverb in formal speech or writing, such as in, "He did good on the test." It should be: "He did well on the test."

Good Book *n.* the Christian Bible

good-bye /gʊdˈbaɪ, gəˈbaɪ/ *n.* an expression used when one is leaving: *When we finished our conversation, I said good-bye to her and left. See:* bye-bye.

good-for-nothing *n.* a lazy, undependable person: *He never keeps his promises; he's a good-for-nothing.*

Good Friday *n.* (in the Christian religion) the day that Christ died; the Friday before Easter

good·heart·ed /ˈgʊdˈhartɪd/ *adj.* kind, (*syn.*) generous: *She is a goodhearted woman.*

good-hu·mored /ˈgʊdˈhyumərd/ *adj.* feeling or sharing happiness, cheerfulness, often about s.t. unpleasant: *My manager was good-humored about the mistakes in my report. -n.* **good humor.**

good·ie or **goody** /ˈgʊdi/ *n.infrml.* s.t. attractive or pleasant, esp. s.t. sweet to eat: *At the party, the hostess had a table full of cookies, cake, and other goodies.*

good-looking *adj.* attractive, handsome: *She is a good-looking woman.*

good luck *n.* said to wish s.o. well: *"Good luck! Call me when you get back from your trip."||He wished me good luck in my new job.*

good·ly /'gʊdli/ *adj.* old usage large in amount, (*syn.*) substantial: *I pay a goodly amount of money in taxes every year.*

good-na·tured /'gʊd'neɪʧərd/ *adj.* **1** having or showing kindness and friendliness: *Our babysitter is very good-natured; all the children love her.* **2** gentle, (*syn.*) docile: *That dog is very good-natured; it has never attacked anybody.*

good·ness /'gʊdnɪs/ *n.* **1** the quality or state of being good: *The goodness of the life in that region was the reason we moved there.* **2** the part of s.t., esp. food, that is good or healthy: *There is a lot of goodness in fresh fruits and vegetables.* **3** kindness
—*exclam.* **My goodness!** or **Goodness!:** used to express surprise: *"My goodness! You're two hours early!"*

goods /gʊds/ *n.pl.* **1** items that can be bought or sold: *The goods that you ordered have arrived in the warehouse.* **2** *fig.* **to deliver the goods:** to do what is expected of you, usu. under difficult circumstances: *We worked all night to finish the job and we delivered the goods at 9:00 A.M.* **3** *fig.* **to get the goods on s.o.:** to prove that s.o. did wrong: *The police got the goods on the bank robber by finding his picture on the bank's video camera.*

Good Sa·mar·i·tan /sə'mærətən/ *n.* a person who helps another in trouble: *We had a car accident and a Good Samaritan stopped and took us to the hospital.*

good-sized *adj.* fairly large: *The portions of food at that restaurant are good-sized.*

good will or **goodwill** *n.* **1** friendliness or good feelings between people: *The negotiations between the two countries took place in an atmosphere of good will.* **2** (in business accounting) the financial value of the popularity of a business: *The price of the business was $80,000, and we paid $25,000 extra for the good will.*

good·y /'gʊdi/ *n.infrml. See:* goodie.

good·y-good·y /'gʊdi'gʊdi/ or **goody-two-shoes** *n.infrml.* **goody-goodies** a person who behaves very well in order to make other people happy, not because he or she is really good, often used negatively: *He's a real goody-goody and so is his sister.*

goo·ey /'gui/ *adj.infrml.* **gooier, gooiest** sticky: *The chocolate became gooey in the sun.*

goof /guf/ *n.infrml.* **1** a stupid, careless mistake: *He made a goof and ordered the wrong part.* **2** a foolish or stupid person: *He's a big goof; he always forgets our meetings.*

—*v.infrml.* **1** to make a stupid mistake, blunder: *He goofed when he ordered the wrong part for the computer.* **2** *phrasal v.* **to goof off:** not to work hard, to waste time: *He goofs off all day when the boss is away.*

goof-off *n.infrml.* a person who does not work hard, (*syn.*) a shirker, loafer: *He's a big goof-off and doesn't study.*

goof·y /'gufi/ *adj.infrml.* **-ier, -iest** silly, often in a strange way: *He wore a goofy yellow tie with a red jacket.*

goon /gun/ *n.infrml.* **1** a violent person, often a criminal employed to attack or frighten people: *The company owner hired goons to try to make the striking employees go back to work.* **2** a silly person: *Stop making that stupid face! Stop being such a goon!*

goon squad *n.infrml.* a group of goons

goose /gus/ *n.* **geese** /gis/ **1** a water bird with a long neck, larger than the duck: *Geese fly south for the winter.* **2** the female of this bird *See:* gander. **3** *infrml.fig.* **to be a silly goose:** to make a mistake or hold a foolish opinion: *He's such a silly goose; he always says the wrong thing to his manager.* **4** *infrml.fig.* **to cook s.o.'s goose:** to ruin s.o., get s.o. in trouble: *A witness cooked the thief's goose by telling the police where the thief was hiding.*

—*v.* **goosed, goosing, gooses 1** *vulg.slang* to touch s.o. on the buttocks: *He goosed her and she hit him.* **2** to cause s.t. to increase suddenly: *High discounts goosed sales this week.*

goose bumps *n.pl.infrml.* very small raised points on the skin caused by cold, fear, or disgust: *The horror movie gave me goose bumps.*

goose pimples *n.pl.* goose bumps

goose-step *v.* **-stepped, -stepping, -steps** a special way of marching in which one does not bend the knees: *Soldiers goose-stepped down the boulevard.* **-n. goose step.**

GOP /ˌʤiou'pi/ *short for* Grand Old Party, the Republican Party in US politics

go·pher /'goufər / *n.* **1** a small animal of North America that makes holes in the ground: *Many gophers live in the flat grasslands of the USA.* **2 Gopher:** a program that makes it easier for computers on the Internet to link to information sources all over the Internet

gore /gɔr/ *v.* **gored, goring, gores** to make a hole and injure with the horn or tusk of an animal: *The bull gored the bullfighter and he had to go to the hospital.*
—*n.* blood from a person or animal, esp. after an accident: *There was a lot of blood and gore in the horror movie.* **-n. goring.**

gorge /gɔrʤ/ *n.* a high, narrow opening between mountains, usu. with a stream: *After the heavy rain, the stream rushed through the mountain gorge.*

—*v.* to fill oneself quickly with a lot of food until one cannot eat anymore, (*syn.*) to stuff oneself: *The hungry children gorged themselves on chocolate until they felt sick.*

gor·geous /'gɔrdʒəs/ *adj.* beautiful, (*syn.*) stunning: *She is a fashion model and a gorgeous woman.‖The flowers in the window have a gorgeous color.*

go·ril·la /gə'rɪlə/ *n.* the largest of the great apes (man-like monkeys) and native to western Africa: *There are only a few mountain gorillas left in the world.*

gor·y /'gɔri/ *adj.* **-ier, -iest** bloody, full of gore: *The accident scene was gory with broken bodies and bloody clothing.* -*n.* **goriness.**

gosh /gɑʃ/ *exclam.* expression of surprise or disappointment: *Gosh, that exam was difficult.*

gos·ling /'gɑzlɪŋ/ *n.* a baby goose

gos·pel /'gɑspəl/ *n.* **1** an idea that cannot be questioned: *In that company, the owner's wishes are the gospel* (or) *gospel truth that everyone must follow.* **2 Gospel:** any of the first four books of the New Testament in the Bible

gospel music *n.* a type of American religious music with strong rhythms and harmonies: *My mother sings gospel music in the church choir.*

gos·sa·mer /'gɑsəmər/ *n.* **1** very thin silky threads made by spiders **2** a very soft, thin material: *The nightgown looks as though it is made of gossamer.*

gos·sip /'gɑsəp/ *v.* to talk or write about other people's actions or lives, sometimes in an untruthful way: *The whole country was gossiping about the recent political scandal.*
—*n.* **1** talk or writing about other people's actions or lives, sometimes untruthful: *"Did you hear the gossip about the new manager?"* **2** a person who likes to gossip: *The old man is the town gossip.* -*adj.* **gossipy.**

gos·sip·mon·ger /'gɑsəp,mʌŋgər, -,mɑŋ-/ *n.* a person who spreads gossip: *She is a gossipmonger; she will tell you about everyone's business.*

got /gɑt/ *v.past tense & part. of* get **1** to be necessary, must do s.t.: *I have got to leave now; it is very late.* **2** to have s.t. or s.o.: *She has got $100 to spend this evening.*

Goth·ic /'gɑθɪk/ *adj.* **1** related to the Goths, an ancient Germanic tribe: *Gothic warriors invaded Rome.* **2** a style of European architecture used in the 12th and 16th centuries: *Notre Dame in Paris is a Gothic cathedral.* **3 gothic:** related to a romantic type of literature with isolated, mysterious settings: *Many gothic novels are set in castles in France.*

got·ten /'gɑtn/ *v.past part. of* get

gouge /gaʊdʒ/ *v.* **gouged, gouging, gouges 1** to press, shape, or force out of s.t.: *The children gouged out a big hole in the old tree and*

played in it. **2** to overcharge: *That storekeeper gouges his customers; I never shop there.* -*n.* **gouger.**

gou·lash /'gu,lɑʃ/ *n.* a stew of vegetables, meat, and seasonings, usu. paprika, cooked together: *We had beef goulash with potatoes for dinner.*

gourd /gɔrd, gʊrd/ *n.* a fruit with a hard outer shell that usu. cannot be eaten: *People use gourds to hold drinking water.*

gour·met /gʊr'meɪ, 'gʊr,meɪ/ *n.adj.* a person who knows a lot about and enjoys fine food and drink: *He is a <n.> gourmet of French food.‖This restaurant serves <adj.> gourmet Italian food.*

gout /gaʊt/ *n.* a disease that makes the joints, esp. toes and fingers, become bigger and painful: *My grandfather suffers from gout in his feet and has difficulty walking.*

gov·ern /'gʌvərn/ *v.* **1** to rule a country, city, etc.: *The President governs the USA.‖The mayor governs any new policies in the city.* **2** to have influence over s.t., (*syn.*) to determine: *The weather governs the prices of fresh fruit and vegetables every year.* **3** to control the actions or behavior of s.t., (*syn.*) to restrain: *She tried to govern her temper when she heard about the car crash.* **4** (in grammar) to require, make necessary

gov·ern·ment /'gʌvərmənt, -ərnmənt/ *n.* **1** a system of political and social representation and control: *Governments are classified by who holds power, such as a dictator.* **2** the people who rule: *The government decided to cut taxes for the middle classes.* -*adj.* **governmental** /,gʌvərn'mɛntl, -ər'mɛn-/.

Government Issue *n.adj.* s.t. that is provided by the government: *The savings bonds are Government Issue. abbr.* GI.

gov·er·nor /'gʌvənər, -ərnər/ *n.* **1** a government official in charge of a state in the USA: *The state governors meet annually to discuss common problems.* **2** a manager or head of a business or institution: *The hospital board of governors decided to open a new building.*

governor-general *n.* a governor of a large territory to whom other governors report

gov·er·nor·ship /'gʌvənər,ʃɪp, -ərnər-/ *n.* the office or term of a governor: *The governorship of our state belongs to a Democrat.*

gown /gaʊn/ *n.* **1** a long, formal evening dress for women: *She wore a blue silk gown to the opera.* **2** a long, usu. black coat worn in special ceremonies by judges, professors, students, etc.

GPA /,dʒipi'eɪ/ *abbr. for* grade point average

grab /græb/ *v.* **grabbed, grabbing, grabs 1** to take quickly and roughly, (*syn.*) to snatch: *A thief grabbed the woman's purse and ran.* **2** to take an opportunity with enthusiasm: *She*

grabbed the chance to work for the company and accepted the job immediately.
—*n.* **1** an attempt to take s.t. roughly: *He made a grab for her purse and ran.* **2** *infrml.* **up for grabs:** available for anyone to take or win: *This election year, the mayor's office is up for grabs because the present mayor is not running for reelection.*

grab bag *n.* **1** a container filled with a mixture of small items that people choose from at a social occasion **2** a collection of varied things: *The economic plan was a grab bag of politicians' favorite projects.*

grace /greɪs/ *n.* **1** beauty of motion or style: *She dances with grace.||He writes with grace.* **2** kindness: *My mother had the grace not to tell my father that I had crashed his car.* **3** a short prayer of gratitude said before a meal: *I said grace before Thanksgiving dinner.* **4** favor, (*syn.*) mercy: *The prisoners asked for the King's grace.* **5** a form of address of a duke, duchess, archbishop, or bishop: *What is your wish, Your Grace?* **6 to be in the good/bad graces of s.o.:** to be on good/bad terms with: *She is an excellent student and in the good graces of all her teachers.* **7 with good grace:** nicely, willingly: *He took his daughter's bad exam results with good grace.*
—*v.* **graced, gracing, graces** to favor, decorate: *The beautiful lady graced us with her company.||Flowers graced the dinner table.*

grace·ful /ˈgreɪsfəl/ *adj.* with beauty of motion or style: *She is a graceful dancer.* -*adv.* **gracefully.**

grace·less /ˈgreɪslɪs/ *adj.* without grace, tasteless

grace period *n.* a time period after a payment is due in which that payment may be made with or without penalty but no legal action: *Most mortgage and insurance contracts have grace periods in which late payments can be made without the contract being canceled.*

gra·cious /ˈgreɪʃəs/ *adj.* kind and polite: *She is a gracious hostess who provides her guests with everything they need.* -*adv.* **graciously;** -*n.* **graciousness.**

grad /græd/ *n.infrml.* short for graduate: *He is a Harvard grad.*

gra·da·tion /greɪˈdeɪʃən/ *n.* gradual progressions or degrees of s.t.: *Different gradations in the strength of steel are needed according to building requirements.* -*v.* **gradate** /ˈgreɪˌdeɪt/.

grade /greɪd/ *n.* **1** an educational class level: *Her son goes into the seventh (first, 12th, etc.) grade this year.* **2** an academic mark, score: *He makes good grades in school.* **3** a level of quality: *That store sells an excellent grade of fruits and vegetables.* **4** a degree of incline or decline as in a road: *The road goes up a steep grade from the valley to the mountaintop.* **5 to make the grade:** to achieve proficiency, prove one-

self, succeed: *She has made the grade as a professional singer.*
—*v.* **graded, grading, grades 1** to score, mark: *The teacher grades tests every week.* **2** to separate into groups according to quality or size: *The chicken farmer grades eggs by color and size.*

grade point average *n.* the average of a student's marks in which 4.0 is considered perfect: *He has a 3.7 grade point average for his four years of college study.*

USAGE NOTE: Abbreviated as GPA. The numbers correspond to these letter grades: 4.0 = A, 3.0 = B, 2.0 = C, 1.0 = D, 0 = F

grade school *n.* in the USA, elementary school; first through fifth or sixth grades: *Her eight-year-old daughter goes to grade school in the neighborhood. See:* secondary school.

USAGE NOTE: *Grade school* or *elementary school* is followed by two or three years of *middle school* or *junior high school;* sixth or seventh through eighth or ninth grades. *High school* begins in ninth or tenth grade and goes through twelfth grade. Tenth, eleventh, and twelfth grades are also called, respectively, *sophomore, junior,* and *senior year: Their son is a senior in high school, but their daughter is only in eighth grade.*

gra·di·ent /ˈgreɪdiənt/ *n.* **1** the degree of change on a slope, as in a road: *The railroad rises in a small gradient.* **2** a rate of change, as in temperature: *The pressure gradient in the water heater is rising.*

grad school *n.short for* graduate school: *Juan is in grad school at Cal State, Fullerton.*

grad·u·al /ˈgrædʒuəl/ *adj.* happening slowly or by small steps: *A gradual increase in prices has slowed inflation.* -*adv.* **gradually;** -*n.* **gradualness.**

grad·u·ate /ˈgrædʒuˌeɪt/ *v.* **-ated, -ating, -ates 1** to receive a degree from an academic institution: *He graduates from high school in June.* **2** to increase or progress gradually: *The housing development graduates up a hillside.*
—*n.* /ˈgrædʒuɪt/ a person who has received a degree: *She is a college graduate.||She is a graduate of UCLA.*

graduate school *n.* an academic institution where students study for a higher degree (M.A., M.S., etc.) after they have received a first college degree: *Sylvia is in graduate school at Georgia State University.*

grad·u·a·tion /ˌgrædʒuˈeɪʃən/ *n.* **1** the awarding of an academic degree; the ceremony at which diplomas are presented to graduating students of colleges or high schools: *My family came to my college graduation in the summer.* **2** a degree of increase or decrease in s.t.

graf·fi·ti /grə'fiti/ *n.pl. used with a sing. or pl.v.* writings and drawings on walls, often rude, funny, or political

graft /græft/ *v.* **1** to join part of one living thing to another: *A farmer grafts branches on fruit trees to produce better crops.||The doctor grafted new skin onto the burned leg.* **2** to gain money or influence by illegal methods often for political purposes
—*n.* **1** an implantation: *Doctors do bone grafts.* **2** money or influence gained illegally: *Graft in the mayor's office is a serious problem.*

grain /greɪn/ *n.* **1** a single seed of a plant (wheat, corn, oats, etc.) **2** [U] the grasses from plants which produce such seeds, esp. wheat and corn: *Europe imports a lot of grain from Russia every year.* **3** a very small, hard piece of s.t.: *Grains of sand form a beach.* **4** a small amount of s.t.: *There is not a grain of truth in what he says.* **5** the natural flow of a surface: *You can feel the grain of the wood (leather, grass, etc.) by its smoothness.* **6 to go against the grain:** to be unnatural, s.t. that one is not comfortable doing: *It goes against the grain for her to accept help from her parents.* **7** *fig.* **to take s.t. with a grain of salt:** not to believe all that is said, to doubt: *You have to take what he says with a grain of salt because he doesn't always tell the truth.*

grain·y /'greɪni/ *adj.* **-ier, -iest** rough, having a grain: *The wood in those shelves is unfinished and very grainy.* -*n.* **graininess.**

gram /græm/ *n.* a measure of weight equal to one 1,000th of a kilogram or, about .04 oz.

gram·mar /'græmər/ *n.* a system of rules that apply to a language: *We study grammar in order to write good sentences.*

gram·mar·i·an /grə'meriən/ *n.* a person who studies and knows a lot about grammar

grammar school *n.old usage* elementary school

gram·mat·i·cal /grə'mætɪkəl/ *adj.* **1** related to the rules of grammar: *My grammatical knowledge of Spanish is very poor.* **2** correct according to the rules of grammar: *This sentence is grammatical.* -*adv.* **grammatically.**

Gram·my /'græmi/ *n.* **-mys** or **-mies** a small statue awarded each year for excellence in many areas of the recording industry, mainly for music: *Aretha Franklin has won many Grammys.*

gra·na·ry /'greɪnəri, 'græ-/ *n.* **-ries** a storage area for grain: *After the harvest, the granaries are full.*

grand /grænd/ *adj.* **1** large and impressive in size: *We had our party in the grand ballroom.* **2** splendid in appearance, wonderful: *There is a grand view of Manhattan from the Empire State Building.* **3** *frml.*pleasant,

enjoyable: *We had a grand time on our vacation.* -*adv.* **grandly.**
—*n. infrml.* **1** a grand piano: *We have a baby grand in our living room.* **2** *slang* $1,000: *That computer cost me two grand.*

grand·dad /'græn,dæd/ *n.infrml.* grandfather

grand·dad·dy /'græn,dædi/ *n.infrml.* **-dies 1** grandfather **2** *fig.* the oldest and most impressive of s.t.: *That huge alligator is the granddaddy of them all.*

grand·daugh·ter /'græn,dɔtər/ *n.* a daughter of one's child

gran·deur /'grændʒər, -,dʒʊr/ *n.* splendor, beauty on a large scale: *The grandeur of the mountain scenery is wonderful.*

grand·fa·ther /'græn,faðər, 'grænd-/ *n.* the father of one's father or mother

grandfather clock *n.* a clock in a tall wooden frame that stands on the floor: *The grandfather clock standing in the corner chimes every hour.*

gran·di·ose /'grændi,ous, ,grændi'ous/ *adj.* **1** magnificent, splendid: *Many palaces in France were built on a grandiose scale.* **2** s.t. that is bigger or more impressive than is necessary, often used negatively, (*syn.*) pretentious: *He has grandiose plans for his future.*

grandfather clock

grand jury *n.* (in law) a group of 12–23 citizens who review evidence against s.o. accused of a crime and decide if a trial is necessary: *The grand jury dismissed the charges against the company because there was not enough evidence.*

grand·ma /'græn,ma, 'græ,ma/ *n.infrml.* grandmother

grand·moth·er /'græn,mʌðər, 'grænd-, 'græm-/ *n.* the mother of one's father or mother: *My grandmother lives in Houston.*

grand·pa /'græn,pa, 'græm-, 'grænd-/ *n.infrml.* grandfather

grand·par·ent /'græn,perənt, -,pær-, 'grænd-/ *n.* a parent of one's father or mother

grand piano *n.* a large, concert-type piano: *When she lifts the top of her grand piano, her playing can be heard at a great distance.*

grand prix /,grã'pri, ,græn-/ *n.* **1** a racing event for sports cars: *Mario won the Grand Prix in Monte Carlo this year.* **2** the top prize: *The pianist won the grand prix in the competition in Moscow.*

grand slam *n.* **1** in baseball, a home run hit with players on all three bases **2** in tennis and golf, the winning of all the major championships in the same year: *The Germans won the grand slam in tennis this year.*

G

grand·son /'græn,sʌn, 'grænd/ *n.* the son of one's daughter or son

grand·stand /'græn,stænd, 'grænd-/ *n.* rows of seats outdoors sometimes covered with a roof, for watching sporting events: *We sat in the grandstand to watch the baseball game.*

gran·ite /'grænɪt/ *n.* a hard, gray rock: *That building is made of granite and will last for centuries.*

gran·ny /'græni/ *n.infrml.* **-nies** grandmother

gra·no·la /grə'noulə/ *n.* a breakfast food or snack made of whole oats, nuts, dried fruits, and honey

grant /grænt/ *v.frml.* **1** to give or allow what is asked for: *The governor granted my request for an interview for my newspaper.* **2** to accept as true: *I grant what you say is correct, but you still owe me the money.*
—*n.* **1** money given for a specific purpose: *The Ford Foundation gave the writer a grant for research.* **2** a formal transfer of ownership: *The king gave the lord a land grant in the new colony.*

gran·u·lar /'grænyələr/ *adj.* shaped in granules: *Sand has a granular texture.*

gran·u·late /'grænyə,leɪt/ *v.* **-lated, -lating, -lates** to form into granules: *Workers granulate sugar so that it will pour easily.* *-n.* **granulation** /,grænyə'leɪʃən/.

gran·ule /'grænyul/ *n.* a tiny, grain-like piece, (*syn.*) particle: *The machine crushes salt into granules.*

grape /greɪp/ *n.* a small round fruit, usu. green or dark purple, that grows in bunches and can be used to make wine: *Grapes are grown in great quantities in California and New York.*

grape·fruit /'greɪp,frut/ *n.* **-fruits** or **-fruit** a large round citrus fruit, usu. yellow with a thick skin, that has a tart taste: *I have a half grapefruit for breakfast.*

grape·vine /'greɪp,vaɪn/ *n.* **1** the climbing plant on which grapes grow **2** *fig.* **to hear s.t through/on the grapevine:** to hear news unofficially: *I heard through the grapevine that you are planning to get married.*

graph /græf/ *n.v.* a drawing that shows changes in quantities: *I made a line <n.> graph that shows sales increases from year to year.*

graph·ic /'græfɪk/ *adj.* **1** related to graphs **2** concerned with drawing *See:* graphics. **3** described in a very clear and detailed way: *The victim explained the attack in graphic detail.* *-adv.* **graphically.**

graph·ics /'græfɪks/ *n.pl.* **1** illustrative, decorative parts of s.t. (photographs, drawings, etc.): *The graphics in that art book (computer program, etc.) are beautiful.* **2** engineering and architectural drawings: *Engineers take a course in graphics in college.*

graph·ite /'græfaɪt/ *n.* a black substance that is a form of carbon: *Graphite is used to make pencil lead.*

gra·phol·o·gy /græ'fɑlədʒi/ *n.* the study of handwriting as a guide to personality: *Some companies use graphology to help them choose new employees.* *-n.* **graphologist.**

graph paper *n.* paper with horizontal and vertical lines on which graphs can be drawn: *We use graph paper to show our monthly sales figures.*

grap·ple /'græpəl/ *v.* **-pled, -pling, -ples 1** to take hold of and fight or struggle with s.o. or s.t.: *The two wrestlers grappled with each other.* **2** to try hard to solve a problem, (*syn.*) to struggle: *The technicians grappled with the broken computers all day.*

grasp /græsp/ *v.* **1** to hold firmly, take hold of: *I grasped the door handle with both hands and pulled hard.* **2** to succeed in understanding s.t. often complex: *After reading the text again, I finally grasped the main points of the story.* **3** *phrasal v.* **to grasp at:** to try to take hold of, to reach for s.t.: *As she fell, she grasped at the window to try to stop her fall.* **4** *fig.* **to grasp at straws:** to hope for miracles: *He is grasping at straws if he thinks his money problems will be solved by winning the lottery.*
—*n.* **1** a firm hold on s.t.: *I got a firm grasp on the stuck faucet and forced it open.* **2** understanding, comprehension: *She has a good grasp of the facts in the situation.‖This problem is beyond her grasp.*

grasp·ing /'græspɪŋ/ *adj.* wanting more, usu. money, (*syn.*) greedy, avaricious: *He is a grasping person, always after money.*

grass /græs/ *n.* **grasses 1** [U] any of a variety of green plant that covers the ground: *I like to play tennis on grass.* **2** [C] a tall green plant with flat leaves **3** *slang* marijuana: *He stopped smoking grass because it made him feel sick.*

grass·hop·per /'græs,hɑpər/ *n.* a plant-eating insect that can jump high and makes a loud noise: *A swarm of grasshoppers got into our flower garden and ruined it.*

grass·land /'græs,lænd/ *n.* flat land covered with wild grass: *The cows feed themselves on the grassland in the summer months.*

grass roots *adj.fig.* located with ordinary people, not with the leaders or those in power: *Some politicians have grass roots support.*

grass·y /'græsi/ *adj.* **-ier, -iest** covered with grass: *The grassy areas around the building make it an attractive place to work.*

grate /greɪt/ *v.* **grated, grating, grates 1** to make a sharp unpleasant sound by rubbing against s.t.: *When one piece of metal grates against another, it produces a terrible noise.* **2** to make into small pieces by rubbing against a rough surface: *The cook grated a piece of cheese.* **3** to make s.o. annoyed, (*syns.*) to irritate, rankle: *That rude fellow grates on my nerves. -n.* **grater.**

—*n.* **1** bars that hold the wood and coal in a fireplace **2** bars put over a window to keep out thieves

grate·ful /'greɪtfəl/ *adj.* thankful, (*syn.*) appreciative: *I am grateful for the help that you have given to me. -adv.* **gratefully.**

grat·i·fi·ca·tion /ˌgrætəfə'keɪʃən/ *n.* **1** a sense of pleasure and satisfaction: *Teachers find gratification in the success of their students.*

grat·i·fy /'grætəˌfaɪ/ *v.frml.* **-fied, -fying, -fies** **1** to give pleasure and satisfaction: *His children's success gratified him.* **2** to satisfy a desire: *She gratified her hunger by eating chocolate cake.*

grat·ing /'greɪtɪŋ/ *adj.* annoying, usu. related to a loud, unpleasant noise: *That singer has a grating voice.*

—*n.* a covering of metal bars over a window, hole, etc.: *The grating over the hole in the road stops large objects from falling in.*

grat·is /'grætɪs, 'grɑ-, 'greɪ-/ *adv.adj.* without charge, free: *He did the work <adv.> gratis.*‖*When he told me that the work was <adj.> gratis, I couldn't believe it.*

grat·i·tude /'grætəˌtud/ *n.* thankfulness, (*syn.*) appreciation: *She showed her gratitude by saying, "Thank you!"*

gra·tu·i·tous /grə'tuətəs/ *adj.* unnecessary, unasked for: *He made gratuitous comments about my clothes that I didn't like at all.*

gra·tu·i·ty /grə'tuəti/ *n.* **-ties** a gift of money for service, (*syn.*) a tip: *The standard gratuity at good restaurants is 15 percent of the bill.*

grave /greɪv/ *adj.* **graver, gravest** serious, worrying: *The patient is very ill and in grave condition.*

—*n.* **1** a place in the ground for placing a dead person: *He is buried in a grave next to his wife's.* **2** *fig.* **to dig one's own grave:** to harm one's own interests: *He is digging his own grave by complaining about his boss so openly.* **3 to drive s.o. to an early grave:** to constantly make s.o. do s.t. that is often bad for the health, (*syns.*) to hound, harass: *His friends are always pushing him to smoke cigarettes with them; they'll drive him to an early grave.* **4** *fig.* **to have one foot in the grave:** to be close to death: *He's 95 and has cancer; he has one foot in the grave.* **5** *fig.* **to turn over in one's grave:** said of a dead person who would not be happy with the actions of the living: *Their mother would be turning over in her grave if she could see how badly her children behave. -adv.* **gravely.**

grave·dig·ger /'greɪvˌdɪgər/ *n.* a person who digs holes in the ground for dead people's graves

grav·el /'grævəl/ *n.* rock crushed into very small pieces: *The gardener put gravel along the walkway.*

grave robber *n.* a person who steals bodies or valuables from graves: *Grave robbers stole gold from many Egyptian tombs.*

grave·stone /'greɪvˌstoʊn/ *n.* a stone over a grave that usu. shows the name and dates of birth and death of the dead person: *My grandmother's gravestone reads: Harriet M. Gundersen 1907-1991.*

grave·yard /'greɪvˌyɑrd/ *n.* an area of land, sometimes near a church, where dead people are buried: *We visited the graveyard where my grandmother is buried on Sunday.*

grav·i·tate /'grævəˌteɪt/ *v.* **-tated, -tating, -tates** **1** to react to the force of gravity: *Objects gravitate naturally downward toward the ground.* **2** to feel attracted to s.t. or s.o.: *The major industries gravitated toward the outer parts of the city where rents were cheap. -n.* **gravitation** /ˌgrævə'teɪʃən/.

grav·i·ty /'grævəti/ *n.* **1** a natural force pulling objects to the ground: *Objects fall to earth because of the force of gravity.* **2** seriousness, severity: *When the shooting started, the gravity of the situation became clear.*

gra·vy /'greɪvi/ *n.* **1** a warm liquid made of the juices and fats from cooked meat, combined with a thickener, such as flour: *I like brown gravy on my mashed potatoes.* **2** *infrml.fig.* extra money, a bonus: *After we pay off our expenses, the rest is gravy for us.* **3** *fig.* **gravy train:** a job requiring little effort and offering good compensation: *He has a gravy train as he works part-time for his father at a full-time salary.*

gray or **grey** /greɪ/ *n.* a dark color like black mixed with a little white: *The lady is dressed in gray.*

—*adj.* **1** colored gray: *She is wearing a gray dress.* **2** sad, depressing: *It is a gray day: rainy and cold.*

—*v.* (of hair) to become gray: *My father's hair is graying.*

gray matter *n.infrml.* intelligence, brain power: *You should use your gray matter to help you solve that problem.*

gray·scale /'greɪˌskeɪl/ *n.* the use of different shades of gray rather than different colors, e.g. in television, computer graphics, etc.

graze /greɪz/ *v.* **grazed, grazing, grazes** **1** to feed on grass: *The sheep graze in the field.* **2** to touch lightly against s.t. and injure the skin: *The child fell and grazed her hand.* **3** to touch s.t. lightly as it passes: *I grazed the side of the car when I tried to park.*

—*n.* a light wound, scrape on the surface of the skin

grease /gris/ n. **1** animal fat that has been softened by cooking: *There was too much grease on the plate; I couldn't eat my dinner.* **2** any thick oily substance, esp. used to make moving parts of machines work more smoothly: *The mechanic put grease on the bike's wheels.*
—v. /gris, griz/ **greased, greasing, greases 1** to put grease on: *He greased the wheels.* **2** *infrml.fig.* **to grease s.o.'s palm:** to give money to s.o. in order to persuade them to do s.t. for you: *I greased the headwaiter's palm and he gave us a good table.*

grease monkey n. *pej.fig.* a mechanic: *Oh, he's just a grease monkey at the local garage.*

grease paint n. makeup used by actors: *Clowns cover their faces with grease paint.*

greas·y /'grisi, -zi/ adj. **-ier, -iest** having grease: *That sausage is very greasy.*

great /greɪt/ adj. **1** large, huge: *A great big bear blocked our path.* **2** renowned, (syn.) monumental: *Alexander the Great never saw the Great Wall of China.* **3** excellent, superior: *That company has a great reputation.* **4** *infrml.* pleasant, wonderful: *We had a great time on our vacation.* -n. **greatness.**

great aunt n. The sister of one's grandparent

great·en /'greɪtn/ v. to increase: *Ill health greatened his financial problems.*

greatly /'greɪtli/ adv. very much: *Crime has increased greatly in the city over the last year.*

great uncle n. a brother of one's grandparent

greed /grid/ n. a strong desire for money, food, etc.: *Greed made the child take the last piece of cake.*

greed·y /'gridi/ adj. **-ier, -iest** wanting more of money, food, etc., than one has or is fair, (syn.) avaricious: *He overcharges customers because he is greedy.*

green /grin/ adj. **1** having the color green, a combination of blue and yellow: *Most leaves are green in the summer.* **2** with little experience or training: *The general sent the green soldiers for more training.* **3** looking pale in the face, usu. from sickness: *She looked green after the rough boat trip.* **4** *fig.* **green with envy:** very envious, jealous: *When he saw my new car, he was green with envy.* **5 to have a green thumb:** to be very good at growing flowers or plants

green·back /'grin,bæk/ n.infrml. old usage the US dollar: *There are $80 billion in greenbacks floating around the world as an unofficial currency.*

Green Beret n. a member of a special US Army commando unit: *Green Berets parachuted behind enemy lines.*

green card n. a small plastic card issued by the US government allowing a non–US citizen to live and work in the USA legally: *I took an exam in order to get my green card.*

USAGE NOTE: A green card may be obtained by the relative or employer of a non-US citizen. Alien residents who have green cards may apply for *citizenship* after living in the USA for 5 years, or after 3 years if they are married to a US citizen. A work permit may be an authorization card or a stamp in a passport from immigration. An F-1 visa is given to students.

green·er·y /'grinəri/ n. plants and trees in general: *We like the greenery in the mountains.*

green-eyed adj. having green eyes: *She has a green-eyed cat.*

green·gro·cer /'grin,grousər/ n. a shop where fruits and vegetables are sold: *I'm going to the greengrocer to buy some carrots.*

green·horn /'grin,hɔrn/ n.infrml. **1** a beginner, esp. in an outdoor activity, such as hiking, riding, etc.: *He doesn't know how to ride a horse; he's a greenhorn.* **2** a young, inexperienced person, usu. a man who can be easily tricked

green·house /'grin,haus/ n. **-houses** /-'hauziz/ a building with glass walls and a glass roof, used to grow and protect plants: *Those flowers were grown in a greenhouse during the winter.*

greenhouse effect n. the gradual increase in the warmth of the air around the earth because the heat cannot leave the atmosphere: *Many people are afraid that the greenhouse effect will cause serious weather problems on earth.*

USAGE NOTE: The *greenhouse effect* can already be seen in the extreme temperatures of recent years. Even areas with usu. moderate climates report much hotter summers and colder winters.

greet /grit/ v. **1** to say hello to s.o.: *When I met the president, she greeted me in a very friendly way.* **2** to meet, welcome: *The host of the party greets his guests at the door.* -n. **greeter.**

greet·ing /'gritɪŋ/ n. **1** the first words or actions used on meeting s.o., such as "Hello" or "Hi": *We passed on the street and gave each other a friendly greeting.* **2** *pl.* **greetings** good wishes, usu. written: *"Greetings on your birthday and Congratulations!"*

greeting card n. a card, usu. folded and printed with a message inside, such as "Get well" or "Happy Birthday": *I sent my friend a greeting card for her birthday.*

gre·gar·i·ous /grɪ'gɛriəs/ adj. liking to be with other people, friendly, (syn.) sociable: *He is a very gregarious fellow who enjoys company.*

grem·lin /'grɛmlɪn/ n. an imaginary little creature who causes problems: *That computer has got gremlins; there is always s.t. wrong with it!*

gre·nade /grə'neɪd/ n. a hand-sized, small bomb: *A soldier threw a grenade into a building.*

grew /gru/ past tense of grow

grey /greɪ/ *n.adj. See:* gray.

grey·hound /'greɪ,haʊnd/ *n.* a thin racing dog with long legs: *People love to watch greyhounds race at the track.*

grid /grɪd/ *n.* **1** a group of vertical and horizontal lines: *In many cities, the streets form a grid.* **2** a group of powerful electrical wires over a region: *The electrical grid was overloaded in hot August weather.*

grid·dle /'grɪdl/ *n.v.* **-dled, -dling, -dles** a flat iron surface used for cooking: *I put some bacon and eggs on the <n.> griddle.*

grid·dle·cake /'grɪdl,keɪk/ *n.* a hotcake, pancake: *We eat griddlecakes for breakfast once a week.*

grid·i·ron /'grɪd,aɪərn/ *n.* **1** a frame of metal bars used to cook (grill) foods over a fire **2** *fig.* an American football field: *In high school, my friend became a hero on the gridiron.*

grid·lock /'grɪd,lɑk/ *n.* the traffic that blocks an intersection: *Cars are blocking the main intersections because of the accident, and the central city is in gridlock.*

grief /grif/ *n.* **1** great sadness, sorrow, (*syn.*) anguish: *Her brother's sudden death caused her grief.* **2 to give s.o. grief:** to make trouble for s.o.: *My boss gives me a lot of grief about my poor computer skills.*

griev·ance /'grivəns/ *n.* a complaint, esp. of being treated unfairly: *Labor has a grievance over low wages.*

grieve /griv/ *v.* **grieved, grieving, grieves** to feel great sadness over s.t., (*syn.*) to mourn: *She grieved for weeks over the death of her mother.*

grie·vous /'grivəs/ *adj.* causing pain, suffering, or sorrow; very serious: *The death of her brother was a grievous loss. See:* barbeque, BBQ.

grill /grɪl/ *n.* a frame of metal bars on which food is cooked, usu. outside: *I put some hamburgers on the grill.*
—*v.* **1** to cook on a grill: *I grilled some burgers for lunch.* **2** to ask s.o. many questions for a long period of time: *Police grilled the suspect for hours until he confessed that he had robbed the bank. See:* barbecue, USAGE NOTE.

grim /grɪm/ *adj.* **grimmer, grimmest 1** serious, (*syn.*) solemn: *The prisoner has a grim look on his face.* **2** expecting the worst, (*syn.*) foreboding: *He suffered a severe injury and his prospects for living are grim. -adv.* **grimly; -***n.* **grimness.**

grim·ace /'grɪməs, grɪ'meɪs/ *v.* **-aced, -acing, -aces** to twist the face, (*syn.*) to wince: *He grimaced at hearing the bad news.*
—*n.* a twisting of the face often in pain, (*syn.*) a wince: *He has a grimace on his face.*

grime /graɪm/ *n.* [U] dirt or grease on the surface of s.t.: *The city's buildings are covered with grime. -adj.* **grimy.**

grin /grɪn/ *n.* a big smile: *He greeted his friend with a big grin. See:* smile, USAGE NOTE.
—*v.* **grinned, grinning, grins 1** to give a big smile: *He grinned at his girlfriend.* **2 to grin and bear it:** to suffer pain or embarrassment without complaining

grind /graɪnd/ *v.* **ground** /graʊnd/, **grinding, grinds 1** to make into small pieces or powder by rubbing: *The worker is grinding metal.*||*I ground the coffee beans.* **2** to rub two hard surfaces together, usu. to make smooth: *He grinds his teeth together when he sleeps.* **3** *fig.*to work very hard, usu. for a long time without pleasure: *She grinds at her studies, day and night.*
—*n.* **1** the process of grinding **2** *infrml.fig.* a tiring job: *Her job is a daily grind; she works on the computer eight hours a day.*

grind·er /'graɪndər/ *n.* **1** any device used to grind substances: *We put leftover pork in a meat grinder to make sausages.* **2** a sandwich on a long crusty roll, often served hot: *I had a steak and cheese grinder for lunch.*

grind·stone /'graɪn,stoʊn, 'graɪnd-/ *n.* **1** a piece of stone or other material used to smooth or sharpen metal **2** *fig.* **to keep one's nose to the grindstone:** to work very hard and steadily

grin·go /'grɪŋgoʊ/ *n.slang* **-gos** a foreigner in Latin America, esp. one who is white and speaks English (usu. used in a negative way)

grip /grɪp/ *n.* **1** a strong hold, (*syn.*) a grasp: *The thief had a firm grip on the money.* **2** command, control: *He has a good grip on his emotions.* **3** *See:* grippe.
—*v.* **gripped, gripping, grips** to hold firmly, (*syn.*) to grasp: *He gripped the club with both hands.*

gripe /graɪp/ *n.infrml.* a complaint, (*syn.*) a grievance: *The worker has a gripe with the boss.*
—*v.* **griped, griping, gripes** to complain: *He gripes all the time about the bad weather.*

grippe or **grip** /grɪp/ *n.* influenza: *I have the grippe and will stay home today.*

gris·ly /'grɪzli/ *adj.* **-lier, -liest** frightening or disgusting, usu. because of the connection with death, (*syn.*) gruesome: *She told a grisly story about a murder.*

gris·tle /'grɪsəl/ *n.* tough part of meat that is difficult to eat: *I don't like meat with a lot of gristle. -adj.* **gristly** /'grɪsli/.

grit /grɪt/ *n.* **1** very small pieces of stone or sand: *The desert sand left a layer of grit on our car.* **2** *infrml.* courage, (*syn.*) spunk: *He broke his finger, but continued to play; he has grit.*

G

—*v.* **gritted, gritting, grits, to grit one's teeth:** to press one's teeth together hard, usu. during difficult moments: *He gritted his teeth and lifted the heavy box.* -*adj.* **gritty.**

grits /grɪts/ *n.pl.* American corn that is ground and boiled into a soft, white food: *In the South, people often eat grits for breakfast.*

USAGE NOTE: A popular southern dish, *grits* are usu. served plain with butter, often with fried eggs and potatoes. They may also be cooked very thick, then cooled, cut into slices, and fried.

griz·zled /'grɪzəld/ *adj.* with gray parts, usu. of hair: *As he became older, his hair became grizzled.*

griz·zly /'grɪzli/ *adj.* **-zlier, -zliest** quite gray, grizzled: *He has a grizzly beard.*
—*n.* **-zlies** *See:* grizzly bear.

grizzly bear or **grizzly** *n.* **-zlies** a large gray and brown bear of western North America: *The grizzly bear frightens people because of its power and aggressive nature.*

grizzly bear

groan /groʊn/ *v.n.* (to make) a deep sound from the throat to show pain, worry, disapproval, etc.: *He <v.> groaned when the other team scored another goal.*

gro·cer /'groʊsər/ *n.* **1** a person who sells food and other household things **2** a grocery store: *I'm going to the grocer to buy some groceries.*

gro·cer·ies /'groʊsəriz, 'groʊsriz/ *n.pl.* food and other household things: *I buy groceries at the supermarket.*

gro·cer·y /'groʊsəri, 'groʊsri/ *n.* **-ies** a food store: *The local grocery (or) grocery store is open seven days a week.*

grog·gy /'grɑgi/ *adj.* **-gier, -giest** unsteady and with an unclear mind, as from illness, shock, etc.: *The hit on the head made her groggy.* -*adv.* **groggily.**

groin /grɔɪn/ *n.* the area of the body around the sex organs: *The athlete pulled a muscle in his groin.*

groom /grum/ *n.* **1** a bridegroom: *The groom wore a tuxedo to the wedding. See:* bride, best man. **2** a man who takes care of horses
—*v.* **1** to dress well, keep the hair neat: *She is a well-groomed woman.* **2** to help s.o. improve, esp. for a better job: *The boss groomed his son to take over the family business.* **3** to brush and care for horses: *The boy grooms the horses every morning.*

groove /gruv/ *n.* a long narrow hole for s.t. to move smoothly in: *The doors on that cabinet slide open on grooves.*

—*v.* **grooved, grooving, grooves 1** to make grooves **2** *slang* to delight in, find appealing: *That band plays well together; they really groove with each other.*

groov·y /'gruvi/ *adj.slang* **-ier, -iest** very good, excellent: *Batman is a groovy movie.*

USAGE NOTE: Slang expressions like *groovy* and *far-out* used to be associated with the drug culture of the '60s and '70s. Today they are common adjectives.

grope /groʊp/ *v.* **groped, groping, gropes** to feel about, search for s.t. with the hands as if in darkness or with difficulty: *The room was completely dark and I groped for the light switch.*

gross (1) /groʊs/ *adj.* **1** disgusting, (*syn.*) repugnant: *He behaved in a gross manner, so I left him.* **2** shocking, (*syn.*) flagrant, blatant: *What she said is a gross lie!*
—*v.slang* **grosses to gross out:** to disgust, (*syn.*) to repel: *He vomited in the living room and grossed everyone out.* -*adv.* **grossly;** -*n.* **grossness.**

gross (2) *n.* **1** *pl.* **gross** 144 pieces of s.t., 12 dozen: *The department store bought a gross of pencils.* **2** *pl.* **grosses** the total amount of money taken in by a business before expenses are taken out
—*v.* to earn money, as measured before expenses are taken out: *With her bonus and salary, she grosses $50,000 a year.*

gross domestic product *n.* a measure of the total value of goods and services produced by a nation

gross national product (GNP) *n.* total value in goods and services in a country's economy, usu. for one year: *The GNP for the United States last year was 4 trillion dollars.*

gro·tesque /groʊ'tɛsk/ *adj.* **1** very ugly, (*syns.*) hideous, repugnant: *The grotesque monster frightened the children.* **2** not natural, (*syns.*) deformed, bizarre: *The burned and leafless trees presented a grotesque landscape.*

grot·to /'grɑtoʊ/ *n.* **-toes** or **-tos 1** a small cave **2** a holy place cut out of rock

grouch /graʊtʃ/ *n.* **grouches** a person who complains often: *That man is an old grouch; he never likes the food I cook.*
—*v.infrml.* **grouched, grouching, grouches** to complain often about s.t., (*syn.*) to grumble: *He grouches at everyone.* -*adj.* **grouchy.**

ground (1) /graʊnd/ *n.* **1** the earth, soil: *The ground is wet from the rain.* **2** a safety wire on an electrical device **3** *pl.* **grounds: a.** outdoor property: *The grounds outside our office building are grassy.* **b.** a basis, a reason: *Not going to work is grounds for dismissal.* **4 to gain ground:** to progress, usu. despite difficulty: *The runner gained ground on his competitor* *and passed him.* **5 to give** or **lose ground:** to move backward, be forced back: *The enemy gave ground under a heavy attack.* **6 to stand** or **hold one's ground:** not to move or surrender: *Despite heavy criticism, she stood her ground and succeeded.*

—*v.* **1** to wire electrically into the earth for safety: *The lightning rod is grounded into the soil.* **2** to deny travel rights: *The manager grounded all salespeople to save money.*

ground (2) *past tense & past part. of* grind
—*adj.* **to be ground down:** to be very tired: *She works seven days a week and is ground down.*

ground crew *n.* workers who support an airline by doing work on the ground at airports, such as reservation agents, baggage handlers, and maintenance workers: *She is a member of the Northwest Airlines ground crew in Seattle.*

ground floor *n.* **1** in the USA, the first floor, one at ground level: *The reception is on the ground floor.* **2** *fig.* **to get in on the ground floor:** to be present at the beginning of an excellent opportunity: *He got in on the ground floor with that small company and grew with it.*

Ground·hog Day /ˈgraʊndˌhɔg, -ˌhɑg/ *n.* in the USA, February 2, when, according to tradition, if a groundhog comes out of its hole and sees its shadow, there will be six more weeks of bad weather, or, if it does not see its shadow, there will be an early spring (good weather)

ground·ing /ˈgraʊndɪŋ/ *n.* education and usu. experience in some area: *She has a good grounding in computers.*

ground·less /ˈgraʊndlɪs/ *adj.* without good reason or basis in fact, *(syn.)* baseless: *He made groundless accusations.*

ground rules *n.pl.* (originally from baseball) a set of rules, such as for a sport or formal discussion, particularly for an specific occasion or place: *As ground rules, the lawyers agreed that each could speak for five minutes without interruption.*

ground·swell /ˈgraʊndˌswɛl/ *n.* **1** a rising or rolling of the ocean as caused by a storm or an earthquake **2** *fig.* a sudden increase of s.t.: *After the politician announced his candidacy, there was a groundswell of support from across the nation.*

group /grup/ *n.* **1** a number of people or things placed together: *A group of people protested against the new law.* **2** two or more singers, musicians, etc.: *A singing group performed at the local theater.* **3** (in mathematics) a type of set: *He is an expert in group theory.*

—*v.* **1** to put together in a group, assemble: *The grocer groups apples by variety: Golden Delicious, McIntosh, etc.* **2** to come together,

gather: *People grouped on the street to watch the parade.*

group·ie /ˈgrupi/ *n.infrml.* a person, esp. a girl, who follows rock stars, movie stars, etc. in a group of admirers: *Groupies shouted with delight as the rock group arrived.*

group·ing /ˈgrupɪŋ/ *n.* **1** a group of s.t.: *A grouping of roses looks pretty by the door.* **2** a category, classification: *The authorities placed immigrants into different groupings by country.*

grouse /graʊs/ *n.* **grouse** **1** a medium-sized bird with dark, spotty coloring: *Grouse run into the woods when frightened.* **2** *infrml.* a complaint
—*v.* **groused, grousing, grouses** to complain, *(syn.)* to gripe: *He grouses all the time about his low salary.*

grove /groʊv/ *n.* a small grouping of trees: *A pine grove grows near the farmhouse.*

grov·el /ˈgrɑvəl, ˈgrʌ-/ *v.* **1** to lie flat on the ground to show fear or obedience before s.o. or s.t.: *The servant groveled before his master.* **2** *fig.* to behave in a way that shows one has no self-respect, usu. in order to obtain s.t.: *He groveled in front of his boss so he could leave work early.*

grow /groʊ/ *v.* **1 grew** /gru/, **grown** /groʊn/, **growing, grows** to plant and harvest: *A farmer grows corn and wheat.* **2** to develop, mature: *The boy has grown into a man.* **3** to become: *She grew impatient (sad, angry, etc.) with the delays.* **4** *phrasal v. insep.* **to grow away from s.o.:** to feel less close to s.o.: *We were friends in school, but we grew away from each other.* **5 to grow by leaps and bounds:** to increase rapidly: *Our business is growing by leaps and bounds.* **6** *phrasal v. insep.* **to grow into s.t.: a.** to develop into, become: *He's grown into a delightful person.* **b.** to become big enough for s.t.: *She's grown into her new bicycle.* **7** *phrasal v. insep.* **to grow on s.o.:** to become more pleasing to s.o. over time: *Living in the country grows on you after a while.* **8** *phrasal v. insep.* **to grow out of s.t.: a.** to become too old for s.t.: *She sucked her thumb as a baby, but she grew out of it.* **b.** to become too large for s.t.: *He has to buy new shoes because he's grown out of the old ones.* **9** *phrasal v. insep.* **to grow to (understand, appreciate, etc.):** to change one' understanding over time: *He grew to understand why his immigrant parents missed the old country.* **10** *phrasal v.* **to grow up: a.** to mature: *Our daughter has grown up now.* **b.** to live in a place during one's youth: *She grew up in the San Francisco area.* **c.** to act responsibly (said in anger): *Oh, why don't you grow up and behave?!*

grow·er /ˈgroʊər/ *n.* a person or business that raises food plants: *He's a coffee grower from Brazil.*

growing pains *n.pl.* difficulties resulting from growth, esp. of a business: *We have growing pains because our warehouse is too small and can't keep up with the orders.*

growl /graʊl/ *n.* a low sound made in anger, (*syn.*) a snarl: *The dog let out a growl when the stranger came near.*
—*v.* to give a growl: *The boss growls when things aren't going well.* -*n.* **growler.**

grown-up /ˈgroʊnˌʌp/ *n.* an adult: *Many grown-ups have dinner after the children are asleep.*

growth /groʊθ/ *n.* **1** the process of growing, development, (*syn.*) maturation: *The growth of trees in this area is slowed by bad weather.* **2** s.t. in the process of growing: *There is a growth of pine trees near the highway.* **3** an abnormal lump on or in the body: *He has a growth on his neck.* **4** an expansion, increase: *There was a growth in US exports overseas last year.*

growth fund *n.* a mutual fund dedicated to growth of capital, instead of its preservation: *Growth funds carry greater risk.*

growth rate *n.* the amount of change in a financial area of a company

grub /grʌb/ *n.* **1** an insect that looks like a small worm: *I killed the grubs in the garbage can.* **2** *infrml.* food: *Let's get some grub for lunch.*

grub·by /ˈgrʌbi/ *adj.* **-bier, -biest** dirty, (*syn.*) grimy: *The children's hands are grubby from playing in the garden.*

grudge /grʌdʒ/ *n.* **1** a feeling of anger toward s.o. for s.t. a person did wrong to you, (*syn.*) resentment: *He has a grudge against me for stealing his girlfriend.:\\He holds a grudge against his former boss for firing him.* -*adj.* **grudging.**

gru·el /ˈgruəl/ *n.* oatmeal that is watery and not tasty: *The prisoner was given only gruel to eat.*

gru·el·ing /ˈgruəlɪŋ, ˈgrulɪŋ/ *adj.* very difficult and tiring, (*syn.*) harsh: *The trip through the desert was grueling.*

grue·some /ˈgrusəm/ *adj.* horrifying, usu. because it is connected with death, (*syn.*) grisly: *The murder scene was gruesome.*

gruff /grʌf/ *adj.* rude, (*syn.*) curt: *That truck driver has a gruff manner.* -*adv.* **gruffly; -***n.* **gruffness.**

grum·ble /ˈgrʌmbəl/ *v.* **-bled, -bling, -bles** *n.* to complain in a quiet, unhappy manner: *He <v.> grumbled about having to clean the bathroom.*

grump /grʌmp/ *n.* a person who complains often: *He's an old grump!*

grump·y /ˈgrʌmpi/ *adj.* **-ier, -iest** bad-tempered, (*syn.*) irritable: *He's grumpy in the morning.*

grunge /grʌndʒ/ *n.adj.* **1** a type of alternative, loud rock music originally from Seattle: *I listen to the Beatles, but my teenage children listen to <adj.> grunge music.* **2** a style of dressing in old, inexpensive clothing, inspired by grunge musicians: *Morton wears a lot of <n.> grunge; he likes flannel shirts and baggy pants.*

grun·gy /ˈgrʌndʒi/ *adj.infrml.* **-gier, -giest** in a dirty and bad condition: *His sweatshirt was grungy from working on his car.*

grunt /grʌnt/ *v.n.* (to make) a short deep sound from the throat, usu. to show great effort, disgust, or boredom: *He <v.> grunted as he lifted the heavy rock.*

G-string /ˈdʒiˌstrɪŋ/ *n.infrml.* a small covering worn over the sex organs

gua·ca·mo·le /ˌgwɑkəˈmoʊli/ *n.* a creamy green food made from avocados: *Guacamole tastes good with tortilla chips. See*: enchilada, **USAGE NOTE.**

gua·no /ˈgwɑnoʊ/ *n.* bird or bat excrement

guar·an·tee /ˌgærənˈti/ *n.* **1** a written promise of satisfaction with a product or service, or that s.t. is genuine: *Under the courier's guarantee, if I send the letter today, he'll have it tomorrow.* **2** a document stating conditions of a guarantee *See*: warranty.
—*v.* **-teed, -teeing, -tees** to give a guarantee: *The shipper guaranteed next-day delivery.*

guar·an·tor /ˌgærənˈtɔr, ˈgærəntər/ *n.* the person or business giving a guarantee: *Ford Motor Corp. is the guarantor of its cars' quality.*

guar·an·ty /ˈgærənti/ *n.* **-ties** *v.* **-tied, -tying, -ties** *See:* guarantee.

guard /gɑrd/ *n.* a protector of property: *The headquarters has guards at each entrance.*
—*v.* **1** to protect property: *They guard against entry by unauthorized persons.* **2** to be very careful: *Banks guard against making risky loans.* **3 to catch s.o. off guard:** to catch s.o. unprepared: *The exam caught me off guard; I hadn't studied at all.* **4 to stand guard: a.** to perform guard duty: *A policeman stood guard at the door.* **b.** to watch carefully for wrongdoing: *The public stands guard against corruption in government.*

guard·ed /ˈgɑrdɪd/ *adj.* **1** protected by a guard: *The President lives in a guarded building.* **2** *fig.* careful, (*syn.*) cautious: *The senator made some guarded comments about the scandal.* -*adv.* **guardedly.**

guard·i·an /ˈgɑrdiən/ *n.* **1** a person legally responsible for another, esp. a child: *After the girl's parents died, her uncle became her guardian.* **2** a guard: *Guardians watch over the museum's galleries.* -*n.* **guardianship.**

guardian angel *n.* **1** an imaginary spirit who protects one from harm **2 Guardian Angel:** a member of a group of volunteer citizens who watch out for crime and often hold criminals for the police to arrest

guard·rail /'gɑrd,reɪl/ *n.* a railing or barrier used to stop falls: *Guardrails on the ship's deck stop people from falling into the water.*

guards·man /'gɑrdzmən/ *n.* **-men** /-mən/ in the USA, a member of the National Guard: *Guardsmen were called in to stop the rioting.*

gu·ber·na·to·ri·al /,gubərnə'tɔriəl/ *adj.* related to governors: *The gubernatorial election is held every four years.*

guck /gʌk, gʊk/ *n.slang* any sticky, messy substance, (*syn.*) goop: *The engine is covered with guck; I have to clean it.*

guer·ril·la /gə'rɪlə/ *n.* a member of a non-regular military group that is trying to attack and defeat the regular military: *Guerrillas hide in the jungle and attack government installations.*

guess /gɛs/ *n.* **guesses 1** a try at saying what might happen or is true: *I made a guess at the cost of that computer.* **2 an educated guess:** an estimate or prediction based on experience or special knowledge: *The sales manager made an educated guess that she would sell 5,000 units next year.*
—*v.* **guessed, guessing, guesses 1** to make a guess, (*syns.*) to predict, speculate: *I guess that will rain today.* **2** to say politely what one will do: *"Oh, I guess I'll go home now."* **3 to keep s.o. guessing:** to not tell s.o. what is true or will happen: *She keeps him guessing by not saying whether she loves him.*

guess·ti·mate /'gɛstəmɪt/ *n.infrml.* an estimate or prediction made mostly by guessing: *He made a guesstimate that he would sell 100 cars this year because he had sold 90 last year.*
—*v.* /'gɛstə,meɪt/ **-mated, -mating, -mates** to make an educated guess

guess·work /'gɛs,wɜrk/ *n.* the process of guessing: *The team did a lot of guesswork before they found the answer.*

guest /gɛst/ *n.* **1** a visitor who comes to s.o.'s home for a short time, or to stay for a short time: *We had guests for dinner last night.* **2** s.o. who stays in a hotel, (*syn.*) patron: *Guests check out of the hotel each morning.* **3** a person who is invited to a restaurant, the movies, etc., and who is paid for by the host: *"I'll pay; you're my guest this evening."*

guff /gʌf/ *n.infrml.* rude talk, (*syn.*) insolence: *Don't give me any of your guff!*

guf·faw /gə'fɔ/ *v.n.* (to give) a loud laugh: *He <v.> guffawed when I told him a joke.*

GUI /'gui/ *n.abbrev.* for Graphical User Interface, a computer operating system that allows a users to use visual images and a mouse to perform tasks, rather than having to type words as commands

guid·ance /'gaɪdns/ *n.* **1** help, advice, (*syn.*) counsel: *The teacher gave the student guidance on how to pass the exam.* **2** an electronic mechanism used to direct space vehicles (weapons, computers, etc.): *The missile operates by the guidance of radar and computers.*

guide /gaɪd/ *n.* **1** a person who shows the way and often gives information, esp. to tourists: *A tour guide gave some history as we passed each important building.* **2** a reference book: *We looked at a map in our city guide to find the museum.* **3** an idea (rule, measure, etc.) used to decide how to do s.t.: *I use a ruler as a guide in drawing a straight line.*
—*v.* **guided, guiding, guides 1** to show the way, give information: *A professor guided us through the museum.* **2** to direct, define: *Religious teaching guides us to be kind to others. See:* guidelines.

guide·book /'gaɪd,bʊk/ *n.* a book with detailed information about a place or subject: *Tourists use guidebooks to find their way around cities.*

guided missile *n.* a rocket directed by such devices as radar, videocameras, and computers: *The pilot fired a guided missile at a target.*

guide·lines /'gaɪd,laɪnz/ *n.pl.* ideas or rules on what to do (or not to do): *The teacher gave us guidelines for writing our paper; it had to be typed, double-spaced, and 10–12 pages long.*

guide·post /'gaɪd,poʊst/ *n. See:* signpost.

guild /gɪld/ *n.* a group of skilled workers organized to control the way their work is practiced: *The guilds controlled business in Northern Europe in the Middle Ages (1400–1700).*

guile /gaɪl/ *n.* clever trickery, (*syns.*) cunning, deceit: *The swindler used guile to cheat people out of their money.*

guile·less /'gaɪllɪs/ *adj.* straightforward, without deceit: *He is guileless, almost childlike in his behavior.*

guil·lo·tine /'gɪlə,tin, 'giə-/ *n.v.* **-tined, -tining, -tines** (to use) a machine that cuts off a criminal's head with a large, sharp blade

guilt /gɪlt/ *n.* **1** the state of having broken the law: *A jury decides the guilt or innocence of an accused person.* **2** fault, blame for doing s.t wrong: *The guilt for the breakdown of the talks lies with the lawyers.* **3** a feeling of having done s.t. wrong or shameful, *(syn.)* remorse

guilt·less /ˈgɪltlɪs/ *adj.* not guilty, innocent

guilt·y /ˈgɪlti/ *adj.* **-ier, -iest 1** having broken a law, at fault, *(syn.)* culpable: *The jury found the man guilty of the murder.* **2** having or showing a feeling of shame, of having done s.t. wrong: *He feels guilty about hurting his friend.* -*adv.* **guiltily.**

guin·ea pig /ˌgɪni/ *n.* **1** a small animal resembling a big rat with short ears and no tail, often kept as a pet **2** *fig.* a person or animal used for scientific or medical tests: *People were used as guinea pigs without their knowledge to test effects of a new drug.*

guise /gaɪz/ *n.* **1** *frml.* appearance, look **2** *fig.* disguise, camouflage: *Under the guise of night, the soldiers marched forward.*

gui·tar /gɪˈtɑr/ *n.* a musical instrument with strings: *She plays the guitar beautifully.*

guitar

gulch /gʌltʃ/ *n.* **gulches** a narrow valley cut by a river: *Cowboys chased cattle down a dry gulch.*

gulf /gʌlf/ *n.* **1** a large area of a sea or ocean surrounded on three sides by land: *The Gulf of Mexico goes from Florida over to Texas and down to Mexico.* **2** a deep, wide hole in the ground, *(syn.)* a chasm **3** *fig.* a wide difference, esp. between opinions: *There was a wide gulf between my ideas for the new plan and my manager's ideas.*

gull /gʌl/ *n.* a type of common seabird usu. white in color with white, gray, or black wings: *Sea gulls stay near the ocean.*

gul·let /ˈgʌlɪt/ *n.* the tube between the throat and the stomach: *A gull swallowed a fish down its gullet.*

gul·li·ble /ˈgʌləbəl/ *adj.* easily tricked, *(syn.)* naive: *My sister is very gullible; she believes everything I tell her.* -*n.* **gullibility** /ˌgʌləˈbɪləti/.

gul·ly /ˈgʌli/ *n.* **-lies** a long, narrow hole in the earth: *Rainwater ran off the hill into the gullies.*

gulp /gʌlp/ *v.n.* to swallow whole mouthfuls, usu. quickly: *The thirsty man <v.> gulped (down) the water.‖The bird swallowed an insect in one <n.> gulp.*

gum /gʌm/ *n.* **1** a sticky substance from inside a tree **2** chewing gum: *He likes to chew gum and watch TV.* **3** the pink flesh surrounding the teeth: *Her gums are swollen.*

—*v.* **gummed, gumming, gums** to stick s.t. together with gum: *A worker gummed the address labels on envelopes.*

gum·bo /ˈgʌmbou/ *n.* **-bos** a thick soup (stew) made with okra and often meat, fish, or vegetables: *I like shrimp gumbo.*

gum·drop /ˈgʌmˌdrɑp/ *n.* a small, sugar-coated, fruit-flavored candy: *I like orange gumdrops.*

gum·my /ˈgʌmi/ *adj.* **-mier, -miest** soft, usu. sticky

gump·tion /ˈgʌmpʃən/ *n.* **1** common sense, *(syn.)* initiative **2** the will to do s.t. difficult, courage: *She had the gumption to start her own business.*

gun /gʌn/ *n.* **1** a weapon that fires bullets or cannon shells: *Hunters use guns to kill animals.* **2** any device with barrels that shoot substances: *A worker used a paint gun to paint the wall.* **3** *infrml.* **big gun:** an important person: *He is a big gun in city government.* **4** *fig.* **to go great guns:** to make great progress: *Our new product is going great guns.* **5** *fig.* **to jump the gun:** to act too soon: *He jumped the gun in advertising the new product because it is not ready for market yet.* **6** **to stick to one's guns:** to keep one's opinion or position in spite of opposition **7** **son of a gun: a.** *exclam.* expression of surprise, gee whiz, gosh: *Son of a gun, what a success!* **b.** rascal, devil: *You son of a gun, I didn't think you could win, but you did.*

—*v.* **gunned, gunning, guns 1** to cause an engine to run very quickly: *Racers gunned the engines of their cars.* **2** :*phrasal v. sep.* **to gun s.o. or s.t. down:** to shoot s.o. or s.t. with a gun, causing a fall to the ground or death: *The police gunned down a criminal in the street.:‖They gunned him down.* **3** *phrasal v. insep.* **to gun for s.o. or s.t.:** to chase, follow, *(syn.)* to pursue: *She's gunning for a promotion.*

gun·fire /ˈgʌnˌfaɪr/ *n.* a shooting of guns (rifles, pistols, etc.): *The sound of gunfire was heard in the hills.*

gung ho /ˈgʌŋˈhou/ *adj.infrml.* very enthusiastic: *He is gung ho to join the army.*

gunk /gʌŋk/ *n.infrml.* any thick, unpleasant greasy substance: *The car leaked oil and made a pool of gunk on the floor.*

gun·man /ˈgʌnmən/ *n.* **-men** /-mən/ a criminal using a gun: *A gunman held up the bank.*

gun·ner /ˈgʌnər/ *n.* a soldier trained to use a heavy gun: *The gunners on our ship fire machine guns.* -*n.* **gunnery.**

gun·ny·sack /ˈgʌniˌsæk/ *n.* a bag used to store and carry materials, such as grain: *The coconuts are in gunnysacks on the ship.*

gun·point /'gʌn,pɔɪnt/ n. **1** the end of a gun **2 at gunpoint:** being forced to do s.t. by s.o. who is pointing a gun at one: *I was robbed at gunpoint in the city.*

gun·pow·der /'gʌn,paʊdər/ n. a mixture of chemicals that explodes to shoot bullets and cannon shells

gun·run·ning /'gʌn,rʌnɪŋ/ n. illegal trade and transport of weapons -n. **gunrunner.**

gun·shot /'gʌn,ʃɑt/ n. **1** the loud sound of a gun (rifle, pistol, etc.) being fired: *The police heard a gunshot and ran after the criminal.* **2** the range of a gun: *She fired the gun when the bear came within gunshot.*

gun·shy /'gʌn,ʃaɪ/ adj. **1** afraid of loud noises, such as the sound of a gunshot: *My horse is gun-shy and runs when a rifle is shot.* **2** fig. fearful about certain situations: *He lost money in the stock market and is gun-shy about investing again.*

gun·sling·er /'gʌn,slɪŋər/ n.infrml. See: gunman.

gun·smith /'gʌn,smɪθ/ n. a person who repairs and sells guns

gur·gle /'gɜrgəl/ v. **-gled, -gling, -gles** n. (to make) a sound of bubbling liquid: *The baby <v.> gurgled when she saw her father.* -n.adj. **gurgling.**

gu·ru /'gu,ru, 'guru/ n. **1** an Indian spiritual leader **2** a leader or expert in a field or cause: *She is a guru to artists from all over the world.*

gush /gʌʃ/ v. **gushed, gushing, gushes 1** (of liquids) to rush or flow out suddenly in large quantities: *Water gushed out of the broken pipe.* **2** to show too much enthusiasm or emotion over s.t.: *Everyone gushed over the new baby.*
—n. **gushes** a sudden rush or flow of s.t.: *a gush of oil, emotion, interest, etc.* -n.adj. **gushing.**

gush·er /'gʌʃər/ n. an oil well that suddenly shoots a lot of oil into the air

gush·y /'gʌʃi/ adj. **-ier, -iest** emotional, (syn.) effusive: *The hostess was gushy in welcoming her guests.*

gus·set /'gʌsɪt/ n. **1** a triangular piece of cloth placed in a garment to make it stronger or bigger **2** fig. **to bust a gusset:** to try very hard, bust a gut: *He busted a gusset to finish the job on time.*

gust /gʌst/ n. a sudden strong wind: *A gust of wind knocked over the sailboat.* -adj. **gusty.**

gus·to /'gʌstoʊ/ n. enthusiasm, (syn.) zest: *He ate the delicious meal with gusto.*

gut /gʌt/ n. **1** the food canal, esp. the intestines or stomach **2** slang stomach area: *He overeats and has a big gut.* **3** a strong thread, esp. used for strings of musical instruments, made from this part of animals **4** pl.infrml. **guts:** the intestines **5** courage, determination: *He's got guts to fight a man bigger than he is.* **6 to hate s.o.'s guts:** to dislike, hate s.o. very much: *I hate his guts because he crashed my new car.*
—v. **gutted, gutting, guts 1** to cut out the inside of s.t., esp. an animal, (syn.) to eviscerate: *The hunter gutted the deer.* **2** to completely empty or destroy the inside or contents of a building: *The fire gutted the office building.*
—adj.infrml. (of a reaction or fleeing) strong, often unexplained, ((syn.)) intuitive: *I can't explain it but I have a gut feeling that she's telling the truth.‖My gut reaction to the news was one of horror.*

gut·less /'gʌtlɪs/ adj. having no courage, (syns.) cowardly, spineless: *He's gutless and won't fight for his rights.*

guts·y /'gʌtsi/ adj.infrml. **-ier, -iest** brave, (syn.) courageous: *She is gutsy; she defended herself against a robber.*

gut·ter /'gʌtər/ n. **1** a low, narrow area on the side of a street, or open pipe on a roof for water to run off: *Water runs along the gutter into the sewer.* **2** a lowly or poor place: *He uses language of the gutter.*

gut·tur·al /'gʌtərəl/ adj. related to the throat: *"Grrr" as in "growl" is a guttural sound.*

guy /gaɪ/ n.infrml. a man: *He is a nice guy; he always helps me with my taxes.*

USAGE NOTE: In speaking informally to a group (male, female, or mixed) of two or more people, you may say, *"Do you guys know what time it is?"* In referring to the group, however, you may say, *"I asked some guys to tell me the time,"* only if they were all men.

---

guz·zle /'gʌzəl/ v. **-zled, -zling, -zles** to drink or eat greedily, often quickly: *He guzzled all the beer at the party before he left.* -n. **guzzler.**

gym /dʒɪm/ n. short for gymnasium: *I'm going to the gym to play basketball.*

gym·na·si·um /dʒɪm'neɪziəm/ n. a large sports hall, usu. with seats for people to watch games: *The college gymnasium has seats for 15,000 spectators.*

gym·nast /'dʒɪm,næst, -nəst/ n. a person who does gymnastics: *She is a gymnast on the Olympic team.*

gym·nas·tics /dʒɪm'næstɪks/ n.pl. used with a sing.v. the sport of doing various acrobatic exercises to develop strength, balance, etc.: *Gymnastics is his favorite sport.*

gy·ne·col·o·gy /,gaɪnə'kɑlədʒi, ,dʒɪ-, ,gaɪ-/ n. the branch of medicine that specializes in

G

human females' sex organs: *Her doctor studied gynecology in medical school.* -*n.* **gynecologist;** -*adj.* **gynecological** /, gaɪnəkə'lɑʤɪkəl, ,ʤɪ-, ,ʤaɪ-/.

gyp /ʤɪp/ *v.infrml.* **gypped, gypping, gyps** to cheat: *That store gypped me by charging me too much.*

gyp·sy or **Gypsy** /'ʤɪpsi/ *n.* -**sies** **1** Gypsy: a people, esp. of Eastern Europe, that live by going from place to place **2** *fig.* a person who does not stay in one place for long
—*adj.* non-union, unlicensed: *Gypsy taxis are not licensed by the government.*

gy·rate /'ʤaɪ,reɪt/ *v.* -**rated, -rating, -rates** to move in circles around a fixed point, (*syn.*) to revolve: *The space rocket gyrated as it returned to earth.* -*n.* **gyration** /ʤaɪ'reɪʃən/.

gy·ro·scope /'ʤaɪrə,skoup/ *n.* a device that helps airplanes and ships to stay level

G

H,h

H, h /eɪtʃ/ *n.* **H's, h's** or **Hs, hs** the eighth letter of the English alphabet

ha or **hah** /hɑ/ *exclam.* **1** used to express laughter, surprise, delight: *Ha, ha, ha, that's a very funny joke!* **2** used to make fun of s.t.: *Ha! What a stupid thing to say.*

hab·er·dash·er·y /'hæbər,dæʃəri/ *n.* [C;U] **-ies** a store that sells men's clothing: *Harry Truman, former President of the USA, once owned a haberdashery.* *-n.* [C] **haberdasher.**

hab·it /'hæbɪt/ *n.* [C;U] a repeated behavior: *He has the bad habit of lighting a cigarette every time that his telephone rings.*

hab·it·a·ble /'hæbɪtəbəl/ *adj.* fit to live in: *Their old cabin in the woods is habitable but not very comfortable.*

hab·i·tat /'hæbə,tæt/ *n.* (in biology) the area in which an animal or plant normally lives: *The habitat for deer is mainly the valley, not the mountains.*

hab·i·ta·tion /,hæbə'teɪʃən/ *n.frml.* [U] **1** the act of making one's home in, (*syns.*) inhabiting, dwelling, occupancy: *The buildings in this area are in bad shape; they are unfit for human habitation.* **2** a place to live, (*syn.*) a dwelling

ha·bit·u·al /hə'bɪtʃuəl/ *adj.* done as a habit; constant: *She is a habitual liar (smoker, drinker).*

ha·bit·u·ate /hə'bɪtʃu,eɪt/ *v.* **-ated, -ating, -ates** to make s.o. used to s.t., (*syn.*) to accustom: *He is habituated to eating breakfast in the morning and does not leave the house without eating it.* *-n.* [U] **habituation** /hə,bɪtʃu'eɪʃən/.

ha·ci·en·da /,hɑsi'ɛndə, 'ɑ-/ *n.* (Spanish for) a large ranch or estate: *Rich families in Latin America own haciendas.*

hack /hæk/ *v.* **1** to cut or chop with sharp blows: *A worker hacked branches off trees with an ax.* **2** to edit writing by chopping it up **3** *infrml.fig.* **to hack it:** to function well or poorly: *He can't hack it at college; he flunked out.*

—n. **1** a horse-drawn taxi **2** a writer who is more interested in selling stories than in their quality

hack·er /'hækər/ *n.* **1** a person who plays golf or tennis poorly: *She plays golf every day, but is still a hacker.* **2** a computer fanatic, often s.o. who illegally enters computer systems: *He's a hacker who often stays up all night working on a project.*

hack·les /'hækəlz/ *n.pl.* **1** hairs that angry animals can raise on their necks and backs: *The dog raised its hackles, growled, and attacked the robber.* **2 to raise the hackles:** to make s.o. feel angry, (*syn.*) to enrage: *When politicians promise to lower taxes and then don't, it always raises my hackles.*

hack·ney /'hækni/ *n.* a horse-drawn carriage that one pays to ride in: *We hired a hackney and rode around the park.*

hack·neyed /'hæknid/ *adj.* dull, uninteresting: *She writes hackneyed stories for a local newspaper.* See: trite.

hack·saw /'hæk,sɔ/ *n.v.* a saw used to cut metal: *The prisoner used a <n.> hacksaw to cut the bars of his cell.||He <v.> hacksawed through the cell's bars.*

had /hæd; *weak form* əd, həd, d/ *past tense & part. of* have **1** *I had a good time at the party.* **2** *infrml.* **to be had:** to be victimized, taken advantage of: *When the cab driver charged me 20 dollars to go one mile, I knew that I had been had.*

had·dock /'hædək/ *n.* [C;U] an edible whitefish

hag /hæg/ *n.pej.* an ugly old woman: *The witch in the movie is an old hag.*

hag·gard /'hægərd/ *adj.* tired and weary, (*syns.*) drawn, gaunt: *The student looked haggard after studying all night.*

hag·gle /'hægəl/ *v.* **-gled, -gling, -gles** to argue about price, (*syn.*) to bargain: *The salesman and customer haggled over the price of a coat.* *-n.* [C] **haggler;** [U] haggling.

hah /hɑ/ *exclam.* See: ha.

hail /heɪl/ n. [U] rain that freezes and falls as balls of ice: *Hail ruined the farmer's wheat crop.*
—v. **1** to greet, esp. with enthusiasm: *The President hailed the astronauts when they returned from space.* **2** to pour down hail: *It hailed this morning for a few minutes.* **3** to speak loudly to get attention: *Standing on the sidewalk, I hailed a passing cab.* **4** phrasal v. insep. **to hail from:** to come from: *The cowboy hails from Texas.* **5** phrasal v. insep. **to hail s.o. or s.t. as s.t.:** to praise s.o. or s.t. for good qualities: *He hailed his new boss as a fair woman.*

hail·stone /'heɪl,stoʊn/ n. a ball of hail, an ice pellet: *Hailstones sounded like small rocks when they fell.*

hair /hɛr/ n. **1** [U] a thin, fine growth on the skin of a person or an animal: *Most people have lots of hair on their heads.* **2** [C] one strand, or piece, of the growth found on the body of a person or an animal: *I found a cat hair in my food.* **3** sing. a very small amount or distance: *Move the picture a hair to the right.* **4 to be** or **get in one's hair:** to annoy: *That boy won't leave me alone; he's really getting in my hair.* **5 to let one's hair down:** to relax, act naturally, not formally: *The business executive let her hair down at the office party and was friendly with everyone.* **6 to make one's hair stand on end:** to frighten: *That horror movie was so scary that it made my hair stand on end.* **7 to split hairs:** to disagree about very small and usu. unimportant differences, (syn.) to quibble: *He likes to argue by splitting hairs.*

hair·brush /'hɛr,brʌʃ/ n. -brushes a brush for taking care of the hair: *She uses a hairbrush every morning to do her hair.*

hair·cut /'hɛr,kʌt/ n. the cutting and usu. styling of hair: *I went to the barber for a haircut today.*

hair·do /'hɛr,du/ n. -dos See: hairstyle.

hair·dress·er /'hɛr,drɛsər/ n. a person who cuts and styles hair: *My brother works as a hairdresser in a local salon.*

hair·line /'hɛr,laɪn/ n. the dividing line between the hair and the face: *His hairline recedes as he grows bald.*
—adj. extremely narrow, fine: *The vase has a hairline crack down its center.*

hair·net /'hɛr,nɛt/ n. a netting or mesh placed over the hair: *Food workers often wear hairnets.*

hair·piece /'hɛr,pis/ n. a covering of hair that is not one's own used to cover baldness or to make one's natural hair look thicker, (syn.) a toupee: *He wears a hairpiece to look younger than he is. See:* wig.

hair·pin /'hɛr,pɪn/ n. a U-shaped wire used to hold hair in place: *When women began to use hair sprays, they stopped using hairpins.*

—adj. (of a road) having a sharp curve like a hairpin: *The road made several hairpin turns going up the mountain.*

hair-raising adj.fig. scary, (syns.) frightening, terrifying: *Being trapped in an elevator was a hair-raising experience.*

hair·split·ting /'hɛr,splɪtɪŋ/ n. [U] adj. arguing over small or unimportant differences, (syn.) quibbling: *He argued with me for four hours about whether we save money with our new phone company; his <n.> hairsplitting drives me crazy!*

hair·style /'hɛr,staɪl/ n. the way that one's hair is cut and shaped, (syns.) hairdo, coiffure: *Her hairstyle is simple, but her clothing is wild! -n.* **hairstylist.**

hair·y /'hɛri/ adj. -ier, -iest **1** covered with hair: *That man has a hairy chest.* **2** fig.slang difficult or dangerous: *The situation got hairy when a bad storm shook the airplane from side to side. -n.* [U] **hairiness.**

hale /heɪl/ adj. **1** healthy, (syn.) vigorous **2 to feel hale and hearty:** *She feels hale and hearty after her long vacation.*
—v. **haled, haling, hales** to order s.o. to go, (syn.) to summon: *She was haled into court to tell the judge what she saw.*

half /hæf/ n. **halves** /hævz/ **1** one of two equal parts of s.t.: *I ate half a sandwich.* **2 half a loaf is better than none:** part of what one wants is better than nothing: *The bank gave me only a small loan, but half a loaf is better than none.* **3 to do s.t. by halves:** to do s.t. halfway, incompletely: *He's lazy; he always does things by halves.* **4 to go halves:** to split s.t. (usu. the price) in half, to go fifty-fifty: *My girlfriend and I went halves on a new TV.*

half-and-half adj. being equal parts of s.t.: *I'd like my tea half-and-half, half milk and half tea.*
—n. [U] a mixture of half milk and half cream: *Put a little half-and-half in my coffee.*

half-baked adj.fig. without good judgment or common sense, (syn.) ill-conceived: *She has these half-baked ideas on how to make money.*

half brother n. a brother with whom s.o. shares only one biological parent: *My half brother and I have the same father but different mothers.*

half-hearted /'hæf'hɑrtɪd/ adj. without interest or energy, (syn.) feeble: *He made a half-hearted attempt at solving the problem, then gave up. -adv.* **halfheartedly.**

half-hour n. 30 minutes: *A flight to New York leaves from Washington every half-hour.*

half-mast n. **1** a position approx. halfway between the top and bottom of a mast or flagpole **2 to fly at half-mast:** to show respect for the dead by lowering the flag: *Flags flew at half-mast when the mayor died.*

half shell *n.* **1** one part of a two-part shell, usu. of an oyster, clam, mussel, etc. **2 on the half shell:** in one part of the opened shell: *She likes to eat oysters on the half shell.*

half sister *n.* a sister related through only one biological parent: *My half sister usually visits her mother in New York for the holidays.*

half-truth *n.* a statement that leaves out some facts: *He told a half-truth when he said that he worked on Saturday; in reality, he worked only for one hour on Saturday morning.*

half·way /ˈhæfˈweɪ/ *adv.adj.* **1** in the middle, between two points: *New York is approximately <adj.> halfway between Boston and Washington, D.C.* **2 to meet s.o. halfway:** to reach an agreement where each person gives up part of what he or she wanted, *(syn.)* to compromise: *You want $1000 for the car, and I offered $500. I will meet you <adv.> halfway; will you take $750?*

half-wit *n.* a stupid person, *(syn.)* an idiot: *He must be a half-wit to suggest such a silly idea!* *-adj.* **half-witted.**

hal·i·but /ˈhæləbət/ *n.* [C;U] **-but** or **-buts** a fish of the North Pacific and Atlantic Oceans: *I like the taste of halibut, but many people do not.*

hal·i·to·sis /ˌhæləˈtoʊsɪs/ *n.frml.* [U] bad breath: *Her dentist suggested that she use a mouthwash because she has halitosis.*

hall /hɔl/ *n.* **1** a large room usu. used for classes, meetings, or entertainment: *The concert hall was filled with people who came to see the show.* **2** a hallway: *Your friend is waiting for you out in the hall.* **3** a large building where students live: *What residence hall do you live in?*

hal·le·lu·jah /ˌhæləˈluyə/ *exclam.* used to express joy, *lit.* Praise to God!: *The church chorus sang "Hallelujah."*‖*Hallelujah! I finally finished my college degree!*

hall·mark /ˈhɔlˌmark/ *n.* **1** a mark to indicate purity in silver or gold: *My grandmother's gold plate has a hallmark on the bottom.* **2** a sign of excellence: *A hallmark of a good tennis player is the ability to hit the ball from both sides.*

Hall of Fame *n.* an institution that honors people who have done very well in their job: *It is a great honor to be part of the Baseball Hall of Fame.*

USAGE NOTE: The Baseball *Hall of Fame* in Cooperstown, New York is a popular destination for baseball fans and their families. Other halls of fame include one for football in Canton, Ohio; for basketball in Springfield, Massachusetts; for track and field in Indianapolis, Indiana; for aviation in Dayton, Ohio; and for rock and roll in Cleveland, Ohio.

hal·lowed /ˈhæloʊd/ *adj.* holy, sacred: *Many people died in battle on this hallowed ground.* *-v.* **hallow.**

Hal·low·een /ˌhæləˈwin, ˌhɑ-/ *n.* (in USA) a folk holiday on October 31, when children dress up in costumes and visit neighbors' houses to ask for candy: *On Halloween, some children dress up as witches.* See: pumpkin.

USAGE NOTE: Asking for candy on *Halloween* is also known as *trick or treating.* At each house children cry, *"Trick or treat!"* to let neighbors know that if they aren't given any candy, they may do some mischief. It's traditional at *Halloween* to decorate the home with a *jack-o'lantern,* a pumpkin carved to look like a head, lit from inside by a candle.

H

hal·lu·ci·nate /həˈlusəˌneɪt/ *v.* **-nated, -nating, -nates** to imagine unreal things, esp. scary or horrifying events: *His high fever made him hallucinate last night.*

hal·lu·ci·na·tion /həˌlusəˈneɪʃən/ *n.* [C;U] unreal events imagined by s.o., esp. scary or horrifying things: *She has hallucinations that demons are chasing her.*

hal·lu·ci·no·gen /həˈlusənədʒən/ *n.* a drug that causes hallucinations: *The drug LSD is a strong hallucinogen.* *-adj.* **hallucinogenic** /həˌlusənənˈdʒɛnɪk/.

hall·way /ˈhɔlˌweɪ/ *n.* a passageway between rooms: *That hallway goes to the president's office.*

ha·lo /ˈheɪloʊ/ *n.* **-los** or **-loes** **1** a circle of light around the head: *Angels are often shown with halos around their heads.* **2 a halo effect:** when one good action makes a person look better in a general, overall way: *The President's visit to the fire victims had a halo effect because now everyone thinks he is a kinder, better person.*

halt /hɔlt/ *v.* to stop: *The marching soldiers halted when their sergeant shouted, "Halt!"*‖*The car halted at the traffic light.* —*n.sing.* **1** an end, *(syn.)* a cessation **2 to bring to a halt:** to stop: *The cowboy brought his horse to a halt.* **3 to put a halt to:** to stop s.t. by using authority: *The police put a halt to robberies in the town.*

hal·ter /ˈhɔltər/ *n.* **1** an article of women's clothing worn around the upper body and tied behind the neck, leaving the shoulders and arms bare: *In summer, she wears a halter and shorts.* **2** a type of strap put on a horse's head: *We put halters on horses' heads to control them.*

halt·ing /ˈhɔltɪŋ/ *adj.* uncertain, *(syn.)* hesitant: *He spoke in a halting way, as if he wasn't sure what to say.* *-adv.* **haltingly.**

halve /hæv/ v. **halved, halving, halves** **1** to cut in half: *He halved the apple with a knife.* **2** to make smaller by half: *The boss halved the budget for this year.*

halves /hævz/ n.pl. *of* half

ham /hæm/ n. **1** [C;U] the meat of a pig, usu. from the thigh: *I would like a sandwich of sliced ham with cheese.* **2** [C] s.o. who overacts or draws attention to himself or herself in a funny way: *My daughter would make a good comedian; she's such a ham!*
—v. **hammed, hamming, hams to ham it up:** to make s.t. funny by overdoing or exaggerating it: *You should see him pretend he's the teacher; he really hams it up!*

ham·burg·er /'hæm,bɜrgər/ n. **1** [C;U] a small cake of chopped beef, usu. served on a roll as a sandwich: *I'd like a hamburger, fries, and a cola.* **2** [U] chopped beef

USAGE NOTE: The *hamburger* contains no ham and was named after a German food called Hamburg steak. It has become a symbol of America's fast-paced, informal way of life. People often entertain friends and family at *cookouts* or *barbecues* in their backyards and serve grilled hamburgers and hot dogs.

ham·let /'hæmlɪt/ n. a little village: *We drove through hamlets in the German countryside.*

ham·mer /'hæmər/ n. a tool with a handle and metal head used for pounding: *Carpenters use a hammer to pound nails.*
—v. **1** to strike with a hammer: *He hammered nails into the plywood.* **2** *phrasal v. sep.* **to hammer s.t. home:** to say something over and over, in different ways: *The speaker hammered home her point by giving us many different facts that showed she was right.||She hammered it home.*

ham·mock /'hæmək/ n. a net or strong material that is hung between two poles or trees and used for sleeping: *After lunch, she likes to nap in her hammock in the yard.*

ham·per /'hæmpər/ v. to make s.t. hard to do, (syn.) to hinder: *Rescue work was hampered by heavy rains.*

ham·ster /'hæmstər/ n. a small animal in the mouse family that some people keep as a pet: *My hamster likes to eat carrots.*

ham·string /'hæm,strɪŋ/ n. a large tendon at the back of the knee
—v. **-strung** /-,strʌŋ/, **-stringing, -strings** **1** to cut the hamstring tendon and prevent from walking (usu. a horse) **2** *fig.* to make s.t. hard to do, (syn.) to impede: *The student president tried to hamstring the school senate because she didn't agree with its decision.||The senate was hamstrung by the president's refusal to help.*

hand /hænd/ n. **1** [C;U] one of two parts of the human body below the wrist made up of four fingers, a palm, and a thumb: *I write with my left hand.* **2** [C] a pointer, as on a dial or clock: *On a watch, when the little hand is on 11 and the big hand is on 12, the time is 11 o'clock.* **3** [U] a promise, esp. in marriage or business, (syn.) a pledge: *She gave her hand in marriage to a wonderful man.* **4** [C] one play in a game of cards: *We played a few hands of cards (poker, bridge, etc.), then went home.* **5** [C] the cards that one is dealt in a game of cards **6** [C] an ordinary worker: *The farmer hires field hands to pick corn.* **7** [U] handwriting: *She is 90 years old, but still writes in a clear hand.* **8** **all hands:** all members of a group, esp. a ship's crew: *All hands on deck!* **9** **at hand:** ready to use, (syn.) nearby: *He keeps a radio close at hand to listen to the news.* **10** **at the hands of:** done by s.o.: *A poor old man died at the hands of a robber, who stabbed him.* **11** **by hand:** done by hand: *He washes his car by hand.* **12** **clean hands:** free of guilt, blameless: *The police chief has clean hands even though some of the police officers are dishonest.* **13** **hand in hand** or **in glove:** closely connected: *A good education goes hand in hand with getting a good job.* **14** **hand over fist:** quickly and in large amounts (handfuls): *He is making money hand over fist in his new business.* **15** **hand over hand:** using one hand after the other hand to hold s.t.: *She climbed up the rope hand over hand.* **16** **Hands up!:** to surrender by putting one's hands in the air: *Police caught the thief and shouted, "Hands up or we will shoot!"* **17** **hand to mouth:** when one spends all of one's pay just on necessities with nothing left for fun: *She lives hand to mouth; all of her salary goes to pay for food and rent.* **18** **off one's hands:** to be free of a responsibility or problem: *I have too much work to do; could you take some of it off my hands?* **19** **on hand: a.** taking part in some activity, to be present: *Thirty guests were on hand to sing "Happy Birthday" at my birthday party.* **b.** (to have) available, (syn.) in stock: *The store has plenty of merchandise on hand for the holiday sale.* **20** **on the one hand . . . on the other hand:** viewed one way, then another way: *On the one hand, he is very intelligent, but on the other hand, he does not work very hard.* **21** **One hand washes the other:** cooperation benefits both parties: *The owner is very good to her employees and, as one hand washes the other, they work hard for her.* **22** **out of hand: a.** immediately, without thinking about s.t.: *He said, "No!" out of hand to my offer.* **b.** out of control, (syn.) disorderly: *The kids were so noisy that order in the classroom got out of hand.* **23** **to bite the hand that feeds you:** to do wrong to s.o. you depend on for your life's basic necessities: *She is hateful* *to her boss, and she is biting the hand that feeds her.* **24 to give s.o. a hand: a.** to help, (*syn.*) to give assistance: *Let me give you a hand with your bags.* **b.** applause, clapping: *The audience gave the singer a big hand.* **25 to have a hand in:** to have a role or part: *His wife had a hand in starting his business.* **26 to have in hand: a.** to control: *Students rioted, but the police now have the situation in hand.* **b.** to own, (*syn.*) to possess: *The store has the art pieces in hand and will sell them.* **27 to have one's hands full:** to have too much to do, (*syns.*) to be overburdened, overwhelmed: *She has her hands full with three unruly children to take care of.* **28 to keep one's hand in:** to stay active in s.t., esp. in a former job or skill: *The owner left the company, but still keeps her hand in by visiting once a month.* **29 to throw up one's hands:** to give up in frustration: *He tried to fix the motor, but threw up his hands and walked away.* **30 upper hand:** power over s.o: *She has the upper hand with her husband because she will leave him unless he does what she wants.* **31 with a heavy hand:** with hard demands, insensitively: *He runs the company with a heavy hand and simply fires anyone who disagrees with him.*

—*v.* **1** to give s.t. to s.o. with your hands, to pass, transfer: *I handed the contract to my lawyer.‖The thief handed the stolen jewels over to the police.* **2** *infrml.fig.* **to hand it to s.o.:** to admire, praise: *I have to hand it to him; he's done a wonderful job!* **3** *phrasal v. sep.* **to hand s.t. down: a.** (in law) to announce, declare: *The judge handed down their decision yesterday.‖She handed it down.* **b.** to transfer to one's children or other heirs upon one's death: *His parents handed down a big house and land to their son.‖They handed it down to him.* **4** *phrasal v. sep.* **to hand s.t. in:** to submit, present: *The student handed in her term paper right on time.‖She handed it in.* **5** *phrasal v. sep.* **to hand s.t. on:** to give s.t. to s.o. else: *When you're finished, please hand on this memo.‖Hand it on.* **6** *phrasal v. sep.* **to hand s.t. out:** to give out, (*syn.*) to distribute: *A person handed out free samples of a "new cigarette on a street corner.* **7** *phrasal v. sep.* **to hand s.o. or s.t. over:** to turn in, surrender: *A criminal handed over his pistol to the police officer.‖He handed it over.*

—*suffix* related to the hand(s): *She is left-handed.*

hand·bag /'hænd,bæg, 'hæn-/ *n.* **1** a woman's purse: *She carries her handbag wherever she goes.* **2** a small carrying case

hand·ball /'hænd,bɔl, 'hæn-/ *n.* [U] a game in which players hit a ball off the wall, using their hands: *In handball, you try to hit the ball in a*

way that makes it hard for your opponent to return it.

hand basket *n.* **1** a basket, usu. woven, used to carry small things: *We filled a hand basket with soda and sandwiches for a picnic.* **2** *fig.* **to go to hell in a hand basket:** to fall apart rapidly: *After the owner died, that company went to hell in a hand basket.*

hand·book /'hænd,bʊk, 'hæn-/ *n.* a manual of information: *The Boy Scout Handbook is sold in many countries.*

hand·craft /'hænd'kræft, 'hæn-/ *v.* to make by hand, not machine: *We handcrafted everything in the store, including the candles, the pottery, and the holiday decorations. See:* handicraft.

hand·cuff /'hænd,kʌf, 'hæn-/ *n.v.* a short chain with round rings on each end that open and close around a prisoner's hand; used to hold a prisoner's hands together: *A policeman put <n.> handcuffs on a criminal. He <v.> handcuffed him.*

handcuff

hand·ful /'hænd,fʊl, 'hæn-/ *n.* **1** an amount of s.t. held in the hand: *I ate a handful of popcorn at the movies.* **2** *fig.* a difficult person: *That child is a handful; he screams all day long!* **3** *fig.* a small number of s.t.: *Only a handful of people attended the concert.*

hand·gun /'hænd,gʌn, 'hæn-/ *n.* a pistol: *Police officers usually carry handguns.*

hand·hold /'hænd,hoʊld/ *n.* a strong hold, (*syn.*) a grip: *The climber got a handhold on a rock and pulled herself up.*

hand·i·cap /'hændi,kæp/ *n.* **1** a disability: *He lost a leg in an accident and now has a handicap.* **2** (in horse racing, golf) a calculation made to give each player a chance to win: *He has a low handicap in golf because he is such a good player.*

—*v.* **-capped, -capping, -caps 1** to cause a disability: *A bad accident handicapped him for life.* **2** to calculate handicaps in sports: *He handicaps the horseraces.* -*adj.* **handicapped** -*n.* **handicapper.**

hand·i·craft /'hændi,kræft/ *n.* **1** skilled work with the hands: *My grandmother does handicrafts.* **2** objects made with skill by hand: *Some of the handicrafts that she makes are woven baskets and holiday decorations.*

hand·i·ly /'hændəli/ *adv.* easily, (*syn.*) effortlessly: *She won the tennis match handily.*

hand·i·work /'hændi,wɜrk/ *n.* [U] **1** work done by hand: *The boy built a doghouse and asked his father to come see his handiwork.* **2** s.t. done or made by s.o.: *Who made such a mess? It must be the cat's handiwork!*

hand·ker·chief /ˈhæŋkərtʃɪf, -ˌtʃif/ *n.* a square of cloth usu. used for cleaning the nose or mouth: *He wiped his nose with a handkerchief.*

hand·knit /ˈhænd'nɪt, 'hæn-/ *v.* **-knit** or **-knitted, -knitting, -knits** to knit by hand: *She handknits sweaters for her children.*
—*adj.* referring to s.t. knit by hand: *That sweater is handknit. See:* knit.

han·dle /ˈhændl/ *n.* a part on an object used to pick it up or open it: *I took hold of the knife handle and cut the meat.*‖*I pulled the handle and opened the refrigerator door.*
—*v.* **-dled, -dling, -dles** **1** to take in one's hands, (*syn.*) to manipulate: *Workers handle objects in the museum very carefully.* **2** to take care of s.t.: *I will handle some business, then go home early today.*‖*She handles all of the billing for the law firm.* **3** *infrml.fig.* **to get a handle on s.t.:** to gain control or understanding of s.t.: *I have to get a handle on the problem before I can do anything about it.*

hand·ler /ˈhændlər/ *n.* a trainer, esp. of animals: *The handler of elephants in the circus is highly skilled.*

hand·made /ˈhænd'meɪd, 'hæn-/ *adj.* fashioned by hand: *Those sweaters are handmade from the best materials.*

hand-me-down /ˈhændmiˌdaʊn, 'hæn-/ *n.adj.* a used article, esp. of clothing, given to another person: *The youngest boy in a big family usually wears <n.> hand-me-downs from his older brothers.*‖*He wears <adj.> hand-me-down clothes.*

hand·out /ˈhænˌdaʊt/ *n.* **1** information given out on paper, usu. informally, such as a flyer or photocopy: *The professor gave the class handouts that explained the homework.* **2** s.t. given free, (*syn.*) charity: *The beggar on the corner receives handouts of money from people who walk by him.*

hand·pick /ˈhænd'pɪk, 'hæn-/ *v.* **1** to gather by hand: *Raspberries are handpicked.* **2** *fig.* to choose with great care: *The manager handpicked each member of the special research team.* -*adj.* **handpicked.**

hand·rail /ˈhændˌreɪl/ *n.* a railing held on to by people for support: *Be sure to hold the handrail when you come down the stairs.*

hand·shake /ˈhændˌʃeɪk, 'hæn-/ *n.* a way people greet or leave each other, or agree on a decision, by grasping each other's hand: *The two men greeted each other with a handshake.*

hands-off *adj.* left alone, not to be touched: *The mayor told the police to have a hands-off policy toward beggars; in other words, not to arrest them.*

hand·some /ˈhænsəm/ *adj.* **1** good-looking, attractive (usu. of a man): *He is a handsome man, tall and slim.* **2** (of things) large, (*syns.*) generous, admirable: *She was paid a handsome price for her jewels.* -*adv.* **handsomely.**

USAGE NOTE:
USAGE NOTE: While many male movie stars are described as *handsome,* female stars are usually called *beautiful* or *pretty.* People who are handsome, beautiful, or pretty may also be called *good-looking.* The word *attractive* may be used to describe anyone who looks nice, but not beautiful: *I wouldn't say she's pretty, but she's a very attractive person. Cute* is often used to describe children or animals, but may also describe an adult whose face has a childlike quality: *Is he handsome? Well, not really, but he's cute.*

hands-on *adj.* active in the day-to-day work of a job or activity: *He is a hands-on manager; he pays close attention to every part of his business.*

hand·stand /ˈhænd,stænd, 'hæn-/ *n.* a movement in which one places one's hands on the ground and feet up in the air: *He does a handstand every morning as part of his exercises.*

hand-to-hand *adj.* involving close body contact, usu. in battle: *Soldiers were fighting in hand-to-hand combat with fists and knives.*

hand·wo·ven /ˈhænd'woʊvən/ *adj.* woven by hand: *He sells small, handwoven rugs.*

hand·writ·ing /ˈhænd,raɪtɪŋ/ *n.* [U] writing produced by hand (rather than by machine): *She has very clear handwriting.*

hand·writ·ten /ˈhænd,rɪtn/ *adj.* written by hand: *She sent a handwritten note of thanks to her boss.*

hand·y /ˈhændi/ *adj.* **-ier, -iest** **1** close at hand, ready for use: *He keeps his tools handy in a toolbox.* **2** *infrml.* good at fixing or making things: *My sister is handy; she always fixes broken things in her house.* **3** **to come in handy:** to be useful: *A map sure would come in handy right now; I'm lost!*

hand·y·man /ˈhændi,mæn/ *n.* **-men** /-,mɛn/ s.o. who knows how to fix many things: *We called the handyman to fix our broken fence.*

hang /hæŋ/ *v.* **hung** /hʌŋ/, **hanging, hangs** **1** to attach s.t. from the top, (*syn.*) to suspend: *I hang my clothes in the closet every night.* **2** to swing while attached from above, (*syn.*) to dangle: *Wires are hanging loose from telephone poles after the storm.* **3** to put on a wall or window: *A worker hung new wallpaper on the living room wall.*‖*I am hanging new curtains on the windows.* **4** *past* **hanged:** to put a rope around the neck to kill s.o., (*syn.*) to execute: *The authorities hanged a murderer.* **5** to stay in one place, (*syn.*) to float: *Smoke hangs in the air in most barrooms.* **6** **to hang around: a.** to attach, (*syn.*) to drape: *A pearl necklace hangs around her neck.* **b.** *fig.* to spend time doing nothing, (*syns.*) to loiter, idle: *He hangs around the street corner every evening.* **7** **to hang back:** to be slow to decide or act, (*syns.*) to hesitate, remain cautious: *She* *does not make decisions quickly, but hangs back before deciding.* **8 to hang in the balance:** to be uncertain about an important situation that must be decided, (*syn.*) to be at stake: *Can the doctor save the sick woman? Her life hangs in the balance.* **9** *infrml.* **to hang in there:** to keep going in a difficult situation, (*syn.*) to persist: *My business is very slow, but I'm hanging in there, hoping it will improve.* **10** *infrml.* **to hang loose:** to relax in a tense situation: *The company will come out of its slow period, so you should hang loose and stop looking for another job.* **11** *phrasal v.* **to hang on: a.** to wait: *Hang on a minute while I change my shoes.* **b.** to continue doing s.t.: *He told me he wasn't sure he could hang on with the project.* **12** *phrasal v.* **to hang on (to):** to hold tightly, (*syns.*) to clutch, grasp: *The swimmer hung on to the rope and was pulled to safety.*||*Hang on! This road is really bumpy!* **13** *phrasal v. insep.* **to hang onto s.o. or s.t.:** to (try to) keep: *She wants to sell their old car, but her husband wants to hang onto it.* **14 to hang out: a.** to put outdoors: *I hung the clothes out to dry in the backyard.* **b.** *infrml.* to spend time with others informally: *He hangs out at the local bar in the evening.* **15 to hang s.o. or s.t. up: a.** to attach s.t. from the top, (*syn.*) to suspend: *He hung his coat up on a hook.* **b.** to stop or delay s.t., (*syn.*) to obstruct: *The owner will simply not decide on the budget, so he's hung up the entire project.* **16 to hang up:** to put down the telephone to end a conversation: *He said good-bye and hung up.*||*She was angry yesterday and hung up on me.* **17 to leave s.o. hanging:** to leave s.o. waiting for an answer: *She promised to marry him but would not set a date, so she left him hanging.*

—*n.* [U] **1** the way in which s.t., esp. clothes or a curtain hangs, (*syn.*) the drape of s.t.: *The hang of that skirt is loose and comfortable.* **2** *slang* **to get the hang of s.t.:** to understand, be able to do: *It took me a while to get the hang of how to do word processing.*

hang·ar /ˈhæŋər, ˈhæŋɡər/ *n.* a large, covered area for airplanes: *The planes in the hangar are being repaired.*

hang·er /ˈhæŋər/ *n.* a device used to suspend clothes from: *She keeps her suits on hangers in the closet.*

hanger-on *n.* **hangers-on** s.o. who stays around a group that he or she is not part of: *He is one of the hangers-on around the university; he wants people to think he belongs here.*

hang gliding *n.* [U] the sport in which a person flies through the

hang glider

air attached to a large set of wings: *She loves the thrill of hang gliding.* -*n.* [C] **hang glider.**

hang·ing /ˈhæŋɪŋ/ *adj.* suspended, dangling: *apples hanging from an apple tree*
—*n.* [C;U] a way of killing by suspending a person from the neck with a rope: *Hanging was a commonly used method of putting people to death in the 1800s.*

hang·out /ˈhæŋˌaʊt/ *n.* a place where people gather informally to talk, drink, and eat: *The café on Main Street has become a hangout for basketball players.*

hang·o·ver /ˈhæŋˌoʊvər/ *n.* headache and sickness from drinking too much alcohol: *The morning after the party, she woke up with a bad hangover.*

hang-up *n.infrml.* s.t. that a person finds very difficult, usu. for emotional reasons: *He has a hang-up about flying; he would rather drive hundreds of miles than get into a plane.*

han·ker /ˈhæŋkər/ *v.infrml.* to desire, (*syn.*) to crave: *Europeans in America often hanker for a good cup of coffee.* -*n.* **hankering.**

han·kie /ˈhæŋki/ *n.infrml.* a handkerchief: *She keeps a hankie in her purse.*

han·ky-pan·ky /ˈhæŋkiˈpæŋki/ *n.* [U] dishonest behavior, usu. related to sex or corruption: *All sorts of hanky-panky are going on in that company.*

hap·haz·ard /hæpˈhæzərd/ *adj.* by chance, without planning: *He works in such a haphazard way that no one can figure out what he has done.* -*adv.* **haphazardly.**

hap·less /ˈhæplɪs/ *adj.frml.* unlucky, (*syn.*) unfortunate: *He drowned in a hapless way, with no one near to help.*

hap·pen /ˈhæpən/ *v.* **1** to take place, (*syn.*) to occur: *The accident happened this morning.* **2** *phrasal v. insep.* **to happen on** or **upon s.o. or s.t.:** to see or discover s.t. by chance: *We happened upon the accident on our way to work.*

hap·pen·ing /ˈhæpənɪŋ, ˈhæpnɪŋ/ *n.* **1** s.t. that happens, an event **2** an informal or improvised performance or event: *The musicians had a happening at a friend's house by playing music together for fun.*

hap·pen·stance /ˈhæpənˌstæns/ *n.* [U] a chance occurrence: *It was just happenstance that I saw her at the party; I didn't know she would be there.*

hap·pi·ness /ˈhæpinɪs/ *n.* [U] **1** a state of contentment: *The U.S. Constitution guarantees people the right to pursue happiness.* **2** delight, joy: *Their wedding was a time of true happiness for both of them.*

hap·py /ˈhæpi/ *adj.* **-pier, -piest 1** joyful, (*syn.*) cheerful: *His birthday party was a happy occasion.* **2** pleased, (*syn.*) gratified: *I am happy to meet you.* -*adv.* **happily.**

USAGE NOTE: A *happy* person is positive, light-hearted, and good-humored: *I'm really happy in my new job; it's just what I wanted.* If you accept things without complaint and don't wish for what you don't have, you are *content:* *Some people look for excitement, but my parents are content to stay at home and read.* Glad describes how we feel about s.t. specific: *I'm glad I brought my umbrella.‖I'm very glad to meet you.* The words *ecstatic* and *overjoyed* both describe extreme happiness: *He was ecstatic when he won the lottery.‖They were overjoyed by the birth of their first grandchild.*

happy-go-lucky *adj.* carefree, easygoing: *He's a happy-go-lucky guy, always relaxed and cheerful.*

happy hour *n.* one or more hours between 4:00 and 7:00 p.m. in which people get together and drink alcoholic beverages, at a lower price than usual

ha·rangue /həˈræŋ/ *n.v.* **-rangued, -ranguing, -rangues** a long, loud speech, (*syn.*) a tirade: *A candidate for mayor <v.> harangued his opponent about governmental injustice.*

ha·rass /həˈræs, ˈhærəs/ *v.* to criticize or attack s.o. again and again, (*syn.*) to badger: *She harassed me for days about the mistake I made.* *-n.* [U] **harassment.**

har·bin·ger /ˈhɑrbɪndʒər/ *n.frml.* s.t. that announces the beginning, (*syn.*) a messenger, forerunner: *Warm weather is a harbinger of spring.*

har·bor /ˈhɑrbər/ *n.* a port: *Ships sail into the harbor at night.*
—*v.* **1** to hide s.o. in order to protect him or her: *She harbored a criminal in her house to hide him from the police.* **2 to harbor a grudge:** to hold a bad feeling about s.o.: *She harbored a grudge against the authorities for putting him in jail.*

hard /hɑrd/ *adj.* **1** firm, solid: *The surface of stone is hard and cold.* **2** difficult: *Poverty is a hard problem to solve.* **3** true, unquestionable: *The hard fact of the case is that a murder was committed.* **4** of s.o. who requires people to work a lot but shows them little kindness, (*syn.*) severe: *The officer is a hard man on his troops.* **5** joyless, (*syn.*) harsh: *She has led a hard life on a small farm.* **6 hard and fast:** unbreakable: *We have a hard and fast rule that no one may smoke in this office.* **7 hard as nails:** an uncompromising, demanding person: *That drill sergeant is as hard as nails.* **8 hard luck:** bad luck: *She had hard luck when she lost her job and then her house burned down.‖She told a hard luck story about her situation.* **9 hard of hearing:** deaf, a hearing loss: *The old man is hard of hearing.* **10 hard times:** when a person or an economy is not doing well: *Many people are jobless in these hard times.* **11 hard to take:** difficult to believe or accept: *The news of her death is very hard to take.* **12 hard up:** to be without money: *He lost everything in a flood and is hard up now.* **13 hard water:** water containing minerals **14 to be hard at it:** working: *He started fixing the roof this morning and has been hard at it all day.* **15 to be hard on: a.** to treat harshly or severely: *Don't be too hard on him; he didn't know any better.* **b.** to be especially difficult or unpleasant for: *The cold weather was hard on the elderly.* **16 to do things the hard way:** to make things more difficult than they need to be: *Why are you retyping your paper instead of just correcting your mistakes? Do you always do things the hard way?* **17 to drive a hard bargain:** to insist on an agreement that meets one's demands: *He always wants lower prices; he drives a hard bargain on everything he buys.* **18 to have hard feelings** or **no hard feelings:** anger, bad feelings, (*syn.*) resentment: *If you decide not to buy my product, I will have no hard feelings toward you.* **19 to play hard to get:** to refuse to respond to flirting or attention: *I have asked her for a date often, but she plays hard to get.* **20 to take a hard line:** to follow rules exactly: *The Congress wanted to increase spending, but the President took a hard line and said, "No."* **21 to take a hard look:** to examine closely and critically: *The top manager took a hard look at the company's budget to see where she could cut costs.*
—*adv.* **1** with much effort: *She works hard every day.* **2** with great force, a large amount: *It was snowing hard last night, and now there are 13 inches of snow on the ground.* **3 to be hard put:** not to know, to be unable to answer: *That question is difficult, and I am hard put to give you an answer.*

hard·ball /ˈhɑrdˌbɔl/ *n.* [U] **1** (in U.S. sports) baseball (versus softball) **2 to play hardball:** to act to destroy an opponent: *Our competitor is playing hardball by lowering his prices below ours and advertising widely.*

hard-bitten *adj.* tough, determined: *She is a hard-bitten fighter against crime.*

hard-boiled *adj.* **1** (said of eggs) cooked solid: *We take hard-boiled eggs on picnics.* **2** *fig.* tough, unsentimental: *He is a hard-boiled police officer.*

hard copy *n.* **copies** a printed copy of computerized or spoken material: *After I edited the report on my computer screen, I printed a hard copy of it.*

hard core *n.* [U] the dedicated people at the center of an activity: *The hard core of the politician's followers stayed with him even after he lost the election.*
—*adj.* **hardcore** /ˈhɑrdˌkɔr/ being the most basic or dedicated form or group, usu. refusing

change or improvement: *Hardcore rock fans won't listen to any other music.*

hard·cov·er /'hard,kʌvər/ *n.adj.* a book bound with a stiff cover: *<adj.> Hardcover books cost more than paperbacks but last longer.||I bought the <n.> hardcover.*

hard drive *n.* (in computers) a disk drive and disk that can store a lot of information

hard·en /'hardn/ *v.* **1** to make hard, firm: *To fix a broken vase, first use glue, then hold the vase together until the glue hardens.* **2** *phrasal v. insep.* **to harden s.o. to s.t.:** to toughen mentally: *Difficulties, like having little money, only hardened her desire to succeed. -n.* **hardener.**

hard hat *n.* **1** in USA, a helmet worn by construction workers to keep them from being hurt **2** *fig.* a construction worker —*adj.n.fig.* having conservative values, esp. patriotism: *<n.> Hard hats place an American flag atop skyscrapers after they finish building them.*

hard hat

hard·head·ed /'hard'hɛdɪd/ *adj.* tough-minded, (*syn.*) stubborn: *The boss is hard-headed about office policies; she will not change the rules for anyone. -n.* **hardhead** /'hard,hɛd/.

hard·heart·ed /'hard'hartɪd/ *adj.* without feelings of kindness, (*syns.*) insensitive, cruel: *He is a hardhearted man who won't even help his own parents.*

hard-hitting *adj.* very effective, forceful: *The journalist wrote a hard-hitting article against government bureaucracy.*

hard-line *adj.* following rules or dogma exactly: *She is a hard-line socialist from the old school. -n.* **hard-liner.**

hard·ly /'hardli/ *adv.* **1** almost no, (*syns.*) scarcely, barely: *We have hardly any money left.* **2** most certainly not: *He's so stupid; I hardly think I'll want to talk with him!*

hard·ness /'hardnɪs/ *n.* **1** firmness: *The hardness of oak wood makes it a good choice for floors.* **2** harshness, grimness: *The hardness of life in the desert is well known.*

hard-nosed /'hard,noʊzd/ *adj.* tough, resistant to pressure: *He is a hard-nosed police captain who allows no joking among his officers.*

hard rock *n.* [U] loud, driving rock music: *I prefer hard rock to soft rock. See:* rock and roll.

hard sell *n.* high-pressure salesmanship: *That car dealership gives everyone the hard sell by making you feel you've made a mistake if you don't buy a car.*

hard·ship /'hard,ʃɪp/ *n.* [C;U] difficulty related to one's living conditions: *He suffered financial hardship after he lost his job.*

hard·ware /'hard,wɛr/ *n.* [U] **1** tools and small building supplies (not wood): *He bought some hardware at a store.* **2** machines, esp. computer equipment: *That store sells computer hardware, such as PCs, printers, and modems. See:* software.

hard·wood /'hard,wʊd/ *n.* [U] *adj.* wood, such as oak, maple, or apple, with a hard surface and texture (versus softwoods like pine): *We have <adj.> hardwood oak floors in our house.*

hard-working *adj.* diligent, industrious: *She is a hard-working employee.*

har·dy /'hardi/ *adj.* **-dier, -diest** strong, able to survive bad weather, illness, etc., (*syn.*) robust: *New Englanders are a hardy people; their winters can be very cold. -n.* [U] **hardiness.**

hare /hɛr/ *n.* **hares** or **hare** an animal that is very similar to a rabbit, but larger: *Hares run rapidly through the fields.*

hare·brained /'hɛr,breɪnd/ *adj.* stupid, foolish: *He has these harebrained ideas for getting rich that always fail.*

hare·lip /'hɛr,lɪp/ *n.* a split upper lip: *The child was born with a birth defect, a harelip.*

har·em /'hɛrəm, 'hær-/ *n.* **1** (in Muslim culture) a part of a house reserved for women, where men are not allowed: *Traditional Muslim households have harems, where men cannot enter.* **2** (popular) a group of women associated with one man: *Romantic stories often involve adventure and harems.*

hark /hark/ *v.frml.* **1** to listen: *"Hark, I hear the sound of horses," shouted a castle guard.* **2** *phrasal v. insep.* **to hark back to s.t.:** to refer to things what happened in the past: *The priest's sermon harked back to biblical days.*

hark·en /'harkən/ *var. of* hearken

har·le·quin /'harləkwɪn, -kɪn/ *n.* a type of clown: *The harlequin is dressed in a costume with black diamond shapes on a white surface.*

har·lot /'harlət/ *n.* a woman who trades sex for money, (*syn.*) prostitute

harm /harm/ *n.* [U] hurt, (*syns.*) injury, damage: *No harm came to the girl as she crossed a busy highway.*
—*v.* to hurt, injure, or damage: *A speeding car could harm her.*

harm·ful /'harmfəl/ *adj.* causing hurt or damage: *Smoking cigarettes can be harmful to your health. -adv.* **harmfully.**

harm·less /'harmlɪs/ *adj.* not harmful, (*syn.*) benign: *Don't be afraid; that snake is harmless. -adv.* **harmlessly.**

har·mon·i·ca /har'manɪkə/ *n.* a musical instrument played with the mouth, (*syn.*) a mouth organ: *He plays the harmonica in a country band.*

har·mo·ni·ous /har'moυniəs/ *adj.* **1** (in music) having harmony: *That music is harmonious and pleasant to listen to.* **2** in agreement, working well together: *The departments within the company have a harmonious relationship.* *-adv.* **harmoniously.**

harmonica

har·mo·nize /'harmə,naιz/ *v.* **-nized, -nizing, -nizes 1** (in music) to play or sing in harmony: *Our school's choral group loves to harmonize.* **2** to blend together well: *She dresses beautifully and harmonizes her colors well.*

har·mo·ny /'harməni/ *n.* **-nies 1** [C;U] (in music) the art and science of relationships among musical sounds: *In her course in harmony, she learned how a Beethoven symphony works.* **2** [U] peaceful cooperation, *(syn.)* accord: *Harmony among the races exists throughout most of the great city.*

har·ness /'harnιs/ *n.* **-nesses** straps and a collar that horses and other animals wear to pull loads: *I put the harness on the horse so he can pull the wagon.*
—*v.* **1** to put a harness on an animal: *Napoleon's army harnessed horses to pull cannon and supplies.* **2** to capture the power of s.t.: *When we built a dam across the river, we harnessed the river's power to produce electricity.*

harp /harp/ *n.* a musical instrument with 46 strings going from top to bottom in a frame and played with the fingers: *She plays the harp in a symphony orchestra.*
—*phrasal v. insep.* **to harp on** or **about s.t.:** to talk about continually, in a way that annoys others: *He keeps harping on how much money he has lost.* *-n.* **harpist.**

har·poon /har'pun/ *n.v.* a type of spear thrown by hand or shot from a cannon to kill fish and whales: *A sailor threw a <n.> harpoon at a whale.||He <v.> harpooned it.*

harp·si·chord /'harpsι,kɔrd/ *n.* a musical instrument like a piano, whose strings are pulled rather than pushed

har·row /'hæroυ/ *n.* a farming tool with spikes used to make the ground smooth after it has been plowed
—*v.* to use a harrow: *The farmer harrowed his fields after he plowed them.*

har·row·ing /'hæroυιŋ/ *adj.* extremely upsetting: *We ran into a bad storm at sea, and it was a harrowing experience.*

har·ry /'hæri/ *v.* **-ried, -rying, -ries** to upset by constant attacks, *(syn.)* to harass: *Fighter planes harried ground troops with continuous attacks.* *-adj.* **harried.**

harsh /harʃ/ *adj.* **1** causing pain or irritation: *The soap is too harsh for my skin.* **2** severe: *Winter in the Arctic is harsh.||The punishment was too harsh for such a young child.* *-adv.* **harshly** *-n.* [U] **harshness.**

har·vest /'harvιst/ *v.* to gather crops: *We harvest corn in the early autumn.*
—*n.* the gathering of crops: *We picked hundreds of oranges in this year's harvest.* *-n.* **harvester.**

has /hæz; *weak form* əz, həz, z, s; *before "to"* hæs/ *v.* third person, present tense of *have*: *He has lots of money.*

has-been /'hæz,bιn/ *n.* a person who was, but is not now, successful: *He was a top manager in banking, but is a has-been now.*

hash /hæʃ/ *n.* [C;U] **1** chopped-up potatoes and meat, usu. beef: *I enjoy eating some corned beef hash once in a while.* **2** *infml.* the drug hashish **3** *fig.* **to make a hash of:** to make a situation complicated and messy: *He has made a hash of that project.*
—*v.infml.fig.* **-es 1** *phrasal v. sep.* **to hash s.t. over:** to discuss, talk about: *We sat down and hashed over what we need to do.||We hashed it over.* **2 to hash things out:** to discuss all sides of a problem until a solution is found: *We met for hours and finally hashed things out.*

hash browns *n.pl.* chopped, fried potatoes: *He likes fried eggs with hash browns for breakfast.*

hash·ish /hæ'ʃiʃ, 'hæ,ʃiʃ/ *n.* [U] a narcotic drug made from marijuana plants: *The authorities put her in jail for smoking hashish.*

has·sle /'hæsəl/ *n.infml.* an unpleasant task or chore that is harder than it should be: *Her car broke down in the country, and getting it fixed was a big hassle.*
—*v.* **-sled, -sling, -sles** to annoy, give s.o. a hard time: *An employee of the bank hassled me about correcting an error in my account.*

haste /heιst/ *n.* [U] **1** speed, *(syn.)* rapidity: *He left in haste to catch a train.* **2** the act of going too fast, *(syn.)* recklessness: *He made that decision in haste and now wishes he could change it.* **3** *frml.* **to make haste:** to move rapidly: *We have to make haste if we are going to catch the train.*

has·ten /'heιsən/ *v.* to move or act quickly: *His mother said she is ill, so he hastened to her house to help.*

hast·y /'heιsti/ *adj.* **-ier, -iest** too fast, done without thought, *(syn.)* reckless: *He made a hasty decision about investing his money and lost thousands of dollars.* *-adv.* **hastily.**

hat /hæt/ *n.* **1** a head covering: *He wears a warm hat in wintertime.* **2 to keep s.t. under one's hat:** to keep s.t. secret: *Keep this under your hat; don't tell the boss, but I am looking for a new job.* **3 to pass the hat:** to collect money: *When Sara left the company, we all* *passed the hat and collected some money for a going-away present.* **4 to take one's hat off:** to praise, admire: *I take my hat off to her; she has done a wonderful job.* **5 to talk through one's hat:** to speak in a stupid way: *He doesn't know what he's talking about; he's talking through his hat.* **6 to toss one's hat in the ring:** to enter a contest: *A local businessman tossed his hat in the ring to run for election.*

hatch /hætʃ/ *v.* **-es 1** (birds, chickens) to bring a bird's eggs to life by sitting on them: *The hen hatched three eggs this week.* **2** to come out of an egg: *Four chicks hatched yesterday.* **3** *fig.* to create, (*syn.*) to conceive (an idea): *He hatched a plan to get more business.*

—*n.* **-es** a door that opens by going up, esp. on boats: *A sailor opened a hatch and climbed onto the deck.*

hatch·back /'hætʃ,bæk/ *n.* a small car with a back door that swings up: *We bought a hatchback because it is so easy to put things in the back.*

hat·check /'hæt,tʃɛk/ *n.adj.* a room for coats in a restaurant or public hall: *I left my hat and coat at the <n.> hatcheck and sat down in the restaurant.‖The <adj.> hatcheck girl gave me a ticket for my coat.*

hatch·et /'hætʃɪt/ *n.* a small ax: *I use a hatchet to chop wood for the fire.*

hatch·way /'hætʃ,weɪ/ *n.* **1** an opening with a hatchdoor: *I opened the hatchway and climbed on deck.* **2** a passageway leading to a hatch

hate /heɪt/ *v.* **hated, hating, hates** to dislike strongly, (*syns.*) to detest, loathe: *The two peoples have hated each other since the war began.*

—*n.* [U] a feeling of strong dislike, (*syn.*) loathing: *Hate between two men can lead to murder.*

hate·ful /'heɪtfəl/ *adj.* causing strong dislike, (*syn.*) odious: *She has a hateful attitude toward anyone who disagrees with her.* *-adv.* **hatefully.**

hate·mon·ger /'heɪt,mɑŋgər, -,mʌŋ-/ *n.* a person who creates and spreads hate: *Hate-mongers are often racists, too.*

ha·tred /'heɪtrɪd/ *n.* [U] hate, (*syn.*) loathing: *The couple lived with feelings of hatred for many years before getting a divorce.*

haugh·ty /'hɔti/ *adj.* **-tier, -tiest** proud in a snobbish way, (*syn.*) arrogant: *That rich, haughty woman thinks she is better than everyone else.* *-n.* [U] **haughtiness** *-adv.* **haughtily.**

haul /hɔl/ *v.* to carry a load: *Trucks haul sand to build a new road.*

—*n.* distance: *It is a long haul between Chicago and San Francisco.*

haunch·es /'hɔntʃɪz, 'hɑn-/ *n.pl.* the buttocks of an animal: *The lion sat on its haunches and looked around.*

haunt /hɔnt, hɑnt/ *v.* **1** to visit in a ghostly form: *When a ghost haunts a house, strange things can happen.* **2** to think about continually and be bothered by continually: *He is haunted by his son's death.*

—*n.* a favorite place, hangout: *When she is home from college, she likes to visit her old haunts, such as restaurants and movie houses.* *-adj.* **haunted; haunting.**

haute cui·sine /,outkwɪ'zin/ *n.* [U] the very best cooking, esp. French: *That restaurant serves only haute cuisine.*

have /hæv; *weak form* əv, həv, v; *before "to"* hæf/ *v.* **had** /hæd; *weak form* əd, həd, d/, **having** /'hævɪŋ/, **has** /hæz; *weak form* əz, həz, z, s; *before "to"* hæs/ **1** to own, (*syn.*) to possess: *I have a new Ford car.* **2** to be sick with: *He has a bad cold.* **3** to experience: *We have fun on weekends.‖Our planners had a meeting on new products.* **4 a.** to hold as a thought: *She has an idea on how to solve the problem.* **b.** to hold as an emotion: *She has a lot of sadness about her mother's death.* **5** to allow, permit to happen: *I can't have a cat eating my plants!* **6** to cause s.t. to happen: *I had my house painted last year.* **7** to order, choose (usually food or drink): *I'll have the chocolate cake for dessert, please.* **8** to give birth: *She had a baby boy.* **9 had better:** must, ought to: *We had better get going, or we will be late.* **10 to be had:** to be cheated: *He bought some gold coins and then learned they are fake—he's been had.* **11** *infrml.fig.* **to have a ball:** to have a wonderful time: *We had a ball at the party.* **12 to have a feel for:** to have a good sense of: *The salesperson has a good feel for what customers like.* **13 to have a fit:** to be angry or lose control: *He had a fit when he heard the bad news.* **14 to have a gift for:** to have a natural ability for s.t.: *She has a gift for playing the piano.* **15 to have a go at:** to try s.t., take a turn: *I can't loosen this screw; you have a go at it.* **16 to have a heart:** to show pity or sympathy: *Have a heart; don't kill that little mouse!* **17 to have a knack for:** to have a special ability: *He has a knack for fixing things around the house.* **18 to have all one's marbles** or **buttons:** to function well mentally: *He may be old, but he still has all his marbles.* **19 to have an eye for: a.** to have a special visual ability: *The artist has an eye for color.* **b.** to enjoy the good looks of members of the opposite sex, esp. a man for women: *He has an eye for the ladies.* **20 to have an eye on: a.** to watch, observe: *I have an eye on that guy to be sure he doesn't cause trouble.* **b.** to desire: *I have my eye on a great pair of shoes at the shoe store.* **21** *phrasal v. insep.* **to have**

at s.o. or s.t.: to attack physically or verbally: *He made a big mistake, and his boss really had at him for it.*‖*When I asked if I could help clean the kitchen, he said, "Have at it!"* **22 to have a way with:** to get along well with: *She has a way with animals.* **23 to have done with:** to finish, esp. s.t. unpleasant: *This project has taken too long, so let's have done with it and move on.* **24 to have had it:** to have reached one's limit, to be disgusted: *I have had it with this old car breaking down all the time!* **25 to have had one's day** or **have seen better days:** to be worse now than before: *She used to be a great lawyer, but she's had her day (or she has seen better days).* **26 to have it:** to possess talent, ability, etc.: *She sings beautifully; she really has it!* **27 to have it coming:** to deserve punishment: *He is mean to everyone, so when that guy hit him, he had it coming.* **28 to have it in for:** to wish to harm s.o.: *Ever since I was robbed, I've had it in for the guy who robbed me.* **29 to have it made:** to be in a good financial situation: *He has it made; he just sold his business for a million dollars and retired.* **30 to have it out with s.o.:** to discuss or argue until agreement is reached: *He says the job must be done his way, but he's wrong—I am going to have it out with him.* **31 to have it your (his, her, etc.) way** or **to have your way:** to get what one wants: *I want to vacation in Spain, but have it your way; we will go to Paris, instead.* **32** *fig.* **to have kittens:** to become upset, panic: *She had kittens when she found out her house was robbed.* **33 to have on: a.** to wear: *He has on a ski jacket and ski boots.* **b.** to have plans for: *What do you have on this evening? I have a party with friends on tonight.* **34 to have one's day in court:** to have one's chance to appear before a judge: *Even a thief should have his day in court.* **35 to have s.t. going: a.** to be close to making a business deal: *He has s.t. going now; two people made offers to buy his house.* **b.** to have a love affair: *The two of them have s.t. going.* **36 to have s.t.** or **be on the ball:** to be intelligent, hard-working: *He's a smart kid and has a lot on the ball.* **37** *phrasal v. sep.* **to have s.t. out (with s.o.): a.** to remove s.t., usu. through surgery: *He had out his appendix last week.*‖*He had it out.* **b.** to resolve a problem, etc. by discussing it openly, often angrily: *She and her roommate had out their disagreement about cleaning.*‖*She had it out.* **38 to have the last laugh:** to win at the end of a struggle: *Her boss gave her a hard time day after day, but she had the last laugh when she found a better job and left.* **39 to have things well in hand:** to have things under control: *She is new on the job, but already has things well in hand.* **40 to have to:** to be required to: *I have to pay the rent on the first of the month.* **41 to have it to do with:** to be about: *That letter has to do with the*

new rental agreement. **42 to have to go:** to need to urinate: *I have to go, or I'll wet my pants.* **43** *infrml.* **to let s.o. have it:** to attack s.o. physically or with words: *I was so angry with him that I wanted to let him have it.* —*auxiliary verb* **1** auxiliary verb used with a past participle to show completed action: *She has learned an important lesson today.* **2 to have been around: a.** to have existed for a long time: *That old chair has been around for many years.* **b.** *fig.* to have experienced a lot in life: *He has been around; he was a truck driver, then a carpenter, and now he's a salesman.*

ha·ven /'heɪvən/ *n.* a place of safety, such as a harbor: *A ship sought a haven from the storm.*

have-not *n.* **1** a person with little or no money **2** *pl.* the poor as a social class: *The have-nots usually vote for the Democrats.*

haves /hævz/ *n.pl.* people with money, the wealthy: *The new government gives to the haves and forgets the poor.*

hav·oc /'hævək/ *n.* [U] **1** general destruction: **2 to wreak havoc:** to cause destruction: *The hurricane wreaked havoc in central Florida.*

haw /hɔ/ *v.* **to hem and haw** *See:* hem, *v.,* **4.**

hawk /hɔk/ *n.* **1** a large bird that hunts animals and birds: *Hawks fly overhead looking for rabbits to catch and eat.* **2** *fig.* a person in favor of military action: *This President is a hawk who believes in using force.* —*v.* to sell, esp. by loud presentation: *To make a living, she hawks jewelry in the street, by shouting, "Bargains, check it out!"* -*n.* **hawker.**

hawk

hawk-eyed /'hɔk,aɪd/ *adj.* able to see at a great distance: *That hunter is hawk-eyed; he can see a deer from a mile away.*

hay /heɪ/ *n.* [U] **1** grass cut and dried for animal food, (*syn.*) fodder: *The horses have plenty of hay to eat this winter.* **2** *infrml.fig.* a small amount of money: *He won $10,000 in the Lotto, and that's not hay!* **3 make hay while the sun shines:** get as much as possible from a good opportunity: *The newspaper just advertised her new products, and she is looking for new customers. She is making hay while the sun shines.*

hay fever *n.* [U] reaction to some trees and flowers, consisting of sneezing and a runny nose: *She has hay fever, and her nose won't stop running.*

hay·stack /'heɪ,stæk/ *n.* a pile of hay: *After mowing the hay, the farmer piled it into haystacks.*

hay·wire /'heɪ,waɪr/ *adj.infrml.fig.* **to go haywire:** to go wrong, badly: *A power outage caused all our computers to go haywire.*

haz·ard /'hæzərd/ *n.* a danger: *A road under construction is full of hazards to drivers.*
—*v.* **to hazard a guess:** to give an opinion that is not based on facts, (*syn.*) to venture: *I hazard a guess that he's right this time.* -*adj.* **hazardous.**

haze /heɪz/ *n.* [C;U] a condition in the air similar to light fog, caused by water, dust, or smoke: *There is always a blue haze on the Virginia mountains.*
—*v.* **hazed, hazing, hazes** to make fun of, embarrass, or hurt people when they join a club or fraternity: *At our school it is illegal to haze freshmen.* -*n.* [C;U] **hazing.**

ha·zel /'heɪzəl/ *n.* a small tree that produces edible nuts called hazelnuts
—*adj.* light brown or greenish brown in color: *She has lovely hazel eyes.*

haz·y /'heɪzi/ *adj.* **-ier, -iest 1** filled with haze: *The air in Los Angeles is nearly always hazy with smog.* **2** vague, unclear: *His memory is hazy about the details of the accident.*

H-bomb /'eɪtʃ,bɑm/ *n.* the hydrogen bomb: *The H-bomb is a powerful weapon.*

he /hi; *weak form* i/ *pron.* third-person singular masculine: *Do you know Antonio? Yes, he and I went to school together. See:* who, USAGE NOTE.

head /hɛd/ *n.* **1** [C] the part of the body that contains the face, ears, hair, skull, and brain: *That boy shaved his head.* **2** [C] the place where thinking happens, (*syn.*) the mind: *I can't seem to get this idea out of my head.* **3** [C] ability: *She has a good head for numbers.* **4** [C] intelligence: *She used her head in solving that difficult problem.* **5** [C] leader, chief: *She is the head of the finance committee.*||*The heads of state met to discuss the peace plan.* **6** [U] the position at the beginning, top, or front: *He is standing at the head of the line.*||*She is at the head of her class.* **7** [U] each person: *The entrance fee is $10.00 per head.* **8** [U] foam on beer: *German beer produces a thick head.* **9 head and shoulders above:** much better than: *He is head and shoulders above the other students.* **10 head over heels: a.** to fall down: *He fell head over heels down the stairs.* **b.** *fig.* to fall in love: *He fell head over heels in love with her.* **11 heads or tails:** the side of a coin showing a person's face and head, as opposed to the other side: *Which do you choose, heads or tails?* **12 Heads up!** Watch out!: *Heads up; I'm coming through with boiling hot water!* **13 not to make head or tail of** or **out of:** not to be able to figure out, comprehend: *This map is so confusing that I can't make head or tail of where we are.* **14 over one's head:** beyond one's abilities: *That project is too technical for him; it's over his head.* **15 to come to a head:** to reach a critical point, require action: *He has not paid his rent, and things have come to a head; his landlord is evicting him.* **16** *fig.* **to give s.o. his or her head:** to give s.o. freedom to act: *He has acted responsibly, and it is time to give him his head to run the business on his own.* **17 to go to one's head: a.** to make s.o. drunk, intoxicated: *The beer has gone to his head.* **b.** to cause s.o. to become overly proud or arrogant: *His promotion has gone to his head; now he thinks he's better than everyone else.* **18 to have a good head on one's shoulders:** to act intelligently: *Many smart people do stupid things, but this girl has a good head on her shoulders.* **19 to keep one's head:** to stay calm: *The doctor keeps her head in an emergency.* **20** *fig.infrml.* **to lose one's head:** to act irrationally, recklessly: *He lost his head and started a fight.*
—*adj.* first or most important: *She is sitting at the head table next to the head man.*
—*v.* **1** to lead, be in charge of: *My father heads a large corporation.* **2** to move in a certain direction: *Let's head for home (Canada, port, etc.).*||*Our ship is headed west.* **3** to move toward a condition or result: *That fellow is headed for trouble.*||*She is a great swimmer and is headed for victory.* **4** *phrasal v. insep.* **to head for s.t.:** to go in the direction of: *Instead of going to the beach, we headed for the mountains.* **5** *phrasal v. sep.* **to head s.o.** or **s.t. off: a.** to leave: *I have to head off now and will see you tomorrow.* **b.** to prevent: *He headed off financial trouble by selling his stocks before the crash.*||*He headed it off.*

head·ache /'hɛd,eɪk/ *n.* **1** a pain in the head: *I have a headache and need to lie down.* **2** a difficult problem: *Fixing the roof is a real headache.*

USAGE NOTE: A *headache* is a common physical complaint. Others are *stomachache, sore throat, stuffy nose,* and *a temperature.* (Everyone has a body temperature, but Americans say, *"He has a temperature,"* when they mean, *"He has a fever."*) None of these ailments is serious in itself, but may suggest another illness: *"My son has a stomachache and a temperature, so I'm keeping him home from school today."*

head·band /'hɛd,bænd/ *n.* a piece of cloth wrapped around one's head: *That tennis player wears a headband to keep sweat out of her eyes.*

headband

head count *n.* the number of people in a group: *The sergeant called the soldiers by name to get a head count of those present.*

head·first /'hɛd'fɜrst/ *adv.* with the head leading the body's movement: *He dove headfirst into the water.*

head·gear /'hɛd,gɪr/ *n.* [C;U] helmets, hats, and other items worn on the head: *Motorcyclists are required to wear headgear to protect themselves.*

head·hunt·er /'hɛd,hʌntər/ *n.* [C] **1** a person who hunts other humans and keeps their heads **2** *fig.infrml.* a person who tries to find good jobs for well-qualified people, (*syn.*) an executive search firm: *The headhunter offered the banker a better job at a different bank.* *-n.* [U] **headhunting.**

head·ing /'hɛdɪŋ/ *n.* **1** [C] the words used to summarize writing, (*syn.*) title: *I can't think of a heading for this page.* **2** [U] a direction: *The ship is on a northeast heading.*

head·land /'hɛdlənd/ *n.* a high, narrow point of land overlooking the sea: *From our ship the headland appeared on the horizon.*

head·light /'hɛd,laɪt/ *n.* a light used for night driving on cars or other vehicles: *The headlights of the cars are very bright.*

head·line /'hɛd,laɪn/ *n.* the title of a news article, esp. a title printed in large type on the front page: *The headline in today's* Times *says "Peace declared!"*

head·lock /'hɛd,lɑk/ *n.* in wrestling, a hold in which one wrestler's arm is locked around the other's head: *He got his opponent in a headlock and threw him to the mat.*

head·long /'hɛd,lɔŋ/ *adv.* **1** headfirst: *He fell headlong down the stairs.* **2** without thought: *She jumped headlong into the project without stopping to think about its high cost.*

head·mas·ter /'hɛd,mæstər, -'mæs-/ *n.* the male principal of a private school: *The headmaster of our prep school comes from a wealthy family.*

head·mis·tress /'hɛd,mɪstrɪs, -'mɪs-/ *n.* the female principal of a private school: *Our headmistress spoke at the graduation ceremony.*

head-on *adv.* with the front parts meeting or hitting: *One car drove head-on into another.* —*adj.* front-to-front: *It was a terrible head-on collision.*

h e a d · p h o n e s /'hɛd,foʊnz/ *n.pl.* two earphones connected over the top of the head with a band, (*syn.*) a headset: *Radio personalities wear headphones while they are on the air.*

headphones

head·quar·ters /'hɛd,kwɔrtərz/ *n.pl.* used with a *sing.* or *pl. v.* **1** a military commander's office: *The military*

headquarters is near the airfield. **2** a central place for an activity: *My office is the headquarters for our company's work on that project.*

head·rest /'hɛd,rɛst/ *n.* the part of a chair or seat that the head rests upon: *She put her head on the headrest, and the dentist cleaned her teeth.*

head·room /'hɛd,rum/ *n.* [U] (in vehicles) the space between an occupant's head and the inside roof: *Some small cars don't have enough headroom for tall people.*

head·set /'hɛd,sɛt/ *n.* two earphones connected by a band, (*syn.*) headphones: *I wore a headset to listen to music.*

head start *n.* **1** an advantage over a competitor or an opponent: *She gave her younger brother a head start in the race.* **2 Head Start:** in USA, a government program for young children: *Head Start has helped many inner city children with early education.*

head·stone /'hɛd,stoʊn/ *n.* a marker for a grave in a cemetery, a gravestone: *Carved on his headstone is "Rest in Peace."*

head·strong /'hɛd,strɔŋ/ *adj.* stubborn, willful: *The boy is headstrong and won't obey his mother.*

heads-up *adj.infrml.* alert, quick acting (from sports): *She made a great catch; what a heads-up ball player.*

head-to-head *adj.* **1** knocking heads: *The two football players are going at each other head-to-head.* **2** direct, (*syn.*) confrontational: *The two politicians are in an intense head-to-head campaign.*

head·wait·er /'hɛd'weɪtər, -,weɪ-/ *n.* the waiter in charge in a restaurant's dining room: *The headwaiter showed us to a cozy table in the corner.* *-n.* **headwaitress** /'hɛd'weɪtrɪs, -,weɪ-/.

head·wa·ters /'hɛd,wɔtərz, -,wɑ-/ *n.pl.* the place where a river begins: *Finding the headwaters of the Nile was a great discovery.*

head·way /'hɛd,weɪ/ *n.* [U] **1** forward movement **2** *fig.* **to make headway:** to progress: *We are making headway in building a new factory.*

head wind *n.* a wind blowing against the direction s.o. or s.t. is moving: *The head wind was so strong that our boat had difficulty sailing against it.*

head·y /'hɛdi/ *adj.* **-ier, -iest** thrilling, exciting: *Winning the championship is a heady experience.*

heal /hil/ *v.* **1** to cure, restore s.o.'s health: *A doctor heals patients.* **2** to become healthy, recover, (*syn.*) to recuperate: *The soldier's wounds gradually healed.* *-n.* **healer.**

health /hɛlθ/ *n.* [U] the condition of a living thing's body and mind: *Although she is 84 years old, my mother is in good health.*

—*adj.* related to well-being: *The drugstore has hundreds of health and beauty products.*

health care *n.* [U] medical care: *Health care in the USA is very expensive. See:* health maintenance organization.

health club *n.* a place where people pay to exercise: *I belong to a health club that has weight machines and two locker rooms.*

health food *n.* [U] natural and specially prepared foods, consumed to improve health

health·ful /'hɛlθfəl/ *adj.* good for the health, wholesome: *Walking and swimming are healthful activities.* -*adv.* **healthfully.**

health maintenance organization *n.* a business that provides a wide range of medical care by doctors, nurses, and others to people who pay a monthly or yearly fee: *Our company pays for medical insurance at a health maintenance organization.* -*abbr.* **HMO.** *See:* health care.

health·y /'hɛlθi/ *adj.* **-ier, -iest** in good health: *His wife had a healthy baby boy.*

heap /hip/ *n.* a pile of s.t., (*syn.*) a mound: *The garbage dump contains heaps of trash.*
—*v.* to pile up: *The party guests heaped gifts on the table.*

hear /hɪr/ *v.* **heard** /hɜrd/, **hearing, hears 1** to receive sound with the ears: *I hear the sound of traffic on the street.* **2** *infrml.* to understand s.o.'s meaning: *I hear what you are saying, but I disagree.* **3** *phrasal v. insep.* **to hear about s.o. or s.t.:** to learn about, become acquainted with: *He was surprised when he heard about my promotion.* **4** *phrasal v. insep.* **to hear from s.o.:** to have news from s.o.: *She heard from her parents this morning.* **5** *phrasal v. insep.* **to hear of s.o. or s.t.:** to know about s.o. or s.t.: *I've never heard of Grand Island before.* **6** *phrasal v. sep.* **to hear s.o. out:** to listen to what s.o. says from beginning to end: *She was very angry, but she agreed to hear out our side of things.‖She heard us out. See:* listen, USAGE NOTE.

hear·ing /'hɪrɪŋ/ *n.* **1** [U] the sense of receiving sound through the ears: *His hearing is not good; he's becoming deaf.* **2** [C] a discussion of a subject, usu. in a formal, public setting: *a hearing on proposed tax increases* **3** [C] a legal session: *The lawyers asked the witness questions during the hearing.*

hearing aid *n.* a very small machine placed in or near the ear to make sound louder: *Since she wears a hearing aid, my grandmother can hear the phone ring in another room.*

hearing aid

hearing-impaired *adj.n.*
1 having a reduced sense of hearing, but not deaf: *Jonah has a very hard time understand-

ing me when I speak; he's <adj.> hearing-impaired.* **2** unable to hear, (*syn.*) deaf: *My mother works as a sign-language interpreter for the <n.> hearing-impaired.*

hear·say /'hɪr,seɪ/ *n.* [U] information heard from s.o. else: *My neighbor said he heard that the burglar drove a blue car, but that is just hearsay.*

hearse /hɜrs/ *n.* the funeral car carrying a dead person: *The black hearse entered the cemetery.*

heart /hɑrt/ *n.* **1** [C] the organ in the chest that pumps blood through the body: *He has a weak heart and must not exercise too hard.* **2** [C;U] kindness, goodness: *She has a kind heart; she helps the poor.* **3** [U] courage, (*syn.*) fortitude: *You must have the heart to overcome difficult situations.* **4** [C;U] the important or central issue: *Let's avoid the minor topics and get to the heart of the matter.* **5** *pl.* a card game **6** [C] one of the four suits of playing cards: *I had three clubs and two spades but no diamonds or hearts.* **7** [C] one's deepest feelings: *He knew in his heart that he was wrong.* **8 a light** or **heavy heart:** happy or sad: *When she heard the good news, she left with a light heart.‖He has a heavy heart after learning of his friend's death.* **9 by heart:** by memory: *She learned the names of all 50 states by heart.* **10 from the heart:** from one's deepest emotions: *She spoke from the heart, but her argument was still logical.* **11 heart and soul:** with total belief, dedication: *She believes heart and soul in her artistic career.* **12 heart of gold:** great human warmth, generosity: *He gives money to poor people; he has a heart of gold.* **13 in one's heart of hearts:** from one's deepest beliefs and desires: *In her heart of hearts, she does not love him enough to marry him.* **14 one's heart goes out to s.o.:** to sympathize deeply with s.o.: *I am so sorry your husband died; my heart goes out to you.* **15 to have a heart:** have compassion, be kind: *Try to have a heart and forgive the impolite child.* **16 to have one's heart in the right place:** to be well-intentioned, decent: *He has rough manners, but his heart is in the right place.* **17 to lose heart:** to become discouraged: *His job became so boring that he lost heart and stopped trying.* **18 to one's heart's content:** as much as one likes: *He is retired now and plays golf to his heart's content.* **19 with all one's heart:** totally, in all sincerity: *With all my heart, I hope you believe me.*

heart·ache /'hɑrt,eɪk/ *n.* [U] sorrow, grief: *They felt such heartache when their daughter ran away.*

heart attack *n.* a heart seizure, (*syn.*) infarction: *He had a mild heart attack but won't need an operation.*

heart·beat /'hɑrt,bit/ *n.* [C;U] the action of the heart: *Her strong heartbeat sounded like "thump, thump" in her chest.*

heart·break /'hɑrt,breɪk/ n. [U] a great disappointment or sorrow: *Their child's death is a heartbreak for them.*

heart·bro·ken /'hɑrt,broʊkən/ adj. emotionally hurt, (syns.) devastated, brokenhearted: *The couple was heartbroken over their dog's death.*

heart·burn /'hɑrt,bɜrn/ n. [U] pain in the chest caused by acid in the stomach, (syn.) indigestion: *Every time he eats spicy food, he later has heartburn.*

heart·en /'hɑrtn/ v. to encourage, to make optimistic: *He was heartened by the good test results.*

heart·felt /'hɑrt,fɛlt/ adj. very sincere, true: *She made a heartfelt apology for her mistake.*

hearth /hɑrθ/ n. 1 a fireplace, esp. used for cooking: *The hearth glowed red from the wood fire.* 2 symbol for the pleasures of daily life: *Away at sea for months, the sailor missed hearth and home.*

heart·i·ly /'hɑrtəli/ adv. strongly, (syn.) earnestly: *I heartily agree with what you say.*

heart·land /'hɑrt,lænd/ n. the part of a country that represents its basic values, typical image, and usu. food production: *The USA's Middle West is the heartland of the country.*

heart·less /'hɑrtlɪs/ adj. unfeeling, cruel: *He is heartless in that he will not talk to his own parents.*

heart-rending adj. causing distress, sadness: *The death of their child is a heart-rending tragedy.*

heart·sick /'hɑrt,sɪk/ adj. very saddened, feeling great pain: *She was heartsick over the death of her husband.*

heart·throb /'hɑrt,θrɑb/ n.fig. s.o. one loves romantically, (syn.) an idol: *Elvis Presley was the heartthrob of millions of people.*

heart-to-heart adj.n. telling one's true feelings, honest: *My boss and I had a <adj.> heart-to-heart talk, and I told him that I'm leaving the company for a better-paying job.*

heart·warm·ing /'hɑrt,wɔrmɪŋ/ adj. causing good feelings, (syn.) gratifying: *The whole family was together for Thanksgiving dinner, and the gathering was heartwarming.*

heart·y /'hɑrti/ adj. -ier, -iest 1 large, plentiful: *We ate a hearty breakfast before starting the trip.* 2 with feeling, warm: *Our friends gave us a hearty welcome when we arrived.*

heat /hit/ n. [U] 1 warmth, high temperature: *The heat from the fire is intense.* 2 intense, busy activity: *In the heat of battle, soldiers fight for their lives.* 3 (of female animals) ovulation: *The dog is in heat; she is ready to become pregnant.* 4 slang the authorities, the police: *The heat is on; the cops are after us.* 5 a stage of an athletic competition to reduce the number of people in the next round: *He*

didn't do well in this heat, so he won't go on in the bicycle race. 6 **dead heat:** a tie, a race with no single winner 7 **If you can't stand the heat, stay out of the kitchen:** If you cannot deal with problems (pressure, criticism, etc.), then do not become involved. 8 **to give** or **throw off heat:** to send out heat: *The fireplace gives off lots of heat.||That engine throws off a lot of heat.* 9 infrml. **to give s.o. heat:** to criticize, pressure, or threaten: *My boss is giving me heat about high expenses.* 10 **to take** or **stand the heat: a.** to be comfortable in high temperatures in the weather: *It is so hot outside that I can't take the heat.* **b.** infrml.fig. to get criticism (disapproval, threats, etc.): *I am taking the heat from the company president over a mistake one of my workers made.*
—v. 1 to warm, raise the temperature: *We heat our house with an oil burner.* 2 phrasal v. sep. **to heat s.t. up: a.** to warm up, reheat: *I'll heat up some coffee for you.||I'll heat it up.* **b.** to increase in temperature: *It was cool outside this morning, but now it is heating up.*

heat·ed /'hitɪd/ adj. 1 warmed: *That empty house is not heated in the winter.* 2 intense: *Two men are having a heated argument.* -adv. **heatedly.**

heat·er /'hitər/ n. a machine that produces warmth: *In winter, we use electric space heaters under our desks.*

heath /hiθ/ n. open fields with small plants: *Hikers love to walk on the heaths of Scotland.*

hea·then /'hiðən/ n. **-thens** or **-then** a person not believing in one's religion, (syn.) a pagan: *The missionaries thought that the natives were heathens because they did not believe in Christianity.*
—adj. pagan: *The missionaries criticized the heathen religious ceremonies.*

heath·er /'hɛðər/ n. [U] a wild, short plant with pink flowers: *When the heather is in bloom in Ireland, it's a beautiful sight.*

heat wave n. a period of unusually hot weather: *Last August we had a heat wave of ten days when temperatures were above 90°.*

heave /hiv/ v. **heaved, heaving, heaves** 1 to lift or throw with great effort: *Two strong men heaved a big rock onto a truck.* 2 slang to vomit, (syn.) to retch: *He was sick and went to the bathroom and heaved.* 3 phrasal v. **to heave to:** (of ships) to stop moving: *The yacht hove to at the harbor entrance.*
—n. 1 a lift, a hurl: *They gave the rock a heave over the cliff.* 2 slang the act of retching

heave-ho /'hiv'hoʊ/ n.infrml. dismissal, ejection: *The nightclub bouncer gave a drunk customer the heave-ho.*

heav·en /'hɛvən/ n. 1 [U] (in some religions) the place of God, angels, and the souls of dead people who have been given eternal life: *The woman died and went to heaven.* 2 [U] s.t.

wonderful: *Our vacation in the mountains was heaven.* **3** *pl.* the sky above the earth: *Astronomers watch the heavens for new stars.* **4 Good Heavens!** or **Heavens to Betsy!:** expression of surprise: *Good heavens! Those children make a lot of noise!* **5 Thank heaven:** Thank God or good fortune: *Thank heaven you haven't left yet.*

heav·en·ly /'hɛvənli/ *adj.* **1** related to God's home **2** wonderful: *The weather during our vacation was heavenly.*

heav·i·ly /'hɛvəli/ *adv.* very seriously, in a large amount: *His business is heavily in debt.‖She drank heavily, but has stopped.‖This part of the city is heavily populated during the day.*

heav·y /'hɛvi/ *adj.* **-ier, -iest 1** having a lot of weight: *The rock is very heavy.* **2** fat, overweight: *He eats too much and has become heavy.* **3** *infrml.* dealing with a serious topic: *We had a heavy discussion about our relationship.* **4** of a large amount: *He's a heavy smoker and drinker.‖There is always heavy traffic in the morning in my town.* -*n.* [U] **heaviness.**

heavy-duty *adj.* **1** strong, durable: *He has heavy-duty tires on his truck.* **2** *slang* serious, impressive: *The lawyers working on the case are heavy-duty.*

heavy-handed *adj.* unkind, insensitive, (*syn.*) overbearing: *She gave orders to people in a heavy-handed manner.*

heavy metal *n.* [U] *adj.* loud rock music: *The words to most <adj.> heavy metal rock groups are hard to understand. See:* rock and roll.

heav·y·weight /'hɛvi,weɪt/ *n.adj.* **1** (in boxing) the heaviest of the classes of weight, at 175 pounds (80 kilos) or more: *Joe Louis was a great <n.> heavyweight, and he was <adj.> heavyweight champion of the world.* **2** *fig.* a person with a lot of knowledge and power: *He is a <n.> heavyweight in the banking business.*

heck /hɛk/ *exclam.* mild expression of dismay: *Ah, heck, I forgot my keys!*

heck·le /'hɛkəl/ *v.* **-led, -ling, -les** to interrupt a public speech by s.o., (*syn.*) to jeer at: *Two protesters heckled the speaker at a political demonstration.* -*n.* **heckler.**

hec·tic /'hɛktɪk/ *adj.* rushed, fast-paced, (*syn.*) frenzied: *I had a very hectic week; I worked late every night, and my child was sick.*

hec·tor /'hɛktər/ *v.frml.* to harass, bully, (*syn.*) to badger: *The mayor was hectored by her critics.*

hedge /hɛʤ/ *n.* **1** a row of bushes, shrubs: *The hedge in front of the house keeps out the sun.* **2** a protection or defense: *Buying real estate is a hedge against bad times.*

—*v.* **hedged, hedging, hedges 1** to withhold information, evade, (*syn.*) to equivocate: *He hedged when asked his opinion about who should be elected President.* **2** (in business) to invest money in various ways to avoid the financial risk of only one investment **3 to hedge one's bets:** (in stock market, gambling, etc.) to take action to prevent a loss: *He hedged his bets by taking two jobs in case one didn't work out well.*

hedge·hog /'hɛʤ,hɔg, -,hɑg/ *n.* a small insect-eating animal covered with sharp hairs: *Hedgehogs make tunnels near fields.*

he·do·nism /'hidn,ɪzəm/ *n.* [U] the placing of great importance on seeking pleasure, (*syn.*) self-indulgence: *Hedonism is a way of life for many people.* -*n.* [C] **hedonist;** -*adj.* **hedonistic** /,hidn'ɪstɪk./.

heed /hid/ *v.* to follow the advice of s.o., obey: *I heeded my doctor's advice and stopped smoking.*
—*n.* **to pay heed:** to give attention: *I paid heed to his advice.*

heed·less /'hidlɪs/ *adj.* not paying attention, reckless

heel /hil/ *n.* **1** the rounded back part of the foot: *My heels hurt from walking so far.* **2** the bottom back part of a shoe or boot: *The heels on my shoes are worn down.* **3** *s.t.* similar to the heel of the foot: *I pushed the door with the heel of my hand.* **4** *infrml.fig.* a bad man, (*syn.*) a scoundrel: *He's a heel who can't be trusted with anything.* **5 (close) on the heels of:** quickly, right after: *The police followed close on the heels of the criminal.* **6 down at the heels:** to look shabby, have hard luck: *Since he lost his job, he looks down at the heels.* **7** *fig.* **to cool one's heels:** to wait for a long time: *I had to cool my heels in the doctor's office while she took care of an emergency patient.* **8** *fig.* **to fall head over heels in love:** to fall suddenly and deeply in love: *He met her just once and fell head over heels in love.* **9 to kick up one's heels:** to dance, have fun: *She went to a party and kicked up her heels.*
—*v.* **1** to put a new heel on a shoe or boot: *I had my shoes heeled.* **2 well-heeled:** to be well dressed, wealthy

heft /hɛft/ *n.* weight, bulk: *Those sacks have a lot of heft.*
—*v.* **1** to check the weight of by lifting: *He hefted a sack of wheat to see how heavy it was.* **2** to lift: *He hefted it onto the truck.* -*adj.* **hefty.**

he·gem·o·ny /hɪ'ʤɛməni, 'hɛʤə,mouni/ *n.* [U] rule, area of influence: *Former colonies lived under the hegemony of Great Britain for more than a century.*

heifer /'hɛfər/ *n.* a young female cow that has not had a calf

height /haɪt/ *n.* **1** [C;U] vertical measurement: *The building has a height of six stories (of 60", approx. 19 meters, etc.).*||*The space capsule flies at a height of 200 miles (320 km) above the earth.* **2** [C] the top, (*syn.*) the apex: *She is at the height of her career in law.* **3** *sing.*the ultimate, extreme: *That action is the height of stupidity.* **4 heights:** (in geography) high points, such as cliffs or hills: *The heights above the city provide a beautiful view.*

height·en /ˈhaɪtn/ *v.* to increase, intensify: *The storyteller heightened the suspense in the mystery story.*||*Workers heightened the building by adding two stories on top of it.*

Heim·lich maneuver /ˈhaɪmlɪk/ *n.* a technique to clear s.t. blocking a person's windpipe by a sharp upward movement into the abdomen: *The dinner guest was choking, and a waiter did the Heimlich maneuver and saved him.*

hei·nous /ˈheɪnəs/ *adj.* bad, wicked, monstrous: *A madman committed a heinous crime when he killed four people in a restaurant.*

heir /ɛr/ *n.* the person legally in line to receive property (or title of nobility) when s.o. dies: *John D. Rockefeller's sons were heirs to a great fortune.*||*Prince William is heir to the British throne.*

heir·ess /ˈɛrɪs/ *n.* a female heir

heir apparent *n.* **heirs apparent 1** the child first in line to become king or queen: *The Prince of Wales is the heir apparent to the British throne.* **2** a person in business most likely to replace the president or CEO: *The company owner's son-in-law is his heir apparent.*

heir·loom /ˈɛr,lum/ *n.* an object of real or sentimental value passed from one generation to another: *The silver tea set is a family heirloom.*

heist /haɪst/ *n.slang* a robbery or holdup
—*v.* to steal at gunpoint, hold up: *Thieves heisted the jewels from the shop.*

held /hɛld/ *past tense & part. of* hold

hel·i·cop·ter /ˈhɛli,kɑptər/ *n.* an aircraft with one or two motorized blades on its top: *A police helicopter rescued passengers on a sinking boat.*

hel·i·port /ˈhɛlə,pɔrt/ *n.* a landing place or airport for helicopters

helicopter

he·li·um /ˈhiliəm/ *n.* [U] a gaseous element lighter than air: *We filled balloons with helium and watched them fly into the sky.*

he·lix /ˈhilɪks/ *n.* **helices** /ˈhɛlə,siz/ or **helixes** a three-dimensional object in the shape of a spiral: *DNA is called "the double helix" because of its shape.*

hell /hɛl/ *n.* [U] **1** (in religion) the place where the souls of bad people are sent to after death **2** *infrml.fig.* a place of suffering or misery: *It was hell working for my old boss because he often lost his temper and shouted at workers.* **3** expression of anger and disgust: *Oh, hell! I lost my watch!* **4** *infrml.* **Come hell or high water:** No matter what happens: *Come hell or high water, he is going to climb Mt. Everest!* **5 for the hell of it:** for no reason, for fun: *I didn't need anything; I just went shopping for the hell of it.* **6** *infrml.* **Go to hell!:** Leave me alone! Go away! **7** *infrml.* **hell-on-wheels:** unstoppable, awesome: *He is a terrific football player; he's hell-on-wheels.* **8** *infrml.* **like a bat out of hell:** very quickly: *When the fire started, he ran like a bat out of hell.* **9** *infrml.* **like hell: a.** very quickly: *When the shooting started, I ran like hell.* **b.** absolutely not: *Like hell I'm going to pay you!* **10** *infrml.* **snowball's chance in hell:** no chance of success: *She doesn't have a snowball's chance in hell of passing that math exam she didn't study for.* **11** *infrml.fig.* **to catch or get hell:** to be punished, reprimanded: *If you come home late, you will catch hell from your mother.* **12** *infrml.* **to give s.o. hell: a.** to criticize severely, (*syn.*) to scold: *My father gave me hell for crashing his car.* **b.** to beat an opponent: *A soccer player shouted to his teammates, "Let's give'em hell!"* **13 to go through hell:** to survive a difficult experience: *She had cancer and went through hell from the radiation and chemotherapy.* **14** *infrml.* **to go to hell and back:** to push oneself to the limit: *He went to hell and back to prove his innocence.* **15 to have a hell of a time: a.** to have much difficulty: *He had a hell of a time finding this place; it's so far away.* **b.** to have fun **16** *infrml.* **to have hell to pay:** to be punished: *You will have hell to pay if you are caught cheating on your taxes.* **17** *infrml.* **to raise hell: a.** to criticize severely, (*syn.*) to upbraid: *The boss raised hell with the staff for working too slowly.* **b.** to make noise, cause a commotion: *On Saturday night, beer drinkers raise hell in the barroom.* **18** *exclam.infrml.* **What the hell:** of surprise, disgust, anger: *What the hell are you doing here?* **19** *infrml.* **when or until hell freezes over:** never, forever: *He can wait until hell freezes over before I forgive him.*

hell-bent *adj.infrml.fig.* totally determined to do s.t., obsessed: *He is hell-bent on joining the Marine Corps.*

hell·fire /ˈhɛl,faɪr/ *n.* [U] **1** the fires of hell **2** *fig.* strong punishment for sin: *The minister warned the congregation about damnation and hellfire if they behaved badly.*

hell·hole /ˈhɛl,houl/ *n.* a place of corruption, decay, and danger: *Areas of drug dealing are hellholes of addiction, poverty, and murder.*

H

hel·lion /'hɛlyən/ n. a wild, devilish person, esp. a bratty child: *That boy is a little hellion and needs discipline.*

hell·ish /'hɛlɪʃ/ adj. similar to hell, terrible, (syn.) dreadful: *Traffic leaving the city on a holiday weekend is hellish.*

hel·lo /hə'lou, hɛ-/ exclam. a greeting: *Hello, how are you today?*

hell·uv·a /'hɛləvə/ adj.slang intensifier used in positive or negative sense: *He is a helluva nice guy.||We had a helluva time getting through traffic.*

helm /hɛlm/ n. 1 the steering mechanism of a ship, (syn.) the tiller 2 at the helm: in control: *Who's at the helm in this office?*

hel·met /'hɛlmɪt/ n. a protective head covering: *Bicyclists wear helmets to protect their heads.*

helms·man /'hɛlmzmən/ n. -men /-mən/ the person at a ship's helm: *The helmsman steered the ship into the wind.*

help /hɛlp/ v. 1 to aid, assist, support: *My neighbor helped me fix my roof.* 2 to improve, make better: *What will help my upset stomach?* 3 to prevent, refrain from: *He is depressed and cannot help crying.* 4 **cannot help but:** to do s.t. unavoidable: *When I think of all my mother has done for me, I cannot help but say I love her.* 5 **It can't be helped:** It's unavoidable: *I don't want to leave early, but it can't be helped.* 6 **not to be able help oneself:** unable to change or stop doing s.t.: *I know I shouldn't eat so much chocolate, but I can't help myself.* 7 phrasal v. insep. **to help oneself to s.t.:** to serve oneself: *She helped herself to food in the refrigerator.* 8 phrasal v. sep. **to help s.o. out:** to aid, support: *My father helped out our neighbors by mowing their lawn.||He helped them out.*
—n. 1 [C;U] aid, support: *I gave my friend help with his homework.* 2 [U] rescue: *Help was sent to the hurricane victims.* 3 [U] employees, esp. servants: *The boss doesn't pay the help very well.*

help·er /'hɛlpər/ n. an assistant: *The plumber's helper passes him tools and gets new parts.*

help·ful /'hɛlpfəl/ adj. aiding, useful: *The lawyer gave me some helpful advice.* -adv. **helpfully.**

help·ing /'hɛlpɪŋ/ n. a portion, serving: *The cook gave me a big helping of mashed potatoes.*
—adj. **to give s.o. a helping hand:** to be supportive: *She gave the old lady a helping hand off the bus.*

help·less /'hɛlplɪs/ adj. unable to do s.t., defenseless: *The accident victim fell helpless on the street.||He's helpless at changing a tire.* -adv. **helplessly.**

hel·ter-skel·ter /,hɛltər'skɛltər/ adj. confused, rushed: *She does things in a helter-skelter way; she should try to be better organized.*

hem /hɛm/ n. 1 the lower edge of a piece of cloth, turned up and sewn: *The hem on her skirt needs sewing.* 2 a short cough
—v. **hemmed, hemming, hems** 1 to sew a hem: *She hemmed her skirt.* 2 to surround, enclose: *The soldiers were hemmed in on all sides.* 3 to cough or clear one's throat 4 **to hem and haw:** to go back and forth in one's ideas about s.t., (syn.) to hesitate: *He hemmed and hawed about which suit to buy.*

he·ma·tol·o·gy /,himə'talədʒi/ n. [U] the medical science and study of blood -n. [C] **hematologist.**

hem·i·sphere /'hɛmə,sfɪr/ n. 1 half of a sphere or a ball 2 half of the earth: *The earth is divided by the equator into the Northern and Southern hemispheres.*

hem·line /'hɛm,laɪn/ n. the bottom edge of a skirt or dress: *Hemlines go up and down depending on the fashion.*

hem·lock /'hɛm,lak/ n. 1 [C;U] a type of evergreen tree 2 [U] the poison made from the hemlock tree: *People drank hemlock to commit suicide in ancient times.*

he·mo·glo·bin /'himə,gloubɪn/ n. [U] the component of blood that carries oxygen

he·mo·phil·i·a /,himə'fɪliə, -'filyə/ n. [U] a disease, usu. of males, in which the blood does not stop flowing after a cut: *People who have hemophilia can bleed to death.* -adj. **hemophilic.**

he·mo·phil·i·ac /,himə'fɪli,æk, -'fi-/ n. a person with hemophilia

hem·or·rhage /'hɛmrɪdʒ, 'hɛmə-/ n. [C;U] a large flow of blood that cannot be stopped: *Because of the car accident, he had a hemorrhage.*
—v. **-rhaged, -rhaging, -rhages** to bleed uncontrollably: *He hemorrhaged to death.*

hem·or·rhoid /'hɛm,rɔɪd/ n. swollen blood vessels in the rectal area: *Her hemorrhoids make sitting uncomfortable.*

hemp /hɛmp/ n. [U] a tall, annual herb grown for the manufacture of rope, cloth (canvas), and as a source of marijuana: *The heavy ropes used in ships are made from hemp.*

hen /hɛn/ n. a female fowl (chicken, pheasant, etc.): *Hens lay the eggs we eat for breakfast.*

hence /hɛns/ adv.frml. 1 therefore, for this reason: *It is raining outside; hence, I will wear my raincoat.* 2 from now, from this time: *Two weeks hence we are meeting at the club.*

hence·forth /'hɛns,fɔrθ, ,hɛns'fɔrθ/ adv.frml. from now on: *Henceforth, all students must have ID cards.*

hench·man /'hɛntʃmən/ n. -men /-mən/ a helper, supporter of an evil person: *The gang-*

ster and his henchmen collected money from shopowners every month.

hen·na /ˈhɛnə/ *n.* [U] a reddish-brown dye made from the leaves of a small Asian tree or shrub: *Henna is used as a hair dye and conditioner.*

hep·a·ti·tis /ˌhɛpəˈtaɪtɪs/ *n.* [U] liver disease, usu. caused by a virus

her /hɜr; *weak form* hər, ər/ *pron.* **1** the objective form of *she: I saw her leave the room.* **2** the possessive form of *she: She took her purse when she left.*

her·ald /ˈhɛrəld/ *n.* a messenger, announcer, (*syn.*) a proclaimer: *Shorter days are the herald of wintertime.*

her·ald·ry /ˈhɛrəldri/ *n.* [U] the study of coats of arms and family history: *Heraldry is still studied in Europe.*

herb /ɜrb, hɜrb/ *n.* **1** a soft-stem plant used as seasoning or medicine: *People use herbs to season food and to heal.* **2** *slang* marijuana

herb·al /ˈɜrbəl, ˈhɜr-/ *adj.* related to herbs: *She loves to drink herbal teas, such as peppermint and cinnamon.*

herb·al·ist /ˈɜrbəlɪst, ˈhɜr-/ *n.* a person who grows and sells herbs for health

her·bi·cide /ˈɜrbəˌsaɪd, ˈhɜr-/ *n.* a weed killer: *We put an herbicide on our lawn to kill the weeds.*

her·bi·vore /ˈhɜrbəˌvɔr, ˈɜr-/ *n.* an animal that eats only plants: *Cows and horses are herbivores.* -*adj.* **herbivorous** /hərˈbɪvərəs, ər-/.

herd /hɜrd/ *n.* **1** a group of animals of one kind: *Herds of horses run wild in the American West.* **2** *pej.* a crowd of people who think the same: *She follows the herd and never thinks for herself.*

herds·man /ˈhɜrdzmən/ **-men** /-mən/ or **herder** *n.* an owner or keeper of a herd of animals, esp. cattle, sheep, or goats: *Herdsmen guard their sheep.*

here /hɪr/ *adv.* **1** at or in this place: *We have lived here (in this house) for ten years.* **2** used to present or show s.t.: *Here are the keys to my car.* **3 here and there:** in different places **4 Here's to:** offering a toast for someone: *Here's to a long and happy life together.* **5 neither here nor there:** not relevant or important: *Who broke the window is neither here nor there; we must fix it.* **6 the here and now:** the immediate, this time and place: *We have to deal with the problems of the here and now before we think about future problems.*

here·a·bouts /ˌhɪrəˈbaʊts, ˈhɪrəˌbaʊts/ *adv.* in this area: *That company has had various offices hereabouts for years.*

here·af·ter /ˌhɪrˈæftər/ *adv.* in the future, at a later date: *I will excuse your mistake this time, but hereafter be more careful.*

—*n.* **in the hereafter:** after death: *In the hereafter, she hopes to go to heaven.*

here·by /ˌhɪrˈbaɪ, ˈhɪrˌbaɪ/ *adv.frml.* by this means, in this manner: *In the marriage ceremony, the minister said, "I hereby pronounce you husband and wife."*

he·red·i·tar·y /həˈrɛdəˌtɛri/ *adj.* **1** (in biology) related to the passing of physical characteristics through genes: *Some disorders, such as hemophilia, are hereditary.* **2** related to the inheritance of property and rights: *The oldest son of a nobleman has a hereditary right to his title.*

he·red·i·ty /həˈrɛdəti/ *n.* [U] the passing of genes and their characteristics from parents to children: *People argue about whether heredity or the environment has more influence on a person's behavior.*

here·in /ˌhɪrˈɪn/ *adv.* in this: *The national debt is too large, and herein lies our worst problem.*

her·e·sy /ˈhɛrəsi/ *n.* [C;U] **-sies** a belief that goes against accepted practice, esp. religious belief: *Her belief that taxes should be higher was heresy.*

her·e·tic /ˈhɛrəˌtɪk/ *n.* a person who commits heresy: *Heretics were burned at the stake long ago.*

he·ret·i·cal /həˈrɛtɪkəl/ *adj.* characterized by heresy, unorthodox: *The minister's beliefs were heretical against the state religion.*

here·to·fore /ˈhɪrtəˌfɔr, ˌhɪrtəˈfɔr/ *adv.frml.* before now: *Heretofore, we sent out bills on the first of each month; now we bill continually.*

here·with /ˌhɪrˈwɪθ -ˈwɪð/ *adv.frml.* with this

her·i·tage /ˈhɛrətɪdʒ/ *n.* [U] **1** beliefs, traditions, history, etc. passed from one generation to the next: *This country has a heritage of freedom and independence.* **2** inheritance: *That family has a heritage of wealth and power.*

her·maph·ro·dite /hərˈmæfrəˌdaɪt/ *n.* a plant or animal with both male and female reproductive organs: *Most flowering plants are hermaphrodites.* -*adj.* **hermaphroditic** /hərˌmæfrəˈdɪtɪk/.

her·met·ic /hərˈmɛtɪk/ *adj.* sealed so that air cannot enter, airtight: *Canned foods have a hermetic seal.*

her·mit /ˈhɜrmɪt/ *n.* a person who avoids society, (*syn.*) a recluse: *The hermit lives in the woods in a log cabin.*

her·ni·a /ˈhɜrniə/ *n.* [C;U] an opening in the muscles of the abdomen: *He had a hernia operated on and is now well.*

he·ro /ˈhɪroʊ/ *n.* **-roes 1** a person admired for bravery or great deeds: *Martin Luther King, Jr., was a hero in the fight for equality for all people.* **2** the main character in a novel, film, play, etc. -*adj.* **heroic.**

her·o·in /'hɛroʊɪn/ *n.* a strong, addictive, narcotic drug that is illegal in the USA

her·o·ine /'hɛroʊɪn/ *n.* **1** a woman who performs great actions: *Amelia Earhart was a courageous pilot and heroine to many.* **2** the main female character in a novel, film, play, etc.: *In the movie* The Color Purple, *the actress Whoopi Goldberg plays the heroine.*

her·o·ism /'hɛroʊ,ɪzəm/ *n.* [U] an act of courage or great skill: *The daily heroism of firefighters is remarkable.*

her·on /'hɛrən/ *n.* a wading bird with a long neck, legs, and beak: *White herons in the pond are graceful.*

hero sandwich *n.* **-es** a large bread roll with cold meats, cheese, and other ingredients: *For lunch today, I ate a hero sandwich with Swiss cheese, cheddar cheese, turkey, salami, pastrami, and bologna! See:* grinder.

her·pes /'hɜrpiz/ *n.* [U] any of several infections of the skin that are sometimes transmitted sexually from one person to another

her·ring /'hɛrɪŋ/ *n.* **-rings** or **-ring** any of a variety of small fishes such as sardines and anchovies: *I enjoy eating pickled herring once in a while. See:* red herring.

hers /hɜrz/ *possessive pron. of* she belonging to her: *The coat in the closet is hers.*‖*Hers was the best test result.*

her·self /hər'sɛlf; *weak form* ər'sɛlf/ *feminine pron. of* she **1** as a reflexive: *She does all the work herself.* **2** for emphasis: *I spoke with the actress herself.* **3** one's usual manner of being: *She doesn't feel herself today.*

hertz /hɜrts/ *n.* **hertz** unit of frequency of one cycle per second: *This computer has a processing speed of 33 megahertz.*

hes·i·tan·cy /'hɛzətənsi/ *n.* [U] reluctance, delay because of doubt or fear: *His hesitancy about buying the house is based on his poor job opportunities.*

hes·i·tant /'hɛzətənt/ *adj.* **1** unsure, reluctant: *She is hesitant about marrying him.* **2** indecisive, *(syn.)* diffident: *He has a hesitant manner in his speech.*

hes·i·tate /'hɛzə,teɪt/ *v.* **-tated, -tating, -tates** **1** to pause, delay: *He hesitated before crossing the street.* **2** to pause out of politeness, doubt, or fear, *(syn.)* to balk: *She hesitated to criticize the child who was trying so hard.* **3 he** or **she who hesitates is lost:** a person who doesn't take an opportunity as it comes up will fail

hes·i·ta·tion /,hɛzə'teɪʃən/ *n.* **1** [C;U] a pause, delay: *Each hesitation in his speech bored the audience even more.* **2** [U] doubt, fearfulness: *Her hesitation about signing the contract was based on financial concerns.*

het·er·o·ge·ne·ous /,hɛtərə'dʒiniəs -'dʒinyəs/ *adj.* mixed, made up of different parts (objects, ideas, etc.): *People of all races made a hetero-* geneous group at the conference. See: homogeneous.

het·er·o·sex·u·al /,hɛtərə'sɛkʃuəl/ *n.adj.* attracted to the opposite sex, *(syn.)* straight: *He is a <n.> heterosexual and dates <adj.> heterosexual women.*

heu·ris·tics /hyʊ'rɪstɪks/ *n.pl.* used with a *sing. verb* learning through investigation and discovery: *Heuristics is called the discovery approach in education. -adj.* **heuristic.**

hew /hyu/ *v.* **hewed, hewed** or **hewn, hewing, hews** **1** to cut, esp. with an ax, to fell: *The woodsman hewed down the tree with his ax.* **2** to follow, conform: *Followers hewed to the political party's program.*

hewn /hyun/ *adj. & past part. of* hew, cut: *Hewn trees lie on the ground.*

hex /hɛks/ *v.* **hexes** to prevent, stop by using witchcraft, *(syn.)* to jinx: *He hexed the deal by saying it would never work.*
—*n.* a spell or curse put on s.o. or s.t. by using witchcraft: *She put a hex on her old boyfriend's new girlfriend.*

hex·a·gon /'hɛksə,gɑn/ *n.* a geometric figure with six sides *-adj.* **hexagonal** /hɛk'sægənəl/.

hey /heɪ/ *exclam.* **1** used to get s.o.'s attention: *Hey, Joe, come look at this.* **2** an expression of surprise, happiness, etc.: *Hey, I didn't know that you won first prize!*

hey·day /'heɪ,deɪ/ *n.* a period of success (health, power, wealth, etc.): *In his heyday, he was the best lawyer in town.*

hi /haɪ/ *exclam.infrml.* a greeting, hello: *Hi, how are you today?*

hi·a·tus /haɪ'eɪtəs/ *n.frml.* **-tuses** a gap, pause, break: *The miners' strike caused a hiatus in coal production.*

hi·ber·nate /'haɪbər,neɪt/ *v.* **-nated, -nating, -nates** to enter a period of long sleep: *Bears hibernate during the winter. -n.* [U] **hibernation** /,haɪbər'neɪʃən/.

hic·cup or **hic·cough** /'hɪkʌp/ *n.v.* a small, involuntary spasm in breathing accompanied by a sharp sound: *He had the <n.pl.> hiccups from eating too fast.*‖*She <v.> hiccuped for a few minutes, then stopped.*

hick /hɪk/ *n.pej.* an unsophisticated country person, *(syn.)* a yokel: *He is a hick with no education.*

hick·ey /'hɪki/ *n.infrml.* a bruise made by sucking or biting in lovemaking: *She had two hickeys on her neck.*

hick·or·y /'hɪkəri, 'hɪkri/ *n.* [C;U] **-ries** a northeastern American tree with edible nuts and useful wood: *We have furniture made out of hickory.*

hid /hɪd/ *past tense & past part. of* hide (1), to conceal: *She hid candy in a closet so the children could not find it.*

H

hid·den /'hɪdn/ *adj. & past part. of* hide, concealed: *Guests were hidden behind the door at the surprise party.*

hide (1) /haɪd/ *v.* **hid** /hɪd/, **hidden** /'hɪdn/ or **hid, hiding, hides** **1** to conceal, secret: *She hides her jewelry in a drawer.* **2** *phrasal v.* **to hide out:** to stay concealed: *Thieves are hiding out in a cabin in the woods.*

hide (2) *n.* [C;U] **1** the tough skin of an animal, such as a cow: *His boots are made of cowhide.* **2 not to see hide nor hair of s.o.:** not to have seen s.o. at all: *I haven't seen hide nor hair of her for weeks.* **3** *infrml.fig.* **to tan s.o.'s hide:** to spank or criticize strongly: *The father tanned his son's hide for running away.* —*v.* **hided, hiding, hides** to spank, beat: *His father hided the boy for misbehaving. -n.* **hiding.**

hide-and-seek *n.* [U] a game in which children hide while one child closes his or her eyes, then tries to find the other children: *The children played hide-and-seek at the birthday party.*

hide·a·way /'haɪdə,weɪ/ *n.* a secluded place, a refuge: *We have a hideaway, a cabin in the mountains, where we go on weekends. See:* hideout.

hid·e·ous /'hɪdiəs/ *adj.* frightening in looks, (*syn.*) repulsive: *The horror film was about a hideous monster. -adv.* **hideously.**

hide·out /'haɪd,aʊt/ *n.* a secret place, (*syn.*) a refuge: *The criminals have a hideout in the swamp.*

hid·ing /'haɪdɪŋ/ *n.* **in hiding:** in concealment: *Bandits are in hiding in the woods.*

hi·er·ar·chy /'haɪə,rɑrki, 'haɪ,rɑr-/ *n.* [C;U] **-chies** organization from higher to lower by rank, social status, or function: *Generals and admirals are at the top of the military hierarchy. -adj.* **hierarchical** /,haɪə'rɑrkɪkəl, ,haɪ'rɑr-/.

hi·er·o·glyph /'haɪərə,glɪf, 'haɪrə-/ *n.* a picture of a word or idea: *Mayan hieroglyphs are difficult to decode.*

hi·er·o·glyph·ic /,haɪərə'glɪfɪk, ,haɪrə-/ *n.adj.* a system of writing using hieroglyphs as symbols: *Some Egyptian <n.pl.> hieroglyphics are beautiful works of art.‖They are <adj.> hieroglyphic symbols for words.*

hi-fi /'haɪ'faɪ/ *n.adj.infrml.* **-fis** short for high fidelity, a set of equipment that reproduces sound with high fidelity See: high fidelity.

high /haɪ/ *adj.* **1** describing vertical measure: *The statue is 10 feet high (3 m).‖She has a high-pitched voice.* **2** related to great intensity: *Emotions at the protest rally were high.* **3** having an elevated rank: *She is a high official in the government.* **4** intoxicated, usu. referring to illegal drug use: *He got high on marijuana last night.* **5 high as a kite:** drunk, intoxi-

cated: *He drank all night and got high as a kite.* **6 high horse:** arrogance, snobbery: *I told him to get off his high horse and act normally.* —*adv.* **1** with an elevated location: *Cliffs stand high above the ocean.* **2 high and dry:** abandoned, deserted, (*syn.*) stranded: *When her secretary quit suddenly, she was left high and dry.* **3 high and low:** everywhere: *I looked high and low for my eyeglasses, but could not find them.* **4 high on the hog:** well, richly: *Since they won the lottery, they have lived high on the hog.* —*n.* **1** a feeling of excitement, elation: *He felt a high from winning the race.‖She won the tennis match and was on a high.* **2** intoxication: *She got a high from drinking wine.* **3 from on high:** from God, heaven, or a person of high rank: *The writer gets inspiration from on high.* **4 highs and lows:** happy and sad times, ups and downs: *He has had highs and lows in his life.* **5 to come off a high:** to return to reality, become normal: *After winning, he came off that high and felt that his usual life was boring.*

high·ball /'haɪ,bɔl/ *n.* a tall glass of liquor and soda or water: *I like a highball before dinner.*

high beams *n.pl.* vehicle headlights that are brighter and more intense than low beams: *I use the high beams on country roads at night.*

high·born /'haɪ,bɔrn/ *adj.* born into the nobility or upper class: *She is a highborn lady from London whose family owns many beautiful houses.*

high·boy /'haɪ,bɔɪ/ *n.* a tall chest of drawers: *We keep clothes in a highboy in our bedroom.*

high·brow /'haɪ,braʊ/ *adj.* well educated and cultured, refined: *He has very highbrow tastes in music and literature. See:* lowbrow.

high chair *n.* a tall chair for feeding a young child: *The baby loves to throw food on the floor from his high chair.*

high-class *adj.* related to upper social classes: *That restaurant has a high-class clientele.*

higher education *n.* [U] education after high school,

high chair

(*syn.*) postsecondary education: *Higher education in the USA is composed mainly of universities, four-year colleges, and two-year colleges.*

higher-up *n.* one's superior in business or government: *He sent the proposal to the higher-ups in his company for approval.*

high·fa·lu·tin /,haɪfə'lutn/ *adj.infrml.* pretentious, affected: *She has the highfalutin idea that she's a great singer, when in reality she's terrible.*

high fidelity *n.adj.* a method of recording sound for the highest quality: *That symphony* *is recorded in* <*n.*> *high fidelity.*||*It is available as a* <*adj.*> *high-fidelity recording. See:* Dolby System; stereo.

high-flown *adj.* unrealistic, (*syn.*) pretentious: *He has high-flown ideas about becoming rich.*

high-grade *adj.* of the purest or highest amounts of s.t.: *High-grade ore produces the most gold.*

high-handed *adj.* overbearing, not thinking of the rights of others: *He speaks to others in a high-handed manner.*

high·jack /'haɪˌdʒæk/ *v. See:* hijack.

high jinks /'haɪˌdʒɪŋks/ *n.pl.* jokes, harmless pranks, and laughter: *The children's high jinks were all in good fun.*

high·land /'haɪlənd/ *n.* hills and level fields in mountain areas: *The Highlands of Scotland are world famous.*

high·land·er /'haɪləndər/ *n.* a person from the highlands

high life *n.* a luxurious lifestyle: *My friend married a rich woman and lives the high life of parties and exotic vacations.*

high·light /'haɪˌlaɪt/ *v.* **-lighted, -lighting, -lights** to single out, emphasize: *Students highlight important parts of their textbooks.*||*The speaker highlighted the important ideas in his talk with a diagram.*

high·light·er /'haɪˌlaɪtər/ *n.* a thick pen with transparent ink, usu. used for marking important parts of text

high·ly /'haɪli/ *adv.* to a high level or degree: *A highly placed source in government gave the newspaper secret information.*||*She is highly respected as an excellent lawyer.*

high-mind·ed /'haɪ'maɪndɪd/ *adj.* devoted to high ideas or principles, such as of religion, civic responsibility, and justice: *He is a high-minded politician and always does what is morally right.*

High·ness /'haɪnɪs/ *n.* a form of address to royal family members: *Her Royal Highness, the Queen of England, visited the U.S. President.*

high noon *n.* **1** exactly 12 o'clock noon **2** a time of decisive confrontation: *The two superpowers reached high noon in their conflict and faced nuclear war.*

high-pitched *adj.* loud and high, (*syn.*) shrill: *The factory whistle lets out a high-pitched signal at noon.*

high-powered *adj.* **1** having much force: *His car has a high-powered engine.* **2** having much power (talent, ability, influence): *She is a high-powered lawyer in Washington; even the President asks her for advice.*

high-pressure *adj.* pushy, insistent: *I don't like to do business with him because he is a high-pressure salesman.*

high-priced *adj.* costly, having a large price

tag: *That store carries only high-priced merchandise.*

high-rise *n.adj.* a tall building: *We live in a* <*n.*> *high-rise* or *a* <*adj.*> *high-rise apartment building in New York.*

high road *n.* **1** a road that goes over hills: *We drove along the high roads to see the scenery.* **2** *fig.* a glamorous, direct path to success: *Her brother took the high road as a successful banker, while she became a high school teacher.*

high roller *n.* (in gambling) a person who takes big financial risks: *He is a high roller in real-estate investing.*

high school *n.* [C;U] in USA, a school for grades 9-12 or 10-12: *He graduated from high school in 1996. See:* grade school, USAGE NOTE.

high-sounding *adj.* lofty, pretentious: *That politician proposes high-sounding solutions to the nation's problems.*

high-spirited *adj.* lively, full of fun: *That horse is very high-spirited, so only experienced riders should ride him.*

high-strung *adj.* tense, energetic in a nervous way: *She is very high-strung and cannot relax.*

high·tail /'haɪˌteɪl/ *v.infrml.* **to hightail it out of here:** to run rapidly: *The students hightailed it out of the classroom when the fire alarm went off.*

high-tech /'haɪ'tɛk/ *adj.* using complex engineering, usu. in the latest technology: *Advances in computer technology need high-tech solutions.*

high-tension *adj.* related to wires carrying high-voltage electricity: *High-tension wires run across miles of open country to big cities.*

high tide *n.* [C;U] the time each day when the ocean is at the highest place on the shore: *Sailors wait for high tide before sailing from the harbor.*

high time *n.* **1** *sing.fun:* *We had a high time at the party.* **2** [U] **It's high time:** an expression of impatience: *It's high time you got a job and started supporting yourself.*

high-toned *adj.* elegant, high-class: *The social gathering was a high-toned party with well-known people.*

high-water mark *n.* the highest point a flood or tide reaches: *The river overflowed and left a high-water mark on the cliffs next to it.*

high·way /'haɪˌweɪ/ *n.* a major, usu. long-distance road: *An interstate highway passes near our town.*

highway patrol *n.* the police who travel in cars on major roads

high-wire *n.* a wire stretched high above the ground, on which acrobats perform
—*adj.* risky, thrilling: *He made some high-wire investments in foreign currencies.*

hi·jack /'haɪ,dʒæk/ v. to control an airplane or vehicle by threatening its pilot, usu. with a gun: *A desperate man hijacked a plane from New York to Cuba.* -n. [C] **hijacker;** [C;U] **hijacking.**

hi·jinks /'haɪ,dʒɪŋks/ n.pl. See: high jinks.

hike /haɪk/ n. **1** a long walk in the country: *We went for a hike* (or) *we took a hike in a national park.* **2** infrml. a sudden increase (in prices): *The manufacturers gave wholesalers a price hike on all products.* **3** infrml.fig. **to take a hike:** (to tell s.o.) to stop, go away: *The salesman tried to get me to buy a car, and I told him to take a hike.* -n. **hiker.**
—v. **hiked, hiking, hikes 1** to take a long walk: *We hiked through the hills of Yosemite Park.* **2** infrml. to raise (prices): *Manufacturers hiked prices this month.*

hi·lar·i·ous /hɪ'lɛriəs/ adj. extremely funny, (syn.) uproarious: *The new comedy was absolutely hilarious.* -n. [U] **hilarity** /hɪ'lærəti, -'lɛr-/.

hill /hɪl/ n. **1** (in geology) an elevation of land shorter than a mountain: *The hills above the city offer a lovely view.* **2** a pile, mound: *A truck deposited a hill of earth in the yard.* **3 a hill of beans:** s.t. unimportant, (syn.) inconsequential: *That political scandal doesn't amount to a hill of beans.* **4 over the hill:** old, ineffective: *He was a great lawyer at one time, but he's over the hill now.*

hill·bil·ly /'hɪl,bɪli/ n.infrml.pej. **-lies** a country person, (syns.) a hick, yokel (esp. from the U.S. southern hill country): *He's a hillbilly from a small mountain town.*

hill·ock /'hɪlək/ n. a small mound or hill: *The hillocks of New England make farming difficult.*

hill·side /'hɪl,saɪd/ n. the side of a hill: *Trees cover the hillsides in this area.*

hill·top /'hɪl,tɑp/ n. the top of a hill: *There is a good view of the lake from the hilltops above the town.*

hill·y /'hɪli/ adj. **hillier, hilliest** having many hills: *Parts of West Virginia are very hilly.*

hilt /hɪlt/ n. **1** the crossbar between the handle and blade of a sword or knife: *He pushed the knife into the animal to the hilt.* **2 to the hilt:** to the extreme, completely: *When she criticizes s.o., she does it to the hilt.*

him /hɪm; *weak form* ɪm/ object pron. of he: *I gave him the book.*

him·self /hɪm'sɛlf; *weak form* ɪm'sɛlf/ masculine pron. of him: **1** as a reflexive: *He did all the work himself* (or) *by himself.* **2** for emphasis: *I spoke with the President himself.* **3** one's usual manner of being: *He doesn't feel himself today; he might have the flu.*

hind /haɪnd/ adj. related to the rear or posterior part: *the hind legs of a dog See:* fore.

—n. the female red deer: *A hunter shot a hind.*

hin·der /'hɪndər/ v. to slow the progress of s.t., (syn.) to impede: *Lack of modern equipment hinders efficient manufacturing.*

hind·most /'haɪnd,moʊst, 'haɪn-/ adj. last, at the farthest end of s.t.: *A worker fixed the hindmost part of the fence.*

hind·quar·ters /'haɪnd,kwɔrtərz, 'haɪn-/ n.pl. posterior of animals, (syn.) the haunches: *The farmer hit the horse's hindquarters to make it move faster.*

hin·drance /'hɪndrəns/ n. obstacle, handicap: *She won't cooperate with us, which is a hindrance in our work.*

hind·sight /'haɪnd,saɪt, 'haɪn-/ n. [U] an opinion about s.t. after it has happened: *The stock market has dropped so badly that in hindsight, I should never have bought stock. See:* foresight.

hinge /hɪndʒ/ n. a metal device with two parts that act like a joint: *The hinges on doors allow them to open and close.*
—v. **hinged, hinging, hinges** phrasal v. insep. **to hinge on** or **upon:** to depend on, result from: *Peace between the two nations hinges on the result of their negotiations.*

hint /hɪnt/ v.n. to make reference to s.t. in an indirect way, (syn.) to intimate: *He <v.> hinted to his wife that he wanted a new watch for his birthday.‖She took the <n.> hint and bought one.*

hin·ter·land /'hɪntər,lænd/ n. a remote region: *We lived in the city, then moved to the hinterland of northern Vermont.*

hip /hɪp/ n. **1** the part of the body where the leg joins the pelvis: *He fell and hurt his hip.* **2** the area around the hip joint: *She has wide hips.*
—adj. slang informed, aware, esp. of youthful fashions: *Hey, man, that guy is real-ly hip!*

hip·pie or **hip·py** /'hɪpi/ n. **-pies** a person, esp. of the 1960s, who is against traditional values and lifestyles: *In the 1960's my father was a hippy who lived in San Francisco, played the guitar on the streets, and cooked food for poor people.*

hip·po /'hɪpoʊ/ n. **-pos** short for hippopotamus

Hip·po·crat·ic oath /,hɪpə'krætɪk/ n. the oath that medical doctors take as a code of conduct: *Hippocrates wrote the Hippocratic oath in the fifth century B.C.*

hip·po·pot·a·mus /,hɪpə'pɑtəməs/ n. **-muses** or **-mi** /-,maɪ/ a large African animal with a heavy body, gray skin, and a very large

hippopotamus

head and mouth: *Hippopotamuses live near rivers.*

hippy *n. var. of* hippie

hire /haɪr/ *v.* **hired, hiring, hires 1** to pay for the services of, employ: *The company hired her last week.* **2** to rent, pay a fee for: *I hired a limousine to take me to the airport.* **3** *phrasal v. sep.* **to hire s.o. out:** to do work for money: *Temporary agencies hire out workers to other companies.‖They hire workers out.*
—*n.* a person who is hired: *New hires go through a training program.*

hired hand *n.* a low-level employee hired for simple jobs: *He is a seasonal hired hand on a ranch.*

hire·ling /'haɪrlɪŋ/ *n. pej.* a low-level employee usu. hired for temporary or unskilled work: *The man brought along several hirelings to clean up the mess.*

hir·sute /'hÆr,sut, hər'sut/ *adj.frml.* hairy: *His chest is hirsute.*

his /hɪz; *weak form* ɪz/ *possessive pron. of* he: *He hung his coat in the closet.‖He tried his hardest on the test.*

His·pan·ic /hɪ'spænɪk/ *n.* a Latino, person of Latin American or Spanish descent: *Hispanics come from all over the world to New York.*
—*adj.* related to Spanish-speaking Latin America

hiss /hɪs/ *n.* **hisses** a low-pitched sound of air forced from the mouth: *The cat hissed at the dog.*
—*v.* **hisses** to make the sound of a hiss: *The snake hissed at the mouse, then attacked it.*

his·tol·o·gy /hɪ'stɑlədʒi/ *n.* [U] the microscopic study of plant and animal tissues: *Dermatologists study the histology of the skin.*

his·to·ri·an /hɪ'stɔriən/ *n.* a person who teaches, studies, and writes about history: *The professor is a historian at the University of Chicago.*

his·tor·ic /hɪ'stɔrɪk, -'stɑr-/ *adj.* important in history, famous: *We visited places of historic interest in Paris.*

his·tor·i·cal /hɪ'stɔrɪkəl, -'stɑr-/ *adj.* related to history: *The French Revolution was of great historical importance. -adv.* **historically.**

his·tor·y /'hɪstəri, 'hɪstri/ *n.* **-ries 1** [C;U] the study of past events (people, civilizations, etc.): *She studied European history at college.* **2** [C] past events, or a written account of past events: *My family history is very interesting; I plan to write it all down some day.‖She read a history of Peru.* **3 that's history** or **past (ancient) history:** s.t. that is no longer important: *His bad behavior is past history; he's a good boy now.* **4 to make history:** to do s.t. memorable, important

his·tri·on·ics /ˌhɪstri'ɑnɪks/ *n.pl. frml.* dramatic emotional behavior used to make others do what one wants: *His histrionics do not work on those who know him; they just ignore his yelling and crying. -adj.* **histrionic.**

hit /hɪt/ *v.* **hit, hitting, hits 1** to strike, pound: *He hit the nail with a hammer.* **2** to punch, slap: *The boxer hit his opponent with his right fist.* **3** to collide with, crash into: *One car hit the other.* **4** to upset emotionally, *(syn.)* to stun: *The death of his mother hit him hard.* **5** to score in sports, such as basketball: *The player hit the basket for two points.* **6** to strike a target: *A bullet hit the soldier in the leg.* **7** *infrml.*to reach, attain: *The stock market hit a new high.* **8** *slang* to kill: *A gangster hit another gang member.* **9 to be hit with:** to be shocked, surprised by: *My father was hit with a big dental bill.* **10 to hit it off:** to like one another: *My two friends met for the first time yesterday and hit it off.* **11** *phrasal v. insep.* **to hit on** or **upon s.o. or s.t.: a.** *slang* to flirt, make a pass at s.o.: *All the men at the party hit on her.* **b.** to discover, find s.t. useful: *My boss hit on a new way of making our product.* **12 to hit pay dirt:** to reach success, be rewarded: *The salesman talked to many possible customers before he hit pay dirt with a big order.* **13 to hit s.o. like a ton of bricks:** to stun, *(syn.)* to overwhelm: *His boss fired him suddenly, and it hit him like a ton of bricks.* **14** *phrasal v. insep.* **to hit s.o. up for s.t.:** to ask s.o. for s.t.: *My friend John hit me up for a loan that I can't really afford.* **15 to hit the books:** to study hard: *I'm going to hit the books this weekend to study for my exams.* **16 to hit the bottle** or **sauce:** to drink too much alcohol: *Since his girlfriend left him, he has been really hitting the bottle.* **17** *infrml.* **to hit the brakes:** To stop a car quickly: *When a dog ran in front of my car, I hit the brakes.* **18 to hit the bull's-eye: a.** to strike a target's center **b.** *fig.* to be accurate, very good in describing s.t. or solving a problem: *She hit the bull's-eye when she described him as a jerk.* **19** *infrml.* **to hit the deck (dirt, floor):** to fall to the ground to avoid danger: *I hit the deck when the shooting started.* **20** *infrml.* **to hit the hay** or **sack:** to go to bed: *I hit the hay early last night.* **21 to hit the nail on the head:** to describe s.t. accurately: *You hit the nail on the head when you said that debt will destroy the economy.* **22** *infrml.* **to hit the panic button:** to panic, alarm others: *When sales went down, the manager hit the panic button and told all the workers to sell more.* **23** *infrml.* **to hit the road:** to leave, go on a trip: *The sales manager told the salespeople to hit the road and sell.* **24** *infrml.* **to hit the roof:** to become mad: *When sales went down,*

H

she hit the roof and started yelling at everyone.
25 to hit the spot: to satisfy well: *A cold drink on a hot August day really hits the spot.*
—*n.* **1** a blow, impact: *The fighter plane got a hit from enemy fire.* **2** a great success: *The new movie was a big hit.* **3** *slang* a murder: *One gang made a hit on the leader of another gang.* **4 to score a hit:** to succeed greatly: *The good food and nice decorations scored a hit with our guests.*
—*adj.* **1 hit-and-run:** leaving the scene of an accident: *I was in a hit-and-run accident where the car that hit me took off right away.* **2 hit-and-miss:** unreliable, (*syn.*) erratic: *The buses never run on time here; their schedules are hit-and-miss.*

hitch /hɪtʃ/ *v.* **-es** **1** to attach, connect, esp. to harness an animal: *The farmer hitched the horse to a wagon.* **2** *phrasal v. sep.* **to hitch s.t. up: a.** to pull up quickly: *She hitched up her pants.* **b.** to attach s.t. by hitching: *The boy hitched up his pony to the cart and rode away.* **3 to hitch a ride:** to hitchhike: *I hitched a ride with a truck driver to get here.* **4** *slang* **to get hitched:** to marry: *Susan and I are planning to get hitched in June.*
—*n.* **hitches** **1** a harness or device used as a hitch: *The railroad cars' hitches locked together.* **2** a difficulty, delay: *The seller is demanding more money and caused a hitch in the sale.*

hitch·hike /'hɪtʃ,haɪk/ *v.* **-hiked, -hiking, -hikes** to stand on the road and ask for a ride from others, to thumb a ride: *I hitchhiked from Baltimore to Washington.* *-n.* **hitchhiker.**

hi-tech /'haɪ'tɛk/ *See:* high tech.

hith·er /'hɪðər/ *adv.frml.* **1** to here, toward s.o. **2 hither and thither** or **yon:** here and there, all over: *We traveled hither and thither on vacation.*

hith·er·to /'hɪðər,tu, ,hɪðər'tu/ *adv.frml.* up to this time, until now: *Hitherto, we used that grammar book, but now we have a new one.*

hit list *n.infrml.* a list of people to be hurt or killed: *That gangster has a hit list of his enemies.*

hit man *n.infrml.* **men** a hired murderer, esp. a gangster: *The mob sent a hit man to kill a police detective.*

hit-or-miss *adj.* by chance, (*syn.*) unpredictable *See:* hit, *adj..* 2.

HIV /,eɪtʃaɪ'vi/ *abbr. for* human immunodeficiency virus: *The HIV virus causes AIDS. See:* AIDS, USAGE NOTE.

hive /haɪv/ *n.* **1** a box-like structure where bees live: *Beekeepers keep bees in hives.* **2** *fig.* a busy place: *The stock exchange is a hive of activity.*
—*v.* **hived, hiving, hives** (of bees) to gather into hives

hives /haɪvz/ *n.pl.* a rash or bumps on the skin: *I have a food allergy that gives me hives.*

HMO /,eɪtʃɛm'oʊ/ *abbr. for* health maintenance organization

ho /hoʊ/ *exclam.* a laugh or expression of disapproval: *Santa Claus laughs, "Ho, ho, ho!"*

hoard /hɔrd/ *v.* to hide a lot of s.t. for future use or sale: *People hoard gold when their national currency is weak.*
—*n.* a group of hoarded items: *They keep their hoard of gold in a safe place.* *-n.* [C] **hoarder;** [U] **hoarding.**

hoarse /hɔrs/ *adj.* **hoarser, hoarsest** having a scratchy, husky voice caused by overuse or a virus: *The politician is hoarse from giving speeches.* *-adv.* **hoarsely;** *-n.* [U] **hoarseness.**

hoar·y /'hɔri/ *adj.* **-ier, -iest** old and gray: *The graveyard has a hoary look.* *-n.* [U] **hoariness.**

hoax /hoʊks/ *n.v.* **hoaxes** s.t. false, a deception, trick: *The bomb threat turned out to be a <n.> hoax.*

hob·ble /'hɑbəl/ *v.* **-bled, -bling, -bles** **1** to restrain, handicap: *Our efforts are hobbled by a lack of funds.* **2** to limp: *He broke his leg and hobbles along on crutches.*
—*n.* **1** a restraint, such as a rope tying a horse's legs together: *The farmer put a hobble on his horse to keep it from walking off.* **2** a limp, an awkward gait: *She walks with a hobble because of a leg injury.*

hob·by /'hɑbi/ *n.* **-bies** an activity done often for pleasure, (*syn.*) an avocation: *His hobby is gardening.*

hob·by·horse /'hɑbi,hɔrs/ *n.* **1** a child's toy rocking horse: *Our little boy loves to ride his hobbyhorse.* **2** *fig.* a subject or idea that s.o. continually talks about

hob·gob·lin /'hɑb,gɑblɪn/ *n.* a scary ghost, evil spirit: *Hobgoblins are said to come out on Halloween.*

hob·nob /'hɑb,nɑb/ *v.* **-nobbed, -nobbing, -nobs** to socialize with, be friendly with: *He hobnobbed with rich friends on vacation last summer.*

ho·bo /'hoʊboʊ/ *n.* **-boes** or **-bos** a homeless wanderer, (*syn.*) a vagabond: *Old Joe is a hobo who rides the trains from place to place.*

hock /hɑk/ *n.* **1** the ankle area of an animal **2** a cut of meat from this area: *My mother cooks a ham hock in the pea soup to give it flavor.* **3 in hock:** in debt: *He looks rich, but he's in hock up to his ears.*
—*v.* to pawn: *He hocked his watch to pay the rent.*

hock·ey /'hɑki/ *n.* [U] a sport played on ice with a puck or on a field with a ball: *The team that makes the most goals in hockey wins the game.*

hock·shop /'hɑk,ʃɑp/ *n.infrml.* a pawnshop

ho·cus-po·cus /ˈhoʊkəsˈpoʊkəs/ *n*. [U] words said to trick or deceive, nonsense: *What she says is just hocus-pocus, pure nonsense.*

hodge-podge /ˈhɑdʒˌpɑdʒ/ *n*. a mixture of different things, (*syn.*) a jumble: *His ideas are a hodgepodge of unproved theories.*

hoe /hoʊ/ *n.v*. **hoed, hoeing, hoes** a digging tool with a metal blade on a long handle: *I use a <n.> hoe to <v.> hoe weeds from my garden.*

hog /hɔg, hag/ *n*. **1** a large domesticated pig: *Hogs are raised for ham, pork, bacon, and lard.* **2** *fig.* s.o. who eats or takes a lot of s.t.: *He's a real hog with the ice cream.* **3** *infrml.fig.* **to go whole hog:** to do s.t. completely
—*v*. **hogged, hogging, hogs** to take more than one's share of s.t.

hog·back /ˈhɔgˌbæk, ˈhag-/ *n*. (in geology) a geologic formation of a sharp ridge with steep sides: *Hogbacks create barriers that can make travel difficult.*

hog-tie *v*. **-tied, -tying, -ties 1** to tie the legs together **2** to prevent from acting, obstruct: *We were hog-tied by laws preventing us from buying the land.*

hog·wash /ˈhɔgˌwaʃ, -ˌwɔʃ, ˈhag-/ *n*. [U] **1** leftover food used to feed pigs **2** *infrml.fig.* nonsense: *His ideas are pure hogwash.*

hog-wild *adj.* **to go hog-wild:** to act crazy, reckless: *She went hog-wild and bought risky stocks.*

ho-hum /ˈhoʊˈhʌm/ *exclam. of* tiredness, boredom
—*v*. **-hummed, -humming, -hums:** to express fatigue or disapproval: *He ho-hummed the idea of building a new house.*
—*adj.* boring: *We attended a ho-hum concert.*

hoi pol·loi /ˈhɔɪpəˈlɔɪ/ *n.pl.* (Greek for) the masses, ordinary people: *He's a snob and doesn't mix with the hoi polloi.*

hoist /hɔɪst/ *v*. to lift and move an object: *The father hoisted his small child onto his shoulders.*
—*n*. a device used to pick up and place s.t.: *A mechanic used a chain hoist to lift an engine from an automobile.*

hoi·ty-toi·ty /ˌhɔɪtiˈtɔɪti/ *adj.* snobbish, snooty: *She puts on hoity-toity airs and thinks she is better than other people.*

hok·ey /ˈhoʊki/ *adj.infrml.* **-ier, -iest 1** corny, unsophisticated: *Her jokes are hokey.* **2** phony, fake: *He has these hokey schemes that never work.*

ho·kum /ˈhoʊkəm/ *n*. [U] nonsense, empty talk

hold (1) /hoʊld/ *v*. **held** /hɛld/, **holding, holds 1** to own, possess: *She holds stocks of 12 companies in her portfolio.* **2** to grasp, grip: *The worker held the hammer in his right hand.* **3** to keep still, in place: *The dancer held his leg*

in the air for five seconds. **4** to embrace, encircle with the arms: *Lovers are holding each other in their arms.* **5** to contain, (*syn.*) to encompass: *That barrel holds 60 gallons of oil.* **6** to continue, keep steady: *Let's hope the good weather holds for the weekend.* **7** to detain: *Police held the thief for the witness to identify.* **8** to have a meeting: *We held a conference in my office.* **9** to believe, affirm: *"We hold these truths to be self-evident, that all men are created equal. . . ."* **10** to decide, judge: *The court held that she must pay a fine.* **11** to keep back, restrain: *He was upset, but held his temper.*‖*The dam held back the flood waters.* **12** **hold it: a.** to stop, (*syn.*) to desist: *Hold it! I don't want any more trouble from you!* **b.** to keep or retain s.t.: *Here's some money; hold it for me for a week.* **13 to hold court: a.** (in law): *Court will be held three days at week at the Municipal Building.* **b.** to be the focus of attention in a social gathering: *She holds court in that restaurant every Sunday night.* **14** *phrasal v.* **to hold forth:** to speak for a long time, (*syn.*) to expound: *The speaker held forth for an hour.* **15** *phrasal v.* **to hold on: a.** to grip, grasp: *Hold on, this is a bad road!* **b.** to struggle against difficulty: *He was very ill, but held on and gradually recovered.* **16 to hold one's breath: a.** to inhale and not breathe: *He held his breath under water for 20 seconds.* **b.** *fig.* (said ironically): *He says that he will pay me next week, but I'm not holding my breath (until then).* **17 to hold one's horses:** to stop s.t. and think about it: *Hold your horses! Don't put all your money into that risky deal!* **18 to hold one's nose:** to smell s.t. bad or show disgust: *The barn smelled so bad that she held her nose.* **19 to hold one's own:** to perform satisfactorily, neither poorly nor well: *Our product is holding its own against the competition.* **20 to hold one's tongue:** not to speak, keep silent: *He wanted to criticize, but he held his tongue.* **21** *phrasal v. insep.* **to hold out for s.t.:** to wait to do s.t. until one is satisfied: *He didn't sell his house right away; he held out for the best offer.* **22 to hold out hope:** to be optimistic: *Her cancer is so advanced that we hold out no hope of recovery.* **23** *phrasal v. sep.* **to hold s.o. or s.t. back: a.** s.o.: to keep s.o. from developing, advancing: *Our boss's attitude holds back workers who want a promotion.*‖*It holds them back.* **b.** s.t.: to keep s.t. secret: *She held back the announcement for a week.*‖*She held it back.* **c.** s.o. or s.t.: to control, keep in place, (*syn.*) to restrain: *The fence held back the crowd at the ball game.*‖*It held them back.* **24** *phrasal v. sep.* **to hold s.o. or s.t. down: a.** *lit.* to restrain: *One cop held down the robber while another handcuffed him.*‖*They held him down.* **b.** to lower or maintain s.t., esp. prices: *In bad times, merchants hold down prices so customers will still*

H

shop at their stores. **25** *phrasal v. sep.* **to hold s.o. or s.t. off: a.** to prevent an action, (*syn.*) to thwart: *Our soldiers held off an enemy attack.||They held it off.* **b.** to wait, delay: *We held off buying a house until prices came down.||We held it off.* **26** *phrasal v. sep.* **to hold s.o. or s.t. up: a.** to delay, obstruct: *She held up payment on the invoice for three months.* **b.** to rob: *He held up a store owner with a gun.* **c.** to show as a model: *Her teacher held her up as an example of a good student.* **27 to hold s.o. to a promise (word, contract, commitment):** to demand that s.o. does what he or she promised: *I held my friend to his promise to pay back the money that I loaned to him.* **28** *phrasal v. insep.* **to hold s.o. to s.t.:** to require s.o. to do s.t. promised: *He held us to our promise to visit him.* **29** *phrasal v. insep.* **to hold s.t. against s.o.:** to feel angry toward s.o. for doing s.t. wrong: *Her father left the family when she was young, and she holds that against him.* **30** *phrasal v. insep.* **to hold s.t. at s.t.:** to keep s.t. steady (a temperature, position, etc.): *The plane is holding its altitude at 5,000 ft. (1,272 m).* **31** *phrasal v. sep.* **to hold s.t. in:** to suck in: *He held in his breath (stomach).||He held it in.* **32** *phrasal v. sep.* **to hold s.t. out:** to put forward, extend: *He held out his hand and shook hands with everyone.||He held it out.* **33** *phrasal v. sep.* **to hold s.t. over:** to keep for later action, postpone: *Discussion of that legislation will be held over to the next session of Congress.||They'll hold it over.* **34** *phrasal v. sep.* **to hold s.t. together:** to keep s.t. unified: *We want to hold together our chess club.||We want to hold it together.* **35 to hold sway:** to be in power: *The dominance of Rome held sway for many centuries.* **36 to hold the fort:** to take care of business while others are away: *My partner is holding the fort while I am on vacation.* **37 to hold the line:** to keep things as they are against pressure to change: *Management held the line against workers' demands for higher wages.* **38 to hold the trump card(s):** to dominate, have the superior position: *The seller holds the trump cards; she has so many offers to choose from.* **39 to hold the upper hand:** to dominate, have a superior position: *The buyer holds the upper hand in negotiations with so many suppliers to choose from.* **40** *phrasal v. insep.* **to hold with s.t.:** to agree with, approve of s.t.: *She doesn't hold with drinking.*
—*n.* **1** [C;U] a grip, grasp: *He has a good hold on the railing.* **2** [U] control over: *She has a hold over him, and he does what she says.* **3 no holds barred:** (from wrestling) to use every way possible to win: *The legal battle was dirty, with no holds barred.* **4 to be on hold: a.** postponed, delayed: *The project is stopped now and is on hold until next year.* **b.** waiting for s.o. on the telephone: *Mr. Jones is*

on hold on line 2. **5 to catch hold of:** to grab, grasp quickly: *He slipped but caught hold of the railing.* **6 to get hold of:** to obtain, usu. by luck: *I was able to get hold of some rare champagne, so let's celebrate.* **7 to get a hold of oneself:** to control one's emotions: *He began to cry, but got a hold of himself and stopped.*

hold (2) *n.* the container area of a ship: *The ship's hold is full of cargo.*

hold·er /'hoʊldər/ *n.* **1** a device to hold s.t.: *I put the pen in the holder on my desk.* **2** the person who controls a place or possessions: *The bank is the mortgage holder on the house.*

hold·ing /'hoʊldɪŋ/ *n.* ownership of an asset, s.t. valuable: *She has holdings (buildings, land) in real estate.*

holding company *n.* **-nies** a company that owns stock in and usu. controls other companies: *The businessman formed a holding company to control all his assets.*

hold·out /'hoʊl,daʊt/ *n.* a person who does not agree to do s.t., usu. waiting for s.t. better: *Everyone agreed to the plan, except for one holdout who wanted more money.*

hold·o·ver /'hoʊl,doʊvər/ *n.* a person or thing from the past that exists in new times: *The whole management team was new except for one holdover from the old group.*

hold·up /'hoʊl,dʌp/ *n.* a robbery with a weapon (gun, knife, etc.), a stickup: *A holdup at gunpoint happened in the local grocery store.*

hole /hoʊl/ *n.* **1** an opening in a surface: *I sewed a hole in my shirt.* **2** an animal's home or nest: *A rabbit jumped into its hole.* **3** an unclear point, (*syn.*) a gap: *The witness's story had holes in it.* **4** *infrml.* an unpleasant place: *His small, messy apartment is a hole.||The police threw the prisoner into a hole.* **5** (in golf) **a.** the cup into which the ball is hit **b.** one of 18 links: *We played 18 holes of golf today.*
—*adj.* **1** *slang* **in the hole:** in debt: *He is in the hole to his landlord for three months' rent.* **2 to poke holes in s.t.:** to criticize too much
—*v.* **holed, holing, holes 1** to make a hole in s.t.: *The workman holed the garden for plants.* **2** *phrasal v.* **to hole out:** to finish a hole in golf **3** *phrasal v.* **to hole up:** to hide: *The criminal holed up in a mountain cabin.*

hole-in-the-wall *n.* a small place, usu. dark and run-down: *His store is a hole-in-the-wall, but he does good business.*

hol·i·day /'hɑlə,deɪ/ *n.* **1** a day of celebration or rest: *Many companies in the USA give their employees ten legal holidays.* **2** *usu. Brit.* a vacation: *We go on holiday in August.*

ho·li·ness /'hoʊlinɪs/ *n.* [U] **1** the quality of being holy: *The holiness of a church is widely respected.* **2 Holiness** a title of the Pope: *His Holiness, Pope John Paul II, visited the cathedral.*

ho·lis·tic /hoʊˈlɪstɪk/ *adj.* related to a total being, such as the body and mind: *Many doctors practice holistic medicine and focus on their patients' emotions as well as their illnesses.*

hol·ler /ˈhɑlər/ *v.infrml.* **1** to yell, shout: *My friend hollered at me to come over to her quickly.* **2** to complain, (*syn.*) to bellyache: *He started hollering that he hurt his ankle. -n.* [U] **hollering.**

hol·low /ˈhɑloʊ/ *n.* (in geology) a shallow depression in the ground: *Deer were eating down in the hollow.*
—*v.* to remove the contents of s.t.: *We hollowed out a pumpkin and made a jack-o'-lantern.*
—*adj.* **1** empty, with no center: *The tree trunk was hollow from insects feeding inside.* **2** *fig.* false, empty: *His arguments are hollow.*

hol·ly /ˈhɑli/ *n.* **-lies** any of a family of trees and shrubs with shiny, pointed leaves and red berries, used for Christmas decorations: *The leaves and berries of holly make beautiful decorations.*

hol·ly·hock /ˈhɑliˌhɑk/ *n.* a tall plant with large flowers along a tall stem

Hol·ly·wood /ˈhɑliˌwʊd/ *n.* a Los Angeles suburb and the center of the USA's film industry: *Hollywood is a symbol of glamour and excitement.*

hol·o·caust /ˈhɑləˌkɔst, ˈhoʊ-/ *n.* **1** great destruction, esp. by fire: *The great fire of London in 1666 was a holocaust that destroyed the city.* **2 the Holocaust** the killing of European Jews and others by the Nazis: *Millions lost their lives in the Holocaust.*

USAGE NOTE: Several American cities, especially those that are home to many survivors of the *Holocaust,* have built monuments to its victims.

ho·log·ra·phy /hoʊˈlɑgrəfi, hə-/ *n.* [U] a process of forming three-dimensional images by using light waves: *Companies use holography to create special images on credit cards. -n.* **hologram** /ˈhoʊləˌgræm, ˈhɑ-/ *-adj.* **holographic** /ˌhoʊləˈgræfɪk/.

hol·ster /ˈhoʊlstər/ *n.* a leather holder for a gun: *The cowboy drew his pistol from his holster.*

ho·ly /ˈhoʊli/ *adj.* **-lier, -liest** sacred, coming from or connected with God: *Christmas is a holy day. See:* holiness.
—*exclam.* **Holy cow** or **Holy smoke:** expression of surprise: *Holy cow! What a great play that team made!*

hom·age /ˈɑmɪʤ, ˈhɑ-/ *n.* [U] **to pay homage:** to show great respect, esp. publicly: *The nobles paid homage to the queen by bowing to her.*

home /hoʊm/ *n.* **1** the place where one lives, (*syn.*) an abode: *My home is an apartment in Manhattan.* **2** one's birthplace: *My home was originally in Boston (in America, North America, etc.).* **3** a place where s.t. comes from: *New Orleans is the home of jazz music.* **4** (in baseball) home plate **5 at home: a.** comfortable and welcome, as you would feel in your own house: *I feel at home at my friend's house.*‖*When she visits me, I tell her to make herself at home.* **b.** comfortable with s.t.: *She's at home working with computers.*‖*He's at home with horses; he's ridden them for years.* **6 there's no place like home** (or) **home sweet home:** related to one's sense of belonging or comfort: *I am so sick of traveling for a month; there's no place like home.*
—*adj.* **1** related to or prepared at home: *When I went away to college, I really missed my mother's home cooking.* **2** related to or being a base of operations: *The company's home office is in Chicago.*
—*adv.* **1 to hit home:** to disturb, affect deeply: *His wife's criticism of his bad habits hit home, and he changed them.* **2 towards home:** *We were driving towards home when we saw the accident.*
—*v.* **homed, homing, homes 1** (said of pigeons) to head to one's place of origin: *Homing pigeons released into the air far away home for their nests.* **2** *phrasal v. insep.* **to home in on s.t.:** to move toward, sight on: *Guided missiles home in on their target and hit it.*

home·bod·y /ˈhoʊmˌbɑdi/ *n.* **-ies** a person who prefers to stay at home and not travel or go out: *He's a real homebody who would rather read a good book than go out at night.*

home·com·ing /ˈhoʊmˌkʌmɪŋ/ *n.* **1** a return to one's home: *After the war, the soldier's homecoming was an emotional event.* **2** the return of graduates to their school at an annual celebration: *The college homecoming weekend is a lot of fun.*

USAGE NOTE: *Homecoming* weekends are usu. held in the fall. A homecoming king and queen may be crowned during the intermission at a football game and later join in the fun at a big dance for students and graduates.

home-grown *adj.* grown locally or in one's garden: *Home-grown tomatoes taste better than any sold in the grocery store.*

home·land /ˈhoʊmˌlænd/ *n.* one's native country: *The USA (China, Poland, etc.) is my homeland.*

home·less /ˈhoʊmlɪs/ *n.pl.* people who have no home, formerly (in USA) called vagrants: *The government built shelters for the homeless.*

—*adj.* without a home: *The earthquake left hundreds of people homeless.*

home·ly /'hoʊmli/ *adj.* **-lier, -liest** not good-looking, ugly: *He is a homely guy; she is a homely girl.*

home·made /'hoʊm'meɪd/ *adj.* made at home or by hand: *That bread is homemade.*

home·mak·er /'hoʊm,meɪkər/ *n.* a person who takes care of his or her family's house and children: *Zora is a homemaker, and her husband is a teacher.*

USAGE NOTE: The term *homemaker* describes anyone who creates and cares for a home. It is a more contemporary term than *housewife* or *househusband.*

ho·me·o·path·ic /,hoʊmiə'pæθɪk/ *adj.* (in medicine) related to the treatment of an illness by giving a small dose of a medicine that, in a larger dose, would cause the feelings of that illness -*n.* [U] **homeopathy** /,hoʊmi'ɑpəθi/.

ho·me·o·sta·sis /,hoʊmioʊ'steɪsɪs/ *n.* [U] a state of balance, esp. in the bodily system of a person or animal: *In hot weather, we stay in homeostasis by sweating and drinking fluids.*

home·own·er /'hoʊm,oʊnər/ *n.* a property owner, esp. of a house or apartment: *She is a homeowner; she owns a condominium.*

home plate *n.* (in baseball) the fourth base, where the batters stand to hit the ball and then cross after they run around all bases to score: *He hit a home run and crossed home plate to win the game.*

home room *n.* in USA, the room to which students go first in a school day

home rule *n.* [U] the self-governing of a former colony: *After World War II, many colonies of European countries voted for home rule.*

home run *n.* (in baseball) hitting a ball within bounds, allowing the batter to run around all the bases and back home; usu. the ball goes over the fence around the outfield: *The batter hit a home run, and the fans started yelling.*

home·sick /'hoʊm,sɪk/ *adj.* feeling sad when away, missing one's home: *After traveling for a month, I began to feel homesick.* -*n.* [U] **homesickness.**

home·spun /'hoʊm,spʌn/ *adj.* **1** referring to thread spun in a home **2** *fig.* folksy, plain: *Her homespun humor is dry, but funny.*

home·stead /'hoʊm,stɛd/ *n.* a piece of land with a simple house, often given by a government to settlers in return for working on the land: *He has a 150-acre homestead in Alaska.* —*v.* to build a house on remote land: *He homesteaded the land for a year and got ownership of it.* -*n.* [C] **homesteader;** [U] **homesteading.**

home·stretch /'hoʊm'strɛtʃ/ *n.* **1** the final distance on a racetrack before the finish line: *The horses have made the final turn and are in the*

homestretch. **2** the time just prior to the end of an activity: *We're almost finished with our work; we're in the homestretch.*

home·town /'hoʊm'taʊn/ *n.* the city or town where one grew up, often one's birthplace: *Seattle is my hometown.*

home·ward /'hoʊmwərd/ *adv.adj.* toward home: *We walked <adv.> homeward after the concert.*

home·work /'hoʊm,wɜrk/ *n.* [U] schoolwork for students to do at home: *Our math teacher gives us a lot of homework.*

hom·ey /'hoʊmi/ *adj.* **-ier, -iest** having the comfort or familiarity of one's home: *That restaurant has a homey atmosphere.* -*n.* [U] **hominess.**

hom·i·cide /'hɑmə,saɪd/ *n.* **1** [C;U] the killing of one person by another, murder: *Her death was a homicide from a knife wound to the heart.* **2** [C] a person who kills s.o., a murderer

hom·i·cid·al /,hɑmə'saɪdl/ *adj.* likely to commit homicide, kill s.o.

hom·i·ly /'hɑməli/ *n.* **-lies** a sermon, talk: *The priest talked about love for one another in his homily.*

ho·mo /'hoʊmoʊ/ *n.* **-mos** *pej.short for* homosexual *See:* gay, USAGE NOTE.

ho·mo·ge·ne·ous /,hoʊmə'dʒiniəs, -'dʒinyəs/ *adj.* **1** of the same kind: *The population of Japan is homogeneous, with few foreigners.* **2** being the same throughout: *The cream is mixed into the milk so that it is homogeneous.* -*n.* [U] **homogeneity** /,hoʊmədʒə'niəti, -'neɪ-/ *See:* heterogeneous.

ho·mog·e·nize /hə'mɑdʒə,naɪz/ *v.* **-nized, -nizing, -nizes** to make the same throughout: *The milk is homogenized so that the cream is mixed evenly throughout the carton.*

hom·o·nym /'hɑmə,nɪm/ *n.* a word spelled the same as another but with different meanings: *"Wind" is a homonym that as a noun means the motion of the air and as a verb means to turn s.t., as in winding a watch.*

hom·o·phone /'hɑmə,foʊn/ *n.* a word that sounds like another but has a different spelling and meaning: *"Ate" and "eight" are homophones.*

ho·mo·sex·u·al /,hoʊmə'sɛkʃuəl/ *n.* a person who is emotionally and sexually attracted to people of the same sex: *Scientists estimate that 10% of the people in the world are homosexual and that 90% of the people are heterosexual. See:* gay, USAGE NOTE..

—*adj.* related to being homosexual or gay: *He has homosexual preferences.* -*n.* **homosexuality** /,hoʊmə,sɛkʃu'æləti/.

hon·cho /'hɑntʃoʊ/ *n.infrml.* **-chos** the boss, head person: *He is the head honcho in that company.*

hone /houn/ *n.* a stone used to sharpen knives, razors, etc.

—*v.* **honed, honing, hones** **1** to sharpen: *He honed the blades on his hunting knife to a fine edge.* **2** *fig.* to improve, sharpen: *She honed her piano playing by practicing eight hours a day.*

hon·est /'anɪst/ *adj.* **1** truthful and trustworthy: *He is honest in his business with others.* **2** solid, real: *She did an honest day's work on the project.* -*adv.* **honestly.**

hon·es·ty /'anəsti/ *n.* [U] truthfulness and trustworthiness: *You can trust her honesty both in what she says and in her business dealings.* See: *dishonesty.*

hon·ey /'hʌni/ *n.* **1** [U] the sweet, syrupy liquid produced by bees from plant nectar: *I like honey on toast in the morning.* **2** [C] a term of affection similar to "dearest" or "sweetheart": *Honey, would you pass me the salt, please?* -*adj.* **honeyed.**

USAGE NOTE: *Honey* is a common term of affection between two people. Names like *sweetie, darling, pumpkin,* and *angel* are also used as affectionate terms by adults or by an adult speaking to a child.

---

hon·ey·bunch /'hʌni,bʌntʃ/ *n.infrml.* a term of affection: *My daughter is my little honeybunch.*

hon·ey·comb /'hʌni,koum/ *n.* a group of cells that bees make of wax to keep honey and to plant pollen and their eggs: *Beekeepers take honeycombs out of the hives to get honey.*

hon·ey·dew melon /'hʌni,du/ *n.* [C;U] a large, light-green sweet fruit: *Honeydew melons are delicious for dessert.*

hon·ey·moon /'hʌni,mun/ *n.* **1** a trip people take after they get married: *We went to Paris on our honeymoon.* **2** *fig.* a period when one's opponents do not attack: *The President went through a month-long honeymoon before the press criticized him.*

hon·ey·suckle /'hʌni,sʌkəl/ *n.* [C;U] any of a variety of climbing plants with small, trumpet-shaped, sweet-smelling flowers: *The honeysuckle shrubs in our backyard flower in June.*

honk /haŋk, hɔŋk/ *v.n.* **1** to make a sound like a goose: *Geese <v.> honk on their way south each autumn.‖You can hear their <n.pl.> honks.* **2** to blow a car horn: *I <v.> honked at a pedestrian to warn him, and he heard my <n.> honk and stopped.*

hon·ky-tonk /'haŋki,taŋk, 'hɔŋki,tɔŋk/ *n.* **1** [C] a cheap nightclub: *She sings in honky-tonks.* **2** [U] a kind of music played at such nightclubs

hon·or /'anər/ *n.* **1** [U] one's good reputation (for honesty, integrity, etc.): *He is a man of honor and is totally trustworthy.* **2** [U] (for a

woman) virtue, morality, (*syn.*) chastity: *Her honor is above question.* **3** [C;U] praise, recognition from others: *She has the honor of being given an award.* **4** *sing.* privilege, distinction: *The mayor has the honor of introducing the President to the audience.* **5** [U] a term of address for a mayor or a judge: *His Honor the Mayor attended the meeting.* **6 on one's honor:** an agreement to do s.t. based on one's word, integrity: *You may take the examination without supervision, and you are on your honor not to cheat.* **7 with honors:** with high academic marks: *He graduated with honors.*

—*v.* **1** to praise, give recognition to: *She was honored by the mayor with a good citizenship award.* **2** to show respect, (*syn.*) to venerate: *The son honors his parents by caring for them.* **3** to fulfill a promise or obligation: *She honored her student loans by paying them.*

honor roll *n.* an academic honor given to students who achieve high enough grades at the end of a school term: *She is an honors student and is on the honor roll.*

hon·or·a·ble /'anərəbəl/ *adj.* respectable, reputable: *He is an honorable man who keeps his promises.* -*adv.* **honorably.**

hon·o·rar·i·um /,anə'rɛriəm/ *n.* **-iums** or **-ia** /-iə/ a one-time fee paid for work: *The company paid the teacher an honorarium for the speech she gave to its workers.*

hon·or·ar·y /'anə,rɛri/ *adj.* **1** elated to an honor given to s.o. who has not earned it the normal way: *The university gave an honorary degree to a politician.* **2** of an unpaid position: *the honorary president of the theater club*

hooch /hutʃ/ *n.slang* [U] homemade alcoholic drinks: *He sold hooch out of his car.*

hood /hʊd/ *n.* **1** a cloth covering for the head and neck (as part of a robe, coat, or jacket): *It started to snow, and she put up the hood on her jacket.* **2** the metal cover of the front of a car **3** *infrml.short for* hoodlum

—*v.* to cover with a hood: *Monks hooded their heads as they left the church.* -*adj.* **hooded.**

hood·lum /'hʊdləm, 'hud-/ *n.* s.o. who is violent and rough, and often young, (*syns.*) a thug, gangster: *Hoodlums robbed the store.*

hood·wink /'hʊd,wɪŋk/ *v.* to trick, deceive, (*syn.*) to swindle: *A swindler hoodwinked an old man into buying counterfeit coins.*

hoo·ey /'hui/ *n.infrml.* [U] nonsense, (*syn.*) hogwash: *What he says is a lot of hooey; don't believe it.*

hoof /huf, hʊf/ *n.* **hooves** /huvz, hʊvz/ or **hoofs** **1** the hard part of certain mammals' feet, such as cattle and horses: *The hooves of horses are protected by horseshoes.* **2 on the hoof:** (of animals) unbutchered, alive: *The price of cattle on the hoof is low.*

H

H

—*v.infrml.* **to hoof it:** to walk: *We could not find a taxi, so we hoofed it to the park.*

hoofed /hʊft, huft/ *adj.* having hooves: *Hoofed animals include cattle, horses, and many wild species.*

hook /hʊk/ *n.* **1** a tool with a shaft and curved end: *We catch fish with hooks and worms.* **2 by hook or by crook:** by one means or another: *I will fix that computer for you by hook or by crook.* **3 hook, line, and sinker:** the whole thing: *The teacher believed my story hook, line, and sinker.* **4 on one's own hook:** by one's own actions: *I paid my way through college on my own hook with no help from anybody.* **5 to be off the hook: a.** to be thought not responsible for s.t., to have a problem fixed: *His father paid his rent, and that got him off the hook with the landlord.* **b.** (said of telephones) to be disconnected: *Her telephone is off the hook; it doesn't ring.*

—*v.* **1** to catch with a hook: *We hooked some fish in the pond.* **2** to close, fasten with a hook: *She hooked her jacket closed.* **3** *phrasal v. insep.* **to hook on to s.t.: a.** to place on, attach to: *He took off his jacket and hooked it onto the coat rack.* **b.** *fig.* to get s.t. good: *Your new job is high paying and interesting; you've really hooked onto something!* **4** *phrasal v. sep.* **to hook s.t. up:** to connect: *He hooked up the radio antenna and listened to broadcasts.‖She hooked two friends up who were both interested in theater.*

hooked /hʊkt/ *adj.* **1** shaped like a hook, curved: *He has a hooked nose.* **2** addicted, obsessed: *She is hooked on television; she watches it 12 hours a day.‖He is hooked on drugs.*

hook·er /ˈhʊkər/ *n.vulg.slang* a prostitute: *Hookers look for customers near the big hotels.*

hook·up /ˈhʊkˌʌp/ *n.* a connection, linkage: *Stock exchanges have a satellite hookup to send data between countries.*

hook·y or **hook·ey** /ˈhʊki/ *n.* [U] **to play hooky:** to stay out of school without permission, (*syn.*) to be truant: *She played hooky so often that the school called her parents.*

hoo·li·gan /ˈhulɪgən/ *n.* a thug, troublemaker: *Hooligans turned over cars and set them on fire.*

hoop /hup/ *n.* a circular tube or band: *Basketball players shoot the ball through a hoop.*

hoop·la /ˈhup,lɑ/ *n.* [U] loud excitement, (*syn.*) ballyhoo: *Band music and speeches created hoopla at the political rally.*

hoo·ray or **hurray** /hʊˈreɪ, hə-/ *exclam.* expression of triumph, delight: *Hooray, our team won the game!*

hoot /hut/ *n.* **1** the cry made by an owl or a ship's horn **2** a shout of contempt **3** *infrml.fig.* **not to give a hoot:** not to care, to disdain: *I don't give a hoot what he says; he's wrong.*

—*v.* **1** to let out such a cry: *Owls hoot at night.* **2** to make a sound of contempt: *The audience hooted the performer off the stage.* -*n.* **hoot owl.**

hooves /huvz, hʊvz/ *n.pl.* of hoof

hop /hɑp/ *n.* **1** a forward jump: *The girl took little hops down the sidewalk.* **2** a quick trip: *San Diego is a short hop from Los Angeles.*

—*v.* **hopped, hopping, hops** to move with a hopping motion: *Rabbits hop very quickly.*

hops /hɑps/ *n.pl.* the dried flowers of a plant of the hemp family: *Hops are used in the brewing of beer.*

hope /hoʊp/ *n.* **1** [C;U] faith that a situation will improve: *He has hope that his cancer will not be fatal.* **2** [C] s.o. or s.t. that can improve a situation: *That doctor is my last hope.* **3** [C;U] desire that s.t. will happen, (*syn.*) an aspiration: *Her hopes center on having a successful career in law.* **4 to have high hopes:** to have high expectations: *He is doing well at college, and he has high hopes of graduating this June.*

—*v.* **hoped, hoping, hopes 1** to wish, desire: *I hope that you feel better soon.* **2** to aspire, desire success: *She hopes to be a doctor someday.*

hope·ful /ˈhoʊpfəl/ *adj.* **1** having faith that s.t. good will happen: *She is hopeful that she will be cured soon.* **2** optimistic, positive: *There are hopeful signs that she will recover completely.* -*adv.* **hopefully;** -*n.* [U] **hopefulness.**

hope·less /ˈhoʊplɪs/ *adj.* without hope, (*syn.*) dire: *The situation with his bad health is hopeless.* -*adv.* **hopelessly;** -*n.* [U] **hopelessness.**

hop·per /ˈhɑpər/ *n.* **1** a container that receives and sends out things: *Farmers pour grain into hoppers, which release the grain into railroad cars.* **2** s.t. that hops: *Grasshoppers and frogs are hoppers.* **3** *fig.* **in the hopper:** in the works, in process: *Our company has some excellent new projects in the hopper for future sales.*

hop·scotch /ˈhɑp,skɑtʃ/ *n.* [U] a children's game of hopping across numbered squares to pick up a stone that has been tossed onto them: *Youngsters play hopscotch on the sidewalk.*

—*v.* **-scotches** to move or act as though playing hopscotch: *Our airplane flight hopscotched at stops all over the Northeast before landing in Boston.*

horde /hɔrd/ *n.* a mass of people: *Hordes of people came to hear the President speak.*

ho·ri·zon /həˈraɪzən/ *n.* **1** the place in one's view where the earth's surface forms a line with the sky: *Sailors could see another ship coming over the horizon.* **2** a person's chances for success, (*syn.*) prospects: *She is so smart that her future holds unlimited horizons.*

hor·i·zon·tal /ˌhɔrəˈzɑntl, ˌhɑr-/ *adj.* parallel to the ground: *He lay horizontal on the bed.* -*adv.* **horizontally.** *See:* vertical.

hor·mone /ˈhɔrˌmoʊn/ *n.* a chemical from body organs that stimulates activity in living systems: *Testosterone is the male sex hormone.*

horn /hɔrn/ *n.* **1** a pointed growth on the heads of some animals: *Goats have horns.* **2** a musical instrument, usu. made of metal, that creates sounds with air: *The French horn has a beautiful sound.* **3** a device that gives a warning sound: *a car horn* **4 to take the bull by the horns:** to take control, struggle: *My father could not solve the difficult problem, so I took the bull by the horns and solved it for him.* —*phrasal v. insep.* **to horn in on s.t.:** to interupt against the wishes of others, (*syns.*) to intrude, butt in: *He horned in on our conversation and monopolized it.* -*adj.* **horned.**

hor·net /ˈhɔrnɪt/ *n.* a type of wasp noted for its aggressiveness and sting

horn·y /ˈhɔrni/ *adj.* **-ier, -iest 1** rough, hard: *His feet were horny from walking barefoot.* **2** *vulg.slang* wanting sex, (*syn.*) lustful

ho·rol·o·gy /hɔˈrɑlədʒi/ *n.* [U] **1** the making of watches and other timepieces **2** the study of time -*n.* **horologist;** -*adj.* **horological** /ˌhɔrəˈlɑdʒɪkəl/.

hor·o·scope /ˈhɔrəˌskoʊp, ˈhɑr-/ *n.* (in astrology) prediction of a person's future by interpreting the positions of the stars and planets around the time she or he was born: *My horoscope for today is full of good news.*

hor·ren·dous /hɔˈrɛndəs/ *adj.* extreme, terrible: *He is having horrendous difficulty with his health.*

hor·ri·ble /ˈhɔrəbəl, ˈhɑr-/ *adj.* **1** causing horror, terrifying: *A horrible snake came out of the jungle.* **2** *infrml.* very unpleasant or annoying: *We had a horrible time getting through traffic.* -*adv.* **horribly.**

hor·rid /ˈhɔrɪd, ˈhɑr-/ *adj.* **1** monstrous, repulsive: *That snake is horrid.* **2** very annoying: *We had a horrid time with customs authorities.*

hor·rif·ic /hɔˈrɪfɪk, hɔ-, hɑ-/ *adj.* **1** *frml.* terrifying **2** *infrml.* very annoying: *We had horrific difficulties in fixing the computer.* -*adv.* **horrifically.**

hor·ri·fy /ˈhɔrəˌfaɪ, ˈhɑr-/ *v.* **-fied, -fying, -fies** to terrify, sicken with fear: *The sight of his murdered friend horrified him.*

hor·ror /ˈhɔrər, ˈhɑr-/ *n.* **1** [U] fear (terror, revulsion) caused by ugliness or s.t. life-threatening: *The sight of that monster created horror in the crowd.* **2** [C] s.t. causing terror: *That monster was a horror to see.* **3** [C] *infrml.* a terrible situation, incident: *Driving through*

terrible traffic was a horror. -*adj.* **horror-stricken.**

hors d'oeuvre /ɔrˈdɜrv/ *n.* **d'oeuvres** /-ˈdɜrvz/ (French for) an appetizer, (*syn.*) a canape: *We served hors d'oeuvres to our guests before dinner.*

horse /hɔrs/ *n.* **1** a large, four-footed, domesticated animal with hard hooves used for riding, work, and in some places for meat: *The Arabian horse is one of the earth's most beautiful creatures.* **2 a dark horse:** s.o., usu. a politician, who has little chance of winning: *She was a dark horse in the race for mayor, but she won.* **3 a horse of a different color:** s.t. different from what one expected: *We wanted to go on vacation in Hawaii, but when the tickets were twice as expensive as we had thought, that was a horse of a different color!* **4 not to look a gift horse in the mouth:** don't examine or criticize s.t. too much if you get it for free: *My parents gave me their old car, and I did not look a gift horse in the mouth by asking if it needed repairs.* **5** *fig.* **straight from the horse's mouth:** directly from the person who said s.t.: *The boss told me she is going to give everyone a good salary increase; I heard it straight from the horse's mouth (the boss).* **6 to be on a high horse:** to be too proud, arrogant: *I wish that he would get off his high horse and act sensibly.* **7** *fig.* **to hold one's horses:** to wait, not act carelessly: *Hold your horses; we're not ready to leave yet!* **8** *fig.* **to put the cart before the horse:** to do s.t. before the right time for it: *At the meeting, our sales manager started talking about the design of the company's product catalog before we decided what to include in it, so he put the cart before the horse.*
—*v.* **horsed, horsing, horses,** *phrasal v. infrml.* **to horse around:** to play, (*syn.*) to roughhouse: *Those boys are always horsing around with each other. See:* horseplay.

horse·fly /ˈhɔrsˌflaɪ/ *n.* **-flies** a kind of large, blood-sucking fly: *Horseflies can really be annoying.*

hors·ey or **horsy** /ˈhɔrsi/ *adj.infrml.* **1** related to horses: *The horsey crowd has horse shows.* **2** *pej.* looking like a horse, esp. in the face or hips: *My boyfriend was a handsome man, but a bit horsey.*

horse·play /ˈhɔrsˌpleɪ/ *n.* [U] noisy play, wild behavior, (*syn.*) roughhousing: *Boys engage in horseplay after school.*

horse·pow·er /ˈhɔrsˌpaʊər/ *n.* [U] *adj.* **1** a force equal to 746 watts or lifting 550 pounds a distance of one foot in one second **2** a measurement of engine power: *His car has a <adj.> 200-horsepower engine.*

horse·rad·ish /ˈhɔrsˌrædɪʃ/ *n.* [U] a plant with a hot-tasting root that is made into a sauce: *He puts horseradish on his sandwiches.*

horse·shoe /'hɔrʃ,ʃu, 'hɔrs-/ *n.* a U-shaped piece of metal nailed to horses' hooves for protection

hors·y /'hɔrsi/ *adj. See:* horsey.

hor·ti·cul·ture /'hɔrtə,kʌltʃər/ *n.* [U] the science of growing plants: *The city's botanical garden is a center of horticulture.* *-adj.* **horticultural** /,hɔrtə'kʌltʃərəl/ *-n.* [C] **horticulturist.**

hose /hoʊz/ *n.* **1** [C;U] a flexible tube: *I use a garden hose to water the lawn.* **2** *pl.* stockings or socks: *That store sells hose for both men and women.‖Her pantyhose are ripped.*
—v. **hosed, hosing, hoses** to use a hose: *I hosed down my car with water.*

ho·sier·y /'hoʊʒəri/ *n.* [U] socks or stockings: *My wife went to the store to buy some hosiery.*

hos·pice /'hɑspɪs/ *n.* **1** a facility or program for the care of terminally ill people: *Hospice work is difficult because people are very sick and usually do not get well again.* **2** a place of rest and healing: *Monks provide hospices for the poor and ill.*

hos·pi·ta·ble /ha'spɪtəbəl, 'hɑspɪ-/ *adj.* friendly, welcoming, esp. with food, drink, and comfort: *They are a very hospitable couple to both friends and strangers.*

hos·pi·tal /'hɑspɪtl/ *n.* a medical institution that gives health care: *He went to the hospital to have an operation.*

hos·pi·tal·i·ty /,hɑspɪ'tæləti/ *n.* [U] friendly treatment of others, esp. in giving food, drink, and a comfortable place to be: *We enjoyed the hospitality of friends at their country home.*

hos·pi·tal·i·za·tion /,hɑspɪtələ'zeɪʃən/ *n.* [C;U] a stay at a hospital: *His hospitalization was necessary so the doctors could perform tests.*

hos·pi·tal·ize /'hɑspɪtl,aɪz/ *v.* **-ized, -izing, -izes** to place in a hospital: *She was hospitalized for appendicitis.*

host /hoʊst/ *n.* **1** a person in charge of a social or other event: *He is the host of a party tonight.‖She is the host of a TV talk show.* **2** the victim of a bacteria: *Humans are the host of the parasite E. coli.*
—v. to act as a host: *He hosts the nightly news program on TV. See:* hostess.

hos·tage /'hɑstɪdʒ/ *n.* **1** a person taken and held for money or other ransom: *He is a political hostage.* **2 to be held** or **to hold hostage: a.** to be kidnapped or to kidnap s.o. for money or other ransom: *He was held hostage to trade for another country's spy.‖The rebels held her hostage until her country met their demands.* **b.** *fig.* having to do things for a special reason: *He is a politician held hostage to his promise not to raise taxes.*

hos·tel /'hɑstəl/ *n.* an inexpensive place to sleep, esp. for youths: *He travels by bicycle and stays at youth hostels.*

hos·tel·ry /'hɑstəlri/ *n.old usage* **-ries** a hotel, hostel

host·ess /'hoʊstɪs/ *n.* **1** a female host **2** *old usage* a worker on an airplane: *She works as a hostess for American Airlines.* **3** a woman who greets customers in a restaurant *See:* flight attendant.

hos·tile /'hɑstəl, -,taɪl/ *adj.* **1** hateful, angry: *That driver has a hostile attitude; he blows his horn and yells at other drivers.* **2** opposing, *(syn.)* antagonistic: *Our troops ran into hostile forces.*

hostile takeover *n.* (in business) taking control of a company against the wishes of its management

hos·til·i·ty /ha'stɪləti/ *n.* **-ties 1** [U] hatred, anger: *You can feel the hostility coming from that man.* **2** [U] strong opposition, *(syn.)* antagonism: *There was open hostility between the political parties.* **3** *pl.* **hostilities** acts of war: *Hostilities continue between the two countries' armies.*

hot /hɑt/ *adj.* **hotter, hottest 1** having a high degree of heat, burning: *The water is very, very hot.* **2** warm, sultry, *(syn.)* torrid: *The weather is hot today.* **3** spicy, highly seasoned: *My food is hot because I added lots of red peppers to it.* **4** angry, agitated: *We started to argue, and tempers got hot.* **5** *infrml.* sexually aroused: *The couple started kissing, then got hot.* **6** popular, sought after: *Short skirts are the hot fashion this season.* **7** selling fast: *Cowboy boots are a hot item in our store.* **8** *infrml.* stolen: *He was arrested for selling hot merchandise.* **9** doing or performing well: *That comedian is really funny; he's hot tonight.* **10 hot and bothered:** easily upset, worried by s.t.: *When she gets lost driving her car, she gets all hot and bothered but won't ask for directions.* **11** *infrml.* **hot on s.o.'s trail:** close behind, in pursuit of s.o.: *The police were hot on the bank robber's trail.* **12** *infrml.* **hot under the collar:** angry, *(syn.)* agitated: *He gets hot under the collar if you don't agree with him.* **13** *infrml.* **in hot water:** in trouble, difficulty: *He stole a car and is in hot water with the law.* **14 to blow hot and cold:** to go back and forth, *(syn.)* to vacillate: *She blows hot and cold about changing jobs. See:* warm, USAGE NOTE.
—n.pl.infrml. **to have the hots:** to be attracted to: *They have the hots for each other.*

hot air *n.* [U] *fig.* nonsense, loose talk: *He doesn't know what he's talking about; he's full of hot air.*

hot·bed /'hɑt,bɛd/ *n.fig.* an environment that helps create s.t.: *That political party is a hotbed of revolution.*

hot·blood·ed /'hɑt'blʌdɪd/ *adj.* easily angered, hotheaded: *She is hotblooded and gets mad at any little thing.*

hot·cake /'hɑt,keɪk/ *n.* **1** a pancake: *I like to eat hotcakes and sausages for breakfast.* **2 to sell like hotcakes:** to sell rapidly: *Those new shoes are selling like hotcakes.*

hot dog *n.* **1** a sausage made of ground, spiced meat: *We had hot dogs for lunch today.* **2** *infrml.fig.* a show-off: *He is a hot dog on the ski slopes.*

ho·tel /hoʊ'tɛl/ *n.* a building with bedrooms for rent and usu. food and other services: *We stayed in a big hotel in Montreal.*

USAGE NOTE: An *inn* is a small hotel, often in the country, offering rooms and food to travelers; *a B&B*, or *bed and breakfast,* is usually a large home with few rooms to rent, that serves only breakfast. A *youth hostel* offers young people military-style accomodations for a low price. A *motel* or *motor inn* is less expensive than a hotel. The rooms often open onto the parking lot. The category of *pension* is not used in the USA.

---

hot flash *n.* **flashes 1** a sudden hot feeling, usu. during menopause: *She told her doctor she often has hot flashes.* **2** a sudden, important news story: *A reporter interrupted the broadcast with a hot flash from Washington.*

hot·foot /'hɑt,fʊt/ *n.infrml.* the prank of lighting a match in a person's shoe
—*v.infrml.* **to hotfoot it:** to run or move quickly: *I hotfooted it over to the department store to go to their one-day sale.*

hot·head /'hɑt,hɛd/ *n.* a person who does things without thinking and gets angry easily: *He's a hothead who starts yelling if you disagree with him.* -*adj.* **hotheaded** /'hɑt'hɛdɪd/.

hot line *n.* a telephone line for emergencies: *The hot line between Moscow and Washington is a red telephone that sits on the President's desk.∥She works at a suicide hot line.*

hot·ly /'hɑtli/ *adv.* **1** heatedly, passionately **2** closely: *The cat was hotly pursued by the dog.*

hot plate *n.* a small stove with a metal burner for heating food: *My small apartment has no kitchen, but I have a hot plate to heat soup.*

hot potato *n.infrml.fig.* -**toes** a difficult situation, sensitive dilemma: *The abortion issue in the USA is a political hot potato.*

hot seat *n.* **to put s.o. in the hot seat** or **to sit in the hot seat:** a position where one must answer difficult and embarrassing questions: *His boss put him in the hot seat because his department was making mistakes and losing money.*

hot·shot /'hɑt,ʃɑt/ *n.adj.infrml.* an excellent performer, esp. one who shows off: *She is a young <n.> hotshot* or *<adj.> hotshot stockbroker.*

hot spot *n.* an area where there is trouble or likely to be trouble: *Hot spots in the world are places where war happens.*

hot-tempered *adj.* related to a person who gets angry easily: *He is a hot-tempered man, always yelling.*

hot tub *n.* a large tub filled with hot water for relaxation: *The couple has a hot tub in their backyard.*

hot water bottle *n.* a rubber bag filled with hot water: *When I hurt my foot, I put a hot water bottle on it to ease the pain.*

hot-wire *v.* **-wired, -wiring, -wires** to go around a vehicle's normal ignition system by connecting starting wires directly to each other: *Thieves hot-wire cars and steal them without using keys.*

hound /haʊnd/ *n.* any of approx. 17 breeds of hunting dogs: *Foxhounds have a sharp sense of smell.*
—*v.* to bother, chase, worry: *My mother hounded me until I washed the dishes.*

hour /aʊər/ *n.* **1** a time period of 60 minutes, 1/24th of a day: *My train ride to work takes an hour.* **2** a special moment in time: *The fall of the Berlin Wall was one of history's finest hours.* **3** *pl.* a time period designated for certain activity: *Our office hours are from 9 to 5.* **4 after hours:** after usual business hours **5 at the eleventh hour:** at the last minute, almost too late **6 on the hour:** at exactly one o'clock, two o'clock, etc.: *A bus leaves for New York on the hour.*

hour·glass /'aʊər,glæs/ *n.* a device for measuring time by the falling of sand from a top globe to a bottom globe: *I use a small hourglass as a timer for boiling eggs.*

hourglass

hour hand *n.* the smaller hand on a watch: *When both the minute hand and hour hand are on 12, it is either noon or midnight.*

hour·ly /'aʊərli/ *adv.* happening every hour: *A train leaves for San Francisco hourly from here.*

house /haʊs/ *n.* **houses** /'haʊzɪz/ **1** a place to live for one or a few families: *Our house is located on the corner.* **2** a building for various purposes: *Firefighters work in the local fire house.* **3** a legislative body or its chambers: *The House of Representatives is located in Washington, D.C.* **4** the audience in a theater: *There was a full house on the opening night of the ballet.* **5** a noble or important family: *Queen Elizabeth II belongs to the House of*

Windsor. **6 like a house afire** or **on fire:** quickly: *He ran out of here like a house afire.* **7 on the house:** paid for by a bar or restaurant (usu. of food, drinks)

—*v.* **housed, housing, houses** to have shelter, stay somewhere: *Refugees are housed temporarily in tents.*

house arrest *n.* [U] forcing s.o. to stay in a house: *Soldiers put the minister under house arrest by surrounding his home.*

house·boat /'haʊs,boʊt/ *n.* a boat that functions as a home: *We turned an old barge into a houseboat with a bedroom, kitchen, etc.*

house·bound /'haʊs,baʊnd/ *adj.* unable to go out, usu. because of age or illness: *My grandmother broke her leg and is housebound.*

house·break·ing /'haʊs,breɪkɪŋ/ *n.* [U] **1** forcing one's way into a house to steal s.t.: *The burglar was convicted of housebreaking.* **2** training an animal to excrete outdoors or in a box

house·bro·ken /'haʊs,broʊkən/ *adj.* (said of an animal) trained to do its excretion outdoors or in a box: *Our cat was housebroken quickly.* -*v.* **housebreak** /'haʊs,breɪk/.

house·clean·ing /'haʊs,klinɪŋ/ *n.* **1** [U] chores needed to keep a house clean: *She has a maid who does the housecleaning.* **2** [C;U] *fig.* a replacement of many employees with new ones: *The new boss did a housecleaning by hiring a whole new staff.*

house·coat /'haʊs,koʊt/ *n.* a casual dress worn around the house: *She wears a thick housecoat to keep warm in winter.*

house·hold /'haʊs,hoʊld, 'haʊ,soʊld/ *n.* the person or people living together in one home: *The national survey counts the number of households in the country.* -*n.* **householder.**

household word *n.* a well-known person or the brand name of a product that is used to mean the product itself: *Coke is a household word for a cola soft drink.*

house·hus·band /'haʊs,hʌzbənd/ *n.* a man who keeps the house while the wife works outside the house: *He is a househusband who cleans, cooks, and takes care of their children.* *See:* homemaker, USAGE NOTE.

house·keep·er /'haʊs,kipər/ *n.* a person hired to take care of a private house or supervise workers in hotel rooms: *Our housekeeper cleans, does the laundry, and makes the beds.*

house·keep·ing /'haʊs,kipɪŋ/ *n.* [U] housecleaning, the chores needed to keep a house or hotel in order: *Housekeeping in a big hotel can involve hundreds of maids and maintenance workers.*

house·lights /'haʊs,laɪts/ *n.pl.* theater lights that can be made brighter or dimmer

house·maid /'haʊs,meɪd/ *n.* a maid, domestic servant

house·moth·er /'haʊs,mʌðər/ *n.* a woman in charge of a group house, usu. in a school: *My aunt is a housemother at a college dormitory.*

house of cards *n.fig.* a fragile, shaky situation or structure: *His business dealings were a house of cards, so his company soon went out of business.*

house of correction *n.* **houses of correction** a prison for people who have committed minor offenses: *The teenage thief was sent to a house of correction by the judge.*

House of Representatives *n.* the lower legislative house of Congress in the USA and of many state legislatures: *Members of the House of Representatives are elected every two years.*

house organ *n.* a newsletter, magazine, etc. published internally by a business or institution: *The museum sends its house organ to employees and members.*

house-sit *v.* **-sat, -sitting, -sits** to stay in a house while its owners or tenants are away -*n.* (person) **house sitter; (act) house-sitting.**

house·wares /'haʊs,wɛrz/ *n.pl.* dishes, glasses, and other articles used in a house, esp. the kitchen: *Large stores have a department that sells housewares.*

house·warm·ing /'haʊs,wɔrmɪŋ/ *n.* a party given for new owners or tenants of a house: *Our neighbors gave us a housewarming when we moved in.*

USAGE NOTE: People may also give themselves a *housewarming* party by inviting friends and family to a party. It is traditional to bring a small gift of s.t. for the house: a potted plant, guest soap, candles, a bottle of wine, or s.t. for the kitchen.

house·wife /'haʊs,waɪf/ *n.* **-wives** /-,waɪvz/ a woman who does not work outside of the home: *She is a housewife who is very active in civic affairs.* *See:* homemaker, USAGE NOTE.

house·work /'haʊs,wɜrk/ *n.* [U] work done to keep a house in order, (*syn.*) chores: *Housework consists of cleaning, cooking, and doing the laundry.*

hous·ing /'haʊzɪŋ/ *n.* [U] a general term for houses, apartments, etc. that people live in, (*syn.*) dwellings: *Housing in this area is expensive.*

hov·el /'hʌvəl, 'hɑ-/ *n.* a small, open, dirty shelter: *A homeless man built a hovel out of tin sheets and cardboard cartons.*

hov·er /'hʌvər, 'hɑ-/ *v.* to stay suspended in the air over an area: *Hawks hover over fields, searching for rabbits and mice.*

how /haʊ/ *adv.* **1** in what manner: *How do you fix this broken faucet?* **2** for what reason: *How can you say such an awful thing?* **3** in what condition: *How do you feel?* **4** to what extent, cost: *How much does this sofa cost?* **5** by what

description, designation: *How do you describe this object?* **6** as part of a greeting: *How do you do?* **7** *infrml.* **how about:** what do you think about (s.t.): *I couldn't decide what to wear, then asked her, "How about this dress?"* **8** *infrml.* **How come?:** Why?: *How come you didn't call me yesterday?*
—*conj.* the way in which: *I remember how she laughed at his joke.*

how·dy /'haʊdi/ *exclam.infrml.* Hello, how are you?: *Cowboys say "Howdy!" when they greet each other.*

how·ev·er /haʊ'ɛvər/ *conj.* in spite of, but: *He is intelligent; however, he is also difficult.*
—*adv.* **1** to whatever degree, extent: *You may stay there however long you wish.* **2** said in surprise: *However did the cat get up that tree?*

how·it·zer /'haʊɪtsər/ *n.* a cannon of intermediate length and firepower: *The army used howitzers against the enemy hiding in the hills.*

howl /haʊl/ *v.* **1** to cry loudly, (*syns.*) to wail, yowl: *Monkeys howl in the treetops.* **2** *infrml.fig.* to laugh heartily: *The audience howled at the comedian's jokes.* **3** to complain loudly: *He's always howling about something.*
—*n.* a howling sound: *The cat gave out a howl* -*n.* **howler.**

howl·ing /'haʊlɪŋ/ *adj.* **1** making the noise of a howl **2** extreme, (*syn.*) glaring: *a howling mistake*

how·so·ever /ˌhaʊsoʊ'ɛvər/ *adv.* in whatever manner: *Howsoever you wish to do the job is up to you.*

how-to /'haʊ'tu/ *adj.* giving the practical steps needed to do s.t.: *a how-to book on home repairs*
—*n.* [U] a set of practical instructions for doing s.t.

hub /hʌb/ *n.* **1** a wheel's center where the axle is inserted **2** a center of much activity: *Chicago is a hub of airline traffic.*

hub·bub /'hʌˌbʌb/ *n.* [U] noisy confusion: *The train station is full of hubbub at Christmastime.*

hub·by /'hʌbi/ *n.infrml.* **-bies** husband

hub·cap /'hʌbˌkæp/ *n.* a decorative and protective metal plate put on a wheel's hub

hu·bris /'hyubrɪs/ *n.frml.* [U] pride and arrogance: *His hubris prevented him from asking for help on the project, so it was late.*

huck·le·ber·ry /'hʌkəlˌbɛri/ *n.* **-ries** a darkblue edible berry: *We had huckleberry pie with ice cream for dessert.*

huck·ster /'hʌkstər/ *n.* s.o. who sells using questionable, tricky methods: *He is a huckster who tells people that the land they are buying is better than it really is.*

hud·dle /'hʌdl/ *v.* **-dled, -dling, -dles** **1** to press closely together: *Baby rabbits huddle together near their mother.* **2** (in U.S. foot-

ball) to meet in a tight group to plan the next move: *The Atlanta Falcons huddled, then threw a long pass.* **3** *fig.* to consult, meet: *Our department huddled on how to meet the deadline.*

hue /hyu/ *n.* graduation of color, as in red to yellow: *The hues of the leaves in autumn are beautiful against a blue sky.*

huff /hʌf/ *v.* to breathe heavily, blow or puff air: *He huffed and puffed as he climbed the mountain.*
—*n.* **in a huff:** in a state of anger or indignation: *She felt insulted and left in a huff.*

huff·y /'hʌfi/ *adj.* **-ier, -iest** angry, indignant: *She gets huffy often.* -*adv.* **huffily.**

hug /hʌg/ *n.* an embrace, the act of putting one's arms around s.o.: *He gives his children a hug and a kiss as they leave for school.*
—*v.* **hugged, hugging, hugs** **1** to encircle s.o. with the arms: *She hugged her children.* **2** to stay near the shoreline: *The sailboat hugged the coast in the strong wind.*

huge /hyudʒ/ *adj.* **huger, hugest** **1** very large, enormous: *The country suffers from a huge debt.* **2** very large, bulky: *Football players are huge men.* -*adv.* **hugely.**

huh /hʌ, hʌ̃/ *exclam.* **1** expressing a question: *Huh? What did you say?* **2** expressing indifference: *Oh, huh, I don't care what we do.* **3** expressing surprise: *Huh! What a great idea!*

hu·la /'hulə/ *n.* [C;U] a Hawaiian dance with movement of the hips and hands

hulk /hʌlk/ *n.* **1** s.t. or s.o. large and awkward: *He is a hulk of a man.* **2** the remains of an abandoned ship: *The hulk lay on its side in the harbor.*
—*v.* to appear as a hulk: *A giant of a man hulked into our living room.* -*adj.* **hulking.**

hull /hʌl/ *n.* **1** the shell of a ship, without its sails and inside rooms: *The ship's hull is made of steel.* **2** the outer shell of some nuts and fruits: *We removed the hulls from the walnuts.*
—*v.* to remove hulls: *We hulled the nuts before eating them.*

hul·la·ba·loo /'hʌləbəˌlu/ *n.infrml.* [U] **-loos** a loud noise, (*syn.*) uproar: *He created a big hullabaloo about being treated unfairly.*

hum /hʌm/ *v.* **hummed, humming, hums** **1** to make a continuous sound of "M": *Bees hum when they fly.* **2** to sing with the mouth closed: *He hummed a tune as he walked to work.* **3** *fig.* to work smoothly and well: *Our business is humming right along.*
—*n.* a humming sound, the sound of a smooth operation: *You can hear the hum of activity in that business.*

hu·man /'hyumən/ or **human being** *n.* a person: *Humans live in almost every part of the earth.*

—*adj.* having human traits, characteristics: *It is only human to cry for dead loved ones.*

hu·mane /hyu'meɪn/ *adj.* concerned for others, (*syn.*) compassionate: *The Humane Society tries to prevent cruelty to animals.*

hu·man·ism /'hyumə,nɪzəm/ *n.* [U] belief in human values and in science, in contrast to religious ideas: *Humanism has flourished in this century. -n.adj.* **humanist.**

hu·man·i·tar·i·an /hyu,mænə'tɛriən/ *n.* [C] **1** a person devoted to improvement of the human condition **2** s.o. who gives money to charity, (*syn.*) a philanthropist
—*adj.* devoted to improvement of humanity: *She has many humanitarian interests and contributes a lot to them. -n.* [U] **humanitarianism.**

hu·man·i·ty /hyu'mænəti/ *n.* **-ties 1** [U] human beings as a group: *Humanity was threatened by nuclear war.* **2** [U] the state or condition of being human: *He showed his humanity by helping his neighbor.* **3** *pl.* **humanities** fields of study such as literature, arts, languages, and history. *See:* man, USAGE NOTE.

hu·man·ize /'hyumə,naɪz/ *v.* **-ized, -izing, -izes** to make kind, humane: *He was a brutal warrior who was humanized by becoming religious. -n.* [C] **humanizer;** [U] **humanization** /,hyumənə'zeɪʃən/.

hu·man·kind /'hyumən,kaɪnd, ,hyumən-'kaɪnd/ *n.frml.* [U] humans as a group

hu·man·ly /'hyumənli/ *adv.* **1** in a human way **2** if at all possible: *She will help you in every way humanly possible.*

human nature *n.* [U] general characteristics both good and bad of human behavior: *It is human nature to want love and affection.*

hu·man·oid /'hyumə,nɔɪd/ *adj.n.* having human characteristics: *That robot is so realistic that it is <adj.> humanoid.*

human resources or **HR** /'eɪtʃ'ɑr/ *n.pl.* personnel, employees: *Large corporations try to develop their human resources by giving educational programs. See:* personnel.

hum·ble /'hʌmbəl/ *adj.* **-bler, -blest 1** meek, weak: *He has a humble manner in the presence of important people.* **2** modest, (*syn.*) unassuming: *She is a great athlete, but is humble about her accomplishments.* **3** poor, unimportant: *He came to power from humble circumstances as a poor boy.*
—*v.* **-bled, -bling, -bles** to lower in self-esteem or position: *Failure humbled her.*

humble pie *n.fig.* [U] **to eat humble pie:** to feel bad (guilty, ashamed) about losing, (*syn.*) to be humiliated: *He boasted that he could win, but he lost, and now has to eat humble pie.*

hum·bug /'hʌm,bʌg/ *n.* [U] **1** nonsense, expression of contempt: *Dickens's Scrooge said*

"Bah, humbug!" to the needs of others. **2** a deception or deceptive person

hum·ding·er /'hʌm'dɪŋər/ *n.infrml.* s.t. excellent, outstanding: *His new guitar is a real humdinger.*

hum·drum /'hʌm,drʌm/ *adj.* boring, (*syn.*) monotonous: *She leads a humdrum life.*

hu·mec·tant /hyu'mɛktənt/ *n.adj.frml.* a moisturizer. *Skin-care specialists recommend the use of <n.pl.>* humectants.

hu·mid /'hyumɪd/ *adj.* having damp air (and uncomfortable weather): *Oh, it's so humid today; it's hard to breathe!*

hu·mid·i·fy /hyu'mɪdə,faɪ/ *v.* **-fied, -fying, -fies** to put moisture into the air: *We humidify the air in winter with a <n.>* humidifier.

hu·mid·i·ty /hyu'mɪdəti/ *n.* [U] the amount of moisture in the air: *The humidity is high today.*

hu·mil·i·ate /hyu'mɪli,eɪt/ *v.* **-ated, -ating, -ates 1** to embarrass, (*syn.*) to humble: *The actor forgot his lines, and that mistake humiliated him.* **2** to disgrace, shame: *A prison sentence humiliated the thief and his family. -n.* [C;U] **humiliation** /hyu,mɪli'eɪʃən/.

hu·mil·i·ty /hyu'mɪləti/ *n.* [U] **1** weakness, (*syn.*) meekness: *His humility before the king was clear.* **2** modesty, lack of self-importance: *The humility of the great artist impressed everyone.*

hum·mer /'hʌmər/ *n.* a person or thing that hums: *That car of mine is beautiful; that little hummer runs like a gem.*

hum·ming·bird /'hʌmɪŋ,bɜrd/ *n.* any of a variety of tiny, colorful birds that beat their wings very quickly:

hummingbird

Hummingbirds move from flower to flower, drinking their nectar.

hum·mock /'hʌmək/ *n.* a hillock, a rise in the landscape: *A hunter stood on a hummock above the field.*

hu·mor /'hyumər/ *n.* **1** [U] s.t. comical in written, oral, or graphic form: *That comedian's humor is often childish, so I don't think he's very funny.* **2 good** or **bad humored:** having a cheerful or irritable state of mind, mood: *He's always smiling and good humored.*
—*v.* to make s.o. happy by doing what he or she wants: *I humored my mother by going shopping with her. -n.* [C] **humorist.**

hu·mor·ous /'hyumərəs/ *adj.* funny, comical: *A reporter wrote humorous comments about the politician. -adv.* **humorously.**

hump /hʌmp/ *n.* **1** a bulge: *He has a hump on his back.* **2 over the hump:** past the hardest part or time of s.t.

—*v.* **1** to form into a bulge: *He humped his shoulders in lifting the weight.* **2** *fig.* to work very hard: *We really humped to finish that job.*

hump·back /'hʌmp,bæk/ or **humpbacked** /'hʌmp,bækt/ *adj.* having a hump on the back: *The humpback whale was hunted almost to extinction.*

hunch /hʌntʃ/ *n.* **hunches** an idea, feeling s.t. is so, (*syn.*) an intuition: *I have a hunch that it will rain this afternoon.*

—*v.* **hunches** to form into a hump: *The student hunched over her desk as she studied.*

hunch·back /'hʌntʃ,bæk/ *n.* a person with a hump on the back

hun·dred /'hʌndrɪd/ *n.* **-dreds** or (after a number) **-dred 1** the cardinal number between 99 and 101: *I have a hundred dollars in my wallet.* **2** *pl.* **hundreds a.** designation of a century: *When we say that the author lived in the eighteen hundreds, we mean between the years 1801 and 1899.* **b.** lots of s.t.: *Hundreds of people were on the beach last weekend.*

hun·dredth /'hʌndrɪdθ, -drɪtθ/ *adj.n.* **1** being the ordinal number between 99th and 101st: *His was the hundredth application for the job.* **2** being one of a hundred equal parts of s.t.

hung /hʌŋ/ *adj.* past tense & past part. *of* hang **1** not unanimous: *A hung jury is one that cannot decide on a verdict.* **2 hung over:** suffering the effects of too much alcohol: *He drank too much beer last night and is hung over this morning.* **3 hung up: a.** delayed, detained: *I got hung up in traffic; sorry I'm late.* **b.** *infrml.fig.* obsessed, psychologically blocked: *She's hung up about working for a big company, and won't take a job at a small firm.*

hun·ger /'hʌŋgər/ *n.* [U] the need for food: *The population of that country suffers from hunger.*

—*v.* to desire s.t. very much: *He hungered for her love.*

hunger strike *n.* the refusal to eat as a protest: *Prisoners went on a hunger strike to protest bad conditions in the prison.* -*n.* **hunger striker.**

hun·gry /'hʌŋgri/ *adj.* **-grier, -griest 1** feeling the lack of food: *I haven't eaten all day and feel very hungry.* **2** *fig.* eager, wanting s.t.: *She is a student hungry for knowledge.* -*adv.* **hungrily.**

hunk /hʌŋk/ *n.* **1** a piece of s.t., chunk: *I put a hunk of earth in a pot.* **2** *infrml.fig.* a big, strong, attractive man: *Some women prefer hunks to intellectual types.*

hun·ker /'hʌŋkər/ *v.* **1** to bend at the knees, (*syn.*) to squat **2** *phrasal v.* **to hunker down:** to work hard: *He hunkered down and studied hard.*

hunt /hʌnt/ *v.* **1** to search for: *I hunted for my hat and finally found it.* **2** to chase and capture

or kill: *Every autumn, many people hunt deer in this area.*

—*n.* **1** a search: *We went on a hunt for the lost document.* **2** a pursuit, such as of game or criminals: *Police started a hunt for the murderer.*

hunt·er /'hʌntər/ *n.* a person who hunts, mainly game: *Hunters kill deer in the fall.*‖*A fortune hunter tries to marry a wealthy person.*

hunt·ing /'hʌntɪŋ/ *n.* [U] the sport of killing game (animals, birds): *Hunting is a popular sport in many areas.*

hur·dle /'hɜrdl/ *n.* **1** a low barrier: *Runners jump over hurdles.* **2** an obstacle, (*syn.*) hindrance: *In starting a new company, many hurdles must be crossed.*

—*v.* **-dled, -dling, -dles** to jump over a hurdle or other barrier: *The runner hurdled the fence.* -*n.* [C] **hurdler;** [U] **hurdling.**

hurl /hɜrl/ *v.* **1** to throw with great force: *Protesters hurled rocks at the police.* **2** *slang* to vomit -*n.* [U] **hurling.**

hur·ly-bur·ly /'hɜrli'bɜrli/ *n.* [U] noisy commotion, (*syn.*) turmoil: *The hurly-burly of a political protest resulted in the arrests of some demonstrators.*

hur·rah /hə'rɑ, -'rɔ/ or **hur·ray** /hə'reɪ/ *exclam.* expression of triumph, pleasure: *Hurrah! Our team won!*

hur·ri·cane /'hɜrə,keɪn, 'hʌr-/ *n.* a large, violent rain and wind storm: *Hurricanes have winds up to 150 miles (240 km) per hour.*

hur·ried /'hɜrid, 'hʌr-/ *adj.* rushed, (*syn.*) harried: *My boss is always hurried; she has too much work and not enough help.* -*adv.* **hurriedly.**

hur·ry /'hɜri, 'hʌri/ *v.* **-ried, -rying, -ries** to rush, (*syn.*) to hasten: *We hurried, so as not to be late.*

—*n.* [U] a rush, fast pace: *He is always in a hurry.*

hurt /hɜrt/ *v.* **1** to feel pain, ache: *I fell, and my leg hurts.* **2** to feel distress or anguish: *They still hurt from the money they lost in the stock market.* **3** to cause pain, injure: *The accident hurt him badly.* **4** to cause pain that isn't mental or physical: *News of the scandal hurt his chances of winning the election.* -*adj.* **hurtful** /'hɜrtfəl/; -*adv.* **hurtfully.**

hur·tle /'hɜrtl/ *v.* **-tled, -tling, -tles** to rush with great speed, plunge: *A meteor hurtled through the night sky.*

hus·band /'hʌzbənd/ *n.* a man who is married: *He became her husband last year.*

—*v.* to save, (*syn.*) to conserve: *The couple husbanded their resources and bought a house.*

hus·band·ry /'hʌzbəndri/ *n.* [U] **1** farming, cultivation: *He majored in animal husbandry in college.* **2** conservative use of resources:

Husbandry of their food reserves prevented starvation.

hush /hʌʃ/ *v.* **-es 1** to become or make quiet: *The mother hushed her noisy children.* **2** *phrasal v. sep.* **to hush s.t. up:** to hide information from the public: *The mayor hushed up the news that $1 million was missing from the city.||She hushed it up.*
—*n sing.;* [U] a quieting of noise: *A hush came over the audience when the play began.*

hush-hush *adj.* secret, confidential: *Our boss told us that the new project is hush-hush.*

husk /hʌsk/ *n.* a dry outer leaf-like covering, esp. on corn: *You shuck the corn's husks before cooking it.*
—*v.* to remove husks, *(syn.)* to shuck: *We husk corn after the autumn harvest.*

husk·y /ˈhʌski/ *adj.* **-ier, -iest** strong and solid, stocky: *He is a husky boy.*
—*n.* **-ies** a type of work dog: *Alaskan huskies pull dogsleds.* -*n.* **huskiness.**

hus·sy /ˈhʌsi, ˈhʌzi/ *n.pej.old usage* **-sies** a woman with low moral standards

hus·tings /ˈhʌstɪŋz/ *n.pl.* platforms, places where speeches are made: *Politicians speak from the hustings at election time.*

hus·tle /ˈhʌsəl/ *v.* **-tled, -tling, -tles 1** to go rapidly, rush: *I hustled over to my friend's place.* **2** to work energetically: *He really hustled to finish the job on time.* **3** to do business in a sneaky or overly aggressive way: *He hustled stolen cars for a living.* **4** *infrml.* to sell one's body as a prostitute
—*n.* **1** [U] energetic action: *She showed a lot of hustle to get that new customer.* **2** [C] a sneaky scheme, *(syn.)* a scam: *That deal is a hustle.* **3 the hustle and bustle:** energy, much activity: *All the hustle and bustle of the big city is too much for me.* -*n.* [C] **hustler;** [U] **hustling.**

hut /hʌt/ *n.* a cabin, a small, shabby shelter: *People live in huts in that poor area. See:* hovel; hutch, **2.**

hutch /hʌtʃ/ *n.* **hutches 1** a box or coop for small animals: *He used chicken wire to make a rabbit hutch.* **2** a makeshift shelter: *She built a hutch from branches and leaves.*

hy·a·cinth /ˈhaɪəsɪnθ/ *n.* **1** a plant with a cluster of sweet-smelling flowers that grows from a bulb: *Hyacinths bloom in the spring.* **2** a bluish color

hy·brid /ˈhaɪbrɪd/ *n.adj.* a combination of two types of plants or animals: *Those <adj.> hybrid tomatoes are bred for big size and good flavor.*

hy·drant /ˈhaɪdrənt/ *n.* a water outlet, fireplug: *Firefighters put hoses on water hydrants to get water to fight fires. See:* fire hydrant.

hy·drau·lics /haɪˈdrɔlɪks/ *n.* [U] the science of fluids and their practical uses: *Engineers use hydraulics in designing brake systems.* -*adj.* **hydraulic.**

hy·dro·e·lec·tric /ˌhaɪdroʊɪˈlɛktrɪk/ *adj.* related to creating electricity from water power: *Huge amounts of hydroelectric power are generated in Canada's St Lawrence River.* -*adv.* **hydroelectrically.**

hydrofoil

hy·dro·foil /ˈhaɪdrəˌfɔɪl/ *n.* **1** a long, narrow blade used to lift a vessel off the water **2** the vessel itself: *Hydrofoils can travel at speeds over 70 miles (112 km) per hour.*

hy·dro·gen /ˈhaɪdrədʒən/ *n.* [U] *adj.* the lightest gaseous chemical element: *The <adj.> hydrogen bomb has huge destructive power.*

hy·drol·o·gy /haɪˈdrɑlədʒi/ *n.* [U] the science of water, its properties, and distribution in the world

hy·dro·plane /ˈhaɪdrəˌpleɪn/ *v.* **-planed, -planing, -planes** to move across the surface of water: *In a rainstorm, cars can hydroplane dangerously and lose control.*
—*n.* **1** a high-powered motorboat: *A hydroplane race is exciting to watch.* **2** an airplane that can land or take off from water

hy·dro·ther·a·py /ˌhaɪdrəˈθɛrəpi/ *n.* [U] use of water for healing

hy·e·na /haɪˈinə/ *n.* a meat-eating, wild, dog-like animal of Africa and southeast Asia that is active at night: *Hyenas feed on small dead animals and birds.*

hy·giene /ˈhaɪdʒin/ *n.* [U] the science of personal and public health: *Personal hygiene includes cleanliness, eating healthy foods, and exercising.* -*adj.* **hygienic** /ˌhaɪdʒiˈɛnɪk, haɪˈdʒɪnɪk, -ˈdʒɛ-/; -*adv.* **hygienically;** -*n.* [C] **hygienist** /haɪˈdʒinɪst, -ˌdʒɛ-, ˈhaɪˌdʒinɪst/.

hy·men /ˈhaɪmən/ *n.* a membrane partly covering the vaginal opening of a virgin: *The hymen can be broken during exercise.*

hymn /hɪm/ *n.* a religious song of praise

hym·nal /ˈhɪmnəl/ *n.* a religious songbook: *The congregation sings hymns from the hymnal.*

hype /haɪp/ *n.* [U] exaggerated advertising claims, *(syn.)* hoopla: *People went to see the movie because of all the hype.*
—*v.* **hyped, hyping, hypes 1** to make excessive advertising claims: *Promoters really hyped the movie.* **2** *phrasal v. sep. slang* **to hype s.o. up: a.** to stimulate with drugs: *The injection hyped up the patient.||It hyped him*

up. **b.** to excite, enthuse: *The prospect of making money hyped up my assistant.*‖*It hyped her up.*

hy·per /'haɪpər/ *prefix* excessive, overly: *He is a hyperactive child.*
—*adj.slang* high-strung, nervously energetic: *Drinking too much coffee makes me hyper.*

hy·per·ac·tive /,haɪpər'æktɪv/ *adj.* nervously energetic, (*syn.*) high-strung: *He was a hyperactive child.* -*n.* [U] **hyperactivity** /,haɪpəræk'tɪvəti/.

hy·per·bo·le /haɪ'pɜrbəli/ *n.frml.* [C;U] exaggeration used for dramatic effect: *He used hyperbole by describing the wrestler as a giant of a man.*

hy·per·bol·ic /,haɪpər'balɪk/ *adj.* **1** having the shape of a hyperbola: *She drew a hyperbolic figure on the blackboard.* **2** *frml.* characterized by exaggeration: *The speaker made hyperbolic claims for his product.*

hy·per·crit·i·cal /,haɪpər'krɪtɪkəl/ *adj.* too critical: *He is so hypercritical that he corrects every mistake his students make.*

hy·per·sen·si·tive /,haɪpər'sensətɪv/ *adj.* **1** (in medicine) overreaction of the body's defenses: *He is hypersensitive to dust.* **2** easily hurt by others, touchy: *She is hypersensitive to criticism of any kind.*

hy·per·son·ic /,haɪpər'sanɪk/ *adj.* related to speeds five or more times the speed of sound: *Jet fighters are hypersonic aircraft.*

hy·per·ten·sion /,haɪpər'tenʃən/ *n.* [U] high blood pressure: *He takes medicine to lower hypertension.*

hy·per·ven·ti·late /,haɪpər'ventl,eɪt/ *v.* **-lated, -lating, -lates** to breathe fast, usu. causing numbness and dizziness: *He started to hyperventilate when he thought he was having a heart attack.* -*n.* [U] **hyperventilation** /,haɪpər,ventl'eɪʃən/.

hy·phen /'haɪfən/ *n.* the punctuation mark (-): *A hyphen connects the parts of many words, such as "how-to."*

hy·phen·ate /'haɪfə,neɪt/ *v.* **-ated, -ating, -ates** **1** to divide into syllables with a hyphen: *I have now hyphenated the word "hy-phen-ate."* **2** to join two words with a hyphen -*adj.* **hyphenated;** -*n.* [C] **hyphenation** /,haɪfə'neɪʃən/.

hyp·no·sis /hɪp'noʊsɪs/ *n.* [U] a sleep-like state where a person's mind is open to suggestions: *Many people use hypnosis to stop bad habits, such as smoking cigarettes.*

hyp·not·ic /hɪp'natɪk/ *adj.* causing hypnosis: *The mother's voice had a hypnotic effect on her baby.*

hyp·no·tize /'hɪpnə,taɪz/ *v.* **-tized, -tizing, -tizes** to put s.o. under hypnosis: *The therapist*

hypnotized her patient. -*n.* [U] **hypnotism** /'hɪpnə,tɪzəm/; [C] **hypnotist.**

hy·po·al·ler·gen·ic /,haɪpou,ælər'dʒenɪk/ *adj.* unlikely to cause allergic reactions: *That brand of cosmetics is hypoallergenic.*

hy·po·chon·dri·a /,haɪpə'kandriə/ *n.* [U] a condition of imagining illness that one does not have: *That patient bothers his doctor with his hypochondria.*

hy·po·chon·dri·ac /,haɪpə'kandri,æk/ *n.* a person who suffers from hypochondria -*adj.* **hypochondriacal** /,haɪpəkən'draɪəkəl/.

hy·poc·ri·sy /hɪ'pakrəsi/ *n.* [U] saying one holds one belief while really believing s.t. else: *Her hypocrisy was clear when she talked about loving old people; I know she never visits her own grandmother.*

hyp·o·crite /'hɪpə,krɪt/ *n.* a person who acts with hypocrisy: *He is a hypocrite, pretending to care and not really doing so.* -*adj.* **hypocritical** /,hɪpə'krɪtɪkəl/; -*adv.* **hypocritically.**

hy·po·der·mic **needle** or **syringe** /,haɪpə'dɜrmɪk/ *n.* a hollow needle used to inject medication or take out fluid: *The nurse used a hypodermic needle to draw a blood sample.*

hy·po·thal·a·mus /,haɪpou'θæləməs/ *n.* **-mi** /-,maɪ/ the basic part of the brain that controls breathing, heartbeat, etc.: *The hypothalamus is located at the brain stem.*

hy·po·ther·mi·a /,haɪpə'θɜrmiə/ *n.* [U] a condition of low body temperature and feeling cold: *You can get hypothermia from being outside too long in cold weather.*

hy·poth·e·sis /haɪ'paθəsɪs, hɪ-/ *n.* **-ses** /-,siz/ **1** a working theory: *Scientists do experiments to see if their hypotheses work.* **2** an unproved assumption: *His statement is simply a hypothesis.* -*v.* **hypothesize** /haɪ,paθə'saɪz, hɪ-/; -*adj.* **hypothetical** /,haɪpə'θetɪkəl/.

hys·ter·ec·to·my /,hɪstə'rektəmi/ *n.* **-mies** the removal of the uterus (womb)

hys·te·ri·a /hɪ'steriə, -'stɪr-/ *n.* [U] **1** uncontrollable emotional outbursts: *He suffers from hysteria occasionally.* **2** panic, excitement: *News of the stock market crash caused hysteria among the population.*

hys·ter·i·cal /hɪ'sterɪkəl/ *adj.* **1** panicked, emotionally out of control: *The mother became hysterical when she realized her child was lost.* **2** *fig.* hilarious, very funny: *The jokes that he tells are hysterical.* -*adv.* **hysterically.**

hys·ter·ics /hɪ'sterɪks/ *n.pl.* **1** an uncontrollable emotional outburst: *The mental patient was overcome with hysterics.* **2** *fig.* an outburst of laughter: *The audience went into hysterics at the clown's tricks.*

H

I, i

I,i /aɪ/ *n.* **I's, i's** or **Is, is** **1** the ninth letter of the English alphabet **2** *fig.* **to dot the i's and cross the t's:** to agree on small details: *The agreement is nearly final, except that we have to dot a few i's and cross a few t's.*
—*pron.* first person singular, used in speaking or writing to refer to oneself: *I wish I could stay longer.*

i-beam /'aɪ,bim/ *n.* a steel beam shaped like the letter "I": *I-beams are used in the construction of buildings.*

ice /aɪs/ *n.* [U] **1** frozen water: *Ice forms on the roads in winter.* **2** *fig.* **to break the ice:** to make people comfortable at a first meeting: *Let's play a game to break the ice. See:* icebreaker. **3 to put on ice: a.** to make cold or freeze: *We put some soda on ice to chill it.* **b.** *infrml.fig.* to stop or delay, *(syn.)* to shelve: *The project has too many problems, so we put it on ice for a while.*
—*v.* **1** to form ice: *When it is very cold, the wings of an airplane ice.* **2** to cover or decorate a cake with icing **3 to ice over** or **up:** to cover with ice: *The windows in our house are icing up in the winter cold.*

USAGE NOTE: It is common for Americans to put ice in drinks. Most restaurants and bars automatically serve ice with water, soft drinks, and many cocktails unless the customer says, "No ice."

---

ice-berg /'aɪs,bɜrg/ *n.* a large piece of frozen ice in the sea: *Most of an iceberg is under water.*

ice-break-er /'aɪs,breɪkər/ *n.* **1** a powerful ship used to break paths in icy seas: *The cruise ship sailed in the path made by an icebreaker.* **2** *infrml.fig.* s.t. said or done to help people start talking or feel comfortable: *John's funny story was a good icebreaker at the party. See:* ice.

ice cap *n.* a large area of ice, such as those found at the North and South Poles: *The polar ice caps are very thick.*

ice cream *n.* [U] a frozen mixture of cream, milk, flavors, and sweeteners: *We enjoy eating vanilla ice cream for dessert.*

ice-cream cone *n.* a cookie-like object used to hold ice cream: *I'd like a chocolate ice-cream cone, please.*

ice-cream cone

ice hockey *n.* [U] an ice-skating sport in which one team uses curved sticks to shoot a small, round disk into the other team's goal: *Ice hockey is a fast and rough sport.*

ice pick *n.* a long, pointed tool used to chip and crack ice: *I broke bits of ice off a block with an ice pick.*

ice skate *n.* a boot with a sharpened steel blade used to move over ice: *I wear my ice skates when I play ice hockey.*
—*v.* to move over ice with ice skates: *I ice skate early each morning in winter.* -*n.* **ice skater.**

ice skates

ice water *n.* [C;U] **1** water made cold with ice cubes: *American restaurants often serve ice water with meals.* **2** *fig.* **to have ice (water) in one's veins:** to be calm or not easily upset: *She is a brave firefighter who has ice water in her veins when she faces danger.*

i-ci-cle /'aɪsəkəl/ *n.* **1** a pointed piece of ice formed by water that freezes as it falls in small drops: *Icicles hang from tree branches in winter.* **2** *infrml.fig.* a person who is cold or unfriendly: *His wife complains that her husband is an icicle.*

ic-ing /'aɪsɪŋ/ *n.* [U] **1** a sweet, creamy covering on cakes, *(syn.)* frosting: *The icing on my birthday cake is made of chocolate.* **2** *infrml.fig.* **the icing on the cake:** s.t. extra, special: *I received a raise in salary, but the extra week of vacation was the icing on the cake.*

ick·y /'ɪki/ *adj.infrml.* **-ier, -iest** **1** sticky in an unpleasant way: *I spilled spaghetti on my shirt, and it was all icky.* **2** unpleasant: *The weather was so icky that I stayed at home.*

i·con /'aɪ,kɑn/ *n.* **1** in Eastern Christianity, a religious painting of a holy person **2** one who is greatly admired, (*syn.*) idol: *Marilyn Monroe is an icon of American popular culture.* **3** a symbol or picture on a computer screen that stands for a command, program, etc.: *Click on the red icon to start the program.* *-n.* [U] **iconography** /,aɪkə'nɑgrəfi/.

ic·y /'aɪsi/ *adj.* **-ier, -iest** **1** covered with ice: *The roads are icy during a snowstorm.* **2** cold and unfriendly: *He has an icy personality.*

ID or **ID card** /'aɪ'di/ *n.* *abbr. for* identity card: a card, such as a driver's license, often with a photograph, that gives personal information, such as one's name, age, and address: *She needed an ID showing that she was 21 before she could buy the wine.*

ID card

i·de·a /aɪ'diə/ *n.* **1** a thought: *The speaker had very interesting ideas.* **2** a plan, a way to do s.t.: *She has an idea of how to solve the problem.* **3** a sudden wish or urge, (*syn.*) whim: *I have an idea; let's go to a movie tonight!* **4** **not to have the faintest idea:** to have no knowledge or information: *We're lost, and I don't have the faintest idea of where we are.* **5** **to have an idea in mind:** to have an uncertain plan

i·de·al /aɪ'diəl, aɪ'dil/ *n.* **1** the highest standard, s.t. perfect: *A great ideal would be for the world to have no disease or hunger.* **2** **to have ideals:** to wish for perfection: *The philosopher has high ideals about saving the world.*
—*adj.* most desirable, perfect: *Good weather has provided ideal conditions for the boat race today.* *-adv.* **ideally**; *-n.* [U] **idealism**; [C] **idealist.**

i·de·al·is·tic /aɪ,diə'lɪstɪk, ,aɪdi-/ *adj.* **1** having ideals **2** wishing for perfection in an imperfect world: *She is very idealistic about bringing peace to the world.*

i·de·al·ize /aɪ'diə,laɪz/ *v.* **1** to think of s.t. as better than it really is: *He idealizes his job, even though it isn't perfect.*

i·den·ti·cal /aɪ'dɛntəkəl/ *adj.* exactly alike: *The boys are identical twins.*

i·den·ti·fi·ca·tion /aɪ,dɛntəfə'keɪʃən/ *n.* **1** [U] s.t., such as a passport or driver's license, that proves who one is: *I showed my passport as identification at the airport.* **2** [C;U] recognition of s.o. or s.t.: *The police officer made an identification of the criminal after talking to witnesses.*

identification card *n. See:* ID.

i·den·ti·fy /aɪ'dɛntə,faɪ/ *v.* **-fied, -fying, -fies** to recognize the identity of s.o. or s.t.: *The children identified the bird from its picture in the book.* **2 to identify with:** to feel connected to s.o. or s.t.: *I identified with the girl in the movie.*

i·den·ti·ty /aɪ'dɛntəti/ *n.* **-ties** **1** who s.o. is or what s.t. is: *The police described his identity as a white male weighing 200 pounds (90 kilos), with gray hair.* **2** a sense of oneself: *When she quit her job to raise her children, she lost her identity as a career woman.*

identity crisis *n.* not being sure about who one is: *When he lost his job and could not find another, he went through an identity crisis.*

i·de·o·log·i·cal /,aɪdiə'lɑʤəkəl, ,ɪdi-/ *adj.* about beliefs, doctrines that influence action in society: *The ideological structure of capitalism is often attacked.* *-n.* **ideologist** /,aɪdi'ɑləʤɪst, ,ɪdi-/; **ideologue** /'aɪdiə,lɑg, -lɔg, 'ɪdi-/.

i·de·ol·o·gy /,aɪdi'ɑləʤi, ,ɪdi-/ *n.* **-gies** [C;U] a set of beliefs shared by a political or social group: *In the USA, Democrats and Republicans have different ideologies.*

id·i·o·cy /'ɪdiəsi/ *n.* **-cies** **1** [U] a mental condition of low intelligence: *The poor child suffers from idiocy.* **2** [C;U] stupidity, foolishness: *The idiocy of war never stops.*

id·i·om /'ɪdiəm/ *n.* **1** an expression that does not mean the same as the individual words: *The words "to hit the roof" say "to hit against the top of a house", but the idiom actually means "to become very angry."* **2** the speech or dialect of a certain area: *They speak the idiom of their small town.* *-adj.* **idiomatic.**

id·i·o·syn·cra·sy /'ɪdiə'sɪŋkrəsi/ *n.* **-sies** an odd habit or characteristic: *One of her idiosyncrasies is that she sleeps in her clothes.* *-adj.* **idiosyncratic** /,ɪdiousɪn'krætɪk/.

id·i·ot /'ɪdiət/ *n.* **1** a person of little intelligence: *The poor child was born an idiot.* **2** *infrml.fig.* a stupid, foolish person: *He was an idiot to go mountain climbing alone in bad weather.* *-n.* [C;U] **idiocy**; *-adj.* **idiotic** /,ɪdi'ɑtɪk/.

i·dle /'aɪdl/ *adj.* **1** not working, unemployed: *The factory has been closed for a year now, leaving its workers idle.* **2** lazy: *She likes to be idle and watch TV all day.* **3** worthless: *Don't listen to that idle talk.*
—*v.* **idled, idling, idles** **1** to run at lowest speed: *She lets her car engine idle to warm it up.* **2** to take it easy, (*syn.*) to loaf: *He idles away his time by watching television.*

i·dle·ness /'aɪdlnɪs/ *n.* [U] **1** inactivity: *The manufacturing plant lies in idleness, with no workers.* **2** laziness: *He spends his days in idleness without work.* *-n.* [C] **idler.**

i·dol /ˈaɪdl/ *n.* **1** an object of religious worship, such as a statue: *Ancient peoples worshiped idols of their gods.* **2** a celebrity, such as a film or music star: *Popular singers are idols for millions of people.*

i·dol·a·try /aɪˈdɑlətri/ *n.* [U] the worship of idols: *Idolatry was practiced in ancient civilizations by making offerings to the gods the idols represented.* -*adj.* **idolatrous.**

i·dol·ize /ˈaɪdl̩ˌaɪz/ *v.* **-ized, -izing, -izes** **1** to worship: *Ancient people idolized gods.* **2** to admire greatly, look up to: *Jane idolizes her older sister.*

idyll or **idyl** /ˈaɪdl̩/ *n.* **1** a short poem or prose piece describing a simple, happy scene: *Her poem was an idyll about her life on a farm.* **2** a happy event of rural life: *Their honeymoon was an idyll of camping and hiking in a national park.* -*adj.* **idyllic** /aɪˈdɪlɪk/.

i.e. /ˈaɪˈi/ *abbr. for* the Latin *id est,* meaning "that is": *I like bright colors, i.e., red and yellow.*

if /ɪf/ *conj.* **1** in case that: *If you want to leave, let's go now.* **2** on the condition that: *I will pay for the movie if you pay for dinner.* **3** whether: *Please see if the children are dressed for school.* **4** assuming that: *If I have enough money, I shall go on vacation this summer.* **5** **as if:** as though: *He acts as if he's smarter than anyone else.* **6** **even if:** accepting that s.t. is true: *Even if he is smarter, he could act nicer.* **7** **if only:** used to state a wish: *If only I had a million dollars!*
—*n.* **no ifs, ands, or buts:** without excuses: *You must finish your homework: no ifs, ands, or buts.*

if·fy /ˈɪfi/ *adj.infrml.* **-fier, -fiest** doubtful, uncertain: *The weather looks iffy today, as though it might rain.*

ig·loo /ˈɪglu/ *n.* **-loos** a house made of icy snow blocks: *Inuits make igloos for shelter.*

ig·nite /ɪgˈnaɪt/ *v.* **-nited, -niting, -nites** to set on fire: *He ignited the wood with a match.*

igloo

ig·ni·tion /ɪgˈnɪʃən/ *n.* **1** [U] setting on fire, (*syn.*) combustion: *Ignition of the rocket's engine took place after a countdown from ten.* **2** [C] a mechanical switch for ignition: *The car's ignition requires a key to operate it.*

ig·no·rance /ˈɪgnərəns/ *n.* [U] **1** lack of education: *Without schooling, children grow up in ignorance.* **2** lack of knowledge: *Her ignorance of the speed limit made her drive faster than 55 miles per hour.*

ig·no·rant /ˈɪgnərənt/ *adj.* **1** without education **2** unknowing, uninformed: *I am totally igno-*

rant of what happened at home while I was on vacation.

ig·nore /ɪgˈnɔr/ *v.* **-nored, -noring, -nores** **1** to pay no attention to, overlook: *The teacher ignored my spelling mistakes and looked only for my meaning.* **2** to avoid, disdain: *She ignored her old boyfriend.*

i·gua·na /ɪgˈwɑnə/ *n.* a large tropical lizard: *Iguanas can look frightening.*

ilk /ɪlk/ *n.* [U] kind or type: *Those men are nasty, and I don't associate with people of that ilk.*

ill /ɪl/ *adj.* **1** sick, unwell: *He is ill; he has a bad cold.* **2 to be ill at ease:** to feel awkward or uncomfortable: *She is often ill at ease with strangers.* **3 to fall** or **be taken ill:** to become sick **4** evil, terrible, used esp. as a prefix: *A bomb exploded, and the ill-fated plane crashed.*
—*adv.* badly, unfavorably: *He is a bad man, and others think ill of him.*

ill-bred *adj.* without good manners, rude: *He is an ill-bred young man who is rude, vulgar, and dirty.*

il·le·gal /ɪˈligəl/ *adj.* against the law: *Stealing is illegal.* -*n.* [C;U] **illegality** /ˌɪliˈgæləti/.

il·leg·i·ble /ɪˈlɛdʒəbəl/ *adj.* difficult to read: *The writing is illegible; I cannot read what it says.* -*n.* [U] **illegibility** /ɪˌlɛdʒəˈbɪləti/.

il·le·git·i·mate /ˌɪləˈdʒɪtəmɪt/ *adj.* **1** not legal: *He is running an illegitimate business.* **2** born to unmarried parents -*n.* [U] **illegitimacy.**

ill-equipped *adj.* **1** badly prepared, poorly equipped: *The campers were ill-equipped, with little food and no warm clothing.* **2** unable, (*syn.*) incompetent: *He is ill-equipped to handle more responsibility.*

il·lic·it /ɪˈlɪsɪt/ *adj.* **1** unlawful, illegal: *Sale of illicit drugs is a problem in that city.* **2** secretive: *The married man ended an illicit love affair.* -*n.* [U] **illicitness.**

il·lit·er·ate /ɪˈlɪtərɪt/ *adj.* unable to read or write: *He once was illiterate, but later he learned to read.* -*n.* [U] **illiteracy.**

USAGE NOTE: The word *illiterate* generally describes someone who can't read or write. Today people also speak of being *computer literate* or *computer illiterate.* People who have a very low level of literacy may be called *functionally illiterate,* because they can't get jobs that involve much reading or writing.

ill-mannered *adj.* rude, (*syn.*) impolite: *He always behaves in an ill-mannered way when he drinks a lot.*

ill·ness /ˈɪlnɪs/ *n.* [C;U] sickness, disease: *Her illness kept her out of work for a month.*

il·log·i·cal /ɪ'lɑʤɪkəl/ *adj.* without logic, (*syn.*) unsound: *The politician lost the debate because his ideas were illogical.*

ill-suited *adj.* not useful for a purpose: *Those heavy clothes are ill-suited for hot weather.*

ill-tempered *adj.* angry, (*syn.*) irritable: *Martin has an ill-tempered dog that barks at strangers.*

il·lu·mi·nate /ɪ'lumɪ,neɪt/ *v.* **-nated, -nating, -nates 1** to give light to: *Streetlights illuminated the roads.* **2** to make clear, explain: *Our teacher illuminates ancient history in his lectures.* **3** to decorate with lights: *We illuminated the lights in the yard for the birthday party.* *-n.* [U] **illumination.**

il·lu·sion /ɪ'luʒən/ *n.* **1** [C;U] a false impression of reality, fantasy: *My 12-year-old daughter is so tall that she gives the illusion of being much older than she really is.* **2** [C] a mistaken idea: *He has this illusion of himself as a great actor.* *-n.* [C] **illusionist.**

il·lu·so·ry /ɪ'lusəri, -zə-/ *adj.* based on a fantasy or illusion: *Her dream of being famous is illusory.*

il·lus·trate /'ɪlə,streɪt/ *v.* **-trated, -trating, -trates 1** to give examples, explain: *The teacher illustrated the history lesson by telling a story about George Washington.* **2** to provide with pictures, drawings, etc.: *The history book was illustrated with many maps and photographs.* *-adj.* **illustrative** /ɪ'lʌstrətɪv, 'ɪlə,streɪ-/.

il·lus·tra·tor /'ɪlə,streɪtər/ *n.* an artist, s.o. who draws: *Illustrators create pictures and charts for magazine articles.*

il·lus·tra·tion /,ɪlə'streɪʃən/ *n.* **1** [C] artwork, photography, or other pictures: *The art book has many beautiful color illustrations.* **2** [C;U] an example: *A teacher gave illustrations of twentieth-century violence by describing several wars.*

il·lus·tri·ous /ɪ'lʌstriəs/ *adj.* famous, (*syn.*) distinguished: *He has had an illustrious career as a writer.*

I'm /aɪm/ *contr. of* I am: *I'm a doctor.*

im·age /'ɪmɪʤ/ *n.* **1** a mental picture of s.o. or s.t.: *He formed an image of the countryside in his mind.* **2** picture, copy: *The image on the photograph is not clear.* **3** one's appearance to others, reputation: *She is very concerned about her image as a good lawyer.*

im·age·ry /'ɪmɪʤri/ *n.* [U] use of images, esp. in art and literature: *The imagery in his writing is so detailed that the characters seem real.*

i·mag·i·na·ble /ɪ'mæʤənəbəl/ *adj.* capable of being imagined: *In her painting, she has used every color imaginable.*

i·mag·i·nar·y /ɪ'mæʤə,nɛri/ *adj.* existing only in the mind, unreal: *The child has an imaginary friend.*

i·mag·i·na·tion /ɪ,mæʤə'neɪʃən/ *n.* **1** [U] the act of forming images in the mind: *His stories show that he has a clever imagination.* **2** [C;U] ability to think creatively: *It will take a lot of imagination to solve the problem.* *-adj.* **imaginative** /ɪ'mæʤənətɪv/

i·mag·ine /ɪ'mæʤɪn/ *v.* **-ined, -ining, -ines 1** to form (a picture, idea) in one's mind: *She imagined what it would be like to be rich and famous.* **2** to fool oneself, fantasize: *The little boy imagined he saw ghosts at night.*

im·bal·ance /ɪm'bæləns/ *n.* a lack of balance or equality: *There is an imbalance in my diet; I should eat more fruit and less fat.*

im·be·cile /'ɪmbəsɪl/ *n.* a stupid or foolish person *-adj.* **imbecilic.**

im·bibe /ɪm'baɪb/ *v.frml.* **-bibed, -bibing, -bibes** to drink: *He only imbibes alcoholic beverages on special occasions.* *-n.* **imbiber.**

im·bue /ɪm'byu/ *v.frml.* **-bued, -buing, -bues** to fill with a strong feeling, inspire: *A preacher imbued his listeners with religious passion.*

im·i·tate /'ɪmə,teɪt/ *v.* **-tated, -tating, -tates 1** to act the same way as another, (*syn.*) to emulate: *The boy imitates his father's way of talking.* **2** to copy, duplicate: *That manufacturer imitates the designs of a competitor.* **3** to mimic, (*syn.*) impersonate: *Some comedians imitate celebrities and make fun of them.* *-n.* **imitator.**

im·i·ta·tion /,ɪmə'teɪʃən/ *n.* **1** [C] a copy, a duplication, esp. a fake copy: *She bought an imitation of a famous painting.* **2** [C;U] copying of s.o.'s behavior: *My friend does a funny imitation of me.* *-adj.* **imitative.**

im·mac·u·late /ɪ'mækyəlɪt/ *adj.* **1** clean, spotless: *She wore an immaculate white dress.* **2** *fig.* without fault, flawless: *She has an immaculate reputation.*

im·ma·te·ri·al /,ɪmə'tɪriəl/ *adj.* **1** not important: *That information is immaterial to solving the problem.*

im·ma·ture /,ɪmə'ʧur, -'tur/ *adj.* **1** not ripe or fully formed: *When oranges are green, they are immature; when they are orange, they are ripe.* **2** childish, not adult: *His immature behavior annoys people.* *-n.* [U] **immaturity.**

im·meas·ur·a·ble /ɪ'mɛʒərəbəl/ *adj.* **1** not capable of being measured, infinite: *Some distances in space are so long that they are immeasurable.* **2** limitless, great: *The consultant was of immeasurable help in solving our problems.*

im·me·di·ate /ɪ'midiət/ *adj.* **1** prompt, right now: *Earthquake victims have an immediate need for help.* **2** nearby, close to: *Damage occurred in the immediate area of the earthquake's starting point.* **3** soon, near: *The victims will also need help in rebuilding their* *houses in the immediate future. -n.* [U] **immediacy.**

im·me·di·ate·ly /ɪ'midiətli/ *adv.* right away, promptly: *We have to help them immediately.*

im·me·mo·ri·al /ˌɪmə'mɔriəl/ *adj.* beyond memory, forever: *Customs practiced by tribes have been handed down from time immemorial.*

im·mense /ɪ'mɛns/ *adj.* huge: *There is an immense statue in the park. -n.* [U] **immensity.**

im·merse /ɪ'mɜrs/ *v.* **-mersed, -mersing, -merses** **1** to put s.t. in water until it's covered: *The cook immersed the potatoes in boiling water.* **2** to become absorbed in, *(syn.)* to delve into: *Students immerse themselves in their studies. -n.* [U] **immersion** /ɪ'mɜrʒən, -ʃən/; *-adj.* **immersible.**

im·mi·grant /'ɪməgrənt/ *n.* a person who moves to another country to live: *Millions of immigrants came to the USA for religious freedom. See:* emigrant, USAGE NOTE.

im·mi·grate /'ɪmə,greɪt/ *v.* **-grated, -grating, -grates** to leave one's own country to live in another: *John F. Kennedy's grandparents immigrated to the USA from Ireland. -n.* [U] **immigration** /ˌɪmə'greɪʃən/.

im·mi·nent /'ɪmənənt/ *adj.frml.* ready to happen soon, *(syn.)* impending: *The wedding date is imminent, so we must send invitations. -n.* [U] **imminence.**

im·mo·bile /ɪ'moubəl, -ˌbaɪl/ *adj.* not capable of being moved, stationary: *The boat is immobile, frozen in the ice. -n.* [U] **immobility** /ˌɪmou'bɪləti/; *-v.* **immobilize** /ɪ'moubə,laɪz/.

im·mod·est /ɪ'madɪst/ *adj.* **1** saying too many good things about oneself, boastful, vain: *An immodest politician brags about his or her accomplishments.* **2** showing too much, *(syn.)* lewd: *The girl's father thinks her bikinis are immodest. -n.* [U] **immodesty.**

im·mor·al /ɪ'mɔrəl, ɪ'mɑr-/ *adj.* **1** against most people's moral principles, evil, sinful: *Murder is immoral and is a crime in almost every country.* **2** sexually wrong, *(syns.)* debauched, degenerate: *The prostitute went to jail for immoral behavior. -n.* **immorality** /ˌɪmɔ'ræləti, ɪmə-/.

im·mor·tal /ɪ'mɔrtl/ *adj.* **1** living forever: *Ancient Greeks believed their gods were immortal.* **2** lasting forever, eternal: *Beauty and truth are immortal qualities. -n.* **immortality** /ˌɪmɔr'tæləti/.

im·mov·a·ble /ɪ'muvəbəl/ *adj.* fixed, not able to be moved: *Mountains are immovable.*

im·mune /ɪ'myun/ *adj.* **1** not affected by disease: *Children are immune to measles after they receive the proper vaccine.* **2** protected from: *The criminal was immune from strong punishment because he helped the police find the bank robber.*

im·mu·ni·ty /ɪ'myunəti/ *n.* **-ties** **1** [C;U] protection from disease: *Today there is more immunity to chicken pox than there was in the 1950s.* **2** [U] protection from (punishment): *U.S. presidents have immunity if they are pardoned by the new president. -v.* **immunize** /'ɪmyə,naɪz/.

im·mu·ta·ble /ɪ'myutəbəl/ *adj.frml.* unchangeable, fixed: *The laws of physics are constant and immutable. -n.* [U] **immutability.**

imp /ɪmp/ *n.* **1** a little devil: *Some people think imps make us lie or steal.* **2** *fig.* a naughty person, usu. young: *That girl is an imp, always up to mischief. -adj.* **impish.**

im·pact /'ɪm,pækt/ *n.* **1** a forceful contact, blow: *The meteor made a large impact when it crashed to earth.* **2** effect, impression: *Poverty has a bad impact on people's health.*
—v.infrml. to affect: *Lack of food impacted the starving nation.*

im·pair /ɪm'pɛr/ *v.* to weaken, damage: *A blow to the ear impaired her hearing. -n.* [C;U] **impairment.**

im·pale /ɪm'peɪl/ *v.* **-paled, -paling, -pales** to make a hole through s.t. with a pointed object: *Warriors impaled their enemies with spears.*

im·pal·pa·ble /ɪm'pælpəbəl/ *adj.* not able to be felt by touch: *The tiny bird's heartbeat was almost impalpable.*

im·part /ɪm'pɑrt/ *v.* **1** to give (information): *The English teacher imparts knowledge of verb tenses to his students.* **2** to give, *(syn.)* to bestow: *Her vast knowledge of history imparts a special richness to her writing.*

im·par·tial /ɪm'pɑrʃəl/ *adj.* treating all sides fairly: *The judge gave an impartial verdict that did not favor either side. -n.* [U] **impartiality** /ˌɪm,pɑrʃi'æləti/; *-adv.* **impartially.**

im·pass·a·ble /ɪm'pæsəbəl/ *adj.* not able to be traveled because of an obstacle, blocked: *A mudslide made the road impassable to cars and people.*

im·passe /'ɪmpæs/ *n.* a lack of agreement, *(syn.)* dilemma: *The two countries tried to divide the land equally, but reached an impasse.*

im·pas·sioned /ɪm'pæʃənd/ *adj.* full of emotion: *The senator had tears in his eyes as he gave an impassioned speech.*

im·pas·sive /ɪm'pæsɪv/ *adj.* showing no emotion: *His face was impassive as the judge sentenced him to death.*

im·pa·tient /ɪm'peɪʃənt/ *adj.* not wanting to wait: *She was impatient to hear where her lost son was. -n.* **impatience** /ɪm'peɪʃəns/.

im·peach /ɪm'pitʃ/ *v.* to accuse a public official of a crime or wrongdoing: *The legislature impeached the governor for lying about her background.*

im·pec·ca·ble /ɪm'pɛkəbəl/ *adj.* without fault, flawless: *The fashion designer was admired for her impeccable clothes.*

im·pede /ɪm'pid/ *v.* **-peded, -peding, -pedes** to get in the way of, slow down: *A large ship in the port impeded the movement of many smaller boats.*

im·ped·i·ment /ɪm'pɛdəmənt/ *n.* s.t. that slows or stops movement or progress, obstacle, *(syn.)* hindrance: *Conflict between the two nations is an impediment to reaching a peace agreement.*

im·pel /ɪm'pɛl/ *v.frml.* **-pelled, -pelling, -pels** **1** to make s.o. do s.t., *(syns.)* to motivate, prompt: *Hunger impelled him to seek food.*

im·pend·ing /ɪm'pɛndɪŋ/ *adj.* about to happen: *The impending law will help poor families by the end of the year.*

im·pen·e·tra·ble /ɪm'pɛnətrəbəl/ *adj.* not able to be gone through or entered: *The castle has thick, impenetrable walls.* *-n.* [U] **impenetrability.**

im·per·a·tive /ɪm'pɛrətɪv/ *adj.* necessary, urgent: *It is imperative that you call home immediately, because your child is ill.*
—*n.* (in grammar) a command form: *"Go home immediately!" shows the imperative of the verb "to go."*

im·per·cep·ti·ble /,ɪmpər'sɛptəbəl/ *adj.frml.* not able to be sensed, very tiny: *The difference between their opinions is imperceptible.*

im·per·fect /ɪm'pɜrfɪkt/ *adj.* **1** having mistakes, flawed: *The diamond is pretty, but that crack makes it imperfect.* **2** a verb tense indicating past action in progress: *"We were talking when you arrived" shows the imperfect tense of "talk."*

im·per·fec·tion /,ɪmpər'fɛkʃən/ *n.* **1** [C] a flaw, defect: *The vase has several imperfections that make it unable to hold water.* **2** [C;U] a general lack of perfection: *Imperfections spoil his writing.*

im·pe·ri·al·ism /ɪm'pɪriə,lɪzəm/ *n.* [U] **1** rule of a nation by an emperor or empress: *Imperialism existed in France under the Emperor Napoleon.* **2** one nation controlling the political or economic life of other nations: *Great Britain's imperialism spread to Africa long ago.* *-adj.* **imperial.**

im·per·il /ɪm'pɛrəl/ *v.frml.* to put in danger, *(syn.)* to jeopardize: *A fierce storm imperiled the passenger ship.*

im·pe·ri·ous /ɪm'pɪriəs/ *adj.frml.* having an attitude of superiority, *(syns.)* arrogant, haughty: *The strict father showed an imperious attitude toward his children.* *-n.* [U] **imperiousness.**

im·per·son·al /ɪm'pɜrsənəl/ *adj.* **1** not showing personal opinion or preference, unemotional, fair: *She is impersonal in her hiring of*

employees. **2** lacking in feeling or compassion, unfriendly: *Many taxpayers feel the IRS is an impersonal government agency.*

im·per·son·ate /ɪm'pɜrsə,neɪt/ *v.* **-ated, -ating, -ates** to imitate, act like s.o. else, sometimes using clothes, voices, or makeup: *That comedian impersonates famous politicians.* *-n.*[C;U] **impersonation** /ɪm,pɜrsə'neɪʃən/.

im·per·ti·nent /ɪm'pɜrtnənt/ *adj.* rude, disrespectful: *His impertinent behavior shocked the nice old lady.* *-n.* [U] **impertinence.**

im·per·vi·ous /ɪm'pɜrviəs/ *adj.* **1** not allowing anything to pass through or cause damage, *(syn.)* impenetrable: *Two coats of paint make the house impervious to bad weather.* **2** not affected by s.o. or s.t. because of inner strength or confidence: *The child seems impervious to the teacher's criticism.*

im·pe·ti·go /,ɪmpə'taɪgoʊ/ *n.* [U] a serious, contagious skin disease: *Impetigo is less common today than in the past.*

im·pet·u·ous /ɪm'pɛtʃuəs/ *adj.* done quickly often without thinking, *(syn.)* impulsive: *She made an impetuous decision in marrying so young.* *-adv.* **impetuously.**

im·pe·tus /'ɪmpɪtəs/ *n.* [C;U] the encouragement needed to do s.t.: *The President's enthusiasm was impetus for Congress to pass the new law.*

im·pinge /ɪm'pɪndʒ/ *v.frml.* **-pinged, -pinging, -pinges 1** to affect, change: *His writings have impinged upon (or) on liberal thinking.* **2** to advance into a new or forbidden area, *(syn.)* to trespass: *That fence impinges on our property.*

im·plac·a·ble /ɪm'plækəbəl/ *adj.frml.* not able to be satisfied or changed: *The parents are implacable enemies, but the children are friends.* *-n.* [U] **implacability.**

im·plant /'ɪm,plænt/ *v.* **1** to insert or place in s.t., usu. a living body: *A doctor implanted a small tube under the patient's skin.* **2** to put (information) firmly into s.o.'s mind: *My teacher implanted ideas that have stayed with me all my life.* *-n.* [C;U] **implantation.**

im·plau·si·ble /ɪm'plɔzəbəl/ *adj.* not believable, unlikely to be true: *His version of the story is implausible because it changes every time he tells it.* *-n.* [C;U] **implausibility.**

im·ple·ment /'ɪmpləmənt/ *v.* to start, put into action: *The meat company implemented a new advertising plan for low-fat beef.*
—*n.* a tool or piece of equipment: *With the right implements, I can unlock a door without a key.* *-n.* [U] **implementation.**

im·pli·cate /'ɪmplə,keɪt/ *v.frml.* **-cated, -cating, -cates** to show that s.o. participated or was involved, esp. in a crime: *The drug addict implicated the man who sold her the cocaine.*

im·pli·ca·tion /,ɪmplə'keɪʃən/ *n.* **1** [U] an indication of participation or involvement of others, esp. in a crime: *The woman's implication of her brother sent him to jail.* **2** [C] an indirect suggestion: *John made implications that Mr. Lu had faked his wife's signature.*

im·plic·it /ɪm'plɪsɪt/ *adj.* understood but not directly written or stated: *Polite conversation is implicit at a formal dinner party.*

im·plode /ɪm'ploʊd/ *v.* **-ploded, -ploding, -plodes** to collapse inwardly from some force: *The volcanic mountain seemed much smaller after it erupted and imploded.* **-n.** [C;U] **implosion.**

im·plore /ɪm'plɔr/ *v.frml.* **-plored, -ploring, -plores** to beg, (*syn.*) to beseech: *He implored his son not to take drugs.*

im·ply /ɪm'plaɪ/ *v.* **-plied, -plying, -plies** to indicate or suggest only indirectly, (*syn.*) to intimate: *The Secretary of the Treasury implied that interest rates would go down.*

im·po·lite /ˌɪmpə'laɪt/ *adj.* showing bad manners, rude: *The clerk was impolite to the customer.* **-n.** [U] **impoliteness.**

im·port /ɪm'pɔrt, 'ɪmˌpɔrt/ *v.* **1** to bring products into one country from another: *The jeweler buys diamonds from Africa and imports them into the USA.* **2** (in computers) to move data from one system to another: *I imported information from WordPerfect to my database.* —*n.frml.* meaning, significance: *It is of little import whether we go by bus or train.* **-n.** [U] **importation.**

im·por·tant /ɪm'pɔrtnt/ *adj.* having great meaning or significance, (*syn.*) weighty: *Important news is broadcast instantly over radio and television.* **-n.** [U] **importance.**

im·pose /ɪm'poʊz/ *v.* **-posed, -posing, -poses** **1** to place upon, burden: *Inheriting money imposes new taxes on people.* **2** to make inconvenient, take advantage of: *Relatives imposed upon us when they stayed for a whole week.*

im·pos·ing /ɪm'poʊzɪŋ/ *adj.* having a strong or powerful effect, grand: *An imposing statue dominates the square.*

im·po·si·tion /ˌɪmpə'zɪʃən/ *n.* **1** [U] placement of s.t., usu. a burden or difficulty: *The imposition of new rules in the middle of the school year confused the children.* **2** [C] inconvenience, burden: *Having to drive 150 miles (240 km) was an imposition on our time.*

im·pos·si·ble /ɪm'pɑsəbəl/ *adj.* **1** not able to be done: *Flying by flapping your arms is impossible.* **2** not acceptable, ridiculous: *He knows our limits, but still makes impossible demands.* **3** extremely difficult, unbearable: *She is impossible to talk to when she's angry.* **-n.** [U] **impossibility; -adv. impossibly.**

im·pos·tor /ɪm'pɑstər/ *n.* a person who pretends to be s.o. else: *The impostor had a false passport, but the customs department knew his real name.*

im·po·tence /'ɪmpətəns/ *n.* [U] **1** (of men) the condition of not being able to have sexual intercourse or activity: *Sometimes doctors can treat impotence so that men can become fathers.* **2** lack of strength: *The tiny country's impotence was extreme when compared to the power of the large country.* **-adj. impotent.**

im·pound /ɪm'paʊnd/ *v.* to seize and keep by law, (*syn.*) to confiscate: *The police impounded a vehicle for blocking the fire exit.*

im·pov·er·ish /ɪm'pɑvərɪʃ/ *v.* to make poor: *The cruel regime's unfair taxes impoverished the people.*

im·prac·ti·cal /ɪm'præktəkəl/ *adj.* not realistic, not sensible: *He has imaginative solutions, but their cost makes them impractical.*

im·pre·cise /ˌɪmprə'saɪs/ *adj.* not exact, vague: *The price of the trip is an imprecise estimate until we know the cost of airplane tickets.*

im·preg·na·ble /ɪm'prɛgnəbəl/ *adj.* not able to be attacked because of strength: *The city was impregnable to the enemy's army because of its high stone walls.*

im·preg·nate /ɪm'prɛgˌneɪt/ *v.* **-nated, -nating, -nates** to fertilize, make pregnant: *The male cat impregnated the female, and she had five kittens.*

im·press /ɪm'prɛs/ *v.* **1** to create and give an image of s.o. or s.t.: *He impresses me as a decent man.* **2** to cause others to admire: *Her brilliant ideas impressed her boss.* **3** to emphasize, stress: *She impressed on us all how important it is to be kind.* **4** to make a mark by stamping or pressing: *Workers impress words and symbols in leather.*

im·pres·sion /ɪm'prɛʃən/ *n.* **1** a feeling about s.o. or s.t., impact: *She makes a good impression on everyone she meets.* **2** a stamp, seal: *The impression of the company's trademark must appear on all letters.* **3** a printing: *The novel went through 20 impressions.*

im·pres·sion·a·ble /ɪm'prɛʃənəbəl/ *adj.* easily influenced (usu. referring to young people): *The impressionable boy was awed by his rich cousins.*

im·pres·sion·ism /ɪm'prɛʃəˌnɪzəm/ *n.* [U] a late nineteenth-century style of painting (mostly French) that used strokes of color to create effects of light: *Monet helped to begin Impressionism with his painting of a sunrise.* **-n.** [C] **impressionist; -adj. impressionistic.**

im·pres·sive /ɪm'prɛsɪv/ *adj.* causing admiration, (*syns.*) awesome, grand: *That athlete's ability is very impressive; she can jump as high as her older brother.*

im·print /ɪm'prɪnt/ *v.* **1** to make a mark by pressing or printing: *A publisher imprints its logo on book covers.* **2** *fig.* to put permanently

in the mind: *The Holocaust imprinted terrible images in the survivors' memories.*
—*n.* /ˈɪmˌprɪnt/ **1** a publishing company that is owned by a larger one: *That publisher has an imprint that produces only cookbooks.* **2** a mark made by pressure: *The new parents made an imprint of their baby's hand in clay.*

im·pris·on /ɪmˈprɪzən/ *v.* to send to jail, (*syn.*) to incarcerate: *The judge imprisoned the criminal for theft.*

im·prob·a·ble /ɪmˈprɑbəbəl/ *adj.* unlikely, (*syn.*) farfetched: *Scientists think that the earth's collision with an asteroid is highly improbable. -n.* [U] **improbability.**

im·promp·tu /ɪmˈprɑmptu/ *adj.* done without preparation, not rehearsed: *We were at a party and had an impromptu sing-along.*

im·prop·er /ɪmˈprɑpər/ *adj.* **1** without good manners, inappropriate, impolite: *The man's improper remarks embarrassed his wife.* **2** incorrect, not suitable: *Jeans are improper for a formal occasion.*

im·pro·pri·e·ty /ˌɪmprəˈpraɪəti/ *n.frml.* [C;U] **-ties** s.t. that lacks proper behavior or standards: *His improprieties include laughing at funerals.*

im·prove /ɪmˈpruv/ *v.* **-proved, -proving, -proves 1** to make better, enhance: *He improved his appearance by dressing more carefully.* **2** to become better: *Her health improved when she began eating fruits and vegetables.* **3** to advance, progress: *He improved himself by getting a better job.* **4 to improve upon:** to make s.t. better: *The actors were already good, but they improved upon their performance by rehearsing more.*

im·prove·ment /ɪmˈpruvmənt/ *n.* [C;U] **1** s.t. that is better or makes s.t. else better, (*syn.*) an enhancement: *They made improvements to the house by building a fancy kitchen and a new roof.* **2** better health: *The patient has shown improvement after her chemotherapy.*

im·pro·vise /ˈɪmprəˌvaɪz/ *v.* **-vised, -vising, -vises 1** to create and perform (a song, speech, etc.) with no preparation or rehearsal, (*syn.*) to extemporize: *A piano player improvised a song using suggestions from the audience.* **2** to make or invent s.t. with what is available: *The hikers improvised by making a tent from tree branches. -n.* [C;U] **improvisation** /ɪmˌprɑvəˈzeɪʃən, ˌɪmprɑv-/.

im·pru·dent /ɪmˈprudnt/ *adj.* unwise, thoughtless, (*syn.*) rash: *He made some imprudent banking decisions and lost money. -n.* [U] **imprudence.**

im·pu·dent /ˈɪmpyədənt/ *adj.* not respectful, rude, (*syn.*) insolent: *The child was impudent to her mother when she stuck out her tongue. -n.* [U] **impudence.**

im·pulse /ˈɪmpʌls/ *n.* **1** a sudden urge, whim: *He had an impulse to run, but he kept on walking.* **2 on impulse:** *People who buy on impulse often return purchases later.*

im·pul·sive /ɪmˈpʌlsɪv/ *adj.* acting on sudden urges, (*syn.*) impetuous: *She is impulsive and often says things that she doesn't mean.*

im·pu·ni·ty /ɪmˈpyunəti/ *n.* [U] without risk or fear of punishment: *The cruel queen ordered killings with impunity, for she knew no one could stop her.*

im·pure /ɪmˈpyʊr/ *adj.* **1** mixed with s.t., usu. bad or dirty, (*syn.*) contaminated: *That gasoline is impure; it's full of sand.* **2** morally or sexually wrong: *The priest didn't want children to read the novel because he thought it contained impure ideas. -n.* [C;U] **impurity.**

in /ɪn/ *prep.* **1** used to show s.t. is contained: *We put the gift in a box.* **2** used to show location: *Students are in the classroom.*
—*adv.* **1** present, here: *Dr. Smith is in today.* **2 in between:** located or existing in the middle of two or more things: *Hartford is in between Boston and New York.* **3 in for: a.** about to experience: *He is in for a big surprise.* **b.** in jail: *The prisoner is in for robbery.* **4 in on:** aware of s.t. others are not: *She is in on the secret.* **5 in the know:** aware of, having information: *Newspaper reporters are always in the know about current events.* **6 in with: a.** *lit.* in the same place or room: *He is in with (the office of) his boss.* **b.** *infrml.fig.* a friend or confidante of: *She is in with important people in the auto industry, so she gets free cars.* **7 to have it in for:** to want to harm s.o.: *She has it in for her old boss, because he fired her.*
—*adj.* **the in crowd:** fashionable social group: *The less popular students cannot join the in crowd.*
—*n.* **1 the ins and outs of:** complications, details of s.t.: *That lawyer is familiar with all the ins and outs of divorce law.* **2** *infrml.* **to have an in with s.o. or s.t.:** to have special privileges because of knowing s.o.: *Her best friend is the mayor, so she has an in with city government.*

in·a·bil·i·ty /ˌɪnəˈbɪləti/ *n.* [U] lack of power or capacity to do s.t.: *He needed a wheelchair because of his inability to walk.*

in·ac·ces·si·ble /ˌɪnækˈsɛsəbəl, ˌɪnək-/ *adj.* impossible or difficult to reach: *The road is blocked, so the town is now inaccessible. -n.* [U] **inaccessibility.**

in·ac·cu·ra·cy /ɪnˈækyərəsi/ *n.* [C;U] **-cies** s.t. that is not correct, an error, mistake: *The inaccuracy of the numbers makes the estimates useless.*

in·ac·cu·rate /ɪnˈækyərɪt/ *adj.* **1** incorrect, (*syn.*) erroneous: *Inaccurate newspaper reports gave the wrong date and time of the fire.*

in·ac·tion /ɪnˈækʃən/ n. [U] lack of activity, doing nothing: *Inaction by the workers left the house half built.*

in·ac·tive /ɪnˈæktɪv/ adj. **1** not working or moving, (*syns.*) idle, dormant: *He has been inactive since his retirement.* **2** not doing military duty: *Although she is in an inactive National Guard unit, she still wears her uniform.*

in·ad·e·quate /ɪnˈædəkwɪt/ adj. **1** not enough, insufficient: *There is an inadequate supply of water, so people are thirsty.* **2** not good enough, unsatisfactory, (*syn.*) deficient: *His homework is inadequate, but it will improve if he asks for help* -n. [C;U] **inadequacy.**

in·ad·mis·si·ble /ˌɪnədˈmɪsəbəl/ adj. (in law) unacceptable: *The evidence submitted by the prosecution is inadmissible.* -n. [U] **inadmissibility.**

in·ad·ver·tent /ˌɪnədˈvɜrtnt/ adj. not on purpose, done without thinking, unintentional: *I'm sorry; not inviting you to the party was an inadvertent mistake.* -n. [U] **inadvertence.**

in·ad·vis·a·ble /ˌɪnədˈvaɪzəbəl/ adj. not a good idea, unwise: *It is inadvisable to spend one's rent money on alcohol.*

in·al·ien·a·ble /ɪnˈeɪlyənəbəl, -ˈeɪliə-/ adj. not able to be taken away: *Freedom is an inalienable right in the USA.*

in·al·ter·a·ble /ɪnˈɔltərəbəl/ adj. not able to be changed, (*syn.*) immutable: *It's an inalterable fact that the sun alway sets in the west.*

in·ane /ɪnˈeɪn/ adj. without sense, stupid: *His inane comments made him seem silly next to his serious sister.* -n. [C;U] **inanity** /ɪˈnænəti/.

in·an·i·mate /ɪnˈænəmɪt/ adj. **1** lifeless: *Rocks and other inanimate objects were placed among the plants in the garden.* **2** not moving: *The actors were inanimate until the music started.*

in·ap·pli·ca·ble /ɪnˈæplɪkəbəl, ˌɪnəˈplɪ-/ adj. not usable for a particular purpose: *The money from state taxes is inapplicable to national education programs.*

in·ap·pro·pri·ate /ˌɪnəˈproupriət/ adj. **1** not suitable for the situation, incompatible: *His dark wool suit was inappropriate in the Florida heat.* **2** not proper, impolite: *Some people thought the film was inappropriate for television because it contained nudity.*

in·ar·tic·u·late /ˌɪnɑrˈtɪkyəlɪt/ adj. not able to speak clearly or express oneself well: *He is intelligent but inarticulate when he tries to explain his ideas.*

in·as·much as /ˌɪnəzˈmʌtʃəz, -æz/ conj.frml. because of the fact that, since, (*syn.*) insofar as: *Inasmuch as the patient is now feeling strong, he can leave the hospital.*

in·au·di·ble /ɪnˈɔdəbəl/ adj. too soft to be heard, almost silent: *The words that he whispered were inaudible.*

in·au·gu·rate /ɪnˈɔgyəˌreɪt/ v. **-rated, -rating, -rates 1** to put in public office with a ceremony: *The governor of Texas was inaugurated two months after her election.* **2** to open, begin with a ceremony: *A jazz band inaugurated the festivities with a lively song.* -adj. **inaugural** /ɪnˈɔgyərəl/.

in·au·gu·ra·tion /ɪnˌɔgyəˈreɪʃən/ n. **1** [C;U] installation of a U.S. president or state governor: *The inauguration brings spectators from all over.* **2** [C] beginning, opening ceremony: *The inauguration of the Independence Day festivities included a speech by the mayor.*

USAGE NOTE: Presidential elections are held every four years in November. The *inauguration* of a US President takes place on the following January 20. It is not a national holiday: *We watched the inauguration on TV at work.*

in·aus·pi·cious /ˌɪnɔˈspɪʃəs/ adj.frml. showing bad luck or difficulty, unfavorable: *His son's death was an inauspicious event to begin the year.*

in·bound /ˈɪnˌbaʊnd/ adj.adv. headed toward or into a place from the surrounding area: *The <adj.> inbound trains to Manhattan from Connecticut run often.*

in·bounds /ˈɪnˌbaʊndz/ adv.adj. (in sports) within a playing area: *The tennis ball landed <adv.> inbounds.*

in·bred /ˈɪnbred/ adj. **1** having (an ability or characteristic) from birth, (*syn.*) innate: *Plow horses have inbred strength.* **2** mated with close relatives, sometimes causing genetic defects or disease: *Popular dog breeds are so inbred that some some puppies are born insane.*

in·cal·cu·la·ble /ɪnˈkælkyələbəl/ adj. **1** not able to be counted, limitless: *The number of stars in the universe is incalculable.* **2** great, immense: *The hurricane did incalculable damage to the coastal area.*

in·can·des·cent /ˌɪnkənˈdesənt/ adj. giving light when heated, glowing: *My family uses incandescent light bulbs in our lamps.* -n. [U] **incandescence.**

in·can·ta·tion /ˌɪnkænˈteɪʃən/ n. [C;U] the repeated speaking or singing of certain words to make magic: *The witches in Shakespeare's* Macbeth *utter incantations that foretell the future.*

in·ca·pa·ble /ɪnˈkeɪpəbəl/ adj. **1** not able: *Our small garage is incapable of holding three cars.* **2** without ability or talent, incompetent: *He is incapable of adding 2 + 2.*

in·ca·pac·i·tate /ˌɪnkəˈpæsəˌteɪt/ v. **-tated, -tating, -tates** to make helpless, cripple: *A*

*head-on collision in an auto accident incapac-
itated her -n.* [U] **incapacity.**

in·car·cer·ate /ɪnˈkɑrsə,reɪt/ *v.* **-ated, -ating,
-ates** (in law) to put in jail, (*syn.*) to imprison:
*They incarcerated the woman, but many peo-
ple believed that she was innocent. -n.* [C;U]
incarceration.

in·car·na·tion /,ɪnkɑrˈneɪʃən/ *n.* **1** [C;U] a living being that represents s.t. else: *Christians
believe Jesus was the incarnation of God.* **2**
[C] a different version or form: *That is the
same story in another incarnation. -adj.* **in-
carnate.**

in·cen·di·ar·y /ɪnˈsɛndieri/ *n.* **-ies** s.o. who
sets fires, (*syn.*) arsonist: *Incendiaries caused
great damage when they started fires in government buildings.*
—*adj.* **1** relating to fire or burning: *Arsonists
planned for the incendiary bombs to blow up
the building.* **2** *fig.* causing anger or excitement: *The parents were upset when the cult
gave incendiary literature to their teenagers.*

in·cense /ˈɪn,sɛns/ *n.* [U] substance (often in a
stick or cone form) that releases a pleasant
smell when burned: *I went to a Catholic funeral where the priest used sweet incense.*
—*v.* /ɪnˈsɛns/ **-censed, -censing, -censes** to
make very angry, (*syns.*) to enrage, infuriate:
*The child's lies incensed his babysitter so
much that she slapped him.*

in·cen·tive /ɪnˈsɛntɪv/ *n.* s.t. that makes s.o.
work harder, motivation: *The man promised
his nephew $100 as an incentive for good
grades.*
—*adj.* causing hard work, motivating, rewarding: *Incentive awards go to salespeople who
sell the most insurance.*

in·cep·tion /ɪnˈsɛpʃən/ *n.* beginning, start: *The
day-care center has been a success since its
inception.*

in·ces·sant /ɪnˈsɛsənt/ *adj.* without stop, continuing, persistent: *Incessant noise makes me
appreciate silence.*

in·cest /ˈɪnsɛst/ *n.* [U] illegal sexual relations
between close family members, such as parent
and child or brother and sister: *When the father
had sex with his daughter, he committed in-
cest. -adj.* **incestuous.**

inch /ɪntʃ/ *n.* **1** a measure of length equal to
1/12 of a foot or 2.54 centimeters: *My ruler is
12 inches long.* **2 If you give him (her) an
inch, he (she) takes a mile:** if you give s.o. a
little opportunity, that person will take too
much: *I loaned him my car for the evening,
and he has kept it for a week. If you give him
an inch, he takes a mile.* **3 inch by inch:** a
short distance at a time: *The soldiers crawled
forward inch by inch.* **4 within an inch of
doing s.t.:** almost, very nearly doing s.t.: *He
has recovered from cancer but came within an
inch of dying.*

—*v.* to move very slowly: *Traffic is so bad that
cars are just inching along.*

USAGE NOTE: There are 12 *inches* in a *foot*
(30.48 cm.) and three feet to a *yard* (91.44
cm.). Today both the US system (inches, feet,
pounds, ounces, etc.) and the metric system
are taught in school, but most Americans are
more comfortable with th US system: *He's six
feet four inches tall, but his mother's only five
foot one.‖I bought ten yards of curtain material.*

in·ci·dence /ˈɪnsədəns/ *n.* [U] frequency of
s.t. happening: *The incidence of terrorism is
increasing in big cities.*

in·ci·dent /ˈɪnsədənt/ *n.* an event, occurrence,
esp. a bad one: *There was an incident in a
downtown bar where two men got into a fist
fight.*

in·ci·den·tal /,ɪnsəˈdɛntl/ *adj.* **1** minor, (*syn.*)
inconsequential: *The budget did not include
incidental costs, such as paper and pens.* **2**
secondary to, less important than: *My new CD
has incidental music along with the main
songs.*

in·ci·den·tal·ly /,ɪnsəˈdɛntli/ *adv.* by the way
(used to introduce a new thought): *Yes, I know
she's from Germany. Incidentally, did you
know that I speak German?*

in·cin·er·ate /ɪnˈsɪnə,reɪt/ *v.* **-ated, -ating,
-ates 1** to burn to ashes, destroy by fire: *Huge
bombs incinerated the enemy village.* **2** to
burn in an incinerator: *Some cities incinerate
large amounts of trash. -n.* [U] **incineration.**

in·cin·er·a·tor /ɪnˈsɪnə,reɪtər/ *n.* a machine
used to burn things, esp. trash: *The smoke from
our town's incinerator causes pollution.*

in·ci·sion /ɪnˈsɪʒən/ *n.* [C;U] a narrow cut,
usu. in the skin: *The patient's incision is healing well. -v.* **incise** /ɪnˈsaɪz/**.**

in·ci·sive /ɪnˈsaɪsɪv/ *adj.* smart and direct,
(*syns.*) sharp, penetrating: *The book critic
made incisive comments about the new novel.*

in·ci·sor /ɪnˈsaɪzer/ *n.* a sharp front tooth used
for cutting: *Rats tore into the meat with their
strong incisors.*

in·cite /ɪnˈsaɪt/ *v.* **-cited, -citing, -cites** to
cause s.t. to happen, make s.o. do s.t., (*syn.*) to
provoke: *The baseball fans' screams incited
the team to play hard and win. -n.* [U] **incite-
ment.**

in·clem·ent /ɪnˈklɛmənt/ *adj.frml.* referring to
bad weather, such as rain or snowstorms:
*Inclement weather forced the graduation cere-
mony to be held inside.*

in·cli·na·tion /,ɪnkləˈneɪʃən/ *n.* desire to do
s.t., preference, leaning: *I have an inclination
to see a movie tonight, but my wife doesn't
want to.*

in·cline /ɪnˈklaɪn/ v. **-clined, -clining, -clines**
1 to tilt at an angle: *He inclined his easy chair to a nearly flat position and rested.* **2** to bend forward or backward: *Listeners inclined forward to better hear the speaker.*
—n. a hill or slope, usu. of land: *A train went up an incline through the mountains.*

in·clined /ɪnˈklaɪnd/ adj. **1** slanted, tilted: *The road is inclined steeply upward.* **2** *fig.* preferring, likely to: *I am inclined to be very careful about what bank I use.*

in·clude /ɪnˈklud/ v. **-cluded, -cluding, -cludes** to make s.t. a part of s.t. else: *She included some of her friends on the party guest list.* **2** to put with, to insert, attach: *She included some chocolate in each child's lunch bag.*

in·clu·sion /ɪnˈkluʒən/ n. [U] the act of making s.t. a part of s.t. else: *The inclusion of her book on the reading list made the author happy.*

in·clu·sive /ɪnˈklusɪv/ adj. **1** allowing everyone or everything to be part of, making no exceptions, (syn.) comprehensive: *This class is inclusive of all ages; one student is 19, another is 45, and a third is 70.* **2** along with: *Send in your application inclusive of the application fee.*

in·cog·ni·to /ˌɪnkɑgˈnitoʊ/ adj.frml. using another name or in disguise: *The rock star wore dark glasses and traveled incognito so no one would bother her.*

in·co·her·ent /ˌɪnkoʊˈhɪrənt/ adj. not able to be understood, (syn.) unintelligible: *The little girl was so scared that her speech was incoherent.* -n. [U] **incoherence.**

in·com·bus·ti·ble /ˌɪnkəmˈbʌstəbəl/ adj. not able to burn or be burned: *Do not throw incombustible materials in this trash can.*

in·come /ˈɪnˌkʌm, ˈɪŋ-/ n. [C;U] money earned from working or investments: *Her income increased when she changed jobs and bought stock.*

income tax n. a percentage of individuals' and businesses' earnings paid to the government: *North Carolina uses state income taxes to build roads and highways.*

in·com·ing /ˈɪnˌkʌmɪŋ/ adj. coming toward a place from farther away: *Incoming mail from other countries arrives in the USA by plane and boat.*

in·com·pa·ra·ble /ɪnˈkɑmpərəbəl/ adj. unlike anything else, unique: *The dinosaur fossil is incomparable to the fossils of all other animals.*

in·com·pat·i·ble /ˌɪnkəmˈpætəbəl/ adj. not able to work or be together: *This new word processing program is incompatible with my computer.* -n. [C;U] **incompatibility.**

in·com·pe·tent /ɪnˈkɑmpətənt/ adj. without the skill or talent to do s.t., (syn.) bungling: *He is an incompetent vice-president; he is not very smart, and he has only two years of experience in the business.* -n. [U] **incompetence.**

in·com·plete /ˌɪnkəmˈplit/ adj. lacking, s.t. unfinished: *My mother feels her life is incomplete without grandchildren.*

in·com·pre·hen·si·ble /ˌɪnkɑmpriˈhɛnsəbəl, ɪnˌkɑm-/ adj. not able to be understood: *I understand algebra, but calculus is incomprehensible.* -n. [U] **incomprehension.**

in·con·ceiv·a·ble /ˌɪnkənˈsivəbəl/ adj. not able to be imagined, shocking: *It is inconceivable that your nice brother would hit his child.*

in·con·clu·sive /ˌɪnkənˈklusɪv/ adj. not leading to a sure result, not complete enough, indefinite: *The results of Angela's medical tests were inconclusive, showing no cause for her pain.*

in·con·gru·ous /ɪnˈkɑŋgruəs/ adj. not matching, not appropriate to the situation, (syn.) incompatible: *His radical ideas are incongruous with his family's conservative traditions.* -n. **incongruity** /ˌɪnkənˈgruəti/.

in·con·se·quen·tial /ˌɪnkɑnsəˈkwɛnʃəl, ɪnˌkɑn-/ adj. not important, insignificant: *A few inconsequential details remain, but most of the book is written.*

in·con·sid·er·ate /ˌɪnkənˈsɪdərɪt/ adj. not polite, rude, (syn.) insensitive: *He is inconsiderate of my feelings when he shouts at me.*

in·con·sis·tent /ˌɪnkənˈsɪstənt/ adj. not matching, different from: *Her statements are inconsistent with the facts.* -n.[C;U] **inconsistency.**

in·con·sol·a·ble /ˌɪnkənˈsoʊləbəl/ adj. not able to be comforted, (syn.) devastated: *The mother was inconsolable after the death of her child.*

in·con·spic·u·ous /ˌɪnkənˈspɪkyuəs/ adj. not obvious or noticeable, unobtrusive: *He is of medium height and weight, quite inconspicuous in a crowd.*

in·con·stant /ɪnˈkɑnstənt/ adj.frml. variable, changeable: *The direction of the wind is inconstant.* -n. [U] **inconstancy.**

in·con·test·a·ble /ˌɪnkənˈtɛstəbəl/ adj. true, certain: *The earth is round, not flat; this is an incontestable fact.*

in·con·ven·ient /ˌɪnkənˈvinyənt/ adj. not at a good time, difficult, (syn.) awkward: *Seeing you tomorrow is inconvenient because I have another appointment.* -n. [C;U] **inconvenience.**

in·cor·po·rate /ɪnˈkɔrpəreɪt/ v. **-rated, -rating, -rates 1** to include, contain: *The spending agreement incorporates ideas from both Democrats and Republicans.* **2** to form a corporation: *Many people incorporate their busi-*

nesses to avoid certain taxes. -adj. **incorporated;** *-n.* [U] **incorporation.**

in·cor·rect /ˌɪnkəˈrɛkt/ *adj.* **1** containing mistakes, wrong: *The sum of those numbers is incorrect; they need to be added again.* **2** not appropriate, improper: *His loud behavior in church was incorrect.*

in·cor·ri·gi·ble /ɪnˈkɔrədʒəbəl, -ˈkɑr-/ *adj.* not able to behave correctly, always bad: *Some criminals are incorrigible and will be in jail all their lives.*

in·crease /ˈɪnˌkris/ *n.* [C;U] a larger amount, *(syn.)* an augmentation: *Mr. Kim got a salary increase of 10 percent; he was earning $40,000 per year, so now he will earn $44,000.*
—*v.* /ɪnˈkris/ **-creased, -creasing, -creases 1** to go up in number, rise: *The temperature increased ten degrees this afternoon.* **2** to make bigger, enlarge: *Architects increased the size of our house by adding a kitchen.*

in·cred·i·ble /ɪnˈkrɛdəbəl/ *adj.* **1** wonderful, fabulous: *We had an incredible time on our vacation!* **2** unbelievable, not true: *He tells incredible lies. -adv.* **incredibly.**

in·cred·u·lous /ɪnˈkrɛdʒələs/ *adj.* not believing, *(syn.)* surprised: *I was incredulous when you told me your cat can swim. -n.* [U] **incredulity.** /ˌɪnkrəˈduləti/.

in·cre·ment /ˈɪnkrəmənt, ˈɪŋ-/ *n.* a small segment of s.t., a step: *Temperature is measured in increments called degrees. -adj.* **incremental** /ˌɪnkrəˈmɛntl/.

in·crim·i·nate /ɪnˈkrɪməˌneɪt/ *v.* **-nated, -nating, -nates** to show that s.o. was involved in a crime: *The woman incriminated her neighbors who were growing marijuana. -n.* [U] **incrimination.**

in·cu·bate /ˈɪnkyəˌbeɪt, ˈɪŋ-/ *v.* **-bated, -bating, -bates 1** to keep eggs warm until babies are born: *Birds incubate eggs by sitting on them.* **2** to put a newborn baby in a special machine so it can grow: *The hospital incubates premature babies until their mothers can take care of them. -n.* [U] **incubation.**

in·cu·ba·tor /ˈɪnkyəˌbeɪtər, ˈɪŋ-/ *n.* a special hospital bed with a cover, used to shelter and warm babies: *The father took his son out of the incubator to hold him.*

in·cum·bent /ɪnˈkʌmbənt/ *n.* a politician who is trying to be elected again: *Senator Chen is an incumbent; he has been in the Senate for six years and wants to be elected for six more years.*

in·cur /ɪnˈkɜr/ *v.* **-curred, -curring, -curs** to take on (responsibilities, obligations, etc.): *He incurred debts when he started a new business.*

in·cur·a·ble /ɪnˈkyʊrəbəl/ *adj.* impossible to heal or cure, fatal: *He has incurable cancer and will die within six months.*

in·cur·sion /ɪnˈkɜrʒən/ *n.* an aggressive or forceful entrance into another country or s.o. else's area: *We don't like the neighbors' incursion when they park their car in our driveway.*

in·debt·ed /ɪnˈdɛtɪd/ *adj.* obligated because of receiving a favor, grateful: *I am indebted to you for saving my life. -n.* [U] **indebtedness.**

in·de·cent /ɪnˈdisənt/ *adj.* **1** not good or proper: *It was indecent of him to lie to his mother.* **2** sexually wrong, *(syns.)* obscene, lewd: *The man took off his clothes in public and was arrested for indecent behavior. -n.* [U] **indecency.**

in·de·ci·sive /ˌɪndəˈsaɪsɪv/ *adj.* not able to choose or make a decision, *(syns.)* vacillating, wavering: *She is indecisive about wearing pants or a skirt. -n.* [U] **indecision** /ˌɪndəˈsɪʒən/.

in·dec·o·rous /ɪnˈdɛkərəs/ *adj.frml.* improper, bad: *Her drunken behavior at the dance was indecorous. -n.* [U] **indecorum.**

in·deed /ɪnˈdid/ *exclam.* used to express surprise or disbelief: *I will earn a million dollars next year—indeed?*
—*adv.* **1** truly, factually: *It was indeed the largest elephant in the world.* **2** used to express s.t. strongly: *Do I love my husband? Yes, indeed!*

in·de·fen·si·ble /ˌɪndəˈfɛnsəbəl/ *adj.* so bad that there is no justification, inexcusable: *She tried to apologize, but we still felt her rude behavior was indefensible.*

in·de·fin·a·ble /ˌɪndəˈfaɪnəbəl/ *adj.* not able to be explained, mysterious: *That slow violin music has a certain indefinable quality to it.*

in·def·i·nite /ɪnˈdɛfənɪt/ *adj.* not specific about time, place, or detail: *We know the meeting is on July 12, but the time is indefinite.*

indefinite article *n.* (in grammar) "a" or "an," used before a noun when "the" is too specific: *A tree fell in the forest.*

indefinite pronoun *n.* a word, such as "either," "any," or "some," that replaces a noun in a nonspecific way: *He needs some (money) because he doesn't have any.*

in·del·i·ble /ɪnˈdɛləbəl/ *adj.* **1** not able to be erased, permanent: *The letter was written in indelible ink.* **2** *fig.* unforgettable, lasting: *Her intelligence makes an indelible impression on others.*

in·del·i·cate /ɪnˈdɛləkɪt/ *adj.frml.* in bad taste, *(syns.)* coarse, tactless: *His indelicate behavior included banging his fist on the table and swearing. -n.* [C;U] **indelicacy.**

in·dem·ni·fy /ɪnˈdɛmnəˌfaɪ/ *v.* **-fied, -fying, -fies** to agree to pay s.o. for loss or damage if loss or damage occurs: *The insurance contract indemnifies my company in case of flood or fire. -n.* [U] **indemnification** /ɪnˌdɛmnəfəˈkeɪʃən/.

in·dem·ni·ty /ɪn,dɛmnəti/ *n.* [C;U] protection or insurance against loss or damage: *I was glad I had an indemnity when my house burned down.*

in·dent /ɪn'dɛnt, 'ɪn,dɛnt/ *v.n.* to start writing or typing a short distance in from the margin: *When I begin a new paragraph, I <v.> indent five spaces.*

in·den·tured /ɪn'dɛntʃərd/ *adj.* having a work contract or agreement with a more powerful person, enslaved: *indentured workers, servants* *-v. n.* [U] **indenture.**

in·de·pend·ence /,ɪndə'pɛndəns/ *n.* [U] **1** freedom: *Many former African colonies fought for independence from France, Portugal, and other European countries.* **2** state of taking care of oneself, (*syn.*) self-sufficiency: *She felt a sense of independence when she left home to go to college.*

Independence Day *n.* in the USA, July 4, the holiday marking independence from Great Britain (also called the Fourth of July): *We celebrate Independence Day with fireworks and a cookout.*

in·de·pend·ent /,ɪndə'pɛndənt/ *adj.* **1** free: *The USA became an independent nation after 1776.* **2** taking care of oneself, (*syn.*) self-sufficient: *He is financially independent of his parents but still asks for their advice.*

in-depth *adj.* very detailed, thorough, (*syn.*) exhaustive: *We had an in-depth discussion of the problem and every possible solution to it.*

in·de·scrib·a·ble /,ɪndɪ'skraɪbəbəl/ *adj.* not able to be put into words, (*syns.*) overwhelming, mind-boggling: *The water in the Caribbean is an indescribable blue!*

in·de·struc·ti·ble /,ɪndə'strʌktəbəl/ *adj.* **1** not able to be destroyed: *That metal ship is indestructible.* **2** durable, lasting: *My boots are nearly indestructible because the leather is so thick.*

in·de·ter·mi·nate /,ɪndə'tɜrmənɪt/ *adj.* not known yet, unspecified: *Telephone lines are still down on the island, so the hurricane damage is indeterminate.*

in·dex /'ɪn,dɛks/ *n.* **-dexes** or **-dices** /-də,siz/ **1** in a book, a list of topics in alphabetical order with page numbers: *Look for "World War II" in the index of your history book.* **2** an indicator, such as labels on a graph or other symbols, esp. about money and economics: *The economic <pl.> indices published in my business magazine suggest that the economy is improving.*
—v. **1** to create an index or include in an index: *An editor indexed the main topics of the book.* *-n.* **indexer.**

In·di·an /'ɪndiən/ *n.* **1** a person born in India or with parents from India: *Many Indians practice the Hindu religion.* **2** a person related to any of the original people of America, (*syn.*) Native American: *Her father is an Indian, a member of the Cherokee tribe.*
—adj. related to Indians: *Indian restaurants serve spicy foods with curry and rice.||Navajo and Cherokee Indians are two different groups of people.*

USAGE NOTE: Christopher Columbus was looking for India when he reached the Americas, which is why the native populations were called *Indians.* The preferred term for American Indians is *Native Americans.*

Indian summer *n.* [C;U] a warm period in the late autumn: *Sometimes Halloween (October 31) falls during Indian summer, and we can wear costumes with no coats.*

in·di·cate /'ɪndə,keɪt/ *v.* **-cated, -cating, -cates** **1** to show where or what s.t. is: *The girl indicated her choice of dessert by pointing to the chocolate cake.* **2** to mean, (*syn.*) to symbolize: *Those black clouds indicate that it might rain soon.*

in·di·ca·tion /,ɪndə'keɪʃən/ *n.* **1** [C] a sign, signal: *The arrows in the elevator give an indication of whether it is going up or down.* **2** [C;U] meaning, hint: *An increase in rain gives us an indication that grass will be greener soon.* *-n.* [C] **indicator** /'ɪndə,keɪtər/; *-adj.* **indicative** /ɪn'dɪkətɪv/.

in·dict /ɪn'daɪt/ *v.* (in law) to formally charge s.o. with a crime or wrongdoing: *The court indicted the man for murder, but he's not in jail yet.* *-n.* [C;U] **indictment.**

in·dif·fer·ent /ɪn'dɪfərənt, -'dɪfrənt/ *adj.* not caring, without feeling, (*syn.*) apathetic: *His indifferent attitude toward food made him lose weight.* *-n.* [U] **indifference.**

in·dig·e·nous /ɪn'dɪdʒənəs/ *adj.* born in, native to: *The Navajo tribes are indigenous to Arizona.*

in·di·gent /'ɪndədʒənt/ *adj.frml.* without money, poor, (*syn.*) destitute: *Some indigent people beg for money and food.*

in·di·ges·tion /,ɪndə'dʒɛstʃən/ *n.* [U] pain in the stomach because of s.t. one has eaten: *He ate three hot dogs with chili and had indigestion.* *-adj.* **indigestible.** /,ɪndə'dʒɛstəbəl/.

in·dig·nant /ɪn'dɪgnənt/ *adj.* angry because s.t. is unfair or not right, (*syns.*) offended, insulted: *She became indignant when a store clerk said she stole a ring.* *-n.* [U] **indignation.**

in·dig·ni·ty /ɪn'dɪgnəti/ *n.* [C;U] **-ties** feeling of shame, (*syns.*) humiliation, affront: *Falling on the ice in public caused him some indignity.*

in·di·go /'ɪndə,goʊ/ *n.* a purple-blue color: *My dark blue jeans have an indigo shade.*

in·di·rect /,ɪndə'rɛkt, -daɪ-/ *adj.* **1** not going straight toward s.t., (*syns.*) circuitous, roundabout: *We left the highway and took an indirect route on little back roads.* **2** not definite, *(syns.)* subtle, implied: *Eva's criticism of her child was indirect but still hurtful.* -*n.* [U] **indirection; indirectness.**

indirect object *n.* (in grammar) a noun receiving indirect action from a verb—for example, "him" in this sentence: *I loaned him money.*

in·dis·creet /ˌɪndəˈskrit/ *adj.* **1** not showing wise or good behavior, esp. in telling the secrets of others, *(syn.)* untrustworthy: *Don't tell private things to an indiscreet person, or everyone will know about them.*

in·dis·cre·tion /ˌɪndəˈskrɛʃən/ *n.* [C;U] bad or unwise behavior, esp. s.t. socially wrong or revealing: *Drinking too much and telling dirty jokes are two of his indiscretions.*

in·dis·crim·i·nate /ˌɪndəˈskrɪmənɪt/ *adj.* lacking care or wisdom, without thought for the future or result, *(syn.)* rash: *His indiscriminate spending on fancy cars left him with no money.* -*n.* [U] **indiscrimination** /ˌɪndəˌskrɪməˈneɪʃən/.

in·dis·pen·sa·ble /ˌɪndəˈspɛnsəbəl/ *adj.* necessary, essential: *Warm clothing is indispensable in cold weather.*

in·dis·posed /ˌɪndəˈspoʊzd/ *adj.frml.* **1** not able to do s.t., usu. because of sickness: *The opera star has a cold and is indisposed today.* **2** not interested: *Those rich people are indisposed toward helping their poor neighbors.*

in·dis·put·a·ble /ˌɪndəˈspyutəbəl/ *adj.* definite, unquestionable: *Police have indisputable proof that the gun is yours.*

in·dis·tinct /ˌɪndəˈstɪŋkt/ *adj.* **1** not easy to be seen or heard, *(syns.)* blurred, fuzzy: *His voice was indistinct because of the loud music.* -*adj.* **indistinctive.**

in·dis·tin·guish·a·ble /ˌɪndəˈstɪŋgwɪʃəbəl/ *adj.* just the same as, alike: *One twin brother is indistinguishable from the other.*

in·di·vid·u·al /ˌɪndəˈvɪdʒuəl/ *n.* one person: *Three individuals walked away from the crowd.*
—*adj.* different from others, single, separate,: *When Frida speaks, she has an individual accent because as a child she lived for five years in Mexico, five years in the USA, and five years in Korea.*

in·di·vid·u·al·ist /ˌIndəˈvɪdʒuəlɪst/ *n.* a person who thinks and behaves according to his or her own beliefs, *(syn.)* a nonconformist: *Be an individualist; don't be a doctor like the rest of your family.* -*adj.* **individualistic;** -*n.* [U] **individualism.**

in·di·vid·u·al·i·ty /ˌIndəˌvɪdʒuˈæləti/ *n.* [U] a separate style, one's way of being different from others: *Her individuality shows in her colorful scarves and interesting jewelry.*

in·di·vid·u·al·ize /ˌIndəˈvɪdʒuəˌlaɪz/ *v.* **-ized, -izing, -izes** to make s.t. for a person's special

needs: *That company is huge, but it individualizes its services for each customer.*

in·di·vis·i·ble /ˌɪndəˈvɪzəbəl/ *adj.* not able to be forced apart, solid, unified: *That family is indivisible; they stay together even during troubled times.*

in·doc·tri·nate /ɪnˈdɑktrəˌneɪt/ *v.* **-nated, -nating, -nates** to teach s.o. that certain opinions and customs are the right ones: *The Marines indoctrinate new soldiers into the ways of military life.*

In·do-Eu·ro·pe·an /ˌIndoʊˌyʊrəˈpiən/ *n.adj.* related to languages spoken in Europe and parts of Asia: *He speaks Arabic, but he wants to learn an <adj.> Indo-European language.*

in·do·lence /ˈɪndələns/ *n.frml.* [U] laziness: *His indolence made him lose his job, since he didn't work hard enough.* -*adj.* **indolent.**

in·dom·i·ta·ble /ɪnˈdɑmɪtəbəl/ *adj.* not able to be discouraged or stopped, *(syns.)* irrepressible, undaunted: *The indomitable spirit of the firefighters helped save many lives.*

in·door /ˈɪnˌdɔr/ *adj.* located inside a building: *Some rich people have indoor swimming pools.*

in·doors /ɪnˈdɔrz/ *adv.* inside a building: *When it started to rain, we moved our picnic indoors.*

in·du·bi·ta·ble /ɪnˈdubətəbəl/ *adj.frml.* without doubt, certain: *Death is an indubitable fact of life.*

in·duce /ɪnˈdus/ *v.* **-duced, -ducing, -duces 1** to make s.o. do s.t., *(syns.)* to persuade, coax: *His wife's love of the ocean induced him to take a vacation at the seashore.* **2** to cause, make happen: *The nurse induced a lower fever by bathing the man in cool water.*

in·duce·ment /ɪnˈdusmənt/ *n.* [C;U] s.t. that makes s.o. want to do s.t., *(syns.)* motive, incentive: *The company promised her a big office as an inducement to take the job.*

in·duct /ɪnˈdʌkt/ *v.* to put in public office or the military with a formal ceremony: *When he was inducted into office, the mayor promised to always tell the truth.||Our son was inducted into the army last week.* -*n.* [C;U] **induction.**

in·duc·tive /ɪnˈdʌktɪv/ *adj.* using logic or math to solve a puzzle or problem: *The police knew the robber's shoe size and used inductive reasoning to connect the footprints to the man.*

in·dulge /ɪnˈdʌldʒ/ *v.* **-dulged, -dulging, -dulges 1** to take or eat s.t. good (sometimes too much): *I indulged and had chocolate cake for dessert.* **2** to allow s.o. to do s.t., even if it is not good or wise: *Carlos indulged his son's wish to learn to fly an airplane.*

in·dul·gence /ɪnˈdʌldʒəns/ *n.* **1** [U] patience, tolerance: *I ask your indulgence while I tell you this long, boring story.* **2** [C] s.t. one enjoys, even though it may be bad or wrong: *Two* *glasses of wine at dinner is my only indulgence.*

in·dul·gent /ɪn'dʌldʒənt/ *adj.* tolerant, *(syn.)* pampering: *He is indulgent in buying his children all that candy.*

in·dus·tri·al /ɪn'dʌstriəl/ *adj.* related to industry (esp. manufacturing): *Industrial production is up this year, but agriculture is weak.*

in·dus·tri·al·ism /ɪn'dʌstriə,lɪzəm/ *n.* [U] the growth or present state of industry within a nation or region: *That developing country changed its economy from farming to industrialism.*

in·dus·tri·al·ize /ɪn'dʌstriə,laɪz/ *v.* **-ized, -izing, -izes** to make a nation or region use and develop industry: *Many developing countries wish to industrialize their economies by building factories.* *-n.* [U] **industrialization** /ɪn,dʌstriəlɪ'zeɪʃən/.

industrial park *n.* a piece of land with buildings for businesses, esp. those that make new products, *(syn.)* office park: *The industrial park on the edge of town has three office buildings and two small factories.*

in·dus·tri·ous /ɪn'dʌstriəs/ *adj.* hardworking, busy: *She started her own business and is now very industrious.*

in·dus·try /'ɪndəstri/ *n.* **-tries 1** [U] the making and selling of products: *Industry grew quickly after the discovery of electricity.* **2** [C] a specific type of manufacturing: *The U.S. auto industry is centered in Detroit.* **3** [U] hard work, *(syn.)* diligence: *His industry in college resulted in high grades.*

in·e·bri·at·ed /ɪn'ibri,eɪtɪd/ *adj.infrml.* drunk: *He drank too much beer and is inebriated.* *-n.* [U] **inebriation** /ɪn,ibri'eɪʃən/.

in·ef·fec·tive /,ɪnɪ'fɛktɪv/ *adj.* **1** not good enough to make s.t. happen, *(syn.)* fruitless: *Yelling at teenagers is ineffective; talking works better.* **2** not good at doing s.t., *(syns.)* ineffectual, incompetent: *She is ineffective at speaking another language and has decided to stop trying to learn one.* *-n.* [U] **ineffectiveness.**

in·ef·fi·cient /,ɪnɪ'fɪʃənt/ *adj.* not using time well: *The factory is inefficient because its machinery is slow and old.* *-n.* [U] **inefficiency.**

in·el·e·gant /ɪn'ɛləgənt/ *adj.* without grace, *(syn.)* awkward: *The young dancers' movements were inelegant.*

in·el·i·gi·ble /ɪn'ɛlɪdʒəbəl/ *adj.* not able to do s.t. for some reason (too young, not skilled, etc.), *(syn.)* unqualified: *He is ineligible to enter college because he has not finished high school.* *-n.* [U] **ineligibility.**

in·ept /ɪn'ɛpt/ *adj.* **1** not good at, *(syns.)* clumsy, awkward: *His inept singing made us put our hands over our ears.* *-n.* [U] **ineptness; ineptitude** /ɪn'ɛptɪ,tud/.

in·e·qual·i·ty /,ɪni'kwɑləti/ *n.* [C;U] **-ties 1** a condition in which s.t. is greater or less than s.t. else: *There is an issue of inequality here; I make $20,000 a year and you make $30,000, but we do the same job.* **2** a different amount of opportunity or resources from s.t. else: *Inequality among nations can cause war.*

in·eq·ui·ta·ble /ɪn'ɛkwɪtəbəl/ *adj.* not equal, unfair, unjust: *Some people believe that Africa receives an inequitable amount of Western support compared to Southeast Asia.*

in·eq·ui·ty /ɪn'ɛkwəti/ *n.* **-ties** an unfair thing: *Many inequities in life are caused by poverty and lack of education.*

in·ert /ɪn'ɜrt/ *adj.* **1** lacking the power to move, *(syns.)* immobile, stationary: *A car without an engine sat inert in the garage.* **2** (in chemistry) not active: *inert gas*

in·er·tia /ɪ'nɜrʃə/ *n.* [U] lack of movement, resistance to change: *Social changes often do not happen due to governmental inertia.*

in·es·cap·a·ble /,ɪnɪ'skeɪpəbəl/ *adj.* not avoidable: *Drug abuse is an inescapable problem that must be solved.*

in·es·sen·tial /,ɪnɪ'sɛnʃəl/ *adj.* not necessary, *(syn.)* dispensable: *Those topics are inessential, so leave them out of the report.*

in·ev·i·ta·ble /ɪn'ɛvətəbəl/ *adj.* definitely going to happen, unavoidable, certain: *Gaining weight is inevitable when you eat too much and don't exercise.*

in·ex·act /,ɪnɪg'zækt/ *adj.* not precise, vague: *Those numbers are too inexact to base decisions on.* *-n.* [U] **inexactness.**

in·ex·haust·i·ble /,ɪnɪg'zɔstəbəl/ *adj.* without end, limitless: *The sun seems to have an inexhaustible supply of energy.*

in·ex·pen·sive /,ɪnɪk'spɛnsɪv/ *adj.* not costly, low-priced, cheap: *The cost of living in Kansas City is inexpensive compared to that of Los Angeles.*

in·ex·pe·ri·ence /,ɪnɪk'spɪriəns/ *n.* [U] **1** lack of experience in the world, *(syn.)* naiveté: *His inexperience with big-city life showed when he didn't know how to use the subway.* **2** limited knowledge: *We laughed at her inexperience in the kitchen; she can't boil water.*

in·ex·pli·ca·ble /,ɪnɪk'splɪkəbəl/ *adj.* not able to be explained, mysterious: *The strange voices you hear are inexplicable; they must be in your mind.*

in·ex·plic·it /,ɪnɪk'splɪsɪt/ *adj.* not clear, inexact, *(syn.)* vague: *His directions are inexplicit; we'll get lost.*

in·fal·li·ble /ɪn'fæləbəl/ *adj.* never making a mistake, faultless: *Calculations from that computer are infallible.*

in·fa·mous /'ɪnfəməs/ *adj.* famous because of s.t. bad: *That murderer is infamous for his cruelty.*

USAGE NOTE: Compare *infamous, notorious, famous,* and *well-known.* Use infamous and notorious to indicate that s.o. or s.t. is famous for a negative reason: *Adolf Hitler was notorious for his cruelty.||The airplane disappeared over the infamous Bermuda Triangle.* Use famous and well-known when s.o. or s.t. is familiar to many people: *Pablo Picasso was a famous Spanish artist.||McDonald's is a well-known chain of fast-food restaurants.*

in·fa·my /'ɪnfəmi/ *n.frml.* [U] evil or bad reputation: *The infamy of Hitler lives on in history books.*

in·fan·cy /'ɪnfənsi/ *n.* [U] **1** the part of a baby's life just after birth and before walking: *Many parents choose to work at home during their child's infancy.* **2** *fig.* early time, beginning: *That business is still in its infancy; it opened last week.*

in·fant /'ɪnfənt/ *n.* a baby: *A mother held an infant in her arms.*

in·fan·tile /'ɪnfən,taɪl/ *adj.* childish, stupid: *His infantile remarks like "Me first!" annoy everyone.* -*n.* [U] **infantilism** /'ɪnfəntl,ɪzəm, ɪn'fæn-/.

in·fan·try /'ɪnfəntri/ *n.* [C;U] **-tries** soldiers who fight on foot: *The infantry moved forward behind tanks.*

in·farc·tion /ɪn'fɑrkʃən/ *n.* (in medicine) clotting and blockage of a blood vessel, esp. in the heart, a heart attack: *That patient died of an infarction before she could have heart surgery.*

in·fat·u·at·ed /ɪn'fæʧu,eɪtɪd/ *adj.* in love in a brief, often unthinking way: *He was infatuated with* (or) *by a model one week, an artist the next.* -*v.* **infatuate;** -*n.*[C;U] **infatuation.**

in·fect /ɪn'fɛkt/ *v.* **1** to give s.o. a sickness or disease: *A flu virus has infected everyone in the office.* **2** *fig.* to spread through a place, (*syns.*) to contaminate, infest: *Crime has infected the entire neighborhood.*

in·fec·tion /ɪn'fɛkʃən/ *n.* [C;U] a disease or sickness received by s.o. or s.t.: *One rat bite can start the spread of infection.* -*adj.* **infectious.**

in·fer /ɪn'fər/ *v.* **-ferred, -ferring, -fers** to guess by having some information, (*syns.*) to surmise, deduce: *I infer from your smile that you are happy.*

in·fer·ence /'ɪnfərəns/ *n.* [C;U] an educated guess based on some information: *I made an inference about the child's height when I met her tall parents.* -*adj.* **inferential** /,ɪnfə'rɛnʃəl/.

in·fe·ri·or /ɪn'fɪriər/ *adj.* lower in quality: *Most wine from Switzerland is inferior to wine from France.*
—*n.* a person of lower rank or ability: *The general is unkind to his inferiors.* -*n.* [U] **inferiority** /ɪn,fɪri'ɔrəti, -'ɑr-/.

inferiority complex *n.* a serious feeling of not being good enough: *That boy has an inferiority complex, but his psychologist helps him feel better about himself.*

in·fer·no /ɪn'fərnou/ *n.* **1** a fiery place, hell: *The inside of a live volcano is an inferno.* **2** a very hot place: *Turn on the air conditioner! This office is an inferno.* -*adj.* **infernal.**

in·fer·tile /ɪn'fərtl/ *adj.* **1** not able to have children, (*syn.*) barren: *She was infertile as a young woman, then had a baby in her forties.* **2** not good for growing plants or crops: *The Sahara Desert is dry and infertile.* -*n.* [U] **infertility** /,ɪnfər'tɪləti/.

in·fest /ɪn'fɛst/ *v.* **1** to fill with insects or animals that cause trouble: *Mosquitoes infested hot, wet areas.* **2** *fig.*to grow in population and have a bad effect: *Crime infests that poor neighborhood.* -*adj.* **infested;** -*n.*[C;U] **infestation** /,ɪnfɛ'steɪʃən/.

in·fi·del /'ɪnfə,dɛl, -dəl/ *n.adj.* a person who doesn't believe in a particular religion: *The radical cult leader called all nonbelievers <n.> infidels.*

in·fi·del·i·ty /,ɪnfə'dɛləti/ *n.* [C;U] **-ties** having sex with s.o. besides a husband or wife: *She divorced her husband for infidelity after she found him in bed with another woman.*

in·field /'ɪn,fild/ *n.* (in baseball) the area within the bases and baselines: *The young boy wasn't strong enough to hit the ball beyond the infield.* -*n.* **infielder.**

in·fil·trate /'ɪnfəl,treɪt/ *v.* **-trated, -trating, -trates** to join or enter s.t. for a secret purpose: *The police infiltrated the drug dealer's house by pretending to want some cocaine.* -*n.* [U] **infiltration.**

in·fi·nite /'ɪnfənɪt/ *adj.* going on forever, never-ending, limitless: *There are an infinite number of stars in the night sky.*

in·fin·i·tes·i·mal /,ɪnfənə'tɛsəməl/ *adj.* extremely small, (*syns.*) minute, tiny: *Those crackers have an infinitesimal amount of salt, so you won't be thirsty.*

in·fin·i·tive /ɪn'fɪnɪtɪv/ *n.* (in grammar) the main form of a verb, usu. used with "to": *"To go" is the infinitive form of the verb "go."*

in·fin·i·ty /ɪn'fɪnəti/ *n.* [U] a limitless number, thing, or place, such as outer space and time: *Astronomers study the infinity of the universe.*

in·firm /ɪn'fərm/ *adj.* physically weak, (*syn.*) feeble: *My 90-year-old uncle is infirm with old age.* -*n.* [C;U] **infirmity.**

in·fir·ma·ry /ɪn'fərməri/ *n.* **-ries** a place where people get medical care, usu. at a university or other institution: *I fell playing hockey and had to go to the infirmary.*

in·flame /ɪn'fleɪm/ *v.* **-flamed, -flaming, -flames** **1** to cause great emotions, usu. anger or excitement: *The king's evil actions inflamed* *the slaves.* **2** to make red and sore: *The boy's knee became inflamed when he scraped it on the ground.*

in·flam·ma·ble /ɪnˈflæməbəl/ *adj.* able to burn, (*syn.*) flammable: *Materials in these rugs and curtains are inflammable, so don't light a match.*

in·flam·ma·tion /ˌɪnfləˈmeɪʃən/ *n.* [C;U] a physical reaction to an injury or disease, usu. with redness, heat, and swelling: *He has an inflammation in his right eye from too much dust.*

in·flam·ma·to·ry /ɪnˈflæməˌtɔri/ *adj.* causing strong emotion, (*syn.*) provocative: *That politician makes inflammatory speeches that people talk about for days.*

in·flate /ɪnˈfleɪt/ *v.* **-flated, -flating, -flates** **1** to fill with air: *A mechanic inflated the car's tires.* **2** to raise above the normal or proper level: *During shortages, some merchants inflate prices.* **3** *fig.* to pump up, swell: *Praise inflates his ego.*

in·fla·tion /ɪnˈfleɪʃən/ *n.* [U] **1** a rise in prices and lowering of currency's value: *Inflation was so great that bread cost twice as much in June as it did in May.* **2** filling with air: *The inflation of the balloon was easy with a gas tank.* *-adj.* **inflationary.**

in·flec·tion /ɪnˈflɛkʃən/ *n.* [C;U] a change in the voice's sound or tone: *The inflection in her voice goes up when she asks a question.*

in·flex·i·ble /ɪnˈflɛksəbəl/ *adj.* **1** rigid, unbending: *The metal bars of a jail are inflexible.* **2** with strong, unchanging opinions, stubborn, (*syn.*) unyielding: *He is very inflexible in his habits, reading the same newspaper every morning.* *-n.* [U] **inflexibility.**

in·flict /ɪnˈflɪkt/ *v.* to cause s.t. bad, give s.o. a problem: *My father inflicts his boring war stories on the whole family.* *-n.* [C;U] **infliction.**

in·flu·ence /ˈɪnfluəns/ *n.* [C;U] the power to change or persuade others: *The President's wife has a strong influence on his thinking.*

—v. **-enced, -encing, -ences** to change s.o.'s mind, have an effect on: *Lenin's ideas influenced the Russians during the 1917 Revolution.* *-adj.* **influential** /ˌɪnfluˈɛnʃəl/.

in·flu·en·za /ˌɪnfluˈɛnzə/ *n.* [U] a contagious illness spread by viruses: *Influenza killed millions in 1918, but now there is a shot that prevents it.*

in·flux /ˈɪnflʌks/ *n.* the sudden arrival of many people or things: *An influx of Cubans and Haitians has made Miami's population grow rapidly.*

in·form /ɪnˈfɔrm/ *v.* **1** to tell s.o., (*syn.*) to notify: *I informed my friends of my new address.* **2** to report s.o.'s wrongdoing: *He is a spy who informs on others to the government.*

in·for·mal /ɪnˈfɔrməl/ *adj.* casual, ordinary: *Dress at the party was informal, with no neck-*

ties or fancy dresses. *-n.* [U] **informality** /ˌɪnfɔrˈmæləti/.

in·form·ant /ɪnˈfɔrmənt/ *n.* a person who collects and gives information about s.o. or s.t.: *Newspaper reporters use informants to gather news.* **2** a spy: *The government informant spied on two people while hiding in the next room.*

in·for·ma·tion /ˌɪnfərˈmeɪʃən/ *n.* [U] knowledge, news, facts: *Newspapers carry useful information about current events.*

information superhighway *n.* a worldwide computer system of facts, news, electronic mail, etc.: *With a computer and a telephone, anyone can get on the information superhighway. See:* E-mail, Internet, World Wide Web.

USAGE NOTE: People travel the *information superhighway* as a car travels on a good road: at top speed. They can get information on their computers from all over the world without leaving their homes or offices by using the *Internet* and *World Wide Web. Many university libraries are popular stops on the information superhighway.*

in·form·a·tive /ɪnˈfɔrmətɪv/ *adj.* providing knowledge: *The stock market report is very informative to businesspeople.*

in·formed /ɪnˈfɔrmd/ *adj.* knowing a lot, esp. about current events: *She reads many books and magazines to stay informed.*

in·form·er /ɪnˈfɔrmər/ *n.* a spy: *He is a police informer about crimes committed in his neighborhood.*

in·frac·tion /ɪnˈfrækʃən/ *n.* the breaking of a rule or law: *He parked his car in a no-parking zone and had to pay a fine for the infraction.*

in·fra·red /ˌɪnfrəˈrɛd/ *adj.* light rays that cannot be seen: *Infrared machines are used in cancer radiation treatments.*

in·fra·struc·ture /ˈɪnfrəˌstrʌktʃər/ *n.* [C;U] roads, water, electricity, and other basic things that help a country's people and economy: *Much of the tax money in the USA pays for its infrastructure, such as the national highway system.*

in·fre·quent /ɪnˈfrikwənt/ *adj.* seldom, not often: *His visits to his parents are infrequent because he lives far away.*

in·fringe /ɪnˈfrɪndʒ/ *v.* **-fringed, -fringing, -fringes** to go where s.o. or s.t. doesn't belong, (*syn.*) to encroach: *Our neighbor's fence infringes on our land.* *-n.* [C;U] **infringement.**

in·fu·ri·ate /ɪnˈfyʊriˌeɪt/ *v.* **-ated, -ating, -ates** to make very angry, (*syns.*) to incense, enrage: *He infuriates me because he won't return my phone calls. See:* angry, USAGE NOTES.

in·fu·sion /ɪnˈfyuʒən/ *n.* [C;U] an inflow, addition: *An infusion of money into the business saved it from bankruptcy.* *-v.* **infuse.**

in·gen·ious /ɪn'dʒinyəs/ *adj.* very good at making things or solving problems, clever, brilliant: *The campers thought of an ingenious way to cross the river without a bridge.*

in·ge·nu·i·ty /ˌɪndʒə'nuəti/ *n.* [U] skill at solving problems, (*syn.*) cleverness: *Great ingenuity goes into building rockets.*

in·gest /ɪn'dʒest/ *v.frml.* to eat, swallow: *A baby ingested poison, and the doctor had to pump her stomach.*

in·grain /ɪn'greɪn/ *v.* to soak into: *Paint becomes ingrained into the surface of wood.*
—*adj.* **ingrained** /'ɪnˌgreɪn/ done so often as to be part of s.o. or s.t., habitual: *Farmers have many ingrained habits: they get up early, they milk the cows, etc.*

in·grate /'ɪnˌgreɪt/ *n.* s.o. who doesn't show thanks, an ungrateful person: *He is an ingrate who takes his parents' money without saying "Thank you."*

in·gra·ti·ate /ɪn'greɪʃiˌeɪt/ *v.* **-ated, -ating, -ates** to get respect by doing nice things (usu. expecting s.t. back): *He ingratiates himself with important people by inviting them to his parties.*

in·grat·i·tude /ɪn'grætɪˌtud/ *n.* [U] not showing thanks, (*syn.*) ungratefulness: *Your son's ingratitude toward his aunt and uncle showed when he didn't send them a thank-you card.*

in·gre·di·ent /ɪn'gridiənt/ *n.* **1** a food item in a recipe: *Flour, milk, butter, and yeast are some ingredients in bread.* **2** a part of s.t.: *Hard work is an ingredient of success.*

in·hab·it /ɪn'hæbɪt/ *v.* to live in an area, (*syn.*) to dwell: *People inhabit even the most difficult climates, such as Siberia.* -*adj.* **inhabited.**

in·hab·i·tant /ɪn'hæbətənt/ *n.* a person who lives in a certain area: *The inhabitants of San Francisco enjoy a view of the Golden Gate Bridge.*

in·hale /ɪn'heɪl/ *v.* **-haled, -haling, -hales** to breathe in: *Patients inhale painkilling medicine before an operation.* -*n.* [U] **inhalation** /ˌɪnhə'leɪʃən/.

in·hal·er /ɪn'heɪlər/ *n.* a small container of medicine, with a hole to breathe through: *She sneezes around cats, but her inhaler helps.*

in·her·ent /ɪn'hɛrənt/ *adj.* naturally belonging to or part of s.t.: *Love is inherent in a good marriage.*

in·her·it /ɪn'hɛrɪt/ *v.* to receive after one dies: *He inherited his grandfather's watch.*

in·her·i·tance /ɪn'hɛrətns/ *n.* [C;U] money, land, etc. received by s.o. when s.o. (usu. a relative) dies: *The uncle left a large inheritance to his nephew.*

in·hib·it /ɪn'hɪbɪt/ *v.* to make an action or behavior difficult: *Her shyness inhibits her social life.* -*n.* **inhibitor;** -*adj.* **inhibitive.**

in·hi·bi·tion /ˌɪnhə'bɪʃən, ˌɪnə-/ *n.* s.t. that makes a certain behavior difficult, usu. psychologically: *He has so many inhibitions about his body that he went on a strict diet.*

in·hos·pi·ta·ble /ˌɪnhɑs'pɪtəbəl/ *adj.* **1** not welcoming, unfriendly: *Some people in this big city are inhospitable to tourists.* **2** difficult to live in because of bad weather or geography: *The climate of the North Pole is inhospitable to humans.*

in-house *adv.adj.* located or performed inside a business: *This publishing company does its artwork <adv.> in-house; it has an <adj.> in-house artist.*

in·hu·man /ɪn'hyumən/ *adj.* without good human qualities, (*syn.*) cold: *Torture of prisoners is inhuman treatment.*

in·hu·mane /ˌɪnhyu'meɪn/ *adj.* not kind to animals or people, cruel, uncivilized: *Some people think that doing scientific experiments on animals is inhumane.* -*n.* [C;U] **inhumanity** /ˌɪnhyu'mænəti/.

in·i·tial /ɪ'nɪʃəl/ *adj.* beginning, first: *My initial good opinion of him changed with time.*
—*n.pl.* **initials** the first letters of one's names: *John Smith's initials are J.S.*
—*v.* to write one's initials on s.t.: *He initialed a page to show that he had read it.*

in·i·ti·ate /ɪ'nɪʃiˌeɪt/ *v.* **-ated, -ating, -ates** **1** to cause s.t. to start, to begin: *The group was quiet until she initiated conversation by asking a question.* **2** to bring s.o. into an organization with a ceremony or activity: *The young man was initiated into a club with a special handshake.* -*n.* **initiation** /ɪˌnɪʃi'eɪʃən/.

in·i·tia·tive /ɪ'nɪʃətɪv/ *n.* [C;U] the first step, usu. showing strength, (*syn.*) ambition: *He showed initiative by learning Spanish before moving to Colombia.*

in·ject /ɪn'dʒɛkt/ *v.* to force a substance, usu. liquid, into a person or thing: *The doctor injected some medicine into the patient with a needle.*

in·jec·tion /ɪn'dʒɛkʃən/ *n.* [C;U] a liquid passed through a needle or small opening: *My car's engine gets an injection of gas when I step on the pedal.*

in·junc·tion /ɪn'dʒʌŋkʃən/ *n.* (in law) a stop, an ending: *A court issued an injunction to stop the man from harassing his former wife.*

in·jure /'ɪndʒər/ *v.* **-jured, -juring, -jures** **1** to hurt, cause damage: *He injured his knee when he ran in a long race.* **2** to hurt (feelings), (*syn.*) to offend: *Her unkind words injured my pride.* -*adj.* **injurious** /ɪn'dʒuriəs/.

in·ju·ry /'ɪndʒəri/ *n.* [C;U] **-ries** a wound, damage: *The basketball player had a foot injury and missed three games.*

in·jus·tice /ɪn'dʒʌstɪs/ *n*. [C;U] an unfair thing, a broken law: *During the Civil War, many fought against the injustice of slavery.*

ink /ɪŋk/ *n*. [U] a colored liquid used in pens: *My teacher uses red ink to correct papers.*
—*v*. to cover with ink: *Long ago, printers had to ink their machines to print newspapers.* -*adj*. **inky.**

ink·blot /'ɪŋk,blɑt/ *n*. a spot of ink, usu. with uneven edges: *His pen leaked and made inkblots on the paper.*

ink·ling /'ɪŋklɪŋ/ *n*. an idea about s.t., (*syns.*) a hint, clue: *I had an inkling that she might be pregnant when she bought some baby clothes.*

in·laid /'ɪn,leɪd/ *adj*. a substance, such as wood or metal, set into another substance: *That jewelry box is made of silver with inlaid gold flowers.*

in·land /'ɪnlənd/ *adv.adj.* away from the seashore: *We moved <adv.> inland, from the California coast to the Nevada desert.*

in·law /'ɪn,lɔ/ *n*. a person related by marriage: *My wife's father and mother are good in-laws; they treat me like a real son.*

in·let /'ɪn,lɛt, -lɪt/ *n*. **1** part of an ocean, lake, or pond that cuts into the land, (*syn.*) a bay: *The water is calmer in the inlet, so we keep our boat there.* **2** a pipe or other opening that allows liquid to enter

in-line skates or **in-line skates** /'ɪn,laɪn/ *n.pl.* boots with one row of rubber wheels and a brake for stopping, used to move quickly over a road or other hard surface: *The kids next door play street hockey on in-*

in-line skates

line skates. -*n*. **in-line skating** or **inline skating.** *See:* roller skates, USAGE NOTE.

in·mate /'ɪn,meɪt/ *n*. a person in jail, a prisoner: *That prison has a section for violent inmates, such as rapists and killers.*

in me·mo·ri·am /'ɪnmə'mɔriəm/ *adv. phr.* (Latin for) in memory of (usu. used to mark graves): *I saw a baby's gravestone that read "In Memoriam Robert White 1950-1951."*

inn /ɪn/ *n*. a small hotel, usu. in the countryside, often serving meals: *We like to stay at small rural inns. See:* bed and breakfast.

in·nards /'ɪnərdz/ *n.pl.infrml.* one's internal body parts, such as intestines or stomach: *My innards hurt from eating too much pie.*

in·nate /ɪ'neɪt, 'ɪn,eɪt/ *adj*. part of s.o. from birth, natural: *He has an innate sense of how to fix things.*

in·ner /'ɪnər/ *adj*. **1** existing or located within: *She doesn't show her inner feelings.* **2** located inside, farther away from walls or doors: *You can walk through six rooms before you reach*

the courtyard.

inner city *n*. a city's central area, esp. a poor area or slum: *Mayor Perez is trying to help the inner city with neighborhood police and better playgrounds.*

in·ner·most /'ɪnər,moʊst/ *adj*. **1** deepest within: *Searchers found the missing child in the innermost part of the cave.* **2** *fig.* most secret, private: *He reveals his innermost feelings only to his best friend.*

in·ning /'ɪnɪŋ/ *n*. (in baseball) a period when each team is allowed three outs: *A baseball game usually has nine innings.*

inn·keep·er /'ɪn,kipər/ *n*. a person who owns or manages an inn: *The innkeeper hired a cook and a maid to help her serve guests.*

in·no·cence /'ɪnəsəns/ *n*. [U] **1** lack of guilt: *You proved your innocence by showing you were at home when the robbery happened.* **2** lack of sin, (*syn.*) naiveté: *Small children have a wonderful innocence before they learn about evil.*

in·no·cent /'ɪnəsənt/ *adj*. **1** not guilty (of a crime): *The lawyer defended the woman because he believed she was innocent.* **2** sinless, pure, (*syn.*) naive: *Innocent children are often harmed during a war.*

in·noc·u·ous /ɪ'nɑkyuəs/ *adj*. harmless, (*syn.*) unobjectionable: *The teacher's innocuous words don't make me angry, but they also don't teach me much.*

in·no·vate /'ɪnə,veɪt/ *v*. **-vated, -vating, -vates** to improve s.t., create s.t. new: *A scientist innovated by creating voice commands for her computer.*

in·no·va·tion /,ɪnə'veɪʃən/ *n*. [C;U] s.t. new made or improved with creativity: *Car telephones were an innovation in the 1980s, but now they are very common.* -*adj*. **innovative** /'ɪnə,veɪtɪv/.

in·nu·en·do /,ɪnyu'ɛndoʊ/ *n*. [C;U] **-does** indirect remark that hints at s.t. bad: *She doesn't say, "You're ugly," but I hear the innuendoes in her voice.*

in·nu·mer·a·ble /ɪ'numərəbəl/ *adj*. very many, countless, frequent: *He has picked me up at the bus station innumerable times.*

in·oc·u·late /ɪ'nɑkyə,leɪt/ *v*. **-lated, -lating, -lates** to give a shot of medicine through a needle to prevent disease: *The nurse inoculated my baby against polio.* -*n*. [C;U] **inoculation.**

in·of·fen·sive /,ɪnə'fɛnsɪv/ *adj*. not causing anger or other bad feelings, (*syns.*) innocuous, unobjectionable: *I let my little boy watch an inoffensive TV show on Saturday morning.*

in·op·er·a·ble /ɪn'ɑpərəbəl, -'ɑprə-/ *adj*. not able to be cured with surgery, fatal: *He has inoperable cancer.*

in·op·er·a·tive /ɪn'ɑpərətɪv, -'ɑprə-/ *adj.* not working, broken: *The telephones are inoperative due to a bad storm.*

in·op·por·tune /ɪn,ɑpər'tun/ *adj.* at a bad or wrong time: *The visitors arrived at an inopportune moment; we were still in bed.*

in·or·di·nate /ɪn'ɔrdnɪt/ *adj.* great, large, more than necessary: *He takes an inordinate amount of time in the morning, so we're always late to school.*

in·pa·tient /'ɪn,peɪʃənt/ *n.* a person who stays overnight for medical care in a hospital: *She is an inpatient, but she's going home Friday.*
—*adj.* related to overnight patients: *That hospital has an inpatient clinic for people with AIDS.*

in·put /'ɪn,pʊt/ *v.* **-putted** or **-put, -putting, -puts** to type information into a computer: *My assistant inputs the conpany's sales figures every month.*
—*n.* **1** [C;U] information typed into a computer: *My daily input includes letters, checks, and dates from my calendar.* **2** [C;U] information or advice from s.o.: *We would like your input, because you always have good ideas.*

in·quest /'ɪn,kwɛst, 'ɪŋ-/ *n.* (in law) a meeting, esp. before a jury, to find out the facts about a death: *At the inquest, we learned that the woman drowned.*

in·quire /ɪn'kwaɪr, ɪŋ-/ *v.* **-quired, -quiring, -quires** **1** to ask about s.t.: *My friend inquired about my health because I was sneezing.* **2** to ask for (public or official) information, to investigate, look into: *A neighborhood group inquired into the plans for a new park. See:* ask, USAGE NOTE.

in·quir·y /ɪn'kwaɪri, ɪŋ, 'ɪŋ,kwaɪri, 'ɪnkwəri, 'ɪŋ-/ *n.* [C;U] **-ries** **1** a question, query: *An old friend made an inquiry about your health.* **2** a request for (public or official) information, *(syn.)* an investigation: *A citizens' group made an inquiry into police behavior.*

in·qui·si·tion /,ɪnkwə'zɪʃən, ,ɪŋ-/ *n.* a formal investigation into s.o.'s beliefs -*n.* **inquisitor** /ɪn'kwɪzətər/.

in·quis·i·tive /ɪn'kwɪzətɪv, ɪŋ-/ *adj.* asking lots of questions, curious, nosy: *My brother is too inquisitive about my private life. -n.* [U] **inquisitiveness.**

in·roads /'ɪn,roʊdz/ *n.pl.* progress toward or into s.t.: *We have made inroads into our painting job; we finished the kitchen already!*

in·sane /ɪn'seɪn/ *adj.* **1** mentally ill, crazy: *The doctors knew the man was insane when he heard voices in an empty room.* **2** *fig.* ridiculous, foolish: *She has insane ideas about how to get rich overnight. -n.* [U] **insanity** /ɪn'sænəti/.

in·sa·tia·ble /ɪn'seɪʃəbəl/ *adj.* not able to get enough of s.t., not satisfied with a normal amount: *His insatiable hunger made him eat three hamburgers and want more.*

in·scribe /ɪn'skraɪb/ *v.* **-scribed, -scribing, -scribes** to write or carve words: *I inscribed my name in the guest book. -n.* **inscription** /ɪn'skrɪpʃən/.

in·scru·ta·ble /ɪn'skrutəbəl/ *adj.* not easy to be understood, mysterious

in·sect /'ɪnsɛkt/ *n.* a small (invertebrate) animal with six legs, three body segments, and sometimes wings: *We have a lot of ants and other insects in our garden in the summer.*

in·sec·ti·cide /ɪn'sɛktə,saɪd/ *n.* a chemical or other substance used to kill insects: *Farmers use insecticides to protect their corn and wheat fields.*

in·se·cure /,ɪnsə'kyʊr/ *adj.* **1** not confident, afraid, uncertain: *He feels insecure about his body, so he wears a shirt at the beach.* **2** not steady, unsafe: *The fire escape is insecure; it moves in the wind.*

in·sem·i·nate /ɪn'sɛmə,neɪt/ *v.* **-nated, -nating, -nates** to make pregnant by putting male semen into a female body: *My aunt was inseminated with her husband's sperm. -n.* [C;U] **insemination.**

in·sen·si·tive /ɪn'sɛnsətɪv/ *adj.* **1** unkind because s.o. is not aware of others' feelings, *(syn.)* tactless: *She said insensitive things to the overweight woman.* **2** not able to feel s.t. physically: *After living in Alaska, I am almost insensitive to cold.*

in·sep·a·ra·ble /ɪn'sɛpərəbəl, -'sɛprə-/ *adj.* unable to be separated: *The two women were best friends in high school and are still inseparable.*

in·sert /ɪn'sɜrt/ *v.* to put s.t. in s.t. else: *She inserted the letter into an envelope. -n.* [C;U] **insertion** /ɪn'sɜrʃən/.

in·service *n.adj.* a short educational course about one's job, taught during the day at work: *The nurses went to an <adj.> in-service class about AIDS.*

in·set /'ɪn,sɛt/ *n.* a small picture or map placed on a larger one: *The map of New York State has an inset of New York City.*

in·side /'ɪn,saɪd/ *n.* **1** the part (of a building) within walls, *(syn.)* the interior: *The inside of the house looks better than the outside.* **2** *pl.* the body's internal parts, esp. near the stomach: *My insides hurt from laughing too much.*
—*prep.* into: *We like the painting inside the museum.*
—*adv.* **1** /ɪn'saɪd/ toward the interior: *We walked inside to get out of the rain.* **2 inside out:** (of clothing) reversed so that the wrong or inner side is showing: *Her jacket was inside out; I could see the label.*
—*adj.* **1** related to the interior of s.t.: *The inside pockets of the coat are made of silk.* **2 the**

inside story: the secret or true information: *The writer heard the inside story of the robbery from a neighbor.* **3** *infrml.* **the inside track:** an advantage: *She is the owner's daughter, so she has the inside track on becoming company president.*

in·sid·er /'ɪn,saɪdɛr/ *n.* a person belonging to a group in power: *Anwar is an insider with the mayor; Anwar and the mayor have been good friends for many years.*

in·sid·i·ous /ɪn'sɪdiəs/ *adj.* bad or harmful without being obvious or easy to see: *The doctor found the insidious cancer before my friend felt pain.* *-n.* [U] **insidiousness.**

in·sight /'ɪn,saɪt/ *n.* [C;U] ability to see or know the truth, intelligence about s.t., (*syn.*) perception: *By moving to Washington, the senator gained insight into how politics really work.* *-adj.* **insightful** /ɪn'saɪtfʊl/.

in·sig·ni·a /ɪn'sɪgniə/ *n.* [C;U] an official mark or design showing membership, rank, or honor: *I have a sweatshirt with my university's insignia.*

in·sig·nif·i·cant /,ɪnsɪg'nɪfəkənt/ *adj.* not important, without meaning: *We thought the book had too many insignificant details about George Washington's life and not enough history.* *-n.* [U] **insignificance.**

in·sin·cere /,ɪnsɪn'sɪr/ *adj.* not showing true feelings or opinions, (*syn.*) hypocritical: *He said he was happy you won the tennis match, but I think he was insincere.* *-n.* [U] **insincerity** /,ɪnsɪn'sɛrəti/.

in·sin·u·ate /ɪn'sɪnyu,eɪt/ *v.* **-ated, -ating, -ates** to hint about s.t. bad in an indirect way: *One worker insinuated that another employee was dishonest.* *-n.* [C;U] **insinuation.**

in·sip·id /ɪn'sɪpɪd/ *adj.* **1** tasteless, (*syn.*) bland: *Oatmeal has an insipid taste, so I add sugar.* **2** not interesting, lacking exciting qualities, (*syn.*) vapid: *That insipid movie had dull characters and no plot.*

in·sist /ɪn'sɪst/ *v.* **1** to demand, show strong opinion: *I insist that you go to the hospital immediately; you are very ill!* **2** *phrasal v.* **insist on:** to accept only certain things, to require: *The cook insists on the finest meat and fish.*

in·sis·tence /ɪn'sɪstəns/ *n.* [U] strong pressure to do s.t.: *Her insistence on quality keeps her employees hard at work.* *-adj.* **insistent.**

in·so·far as /,ɪnsoʊ'fɑrəz, -æz/ *conj.* as much or as long as (possible): *Insofar as my grandfather is able to walk, he won't use a wheelchair.*

in·sole /'ɪn,soʊl/ *n.* **1** the part of a shoe that one's foot rests on: *My shoes are very old; there is a hole in my insole.* **2** a piece of leather or other material placed inside a shoe for comfort: *I wear insoles so my feet don't get so tired.*

in·so·lent /'ɪnsələnt/ *adj.* too bold for one's age or situation, rude: *The insolent daughter slammed the door in her parents' face.* *-n.* [U] **insolence.**

in·sol·u·ble /ɪn'sɑlyəbəl/ *adj.* **1** not able to be dissolved in liquid: *Oil is insoluble in water.* **2** not able to be solved: *That math problem is insoluble.*

in·sol·vent /ɪn'sɑlvənt/ *adj.* with no money left, (*syn.*) bankrupt: *My friend lost her job and became insolvent.* *-n.*[C;U] **insolvency.**

in·som·ni·a /ɪn'sɑmniə/ *n.* [U] not able to sleep on a regular basis: *My father's insomnia went away when he stopped drinking coffee.* *-n.* [C] **insomniac.**

in·spect /ɪn'spɛkt/ *v.* **1** to look at s.t. closely, examine, (*syn.*) to scrutinize: *Automakers inspect their cars to make sure they are safe.*

in·spec·tion /ɪn'spɛkʃən/ *n.* [C;U] **1** a close, careful look, examination, (*syn.*) scrutiny: *Inspection of the new house shows that it needs a new roof.* **2 to pass inspection:** to receive approval: *Soldiers must pass inspection to make sure their uniforms are clean.*

in·spec·tor /ɪn'spɛktər/ *n.* **1** a person who has a job looking for mistakes or flaws: *The electrical inspector looked at our outlets and fuses.* **2** a high-level police officer or firefighter: *We called the inspector with facts about a murder case.*

in·spi·ra·tion /,ɪnspə'reɪʃən/ *n.* [C;U] **1** s.o. or s.t. that makes a person work hard or be creative, (*syn.*) motivation: *She is a writer who gets her inspiration from the novels of Hemingway and Fitzgerald.* *-adj.* **inspirational.**

in·spire /ɪn'spaɪr/ *v.* **-spired, -spiring, -spires** to cause to work hard or be creative, to motivate, stimulate: *My grandmother inspires us with stories of her difficult childhood.*

in·sta·bil·i·ty /,ɪnstə'bɪləti/ *n.* [U] **1** lack of firmness, (*syn.*) shakiness: *The instability of that old bridge caused it to fall.* **2** *fig.* emotional weakness, lack of unity, (*syn.*) unpredictability: *The instability of the government may lead to war. See:* unstable.

in·stall /ɪn'stɔl/ *v.* **1** to put s.t. (such as a piece of machinery) in place and make it work: *Our technical expert installed a new computer Wednesday, and we began using it Friday.* **2** to employ s.o., put s.o. in a job: *The new mayor was installed in office last week.* *-n.* **installer;** *-n.*[C;U] **installation.**

in·stall·ment /ɪn'stɔlmənt/ *n.* **1** s.t. divided into parts: *The biography of Elizabeth Taylor appeared in three installments in three separate issues of the magazine.* **2** a partial payment: *He is paying off a $1,200 debt in twelve monthly installments of $100.*

in·stance /'ɪnstəns/ n. **1** a single occurrence or happening, a situation, case: *In this instance, we will lend you money, but usually we can't.* **2 for instance:** for example: *There are many things I would like to learn; for instance, how to swim.*

in·stant /'ɪnstənt/ n. a very quick period of time, less than a second: *Lightning struck a tree, and it fell in an instant.*
—*adj.* **1** very fast, immediate: *We can't give instant answers to such difficult questions.* **2** easily mixed or prepared: *He added water and ice to the instant tea. -adv.* **instantly.**

in·stan·ta·ne·ous /ˌɪnstən'teɪniəs/ adj. with no delay, sudden, immediate (occurrence, reaction, etc.): *The pain was instantaneous when I bumped my head.*

instant replay n. (in television) a filmed or taped moment, esp. in sports, shown just after it happens: *You were in the kitchen when the goal was scored in the soccer game, but you can see the instant replay.*

in·stead /ɪn'stɛd/ prep. in place of, rather than: *The bride chose roses instead of tulips for her bouquet.*

in·step /'ɪn,stɛp/ n. the top part of a shoe or foot between the toes and the ankle

in·sti·gate /'ɪnstə,geɪt/ v. **-gated, -gating, -gates** to make s.t. happen, (syn.) to incite: *In the 1960s, students instigated demonstrations against the Vietnam War. -n.* [U] **instigation.**

in·still /ɪn'stɪl/ v. **1** to give (an emotion or quality) by example or teaching: *Her athletic parents instilled the girl with a love of baseball. -n.* [U] **instillation** /ˌɪnstə'leɪʃən/.

in·stinct /'ɪn,stɪŋkt/ n. [C;U] **1** a natural, unlearned behavior or ability: *Birds migrate south each winter by instinct.* **2** often pl. feelings, not thoughts: *She used her instincts in deciding which man to date.*

in·stinc·tive /ɪn'stɪŋktɪv/ adj. done from feeling, not from reason or learned behavior: *His instinctive reaction to the falling rock was to run from it.*

in·sti·tute /'ɪnstə,tut/ v.frml. **-tuted, -tuting, -tutes** to begin, (syn.) to initiate: *Since we instituted the new rule, fewer people have been late to work.*
—*n.* an organization, esp. one for education or research: *The Massachusetts Institute of Technology has courses in engineering and computing.*

in·sti·tu·tion /ˌɪnstə'tuʃən/ n. **1** [C] an organization that helps or serves people in the area of health, education, or work: *My aunt cannot pay for a private nurse, so she lives in a state institution.* **2** [C;U] a function in society: *The institution of marriage is important in most Western religions.* **3** [C] s.t. or s.o. that is a

necessary, longtime part of s.t.: *Big Sunday dinners are an institution at Mom's house.*

in·sti·tu·tion·al·ize /ˌɪnstə'tuʃənə,laɪz/ v. **-ized, -izing, -izes** to put s.o. in an institution: *After his car accident, he was institutionalized in a special hospital.*

in·struct /ɪn'strʌkt/ v. **1** to teach: *The Spanish professor instructs her students in the language and culture of Mexico.* **2** to direct, tell s.o. what to do: *My sister instructed me to take out the garbage.*

in·struc·tion /ɪn'strʌkʃən/ n. **1** [U] education, teaching: *Hearing-impaired students receive instruction in sign language.* **2** pl. information about how to do s.t., directions: *The mechanic gave us instructions on how to fix our car's brakes.*

in·struc·tive /ɪn'strʌktɪv/ adj. with useful information, educational: *I saw a TV show about the U.S. Civil War that was very instructive.*

in·struc·tor /ɪn'strʌktər/ n. **1** a teacher: *My swimming instructor showed us how to dive into the water.* **2** the lowest level of college teacher: *When she completes her Ph.D., her title will change from instructor to assistant professor. See:* teacher, **USAGE NOTE.**

in·stru·ment /'ɪnstrəmənt/ n. **1** a tool that helps s.o. do work: *The doctor used an instrument to look in the girl's ears.* **2** an object for making music, such as a violin, piano, or horn: *She plays two musical instruments and is now learning to sing.*

in·stru·men·tal /ˌɪnstrə'mɛntl/ adj. **1** helpful, causing s.t. to happen: *Her good grades were instrumental in getting her a scholarship to Harvard.* **2** of or for musical instruments, not voices: *Mozart wrote instrumental music as well as operas. -n.* **instrumentalist.**

in·sub·or·di·na·tion /ˌɪnsə,bɔrdn'eɪʃən/ n. [U] not following directions or orders from a high-ranking person, (syn.) disobedience: *The young soldier did not salute the general and was punished for insubordination. -adj.* **insubordinate** /ˌɪnsə'bɔrdnɪt/.

in·sub·stan·tial /ˌɪnsəb'stænʃəl/ adj. not strong or solid, (syn.) flimsy: *A headache is an insubstantial reason for missing a week of school.*

in·suf·fer·a·ble /ɪn'sʌfərəbəl, -'sʌfrə-/ adj. extremely annoying, (syns.) unbearable, intolerable: *When that insufferable man speaks, I get so angry that I have to leave the room.*

in·suf·fi·cient /ˌɪnsə'fɪʃənt/ adj. not enough, (syn.) inadequate: *We had an insufficient amount of flour to bake bread. -n.* [C;U] **insufficiency.**

in·su·lar /'ɪnsələr, -syə-/ adj. **1** related to islands: *Hawaii is an insular state.* **2** having certain ideas because of being alone or isolated, provincial: *His insular opinions come* *from growing up in a small town. -n.* [U] **insu-larity** /ˌɪnsəˈlærəti, -syə-/.

in·su·late /ˈɪnsəˌleɪt/ *v.* **-lated, -lating, -lates 1** to put material in walls and roofs to keep buildings warmer: *After we insulated the walls and attic, our heating costs went down.* **2** *fig.* to keep s.o. away from, to protect: *Some city parents insulate their children by sending them to private schools. -n.* **insulator.**

in·su·la·tion /ˌɪnsəˈleɪʃən/ *n.* [U] any material that keeps out cold, heat, and/or sound: *My winter jacket has goose feathers as insulation.*

in·su·lin /ˈɪnsəlɪn/ *n.* [U] a hormone from a person's pancreas that helps control sugar in the bloodstream and is taken as medicine by people with diabetes: *My diabetic sister gets insulin shots and follows a low-sugar diet.*

in·sult /ˈɪnˌsʌlt/ *n.* a very unkind remark about s.o.: *It was an insult to tell your brother that he's stupid.*
—*v.* /ɪnˈsʌlt/ do or say bad, unkind things to s.o.: *You insulted me by saying I have ugly clothes. -adj.* **insulting.**

in·sur·ance /ɪnˈʃʊrəns/ *n.* [U] **1** an agreement with a company in which the company will pay for a loss or accident in exchange for regular premiums (payments): *I have insurance, so I can buy another car if mine is stolen.* **2** any protection against a possible problem: *Do you carry an umbrella as insurance against getting wet?*

insurance policy *n.* the legal contract or agreement that explains the type, details, and conditions of insurance: *I have a health insurance policy that tells me which doctors I can use.*

in·sure /ɪnˈʃʊr/ *v.* **-sured, -suring, -sures 1** to buy insurance for protection: *The company has insured all the workers who use dangerous machines.* **2** to make sure, make certain: *I insured that the house was protected by locking all the doors. See:* ensure.

in·sured /ɪnˈʃʊrd/ *adj.* having insurance: *Our house is insured against fire and flood.*
—*n.* the person or business having insurance: *My life insurance policy shows me as the insured and my wife as the person who will receive money if I die.*

in·sur·er /ɪnˈʃʊrər/ *n.* the company providing insurance: *My insurer is a big company in Boston.*

in·sur·gen·cy /ɪnˈsɜrdʒənsi/ *n.* [C;U] the state of being or acting against a government or political power, (*syns.*) a rebellion, revolt: *Radical party members started an insurgency against their leaders. -n.* [C;U] **insurgence;** *-adj.* **insurgent.**

in·sur·mount·a·ble /ˌɪnsərˈmaʊntəbəl/ *adj.* too difficult, impossible: *The man thought his problems were insurmountable, so he killed himself.*

in·sur·rec·tion /ˌɪnsəˈrɛkʃən/ *n.* [C;U] the act of going against a government, (*syns.*) a revolt, rebellion: *The people started an insurrection against the king.*

in·tact /ɪnˈtækt/ *adj.* whole, not in pieces: *The eggs were in the bottom of the bag, but they did not break; they remained intact.*

in·tan·gi·ble /ɪnˈtændʒəbəl/ *adj.* not able to be felt with touch, sight, or hearing, but still sensed: *My grandmother, who died last year, is an intangible presence in my life.*

in·te·ger /ˈɪntədʒər/ *n.* any positive or negative whole number, including 0 (zero), but not fractions: *If you add 1.5 and 1.5, you will get an integer, 3.*

in·te·gral /ˈɪntəgrəl/ *adj.* necessary, essential: *Rice is an integral part of the Chinese diet.*

in·te·grate /ˈɪntəˌgreɪt/ *v.* **-grated, -grating, -grates** to put different groups of people together: *My school is integrated; I have African American, Caucasian, and Hispanic classmates. -n.* [U] **integration.**

in·teg·ri·ty /ɪnˈtɛgrəti/ *n.* [U] **1** strong morals, honesty: *Her integrity made her call the police when she found drugs in her son's room.* **2** completeness, strength: *The integrity of our nation depends on working together.*

in·tel·lect /ˈɪntəˌlɛkt/ *n.* [C;U] the ability to think logically and remember knowledge: *My sister has a great intellect; she teaches economics and advises the President.*

in·tel·lec·tu·al /ˌɪntəˈlɛktʃuəl/ *adj.* related to thinking (not emotion) and learned knowledge: *If you read more books, you will have more intellectual powers.*
—*n.* a thinker, person who studies and uses his or her mind: *That bar near the university is full of intellectuals talking about politics. -n.* [U] **intellectualism;** *-v.* **intellectualize.**

in·tel·li·gence /ɪnˈtɛlədʒəns/ *n.* [U] **1** the ability to learn, understand, and use information; smartness: *He used his intelligence to win the chess game.* **2** secret information about a country or an enemy: *The USA has intelligence about other countries' nuclear weapons.*

in·tel·li·gent /ɪnˈtɛlədʒənt/ *adj.* **1** able to learn, understand, and use information well; smart: *We knew you were very intelligent when you wrote two music books and an opera in one year.* **2** showing good judgment, wise: *Eating well and exercising are intelligent things to do.*

in·tel·li·gi·ble /ɪnˈtɛlədʒəbəl/ *adj.* able to be heard and understood: *There was loud noise from the burning building, but the firefighters' shouts were still intelligible.*

in·tem·per·ate /ɪnˈtɛmpərɪt, -prɪt/ *adj.* **1** not wise, out of control, (*syn.*) hotheaded: *His intemperate opinions were too strong for small-town politics.* **2** drinking too much: *Alcoholics* *are often sorry about their intemperate habits.* *-n.* [U] **intemperance.**

in·tend /ɪn'tɛnd/ *v.* **1** to plan to do s.t.: *I intend to visit Australia this year.* **2** to mean to be: *Don't read that letter; it is intended for my boyfriend.*

in·tense /ɪn'tɛns/ *adj.* **1** strong (in feeling or emotion), *(syn.)* concentrated: *She felt intense pain when the bone broke in her leg.* **2** bright, rich: *an intense red\\intense sunlight*

in·ten·si·fi·er /ɪn'tɛnsə,faɪər/ *n.* words that give strength or intensity to meanings, such as "very" or "awfully," as in: *I am awfully sorry.*

in·ten·si·fy /ɪn'tɛnsə,faɪ/ *v.* **-fied, -fying, -fies** to get stronger, make s.t. stronger, to increase: *The noise from the party intensified as the clock struck midnight.*

in·ten·si·ty /ɪn'tɛnsəti/ *n.* [U] the degree, strength of s.t.: *He showed the intensity of his love with roses and poems.*

in·ten·sive /ɪn'tɛnsɪv/ *adj.* a lot in a short time, *(syn.)* concentrated: *I took an intensive Russian course and learned the language in three months.*

in·tent /ɪn'tɛnt/ *n.* **1** [U] purpose, plan, *(syn.)* intention: *It was his intent to leave at 6:30, but he stayed until 8:00.* **2 to all intents and purposes:** as things really are: *To all intents and purposes, the company lost money last year.*

in·ten·tion /ɪn'tɛnʃən/ *n.* [C;U] purpose, plan, *(syn.)* intent: *He had no intention of wearing a tie to the casual party.*

in·ten·tion·al /ɪn'tɛnʃənəl/ *adj.* done on purpose, *(syn.)* deliberate: *Meeting for dinner at a vegetarian restaurant was intentional; I am a vegetarian.*

in·ter /ɪn'tɜr/ *v.* **-terred, -terring, -ters** to bury, put in a grave: *My friend died Friday and was interred yesterday.* *-n.* [C;U] **interment.**

in·ter·act /,ɪntər'ækt/ *v.* to communicate with s.o. through conversation, looks, or action: *The couple interacted wordlessly with their eyes.* *-adj.* **interactive;** *-n.* **interaction.**

in·ter·cede /,ɪntər'sid/ *v.* **-ceded, -ceding, -cedes** to do s.t. for or act on behalf of s.o., *(syn.)* to intervene: *You are telling lies about my sister; I must intercede on her behalf.*

in·ter·cept /,ɪntər'sɛpt/ *v.* **1** to stop or catch s.t. while it is in the air or going toward s.t.: *She intercepted the mail before her parents could find the letter.* *-n.* [C;U] **interception.**

in·ter·change /'ɪntər,tʃeɪndʒ/ *n.* a place where highways meet and cars can go from one highway to another: *I drove onto Route 66 at an interchange.*

in·ter·change·a·ble /,ɪntər'tʃeɪndʒəbəl/ *adj.* able to be used in the same way: *The keyboard for that computer is interchangeable with mine.*

in·ter·com /'ɪntər,kɑm/ *n.* a small machine that lets people talk to each other from different rooms or areas of a building: *From the kitchen, I heard my baby cry on the intercom.*

in·ter·con·nect /,ɪntərkə'nɛkt/ *v.* to relate to s.t., connect: *Railroad tracks interconnect at the train station.* *-n.* [C;U] **interconnection.**

in·ter·con·ti·nen·tal /,ɪntər,kɑntə'nɛntl/ *adj.* between or relating to more than one continent: *Intercontinental airplane flights between the USA and Europe take about six hours.*

in·ter·course /'ɪntər,kɔrs/ *n.* [U] **1** the act of having sex, *(syn.)* copulation: *That couple is trying to have a baby, so they have intercourse often.* **2** *frml.* talk or discussion between people or groups: *Before television, families spent more time in social intercourse.*

in·ter·de·pend·ent /,ɪntərdə'pɛndənt/ *adj.* needing s.t. from s.o. who also needs s.t. in return: *The farmer and his cows have an interdependent relationship; he gives them food and shelter, and they give them milk.* *-n.* [U] **interdependence.**

in·ter·est /'ɪntrɪst, -tərɪst, -trɛst/ *n.* **1** [C;U] s.t. one wants to know more about, curiosity: *I have an interest in learning about computers.* **2** [C;U] an activity or thing that one likes, *(syns.)* a pastime, hobby: *He plays piano because he has an interest in music.* **3** [U] right to know, concern: *She is my daughter, so I have an interest in where she goes to college.* **4** [U] a percentage paid on an amount of money: *The bank paid me 3% on my savings of $100, so I made $3 in interest.* **5** [C;U] financial relationship, part ownership: *Along with several other families, they have an interest in an ice-cream shop and a bakery.*
—*v.* to make s.o. curious, attract s.o.'s attention: *Does chemistry interest you, or do you prefer biology?*

in·ter·est·ed /'ɪntrɪstɪd, -tərɪs-, -,trɛs-/ *adj.* having curiosity, wanting to know more: *He is interested in travel, so he visits a different country every year.*

USAGE NOTE: If s.o. or s.t. excites your interest, you are *interested: I'm interested in reading more of her books.* The person or thing itself is *interesting: Her ideas are interesting.\\She's an interesting writer.*

in·ter·est·ing /'ɪntrɪstɪŋ, -tərɪs-, -,trɛs-/ *adj.* causing curiosity or a wish to know more: *I think American kids find TV to be more interesting than books.*

in·ter·face /'ɪntər,feɪs/ *n.* the place where objects, people, or ideas connect: *The only interface between the girls' school and boys' school is at dances.*

—*v.* **-faced, -facing, -faces** to connect, interact: *Our two computers can interface because we have the same software.*

in·ter·fere /ˌɪntərˈfɪr/ *v.* **-fered, -fering, -feres** to enter or interrupt a situation or discussion, usu. without permission, (*syns.*) to disrupt, meddle: *Sandra didn't want to interfere in family problems, but she had important information about Shu-min's sick son.*

in·ter·fer·ence /ˌɪntərˈfɪrəns/ *n.* [U] **1** the entering or interruption of a situation or discussion, usu. without permission, (*syn.*) disruption: *His interference in our lives includes calling every day and visiting every week.* **2** noise on an electrical line, static: *Interference on the telephone line was caused by a storm.*

in·ter·ga·lac·tic /ˈɪntərgəˈlæktɪk/ *adj.* between or about other regions of space and our galaxy: *Intergalactic space travel is not yet possible.*

in·ter·im /ˈɪntərəm/ *n.* **1** a time period between events: *There was an interim between the time he received the money and spent it.* **2 in the interim:** meanwhile, in the meantime: *I shall see you again next week; in the interim, write to me.*

in·te·ri·or /ɪnˈtɪriər/ *n.* **1** the inside of s.t.: *From the outside, the house looks terrible, but the interior is beautiful.* **2** an area of land away from the ocean or a border: *Australia's interior is almost all desert.*
—*adj.* of or about the inside of s.t.: *The interior walls are painted white.*

interior decorator *n.* a person who gives ideas about color, style, and placement of furniture, art, and other items in a building: *An interior decorator helped us choose our couch and curtains.*

interior design *n.* [U] **1** the way furniture, art, and other items are arranged, with a focus on color, style, and placement: *Some modern interior design uses a lot of mirrors and metal.* **2** the profession or subject: *He studied interior design at an art school.*

in·ter·ject /ˌɪntərˈdʒɛkt/ *v.* to make a comment in the middle of a discussion, interrupt: *She was quiet for a long time, then interjected a few remarks at the end of the day.*

in·ter·jec·tion /ˌɪntərˈdʒɛkʃən/ *n.* **1** [C;U] a comment in the middle of or that interrupts a conversation: *My teacher likes our questions and interjections during class.* **2** [C] an exclamation, such as *Oh!* or *Ouch!*

in·ter·lace /ˌɪntərˈleɪs/ *v.* **-laced, -lacing, -laces** to join by placing any long, thin items (such as shoelaces) one over the other: *The lovers' fingers interlaced as they held hands.*

in·ter·lock /ˈɪntərˌlɑk/ *v.* to connect items so that one can't move without the other: *The children interlocked arms and crossed the street as a group.* -*adj.* **interlocking.**

in·ter·lop·er /ˈɪntərˌloupər/ *n.* a person who goes where he or she has no right to go or doesn't belong, (*syn.*) an intruder: *Who are these interlopers? They weren't invited!*

in·ter·lude /ˈɪntərˌlud/ *n.* **1** a period of time between two events: *There was an interlude of good weather between the two snowstorms.* **2** a short piece of music played between longer parts of a play, concert, church service, etc.: *There was a brief musical interlude before each new group of singers appeared on stage.*

in·ter·mar·ry /ˌɪntərˈmæri/ *v.* **-ried, -rying, -ries** to marry s.o. of a different race, religion, etc.: *A Jewish man and a Catholic woman intermarried against their parents' wishes.* -*n.* [U] **intermarriage** /ɪntərˈmærɪdʒ/.

in·ter·me·di·ar·y /ˌɪntərˈmidieri/ *n.* **-ies** a person who acts as the communicator between people or groups, (*syns.*) a go-between, mediator: *My lawyer was the intermediary between my former wife and me during our divorce.*

in·ter·me·di·ate /ˌɪntərˈmidiɪt/ *adj.* between or in the middle of two extreme points, such as highest and lowest, or beginning and end: *She took swimming lessons last year and is now in an intermediate class.*

in·ter·mi·na·ble /ɪnˈtɜrmənəbəl/ *adj.* seemingly endless because of being boring or tedious: *The play was interminable; we all fell asleep in Act II.*

in·ter·min·gle /ˌɪntərˈmɪŋgəl/ *v.* **-gled, -gling, -gles** to mix together, mingle: *The guests at the large party intermingled with friends and strangers.*

in·ter·mis·sion /ˌɪntərˈmɪʃən/ *n.* [C;U] the time between acts (of a play, opera, etc.): *During intermission, I went to the lobby for a drink of water.*

in·ter·mit·tent /ˌɪntərˈmɪtnt/ *adj.* happening with stops and starts, periodic: *There will be intermittent rain showers today in Los Angeles.*

in·tern /ˈɪnˌtɜrn/ *n.* **1** a new or young doctor: *The interns learned a lot from doctors who had worked for many years.* **2** a person who works for little or no money in order to gain experience in a business or profession: *During her college years, she was a summer intern in a Washington law office.*
—*v.* /ɪnˈtɜrn/ to contain in an area, usu. as a prisoner of war: *Japanese Americans were interned in California during World War II.* -*n.* [U] **internment.**

in·ter·nal /ɪnˈtɜrnəl/ *adj.* **1** inside, within: *His internal organs, including his heart and liver, are damaged from smoking and drinking.* **2** related to an organization's or country's own rules and interests: *This President thinks more about internal affairs, such as unemployment and education, than about foreign policy.*

in·ter·nal·ize /ɪn'tɜrnə,laɪz/ v. **-ized, -izing, -izes** **1** to keep things (ideas, teaching, values) inside oneself and make them part of one's life: *She internalized religious lessons so strongly as a child that she later became a nun.* **2** to keep thoughts or feelings inside and not let them out: *Don't internalize your anger; if you are angry with your mother, tell her.* -n. [U] **internalization** /ɪn,tɜrnələ'zeɪʃən/.

Internal Revenue Service n. in the USA, the government agency that collects taxes and makes sure that tax laws are followed: *The Internal Revenue Service is very busy in the spring while people are paying their yearly income taxes. See:* IRS.

in·ter·na·tion·al /,ɪntər'næʃənəl/ adj. of or about two or more nations: *At an international conference on the environment, five South American leaders discussed the rain forest.* -adv. **internationally.**

in·ter·na·tion·al·ism /,ɪntər'næʃənə,lɪzəm/ n. [U] a view toward cooperation among nations: *The United Nations promotes internationalism around the world.* -v. **internationalize.**

International Phonetic Alphabet n. abbr. IPA, symbols that show how to pronounce all human sounds for any language: *The IPA is used in most bilingual dictionaries.*

In·ter·net /'ɪntər,nɛt/ n. [U] a huge computer network of electronic mail and information, used by millions of people and organizations all over the world: *On my business trip, I used the Internet to receive a note from my boss and send a birthday message to my daughter. See:* E-mail, information superhighway, World Wide Web, USAGE NOTE.

in·ter·nist /ɪn'tɜrnɪst/ n. a doctor who practices general medicine, esp. treatment of the internal organs: *Their family doctor is an internist.*

in·ter·per·son·al /,ɪntər'pɜrsənəl/ adj. between people: *She makes her friends happy by using her good interpersonal skills, such as smiling and asking questions.*

in·ter·plan·e·tar·y /,ɪntər'plænə,tɛri/ adj. of or among planets: *She wants to be an astronaut and make interplanetary flights between Earth and Mars.*

in·ter·play /'ɪntər,pleɪ/ n.v. [U] action between people or things: *The interplay of different spices gives Indian food a special flavor.*

interpolate /ɪn'tɜrpə,leɪt/ v.frml. **-lated, -lating, -lates** to add information to a written work: *The newspaper writer interpolated incorrect facts into her story.* -n. [C;U] **interpolation.**

in·ter·pose /,ɪntər'pouz/ v.frml. **-posed, -posing, -poses** **1** to go or place oneself between, (syn.) to insert: *The soldier interposed his body between his friend and a flying bullet.* **2** to put in the middle of: *Stop talking so I can interpose a different idea.*

in·ter·pret /ɪn'tɜrprɪt/ v. **1** to translate (usu. orally) from one language into another: *She interprets the French museum guide's words for American tourists.* **2** to decide on the meaning of s.t. that is not very clear: *I interpret your nod to mean that you agree with me.* **3** to show one's own artistic ideas and ability through painting, music, writing, etc.: *She is a violinist who interprets Bach brilliantly.* -adj. **interpretative; interpretive.**

in·ter·pre·ta·tion /ɪn,tɜrprə'teɪʃən/ n. **1** [C;U] an explanation, decision about what s.t. means: *My interpretation of the Bible is different from my priest's.* **2** [C;U] performance or other piece of art showing one's own ideas and ability: *His interpretation of Shakespeare's Hamlet made the audience cry.*

in·ter·pret·er /ɪn,tɜrprətər/ n. **1** a person who translates (usu. orally) from one language into another: *This interpreter hears Chinese in one moment and gives the Spanish words in the next.* **2** an artist: *That painter is a fine interpreter of the human face.*

in·ter·re·late /,ɪntərə'leɪt/ v. **-lated, -lating, -lates** **1** to connect or relate to one another: *The families are interrelated by marriage.* **2** to have s.t. in common, interconnect: *The social problems of poverty and disease are interrelated.* -n. [C;U] **interrelation.**

in·ter·re·la·tion·ship /,ɪntərə'leɪʃən,ʃɪp/ n. a connection, link: *There is an interrelationship between exercising and good health.*

in·ter·ro·gate /ɪn'tɛrə,geɪt/ v. **-gated, -gating, -gates** to ask questions, often in a strong or aggressive way: *The police officer interrogated the man in a very loud voice.* -n. [C;U] **interrogation;** [C] **interrogator.**

in·ter·rupt /,ɪntə'rʌpt/ v. **1** to stop s.t. from continuing: *A bad storm interrupted telephone communications between the two islands.* **2** to start talking or doing s.t. in the middle of s.o.'s conversation or activity, to break in: *Our little boy always interrupts our conversations by asking questions.* -n. [C;U] **interruption.**

in·ter·scho·las·tic /,ɪntərskə'læstɪk/ adj. of or between schools: *Our school plays interscholastic volleyball against teams from other towns.*

in·ter·sect /,ɪntər'sɛkt/ v. to join by passing through, to cross one another: *Ninth Street and Elm Avenue intersect near the park.*

in·ter·sec·tion /'ɪntər,sɛkʃən/ n. **1** a crossing of roads: *Traffic lights control the movement of cars at intersections.* **2** a point or area that two geometric figures share: *The intersection of two lines can form four angles.*

in·ter·sperse /,ɪntər'spɜrs/ v. **-spersed, -spersing, -sperses** to place or mix s.t. among other things: *A few apartment buildings were interspersed among the houses.*

in·ter·state /'ɪntərˌsteɪt/ *adj.* in the USA, of or between states: *You can travel on Interstate Highway 20 from Atlanta, Georgia, to Columbia, South Carolina.*
—*n.* a numbered superhighway: *We drove off a small country road onto the interstate.*

in·ter·twine /ˌɪntər'twaɪn/ *v.* -twined, -twining, -twines to wind around each other, (*syn.*) to twist: *The tree's branches intertwined as they grew.* -*n.* [U] **intertwining.**

in·ter·val /'ɪntərvəl/ *n.* **1** a time period between events: *I always get hungry in the interval between breakfast and lunch.* **2** an amount of distance or time, occurring regularly: *We stopped at 100-mile intervals to use the bathroom.*

in·ter·vene /ˌɪntər'vin/ *v.* -vened, -vening, -venes to stop an action happening between other people: *Would you intervene if you saw a parent hit a child?* -*n.* [C;U] **intervention** /ˌɪntər'vɛnʃən/.

in·ter·view /'ɪntərˌvyu/ *v.* **1** to get information by questioning s.o.: *A TV reporter interviewed the mayor about the city's problems.* **2** to meet with and question s.o. to decide if that person is right for a job: *She interviewed 12 people before she found a good secretary.*
—*n.* **1** a meeting where information is gathered from s.o.: *In the interview, the writer said he was working on a new book.* **2** a published report of such a meeting: *Did you read the interview with Princess Diana in this magazine?*

in·ter·view·er /'ɪntərˌvyuər/ *n.* a person who asks people questions to gain information: *The interviewer asked me when and where I was born.*

in·ter·weave /ˌɪntər'wiv/ *v.* -wove /'wouv/, -woven /'wouvən/, -weaving, -weaves to blend together, (*syn.*) to entwine: *The author interweaves actual historical events into her novels.*

in·tes·tate /ɪn'tɛsteɪt/ *adj.* (in law) without a will at death: *The old man died intestate, so a court had to decide how to divide his money.*

in·tes·tine /ɪn'tɛstɪn/ *n.* the part of the body that carries food from the stomach to the anus (including the small and large intestines): *Drinking water helps your food move more easily through the intestines.* -*adj.* **intestinal.**

in·ti·ma·cy /'ɪntəməsi/ *n.* -cies **1** [U] emotional closeness: *I feel great intimacy with my brother; I tell him everything.* **2** [U] a good feeling of warmth and privacy, (*syn.*) coziness: *I like the intimacy of candlelight and soft music in restaurants.*

in·ti·mate /'ɪntəmɪt/ *adj.* **1** emotionally close: *We have had an intimate friendship since we were young.* **2** warm and private, (*syn.*) cozy: *That little café has an intimate atmosphere.* **3**

involved sexually: *I just want to be a friend; I don't want to be intimate with you.* **4** deep, profound: *He has an intimate knowledge of plants and how to grow them.*
—*n.* /'ɪntəˌmeɪt/ -mated, -mating, -mates to hint, suggest: *By not letting me speak, he intimated that my ideas aren't important.*

in·tim·i·date /ɪn'tɪməˌdeɪt/ *v.* -dated, -dating, -dates to make s.o. fearful or timid by showing power or making threats: *An older boy intimidated the little children when he took their lunch money.* -*n.* **intimidation.**

in·to /'ɪntu/ *prep.* **1** to the inside of s.t.: *We walked down the street and into the movie theater.* **2** applied to s.t., showing involvement: *She puts a lot of effort into her piano playing.* **3** showing a change toward a condition or state: *The seed grew into a huge tree.* **4** against, having contact with: *The car ran into a fence.* **5** (in math) showing division: *4 into 12 is 3.* **6** *infrml.* very interested in: *He is really into playing basketball.*

in·tol·er·a·ble /ɪn'tɑlərəbəl/ *adj.* **1** too difficult, painful, unbearable: *The heat in August is intolerable.* **2** objectionable, offensive: *Her bad language is intolerable to her parents.*

in·tol·er·ance /ɪn'tɑlərəns/ *n.* **1** [U] lack of kindness or understanding toward people who are different, (*syns.*) bigotry, prejudice: *The parents' intolerance made the children hate foreigners, too.* **2** [C;U] physical sensitivity to s.t., such as food: *He has an intolerance for milk and cheese; they make him sick.* -*adj.* **intolerant.**

in·to·na·tion /ˌɪntə'neɪʃən, -tou-/ *n.* [U] **1** the level of the voice (high or low): *Even though they both speak English, their intonation is different because Mary comes from London and Gina comes from New York.* **2** the ability to sing the right note: *Your intonation is terrible; you're hurting my ears!* -*v.* **intone.**

in to·to /ɪn'toutou/ *adv.frml.* in all, in sum: *In toto, we have everything that we need.*

in·tox·i·cate /ɪn'tɑksəˌkeɪt/ *v.* -cated, -cating, -cates **1** to make drunk, (*syn.*) to inebriate: *Drinking beer and whiskey intoxicates him.* **2** to excite greatly: *The queen was intoxicated with her own power.* -*n.* [U] **intoxication.**

in·trac·ta·ble /ɪn'træktəbəl/ *adj.* **1** not able to be changed or persuaded: *You keep saying, "No, no"; you're intractable.* **2** hard to control: *We couldn't teach the intractable dog to sit or come.* -*n.* [U] **intractability.**

in·tra·mu·ral /ˌɪntrə'myurəl/ *adj.* within an organization, esp. a school or college: *The freshmen played intramural football against the sophomores.*

in·tran·si·tive /ɪn'trænsətɪv, -zə-/ *n.adj.* related to a verb that does not take a direct object: *The verb "to go" is <adj.> intransitive:*

In the summer, we go to the beach every chance we get. See: transitive.

in·tra·ve·nous /ˌɪntrə'vinəs/ *adj.* into or within a vein: *The patient got food through an intravenous tube because he couldn't swallow.*

in·trep·id /ɪn'trɛpɪd/ *adj.frml.* without fear, brave: *The intrepid hunter lived alone in Africa.*

in·tri·ca·cy /'ɪntrəkəsi/ *n.* [C;U] **-cies** the condition of being detailed, complicated, and difficult to understand: *In medical school, aspiring doctors learn about the intricacies of brain surgery.*

in·tri·cate /'ɪntrɪkɪt/ *adj.* **1** complex, sometimes with many small details: *My sweater has an intricate design.* **2** difficult because of detail and depth: *The mystery novel has an intricate plot.*

in·trigue /'ɪn,trig/ *n.* [C;U] secret, interesting plans: *There was intrigue in the palace when the queen decided to steal power from the king.*
—*v.* /ɪn'trig/ **-trigued, -triguing, -trigues** to cause interest or curiosity: *The man intrigued me, so I asked him to my house for dinner.*

in·trigu·ing /ɪn'trigɪŋ/ *adj.* interesting, causing curiosity, (*syn.*) fascinating: *Psychologists find human emotions intriguing.*

in·trin·sic /ɪn'trɪnzɪk/ *adj.* belonging naturally to s.o. or s.t., (*syn.*) inherent: *Hunting mice is intrinsic behavior in most cats.*

in·tro·duce /ˌɪntrə'dus/ *v.* **-duced, -ducing, -duces 1** to present one person to another for the first time: *A friend introduced me to the woman I later married.* **2** to put in s.t. new: *The math teacher introduced some geometry into the lesson.*

in·tro·duc·tion /ˌɪntrə'dʌkʃən/ *n.* **1** [C] a first meeting, in which people learn each other's names: *She wants to meet that guest; will you make the introduction?* **2** [C;U] s.t. new put in or presented: *The introduction of new car engines caused excitement in the automobile business.* **3** [C] an opening statement before a speech or performance: *The vice president made an introduction before the president spoke.* -*adj.* **introductory.**

in·tro·spec·tion /ˌɪntrə'spɛkʃən/ *n.* [U] looking inside oneself and thinking carefully: *After long introspection, we decided to have a baby.* -*v.* **introspect;** -*adj.* **introspective.**

in·tro·vert /'ɪntrə,vɜrt/ *n.* a shy, quiet person: *He is an introvert who goes to movies alone and doesn't like parties.* -*n.* [U] **introversion.**

in·trude /ɪn'trud/ *v.* **-truded, -truding, -trudes 1** to break into the conversation or activity of others, to interrupt: *My mother often intrudes on my work by phoning me at my office.* **2** to enter without permission, (*syns.*) to trespass, encroach: *A stranger intruded by*

climbing over our fence and into our yard. -*n.* [C;U] **intrusion;** -*adj.* **intrusive.**

in·trud·er /ɪn'trudər/ *n.* a person who goes somewhere he or she doesn't belong: *An intruder entered our house and took our TV.*

in·tu·it /ɪn'tuɪt/ *v.frml.* to guess, feel s.t. will happen without certain facts: *My friend intuited that the weather would turn bad, and the next day it rained.*

in·tu·i·tion /ˌɪntu'ɪʃən/ *n.* [U] a feeling, a guess about s.t. without certain facts: *He used his intuition, not a map, to find my house.*

in·tu·i·tive /ɪn'tuətɪv/ *adj.* related to feeling, not learned knowledge: *He never took lessons, but he has an intuitive knack for playing the piano.*

in·un·date /'ɪnən,deɪt/ *v.* **-dated, -dating, -dates 1** to cover with water, (*syns.*) to flood, overflow: *The river inundated the farmland after too much rain.* **2** to give too much or too many, (*syn.*) to overwhelm: *The post office was inundated with thousands of holiday cards in December.* -*n.* [U] **inundation** /ˌɪnən'deɪʃən/.

in·ure /ɪn'yʊr/ *v.frml.* **-ured, -uring, -ures 1** to get used to (usu. s.t. bad or difficult): *Garbage collectors become inured to the smell of trash.* **2** (in law) to take effect

in·vade /ɪn'veɪd/ *v.* **-vaded, -vading, -vades 1** to enter by force: *Napoleon's armies invaded Russia.* **2** to enter without permission, (*syn.*) to intrude: *Loud music from next door invaded the privacy of our home.* -*n.* **invader.**

in·va·lid /ɪn'vælɪd/ *adj.* **1** not correct, lacking proof: *Your ideas about the first humans are interesting but invalid.* **2** not able to be used, illegal: *His driver's license is too old and hence invalid.*
—*n.* /'ɪnvəlɪd/ a person unable to care for himself or herself because of sickness or disability: *A bad car accident made him an invalid.*

in·val·i·date /ɪn'vælə,deɪt/ *v.* **-dated, -dating, -dates 1** to make illegal or unusable: *Airport workers invalidated the drug dealer's passport so she could not leave the country.* **2** to show to be wrong: *People who saw you steal the money invalidated your story about being home at the time.* -*n.* [U] **invalidation.**

in·val·u·a·ble /ɪn'vælyuəbəl/ *adj.* extremely valuable, worth a great deal: *Your help in moving the big refrigerator was invaluable.*

in·var·i·a·bly /ɪn'vɛriəbli/ *adv.* without exception or change: *Invariably, her advice is excellent; we always do what she says.* -*adj.* **invariable.**

in·va·sion /ɪn'veɪʒən/ *n.* [C;U] **1** an attack, entrance by force: *Napoleon's invasion of Russia was stopped by the bad winter.* **2** s.t. bad or hurtful coming in, (*syn.*) intrusion: *It was an invasion of my rights for the police to arrest me without cause.*

in·va·sive /ɪn'veɪsɪv/ *adj.* **1** having to do with entering or cutting into the body, esp. by surgery: *The doctors need to do an invasive operation to find the cancer.* **2** too personal and probing, *(syn.)* intrusive: *The newspaper article was invasive; we don't need to know those private things about the senator.*

in·vent /ɪn'vɛnt/ *v.* **1** to create s.t. new: *Trains were invented long before cars.* **2** to make up a story, to lie: *A little girl invented an imaginary friend to play with. -n.* **inventor.**

in·ven·tion /ɪn'vɛnʃən/ *n.* **1** [C;U] s.t. useful created by s.o.: *After the invention of the wheel, people could travel faster.* **2** [C] an untrue story, a lie: *His stories about his adventure in Rome are inventions; he's never been there.*

in·ven·tive /ɪn'vɛntɪv/ *adj.* able to make things or solve problems in a smart, clever way, *(syns.)* creative, resourceful: *Her way of fixing her kids' toys is often quite inventive.*

in·ven·to·ry /'ɪnvən,tɔri/ *n.* **-ries** the items that are available for sale in a store: *The bookstore has a large inventory of novels and cookbooks.* *—v.* **-ried, -rying, -ries** (or) **to take inventory** to count the items in a store to find out what has been sold and what needs to be replaced: *When I worked in a grocery store, I inventoried spices and canned foods.*

in·verse /'ɪn,vɜrs/ *n.adj.* in a different position, direction, or order; opposite: *2/3 is the <n.> inverse of 3/2.||Your pay is in <adj.> inverse proportion to your work; you work too much and earn too little.*

in·vert /ɪn'vɜrt/ *v.* to turn upside down or inside out: *The baby inverted the cup and spilled her juice. -n.* [C;U] **inversion.**

in·ver·te·brate /ɪn'vɜrtəbrɪt, -,breɪt/ *n.adj.* an animal without a backbone: *Ants are <n.pl.> invertebrates or <adj.> invertebrate animals.*

in·vest /ɪn'vɛst/ *v.* **1** to put money into a business idea or activity in the hope of making more money if it is successful: *We invested in a hamburger restaurant and became rich when it expanded to Europe.* **2** to put effort (time, money, energy, etc.) into s.t.: *We invested a lot in our garden, and now we have flowers and vegetables.*

in·ves·tor /ɪn'vɛstər/ *n.* a person who puts money into a business idea or activity in the hopes of making more money if the idea is successful: *We need three other investors before we can buy that computer company.*

in·ves·ti·gate /ɪn'vɛstə,geɪt/ *v.* **-gated, -gating, -gates** **1** to look at s.t. carefully, examine: *My car was stolen last week; the police are investigating.* **2** to look at (choices), *(syn.)* to evaluate: *We investigated various towns before we decided where to buy a house.*

in·ves·ti·ga·tion /ɪn,vɛstə'geɪʃən/ *n.* [C;U] **1** a search for facts and information, esp. by people with power: *Police began an investigation*

of the rape. **2** a close look, *(syn.)* an evaluation: *An investigation of various investment possibilities suggested real estate as a good choice now.*

in·ves·ti·ga·tor /ɪn'vɛstə,geɪtər/ *n.* a person (esp. the police) who investigates: *An investigator questioned the family of the dead person.*

in·vest·ment /ɪn'vɛstmənt/ *n.* **1** [C;U] money spent on s.t. in the hope of making more money: *His investments in the stock market have made him a millionaire.* **2** [C;U] s.t. one pays for with the future in mind: *The diamond was a good investment; it is worth more now than when I bought it.* **3** [U] money, time, energy, etc. toward s.t.: *Her investment of hard work and love has made her children good, honest people.*

in·vet·er·ate /ɪn'vɛtərɪt/ *adj.frml.* longtime, habitual: *He is an inveterate sailor who spends all his time on his boat.*

in·vig·or·ate /ɪn'vɪgə,reɪt/ *v.* **-ated, -ating, -ates** to give s.o. energy, *(syn.)* to stimulate: *Cold weather invigorates my brother and makes him work harder. -n.* [U] **invigoration.**

in·vin·ci·ble /ɪn'vɪnsəbəl/ *adj.* too strong (smart, etc.) to be beaten: *The invincible soccer team won every game. -n.* [U] **invincibility.**

in·vi·o·late /ɪn'vaɪəlɪt/ *adj.frml.* very well respected, secure, *(syn.)* sacred: *My garden is inviolate; children and dogs must stay out of it.*

in·vis·i·ble /ɪn'vɪzəbəl/ *adj.* not able to be seen: *Music is invisible; we can hear it and feel it, but not see it. -n.* [U] **invisibility.**

in·vi·ta·tion /,ɪnvə'teɪʃən/ *n.* a card or spoken request asking s.o. to come to an event: *The couple sent out wedding invitations to family and friends.*

in·vi·ta·tion·al /,ɪnvə'teɪʃənəl/ *n.adj.* an event, esp. in sports, to which participants are invited: *Tennis has a number of <n.pl.> invitationals or <adj.> invitational tournaments to which players are asked to attend.*

in·vite /ɪn'vaɪt/ *v.* **-vited, -viting, -vites** **1** to ask s.o. to come to an event: *I invited my friends to a birthday party.* **2** to attract attention and a reaction: *The violin player's beautiful solo invited loud applause.*

in·vit·ing /ɪn'vaɪtɪŋ/ *adj.* causing desire, tempting, *(syn.)* alluring: *The chocolate cake looked inviting, but it was also very fattening.*

in·vo·ca·tion /,ɪnvə'keɪʃən/ *n.* an opening prayer: *A minister gave the invocation at the university graduation ceremony.*

in·voice /'ɪn,vɔɪs/ *n.* (in business) a list of items or services and their cost, a bill: *Our company sends invoices to customers after they order from us.* *—v.* **-voiced, -voicing, -voices** to prepare and send a bill: *We invoice our customers after we send them the books they have ordered.*

in·voke /ɪn'voʊk/ *v.* **-voked, -voking, -vokes**
1 to call upon for help, (*syn.*) to summon:
*Through prayer, she invoked the help of God to
cure her sick brother.* **2** to put into effect, to
use: *When they saw the girl buy wine, the police invoked a law that forbids the sale of alcoholic beverages to people under 21.*

in·vol·un·tar·y /ɪn'vɑlən,tɛri/ *adj.* **1** not done
by choice, forced: *He didn't want to move
when his wife got a new job, so his leaving was
involuntary.* **2** done without thinking, automatic: *The heartbeat is involuntary.* *-adv.* **in-
voluntarily.**

in·volve /ɪn'vɑlv/ *v.* **-volved, -volving, -volves**
1 to need s.t. in order to complete an action:
*Getting a driver's license involves learning
how to drive, studying the rules of the road,
and taking a test.* **2** to cause to participate,
(*syns.*) to implicate, entangle: *If you have
problems with money, don't involve your relatives by borrowing from them. -n.* [U] **involvement.**

in·volved /ɪn'vɑlvd/ *adj.* **1** with many complex details, (*syn.*) intricate: *That mystery
novel is very involved; I can't explain the plot
in five minutes.* **2** with s.o. romantically: *Are
you two involved? I thought you were just
friends!* **3** participating in: *He was involved in
a car accident in which the other driver was
drunk.*

in·vul·ner·a·ble /ɪn'vʌlnərəbəl/ *adj.* not able
to be conquered, or hurt: *That fortress is invul-
nerable to attack. -n.* [U] **invulnerability.**

in·ward /'ɪnwərd/ *adv.* toward the inside:
*When he read the hate-filled letter, he stayed
quiet and directed his anger inward.*
—*adj.* located on the inside, within s.t.: *The inward side of the fence needs painting. -n.* [U]
inwardness.

in·ward·ly /'ɪnwərdli/ *adv.* within oneself, privately: *Inwardly, he loves her, but he can't tell
her.*

i·o·dine /'aɪə,daɪn, -,dɪn/ *n.* a chemical element used in medicine and photography: *Some
people put iodine on their cuts to prevent infection. -v.* **iodize;** *-adj.* **iodized.**

i·o·ta /aɪ'oʊtə/ *n.* a tiny amount (usu. used in
the negative): *That man does not care one iota
about other people's feelings.*‖*There is not one
iota of salt in this food.*

IOU /'aɪoʊ'yu/ *n.abbr. of* I owe you, a written
promise to pay back money: *I loaned my
friend $100, and he gave me an IOU.*

IPA /'aɪpi'eɪ/ *See:* International Phonetic
Alphabet.

i·ras·ci·ble /ɪ'ræsəbəl/ *adj.* easily angered,
(*syn.*) hot-tempered: *The old man is irascible,
shouting and waving his cane when kids ride
bicycles on his lawn. -n.* [U] **irascibility.**

i·rate /aɪ'reɪt, 'aɪ,reɪt/ *adj.* very angry, (*syns.*)
infuriated, incensed: *The governor received
irate letters and phone calls from people who
didn't want higher taxes. -n.* [U] **irateness.**

ire /aɪr/ *n.frml.* anger, (*syns.*) fury, wrath: *The
queen's ire was so great that she had her
nephew's head cut off.*

i·ri·des·cent /,ɪrə'dɛsənt/ *adj.* showing colors
of the rainbow, usu. shiny: *She wore an irides-
cent dress that seemed to change color in the
lamplight.*

i·ris /'aɪrɪs/ *n.* **1** the colored part of the eye
around the pupil: *His irises are a pretty blue.*
2 a tall plant with a large flower, often yellow
or purple: *We planted irises in our flower garden.*

I·rish coffee /'aɪrɪʃ/ *n.* [C;U] a hot drink made
of coffee, Irish whiskey, and sugar, topped
with whipped cream: *He likes an Irish coffee
after a nice meal.*

Irish setter *n.* a breed of
dog with long, silky,
brownish-red fur

irk /ɜrk/ *v.* to make angry
(but not extremely
angry), irritate, annoy: *I
was irked by the loud
talk at the dining table
next to mine. -adj.* **irk-
some.**

Irish setter

i·ron /'aɪərn/ *n.* **1** [U] a
common metal, used in making tools, machinery, furniture, and other strong, durable items;
also present in small amounts in the blood and
some foods: *Eat more spinach to get more
iron.* **2** [U] *n.adj. fig.* great strength and
courage: *The brave hunter had a will of <n.>
iron or an <adj.> iron will.* **3** [C] a small
household machine used to smooth wrinkles:
*My mother uses an iron to press my cotton
shirts.* **4** *pl.* chains, shackles: *The prisoners
were put into irons and thrown into jail.* **5** *infrml.* **to have irons in the fire:** to have a number of projects or interests happening now:
*Sam doesn't have a job, but four companies
are interested in interviewing him; he has several irons in the fire.* **6** *infrml.* **to pump iron:**
to lift weights to get stronger: *She goes to the
gym to pump iron every day.* **7 to strike while
the iron is hot:** to act while the opportunity is
there: *The movie is leaving that theater tomorrow, so let's strike while the iron is hot and go
tonight.*
—*v.* **1** to smooth with an iron: *She irons sheets
and pillow cases.* **2** *infrml.phrasal v. sep.* **to
iron s.t. out:** to solve problems, reach agreement: *My sister and I were angry, but we
ironed out our differences.*‖*We ironed them
out.*
—*adj.fig.* **with an iron hand:** with strength,
with strict rules: *The father ran the house with*

an iron hand, and his wife and children were always afraid.

i·ron·clad /'aɪərn,klæd/ *adj.* **1** covered with iron plates **2** *fig.* firm, unchangeable, *(syn.)* guaranteed: *We wanted an ironclad agreement, in writing, before we bought the house.*

Iron Curtain *n.fig.* the political and philosophical barriers or separation between Communist countries and democracies that began after World War II and ended in 1989 with the fall of the Berlin Wall: *She lived behind the Iron Curtain in Poland all her life, so she didn't know about Western political systems.*

i·ron·ic /aɪ'rɑnɪk/ *adj.* having a meaning opposite to what actions or words are showing: *I find it ironic that you don't like children, but you teach kindergarten. See:* irony.

i·ron·ing /'aɪərnɪŋ/ *n.* [U] the activity of smoothing out clothes, etc. with an iron: *My mother did the washing and ironing once a week.*

ironing board

ironing board *n.* a flat, covered surface on legs, used to spread out items for ironing: *After ironing the sheets, I folded the ironing board's legs and put it in a closet.*

i·ron·y /'aɪrəni/ *n.* **-ies** **1** [C;U] the use of words or actions that mean the opposite of what they say literally: *My friend used irony when he said, "You were so smart to paint your fence on a rainy day!"* **2** [C;U] a situation that shows the opposite of what one would expect: *There is irony in the fact that the USA is a rich country with so many poor people.* **3** [U] the use of irony in writing or theater for humorous or dramatic reasons: *The reader understands the irony, but the book's characters don't.*

ir·ra·tion·al /ɪ'ræʃənəl/ *adj.* **1** done without thinking, *(syn.)* illogical: *I had the irrational wish to laugh loudly in church.* **2** crazy, insane: *Your fears are irrational; no one is going to hurt you.* *-n.* [U] **irrationality** /ɪ,ræʃə'næləti/.

ir·re·con·cil·a·ble /ɪ,rɛkən'saɪləbəl/ *adj.* not able to be agreed upon: *The couple had irreconcilable differences about money and children, so they got a divorce.*

ir·ref·u·ta·ble /ɪ,rɪ'fyutəbəl/ *adj.* definitely true, convincing: *Police found her fingerprints on the knife, which is irrefutable proof that she was in the kitchen.*

ir·reg·u·lar /ɪ'rɛgyələr/ *adj.* **1** below normal or accepted standards, perhaps wrong or illegal: *Taking money from your father's wallet was quite irregular.* **2** not smooth or even, crooked, bumpy: *The paper was torn, not cut, with an irregular edge.* **3** not perfect, flawed: *That store sells irregular blue jeans; some are miss-*

ing zippers and buttons. *-n.*[C;U] **irregularity** /ɪ,rɛgyə'lærəti/.

ir·rel·e·vant /ɪ'rɛləvənt/ *adj.* not important to the situation, *(syn.)* extraneous: *It is irrelevant to me whether you are rich or poor, as long as you are kind.* *-n.* [U] **irrelevance.**

ir·rep·a·ra·ble /ɪ'rɛpərəbəl/ *adj.* not able to be fixed or repaired: *The storm did irreparable damage to the little houses near the beach.*

ir·re·place·a·ble /,ɪrə'pleɪsəbəl/ *adj.* without equal, so special as to be unlike any other: *My antique Chinese vase is irreplaceable.*

ir·re·press·i·ble /,ɪrə'prɛsəbəl/ *adj.* not able to be controlled or kept down, *(syn.)* unrestrained: *Her happiness was irrepressible at her wedding; she smiled and laughed all day.*

ir·re·proach·a·ble /,ɪrə'proʊtʃəbəl/ *adj.* extremely good (behavior, etc.), faultless: *The way you do business is irreproachable; you're always smart, honest, and on time.*

ir·re·sis·ti·ble /,ɪrə'zɪstəbəl/ *adj.* not able to be refused, very tempting: *That apple pie is irresistible; I had three slices.*

ir·re·spec·tive /,ɪrə'spɛktɪv/ *adj.* regardless: *Irrespective of his strange way of talking, he's an excellent worker.*

ir·re·spon·si·ble /,ɪrə'spɑnsəbəl/ *adj.* not wise about one's tasks, obligations, or behavior, *(syns.)* reckless, careless: *The irresponsible mother left her baby alone for two hours.* *-n.* [U] **irresponsibility.**

ir·re·triev·a·ble /,ɪrə'trivəbəl/ *adj.* not able to be gotten back or recovered: *Live life well, because the past is irretrievable.*

ir·rev·er·ent /ɪ'rɛvərənt/ *adj.* not showing respect, esp. for religious beliefs: *The rabbi thought his daughter was irreverent when she didn't go to temple on Yom Kippur.* *-n.* [U] **irreverence.**

ir·re·vers·i·ble /,ɪrə'vɜrsəbəl/ *adj.* not able to be changed or put back to original form, *(syn.)* irrevocable: *My decision to move to Italy is irreversible; I have bought my ticket and left my job.*

ir·ri·gate /'ɪrə,geɪt/ *v.* **-gated, -gating, -gates** **1** to supply with water collected in another location: *Farmers irrigated their corn by sending river water through pipes to their fields.* **2** to fill with water in order to remove s.t.: *A doctor irrigated my eye because there was dirt in it.* *-n.* [U] **irrigation** /,ɪrə'geɪʃən/.

ir·ri·ta·ble /'ɪrɪtəbəl/ *adj.* annoyed, bothered by s.t., *(syn.)* irascible: *She felt impatient and irritable after waiting an hour for a bus in the rain.* *-n.* [U] **irritability.**

ir·ri·tant /'ɪrətənt/ *n.* **1** s.t. that bothers or annoys: *Loud noise outside my window was an irritant when I was trying to sleep.* **2** s.t. that makes a physical condition bad or worse: *This wool sweater is an irritant to my sensitive skin.*

ir·ri·tate /ˈɪrəˌteɪt/ *v.* **-tated, -tating, -tates 1** to annoy, bother: *Your messy bedroom irritates your mother.* **2** to make s.t. worse, esp. a physical condition: *She irritated her skin by scratching too much.* *-n.* **irritation.** *See:* angry, USAGE NOTE.

IRS /ˈaɪɑrˈɛs/ *abbr. for* Internal Revenue Service, the USA's national tax collection agency: *The IRS sent me a letter saying I made a mistake on my tax form.*

Is·lam /ɪsˈlɑm, ɪz-, ˈɪsˌlɑm, ˈɪz-/ *n.* **1** the Muslim religion: *Our cousin in Morocco is a follower of Islam.* **2** the Muslim nations *-adj.* **Islamic.**

is·land /ˈaɪlənd/ *n.* a piece of land completely surrounded by water: *She lived on an island that was connected to the coast by a bridge.*

isle /aɪl/ *n.* an island: *He is from the Isle of Man in the Irish Sea.*

ism /ˈɪzəm/ *n.infrml.* a collection of knowledge and/or beliefs ending with the suffix "ism": *Socialism is one of the twentieth-century isms.*

i·so·late /ˈaɪsəˌleɪt/ *v.* **-lated, -lating, -lates** to separate from others, cause to be alone: *The snobby students isolated themselves from the rest of the class.* *-n.* [U] **isolation** /ˌaɪsəˈleɪʃən/.

i·so·la·tion·ism /ˌaɪsəˈleɪʃəˌnɪzəm/ *n.* [U] a political idea of ignoring or not getting involved with other countries: *Isolationism is easier for countries that are surrounded by water.*

is·sue /ˈɪʃu/ *v.* **-sued, -suing, -sues 1** to give or send out, (*syn.*) to distribute: *Between 1941 and 1945, the White House issued news about the war nearly every day.* **2** to give or provide in a formal or official way: *The motor vehicle office issues drivers' licenses after people pass a test.*
—n. **1** [C] a topic or matter of concern: *The main issues we are discussing today are tax increases and military spending.* **2** [C] a dated copy of a magazine or newspaper: *The Sunday issue of the newspaper has the comics in color.* **3** [C;U] a special supply of s.t., given out or made available at a certain time: *The government will put on sale a special issue of coins today.* **4 to be at issue:** to be of present concern: *We know you're going to Florida; what is at issue is whether you are driving or flying.* **5 to force the issue:** to force a decision: *If they can't decide between planting beans or tomatoes, you should force the issue by buying the seeds yourself.* **6 to make an issue of s.t.:** to take a problem or topic and make it bigger by talking and arguing: *This is just a small decision; don't make an issue out of it.* **7 to take issue with:** to disagree, argue: *The Republican senator took issue with the Democrat senator's speech.* *-n.* [U] **issuance.**

isth·mus /ˈɪsməs/ *n.* a narrow strip of land connecting two larger pieces of land: *The Isthmus of Panama connects North and South America.*

it /ɪt/ *pron.* **1** third person singular pronoun, used to refer to s.t. that is neither male nor female, and usually not alive: *We just had a vacation, and it was very relaxing.* **2** the subject of an impersonal verb: *It is raining today.* **3** the subject or object of a verb, often introducing a more important part of the sentence: *It was in this room that I first saw you.* **4** the object of a verb referring to s.t. mentioned before: *I explained the grammar, so he understands it now.* **5** *slang* **don't knock it:** don't complain about it: *Hey, this is the best job you've had; don't knock it!* **6 That's it!: a.** that's all I can take (showing anger, frustration): *That's it; I'm leaving if you don't be quiet!* **b.** Yes! (showing delight, discovery): *That's it; what a wonderful idea!* **7 to be "it":** in children's games, to be the one who chases or finds others: *In tag, children take turns being "it."* **8** *infrml.* **to get it:** to understand: *He didn't laugh at your joke because he didn't get it.‖This homework is hard; I don't get it.* **9** *infrml.* **to have had it:** to have suffered too much in a situation, (*syn.*) to be fed up: *I have had it with this party; let's get out of here!* **10 to have it:** to be good at s.t. (such as work or a sport): *In tennis, she really has it.*

i·tal·ic /aɪˈtælɪk ɪˈtæl-/ *n.adj.* a style of type in which the letters slant to the right: *The sentence you are reading is in <adj.> italic type or in <n.> italics.* *-v.* **italicize** /aɪˈtæləˌsaɪz, ɪˈtæl-/.

itch /ɪtʃ/ *n.* **1** a feeling on the skin causing an urge to scratch: *He has an itch on his leg from a flea bite.* **2** a desire, a wish: *I have an itch to play softball tonight.*
—v. **1** to have an itch: *His head itches from the new shampoo.* **2 to be itching (to do s.t.):** to have a strong wish or desire to do s.t.: *After reading a book about Africa, I was itching to go there.* *-adj.* **itchy.**

i·tem /ˈaɪtəm/ *n.* **1** a general term for a thing or objects: *Department stores have a wide choice of items for sale.* **2** s.t. on a list, a separate topic: *We have four items to discuss today; we'll start with item one.* **3** a short piece of news: *an item in the newspaper* **4** *slang* a couple in love: *They met last year and have been an item for six months.*

i·tem·ize /ˈaɪtəˌmaɪz/ *v.* **-ized, -izing, -izes** to list thing by thing: *I itemized the equipment that we will need for the new office.*

i·tin·er·ant /aɪˈtɪnərənt/ *n.* s.o. who travels from place to place and job to job: *That guy is an itinerant who does odd jobs all over the state.*

—*adj.* traveling from place to place or job to job: *My mother was an itinerant farm worker, in California one month and Oregon the next.*

i·tin·er·ar·y /aɪˈtɪnəˌrɛri/ *n.* **-ies** a travel plan, showing places to visit and transportation times: *Look on our vacation itinerary to find out when we are flying to London.*

it·self /ɪtˈsɛlf/ *pron.* **1** third person singular pronoun used to refer back to a subject: *The problem solved itself; we did nothing.* **2** used to make a noun stronger or more definite: *The neighborhood is dangerous, but the house itself is safe.* **3 in and of itself:** without being affected by other things: *Money in and of itself is not bad, but too much of it can ruin some people.*

i·vo·ry /ˈaɪvəri/ *n.* [C;U] **-ries** the hard, white-yellow substance of elephant, walrus, and other animal tusks: *My grandmother has some jewelry made of ivory.*
—*n.* [U] *adj.* a white-yellow color: *My shirt is more <n.> ivory (or) more of an <adj.> ivory color than white.*

ivory tower *n.fig.* a place or attitude removed from practical, everyday life, usu. referring to a college or university: *You live in an ivory tower; you read about poverty and war, but you never see them.*

i·vy /ˈaɪvi/ *n.* [C;U] **ivies** a green plant with shiny leaves that can cover the ground or climb the walls of buildings: *The walls of my cousin's brick house are green with ivy.*

Ivy League *n.* in the USA, eight northeastern universities known for strong academics, competing sports teams, tradition, and wealth; they are Brown, Columbia, Cornell, Dartmouth, Harvard, Princeton, the University of Pennsylvania, and Yale: *My father played football in the Ivy League when he was at Yale.*
—*adj.* having to do with the Ivy League, usu. meaning a fine education, traditional behavior, and wealth: *He acts like an Ivy League snob, but he never graduated from high school.*

J, j

J, j or **J's, j's** or **Js, js** /ʤeɪ/ the tenth letter of the English alphabet

jab /ʤæb/ *v.* **jabbed, jabbing, jabs** to hit with a quick, sharp blow: *She jabbed me in the arm with her umbrella.*
—*n.* a quick, sharp blow: *The boxer threw a jab at his opponent's face. See:* poke.

jab·ber /ʤæbər/ *v.n.* to talk quickly without making much sense: *Some people <v.> jabber about nothing. See:* chatter.

jack /ʤæk/ *n.* **1** a tool for lifting: *We carry a jack in our car in case we have a flat tire.* **2** a small electrical device: *a telephone jack*
—*v.phrasal v. sep.* **to jack s.t. up 1** to lift with a jack: *She jacked up the car to fix the flat tire.* ‖*She jacked it up.* **2** *fig.* to raise: *to jack up prices*

jack·al /ʤækəl/ *n.* a type of wild dog found in Africa and Asia: *Jackals hunt mostly at night.*

jack·ass /ʤæk,æs/ *n.* **-asses 1** a male donkey **2** *infrml.fig.pej.* a stupid, usu. offensive person: *That jackass delivered the wrong box again!*

jack·et /ʤækɪt/ *n.* **1** a short coat made of cloth or leather, etc.: *He wears a leather jacket every day.* **2** a cover: *a book jacket*

Jack Frost /ʤæk'frɔst/ *n.* an imaginary man associated with frost and cold weather: *It is so cold outside that Jack Frost is biting my nose; it's all red.*

jack·ham·mer /ʤæk,hæmər/ *n.* a powerful, handheld tool used to break up rocks and cement: *The sound of a jackhammer is very loud.*

jack-in-the-box *n.* **-boxes** a toy made of a doll-like figure that pops out of a box when it is opened: *The child laughed when the jack-in-the-box jumped out at him.*

jack-in-the-box

jack·knife /ʤæk,naɪf/ *n.* **-knives** a knife with one or more blades that fold into the handle
—*v.fig.* **-knifed, -knifing, -knifes** to bend like a blade folding into a knife handle: *A truck jackknifed on the highway in the rain.*

jack-of-all-trades *n.* **jacks-** a person who can do many different jobs, such as repair cars and wash windows: *He is a jack-of-all-trades but does none of them well.*

jack-o'-lan·tern /ʤækə,læn-tərn/ *n.* an empty pumpkin shell with a funny or ugly face cut into it: *The Halloween jack-o'lantern contains a lighted candle to show its funny eyes and teeth. See:* pumpkin.

jack-o'lantern

jack·pot /ʤæk,pɑt/ *n.* **1** a sum of money won as the biggest prize in many forms of gambling, such as a slot machine or lottery **2 to hit the jackpot:** to win the big prize: *Many gamblers try to hit the jackpot in Las Vegas.*

jack rab·bit *n.* a large, fast rabbit with long ears, found in the southwestern USA: *That boy can run fast like a jack rabbit.*

jade /ʤeɪd/ *n.* [U] a usu. green or white semi-precious stone used for jewelry or ornaments: *She wears earrings made of jade.*

jaded /ʤeɪdɪd/ *adj.* **1** tired, (*syn.*) worn-out: *She is jaded from too much work.* **2** tired from doing s.t. too much: *He felt jaded after visiting 25 countries in 15 days.*

jag /ʤæg/ *n.slang* a period of doing s.t. without being able to stop, (*syns.*) a binge, spree: *He's on a jag, buying everything that he likes in the store.*

jag·ged /ʤægɪd/ *adj.* having an uneven, pointed edge: *I cut my finger on the jagged edge of a broken mirror. -n.* **jaggedness.**

jag·uar /ʤæg,wɑr/ *n.* a large wild cat of Latin America that has a tan coat with black spots: *Jaguars are strong and fast hunters.*

jail /ʤeɪl/ *n.* a building where criminals are kept as punishment, a prison: *The thief was sent to jail.*
—*v.* to put s.o. in a jail, to sentence s.o. to jail: *The criminal was jailed by the police. See:* penitentiary.

jail·break /ʤeɪl,breɪk/ *n.* an escape from prison: *There was a jailbreak last night, and two prisoners ran away.*

463

jail·er /'dʒeɪlər/ n. a person who guards prisoners, a jailkeeper: *That jailer treats the prisoners badly.*

ja·lop·y /dʒə'lɑpi/ n.infrml. **-ies** an old car that does not run well: *He drives a jalopy to work each day.*

jam (1) /dʒæm/ n. [U] a sweet fruit topping made by boiling fruit with sugar: *He put strawberry jam on his breakfast toast.*

jam (2) n. **1** a crowd (of people, cars, etc.): *Our bus was stuck in a traffic jam.* **2 to be in a jam:** to be in a difficult situation: *She is in a jam with the police, who think she stole s.t.*
—v. **jammed, jamming, jams 1** to push hard into s.t., force: *He jammed a metal bar under a window that was stuck.* **2** to break s.t., get s.t stuck: *She jammed the key into the lock, and now it won't come out.* **3** to fill with many people, cars, etc., to crowd: *People jammed into the stadium to see the game.* **4** to create a piece of music, esp. jazz, while one is playing it **5** to block a radio signal by making it difficult to understand **6 to jam on the brakes:** to stop a car suddenly

jamb /dʒæm/ n. the sides of a window or door frame: *The door jamb is too small, so the door won't close.*

jam·bo·ree /,dʒæmbə'ri/ n. an enjoyable time for a large crowd, a festival: *Thousands of Boy Scouts get together each summer to have a jamboree.*

Jane Doe /'dʒeɪn'dou/ n. **1** a name used for an imaginary average woman **2** a woman with no known name: *The dead woman was a Jane Doe. See:* John Doe.

jan·gle /'dʒæŋgəl/ n. the sound of metal hitting metal
—v. **-gled, -gling, -gles 1** to make a sharp, unpleasant noise, as of metal hitting metal **2** to make s.o. angry, nervous, or impatient: *The sound of car horns jangles his nerves.*

jan·i·tor /'dʒænətər/ n. a person in charge of cleaning and fixing things in a building, (*syn.*) custodian: *In many parts of the USA, a janitor is called a "super" or "superintendent."*

Jan·u·ar·y /'dʒænyuˌɛri/ n. the first month of the year: *It started to snow in January.*

jar /dʒɑr/ n. **1** a round container made of glass, plastic, etc. with a removable top: *a jar of grape jelly (face cream, mustard, etc.)* **2** a forceful hit, (*syn.*) a jolt
—v. **jarred, jarring, jars 1** to bump hard against s.t., to bang: *She moved her chair backwards, and it jarred against the wall.* **2** to shock: *to jar s.o. back to reality* **3** to make s.o. angry, nervous, or impatient: *Loud talk jars her nerves* (or) *on her nerves.*

jar·gon /'dʒɑrgən/ n. [C;U] the special words used in many areas of work or study, often difficult for outsiders to understand: *People who work with computers use jargon, such as "log on" and "on line."*

jas·mine /'dʒæzmɪn/ n. [C;U] a plant with sweet-smelling white flowers: *Most people like the sweet smell of jasmine.*

jaun·dice /'dʒɔndɪs/ n.v. a yellow coloring of the skin caused by liver disease

jaun·diced /'dʒɔndɪst/ adj. **1** colored yellow by liver disease **2** fig. a bad opinion about s.o. or s.t.: *He has a jaundiced view* (or) *attitude toward popular music.*

jaunt /dʒɔnt/ n.v. a short trip for pleasure: *I took a <n.> jaunt to the Caribbean to relax for a few days.*

jaun·ty /'dʒɔnti/ adj. **-tier, -tiest** feeling confident, happy: *The well-dressed man gave a jaunty laugh. -adv.* **jauntily.**

jav·e·lin /'dʒævlɪn, 'dʒævə-/ n. a type of spear used in sports: *An athlete threw the javelin 100 meters.*

jaw /dʒɔ/ n. the lower and upper bones of the mouth, including the teeth: *She couldn't eat because of her broken jaw.*
—v.infrml. to gossip, chat: *We jawed about the stock market all afternoon.*

jaw·bone /'dʒɔˌboun/ n. the jaw in the skull
—v.infrml. **-boned, -boning, -bones** to demand that s.o. do s.t., to bully verbally: *The President jawboned Congress into not raising taxes.*

jay /dʒeɪ/ or **jay·bird** /'dʒeɪˌbɜrd/ n. a blue and gray bird common in North America: *Jays have a loud, unpleasant cry.*

Jay·cees /,dʒeɪ'siz/ n.pl. abbr. of Junior Chamber of Commerce (an organization for young adults): *Jaycees encourage young people to start businesses.*

jay·walk /'dʒeɪˌwɔk/ v. to cross a street illegally: *A police officer stopped her when she jaywalked across Main Street. -n.* **jaywalker.**

jazz /dʒæz/ n. [U] **1** a form of American popular music, such as slow New Orleans jazz or fast Dixieland jazz **2** infrml.fig. **all that jazz** and everything else: *We talked about our vacation, the places we went, and all that jazz. -n.* **jazzman.**
—phrasal v.sep. **to jazz s.t. up:** to make s.t. look more attractive or bright: *The company jazzed up its offices by painting the walls.‖It jazzed them up.*

jazz·y /'dʒæzi/ adj.infrml. **-ier, -iest 1** lively, exciting: *They gave a really jazzy party.* **2** bright, showy: *She is wearing a jazzy dress.*

jeal·ous /'dʒɛləs/ adj. **1** afraid of having a loved one taken away by another, (*syn.*) possessive: *He gets jealous when other men talk to his girlfriend.* **2** wanting s.o. or s.t. belonging to another person, (*syn.*) envious: *She is jealous of her friend's wealth. -adv.* **jealously.**

jeal·ous·y /'dʒɛləsi/ n. [C;U] **-ies 1** fear that another person will take away a loved one **2**

the feeling of envy, of wanting what another person has: *Jealousy over his neighbor's wealth made him angry.*

jeans /ʤinz/ *n.pl.* pants made of cotton denim and worn informally: *Blue jeans are worn by people of all ages.*

Jeep /ʤip/ *n.TM* a type of strongly built car made to travel over rough ground: *We drove our Jeep up a mountain road.*

jeer /ʤɪr/ *v.* to hurt s.o.'s feelings by laughing rudely, *(syn.)* to mock: *The crowd jeered when the boxer was knocked down.*
—*n.* a loud insult: *They shouted jeers at him.*
-*n.* **jeering.**

jell /ʤɛl/ *v.* **1** to become firm, harden **2** *fig.* to take shape, to become definite: *Her plans for a summer vacation finally jelled today. See:* gel.

Jell-O or **jel·lo** /ˈʤɛloʊ/ *n.TM* a light dessert made of gelatin, usu. with a fruit flavor: *orange-flavored Jell-O*

jel·ly /ˈʤɛli/ *n.* [U] **1** a soft, sweet food made from fruit juice and sugar boiled together, used as a topping: *She spread grape jelly on her toast.* **2** any jelly-like substance: *petroleum jelly See:* jell, jam (1).

jel·ly·bean /ˈʤɛli,bin/ *n.* a small, fruit-flavored candy in the shape of a bean: *He keeps a jar of jellybeans on his desk.*

jel·ly·fish /ˈʤɛli,fɪʃ/ *n.* **-fish** or **-fishes 1** a sea animal with a soft body and no internal skeleton: *A dangerous jellyfish floated near the beach.* **2** *fig.* a weak or cowardly person

jeop·ard·ize /ˈʤɛpər,daɪz/ *v.* **-ized, -izing, -izes** to make it easy for s.t. bad to happen, to put in danger, *(syn.)* to endanger: *She jeopardized her job by always being late.*

jeop·ard·y /ˈʤɛpərdi/ *n.* [U] danger, risk: *He put his health in jeopardy by smoking too many cigarettes.*

jerk /ʤɜrk/ *n.* **1** a quick, sharp pull on s.t.: *The rope was stuck, and he gave it a jerk to loosen it.* **2** *fig.slang* a stupid, annoying person, an idiot: *He's a real jerk!*
—*v.* **1** to pull sharply on s.t.: *He jerked on the fishing line.* **2** to move s.t. away suddenly: *She jerked her hand away from the fire.* **3** *infrml.fig.* **to jerk s.o. around:** to mislead and confuse s.o.: *The airline really jerked us around by canceling our flight, putting us on another one, and canceling that one too.*

jerk·wa·ter /ˈʤɜrk,wɔtər, -,wɑ-/ *adj.slang* small, unimportant, and uncivilized: *They live in some jerkwater town.*

jerk·y /ˈʤɜrki/ *adj.* **-ier, -iest 1** s.t. done with short, jumpy movements: *She walks with jerky steps.* **2** foolish, stupid: *Making a funny face at the teacher was a jerky thing to do.*

jer·ry·built /ˈʤɛri,bɪlt/ *adj.* cheaply and poorly built: *That jerrybuilt house is falling apart.*

jer·sey /ˈʤɜrzi/ *n.* a light, soft shirt worn informally: *He wears a cotton jersey when he plays football.*

jest /ʤɛst/ *v.frml.* to say s.t. funny, to joke
—*n.* a funny remark, a joke: *I said you look terrible in jest; actually, you look very pretty.*

jest·er /ˈʤɛstər/ *n.* a person paid to tell jokes: *A long time ago, kings had jesters to tell them funny stories.*

jet /ʤɛt/ *v.* **jetted, jetting, jets 1** to fly by jet airplane **2** to come out of a small opening with great force: *Water jets from the fountain.*
—*n.* **1** a jet-propelled airplane: *He takes a jet from London to Paris.* **2** a steady, controlled stream of gas, steam, liquid, etc.
—*adj.* (said of colors) completely, deep: *jet black hair*

jet en·gine *n.* an engine that moves an airplane by shooting streams of hot gas backwards: *Jet engines are powerful enough to carry huge planes.*

jet lag *n.* a tired feeling caused by long-distance travel into different time zones: *Every time that I travel from London to Asia, I suffer from jet lag.*

jet-pro·pelled *adj.* having jet engines: *Jet-propelled airplanes travel very fast.* -*n.* **jet propulsion.**

jet·sam /ˈʤɛtsəm/ *n.* [U] **1** items of cargo thrown overboard to lighten a ship in danger of sinking **2 flotsam and jetsam:** useless garbage from some activity: *A huge storm left the water full of flotsam and jetsam—trees, mud, and wood.*

jet set *n.* [U] rich people who travel internationally in search of pleasure: *As a member of the jet set, she goes to parties all over the world.* -*n.* [C] **jet setter.**

jet stream *n.* a high speed wind very high in the sky: *Our plane had the jet stream pushing it, so we arrived an hour early.*

jet·ti·son /ˈʤɛtəsən, -zən/ *v.frml.* to throw s.t. away, esp. over the side of a ship or from an airplane: *Sailors jettisoned big boxes in the storm to make the ship lighter.*

jet·ty /ˈʤɛti/ *n.* **-ties** a wall usu. made of large rocks built into the water and used as a place to get on and off boats, or to protect a harbor from storm waves: *People waited on the jetty for their boat to arrive.*

Jew /ʤu/ *n.* **1** a member of the Jewish faith **2** a person of Jewish descent: *The religion of the Jews is Judaism.* -*adj.* **Jewish.**

jew·el /ˈʤuəl/ *n.* **1** a precious or semi-precious gemstone: *Diamonds, rubies, and emeralds are beautiful jewels.* **2** *fig.* a person or thing of very special qualities: *He gave me a surprise party for my birthday; he's such a jewel!* -*adj.* **jeweled.**

J

jew·el·er /'ʤuələr/ *n.* **1** a person who makes, repairs, and/or sells jewelry **2** a jewelry store: *I am taking my watch to the jeweler to be fixed.*

jew·el·ry /'ʤuəlri/ *n.* [U] body decorations, such as rings, bracelets, and necklaces: *Her favorite piece of jewelry is her diamond ring.*

jib /ʤɪb/ *n.* a triangular sail on a boat: *The storm tore the boat's jib.*

jibe /ʤaɪb/ *v.* **jibed, jibing, jibes** to agree with s.t.: *What he says happened does not jibe with what others say.*

jif·fy /'ʤɪfi/ *n.infrml.* [U] a brief moment, an instant: *Please stay on the phone; I'll be back to you in a jiffy.*

jig /ʤɪg/ *n.* **1** a quick, lively dance **2 in jig time:** quickly, rapidly: *He did that job in jig time!*
—*v.* **jigged, jigging, jigs** to dance a jig

jig·ger /'ʤɪgər/ *n.* a small glass for measuring liquor, usu. 1 to 1 oz: *He poured a jigger of rum in the glass.*

jig·gle /'ʤɪgəl/ *v.* **-gled, -gling, -gles** to move up and down or from side to side: *The fat man's stomach jiggles as he walks.*

jig·saw /'ʤɪg,sɔ/ *n.* a handheld tool with a thin, narrow blade, used to cut curves: *He cut a toy out of wood with a jigsaw.*

jig·saw puz·zle *n.* **1** a game made of a picture on cardboard or wood, cut into pieces and put back together again for fun **2** *fig.* a problem or situation not easily understood: *Our company has to find all the possible customers for our new product, and that task is a real jigsaw puzzle.*

ji·had /ʤɪ'had/ *n.* an Islamic holy war: *The leader started a jihad against a neighboring country.*

jilt /ʤɪlt/ *v.* to desert a friend or loved one without warning: *He saw her every day, then jilted her.*

jim·my /'ʤɪmi/ *n.* **-mies** a short metal bar used to force open windows (doors, etc.)
—*v.* **-mied, -mying, -mies** to use a jimmy: *The burglar jimmied open the window and stole my TV.*

jin·gle /'ʤɪŋgəl/ *v.* **-gled, -gling, -gles** to make a light, metallic ringing sound: *Small bells jingled as the door opened.*
—*n.* **1** a short advertising message, usu. with music and rhyming words **2** the sound of jingling: *My keys make a jingle in my pocket when I walk.*

jin·go·ism /'ʤɪŋgou,ɪzəm/ *n.* [U] a feeling of strong love for one's country, usu. with a hatred of foreigners: *Jingoism is a problem in many parts of the world.* -*n.* **jingoist;** -*adj.* **jingoistic** /,ʤɪŋgou'ɪstɪk/.

jinx /ʤɪŋks/ *v.* **jinxes** to cause s.o. or s.t. to have bad luck: *John has jinxed his football team; they have lost every game this season.*

—*n.* **jinxes 1** a person or thing that brings bad luck **2** a mild curse: *He has a jinx.* **3 to put a jinx on s.o.:** to bring bad luck to s.o.: *I could not give my speech because my friend made me laugh and put a jinx on me.*

jit·ters /'ʤɪtərz/ *n.pl.* nervousness, worry: *He has the jitters about going to a job interview.* -*adj.* **jittery.**

jive /ʤaɪv/ *n.infrml.* [U] **1** empty, often boastful talk, nonsense **2** a type of popular music from the 1940s and 1950s
—*v.* **jived, jiving, jives** to play, dance, or sing jive music: *That band really jives!*

job /ʤab/ *n.* **1** work that one is paid to do every day, permanent employment: *She has a good job.* **2** a specific task, piece of work: *I have a job to do now, a long report.* **3** *slang* **to do a job on s.o.:** to make others think badly of s.o., to criticize s.o.: *The people at his former company really did a job on him by saying bad things about his past.*
—*v.* **jobbed, jobbing, jobs: to job s.t. out:** to have a job done outside of a business by another business, (*syn.*) to subcontract: *Our company does not do any of its own printing; we job it out to local printers.*

job ac·tion *n.* a workers' protest, such as stopping work for a short time: *The union started a job action to force management to pay the workers more.*

job·less /'ʤablɪs/ *adj.* without a job, unemployed: *She has been jobless for two months now.*

job lot *n.* a number of cheap goods, usu. mixed items: *Stores that buy in job lots often have low prices.*

jock /ʤak/ *n.slang* **1** an athlete: *In college, he was a jock because he played football and baseball.* **2** a jockstrap

jock·ey /'ʤaki/ *n.* a person who rides horses in races: *Jockeys try to win every race.*
—*v.* **1** to ride horses in races **2** to go around things that are in the way: *He jockeyed his car around holes in the road. See:* disc jockey.

jock·strap /'ʤak,stræp/ *n.* tight-fitting underwear worn around a man's sexual organs for support and protection: *When he plays football, he wears a jockstrap.*

joc·u·lar /'ʤakyələr/ *adj.frml.* full of fun, joking: *He is a man with a jocular attitude.* -*n.* **jocularity** /,ʤakyə'lærəti/.

jog /ʤag/ *v.* **jogged, jogging, jogs 1** to run at a slow pace: *He jogged around the park.* **2 to jog s.o.'s memory:** to cause s.o. to remember s.t.: *I jogged his memory by reminding him of our meeting tomorrow.*
—*n.* a slow run: *I go for a jog every evening.*

jog·ging /'ʤagɪŋ/ *n.* [U] the sport of running at a slow pace: *go jogging* -*n.* **jogger.**

john /ʤɑn/ *n.slang* **1** a bathroom, toilet **2** a prostitute's male customer

John Doe /ˌʤɑnˈdoʊ/ *n.* **1** a name used for an imaginary average man **2** a name used for a man who has no known name or identity: *The police captured a thief who would not give his name, so they called him John Doe. See:* Jane Doe.

John Han·cock /ˈʤɑnˈhænkɑk/ *n.* **1** *lit.* a signer of the USA's Declaration of Independence **2** *fig.*a signature **3** *infrml.fig.* **to put** or **sign your John Hancock:** to sign a document with your name: *The contract is ready; just put your John Hancock on it.*

John·ny-come-late·ly /ˈʤɑnikʌmˈleɪtli/ *n.* **-lies** a person who joins a cause or adopts a fashion (trend, idea, etc.) after it is well established, a latecomer: *Everyone uses computers, and he is just now starting to learn; he's a Johnny-come-lately.*

John·ny-on-the-spot *n.* an eager, helpful person: *The television salesman became ill, so his helper was Johnny-on-the-spot and sold many TVs for him.*

join /ʤɔɪn/ *v.* **1** to become a member of an organization, (*syn.*) to enroll in: *She joined a health club (a church, Girl Scouts, the American Medical Association, etc.).* **2** to get together with others: *I joined my friends for a party.* **3** to put s.t. together, (*syn.*) to assemble: *A worker joined two pieces of wood with glue.* **4** *phrasal v. insep.* **to join in s.t.:** to do s.t. with others, to participate: *She joins in the fun (conversation, task, etc.) with the others.* **5** *phrasal v. sep.* **to join s.o. together:** to marry: *A judge joined the man and woman together in marriage.* **6** *phrasal v.* **to join up:** to go into military service, (*syn.*) to enlist: *After talking with an Army officer, he joined up.*

joint /ʤɔɪnt/ *adj.* **1** used by several people together, shared: *They have a joint checking account; both can sign checks.* **2** done together, (*syn.*) united: *Many countries made a joint effort to fight hunger.*
—*n.* **1** a point at which two pieces of material (wood, metal, etc.) come together: *You can see the joints in that wooden bookcase.* **2** the connection point between moving parts in a living body: *The leg has the knee joint.* **3** *slang* a cheap nightclub or restaurant, (*syn.*) a dive: *There is a beer joint on the corner.* **4** *infrml.* a marijuana cigarette **5 out of joint:** out of the correct position, (*syn.*) dislocated: *He hurt himself playing football; his knee is out of joint.* **6** *infrml.fig.* **to have one's nose out of joint:** to be annoyed: *He did not get what he wants, so his nose is out of joint.*

Joint Chiefs of Staff *n.pl.* in the USA, a group of military officers in charge of the Army, Navy, Air Force, and Marines, located in Washington, D.C.: *The Joint Chiefs of Staff make important military decisions.*

joint·ly /ˈʤɔɪntli/ *adv.* **1** together, (*syn.*) mutually: *We hold a checking account jointly.* **2** acting together: *The two countries acted jointly to fight hunger.*

joint ven·ture *n.* a business arrangement made by two or more companies: *An American and a Japanese auto maker agreed to form a joint venture to build trucks.*

joke /ʤoʊk/ *n.* **1** a funny idea or story with a surprise ending: *He has a great sense of humor and loves to tell jokes.* **2 to play a joke on s.o.:** to trick, (*syn.*) to play a prank: *His friends played a joke on him by sewing his pant legs together.* **3** a ridiculous, situation: *That salary increase was so small that it was a joke!*
—*v.* **joked, joking, jokes 1** to tell a joke: *When she gets together with her friends, they joke a lot.* **2** to act playfully: *They dance and sing and joke around together.* *-adv.* **jokingly.**

jok·er /ˈʤoʊkər/ *n.* **1** a playing card of no use in most card games and given special importance in others **2** a person who likes to joke

joker

jol·ly /ˈʤɑli/ *adj.* **-lier, -liest** happy, cheerful: *He is a jolly old man.*
—*n.pl.* **-lies 1** pleasure, fun **2** *slang* **to get one's jollies:** to have fun: *They get their jollies by driving very fast on the highway. -n.* **jolliness.**

jolt /ʤoʊlt/ *v.* **1** to strike with a heavy, sudden blow: *Earthquakes jolt buildings.* **2** *fig.* to fill with fear, to shock: *She was jolted by the bad news.*
—*n.* **1** a blow: *The jolt of an earthquake shook the house.* **2** *fig.* an emotional shock: *He got a jolt on learning of his friend's death.* **3** *fig.* a sudden shock of electricity: *If you stick s.t. into an electrical socket, you will get a jolt.*

josh /ʤɑʃ/ *v.infrml.* **joshes** to joke with s.o., (*syn.*) to tease: *He joshes his friend about her green hair.*

jos·tle /ˈʤɑsəl/ *v.* **-tled, -tling, -tles** to knock off balance, push, esp. in a crowd of people: *People jostled me on the bus, and I nearly fell.*

jot /ʤɑt/ *v.* **jotted, jotting, jots** to write short notes quickly: *I jotted down her name and telephone number.*

jour·nal /ˈʤɜrnl/ *n.* **1** a written record, a diary: *He keeps a journal of daily events.* **2** a magazine, periodical: *The New England Journal of Medicine is for doctors and nurses.* **3** a newspaper: *The Wall Street Journal has news about business.* **4** an accounting ledger: *He keeps a journal of expenses.*

J

jour·nal·ese /ˌdʒɜrnl'iz, -'is/ *n.* [U] special words and phrases used often by journalists: *"Have the politicians begun to address the issues?"* is journalese for *"Are politicians doing s.t. about the country's problems?"*

jour·nal·ism /'dʒɜrnl,ɪzəm/ *n.* [U] **1** the gathering and reporting of news **2** the study of that field: *She is studying journalism so that she can write for a newspaper.*

jour·nal·ist /'dʒɜrnlɪst/ *n.* a person whose job is to gather and report the news: *Journalists write news stories for magazines and newspapers.* -adj. **journalistic.**

jour·ney /'dʒɜrni/ *n.* a trip, esp. a long one —*v.* to take a long trip: *Many Irish immigrants journeyed to America by sea in the 1840s.*

jour·ney·man /'dʒɜrnimən/ *n.* **-men** a worker whose work is acceptable but not the best: *He is a good journeyman, but his partner's work is better.*

joust /dʒaʊst/ *v.frml.* (long ago) to ride a horse toward an opponent and knock him off his horse with a lance (a long stick): *Knights jousted against each other centuries ago.* -n. **jouster; jousting.**

jo·vi·al /'dʒoʊviəl/ *adj.* full of laughter, cheerful: *He is a jovial person who makes others feel happy, too.* -adv. **jovially.**

jowls /dʒaʊlz/ *n.pl.* loose skin on the cheeks that hang down below the chin, usu. on a fat person or animal

joy /dʒɔɪ/ *n.* [U] **1** a moment of great happiness, delight: *The parents felt joy at seeing their child begin to walk.* **2** having a good time: *We experienced the joy of having a wonderful vacation.* **3** well-being over a long period, happiness: *She knew the joy of being in good health and having no problems in life.*

joy·ful /'dʒɔɪfəl/ *adj.* **1** causing happiness, delightful: *We had a joyful experience at seeing an old friend.* **2** full of laughter, merry: *a joyful family dinner* **3** happy: *The first months of our marriage were a joyful time.* -adv. **joyfully.**

joy·less /'dʒɔɪlɪs/ *adj.* without pleasure: *That job turned into a joyless, boring experience.* -adv. **joylessly.**

joy·ous /'dʒɔɪəs/ *adj.* happy, cheerful: *Our first family reunion after many years was a joyous occasion.* -adv. **joyously;** -n. **joyousness.**

joy ride *n.v.infrml.* a ride, often fast and dangerous, sometimes in a stolen car for fun: *Someone took our car for a <n.> joy ride and left it in a parking lot.* -n. **joy riding.**

joy stick *n.* device used to control the movements and direction of a model airplane, a video-game character, etc.: *The first airplanes were controlled with joy sticks.*

ju·bi·lant /'dʒubələnt/ *adj.* full of great joy, *(syn.)* ecstatic: *She was jubilant when she won the race.* -adv. **jubilantly.**

ju·bi·la·tion /ˌdʒubə'leɪʃən/ *n.* [U] a joyful celebration: *When the war ended, there was jubilation all over the country.*

ju·bi·lee /'dʒubə,li, ˌdʒubə'li/ *n.* a celebration, esp. of an anniversary: *The couple celebrated their golden jubilee, 50 years of marriage.*

judge /dʒʌdʒ/ *n.* **1** a public official in charge of a court of law who determines what the law is and gives penalties to guilty persons and rewards those who have been wronged: *Alexander Smith is a judge on the State Supreme Court.* **2** an expert whose opinion is accepted by others as official: *Ms. Jones is an expert on French paintings and an excellent judge of their value.* **3** s.o. who enforces the rules, esp. of a sporting event, *(syn.)* a referee: *the line judge in football* **4** a person who evaluates others: *Your father is a good judge of your character.*
—*v.* **judged, judging, judges 1** to make an official decision in a court of law: *The jury judged the man to be guilty.* **2** to consider s.t. and give an opinion as an authority or expert: *She judged the painting to be authentic, not a fake.* **3** to make decisions in a game, to referee: *He judged that the ball was out.* **4** to express a personal opinion: *I judge the contract to be a good one for us.*

judge·ship /'dʒʌdʒ,ʃɪp/ *n.* the position or job of a judge in the public legal system: *Judge Smith has held a judgeship for over 20 years.*

judg·ment or **judge·ment** /'dʒʌdʒmənt/ *n.* **1** a decision (verdict, ruling) in a court of law: *The judgment of the court is that she is not guilty.* **2** knowledgeable opinion, *(syn.)* estimation: *The judgment of the experts is that the vase is authentic, not a fake.* **3** personal evaluation, decision about what to do: *She made a judgment to buy a new car.* **4 to have good judgment:** the ability to decide well and correctly: *She does excellent work because she has good judgment on what is important and what is not important.*

judg·men·tal /dʒʌdʒ'mɛntl/ *adj.* quick to make decisions about s.o. or s.t., usu. negative: *Don't be so judgmental; today is his first day on the job.*

Judg·ment Day *n.* **1** in some religions, the end of the world, the day when God judges all people as good or bad **2** *fig.*the day when a very important event takes place: *Tomorrow is judgment day for me because I will know whether I passed my final exams.*

ju·di·cial /dʒu'dɪʃəl/ *adj.* related to laws, law courts, and judges: *The judicial system settles arguments between people.* -adv. **judicially.**

ju·di·ci·ar·y /dʒu'dɪʃi,ɛri, -'dɪʃəri/ *n.* **-ies 1** the court system: *The judiciary is a branch of government.* **2** judges as a group

ju·di·cious /dʒu'dɪʃəs/ *adj.frml.* showing good sense, *(syn.)* wise: *She made a judicious* *decision to save money for her old age.* -adv. **judiciously.**

ju·do /ˈʤudoʊ/ *n.* [U] a type of self-defense that uses one's body, a modern type of jujitsu: *Judo can be used to defend oneself. See:* jujitsu.

judo

jug /ʤʌg/ *n.* a container for liquid with a handle: *She put a jug of milk on the table.*

jug·ger·naut /ˈʤʌgərˌnɔt/ *n.* a great, unstoppable force: *That army is a juggernaut that crushes its enemies.*

jug·gle /ˈʤʌgəl/ *v.* **-gled, -gling, -gles 1** *lit.* to throw and catch two or more objects in the air quickly: *He juggled five tennis balls.* **2** *fig.*to deal with many things at the same time: *She juggled six college classes and a job.* **3** *fig.*to change s.t. in order to give a false impression or to cheat: *He juggled the company's accounts to show a profit.* **4** *fig.*to put things in a different order, such as to change meeting times: *I juggled my schedule in order to see a surprise visitor.*

jug·gler /ˈʤʌglər/ *n.* a person who juggles for entertainment: *Jugglers perform in a circus.*

juggler

jug·head /ˈʤʌgˌhɛd/ *n.infrml.fig.* a stupid person: *That jughead sent our baggage to the wrong hotel.*

jug·u·lar /ˈʤʌgyələr/ *adj.* **1** related to the throat and neck: *the jugular vein* **2 to go for the jugular:** to try to destroy s.o. or s.t.: *A wolf goes for the jugular to kill a deer.*

jug·u·lar vein *n.* the large neck vein: *Jugular veins return blood from the head to the heart.*

juice /ʤus/ *n.* [C;U] **1** the liquid in fruits, vegetables, or meat: *orange juice* **2** *slang* gas, electricity, etc.: *There is no juice in that electrical wire.*

juic·er /ˈʤusər/ *n.* a machine used to make juice from fruit: *She put some oranges in the juicer.*

juic·y /ˈʤusi/ *adj.* **-ier, -iest 1** full of juice, (*syn.*) succulent: *He bit into a juicy pear.* **2** *fig.* causing embarrassment, (*syn.*) scandalous: *Newspapers love to print juicy stories about movie stars.*

ju·jit·su or **jiu·jit·su** /ʤuˈʤɪtsu/ *n.* [U] a Japanese way of fighting in self-defense: *Jujitsu uses an opponent's movements and body weight to the fighter's advantage. See:* judo.

juke·box /ˈʤukˌbɑks/ *n.* **-boxes** a machine that plays recorded music: *If you put four quarters in this jukebox, you can choose three songs.*

ju·lep /ˈʤuləp/ *n.* a sweet alcoholic drink, (*syn.*) mint julep: *Juleps have mint leaves and bourbon whiskey in them.*

Ju·ly /ʤuˈlaɪ, ʤə-/ *n.* the seventh month of the year, between June and August: *In the USA, Independence Day is July 4.*

jum·ble /ˈʤʌmbəl/ *v.* **-bled, -bling, -bles 1** to mix things up, (*syn.*) to disarrange: *He jumbled the pages in the report.* **2** to confuse: *He does not understand; he has the instructions all jumbled up.*
—*n.* a mess: *He has a jumble of papers on his desk.*

jum·bo /ˈʤʌmboʊ/ *adj.* very large, huge: *Jumbo jets carry hundreds of people.*

jump /ʤʌmp/ *v.* **1** to push one's feet against the ground to go into the air, (*syns.*) to leap, spring: *The basketball player jumped up to catch the ball.* **2** to go down, descend: *She jumped off/down from the horse and walked away.||There was a fire in the building, and the man jumped out of the window.* **3** to go up quickly and suddenly: *The price of oil jumped when the war started.* **4** to make a quick movement when one is frightened suddenly: *I jumped when I heard the gunshot.* **5** *fig.* to follow orders, obey immediately: *He jumps when the boss gives an order.* **6** to jump horses (over fences, streams, etc.) **7** *fig.* to attack s.o. without warning: *A thief jumped me yesterday and took all my money.* **8** *phrasal v. insep.* **to jump at s.o. or s.t.: a.** to attack: *The guard dog jumped at the stranger.* **b.** to accept s.t. eagerly: *When she was offered a new job, she jumped at the chance/opportunity and took it immediately.* **9** *fig.infrml.* **to jump down s.o.'s throat:** to answer s.o. angrily before he or she has finished speaking **10** *phrasal v. insep.* **to jump on s.o.:** to speak angrily to s.o., criticize severely: *Her father jumped on her when he learned she had failed her exam.* **11** *fig.* **to jump out of one's skin:** to be frightened suddenly, to be startled: *When the alarm bell started to ring, I nearly jumped out of my skin.* **12** *fig.* **to jump to (the) conclusion:** to make a decision about s.t. quickly and without thinking carefully: *She jumped to the conclusion that the boy was crying, but he only had s.t. in his eye.*
—*n.* **1** an increase: *There was a big jump in prices.* **2 to get the jump on s.o. or s.t.:** to do s.t. faster than s.o. else: *Our company got the jump on our competitors by getting our product into the market first.*

jump·er /ˈʤʌmpər/ *n.* **1** a sleeveless dress worn over other clothes: *She wore a blue jumper over a white shirt.* **2** a person or horse that jumps

jump·er ca·ble *n.* a thick wire that transfers electricity from a live car battery to help start a dead one: *I used a jumper cable to start my friend's car. See:* jumpstart.

jump·ing /'ʤʌmpɪŋ/ *n.* [U] **1** (in sports) jumping out of a plane with a parachute **2** horse jumping: *Some horse riding contests include jumping.*
—*adj.infrml. fig.* lively, exciting: *After the band started to play, the nightclub was a jumping place.*

jump·ing bean *n.* a bean that moves because a live insect is inside it: *Children have fun playing with Mexican jumping beans.*

jump·ing-off place *n.* a meeting location, a place where people gather to move off as a group: *Soldiers gathered on the beach as a jumping-off place for their attack.*

jump rope *n.* a strong cord, often with handles, used for recreation or exercise: *Children have fun playing with a jump rope.*

jump seat *n.* a small seat that folds down in a limousine or airplane: *An airline attendant sits in a jump seat as the plane is landing.*

jump·start /'ʤʌmp,stɑrt/ *v.* to start a car by pushing it or by using a jumper cable
—*n. fig.* **to give s.o. or s.t. a jumpstart:** to help s.t. or s.o. get started: *The teacher gave her students a jumpstart on their homework by doing the first two problems for them.*

jump·suit *n.* light, one-piece clothing that covers the entire body from neck to ankle: *She wears a jumpsuit because it is comfortable.*

jump·y /'ʤʌmpi/ *adj.* **-ier, -iest** nervous, (*syn.*) jittery: *She is very jumpy today because she's worried about her sick father.*

junc·tion /'ʤʌŋkʃən/ *n.* a place where two roads or railroad lines meet: *The train stopped at the junction.*

junc·ture /'ʤʌŋktʃər/ *n.* **1** a point in time, esp. a turning point **2 at this juncture:** at this important time: *Our store is doing well, and at this juncture we want to hire more people.*

June /ʤun/ *n.* the sixth month of the year, between May and July: *My birthday is in June.*

jun·gle /'ʤʌŋgəl/ *n.* **1** a hot, humid area with many trees and plants close together: *He visited the jungles of Guatemala.* **2** *fig.* a crowded and highly dangerous place: *This city is so full of crime that it is a jungle.*

jun·ior /'ʤunyər/ *adj.* **1** abbreviated as **Jr.** to show that the son has the same first and last names as his father: *Philip Jones, Jr. is the son of Philip Jones, Sr.* **2** with fewer years of service: *He is a junior employee.*
—*n.* a student in his or her third year (out of four years) of college or high school: *Phil is a junior in high school. See:* freshman.

Jun·ior Cham·ber of Com·merce *n. See:* Jaycees.

jun·ior col·lege *n.* in the USA, a two-year college that offers the first two years of a four-year curriculum along with other courses of study: *My son attends Santa Rosa Junior College.*

jun·ior high school *n.* **1** in USA, usu. grades seven through nine in a 12-year curriculum **2** a building used as a junior high school: *Our 13-year-old son goes to Kennedy Junior High School. See:* grade school, secondary school.

jun·ior var·si·ty *n.* **-ties** a team that plays at an easier level of competition than varsity: *Last year, she played soccer on the junior varsity.*

ju·ni·per /'ʤunəpər/ *n.* types of bushes and shrubs with gray berries: *Junipers have berries that smell good.*

junk (1) /ʤʌŋk/ *n.* [U] **1** items no longer valuable or useful to their owners: *Their yard is full of junk, such as old refrigerators and broken lamps.* **2** poorly made, cheap items: *That store only sells junk.* **3** *fig.* worthless ideas, nonsense **4** *slang* illegal drugs, esp. heroin

junk (2) *n.* a type of Chinese boat

jun·ket /'ʤʌŋkɪt/ *n.* a trip or tour, esp. one made by a politician at government expense: *The politician went on a junket to England.*

junk food *n.* [U] food that tastes good but is bad for your health: *He eats junk food, such as potato chips and ice cream.*

junk·ie or **junk·y** /'ʤʌŋki/ *n.slang* **-ies 1** s.o. who cannot stop taking an illegal drug, (*syn.*) a drug addict: *Some junkies take heroin.* **2** a person who very much likes s.t. that is not good for him or her: *a fast-food junkie*

junk mail *n.* [U] advertising pieces (flyers, brochures) selling things not asked for: *Some people find junk mail annoying.*

junk·yard /'ʤʌŋk,yard/ *n.* **1** a business that re-sells unwanted items, esp. car parts and other items made of metal **2** a place where people leave their junk **3** *fig.* an untidy, messy place: *His garage is so full of old furniture that it looks like a junkyard.*

jun·ta /'hʊntə, 'ʤʌntə/ *n.* a group of military officers that rules a country, usu. after a takeover of the government: *The junta rules the country by military law.*

Ju·pi·ter /'ʤupətər/ *n.* the fifth planet from the sun: *Jupiter is the largest planet in the solar system.*

ju·ris·dic·tion /,ʤʊrɪs'dɪkʃən/ *n.* [C;U] **1** the right or the authority to say what the law means and require that it be obeyed: *The Supreme Court holds jurisdiction over lower court decisions.* **2** a specific area of such authority: *The city police have jurisdiction only in the city where they work.*

ju·ris·pru·dence /,ʤʊrɪs'prudns/ *n.* [U] the study of law: *Lawyers study jurisprudence in law school.*

ju·rist /'ʤʊrɪst/ *n.* s.o. who has studied the law, such as a judge or lawyer: *Mr. Smith is a jurist, first as a lawyer and now as a judge.*

ju·ror /ˈʤʊrər/ n. a person who serves on a jury to decide the guilt or innocence of a person, business, or institution: *The jurors in a trial meet in the jury room to make their decision.*

ju·ry /ˈʤʊri/ n. **-ries 1** a group of usu. 12 citizens who are asked to sit in a court of law, listen to information about the problem or crime, receive instructions from the judge, and decide the guilt or innocence of the person, business, or institution (defendant) on trial: *The jury decided that the defendant was not guilty.* **2** a group of people who judge a competition: *The jury gave her painting first prize.*

ju·ry du·ty n. the duty of a citizen to act as a juror when called and chosen to do so by a court of law: *I was called for jury duty, and I will have to go for a week. See:* juror.

just (1) /ʤʌst; *weak form* ʤəst/ adv. **1** a very short time ago: *The train just left.* **2** exactly, perfectly: *The cake was cooked just right; it is delicious.*‖*He arrived just at two o'clock.* **3** at this particular moment: *We're just having dinner* (or) *just about to have dinner; can you call later?* **4** barely, only: *I have just enough money to pay the bills and nothing else.* **5** by a little bit, by a moment of time: *You just missed him; he left five minutes ago.*‖ *We arrived just in time to catch the airplane.* **6** only, simply: *I want to make just a brief statement* (or) *I just want to make a brief statement; you can find all the details in the report.* **7** at a short distance: *The store is just across the street.* **8** maybe, possibly: *I may just want to go on vacation, but I haven't decided yet.* **9 just about:** almost, nearly: *Can you wait a minute? I have just about finished my homework.* **10 just as: a.** exactly the same as: *Leave the kitchen just as clean as you found it.* **b.** when: *Just as we arrived at the station, the train was leaving.* **11 just now:** at this moment: *The baby is sleeping just now.*

just (2) /ʤʌst/ adj. **1** fair and reasonable: *She is a just person.* **2** well deserved: *The criminal was given a just punishment.* **3** s.t. that should be done, (syn.) worthy: *Feeding the poor is a just cause.* **4** *fig.* **just deserts** /dɪˈzɜrts/ morally deserved punishment: *The criminal got his just desserts by being sent to jail for a long time.*

jus·tice /ˈʤʌstɪs/ n. [U] **1** the law when it is applied or carried out in a fair way, fairness: *The judge seeks justice for everyone.* **2** *fig.* **to do justice to:** to do s.t. well, the right way: *He* has two jobs, but he cannot do justice to them both.

jus·tice of the peace n. **-tices** a low-level official who can marry people, judge small offenses (such as driving too fast), and send more serious crimes to higher courts: *My wife and I were married by a justice of the peace.*

jus·ti·fi·able /ˈʤʌstəˌfaɪəbəl, ˌʤʌstəˈfaɪ-/ adj. **1** having a good reason for doing s.t., (syn.) valid: *Spending a lot of time on doing a good job is justifiable.* **2** lawful, (syn.) ethical **-adv. justifiably.**

jus·ti·fi·ca·tion /ˌʤʌstəfəˈkeɪʃən/ n. [U] **1** having a good reason for doing s.t.: *We have justification for moving to a larger house, because this house is too small for us.* **2** proof that an action is not against the law: *The police officer shot the man with justification because the man shot at him first.*

jus·ti·fy /ˈʤʌstəˌfaɪ/ v. **-fied, -fying, -fies 1** to give acceptable reasons for an action: *He justified buying a car by showing how useful it would be.* **2** not to blame s.o., (syn.) to absolve: *The law justifies killing s.o. to defend oneself.* **3** to line up typewritten words so that each line is the same length: *to justify a page on both the left and right sides*

jut /ʤʌt/ v. **jutted, jutting, juts** to stick out or rise sharply: *Mountain peaks jut into the sky.*

jute /ʤut/ n. a plant woven into a type of thread and used to make ropes and sacks: *Coffee sacks are made of jute.*

ju·ve·nile /ˈʤuvəˌnaɪl, -nl/ adj. **1** childlike, (syn.) immature: *The actions of some adults are juvenile.* **2** related to young people: *The 15-year-old thief was sent to juvenile court.*
—n. a youth or child, esp. one under the age of 16: *Juveniles must have an adult to take care of them.*

USAGE NOTE: "Young adult" is a more common way fo referring to people aged 12-18: *My 14-year old daughter reads books from the young adult section of the library.*

ju·ve·nile de·lin·quent n. a youth, usu. under the age of 16, who has done an illegal act: *Juvenile delinquents have painted obscene words on the school walls.*

jux·ta·pose /ˈʤʌkstəˌpoʊz, ˌʤʌkstəˈpoʊz/ v. **-posed, -posing, -poses** to place side-by-side, esp. for comparison: *She juxtaposed two dresses to decide which one she liked better.*
—n. **juxtaposition** /ˌʤʌkstəpəˈzɪʃən/.

J

K,k

K, k /keɪ/ n. **K's, k's** or **Ks, ks 1** the 11th letter of the English alphabet **2** *sing.infrml.* 1,000: *That house costs $100K* (or) *$100k ($100,000).* **3** (in computers) *abbr. of* kilobyte: *He has an old computer with 640k of memory.* **4** kilometer: *She entered a 10k road race.*

ka·lei·do·scope /kə'laɪdə,skoʊp/ n. **1** a toy you look into, made of a small tube in which mirrors and colored pieces of glass are used to make patterns: *If you turn the tube of the kaleidoscope, you can make the patterns change.* **2** *fig.* s.t. with many bright and changing colors: *During the fall, the leaves in New England are a beautiful kaleidoscope of orange, red, and brown.*

kan·ga·roo /,kæŋgə-'ru/ n. **-roos** a two-legged animal from Australia that hops very fast and has a long tail: *Baby kangaroos live in a pocket or "pouch" on their mothers' stomachs.*

kangaroo

kangaroo court *n.fig.* an illegal court quickly set up to punish s.o.: *A person judged by a kangaroo court will not be treated fairly.*

ka·put /kɑ'pʊt, kə-/ *adj.infrml.* **1** not working, (*syn.*) broken: *Our refrigerator is kaput, and all the food is getting warm.*

kar·at /'kærət/ n. a unit of measurement of pure gold; one karat equals 1/24th of the total weight of the object: *Pure gold is 24 karat gold, but an 18 karat gold ring has 18 karats of gold and 6 karats of another metal mixed in.* See: carat.

ka·ra·te /kə'rɑti/ n. [U] a traditional Asian way of fighting: *He used karate to defend himself from the thieves who attacked him.*

kar·ma /'kɑrmə/ *n.fig.* **1** [C;U] in Buddhism and Hinduism, the total effect of one's behavior during one's life: *If you have done good things, your karma will be good.* **2** [U] *infrml.* a feeling caused by a person, place, or situation: *People enjoy being around her because she's nice; she has good karma.*

kay·ak /'kaɪ,yæk/ *n.v.* **1** a light, narrow, covered Eskimo boat: *There is an opening in the middle of a <n.> kayak where one person can sit and paddle.* **2** a store-bought variety of this boat, usu. made from fiberglass: *In the summer, we <v.> kayak on rivers and lakes. -n.* **kayaking**.

kayak

keel /kil/ n. **1** a strong piece of metal or wood that runs along the bottom of a boat and supports its sides: *The keel of our boat hit a rock when we were sailing in shallow water.* **2** *fig.* **on an even keel:** stable, working well: *We are so busy that we had to hire more workers to keep our office on an even keel.*
—v. *phrasal v. insep.* **to keel over: a.** *fig.*to fall down, (*syn.*) to collapse: *The poor man keeled over from a heart attack.* **b.** to turn over, (*syn.*) to capsize: *The sailboat keeled over in the wind.*

keen /kin/ *adj.* **-er, -est 1** intelligent, (*syn.*) shrewd: *She has a keen mind (intellect, wit, etc.).* **2** fine-edged, sharp: *That knife has a keen edge.* **3** strong, (*syn.*) intense: *She has a keen desire to get a job with our company.* **4** *infrml.* **to be keen on:** to desire greatly: *I am keen on going to the party tonight. -adv.* **keenly**.

keep /kip/ v. **kept** /kɛpt/ , **keeping, keeps 1** to save s.t. for oneself, (*syn.*) to retain: *I kept $20 for myself and gave $10 to my friend.* **2** to put away, (*syn.*) to store: *He keeps his tools in his garage.‖She keeps her money in a savings account.* **3** to keep alive and healthy, (*syn.*) to raise: *That farmer keeps chickens and cattle.* **4** to maintain, care for: *He keeps his clothes very clean.* **5** to write down information, (*syn.*) to maintain records: *She kept a diary of what she did every day.* **6** to continue doing s.t., stay in the same place or condition: *He keeps working while the children play.* **7** not to tell s.t.: *She kept her marriage (a secret) from her parents.* **8** to stop s.t. from happening, (*syn.*) to prevent: *He kept his son from falling into the lake.* **9** to stay fresh: *Put the milk in the refrigerator to*

472

keep it from spoiling. **10 to keep at it:** to continue doing s.t., (*syn.*) to persist: *She is an excellent worker; she keeps at it day after day.* **11** *phrasal v. insep.* **to keep at (s.o. or s.t.):** to ask s.o. to do s.t. repeatedly, (*syn.*) to nag: *The mother kept after him until he cleaned his room.* **12** *phrasal v. insep.* **to keep at (s.o. or s.t.):** **a.** *See:* keep after. **b. s.t.:** to continue doing s.t., (*syn.*) to persist: *She is an excellent student; she keeps at her assignments day after day.||She keeps at them.* **13** *phrasal v. sep.* **to keep s.t. back:** to refuse to tell or give s.t., (*syn.*) to withhold: *He kept back the whole story because he didn't want to offend us.||He kept it back.* **14** *phrasal v. sep.* **to keep s.o. or s.t. down:** **a.** to control, prevent from spreading or increasing: *Doctors are trying to keep down the epidemic.||They are keeping it down.* **b.** to keep in a degraded state, (*syn.*) to oppress: *I think management is keeping down some of the best workers at this factory.||They are keeping them down.* **15 to keep house:** to be responsible for the cooking, cleaning, etc. in s.o.'s home: *He keeps house for the family.* **16** *phrasal v. insep.* **to keep on s.t.:** to continue to do s.t., esp. despite difficulties, (*syn.*) to persevere: *She kept on driving, even though she didn't know where she was.* **17** *phrasal v. sep.* **to keep s.o. or s.t. out:** to prevent from entering or joining: *We had a hard time keeping strangers out of our yard.* **18** *fig.* **to keep one's head above water:** to barely be able to do s.t., (*syn.*) to struggle to do s.t.: *I have a great deal of work, but I manage to keep my head above water.* **19 to keep one's sanity:** to stay calm, in control: *I have so much work to do that it's difficult to keep my sanity.* **20 to keep safe:** to avoid harm: *The enemy invaded the city, but we kept safe by hiding from them.* **21 to keep the ball rolling:** to make sure that s.t. continues to do well: *You're doing well in school, so keep the ball rolling by studying hard.* **22 to keep the books:** to work as a bookkeeper, writing down how a company spends its money: *He keeps the books for a small business.* **23 to keep the faith:** to remain dedicated, to not give up: *I have to leave you now, but keep the faith while I'm away.* **24 to keep to oneself:** to avoid others: *She is very shy and keeps to herself most of the time.* **25** *phrasal v.* **to keep up:** **a.** *insep.* **with s.t.:** to stay equal with: *You must keep up with your work so that it is finished on time.* **b.** *sep.* **s.t.:** to maintain in good condition: *We keep our house up by having things fixed when they break.* **c.** to continue doing s.t., either good or bad: *You are doing wonderful work; keep it up!* **26 to keep well:** to wish that s.o. stays in good health: *I'll see you next week; until then, keep well.* **27** *infrml.* **to keep your eyes peeled:** to watch for s.o. or s.t., stay alert: *Our friend should arrive any minute, so keep your eyes*

peeled for her. **28** *infrml.* **to keep your nose clean:** to avoid trouble, to remain honest: *When he left for college, his mother told him to keep his nose clean and to stay away from trouble.*

—*n.* **to earn one's keep:** to pay for the cost of meals and a room: *He earned his keep by cleaning the house.*

—*adv.* **for keeps: 1** forever, permanently: *She has left her boyfriend for keeps.* **2** seriously, with great desire: *Our team is trying hard to win; they are playing for keeps.*

keep·er /'kipər/ *n.* **1** a person in charge of s.t.: *A goal keeper stops the ball from going into the goal.* **2** a person paid to take care of s.t. (a house, park, etc.): *A grounds keeper cuts the grass and keeps the flowers healthy.*

keep·ing /'kipɪŋ/ *n.* [U] **1** care, control: *He left his gold coins in the bank's keeping.* **2** agreement, accord **3 in keeping with:** right for the situation: *In keeping with the blue color of his room, he bought a blue table.*

keep·sake /'kip,seɪk/ *n.* s.t. kept because it reminds of a loved one or an enjoyable event, (*syn.*) a memento: *That bracelet is a keepsake from her husband.*

keg /kɛg/ *n.* a small barrel made of metal or wood: *He bought a keg of beer for the party.*

kelp /kɛlp/ *n.* [U] large, brown plants that grow below the sea: *People and animals can eat kelp.*

kel·vin /'kɛlvɪn/ *n.* [U] a unit of temperature measurement: *Water freezes at 273 degrees kelvin (273 K).*

ken·nel /'kɛnəl/ *n.* a place where dogs are kept, usu. while their owners are away: *When I go on vacation, I put my dog in a kennel.*

kept /kɛpt/ *v.past tense & past part. of* keep: **1** held, retained for oneself: *He kept the money that he found on the street.* **2 a kept woman** or **man:** a person supported by another: *Since he only stays with her because she is rich, he is a kept man.*

ker·chief /'kɜrtʃɪf, -'tʃif/ *n.* a small, square scarf, usu. made of cotton: *The cowboy wore a kerchief around his neck.*

ker·nel /'kɜrnəl/ *n.* **1** a seed, esp. one that can be eaten: *a kernel of corn (wheat, rice, etc.)* **2** *fig.* a bit, (*syn.*) a trace: *There is not a kernel of truth in what she says.*

ker·o·sene /'kɛrə,sin, ,kɛrə'sin/ *n.* [U] a thin, colorless oil made from petroleum and used for fuel: *People used kerosene lamps before the light bulb was invented.*

ketch·up /'kɛtʃəp, 'kætʃ-/ *n.* [U] *var. of* catsup, a thick, red sauce made from tomatoes and spices: *He poured ketchup on his hamburger.*

ket·tle /'kɛtl/ *n.* **1** a large cooking pot, usu. with a lid: *The water in the tea kettle is boiling.* **2** *fig.* **a fine kettle of fish:** an awkward

K

situation that is difficult to fix: *We just spent the last of our money fixing the car and now it has broken down again. That's a fine kettle of fish!*

ket·tle·drum /'kɛtl,drʌm/ *n.* a large bowl-shaped copper or brass drum tightly covered with a thin material (parchment): *The kettledrum sounds like thunder when you hit it hard.*

key /ki/ *n.* **1** a thin piece of metal used to lock or unlock a door, start or stop an engine, etc.: *I opened the front door with my key.* **2** *fig.* the most important part of s.t.: *The key to success is hard work.* **3** a written guide that explains the meaning of s.t.: *This key explains how to read the symbols on the map.* **4** in music, a group of notes related to and named after the lowest note in the group: *That song is written in the key of B flat.* **5** a part of a machine or musical instrument that is pressed down to make it work: *She pressed a computer key and typed a letter.* **6** a small low island: *We went camping in the Florida Keys last summer.*
—*v.* **1** to test musical instruments to make sure that they will sound good together: *Musicians in the band keyed their guitars before playing.* **2 to be keyed up:** to be excited or nervous: *She is always keyed up before a test.*
—*adj.* very important, essential: *Cotton is a key industry in the South.*

key·board /'kibɔrd/ *n.* a row or rows of keys (on a piano, computer, etc.): *The row of black and white keys on a piano is called a keyboard.*
—*v.* to type information on a keyboard: *He keyboarded his report into the computer.*

keyboards

key·hole /'ki,hoʊl/ *n.* the hole for the key in a lock: *In some old locks, the keyholes are so large that you can look through them.*

key·note address /'ki,noʊt/ *n.* **-es** the first speech, made by the guest of honor, describing the main ideas of the event: *Our business college asked a successful businesswoman to give the keynote address at our graduation.*

key ring *n.* a ring on which keys are kept: *I keep my car keys on a key ring.*

key·stone /'ki,stoʊn/ *n.* the top, center stone in an arch: *The keystone in an arch keeps the other stones in place.*

key·stroke /'ki,stroʊk/ *n.* **1** the pressing down of a key on a machine **2** a basic unit of measurement of information going into a computer: *Our typist does 20,000 keystrokes a day.*

khak·i /'kæki/ *adj.n.* [C;U] the tan or light brown color typical of khaki cloth: *She is wearing <adj.> khaki pants.*

—*n.pl.* **khakis** light brown, loose-fitting pants that men and women wear when dressing casually: *My 20-year-old brother often wears a blue shirt, khakis, and sneakers.*

USAGE NOTE: *Khakis* are worn by Americans of all ages on informal occasions, but are especially popular among college students and other young people. A typical college student's wardrobe includes jeans, T-shirts, sweatshirts, sweaters, and khakis. Today some businesses encourage employees to dress casually on Fridays, and many people wear *khakis* to the office on these days.

---

kib·butz /kɪ'bʊts/ *n.* a farm in Israel where a group of people live and work together: *My sister and her family live on a kibbutz.*

kib·itz /'kɪbɪts/ *v.infrml.* **-itzes** to look over the shoulder of others and give unwanted advice: *My friend kibitzes when we play cards.*

ki·bosh /'kaɪ,bɑʃ, kɪ'bɑʃ/ *n.sing.infrml.* **1** a halt, a stop **2 to put the kibosh on:** to put a stop to s.t.: *When his mother learned how dangerous her son's plans were, she put the kibosh on them.*

kick /kɪk/ *n.* **1** a blow with the foot or feet: *He gave the football a kick.* **2** strength, force: *That coffee is strong; it has a real kick.* **3** a sudden, hard move backwards, (*syn.*) a recoil: *Be careful, this rifle has a strong kick.* **4** *infrml.fig.* **for kicks** or **just for kicks:** just for fun: *We go to Las Vegas once a year just for kicks.* **5** *infrml.fig.* **to get a kick out of s.t.:** to enjoy doing s.t.: *He gets a kick out of listening to rock music (seeing a good movie, eating hamburgers, etc.).*
—*v.* **1** to strike with the foot or feet: *The football player kicked the ball down the field.* **2** *phrasal v. sep.* **to kick s.o. or s.t. around: a.** to treat s.o. badly, (*syn.*) to abuse: *The older men kick the boy around by giving him all the dirty jobs to do.* **b.** to talk about s.t. informally: *We kicked the idea of moving to California around, but we were never serious about it.* **3 to kick back: a.** *sep. s.t.:* to pay money to s.o., often in a dishonest situation, (*syn.*) to bribe: *If you want my company to buy paper only from you, you will have to kick back 7 percent of what we pay you.* ||*You will have to kick it back.* **b.** to relax by stopping work: *She likes to kick back and read the newspaper when she gets home from work.* **4** *phrasal v. sep.* **to kick s.t. in:** to join others in giving to s.o. or s.t., (*syn.*) to contribute: *Each of the four children kicked in $10 to buy their mother a gift.* ||*They kicked it in.* **5** *phrasal v. insep.* **to kick off:** to start s.t., esp. a game: *The team captain kicked off to the opposing team.* **6** *phrasal v. sep.* **to kick s.o. out:** to throw s.o. out, (*syn.*) to eject: *Our landlord kicked out the people downstairs because they weren't paying*

the rent.||He kicked them out. **7** *infrml.fig.* **to kick the bucket:** to die: *The old man finally kicked the bucket last year.* **8 to kick the habit:** to stop doing s.t. that is bad for you, such as using drugs, alcohol, or tobacco: *He smoked cigarettes for thirty years, but finally kicked the habit.* **9** *phrasal v. insep.* **to kick up: a.** to start hurting, become aggravated: *My arthritis has kicked up again; it's painful.* **b. s.t.:** to make trouble: *When she discovered that her food was burnt, she kicked up a fuss by shouting at the cook.* **11** *infrml.fig.* **to kick up one's heels:** to spend a lot of money having a good time: *The couple flew to an island hotel and kicked up their heels for a week.* *-n.* **kicker.**

kick·back /ˈkɪkˌbæk/ *n.* money paid dishonestly to a person, usu. in a business or government situation, *(syn.)* a bribe: *If your company buys all of its office supplies from me, I'll give you a kickback of 5 percent of all the money your company pays me.*

kick·off /ˈkɪkˌɔf/ *n.* **1** the kicking of a football to start play **2** *fig.* the beginning of s.t., esp. an exciting project: *Every fall, the football players celebrate the kickoff of a new season.*

kid /kɪd/ *n.* **1** *infrml.fig.* a child: *That family has three kids.* **2** a young goat
—*v.* **kidded, kidding, kids** to make jokes, *(syn.)* to tease: *She often kids him about his bright red hair.*
—*adj. infrml.* younger: *She tells her kid brother what to do.*

USAGE NOTE: Adults in the USA often refer to young people as *kids* and college students as *college kids* in a friendly way.

kid·do /ˈkɪdoʊ/ *n.infrml. pl.* **-dos** or **-does** a good friend: *How are you today, kiddo?*

kid·dy /ˈkɪdi/ *n.infrml.* **-dies** a child: *Look at all the little kiddies playing on the playground.*
—*adj.* related to children: *They play kiddy games, like jump rope or playing with dolls.*

kid glove *n.* **1** fine gloves made of leather from the skin of young goats (kidskin) **2** *fig.* **to handle** or **treat s.o. with kid gloves:** to treat s.o. with special care, delicately: *She is very rich and everyone handles her with kid gloves.*

kid·nap /ˈkɪdˌnæp/ *v.* **-napped, -naps** to illegally take s.o. away by force, and usu. to demand money for that person's safe return: *A young woman kidnapped the baby while the baby's mother was not looking.||The story of the <n.> kidnapping was in all the newspapers. -n.* **kidnapping.**

kid·ney /ˈkɪdni/ *n.* one of the two organs that clean our blood and are located in the lower back near the hips

kidney bean *n.* a red, oval-shaped bean: *People often put kidney beans in a spicy meat dish called chili.*

kid or **kids' stuff** *n.infrml.* a task or entertainment meant for children, not adults: *That movie is so childish; its kids' stuff.*

kill /kɪl/ *v.* **1** to cause the death of any living thing: *Soldiers killed the enemy.* **2** to stop, *(syn.)* to cancel: *She killed our weekend plans to go to the beach when she decided she wanted to stay home.* **3** *fig.* to hurt badly: *My back (tooth, foot, etc.) is killing me.* **4** *fig.* to cause to laugh loudly: *Your jokes are killing me.* **5** to use s.t. up, esp. time: *It's 7:00; we have two hours to kill before the movie starts at 9:00.||He killed the whole bottle of wine in two hours.* **6** *phrasal v. sep.* **to kill s.o.** or **s.t. off:** to kill in large numbers, usu. one at a time: *The hot summer killed off my roses.||It killed them off.*
—*n.* an animal that has been killed: *A lion eats its kill.*

kill·er /ˈkɪlər/ *n.* **1** s.o. who kills other people, *(syn.)* a murderer: *A killer is on the loose in the city.* **2** an animal that attacks others, *(syn.)* a predator: *Lions are killers.* **3** a disease that kills people: *Cancer is a killer.* **4** *fig.* a difficult task or situation: *He has a job that is a killer; it's so difficult.*

kill·ing /ˈkɪlɪŋ/ *n.* **1** [U] the act of ending a life: *In a war, the killing continues day after day.* **2** [C;U] murder: *The killing of the young woman happened yesterday.* **3** *fig.* **to make a killing:** to make a lot of money very quickly: *He makes a killing selling umbrellas when it rains.*

kill·joy /ˈkɪlˌdʒɔɪ/ *n.* a person who ruins the happiness and fun of others: *At my party, my father shut off the music and sent everyone home. What a killjoy!*

kiln /kɪln, kɪl/ *n.* a special oven used esp. for baking clay objects (pots, vases, etc.): *She put the pot in the kiln for two hours.*

ki·lo /ˈkiloʊ/ *n.* short for kilogram

kil·o·byte /ˈkɪləˌbaɪt/ *n. abbr.* k. approx. 1,000 bytes, a measure of computer memory space: *The size of a computer file can be measured in kilobytes. See:* megabytes.

kil·o·gram /ˈkɪləˌgræm/ *n.* 1,000 grams, or 2.2 pounds (lbs.): *She bought two kilograms (kg)* (or) *kilos of bananas.*

ki·lo·met·er /kɪˈlɑmɪtər, ˈkɪləˌmitər/ *n.* 1,000 meters, or 0.62137 mile: *The distance to the next town is 10 kilometers (km).*

kil·o·watt /ˈkɪləˌwɑt/ *n.* 1,000 watts

kilt /kɪlt/ *n.* a knee-length, plaid skirt worn traditionally by Scottish men: *When he is in Scotland, the Prince of Wales wears a kilt.*

K

kil·ter /ˈkɪltər/ n. [U] **to be out of kilter:** to be out of order, or not working properly: *The clock is not running right; it is out of kilter.*

ki·mo·no /kəˈmoʊnoʊ/ n. **-nos** a long Japanese dress: *Some traditional Japanese women wear colorful, pretty kimonos.*

kin /kɪn/ n.pl. relative: *My mother is my next of kin; my father's dead.*

kind /kaɪnd/ n. **1** a similar type of person or thing: *He has the same kind of leather jacket as mine.* **2 in kind:** to pay with s.t. other than money, such as service, food, etc.: *He fixed my roof and I fixed his car; we paid each other in kind.* **3 kind of:** a little bit, somewhat: *I am kind of tired; let's go home.* **4 to be with one's own kind:** to prefer people similar to oneself: *She is an actor, and she feels most comfortable with her own kind: other actors.*
—adj. **1** friendly, helpful, and generous: *She is very kind to her friends and helps them with their problems.* **2** feeling sorry for those in trouble, (syn.) tenderhearted: *He is kind to lost and hurt animals by taking care of them. -n.* [C;U] **kindness.**

USAGE NOTE: Both *kind of* and *sort of* mean "a little bit" before adjectives: *That restaurant is kind of expensive.*||*His grammar is good, but his intonation is strange, so he's sort of difficult to understand.* The words *fairly* and *rather* mean "moderately": *I got up fairly early, so I had time to eat a good breakfast.* ||*It's rather cool this morning.*

kin·der·gar·ten /ˈkɪndərˌgɑrtn, -ˌgɑrdn/ n. classes that four- and five-year-old children go to the year before the first grade of school: *Our little boy goes to kindergarten.*

kind·heart·ed /ˈkaɪndˌhɑrtɪd/ adj. feeling friendly and helpful toward others, (syn.) compassionate: *She is a kindhearted woman; she takes care of sick neighbors.*

kin·dle /ˈkɪndl/ v. **-dled, -dling, -dles 1** to light a fire: *He used paper to kindle a fire in the stove.* **2** to excite: *His kindness and intelligence kindled love in her heart.*

kind·li·ness /ˈkaɪndlinɪs/ n. [U] kindness and concern for others, (syn.) compassion: *His kindliness toward animals is well known.*

kin·dling /ˈkɪndlɪŋ/ n. [U] s.t. that burns easily (sticks, leaves, paper, etc.) and is used to start a fire: *She started the fire with kindling before adding a big piece of wood.*

kind·ly /ˈkaɪndli/ adj. **-lier, -liest** friendly and gentle: *He is a kindly old man.*
—adv. **1** please: *Would you kindly hold the door for me?* **2 to take kindly to s.t.:** to feel agreeably about: *I do not take kindly to people who scream and shout at me.*

kin·dred /ˈkɪndrɪd/ adj. **1** belonging to the same family or group: *Wolves and dogs are*

kindred species. **2 kindred spirits:** people who have the same interests or goals: *My friend and I are kindred spirits who love books.*

ki·net·ic /kɪˈnɛtɪk/ adj. moving, (syn.) dynamic: *Kinetic art is made of parts that move, such as motors and lights. -adv.* **kinetically.**

kin·folk /ˈkɪnˌfoʊk/ n.pl. one's family, people who are related: *Some people call their relatives "kinfolk."*

king /kɪŋ/ n. **1** the male ruler of a country: *the King of England* **2** the main person (usu. male) in a field of activity: *That actor is the king of the entertainment business.* **3** a playing card with a picture of a king **4** the most important piece in chess -n.[C;U] **kingship.**

king·dom /ˈkɪŋdəm/ n. **1** a country ruled by a king and/or queen: *The Queen of England rules the kingdom of Great Britain.* **2** a group of living things: *the animal kingdom* **3 to blow s.o.** or **s.t. to kingdom come:** to completely and violently destroy: *She pointed a gun at the bottle and blew it to kingdom come.* **4 until kingdom come:** forever, (syn.) for an eternity: *You can work on that job until kingdom come and never get it done.*

king·fish /ˈkɪŋˌfɪʃ/ n. **-fish** or **-fishes 1** a type of fish that lives in the Atlantic Ocean and can be eaten **2** infrml.fig. a powerful person who can influence what others do: *The President is a kingfish in US politics.*

king·fish·er /ˈkɪŋˌfɪʃər/ n. a type of colorful bird: *Kingfishers dive into the water to catch fish.*

king·pin /ˈkɪŋˌpɪn/ n. the most important person in a certain field or area: *He owns several large oil companies and is the kingpin of the oil business.*

king-size /ˈkɪŋˌsaɪz/ or **king-sized** /-ˌsaɪzd/ adj. **1** larger than queen-sized: *A king-sized bed is large enough to hold three people.* **2** larger than the regular size: *He smokes king-sized cigars.*

kink /kɪŋk/ n. **1** a sharp curve or curl in a piece of hair, rope, thread, etc.: *There is a kink in the rope that I can't straighten out.* **2** a sudden tightening of a muscle, (syn.) a spasm: *I have a kink in my leg.* **3** fig. a small problem or difficulty: *My project is almost done, but it still has some kinks in it.* **4 to get** or **to (iron) the kinks out of s.t.: a.** to straighten or stretch s.t. out: *Stretch your arms to get the kinks out of your muscles.* **b.** to remove problems: *There are problems with our new computer system; we need to get the kinks out of it.*

kink·y /ˈkɪŋki/ adj. **-ier, -iest 1** tightly curled, having lots of wiggles: *That man has kinky hair.* **2** infrml. having to do with unusual sexual activities

kin·ship /ˈkɪnˌʃɪp/ n. **1** [U] relationship by blood or marriage: *The two sisters proved their*

kinship by showing their identification cards.
2 [C] a friendship, based esp. on common interests, *(syn.)* a fellowship: *A strong kinship grew between the two children.*

ki·osk /'ki,ɑsk/ *n.* **1** a stand or stall where newspapers or food and drink are sold, esp. in Europe: *I bought a newspaper at the kiosk.* **2** a thick, round pole on which notices, advertisements, etc. can be put up

kis·met /'kɪz,mɛt, -mɪt/ *n.* [U] s.t. that was meant to happen, *(syn.)* destiny: *It was kismet that the couple met, then fell in love.*

kiss /kɪs/ *n.* **-es 1** a touch with the lips to show that one likes or loves s.o. or s.t., or as a sign of greeting, etc.: *He gave her a kiss on the cheek (lips, hand, etc.).* **2** a small candy: *He brought a bag of chocolate kisses.*
—*v.* **kisses 1** to press the lips against s.o. or s.t.: *She kissed the baby's cheek.* **2** to touch lightly: *The wind kissed her hair.* **3 to kiss good-bye: a.** to kiss s.o. as he or she leaves: *Before she left on the airplane, her friend kissed her good-bye.* **b.** *fig.* to think of as lost forever: *When he forgot his wallet on the bus, he kissed the money that was in it good-bye.*

kiss·er /'kɪsər/ *n.* **1** s.o. who kisses: *He's a really good kisser.* **2** *infrml.* the face, esp. the mouth: *The boxer hit his opponent in the kisser.*

kiss of death *n.fig.* an act that ruins or could ruin another event: *Our team dropped the ball in the last few seconds of the game, and that mistake was the kiss of death. We lost.*

kiss·off /'kɪs,ɔf/ *n.* a sudden, harsh way of telling s.o. to leave you alone: *She gave her boyfriend the kissoff. See:* kiss, *v.,* **4.**

kit /kɪt/ *n.* **1** a group of tools, supplies, etc. kept together, often in a box, and used for a certain purpose: *a mechanic's kit, a carpenter's kit, a make-up kit* **2** a group of parts or materials to be put together to make s.t.: *We sell model airplane (car, train, etc) kits.*

kitch·en /'kɪtʃən/ *n.* a room where meals are prepared, usu. having a stove, sink, and refrigerator: *Some kitchens also have a table and chairs where people eat their meals.*

kitch·en·ette /,kɪtʃən'ɛt/ *n.* a small kitchen: *Some hotel rooms have kitchenettes.*

kitch·en·ware /'kɪtʃən,wɛr/ *n.* [U] utensils used for cooking (pots, pans, etc.): *That store is having a sale on kitchenware.*

kite /kaɪt/ *n.v.* a toy made of a light wooden frame covered with brightly colored paper, plastic, etc.: *Children fly <n.> kites in the air for fun.*

kit·ten /'kɪtn/ *n.* a baby cat: *Our cat just gave birth to four kittens.*

kit·ty /'kɪti/ *n.* **-ties 1** *infrml.* a cat **2** money set aside for some purpose: *My wife and I are*

putting money in a vacation kitty, so we can go to Disneyworld.

ki·wi /'kiwi/ *n.* **1** [C] a flightless bird of New Zealand: *The kiwi has brown, hairlike feathers and a long beak.* **2** [C;U] a fruit that is fuzzy and brown on the outside and green on the inside: *Kiwis are a good source of vitamin C.*

KKK *abbr.for* Ku Klux Klan

Klee·nex /'kli,nɛks/ *n.* TM **-nexes** a brand of soft paper tissue: *People use Kleenex to wipe their eyes (nose, glasses, etc.).*

klep·to·ma·ni·a /,klɛptə'meɪniə/ *n.* [U] an uncontrolled desire to steal: *He is always stealing things; I think he has kleptomania. -n.* **kleptomaniac** /,klɛptə'meɪni,æk/.

klutz /klʌts/ *n.infrml.* **klutzes** a clumsy person: *That klutz spilled soup on me.*

knack /næk/ *n.* **to have a knack for: a.** a special talent or ability, but not necessarily a great talent: *She has a knack for painting (cooking, drawing, making people laugh).* **b.** a quick, clever way of doing s.t.: *He has a knack for getting the baby back to sleep; when he holds the baby, she stops crying and falls asleep.*

knap·sack /'næp,sæk/ *n.* a closed bag carried on one's back, *(syn.)* a backpack: *When I go to the beach, I carry my lunch, a book, and a towel in my knapsack.*

knead /nid/ *v.* to press with the fingers and hands: *A baker kneads flour and milk together to make bread dough.*

knee /ni/ *n.* the joint that connects the upper and lower parts of the leg: *She fell and twisted her knee.*
—*v.* **kneed, kneeing, knees** to strike s.o. with the knee: *She kneed him in the stomach.*

knee·cap /'ni,kæp/ *n.* a small movable bone in the front of the knee, *(syn.)* the patella: *He hurt his kneecap when he fell.*

knee-deep *adj.* **1** being in s.t. up to one's knees: *The fisherman was knee-deep in the water.* **2** *fig.* **knee-deep in trouble:** to be in a lot of trouble: *She is going to be knee-deep in trouble when her parents find out where she's been.*

knee-high *adj.* approx. two feet high: *The grass has grown knee-high.*
—*n.pl.* **knee-high socks** or **knee-highs:** a type of stocking that usu. fits up to the knee

kneel /nil/ *v.* **knelt** /nɛlt/ or **kneeled, kneeling, kneels** to place the weight of the body upon the knees: *Gardeners kneel on the ground.*

knell /nɛl/ *n.* the sound of a bell, esp. at a funeral: *The bells tolled a death knell.*

knelt /nɛlt/ *v.past tense & past part. of* kneel

knew /nu/ *v.past tense of* know

knick·ers /'nɪkərz/ *n.pl.* a pair of pants worn from the waist to just below the knee, usu. with long socks: *When he was a boy, he wore knickers to school.*

knick·knack or **nick·nack** /'nɪk,næk/ *n.* an inexpensive decorative object, such as a little animal or vase made of china: *My grandmother keeps knickknacks on tables in her living room.*

knife /naɪf/ *n.* **knives** /naɪvz/ a tool with a handle and sharp blade for cutting things: *He used a knife to cut the vegetables.*
—*v.* **knifed, knifing, knifes** to stab or cut s.o. with a knife: *The murderer knifed the man and ran away.*

knight /naɪt/ *n.* **1** a gentleman who, hundreds of years ago, was a soldier on horseback in the service of another noble (baron, duke, etc.) or a king: *The Knights of the Round Table* **2** a chess piece, usu. with a horse's head
—*v.* to make s.o. a knight: *The King knighted several brave soldiers. See:* chess.

knit /nɪt/ *v.* **knit** or **knitted, knitting, knits** **1** to make clothes by connecting loops of yarn (thick, twisted thread) with long needles: *She knitted socks for her grandson.* **2** to grow together: *He broke his arm and the broken bone knit back together slowly.*
—*n.* **1** [U] the pattern made by knitting: *This sweater has a tight knit.* **2** *n.pl.* **knits:** a type of clothing that is knitted, such as sweaters and socks: *I like to wear knits.* **3 close-knit:** closely related and helpful to each other: *They are a close-knit family who take good care of each other.*

knit·ting /'nɪtɪŋ/ *n.* s.t. being knitted: *Her knitting is stored in a bag.* -*n.* **knitting needle.**

knives /naɪvz/ *n.pl. of* knife

knob /nɑb/ *n.* **1** a round handle, usu. on a door: *He turned the door knob and opened the door.* **2** a bump: *She fell and has a knob on her head now.* -*adj.* **knobby.**

knock /nɑk/ *n.* **1** a light hit, such as a tap with the knuckles or a tool: *He gave a knock on the door.* **2** the sound of a tap: *I hear the sound of a knock at the door.* **3** a cracking, banging sound in a car engine: *That old engine has a knock.* **4** a criticism, (*syn.*) a barb: *She's been getting knocks all day about that ugly hat.* **5** *infrml.fig.* **the school of hard knocks:** to learn from life's difficult experiences: *As a youth, he was in trouble frequently; but he learned from the school of hard knocks and he is a good citizen now.*
—*v.* **1** to hit lightly, as with the knuckles or a tool: *He knocked on the door.* **2** to strike with a sharp, heavy blow: *The worker knocked through a wall with a heavy hammer.* **3** to criticize, (*syn.*) to disparage: *He knocks his company for paying him too little.* **4** to make a cracking, banging sound: *The car's oil ran out and the engine began to knock.* **5 to knock against:** to hit against, (*syn.*) to collide: *She tripped and knocked her head against the wall.* **6** *phrasal v.* **to knock around: a.** *insep.* to

wander: *As a young woman, she knocked around, doing odd jobs all over the country.* **b.** *sep.* **s.o.:** to hit, treat badly, (*syn.*) to abuse: *He worked with rough men, who knocked him around because he was new.* **7** *phrasal v. sep.* **to knock s.t. back:** to drink, usu. alcohol, quickly: *He's really knocking back those drinks.* ‖*He's knocking them back.* **8** *fig.* **to knock dead:** to please very much, often with surprise: *She is a beautiful and talented actress; she knocks her audiences dead.* **9** *fig.* **to knock for a loop:** to make speechless, to shock: *When he heard the bad news, it knocked him for a loop.* **10** *infrml.fig.* **to knock heads:** to criticize in order to persuade s.o.: *Those two people would not listen to me, so I knocked heads and now they do.* **11 to knock into:** to bump, (*syn.*) to collide with: *He slipped and knocked into another person.* **12** *phrasal v.* **to knock off: a.** *insep.* **s.t.:** to stop doing s.t., such as working: *We knocked off work at two o'clock today.* **b.** *sep.* **s.t.:** to make an illegal copy of s.t., (*syn.*) to fake: *They knocked off copies of videotapes of famous movies.* **c.** *sep.* **s.o.:** to kill: *The gangster knocked off his rival.*‖*He knocked him off.* **d.** to rob: *The robber knocked off a bank.* **13 to knock oneself out:** to work very hard: *He knocked himself out by staying up all night to finish the job.* **14** *phrasal v. sep.* **to knock s.o. out: a.** (of drugs, etc.) to cause sleep: *My cold medication knocks me out.* **b.** (in boxing, etc.) to cause s.o. to become unconscious: *After he was knocked out in a fight, he was taken to a hospital.* **c.** to be removed from competition: *We were knocked out of the band contest by a group from Indiana.* **15** *phrasal v. sep.* **to knock over:** to cause to fall down, (*syn.*) to upset: *The baby knocked his cup over and spilled the milk.* **16** *phrasal v. sep.* **to knock s.o.** or **s.t. down:** to cause s.o. to fall on the ground: *The big dog knocked down the little boy.*‖*It knocked him down.* **17** *fig.* **to knock (some) sense into s.o.'s head:** to tell s.o. strongly that what that person is doing is foolish and wrong: *She is going to parties instead of studying; you should knock some sense into her head.* **18** *phrasal v. sep.* **to knock s.t. together:** to build quickly and carelessly: *Those houses were knocked together in only two weeks.* **19** *phrasal v. sep. slang* **to knock s.o. up:** to make a woman pregnant

knockdown-dragout *adj.* related to a long, angry disagreement or fight: *The two men had a knockdown-dragout fight.*

knock·er /'nɑkər/ *n.* a door knocker, usu. pieces of metal hung on a door used to show s.o. is at the door: *She tapped the door knocker to let him know that she had arrived.*

knock-kneed *adj.* having knees that rub together when a person walks: *That knock-kneed man can't run fast.*

knock·off /'nɑk,ɔf/ *n.infrml.* an imitation, usu. a cheap one: *That watch is a knockoff of an expensive one.*

knock·out /'nɑk,aʊt/ *n.* **1** (in boxing) the hitting of an opponent to the floor to end the fight, (*syn.*) a victory *See:* kayo, KO. **2** *infrml.fig.* a very attractive or impressive person: *That lady is an absolute knockout.*

knock·wurst /'nɑk,wɜrst/ *n.* [U] spicy, finely chopped meat stuffed into a casing and sold in sections linked together like a sausage: *Many people like to eat knockwurst with sauerkraut.*

knoll /noʊl/ *n.* a small hill, (*syn.*) a hillock: *The farmer stood on a knoll and looked out over his fields.*

knot /nɑt/ *n.* **1** a fastening made of pieces of thread (rope, wire, etc.) purposely wrapped around each other in tight loops: *She wrapped the box with string and tied it with a knot.* **2** string, etc., twisted and tied in many tight loops, (*syn.*) a tangle: *It's impossible to sew if there are knots in the thread.* **3** a round, dark spot on a tree where a branch used to come out: *There are quite a few knots in the wood of this table.* **4** *infrml.fig.* **to be tied up in knots: a.** to be in a difficult situation, a tangle: *This project is tied up in knots; there are many problems with it.* **b.** to be emotionally upset: *The person responsible for the accident is all tied up in knots; she is sick to her stomach.* **5** *infrml.fig.* **to tie the knot:** to get married: *Those two have been dating for years, and now they're finally tying the knot.*

knot

—*v.* **knotted, knotting, knots** to tie a knot, make s.t. secure so it won't move: *The cowboy knotted the reins of his horse around a tree branch.*

knot·ty /'nɑti/ *adj.* **-tier, -tiest** having many knots: *That cabin is made of knotty pine.*

know /noʊ/ *v.* **knew** /nu/, **known** /noʊn/ **knowing, knows 1** to understand the importance of s.t., (*syn.*) to comprehend: *She knows that she is intelligent, and she uses her mind to solve problems.* **2** to have information about s.t.: *The police know how the robbery happened.* **3** to have met s.o.: *She knows the people who live next door.* **4** to have learned a lot about and to enjoy, (*syn.*) to appreciate s.t.: *He knows fine wines (modern art, old coins, etc.).* **5** *infrml.* **to be in the know:** to be well-informed: *She is always in the know because her friends tell her everything.* **6 to know a thing or two** or **to know one's p's and q's:** to have learned a great deal about a certain area, to be an ex-

pert: *The people in our computer department know their p's and q's; you can ask them about that problem.* **7 to know how to:** to be skilled at: *She knows how to run computers (speak French, fly airplanes, etc.).* **8** *phrasal v. insep.* **to know of:** to be familiar with but not know everything about s.t. or s.o.: *I know of the man, but I have never met him.* **9 to know one's own mind:** to know what one wants: *He knows his own mind; he will not change his decision.* **10 to know right from wrong:** to understand the difference between good and evil: *The boy stole money, but is too young to know right from wrong.* **11 to know s.t. cold:** to have learned everything one can about a subject: *He has been doing that job for twenty years and knows his work cold.*

know-how *n.* [U] the knowledge, skills, and ability to do s.t. well, (*syn.*) expertise: *Our company has the know-how to make great computers.*

know·ing /'noʊɪŋ/ *adj.* having learned a great deal about many things, (*syns.*) knowledgeable, wise: *Everyone asks her questions because she is a knowing person.* **-adv. knowingly.**

know-it-all *n.* a self-important person who thinks he or she knows everything: *He is such a know-it-all that it is impossible to tell him anything.*

know·ledge /'nɑlɪʤ/ *n.* [U] **1** an area of learning: *The study of English (math, history, etc.) is a field of knowledge.* **2** an understanding of s.t. and the ability to use that understanding through study and experience: *She has a knowledge of mechanical things and knows how to fix cars.* **3** information about or familiarity with s.t.: *He has knowledge of the accident and how it happened.* **4 to one's knowledge:** according to the information that one has: *Has he finished the report? To my knowledge, he has.* ‖*Not to my knowledge; I don't think he has.* **5 with my knowledge** or **without my knowledge:** with or without s.o.'s awareness: *She left on vacation without my knowledge, so I don't know where she is.* **-adj. knowledgeable.**

known /noʊn/ *v.past part. of* know
—*adj.* recognized: *He is a known criminal.*

knuck·le /'nʌkəl/ *n.* any of the joints in the finger: *He knocked on the door with his knuckles.* — **1** *phrasal v.* **to knuckle down:** to begin working hard at a task: *She knuckled down and finished her paper quickly.* **2** *phrasal v.* **to knuckle under:** to do what s.o. demands, give in: *When the teacher told the boy to be quiet, he knuckled under and was silent.*

KO /'keɪ'oʊ/ *n. abbr. for* knockout: *The boxing match ended with a tenth round KO.*

K

—*v.* to hit s.o., esp. a boxer, so hard that the person loses consciousness: *The boxer was KOed in the 10th round.*

ko·a·la /kou'ɑlə/ *n.* a small furry animal from Australia that looks like a little bear and lives in trees: *The koala, with its sweet eyes and big ears, is a symbol of Australia.*

Ko·dak /'kou,dæk/ *adj.TM* name of a photographic company: *a Kodak camera, Kodak film*
—*n.TM* a camera made by Eastman Kodak Company: *I bought a Kodak to take pictures on our trip.*

kook /kuk/ *n.infrml.* a person with strange behavior, (*syn.*) a weirdo: *That man acts like a* <*n.*> *kook.*||*He does* <*adj.*> *kooky things like shout nonsense.* -*n.* **kookiness;** -*adj.* **kooky.**

USAGE NOTE: We use terms like *kook, nut,* and *weirdo,* to describe s.o. whose behavior is a little crazy: *He's a real nut about cleanliness; he takes five showers a day.* We use *moron, idiot, fool,* and *jerk* to suggest that s.o. is stupid: *That idiot doesn't know who the President of the country is.*

Ko·ran /kə'ræn, -'rɑn, kɔ-/ *n.* the sacred scrip-

tures of Islam: *Muslims believe that the Koran contains the things that Allah told Mohammed.*

ko·sher /'kouʃər/ *adj.* **1** (from Jewish religious law, esp. regarding food) clean, pure: *He eats only kosher meat.* **2** *infrml.* honest, done according to correct behavior: *That business is not kosher; it sells cheap clothes, but charges high prices.*

kow·tow /'kau,tau/ *v.* to obey s.o. without question, often unwillingly: *He kowtows to his older brother's wishes.*

ku·dos /'ku,douz, -,dous/ *n.sing.* praise, (*syn.*) acclaim: *The manager received kudos for his outstanding work.*

Ku Klux Klan /'ku'klʌks'klæn/ also **KKK** or **the Klan** *n.* a secret society whose members think white people are superior, located mainly in the southern USA: *The KKK is devoted to having white Christian people rule the world.*

kum·quat /'kʌm,kwɑt/ *n.* the tree and its small, orange fruit: *The inside of a kumquat is sour, but its skin is sweet.*

kung fu /'kʌŋ'fu/ *n.* [U] a Chinese method of fighting with the hands and feet: *He is a master of kung fu.*

kw /'keɪ'dʌbəl,yu/*abbr. of* kilowatt(s)

L, l

L, l /ɛl/ *n.* **L's, l's** or **Ls, ls 1** the 12th letter of the English alphabet **2** in Roman numerals, the symbol for 50 **3 L-shaped:** in the form of an L: *The building is L-shaped, with a long wing for offices and the short wing for the entrance area.*

la /lɑ/ *n.* the name for the sixth note of the musical scale: *She sang up the scale from do to la.*

lab /læb/ *n. See:* laboratory.

la·bel /ˈleɪbəl/ *n.* **1** any of a variety of markers, such as a small piece of paper or cloth attached to s.t. to identify it: *The label on this shirt says, "Made in USA."* **2** a marker on a product used to give its name and contents: *Labels on cans of soup give the brand name, ingredients, and nutritional values.* **3** any word or phrase describing or classifying s.o. or s.t.
—*v.* **1** to mark with a label: *The teacher labeled file folders by attaching a label with a student's name on each one.* **2** *fig.* to apply a descriptive word or phrase to s.o. or s.t.: *His teachers have labeled him a troublemaker.*

la·bor /ˈleɪbər/ *n.* **1** [C;U] work, esp. difficult or tiring physical work, (*syn.*) toil: *He is well paid for his labor.* **2** [U] the work force, workers in general **3 a labor of love:** work done not for pay but out of dedication to s.o. or s.t.
—*v.* to work, (*syn.*) to toil: *We labored for weeks on a big project.* **4** *sing.* [U] **to go into** or **be in labor:** to begin or be in the process of giving birth: *Her baby was born ten hours after she went into labor.*

lab·o·ra·to·ry /ˈlæbrəˌtɔri/ *n.* **-ries** a specially equipped room for doing experiments and other exploratory work: *Scientists develop new products in the laboratory.*

labor camp *n.* a type of prison where prisoners (inmates) work: *During the war, prisoners were sent to work in labor camps.*

Labor Day *n.* in the USA and Canada, a holiday observed on the first Monday in September in honor of workers: *Labor Day is the last big holiday of summer.*

la·bored /ˈleɪbərd/ *adj.* forced, (*syn.*) strained: *After she climbed the stairs, her breathing was labored.*

la·bor·er /ˈleɪbərər/ *n.* a worker who does unskilled physical work: *The farmer hired several day laborers.*

la·bo·ri·ous /ləˈbɔriəs/ *adj.* requiring a lot of effort or work: *Preparing fields for planting without using machines is a laborious job.*

labor-saving *adj.* reducing the amount of work necessary to do a job: *Washing machines and computers are labor-saving devices.*

labor union *n.* an organization of workers dedicated to the interests of its members: *Officials of the labor union bargain with management for better pay and benefits.*

lab·y·rinth /ˈlæbəˌrɪnθ/ *n.* a complicated set of paths or passages where s.o. is easily lost, (*syn.*) maze: *Just for amusement, a rich man had a labyrinth made of bushes in his garden.*

lace /leɪs/ *n.* **1** [U] material, such as silk, woven by hand or machine into fine decorative patterns: *She has a tablecloth made of beautiful lace for her dining room table.* **2** [C] strings used to fasten shoes and boots: *The little boy is learning to tie the laces on his shoes.*
—*v.* **laced, lacing, laces** to close together or fasten with laces: *I laced up my boots and went out into the rain.*

lac·er·a·tion /ˌlæsəˈreɪʃən/ *n.* a cut, (*syn.*) a slash: *He received lacerations on his face in the accident.* -*v.* **lacerate.**

lack /læk/ *n.sing.* [U] **1** to be without s.t., an absence, (*syn.*) dearth: *There has been no rain, and the lack of it has ruined the crops.* **2** not enough of s.t., a shortage, (*syn.*) deficiency: *A lack of attention to his diet resulted in a heart attack.*
—*v.* **1** to be without (s.t. needed): *The villagers lacked food and medicine during the war.* **2** to have too little of (s.t. desirable): *He lacks care in his work; it's never well-done.* **3** *phrasal v. insep. frml.* **to lack for s.t.:** to have a need for s.t.: *His parents are very wealthy; they lack for nothing.*

lack·a·dai·si·cal /ˌlækəˈdeɪzɪkəl/ *adj.* lacking interest, careless: *A lackadaisical attitude toward her studies brought low grades.*

lack·lust·er /ˈlækˌlʌstər/ *adj.* ordinary, dull: *The performance of the symphony was not good, it was lackluster.*

lac·quer /ˈlækər/ *n.* [C;U] a liquid that hardens into a shine: *That beautiful tray was painted with black lacquer.*

la·crosse /ləˈkrɔs/ *n.* [U] a ball game played on a field by two ten-player teams using sticks with nets for catching and throwing the ball: *Lacrosse is a very fast and often rough sport.*

lac·tate /ˈlækˌteɪt/ *v.frml.* **-tated, -tating, -tates** to produce milk: *Female mammals lactate and nurse their young.* *-n.* [U] **lactation** /ˌlækˈteɪʃən/.

lac·y /ˈleɪsi/ *adj.* **-ier, -iest** looking like or made of lace: *She likes to wear beautiful lacy dresses.*

lad /læd/ *n.infrml.old usage* a boy or young man: *He was just a lad when he went to sea as a cabin boy.*

lad·der /ˈlædər/ *n.* **1** a piece of equipment used for climbing: *A carpenter climbed a ladder to fix the roof.* **2** *fig.* a series of upward steps: *She climbed the ladder of success at her company.*

lad·en /ˈleɪdn/ *adj.frml.* full of, *(syn.)* burdened with: *The truck is laden with goods for market.*

la·dies' man /ˈleɪdiz/ *n.* a man who likes women, esp. one liked by women: *He is a real ladies' man who loves to be with women.*

ladies' room *n.* a toilet facility for women: *She asked the waiter where to find the ladies' room.* See: bathroom, USAGE NOTE.

la·dle /ˈleɪdl/ *n.v.* **-dled, -dling, -dles** a type of large spoon: *I used a <n.> ladle to pour soup from the pan into my dish.*

la·dy /ˈleɪdi/ *n.* **-dies 1** (polite word for) a woman, esp. of good social standing: *"Ladies and gentlemen, may I have your attention, please."* **2** a title for women of British nobility: *Lady Walpole visited the Queen.*

la·dy·bug /ˈleɪdiˌbʌg/ *n.* a small beetle, usu. with red wings and black spots: *People say that when a ladybug lands on you, it brings good luck.*

la·dy·like /ˈleɪdiˌlaɪk/ *adj.* having the polite manners of a lady: *That little girl is ladylike.*

lag /læg/ *n.* a delay, slowness: *There was a lag in communications, so he did not hear the news until many days later.*
—*v.* **lagged, lagging, lags** to not keep up, to delay, *(syn.)* to straggle: *The little boy lagged behind the others on the walk.*

la·ger /ˈlɑgər/ *n.* [C;U] a German-type beer: *Lager has a stronger taste than American beer.*

lag·gard /ˈlægərd/ *n.* a person who is usually slower than others: *He is a laggard in his work.*

la·goon /ləˈgun/ *n.* an area of sea water nearly surrounded by land: *The lagoon acted as a harbor for small boats.*

laid /leɪd/ *past tense & past part. of* lay

laid-back *adj.infrml.* relaxed, easygoing: *The employees liked their boss's laid-back style of management.*

lain /leɪn/ *past part. of* lie (2)

lair /lɛr/ *n.* a wild animal's home: *The fox escaped from the dogs by hiding in its lair.*

lais·sez-faire /ˌlɛseɪˈfɛr/ *adj.n.* [U] a policy of little or no interference by government in the functioning of the free market: *The USA is known for <adj.> laissez-faire capitalism.*

lake /leɪk/ *n.* a large body of fresh water: *The lakes of Minnesota and Maine are famous vacation spots.*

lake·front /ˈleɪkˌfrʌnt/ *n.* land next to and around a lake: *They have a cottage on the lakefront.*

lam /læm/ *n.slang* **to be on the lam:** to run away, escape: *When the police caught the robber, he had been on the lam for three weeks.*

lamb /læm/ *n.* [C;U] a young sheep or the meat from one: *The family had roast leg of lamb for dinner.*

lam·baste /læmˈbeɪst, -ˈbæst/ *v.* **-basted, -basting, -bastes** to criticize strongly: *A newspaper editorial lambasted the government program as useless.* *-n.* [U] **lambasting.**

lamb·skin /ˈlæmˌskɪn/ *adj.n.* **1** a soft leather: *She wears <adj.> lambskin gloves.* **2** the soft, fleecy fur of lamb: *She also wears a gray coat made of <n.> lambskin.*

lame /leɪm/ *adj.* **lamer, lamest 1** unable to walk normally due to some injury or disability: *The lame horse walks with a limp.* **2** *fig.* weak, unsatisfactory, *(syn.)* feeble: *He makes lame excuses for being late for work, like saying the train was late.*

lamebrain /ˈleɪmˌbreɪn/ *n.infrml.* a stupid person, idiot: *He is such a lamebrain that he locked his car keys inside his car.*

lame duck *n.* See: duck (1).

la·ment /ləˈmɛnt/ *v.frml.* to feel sadness or cry for, *(syn.)* to mourn: *Her friends lamented the death of the dear old lady.*
—*n.* an expression of sorrow, esp. a song: *He wrote a lament for his dead friend.* *-n.* [C;U] **lamentation.**

la·men·ta·ble /ləˈmɛntəbəl/ *adj.frml.* involving sadness, regret, or sorrow: *His accidental death was most lamentable.*

lam·i·nate /ˈlæməˌneɪt/ *v.* **-nated, -nating, -nates** to join together thin layers of material: *In the factory, they laminate layers of wood to make strong plywood.*
—*n.* [C;U] /ˈlæmənɪt/ material made from thin layers joined together: *Plastic laminate is used for kitchen countertops.* *-n.* [U] **lamination.**

lamp /læmp/ *n.* any of a variety of lighting devices using electricity, oil, or gas: *We have lamps on the end tables next to our sofa.*

lam·poon /læm'pun/ *n.* a piece of writing or a cartoon that attacks s.o. or s.t. with humor or ridicule, *(syns.)* satire, spoof: *The magazine's lampoon of the rock star was very funny.*
—*v.* to attack with humor, *(syns.)* to spoof, satirize: *The magazine lampooned him.*

lance /læns/ *n.* **1** a long spear: *Men on horses used to charge the enemy with lances.* **2** a sharp medical tool used to cut the skin open: *The doctor used a lance to draw blood.*
—*v.* **lanced, lancing, lances** to cut with a lance: *Doctors lance boils.*

land /lænd/ *n.* **1** [U] soil, earth: *The land in this area is good for farming.* **2** [U] an area owned as property: *We own our house and the four acres of land around it.* **3** [C] a nation, country: *The boy dreamed of travel to a foreign land.* **4** *n.pl.* (in law) property: *The parks in the town are public lands—open to all.*
—*v.* **1** to reach land: *Our airplane landed at New York's Kennedy Airport.* **2** *infrml.* to put or be put: *The boy's joke about the teacher landed him in trouble.* **3** *fig.* **to land on one's feet:** to be in difficulty, then succeed: *He lost his job but landed on his feet by finding a better one.* **4 to land s.t.: a.** *lit.* to bring to land: *He landed the plane.* **b.** *fig.* to secure or win: *She landed a new job (a big contract, a special assignment, etc.).* -*adj.* **landed.**

land·fill /'lænd,fɪl/ *n.* a low-lying area filled in, often with garbage: *The landfills in many big cities are already full.*

land·hold·er /'lænd,houldər/ *n.* a person who owns property: *Any landholder in the center of town must be rich.*

land·ing /'lændɪŋ/ *n.* **1** [C;U] touchdown of an aircraft or a boat on land: *The landing of our airplane was smooth and on time. See:* takeoff. **2** [C] a place on shore where boats land, such as a pier, wharf, or shallow area: *People walked to the landing to get on the ferryboat.* **3** [C] a platform set into a staircase or the area at the top or bottom of a flight of stairs: *Climbing the stairs with our suitcases, we stopped to rest on the landing.*

landing strip *n.* a long, narrow area used for landing aircraft: *A small airplane touched down on the dirt landing strip.*

land·la·dy /'lænd,leɪdi/ *n.* a woman who owns or manages real estate, esp. that is rented to others: *The landlady lives downstairs in our apartment building. See:* landlord.

land·locked /'lænd,lakt/ *adj.* surrounded on all sides by land: *A landlocked country like Switzerland has no seaports.*

land·lord /'lænd,lɔrd/ *n.* a man or business that owns real estate, esp. that is rented to others: *The landlord of our apartment building is a huge real estate company. See:* landlady.

called *tenants,* and they have certain rights that *landlords* must honor. Landlords must for example, supply (but not necessarily pay for) electricity, heat, and water, keep the property in good condition; and provide light in the halls outside the apartments.

land·lub·ber /'lænd,lʌbər/ *n.* a person not used to boats or the sea: *Don't ask me about sailing; I'm a complete landlubber!*

land·mark /'lænd,mɑrk/ *n.* **1** s.t. easily seen, such as a tall building or mountain: *The tallest mountain in the area is a famous landmark.* **2** a historical building or other point of interest: *The old church in the center of town is a historical landmark.* **3** *fig.* an important event: *The invention of the radio is a landmark in technology.*

land·own·er /'lænd,ounər/ *n.* a person who owns land, esp. undeveloped land or farmland: *He is a large landowner in Louisiana.*

land·scape /'lænd,skeɪp/ *n.* **1** a broad view of the land: *The landscape seen from the mountains is green and beautiful.* **2** a picture showing such a view: *She paints landscapes.* **3** *fig.* a field of activity: *The political landscape in this city is varied and ever-changing.*
—*v.* **-scaped, -scaping, -scapes** to improve (the ground around a building) with trees, plants, etc.: *Construction of their new house is complete, so they can start landscaping.*

landscape gardener *n.* a skilled worker who designs and works on landscaped areas: *The landscape gardener planted a new lawn, trees, and flowers around our house.*

land·slide /'lænd,slaɪd/ *n.* **1** a large collapse of rocks and earth down a slope: *A landslide blocked the coastal road.* **2** *fig.* a very big win, esp. in an election: *The new President won by a landslide.*

lane /leɪn/ *n.* **1** a short street, often narrow with little traffic: *They live on a little country lane outside of town.* **2** one of several paths marked by painted lines on a highway: *He drives slowly in the right lane of the highway.* **3** one pathway in a swimming pool or bowling alley: *The swimmer in lane four won the race. See:* street, **USAGE NOTE.**

lan·guage /'læŋgwɪdʒ/ *n.* **1** [U] human communication by systems of written symbols, spoken words, and movements: *She is a psychologist who studies language development in children.* **2** [C] a particular communication system shared by a people: *He knows three languages: French, English, and American Sign Language.* **3** [U] a type of speech or wording: *He uses bad language.* **4** [C;U] any system for giving instructions to a computer: *PASCAL and COBOL are computer programming languages.*

L

lan·guid /'læŋgwɪd/ *adj.* with little energy or spirit, (*syn.*) listless: *Tropical climates can make you feel languid.* *-n.* [U] **languor** /'læŋgər/ *-adj.* **languorous.**

lan·guish /'læŋgwɪʃ/ *v.frml.* **1** to be without energy or spirit: *He languishes in the noonday heat.* **2** to suffer in terrible conditions: *He languished in prison for years before his release.*

lank·y /'læŋki/ *adj.* **-ier, -iest** thin, ungraceful, and usu. tall: *He is a tall and lanky basketball player.* *-n.* [U] **lankiness.**

lan·o·lin /'lænəlɪn/ *n.* [U] fat taken from sheep's wool and used in cosmetics and ointments: *I use lanolin on my dry skin in winter.*

lan·tern /'læntərn/ *n.* a light or flame inside a container usu. of metal and glass: *They took a lantern on their camping trip. See:* jack-o'-lantern.

lap /læp/ *v.* **lapped, lapping, laps** **1** to lick with the tongue as in taking up liquid: *A cat laps milk from a bowl.* **2** (in racing) to go ahead of a competitor by a complete circuit: *The leader lapped the others.* **3** (of water) to hit against s.t. with small movements and soft sounds: *The waves lapped against the side of the ship.* **4** *phrasal v. sep.infrml.* **to lap s.t. up:** to receive eagerly, (*syn.*) to relish: *She lapped up all his flattery.‖She lapped it up.*
—n. **1** the area formed by the top of the legs in a seated position: *The baby sat on his mother's lap.* **2** a circuit around a track or a length of a swimming pool: *The runner (or swimmer) did 20 laps for practice.* **3** *fig.* **in the lap of luxury:** to be in a position of great wealth: *We stayed in the lap of luxury in our expensive deluxe hotel.*

la·pel /lə'pɛl/ *n.* the front area of a jacket, blouse, etc. that is folded back, then extends to the back collar: *He wears a flower in his lapel.*

lapel

lapse /læps/ *v.* **lapsed, lapsing, lapses** **1** to fall gradually: *The patient lapsed into unconsciousness.* **2** to make a mistake, esp. a fall from good behavior: *He lapsed when he spoke too freely.* **3** (of agreements, rights, benefits) to end or be no longer valid: *It's too late to take the problem to the manufacturer because the car's warranty has lapsed.*
—n. **1** a fall from correct behavior: *It was a lapse on his part when he forgot to pay the rent.* **2** the passing of a period of time: *There was a lapse of 9 years before he saw her again.*

laptop computer or **laptop** /'læp,top/ *n.* a small, portable computer: *The reporter used a laptop to write the story while she was at the scene of the accident. See:* desktop.

lar·ce·ny /'lɑrsəni/ *n.* [C;U] (in law) stealing of property: *The fellow stole a car and was arrested for grand larceny. -adj.* **larcenous.**

lard /lɑrd/ *n.* [U] **1** pig fat used for cooking: *Some people fry foods in lard.* **2** *fig.* human fat: *He has a lot of lard around his waistline.*

large /lɑrdʒ/ *adj.* **larger, largest** **1** big in size, amount, etc.: *He wears extra large shirts.* **2** important, on a grand scale: *That company is a large computer maker.* **3** **at large: a.** free to move around, uncontrolled: *The escaped prisoners are still at large.* **b.** in general, as a whole: *The country at large supports the peace plan.* **4** **by and large:** in general, speaking generally: *By and large, I think that the economy is doing well.*

large intestine *n. See:* intestine.

large·ly /'lɑrdʒli/ *adv.* mostly, to a great degree: *He is largely responsible for the success of the business.*

large-scale *adj.* big, broadly planned or made: *Auto makers are large-scale manufacturers with many big operations.*

lar·gess or **lar·gesse** /lɑr'ʒɛs, -'dʒɛs/ *n.* [U] great generosity, esp. with money: *The university built its new science center thanks to the largess of a rich industrialist.*

lar·i·at /'læriət/ *n.* a rope for capturing horses and cattle, (*syn.*) lasso: *Cowboys carry lariats on their saddles.*

lark /lɑrk/ *n.* **1** a songbird with gray and brown markings **2** *fig.* a carefree good time, (*syn.*) fling: *They decided just this morning to go on a weekend lark in the mountains.*

lar·va /'lɑrvə/ *n.* **-vae** /-vi/ the second stage between egg and pupa in the development of many types of insects: *Ugly larvae later become beautiful butterflies.*

lar·yn·gi·tis /,lærən'dʒaɪtɪs/ *n.* [U] a painful condition caused by inflammation of the larynx in the throat and affecting speech: *The speaker had laryngitis and canceled his talk.*

lar·ynx /'lærɪŋks/ *n.* **larynges** /lə'rɪndʒiz/ the voice box, located in the throat: *The larynx is vital to human communication.*

las·civ·i·ous /lə'sɪviəs/ *adj.frml.* related to strong sexual desire, lustful: *His lascivious desires lead to disgusting behavior.*

la·ser /,leɪzər/ *n.* a device that focuses a powerful light in a specific place for many uses, from surgery to metal cutting: *The operation on his eye was done with a laser.*

lash /læʃ/ *v.* **1** to hit with a whip: *The man lashed the horse to make it run faster.* **2** to tie down, bind: *Sailors lashed down boxes with strong ropes before the storm.* **3** *phrasal v. insep.* **to lash out at s.o. or s.t.: a.** *lit.* to suddenly strike or hit violently with a hand or weapon: *The prisoner lashed out at the guard.*

b. *fig.* to attack with words: *She lashes out at anyone who criticizes her.*
—*n.* **1** a type of short whip: *He used a lash to punish the prisoner.* **2** a stroke of a whip or lash: *The captain ordered the sailor to get 20 lashes as punishment for stealing.* **3 a tongue-lashing:** a severe scolding: *Her mother gave her a tongue-lashing for coming home so late.* **4 lashes:** *See:* eyelash.

lass /læs/ *n.infrml.old usage* a girl or young woman: *The old song described "the lass he loved."*

las·si·tude /ˈlæsə,tud/ *n.frml.* [U] tiredness, lack of energy, *(syn.)* listlessness: *His lassitude was because of a long illness.*

last /læst/ *adj.* **1** behind all others in position: *He was the last in line because he arrived very late.* **2** (of a time period) the most recently passed: *All the bills were paid last month (week, year).* **3** final, at the end: *His last days before his death were peaceful.* **4** least desirable: *Washing windows is the last thing that I want to do.* **5** said of the only one left: *He spent his last dollar.* **6 last but not least:** at the end but still important
—*adv.* **1** behind all others: *My favorite horse ran last in the race.* **2** in the recent past: *When he last visited his mother, she was well.* **3** at the end: *You should answer each question on the test, check your answers, and, last, hand the test in to the teacher.*
—*n.* **1** a person or thing after all others: *He was the last to arrive.* **2** the last moment: *He fought to save his life right up until the last.* **3** [C] a form used to make things: *Shoes are made on a last.* **4 at (long) last:** after a long wait or delay: *They're here at last!*
—*v.* **1** to continue to exist, *(syn.)* to endure: *The pyramids have lasted for thousands of years.* **2** to remain in good condition: *Well-made shoes last a long time.* **3** to survive, live: *The sick patient is not expected to last the night.* **4** to remain in supply, *(syn.)* to suffice: *That supply of wood should last the winter.*

last-ditch *adj.* done or made as a frantic final attempt: *Negotiators made a last-ditch effort to reach agreement before fighting began again.*

last hurrah *n.infrml.fig.* a last appearance or moment of glory at the end of a sporting event, political term, career, or life: *The President's last hurrah was a farewell speech to the nation.*

last·ing /ˈlæstɪŋ/ *adj.* continuing for a long time, *(syn.)* enduring: *She makes a good, lasting impression on people.*

last minute *adj.* at the final moment before an important event: *He made a last minute effort to make her stay, but she left him.*

last name *n.* a surname, family name: *His last name is Jones.*

last straw *n.fig.* the final displeasing event in a series of events that causes s.o. to take action: *He is always late, and when he was late for a very important meeting, that was the last straw; he was asked to leave the company.*

last word *n.sing.* **1** the final statement: *He must have the last word in every discussion.* **2** the final decision: *She insists on having the last word on which person we hire.*

latch /lætʃ/ *n.* a type of lock, such as for a door or cabinet: *The latch on the gate is broken.*

latch·key child /ˈlætʃ,ki/ *n.* a child who is home alone after school: *Latchkey children learn to take care of themselves while their parents are at work.*

USAGE NOTE: Since both parents in the majority of American couples and many single parents work full-time, there are more and more *latchkey children.* Some businesses now provide daycare for their employees' kids, and many schools have *afterschool* programs so that children don't have to go home to an empty house.

late /leɪt/ *adj.* **later, latest 1** arriving after the expected time, *(syn.)* tardy: *She was late for our meeting.* **2** happening near the end (of a period of time): *in the late afternoon, the late 1800s* **3** dead, *(syn.)* deceased: *A church service was held for the late Mr. Jones.*
—*adv.* after the expected time: *The movie started five minutes late.*

late·ly /ˈleɪtli/ *adv.* recently: *Lately, her health has been much better.*

la·tent /ˈleɪtnt/ *adj.* **1** present but inactive, *(syn.)* dormant: *The boy has latent athletic ability that is not yet developed.* **2** present but not seen, *(syn.)* concealed: *The virus lies latent for years before the person becomes sick from it.* -*n.* [U] **latency.**

lat·er·al /ˈlætərəl/ *adj.* **1** to the side: *The ballerina made a lateral movement.* **2** located on the side of s.t.: *The lateral section of the upper body contains the ribs.*

lat·est /ˈleɪtɪst/ *adj.infrml.* **1** most recent: *We just heard the latest news.* **2** most modern or current: *She wears the latest fashions.*

la·tex /ˈleɪ,tɛks/ *n.* [U] **1** a thick liquid, such as from the rubber tree, that produces natural rubber **2** a rubbery liquid, such as used in paint: *We painted our house with a <adj.> latex paint.*

lathe /leɪð/ *n.v.* **lathed, lathing, lathes** a machine used to cut out objects with precision: *He makes machine parts on a <n.> lathe.||He <v.> lathes percision parts for machines.*

lath·er /ˈlæðər/ *n.* [U] a foamy substance, such as soapsuds or sweat on a horse: *He covers his beard with lather in order to shave it.*

—*v.* **1** to cover with lather: *He lathered his face with soap.* **2** to produce a lot of sweat: *Racehorses lather as they run.*

Lat·in /'lætn/ *n.* [U] the language of Romans: *Latin was spoken throughout the Roman Empire.*
—*n.* [C] *adj.* referring to the peoples of France, Italy, Spain, Mexico, and Central and South America, whose languages come from Latin: *<n.pl.> There are ten Latins and ten Asians in my English class.*

Latin America *n.* the countries of Central and South America: *Spanish is the main language spoken in Latin America.*

La·ti·no /lə'tinou/ *n.adj.* a Latin American person living in the USA. *The <adj.> Latino Student Association organized a debate.*

lat·i·tude /'lætə,tud/ *n.* **1** [C;U] an imaginary line of measurement of the earth's surface running parallel to the equator: *New York City is located at a latitude of about 41 degrees north of the equator and at a longitude of 74 degrees west of Greenwich, England.* **2** *pl.* regions of the world: *Many Canadians travel to the southern latitudes in winter.* **3** [U] freedom to act: *Her boss gives her wide latitude to do her job as she thinks best.*

la·trine /lə'trin/ *n.* a toilet, esp. in the military: *The sergeant ordered the men to dig a latrine.*

lat·ter /'lætər/ *n.sing.* the second of two people or things named: *We eat lots of fish and poultry, but we prefer the latter. See:* former.
—*adj.* **1** later, nearer the end: *I disliked the latter part of the book.* **2** **latter-day:** of recent times: *Some long-time conservatives distrust the latter-day conservatives now coming into power.*

lat·tice /'lætɪs/ *n.* [U] a pattern of crossed lines (wood, metal, crystals, etc.)

laud /lɔd/ *v.frml.* to praise: *The teacher lauded the student for her excellent work.* -*adj.* **laudatory.**

laud·a·ble /'lɔdəbəl/ *adj.frml.* deserving of praise, (*syn.*) praiseworthy: *Helping an old person cross the street is a laudable act.*

laugh /læf/ *n.* **1** a sound of amusement, happiness, disrespect, etc. made with the voice: *When he heard my funny story, he gave a loud laugh.* **2** *fig.* s.t. that deserves no respect: *That performance was so bad that it was a laugh.* **3** **to have the last laugh:** to succeed after seeming to have lost: *My competitor took my customer away from me, but then that customer did not pay him, so I had the last laugh.*
—*v.* **1** to voice sounds of amusement, happiness, disrespect, etc.: *I laughed when I heard about his crazy plan.* **2** **no laughing matter:** serious: *This letter from their lawyer is no laughing matter.* **3** *fig.* **to die laughing:** to laugh uncontrollably: *That comedian was so funny that the audience nearly died laughing.*

4 *phrasal v. insep.* **to laugh at s.o. or s.t.: a.** to respond with sounds of amusement, delight, etc.: *She laughs at funny jokes.* **b.** to express disrespect for, ridicule, (*syns.*) to scoff at, mock: *He laughed at the stupid idea.* **5** *phrasal v. sep.* **to laugh s.t. off:** to make (s.t. bad) seem unimportant by laughing: *He slipped on some ice but got up and laughed off his fall.||He laughed it off. See:* smile, USAGE NOTE.

laugh·a·ble /'læfəbəl/ *adj.* deserving no respect, ridiculous: *The offer to buy that he made was so low that it was laughable.*

laughingstock /'læfɪŋ,stak/ *n.* a person laughed at for doing s.t. bad or stupid: *His poor acting made him the laughingstock of the theater.*

laugh·ter /'læftər/ *n.* [U] the sound of laughing: *Laughter from the audience inspired the comedian.*

launch /lɔntʃ/ *v.* **1** to push into the water: *We launched our boat into the lake.* **2** to send up into the air: *The spacecraft will be launched tomorrow.* **3** *fig.* to start, put into operation, etc.: *Our company launched an advertising campaign for our new product.*
—*n.* **1** *sing.* the start, the process of putting into action: *The launch of the new advertising campaign will be next week.* **2** [C] the sending of s.t. up into the air: *The space launch took place this morning.* **3** [C] a small powerboat used for travel between land and other boats: *The captain took a launch from shore to his ship.*

launch pad *n.* an area with a hard surface and supporting equipment from which spacecraft are launched: *The missile roared off the launch pad into the sky.*

laun·der /'lɔndər/ *v.* **1** to clean with soap and water: *She launders her clothes at the Laundromat each week.* **2** *fig.* to hide the source of money gotten illegally by passing it through a legitimate business: *A large bank laundered money from drug sales.*

Laun·dro·mat /'lɔndrə,mæt/ *n.TM* a self-service laundry, (*syn.*) launderette: *The Laundromat is crowded with people washing their clothes.*

laun·dry /'lɔndri/ *n.* -**dries 1** [C] a business where clothes and linen are washed, dried, and pressed: *A big commercial laundry supplies restaurants with uniforms and table linen.* **2** [U] clothes and linen that need to be washed or have just been washed: *She put the dirty laundry into the washer.*

lau·re·ate /'lɔriɪt, lɑr-/ *n.* a person honored with an award: *The professor is a Nobel laureate in chemistry.*

lau·rel /'lɔrəl, lɑr-/ *n.* **1** a family of mostly evergreen trees and shrubs prized for their fruits, bay leaves, and oils **2** [C] a symbol of victory and honor, often shown as a crown of laurel **3 to rest on one's laurels:** to be satisfied with what one has achieved already: *She does not rest on her laurels but rather is always working towards new goals.*

la·va /ˈlɑvə/ *n.* [U] hot liquid volcanic rock: *Lava flowed down the sides of the volcano.*

lav·a·to·ry /ˈlævəˌtɔri/ *n.frml.* **-ries** a room with toilets and sinks, bathroom: *The school has lavatories on each floor.*

lav·en·der /ˈlævəndər/ *adj.* a pale violet color: *She writes letters on lavender paper.*
—*n.* [U] any of a variety of Mediterranean shrubs belonging to the mint family, used for its scent and as a flavoring: *This soap has a lovely smell of lavender.*

lav·ish /ˈlævɪʃ/ *adj.* done in very large and generous amounts: *She gives lavish parties with wonderful food, flowers, and music.*
—*v.* to give (affection, gifts, etc.) in large amounts: *He lavishes affection on his wife.*

law /lɔ/ *n.* **1** [C] a rule made by a government body that must be followed by the people in a nation, state, etc.: *In the USA, laws are written by Congress and by state legislatures.* **2** [U] such rules as a group: *Lawyers must know the law.* **3** [U] the officials and courts of the legal system: *The man is in jail because he got into trouble with the law.* **4** [C] (in many religions) a commandment from God **5** [C] a statement describing what happens under certain conditions: *the law of gravity* **6** *fig.* **to lay down the law:** to demand obedience to one's rules: *He laid down the law to his children that they had to be home by 11:00 p.m.* **7** *fig.* **to take the law into one's own hands:** to take for oneself the power of a legal authority: *Instead of waiting for the police, an angry group took the law into their own hands by catching and beating the thief.*
—*adj.* related to law: *She has a law degree.*

law-abiding *adj.* well behaved, respectful of the law: *Law-abiding citizens are the backbone of a community.*

law·break·er /ˈlɔˌbreɪkər/ *n.* a person who disobeys a law: *The police want to catch lawbreakers.*

law·ful /ˈlɔfəl/ *adj.* permitted by law, according to law: *Citizens have the lawful right to use public places.*

law·less /ˈlɔlɪs/ *adj.* full of crime, without effective legal action: *In the USA in the 1800s, parts of the Wild West were lawless areas where crimes went unpunished.*

law·mak·er /ˈlɔˌmeɪkər/ *n.* a legislator: *Lawmakers in Washington, D.C., pass new laws in Congress.*

lawn /lɔn/ *n.* an area of cut grass: *The lawn in the front yard is kept very neat.*

lawn mower *n.* a machine used to cut grass: *He uses a riding lawn mower to cut his large yard.*

law·suit /ˈlɔˌsut/ *n.* a legal action bringing a problem or claim to a court of law: *John's lawyer filed a (law)suit against the company where he had an accident.*

law·yer /ˈlɔyər/ *n.* a professional who practices law, (*syn.*) attorney: *I depend on my lawyer for her sharp mind and knowledge of law.*

lax /læks/ *adj.* **1** lacking in strict attention to details: *His bookkeeping is lax.* **2** careless, lacking control, (*syn.*) negligent: *Enforcement of some laws in this city is lax.* -*n.* [U] **laxity.**

lax·a·tive /ˈlæksətɪv/ *n.adj.* a medicine to relieve constipation: *The doctor recommended an effective <n.> laxative with a gentle <adj.> laxative effect.*

lay (1) /leɪ/ *past tense of* lie

lay (2) *v.* **laid** /leɪd/, **laying, lays 1** to put down: *I laid my keys on the table.* **2** to prepare, set: *She lays the table for dinner each evening.* **3** to form, create: *He's laying plans for a new business.* **4** to put in place: *He laid bricks to form a wall, then laid a coat of white paint over them.* **5** to produce (eggs): *Birds and insects lay eggs. See:* to lay an egg. **6 to lay a finger** or **a hand on s.o.:** to touch (with the intention of doing harm): *If he even lays a finger on my girlfriend, I'll punch him in the nose.* **7** *infrml.fig.* **to lay an egg:** to fail badly: *That new play was terrible; the producers really laid an egg.* **8 to lay at s.o.'s feet:** to give s.o. (an honor), (*syn.*) to bestow on s.o.: *He was so in love with her that he offered to lay everything he owned at her feet.* **9 to lay down the law:** *See:* law. **10** *infrml.* **to lay eyes on:** to see: *I have not laid eyes on John for several weeks* **11** *phrasal v. insep.infrml.* **to lay into s.o.:** to criticize severely: *The boss really laid into me for coming to work late.* **12** *infrml.* **to lay it on the line:** to state clearly how one feels: *The boss laid it on the line that anyone who argues with him gets fired.* **13** *infrml.* **to lay it on thick, heavy, etc.:** to flatter or compliment too much: *He laid it on thick by telling her that he couldn't live without her.* **14** *phrasal v.* **to lay off s.o. or s.t.: a.** *sep.* to dismiss workers from their jobs, esp. temporarily: *My company laid off 200 workers due to the economic recession. ||It laid them off.* **b.** *insep. infrml.* to stop: *I told you to lay off bothering my little brother!* **15** *fig.* **to lay one's cards on the table:** to state one's intentions clearly, usu. after negotiating for a while: *He finally laid his cards on the table and said he badly needed money.* **16** *infrml.* **to lay** or **get one's hands on:** to get, (*syns.*) to acquire, grasp: *I'll buy it if I can lay my hands on enough money.* **17** *phrasal v. insep.* **to lay over** or **stop over:** to wait for a plane (train,

L

bus, etc.) to continue one's journey: *We laid over for an hour in Chicago before continuing our flight to Seattle.* **18** *phrasal v. sep.* **to lay s.o. or s.t. out: a.** to prepare for burial: *They laid out the body in the bedroom.||They laid it out.* **b.** to arrange: *He laid out the table in style for the party.||He laid it out in style.* **c.** *infrml.fig.* to spend a sum of money: *I laid out $21,000 for that new car.|| I laid it out.* **19** *phrasal v. sep.infrml.* **to lay s.o. or s.t. up:** to keep at home or in bed because of sickness or injury: *The accident laid up my brother for two months.||It laid him up.* **20** *phrasal v. sep.* **to lay s.t. aside: a.** to no longer consider important, put down: *They laid them aside.||The two enemies agreed to lay aside their differences and stop fighting.* **b.** to put away for the future: *We lay aside as much money as we can.||We lay it aside.* **21** *fig.* **to lay s.t. at s.o.'s doorstep:** to place blame for s.t. on s.o.: *The opposition party lays all the nation's problems at the doorstep of the President.* **22** *phrasal v. sep.* **to lay s.t. away:** to save (money): *She lays away part of her paycheck each month. ||She lays it away.* **23** *phrasal v. sep.* **to lay s.t. down: a.** to put s.t., such as a weapon, down in a sign of peace: *The generals laid down their swords.||They laid them down.* **b.** *fig.* to say s.t. firmly or clearly: *The union negotiator laid down the workers' terms.||He laid them down.* **24** *phrasal v. sep.* **to lay s.t. in:** to save, store: *The farmer lays in food for his animals for the winter. ||He lays it in.* **25 to lay to rest: a.** to bury: *The old man was laid to rest in the town where he was born.* **b.** *fig.* to stop or make disappear: *The politician announced his plans to retire and laid the recent rumors to rest.* **26 to lay waste to:** to destroy, (*syn.*) to annihilate: *The enemy laid waste to the town by bombing it.*
—*n.* **the lay of the land: a.** the nature or condition of the land, landscape: *The lay of the land around here is hilly.* **b.** *infrml.* the general situation: *I talked with several investors to get the lay of the land before I invested my own money.*

lay (3) *adj.* **1** not expert in a field of knowledge: *She's a lay therapist working with a team of professionals.* **2** not of the clergy (officials of a religion): *The minister's lay assistants organize many church events.* See: layman, layperson.

lay·a·way /'leɪə,weɪ/ *n.adj.* system of making payments to hold s.t. for future purchase: *I used a <adj.> layaway plan to pay for our living room furniture; I put it on <n.> layaway.*

lay·er /'leɪər/ *n.* **1** a coating, covering: *A layer of mud lies on the lake bottom.* **2** a thickness, usu. one of several: *The birthday cake had two layers of chocolate cake with chocolate icing between them.*
—*v.* to arrange in layers: *She layered a vest over two shirts for a stylish look.* -*n.* [U] **layering.**

lay·man /'leɪmən/ *n.* **-men** /-mən/ **1** a person who is not expert in a field: *He is a complete layman in the computer field.* **2** a member of the laity within a religion (not a religious official): *Laymen perform important functions in churches.*

lay·off /'leɪ,ɔf/ *n.* a dismissal from employment, esp. temporary: *In a recession, there are often mass layoffs of factory workers.*

lay·out /'leɪ,aʊt/ *n.* **1** a drawing or design, such as for a building or advertisement, (*syn.*) a schematic: *The artist showed me the layout for the magazine cover.* **2** an arrangement, such as of rooms or furniture etc: *The layout of that apartment is spacious.*

lay·o·ver /'leɪ,oʊvər/ *n.* a short stay, such as to change airplanes, (*syn.*) stopover: *We had a two-hour layover in Chicago between flights.*

lay·wom·an /'leɪ,wʊmən/ *n.* See: layman.

la·zy /'leɪzi/ *adj.* **-zier, -ziest 1** disliking and avoiding work, (*syn.*) indolent: *He's so lazy that he avoids any kind of work.* **2** lacking energy or activity: *He spent a lazy afternoon reading and sleeping.*

la·zy·bones /'leɪzi,boʊnz/ *n.infrml.* a lazy person: *He is a lazybones with no plans to look for work.*

lb. /paʊnd/ *abbr. for* pound(s): *I bought a 2- lb. cut of beef.*

USAGE NOTE: A *pound* is equal to 16 ounces, which is abbreviated as *oz.*: *She gave birth to a healthy baby girl, who weighed seven pounds and six ounces (7 lbs. 6 oz.).*

---

leach /litʃ/ *v.* **leached, leaching, leaches** to pass from s.t. or cause (elements) to pass from s.t. because of liquid moving through: *Valuable minerals leached from the soil because of heavy rains.*

lead /lɛd/ *n.* **1** [U] a heavy soft basic metal used in industry as a sealant, as a shield against X-rays, etc.: *Plumbers use lead to seal the joints in pipes.* **2** [C;U] the gray carbon in a pencil: *I need a pencil with a softer lead.* **3** *infrml.fig.* **to get the lead out:** to move (work, act, etc.) more quickly: *C'mon, get the lead out and let's start working!*
—*v.* to apply lead: *The plumber leaded the pipe joint.*

lead /lid/ *v.* **led** /lɛd/**, leading, leads 1** to go first to show the way: *She led the visitors on a tour through the museum.* **2** to be ahead of, in front of: *He leads the others in the race by several meters.* **3** to direct, control: *She led the orchestra (the discussion, the team, etc.).* **4** to be a route to: *That road leads to the river.* **5** to experience, live (a life): *He leads an exciting*

life. **6** to influence or cause (s.o. to do s.t.): *Her expression led me to believe there was some problem.* **7** *phrasal v. sep.* **to lead off with s.t.:** to start, begin: *The speaker led off with a funny story.* **8** *infrml.fig.* **to lead s.o. by the hand:** to instruct s.o. step-by-step: *The teacher led the students by the hand through the math problem.* **9** *phrasal v. sep.* **to lead s.o. on:** to make s.o. believe s.t. that is not true, (*syn.*) to deceive: *He led on his victims by promising to make them rich.||He led them on.* **10** *fig.* **to lead s.o. on a wild goose chase:** to cause s.o. a lot of trouble, esp. in looking for s.t.: *Our horse got loose and led us on a wild goose chase through town until we caught him.* **11** *phrasal v. insep.* **to lead to s.t.:** to result in: *Use of illegal drugs can lead to disability and death.* **12** *phrasal v. insep.* **to lead up to s.t.:** to present (or serve as) an introduction to: *After my brother told me a long story, I found that he was leading up to a request to borrow some money.*
—*n.* **1** a distance one is ahead: *That racehorse has a big lead over the others.* **2** a piece of information useful in a search, a clue: *My friend gave me a lead on a new job opening.* **3** an important part, esp. in a theatrical role: *She has the lead in the new play.* **4 in the lead:** in first position (in a race) **5 to follow s.o.'s lead:** to follow s.o.'s example: *His younger brothers followed his lead and also became dentists.*
—*adj.* in the first or an important position: *the lead singer in a group, the lead car in a race*

lead·en /ˈlɛdn/ *adj.* **1** made of lead: *Leaden pipes are used at the work site.* **2** *fig.* heavy, from tiredness, sadness, etc.: *After he walked three miles, his legs felt leaden.* **3** *fig.* gray like lead: *leaden skies*

lead·er /ˈlidər/ *n.* **1** a person who directs others: *Our leader tells us what to do.* **2** one who is in front of others: *The Senator is the leader in the Presidential race. -n.* [U] **leadership.**

lead-in /ˈlid,ɪn/ *n.* an introduction: *He told a funny story as a lead-in to his speech.*

lead·ing (1) /ˈlidɪŋ/ *adj.* **1** ahead of others: *The Senator is the leading candidate for President.* **2** important, (*syn.*) prominent: *The soprano has the leading role in the opera.* **3 leading lady** or **man:** person playing an important role in a play or film **4 leading question:** a question formed so as to control or direct the answer: *The judge stopped the lawyer from asking the witness leading questions.*

lead·ing (2) /ˈlɛdɪŋ/ *n.* **1** (in printing) the distance between lines of type: *The leading in dictionary type is very narrow.* **2** (in metalwork) the use of lead as a border: *The leading in the stained-glass windows has loosened.*

lead time /lid/ *n.* [C;U] the amount of time between the start of s.t. and when it must be fin-

ished: *We have several weeks' lead time to finish the advertisement.*

leaf /lif/ *n.* **leaves** /livz/
1 [C] a part of a plant, usu. flat and green, growing from its stem or a branch **2** [C] a sheet of paper with both sides used: *The front*

leaf

leaf in the book has the title and author on one side and the copyright notice on the back side. **3** [U] a thin sheet of metal, such as gold: *The frame of the mirror is covered with rich-looking gold leaf.* **4 in full leaf:** fully grown, with complete foliage: *In mid-summer, trees are in full leaf. See:* turn (over a new leaf).
—*v. phrasal v. insep.* **to leaf through s.t.:** to turn the pages of: *He leafs through books before he buys them.*

leaf·let /ˈliflɪt/ *n.* a folded paper printed with information or advertising, (*syns.*) flyer, pamphlet: *I got a leaflet in the mail about a sale at a neighborhood store.*

leaf·y /ˈlifi/ *adj.* having leaves, esp. in large amounts: *Oaks and maples are leafy trees.*

league /lig/ *n.* **1** a group of sports teams that compete against each other: *Our local team belongs to the National Football League.* **2** a group of people, businesses, or nations joined together in a shared interest: *The League of Nations was founded in 1919 to promote world peace.* **3 in league with:** in connection with, esp. in s.t. illegal or immoral: *The terrible crimes that man has committed put him in league with the devil.* **4** *fig.* **in the same league with s.o.** or **in s.o.'s league:** at the same level of excellence: *He plays the piano very well, and I am just not in his league.*

leak /lik/ *n.* **1** an unwanted drip or rush of liquid or gas: *The boat has a leak and is filling up with water.* **2** a letting out of secret information: *A leak from inside the government spread the news of the President's decision.*
—*v.* **1** to let in or out a drip or rush of liquid or gas: *The kitchen sink leaks water onto the floor.* **2** to reveal information secretly: *An official inside the government leaked a story to journalists. -n.* [U] **leakage** *-adj.* **leaky.**

lean /lin/ *v.* **1** to rest against for support: *He leaned against a wall.* **2** to bend from the waist: *He then leaned over and picked a flower.* **3** *phrasal v. insep.* **to lean on upon s.o.:** to depend on for help: *Her children lean on her, even though they are adults.* **4** *phrasal v. insep.* **to lean toward(s):** to favor, prefer: *She leans toward going on vacation in July, not August.*
—*adj.* **-er, -est 1** (of a person) thin, not fat: *Professional dancers are usually lean.* **2** (of meat) with little fat: *They eat lean meat with*

L

the fat cut off. **3** producing little, (*syn.*) meager: *The country is going through lean times now because of the recession.* **4** *infrml.fig.*
lean and mean: hungry and aggressive, esp. to increase business or to win a sports competition: *The company laid off 1,000 workers and is now lean and mean and ready to make money.*

lean·ing /ˈliniŋ/ *n.* a preference, (*syn.*) inclination: *She has a leaning toward vacationing in Europe this summer.*

lean-to /ˈlintu/ *n.* **-tos** a shelter made of tree branches leaned against a rectangular frame: *The hunter made a lean-to in the forest.*

lean-to

leap /lip/ *n.* **1** a jump into the air, bound, spring: *The dancer made a series of leaps around the stage.* **2 by leaps and bounds:** with fast progress: *That company is growing by leaps and bounds.*
—*v.* **leaped** or **leapt** /lɛpt, lipt,/ **leaping, leaps 1** to spring into or through the air: *Monkeys leaped from branch to branch.* **2** to jump over: *The boy leaped the puddle.* **3** *phrasal v. insep.* **to leap at s.t.:** to accept quickly, (*syn.*) to seize: *She leaped at the opportunity to take a new job.*

leap·frog /ˈlip,frag, -,frɔg/ *v.fig.* to progress rapidly, jump over s.t. that blocks the way: *She leapfrogged over her co-workers to become the general manager of the company.*
—*n.* [U] a children's game of one jumping over the other: *Children like to play leapfrog.*

leap year *n.* a year of 366 days (by adding February 29) occurring every fourth year: *The year 2004 will be a leap year.*

learn /lɜrn/ *v.* **learned** /lɜrnd/ or **learnt** /lɜrnt,/ **learning, learns 1** to gain knowledge of: *She learned some American history in high school.* **2** to gain skill in: *He is learning how to use a computer.* **3** to become informed about, find out: *They learned about the accident from a friend.* **4 to learn a lesson** or **to learn the hard way:** to learn by suffering from a mistake: *She lost so much money in the stock market that she learned a lesson (or) she learned the hard way about avoiding high risks.* **5** *fig.* **to learn the ropes:** to learn how to do a job by doing it

learn·ed /ˈlɜrnɪd/ *adj.* having much knowledge, (*syn.*) erudite: *Great universities have many learned professors.*

learn·ing /ˈlɜrnɪŋ/ *n.* [U] knowledge or understanding gained through study: *He is a man of great learning.*

learning curve *n.* the amount of time and effort required to learn to do s.t.: *The learning curve for mastering a complicated computer program is long and steep.*

learning disability *n.* a condition related to the functioning of the brain that makes learning difficult: *He was slow to learn to read because of a learning disability.*

lease /lis/ *n.v.* **leased, leasing, leases 1** a contract to pay to use property (a building, equipment, etc.) for a period of time: *Our business has <v.> leased its offices for five years.* **2 a new lease on life:** an improved situation: *Bypass surgery on his heart gave him a new lease on life.*

leash /liʃ/ *n.* a cord used to hold a dog: *She walks her dog on a leash.*
—*v.* to tie up with a leash: *She leashed her dog to a tree while she shopped.*

leash

least /list/ *n.* [U] *adj.* **1** the smallest amount of s.t.: *She is paid the <n.> least* (or) *the <adj.> least amount of all the office employees.* **2 in the least:** in the smallest amount, at all: *I don't care about that matter in the least.*

least common denominator *n.* See: lowest common denominator (1).

leath·er /ˈlɛðər/ *n.* the skin of cattle, sheep, etc.: *His shoes are made of leather.* -*adj.* **leathery.**

leave /liv/ *v.* **left** /lɛft/, **leaving, leaves 1** to go away (from), (*syn.*) to depart: *I leave at 8:00 to go to work.* **2** to go away from permanently: *He has left his wife (his job, college, etc.).* **3** to cause to stay where one goes away: *They left their children with a babysitter.* **4** to fail to bring when one goes away: *Oh, no, I left the keys inside the car!* **5** to put in the care of, (*syn.*) to entrust: *I'll leave a message with your secretary.* **6** to have as a result: *Coffee will leave stains on your teeth.* **7** *fig.* **to leave a bad taste in s.o.'s mouth:** to leave s.o. feeling annoyed or disturbed: *While on vacation, he was cheated several times, and that left a bad taste in his mouth.* **8 to leave for:** to leave to go to (a destination): *The plane leaves for New York at 9:15.* **9 to leave much to be desired:** to be lacking in quality: *I can't recommend that hotel because the service there leaves much to be desired.* **10** *fig.* **to leave no stone unturned:** to make every possible effort: *The police left no stone unturned to solve the crime.* **11** *phrasal v.* **to leave off s.t.: a.** *sep.* not to include, (*syn.*) to omit: *The airline left off several passengers' names, so they had no seats.‖It left them off.* **b.** *insep.* to stop (talking, reading, writing, etc.): *He surprised me by leaving off in mid-sentence.* **12** *fig.* **to leave oneself wide open:** to make oneself vulnerable, such as to

criticism, loss, or harm: *He makes unneces-sary mistakes and leaves himself wide open to being fired.* **13** *phrasal v. sep.* **to leave s.o. or s.t. alone:** to keep from touching, bothering s.o. or. s.t.: *Please leave the cat alone; she doesn't feel well.* **14** *fig.* **to leave s.o. cold:** to fail to interest s.o.: *The idea of a longer work day leaves me cold.* **15** *fig.* **to leave s.o. hang-ing, swinging** or **twisting in the wind:** to fail to complete an agreement, arrangement, etc.: *Two businessmen signed a contract, but one disappeared and left the other hanging.* **16** *fig.* **to leave s.o. in the dark:** *See:* dark. **17** to **leave s.o. in the lurch:** *See:* lurch. **18** *fig.* **to leave s.o. out in the cold:** to abandon or ex-clude so: *He was due for a promotion, but his boss decided against it and left him out in the cold without any explanation.* **19** *phrasal v. sep.* **to leave s.o. or s.t. behind:** to fail to bring or take, usu. by accident: *I can't believe I left behind my reading glasses!||I left them behind.* **20** *phrasal v. sep.* **to leave s.o. or s.t. out:** not to include, (*syn.*) to omit: **a.** *To shorten the lec-ture, the professor left out the less important parts.||He left them out.* **b.** to fail to take s.o. or s.t., (*syn.*) to abandon: *The plane took off and left him behind.* **21 to leave s.t. at that:** to keep from continuing with s.t.: *The two friends argued over whose turn it was to pay for lunch, but finally they agreed to split the bill and left the matter at that.* **22 to leave s.t. on** or **running:** to allow a machine to continue working: *I left the lights on all night.* **23 to leave s.t. to s.o.: a.** to give s.t. to s.o. after one's death: *In her will, she left all her prop-erty to her children.* **b.** to depend on s.o. to manage s.t.: *Just leave the travel arrange-ments to me.* **24** *phrasal v. insep.* **to leave s.t. up to s.o.:** to allow s.o. else to decide: *He often leaves matters involving the children up to his wife.* **25 to leave the best for last:** to present the best of s.t. after everything else has been done: *The comedian left the best for last, telling his funniest jokes at the end of his act.* **26 to leave well enough alone:** to avoid inter-fering when s.t. is satisfactory: *The children were playing quietly, so their parents decided to leave well enough alone and not suggest going for a walk.* **27 to leave word:** to leave a message: *I telephoned Jane, but she wasn't in, so I left word with her secretary for Jane to return my call.*
—*n.* **1** [C] a period away from work or the military: *She took a leave (of absence) when she had her baby.* **2** *frml.* [U] permission: *He has been given leave to speak to the Queen.* **3 on leave:** temporarily away from work or the military by official permission: *The soldier went on leave for two weeks.* **4** *frml.* **to take one's leave:** to say good-bye and go away

leav·en /ˈlɛvən/ *v.* **1.** to add an agent such as yeast that lightens and expands dough: *A baker leavens bread with yeast.* **2** *fig.* to improve by making livelier, (*syn.*) to enhance: *Her speeches are leavened with humor.* -*n.* [U] **leavening.**

lech·er /ˈlɛtʃər/ or **lech** /lɛtʃ/ *n.* a man with con-tinual thoughts of sex -*adj.* **lecherous** -*n.* **lech-ery.**

lec·tern /ˈlɛk,tərn/ *n.* a type of tall table at which a speaker stands: *The professor stood at the lectern and gave her lecture.*

lec·ture /ˈlɛktʃər/ *n.v.* **-tured, -turing, -tures 1** (to give) a speech on a topic: *The professor de-livered a one-hour <n.> lecture on modern art.* **2** (to give) a long, serious talk with a warning, (*syns.*) scold, reprimand: *The boy's mother <v.> lectured him on bicycle safety.* -*n.* **lecturer.** *See:* teacher, USAGE NOTE.

ledge /lɛdʒ/ *n.* **1** a narrow platform below the window areas of a building: *Birds often land on my window ledge.* **2** a flat area like a shelf in rock formations: *Climbers reached a nar-row ledge on the cliff.*

ledg·er /ˈlɛdʒər/ *n.* a journal in which numbers are recorded: *Every business should keep a ledger of its income and expenses.*

leech /litʃ/ *n.* **1** any bloodsucking worm: *He walked through the swamp and came out of the water with several leeches on his legs.* **2** *fig.* a person who takes from others and gives noth-ing in return: *He is a leech who uses his friends when they let him do so.*
—*v.infrml.* **to leech off:** to take from without giving in return: *He leeches off his friends by staying with them without paying any rent.*

leek /lik/ *n.* a vegetable of the onion family: *I like leeks in my salads.*

leer /lɪr/ *n.* a look that shows sexual desire or cruel satisfaction: *He looked at her with a leer and laughed.*
—*v.* to look at s.o. with a leer: *He leered at her and whispered dirty words.*

leer·y /ˈlɪri/ *adj.* **-ier, -iest** cautious and dis-trustful, (*syns.*) wary, suspicious: *She is leery of investing in stocks.*

lee·ward /ˈliwərd/ *adj.* protected from the wind, rain, etc.: *We camped on the leeward side of the hill.*

lee·way /ˈli,weɪ/ *n.* [U] **1** extra time in which to act: *We have several weeks of leeway in the production schedule in case of delays.* **2** lib-erty to act: *The boss gave us plenty of leeway on how we want to handle the problem.*

left (1) /lɛft/ *adj.* on or by the side of the body containing the heart: *Fewer people write with the left hand than with the right.*
—*adv.* toward the left: *We headed to the cor-ner and turned left.*

L

—*n.* **1** [C] a left-hand turn: *We made a left at the corner.* **2** *sing.*the liberal or socialist parties in politics: *He believes the New Left will lose to the Conservatives.* -*adj.* **leftist.**

left (2) *past tense & past part. of* leave

left field *n.* **1** (in baseball) the left part of the outfield: *He caught the ball in left field.* **2** *infrml.fig.* **way out in left field:** wrong, impractical, far from the truth or reality: *His ideas on how to do things are way out in left field.*

left-handed *adj.* favoring the use of the left hand: *She is a left-handed tennis player.* -*n.* **left-hander.**

left·ie /'lɛfti/ *n.infrml. See:* lefty.

left·o·vers /'lɛft,ouvərz/ *n.pl.* what remains, such as some food after a meal: *We eat leftovers on Sunday evening.*

left wing *n.* [U] *adj.* the liberal to radically liberal side of politics: *She belongs to the <n.> left wing or a <adj.> left wing political party.*

left·y /'lɛfti/ *n.infrml.* a person who tends to use the left hand: *He's a lefty and cannot write with his right hand.*

leg /lɛg/ *n.* **1** one of the lower limbs of humans and many animals, used for walking, running, etc.: *Runners need strong legs.* **2** one of the supports of a piece of furniture: *Don't sit on that chair; one of the legs is broken.* **3** a part of a journey: *She flew first to Rome, then to Pisa, then made the last leg of her trip by taxi.* **4** *infrml.fig.* **Break a leg!:** Good luck! **5** *infrml.fig.* **not to have a leg to stand on:** to have no basis for a claim, demand, etc.: *The law is entirely against him; he doesn't have a leg to stand on.* **6** *infrml.* **to be on one's last legs:** to be worn out or used up, close to failure or death: *This old car is on its last legs.* **7** *infrml.fig.* **to cost an arm and a leg:** to cost much more than expected: *The lawsuit cost her an arm and a leg, but she won.* **8** *infrml.fig.* **to give s.o.** or **to have a leg up (on s.t.):** to put s.o. or be in a good position (in a competition): *He has a leg up on getting that job because he has a friend in the personnel section who recommended him.* **9** *infrml.fig.* **to pull s.o.'s leg:** to play a trick on s.o., to tease s.o.: *She was pulling my leg when she said she had won $1 million in the lottery.* **10** *infrml.fig.* **to shake a leg: a.** to hurry, move fast: *His boss told him to shake a leg and deliver the package.* **b.** to dance: *Tonight, we're going to shake a leg.* **11** **to stretch one's legs:** to take a walk, esp. after sitting or staying indoors a long time: *I'm going outside to stretch my legs.*

leg·a·cy /'lɛgəsi/ *n.* **1** money, property, etc. given in the will of s.o. who has died, (*syn.*) inheritance: *His uncle left him a generous legacy when he died.* **2** s.t. passed on or left by an earlier generation, event, etc.: *We must not let destruction of the environment be our legacy to the next generation.*

le·gal /'ligəl/ *adj.* **1** related to law: *The legal system is slow to function.* **2** permitted or created by law, (*syn.*) lawful: *He has a legal right to vote.* **3** *slang* **to make it legal:** to marry s.o. with whom one has been living: *He lived with his girlfriend for eight years, and now they are going to make it legal.*

le·gal·ese /,ligə'liz/ *n.* written material full of legal terms that make it hard to understand: *That contract is full of legalese.*

legal holiday *n.* a holiday declared by the federal or state government on which businesses, institutions, etc. often close: *Christmas and New Year's Day are legal holidays in the USA.*

le·gal·i·ty /li'gæləti/ *n.* **-ties 1** the state or quality of being legal: *I question the legality of that contract.* **2** *n.pl.* **legalities** legal requirements: *We must take care of the legalities before we buy the land.*

le·gal·ize /'ligə,laɪz/ *v.* **-ized, -izing, -izes** to make legal that which was illegal: *Many states in the USA have legalized gambling.*

leg·end /'lɛdʒənd/ *n.* **1** a story from the distant past, (*syn.*) myth: *Each country has its legends about the past.* **2** an explanation of the symbols used on a map: *The legend on this map shows that a star is the symbol for a capital city.*

leg·en·dar·y /'lɛdʒən,dɛri/ *adj.* **1** based on legend, (*syn.*) mythical: *Legendary stories are passed down from parents to children.* **2** famous, (*syn.*) renowned: *Great Olympic athletes have become legendary.*

leg·gings /'lɛgɪnz/ *n.pl.* coverings for the legs: *In winter, she wears woolen leggings to keep warm.*

leg·gy /'lɛgi/ *adj.* having long legs: *Newborn horses are leggy.*

leg·i·ble /'lɛdʒəbəl/ *adj.* capable of being read, clear: *The photocopy is faint but legible.*

le·gion /'lidʒən/ *n.* **1** a Roman fighting unit of up to 6,000 men with cavalry **2** a mass of people or things: *Legions of people filled the streets to celebrate independence.* **3** a fighting unit, social group, or honorary society: *He belongs to the French Legion of Honor.*

leg·is·late /'lɛdʒɪs,leɪt/ *v.* **-lated, -lating, -lates** to write, debate, and pass laws: *Congress has legislated a new minimum wage for workers.*

leg·is·la·tion /,lɛdʒɪs'leɪʃən/ *n.* **1** a proposed law or laws: *Congress is debating legislation on a new trade agreement.* **2** a law or laws already passed: *New legislation has raised taxes on people's incomes and on businesses.* **3** the act of making laws: *Legislation of a new trade agreement will take time.*

leg·is·la·tive /'lɛdʒɪs,leɪtɪv/ *adj.* related to making laws: *Congress is the legislative branch of the U.S. government.*

leg·is·la·tor /ˈlɛdʒɪsˌleɪtər/ n. a person elected to propose and vote on new laws: *In the U.S. Congress, the legislators are Senators and Representatives.*

leg·is·la·ture /ˈlɛdʒɪsˌleɪtʃər/ n. a governmental body with the power to make laws for a nation or state: *The state legislature meets to pass laws affecting only the state and not the nation.*

le·git /ləˈdʒɪt/ adj.slang short for legitimate

le·git·i·mate /ləˈdʒɪtəmɪt/ adj. 1 legal, lawful: *He has a legitimate claim to part of the profits.* 2 honest, genuine: *She runs a legitimate business.* 3 reasonable, justified: *She has a legitimate concern about her daughter's health.* 4 born to parents legally married to each other -n. **legitimacy.**

le·git·i·mize /ləˈdʒɪtəˌmaɪz/ v. **-mized, -mizing, -mizes** to make legitimate: *By getting married, the couple legitimized their young child.* -v. **legitimate** /ləˈdʒɪtəˌmeɪt/.

leg·room /ˈlɛgˌrum/ n. space to stretch out one's legs when sitting in an airplane, car, etc.: *There is lots of legroom in a big car.*

leg·ume /ˈlɛgˌyum, ləˈgyum/ n. a plant such as beans, peas, and related seed foods: *Legumes are healthy foods.*

leg·work /ˈlɛgˌwɜrk/ n. work requiring looking for and collecting information, such as by a reporter or detective: *Lawyers hire detectives to do legwork in investigating crimes.*

lei·sure /ˈliʒər, ˈlɛ-/ n.adj. 1 relaxation free from work: *They enjoy their <n.> leisure or <adj.> leisure time at the seashore.* 2 **at s.o.'s leisure:** in an unhurried way: *There's no need to rush that report, so you can write it at your leisure.*

lei·sure·ly /ˈliʒərli, ˈlɛ-/ adj. without hurry: *She enjoyed a leisurely bath.*

lem·ming /ˈlɛmɪŋ/ n. a mouselike rodent: *Sometimes migrating lemmings run into the sea and drown.*

lem·on /ˈlɛmən/ n. 1 a sour yellow citrus fruit: *Lemons are squeezed for juice to make lemonade.* 2 infrml.fig. a badly made machine that constantly breaks down and needs repair: *In some states "lemon laws" protect buyers from defective products, such as cars.* -adj. **lemony.**

lem·on·ade /ˌlɛmənˈeɪd/ n. a drink made of lemon juice, water, and sugar: *We like lemonade on hot days.*

le·mur /ˈlimər/ n. an animal with a monkeylike body and long bushy tail, found only in Madagascar: *Lemurs leap through the trees in search of food.*

lend /lɛnd/ v. **lent** /lɛnt/, **lending, lends** 1 to permit the use of for a period of time, loan: *Banks lend money to people.* 2 fig. **to lend a hand:** to help: *When they moved to another apartment, their friends came to lend a hand.*

3 fig. **to lend an ear:** to listen: *She lends an ear to her friends' troubles.*

lending library n. a library that loans books, esp. a public library: *The USA has public lending libraries nationwide.*

length /lɛŋθ, lɛnθ/ n. 1 the measurement of s.t. from end to end: *The length of the highway is 100 miles (160 km). See:* width, depth. 2 the duration of s.t.: *The length of the trip was four hours.* 3 **arm's length:** on strict legal or financial terms, not personal terms: *I now keep my neighbor at arm's length because he has been rude to me many times in the past.* 4 **at length:** in great detail, over a long time: *The speaker talked at length about his political views.* 5 **to go to any length** or **great lengths:** to do anything necessary: *She's so afraid of him that she'll go to any length to avoid him.*

length·en /ˈlɛŋkθən, ˈlɛnθən/ v. to become or make longer (in space or time): *In summer, the number of daylight hours lengthens.*

length·wise /ˈlɛŋkθˌwaɪz, ˈlɛnθ-/ adv. in the direction of the length of s.t.: *We measured the table lengthwise at six feet and across at three.*

length·y /ˈlɛŋkθi, ˈlɛnθi/ adj. **-ier, -iest** long in distance, time, or coverage: *The professor wrote a lengthy book on Napoleon.*

le·ni·en·cy /ˈliniənsi, ˈlinyən-/ n. 1 tolerance of misbehavior: *The judge treated the young man with leniency.* 2 mildness of punishment: *The leniency of the sentence the judge gave him surprised many people.*

le·ni·ent /ˈliniənt, ˈlinyənt/ adj. mild in responding to bad behavior: *That mother is too lenient with her noisy children.*

lens /lɛnz/ n. **lenses** a circular or rectangular device made of glass, plastic, etc., with curved surfaces designed so that it forms images: *Cameras and eyeglasses have lenses.*

len·til /ˈlɛntl/ n. a legume plant whose seeds are cooked and eaten: *Lentil soup is very thick and nourishing.*

leop·ard /ˈlɛpərd/ n. 1 a large member of the cat family, often tan with black spots 2 fig. **leopard can't change its spots:** a person can't change his character: *That criminal is in jail again, which proves that a leopard can't change his spots.*

le·o·tard /ˈliəˌtɑrd/ n. a tight, stretchy piece of clothing for the upper body, worn esp. by dancers: *She exercises in a white leotard.*

lep·er /ˈlɛpər/ n. a person who has leprosy: *In the past, lepers were isolated from other people.*

lep·re·chaun /ˈlɛprəˌkɑn/ n. in stories about Ireland, a little elf-like man: *It is said that leprechauns have hidden pots of gold.*

lep·ro·sy /ˈlɛprəsi/ n. a disease that destroys skin and nerves: *Leprosy is usually found in tropical countries.* -adj. **leprous.**

L

les·bi·an /ˈlɛzbiən/ *n.adj.* a female homosexual: <*n.*> *Lesbians are physically and romantically attracted to other women.* -*n.* [U] **lesbianism.** *See:* gay, USAGE NOTE.

le·sion /ˈliʒən/ *n.* a diseased or injured area of tissue: *Her skin lesions showed where she hit the ground when she fell.*

less /lɛs/ *adj.adv.* not so much (in amount): *She makes* <*adj.*> *less money at her new job but also has to work* <*adv.*> *less.*

less·en /ˈlɛsən/ *v.* to make less, reduce, (*syn.*) to diminish: *The medicine lessened the patient's pain.*

less·er /ˈlɛsər/ *adj.comp. of* less **1** not as much: *We ordered a lesser amount of goods this month.* **2 the lesser of two evils:** the one that is not so harmful, bad, etc. as the other choice: *We could lay off employees, but cutting everyone's hours seems the lesser of two evils.*

les·son /ˈlɛsən/ *n.* **1** s.t. to be learned: *Pupils learn lessons in reading, writing, and arithmetic.* **2** a class or period of instruction: *Her piano lesson is at 4:00.* **3 to learn a lesson** or **to teach s.o. a lesson:** to learn or to teach s.o. correct behavior from a bad experience: *He was nearly hit by a car and learned a lesson about being careful when crossing the street.*

les·sor /ˈlɛsɔr, lɛˈsɔr/ *n.frml.* the person or business that leases property to a lessee: *The lessor offered a five-year lease on the office.*

lest /lɛst/ *conj.frml.* for fear that: *Hold on to the railing lest you fall.*

let /lɛt/ *v.* **let, letting, lets 1** to allow, permit: *I let my dog run free in the yard.* **2** to rent, lease: *The landlord lets apartments to tenants.* **3 let alone:** even less: *I can't afford a nice apartment, let alone a house!* **4 to let go: a.** to set free, release: *Because they had no evidence, the police had to let the suspect go.* **b.** *infrml.* to release emotions, act freely: *She let go and danced wildly to the music.* **5 to let go of:** to release one's hold on: *A monkey let go of a branch and dropped to the ground.* **6** *slang* **to let it all hang out:** to act without reserve, show all that is on one's mind: *My friend was deeply troubled, and she finally let it all hang out.* **7** *slang* **to let it rip:** to allow s.t. (forceful, dangerous, loud, etc.) to happen: *We wanted loud music to dance to, so I told the band leader to let it rip.* **8** *infrml.fig.* **to let off steam:** to release one's frustrations: *She had a hard day at the office and let off steam at home by talking about it.* **9** *phrasal v.* **to let on:** to tell that one knows s.t. secret: *She learned about the surprise party planned for her but didn't let on that she knew.* **10 to let oneself go:** to stop taking care of one's appearance: *Since he lost his job, he has stopped shaving and has generally let himself go.* **11** *phrasal v.* **to let out: a.** to allow to go out: *I let the cat out at night.* **b.** to allow (a sound) to come out, ex-

press: *I let out a yell when I hurt my finger.* **c.** (in sewing) to make larger: *The waist in these pants needs to be let out. See:* take in. **12 to let s.o. in on: a.** to allow s.o. to participate: *We let a friend in on a good business deal.* **b.** to tell s.o. a secret: *I let others in on the fact that the factory is closing down soon.* **13 to let s.o. know:** to tell or inform s.o.: *Please let me know if you'll be late.* **14 to let s.o. off:** to release with little or no punishment: *The judge let the young man off with a short prison sentence.* **15 to let s.o. or s.t. down: a.** to disappoint, fail to meet the expectations of: *When they lost, the players felt they had let their coach down.* **b.** (in sewing) to make longer: *These pants need to be let down an inch. See:* take up. **16 to let s.o. or s.t. go by: a.** to allow to pass: *I stepped aside and let others go by me.* **b.** to pay no attention to, (*syn.*) to ignore: *I just let his stupid insult go by.* **17 to let s.o.** or **s.t. in:** to allow to enter: *She opened a window to let some fresh air in.* **18** *phrasal v. infrml.* **to let up:** to become less intense or forceful: *The rain is letting up now.*
—*n.* (in tennis) a serve that touches the net and is invalid

let·down /ˈlɛtˌdaʊn/ *n.* a disappointment, discouragement: *She was not offered the job after two good interviews, and that was a big letdown.*

le·thal /ˈliθəl/ *adj.* able to kill, (*syns.*) deadly, fatal: *Nuclear weapons are lethal to whole populations.*

le·thar·gic /ləˈθardʒɪk/ *adj.* **1** sleepy, tired, (*syns.*) drowsy, listless: *Some medicines make people lethargic.* **2** slow, with little energy, (*syn.*) sluggish: *That organization acts in a lethargic manner.*

leth·ar·gy /ˈlɛθərdʒi/ *n.* **1** sleepiness, (*syn.*) drowsiness: *The patient's lethargy after surgery is normal.* **2** lack of energy, (*syn.*) sluggishness: *That fellow's lethargy is in fact laziness.*

let's /lɛts/ *contr. of* let us (used to make a suggestion or proposal): *Let's go out for lunch!*

let·ter /ˈlɛtər/ *n.* **1** a symbol of an alphabet: *The letter* M *follows the letter* L. **2** a written message, usu. sent by mail: *She sent a letter to her mother.* **3** a formal document ensuring certain conditions: *The king gave the ambassador a letter of safe passage for his trip home.* **4** *pl.* distinction in learning: *The professor is a man of letters.* **5 the letter of the law:** the exact written requirements of s.t. (as opposed to its intent or purpose): *The judge decided the case according to the letter of the law.* **6 to follow to the letter:** to obey precisely, with attention to detail: *He told me to follow the instructions to the letter.*

—*v.* **1** to draw or write letters on **2** to earn an athletic award: *He lettered in three sports in high school.*

letter carrier *n. See:* mail carrier.

let·ter·head /'lɛtər,hɛd/ *n.* sheets of writing paper with a person's or business's name, address, and telephone number printed at the top: *I write letters to customers on the company letterhead.*

let·ter·ing /'lɛtərɪŋ/ *n.* **1** the writing of letters and numbers: *Children learn to do lettering in school.* **2** letters as a group: *The lettering on the office door gave the doctor's name and specialization.*

letter of credit *n.* a bank document guaranteeing to a supplier that its bill will be paid (up to a certain amount for a specified period): *Our company bought a letter of credit to guarantee payment for supplies from China.*

let·tuce /'lɛtəs/ *n.* any of a variety of leafy salad plants: *I like a salad made with romaine lettuce.*

let·up /'lɛt,ʌp/ *n.* a slowdown, lessening of intensity: *It has been raining steadily all day with no letup.*

leu·ke·mi·a /lu'kimiə/ *n.* cancer of the white blood cells, often leading to death: *The unfortunate child died of leukemia.*

lev·ee /'lɛvi/ *n.* a raised area beside a river designed to prevent flooding: *A levee burst on the Mississippi River, and much farmland was flooded.*

lev·el /'lɛvəl/ *adj.* **1** horizontal, flat: *We can't put the picnic table here because the ground isn't level.* **2** at the same height, even: *The building is level with its neighbor.* **3 to do** or **try one's level best:** to try hard (to do s.t. well): *I'll try my level best to do a good job.*
—*n.* **1** height, vertical distance: *The land around here is mainly at sea level.* **2** a position on a scale or in relation to others: *a low level of production, a government official at a very high level* **3** a worker's tool used to test if s.t. is horizontal: *Bricklayers use a level to see if their work is level.* **4** *fig.* **to be on the level:** to be honest and sincere: *He is not on the level when he says that he'll be able to pay because he owes everyone money.*
—*v.* **1** to pull down to the ground, flatten, (*syn.*) to raze: *Bulldozers leveled houses to make way for a new building.* **2** to direct an accusation or criticism: *He has leveled charges of dishonesty against the other candidate.* **3** *infrml.* **to level with s.o.:** to tell s.o. what the real situation is, frankly and completely: *He finally leveled with me that he has no money and is desperate.*

lev·el·head·ed /ˈlɛvəl,hɛdɪd/ *adj.* sensible and calm, (*syn.*) prudent: *She is a levelheaded girl and won't do anything foolish.*

lev·er /'lɛvər, 'li-/ *n.* **1** a bar positioned on a fixed point (the fulcrum) and pressed to move s.t.: *A worker used a crowbar as a lever to lift a rock.* **2** *fig.* a means to apply pressure or influence: *A politician used his vote as a lever to get what he wanted from the party's leaders.*
—*v.* to use a lever: *The worker levered the rock out of the ground.*

lev·er·age /'lɛvərɪdʒ, 'li-/ *n.* **1** use, action, or power of a lever: *A longer lever will give us more leverage.* **2** *fig.* power to accomplish s.t.: *Unions have the leverage of a strike in negotiations with management.*
—*v.* **-aged, -aging, -ages** **1** to use s.t. to force a change or movement: *Union leaders were able to leverage a wage increase in the new contract.* **2** *fig.* to buy securities or property by using borrowed money to purchase them: *He leveraged his investment in stock by borrowing lots of money to buy it.*

lev·i·tate /'lɛvə,teɪt/ *v.* **-tated, -tating, -tates** to (cause to) rise in the air: *A magician levitated a chair on the stage by waving his hands. -n.* [U] **levitation** /,lɛvə'teɪʃən/.

lev·i·ty /'lɛvəti/ *n.frml.* lack of seriousness, (*syns.*) frivolity, merrymaking: *Levity at the party grew louder and louder.*

lev·y /'lɛvi/ *v.* **-ied, -ying, -ies** to require to pay (taxes, customs duties, etc.), (*syn.*) to assess: *The government levied a new tax on the people.*
—*n.* **-ies** a tax or other assessment: *The new customs levies on travelers go into effect now.*

lewd /lud/ *adj.* related to sex in an offensive way, (*syn.*) obscene: *Pornographic magazines are full of lewd pictures. -n.* [U] **lewdness.**

lex·i·cog·ra·pher /,lɛksə'kɑgrəfər/ *n.* a person who compiles dictionaries: *Lexicographers define the meanings of words. -n.* [U] **lexicography.**

lex·i·con /'lɛksə,kɑn/ *n.* **1** a dictionary: *He has an old lexicon of Latin words and their English equivalents.* **2** a group of words of a particular field: *"Liberal" and "Conservative" are words with different interpretations in the lexicon of politics. -adj.* **lexical.**

li·a·bil·i·ty /'laɪə'bɪləti/ *n.* **1** a legal obligation, such as to pay debts and damages: *Insurance companies had huge liabilities to pay because of the hurricane damage.* **2** disadvantage, drawback: *That business has excellent products, but its debt is a big liability. See:* asset.

li·a·ble /'laɪəbəl/ *adj.* **1** legally obligated, responsible: *Rental contracts state that tenants are liable for damages that they cause to the property.* **2** likely (to do or experience): *If you drive in a bad storm, you are liable to have an accident.*

L

li·ai·son /ˈlieɪˌzɑn, liˈeɪ-/ *n.* **1** a coordination, an exchange between individuals, businesses, or governments, esp. of information: *The liaison between the two governments is carried out personally by the Prime Minister and the President.* **2** a love affair: *The two enjoyed their liaison while it lasted.* -*v.* **liaise.**

li·ar /ˈlaɪər/ *n.* a person who doesn't tell the truth: *He's such a liar that you can't believe a word he says.*

lib /lɪb/ *n. short for* liberation.

li·bel /ˈlaɪbəl/ *n.* (in law) a published statement or picture that unfairly damages a person's good name or reputation: *The newspaper story about the movie star was false, and she sued for libel.*
—*v.* to print libel about, (*syn.*) to defame: *The tabloid newspaper libeled a movie star.* -*adj.* **libelous.**

lib·er·al /ˈlɪbərəl, ˈlɪbrəl/ *adj.* **1** generous, large: *She puts liberal amounts of food on the table.* **2** (in politics) proposing change, progressive: *The liberal politicians wanted to expand the welfare system.*
—*n.* a person or politician of liberal views: *The Liberals won the last election.*

USAGE NOTE: The two largest political parties in the USA are the *Democrats* and the *Republicans,* but their members are also described by the labels *liberal* and *conservative,* respectively. Members of each party can be categorized from most to least progressive, as *liberal, moderate,* or *conservative: She's a moderate Republican and her husband's a conservative Democrat, so they agree on some important issues.*

liberal arts *n.pl.* (in education) study of the humanities, social and natural sciences, and mathematics: *She studied liberal arts at college before beginning her professional training.*

lib·er·al·ism /ˈlɪbərəˌlɪzəm, ˈlɪbrə-/ *n.* a set of beliefs favoring change in politics, religion, etc.: *His liberalism led him to join a community action group.*

lib·er·al·ize /ˈlɪbərəˌlaɪz, ˈlɪbrə-/ *v.* **-ized, -izing, -izes** to make more liberal and less strict, such as to extend government programs to benefit more people: *The tax laws have been liberalized to make it easier to save money for retirement.*

lib·er·ate /ˈlɪbəˌreɪt/ *v.* **1** to free from oppression: *The American Civil War liberated many people from slavery.* **2** *slang* (said ironically) to steal, (*syn.*) to make off with: *Thieves liberated goods from stores during a riot.*

lib·er·a·tion /ˌlɪbəˈreɪʃən/ *n.* an act of freedom from oppression: *The peace agreement called for the liberation of all prisoners of war.*

lib·er·tar·i·an /ˌlɪbərˈtɛriən/ *n.adj.* a person who believes in freedom of thought and responsibility for one's own path in life: *The* <*n.*> *Libertarians are a small political party.*

lib·er·tine /ˈlɪbərˌtin/ *n.* a person of unrestrained desires: *He was a libertine, always chasing after women.* -*n.* [U] **libertinism.**

lib·er·ty /ˈlɪbərti/ *n.* **-ties 1** freedom, right: *Peoples of many countries enjoy liberties guaranteed by their constitutions.* **2** freedom from prison, control, etc.: *Prisoners gain their liberty after serving their sentences.* **3 at liberty: a.** free to act, speak, etc.: *He is not at liberty to reveal secret information.* **b.** free from duty: *The sailors were at liberty in the port.* **4 to take liberties (with): a.** *frml.* to behave in a way that offends by being too friendly: *He made a serious mistake by taking liberties with the boss's daughter.* **b.** to make changes in too freely: *That English translation was criticized for taking liberties with the original French novel.*

li·bi·do /lɪˈbidoʊ/ *n.* **-dos** sexual desire, sex drive: *He has a very strong libido.* -*adj.* **libidinous** /lɪˈbɪdnəs/.

li·brar·i·an /laɪˈbrɛriən/ *n.* a person who directs or works in a library, esp. s.o. with a degree in library science: *The head librarian approves all book purchases.*

li·brar·y /ˈlaɪˌbrɛri/ *n.* **1** a collection of books and other reference materials: *The couple has a library of novels and reference books in their house.* **2** a building that houses books and other reference materials: *Public libraries are found all over the USA.*

library science *n.* the academic discipline concerned with the management and development of libraries: *Library science requires several years of academic training.*

li·bret·to /lɪˈbrɛtoʊ/ *n.* **-tos** or **-ti** /-ti/ the words of a musical piece that is sung, esp. an opera: *He has written both the music and the libretto for an opera.* -*n.* **librettist.**

lice /laɪs/ *n.pl.* of louse. blood-sucking insects: *The child had lice in his hair.*

li·cense /ˈlaɪsəns/ *n.* **1** a permit given by an official body, usu. to s.o. who passes an examination: *She has a driver's license (hairdresser's license, license as a registered nurse, etc.).* **2** *fig.* liberty to break accepted norms, such as the license to break rules of grammar when writing poetry: *He used poetic license in describing the dictator as the greatest hero since Julius Caesar.*
—*v.* to give a permit to or for, (*syn.*) to authorize: *This restaurant is licensed to sell alcohol.* -*n.* [U] **licensure** /ˈlaɪsənʃər/.

licensed practical nurse *n. abbr.* **LPN** a nurse who has passed an examination and can provide nursing care if supervised by a doctor or registered nurse: *She works in a local hospital as a licensed practical nurse.*

li·cens·ee /ˌlaɪsənˈsi/ *n.* a person or business that has received a license: *All barber shops in the city are licensees of the City Board of Health. See:* franchisee.

li·chen /ˈlaɪkən/ *n.* a very small plant formed of fungus and algae: *Lichen can live even under snow and provide food for animals in winter.*

lick /lɪk/ *v.* **1** to rub the tongue over: *Children like to lick ice cream cones.* **2** *infrml.fig.* to beat decisively: *The hockey team licked their opponents 5 to 0.* **3** *infrml.fig.* **to lick one's chops** or **lips:** to look ahead with delight: *He is just licking his chops to go out with that pretty girl.* **4** *fig.* **to lick one's wounds:** to recover from a defeat (like an animal that has been hurt in a fight): *He lost the election and is licking his wounds at home.*
—*n.* **1** a stroke of the tongue: *I gave the stamp a lick and stuck it on the envelope.* **2** *infrml.fig.* a punch, blow: *The boxers gave each other some hard licks.* **3** *infrml.fig.* **to get one's licks in:** to take the chance to fight for one's cause: *The politician gave an impassioned speech to get his licks in against the tax legislation.* **4 to give s.t. a lick and a promise:** to do a job quickly and carelessly: *He did a poor job of repairing the stove; he just gave it a lick and a promise, then left.*

lick·e·ty-split /ˈlɪkətiˈsplɪt/ *adv.infrml.* very fast, quickly: *The children ran lickety-split to the ice cream truck.*

lick·ing /ˈlɪkɪŋ/ *n.infrml.fig.* a beating in a fight: *Someone should give that big bully a good licking.*

lic·o·rice /ˈlɪkərɪs, -rɪʃ/ *n.* a substance used in medicine and in a red or black candy: *Children love to suck and chew on licorice.*

lid /lɪd/ *n.* **1** a covering of a container, a top: *I took the lid off the coffee can and scooped some out.* **2** *short for* eyelid, the skin over the eye: *The baby closed her lids and went to sleep.* **3** *infrml.fig.* **to blow the lid off:** to suddenly expose (s.t. that was secret): *The story in the newspaper blew the lid off the company's plan to buy the land.* **4** *infrml.fig.* **to keep the lid on:** to prevent (rioting, trouble, scandal, etc.): *The police patrolled the city to keep the lid on any rioting or looting.*

lie (1) /laɪ/ *n.* **1** a statement that is not true, (*syn.*) a falsehood: *She told a lie about how old she is.* **2 a little white lie:** a small lie told to save s.o.'s feelings from hurt
—*v.* **lied, lying, lies** **1** to tell s.t. that is not true: *He lied when he said he didn't steal.* **2 to lie through one's teeth:** to lie openly: *He lied through his teeth in denying he stole; four people saw him do it.*

lie (2) *v.* **lay** /leɪ/, **lain** /leɪn/, **lying, lies** **1** to rest in a horizontal position: *She lay down on the grass to take a nap.* **2** to be located: *The river lies near the town.* **3 to lie down on the job:** to be lazy and work little: *He lies down on the job by talking all the time.* **4** *fig.* **to lie low:** to wait in hiding or to avoid notice: *She lay low until the time was right to present her idea.* **5** *fig.* **to take s.t. lying down:** (usu. used negatively) to accept an insult without protest: *The boss cut his pay for no reason, but John did not take it lying down; he protested.*

lie detector *n.* a device that registers changes in blood pressure and breathing in response to questions to determine if s.o. is telling the truth: *The accused murderer passed two lie detector tests, indicating that she was not the killer.*

lien /lin/ *n.* a creditor's legal claim on property that may be seized if the principal and interest are not paid: *A mortgage on a house is a lien owned by the bank that loaned the buyer the money to purchase the house.*

lieu /lu/ *n.* place, usu. in place of: *In lieu of cash, the buyer offered to trade another property for the new house.*

lieu·ten·ant /luˈtɛnənt/ *n.* **1** (in the USA) an officer of the lowest military rank **2** (in many civil positions) a rank below: *He was elected Lieutenant Governor of Louisiana.*

life /laɪf/ *n.* **lives** /laɪvz/ **1** the state of being of a functioning plant or animal: *When the doctor arrived, the life had already gone out of the old man.* **2** living things: *Is there life on other planets?* **3** one's existence from birth to death: *He lived a long and productive life.* **4 a dog's life:** a boring, hard existence: *He leads a dog's life, with a demanding job and no friends.* **5** *fig.* **for dear life:** as if one's life depended on it: *When the alligator charged at us, we ran for dear life.* **6** *fig.* **for the life of me:** (an expression of extreme disbelief): *For the life of me, I can't understand why he continues to gamble away his money!* **7 life (and soul) of the party:** a person who is the center of activity and enjoyment in a group, providing laughter, jokes, stories, etc.: *George was really the life of the party last night when he danced on the piano.* **8 life (in prison)** or **a life sentence:** the punishment of spending the rest of one's life in prison: *The judge gave him a life sentence for the killings.* **9** *fig.* **not on your life:** (an expression of strong disapproval): *My young daughter asked if she could go out in a bad storm, and I said, "Not on your life!"* **10 to bring to life: a.** to bring back to consciousness, (*syn.*) to resuscitate: *The old man fell unconscious, and a paramedic brought him to life.* **b.** to create, make possible: *The product lay untouched for years until a new engineer brought it to life with a new design.* **11 to**

come to life: to awaken, spring into being: *He was quiet at first, then came to life with a joke and laughter.* **12 to risk life and limb:** to put one's life in danger: *He risked life and limb to save the drowning child.* **13 exclam. What a life!:** (an expression of sorrow or happiness): *What a life; I love it here in the Caribbean!*

life-and-death *adj.* with living or dying as the result: *He has cancer and is in a life-and-death struggle to survive.*

life·blood /ˈlaɪfˌblʌd/ *n.fig.* s.t. basic to sustain and give strength to a business, economy, culture, etc.: *A constant flow of successful new products is the lifeblood of most businesses.*

life·boat /ˈlaɪfˌboʊt/ *n.* a small boat used in emergencies: *The ship started to sink, so the passengers climbed into the lifeboats to save themselves.*

life buoy *n.* flotation equipment used to hold s.o. up in water: *A sailor threw a life buoy to the man who fell off the ship.*

life expectancy *n.* the average age to which people can expect to live: *In the USA, the life expectancy of women is longer than that for men.*

life·guard /ˈlaɪfˌgɑrd/ *n.* a person whose job it is to save swimmers from drowning: *Lifeguards patrol the beaches and rescue swimmers in trouble.*

life history *n.* a person's story from birth to the present: *I asked him where he was from, but he gave me his entire life history!*

life insurance *n.* a contract paying money after the death of its owner: *His life insurance provided for his family after he died.*

life jacket *n.* a piece of equipment worn around the upper body to keep a person afloat in water

life·less /ˈlaɪflɪs/ *adj.* dead: *Lifeless bodies from the airplane crash lay on the ground.*

life·like /ˈlaɪfˌlaɪk/ *adj.* so real as to seem alive: *The painter's portraits are so lifelike that they seem like photographs.*

life jacket

life·line /ˈlaɪfˌlaɪn/ *n.* **1** a rope used to save people and animals in danger of death: *A sailor threw a lifeline to passengers washed off the ship in the storm.* **2** *fig.* any form of life-giving help: *International food supplies provide a lifeline for starving refugees.*

life·long /ˈlaɪfˌlɔŋ/ *adj.* lasting through one's lifetime: *Jane and June have been lifelong friends.*

life preserver *n.* equipment, esp. a doughnut-shaped ring, used to keep a person above water: *He held onto a life preserver until he could be pulled into the boat.*

lif·er /ˈlaɪfər/ *n.* a prisoner sentenced to life in prison: *That murderer is a lifer and will never be released.*

life raft *n.* an air-filled lifeboat: *When the ship hit the rocks, the crew took to life rafts for safety.*

life·sav·er /ˈlaɪfˌseɪvər/ *n.* **1** anything that preserves life: *A supply of food from the Red Cross was a lifesaver for the starving population.* **2** *TM* **Lifesaver** a small, ring-shaped candy *-adj.* **lifesaving.**

life-size *n.* equal in size to a living thing: *The artist painted a life-size portrait of my mother.*

life·style /ˈlaɪfˌstaɪl/ *n.* the manner in which one lives: *Her lifestyle changed greatly when she left New York to live in the country.*

USAGE NOTE: The term *alternative lifestyle* often refers to people in *gay* relationships and others who follow less traditional paths in life: *She joined a community of artists, shaved her head, and moved to the desert; sadly, her parents couldn't accept her alternative lifestyle.*

life-support system *n.* **1** any combination of oxygen, food, or light systems, used to enable (plant or animal) life to continue: *Astronauts depend on life-support systems in space.* **2** any of a number of devices used to sustain life for the sick, such as heart-lung, kidney dialysis, or oxygen machines: *Doctors removed the life-support system from the dying patient.*

life-threatening *adj.* capable of killing s.o.: *Wars are life-threatening situations.*

life·time /ˈlaɪfˌtaɪm/ *n.* the duration of a person's life: *During his lifetime, he experienced two world wars and the Great Depression.*

life vest *n.* See: life jacket.

lift /lɪft/ *v.* **1** to raise to a higher level, (*syn.*) to elevate: *He lifted his little girl up to his shoulders.* **2** to remove, end: *The government lifted some restrictions on imported goods.* **3** to go up and disappear: *The fog lifted in the morning sun.* **4** *infrml.fig.* to steal, (*syn.*) to make off with: *Someone lifted my coat from the rack.* **5 to not lift a finger:** not to make any effort at all: *He did not lift a finger to help his hurt neighbor.*
—*n.* **1** an act of raising to a higher level: *A worker gave the box a lift onto a shelf.* **2** *fig.* a raising of spirits, (*syn.*) a boost: *The good news gave us all a lift.* **3** *infrml.* a free ride in a vehicle: *My friend gave me a lift to the store in his car.* **4** *Brit.* an elevator

lift-off *n.* the launching of a space vehicle from Earth: *The space probe is scheduled for lift-off at 7:03 A.M.*

lig·a·ment /ˈlɪgəmənt/ *n.* a strong, flexible band holding bones or other body parts in place: *The football player hurt the ligaments of his right knee.*

li·ga·tion /laɪˈgeɪʃən/ *n.* the surgical tying of a vein, artery, etc.: *The doctor made ligations to repair the artery.* -*v.* **ligate;** -*n.* **ligature** /ˈlɪgəʧər/.

light /laɪt/ *n.* **1** radiation, as from the sun or electric lights, that allows vision: *I need more light to take a picture with this camera.* **2** sunshine, daylight: *He walked out of the house and into the light.* **3** s.t. that produces light, such as lightbulbs or lamps: *When it is dark, we turn on the lights.* **4** s.t. that can start a fire, such as a match: *She took out a cigarette and asked her friend for a light.* **5** a traffic signal: *Turn right at the next light.* **6** *fig.* a way of understanding: *He now looks back on his life and sees it in a new light.* **7** *fig.* **in light of:** considering, in relationship to: *We need to rethink our plan in light of this new information.* **8** *fig.* **not to see the light of day:** not to appear or happen: *That project is so slow and costly that it will never see the light of day.* **9** *fig.* **to bring** or **come to light:** to make or become known, bring or come to public attention: *New information about the presidential candidate's past has come to light.* **10 to make light of:** to treat as if unimportant: *He made light of his illness, but we knew it was serious.* **11** *infrml.fig.* **to see the light:** to realize that action needs to be taken, usu. in a situation where it was already obvious to others: *His stomach hurt for weeks before he finally saw the light and visited a doctor.* **12 to throw** or **shed (some) light on:** to make clear, explain: *She saw the accident happen, so maybe she can throw some light on what caused it.*

—*v.* **lighted** or **lit** /lɪt/, **lighting, lights 1** to set on fire, (*syn.*) to ignite: *We light a fire in the fireplace on cold winter nights.* **2** to give light to, (*syn.*) to illuminate: *At night, we light the sides of the house to keep burglars away.* **3** to land gently, (*syn.*) to alight: *The bird lighted on a tree branch.* **4** *phrasal v. infrml.* **to light into:** to attack with words or blows: *He'll light into anyone who criticizes his work.* **5** *phrasal v. slang* **to light out:** to leave quickly: *When the police arrived, the thief lit out down the street, but they lit out right after him.* **6** *phrasal v.* **to light up: a.** to brighten up, as with happiness: *Her eyes lit up at the good news.* **b.** *phrasal v. infrml.* to ignite a cigarette: *He waited to light up until after everyone had finished eating.*

—*adj.* **-er, -est 1** having little weight, not heavy: *An empty suitcase is light.* **2** pale in color, not dark: *She wore a light blue dress.* **3** not forceful, intense, or serious: *a light rain, a*

light sleep, light reading **4** gentle, delicate: *Ballet dancers move with light steps.*

—*adv.* **to travel light:** to take few possessions when traveling: *She usually travels light.*

light bulb *n.* **1** the round glass part of an electric light: *The light bulb in the lamp is burned out.* **2** *infrml.fig.* **to have a light bulb go on:** a sudden understanding: *A light bulb went on when she found the solution to the math problem.*

light·en /ˈlaɪtn/ *v.* **1** to reduce the weight of: *He lightened the horse's load by using a smaller saddle.* **2** to become or make a lighter color or less dark: *The painter lightened the color by adding some white.* **3** to reduce the intensity of s.t., esp. worry: *The arrival of springtime lightens people's spirits.*

light·er /ˈlaɪtər/ *adj. comp* of light: not as heavy in weight or dark in color as s.t. else
—*n.* a device for igniting cigarettes, etc.: *She carries a cigarette lighter in her purse.*

light-headed *adj.* feeling faint or dizzy: *The hot weather sometimes makes him feel light-headed.*

light·heart·ed /ˈlaɪtˌhɑrtɪd/ *adj.* cheerful, carefree: *He is a lighthearted boy, always joking.*

light·house /ˈlaɪtˌhaʊs/ *n.* a tall building housing a light to guide ships

lighthouse

light housekeeping *n.* the less difficult work in a house, such as washing dishes, vacuuming, and dusting furniture: *She does the light housekeeping herself and has her children do the rest.*

light·ing /ˈlaɪtɪŋ/ *n.* **1** the system for producing light in a room or the quality of that light, (*syn.*) illumination: *The lighting in that restaurant is soft and romantic.* **2** starting of a fire: *The lighting of a wood fire begins with small pieces of wood.*

light·ly /ˈlaɪtli/ *adv.* **1** with gentleness: *She touched the cat's fur lightly.* **2 to take s.t. lightly:** to treat with a lack of seriousness or concern: *He took his illness lightly.*

light·ness /ˈlaɪtnɪs/ *n.* **1** a small degree of weight or color: *The lightness of furnishings in the room made it cheerful.* **2** lack of seriousness, (*syn.*) frivolity: *The lightness of the conversation pleased everyone.*

light·ning /ˈlaɪtnɪŋ/ *n.* **1** an electrical discharge in the sky or between sky and earth, esp. during a thunderstorm: *Lightning streaked across the sky, and thunder clapped.* **2 lightning never strikes twice in the same place:** very unusual accidents never happen a second time to the same person: *You have had a bad accident, but remember that lightning never strikes twice in the same place.* **3 like** or **as fast as lightning:** extremely fast: *Those jet planes flew over the battlefield like lightning.*

lightning rod *n.* a device for directing lightning harmlessly into the ground: *Houses and barns in rural areas have lightning rods on their roofs.*

light opera *n.* opera with a light, comical theme: *Straus's is my favorite light opera.*

lights-out *n.* a time when lights are turned off: *Eleven o'clock is lights-out in that prison.*

light·weight /'laɪt,weɪt/ *n.* **1** a boxer between a featherweight and a welterweight (127 to 135 pounds): *He boxed in the Olympics as a lightweight.* **2** a person of little ability, influence, or intelligence: *The other editors at his newspaper consider him a lightweight.*

light-year *n.* **1** the distance that light travels in a year, or approx. 5.88 trillion miles (9.46 trillion km): *Astronomers measure the distance to stars in light-years.* **2** *fig.* (indicating superiority) a great distance: *That company's product is light-years ahead of the competition in quality.*

lik·a·ble /'laɪkəbəl/ *adj.* (of a person) easy to like, pleasant: *He's a likable boy, always friendly.*

like /laɪk/ *v.* **liked, liking, likes 1** to enjoy, find pleasant: *He likes to watch television.* **2** to be fond of: *The boy and girl like each other very much.* **3 would like:** want, desire: *I would like coffee, please.*
—*adj.* **1** similar to: *The girl is like her mother.* **2** *suffix* **-like** seeming to be, typical of: *homelike, childlike*
—*n.pl.* **likes and dislikes:** personal preferences: *We all have our likes and dislikes.*

like·li·hood /'laɪkli,hʊd/ *n.* probability (of s.t. happening): *In all likelihood, it will rain today.*

like·ly /'laɪkli/ *adj.* **-lier, -liest** probable, to be expected: *Accidents are likely to happen.*

like-minded *adj.* (of people) sharing the same values: *Some like-minded people got together and formed a political discussion group.*

lik·en /'laɪkən/ *v.* to think of as being similar to, compare: *She admired her father so much that she likened him to a saint.*

like·ness /'laɪknɪs/ *n.* **1** sameness or similarity, (*syn.*) resemblance: *The daughter has a likeness to her mother.* **2** image, as in painting: *That painting of your uncle is a good likeness of him.*

like·wise /'laɪk,waɪz/ *adv.* **1** in addition, also: *My friend ordered a lemonade, and I did likewise.* **2** in the same way or manner: *I told my friend to enjoy her vacation, and she said, "Likewise, I hope you enjoy yours, too."*

lik·ing /'laɪkɪŋ/ *n.* [C;U] fondness, taste: *She has a liking for French perfume.*

li·lac /'laɪ,læk, -,lɑk, -lək/ *n.* [C] a bush or shrub, noted for its white or purple flowers and pleasant smell: *Lilacs are popular in the USA as a yard flower.*

lilt /lɪlt/ *n.v.* a pleasing rhythmic style in singing or speech: *Her musical style has a pleasing <n.> lilt.* **-adj. lilting.**

lil·y /'lɪli/ *n.* **lies** any of over 2,000 flowering plants that usu. have trumpet-shaped flowers

lily pad *n.* leaf of a water lily: *A tiny frog sat on a lily pad.*

limb /lɪm/ *n.* **1** *frml.* an arm, leg, or wing of an animal: *Diabetes limits blood circulation in the limbs.* **2** a tree branch: *A broken limb fell on the road.* **3 out on a limb:** alone in a risky position (in a discussion, argument, etc.): *I don't dare go out on a limb to predict a winner in this election.* **4** *frml.suffix* **-limbed** /-lɪmd/ having limbs, such as legs: *He's a long-limbed basketball player. See:* life (and limb).

lim·ber /'lɪmbər/ *adj.* (of a person) able to move easily, (*syns.*) supple, flexible: *She is limber from regular exercise.*
—*phrasal v. sep.* **to limber up s.t.:** to loosen, make flexible: *She limbers up her muscles by stretching before she runs.||She limbers them up.*

lim·bo (1) /'lɪmboʊ/ *n.* [U] in limbo· in a state of uncertain waiting: *His visa application is in limbo; no one at the consulate can tell him its status.*

limbo (2) *n. sing.* a West Indian dance: *She loves to do the limbo.*

lime /laɪm/ *n.* **1** [C;U] a small green citrus fruit: *He drinks soda with a dash of lime (juice).* **2** [U] calcium oxide in a whitish earthy form, often mixed in cements: *Bricklayers put lime in mortar to cement bricks.*

lime·light /'laɪm,laɪt/ *n.* [U] **1** the strong light directed onto a performer on stage: *The stage was dark except for a singer in the limelight.* **2** *fig.* the center of attention: *He is a well-known athlete and enjoys being in the limelight.*

lim·er·ick /'lɪmərɪk/ *n.* a short, humorous poem of five lines: *He writes and recites limericks for fun.*

lime·stone /'laɪm,stoʊn/ *n.* [U] a type of rock composed of calcium carbonate: *Limestone is often used in building construction.*

lim·it /'lɪmɪt/ *n.* **1** the greatest amount or extent allowed: *The speed limit is 55 MPH in many states.* **2** the farthest point of, border: *The limits of the property are marked by a fence.* **3 off limits:** where s.o. is not permitted to go: *The children understand that the river is off limits when there's no adult with them.* **4** *fig.* **the limit:** s.o. or s.t. shocking or unacceptable: *That's the limit! That child is so badly behaved he'll have to stay home!* **5 (to go) to the limit:**

(to go) to the greatest extent, esp. of one's ability: *He ran to the limit of his strength and then dropped, exhausted.*
—*v.* to keep within limits, restrict: *The committee limited spending for the project to $1 million.* -*adj.* **limiting.**

lim·i·ta·tion /ˌlɪmɪˈteɪʃən/ *n.* **1** [C;U] a restriction in amount or extent: *The limitation on spending for new equipment is now set.* **2** [C] restrictions in one's ability: *That employee has limitations on what work he can do.*

lim·it·ed /ˈlɪmɪtɪd/ *adj.* **1** restricted in extent or amount: *He is old and has limited use of his legs.* **2** *frml.* a train or bus that makes few stops: *He takes the limited bus on long trips.*

limited edition *n.* a manufacturing run of a fixed, small number to increase the value of each copy: *The artist did a limited edition of his prints and signed each of them.*

lim·o /ˈlɪmoʊ/ *n.short for* limousine

lim·ou·sine /ˌlɪməˈzin, ˈlɪməzɪn/ *n.* a large, expensive car, usu. with a driver: *The movie star arrived at the theater in a chauffeured limousine.*

limp /lɪmp/ *adj.* **-er, -est** lacking firmness or stiffness: *The flowers are limp from lack of water.*
—*n.* an uneven walk as from an injury to the leg or foot: *After the truck ran over his foot, he walked with a limp.*
—*v.* **1** to walk with a limp, (*syn.*) to hobble: *He limped after his skiing accident.* **2** *phrasal v.* **to limp along:** to progress slowly and weakly: *The project is in bad shape and just limps along from day to day.*

lim·pid /ˈlɪmpɪd/ *adj.frml.* clear, (*syn.*) lucid: *The author wrote in a limpid style.*

linch·pin /ˈlɪntʃˌpɪn/ *n.* **1** a strong pin used to hold a wagon or carriage wheel in place: *The linchpin came loose, and the wheel fell off.* **2** *fig.* s.t. very important that holds other things together, such as a key person or part of a plan: *She is the linchpin of her organization.*

line /laɪn/ *n.* **1** a narrow, continuous mark, such as on a piece of paper: *My notebook has thin blue lines printed on each page.* **2** a stripe: *Two yellow lines painted on a highway means that drivers should not pass cars ahead of them.* **3** a row of people or things: *A line of people waited outside the passport office.* **4** a limit or border: *A sign at the state line said, "Welcome to Florida."* **5** a rope or cord: *We hang clothes on the line to dry them in the sun.* **6** a wire: *Transmission lines carry electricity.* **7** an electronic connection, such as a telephone line: *Mr. Jones is on the line and wants to talk with you.* **8** a wrinkle in the skin: *She has lines in her forehead.* **9** a manufacturer's product: *The store carries several different lines of shoes from Italy.* **10** a connected series of ideas: *a line of thought, a line of questioning*

11 a series of members of a family: *The king's line ended when he died with no son or daughter to take his place.* **12** a direction, course: *The line for the parade was down Fifth Avenue.* **13** a written sentence or phrase for an actor to speak: *Actors sometimes forget their lines.* **14** a company running a system of ships, planes, or buses: *She works for Delta Air Lines.* **15** *infrml.* a factory assembly line: *He works on the line at General Motors.* **16 between the lines:** in an indirect way, not written or said openly: *The memo from his boss didn't say he was fired, but reading between the lines he knew his job was not secure.* **17 in line for:** likely to get, (*syn.*) destined for: *She is an excellent employee and is in line for a promotion.* **18 in the line of duty:** while performing one's work, esp. as a police officer or firefighter: *A firefighter was injured in the line of duty.* **19 on line:** *See:* online. **20** *infrml.* **on the line:** in a dangerous position, at risk: *Her plan had better succeed, or her job will be on the line.* **21 out of line:** (of words or actions) unexpected and unacceptable, (*syn.*) improper: *His rude remark was out of line, and he should apologize.* **22 to bring into line:** to change s.t. so as to make it agree, (*syn.*) to align: *The company lowered its costs and brought them into line with the budget.* **23 to draw the line:** *See:* draw. **24** *infrml.* **to drop s.o. a line:** to write s.o. a short letter **25** *infrml.* **to feed, give,** or **hand s.o. a line:** to speak to s.o. in a way that is meant to trick or mislead: *He loves to feed girls a line about how much money he has, when in fact he has very little.* **26** *infrml.* **to get a line on:** to find information about: *A reporter got a line on the politician's plans from a secret source within the government.* **27 to get in line: a.** to join with others in a line: *I got in line and waited to buy my ticket for the movie.* **b.** *fig.* to act in the desired or approved way, (*syn.*) to conform: *After the teacher punished the student, he got in line and behaved well.* **28 to hold the line: a.** to wait for s.o. on the telephone: *The bank clerk asked the customer to hold the line while he checked the account.* **b.** *fig.* to make strong efforts (against s.t.): *The company is trying to hold the line on production costs and not let them rise.*
—*v.* **lined, lining, lines 1** to mark lines on: *I lined the page so that my young son could practice forming his letters.* **2** to form a border: *Tall trees line the street.* **3** to put an inner layer on: *Her fur coat is lined with silk.* **4** *infrml.* **to line one's pockets:** to make money by cheating: *The politician lined his pockets by taking bribes.* **5** *phrasal v. sep.* **to line s.t. up: a.** to place s.t. in line with s.t. else: *A worker lined up rows of chairs for the audience.‖They lined them up.* **b.** *fig.* to organize and make ready, (*syn.*) to arrange: *Personnel agencies*

L

line up job interviews for their clients. **6** *phrasal v.* **to line up:** to form a line: *People lined up to buy tickets to the concert.*

lin·e·age /'lɪniɪdʒ/ *n.frml.* members of a family through history, *(syn.)* ancestry: *She is a New Yorker who traces her lineage back to England.*

lin·e·ar /'lɪniər/ *adj.* **1** of (or) in a line (or) lines: a linear measurement of one meter **2** direct, connected: *There is a linear relationship between the company's losses and its poor-quality products.* *-n.* [U] **linearity.**

lin·en /'lɪnən/ *n.adj.* **1** cloth woven of flax: *She wore a summer dress made of <n.> linen.* **2** fabric product such as bedsheets and table-cloths: *You can buy towels in the <adj.> linen department of this store.* **3** *infrml.* **to wash one's dirty linen in public:** to tell one's personal and embarrassing problems in public: *The two movie stars washed their dirty linen in public when they talked to reporters about their divorce.*

line of credit *n.* a fixed amount of money that can be borrowed by a business: *Our business has a line of credit at the local bank to pay for new shipments of goods.*

lin·er /'laɪnər/ *n.* **1** a ship or airplane: *An ocean liner can carry hundreds of people.* **2** an inner layer in clothing: *In winter, he puts the liner into his coat for warmth.*

line·up /'laɪn,ʌp/ *n.* **1** (in baseball) a list of players in the order in which they will come to bat: *The starting lineup includes the team's best players.* **2** *fig.* any listing of people, events, products, etc.: *The fall lineup of television programs (new fashions, social events, etc.) looks interesting.* **3** a group of people, including criminal suspects, presented by police to witnesses who try to identify the criminal(s) in the group: *The man who was robbed picked out the thief from the police lineup.*

lin·ger /'lɪŋgər/ *v.* **1** to remain, as if not wanting to go: *Some guests lingered after the others had left.* **2** to stay, persist: *Her perfume lingered even after she had gone.* **3** to continue living but in a weak condition: *He was badly hurt in the crash but lingered a day before dying.* *-adj.* **lingering.**

lin·ge·rie /,lɑnʒə'reɪ, 'lɑnʒə,ri, ,lænʒə'ri/ *n.* [U] women's bras, slips, panties, and stockings: *She buys her lingerie at an expensive store.*

lin·go /'lɪŋgoʊ/ *n.infrml.* **-goes** or **-gos** language difficult for outsiders to understand: *The computer experts spoke to each other in a lingo I couldn't decipher.*

lin·gua fran·ca /'lɪŋgwə'fræŋkə/ *n.* **lingua francas** /-'fræŋkəz/ a language of words taken from many languages and used by foreigners to communicate with each other: *Sailors of many lands speak a lingua franca in foreign ports.*

lin·guist /'lɪŋgwɪst/ *n.* **1** a person who knows several languages and their structure: *She is a linguist on the faculty at Harvard University* *-adj.* **linguistic.**

lin·guis·tics /lɪŋ'gwɪstɪks/ *n.* [U] *used with a sing. verb:* the study of the nature and structure of languages: *She studied linguistics in college.*

lin·i·ment /'lɪnəmənt/ *n.* [C;U] a liquid or cream pain reliever spread on the skin: *After exercise, he spreads liniment on his legs to ease the pain.*

lin·ing /'laɪnɪŋ/ *n.* **1** an internal layer, such as in a jacket or coat: *She has a wool lining in her winter coat.* **2 every cloud has a silver lining:** an expression that means that a source of hope or a benefit can be found in a bad situation: *My car got a new paint job because of the accident; every cloud has a silver lining.*

link /lɪŋk/ *n.* **1** one connection in a series, such as a ring in a chain: *Links in a chain can break.* **2** part of a communication or transport system: *The company has telephone links to its branch offices.* **3** a relationship: *That crime has a link to other crimes committed by the same person.* **4** *pl.* **links** a golf course **5 missing link: a.** (in human history) a species linking apes to human beings: *Anthropologists continue to look for the missing link.* **b.** a missing part or idea needed to complete a function: *An experienced marketing manager is the missing link in our company.* **6** *infrml.* **weak link:** a connection likely to break and thus endanger a whole process: *Our accounting system is slow; it's a weak link in our business.*
—*v.* **1** to connect: *Workers linked the railroad cars together.* **2** *phrasal v. sep.* **to link s.t. up:** to form a business venture: *We linked up our business with a distributor in Hong Kong.*

link·age /'lɪŋkɪdʒ/ *n.* **1** [U] the act or process of connecting: *Steel provides strong linkage in a chain.* **2** [C] a connection between two points: *The rail linkages between Boston and New York are used by passenger traffic.* **3** *fig.* [U] (in diplomacy) agreement on shared interests between nations: *The USA and China achieved linkage on mutual trade.*

link·up /'lɪŋk,ʌp/ *n.* a connection, *(syn.)* a hookup: *Technicians achieved a communications linkup between the ground and the satellite.*

li·no·le·um /lɪ'noʊliəm/ *n.* [U] a smooth, strong floor covering: *We have linoleum on our kitchen floor.*

lint /lɪnt/ *n.* [U] very small bits of cloth, fluff: *She tried to brush the lint from her jacket.*

li·on /'laɪən/ *n.* **1** a large member of the cat family, found mainly in Africa **2** *infrml.* **the lion's share:** the most of s.t.: *The owner takes the lion's share of profits from the company.*

li·on·heart·ed /ˈlaɪənˌhɑrtɪd/ *adj.fig.* courageous, fearless like a lion: *For his bravery, King Richard of England was called "the Lionhearted."*

li·on·ize /ˈlaɪəˌnaɪz/ *v.frml.* **-ized, -izing, -izes** to honor, raise s.o. to the stature of a great person: *The prime minister was lionized in newspapers for his success with the economy.*

lip /lɪp/ *n.* **1** one of two fleshy borders of the human mouth: *She put red lipstick on her lips.* **2** the top edge of s.t.: *There is gold trim around the lip of the teacup.* **3** *suffix* **-lipped:** having lips as described: *She was white-lipped with fear.* **4** *infrml.* **to give s.o. lip:** to speak to s.o. without respect, (*syn.*) to sass: *The supervisor criticized the worker, who then gave the supervisor a lot of lip.* **5 to keep a stiff upper lip:** to hold in one's feelings during a difficult time: *Through all his bad luck, he kept a stiff upper lip.* **6 to smack one's lips: a.** to press together and open one's lips noisily: *He smacked his lips when he saw the delicious food.* **b.** *fig.* to express delight: *He smacked his lips over the big profit he would make.*

lip-read /ˈlɪpˌrid/ *v.* **-read** /-rɛd/, **-reading, -reads** to watch the words formed on s.o.'s lips so as to understand without hearing them, as hearing-impaired people often do: *He lipreads what others say.*

lip service *n. infrml.* [U] **to pay lip service to s.t.:** to agree with s.t. in words but not in actions: *He pays lip service to his need for exercise but does nothing about it.*

lip·stick /ˈlɪpˌstɪk/ *n.* [C;U] a cosmetic coloring for the lips: *She wears pink lipstick.*

lip-synch /ˈlɪpˌsɪŋk/ *v.* to move the lips along with recorded music as if singing the words: *He did a funny imitation of the singer while lip-synching one of her songs.*

liq·ue·fy or **liq·ui·fy** /ˈlɪkwəˌfaɪ/ *v.* **-fied, -fying, -fies** to change into liquid form: *Ice liquefies as it melts.*

li·queur /lɪˈkʊr, -ˈkyʊr, -ˈkɜr/ *n.* a sweet alcoholic drink with a flavoring such as fruit: *She likes an orange liqueur after dinner.*

liq·uid /ˈlɪkwɪd/ *n.* [C;U] the fluid state of matter that is neither a gas nor a solid: *Water is a liquid that covers most of the earth.*
—*adj.* **1** free-flowing, fluid: *When it is frozen, water is no longer liquid.* **2** (in finance, said of assets) readily available and usable as cash: *That company has no liquid assets.*

liq·ui·date /ˈlɪkwəˌdeɪt/ *v.* **-dated, -dating, -dates 1** to sell off, get rid of: *The storekeeper liquidated her inventory by offering it for sale at a big discount.* **2** to end, esp. to close a business: *The owner liquidated his business and retired.* **3** *fig.* to kill, put to death: *The military government liquidated its opponents.* -*n.* [U] **liquidation.**

USAGE NOTE: Often, to *liquidate* a business is directly associated with declaring bankruptcy (when one cannot pay money owed): *Our largest creditor ordered us to liquidate and close the business.*

liq·uor /ˈlɪkər/ *n.* a strong alcoholic drink: *Vodka, whiskey, and scotch are types of liquor.*

lisp /lɪsp/ *n.* a speech abnormality in which the sound /θ/ is pronounced as /s/: *Because of her lisp, the word "sing" sounds like "thing."*
—*v.* to speak with a lisp: *She lisped as a child but doesn't now.*

list /lɪst/ *n.* **1** a series of items written in a column: *I made a list of things to buy at the supermarket.* **2** a tilt to one side: *The ship has a list to the starboard side because the cargo is not balanced.*
—*v.* **1** to make a list of: *I listed the terms to be included in the contract.* **2** to lean to one side, tilt: *The ship listed during the storm.* **3** *phrasal v. insep.* **to list for s.t.:** to have a regular price of: *That item lists for $20 but is now on sale at $14. See:* list price.

lis·ten /ˈlɪsən/ *v.* **1** to hear, sense with the ears: *I like to listen to birds sing in the trees.* **2** to pay attention to and act in accord with: *I listened to the advice of my friend.* **3** *phrasal v. insep.* **to listen in (on s.t.): a.** to listen to, (*syn.*) to eavesdrop: *She listens in on the private conversations of others.* **b.** to listen, such as to a radio program: *Thousands listen in each morning to their favorite radio program.* **4** *phrasal v. slang* **to listen up:** to pay attention: *Listen up, children! See:* hear.

USAGE NOTE: We *hear* (passively) because we have ears, and we *listen* (actively) when we focus our attention on s.t.: *I was listening to the radio, so I didn't hear you come in.*

lis·ten·er /ˈlɪsənər, ˈlɪsnər/ *n.* **1** a member of an audience, such as for a radio program: *Classical music stations have a limited number of listeners.* **2 a good listener:** a sympathetic, supportive person: *Her friends love her; she is a good listener to their problems.*

list·ing /ˈlɪstɪŋ/ *n.* **1** a list of items: *I made a listing of the new clothes that I need.* **2** an advertisement: *We looked through the newspaper listings of apartments for rent.*

list·less /ˈlɪstlɪs/ *adj.* lacking energy or interest: *The summer heat makes people feel listless.* -*n.* [U] **listlessness.**

list price *n.* the regular retail price of an item: *No one likes to pay the list price for an item; everyone wants a discount.*

lit·a·ny /ˈlɪtni/ *n.* **1** [U] a form of prayer spoken by a priest or minister and answered by the churchgoers: *The familiar litany of the church service comforted her.* **2** [C] a long speech

L

listing complaints: *He was forced to listen to a litany of the old man's aches and pains.*

lite /laɪt/ *adj.slang* a nonstandard spelling of **light** used mainly in advertising low-calorie products: *lite beer, lite yogurt*

li·ter /'litər/ *n.* or *Brit.* **litre** **1** a liquid measure equal to 33.824 ounces or 1.057 quarts: *He bought a liter of milk for the children.* **2** a metric measure of capacity equal to the volume of one kilogram of water at four degrees Celsius under normal pressure: *That motor has a five-liter capacity.*

lit·er·a·cy /'lɪtərəsi/ *n.* [U] the ability to read and write: *The literacy rate in that country is low.*

lit·er·al /'lɪtərəl/ *adj.* **1** keeping to the exact meaning of a word or words: *We translate the French "S'il vous plaît" as "Please," but a literal translation would be "If it pleases you."* **2** (of word meanings) basic, usual: *The literal meaning of "dawn" is "sunrise," but it is used figuratively to mean "a beginning."* **3** concerned with facts and lacking in imagination: *literal-minded*

lit·er·al·ly /'lɪtərəli/ *adv.* according to the exact words: *I know he told you to get lost, but he didn't mean it literally; he just wanted you not to bother him.*

USAGE NOTE: *Literally* is sometimes used to give force to words when the meaning is not literal, as in "Her eyes literally popped out of her head at the sight of all that money."

lit·er·ar·y /'lɪtə,rɛri/ *adj.* related to literature and writing: *Literary magazines have few readers compared to news magazines.*

lit·er·ate /'lɪtərɪt/ *adj.* **1** able to read and write: *The percentage of literate adults in that country is approximately 60 percent.* **2** well-educated, (*syns.*) well-read, learned: *She is a very literate woman.*

lit·er·a·ti /,lɪtə'rati/ *n.pl.* the writers, critics, and learned people of a city, nation, or era: *The class studied the literati of nineteenth-century London.*

lit·er·a·ture /'lɪtərətʃər/ *n.* [U] **1** written works, such as novels, poems, and plays, and commentary about them: *She is a professor of French literature.* **2** written information about a specific field: *The current literature on medicine is highly technical.*

lithe /laɪð/ *adj.* **lither, lithest** able to move and bend easily, (*syns.*) flexible, supple: *Dancers are lithe.*

li·thog·ra·phy /lɪ'θɑgrəfi/ *n.* [U] a printing process using a smooth stone or metal surface treated so image areas can absorb ink and surrounding areas cannot: *Lithography is a popular type of printing.* *-n.* [C] **lithograph** /'lɪθə,græf/.

lit·i·gant /'lɪtəgənt/ *n.* (in law) a person involved in a legal action as a defendant or plaintiff: *Litigants met in court before the judge.*

lit·i·gate /'lɪtə,geɪt/ *v.* **-gated, -gating, -gates** (in law) to argue (a case) in court: *We litigated the dispute in Superior Court.*

lit·i·ga·tion /,lɪtə'geɪʃən/ *n.* **1** [C] a lawsuit: *We began a litigation against that company.* **2** [U] the process of litigating: *The litigation finally came to an end after several years.* *-adj.* **litigious** /lɪ'tɪdʒəs/.

lit·mus test /'lɪtməs/ *n.* **1** a chemical test for acidity: *The paper used in the litmus test turned red, showing a high level of acid in the soil.* **2** *fig.* a test for truth, genuineness, or sincerity: *Belief in the role of government in solving social problems is a political litmus test.*

li·tre /'litər/ *Brit. See:* liter.

lit·ter /'lɪtər/ *n.* **1** [U] pieces of trash on the ground: *Empty bottles, newspapers, and other litter lay on the sidewalks.* **2** [C] a group of animals born together: *Our dog had a litter of puppies.* **3** [C] a frame covered with strong cloth for carrying s.o., a stretcher: *Soldiers carried the injured man on a litter.*
—*v.* to drop trash on the ground: *People who litter may have to pay a fine.*

lit·ter·bag /'lɪtɚ,bæg/ *n.* a small bag used to collect trash: *We keep a litterbag in our car.*

lit·ter·bug /'lɪtər,bʌg/ *n.infrml.* a person who litters: *Litterbugs leave cans and cigarette butts on the beach.*

lit·tle /'lɪtl/ *adj.* **1** small in size, (*syn.*) diminutive: *Little children played in the school yard.* **2** small in amount, (*syn.*) meager: *He gets little pay for the work he does.* **3** short in time: *a little while* **4** young or younger: *their little boy, her little brother* **5** unimportant, (*syn.*) trivial: *She leaves the little decisions to her assistants.* **6 the little guy** or **man:** an ordinary citizen, esp. a low-level employee or single investor as opposed to s.o. with power or influence *See:* few.
—*adv.* **less** /lɛs/, **least** /list/ **1** not much: *He cared little about his job.* **2** not at all: *Little did I know what trouble lay ahead.* **3** to some degree, (*syns.*) rather, somewhat: *I was a little upset.* **4 little by little:** in small amounts or by small steps, gradually: *They have added rooms on to their house little by little.* **5 to make little of:** to treat as unimportant: *He is very modest and makes little of the prizes he has won.* **6 to think little of: a.** to consider unimportant: *She thinks little of driving two hours to work each day.* **b.** to consider as not deserving respect: *The boss thought little of my idea and refused to discuss it.*
—*pron.* **1** a small amount: *She has little to do.* **2** a short distance or time: *I moved my chair a little to the left.*

Little League *n.* a group of children's baseball teams supported by local families and businesses: *Our son plays in the Little League.*

little toe *n.* the outer toe on the foot: *She has a blister on her little toe from walking.*

lit·ur·gy /ˈlɪtərdʒi/ *n.* the prayers, songs, etc. of a church service: *The minister plans the liturgy for each Sunday's service.* -*adj.* **liturgical** /lɪˈtɜrdʒɪkəl/.

liv·a·bil·i·ty /ˌlɪvəˈbɪləti/ *n.* the degree of comfort and convenience of a place: *That small city is known for its livability.*

liv·a·ble /ˈlɪvəbəl/ *adj.* **1** comfortable and convenient: *With hard work, they made the old house livable.* **2** acceptable, bearable: *He's depressed and feels his life is not livable.*

live /lɪv/ *v.* **1** lived, living, lives to have life, be or stay alive, exist: *He is badly hurt, but the doctors say he'll live.* **2** to have one's home located (in a place), (*syn.*) to reside: *She lives in Boston.* **3** to lead one's life in a certain way: *He's a racecar driver who likes to take risks and live dangerously.* **4 to live and learn:** to learn from one's mistakes: *After losing money on his first venture into the stock market, he sighed and said, "Live and learn!"* **5 to live and let live:** to have tolerance for others: *She criticized the lifestyle of the new neighbors, but her sister advised her to live and let live.* **6** *phrasal v.* **to live in:** (of a servant) to live in the house where one works: *They have a woman who lives in and takes care of the children.* **7** *infrml.* **to live it up:** to enjoy oneself, esp. in spending freely: *We decided to really live it up on vacation and stay in an expensive hotel.* **8** *phrasal v. insep.* **to live off s.o. or s.t.:** to get money for one's support: *He lives off his friends (his savings, etc.).* **9** *infrml.fig.* **to live off the fat of the land:** to live in comfort without effort: *After winning the lottery, they retired to live off the fat of the land.* **10** *phrasal v. insep.* **to live on s.t.: a.** to have as one's only means of support, (*syn.*) to subsist on: *The refugees lived on little food.* **b.** *fig.* to continue to live: *After her death, she lived on in our hearts.* **11** *fig.* **to live or die by s.t.:** to believe in s.t. very strongly: *He is so religious that he lives or dies by what his minister says.* **12** *phrasal v. sep.* **to live s.t. down:** to have a bad action from one's past be forgiven or forgotten: *He has never been able to live down wrecking his father's car.||He can't live it down.* **13** *phrasal v. insep.* **to live up to s.t.: a.** to satisfy, not disappoint: *She was an excellent student and lived up to her parents' expectations for her.* **b.** to fulfill, carry out (responsibilities, obligations, etc.): *He lived up to his promises and paid the money he owed.*

—*adj.* /laɪv/ **1** living, alive: *The cook dropped the live lobsters into boiling water.* **2** capable of exploding: *live ammunition* **3** (of a perfor-mance) viewed or heard by an audience as it happens, not prerecorded: *We watched a live broadcast of the opera on TV.* **4** *infrml.fig.* **a live one: a.** a fool easily tricked: *The card cheat knew he had a live one when the young stranger started losing heavily.* **b.** s.o. who is excited and enthusiastic: *She is a live one who can dance all night.* **5 a live wire: a.** a dangerous wire carrying electricity: *That's a live wire, so don't touch it.* **b.** *infrml.fig.* s.o. full of energy and spirit: *He's a live wire and a super salesman.*

live-in /ˈlɪvˌɪn/ *adj.* (of domestic employees) living in the house where one works: *The couple has a live-in maid who cleans and cooks.*

live·li·hood /ˈlaɪvliˌhʊd/ *n.* way of earning money to live: *He makes his livelihood as a carpenter.*

live·ly /ˈlaɪvli/ *adj.* quick and full of energy, spirited: *She is a lively young girl, always laughing and doing things.*

li·ven /ˈlaɪvən/ *phrasal v. sep.* **to liven s.t. up:** to make spirited, joyful: *She livened up the party by putting on fast music.||She livened it up.* See: enliven.

liv·er /ˈlɪvər/ *n.* **1** the organ in the body that helps in digestion and cleaning the blood: *The liver is a vital organ.* **2** this organ from certain animals as a food: *calf's liver, chicken livers*

liv·er·wurst /ˈlɪvərˌwɜrst/ *n.* ground liver in roll form: *Liverwurst is used in sandwiches.*

liv·er·y /ˈlɪvəri/ *n.* **-ies** [C;U] **1** uniforms, esp. those of servants: *The English lord's footmen wore colorful livery.* **2** a place where horses are cared for: *Our friend keeps his riding horse at a livery stable.* -*adj.* **liveried.**

live·stock /ˈlaɪvˌstɑk/ *n.* [U] farm animals, such as cattle, sheep, and chickens: *In winter, the farmer keeps his livestock in the barn.*

liv·id /ˈlɪvɪd/ *adj.* **1** extremely angry, furious: *He was livid when he was refused entry to the building.* **2** pale, esp. from anger: *He turned livid when the guard stopped him.* **3** bluish gray: *There was a livid bruise on her face where he had hit her.*

liv·ing /ˈlɪvɪŋ/ *n.* **1** *sing.* way of making money to live on, (*syn.*) livelihood: *He earns his living as a plumber.* **2** [U] the getting of things necessary for life, such as food and housing: *the high cost of living, a rising standard of living*

—*adj.* alive: *Who is the world's greatest living artist?*

living room *n.* the room in a home where people sit, often to talk, read, or entertain: *He sits in the living room and watches TV.*

living will *n.* a written request not to be kept alive by any medical life-support system when one is dying: *Before her illness became serious, she wrote a living will.*

L

liz·ard /'lɪzərd/ n. a type of four-legged reptile: *Lizards include the chameleon, which changes colors, and the 10-foot Komodo dragon of Southeast Asia.*

lla·ma /'lɑmə/ n. a South American animal, like a small camel without a hump, used to carry loads: *Llamas can work at high altitudes in the Andes.*

llama

load /loʊd/ n. **1** an amount to be carried, lifted, etc., (*syn.*) cargo: *Trucks can carry heavy loads of materials.* **2** an amount of work, responsibility, etc., (*syn.*) burden: *That department has a heavy load of paperwork.* **3** (of explosives) the amount to be exploded at one time, (*syn.*) charge: *A sailor got a load of powder for the cannon.* **4** the amount of electricity from a power source **5** *slang* **to get a load of:** to look at (s.o. or s.t.) with admiration or disgust: *As the photographer developed the film for the news story, she said to the editor, "Get a load of this!"* **6** *infrml.fig.* **loads of:** a lot of, plenty: *Don't hurry; we have loads of time.*
—*v.* **1** to put a load into or on: *Workers loaded the truck with sand.* **2** to put ammunition into a weapon or film into a camera: *Soldiers loaded their guns.* **3** to put into position, (*syn.*) to install: *A programmer loads software onto a computer.* **4** *phrasal v. insep.* **to load (s.o. or s.t.) up: a.** to fill (with cargo): *The driver loaded up his van and left.||He loaded it up with his tools.* **b.** to give too much work, (*syn.*) to overload: *The boss loaded her up with extra work.* **5** *phrasal v. insep.* **to load up on s.t.:** to get a large supply of: *The store manager was afraid of shortages, so he loaded up on extra inventory.* -*adj.* **loading.**

load·ed /'loʊdɪd/ adj. **1** filled with s.t. to carry: *The heavily loaded truck carried sand.* **2** (of a weapon) filled with ammunition: *The gun is loaded and ready to fire.* **3** *infrml.fig.* very rich: *She is loaded (with money, dough, etc.).* **4** *slang* drunk: *He got loaded on beer.* **5 a loaded question:** a question that is unfairly worded to trick s.o.: *He saw that it was a loaded question and refused to answer it.* **6 loaded dice:** dice that are weighted to give the owner an unfair advantage

loading dock n. a platform onto which cargo is unloaded and moved into or out of a warehouse: *Trucks pull up and unload their freight onto the loading dock.*

load·stone /'loʊd,stoʊn/ n. See: lodestone.

loaf /loʊf/ n. **loaves** /loʊvz/ a standard portion of baked bread: *We buy loaves of bread at the bakery.*
—*v.* **1** to spend time in a carefree way, (*syns.*) to idle, dawdle: *During vacation we loafed at*

the beach a lot. **2** to waste time instead of working: *He loafs on the job by talking all day.*

loaf·er /'loʊfər/ n.*infrml.* **1** a person who avoids work: *She is a loafer who works as little as she can.* **2** *TM* for a type of shoe with no laces: *Loafers are comfortable footwear.*

loam /loʊm/ n. [C;U] a type of soil rich in oxygen and nutrients for growing crops: *The loam in some farmlands is deep and fertile.*

loan /loʊn/ n. **1** [C] a sum of money borrowed at a rate of interest: *I applied at the bank for a mortgage loan at 7% interest.* **2** [C;U] the act of lending s.t.: *I thanked him for the loan of his car.*
—*v.* to lend: *I loaned my car to a friend for the weekend.*

loan·er /'loʊnər/ n. a car or other piece of equipment given to s.o. to use while his or hers is being repaired: *My auto dealership gives me a loaner when it keeps my car overnight for repair.*

loan shark n. a person or business that lends money at extremely high interest rates, esp. money provided by organized crime: *Loan sharks operate outside the law.* -n. [U] **loan sharking.**

loath /loʊθ, loʊð/ adj.frml. **loath to:** unwilling to, (*syn.*) reluctant to: *He is loath to lend anyone money.*

loathe /loʊð/ v. to hate, detest: *Those two people loathe each other.*

loath·ing /'loʊðɪŋ/ n. [U] hatred, detestation: *The loathing between the two people is clear.*

loath·some /'loʊðsəm, 'loʊθ-/ adj. extremely unpleasant, (*syns.*) abhorrent, repugnant: *His behavior is so loathsome that people can't stand him.*

lob /lɑb/ v. **lobbed, lobbing, lobs** n. to hit or throw (a ball) high and gently: *The father <v.> lobbed the ball to the child.*

lob·by /'lɑbi/ n. **-bies 1** an entrance area to a building, such as where people are greeted and wait to be seen, etc.: *We sat in the lobby until we were led to an office by a secretary.* **2** a person or group working to influence people (esp. politicians) whose decisions affect their special interests: *Our union's lobby is very active in Washington, D.C.*
—*v.* **-bied, -bying, -bies** to try to influence s.o. in power (esp. politicians) to support one's interests and needs: *All major industries lobby for favor in the nation's capital.* -n. **lobbyist.**

lobe /loʊb/ n. a rounded part, as of the human ear: *She had the lobes of her ears (or) her earlobes pierced for earrings.*

lo·bot·o·my /lə'bɑtəmi/ n. **-mies** an operation now not often performed that cuts away parts of the brain to relieve mental disorders: *He had a lobotomy in 1947 to stop his psychotic behavior.*

lob·ster /'labstər/ *n.* [C;U] any of a variety of ocean shellfish with large claws and an extended abdomen: *New England lobsters are delicious.*

lo·cal /'loukəl/ *adj.* **1** located nearby, as in a neighborhood, town, or area: *We have plenty of local stores to choose from.* **2** affecting or limited to a certain area: *a local anesthetic* —*n.* **1** a train or bus that makes all stops: *That train is a local.* **2** *infrml.* s.o. who lives in a certain area: *The tourists asked one of the locals for directions to the best beach.*

local color *n.fig.* buildings, people, and customs that make an area special: *The narrow streets, old buildings, and people with strong accents are part of the local color in Boston.*

lo·cale /lou'kæl/ *n.* a place, location for s.t. that happens: *The movie director chose a new locale to shoot the final scenes of the film.*

lo·cal·i·ty /lou'kæləti/ *n.* -ties a location, area: *The rich people live in a locality north of town.*

lo·cal·ize /'loukə,laɪz/ *v.* -ized, -izing, -izes **1** to limit to a local area: *Police localized the riot to a small area of the city.* **2** (in medicine) to limit to an area or part of the body: *The infection was localized around the knee joint.*

lo·cate /'lou,keɪt/ *v.* -cated, -cating, -cates **1** to find the location of, (*syn.*) to pinpoint: *The student located Moscow, Paris, and London on a map.* **2** to place, (*syns.*) to establish, situate: *The company located its new office building in a suburb.*

lo·ca·tion /lou'keɪʃən/ *n.* **1** the place where s.t. is located: *The location of the capital is in the center of the state.* **2** a piece of property: *We moved our offices to a new location in the city.* **3 on location:** (of a film) in a city, town, outdoors, etc., instead of in a film studio: *The movie was filmed on location in Canada.*

lock /lak/ *n.* **1** a mechanism for securing a door, suitcase, etc. so that only a key or a code will open it: *The lock on our front door opens with an ordinary key.* **2** an area in a waterway where the water level can be raised and lowered so that ships can pass through it: *They opened the gates to the next lock in the canal.* **3** a curling group of hairs: *The child had curly blond locks.* **4 lock, stock, and barrel:** everything included, completely: *Thieves broke in and stole everything, lock, stock, and barrel.* **5 to have a lock on s.t.:** to have control or a guarantee of s.t.: *That candidate has a lock on his party's nomination for President.* **6 under lock and key: a.** safely put away: *She keeps important papers under lock and key.* —*v.* **1** to secure with a lock: *I locked my apartment door before leaving for work.* **2 locked itself into:** unable to change one's situation or an agreement, etc.: *Our business locked itself*

into a contract to buy the merchandise even though the market price has fallen. **3** *phrasal v. sep.* **to lock s.o. or s.t. away: a.** to put s.o. in jail: *The judge locked away the murderer for life.||He locked him away.* **b.** to store s.t. safely: *She locked away her jewels in a safe.||She locked them away.* **4** *phrasal v. sep.* **to lock s.o. or s.t. in:** to put s.o. or s.t. into an enclosure, a room, etc. and lock it: *She locks in the animals at night.||She locks them in.* **5** *phrasal v. sep.* **to lock s.o. out: a.** to keep s.o. from entering a place: *She locked out her brother because she was mad at him.||She locked him out.* **b.** to keep employees from entering their place of work so as to force them to accept an agreement: *Management responded to a protest about low wages by locking out the workers.||Management locked them out.* **6** *phrasal v. sep.* **to lock (s.o. or s.t.) up: a.** to close and lock a house, office, store, etc.: *I was the last to leave the warehouse, so I locked up.* **b.** to put s.o. in jail: *The judge ordered the thief locked up.||She locked him up.* **c.** to gain complete control over s.t., such as a business deal, the market for a product, etc.: *That company has the market for supercomputers locked up.||The company has locked it up.*

lock·er /'lakər/ *n.* **1** a storage compartment, such as one in a row of metal cabinets used for keeping work clothes, athletic equipment, etc.: *Each student at the high school has a locker.* **2** any of a great variety of storage containers, such as food lockers or military uniform lockers:

locker

The crew of the fishing boat stored the fish in food lockers.

locker room *n.* a room with lockers for athletes: *The team changes clothes in a locker room.*

lock·et /'lakɪt/ *n.* small case, usu. containing a picture or message from a loved one, worn on a necklace: *She wears a gold locket from her boyfriend.*

lock·out /'lak,aʊt/ *n.* a management action of locking protesting employees out of a business to force a settlement: *After the wage protest, management began a lockout of labor.*

lock·smith /'lak,smɪθ/ *n.* s.o. who installs and repairs locks: *When the lock on our front door broke, we called a locksmith to fix it.*

lock·step /'lak,stɛp/ *n. sing.* **in lockstep:** *fig.* in accord with rules so rigid that people must follow them closely and in exact order: *The school curriculum requires the students to follow lessons in lockstep without any changes.*

L

lock·up /'lak,ʌp/ *n.infrml.* a jail: *The sheriff put the suspect in the lockup for the night.*

lo·co /'loukou/ *adj.slang* crazy: *He's loco to think he can walk on water.*

lo·co·mo·tive /,louka'moutɪv/ *n.adj.* a large railroad vehicle with an engine: *Several <n.> locomotives can pull a string of freight cars a mile long. -n.* [U] **locomotion.**

lo·cus /'loukas/ *n.* **-ci** /-saɪ, -kaɪ, -ki/ a point on a line, in space, etc.: *Two lines cross at a locus on the chart.*

lo·cust /'loukast/ *n.* an insect of the grasshopper family noted for flying in large groups and destroying crops: *Historical records describe terrible plagues of locusts.*

lo·cu·tion /lou'kyuʃən/ *n.frml.* [U] a person's style of speaking: *She has excellent locution.*

lode /loud/ *n.* **1** a deposit of gold, silver, etc. in harder surrounding rock: *Geologists discovered a lode of lead.* **2 the mother lode:** a source of great natural riches: *The adventurers were in search of the mother lode of gold to make them rich.*

lode·star /'loud,star/ *n.* a star used as a guide to navigation, esp. the North Star: *The North Star served as the lodestar for sailing for centuries.*

lode·stone /'loud,stoun/ *n.* **1** magnetite, which points to magnetic north as a guide to navigation: *Sailors used a lodestone as a compass to help find their way at sea.* **2** *fig.* s.t. that attracts, s.t. magnetic: *The chance to find gold was the lodestone that drew people to California in the 1800s.*

lodge /ladʒ/ *n.* **1** a cabin or other small country house: *On vacation, we stayed at a ski lodge in the woods.* **2** a hotel, motel, etc.: *Yosemite National Park has some wonderful old lodges.* **3** a local group of certain organizations or the building used for the group's meetings: *The Odd Fellows lodge is a big, old building.*
—v. **lodged, lodging, lodges 1** *frml.* to stay for a short while: *The travelers lodged in an old inn for the night.* **2** to enter and stop: *Bullets lodged in the walls.* **3** to present formally or officially: *A dissatisfied customer lodged a complaint about a faulty product.* **4** *frml.* to place in the control of, (*syn.*) to confer upon: *Power was lodged with the new head of state.*

lodg·er /'ladʒər/ *n.* a paying guest, esp. of a rooming house: *The professor and his wife have three students as lodgers in their house.*

lodg·ing /'ladʒɪŋ/ *n.* **1** [C;U] a temporary place to stay for pay (as in a hotel or motel): *We found lodging for the night in a small motel.* **2** *n.pl.frml.* one's place of living (room, apartment): *His lodgings are in a quiet section of town.*

loft /lɔft/ *n.* **1** an open work area or part of one in a factory: *Many lofts in New York have been* changed to artists' apartments. **2** a platform area above a main floor, such as a sleeping loft in an apartment: *A narrow staircase leads to a loft with a bed.* **3** a space under the roof of a barn: *The farmer keeps hay for his cows in the loft.*
—v. to send or be sent into the air: *The golf ball lofted into the air.*

lof·ty /'lɔfti/ *adj.* **1** high in elevation: *The eagle's nest is on a lofty perch on the mountain.* **2** *fig.* high in relation to others, (*syn.*) elevated: *She has lofty ambitions to be rich and famous. -n.* [U] **loftiness.**

log /lɔg, lag/ *n.* **1** a tree trunk or large branch that has either fallen or been cut: *The man cut trees into logs with a chain saw.* **2** a journal or other record of information: *He keeps a computerized log of all shipments that enter and leave the warehouse.* **3** *infrml.* **a bump on a log:** a stupid, lazy person: *He just sat in class like a bump on a log and never passed the course.*
—v. **logged, logging, logs 1** to cut trees into logs: *He works as a lumberjack, logging trees for a big paper company.* **2** to enter into a written record: *The sergeant logs (in) the name of each soldier as he arrives at camp.* **3** to earn credit for time spent working, distance traveled, etc.: *During her training, the pilot logged 100 hours on planes of this type.* **4** *phrasal v. insep.* **to log on to s.t.:** to enter into a computer system, usu. with a password: *I logged on to an information service by using my modem.*

log·a·rithm /'lɔgə,rɪðəm, la-/ *n.* the power to which a base number must be raised to produce a given number: *Logarithms are shown in long numerical tables. -adj.* **logarithmic.**

loge /louʒ/ *n.* a section of the balcony in a theater or stadium: *We sat in the left loge and had a good view of the baseball field.*

log·ger·head /'lɔgər,hɛd, -'la-/ *n.fig.* **at loggerheads:** arguing, in disagreement: *The two partners are always at loggerheads with each other and may split up.*

log·ging /'lɔgɪŋ, 'la-/ *n.* [U] the work or industry of cutting trees: *Logging can be a dangerous job.*

log·ic /'ladʒɪk/ *n.* [U] **1** a system of reasoning: *She uses logic—not emotion—in all her decisions.* **2** the study of principles of inference and reasoning: *A course in mathematical logic can be quite difficult.*

log·i·cal /'ladʒəkəl/ *adj.* **1** using a system of reasoning: *She has a very logical mind.* **2** showing good sense, reasonable: *It is logical that people protect themselves when they feel threatened.*

lo·gis·tics /lə'dʒɪstɪks, lou-/ *n.pl. sometimes used with a sing. verb* the organization and distribution of goods, services, and personnel, esp. in large amounts: *The logistics of moving*

an army into combat are very complex. -*adj.*
logistical.

log·jam /ˈlɔɡˌdʒæm, ˈlɑɡ-/ *n.* **1** a mass of logs that does not move in a stream: *A logjam formed from logging operations near the river.* **2** *fig.* a blockage, such as from an overload of work: *Complicated new tax laws caused a logjam in the accounting department.*

lo·go /ˈloʊˌɡoʊ/ -**gos** *n.* a design symbol of a business, an institution, or a product: *IBM's logo, with its silver streaks, is recognized the world over.*

log·o·type /ˈlɔɡəˌtaɪp, ˈlɑ-/ *n. See:* logo.

log·roll·ing /ˈlɔɡˌroʊlɪŋ, ˈlɑɡ-/ *n.* [U] **1** transport of logs by water: *Lumbermen use logrolling down a river to move logs to a port.* **2** a sport between two opponents, each one trying to roll the other off a log placed in water

loin /lɔɪn/ *n.adj.* (in animals) the section from the lower back to the upper leg: *The butcher cut a section of the <n.> loin for the restaurant to serve as <adj.> loin chops.*

loin·cloth /ˈlɔɪnˌklɔθ/ *n.* a cloth wrapped around the groin and hips: *In hot climates, some men wear loincloths.*

loi·ter /ˈlɔɪtər/ *v.* to stand or sit doing nothing, esp. in a public place, (*syn.*) to idle: *Homeless men loitered in the park.* -*n.* **loiterer.**

loll /lɑl/ *v.* **1** to hang loosely, esp. the tongue: *The dog's tongue lolled out of its mouth during the hot weather.* **2** to lie or sit in a lazy manner: *Vacationers lolled (about) on the beach.*

lol·li·pop /ˈlɑliˌpɑp/ *n.* a ball or flat round piece of hard candy on a stick: *Children enjoy lollipops.*

lone /loʊn/ *adj.* only, (*syns.*) solitary, sole: *He was the lone person to discover the secret.*

lone·li·ness /ˈloʊnlinɪs/ *n.* [U] a condition of being alone and feeling sad: *Most people experience loneliness sometimes.*

lone·ly /ˈloʊnli/ *adj.* -**lier,** -**liest** **1** alone and feeling sad, lonesome: *Without friends, he felt lonely in a new city.* **2** empty of people, deserted: *The desert can be a lonely place.*

lonely hearts *n.pl.* lonely people looking for love, esp. by advertising in the personal sections of newspapers: *Many people read the column for lonely hearts in the local newspaper.*

lon·er /ˈloʊnər/ *n.* a person who avoids the company of others and prefers to be and act mostly alone: *John is a loner and keeps apart from his co-workers.*

lone·some /ˈloʊnsəm/ *adj.* feeling sad and in need of a friend: *She was alone on Saturday night and feeling lonesome.*

lone wolf *n.fig.* a person who lives and acts alone: *George is a lone wolf who keeps to himself.*

long /lɔŋ/ *adj.* -**er,** -**est** **1** having a certain length: *The table is six feet long, or about two meters long.* **2** lasting a certain amount of time: *Our conversation was only five minutes long.* **3** (in distance or time) having great length or duration: *It is a long way from New York to Hong Kong.‖The senator made a long speech on taxes.* **4 in the long run:** over many months or years: *The economy is weak now, but in the long run it will improve.* **5** *fig.* **to be long on** or **short of:** to have (too) much of or (too) little of: *That young company is long on ideas but short of the money to put them into production.*
—*adv.* **1** (for) a long time: *Have you been waiting long?* **2 all day (morning, night, etc.) long:** for or throughout a certain amount of time without stopping: *Noise from the construction site continued all day long.* **3 as** or **so long as:** if, provided that, on condition that: *So long as it does not rain, we can have a picnic.* **4** *exclam.* **Long live (the King, the Republic, etc.)!:** May (the King, etc.) endure for a long time: *The crowd outside the palace shouted, "Long live the Queen!"* **5** *infrml.* **So long:** Good-bye: *So long for now! See you tomorrow!*
—*n.* **1** (in clothes) a length and cut for a tall person: *In suits, he wears a long.* **2 before long:** soon, shortly: *Clouds appeared, and before long it began to rain.* **3 the long and short of s.t.:** the main point, the substance, (*syn.*) the gist: *We talked for an hour, but the long and short of it is that he won't lower the price.*
—*v.* to want very much (s.o. or s.t. that is not available): *He longed for his girlfriend, who lived far away.‖She longs to take a vacation.*

long ago *adv.* in the distant past: *Long ago, people believed the earth was flat.*

long-distance *adj.* between distant places: *Long-distance moves from one part of the country to another are difficult.‖I had to make many long-distance (telephone) calls when I was in college.*

long·er /ˈlɔŋɡər/ *adj.adv.* **1** *comp.* of long **2** *adv.* **no longer** or **not any longer:** not now, not anymore: *He no longer works there; he retired.‖I won't wait any longer; I'm leaving.*

lon·gev·i·ty /lɔnˈdʒɛvəti, lɑn-/ *n.* [U] **1** the length of life: *The marine biologist studied the longevity of sea turtles.* **2** a long lifetime: *The people in that family live a long time; they are known for their longevity.*

long face *n.fig.* an expression of sadness or disappointment: *She had a long face after she failed the examination.*

long·hand /ˈlɔŋˌhænd/ *n.* [U] ordinary writing by hand: *She writes letters in longhand to her friends.*

long haul *n.* **over the long haul:** during or after a long period of time: *Real estate is a good investment over the long haul.*

long·ing /'lɔŋɪŋ/ *n.* [C;U] a strong desire or emotional need, (*syn.*) yearning: *She has a longing to see her old friends.*

lon·gi·tude /'lɑndʒə,tud, 'lɑn-/ *n.* [C;U] the distance from an imaginary line of measurement called the Prime Meridian, which runs north and south from pole to pole and divides the earth's surface into east and west: *Sailors can measure their location by determining their exact longitude and latitude.* *-adj.* **longitudinal.**

long johns /dʒɑnz/ *n.pl.* underwear covering the entire body from neck to wrists and ankles: *People wear long johns under their clothes during cold winters.*

long-lived /'lɔŋ'laɪvd, -'lɪvd/ *adj.* living a long time: *His parents were long-lived; they died when they were well into their nineties.*

long-range *adj.* **1** covering a time period lasting far into the future: *The company must make long-range plans.* **2** operating over long distances: *long-range missiles*

long·shore·man /lɔŋ'ʃɔrmən/ *n.* **-men** /-mən/ a dock worker responsible for moving cargo on and off ships: *Longshoremen use machines to move heavy loads.*

long shot *n.infrml.fig.* **1** s.t. that has little chance of success, esp. a horse with a weak record of winning: *At the racetrack, she bet on a long shot and lost.* **2 not by a long shot:** not at all, not even close: *He didn't pass the test, not by a long shot.*

long-standing *adj.* in effect for a long time, (*syn.*) customary: *The celebration of Thanksgiving is a long-standing tradition in North America.*

long-suffering *adj.* patient in spite of suffering for a long time, (*syn.*) oppressed: *The long-suffering poor people were helped by the new government.*

long-term *adj.* extending over a long period, lasting: *He suffers from a long-term disability.* *—n. sing.* **in** or **over the long term:** after several years: *Over the long term, the economy will be healthy.*

long-winded /'lɔŋ'wɪndɪd/ *adj.* speaking for a long period of time: *Politicians can make long-winded speeches.*

look /lʊk/ *v.* **1** to use one's eyes to see: *Look! There's a beautiful bird in that tree.* **2** to inspect, examine: *The accountant looked closely at the company's financial records.* **3** to appear, seem to be: *She looked tired after the race.* **4** to face, have a view of: *These windows look south.* **5 It looks like** or **It looks as if:** it seems probable that: *It looks like (it's going to) rain.* **6** *exclam.* **Look** or **Look here:** an ex-

pression used in anger to get s.o.'s attention: *Look here, stop making so much noise!* **7** *phrasal v. insep.* **to look after s.o. or s.t.:** to take care of s.o. or s.t.: *She stayed home to look after the baby.* **8** *phrasal v.* **to look ahead:** to think about and plan for the future: *The company president asked the management team to look ahead.* **9** *infrml.* **to look alive:** to move or act quickly or energetically: *We'll have to look alive if we want to catch that train!* **10** *phrasal v. insep.* **to look around (s.t.):** **a.** to examine an area: *Getting off the train, he looked around to see if his friends were there.* **b.** *infrml.* **s.t.:** to consider a number of choices, esp. before buying s.t.: *We looked around at many houses before we found this one.* **11** *phrasal v. insep.* **to look at s.o. or s.t.:** **a.** to examine or give one's close attention to s.o. or s.t.: *She wanted the doctor to look at her son.* **b.** to think about and form an opinion of s.o. or s.t., (*syns.*) to regard, view: *His father said, "You'll look at things differently when you're older."* **12** *phrasal v.* **to look back:** to think about or remember the past: *She looked back at her childhood.* **13** *phrasal v. insep.* **to look down on s.o.** or **down one's nose at s.o.:** to feel or show a lack of respect for s.o.: *Some rich people look down on the poor as inferior.* **14 to look for trouble:** *See:* trouble. **15** *phrasal v. insep.* **to look forward to s.t.:** to be eager for s.t. enjoyable in the future: *I'm looking forward to my vacation next month.* **16 to look high and low:** to search everywhere: *He looked high and low for his keys until he found them.* **17** *phrasal v. insep.* **to look in on s.o.:** to visit so s.o. as to check his or her condition: *Nurses look in on patients regularly.* **18** *phrasal v. insep.* **to look into s.t.:** to try to find the truth about s.t,, (*syn.*) to investigate: *The police looked into the crime and solved it.* **19** *infrml.fig.* **to look like death warmed over:** to appear very sick or upset: *He has a bad case of the flu and looks like death warmed over.* **20** *infrml.fig.* **to look like hell:** to be badly disordered: *I've had no sleep, and I look like hell!* **21** *phrasal v.* **to look on:** to stand by and watch: *A crowd looked on as two men fought.* **22** *phrasal v. insep.* **to look on** or **upon s.o. or s.t.:** to think of or consider s.o. or s.t., (*syns.*) to view, regard: *His new job pays poorly, but he looks on it as a learning experience.* **23** *phrasal v. insep.* **to look out (for s.o. or s.t.):** **a.** to be careful: *Look out! You'll fall!* **b.** to be careful about s.o. or s.t. dangerous: *Look out for that car!* **c.** to care for or protect s.o. or s.t.: *A mother needs to look out for her children when they play outside.* **24** *infrml.* **to look out for Number One:** to think of one's own interests (not those of others): *He's a selfish man, always looking out for Number One.* **25** *phrasal v. insep.* **to look out on** or **over s.t.:** to face or have a view of s.t.: *Our apartment*

L

looks out on a park. **26** *phrasal v. sep.* **to look over s.t.:** to examine s.t.: *We looked over the contract before signing it.||We looked it over.* **27 to look the other way:** to permit s.t. illegal or immoral by pretending not to see it or know about it: *The authorities knew about the illegal drug traffic, but they looked the other way.* **28** *phrasal v. insep.* **to look to s.o. or s.t.: a.** to depend on or rely on s.o.: *The boy looks to his big brother for help.* **b.** to take care of or attend to an obligation: *The girl looked to finishing her homework before going out to play.* **29** *phrasal v. sep.* **to look (s.o. or s.t.) up: a.** *fig.* to improve: *Now that I have a better job, things are looking up.* **b.** *infrml.fig.* to locate s.o. and then call or visit: *When I was in Chicago, I looked up an old school friend.||I looked him up.* **c.** to try to find s.t. in a dictionary or other reference: *Look up the number in the telephone book.||Look it up.* **30** *phrasal v. insep.* **to look up to s.o.:** to respect or admire s.o.: *The boy looks up to his father as a kind man and a good coach.*
—*n.* **1** an act of looking, *(syn.)* a glance: *The girl gave a look in my direction.* **2** an appearance: *That couple has a fashionable look.* **3** a facial expression, esp. one used to communicate a feeling: *He gave me an angry look.* **4** *pl.* one's general appearance, esp. a good one: *That actor is known more for his looks than for his acting ability.* **5** *infrml.fig.* **a dirty look:** a facial expression that shows anger directed at s.o.: *When the man said something rude to her, she gave him a dirty look.* **6 a good look:** a careful examination: *We'll take a good look at the house before we decide whether to buy it.*

look-alike *n.* a person who closely resembles another, a double: *She is a look-alike for a famous movie star.*

look·out /'lʊk,aʊt/ *n.* **1** a person who watches and warns others of danger: *The thief has a lookout to warn him if the police arrive.* **2** a place to watch from: *The church tower made a good lookout.* **3 to be on the lookout for:** to expect and watch for: *You should be on the lookout for that dangerous storm to arrive soon.*

loom /lum/ *v.* **1** to appear large and dangerous: *The storm loomed on the horizon and then struck.* **2** to weave on a loom: *Workers loomed fabric made of cotton.* **3** *fig.* **to loom large:** to be important, have great influence: *That senator looms large in national politics.*
—*n.* a frame or machine used to weave cloth and rugs: *She makes pretty things on her loom.*

loon /lun/ *n.* **1** a water bird with a laugh-like cry: *We sat at the edge of the lake and listened to the strange cry of the loon.* **2** *infrml.fig.* **crazy as a loon:** not sensible, mad: *That fool is as crazy as a loon.*

loon·y /'luni/*infrml.fig. adj.* **-ier, -iest** *n.* **-ies** crazy, mad: *He's <adj.> loony, always talking and laughing to himself.*

loony bin *n. slang.fig.pej.* a hospital for mentally ill people: *He's so crazy that his family sent him off to a loony bin.*

loop /lup/ *n.* **1** a circular shape formed by a line, string, wire, etc.: *The cowboy threw a loop of his rope over the horse's neck.* **2** *fig.* **in the loop:** informed, consulted, participating in a discussion (decision, project, etc.): *My boss is very good about keeping me in the loop on what's happening.* **3** *infrml.fig.* **to throw s.o. for a loop:** to shock and confuse s.o.: *When he heard the bad news, it threw him for a loop.*
—*v.* to make a loop (in, over, or with): *The cowboy looped his rope over the cow's horns.*

loop·hole /'lup,hoʊl/ *n.fig.* a way out (of an agreement), esp. a fault in a law that allows people to avoid following it: *There is a loophole in the new tax law that allows the rich to escape paying higher taxes.*

loose /lus/ *adj.* **looser, loosest 1** not firmly fixed or attached, *(syn.)* unfastened: *A button came loose and fell off my jacket.* **2** escaped, free, *(syn.)* unconfined: *The farmer's horse got loose, and he had to catch it.* **3** not tight-fitting: *She wears loose clothing in summer.* **4** careless, too relaxed: *The bookkeeping (attendance, discipline, etc.) in that company is loose.* **5** without strict morals, *(syn.)* promiscuous: *He called her a loose woman.* **6 a loose cannon:** a careless person who is a danger to others in a group, institution, etc.: *The other officers saw him as a loose cannon and wanted him off their ship.* **7 a loose end:** a point that has not yet been agreed on: *We just need to tie up a few loose ends before we can write up the contract.* **8 on the loose:** escaped and moving freely, esp. a prisoner or an animal: *He escaped from jail and is on the loose in the city.* **9** *infrml.* **to be at loose ends: a.** to be without a job or anything useful to do: *She is at loose ends and does little all day.* **b.** confused, not knowing what to do: *She is at loose ends, not knowing whether to look for a job or go to school.* **10** *infrml.* **to have a screw loose:** to be crazy, not sensible: *You can't depend on him; sometimes he acts as though he has a screw loose.* **11 to let loose: a.** to release, set free: *She let loose a cry of excitement when her team won.* **b.** *infrml.* to act without reserve or restraint: *It's the weekend at last, and we're going to let loose tonight!*
—*v.frml.* to release, untie: *He believes no one can ever loose the bonds of marriage.* **-n.** [U] **looseness.**

loose-leaf *adj.* containing individual sheets of paper that can usu. be removed or replaced: *Students keep their class notes in a loose-leaf binder.*

L

loos·en /ˈlusən/ v. **1** make or become less tight or firm: *A technician loosened the screws on the TV and opened the back of it.*‖*My hold on the rope loosened, and it slipped through my hands.* **2** *phrasal v. sep.* **to loosen s.o.** or **s.t up: a.** to get ready for an activity: *Athletes need to loosen up their muscles before competing.*‖*They loosen them up.* **b.** to relax: *After that six-hour meeting, I felt the need to loosen up.*

loot /lut/ v. to rob, steal from: *People looted stores during the riot.*
—n. [U] stolen goods or money: *Thieves hid their loot in an empty building.*

lop /lɑp/ v. **lopped, lopping, lops** to cut, chop: *A farm worker lopped the green tops off carrots with a knife.*

lope /loup/ v.n. to run in a smooth, graceful way: *A dog <v.> loped through the field toward home.*‖*He ran with an easy <n.> lope.*

lop·sid·ed /ˈlɑpˌsaɪdɪd/ adj. with one side much larger or heavier than the other: *Our team had a lopsided victory of 10 to 0 over our opponent.*

lord /lɔrd/ n. **1** a nobleman: *She reads books about English lords and their ladies.* **2 the Lord:** term for the Christian God: *O Lord, hear my prayer.*
—v. *phrasal v. insep.* **to lord it over s.o.:** to act like s.o.'s master, *(syn.)* to domineer: *After winning the competition, he tried to lord it over his classmates, but they refused to listen.*

lord·ly /ˈlɔrdli/ adj. **1** formal and dignified: *He manages his business with a lordly air.* **2** showing too high an opinion of one's importance, *(syn.)* haughty: *The workers disliked their supervisor's lordly manner.*

lore /lɔr/ n. [U] informal history, often stories, customs, and beliefs: *The sportswriter is an expert on the lore of baseball.*

lor·ry /ˈlɔri, ˈlɑ-/ n.Brit. **-ries** a truck: *In England, lorries carry freight.*

lose /luz/ v. **lost** /lɔst/, **losing, loses 1** to become unable to find, misplace: *He lost his wallet.* **2** to be defeated (in a competition or war): *Our team lost the basketball game.* **3** to have s.t. valuable taken away: *Because of the storm, they lost time (their ship, their lives, etc.).* **4** to be unable to keep, no longer control (one's balance, patience, etc.): *She lost her temper and began shouting.* **5** to have less of: *lose weight, lose interest in s.t.* **6** to escape from: *(s.o. who is following): The thief managed to lose the police in the crowded street.* **7** to fail to make s.o. understand: *I'm afraid you've lost me; would you repeat the instructions?* **8 a losing battle:** an effort that cannot succeed: *She stopped trying to change his mind when she saw that it was a losing battle.* **9 to lose heart:** to have less hope, become discouraged: *After the other team scored, our team lost heart and*

played poorly. **10** *infrml.* **to lose one's cool:** to become angry, upset, emotional, etc.: *The thief lost his cool and started fighting with the police.* **11** *infrml.* **to lose one's shirt:** to suffer a large financial loss: *He invested his money foolishly, and when stock prices dropped, he lost his shirt.* **12 to lose one's touch:** to no longer have the same high level of skill (as a performer, an artist, etc.): *She has been a very successful writer, but her newest book is selling poorly; maybe she's losing her touch.* **13** *phrasal v. insep.* **to lose out (on s.t.):** to miss an opportunity: *He arrived too late for the interview and lost out on any chance at the job.* **14 to lose sight of: a.** to become unable to see: *We lost sight of land as our ship moved out to sea.* **b.** *fig.* to no longer consider, forget: *She is following her own idea and has lost sight of what her boss wants her to do.*

los·er /ˈluzər/ n. **1** a person or team that has lost a competition: *Our team was the loser in the volleyball game.* **2** *infrml.pej.* a person who is a failure, esp. one whose actions harm others: *He is a loser who won't get off drugs.*

loss /lɔs/ n. **-es 1** [C] a failure to win: *Our team has a record of five wins, two losses, and one tie.* **2** [C] an amount of money that is lost or taken away: *She suffered large losses when stock prices dropped.* **3** [C;U] the fact of losing s.o. or s.t. valued, esp. because of a death: *The loss of his mother caused him great pain.* **4 at a loss:** not knowing what to do or say: *When his business failed, he was at a loss as to what to do.* **5 to be at a loss for words:** to not know what to say: *When she learned she had won a big prize, she was at a loss for words and could only smile.*

lost /lɔst/ v. *past tense & part. of* lose
—adj. **1** unable to be found, misplaced: *His wallet is lost.* **2** not knowing where one is located: *The lost child asked a police officer for help.* **3** killed or destroyed: *Several seamen were lost at sea in the storm.* **4 a lost cause:** a project or effort that cannot be successful: *He decided that losing weight was a lost cause and stopped trying to diet.* **5** *exclam.slang* **Get lost!:** angry request for others to leave: *Get lost and stop annoying me!* **6 lost in thought:** thinking deeply and so not aware of people or things around one: *She was lost in thought and didn't hear my question.*

lot /lɑt/ n. **1** [C] a piece of land: *We own a small lot next to our house.* **2** [U] one's condition in life, *(syn.)* fate: *It was his lot to become priest.* **3** *infrml.* **a lot (of)** or **lots (of):** a large amount or number: *I like her a lot.*‖*He has lots of money, problems, etc.* **4 to draw lots:** to use chance to make a choice, such as by picking straws of differing lengths: *We drew lots to decide who would go first, second, and third.*

lo·tion /'louʃən/ n. [C;U] a liquid used to clean, soften, moisturize, or protect skin: *People use suntan lotion to protect against sunburn.*

lot·ter·y /'lɑtəri/ n. **-ies** a game of chance in which people buy tickets with numbers and the winner is the one whose numbers match those drawn by the lottery organizer: *Many states have a lottery to raise money.*

lot·to /'lɑtou/ n. a lottery: *I play lotto once a week.*

lo·tus /'loutəs/ n. **-es** any of a variety of land or water plants having large white, pink, or yellow flowers: *The lotus is a beautiful plant with special religious meaning.*

loud /laud/ adj. **-er, -est** **1** having an intense sound, noisy: *The sound of city traffic is loud.* **2** unpleasantly bright in color: *He wears bright reds and other loud colors.* -n. **loudness.**

loud·mouth /'laud,mauθ/ n.infrml. **-mouths** /-,mauðs, -,mauθs/ **1** a person who speaks in a loud voice: *That loudmouth is always saying how tough he is.* **2** s.o. who tells the secrets of others: *Don't tell that loudmouth anything that you want to keep secret.* -adj. **loudmouthed** /'laud,mauðd, -,mauθt/.

loud·speak·er /'laud,spikər/ n. a device for amplifying sound: *Loudspeakers in the train station are used to announce departures and arrivals.*

lounge /laundʒ/ n. **1** a place with seats where people can wait, read, etc.: *We waited in the airline's lounge.* **2 (cocktail) lounge:** a barroom often with comfortable seats and tables: *We met in the lounge for a drink before dinner.* —v. **lounged, lounging, lounges** to rest in a relaxed position: *We lounged on the beach.*

louse /laus/ n. **lice** /lais/ **1** any of a variety of bloodsucking insects that live on people and animals: *Lice cause itching and carry diseases.* **2** infrml.fig. a bad person who cannot be trusted: *She finally divorced that louse!* —v. **loused, lousing, louses** phrasal v. sep. slang **to louse s.t. up:** to make a mess of, spoil: *That idiot loused up all our plans!‖ He loused them up!*

lous·y /'lauzi/ adj.infrml.fig. **1** awful, no good: *That repair shop did a lousy job of fixing my car.* **2** in poor health, miserable: *She has the flu and feels lousy.*

lout /laut/ n. stupid, offensive man: *That lout annoys everyone he meets.* -adj. **loutish.**

lov·a·ble /'lʌvəbəl/ adj. easy to love, (syns.) adorable, endearing: *That little girl is a lovable child.*

love /lʌv/ v. **loved, loving, loves** **1** to like with great intensity: *I love my wife with all my heart.* **2** to enjoy very much, take great pleasure in: *He loves to play golf, but his wife loves gardening.*

—n. **1** [U] very strong liking and affection: *She shows her love for her children every day.* **2** [C] strong enjoyment or pleasure: *a love of music* **3** [C] an endearing person: *That little boy is such a love!* **4** [U] sexual desire or passion: *He is full of love for his new wife.* **5** [U] (in tennis) a score of zero **6 a labor of love:** a job or project done for idealistic reasons rather than for money: *The professor wrote his book on Shakespeare as a labor of love.* **7 a love-hate relationship:** a strong emotional connection that involves both caring for and disliking s.o.: *That couple has a love-hate relationship.* **8 Give s.o. my love:** say hello for me in a loving way: *Give my love to your mother when you see her.* **9 neither for love nor money:** not for any reason: *Neither for love nor money will he give up smoking.* **10 to fall** or **be in love (with s.o.):** to begin to feel or to have strong romantic feelings for s.o.: *He fell in love with her the moment he saw her; it was love at first sight.* **11 to make love:** to have sexual intercourse: *They made love on their wedding night.*

love·bird /'lʌv,bɜrd/ n. **1** any of several small parrots that seem to talk to and touch each other with affection **2** fig. an affectionate couple: *The lovebirds kissed in public on their honeymoon.*

love child n.old usage a child born to a couple not married to each other: *The king kept his love child a secret from the public.*

love·less /'lʌvlɪs/ adj. without love: *That couple suffers from a loveless marriage.*

love·lorn /'lʌv,lɔrn/ adj.frml. sad from lack of love or the absence of one's lover: *He is lovelorn; his wife has left him.*

love·ly /'lʌvli/ adj. **-lier, -liest** **1** attractive, pretty: *The girl on the magazine cover is lovely.* **2** pleasant, delightful: *We had a lovely time at the wedding.* -n. [U] **loveliness.**

lov·er /'lʌvər/ n. **1** a person in a sexual relationship outside marriage: *Two lovers met for dinner at a cozy restaurant.* **2** s.o. who very much enjoys s.t.: *a music lover* **3** a gay person's romantic partner

love seat n. a small sofa seating two people: *We have a love seat against the wall opposite the sofa.*

love·sick /'lʌv,sɪk/ adj. sad and depressed from love that is not returned: *He is so lovesick since his girlfriend left him that he can't eat or sleep.*

lov·ing /'lʌvɪŋ/ adj. showing love, esp. attentive and affectionate: *The children's mother is a loving woman.*

low /lou/ adj. **-er, -est** **1** below s.t. else in level: *The land is low in this area; it is near sea level.‖ I was glad to pay such a low price for the car.* **2** near the floor or ground: *There*

was a low table in front of the sofa. **3** (of a sound) quiet or deep: *They spoke in low voices so as not to disturb anyone.||The radio announcer had a low voice.* **4** *fig.* morally bad, dishonest, (*syn.*) base: *He stole from his friend, and that was a low thing to do.* **5** *fig.* sad, depressed: *She is feeling low about the death of her father.* **6 to be low on s.t.:** to have only a little of s.t. left: *We were low on gas, so we drove into a gas station to buy some.*
—*adv.* **1** in, at, or to a negligible position or level: *She scored low on the test.* **2** near the floor or ground: *He bent low to pick up the child.*
—*n.* **1** a depth: *Winter temperatures there reach extreme lows.* **2 to hit a new low:** to reach the lowest point so far: *The price of that stock hit a new low yesterday.*
—*v.* to make a sound like a cow, to moo: *The cows are lowing in the field.*

low·brow /'lou,brau/ *adj.n.* common, not cultured, (*syn.*) undiscriminating: *He has <adj.> lowbrow tastes and is happiest when drinking beer and watching football.*

low-cal /'lou,kæl/ *adj.infrml.* low in calories: *She drinks low-cal diet sodas.*

low-down /'lou,daun/ *adj.infrml.* lacking honor or fairness, mean: *He did a lowdown, nasty thing when he cheated his friend.*
—*n. sing.infrml.fig.* the most recent information about s.t.: *My friend gave me the lowdown on the current office rumors.*

low·er /'louər/ *adj. comp.* of low
—*v.* **1** to let down to a reduced level or position: *A sailor lowered a rope over the side of the ship.* **2** to make less in amount, degree, or intensity: *The dealer lowered the price of the car.* **3 to lower oneself:** to act beneath one's dignity or self-respect: *He needed money but would not lower himself to picking up coins on the street.*

low·er·case /'louər,keis/ *adj.n.* [U] in small rather than capital letters: *This sentence is in <adj.> lowercase letters, except for the capital "T" of "This."*

lowest common denominator *n.* **1** (in mathematics) the lowest number that is a multiple of each denominator in a set of fractions **2** *fig.* the people lowest in ability in a society: *Critics claim that the public school system is run for the benefit of the lowest common denominator.*

low-grade *adj.* poor in quality: *The ore from that mine is low-grade and yields little gold.*

low-key *adj.* quiet, calm, and controlled: *He is a low-key guy who never raises his voice.*

low·lands /'loulandz/ *n.pl.* a region near sea level: *The mountains slope down into lowlands near the ocean.*

low·ly /'louli/ *adj.* **-lier, -liest** from a low or humble position: *She comes from lowly origins but is a brilliant student.*

low-pressure *adj.* calm, not pushing people to work faster: *She has a low-pressure job and friendly co-workers.*

low profile *n.* a way of behaving that does not draw attention: *He is a diplomat who maintains a low profile and works quietly with others.*

low tide *n.* [C;U] one of two daily periods during which the tide is lowest: *Small fishing boats lie in the mud during low tide.*

lox /laks/ *n.* [U] smoked salmon: *Many people enjoy lox and cream cheese on bagels.*

loy·al /'lɔɪəl/ *adj.* faithful to others, esp. one's friends or country: *He is a loyal soldier.*

loy·al·ist /'lɔɪəlɪst/ *n.* a person loyal to a government, king, or queen: *Many loyalists were driven out of the country during the revolution.*

loy·al·ty /'lɔɪəlti/ *n.* [C;U] **-ties** faithfulness, devotion, (*syn.*) allegiance: *The loyalty of dogs to their owners is well-known.*

loz·enge /'lazəndʒ/ *n.* a small medicated candy: *He sucked on a throat lozenge to relieve his sore throat.*

LPN /'ɛlpi'ɛn/ *n. See:* licensed practical nurse.

LSD /'ɛlɛs'di/ *n.* [U] *abbr. for* lysergic acid diethylamide, a powerful drug that makes people see things in strange ways: *In the 1960s, many young people experimented with LSD.*

lu·bri·cant /'lubrəkənt/ *n.* [C;U] an oil, grease, or other substance used to smooth friction between rubbing surfaces: *Oil is used as a lubricant in engines.*

lu·bri·cate /'lubrə,keit/ *v.* **-cated, -cating, -cates** to apply a lubricant to: *Oils lubricate moving parts of engines and other machines.* -*adj.* **lubricating.**

lu·cid /'lusid/ *adj.* **1** clear, easily understood: *She wrote a lucid explanation of the problem.* **2** clear-headed, not confused: *That man is very old, but he is still lucid in conversation.* -*n.* **lucidity.**

luck /lʌk/ *n.* [U] **1** chance, fortune: *She had good luck in finding a new job quickly.* **2** good fortune, success: *He wished me luck.* **3 as luck would have it:** by chance or fate, (*syn.*) coincidentally: *Our car broke down, but as luck would have it, a police car was nearby and helped us.* **4** in or out of luck: to have or not have good fortune **5** *infrml.* **to luck out:** to have good fortune **6 to push (one's) luck:** to act too confidently

luck·y /'lʌki/ *adj.* **-ier, -iest** having or bringing good luck, (*syn.*) fortunate: *He was lucky not to hurt himself when he fell.||Seven is my lucky number.*

lu·cra·tive /'lukrətɪv/ *adj.* producing a lot of money, profitable: *The business of selling lux-*

ury goods, such as furs and fancy cars, can be quite lucrative when the economy is strong.

lu·di·crous /'ludəkrəs/ *adj.* causing laughter, ridiculous, (*syn.*) absurd: *What a ludicrous idea that such an idiot could become President!*

lug /lʌg/ *v.infrml.* **lugged, lugging, lugs** to carry or pull with difficulty, haul: *I lugged two heavy suitcases to the train station.*
—*n.* **1** *short for* lug nut, a small piece of metal used as a fastener: *The mechanic used a lug wrench to loosen the lugs and remove the tire.* **2** *slang* a big, fool: *He is a friendly lug.*

lug·gage /'lʌgɪʤ/ *n.* [U] suitcases and bags used to carry clothing while traveling, (*syn.*) baggage: *We checked our luggage in at the airport ticket counter.*

lu·gu·bri·ous /lʊ'gubriəs/ *adj.frml.* sad, (*syns.*) sorrowful, mournful: *The losing players sat with lugubrious faces while the winners celebrated.*

luke·warm /'luk,wɔrm/ *adj.* **1** (of a liquid) mildly warm, (*syn.*) tepid: *The tea is lukewarm and not very tasty.* **2** lacking strong interest or admiration: *The critics gave the new play lukewarm reviews. See:* warm, USAGE NOTE.

lull /lʌl/ *n.* a lessening or temporary stopping of activity: *The store was very busy, but now there is a lull.*
—*v.* **1** to quiet, calm, (*syn.*) to soothe: *She lulled her baby to sleep by singing a lullaby.* **2** *fig.* **to lull s.o. (into doing s.t.):** to dishonestly gain s.o.'s trust (so he or she will do s.t.), as by giving false assurances: *The company treasurer lulled creditors into thinking that he would pay overdue bills, but then he declared bankruptcy and cheated them.*

lull·a·by /'lʌlə,baɪ/ *n.* **-ies** a quiet song for lulling a child to sleep: *She sang sweet lullabies to her baby at bedtime.*

lum·ber /'lʌmbər/ *n.* [U] wood cut to various lengths and sizes for building houses, furniture, etc.: *I bought some lumber at the lumberyard to make bookshelves.*
—*v.* **1** to cut trees for lumber: *People lumber for a living in the Pacific Northwest.* **2** to walk or run in an awkward, heavy way: *The bear lumbered along the forest trail. -n. adj.* **lumbering.**

lum·ber·jack /'lʌmbər,ʤæk/ *n.* a person who cuts down trees or transports them: *His father was a Canadian lumberjack.*

lum·ber·man /'lʌmbərmən/ *n.* **-men** /-mən/ a person working in the lumber industry, such as a mill owner or lumberjack: *Lumbermen gather at the local coffee shop each morning before work.*

lum·ber·yard /'lʌmbər,yard/ *n.* a business that sells lumber: *I bought shingles at the lumberyard to repair my roof.*

lu·mi·nar·y /'lumə,nɛri/ *n.frml.* **-ies** a respected person, esp. in the arts or academia: *That professor is a luminary in the field of biology.*

lu·mi·nes·cence /lumə'nɛsəns/ *n.* [U] light without heat, a glow: *The glow in the sea at night was produced by the luminescence of certain algae. -adj.* **luminescent.**

lu·mi·nous /'lumənəs/ *adj.* giving or reflecting light: *The full moon is luminous in the night sky. -n.* [U] **luminosity** /,lumə'nɑsəti/.

lump /lʌmp/ *n.* **1** a round mass: *An artist molded a lump of clay.* **2** a hard abnormal growth: *She felt a lump in her breast and called the doctor.* **3** a small block of sugar: *One lump or two in your coffee?* **4** *fig.* **a lump in the throat:** a tight feeling in the throat caused by strong emotion **5** *fig.* **to take one's lumps:** to suffer punishment or bad luck when trying s.t. difficult: *If you play ice hockey, you have to take your lumps; it's a rough sport.*
—*v.* **1** to put together and treat as the same: *He lumps all those who disagree with him into one category: stupid.* **2** *infrml.fig.* **to like it or lump it:** to accept s.t. that one dislikes: *Like it or lump it, we have to follow orders.* **3** *phrasal v. sep.* **to lump s.t. together:** to put two or more things together, usu. randomly: *She lumped together all the files on her desk.||She lumped them together.*
—*adj.* **a lump sum:** an amount of money paid at one time : *We paid for the car on the installment plan because we couldn't afford to pay in a lump sum.*

lump·y /'lʌmpi/ *adj.* **-ier, -iest** having lumps, not smooth or even: *The mashed potatoes are terribly lumpy.*

lu·na·cy /'lunəsi/ *n.* [U] **-cies 1** madness, insanity: *The poor man suffers from lunacy.* **2** foolishness, stupidity: *It was lunacy to go out in that storm!*

lu·nar /'lunər/ *adj.* related to a moon, esp. the earth's: *The astronauts returned from the moon with lunar rocks.*

lu·na·tic /'lunətɪk/ *adj.n.* crazy, insane: *He has these <adj.> lunatic ideas about becoming rich; he's a <n.> lunatic!*

lunatic fringe *n.infrml.* the most extreme members of a political group or believers in a cause: *The people responsible for the bombing belong to the lunatic fringe.*

lunch /lʌnʧ/ *n.* [C;U] **-es** the midday meal: *I have just a sandwich for lunch.*
—*v.frml.* to have lunch: *We lunched at a fine restaurant today.*

L

USAGE NOTE: Most workers in the USA have only 30 minutes to one hour for *lunch,* so they usually eat a small, informal meal, often just a sandwich. Typically, people eat lunch any time between noon and 2:00 p.m. Dinner, usually the big meal of the day, is served between 6:00 and 7:30 pm in most American homes.

lunch counter *n.* a restaurant counter with stools where one sits for quick service: *We sat at the lunch counter today rather than at a table.*

lunch·eon /'lʌntʃən/ *n.frml.* **1** lunch **2** an event that includes lunch and usu. speeches: *We went to a luncheon given in honor of the ambassador.*

lunch·eon·ette /ˌlʌntʃə'nɛt/ *n.* a restaurant that serves inexpensive meals: *We stopped for a sandwich at a luncheonette and then went right back to work.*

lunch·room /'lʌntʃˌrum/ *n.* an area in a business or school where employees or students can eat: *We had lunch in the company lunchroom today.*

lung /lʌŋ/ *n.* **1** one of two breathing organs in the chest that supply oxygen to the blood: *Her lungs are in bad condition from smoking.* **2 at the top of one's lungs:** very loudly: *He yelled at the top of his lungs when cheering for his favorite team.*

lunge /lʌndʒ/ *v.* **lunged, lunging, lunges** to move forward with sudden force: *She lunged at the basketball and stole it from the opposing player.*
—*n.* a fast, forward movement: *The criminal made a lunge with a knife at his victim.*

lu·pus /'lupəs/ *n.* [U] any of several serious diseases that involve the skin: *She suffers from lupus.*

lurch /lɜrtʃ/ *n.* **-es 1** a sudden, awkward motion: *The drunken man moved with a lurch and fell.* **2** *fig.* **to leave s.o. in the lurch:** to desert s.o., putting him or her in a difficult situation: *His fiancée left him in the lurch by failing to come to their wedding.*
—*v.* to move with a sudden, unsteady motion: *The ship lurched from side to side in the storm's waves.*

lure /lʊr/ *n.* **1** [C] bait used to attract and catch animals: *Fisherman use lures to attract and hook fish.* **2** *sing.* the power of s.t. that attracts: *the lure of money*
—*v.* **lured, luring, lures** to attract, usu. with dishonest promises, (*syn.*) to entice: *People were lured to invest in the scheme with promises of huge profits.*

lu·rid /'lʊrɪd/ *adj.* shocking, causing horror: *Today's newspaper has the lurid details of the murder.*

lurk /lɜrk/ *v.* **1** to wait in hiding: *The robbers lurked in the woods near the house as they waited for darkness to fall.* **2** to read computer messages on an electronic news group or mailing list, esp. on the Internet, without stating one's presence or adding to the discussion: *He never shares his opinions in the online discussion; he just lurks.* -*n.* **lurker.**

lus·cious /'lʌʃəs/ *adj.* juicy and delicious: *Ripe pears have a luscious taste.*

lush /lʌʃ/ *adj.* (of plants) having thick, healthy growth: *The garden is lush with new spring growth.*
—*n.slang* a person who is often drunk: *The poor woman has become a lush.*

lust /lʌst/ *n.* [U] **1** strong sexual desire: *Some people confuse love with lust.* **2** [C;U] an intense desire: *Dictators have a lust for power.*
—*v.* **1** to desire sexually: *That man constantly lusts after women.* **2** to have a strong desire: *Some people lust for power and riches.* -*adj.* **lustful; lusty.**

lust·er /'lʌstər/ *n.* [U] **1** *sing.* a shine, such as bright polish on a surface: *The luster of wax made the table shine.* **2** a special quality, (*syns.*) brilliance, splendor: *Wonderful costumes and scenery added luster to the performance of the opera.* -*adj.* **lustrous.**

lute /lut/ *n.* a stringed musical instrument from the past, having a softer, sweeter tone than the guitar

lux·u·ri·ant /lʌg'ʒʊriənt, lʌk'ʃʊr-/ *adj.* **1** having dense, full texture or growth: *Expensive oriental rugs have a luxuriant feel and look.* **2** abundant

lux·u·ri·ate /lʌg'ʒʊriˌeɪt, lʌk'ʃʊr-/ *v.* **-ated, -ating, -ates** to enjoy oneself very much, esp. in a costly way: *She luxuriated in her beautiful new apartment overlooking the ocean.*

lux·u·ri·ous /lʌg'ʒʊriəs, lʌk'ʃʊr-/ *adj.* characterized by luxury, wasteful spending, and great comfort: *Their house is full of luxurious furniture.*

lux·u·ry /'lʌgʒəri, 'lʌkʃə-/ *n.* **-ries 1** [U] great comfort at great expense: *That family lives in luxury, enjoying costly clothes, high-priced cars, and a beautiful house.* **2** [C] s.t. pleasant that is expensive and not a necessity: *We can't afford luxuries, such as overseas vacations.*

lye /laɪ/ *n.* [U] a strong alkaline liquid: *Lye has a very strong cleaning action.*

ly·ing /'laɪɪŋ/ *v. pres. part. of* lie
—*n.* [U] saying s.t. that is not true: *His lying will get him into trouble someday.*

lymph /lɪmf/ *n.* [U] *adj.* the clear fluid in the lymphatic system, used mainly to eliminate bacteria from the body: *<n.> Lymph passes through <adj.> lymph nodes throughout the body.* -*adj.* **lymphatic** /lɪm'fætɪk/.

lynch /lɪntʃ/ v. (of a crowd) to attack and hang s.o. accused of a crime, without any legal process: *Cowboys lynched the cattle thief after they caught him.*

lyre /laɪr/ n. an ancient type of musical instrument like a harp with a U-shaped frame in which strings are fixed

lyr·ics /ˈlɪrɪks/ n.pl. the words of a song: *The lyrics to that song are clever.*
—*adj.* **1** having a light quality: *That singer has a lyric tenor voice.* **2** related to expression of feelings in poetry: *Much of romantic poetry is lyric in quality.*

lyr·i·cist /ˈlɪrɪsɪst/ n. a person who writes words for songs: *He was a lyricist for Broadway musicals.*

L

M,m

M, m /ɛm/ *n.* **M's, m's** or **Ms, ms** **1** the 13th letter of the English alphabet **2** the Roman numeral for 1,000: *The printer printed 5M copies of the book.*

M.A. /ˌɛm'eɪ/ *abbr. for* the academic degree of Master of Arts: *He has an M.A. in English literature. See:* B.A.

USAGE NOTE: An *M.A.*, like an *M.S.* (Master of Science) is often called a master's degree. This graduate degree is awarded after a *B.A.* (bachelor's) but before a *Ph.D.* (doctorate). Other types of *M.A.s* include *M.B.A.* (master of business administration), *M.S.W.* (master of social work), and *M.Ed.* (master in education)

---

ma'am /mæm/ *n. See:* madam.

ma·ca·bre /mə'kɑbrə, -'kɑbər/ *adj.* frightening, because of showing death and decay: *The car accident scene with dead bodies on the road was macabre.*

mac·a·ro·ni /ˌmækə'roʊni/ *n.* [U] a type of pasta made from flour in the shape of small tubes, boiled, and often mixed with cheese: *I like to eat macaroni and cheese with a hamburger for dinner. See:* spaghetti, USAGE NOTE.

mace /meɪs/ *n.* **1** [C] a metal club: *Soldiers used maces to kill each other in the Middle Ages.* **2** [U] **Mace** *TM* a name for a powerful spray that forces away people or dogs: *She sprayed Mace in the dog's face when he attacked her, and he ran away.*

ma·che·te /mə'ʃɛti, -'tʃɛ-/ *n.* a long knife with a heavy blade used in farm work or as a weapon: *Workers cut sugarcane with machetes.*

Mach·i·a·vel·li·an /ˌmækiə'vɛliən/ *adj.* related to getting and keeping power, esp. by tricking others: *That politician uses Machiavellian methods to stay in office.*

mach·i·na·tions /ˌmækə'neɪʃənz/ *n.pl.frml.* methods used to trick others, esp. in business and politics: *The cheat used various machinations, such as fake addresses and documents, to fool people and steal their money.*

ma·chine /mə'ʃin/ *n.* **1** a piece of equipment that uses power to do work: *An automobile is a machine used for transportation.* **2** a powerful organization: *The political machine in New York has a lot of influence in the elections.*
—*v.* **-chined, -chining, -chines** to make or change s.t. on a machine, esp. parts of things: *That factory machines metal parts for tractors.* *-n.* **machinist.**

machine gun *n.* a weapon that fires bullets in a fast, constant action when its trigger is pressed: *Soldiers shoot machine guns at the enemy.*

ma·chin·er·y /mə'ʃinəri, -'ʃinri/ *n.* [U] machines as a group: *Machinery in that textile mill is used to make fabric.*

ma·chis·mo /mɑ'tʃizmoʊ, mə'tʃɪz-/ *n.* [U] an attitude or behavior that values male strength and courage: *He believes in machismo and acts like a tough guy.*

ma·cho /'mɑtʃoʊ/ *adj.* strong, tough, (*syn.*) virile (said of men): *He is a big macho man from a tough neighborhood.*

mack·er·el /'mækərəl, 'mækrəl/ **-el** or **-els** *n.* [C;U] any of some 60 types of edible deepocean fishes, such as the Atlantic mackerel

mac·ro /'mækroʊ/ *n.* **-ros** (in computers) a stroke or group of strokes on a keyboard or group of them used to do frequent but long functions: *The typist uses a macro to tell the computer when to exit.*
—*adj.* general, (*syn.*) overall: *Many economists take a macro view of the economy and don't look at individual business performance.*
—*prefix* indicating largeness or length: *Some environmentalists take a macroscopic view of the world's pollution.*

mac·ro·bi·ot·ics /ˌmækroʊbaɪ'ɑtɪks/ *n.* [U] *pl.* **1** natural foods, esp. whole grain cereals and vegetables grown without chemicals **2** the philosophy of eating such foods to be healthy: *She studied macrobiotics and became a vegetarian. -adj.* **macrobiotic.**

mac·ro·cosm /'mækrə,kɑzəm/ *n.* a large system, such as the world or the universe:

Scientists study the earth's atmosphere as a macrocosm.

mac·ro·ec·o·nom·ics /ˈmækroʊˌɛkəˌnɑmɪks, -ˌikə-/ n. [U] the study of national economies: *Macroeconomics is an important field to help countries' governments improve their economies.*

mad /mæd/ adj. **madder, maddest 1** angry, upset: *She was mad when her boyfriend was late without calling her.* **2** strongly attracted to s.t.: *He is mad about fast cars.* **3** crazy, (*syn.*) insane: *He went mad when his wife died.*

mad·am /ˈmædəm/ also **ma'am** /mæm/ n. **1** pl. **mesdames** /meɪˈdɑm, -ˈdæm/ a polite way to speak to a woman: *The store clerk said, "Madam, how may I help you?"* **2** a woman who runs a house of prostitution

mad·cap /ˈmædˌkæp/ adj. funny and foolish, (*syn.*) absurd: *That comedian does madcap tricks on stage.*

mad·den /ˈmædn/ v. to make angry, (*syn.*) to enrage

mad·den·ing /ˈmædnɪŋ/ adj. annoying: *I find it maddening that my car breaks down a lot.*

made /meɪd/ adj. & past part. of make **1** manufactured: *My TV set was made in the USA.* **2** composed of s.t.: *Those new sheets are made of cotton.* **3** infrml. **to have it made:** to be successful, secure, free from worry: *When you win the big prize in the lottery, you have it made for life.*

made-to-order adj. **1** created to a customer's specifications: *His suits are made-to-order to fit his measurements.* **2** just right, perfect: *We found a lamp made-to-order for our furniture; it has the same color.*

made-up adj. **1** false, untrue: *Her story about where she was last night was made-up.* **2** having cosmetics put on, usu. on the face: *The actor was made-up and ready to perform.*

mad·house /ˈmædˌhaʊs/ n.infrml. **1** old usage an insane asylum: *His family sent their insane relative to live in a madhouse.* **2** fig. a confusing, noisy place: *Our apartment was a madhouse on the weekend; there were ten children playing games in one room.*

mad·ly /ˈmædli/ adv. totally, (*syn.*) obsessively: *He is madly in love with her.*

mad·man /ˈmædˌmæn, -mən/ or **mad·wom·an** /ˈmædˌwʊmən/ n. **-men** /-ˌmɛn, -mən/ or **-women** /-ˌwɪmən/ a crazy, dangerous person, (*syn.*) a maniac: *A madman is loose in the city.*

mad·ness /ˈmædnɪs/ n. [U] **1** severe mental disorder, (*syn.*) insanity: *In his madness, he thought he was the President.* **2** fig. a foolish, crazy idea: *It was madness to drive in that terrible snowstorm.*

mael·strom /ˈmeɪlstrəm/ n.frml. **1** a powerful whirlpool **2** fig. a dangerous situation: *Soldiers fight in the maelstrom of war.*

mae·stro /ˈmaɪstroʊ/ n. **-stros** a master in the arts, esp. music: *Mozart was a maestro of classical music.*

Ma·fi·a /ˈmɑfiə/ n. a violent, criminal organization most active in Italy and the USA: *The Mafia is said to control the casinos in many big cities.*

mag·a·zine /ˌmægəˈzin, ˈmægəˌzin/ n. **1** a small weekly, or monthly, publication that usu. includes news articles, stories, essays, and photos, (*syn.*) a periodical: *We read Time, a weekly news magazine.* **2** a storage place for bullets and weapons

ma·gen·ta /məˈdʒɛntə/ n. [U] a red color mixed with purple: *Some plants have magenta flowers.*

mag·got /ˈmægət/ n. a creature that looks like a worm, esp. the larva of the common housefly: *Maggots live in the garbage in the heat of summer.*

mag·ic /ˈmædʒɪk/ n. [U] adj. **1** the use of supernatural forces to control s.t.: *She used magic to create a thunderstorm.* **2** the use of tricks to entertain people: *That magician uses <n.> magic to pull rabbits out of a hat.‖He does <adj.> magic tricks.* **3** an enchanting quality about s.t.: *The singer filled the evening with the magic of her voice.* -adj. **magical.**

ma·gi·cian /məˈdʒɪʃən/ n. **1** a person who does magic tricks: *Magicians make impossible things seem real, such as cutting people in half.* **2** fig. a person who can do wonderful things, (*syn.*) a whiz: *She is a magician with food and can turn simple ingredients into delicious meals.*

Magic Marker n.TM a type of thick, felt-tip pen used to mark a text, draw a picture, or write in big letters: *We used a Magic Marker at our meeting to write our ideas on a board so everyone could see. See:* marker, **2**.

mag·is·te·ri·al /ˌmædʒəˈstɪriəl/ adj.frml. **1** related to a magistrate's power: *The judge put on her black robe and did her magisterial duties.* **2** haughty, arrogant

mag·is·trate /ˈmædʒəˌstreɪt, -strɪt/ n. a low-level government official with power to enforce the law: *The traffic magistrate heard the man's explanation for getting a parking ticket.*

mag·ma /ˈmægmə/ n. [U] hot, liquid rock below the earth's surface: *Magma moves up to the surface and becomes lava in volcanoes.*

mag·nan·i·mous /mægˈnænəməs/ adj.frml. generous in spirit, not showing resentment or meanness: *He was magnanimous in forgiving those who injured him.* -adv.frml. **magnanimously;** -n. [U] frml. **magnanimity** /ˌmægnəˈnɪməti/.

M

mag·nate /'mæg,neɪt, -nɪt/ *n.* an important businessperson, a big industrialist: *She is a coal and iron magnate from Australia.*

mag·net /'mægnɪt/ *n.* **1** an object, esp. metal, with a magnetic field that attracts iron and steel: *I have a magnet on my desk that holds paper clips.* **2** anything that attracts people: *The Caribbean is a magnet for tourists in the winter.* -*v.* **magnetize** /'mægnə,taɪz/; -*adj.* **magnetic** /mæg'nɛtɪk/.

mag·net·ism /'mægnə,tɪzəm/ *n.* [U] **1** the study of magnets and their forces **2** personal attractiveness: *He is an actor with a lot of personal magnetism. See:* magnet.

mag·ni·fi·ca·tion /,mægnəfə'keɪʃən/ *n.* the power to make s.t. appear larger: *With the magnification on the photocopier, you can make a document up to 125 percent larger than its original size.*

mag·nif·i·cent /mæg'nɪfəsənt/ *adj.* very beautiful or impressive, (*syn.*) splendid: *The Taj Mahal in India is a magnificent building.* -*n.* [U] **magnificence.**

mag·ni·fy /'mægnə,faɪ/ *v.* **-fied, -fying, -fies 1** to make s.t. look larger: *His eyeglasses magnify words so he can read them.* **2** to make s.t. seem greater than it is: *Nervousness magnified her fears about failing the exam.*

magnifying glass *n.* an optical lens, usu. framed, used to make images look larger, esp. for reading: *He uses a magnifying glass to look at his stamp collection.*

mag·ni·tude /'mægnə,tud/ *n.* [U] **1** the size or importance of s.t.: *The economy is slowing down, but economists don't know the magnitude of this change yet.* **2** (in science) the degree of brightness of a star or force of an earthquake: *The magnitude of the earthquake in California was 5.0 on the Richter scale.*

mag·no·lia /mæg'noʊlyə/ *n.* a tree with large flowers, esp. in the USA, from lower New York state down through the South: *The white and pink magnolia blossoms in the spring are beautiful.*

mag·num /'mægnəm/ *n.* a bottle containing 1.5 liters of wine or liquor: *We celebrated my wife's birthday with a magnum of champagne.*

mag·pie /'mæg,paɪ/ *n.* a bird with a loud, rapid call, of black color with white, blue, or green markings and a long tail: *Magpies annoy people with their loud call.*

ma·hog·a·ny /mə'hɑgəni/ *n.* [U] the hard, reddish brown wood of a Caribbean tree: *Furniture made of mahogany was popular in the 19th century.*

maid /meɪd/ *n.* **1** a female servant, esp. a cleaning woman: *Maids clean the rooms and make the beds in hotels.* **2** *pej.* **an old maid:** an older woman who has never married: *She never married and is now an old maid.*

maid·en /'meɪdn/ *n.frml.* **1** an unmarried girl or woman: *Maidens were summoned to the royal court.* **2** *old usage* a virgin **3 maiden voyage:** a first trip: *A new passenger ship made her maiden voyage across the Atlantic.* -*n.* **maidenhood.** *See:* maiden name.

maiden name *n.* a woman's family name before she marries: *Mrs. Silveri's maiden name was Rodriguez.*

maid of honor *n.* a bride's main unmarried attendant at her wedding: *I asked my best friend to be the maid of honor at my wedding. See:* matron of honor, best man.

mail (1) /meɪl/ *n.* [U] **1** letters, postcards, packages, etc., sent through the postal system: *The mail arrives at noon every day except Sunday.* **2** the postal system: *I put letters into the mail every evening.*
—*v.* to send by mail: *I mailed a package to my friend in Seattle. See:* electronic mail.

mail (2) *n.* [U] metal covering worn over the body by soldiers long ago to protect themselves

mail·box /'meɪl,bɑks/ *n.* **-boxes** blue metal box in which people put mail: *She dropped a letter into the mailbox.*

mail carrier *n.* a person who delivers mail: *Our mail carrier arrives around 10:00 A.M. See:* letter carrier.

mail·er /'meɪlər/ *n.* **1** a large envelope, usu. strong, used for mailing things: *I put the computer diskette into a cardboard mailer and sent it.* **2** a person or business that mails things: *Businesses are big mailers of brochures that describe their products.* **3** (in computers) a program that sends electronic mail

mail·ing /'meɪlɪŋ/ *n.* [C;U] a group of the same letters, brochures, etc., sent to customers at the same time: *Our company did a mailing about our new products on sale.*

mailing list *n.* a list of names, addresses, etc., esp. of possible customers: *Our mailing list has 5,000 names and addresses.*

mail·man /'meɪl,mæn/ *n.* **-men** /-,mɛn/ a male letter carrier. *See:* letter carrier.

mail order *n.* the system of selling products by mail: *She shops for clothes by mail order.*

maim /meɪm/ *v.* to injure and ruin the looks of s.o. or s.t. so that some part of it cannot be used: *The car accident maimed him; he will not be able to walk again.*

main /meɪn/ *adj.* central, most important: *Our teacher talked about the main idea in the essay.*
—*n.* a large pipe that carries water or gas under a street: *The water main broke and flooded the street.*

main clause *n.* The main clause in a sentence is a clause with a subject, verb, and often an object that can stand by itself as a sentence:

The main clause in the above sentence goes from: "The main clause" to "an object."

main·frame /'meɪn,freɪm/ *n.* a powerful, central computer: *The mainframe* (or) *mainframe computer serves the company's entire headquarters.*

main·land /'meɪn,lænd, -lənd/ *n.sing.adj.* land on a continent, not including islands: *People from Taiwan visit the <n.> mainland* (or) *<adj.> mainland China.*

main line *n.* the main railway track on a railroad: *The main line from Grand Central Terminal in New York heads north.*

main·ly /'meɪnli/ *adv.* usually, for the most part: *Farmers plant seeds mainly in the spring.*

main·stay /'meɪn,steɪ/ *n.* the key person or activity that supports others in a family, team, or organization: *The mother takes care of her five children and is the mainstay of the family.*

main·stream /'meɪn,strim/ *n.* the group of ideas accepted by the majority of people, the most popular way of thinking: *Her ideas are in the mainstream of American political thought.* —*adj.* accepted by most people, *(syn.)* conventional: *The politician has a <adj.> mainstream political view* (or) *her ideas are in the <n.> mainstream.* —*v.* to mix a person into a main group: *Some non-native students take bilingual classes and are mainstreamed into regular classes later.*

Main Street *n.* the principal street and business center of a town: *The bank, post office, and library are all on Main Street in our town.* —*adj.* typical of ordinary America and Americans: *Cars made by Ford and Chevrolet are as Main Street as you can find.*

main·tain /meɪn'teɪn/ *v.* **1** to keep in good condition, good repair: *People maintain their houses well in this neighborhood.* **2** to keep s.t. going, continue: *She maintains a friendship with her college friend who lives in another state.* **3** to say that s.t. is true, believe: *The man who saw the accident maintains that he told the truth about what happened.*

main·te·nance /'meɪntənəns/ *n.* [U] keeping s.t. in good condition, such as by cleaning, painting, and fixing it: *The maintenance in that building is excellent, as the paint is new and the halls are always clean.*

maître d' /,meɪtrə'di, ,meɪtər-/ *n.* **maître d's** /-'diz/ *short for* maître d'hôtel, a headwaiter: *The maître d' at the restaurant gave us a table near the window.*

maize /meɪz/ *n.* [U] *See:* corn.

ma·jes·tic /mə'dʒɛstɪk/ *adj.* **1** magnificent, spectacular: *The Rocky Mountains in the western United States are majestic.* **2** proud, dignified, *(syn.)* regal: *The Queen acts in a majestic manner.* -*adv.* **majestically.**

maj·es·ty /'mædʒəsti/ *n.* -**ties** **1** [U] magnificence, splendor: *The majesty of the Alps in Switzerland takes people's breath away.* **2** [C] a title for a king or queen and the power connected to the position: *Her Majesty the Queen will visit a hospital today.*

ma·jor /'meɪdʒər/ *adj.* main, most important: *The major reason for working is to make money to live.* —*n.* **1** a military rank above captain and below colonel: *She is a major in the Air Force.* **2** one's primary subject of study in college: *My major is Spanish literature.* —*v.* to study as one's major field in college: *He majored in economics at the university.*

ma·jor·i·ty /mə'dʒɔrəti, -'dʒɑr-/ *n.* [C] **1** more than half, but not all of s.t.: *A majority of the people voted for the President.* **2** [U] the age of legal adulthood and responsibility: *All of their children have reached their majority.*

major league *n.* **1** (in baseball) the highest-level organization of teams in professional baseball: *He plays baseball in the major league.* **2** *fig.* **in the major league(s):** a high level of success or importance in a field: *In her important new job, she's really in the major leagues now.* -*adj.* **major-league.**

make /meɪk/ *v.* **made** /meɪd/ **making, makes** **1** to manufacture, create: *Our company makes computers.‖That shop makes toys of wood.* **2** to do, perform: *The businesswoman made contact with a new customer.‖A surgeon made a cut in the patient's stomach.* **3** to earn a living: *She makes a good salary (living, income) as an accountant.‖That company makes a big profit.* **4** to cook, prepare: *He made chicken with rice for dinner.* **5** to appoint, promote s.o.: *The boss made her assistant national sales manager.* **6** to reach, *(syn.)* to attain: *The army private made the rank of sergeant.* **7** to make, *(syn.)* to enact: *Congress makes the laws of the country.* **8** to force, order s.o. to do s.t.: *Her mother made her brush her teeth.* **9** to deliver, give: *He made a speech before an audience.* **10 to make a big deal of s.t.:** to make s.t. seem more important than it is, *(syns.)* to exaggerate, blow out of proportion: *He makes a big deal out of everything and is always in a panic.* **11 to make a decision:** to decide: *He made a quick decision to buy the TV.* **12 to make a difference:** to change s.t. in an important way: *Her volunteer work at the hospital makes a difference to the children she helps.* **13 to make a go of s.t.:** to succeed: *The couple opened a new restaurant and is making a go of it.* **14** *slang* **to make as if** (or) **as though:** to act as though s.t. is so: *He doesn't speak French, but he makes as though he does.* **15** *phrasal v. insep.* **to make away with s.t.:** to steal s.t.: *Thieves made away with our silver and china.* **16 to make believe:** to pretend

M

that s.t., usu. s.t. unrealistic, is true: *The father makes believe that he is a dog and tells his children stories in a funny voice.* **17 to make by hand** or **machine:** referring to how s.t. is made: *All her sweaters are made by hand by her grandmother.* **18 to make do:** to function at a minimum level: *He makes do on a small income.* **19 to make ends meet:** to have enough money to pay one's bills, but with little left over: *She makes ends meet by working two jobs.* **20** *phrasal v. insep.* **to make for s.t.: a.** to create, make possible: *She earns a big salary, and that makes for a good life for her family.* **b.** to go in a certain direction: *The ship made for home port.* **21 to make fun of s.o.:** to ridicule, tease s.o. *Comedians like to make fun of politicians.* **22 to make good: a.** to succeed: *He graduated from college, then made good as a salesperson.* **b.** to fulfill a promise: *A customer returned a broken radio and the store made good on it by giving him a new one.* **23 to make good time:** to travel rapidly: *Our airplane flight made good time from Seattle to Chicago.* **24 to make hay:** to take advantage of a good opportunity while one can: *The singer became successful, and she made hay by giving many performances while she was popular.* **25** *infrml.* **to make it:** to succeed: *She owns a good business and has made it* (or) *made it big in life.* **26 to make love:** to have sex with s.o.: *The couple made love on their wedding night.* **27** *phrasal v.* **to make off with s.t.:** *See:* to make away with s.t. **28** *phrasal v.* **to make out: a.** to see s.t. and recognize it: *The sailors could not make out the shore through the fog.* **b.** to result in s.t., succeed: *A woman had a job interview and later her husband asked how she made out.* **c.** *infrml.fig.* to kiss and hug: *A couple was making out on a park bench.* **29** *phrasal v.* **to make over:** to renew, (*syn.*) to renovate: *Workers made over the inside of the house.* **30 to make sense:** to be reasonable, logical: *Teachers create lesson plans that make sense for teaching the subject.* **31 to make time for:** to set aside time for s.o. or s.t.: *Although the father is the president of a large company, he always makes time for his kids.* **32** *phrasal v. sep.* **to make s.t. up:** to lie, say s.t. untrue: *The criminal made up a story about where he was when the crime happened.||He made it up.* **33 to make it up to s.o.:** to do s.t. good for s.o. after having done s.t. bad: *The husband could not take his wife out to dinner on her birthday, so he made it up to her later by taking her on a weekend vacation.* **34** *phrasal v.* **to make up: a.** to agree to be friends again, (*syn.*) to reconcile: *The couple had a fight, but then made up and kissed.* **b.** to apply cosmetics: *The model makes up her face before a job.* **35 to make up for lost time: a.** to tell stories about one's past: *Two friends had not seen*

each other for ten years and made up for lost time by talking all night. **b.** to do s.t. faster: *He had a flat tire that delayed his trip, so he made up for lost time by driving faster.*
—*n.* **1** the name of a product: *Ford is the make of my car.* **2** *infrml.* **to be on the make: a.** to be aggressive about business, improving one's situation: *She works very hard at her job and is on the make for a salary increase.* **b.** to seek sex: *He is on the make with every woman he meets.*

make-believe *n.* [U] not real, pretend: *The boy told make-believe stories to his sister.*

mak·er /ˈmeɪkər/ *n.* **1** a manufacturer: *That company is a furniture maker.* **2 to meet one's Maker:** to die: *The old man died and went to meet his Maker.*

make·shift /ˈmeɪkˌʃɪft/ *adj.* done in a temporary way, sloppy: *The cabin was made in a makeshift way of old cartons and pieces of tin.*

make·up /ˈmeɪkˌʌp/ *n.* **1** [C;U] cosmetics, esp. used by women and actors: *She wears light makeup that looks natural.* **2** [C] character, personality: *He has a very relaxed makeup.*

mak·ing /ˈmeɪkɪŋ/ *n.* [U] **1** the process of doing or manufacturing s.t.: *The making of toys is a big business.||Bread making requires a lot of time.* **2 in the making:** in process, being done now: *The plan is in the making and will be finished tomorrow.*

mal·ad·just·ed /ˌmæləˈdʒʌstɪd/ *adj.* poorly adapted: *The boy is maladjusted to school and cannot concentrate on his work.||The gear shift on my bicycle is maladjusted.* -*n.* **maladjustment.**

mal·a·dy /ˈmælədi/ *n.frml.* -**dies** a sickness, illness: *She suffers from a rare malady.*

mal·aise /mæˈleɪz, -ˈlɛz/ *n.* [C;U] *frml.* **1** a feeling of illness, unhappiness: *He suffers from a general malaise with pains and depression.* **2** a social problem: *Poverty and crime are two social malaises.*

mal·a·prop·ism /ˈmæləprɑˌpɪzəm/ *n.frml.* a funny misuse of language, esp. a word (or words) that sounds similar to the correct word but means something different: *It was a malapropism when he said he was afraid of "revolting doors" instead of "revolving doors."*

ma·lar·i·a /məˈlɛriə/ *n.* [U] a tropical disease, transmitted by a type of mosquito, that causes weakness, fever, etc.: *Malaria is still a dangerous disease in some parts of the world.*

male /meɪl/ *n.* the member of any species that produces sperm to fertilize eggs: *Human males mature physically at approximately 13 years of age.*
—*adj.* **1** related to the male: *Male goats are called billy goats.* **2** the part of a machine designed to be put inside another part **3** *infrml.* **male chauvinist (pig):** a man who oppresses

women: *He is a male chauvinist who thinks women cannot be as good as men in business and politics. See:* man, USAGE NOTE.

ma·lev·o·lence /mə'lɛvələns/ *n.* [U] *frml.* an evil desire or act: *He stole money from a homeless person in an act of malevolence.* *-adj.* **malevolent.**

mal·func·tion /mæl'fʌŋkʃən/ *v.* to work improperly: *A rocket malfunctioned and exploded in the air.*
—*n.* [C;U] an act of working improperly: *The rocket's malfunction caused a big explosion.*

mal·ice /'mælɪs/ *n.* [U] **1** an evil attitude, desire to hurt others: *The boy broke his neighbor's window out of malice.* **2 to bear s.o. malice:** to want to harm s.o.: *She bore her boss malice after she was fired.* *-adj.* **malicious** /mə'lɪʃəs/; *-adv.* **maliciously.**

ma·lign /mə'laɪn/ *v.* to speak or write evil things about s.o., to defame s.o.'s character, (*syn.*) to slander: *The politician maligned her opponent as dishonest.*

ma·lig·nan·cy /mə'lɪgnənsi/ *n.* [C;U] *-cies* a cancerous tumor or condition: *Doctors found a malignancy in the patient's stomach.* *-adj.* **malignant.**

mall /mɔl/ *n.* **1** a building or group of buildings with connected hallways with shops, restaurants, theaters, etc.: *We can shop at many different stores at the mall.* **2** often called a pedestrian mall, a street with shops, restaurants, theaters, etc., closed to automobile traffic: *Main Street has been turned into a pedestrian mall.*

mal·lard /'mælərd/ *n.* a type of wild duck: *There are mallards in the lake at the center of town.*

mal·le·a·ble /'mæliəbəl/ *adj.frml.* **1** referring to s.t. that can be shaped, such as gold or silver: *Silver is malleable and can be shaped into jewelry.* **2** referring to a person whose opinions can be changed: *He is malleable and will change his ideas when you talk to him.* *-n.* **malleability** /,mæliə'bɪləti/.

mal·let /'mælɪt/ *n.* a type of hammer with a short handle

mal·nour·ished /mæl'nɜrɪʃt, -'nʌr-/ *adj.* poorly fed, starved: *The children were malnourished and got sick often.*

mal·nu·tri·tion /,mælnu'trɪʃən/ *n.* [U] a condition of lack of food: *Malnutrition is common in some poor countries.*

mal·prac·tice /mæl'præktɪs/ *n.* [U] wrong treatment by a professional, esp. a doctor: *The physician was sued for malpractice after the patient died.*

malt /mɔlt/ *n.* [U] *adj.* grain, usu. barley, esp. used in brewing beer and distilling alcoholic beverages: <*n.*> *Malt is used to make whiskey and other* <*adj.*> *malt liquors.*

ma·ma or **mam·ma** /'mɑmə/ *n.infrml.* **1** mother: *Mama, would you please hold my hand to cross the street?* **2 mama's boy:** a man thought to be spoiled by his mother: *Joe is a mama's boy who won't leave home.*

mam·bo /'mɑmboʊ/ *n.* a Latin American dance: *I like to dance the mambo and the samba.*

mam·mal /'mæməl/ *n.* a warm-blooded animal, the female of which feeds its own milk to its young: *Mammals range from whales at sea to mice and humans on land.* *-adj.* **mammalian** /mə'meɪliən/.

mam·ma·ry /'mæməri/ *adj.* related to the milk-producing organ of mammals, such as breasts, used to feed the young: *The mammary glands in humans are located in the chest area.*

mam·mo·gram /'mæmə,græm/ *n.* a picture made by x-ray of the breast, esp. to find cancer: *A mammogram can show a cancer early so it can be treated.* *-n.* [U] **mammography** /mə'mɑgrəfi/.

mam·moth /'mæməθ/ *n.* a type of extinct hairy elephant: *Mammoths once lived in parts of the USA.*
—*adj.* huge in size: *The national debt is mammoth.*

man /mæn/ *n.* **men** /mɛn/ **1** the adult male of the human species: <*n.pl.*> *Men sometimes grow beards and mustaches.* **2** an older term, now questioned by many people, for people in general: *Man lives in almost all parts of the earth.* **3** a piece in a board game, such as chess **4** a husband or lover: *My man works hard.* **5** a servant: *His man took his clothes to be cleaned.* **6** soldier, enlisted man **7** *slang exclam.* of surprise, admiration, or discontent: *Man! It's cold outside today!||Man! She can really sing!* **8 man in the street:** the average, ordinary person: *The television reporter interviewed the man in the street about the elections.* **9 man of God** or **of the cloth:** a religious man, clergyman, pastor, priest **10 man of letters:** a scholar, a learned man: *He is a professor at Harvard and a man of letters.* **11 man-to-man:** honest, frank interaction: *He had a* <*n.*> *man-to-man* (or) <*adj.*> *man-to-man talk with his boss.* **12 one's own man:** an independent thinker or person: *He is really his own man and doesn't worry about what the neighbors think.*
—*v.* **manned, manning, mans** to operate s.t. (guns, machinery): *Soldiers man guns and shoot at the enemy. See:* staff.

M

USAGE NOTE: Many people consider the use of *man* for all people offensive because it does not include women; they prefer to use the term *humanity* as more inclusive.

man·a·cle /'mænɪkəl/ *n.v.* **-cled, -cling, -cles** s.t. used as a restraint, such as a chain or handcuffs, a shackle: *Police <v.> manacle criminals so they cannot escape.*

man·age /'mænɪʤ/ *v.* **-aged, -aging, -ages** **1** to direct the business of an organization: *She manages a legal department in a large company.* **2** to struggle but succeed at doing s.t.: *He managed to carry the heavy suitcase into the house alone.*

man·age·a·ble /'mænɪʤəbəl/ *adj.* able to be done, doable: *Cleanup after a hurricane is difficult, but manageable.* *-n.* [U] **manageability** /ˌmænɪʤə'bɪləti/.

man·age·ment /'mænɪʤmənt/ *n.* **1** [U] the art and science of directing the business of an organization: *Some types of management need a scientific education.* **2** [C] the people who make up the management group in an organization: *Management and the labor union meet yearly to negotiate about workers' wages and benefits.*

man·ag·er /'mænɪʤər/ *n.* **1** a person who sets or works to achieve goals and policies in an organization: *Some managers are strict; others are more relaxed.* **2** a person who runs a business on a day-to-day basis for the owner(s), or manages the career of a performer, athlete, etc.: *Customers complain to the manager of the store when the owner is away.* *-adj.* **managerial** /ˌmænə'ʤɪriəl/.

man·da·rin /'mændərɪn/ *n.* [C] **1** a high official, originally in old China **2** [U] **Mandarin** the official language of China: *Mandarin is taught in the schools.*

man·date /'mæn,deɪt/ *n.* a written order or command
—v. **-dated, -dating, -dates** to order: *The voters mandated change in the last election.*

man·da·to·ry /'mændə,tɔri/ *adj.* required, dictated by law, (*syn.*) compulsory: *The law makes it mandatory for students to go to school until they reach the age of 16.*

man·di·ble /'mændəbəl/ *n.* (in anatomy) a jaw that can move, esp. the lower jaw in humans and apes: *The archaeologists are studying the mandible and skull of prehistoric man.*

man·do·lin /ˌmændə'lɪn, 'mændəlɪn/ *n.* a high-pitched six- or eight-stringed musical instrument like the lute: *The mandolin has a high sweet sound.*

mane /meɪn/ *n.* a strip of long hair on the neck of some animals, such as the lion or horse: *The mane around the head of male lions makes them look scary.*

ma·neu·ver /mə'nuvər/ *n.* **1** a motion made in a particular direction: *The pilot turned the jet to the west in a maneuver to get back on course.* **2** an act meant to deceive or defeat s.o. else: *He made maneuvers to get the best assignments at work.* **3** **to go on maneuvers:** to

do a military exercise: *Each summer, the army goes on maneuvers to test its equipment and its readiness to fight.*
—v. to make a maneuver: *The basketball player maneuvered around the other team's players.*

mange /meɪnʤ/ *n.* [U] a contagious skin disease of animals caused by insects: *We took our dog to the veterinarian to get medication for mange.* *-adj.* **mangy.**

man·ger /'meɪnʤər/ *n.* a long box or container for animal feed, (*syn.*) trough: *The farmer puts hay in the manger for her cows each day.*

man·gle /'mæŋgəl/ *v.* **-gled, -gling, -gles** to damage badly, (*syns.*) to mutilate, deform: *Our photocopy machine mangles pieces of paper when it is not working correctly.*

man·go /'mæŋgoʊ/ *n.* **-goes** a sweet, slightly acid, tropical fruit with yellow flesh: *Scientists say that mangoes have many nutrients.*

man·grove /'mæŋˌgroʊv/ *n.adj.* a large tropical tree found along ocean shorelines and swamps: *Wood from the <n.> mangrove is so heavy that it won't float.*

man·han·dle /'mæn,hændl/ *v.* **-dled, -dling, -dles** to treat s.o. roughly, use force: *Police manhandled the criminal by pushing him against a wall.*

man·hole /'mæn,hoʊl/ *n.* a hole in a street used to reach utilities, such as gas and water pipes or telephone lines: *Workers went down a manhole to fix a leak in the gas pipeline.*

man·hood /'mæn,hʊd/ *n.* [U] the age and condition of being an adult human male: *He reached manhood after he finished high school.*

man·hunt /'mæn,hʌnt/ *n.* a search by police for s.o: *When a prisoner escaped, police began a manhunt for him.*

ma·ni·a /'meɪniə/ *n.* [U] **1** a mental disorder shown by great excitement: *In his mania, he sang and shouted at people in the library.* **2** [C;U] *infrml.fig.* an obsession for s.t., an uncontrollable desire: *She has a mania for chocolate; she eats a chocolate bar every day.* *-adj.* **manic** /'mænɪk/.

ma·ni·ac /'meɪni,æk/ *n.* an insane person; a wild, dangerous person: *A maniac broke out of jail and killed a man.* *-adj.* **maniacal** /mə'naɪəkəl/.

manic depressive *n.* a person with mental depression, sometimes suicidal, who also experiences periods of extreme excitement: *She was a manic depressive, overly excited one day and very unhappy the next day.*

man·i·cure /'mænɪ,kyʊr/ *n.v.* **-cured, -curing, -cures** care and beautification of the fingernails and hands: *My wife had a <n.> manicure at the beauty salon.* *-n.* **manicurist.**

man·i·fest /'mænə,fɛst/ *v.frml.* to appear, arrive: *The illness manifested itself with a high fever and a cough.*
—*n.* a shipping document listing passengers, items, and destinations: *A clerk checked off the items on the manifest that she had received.*

man·i·fes·ta·tion /,mænəfə'steɪʃən, -fɛ-/ *n.* [C;U] *frml.* a sign, symbol: *Warm temperatures and budding flowers are manifestations of spring.*

man·i·fes·to /,mænə'fɛstoʊ/ *n.v.* **-tos** or **-toes** a public statement of the political or economic principles of a group: *Revolutionaries issued a manifesto for political change.*

man·i·fold /'mænə,foʊld/ *n.* the part of an exhaust pipe that lets gases escape from an engine: *I had my car repaired, then a crack developed in the engine manifold.*
—*adj.frml.* many: *Society faces manifold problems.*

man·i·kin /'mænɪkɪn/ *n. See:* mannequin.

ma·nip·u·late /mə'nɪpyə,leɪt/ *v.* **-lated, -lating, -lates** **1** to handle, change the position of s.t.: *A worker manipulates the levers of the bulldozer.‖A musician manipulated the strings of a guitar.* **2** to influence s.o. or s.t. secretly, esp. for one's own advantage: *He manipulated the price of a stock so he could buy it cheaply.* -*n.* [C;U] **manipulation** /mə,nɪpyə'leɪʃən/; -*adj.* **manipulative** /mə'nɪpyələtɪv, -,leɪtɪv/.

man·kind /,mæn'kaɪnd/ *n.* [U] humanity, people in general: *Mankind has existed for thousands of years. See:* man, 2.

USAGE NOTE: Many people consider the use of *mankind* (meaning all people) to be sexist because it does not include women; a more general term is *humankind* or *humanity.*

---

man·ly /'mænli/ *adj.* **-lier, -liest** having positive characteristics, such as strength and courage, that are associated with men, (*syn.*) virile: *The boy performed a manly act by saving an old woman from a robber.*

man-made *adj.* artificial, not natural: *Plastic is a man-made substance.*

man·na /'mænə/ *n.* [U] **1** food from heaven **2** *fig.* an unexpected gift or good event: *When the poor man won the lottery, the money was like manna from heaven to him.*

man·ne·quin /'mænɪkɪn/ *n.* a plastic model of a human body: *Mannequins in department store windows are dressed in clothes in the latest styles.*

man·ner /'mænər/ *n.* [C] **1** behavior, a way of acting: *Some children have good (or bad) manners.* **2** *sing.* a type of action, a way of doing s.t.: *"Hit the ball in this manner," said the tennis coach as she showed her student*

how to do it. **3 all manner of:** all kinds of: *There was all manner of food at the party.*

man·ner·ism /'mænə,rɪzəm/ *n.* a particular gesture, facial expression, etc., that s.o. often uses: *His special mannerism is waving his hands when he talks.*

man·ner·ly /'mænərli/ *adj.frml.* having good manners, (*syn.*) courteous

man·nish /'mænɪʃ/ *adj.* (of a woman) having the characteristics of a man: *She has a short, mannish hair style.*

man·or /'mænər/ *n.* a large, elegant house and land: *Wealthy English people live in manors.*

man·pow·er /'mæn,paʊər/ *n.* [U] labor, workers as a group: *Building the railroads required a lot of manpower. See:* workforce.

man·sion /'mænʃən/ *n.* a large, expensive house with land: *Mansions in rich neighborhoods have a lot of land around them.*

man-sized *adj.* large, big enough for a large man: *That restaurant serves man-sized meals.*

man·slaugh·ter /'mæn,slɔtər/ *n.* [U] an act of killing s.o., usu. by accident: *He killed two people in an automobile accident and was sent to jail for manslaughter.*

man·tel /'mæntəl/ *n.* a shelf and any of its supporting parts on a fireplace: *They keep pictures of their family on the mantel.* -*n.* **mantelpiece** /'mæntəl,pis/.

man·tle /'mæntəl/ *n.* a covering, such as a scarf worn over the shoulders: *A mantle of snow covers the mountaintop.*

man·tra /'mɑntrə/ *n.* a word or saying repeated in meditation or prayer: *She meditates every morning by repeating the word "om" as a mantra.*

man·u·al /'mænyuəl/ *n.* a handbook or guidebook often of step-by-step procedures on how to do s.t.: *The manual for my computer shows how to set it up and program it.*
—*adj.* done using the hands rather than by machine: *My car has a manual gear shift, not an automatic transmission.* -*adv.* **manually.**

man·u·fac·ture /,mænyə'fæktʃər/ *v.* **-tured, -turing, -tures** **1** to make s.t. for sale, (*syn.*) to fabricate using machinery: *Our company manufactures furniture.* **2** to deceive, make up false information: *She manufactured her previous work history that she wrote on her résumé.*
—*n.* [U] the act of making products using machinery: *The manufacture of that type of gun is illegal now.*

man·u·fac·tur·er /,mænyə'fæktʃərər/ *n.* a business that makes things: *That corporation is a manufacturer of medicines.*

man·u·fac·tur·ing /,mænyə'fæktʃərɪŋ/ *n.* [U] the part of industry that makes things: *Manufacturing has left the big cities and relocated overseas.*

M

ma·nure /mə'nʊr/ n. [U] animal waste, (syn.) dung: *Farmers use cow manure as fertilizer.*

man·u·script /'mænyə,skrɪpt/ n. a handwritten or typed document before it is printed: *The author's book manuscript was sent to the editor.*

man·y /'mɛni/ adj. **more** /mɔr/, **most** /moʊst/ **1** related to a lot of s.t., (syn.) numerous: *Many people attended the concert.* **2 a good** or **great many:** a lot of: *A good many people should exercise more.* **3 how many:** used with countable nouns to ask about the number of s.t.: *How <adj.> many books do you have?||How <pron.> many do you have?*
—n. *sing.* used with a pl.v. used with *of,* a large number of s.t.: *Many of us eat too much sugar.*
—pron. a large number of s.t.: *When the babies heard a loud noise, many began to cry.||How many cried?*

USAGE NOTE: *Many* is used with or in place of countable nouns: *many books.* Use *much* with or in place of uncountable nouns: *much work.*

map /mæp/ n. a graphic representation or plan of geographic locations: *We looked at a map to find the best roads from Boston to Chicago.*
—v. **mapped, mapping, maps 1** to make a map of s.t.: *Engineers mapped the area for a road.* **2** *phrasal v. sep.* **to map s.t. out:** to plan in detail: *They mapped out exactly what to study for the examination.||They mapped it out.*

ma·ple /'meɪpəl/ n. a tall shade tree that produces a sugary liquid: *The maple next to our house protects it from the afternoon sun.*

maple leaf n. **1** a symbol for the country of Canada: *The red maple leaf is on the Canadian national flag.* **2** a gold coin minted in Canada

maple syrup n. [U] a sweet, brown syrup made by boiling maple sap (liquid that comes out of maple trees): *We pour maple syrup on pancakes.*

mar /mɑr/ v. **marred, marring, mars** to damage; to make a cut, bruise, or dent in s.t., (syn.) to deface: *A scratch in the side of the car marred its appearance.*

mar·a·thon /'mærə,θɑn/ n. **1** a foot race of over 26 miles (41.3 km): *Thousands of runners come to the Boston Marathon every April.* **2** any event or test that lasts a long time: *To meet the deadline, negotiators held marathon meetings all night long. -n.* **marathoner.**

mar·ble /'mɑrbəl/ n. [U] **1** a type of stone that is cut and polished for use in floors, walls, statues, and decoration: *The floors of the Capitol building are made of different colored marble.* **2** [C] *pl.* **marbles** a game children play by rolling small balls of marble or glass on the floor: *When it rains, the children stay in and play marbles.* **3 to lose one's marbles:** to go insane: *I almost lost my marbles studying for that test.*

mar·bling /'mɑrblɪŋ, -bəlɪŋ/ n. [U] a pattern of stripes and spots in different colors, made to look like marble: *The cover of the book had green and blue marbling on it.*

march /mɑrtʃ/ v. **marches 1** to step in a formal way, such as soldiers or musical band members in a parade: *My high school band marched in a parade.* **2** to progress, move ahead: *The seasons march on.* **3 to be given one's marching orders: a.** to be told exactly where to go: *The colonel gave the soldiers their marching orders to the battlefront.* **b.** *infrml.* to be fired, to be told to leave: *When he made a lot of mistakes, his boss gave him his marching orders. See:* walk, USAGE NOTE.
—n. **marches 1** a military piece of music with an upbeat tempo: *The band played marches that cheered everyone up.* **2** a journey made on foot by soldiers: *Soldiers made a long march from their camp to the mountains. -n.* **marcher.**

March /mɑrtʃ/ n. the third month of the year, between February and April: *A common expression about the weather in March is, "March comes in like a lion and goes out like a lamb."*

Mar·di Gras /'mɑrdi,grɑ/ n. the Tuesday before the beginning of Lent and a time of carnival in many countries: *Mardi Gras in New Orleans is a big party with dancing, music, and fun.*

mare /mɛr/ n. a mature, female horse or donkey: *A mare won the horse race.*

mar·ga·rine /'mɑrdʒərɪn/ n. [U] a substitute for butter made from vegetable oils: *Margarine spreads easily on toast.*

mar·ga·ri·ta /,mɑrgə'ritə/ n. an alcoholic drink of tequila and lime juice: *She likes to drink a margarita with Mexican food.*

mar·gin /'mɑrdʒɪn/ n. **1** the side border of a printed page: *The margins on a newspaper are blank.* **2** the amount of profit that a business earns: *Last quarter, our company had a high profit margin.* **3** the degree or amount more than what is needed: *She won the election by a margin of 5,000 votes.*

mar·gin·al /'mɑrdʒənəl/ adj. **1** located on a margin: *Authors make marginal corrections to their writing.* **2** of little importance or worth: *Desert is marginal land for farming because its soil is poor quality.*

mar·gi·na·li·a /,mɑrdʒə,neɪliə/ n.pl. comments or notes written in the margin, esp. of a book: *Professors write marginalia in textbooks to use in their lectures.*

mar·gin·al·ize /'mɑrdʒənə,laɪz/ v. **-ized, -izing, -izes** to make s.o. less important or s.t. less valuable: *The new computers marginalize the value of older, slower ones.*

mar·i·gold /'mærə,goʊld/ n. a small orange or yellow flower: *Marigolds keep insects away from the tomato plants in our garden.*

mar·i·jua·na /ˌmærəˈwɑnə/ *n.* [U] a hallucinogenic drug that comes from the hemp plant: *It is illegal to smoke marijuana in the USA.*

ma·ri·na /məˈrinə/ *n.* [C;U] a boatyard or harbor that has docks and other facilities for boats: *We keep a small sailboat at the marina on the river.*

mar·i·nade /ˌmærəˈneɪd, ˈmærəˌneɪd/ *n.* a flavoring sauce used to soak meat, fish, and other food in before cooking: *My brother soaks chicken in a marinade of soy sauce and herbs before he barbecues it. See:* barbecue.

mar·i·nate /ˈmærəˌneɪt/ *v.* **-nated, -nating, -nates** to soak (food) in a marinade

ma·rine /məˈrin/ *adj.* related to the ocean and ships: *She studied marine biology in college.*
—*n.* **marine** or **Marine** a member of the Marine Corps

Marine Corps *n.* a branch of the US military known for its toughness and heroism: *My sister is an officer in the Marine Corps.*

mar·i·ner /ˈmærənər/ *n.frml.* a sailor

mar·i·o·nette /ˌmæriəˈnɛt/ *n.* a doll or figure moved by strings to entertain people: *Marionettes make people laugh.*

mar·i·tal /ˈmærətl/ *adj.* related to marriage: *He is not married, so his marital status is single.*

mar·i·time /ˈmærəˌtaɪm/ *adj.* related to the sea: *Maritime laws govern international shipping.*

mark /mɑrk/ *n.* **1** a scrape, stain, or spot: *There is a mark on the wall where I hit it with a ball.‖Fighting in the war left its mark on him.* **2** a grade, such as on an examination or for a course: *She got high marks in high school.* **3** a symbol, a sign of distinction: *Chanel™ is a mark of perfume known all over the world.‖Young people stand up as older people enter the room as a mark of respect.* **4** a target, such as a bull's-eye: *He shot an arrow and it hit the mark.* **5** a place where racers begin: *The starter for the race said to the runners, "On your mark, get set, go!"* **6** a symbol used by an illiterate person as a signature: *He made his mark as an "X" on the contract.* **7 off the mark** or **miss the mark:** wrong, inaccurate: *The weather reporter missed the mark when she said it would rain today, because it's sunny!* **8 to give s.o. high marks:** to praise, admire s.o. for doing s.t. well: *She did excellent work and I give her high marks for it!* **9 to make one's mark:** to prove oneself as very good at s.t., to accomplish good things: *He made his mark as a super salesperson at his company.* **10** the currency of Germany: *My change at the restaurant in Munich included a ten-mark note and a five-mark coin.*
—*v.* **1** to stain, leave a mark: *The broken plate marked the floor where it broke.* **2** to show a specific place: *I marked my page in the book with a bookmark.* **3** to write down, note: *He*

marked the price on a piece of paper. **4** to grade homework or examinations: *The teacher marked the students' exams.* **5** to celebrate: *The USA marks its independence from Britain with Fourth of July celebrations.* **6** *phrasal v. sep.* **to mark s.t. down: a.** to note down: *I marked down her telephone number on a piece of paper.‖I marked it down.* **b.** to lower the price of s.t., discount: *That store marked down prices on its shoes by 40 percent.‖It marked them down.* **7** *phrasal v. sep.* **to mark s.t. up:** to increase the price of s.t.: *In that business, he marks up all his products by 100 percent.*

mark·down /ˈmɑrkˌdaʊn/ *n.* a lowered price of s.t., esp. to put it on sale: *The markdown on shoes on sale is 20 percent off the regular price.*

marked /mɑrkt/ *adj.* **1** clear, definite: *Colder weather in the fall is a marked difference from the heat of summer.* **2** *fig.* singled out for punishment: *He is a marked man for criticizing his boss who will fire him as soon as she can.*

mark·er /ˈmɑrkər/ *n.* **1** a post, sign, or other noticeable object: *Workers placed little orange flags as markers to show where the road will be built.* **2** a thick pen or other tool to make marks: *The girl has markers in all colors to draw pictures with.*

mar·ket /ˈmɑrkɪt/ *n.* **1** a place or store that sells things: *Supermarkets are large stores that sell food.* **2** the combination of makers, sellers, and buyers of a product or service on a local, national, or international level: *There is a good market for healthy foods these days.* **3 buyer's** or **seller's market:** conditions good for the buyer or seller: *Real estate is a buyer's market right now, because there are many houses and apartments available to choose from.*
—*v.* **1** to offer goods and services for sale: *That company markets cosmetics in the New York area.* **2** to promote goods and services: *Our marketing department markets our products nationally.* **3 to be in the market for:** to want to purchase s.t.: *I am in the market for a new car and have looked at many different models.* **4 to play the market:** to look for the highest profit by buying and selling stocks: *She is comfortable with taking risks to play the market.*

mar·ket·a·ble /ˈmɑrkɪtəbəl/ *adj.* capable of being sold, salable: *That new computer is highly marketable because there are no competing products for it. -n.* **marketability.**

market economy *n.* an economy that depends on market forces, such as supply and demand, to determine how many goods will be produced and at what price they will be sold

mar·ket·er /ˈmɑrkɪtər/ *n.* a person, department, or business that sells goods or services:

M

That huge corporation is a marketer of soap and other personal care products.

mar·ket·ing /ˈmɑrkɪtɪŋ/ *n.* [U] **1** the purchase of daily food and household items: *My husband does the marketing for our family once a week.* **2** the art and science of designing, advertising, and selling goods and services: *She has a master's degree in marketing from Stanford University.*

mar·ket·place /ˈmɑrkɪtˌpleɪs/ *n.* **1** an open area in a city or town for selling products, esp. food: *Marketplaces in many European cities are located in central places.* **2** the combination of all makers, sellers, and buyers of a product or service: *Our new product was well received in the marketplace.*

market research *n.* [U] the study of what products and services customers might like to buy: *Market research helped us design our products to sell better.*

market share *n.* the percentage of industry sales of a certain product or company

mark·ing /ˈmɑrkɪŋ/ *n.* [U] a mark of some kind or coloring, esp. of an animal: *Our dog has brown and white markings.*

mark·up /ˈmɑrkˌʌp/ *n.* an increase in the price of s.t. above its cost: *The markup on clothes can be five times their cost.*

mar·ma·lade /ˈmɑrməˌleɪd/ *n.* [U] a fruit mixture that is spread on bread, rolls, etc.: *I put orange marmalade on my toast for breakfast.*

ma·roon /məˈrun/ *adj.n.* [U] a dark purplish red: *He wears a <adj.> maroon baseball cap.*
—*v.* to leave s.o. in a distant place with no or little hope of escape: *Our ship was wrecked and we were marooned on an island.*

mar·quee /mɑrˈki/ *n.* a large display above the front entrance to a theater that tells what is playing: *The theater's marquee said that the movie* Casablanca *was playing.*

mar·riage /ˈmærɪdʒ/ *n.* [C;U] **1** a legal union of a man and woman: *The couple enjoyed a long and happy marriage.* **2** a wedding: *My sister had a private marriage with only a small ceremony.* **3** *fig.* a strong bond between people or things: *One business bought another in a marriage of similar interests.*

marriage broker *n.* a person who sets up marriages: *A man went to a marriage broker and asked her to find him a wife.*

mar·ried /ˈmærɪd/ *adj.* having a husband or wife: *She is married with two children.*

mar·row /ˈmæroʊ/ *n.* a soft jelly-like substance inside bones that makes new blood cells: *Dogs love to chew on bones to taste the marrow.*

mar·ry /ˈmæri/ *v.* **-ried, -rying, -ries** to join in marriage: *Jane and Joe were married last Saturday.*

Mars /mɑrz/ *n.* the fourth planet in the solar system, between Earth and Jupiter: *Space vehicles have explored Mars.*

marsh /mɑrʃ/ *n.* [C;U] **marshes** a wet, low-lying area with thick plant growth: *Marshes have ponds where ducks and geese build nests and feed.* -*n.* **marshland** /ˈmɑrʃˌlænd/; -*adj.* **marshy.**

mar·shal /ˈmɑrʃəl/ *n.* **1** a sheriff or officer of the US government: *A US marshal arrested a criminal.* **2** the leader of an event: *The mayor was the grand marshal leading the parade.*
—*v.* to gather one's forces together: *The old man marshaled his strength to endure major heart surgery.*

marsh·mal·low /ˈmɑrʃˌmɛloʊ/ *n.* a soft, white candy made of sugar: *We toasted marshmallows over a fire when we camped in the woods.*

mar·su·pi·al /mɑrˈsupiəl/ *n.* an animal, such as a kangaroo or an opossum, whose female members have a pouch to carry their young in: *Marsupials are common in Australia.*

mart /mɑrt/ *n.frml.* a market or trading place: *The convenience store on the corner is called Mini Mart.*

mar·tial /ˈmɑrʃəl/ *adj.* related to the military and war: *A court-martial is a military court that tries soldiers for crimes.*

martial art *n.* a skill used for self-defense and military attack, such as karate or judo: *He is an expert in the martial arts and has a black belt in karate.*

martial law *n.* [U] emergency powers of the military to govern the civilian population to maintain order: *After mass demonstrations, martial law was imposed on the country to prevent rioting.*

mar·ti·ni /mɑrˈtini/ *n.* an alcoholic drink made of gin or vodka and a small amount of vermouth: *They drink dry gin martinis before dinner.*

mar·tyr /ˈmɑrtər/ *n.* a person who dies for a cause and whose death inspires others to continue it: *Joan of Arc (1412–1431) was a French martyr who tried to save France from the English.*
—*v.* to kill s.o. and make a martyr of that person: *The Romans martyred early Christians for their religious beliefs.*

mar·tyr·dom /ˈmɑrtərdəm/ *n.* [U] an act or condition of being a martyr: *The martyrdom of early Christians inspired others to bear suffering.*

mar·vel /ˈmɑrvəl/ *v.* to regard with wonder and admiration: *He marvels at the strength of professional athletes.*
—*n.* a wonder, amazement: *The girl is so smart that she is a marvel to her teachers.*

mar·vel·ous /ˈmɑrvələs/ *adj.* **1** wonderful, excellent: *We had a marvelous time on vacation.*

2 amazing, admirable: *He has a marvelous ability to play the violin.*

Marx·ism /'mɑrk,sɪzəm/ *n.* a type of communism based on the writings of Karl Marx that sees the struggle between social classes as a major cause of historical change: *Marxism was developed in 19th-century Europe.* *-n.adj.* **Marxist.**

mar·zi·pan /'mɑrzə,pæn/ *n.* [U] a soft candy made from almonds and sugar: *Marzipan is made into shapes of animals and fruits.*

mas·car·a /mæ'skærə/ *n.* [U] a dark cosmetic applied to the eyelashes: *Mascara makes her eyes look bigger.*

mas·cot /'mæs,kɑt/ *n.* a person or an animal or its image kept for good luck by a sports team or other organization: *Our football team keeps a mule as its mascot to show its strength and determination.*

mas·cu·line /'mæskyəlɪn/ *adj.* **1** related to male qualities: *That actor projects a masculine image in his films.* **2** related to the male gender of nouns in some languages: *The words for "work" in French and Spanish are masculine:* le travail *and* el trabajo. *See:* feminine.

mash /mæʃ/ *v.* **mashes** to press into a mass: *She mashed bananas to feed to her baby.‖Mashed potatoes taste good with butter or gravy.*
—*n.* [C;U] **mashes** a wet mixture, such as grain and water: *Distillers use a mash to make alcohol.*

mask /mæsk/ *n.* a covering for the face used esp. to hide one's identity or for a ceremony: *Skiers use masks to keep their faces warm in the cold.*
—*v.* **1** to hide one's identity: *Robbers masked themselves to avoid being identified.* **2** to hide one's feelings: *She masked her unhappiness when she was not invited to the party.*

masking tape *n.* [U] a tape used to mark areas, such as places not to be painted, that is easy to remove: *A worker put masking tape over the door frame in the room to be painted.*

mas·o·chism /'mæsə,kɪzəm/ *n.* [U] any pain or discomfort deliberately experienced for pleasure: *The masochism of running every day in cold and heat gives joggers satisfaction.* *-n.* **masochist;** *-adj.* **masochistic** /,mæsə'kɪstɪk/.

ma·son /'meɪsən/ *n.* **1** a skilled worker in brick or stone: *A stonemason is repairing the old church.* **2 Mason** a member of the Freemasons, a secret organization of men

ma·son·ry /'meɪsənri/ *n.* [U] brickwork or stonework in buildings: *The masonry on the outside of the school needs to be fixed.*

mas·quer·ade /,mæskə'reɪd/ *n.adj.* **1** a party or dance where people wear costumes and masks **2** a costume worn to pretend to be s.o.

else: *We went to a <n.> masquerade* (or) *a <adj.> masquerade party.*
—*v.* **-raded, -rading, -rades** to pretend to be s.o. else: *He masquerades as a big businessman, but he really isn't one.*

mass /mæs/ *n.* [U] **masses 1** the amount of matter of an object: *Spaceships have no weight in space but do have mass and could cause damage if they hit each other.* **2** [C] a group of people, things, etc.: *A mass of people were in the town square for the concert.* **3** [C] a shapeless amount of similar matter: *A mass of rock fell down the mountain.*
—*v.* **masses** to come together in a mass: *Sports fans massed in front of the stadium before the game.*

mas·sa·cre /'mæsəkər/ *n.* [C;U] the brutal killing of many people or animals, *(syn.)* slaughter: *The massacre of the American buffalo almost made them extinct.*
—*v.* **-cred, -cring, -cres** to slaughter, kill brutally: *Hunters massacred elephants to get ivory from their tusks.*

mas·sage /mə'sɑʒ, -sɑdʒ/ *n.* [C;U] the act of rubbing and moving the muscles of the body for relaxation and relief of pain: *A masseuse gave me a relaxing massage for half an hour.*
—*v.* **-saged, -saging, -sages** to give a massage: *She massaged me skillfully. See:* caress.

mas·seur /mə'sɜr, -sʊr/ *n.* a man who gives massages professionally: *Masseurs have to go to school and be licensed to work in most states.*

mas·seuse /mə'sus, -'suz, -'sɜz/ *n.* a woman who gives massages professionally: *That masseuse has a firm, but gentle touch.*

mas·sive /'mæsɪv/ *adj.* huge, great: *A massive amount of information is available now with computers.*

mass media *n.* [U] *used with a sing. or pl.v.* television, radio, and large urban newspapers used to communicate with people daily: *The mass media is constantly watching what the President says and does.*

mass production *n.* [U] the manufacture of products in large amounts using modern machinery: *Mass production of automobiles means that almost everyone can own one.* *-v.* **mass-produce.**

mast /mæst/ *n.* on a ship, a vertical pole to which sails are connected: *The main mast on old ships was made from tall trees.*

mas·tec·to·my /mæ'stɛktəmi/ *n.* **-mies** the surgical removal of a breast: *She had a mastectomy to remove a cancerous tumor from her breast.*

mas·ter /'mæstər/ *n.* **1** a person who can order others: *The dog's master ordered it to lie down.* **2** a very competent, skilled person: *He is a*

M

master at the game of tennis.||She is a master of intrigue.
—*v.* to learn how to do s.t. well: *He finally mastered typing.*

mas·ter·ful /'mæstərfəl/ *adj.* **1** able to do things well, very competent, (*syn.*) masterly: *He is masterful at handling horses.* **2** having a strong personality, able to dominate others -*adv.* **masterfully.**

mas·ter·ly /'mæstərli/ *adj.* showing the skill of a master: *He is a masterly tennis player.*

mas·ter·mind /'mæstər,maɪnd/ *n.v.* a person who plans s.t. completely: *She was the <n.> mastermind behind the plan to rob the museum of famous paintings.||She <v.> masterminded the robbery.*

master of ceremonies *n.* a person who introduces others, esp. entertainers at a public event: *The master of ceremonies introduced each singer in the voice contest.*

mas·ter·piece /'mæstər,pis/ *n.* one of the best works of art, music, literature, etc.: *The painting* Mona Lisa *by Leonardo da Vinci is considered a masterpiece.*

master's or **master's degree** *n.sing. abbr.* **M.A.** a college degree above a Bachelor's and below a Ph.D.: *Her master's degree is in literature. See:* B.A., M.A., USAGE NOTE.

mas·ter·work /'mæstər,wɜrk/ *n.* the best work done by an artist, composer, etc.: *I think Beethoven's Fifth Symphony is his masterwork.*

mas·ter·y /'mæstəri/ *n.* [U] the ability to do s.t. extremely well, complete competence: *She has complete mastery of using a computer to do accounting.*

mast·head /'mæst,hɛd/ *n.* **1** the top of a mast: *The sailor climbed up to the masthead to look for land.* **2** a list of a newspaper's or magazine's owners, editors, other employees, and address: *The masthead of the local newspaper is on the second page.*

mas·ti·cate /'mæsti,keɪt/ *v.frml.* **-cated, -cating, -cates** to chew: *Cows masticate their food.*

mas·tiff /'mæstɪf/ *n.frml.* a large, strong dog with short tan fur: *Mastiffs are good guard dogs.*

mat /mæt/ *n.* a piece of material often of rectangular shape with many uses, such as under plates on tables, in front of doors, on floors, etc.: *We wipe our feet on the mat in front of our door to remove dirt from our shoes.*
—*v.* **matted, matting, mats** to tangle, press down: *The rain matted the dog's hair.*

match /mætʃ/ *n.* **matches 1** a contest, game between participants: *We played a tennis match and then watched a soccer match on TV.* **2** a similarity, harmony: *There is a nice match between the color of his suit and his tie.* **3** a unity, bond: *The couple started dating and*

found that they have a love match. **4** a small stick used to light fires: *He struck a match and lit a candle.* **5 to meet one's match:** to compete with s.o. equal to or better than you are: *The boxer met his match as his opponent knocked him out in the first round.*
—*v.* **matches 1** to be similar to s.t. else: *One of his socks is blue and the other is brown; they don't match.* **2** to equal: *Federal governments match funds to those given by states for large construction projects.*

match·book /'mætʃ,bʊk/ *n.* a thin piece of cardboard covering a set of matches: *Businesses advertise their products on matchbook covers.*

matchbook

match·box /'mætʃ,bɑks/ *n.* **-boxes 1** a small box containing matches **2** *fig.* a small house

match·less /'mætʃlɪs/ *adj.* without equal, unique: *That opera singer has a matchless voice.*

match·mak·er /'mætʃ,meɪkər/ *n.* a person who makes introductions between people interested in marriage: *A matchmaker interviews men and women, then matches them with the kind of person they like.* -*n.* **matchmaking.**

mate /meɪt/ *n.* **1** one of a pair of animals: *The male bird found food for its mate.* **2** a husband or wife: *The elderly woman's mate died last week.* **3** either of a matched pair: *I lost the mate to my glove.* **4 (-)mate:** friend, companion, usu. with other words: *roommate, classmate, housemate*
—*v.* **mated, mating, mates** to become a pair to produce offspring: *Animals mate in the springtime.*

ma·te·ri·al /mə'tɪriəl/ *n.* [C;U] **1** cloth, fabric: *Her suit is made out of fine wool material.* **2** [C;U] any physical substance, such as rock, wood, glass, plastic, etc.: *Building materials, including wood, bricks, and pipes, are available at lumber yards.* **3** [C;U] tools and supplies: *Art materials include paint, brushes, and canvas.* **4** [U] information in many forms that can be used, such as for a book or a speech: *Our teacher put together material for a textbook.*
—*adj.* **1** related to the physical, not the spiritual: *The material world makes a lot of demands on us.* **2** related to a situation in an important way, (*syn.*) crucial: *Evidence by a witness is material to the prosecution of a crime.*

ma·te·ri·al·ism /mə'tɪriə,lɪzəm/ *n.* [U] **1** a philosophy that physical reality is most important, not spirituality: *She did not go to church* *because she believed in materialism.* **2** the idea that having a lot of wealth is the goal in life: *Materialism is an important part of western culture. -n.* **materialist;** *-adj.* **materialistic** /mə,tɪriə'lɪstɪk/.

ma·te·ri·al·ize /mə'tɪriə,laɪz/ *v.* **-ized, -izing, -izes** to happen, become real: *Her plans to become a professional singer materialized when she received offers to give performances.*

ma·ter·nal /mə,tɜrnl/ *adj.* **1** related to a mother: *Maternal instinct makes mothers protect their children.* **2** related through one's mother: *My maternal grandparents raised my mother in Idaho.*

ma·ter·ni·ty /mə'tɜrnəti/ *adj.n.* related to the condition of pregnancy and caring for a child: *She took three months' <adj.> maternity leave from work to have a baby.*

math /mæθ/ *n.* [U] *short for* mathematics: *I have a math exam today at school.*

math·e·mat·i·cal /,mæθə'mætɪkəl/ *adj.* related to mathematics: *Computers can do mathematical calculations very quickly. -adv.* **mathematically.**

math·e·mat·ics /,mæθə'mætɪks/ *n.* [U] *pl.used with a sing.v.* the study of numbers, symbols, and forms that follow strict rules and laws: *Mathematics is a difficult field of study. -n.* **mathematician** /,mæθəmə'tɪʃən/.

mat·i·nee /,mætn'eɪ/ *n.* an afternoon film or theater performance: *We saw the Wednesday matinee of a new musical comedy.*

ma·tri·arch /'meɪtri,ɑrk/ *n.* the female head of a family or society: *After grandfather died, grandmother became the matriarch of our family. -adj.* **matriarchal** /,meɪtri'ɑrkəl/.

ma·tri·ar·chy /'meɪtri,ɑrki/ *n.* **-chies** a family or society in which women have most of the power: *Long ago, some societies were matriarchies led by women.*

ma·tric·u·late /mə'trɪkyə,leɪt/ *v.* **-lated, -lating, -lates** to enroll officially as a student in an educational institution, esp. a college: *She matriculated into the state university last fall.*

mat·ri·mo·ny /'mætrə,mouni/ *n.* [U] **1** the state of marriage: *Religions see matrimony as a relationship blessed by God.* **2** the marriage ceremony: *The couple went through matrimony in a church wedding. -adj.* **matrimonial** /,mætrə'mouniəl/.

ma·trix /'meɪtrɪks/ *n.* **matrices** /'meɪtrə,siz, 'mæ-/ or **matrixes 1** an arrangement of numbers, symbols, items, etc., that have a relationship to each other and are often arranged in columns and rows: *If supplies cost too much in the matrix of production expenses to make a profit, then other costs must be reduced.* **2** material that surrounds minerals, etc.: *Gold ore is sometimes found in a matrix of rock.*

ma·tron /'meɪtrən/ *n.* **1** a respected older, married woman: *My aunt is a matron who organizes volunteers to read to children in the schools.* **2** a female guard in a court or prison: *A matron escorted a female prisoner into court.* **3** a housekeeper in a hospital or prison: *The matron has the keys to the laundry room in the hospital.*

ma·tron·ly /'meɪtrənli/ *adj.* **1** (about women) dignified, stately: *My grandmother has a matronly air about her.* **2** euphemism for fat or middle-aged: *That dress makes you look matronly.*

matron of honor *n.* a bride's main married attendant at her wedding: *The bride's matron of honor was her best friend. See:* maid of honor.

mat·ted /'mætɪd/ *adj. & past part of* mat, tangled, pressed down: *Her hair was matted after she got caught in rain.*

mat·ter /'mætər/ *n.* [U] **1** physical substance that has weight and takes up space: *Matter is composed of atoms and molecules.* **2** [C] a concern, subject of interest: *We met to discuss business matters.* **3** [U] *s.t.* to read: *The doctor's office has reading matter (magazines, books) in the waiting room.* **4 a matter of: a.** an unknown but small amount: *The train arrives in a matter of minutes.* **b.** a decision, a situation: *It's a matter of whether you want to get home early or late.* **5 for that matter:** as far as (a topic being discussed) is concerned: *My sister doesn't like television, and for that matter, neither do I.* **6** *n.adj.* **matter of fact: a.** based on fact, not dreams: *Police detectives have a <adj.> matter-of-fact attitude to finding information about crimes.* **b.** actually, in reality: *As a matter of fact, I do speak Spanish.* **7 matter of life and death:** a serious situation that could end in death: *Whether enough blood is donated could be a matter of life and death for the accident victims.* **8 matter of opinion:** a question open to different ideas: *It's a matter of opinion whether chemistry or physics is more difficult.* **9 no laughing matter:** *s.t.* serious: *Dressing warmly in winter is no laughing matter.* **10 no matter:** without regard to, *(syn.)* irrespective of: *No matter what my boss says, I'm still going to check these numbers twice.* **11 What's the matter?:** What's the problem?: *"You're crying; what's the matter?" "Oh, my dog just died."*
—*v.* to be of importance, concern: *What you think matters.*

mat·ting /'mætɪŋ/ *n.* [U] a rough mat or combination of them: *We put matting on the floor under the kitchen table.*

mat·tress /'mætrɪs/ *n.* **-tresses** a rectangular pad of wool, cotton, etc., to put on a bed for sleeping: *I like a firm mattress to support my back.*

M

ma·ture /mə'tʃur, -'tur/ v. **-tured, -turing, -tures** to grow to full size and full mental abilities: *Human babies mature slowly.*
—*adj.* **1** adult, fully grown: *There are mature oak trees on each side of our street.* **2** capable of doing what is right, responsible: *Mature teenagers can be excellent caretakers for small children.*

ma·tu·ri·ty /mə'tʃurəti, -'tur-/ n. [U] **1** the state of being fully grown, adulthood: *Girls reach sexual maturity earlier than boys do.* **2** (in finance) the state of being ready to be collected or due: *The bank charges a penalty fee if you withdraw money from a certificate of deposit before its maturity date.*

maud·lin /'mɔdlɪn/ adj. extremely sentimental, tearful: *Romantic novels can be maudlin if the hero dies.*

maul /mɔl/ v. to treat roughly, beat: *A bear mauled a tourist in the woods.*
—*n.* a type of hammer with a wooden head

mau·so·le·um /,mɔsə'liəm, -zə-/ n. a large burial tomb: *Wealthy families used to build mausoleums.*

mauve /mouv, mɔv/ n. [U] adj. a light purple color: *Her favorite color is <n.> mauve, and she is wearing a <adj.> mauve dress.*

ma·ven /'meɪvən/ n. an expert: *He is a computer maven.*

mav·er·ick /'mævrɪk, -vərɪk/ n. **1** cattle or a horse without its owner's brand: *The cowboy tried to catch the mavericks on his land.* **2** fig. a very independent person, (syn.) an eccentric: *That scientist is a maverick who doesn't care what others think.*

mawk·ish /'mɔkɪʃ/ adj. maudlin, very sentimental

max·im /'mæksɪm/ n. a saying that states a principle of behavior or living: *"Birds of a feather flock together" is a maxim that similar people like to be with each other.*

max·i·mize /'mæksə,maɪz/ v. **-mized, -mizing, -mizes** to get or demand the most from s.t.: *The boss maximizes profits by paying his employees very little.* -n. **maximization** /,mæksəmə'zeɪʃən/.

max·i·mum /'mæksəməm/ n.adj. the ultimate, most of s.t.: *Race cars speed at the <n.> maximum* (or) *<adj.> maximum speed.*

may /meɪ/ auxiliary verb used with other verbs without the infinitive "to" **might** /maɪt/ or **may have, may 1** expressing possibility of s.t. happening: *I may go to the movies tonight if I'm not too tired.* **2** asking or giving permission: *May I go to the movies?‖You may go to the movies, but you have to wash the dishes first.* **3 may as well:** having no reason not to do s.t.: *We may as well go home, this party is so boring. See:* can, might, modal auxiliary.

USAGE NOTE: *May* is used with the base form of another verb (for example, "go") to express the possibility that something *might* happen. *I may go away for the weekend.*

May /meɪ/ the fifth month of the year, between April and June: *In the Northern Hemisphere, May is a month of springtime.*

may·day /'meɪ,deɪ/ n.infrml. **1** a call for help sent over a radio from boats and planes in trouble: *The pilot shouted, "Mayday, mayday, this is flight 101 and we are going to crash into the sea!"* **2 May Day** a holiday that celebrates labor in many countries: *May Day is a festival of workers.*

May·flow·er /'meɪ,flauər/ n. the name of a ship that brought early European colonizers to North America in 1620: *Her family came to New England on the Mayflower.*

may·hem /'meɪ,hɛm/ n. [U] serious destruction of property or harm to s.o.: *He drank too much alcohol and committed mayhem in nearly destroying the furniture in the bar.*

may·o /'meɪou/ n. [U] *slang short for* mayonnaise

may·on·naise /'meɪə,neɪz, ,meɪə'neɪz/ n. [U] a food sauce made of eggs, oil, and lemon juice: *She puts mayonnaise on her turkey sandwich.*

may·or /'meɪər, mɛr/ n. the elected head of a city's government: *The mayor holds a regular news conference with newspaper reporters.*

may·pole /'meɪ,poul/ n. a pole, symbol of fertility, decorated with ribbons and flowers around which children dance on May 1: *Maypoles are fun at May Day festivals.*

maze /meɪz/ n. a system of passages designed to confuse people or animals as they move through it, (syn.) a labyrinth: *Psychologists test the ability of rats to go through a maze.*

Mc·Coy /mə'kɔi/ n.infrml.fig. **the real McCoy:** an expression that describes s.t. genuine: *Those gold coins are the real McCoy; they are worth a lot of money.*

MD /'ɛm'di/ abbr. for Doctor of Medicine: *Jerry Christopher, MD*

me /mi/ pron. the object form of "I": *The teacher praised me for my speech.*

me·a cul·pa /'meɪə'kulpə, -'kʌl-/ n.frml. (Latin for) a formal expression of guilt, when s.o. does s.t. wrong: *The vase broke and I said, "Mea culpa."*

mead·ow /'mɛdou/ n. a pasture, land with grass and few trees: *Cows eat grass in the meadows near the farm.*

mea·ger /'migər/ adj. very little, (syn.) skimpy: *He makes a meager living from his small farm.*

meal /mil/ *n.* **1** a daily time for eating, known as breakfast, lunch, supper, or dinner, or all the food served at such a time: *Everyone in our family gets together for the evening meal.||I feel tired after a large meal.* **2** [U] coarsely ground grain: *I make corn bread with cornmeal.* **3 meal ticket: a.** a ticket permitting s.o. to eat a meal: *Students give their meal tickets to the cashier in the cafeteria.* **b.** *fig.* a means of living: *He doesn't work and lives off his girlfriend; she's his meal ticket.*

meal·time /'mil,taɪm/ *n.* a time at which meals are eaten: *Noon is our usual mealtime for lunch.*

meal·y /'mili/ *adj.* having a coarse, grainy texture: *I expected the custard to be smooth, but it was mealy.*

mealy-mouthed /'mili,mauðd, -,mauθt/ *adj.infrml.fig.* not stating matters clearly and directly, (*syn.*) equivocal: *He would not say if he would pay for dinner; he just got mealy-mouthed and didn't say "yes" or "no."*

mean /min/ *v.* **meant** /mɛnt/, **meaning** /'minɪŋ/, **means** **1** to indicate, have significance: *That flashing red light means to stop your car and wait for the train to go by.* || *What does this word mean?* **2** to intend to, want to do s.t.: *I meant to call home, but forgot to do it.* **3 to mean business:** to be serious, ready to do s.t.: *The frustrated mother said, "I mean business" to her children who wouldn't go to sleep.* **4 to mean well:** to make a mistake, do s.t. wrong, but not plan to harm s.o.: *She uses rough language, but she means well.*
—*n.* a number in the middle between two extremes of numbers: *The age of students in our class ranges from 18 to 30; the mean age is 24. See:* means.
—*adj.* **1** wanting to hurt s.o., (*syn.*) vicious: *That boy is mean, a real bully.* **2** poor, (*syn.*) wretched: *During dry periods, poor farmers can lead a mean existence.*

me·an·der /mi'ændər/ *v.* to move and turn slowly: *The river meanders through the countryside. -n.* [U] *adj.* **meandering.**

mean·ie /'mini/ *n.infrml.* an aggressive person, who likes to hurt others: *That bully is a meanie.*

mean·ing /'minɪŋ/ *n.* [C] **1** interpretation, explanation: *Can you tell me the meaning of that sentence?* **2** [U] significance, importance of s.t.: *The meaning of the President's speech is that taxes are going to go up.*

mean·ing·ful /'minɪŋfəl/ *adj.* **1** significant, important: *That scientist has made meaningful contributions to her field of science.* **2** having a powerful effect on the mind, (*syn.*) weighty: *Poetry contains meaningful images.*

mean·ing·less /'minɪŋlɪs/ *adj.* **1** without meaning, unimportant: *Those birds make meaningless sounds.* **2** without effect or impact on the mind: *The speaker made a few meaningless comments and left the meeting.*

means /minz/ *n.* **1** *pl.* wealth, resources, and influence: *They are a family of means in this town.* **2** [C] the skill, tools, money, etc., necessary to do s.t.: *Our company has the means to develop new products and market them well.* **3 by all means: a.** definitely, absolutely: *By all means, I would like to see you this evening!* **b.** using everything and everyone available to get s.t. done: *Citizens of the town put out the fire by all means available.* **4 by any means: a.** often used negatively to mean absolutely not: *Not by any means will I allow you to travel across the country alone; it's dangerous!* **b.** using everything available to get s.t. done: *We have to put that fire out by any means that we can.* **5 by no means:** certainly not: *He is by no means poor; in fact, he's rich.*

mean·time /'min,taɪm/ *n.* [U] the period between two events, meanwhile: *I'll talk to you tomorrow; in the meantime, have a good evening.*

mea·sles /'mizəlz/ *n.* [U] *used with a sing.v.* rubeola, a contagious viral disease that causes red spots on the body: *Measles makes children very uncomfortable and itchy.*

meas·ly /'mizli/ *adj.* very little, of poor quality, (*syn.*) miserly: *He received a measly raise in his salary.*

meas·ure /'mɛʒər/ *v.* **-ured, -uring, -ures** **1** to calculate, find the size, weight, speed, etc., of s.t.: *I measured the size of the floor for a new rug.* **2** *phrasal v. sep.* **to measure s.t. out:** to measure s.t. carefully step-by-step: *I measured out the room with a yardstick.||I measured it out.* **3** *phrasal v. insep.* **to measure up to s.t.:** to meet standards: *The new student's work measures up to the level of the other students.*
—*n.* **1** determination of the size, weight, speed, etc., of s.t.: *The measure of the floor is 15' by 20' (approx. 4.6 m x 6.1 m).* **2** a portion of s.t.: *I asked the worker at the garden store to give me a ten-pound (approx. 4.5 kilos) measure of grass seed.* **3** a legislative act: *Our state legislature passed a measure to increase property taxes.* **4 for good measure:** for additional safety, insurance: *The weather looked as though it might rain, so for good measure, I took my umbrella.* **5 to take measures:** to perform a specific action, a step to do s.t.: *Officials took the measures of placing police and emergency vehicles in the park to help people during a huge outdoor concert. -adj.* **measurable.**

M

meas·ure·ment /ˈmɛʒərmənt/ *n.* [C;U] a determination of the size, weight, speed, etc., of s.t.: *A tailor took the man's measurements for a new suit.*

meat /mit/ *n.* **1** the muscle and flesh of animals: *We eat meat, either pork or beef, for dinner.* **2** *fig.* s.t. important, meaningful: *Our meetings were not just talk; there was some meat to them. See:* meaty.

meat·ball /ˈmit,bɔl/ *n.* **1** a small ball of chopped beef often mixed with bread crumbs: *We had spaghetti and meatballs for lunch.* **2** *fig.slang* a stupid person, (*syn.*) a jerk: *That guy is a real meatball.*

meat·head /ˈmit,hɛd/ *n.infrml.fig.* a stupid person: *My sister's last boyfriend was a meathead.*

meat·loaf /ˈmit,louf/ *n.* [C;U] ground beef with spices formed into a loaf, baked, and served in slices: *We ate meatloaf and gravy with mashed potatoes and carrots for dinner.*

meat·pack·ing /ˈmit,pækɪŋ/ *n.* [U] the industry of slaughtering and preparing meat for market: *Meatpacking is a big industry in the USA.*

meat·y /ˈmiti/ *adj.* **-ier, -iest** **1** containing lots of meat: *That lamb stew is very meaty with few vegetables.* **2** *infrml.fig.* meaningful, having substance: *His suggestions are meaty and worth considering.*

Mec·ca /ˈmɛkə/ *n.* **1** a city in western Saudi Arabia considered the most holy city to Muslims: *Religious pilgrims visit Mecca each year.* **2** *fig.* a place that attracts people: *Paris is a mecca for tourists who love food, history, and culture.*

me·chan·ic /məˈkænɪk/ *n.* a person who repairs and maintains machinery: *Do you know a good car mechanic?*

me·chan·i·cal /məˈkænɪkəl/ *adj.* **1** related to machines and systems: *The air conditioning system stopped because of a <adj.> mechanical breakdown.* **2** automatic, done without thinking: *She danced <adv.> mechanically, with no sense of style.*

me·chan·ics /məˈkænɪks/ *n.* [U] **1** *used with a sing.v.* any of a variety of scientific fields that study the laws of motion and the design and manufacture of mechanical devices: *The study of mechanics is basic to science and engineering students.* **2** *used with a pl.v.* the motions and technical aspects of an activity: *The mechanics of sports, such as running or hitting a baseball, are studied scientifically.*

mech·a·nism /ˈmɛkə,nɪzəm/ *n.* **1** parts of a machine that move and perform a function: *A lock has a mechanism that opens and closes.* **2** a means of doing s.t.: *A stock exchange is a mechanism that brings investors and companies together to provide capital to businesses.*

mech·a·nize /ˈmɛkə,naɪz/ *v.* **-nized, -nizing, nizes** to change tasks done by hand to having machines do them: *A shoe manufacturer mechanized the factory by installing power machinery.*

med·al /ˈmɛdl/ *n.* an award shaped in a circle: *Olympic athletes can win gold, silver, or bronze medals.* **-n. medalist.**

medal

me·dal·lion /məˈdælyən/ *n.* **1** a metal shield usu. shaped like a medal: *Taxicabs have medallions on their hoods to show they are legally registered.* **2** a circular portion of food: *We had medallions of veal for dinner.*

Medal of Honor *n.* the USA's highest military award for great bravery in combat: *Winners of the Medal of Honor are national heroes.*

med·dle /ˈmɛdl/ *v.* **-dled, -dling, -dles** to interfere in the affairs of others, (*syn.*) to butt in: *He meddles in his neighbors' business.* **-n. meddler.**

med·dle·some /ˈmɛdlsəm/ *adj.* related to s.o. who interferes with others: *Meddlesome people are often told to mind their own business.*

me·di·a /ˈmidiə/ *n.* [U] **1** *used with a pl.v.* means of sending information or expressing ideas: *She is an artist whose media are painting and sculpture.* **2** *used with a sing. or pl.v.* used with "the" to mean the combination of television, radio, news magazines, and large circulation newspapers: *The media report on every little thing that the President does.* —*adj.* related to communications media: *Media relations are often handled by professional press agents.*

media event *n.* an event that attracts media attention: *Whenever the President travels, it is a media event.*

me·di·an /ˈmidiən/ *n.* **1** the halfway point in an ordered array of numbers: *The income of people in this city ranges from zero to $250,000 per year; the median is $125,000.* **2** a center strip on a highway: *The median* (or) *median strip on the expressway helps prevent accidents.*

me·di·ate /ˈmidi,eɪt/ *v.* **-ated, -ating, -ates** to help both sides in negotiations reach agreement: *The mayor mediated in a salary dispute between the teachers' union and the board of education.* **-n.** [U] **mediator; mediation** /ˌmidiˈeɪʃən/.

med·ic /ˈmɛdɪk/ *n.* a person trained to give emergency medical help to the sick or injured until they can see a doctor: *Medics bandaged the injuries of the accident victim, then drove him to the hospital.*

Med·i·caid /ˈmɛdɪ,keɪd/ *n.* [U] in the USA, a health-care program for poor people paid for by public funds: *Medicaid provides millions of people with medical care that they could not afford without the program.*

med·i·cal /'mɛdɪkəl/ *adj.* related to medicine: *She visited a medical clinic for a flu shot.* -*adv.* **medically.**

medical examiner *n.* an official who guards public health and performs autopsies on corpses to find the cause of death: *The chief medical examiner has many physicians working for her.*

Med·i·care /'mɛdɪˌkɛr/ *n.* [U] in the USA, a government-funded public health care program for the elderly: *Medicare provides doctor and hospital care for old people.*

med·i·ca·tion /ˌmɛdɪ'keɪʃən/ *n.* [C;U] drugs, such as pills, shots, or ointments, used to treat or cure an illness: *He has to take medication for high blood pressure twice a day.* -*v.* **medicate** /'mɛdɪˌkeɪt/.

me·dic·i·nal /mə'dɪsənəl/ *adj.* related to the healing properties of medicine and natural substances, (*syn.*) curative: *The medicinal effects of many plants have been known for centuries.*

med·i·cine /'mɛdəsən/ *n.* [U] **1** the art and science of curing sick people and preventing disease: *Modern medicine can cure many diseases that used to kill many people.* **2** [C] medication: *She gave her baby cough medicine.*

me·di·e·val /ˌmidi'ivəl, ˌmɛ-, ˌmɪ-/ *adj.* related to the Middle Ages: *Medieval times lasted approx. 1,000 years, from about 476 to 1450 A.D.*

me·di·o·cre /ˌmidi'oʊkər/ *adj.* second-rate, not good or bad: *He got mediocre grades in high school.* -*n.* [C;U] **mediocrity** /ˌmidi'ɑkrəti/.

med·i·tate /'mɛdəˌteɪt/ *v.* -**tated,** -**tating,** -**tates** to sit quietly and think freely: *She meditates each morning to relax and clear her mind.* -*n.* [C;U] **meditation** /ˌmɛdə'teɪʃən/.

me·di·um /'midiəm/ *n.* -**iums** or -**ia** /-iə/ **1** a means of doing s.t.: *Language is a medium of expression. See:* media. **2** an environment in which s.t. develops or lives: *Our classroom is a comfortable medium in which to work.* **3** s.o. who claims to be able to speak with spirits: *The police sometimes use mediums to look for missing children.* **4 to strike a happy medium:** to find a balance: *He strikes a happy medium in exercising by taking fast walks, but not jogging or just sitting at home.* —*adj.* average-sized: *He wears medium-sized sweaters.*

med·ley /'mɛdli/ *n.* **1** melodies from different tunes that are played one after the other: *The orchestra played a medley of songs from great Broadway musicals.* **2** a mixture of things or people: *She served a fruit medley for dessert.*

meek /mik/ *adj.* mild, passive: *When he was young, he was loud and outspoken; now he is old and meek.* -*adv.* **meekly;** -*n.* [U] **meekness.**

meet /mit/ *v.* **met** /mɛt/, **meeting, meets 1** to see s.o. accidentally: *On the street, I met an old friend whom I had not seen in years.* **2** to see s.o. at a certain time and place: *I will meet you tonight at your place at 8 (8:00 P.M.).* **3** to wait for s.o., greet s.o.: *I met my friends at the airport and took them to their hotel.* **4** to join, come together: *Two highways meet near the town.* **5** to be introduced to s.o. for the first time: *You will meet some new people at school.* **6** to reach a desired goal: *Our department met its sales goal for the year.* **7** to satisfy: *Governments try to meet the needs of their people for law and order.* **8** to pay a debt: *He couldn't meet all of the expenses of a large house.* **9** *phrasal v. insep.* **to meet on s.t.:** to discuss a specific topic: *Let's meet on how we can improve profits in our company.* **10** *infrml.* **to meet s.o. halfway:** to compromise with s.o., try to agree: *He wanted to buy the plants for $5 each and I wanted $10 for them, so we met each other halfway at $7.50 each.* **11 to meet the competition:** to do s.t. equal to or better than a competitor: *She lowered her prices, so we'll meet the competition by reducing our prices, too.* **12** *phrasal v. insep.* **to meet up with s.o.** or **s.t.: a. s.o.:** to see s.o. at a specific place and time: *I'm going home now, but I'll meet up with you at 8:00 tonight at the restaurant.* **b. s.t.:** to encounter, experience: *As we got close to the city, we met up with a huge traffic jam.*
—*n.* an athletic competition, match, or event: *Our college had a track meet with another college.*

meet·ing /'mitɪŋ/ *n.* **1** a conference or encounter of two or more people: *Our department holds a meeting every Monday morning.* **2 to have** or **reach a meeting of the minds:** to agree, come to an understanding: *Two businesspeople met and had a meeting of the minds on a new project.*

meet·ing·house /'mitɪŋˌhaʊs/ *n.* -**houses** /-ˌhaʊzɪz/ a place where religious and public meetings are held: *Old New England towns have buildings that serve as meetinghouses for the townspeople to vote on town business.*

meg·a·bucks /'mɛgəˌbʌks/ *n.pl.slang* large sums of money, thousands to millions of dollars: *She's earning megabucks in her new job.*

meg·a·byte /'mɛgəˌbaɪt/ *n.* a unit of computer memory capacity of approx. one million bytes: *That computer has a hard disk memory of 500 megabytes. See:* megs, kilobyte.

M

meg·a·hertz /ˈmɛgəˌhɜrts/ *n.* **-hertz** one million cycles per second, esp indicating the processing speed of a computer: *My computer is extremely fast at 125 megahertz.*

meg·a·lith /ˈmɛgəˌlɪθ/ *n.* a large stone, esp. one used by ancient peoples: *Priests in ancient England placed megaliths in a circle for religious worship.*

meg·a·lo·ma·ni·a /ˌmɛgəloʊˈmeɪniə/ *n.* [U] false ideas of grandeur and power: *The dictator suffers from megalomania in planning to construct large palaces with armies that he does not have* -*n.* **megalomaniac** /ˌmɛgəloʊˈmeɪniˌæk/; -*adj.* **megalomaniacal** /ˌmɛgəloʊməˈnaɪəkəl/.

meg·a·phone /ˈmɛgəˌfoʊn/ *n.* a hollow tube placed against the mouth used to make the voice louder: *The politician used a megaphone to speak to a large crowd of people.*

meg·a·ton /ˈmɛgəˌtʌn/ *n.* the explosive force of one million tons of TNT, used as a measure of nuclear bombs: *One nuclear warhead of several megatons can destroy a whole city.*

megs /mɛgz/ *n.pl.* short for megabytes: *My computer has 30 megs of memory. See:* megabytes, kilobytes.

mel·an·chol·y /ˈmɛlənˌkɑli/ *n.* [U] *adj.* a deep sadness, depression: *Listening to the sad music on a rainy day made her feel melancholy.*

mé·lange /meɪˈlɑnʒ, -ˈlɑndʒ/ *n.frml.* (French for) a mixture, esp. of different things, (*syn.*) infrml. a mixed bag: *That restaurant serves a mélange of American and Chinese food.*

meld /mɛld/ *v.* to blend together: *Two groups of workers were melded together to help each other finish a job.*

me·lee /ˈmeɪˌleɪ, meɪˈleɪ/ *n.* a disorderly, noisy fight, (*syn.*) a brawl: *Two men started an argument in a bar, and their fight turned into a melee with lots of people punching each other.*

mel·low /ˈmɛloʊ/ *adj.* **1** smooth and rich-tasting: *Some coffees have a mellow taste.* **2** *infrml.* in a relaxed, friendly mood: *After a good meal, the couple feels mellow and contented.* -*n.* [U] **mellowness.**

me·lod·ic /məˈlɑdɪk/ *adj.* having melody, pleasant: *The violin piece they played was melodic.*

me·lo·di·ous /məˈloʊdiəs/ *adj.* pleasing to the ear: *She has a melodious voice.*

mel·o·dra·ma /ˈmɛləˌdrɑmə, -ˌdræ-/ *n.* [C;U] a play, film, novel, or situation of intense emotion usu. about love, danger, and death: *We saw a melodrama on TV where war separates a couple forever.*

mel·o·dra·mat·ic /ˌmɛlədrəˈmætɪk/ *adj.* showing strong emotions about love, danger, death, etc.: *The boss makes melodramatic announcements about how sales must go up or* everyone will lose their jobs. -*n.pl.* **melodramatics.**

mel·o·dy /ˈmɛlədi/ *n.* **-dies** **1** [C] a tune or song: *He plays Irish melodies on the flute.* **2** [U] a musical idea expressed in notes: *The soprano sang the melody while the tenor sang in harmony with her.*

mel·on /ˈmɛlən/ *n.* a sweet, juicy, thick-skinned fruit of the gourd family, such as cantaloupe, honeydew, or watermelon: *A cool slice of melon makes an excellent dessert in hot weather.*

melt /mɛlt/ *v.* **1** to change from a solid to liquid state, liquefy: *Ice melts to water quickly in warm weather.* **2** *fig.* to feel affection: *He melts when he sees a beautiful baby.* **3** *phrasal v.* **to melt away:** to disappear, leave: *Her fatigue melted away when she reached the top of the mountain.* **4** **to melt in one's mouth:** to taste smooth and wonderful: *The steak is so tender that it almost melts in your mouth.*
—*n.* a period of melting, such as winter ice turning to water, (*syn.*) a thaw: *a spring melt See:* meltdown.

melt·down /ˈmɛltˌdaʊn/ *n.* (in nuclear reactors) the melting down of uranium rods and safety walls, releasing nuclear radiation: *Cooling water escaped accidentally from the reactor, leading to a meltdown.*

melting pot *n.* **1** a container in which metals are melted **2** *fig.* a place in which immigrants mix into the main culture: *New York City is called a melting pot where people from all over the world live together.*

USAGE NOTE: The *melting pot* has traditionally been an image for the blending and mixing of immigrant cultures into American society. Recently, with new immigrants who want to keep their own culture and take on parts of American culture, people also use the image of American society as a *tossed salad* or a *mosaic.*

mem·ber /ˈmɛmbər/ *n.* **1** a person who belongs to an organization, club, family, etc.: *She is a member of a tennis club.* **2** *frml.* a limb, such as an arm or leg

mem·ber·ship /ˈmɛmbərˌʃɪp/ *n.* [C] **1** the state of being a member: *My membership in the health and fitness club ends next month.* **2** all members of a group: *The president asked the club membership to vote on a fee increase.*

mem·brane /ˈmɛmˌbreɪn/ *n.* a thin covering of living tissue: *Membranes of cells allow food to go in and waste to go out.*

me·men·to /məˈmɛntoʊ/ *n.* **-tos** or **-toes** an object that reminds one of s.o. or s.t., (*syn.*) a souvenir: *The couple has maps and photos as mementos of their vacation in London.*

mem·o /ˈmɛmoʊ/ *n.* **-os** short for memorandum

mem·oir /'mɛm,wɑr/ n.frml. the written account of one's life: *Famous men and women often write memoirs about their lives and accomplishments.*

mem·o·ra·bil·i·a /,mɛmərə'bɪliə, -'bɪlyə, -bil-/ n.pl. things that remind one of past events or famous people, such as photos, souvenirs, etc.: *She has a collection of memorabilia of her grandfather, who was a famous general.*

mem·o·ra·ble /'mɛmərəbəl/ adj. unforgettable, worthy of being remembered: *We took some memorable vacations in Alaska in the past.* -adv. **memorably.**

mem·o·ran·dum /,mɛmə'rændəm/ n. **-dums** or **-da** /-də/ a written note used inside a company to inform others, ask for information, record meetings, etc.: *I sent my boss a memorandum asking for a larger office.*

me·mo·ri·al /mə'mɔriəl/ n. **1** a monument dedicated to the memory of the dead: *The Lincoln Memorial in Washington, D.C., has a big statue of President Abraham Lincoln.* **2** a service held to remember the dead: *He went to a memorial for the president of the company, who died last week.*
—adj. related to remembrance of the dead: *Memorial services were held at the church for the man killed in the accident.* -v. **memorialize.**

Memorial Day n. in the USA, a national holiday on the last Monday in May in remembrance of people killed in wars and other dead: *People often visit cemeteries and decorate their relatives' graves on Memorial Day.*

mem·o·rize /'mɛmə,raɪz/ v. **-rized, -rizing, -rizes** to remember s.t. exactly, learn s.t. by heart: *Students memorize the verb forms of a new language.*

mem·o·ry /'mɛməri, 'mɛmri/ n. [C;U] **-ries 1** the ability of the brain to remember: *He has an excellent memory for faces.* **2** [C] recollection of past events: *She has pleasant memories of her summer vacations as a child.* **3** [C] the capacity of a computer to hold information: *My computer has a 500-megabyte memory.* **4** in **memory of s.o.** or **to the memory of:** to pay respect to s.o. who is dead: *Many university buildings are dedicated in memory of important people.*

men /mɛn/ n.pl. of man: human males in general: *Men wear suits to work.*

men·ace /'mɛnɪs/ v. **-aced, -acing, -aces 1** to threaten s.o. with harm: *A thief menaced the store owner with a gun.* **2** to endanger, be harmful: *Heavy rainstorms menace the farmers' crops.*
—n. s.t. that threatens with danger: *That nasty dog is a menace to the children in the neighborhood.*

me·nag·er·ie /mə'nædʒəri, -næʒə-/ n. a group of animals held in captivity: *That family keeps a menagerie of dogs, cats, ducks, goats, and other animals.*

mend /mɛnd/ v. **1** to fix, repair, such as holes in fences or clothes: *He mended a hole in his sock with a needle and thread.* **2 to be on the mend:** to heal, esp. after surgery or an accident: *My friend is on the mend after his auto accident.* **3 to mend fences:** to become friendly to s.o. whom you wronged: *A politician visited voters to mend fences after he voted for a tax increase.* **4 to mend one's ways:** to show better behavior, improve: *After she failed the math quiz, she mended her ways and studied more.*

mend·ing /'mɛndɪŋ/ n. [U] sewing, repair of holes in clothes with needle and thread: *These old clothes need mending and ironing.*

men·folk /'mɛn,foʊk/ n.pl.infrml. men in a family or gathering: *At the party, the menfolk gathered near the barbecue grill while the women went for a walk.*

me·ni·al /'miniəl, 'minyəl/ adj. lowly, related to boring or unpleasant tasks: *He does menial chores, such as sweeping floors and washing windows.*

men·in·gi·tis /,mɛnɪn'dʒaɪtɪs/ n. [U] a life-threatening infection of the membranes covering the brain and spinal cord: *The baby had a mild case of meningitis but is better now.*

men·o·pause /'mɛnə,pɔz/ n. [U] the time of the permanent stopping of menstruation of women around ages 45 to 50: *She went through menopause recently.*

me·no·rah /mə'nɔrə, -'noʊrə/ n. a candlestick with seven branches: *Jewish people light the menorah at Chanukah, the festival of lights.*

mensch /mɛntʃ/ n.infrml. (Yiddish for) a nice, sensitive person: *My dad helps everyone in the neighborhood; he's a real mensch.*

men's room n. a public toilet for men: *After the movie, he went to the men's room.*

USAGE NOTE: *Men's room* is a polite term for *restroom*, a bathroom in a public place. *Bathroom* and *toilet* are considered less polite terms.

men·stru·ate /'mɛnstru,eɪt/ v. **-ated, -ating, -ates** to have one's period, menstruation: *Women menstruate about once a month.* -adj. **menstrual.**

men·stru·a·tion /,mɛnstru'eɪʃən/ n. [U] in females, the monthly discharge of the lining of the uterus and accompanying bleeding: *Menstruation begins in many girls at the age of 11 or 12.*

men·tal /'mɛntl/ adj. **1** related to the mind: *He's old, but his mental abilities are still strong.* **2** slang **a mental case:** a troubled or

M

crazy person: *She was exhausted and a mental case after taking final examinations. -adv.* **mentally.**

men·tal·i·ty /mɛn'tæləti/ *n.* [C;U] **-ties 1** a way of thinking, attitude toward life or a situation: *She has a very positive mentality about the future.* **2** [U] level of intelligence: *Students in that class are of average mentality.*

mental retardation *n.* [U] a condition of lowered mental abilities caused by birth defects, disease, genetics, etc.: *The baby has mental retardation because of a birth defect. -adj.* **mentally retarded.**

men·thol /'mɛn,θɔl, -,θɑl/ *n.* [U] *adj.* a substance from peppermint with a refreshing coolness used in medications, to flavor cigarettes, etc.: *He smokes <n.pl.> menthols (or) <adj.> menthol cigarettes.*

men·tion /'mɛnʃən, -tʃən/ *v.* **1** to say or write s.t. briefly or casually: *I mentioned to my friend that he needed a haircut.* **2 Don't mention it.:** You're welcome; it's no trouble: *He thanked the librarian for her help and she said, "Don't mention it."* **3 not to mention:** s.t. obvious: *He's rich and not to mention, he's handsome, too!* **4 to make mention of:** to speak of in passing: *She made mention of how much she likes living in Florida, but didn't give any details.*

men·tor /'mɛn,tɔr, -tər/ *n.* a teacher and friend: *My former boss is my mentor, who gives me advice in my career.*

men·u /'mɛnyu/ *n.* **-us 1** a list of foods available in a restaurant: *We read the menu and chose an appetizer and a main dish.* **2** (in computers) a display of functions or files: *I chose a file from the main menu.* **3 to be** or **have on the menu:** to have s.t. planned: *What do you have on the menu for this weekend? Fishing? Hiking?*

me·ow /mi'aʊ/ *n.v.* **1** a sound made by a cat: *Her cat makes a loud <n.> meow when he is hungry.* **2** *infrml.* **the cat's meow:** s.t. excellent: *Your new hat is the cat's meow.*

mer·can·tile /'mɜrkən,taɪl, -,til/ *adj.n.* a system of business by merchants, esp. in foreign trade: *Cotton, wheat, corn, etc., were traded on the mercantile exchange. -n.* [U] **mercantilism.**

mer·ce·nar·y /'mɜrsə,nɛri/ *adj.frml.* greedy, concerned mainly with money: *He's very mercenary and won't do anything unless he gets paid for it.*

—n. **-ies** a professional soldier paid to fight for another country's army: *Britain hired German mercenaries to fight the Americans in the Revolutionary War.*

mer·chan·dise or **-dize** /'mɜrtʃən,daɪz, -,daɪs/ *n.* [U] items, goods made for sale at the retail level, (syn.) wares: *That department store has a large selection of merchandise for sale.*

—v. /'mɜrtʃən,daɪz/ **-dised, -dising, -dises** to buy, display, advertise, and sell goods at retail: *Department stores merchandise clothes by advertising them in newspapers. -n.* [U] **merchandising.**

mer·chant /'mɜrtʃənt/ *n.* a person or business that buys and sells goods at wholesale, to other businesses, or at retail, to customers: *Clothing merchants often have their stores in shopping malls.*

—adj. related to buying and selling goods: *Merchant ships travel to Asia and return with products to sell in western countries.*

mer·ci·ful /'mɜrsɪfəl/ *adj.* showing mercy, kind: *He suffered so much pain from cancer that his death was merciful. -adv.* **mercifully.**

mer·ci·less /'mɜrsɪlɪs/ *adj.* without mercy, cold-blooded: *The cat was merciless, playing with the mouse until he killed it. -adv.* **mercilessly.**

mer·cu·ry /'mɜrkyəri/ *n.* [U] a metallic element, known as quicksilver for its liquid shiny appearance at room temperature: *In thermometers, the level of mercury rises as the temperature goes up.*

Mercury /'mɜrkyəri/ *n.* [U] the closest planet to the sun: *The surface of Mercury is very hot in the daytime.*

mer·cy /'mɜrsi/ *n.* **1** forgiveness, willingness to let s.o. avoid punishment: *The governor showed mercy to the prisoner on death row and allowed him to live.* **2 at the mercy of:** in a situation where s.o. or s.t. can harm you and you are helpless: *Farmers are at the mercy of bad weather that can destroy their crops.* **3 It's a mercy:** a piece of good luck, a fortunate event: *It was a mercy that the old woman died before she could see her farm turned into a shopping mall.*

mercy killing *n.* [U] the killing of a person or animal who is suffering greatly and unlikely to recover, (syn.) euthanasia: *A race horse broke its leg, and its owner did a mercy killing by shooting it.*

mere /mɪr/ *adj.* **1** only, nothing more than: *She was a mere child when she learned to sing beautifully.* **2 the merest:** the smallest, the least thing: *The merest noise makes her dog bark.*

mere·ly /'mɪrli/ *adv.* only, just, nothing more than: *I merely asked how he felt, and he started yelling at me.*

me·ren·gue /mə'rɛŋgeɪ/ *n.* [C;U] a fast Caribbean dance: *I like to dance the merengue even more than the rumba.*

merge /mɜrdʒ/ *v.* **merged, merging, merges 1** to combine: *Our company merged two sales forces into one.* **2** to blend together: *The col-*

ors of the sunset merged gradually into each other.

merg·er /ˈmɜrdʒər/ *n.* (in business) combining two companies into one larger company: *Two banks underwent a merger and combined into one huge operation.*

me·rid·i·an /məˈrɪdiən/ *n.* on a map or globe, a line of longitude that makes a half circle of the earth from the North to the South Pole: *The prime meridian runs through Greenwich, England.*

me·ringue /məˈræŋ/ *n.* [C;U] a topping made of whipped egg whites, sugar, and flavoring for pies and cakes: *She loves lemon meringue pie for dessert.*

mer·it /ˈmɛrɪt/ *v.* to be worthy of, deserve attention because of the quality of s.o. or s.t.: *That business proposal merits careful consideration.*
—*n.* [U] **1** high quality, excellence: *Her poetry is of great merit.* **2** [C] an award for excellence: *Boy and Girl Scouts earn badges for merit.* ‖ *Employees receive merit increases in their salaries.* **3 on one's** or **its own merits:** judged by itself: *Teachers judge students on their own merits and not on how rich their parents are.* -*adj.* **meritorious** /ˌmɛrəˈtɔriəs/.

mer·i·toc·ra·cy /ˌmɛrəˈtɑkrəsi/ *n.* an organization or society in which success and rewards are based on performance: *Our company is a meritocracy in which young employees who work well can be promoted over older ones.*

mer·maid /ˈmɜrˌmeɪd/ *n.* a mythical being that is half woman, half fish: *Mermaids are described in stories about the sea.*

mer·ry /ˈmɛri/ *adj.* **-rier, -riest 1** happy, lively: *We had a merry time at the party last night.* **2 to make merry:** to celebrate cheerfully: *We made merry at my brother's wedding.* -*n.* [U] **merriment.**

merry-go-round *n.* **1** a carousel, a type of carnival ride with models of horses on a platform that goes around to music: *Children and adults love the motion of a merry-go-round.* **2** *fig.* any busy activity that leads nowhere: *The diplomatic negotiations were just a merry-go-round that got nothing done.*

merry-go-round

mer·ry·mak·ing /ˈmɛriˌmeɪkɪŋ/ *n.* [U] *frml.* laughter, singing, having a good time: *On New Year's Eve, merrymaking lasts all night.*

mesh /mɛʃ/ *n.* [U] a loose woven material of string, rope, wire, etc.: *Fishers use nets made of mesh to catch fish.*
—*v.* **meshes** to fit together: *Gears in a machine mesh together.*

mes·mer·ize /ˈmɛzməˌraɪz/ *v.* **-ized, -izing, -izes** to hypnotize, entrance: *The birds in the tree mesmerized the cat.* -*n.* [U] **mesmerism.**

mess /mɛs/ *n.* [C;U] **1** a clutter, disorder: *His office is always a mess because he never throws anything away.* **2** [C;U] a dirty condition, filth: *An egg fell on the floor and made a mess.* **3** [C] trouble, a difficult situation: *She's in a mess because she quit school but has to pay off her student loans.*
—*v.* **messes 1** *infrml.* **to mess around:** to loaf, goof off: *She doesn't work and just messes around watching TV and reading magazines.* **2** *phrasal v.* **to mess around with s.o.** or **s.t.: a.** to deal with s.o. or s.t. casually, play around with it: *He messed around with trying to fix his car himself, then took it to a mechanic.* **b.** to get sexually involved with s.o.: *She won't mess around with married men.* **3** *phrasal v. sep.* **to mess up s.o.** or **s.t.: a. s.t.:** to dirty, spoil: *He messed up his report by spilling coffee on it.* **b. s.t.:** to make a mistake, spoil, (*syn.*) to goof up: *She messed up her report by leaving a lot of mistakes in it.*

mes·sage /ˈmɛsɪdʒ/ *n.* **1** a short written or spoken note: *I left a message on her answering machine to call me.* **2** the central meaning: *The message of that lecture was that drugs are dangerous.* **3** *infrml.* **to get the message:** to understand s.t., esp. s.t. implied: *He finally got the message (that she did not like him) when she refused many times to go out with him.*

mes·sen·ger /ˈmɛsəndʒər/ *n.* a person who brings a message, letter, package, etc.: *A messenger came to my door with a package from my office.*

mess hall *n.* a building used as an eating place for soldiers or children at summer camp: *Soldiers go to the mess hall to eat.*

mes·si·ah /məˈsaɪə/ *n.* any savior of humanity; to Christians, Jesus Christ: *Jews believe that the messiah has not come to Earth yet.*

mess·y /ˈmɛsi/ *adj.* **-ier, -iest 1** cluttered, disorderly: *Her room is always messy with magazines and clothes everywhere.* **2** dirty, soiled: *The kitchen floor is messy with spilled food.* **3** troubled, difficult: *Their divorce was a messy legal battle.*

met /mɛt/ *v.* past tense & past part. of meet: *We met in the park last week.*

me·tab·o·lism /məˈtæbəˌlɪzəm/ *n.* all the processes in the body that digest, use, and expel nourishment: *She has a fast metabolism that burns food quickly.* -*adj.* **metabolic** /ˌmɛtəˈbɑlɪk/; -*v.* **metabolize** /məˈtæbəˌlaɪz/.

met·al /ˈmɛtl/ *n.* [C;U] any of the basic metallic elements, usu. hard, shiny substances that can be melted, shaped, and cut to make things: *Steel is a metal that is used a lot in building and manufacturing.*
—*adj.* made of metal: *Ships are made of metal plates welded together.*

me·tal·lic /mə'tælɪk/ *adj.* related to metal (iron, steel, copper, etc.): *He painted his car with metallic paint.*

met·al·lur·gy /'mɛtl,ɜrʤi/ *n.* [U] the study of metals, the extraction of them from ores and their preparation for use: *Metallurgy is a field of engineering. -n.* **metallurgist.**

met·al·work /'mɛtl,wɜrk/ *n.* [U] metal shaped for particular uses, such as ventilation ducts, or decorative shapes, such as wrought iron fences *-n.* [U] **metalworker; metalworking.**

met·a·mor·pho·sis /,mɛtə'mɔrfəsɪs/ *n.* [U] **-ses 1** (in biology) a dramatic change from one stage of life to another, as in the butterfly's change from a cocoon to a winged insect: *Ancient people believed that humans could undergo metamorphosis from human form to animal form.* **2** [C] *fig.* a dramatic change in character, appearance, etc.: *He underwent a real metamorphosis in his teenage years from a weak boy to a strong young man. -v.* **metamorphose** /,mɛtə'mɔr,fouz/.

met·a·phor /'mɛtə,fɔr/ *n.* [C;U] a figure of speech that suggests similarity between one thing and another: *"All that glitters is not gold" is a metaphor for saying that things are not always what they appear to be. -adj.* **metaphorical** /,mɛtə'fɔrɪkəl, -'fɑr-/.

met·a·phys·ics /,mɛtə'fɪzɪks/ *n.* [U] *pl.* used with a sing.v. (in philosophy) the study of the nature of reality and knowledge: *Metaphysics is a difficult and deep field of study. -adj.* **metaphysical.**

me·tas·ta·size /mə'tæstə,saɪz/ *v.* **-sized, -sizing, -sizes** usu. of cancer, to spread from a local tumor throughout an organism: *Her cancer has metastasized from the lungs all through her body. -n.* [U] **metastasis** /mə'tæstəsɪs/.

mete /mit/ *v.* **meted, meting, metes** to give out, (*syn.*) to dispense: *The father meted out punishment when his son came home late at night.*

me·te·or /'mitiər, -ɔr/ *n.* a small body of matter from outer space that burns up when it enters the earth's atmosphere: *On clear nights, meteors often can be seen streaking across the sky.*

me·te·or·ic /,miti'ɔrɪk, -'ɑr-/ *adj.* **1** related to meteors: *Geologists found pieces of meteoric rock in a field.* **2** *fig.* speedy, rapid: *He had a meteoric rise in politics, from local mayor to President.*

me·te·or·ite /'mitiə,raɪt/ *n.* a small meteor that lands on Earth: *Meteorites have been found and studied by scientists.*

me·te·or·ol·o·gy /,mitiə'rɑləʤi/ *n.* [U] the study of the earth's atmosphere and weather conditions: *Meteorology includes the study of weather. -n.* **meteorologist;** *-adj.* **meteorological** /,mitiərə'lɑʤɪkəl/.

me·ter /'mitər/ *n.* **1** a linear measurement of 39.37 inches (3.37 inches more than a yard): *Most countries measure distance in meters and kilometers.* **2** a machine that measures things, such as the use of water, electricity, and gas: *A parking meter shows how much time a car can stay in a parking space.* **3** the rhythmic pattern of music or poetry: *Poetry is written in different meters.*
—*v.* to measure with a meter: *The use of electricity is metered in each house.*

meter maid *n.* a civil employee (often female) who checks parking meters and writes tickets if the meter is not paid: *Meter maids walk up and down the streets looking for parking violations.*

meth·a·done /'mɛθə,doun/ *n.* [U] a substitute for heroin that can help cure drug addiction: *She takes methadone in a program to stop using drugs.*

meth·ane /'mɛ,θeɪn/ *n.* [U] a colorless, odorless, flammable gas: *Methane is widely used for cooking and heating.*

meth·a·nol /'mɛθə,nɔl/ *n.* wood alcohol, a colorless liquid used for fuel and as a solvent: *Methanol is a very flammable liquid.*

meth·od /'mɛθəd/ *n.* a way of doing s.t., a means, technique: *That business uses trucks as its method of moving goods.*

me·thod·i·cal /mə'θɑdɪkəl/ *adj.* systematic, careful, in a step-by-step manner: *He is very methodical in his work habits.*

meth·od·ol·o·gy /,mɛθə'dɑləʤi/ *n.* the manner in which tasks are performed, methods as a group: *Teachers use different methodologies to teach language to students. -adj.* **methodological** /,mɛθədə'lɑʤəkəl/.

me·tic·u·lous /mə'tɪkyələs/ *adj.* careful and thorough, painstaking: *She is meticulous in spelling every word correctly in her papers.*

me·tier /mɛ'tyeɪ, meɪ-/ *n.frml.* (French for) one's occupation, specialty: *Her metier is painting portraits of children.*

met·ric /'mɛtrɪk/ *adj.* **1** related to the metric system: *Most of the world uses the metric system of measurement.* **2** related to a rhythmic pattern of poetry: *Iambic pentameter is a metric pattern in much of Shakespeare's poetry.*

metric system *n.* the system of measurement based on the meter, kilogram, and second: *The metric system is based on the use of decimals and is easier to use than the English system.*

met·ro /'mɛtrou/ *adj.infrml.* short for metropolitan, referring to a city and its surrounding area: *Rain showers will cross the metro area today.*
—*n.* **-ros** (French for) subway: *People in Paris go to work on the metro.*

me·trop·o·lis /mə'trɑpəlɪs/ *n.frml.* a large, important city: *New York City is a metropolis.*

met·ro·pol·i·tan /ˌmɛtrə'pɑlətən/ *adj.* related to a city and its suburbs: *Metropolitan Miami covers a much larger area than the city of Miami itself.*

met·tle /'mɛtl/ *n.* [U] courage and endurance, character: *She takes the hardest courses that she can to test her mettle as a good student -adj.* **mettlesome** /'mɛtlsəm/.

mew /myu/ *n.v. var. of* meow: *The kitten* <*v.*> *mews when it is hungry.*

mez·za·nine /'mɛzəˌnin, ˌmɛzə'nin/ *n.* the floor or balcony above the main floor in a store or hotel: *Business offices of the hotel are located on the mezzanine.*

mgr /'mænɪdʒər/ *n.abbr. for* manager: *She signs her letters, Jane Wong, General Mgr.*

mica /'maɪkə/ *n.* [U] a mineral found in thin layers, used as insulating material

mice /maɪs/ *n.pl. of* mouse

mi·crobe /'maɪˌkroʊb/ *n.* germs, bacteria, or viruses too small to be seen without a microscope: *Microbes cause disease.*

mi·cro·bi·ol·o·gy /ˌmaɪkroʊbaɪ'ɑlədʒi/ *n.* [U] the study of microorganisms: *Biology students must take at least one course in microbiology.*

mi·cro·chip /'maɪkroʊˌtʃɪp/ *n.* a tiny integrated circuit used in computers and other electrical equipment: *Microchips are manufactured in Silicon Valley, California.*

mi·cro·com·puter /'maɪkroʊkəmˌpyutər/ *n.* a category of small computers smaller than minicomputers: *Microcomputers are used in many businesses.*

mi·cro·cosm /'maɪkroʊˌkɑzəm/ *n.* a small, complete version of s.t. larger, a sample: *The style of life in Pittsburgh is a microcosm of how people live in America in general.*

mi·cro·ec·o·nom·ics /ˌmaɪkroʊˌɛkə'nɑmɪks, -ˌikə-/ *n.* [U] *v.* the study of types of businesses in an economy, rather than the overall economy: *The study of microeconomics is done with computers and mathematics. See:* macroeconomics.

mi·cro·fiche /'maɪkrəˌfiʃ/ *n.* [C;U] the photographic reduction, storage, and retrieval of information, esp. copies of printed documents on film: *Our business has all our old accounting documents on microfiche.*

mi·cro·film /'maɪkrəˌfɪlm/ *n.* [C;U] a small film of highly reduced images of things: *In spy novels, secret documents are saved on microfilm.*

mi·cro·man·age /ˌmaɪkroʊ'mænɪdʒ/ *v.* **-aged, -aging, -ages** to tell s.o. else what to do step-by-step: *Her boss micromanages every task he gives her to do.*

mi·crom·e·ter /maɪ'krɑmətər/ *n.* a machine used to measure distances in fractions of an inch: *A micrometer can measure the accuracy of parts of a machine.*

mi·cro·or·ga·nism /ˌmaɪkroʊ'ɔrgəˌnɪzəm/ *n.* a tiny creature, such as viruses and bacteria, so small that it can be seen only under a microscope: *There are many thousands of kinds of microorganisms.*

mi·cro·phone /'maɪkrəˌfoʊn/ *n.* an electronic device that changes sound into electric current, usu. for recording on magnetic or digital tape, or for making the sound louder through amplifiers and speakers: *The rock singer picked up a microphone and started to sing.*

microphone

mi·cro·proc·es·sor /'maɪkroʊˌprɑsɛsər/ *n.* a computer chip that performs the basic calculations and processing of a computer: *Micro-processors are used in digital wristwatches, as well as computers.*

mi·cro·scope /'maɪkrəˌskoʊp/ *n.* an optical instrument that uses lenses to make small objects appear larger: *Under the microscope, the students could see tiny organisms. -n.* [U] **microscopy** /maɪ'krɑskəpi/.

microscope

mi·cro·scop·ic /ˌmaɪkrə'skɑpɪk/ *adj.* very small, visible only with a microscope: *Viruses are microscopic in size.*

mi·cro·sur·ger·y /'maɪkroʊˌsɜrdʒəri/ *n.* [U] surgery done with small instruments and laser beams while the doctor views the process on a television screen: *Microsurgery reduces the size of the wound created when the surgeon cuts the skin.*

mi·cro·wave /'maɪkrəˌweɪv/ *n.* **1** a short frequency electromagnetic wave: *Radar uses microwaves.* **2** a microwave oven
—*v.* **-waved, -waving, -waves** to cook with a microwave oven: *She microwaved her dinner when she came home from work. See:* nuke, USAGE NOTE.

mid or **mid-** /mɪd/ *prefix* referring to the middle of s.t.: *The temperature was in the mid-90s.*||*She paused in mid-sentence.*

mid·air /'mɪd'ɛr/ *n.* a location in the air: *Two airplanes hit each other in midair.*

mid·day /'mɪdˌdeɪ/ *adj.* around noon, the middle of the day: *The man eats a midday meal.*

mid·dle /'mɪdl/ *n.* **1** the center of s.t.: *The core of an apple is in its middle.* **2** *infrml.* the

waistline: *He wears a belt around his middle.*
3 in the process of doing s.t., (*syn.*) the midst:
We were in the middle of a meeting when the phone rang.
—adj. between two other things: *The girl is the middle child in her family.*

middle age *n.* [U] the period of human life approx. between the ages of 40 and 65: *In middle age, the body slows down.* *-adj.* **middle-aged.**

Middle Ages *n.pl. used with a sing.v.* the medieval period of history from the fall of Rome in 476 A.D. to approx. 1450: *The Middle Ages lasted for about 1,000 years.*

Middle America *n.fig.* people who are middle-class and who reflect typical American culture and attitude: *The President visited Kansas and Iowa to learn what Middle America thinks of his policies.*

middle class *n.* the social level of people between the working class and upper class: *The USA has a large middle class.*

Middle East or **Mid-east** /ˌmɪdˈist/ *n.* countries located from the southern and eastern Mediterranean, east to Iran: *The Middle East was home to many ancient civilizations.*

mid·dle·man /ˈmɪdlˌmæn/ *n.* **-men** /-ˌmɛn/ a person or business that negotiates or buys products from a manufacturer and sells with a price increase to retailers: *Our company sells only through middlemen and not at retail.*

middle-of-the-road *adj.fig.* having moderate opinions: *He's a middle-of-the-road kind of guy without strong beliefs.*

middle school *n.* in USA, a school between elementary and high school, usu. with grades five through eight: *Our town has several middle schools but only one high school. See:* grade school, secondary school, USAGE NOTE.

mid·get /ˈmɪdʒɪt/ *n.* a very small, short person: *Children do not like to be called midgets.*

mid·life /ˈmɪdˌlaɪf/ *n.* [U] middle age: *At midlife, she felt as healthy as she had felt in her youth.*

mid·night /ˈmɪdˌnaɪt/ *n.* **1** 12:00 P.M., the end of the day: *A new day begins at one second after midnight.* **2 to burn the midnight oil:** to work through the night: *I burned the midnight oil getting my presentation ready for the meeting.*

mid·riff /ˈmɪdrɪf/ *n.* the area from the waist to the chest: *She wore a shirt that showed her midriff.*

mid·ship·man /ˈmɪdˌʃɪpmən, ˌmɪdˈʃɪp-/ *n.* **-men** /-mən/ a student in school to become a naval officer: *Midshipmen throw their hats in the air when they graduate from the US Naval Academy.*

midst /mɪdst/ *n.* [U] **1** the middle of a place or activity: *We were in the midst of discussing a contract when the fire alarm rang.* **2** a position

among or with others: *We have a new student in our midst.*

mid·stream /ˈmɪdˈstrim/ *n.* [U] **1** the middle of a river: *We stopped our boat in midstream.* **2** *fig.* the midst of an activity: *The project was canceled in midstream.*

Mid·west /ˌmɪdˈwɛst/ *n. short for* the Middle West of the USA, the middle northwestern states of the USA, from Ohio, Michigan, and Indiana in the east to Kansas and Nebraska in the west: *The Midwest is known for its farmland and industries. -n.* **Midwesterner** /ˌmɪdˈwɛstərnər/.

mid·wife /ˈmɪdˌwaɪf/ *n.* **-wives** /-ˌwaɪvz/ a person who is not a doctor but is trained to assist women in giving birth to babies: *Some people prefer to have a midwife rather than a doctor present when their babies are born. -n.* [U] **midwifery** /ˌmɪdˈwɪfəri, ˈmɪdˌwaɪfəri/.

mien /min/ *n.frml.* a person's expression and general appearance, (*syn.*) demeanor: *The nurse has a kind-looking mien.*

miffed /mɪft/ *adj.* annoyed, mildly angry: *He was miffed that his girlfriend did not show up for a date.*

might /maɪt/ *auxiliary verb & past tense of* may **1** helping verb used to express possibility: *I might go shopping this afternoon if I have time.‖She might have been a good doctor if she hadn't quit school.* **2** as a suggestion: *You might visit the Metropolitan Museum when you go to New York. See:* modal auxiliary.
—n. strength, power: *The might of that athlete is impressive.*

USAGE NOTE: *Might* is used with the base form of another verb (for example, "go") to express possibility in the present, future, or past. It shows that something is less likely to happen than using *may* does. Also *might* can be used as a polite alternative to *may, should,* or *ought to. I might go to the beach tomorrow, if my friends don't come from out of town.*

might·y /ˈmaɪti/ *adj.* **-ier, -iest** having great strength, power: *Mighty armies fought in World War II.*
—adv.infrml.fig. very, greatly: *I'm mighty pleased to see you*

mi·graine /ˈmaɪˌgreɪn/ *n.* a severe headache that some people get frequently: *She gets <n.pl.> migraines once a week.*

mi·grant /ˈmaɪgrənt/ *n.* an animal, bird, or person who moves from one place to another, esp. workers who harvest seasonal crops: *Migrant workers pick fruit in Florida each year.*

mi·grate /ˈmaɪˌgreɪt/ *v.* **-grated, -grating, -grates** to move from one place to another, as animals, birds, and fish do: *Some whales migrate from the northern Pacific Ocean to the*

M

waters near Baja, California, each winter. -n.
migration /maɪˈgreɪʃən/. *See:* emigrate.

mi·gra·to·ry /ˈmaɪgrəˌtɔri/ *adj.* related to migration: *The migratory routes of birds go on for thousands of miles.*

mike /maɪk/ *n.infrml. short for* microphone

mild /maɪld/ *adj.* **1** moderate, not cold or hot: *We have had mild weather this summer, except for one week of heat.* **2** not sharp or strong-tasting: *That mustard is mild, not spicy or hot.* **3** gentle, calm: *She is good with children because she has a mild nature.*
—*adv.* **to put it mildly:** to state s.t. that is very obvious: *The temperature is warm today, to put it mildly; it's over 100 degrees.*

mil·dew /ˈmɪlˌdu/ *n.* [U] *v.* a small fungus that can destroy things (clothes, food, plants, etc.): *<n.> Mildew has ruined the potatoes in our basement; they have <v.> mildewed.*

mile /maɪl/ *n.* a distance equal to 5,280 feet (1.6 km): *A marathon is 26.8 miles (1,852 km) long.‖A nautical mile of 6,076 feet is used in air and sea navigation.*

mile·age /ˈmaɪlɪdʒ/ *n.* [U] **1** the distance in miles between two points: *The mileage between San Francisco and L.A. is approx. 400 (640 km).* **2** an accumulation of use, as in a car: *She got a lot of mileage out of that old coat.*

mile·stone /ˈmaɪlˌstoʊn/ *n.* **1** a marker, such as a stone that indicates the distance in miles: *Many years ago, the main road between Boston and New York had milestones next to it.* **2** *fig.* an important achievement, event: *Getting her college degree was a milestone in her life.*

mi·lieu /mɪlˈyu, -ˈyɜ, mil-/ *n.frml.* **-lieus** or **-lieux** /-ˈyu, -ˈyɜ/ (French for) environment, surroundings: *A city milieu is too noisy and crowded for him. See:* ambiance.

mil·i·tant /ˈmɪlətənt/ *adj.* **1** aggressive, strongly dedicated as to a cause: *Militant labor unions will go on strike to support their demands.* **2** aggressive militarily: *Militant nations often start wars.*
—*n.* a dedicated, aggressive person: *He is a militant in the cause for government reform. -n.* [U] **militancy.**

mil·i·ta·rism /ˈmɪlətəˌrɪzəm/ *n.* [U] a government policy of military aggression *-adj.* **militarist.**

mil·i·ta·rize /ˈmɪlətəˌraɪz/ *v.* **-rized, -rizing, -rizes 1** to build up military capability (army, navy, air force, weaponry, etc.): *The country militarized to get ready for making war.* **2** to control an area with the military: *After World War II, Germany was divided into several militarized zones.*

mil·i·tar·y /ˈmɪləˌtɛri/ *n.* [U] a group of armed forces (army, air force, navy, etc.) of a nation: *In the USA, the military is headed by civilians.*
—*adj.* related to armed forces: *Military bases are located all over the country.*

mil·i·tate /ˈmɪləˌteɪt/ *v.* **-tated, -tating, -tates** to work against s.t., make s.t. worse: *The prisoner's past crimes militated against his getting early release.*

mi·li·tia /məˈlɪʃə/ *n.* a military force, with local, volunteer members: *In colonial times, a town's militia gathered to fight invaders.*

milk /mɪlk/ *n.* [U] a white liquid produced from the breasts of female mammals: *Cows' milk nourishes their young and is food for humans, too.*
—*v.* **1** to take milk from (cows, goats, etc.): *Farmers milk their cows every morning.* **2** to drain, draw s.t. valuable from s.t. usu. in a bad way: *The owners milked their company of its profits then sold it.* **3 to cry over spilled milk:** to be angry over s.t. one cannot change: *A flood ruined our furniture, but there's no use crying over spilled milk; we'll buy some new furniture.*

milk·man /ˈmɪlkˌmæn/ *n.* **-men** /-ˌmɛn/ a man who delivers milk: *The milkman left bottles of milk at the door of our house.*

milk of magnesia *n.* [U] a medication made from magnesium hydroxide used as an antacid and laxative: *He took milk of magnesia to calm his upset stomach.*

milk shake *n.* a drink made with milk and ice cream: *A chocolate milk shake is delicious in the summer.*

milk·y /ˈmɪlki/ *adj.* **-ier, -iest** having the whitish color or consistency of milk: *I cleaned my paintbrush in water and the water turned milky.*

Milky Way *n.* the galaxy of 100 billion stars in which our sun and Earth are located: *On a clear night, you can see part of the Milky Way in the sky.*

mill /mɪl/ *n.* **1** a factory where grain is ground into meal or metal is made: *The steel mills in Pittsburgh were famous for their large size.* **2** a small machine for grinding: *She puts beef through a mill to make hamburger meat.* **3 the rumor mill:** a group of people who gossip about others: *News that the TV actress was pregnant went through the rumor mill but was found to be false. See:* (the) grapevine.
—*v.* **1** to grind grain into flour or meal, to refine metal: *A worker milled wheat into flour for making bread.* **2** *phrasal v.* **to mill about** or **around:** to move around at random: *The party was filled with people milling about.* **3 to put s.o. through the mill:** to require a lot of effort and trouble from s.o.: *A man was accused of war crimes, and the legal system put*

M

him through the mill for seven years before he was found not guilty. -*n.* **miller.**

mil·len·ni·um /məˈlɛniəm/ *n.* **-niums** or **-nia** /-niə/ **1** one thousand years: *On January 1, 2000, this millennium will end.* **2** (in Christianity) a period of paradise of 1,000 years after the second coming of Christ: *Many Christians hope to see the millennium.*

mil·li·gram /ˈmɪləˌgræm/ *n.* 1/1,000th of a gram: *Salt in foods is measured in milligrams.* -*abbr.* **mg.**

mil·li·li·ter /ˈmɪləˌlitər/ *n.* 1/1,000th of a liter: *Some medicines are measured in milliliters.* -*abbr.* **ml.**

mil·li·me·ter /ˈmɪləˌmitər/ *n.* 1/1,000th of a meter: *Tiny distances are measured in millimeters.* -*abbr.* **mm.**

mil·li·ner /ˈmɪlənər/ *n.* a hat maker and seller: *Milliners are located in the garment district.*

mil·li·ner·y /ˈmɪləˌnɛri/ *n.* [U] *adj.* **1** the business of making hats **2** a hat shop: *She works as a clerk in a <n.> millinery (or) <adj.> millinery shop.*

mill·ing /ˈmɪlɪŋ/ *n.* [U] **1** the measurement and cutting of metals, cloth, etc.: *Milling is an exact, skilled craft.* **2** the grinding of grain into flour or meal: *Milling wheat into bread flour is a big industry.*

mil·lion /ˈmɪlyən/ *n.adj.* **-ion** or **-ions** 1,000,000 of s.t.: *She made a <adj.> million dollars (or) $1,000,000 last year.* -*adj.* **millionth.**

USAGE NOTE: The plural of *million* is not used after a number: *He has six million dollars.* BUT *Millions of people love rock and roll.*

mil·lion·aire /ˌmɪlyəˈnɛr, ˈmɪlyəˌnɛr/ *n.* a rich person who has a million dollars or more: *He is a millionaire from Texas.*

mil·li·sec·ond /ˈmɪləˌsɛkənd/ *n.* 1/1,000 of a second: *A millisecond is a very brief period of time.*

mill·stone /ˈmɪlˌstoʊn/ *n.* **1** one of two round, flat stones between which grain is ground into flour: *Millstones turn rapidly as they grind.* **2** *fig.* a burden: *His debts that he can't pay are a millstone around his neck.*

mill·stream /ˈmɪlˌstrim/ *n.* a stream that gives power to a mill: *His farm has an old mill built over a millstream.*

mime /maɪm, mim/ *n.* **1** [C] an entertainer who imitates actions and moods without speaking **2** [U] the art of acting without language: *There is a famous school of mime (or) for mimes in Paris.*

—*v.* **mimed, miming, mimes** to imitate, act as a mime: *The children laughed when he mimed being inside a room with no door.* See: mimic.

mim·ic /ˈmɪmɪk/ *n.v.* **-icked, -icking, -ics** a person who imitates the speech and manner-

isms of others, esp. to make fun of them: *My sister is a very funny <n.> mimic; she <v.> mimics our friends and famous people.* -*n.* [U] **mimicry.**

mince /mɪns/ *v.* **minced, mincing, minces 1** to cut, chop, or grind s.t. into little pieces: *My mother minces onions and mixes them with tomatoes for a pasta sauce.* **2** to walk with short steps **3 not to mince words:** to speak directly, to the point: *He is very outspoken; he's a man who does not mince words.*

mince·meat /ˈmɪnsˌmit/ *n.* [U] **1** finely chopped meat or fruit and spices used as a pie filling: *We had pies filled with mincemeat after Christmas dinner.* **2 to make mincemeat of:** to defeat s.o. easily: *Our basketball team made mincemeat of the other team by winning with a score of 110 to 75.*

mince pie *n.* [C;U] a pastry filled with finely chopped fruit and spices: *Mince pie tastes very rich and sweet.*

mind /maɪnd/ *n.* **1** the awareness of being alive and of one's surroundings: *He is very old, but his mind is still clear.* **2** the mental processes of learning, thinking, and applying knowledge: *She has a good mind and is an excellent student.* **3** beliefs, ideas, feelings: *He speaks his mind and lets you know what he thinks.* **4** *infrml.* **to blow s.o.'s mind:** to shock, overwhelm: *He tells lies so often that he blows people's minds.* **5 to change one's mind:** to change a plan, intention: *He keeps changing his mind about which car to buy.* **6 to give s.o. a piece of one's mind:** to criticize s.o., tell s.o. off: *He tried to cheat me twice, and I really gave him a piece of my mind.* **7 to have a mind of one's own:** to be an independent thinker: *She may be young, but she has a mind of her own.* **8** *infrml.* **to have a mind to do s.t.:** to want to do s.t., lean toward: *I have a mind to go to the movies tonight.* **9 to have a one-track mind:** *infrml.* to think only of one thing, usu. sex or money: *He'll do anything to earn money; he has a one-track mind.* **10 to keep in mind:** to remember: *Keep in mind what I'm telling you.* **11 to know one's own mind:** to stay with one's beliefs and values and not change one's opinion: *She knows her own mind and will not go out with any man she does not like.* **12 to lose one's mind: a.** to go insane, crazy: *He lost his mind and is in a mental hospital now.* **b.** to like or desire greatly: *He has lost his mind over his new girlfriend; he acts crazy about her.* **13** *infrml.* **to take a load off one's mind:** to stop worrying: *He was unemployed and when he finally found a new job, it took a load off his mind.*

—*v.* **1** to take care of, watch over: *I mind the children at home while my wife goes shopping.* **2** to pay attention to s.t.: *Mind how you pronounce your words; say them correctly.* **3** not to like s.t., be annoyed at: *He minds the noise of sirens and trucks in the street; but I don't mind it at all.* **4** to obey, do as one is told: *The boy's mother told him to mind the teacher while he was at school.* **5 never mind:** it doesn't matter; don't worry: *Never mind the dishes, we'll wash them later.* **6** *infrml.* **to mind one's P's and Q's:** to behave properly, pay attention to detail: *The children minded their P's and Q's at the formal party their parents took them to.*

mind-blowing *adj.slang* **1** incredible, unbelievable: *The crazy things that guy says are mind-blowing.* **2** (said of drugs) hallucinogenic, harmful: *Taking acid can be mind-blowing.*

mind-boggling *adj.* difficult to imagine or understand: *There are 100 billion stars in our galaxy, which I find mind-boggling.*

mind·ful /ˈmaɪndfəl/ *adj.* attentive, careful in doing things: *She is mindful of her need to study hard, and she does so every evening. -n.* **mindfulness.**

mind·less /ˈmaɪndlɪs/ *adj.* **1** thoughtless, stupid: *He says mindless things once in a while.* **2** not paying attention to danger, (*syn.*) heedless: *He is mindless of the dangers of driving too fast. -adv.* **mindlessly.**

mind·set or **mind-set** /ˈmaɪndˌsɛt/ *n.* a general attitude, belief(s) about s.t.: *The mindset of people who live in the big city is that they know everything; that's simply not true!*

mine (1) /maɪn/*poss.pron.* belonging to me: *That umbrella is mine.‖Those boots are mine.*

mine (2) *n.* a hole made in the ground to remove minerals: *Some big gold mines run for miles under the earth.* —*v.* **mined, mining, mines 1** to remove minerals from under the earth's surface, (*syn.*) to excavate: *South Africans mine gold and diamonds.* **2** to extract information from s.t.: *When the government opened its secret files, scholars mined historical information. -n.* **miner.** *See:* gold mine.

mine (3) *n.v.* a hidden bomb or explosive device, land mine: *Roads to the battlefield are loaded with <n.pl.> mines.‖Soldiers <v.> mined the roads with explosives.*

mine·field /ˈmaɪnˌfild/ *n.* **1** an area where explosives are hidden: *Minefields are very dangerous places to cross.* **2** *fig.* a situation that can lead to conflicts, lawsuits, etc.: *Any politician who talks about taking away programs for elderly people is walking on a political minefield.*

min·er·al /ˈmɪnərəl, ˈmɪnrəl/ *n.* an inorganic substance, such as copper, iron, sulfur, etc., found naturally in the earth: *Discovering minerals in the soil can make a country wealthy.*

mineral water *n.* [U] a natural or prepared water containing minerals: *He drinks mineral water because he thinks it's good for his health.*

min·e·stro·ne /ˌmɪnəˈstrouni/ *n.* [U] a type of Italian vegetable soup with pasta and beans: *A bowl of minestrone for lunch is good on a cold day.*

min·gle /ˈmɪŋgəl/ *v.* **-gled, -gling, -gles 1** to move around in a group of people: *I mingled at the party and talked with many people.* **2** to blend together, mix: *A businessperson should not mingle business funds with personal funds.*

min·i /ˈmɪni/ *n.* a small version of s.t., such as a miniskirt: *In winter, she wears long skirts and in summer, she wears minis.*

—*prefix* **mini-** miniature, referring to a small or short version of s.t.: *We took a minicourse on English grammar.*

min·i·a·ture /ˈmɪniətʃər, ˈmɪnətʃər/ *n.adj.* a small original or copy of s.t.: *She paints <n.pl.> miniatures (or) <adj.> miniature portraits of people. -v.* **miniaturize.**

min·i·com·put·er /ˈmɪnikəmˌpyutər/ *n.* a small, powerful computer larger than a personal computer, but smaller than a mainframe computer: *Our accounting department uses a minicomputer to keep track of expenses.*

min·i·mal /ˈmɪnəməl/ *adj.* related to a least amount of s.t.: *He spends a minimal amount of time watching television because he needs to study. -adv.* **minimally.**

min·i·mize /ˈmɪnəˌmaɪz/ *v.* **-mized, -mizing, -mizes 1** to reduce s.t. to the limit, lessen: *She minimizes the amount of money that she spends on clothes in order to pay for her college tuition.* **2** to make s.t. seem unimportant, downplay: *The teacher minimized the importance of the quiz.*

min·i·mum /ˈmɪnəməm/ *n.adj.* the least amount of s.t.: *The couple cut their household expenses to the <n.> minimum.*

minimum wage *n.sing.* in the USA, the minimum hourly rate that employers must pay to workers: *It is difficult to support a family on the minimum wage.*

min·ing /ˈmaɪnɪŋ/ *n.* [U] the business and process of taking minerals out of the earth: *Mining requires a big investment in land, equipment, and labor.*

min·i·se·ries /ˈmɪniˌsɪriz/ *n.* **-ries** a television program with a limited number of shows: *Public television showed a miniseries of five episodes on the Civil War.*

min·i·skirt /ˈmɪniˌskɜrt/ *n.* a short skirt from the waist to above the knee: *Miniskirts have been in fashion for the past few years.*

min·is·ter /ˈmɪnəstər/ *n.* **1** a Protestant clergyman or clergywoman: *The new minister of the local Episcopal church is a woman.* **2** a high

M

government official (not in the USA): *The Minister of Public Housing belongs to the Prime Minister's Cabinet.*
—*v.frml.* to help, take care of: *Volunteers ministered to the needs of the flood victims.* -*adj.* **ministerial** /ˌmɪnəˈstɪriəl/.

min·is·try /ˈmɪnəstri/ *n.* -**tries** **1** [U] the profession of the Christian clergy: *He wanted to join the ministry at an early age.* **2** [C] a branch of government (not in the USA): *The Ministry of Housing oversees public and low-income housing in that government.*

mink /mɪŋk/ *n.* [C;U] **minks** or **mink** **1** a small animal, a type of weasel, with soft, shiny fur used to make fur coats: *Minks in captivity are raised on mink farms.* **2** the fur of minks: *She owns an expensive mink coat.*

min·now /ˈmɪnoʊ/ *n.* a small fish often used as bait to catch larger fish: *Minnows swim together in groups (schools) in fresh water.*

mi·nor /ˈmaɪnər/ *adj.* **1** not important, (*syn.*) inconsequential: *We agreed on everything in the contract, even minor points.* **2** not well known, obscure: *Minor poets are not read much by students.* **3** related to the minor key in music: *Sad music is often written in a minor key.*
—*n.* a person under a legal age, such as 18, to vote, drink alcohol in bars, etc.: *In the USA, minors may not purchase or drink alcoholic beverages in public places.*

mi·nor·i·ty /məˈnɔrəti, -ˈnɑr-, maɪ-/ *n.* -**ties** **1** [C] a number or group that is less than half of the total: *The Senator's "no" vote was in the minority, as the law was passed by a vote of 63 to 37.* **2** [C] people of a different race, ethnic background, or religion from those of the majority of people in a nation: *New York City has been a home to minorities for centuries.* **3** [U] old usage the state of being under legal age: *As long as the children are in their minority, they must obey their parents.*
—*adj.* related to a minority: *Blacks in the city formed a minority political party.*

USAGE NOTE: As American society becomes more and more ethnically diverse, many people think the term *minority*—often used to refer to blacks, Asians, Hispanics, and others— is inaccurate. Some people use *people of color* instead of *minority* to refer to non-white Americans. Note that some Hispanics do not consider themselves to be *of color.*

minor league *n.* a sports organization, such as baseball, that ranks below the highest professional level: *A friend of mine from high school plays baseball in the minor leagues.*
—*adj. fig.* **minor-league** unimportant, not very good: *He thinks he's very powerful, but he's minor league. See:* major league.

min·strel /ˈmɪnstrəl/ *n.* **1** in medieval times, a singer and poet who traveled around to perform: *The minstrel entertained the people with his songs and guitar playing.* **2** a song-and-dance entertainer: *Al Jolson was a 20th-century minstrel.*
—*adj.* old usage related to light entertainment from the African American culture by (usu. white) performers made up to look black: *Singers and dancers put on minstrel shows in the early 20th century.*

mint (1) /mɪnt/ *n.* **1** [C;U] a plant with a cool, refreshing taste: *Mint is often used in tea to help digestion.* **2** [C] a candy made of sugar and mint, sometimes covered with chocolate: *We had a mint* (or) *mint candy after dinner.* -*adj.* **minty.**

mint (2) *n.* a building owned by the government where coins are manufactured and paper money is printed: *The USA has mints in Denver and other cities.*
—*v.* to manufacture money (stamp coins, print paper currency): *The US government mints pennies, nickels, dimes, and quarters in its mints.*
—*adj.fig.* in new, excellent condition: *The car I bought is old, but it's in mint condition.* -*n.* [U] **mintage** /ˈmɪntɪdʒ/.

min·u·et /ˌmɪnyuˈɛt/ *n.* a slow, graceful 17th-century French dance and its music: *Long ago, people danced the minuet.*

mi·nus /ˈmaɪnəs/ *n.* -**nuses** **1** a minus sign (–): *The accountant put a minus beside the $100 expense.* **2** s.t. missing or bad, (*syn.*) a deficiency: *Not having a college degree is a minus for him in looking for a job.*
—*prep.* to subtract, take away s.t.: *Seven minus three equals four.‖4 – 2 = 2.*

min·us·cule /ˈmɪnəˌskyul/ *adj.* related to the least, minimal amount of s.t.: *The pay for working as a clerk in that store is minuscule.*

minus sign *n. See:* minus, **1.**

min·ute /ˈmɪnɪt/ *n.* **1** 60 seconds: *I like an egg boiled for three minutes.* **2** a moment, brief time period: *When you have a minute, I would like to talk with you.* **3** a unit of measurement equal to 1/60th of a degree, in an angle. **4** *pl.* **minutes** the official record of a meeting: *The secretary took minutes at the town meeting.* **5 hold on** or **wait a minute!:** to stop or wait: *Hey, wait a minute; don't leave without me!*
—*adj.* /maɪˈnut/ very small, tiny: *Bacteria are minute organisms.*

minute hand *n.* the larger hand on a clock or watch that shows minutes: *When the minute hand is on six, it is half past the hour.*

min·ute·man /ˈmɪnɪtˌmæn/ *n.* -**men** /-ˌmɛn/ during the American Revolution, a citizen who was ready to fight the British on a minute's notice: *Minutemen fought the British all over New England.*

mi·nu·tia /mɪ'nuʃə, -ʃiə/ *n.* **-tiae** /-ʃi,i, -,aɪ/ a small detail: *We agreed on everything, including the <n.pl.> minutiae of the contract.*

mir·a·cle /'mɪrɪkəl/ *n.* an event that cannot be explained by the laws of nature: *All the passengers in a sinking boat drowned except one who was saved by a miracle. -adj.* **miraculous** /mɪ'rækyələs/; *-adv.* **miraculously.**

mi·rage /mɪ'rɑʒ/ *n.* the sight of s.t. that does not exist created by hot-air conditions, (*syn.*) optical illusion: *The thirsty travelers saw a mirage of a water hole in the desert.*

mire /maɪr/ *n.* **1** a muddy, wet place where it is easy to become stuck, (*syn.*) a bog: *Dirt roads in the valleys turn into mires in the spring rains.* **2** a difficult situation: *He spent too much on his credit cards and got into a mire of debt.*
—*v.* **mired, miring, mires** to become stuck, (*syn.*) to bog down: *Trucks got mired in the mud.*

mir·ror /'mɪrər/ *n.* a highly polished surface or glass that reflects light and images: *She looks in the mirror each morning as she puts on makeup.*
—*v.* to copy, agree with: *He mirrors his wife's opinions about most things.*

mirth /mɜrθ/ *n.frml.* laughter, fun: *As the party went on, you could hear the mirth coming from the house. -adj.* **mirthful** /'mÆrθfəl/.

mis- /,mɪs/ *prefix* indicating s.t. negative: *The clerk miscalculated the customer's bill.*

mis·ad·ven·ture /,mɪsəd'vɛntʃər/ *n.* a bad experience, bad luck: *I wanted to spend a weekend playing golf in the country, but my car broke down, the hotel lost my reservation, and it rained; what a misadventure!*

mis·a·lign·ment /,mɪsə'laɪnmənt/ *n.* [U] a mismatch of two things: *The front wheels on my car point to the right, causing a misalignment. -adj.* **misaligned** /,mɪsə'laɪnd/.

mis·al·li·ance /,mɪsə'laɪəns/ *n.* a connection between nations, organizations, or people in a marriage that does not work well: *That marriage is really a misalliance, as the husband and wife do not get along well.*

mis·ap·pro·pri·ate /,mɪsə'proʊpri,eɪt/ *v.* **-ated, -ating, -ates** to use wrongly, steal, (*syn.*) to embezzle: *He misappropriated company funds and was arrested on vacation in the Caribbean. -n.* [C;U] **misappropriation** /,mɪsə,proʊpri'eɪʃən/.

mis·be·got·ten /,mɪsbɪ'gɑtn/ *adj.frml.* illegitimate: *A misbegotten child has unmarried parents.*

mis·be·have /,mɪsbɪ'heɪv/ *v.* **-haved, -having, -haves** to act badly, be impolite: *When her son misbehaves, she yells at him instead of telling him why his actions are wrong. -n.* [U] **misbehavior** /,mɪsbɪ'heɪvyər/.

misc. *adj. abbr. for* miscellaneous

mis·car·riage /mɪs'kærɪdʒ, 'mɪs,kær-/ *n.* **1** accidental birth of a fetus (a baby before it is born) before the proper time, whereby the fetus does not survive: *Sadly, Yvonne had a miscarriage last year when she was four months pregnant.* **2** an injustice, a wrong done to s.o.: *He was innocent, but sent to jail in a miscarriage of justice. -v.* **miscarry** /mɪs'kæri, 'mɪs,kæri/.

mis·cel·la·ne·ous /,mɪsə'leɪniəs/ *adj.* referring to various objects or ideas: *She keeps all sorts of miscellaneous items in her garage, such as a statue, a shovel, and a broken TV. -n.* **miscellany** /'mɪsə,leɪni/.

mis·chief /'mɪstʃɪf/ *n.* [U] small, irritating acts or behavior, usu. by children: *On April Fools' Day, children make mischief by changing the salt and sugar on the kitchen table. -adj.* **mischievous** /'mɪstʃəvəs/.

mis·con·cep·tion /,mɪskən'sɛpʃən/ *v.frml.* a misunderstanding: *The sculptor had a misconception of what the city wanted and made a sculpture that the city rejected. -v.* **misconceive** /,mɪskən'siv/.

mis·con·duct /mɪs'kɑn,dʌkt/ *n.* [U] misbehavior, not acting according to the rules: *The student fought with other students and was expelled from school for misconduct.*

mi·con·strue /,mɪskən'stru/ *v.frml.* **-strued, -struing, -strues** to misunderstand, to be confused by: *I misconstrued what the teacher said to me and did the wrong assignment.*

mis·cue /mɪs'kyu, 'mɪs,kyu/ *n.v.frml.* **-cued, -cuing, -cues** a mistake, s.t. done wrong accidentally: *I made a <n.> miscue when I told a friend to meet me at two o'clock and I went there at three o'clock.‖I <v.> miscued when I said that.*

mis·de·mean·or /,mɪsdɪ'minər/ *n.* a minor legal offense usu. punished by a fine, not prison: *Parking violations are misdemeanors.*

mis·di·ag·nose /mɪs'daɪəg,noʊs, -,daɪəg'noʊs/ *v.* **-nosed, -nosing, -noses** to identify a disease or injury incorrectly: *The doctor misdiagnosed the patient's stomach pain as cancer, but it was only an ulcer. -n.* [C;U] **misdiagnosis** /,mɪsdaɪəg'noʊsɪs/.

mi·ser /'maɪzər/ *n.* a person who tries not to spend any money, even on necessities, (*syn.*) a tightwad: *When the old miser died, his relatives found a million dollars in a box under his bed. -adj.* **miserly.**

mis·er·a·ble /'mɪzrəbəl, 'mɪzərə-/ *adj.* **1** sad, heartbroken: *After their dog died, the couple felt miserable for weeks.* **2** feeling physical pain: *She feels miserable with a bad cold.* **3** poor quality or bad conditions, (*syn.*) wretched: *Poor children lead miserable lives.*

||*She made a miserable attempt at passing the mathematics exam.* -adv. **miserably.**

mis·er·y /ˈmɪzəri/ n. [U] **-ies 1** sadness, a state without hope: *Ever since his wife died, he's been in misery.* **2** physical suffering, bad conditions: *Starving people live in misery.*

mis·fit /ˈmɪsˌfɪt/ n. a person who does not fit in with other people or in a job, (*syn.*) an oddball: *With his elitist attitudes, he is a misfit among construction workers.*

mis·for·tune /mɪsˈfɔrtʃən/ n. **1** [U] bad luck: *Misfortune follows her wherever she goes.* **2** [C] a terrible event, (*syn.*) a calamity: *The earthquake was a misfortune for thousands of people.*

mis·giv·ings /mɪsˈgɪvɪŋz/ n.pl. doubt, suspicion: *He has misgivings about the man his daughter wants to marry, but he says nothing.*

mis·hap /ˈmɪsˌhæp/ n. [C;U] frml. an accident, misfortune: *He had a mishap with his car during his vacation.*

mish·mash /ˈmɪʃˌmæʃ, -ˌmɑʃ/ n.infrml. a mess, confused situation: *Negotiations broke down into a mishmash of disagreements.*

mis·lead /mɪsˈlid/ v. **-led** /-ˈlɛd/, **-leading** /-ˈlidɪŋ/, **-leads** to lead one to the wrong idea, action, or direction, (*syn.*) to deceive: *The book's title misled me into thinking it was a mystery novel, but it was about cars.* -adj. **misleading.**

mis·match /mɪsˈmætʃ/ n. /ˈmɪsˌmætʃ/ **-matches** s.t. unequal in ability, personality, strength, etc.: *The champion boxer knocked out the younger boxer in 30 seconds; it was a total mismatch.*

mis·no·mer /mɪsˈnoʊmər, ˈmɪsˌnoʊ-/ n. a wrong name for s.t. or s.o.: *Her name is Joy, but it's a misnomer; she's a very unhappy person.*

mi·sog·y·nist /mɪˈsɑdʒənɪst/ n.frml. a person who hates women: *He is a misogynist who is openly hostile to women.* -n. **misogyny.**

mis·per·cep·tion /ˌmɪspərˈsɛpʃən/ n. misunderstanding of what is true: *He has a misperception about how intelligent he is, because he's not.* -v. **misperceive** /ˌmɪspərˈsiv/.

mis·place /mɪsˈpleɪs/ v. **-placed, -placing, -places** to put s.t. where you can't find it, (*syn.*) to mislay: *I misplaced my keys somewhere in the house.*

mis·print /ˈmɪsˌprɪnt/ n. a printed error, as in spelling or typing: *The newspaper article has many misprints.*
—v. /mɪsˈprɪnt/ to make a mistake in printing: *They misprinted "times" as "tomes."*

mis·quote /mɪsˈkwoʊt/ n.v. **-quoted, -quoting, -quotes** an incorrect reporting or copying of s.o. else's words: *The newspaper <v.> misquoted what the mayor said about*

taxes.||*He complained about a <n.> misquote in the newspaper.*

mis·read /mɪsˈrid/ v. **-read** /-ˈrɛd/, **-reading** /ˈridɪŋ/, **-reads 1** to read s.t. incorrectly, misunderstand: *I misread today's date on my calendar as August 23 when it is in fact the 24th.* **2** to misjudge a person or situation: *I misread her because I thought she could do the job well, but she apparently can't.* -n. **misreading.**

mis·rep·re·sent /ˌmɪsˈrɛprɪˈzɛnt/ v. to mislead s.o., say s.t. incorrect or untrue on purpose: *He misrepresented the job as working in an office when it is actually an outside sales position.* -n. [C;U] **misrepresentation** /ˌmɪsˈrɛprɪzənˈteɪʃən/.

miss /mɪs/ v. **misses 1** to fail to hit s.t.: *The baseball player missed hitting the ball.* **2** to fail to catch or stop s.t.: *The goaltender missed stopping the ball.* **3** to fail to understand: *She missed the main point the teacher made.* **4** to feel a sense of loss: *When the student went to college in a new city, he missed his family.* **5** not to recognize or notice s.t.: *The shoe store is on the corner straight ahead; you can't miss it.* **6** phrasal v. **to miss out:** not to participate in s.t., not enjoy: *Be sure to come to the picnic because if you don't, you will miss out on the fun.* **7 to miss the boat:** to lose an opportunity to benefit: *He missed the boat by buying stocks well after the prices went up. See:* hit-and-miss.
—n. **1** the failure to hit s.t. **2 miss** or **Miss** a form of address for an unmarried woman or girl, used alone or before her last name: *The store clerk said, "How may I help you, miss?"||How do you do, Miss Jones? See:* Ms., USAGE NOTE.

mis·sile /ˈmɪsəl/ n. **1** an object that is thrown or shot, such as a bullet, arrow, stone: *The missile that broke the window turned out to be a rock.* **2** a cigar-shaped rocket with explosives: *A missile struck the ship and sank it.* -n. [U] **missilery** /ˈmɪsəlri/.

miss·ing /ˈmɪsɪŋ/ adj. not there, absent: *He is missing from class; maybe he's sick.*

mis·sion /ˈmɪʃən/ n. **1** the purpose of the business that a person or organization conducts: *The ambassador's mission is to work for peace with other countries.* **2** a group of people sent to another country for a specific purpose: *A trade mission left Washington to conduct negotiations about business in China.* **3** a religious settlement: *Many towns in California were originally missions of the Catholic church.*
—v.frml. to send on a mission

mis·sion·ar·y /ˈmɪʃəˌnɛri/ n. **-ries** a person, esp. a member of the clergy, sent on a religious mission to convert others to a faith: *Christian missionaries are sent all over the world.*

mis·sive /ˈmɪsɪv/ *n.frml.* a letter or document, usu. formal: *She received a missive from the tax collector asking for the payment of an overdue bill.*

mis·step /mɪsˈstɛp, ˈmɪsˌstɛp/ *n.* **1** a wrong step, (*syn.*) a false step: *If you make a mis-step when you climb a mountain, you can fall.* **2** *fig.* a social mistake, (*syn.*) a faux pas: *He made a misstep at the party when the hostess heard him say her food was bad.*

mis·sus /ˈmɪsəz, -səs/ *n.infrml.* old usage one's wife: *My missus and I went to the movies last night.*

miss·y /ˈmɪsi/ *n.infrml.* old usage **1** a form of address to a girl: *"It's nice to meet you, young missy," said the girl's neighbor.* **2** a girl's nickname: *Missy, that's a pretty dress you have on today.*

mist /mɪst/ *n.* **1** [U] fog, very fine drops of water forming a cloud near the ground: *Mist rises from the fields in the morning.* **2** [C] a fine spray: *She sprayed a mist of perfume on her arms.*
—*v.* to form mist, esp. a very fine rain: *It is misting outside now.* *-adj.* **misty.**

mis·take /mɪˈsteɪk/ *n.* an error, (*syn.*) an inaccuracy: *The waiter made a mistake in adding up the bill.*
—*v.* **mistook** /mɪˈstʊk/, **mistaken, mistaking, mistakes** to have a wrong idea, to identify s.o. incorrectly: *I mistook that woman for a friend of mine, but she's a stranger.*

mis·tak·en /mɪˈsteɪkən/ *adj.* & *past.part* of mistake, incorrect, wrong: *He was mistaken when he thought I was on vacation; I wasn't.*

mis·ter /ˈmɪstər/ *n.abbr.* **Mr.** a form of address for a man: *Excuse me, mister, can you tell me what time it is?||Mr. Smith is in his office.*

mis·tle·toe /ˈmɪsəlˌtoʊ/ *n.* [U] an evergreen parasitic plant with poisonous pearl-like berries: *At Christmastime in some countries, people must kiss when they walk under the mistletoe.*

mis·tress /ˈmɪstrɪs/ *n.* **-tresses 1** the female head of a household: *Is the mistress of the house at home?* **2** a woman in a sexual relationship with a man who is not her husband: *She is the mayor's mistress, but no one knows it.*

mis·tri·al /ˈmɪsˌtraɪəl, -ˌtraɪl/ *n.* a trial that a judge says is not valid and must be canceled because of mistakes or misconduct: *Several witnesses lied about the defendant's guilt, so the judge declared the case a mistrial.*

mis·un·der·stand·ing /ˌmɪsʌndərˈstændɪŋ/ *n.* **1** a mistaken idea, (*syn.*) a misinterpretation: *We had a misunderstanding about the time of our meeting.* **2** an argument, disagreement: *We had a misunderstanding over salary, but later agreed.*

mite /maɪt/ *n.infrml.* **1** a bit, small amount: *There's a mite of coldness in the air today.* **2** a tiny parasitic insect: *That cat has mites in its ears.*

mi·ter /ˈmaɪtər/ *n.* a pointed religious ceremonial hat: *The bishop wore his miter to Christmas mass.*

mit·i·gate /ˈmɪtəˌɡeɪt/ *v.frml.* **-gated, -gating, -gates** to lessen, reduce the intensity or pain of s.t.: *Cool weather from Canada mitigated the heat wave in New York.* *-adj.* **mitigating;** *-n.* [U] **mitigation** /ˌmɪtəˈɡeɪʃən/.

mitt /mɪt/ *n.* **1** a baseball glove: *The catcher held up his mitt to show he was ready to play baseball.* **2** a mitten **3** *slang* one's hand: *When I get my mitts on my paycheck this week, I'll have some fun.*

mit·ten /ˈmɪtn/ *n.* a glove that covers the fingers together and the thumb separately: *Children wear mittens in winter because they are easier to put on their hands.*

mix /mɪks/ *v.* **mixes 1** to blend together, stir: *I mixed the lettuce and tomatoes with salad dressing.* **2** to mingle with other people, socialize: *Guests mixed with each other at the party.* **3 to get mixed up with** or **in:** to be involved, esp. in s.t. that gets one into trouble: *She got mixed up with some bad people and almost went to jail.* **4** *phrasal v.* **to mix it up:** to fight: *Two football players mixed it up and were thrown out of the game.* **5** *phrasal v. sep.* **to mix s.o. or s.t. up:** to confuse, replace one thing with another by mistake: *My teacher mixed my test up with another person's who has the same last name.||She mixed them up! See:* mix-up.
—*n.* **mixes 1** a blend of different things: *That bread is made of a mix of wheat and oatmeal.* **2** a food preparation that is sold already packaged: *She made a cake from a mix by adding water and an egg and then baking it.*
—*adj.* **mixed up:** confused: *In a hurry, I got all mixed up and left my keys at home.*

mixed bag *n.slang* a combination of good and bad ideas or things: *College is a mixed bag for him; he likes some of his courses, but not others.*

mixed marriage *n.* a marriage between two people of different races, religions, or cultures: *He is African American and she is Asian; they have a mixed marriage.*

M

mix·er /'mɪksər/ *n.* **1** a drink, such as cola or soda water, to mix with alcoholic beverages: *He uses tonic water as a mixer with vodka.* **2** a machine used in cooking to mix or blend ingredients: *She uses a hand mixer to make bread.* **3** a social event, usu. a dance where men and women socialize: *Our college has a mixer every two weeks.*

mix·ture /'mɪkstʃər/ *n.* a combination of elements: *That salad is a mixture of fruits on lettuce.*

mix-up *n.* a confused situation: *There was a mix-up at the hospital where two babies were given to the wrong mothers.*

mmm /mm/ an expression of pleasure, used especially when s.t. tastes good: *Mmm, that ice cream is delicious!*

mne·mon·ic /nɪ'manɪk/ *n.* [C;U] s.t., as a phrase or short poem, that helps you to remember s.t. else: *"Every Good Boy Does Fine" is a mnemonic for the order of the musical notes E G B D F.*

moan /moʊn/ *v.* **1** to make low sounds of pain or pleasure: *He cut his thumb with a knife and moaned in pain.* **2** to complain: *She is always moaning about how much work she has.*
—*n.* the sound of moaning: *He let out a moan when he hit his thumb.*

moat /moʊt/ *n.* a ditch filled with water for defense of a building, such as a castle: *A bridge goes over the castle's moat.*

mob /mab/ *n.* a disorderly, violent mass of people: *A mob gathered in the town square to protest new tax increases.*
—*v.* **mobbed, mobbing, mobs** to act like a mob: *Shoppers mobbed the stores for big holiday sales.*

mobbed /mabd/ *adj. & past part. of* mob, crowded: *The grocery store was mobbed on Saturday morning.*

mo·bile /'moʊˌbil, moʊ'bil/ *n.* a hanging sculpture or toy: *A mobile of paper birds hangs over the baby's bed.*
—*adj.* /'moʊbəl, -ˌbil, -ˌbaɪl/ movable, capable of going from one place to another: *She broke her leg but is now mobile and can walk with a cane.*

mobile home /'moʊbəl, -ˌbil, -ˌbaɪl/ *n.* a small house made of metal that can be pulled by a car or truck: *The retired couple lives in a two-bedroom mobile home near a lake. See:* trailer, motor home.

mobile home

mo·bil·ity /moʊ'bɪləti/ *n.* [U] the ability to be mobile: *Gradually old age limited his mo-*

bility, *and he became more dependent on others.*

mo·bi·lize /'moʊbəˌlaɪz/ *v.* **-lized, -lizing, -lizes** to organize and get ready to move: *After the earthquake, the Red Cross mobilized many workers to help people* -*n.* **mobilization** /ˌmoʊbələ'zeɪʃən/.

moc·ca·sin /'makəsən/ *n.* a soft shoe without a heel: *Moccasins are often decorated with pretty beads.*

moccasins

mock /mak/ *v.* to make fun of s.o., usu. by imitating, (*syn.*) to ridicule: *The older children mocked the way the baby tried to speak.*
—*adj.* in imitation, fake: *Soldiers fought a mock battle in training exercises.*

mock·er·y /'makəri/ *n.* **1** [U] ridicule, expressed with disrespect: *The crowd's mockery of the speaker made him leave the room.* **2** *sing.* an insincere imitation: *His trial was a mockery of justice; everyone knew he was guilty, yet he was found innocent.*

mock·ing·bird /'makɪŋˌbərd/ *n.* a North American songbird with grayish tan feathers: *Mockingbirds imitate the songs of other birds.*

mock-up *n.* a model of what s.t. will look like: *Architects make mock-ups of what their buildings will look like.*

mod·al auxiliary /'moʊdl/ *n.* (in grammar) a verb that indicates a mood (the likelihood or factuality of s.t.) or a tense and is always used with another verb: *Some modal auxiliaries are "can," "may," and "might." See:* mood, **2**; tense.

USAGE NOTE: The modal auxiliaries in English are: *can, could, may, might, must, shall, should, will, would.* The modal auxiliary is used before the base form of the main verb: *I will be home late tonight. Can you make dinner for me?*

mode /moʊd/ *n.* [C;U] **1** a manner, way, condition of doing s.t.: *We were in panic mode when the computer crashed.* **2** [U] fashion: *She always dresses in the latest mode; she's very stylish.*

mod·el /'madl/ *n.* **1** a small version of s.t.: *An architect made a one-foot-tall model of the new office building.* **2** a person who poses for artists or with products for sale: *She is a model and often appears in fashion magazines.*
—*adj.* a good example: *He is a model student and always does his homework.*
—*v.* **1** to serve as a model for artists' products: *He models for painting students.* **2** to shape as

with the hands: *She models clay into pots.* **3** to make a model of s.t.: *He models designs of buildings for architects.* **4 to model on** or **after:** to take s.o. as an example: *She modeled herself after her successful mother. See:* role model.

mo·dem /ˈmoʊdəm, -ˌdɛm/ *n.* (in computers) an electronic device for sending or receiving computer data over telephone lines: *We send product orders from our office to the warehouse via modem.*

mod·er·ate /ˈmɑdəˌreɪt/ *v.* **-ated, -ating, -ates** **1** to become less in strength or severity: *The hurricane's high winds moderated as it reached the shore.* **2** to be in charge of a discussion group: *The senior news reporter moderated a discussion between politicians. -n.* **moderator.**
—*adj.* /ˈmɑdərɪt/ **1** in the middle, not large or small, (*syn.*) modest: *He makes a moderate income.* **2** not high or low, comfortable

mod·er·a·tion /ˌmɑdəˈreɪʃən/ *n.* [U] non-extreme behavior: *She drinks alcohol only in moderation.*

mod·ern /ˈmɑdərn/ *adj.* **1** related to today's life, current: *Most modern women work outside the home.* **2** new, (*syn.*) avant garde: *Modern computers keep getting faster and faster.*
—*n.* a person, esp. an artist, doing what is new: *The moderns in art paint mostly abstractions. -n.* [U] **modernism; modernity** /məˈdɜrnəti, mɑ-/.

mod·ern·ize /ˈmɑdərˌnaɪz/ *v.* **-ized, izing, izes** to improve s.t., bring up to date: *We modernized our computer systems with the newest equipment. -n.* [U] **modernization** /ˌmɑdərnəˈzeɪʃən/.

mod·est /ˈmɑdɪst/ *adj.* **1** describing a person who does not brag or boast: *She has won many athletic prizes, but she is so modest that she rarely talks about them.* **2** not large, (*syn.*) moderate: *He lives on a modest income in a modest house. -n.* [U] **modesty.**

mod·i·cum /ˈmɑdɪkəm/ *n.frml.* a small amount of s.t.: *He gives only a modicum of attention to his studies.*

mod·i·fi·ca·tion /ˌmɑdəfəˈkeɪʃən/ *n.* [C;U] a change, (*syn.*) alteration: *Architects made modifications in the building by taking down walls to make larger rooms.*

mod·i·fi·er /ˈmɑdəˌfaɪər/ *n.* (in grammar) a word or phrase that describes another: *Adjectives are modifiers that describe nouns, such as "good" in "We had a good time."*

mod·i·fy /ˈmɑdəˌfaɪ/ *v.* **-fied, -fying, -fies** **1** to change s.t., alter: *He was loud and angry, and his friends told him to modify his behavior.* **2** (in grammar) to describe s.t.: *An adjective*

such as *"blue" modifies a noun, such as "dress."*

mod·ish /ˈmoʊdɪʃ/ *adj. old usage* stylish, well dressed in the latest fashions: *She loves new clothes and is always modish.*

mod·u·late /ˈmɑdʒəˌleɪt/ *v.* **-lated, -lating, lates** to change the level, strength, or tone of s.t.: *Her teacher taught the singer how to modulate her voice in singing a difficult passage.*

mod·u·la·tion /ˌmɑdʒəˈleɪʃən/ *n.* [C;U] the change in the type of radio waves: *I listen to both AM (amplitude modulation) and FM (frequency modulation) radio programs.*

mod·ule /ˈmɑdʒul/ *n.* **1** a part of a whole, such as a section in a course: *Our English course is divided into modules on poetry, drama, and novels.* **2** a section of a space vehicle: *The passenger module released from the rocket after takeoff. -adj.* **modular** /ˈmɑdʒələr/.

mo·gul /ˈmoʊgəl/ *n.* an important, powerful, person, (*syn.*) a magnate: *Years ago, moguls ran the movie studios in Hollywood.*

mo·hair /ˈmoʊˌhɛr/ *n.* [U] the soft hair of the Angora goat and wool cloth made from it: *In winter, he wears a warm mohair scarf.*

moist /mɔɪst/ *adj.* slightly wet, damp: *From working hard, her face was moist with sweat.*

moist·en /ˈmɔɪsən/ *v.* to make a little bit wet, dampen: *He moistened a sponge with water and wiped the table.*

mois·ture /ˈmɔɪstʃər/ *n.* [U] dampness, small amount of liquid on s.t.: *The moisture in the air makes it humid today.*

mois·tur·ize /ˈmɔɪstʃəˌraɪz/ *v.* **-ized, -izing, -izes** to add liquid: *She moisturizes her hands with cream. -n.* **moisturizer.**

mo·lar /ˈmoʊlər/ *n.* a large back tooth, used for chewing: *The dentist took a bad molar out of my mouth.*

mo·las·ses /məˈlæsɪz/ *n.* [U] **1** a thick, dark sweet liquid made from sugarcane: *He adds molasses to the bread he bakes.* **2 as slow as molasses:** very slowly: *He walks as slow as molasses.*

mold (1) /moʊld/ *n.* a hollow form into which materials are put to shape objects, such as tools, toys, candy, etc.: *Workers pour hot plastic into molds to make toys.*
—*v.* **1** to form into a shape: *She molded the clay into a pot with her hands.* **2** to develop one's character: *Her personality was molded by her strict parents.*

mold (2) *n.* [U] a fungus that grows on materials, such as cloth, rubber, plants, etc.: *Mold has formed on the bread, so we cannot eat it. -adj.* **moldy.**

mold·ing /ˈmoʊldɪŋ/ *n.* [U] a strip of decorative wood or plaster at the tops and bottoms of walls

M

mole /moʊl/ *n.* **1** a small, dark, raised growth on the skin: *A mole on one's cheek is sometimes called a beauty mark.* **2** a small rodent that digs in the earth: *Moles dig little tunnels in the ground.* **3** a chemical measurement **4** *infrml.fig.* a spy: *There is a mole in the intelligence agency who is sending secrets to the enemy.*

mol·e·cule /'malɪ,kyul/ *n.* (in chemistry) the smallest unit of the elements of a substance: *The structure of molecules can be seen under an electron microscope.* -*adj.* **molecular** /mə'lɛkyələr/.

mo·lest /mə'lɛst/ *v.* **1** to annoy, bother with comments, etc.: *The bigger children in the neighborhood molested the younger ones.* **2** to abuse sexually: *He molested children and was sent to jail for 30 years.* -*n.* [U] **molestation** /,moʊlɛ'steɪʃən, ,ma-/.

mol·li·fy /'malə,faɪ/ *v.frml.* **-fied, -fying, -fies** to calm, reduce s.o.'s anger or discomfort: *A customer was unhappy, and the store manager mollified her by returning her money.*

mol·lusk /'maləsk/ *n.* any of a class of soft, boneless animals living inside hard shells, such as clams, oysters, and scallops: *Fishermen can make a good living by fishing for mollusks.*

molt /moʊlt/ *v.n.* in animals, to lose old skin, feathers, shells, etc.: *Birds <v.> molt in the late summer and grow their winter feathers.||Their summer <n.> molt (or) <adj.> molting season has passed.*

mol·ten /'moʊltn, -tən/ *adj. past part. of* melt, melted by a great heat: *Molten lava flows from the volcano.*

mom /mam/ *n.infrml.* short for mommy, mother: *Mom, can I go to the movies tonight?*

mom-and-pop store *n.infrml.fig.* a small family business: *He runs the mom-and-pop drugstore on the corner.*

mo·ment /'moʊmənt/ *n.* **1** a brief period of time, such as a few seconds to several minutes: *I am on the telephone, but will be with you in a moment.* **2** a short period: *World War II was a terrible moment in world history.* **3** moment of truth: when s.t. important will be known: *The moment of truth came when the jury gave its verdict.* -*adv.* **momentarily** /,moʊmən'tɛrəli/; -*adj.* **momentary** /'moʊmən,tɛri/.

mo·men·tous /moʊ'mɛntəs, mə-/ *adj.* greatly significant, very important: *Presidents of countries make momentous decisions that affect the lives of millions of people.*

mo·men·tum /moʊ'mɛntəm, mə-/ *n.* [U] the speed at which s.t. moves, (*syn.*) impetus: *The big ship started to move, then gradually reached full momentum.*

mom·ma /'mamə/ *n.infrml.* mother

mom·my /'mami/ *n.infrml.* **-mies** mother

mon·arch /'manərk, -,nark/ *n.* a ruler by birth, such as a king or queen: *Monarchs ruled England for centuries.* -*adj.* **monarchal** /mə'narkəl/; **monarchical** /mə'narkɪkəl/.

mon·ar·chism /'manər,kɪzəm/ *n.* [U] the belief in government by monarchs: *Monarchism is less common now than it used to be.*

mon·ar·chy /'manərki/ *n.* a government run by a monarch usu. with limited powers: *The monarchy in England plays an important role in British culture.*

mon·as·ter·y /'manə,stɛri/ *n.* **-ies** a place where monks live, work, and pray: *Some monasteries are open to the public as a place to rest and meditate. See:* convent.

mo·nas·tic /mə'næstɪk/ *adj.* **1** related to monks: *He joined a monastic order.* **2** referring to a plain, simple lifestyle: *He leads a monastic life; he works hard and doesn't go out.*

Mon·day /'mʌn,deɪ, -di/ *n.* the day of the week between Sunday and Tuesday: *Many people do not like to go to work on Mondays after having the weekend off.*

mon·e·tar·ism /'manətə,rɪzəm/ *n.* [U] a policy of influencing a nation's economy by the government's controlling its money supply: *Monetarism is a controversial economic theory.* -*n.adj.* **monetarist.**

mon·e·tar·y /'manə,tɛri/ *adj.* related to money, fiscal: *He doesn't have much monetary sense; he's always wasting his money.*

mon·e·tize /'manə,taɪz/ *v.* **-tized, -tizing, -tizes** **1** to print or coin money **2** to convert government bonds and other debt into currency, liquidate: *The government monetized its bonds and spent the money on new projects.*

mon·ey /'mʌni/ *n.* [U] **1** a medium of exchange, such as paper currency: *Money can't buy you love.* **2** *infrml.* **for my money:** in my opinion: *For my money, that movie we saw last night was great.* **3** money's worth: to receive good value: *I have worn these shoes for two years and really got my money's worth.* **4** to make money: to earn money or profit: *Her investments make money every year.*

money belt *n.* a belt with pockets for money to hide under clothes: *When he travels, he keeps his cash in a money belt around his waist. See:* fanny pack.

mon·eyed /'mʌnid/ *adj.* having money, rich: *She married a man from a moneyed family.*

mon·ey-grub·ber /'mʌni,grʌbər/ *n.infrml.* a greedy person who tries to make money from every activity: *He is such a money-grubber that he won't answer a question unless you tell him how much you will pay him.* -*adj.n.* **money-grubbing.**

mon·ey·mak·er /'mʌni,meɪkər/ *n.* a product or person who makes a good profit for a business: *That new saleswoman is already a moneymaker for our company.*

money market *n.* a financial market where short-term debt instruments, such as government treasury bonds, are traded: *Big money-market centers are New York, London, and Tokyo.*

money-market fund *n.* a fund that sells shares invested in short-term debt and pays interest to buyers: *Many people put money in money-market funds to get higher interest payments than banks offer. See:* mutual fund.

money order *n.* a check to a specific person, business, etc., that one can buy with cash: *I bought a $300 money order at the post office and sent it to my mother.*

mon·grel /ˈmaŋgrəl, ˈmʌŋ-/ *n.adj.* a dog of mixed breed: *Our family dog is a mongrel we got at the animal shelter.*

mon·i·ker /ˈmanɪkər/ *n.slang* a nickname: *One cowboy told another that his moniker was Red.*

mon·i·tor /ˈmanətər/ *n.* **1** a screen, as on a television or computer, that displays information: *I looked at the monitor in the airport to see when my plane leaves.* **2** a person or machine that checks on the performance of s.t.: *When the teacher leaves the room, she tells a student to be a monitor so all the children will behave well.*
—*v.* to observe the actions of others: *The boss monitors the quality of her employees' work.*

monk /mʌŋk/ *n.* a member of an all-male religious order who lives in a monastery: *The Buddhist monk meditated all day.*

mon·key /ˈmʌŋki/ *n.* **1** any of a variety of primates with human-like faces, long tails, and excellent climbing ability: *Monkeys spend most of their lives in trees.* **2 to have a monkey on one's back: a.** to be addicted to drugs: *He has a monkey on his back and can't get it off.* **b.** to be greatly troubled and burdened: *She has a monkey on her back, because she's in a bad marriage and poor health.* **3** *infrml.* **to make a monkey out of s.o.:** to make a fool of s.o., embarrass: *One lawyer made a monkey out of another by showing that he did not know the law.*
—*v.* **-keyed, -keying, -keys** *phrasal v. infrml.* **to monkey around:** to handle s.t. in a casual way, to play with: *I monkeyed around with trying to fix my car, but I finally took it to a mechanic.*

monkey business *n.infrml.* illegal or dishonest actions: *There is monkey business with tax money going on in the state capitol.*

monkey wrench *n.* **1** a tool with one fixed end and one movable end **2** *infrml.* **to throw a monkey wrench into s.t.:** to mess s.t. up

badly: *A snowstorm threw a monkey wrench into our vacation plans; we could not leave.*

mon·o /ˈmanoʊ/ *adj. prefix* single, one
—*n.infrml. short for* mononucleosis

mon·o·chrome /ˈmanəˌkroʊm/ *n.* [U] *adj.* s.t. in only one color or shades of it: *Early photographers worked only in <n.> monochrome* (or) *<adj.> monochrome film. -adj.* **monochromatic** /ˌmanəkroʊˈmætɪk/.

mo·nog·a·mist /məˈnagəmɪst/ *n.* a person who has only one husband or wife at a time: *In California, the law says that you must be a monogamist.*

mo·nog·a·my /məˈnagəmi/ *n.* [U] having only one husband or wife at one time: *Catholic tradition requires monogamy. -adj.* **monogamous.** *See:* polygamy.

mon·o·gram /ˈmanəˌgræm/ *n.v.* **-grammed, -gramming, -grams** a symbol of identity, usu. one's initials, (*syn.*) an insignia: *He has his <n.> monogram on his bath towels.*

mon·o·lin·gual /ˌmanəˈlɪŋgwəl/ *adj.* having only one language: *Most Americans are monolingual in English. See:* bilingual.

mon·o·lith /ˈmanəˌlɪθ/ *n.* **1** a large, thick piece of rock that stands alone: *Ancient peoples put up monoliths as religious monuments.* **2** *fig.* referring to s.t. large, solid, and hard to get inside: *The government is such a monolith that I don't want to deal with it. -adj.* **monolithic** /ˌmanəˈlɪθɪk/.

mon·o·logue /ˈmanəˌlɔg, -lag/ *n.* a long talk by only one person, usu. in drama: *The comedian gave a long monologue of jokes. See:* dialogue.

mon·o·nu·cle·o·sis /ˌmanəˌnukliˈoʊsɪs/ *n.* [U] an infectious viral disease with fatigue and swollen glands, called the "kissing disease": *Many students get mononucleosis and must rest in bed.*

mo·nop·o·lize /məˈnapəˌlaɪz/ *v.* **-lized, -lizing, -lizes 1** to control a market completely: *An electric power company monopolizes the power supply in this area.* **2** *infrml.fig.* to dominate s.o. or s.t.: *When she is at a party, she monopolizes the conversation and won't let others speak. -n.* **monopolization** /məˌnapələˈzeɪʃən/.

mo·nop·o·ly /məˈnapəli/ *n.* **-lies** the control of an entire market by only one person, business, or organization: *The government has laws against monopolies in many industries.*

mon·o·rail /ˈmanəˌreɪl/ *n.* a train that moves on a single rail: *A monorail takes people up the mountain.*

mon·o·syl·la·ble /ˈmanəˌsɪləbəl/ *n.* a word that has one syllable: *She used three important monosyllables: I love you. -adj.* **monosyllabic** /ˌmanəsɪˈlæbɪk/.

M

mon·o·the·ism /'manǝθi,ızǝm/ n. [U] belief in a single supreme god: *Monotheism is a fundamental belief of Judaism.* -adj. **monotheistic** /,manǝθi'ıstık/.

mon·o·tone /'manǝ,toʊn/ n. a tone of voice that stays the same: *The speaker's monotone bored the audience and many people fell asleep.*

mo·not·o·nous /mǝ'natnǝs/ adj. boring and without change: *She thought life in a small town was monotonous.* -adv. **monotonously;** -n. [U] **monotony.**

mon·soon /man'sun/ n. **1** a heavy rain storm, esp. of southeast Asia: *A monsoon struck the coastline.* **2** a seasonal wind in southeastern Asia that changes direction: *The monsoons from April to October bring rain to the area.*

mon·ster /'manstǝr/ n. **1** a scary, imaginary creature, usu. a person, animal, or plant: *Some films show monsters, such as a giant lizard or gorilla.* **2** a very cruel person or animal: *The murderer is a monster who cuts his victims up.* —adj.fig. s.t. unusually big or violent: *A monster hurricane destroyed the coastline.*

mon·strous /'manstrǝs/ adj. **1** extremely ugly, (syn.) hideous: *Monstrous reptiles lived millions of years ago.* **2** outrageously bad: *The killer committed monstrous acts.* **3** very large, huge -n. **monstrosity** /man'strasǝti/.

mon·tage /man'taʒ, moʊn-/ n. **1** (in art) things, such as pictures, cut out and placed near or overlapping each other, (syn.) a collage: *An artist did a montage of pictures from city life.* **2** a collection of short pieces of film: *The movie was a montage of scenes of life in New York City.*

Mon·te·zu·ma's revenge /,mantǝ'zumǝz/ n.infrml.fig. diarrhea and stomach pains: *North American tourists in Mexico often suffer Montezuma's revenge.*

month /mʌnθ/ n. a time period of approx. 30 days as one of 12 months that make a year: *His rent costs $500 a month, and he pays it on the first of the month.*

month·ly /'mʌnθli/ adv. done each month: *She washes her car monthly.* —n. adj. **-lies** a magazine published monthly: *I subscribe to several <n.> monthlies* (or) *<adj.> monthly magazines.*

mon·u·ment /'manyǝmǝnt/ n. a statue, building, etc., built in memory of a person or historical event: *The Vietnam Memorial in Washington, D.C. is a monument to the soldiers who died in the Vietnam War.*

mon·u·men·tal /,manyǝ'mɛntl/ adj. having large proportions, endurance, or importance: *Tolstoy's* War and Peace *is a monumental book.*

moo /mu/ n. the sound made by a cow —v. to make a sound like a cow's moo: *Cows mooed in the pasture.* -adj. n. **mooing.**

mooch /mutʃ/ n.infrml. **mooches** a person who always asks for money, food, and things from other people: *He is a real <n.> mooch who is always asking for money and cigarettes.* -n. **moocher.**

mood /mud/ n. **1** an emotional state or feeling, such as happiness or sadness: *She is in a good mood today and smiles a lot.* **2** (in grammar) verb forms that show if the speaker regards s.t. as a fact, possibility, or command, etc.; the moods include the indicative, imperative, and conditional: *"Do your homework every day" expresses the imperative mood.*‖*"It might rain tomorrow" is in the conditional or subjunctive mood.*

mood·y /'mudi/ adj. **-ier, -iest** changing one's moods often, including feeling sad, irritable, or angry: *He is a moody guy, one day happy, the next day sad.* -adv. **moodily.**

moon /mun/ n. **1** the natural satellite that orbits earth: *The moon is Earth's nearest neighbor in space.* **2** any celestial body that orbits **3 once in a blue moon:** rarely, almost never: *She works all the time and takes a vacation once in a blue moon.* **4 to ask for the moon:** to ask for too much: *All I want is a small salary increase; I'm not asking for the moon.* —v. to miss s.o., (syn.) to pine for s.o.: *He moons for his girlfriend while she's away.*

moon·beam /'mun,bim/ n. a ray of light from the moon: *Moonbeams shine in through my window at night.*

moon·light /'mun,laıt/ n. [U] light from the moon, esp. a full moon: *When the moon is full, you can see well in the moonlight.* -adj. **moonlit** /'mun,lıt/.

—v.infrml. **-lighted, -lighting, -lights** to have a second job (often at night) in addition to regular work: *She works for a company as a computer technician and she moonlights for individual computer owners.* -n. [U] **moonlighting.** See: freelance.

moon·shine /'mun,ʃaın/ n. **1** moonlight: *He kissed her under the moonshine.* **2** infrml.fig. whisky made and sold illegally: *Moonshine was made when alcohol was illegal in the USA.* -n. **moonshiner.**

moor /mʊr/ v. to tie a boat or other vehicle to a pier, to drop anchor, etc.: *Sailors moored their boat to a dock and went onshore.*

moor·ing /'mʊrıŋ/ n. a place where s.t., esp. a boat, can be tied and made secure: *In the harbor, there are moorings at docks and buoys.*

moose /mus/ n.pl. **moose** the largest member of the deer family with dark brown coat, short neck, and long nose, living in northern North America, Europe, and Asia: *A male moose is over 2 meters (6') high at the shoulder.*

moot /mut/ adj. **a moot point** or **question:** open to discussion: *It's a moot question where to go on vacation this year.*

M

mop /map/ *n.* cleaning equipment made of a sponge or rope-like pieces at the end of a long handle: *A worker wet the <n.> mop and <v.> mopped the floor to clean up the spill.*
—*v.* **mopped, mopping, mops** *phrasal v. sep.*
to mop s.t. up: a. to use a mop: *A worker mopped up the floor this morning.||He mopped it up.* **b.** *fig.* to finish a job: *The army won the battle, and soldiers mopped up a few areas of resistance that were left.||They mopped them up.*

mope /moup/ *v.* **moped, moping, mopes** to act dull, without energy, in low spirits: *He feels sad and mopes around his apartment all day.*
—*n.* a person who mopes: *She has become a mope lately.*

mo·ped /'mou,pɛd/ *n.* a type of bicycle with a small motor: *He rides a moped to work.*

mor·al /,mɔrəl, 'mar-/ *adj.* related to what is right or wrong: *She is a very moral person who acts correctly all the time; she never steals or lies.* -*adv.* **morally.**
—*n.* an idea about correct living, esp. an idea shown by a story: *"The truth will out" is a moral that means that the truth will eventually be told.*

mo·rale /mə'ræl/ *n.* [U] the level of enthusiasm and confidence a person or group has for what they are doing: *Morale in our company is high after good sales last year.*

mor·al·ist /'mɔrəlɪst, 'mar-/ *n.* **1** a person who teaches morals and ethics **2** a person concerned about the moral behavior of other people: *That minister is a moralist with strict standards of behavior.* -*adj.* **moralistic** /,mɔrə'lɪstɪk, ,mar-/.

mo·ral·i·ty /mə'ræləti, mɔ-/ *n.* [U] standards, beliefs about what is right and wrong behavior, esp. regarding sex: *Religious people talk about the need for greater morality in every era.*

mo·rass /mə'ræs/ *n.* **-rasses 1** a swampy area where it is easy to get stuck: *The dog got caught in a morass and had to be saved.* **2** *fig.* a difficult or dangerous situation like a swamp: *Congress turned into a legislative morass where nothing could become law.*

mor·a·to·ri·um /,mɔrə'tɔriəm/ *n.* **-riums** or **-ria** /-riə/ a delay or ban on s.t.: *A group of nations agreed on a moratorium on the sale of nuclear weapons.*

mor·bid /'mɔrbɪd/ *adj.* **1** referring to a person who has sad or bad thoughts, esp. about death: *He has a morbid sense of humor about human nature.* **2** related to disease: *The stray dog was taken to the animal hospital because of its morbid condition.* -*n.* [U] **morbidity** /mɔr'bɪdəti/.

mor·dant /'mɔrdnt/ *adj.frml.* biting, bitter: *The critic writes mordant reviews about the plays he sees.*

more /mɔr/ *adj.comp.* of many *and* much: additional, added: *She needs to make more money if she wants to buy a car.*
—*adv.* **1** additionally, to a greater degree: *He should study more than he does.* **2 more and more:** to an increasing degree: *She is becoming more and more interested in going into politics.* **3 more often than not:** usually, frequently: *More often than not, he goes to church on Sunday.* **4 more or less:** approximately, about: *That table is more or less 6 feet (2 m) long.*
—*n.* a greater number, degree, etc.: *The <n.> more who come to the party, the <adj.> more fun we'll have, or as they say, "The more, the merrier." See:* less, fewer.

more·o·ver /mɔr'ouvər/ *adv.* in addition: *She is rich; moreover, she is beautiful and generous.*

mo·res /'mɔr,eɪz/ *n.pl.frml.* customs of a people or culture, such as ideas about the family, sex, etc: *Anthropologists study the mores of various cultures.*

morgue /mɔrg/ *n.* a public place where the bodies of people found dead are kept for identification before burial: *The police took an unidentified dead man to the morgue for an autopsy to discover the cause of death. See:* mortuary.

morn /mɔrn/ *n.litr.* morning

morn·ing /'mɔrnɪŋ/ *n.* [C;U] *adj.* the hours between sunrise and noon: *Children go to school in the <n.> morning.*

morning sickness *n.* [U] sickness to the stomach and vomiting in the first few months of pregnancy: *She is two months pregnant and has morning sickness when she gets up each day.*

mo·ron /'mɔr,an/ *n.slang* a stupid, foolish person: *That moron drove past a stop sign and almost hit us!* -*adj.* **moronic** /mə'ranɪk, mɔ-/.

mo·rose /mə'rous/ *adj.* sad, angry, (*syn.*) sullen: *He is a morose man who can find no good in the world.*

mor·phine /'mɔr,fin/ *n.* [U] a strong drug made from opium: *The doctor gave her patient morphine to kill the pain.*

mor·phol·o·gy /mɔr'faləʤi/ *n.* [U] **1** the structure of living organisms and the study of it: *Medical students study human morphology.* **2** the study of word formations: *Linguists study morphology and syntax.* -*adj.* **morphological** /,mɔrfə'laʤɪkəl/.

Morse code /mɔrs/ *n.* a system of communication that uses dots and dashes to replace letters of the alphabet: *Morse code uses signals to send messages.*

mor·sel /'mɔrsəl/ *n.* a small piece of s.t., usu. food: *A morsel of cake was left on the plate.*

M

mor·tal /'mɔrtl/ *adj.* subject to death: *All of us are mortal and will die one day.* -*adv.* **mortally.**

mor·tal·i·ty /mɔr'tæləti/ *n.* [U] **1** the condition of being mortal: *In middle age, he felt his own mortality and became religious.* **2** *sing.* [U] the rate of death from illness or disaster: *The infant mortality rate in some countries is very high.*

mor·tar /'mɔrtər/ *n.* [U] **1** cement, plaster, etc., used to hold stone or brick together: *The library is made of red brick and white mortar.* **2** [C] a type of weapon: *Soldiers fired mortars at the enemy.*
—*v.* **1** to join with mortar **2** to shoot mortars: *Soldiers mortared enemy lines.*

mor·tar·board /'mɔrtər,bɔrd/ *n.* a flat black hat worn for graduation ceremonies: *Students rent their mortarboards and robes for graduation.*

mortarboard

mort·gage /'mɔrgɪʤ/ *n.* a long-term loan from a bank for buying property, which is used as security: *We make monthly payments on our house mortgage.*
—*v.* **-gaged, -gaging, -gages 1** to borrow money against one's house: *Our house is mortgaged.* **2** to put oneself into heavy debt: *She mortgaged her future by having to repay big debts for many years.*

mor·ti·cian /mɔr'tɪʃən/ *n.* a person who organizes funerals and prepares the dead body, (*syn.*) an undertaker: *Most morticians work in funeral homes.* See: undertaker.

mor·ti·fy /'mɔrtə,faɪ/ *v.* **-fied, -fying, -fies** to make s.o. feel shame or embarrassment: *He was mortified when he called his wife by the wrong name* -*n.* [U] **mortification** /,mɔrtəfə'keɪʃən/.

mor·tu·ar·y /'mɔrʧu,ɛri/ *n.* **-ies** a place, usu. in a hospital, where dead bodies are kept before burial: *When the patient died, her body was sent to the mortuary.* See: morgue.

mo·sa·ic /mou'zeɪɪk/ *n.* [C;U] a picture or design made of little colored stones: *Old mosaics show scenes from ancient Greece and Rome.*

mosque /mask/ *n.* a Muslim building of worship: *Muslims pray in the mosques five times a day.*

mos·qui·to /mə'skitou/ *n.* **-toes** or **-tos** small, biting, blood-sucking insects: *Mosquitoes spread malaria in some parts of the world.*

moss /mɔs/ *n.* [C;U] a short, soft plant that grows on the ground and on trees: *Moss grows on trees in our backyard.* -*adj.* **mossy.**

most /moust/ *n.* **1** the highest degree, amount, number, etc.: *I like to vacation in Paris the most of all the cities I have visited.* **2 at most:** at the greatest degree, amount, etc.: *Those fancy shoes should cost at most $100.* **3 to make the most of s.t.:** to take advantage of an opportunity: *I had not been to Tokyo in ten years, so I made the most of my trip and saw everything.*
—*adj. superlative of* many, much, more **1** related to the highest degree, amount, number, etc.: *Last year, he made the most money that he has ever made.* **2 most of all:** regarding the greatest amount, degree, etc.: *I like to eat ice cream most of all.* -*adv.* **mostly.**
—*adv.* for the most part, usually: *I like to vacation mostly in the fall.*

mo·tel /mou'tɛl/ *n.* a hotel next to a highway where motorists park their cars in front of the rooms: *On our vacation, we stayed at a new motel every night.* See: USAGE NOTES: at bed and breakfast, hotel.

moth /mɔθ/ *n.* **moths** any of many insects with wings that are active at night: *Moths got into the closet and made holes in the wool clothes.*

moth·ball /'mɔθ,bɔl/ *n.* a small ball of chemicals that keeps moths away: *I put mothballs in the closet to keep the moths away from the clothes.*

moth-eaten *adj.* **1** with holes eaten by moths: *My best woolen shirt is moth-eaten.* **2** *fig.* old, out of style: *That couch is moth-eaten and stained.*

moth·er /'mʌðər/ *n.* **1** the female parent: *My mother lives in New Hampshire.* **2** the head of a female religious order or organization **3** *infrml. fig.* the greatest, most important of s.t.: *The she-bear that we saw in the park was the mother of all bears; she was so big!*
—*v.* to care for, nurture: *She mothers her two children with loving care.* -*adj.* **motherly.**

moth·er·board /'mʌðər,bɔrd/ *n.* (in computers) a board that holds the main circuit of a computer: *To upgrade my computer, I have to replace the expensive motherboard.*

Mother Goose *n.* the imaginary author of a collection of children's rhymes in 18th-century England: *Children have loved Mother Goose poems for centuries.*

moth·er·hood /'mʌðər,hud/ *n.* [U] the state of being a mother: *Motherhood came late to her, as she had her first child at age 40.*

moth·er·ing /'mʌðərɪŋ/ *n.* [U] care and nurturing given by mothers: *Her child is sickly, so he needs a lot of mothering.*

moth·er-in-law /'mʌðərɪn,lɔ/ *n.* **mothers-in-law** the mother of one's spouse: *His mother-in-law comes to visit every year.*

Mother Nature *n.* a term for nature and its power: *The powerful storms that Mother*

Nature sends across land and sea cause much damage.

Mother's Day *n.* in USA, a holiday on the second Sunday in May that honors mothers: *I sent flowers to my mother for Mother's Day.*

mother superior *n.* a woman in charge of a religious organization, such as a convent or school: *Mothers superior are often teachers as well as religious leaders.*

mother tongue *n.* the first language one speaks as a child: *Her mother tongue is Spanish.*

mo·tif /mou'tif/ *n.frml.* a theme or design element used repeatedly in literature, music, art, and architecture: *The building was decorated with a motif of flowers and circles.*

mo·tion /'mouʃən/ *n.* **1** [U] movement, going from one place to another: *That child is always in motion; she never sits still.* **2** [C] a gesture, movement of the hand, arm, etc.: *I made a motion with my hand to get the attention of the waiter.* **3** [C] a formal request to suggest a proposal to be voted on at a meeting: *The moderator at the town meeting made a motion to vote on new taxes.*
—*v.* to move the hand, arm, etc.: *The queen motioned with her hand to dismiss her visitors.*

motion sickness *n.* [U] feelings of upset stomach, dizziness, etc., when riding in a moving vehicle: *He takes pills for motion sickness when he rides in a car.*

mo·ti·vate /'moutə,veit/ *v.* **-vated, -vating, -vates** to give a reason to do s.t.: *A desire to go to medical school motivates her to study hard every day.* *-n.* **motivation** /,moutə'veiʃən/; *-adj.* **motivational.**

mo·tive /'moutiv/ *n.* a reason, purpose for doing s.t.: *Money was the thief's motive in robbing the bank.*

mot·ley /'matli/ *adj.frml.* varied in color, type, etc.: *The party was a motley mixture of well-dressed businesspeople and poor students.*

mo·tor /'moutər/ *n.* a machine that creates power, such as the engine in a car: *An air conditioner uses an electric motor to cool the air and turn a fan.*
—*v.* to travel in a vehicle: *For our vacation, we motored through Calfornia.*
—*adj.* related to movement of the muscles: *She has good motor coordination.*

mo·tor·bike /'moutər,baik/ *n.* a lightweight motorcycle similar to a bicycle, often with a powerful motor: *Bikers race motorbikes over rough ground.*

mo·tor·boat /'moutər,bout/ *n.* a boat powered by motors usu. without sails: *Our friends have a motorboat that they take on the lake on weekends.*

mo·tor·cade /'moutər,keid/ *n.* a line of cars for important people: *The President rides in a motorcade surrounded by Secret Service agents.*

mo·tor·cy·cle /'moutər,saikəl/ *n.v.* **-cled, -cling, -cles** a two-wheeled vehicle larger than a motorbike, with a powerful engine: *To ride on a <n.> motorcycle gives you a feeling of freedom and speed.*

motorcycle

motor home *n.* a metal house on wheels pulled by another vehicle or driven by itself: *We traveled across the country in a motor home. See:* mobile home.

motor inn *n.* a motel, where motorists stay overnight: *On our trip, we stayed at motor inns along the route. See:* hotel, USAGE NOTE.

mo·tor·ist /'moutərist/ *n.* a person who drives or rides in a car, truck, or motorcycle: *Motorists crowd the highways during rush hour.*

mo·tor·ize /'moutə,raiz/ *v.* **-ized, -izing, -izes** to equip with engines or motor vehicles: *Armies switched to motorized weapons, such as tanks and airplanes, in World War I.*

motor mouth *n.infrml.fig.* a talkative person, esp. one who won't let others talk: *She is a real motor mouth; once she starts talking, she won't let anyone else say anything.*

motor vehicle *n.* a general term for a car, bus, truck, etc: *All motor vehicles must be registered with the state.*

mot·tled /'matld/ *adj.* having different colored marks: *Our dog is mottled with white and brown spots.*

mot·to /'matou/ *n.* **-toes** or **-tos** a short saying that states a basic belief of a nation, organization, etc.: *The motto on the US dollar says "in God we trust."*

mound /maund/ *n.* a rounded pile, heap: *A mound of dirt is in the garden waiting to be spread for planting.*
—*v.* to pile into a mound: *A gardener mounded soil around each plant.*

mount /maunt/ *v.* **1** to increase, go up: *Costs of products are mounting every week.* **2** to climb on: *The cowboy mounted his horse and rode away.* **3** to put on display, hang up: *We mounted new pictures on the wall.‖The theater mounted a production of Romeo and Juliet.* **4** (of animals) to mate, make babies: *The bull mounted the cow.*
—*n.* **1** a horse: *"Where is my mount?" asked the jockey.* **2 Mount** mountain (used in place names): *Mount McKinley*

M

moun·tain /'maʊntn/ n. **1** a tall formation of land and rock higher than a hill: *The mountains south of San Francisco make a pretty picture.* **2** *fig.* a large amount: *There is a mountain of dishes to wash.* **3** *infrml.* **to make a mountain out of a molehill:** to become angry over a small issue: *She made a mountain out of a molehill about getting a B on her paper instead of an A . -adj.* **mountainous.**

moun·tain·eer /ˌmaʊntn'ɪr/ n. a mountain guide or person who climbs mountains for fun: *She is a mountaineer who lives in the Rockies.*

mountain lion n. a large cat with a long tail and tan coat, found from western Canada to the tip of South America, (*syn.*) a cougar: *Mountain lions avoid humans as their greatest natural enemy.*

mountain range n. **1** a group of mountains in a general area: *New York state has several mountain ranges, including the Adirondacks.* **2** a mountain chain

mount·ing /'maʊntɪŋ/ n. **1** [U] the act of climbing on s.t.: *Mounting a horse from the ground requires strength.* **2** [C] the support structure, such as metal bars for a motor or backing for a picture: *The mounting for the motor has rusted and needs to be replaced.*

mourn /mɔrn/ v. **1** to feel sad at the death of s.o.: *The family mourned the death of their grandfather.* **2** to show one's sadness through a traditional act of sorrow for the dead: *Jewish people mourn by reading a prayer called the Kaddish. -n.* **mourner.**

mourn·ful /'mɔrnfəl/ adj. **1** of mourning, sorrow for the dead: *Funerals are mournful events.* **2** having a sad sound: *The boat's horn gave off a low, mournful sound. -adv.* **mournfully.**

mourn·ing /'mɔrnɪŋ/ n. [U] adj. **1** a traditional way of expressing sorrow for a dead person: *Wearing black clothes is a sign of <n.> mourning.* **2** [C] a time of sorrow for the dead: *He went through a long period of <n.> mourning (or) a <adj.> mourning period after the death of his wife.*

mouse /maʊs/ n. **mice** /maɪs/ **1** any of many types of small gray or brown rodents, found worldwide: *<n.pl.> Mice steal food and carry diseases.* **2** *fig.* a quiet, shy person: *He is a little mouse who can't talk to anyone.* **3** (in computers) a small device for controlling computer functions: *I use a mouse to choose documents from my files.*

mouse·trap /'maʊsˌtræp/ n. a device used to catch mice: *We put mousetraps in the kitchen to catch a mouse that was eating our food.*

mousse /mus/ n. [C;U] a cold dessert usu. made of whipped cream, eggs, and flavorings: *I love chocolate mousse.*

mous·y /'maʊsi, -zi/ adj.fig. **-ier, -iest** dull, shy, unattractive: *One of my sisters is lively and cute, the other is mousy.*

mouth /maʊθ/ n. **mouths** /maʊðz/ **1** the opening on the face used for eating food: *With a spoon, the mother put food in her baby's mouth.* **2** an entrance or opening: *People entered the mouth of the cave.* **3** **by word of mouth:** through oral communication: *That new store has not advertised; its business comes by word of mouth.* **4** *infrml.* **to have a big mouth:** to annoy by speaking loudly and offensively: *He has a big mouth and is always telling his friends what to do.* **5** *infrml.* **to open one's big mouth:** to tell secrets or say s.t. harmful: *My boss was going to give me a raise, but I opened my big mouth and said I didn't need it, so she didn't give it to me!* **6 to put words into s.o.'s mouth:** to speak for s.o. else **7 to take the words out of s.o.'s mouth:** to say the same thing s.o. else is about to say
—v. /maʊð/ **1** to move one's mouth as if speaking, but without making any sound: *He could not hear her through the glass, so she mouthed the words.* **2** to speak insincerely: *She mouthed the words her mother told her to say as an apology.*

mouth·ful /'maʊθˌfʊl/ n. **1** an amount equal to the size of one's mouth: *The little boy took mouthfuls of cereal and chewed them one after another.* **2** *fig.* s.t. difficult to pronounce: *The teacher's last name is a mouthful, so the children call her Mrs. B.* **3 to say a mouthful:** to say s.t. important: *When the teacher told us what would be on the test, he said a mouthful.*

mouth·piece /'maʊθˌpis/ n. **1** a part of s.t., such as a musical instrument, that is placed in or near the mouth **2** *fig.* a spokesperson, representative: *The mayor sent his mouthpiece to talk to the reporters.*

mouth-to-mouth adj. related to putting one's mouth on s.o. else's: *A woman almost drowned and a firefighter did mouth-to-mouth resuscitation to revive her.*

mouth·wash /'maʊθˌwɑʃ, -ˌwɔʃ/ n. [C;U] washes a rinse that cleans and freshens the mouth: *I use a mint-flavored mouthwash each morning.*

mouth·wa·ter·ing /'maʊθˌwɔtərɪŋ, -ˌwɑ-/ adj. stimulating the appetite: *The smell of good food cooking on the stove is mouthwatering.*

mov·a·ble /'muvəbəl/ adj. capable of being moved: *Those heavy boxes on wheels are movable.*

move /muv/ v. **moved, moving, moves 1** to go from one place to another: *Traffic moved slowly out of the city at rush hour.* **2** to change a home or office: *We moved from Chicago to New Orleans.* **3** to shift the position of s.t.: *I moved my arms over my head.* **4** to create strong emotions in s.o.: *The singer moved the*

audience to tears. **5** to take a step in a game: *In chess, I moved my queen down the board.* **6** to sell: *Air conditioners move quickly in the summer.* **7** to work or socialize with a certain group: *She moves among the famous in Hollywood.* **8** (in a formal meeting or court of law) to make a motion: *I move that this meeting be adjourned. See:* motion. **9** to empty the bowels: *The hospital patient moved his bowels this morning.* **10** *phrasal v. sep.* **to move (s.o.) along: a.** to move farther away: *After a few weeks, we decided to move along on our trip.* **b. s.o.:** to force s.o. to move: *Police moved the protesters along.* **11** *phrasal v. sep.* **to move (s.o. or s.t.) around: a.** to (cause to) move without stopping: *She makes me nervous because she moves around so much.* **b. s.o.** or **s.t.:** to rearrange: *He decided to move his books around so he could find the ones he needed.* **12** *phrasal v.* **to move away: a.** to live someplace else: *We moved away from New York and live in Florida now.* **b.** to step back: *Firefighters told people to move away from the fire.* **13** *infrml.* **to move heaven and earth:** to try with all one's power: *The son got sick and his parents moved Heaven and Earth with the hospital to try to save him.* **14** *phrasal v.* **to move in:** to go live in: *We bought a new house and moved in last week.* **15** *phrasal v. insep.* **to move in on s.o. or s.t.: a.** to go closer to s.o. or s.t., approach: *The police moved in on the criminal and captured her.* **b.** to take s.o. or s.t. away from s.o., displace: *Another guy moved in on my girlfriend and now she and he are dating.* **16** *phrasal v.* **to move off:** to go away, leave, *(syn.)* to depart: *As we walked closer, the deer moved off.* **17** *phrasal v. insep.* **to move on s.t.:** to finish s.t., conclude it: *The deal is all clear and settled, so we can move on it now.* **18** *phrasal v.* **to move out:** to leave a place permanently, usu. a home: *We moved out of our old house into a small apartment.* **19** *phrasal v. sep.* **to move s.t. up:** to advance, improve one's position: *She is moving up in that company to a better job.*
—*n.* **1** a change of position: *The policeman told the thief not to make a move or he would shoot.* **2** a change of homes: *We made a move from a city apartment to a suburban house.* **3** a player's action: *In chess, each player makes one move at a time.* **4 Don't make a move!:** Stand still!: *The police officer told the criminal, "Don't make a move while I handcuff you!"* **5 on the move: a.** to go to different places: *I have been on the move all day, from work to the supermarket to the post office to the cleaners.* **b.** to be functioning well, in action: *Our plans are really on the move now for marketing our new product.* **6** *infrml.* **to get a move on:** to hurry, move fast: *We should get a move on, or we'll be late*

for the movie. **7 to make a move: a.** to take action: *We should make a move now and offer money for that house.* **b.** to change space: *We made a move downtown to a new set of offices.* **8 to make the move: a.** to change jobs: *I made the move to a new job* (or) *company last month.* **b.** to take a specific action: *I am thinking about going back to school and I should make the move now.* **9** *slang* **to put a move on s.o.:** to make sexual advances to s.o.: *This guy put a move on my girlfriend and asked her for a date, but she said, "No!"*

move·ment /'muvmənt/ *n.* [C;U] **1** going from one place to another, motion: *Movement of traffic is very slow during rush hour.* **2** [U] the ability to move, *(syn.)* mobility: *The worker injured his hand and has no movement in it.* **3** [C] a political or social cause: *A reform movement is underway in government.* **4** [C] (in music) a major division of a symphony or sonata: *The second movement of that symphony is slow and sounds sad.* **5** [U] emptying of the bowels: *The patient had a bowel movement this morning.*

mov·er /'muvər/ *n.* **1** a business or person who moves furniture, etc.: *Movers came in and moved our things to a new apartment.* **2** *infrml.* an important person who makes things happen, a doer: *She is a mover in finance, always working on some big deal.*

mover and shaker *n.infrml.fig.* an important person with the power to make big deals happen: *He is a mover and shaker who wants to build a big new convention center in Chicago.*

mov·ie /'muvi/ *n.* **1** a motion picture, film: *I saw a great movie last night about cowboys.* **2** *pl.* **the movies:** films in general: *We like to go to the movies once a week.*

mov·ing /'muvɪŋ/ *adj.* **1** in motion: *The planets are moving objects in the sky.* **2** creating strong emotions: *The preacher's sermon was very moving.*

moving picture *n. old usage* a motion picture: *"Moving picture" is an old-fashioned term for a movie or film.*

mow /moʊ/ *v.* **mowed, mowed** or **mown** /moʊn/, **mowing, mows** **1** to cut with a mower or blade: *Farmers mow hay to feed cattle.||I mowed the lawn yesterday.* **2** *phrasal v. sep.* **to mow s.t. down:** to kill in great numbers, slaughter: *A machine gun mowed down soldiers by the dozens.||It mowed them down.*

mow·er /'moʊər/ *n.* a machine with sharp blades used to cut grass

mower

or hay: *I use an electric mower to cut my lawn.*

mox·ie /'mɑksi/ *n.infrml.* energy, courage, enthusiasm: *She has a lot of moxie and gets things done quickly and well.*

moz·za·rel·la /ˌmɑtsəˈrɛlə/ *n.* [U] a soft, mild cheese: *I like my pizza made with mozzarella.*

MPH *abbr. for* miles per hour: *The speed limit is 55 MPH.*

USAGE NOTE: Said as "miles per hour," not "MPH."

Mr. /'mɪstər/ *abbr.for* Mister **Messrs.** /'mɛsərz/: *Mr. Jones is here to see you.*

Mr. Right *n.infrml.* a nickname for the perfect man: *Mary Jane finally met Mr. Right and they got married.*

Mrs. /'mɪsɪz/ *abbr.for* Mistress **Mmes.** /meɪˈdɑm, -ˈdæm/ a courtesy title before the name of a married woman: *Mrs. Jones visited the doctor. See:* Ms., USAGE NOTE.

Ms. /mɪz/*abbr.for* Miss or Mrs., a title for a woman that does not indicate marital status: *Ms. Smith is the director of accounting here.*

USAGE NOTE: Use of the title *Ms.* avoids mistakenly calling a married woman *Miss* or a single woman *Mrs.* Many people prefer *Ms.* because it does not refer to marital status, as *Mr.* does not for men.

M

much /mʌtʃ/ *adj.* **more** /mɔr/, **most** /moʊst/ **1** related to a lot of s.t.: *We haven't had much snow this winter.* **2 a bit much:** too much, excessive: *Sometimes he finds the summer heat a bit much and must stop playing.* **3 how much:** used with uncountable nouns to ask about the amount of s.t.: *How much jam is left?||How <pron.> much is left?* **4 not much of a s.t.:** not very good at s.t.: *She likes golf, but is not much of a player.* **5 to make much of:** to give importance to: *He made much of how happy he is to be retired.*
—*n.* a lot, plenty of s.t.: *There was <adj.> much food on the table at the party; I had too <n.> much to eat!*
—*adv.* **1** a great deal, a lot: *She is feeling much better.* **2** often, frequently: *I asked him if he played golf much.* **3** to the degree, extent that: *He said that he plays as much as he wants to.*

USAGE NOTE: *Much* is used with or about uncountable nouns: *much fun.* Use *many* with or about countable nouns: *many boys.*

muck /mʌk/ *n.* [U] **1** deep, sticky mud: *Our car got stuck in the muck on a country road.* **2** mud and manure mixed together: *The barnyard is full of muck when it rains.*

muck·rake /'mʌkˌreɪk/ *v.* **-raked, -raking, -rakes** to search for and publish scandals about public officials: *Reporters from that newspa-*

per muckrake about the candidates for mayor to sell more newspapers. -n. **muckraker.**

mu·cous /'myukəs/ *adj.* **1** related to mucus **2** moist, slippery: *Mucous membranes line the lungs. See:* mucus.

mu·cus /'myukəs/ *n.* [U] a moist substance that protects mucous membranes, lining the nasal passages, lungs, etc: *When you have a chest cold, you cough up mucus from the lungs.*

mud /mʌd/ *n.* [U] **1** a sticky mixture of water and dirt: *In the springtime, dirt roads turn to mud when it rains.* **2 one's name is mud:** to be disgraced: *His name is mud since he cheated on his math exam.*

mud·dle /'mʌdl/ *n.* a mix-up, confused situation: *My taxes are in such a muddle, I'll have to get help with them.*
—*v.* **-dled, -dling, -dles** to act in a confused way: *Computers are difficult to learn to use, but we muddle through and get the job done.* -*adj.* **muddled.**

mud·dy /'mʌdi/ *adj.* **-dier, -diest** **1** full of or covered with mud: *My boots are muddy after walking in the woods.* **2** unclear, confused: *Her writing is muddy and difficult to understand.*
—*v.* **-died, -dying, -dies** **1** to stain, make dirty with mud: *The little girl muddied the kitchen floor after walking in the rain.* **2** *infrml.* **to muddy the waters:** to confuse, make unclear: *He muddied the waters by saying that many new conditions must be added to the contract that we had agreed to sign.*

mud·slide /'mʌdˌslaɪd/ *n.* the falling of a dirt cliff or hillside after rain has turned it to mud: *A mudslide blocked the road.*

mud·sling·ing /'mʌdˌslɪŋɪŋ/ *n.* [U] accusing an opponent, esp. another politician, of doing s.t. wrong: *Both Democrats and Republicans engage in mudslinging in campaigns for mayor in New York.*

muff /mʌf/ *n.* a piece of fur worn to warm the hands: *Women don't wear muffs anymore.*
—*v.infrml.* to do s.t. badly, (*syn.*) to flub: *The actor muffed his lines and needed help.*

muf·fin /'mʌfɪn/ *n.* a small, sweet bread often made of a grain, such as corn, bran, oats, etc.: *I had a bran muffin for breakfast. See:* English muffin.

muf·fle /'mʌfəl/ *v.* **-fled, -fling, -fles** to quiet, lower the sound of s.t.: *I put my hand over my mouth to muffle my words, so only my friend could hear.*

muf·fler /'mʌflər/ *n.* **1** a device that lowers sound as in a motor's exhaust system: *The muffler on my car has a hole and makes a loud noise.* **2** a warm, woolen scarf: *My neck gets cold in winter, so I wear a muffler.*

mug /mʌg/ *n.* **1** a thick cup with a handle: *She drinks a mug of beer at lunch.* **2** *infrml.* one's face: *When you are arrested, the police take a mug shot—a photograph—of you.*

—*v.* **mugged, mugging, mugs** to attack s.o. to rob him or her: *He was mugged in the park.* -*n.* [U] **mugging.**

mug·ger *n.* a criminal who robs others in public: *A mugger in the park hit me on the head and stole my wallet.*

mug·gy /'mʌgi/ *adj.* **-gier, -giest** of damp, warm air, (*syn.*) very humid: *Muggy weather makes people feel uncomfortable.*

mu·lat·to /mə'lɑtoʊ, -'læ-, myʊ-/ *n.adj.* old usage **-toes** or **-tos** a person of mixed racial parentage, usu. one black and one white parent, (*syn.*) biracial: *Angela is a mulatto whose mother is African American and whose father is white.*

USAGE NOTE: *Mulatto* is old usage. If race needs to be mentioned, the term *biracial* is preferable.

---

mul·ber·ry /'mʌl,beri, -bəri/ *n.* **-ries** any of a variety of trees used for their wood, fiber, and fruit, in much of the world: *The leaves of mulberries are food for the worms that spin silk.*

mulch /mʌltʃ/ *n.* [U] *sing.* a layer of material, usu. leaves, grass clippings, etc., put on the earth around plants to protect them: *I put mulch around my tomato plants to protect them from weeds and freezing.*

mule /myul/ *n.* an animal that comes from a female horse bred with a donkey: *Mules are very strong and surefooted.*

mull /mʌl/ *v.* **1** to heat a drink with spices: *We mull wine and spices in the winter.* **2 to mull over:** to think about s.t. long and seriously, (*syn.*) to ponder: *I mulled over the idea of going back to college for weeks.*

multi- /,mʌlti/ *prefix* indicating many of s.t.: *Her cosmetics business has made her a multi-millionaire.*

mul·ti·fac·et·ed /,mʌlti'fæsɪtɪd, ,mʌltaɪ-/ *adj.* having many sides or aspects: *She has multi-faceted talents as both a singer and a dancer.*

mul·ti·lat·er·al /,mʌlti'lætərəl/ *adj.* of s.t. done by or involving many sides: *Multilateral peace talks took place among five nations.*

mul·ti·me·di·a /,mʌlti'midiə, ,mʌltaɪ-/ *adj.n.* **1** a combination of several media, such as newspapers, radio, and TV **2** (in computers) the use of text, sound, graphics, and video in a single computer program: *Ordinary computers can play <n.pl.> multimedia (or) <adj.> multimedia programs on laser discs.*

multimedia player *n.* a device used to play sound, graphics, and video, such as from a laser disc

mul·ti·ple /'mʌltəpəl/ *adj.* many, numerous: *She has multiple reasons for not marrying him.*

multiple-choice *adj.* having many choices for answers, as on a test: *The multiple-choice questions on that test had four possible answers.*

multiple scle·ro·sis /sklə'roʊsɪs/ *n. abbr.* **MS** /'ɛm'ɛs/ [U] a disease of the nervous system that can cause muscle weakness, loss of feeling in part of the body, and problems with speech or vision

mul·ti·plex /'mʌltə,plɛks/ *adj.* of an electronic system that sends and receives multiple messages over the same wire: *Some military communications equipment is multiplex.*

—*n.* **-plexes** a theater with many separate movie theaters within it

mul·ti·pli·ca·tion /,mʌltəplə'keɪʃən/ *n.* [U] **1** the arithmetic operation of multiplying one number by another: *2 times 2 equals 4 is an act of multiplication.* **2** an increase in number, intensity, variety, etc.: *The multiplication of problems at the company continues.*

mul·ti·plic·i·ty /,mʌltə'plɪsəti/ *n.sing.frml.* a great number, a variety: *The new government has a multiplicity of problems to solve.*

mul·ti·pli·er /'mʌltə,plaɪər/ *n.adj.* a number used to multiply another number

mul·ti·ply /'mʌltə,plaɪ/ *v.* **-plied, -plying, -plies** **1** in arithmetic, to increase a number (the multiplicand) by a certain number of times (the multiplier) for a result (the product): *If you multiply 20 five times, you get 100.* **2** to increase in number: *Mice multiply very rapidly by having babies every three weeks.* See: divide.

mul·ti·task·ing /,mʌlti'tæskɪŋ, ,mʌltaɪ-/ *n.* [U] *adj.* the ability of a computer to operate two or more programs at one time: *Her computer is capable of multitasking, so she can run an accounting program at the same time as a word processing program.*

mul·ti·tude /'mʌltə,tud/ *n.* a large number of st, esp. people: *The politician spoke to a multitude of 300,000 gathered to hear her.* -*adj.frml.* **multitudinous** /,mʌltə'tudnəs/.

mum /mʌm/ *adj.* **1** quiet, silent: *I have a secret to tell you, and I'd like you to stay mum about it.* **2 mum's the word:** a request or a promise to keep silent

—*n.* **1** *short for* chrysanthemum, a flower: *For her birthday, I sent a bunch of mums.* **2** *n.infrml.Brit.* mother

—*v.* **-mummed, -mumming, -mums** to pantomime: *He mums for the fun of it.* -*n.* **mummer.**

mum·ble /'mʌmbəl/ *v.n.* **-bled, -bling, -bles** to speak unclearly in a low voice, mutter: *He <v.> mumbles (or) speaks in a <n.> mumble when he talks, so it's hard to understand him.* -*n.* **mumbler.**

M

mum·bo jum·bo /ˈmʌmboʊˈdʒʌmboʊ/ *n.infrml.* [U] meaningless talk, nonsense, *(syn.)* gibberish: *I asked her a question and all that she said to me was mumbo jumbo.*

mum·my /ˈmʌmi/ *n.* **-ies 1** a dead body that has been preserved by an injection of chemicals and wrapped in material: *We saw an ancient Egyptian mummy at the museum.* **2** *infrml.* mother *-v.* **mummify** /ˈmʌmə‚faɪ/.

mumps /mʌmps/ *n.* [U] a contagious viral disease of the glands: *The mumps are a very painful disease that makes your face and throat swell.*

munch /mʌntʃ/ *v.infrml.* **munches** to chew strongly on s.t.: *He munches on potato chips while he watches TV.*

munch·ies /ˈmʌntʃiz/ *n.pl.infrml.* **1** snack foods, such as potato chips, pretzels, raw carrots, etc.: *He served beer and munchies at his party.* **2** a craving, sudden hunger: *At midnight, we got the munchies and ordered a pizza. See:* junk food.

mun·dane /mʌnˈdeɪn/ *adj.frml.* referring to the events of everyday living, *(syn.)* commonplace: *Her life is filled with mundane work.*

mu·nic·i·pal /myuˈnɪsəpəl/ *adj.* related to a city, town, etc.: *There is a municipal parking lot near the town hall.*

mu·nic·i·pal·i·ty /myu‚nɪsəˈpæləti/ *n.* **-ties** a city, village, or town legally organized for self-government: *This municipality has a professional city manager.*

mu·ral /ˈmyʊrəl/ *n.* a painting or mosaic done directly on a wall: *Two huge murals were painted by Marc Chagall on the walls of the opera house. -n.* **muralist.**

mur·der /ˈmɜrdər/ *n.* [C;U] **1** the intentional killing of s.o. illegally: *A criminal committed murder when he shot his victim.* **2** *infrml.* **to get away with murder:** to escape punishment for doing s.t. outrageous: *The mayor did not pay his income taxes, but got away with murder because the people re-elected him anyway. See:* assassination, manslaughter.
—v. to kill s.o. (not in military battle): *The criminal murdered his victim for her money and jewels. -n.* **murderer;** *-adj.* **murderous.**

murk·y /ˈmɜrki/ *adj.* **-ier, -iest** unclear and dark: *I looked into the murky water of the river and could see nothing but mud. -n.* **murk;** *-adv.* **murkily.**

mur·mur /ˈmɜrmər/ *n.* **1** a low, unclear sound: *A murmur of conversation went through the classroom after the teacher announced the date of the exam.* **2** (in medicine) an irregular beating of the heart: *The doctor says that the child has a heart murmur.*
—v. to sound or speak with a low unclear tone: *My husband murmured, "Let's leave this boring party."*

Mur·phy's Law /ˈmɜrfiz/ *n.infrml.* the idea that if s.t. can go wrong, it will go wrong: *I had a very important meeting and Murphy's Law was working; my car got a flat tire and I forgot to bring my briefcase.*

mus·cle /ˈmʌsəl/ *n.* [C;U] **1** body tissues on the bones that make the body move and give it bulk: *The muscles in my legs ache after walking a long distance.* **2** [U] *fig.* power, force: *Help me move this sofa, and let's put some muscle into it!* **3 Don't move a muscle.:** stay still, don't move
—v. **-cled, -cling, -cles** to force one's way into s.t.: *A coworker muscled in on a conversation I was having with my boss.*

muscle-bound *adj.* awkward and stiff from having overdeveloped muscles: *His arms are so muscle-bound from lifting weights that he can hardly comb his hair.*

mus·cu·lar /ˈmʌskyələr/ *adj.* having well developed, strong muscles: *She is a strong, muscular athlete.*

muscular dys·tro·phy /ˈdɪstrəfi/ *n.* a disease that weakens the muscles so a person gradually cannot move: *Muscular dystrophy is an uncommon hereditary disease.*

muse /myuz/ *n.* **1** (with a capital M, in Greek mythology) any one of the nine sisters who inspired the arts and sciences: *Erato was the Muse of love poetry.* **2** an inspiration: *His wife served as the painter's muse.*
—v.frml. **mused, musing, muses** to think about s.t., imagine what it would be like: *He mused about his life and his future. See:* musing.

mu·se·um /myuˈziəm/ *n.* a place that displays rare, valuable, and important art or historical objects: *The art museum has a beautiful collection of ancient gold and silver coins.*

mush /mʌʃ/ *n.* [U] **1** a soft, wet mass, esp. corn or oat meal: *The farmer had cornmeal mush and coffee for breakfast.* **2** *infrml.* s.t. sentimental, such as a soap opera, novel, etc.: *That play was full of mush.*
—v. **mushes 1** to travel by dog sled: *An Eskimo mushed across the snow.* **2** the command that tells sled dogs to move: *"Mush!" said the sled driver to her dogs.*

mush·room /ˈmʌʃ‚rum/ *n.* any of the thousands of kinds of small fungi with a stem and fleshy cap: *The morel is a popular, edible mushroom.*
—v.fig. to grow rapidly and in great numbers: *In an economic boom, houses mushroomed in the desert near Las Vegas.*

mush·y /ˈmʌʃi, ˈmʊ-/ *adj.* **-ier, -iest 1** soft, wet, and grainy: *In the sunlight in winter, snow on the sidewalks becomes mushy.* **2** very sentimental: *I saw a mushy movie about a couple in love.*

mu·sic /'myuzɪk/ *n.* [U] *adj.* **1** the art of putting sounds in a rhythmic sequence: *I prefer classical <n.> music to jazz.* **2 music to my ears:** to learn good news: *When my wife told me we were going to have a baby, I told her it was music to my ears.*

mu·si·cal /'myuzɪkəl/ *adj.* **1** related to music: *Mozart wrote many musical compositions in his short life.* **2** pleasant-sounding: *Her voice has a musical quality.*

mu·si·cian /myu'zɪʃən/ *n.* a person who writes, sings, or plays music: *One hundred musicians play in that orchestra.*

mus·ing /'myuzɪŋ/ *n.* [C;U] deep thought, meditation: *He spent a lot of time in musing about his career.*

musk /mʌsk/ *n.* [U] a sticky substance with a rich, strong smell, used in making perfume: *Many people like the scent of musk.*

mus·ket /'mʌskɪt/ *n.* an old-fashioned gun: *George Washington's troops used muskets to fight the British. -n.* **musketeer** /,mʌskə'tɪr/; [U] **musketry** /'mʌskətri/.

musk·rat /'mʌsk,ræt/ *n.* a North American rodent with brown, shiny fur living in wetlands: *The fur of muskrats is made into fur coats.*

mus·lin /'mʌzlɪn/ *n.* [U] *adj.* a type of plain cotton fabric: *My bed sheets are of <n.> muslin* (or) *<adj.> muslin fabric.*

muss /mʌs/ *v.* **musses** to mess up, esp. hair: *The wind mussed her hair. -adj.* **mussy.**

mus·sel /'mʌsəl/ *n.* any of a variety of shellfish, some of which are edible: *Mussels are found on the sea rocks on the shores of America and Europe.*

must (1) /mʌst; *weak form* məst/ *auxiliary verb* used with other verbs without the infinitive "to" **1** expressing obligation: *I must go to work tomorrow.* **2** express the likelihood of s.t.: *Her car is gone, so she must have left already. See:* modal auxiliary.
—*n.* s.t. necessary, a necessity: *A warm winter coat is a must in Toronto.*

USAGE NOTE: Compare *ought to, would, should,* and *might.* The past tense of *must* is usu. *had to: I had to go to work yesterday.* Use *must have & past part.* to indicate that you are quite sure s.t. happened: *If the books are gone, Diane must have taken them.*

must (2) /mʌst/ *n.* [U] dustiness, mold, mildew, and their smell: *A smell of must came from the basement as I opened the door. -adj.* **musty.**

mus·tache /'mʌ,stæʃ, mə'stæʃ/ *n.* hair growing above the mouth: *He wears a mustache because he thinks it makes him look handsome. See:* sideburns, USAGE NOTE.

mus·tang /'mʌ,stæŋ/ *n.* a strong, small wild horse of the American West: *Mustangs run in herds.*

mus·tard /'mʌstərd/ *n.* [U] **1** a strong herb, usu. two to three feet (1 m) tall with yellow flowers and seeds that are crushed and mixed with liquid and spices to make table mustard: *I like to put mustard on my hot dogs.* **2** *infrml.* **to cut the mustard:** to do s.t. well: *She can really cut the mustard since she brings in a lot of business to the company.*

mus·ter /'mʌstər/ *v.* to collect, gather, summon: *The diver mustered his courage and dove off a high cliff.*
—*n.* **1** a gathering, as of troops, for inspection or battle **2 to pass muster:** to be thought acceptable: *She passed muster in a job interview and got the job.*

mu·ta·ble /'myutəbəl/ *adj.frml.* capable of being changed: *Some parts of the contract are mutable; others are not. -n.* **mutability** /,myutə'bɪləti/.

mu·tant /'myutnt/ *n.adj.* a person or organism with an accidental change from its species, *(syn.)* a freak: *Science-fiction stories describe <n.> mutants who have two heads. -v.* **mutate** /'myu,teɪt/; -*n.* [C;U] **mutation** /myu'teɪʃən/.

mute /myut/ *n.adj.* **1** unable or unwilling to speak: *He was born <adj.> mute, and he has been a <n.> mute since birth.* **2** silent: *She was <adj.> mute when the teacher asked her a question. -adv.* **mutely.**
—*v.* **muted, muting, mutes** to reduce or stop the sound of s.t.: *A jazz musician muted her horn by putting her hand over its opening.*

mu·ti·late /'myutl,eɪt/ *v.* **-lated, -lating, -lates** to cut, rip s.o. or s.t. apart, disfigure: *A madman mutilated his victims by cutting off their hands. -n.* [C;U] **mutilation** /,myutl'eɪʃən/.

mu·ti·ny /'myutni/ *n.* [C;U] **-nies** a revolt against authority, esp. by sailors against their captain: *In the mutiny aboard a battleship, the captain was killed.*
—*v.* **-nied, -nying, -nies** to revolt against authority: *The ship's sailors mutinied and took over the ship. -adj.* **mutinous.**

mutt /mʌt/ *n.infrml.* a dog with parents of different breeds, *(syn.)* a mongrel: *They have a funny-looking mutt for a pet.*

mut·ter /'mʌtər/ *v.n.* to speak unclearly and quietly, usu. to complain: *The taxi driver <v.> muttered about the bad traffic. -n.* **muttering.**

mut·ton /'mʌtn/ *n.* [U] meat from a mature sheep (not lamb): *Mutton can be tough, but it tastes good with gravy.*

mu·tu·al /'myutʃuəl/ *adj.* **1** having similar feelings, ideas, tastes: *I was happy to see my friend, and he said the feeling was mutual.* **2** sharing business or other interests: *We have a mutual interest in a bakery that is managed by a mutual friend.*

M

mutual fund *n.* a type of financial investment run by a company that sells shares and invests the money in stocks, bonds, etc.: *In the USA, thousands of mutual funds are offered to the public. See:* money-market fund.

Mu·zak /'myu,zæk/ *n.TM* prerecorded music played in hotels and elevators, etc: *Our hotel has Muzak playing in the lobby to relax the guests.*

muz·zle /'mʌzəl/ *n.* **1** the nose and jaw of a dog, bear, or other animal: *Our dog stuck his muzzle in his food dish to eat.* **2** a piece of leather put around a muzzle to keep an animal from biting or eating: *In some places, dogs must wear a muzzle in public.* **3** *fig.* s.t. that prevents s.o. from telling the truth: *The government put a muzzle on the newspapers to keep them quiet about the scandal.* **4** the end of the barrel of a gun: *Smoke came out of the rifle's muzzle after it was fired.*
—*v.* **-zled, -zling, -zles 1** to put a muzzle on an animal **2** to prevent s.o. from expressing opinions: *During the war, officials muzzled the newspaper, TV, and radio.*

my /maɪ/ *poss.pron. of* I: *My head aches; I'm going to my room.*
—*exclam.* to express surprise: *My goodness, (my word, oh my, etc.) it's starting to rain again!*

my·op·ic /maɪ'ɑpɪk, -'ou-/ *adj.* **1** unable to see things in the distance, (*syn.*) near-sighted: *He is myopic but can see well with glasses.* **2** *fig.* unable to plan ahead, (*syn.*) short-sighted: *The building's owner is myopic; he will only make small repairs while the building is slowly falling apart.*

myr·i·ad /'mɪriəd/ *adj.n.frml.* many, referring to a great number of things: *An accounting department must take care of a <n.> myriad of details.*

myrrh /mɜr/ *n.* [u] a sticky gum or resin used in making perfume and incense: *Myrrh is burned as incense in church services.*

myr·tle /'mɜrtl/ *n.* [C;U] any of various tropical trees with good-smelling leaves: *Myrtles sometimes have large, fancy blossoms.*

my·self /maɪ'sɛlf/ *reflexive pron. of* I **1** without help: *I poured myself a glass of milk.||After my promotion, I gave myself a present.* **2** alone: *I live by myself.* **3** one's usual condition: *I'm not feeling myself today; I didn't sleep well last night.*

mys·te·ri·ous /mɪ'stɪriəs/ *adj.* having no known cause, such as s.t. supernatural or secret: *For some mysterious reason, she left last week without saying good-bye to anyone.*

mys·ter·y /'mɪstəri, -stri/ *n.* **1** [C;U] an event that has no known cause, a supernatural event, a problem with no solution: *How the universe was created is still a mystery.* **2** [C] a secret: *Why she left home without saying where she was going is still a mystery.* **3** [C] a crime story that leaves the reader in suspense until the end: *My friend likes to read murder mysteries* (or) *<adj.> mystery stories.*

mys·tic /'mɪstɪk/ *n.* a person who through meditation communicates directly with the spiritual: *Mystics can see visions and hear voices. -adj.* **mystical** /'mɪstɪkəl/.

mys·ti·cism /'mɪstə,sɪzəm/ *n.* [U] the practice of placing oneself in direct relationship with the spiritual: *Mysticism is practiced by many people all over the world. -adj.* **mystical** /'mɪstɪkəl/.

mys·ti·fy /'mɪstə,faɪ/ *v.* **-fied, -fying, -fies,** to confuse, puzzle: *Everyone was mystified by his sudden disappearance. -n.* **mystification** /,mɪstəfə'keɪʃən/.

mys·tique /mɪ'stik/ *n.sing.* a mysterious and usu. attractive image: *That island has a mystique about it as a vacation spot of the rich.*

myth /mɪθ/ *n.* [C;U] **1** stories from ancient cultures about history, gods, and heroes: *Students learn about the myths of ancient Greece and Rome.* **2** [C] an untrue or unproved story: *His stories about his great successes in sports are myths.*

myth·i·cal /'mɪθɪkəl/ *adj.* related to mythology, unreal: *Many mythical creatures were ugly, like the giant one-eyed Cyclops.*

my·thol·o·gy /mɪ'θɑlədʒi/ *n.* [U] **1** the stories of ancient peoples: The Iliad *is one of the most famous stories in Greek mythology.* **2** the study of myths and cultures: *She took a course in Roman mythology. -v.frml.* **mythologize;** *-adj.* **mythological** /,mɪθə'lɑdʒɪkəl/.

M

N, n

N, n /ɛn/ **N's, n's** or **Ns, ns** the 14th letter of the English alphabet

NAACP /ˈɛnˌdʌbəlˌeɪsiˈpi/ *abbr.for* National Association for the Advancement of Colored People, an organization dedicated to protecting the rights of African-Americans and to providing them with equal opportunities for educational and career advancement

---

USAGE NOTE: The *NAACP* is an interracial organization formed in 1909. It has focused on making changes in American society by changing discriminatory laws. The NAACP helped change the laws that discriminated against African-Americans in schools, government, and employment. Also pronounced "N-double A-C-P."

---

nab /næb/ *v.infrml.* **nabbed, nabbing, nabs** to seize s.o., esp. a criminal, (*syn.*) to capture: *The police nabbed the thief after he robbed the bank.*

na·chos /ˈnɑtʃoʊz, ˈnæ-/ *n.pl.* a snack food made of small corn chips covered with cheese or salsa and heated: *People often put spicy beef and vegetables, such as tomatoes and peppers, on top of their nachos. See:* enchilada, USAGE NOTE.

na·dir /ˈneɪdər, -ˌdɪr/ *n.frml.* [C] the lowest and usu. the worst point, as in one's life, career, etc.: *The day his wife died was the nadir of his life.*

nag (1) /næg/ *n.* a horse, esp. one that looks old and tired: *An old nag slowly pulled the carriage up the road.*

nag (2) *v.* **nagged, nagging, nags** to remind s.o. repeatedly to do s.t. in an annoying way, (*syn.*) to pester: *She's always nagging her son to get a haircut.*
—*adj.* **nagging** constantly bothered by s.t.: *a nagging backache*
—*n.* a person who nags another, (*syn.*) a pest: *Don't be such a nag!*

nail /neɪl/ *n.* **1** a small, thin, metal rod with a sharp point on the end, used to hold things together or to keep them in place: *She used nails*

to put the bookshelves up on the wall. **2** the hard smooth surface at the end of a finger or toe: *She has long nails.* **3** the claws of an animal: *The nails in a cat's paw are sharp.* **4 hard as nails:** tough, not sensitive or sympathetic: *Her son complained*

nails

that she was hard as nails when she refused to help him.
—*v.* **1** to attach with a nail: *Carpenters nailed wooden boards together to build a fence.* **2** *infrml.* **to nail s.o.:** to prove s.o. guilty of a crime: *The police nailed the thieves by finding the stolen money in their car.* **3** *phrasal v. sep.* **to nail s.o. down:** to get s.o. to make a definite statement: *His wife seemed interested in selling the boat, but we couldn't nail the Captain down as to an exact price.||We couldn't nail him down.* **4** *phrasal v. sep.* **to nail s.t. down:** to make certain, to make sure s.t. isn't going to change: *Please repeat the price of those items; I want to nail down the cost before I commit to buying them.||I want to nail it down.*

nail clipper *n.* a small steel tool with sharp edges for cutting fingernails or toenails

nail file *n.* a thin, flat piece of metal with a rough surface used to smooth and shape fingernails

nail polish *n.* [U] paint used to cover and beautify fingernails and toenails: *She put red nail polish on before she went out to dinner.*

na·ive /nɑˈiv/ *adj.* having or showing a childlike, simple view of the world, due to a lack of experience, (*syn.*) unsophisticated: *She was naive to trust even a friend with so much money. -adv.* **naively.**

na·ive·té /ˌnɑivˈteɪ, nɑˌivəˈteɪ, nɑˈivˌteɪ, -ˈivə-/ *n.* [U] the act or condition of being naive: *He loved her with such naiveté that he could not believe it when she left him.*

na·ked /ˈneɪkɪd/ *adj.* **1** without clothes, bare: *He was as naked as a newborn baby.* **2** *fig.* not

N

hidden or disguised: *naked ambition*||*naked greed*

naked eye *n.* [U] normal eyesight without a device to make things look larger (such as a microscope) or closer (such as a telescope): *Most stars and planets are too far away to be seen with the naked eye.*

name /neɪm/ *n.* **1** [C] a word by which a person, place, or thing is known: *Her name is Diane Daniel.*||*What is the name of that flower?* **2** [C, usu. *sing.*] an important person: *He is a big name in banking (entertainment, city politics, etc.)* **3** [C, usu. *sing.*] the way in which one is thought of by others, (*syn.*) reputation: *She has a good name in the local community.* **4 in name only:** giving only the appearance of, (*syn.*) superficially: *The young man is president of the company in name only; his father makes all the decisions.* **5 in the name of:** by the authority of: *You are under arrest in the name of the law.* **6 not a penny to one's name:** very poor: *Born with not a penny to his name, he's now a rich man.* **7 the name of the game:** the most important thing: *In this business, increasing sales is the name of the game; everything else is less important.* **8 to call s.o. names:** to address s.o. using an offensive word, (*syn.*) to insult: *He became angry and called me names like "stupid" and "jerk."* **9 to drop names:** to talk about important or famous people as if one knew them personally: *He drops the names of actors and politicians that he has never met.*

—*v.* **named, naming, names 1** to give s.o. a name: *She named her daughter Mary.* **2** to put s.o. in a certain job or position, (*syn.*) to appoint: *The governor named a judge to a court.* **3** to identify, call by name, (*syn.*) to label: *Police named him as the killer.*||*She can name all the state capitals.* **4 to name names:** to tell about (or) accuse people whose names one was supposed to have kept secret: *Under police questioning, he started to name names.*

name brand *n.* a product by a well-known maker (as opposed to an unknown brand): *He only buys name brands like Kodak™ film.*

USAGE NOTE: The *brand names* of some products are sometimes used to refer to all products of that type. For example, adhesive tape is called by the name brand Scotch Tape™, and tissue is called by the name brand Kleenex™. *Please hand me a Kleenex. I have to blow my nose.*

name-dropping *n.* the practice or habit of mentioning important or famous people as if one knew them personally: *She tries to impress people by name-dropping.* -*n.* **name-dropper.**

name·less /ˈneɪmlɪs/ *adj.* **1** without a name or with an unknown name: *A nameless man without any identification was brought into the*

hospital. **2** impossible to describe: *a nameless fear* **3 to remain nameless:** to not identify by name: *Some members of the group, who shall remain nameless, refused to help in any way.*

name·ly /ˈneɪmli/ *adv.* to be exact, specifically: *I would like to buy a new car, namely a Mercedes.*

name·plate /ˈneɪmˌpleɪt/ *n.* a plastic or metal plate with the name of a person, location, or company on it: *The company nameplate is on the door.*

name·sake /ˈneɪmˌseɪk/ *n.* a person named after or with the same name as another person: *He left all his money to his only child and namesake, Charles Randall III.*

nan·a /ˈnænə/ *n.infrml.* grandmother: *The children just love their nana.*

nan·ny /ˈnæni/ *n.* **-nies** a person hired to take care of a child: *She works as a nanny for a wealthy family.*

USAGE NOTE: Compare *nanny, babysitter, au pair.* A nanny is a professional child care provider who gives full-time child care and often lives with the family. A babysitter provides part-time child care and does not live with the family. Teenagers often work as babysitters for families in their neighborhood. An au pair comes from another country to live with an American family and learn English. The au pair takes care of the children in exchange for a room, meals, and a little money.

nanny goat *n.* a mature female goat: *Nanny goats are popular in children's stories.*

nan·o·sec·ond /ˈnænəˌsɛkənd/ *n.* one billionth (1/1,000,000,000) of a second: *The speed at which computers work is measured in nanoseconds.*

nap /næp/ *v.* **napped, napping, naps** to sleep for a short period of time, (*syn.*) *infrml.* to snooze: *I napped for a while this afternoon.*
—*n.* a short sleep, (*syn.*) *infrml.* a snooze: *I took a short nap.*

na·palm /ˈneɪˌpɑm/ *n.* [U] gasoline in jelly form used in flamethrowers and bombs: *Buildings burst into flames as the enemy plane dropped napalm.*

nape /neɪp/ *n.* the back of the neck: *The mother cat carried her kittens by the nape of the neck.*

nap·kin /ˈnæpkɪn/ *n.* a square piece of paper or cloth used when eating to wipe the mouth, protect the lap, and clean up spills: *Take some paper napkins for the picnic.*

narc or **nark** /nɑrk/ *n.slang* a narcotics agent: *Narcs arrest drug dealers.*

nar·cis·sist /ˈnɑrsəsɪst/ *n.* a person who is only concerned with his or her own feelings, ideas, experiences, or appearance: *The famous artist was a narcissist who neglected his fam-*

ily. -n. [U] **narcissism;** *-adj.* **narcissistic** /ˌnɑrsə'sɪstɪk/.

nar·cis·sus /nɑr'sɪsəs/ *n.* **-cissus** or **-cissi** /'sɪˌsaɪ/ or **-cissuses** a plant with white or yellow flowers that grows from a bulb in the spring: *A daffodil is a type of narcissus.*

nar·co·lep·sy /'nɑrkəˌlɛpsi/ *n.* [U] a disease causing an uncontrollable desire for sleep: *He suffers from narcolepsy.*

nar·co·sis /nɑr'koʊsɪs/ *n.* [U] a state of unconsciousness caused by drugs: *He suffered from narcosis after taking too many drugs.*

nar·cot·ic /nɑr'kɑtɪk/ *n.* a drug that reduces pain and causes sleep: *He is on narcotics.*
—adj. related to drugs: *Marijuana has a narcotic effect.*

nar·rate /'nærˌeɪt, næ'reɪt/ *v.* **-rated, -rating, -rates** to tell a story in writing or speech: *He narrated a television show on the history of Mexico. -n.* [C;U] **narration** /næ'reɪʃən; / **narrator** /'nærˌeɪtər, næ'reɪ-, 'nærə-/.

nar·ra·tive /'nærətɪv/ *adj.* related to storytelling, in the form of a story: *a narrative tale*
—n. a story, a description of events: *The police asked her for a narrative of her activities the day of the murder.*

nar·row /'næroʊ/ *adj.* **1** not wide, less wide than usual: *The big truck could hardly fit in the narrow street.||Little light came through the narrow windows.* **2** thin, slim: *That fence is made of narrow pieces of metal.* **3** limited in number: *a narrow choice of desserts* **4** almost unsuccessful: *a narrow escape*
—v. **1** to make or become less wide: *The growth of bushes narrowed the path to the garden.* **2** to reduce, limit: *They talked and narrowed the differences between the two parties.||Having no education narrows the opportunities available to us. -adv.* **narrowly;** *-n.* **narrowness.**

nar·row-mind·ed /'næroʊ'maɪndɪd/ *adj.* showing or having no interest in the ideas and opinions of others: *No one accepted his narrow-minded political views.*

nar·y /'nɛri/ *adj.infrml.* not one, no: *We walked in the woods and nary a person was there.*

NASA /'næsə/ *abbr. for* National Aeronautics and Space Administration, the agency of the US federal government responsible for space exploration

na·sal /'neɪzəl/ *adj.* **1** related to the nose: *My nasal passages are stuffed up from a cold.* **2** having a sound that comes through the nose: *He kept complaining in a nasal voice. -adv.* **nasally.**

nas·cent /'neɪsənt/ *adj.frml.* about beginning to form or grow: *The author had only a few ideas written down; his book was still in its nascent stages.*

NASDAQ /'næsˌdæk, 'næz-/ *abbr. for* National Association of Securities Dealers Automated Quotations, an organization that provides a marketplace for the sale of stocks for mostly newer and smaller companies *See:* stock market, Wall Street.

nas·ty /'næsti/ *adj.* **-tier, -tiest 1** unkind, offensive: *a nasty person||a nasty comment* **2** harsh, unpleasant: *nasty weather||a nasty temper||a nasty smell* **3** harmful, *(syn.)* injurious: *I have a nasty cut (injury, burn, etc.) on my hand. -adv.* **nastily;** *-n.* [U] **nastiness.**

na·tal /'neɪtl/ *adj.* (in medicine) related to birth: *The child suffered a natal injury.*

natch /nætʃ/ *adv.infrml.* short for *naturally;* yes, of course: *"Would you like to go to the show tonight?"—"Natch, let's go!"*

na·tion /'neɪʃən/ *n.* **1** a people living in and having a common loyalty to a country or region: *When the war ended, there was joy throughout the nation.* **2** an independent country with its own government, esp. considered together with its people, culture, government, etc.: *Spain is one of many nations in the European Union.* **3** a group of Native American tribes that together form a union: *the Sioux nation*

na·tion·al /'næʃənəl, 'næʃnəl/ *adj.* **1** related to a nation: *national pride||national holidays* **2** all over the country, *(syn.)* nationwide: *The story about the murder received national coverage on the news.*
—n. a person who is a citizen of a particular country: *She is an American national living in Brazil. -adv.* **nationally.**

na·tion·al·ism /'næʃənəˌlɪzəm, 'næʃnə-/ *n.* [U] **1** a feeling of loyalty to a country on the part of its people and leaders: *Nationalism reached its peak when war was declared.* **2** a movement for political independence by an ethnic or religious group within a country or by a country under the control of another: *There has been a rise in nationalism in the former Soviet republics. -n. adj.* **nationalist;** *-adj.* **nationalistic** /ˌnæʃənə'lɪstɪk, ˌnæʃnə-/.

na·tion·al·i·ty /ˌnæʃə'næləti/ *n.* **-ties** [C;U] the state of being a citizen of a particular country: *"What nationality is she?"—"Peruvian."*

na·tion·al·ize /'næʃənəˌlaɪz, 'næʃnə-/ *v.* **-ized, -izing, -izes** to transfer ownership of a private business to the government with or without paying the owners: *Britain nationalized the steel industry. -n.* **nationalization** /ˌnæʃənələ'zeɪʃən, ˌnæʃnə-/.

national monument *n.* a structure with historical importance, such as a statue or building, owned and managed by the national government for the people: *The Lincoln Memorial in Washington, D.C., is a national monument.*

national park *n.* a large park kept by the national government in its natural condition for limited public use (hiking, camping, etc.): *Yellowstone and Yosemite are famous national parks in the USA.*

USAGE NOTE: There are about 375 *National Parks* and monuments in the USA, and about 175 National Forests, equaling three percent of the total US land area. The public can use the National Parks for free or a very low fee. The parks are cared for by park rangers, who act as police, guides, and caretakers.

na·tion·hood /'neɪʃən,hʊd/ *n.* the condition of being a nation: *The people on that island are fighting to keep their nationhood.*

na·tion·wide /,neɪʃən'waɪd/ *adj.* national, across a whole country: *The phone company has a nationwide network of phone lines.*

na·tive /'neɪtɪv/ *n.* **1** a person who is born in a certain place: *She is a native of Texas.* **2** *pej.* one of a group of people living in a place before the arrival of Europeans, (*syn.*) an aborigine: *They forced the natives to leave their land by burning their villages.*
—*adj.* **1** born in a certain place: *She's a native New Yorker.* **2** coming from or belonging to a particular place: *Those beautiful flowers are native to South America.* **3** belonging to a person naturally or from birth: *The teacher tried to encourage the boy's native musical talent.* **4** being the language one first learned as a child: *She speaks English fluently, but her native language is Italian.* **5 native speaker:** a person who speaks a particular language as his or her first language: *a native speaker of Chinese*

USAGE NOTE: The opposite of a *native speaker* is a *nonnative speaker*, a person who does not speak a particular language as his or her first language: *Since Han immigrated to the US from Taiwan at age 20, he's a nonnative speaker of English.*

Native American *adj.* of or related to American Indians: *Native American history‖a Native American poet*
—*n.* an American Indian: *She's a Native American born and brought up in Tucson, Arizona. See:* Indian, USAGE NOTE.

na·tiv·i·ty /nə'tɪvəti, neɪ-/ *n.frml.* **-ties 1** an act of birth **2 the Nativity:** *The birth of Jesus Christ is called the Nativity.*

NATO /'neɪtoʊ/ *abbr. for* North Atlantic Treaty Organization, an association of North American and European countries formed for military defense

nat·ty /'næti/ *adj.* **-tier, -tiest** stylish, well-dressed (said usu. of men): *He is a natty dresser in his well-designed suit and blue hat.* -*adv.* **nattily.**

nat·u·ral /'næʧərəl, 'næʧrəl/ *adj.* **1** related to or formed by nature, not made or changed by humans: *We admired the natural beauty of the forest.* **2** as in nature: *The zoo displayed animals in their natural surroundings.* **3** true to life, not fake: *The star of the show was praised for her natural acting style.* **4** born with a particular ability, without need of education or training: *He is a natural athlete who excels at many sports.* **5** understood and accepted as normal: *They are in love, and it is natural that they should marry.*
—*n.* s.o. who is just right or well-suited for s.t. -*n.* **naturalness.**

natural childbirth *n.* [U] the method of giving birth to a child with a minimum of modern medical procedures and usu. without anesthesia: *She had both of her children by natural childbirth.*

natural food *n.* [C;U] food grown without the use of chemicals (fertilizer or pesticides): *Many people enjoy the fresh taste of natural foods. See:* organic food, USAGE NOTE.

natural history *n.* the study of animals, plants, and natural objects, such as rocks: *My children love to look at the dinosaurs in the Museum of Natural History.*

nat·u·ral·ist /'næʧərəlɪst, 'næʧrə-/ *n.* a person who studies plants and animals *See:* biologist.

nat·u·ral·ize /'næʧərə,laɪz, 'næʧrə-/ *v.* **-ized, -izing, -izes** to become a citizen of a country
—*adj.* Born and raised in Hong Kong, she has become a naturalized citizen of the USA. -*n.* **naturalization** /,næʧərələ'zeɪʃən, 'næʧrə-/.

nat·u·ral·ly /'næʧərəli, 'næʧrə-/ *adv.* **1** in a natural way: *Animals grow up naturally in a forest (not in a zoo).* **2** as to be expected, of course: *Naturally, I would like to go to bed; I'm tired.*

natural number *n.* a whole number without a minus sign in front of it: *The numbers 1, 2, 3, 4, etc., are natural numbers.*

natural resources *n.pl.* raw materials found in nature, such as minerals, trees, fresh water, and oil that are useful to humans: *Some countries are rich in natural resources.*

na·ture /'neɪʧər/ *n.* **1** [U] the part of our world not made by humans, such as the sky, trees, fields, streams, plants, animals, etc. **2** [U] the forces that control this part of the world: *Hurricanes and earthquakes show the destructive power of nature.* **3** [C;U] a person's character, personality: *It is his nature to be kind and forgiving.* **4** [C, usu. *sing.*] type, kind: *The discussion was of a personal nature.* **5 Mother Nature:** the forces that control the natural environment: *We had bad weather this year; Mother Nature has not been kind to us.* **6 second nature:** a habit, s.t. done without thinking: *Driving (a car) has become second nature to her.*

naught /nɔt/ *n.frml.* [C;U] zero, nothing: *All his work has come to naught.*

naugh·ty /'nɔti/ *adj.* **-tier, -tiest 1** badly behaved, (*syn.*) mischievous: *That boy is a naughty child.* **2** showing or describing sex acts, (*syn.*) bawdy: *That is a naughty magazine.* *-n.* [U] **naughtiness.**

nau·se·a /'nɔziə, 'nɔʒə, 'nɔʃə, 'nɔsiə/ *n.* [U] a feeling that one is going to vomit, sick to one's stomach: *She has a feeling of nausea from eating too much.*

nau·se·ate /'nɔzi,eɪt, -ʒi-, -ʃi-, -si-/ *v.* **-ated, -ating, -ates 1** to cause nausea: *The smell of paint nauseated him.* **2** *infrml.fig.* to be very distasteful to s.o., (*syn.*) to disgust: *It was nauseating to see my ex-husband with his new wife.*

nau·seous /'nɔʃəs, 'nɔziəs/ *adj.* **1** *infrml.* feeling nausea, (*syn.*) nauseated: *She felt nauseous from the boat ride.* **2** causing nausea: *The nauseous smell of the garbage made me feel sick.*

nau·ti·cal /'nɔtɪkəl/ *adj.* related to ships, sailors, or navigation: *a nautical map||a nautical design*

nautical mile *n.* 6,076 feet or 1,852 meters, used in sea and air travel: *The airplane is traveling at 600 nautical miles per hour.*

nau·ti·lus /'nɔtələs/ *n.* **-luses** or **-li** /-,laɪ/ a sea animal with a beautifully curved shell

na·val /'neɪvəl/ *adj.* related to the navy and sailors: *He is in charge of the naval officers.*

nave /neɪv/ *n.* the main part of a church where people sit: *She joined her family in the nave.*

na·vel /'neɪvəl/ *n.* the little hole in the stomach area, (*syn.*) *infrml.* belly button: *He had a stomach pain and rubbed his navel.*

nav·i·ga·ble /'nævəgəbəl/ *adj.* capable of being used by boats: *A navigable river is deep and wide enough for boats to pass through it.*

nav·i·gate /'nævə,geɪt/ *v.* **-gated, -gating, -gates 1** to figure out the course of a ship or airplane, using maps and mechanical aids **2** to steer a ship or airplane: *The captain navigated his boat carefully up the river.*

nav·i·ga·tion /,nævə'geɪʃən/ *n.* [U] the science or practice of figuring out a correct course (path, route) for a ship or airplane: *Navigation of a ship across the ocean requires skill. -adj.* **navigational.**

nav·i·ga·tor /'nævə,geɪtər/ *n.* a person who navigates ships or airplanes: *The navigator tells the pilot when he is not on the correct course.*

na·vy /'neɪvi/ *n.* **-vies** a country's sailors and fighting ships with their related equipment: *The US Navy played an important role in World War II.*
—*adj. See:* navy blue.

navy blue or **navy** *adj.* dark blue: *Many businesspeople wear navy blue suits.*

nay /neɪ/ *n.* [C] *adv.* no, esp. in voting: *Fifty-one senators voted <adv.> nay and defeated the proposal.*

Na·zi /'natsi, 'næt-/ *n.* **-zis** [C] *adv.* a member of the National Socialist German Workers' Party, the political party headed by Adolf Hitler that ruled Germany from 1933 to 1945 —*adj.* related to the Nazis: *a Nazi submarine* *-n.* [U] **Nazism** /'nat,sɪzəm, 'næt-/ or **Naziism.**

near /nɪr/ *adj.* **1** close in distance or time: *Go to the nearest hospital.||I'll see you in the near future.* **2** almost happening: *a near accident (loss, disaster, etc.)* **3 to have a near miss:** to barely escape harm or injury: *I had a near miss when a speeding car almost hit me as I crossed the street.* **4 one's nearest and dearest:** (often used humorously) one's closest friends and relatives: *I invited only my nearest and dearest to the wedding.* **5 to be so near and yet so far:** to almost but not quite reach a goal: *She lost the election by only three votes; she was so near and yet so far.*
—*adv. prep.* **1** close to: *As he came <adv.> nearer, I could see he had changed.||There's a supermarket <prep.> near my house.||It was <prep.> near midnight when we arrived.||She received the news that her brother was <prep.> near death.* **2 near at hand:** close by in distance or time: *When I am ill, I want you near at hand to help me.||Their arrival is near at hand.*
—*v.* to come close or closer to a point in space or time, (*syn.*) to approach: *As we neared the shore, I saw that there was no one there to greet us.||He is nearing the end of his story (task, life, etc.).*

near·by /,nɪr'baɪ/ *adj.adv.* close: *We walked to a <adj.> nearby town.||Is there a post office <adv.> nearby?*

near·ly /'nɪrli/ *adv.* almost, not quite or completely: *He has nearly finished his meal.||That item cost nearly $500.*

near·sight·ed /'nɪr,saɪtɪd/ *adj.* unable to see things that are far away, (*syn.*) myopic: *She always wears glasses because she's very nearsighted.*

neat /nit/ *adj.* **1** in good order, (*syn.*) tidy: *His house is always neat and clean.* **2** skillfully done: *a neat phrase* **3** *infrml.* great, wonderful: *We had a neat time at the party. -adv.* **neatly; -n.** **neatness.**

neat·en /'nitn/ *v.* to put in order, (*syn.*) to tidy: *She neatened her living room.*

neb·u·la /'nɛbyələ/ *n.* [C] **-las, -lae** /-,li/ in space, a cloud of gas or dust that sometimes appears bright

N

neb·u·lous /ˈnɛbyələs/ *adj.frml.* not clear, (*syn.*) vague: *What he said was too nebulous to understand.*

nec·es·sar·i·ly /ˌnɛsəˈsɛrəli/ *adv.* as is always true, as must be: *Traveling in that country isn't necessarily expensive; you can find moderately priced hotels and restaurants.*

nec·es·sar·y /ˈnɛsəˌsɛri/ *adj.* **1** required, (*syn.*) obligatory: *It is necessary that you attend the meeting today.* **2** needed, (*syn.*) sufficient: *You must provide the necessary money to do the project.*

ne·ces·si·tate /nəˈsɛsəˌteɪt/ *v.frml.* **-tated, -tating, -tates** to make necessary, to require: *The changes in the contract necessitate that you sign a new one.*

ne·ces·si·ty /nəˈsɛsəti/ *n.* **-ties 1** a basic need or requirement in order to live: *Water is a necessity for all life.* **2** s.t. that must be done: *It is a necessity that he have an operation to remove his appendix.* **3 by** or **of necessity:** unavoidably: *By necessity, I must have a car because there is no other way that I can go to work.*

neck /nɛk/ *n.* **1** the part of the body that joins the head and the shoulders: *She wore a scarf around her neck.* **2** a narrow part of s.t.: *This bottle has a long neck.* **3** *infrml.* **a pain in the neck:** a bother, an annoyance: *That job is a pain in the neck.||That guy is a pain in the neck with his constant demands.* **4 neck and neck:** even or very close in a competition, such as a race: *The horses ran neck and neck toward the finish line.||Both toy companies are doing well; their sales are neck and neck.* **5** *infrml.* **neck of the woods:** the area where one lives: *There are no public buses in my neck of the woods.* **6 to nearly break one's neck:** to nearly get seriously hurt: *I tripped on the stairs and nearly broke my neck.* **7 to risk one's neck:** to put oneself in danger, esp. physical harm: *That man jumped into a frozen lake to save a drowning boy; the man risked his neck to save him.* **8** *infrml.* **up to one's neck in:** very occupied with, struggling to manage: *She's up to her neck in financial problems.*
—*v. old usage* to kiss and touch lovingly: *A young couple is necking in the car over there.*

neck·er·chief /ˈnɛkərtʃɪf, -ˌtʃif/ *n.* a light scarf often made of silk

neck·lace /ˈnɛklɪs/ *n.* a string of beads, pearls, etc. or a chain of gold, silver, etc., worn around the neck: *She always wears pearl necklaces when she goes out in the evening.*

necklace

neck·line /ˈnɛkˌlaɪn/ *n.* a line formed by clothing about the neck: *She likes sweaters with a V-shaped neckline.*

neck·tie /ˈnɛkˌtaɪ/ *n.* a long, narrow piece of cloth placed under one's shirt collar and knotted in front, a tie: *She bought him some neckties for Christmas.*

nec·tar /ˈnɛktər/ *n.* [U] **1** a sweet liquid made in plant flowers and collected by bees to make honey **2** a fruit juice: *I had some peach nectar for breakfast.*

nec·tar·ine /ˌnɛktəˈrin/ *n.* a type of peach with a smooth skin

née /neɪ/ *adj.* born (said of a married woman to show her original family name): *Mrs. Marilyn Woods, née Hunter, was married on Sunday.*

need /nid/ *n.* **1** usu. *sing.* [C] a lack of s.t. that is required or wanted: *The company has a need for computer programmers.||The country is badly in need of rain now.* **2** usu. *sing.* [C] a desire, wish: *He feels a need for love (a new car, vacation, etc.).* **3** usu. *sing.* [C] a duty, requirement: *There's no need for you to sign this.* **4** necessities of life (food, clothes, etc.): *Our needs are simple.* **5 if need be:** if necessary: *If need be, I'll lend you the money.* **6** [U] **in need:** requiring help, usu. because of poverty: *She always sends money to children in need.* See: friend (in need, etc.).
—*v.* **1** to require as a necessity for life: *Everyone needs food.* **2** to want, desire: *The baby needs love and affection.*

nee·dle /ˈnidl/ *n.* **1** a thin, pointed piece of metal or plastic for sewing or knitting: *She looked for a needle and thread to sew the button.* **2** any of various objects shaped like a needle, such as on a measurement dial, a record player, etc.: *The needle on my stereo is broken, so I can't listen to music.* **3** a hypodermic needle, used to put liquid into or take liquid out of one's body: *The nurse used one hypodermic needle to give the patient some medicine, and another to take a sample of her blood.* **4** the pointed leaf of a pine tree
—*v.* **-dled, -dling, -dles** *infrml.fig.* to make fun of s.o., (*syns.*) to tease, mock: *They needle him about the way he always gets lost.* See: pins (and needles).

need·less /ˈnidlɪs/ *adj.* **1** unnecessary, (*syn.*) pointless: *This long meeting is a needless waste of time.* **2 needless to say:** unnecessary to say, obviously: *It rained while we were at the picnic; needless to say, we went home.* -*adv.* **needlessly.**

nee·dle·work /ˈnidlˌwɜrk/ *n.* [U] sewing: *The tailor does fine needlework.*

need·y /ˈnidi/ *adj.* **-ier, -iest 1** lacking the basic necessities, such as food, clothing, and housing; poor, (*syn.*) impoverished: *That needy man has no money, food, medicine, or clothes.* **2** *pl.* **the needy:** poor people in general: *The needy are helped by the charities in our town.*

ne·er-do-well /'nɛrdu,wɛl/ *n.pej.* **-wells** a lazy, unsuccessful person, (*syn.*) a loafer: *He's a ne'er-do-well who can't keep a job.*

ne·far·i·ous /nɪ'fɛriəs/ *adj.frml.* evil, wicked: *One of his nefarious crimes was the bombing of a busy train station.*

ne·gate /nɪ'geɪt/ *v.* **-gated, -gating, -gates** **1** to make s.t. useless, (*syn.*) to nullify: *By suddenly leaving the discussions about wages, the workers negated all of the work done up to that point.* **2** to say that s.t. is not true (real, in existence, etc.), to deny: *She negated the accusations of murder.* -*n.* [U] **negation.**

neg·a·tive /'nɛgətɪv/ *adj.* **1** against s.t., not for it: *He received a negative response to his question.* **2** doubtful about the value of s.t., critical: *The film received mostly negative reviews.* **3** showing a dislike of s.o. or s.t., (*syn.*) antagonistic: *She has a negative attitude toward other people.* **4** always feeling that s.t. bad will happen, (*syn.*) pessimistic: *He has a negative way of looking at life.* **5 negative number:** a number less than zero
-*n.* **1** saying "no" to a request, a refusal, denial: *She received a negative in response to her request.* **2** a problem, (*syn.*) a drawback: *One of the negatives of this plan is that it costs a great deal of money.* **3** (in photography) film that shows light images as dark and dark images as light: *Photographs are made from negatives.* -*adv.* [U] **negatively.**

ne·glect /nɪ'glɛkt/ *v.* **1** to not give enough care or attention to s.o. or s.t.: *Working every weekend, he neglected his family.* **2** to forget to do s.t., (*syn.*) to overlook: *She neglected to pay a bill (mail a letter, telephone her mother, etc.).* **3** to not do s.t. out of laziness, irresponsibility: *He neglected to make repairs in his house.*
-*n.* [U] a state of neglect: *That house stands in neglect, with peeling paint and broken windows.* -*adj.* **neglectful.**

neg·li·gee /,nɛglɪ'ʒeɪ, 'nɛglɪ,ʒeɪ/ *n.* a light nightgown worn by women: *She wore a lacy negligee to bed.*

neg·li·gence /'nɛglɪdʒəns/ *n.* [U] a lack of care or attention, irresponsibility: *She is guilty of negligence for driving while she was drunk.||Their negligence resulted in a forest fire.* -*adj.* **negligent;** -*adv.* **negligently.**

neg·li·gi·ble /'nɛglɪdʒəbəl/ *adj.* small, not important: *The cost of fixing your shoes will be negligible.*

ne·go·ti·a·ble /nɪ'gouʃəbəl, -ʃiə-/ *adj.* **1** capable of being talked about and changed: *The owner says that the price of his house is negotiable.* **2** capable of being changed into cash: *Traveler's checks are negotiable in foreign countries.*

ne·go·ti·ate /nɪ'gouʃi,eɪt, -si-/ *v.* **-ated, -ating, -ates** **1** to talk in order to reach an agreement on prices, wages, conditions, etc.: *The labor union is currently negotiating with the company.* **2** to reach an agreement through discussion: *The labor union negotiated a wage increase.* -*n.* **negotiator.**

ne·go·ti·a·tion /nɪ,gouʃi'eɪʃən, -si-/ *n.* [C;U] a talk between people to reach an agreement on s.t.: *The negotiations between the two countries resulted in a new trade agreement.*

neigh /neɪ/ *n.v.* a loud, high sound made by a horse, (*syn.*) a whinny.

neigh·bor /'neɪbər/ *n.* **1** a person or family that lives next to or near one's house, apartment, etc.: *Our neighbors are very friendly.* **2** the person next to another person: *Please pass the paper to your neighbor.* **3** a country sharing a border with another country: *Mexico is our neighbor to the south.*
-*v.* to be next to, (*syn.*) to border on: *The countries that neighbor the USA are Canada and Mexico.* -*adj.* **neighboring.**

neigh·bor·hood /'neɪbər,hʊd/ *n.* **1** [C] the people, buildings, land, etc., where one lives: *We are friends with many of the families who live in our neighborhood.* **2 in the neighborhood of:** about, (*syn.*) approximately: *That item costs in the neighborhood of $100.*

neigh·bor·ly /'neɪbərli/ *adj.* friendly, helpful: *Helping elderly people do their shopping is a neighborly thing to do.*

nei·ther /'niðər, 'naɪ-/ *conj.* **1 neither...nor:** not one and not the other: *Neither you nor I can attend tonight's meeting.||She has neither friends nor relatives to help her.* **2** not also: *"I don't know the answer."—"Neither do I."* **3 neither here nor there:** not important, (*syn.*) irrelevant: *We haven't received the official report yet, but that's neither here nor there; we all know what it's going to say.*
-*adj. pron.* not either of two: *<adj.> Neither plan is acceptable.||We invited both of them, but <pron.> neither can come.||<pron.> Neither of us prepared for the exam.*

nem·e·sis /'nɛməsɪs/ *n.* **-ses** /-,siz/ **1** [U] a source of great difficulty, frustration, or harm to s.o.: *Chemistry was my nemesis in college.* **2** [C] an opponent who cannot be defeated: *The tennis champion's nemesis was a 16-year-old newcomer from Florida.*

ne·on /'ni,ɑn/ *n.* [U] a rare natural gas used to light up gas tube signs: *The centers of many cities are full of neon signs for restaurants, bars, and clubs.*

ne·o·phyte /'niə,faɪt/ *n.frml.* a beginner: *He is a neophyte at playing the piano.*

neph·ew /'nɛfyu/ *n.* the son of one's brother or sister, or the son of one's husband or wife's brother or sister: *My nephew Luke is my sister's son.*

nep·o·tism /'nɛpə,tɪzəm/ *n.* [U] favoritism shown to relatives in giving them jobs, whether or not they are qualified: *She was guilty of nepotism when she hired her son over other applicants who were more experienced and better educated.*

nerd /nɜrd/ *n.infrml.* a socially unskilled person: *Why did you invite that nerd to the party? -adj.* **nerdy.**

nerve /nɜrv/ *n.* **1** [C] a long fiber that carries messages between the brain and other parts of the body: *Nerves can carry messages from the brain to move a muscle, or send feelings of pleasure or pain back to the brain.* **2** [U] courage, (*syn.*) backbone: *She has nerves of steel; nothing seems to scare her.* **3 to have a lot of** or **some nerve:** to act in a rude way, take advantage: *He had a lot of* (or) *some nerve stealing my parking space.* **4 to get on s.o.'s nerves:** to annoy, irritate s.o.: *His constant complaining gets on my nerves.* **5 to hit a nerve:** to bring up a painful subject for s.o.: *I hit a nerve when I asked him how his wife was; she divorced him last month.*

nerve gas *n.* **gases** [U] a poisonous gas used as a weapon in war: *They bombed the village with nerve gas.*

nerve-rack·ing /ˈnɜrvˌrækɪŋ/ *adj.* stressful, causing fear and tiredness: *The flight was nerve-racking because of the storm.*

nerv·ous /ˈnɜrvəs/ *adj.* **1** worried about a future event, (*syns.*) anxious, jittery: *The student is very nervous about taking her exams next week.* **2** easily upset, always worried and tense: *He's a nervous person who can't sit still for a minute.* **3** related to the nerves: *the nervous system||a nervous disorder* **4** *infrml.* **nervous Nelly:** a person who is always worried that s.t. will go wrong: *She's such a nervous Nelly that she refused to let her daughter go away to college. -adv.* **nervously;** *-n.* **nervousness.**

nervous breakdown *n.* [C] a medical condition in which a person cannot work or live normally due to worry, sadness, and tiredness: *She suffered a nervous breakdown after losing her family in a plane crash.*

nervous system *n.* also called the central nervous system, the system of the body made up of the brain, the spine, and nerves that send messages to the brain about pain, pleasure, movement, etc.

nerv·y /ˈnɜrvi/ *adj.* **-ier, -iest** taking advantage of other people, (*syn.*) pushy: *Stepping ahead of everyone else in line is a nervy thing to do.*

nest /nɛst/ *n.* **1** a place made of twigs, grass, or leaves where birds or other animals, such as squirrels, raise their young: *Nests are often located in places where it is difficult for the animal's enemies to reach them.* **2** *infrml.fig.* a person's home, esp. one's parents' house: *Just when their youngest child had moved out, their oldest decided to return to the nest for a while.*

—v. to build a nest and raise young in it: *Birds nest in the spring.*

nest egg *n.* a sum of money saved for a specific purpose, such as retirement: *The young man started to build a nest egg when he was in his 30's.*

nes·tle /ˈnɛsəl/ *v.infrml.fig.* **-tled, -tling, -tles** to lie close and comfortably: *The baby nestled in her mother's arms.*

net (1) /nɛt/ *n.* [C;U] a material made of string, wire, etc., knotted or twisted together, used for a specific purpose: *A fisherman uses a net to catch fish.||A hair net is used to hold hair in place.||In tennis, a player must hit the ball over a net.*

—v. **netted, netting, nets** to catch with a net: *The fisherman nets fish in the river.*

net (2) *adj.* related to the amount remaining after subtractions (for expenses, taxes, etc.) have been made: *After taxes, her net salary comes to $850 a week.||The net weight of the cereal (without the box) is 12 ounces.||Net sales were down this year.*

—v. **netted, netting, nets** to gain, have left after subtractions: *Our company netted a ten-percent profit after paying taxes. See:* net profit, gross.

net assets *n.pl.* the value of all of a company's property, minus what it owes: *That company's assets are $1 million, and it owes $700,000, so its net assets are $300,000.*

neth·er /ˈnɛðər/ *adj.frml.* below, underneath: *That cave extends to the nether reaches of the earth.*

neth·er·world /ˈnɛðərˌwɜrld/ *n.* usu. *sing.* [C] hell, world of the dead: *a tale of the netherworld*

net profit *n.* a sum of money left after all expenses, including taxes, are subtracted from the total sales: *Our company made a ten-percent net profit for the year.*

net·ting /ˈnɛtɪŋ/ *n.* [U] a net or series of nets: *The workmen hung netting under the bridge to catch anything that might fall while they were repairing it.*

net·tle /ˈnɛtl/ *n.* a type of plant with needles that can irritate and hurt the skin

—v. **-tled, -tling, -tles** to irritate, anger s.o.: *His criticism of the project nettled me. -adj.* **nettlesome** /ˈnɛtlsəm/.

net·work /ˈnɛtˌwɜrk/ *n.* **1** a system of connected travel routes or communication lines: *a network of highways (railways, telephone lines)||a computer network* **2** a large television or radio company with stations across the country: *ABC, CBS, and NBC are the three major television networks.*

—v. to meet and exchange information with people in one's business or profession, esp. in order to further one's career: *She networked at*

a conference and learned about several new job openings.

net worth *n.* the value of all of one's property (house, car, money, etc.) minus what one owes in debts: *According to the newspaper, her net worth is in the millions.*

neu·ral /'nʊrəl/ *adj.* related to nerves: *He has a neural disease.*

neu·rol·o·gy /nʊ'raləʤi/ *n.* [U] the study of the nervous system and its disorders: *He is a doctor in neurology. -adj.* **neurological** /,nʊrə'laʤɪkəl/; *-n.* **neurologist.**

neu·ron /'nʊr,an/ *n.* a nerve cell: *A neuron is the basic unit of the nervous system.*

neu·ro·sis /nʊ'roʊsɪs, nə-/ *n.* **-ses** /-,sɪz/ [C] a mental illness whose symptoms include anxiety, irrational fears, recurrent disturbing thoughts, and repetitive behavior: *Her neurosis causes her to have a fear of small spaces.*

neu·rot·ic /nʊ'ratɪk, nə-/ *adj.* related to neurosis: *Brushing one's teeth every 10 minutes can be neurotic behavior.*
—*n.* a person with a neurosis: *My boss is a neurotic who is difficult to work with.*

neu·ter (1) /'nutər/ *v.* to cut off the sex organs of an animal, (*syns.*) to castrate or spay: *She neutered her dog so that it can't have puppies.*

neuter (2) *adj.* (in the grammar of some languages) referring to nouns that are neither feminine nor masculine: *In Latin, "opus" is a neuter noun meaning "work."*

neu·tral /'nutrəl/ *adj.* **1** not on either side in a disagreement, debate, war, etc., (*syn.*) impartial: *That politician is neutral, neither for nor against a tax increase.* **2** not clearly one thing or another: *Her face has a neutral expression.* **3** (of colors) dull: *Gray is a neutral color.*
—*n.* [U] (in a car or other vehicle) a position of the gears in which the engine gives no power to the wheels: *Put the car in neutral.*

neu·tral·i·ty /nu'trælət̬i/ *n.* [U] a position of being neither for nor against s.t., (*syn.*) impartiality: *Switzerland maintained its position of neutrality during World War II.*

neu·tral·ize /'nutrəlaɪz/ *v.* **-ized, -izing, -izes** to stop s.t., to prevent the effects of s.t.: *He neutralized an upset stomach with an antacid. -n.* [U] **neutralization** /,nutrələ'zeɪʃən/.

neu·tron /'nu,tran/ *n.* one of the tiny particles with no electric charge that together with protons forms most atoms

nev·er /'nɛvər/ *adv.* **1** at no time, not ever: *My husband and I never go to the opera.‖She's never been to China.‖I'll never see you again.*

never-never land *n.* a beautiful imaginary place, (*syn.*) a paradise: *The prince married her and took her off to never-never land.*

nev·er·the·less /,nɛvərðə'lɛs/ *adv.* in spite of that, however: *We spent too much money on our vacation; nevertheless, we had fun.*

new /nu/ *adj.* **1** recently made, bought, arrived, etc.: *Is that a new shirt you're wearing?‖I'm new in the neighborhood.‖There are some new leaves on the plant.* **2** of the latest type, design, etc.: *Have you seen the new car that company is selling?* **3** not known, not existing before: *a new cure for the disease‖the formation of a new company* **4** not previously owned by anyone: *That store sells new and used books. -n.* **newness.**

new·born /'nu,bɔrn/ *n.adj.* a child or animal that has just been born: *They have a <adj.> newborn baby.‖The <n.> newborns are well treated at that hospital. See:* infant.

new·com·er /'nu,kʌmər/ *n.* a recent arrival: *He is a newcomer to our town.*

new·fan·gled /,nu'fæŋgəld, 'nu,fæŋ-/ *adj.infrml.* (often used humorously of ideas or equipment) newly made, technologically up-to-date: *She just bought one of those newfangled computers that can talk.*

new·ly /'nuli/ *adv.* **1** just recently: *He is newly arrived in town.* **2** freshly: *Newly made cookies taste good.*

new·ly·wed /'nuli,wɛd/ *n.* a person who has just been married: *The newlyweds left to go on their honeymoon.*

news /nuz/ *n.pl. used with a sing. v.* [U] **1** a report on the latest major events in one's own city and nation and in other parts of the world, on television, on the radio, in a newspaper, etc.: *I watched the evening news on television.* **2** information about recent events or changes in s.o.'s personal or business life: *She read a letter with news from her son.* **3 That's news to me:** a surprise: *"Did you hear that George was fired today?"—"No. That's news to me!"*

news·break /'nuz,breɪk/ *n.* an interruption of a regular radio or television program to give a brief news report: *We interrupt our regular show for this important newsbreak.*

news·cast /'nuz,kæst/ *n.* a radio or TV program reporting current events: *This newscast is coming to you direct from Tokyo. -n.* **newscaster.**

news conference *n.* a gathering of reporters to hear an important person make a statement and usu. answer questions asked by them, (*syn.*) a press conference: *The President held a news conference to discuss the crisis.*

news·let·ter /'nuz,lɛtər/ *n.* a few pages of information on a certain topic sent weekly (or monthly, quarterly, etc.) to people with an interest in that topic: *Each month our company sends a four-page newsletter about new products to all of its employees.*

news·pa·per /'nuz,peɪpər, 'nus-/ *n.* a printed paper containing daily or weekly news: *We read the newspaper every morning.*

N

news·per·son /'nuz,pɜrsən/ *n.* a person who gathers and reports the news for a newspaper, magazine, etc.: *The newsperson for the local paper reported on the fire.*

news·print /'nuz,prɪnt/ *n.* [U] the paper used to print newspapers: *Most of the newsprint comes from Canada.*

USAGE NOTE: Many cities in the USA require that newsprint be made partly of *recycled* paper to encourage recycling and reduce the number of trees that are cut down to make paper.

news release *n.* new information written in a brief style, which is given to newspeople to use in their reporting, (*syn.*) a press release: *The White House issued a news release with the latest information on the nation's economy.*

news·room /'nuz,rum/ *n.* a place where news is received and written for use by newspapers, magazines, radio, and television: *The reporters and writers are in the newsroom preparing for tonight's broadcast.*

news·stand /'nuz,stænd/ *n.* a small store often with one side open, that sells newspapers and magazines: *The newsstand on the corner also sells candy.*

newsstand

news·wor·thy /'nuz,wɜrði/ *adj.* considered of sufficient interest to people to be reported by the news media: *Fires and murders are always newsworthy items.*

news·y /'nuzi/ *adj.infrml.* **-ier, -iest** full of news, esp. about one's personal life: *My sister sent me a long, newsy letter.*

newt /nut/ *n.* a small lizard-like creature that can live both in water and on land: *The children caught some newts near the pond.*

New Testament *n.* the section of the Bible that contains the earliest Christian writings, including the story of the life of Christ: *In his speech, he made several references to the New Testament. See:* Old Testament.

New World *n.* the Western Hemisphere (North, Central, and South America): *Columbus sailed to the New World from Spain.*

new year *n.* the coming year (as viewed from the end of the previous one): *We are making vacation plans for the new year.*

New Year's Day *n.* January 1: *We relax on New Year's Day. See:* resolution.

New Year's Eve *n.* the evening up to 12 midnight of December 31: *We're going to attend a party on New Year's Eve.*

USAGE NOTE: The most well-known *New Year's Eve* celebration in the USA takes place in Times Square in New York City. Thousands of people gather at midnight to watch "the Big Apple"—a ball of lights—slowly fall down the side of a large building. People all over the world watch on TV.

next /nɛkst/ *adj.* **1** the one after the present or a previous one: *The next time that you're late, you'll be in trouble.||Her next book was a great success.* **2** closest to where one is: *Turn right at the next traffic light.* **3 next best:** second choice: *The best person for the job is Susan; the next best is Paul.* **4 next to nothing:** very little: *She has next to nothing in the bank.*
—*adv.* after the present one: *I will answer your question next.*
—*prep.* **next to:** beside: *He's sitting next to his sister.*

next door *adv.adj.* located beside, to the left or right of a building, office, apartment, etc.: *The shop <adv.> next door always looks busy.*

next of kin *n.* [U] one's closest living relative: *When she died, the hospital called her nephew (husband, brother, etc.), because he was her next of kin.*

nex·us /'nɛksəs/ *n.* **nexus** or **nexuses** a connected group of people, objects, or ideas: *The president, vice-president, and marketing director form the nexus of power in that company.*

nib /nɪb/ *n.* the point of a pen: *The nib of my pen is broken.*

nib·ble /'nɪbəl/ *v.* **-bled, -bling, -bles** to eat lightly in small bites: *Sheep nibbled at the grass.*
—*n.* a small amount of food: *She ate just a nibble.* *-n.* **nibbler.**

nice /naɪs/ **nicer, nicest** *adj.* **1** kind, friendly, pleasant: *She has a nice personality.||It was nice of you to drive me home.* **2** pretty, attractive: *That is a nice dress (hat, suit, house, car, etc.).* **3** proper, well-behaved: *Your son is such a nice boy.* **4** pleasing, enjoyable: *We had a very nice time on our vacation. -n.* **niceness.**

nice·ly /'naɪsli/ *adv.* **1** well, excellently: *The patient was sick, but is now doing nicely.* **2** properly, politely: *Speak nicely to your mother.*

niche /nɪʧ, niʃ/ *n.* **1** a hollow area in a wall usu. for showing art: *The statue stood in a niche.* **2** a position or place that is just right for a person: *She is very happy with her new job; it sounds like she found her niche.*

nick /nɪk/ *n.* **1** a small cut: *He has a nick on his cheek from shaving.* **2 in the nick of time:** (in an urgent situation) at the very last moment: *The ambulance arrived in the nick of time.*
—*v.* to make a small cut or mark: *She nicked the table (her hand, the paint on her car, etc.).*

nick·el /ˈnɪkəl/ n. **1** [U] a hard, silver-colored metallic element that is often used to mix with or cover other metals, since it is easy to shape and resists wear well **2** [C] in the USA and Canada, a five-cent coin

nickel-and-dime /ˌnɪkələn'daɪm/ v. **nickel-and-dimed** or **nickeled-and-dimed, nickel-and-diming,** or **nickeling-and-diming, nickel-and-dimes** or **nickels-and-dimes** to force s.o. to bargain over small amounts of money, (syn.) to haggle: *The buyer nickel-and-dimed us over every little item, so we decided not to sell our house to him.*

nick·nack /ˈnɪk,næk/ n. See: knicknack.

nick·name /ˈnɪk,neɪm/ n.v. **-named, -naming, -names** an informal name given to a person in addition to a legal one: *James's <n.> nickname is Jim.‖His mother <v.> nicknamed him "Speedy" because he was always in a hurry.*

nic·o·tine /ˈnɪkə,tin/ n. [U] the poisonous chemical in tobacco: *It is difficult for people to stop smoking because nicotine is addictive.*

niece /nis/ n. the daughter of one's brother or sister, or the daughter of one's husband or wife's brother or sister: *My niece Michelle is my brother's daughter.*

nif·ty /ˈnɪfti/ adj.infrml. **-tier, -tiest** excellent, wonderful: *He owns a nifty new motorcycle.*

nig·gard·ly /ˈnɪgərdli/ adj.pej. always unwilling to spend money, cheap: *He gave a niggardly contribution to the cause.*

nig·gle /ˈnɪgəl/ v. **-gled, -gling, -gles** to argue over details, (syn.) to quibble: *They niggled over the price.*

nig·gling /ˈnɪglɪŋ/ adj. unimportant, (syn.) petty: *That's a niggling detail; stop worrying about it.*

night /naɪt/ n. **1** [U] the time without sunlight between sunset and sunrise in a 24-hour period: *I couldn't sleep all night.‖We walked in the dark of night.* **2** [C] evening: *We went to the movies last night.* **3 night after night:** every night for a period of time: *She lay awake worrying night after night.* **4 night and day: a.** without stopping: *I'm working night and day to finish the project on time.* **b.** completely changed: *The difference in his grades at school between last year and this year is like night and day.* **5 make a night of it:** to spend all or most of the night out having fun: *After dinner at a restaurant, we decided to make a night of it and go to a discotheque.*

night·cap /ˈnaɪt,kæp/ n. **1** an alcoholic drink taken before bedtime: *Some people like to have a nightcap before going to sleep.* **2** a cap worn in bed at night for warmth

night·club /ˈnaɪt,klʌb/ n.v. **-clubbed, -clubbing, -clubs** a place of entertainment where people can eat, drink, and dance or watch a show: *We go to a <n.> nightclub on Saturday nights.‖Our friends go <v.> nightclubbing, too. See:* bar, USAGE NOTE.

night·fall /ˈnaɪt,fɔl/ n. [U] the time of day when the sun goes down: *I must be home before nightfall.*

night·gown /ˈnaɪt,gaʊn/ n. a loose, comfortable dress that women or girls wear for sleeping: *Put on your nightgown and go to bed.*

night·ie or **nighty** /ˈnaɪti/ n. **-ies** short for nightgown: *She wears a pink nightie to bed.*

night·in·gale /ˈnaɪtn,geɪl, ˈnaɪtɪŋ-/ n. a small brown European bird noted for its beautiful singing

night·life /ˈnaɪt,laɪf/ n. [U] night entertainment (nightclubs, theater, movie houses, restaurants, etc.) in a community: *There is much more nightlife in big cities than in small towns.*

night·light /ˈnaɪt,laɪt/ n. a dim light left on in a house during the night: *Our daughter is afraid of the dark, so we have a nightlight in her room.*

night·long /ˈnaɪt,lɔŋ/ adj. during the whole night: *He made a nightlong visit to help his sick friend.*

night·ly /ˈnaɪtli/ adj.adv. every night: *Her <adj.> nightly trip home from work takes one hour.‖The store is open <adv.> nightly until eight.*

night·mare /ˈnaɪt,mɛr/ n. **1** a frightening dream: *The poor child had a nightmare.* **2** a terrible experience: *The terrible accident turned the vacation into a nightmare.* -adj. **nightmarish.**

night owl n. fig. a person who likes to stay up late or work at night rather than sleep: *He's a night owl who doesn't go to bed before 3:00 A.M.*

nights /naɪts/ adv. during each night: *She stays up nights to study.‖He works nights at a factory. See:* night shift.

night shift n. **1** a work period that occurs at night: *She's a nurse who works on the night shift at a local hospital.* **2** the people who work at this time: *The night shift completed the job.*

USAGE NOTE: The *night shift* is also called the *graveyard shift. She sleeps during the day because she works the graveyard shift.*

night school n. a division of a school or college that gives classes in the evenings and on weekends: *After work she goes to night school to finish her degree in English.*

night·stick /ˈnaɪt,stɪk/ n. a thick stick carried by police officers, (syn.) a billyclub: *The police officer used his nightstick to defend himself against the attackers.*

N

night table *n.* a small table near a bed with a lamp and other useful items (telephone, clock, etc.): *I keep books and magazines on my night table.*

night·time /ˈnaɪtˌtaɪm/ *n.* [U] the period of darkness between sunset and sunrise: *It was nighttime and the children were asleep.*

nil /nɪl/ *n.* [U] nothing, zero, (*syn.*) naught: *Our interest in that project is nil, because there is little chance of making a profit.*

nim·ble /ˈnɪmbəl/ *adj.* **-bler, -blest 1** able to move easily and quickly, (*syn.*) agile: *She played the piano with nimble fingers.* **2** clever, quick-thinking: *Her nimble mind immediately came up with a solution to the problem.* **-adv. nimbly.**

nin·com·poop /ˈnɪnkəmˌpup, ˈnɪŋ-/ *n.infrml.* a stupid person, (*syn.*) an idiot: *That nincompoop gave me the wrong information again.*

nine /naɪn/ *adj.n.* the cardinal number 9: <*adj.*> *nine apples*||<*n.*> *Nine of the children were at the park.*

nine·teen /ˌnaɪnˈtin/ *adj.n.* the cardinal number 19: *She's* <*adj.*> *19 years old.*||<*n.*> *Nineteen of the soldiers were killed.* **-adj. n. nineteenth** /ˌnaɪnˈtinθ/.

nine·ty /ˈnaɪnti/ *adj.n.* **-ties** the cardinal number 90: *The film is* <*adj.*> *90 minutes long.*||<*n.*> *Ninety out of a hundred people voted for her.* **-adj. n. ninetieth** /ˈnaɪntiiθ/.

nin·ny /ˈnɪni/ *n.infrml.* **-nies** a silly, stupid person: *What a bunch of ninnies we have working here!*

ninth /naɪnθ/ *adj.n.* the ordinal number 9: *She was my* <*adj.*> *ninth customer today.*||*She is the* <*n.*> *ninth in line.*

nip /nɪp/ *n.* [C, usu. *sing.*] **1** a sharp, shallow bite: *The little boy got a nip on the hand from an ill-tempered dog.* **2** a small drink, esp. of liquor: *She took a nip of whiskey.* **3 nip and tuck:** racing against time, esp. in a difficult or dangerous situation: *It was nip and tuck, but we got him to the hospital in time to save him.* —*v.* **nipped, nipping, nips 1** to bite in a quick, shallow fashion: *As she walked, the little dogs nipped at her heels.* **2** to drink small amounts of alcohol: *He nipped at a bottle of Scotch.* **3 to nip s.t. in the bud:** to stop s.t. before it can develop: *His dream of becoming an actor was nipped in the bud by his parents.*

nip·ple /ˈnɪpəl/ *n.* **1** the tip of the breast, through which mother's milk is passed to babies **2** the top rubber part of a baby's bottle **3** a device in the shape of a nipple: *the nipple on a special telephone earplug*

nip·py /ˈnɪpi/ *adj.* **-pier, -piest** unpleasantly cold: *Put a coat on; it's nippy outside.*

Nir·va·na /nɪrˈvɑnə, nər-/ *n.* **1** (in Hinduism and Buddhism) the state of spiritual perfection in which one has no needs or desires: *How does one reach Nirvana?* **2** a state of great happiness and complete contentment: *When she listened to the beautiful music, she was in nirvana.*

nit /nɪt/ *n.* the egg of a tiny insect (louse) that can sometimes be found in people's hair

nit·pick /ˈnɪtˌpɪk/ *v.* to criticize by finding fault with small, unimportant details: *Instead of helping us write the report, he just kept nitpicking.* **-n. nitpicker.**

ni·trate /ˈnaɪˌtreɪt/ *n.* [C;U] an important chemical with many uses, esp. as fertilizer

ni·tro·gen /ˈnaɪtrədʒən/ *n.* [U] a gaseous chemical element which makes up most of the earth's air and is essential to plant and animal life

nit·ty-grit·ty /ˌnɪtiˈgrɪti/ *n.infrml.* [U] **1** the specific details or basic facts of a situation **2 to get down to the nitty-gritty:** to begin discussing the most important issues or specific details in the process of reaching an agreement: *Let's get down to the nitty-gritty so that we can have the contract signed by Friday.*

nit·wit /ˈnɪtˌwɪt/ *n.infrml.* a stupid person, (*syn.*) an idiot: *Those nitwits keep sending shipments to the wrong address! See:* kook, USAGE NOTE.

nix /nɪks/ *v.infrml.* **nixes** to turn down a proposal (idea, plan, etc.), (*syn.*) to veto: *The boss nixed the project as too expensive.*

no /noʊ/ *adv.* used to express a negative response: *"Do you want to go?"—"No, I don't."*||*No, don't say that because it's not true.* —*adj.* **1** not any: *to have no time (no money, no fear, etc.)* **2** not at all: *She's no fool.*||*The sign says "No smoking."*||*We are no closer to the truth.*

—*n.* an answer to a question: *She gave my request a solid no.*

no-account *adj.* untrustworthy, worthless: *He's a no-account fool who tries to borrow money all the time.*

—*n.* a worthless person: *that no-account who keeps pestering us for money*

No·bel Prize /noʊˈbɛl, ˈnoʊˌbɛl/ *n.* an annual prize awarded in the physical sciences, medicine, economics, literature, and for contributions to peace: *She won the Nobel Prize in chemistry.*

no·bil·i·ty /noʊˈbɪləti/ *n.* [U] **1** the group of people of high social rank, (*syn.*) aristocracy: *a member of the French nobility* **2** the quality of being noble

noble /ˈnoʊbəl/ *adj.* having or showing strength of character, high ideals, and honorable intentions: *noble ambitions to help the poor*||*a noble cause*

—*n.* a member of the nobility: *the nobles of England* **-adv. nobly.**

no·ble·man /'noʊbəlmən/ n. **-men** /-mən/ a male member of the nobility: *The hero was a French nobleman in the romantic novel.*

no·blesse o·blige /noʊ'blɛsə'bliʒ/ n. the obligation of a person of high rank or privilege to behave graciously toward or help others, esp. social inferiors: *When the millionaire's son went to help build a community center for the inner-city poor, everyone called it a case of noblesse oblige.*

no·ble·wom·an /'noʊbəl,wʊmən/ n. **-women** /,wɪmən/ a female member of the nobility: *The noblewoman lived on a country estate.*

no·bod·y /'noʊ,badi, -,bʌdi, -bədi/ n.pron. no one, no person: *The house was empty; nobody was there.*

—n. **-ies** an insignificant person, one without money, education, or social position: *How did that nobody get to be president of a company?*

no-brain·er /,noʊ'breɪnər/ n.slang s.t. that needs little or no thought or attention: *Making hamburgers is easy, a real no-brainer.*

noc·tur·nal /nak'tɜrnl/ adj. **1** during or relating to the night: *her nocturnal walks around the city* **2** (of animals) awake and active at night: *Cats are nocturnal animals.*

noc·turne /'nak,tɜrn/ n. a soft piece of music, usu. for the piano

nod /nad/ v. **nodded, nodding, nods 1** to move the head up and down slightly to express agreement, approval, or greeting: *When the waiter asked if he wanted more coffee, he nodded Yes.||I nodded to my friend as she entered the room.* **2** to signal the presence or location of s.o. or s.t. with a movement of the head: *She asked him to sit as she nodded toward a chair.* **3** to let the head fall forward heavily out of sleepiness: *The baby's head was starting to nod.* **4** to bend slowly up and down: *The flowers nodded in the breeze.* **5** phrasal v. **to nod off:** to fall asleep: *I nodded off during class.*
—n. an up and down movement of the head: *She gave him a nod in response to his question.*

node /noʊd/ n. **1** a swelling or small lump: *a node on the skin* **2** a mass of tissue inside the body: *a lymph node* **3** a point on the stem of a plant from which a leaf grows **4** a device, such as a terminal or printer, in a computer network

no-fault adj. **1** referring to automobile insurance that pays for damages regardless of who is responsible for the accident: *Some states require no-fault auto insurance by law.* **2** referring to a type of divorce made legal without assigning blame to either partner

no-frills adj. basic, with no extras or luxuries: *That airline offers a no-frills flight to California for a very low price.*

nog·gin /'nagɪn/ n.infrml. the head: *I bumped my noggin on the low ceiling.*

no-go n. adj.infrml. stopped (from proceeding further), (syn.) halted: *The flight was <adj.> no-go due to bad weather.*

no-good n.adj.infrml. a worthless, often dangerous person, (syn.) a good-for-nothing: *He is a <n.> no-good; stay away from him!*

noise /nɔɪz/ n. [C;U] **1** a sound, esp. an unpleasant one: *We heard a strange noise.||Street noise kept me awake all night.||The children were told not to make any noise.* **2 to make noise about s.t.:** to make a public complaint: *The community group was making noise about the broken streetlights.*

noise·less /'nɔɪzlɪs/ adj. without noise: *The fan was almost noiseless.* **-adv. noiselessly; -n.** [U] **noiselessness.**

noise·mak·er /'nɔɪz,meɪkər/ n. a hand-held device used to make noise during celebrations: *We brought noisemakers and champagne to the New Year's Eve party.* **-n.** [U] **noisemaking.**

noise pollution n. [U] a noise level harmful to human health, caused by motor vehicles, airplane traffic, construction equipment, etc.: *We need stricter city regulations to control noise pollution.*

noi·some /'nɔɪsəm/ adj. **1** bad-smelling: *The chemical had a noisome odor.* **2** harmful: *The rotting meat caused a noisome health hazard.*

nois·y /'nɔɪzi/ adj. **-ier, -iest 1** full of noise and sounds: *a noisy restaurant (party, street, etc.)* **2** making loud noise, (syn.) raucous: *a noisy machine (dog, child, etc.)*

no·mad /'noʊ,mæd/ n. **1** a member of a tribe which has no permanent home, but moves constantly in search of water and grassy land for its animals: *We passed desert nomads with tents and flocks of goats.* **2** a person without a permanent home: *After years as a nomad, she finally settled in Miami and opened a business.* **-adj. nomadic** /noʊ'mædɪk/.

no-man's-land /'noʊmænz,lænd/ n. **1** an area of land separating two warring armies: *Any soldier who tried to cross the no-man's-land would be killed.* **2** land that is not owned by any person or country: *The remote mountainous area was a no-man's-land.*

nom de plume /,namdə'plum/ n. **noms de plume** /,namdə'plum/ a false name used by an author, (syns.) a pen name, pseudonym: *Mark Twain is the nom de plume for Samuel Clemens, the American writer.*

no·men·cla·ture /'noʊmən,kleɪʧər, noʊ'mɛn-klə-/ n.frml. [U] names used in a systematic way in science and other fields: *The names of bones on a picture of a skeleton represent part of the nomenclature in biology.*

nom·i·nal /'namənəl/ adj. **1** small, very little: *She bought the house for a nominal amount of* money. **2** in name only: *He is the nominal head of a government that is actually run by the Prime Minister. -adv.* **nominally.**

nom·i·nate /'nɑmə,neɪt/ *v.* **-nated, -nating, -nates 1** to propose s.o. for election to a position: *The Republican Party nominated him for President.* **2** to appoint s.o. to a position: *The director nominated me to attend the conference.*

nom·i·na·tion /,nɑmə'neɪʃən/ *n.* [C;U] a proposal of s.o. for a position: *the nomination of Jane Smith for Treasurer of the garden club.*

nom·i·na·tive /'nɑmənətɪv/ *n.* [C] a grammatical word form referring to the subject of s.t.: *The pronoun "we" is nominative.*

nom·i·nee /,nɑmə'ni/ *n.* the person who is nominated: *Jane Smith is the nominee for Treasurer.*

non- /nɑn/ *prefix* not or lack of: *Noncontributing means not contributing·*

non·ag·gres·sion pact /,nɑnə'grɛʃən/ *n.* a formal agreement by two or more countries not to attack each other: *The representatives of the two countries met and worked out a nonaggression pact.*

non·call·a·ble /,nɑn'kɔləbəl/ *adj.* referring to a bond or preferred stock that cannot be redeemed by the corporation or government agency that offered it before a specific date: *My financial advisor recommended buying noncallable government bonds.*

non·ca·lor·ic /,nɑnkə'lɔrɪk/ *adj.* containing no or almost no calories: *Some diet sodas are noncaloric, with only one calorie per serving.*

non·cha·lance /,nɑnʃə'lɑns/ *n.* usu. *sing.* [C;U] a relaxed, carefree, unconcerned manner and attitude: *We were surprised by her nonchalance during the crisis.*

non·cha·lant /,nɑnʃə'lɑnt/ *adj.* relaxed, carefree, unconcerned: *He was quite nonchalant about losing his job. -adv.* **nonchalantly.**

non·com·mit·tal /,nɑnkə'mɪtl/ *adj.* indefinite about a decision or opinion: *When we offered him a partnership in the company, his response was noncommittal. -adv.* **noncommittally.**

non·com·pet·i·tive /,nɑnkəm'pɛtətɪv/ *adj.* **1** not involving or requiring competition: *a noncompetitive contract‖She enjoys noncompetitive sports, such as jogging and ice skating.* **2** inferior, undesirable: *a product that is noncompetitive in the marketplace*

non·com·pli·ance /,nɑnkəm'plaɪəns/ *n.* [U] failure to meet the requirements of a contract: *A manufacturer fell into noncompliance by failing to deliver the goods on time.*

non·con·form·ist /,nɑnkən'fɔrmɪst/ *n.adj.* a person who does not behave according to ordinary standards of conduct, (*syn.*) a maverick: *Ever since his college days as a political radical, he has been a <n.> nonconformist.‖*

People are often shocked by his <adj.> nonconformist ideas. -n. [U] **nonconformity.**

non·co·op·er·a·tion /,nɑnkou,ɑpə'reɪʃən/ *n.* [U] failure to work together to achieve a goal: *Your department's noncooperation prevented us from completing the project on time.*

non·cred·it /,nɑn'krɛdɪt/ *adj.* (in education) referring to a course offered for no academic credit: *My adviser suggested that I take the noncredit reading course.*

non·dair·y /,nɑn'dɛri/ *adj.* containing no milk or milk products, such as cheese: *The restaurant offers a variety of nondairy dishes.*

non·de·duct·i·ble /,nɑndɪ'dʌktəbəl/ *adj.* referring to expenses, such as for travel or entertainment, that cannot be subtracted from one's income on a tax return: *Medical expenses under a certain amount are nondeductible on your tax return.*

non·de·nom·i·na·tion·al /,nɑndɪ,nɑmə'neɪʃənəl/ *adj.* not related or restricted to a specific religion or religious group: *The chapel at the airport is nondenominational; everyone may enter.*

non·de·script /,nɑndɪ'skrɪpt/ *adj.* common, ordinary, with no outstanding features: *Her office is in a nondescript building on the main street.*

non·dis·crim·i·na·to·ry /,nɑndɪ'skrɪmənə,tɔri/ *adj.* not favoring or excluding any race, religion, sex, or ethnic background: *The company was praised for its nondiscriminatory hiring practices. -n.* **nondiscrimination** /,nɑndɪ,skrɪmə'neɪʃən/.

non·drink·er /,nɑn'drɪŋkər/ *n.* a person who does not drink alcoholic beverages, (*syn.*) a teetotaler: *He has been a nondrinker all his life.*

none /nʌn/ *pron.* **1** not any: *We wanted some coffee, but there was none left.* **2** no one: *None of the children had enough to eat.* **3 none but:** only: *They wanted none but the best (employees, furniture, etc.).* **4 none other:** not another person: *It was none other than my old friend Jack, whom I hadn't seen in 20 years.*
—*adv.* **1 none too:** not very: *They were none too happy about that.* **2 none the:** not at all: *She is none the worse for her difficult journey.*

non·en·ti·ty /nɑn'ɛntəti/ *n.* **-ties** a person with no personality, ambition, or social position: *I spoke to some nonentity at the company who couldn't give me any information.*

none·such /'nʌn,sʌtʃ/ *n.* [U] s.o. or s.t. without equal, (*syn.*) a nonpareil: *She is a nonesuch in computer design; she is the best.*

none·the·less /,nʌnðə'lɛs/ *adv.frml.* however, in spite of that, (*syn.*) nevertheless: *The soldiers were cold, tired, and hungry; nonetheless, they continued to march.*

non·e·vent /ˌnɑnɪˈvɛnt, ˈnɑnɪˌvɛnt/ *n.* an event of no substance or real importance: *The meeting of the finance ministers was a nonevent because they could not come to an agreement on the important issues.*

non·ex·clu·sive /ˌnɑnɪkˈsklusɪv, -zɪv/ *adj.* not obligated to only one agent: *Our company has a nonexclusive distribution policy, so anyone can sell our product.*

non·ex·is·tent /ˌnɑnɪgˈzɪstənt/ *adj.* missing, absent: *nonexistent funds in the account‖nonexistent people on the voter list* **-n.** [U] **nonexistence.**

non·fat /ˌnɑnˈfæt, ˈnɑnˌfæt/ *adj.* containing no fat: *Athletes often buy nonfat milk.*

non·fic·tion /ˌnɑnˈfɪkʃən/ *n.* [U] a category of literature based on fact, about real people and events: *The author writes only historical nonfiction. See:* fiction, USAGE NOTE.

non·flam·ma·ble /ˌnɑnˈflæməbəl/ *adj.* not capable of being set on fire or burning: *The furniture is covered with nonflammable material.*

non·in·ter·ven·tion /ˌnɑnɪntərˈvɛnʃən/ *n.* [U] **1** the act of not interfering in a situation: *the nonintervention of police in a family argument* **2** a policy of not interfering, esp. in the internal affairs of another nation or in its disputes with other nations: *The foreign minister favored the nonintervention of Russia in Mideast disputes.*

non·in·va·sive /ˌnɑnɪnˈveɪsɪv/ *adj.* (in medicine) not involving the use of instruments that cut or enter the body: *She is receiving a new noninvasive cancer treatment.*

non·judg·men·tal /ˌnɑndʒʌdʒˈmɛntl/ *adj.* about not expressing either approval or disapproval: *The priest has a nonjudgmental attitude toward the prison inmates; he doesn't say anything positive or negative about them.*

non·lin·e·ar /ˌnɑnˈlɪniər/ *adj.* not in a straight line, not having direct connection points: *a nonlinear problem‖nonlinear equations*

non·mem·ber, /ˌnɑnˈmɛmbər, ˈnɑn-/ *n.* a person who does not belong, esp. to a club or other organization: *Nonmembers may play at the golf club by invitation only.*

non·me·tal·lic /ˌnɑnməˈtælɪk/ *adj.* not made of metal: *nonmetallic elements or materials*

no-no /ˈnoʊˌnoʊ/ *n.infrml.* **-nos** or **-no's** *s.t.* forbidden, (*syn.*) a taboo: *Walking on the grass (stealing money, hitting s.o.) is a no-no.*

no-non·sense *adj.* direct, serious, (*syn.*) businesslike: *The teacher has a no-nonsense attitude in the classroom and doesn't tolerate misbehavior.*

non·ob·jec·tive /ˌnɑnəbˈdʒɛktɪv/ *adj.* influenced by one's personal feelings, (*syn.*) biased: *a nonobjective evaluation*

non·pa·reil /ˌnɑnpəˈrɛl/ *n.* [C] *adj.* a person without equal, (*syn.*) a nonesuch: *She is a <n.> nonpareil on the tennis court.*

non·par·ti·san /ˌnɑnˈpɑrtəzən, -sən/ *adj.* about not representing or favoring a particular group, esp. a political party: *A congressional nonpartisan committee was formed to examine the problem.*

non·per·form·ance /ˌnɑnpərˈfɔrməns/ *n.* [U] failure to fulfill the demands of a contract: *The landlord sued a tenant for nonperformance because the tenant did not pay his rent.*

non·per·form·ing /ˌnɑnpərˈfɔrmɪŋ/ *adj.* referring to assets that are not producing income: *The company has 1,000 acres of undeveloped land as a nonperforming asset.*

non·per·son /ˌnɑnˈpɜrsən/ *n.* a person whom the government seeks to make nonexistent by banishing him or her from public life and removing all mention of him or her from public records: *The scientist became a nonperson in his country after criticizing the government.*

non·plussed /ˌnɑnˈplʌst/ *adj.* to be so puzzled and shocked by an occurrence that one is speechless: *She was nonplussed by his offer of marriage; they had only known each other a short time.*

non·pol·lut·ing /ˌnɑnpəˈlutɪŋ/ *adj.* (of products and industrial processes) not causing environmental pollution: *Solar and wind power are nonpolluting sources of energy.*

non·pre·scrip·tion /ˌnɑnprɪˈskrɪpʃən/ *adj.* (of medicine) not requiring a doctor's prescription, (*syn.*) over-the-counter: *Aspirin is a nonprescription drug.*

non·pro·duc·tive /ˌnɑnprəˈdʌktɪv/ *adj.* producing no positive results: *The meeting was nonproductive because neither side was willing to compromise.*

non·pro·fes·sion·al /ˌnɑnprəˈfɛʃənəl/ *adj.n.* referring to a person who works at, but is not an official member of, a particular profession or trade, (*syn.*) amateur: *We hired <adj.> nonprofessional electricians to save money.‖The actors in the film were <n.> nonprofessionals.*

non·prof·it /ˌnɑnˈprɑfɪt/ *adj.* (of businesses and organizations) not intended to make money: *Many nonprofit organizations, such as charities, rely on public donations.*

USAGE NOTE: *Nonprofit organizations* do not have to pay tax on money they raise from donations. Churches, charities, museums, and schools are usually nonprofit.

non·pro·lif·er·a·tion /ˌnɑnprəˌlɪfəˈreɪʃən/ *n.* [U] *adj.* restriction on the spread of s.t., esp. nuclear weapons: *One country refused to sign the nonproliferation treaty.*

non·re·fund·a·ble /ˌnɑnrɪˈfʌndəbəl/ *adj.* (referring to money, esp. a deposit) that will not be returned: *We made a nonrefundable deposit toward the purchase of a house.*

non·re·new·a·ble /ˌnɑnrɪ'nuəbəl/ *adj.* (referring to natural resources such as oil and coal) that cannot be replaced: *We must conserve our nonrenewable resources.*

non·rep·re·sen·ta·tion /ˌnɑn,rɛprɪzɛn'teɪʃən, -zən-/ *n.* [U] absence of representation, esp. in government: *The nonrepresentation of our party in Parliament resulted from our being voted out of office in the last election.*

non·rep·re·sen·ta·tive /ˌnɑn,rɛprɪ'zɛntətɪv/ *adj.* not typical: *He is a hardworking, disciplined employee who occasionally drinks too much; his drinking is nonrepresentative of his general behavior.*

non·res·i·dent /ˌnɑn'rɛzədənt, -ˌdɛnt/ *n.adj.* a person who does not permanently live in an area, esp. related to one's legal address or foreign citizenship: *She is a <adj.> nonresident alien living in New York on a student visa.||As a <n.> nonresident (of this city), I have to pay to use the community pool.*

non·re·sis·tance /ˌnɑnrɪ'zɪstəns/ *n.* [U] the belief or practice of deliberate passivity by individuals or a nation in the face of force: *The TV newscast showed the nonresistance of demonstrators to police arrest.*

non·re·stric·tive /ˌnɑnrɪ'strɪktɪv/ *adj.* **1** not placing restrictions, esp. in contracts: *The warehouse lease contains a nonrestrictive clause regarding the type of goods that can be stored there.* **2** (in grammar) relating to a descriptive word, clause, or phrase that is not essential to the basic meaning of what it describes: *In the sentence, "My sister, who is a teacher, has a degree in Fine Arts," "who is a teacher," is a nonrestrictive clause.*

non·re·turn·a·ble /ˌnɑnrɪ'tɜrnəbəl/ *adj.* referring to goods that may not be returned after purchase for a refund or exchange: *We threw away the nonreturnable beer and soda cans.*

non·sched·uled /ˌnɑn'skɛdʒuld, -dʒuəld, -dʒəld/ *adj.* not planned on a regular basis: *World Air is a nonscheduled airline that provides charter flights to the Caribbean.*

non·sense /'nɑn,sɛns, -səns/ *n.* [U] **1** words that have no meaning, (*syn.*) gibberish: *The baby spoke nonsense.* **2** speech or writing that is absurd or untrue: *His ideas are pure nonsense.* **3** an act or behavior that doesn't make sense: *That company demands that we pay a bill that we've already paid. Why do we have to put up with that nonsense?*

non·sen·si·cal /nɑn'sɛnsɪkəl/ *adj.* making no sense, foolish, absurd, (*syn.*) inane: *a nonsensical report||nonsensical behavior*

non se·qui·tur /nɑn'sɛkwɪtər/ *n.frml.* [C] (Latin for) it does not follow; a break in the logical development of s.t., such as a series of

facts, dates, events, or ideas: *His next statement seemed to be a non sequitur.*

non·sex·ist /ˌnɑn'sɛksɪst/ *adj.* free of negative references to gender, esp. regarding women: *She writes nonsexist children's books.*

non·skid /ˌnɑn'skɪd/ *adj.* (usu. of tires) with a surface that resists sliding

non·stand·ard /ˌnɑn'stændərd/ *adj.* **1** not conforming to a specified set of measurements: *It's a nonstandard part that must be made specially for that machine.* **2** (of language) not considered acceptable by most educated people: *"Ain't" is nonstandard English, as in "I ain't going to the movies."*

non·stop /ˌnɑn'stɑp/ *adj.adv.* without pause, without stopping: *He worked <adv.> nonstop for 24 hours.||We took a <adj.> nonstop flight to Los Angeles.*

non·sup·port /ˌnɑnsə'pɔrt/ *n.* [U] (in law) nonpayment of living expenses, esp. in a divorce: *He divorced his wife, but did not send money for their children as agreed; she is suing him for nonsupport.*

non·un·ion /ˌnɑn'yunyən/ *adj.* **1** not a member of a trade union: *The factory hires nonunion workers.* **2** not employing trade union members: *a nonunion company*

non·us·er /ˌnɑn'yuzər/ *n.* a person who does not use drugs, alcohol, or other harmful substances: *He is a former addict who has been a nonuser for ten years.*

non·ver·bal /ˌnɑn'vɜrbəl/ *adj.* related to gestures, such as hand movements, and other body language: *Because they spoke different languages, they expressed themselves through nonverbal communication.*

non·vi·a·ble /ˌnɑn'vaɪəbəl/ *adj.* not workable, not practical: *The company decided it was a nonviable project because of the high cost of materials.*

non·vi·o·lence /ˌnɑn'vaɪələns/ *n.* [U] a doctrine that prohibits the use of force in bringing about political reform: *Mahatma Gandhi preached nonviolence in seeking the independence of India from Great Britain.*

USAGE NOTE: Following the ideas of Mahatma Gandhi, Dr. Martin Luther King Jr., led *nonviolent* protests during the *civil rights* movement in the 1950s and 1960s. Later the antiwar, ecology, and women's movements also held nonviolent protests. One popular type of protest was the *sit-in*, in which people would sit down somewhere and refuse to move. Police had to drag or carry the people away from the protest site.

non·vi·o·lent /ˌnɑn'vaɪələnt/ *adj.* peaceful, without the use of force: *The 1974 revolution in Portugal was nonviolent.*

noo·dle /'nudl/ *n.* **1** a long, narrow or wide flat strip of pasta made from a mixture of flour, egg, and water: *Boil the noodles first.* **2** *infrml.* head: *You can figure it out; just use your noodle!*
—*v.* **-dled, -dling, -dles 1** *infrml.* to take a light interest in s.t.: *He noodles in the stock market.* **2** *infrml.* to adjust with the hand, (*syn.*) to fiddle with: *She noodled with the lock that was stuck.*

nook /nʊk/ *n.* **1** a small area, a small space set back from the rest of a room: *The kitchen has a sunny breakfast nook.* **2** a private, hidden spot: *a nook among the trees in the park* **3 nook(s) and crannie(s):** small, hard to reach places: *She lost her ring and searched for it in every nook and cranny (or) in all the nooks and crannies in the house.*

noon /nun/ *n.* [U] *adj.* 12 o'clock during the day: *We stopped work at <n.> noon for lunch.*‖*a <adj.> noon walk (break, meal, etc.)*

noon·day /'nun,deɪ/ *adj.* related to noontime: *a noonday meal*

no one *pron.* not one person, nobody: *No one is in the office; everyone has left.*

noon·time /'nuntaɪm/ *n.* [U] *adj.* the period surrounding 12 o'clock during the day, (*syn.*) midday: *I go out for lunch at <n.> noon-time.*‖*a <adj.> noontime lunch date*

noose /nus/ *n.* **1** a rope tied at one end in a loop with a knot that allows the loop to tighten for the purpose of hanging s.o. by the neck: *The hangman put the noose on the murderer.* **2 to put a noose around one's own neck:** to put oneself in danger often unnecessarily: *By criticizing his boss so openly, he is putting a noose around his own neck.*

nope /noʊp/ *adv.infrml.* no: *"Are you coming with me?"—"Nope, I can't leave now."*

nor /nɔr; *weak form* nər/ *conj.* **1 neither...nor:** not that one either: *Neither you nor she plans to attend the meeting.* **2** and not: *I can't afford to buy a house, nor can you.*

norm /nɔrm/ *n.* **1** a standard of behavior, that is typical of a group: *Saving five percent of one's income is the norm for the middle class.* **2** an average, an expected result: *The norm on the exam was a grade of C.*

nor·mal /'nɔrməl/ *adj.* as expected, typical, average: *Hot weather is normal for the summer.*‖*My temperature was above normal this morning.*‖*She had a normal childhood.* -*n.* [U] normality /nɔr'mælәti/.

nor·mal·cy /'nɔrməlsi/ *n.* [U] a state in which life is functioning as it usually does: *After the war, there was a return to normalcy.*

nor·mal·ize /'nɔrməl,aɪz/ *v.* **-ized, -izing, -izes** to make normal, peaceful: *The leaders met to normalize relations between the two countries.* -*n.* **normalization** /,nɔrmәlә'zeɪʃәn/.

nor·mal·ly /'nɔrməli/ *adv.* ordinarily, usually: *Normally, I would go fishing, but the weather is bad.*

nor·ma·tive /'nɔrmәtɪv/ *adj.* related to a standard or average: *a normative code of behavior*

north /nɔrθ/ *n. sing.* **1** the direction to the right when facing a sunset **2** the northern part of a country: *Minnesota is in the north; Texas is in the south.* **3 The North:** in the USA the former Union states in the Civil War: *The North defeated the South in the Civil War.*
—*adj.* **1** referring to the area towards the north: *the north side of the street (park, building, city, etc.)* **2** (of wind) coming from the north: *a bitter north wind*
—*adv.* in a northerly direction: *The plane (car, boat, etc.) is headed north.*

north·bound /'nɔrθ,baʊnd/ *adj.* toward the north: *She drove northbound from San Diego to L.A.*

north·east·er /,nɔrθ'istәr, ,nɔr'istәr/ *n.* a storm, often severe, that comes out of the northeast: *A northeaster lasted for three days and destroyed many homes.*

north·er·ly /'nɔrðәrli/ *adj.adv.* located in the north

north·ern /'nɔrðәrn/ *adj.* located in the north: *the northern part of the United States*‖*northern California* -*adj.* **northernmost** /'nɔrðәrn,moʊst/.

north·ern·er /'nɔrðәrnәr/ *n.* s.o. originally from or living in the northern part of a country: *He was a northerner from New England traveling in the southwest.*

Northern Hemisphere *n.* the part of the world that is north of the equator

northern lights *n.pl.* the aurora borealis, the lights that appear at night in the sky of the far north: *We saw the northern lights on our trip to Alaska.*

North Pole *n.* the northernmost point on earth and the land that surrounds it: *The scientist joined a research team stationed at the North Pole.*

nose /noʊz/ *n.* **1** the part of a human or animal face above the mouth that contains two holes (called nostrils) for smelling and breathing: *She has a long straight nose.* **2** sense of smell: *Dogs have good noses.* **3** *fig.infrml.* excessive interest or interference in the affairs of others: *He'd better keep his nose out of my business.* **4** *fig.* special ability, esp. to find s.t. hidden: *The detective had a nose for tracking criminals.* **5** the forward part of certain things: *the nose of a plane (boat, gun, etc.)* **6 on the nose:** exactly right: *His estimate of the cost of the project was on the nose.* **7 to follow one's nose:** to move directly ahead: *The store is across the street; just follow your nose.* **8** *infrml.* **to keep one's nose clean:** to stay out of trouble: *The prison inmate was warned to keep*

N

his nose clean. **9 to lead s.o. around by the nose:** to have complete control over s.o.: *Although her son is now an adult, she's still leading him around by the nose.* **10 to look down one's nose at s.o.:** to feel socially superior to s.o.: *She looks down her nose at her poorer relatives.* **11** *infrml.* **to pay through the nose:** to pay too high a price for s.t.: *He paid through the nose for his new boat.* **12 to pick one's nose:** (a rude and offensive act) to clean the inside of one's nose with one's finger: *The mother told her son to stop picking his nose.* **13** *infrml.* **to put s.o.'s nose out of joint:** to offend or insult s.o.: *Her supervisor's criticism of her work put her nose out of joint.* **14** *infrml.* **to stick** or **poke one's nose in s.t.:** to interfere in the affairs of others in an inappropriate way: *He has a habit of poking his nose in where it doesn't belong.* **15 to thumb one's nose at s.o.** or **s.t.:** to show disregard or disrespect for s.o. or s.t.: *She thumbs her nose at school regulations.* **16 to turn one's nose up at s.t.:** to reject with contempt: *He turned his nose up at the job offer.* **17 under one's nose:** very near s.o., easily seen: *Your keys are right under your nose!*
—*v.* **nosed, nosing, noses 1** to move ahead carefully: *The boat nosed around the rocks.* **2** *phrasal v.* **to nose around** or **about:** to search, gather information, (*syn.*) to investigate: *The detective nosed around the neighborhood for witnesses to the crime.*

nose·bleed /'noʊzblid/ *n.* a condition of blood running from the nose: *He got a nosebleed after being hit in the face by a baseball.*

nose cone *n.* the forward part of a missile or space vehicle: *The nose cone of the plane was badly damaged in the crash.*

nose·dive /'noʊzdaɪv/ *v.* **-dived** or **dove** /-,doʊv/, **-diving, -dives** to move downward quickly, front first: *A fighter plane nosedives in an attack.*
—*n.* a sharp drop: *Stock prices took a nosedive last week.*

nose job *n.infrml.* surgery performed on the nose to improve its appearance: *She had a nose job when she was in high school.*

nosh /nɑʃ/ *n.v.infrml.* **noshes** a small amount of food eaten between meals, (*syn.*) a snack: *She's <v.> noshing on some raisins.||She's having a <n.> nosh.*

no-show *n.infrml.* a person with a reservation who does not show up or call to cancel it: *There were ten no-shows on our flight to Paris.*

nos·tal·gia /nɑ'stældʒə, nə-/ *n.* [U] sentimental remembrance of and desire to return to the past: *When the old friends get together, the talk is full of nostalgia for their college days.* -*adj.* **nostalgic;** -*adv.* **nostalgically.**

nos·tril /'nɑstrəl/ *n.* one of the openings in the nose

nos·trum /'nɑstrəm/ *n.* [C] **-trums, -tra** a remedy usu. of no real value: *Society's nostrums for social problems are often ineffective.*

nos·y /'noʊzi/ *adj.* **-ier, -iest** overly curious about the affairs of others, (*syn.*) intrusive: *She's so nosy; she's always asking me personal questions which I refuse to answer.* -*n.* **nosiness.**

not /nɑt/ *adv.* **1** (used to express negation, refusal, or denial, often shortened to *n't* after auxiliary verbs): *He will not pay his bill.||You shouldn't say that.||"Are you ready?"—"No, I'm not."||Don't leave yet.||She doesn't believe that he's guilty.* (= *She believes that he isn't guilty.*) **2 not at all:** (a response to an expression of gratitude): *"I really appreciate your help."—"Not at all, it was no trouble."* **3** *conj.* **not that:** (used to begin a phrase expressing negation) *He said he was sorry—not that it matters.*

no·ta·ble /'noʊtəbəl/ *adj.* **1** important, impressive, (*syns.*) outstanding, remarkable: *She received an award for her notable achievements in cancer research.* **2** attracting attention: *He was notable by his absence.||a notable exception*
—*n.* an important person: *Many notables from the entertainment world attended the actor's funeral.* -*n.* **notability;** -*adv.* **notably.**

no·ta·rize /'noʊtə,raɪz/ *v.* **-rized, -rizing, -rizes** to have a notary public state that a signature on a document is authentic: *I had my signature on the contract notarized at the bank.* -*n.* [U] **notarization** /,noʊtərə'zeɪʃən/.

no·ta·ry public or **notary** /'noʊtəri/ *n.* **notaries public** or **notary publics** a person with the legal authority to state that a signature on a document is authentic: *The pharmacist is also a notary public.*

no·ta·tion /noʊ'teɪʃən/ *n.* [C;U] **1** a short written note: *I made a notation on my calendar to call you in two weeks.* **2** a set of symbols used to represent musical notes, numbers, etc.: *In 53, the 3 is a notation that represents 5 multiplied by itself three times.* -*v.* **notate.**

notch /nɑtʃ/ *n.* **notches 1** a shallow cut in a surface: *He cut a notch on the pole to tie a rope around it.* **2** *fig.* a level of quality, intensity, or degree: *to move up a notch in a company*
—*v.* **notches** to cut a notch in s.t.: *He notched the tree to mark where it should be cut.*

note /noʊt/ *n.* **1** a short written message: *She sent me a thank-you note for the gift.* **2** usu. pl. **notes** words, phrases, or short sentences serving as a reminder of what one heard or read: *I studied my lecture notes before the biology exam.* **3** a piece of paper representing a promise to pay a sum of money: *She received a bank note for $1000.* **4** additional information about a text found at the bottom of a page or in the back of a book: *The book provided* notes explaining some of the technical words.

notes

5 (in music) a single sound of a certain pitch or length or the symbol used to represent it: *She played the first few notes of the song.* **6** a quality of expression: *There was a note of resentment in his voice.* **7** *frml.* **of note:** important, famous: *Several actors of note appeared in the play.* **8 to compare notes:** (of two people) to share ideas and opinions about s.t.: *Let's compare notes about the party.* **9 to make a mental note of s.t.:** to try to remember s.t.: *I made a mental note to make a donation to that organization.* **10 to take note of:** to pay special attention to: *I took note of the fact that the company has expansion plans.* **11 to take** or **make notes:** to write down words, phrases, or short sentences to remember what one heard or read: *He took notes during the meeting.*

—*v.* **noted, noting, notes** **1** to write down: *I noted the most important information on a piece of paper.* **2** to observe, pay attention to: *Note the "For Sale" signs in front of many of the houses.||I noted that he seemed unhappy about the plan.*

note·book /'noʊtbʊk/ *n.* a book with blank or lined pages to make notes in: *Students carry their notebooks to class.*

not·ed /'noʊtɪd/ *adj.* well-known and respected, (*syns.*) eminent, prominent: *She is a noted authority on tropical diseases.*

notebook

note·wor·thy /'noʊt,wɜrði/ *adj.* important, significant: *He gave a noteworthy speech on poverty in America.*

not-for-profit *adj.* nonprofit: *He works for a not-for-profit human rights organization.*

noth·ing /'nʌθɪŋ/ *n.* **1** [U] not anything: *There is nothing to eat in the refrigerator.||She said nothing to me about the problem.* **2** [U] the absence of substance (quality, interest, value, etc.): *There is nothing in the newspaper (on TV, the radio, etc.) today.* **3** [U] s.t. unimportant, insignificant: *The item costs nothing, only a few cents.* **4 a big nothing:** an event of expected importance that turns out to be of little significance: *The town meeting was a big nothing.* **b.** a person who acts more important than he or she really is: *Although he talks as if he owned the company, he's just a big nothing.* **5 for nothing: a.** without payment: *He works weekends at the community center for nothing.* **b.** without achieving anything: *Our trip had to be cancelled; we spent all that time planning it for nothing.* **c.** for no money, for a very low

price: *She bought the house for nothing because the owner needed to sell it quickly.* **6 nothing but:** only, (*syn.*) solely: *The company makes nothing but mattresses.||That child is nothing but trouble.* **7 nothing doing: a.** the absence of any interesting activity: *There is nothing doing in town tonight.* **b.** *infrml.* absolutely not!: *"Will you loan me $100?"—"Nothing doing!"* **8 nothing less than** or **nothing short of:** a minimum requirement: *Nothing short of bribery will get him to go to the concert tonight; he hates classical music.* **9 to have nothing to do with s.o.** or **s.t.:** to avoid completely: *She will have nothing to do with her former husband.* **10 to make nothing of s.t.:** to minimize the importance of s.t., (*syn.*) to downplay: *He spilled tomato sauce on her dress, but she kindly made nothing of it.*

no·tice /'noʊtɪs/ *v.* **-ticed, -ticing, -tices** to observe, to look at with interest: *I noticed that there was a leak in the ceiling.||She noticed him as soon as she entered the room.*

—*n.* **1** [C] a written announcement: *I received a notice that the rent was unpaid.||There was a notice on the door that the store had moved.* **2** [C] an announcement or warning about a future event: *When she decided to quit her job, she gave the company two weeks' notice.||I gave my landlord a month's notice before I moved out.* **3** [C;U] public attention: *The movie star has been receiving a lot of notice in the press recently.* **4 at (such) short notice:** with little or no advance warning: *I can't give a speech at such short notice.* **5 until further notice:** until the next announcement: *This building is closed until further notice.*

no·tice·a·ble /'noʊtɪsəbəl/ *adj.* easily observed, obvious, (*syns.*) conspicuous, evident: *There has been a noticeable increase in sales.||His weight loss is noticeable.* -*adv.* **noticeably.**

no·ti·fi·ca·tion /,noʊtəfə'keɪʃən/ *n.* [C;U] an announcement, esp. a written one of s.t.: *They received notification from their landlord of a rent increase.*

no·ti·fy /'noʊtə,faɪ/ *v.* **-fied, -fying, -fies** to inform, to announce officially: *A man notified the police that his store had been robbed.||The telephone company notifies customers when there is a rate increase.*

no·tion /'noʊʃən/ *n.* **1** an idea or belief, esp. one that is unclear or unreasonable: *He has a silly notion about making a million dollars without working.* **2** *pl.* **notions** small useful items, such as buttons, thread, hairpins, etc.

no·to·ri·e·ty /,noʊtə'raɪəti/ *n.* [U] fame, esp. for s.t. bad: *Notoriety from the scandal led to the politician's resignation.*

no·to·ri·ous /noʊ'tɔriəs/ *adj.* well-known, famous, esp. for s.t. bad: *The film star was noto-*

N

rious for her wild living.||*A notorious criminal escaped from prison.* -*adv.* **notoriously.** *See:* infamous, USAGE NOTE.

not·with·stand·ing /ˌnɑtwɪθ'stændɪŋ, -wɪð-/ *prep.frml.* in spite of: *We will proceed with our plan, notwithstanding any objections.*
—*adv.frml.* in spite of this, (*syn.*) nevertheless: *Many political leaders expressed opposition to the proposal, but it was passed by Congress notwithstanding.*

nou·gat /'nugət/ *n.* [U] a sweet candy made of honey or sugar and nuts

nought /nɔt/ *n.* zero, nothing: *All his hard work came to nought.*

noun /naʊn/ *n.* (in grammar) a name of a person, place, thing, action, or quality that is used as the subject or object of a sentence or the object of a preposition: *In the sentence, "People buy stamps at the post office," "People," "stamps," and "post office" are nouns.*

nour·ish /'nɜrɪʃ, 'nʌr-/ *v.* **-ishes 1** to feed, esp. with healthful food: *Children should be nourished with a balanced diet.* **2** *fig.*(of a plan, belief, emotion) to keep alive or cause to grow: *The child's fear of the dark was nourished by her brother's frightening bedtime stories.*

nour·ish·ing /'nɜrɪʃɪŋ, 'nʌr-/ *adj.* healthy, (*syn.*) nutritious: *We were served a nourishing breakfast.*

nour·ish·ment /'nɜrɪʃmənt, 'nʌr-/ *n.* [U] food, esp. healthy things to eat: *A child needs nourishment to grow strong.*

nou·veau riche /ˌnuvoʊ'riʃ/ *adj.n.* **nouveaux riches** newly rich, esp. in a showy way: *They act very <adj.> nouveau riche with their matching fur coats and foreign cars.*

nou·velle cui·sine /ˌnuvɛlkwɪ'zin, nu'vɛl-/ *n.* [U] a type of French cooking that uses very little cream sauce or butter: *The local French restaurant features nouvelle cuisine.*

nov·el (1) /'nɑvəl/ *n.* a full-length work of fiction: *She wrote a novel about the Civil War. See:* fiction, USAGE NOTE.

novel (2) *adj.* new and different, (*syn.*) unusual: *He thought of a novel solution to the problem.*

nov·el·ist /'nɑvəlɪst/ *n.* a person who writes novels: *The novelist has written several best-sellers.*

no·vel·la /noʊ'vɛlə/ *n.* a piece of fiction that is longer than a short story, but shorter than a novel: *The movie is based on a famous novella.*

nov·el·ty /'nɑvəlti/ *n.* **-ties 1** [C] s.t. new and unusual: *It is a novelty to visit Disney World for the first time.* **2** [U] the quality of being novel: *She was excited by the novelty of being in a foreign country for the first time.* **3** [C] a small, unusual item: *The store sold novelties to tourists.*

No·vem·ber /noʊ'vɛmbər, nə-/ *n.* the eleventh month of the year: *November has 30 days.*

nov·ice /'nɑvɪs/ *n.* **1** a beginner at s.t. that requires skill: *a novice in skiing (playing the piano, learning to paint, etc.)* **2** a person who is studying to become a nun or monk: *He is one of the novices at the monastery.*

no·vi·ti·ate /noʊ'vɪʃiət, -ˌeɪt, -'vɪʃət/ *n.* **1** a place where religious novices live **2** a novice in a religious order

No·vo·cain /'noʊvəˌkeɪn/ *n.TM* a pain killer used by dentists: *I was given Novocain when my tooth was pulled.*

now /naʊ/ *adv.* **1** at this time: *I used to take the bus, but now I take the subway.* **2** immediately, at once: *Go now, or you'll be late to work.* **3** (used in telling or writing stories) then, next: *She heard a knock at the door.—now she was frightened.* **4** (used to emphasize a warning, command, or request, or to introduce a new topic into a conversation): *Now don't start complaining again.||Now tell me how it happened.* **5 it's now or never:** Take advantage of the opportunity; it will never happen again: *This is our only chance to escape; it's now or never.* **6 now and then** or **now and again:** occasionally, once in a while: *I still see him now and then.* **7 now and forever:** for all time: *We will be together now and forever.* **8 now, now:** (used to express sympathy): *Now, now, don't cry; everything is going to be fine.*
— *conj.* **now that:** since: *Now that everyone's here, we can begin the meeting.*

NOW /naʊ/ *n. abbr. for* National Organization for Women, an organization in the USA dedicated to promoting the interests and protecting the rights of women

NOW account *n. short for* Negotiable Order of Withdrawal, a type of checking account that pays interest: *I opened a NOW account at the local bank.*

now·a·days /'naʊəˌdeɪz/ *adv.* now, at this time: *Nowadays, inflation is under control.*

no way *interj.infrml.* no, definitely not: *He wants me to lend him $1,000—no way!*

no·where /'noʊˌwɛr/ *adv.* **1** not anywhere, in no place: *My wallet is nowhere to be found.* **2 nowhere near: a.** not close to, far away from: *The hotel is nowhere near the train station.* **b.** not at all: *We have nowhere near enough money to buy a house.* **3 to get nowhere:** to make no progress, to gain nothing: *Yelling at me will get you nowhere.* **4 to go nowhere:** (in a career) to make no advancement: *She's going nowhere at that company.*
—*n.* **in the middle of nowhere:** in a place where few people live: *Our car broke down in the middle of nowhere and we couldn't find a phone.*

no-win *adj.* referring to a situation in which no matter what one does, the result will be negative: *I love her, but she won't see me very often; if I date other women, she won't see me at all. It's a no-win situation!*

nox·ious /'nɑkʃəs/ *adj.* poisonous, harmful: *Noxious fumes were rising from the fire.*

noz·zle /'nɑzəl/ *n.* a narrow part at the end of a hose or pipe through which substances, such as water or air, are forced: *the nozzle on a garden hose (air hose, carburetor, etc.)*

nth /ɛnθ/ *adj.* **1** the latest in a long series: *This is the nth time I've heard the story.* **2 to the nth degree:** to the greatest extent possible: *As an artist, she is a perfectionist to the nth degree.*

nu·ance /'nu,ɑns, nu'ɑns/ *n.* a detail or a quality that is not obvious, (*syn.*) a subtlety: *the nuances of meaning in a poem*||*the nuances of an actor's performance*

nub /nʌb/ *n.* **1** a small bump or lump: *an eraser worn down to a nub* **2** the central point: *The nub of the matter is how much it will cost.*

nu·bile /'nu,baɪl, -bəl/ *adj.* (of a woman) young and sexually mature: *His nubile daughter had many admirers.*

nu·cle·ar /'nukliər/ *adj.* **1** related to a nucleus **2** related to the production of atomic energy or weapons: *nuclear physics*||*nuclear bombs*

nuclear energy *n.* [U] power generated by the splitting of the atom: *Nuclear energy is used to produce electricity.*

nuclear family *n.* **-lies** a family of two parents and their children living together in a household: *The rising divorce rate is causing the breakup of the nuclear family.* See: extended family.

nuclear freeze *n.* an end to the further building of nuclear weapons: *The superpowers agreed to a nuclear freeze.*

nuclear missile *n.* a military rocket with nuclear weapons: *A country with nuclear missiles threatens world peace.*

nuclear reaction *n.* the chain reaction caused in splitting an atom: *Nuclear reactions generate great power.*

nuclear reactor *n.* a machine used to make and contain nuclear reactions: *Nuclear reactors are used to produce electricity.*

nuclear rocket *n.* a nuclear missile

nuclear warhead *n.* the nuclear explosive device located in the front end of nuclear missiles: *Some missiles carry multiple nuclear warheads.*

nu·cle·us /'nukliəs/ *n.* **-clei** /-kli,aɪ/ **1** the center of s.t.: *Those three individuals are the nucleus of the organization.* **2** the beginning or seed: *The donated set of paintings formed the nucleus of the museum's collection.* **3** (in physics) the center of an atom: *The nucleus of an atom is composed of protons and neutrons.*

4 (in biology) the central part of a cell: *The nucleus of a cell controls its vital functions.*

nude /nud/ *adj.* without any clothes, (*syn.*) naked: *There was a nude couple on the beach.* —*n.* **1** [C] (in a painting, picture, or sculpture) a person without clothes: *The artist was famous for his nudes.* **2** [U] **in the nude:** without any clothes: *Some people like to sleep in the nude.* -*n.* **nudity.**

nudge /nʌdʒ/ *n.* **1** a light push: to give s.o. a nudge to be still: *She gave the child a nudge to get her to stop talking during the movie.* **2** *infrml.* a persistent, often annoying person: *He's such a nudge, always asking me the same question.*
—*v.* **nudged, nudging, nudges 1** to push in a gentle manner: *I nudge him to get his attention.* **2** to repeatedly try to persuade s.o. to do s.t.: *She nudged him to get a haircut.*

nud·ist /'nudɪst/ *n.* a person who wears no clothes on a regular basis
—*adj.* related to nudists: *He joined a nudist colony deep in the woods.* -*n.* [U] **nudism** /'nudɪzəm/; [U] **nudity.**

nud·nick /'nʊdnɪk/ *n.infrml.* a tiresome, annoying person: *He's a nudnick who is always trying to borrow money.*

nug·get /'nʌgɪt/ *n.* **1** a small piece of gold **2** s.t. small and desirable: *a nugget of information*

nui·sance /'nusəns/ *n.* a bother, s.o. or s.t. that causes irritation or frustration: *It's a nuisance, but we need to redo the report and correct the errors.*||*She's a real nuisance, always calling when we're about to eat dinner.*

nuke /nuk/ *n.infrml.* a nuclear weapon: *The protesters carried signs saying "No Nukes."*
—*v.infrml.* **nuked, nuking, nukes 1** to attack with nuclear weapons **2** *fig.* to heat or cook food in a microwave oven

N

USAGE NOTE: When used informally as a verb, *to nuke* means to heat something in a *microwave* oven. *It only takes three minutes to nuke a frozen dinner.*

null /nʌl/ *adj.* **null and void:** legally invalid, no longer in effect: *That contract is null and void.*

nul·li·fy /'nʌlə,faɪ/ *v.* **-fied, -fying, -fies** to make legally invalid, cancel: *It became necessary to nullify the law (contract, agreement, etc.).* -*n.* **nullification** /,nʌləfə'keɪʃən/.

numb /nʌm/ *adj.* **1** without feeling, sensation: *My hands are numb from the cold.* **2** unable to feel any emotion: *After the funeral, I felt numb.* -*adv.* **numbly;** -*n.* **numbness.**

num·ber /'nʌmbər/ *n.* **1** [C] a symbol, such as "3," or a word, such as "five," that expresses a quantity or a position in a series: *The average number of students in a class is 25.*||*She is*

number 21 on the waiting list. **2** [C] a group of people or things: *A large number of people visit this museum every year.||She gave me a number of (=several) suggestions.* **3** [C;U] a total: *The number of inches in a foot is 12.* **4** [C] a numeral used for identification: *a social security number||a checking account number* **5** [C] a performance of a song, dance, piece of music, etc. in a series: *Her first number was a song from a popular musical.* **6** *infrml.* **one's number is up:** one is going to die soon: *From the expression on the doctor's face, he knew that his number was up.* **7 the numbers game** or **the numbers:** a type of lottery in which a person bets on a series of numbers which are later published in a periodical: *He loses a lot of money playing the numbers every week.* **8** *infrml.* **to do a number on s.o.: a.** to tease or play a joke on s.o.: *When the young boy fell off the boat, his friends did a number on him by refusing at first to help him back on board.* **b.** to behave cruelly toward s.o.: *Instead of helping him, they did a number on him and started to drive the boat away.* **9 to do s.t. by the numbers:** to follow a procedure exactly: *The credit manager does everything by the numbers; he checks a company's credit references, its credit rating, its bank statement, and so on.* **10** *infrml.* **to have s.o.'s number:** to know s.o.'s true character or motives: *The car dealer appears to be friendly and helpful, but I have his number; he just wants to make a sale.* **11** *infrml.* **to look out for Number One:** to put one's own interests first: *She is nice to people when it is to her advantage; she is always looking out for Number One.*
—*v.* **1** to assign a number to s.t.: *I numbered the pages of the report.* **2** to include, consider: *She numbered him among her closest friends.* **3** to total: *The crowd numbered in the thousands.* **4 one's days are numbered:** one is going to die soon or a particular stage of one's life will soon end: *When she reached 35, she knew that her days as a professional athlete were numbered.*

number cruncher *n.infrml.* **1** a person, usu. a junior employee in management, who devotes a lot of time to processing numbers on a calculator or computer for interpretation and use by senior management: *He is a young number cruncher for an investment company.* **2** a computer dedicated to lengthy computations

numb·skull or **num·skull** /ˈnʌmˌskʌl/ *n.infrml.* a stupid person, (*syns.*) an idiot, a blockhead: *What numbskull thought of that stupid idea?*

nu·mer·al /ˈnumərəl, ˈnumrəl/ *n.* a symbol that represents a number: *The Roman numeral for "9" is "IX."*

nu·mer·ate /ˈnuməˌreɪt/ *v.* **-ated, -ating, -ates** *See:* enumerate.

nu·mer·a·tion /ˌnuməˈreɪʃən/ *n.* [U] the process of counting: *Some five-year-olds excel in numeration.*

nu·mer·a·tor /ˈnuməˌreɪtər/ *n.* the symbol over the line in a common fraction: *The numerator in the fraction 2/3 is 2. See:* denominator.

nu·mer·i·cal /nuˈmɛrɪkəl/ *adj.* related to numbers: *The report provided us with the necessary numerical information -adv.* **numerically.**

nu·mer·ous /ˈnumərəs, ˈnumrəs/ *adj.* many: *Numerous people attended the concert.||We did not buy the product for reasons too numerous to mention.*

nu·mis·mat·ics /ˌnumɪzˈmætɪks, -mɪs-/ *n.pl.* the study of coins: *His hobby is numismatics and he has a large collection of old coins -adj.* **numismatic.**

nun /nʌn/ *n.* a female member of a religious order: *She is a nun who is studying to be a nurse.*

nun·ci·o /ˈnʌnsiˌoʊ, ˈnʊn-/ *n.* **-os** an ambassador or representative of the Pope: *A papal nuncio was sent from Rome to meet with government officials.*

nun·ner·y /ˈnʌnəri/ *n.old usage* **-ies** a building where nuns live, (*syn.*) a convent

nup·tial /ˈnʌpʃəl, -tʃəl/ *adj.frml.* related to a wedding ceremony or marriage: *The nuptial celebration was held at a local restaurant.*

nup·tials /ˈnʌpʃəlz, -tʃəlz/ *n.pl.frml.* a marriage ceremony: *The nuptials were held at a local church.*

nurse /nɜrs/ *n.* **1** a person specially trained to take care of sick, injured, or old people: *The nurse gave the patient some pills.* **2** a person employed to take care of young children: *The wealthy family hired a nurse for their child.*
—*v.* **nursed, nursing, nurses 1** to give care to sick or old people: *He nursed his wife back to health.* **2** to feed a baby through the breast: *She nursed the baby for six months.* **3** *fig.* to keep alive for a long period of time: *He nursed his desire for revenge during his long years in prison.*

nurse·maid /ˈnɜrsˌmeɪd/ *n.* a woman who is employed to take care of children: *The nursemaid read the child a bedtime story.*

nurs·er·y /ˈnɜrsəri, ˈnɜrsri/ *n.* **-ies 1** a room specially set up for children: *The children were playing in the nursery.* **2** a garden where young plants are raised for general sale or for future transplanting: *a tree nursery*

nursery rhyme *n.* a story for children in the form of a short poem: *The nursery rhymes of Mother Goose are popular with children.*

nursery school *n.* a school for children before they enter kindergarten

nurs·ing /ˈnɜrsɪŋ/ *n.* [U] *adj.* the profession of caring for the ill: *Many students choose a career in <n.> nursing after finishing high* *school.*‖A *<adj.> nursing career can be very rewarding.*

nursing care *n.* [U] the care provided by a nurse: *My mother is ill and requires part-time nursing care at home.*

nursing home *n.* a private institution dedicated to the care of the elderly: *My eighty-year-old father went into a nursing home last fall.*

nur·ture /'nɜrtʃər/ *v.* **-tured, -turing, -tures 1** to feed and care for: *A mother should nurture her child.* **2** to help develop: *The famous musician nurtured young talent.*

nut /nʌt/ *n.* **1** a fruit with a hard shell or its seed: *a candy made from fruit and nuts* **2** *infml.* a person who seems very odd or crazy: *Stop acting like a nut!* **3** *infml.* a person with a strong or excessive interest in s.t.: *I've got to get to work on time; my boss is a nut about lateness.* **4** a small piece of metal with a hole in the middle used with a bolt **5** *infml.* the head: *I fell and bumped my nut.* **6 a hard** or **tough nut to crack:** a difficult problem or person that one must deal with: *We spent many hours searching for a solution to the problem; it was a tough nut to crack. See:* kook, USAGE NOTE.

nut·crack·er /'nʌt,krækər/ *n.* a hand-held device for cracking the shell of nuts in order to eat the part inside

nut·meg /'nʌt,mɛg/ *n.* [C;U] a brown spice made from seeds: *I'll need nutmeg for the apple pie.*

nu·tri·ent /'nutriənt/ *n.adj.* any of the substances contained in food that are essential to life, such as protein, vitamins, and minerals: *Fruit and vegetables are high in <n.> nutrients.*‖*The <adj.> nutrient value of candy is generally low.*

nu·tri·ment /'nutrəmənt/ *n.* [U] food needed for growth, health, etc., (*syn.*) nourishment: *Milk is an excellent source of nutriment.*

nu·tri·tion /nu'trɪʃən/ *n.* **1** [U] the study of how the body needs and uses food: *She's taking a course in nutrition in college.* **2** the processes by which the body uses food: *The body requires proper nutrition in order to maintain itself. -adj.* **nutritional.**

nu·tri·tion·ist /nu'trɪʃənɪst/ *n.* a trained person who supervises the nutrition of others, esp. in institutions, such as hospitals: *My mother works as a nutritionist at the local college.*

nu·tri·tious /nu'trɪʃəs/ *adj.* (of food) containing substances essential to good health, (*syn.*) nourishing: *You should eat nutritious meals to keep yourself healthy.*

nuts /nʌts/ *adj.infml.* **1** crazy, foolish: *You're nuts to try to climb that mountain; it's too dangerous.* **2 to be nuts about** or **over** very enthusiastic about, very fond of, (*syn.*) crazy about: *She's just nuts about her new boyfriend.*

nuts and bolts *n.pl.fig.* the practical details, the basic operating procedures: *The course taught me the nuts and bolts of computer programming.*

nut·shell /'nʌt,ʃɛl/ *n.* **1** the hard outer covering of a nut **2 in a nutshell:** in the fewest possible words: *The situation in a nutshell is that sales have fallen and we have to sell the company.*

nuts and bolts

nut·ty /'nʌti/ *adj.* **-tier, -tiest 1** tasting like or containing nuts: *The almonds give the pie a nutty flavor.* **2** crazy, foolish: *What a nutty idea!* **3 as nutty as a fruitcake:** (used humorously) crazy: *He's a nice guy, but as nutty as a fruitcake. -n.* **nuttiness.**

nuz·zle /'nʌzəl/ *v.n.* **-zled, -zling, -zles** to push or rub gently with the nose: *The dog <v.> nuzzled its owner's cheek.*

ny·lon /'naɪ,lɑn/ *n.* [U] **1** a strong, artificial fiber used in making cloth, thread, and stockings: *Women wear stockings made of nylon.* **2 nylons:** stockings, usu. worn by women with a skirt or dress: *I always wear black nylons under my black dress.*

nymph /nɪmf/ *n.* (in ancient stories) a minor goddess of nature resembling a young woman: *He met a wood nymph in the forest.*

nymph·et /nɪm'fɛt, 'nɪmfɪt/ *n.* a sexually desirable adolescent girl

nym·pho·ma·ni·ac /,nɪmfə'meɪni,æk/ *n.* a woman with an abnormally high sex drive *-n.* [U] **nymphomania.**

N

O, o

O, o /oʊ/ *n*. **O's, o's** or **Os, os** **1** the 15th letter of the alphabet **2** *s.t.* shaped like an O: *Doughnuts and circles are O-shaped.* **3** zero (esp. in saying numbers): *My telephone number is 456-00 (oh-oh) 22.*

oaf /oʊf/ *n*. [C] a stupid person, (*syn.*) a simpleton: *That oaf made another stupid mistake!* *-adj.* **oafish; -***n*. [U] **oafishness.**

oak /oʊk/ *n*. **1** [C] tall hardwood tree that grows small nuts called acorns: *The park has many oaks in it.* **2** [U] the wood of oak trees: *Bookshelves made of oak last for many years.*

oar /ɔr/ *n*. a pole with a flat blade pulled by hand to row a boat: *The fisherman pulled on the oars as he left the dock.*

o·a·sis /oʊˈeɪsɪs/ *n*. **oases** /oʊˈeɪˌsiz/ **1** a place usu. with trees and water in the desert: *The camels stopped at an oasis for the night.* **2** *fig.* a pleasant place in a dull area

oar

oath /oʊθ/ *n*. **oaths** /oʊðz, oʊθs/ **1** a promise to do s.t., such as remain loyal to one's country or tell the truth in a court of law: *The soldiers took an oath of loyalty to their country.* **2 to be under oath:** (in law) to have promised to tell the truth: *When the witness began to answer questions, the judge reminded her that she was under oath.*

oat·meal /ˈoʊtˌmil/ *n*. [U] crushed oats made into cookies and breakfast cereal: *He eats oatmeal with milk for breakfast. See:* scrambled eggs, USAGE NOTE.

oats /oʊts/ *n.pl*. **1** a type of grain eaten by animals and people: *My mother baked bread made with oats and raisins.* **2** *infrml.fig.* **to feel one's oats:** to feel full of energy, said esp. of horses: *That horse is feeling his oats; he's been running and kicking up his heels.* **3** *fig.* **to sow one's wild oats:** to pursue pleasure or do very adventurous things, esp. when one is young: *She sowed her wild oats when she was*

a teenager by driving across the country alone. *-adj.* **oat.**

ob·du·rate /ˈɑbdərɪt, -dʒər-/ *adj.frml.* unwilling to change one's opinion or belief, (*syn.*) stubborn: *He is obdurate and will not change his mind about anything. -adv.* **obdurately.**

o·be·di·ence /əˈbidiəns, oʊ-/ *n*. [U] willingness to follow or obey (rules, orders, etc.): *The teacher was pleased by his pupils' obedience.*

o·be·di·ent /əˈbidiənt, oʊ-/ *adj*. willing to follow or obey (rules, orders, etc.): *Good children are obedient to their parents. -adv.* **obediently.**

o·be·lisk /ˈɑbəlɪsk/ *n*. a tall stone pillar built in honor of *s.t.* or *s.o.*: *An obelisk celebrating the revolution stands in the square.*

o·bese /oʊˈbis/ *adj.frml.* very fat, (*syn.*) corpulent: *That man who weighs 350 pounds is obese. -n.* [U] **obesity.**

o·bey /oʊˈbeɪ, ə-/ *v*. **obeyed, obeying, obeys** to do what is asked or ordered, (*syn.*) to comply with: *Soldiers obey their commander's orders.*

o·bit·u·ar·y /əˈbɪtʃuˌɛri, oʊ-/ *n*. **-ies** a printed announcement of *s.o.*'s death, often with an account of his or her life and accomplishments: *The obituary of the famous writer is in today's newspaper.*

ob·ject /ˈɑbdʒɪkt, -ˌdʒɛkt/ *n*. **1** a physical thing, (*syn.*) an entity: *A pencil was one of the objects left on the table.* **2** the subject of *s.o.*'s attention: *Her next-door neighbor is the object of her love.* **3** (in grammar) the focus of a verb's action: *The word "answers" is the object in the sentence "Students give answers to questions."* **4** a goal, purpose: *The object of this study is to research energy use.*
—*v.* /əbˈdʒɛkt/ **1** to be against *s.t.*, (*syn.*) to protest: *She objects to the death penalty.* **2** to give as an objection: *They objected to eating dinner at 10 P.M. -n.* **objector.**

ob·jec·tion /əbˈdʒɛkʃən/ *n*. **1** a statement or feeling of dislike, disapproval, or opposition: *I have an objection to the high cost of government.* **2** a reason against *s.t.*: *They had objections to our plan and so we changed it.*

ob·jec·tion·a·ble /əbˈdʒɛkʃənəbəl/ *adj*. **1**

causing an objection or protest: *The committee found the plan objectionable and voted against it.* **2** shocking, (*syn.*) offensive: *People found his rude behavior objectionable.*

ob·jec·tive /əb'dʒɛktɪv/ *adj.* **1** not influenced by emotions or personal beliefs, fair, (*syn.*) impartial: *The economist gave an objective report of the economy's problems.* **2** existing outside the mind, real: *People, buildings, and streets are part of objective reality, not imagined.* *-adv.* **objectively;** *-n.* **objectivity** /ˌɑbdʒɛk'tɪvəti/.
—*n.* a goal, purpose: *Our objective in doing market research is to develop useful new products.*

ob·jet d'art /ˌoʊbʒeɪ'dɑr, ˌɑb-/ *n.* **objets d'art** /ˌoʊbdʒeɪ'dɑr, ˌɑb-/ (French for) an art object, (usu. small) piece of art: *She gave her collection of objets d'art to the museum.*

ob·li·gate /'ɑblə,geɪt/ *v.* **-gated, -gating, -gates** to make s.o. feel he or she must do s.t.: *His boss obligated him to work on weekends.* *-adj.* **obligated.**

ob·li·ga·tion /ˌɑblə'geɪʃən/ *n.* [C;U] a legal or moral requirement to do s.t., a feeling one must do s.t.: *She has a family obligation to visit her sick aunt.*

o·blig·a·to·ry /ə'blɪgə,tɔri/ *adj.* required by law, custom, rules, etc.: *In order to get a driver's license, it is obligatory to first pass an eye test.*

o·blige /ə'blaɪdʒ/ *v.* **obliged, obliging, obliges** **1** to require because of law, custom, etc.: *We are obliged to stop the car at a red light.* **2** to help, do a favor for s.o.: *He obliged his wife by driving her to the store.* **3 to be much obliged (to s.o.):** to be very thankful, grateful: *I'm much obliged to you for your help.*

o·blig·ing /ə'blaɪdʒɪŋ/ *adj.* helpful, (*syn.*) accommodating: *He is a very obliging man who does many favors for others.* *-adv.* **obligingly.**

o·blique /oʊ'blik, ə-/ *adj.* **1** slanted usu. at a sharp angle, (*syn.*) sloping: *The roof of that house has an oblique slant, so snow falls off of it in winter.* **2** not clear, indirect: *The criminals' answers to the police were oblique.* *-adv.* **obliquely.**

ob·lit·er·ate /ə'blɪtə,reɪt/ *v.* **-ated, -ating, -ates** to remove all signs of s.t., destroy, (*syn.*) to eradicate: *Sand blown by the wind obliterated the writing on the temple walls.* *-n.* [U] **obliteration** /ə,blɪtə'reɪʃən/.

ob·liv·i·on /ə'blɪviən/ *n.* [U] **1** the state of being forgotten, nothingness: *The broken spaceship flew far into the oblivion of outer space.* **2** the state of having forgotten, unconsciousness: *She can remember nothing; her memory has gone into oblivion.*

ob·liv·i·ous /ə'blɪviəs/ *adj.* not noticing s.t., unaware, (*syn.*) inattentive: *She was oblivious*

to the fact that the music had stopped, and she continued dancing. *-adv.* **obliviously;** *-n.* [U] **obliviousness.**

ob·long /'ɑb,lɔŋ/ *n.adj.* a figure or shape that is longer than it is wide: *They bought an <adj.> oblong table for the classroom.*

ob·nox·ious /əb'nɑkʃəs/ *adj.* very unpleasant or annoying, (*syn.*) offensive: *He has an obnoxious habit of picking his teeth during meals.* *-adv.* **obnoxiously.**

o·boe /'oʊboʊ/ *n.* a musical wind instrument made of wood: *Oboes are similar in size and shape to clarinets.*

ob·scene /əb'sin/ *adj.* **1** offensively sexual, indecent, (*syn.*) lewd: *He made some obscene remarks to a woman at a party.* **2** offensive, shocking, (*syn.*) repugnant: *Pornography is obscene to most people.* *-adv.* **obscenely.**

ob·scen·i·ty /əb'sɛnəti/ *n.* **-ties** **1** [U] the quality of being obscene or indecent, (*syn.*) lewdness **2** [C] an indecent act or word: *A woman shouted obscenities at the speaker.*

ob·scure /əb'skyʊr/ *v.* **-scured, -scuring, -scures** **1** to block from view, hide, (*syn.*) to conceal: *Fog obscured the airport, so our plane could not land.* **2** to confuse, make unclear: *Her bad memory obscured the facts about the accident.*
—*adj.* **1** difficult to understand, unclear: *That professor's writing is so obscure that it is very hard to understand.* **2** difficult to see: *Heavy rain made the view of the mountain obscure.* *-adv.* **obscurely.**

ob·scu·ri·ty /əb'skyʊrəti/ *n.* **-ties** **1** [U] a place or condition that cannot be seen or is not well known: *She is a little known painter living in obscurity on a farm.* **2** [C] s.t. that cannot be understood: *My professor said that my essay was full of obscurities.*

ob·se·qui·ous /əb'sikwiəs/ *adj.frml.* too obedient, overly eager to please: *He is a young employee who is obsequious with the boss.* *-adv.* **obsequiously;** *-n.* [U] **obsequiousness.**

ob·serv·a·ble /əb'zɜrvəbəl/ *adj.* able to be seen or noticed, in view: *The parade was observable to all except those far from the street.* *-adv.* **observably.**

ob·serv·ance /əb'zɜrvəns/ *n.frml.* **1** [C;U] the celebration of an event, such as one of religious or civic importance: *The observance of Independence Day includes fireworks and patriotic speeches.* **2** [U] behavior according to laws, rules, holidays, and customs: *Observance of the tax laws is required of everyone.*

ob·serv·ant /əb'zɜrvənt/ *adj.* **1** quick to notice or see, aware, (*syn.*) perceptive: *She is very observant of what is happening around her.* **2** behaving according to law or custom, respectful, (*syn.*) dutiful: *Religious people are obser-*

vant of religious laws and customs. **-adv. ob-servantly.**

ob·ser·va·tion /ˌɑbzər'veɪʃən, -sər-/ *n.* **1** [U] viewing, watching: *A soldier climbed the church tower for observation of the whole town.* **2** [C] a remark, opinion: *My friend made an observation that I seem nervous today.* **3** **under observation:** under close care or supervision: *The heart patient is under observation by a trained nurse.*

ob·serv·a·to·ry /əb'zɜrvəˌtɔri/ *n.* **-ries** a place for the scientific study of space, weather, etc.: *The observatory is located on a mountain top.*

observatory

ob·serve /əb'zɜrv/ *v.* **-served, -serving, -serves 1** to view, watch, esp. for anything unusual: *A policeman observed the activity on the street.* **2** to remark, express an opinion: *Our professor observed that we all did well on the examination.* **3** to see, notice: *She observed a man with a large suitcase getting into a car.||Did you observe anything unusual?* **4** to respect or follow laws, rules, or customs: *We observed Memorial Day by going to church and praying for the dead.*

ob·serv·er /əb'zɜrvər/ *n.* a person who observes s.t. without participating, such as a spectator, official, etc.: *Foreign governments sent observers to watch the US military exercises.*

ob·sess /əb'sɛs/ *v.* **-sesses** to have s.t. control one's mind or behavior: *He is obsessed with being clean; he's always washing his hands.* **-adj. obsessed.**

ob·ses·sion /əb'sɛʃən/ *n.* [C] an idea or habit that controls the mind: *She has an obsession about always being right.*

ob·ses·sive /əb'sɛsɪv/ *adj.* of or like an obsession: *His obsessive behavior about cleanliness drives others crazy.* **-adv. obsessively.**

ob·so·les·cence /ˌɑbsə'lɛsəns/ *n.* [U] the process of becoming no longer useful: *The obsolescence of buildings happens over many years, as they become too old to use.* **-v. obsolesce; -adj. obsolescent.**

ob·so·lete /ˌɑbsə'lit/ *adj.* no longer used, replaced by s.t. better: *Vinyl records will soon be obsolete, now that compact discs are popular.*

ob·sta·cle /'ɑbstɪkəl/ *n.* s.t. that gets in the way and stops action or progress, *(syns.)* a hindrance, hurdle: *A tree fell across the road and became an obstacle for cars and trucks.*

ob·stet·rics /əb'stɛtrɪks/ *n.pl.* used with a *sing.v.* the branch of medicine dealing with pregnancy and childbirth: *That doctor decided*

to practice obstetrics after working with children. **-n. obstetrician** /ˌɑbstə'trɪʃən/.

ob·sti·nate /'ɑbstənɪt/ *adj.* refusing to cooperate, *(syn.)* stubborn: *He is obstinate in refusing to stop smoking as his doctor ordered him.* **-adv. obstinately; -n. obstinacy** /'ɑbstənəsi/.

ob·struct /əb'strʌkt/ *v.* **1** to form a barrier, block: *A tree fell across the road and obstructed traffic.* **2** to prevent from happening, *(syn.)* to impede: *One political party obstructed the passage of laws proposed by another.* **-n. obstruction; -adj. obstructive; -adv. obstructively.**

ob·tain /əb'teɪn/ *v.* to acquire, get, such as by purchase, loan, or gift: *She obtained the property with a bank loan.*

ob·tain·a·ble /əb'teɪnəbəl/ *adj.* capable of being acquired, available: *Loans are obtainable at banks.*

ob·tru·sive /əb'trusɪv/ *adj.frml.* very noticeable, intruding, *(syn.)* forward: *His obtrusive manners made him unpopular with his coworkers.* **-adv. obtrusively.**

ob·tuse /əb'tus/ *adj.frml.* **1** slow to understand, *(syn.)* dull: *He was being obtuse when he said he didn't understand the problem.* **2** (in mathematics, of an angle) between 90° and 180° **-adv. obtusely.**

ob·vi·ous /'ɑbviəs/ *adj.* easy to see or understand, clear: *It is obvious that that woman has had too much to drink.* **-adv. obviously; -n.** [U] **obviousness.**

oc·ca·sion /ə'keɪʒən/ *n.* **1** a time when s.t. happens: *We'll present the new product on the occasion of our next conference.* **2** a special event or ceremony, *(syn.)* a happening: *Their wedding was a happy occasion.* **3** an opportunity, chance: *I had the occasion to make some new friends on vacation.* **4** a reason, cause for s.t.: *His sudden death was occasion for much sadness.* **5 on occasion:** once in a while, *(syn.)* periodically: *On occasion, he smokes a cigar after dinner.* **6 to have no occasion:** to have no reason, opportunity, etc.: *She was never in the house, so she had no occasion to steal anything from it.* **7 to rise to the occasion:** to perform well when circumstances encourage: *The guest of honor rose to the occasion by making a good speech.* **8 to take the/this occasion:** to make good use of an opportunity: *She took the occasion to thank all the guests for listening to her speech.*

oc·ca·sion·al /ə'keɪʒənəl/ *adj.* once in a while, *(syn.)* periodic: *He smokes an occasional cigar, but he doesn't smoke regularly.* **-adv. occasionally.**

oc·cult /ə'kʌlt/ *adj.* hidden from ordinary people, *(syns.)* supernatural, mysterious: *That shop sells books on the occult sciences.*

—*n.* the supernatural world of ghosts, witches, etc.: *Some people study the occult to learn its mysteries.*

oc·cu·pan·cy /'ɑkyəpənsi/ *n.* [U] being or living in a certain place: *Our company took occupancy of that new building last month.*

oc·cu·pant /'ɑkyəpənt/ *n.* a person, business, or institution that occupies a place: *The car's occupants were not hurt in the accident.*

oc·cu·pa·tion /,ɑkyə'peɪʃən/ *n.* **1** one's means of making a living, job: *Her occupation is as a doctor.* **2** any activity on which you spend time: *Her chief occupation at that time was reading.* **3** taking possession of s.t.: *The enemy's occupation of the city lasted a year.*

USAGE NOTE: The most common way to ask about a person's *occupation* is, "What do you do?," not "What is your occupation?"

oc·cu·pa·tion·al /,ɑkyə'peɪʃənəl/ *adj.* related to one's job: *His occupational duties require him to travel a lot.*

oc·cu·py /'ɑkyə,paɪ/ *v.* **-pied, -pying, -pies 1** to be, live, or work in a place: *Our company occupies three floors in an office building.* **2** to take control of, esp. in wartime: *Soldiers occupied the town.* **3** to fill (time, space, etc.): *Children occupy their free time with their toys and games.* **-n.** **occupier.**

oc·cur /ə'kɜr/ *v.* **-curred, -curring, -curs 1** to happen, take place, esp. without planning: *The accident occurred at 10:00 A.M.* **2** to exist, be found (esp. of objects, concepts, etc.): *The image of a flower often occurs in his paintings.* **3** *phrasal v. insep.* **to occur to s.o.:** to come to mind: *It suddenly occurred to me that I knew how to solve that problem!*

oc·cur·rence /ə'kɜrəns/ *n.* **1** [C] an event, incident: *The occurrence of that illness worried everyone.* **2** [U] how many times s.t. happens, *(syn.)* rate: *The occurrence of crime in this city is on the rise.*

o·cean /'oʊʃən/ *n.* **1** the great body of salt water covering more than 70 percent of the earth's surface: *I like swimming in the ocean.* **2** any of the five oceans: *She has sailed on the Pacific and Indian Oceans.* **-adj.** **oceanic** /,oʊʃi'ænɪk/.

o·cean·og·ra·phy /,oʊʃə'nɑgrəfi/ *n.* [U] the study of oceans: *Many universities teach courses in marine biology and oceanography.*

o'clock /ə'klɑk/ *adv.* **1** indicating time on a watch or clock: *It is now 11 o'clock in the morning.* **2** referring to a position in space like that of one of the 12 hours on a clock face: *Ducks are flying overhead at 12 o'clock.*

oc·ta·gon /'ɑktə,gɑn, -gən/ *n.* a flat, eight-sided figure: *Old coins were shaped as octagons and called "pieces of eight." -adj.* **octagonal** /ɑk'tægənəl/.

oc·tane /'ɑk,teɪn/ *n.* a measure of how well gasoline and other motor fuels burn in an engine: *I use regular 88 octane in my car, rather than a high octane gasoline.*

oc·tave /'ɑktɪv/ *n.* a series of eight notes between two tones on a musical scale: *Men's singing voices are often an octave lower than women's.*

oc·tet /ɑk'tɛt/ *n.* a group of eight musicians or singers, or a composition written for them: *My friends and I formed an octet of singers.*

Oc·to·ber /ɑk'toʊbər/ *n.* the 10th month of the year: *October is harvest time in many parts of the USA.*

oc·to·pus /'ɑktəpəs/ *n.* **-puses** or **-pi** /-,paɪ/ a sea animal with eight arms and a soft body like a bag: *Octopus is eaten in many parts of the world.*

octopus

oc·u·lar /'ɑkyələr/ *adj.* related to the eyes: *Optometrists take ocular measurements to make eyeglasses.*

OD /,oʊ'di/ *v.n.abbr.slang* **OD'd** or **ODed, OD'ing, OD's 1** to overdose on, take too much of a drug: *The addict <v.> OD'd on heroin; he took an <n.> OD.* **2** to take too much of s.t.: *I really OD'd on that chocolate cake; I feel sick.*

odd /ɑd/ *adj.* **1** (of numbers) not evenly divisible by two, such as 1, 3, 5, 7, etc.: *The houses with odd numbers are on the left side of the street.* **2** strange, unusual: *He is never late and it's odd that he's not here now.* **3** being one of an incomplete pair or set: *There is a box of odd socks in the laundry room.* **4** (used after round numbers) in addition, more than: *Fifty-odd people attended the funeral.* **5 at odd times:** at irregular times, *(syn.)* periodically: *It has been raining today at odd times.* **6 odd jobs:** small jobs that are not full-time or regular: *She does odd jobs, such as painting rooms and fixing cars.* **7 odd man out:** a person who, because of unusual behavior or appearance, stands out from others in a group: *That man in the motorcycle jacket is an odd man out at the opera.* **8 That's odd!** or **How odd!:** expressing doubt and surprise: *That's odd! My wallet is missing! See:* oddly, odds.

odd·ball /'ɑd,bɔl/ *n. slang* a person who behaves strangely, *(syn.)* a kook: *That woman is an oddball who dresses in funny clothes and sings to the people on our street.*

odd·i·ty /'ɑdəti/ *n.* **-ties** s.t. unusual, not typical of its kind: *Black roses are oddities.*

odd lot *n.* **1** a purchase of securities in fewer than 100 shares for which an extra charge is usually made: *I bought an odd lot of 25 shares of IBM stock.* **2** a nonstandard amount of any merchandise: *That store sells odd lots of household items at low prices.*

odd·ly /'adli/ *adv.* **1** in a strange or peculiar manner, strangely: *That man who is shouting at passing cars often behaves oddly.* **2** curiously, unusually: *She loves to travel, but oddly, this year, she doesn't want to.*

odds /adz/ *n.pl.* **1** the likelihood or probability that s.t. will happen: *The doctors have given him good odds for a full recovery.* **2** the chances against or for a certain result: *The odds are against* (or) *for our company's being given the order.* **3 by all odds:** probably, (*syn.*) in all likelihood: *By all odds, our team should win today because we're the better team.* **4 The odds are that:** it is likely that: *The odds are that it will rain today.* **5 to be an odds-on favorite:** to be the likely winner: *Even though she wasn't the odds-on favorite, she won the tennis match easily.* **6 to be at odds with s.o.:** to disagree, dispute with s.o.: *Those two employees argue and are always at odds with each other.* **7 to fight against the odds:** to try to succeed although the chances of success are not good: *She is fighting against the odds of dying from cancer.* **8 to give odds:** to give points to weaker competitors to make their chances of winning better or to make it worth more money to bet against stronger ones: *Good golfers give odds to new players so that they have an equal chance to win a round of golf.*

odds and ends *n.pl.* a mix of items, bits and pieces: *We moved all our things from one apartment to another, except for a few odds and ends, like an old lamp.*

ode /oʊd/ *n.* a poem addressed to s.o. or s.t., usu. with a grand subject and tone: *Many countries have odes that praise the bravery of their heroes of long ago.*

o·di·ous /'oʊdiəs/ *adj.* creating hate and anger: *He is an odious man, always attacking others.* *-adv.* **odiously.**

o·dom·e·ter /oʊ'dɑmətər/ *n.* a device that measures the distance a motor vehicle has traveled: *The odometer in my car reads: 53,432.8 miles.*

o·dor /'oʊdər/ *n.* a smell or scent, usu. an unpleasant one: *The odor of old fish filled the air.* *-adj.frml.* **odoriferous** /,oʊdə'rɪfərəs/.

od·ys·sey /'adəsi/ *n.* **-seys** a long, adventurous journey: *His youth was spent in an odyssey of working in Canada, the USA, and then Latin America.*

of /ʌv, *weak form* əv, ə/ *prep.* **1** indicating possession: *That old car of mine gives me trouble all the time.* **2** indicating material from which s.t. is made: *That necklace is made of pearls.* **3** indicating time before the hour: *It is five minutes of eight (o'clock).* **4** indicating date: *The opening ceremonies will be held on the 30th of July.* **5** indicating authorship or origin: *People of this area rush to and from work every day.* **6** indicating direction, toward or away from: *The lake is located ten miles north of here.* **7** in reference to, in regard to: *A publisher contacted the writer on a matter of great importance.* **8** on the part of: *Lawyers act on behalf of their clients.* **9** indicating relief, cure, etc.: *Radiation treatment cured him of cancer.* **10** describing, naming, characterizing: *They spent their vacation sailing in the Gulf of Mexico.* **11** indicating reason or cause: *She nearly died of pneumonia.* **12** indicating the contents of s.t.: *I bought a box of rice and a bottle of oil at the market.* **13** indicating association: *We expected a serious answer from a man of his profession.* **14** indicating the object of an action: *Children have a great love of animals.* **15** indicating a smaller unit out of a total: *Most of the cars she looked at were too expensive.*

off /ɔf/ *prep.* **1** from, away from: *He took his coat off the hanger.* **2** down from: *Water drips off the roof in a rain storm.* **3** branching from: *A narrow road leads off the main highway.* **4** located at a distance from: *Ships fish off the coastline.*

—*adv.* **1** going away: *The farmer shouted at the hunters to leave, and they moved off.* **2** far away, distant: *That family lives off in the mountains.* **3** indicating distance: *Her cabin is located ten miles (16 km) off, down that dirt road.* **4** indicating time: *Our vacation is still a month off.* **5** making smaller, reducing: *The sales clerk took 20 percent off on our purchase.* **6** completely, (*syn.*) thoroughly: *He finished off his dinner in a hurry.* **7** in order to disconnect: *Shut off the computer when you've finished.* **8** away from work or duty: *She's been working too hard; she should take off for a week or two.*

—*adj.* **1** not operating, switched off (said of machines, lights, etc.): *The lights in the office are off all night.* **2** away from work, on one's free time: *I am off on weekends.* **3** postponed or canceled: *The meeting today is off and rescheduled for tomorrow.* **4** reduced, less: *Sales are off this month.* **5** poor, (*syn.*) inferior: *The quality of her performance (that merchandise, his work, etc.) was off.* **6** inaccurate, wrong: *His estimate of the cost is off by a large amount.* **7** less busy, dull: *Most airlines offer lower prices during the off season.* **8** no longer wanting or interested in something: *I think the dog is sick; his appetite is off.* **9 to be better off: a.** having a better life: *She has a good job and is better off now than she was when unemployed.* **b.** preferable, choosing an alternative that is better for you: *I am better off wearing old clothes when I get dirty working in the garden.* **10 to be well off:** to be wealthy and usu. in good health: *That couple is very well off, with a big house, fine jobs, and three cars.* **11 to have an off day: a.** to feel ill or depressed:

He has a bad cold and is having an off day. **b.** to perform poorly for a day: *The tennis star lost all her matches during an off day.*

off and on *adv. See:* on and off.

off·beat /ˌɔfˈbit/ *adj.fig.* different from the usual or expected, unusual: *That writer has an offbeat style of using very short sentences.*

off-color *adj.* offensive, dirty (jokes, remarks, etc.): *He makes off-color jokes at parties that makes me feel uncomfortable.*

of·fend /əˈfɛnd/ *v.* **1** to hurt the feelings of people: *She was offended that we didn't accept her invitation to dinner.* **2** to displease, disgust, (*syn.*) to annoy: *His constant lateness to work offends his coworkers.* -*n.* **offender.**

of·fense /əˈfɛns/ *n.* **1** the breaking of a law or rule: *He committed a minor offense by parking his car on the wrong side of the road.* **2** s.t. that hurts others' feelings, (*syn.*) an affront: *Her bad behavior was an offense to others attending church.* **3** /ˈɔ,fɛns, ˈɑ-/ (in sports) action by the team controlling the ball or hockey puck to try to score: *Our basketball team has an excellent offense.* **4 the best defense is a good offense:** /ˈɔ,fɛns, ˈɑ-/ the best way to defend yourself is to attack your opponent vigorously **5 to give offense:** to hurt or upset s.o. **6 to take offense:** to be annoyed or offended by s.o.'s actions or words

of·fen·sive /əˈfɛnsɪv/ *adj.* **1** causing suffering of the body or the mind, disgusting: *An offensive smell came from the garbage.* **2** rude, (*syn.*) insulting: *Her offensive words made her friend cry.* **3** aggressive, on the attack: *Our team's offensive moves won the game.* -*adv.* **offensively.**
—*n.* an attack, assault: *The army mounted an offensive against the enemy.*

of·fer /ˈɔfər, ˈɑ-/ *v.* **1** to propose s.t., express willingness to do s.t.: *I offered to take my friend to dinner.* **2** to present s.t. that may be accepted or not: *She offers me a cigarette every time I see her.* **3** to show signs of, to present: *She offered no explanation for the mistakes in the report.* **4** to happen, occur: *He decided to leave at the first chance that offered itself.* **5** *phrasal v. sep.* **to offer s.t. up:** to present in a formal way: *I offered up prayers to God.‖I offered them up.*
—*n.* **1** a business deal: *Car dealers have good offers at this time of year.* **2** a personal proposal: *He made her an offer of marriage.* **3 to put up s.t. for offers:** to present for sale: *We put up our house for offers last week.*

of·fer·ing /ˈɔfərɪŋ, ˈɑ-/ *n.* [C;U] an offer, esp. of a religious nature: *At church, I make an offering of money to help the poor.*

off·hand /ˌɔfˈhænd/ *adj.adv.* without research or much thought, (*syn.*) extemporaneous: *I don't recall <adv.> offhand how much I paid*

for the TV.‖The teacher made some <adj.> offhand remarks after class.

off·hand·ed /ˌɔfˈhændɪd/ *adj.* without thinking ahead or planning, (*syn.*) offhand: *The politician made some offhanded remarks to reporters and left.* -*adv.* **offhandedly.**

of·fice /ˈɔfɪs, ˈɑ-/ *n.* **1** a place of business with desk, chair, telephone, etc.: *His office is in a skyscraper.* **2** an official position, esp. in an organization, government, etc.: *The President holds the highest office in government.* **3** *pl.frml.* **offices:** through s.o., (*syn.*) under the auspices of: *Many poor people were helped by the mayor's good offices.*
—*adj.* related to offices: *He does office work in an insurance company.*

USAGE NOTE: A growing number of Americans work from a *home office* instead of going to their company's office every day. They *telecommute* to work from home, doing their jobs by using computers, fax machines, and telephones to communicate.

of·fice·hold·er /ˈɔfɪs,houldər, ˈɑ-/ *n.* a politician holding an elected position, an official: *Officeholders in the city government met yesterday.*

of·fic·er /ˈɔfəsər, ˈɑ-/ *n.* **1** a person with a position of command in the military or on a merchant ship: *She is an officer in the Air Force.* **2** a member of the police: *Police officers came to take the thief to jail.* **3** a person with a position of power or responsibility in a business or public institution: *He is a bank officer who makes decisions about loans.*

of·fi·cial /əˈfɪʃəl/ *n.* a person who works for a government or other organization: *Labor officials met to discuss a new contract.*
—*adj.* of or related to a position of power or authority: *Presidents of two nations signed the official documents for a peace agreement.* -*adv.* **officially.**

of·fi·ci·ate /əˈfɪʃiˌeɪt/ *v.* **-ated, -ating, -ates 1** to judge in a competition, (*syn.*) to referee: *Four officials officiate at football games.* **2** to be in charge of an event, carry out official duties, (*syn.*) to preside: *The mayor officiated at the spring festival.*

of·fi·cious /əˈfɪʃəs/ *adj.pej.* self-important, (*syn.*) bossy: *He is so officious that he tries to tell everyone what to do.* -*adv.* **officiously;** -*n.* [U] **officiousness.**

off·ing /ˈɔfɪŋ/ *n.* **in the offing:** in the near future, happening soon: *It's Friday and a relaxing long weekend is in the offing.*

off-limits *adj.* referring to places where certain people are not allowed to go, (*syn.*) prohibited: *Barrooms are off-limits to military personnel.*

off-line *adj.* **1** not having, offering, or using a connection to a network of computers (by direct wiring or modem): *The bank couldn't process my deposit because its computers were off-line.* **2** (of computers and electronic equipment) not working properly: *Her term paper was late because her printer was off-line.*

off-peak *adj.* not during a traffic rush hour, less busy: *I bought an off-peak round trip ticket for evening travel.*

off-season *adj.n.* not during the height of the tourist season: *We took a less costly, <adj.> off-season cruise in the Caribbean during the <n.> off-season.*

off·set /'ɔf,sɛt, ,ɔf'sɛt/ *v.* **-set, -setting, -sets** to balance, (*syn.*) to compensate for: *His bad behavior is offset by his hard work.*

off·shoot /'ɔf,ʃut/ *n.* **1** (in biology) a new part of a plant growing from the main part: *In the spring, offshoots of branches grow longer.* **2** *fig.* a new development or direction of s.t.: *That computer company is an offshoot of an electronics company.*

off·shore /,ɔf'ʃɔr/ *adv.adj.* **1** away from the shoreline in the water: *That <adj.> offshore island is two hundred miles away in the ocean.* **2** (in business) related to business activity that is outside of the country, usu. to avoid taxes. *See:* onshore.

off-site /,ɔf'saɪt/ *adj.* away from the place of business: *I won't be in my office today; I'll be at an off-site meeting.*

off·spring /'ɔf,sprɪŋ/ **-spring** *n.* [U] child or children, (*syn.*) progeny: *That couple's four offspring all live in different cities.*

off·stage /,ɔf'steɪdʒ/ *adj.adv.* not on the stage, in the wings: *The actors walked <adv.> offstage when the play finished.*

off-the-rack *adv.adj.* ready to wear: *He buys his suits <adv.> off-the-rack.*

off-the-record *adj.adv.* referring to important information given privately and without the name of the person giving it: *The mayor spoke to the reporters <adv.> off-the-record.‖She made <adj.> off-the-record comments on the crime problem.*

off-the-wall *adj.infrml.* crazy or foolish: *Most of his ideas are off-the-wall and therefore useless.*

off-white *adj.* not quite white in color: *Her teeth were off-white from smoking.*

off year *n.* a year of less than good performance: *Football players have off years when they do not play as well as in others.*

of·ten /'ɔfən/ *adv.* **1** many times, frequently: *He often likes to tell jokes.* **2 as often as not:** at least 50 percent of the time: *As often as not, she calls us on Sunday.* **3 every so often:** occasionally, (*syn.*) infrequently: *He only washes his car every so often.* **4 more often than not:** more than 50 percent of the time, (*syn.*) frequently: *More often than not, we take the bus to work.* **5 once too often:** more than is safe, recommended, etc.: *They've lied to us once too often; we're not going to trust them anymore.*

o·gle /'ougəl/ *v.* **ogled, ogling, ogles** to look at s.o. with interest, esp. with sex in mind: *The man ogled the woman so hard that she became angry.* **-n. ogler.**

o·gre /'ougər/ *n.* **1** in children's fairy tales, a giant who eats people **2** a person who causes fear: *The boss can be an ogre sometimes.*

oh /ou/ *exclam.of* surprise, recognition, or disgust: *Oh, I forgot my eyeglasses!*

ohm /oum/ *n.* one ampere of resistance in an electrical conductor: *Ohms are used to measure electrical resistance.* **-n. ohmmeter** /'oum,mitər/.

oil /ɔɪl/ *n.* **1** [U] petroleum: *Companies drill for oil in the desert.* **2** [U] a lubricant from petroleum that makes machines work more easily: *We change the motor oil in our car regularly.* **3** [C;U] the fatty juice of some plants, like corn or olives: *People cook with olive oil.* **4 to burn the midnight oil:** to stay up late at night to study, work, etc.: *She was tired after burning the midnight oil last night.* See: oily.
—*v.* to put oil into or onto s.t., (*syn.*) to lubricate: *I oiled the squeaky wheel on my bicycle.* *See:* grease.

oiled /ɔɪld/ *adj.* **1** treated or covered with oil: *The engine is oiled and ready to run.* **2** *fig.slang* drunk: *He's too oiled to drive home.*

oil painting *n.* **1** [C] a painting produced with oil-based paints: *I have an old oil painting on the wall.* **2** [U] the art of painting with oil-based paints: *She prefers oil painting to watercolors.*

oil well *n.* a well dug for oil: *Oil wells cover the landscape in parts of Texas.*

oil·y /'ɔɪli/ *adj.* **-ier, -iest 1** covered by or containing oil: *The salad was very oily.* **2** of or like oil: *There was s.t. oily on the kitchen floor.*

oink /ɔɪŋk/ *v.n.* a sound made by pigs: *Pigs go, <n.> "Oink, oink!"*

oint·ment /'ɔɪntmənt/ *n.* [C;U] medicine in cream form: *An athlete rubbed ointment on her sore muscles.*

OK or **o·kay** /ou'keɪ/ *adj.adv.infrml.* **1** all right, well: *I feel <adj.> OK today.* **2** that's acceptable, agreeable: *<adv.> Okay, I'll accept $10 for it.*
—*v.infrml.* **OK'd, OK'ing, OK's** or **okayed, okaying, okays** to give approval: *They okayed the proposal in just five minutes.*
—*n.infrml.* [U] permission, approval

o·kra /'oukrə/ *n.* [U] a vegetable with long green pods used in soups, stews, etc.: *Okra makes a healthy soup.*

old /oʊld/ *adj.* **1** indicating a specific age: *His brother is 20 years old.* **2** indicating long life or existence: *Their grandfather is very old.* **3** old-fashioned, (*syn.*) outmoded: *Many stay with the old ways of doing things.* **4** in use for a long time: *She was wearing an old hat.* **5** past, former: *He met his old roommate for dinner last week.* **6** known for a long time, familiar: *It was good to see my old friends again.* **7** *fam.infrml.* **a good old boy:** a man, usu. from the Southern USA, who is an ordinary, simple, and friendly fellow: *Some of the good old boys love to discuss politics over a cup of coffee.* **8** *frml.* **of old:** in past times: *People of old lived more simply than we do today.* **9 old boy network:** a network of male friends and colleagues from college years and past associations: *He found his new job through the old boy network.* **10 the same old (stuff, nonsense, etc.):** referring to a repetition of offensive, boring behavior, propaganda, etc.: *The government keeps telling the people the same old nonsense about how good things are, when they are not.* **11 to have a good (great, high, wonderful, etc.) old time:** to enjoy oneself: *We had a great old time at the convention. See:* elderly.
—*n.* **1** *pl.* **the old:** elderly people, the aged: *The old have special medical needs.* **2** a person or animal of a specific age (used in combination): *Our school runs a day-care program for three-year-olds.*

USAGE NOTE: When describing people, it is more common and polite to use the word *elderly. She takes care of two elderly women.*

old country *n. sing.* the country of an immigrant's birth or origin: *My Italian neighbor arrived in New York as a child and visits the old country (Italy) every year.*

old·en /ˈoʊldən/ *adj.* old usage **in (the) olden days** or **in olden times:** old, past, long ago: *In the olden days, the pace of life was slower.*

old-fash·ioned /ˌoʊldˈfæʃənd/ *adj.* no longer in common use, out-of-date, (*syn.*) outmoded: *His clothes are old-fashioned and worn.*

Old Glory *n.fig.* the flag of the USA: *Each professional baseball game starts with a salute to Old Glory.*

old guard *n.* [U] a conservative, often older group in a political party or other organization: *The old guard in the Senate votes for rights for the elderly.*

old hand *n.infrml.* a person who is very experienced at doing s.t.: *She is an old hand at solving problems with computers.*

old hat *adj.infrml. fig.* no longer of particular interest, (*syn.*) passé: *That scandal is now old hat; no one is interested anymore.*

old·ie /ˈoʊldi/ *n.infrml.* s.t. old and widely known, esp. a song: *That tune is an oldie* (or) *a golden oldie.*

old maid *n. pej.* a middle-aged or older woman who has never married

old man *n.sing.slang* **1** one's father: *His old man is 90 years old.* **2** an older man in charge of anything, such as a ship's captain or a business owner: *The old man is in his office.* **3** *old usage* a woman's husband: *Her old man earns a big salary.*

old school *n.sing.adj.* referring to conservative, often old-fashioned ways: *He comes from the <n.> old school and will address a woman only by her last name.*

Old Testament *n.* the Holy Scripture of the Jews, the first part of the Christian Scripture, containing ancient Hebrew writings: *The Old Testament is the longer of the two parts of the Christian Bible. See:* New Testament.

old-timer *n.infrml.* **1** a person who has a long connection with a place, activity, etc.: *We watched the old timers' golf tournament on TV.* **2** an elderly person, esp. an old man: *Old-timers meet to play checkers in the park.*

old wives' tale *n.* s.t. which is widely believed, but untrue: *The idea that peach pits can cure cancer is an old wives' tale.*

Old World *n.* Europe with parts of Asia and North Africa: *Greek and Roman civilizations were part of the Old World.*

old world *adj.* of or like the Old World, esp. European: *My favorite restaurant has an old world atmosphere.*

o·le·an·der /ˈoʊliˌændər, ˌoʊliˈæn-/ *n.* a poisonous evergreen plant with sweet-smelling red, white, or pink flowers: *We have several oleanders growing in our front yard.*

ol·fac·to·ry /ɑlˈfæktəri, oʊl-/ *adj.* related to the sense of smell: *People with a limited olfactory sense also often have a poor sense of taste.*

ol·i·gar·chy /ˈɑləˌgɑrki, ˈoʊl-/ *n.* **-chies** [C;U] a form of government run by a few people, often a form of dictatorship: *The ruling oligarchy in that country is composed of one family and their friends.* **-adj. oligarchical** /ˌɑləˈgɑrkɪkəl, ˈoʊl-/. *See:* dictatorship.

ol·ive /ˈɑlɪv/ *n.* **1** (the small green or black oval fruit of) a tree that grows in southern Europe: *Olive oil has been used for cooking for thousands of years.* **2** a yellow-green color: *Army uniforms are often olive green.* **3 an olive branch:** a symbol of peace: *One nation handed an olive branch to another to seek peace.*

O·lym·pic Games /əˈlɪmpɪk/ or **Olympics** *n.pl.* **1** the international sports competitions held every four years: *The Olympics always draw huge crowds of spectators.* **2** the original ancient Greek games: *This Greek vase shows a scene from the ancient Olympics.*

USAGE NOTE: The *Special Olympics* is an international sports competition for mentally challenged children and adults. There is an international Special Olympics competition every two years.

om·buds·man /'ambədzmən, -,bʊdz-/ *n. gender neutral* **-men** /-mən/ a person, often a public official, who deals with citizens' complaints against an organization, esp. the government: *She acts as an ombudsman for complaints against the Social Security System.*

o·me·ga /oʊ'meɪgə, -'mi-/ *n.* **1** the last (24th) letter of the Greek alphabet **2** the last or the best of s.t.: *His knowledge was so great that it ran from the alpha (beginning) to the omega of that field.*

om·e·let or **om·e·lette** /'amlɪt/ *n.* a fried dish made of eggs often served folded over a filling, such as cheese: *I had a vegetable omelet for lunch. See:* scrambled eggs, USAGE NOTE.

o·men /'oʊmən/ *n.* a sign of s.t. that is going to happen in the future: *Dark clouds in the sky were an omen of a violent storm about to arrive.*

om·i·nous /'amənəs/ *adj.* being a sign of s.t. evil, bad, (*syn.*) threatening: *That man's angry threats are ominous; he may hurt s.o.* **-adv. ominously.**

o·mis·sion /oʊ'mɪʃən, ə-/ *n.* **1** [C] s.t left out, forgotten: *There were so many omissions on her test that she got an F.* **2** [U] the act of leaving s.t. out: *He was angry when he discovered the omission of his name from the list.*

o·mit /oʊ'mɪt, ə-/ *v.* **omitted, omitting, omits** **1** to leave out, not include: *I omitted milk from my shopping list by mistake.* **2** to not do s.t. on purpose: *She omitted several steps in the experiment and it failed.*

om·nip·o·tent /am'nɪpətənt/ *adj.* having total power: *That country is ruled by an omnipotent dictator.* **-n.** [U] **omnipotence.**

om·ni·pres·ent /,amnɪ'prezənt/ *adj.* present everywhere, (*syn.*) ubiquitous: *Many religious people believe that God is omnipresent.* **-n.** [U] **omnipresence.**

om·nis·cient /am'nɪʃənt/ *adj.* knowing all, understanding all: *That man thinks that he is omniscient, but he isn't.* **-n.** [U] **omniscience.**

om·niv·o·rous /am'nɪvərəs/ *adj.* eating both meat and plant foods: *Bears are omnivorous; they eat berries, fish, and meat.*

on /an, ɔn/ *prep.* **1** on the surface of (supported by, touching, connected to): *We have an Oriental rug on the floor.* **2** indicating location: *Their cottage is located on the seashore.* **3** indicating direction: *The new house is on the right of mine.* **4** indicating days or dates: *We'll*

be there on Sunday, June 19th. **5** indicating an object of some action: *The army began its attack on the enemy.* **6** indicating s.t. that is in process, happening: *I'm on vacation now.* **7** indicating a means of transportation: *We went to church on foot.* **8** referring to a subject, about: *We watched a video tape on exercise.* **9** indicating that s.o. is taking medication or drugs: *She is on penicillin.* **10** indicating membership or association: *She is serving on the Board of Directors.* **11** indicating the reason for s.t.: *He refused to sign the contract on the advice of his lawyer.* **12** by means of, using: *I talked to the doctor on the phone.*||*The clock runs on batteries.* **13** *infrml.* paid for by: *Dinner is on my dad tonight; he's celebrating his promotion.*

—*adv.* **1** functioning, operating: *He turned the television on.* **2** more distant, farther: *He arrived in Newark and drove on to Baltimore.* **3** in place, covering, esp. referring to clothing: *She put her shoes on.* **4** without stopping, continuously: *Despite doctor's orders, he went on smoking.* **5 and so on:** and more, (*syn.*) et cetera (etc.): *We did some cleaning, such as vacuuming the rugs, washing the windows and so on.* **6 on and on:** for a long time, at great length: *The speaker talked on and on.*

—*adj.* **1** operating, functioning: *The TV is on.* **2** planned, happening: *I have s.t. on for this weekend; I'm going to a party.* **3** acting artificially and being aware of others' reactions: *He's on all the time with an act about how smart he is.*

on-again, off-again *adj.* switching between functioning and not functioning, happening and not happening: *That couple has an on-again, off-again relationship where they see each other frequently for a couple of weeks, then not at all for months.*

on and off or **off and on** *adv.* periodically, sometimes *It rained on and off all night long.*

once /wʌns/ *adv.* **1** occurring one time only: *I told him what to do just once.* **2** occurring in the past: *I once visited California many years ago.* **3 all at once:** happening all at one time: *Customers came into the restaurant all at once.* **4 at once:** immediately, right now: *That matter must be taken care of at once.* **5 just for once:** for this one time only, as an exception: *Just for once, will you clean your room?* **6 once and for all:** with certainty, for sure: *The question of who owns that property must be settled once and for all.* **7 once in a while:** periodically, sometimes: *He likes to go to the movies once in a while.* **8 once more** or **once again:** one more time, again: *He decided to try the recipe once more.* **9 once upon a time:** a long time ago: *Children's stories often begin: "Once upon a time, there lived a beautiful princess."*

—*conj.* when, as soon as: *Once he understood, he did what he was told to do.*

once-over *n.infrml.* a quick look, rapid examination: *Doctors give accident victims a once-over to see which ones need immediate attention.*

on·col·o·gy /ɑŋˈkɑlədʒi, ɑn-/ *n.* [U] the study and treatment of tumors, esp. cancerous ones: *Oncology is studied by all medical students.* -*n.* **oncologist.**

on·com·ing /ˈɑnˌkʌmɪŋ, ˈɔn-/ *adj.* approaching, nearing: *The headlights of oncoming cars at night can hurt your eyes.*

one /wʌn/ *n.pron.* **1** the cardinal number 1: *Turn to page <n.> one.* **2** *personal pron.* any person, you: *One can only try.* **3** *s.o. or s.t.* that has been mentioned: *He looked for a pen and found one in his pocket.* **4** a single person, thing, or animal: *She's the one he wants to meet.* **5 one and all:** everyone, all those involved: *The host wished one and all (of his guests) a Happy New Year.* **6 one another:** each other: *She told her children to be kind to one another.* **7 to be one up on s.o.:** to have an advantage over s.o.: *They got the contract because they were one up on their competition.* —*adj.* **1** being a single person, thing, or animal: *He has only one dollar in his wallet.* **2** related to a unified group: *Our children returned home and we are one family again.* **3 all in one:** included in one group: *I bought a sound system with a radio and CD player all in one.* **4 at one:** in agreement, in accord: *After negotiating, the two parties were at one on an agreement.* **5 one-and-only: a.** unique: *That was our one-and-only chance to get the contract.* **b.** most beloved: *After his one-and-only love left him, he was depressed.* **6 one by one:** in single file, one at a time: *Soldiers turned in their weapons one by one.* **7 one day** or **one of these days:** referring to an indefinite time in the future: *One day you'll understand.* **8 one of:** One item that is part of a larger group: *That's one of my favorite movies.* **9 one-of-a-kind:** unique, (*syn.*) irreplaceable: *She was very embarrassed when she broke her host's one-of-a-kind statue.* **10 one-on-one:** directly with another person: *We had a one-on-one discussion and solved a lot of problems.*

one-night stand *n.* **1** a performance on a single evening by an entertainer: *She's a singer who does one-night stands around the state.* **2** *slang* a one-time sexual act: *They met in a bar, had a one-night stand, and never saw each other again.*

on·er·ous /ˈɑnərəs, ˈoʊ-/ *adj.* difficult, heavy, (*syn.*) burdensome: *The presidency is an onerous job.* -*adv.* **onerously;** -*n.* **onerousness.**

one·self /wʌnˈsɛlf/ *reflexive pron.* **1** (used as the object of a verb or preposition) **a.** alone **b.** without assistance: *There are many things one must do by oneself without depending on others.* **2** (used to intensify): *One must believe oneself that anything is possible.* **3 to be oneself:** to act normally or in a relaxed manner: *The best friends are those with whom one can feel comfortable, at home, and like oneself.*

one-shot *adj.infrml.* referring to s.t. done only once, one-time: *Our company bought out our only competitor in a one-shot deal.*

one-sided *adj.* **1** being stronger on one side than on the other: *It was a one-sided match between the champions and the new team; the champions won 10—0.* **2** unfair, seeing only one side of a problem (issue, argument, etc.), (*syn.*) biased: *The report was one-sided and didn't show any other opinions.*

one-time *adj.* **1** occurring or done only once: *We made an exception to our rules as a one-time thing.* **2** former, previous: *She was the one-time mayor of the town and is now retired.*

one-to-one *adj.* direct with another person: *The two ministers had a one-to-one discussion that was friendly and useful.*

one-track mind *n.* a mind with only one idea or goal, esp. used with reference to a man with sex on his mind: *That guy has a one-track mind; all that interests him is women.*

one-up·man·ship /ˌwʌnˈʌpmənˌʃɪp/ *n.* [U] a way to get superiority over others, esp. in power or wealth, by trying to seem better than them: *He drives the most expensive car in a show of one-upmanship over his neighbors.*

one-way *adj.* permitting movement in only one direction: *The police stopped her for driving the wrong way on a one-way street.*

on·go·ing /ˈɑnˌgoʊɪŋ, ˈɔn-/ *adj.* continuing, happening: *There is an ongoing discussion in my company about working conditions.*

on·ion /ˈʌnyən/ *n.* [C;U] a round, white vegetable with a strong smell and taste: *I like liver and onions for dinner.*

on·line or **on-line** /ˌɑnˈlaɪn, ɔn-/ *adj.* **1** having, offering, or using a connection to a network of computers (by direct wiring or modem): *While I was using the computer, I looked up a word in an online dictionary.* **2** (of computers and electrical equipment) working properly: *The radar system was down earlier, but now it's online again.* See: off-line.

on·look·er /ˈɑnˌlʊkər, ˈɔn-/ *n.* a spectator, s.o. who sees s.t.: *Onlookers stared at the accident scene*

on·ly /ˈoʊnli/ *adj.* **1** with no others in its group, (*syn.*) sole: *I loaned my only tennis racket to a friend.* **2** in a subgroup of a whole: *They were the only students who passed the exam.* **3** most worthy of consideration, (*syn.*) superior: *She's the only candidate for this position.* **4 an only child:** having no brothers or sisters: *She is an only child.*

—adv. **1** with nobody or nothing else, (*syn.*) solely: *I can only say how sorry I am.* **2** at the least: *If they would only try to understand.* **3** restricted in authority or importance: *I am only the secretary here, not the boss.* **4** restricted in time: *He had only a minute to talk.* **5** in the recent past: *We talked only yesterday.* **6** in the final analysis: *Her attempts to explain only confused us more.* **7** contradictory to the expected result: *He rushed to the airport only to miss his flight by two minutes.* **8 not only . . . but also:** not just, but in addition: *We were not only hungry, but also tired.* **9 to be only too glad, happy, etc., to:** willing to do s.t.: *I am only too happy to drive you to the store.*
—conj. **1** except, however: *The sky is clear, only it is too hot to go for a walk.* **2** with the restriction that: *You may go bicycle riding, only watch out for cars.*

on·o·mat·o·poe·ia /ˌɑnəˌmætəˈpiə, -ˌmɑ-/ *n.* [U] the use of words to imitate sounds: *The teacher used onomatopoeia to teach the children animal sounds such as "moo" and "meow". -adj.* **onomatopoeic.**

on·rush /ˈɑnˌrʌʃ, ˈɔn-/ *n.* **-rushes** a sudden move forward, (*syn.*) a surge: *The onrush of the crowd into the stadium happened when guards opened the gates.*

on·set /ˈɑnˌsɛt, ˈɔn-/ *n.sing.* the beginning of s.t., such as an illness: *The onset of the disease began in October.*

on·shore /ˌɑnˈʃɔr, ˌɔn-/ *adv.adj.* **1** headed toward the shore: *The wind is blowing <adv.> onshore.||An <adj.> onshore breeze cooled the beach.* **2** located on a coastline: *Boats are stored <adv.> onshore for the winter. See:* offshore.

on·side /ˌɑnˈsaɪd, ˌɔn-/ *or* **onsides** *adj. adv.* (in sports) within the lines of a sports field, court, rink, etc: *He kicked the ball <adv> onside (or) onsides. See:* offside.

on·slaught /ˈɑnˌslɔt, ˈɔn-/ *n.* a violent attack, either physically or with words, (*syn.*) an assault: *When the governor said he was raising taxes, there was an onslaught of criticism.*

on·stage /ˌɑnˈsteɪdʒ, ˈɔn-/ *adj.adv.* located on a stage: *The opera singer is <adj.> onstage now. See:* offstage.

on-the-job *adj.* happening during work, such as learning a skill: *She received on-the-job training on how to use a computer*

on·to /ˈɑntu, -tə, ˈɔn-/ *prep.* **1** on top of, upon s.t.: *The tractor left the field and drove onto the road.* **2** *infrml.* in a state of understanding: *She's onto your plan to trick her.*

o·nus /ˈoʊnəs/ *n.sing.frml.* a responsibility, (*syn.*) a burden: *The onus of caring for her elderly, sick parents was on her brother while she was on vacation.*

on·ward /ˈɑnwərd, ˈɔn-/ *or* **onwards** *adv.adj.* in a forward direction: *After landing in Los Angeles, the plane flew <adv.> onwards to Hawaii.*

on·yx /ˈɑnɪks/ *n.* **-yxes** [C;U] a semi-precious gemstone with layers of colors in white, brown, or black: *He wears a gold ring with a black onyx.*

oo·dles /ˈudlz/ *n.pl.infrml.* a great deal, much, (*syn.*) *fig.* tons: *That couple has oodles of money.*

ooh /u/ *exclam.* an expression of pleasure, surprise, or disgust: *Ooh, I think he's a terrific actor!*

oops /ʊps, ups/ *exclam.* an expression of surprise or apology said after making a mistake, dropping s.t., etc.: *Oops, I spilled some coffee on my shirt.*

ooze /uz/ *n.* [U] **1** soft mud, (*syn.*) slime: *The ooze on the bottom of the river is very deep.* **2** anything like soft mud, such as oily dirt: *There was ooze on the ground where he had worked on the car.*
—v. **oozed, oozing, oozes** (of liquids) to pass slowly out, as through small openings: *Blood was oozing through the bandage.*

o·pac·i·ty /oʊˈpæsəti/ *n.* [U] the quality of not permitting the passage of light: *The paper in that book is thick and has a high opacity. See:* opaque, **1.**

o·pal /ˈoʊpəl/ *n.* a gemstone with bright colors in a milky base: *Opals are made into jewelry. -adj.* **opalescent** /ˌoʊpəˈlɛsənt/.

o·paque /oʊˈpeɪk/ *adj.* **1** not permitting the passage of light: *Some glass is so thick that it is opaque.* **2** dense, difficult to understand: *His writing style can be opaque in places. -adv.* **opaquely; -***n.* [U] **opaqueness.**

op ed page /ˈɑpˈɛd/ *n.* short for opposite the editorial page, a page in a newspaper with columns or articles giving opinions: *The op ed page in today's newspaper has one column criticizing the mayor and another praising her. See:* editorial, USAGE NOTE.

o·pen /ˈoʊpən/ *adj.* **1** not closed or locked, (*syn.*) unfastened: *The front door is open; please come in!* **2** not enclosed, unprotected: *They built their house in an open field.* **3** not covered, without a top, lid, etc.: *He took us for a ride in an open sports car.* **4** spread out, unfolded: *There was an open magazine on the table.* **5** free to all, public: *The mayor has held open meetings to discuss city problems.* **6** without a final decision, available: *The position of assistant manager is still open.* **7** willing to listen to new ideas, opinions, etc.: *He has an open mind. See:* open-minded. **8** without secrets, honest, (*syn.*) frank: *I want you to be open with me about your money problems, so I can help you.* **9** ready for business: *She looked everywhere before she found a drugstore that was open.* **10 open to: a.** unprotected, (*syn.*) vulnerable: *After winning*

$10,000, he was open to many people asking him for money. **b.** willing to receive: *That company is open to suggestions from customers and employees.* -adv. **openly.** See: open-minded.

—*v.* **1** to make or become open, (*syn.*) to unfasten: *She opened the door before I could knock.* **2** to make a passage through: *Workers opened a road into the jungle.* **3** to spread apart, unfold: *She opened the map on her knees.* **4** to start, begin: *The movie opens in a theater next week.* **5** to make ready for business: *Most stores open at noon on Sundays.* **6** to be accessible to: *The living room doors open onto the garden.* **7** to cause understanding, sympathy, etc.: *The minister asked us to open our hearts to the flood victims.* **8** *phrasal v. insep.* **to open at s.t.:** (in stock markets, etc.) to have an initial price of: *IBM opened at $100 per share this morning.* **9** *phrasal v. insep.* **to open fire on s.o. or s.t.:** to begin shooting at: *The enemy opened fire on our position.* **10** *phrasal v.* **to open up:** to tell everything, (*syn.*) to confide in: *She opened up and told her friend all her troubles.*

—*n.* **1** the outdoors, outside: *I like sleeping in the open.* **2** general knowledge, public view: *I didn't want to keep our marriage secret any longer, so I brought it into the open and told my parents.* **3** a competition where professionals and amateurs can play together: *The US tennis Open is held in New York.*

open-air *adj.* located outdoors: *In summertime, open-air concerts are held in the park.*

open-and-shut *adj.* easily settled, quickly determined: *His death is an open-and-shut case of murder committed by his wife.*

open-door *adj.* available to all on an equal basis, freely accessible: *The boss has an open-door policy of encouraging any employee to talk to her.*

open-ended *adj.* continuing without stopping, ongoing: *The two nations are having open-ended discussions on a trade agreement.*

o·pen·er /'oupənər/ *n.* **1** a person or thing that opens: *She uses an electric can opener to open cans.* **2** a beginning statement (joke, proposal, etc.): *As an opener, the comedian made a joke about himself.*

o·pen·hand·ed /,oupən'hændɪd/ *adj.* generous: *She is kind and openhanded to people less fortunate than she is.*

open house *n.* a social event for all who wish to attend: *On New Year's Eve, my wife and I have an open house for anyone in our neighborhood who wants to visit us.*

o·pen·ing /'oupənɪŋ, 'oupnɪŋ/ *n.* **1** a passage through s.t., a path: *An opening in the trees leads to a large garden.* **2** a job vacancy: *We have an opening in our sales department.* **3** the act of becoming or causing to become

open: *There were many changes in China after its opening to the West.*

—*adj.* beginning, starting: *Her opening remarks at the meeting were brief.*

open-market *n.* a market that is open to imports with few government regulations.

open-minded *adj.* willing to listen to or consider the opinions and ideas of others, (*syn.*) broadminded: *He is open-minded about new ways of doing things.* -adv. **open-mindedly.**

o·pen·ness /'oupənnɪs/ *n.* the quality of telling the truth, (*syn.*) frankness: *The committee chairwoman said she appreciated our openness in saying exactly what we thought.*

open season *n.* [C;U] **1** a time period when hunting and fishing is permitted: *For three weeks in the autumn, it is open season for hunters.* **2 to declare open season on s.o.:** to attack freely: *The news media declared open season on the President and attacked him daily in the newspaper.*

open shop *n.* a workplace where it is not necessary to be a union member in order to get a job: *The hospital workers voted to have an open shop.*

op·er·a /'aprə, 'apərə/ *n.* **1** [C;U] a theater art in which a story is set to music: *He listens to opera for relaxation.* **2** [C] an opera house: *The opera is located up the avenue from our offices.* **3** *pl.* of opus -*n.* **opera-goer** /'aprə,gouər, 'apərə-/; -*adj.* **operatic** /,apə'rætɪk/.

op·er·a·ble /'apərəbəl, 'aprə-/ *adj.* **1** (in medicine) treatable by surgery: *He has an operable type of cancer.* **2** in working condition: *Our car is in operable condition.*

op·er·ate /'apə,reɪt/ *v.* -ated, -ating, -ates **1** to function, work: *Her new computer operates at a high speed.||That company operated in an old-fashioned way.||He operates out of his home.* **2** to be in charge of, manage: *He operates a food business in the city.* **3** to perform surgery: *The doctor operated on her this morning and removed her appendix.*

op·er·at·ing /'apə,reɪtɪŋ/ *adj.* **1** functioning, working: *That machine was broken, but is operating now.* **2** of or related to surgery: *She is famous for her new operating techniques.*

operating expense *n.* the cost of keeping a business going

operating room or **OR** *n.* a room specially equipped for surgery: *Surgeons and nurses perform surgery in an operating room.* See: recovery room.

operating system *n.* (in computers) the main software, such as DOS or Windows 95™, used to run a computer's more specialized programs: *The operating system in my computer is the most popular one available today.*

O

op·er·a·tion /ˌɑpəˈreɪʃən/ n. **1** [C;U] a way or process of working s.t., such as a machine: *The operation of that machine is simple; just press the green buttons to make it work.* **2** [C] a surgical procedure: *She had an operation to remove her appendix.* **3** [C] s.t. that needs to be done: *The company carried out a secret operation to improve its products.* **4** [C] (in mathematics) a process, such as addition or subtraction, carried out on numerals, following certain rules: *Addition is one of the simplest mathematical operations.* **5** *pl.* **operations:** the main internal workings of business, military, or government: *Military operations are based in a command center in its headquarters.*

op·er·a·tion·al /ˌɑpəˈreɪʃənəl, -ˈreɪʃnəl/ adj. working effectively, functioning: *Repairs were made to the machine and now it is operational.* **-adv.** **operationally.**

op·er·a·tive /ˈɑpərətɪv, ˈɑprə-/ adj. operating, producing certain effects: *Her computer is now operative after a breakdown.*
—n. a special worker, esp. a spy or agent: *That secret agency has operatives who gather information on other governments.*

op·er·a·tor /ˈɑpəˌreɪtər/ n. **1** a person who operates equipment: *The operator of a big truck must be careful not to injure others.* **2** a person who handles telephone calls at a switchboard: *I didn't know how to make an overseas call, so I asked an operator to help me.* **3** *infrml.fig.* a person who gets what he or she wants through dishonest behavior: *He's an operator who gets women by pretending to be rich.*

op·er·et·ta /ˌɑpəˈrɛtə/ n. an opera sung with light, often comical moments and some spoken dialogue

oph·thal·mol·o·gist /ˌɑfθəlˈmɑlədʒɪst, -θəlˈmɑ-, ˌɑp-/ n. a doctor who specializes in diseases of the human eye: *An ophthalmologist treated the old man's blindness.* **-n.** [U] **ophthalmology.**

o·pin·ion /əˈpɪnyən/ n. **1** [C;U] what s.o. believes, s.t. not proven in fact: *His opinion is that life on earth will improve year by year.* **2** [U] any widely held views: *Public opinion indicates that the people think the President is doing a good job.* **3** [C] a professional judgment, such as one made by a doctor, court, or judge: *His doctor's medical opinion is that he has curable cancer.* **4 to be of the opinion:** to believe, possibly with a willingness to change one's mind: *He is of the opinion that environmental pollution can be fixed.* **5 to hold the opinion:** to believe strongly: *She holds the opinion that there is no cure for that disease.*

o·pin·ion·at·ed /əˈpɪnyəˌneɪtɪd/ adj. convinced that only one's own opinions are true: *He is so opinionated that he insists only his views are correct.*

opinion poll n. a scientific survey in which questions are asked of people to know what they think about a particular subject, esp. politics: *Opinion polls show that people think crime is the nation's biggest problem.*

o·pi·um /ˈoupiəm/ n. [U] a narcotic drug made from the seeds of a type of poppy: *Opium supplies other strong drugs like morphine and heroin.*

o·pos·sum /əˈpɑsəm, ˈpɑsəm/ n. **-sums** or **-sum** an American marsupial animal with a pointed nose and a long bare tail that is active mostly at night and may pretend to be dead when in danger

op·po·nent /əˈpounənt/ n. a person who takes the opposite side in a fight, game, contest, etc.: *She was the mayor's opponent in the last election and she won.*

op·por·tune /ˌɑpərˈtun/ adj. correct for a moment or purpose, *(syns.)* timely, advantageous: *Early spring is the opportune time to plant crops.*

op·por·tun·ism /ˌɑpərˈtuˌnɪzəm/ n. [U] an opportunity for self-advancement usu. with no respect for right or wrong: *In an act of opportunism, he eliminated his political opponent by spreading false stories about him.* **-n.** **opportunist;** **-adj.** **opportunistic** /ˌɑpərtuˈnɪstɪk/.

op·por·tu·ni·ty /ˌɑpərˈtunəti/ n. **-ties 1** an advantageous time to act: *I had the opportunity to visit my relatives this summer.* **2** an occasion for personal advancement or financial gain: *Her new job represents an excellent opportunity to make much more money.*

op·pose /əˈpouz/ v. **-posed, -posing, -poses 1** to be against s.t. or s.o.: *The radicals opposed the government's plan for reform.* **2** to contrast two ideas, concepts, etc.: *When the two plans were opposed, it was easy to see their advantages and disadvantages.* **3 as opposed to:** in complete contrast to: *This city, as opposed to the state capital, is small and friendly.* **4 to be opposed to:** to take an active position against: *She is opposed to the death penalty.*

op·po·site /ˈɑpəzɪt, -sɪt/ prep. in a position across from s.o. or s.t.: *My friend sat opposite me at dinner.*
—adj. **1** across from one another, facing each other: *The restaurant and my apartment are on opposite sides of the street.* **2** in contrast to, completely different, disagreeing: *The two experts hold opposite opinions as to how to stop poverty.*
—n. a totally different opinion or action: *The two experts think just the opposite.*

op·po·si·tion /ˌɑpəˈzɪʃən/ n. **1** [U] in the state of being against s.o. or s.t.: *The Liberals are the opposition to the Conservatives.* **2** disagreement, protest: *Opposition to companies that pollute comes from environmental groups.*

op·press /ə'prɛs/ v. **-es** **1** to govern or treat cruelly and unjustly, (syn.) to subjugate: *The upper classes oppress the poorer people by taking land away from them.* **2** fig. to worry, (syn.) to burden: *Ill health and financial problems oppress him.* -n. **oppression, oppressor.**

op·pres·sive /ə'prɛsɪv/ adj. **1** limiting one's freedoms: *Oppressive officials will not allow the poor to work.* **2** fig. difficult to endure, (syn.) weakening: *The heat in summer is oppressive.*

opt /ɑpt/ v. **1** to choose, decide on: *She opted for a winter vacation, instead of one in the summer.* **2 to opt out:** to remove oneself from, decide against: *She opted out of going to the wedding and stayed at home.*

op·tic /'ɑptɪk/ adj. of or belonging to the eye: *The accident injured the optic nerve in his eye.*

op·ti·cal /'ɑptɪkəl/ adj. of the eye or the sense of sight: *Optical lenses are used in many applications from eyeglasses to telescopes.* -adv. **optically.**

optical illusion n. s.t. that looks real, but is not: *A mirage is an optical illusion of trees and water appearing in the desert when they do not exist.*

op·ti·cian /ɑp'tɪʃən/ n. **1** a skilled person who makes lenses for eyeglasses **2** a person or business that sells eyeglasses: *I went to the optician for eyeglasses.* See: optometry.

op·tics /'ɑptɪks/ n. [U] the science of light, vision, and lenses

op·ti·mal /'ɑptəməl/ adj. referring to the best (conditions, circumstances, etc): *Clear skies and no wind are optimal conditions for a picnic.*

op·ti·mism /'ɑptə,mɪzəm/ n. [U] **1** the belief that good things will happen: *Despite her health problems, she has kept her optimism.* **2** the belief that the future will be good: *Our company is full of optimism about the future.* -n. **optimist;** -adj. **optimistic** /,ɑptə'mɪstɪk/; -adv. **optimistically.**

op·ti·mum /'ɑptəməm/ n.adj. **-mums** or **-ma** /-mə/ the best outcome (use, condition, etc.) possible: *The <n.> optimum that we can expect is a 7 percent return on money invested.||That is the <adj.> optimum rate possible at this time.* -v. **optimize** /'ɑptə,maɪz/.

op·tion /'ɑpʃən/ n. **1** [C;U] a choice, (syn.) an alternative: *She has two options: she can stay here or leave.* **2** [C] a right to buy s.t. at a stated price: *He has a 90 day option to buy that house for $170,000.*
—v. to offer or get an option to buy s.t.: *He optioned his cottage to a potential buyer for a month.*

op·tion·al /'ɑpʃənəl/ adj. referring to s.t. that can be done or not done freely, (syn.) volun- tary: *If you want to give money to the church, that is optional.* -adv. **optionally.**

op·tom·e·try /ɑp'tɑmətri/ n. [U] the profession of examining the eyes for problems and writing prescriptions for eyeglasses: *Optometry requires advanced study of the eyes and a license.* -n. **optometrist.**

op·u·lence /'ɑpyələns/ n. [U] great wealth and luxury: *The king of France lived in opulence in his palace.* -adj. **opulent;** -adv. **opulently.**

o·pus /'oupəs/ n. **opera** /'oupərə, 'ɑ-/ or **opuses** an artistic work such as a musical composition or group of compositions: *This sonata is the composer's opus one.*

or /ɔr; weak form ər/ conj. **1** referring to choices or alternatives: *You can go today or tomorrow.* **2** if not, (syn.) otherwise: *Take care of your car or else you'll have problems.* **3** introducing a word with the same meaning: *I'll have half a dozen, or six, of those.* **4 or so:** more or less, (syn.) approximately: *The car cost $19,000 or so.*

or·a·cle /'ɔrəkəl, 'ɑr-/ n. a wise person who tells the future, (syn.) a soothsayer: *The ancient Greeks tried to learn the future from oracles.* -adj. **oracular** /ɔ'rækyələr/.

o·ral /'ɔrəl/ adj. **1** related to the mouth, its opening and inside: *Dentists give their patients oral examinations.* **2** not written, spoken: *He had to give an oral report at the meeting.* -adv. **orally.**

or·ange /'ɔrɪndʒ, 'ɑr-/ n.adj. **1** a round, orange-colored fruit with thick skin and sweet, juicy flesh, or the tree it grows on: *He likes to eat <n.> oranges and to drink orange juice for breakfast.* **2** the color made by mixing red and yellow: *She wore an <adj.> orange bathing suit to the beach.*

or·ange·ade /,ɔrɪn'dʒeɪd, ,ɑr-/ n. [C;U] an orange-flavored drink with bubbles: *I like a cold orangeade on a hot day.*

o·rang·u·tan /ə'ræŋə,tæŋ, -,tæn/ n. a large monkey with a reddish brown coat and no tail, found in Sumatra and Borneo: *Orangutans have humanlike faces.*

o·ra·tion /ɔ'reɪʃən/ n.frml. [C;U] a formal public speech often in dignified language: *The priest gave an oration on the value of not drinking alcohol.* -v. **orate** /ɔ'reɪt, 'ɔr,eɪt/.

or·a·tor /'ɔrətər, 'ɑr-/ n. [U] **1** a person who gives an oration: *Each orator took a turn speaking in the Senate.* **2** a skilled public speaker: *Sir Winston Churchill was famous as an orator; he gave wonderful speeches.* -n. **oratory** /'ɔrə,tɔri, 'ɑr-/.

or·bit /'ɔrbɪt/ n. **1** a path in space followed by a planet, moon, or spacecraft: *The space vehicle settled into an orbit around Mars.* **2** old usage the range of a person's activity or influ-

ence: *I'd like to help you, but I'm afraid that's out of my orbit.*
—*v.* to move in an orbit: *Planets orbit the sun.*
-adj. **orbital.**

or·chard /'ɔrtʃərd/ *n.* **1** a piece of land on which fruit trees grow: *Farmers pick apples from their orchards in autumn.* **2** a group of trees grown for their crops, such as fruits and nuts

or·ches·tra /'ɔrkəstrə, -ˌkɛs-/ *n.* **1** a usu. large group of musicians who play music on instruments, such as the violin and horns: *That orchestra plays classical music.* **2** the seats on the floor of a theater (not in the balconies) closest to the stage **3 orchestra pit:** the part of a theater where the orchestra sits *-adj.* **orchestral** /ɔr'kɛstrəl/.

or·ches·trate /'ɔrkəˌstreɪt/ *v.* **-trated, -trating, -trates 1** to write or arrange music for an orchestra **2** *fig.*to organize an event: *My mother orchestrated a big party for charity.* *-n.* **[C;U] orchestration** /ˌɔrkə'streɪʃən/.

or·chid /'ɔrkɪd/ *n.* **1** any of a large variety of plants with beautiful flowers: *Some women wear orchids in their hair on formal occasions.* **2** a purplish-red color

or·dain /ɔr'deɪn/ *v.* **1** to make s.o. a priest or minister: *The student of religion was ordained a minister* (or) *as a minister last month.* **2** *frml.*to order by one's authority or by law: *The king ordained that all his citizens must pay taxes.*

or·deal /ɔr'dil, -'diəl/ *n.* a painful experience or a struggle that tests one's abilities: *Her treatment for cancer was a long, hard ordeal for her.*

or·der /'ɔrdər/ *n.* **1** [U] the way in which things are arranged in time or space, organization: *She arranged the newspapers in order by their dates.* **2** [U] the condition of being neatly arranged: *He always keeps his office in order.* **3** [U] the condition of working or functioning, esp. of machines: *We had to walk up the stairs because the elevator was out of order.* (=not functioning) **4** [U] the condition that results from laws, rules, etc. being obeyed: *The judge asked for order in the court.* **5** [C] a direction, command: *The captain gave the sailor an order.* **6** [C] **a.** a request for goods or services: *She placed an order with our company for five new computers.* **b.** the goods that were requested: *Their order of office supplies was delivered this morning.* **7** [C] a written or printed paper that gives s.o. permission to do s.t., such as collect money: *He paid his rent with a money order.* **8** [C] (in biology) a division of plants or animals classified by similarity: *Orchids belong to the order Orchidales.* **9** [C] a religious organization, esp. a group of monks or nuns: *He was a member of the Dominican order.* **10** [C] **a.** a group of people who have

been honored for bravery, service, etc. **b.** the badge, emblem, they wear to show membership in this group: *She was given the Order of the Silver Star.* **11** *fig.* **a tall order:** a request to do s.t. very difficult: *She wants the job done tomorrow, and that's a tall order!* **12 in order to/that:** for, with the purpose of: *He moved to a smaller apartment in order to save money.* **13 in short order:** very quickly, soon: *She needs to act in short order if she wants to avoid penalties.* **14 on order:** requested but not yet made, shipped, or delivered: *The shoes are on order and will be shipped next week.* **15 on/by the order of:** by the authority of, command of: *On the order of the judge, the man paid a $500 fine.* **16 to keep order:** to maintain conditions of daily life, obedience of laws, rules: *During the war, the soldiers tried to keep order.* **17 to make to order:** to make s.t. specially for a customer: *He has his suits made to order by a tailor.* **18 under orders:** having been commanded to do s.t.: *Our platoon was under orders to take the city. See:* disorder.
—*v.* **1** to give a command: *The captain ordered the soldiers to clean their guns.* **2** to request that s.t. be supplied: *I've ordered new curtains for the kitchen.* **3** to arrange, manage in a logical way: *The accountant ordered the figures by month and year.* **4** *phrasal v. sep.* **to order s.o. around:** to tell s.o. what to do: *The boss likes to order her employees around.*

or·der·ly /'ɔrdərli/ *n.* **-lies** a worker who cleans and does chores: *An orderly cleans floors and bathrooms in the hospital.*
—*adj.* neatly arranged, organized: *Her office is very orderly and clean.*

or·di·nal /'ɔrdnəl/ *adj.* referring to ranking or place in a series: *First, second, third, and fourth, etc. (also written 1st, 2nd, 3rd, 4th) are ordinal numbers. See:* cardinal.

or·di·nance /'ɔrdnəns/ *n.* a regulation or law, esp. one passed by a state or local government: *A city ordinance requires that garbage must be collected once a week.*

or·di·nar·i·ly /ˌɔrdn'ɛrəli/ *adv.* under normal conditions, usually: *Ordinarily the library is open, but it is closed because of the storm.*

or·di·nar·y /'ɔrdnˌɛri/ *adj.* **1** common, regular: *She wears an ordinary pair of shoes to go for a walk.* **2** of average quality, (*syn.*) mediocre: *That singer has an ordinary voice; she won't be very successful.*

or·di·na·tion /ˌɔrdn'eɪʃən/ *n.* [C;U] the act or ceremony of ordaining s.o. as a priest or minister *See:* ordain.

ore /ɔr/ *n.* [C;U] earth, rock, etc., from which metals can be processed: *Workers find gold in ore taken from deep in the earth.*

o·reg·a·no /ə'rɛgəˌnoʊ/ *n.* [U] a green herb plant with small leaves, used in cooking:

Oregano is a popular spice in Mexico and the Philippines.

or·gan (1) /ˈɔrgən/ *n.* a part of an animal or plant that has a specific function: *The eyes, tongue, and heart are human organs.*

organ (2) *n.* a musical instrument played like a piano that makes music by electronic sounds or by wind blowing through pipes: *Most churches have an organ. -n.* **organist.**

organ (3) *n.* a newspaper, magazine, etc., that publishes the official views of a group or organization: *He didn't believe the news he read in the Republican party organ.*

organ grinder *n.* a person who plays a portable organ, usu. outdoors and often with a monkey to amuse people: *The organ grinder's monkey accepts coins from spectators.*

or·gan·ic /ɔrˈgænɪk/ *adj.* **1** of or related to living things: *Organic fertilizer is made from natural products, like cow or horse manure.* **2** (of food) produced without chemicals: *organic fruits and vegetables* **3** (in chemistry) of or related to compounds containing carbon *-adv.* **organically.**

USAGE NOTE: *Organic food* is also called *natural* food. Organic food is often sold in natural food stores, which also sell shampoo, cleaning supplies, and other products made without a lot of harmful chemicals.

---

or·ga·nism /ˈɔrgəˌnɪzəm/ *n.* a living creature: *Bacteria are very small organisms.*

or·ga·ni·za·tion /ˌɔrgənəˈzeɪʃən/ *n.* **1** [C] a group of people working together for a purpose, such as a business or a hobby: *People give money to charitable organizations.* **2** [U] an arrangement of people, things, or functions for a specific purpose: *The organization of books in that library is by subject matter.*

or·ga·ni·za·tion·al /ˌɔrgənəˈzeɪʃənəl/ *adj.* related to organizing, arranging: *Her organizational abilities keep our office in order. -adv.* **organizationally.**

or·ga·nize /ˈɔrgəˌnaɪz/ *v.* **-nized, -nizing, -nizes** **1** to make a group for a specific purpose: *Workers organized into labor unions to protect their rights.* **2** to put in order, arrange: *She organizes meetings by asking people to come, getting the meeting room, etc.*

or·ga·niz·er /ˈɔrgəˌnaɪzər/ *n.* **1** a person who arranges activities: *She is a good organizer of meetings and parties.* **2** a device, such as a cabinet or a notebook, used to arrange books, papers, etc. **3** a person who persuades workers to join a labor union

or·gasm /ˈɔrˌgæzəm/ *n.* [C; U] the moment of feeling the greatest pleasure in sex

or·gy /ˈɔrdʒi/ *n.* **-gies** **1** a wild party, usu. with sex, drugs, and/or alcohol: *After graduation,* my roommates held a party; it was so wild, it reminded me of an ancient Roman orgy.

o·ri·ent /ˈɔriˌɛnt, -ənt/ *v.* **1** to find a geographic location using a map, compass, etc.: *During our walk in the woods, we got lost and had to orient ourselves with a compass.* **2** *fig.* to become familiar with a new city, neighborhood, etc.: *Volunteers orient new students to the campus every semester.* **3** to locate s.t. in a specific direction: *Mosques are oriented toward Mecca. See:* orientation.

—*n.sing.old usage* /ˈɔriənt, -ˌɛnt/ **the Orient:** the East, esp. Asian countries such as Japan, China, Vietnam, etc.: *The explorer wrote a book about her travels to the Orient.*

O·ri·en·tal or **o·ri·en·tal** /ˌɔriˈɛntəl/ *adj.* related to Asian countries, eastern: *He studied Oriental languages. See:* Asian, USAGE NOTE.

o·ri·en·ta·tion /ˌɔriənˈteɪʃən, -ɛn-/ *n.* **1** [C;U] the direction in which s.t. is pointed: *The orientation of the building is facing south.* **2** [C;U] a person's desires in religion, politics, or sexuality: *Her political orientation is toward the Left.* **3** [C;U] a period of becoming familiar with a new neighborhood, job, etc.: *The company gives a three-day orientation to all new employees.*

or·i·fice /ˈɔrəfɪs, ˈɑr-/ *n.frml.* an opening, hole: *The mouth is an orifice.*

or·i·gin /ˈɔrədʒɪn, ˈɑr-/ *n.* **1** [C;U] the location of where s.t. begins or began, the source: *The origin of that folk song is France.* **2** [C;U] one's childhood and one's family's social class, (*syn.*) ancestry: *He comes from working-class origins.*

o·rig·i·nal /əˈrɪdʒənəl/ *adj.* **1** first, earliest: *The original draft of her novel has been lost.* **2** new, different from what has come before, (*syns.*) unique, creative: *There wasn't a single original idea in the book.* **3** not being a copy or translation: *The original painting is in a museum; this is just a copy.*

—*n.* [C] s.t. that can be or has been copied or translated: *She wants to study English, so she can read Shakespeare's plays in the original.*

o·rig·i·nal·i·ty /əˌrɪdʒəˈnæləti/ *n.* [U] the quality of being new or different, (*syn.*) freshness: *Her style of writing has an originality all its own.*

o·rig·i·nal·ly /əˈrɪdʒənəli/ *adv.* previously, before: *He originally came from Florida but lives in Chicago now.*

o·rig·i·nate /əˈrɪdʒəˌneɪt/ *v.* **-nated, -nating, -nates** to (cause to) begin, come from: *Automobiles originated in the 19th century. -n.* **originator,** [U] **origination** /əˌrɪdʒəˈneɪʃən/.

o·ri·ole /ˈɔriˌoʊl/ *n.* a small, colorful North American bird with males having black and orange markings: *Orioles use pieces of string and hair to make their nests.*

or·na·ment /'ɔrnəmənt/ *n. s.t.* that is decorative rather than useful, (*syn.*) an adornment: *His grandmother's living room is full of little china ornaments.*||*Christmas tree ornaments* —*v.* /'ɔrnəˌmɛnt/ to add decorations to *s.t.*, (*syn.*) to adorn: *We used white flowers and green leaves to ornament the church door for the wedding.* -*adj.* **ornamental** /ˌɔrnə'mɛntl/; -*n.* **ornamentation** /ˌɔrnəmən'teɪʃən, -mɛn-/.

or·nate /ɔr'neɪt/ *adj.* having lots of decorations: *The frames on the pictures are ornate with flowers and fruit painted in gold.* -*adv.* **ornately;** -*n.* [U] **ornateness.**

or·ni·thol·o·gy /ˌɔrnə'θɑlədʒi/ *n.* [U] the science and study of birds: *He studied ornithology in college.* -*n.* **ornithologist.**

or·phan /'ɔrfən/ *n.* a child whose parents have died: *When his parents were killed in an accident, he was left an orphan (or) their little boy became an orphan.* —*v.* to become an orphan: *He was orphaned at an early age.*

or·phan·age /'ɔrfənɪdʒ/ *n.* a place where orphans live and are cared for: *She was brought up in an orphanage after her parents died.*

or·tho·don·tics /ˌɔrθə'dɑntɪks/ *n.pl. used with a sing.v.* (in dentistry) the science of correcting irregular teeth: *Advances in orthodontics help children to have straight teeth.* -*n.* **orthodontist.**

or·tho·dox /'ɔrθəˌdɑks/ *adj.* **1** having generally accepted or approved beliefs, ideas, etc.: *She follows orthodox Muslim teaching in her daily life.* **2** common, traditional (*syn.*) conventional: *We were surprised by his orthodox taste in clothes.* **3 Orthodox: a.** of or related to the Christian churches (Russian, Greek, etc.) that originated in the Byzantine empire **b.** of or related to the branch of Judaism that follows traditional customs and teachings -*n.* **orthodoxy.**

or·tho·pe·dics /ˌɔrθə'pidɪks/ *n.pl. used with a sing.v.* the branch of medicine that specializes in (the correction and prevention of injuries in) bones: *She studied orthopedics in medical school.* -*n.* **orthopedist.**

Os·car /'ɑskər/ *n.*™ an award and small statue given each year to actors, directors, and other people for great work in American movie making: *Tom Hanks got an Oscar for his performance in the movie* Philadelphia. *See:* Emmy.

USAGE NOTE: Also called the *Academy Awards,* the *Oscars* are given every spring for best picture (movie), best actor and actress, and best director. They are also awarded for the best documentary, short animation, movie soundtrack, makeup, special effects, etc. "Oscar" is the name of the gold statue that is given for the award.

os·cil·late /'ɑsəˌleɪt/ *v.* **-lated, -lating, -lates 1** to move constantly up and down, or side to side, between two points: *On an oscilloscope, you can see an electrical current oscillate up and down.* **2** *fig.* to be undecided, (*syn.*) to vacillate -*n.* **oscillator;** [U] **oscillation** /ˌɑsə'leɪʃən/. *See:* vacillate.

os·mo·sis /ɑs'moʊsɪs, ɑz-/ *n.* [U] **1** a transfer of liquid through the wall of a cell **2 by osmosis:** learning *s.t.* by experience or observation, rather than by formal study: *She learned computers by osmosis from watching her friends work on them.*

os·prey /'ɑspri, -preɪ/ *n.* **-preys** a large North American fish-eating bird: *The osprey flew close to the water and caught a fish.*

os·si·fy /'ɑsəˌfaɪ/ *v.* **-fied, -fying, -fies 1** to form into bone: *Babies' skeletons ossify.* **2** *fig.* to be unchanging and conventional in one's ideas: *His thinking has ossified as he's grown older; he won't consider new ideas.* -*n.* [U] **ossification** /ˌɑsəfə'keɪʃən/.

os·ten·si·ble /ɑ'stɛnsəbəl, ə-/ *adj.* seeming to be, pretended: *His ostensible reason for calling her was to ask for a friend's telephone number; his real reason was to invite her to a party.* -*adv.* **ostensibly.**

os·ten·ta·tion /ˌɑstən'teɪʃən/ *n.frml.* [U] an unnecessary or showy display of wealth, learning, skill, etc. which is meant to impress *s.o.*: *Fur coats, diamonds, and a Rolls Royce are all part of the ostentation of Hollywood.* -*adj.* **ostentatious** /ˌɑstən'teɪʃəs/; -*adv.* **ostentatiously.**

os·tra·cize /'ɑstrəˌsaɪz/ *v.frml.* **-cized, -cizing, -cizes** to refuse to have a social relationship with *s.o.*: *They were ostracized by the members of their political party because they voted against a party proposal.* -*n.* [U] **ostracism** /'ɑstrəˌsɪzəm/.

os·trich /'ɑstrɪʃ, 'ɔ-/ *n.* **-triches** a large African bird with long legs and neck, which cannot fly: *Ostriches are believed to bury their heads in the sand when frightened.*

ostrich

oth·er /'ʌðər/ *adj.* **1** identifying the one that remains out of two or more: *I don't like this book, so I'm going to read the other one first.* **2** second, (*syn.*) alternate: *We play cards every other Tuesday night.* **3** more of the same kind, (*syn.*) additional: *He was at the library with two other students.* **4** not the same, not one's own, different: *She likes to visit other people's families, but not her own.* **5 on the other hand:** from a different point of view: *I like taking my vacation in the summer; on the other hand, a winter vacation can also*

be relaxing. **6 other than:** except for, besides: *There isn't anything to do other than to wait to see what happens.* **7 the other day/morning/afternoon/night:** on a day/morning/afternoon/night in the recent past: *He called me just the other day.*
—*pron.* **1** s.t. that remains: *You take one end, and I'll take the other.* **2** s.o. or s.t. that is indefinite or uncertain: *They promised to take us out to dinner sometime or other.* **3 one after the other:** in sequence, not in a group: *Her dinner guests arrived one after the other.*

oth·er·wise /ˈʌðərˌwaɪz/ *adv.* **1** differently: *I can't say otherwise or I would be lying.* **2** in every other way, except for: *Their plane was late, but otherwise they had a good trip.* **3** if not, or else: *You must pay your taxes on time; otherwise, you will be punished.*

ot·ter /ˈɑtər/ *n.* a water mammal with brown fur and a playful nature: *Sea otters float on their backs and eat fish and clams.*

ouch /aʊtʃ/ *exclam. of* pain and surprise: *Ouch! I hit my finger with the hammer!*

ought /ɔt/ *auxiliary v.* **1** (used to express a moral or legal duty or obligation): *You ought to drive more slowly.* **2** (used to express what is advisable): *It's after 11:00; I ought to go to bed.* **3** (used to express what is logical to expect): *The wind has stopped blowing; it ought to be warmer. See:* might, must, should.

ounce /aʊns/ *n.* **1** a unit of weight equal to 1/16 of a pound (approx. 28 g): *Several ounces of pepper will last a long time.* **2** a unit of liquid measure equal to 1/16 of a pint (approx. 29.6 ml): *A drink of whiskey contains several ounces of alcohol.* **3** *fig.* a very small amount: *She told me the news without an ounce of emotion. -abbr.* **oz.**

our /ˈaʊər, ˈɑr/ *poss.adj.* of, relating to, belonging to us: *Our house is on the corner.*
—*poss.pron.* **ours:** *That house is ours.*

our·selves /ɑrˈsɛlvz, aʊər-/ *reflexive pron.* **1** referring to us: *We don't need to concern ourselves with the details of the project.* **2** used to give emphasis: *We didn't believe his story ourselves.* **3 by ourselves: a.** alone: *We went there by ourselves because nobody wanted to go with us.* **b.** without help, (*syn.*) unassisted: *We were surprised to be able to finish the work by ourselves.*

oust /aʊst/ *v.frml.* to send s.o. out, usu. with physical or legal force, (*syn.*) to expel: *The politician was ousted from office by a vote from members of her own party.*

oust·er /ˈaʊstər/ *n.* [C;U] an act of ousting, forcing s.o. out of a job, place, etc., (*syn.*) an expulsion

out /aʊt/ *adj.* **1** not in one's office, house, etc., (*syn.*) absent: *The boss is out now, but will be back in an hour.* **2** not in power or fashion:

Miniskirts and the color green are out this year; long black dresses are in. **3** not in operation, broken: *The electricity was out for a week after the hurricane.* **4** not possible or selected: *A winter vacation is out; we don't have enough money.* **5** (in baseball) unsuccessful in reaching a base **6 out-and-out:** complete, total: *He's an out-and-out cheat!* **7** *fig.* **out of it: a.** insensitive to others, stupid: *Don't talk to him about your problems; he's out of it!* **b.** very tired, (*syn.*) exhausted: *After taking those final exams, I'm really out of it!* **8 to be out for s.t.:** to try to get s.t.: *She's not interested in him as a person; she's only out for his money.* **9 to be out to do s.t.:** to try, be determined to do s.t.: *He's very ambitious; I'm sure he's out for his boss's job.*
—*adv.* **1** away from the inside, middle, or center: *The children ran out of the house to play in the yard.* **2** at a distance from a particular place: *We drove out in the desert.* **3** away from the usual place: *He went out to dinner.* **4** in(to) the open: *The secret came out and surprised everyone.* **5** completely, totally: *I'm just worn out!* **6** loudly: *He called out to me just as I walked in front of the car.* **7 to lose out:** not to be included, to fail: *She was disappointed when she lost out on getting the job.*
—*prep.* **1** from inside, away from: *Our cat jumped out the window.* **2 out of: a.** out **b.** from among: *In six cases out of ten, patients make a complete recovery.* **c.** not within the limits, boundaries of: *He's out of power now.* **d.** no longer possessing, lacking, missing: *I'd like to talk longer, but I'm out of time.* **3 to talk s.o. out of s.t.:** to get s.o. to change an opinion on s.t.: *We talked them out of moving to a larger house.*
—*v.* **1** to fail, break down: *The city was dark after the electrical power outed.* **2** to go public with s.t.: *"The truth will out."* **3** *infrml.* to reveal s.o.'s homosexuality: *A reporter outed the movie star by writing a story about the actor's romantic relationship with another man.*
—*n.* **1 to be on the outs with:** to be quarreling or on unfriendly terms with s.o. **2 to have an out:** to have an excuse or reason: *That politician has an out with her followers because she did not vote for an increase in taxes.* **3 ins and outs:** the details of a situation: *She doesn't remember all of the ins and outs of the situation, just the general idea.*

out- /aʊt/ *prefix* added to verbs to give the meaning in a superlative way: *"Outrun"* means to run faster or farther than all others.

out·age /ˈaʊtɪdʒ/ *n.* an interruption, esp. in electrical power, (*syn.*) a stoppage: *A power outage darkened the city last night.*

out·bid /ˌaʊtˈbɪd/ *v.* **-bid, -bidding, -bids** to offer to pay more money than s.o. else for s.t.:

0

Another person outbid me for a painting at an auction.

out·board motor /'aʊt,bɔrd/ *n.* a motor on the back of a boat, not one inside it: *His boat has two powerful outboard motors.*

out·bound /'aʊt,baʊnd/ *adj.adv.* moving away from a beginning point: *At night, she takes the <adj.> outbound train to go home.‖He was headed <adv.> outbound at that time.*

out·break /'aʊt,breɪk/ *n.* a sudden appearance of a disease or s.t. negative, such as crime: *There was an outbreak of influenza last week in the city's schools.*

out·burst /'aʊt,bɜrst/ *n.* a sudden expression of feeling (anger, laughter, etc.) or activity: *His outbursts of anger shock people.*

out·cast /'aʊt,kæst/ *n.* s.o. avoided by friends or forced to leave home: *After she was found guilty of cheating, she became an outcast among her friends at college.*

out·class /,aʊt'klæs/ *v.* **-classes** to be much better than s.o. or s.t., outperform, *(syn.)* to surpass: *The tennis star outclassed his opponents by beating all of them easily.*

out·come /'aʊt,kʌm/ *n.* the effect, result, *(syn.)* the consequence: *The outcome of the election will be known today.*

out·crop /'aʊt,krɑp/ *n.* a rock that sticks out, such as from the ground: *Climbers rested on an outcrop on the face of a cliff.* *-n.* [U] **outcropping.**

out·cry /'aʊt,kraɪ/ *n.* **-cries 1** a show of anger, protest: *An increase in taxes produced an outcry from the voters.* **2** a loud shout or scream

out·dat·ed /,aʊt'deɪtɪd/ *adj.* no longer useful, *(syn.)* obsolete: *That list of addresses is outdated; many have changed.*

out·dis·tance /,aʊt'dɪstəns/ *v.* **-tanced, -tancing, -tances** to go farther or faster than s.o. else: *The star runner outdistanced her competitors early in the race.*

out·do /,aʊt'du/ *v.* **-did** /-'dɪd/, **-done** /-'dʌn/, **-doing, -does** /-'dʌz/ to do more or better than, *(syn.)* to outperform: *We outdid our competitors by offering a better product at a lower price than theirs.*

out·door /'aʊt,dɔr/ *adj.* located outside or intended for outside use: *That singer gives outdoor concerts in the summer.*

out·doors /,aʊt'dɔrz/ *adv.* in the open air: *The weather was good, so they held the concert outdoors.*
—n. [U] **the outdoors:** the world of nature (forests, lakes, etc.): *She likes to hike in the outdoors.*

out·door·sy /,aʊt'dɔrzi/ *adj.infrml.* enjoying the outdoors: *That couple is very outdoorsy and enjoys hiking all year round.*

out·er /'aʊtər/ *adj.* at a greater distance, farther from the middle or center: *Tourists travel to the outer islands by ferry boat.*

out·er·most /'aʊtər,moʊst/ *adj.* at the greatest distance, farthest from the middle or center: *A space vehicle is exploring the outermost planets of the solar system.*

outer space *n.* [U] the area where the planets and stars are, esp. the area beyond the earth's atmosphere or beyond the solar system: *The government sent a spaceship to outer space.*

out·field /'aʊt,fild/ *n.* (in baseball) the part of a baseball field that is farthest from home plate: *He caught a ball in the outfield.* *-n.* **outfielder.**

out·fit /'aʊt,fɪt/ *n.* **1** a set of clothing worn for an occasion: *She wore a beautiful outfit of a silk dress with matching shoes and handbag.* **2** clothing intended for a special use: *A firefighter's outfit includes a helmet, heavy raincoat, and boots.* **3** a group of people, such as in the military, working together: *Our outfit was in charge of the cleanup operations.*
—v. **-fitted, -fitting, -fits 1** to provide with clothing and other things: *The mother outfitted her daughter with new clothes for school.* **2** to supply with equipment, food, water, etc. for a special purpose: *Explorers outfitted a ship to explore the North Pole.*

out·fox /,aʊt'fɑks/ *v.* **-foxes** to be smarter than an opponent: *The tennis player outfoxed her opponent by hitting the tennis ball close to the net.*

out·go /'aʊt,goʊ/ *n.* [U] an outflow, such as a payment of money for expenses: *Our outgo this month is greater than our income.*

out·go·ing /'aʊt,goʊɪŋ/ *adj.* **1** active in seeking the company of others, friendly: *He is an outgoing and lively person.* **2** leaving s.t., such as an official post, retiring: *She is the outgoing head of a large corporation.*

out·grow /,aʊt'groʊ/ *v.* **-grew** /-'gru/, **-grown** /-'groʊn/, **-growing, -grows 1** to grow too large for s.t.: *That boy outgrows his clothes every few months.* **2** to grow faster than: *This variety of tomato outgrows all others.* **3** to grow or progress beyond s.o. or s.t.: *She outgrew the company she worked for and found a better job somewhere else.*

out·growth /'aʊt,groʊθ/ *n.* **1** [C;U] a result of s.t. else, a development: *Hunger in that country is an outgrowth of a lack of rain to grow food.* **2** [C] s.t. that grows out of a plant, etc.: *an outgrowth on a rosebush*

out·house /'aʊt,haʊs/ *n.* **-houses** /-,haʊzɪz/ an outdoor toilet in a little house

out·ing /'aʊtɪŋ/ *n.* a short trip to have fun, *(syn.)* an excursion: *We went for an outing that included a picnic and a volleyball game.*

out·land·ish /aʊt'lændɪʃ/ *adj.* shocking or strange in style or behavior, *(syn.)* ridiculous:

He wore an outlandish outfit of pink pants and green sneakers. **-adv. outlandishly.**

out·last /ˌaʊtˈlæst/ *v.* **1** to perform longer, (*syn.*) to outwear: *Even though my new boots are expensive, I'm not sure they will outlast the old ones.* **2** to live longer than s.o. else, (*syn.*) to outlive: *The old woman outlasted her three husbands, who are all dead now.*

out·law /ˈaʊtˌlɔ/ *n.* a criminal being chased by the police, (*syn.*) a fugitive: *Sheriffs chased outlaws on horseback in the old West.*
—*v.* to make s.t. illegal, (*syn.*) to ban: *Most states have outlawed the use of marijuana.*

out·lay /ˈaʊtˌleɪ/ *n.* money spent for s.t.: *You can expect a higher outlay for rent in a city than in the country.*

out·let /ˈaʊtˌlɛt, -lɪt/ *n.* [C] **1** a wall socket for electricity: *He plugged the vacuum cleaner plug into an outlet.* **2** a store that sells discount merchandise: *She shopped at a clothing outlet to buy shorts.* **3** a way out or opening for s.t.: *The dam broke because there was no outlet for the flood waters.* **4** a release for emotions, energy: *He talks to his best friend as an outlet for his anger.*

out·line /ˈaʊtˌlaɪn/ *n.* [C] **1** the outer shape of s.t.: *The children drew the outline of flowers on paper, then colored them.* **2** a summary of the main ideas of s.t., such as a book, lecture, etc.: *She made an outline of ideas she wanted to present in her talk. See:* flow chart.
—*v.* **-lined, -lining, -lines 1** to draw an outline of s.t. **2** to give the main ideas of s.t.: *He outlined his plans for the new kitchen.*

out·live /ˌaʊtˈlɪv/ *v.* **-lived, -living, -lives 1** to live longer than, die after s.o. else: *The old couple outlived several of their children.* **2 to outlive one's usefulness:** to be no longer useful, (*syn.*) to be obsolete: *That computer never works properly; it has outlived its usefulness.*

out·look /ˈaʊtˌlʊk/ *n.* [C] **1** a view that one sees from a place: *The hotel had a beautiful outlook on the bay.* **2** a prediction for the future, (*syn.*) a prospect: *The outlook for the economy is good for this year.* **3** one's point of view, (*syn.*) an attitude: *She always has a cheerful outlook on life.*

out·ly·ing /ˈaʊtˌlaɪɪŋ/ *adj.* far from the center of a town or city: *She lives in an outlying area of Los Angeles.*

out·ma·neu·ver /ˌaʊtməˈnuvər/ *v.* to act more skillfully than s.o., (*syn.*) to outwit: *The soccer player outmaneuvered her opponents and scored a goal.*

out·match /ˌaʊtˈmætʃ/ *v.* **-matches 1** to perform better than: *The tennis star outmatched his opponent and won.* **2** to offer s.t. better: *Our company outmatched a competitor by offering lower prices and selling more of our product.*

out·mod·ed /ˌaʊtˈmoʊdɪd/ *adj.* no longer useful or fashionable, (*syn.*) outdated: *We got rid of our outmoded computers and bought fast new ones.*

out·num·ber /ˌaʊtˈnʌmbər/ *v.* to be greater in number than: *Reporters outnumbered guests at the political gathering.*

out-of-bounds *adv.* **1** (in sports) beyond the official limits of a playing area: *The tennis player hit the ball out-of-bounds.* **2** *fig.* not within accepted standards of behavior, impolite: *He made some nasty comments that were out-of-bounds in a polite talk.*

out-of-date *adj.* no longer useful, (*syn.*) obsolete: *Your information on that subject is out-of-date.*

out-of-doors *adv.* located outside, outdoors: *We left the building and went out-of-doors.*

out-of-pocket *adj.* paying cash for small items: *His out-of-pocket expenses for his trip were for the bus fare and for food.*

out-of-the-way *adj.* **1** far away from cities and difficult to reach, (*syn.*) remote: *Her parents live in a little, out-of-the-way town in the country.* **2** not well-known, unusual: *We had dinner in an out-of-the-way restaurant.*

out·pa·tient /ˈaʊtˌpeɪʃənt/ *n.* a patient who receives treatment at a hospital or clinic and does not stay there: *He cut his hand and was treated as an outpatient at a local hospital.*

out·per·form /ˌaʊtpərˈfɔrm/ *v.* to do better than others, (*syn.*) to excel: *The growth of that company has outperformed all of its competitors'.*

out·place·ment /ˈaʊtˌpleɪsmənt/ *n.* [C;U] an employment service provided by a company to help workers it has laid off to find another job: *He was let go, but the outplacement department found him a new job quickly.*

out·play /ˌaʊtˈpleɪ/ *v.* to play a sport, an instrument, etc., better than s.o.: *She won the piano competition by outplaying all the other musicians.*

out·post /ˈaʊtˌpoʊst/ *n.* **1** a station far from a military center: *Some soldiers waited at an outpost deep in the forest.* **2** any distant settlement: *That little store was the last outpost for motorists before they entered the desert.*

out·pour·ing /ˈaʊtˌpɔrɪŋ/ *n.* [C;U] **1** *fig.* the expression of a rush of emotion or feeling: *In an outpouring of sorrow, she cried and cried after her grandmother died.* **2** a rush of liquid: *An outpouring of water filled the fountain.*

out·put /ˈaʊtˌpʊt/ *n.* [U] **1** s.t. produced for use, such as manufactured goods, esp. during a specific time period: *That state's annual agricultural output has increased.* **2** electricity, etc., produced by a system or device: *Electrical output sometimes doesn't meet demand during hot weather.* **3** information, data, produced by a computer: *I can't finish this project without the accounting output. See:* input.

out·rage /'aʊt,reɪʤ/ *n.* [C;U] **1** a cruel or evil act, serious offense: *The mayor's decision to close the clinic is an outrage.* **2** great anger, (*syn.*) fury, caused by such an act: *I felt a great outrage when I heard about the murder.*
—*v.* **-raged, -raging, -rages** to make very angry or resentful: *Residents of our state were outraged when the governor stopped free school lunches.*

out·ra·geous /aʊt'reɪʤəs/ *adj.* **1** very offensive, insulting: *Her outrageous behavior at the party offended everyone.* **2** ridiculous, shocking: *That hotel charges outrageous prices.* -*adv.* **outrageously.**

out·reach /'aʊt,riʧ/ *n.adj.* a program that provides services which help others: *Our church has an <adj.> outreach program to provide food and shelter to the poor.*

out·right /'aʊt,raɪt/ *adj.* complete, total: *When Ross said "My brother and I went to Thailand," he told an outright lie. Ross doesn't have a brother and he's never been to Asia.*
—*adv.* /,aʊt'raɪt, 'aʊt,raɪt/ **1** with nothing held back, openly, (*syn.*) frankly: *If you have a complaint, you should tell me outright.* **2** completely, totally: *His mother gave him the car outright (for no money).* **3** immediately: *Three people were killed outright in the accident.*

out·run /,aʊt'rʌn/ *v.* **-ran** /-'ræn/ , **-run, -running, -runs** **1** to run faster than, (*syn.*) to outdistance: *The track star outran all of his competitors.* **2** to avoid capture, escape: *Criminals sometimes outrun the police.* **3** to be greater in number than, (*syn.*) to exceed: *Orders are outrunning production.*

out·score /,aʊt'skɔr/ *v.* **-scored, -scoring, -scores** to score more points than a competitor: *Our team outscored our rivals and won the game.*

out·set /'aʊt,sɛt/ *n.sing.* the beginning, start: *At the outset, the weather was bad, but we had sunny skies later in our trip.*

out·shine /,aʊt'ʃaɪn/ *v.* **-shone** /-'ʃoʊn/ , **-shining, -shines** **1** to shine more brightly than: *Halogen bulbs outshine regular ones.* **2** *fig.* to perform better than s.o. else, (*syn.*) to excel: *Her performance on the violin outshone everyone else's.*

out·side /,aʊt'saɪd, 'aʊt,saɪd/ *n.* **1** the outdoor or exterior surface of s.t.: *The outside of the house needs painting.* **2** outdoors: *He stood on the outside of the house and looked in.* **3 at the outside:** at the most: *At the outside, you can expect to pay $1,000 for that used car.* **4 to be on the outside looking in:** to be excluded, esp. not to have a job: *He was a manager for years, then was laid off and now he's on the outside looking in.*

—*adv.* **1** to or toward the outside: *She stepped outside and breathed the fresh air.* **2 outside of:** except for, other than: *Outside of you and me, no one else knows the secret.*
—*adj.* **1** outdoor, exterior in location: *The paint on the outside walls of the house is falling off.* **2 an outside chance:** a very small chance that s.t. will happen: *There is an outside chance that it might rain, so bring an umbrella.*
—*prep.* **1** on or to the outside of: *Leave my mail outside my door.* **2** except, other than: *He has no interests outside his family.*

out·sid·er /,aʊt'saɪdər, 'aʊt,saɪ-/ *n.* **1** a person not thought of as a member of a group, (*syn.*) a stranger: *People in that small town avoid talking to outsiders.* **2** a person or animal who is not believed to have a chance of winning a race, contest, etc.: *People were surprised when an unknown outsider won the marathon.*

out·skirts /'aʊt,skɜrts/ *n.pl.* the outer area of s.t.: *Our car broke down on the outskirts of the city.*

out·smart /,aʊt'smart/ *v.* **1** to act more cleverly or skillfully than s.o. else, (*syn.*) to outwit: *She outsmarted her competitors by offering customers a better product for less money.* **2 to outsmart oneself:** to act foolishly, while believing oneself to be intelligent: *He outsmarted himself by thinking that he could cheat on his taxes and not get caught.*

out·sourc·ing /'aʊt,sɔrsɪŋ/ *n.* [U] the purchase of services outside one's company in order to save money, be more efficient, or simply get all the work done: *We have a policy of outsourcing; for example, we once had our accounting department do our payroll, but now an outside specialist does it.*

out·spend /,aʊt'spɛnd/ *v.* **-spent** /-'spɛnt/, **-spending, -spends** to spend more than s.o. else: *The politician outspent her opponent on advertising and won the election.*

out·spo·ken /,aʊt'spoʊkən/ *adj.* saying clearly what one thinks, (*syn.*) frank: *She is an outspoken critic of the school system in this city.* -*adv.* **outspokenly; -*n.* outspokenness.**

out·stand·ing /,aʊt'stændɪŋ/ *adj.* **1** excellent, extraordinary: *He is an outstanding worker.* **2** not yet paid, settled, etc: *I still have an outstanding balance of 50 dollars on my credit card account.*

out·stay /,aʊt'steɪ/ *v.* **1** to stay longer than s.o. else: *They outstayed all the other audience members.* **2 to outstay one's welcome:** to stay so long that one is no longer a welcome guest: *After he outstayed his welcome, we decided not to invite him back. See:* outwear, **2;** overstay.

out·stretched /,aʊt'strɛʧt/ *adj.* reaching out, extended: *The girl's arms were outstretched as she tried to catch the ball.*

O

out·strip /ˌaʊt'strɪp/ v. **-stripped, -stripping, -strips** to do better than or get ahead of s.o. or s.t. else, (syn.) to surpass: *That manufacturer outstripped all his competitors in sales last year.*

out·think /ˌaʊt'θɪŋk/ v. **-thought** /-'θɔt/, **-thinking, -thinks** to perform better than others by thinking carefully and cleverly, (syn.) to outsmart: *Our lawyer outthinks those lawyers who oppose her.*

out·ward /'aʊtwərd/ adj. **1** moving away from, going out: *The weather during our outward journey was beautiful.* **2** on the outside: *During her interview, she showed outward calm. -n.* **outwardness.**
—adv. (or **outwards**) away from the center, toward the outside: *Move your arms outward as you breathe out.*

outward-bound adj. going away from the center of a city or from shore: *Each evening, he takes an outward-bound train home to his house.*

out·ward·ly /'aʊtwərdli/ adv. on the surface, seeming to be, (syn.) apparently: *Although she was outwardly amused, I'm sure she was really very angry.*

out·wear /ˌaʊt'wɛr/ v. **-wore** /-'wɔr/, **-worn** /-'wɔrn/, **-wearing, -wears** **1** to last longer than s.t. else: *My nylon jacket has outworn my other clothes.* **2 to outwear one's welcome:** to stay so long that one becomes unwelcome: *He has stayed at his friends' house for three weeks; he has really outworn his welcome. See:* outstay, **2.**

out·weigh /ˌaʊt'weɪ/ v. **1** to weigh more than s.t. else: *One boxer outweighed the other by 20 lbs.* **2** fig. to be more important than s.t. else: *Her need to save money outweighs her desire to spend it on fun.*

out·wit /ˌaʊt'wɪt/ v. **-witted, -witting, -wits** to defeat by being more intelligent than, (syns.) to outsmart, outmaneuver: *The criminal outwitted the police and escaped.*

out·work /ˌaʊt'wɜrk/ v. to work harder than s.o.: *He outworks his coworkers and they dislike him for doing it.*

o·va /'oʊvə/ n.pl. of ovum

o·val /'oʊvəl/ n.adj. anything that is shaped like an egg or an ellipse: *She put her photograph in an <adj.> oval frame.||His face was a perfect <n.> oval.*

o·va·ry /'oʊvəri/ n. **-ries** **1** the organ of a woman or a female animal that produces eggs **2** the part of a flowering plant that produces seeds -adj. **ovarian** /oʊ'vɛriən/.

o·va·tion /oʊ'veɪʃən/ n. enthusiastic applause showing approval or welcome: *The audience gave the singer a standing ovation after her wonderful performance. See:* encore.

ov·en /'ʌvən/ n. any usu. box-shaped device used for cooking, baking, and heating food and other things: *The cook put some bread in the oven.*

o·ver /'oʊvər/ adv. **1** from an upright position: *She stood up quickly and knocked the chair over.* **2** so as to show another side: *Turn the steaks over or they will burn.* **3** across a distance, open space, edge, barrier, etc.: *Come over here and sit with me!* **4** above the surface or top of s.t.: *A hot air balloon flew over early this morning.* **5** from one person, group, etc., to another: *She signed the rights to her book over to a publishing company.* **6** from beginning to end, thoroughly: *He didn't want to do anything until he had thought all of our suggestions over.* **7** so as to cover completely: *She painted over the ugly wallpaper.* **8** another time, again: *My homework assignment was so bad that my instructor made me do it over.* **9** in addition, in excess of s.t.: *We were supposed to leave on Thursday, but the good weather convinced us to stay over (the weekend).* **10 over and over:** many times, (syn.) repeatedly: *He has applied to medical school over and over, but he is always rejected.*
—adj. **1** done, ended, finished: *By the time they arrived, the party was over.* **2** in excess of: *Our trip cost over $2,000.* **3 all over:** completely finished: *Even though the movie was terrible, he stayed in the theater until it was all over.* **4 "It's not over till it's over":** (said by a famous baseball player, Yogi Berra) a situation can change even at the last minute: *Even though things look difficult, you should be optimistic; remember, "It's not over until it's over."* **5 over with:** finished, completed, usu. of s.t. unpleasant: *I have to have a tooth pulled and I want to get it over with as soon as possible.*
—prep. **1** at a higher level than, above, but not touching: *The flag was flying over the entrance to the building.* **2** in order to cover: *We put plastic over the furniture to protect it.* **3** from one side to the other, across: *A dog jumped over the fence.* **4** on the opposite side of: *She's from a town that's just over the state line.* **5** in every part of, (syn.) throughout: *He is famous all over the world.* **6** in control of, commanding: *Her new position gives her authority over the whole department.* **7** more than, in excess of: *He has been reading that book for over a year.* **8** using, through: *The government made the announcement over the TV and the radio.* **9** during: *I plan to finish writing these letters over my vacation.* **10** in connection with, (syn.) regarding: *My professor and I talked over my new research project.* **11 over against:** in a direction against a barrier: *I moved the desk over against the wall.* **12 over and above:** in addition to, as well as,

O

besides: *She has to take care of her parents over and above her children.*

o·ver·a·bun·dance /ˌouvərə'bʌndəns/ *n.sing.* [U] too much of s.t.: *There is an overabundance of wheat on the market now.* -*adj.* **overabundant.**

o·ver·a·chiev·er /ˌouvərə'ʧivər/ *n.* a person who works harder and achieves more than is necessary: *She is an overachiever with two Master's degrees.* -*v.* **overachieve.**

o·ver·act /ˌouvər'ækt/ *v.* to act in an obviously exaggerated way: *The actor overacted in the play; it was a terrible performance.*

o·ver·ac·tive /ˌouvər'æktiv/ *adj.* too active, (*syn.*) hyperactive: *That child is overactive and runs around all day.*

o·ver·age /ˌouvər'eɪʤ/ *adj.* too old for a specific purpose: *At 50 years old, he is overage to join the army.*
—*n.* /'ouvərɪʤ/ an extra amount, excess, esp. in inventory or funds: *Our warehouse received an overage in a shipment and returned it.*

o·ver·ag·gres·sive /ˌouvərə'gresɪv/ *adj.* too aggressive, (*syn.*) hostile: *She is an overaggressive child who hurts her playmates.*

o·ver·all /ˌouvər'ɔl/ *adv.* **1** in general, considering everything: *Overall, his job performance is quite good.* **2** completely, totally: *The bill for the furniture overall is quite a lot of money.*
—*adj.* /'ouvər,ɔl/ including everything, total: *The overall length of that table is eight feet.*

o·ver·alls /'ouvər,ɔlz/ *n.pl.* loose work pants with straps over the shoulders, usu. worn over other clothes: *He is a painter and wears overalls to work. See:* dungarees, jeans.

o·ver·awe /ˌouvər'ɔ/ *v.* **-awed, -awing, -awes** to control through respect or fear: *The school principal overawed the troublemakers by speaking to them in her office.*

over·bal·ance /ˌouvər'bæləns/ *v.* **-anced, -ancing, -ances** to have more weight or importance than, to outweigh: *She thinks that the pleasures of mountain climbing overbalance the dangers.*

o·ver·bear·ing /ˌouvər'berɪŋ/ *adj.* trying to force others to do one's will without considering their ideas or feelings: *His overbearing behavior makes people stay away from him.* -*adv.* **overbearingly.**

o·ver·board /'ouvər,bɔrd/ *adv.* **1** over the side of a boat or ship and into the water: *A sailor fell overboard and was rescued.* **2** *infrml.fig.*
to go overboard: to do too much of s.t.: *They went overboard and spent $30,000 on their wedding.*

o·ver·book /ˌouvər'buk/ *v.* to sell more tickets than there are seats available, as on an airline flight: *That airline overbooked, then had to cancel some passengers' reservations because they had too few seats. See:* oversell.

o·ver·build /ˌouvər'bɪld/ *v.* **-built** /-'bɪlt/, **-building,** or **-builds** to construct too many houses or offices in one area: *Houses are relatively inexpensive in Texas now because of overbuilding during the good economic times of the '70's and '80's.*

o·ver·bur·den /ˌouvər'bərdn/ *v.* to make s.o. or s.t. do or carry too much, place too many worries on s.o.: *Her husband's ill health overburdens her; she takes care of him 24 hours a day.*

o·ver·cast /'ouvər,kæst/ *adj.* **1** (of weather, skies) very cloudy but not raining: *The sky is overcast today; we should take an umbrella in case it rains.* **2** *fig.* depressed, (*syn.*) gloomy: *His overcast expression matched his sadness.*
-*n.* **overcast.**

o·ver·charge /ˌouvər'ʧarʤ/ *v.* **-charged, -charging, -charges** to charge s.o. too much for s.t.: *That store overcharges tourists.*
—*n.* /'ouvər,ʧarʤ/ [C] a price, load, etc. that is too high or large: *I am going to call the gas company about this overcharge on my bill.*

o·ver·coat /'ouvər,kout/ *n.* a long winter coat, worn over other clothes: *In winter, he wears a heavy, wool overcoat to work.*

o·ver·come /ˌouvər'kʌm/ *v.* **-came** /-'keɪm/, **-come, -coming, -comes** **1** to fight against successfully, (*syn.*) to defeat: *The girl with broken legs overcame her medical problems and learned to walk again.* **2** (of emotions, will) to take control of: *He was overcome with happiness when his daughter was born.*

o·ver·com·pen·sate /ˌouvər'kampən,seɪt/ *v.* **-sated, -sating, -sates** to try to correct a weakness by making too strong an effort in the opposite direction: *He overcompensates for time away from his children, by buying them too many toys.* –*n.* [U] **overcompenstion** /ˌouvər,kampən'seɪʃən/.

o·ver·crowd /ˌouvər'kraud/ *v.* **-crowded, -crowding, -crowds** to allow too many people; to put too many things in one place: *The managers of that theater created a dangerous situation by allowing people to overcrowd the balcony.* -*adj.* **overcrowded;** -*n.* [U] **overcrowding.**

o·ver·do /ˌouvər'du/ *v.* **-did** /-'dɪd/, **-done** /-'dʌn/, **-doing, -does** /-'dʌz/ **1** to do too much of s.t., (*syn.*) to exaggerate: *She overdid it by rushing around in the summer heat and is ill now.* **2** to cook too long, (*syn.*) to overcook: *We overdid the meat and it didn't taste good.* **3** to use too much of s.t.: *I can't eat her cooking; she always overdoes the hot spices.*

over·done /ˌouvər'dʌn, 'ouvər,dʌn/ *adj. & past part.* of overdo, cooked too long: *The fish was overdone and dry.*

o·ver·dose /'ouvər,dous, ˌouvər'dous/ *v.* **-dosed, -dosing, -doses** to give or take too much of a drug: *The drug addict overdosed on heroin and died. See:* OD.

—*n.* /'ouvər,dous/ too much of a drug: *He took an overdose and was in the hospital for weeks.*

o·ver·draft /'ouvər,dræft/ *n.* an amount of money taken from a bank account that is greater than the amount actually available in it: *An overdraft resulted when a $1,000 check was drawn against only $900 in the account.*

o·ver·draw /,ouvər'drɔ/ *v.* **-drew** /-'dru/, **-drawn** /-'drɔn/, **-drawing, -draws 1** to take more money from a bank account than it has in it: *She forgot to deposit her paycheck in her account and overdrew it by $200 when she paid the bills.* **2** to create characters, situations, which are unrealistic, (*syn.*) to exaggerate: *Generally I enjoy his novels, but I find that he tends to overdraw his characters.* -*adj.* **overdrawn.**

over·dressed /,ouvər'drɛst/ *adj.* **1** wearing clothes that are too formal for the situation: *He felt overdressed in his suit and tie when he saw that everyone else at the party was wearing jeans.* **2** wearing too many clothes: *She was overdressed for the warm weather with her hat and scarf.*

o·ver·due /,ouvər'du/ *adj.* **1** not arriving at a scheduled, expected time; late: *The plane is overdue and has been delayed by bad weather.* **2** not paid on time, late: *His rent payment is overdue.*

o·ver·eat /,ouvər'it/ *v.* **-ate** /-'eɪt/, **-eaten** /-'itn/, **-eating, -eats** to eat too much food

o·ver·es·ti·mate /,ouvər'ɛstə,meɪt/ *v.* **-mated, -mating, -mates 1** to give too high a value to s.t. or s.o.: *She overestimates her importance in that business.* **2** to calculate too high a number of: *He overestimated the number of people attending the party and ordered too much food.*
—*n.* /,ouvər'ɛstə,mɪt/ an estimate, projection, that is too high: *She apologized for sending an overestimate on the project.*

o·ver·ex·pose /,ouvərɪk'spouz/ *v.* **-posed, -posing, -poses 1** to show too much and lose popularity: *That star's manager ruined his career by overexposing him.* **2** to apply too much light to photographic film: *She overexposed the photographs by opening the back of the camera before the film was finished.* -*n.* [U] **overexposure** /,ouvərɪk'spouʒər/.

o·ver·ex·tend /,ouvərɪk'stɛnd/ *v.* to stretch s.t. beyond its limits: *You can injure your muscles if you overextend them by running too fast.*

o·ver·ex·tend·ed /,ouvərɪk'stɛndɪd/ *adj.* **1** stretched beyond limits: *The cable was overextended and it snapped.* **2** *fig.* too deeply in debt, owing money beyond one's ability to pay: *He owes too many payments on his bills and is now overextended.*

o·ver·flow /,ouvər'flou/ *v.* **1** to spill, flow over or beyond the edges of s.t.: *After the heavy rains, the flooded river overflowed its banks.* **2** to go beyond the usual limits: *There were so many guests at the party that it overflowed into the hallway.*
—*n.* /'ouvər,flou/ [C;U] **1** the act of overflowing: *The blocked drain in the kitchen caused an overflow.* **2** an excess amount of s.t. (liquid, people, etc.): *So many people attended the concert that chairs were set up in the lobby for the overflow.*

o·ver·grown /,ouvər'groun, 'ouvər,groun/ *adj.* covered with plants, often in an uncontrolled way: *When I came back from my long vacation, I found my garden overgrown.* -*v.* **overgrow; -***n.* [U] **overgrowth** /'ouvər,grouθ/.

o·ver·hand /'ouvər,hænd/ *adj.adv.* (in sports) with the arm moving from a position above the shoulder, then forward and downward: *The ball will go farther if you throw it <adv.> overhand.*

o·ver·hang /,ouvər'hæŋ, 'ouvər,hæŋ/ *v.* **-hung** /-'hʌŋ/ , **-hanging, -hangs** to hang over, (*syn.*) to project over: *A balcony overhangs the door below it.* -*n.* [C] **overhang** /'ouvər,hæŋ/.

o·ver·haul /,ouvər'hɔl, 'ouvər,hɔl/ *v.* to examine s.t. thoroughly, in order to evaluate its condition and to repair if necessary: *A mechanic overhauled the car's motor with new parts.* -*n.* **overhaul** /'ouvər,hɔl/.

o·ver·head /,ouvər',hɛd 'ouvər,hɛd/ *adj.adv.* above one's head: *I put my luggage on the <adj.> overhead bin on the airplane.||Birds flew <adv.> overhead on their way south.*
—*n.* /'ouvər,hɛd/ [U] the money spent to run a business, such as rents, salaries, etc.: *When we moved our offices out of the city, our overhead was cut in half.*

overhead projector *n.* a device that shines information on a wall or screen for people to see: *Teachers use overhead projectors as an aid to their lectures.* -*abbr.* **OHP**

o·ver·hear /,ouvər'hɪr/ *v.* **-heard** /-'hɜrd/, **-hearing, -hears** to hear s.t. by accident: *The next table was so close to me that I overheard the conversation of the couple eating there.*

USAGE NOTE: Compare *overhear* and *eavesdrop.* When you overhear a conversation, you hear it by accident. When you eavesdrop, you try to hear s.o.'s conversation without letting them know you are listening.

o·ver·heat /,ouvər'hit/ *v.* to become too hot: *My car overheated and broke down.*

o·ver·in·dulge /,ouvərɪn'dʌldʒ/ *v.* **-dulged, -dulging, -dulges** to eat, drink, or play too much: *The little boy overindulged in chocolate cake and has a stomachache now.*

o·ver·joyed /,ouvər'dʒɔɪd/ *adj.* very happy, pleased, (*syn.*) ecstatic: *She was overjoyed* *when the doctor told her that her newborn baby is healthy and normal. See:* happy.

o·ver·land /'ouvər,lænd, -lənd/ *adj.adv.* across or by land (not by sea or air): *<adj.> Overland trucks carry food to market.||They travel <adv.> overland quickly.*

o·ver·lap /,ouvər'læp/ *v.* **-lapped, -lapping, -laps** **1** to have a part of one object over another, to cover s.t. partly: *His sweater overlaps the top of his pants.* **2** *fig.*to have s.t. in common, *(syn.)* to coincide: *Our visits overlapped by a few days.*

o·ver·lay /,ouvər'leɪ/ *v.* **-laid** /-'leɪd/, **-laying, -lays** to cover one thing with another: *A carpet overlays the wood floor.*
—*n.* /'ouvər,leɪ/ an object that covers another: *An overlay of wood covers the brick wall.*

o·ver·load /,ouvər'loud/ *v.* **1** to place too much work, weight, etc., on s.o. or s.t.: *She has overloaded her schedule with work, study, and family responsibilities.* **2** to use too much power, electricity, etc.: *During hot weather, the city's electrical system is often overloaded by fans and air conditioners.* *-n.* **overload** /'ouvər,loud/.

o·ver·look /,ouvər'luk/ *v.* **1** to look upon, face: *The cabin on the hill overlooks the valley below.* **2** to miss, not see or do s.t.: *He overlooked several important points in his report.* **3** to act as if one does not see, ignore: *The mother overlooks her little boy's bad behavior.*
—*n.* /'ouvər,luk/ a viewing point, a place to look down: *We stopped at the overlook on the mountain road to see the view.*

o·ver·ly /'ouvərli/ *adv.* too much, greatly: *He is overly worried about his health; his doctor said he is very healthy.*

o·ver·night /,ouvər'naɪt/ *adv.adj.* **1** during or for a single night: *He stayed <adv.> overnight at his friend's house.||He took an <adj.> overnight train to Canada.* **2** without warning, suddenly: *She won the lottery and her life changed <adv.> overnight.*

overnight bag *n.* a small, light bag to hold some clothes, toothbrush, etc.: *She brought her overnight bag to stay overnight with her friend. See:* garment bag.

o·ver·op·ti·mis·tic /,ouvər,aptə'mɪstɪk/ *adj.* feeling that s.t. good will happen when it will not, false hope: *He was overoptimistic about finding a cure for cancer. -n.* **overoptimism** /,ouvər'aptə,mɪzəm/.

o·ver·pass /'ouvər,pæs/ *n.pl.* **-es** a road that passes over another road, railroad, etc. by a kind of a bridge: *We left the main highway and used the overpass to the other side.*

o·ver·pop·u·la·tion /,ouvər,papyə'leɪʃən/ *n.* [U] a condition of too many people (or animals), esp. with not enough housing or food: *Overpopulation leads to overcrowding in*

housing. *-v.* **overpopulate** /,ouvər'papyə,leɪt/; *-adj.* **overpopulated.**

o·ver·pow·er /,ouvər'pauər/ *v.* **1** to defeat s.o. by greater power: *Police overpowered the criminal and took him away.* **2** to be too strong for one's feelings or senses, make one feel helpless: *The smell of the garbage overpowered me. -adj.* **overpowering.**

o·ver·price /,ouvər'praɪs/ *v.* **-priced, -pricing, -prices** to place too high a price on s.t., *(syn.)* to overvalue: *The owner has overpriced that house and no one will buy it.*

o·ver·pro·duce /,ouvərprə'dus/ *v.* **-duced, -ducing, -duces** to produce too much of s.t.: *Farmers overproduced wheat and now there is too much on the market. -n.* **overproduction** /,ouvərprə'dʌkʃən/.

o·ver·pro·tect /,ouvərprə'tɛkt/ *v.* to take too much care of s.o., esp. a child: *She overprotects her children; they never go out by themselves. -adj.* **overprotective.**

o·ver·qual·i·fied /,ouvər'kwalə,faɪd/ *adj.* referring to a worker whose experience and abilities are too great for a new job: *As a former manager, now unemployed, he is overqualified for an ordinary salesman's job.*

o·ver·rate /,ouvər'reɪt/ *v.* **-rated, -rating, -rates** to give too much praise or value to s.o. or s.t.: *That music is overrated; it is not very good.*

o·ver·reach /,ouvər'riʧ/ *v.* **-reaches** **1** to reach beyond or over **2** *fig.* to try to do s.t. beyond one's ability: *She overreached herself when she became a manager before she was able to do the work.*

o·ver·re·act /,ouvərri'ækt/ *v.* to react to s.t. in a way that is stronger than necessary, out of panic, fear, anger, etc.: *When his stomach hurt, he overreacted and went to the hospital when it was only gas pains.*

o·ver·ride /,ouvər'raɪd/ *v.* **-rode** /-'roud/, **-ridden** /-'rɪdn/, **-riding, -rides** **1** to set aside, ignore, *(syn.)* to overrule: *The Congress overrode the President's objection and passed the law.* **2** to be more important than, *(syn.)* to take precedence over: *A concern for safety overrode all other considerations. -adj.* **overriding.**

o·ver·rule /,ouvər'rul/ *v.* **-ruled, -ruling, -rules** to change a previous decision, *(syn.)* to nullify: *A higher court of law overruled a lower court and set the accused person free.*

o·ver·run /,ouvər'rʌn/ *v.* **-ran** /-'ræn/, **-run, -running, -runs** **1** to spread over in large numbers, usu. causing harm: *Because the kitchen was dirty, it was overrun by insects.* **2** to go beyond a limit: *The advertising department has overrun its budget three years in a row.*

—*n.* /'oʊvər,rʌn/ s.t. in excess of a limit or requirement: *That store sells books at a discount by buying publishers' overruns.*

o·ver·seas /,oʊvər'siz/ *adv.adj.* of, from, across, or beyond an ocean, in a foreign land, (*syn.*) abroad: *That business ships its products <adv.> overseas to foreign countries.||They make <adj.> overseas shipments every week.*

o·ver·see /,oʊvər'si/ *v.* **-saw** /-'sɔ/, **-seen** /-'sin/, **-seeing, -sees** to make sure that people do their work properly, (*syn.*) to supervise: *She oversees both the research and the manufacturing departments.* *-n.* **overseer** /'oʊvər,siər, -,sɪr/.

o·ver·sell /,oʊvər'sɛl/ *v.* **-sold** /-'soʊld/, **-selling, -sells** to sell more tickets than there are seats available for a flight, etc.: *Airlines regularly oversell flights during popular travel periods.* *-adj.* **oversold.** *See:* overbook.

o·ver·sen·si·tive /,oʊvər'sɛnsətɪv/ *adj.* easily upset by remarks or actions of others, (*syn.*) hypersensitive: *He is oversensitive and becomes angry when people make fun of him about losing his hair.*

o·ver·shad·ow /,oʊvər'ʃædoʊ/ *v.* **1** to throw a shadow over **2** *fig.* to seem more important than s.o. or s.t. else, (*syn.*) to dwarf: *The famous father overshadowed his less talented sons.*

o·ver·shoes /'oʊvər,ʃuz/ *n.pl.* rubber boots worn over shoes to protect them in wet weather: *Overshoes keep your feet dry in winter snow.*

o·ver·shoot /,oʊvər'ʃut/ *v.* **-shot** /-'ʃɑt/, **-shooting, -shoots** to miss or go beyond a target or limit: *The airplane overshot the runway and landed in a field.*

o·ver·sight /'oʊvər,saɪt/ *n.* **1** [C] an unintended mistake, error: *It was an oversight when he forgot to buy his plane ticket.* **2** [U] supervision, control, (*syn.*) guardianship: *A committee has oversight on how the bank invests its depositors' money.*

o·ver·sim·pli·fy /,oʊvər'sɪmplə,faɪ/ *v.* **-fied, -fying, -fies** to explain s.t. too simply so that its true meaning is lost or changed, sometimes in order to mislead: *The politician oversimplified the explanation of the new tax law to make it look like a good idea.* *-n.* **oversimplification** /,oʊvər,sɪmpləfə'keɪʃən/.

o·ver·sized /'oʊvər,saɪzd, ,oʊvər'saɪzd/ *adj.* bigger than life-sized, larger than normal size: *An oversized statue of the king stands in the square.*

o·ver·sleep /,oʊvər'slip/ *v.* **-slept** /-'slɛpt/, **-sleeping, -sleeps** to sleep too long or too late: *She overslept and missed her appointment.*

o·ver·spend /,oʊvər'spɛnd/ *v.* **-spent** /-'spɛnt/, **-spending, -spends** to spend too much money: *The government has overspent its budget and has had to borrow funds.*

o·ver·state /,oʊvər'steɪt/ *v.* **-stated, -stating, -states** to say s.t. is bigger, better, worse, etc. than it is, (*syn.*) to exaggerate: *He overstated the value of his company and no one would buy it.* *-n.* **overstatement.**

o·ver·stay /,oʊvər'steɪ, 'oʊvər,steɪ/ *v.* to stay longer than necessary or wanted: *We knew we had overstayed our welcome when we noticed that our hosts were very tired. See:* outstay; outwear, **2.**

o·ver·step /,oʊvər'stɛp/ *v.* **-stepped, -stepping, -steps** to go beyond a limit, (*syn.*) to exceed: *She overstepped her duties when she made that important decision.*

o·vert /oʊ'vɜrt, 'oʊ,vɜrt/ *adj.* public, not hidden, (*syn.*) obvious: *Two politicians who hated each other shook hands as an overt act of showing they are now friendly.* *-adv.* **overtly.**

o·ver·take /,oʊvər'teɪk/ *v.* **-took** /-'tʊk/, **-taken** /-'teɪkən/, **-taking, -takes** to catch up to and pass s.o.: *One runner overtook another runner and passed him.*

o·ver·tax /,oʊvər'tæks/ *v.* **-taxes** **1** to burden s.o. with too many taxes: *Officials overtaxed workers in the big cities.* **2** to do too much of s.t., (*syn.*) to strain: *She overtaxed herself by running in the hot weather and fainted.*

over-the-counter *adj.* **1** available without a doctor's prescription: *Most types of aspirin are available in over-the-counter form.* **2** in USA, a type of stock market called NASDAQ for smaller companies: *Small company stocks are traded in the over-the-counter market.*

o·ver·throw /,oʊvər'θroʊ/ *v.* **-threw** /-'θru/, **-thrown** /-'θroʊn/, **-throwing, -throws** to remove from a position of power by force: *The military overthrew the dictator.*
—*n.* /'oʊvər,θroʊ/ removal of a leader, (*syn.*) a coup: *The dictator's overthrow was carried out by the military.*

o·ver·time /'oʊvər,taɪm/ *n.* [U] *adv.* time worked above normal working hours, usu. beyond 40 hours per week: *<n.>Overtime (pay) is paid at a higher hourly rate.||I worked <adv.> overtime on the weekend.*

USAGE NOTE: Many employees get paid time and a half when they work *overtime.* For example, an employee who normally earns $10.00 an hour will earn $15.00 dollars an hour when working overtime.

o·ver·ture /'oʊvərtʃər, -,tʃʊr/ *n.* **1** an introductory piece of music: *The orchestra played the overture to the opera.* **2 to make overtures:** to make an initial offer, proposal, with the hope of reaching an agreement: *He made overtures of marriage to her.*

o·ver·turn /,oʊvər'tɜrn/ *v.* **1** to cause to turn over, (*syn.*) to upset: *The boat overturned and sank in the storm.* **2** to change a decision, policy, etc. (*syn.*) to reverse: *The higher court overturned the decision of the lower one.*

o·ver·view /ˈouvərˌvyu/ *n.* a general picture of s.t., (*syn.*) a summary: *Our teacher gave us an overview of the course on the first day of class.*

o·ver·weight /ˌouvərˈweɪt, ˈouvərˌweɪt/ *adj.* heavier than the normal or permitted weight: *He is a little overweight and needs to eat less.*

USAGE NOTE: In the USA, it is considered impolite to say that someone is *fat* or *obese*. It is more polite to say that someone is *overweight.*

o·ver·whelm /ˌouvərˈwɛlm/ *v.* **1** (of emotions) to go beyond one's ability to control s.t., (*syn.*) to upset: *The death of his best friend overwhelmed him with sadness.* **2** to defeat or crush with great power, (*syn.*) to overcome: *The huge army overwhelmed its enemy.* -*adj.* **overwhelming;** -*adv.* **overwhelmingly.**

o·ver·work /ˌouvərˈwɜrk, ˈouvərˌwɜrk/ *v.* to (cause to) work too hard or too long: *The new manager is overworking his employees.*
—*n.* /ˈouvərˌwɜrk/ [U] too much work: *She suffers from overwork.*

o·ver·wrought /ˌouvərˈrɔt/ *adj.* very upset or excited, nervous, (*syn.*) hysterical: *His child is missing and the father is overwrought with fear.*

ov·u·late /ˈɑvyəˌleɪt, ˈouv-/ *v.* **-lated, -lating, -lates** to produce an egg (ovum): *Women ovulate once a month.* -*n.* [U] **ovulation** /ˌɑvyəˈleɪʃən, ˌouv-/.

o·vum /ˈouvəm/ *n.* **ova** /ˈouvə/ a female reproductive cell: *Human females release one ovum a month.*

ow /aʊ/ *exclam.* an expression of pain: *Ow! I hurt my finger.*

owe /ou/ *v.* **owed, owing, owes** **1** to need to pay money to s.o., (*syn.*) to be indebted to s.o.: *He owes the landlord last month's rent.* **2** to feel a sense of obligation: *She owes her parents thanks for encouraging her career.* **3 owing to:** because of, due to: *Owing to the bad weather, classes were canceled.*

owl /aʊl/ *n.* **1** a meat-eating bird with a flat face, large front-facing eyes, a hooked beak, and sharp claws, usu. active at night: *Owls catch mice at night.* **2** *infrml.* **night owl:** a person who is active at night and sleeps days: *His girlfriend is a night owl who plays guitar in a rock band.* -*adj.* **owlish.**

own /oun/ *adj.* (used with *possessive adjectives*) **1** belonging to oneself: *This is my own*

recipe for apple pie. **2** (used to emphasize): *She found the answer by her own efforts; no one helped her.*
—*pron.* **1** belonging to oneself: *He said the car was his own.* **2 on one's own:** without help: *She built her business on her own.* **3 to be on one's own:** to be independent: *Their daughter has a good job and lives on her own now.* **4 to come into one's own:** to become successful, to receive credit, fame, etc., for s.t. one has done: *He has come into his own now that he is running the business successfully.* **5 to hold one's own:** to remain strong despite difficulties: *He is sick, but he is holding his own and is getting better.*
—*v.* **1** to have as property, (*syn.*) to possess: *She owns a bookstore.* **2** to admit, acknowledge: *The judge owned that the juror was biased.* **3** *phrasal v. insep.* **to own up to s.t.:** to confess, admit to s.t.: *The little boy finally owned up to the fact that he ate all the cookies.*

own·er /ˈounər/ *n.* a person or business that owns s.t.: *The owner of that car bought it at an auto dealer.* -*n.* **ownership.**

ox /ɑks/ *n.* **oxen** /ˈɑksən/ any of the large domesticated cattle, esp. a castrated bull used for farm work: *Oxen pull plows on many farms in the world.*

ox·ide /ˈɑkˌsaɪd/ *n.* a compound of a chemical element plus oxygen

ox·i·dize /ˈɑksəˌdaɪz/ *v.* **-dized, -dizing, -dizes** to (cause to) combine with oxygen: *Most metals darken when they oxidize.* -*n.* **oxidation** /ˌɑksəˈdeɪʃən/.

ox·y·gen /ˈɑksɪdʒən/ *n.* [U] a colorless, odorless gas (chemical symbol O) present in air, which is necessary for all forms of life: *People must breathe oxygen in order to live.* -*v.* **oxygenate** /ˈɑksɪdʒəˌneɪt/.

oxygen mask *n.* a device attached to an oxygen supply and worn over the nose and mouth: *Patients with pneumonia have oxygen masks placed over their faces to help them breathe.*

oys·ter /ˈɔɪstər/ *n.* an edible sea animal in a rough, flat grayish shell: *Some oysters taste good and others produce pearls.*

oz *abbr. for* ounce: *Baby José weighed 8 lbs., 3 ozs. when he was born.*

o·zone /ˈouˌzoun/ *n.* [U] a poisonous gas found in parts of the earth's upper atmosphere, which is a form of oxygen: *If ozone is lost in the atmosphere, earth will be subjected to the sun's harmful rays.*

P,p

P,p /pi/ *n.* **P's, p's** or **Ps, ps** the 16th letter of the English alphabet

pa /pɑ, pɔ/ *n.infrml. short for* papa, father: *My pa turns 90 years old this month.*

Pab·lum /ˈpæbləm/ *n.* [U] **1** ™ a light, bland cereal made to feed babies **2 pablum:** anything that is weak and dull, esp. writing: *The stories in that book are pablum.*

pace /peɪs/ *v.* **paced, pacing, paces 1** to walk back and forth in a worried manner: *He paced in the hospital room, waiting for the birth of the baby.* **2 to pace oneself:** to moderate one's rate or speed: *She had many miles to walk, so she paced herself carefully.* **3** *phrasal v. sep.* **to pace s.t. off:** to measure s.t. by taking steps: *She paced off an area for her new flower garden.*‖*She paced it off.*
—*n.* **1** [C] a single step or stride: *He slowly took five paces toward the edge of the bridge.* **2** [U] speed, tempo of an activity: *Runners in a long race kept up a steady pace.* **3 to keep (up) the pace:** to maintain a steady level of activity; to meet expected standards: *I have worked seven days a week for several months, but I can't keep up that pace forever!*

pace·mak·er /ˈpeɪsˌmeɪkər/ *n.* **1** s.o. who sets the pace by taking an early lead in a race or competition, (*syn.*) a pacesetter: *The young runner from Kenya started quickly and became the pacemaker.* **2** s.o. who sets a good example for others: *Her hard work made her the pacemaker among her schoolmates.* **3** a small electronic device placed near the heart to keep it beating smoothly: *After his heart attack, my father wore a pacemaker.*

pace·set·ter /ˈpeɪsˌsɛtər/ *n.* a leader

pa·cif·ic /pəˈsɪfɪk/ *adj.* calm, peaceful: *They were a pacific people who settled disagreements by talking rather than going to war.*
—*n. adj.* **Pacific:** the ocean located between eastern Asia and Australia on one side and North and South America on the other

pac·i·fi·ca·tion /ˌpæsəfəˈkeɪʃən/ *n.* [U] a process of making a person or region peaceful, not warlike

pac·i·fi·er /ˈpæsəˌfaɪər/ *n.* a small round object made of rubber or plastic for babies to bite or suck: *The baby cried until his mother gave him a pacifier.*

pac·i·fism /ˈpæsəˌfɪzəm/ *n.* [U] a philosophy against the use of violence to settle conflicts: *Some religions teach pacifism as a way of life.*

pac·i·fist /ˈpæsəfɪst/ *n.* a person who practices pacifism: *He refused to join the army because he is a pacifist.*

pac·i·fy /ˈpæsəˌfaɪ/ *v.* **-fied, -fying, -fies 1** to calm, soothe: *The mother pacified the child by feeding her some milk.* **2** to make peaceable: *The government pacified the workers by raising wages for labor.*

pack /pæk/ *v.* **1** to place, wrap, or seal objects in a container for transport or storage: *She packed two suitcases for her trip.* **2** to crowd together or force things into a small space: *She packed the drawer so tightly she could not close it.*‖*Thousands of people packed the stores during the holiday season.* **3** to process and package food products: *They pack peaches and oranges in that building.* **4** *phrasal v. sep.* **to pack s.o. or s.t. in: a** to eat s.t. in large quantities: *Before she has a race she packs in bread and pasta.*‖*She packs it in.* **b** s.o. or s.t.: to attract or fill in large numbers: *That play has been packing in big audiences.*‖*It's packing them in.* **5** *infrml.* **to pack it in:** to stop doing s.t., cease: *We worked all day, then packed it in around seven o'clock.* **6** *phrasal v.* **to pack up:** to prepare to leave: *After the convention, we packed up and left the hotel.* **7 to send s.o. packing:** to send s.o. away suddenly and firmly: *I asked the boss for a raise, and he sent me packing. -n.* **packer.**
—*n.* **1** a group of several similar things wrapped together: *He bought a pack of cigarettes at the store.* **2** a group of animals: *A pack of wolves chased the deer.* **3** a crowd of people (used negatively): *A pack of students filled the room.* **4** a bag of cloth or leather for carrying personal items: *He carries a pack on his back for his schoolbooks. See:* packing.

P

pack·age /'pækɪʤ/ *n.* **1** a container, esp. one wrapped up and sealed: *a package of cookies‖The mail carrier delivered a package for you.* **2** a group of things that are taken or offered together: *The government provides a package of health services for poor people.*
—*v.* **-aged, -aging, -ages** to wrap in a package: *Manufacturers package their products to make them appeal to customers. See:* packaging.

package deal *n.* a group of products or services offered for a single price: *The travel agency offered us a package deal of airfare, hotel, and sightseeing on a trip to Japan.*

package store *n.* a store that sells liquor in sealed bottles

pack·ag·ing /'pækɪʤɪŋ/ *n.* [U] the material, design, and style of containers for goods to be sold: *The packaging of perfumes and cosmetics is very attractive.*

packed /pækt/ *adj.* crowded or filled with people or things: *The stadium was packed with people for the championship game.‖The boxes were packed and ready for shipment.*

pack·et /'pækɪt/ *n.* a small group of items often placed in an envelope: *Travel bureaus put together packets of information for tourists.*

pack·ing /'pækɪŋ/ *n.* [U] **1** the act of putting objects into a container to move or store them: *I have to do the packing for my vacation now.* **2** material, such as cardboard, brown paper, and stuffing, used to protect objects when packed: *When we shipped the wine, we used lots of packaging to keep the bottles from breaking.* **3** the processing and packaging of food products: *Meat packing is a big industry.*

pack rat *n.* **1** a type of rat known for collecting odd objects in its nest **2** *fig.* a person who holds on to old things, often of no value: *She is a real pack rat; she never throws anything away.*

pact /pækt/ *n.* an agreement, accord: *Two nations entered into a pact to improve foreign relations.*

pad /pæd/ *n.* **1** a flat, thin cushion made of soft, flexible material used for comfort or protection: *He put a pad on the garage floor to kneel on while he fixed his car.‖The bicycle rider put a pad on her seat.* **2** a stack of paper glued together at one end: *Each student was given a pad of paper to write on.* **3** *slang.* one's home: *I'm going back to my pad now; see you later.*
—*v.* **padded, padding, pads** **1** to fill s.t. with extra material: *The furniture maker padded the chair with thick cotton.* **2** *fig.* to fill with unnecessary or untrue things: *She pads her speeches with boring stories.*

pad·ding /'pædɪŋ/ *n.* [U] soft, flexible material used to stuff cushions or furniture: *Thick padding in that chair makes it very comfortable.*

pad·dle /'pædl/ *n.* a tool with a handle attached to a broad, flat, or slightly curved surface: *The baker used a paddle to mix flour and butter together.‖They steered the boat with paddles.*
—*v.* **1** to move a canoe or other boat with a paddle: *He paddled up the river for ten miles.* **2** *infrml.fig.* **to paddle one's own canoe:** to be self-sufficient, pay one's own expenses: *She has a good-paying job now and can paddle her own canoe.*

pad·dock /'pædək/ *n.* a small area enclosed by fences and used to keep horses: *After the ride, they returned their horses to the paddock.*

pad·dy /'pædi/ *n.* **-dies** wet land where rice is grown: *The winter snows froze the farmer's paddies and damaged his crops.*

pad·lock /'pæd,lak/ *n.v.* a lock with a movable U-shaped rod released by turning a key or combination dial: *She locked her bike to the fence with a* <*n.*> *padlock.*

pa·dre /'padreɪ, -dri/ *n.infrml.* (Spanish for) father; a priest: *He went to the church to talk to the padre.*

pa·gan /'peɪgən/ *n.adj.* s.o. who does not believe in a religion with a single god: *In the ancient world,* <*n.*> *pagans prayed to the sun and the stars. -n.* **paganism.**

padlock

page /peɪʤ/ *n.* **1** one side of a single sheet of paper in a book, report, etc.: *People turn the pages of a book as they read.* **2** a young employee (in a hotel or office) who carries messages or performs other tasks: *He sent a page to buy newspapers and pick up his mail.* **3** a call over a loudspeaker system for s.o.: *I heard a page for me in the hotel lobby.*
—*v.* **paged, paging, pages** **1** to call s.o. by loudspeaker or electronic device: *The executive's secretary paged her to remind her of a meeting.* **2** **to page through:** to turn the pages of: *I paged through the magazine, looking for an interesting article to read.*

pag·eant /'pæʤənt/ *n.* a colorful public entertainment, usu. with a theme from history: *Each year they put on a pageant that portrays the American Revolution.*

pag·eant·ry /'pæʤəntri/ *n.* [U] a wonderful show with costumes and scenery: *On holidays, the streets were filled with pageantry.*

pag·er /'peɪʤər/ *n.* a device used to contact s.o. quickly with an electronic signal: *The doctor wears his pager on his belt so the hospital can reach him.*

pager

pa·go·da /pə'goudə/ n. an Asian religious building: *Monks pray in the pagoda.*

paid /peid/ v. past tense & past part. of pay

pail /peil/ n. a large metal or plastic container, (*syn.*) a bucket: *A worker filled a pail with water to clean the floor.*

pagoda

pain /pein/ n. [U] **1** a hurt, a bad feeling ranging from a mild ache to extreme hurt caused by disease, injury, or mental distress: *After the car accident, he had a pain in his right side.||The memory of her mother's illness caused her great pain.* **2** *fig.* an annoying person or a situation: *Commuting to work in big cities is a pain* (or) *a pain in the neck.* **3 to take pains with s.t.** or **to do s.t.:** to take great care in doing s.t.: *The worker took great pains in building the stairway.*
—v. to hurt: *My hand pains me from a fall.||It pains me to see food wasted.*

pain·ful /'peinfəl/ adj. causing pain, hurting: *Her broken ankle is a painful injury.* -adv. **painfully.**

pain·kill·er /'pein,kilər/ n. a medicine or drug for relieving pain: *The dentist gave me a painkiller before he pulled my tooth.*

pain·less /'peinlis/ adj. without pain, not causing hurt or difficulty: *To his surprise, the examination was painless.* -adv. **painlessly.**

pains·tak·ing /'pein,steikiŋ, 'peinz,tei-/ adj. careful to do things exactly right: *That painter is very painstaking in making her works look real.*

paint /peint/ n. [U] a liquid mixture of coloring matter (pigment) and oil or water, used to cover and color surfaces: *Workmen covered the floors with white paint.*
—v. **1** to apply paint: *She painted her room green.* **2** to create a picture or work of art: *She paints portraits for a living.* **3** *infrml.* **to paint the town red:** to have a wonderful time eating, drinking, dancing, etc., without concern for money: *When she found a new job, she and her boyfriend painted the town red.*

paint·brush /'peint,brʌʃ/ n. **-brushes** a brush used to apply paint: *House painters use large paintbrushes.*

paint·er /'peintər/ n. a person who paints, such as a worker or artist: *A painter is painting our house this week.*

paint·ing /'peintiŋ/ n. [U] **1** the process of painting: *Painting our house will take a long time.* **2** [C] a painted work of art: *Paintings hang in museums.*

pair /per/ n. **pairs** or **pair 1** two similar things that go together, such as a pair of shoes: *She bought a pair of gloves to wear in winter.* **2** two people in close relation: *That man and woman make a handsome pair.*
—v. **1** to match, put together as a pair: *The teacher paired me with the student next to me to do a project.* **2** *phrasal v. sep.* **to pair s.o. up:** to form pairs, usu. for work or sport: *The director paired up men and women for the dance rehearsal.||She paired them up.*

pais·ley /'peizli/ adj.n. a colorful, curved pattern, usu. on soft wool or silk: *He is wearing a <adj.> paisley tie.*

pa·ja·mas /pə'dʒɑməz, -'dʒæ-/ n.pl. loose pants with a jacket made for sleeping and relaxing: *His pajamas are made of cotton.*

pal /pæl/ n.infrml. a good friend, (*syn.*) a buddy: *My pals and I are going to the movies tonight.*

pal·ace /'pælis/ n. **1** the official home of a king, queen, or other rich and powerful person: *The palace was filled for the prince's wedding.* **2** a large and grand house: *The poor boy thought the big house was a palace.*

pal·at·a·ble /'pælətəbəl/ adj. satisfactory to the taste: *Food in the college cafeteria is palatable, not fancy.*

pal·ate /'pælit/ n. **1** [C] the roof of the mouth: *The ice cream felt cold against his palate.* **2** [C, usu. *sing.*] *fig.* refined judgment about the taste and quality of food: *He loves good food and has a fine palate.*

pa·la·tial /pə'leiʃəl/ adj. like a palace in size and grandeur: *The new art museum is palatial.*

pale /peil/ adj. **paler, palest 1** light in color: *That wall is painted in a pale green.* **2** unhealthy-looking, (*syn.*) pallid: *She looks pale and sick.* -n. **paleness.**
—v. **paled, paling, pales 1** to turn pale: *He paled at the thought of seeing his enemy.* **2** to be of lesser value (importance, worth) than s.t. else: *Country life pales in comparison with life in Paris.*

pa·le·on·tol·o·gy /,peiliən'tɑlədʒi/ n. [U] the science of fossils: *Paleontology is the study of old bodies of living things in stone.* -n. **paleontologist.**

pal·ette /'pælit/ n. **1** a flat plate made of wood or plastic, often with a thumb hole, used by artists to mix paints: *When she dropped her palette, the colors ran together.* **2** a range of colors typical of an artist's style: *That artist paints with a light palette.*

pal·i·sade /,pælə'seid/ n. a row of cliffs: *Palisades run for miles along the Hudson River valley north of New York City.*

pall /pɔl/ n. **1** a dark cloth for covering a coffin: *They removed the pall before opening the coffin.* **2** a saddening effect: *The mother's death cast a pall over the family for months.*

P

pal·la·di·um /pə'leɪdiəm/ n. [U] a silvery-white metallic element: *Palladium is used to make white gold for rings.*

pall·bear·er /'pɔl,bɛrər/ n. s.o. who helps carry the coffin of a dead person: *Six strong pall-bearers carried the dead soldier's coffin from the church.*

pal·lid /'pælɪd/ adj. having a pale, unhealthy-looking complexion: *Her complexion was pallid when she was ill.*

pal·lor /'pælər/ n. [U] lack of healthy color, (syn.) paleness: *From the pallor of his skin, they could tell he had been in prison a long time.*

palm (1) /pɑm/ n. a type of tree found in tropical climates with no branches and large, long leaves at the top: *Palms shaded their house in California.*

palm (2) n. the inside of the central part of the hand: *He touched her forehead with his palm.* —v. **1** to hide with or in the hand: *She palmed the candy to hide it from her mother.* **2** phrasal v. sep. **to palm s.t. off:** to get rid of s.t. by deceiving s.o.: *He palmed off his broken watch on the stranger.‖He palmed it off.*

Palm Sunday n. a Christian holiday on the Sunday before Easter: *On Palm Sunday, they went to church.*

pal·o·mi·no /,pælə'minou/ n. **-nos** a horse with a golden tan coat and white mane

pal·pa·ble /'pælpəbəl/ adj. **1** capable of being felt: *Bumps on his head from a fall were palpable to the touch.* **2** easy to see or notice, obvious: *The soldier's fear was palpable. -adv.* **palpably.**

pal·pi·tate /'pælpə,teɪt/ v. **-tated, -tating, -tates** to beat rapidly, throb: *The sight of the lion caused their hearts to palpitate with fear. -n.*[C,U] **palpitation** /,pælpə'teɪʃən/.

pal·sy /'pɔlzi/ n. [U] a condition involving poor muscle control due to brain or nerve damage

pal·try /'pɔltri/ adj.frml. small, worthless, unimportant: *He gave the waiter a paltry tip (only 5%) for his service.*

pam·per /'pæmpər/ v. to take more care of s.o. than is necessary: *She pampers her child by picking her up every time she cries.*

pam·phlet /'pæmflɪt/ n. a small book of a few pages containing advertising or useful information: *The hospital gives its patients a pamphlet that describes its services.*

pan /pæn/ n. **1** a flat, round, metal container with low sides and a handle, used in cooking: *He uses a frying pan to cook eggs each morning.* **2** a container for holding liquid: *a dishpan‖a paint pan*
—v. **panned, panning, pans 1** to turn a movie camera slowly to film a wide area or a moving object: *She panned the camera to follow the*

flying birds. **2** to judge s.t. for its failures: *Critics panned the new play because the actors were not good.*

pan·a·ce·a /,pænə'siə/ n. s.t. that is believed to cure all ills and problems: *Aspirin is considered a panacea for aches and pains.*

pa·nache /pə'næʃ, -'nɑʃ/ n.frml. [U] the ability to perform with style and ease: *She played the piano with great panache.*

Pan-A·mer·i·can /,pænə'mɛrɪkən/ adj. related to or involving North, Central, and South America: *Interested countries held a Pan-American conference on economic problems.*

pan·cake /'pæn,keɪk, 'pæŋ-/ n. a flat, round cake cooked until brown and made of flour, milk, eggs, and butter: *He likes pancakes with maple syrup for breakfast. See:* scrambled eggs, USAGE NOTE.

pancakes

pan·cre·as /'pæŋkriəs, 'pæn-/ n. **-ases** an organ of the digestive system near the stomach: *When the pancreas doesn't function properly, one may have diabetes. -adj.* **pancreatic** /,pæŋkri'ætɪk, ,pæn-/.

pan·da /'pændə/ n. a large mammal from China that looks like a bear with black-and-white fur: *They went to see the pandas at the zoo.*

pan·dem·ic /pæn'dɛmɪk/ adj. (said of a disease) spreading throughout an entire region, country, population, or the world: *Pandemic influenza outbreaks can kill millions.*

pan·de·mo·ni·um /,pændə'mouniəm/ n. [U] a condition of chaos, wild panic, or uproar: *When a fire started in the theater, there was pandemonium with people screaming and running.*

pan·der /'pændər/ v. to offer or sell s.t. that appeals to low or evil desires, such as for sex, scandal, or easy money: *Those pornographic magazines pander to people's interest in pictures about sex. -n.* **panderer.**

pane /peɪn/ n. a piece of glass used as a section of a window, or one of those sections: *The window took a long time to clean because it had many panes.*

pan·el /'pænəl/ n. **1** a distinct part of a surface or flat area: *The wall was made from panels of wood.* **2** a surface area that contains buttons, levers, switches, dials, etc., for operating a machine or a system: *The pilot faced the airplane's control panel to prepare for take off.* **3** a group of people chosen for a project or discussion of issues: *The mayor formed a panel of important citizens to study the city's schools.*
—v. to cover a surface, such as a wall, with panels, esp. of wood: *The dining room was*

paneled in oak.

panel discussion *n.* an event where a group of people meet to talk about one or several topics: *The TV station held a panel discussion about the election.*

pan·el·ing /ˈpænəlɪŋ/ *n.* [U] a series of panels: *The wood paneling in this room is made of walnut.*

pan·el·ist /ˈpænəlɪst/ *n.* a person who takes part in a panel discussion or study: *Each panelist presented his or her view on the economy.*

pang /pæŋ/ *n.* a brief but sharp feeling of pain in the body or mind: *He had hunger pangs that went away after he ate breakfast.||She had a pang of guilt because she had hurt her brother.*

pan·han·dle /ˈpæn,hændl/ *v.infrml.* **-dled, -dling, -dles** to beg or ask for money on the street: *He panhandles near a restaurant entrance each morning.* *-n.* **panhandler.**

pan·ic /ˈpænɪk/ *n.* [C;U] **1** a condition of uncontrolled fear in response to danger: *The fire in the subway caused a panic.* **2 to hit the panic button:** to do s.t. that causes a state of emergency; to go into a state of panic: *She thought the man was going to steal her purse, so she hit the panic button and screamed for help.*
—*v.* **-icked, -icking, -ics** to experience uncontrolled fear: *She panicked and ran out the door.* *-adj.* **panicky.**

panic-stricken *adj.* overcome with panic, afraid: *When the earthquake struck, he became panic-stricken and ran into the street.*

pan·o·ram·a /ˌpænəˈræmə, -ˈrɑ-/ *n.* [C] **1** a broad, open view of a wide range: *We stood on a mountaintop and viewed the panorama of sea and sky.* **2** a full view or complete picture: *That book presents a panorama of American history.* *-adj.* **panoramic** /ˌpænəˈræmɪk/.

pan·sy /ˈpænzi/ *n.* **-sies 1** a type of short garden flower with broad, colorful petals: *He gave her a bunch of pansies for her birthday.* **2** *infrml.pej.* an effeminate man or boy

pant /pænt/ *v.n.* to breathe quickly, gasp for breath: *Dogs <v.> pant with their tongues hanging out after running fast.*

pan·the·ism /ˈpænθi,ɪzəm/ *n.* [U] a belief that God or many gods live in nature: *Pantheism was common in many ancient societies and religions.* *-n.* **pantheist;** *-adj.* **pantheistic** /ˌpænθiˈɪstɪk/.

pan·the·on /ˈpænθi,ɑn, -ən/ *n.* [C] a public building with busts, statues, etc., of great heroes

pan·ther /ˈpænθər/ *n.* a large, wild type of cat, usually with black fur, known for its ability to hunt: *The hungry panthers attacked the herd of deer.*

pant·ies /ˈpæntiz/ *n.pl.* underpants worn by women or girls: *She wore white panties under her dress.*

pan·to·mime /ˈpæntə,maɪm/ *n.* [C;U] a form of acting (in plays) by expressing feelings and actions without using words: *The clown performed a pantomime about how to ride a horse.*

pan·try /ˈpæntri/ *n.* **-tries** a small room next to the kitchen, used to store food, dishes, and cooking equipment: *He went to the pantry to get flour and sugar for baking a cake.*

pants /pænts/ *n.pl.* **1** trousers, a man's or woman's garment that runs from the waist to the ankles with two long sections for the legs: *Her legs were cold, so she put on a pair of pants.* **2** *infrml.* **to wear the pants:** to be the boss: *His wife wears the pants in their house; she tells him what to do.*

pant·y·hose /ˈpænti,hoʊz/ *n.* used with a *pl.v.* [U] a tight, thin stocking that goes from the waist, down the legs, and over the feet and is worn by women under other clothes: *Many women wear pantyhose for extra warmth in winter. See:* nylons.

pa·pa /ˈpɑpə/ *n.infrml.* father, daddy: *My papa is 90 years old today.*

pa·pa·cy /ˈpeɪpəsi/ *n.* [C; usu. *sing.*] the office and functions of the Pope: *The power of the papacy reaches around the world.* *-adj.* **papal.**

pa·pa·ya /pəˈpaɪə/ *n.* [C;U] a tropical tree with large, greenish-yellow fruit, or the fruit itself: *Papayas are tasty and full of vitamins.*

pa·per /ˈpeɪpər/ *n.* **1** [U] thin, smooth material made from the fibers of wood or cotton and cut into sheets to be used for writing, wrapping, or covering: *I wrote a letter on a piece of paper.* **2** [C] a newspaper: *Have you read this morning's paper?* **3** [C] a written document, such as a scholarly report: *My professor wrote a paper on Shakespeare.* **4** *pl.* **papers:** a collection of personal documents: *He went through his papers to find information he needed to pay his taxes.*
—*v.* to cover with paper: *We papered our bathroom with new wallpaper.*

pa·per·back /ˈpeɪpər,bæk/ *n.* a book with a cover made of stiff or coated paper: *Paperbacks are small and handy to read. See:* hardcover.

paper money *n.* [C] currency made out of paper rather than metal coins: *Paper money is issued by governments in each country.*

pa·per·weight /ˈpeɪpər,weɪt/ *n.* any small, heavy object used to hold down papers: *He used a rock as a paperweight to keep the wind from blowing the letters off his desk.*

pa·per·work /ˈpeɪpər,wɜrk/ *n.* [U] **1** government or legal forms that must be filled out to complete some action or process: *Buying a house involves a lot of paperwork.* **2** work that

P

requires a lot of time for reading and writing reports, letters, or other documents: *She stayed up late to go through paperwork that she had brought home from the office.*

pa·per·y /'peɪpəri/ *adj.* like paper, esp. in being thin or dry: *The old woman's skin was dry and papery.*

pa·pier-mâ·ché /ˌpeɪpərmə'ʃeɪ/ *n.adj.* a material made from wet paper mixed with glue that becomes hard when dry, used for making boxes, small figures, etc.

pa·pri·ka /pæ'prikə, pə-/ *n.* [U] a seasoning powder made from sweet red peppers: *He added some paprika to the soup.*

Pap smear or **Pap test** /pæp/ *n.* a medical test for women to find any early signs of cancer of the cervix: *Her employer's medical benefits included a yearly Pap test.*

pa·py·rus /pə'paɪrəs/ *n.* [C] a type of paper invented in ancient Egypt, made from a tall water plant: *Egyptians wrote on papyrus.*

par /pɑr/ *n.* [C; usu.*sing.*] **1** an amount or status that is equal or to roughly the same level: *The quality of that hotel is on a par with the best in the city.* **2** an average or normal standard score: *After nine holes of golf, her score was three strokes below par.* **3 below par** or **above par:** not equal to normal status or expectations: *He was feeling below par and went to bed early.*‖*She felt above par and ran an extra mile for exercise.* **4 par for the course:** a normal experience; what one would expect: *His jokes were not funny, but that was par for the course.*

par·a·ble /'pærəbəl/ *n.* a brief, simple story told to illustrate a moral or religious truth: *He tells parables that are meant to make you think.*

pa·rab·o·la /pə'ræbələ/ *n.* the shape of a curved line that rises and falls like a ball thrown in the air: *The flight of the rocket formed a giant parabola from start to finish.*

par·a·chute /'pærəˌʃut/ *n.* a large, lightweight sheet, attached to a falling person or thing, that unfolds in the wind and causes the person or thing to fall slowly: *Skydivers use parachutes to float to earth.* —*v.* **-chuted, -chuting, -chutes** to use a parachute: *They parachuted from the aircraft.*

parachute

pa·rade /pə'reɪd/ *n.* [C;U] an orderly movement of people in fanciful or formal dress or uniforms, usu. to show pride or to honor a special day or event: *On Memorial Day, we saw a parade of soldiers marching in honor of those who died in war.* —*v.* **-raded, -rading, -rades** to march in a parade, to celebrate: *On Thanksgiving Day, clowns, horses, children, and bands parade down Fifth Avenue in New York City.*

par·a·digm /'pærəˌdaɪm, -ˌdɪm/ *n.* a model or concept used as a standard by which people evaluate, understand, and often act: *The computer is a popular paradigm for how the brain works.*

par·a·dise /'pærəˌdaɪs, -ˌdaɪz/ *n.* [C; usu.*sing.*] **1** in the Bible, the original home of humankind, a blessed place: *Adam and Eve were sent out of paradise because they disobeyed God.* **2** any place where everything is beautiful, delightful, and peaceful: *Parts of California seem like paradise to me.*

par·a·dox /'pærəˌdɑks/ *n.* **-doxes** a puzzling statement that states two opposing truths or an impossible state of affairs: *He tried to explain the paradox that on his vacation, he had the best and the worst time of his life.* -*adj.* **paradoxical** /ˌpærə'dɑksɪkəl/; -*adv.* **paradoxically.**

par·af·fin /'pærəfɪn/ *n.* a type of wax used to make candles and waxed paper: *He used paraffin from the candle to seal his letter.*

par·a·gon /'pærəˌgɑn, -gən/ *n.* an example of the best: *She is so good that she is a paragon of virtue.*

par·a·graph /'pærəˌgræf/ *n.v.* a part of a piece of writing, signaled by a space or other break, that introduces a new thought or idea: *Newspaper articles use very short paragraphs to make reading easier and faster.*

par·a·keet /'pærəˌkit/ *n.* a type of small parrot often kept in a cage: *We keep a pair of light-green parakeets as pets.*

par·a·le·gal /ˌpærə'ligəl/ *n.* an assistant in a law office who performs many of the lawyers' lesser duties: *My sister worked as a paralegal before going to law school.* —*adj.* related to paralegals and their work: *He works as a paralegal secretary in a big law firm.*

par·al·lel /'pærəˌlɛl, -ləl/ *adj.* running side by side at an equal distance apart: *Railroad tracks are parallel to each other.* —*n.* a likeness or connection between two or more events: *The police officer saw a parallel between the two murder cases.* —*v.* to be similar or to occur at the same time: *The histories of the two countries closely parallel each other.*

pa·ral·y·sis /pə'ræləsɪs/ *n.* **-ses** /-ˌsiz/ [C;U] **1** a loss of ability to move or feel part of the body: *After the car accident, he suffered from paralysis of both his legs.* **2** an inability to act -*adj.n.* **paralytic** /ˌpærə'lɪtɪk/.

par·a·lyze /'pærəˌlaɪz/ *v.* **-lyzed, -lyzing, -lyzes** to cause a state of paralysis: *A strike by transportation workers paralyzed the city.*

par·a·med·ic /ˌpærə'mɛdɪk/ *n.* a person trained to provide emergency medical help when a doctor is not present: *Paramedics were standing ready by the racecourse in case of an accident.*

pa·ram·e·ter /pə'ræmətər/ *n.* **1** a part of s.t. that makes it what it is: *The scientist studied one of the parameters of the disease.* **2** a limit that defines an activity: *Her boss set the parameters for her next project.*

par·a·mount /'pærə,maʊnt/ *adj.* supreme, foremost: *Having food and shelter is of paramount importance to everyone.*

par·a·noi·a /ˌpærə'nɔɪə/ *n.* [U] **1** a sick state of mind in which s.o. believes, without good reasons, that everyone is trying to harm him or her **2** a general feeling of fear and distrust of other people: *She had few friends because her paranoia made her unpleasant to be with.*

par·a·noid /'pærə,nɔɪd/ *adj.* fearful and mistrusting, *(syn.)* overly suspicious: *When the army took control of the government, he became very paranoid.*
—*n.* a person who suffers from paranoia: *He is a paranoid.*

par·a·pet /'pærəpɪt, -,pɛt/ *n.* a low wall to protect soldiers standing on a rooftop, a bridge, or a hill: *She leaned over the parapet of the old castle to take a picture of the countryside.*

par·a·pher·na·lia /ˌpærəfər'neɪlyə, -fə'neɪl-/ *n.* [U] **1** a loose collection of personal belongings: *When she left home to go to college, she threw all her paraphernalia into the car and drove away.* **2** various tools used to perform a function: *The doctor's black bag was filled with medical paraphernalia.*

par·a·phrase /'pærə,freɪz/ *v.* **-phrased, -phrasing, -phrases** **1** to explain the meaning of s.t. that has been said or written by using different words or phrases: *The teacher asked his students to paraphrase the poem.* **2** to give a brief, simple statement of s.t. that is difficult: *He asked me to paraphrase the president's speech.*
—*n.* a brief explanation

par·a·ple·gic /ˌpærə'plidʒɪk/ *n.adj.* a person who cannot move the lower half of his or her body, including the legs: *As the result of a bad accident, he is now a paraplegic. -n.* [U] **paraplegia** /ˌpærə'plidʒə, -dʒiə/.

par·a·site /'pærə,saɪt/ *n.* **1** a small animal or plant that lives on or inside a larger one and feeds on it: *He bought a drug to kill the parasites that were making his dog sick.* **2** s.o. who lives at the expense of others without giving anything in return: *The new senator said that poor people are parasites on society. -adj.* **parasitic** /ˌpærə'sɪtɪk/.

par·a·sol /'pærə,sɔl, -,sal/ *n.* a type of light umbrella used to shield women from the sun

par·a·troop·er /'pærə,trupər/ *n.* a soldier trained to use a parachute to jump from airplanes in war: *The battle began when the paratroopers landed behind enemy lines. -n.pl.* **paratroops.**

par·cel /'parsəl/ *n.* **1** a package or carton that has been wrapped and tied or taped tightly: *I have sent a parcel containing Christmas presents to my parents.* **2** a plot of land: *She owns a parcel of land near the lake.*
— *phrasal v. sep.* **to parcel s.t. out:** to divide into pieces to be given out: *After his death, his relatives parcelled out his property.||They parcelled it out.*

parcel post *n.* [U] in USA, fourth-class mail, a low-cost way of sending packages over long distances by means of trucks and trains: *She sent a package of clothes to relatives by parcel post.*

parch /partʃ/ *v.* **parches** to make very hot and dry: *The hot, dry winds parched the farmland.*

parch·ment /'partʃmənt/ *n.* [U] **1** sheepskin or goatskin that is treated so that it can be written or painted on: *Paper was invented to replace parchment.* **2** paper made to seem like parchment: *College diplomas are printed on parchment.*

par·don /'pardn/ *v.* to forgive or excuse s.o.: *He asked me to pardon him for being late for the meeting.*
—*n.* [C;U] **1** an act of forgiving s.o. and excusing him or her from punishment: *The governor granted the thief a pardon, and he was released from prison.* **2 pardon me** or **I beg your pardon:** a polite way of saying "I am sorry. Please excuse me": *When the waiter bumped into our table, he cried out "Oh! pardon me, madam!"*

par·don·a·ble /'pardnəbəl/ *adj.* worthy of being forgiven or excused

pare /pɛr/ *v.* **pared, paring, pares** **1** to cut off the surface, skin, or edge of s.t.: *He pared the carrots with a knife.||She cut her finger while paring a potato.* **2** to reduce in amount or size: *She pared down her expenses by getting rid of her car and not eating in restaurants.*

par·ent /'pɛrənt, 'pær-/ *n.* the mother or father of s.o.: *His parents raised him in New Hampshire. -n.* [U] **parenthood.**
—*v.* to act as a parent by raising children: *That couple parented four kids through college. See:* parenting.

par·ent·age /'pɛrəntɪdʒ, 'pær-/ *n.* [U] the origins of a person's or animal's parents; family background: *Her parentage was mixed; her grandparents came from several different countries.*

pa·ren·tal /pə'rɛntl/ *adj.* of or related to parents: *The boy was hospitalized after the acci-*

P

dent, but now he is under parental care at home.

pa·ren·the·sis /pə'rɛnθəsɪs/ *n.* **-ses** /-ˌsiz/ **1** a word, phrase, or sentence added within another sentence to explain or comment on s.t.: *He added a parenthesis (like this one) to give an example of what he meant.* **2** *pl.* **parentheses** in writing, the curved signs ( ) that mark off such an addition

par·en·thet·i·cal /ˌpærən'θɛtɪkəl/ *adj.* done or said in addition to the main purpose: *She added many parenthetical remarks to her speech.*

par·ent·hood /'pɛrənt,hʊd, 'pær-/ *n.* the state of being a parent: *The couple found that parenthood brought unexpected joys as well as responsibilities.*

par·ent·ing /'pɛrəntɪŋ, 'pær-/ *n.* [U] the act of taking care of children by providing for their needs, such as food, clothing, shelter, guidance, and education: *She was a good mother and devoted a lot of time to parenting.*

par ex·cel·lence /'par,ɛksə'lans/ *adj.* (French for) of the highest quality: *He is a cook par excellence.*

pa·ri·ah /pə'raɪə/ *n.* a person who is not welcome in society: *His unpopular ideas make him a pariah in his town.*

paring knife *n.* **knives** a short, sharp knife used in the kitchen to prepare food: *She sliced the apple with a paring knife.*

par·ish /'pærɪʃ/ *n.* **-ishes** **1** the local area served by a single church: *The priest was sent to a parish in Florida.* **2** the members of a local church: *The parish planned to raise money for charity.* **-n.** **parishioner** /pə'rɪʃənər/.

par·i·ty /'pærəti/ *n.* [U] an equal level in status, value, or amount: *Women's salaries are not at parity with men's salaries.*

park /park/ *n.* **1** an area of land where people can exercise, play, or relax: *He took his dog for a walk in the park.* **2 ball park:** a field where the game of baseball is played: *They went to the ball park to see the game.*
—*v.* to bring a car to rest in one place and leave it for a limited amount of time: *She parked her car in front of the store.*

par·ka /'parkə/ *n.* a short coat with a hood that covers the head to keep out the wind and rain: *He carried a parka on the boat trip in case the weather turned bad.*

parka

park·ing /'parkɪŋ/ *n.* [U] **1** the activity of bringing a car to rest and leaving it: *She was good at parking large cars in small spaces.* **2** the supply of space in which to park: *The lack of parking in big cities is almost always a problem.*

parking lot *n.* a flat area used for parking cars, often guarded by an attendant: *That shopping mall has a huge parking lot in front of the stores.*

parking meter *n.* a time clock set on a pole next to a parking space into which one puts coins to pay for parking: *He forgot to put money in the parking meter, so he had to pay a fine.*

parking meter

Par·kin·son's disease /'parkɪnsənz/ *n.* [U] an illness in the body's nervous system that causes weakness and shaking in the arms and legs: *Parkinson's disease is a problem for many old people.*

park·way /'park,weɪ/ *n.* a broad highway with grass and trees in the middle and/or along the sides: *They liked to drive on the parkway because it was beautiful.*

par·ley /'parli, -leɪ/ *v.* **-leys** to meet with an enemy or opponent to talk about how to solve problems or end the conflict: *Generals from the two armies parleyed about how to return each other's prisoners.*

par·lia·ment /'parləmənt/ *n.* the national assembly that makes or changes laws in some countries, such as Great Britain: *The British Parliament has two divisions, the House of Lords and the House of Commons.* **-adj. parliamentary** /ˌparlə'mɛntri, -təri/.

par·lia·men·tar·i·an /ˌparləmen'tɛriən/ *n.* a person who is an expert on the rules and procedures of a parliament or other assembly

par·lor /'parlər/ *n.* **1** a room in a house used for sitting and talking: *Big old houses have a parlor near the front door.* **2** a type of business furnished for a particular purpose: *She went to the ice-cream parlor after having her hair done at the beauty parlor.*

Par·me·san /'parmə,zan, -zən/ *n.* [U] a type of nutty-tasting, dry, hard Italian cheese that is usu. grated: *I like to put Parmesan on my spaghetti. See:* **cheddar,** USAGE NOTE.

pa·ro·chi·al /pə'roukiəl/ *adj.* **1** of or belonging to a church parish: *She sends her two children to a parochial school run by the church.* **2** limited by narrow, local interests: *That politician has a parochial view of the government's duty.* **-n.** [U] **parochialism.**

par·o·dy /'pærədi/ *v.* **-died, -dying, -dies** to copy the way s.o. or s.t. looks or behaves in order to make fun of it, *(syn.)* to mock: *A clown parodied a rock musician by dressing up like him and pretending to play a guitar.*
—*n.* **-dies** a work of art that parodies a person, event, or another work for the purpose of pleasure or criticism: *The actors performed a parody of the new TV program.*

P

pa·role /pə'roʊl/ n. [U] the early release of a prisoner who promises to be good and report regularly to a law officer: *After two years in prison, she was given parole, but she had to stay in this country.*
—v. **-roled, -roling, -roles** to give s.o. limited freedom; to put on parole: *He was paroled because he had been a good prisoner.*

pa·rol·ee /pə,roʊ'li, -'roʊli/ n. a person who is on parole from prison: *Parolees must report to a government parole officer.*

par·ox·ysm /'pærək,sɪzəm/ n.frml. a sudden or violent burst of expression: *When the queen died, the people broke into paroxysms of tears.*

par·quet /par'keɪ/ n.adj. [U] a floor covering of narrow strips of wood arranged in patterns: *The <n.> parquet on the living room floor is made of walnut. It is a <adj.> parquet floor.* -n. [U] **parquetry** /'parkətri/.

par·rot /'pærət/ n. any of a variety of tropical birds with a curved beak and colorful feathers, some of which have the ability to copy human speech: *He keeps a parrot in a birdcage in his living room.*
—v. to repeat s.t. without thinking or understanding: *The little boy parrots everything that his parents say.*

par·si·mo·ni·ous /,parsə'moʊniəs/ adj.frml. extremely careful not to spend too much money: *His father was very parsimonious and never wasted a penny.* -n. [U] **parsimony** /'parsə,moʊni/.

pars·ley /'parsli/ n. [U] a small, green herb used to flavor or decorate food: *The cook sprinkled some chopped parsley on the mashed potato.*

pars·nip /'parsnɪp/ n. a plant with a long white or yellowish root that is cooked and eaten as a vegetable: *Parsnips taste sweet and are full of vitamins.*

par·son /'parsən/ n. a Protestant minister: *The congregation listens to the parson's sermon on Sunday.*

par·son·age /'parsənɪdʒ/ n. the residence of a parson: *The parsonage is located right next to the church.*

part /part/ n. **1** [C;U] a segment, piece, or portion of s.t.: *Part of that wall is falling down.‖Part of what he says is true; the rest is not.‖His story had many different parts to it.‖She hurt in every part of her body.* **2** [C] one of many other things that are put together to make a machine: *He bought some new parts for his bicycle.* **3** [C] a role or duty to perform in some activity or event: *She has a part in a new movie.‖He did his part to help his friend.* **4** [U] one side of a conflict or disagreement: *He took her part because he thought she was right.* **5** [C] a line that separates the hair on a person's head: *She used a comb to make a part*

in her hair. **6 for my part:** to speak for myself: *For my part, I plan to go to the party even if you decide not to go.* **7 in good part/for the most part:** to an important degree, large amount: *What he says is in good part* (or) *for the most part true.* **8 on the part of:** on behalf of, for s.o.: *That lawyer is acting on the part of several people who have a complaint about that company.* **9 private parts:** a person's sex organs **10 to be part and parcel of s.t.:** to be an important part of s.t.: *Good health is part and parcel of happiness.* **11 to take part in s.t.:** to participate in s.t.: *She takes part in after-school programs, like playing in the band.*
—v. **1** to pull apart, separate, or divide: *She parted the curtains to let in the sunlight.* **2** to go away from or leave a person or place: *After the party, my friend and I parted to go to our separate homes.* **3** to divide into separate sections: *He parted his hair with a comb.* **4 to part company with:** to end a relationship: *She and her first husband parted company after two years of marriage.* **5** phrasal v. insep. **to part with:** to let go of, often against one's will: *He can't part with his favorite old car even though it won't run anymore.*
—adv. in part, partially: *This shirt is part cotton and part polyester.*

par·take /par'teɪk/ v.frml. **-took** /-'tʊk/ , **-taken** /-'teɪkən/ , **-taking, -takes** to take part, share, or participate in s.t., such as a meal or an activity: *He asked us to partake in the ceremony.*

part·ed /'partɪd/ adj. & past part. of part, not together, separated: *His hair was neatly <adj.> parted down the middle.*

par·tial /'parʃəl/ adj. **1** incomplete, only a part of s.t.: *He owed me $1,000, and he made a partial payment of $500.* **2** about giving special or unfair treatment to s.o. or s.t.: *The judge of the contest was partial to her son.* **3** fond of, having a special liking for s.t.: *She is very partial to chocolate ice cream.* -n. [U] **partiality** /,parʃi'æləti/.

par·tial·ly /'parʃəli/ adv. in part, not fully: *That window is partially open.*

par·tic·i·pant /par'tɪsəpənt, pər-/ n. a person who takes part in s.t.: *He was a participant in the discussion.*

par·tic·i·pate /par'tɪsə,peɪt, pər-/ v. **-pated, -pating, -pates** to take part or have a role in an activity or event: *She likes to participate in political campaigns.* -n. **participation** /par,tɪsə'peɪʃən/ -adj. **participatory** /par'tɪsəpə,tɔri, pər-/.

par·ti·ci·ple /'partə,sɪpəl, -səpəl/ n. a grammatical form of a verb that may also be used as another part of speech **a.** used with an auxiliary verb to show past or present tense: *The past participle of "to cook" is "cooked," as in "The meat is cooked." The present participle*

P

is "cooking," as in, "The food is cooking." **b.** used as an adjective: *Cooked meat tastes better than uncooked meat.*

par·ti·cle /'pɑrtɪkəl/ *n.* a very small piece of s.t., (*syn.*) a speck: *Particles of sand cover the road.*

par·tic·u·lar /pər'tɪkyələr, pə'tɪk-/ *adj.* **1** relating to a specific person, idea, item, etc.: *I like classical music in general, but not that particular composer.* **2** special, unusual: *There is nothing of particular interest on TV tonight.* **3** very exact and demanding about what one wants, (*syn.*) fussy: *He is very particular about the food he eats; everything has to be cooked just right.*
—*n.* **1** *usu.pl.* **particulars:** a specific fact or detail: *I can tell you briefly what happened, but I'll save the particulars for later.* **2 in particular: a.** specifically, especially: *I thought the whole meal was good, but the soup in particular was delicious.* **b.** specific, special: *The salesclerk asked if I was looking for anything in particular.*

par·tic·u·lar·ly /pər'tɪkyələrli, pə'tɪk-/ *adv.* especially, greatly: *She is particularly interested in modern art.*

part·ing /'pɑrtɪŋ/ *n.* [C;U] **1** the act of separating or taking leave: *He found that parting from home was very difficult.* **2** the moment of going away or taking leave: *The lovers' parting was filled with sighs and tears.*
—*adj.* done at the moment of parting: *Her father gave her a parting kiss.*

par·ti·san /'pɑrtəzən, -sən/ *n.* **1** a person who believes strongly in a plan of action or an idea, (*syn.*) an activist: *He is a partisan for socialism.* **2** s.o. who joins a secret army to fight against an enemy that has taken over his or her country: *The partisans attacked at night.*
—*adj.* strongly in favor of a single cause without concern for any others: *Her partisan manner made many people angry.*

par·ti·tion /pɑr'tɪʃən, pər-/ *n.* **1** [C] a wall that divides the parts of an area or room: *A carpenter built a partition between the living room and dining area.* **2** [U] a division of a country or other area: *The partition of North Korea from South Korea has lasted for many decades.*
—*v.* **1** to divide a nation or other area: *Korea was partitioned in 1948.* **2** *phrasal v. sep.* **to partition s.t. off:** to divide into areas: *We partitioned off the living room from the dining room.*

part·ly /'pɑrtli/ *adv.* somewhat, in part: *He is partly right in what he says.*

part·ner /'pɑrtnər/ *n.* **1** a person who joins together with one or more people for a common purpose: *A husband and wife are partners in marriage.||My partner and I play tennis together.* **2** one of the owners of a business: *The partners in that company work hard.* **3** a per-

son with whom one dances: *His partner can really dance well.* **4 silent partner:** an inactive investor in a business
—*v.* to become a partner: *The companies partnered to make a new kind of computer.*

part·ner·ship /'pɑrtnər,ʃɪp/ *n.* **1** [U] a group of two or more partners: *Two writers formed a partnership to write textbooks.* **2** [C] a form of business with two or more owners: *A good partnership depends on the ability of the partners to work well together.*

part of speech *n.* **parts of speech** (in grammar) a class of words, such as noun, verb, adjective, or adverb, based on the way words are used in a sentence: *It is helpful to know the parts of speech to learn a new language.*

par·took /pɑr'tʊk/ *v.frml.* past tense of partake

par·tridge /'pɑrtrɪʤ/ *n.* [C;U] **-tridges** or **-tridge** a short, fat bird, often hunted for sport and food: *The dogs led the hunters to where the shot partridge had fallen.*

part-time *adj.* taking up only part of a normal workday or workweek: *She has three part-time jobs.*
—*adv.* for less than a full workday or workweek: *While in school, he worked part-time as a waiter.*

part·way /'pɑrt,weɪ/ *adv.* partly, somewhere between: *He had reached partway between work and home when the storm hit.*

par·ty /'pɑrti/ *n.* **-ties 1** a social event to which people come to talk, drink, eat, and have fun: *We have a party at our house on New Year's Eve.* **2** a political group with a set of beliefs for the public good: *Their party wants to raise taxes.* **3** a person or group that takes part in a legal, business, or social event: *Each party in the deal had its own goals and interests.||She went to the opera with another party, not her husband.* **4** a group of people who do s.t. together: *They formed a party to go out to dinner.* **5 a search party:** a group that looks for s.o. who is lost or missing: *The search party went to look for the missing hikers.*
—*v.* **-tied, -tying, -ties** to participate in a social party: *Starting Saturday evening, we partied until four o'clock in the morning.*

party animal *n.infrml. fig.* a person who loves to attend parties: *He's a party animal who parties all weekend.*

party-poop·er /'pɑrti,pupər/ *n.infrml. fig.* a person who spoils the fun of others by refusing to take part in it: *They called her a partypooper because she decided to stay home for the weekend.*

pass /pæs/ *v.* **passes 1** to go forward or move along in a steady movement: *Many boats passed us while we stood on the riverbank.* **2** to move toward or catch up to s.t. and then continue to go beyond it: *He drove faster in order to pass the truck in front of him on the

highway. **3** to go or move through, by, over, or under s.t.: *She passed through the gate on the way to catch her train.||I always look in the windows when I pass that store.* **4** to succeed at or meet the standards of a test: *He passed the test at school.* **5** to give official approval to s.o. or s.t.: *Congress passed a law that will raise taxes.||The teacher passed all the students to the next grade.* **6** to move s.t. from one place to another or give it to s.o.: *She asked me to pass her the dish of fruit.||I passed copies of the book to everyone in the room.* **7** (in sports) to throw or kick a ball from one player to another: *The team spent many hours learning to pass well.* **8** to change from one condition to another: *The season passed slowly from winter to spring.* **9** to keep busy or fill the time with s.t. to do: *While waiting for the plane, they passed the time playing games with the children.* **10** to go away after a while, (*syn.*) to cease: *He had a terrible stomachache, but he knew the pain would pass.* **11 to bring to pass:** to cause to happen: *He thought we could never bring to pass such a big event as a rock concert, but we did!* **12 to come to pass:** to happen: *I fear it will come to pass that the poor will always go hungry.* **13** *phrasal v. sep.* **to pass s.t. along** or **down:** to give s.t., esp. as an inheritance: *My grandmother passed along her engagement ring to me.||She passed it along.* **14** *phrasal v. insep.* **to pass away** or **on:** to die: *Her father passed away just last week.* **15** *phrasal v. insep.* **to pass for s.o. or s.t.:** to look like, seem to be: *The teenage girl was tall enough to pass for an adult.* **16 to pass judgment:** to give an opinion: *He did not want to pass judgment on what was right in the conflict between his friends.* **17** *phrasal v.* **to pass out:** to lose mental awareness, as from fear, fatigue, or too much alcohol: *He had too many drinks at the party and passed out on the couch.* **18** *phrasal v. sep.* **to pass s.o. or s.t. off:** to present s.o. or s.t. as that which they are not: *She passed off her ring as a real diamond.||She passed it off as real.* **19 to pass s.o. or s.t. over:** to ignore: *She made a big mistake, but he passed over that.||He passed it over.* **20** *phrasal v. sep.* **to pass s.t. up:** to miss s.t., let s.t. go: *We were sorry we passed up their invitation to dinner.||We passed it up.*
—*n.* **passes 1** the act of moving by or through s.t.: *The boy took* (or) *made a pass by the playground to see if any of his friends were there.||They made a pass through town late at night.* **2** an attempt or try at doing s.t.: *She made a pass at writing the report.* **3** a gap or break in a mountain range that allows travel from one side to another: *The hikers walked over the mountain pass into the valley.* **4** a written or printed notice that gives one the right to enter some place: *He showed his pass*

to the guard, who let him enter the building.||She gave us a free pass to see the new movie. **5** a result on a test that allows you to do s.t.: *I earned a pass on my driver's test and was allowed to get my license.* **6** (in sports) the act of passing a ball from one player to another: *He made a good pass to help score the goal.* **7 to make a pass at s.o.:** to make a bold attempt to attract s.o.'s sexual interest: *She made a pass at him during the office party.*

pass·a·ble /ˈpæsəbəl/ *adj.* **1** just satisfactory, acceptable: *His work at school is passable, but not outstanding.* **2** capable of being crossed: *Despite heavy snowfalls, the road over the mountain is still passable.*

pas·sage /ˈpæsɪdʒ/ *n.* **1** [C] a narrow opening or way between two places: *He walked through the passage to the garden.* **2** [U] the act of moving from one place to another: *The constant passage of big trucks made the street noisy.* **3** [C] **a.** travel onboard a ship or airplane: *We made reservations for passage from New York to London.* **b.** space and provisions for such travel **c.** the fare for such travel **4** [C] a brief section of writing or music: *The priest read a passage from the Bible.* **5** [U] the flow, continuation, usu. of time

pas·sage·way /ˈpæsɪdʒˌweɪ/ *n.* a hallway, a walkway inside a ship or between buildings: *The narrow passageway between the two buildings is used as a shortcut.*

pass·book /ˈpæsˌbʊk/ *n.* a small book in which deposits to and withdrawals from a savings account are recorded: *She handed her passbook to the bank teller along with her deposit.*

pas·sé /pæˈseɪ/ *adj.frml.* old-fashioned, outmoded: *This season's fashions will be passé in a few months.*

pas·sen·ger /ˈpæsəndʒər/ *n.* a person (other than the driver) who rides in a bus, boat, car, taxi, etc. esp. one not steering it: *The bus that crashed was carrying 20 passengers.*

pass·er·by /ˌpæsərˈbaɪ/ *n.* **passers-by** a person who passes by: *The passers-by took no notice of the lovers who were kissing.*

pass·ing /ˈpæsɪŋ/ *n.* [U] **1** a movement that goes by, along, or through; flow: *The passing of time goes slowly in the hospital.* **2** death: *The old man's passing saddened his family.* **3 in passing:** said in the course of saying s.t. else: *While talking to his mother, he said in passing that he was feeling ill.*
—*adj.* **1** brief, short-lived: *Wearing that type of silly hat is just a passing fad.* **2 passing grade:** success in an examination or course: *I received a passing grade in my math course.*

pas·sion /ˈpæʃən/ *n.* [C;U] **1** a strong, overpowering feeling, such as love, anger, or hatred: *He felt such a passion that he forgot where he was.||She spoke with passion about*

P

the love of freedom. **2** strong devotion to some activity: *She has a passion for painting.* **3** **Passion:** (in Christianity) the suffering and death of Jesus: *Christians honor the Passion at Easter.*

pas·sion·ate /'pæʃənɪt/ *adj.* about feeling or expressing passion: *She made a passionate speech in favor of the peace plan.*

pas·sive /'pæsɪv/ *adj.* **1** accepting without resistance, (*syn.*) submissive: *She always had a passive response to her husband's anger.* **2** existing without active expression or display: *He took a passive interest in his father's business.* **3** unwilling to take action, easily influenced by others: *He took a passive attitude toward his job and just did what he was told.* **4** (in grammar) relating to or being a verb form or sentence in which the subject is affected by, rather than the performer of, the action, as in "He was hit by a car," or "The proposal was accepted." *-adv.* **passively;** *-n.* [U] **passivity** /pæ'sɪvəti/.

passive resistance *n.* [U] a form of nonviolent protest against an official policy, usu. by obstructing normal activities or special events: *Protesters sat on the road in passive resistance to the army trucks that were trying to pass.*

pass·key /'pæs,ki/ *n.* **-keys** a key that opens all doors in a given place, such as a hotel: *Maids have passkeys so they can clean guests' rooms.*

Pass·o·ver /'pæs,ouvər/ *n.* [U] a Jewish holiday that celebrates the Jews' release from captivity in Egypt and return to their homeland: *She always goes home to celebrate Passover with her parents.*

pass·port /'pæs,pɔrt/ *n.* a booklet issued by a government to a citizen as proof of nationality and permission to leave and reenter the country: *Before leaving on vacation, I had to have my passport renewed.*

pass·word /'pæs,wɜrd/ *n.* a secret word or phrase used to gain access to a guarded place or a protected system: *I forgot my password, so I couldn't operate the computer.*

past /pæst/ *n.* [C; usu.*sing.*] **1** the time gone by, before the present: *In the past, he wrote with a pen; now he uses a computer.* **2** history: *When she moved to America, she made an effort to study its past.* **3** s.o.'s personal history as evidence of his or her character: *Before we hire him, we must learn about his past.*
—*adj.* **1** gone by in time: *In the past century, many things have changed.*||*It is 10:10 A.M.; that is, 10 past 10 in the morning.* **2** having just finished or ended: *Now that the danger is past, we can relax.*||*In the past few days I've been very busy.* **3** former, earlier: *His past wife lives in California.*
—*adv.* so as to go by or beyond: *He drove past at a fast speed.*

—*prep.* **1** later than: *It is past midnight now.* **2** beyond in distance: *We have driven past the store we want to visit.*

pas·ta /'pɑstə/ *n.* [U] **1** a general term for food made of flour, eggs, and water, formed in many shapes and cooked in boiling water: *Athletes often eat pasta because it is a good source of quick energy.* **2** a dish of food made from pasta: *My favorite pasta is lasagne.* See: spaghetti, USAGE NOTE.

paste /peɪst/ *n.* **1** [U] a thin, moist substance used to stick pieces of paper together or to other things, glue: *She used paste to put pictures in her notebook.* **2** a soft, smooth substance made of liquid and powder mixed so as to be easily spread, formed, or poured: *He made a paste for pasta from flour, eggs, and water.*
—*v.* **pasted, pasting, pastes** to stick things together with paste: *A child pasted her drawings onto a large sheet of paper.*

pas·tel /pæ'stɛl/ *n.* **1** [U] a paste made of colored powder **2** [C] an artist's crayon made of such a dried paste: *That artist works with pastels to achieve a soft style.* **3** [C] a work of art done with pastels: *She creates light, airy pastels.* **4** a light, soft color: *The room was decorated in lavender, pink, and other pastels.*
—*adj.* light and soft in color: *She works in pastel shades in her drawings.*

pas·teur·i·za·tion /,pæstʃərə'zeɪʃən/ *n.* [U] the process of heating foods, such as milk, to kill harmful bacteria: *Pasteurization changes the taste of foods, but it prevents diseases.* *-v.* **pasteurize** /'pæstʃə,raɪz/.

pas·time /'pæs,taɪm/ *n.* a pleasurable activity, hobby: *His favorite pastimes are playing golf by day and watching TV by night.*

pas·tor /'pæstər/ *n.v.* a minister in charge of a church or parish: *She is the <n.> pastor at St. John's Episcopal Church.*

pas·to·ral /'pæstərəl/ *adj.* **1** of or related to a simple, quiet country life: *They lived a pastoral life in the mountains.* **2** related to a pastor's duties toward the church and its members: *A large part of his pastoral work was visiting the poor, the sick, and the elderly.*

past participle *n.* a form of a verb indicating past action and used to form perfect tenses and the passive or as an adjective: *The verb "seen" in "I have already seen that movie" is a past participle.*||*The "fried" in "fried eggs" is a past participle used as an adjective.*

pas·tra·mi /pə'strɑmi/ *n.* [U] a highly seasoned, smoked cut of beef: *I had a hot pastrami sandwich on rye bread with mustard.*

pas·try /'peɪstri/ *n.* **-tries** **1** [U] a rich dough shaped into an open or closed shell to contain sweet foods, such as fruit pies, and savory foods, such as chicken, cheese, or cream fillings: *She rolled out the pastry to make apple* *pie.* **2** [C] a small, sweet cake baked from pastry dough: *We had cream-filled pastries for dessert.*

past tense *n.* a verb form used to express an action or a state in the past: *The past tense of "to go" is "went," as in, "Yesterday I went to class in the evening."*

pas·ture /'pæstʃər/ *n.* **1** [C;U] a field or other large open area where livestock such as sheep and cattle feed on the grass: *We keep our cows in the pasture behind the barn.* **2** *infrml.* **to put s.o. out to pasture:** to retire s.o.: *When he reached 65, his company put him out to pasture.*
—*v.* **-tured, -turing, -tures** to put animals in a pasture: *In summer, farmers pasture their sheep up in the hillsides.*

past·y /'peɪsti/ *adj.* **-ier, -iest 1** having a thick, moist consistency: *Pie dough is pasty in texture.* **2** having a sick, pale look: *During her illness, she developed a pasty complexion.*

pat /pæt/ *n.* **1** a soft, light touch: *The mother gave her son a pat on the head.* **2** a flat portion of s.t.: *He spread a pat of butter on his bread.* **3 a pat on the back:** an expression of encouragement or praise: *The teacher gave me a pat on the back for getting an "A" on the test.*
—*v.* **patted, patting, pats 1** to tap with a soft, light touch: *She patted the laundry after she folded it.* **2** to caress, pet: *The boy patted his dog on its head.*

patch /pætʃ/ *n.* **patches 1** a piece of material used to cover a hole or a weak spot: *She glued a patch over the hole in her bicycle tire.* **2** a small piece of land: *We have a vegetable patch behind our house.* **3** a small area or piece of s.t. that stands out from the rest: *That patch of road is very rough.* **4 bad patch:** a difficult period of time: *With no job and a bad back, he is going through a bad patch now.* -*adj.* **patchy.**
—*v.* **patches 1** to cover with a patch: *My favorite old jacket was torn, so I patched it.* **2 to patch s.t. up:** to mend a relationship or settle one's differences with s.o.: *He had a quarrel with his girlfriend and has gone to see her to patch things up.*

patch·work /'pætʃ,wɜrk/ *n.* [U] **1** s.t. sewn together from many pieces differing in color, size, pattern, and texture: *The blanket was a patchwork made from many older blankets.* **2** s.t. that appears to be made of many odd things: *Her book was a patchwork of old stories and sayings pieced together. See:* quilt.

USAGE NOTE: *Patchwork quilts* are a traditional American craft. Small pieces of cloth are sewn together to make beautiful patterns. In the past, patchwork quilts were popular because people could reuse old clothing to make something useful. Today, handmade patchwork quilts are very expensive.

pâ·té /pɑ'teɪ, pæ-/ *n.* [C;U] a paste or spread made of finely ground meat or fish: *I ate some duck liver pâté on crackers before dinner.*

pate /peɪt/ *n.* the head, esp. the top: *That man has a bald pate.*

pat·ent /'pætnt/ *n.* the exclusive right given by a government to make, use, and sell an invention for a limited number of years: *He wanted a patent for his invention so no one else could copy it.*
—*v.* to obtain a patent: *He patented his invention to protect his rights.*
—*adj.* clear and easy to see, obvious: *She was a patent fool to fall in love with him.* -*adv.* **patently.**

pat·ent leather /'pætnt, 'pætn/ *n.* [U] leather with a shiny, black finish: *She wears patent leather shoes to work.*

pa·ter·nal /pə'tɜrnəl/ *adj.* **1** of or from a father: *His paternal duty is to protect his children from harm.* **2** related through a father: *My father's father is my paternal grandfather.*

pa·ter·nal·ism /pə'tɜrnə,lɪzəm/ *n.* [U] the practice of treating a group, business, or country in the way a father treats his children: *The company president's paternalism made some of his employees happy and some of them angry.* -*adj.* **paternalistic** /pə,tɜrnə'lɪstɪk/.

pa·ter·ni·ty /pə'tɜrnəti/ *n.* [U] **1** the state of being a father, fatherhood: *When my first child was born, my paternity made me proud.* **2** origin or descent from a father: *The child was found after the war, and her paternity was unknown.*

paternity suit *n.* a lawsuit started by a woman to establish that a certain man is the father of her child: *He denied that he was the child's father, so she filed a paternity suit against him.*

path /pæθ/ *n.* **paths** /pæðz, pæθs/ **1** a narrow way or trail for walking or cycling, either built or made by repeated use: *Paths made by animals go through the woods.* **2** a way of doing s.t., or of living: *She is following the path of a deeply religious person.* **3** the direction of a movement: *He stood in the path of a moving truck.* **4 off the beaten path:** in an unusual place or manner: *They vacation in places that are off the beaten path, deep in the mountains.* **5 to make a path for:** to move quickly to do s.t.: *After work, he made a path for the hotel to meet his friend.*

pa·thet·ic /pə'θɛtɪk/ *adj.* **1** full of or causing feelings of pity or compassion, (*syn.*) emotional: *The final scene in the movie was very pathetic.* **2** not worthy of respect, worthless: *The lawyer made a pathetic effort to help his client.* -*adv.* **pathetically.**

P

path·o·gen /ˈpæθədʒən/ n. a tiny organism that causes disease, a germ: *Pathogens will grow in unclean places.* -adj. **pathogenic** /ˌpæθəˈdʒɛnɪk/.

path·o·log·i·cal /ˌpæθəˈlɑdʒɪkəl/ adj. **1** related to pathology **2** causing or caused by a disease, sick: *They believed that his odd behavior was pathological.*

pa·thol·o·gist /pəˈθɑlədʒɪst, pæ-/ n. a specialist in the study of disease

pa·thol·o·gy /pəˈθɑlədʒi, pæ-/ n. [U] **1** the science of disease: *Medical students take a basic course in pathology.* **2** a state, condition, or pattern of illness: *The doctors could not determine the cause of her pathology.*

pa·thos /ˈpeɪˌθɑs, -ˌθoʊs, -ˌθɔs/ n.frml. a quality in life or art that brings out feelings of tenderness, sympathy, or sorrow: *That music is full of pathos.*

path·way /ˈpæθˌweɪ/ n. a path: *A pathway leads through the woods to a cabin.*

pa·tience /ˈpeɪʃəns/ n. [U] the ability to accept discomfort, pain, or troubles while waiting calmly for s.t.: *She waited with patience until her baby stopped crying.*

pa·tient /ˈpeɪʃənt/ adj. having or showing patience, calm, or being undisturbed: *His train was late, but he was patient.* -adv. **patiently.**
—n. a person cared for or treated by a doctor: *The doctor visited her patients in the hospital.*

pat·i·o /ˈpætiˌoʊ/ n. **-os** an open area next to a house paved with slate, cement, or brick and used for outdoor eating, sitting, etc. in good weather: *We barbecue hamburgers on our patio in summer.*

pa·tois /ˈpæˌtwɑ, pæˈtwɑ/ n. [U] **patois** /ˈpæˌtwɑz, pæˈtwɑz/ (French for) a local or regional dialect: *In Haiti, people speak a French patois.*

pa·tri·arch /ˈpeɪtriˌɑrk/ n. **1** the male head of a family, tribe, or kingdom **2** a much respected old man: *The patriarch ruled his country as if it were his family.*

pa·tri·arch·y /ˈpeɪtriˌɑrki/ n. [C;U] **-ies** a social system in which men hold the power to rule or govern: *Most ancient societies were patriarchies.* -adj. **patriarchal** /ˌpeɪtriˈɑrkəl/. See: matriarchy.

pa·tri·cian /pəˈtrɪʃən/ n. old usage a person of high social rank, usu. by birth, (syn.) an aristocrat: *That club is very exclusive and only takes patricians as members.*
—adj. elegant or noble in appearance, behavior, or circumstances: *The elderly lady has very patrician tastes.*

pat·ri·cide /ˈpætrəˌsaɪd/ n. **1** the act of killing one's father: *The boy claimed that he committed patricide to defend himself against his father's cruelty.* **2** s.o. who kills his or her father

pat·ri·mo·ny /ˈpætrəˌmoʊni/ n. [C] **-nies** money or property received from one's father or ancestors, (syn.) an inheritance: *She used her patrimony to buy a farm.* -adj. **patrimonial** /ˌpætrəˈmoʊniəl/.

pa·tri·ot /ˈpeɪtriət, -ˌɑt/ n. a person who is proud of his or her country and eager to defend it: *The patriots formed an army to fight the invading army.*

patriotic /ˌpeɪtriˈɑtɪk/ adj. loyal to and proud of one's country: *He is very patriotic and flies the flag on Independence Day.* -adv. **patriotically.**

pa·tri·ot·ism /ˈpeɪtriəˌtɪzəm/ n. [U] a feeling of love, loyalty, and support for one's country, esp. in defense against its enemies: *Patriotism caused him to join the army and fight for his country.*

pa·trol /pəˈtroʊl/ v. **-trolled, -trolling, -trols** to make regular trips around an area or along a boundary line to guard against trouble or crime: *A policeman patrols the park to prevent robberies.*
—n. **1** [U] the act of patrolling: *Police went on patrol, looking for illegal immigrants.* **2** [C] a person or a group of people on patrol: *The patrol became lost in the snowstorm.*

pa·tron /ˈpeɪtrən/ n. **1** a wealthy or powerful person who encourages and supports the activity of others (an artist, politician, charity, or institution), esp. by giving money: *She is a patron of the arts and gives money to support the symphony.* **2** frml. a regular customer: *Patrons of the store come from all over town.*

pa·tron·age /ˈpeɪtrənɪdʒ, ˈpæ-/ n. [U] **1** the favor and support given by a patron: *The government's patronage was important to the artist's career.* **2** the power to award government jobs: *After he won the election, he used his patronage to reward his friends and supporters.* **3** the business that comes from customers: *The restaurant owner was grateful for our patronage.*

pa·tron·ize /ˈpeɪtrəˌnaɪz, ˈpæ-/ v. **-ized, -izing, -izes 1** to act in a superior manner toward s.o., (syn.) to be condescending: *He patronizes his students by telling them that they know nothing.* **2** frml. to be a customer of: *She patronizes only the finest stores.* -adj. **patronizing.**

pat·sy /ˈpætsi/ n. slang **-sies** a person who is easily cheated, deceived, and blamed, (syn.) a dupe: *The older boys always made him the patsy because he was young and naive.*

pat·ter /ˈpætər/ n. **1** the sound of a quick but light series of taps or steps on a hard surface: *the patter of rain on the street‖the patter of little feet* **2** fast talk: *The comedian's patter was very funny.*
—v. **1** to make a pattering sound: *His feet patter as they tap against the floor.* **2** to move

with quick, light steps: *She pattered about the kitchen.*

pat·tern /'pætərn/ *n.* **1** an example or model to be followed: *Her writing shows a pattern of excellence.* **2** a form or guide to follow when making s.t.: *She made the dress herself from a pattern.* **3** a design of regular shapes and lines: *The flower pattern in that dress is very pretty.* **4** a repeated set of events, characteristics, or features: *There is a pattern to his behavior, in that he grows quiet when he's sad.*
—*v.* to make by following a pattern: *She patterned her wedding dress after her mother's.||He patterns himself after his father, who is athletic and very serious.*

pat·ty /'pæti/ *n.* **-ties** a small, flat cake of ground meat, fish, etc.: *Hamburger patties are cooking on the grill.*

pau·ci·ty /'pɔsəti/ *n.frml.* [U] a small number or amount of s.t.: *The paucity of their savings kept them from returning to their homeland.*

paunch /pɔntʃ/ *n.* **paunches** a fat stomach, big belly, (*syn.*) pot belly: *He drinks lots of beer and has a big paunch. -adj.* **paunchy.**

pau·per /'pɔpər/ *n.frml.* a very poor person who must live on charity: *He ran out of money and died a pauper. -v.* **pauperize.**

pause /pɔz/ *n.* a short break or moment of rest in the midst of an action or movement: *She took a brief pause in her speech while she drank some water.*
—*v.* **paused, pausing, pauses** to stop doing s.t. for a brief moment of time: *We paused to stop and look at the scenery for a few minutes.*

pave /peɪv/ *v.* **paved, paving, paves** **1** to cover over a road, a path, or other area with tar, cement, etc., to make a hard, flat surface: *They paved the field with cement to make a parking lot.* **2 to pave the way:** to make s.t. easier to do, to make progress: *Early settlers paved the way for those who arrived later.*

pave·ment /'peɪvmənt/ *n.* [U] **1** the covering of cement, tar, etc., on a sidewalk or roadway: *The pavement on the road is black tar.* **2** *infrml.* **to pound the pavement:** to walk for hours in search of business, work, etc.: *He is a new salesman, and he really pounds the pavement looking for new customers.*

pa·vil·ion /pə'vɪlyən/ *n.* **1** a large, fancy tent: *The workers put up a pavilion for the wedding party.* **2** a light, tent-like, open building in a garden or park, used for festivals or fairs: *At night in the summer, a band played in the pavilion.* **3** a fancy part of a building that juts out: *People stood on the pavilion and watched the parade below.*

pav·ing /'peɪvɪŋ/ *n.* [U] the material (stone, cement, asphalt, etc.) used to pave a surface: *They stopped work because they ran out of paving.*

paw /pɔ/ *n.* **1** the foot of an animal: *The dog licked its paws.* **2** *infrml.fig.* the human hand: *The woman told the man to keep his paws off her.*
—*v.* **1** to touch, scrape, or strike with a paw: *The lion pawed at its food.* **2** *infrml.fig.* to feel or touch in a rude or clumsy manner, esp. sexually: *She pushed him away because he was pawing at her.*

pawn /pɔn/ *n.* **1** in the game of chess, the least valuable piece **2** a person used by others to serve their own purposes: *The poor people were just pawns in the politicians' fight for power.*
—*v.* to deposit personal valuables, such as watches and rings, with a pawnbroker in exchange for a loan: *She pawned her diamond ring for a week and then got it back when she paid off the loan.*

pawn·bro·ker /'pɔn,broukər/ *n.* a person who makes loans with interest against the value of personal valuables: *The pawnbroker offered me 50 dollars for my watch.*

pawn·shop /'pɔn,ʃɑp/ *n.* the place of business of a pawnbroker: *I went to the pawnshop to pawn my watch.*

pay /peɪ/ *v.* **paid** /peɪd/, **paying, pays** **1** to give money to s.o. in return for regular work: *That company pays its employees every two weeks.* **2** to settle a bill, debt, or loan by giving what is owed: *She paid the doctor's bill by writing a check.* **3** to be worthwhile, to one's advantage: *It pays to brush your teeth to prevent cavities.* **4 to pay attention:** to observe and listen closely: *The teacher told the students to pay attention to her in class.* **5 to pay a compliment:** to say nice things about s.o. or s.t.: *I want to pay my compliments to you on your new home.* **6 to pay a visit:** to go to see and talk with s.o.: *When I went to my homeland, I paid a visit to my old friend.* **7** *phrasal v. insep.* **to pay for (s.t.):** to suffer from the results of one's actions: *I walked five miles (8 km) on Sunday and am paying for it now; my legs hurt!* **8 to pay one's dues: a.** to pay for membership in a club or union **b.** *fig.* to earn one's place in an organization through long and patient service: *He paid his dues as a traveling salesman, and now he has a good office job.* **9 to pay one's way:** to support oneself, pay for food, rent, clothing, etc.: *She has a good job and pays her own way in life.* **10 to pay s.o.:** to be good/profitable for s.o. to do s.t.: *That company has job openings, so it would pay you to look for one there.* **11** *phrasal v. sep.* **to pay s.o. or s.t. back: a. s.o.** to return an insult or injury: *He yelled at her, and she paid him back by not speaking to him for a week.* **b. s.t.** to repay a loan, return money: *I paid back the $10 that my friend loaned to me.* **12** *phrasal v. sep.* **to pay s.o or**

s.t. off: a. s.o. to bribe: *The criminals paid off the judge and got away free.*||*They paid her off.* **b.** s.t. to finish paying for s.t.: *I finally paid off the 30-year mortgage on my house.*||*I paid it off.* **c.** to produce good results: *Her hard work paid off when she got a big raise.* **13** phrasal v. sep. **to pay s.t. down: a.** to reduce the amount of a debt: *I am paying down my car loan each month.*||*I am paying it down.* **b.** to make a first partial payment: *I paid some money down on a new TV and will pay off the rest monthly.* **14** infrml. **to pay the piper:** to pay for doing s.t. that you thought you could avoid paying for: *She cheated on her taxes for years, but she was caught; now it's time to pay the piper by going to jail.* **15** infrml. **to pay through the nose:** to pay a very high price for s.t.: *He only shops at fancy stores, and so ends up paying through the nose.* **16** phrasal v. **to pay up:** to pay money that is due: *He was three months overdue in paying the rent, and the landlord told him to pay up.*
—*n.* [U] **1** money paid in return for work done, (syns.) wages, salary: *She refused to take the job because the pay was too low.*

pay·a·ble /'peɪəbəl/ *adj.* that is to be paid (by a certain date or to a certain party): *The loan is payable on the first of each month.*

pay·back /'peɪ,bæk/ *n.* the time period or amount of money required to get back one's investment in a business or project: *Before he bought the business, he wanted to know how long payback would take.*

pay·check /'peɪ,tʃɛk/ *n.* **1** a salary or wage check: *The bookkeeper handed me my paycheck.* **2** a symbol for making a living, one's source of income: *I don't want to risk my paycheck by being late or doing bad work.*

pay·day /'peɪ,deɪ/ *n.* the regular day when one is paid one's wage or salary: *Our payday is on the Thursday of every second week.*

pay dirt *n.* [U] **1** earth containing minerals or metals worth mining **2** *fig.* a discovery or achievement that promises to be very profitable: *He hit pay dirt when he won the big race.*

pay·ee /peɪ'i/ *n.* the person or business to whom money is to be paid: *My name is typed on the check as the payee.*

pay·er /'peɪər/ *n.* the person or business that pays money to s.o.: *You are the payer of the checks you sign.*

pay·load /'peɪ,loʊd/ *n.* in transportation, the cargo carried by a ship, truck, etc., for which the carrier is paid: *Bigger trucks can carry bigger payloads.*

pay·ment /'peɪmənt/ *n.* **1** [U] the act of paying: *I make a payment on my car loan each month.* **2** [C] the money paid: *The payment amounts to $300.*

pay·off /'peɪ,ɔf/ *n.* **1** the reward or profit from some event or business: *The new business promised a big payoff.* **2** *slang* a bribe, made esp. to avoid harmful acts: *The builder made payoffs to the criminals to avoid strikes on his construction project.*

pay·out /'peɪ,aʊt/ *n.* an amount paid as a return on an investment, (syn.) a dividend: *The payout on that stock is $5.00 per share.*

pay phone *n.* a public telephone operated by inserting coins or credit cards: *I called my friend from a pay phone in the hotel lobby.*

pay phone

pay·roll /'peɪ,roʊl/ *n.* **1** [C] a list of employees to be paid and the amounts due to each: *We hired him and put him on the payroll.* **2** [C; usu. sing.] the total amount paid to employees: *That company has a payroll of one million dollars.*

pay telephone *n. See:* pay phone.

pay television *n.* a system for delivering television programs in which viewers select and pay for programs individually: *Most hotels offer pay television in their guestrooms.*

pay toilet *n.* a coin-operated toilet: *The city government put some pay toilets in major tourist areas.*

pay-TV *n.infrml. See:* pay television, cable TV.

PC /,pi'si/ *n.* **PCs** or **PC's** *abbr.for* personal computer: *I have a PC at home and one at the office. See:* desktop, laptop.

pea /pi/ *n.* **1** a small, round, green seed that grows in long pods and is eaten as a vegetable **2** the creeping and climbing plant on which peas grow: *We plant peas in early spring.* **3 as like as** (or) **like two peas in a pod: a.** exactly alike: *Those twins are as like as two peas in a pod.* **b.** close together, friendly: *Those old friends are like two peas in a pod.*

peace /pis/ *n.* [U] **1** a condition or time without war: *After the last war, the country returned to peace.* **2** a state of harmony and cooperation between peoples or nations: *The neighboring countries prefer to live in peace.* **3** a condition of quiet or stillness: *We enjoyed the peace in the late evening.* **4 peace of mind:** a serenity of mind, freedom from worry, or guilt: *After years of struggle, she finally found peace of mind in a small village in France.* **5 to keep the peace:** to prevent the outbreak of war or rebellion: *The United Nations sent troops to that country to keep the peace among warring tribes.* **6 to make peace:** to end argument or war: *Two countries in the Middle East made peace with each other.*||*After years of quarreling, the two brothers made peace with each other.*

peace·a·ble /'pisəbəl/ *adj.* preferring peace, not violent or hostile: *She had a peaceable at-*

titude and made people feel comfortable.

peace·a·bly /'pisəbli/ *adv.* calmly or quietly, without protest or conflict: *A criminal went peaceably with the police after they arrested him.*

Peace Corps *n.* [U] an agency of the US government that provides skilled volunteers to assist economic development in underdeveloped countries

USAGE NOTE: The *Peace Corps* was started in 1961. Volunteers, who must be 18 years old and US citizens, sign up for two years of service. Some Peace Corps volunteers are involved in construction and agriculture, while others teach English. The US government gives volunteers an allowance to live on in the host country and provides language training.

peace·ful /'pisfəl/ *adj.* calm, quiet, without troubles: *My life in a little cottage by a pond was peaceful. -adv.* **peacefully; -n. peacefulness.**

peace·keeping /'pis,kipɪŋ/ *n.adj.* [U] maintenance of peace through the use of military force to prevent conflict: <*adj.*> *Peacekeeping forces are often caught between armies at war.*

peace·mak·er /'pis,meɪkər/ *n.* a person or country that brings about peace between warring groups: *The USA played the role of peacemaker between two warring countries.*

peace offering *n.* an action showing a wish to make peace: *The army returned some of its prisoners as a peace offering.*

peace officer *n.* a civil officer responsible for keeping peace in a community: *The peace officer stopped a fight between angry neighbors.*

peace pipe *n. old usage* a pipe smoked by Native Americans as a sign of making peace with enemies

peace·time /'pis,taɪm/ *n.* [U] a period of time without war: *Peacetime lasted between 1917 and 1939, when World War II started.*

peach /pitʃ/ *n.* **peaches 1** [C] a juicy, round, yellowish pink color fruit with a fuzzy skin and a large, rough seed: *Peaches grow well in hot weather.* **2** [U] *infrml.fig.* a wonderful person, esp. a very likable woman: *She is so cheerful and kind; she's a real peach!* **3** [C] *infrml.* **peaches and cream:** without trouble or evil: *She has had such an easy childhood that she thinks life will always be peaches and cream.*

peach·y /'pitʃi/ *adj.* **-ier, -iest 1** having the softness or light orange color or juicy sweet taste of a peach: *She has a beautiful peachy complexion.* **2** *infrml.fig.* excellent, wonderful: *I think it's just peachy that I got a big raise.*

pea coat *n. See:* pea jacket.

pea·cock /'pi,kɑk/ *n.* **1** a large male bird with a large, showy, blue-green set of tail feathers **2 proud as a peacock:** very pleased with oneself: *When he won the awards, he was as proud as a peacock.*

peacock

pea jacket *n.* a heavy woolen jacket with two rows of buttons in the front

peak /pik/ *n.* **1** the pointed top of a mountain: *The peak of the mountain is covered with snow.* **2** the pointed end of s.t., such as the top of a roof: *Two birds were sitting on the peak of the barn.* **3** the point of greatest activity, strength, or success: *That singer is now at the peak of her career.* **4** the front part of a cap that extends over the eyes
—*v.* to reach the highest point: *The price of gas has peaked and is now going down.*
—*adj.* the highest level: *That racehorse is in peak condition.*

peak·ed /'pikɪd/ *adj.* pale and thin due to bad health: *He was looking peaked, so they called a doctor.*

peal /pil/ *n.* **1** the sound of bells ringing loudly: *On Sunday morning, the peal of church bells was heard for miles.* **2** a loud series of rolling sounds: *Peals of laughter came from the audience.*
—*v.* to sound or ring long and loudly: *Church bells pealed all morning long.*

pea·nut /'pi,nət/ *n.* **1** a small, light-brown nut about the size of a pea, that grows underground and is a popular snack food: *She always eats peanuts at baseball games.* **2** *pl.* **peanuts:** *infrml.fig.* very little money: *He works for peanuts as a clerk in a grocery store.*

peanut brittle *n.* [U] a hard, flat candy made with peanuts

peanut butter *n.* [U] a soft, creamy food made from crushed peanuts: *Sandwiches made with peanut butter are very popular for lunch.*

USAGE NOTE: *Peanut butter* was invented by African-American scientist George Washington Carver in the early 1900s. Today about one half of the peanuts in the USA are made into peanut butter. Peanut butter and jelly sandwiches are a favorite food of American children.

peanut oil *n.* [U] oil made from crushed peanuts, used for cooking

pear /pɛr/ *n.* a sweet, juicy fruit with a green, yellow, or brownish skin that is narrow at the top and wide at the bottom: *Bartlett pears are very popular and turn bright yellow when ripe.*

P

pearl /pɜrl/ *n.* **1** [C] a smooth, white, round object formed naturally within oysters and valued as a jewel: *She wears earrings made of pearls.* **2** [U] a very light bluish-gray color

pearl·y /'pɜrli/ *adj.* having a smooth, white, shiny appearance, similar to pearls: *His teeth are pearly white.*

peas·ant /'pɛzənt/ *n.* **1** a farmer of low social rank who lives and works on a small piece of land: *The peasant worked from sunrise to sunset.* **2** *pej.* a person with little education and poor manners: *She called him a peasant because of his behavior at the dinner table.*
—*adj.* of or like a peasant: *Peasant food is often simple, but delicious.*

peas·ant·ry /'pɛzəntri/ *n.pl. used with a sing. or pl.v.* the class of peasants: *The peasantry were angry about the increase in land taxes.*

pea soup *n.* [U] a thick soup made from boiled dried peas: *Pea soup is my favorite dish to start a dinner.*

peat /pit/ *n.* [U] decayed plant matter found in wet land, used in gardening and as fuel: *He burns peat in his stove to keep warm in winter.*

peb·ble /'pɛbəl/ *n.* a small stone made round and smooth by the action of water: *We threw pebbles into the ocean.*

pe·can /pɪ'kɑn, -'kæn, 'pi,kæn/ *n.* a nut with a smooth, hard shell that grows on hickory trees, common in the southern states of the USA: *She uses many pecans in a pecan pie.*

pec·ca·dil·lo /,pɛkə'dɪloʊ/ *n.* **-loes** or **-los** a minor fault: *One of her peccadilloes is that she sometimes spends money too easily.*

peck (1) /pɛk/ *v.* **1** to strike or pick up s.t. with the beak: *Chickens peck at grain on the ground.* **2** to eat small bits of a meal without interest: *She was worried and only pecked at her dinner.*
—*n.* **1** a stroke or small hole made with the beak: *The bird broke the seed with a peck.* **2** *infrml.fig.* a quick, light kiss: *He gave his girlfriend a peck on the cheek.*

peck (2) *n.* formerly a measure for grain, equal to approx. nine liters: *Farmers sold wheat by the peck.*

pecking order *n. fig.* the order of importance and privilege among people in a group: *To do well in that company, you must know the pecking order.*

pec·to·ral /'pɛktərəl/ *adj.* related to the chest: *Some athletes have very large pectoral muscles.*

pe·cu·liar /pɪ'kyulyər/ *adj.* **1** odd, strange: *His peculiar behavior puzzles everyone who knows him.* **2** belonging only to one specific person, group of people, place, etc.: *Bright orange tail feathers are peculiar to that type of bird.* **3** unique, unusual, different: *Her peculiar strength is her great courage. -adv.* **peculiarly.**

pe·cu·li·ar·i·ty /pɪ,kyuli'ærəti, -,kyul'yær-/ *n.* **-ties** **1** [C;U] s.t. odd or strange: *The old house has many peculiarities.* **2** [C] odd behavior, an unusual habit, *(syn.)* an eccentricity: *One of his peculiarities is wearing an old baseball cap wherever he goes.* **3** [C] s.t. belonging only to one person, group of people, place, etc.: *That form of greeting is a peculiarity of the region.*

pe·cu·ni·ar·y /pɪ'kyuni,ɛri/ *adj.frml.* related to money: *The pecuniary rewards of the job are small.*

ped·a·gogue /'pɛdə,gɑg, -,gɔg/ *n.frml.* **1** a teacher **2** a demanding, difficult teacher: *A pedagogue is very particular about details.*

ped·a·go·gy /'pɛdə,goʊʤi, -,gɑ-/ *n.* [U] the theory and method of teaching: *The school of education teaches pedagogy. -adj.* **pedagogical** /,pɛdə'gɑʤɪkəl, -'goʊ-/.

ped·al /'pɛdl/ *n.* a lever pushed with the foot to operate a machine or tool: *He stepped on the brake pedal to stop the car.‖She worked the pedals to play the organ.*
—*v.* to move by using pedals: *He pedals his bike to work every day.*

ped·ant /'pɛdnt/ *n.* **1** a person who gives too much attention to rules and details: *The instructor was a pedant who took all the fun out of learning.* **2** a person who makes a showy display of his or her knowledge *-adj.* **pedantic** /pə'dæntɪk/; *-n.* [U] **pedantry** /'pɛdntri/.

ped·dle /'pɛdl/ *v.* **-dled, -dling, -dles** to sell small items from door to door or on the street: *He peddles watches on the street.*

ped·dler /'pɛdlər/ *n.* a person who peddles: *The peddler sold newspapers by the subway station.*

ped·es·tal /'pɛdəstəl/ *n.* **1** the short, wide base or foundation for a column of a building: *He sat on a pedestal outside the courthouse.* **2** the support on which to place a statue or other work of art to lift it up for display: *The teenagers pushed a statue off its pedestal.* **3 to put s.o. on a pedestal:** to admire s.o. greatly or too much and never see his or her faults: *He adores his wife and puts her on a pedestal.*

pe·des·tri·an /pə'dɛstriən/ *n.* any person walking on a sidewalk, across a street, or down a road: *Pedestrians crowd the sidewalks at noon.*
—*adj.* **1** related to walking: *pedestrian traffic ‖ a pedestrian crossing* **2** uninteresting, ordinary: *She is a very rich woman and she would never wear anything off-the-rack that might suggest pedestrian taste in clothing.*

pe·di·a·tri·cian /,pidiə'trɪʃən/ *n.* a doctor who treats children: *The pediatrician cured my baby's illness. See:* physician.

pe·di·at·rics /,pidi'ætrɪks/ *n.pl. used with a sing.v.* the field of medical science concerned with the care of children and their illnesses: *Her love of children led her to study pediatrics.*

ped·i·gree /'pɛdə,gri/ n. **1** [C;U] a recorded list of ancestors, esp. for an animal, (*syns.*) lineage, ancestry: *His horse has a long pedigree.* **2** [C] the quality of an animal's breeding (esp. a dog or horse), the purity of its line of descent: *My dog has a very good pedigree.*
—*adj.* or **pedigreed** /'pɛdə,grid/ recorded as having a pure line of descent from a single breed: *a pedigree poodle*

pee /pi/ v.n. *slang* [U] **peed, peeing, pees** to urinate: *He <v.> peed behind a tree.||He went outside to take a pee.*

peek /pik/ v. to look secretly at s.o. or s.t., esp. when one is not supposed to: *A student peeked at the test questions before the test started.||He peeked through the crack in the door to see who was inside.*
—*n.* a quick look: *Let's take a peek at this new video. See:* peep (**1**).

peek·a·boo /'pikə,bu/ n. a game played with a baby in which an adult hides his or her face, then suddenly shows it while saying "peekaboo!" and then hides it again
—*adj.* designed to let one see through: *She wore a peekaboo sweater over a silk blouse.*

peel /pil/ v. **1** to take the skin off a piece of fruit or vegetable: *She peeled the apples before cooking them.* **2** to strip off the outer layer of anything: *He peeled off his shirt in a hurry.* **3** to loosen, pull away, or fall from a surface: *The paint on the house was peeling.*
—*n.* [U] the skin of a fruit or vegetable: *She threw the orange peel in the garbage.*

peep (1) /pip/ n. a brief look at s.t., esp. through a hole or crack (in a wall, door, curtain, etc.) taken by s.o. who does not want to be seen: *The school principal took a peep at the class through the window. See:* peek.
—*v.* **1** to take a peep: *The mother peeped into the bedroom to see if her child was asleep.* **2** to begin to show or appear, come into view: *The sun peeped through my window at dawn.||The first flowers of spring peeped through the snow.*

peep (2) n. **1** the short, weak, high-pitched sound of a young bird or a mouse: *The peeps of baby birds wake me up in the morning.* **2** *fig.* the sound of children talking: *Sit quietly and don't make a peep.*
—*v.* to make a peep: *Little birds peep when they are hungry.*

peep·hole /'pip,hoʊl/ n. a small hole in a door or wall that allows one to look through it: *He looked through the peephole in his hotel room door to see who had knocked.*

peeping Tom /tɑm/ n. a person who secretly watches others who are not aware of being seen, esp. as they are dressing or undressing: *That peeping Tom uses binoculars to look into people's windows.*

peep·show /'pip,ʃoʊ/ n. a pornographic show with adult movies or live dancers: *To go to a peep show, you have to be over 21.*

peer /pɪr/ n. **1** a person who is one's equal in age, rank, ability, or other quality: *I want to discuss that business offer with my peers at work.* **2 to have no peer:** to be the best: *In sports, he has no peer.*
—*v.* to take a long, slow look as if to discover s.t. (an object, an answer to a question) that is not at first clear: *He peered out the window to see who was coming.*

peer·age /'pɪrɪdʒ/ n. [U] the group of nobles in a country

peer·less /'pɪrlɪs/ adj. without equal, excellent: *The singer gave a peerless performance in the opera.*

peeve /piv/ v. **peeved, peeving, peeves** to annoy, irritate s.o.: *People who chew gum and talk at the same time peeve me. See:* pet peeve.

pee·vish /'pivɪʃ/ adj. easily angered or annoyed, irritable: *He's peevish today because he is not feeling well. -adv.* **peevishly.**

pee·wee /'pi,wi/ n. a small person, esp. a little boy: *He is the peewee in the family of five boys.*
—*adj.* small, or for small people: *They gave the boy a peewee bicycle.*

peg /pɛg/ n. **1** a small rod made of metal or wood that fits in a hole and is used to hang things on, hold things together, or mark a place: *He hung his hat on a peg in the door.||The door hinge has a peg in it.* **2** a **square peg in a round hole:** s.o. or s.t. that does not fit in: *At school, she felt like a square peg in a round hole.* **3 to take s.o. down a peg:** to show that s.o. is less important than he or she thought: *He was rude to her, so she took him down a peg by criticizing his work.*
—*v.* **pegged, pegging, pegs 1** to attach or fasten using pegs: *He pegged a poster to the wall.* **2** to set a value for s.t.: *He pegged the price of his house at $200,000.* **3** *infrml.fig.* to evaluate s.o., know what they are like: *I have him pegged as a lazy fellow.*

pe·jor·a·tive /pɪ'dʒɔrətɪv, -'dʒɑr-/ adj. expressing a critical or negative judgment: *"Fag" is a pejorative word for a male homosexual; it's not used in polite conversation.*

pel·i·can /'pɛlɪkən/ n. a large bird that lives near water and stores the fish it catches in a pouch under its beak: *Pelicans dive into the ocean for fish.*

pel·let /'pɛlɪt/ n. **1** a small metal ball made to be shot from a gun: *Hunters use shotguns to shoot pellets at game birds.* **2** a small round mass (of wax, paper, food, etc.) shaped by the fingers: *The boys threw pellets of food at each other.* **3** food or medicine made into pellets: *Feed for chickens is available in pellets.*

P

pell-mell /ˌpɛl'mɛl/ *adv.frml.* in a hurried, confused way: *Schoolchildren ran down the steps pell-mell after school let out.*

pelt /pɛlt/ *v.* **1** to attack by throwing things: *Protesters pelted the police with bottles and rocks.* **2** to hit forcefully with repeated strokes: *He pelted the rug with a big stick.* **3** to come down hard and continuously: *The rain pelted against the window. -adj.* **pelting.**
—*n.* the fur and skin of an animal: *The hunters returned from the forest with beaver pelts.*

pel·vis /'pɛlvɪs/ *n.* **-vises** the area of the body between the backbone and the legs, framed by the hip bones: *A woman's pelvis is wider than a man's. -adj.* **pelvic.**

pen (1) /pɛn/ *n.* an instrument used to write or draw in ink: *She looked in her purse for a pen to sign her check.*
—*v.* **penned, penning, pens** to write with a pen: *She penned a personal letter to her lawyer.*

pen (2) *n.* a small area of land surrounded by a fence and used to keep animals in: *He built a pen for his sheep.*
—*v.* **penned, penning, pens** to enclose in a pen: *The farmer penned his sheep for the night.*

pe·nal /'pinəl/ *adj.* related to punishment: *The penal laws in that country are very cruel.*

pe·nal·ize /'pinəˌlaɪz, 'pɛ-/ *v.* **-ized, -izing, -izes** **1** to punish **2** to force penalties that seem unfair on a person or group: *The students complained that they were being penalized by the new rules.* **3** to give a penalty to a player or team for breaking a rule: *He was penalized for kicking another player.*

pen·al·ty /'pɛnəlti/ *n.* [C;U] **-ties** a punishment, such as a fine or prison term, imposed for breaking rules or laws: *She paid the penalty of a large fine for cheating on her income tax returns.*

pen·ance /'pɛnəns/ *n.* [U] **1** the punishment one must suffer or the sacrifice one must make to be forgiven for doing s.t. bad or wrong: *His father made him stay home as penance for fighting.* **2** in religion, the act of confessing and atoning for sins

pence /pɛns/ *n.pl.* of penny (British)

pen·chant /'pɛntʃənt/ *n.* a special fondness for s.t. or a habit of doing s.t.: *She has a penchant for silver jewelry.||He has a penchant for saying stupid things at the wrong time.*

pen·cil /'pɛnsəl/ *n.* a narrow, pointed instrument, usu. made of wood with a carbon center, used for writing or drawing: *He used a pencil to add up the total of his monthly bills.*
—*v.* to write, mark, or draw with a pencil: *He penciled some notes in the back of the book.*

pend·ant /'pɛndənt/ *n.* a piece of jewelry or a religious object that hangs on a necklace worn around the neck: *She wears a heart-shaped pendant that hangs on a chain around her neck.*

pend·ing /'pɛndɪŋ/ *adj.* waiting for a final action or decision: *Legislation pending in the Congress must wait until the holidays are over.*
—*prep.* until: *The legislation will be delayed pending the new session of Congress.*

pen·du·lous /'pɛndʒələs, -dyə-/ *adj.frml.* hanging down loosely and free to swing: *Pendulous vines hang in the tropical jungle.*

pen·du·lum /'pɛndʒələm, -dyə-/ *n.* a heavy weight, such as a ball, that hangs from a fixed point and swings back and forth in a regular motion, esp. one found in a clock: *The clock ticked with each swing of the pendulum.*

pen·e·trate /'pɛnəˌtreɪt/ *v.* **-trated, -trating, -trates** **1** to pass or cut a way into or through: *The child cried as the doctor's needle penetrated his skin.||Searchlights penetrated the darkness.* **2** to break or enter into with force: *The army penetrated the city's walls.* **3** to see into, understand, esp. s.t. difficult: *A spy penetrated the secrets of the defense department.* **4** to spread through s.t., (syn.) to permeate: *The smell of frying fish penetrated the hallway. -adj.* **penetrable** /'pɛnətrəbəl/.

pendulum

pen·e·trat·ing /'pɛnəˌtreɪtɪŋ/ *adj.* **1** capable of or showing great understanding, intelligent, (syns.) keen, insightful: *a penetrating mind||penetrating comments* **2** sharp, piercing: *the penetrating sound of children's voices*

pen·e·tra·tion /ˌpɛnə'treɪʃən/ *n.* [U] **1** an entry into s.t.: *He made a penetration into the forest.* **2** ability to understand: *Her penetration into the cause of the problem helped her to solve it quickly.*

pen·guin /'pɛŋgwɪn, 'pɛn-/ *n.* a large black-and-white seabird, found mainly in the Antarctic, that stands upright on short legs and has wings for swimming, not flying

pen·i·cil·lin /ˌpɛnə'sɪlɪn/ *n.* [U] a medicine that fights germs or bacteria that cause infection or diseases: *His doctor gave him a shot of penicillin to cure a sore throat.*

pe·nin·su·la /pə'nɪnsələ, -syə-/ *n.* a long, usu. narrow strip of land surrounded by water and connected to the mainland: *Florida is a peninsula.*

penguin

pe·nis /'pinɪs/ *n.* **-nises** or **-nes** /-niz/ the male sex organ, located between the legs

pen·i·tence /'pɛnətəns/ n. [U] the feeling of sorrow and regret for having done wrong: *His penitence caused her to feel pity.*

pen·i·tent /'pɛnətənt/ adj. of or about showing or expressing penitence and being willing to seek forgiveness through penance: *Penitent acts include prayer, fasting, and good works.* —n. a person who is penitent and seeks forgiveness: *The penitents pray often in church.*

pen·i·ten·tia·ry /,pɛnə'tɛnʃəri/ n. -ries a state or federal prison: *The thief was sent to the state penitentiary.*

pen·knife /'pɛn,naɪf/ n. -knives /-,naɪvz/ a small pocketknife with a folding blade: *He carries a penknife to open his mail.*

pen·light /'pɛn,laɪt/ n. a flashlight shaped like a large pen: *She used a penlight to look into her purse.*

pen·man·ship /'pɛnmən,ʃɪp/ n. [U] **1** the skill of writing by hand **2** one's style or manner of writing by hand: *Her penmanship is round and clear.*

pen name n. a name used by an author in place of his or her real name: *She used a pen name to protect her privacy.*

pen·nant /'pɛnənt/ n. a long, narrow, and usu. colorful flag with a pointed end: *They waved pennants to cheer the football team.*

pen·ni·less /'pɛnilɪs/ adj. having no money, poor: *a penniless beggar*

pen·ny /'pɛni/ n. -nies or Brit. **pence** /pɛns/ **1** a small coin worth one cent, or 1/100 of a US, Canadian, or Australian dollar or British pound: *Pennies in the USA are made of copper.* **2 a penny for your thoughts:** a phrase used to ask s.o. what he or she is thinking **3 a pretty penny:** a fairly large sum of money: *She paid a pretty penny for that dress.* **4 penny-wise and pound-foolish:** referring to a person who saves money on little things but by doing so has to spend much more later: *The building owner is penny-wise and pound-foolish; he refuses to replace the old windows, so his heating bill is very high every winter.*

penny-an·te /'pɛni'ænti/ adj. related to a card game of poker in which bets are limited to pennies, the least amount of money

penny pinch·er /'pɪntʃər/ n. fig. a person who is overly careful about spending money: *Penny pinchers argue over the cost of everything.* -n. adj. **penny-pinching.**

pen pal n. a person, usu. in a foreign country, to whom one writes letters but whom one has never met in person: *When I was a boy in Boston, I had a pen pal in Paris.*

pen·sion /'pɛnʃən/ n. a regular payment made by a business or government to a person who has retired from a job: *She is 70 years old and receives a pension from her former employer.*

pen·sion·er /'pɛnʃənər/ n. a person who receives a pension

pen·sive /'pɛnsɪv/ adj. having deep and serious thoughts, often about sad or worrisome matters: *She looked pensive, so I asked what was bothering her.* -adv. **pensively.**

pen·ta·gon /'pɛntə,gɑn/ n. **1** in geometry, a figure with five sides and five angles **2 the Pentagon:** the office building in Arlington, VA, which is the headquarters for US military forces

pent·house /'pɛnt,haʊs/ n. -houses /-,haʊzɪz/ an apartment built on the roof of a tall building, often set back from the outer walls: *Stephanie's penthouse in New York has a wonderful view of Central Park.*

pentagon

pent-up /,pɛnt'ʌp/ adj. closed in and blocked from escaping, (syn.) frustrated: *They were feeling pent-up indoors because of the bad weather.*

pe·nul·ti·mate /pɪ'nʌltəmɪt/ adj. next to the last: *They rested at the penultimate stop before finishing their journey.*

pe·nu·ri·ous /pə'nʊriəs, -'nyʊr-/ adj.frml. **1** hating to spend or give money, (syns.) stingy, miserly: *The penurious old man refused to lend his children any money.* **2** very poor: *The sight of penurious children in the street made us very sad.* -n. [U] **penury** /'pɛnyəri/.

pe·on /'pi,ɑn, -ən/ n. **1** a poor farmworker in Latin America **2** fig. any low-level, powerless employee: *He is just a peon working in a warehouse.*

pe·o·ny /'piəni/ n. -nies a garden plant with large, showy, round flowers, usu. pink, red, or white in color

peo·ple /'pipəl/ n. **1** pl. human beings in general: *People often have difficulty admitting they are wrong.* **2** pl.the common persons of a nation, (syn.) the populace: *The people are in favor of the government's policies.* **3** [C] the members of a nation or race as a group: *The peoples of Africa have a rich history.* **4** pl.any group of persons: *Those people are in a hurry to catch the train.* **5** pl.one's family or relations: *My people came from China.* —v. -pled, -pling, -ples to fill with people, (syn.) to populate: *During the war, the island was peopled by refugees.*

pep /pɛp/ n.infrml. cheerful, active energy, (syn.) vigor: *She leads the team with a lot of pep.* -adj. **peppy.** —v. **pepped, pepping, peps** phrasal v. sep. **to pep s.t. up:** to make things happy, full of energy: *Whenever she comes to our house, she peps up the party.||She peps things up.*

P

pep·per /'pɛpər/ *n.* **1** [U] a common hot-tasting powder used to flavor food and improve taste, made from the dried berries of a tropical plant: *You always find salt and pepper on a restaurant table.* **2** [C;U] **hot pepper:** a short or long, usu. narrow pepper with a very hot taste, often used in sauces, *(syn.)* chili pepper **3** [C] **sweet pepper:** a common green or red garden vegetable with a hollow inside, often used in salads
—*v.* **1** to add pepper to a dish of food **2** *fig.* to add in small amounts throughout s.t.: *He peppered his speech with little jokes.*

USAGE NOTE: Hot *pepper* is also called chili pepper.

pepper mill *n.* a device used to grind peppercorns into powdered form: *A waiter turned the top of a pepper mill and ground pepper onto my salad.*

pep·per·mint /'pɛpər,mɪnt/ *n.* **1** [U] an herb plant whose leaves are crushed for oils used in medications and as flavoring **2** [U] the cool, fresh taste of this oil: *This ice cream tastes like peppermint.* **3** [C] a candy flavored with peppermint oil: *He gave out peppermints to all the children.*

pep·per·o·ni /,pɛpə'roʊni/ *n.* [U] a hard, fatty, spicy Italian sausage: *I ordered a pizza with pepperoni.*

pep·per·y /'pɛpəri/ *adj.* flavored with pepper, spicy, hot: *That red sauce is peppery.*

pep rally *n.* **-lies** a gathering with inspiring speeches to build enthusiasm and morale for some cause: *We attended a pep rally for the political candidate.*

pep talk *n.* a speech given to encourage s.o. or a group to try hard and do their best: *Before the game, the coach gave the team a pep talk.*

per /pər; *weak form* pər/ *prep.* **1** for one, for each: *That bread costs $3.00 per pound.* **2 as per:** according to, in agreement with: *As per your instructions, we are sending the package to your home address.*

per an·num /pər'ænəm/ *adv.* (Latin for) for each year, annually: *That $1,000 bond pays 7 percent interest per annum.*

per·cale /pər'keɪl/ *n.adj.* [U] a closely woven, smooth cotton cloth often used for bedsheets: *<n.> Percale makes cool, comfortable bedsheets.*

per cap·i·ta /pər'kæpɪtə/ *adj.* (Latin for) per person, by or for each individual: *The per capita income in that town is very high.*

per·ceive /pər'siv/ *v.frml.* **-ceived, -ceiving, -ceives** **1** to become aware of s.t. through the senses (sight, hearing, touch, etc.) or by thinking: *We could just perceive the first light of dawn.* **2** to understand or comprehend: *She perceived my meaning right away.*

per·cent /pər'sɛnt/ *adv.adj.* for each hundred of s.t.: *That loan charges 7 <adj.> percent interest per year.*
—*n.* **-cent** one part in, for, or of each hundred: *The salesperson gave me a discount of 20 percent (20%) off the regular price.*

per·cent·age /pər'sɛntɪdʒ/ *n.* an amount of s.t. understood as a numerical part of a whole that equals 100: *A large percentage of the people favor the new President's policies.*
—*adj.* related to parts per hundred: *The interest rate on that loan is 7 percentage points.*

per·cep·ti·ble /pər'sɛptəbəl/ *adj.frml.* capable of being seen, heard, smelled, or tasted: *The smell of smoke was barely perceptible in the air.* *-adv.* **perceptibly.**

per·cep·tion /pər'sɛpʃən/ *n.* **1** [U] the mental act or process of becoming aware of a thought or sensation: *That scientist studies perception in animals.* **2** [C] the way a person sees s.t.; a point of view: *My perception of the accident was very different from hers.* **3** [U] natural ability to understand or judge things: *She showed great perception in the way she helped her friends.* *-adj.* **perceptual** /pər'sɛptʃuəl/.

per·cep·tive /pər'sɛptɪv/ *adj.* capable of or showing deep understanding, esp. of s.t. complex, *(syn.)* observant: *That child is very perceptive about the moods of adults.* *-adv.* **perceptively;** *-n.* **perceptiveness.**

perch (1) /pərtʃ/ *n.* **perches** **1** a place where a bird lands and rests: *Pigeons use the sunny side of the roof as a perch.* **2** a seat or position high above its surroundings: *From his perch on the ladder he watched the parade below.*
—*v.* **perches** **1** to land and rest: *Birds perch on the roof of the house.* **2** to sit, esp. in a high position: *He perched on the top of the steps and waited for his taxi.*

perch (2) *n.* **perch** or **perches** a small freshwater fish used for food: *Perch are found in lakes and streams.*

per·chance /pər'tʃæns/ *adv. old usage* perhaps: *If, perchance, we meet again, I'll tell you the rest of the story.*

per·co·late /'pərkə,leɪt/ *v.* **-lated, -lating, -lates** (of liquid) to pass through a loose substance or a filter, *(syn.)* to penetrate: *Water percolates through the ground into the well.* *-n.* [U] **percolation.**

per·co·la·tor /'pərkə,leɪtər/ *n.* a coffeepot in which water percolates through ground coffee beans to make a cup of coffee

per·cus·sion /pər'kʌʃən/ *n.* [U] **1** the striking of one object against another to make a sound: *Percussion is one of the oldest methods of making music.* **2** the group of musical instruments played by tapping, hitting, or beating: *The percussion in an orchestra are in the back row.‖Percussion instruments include drums,* *cymbals, castanets, and bells. -n.* **percussion-ist.**

per di·em /pər'diəm/ *n.* [U] (Latin for) a daily expense allowance: *Our company gives a per diem for hotel and meals.*
—*adj.adv.* per day, daily: *My <adj.> per diem allowance is very small.*

pe·remp·to·ry /pə'rɛmptəri/ *adj.* **1** showing disregard for the opinions or wishes of others, (*syns.*) haughty, arrogant: *His peremptory manner made many enemies.* **2** absolute, final: *the judge's peremptory decision*

pe·ren·ni·al /pə'rɛniəl/ *adj.* **1** long-lasting, constant: *Poverty is a perennial social problem.* **2** (of plants) having roots that live for more than two years: *I planted perennial lilies and daisies in the garden.*
—*n.* a perennial plant: *She grows roses and perennials in the garden.*

per·fect /'pərfɪkt/ *adj.* **1** the best possible: *a perfect score* (or) *record*||*If only the world were perfect!* **2** complete and faultless, with nothing wrong or missing: *This car is in perfect condition.* **3** appropriate and satisfactory in every respect: *The holiday decorations were perfect.* **4** total, complete, thorough: *a perfect fool*||*a perfect stranger*
—*v.* /pər'fɛkt/ to make perfect, flawless, excellent: *She perfected her style of playing the piano by practicing eight hours a day.*
—*n.* /'pərfɪkt/ (in grammar) a verb tense that shows action completed at a certain time: *In the sentence, "I had finished my dinner when she phoned," the verb "had finished" is in the past perfect.*

per·fect·i·ble /pər'fɛktəbəl/ *adj.* capable of being improved or made perfect: *His writing is perfectible if he works hard.*

per·fec·tion /pər'fɛkʃən/ *n.* [U] **1** the state of being perfect: *She demanded perfection from her employees.* **2** the process of making s.t. perfect: *They are working on the perfection of the new solar engine.* **3** a perfect example of s.t.: *This garden is wonderful; it's perfection!* **4 to perfection:** excellently, the best way possible: *The Thanksgiving turkey was cooked to perfection.*

perfectionist /pər'fɛkʃənɪst/ *n.* a person who expects or tries to achieve perfection, as in work: *She is such a perfectionist that she finds it hard to finish anything.* -*n.* **perfectionism.**

per·fect·ly /'pərfɪktli, -fɪkli/ *adv.* **1** flawlessly, with excellence: *The space flight went perfectly, without a problem.* **2** *fig.* completely, absolutely, without question or doubt: *perfectly happy*||*a perfectly good reason*

per·fo·rate /'pərfə,reɪt/ *v.* **-rated, -rating, -rates** **1** to make a hole or holes in s.t.: *The bullets perforated the side of the building.* **2** to make a line of small holes in paper so that it can be torn easily: *The telephone bill was per-*

forated in the middle of the page. -n. [C;U] **perforation** /,pərfə'reɪʃən/.

per·form /pər'fɔrm/ *v.* **1** to do or complete a task: *He performed his regular duties quickly and quietly.* **2** to fulfill, satisfy: *The builder performed all the conditions of his contract.* **3** to act, operate, or behave: *She performs well under pressure.* **4** to give, act out, or present a performance (of a play, piece of music, dance, etc.): *The actors performed a play for the queen.*

per·form·ance /pər'fɔrməns/ *n.* **1** [U] the action of doing or completing s.t.: *The performance of his duties took all day.* **2** [C] the presentation before an audience of a ceremony or work of art (drama, music, dance, etc.): *The performance of the play lasted two hours.* **3** [C] the behavior or operation of a person or machine: *Her performance at school was excellent.*||*The computer's performance was better than we expected.*

per·form·er /pər'fɔrmər/ *n.* a person who performs for an audience, such as a singer, dancer, actor, musician, etc.: *The circus performers delighted the children.*

per·fume /'pərfyum, pər'fyum/ *n.* [C;U] **1** a pleasant, attractive odor, (*syn.*) a fragrance: *The flowers had a strong perfume.* **2** a pleasant-smelling liquid made from flowers used on the body to create an attractive impression: *He gave her some perfume for her birthday.*
—*v.* **-fumed, -fuming, -fumes** to apply perfume: *She perfumed her neck and wrists.*

per·fum·er /pər'fyumər, 'pər,fyu-/ *n.* a maker of perfumes: *Many famous perfumers are in Paris and New York.*

per·func·to·ry /pər'fʌŋktəri/ *adj.* done as a matter of habit or routine, without interest, care, or imagination: *The actor gave a perfunctory reading of the speech. -adv.* **perfunctorily.**

per·haps /pər'hæps/ *adv.* maybe, possibly: *Perhaps I'll go to the movies tonight; I'm not sure yet.*

per·il /'pɛrəl/ *n.frml.* **1** [U] danger, a possibility of serious harm or death: *Your life will be in peril if you try to swim across that river.* **2** [C] s.t. that is a source of danger: *Forest fires are a great peril to nearby homeowners. -adj.* **perilous** /'pɛrələs/ -*adv.* **perilously.**

pe·rim·e·ter /pə'rɪmətər/ *n.* the outer edge of a figure or area of property: *They walked on the path around the perimeter of the pond.*

pe·ri·od /'pɪriəd/ *n.* **1** any segment of time, long or short, that forms part of a longer segment and is notable for particular qualities or characteristics: *the dangerous period of an illness*||*a rainy period in spring*||*a happy period in my life* **2** a very long segment of time in the history of the earth: *The Jurassic period lasted* *for millions of years.* **3** a segment of time in the history of a person's life, a country, etc.: *the revolutionary period in American history* **4** a regular division of time in a school day or a game: *the lunch period||The team scored in the second period.* **5** a woman's monthly menstruation: *She occasionally has cramps when she gets her period.* **6** a punctuation mark of a dot ending a sentence: *This sentence ends with a period.* **7 period piece:** a costume or work of art representative of the style of a particular historical time: *That old movie is a period piece, set in medieval France.*

pe·ri·od·ic /ˌpɪriˈadɪk/ *adj.* **1** occurring at regular intervals of time: *I receive periodic reports each month from our representative in Taiwan.* **2** occurring at repeated but irregular intervals: *She gets periodic headaches, but she doesn't know why.* -*adv.* **periodically.**

pe·ri·od·i·cal /ˌpɪriˈadɪkəl/ *n.* a magazine or other publication that comes out at regular intervals (e.g., weekly, monthly): *She subscribes to several periodicals.*

periodic table *n.* a chart of chemical elements arranged according to their atomic number: *Students of chemistry study the periodic table.*

per·i·o·don·tal /ˌpɛriəˈdɑntl/ *adj.* related to the tissue of the mouth that holds the teeth in place: *That dentist specializes in periodontal disease.*

per·i·pa·tet·ic /ˌpɛrəpəˈtɛtɪk/ *adj.frml.* traveling around, on the move from place to place: *A person in his line of business must be peripatetic and willing to travel on airplanes.*

pe·riph·er·al /pəˈrɪfərəl/ *adj.* **1** of or related to a periphery: *I didn't see the car coming because I have bad peripheral vision.* **2** not of central importance or concern: *The cost of the trip was a peripheral matter for him.*
—*n.* a piece of extra equipment attached to a computer and controlled by it: *That printer is a peripheral wired to the main computer.*

pe·riph·er·y /pəˈrɪfəri/ *n.* **-ies** the outer edge of s.t.; a boundary or the area just inside or outside of it: *A fence goes around the periphery of the army post. She stood on the periphery of the group and watched them dance.*

per·i·scope /ˈpɛrəˌskoʊp/ *n.* a device constructed from a long tube with mirrors and lenses at either end, which allow one to see around or over obstructions; often used in submarines to see above water level

per·ish /ˈpɛrɪʃ/ *v.frml.* **-ishes** to die, be killed in a sudden or dramatic manner: *He fell from the ship and perished in the ocean.*

per·ish·a·ble /ˈpɛrɪʃəbəl/ *adj.* likely to decay or spoil quickly: *Perishable goods last longer if kept in a refrigerator.*
—*n.pl.* **perishables** food that is perishable: *Perishables become rotten very quickly in the heat of summer.*

per·jure /ˈpɜrdʒər/ *v.* **-jured, -juring, -jures** to lie deliberately in a court of law after taking an oath to tell the truth: *The witness perjured himself by lying about what he saw.* -*n.* **perjury** /ˈpɜrdʒəri/

perk /pɜrk/ *v.* **1** short for percolate: *We could hear the coffee perking.* **2** *phrasal v. sep.* **to perk s.o. or s.t. up: a. s.o.:** to become lively and happy: *Let's go next door and perk up Mary; she's a little depressed.||Let's perk her up.*
—*n.* short for perquisite

perk·y /ˈpɜrki/ *adj.* **-ier, -iest** lively, cheerful: *a perky personality*

perm /pɜrm/ *n.infrml.* short for permanent: *She had a perm today.*
—*v.infrml.* to give hair a permanent: *A hairdresser permed her hair.*

per·ma·nence /ˈpɜrmənəns/ *n.* [U] the state of being permanent or lasting a long time: *He seeks permanence in a job because he wants to settle down and raise a family.*

per·ma·nent /ˈpɜrmənənt/ *adj.* **1** lasting, or meant to last, forever or for a long time: *They hoped their marriage would be permanent.* **2** firmly set, not expected to change soon: *This house is now my permanent address.* -*adv.* **permanently.** *See:* temporary.
—*n.* treatment of the hair with chemicals and often heat and curlers designed to produce curls and waves: *She had a permanent at the beauty parlor this morning. See:* perm.

permanent press *adj.* requiring no ironing, referring to clothing treated to prevent it from wrinkling after washing: *These slacks are permanent press.*

per·me·a·ble /ˈpɜrmiəbəl/ *adj.* allowing liquids, materials, etc, to pass through: *A cigarette filter is permeable by smoke.*

per·me·ate /ˈpɜrmiˌeɪt/ *v.* **-ated, -ating, -ates** to flow into and spread through every part of s.t.: *Shoe polish permeated the leather and kept it soft.* -*n.* [U] **permeation.**

per·mis·si·ble /pərˈmɪsəbəl/ *adj.* allowable, permitted: *The teacher said that it was not permissible to talk in class.*

per·mis·sion /pərˈmɪʃən/ *n.* [U] consent, agreement, approval: *She asked for permission to leave work early.||The bookstore has written permission to return unsold textbooks to the publishers.*

per·mis·sive /pərˈmɪsɪv/ *adj.* allowing too much freedom, esp. in matters of pleasure that could lead to harm, (*syn.*) indulgent: *permissive parents||a permissive society* -*n.* [U] **permissiveness.**

per·mit /pərˈmɪt/ *v.* **-mitted, -mitting, -mits 1** to allow, let: *He would not permit us to leave the building.* **2** to make possible or offer the opportunity: *If time permits, I will visit my uncle in Miami.*

—*n.* /'pɜr,mɪt, pər'mɪt/ an official document giving s.o. the freedom to do s.t. or go somewhere, such as a gun permit, driving permit, etc.

per·mu·ta·tion /,pɜrmyʊ'teɪʃən/ *n.frml.* a change in a set of things ordered as a group: *The permutations of 123 are 321, 213, 312, 231, 132, and 123.*

per·ni·cious /pər'nɪʃəs/ *adj.frml.* **1** causing or leading to injury, destruction, or ruin in an evil or hidden way: *Pernicious lies can ruin a person's reputation.* **2** causing death: *a pernicious poison*

per·ox·ide /pə'rɑk,saɪd/ *n.* [U] a colorless liquid chemical used to lighten hair and to kill germs: *He used some peroxide to make his hair blond.*

per·pen·dic·u·lar /,pɜrpən'dɪkyələr/ *adj.* **1** at an angle of 90°: *The connected sides of a square are perpendicular to each other.* **2** standing straight up, (*syns.*) vertical, upright: *A flagpole is perpendicular.*

per·pe·trate /'pɜrpə,treɪt/ *v.frml.* **-trated, -trating, -trates** to commit (a crime): *She has neither the courage nor the stupidity to perpetrate a bank robbery. -n.* [U] **perpetration.**

per·pe·tra·tor /'pɜrpə,treɪtər/ *n.* a person who commits a crime: *Police arrested the perpetrator right after he stole the watch.*

per·pet·u·al /pər'pɛtʃuəl/ *adj.* **1** continuing forever: *a heaven of perpetual joy||a perpetual motion machine* **2** constant, occurring all the time: *She became annoyed with his perpetual questions. -adv.* **perpetually.**

per·pet·u·ate /pər'pɛtʃu,eɪt/ *v.* **-ated, -ating, -ates** to keep alive or preserve in memory for a long time: *He worked hard to perpetuate the name of his family's business. -n.* **perpetuation** /pər,pɛtʃu'eɪʃən/.

per·pe·tu·i·ty /,pɜrpə'tuəti/ *n.* esp. in the phrase **in perpetuity:** forever: *He will receive a company pension in perpetuity.*

per·plex /pər'plɛks/ *v.* **-plexes** to make s.o. confused and worried by being hard to understand: *She perplexed all of her teachers.||The new tax laws perplex me. -adj.* **perplexing;** *-n.* [U] **perplexity.**

per·qui·site /'pɜrkwɪzɪt/ *n.frml.* a special benefit given to an employee of a company in addition to pay and normal benefits like health insurance: *One of the perquisites of working for the phone company was a special discount on long-distance calls. See:* perk, *n.*

per se /pər'seɪ/ *adv.frml.* considered by itself alone: *The salary per se is low, but the pension it leads to is excellent.*

per·se·cute /'pɜrsɪ,kyut/ *v.* **-cuted, -cuting, -cutes** to treat people unjustly or cruelly, causing hardship and suff[...] in belief or racia[...] were persecuted of their reli[...] /,pɜrsɪ'kyuʃən['...]

per·se·ver·[...] tent and dete[...] *After much perse[...] match.*

per·se·vere /,pɜrsə'vɪr/ *v.* **-veres** to continue working tow[...] spite difficulties or obstacles, (*syn.*) [...] *My teacher encouraged me to persevere [...] studies. -adj.* **persevering.**

per·sim·mon /pər'sɪmən/ *n.* the reddish-orange colored fruit of a tree native to the tropics

per·sist /pər'sɪst, -'zɪst/ *v.* **1** to continue steadily in the same manner in spite of obstacles or opposition: *He persisted in asking her to marry him until she finally said, "Yes."* **2** to continue to exist longer than usual or expected: *The rain persisted all night.*

per·sist·ence /pər'sɪstəns, -'zɪs-/ *n.* [U] the quality of being persistent, steady pursuit of one's goals: *Her persistence in looking for a job was finally rewarded.*

per·sist·ent /pər'sɪstənt, -'zɪs-/ *adj.* **1** continuing steadily in a belief, activity, or purpose, (*syn.*) tenacious: *He made a persistent effort to finish the big project.* **2** continuing to exist for a long time: *a persistent problem||a persistent noise -adv.* **persistently.**

per·snick·e·ty /pər'snɪkəti/ *adj.infrml.* overly concerned in an annoying way about small, unimportant details, (*syn.*) fussy: *He is very persnickety about how he dresses; his socks and necktie always match.*

per·son /'pɜrsən/ *n.* **1** a single human being, an individual: *There was just one person in the restaurant.* **2** s.o. whose identity is not known: *That person stole my purse.* **3** one's body and its appearance: *She takes great care about her person.* **4** (in grammar) any of the three classes of pronouns or verb forms that indicate the speaker (first person), the one spoken to (second person), or the one spoken about (third person) **5 in person:** physically present, face-to-face: *I have to go to New York to see him in person.*

per·so·na /pər'sounə/ *n.* [C] **-nas** or **-nae** /-ni/ **1** the role or character s.o. adopts in public or for a performance: *She has an attractive persona when she speaks at meetings.* **2** the fictional speaker in a literary work: *The persona in this story is a young boy who has run away from home.*

per·son·a·ble /'pɜrsənəbəl, 'pɜrsnə-/ *adj.* likable, attractive, pleasant to others: *She is a very personable woman with a warm heart.*

P

ₚ rsənɪʤ/ *n.frml.* an important ... *personages entered the castle.*

... pɜrsənəl, 'pɜrsnəl/ *adj.* **1** related ... ging to a particular person; individ- ... ate: *He receives personal telephone* ... *the office.* **2** done or carried out in per- ... *personal visit*||*a personal conversation* ... rected toward a particular person: *a per-* ... *al letter*||*a personal favor* **4** of the body or ... ℓothing: *His personal appearance was very neat.*

personal computer or **PC** *n.* a small, compact computer that can easily be moved, designed mainly for home use

per·son·al·i·ty /ˌpɜrsə'næləti/ *n.* **-ties** **1** the total effect or character of a person's qualities (habits, traits, moods, attitudes, etc.): *She has a warm, lively personality.* **2** a pleasing or exciting quality in a person: *He is fun to be with because he has a lot of personality.* **3** an important or well-known person, esp. in the entertainment business: *Movie personalities filled the audience at the award ceremony.*

per·son·al·ize /'pɜrsənəˌlaɪz, 'pɜrsnə-/ *v.* **-ized, -izing, -izes** **1** to make a subject or event personal by focusing on individual or private concerns: *He talks only about himself and personalizes everything.* **2** to mark a possession with one's name and address or initials: *She had her stationary personalized.*

per·son·al·ly /'pɜrsənəli, 'pɜrsnə-/ *adv.* **1** by oneself, not through others: *The President congratulated the astronauts personally by telephoning them.* **2** in one's own opinion: *I, personally, am opposed to the plan, but my company is going ahead with it.* **3** as a person: *I don't know him personally, but others speak well of him.* **4 to take s.t. personally:** to react to s.t. as if one's skill, ability, or character has been attacked: *He took it personally when his supervisor gave the promotion to another salesperson who had been with the company only a short time.*

personal pronoun *n.* pronoun that refers to a person or thing that is speaking, is spoken to, or is spoken about: *The personal pronouns are I, me, you, he, him, she, her, it, we, us, they, and them.*

per·son·i·fy /pər'sɑnəˌfaɪ/ *v.* **-fied, -fying, -fies** **1** to represent an idea or thing as a person: *The writer personified love as a beautiful young girl.* **2** to be an example of: *He personifies the values of his church. -n.* [U] **personification** /pərˌsɑnəfə'keɪʃən/.

per·son·nel /ˌpɜrsə'nɛl/ *n.* [U] **1** all the people working in an organization (a business, school, etc.): *The company had to fire half of its personnel to save money.* **2** the office in a business that handles employee affairs, such as hiring, records, and benefits: *I went to person-nel to ask about the company retirement program.*

USAGE NOTE: The term *Human Resource Department* is often used instead of *Personnel Department.*

---

per·spec·tive /pər'spɛktɪv/ *n.* [U] **1** in art, a manner of drawing objects to create a realistic sense of depth and distance in space: *A painter uses perspective to make a hallway look long and narrow.* **2** [C;U] a way of seeing things, point of view, opinion, *(syns.)* an angle, slant: *Everyone had a different perspective on the election, and no one agreed.* **3** [C;U] the set of beliefs, interests, attitudes, etc., that contribute to one's judgment on issues and events: *She has a unique perspective on the economic problems of Southeast Asia.* **4** [C] a position (on a mountain or hill) from which one can see a long way off: *The perspective gave us a good view of the sunset.*

per·spi·ra·tion /ˌpɜrspə'reɪʃən/ *n.* [U] sweat: *His shirt was dark from perspiration.*

per·spire /pər'spaɪr/ *v.* **-spired, -spiring, -spires** to sweat: *She perspires when she is nervous.*

per·suade /pər'sweɪd/ *v.* **-suaded, -suading, -suades** to lead a person or group to believe or do s.t. by arguing or reasoning with them, *(syn.)* to convince: *I persuaded my friend to stop drinking alcohol.*

per·sua·sion /pər'sweɪʒən/ *n.* **1** [U] the act of persuading: *Instead of fighting, try persuasion to get what you want.* **2** [U] the power to persuade: *She used persuasion to change his mind.* **3** [U] a strong personal belief: *It is my persuasion that telling the truth is always best.* **4** [C] a particular set of beliefs: *people of different persuasions*||*the Marxist (capitalist, socialist) persuasion*

per·sua·sive /pər'sweɪsɪv/ *adj.* **1** good at persuading others: *He is a persuasive salesman.* **2** reasonable, sensible, convincing: *a persuasive argument -adv.* **persuasively.**

pert /pɜrt/ *adj.* bold, smart, and stylish in a manner that attracts attention and risks disapproval: *She wore a very pert outfit to the dance. -adv.* **pertly.**

per·tain /pər'teɪn/ *v.* to belong or be related to s.t.: *These financial records pertain to this year's tax returns.*

per·ti·nent /'pɜrtnənt/ *adj.frml.* directly related, *(syn.)* relevant: *His skills were not pertinent to the job he applied for. -n.* [U] **pertinence.**

per·turb /pər'tɜrb/ *v.frml.* to trouble, bother, or upset s.o.'s peace of mind: *The bad news perturbed her for days. -n.* [U] **perturbation** /ˌpɜrtər'beɪʃən/.

pe·ruse /pə'ruz/ v. **-rused, -rusing, -ruses** to read or examine s.t. carefully: *He perused the newspaper looking for news of his home town.* -n. [C;U] **perusal** /pə'ruzəl/.

per·vade /pər'veɪd/ v. **-vaded, -vading, -vades** to spread through every part of, (syn.) to permeate: *The smell of burnt toast pervaded the kitchen.*

per·va·sive /pər'veɪsɪv/ adj. **1** tending to pervade or spread: *a pervasive odor* **2** widespread, common, influential: *There is a pervasive trend toward casual dress in businesses.* -n. **pervasiveness.**

per·verse /pər'vɜrs/ adj. **1** unnatural, offensive: *He has a perverse sense of humor, telling jokes about death and destruction.* **2** turned away from what is good, morally bad: *It is perverse to mistreat children.* -adv. **perversely.**

per·ver·sion /pər'vɜrʒən, -ʃən/ n. **1** [C;U] a perverted form of s.t.: *His nasty stories are perversions of the truth.* **2** [C] a form of sexual behavior considered to be abnormal or unnatural

per·ver·si·ty /pər'vɜrsəti/ n. **-ties 1** [U] the state or quality of being perverse: *His perversity caused his parents to worry.* **2** [C] a perverse act: *A perversity committed on stage offended the audience.*

per·vert /pər'vɜrt/ v. **1** to turn s.o. away from what is considered to be natural or truthful, (syn.) to corrupt: *They said he was perverted by sex, money, and power.* **2** to misuse or represent falsely: *That liar perverts the truth.* -adj. **perverted** /pər'vɜrtɪd/.
—n. pej. /'pɜr,vɜrt/ a person whose sexual behavior is considered unnatural or abnormal

pe·se·ta /pə'seɪtə/ n. the basic unit of money in Spain: *In Madrid, she converted her dollars to pesetas.*

pes·ky /'pɛski/ adj.infrml. **-kier, -kiest** annoying, irritating: *The restaurant was filled with pesky flies.*

pe·so /'peɪsoʊ/ n. **-sos** the basic unit of money in many countries of Latin America and in the Philippines: *How many pesos does this hat cost?*

pes·si·mism /'pɛsə,mɪzəm/ n. [U] the tendency to see only the bad things in life and to expect that they are more likely to get worse than better: *His pessimism keeps him from trying new things.* -n. **pessimist.**

pes·si·mis·tic /,pɛsə'mɪstɪk/ adj. expecting s.t. to become worse than it is: *a pessimistic forecast* -adv. **pessimistically.**

pest /pɛst/ n. **1** a small animal or an insect that causes damage to food or crops, or otherwise bothers human beings: *Rats, mice, and flies are regarded as pests.* **2** an annoying person:

The little girl who demands attention all the time is a pest.

pes·ter /'pɛstər/ v. to annoy, irritate s.o. by making repeated demands: *The fund raisers pestered us with telephone calls.||The children pestered her for more candy.*

pes·ti·cide /'pɛstə,saɪd/ n. [C;U] a chemical used to kill pests: *Airplanes spread pesticides on crops.*

pes·ti·lence /'pɛstələns/ n.frml. [C;U] any disease that spreads widely and kills quickly, (syn.) a plague: *The doctors could not stop the pestilence.* -adj.frml. **pestilent.**

pes·to /'pɛstoʊ/ n. an uncooked sauce of Italian origin usu. made from ground fresh basil (a sweet herb), olive oil, garlic, nuts, and cheese: *I made spaghetti with pesto for dinner.*

pet /pɛt/ n. **1** a tame animal kept in the home and treated with kindness and affection: *Dogs are very popular as pets.* **2** a favorite person: *That bright girl is the teacher's pet.*
—adj. **1** kept or treated as a pet: *She has six pet cats.* **2** favorite, special: *His pet topic is politics.||a pet theory* **3** showing affection: *My pet name for her is "Pumpkin." See:* pet peeve.
—v. **petted, petting, pets 1** to stroke lightly and fondly with the hand: *She pets her cat on its back.* **2** to kiss and caress for sexual pleasure: *Teenagers at the party petted on the couch.* -n. [U] **petting.**

pet·al /'pɛtl/ n. the colored or white leaf-like part of a flower: *The petals of a rose are soft.*

pe·ter /'pitər/ phrasal v. **to peter out:** to lessen in number until gone: *The demand for those old computers has petered out.*

pe·tite /pə'tit/ adj. (said of women) small, trim: *She is too petite to reach that high.*
—n. a special size of women's clothing: *The dress shop had a separate section for petites.*

pe·ti·tion /pə'tɪʃən/ n. **1** a formal request signed by many people to change a law: *Voters signed a petition to remove the governor.||The petition called for a special election.* **2** a legal request for action by a court: *I made a petition to have my case heard in court.*
—v. to make a petition: *They petitioned the legislature to pass laws protecting the environment.* -n. **petitioner.**

pet peeve n. s.t. or s.o. that most annoys you: *People who chew gum and talk at the same time are my pet peeve.*

pet·ri·fy /'pɛtrə,faɪ/ v. **-fied, -fying, -fies 1** to turn into stone: *It takes many centuries for dead plants and trees to petrify.* **2** to shock or scare s.o., esp. so that fear makes the person unable to move: *A monster in the movie petrified our child.* -n. [U] **petrifaction** /,pɛtrə'fækʃən/.

P

pe·tro·le·um /pə'troʊliəm/ n. [U] a dark, thick, oily liquid usu. found between layers of rock in the earth and used to make fuels for heating, lighting, or engines: *Gasoline is made from petroleum.*

petroleum jelly n. [U] a soft, smooth, greasy substance made from petroleum and used on skin to heal cuts, burns, or scrapes: *He put some petroleum jelly on his skin to soothe a sunburn.*

pet·ti·coat /'pɛti,koʊt/ n. a woman's skirt worn under another skirt or dress, often with a fancy trim at the bottom: *She wore a petticoat under her dress.*

pet·ty /'pɛti/ adj. **-tier, -tiest 1** unimportant, trivial: *He wastes his time on petty problems that no one else cares about.* **2** (of a person) limited or narrow in interests or kindness toward others, (syn.) small-minded: *Her petty complaints showed her to be selfish. -n.* **pettiness.**

petty cash n. [U] a small amount of money kept in an office to pay for small purchases: *I paid for some pencils with money from petty cash.*

pet·u·lant /'pɛtʃələnt/ adj. easily upset or angered over unimportant matters, having a bad temper, (syn.) irritable: *The petulant man was always starting quarrels with people. -n.* [U] **petulance; -adv. petulantly.**

pe·tu·nia /pɪ'tunyə/ n. a small garden plant with bright, showy flowers: *She placed a vase of petunias on the dining room table.*

pew /pyu/ n. a bench (a long seat with a back) in a church: *We sat in the third pew.*

pew·ter /'pyutər/ n. [U] **1** a grayish metal made of tin and lead **2** dishes, plates, cups, etc., made of this metal: *They served dinner on pewter made in early America.*

pha·lanx /'feɪ,læŋks/ n. **phalanxes** or **phalanges** /fə'lændʒiz/ **1** an ancient military formation of 100 soldiers **2** a group of people dedicated to a common cause: *The President's followers include a phalanx of reporters.*

phal·lus /'fæləs/ n. **-li** /-laɪ/ or **-luses 1** an image of the male sex organ, in some cultures believed to be a sign of sexual power **2** the male sex organ (penis) -adj. **phallic.**

phan·tom /'fæntəm/ n. a ghost, esp. one that flies away quickly: *He thought he saw phantoms in the cemetery.*

phar·aoh /'fɛroʊ, 'færoʊ, 'feɪroʊ/ n. a ruler of ancient Egypt: *The pharaoh was believed to be a god.*

phar·ma·ceu·ti·cal /,fɑrmə'sutɪkəl/ adj. of a pharmacy or pharmacists: *the pharmaceutical industry* (or) *profession*
—n.pl. a drug or medicine: *Pharmaceuticals are sold through drugstores.*

phar·ma·cist /'fɑrməsɪst/ n. a person who has studied pharmacy and is licensed to prepare and sell drugs, (syn.) a druggist: *The pharmacist sold me some medicine for my cold.*

phar·ma·col·o·gy /,fɑrmə'kɑlədʒi/ n. the study of drugs -n. **pharmacologist.**

phar·ma·cy /'fɑrməsi/ n. **-cies 1** [U] the study and profession of making and selling or giving out medicine and drugs: *He studied pharmacy in college.* **2** [C] a drugstore, or the place where drugs are prepared and sold within a store: *She pointed me to the pharmacy in the back of the store.*

phase /feɪz/ n. **1** a period of time within a longer process of change, a stage of development: *The time you spend in high school is an important phase of your education.* **2** a stage in the regularly changing appearance of the moon: *We studied the phases of the moon in school.* **3 to go through a phase:** to behave in an unusual way for a brief time while growing up: *She is going through a phase in which she is always impatient.*
—v. **phased, phasing, phases 1** to plan to do s.t. in phases: *They phased the project in three sections.* **2** *phrasal v. sep.* **to phase s.t. in** or **out:** to introduce or remove s.t. in gradual steps: *They are phasing out that old model of TV.||They are phasing it out.*

Ph.D. /,piɛɪtʃ'di/ n.abbr. for Doctor of Philosophy, an advanced university degree above a master's degree: *She has a Ph.D. in English from Berkeley. See:* M.A., USAGE NOTE.

pheas·ant /'fɛzənt/ n. a large, colorful bird with a long tail, hunted for food and sport: *My dog chased pheasants in the bushes.*

phe·nom·e·nal /fə'nɑmənəl/ adj. **1** unusual, remarkable: *The results of the test were phenomenal.* **2** great, terrific, wonderful, amazing: *That singer's new recording is a phenomenal success. -adv.* **phenomenally.**

phe·nom·e·non /fə'nɑmə,nɑn, -nən/ n. **-na** /-nə/ or **-nons 1** a fact, event, or image that strikes one's attention and attracts interest: *Snow was a phenomenon he had never seen before.* **2** a highly unusual event or person that attracts a lot of attention: *The new movie star was a phenomenon.*

phi·lan·thro·pist /fɪ'lænθrəpɪst/ n. [U] a person who helps or gives to good causes: *The rich woman was a philanthropist who gave money to the museum.*

phi·lan·thro·py /fɪ'lænθrəpi/ n. **1** the feeling of love for all human beings and the desire to help them: *He chose to make philanthropy his guide in life.* **2** the practice of working for or giving money to groups that help the poor, the arts (museums, symphonies, etc.), and other good causes: *The rich woman engages in phil-*

anthropy by giving money to charities. -adj. **philanthropic** /ˌfɪlən'θrɑpɪk/.

phi·lat·e·ly /fə'lætəli/ *n.frml.* [U] stamp collecting: *He engages in philately by collecting stamps from foreign countries. -n.* **philatelist.**

phil·is·tine /'fɪlə,stin, fɪ'lɪstɪn/ *n.* a person who lacks feeling for or understanding of the fine arts and culture: *The actors did not like to perform for philistines.*

phi·los·o·pher /fə'lɑsəfər/ *n.* **1** a person who studies or teaches philosophy

phil·o·soph·i·cal /ˌfɪlə'sɑfɪkəl/ *adj.* **1** related to philosophy: *philosophical books* **2** calm and undisturbed when faced with pain, loss, or hardship, (*syn.*) stoic: *She was philosophical about the death of her son. -adv.* **philosophically.**

phi·los·o·phize /fə'lɑsə,faɪz/ *v.* **-phized, -phizing, -phizes** to speak or write in a philosophical manner

phi·los·o·phy /fə'lɑsəfi/ *n.* **-phies 1** [U] the study of the most general truths and beliefs about the nature and meaning of humankind, the world, and the conduct of life: *Philosophy is a difficult subject.* **2** [C] the unique system of knowledge developed by a particular philosopher: *the philosophy of Plato* **3** [C] the basic principles of a particular field of knowledge: *the philosophy of science* **4** [U] a way of living, esp. a calm, patient attitude toward life: *His philosophy brings him peace of mind.*

phlegm /flɛm/ *n.* [U] a thick, sticky bodily fluid formed in the nose and throat, esp. during a cold: *When she was ill, the phlegm made it hard for her to breathe.*

phleg·mat·ic /flɛg'mætɪk/ *adj.frml.* slow, inactive, unresponsive: *He was too phlegmatic to get excited about the football game.*

pho·bi·a /'foʊbiə/ *n.* [C] a strong fear or anxiety without a good reason about a thing, activity, or situation: *She has a phobia about flying and will not travel in airplanes. -adj.* **phobic.**

phoe·nix /'finɪks/ *n.* **-nixes** (in mythology) a bird that lives for 500 years, sets itself on fire, and is born again from its ashes: *The phoenix is a symbol of hope.*

phone /foʊn/ *n.v.* **phoned, phoning, phones** short for telephone: *I picked up the <n.> phone to <v.> phone my friend.*

phone book *n.* a book listing names, addresses, and telephone numbers of people, businesses, and institutions: *I looked in the phone book for the number for the police.*

phone booth *n. See:* telephone booth.

pho·net·ic /fə'nɛtɪk/ *adj.* related to the sounds of words in human speech: *Phonetic spellings help students learn new languages. -adv.* **phonetically.**

pho·net·ics /fə'nɛtɪks/ **1** *n.pl.* used with a *sing.v.* the science and study of speech sounds **2** used with a *sing. or pl. v.* the sounds of a lan-

guage and their symbols: *The phonetics of English are very different from those of Japanese.*

phon·ics /'fɑnɪks/ *n.pl.* used with a *sing.v.* a system of learning to pronounce words by recognizing sounds that letters or groups of letters represent: *Phonics is taught in schools to help children learn to read.*

pho·no·graph /'foʊnə,græf/ *n.* a record player, machine used to reproduce sounds, esp. music from records: *Our old phonograph doesn't play anymore.*

pho·ny /'foʊni/ *adj.* **-nier, -niest** not real or genuine, (*syns.*) false, fake: *This ring was made with phony diamonds.*
—*n.* **-nies** a person who is not sincere, or pretends to be different than he or she really is: *He says he is a rich businessman, but he is really a phony.*

phoo·ey /'fui/ *exclam.* of disgust, rejection: *Phooey! That milk tastes sour!*

phos·phate /'fɑs,feɪt/ *n.* [U] a mineral with many commercial uses, such as for fertilizer and in detergents: *My mother uses phosphate in her garden to make her flowers grow.*

phos·pho·res·cence /ˌfɑsfə'rɛsəns/ *n.* [U] the natural effect of an object giving off light without heat after the object has been exposed to another source of light: *Phosphorescence causes things to glow in the dark. -adj.* **phosphorescent.**

phos·pho·rus /'fɑsfərəs/ *n.* [U] a yellowish, solid, nonmetallic, and poisonous element that glows in the dark, catches fire easily, and is used to make matches, fertilizers, etc.

pho·to /'foʊtoʊ/ *n.* **-tos** short for photograph: *I took some photos of my kids.*

pho·to·cop·i·er /'foʊtə,kɑpiər/ *n.* a machine that makes duplicate copies of documents and pictures by a photographic process: *The library in my town has three photocopiers for public use.*

pho·to·cop·y /'foʊtə,kɑpi/ *n.* **-ies** a photographic copy of a document, picture, etc., made by a photocopier: *I made a photocopy of a letter that I wrote.*
—*v.* **-ied, -ying, -ies** to make photocopies of s.t.: *I photocopied my letter.*

USAGE NOTE: The brand name *Xerox* ™ is also used as a verb to mean photocopy: *I need to Xerox* ™ *these papers.*

photo finish *n.* any contest in which it is hard to determine the winner: *They expect the election to be a photo finish.*

pho·to·gen·ic /ˌfoʊtə'dʒɛnɪk/ *adj.* having the quality of always looking good in photographs, attractive: *Most movie stars and fashion models are very photogenic.*

pho·to·graph /'foʊtə,græf/ *n.* a picture made from light passing through a camera onto film:

We took photographs of the children while on vacation.
—v. to take a photograph (or photographs) of s.t.: *He photographed our wedding.*

pho·tog·ra·pher /fəˈtɑgrəfər/ *n.* **1** a person who takes photographs: *My sister is the best photographer in my family.* **2** a person who practices photography as an art or business: *She is a photographer for the local newspaper.*

pho·to·graph·ic /ˌfoutəˈgræfɪk/ *adj.* **1** related to photography: *Making movies is a photographic art.* **2 photographic memory:** the ability to remember things in very exact detail

pho·tog·ra·phy /fəˈtɑgrəfi/ *n.* [U] the art and science of making pictures from light that passes through the lens of a camera and forms an image on a film, which is then used to recreate the image on paper, a screen, or some other surface: *Photography plays an important role in the printing industry.*

pho·to·jour·nal·ism /ˌfoutouˈdʒɜrnəˌlɪzəm/ *n.* [U] journalism that relies more on photographs or film than on writing or speech: *Television news is a good example of photojournalism.* **-n. photojournalist.**

pho·ton /ˈfoutɑn/ *n.* (in physics) a unit of energy

pho·to·syn·the·sis /ˌfoutouˈsɪnθəsɪs/ *n.* [U] the process by which plants convert water and carbon dioxide into food using sunlight for energy: *Photosynthesis produces oxygen as a by-product.*

phras·al verb /ˈfreɪzəl/ *n.* a short phrase, made of a verb plus an adverb or a preposition, that acts like a verb and has a special meaning different from the words it is made of, such as *put up with, get by,* or *pass away*

phrase /freɪz/ *n.* a usu. brief group of words that is not a sentence but may form part of a sentence: *"Down the hill" is a phrase in "The ball rolled down the hill."*
—v. **phrased, phrasing, phrases** to express s.t. with carefully chosen words: *She phrased her question politely, using the word "please."*

phra·se·ol·o·gy /ˌfreɪziˈɑlədʒi/ *n.* [U] the choice of words and how they are used in writing or speech: *The legal phraseology in that book is hard to understand.*

phras·ing /ˈfreɪzɪŋ/ *n.* [U] word order, the way in which s.t. is said: *The phrasing of ideas in that report is very awkward.*

phys·i·cal /ˈfɪzɪkəl/ *adj.* **1** of or related to matter and material things (as opposed to mental or spiritual things): *She studies the brain as a physical organ that works like a computer.* **2** of or related to the body: *After falling from a ladder, he had many physical aches and pains.* **3** of or related to the laws of nature: *There are physical limits to how fast we can travel.* **4** involving rough body contact: *American football and rugby are very physical sports.*

—n. *short for* physical examination, a medical examination performed by a doctor: *I had to have a physical before starting my new job.*

physical education *n.* [U] a school or college program designed to teach students how to play sports, exercise, and maintain good health: *Some participation in physical education is required at most schools.*

physical examination *n.* a medical examination *See:* physical, *n.*

phys·i·cal·ly /ˈfɪzɪkli/ *adv.* **1** according to natural laws: *It is not physically possible for humans to breathe under water.* **2** in or of the body: *The sight of blood makes her physically ill.*

physical sciences *n.pl.* the group of sciences including physics, astronomy, and chemistry: *All students must take four courses in the physical sciences.*

physical therapy *n.* [U] the treatment of diseases and injuries (esp. of nerves and muscles) by means of careful exercise and massage: *After the accident, he had physical therapy to learn to walk again.* **-n. physical therapist.**

phy·si·cian /fɪˈzɪʃən/ *n.* a doctor, person with a medical degree licensed to practice medicine: *My physician told me to stop smoking cigarettes.*

phy·si·cian's assistant /fɪˈzɪʃənz/ or **PA** *n.* a person who provides basic medical services, usu. working closely with a doctor.

phys·i·cist /ˈfɪzəsɪst/ *n.* a person who studies physics: *Physicists must know a lot of mathematics.*

phys·ics /ˈfɪzɪks/ *n.pl. used with a sing.v.* the study of the most basic forms of matter, energy, and motion, including heat, light, sound, and electricity: *The laws of physics are true throughout the universe.*

phys·i·ol·o·gy /ˌfɪziˈɑlədʒi/ *n.* [U] the scientific study of living bodies (humans, animals, plants) and how they work: *An important subject in physiology is how living things digest food.* **-adj. physiological** /ˌfɪziəˈlɑdʒɪkəl/.

phys·i·o·ther·a·py /ˌfɪziouˈθerəpi/ *n.* [U] physical therapy: *She takes physiotherapy to heal the muscles of her arm.*

phy·sique /fɪˈzik/ *n.* [U] the shape and appearance of the body: *He has a strong physique from playing sports.*

pi·an·ist /piˈænɪst, ˈpiənɪst/ *n.* a person who plays the piano, esp. a professional piano player: *A pianist played old songs at the party.*

pi·an·o /piˈænou, ˈpyænou/ *n.* **-os** a large musical instrument built with a wooden frame and many  small black and white levers (called "keys")

piano

that are struck by the player's fingers, causing long wire strings to vibrate with sound: *The piano can produce a great range of tones and has become one of the most popular of instruments.*

piano bar *n. See:* bar.

pic·a·yune /,pɪki'yun/ *adj.* of little value or importance: *She runs a big business and cannot concern herself with picayune details.*

pic·co·lo /'pɪkə,loʊ/ *n.* **-los** a small flute: *Piccolos have a high-pitched sound.*

pick /pɪk/ *v.* **1** to choose or select: *She picked a bright yellow dress to wear to the wedding.‖They picked her to play on their team.* **2** to pull off or detach part of a plant, to gather fruits, flowers, vegetables, etc., by breaking them off from the plants they grow on: *He picked an apple from the tree.‖She went into the garden to pick flowers.* **3** to take hold of and pull (with the fingers or a sharply pointed instrument) in order to remove, esp. in small pieces: *Be careful to pick the bones from that fish before you eat it.* **4** to dig, scratch, or poke at s.t. with a finger or a pointed instrument: *Her mother told her not to pick her nose.‖After dinner, he picked his teeth with a toothpick.* **5** to start, bring about, or provoke: *He picked a fight with his brother.* **6** to steal valuables from s.o.'s purse or pocket: *A thief picked my wallet from my pocket.* **7** to open a lock using a pointed instrument instead of a key: *She lost the key to her car door, so a mechanic had to pick the lock.* **8** to pluck the strings of a musical instrument with either the fingers or a small, flat piece of plastic or wood: *She picked her guitar with skill.* **9** *phrasal v. sep.* **to pick at s.o. or s.t.: a. s.o.:** to point out s.o.'s faults: *A good boss never picks at her employees.* **b. s.t.:** to eat (a meal) in small bits and without interest: *She picked at her dinner because she wasn't hungry.* **10** *fig.* **to pick holes in:** to point out the mistakes or errors of: *We picked holes in his plan for the business.* **11** *phrasal v. insep.* **to pick on s.o.:** to single s.o. out in order to bother, hurt, or make fun of the person: *The older boys picked on him because he was new to the school.* **12** *phrasal v. sep.* **to pick over s.t.** to look among carefully in order to make a selection: *She picked over the apples to be sure they were fresh.* **13 to pick (s.o.'s) brains:** to get ideas or opinions from talking with s.o. smart: *He has good ideas; let's pick his brains about our business plan.* **14** *phrasal v. sep.* **to pick s.o. or s.t. out: a. s.o.:** to spot, see clearly: *She picked out her friend in the crowd.* **b. s.t.:** to choose: *Will you pick out a book for me?‖Please pick one out.* **15** *phrasal v. sep.* **to pick s.o. or s.t. up: a.** to go and get s.t. or meet s.o.: *He picked up his date at her house.* **b.** to take passengers in a vehicle: *The bus picked us up on time.* **c.** to try to become intimate with s.o. one has just met: *He*

tried to pick up someone at the party, but he had no luck. **d.** to lift or raise up: *I picked up a rock.‖Pick up your feet!* **e.** to set in order, arrange: *Guests were coming, so I picked up the living room.* **f.** to get, gain, or learn casually: *While I was shopping, I picked up some flowers for my wife.‖She picks up new languages easily.* **g.** to get better or increase: *The hotel business picked up in the summer.‖Traffic picked up as we neared the city.* **h.** to hear or receive signals from: *We can't pick up that radio station from here.* **16** *phrasal v. sep.* **to pick s.t. apart:** to criticize piece by piece: *My writing instructor picked apart my essay.‖He picked it apart.* **17** *phrasal v. sep.* **to pick s.t. off:** to take careful aim at and shoot a person or animal: *The hunter picked off the bird as it flew away.‖He picked it off.* **18** *phrasal v. insep.* **to pick up on s.t.:** to understand, catch on to: *She was trying to get his attention, but he was slow to pick up on it.*

—*n.* **1** a choice or selection: *What's your pick from all the movies we can see tonight?* **2** the best or finest choice among a group: *She's the pick of all the girls.* **3** a small, sharp, pointed instrument: *an ice pick‖a dentist's pick* **4** a small, flat piece of wood or plastic used to pluck the strings of a musical instrument **5** a pickax

pick·ax or **pickaxe** /'pɪk,æks/ *n.* **-axes** a large tool with a long wooden handle and a heavy iron head that is long and pointed at both ends, used to break apart earth, stones, roads, etc.: *He used a pickax to loosen the ground for his garden.*

pick·er /'pɪkər/ *n.* a farm worker who picks (harvests) fruits, vegetables, etc.: *The grape pickers traveled for miles to find work.*

pick·et /'pɪkɪt/ *n.* **1** a long, firm, and usu. flat wooden stick with a pointed end sunk in the ground: *The old fence had many broken pickets in need of repair.* **2** one or more workers who stand in front of an office, factory, etc. to prevent others from entering to work, as part of a strike: *The striking workers formed a picket early in the morning.* **3** a person or group that stands or marches in a public place in order to protest against a decision, law, policy, etc.: *Many people joined the anti-war picket as it passed by.*

—*v.* to protest by standing or walking outside a company's premises: *Protesters picketed outside the main entrance.*

picket fence *n.* a fence made of pickets, or flat wooden stakes: *The boy painted the picket fence in front of the cottage.*

picket line *n.* **1** in a labor dispute, a line of workers that blocks entry to a place of work **2** the imaginary boundary line around that place:

P

To support the workers, we refused to cross the picket line.

USAGE NOTE: People who cross a *picket line* to work during a strike are called *scabs: The striking workers yelled at the scabs when they crossed the picket line.*

pick·le /ˈpɪkəl/ *n.* **1** [U] a cucumber soaked in vinegar and spices: *I like a slice of pickle with my sandwich.* **2** [U] a liquid containing salt, spices, and vinegar, used to preserve and flavor meat, fish, or vegetables: *She made a tasty pickle for the fish.* **3** [C] *infrml.fig.* a difficult or awkward situation: *He is in a pickle now, with no job and no money to pay his bills.*
—*v.* **-led, -ling, -les** to preserve in a pickle: *My grandmother used to pickle corn and peas.*

pick·led /ˈpɪkəld/ *adj.* **1** soaked in vinegar and spices: *Pickled herring tastes good.* **2** *infrml.fig.* drunk: *He's so pickled that he can hardly walk.*

pick·pock·et /ˈpɪkˌpakɪt/ *n.* a person who steals from the pockets or purses of people in crowds or public areas: *A pickpocket on the bus stole his wallet.*

pick·up /ˈpɪkˌʌp/ *n.* **1** [C] a pickup truck **2** [C] the act of picking s.t. up: *The truck driver had three more pickups to make before she could go home.* **3** [C] *infrml.* an unknown person met at a public place or social event for the purpose of casual sex: *He went to the party looking for an easy pickup.* **4** [U] power to speed up fast: *This car has a lot of pickup.* **5** [C] an improvement: *a pickup in sales*

pickup truck *n.* a light truck of medium size, with a driver's cabin in front, an open space in back, low side walls, and a rear gate that folds down; often used in everyday work: *The gardener carried tools in her pickup truck.*

pick·y /ˈpɪki/ *adj.* **-ier, -iest** fussy, difficult to please about small, often unimportant details: *He is very picky about how his shirts are laundered.*

pic·nic /ˈpɪknɪk/ *n.* **1** a trip taken by a friendly group of people to a pleasant outdoor place to eat a meal that has been prepared ahead of time and carried along: *We went for a picnic in the park.* **2** an outdoor meal had on a holiday or special occasion: *Our company gave a picnic for all employees.*
—*v.* **-nicked, -nicking, -nics** to have a picnic: *We picnicked in the park.*

pic·to·ri·al /pɪkˈtɔriəl/ *adj.* showing or presented in pictures: *a pictorial exhibit‖a pictorial history*

pic·ture /ˈpɪktʃər/ *n.* **1** a drawing, painting, or photograph: *The children draw pictures with crayons.‖His picture is in the paper.* **2** an example or perfect model: *She is a picture of good manners.* **3** a movie: *We went to the cin-*

ema to see a picture (or) the pictures. **4** the outlook or future: *The picture looks good for the success of our business.* **5** an explanation or mental image: *She tried to give us a picture of how a computer works.* **6** (the quality of) an image on a TV or movie screen: *This TV gets a really good picture.* **7** *infrml.* **to get the picture:** to understand, see the meaning after some difficulty, (*syn.*) to catch on: *After she explained the solution to the math problem, I said, "Oh, now I get the picture."* **8** *infrml.* **to be in or out of the picture:** to know or not to know the real situation: *When she came back from vacation, she was out of the picture of what happened while she was away.*
—*v.* **-tured, -turing, -tures** **1** to give a certain image of: *The drawing pictured the man in an old chair with his dog.* **2** to imagine: *I pictured myself in a boat on a river.*

pic·tur·esque /ˌpɪktʃəˈrɛsk/ *adj.* **1** like a picture, pleasing to the eye, charming: *That little fishing village by the sea is quite picturesque.* **2** (of writing or speech) colorful, descriptive, expressive: *The old sailor told a picturesque tale of his youth.*

picture window *n.* a large window in a house or apartment, esp. one with a good view: *We can see the park and trees through our picture window.*

pid·dle /ˈpɪdl/ *v.* **-dled, -dling, -dles** to waste time or money on worthless or unimportant things: *I piddled away the morning playing computer games.*

pid·dling /ˈpɪdlɪŋ/ *adj.* insignificant, very little: *That poor fellow gets paid a piddling wage for his work.*

pidg·in /ˈpɪdʒən/ *n.* a simplified language, usu. a mixture of words from two or more languages: *The pidgin spoken by some people in Hawaii is a combination of words from English and native Hawaiian languages.*

pie /paɪ/ *n.* **1** [C;U] a food dish of fruit, meat, or other foods cooked in a pastry crust: *Would you like some apple pie for dessert?* **2** *infrml.fig.* **as easy as pie:** very easy: *Riding a bike is as easy as pie.* **3** *fig.* **to have a finger in every pie:** to be involved in many different projects: *She is a very active manager and has a finger in every pie.* **4** *infrml.fig.* **pie in the sky:** a desirable but unrealistic idea or plan: *They say we will build a new office, but I think that's pie in the sky.*

USAGE NOTE: Apple *pie* is a traditional American dessert. People say "as American as apple pie" to refer to something that is very American: *Baseball was invented in the United States; it's as American as apple pie.*

piece /pis/ *n.* **1** a part of a whole thing that is separate from the rest: *A piece of the house* *roof fell off during the storm.*‖*He dropped the glass and it broke in pieces.* **2** a separate amount or portion of s.t. that is the same in substance or form: *a piece of wood/rock/candy/butter*‖*Would you hand me a piece of wood?* **3** an example of a general kind of thing: *a piece of news/information/furniture/good luck*‖*This morning I heard a sad piece of news.* **4** one of several parts in a related set that are meant to fit or work together as a whole and for a purpose: *the pieces of a bicycle/puzzle/clock*‖*She laid out all the pieces of the clock before she put them together.* **5** one of the objects moved about on a board to play a game, such as chess: *I lost one of the pieces for that game.* **6** a unique product of an activity that requires skill, esp. a work of art: *a piece of music/poetry/work*‖*That essay was an excellent piece of writing!* **7** a firearm, gun: *Soldiers are taught to keep their pieces clean.* **8** *infrml.fig.* **a piece of cake:** something very easy to do: *It will be a piece of cake to win this game.* **9 to give s.o. a piece of one's mind:** to criticize harshly, (*syn.*) to scold: *She was rude to my father, so I gave her a piece of my mind.* **10** *fig.* **to go to pieces:** to break down and lose control of oneself from grief or sorrow: *He went to pieces when she left him.*

—*phrasal v. sep.* **pieced, piecing, pieces to piece s.t. together: a.** to put together, repair, or assemble: *She pieced together the broken chair.* **b.** to make sense of s.t. by putting together separate facts: *He tried to piece together what happened to all his money.*

piece·meal /ˈpis,mil/ *adj.adv.* (done or made) piece by piece, or one piece at a time, without concern for a set or sequence: *He rebuilt the old house <adv.> piecemeal over many years, whenever he had the time.*

piece·work /ˈpis,wɜrk/ *n.* [U] work for which one's pay is measured by the amount done, or number of things produced, rather than the time spent: *She does piecework at home, getting five dollars for each doll that she makes.*

pie chart *n.* a circular chart divided into sections by percent of each activity: *A pie chart of sales shows half comes from overseas.*

pier /pɪr/ *n.* **1** a large, long, flat structure of wood or iron built on pillars and extending like a bridge out from land and over water, at which boats can load or unload passengers and cargo, (*syn.*) a wharf: *She waved goodbye from the boat to her friends who stood on the pier.* **2** a pillar (or large post) that supports such a structure: *At the beach you can see many old piers sticking out of the water.*

pierce /pɪrs/ *v.* **pierced, piercing, pierces 1** to cut a hole in or through s.t. with a pointed object: *The needle pierced my skin.*‖*She had her ears pierced for earrings.* **2** to break through the surface or into the depths of s.t., (*syn.*) to

penetrate: *The boat pierced the waves of the sea.*‖*The searchlight pierced the darkness of night.*

pierc·ing /ˈpɪrsɪŋ/ *adj.* **1** sharp and painful: *a cold, piercing wind*‖*a piercing scream* **2** searching, penetrating: *He has a piercing look that sees through you.* -*adv.* **piercingly.**

pi·e·ty /ˈpaɪəti/ *n.* [U] devotion to God and obedience to his teachings: *The priest was very impressed by the young girl's piety.*

pig /pɪg/ *n.* **1** a common farm animal of the swine family, valued for its meat, with a fat round body, thick skin, short nose, legs, and tail: *A big, fat pig cannot run fast.* **2** the meat of a pig: pork, ham, or bacon **3** a fat, impolite, or offensive person who eats too much: *I will never invite that man to dinner because he is a pig.* **4 to make a pig of oneself:** to behave like a pig in public, causing others to be embarrassed: *She drank too much at the party and made a pig of herself at dinner, so I asked her to leave.*

—*phrasal v. insep.* **to pig out on s.t.:** to take pleasure in eating too much: *After school, he pigged out on pizza and ice cream.*

USAGE NOTE: When pigmeat is eaten, it is called *pork, ham,* or *bacon;* it is not called pig.

pi·geon /ˈpɪdʒən/ *n.* a bird with a round body, small head, and usu. a gray or white color: *People in the park threw bread crumbs to the pigeons.*

pi·geon·hole /ˈpɪdʒən,houl/ *n.* one of a number of open-ended, box-like sections of a desk or cabinet arranged in rows and used for sorting and keeping papers, letters, etc.: *I keep all my old medical bills in one pigeonhole in my desk.*

—*v.* **-holed, -holing, -holes** to put s.t. in a specific group, (*syn.*) to classify: *She pigeonholed me as being from the South because of my accent.*

pig·gish /ˈpɪgɪʃ/ *adj.* greedy, gross, or sloppy like a pig: *His piggish table manners embarrass everyone he knows.*

pig·gy /ˈpɪgi/ *n.infrml.* **-gies** a little pig: *The newborn piggy was cute. See:* piglet.

—*adj.infrml.* **-gier, -giest** piggish

pig·gy·back /ˈpɪgi,bæk/ *adv.adj.* **1** on the back or shoulders: *The little girl loved to ride <adv.> piggyback on her father.*‖*My uncle gave me a <adj.> piggyback ride.* **2** carried by a larger or more powerful vehicle: *We saw a railroad train go by with several trucks riding <adv.> piggyback on top.*

piggy bank *n.* a small container often shaped like a pig and used by a child for saving coins: *When my son's piggy bank is full, he will use his money to buy a new toy.*

pig·head·ed /'pɪgˌhɛdɪd/ *adj.infrml. fig.* stubborn, unwilling to change one's opinion or behavior: *He is pigheaded and refuses to take medicine despite his doctor's orders.*

pig·let /'pɪglɪt/ *n.* a baby pig

pig·ment /'pɪgmənt/ *n.* **1** [C;U] a powder or paste of concentrated color, mixed with other substances to create colored paints or dyes: *We added a yellow pigment to the blue paint to make it green.* **2** [U] the natural coloring of a plant or animal: *Her skin has a beautiful brown pigment.*

pig·men·ta·tion /ˌpɪgmən'teɪʃən/ *n.* [U] the color of s.t., esp. the skin: *His skin has a light pigmentation; he burns easily when he goes to the beach in the summer.*

pig·my /'pɪgmi/ *n.* **-mies** *See:* pygmy.

pig·pen /'pɪgˌpɛn/ *n.* **1** an enclosed area in which pigs are kept and fed **2** *fig.* any dirty, disordered place: *That young woman's room is a pigpen.*

pig·skin /'pɪgˌskɪn/ *n.adj.* **1** [U] a tough leather made from the skin of a pig: *He wears pigskin gloves in winter.* **2** *infrml.* an American football: *Let's go outdoors and throw the pigskin around.*

pig·sty /'pɪgˌstaɪ/ *n.* **-sties** a pigpen

pig·tail /'pɪgˌteɪl/ *n. fig.* a length of hair that hangs down the back of the neck and shoulders, formed by folding two or more strands around each other, *(syn.)* a braid: *She made her hair into a pigtail before she went swimming.*

pike (1) /paɪk/ *n.* **pike** or **pikes** a long, thin, freshwater fish with sharp teeth

pike (2) *n.* **pikes 1** a long, wooden spear with a pointed end made of iron or steel, used by foot soldiers before the invention of modern firearms **2** *short for* turnpike: *I drive the pike to work.*

pi·laf /'pi,lɑf, pɪ'lɑf/ *n.* [U] a rice dish cooked in broth, often with pieces of meat, fish, or vegetables: *For dinner I had rice pilaf mixed with shrimp.*

pile (1) /paɪl/ *n.* **1** a mass or collection of similar material or things laid or thrown together, forming the shape of a small hill, *(syn.)* a heap: *A truck dumped a pile of sand near the road.‖His clothes lay in a pile on the floor.* **2** a collection of similar things laid one on top of the other, *(syn.)* a stack: *a pile of magazines‖a pile of plates* **3** *often pl.* **piles** a lot, very much: *She has piles (or) a pile of homework to do this weekend.* **4** *infrml.* a large amount of money: *She made a pile in real estate.*

—*v.* **piled, piling, piles 1** to make into a pile: *He piled the newspapers on his desk.* **2** to load or fill in large amounts: *She piled the truck with hay.* **3** to go in or out in a disorderly group: *The kids piled into the bus.* **4 pile up:** to become greater in quantity, *(syns.)* to accumulate, add up: *His debts keep piling up.*

pile (2) *n.* [U] the soft, dense layer of upright threads on the surface of a rug or woven fabric such as velvet: *He liked to walk barefoot on the rug with the thick pile.*

pile (3) *n.* a large, long, heavy piece of wood, metal, or cement sunk deep into the ground (esp. wet ground or under water) to provide support for buildings, bridges, or piers: *Close to the river, houses were built on piles that went 30 feet below ground level.*

pile·up /'paɪl,ʌp/ *n.* an accident in which many vehicles crash into each other one after another: *Pileups often happen because the roads are slippery and drivers are unable to stop fast.*

pil·fer /'pɪlfər/ *v.frml.* to steal, esp. small things in small amounts: *The children pilfered apples from the fruit stand.* -*n.* **pilferer.**

pil·grim /'pɪlgrəm/ *n.* a person who travels a long way to visit a holy place: *Pilgrims often travel together for comfort and support when faced with difficulties.* -*n.* [C] **pilgrimage** /'pɪlgrəmɪdʒ/.

USAGE NOTE: In 1620, a group of English settlers established Plimoth Colony (now spelled Plymouth) in Massachusetts. These people are often referred to as the *Pilgrims* (with a capital P). The *Thanksgiving* holiday in the USA celebrates a 1621 harvest feast that the Pilgrims shared with Native Americans of the Massachusetts coast.

pil·ing /'paɪlɪŋ/ *n.* a pile(3): *The wooden pilings under the bridge need to be repaired.*

pill /pɪl/ *n.* **1** a small, round piece of medicine meant to be swallowed: *He takes a pill to reduce his high blood pressure.* **2** a difficult or unpleasant person: *If you're going to be a pill, you can't go to the movies with us because we won't have any fun.* **3 a bitter pill (to swallow):** a blow to one's pride and self-respect: *Being turned down again for a promotion was a bitter pill for her to swallow.* **4 the pill:** a method of birth control for women, taken once each month: *She doesn't want to have children yet, so she's on the pill.*

pil·lage /'pɪlɪdʒ/ *v.frml.* **-laged, -laging, -lages** to steal property using violence, as during a war: *Invaders pillaged the villages along the coast 1,000 years ago.* -*n.* **pillager.**

pil·lar /'pɪlər/ *n.* **1** a tall column of wood, stone, or metal used to support a building: *Marble pillars stood on either side of the doorway.* **2** *fig.* a member of a group who is an important source of its strength and purpose: *Her long years of service made her a pillar of the community.*

pil·low /'pɪloʊ/ *n.* a square or rectangular cloth bag filled with soft material, used to support the back or head for comfort, esp. the head when lying in bed: *He sleeps with a soft pillow under his head.*

pil·low·case /'pɪlou,keɪs/ *n.* a thin, removable covering for a pillow

pi·lot (1) /'paɪlət/ *n.* **1** a person who flies an aircraft: *The pilot spoke to the passengers during our flight.* **2** a person with detailed knowledge of the waters in a particular harbor, river, or canal who guides boats into and out of such areas: *When we arrived at the port, a pilot came on board to take us to the dock.* **3** any guide or leader in a difficult task: *Our teacher was our pilot as we learned to solve the math problem.*
—*v.* to act as a pilot: *She piloted the ship to land.*‖*I was lost but he piloted me back to my hotel.*

pilot (2) *adj.* meant to serve as a test, (*syns.*) trial, experimental: *We designed a pilot program to see if the new computer system would work.*
—*v.* to test s.t. by conducting a pilot program: *My company piloted the new computer software before selling it in stores.*

pilot light *n.* a small gas flame in a stove or furnace, used to light the main gas burners: *A gust of wind blew out the pilot light.*

pi·men·to /pɪ'mɛntou/ *n.* **-tos** a sweet, mild red pepper used in cooking and as a stuffing for olives: *Pimentos add color to a meal.*

pimp /pɪmp/ *n.v.* a person who takes money for offering the services of other people (prostitutes) to satisfy the sexual needs of customers: *He acts as a <n.> pimp for ten prostitutes.*

pim·ple /'pɪmpəl/ *n.* a small, red swelling on the skin: *That young man has pimples on his face.* -*adj.* **pimply.**

pin /pɪn/ *n.* **1** a short, straight, very thin piece of metal with a sharp point and a flat, round head, used to hold together things (made of cloth, paper, etc.) by sticking through them: *She kept a box of pins with her needles and thread for sewing.* **2** a piece of jewelry attached to clothing with a pin: *She wore a diamond pin on her coat.* **3** any object used to hold things in place by piercing or clasping them: *She wore a hair pin to hold back her hair.* **4 on pins and needles:** feeling worried and tense: *He was on pins and needles while waiting for the doctor.*
—*v.* **pinned, pinning, pins 1** to fasten or attach with a pin or pins: *He pinned a flower to her dress.*‖*She pinned up a notice on the board.* **2** to hold s.t. or s.o. in one place and unable to move: *She was pinned against the door by the crowd.*‖*They were pinned down by enemy gunfire.* **3 to pin one's hope on:** to wish for or depend on: *He pinned his hopes on good luck.* **4** *phrasal v. sep.* **to pin s.o. or s.t.**

down: a. s.o.: to force s.o. to give an opinion or make a decision: *His plans were not clear, so we tried to pin down our accountant in the meeting.*‖*We pinned him down.* **b. s.t.:** to make s.t. certain: *She wanted to pin down a date for her wedding.* **5** *phrasal v. insep.* **to pin s.t. on s.o.:** to place responsibility or blame: *They tried to pin the murder on the stranger.*

pin·ball machine /'pɪn,bɔl/ *n.* a coin-operated mechanical game, played by one person on a long glass-covered slanted table, in which a metal ball is struck against pins to score points: *The snack bar has pinball machines in the back.*

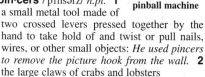
pinball machine

pin·cers /'pɪnsərz/ *n.pl.* **1** a small metal tool made of two crossed levers pressed together by the hand to take hold of and twist or pull nails, wires, or other small objects: *He used pincers to remove the picture hook from the wall.* **2** the large claws of crabs and lobsters

pinch /pɪntʃ/ *v.* **pinches 1** to grasp or press tightly between the thumb and a finger: *She pinched (the skin of) his arm to get his attention.*‖*He pinched some salt to put on his meat.* **2** to be caught and squeezed between two hard objects that come together: *She pinched her finger in the desk drawer.* **3** to cause pain from being too tight: *His shoes pinched his feet.* **4** *slang* to take or steal: *My girlfriend pinched my last cigarette.* **5** *slang* to arrest: *The police pinched him on the street corner.* **6 to be** or **feel pinched:** to feel pressure and distress from the lack of money or other hardship: *He was out of work and (felt) pinched for money.* **7 to pinch pennies:** to be very careful about spending money: *When she was a student, she had to pinch pennies.*
—*n.* **pinches 1** a tight squeeze between the thumb and a finger, esp. of the skin to cause sharp pain: *My mother gave me a pinch to make me be good.* **2** an amount that can be grasped between the thumb and a finger: *a pinch of salt* **3** a pain from a tight muscle or nerve: *He has a pinch in his neck.* **4 in a pinch: a.** in a difficult situation or crisis: *Without his car, he was in a pinch.* **b.** if necessary: *In a pinch, we will have to go ahead without her.*

pinch-hit *v.* **-hit, -hitting, -hits 1** (in baseball) to enter the game as a batter in the place of another player **2** *infrml.* to take s.o. else's place for a brief period of time: *She pinch-hit for me while I was on vacation.* -*n.* **pinch hitter.**

pin cushion *n.* a very small pillow into which pins are stuck when not in use: *Pin cushions should be kept out of the reach of children.*

P

pine /paɪn/ *n.* **1** [C] a tall, straight tree, found mainly in cool climates, with small, thin, sharp leaves (called "needles") that remain green throughout the year and woody, brown fruit (called "cones"): *We built a summer house among the pines* (or) *pine trees.* **2** [U] the soft, yellowish wood of this tree, very commonly used for furniture and houses: *We built our house out of pine.*

—*v.* **pined, pining, pines** **1** to lose one's health and strength from sorrow and grief: *He pined away after the death of his wife.* **2** to feel a lonely desire for s.t. or s.o. one has lost or become separated from, *(syns.)* to long for, to yearn: *He pined for his girlfriend when she moved away.*

pine·ap·ple /ˈpaɪ,næpəl/ *n.* [C;U] a tropical plant with a fruit that is brown and rough on the outside and has a sweet, yellow, juicy flesh on the inside

pine·y /ˈpaɪni/ *adj.* See: piny.

ping /pɪŋ/ *n.* a short, sharp, ringing sound made

pineapple

by striking metal or glass: *After dinner he struck his glass with a knife to make a ping and got everyone's attention.*

—*v.* to make such a sound: *He pinged his glass to get everyone's attention.*

ping-pong /ˈpɪŋ,pɑŋ, -,pɔŋ/ *n.* See: table tennis.

pin·head /ˈpɪn,hɛd/ *n.* **1** the round top of a pin: *A pinhead is very small.* **2** *infrml.fig.* a stupid person: *I never listen to those pinheads; they don't know anything.*

pin·ion /ˈpɪnyən/ *v.* to prevent s.o. from moving by physical force: *I was pinioned to my chair while they searched the room.*

pink /pɪŋk/ *n.* **1** [U] a light red color: *Pink roses are pretty.* **2 in the pink:** in good condition, healthy: *After a long period of rest, he looked in the pink.*

pink·ie or **pinky** /ˈpɪŋki/ *n.infrml.* **-kies** the little finger: *When she holds a teacup, she raises her pinkie.*

pink·o /ˈpɪŋkoʊ/ *n. pej.slang* **-os** a person who sympathizes with left-wing (e.g., socialist, communist) political beliefs: *He thought that the colleges and unions were filled with pinkos.*

pin·na·cle /ˈpɪnəkəl/ *n.* **1** the pointed top of a mountain: *Climbers finally reached the mountain's pinnacle.* **2** the highest point of s.t.: *That lawyer is at the pinnacle of her career.* **3** a pointed ornamental structure set on or rising above a roof: *The grand old church had many small pinnacles and one large one.*

pi·noch·le /ˈpi,nɑkəl, -,nʌ-/ *n.* [U] a card game: *He plays pinochle with friends every week.*

pin·point /ˈpɪn,pɔɪnt/ *n.* the sharp point of a pin

—*v.* **1** to locate exactly: *She pinpointed her street on the map.* **2** to determine the exact nature or cause of: *Let's see if we can pinpoint the problem here.*

pin·prick /ˈpɪn,prɪk/ *n.* a small mark made by a pin or pointed instrument: *He made a pinprick next to my name with his pencil.*

pin·stripe /ˈpɪn,straɪp/ *n.* a thin line of white or colored thread in cloth: *She wore a shirt with blue pinstripes.*

—*adj.* fabric with a pattern of pinstripes: *He wears conservative pinstripe suits.*

pint /paɪnt/ *n.* a unit of measure for liquids, equal to 16 ounces or one half quart (.47 liter): *He bought a pint of beer.*

pin·up /ˈpɪn,ʌp/ *n. old usage* a picture of a sexually attractive person (such as a fashion model, movie star, or popular singer), or of a person wearing little or no clothing, that is put up on a wall for display: *She has pinups from movie magazines on her bedroom wall.*

pin·wheel /ˈpɪn,wil/ *n.* a toy with colorful curved wings rotating on a stick: *The child waved the pinwheel to make it spin.*

pin·y or **piney** /ˈpaɪni/ *adj.* **-ier, -iest** related to pine trees: *The woods have a nice, piny smell.*

pi·o·neer /ˌpaɪəˈnɪr/ *n.* **1** one of the first people to enter new or undeveloped land to live and work there: *Pioneers crossed America to find new farm land.* **2** a person who leads the way for others into a new area of knowledge or invention: *He was a pioneer in computer science.*

—*v.* to develop, explore, or settle s.t. new: *She pioneered the political campaign for women's rights.*

pi·ous /ˈpaɪəs/ *adj.* **1** feeling and showing love and duty to God and religion: *She is a very pious churchgoer.* **2** pretending to be religious and pure while serving one's own interests and hurting other people: *Her husband is fond of making pious accusations about others.* **-adv.** **piously.**

pipe /paɪp/ *n.* **1** a tube through which liquids or gases pass from one place to another: *Pipes are used to carry water and gas into homes and buildings.* **2** a small tube with a bowl at one end and a mouthpiece at the other, for smoking tobacco: *Smoking a pipe is not allowed in this restaurant.* **3** a musical instrument, similar to a flute, played by blowing air through it: *She played a song on her pipe.* **4** one of the many tubes that make the sound of a musical organ: *The pipes in that church's organ have a beautiful tone.*

—*v.* **piped, piping, pipes** **1** to carry, esp. liquids and gas, through pipes: *Water and gas are piped into the house.* **2** to play a musical tune

P

on a pipe or flute: *She piped a song to please the children.* **3** *phrasal v.* **to pipe down:** to become quiet, stop making noise: *The children were screaming, so I told them to pipe down.* **4** *phrasal v.* **to pipe up:** to start speaking or speak louder: *He told me to pipe up so everyone could hear.*

pipe dream *n. fig.* a wish or hope that has little or no chance of coming true: *He has a pipe dream about being President someday.*

pipe·line /'paɪp,laɪn/ *n.* **1** a long system of connected pipes that carry gas, water, or oil over long distances: *The city's pipelines bring us water from the surrounding mountains.* **2** **in the pipeline:** currently being developed, to be available in the near future: *That company has a new computer system in the pipeline for next year.*

pip·ing /'paɪpɪŋ/ *n.* **1** [U] an amount or system of pipes used for water, gas, etc.: *Plumbers are installing piping in the new building.* **2** the sound of musical pipes being played: *We could hear piping coming from the house next door.* **3** a narrow cord used to trim edges and cover seams in clothing or furniture: *The girl's coat had red piping.*
—*adv.* **piping hot:** (of food or drink) very hot: *The mashed potatoes are served piping hot.*

pip-squeak /'pɪp,skwik/ *n.* a small, unimportant person: *Don't be afraid of him; he's a pip-squeak!*

pi·quant /'pikənt, -,kant, pi'kant/ *adj.frml.* **1** sharp and pleasant to taste: *She added spices to the soup to give it a piquant taste.* **2** interesting in an odd way, (*syn.*) stimulating: *His piquant stories of the old days made us want to hear more.* -*n.* **piquancy** /'pikənsi/.

pique /pik/ *v.* **piqued, piquing, piques 1** to annoy, irritate: *We piqued our waiter because we took so long to order our food.* **2** to arouse interest, stimulate: *The mere mention of food piques her appetite.*

pi·ra·cy /'paɪrəsi/ *n.* [U] **1** robbery (of boats or airplanes) that takes place at sea or in the air: *They would not sail across the ocean because they feared piracy.* **2** copying and selling the work of others without permission: *The use of computers has made piracy an important issue.*

pi·ra·nha /pə'ranə, -'ranyə, -'ræ-/ *n.* a small freshwater South American fish with sharp teeth and powerful jaws: *Piranhas are capable of killing people and cattle.*

pi·rate /'paɪrɪt/ *n.* **1** a person who steals sailing ships or airplanes or the cargo they carry: *The pirates threatened to kill anyone who tried to stop them.* **2** a person who reproduces and sells the work of others without permission: *My book was copied illegally and sold by pirates in another country.*

—*v.* **-rated, -rating, -rates** to violate the laws that protect property rights by reproducing, for profit and without permission, the published work (a book, performance, invention, etc.) of another person or company: *The police caught him trying to pirate computer software and sell it in other countries.*

pir·ou·ette /,pɪru'ɛt/ *n.v.* **-etted, -etting, -ettes** a movement in formal dance (such as ballet) in which the dancer spins around in one place while standing on the ball or toes of one foot: *It is hard to keep one's balance when performing a <n.> pirouette.*

Pi·sces /'paɪ,siz/ *n.* the 12th sign of the zodiac

piss /pɪs/ *n. vulg.* **1** urine **2** the act of urinating: *He took a piss behind a tree.*
—*v. vulg.* **pisses 1** to urinate **2** *phrasal v. sep.* **to piss s.o. off:** to make s.o. angry: *He pissed me off; he borrowed my bicycle and then lost it.*

pissed /pɪst/ or **pissed off** *adj. slang* angry: *My father was pissed* (or) *pissed off because I broke the living room window.*

pis·tach·i·o /pɪ'stæʃi,ou, -'sta-/ *n.* **-os 1** [C] small tree that grows in warm climates and produces a small green nut used as a food: *Her favorite ice cream is made with pistachio nuts.* **2** [U] a pale green color

pis·tol /'pɪstəl/ *n.* a small gun that can be held and shot in one hand: *Most police officers on patrol carry a pistol.*

pis·ton /'pɪstən/ *n.* in an engine or pump, a solid, deep metal disk that moves up and down within a tight cylinder and moves other parts of a machine: *An automobile engine with eight pistons has a lot of power.*

pit (1) /pɪt/ *n.* **1** a large, open (shallow or deep; natural or artificial) hole in the ground: *The builders dug a deep pit for the foundation of the new office building.* **2** a large hole in the ground where people dig for coal, (*syn.*) a coal mine: *He has spent years working deep in the pit where it is hard to breathe.* **3** a shallow or hollow area set lower than its surroundings: *The children played in the sandpit.* **4** a hollow part of the body, such as the armpit (under the shoulder, where the arm joins the body) **5** a small scar, dent, or mark in the surface of s.t. smooth, such as skin or sheet metal: *Her car was covered with little pits caused by air pollution.* **6** an enclosed area in which animals are placed to fight each other: *Men gathered around the pit to watch the cocks fight.* **7** an area by the side of a racetrack where race cars enter to be refueled and repaired during the race: *The driver drove into the pit for a new set of tires.* **8 orchestra pit:** the low area in front of a theatrical stage where the musicians in an orchestra sit and perform: *When the conductor entered the (orchestra) pit, the audience applauded.* **9 pit stop: a.** a race car's brief pe-

riod in the pit at a racetrack **b.** any brief stop for fuel or refreshment while traveling: *We turned off the highway for a pit stop at a gas station.* **c.** *slang* a brief stop to use a bathroom: *Wait for me; I have to make a pit stop!* **10** *infrml.* **the pits:** s.t. extremely bad, the worst: *This restaurant is the pits.*
—*v.* **pitted, pitting, pits 1** to mark with pits: *The front of his truck was pitted by stones from the road.* **2** to put in opposition to or competition with: *In the tennis match, I was pitted against my best friend.*

pit (2) *n.* the hard seed of some fruits: *Cherries and peaches have pits.*
—*v.* **pitted, pitting, pits** to remove the pit: *I pitted some peaches before we ate them.*

pi·ta or **pita bread** /'pita/ *n.* a round, flat bread, originally from the Middle East, that can be split open to form a pocket and filled to make a sandwich

pitch (1) /pɪtʃ/ *v.* **pitches 1** to throw or toss: *She pitched her bags into the trunk of the car.||They pitched hay onto the wagon.* **2** (in baseball) to throw the ball to the batter: *My father taught me how to pitch when I was young.* **3** (in baseball) to play the role of pitcher: *Who is going to pitch in tonight's game?* **4** to set up, (*syn.*) to erect: *They pitched their tent near the river.* **5** (of a ship) to roll back and forth in the waves: *Our boat pitched heavily during the storm.* **6** to fall or be thrown suddenly and forcefully: *He hit a bump and was pitched from his bicycle.* **7** to set a piece of music on a particular scale: *This song has been pitched too high for the men in the choir.* **8** to change the way one writes or speaks in order to communicate to a particular group of people: *She pitched her speech to the elderly people in the audience.* **9** *phrasal v.* **to pitch in:** to join with others or contribute to an activity: *We all pitched in to help homeless people.*
—*n.* **pitches 1** (in baseball) a single throw of the ball by a pitcher: *That was a fast pitch.* **2** the degree of highness or lowness of a musical note or a voice: *She sang in a high pitch.* **3** the angle or slope of a building or roof: *Our roof has a very steep pitch.* **4** a level or degree (of activity, energy, etc.): *During summer, activity at school is at a low pitch.* **5** the forward and backward rocking movement of a boat: *The pitch of the boat was so great that everyone was scared.* **6 sales pitch:** a forceful speech or talk meant to persuade people to buy s.t.: *We listened to the car dealer's sales pitch.*

pitch (2) *n.* [U] a dark, sticky substance made from wood, coal, or petroleum, used to cover surfaces and cracks to prevent water from getting through: *After I repaired the roof of my house, my pants were covered with pitch.*

pitch-black *adj.* **1** so dark as to make it impossible to see: *Inside the cave, it was pitch-*

black. **2** very densely black: *That coal is pitch-black.*

pitch·er (1) /'pɪtʃər/ *n.* a tall, round container with an open top and large handle, used for holding and pouring liquids: *A waiter poured water from a pitcher into my glass.*

pitcher (2) *n.* (in baseball) the player who throws the ball toward the batter, who tries to hit it: *Pitchers must have strong and flexible arms.*

pitcher

pitch·fork /'pɪtʃ,fɔrk/ *n.* a large fork with two or three prongs and a long wooden handle, used on farms to lift and move hay: *They used pitchforks to toss the hay onto the truck.*

pit·e·ous /'pɪtiəs/ *adj.* of or about causing pity or sympathy: *The caged dog let out a piteous cry.* -*adv.* **piteously.**

pit·fall /'pɪt,fɔl/ *n.* an unseen danger or difficulty that is a common cause of mistakes or errors: *Starting a new business has many pitfalls.*

pith·y /'pɪθi/ *adj.* -**ier, -iest** brief but full of meaning: *Proverbs in the Bible contain pithy sayings.*

pit·i·ful /'pɪtɪfəl/ *adj.* **1** worthy of pity, sad: *Many poor people live in pitiful conditions.* **2** hopelessly bad, not worthy of much attention, (*syn.*) contemptible: *His attempts to win her love were pitiful.* -*adv.* **pitifully.**

pit·i·less /'pɪtɪlɪs/ *adj.* without pity or mercy, cold and harsh: *The pitiless soldiers killed innocent civilians.* -*adv.* **pitilessly.**

pit·tance /'pɪtns/ *n.* a very small amount of money: *She expects her employees to work for a pittance.*

pit·ter-pat·ter /'pɪtər,pætər, ,pɪtər'pæ-/ *n.* [U] the sound and movement of a rapid succession of light taps or beats, as of rain or feet: *the pitter-patter of rain on the window*
—*adv. adj.* related to having or making such a sound or movement: *My heart went <adv.> pitter-patter when she agreed to marry me.*

pi·tu·i·tar·y gland /pɪ'tuə,teri/ *n.* a small organ at the base of the brain that regulates the body's growth

pit·y /'pɪti/ *n.* [U] **1** the feeling of sorrow, tenderness, or sympathy caused by the suffering or hardships of others: *She feels pity for the poor and the sick.* **2** a cause for regret: *It is a pity that your husband is ill.* **3 to have pity on s.o.:** to help s.o. out of sympathy or mercy: *A soldier had pity on a wounded enemy and helped him to safety.*
—*v.* -**ied, -ying, -ies** to feel sorry for s.o.: *He pities the poor and gives money to them.*

piv·ot /'pɪvət/ *n.* **1** a fixed point, such as a pin, short rod, or ball on which something turns or swings: *My desk lamp has three different pivots for changing its position.* **2** a person or thing on which something else depends: *She is the key pivot in our plan to win the game.* -adj. **pivotal.**

—v. to turn on or as if on a pivot: *A basketball player pivoted and shot the ball.*

pix·el /'pɪksəl, -sɛl/ *n.* a single point of light on a computer or TV screen: *The higher the number of pixels on a screen, the finer the picture.*

pixi·e or **pixy** /'pɪksi/ *n.* **-ies** in folklore, a small imaginary creature that looks human, who is fond of playing tricks: *That little girl behaves like a pixie.*

piz·za or **pizza pie** /'pitsə/ *n.* [C;U] a flat, wide circle of bread dough, usu. baked with tomato sauce and cheese and often topped with sausage, mushrooms, etc.: *I ordered a slice of pizza and a soda.*

piz·zazz /pə'zæz/ *n.infrml.* [U] the quality of being exciting, energetic, and glamorous: *That new Broadway musical has a lot of pizzazz.*

piz·ze·ri·a /ˌpitsə'riə/ *n.* a restaurant that makes and sells pizza

pj's or **PJ's** /'piˌdʒeɪz/ *n.infrml. abbr. for* pajamas

plac·ard /'plækərd, -ˌkɑrd/ *n.* a printed or written poster or sign, such as carried by a protester: *Union members carried placards protesting their low wages.*

pla·cate /'pleɪˌkeɪt/ *v.frml.* **-cated, -cating, -cates** to settle or soothe s.o.'s anger, esp. through special attention or favors: *Our boss was angry at us, so we placated him by working late.*

place /pleɪs/ *n.* **1 a.** a spot or position in space that is or can be occupied by a person or thing: *Here is a good place to hang the picture.* **b.** *fig.* a position in relation to certain thoughts, ideas, feelings, etc.: *She has no place for him in her heart.||He has a place of honor in his country's history.* **2** a particular location, area, or region on the earth, such as a city, state, island, etc.: *Buenos Aires is a great place to visit.* **3** a position in line: *He asked me to save him a place while he parked the car.* **4** a final position in a race or competition: *She came in second place in the diving contest.* **5** a room, building, or piece of land used for a particular purpose: *the workplace||a marketplace||a holy place* **6** *infrml.* a room, apartment, house, or other residence: *After the movie, let's go back to my place.* **7** any part or spot in a body or thing: *I have a sore place in my throat.||Show me the place where the chair is broken.* **8** a space or seat for a person: *Did you get a place at the table?* **9** a function or duty: *It is not his place to tell us what to do.* **10** a short street: *They live on Brentwood Place.* **11 all over the place:** everywhere: *They have traveled all*

over the place.||*The pipe broke and oil went all over the place.* **12 in** or **out of place:** in or not in the position where (s.o. or s.t.) belongs: *Everything is in place, so we are ready to go.||On his first trip overseas, he felt out of place.* **13 in place of:** instead of, as a substitute for: *If you are sick, she will have to go in place of you.* **14 people in high places:** people in important positions with power and influence: *She knows people in high places, including her country's ambassador to Washington.* **15 to go places:** to be successful: *He's so smart; he is really going to go places.* **16 to know one's place:** to know the limits of one's power or position in society and behave accordingly **17 to put s.o. in his** or **her place:** to scold s.o. for claiming rights that are not theirs: *She spoke at the meeting without being asked, and the boss put her in her place.* **18 to take place:** to happen: *The dance will take place on Saturday night.*

—v. **placed, placing, places 1** to put in a specific location or position: *I placed the groceries on the kitchen table.||She was placed on the school's board of directors.* **2** to rank or value: *He placed her among the best students.* **3** to find employment for: *The employment agency placed him in a large computer company.* **4** to remember how, where, or when one came to know s.o. or s.t.: *I know that woman from somewhere, but I can't place her.* **5 to place an order:** to request s.t. with the purpose of buying: *She placed an order for a new refrigerator.*

pla·ce·bo /plə'sibou/ *n.* **-bos** a substance that looks like real medicine, but has no real effects; used for comparison when testing new drugs or to treat patients whose illnesses may be imaginary

place·ment /'pleɪsmənt/ *n.* [C;U] **1** the act of placing or state of being placed: *The company made an official announcement about his placement in the Paris office.* **2** location or arrangement: *She was very careful about the placement of her guests at the dinner table.* **3** the process of matching people who are looking for jobs with opportunities for employment: *She was a specialist in placement for recent college graduates.* **4 placement office:** the office in a college or university that helps students find jobs: *He went to the placement office for a job interview.*

pla·cen·ta /plə'sɛntə/ *n.* **-tas** or **-tae** /-ti/ the organ that is formed during pregnancy in female mammals and that contains and nourishes the fetus, *(syn.)* the afterbirth: *The placenta comes out after the baby has been born.*

plac·id /'plæsɪd/ *adj.* calm, peaceful: *After the storm, the sea was placid and smooth.* **-adv.** **placidly;** **-n.** [U] **placidity** /plə'sɪdəti/.

pla·gia·rism /'pleɪʤə,rɪzəm/ *n.* **1** the act of plagiarizing: *A student was expelled for plagiarism.* **2** a work that is the result of plagiarizing: *His new book is a plagiarism.* -*n.* [U] **plagiarist, plagiary** /'pleɪʤəri/.

pla·gia·rize /'pleɪʤə,raɪz/ *v.* **-rized, -rizing, -rizes** to take the words or ideas of someone else and use them as if they were one's own: *Students must not plagiarize other people's work.*

USAGE NOTE: *Plagiarizing* someone else's writing is a serious offense in the USA. Students who plagiarize in colleges or universities can be expelled from school, and writers or journalists who plagiarize can lose their jobs.

plague /pleɪg/ *n.* [C;U] **1** a dangerous disease that spreads very fast and kills its victims quickly: *Before the modern age, the plague killed millions of people.* **2** *fig.* **a.** any widespread cause of misery, suffering, or death: *The plagues of the modern world are poverty and war.* **b.** a great and bothersome number (of pests): *A plague of flies has invaded our garden.* **3 to avoid s.o. or s.t. like the plague:** to try very hard not to do s.t. or come in contact with s.o.: *He avoids exercise like the plague.*
—*v.* **plagued, plaguing, plagues** to upset with repeated disturbances or interruptions: *Her vacation was plagued by telephone calls from her boss.*

plaid /plæd/ *n.* [C;U] **1** a pattern of light- and dark-colored lines and rectangles often used for the fabric of casual or sports clothes: *He wore a pair of pants with a bright plaid on the boat trip.* **2** a long piece of woolen cloth with a colorful pattern, worn by people in the Scottish highlands

plaid

—*adj.* with a pattern like plaid: *She wore a plaid shirt.*

plain /pleɪn/ *n.* **1** a broad area of flat land: *We drove over a plain that lay between two sets of hills.* **2** *pl.* **plains** a vast expanse of flat land: *In North America, the plains stretch for hundreds of miles.*
—*adj.* **1** easy to see, hear, or understand: *in plain sight*(or) *language*||*Try to make your instructions plain.* **2** simple, ordinary, not fancy: *He likes plain cooking.*||*They had a very plain wedding ceremony.* **3** clear and direct in expression or style, (*syn.*) frank: *She is a plain speaker who says what she means.* **4** not pretty or handsome: *She felt plain next to her beautiful sister.* **5** complete or obvious: *That is plain nonsense!* -*n.* **plainness.**

plain·ly /'pleɪnli/ *adv.* **1** clearly, obviously: *That is plainly the wrong way to do things.* **2** in a plain manner: *They were dressed very plainly.*

plain·tiff /'pleɪntɪf/ *n.* a person or business that files a lawsuit against an opposing party (the defendant): *The plaintiff sat with her lawyer at a table in the courtroom.*

plain·tive /'pleɪntɪv/ *adj.* **1** expressing distress and a desire for relief: *The trapped bird made a plaintive cry.* **2** expressing a lonely sadness and a desire for sympathy: *He listened to plaintive songs on the radio.* -*adv.* **plaintively.**

plan /plæn/ *n.* **1** a design or program of action to do s.t. in the future, usu. including a series of steps toward a goal: *We made a plan for raising money to build a new library.* **2** a drawing of s.t. to be made, showing all its parts and their relations: *She drew a detailed plan of the house she wanted to build.* **3** a map: *He made a plan of the city's subway lines.* **4 according to plan:** as intended or expected, without problems or surprises: *The parade went according to plan.* **5 to have plans: a.** to have a date or appointment: *I'm not free; I have plans for this evening.* **b.** to have goals, dreams, etc.: *She has big plans for her future as a doctor.*
—*v.* **planned, planning, plans 1** to make a plan for: *They planned a big meeting to be held next year.* **2** to intend to do s.t.: *He planned to take a vacation in June.* **3** to prepare drawings, blueprints, or designs for s.t. to be made or constructed: *An architect planned the new shopping center.*

plane /pleɪn/ *n.* **1** an airplane: *Our plane landed at the airport.* **2** a tool with a sharp blade, used to smooth the surface of wood
—*v.* **planed, planing, planes** to use a plane to smooth wood: *He planed the boards to make them fit closely.*

plan·et /'plænɪt/ *n.* a very large ball-shaped body (such as the earth) that moves around a star (such as the sun) in outer space: *People have long wondered whether there is life on other planets.* -*adj.* **planetary** /'plænə,tɛri/.

plan·e·tar·i·um /,plænə'tɛriəm/ *n.* **-iums** or **-ia** /-iə/ **1** a large room with a curved roof on which is shown images of the heavens (the planets, stars, etc.) and how they move in relation to each other **2** a museum with exhibits and displays that show the planets, moons, and other subjects of astronomy: *Children love to visit the planetarium to learn about space.*

plank /plæŋk/ *n.* **1** a wide, flat wooden board, often long and heavy: *The floor of the cabin is made of wooden planks.* **2** a basic principle or position in a political party's statement of its purpose (platform): *An important plank in their platform is to reduce taxes.*

P

plank·ton /'plæŋktən/ n. [U] tiny plants and animals that live in oceans and fresh water: *Many types of fish and some giant whales feed on plankton.*

plan·ner /'plænər/ n. **1** a person who makes plans for the development of towns, cities, highways, ports, etc.: *He is a planner for the state's department of transportation.* **2** anyone who makes plans for business or other large projects

plant /plænt/ n. **1** a living organism that usu. grows in the earth and has roots, stems, leaves, and seeds, and which differs from animals in not being able to move on its own and in making its own food from sunlight, soil, and water: *Humans and animals could not live without plants.* **2** a factory, or the land, buildings, and machinery used for industrial manufacturing: *My father worked in an automobile plant.* **3** a person placed secretly among others to gather information about them: *The police have a plant inside a criminal organization.*
—v. **1** to put seeds, plants, bushes, or trees in the ground to grow: *Farmers planted crops of wheat and corn this spring.||I planted my garden in April.* **2** *fig.* to give s.o. an idea with the hope that it will be acted on: *I planted a seed in her mind that she should look for a job.* **3** to take a firm position, place, or attitude: *He planted himself in the doorway and waited for her to return.* **4** to place stolen goods on someone else's property to make him or her appear guilty of a crime: *They planted drugs in his car and then called the police.*

plan·tain /'plæntən/ n. a tropical plant with a fruit similar to a banana: *Fried plantains with rice is a popular dish in the Dominican Republic.*

plan·ta·tion /plæn'teɪʃən/ n. a large farm, usu. in a warm climate, on which is grown a single major crop, such as tea, coffee, cotton, rubber, etc.: *There were many cotton plantations in the southern USA.*

plant·er /'plæntər/ n. **1** the owner of a plantation: *He was a wealthy coffee planter from Kenya.* **2** a machine for planting seeds in the ground: *The planter was pulled by a large tractor.* **3** an attractive pot used for growing flowers or decorative plants: *She had two large planters for flowers on her doorstep.*

plant·ing /'plæntɪŋ/ n. **1** [U] the seasonal activity of starting a new crop by putting seeds in the ground: *The planting of wheat and corn is going well this spring.* **2** [C;U] a crop of plants that were seeded at the same time: *The spring planting of corn is three feet tall now.*

plaque /plæk/ n. **1** a flat metal or stone plate with writing on it, fixed to a wall or object (such as a statue or tombstone) in memory of a person or event: *Tourists were reading the plaque on a statue in the park.* **2** material that

forms on the teeth and causes decay: *The dentist scraped the plaque off my teeth.*

plas·ma /'plæzmə/ n. [U] the clear liquid part of blood which carries the blood cells: *Hospitals keep supplies of plasma to give to patients who have lost blood.*

plas·ter /'plæstər/ n. [U] a mixture of water, lime, and sand spread on walls to make a smooth surface after it dries: *The plaster on that old wall is yellow and cracked.*
—v. **1** to cover walls with plaster: *They plastered the wall before painting it.* **2** to cover an area (usu. a wall or walls) with a large amount or number of s.t.: *He plastered his office with maps of the world.* -n. **plasterer.**

plas·ter·board /'plæstər,bɔrd/ n. [U] a building material of flat rectangular boards made of plaster covered with heavy paper: *Workers nailed plasterboard to upright boards to make walls in the new house.*

plas·tered /'plæstərd/ adj.infrml. very drunk: *He drank beer all evening and got plastered.*

plas·tic /'plæstɪk/ n. [C;U] a strong, lightweight material, manufactured in a chemical process from organic matter (oil, coal), which can be shaped and hardened into many forms and is commonly used as a substitute for metal or wood: *Many things, such as toys, furniture, and computers, are made of plastic.*
—adj. **1** easily shaped or formed by pressing: *Wet clay is very plastic.* **2** made from plastic: *We ate with plastic forks and spoons.*

plastic surgery n. [U] an operation on (parts of) the body to alter or improve its shape or appearance, often to repair damage from burns, wounds, or the effects of disease: *After the explosion, he needed plastic surgery to replace the skin on his face.*

plate /pleɪt/ n. **1** a flat dish with raised border, used to hold food: *I put plates on the table for lunch.* **2** a serving of food: *He had a plate of noodles for lunch.* **3** a flat sheet of hard material: *She replaced a broken plate of glass in the window.* **4** artificial teeth: *He wears a plate as his upper teeth.* **5** a thin metal covering, esp. a layer of a more valuable metal over an ordinary metal: *The spoons are silver plate, not solid silver.*
—v. **plated, plating, plates** to cover s.t. with a coating of metal: *Those utensils are plated with silver.* -adj. **plated.**

pla·teau /plæ'toʊ/ -teaus or -teaux /-'toʊz/ **1** a raised area of flat land with a steep drop on at least one side: *Plateaus can be hundreds of miles long.* **2** *fig.* a stage or period in which there is no change or progress: *The economy kept improving, and then reached a plateau.*
—v.fig. to reach a stage of little or no change, (*syn.*) to level off: *Sales rose fast and then plateaued.*

P

plat·form /'plæt,fɔrm/ *n.* **1** a flat raised structure, such as used for making speeches and boarding or exiting trains: *I stepped from the platform into the train.* **2** a statement of beliefs and goals made by politicians: *Our candidate ran for re-election on a platform calling for political reform.*

plat·ing /'pleɪtɪŋ/ *n.* [U] a thin covering of metal: *The silver plating on that knife is very shiny.*

plat·i·num /'plætnəm/ *n.adj.* [U] a silvery white metallic element used in jewelry and traded as a valuable commodity: *She collects antique <adj.> platinum rings.*

plat·i·tude /'plætə,tud/ *n.* a boring saying heard frequently: *We have to listen to more platitudes about how we should lower the national debt.*

pla·ton·ic /plə'tɑnɪk/ *adj.* related to a close personal relationship without sex: *She and he have had a platonic friendship for many years. See:* boyfriend, girlfriend, USAGE NOTE.

pla·toon /plə'tun/ *n.* (in the military) a grouping of soldiers within a company: *That army company contains 100 men grouped into four platoons of 25.*

platter /'plætər/ *n.* a large, flat dish with a raised border, used to hold food: *He put the platter holding the roast turkey on the table.* -*n.* **platterful** /'plætər,fʊl/.

plausible /'plɔzəbəl/ *adj.* referring to s.t. that seems true, logical or reasonable: *His car broke down, so he has a plausible explanation as to why he is late.* -*adv.* **plausibly;** -*n.* [U] **plausibility** /,plɔzə'bɪləti/.

play /pleɪ/ *n.* **1** [U] fun, amusement: *Children are at play in the park.* **2** [C] a theatrical production, such as a drama or musical: *Shakespeare's plays have been performed for centuries.* **3** [C;U] one's turn in a sport, game, or gambling: *I told my card partner that it was her play.* **4** [C;U] action in a game or event: *The play in that ping-pong match is very fast.* **5 a play on words:** a word or phrase used with a double meaning: *A manufacturer of calculators used a play on words in its ads: "You can count on our products", meaning that you can rely on their quality and you can count with them.* **6 to bring into play:** to involve s.o. or s.t. in the action: *The soldiers marched toward the enemy, and then the general brought his cavalry into play against them.* **7 to come into play:** to become involved in, be a factor in: *Two countries tried to make peace but radical groups came into play and tried to stop the peace process.*

—*v.* **1** to have fun, amuse oneself: *Children played with a ball on the beach.* **2** to participate in a sport or game: *She plays tennis, and he plays cards.* **3** to compete

against in a sport or game: *Our basketball team played against the state champions.* **4** to perform on a musical instrument: *She played the piano while he played the violin.* **5** to act a part in a movie or stage production: *She played the lead role in the film.* **6** to function, take part in: *Education of the workforce plays an important role in a healthy economy.* **7** to gamble, bet money: *He plays the horses; she plays poker.* **8** to cause a radio, TV, tape player, etc., to produce sounds: *He plays his stereo loudly.* **9** *phrasal v.* **to play along:** to cooperate with s.o. or make believe to: *He pretended to be a big movie star, and his friends played along with him.* **10 to play a role in s.t.:** *fig.* to be involved in s.t., to be a factor: *Lack of education plays a big role in poverty.* **11** *phrasal v.* **to play around:** *infrml.fig.* to cheat on one's spouse: *He plays around with other women.* **12** *phrasal v. insep.* **to play at s.t.:** to do s.t. but not in a serious way: *She plays at being an actress but is interested in lots of other things, too.* **13** *infrml.fig.* **to play by the rules:** to act in a correct, proper way: *She plays by the rules and does not cheat on her tests.* **14** *infrml.fig.* **to play for keeps:** to act seriously, esp. about money and death: *He is a big gambler who plays for keeps and won't give you your money back if you lose to him.* **15 to play hard to get:** to be coy, unwilling to be friendly and date s.o.: *She likes to play hard to get to make the boys really chase after her.* **16** *infrml.fig.* **to play it by ear:** to act according to the situation, rather than planning ahead: *We did not know the agenda for the meeting, so we just played it by ear and answered their questions.* **17 to play it cool:** to not get excited, remain dignified and calm: *When they offered her a salary higher than she expected, she just played it cool and accepted it.* **18 to play it safe:** to take no risk, do the safest thing: *It's not supposed to rain, but I think I'll play it safe and take my umbrella.* **19** *phrasal v.* **to play off:** to take part in a play-off: *Two teams will play off tomorrow to determine the champion.* **20** *phrasal v. insep.* **to play on** or **upon s.t.:** to manipulate others to do what one wants: *She played on the sympathy of her friends by crying about her bad luck so they would give her money.* **21** *infrml.fig.* **to play one's cards right** or **well:** to act intelligently: *That young man's boss will retire soon and, if he plays his cards right and behaves, he will replace him.* **22 to play s.o. off against s.o.:** to set two people against each other for one's own benefit, to manipulate others: *She plays her boyfriends off against each other to make them jealous, so they will treat her well.* **23** *phrasal v. sep.* **to play s.t. back:** to play s.t.

again, esp. a tape recording: *The singers made a recording, then played back their song to listen to it.* ||*They played it back.* **24** *phrasal v. sep.* **to play s.t. down:** to treat s.t. as unimportant, to minimize: *The prime minister played down her importance and stressed the role of her cabinet.* ||*She played it down.* **25** *infrml.fig.* **to play the field:** to date many men or women: *She plays the field by dating five different guys.* **26** *infrml.fig.* **to play the game:** to act according to the rules of a business or social set: *He plays the game by acting enthusiastic about company products when he couldn't care less.* **27 to play up to s.o. or s.t.:** to seek favor with s.o., flatter: *He plays up to his boss because he wants a raise in salary.* **28 to play with fire:** to do s.t. enjoyable, but dangerous: *She experimented with taking drugs, but decided that she was playing with fire and stopped.*

play·act /'pleɪˌækt/ *v.* to pretend, make believe: *He is play-acting that he is hurt, when he is not.*

play·boy /'pleɪˌbɔɪ/ *n.* a wealthy man who does not work and whose life is devoted to pleasure: *Playboys like to chase after women.*

play-by-play *adj. n.* referring to a radio or TV report of the action as it happens in a sporting event: *An announcer gave a <adj.> play-by-play description of the football game.*

play·er /'pleɪər/ *n.* **1** a person who participates in a game: *A basketball team has five players.* **2** an electronic machine used to play audio or video recordings: *I listen to music on my compact disc player.*

play·ful /'pleɪfəl/ *adj.* **1** liking to play, (*syn.*) frisky: *That puppy is a playful little puppy.* **2** not serious, joking in a friendly way: *She gave him a playful tap on the arm.* -*adv.* **playfully;** -*n.* **playfulness.**

play·ground /'pleɪˌɡraʊnd/ *n.* **1** an area used by children to play in, esp. one with such things as swings and slides: *Parents take children to the playground to have fun.* **2** a resort area: *The French Riviera is a playground for the rich.*

play·house /'pleɪˌhaʊs/ *n.* -**houses** /-ˌhaʊzɪz/ **1** a theater: *In summer, we go to a playhouse by the seashore.* **2** a little house that children can play in: *The children made a playhouse by covering a small table with a sheet.*

playing card *n.* one of a set of usu. 52 cards marked with the numbers one through ten or a picture and a suit (spades, clubs, hearts, or diamonds), used for playing various games: *I bought a pack of playing cards to play poker with.*

playing field *n.* a field on which sports events are played: *Football fans ran onto the playing field after the game.*

play·mate /'pleɪˌmeɪt/ *n.* a child who plays with another child: *The little girl and her two playmates played in the yard.*

play-off /'pleɪˌɔf/ *n.adj.* a game or series of competitions to determine a champion: *The National League football <n.> play-off* (or) *<adj.> play-off game will be held this Sunday.*

play·pen /'pleɪˌpɛn/ *n.* a cage-like enclosure without a top in which infants can be left to play: *The baby plays with toys in her playpen.*

play·room /'pleɪˌrum/ *n.* a room in a house in which games are played: *We have a ping-pong table in our playroom in the basement.*

play·thing /'pleɪˌθɪŋ/ *n.* a toy or other object of amusement: *The child keeps her playthings in a wooden chest.*

play·wright /'pleɪˌraɪt/ *n.* a person who writes plays: *Playwrights write dialogue for actors.*

pla·za /'plazə, 'plæ-/ *n.* a public square: *The town is built around a large plaza with a fountain in the middle.*

plea /pli/ *n.* **1** an urgent request, appeal: *The hungry man's pleas for food were answered.* **2** (in law) a defendant's answer to a plaintiff's accusation: *The man's lawyer entered a plea of not guilty before the court. See:* plead.

plea-bargain *n.v.* an agreement by a criminal to plead guilty to a lesser charge in return for a lighter punishment than he or she would have otherwise: *The thief <v.> plea-bargained a ten-year jail sentence down to three years*

plead /plid/ *v.* **pleaded** or **pled** /plɛd/**, pleading, pleads 1** to request s.t. urgently, to appeal: *A hungry man pleaded for food.* **2** (in law): to answer a complaint: *The defendant pleaded not guilty.* -*n.* [C;U] **pleading.**

pleas·ant /'plɛzənt/ *adj.* **1** enjoyable, pleasing: *This is a pleasant, sunny day.*||*The ice cream has a pleasant taste.* **2** friendly, cordial: *She has a pleasant personality.* -*adv.* **pleasantly;** -*n.* [U] **pleasantness.**

pleas·ant·ry /'plɛzəntri/ *n.frml.* -**ries** a friendly or witty remark: *We made a few pleasantries, and then got down to business.*

please /pliz/ *v.* **pleased, pleasing, pleases 1** to make s.o. feel happy, satisfy: *It pleases me that you are making such a big effort in this class.* **2** to want, like, feel: *You should feel free to do what you please.* **3 if you please: a.** to express disapproval: *If you please, would you be quiet!* **b.** if you want to: *"May I go to the movies Mom?" "If you please."* **4 to aim to please:** to make every effort to satisfy s.o.: *In this store, we aim to please our customers.*

—*interj.* **1** a polite request, way of asking s.o. to do s.t.: *Please sit down and take your coat off.* **2** a polite way of saying, yes: *"Would you like some butter?" "Please."*

—*adj.* **pleased** a polite greeting on first meeting s.o.: *I am pleased to meet you.*

pleas·ing /'plizɪŋ/ *adj.* pleasant, enjoyable: *That food has a pleasing taste (smell, look).* -*adv.* **pleasingly.**

pleas·ur·a·ble /'plɛʒərəbəl/ *adj.frml.* pleasant, enjoyable: *Eating is one of life's pleasurable activities.* -*adv.* **pleasurably.**

pleas·ure /'plɛʒər/ *n.* **1** [U] enjoyment, feeling of happiness: *The relaxation and beautiful scenery made her vacation a real pleasure.* **2** [C] an activity that is pleasant: *Good food is one of life's great pleasures.*

pleat /plit/ *n.* a fold doubled over on itself in cloth: *The pleats in her skirt need pressing.*

—*v.* to make pleats: *She wears a pleated skirt.*

ple·be·ian /plɪ'biən/ *adj.n.frml.* **1** of or associated with the common people, ordinary: *Snobs say they don't enjoy the <adj.> plebeian pastimes of drinking beer and watching tv.* **2** crude, coarse: *He lives in a <adj.> plebeian neighborhood.*

pledge /plɛdʒ/ *n.* a formal promise, oath to do s.t.: *He signed a pledge to stop drinking.*

—*v.* **pledged, pledging, pledges** to promise, vow formally to do s.t.: *I pledge allegiance to the flag of the United States of America.*

ple·na·ry /'plinəri, 'plɛ-/ *n.adj.* **-ries 1** a meeting of all fully qualified members of an organization: *The United Nations is in a <adj.> plenary session today.* **2** a major speech at a professional conference: *Professor Pless is giving a <adj.> plenary address on some new research in physics today at 2:00.*

plen·ti·ful /'plɛntɪfəl/ *adj.* **1** abundant, in good supply: *Food is plentiful in the USA.* **2** great, bountiful: *We had a plentiful harvest of wheat this fall.* -*adv.* **plentifully.**

plen·ty /'plɛnti/ *n.adj.* **1** a good supply, abundance: *We have plenty of food for the party today.* **2** more than enough: *You have plenty of time to catch your train.* **3** a state of having more than enough food, wealth, etc.: *The USA is often called the "land of plenty."*

pleth·o·ra /'plɛθərə/ *n.frml.* [C;usu. *sing.*] an overabundance, excessive amount: *There is a plethora of cookbooks published each year.*

Plex·i·glas /'plɛksɪ‚glæs/ *n.*™ a transparent, hard material used often as a substitute for plate glass, such as for windowpanes: *The Plexiglas™ windows in the airplane won't shatter or crack.*

pli·a·ble /'plaɪəbəl/ *adj.* **1** flexible, capable of being bent or shaped: *Heating metal makes it pliable so that it can be shaped into useful*

things. **2** easily persuaded or ruled by others: *He is pliable and will do what he is told.*

pli·ant /'plaɪənt/ *adj.frml.* **1** (of a thing) capable of being bent without breaking **2** (of a person) willing to change one's self or ideas to suit others: *She doesn't like baseball but she's pliant and will play if everyone else wants to.*

pli·ers /'plaɪərz/ *n.pl.* a pair of pincers used for holding, twisting, or cutting: *I used a pair of pliers to cut a small nail and pull it out of the wood.*

pliers

plight /plaɪt/ *n.* a difficult situation, predicament: *His plight is that he has no money.*

plod /plɑd/ *v.* **plodded, plodding, plods 1** to walk slowly and heavily: *A farmer plodded through his muddy field.* **2** *fig.* to act or work very slowly: *Work in that government department plods along.* -*n.* [U] **plodding.**

plop /plɑp/ *v.* **plopped, plopping, plops 1** to let s.t. drop, toss lightly: *He plopped a coin into the wishing well.* **2** to sit down heavily: *She plopped herself (or) plopped onto the sofa and rested.*

plot /plɑt/ *v.* **plotted, plotting, plots 1** to scheme, plan in secret a way to overthrow, rob or harm s.o.: *Several generals plotted to overthrow the government.* **2** to mark a curve, or draw points of activity: *The treasurer plotted the growth of company sales on a chart.* **3** to construct the main story in a novel or play: *He plots out his mystery novels in the bath.*

—*n.* **1** the main story in a novel or play: *The plot concerns a poor boy who moves to California and becomes an actor.* **2** an area of land: *Her house is located on a small plot of land.*

plow /plaʊ/ *n.* **1** a farm implement used to turn over ground for planting crops: *Farmers walk behind a plow pulled by a mule.* **2** an implement used to move snow, sand, etc.: *Snowplows scrape snow from the streets.*

plow

—*v.* **1** to turn over earth, push snow, sand, etc. with a plow: *Farmers plowed their fields in the spring.* **2** *phrasal v. insep.* **to plow into s.o. or s.t.:** to strike violently, crash into: *Cars skidded on the icy road and plowed into each other.* **3** *phrasal v. insep.* **to plow through s.t.:** to force one's way through s.t.: *He came back from vacation and plowed through a small mountain of work.* **4** *phrasal v. sep.* **to plow s.t. up:** to turn over earth: *We plowed up our* *garden in the spring to do planting.||We plowed it up.*

plow·share /'plau,ʃer/ *n.* one blade among many on a plow: *Diplomats speak of turning swords into plowshares, to stop war and grow food.*

ploy /plɔɪ/ *n.* a trick, a maneuver to gain advantage or to disguise one's true intent: *He said on the telephone that he was conducting a survey, but that was just a ploy to sell me life insurance.*

pluck /plʌk/ *v.* **1** to pull quickly, to yank: *She plucked flowers in the field.* **2** to remove feathers from: *Workers pluck chickens to sell in the market.* **3** to vibrate the strings of a guitar, banjo, etc. with a pick or the fingers: *He plucked the guitar and sang.*

plug /plʌg/ *n.* **1** a stopper, s.t. made of rubber, wood, etc. used to block an opening: *He hammered a wooden plug into the opening in the wine barrel.* **2** a small plastic device at the end of an electrical cord with metal prongs that can be connected to an electrical supply: *I stuck the plug into the socket and turned on the TV.* **3** a favorable mention of a product or service, such as on a TV or radio show: *The author was able to give his book a plug when interviewed on a talk show.* **4 to pull the plug on s.t.: a.** to unplug s.t. from an electrical outlet: *I pulled the plug on the TV and moved it to the bedroom.* **b.** *fig.* to stop s.t. abruptly, cancel it: *Management pulled the plug on that project because it cost too much.*
—*v.* **plugged, plugging, plugs 1** to block s.t. with a plug: *Workers plugged the hole in the dam with cement.* **2** to talk about a product or service favorably: *The author plugged her new book on a TV talk show.* **3** *phrasal v. insep.* **to plug away at s.t.:** to work hard and regularly on s.t.: *She plugs away at her studies and makes good grades.* **4** *phrasal v. sep.* **to plug s.t. in:** to connect s.t. to a power supply by pushing a plug into an electrical socket: *Plug in the TV over here.||Plug it in.* **5** *phrasal v. sep.* **to plug s.t. up:** to become blocked: *A piece of meat has plugged up the sink.||It plugged it up.*

plum /plʌm/ *n.* **1** [C;U] a round fruit with smooth, often deep purple skin and juicy flesh, or the tree it grows on: *My grandmother made delicious plum jelly.* **2** *fig.* s.t. very desirable, special: *He received a plum of a high-paying job.* **3** a deep reddish-purple color

plum·age /'plumɪʤ/ *n.* [U] the covering of feathers on a bird: *The male peacock has gorgeous plumage.*

plumb·er /'plʌmər/ *n.* a worker who installs and fixes pipes, drains, bathroom and kitchen fixtures, etc.: *He works as a plumber on a construction site.*

plumb·ing /'plʌmɪŋ/ *n.* [U] **1** pipes, faucets, and fixtures for water and gas: *The plumbing in that old house does not work well.* **2** the work that a plumber does

plume /plum/ *n.* a showy feather, usu. long, brightly colored, and prominently displayed: *The dancer wore a headdress of pink ostrich plumes.*

plum·met /'plʌmɪt/ *v.* to plunge, go downward rapidly and far: *An airplane caught fire and plummeted to earth.*

plump /plʌmp/ *adj.* (referring esp. to women and children) round in shape, chubby or full-figured: *You can say that a woman is pleasingly plump, but it is not polite to call her chubby or fat.* -*adj.* **plumpish;** -*n.* [U] **plumpness.**

plun·der /'plʌndər/ *v.* to steal, take others' property by force and in large quantity: *The invading army plundered the town of food, money, jewels, and valuables.* -*n.* **plunderer.**
—*n.* [U] the property stolen by force: *Soldiers took the plunder to their camp.*

plunge /plʌnʤ/ *v.* **plunged, plunging, plunges** to plummet, dive, or fall fast and far: *A diver plunged into the water from a cliff.*
—*n.* **1** a dive or fall: *She took a plunge into the ocean.* **2 to take the plunge:** to do s.t. risky after hesitating: *He took the plunge by investing all his savings in the stock market.*

plung·er /'plʌnʤər/ *n.* a rubber suction cup on a long handle used for clearing blocked pipes: *She used a plunger to unblock the kitchen sink.*

plunk /plʌŋk/ *v.* to plop, drop s.t. heavily: *He plunked down a pile of cash on the counter and bought the diamond ring.*
—*n.* the sound of s.t. dropping: *You can hear the plunk of a stone dropped in the water.*

plu·per·fect /,plu'pərfɪkt/ *n.adj.* (in grammar) the past perfect tense: *In the sentence, "I just started to eat when the phone rang," the verb "had started" is in the pluperfect. See:* perfect.

plu·ral /'plʊrəl/ *adj.n.* indicating more than one of s.t.: *Potatoes is the <n.> plural of potato.||"Potatoes" is a <adj.> plural noun.* -*v.* **pluralize.**

plu·ral·ism /'plʊrə,lɪzəm/ *n.* [U] a social doctrine and condition in which people of different ethnic and religious backgrounds participate on an equal basis in society but maintain their separate group identities -*n.* **pluralist;** -*adj.* **pluralistic** /,plʊrə'lɪstɪk/.

plu·ral·i·ty /plu'ræləti/ *n.* **-ties** (in an election) the largest number of votes among the candidates: *The winner had a plurality of 15,000 votes, while the other two candidates got 10,000 and 8,000 votes respectively.*

P

plus /plʌs/ *prep.* increased by adding: *Five plus nine is fourteen (5+9=14).||The bill came to thirty dollars plus tax.*
—*conj.* in addition, and: *The job calls for patience plus an interest in children.*
—*n.* **pluses 1** the symbol (+), the plus sign **2** an advantage: *One of the pluses of the job would be the opportunity to travel.*
—*adj.* **1** greater or more than indicated: *a grade of B plus (B+).||He has 20 plus years of experience.* **2** indicating an advantage, positive: *The apartment has a lot of disadvantages, but on the plus side, it has a great view.* **3** indicating a positive number

plush /plʌʃ/ *adj.* **1** soft, (*syn.*) cushy: *She has a plush sofa in her living room.* **2** luxurious, expensive: *She has a plush apartment in a fancy area.* -*adj.* **plushy.**

plus sign *n.* the symbol (+), used to indicate addition (100+10=110) or a number above zero (+5)

Plu·to /'plutoʊ/ *n.* in the earth's solar system, the ninth planet farthest from the sun: *Pluto is 3674.5 million miles from the sun.*

plu·to·cra·cy /plu'tɑkrəsi/ *n.* **-cies** a system of government run by the wealthy: *Some countries have a plutocracy that governs the poor.* -*n.* **plutocrat** /'plutə,kræt/; -*adj.* **plutocratic** /,plutə'krætɪk/.

plu·to·ni·um /plu'toʊniəm/ *n.* a radioactive chemical, element No. 94: *Plutonium can be used to make atomic bombs.*

ply /plaɪ/ *n.* a layer of material: *Two-ply paper towels are stronger than single-ply towels.*
—*v.* **plied, plying, plies 1** to work at a trade: *He plies his trade as a locksmith.* **2** to travel over: *Merchant ships ply the waters between the Americas and Europe.*

ply·wood /'plaɪ,wʊd/ *n.* [U] material made of layers of wood pressed over each other for strength: *Plywood is widely used in making walls of new houses.*

P.M. or **p.m.** /,pi'ɛm/ *abbr. for* post meridiem (after noon), used to indicate the time period between noon and midnight: *The plane leaves at 7:45 p.m.*

PMS /piɛm'ɛs/ *n. abbr.* for premenstral syndrome

pneu·mat·ic /nʊ'mætɪk/ *adj.* **1** related to air, esp. air under pressure: *Pneumatic tires replaced wooden and iron wheels many years ago.* **2** run by compressed air: *Trucks have air brakes activated by a pneumatic system.*

pneu·mo·nia /nʊ'moʊnyə/ *n.* [U] a serious, viral or bacterial disease of the lungs: *She nearly died of pneumonia.*

P.O. /,pi'oʊ/ *abbr. for* post office

poach /poʊtʃ/ *v.* **poaches 1** to cook gently in a hot liquid: *poached eggs, poached salmon* **2** to trespass on s.o.'s land to hunt or trap game ani-

mals: *Two hunters poached deer on the farmer's land.*

poach·er /'poʊtʃər/ *n.* a hunter or trapper who takes game animals illegally on the land of another: *In the old day, poachers were hanged in England.* -*n.* [U] **poaching.**

P.O. Box *n. See:* post office box.

pock·et /'pɑkɪt/ *n.* **1** a type of sack sewn into garments for holding things: *He keeps his wallet in the back pocket of his jeans.* **2** *infrml.fig.* **to line one's pocket:** to obtain money illegally: *The buyer for the company lines his pockets with bribes and kickbacks.* **3 to pick s.o.'s pocket:** to steal from s.o.: *A pickpocket picked my pocket and stole my wallet.*
—*v.* to put s.t. into one's pocket, to take for oneself: *My lunch cost $8. I left the waiter a ten-dollar bill and he pocketed the difference.*

pock·et·book /'pɑkɪt,bʊk/ *n.* **1** a woman's purse, a handbag: *She carries her wallet, keys, and makeup in her pocketbook.* **2** *fig.* [U] one's financial situation: *He lost money in the stock market and that hurt him in his pocketbook.*

pocket edition *n.* a small version of a book capable of being carried in one's pocket: *She carries a pocket edition of an English dictionary.*

pock·et·ful /'pɑkɪt,fʊl/ *n.* **-fuls** the amount that a pocket can hold, a large amount: *He always carries a pocketful of change with him.*

pock·et·knife /'pɑkɪt,naɪf/ *n.* **-knives** /-,naɪvz/ a knife with one or more blades that fold into the handle, a small jackknife: *He uses a pocketknife to clean out his tobacco pipe.*

pocket veto *n.* **-toes** *v.* **-toed, -toing, -toes** a rejection of a piece of legislation by the President by his simply not acting on it within the ten days required by law: *The President exercised a pocket veto on the new tax legislation from Congress.*

pock·mark /'pɑk,mɑrk/ *n.v.* a shallow pit in the skin: *Infected pimples can leave <n.> pockmarks in the skin.* -*adj.* **pockmarked.**

pod /pɑd/ *n.* a long, narrow case in which seeds grow on certain plants, such as peas and beans: *I took the peas out of their pods before I cooked them.*

po·di·a·try /pə'daɪətri/ *n.* [U] the medical study and care of the feet: *To practice podiatry, one needs a college degree and a license.* -*n.* **podiatrist.**

po·di·um /'poʊdiəm/ *n.* **-diums** or **-dia** /-diə/ a rectangular, raised speaking desk: *Speakers stand at the podium and deliver their speeches.*

po·em /'poʊəm/ *n.* a literary composition, usu. arranged in short lines using carefully chosen words and expressing rich images and often deep thoughts or feelings: *The subject of the poem was the nature of beauty.*

po·et /'pouɪt/ *n.* a person who composes poetry: *Poets work hard to make their images powerful and unique.*

po·et·ic /pou'ɛtɪk/ *adj.* **1** related to poetry: *Poetic works have survived from thousands of years ago.* **2** involving strong sentiment, powerful imagination, and beautiful insights or thoughts: *Her thoughts are poetic and inspiring.* *-adj.frml.* **poetical;** *-adv.* **poetically;** *-n.pl.* used with a sing. or pl.v. **poetics.**

poetic justice *n.* [U] punishment of wrongdoing or reward of goodness in a way that seems especially appropriate or ironic: *It was poetic justice that the bomber blew himself up with a bomb intended to kill others.*

poetic license *n.* [U] a use of nonstandard language or the changing of facts to achieve a special, literary effect: *The writer used poetic license when she wrote a historic novel, by creating a character who was supposed to be President Lincoln's close friend.*

poet laureate /'lɔriɪt/ *n.* **poets laureate** or **poet laureates** a title of honor given to a poet of distinction by a monarch, country, or institution: *Robert Penn Warren was named poet laureate of the USA by the President.*

po·et·ry /'pouətri/ *n.* [U] a written and oral literary form composed in verse, usu. with rich images; poems in general: *Poetry has been composed since ancient times.*

po·grom /pə'grʌm, -'grɑm, 'pougrəm/ *n.* a killing of people, often by a government, esp. a massacre of Jews: *A pogrom caused many Jews to flee the country.*

poi·gnant /'pɔɪnyənt/ *adj.* deeply moving, highly emotional: *The sudden death of the little girl was a poignant experience for the entire community.* *-n.* **poignancy;** *-adv.* **poignantly.**

poin·set·ti·a /pɔɪn'sɛtiə, -ˌsɛtə/ *n.* a tropical plant with bright red, showy flowers: *Poinsettias are a favorite decoration at Christmas time.*

point /pɔɪnt/ *n.* **1** the sharp tip of a knife, needle, or other tool or weapon: *She stuck the point of the needle through the cloth.* **2** a location, spot: *We located Paris at a specific point on the map.* **3** a mark, dot, or period: *A period is a point at the end of a sentence.* **4** an item of information, fact: *He made the point that the project cannot be done without proper government funding.* **5** a particular moment: *At this point in time, we must cut expenses.* **6** a characteristic, ability of a person: *Math is not her strong point.* **7** a unit of scoring in games: *Our team scored seven points in the first quarter.* **8** the value of stocks and bonds: *The stock market went up 20 points today.* **9** one percent of a loan paid in advance: *Two points on a $100,000 mortgage equal $2,000.* **10** a decimal point: *She made a 4.0 (pron.: four-point-*

oh) average this semester. **11** a strip of land stretching out into a body of water: *They have a house located on the point in the lake.* **12 all points:** everywhere, in all directions: *The police sent out an all points bulletin to capture the escaped criminal.* **13 beside the point:** irrelevant, not connected to the topic: *We were talking about money that he owed me and what he said about the bad economy was beside the point.* **14 to get to the point:** to conclude, reach the substance of s.t.: *To get to the point, he cannot repay the loan because he has no job and no money.* **15 to keep to the point:** to say only those things related to the central idea: *He talked and talked, and we had trouble keeping him to the point of our discussion.* **16 to make a point:** to say s.t. important, relevant: *He made the point that he was unemployed along with thousands of others.* **17 to make a point of s.t.: a.** to stress, emphasize: *He made a point of promising he would repay me soon.* **b.** to do s.t. habitually, often: *He said that he has always made a point of repaying his debts.*
—v. **1** to indicate the direction of s.t.: *We asked her the way and she pointed toward the town.* **2** to bring to s.o.'s attention or notice: *She pointed out an error in the report.* **3** to give a reason or conclusion: *She pointed out that the company cannot continue to lose money.* **4** *fig.* **to point the finger:** to accuse, blame s.o., often unfairly **5** *phrasal v. insep.* **to point to** or **toward s.t.:** to indicate, suggest: *An increase in jobs points toward an upturn in the economy.*

point-blank *adv.adj.* **1** (with a firearm) at very close range, so close that one cannot miss the victim: *A soldier shot an enemy at <adj.> point-blank range* (or) *he shot him <adv.> point-blank.* **2** bluntly, leaving no room for doubt: *I asked him <adv.> point-blank to help us on the project.*

point·ed /'pɔɪntɪd/ *adj.* **1** having a point: *Needles are pointed.* **2** aimed, directed: *The arrow on the compass is pointed north.* **3** direct, biting: *She made pointed criticisms about her opponent's mistakes.*

point·er /'pɔɪntər/ *n.* **1** a long, narrow stick used to indicate points, such as on a map: *The teacher used a pointer to show where Moscow and New York are located on the map.* **2** a needle on a gauge: *The pointer of the gas gauge is on empty.* **3** a piece of advice, esp. on specific techniques of doing s.t.: *A tennis instructor gave me some pointers on how to improve my swing.* **4** a type of hunting dog: *He hunts with an old pointer who's good at finding birds and rabbits.*

point·less /'pɔɪntlɪs/ *adj.* meaningless, not worth doing: *The storm was so bad that it was*

P

pointless to try to travel in it. -adv. **pointlessly;** -n. [U] **pointlessness.**

point man or **point person** n. a person out in front of others, lead person: *The mayor used his deputy as the point person to go see what the riot was about.*

point of view n. **points of view** an attitude or set of beliefs, s.o.'s way of looking at s.t.: *The liberal point of view is that the government should own the means of production, but conservatives think otherwise.*

point·y /'pɔɪnti/ adj. **-ier, -iest** shaped like a point: *He is bald and has a pointy head.*

poise /pɔɪz/ n. [U] **1** calm self-confidence, dignity: *She answered the criticisms with a great deal of poise.* **2** balance, equilibrium: *Acrobats must maintain their poise at all times.* —v. **poised, poising, poises 1** to be ready to act: *The army is poised for an attack.* **2** to be balanced, in equilibrium: *The pigeon was poised on a small branch.*

poi·son /'pɔɪzən/ n. [C;U] **1** any substance that harms or kills people, animals, or plants if it is swallowed or touched, (*syn.*) a toxin: *She tried to kill herself by swallowing poison.* **2** anything that harms or corrupts: *Gossip and lies are poison to friendships.* —v. **1** to harm or kill with a poison: *Workers poisoned rats in the city's sewers.* **2** to have a bad influence on s.o. or s.t.: *Disagreements over money poisoned the couple's marriage.* -n. **poisoner.**

poi·son·ing /'pɔɪzənɪŋ/ n. [C;U] an act of harming or killing with poison; a harmful condition produced by a poison

poison ivy n. a plant or shrub having groups of three shiny leaves with oil that can cause blisters and severe itching to those who touch it: *When the oil from poison ivy gets on your skin, it really hurts.*

poi·son·ous /'pɔɪzənəs/ adj. **1** causing harm or death by poison: *The venom of a rattlesnake is poisonous.* **2** spoiling relationships among people, malicious: *Lies are poisonous to friendships.*

poke /poʊk/ v. **poked, poking, pokes** to jab, press as with the finger or a stick: *His wife poked him with her elbow to wake him up.* **2** phrasal v. insep. **to poke fun at s.o. or s.t.:** to tease, make fun of s.o.: *She poked fun at her friend by imitating her complaints.* —n. a jab, thrust: *She gave him a poke with her elbow.*

pok·er (1) /'poʊkər/ n. a pointed metal rod: *I used a poker to move logs and coals in the fire.*

poker (2) n. a popular card game played for money, often with five or seven cards per hand: *Many people play poker for lots of money.*

pok·ey or **poky** /'poʊki/ adj. **-ier, -iest** slow, not in a hurry: *The traffic is pokey this morning.* —n.infrml.slang **-eys** or **-ies** a jail, prison: *He got drunk and a cop put him in the pokey.*

po·lar /'poʊlər/ adj. **1** related to a pole, esp. the earth's North or South Pole: *The polar climate is very cold, windy, and icy.* **2** opposite, at extremes: *The conservatives and liberals hold polar views on politics.*

polar bear n. a large white bear inhabiting the coasts of the northern arctic: *Polar bears feed mainly on seals.*

polar bear

polar cap n. the masses of ice extending from the North and South Poles: *The polar caps are made of very deep ice.*

Po·lar·is /pə'lærɪs/ n. the North Star: *For centuries, sailors navigated by looking at Polaris.*

po·lar·i·ty /pə'lærəti/ n. [U] **-ties** a condition of opposite extremes, such as opposing ideas, opinions, etc.: *The polarity of opinion between the two politicians is very clear.*

po·lar·ize /'poʊlə,raɪz/ v. **-ized, -izing, -izes** to develop into opposite views: *Public opinion polarized into completely opposite opinions on the issue of abortion.* -n. **polarization** /,poʊlərə'zeɪʃən/

Po·lar·oid /'poʊlə,rɔɪd/ n.™ a type of camera that develops its own pictures in seconds: *He used a Polaroid to take pictures at the party.*

pole (1) /poʊl/ n. a long wooden or metal rod: *She raised a flag up the pole.* —v. **poled, poling, poles** to use a pole to move a boat: *A fisherman poled his boat down the river.*

pole (2) n. **1** either end of an imaginary line drawn through the earth's north and south axes: *The North Pole is a cold and icy place.* **2 to be poles apart:** to have completely opposite views: *The liberals and conservatives are poles apart in their views.*

po·lem·ic /pə'lɛmɪk/ n. severe criticism, esp. a speech against s.t.: *A senator gave a long polemic against the new tax bill. Her polemics lasted an hour.* -adj. **polemical.**

pole vault n.v. (in sports) a competition between individuals who try to jump the highest over a bar with the aid of a long, flexible pole: *He does the <n.> pole vault.||He <v.> pole vaulted the highest of all.*

po·lice /pə'lis/ n. [C; usu. *sing.*] a branch of city and state governments whose men and women in uniform enforce the law, prevent crime, catch and jail criminals, etc.: *The police use force when necessary to stop criminals.*

—*v.* **-liced, -licing, -lices** to maintain law and order: *American soldiers policed a cease fire between two warring nations.*

police force *n.* uniformed and plainclothes police officers as a group: *The police force is made up of men and women trained in police methods.*

po·lice·man /pə'lismən/ *n.* **-men** /-mən/ a male police officer: *Policemen patrolled the streets in police cars.*

police officer *n.* a member of the police, a man or woman trained in police methods for maintaining law and order: *Police officers in this city must have six months of intensive training.*

police state *n.* a nation or area where the government controls the activity of the people mainly by use of secret police: *In a police state, the political, business, and social activities of the people are tightly controlled.*

police station *n.* a local building for police business: *Police officers report to the local police station and go on patrol from there.*

po·lice·wom·an /pə'lis,wumən/ *n.* **-women** /-,wimən/ a female police officer: *A policewoman wrestled the criminal to the ground.*

pol·i·cy (1) /'pɑləsi/ *n.* **-cies 1** a rule or group of rules for doing business by industry and government: *The policy of that store is that customers may return merchandise for an exchange or credit, but not for a refund.* **2** a general plan, strategy: *The government wrote up a policy of providing health care to everyone in the country.* **3** a practical or prudent course of action: *It is never a good policy to drive after drinking.*

policy (2) *n.* **-cies** an insurance contract: *I keep my life insurance policy in my desk.*

po·li·o /'pouli,ou/ *n.* [U] *short for* poliomyelitis, an infectious viral disease, esp. of children, that attacks the spinal cord and brain and, in serious cases, causes paralysis: *He had polio as a child.*

pol·ish /'pɑlɪʃ/ *v.* **polishes 1** to rub s.t. until it is smooth and shiny: *I polished my shoes.* **2** to refine, perfect s.t.: *Her manners are very polished.*

—*n.* **polishes 1** [C;U] a waxy substance used to shine objects: *I rubbed polish on my shoes.* **2** [U] perfection, refinement of s.t.: *His singing style has a lot of polish; it's very smooth.*

po·lit·bu·ro /'pɑlɪt,byurou, 'pou-/ *n.* the former ruling committee of the Communist Party in the USSR: *The politburo ran the country until the end of communism in the Soviet Union.*

po·lite /pə'laɪt/ *adj.* **-liter, -litest 1** having good manners, courteous: *He is a polite little boy who says "Thank you" and "Excuse me"*

often. **2** refined, polished: *People should not tell dirty jokes in polite company.* -*adv.* **politely;** -*n.* [U] **politeness.**

pol·i·tic /'pɑlə,tɪk/ *adj.frml.* diplomatic, tactful: *She does not like her boss, but it would not be politic for her to show it.*

po·lit·i·cal /pə'lɪtɪkəl/ *adj.* **1** related to politics: *The President's political views are liberal.* **2** scheming, jockeying for power, prestige, money, etc.: *The way people work in that company is political; everyone is scheming for power.* -*adv.* **politically.**

politically correct or **PC** *adj.* conforming to progressive attitudes, such as supporting the rights of women, ethnic minorities, and homosexuals, and avoiding language that might offend such groups: *He was careful to use politically correct language, using terms like "mail carrier" rather than "mailman" and "chairperson" rather than "chairman."* -*n.* [U] **political correctness.**

pol·i·ti·cian /,pɑlə'tɪʃən/ *n.* **1** a person who runs for elected office, such as president, governor, mayor, or congress: *She is a career politician and mayor of the city.* **2** a schemer, s.o. who tries to manipulate power: *He is a real politician; he's only nice to people who can help his career.*

po·lit·i·cize /pə'lɪtə,saɪz/ *v.* **-cized, -cizing, -cizes** to give a political tone, nature to s.t.: *The issue of abortion has been politicized.* -*n.* [U] **politicization** /pə,lɪtəsə'zeɪʃən/.

pol·i·tick·ing /'pɑlə,tɪkɪŋ/ *n.* [U] engaging in political activity, esp. in getting votes: *The mayor did some politicking by speaking to citizens' groups.*

pol·i·tics /'pɑlə,tɪks/ *n.pl.* used with a sing. or pl.v. **1** the art or science of conducting government: *Politics requires compromise between opposing political parties.* **2** the profession of politics: *The mayor has been in politics all his life.* **3** used with a pl.v. a person's political views: *His politics are far to the right.* **4** intrigue, scheming, and maneuvering in order to gain power, prestige, money, etc.: *She refused to get involved in office politics.*

pol·ka /'poulkə, 'poukə/ *n.* a lively dance of Eastern European origin done by couples moving in a circle: *Dancing the polka is a lot of fun.*

polka dot /'poukə/ *n.adj.* a pattern of light dots on a dark background or the reverse: *He wears polka-dot neckties.*

poll /poul/ *n.* **1** a survey of opinion among people: *Pollsters conducted a poll on the popularity of the political candidates.* **2** *pl.* **the polls:** the places where votes are cast: *People go to the polls to vote.*

P

—*v.* to conduct a poll: *Pollsters polled 1,000 families on their preferences in TV programs.* See: polling.

pol·len /'palən/ *n.* [U] fine grains of fertilizing material of plants: *Many plants drop their pollen in the fall as it grows cold* See: pollinate.

pol·li·nate /'palə,neɪt/ *v.* **-nated, -nating, -nates** to transfer pollen to the stigma of a plant so that it can reproduce: *Bees pollinate a lot of plants by transferring pollen from plant to plant.* -*n.* [U] **pollination** /,palə'neɪʃən/.

poll·ing /'poʊlɪŋ/ *n.* [U] a gathering of opinions: *Telephone polling requires that pollsters call people to get their opinions.*
—*adj.* related to voting: *People are going to the polling place to vote today.*

pol·li·wog or **pollywog** /'pali,wag/ *n.* a baby frog, a tadpole: *Polliwogs swim in the ponds in the springtime.*

poll·ster /'poʊlstər/ *n.* a person who conducts polls: *Pollsters ask people questions and record their answers.*

pol·lut·ant /pə'lutnt/ *n.* a contaminant, an impure or dirty substance that makes air, water, or soil polluted: *Cars emit air pollutants.*

pol·lute /pə'lut/ *v.* **-luted, -luting, -lutes** to contaminate, make impure or dirty: *Industries pollute rivers by dumping poisonous chemicals into them.*

pol·lu·tion /pə'luʃən/ *n.* [U] contamination of air, earth, or water by pollutants: *Many countries battle constantly to reduce pollution.*

po·lo /'poʊloʊ/ *n.* [U] a sport played by two teams of four players each on horseback who win by knocking a ball with a mallet through the opponent's goal: *Polo is known as a sport for the rich.*

polo shirt *n.* a tight-fitting knit shirt that is pulled on over the head and usu. has a collar and buttons at the neck: *He wears polo shirts to play golf.*

pol·ter·geist /'poʊltər,gaɪst/ *n.* a ghost that is thought to be responsible for strange noises, mysterious moving of objects, etc.

pol·y·es·ter /,pali'estər, 'pali,estər/ *n.* [U] *adj.* **1** a synthetic resin that is widely used in the production of textiles and plastics **2** a type of light, strong fabric made from this: *He wears cheap <adj.> polyester suits.*

po·lyg·a·mist /pə'lɪgəmɪst/ *n.* a person with more than one spouse: *He is a polygamist with three wives.* -*adj.* **polygamous** /pə'lɪgəməs/; -*n.* [U] **polygamy.**

pol·y·glot /'pali,glat/ *n.adj.frml.* a person who speaks several languages: *Our French teacher is a polyglot; she speaks French, English, Japanese, and Korean.*

pol·y·gon /'pali,gan/ *n.* a closed, flat geometric figure: *A polygon is a geometric figure such as a triangle, rectangle, or pentagon.*

pol·y·graph /'pali,græf/ *n.* a machine that detects changes in pulse and blood pressure, used as a lie detector: *A technician gave the thief a polygraph (or) a polygraph test.*

pol·y·mer /'paləmər/ *n.adj.* [C;U] any of a great variety of natural and artificial substances with wide industrial uses: *Plastics and artificial fibers, such as polyester, are polymers.*

pol·yp /'palɪp/ *n.* an abnormal growth, such as found in the nose or rectum: *He had polyps removed from his lower intestine.*

pol·y·syl·lab·ic /,palɪsɪ'læbɪk/ *adj.* (of a word) having several, usu. more than three, syllables: *"Dictionary" and "encyclopedia" are polysyllabic words.*

pol·y·tech·nic /,pali'tɛknɪk/ *n.adj.* a school or university that teaches technical and scientific subjects: *My friend studied engineering at Brooklyn <n.> Polytechnic.*

pol·y·the·ism /'paliθi,ɪzəm/ *n.* [U] worship of more than one god: *Polytheism existed before such monotheistic religions as Judaism and Christianity.* -*adj.* **polytheistic** /,paliθi'ɪstɪk/.

pol·y·un·sat·u·rat·ed /,palɪən'sætʃə,reɪtɪd/ *adj.* referring to fats, such as vegetable oils, that do not contribute to hardening of the arteries as the saturated fats of red meat do: *They cook food in corn oil and other polyunsaturated fats.*

pom·e·gran·ate /'pamə,grænɪt, 'pam,grænɪt/ *n.* a round fruit with reddish skin, many juicy red seeds, and white flesh with a slightly acid taste

pomp /pamp/ *n.* [U] grand ceremony, stately spectacle: *The coronation of a British king or queen is a ceremony of great pomp.*

pom·pa·dour /'pampə,dɔr/ *n.* a person's hairdo, swept high above the forehead: *Women in the French court wore their hair in pompadours.*

pom·pom /'pam,pam/ *n.* **1** a little round ball of cotton used as a decoration on clothing or curtains: *The child wore a white cap with a red pompom on it.* **2** a large puff of showy material: *Cheerleaders shake pompoms at football games.*

pomp·ous /'pampəs/ *adj.* self-important, having or showing an exaggerated opinion of one's own importance or seriousness: *He acts in a pompous manner toward his employees.* -*adv.* **pompously;** -*n.* [U] **pomposity** /pam'pasəti/.

pon·cho /'pantʃoʊ/ *n.* **-chos** an outer garment shaped like a

poncho

blanket with a hole for one's head: *He wears a plastic poncho in the rain.*

pond /pɑnd/ *n.* a body of water smaller than a lake: *There are fish in the pond near our camp.*

pon·der /'pɑndər/ *v.* to think about s.t. carefully and deeply: *She pondered his marriage proposal for weeks.* -adj. **ponderable;** -n. **ponderer.**

pon·der·ous /'pɑndərəs/ *adj.* slow moving, awkward, dull: *Bureaucracies move in a ponderous way.*||*He wrote a long, ponderous paper on a subject of no interest.* -adv. **ponderously.**

pon·tiff /'pɑntɪf/ *n.* the Pope: *The Pontiff is head of the Roman Catholic Church.* -adj. **pontifical** /pɑn'tɪfɪkəl/.

pon·tif·i·cate /pɑn'tɪfɪ,keɪt/ *v.* -cated, -cating, -cates to speak in a pompous, dictatorial way: *Our boss pontificates about company rules at our meetings.*

pon·toon /pɑn'tun/ *n.* **1** a float on a seaplane: *An airplane with pontoons landed on the lake.* **2** a floating structure: *The army built a bridge of pontoons across a river.*

po·ny /'poʊni/ *n.* -nies any of a variety of small horses: *The little girl wanted to ride the pony.* —*phrasal v. sep.* **to pony s.t. up:** -nied, -nying, -nies to pay for s.t.: *He ponied up his share of the expenses.*||*He ponied them up.*

pony express *n.* a network of riders who carried the mail in the 19th century USA: *The pony express carried the mail from coast to coast.*

po·ny·tail /'poʊni,teɪl/ *n.* a hairstyle where the hair is gathered at the back of the head and hangs down: *She wears her long, red hair in a ponytail.*

ponytail

pooch /putʃ/ *n.infrml.* **pooches** a dog: *She takes her pooch for a walk each morning.*

poo·dle /'pudl/ *n.* a breed of dog with curly hair, usu. black, gray, or white in color and often cut and shaved in fancy patterns

pooh-pooh /,pu'pu/ *v.* to reject, show contempt for s.t.: *She pooh-poohed his attempt to impress her.*

poodle

pool /pul/ *n.* **1** a swimming pool, usu. made of cement or stone: *They have a pool in their back yard. See:* swimming pool. **2** any still body of water or other liquid: *A pool of oil lies beneath the oil field.* **3** a fund of money: *Banks form a pool of funds to be loaned out.* **4** a fund formed by individuals for

betting, esp. on sports, where the winner(s) take the amount put in, minus expenses: *I won the football pool in my office last week.* **5** a game played with 15 balls that are knocked into side pockets on a special table with a cue ball and stick, (syn.) billiards: *He likes to play pool once a week.*

—*v.* **1** to form into a pool: *Rainwater pooled to form puddles on the street.* **2** to contribute money, knowledge, or other resources as a group for a common purpose: *Our friends pooled their money to buy the couple an expensive wedding gift.*

pool·room /'pul,rum/ *n.* a room or hall with pool tables for playing pool: *He runs a poolroom located above a store.*

pool table *n.* a table with four pockets (holes) in the corners and two along the sides, used to play pool: *A pool table is covered with green felt and has raised sides.*

poop /pup/ *n.slang* [U] **1** *infrml.* news: *He rushed in to tell us the latest poop.* **2** *vulg.* excrement: *There is dog poop on the sidewalk.*

—*v.slang* **1** to tire, become worn out: *After walking all day, I am pooped!* ||*He pooped out and sat down to rest.* **2** *vulg.* to defecate: *That dog pooped on the sidewalk.*

poor /pʊr/ *adj.* **1** with little or no money, (syn.) impoverished: *That family is so poor, they can't afford to buy food.* **2** inferior, not good quality: *The quality of those shoes is poor.* **3** worthy of pity, compassion: *Poor Jane, her mother just died!* **4** without the necessary characteristics: *The land around here is poor, crops won't grow.* -adv. **poorly.**

—*n.pl.* **the poor:** the class of people with little or no money: *Religions urge that people with money should give some to the poor.*

poor box *n.* **boxes** a box in a church into which money for the poor is put: *Each time he goes to church, he drops coins in the poor box.*

poor·boy or **po'boy** /'pʊr,bɔɪ, 'poʊ,bɔɪ/ *n.* a long, thick sandwich made with meat, cheese, etc., (syns.) a submarine, a hero sandwich, a hoagie: *The truck driver had a poorboy of ham and salami for lunch.*

poor·house /'pʊr,haʊs/ *n.old usage* -houses /-,haʊzɪz/ in former times, a public institution housing poor people

pop /pɑp/ *n.* **1** the sharp sound of s.t. bursting or exploding: *You could hear the pop of firecrackers during the celebration.* **2** *infrml.* a friendly term for one's father or an elderly man: *My pop recently retired from work.* **3** a soft drink. *See:* soda, USAGE NOTE.

—*v.* **popped, popping, pops 1** to burst suddenly with a loud noise: *The popcorn popped as it cooked.* **2** to open or burst abruptly: *A button on his shirt popped off.* **3** *infrml.* **to**

P

pop the question: to ask s.o. to marry you: *He finally got up enough courage to pop the question to his girlfriend.*

—*adj.* short for popular, related to ordinary people: *Pop culture includes television, movies, sports, and rock and roll music.*

pop·corn /'pap,kɔrn/ *n.* [U] a type of corn whose kernels burst into white puffs when cooked: *I like to eat popcorn at the movies.*

Pope /poup/ *n.* the head of the Roman Catholic Church: *The Pope lives in the Vatican in Rome.*

pop·lar /'paplər/ *n.* **1** [C] a type of softwood tree that is tall and thin with light green bark: *Poplar trees fall over easily in high winds.* **2** [U] the wood of this tree

pop·lin /'paplɪn/ *n.* [U] a type of finely woven fabric: *My trench coat is made of waterproof cotton poplin.*

pop·o·ver /'pap,ouvər/ *n.* a hollow muffin made with light flour, milk, and eggs: *He eats popovers with gravy with his roast beef.*

pop·py /'papi/ *n.* **-ies** any of a variety of plants with large, showy, delicate flowers, typically bright red, white, pink, or orange in color: *One type of poppy is the source of the narcotic drug opium.*

Pop·si·cle /'papsɪkəl/ *n.*™ a type of sweetened, fruit-flavored crushed ice, frozen onto one or two sticks: *In summer, an orange Popsicle tastes very refreshing.*

pop·u·lace /'papyələs/ *n.frml.* [C] the common people of a nation, region, or local area, such as a city: *Many of the city's populace travel to work by subway and bus.*

pop·u·lar /'papyələr/ *adj.* **1** well-liked, admired by a group of people: *She is very popular with her college classmates.* **2** having widespread acceptance: *The Mercedes automobile is popular among the rich.* **3** typical of the interests of ordinary people: *Soap operas and country music are forms of popular entertainment.* -*adv.* **popularly.**

pop·u·lar·i·ty /,papyə'lærəti/ *n.* [U] **1** widespread acceptance: *The popularity of that new electronic device is growing daily.* **2** widespread admiration: *The President's popularity resulted in his re-election.*

pop·u·lar·ize /'papyələ,raɪz/ *v.* **-ized, -izing, -izes** to make widely known, accepted among many people: *The USA popularized the wearing of jeans around the world.* -*n.* **popularization** /,papyələrə'zeɪʃən/.

pop·u·late /'papyə,leɪt/ *v.* **-lated, -lating, -lates 1** to fill an area with people: *Colonists from Europe populated many parts of the Americas.* **2** to live in an area, inhabit it: *Immigrants from all over the world populate New York City.*

pop·u·la·tion /,papyə'leɪʃən/ *n.* [C;U] all of the people living in a specific area: *The population of this city is eight million.*

population explosion *n.* a rapid increase in the number of people in an area: *A population explosion in the country resulted in a food shortage.*

Pop·u·lism /'papyə,lɪzəm/ *n.* [U] an American political philosophy of dedication to the interests of ordinary people with a minimum amount of government interference: *Populism, with its emphasis on individual freedom, is a very American approach to politics.* -*n.adj.* **Populist.**

pop·u·lous /'papyələs/ *adj.* having many people, heavily populated: *Beijing and Tokyo are very populous cities.*

por·ce·lain /'pɔrslɪn, 'pɔrsə-/ *n.* [U] chinaware, fine cups, saucers, plates, vases, etc. made from hard, white material often beautifully colored: *Porcelain was invented by the Chinese in the 8th century A.D.*

porch /pɔrtʃ/ *n.* **porches** a covered structure outside the front or back entrance to a house: *We sit outside on the porch on summer evenings.*

porch

por·cu·pine /'pɔrkyə,paɪn/ *n.* an animal of the rodent family, found widely in the Americas, that moves slowly and has stiff, sharp quills that can be raised to drive off enemies: *Porcupine quills stuck in the nose of a dog can cause it great pain.*

pore /pɔr/ *phrasal v. insep.* **pored, poring, pores to pore over s.t.:** to study carefully, examine long and carefully: *People pore over the Bible, reading it day after day.*

—*n.* a tiny opening: *Pores in the skin allow you to sweat.*

pork /pɔrk/ *n.* **1** [U] the meat of a pig: *I enjoy roast pork for dinner.* **2** *infrml.fig.* also known as **pork barrel** or **pork barrel legislation:** government jobs and projects obtained by politicians for the benefit of their voters: *That new shipyard is pork for New York.*

por·no /'pɔrnou/ or **porn** /pɔrn/ *n.infrml.* [U] short for pornography: *That store sells porno.*

—*adj.infrml.* related to pornography, pornographic: *He is the porno king of dirty magazines.*

por·nog·ra·phy /pɔr'nagrəfi/ *n.* [U] obscene writings, pictures, or films intended to arouse sexual desire: *Pornography is banned by some state and local governments.* -*n.* **por nographer;** -*adj.* **pornographic** /,pɔrnə'græfɪk/.

po·rous /'pɔrəs/ *adj.* allowing liquid, gases, etc. to pass through, (*syn.*) permeable: *Sand is porous, and water can pass through it.* -*n.* [U] **porosity** /pɔ'rasəti, pə-/.

por·poise /ˈpɔrpəs/ *n.* an air-breathing sea animal with a rounded head, similar to a dolphin: *A school of porpoises swam alongside our boat.*

port (1) /pɔrt/ *n.* **1** a harbor, safe place for ships to load and unload cargoes: *Boats head for port when a storm arises.* **2** a place on the outside of a computer where you plug in a cable that connects the computer to other devices, such as a printer: *You've connected your mouse to the wrong port.* **3** the left side of a boat or airplane: *The captain told the pilot to steer to port.*
—*adj.* on or related to the left side of a boat or airplane: *The captain is standing on the port side of the ship. See:* port of call, port of entry.

port (2) *n.* a type of sweet Portuguese wine: *Port is often served after dinner.*

port·a·ble /ˈpɔrtəbəl/ *adj.n.* movable, capable of being carried or moved around: *She uses a <adj.> portable computer when she travels.* -*n.* **portability** /ˌpɔrtəˈbɪləti/.

por·tage /ˈpɔrtɪdʒ, pɔrˈtɑdʒ/ *n.v.* **-taged, -taging, -tages** the act of carrying boats and supplies over an area where boats cannot be used: *The <n.> portage of our canoes between the two lakes took four hours.*

por·tal /ˈpɔrtl/ *n.* a large, impressive gate, door, or entrance: *The portal to the city was a huge arch with columns and decorations.*

por·tend /pɔrˈtɛnd/ *v.frml.* to warn of future danger: *Mass demonstrations portend an armed rebellion.*

por·tent /ˈpɔrˌtɛnt/ *n.frml.* a warning about future danger: *The riot was a portent of the revolution to come.* -*adj.frml.* **portentous** /pɔrˈtɛntəs/.

por·ter /ˈpɔrtər/ *n.* **1** a person employed to carry luggage, as at a train station or hotel: *Porters carry passengers' baggage from the airport to a taxi outside.* **2** a cleaning person: *A porter mopped the hallway.*

port·fo·li·o /pɔrtˈfouliˌou/ *n.* **-os 1** a flat case, sometimes closed with a zipper, used to carry loose papers, drawings, etc.: *Artists carry a portfolio to hold and display their drawings.* **2** a symbol of a high government office: *He was named minister without portfolio in the last government.* **3** a set of different investments by a person: *She has a large portfolio of stocks and bonds.*

port·hole /ˈpɔrtˌhoul/ *n.* a round window in a ship: *A sailor opened the porthole to let some air in.*

por·ti·co /ˈpɔrtɪˌkou/ *n.* **-coes** or **-cos** a walkway with a roof supported by columns leading to a building's entrance: *A portico makes an impressive entrance to any building.*

por·tion /ˈpɔrʃən/ *n.* **1** a small piece or section of a larger thing: *I put a portion of my salary* in a savings account each month. **2** a piece of s.t. larger that is given to one person to one group, as in an inheritance: *When her father died, she received a larger portion than her sister did.* **3** a serving of food: *That restaurant serves large portions of meat and potatoes.*
—*phrasal v. sep.* **to portion s.t. out:** to divide into peices and give them to others: *My grandmother portioned out her property among her five children before she died.‖She portioned it out.*

port·ly /ˈpɔrtli/ *adj.* **-lier, -liest** fat, yet dignified (said esp. of men): *He is a portly man who wears fine clothes.*

port of call *n.* **ports of call** a regular stop on an ocean voyage: *Our cruise ship had eight ports of call in the Caribbean.*

por·trait /ˈpɔrtrɪt/ *n.* **1** a painting, photograph, or other picture of a person: *The king posed for a portrait painted by a famous artist.* **2** a written or spoken description of s.t., esp. of a person: *The reporter painted a portrait of the killer as a crazy animal.*

por·tray /pɔrˈtreɪ, pər-/ *v.frml.* **1** to describe s.o. or s.t. in a certain way, to characterize them: *The writer portrays Americans after the war as happy and rich.* **2** to act, play the part of s.o.: *The movie star portrays a beautiful woman gone mad.* -*n.frml.* **portrayal.**

pose /pouz/ *n.* **1** a particular way of holding one's head and body, esp. for a picture: *The model held a pose sitting on a chair.* **2** a false representation of oneself: *The swindler's pose as a rich man was uncovered by the police.*
—*v.* **posed, posing, poses 1** to hold still in a pose, so one's picture can be painted, drawn, or photographed: *The mayor posed for an oil portrait.* **2** to present s.t. that confuses, such as a question, an idea or a possible danger: *The teacher posed a question to the class.‖The police said the escaped convict might pose a threat to people.* **3** to pretend, make believe: *He posed as a rich man when he was not. See:* posture.

posh /pɑʃ/ *adj.* luxurious, displaying comfort and wealth: *a posh hotel*

po·si·tion /pəˈzɪʃən/ *n.* **1** a location, a point where s.t. exists or belongs: *The best position for that desk is against the wall.* **2** posture, the way in which s.o or s.t. is arranged: *He was sitting in an uncomfortable position.‖I moved the bolt on the door into the locked position.* **3** a job, employment: *She has an excellent position as head of a school.* **4** a rank among others, place in an order: *That student holds the top position in his class.* **5** a point of view, opinion: *The President's position is that taxes must be cut.* **6** a condition, situation: *He is in a good (bad, strong, weak, etc.) position to see his tax program succeed.* **7** a situation, a location and arrangement of a military force:

Soldiers took up a position in front of the presidential palace. **8** (in finance) an amount of money, securities, real estate: *She holds a large position (of stock) in the company.* **9 in a position to do s.t.:** able or not able to do s.t.: *I have very little money now, so I am not in a position to loan you any.* **10 in** or **out of position:** located correctly or not: *That desk is out of position now and should be in position against the wall.*
—*v.* to place in a location: *The soldiers positioned themselves in front of the palace.*

pos·i·tive /'pɑzətɪv/ *adj.* **1** optimistic, hopeful: *He has a positive attitude toward his work; he likes it and does it well.* **2** certain, definite, without doubt: *The police are positive that they have the right man in jail.* **3** affirmative, indicating yes: *I received a positive reply to my application to enter that college.* **4** helpful, beneficial, (syn.) constructive: *She received positive advice (criticism, insights, etc.) on how to study for exams.* **5** (of the results of a medical test) showing that a condition, disease, etc., exists: *She had a pregnancy test and the result was positive.* **6** indicating a (+) sign for an electrical charge: *I hooked the starter cable to the positive post on the car battery.* -*adv.* **positively** /'pɑzətɪvli, ,pɑzə'tɪvli/.
—*n.* **1** a beneficial, hopeful thing: *The sick man feels better today, so that is a positive.* **2** (in math) a number above zero: *A negative multiplied by a negative makes a positive, as in (−2) x (−3) = 6.*

pos·se /'pɑsi/ *n.* a group of citizens called together by a police authority, usu. to chase and capture a criminal: *In old cowboy movies, the sheriff picked a posse to help him chase the bad guy.*

pos·sess /pə'zɛs/ *v.* **-sesses 1** to own, have possession of s.t.: *She possesses wealth and power.* **2** to have as a characteristic, trait: *He possesses a fine mind.* **3** to be dominated by s.t.: *She is possessed by ambition.‖I don't know what possessed me to say something so stupid!*

pos·sessed /pə'zɛst/ *adj.* dominated by crazy or irrational impulses: *He ran out of the building screaming like a man possessed.*

pos·ses·sion /pə'zɛʃən/ *n.* **1** [U] ownership, control over s.t.: *They will lose possession of their house if they don't pay the mortgage.* **2** [C] *often pl* **possessions** a piece of property, a belonging: *He lost most of his personal possessions in the fire.‖Her most valuable possession is a car worth $40,000.*

pos·ses·sive /pə'zɛsɪv/ *adj.* **1** having a strong desire to control things or people: *She is possessive about her money and won't even share it with her husband.* **2** indicating ownership or a similar relationship: *The "my" and "'s" in "my friend's house" are possessive forms.* -*n.* [U] **possessiveness.**

—*n.* (in grammar) a possessive word or form

pos·si·bil·i·ty /,pɑsə'bɪləti/ *n.* [C;U] **-ties** an occurrence, situation, etc. that could happen, be true, or exist: *There is a possibility that it will rain tomorrow.*

pos·si·ble /'pɑsəbəl/ *adj.* **1** capable of existing, happening, or being done, (syn.) feasible: *Is it possible to get there by bus?* **2** reasonable, probable: *There are several possible solutions to the problem.* **3 as . . . as possible:** to the greatest degree that one is able: *Please come as soon as possible.* **4 if possible:** if it can be arranged: *If possible, come by at 10:00 this morning.*

pos·si·bly /'pɑsəbli/ *adv.* **1** perhaps, maybe: *This is possibly the coldest winter we've ever had.‖The package should arrive next week, possibly sooner.* **2** by any possibility or chance: *I got here as soon as I possibly could.‖What could she possibly have meant?*

pos·sum /'pɑsəm/ *n.* **1** *var. of* opossum **2 to play possum:** to make believe one is dead or asleep: *A wounded soldier played possum and the enemy passed him by, thinking he was dead.*

post (1) /poust/ *n.* **1** the place where the members of the military live, (syn.) a military base: *That sergeant lives on his army post.* **2** a diplomatic mission: *Paris is a very desirable post in the foreign service.* **3** a job, esp. in government **4** a place where one must stay as part of one's job: *The prison guard was told never to leave his post near the cells.*

post (2) *v.* **1** to make a bookkeeping entry: *She posted the wages in the ledger.* **2** to put up public notices about s.t.: *The school principal posted a notice on the bulletin board.* **3** *chiefly Brit.* to mail s.t.: *I posted a letter to my friend.* **4 to keep s.o. posted:** to keep s.o. informed: *Be sure to keep me posted on what is happening with you.* -*n.* [C;U] **posting.**

post (3) *n.* a long, strong piece of metal or wood stuck upright in the ground: *Those posts hold up the fence.*

post·age /'poustɪʤ/ *n.* [U] the cost of sending s.t. by mail: *The postage for that letter is $1.00.*

postage stamp *n.* a piece of paper with a picture and postage amount on it, glued to mail: *Postage stamps are sold at the post office.*

post·al /'poustəl/ *adj.* related to the mail: *The postal system employs thousands of workers.*

postal service *n.* [U] the government system that processes and delivers mail, the post office: *She works for the postal service as a letter carrier.*

post·card /'poust,kɑrd/ *n.* a small paper card often with a picture on one side and space for a message, address, and stamp on the other:

When I am on vacation, I send my friends postcards from the places I visit.

post·date /ˌpoʊst'deɪt, 'poʊst,deɪt/ *v.* **-dated, -dating, -dates** to write a date on s.t. that is later than the actual date: *I postdated a check for a week from today.*

post·doc·tor·al /ˌpoʊst'dɑktərəl/ *adj.* related to studies or research done after receiving a doctoral degree (Ph.D.): *She did her postdoctoral work at Harvard University.*

post·er /'poʊstər/ *n.* a large sheet of paper, usu. with a picture and writing, publicly announcing some event: *Political workers put up posters around town with their candidate's name and picture on it.*

pos·te·ri·or /pɑ'stɪriər, poʊ-/ *n.* the buttocks: *That fellow has a large posterior.*

pos·ter·i·ty /pɑ'stɛrəti/ *n.* [U] **1** one's children and grandchildren etc., (*syn.*) descendants: *He built an empire for himself and his posterity.* **2** future generations of people alive after one's death: *He's famous today, but his name will mean little to posterity.*

post·grad·u·ate /ˌpoʊst'grædʒuɪt/ *n.adj.* a student involved in a program of study after a bachelor's degree: *She is a <n.> postgraduate or <adj.> postgraduate student at the University of Chicago.*

post·hu·mous·ly /'pɑstʃəməsli/ *adv.* after one's death: *The writer's novel was published posthumously. -adj.* **posthumous.**

post·man /'poʊstmən/ *n.* **-men** a male letter carrier, mailman: *The postman usually delivers the mail around 10:00 every morning. See:* letter carrier.

post·mark /'poʊst,mɑrk/ *n.v.* a stamped mark over postage usu showing the date and location of mailing: *The <n.> postmark showed that the letter was mailed on October 6 from New York City.||It was <v.> postmarked October 6.*

postmaster general *n.* **postmasters general** the person in charge of the US postal system: *The office of the postmaster general is located in Washington, D.C.*

post me·rid·i·em /ˌpoʊstmə'rɪdiəm/ *adv. long form for abbr.* **p.m.**, the time from 12:00 p.m. (noon) until 11:59 p.m. *See:* ante meridiem, a.m.

post·mor·tem /ˌpoʊst'mɔrtəm/ *n.* **1** an examination of a dead body to determine the cause of death, an autopsy **2** an analysis of a failure: *Investigators did a postmortem on the train accident after it happened.*

post office *n.* **1** a government building where mail is processed: *I'm going to the post office to mail a package.* **2** the entire mail system of a country: *The post office employs hundreds of thousands of people to move the mail. -abbr.* **P.O.**

post office box *n.* **boxes** a rented box where people can receive mail: *The advertisement said to send your order to P.O. Box 123, Radio City Station, New York 10019. -abbr.* **P.O. Box.**

post·paid /ˌpoʊst'peɪd/ *adj.* with the postage paid by the sender

post·pone /poʊst'poʊn, poʊs'poʊn/ *v.* **-poned, -poning, -pones** to move s.t. to a later time: *Our meeting for today was postponed until next week. -n.* [C;U] **postponement.**

post·script /'poʊst,skrɪpt, 'poʊs,skrɪpt/ *n.* an afterthought, addition to the end of a document: *She added a postscript (or) a P.S. at the bottom of her letter. -abbr.* **P.S.**

pos·tu·late *v.* /'pɑstʃə,leɪt/ **-lated, -lating, -lates** to state s.t. as true without proof: *Scientists postulate that there is a tenth planet in the solar system, but they can't prove its existence.*

pos·ture /'pɑstʃər/ *n.* the way the body is held, often referring to how well one sits or stands: *He has poor posture; he doesn't stand up straight.*

—v.fig. **-tured, -turing, -tures** to hold oneself or to behave in a certain, often artificial way, esp. to impress others: *He postures as an important man, when he is really a nobody. -n.* [U] **posturing.** *See:* pose.

post·war /ˌpoʊst'wɔr/ *adj.* related to a time after a war: *Postwar Europe recovered slowly fromWorld War II.*

po·sy /'poʊzi/ *n.old usage* **-sies** a flower: *He gave his girlfriend a bunch of posies.*

pot /pɑt/ *n.* **1** a container made of metal, glass, or ceramic and used for cooking: *The potatoes are boiling in a pot of water.* **2** a round container, esp. made of clay: *She has pots on her balcony to hold flowers.* **3** *slang* marijuana **4** *infrml.* **the pot:** all the money bet by the players at one time in a card game: *He won the pot at poker.* **5** *infrml.* **to go to pot:** to fall apart: *That company has gone to pot; it will probably go out of business soon.*

—v. **potted, potting, pots** to put live plants in a pot: *She pots plants from her garden to put on her balcony.*

po·ta·ble /'poʊtəbəl/ *adj.frml.* drinkable: *Potable water is pure enough to drink; it won't harm anyone.*

pot·ash /'pɑt,æʃ/ *n.* [U] a chemical compound found in burnt ashes: *Potash is used to manufacture soap and glass.*

po·tas·si·um /pə'tæsiəm/ *n.* [U] a chemical element, a silver-white, soft metal that is found in compounds: *Potassium compounds are widely used in industry and agriculture.*

po·ta·to /pə'teɪtoʊ, -tə/ *n.* **-toes 1** a round or oval, starchy root vegetable, usu. with white flesh and brown, red, or yellow skin: *Potatoes*

P

are one of the most popular foods in the Western world. **2** *infrml.* **hot potato:** a dangerous situation or controversial issue: *The topic of abortion rights is a hot potato for politicians.* **3** *infrml.* **small potatoes:** an unimportant matter, a small amount of money: *That lawyer deals only with big lawsuits, so my case about a stolen watch was small potatoes.* **4 to drop s.t.** or **s.o. like a hot potato:** to suddenly stop dealing with or abandon: *When a voter asked the politician about her opinion on abortion rights, she dropped the matter like a hot potato.*

potato chip *n.* a thin slice of potato fried in oil

pot belly *n.infrml.* **-lies** a big stomach: *He's got a pot belly from drinking too much beer.* *-adj.* **pot-bellied** /'pɑt,bɛlid/.

po·ten·cy /'poutnsi/ *n.* [C;U] power, strength: *Medicines can lose their potency over time.*

po·tent /'poutnt/ *adj.* powerful or effective, having a strong effect or influence: *a potent drug||The senator is a potent force in her political party.*

po·ten·tate /'poutn,teɪt/ *n.* a ruler, s.o. with great power: *The sheik is a potentate who rules his people with a firm hand.*

po·ten·tial /pə'tɛnʃəl/ *n.* **1** [C] the possibility of being or doing s.t., the unrealized capability for s.t.: *That business has the potential to be very profitable next year.* **2** [U] talent, ability: *She has the potential to be a top figure skater.* **3** [U] a measure of electrical capacity *—adj.* possible, capable of s.t.: *I think the governor is a potential candidate for president.* *-adv.* **potentially.**

pot·ful /'pɑt,ful/ *n.* **1** an amount of s.t. that can be held in a pot: *His guests ate the whole potful of spaghetti sauce.* **2** *infrml.fig.* a large amount of s.t.: *That rich man has potfuls of money.*

pot·head /'pɑt,hɛd/ *n.slang* a person who smokes marijuana regularly

pot·hole /'pɑt,houl/ *n.* a hole in a street caused by heavy traffic and cold weather: *City workers repair potholes by filling them with tar.*

po·tion /'pouʃən/ *n.* strong liquid medicine, poison, or magic formula: *A witch gave the princess a magic potion and turned her into a frog.*

pot·luck /'pɑt,lʌk/ *n.* a group meal where everyone brings food and shares it with each other *I will make a large salad to bring to the potluck on Saturday.*

pot·pour·ri /,poupu'ri/ *n.* [C;U] **1** a mixture of flowers, herbs, and spices used as fragrance: *She uses potpourri to keep her bathroom sweet-smelling.* **2** a mixture of odd, different things, (*syn.*) a mishmash: *That dish is a potpourri of meat, fish, vegetables, and rice.*

pot roast *n.* a piece of beef cooked slowly in liquid in a covered pot: *Pot roast is usually made with a tough cut of meat that is made tender by cooking.*

pot·ted /'pɑtɪd/ *adj.* located, planted, or grown in a pot: *Potted plants decorate the hotel lobby.*

pot·ter /'pɑtər/ *n.* a person who makes pottery: *The potter shaped the clay into a bowl.*

pot·ter·y /'pɑtəri/ *n.* [U] **1** objects made of soft clay and then baked until hard: *Vases and bowls are common types of pottery.* **2** the activity or skill of making such objects: *I'm taking a pottery class at the art institute.*

pot·ty /'pɑti/ *n.infrml.* **-ties** a toilet, or a container with a seat on it that is used as a toilet by a young child

pouch /pautʃ/ *n.* **pouches** **1** a flexible bag: *Bank guards bring money into the bank in pouches.* **2** a bag-like pocket of skin: *A baby kangaroo lives in its mother's pouch.*

poul·try /'poultri/ *n.* [U] fowl, such as chickens, turkeys, and ducks: *Poultry are raised on farms for their eggs or meat.*

pounce /pauns/ *v.* **pounced, pouncing, pounces** to attack by jumping quickly on s.t. or s.o.: *The cat pounced on the mouse.*

pound (1) /paund/ *v.* **1** to hit s.t. repeatedly with force, to hammer: *The worker pounded nails into the wall with a hammer.* **2** to beat or throb strongly: *My head is pounding from a headache.*

pound (2) *n.* **1** a weight of 16 ounces or 453.6 grams: *She bought a pound of butter at the store.* **2** the basic unit of currency in Britain and several other countries: *He exchanged dollars for pounds in London.* **3** *fig.* **pound of flesh:** a very large price: *When the farmer couldn't pay his mortgage, the bank got its pound of flesh by taking away the farmer's farm. See:* **penny, 4.**

pound (3) *n.* a place where lost or unwanted dogs and cats are kept by a town until s.o. claims them

pound cake *n.* [C;U] a rich, smooth cake originally made with a pound each of butter, flour, sugar, and eggs

pound·ing /'paundɪŋ/ *n.* [U] the act of hammering or hitting s.t. with force: *The boxer gave his opponent a brutal pounding.*

pour /pɔr/ *v.* **1** to let flow, make s.t. stream out: *She poured cream into her coffee.||Curses poured from the thief's lips when he was caught by police.* **2** to give or make in large amounts: *Investors poured money into a new company.* **3** to rain hard: *Wear your boots and take an umbrella; it's pouring out!*

pout /paut/ *v.n.* to show sadness or anger by pressing one's lips together so they move outward: *When the child could not have any candy, she <v.> pouted.*

pov·er·ty /'pavərti/ *n.* [U] **1** the lack of money and material possessions, the state of being poor: *Poverty often goes hand in hand with disease.||There were very few jobs in the town, and many families lived in poverty.* **2** a lack, esp. of s.t. desirable: *The length of the report did not hide the poverty of the writer's ideas.*

poverty level or **poverty line** *n.* [U] the level of income below which the government considers a family to be legally poor and eligible for social services: *The number of people below the poverty level is increasing.*

poverty-stricken *adj.* very poor: *The poverty-stricken family had no place to live.*

POW /,piou'dʌbəlyu/ *n.abbr.* for prisoner of war

pow·der /'paudər/ *n.* [U] **1** fine particles, s.t. ground or crushed into tiny grains: *She always puts baby powder on herself after a bath.* **2** gun powder used as part of ammunition *-adj.* **powdery.**

—*v.* to use powder: *The mother powdered her baby's bottom.*

powder room *n.* a women's bathroom, esp. one with mirrors for freshening makeup: *She went to the powder room to powder her nose.*

pow·er /'pauər/ *n.* **1** [U] the authority and ability to do s.t. important: *As a manager, she has the power to hire and fire employees.* **2** [C;usu. *sing.*] one's ability to function or to do s.t.: *He's 90 years old, but his mental powers are as strong as ever.* **3** [U] a supply of energy, esp. electricity: *The electric company has shut the power off.* **4** [C] (in mathematics) the number of times a number is multiplied by itself, such as a square: 10^2, cube: 10^3, etc.: *10 to the power of 2= 10^2= 100.* **5** [U] strength: *As a bodybuilder he has extreme physical power.*

—*adj.* related to the use of power: *He owns a power lawn mower that is run by gas.*

—*v.* to give power to s.t.: *This toy truck is powered by AAA batteries.*

pow·er·boat /'pauər,bout/ *n.* a boat run by motors, a motorboat, esp. a fast one: *He owns a powerboat that will go up to 40 MPH.*

pow·er·ful /'pauərfəl/ *adj.* **1** having a lot of power and influence: *He is a powerful man in the Senate.* **2** strong or effective, having great force: *That racing car has a powerful engine.* *-adv.* **powerfully.**

pow·er·house /'pauər,haus/ *n.* **-houses** /-,hauzɪz/ **1** *fig.* a powerful person or organization: *That football team is a powerhouse; they beat everybody.* **2** a power plant, such as one generating electricity: *A powerhouse is located at the base of the dam.*

pow·er·less /'pauərlɪs/ *adj.* **1** having no power, weak: *Poor people are often powerless*

in the political process. **2** defenseless, unarmed: *A thief demanded a man's wallet and he was powerless to resist.* *-n.* [U] **powerlessness.**

power of attorney *n.* a formal document that gives one person the right to act and sign documents for another: *I gave my stockbroker the power of attorney to trade stocks in my account without consulting me.*

power pack *n.* a battery or group of batteries used to make a device work: *The power pack for her small computer can be recharged easily.*

power plant *n.* a building or station where power, esp. electricity, is generated: *That nuclear power plant generates electricity for this area.*

power play *n.* **1** (in sports) the use of many players against a key spot in the opposing team: *The team's surprise power play against their defense cost them the game.* **2** *fig.* the use of power to force change: *The union threatened to strike in a power play to force management to raise wages.*

power politics *n.pl.* used with a *sing.* or *pl.v.* the threat of using force or economic power in international affairs: *The USA engaged in power politics by threatening to bomb the other country if it didn't end its war.*

power steering *n.* [U] a steering system in a car that uses the engine's power to make steering the car easier for the driver

power structure *n.* the people and institutions that hold power, esp. political and financial power: *The power structure in that country is made up of a military government cooperating with rich landowners.*

power trip *n.infrml.fig.* the use of power to impress and control others: *The boss was on a power trip when he fired his secretary for not making coffee.*

pow·wow /'pau,wau/ *n.infrml.* a meeting: *The employees had a powwow to discuss the big new project.*

USAGE NOTE: *Powwow* is originally a Native American word. It refers to a Native American dance ceremony, and to a meeting of the group's members to discuss problems.

pox /paks/ *n.* [U] a disease, such as chicken pox or smallpox, that causes sores on the skin

PR /,pi'ar/ *abbr. for* public relations

prac·ti·ca·ble /'præktɪkəbəl/ *adj.* capable of being done, (*syn.*) feasible: *Their marriage was so bad that divorce seemed the only practicable solution.*

prac·ti·cal /'præktɪkəl/ *adj.* **1** realistic, sensible, not acting foolishly: *They wanted to buy a white couch, but with three small children, it just wasn't practical.* **2** useful, handy: *That* *dictionary would be a practical gift for the student.* **3** relating to actual practice or real situations rather than to theory: *She felt that most of what she learned in the course was of no practical use.* -*n.* **practicality** /ˌpræktɪˈkæləti/.

practical joke *n.* a trick or act of embarrassing s.o. done to amuse oneself or others: *He played a practical joke on his friend by tying the friend's shoelaces together.*

prac·ti·cal·ly /ˈpræktɪkli/ *adv.* **1** nearly, almost: *He has practically finished his term paper.* **2** in a practical way

practical nurse *n.* a nurse who takes care of patients and is licensed by the state and supervised by a registered nurse: *Practical nurses can give injections. See:* licensed practical nurse.

prac·tice /ˈpræktɪs/ *v.* **-ticed, -ticing, -tices 1** to do s.t. repeatedly to perfect it: *She practices the piano eight hours a day.* **2** to work in the professions of medicine, law, or accounting: *That doctor has practiced medicine for many years.* **3** to do s.t. regularly or as a habit: *to practice moderation in drinking* **4 to practice what one preaches:** to do yourself what you tell others to do: *The doctor stopped smoking cigarettes and started exercising when he decided to practice what he preaches to his patients.*
—*n.* **1** [U] regular repetition of an activity, art, sport, etc.: *It takes practice to do almost anything well.* **2** [C;usu. *sing.*] a meeting for this purpose: *The school band has practice at 8 a.m., before classes start.* **3** [U] s.t. that is done regularly, the usual way of doing s.t., (*syns.*) a habit, a custom: *It is standard business practice to keep a copy of every letter sent out.||He made a practice of always telling the truth.* **4** [U] the carrying out of s.t. in a real situation, actual performance: *The method worked in theory but not in practice.* **5** [U] work in a profession: *She is engaged in the practice of law.* **6** [C] the business of a person in a profession: *She has a large law practice with many clients.* **7 in practice** or **out of practice:** having or not having the skill produced by doing s.t. repeatedly: *I used to play tennis pretty well, but I'm out of practice now.* **8 practice makes perfect:** repetition leads to excellence: *She plays the violin every day because practice makes perfect.*

prac·tic·ing /ˈpræktɪsɪŋ/ *adj.* actively doing s.t.: *She is a practicing accountant.||He is a practicing Christian (Jew, Muslim, etc.).*

prac·ti·tion·er /prækˈtɪʃənər/ *n.* a person who does skilled work: *He is a legal practitioner.*

prag·mat·ic /prægˈmætɪk/ *adj.* using common sense to solve problems, (*syn.*) practical: *He would like to be a doctor, but he has a pragmatic attitude and realizes that he cannot afford medical school.*

prag·ma·tism /ˈprægməˌtɪzəm/ *n.* [U] a philosophy of dealing with events and solving problems in practical ways: *Americans are known for their pragmatism in business affairs.* -*n.* **pragmatist.**

prai·rie /ˈprɛri/ *n.* a large area of flat or slightly hilly grassland with tall grasses and few trees, esp. in the central part of North America

praise /preɪz/ *v.* **praised, praising, praises 1** to express admiration and respect: *A supervisor praised the employee for her good work.* **2** to worship, (*syn.*) to revere: *Survivors of the crash praised God for saving them.*
—*n.* [C;U] an expression of admiration and respect: *The mayor gave praise to the firefighters for saving people from the burning building.*

praise·wor·thy /ˈpreɪzˌwɜrði/ *adj.* worthy of being praised, (*syn.*) admirable: *Firefighting is a praiseworthy profession.* -*n.* [U] **praiseworthiness.**

prance /præns/ *v.* **pranced, prancing, prances** to move in a spirited way, like a horse or a dancer, picking the feet up high, (*syn.*) to strut: *The child pranced about in her new party dress.* -*n.* **prancer.**

prank /præŋk/ *n.* a practical joke, (*syn.*) a trick: *He played a prank on his friend when he set the clock back an hour.* -*n.* **prankster** /ˈpræŋkstər/.

prawn /prɔn/ *n.* a shellfish similar to a shrimp, but larger

pray /preɪ/ *v.* **1** to speak to God or other gods: *He prays every night for the safety of his family.* **2** *frml.* to ask s.o. for s.t. serious: *I pray that you'll be careful driving in this storm.*

prayer /prɛr/ *n.* [C;U] **1** an act of speaking to God or other gods: *She said a prayer that her sick mother would be healed.* **2 not to have a prayer:** to have no chance: *Our team is so bad that it doesn't have a prayer of winning the game.* -*adj.* **prayerful** /ˈprɛrfəl/.

prayer beads *n.pl.* a rosary: *He says his prayers while counting his prayer beads.*

pre- /pri/ *prefix* indicating s.t. in front of (in space) or before (in time) s.t. else

preach /pritʃ/ *v.* **preaches 1** to give a sermon or talk: *The minister preached the word of God to the people in the church.* **2** to give advice, (*syn.*) to moralize: *She is always preaching to her children about not talking to strangers.* -*adj.pej.* **preachy.**

preach·er /ˈpritʃər/ *n.* a person who preaches, usu. a member of the clergy, minister: *He is a preacher in a Protestant church.*

pre·am·ble /ˈpriˌæmbəl, priˈæm-/ *n.frml.* a formal introduction to a document or speech about its purpose: *The legislators wrote a short preamble to the constitution.*

pre·car·i·ous /prɪˈkɛriəs/ *adj.* **1** unstable, shaky: *The tragedy left her in precarious men-*

tal health. **2** dangerous, not secure or safe: *He has all his money in the stock market and would be in a precarious financial situation if stock prices went down.* *-adv.* **precariously.**

pre·cau·tion /prɪˈkɔʃən/ *n.* [C;U] a step taken in advance to prevent harm, (*syn.*) a safeguard: *She took the precaution of bringing a sweater in case it got cold on the boat trip.* *-adj.* **precautionary** /prɪˈkɔʃəˌnɛri/.

pre·cede /prɪˈsid/ *v.* **-ceded, -ceding, -cedes** to come before, appear earlier: *The dark skies preceded a thunderstorm.*

prec·e·dence /ˈprɛsədəns/ *n.* [U] greater importance, (*syn.*) priority: *My family's health takes precedence over my job.*

prec·e·dent /ˈprɛsədənt/ *n.* [C] an example that allows similar future actions, a custom: *When the principal wore blue jeans to school on Friday, it set a precedent for others to do that, too.*

pre·ced·ing /prɪˈsidɪŋ/ *adj.* coming before s.t., appearing earlier: *The preceding entry in this dictionary is "precedent."*

pre·cept /ˈpriˌsɛpt/ *n.* a rule to use for action: *"Haste makes waste" is a precept that means one should work carefully and accurately.*

pre·cinct /ˈpriˌsɪŋkt/ *n.* **1** one of a number of districts in a city or town under the authority of its own police unit: *He lives in the 112th precinct.* **2** a local police station: *He went to the precinct to report a burglary.*

pre·cious /ˈprɛʃəs/ *adj.* **1** extremely valuable, costly: *Precious metals include gold and platinum.* **2** *fig.* beloved, darling: *That child is so sweet and precious.* **3** artificial, exaggerated in style: *He uses fancy words that give his speech a precious quality.*
—*n.* loved one, darling: *Precious, do you love me?* *-n.* [U] **preciousness.**

prec·i·pice /ˈprɛsəpɪs/ *n.frml.* **1** a steep decline, cliff: *A rock fell over the precipice.* **2** the edge of danger: *The two countries were on the precipice of war with each other.*

pre·cip·i·tate /prɪˈsɪpəˌteɪt/ *v.* **-tated, -tating, -tates** to cause to happen, esp. suddenly or sooner than expected: *His climbing 15 flights of stairs precipitated his heart attack.*
—*adj.* /prɪˈsɪpətɪt/ done suddenly or in a hurry, (*syn.*) hasty: *Her decision to leave her job seemed overly precipitate.* *-adv.* **precipitately.**

pre·cip·i·ta·tion /prɪˌsɪpəˈteɪʃən/ *n.* [U] rain, snow, sleet, or hail, or the amount of this that has fallen: *Precipitation was low this summer.*

pre·cip·i·tous /prɪˈsɪpətəs/ *adj.* **1** steep, dropping down sharply: *There is a precipitous drop off that cliff.* **2** *fig.* declining fast: *The stock market took a precipitous drop yesterday.*

pre·cise /prɪˈsaɪs/ *adj.* **1** exact, accurate: *I need the precise street address of the doctor's*

office. **2** meaning s.t. exactly and not different: *She arrived at the precise moment that we heard the scream.* **3** with special care, (*syn.*) meticulous: *He spoke in a very precise manner.* *-adv.* **precisely.**

pre·ci·sion /prɪˈsɪʒən/ *n.* [U] attention to accuracy, (*syn.*) exactness: *Parts of machines are made to precision.‖The professor spoke with precision.*
—*adj.* made with or producing accurate measurements: *Computers are precision instruments.*

pre·clude /prɪˈklud/ *v.* **-cluded, -cluding, -cludes** to prevent, make impossible: *The accident precluded his participation in the race.* *-n.* [U] **preclusion** /prɪˈkluʒən/.

pre·co·cious /prɪˈkoʊʃəs/ *adj.* (of a child) advanced in intelligence or development: *She was a precocious child who could read and write at the age of three.* *-adv.* **precociously;** *-n.* [U] **precociousness** or **precocity** /prɪˈkɑsəti/.

pre·co·lo·ni·al /ˌprikəˈloʊniəl/ *adj.* before colonial times: *In precolonial times North America was populated by native tribes.*

pre·con·ceived /ˌprikənˈsivd/ *adj.* referring to beliefs (opinions, attitudes, etc.) formed before seeing a situation, prejudiced: *He had the preconceived idea that New Yorkers were unfriendly before he visited the city.* *-v.* **preconceive;** *-n.* [C] **preconception** /ˌprikənˈsɛpʃən/.

pre·con·di·tion /ˌprikənˈdɪʃən/ *n.* [C] a requirement that must be agreed to in advance: *The union has a 5% wage increase as a precondition before it will negotiate.*

pre·cur·sor /prɪˈkɜrsər, ˈpriˌkɜr-/ *n.frml.* [C] s.t. or s.o. that comes before the arrival of another, such as an early model of a machine, (*syn.*) a forerunner: *The quartz radio was a precursor of the modern radio.* *-adj.* **precursory** /prɪˈkɜrsəri/.

pre·date /ˌpriˈdeɪt/ *v.* **-dated, -dating, -dates** to happen before s.t. else: *The Vikings' visit to North America in about 1,000 a.d. predated the visit of Columbus by nearly 500 years.*

pred·a·tor /ˈprɛdətər, -ˌtɔr/ *n.* **1** an animal that lives by killing and eating others: *Hawks and lions are predators.* **2** *fig.* a person who harms others for his or her own benefit: *A swindler is a predator who cheats others.* *-adj.* **predatory** /ˈprɛdəˌtɔri/.

pred·e·ces·sor /ˈprɛdəˌsɛsər/ *n.* **1** a person who worked in a job before the person working in it now: *My predecessor left to start her own company.* **2** an ancestor

pre·des·ti·na·tion /ˌpridɛstəˈneɪʃən, prɪˌdɛs-/ *n.* [U] **1** (in religion) the belief that God chooses which people will be saved, esp. through Christ: *Predestination is one of the*

P

main beliefs of the Presbyterian Church. **2** the belief that one's life is determined in advance by God or fate: *He believes in predestination, or that whatever happens to him is the will of God.*

pre·des·tine /pri'dɛstɪn/ v. **-tined, -tining, -tines** to determine s.t. beforehand: *He believes that God predestined him to be a priest.*

pre·de·ter·mine /ˌpridɪ'tɜrmɪn/ v. **-mined, -mining, -mines** to decide before an action, determine beforehand: *The man and his attorney predetermined that he would plead "not guilty" in court.*

pre·dic·a·ment /prɪ'dɪkəmənt/ n. [C] a difficult situation, dilemma: *Her predicament is that she has run out of money, but does not want to leave her nice apartment.*

pred·i·cate /'prɛdɪˌkeɪt/ v. **-cated, -cating, -cates** to base an action or belief, on s.t.: *He predicated his argument that there is life after death on his belief in God.*
—n. /'prɛdɪkɪt/ in grammar, the part of a sentence that says s.t. about the subject and that consists of a verb and words connected to the verb: *In the sentence, "We bought a new car," "bought a new car" is the predicate.* -n. [U] predication /ˌprɛdɪ'keɪʃən/.

pre·dict /prɪ'dɪkt/ v. to say what will happen in the future, (syn.) to foretell: *Scientists are not able to predict earthquakes very well.*

pre·dict·a·ble /prɪ'dɪktəbəl/ adj. able to be predicted: *Her car accident was predictable because she was drunk and driving much too fast on a wet road at night.* -adv. **predictably.**

pre·dic·tion /prɪ'dɪkʃən/ n. [C;U] a statement about what will happen in the future, forecast: *The meteorologist's prediction that it would rain today was correct.*

pred·i·lec·tion /ˌprɛdl'ɛkʃən, prid-/ n.frml. a liking, tendency: *He has a predilection for drinking alcohol.*

pre·dis·pose /ˌpridɪ'spouz/ v.frml. **-posed, -posing, -poses** **1** to make more likely to suffer from, (syn.) to make vulnerable: *Her family history may predispose her to heart disease.* **2** to incline s.o. in advance to do s.t. or to have a particular attitude: *She is predisposed to taking a vacation in Mexico, not Canada.* -n. [U] **predisposition** /ˌpridɪspə'zɪʃən/.

pre·dom·i·nance /prɪ'dɑmənəns/ n. [U] dominance, the state of having more power or importance or of existing in larger amounts or numbers: *Christianity has predominance over other religions in the USA.* -adj. **predominant;** -adv. **predominantly.**

pre·dom·i·nate /prɪ'dɑmən,neɪt/ v. **-nated, -nating, -nates** to dominate, overshadow others: *Pine forests predominate in this area, not oak or open fields.*

pre·em·i·nent /pri'ɛmənənt/ adj.frml. outstanding, most famous: *She is the preeminent soprano in the opera today.* -n. [U] **preeminence;** -adv. **preeminently.**

pre·empt /pri'ɛmpt/ v. to take the place of s.t., take precedence over: *News of the earthquake preempted regular TV shows.* -n.frml. [U] **preemption;** -adj. **preemptive.**

preen /prin/ v. **1** (of birds) to clean feathers with the beak: *A bird preened its feathers.* **2** fig. to spend a lot of time grooming oneself, esp. in public

pre·ex·ist /ˌpriɪg'zɪst/ v. to exist before s.t. else, (syn.) to antedate: *a preexisting medical condition* -n. [U] **preexistence.**

pre·fab /'pri,fæb/ adj.infrml. short for prefabricated
—n.infrml. a prefabricated building

pre·fab·ri·cate /pri'fæbrɪ,keɪt/ v. **-cated, -cating, -cates** to make, build s.t. beforehand: *That company prefabricates sections of houses and moves them to building sites for carpenters to assemble.* -adj. **prefabricated.**

pref·ace /'prɛfɪs/ n. an introduction to a book or speech: *The preface gave an overview of the book's contents.* -adj. **prefatory** /'prɛfə,tɔri/.
—v. **-aced, -acing, -aces** to introduce, say or write as a preface: *The speaker prefaced her remarks with a joke.*

pre·fer /prɪ'fɜr/ v. **-ferred, -ferring, -fers** to like one thing better than another: *He prefers chocolate ice cream to vanilla.*

pref·er·a·ble /'prɛfərəbəl, 'prɛfrə-, prɪ'fɜrə-/ adj. better or more suitable, to be preferred: *She found life in the city preferable to her quiet life in the country.* -adv. **preferably.**

pref·er·ence /'prɛfrəns, 'prɛfərəns/ n. [C;U] a choice of one thing as better, more suitable than another: *She has a preference for vegetarian dishes over meat.*

pref·er·en·tial /ˌprɛfə'rɛnʃəl/ adj. showing a preference, giving special advantage to a person, group, etc.: *The restaurant gives preferential treatment to its regular customers, giving them the best tables and service.* -adv. **preferentially.**

pre·fix /'pri,fɪks/ n. **-fixes** a letter or group of letters that has no meaning when used alone but, when it is put at the beginning of a word, it can change the word's meaning: *"Un-" is a common prefix meaning "not," as in "unnecessary" or "unfair."*

preg·nan·cy /'prɛgnənsi/ n. [C;U] **-cies** a condition of growing a child in the womb: *Her first pregnancy was not difficult.*

preg·nant /'prɛgnənt/ adj. **1** with a child in the womb: *She is six months pregnant.* **2** full of meaning that is not said, but implied: *a pregnant pause‖pregnant with meaning*

pre·his·tor·ic /ˌprihɪˈstɔrɪk, -ˈstɑr-/ adj. of or relating to a time before history was recorded through pictures or writing: *Dinosaurs lived in prehistoric times.* -n. [U] **prehistory** /priˈhɪstəri, -ˈhɪstri/.

pre·judge /priˈdʒʌdʒ/ v. **-judged, -judging, -judges** to judge s.t. or s.o. without knowing all the facts, jump to conclusions: *The new boss prejudged a good worker as bad because of his odd appearance.* -n. [U] **prejudgment.**

prej·u·dice /ˈprɛdʒədɪs/ n. [C;U] an unfair bias against or for s.o. or s.t., an opinion based on general dislike or good feelings, rather than fact or reason: *Racial prejudice is one of society's great problems.*
—v. **-diced, -dicing, -dices** to cause to judge unfairly or beforehand, cause a person to dislike or to like s.o. or s.t. without looking at the facts: *He prejudiced his co-workers against the new manager by telling them she was very strict.*

prej·u·di·cial /ˌprɛdʒəˈdɪʃəl/ adj. related to or causing harm by holding a biased opinion not based on fact

prej·u·diced /ˈprɛdʒədɪst/ adj. feeling or showing unfair dislike or preference based on s.o.'s race, religion, sex, etc.: *She never hires men because she is prejudiced.*‖*The defendants's mother was not allowed to be a witness because the judge thought she would be prejudiced (in her son's favor).*

pre·lim·i·nar·y /prɪˈlɪməˌnɛri/ n. **-ies** a preparation for some event: *Before the test began, our teacher went through the preliminaries of explaining how long it would take, where to write your name, etc.*
—adj. related to preparations: *Diplomats held preliminary meetings before the presidents of their countries met to sign the treaty.*

prel·ude /ˈprɛlˌyud, ˈpreɪˌlud/ n. an introductory part, esp. in music: *The orchestra played a short prelude before the ballet began.*

pre·mar·i·tal /priˈmærətl/ adj. before marriage: *The couple engaged in premarital sex.*

pre·ma·ture /ˌpriməˈtʃʊr, -ˈtʊr/ adj. too early: *The baby was premature, born at seven months instead of nine.* -adv. **prematurely.**

pre·med·i·cal student /priˈmɛdɪkəl/ or **premed** n. a student in an undergraduate program that prepares students for medical school -adj.abbr. **premed** /priˈmɛd/.

pre·med·i·tat·ed /priˈmɛdəˌteɪtɪd/ adj. planned in advance (said of a crime): *He committed premeditated murder.* -v. **premeditate;** -n. [U] **premeditation** /priˌmɛdəˈteɪʃən/.

premenstrual syndrome /priˈmɛnstruəl, -strəl/ n. a combination of physical and emotional symptoms, such as headaches, depression, backaches, that are felt in the week or two before a menstrual period. abbr. **PMS** /ˌpiɛmˈɛs/.

pre·mier /prɪˈmɪr, -ˌmyɪr/ n. the head of the government in some countries: *The premier of Italy visited Malaysia.*
—adj. best, foremost: *She is the premier pianist of her generation.*

pre·miere /prɪˈmɪr, -ˌmyɛr/ n. the first performance, opening night: *Many celebrities attended the premiere of the new movie.*

prem·ise /ˈprɛmɪs/ n. a basis for a line of reasoning, an assumption: *His major premise for arguing there is life after death is that people have souls as well as bodies.*
—v. **-ised, -ising, -ises** to base on s.t.: *The President premised his speech on the belief that Americans want to help the poor.*

prem·is·es /ˈprɛmɪsɪz/ n.pl.frml. building(s) and the land they occupy: *A guard asked the stranger to leave the premises.*

pre·mi·um /ˈprimiəm/ n. **1** the monthly, quarterly, etc. payment for an insurance policy: *The monthly premium on my car insurance is very high.* **2** an extra amount, esp. for s.t. special: *He paid a premium for that house because of its beautiful view.* **3** a piece of merchandise used as a gift with the purchase of s.t. else: *A mail order company offered an inexpensive watch as a premium to customers who bought clothes from them.*
—adj. of high quality: *I always buy premium gas for my car.*

pre·mo·ni·tion /ˌpriməˈnɪʃən, ˌprɛ-/ n.frml. a fear about the future: *He has a premonition that something bad will happen on their camping trip.*

pre·na·tal /priˈneɪtl/ adj. before birth, while a baby is in the mother's womb: *Prenatal health care is recommended to produce a healthy baby.*

pre·oc·cu·pa·tion /priˌɑkyəˈpeɪʃən, ˌpriɑk-/ n. [C;U] **1** a worry, concern **2** s.t. that absorbs one's time and interest: *His major preoccupation is playing golf.* -v. **preoccupy** /priˈɑkyəˌpaɪ/.

pre·oc·cu·pied /priˈɑkyəˌpaɪd/ adj. (of a person) absorbed in thinking about s.t.: *She is preoccupied with moving to Seattle and neglects everything else.*

prep /prɛp/ v. **prepped, prepping, preps** short for prepare, to get ready: *He is prepping for his exams next week.*
—adj. related to preparation: *She is doing the prep work of reading books before writing her term paper.* See: preppie.

pre·pack·age /priˈpækɪdʒ/ v. **-aged, -aging, -ages** to package or put s.t. together in advance: *The travel agency sells prepackaged tours of Europe with all stops and hotels arranged in advance*

P

prep·a·ra·tion /ˌprɛpə'reɪʃən/ *n.* **1** [C] arrangements necessary for s.t., making s.t. ready: *She is buying food and baking a cake in preparation for the dinner tonight.* **2** [C] a combination of ingredients, compound: *A pharmacist made a preparation of two medicines to treat a skin rash.* **3** [U] education, background: *Her academic preparation includes two advanced university degrees.*

pre·par·a·to·ry /prɪ'pærəˌtɔri, -ˌpɛr-, 'prɛpərə-/ *adj.* related to the process of preparing s.t., arranging s.t.: *Our teacher made preparatory remarks before giving the test.*

preparatory school *n.frml.* a private elementary or secondary school that prepares students to go to college, a prep school: *Tuition at most preparatory schools is very high. See:* coed, USAGE NOTE.

pre·pare /prɪ'pɛr/ *v.* **-pared, -paring, -pares 1** to make arrangements for s.t., put in readiness: *He prepared for his trip by packing his clothes.* **2** to combine ingredients: *The chemist prepared some chemicals to test as a new product.* **3** to plan, rehearse mentally or emotionally: *He prepared himself for his mother's funeral. -adj.* **prepared.**

pre·par·ed·ness /prɪ'pɛrɪdnɪs, prɪ'pɛrd-/ *n.frml.* a state of being ready, having arrangements made: *The nation was in a state of preparedness for war.*

pre·pon·der·ance /prɪ'pɑndərəns/ *n.frml.* a greater amount, most of s.t.: *A preponderance of the evidence is against the defendant. -adj.frml.* **preponderant.**

prep·o·si·tion /ˌprɛpə'zɪʃən/ *n.* [C] (in grammar) a word that indicates relationship to another part of speech, esp. to a noun: *In "I went to the movie with my friend," "to" and "with" are prepositions. -adj.* **prepositional.**

pre·pos·sess·ing /ˌpripə'zɛsɪŋ/ *adj.* pleasing, attractive: *She has a prepossessing personality.*

pre·pos·ter·ous /prɪ'pɑstərəs, -trəs/ *adj.* completely unbelievable, totally absurd: *The idea that it will snow in Chicago in August is preposterous. -adv.* **preposterously.**

prep·pie or **preppy** /'prɛpi/ *n.infrml.* **-pies 1** a person who attends or attended a private preparatory school **2** a person who dresses or behaves in a conservative, upper-class manner associated with preparatory students. *See:* coed, USAGE NOTE.

prep school *n.short for* preparatory school: *He went to prep school at Phillips Exeter in New Hampshire. See:* preppie.

pre·pu·bes·cent /ˌpripyu'bɛsənt/ *adj.frml.* related to the years before sexual maturity (puberty): *prepubescent children -n.frml.* **prepubescence.**

pre·reg·is·tra·tion /ˌpriˌrɛdʒə'streɪʃən/ *n.* [U] an early registration period before the regular registration period, as for returning students at a college or school, when students choose courses for the next term: *During preregistration I signed up for math, science, history, and French -v.* **preregister.**

pre·req·ui·site /pri'rɛkwəzɪt/ *n.* a requirement, s.t. that must be done before doing s.t. else: *The prerequisite for the advanced course in math is basic math.*

pre·rog·a·tive /prɪ'rɑgətɪv/ *n.* a right, privilege: *It is her prerogative to travel first class if she wants to.*

pres·age /'prɛsɪdʒ/ *v.frml.* **-aged, -aging, -ages** to foretell, indicate s.t. that will happen in the future: *Disagreements between the two nations presaged a war.*

pre·school /'priˌskul, ˌpri'skul/ *adj.* related to the time before a child is old enough to go to elementary school, usu. up to the age of five or six: *The children did preschool activities that would help make them ready to read. -n.* **preschooler.**
—*n.* /'priˌskul/ nursery school, a school for children usu. of ages three or four who are too young for kindergarten: *My daughter goes to* (or) *is in preschool.*

pre·science /'prɛʃəns, -ʃiəns, 'pri-/ *n.frml.* [U] knowledge of the future -*adj.frml.* **prescient.**

pre·scribe /prɪ'skraɪb/ *v.* **-scribed, -scribing, -scribes 1** (of a doctor) to write an order (prescription) for medication: *My doctor prescribed penicillin for my sore throat.* **2** to tell s.o. what to do: *The supervisor prescribed the steps in which orders must be filled out.*

pre·scrip·tion /prɪ'skrɪpʃən/ *n.* [C;U] **1** an order for medication: *Her doctor wrote her a prescription for blood pressure medicine.* **2** a formula, set of steps: *Political analysts wrote a prescription for reform in government.*

prescription drug *n.* [U] medicine that can only be obtained by a doctor's order, not available on the shelves of a drugstore: *Prescription drugs are sold in drug stores. See:* pharmacy.

pre·scrip·tive /prɪ'skrɪptɪv/ *adj.* authoritative, telling exactly what to do: *His boss is very prescriptive and wants her orders followed exactly.||a prescriptive grammar*

pres·ence /'prɛzəns/ *n.* [U] **1** attendance: *Your presence at the wedding is important to the bride and groom.* **2** a dignified appearance: *The general has great presence.*

presence of mind *n.* [U] the ability to act quickly and sensibly in an emergency: *She had the presence of mind to throw a blanket over the fire and put it out.*

pre·sent (1) /prɪ'zɛnt/ *v.* **1** to offer, put forth for consideration: *She presented her idea for a new product at the last sales meeting.* **2** to give: *The mayor presented him with an award for good citizenship.||The doctor presented his* *bill.* **3** to bring to meet s.o., esp. of greater importance, introduce: *The ambassador was presented to the Queen at court.* **4** to cause or represent: *The snow was so deep that it presented a problem to people trying to walk.* **5** to perform: *to present a play*

pres·ent (2) /ˈprɛzənt/ *adj.* **1** at this time, now: *The present situation is peaceful.* **2** physically located here: *All students were present in today's class.*
—*n.* the here and now, at this time: *The present is peaceful, but in the past there was trouble in this area. See:* present tense.

pres·ent (3) /ˈprɛzənt/ *n.* a gift: *He gave me this nice pen as a birthday present.*

pre·sent·a·ble /prɪˈzɛntəbəl/ *adj.* suitable, in proper condition to meet others: *He shaved his beard and put on clean clothes to make himself presentable for visitors.*

pres·en·ta·tion /ˌprɛzənˈteɪʃən, ˌprizən-/ *n.* [C;U] **1** an explanation, description: *He gave a presentation of his marketing plan to the sales representatives.* **2** a demonstration, display: *The jewelry store has a presentation of new watches in the window.*

pres·ent-day /ˈprɛzəntˈdeɪ/ *adj.* current, at this time: *The present-day problems of society are different from those of many years ago.*

pres·ent·ly /ˈprɛzəntli/ *adv.* **1** currently, at this time: *He is presently employed.* **2** soon, in a short time: *I will tell you the answer presently.*

pres·ent participle /ˈprɛzənt/ *n.* (in grammar) a form of a verb, in English ending in -*ing,* that typically shows that an action is continuing, used with *be* to form progressive tenses or used as an adjective: *In the sentences "The dog is sleeping" and "Let sleeping dogs lie," "sleeping" is a present participle.*

present perfect *n.* (in grammar) a compound verb tense formed in English with *have + a past participle* and typically used to indicate an event or state that began in the past and continues up to the present or has results continuing up to the present: *In the sentence "I have lived here for five years," "have lived" is in the present perfect.*

present tense *n.* (in grammar) a verb tense representing the current time, not past or future: *In, "Today is Monday," "is" is the present tense of the verb "be."*

pre·serv·a·tive /prɪˈzɜrvətɪv/ *n.* [C;U] a chemical that keeps food from going bad: *That bread has a lot of preservatives in it; it will stay fresh for days.*

pre·serve /prɪˈzɜrv/ *v.* **-served, -serving, -serves** **1** to guard, protect from harm or change: *The government preserves the rights of the individual person.* **2** to maintain, keep in good condition: *She preserves her health by eating sensibly and exercising.* **3** to prevent food from spoiling: *Keeping food in the refrigerator preserves its freshness.* -*n.* [U] **preservation** /ˌprɛzərˈveɪʃən/.
—*n.* **1** an area of land or seashore used to protect wildlife from people, esp. hunters, a reserve: *Huge game preserves in Africa help protect wild animals.* **2** *pl.* **preserves** fruit, usu. in large pieces, cooked with a lot of sugar and stored in a jar: *peach preserves*

pre·set /ˌpriˈsɛt/ *v.adj.* **-set, -setting, -sets** to set s.t. in advance, esp. a device, to a level or number: *I <v.> preset the thermostat to 70 degrees.‖It is <adj.> preset at that temperature.*

pre·side /prɪˈzaɪd/ *v.* **-sided, -siding, -sides** to direct an activity, (*syn.*) to chair: *The chairwoman presided over a meeting of the finance committee.*

pres·i·den·cy /ˈprɛzədənsi/ *n.* [C;U] **-cies** **1** the office and duties of a president: *He was nominated for the presidency of the United States.* **2** the term during which a person is president: *A great deal was accomplished during his presidency.*

pres·i·dent /ˈprɛzədənt/ *n.* **1** a head of some governments, including that of the USA: *The president must handle many problems.* **2** the head of a business or institution, usu. ranking below chair of the board: *The president of that company (university, corporation) travels often.* -*adj.* **presidential** /ˌprɛzəˈdɛnʃəl/.

President's Day *n.* the third Monday in February, observed as a holiday in the US in honor of the birthdays of Abraham Lincoln and George Washington

press /prɛs/ *v.* **presses** **1** to push against, apply force: *She pressed the number keys on the telephone.* **2** to squeeze, crush: *A winemaker presses grapes to make wine.* **3** to smooth wrinkles from clothes, iron: *He has his suits cleaned and pressed at the cleaners.* **4** *fig.* to pressure s.o. to do s.t., to ask for action: *She pressed her supervisor for a raise in salary.* **5** to move ahead despite difficulty: *He pressed ahead with (or) pressed on with his work despite having a cold.* **6** to lift weights: *He goes to the gym and presses weights.* **7 to be pressed for:** to experience pressure because of not having enough of s.t.: *I'm pressed for time right now.‖She is pressed for money.*
—*n.* **presses** **1** a pushing motion: *The door opened at the press of a button.* **2** a smoothing of clothes: *The cleaner gave her skirt a press.* **3** a machine or device for squeezing or crushing s.t.: *A wine press crushes grapes and separates the juice from them.* **4** a machine for printing books, newspapers, magazines, etc.: *The newspaper is on the press now being printed.* **5 good** or **bad press:** positive or negative comments, esp. in the news media: *The political candidate received bad press about not paying his taxes for three years.* **6 the**

P

press: newspapers, magazines, and their reporters, and often radio and television editors, etc.: *The press covers the president's every move.*

press agent *n.* a person who arranges publicity, such as for actors: *Her press agent arranged for the actress's picture to appear in the newspaper with an article about her.*

press box *n.* **boxes** a section of seats for reporters at an event, esp. in a sports arena: *Reporters watched the football game from the press box.*

press conference *n.* a meeting with reporters at which a well-known person, such as a politician, makes an announcement or answers questions: *The President held a press conference to discuss his new economic policy.*

press·ing /'prɛsɪŋ/ *adj.* urgent, demanding attention: *The roof is leaking, so fixing it is a pressing problem.*

press release *n.* a written announcement of an event to the news media: *The White House issued a press release on improvement in the economy.*

pres·sure /'prɛʃər/ *n.* **1** [U] application of force against s.t.: *Air pressure in the tire keeps it inflated.* **2** [U] measurement of that force: *The pressure in that tire should be 32 pounds.*||*He has high blood pressure.* **3** [U] atmospheric pressure: *A low-pressure front moved into our area, bringing rain.* **4** [U] application of influence on s.o., sometimes with the threat of a penalty: *The people put pressure on the government to lower taxes or be voted out of office.* **5** [C] tension, a feeling of being pushed to do things: *The pressure of meeting deadlines in her job causes her to sleep poorly.* **6 under pressure:** in an atmosphere of tension: *Some people perform well under pressure, but I don't.*
—*v.* **-sured, -suring, -sures** to apply pressure to s.o., (*syn.*) to coerce: *Her boss pressured her to finish the report by Friday.*

pressure cook·er /'kʊkər/ *n.* **1** a tightly sealed pot that cooks foods quickly under steam pressure: *He steamed some vegetables in the pressure cooker.* **2** *fig.* a tense, irritating work atmosphere: *Her office is a pressure cooker.*

pres·sur·ize /'prɛʃə,raɪz/ *v.* **-ized, -izing, -izes** to adjust the air pressure in an airplane, spacecraft, or submarine: *The airplane cabin has been pressurized, so you won't get a headache.* -*n.* [U] **pressurization** /,prɛʃərə'zeɪʃən/.

pres·tige /prɛ'stiʒ, -'stiʤ/ *n.* [U] qualities, such as excellent reputation, wealth, and power, that bring admiration or honor: *Her job as a lawyer for a big corporation has a lot of prestige.* -*adj.* **prestigious** /prɛ'stɪʤəs, -'sti-/.

pres·to /'prɛstoʊ/ *adv.exclam.* quickly, suddenly: *I was walking in a field and presto! a beautiful bird flew into the air.*

pre·sum·a·bly /prɪ'zuməbli/ *adv.* proba-bly, as can be assumed: *Presumably he has received the letter by now, since I mailed it last week.*

pre·sume /prɪ'zum/ *v.* **-sumed, -suming, -sumes 1** to suppose s.t. is true, assume: *I presumed that my friend would be at home when I called but she wasn't.* **2** to impose on s.o., take advantage of s.o.: *She presumed on her father's generosity by borrowing money from him and not repaying it.*

pre·sump·tion /prɪ'zʌmpʃən/ *n.* **1** [C] an assumption, thinking s.t. is true: *He got an advanced university degree on the presumption that he would get a better job, which he did.* **2** [U] an imposition, taking advantage of s.o.: *Her father was annoyed by her presumption in borrowing money from him and not repaying it.*

pre·sump·tu·ous /prɪ'zʌmptʃuəs/ *adj.* taking advantage, imposing on s.o.: *It was presumptuous of her to borrow money from her father and not repay him.* -*adv.* **presumptuously;** -*n.* [U] **presumptuousness.**

pre·sup·pose /,prisə'poʊz/ *v.frml.* **-posed, -posing, -poses** to assume s.t. is true, to base s.t. on s.t. else: *Admission to the course presupposes that a student has completed high school.* -*n.* [U] **presupposition** /,prisʌpə'zɪʃən/.

pre·tax /,pri'tæks/ *adj.* referring to money (profits, salary, company earnings) before taxes are paid: *The company had a pretax profit of $1 million and a profit of $500,000 after taxes.*

pre·teen /,pri'tin/ *n.adj.* a child a little younger than a teenager, usu. from 10 to 12 years old: *The rock star was very popular with <n.> preteens.*

pre·tend /prɪ'tɛnd/ *v.* **1** to make believe: *He pretended that he did not hear the insult.* **2** to act in a way that gives a false appearance, to fake: *They pretend to be wealthy when they are not.*

pre·tend·er /prɪ'tɛndər/ *n.* a person who makes a claim to a monarch's throne: *The prince is a pretender to the throne of England.*

pre·tense /'pri,tɛns, prɪ'tɛns/ *n.* [C;U] **1** a reason or act that hides the real reason for doing s.t.: *She called me on the pretense of asking about my health when she really wanted to sell me life insurance.* **2 false pretenses:** reasons used to deceive s.o.: *He entered her house under false pretenses, saying that he was a detective when his real purpose was to steal her jewelry.*

pre·ten·sion /prɪ'tɛnʃən/ *n.* [C;U] a false appearance, action, or statement intended to make one seem better than one is: *It's clear that his pretensions about being a great actor are phony.*

pre·ten·tious /prɪˈtɛnʃəs/ *adj.* acting in a showy or affected manner: *His pretentious show of money annoys his friends.* -*adv.* **pretentiously;** -*n.* [U] **pretentiousness.**

pre·text /ˈpriˌtɛkst/ *n.* an excuse, pretense: *He called me on the pretext that he was taking a survey, but he was actually selling stocks.*

pret·ty /ˈprɪti/ *adj.* **-tier, -tiest** lovely, attractive, pleasing to the eye, but not beautiful: *She has a pretty face. See:* handsome, **USAGE NOTE.** -*adv.* **1** to a certain degree, somewhat, fairly: *We had a pretty good time at the party.* ||*I was pretty happy living in Boston, but New York is more exciting.* **2 pretty much:** almost entirely **3 sitting pretty:** in an excellent position: *He has a high-paying job now and is sitting pretty.*

pret·zel /ˈprɛtsəl/ *n.* a crisp or chewy bread-like food, usu. shaped like a knot and sprinkled with salt: *He likes to snack on pretzels.*

pretzels

pre·vail /prɪˈveɪl/ *v.* **1** to win, triumph: *Our team prevailed over our rival in a tough game.*||*I was going to have dessert, but good sense prevailed and I didn't eat it.* **2** to be common: *A love of fried foods prevails in North America.* **3 to prevail upon** or **on:** to influence or persuade s.o.: *They prevailed on their son to finish college.*

pre·vail·ing /prɪˈveɪlɪŋ/ *adj.* **1** usual, frequent: *The prevailing wind is from the west in this area.* **2** dominant, generally exclusive: *The prevailing opinion now is that the president is doing a good job.*

prev·a·lent /ˈprɛvələnt/ *adj.* common, observed frequently: *Pine trees (small cars, etc.) are prevalent in this part of the country.* -*n.* [U] **prevalence.**

pre·var·i·cate /prɪˈværəˌkeɪt/ *v.frml.* **-cated, -cating, -cates** to hide the truth, misrepresent s.t.: *He prevaricated when he spoke in court.* -*n.* [U] **prevarication** /prɪˌværəˈkeɪʃən/.

pre·vent /prɪˈvɛnt/ *v.* **1** to stop from happening, avoid: *He prevented an accident by braking his car just in time.* **2** to stop s.o. from doing s.t.: *The rain prevented me from going.*

pre·vent·a·ble /prɪˈvɛntəbəl/ *adj.* able to be prevented, (*syn.*) avoidable: *Vaccines have made measles, polio, and smallpox preventable diseases.*

pre·ven·tion /prɪˈvɛnʃən/ *n.* [U] the acting of preventing s.t. from happening, (*syn.*) avoidance: *prevention of disease*

pre·ven·tive /prɪˈvɛntɪv/ or **preventative** /prɪˈvɛntətɪv/ *adj.* related to actions taken to prevent s.t.: *As a preventive measure against fire, he threw away all the paint cans in his house.*

pre·view /ˈpriˌvyu/ *n.* an advance showing of s.t.: *Movie critics watched a preview of the new film before it was shown to the public.* —*v.* to see s.t. beforehand, view in advance: *Critics previewed the movie.*

pre·vi·ous /ˈpriviəs/ *adj.* **1** occurring before s.t. else, preceding: *On the previous day, we had visited Notre Dame cathedral.* **2 previous to:** before, earlier than: *Previous to that, we had traveled by car to Paris.* -*adv.* **previously.**

pre·war /ˌpriˈwɔr/ *adj.* before a war, esp. World War I or II: *Prewar apartments have high ceilings and big windows.*

prey /preɪ/ *n.* **1** [U] animals killed for food by other animals: *Rabbits and squirrels are prey for hawks and coyotes.* **2** a victim: *The thief thought the rich man would be an easy prey.* **3 to fall prey to:** to become a victim, preyed upon by s.o.: *The old woman fell prey to a swindler who stole her savings.* —*v.* **1** to kill animals for food: *Hawks prey on rabbits.* **2** to victimize, exploit: *Pickpockets prey on innocent tourists.*

price /praɪs/ *n.* **1** an amount of money charged for goods or services, cost: *The price of milk has gone up.* **2** an amount of money high enough to make a person accept it as a bribe, as to do s.t. wrong: *"Everyone has their price,"* he said cynically. **3 a price on one's head:** money offered as a reward for capturing s.o., either dead or alive: *The escaped murderer had a price on his head.* **4 asking price:** a price asked for s.t. by an owner, but not necessarily expected: *The asking price for the apartment is $200,000.* **5** *fig.* **at any price:** no matter how great the suffering or loss needed to get s.t.: *The general wanted victory at any price.* **6 offering price:** a price offered by a buyer: *His offering price for the apartment was $150,000.* **7 selling price:** a price agreed to by buyer and seller: *The selling price was $175,000.* **8 to pay a price:** to suffer s.t. unpleasant in order to gain s.t. else: *He paid a high price in unhappiness when he left his wife for another woman.* —*v.* **priced, pricing, prices** **1** to put a price on s.t.: *The company priced its new products lower than its competitors.* **2** to find out the price of, determine prices: *We visited car dealers and priced cars.*

price index *n.* the average price of a group of products or services compared periodically, such as quarter by quarter or year by year: *The consumer price index on groceries has risen 5% from last year.*

P

price·less /'praɪslɪs/ *adj.* **1** having such great value that no price would be high enough: *Paintings by great masters are priceless and irreplaceable.* **2** *fig.* excellent, unbelievable: *She told one funny joke after another; her performance was priceless.*

price tag *n.* a label on merchandise that notes its price: *How much is this suit? I can't find a price tag on it.*

price war *n.* a series of price reductions intended to put one's competitors out of business: *Price wars between computer makers led to many of them going out of business.*

pric·ey /'praɪsi/ *adj.infrml.* **-ier, -iest** expensive: *The clothes in that store are pricey.*

prick /prɪk/ *n.* **1** a slight stabbing pain made by a sharp point: *I felt a prick from the doctor's hypodermic needle.* **2** the hole made by a sharp point: *The dressmaker's pins left tiny pricks in the silk.* **3** *vulg.slang* the penis **4** *vulg.slang* an obnoxious, difficult man: *That prick makes trouble for everyone!*
—*v.* **1** to stab the skin lightly: *I pricked my finger on the needle.* **2 to prick up one's ears: a.** (of an animal) to raise the ears upward in order to listen: *The dog pricked up his ears at the sound of the car door.* **b.** to begin to listen attentively: *I pricked up my ears when I heard them mention my name.*

prick·ly /'prɪkli/ *adj.* **-lier, -liest 1** having thorns, spines: *Thorn bushes are prickly.* **2** having a feeling of needles on the skin caused by numbness: *My foot has gone to sleep and is all prickly.* **3** difficult, troublesome: *The diplomat handled a prickly political situation. -v.* **prickle** /'prɪkəl/.

pride /praɪd/ *n.* [U] **1** self-esteem, self-respect: *When she failed her exams, her pride was hurt.* **2** satisfaction with personal characteristics and abilities: *He takes great pride in his ability to fix things.* **3** the feeling that one is better than other people, *(syn.)* arrogance: *His own pride is his worst enemy.*
—*v.* **prided, priding, prides to pride oneself on s.t.:** to feel good about oneself for s.t.: *He prides himself on his talent for writing.*

priest /prist/ *n.* **1** a member of the clergy in many religions of the world: *Buddhist priests wear brightly colored robes.* **2** in some Christian denominations, a member of the clergy ranking below a bishop, above a deacon and often in charge of a church: *Catholic priests dress in black. -adj.* **priestly.**

priest·ess /'pristɪs/ *n.* a holy woman in many religions, esp. ancient ones: *She was a priestess in the Greek temple of Apollo.*

priest·hood /'prist,hʊd/ *n.* [U] priests as a group: *Members of the priesthood gathered in Rome.*

prig /prɪg/ *n.* a conceited, formal person: *Prigs are usually very critical of others. -adj.*

priggish.

prim /prɪm/ *adj.* **primmer, primmest** very proper, formal in manner: *She is old-fashioned and rather prim and disapproves of her loud, rough nephew. -adv.* **primly.**

pri·ma·cy /'praɪməsi/ *n.* [U] the state of being the most important, a first concern: *Everyone understands the primacy of education in a person's life.*

pri·ma don·na /ˌprimə'dɑnə, ˌprɪ-/ *n.* **1** a diva, leading female soloist in an opera company: *The prima donna was too ill to finish the performance.* **2** an irritable, haughty person: *The owner acts like a prima donna when anyone disagrees with him.*

pri·mal /'praɪməl/ *adj.* very basic as if originating in the distant past, *(syn.)* primeval: *primal instincts, such as hunger*

pri·mar·i·ly /praɪ'mɛrəli/ *adv.* mainly, first of all: *He is primarily concerned with his work, not his family.*

pri·mar·y /'praɪ,mɛri, -məri/ *adj.* main, greatest: *My primary concern is about my wife's health, since she has cancer.*
—*n.* **-ies** or **primary election** (in the USA) an election by a political party to choose its candidate to run in a general election: *Four candidates ran in the Democratic primary for governor and two in the Republican primary.*

primary care *n.* the first medical care that a patient receives before referral to a specialist: *My primary care physician listened to my heart and then referred me to a heart specialist.*

primary school *n.* (in the USA) the first three to six grades of elementary school: *My grandson is in the first grade in primary school. See:* grade school, **USAGE NOTE.**

pri·mate /'praɪ,meɪt/ *n.* any member of the highest order of animals, including humans, apes, monkeys, and lemurs

prime /praɪm/ *n.* the period in which a person is at the height of his or her abilities, personal powers, and usu. ability to earn money: *He is in the prime of life now in his 40s.*
—*adj.* **1** main, greatest: *Her prime concern now is finding another job.* **2** the highest US government grade of meat, ranked above "choice": *Most prime steak goes to restaurants, not to supermarkets.*
—*v.* **primed, priming, primes 1** to make s.t. ready, to prepare: *The director primed the actors for their roles in the play.* **2** to cover a surface with a special paint before painting it: *I've primed all the woodwork and will put on the paint tomorrow.*

prime minister or **PM** *n.* (in many countries outside the USA) the chief officer of a government: *The prime minister held a cabinet meeting to discuss policy.*

prim·er (1) /'praɪmər/ *n.* **1** a small explosive used to detonate a large one: *The explosion of a primer in a bundle of dynamite sets it off.* **2** a special paint or liquid put on a surface in preparation for painting: *I gave the door one coat of primer and one of paint.*

prim·er (2) /'prɪmər/ *n.* **1** a basic textbook for teaching school children to read **2** a manual that covers the basics of a subject: *He wrote a primer on sales techniques.*

prime rate *n.* the interest rate set by the Federal Reserve Bank, the lowest rate that a bank will charge its best large customers for loans: *His brokerage house charges him 1% above the prime rate for loans.*

prime time *n.adj.* the hours from about 7:00 to 11:00 p.m. when the largest number of people are available to watch television: *The championship football game will be broadcast on <adj.> prime-time television* (or) *during <n.> prime time.*

pri·me·val /praɪ'mivəl/ *adj.* ancient, prehistoric: *Primeval creatures live in the ocean depths.*

prim·i·tive /'prɪmətɪv/ *adj.* **1** native, unchanged since ancient times: *Primitive tribes live in the Amazon River basin.* **2** belonging to an early stage of development: *primitive tools||primitive forms of life* **3** simple, rough, (*syns.*) unsophisticated, crude: *We built a primitive shelter to sleep in.*

pri·mor·di·al /praɪ'mɔrdiəl/ *adj.* characteristic of the earliest beginnings of s.t., ancient: *Life formed in the primordial oceans millions of years ago.*

primp /prɪmp/ *v.* to dress with excessive attention to detail, groom oneself to excess: *She sits before the mirror and primps for hours.*

prim·rose /'prɪm,rouz/ *n.* **1** a small wild and garden flower: *Primroses appear in the springtime.* **2 primrose path:** the illusion that s.t. will be wonderful but that ends in trouble: *He led investors down the primrose path by promising them big profits and then stealing all their money.*

prince /prɪns/ *n.* **1** a son of a monarch: *The prince is in line to inherit the throne.* **2** any nobleman with the title of prince **3** *fig.* a wonderful man: *He was a wonderful friend and a prince of a man!*

prince·ly /'prɪnsli/ *adj.* **1** of or related to a prince: *His princely duties include attending ceremonial functions.* **2** great, very large: *The couple paid a princely sum for their beautiful house.*

prin·cess /'prɪnsɪs, -,sɛs/ *n.* **-cesses** **1** a daughter of a monarch: *The princess has private tutors.* **2** any noblewoman with the title of princess **3** the wife of a prince **4** a woman or girl who gets special treatment from others:

She is such a princess that she refuses to do any cooking or cleaning.

prin·ci·pal /'prɪnsəpəl/ *n.* **1** the head of a school: *Ms. Wu is the principal of our local high school.* **2** any person who can make important decisions in a business: *The principals include the owner and his wife.* **3** the amount remaining on a debt: *The principal remaining on the mortgage is $20,000 at 7% interest.* **4** money invested: *He can live on the interest from his savings and never touch the principal.* —*adj.* main, most important: *The principal reason they visited was to make an offer to buy your business.*

prin·ci·pal·i·ty /,prɪnsə'pæləti/ *n.* **-ties** an area or nation ruled by a prince or princess: *The principality of Liechtenstein is a small country.*

prin·ci·ple /'prɪnsəpəl/ *n.* **1** [C;U] a standard, such as a guide to behavior, rule: *It is a matter of principle with him to have no debts.* **2 in principle:** regarding a principle, in theory: *In principle, he has no debts, but in actual fact he has a mortgage on his house.*

prin·ci·pled /'prɪnsəpəld/ *adj.* having strict standards of behavior: *She is very principled and never lies or cheats.*

print /prɪnt/ *v.* **1** to put words or images onto paper or other material, using a mechanical process: *He printed a letter on his computer's printer.* **2** to make available in print, usu. in many copies, by such a process, (*syn.*) to publish: *The newspaper printed an interview with the governor.* **3** to write by hand using letters similar to those in printed material: *He printed his name on the application.* **4** *phrasal v. sep.* **to print s.t. out:** to print from a computer: *She printed out her report and made 10 copies of it.||She printed it out.* -*adj.* **printable.** —*n.* **1** [U] letters printed on paper or other material: *I can't read the small print on the package.* **2** [U] a pattern or design printed on cloth, or the cloth itself: *Her dress has a black and white print.* **3** [C] a picture printed from a wood block, metal plate, etc., as a reproduction of an original work of art: *The museum store sold prints of many of its paintings.* **4** [C] a photograph produced on paper **5** [C] a mark made by s.t. pressing on s.t. else: *They followed the paw prints of the animal through the woods.* **6 in print: a.** in printed form: *It was exciting to see my name in print in the newspaper.* **b.** (of a book) available for sale by the publisher: *The book was written a long time ago, but it's still in print.* **7 out of print:** no longer available for sale by the publisher: *She couldn't find the book in stores because it is out of print. See:* fine, fine print.

print·er /'prɪntər/ *n.* **1** a person or business engaged in printing: *He buys his stationery from a printer.* **2** a device attached to a computer, used for making paper copies of material produced on the computer: *a laser printer||The printer sits on her desk next to her computer.*

print·ing /ˈprɪntɪŋ/ *n.* [U] **1** the art or process of putting words and images on paper or other materials by a mechanical process: *Printing is a big business, including everything from newspapers and catalogs to labels in clothes.* **2** all the copies of a book printed at one time: *The first printing of the book sold out quickly.*

print·out /ˈprɪntˌaʊt/ *n.* a document printed from a computer: *He did a printout of the budget.*

pri·or /ˈpraɪər/ *adj.frml.* **1** earlier, previous: *A prior engagement prevented me from accepting the invitation.||No prior knowledge of Spanish is required for this course.* **2 prior to:** before, earlier than s.t. else: *Prior to becoming a lawyer, he worked as a legal secretary.*

pri·or·i·tize /praɪˈɔrəˌtaɪz, -ˈɑr-/ *v.* **-tized, -tizing, -tizes** to put tasks, events, etc. in their order of importance: *She prioritized her day by listing what she had to do.*

pri·or·i·ty /praɪˈɔrəti, -ˈɑr-/ *n.* **-ties 1** the tasks, or beliefs that are most important and require attention: *His priorities include working at his job, studying for his classes, and keeping his girlfriend happy.* **2 to have priority over:** to have greater importance than s.t. else, take precedence: *Studying for the test has priority over listening to music.*

pri·or·y /ˈpraɪəri/ *n.* **-ries** a monastery smaller than an abbey: *Monks live in the priory on the hill.*

prism /ˈprɪzəm/ *n.* a piece of glass that separates the colors of sunlight into blue, green, yellow, red, etc. *-adj.* **prismatic** /prɪzˈmætɪk/.

pris·on /ˈprɪzən/ *n.* [C;U] a jail, a place where people found guilty or accused of a crime are confined: *He was sent to prison for robbing a bank.*

prison camp *n.* a jail for prisoners of war: *Prisoners in prison camps were often forced to work on enemy projects.*

pris·on·er /ˈprɪzənər, ˈprɪznər/ *n.* anyone placed in forced confinement: *The prisoner was jailed for committing a crime.*

prisoner of war *n.* **prisoners of war** a person, esp. a soldier, captured by the enemy during a war: *Prisoners of war were exchanged for enemy prisoners. n.abbr.* **POW.**

pris·sy /ˈprɪsi/ *adj.* **-sier, -siest** excessively concerned with correct thought, behavior, or appearances, (*syn.*) priggish: *She is very prissy about her children using slang expressions.*

pris·tine /ˈprɪsˌtin, prɪˈstin/ *adj.* pure, esp. in nature, unspoiled: *We hiked through pristine wilderness in Alaska.*

pri·va·cy /ˈpraɪvəsi/ *n.* [U] **1** the state of being away from the unwanted presence of others,

seclusion: *After meeting with many people, she looked forward to the privacy of her hotel room.* **2** secrecy, confidentiality: *Lawyers and doctors are required to guard the privacy of their clients.*

pri·vate /ˈpraɪvɪt/ *adj.* **1** secret, keeping personal matters exclusively to oneself: *Her sex life is private; no one else has the right to know about it.* **2** not public, away from other people and their observation: *She had a private room at the hospital.* **3** owned by a person or business rather than a government: *The land is private property and no one is allowed to trespass on it. -adv.* **privately.**
—*n.* a soldier of the lowest rank in the army: *He was a private for six months, and then was promoted to corporal.*

private enterprise *n.frml.* business owned and conducted with private money, not by governmental agencies: *The automobile companies are at the center of American private enterprise.*

private investigator *n.* a detective: *The film star hired a private investigator to find out who was following her.*

private parts *n.pl.* the sex organs, genitals

private school *n.* a school run by a private group, not by the government: *The Catholic church runs private schools throughout the USA. See:* coed, **USAGE NOTE.**

pri·va·tion /praɪˈveɪʃən/ *n.* [U] lack of the basic necessities of life, such as food, clothes, and shelter: *The homeless woman is suffering from privation.*

pri·vat·ize /ˈpraɪvəˌtaɪz/ *v.* **-ized, -izing, -izes** to sell a business or service owned by the government to private owners: *England has privatized industries by selling them to private owners. -n.* [U] **privatization** /ˌpraɪvətəˈzeɪʃən/.

priv·i·lege /ˈprɪvəlɪdʒ, ˈprɪvlɪdʒ/ *n.v.* **1** a special right or benefit granted to a person: *As a top manager, she has the special privileges of a big office and a private bathroom.* **2** rights held by some but not all, because of their wealth and status in society: *For centuries the nobility led lives of privilege, free from having to work.* **3** something enjoyable that you are honored to have the chance to do: *It is a great privilege to accept this award.*

priv·i·leged /ˈprɪvəlɪdʒd, ˈprɪvlɪdʒd/ *adj.* **1** private, secret between individuals: *Discussions between a lawyer and client are privileged communications.* **2** having special rights or benefits: *Only the privileged few could afford to send their children to private schools.*

priv·y /ˈprɪvi/ *n.infrml.* **-ies** an outdoor toilet, (*syn.*) an outhouse: *Old farmhouses had privies behind them.*
—*adj.frml.* allowed to know s.t. secret: *I am not privy to what the President thinks.*

prix fixe /'pri'fiks/ *n.* (French for) a fixed price for a restaurant meal with two or three courses: *The prix fixe of $35 included an appetizer, a main dish, and dessert.*

prize /praɪz/ *v.* **prized, prizing, prizes** to appreciate s.t. greatly, cherish: *He prizes his new car above all his other possessions.*
—*n.* an award presented in recognition of winning a contest or lottery: *She won first prize of a college scholarship in a writing contest.*
—*adj.* outstanding, champion: *His prize roses bloom in June.*

prize·fight·er /'praɪz,faɪtər/ *n.* a professional boxer who fights for money: *Prizefighters can become millionaires if they win often. -n.* [U] **prizefighting.**

pro (1) /proʊ/ *n.adj.infrml.* short for professional

pro (2) *prefix & adj.* for, in favor of: *The senator is pro-choice on the issue of abortion.*

prob·a·bil·i·ty /,prɑbə'bɪləti/ *n.* **-ties** the likelihood, chance that s.t. will or did happen: *The probability that it will rain today is high.*

prob·a·ble /'prɑbəbəl/ *adj.* **1** likely to happen, having a good chance of occurring: *It is probable that it will snow tomorrow.* **2** reasonable to believe, likely: *The probable cause of that accident was that the driver was drunk.*

prob·a·bly /'prɑbəbli/ *adv.* likely, believably: *He was probably drunk and that caused him to drive off the road.*

pro·bate /'proʊ,beɪt/ *n.* [U] a legal procedure that proves the validity of a will: *When someone dies, their will can go through probate.*
—*v.* **-bated, -bating, -bates** to go through probate: *The old woman's will was probated in probate court.*

pro·ba·tion /proʊ'beɪʃən/ *n.* [U] **1** a period of time in which a lawbreaker is allowed to go free under supervision: *The judge did not jail the young man, but put him on probation for a year.* **2** a period of testing the ability of a new employee or seeing if a student improves: *That company puts all new employees on a three-month probation.*

probe /proʊb/ *n.* **1** an instrument used to explore inside s.t.: *A doctor used a probe to remove metal fragments from a wound.* **2** a space vehicle, special aircraft, or submarine: *Our space agency sent out a probe with cameras to explore the planet Mars.* **3** an inquiry, questioning: *The police probe into organized crime led to several arrests.*
—*v.* **probed, probing, probes** to explore with questions or a probe: *A lawyer probed the witness' truthfulness by asking questions.‖The doctor probed inside my ear to see if it was infected.*

prob·ing /'proʊbɪŋ/ *n.* [U] an act of exploring: *The lawyer's probing caused the witness to tell the truth.*
—*adj.* searching, far-reaching: *The lawyer asked probing questions.*

prob·lem /'prɑbləm/ *n.* **1** a difficult situation or person: *He has a problem with understanding mathematics.* **2** an obstacle, hurdle: *A tree that fell across the road presented a problem to drivers.*
—*adj.* presenting difficulties: *That bad boy is a problem child. -adj.* **problematical.**

pro·ce·dure /prə'siʤər/ *n.* [C;U] **1** a detailed method of doing s.t.: *He told me the procedure for changing the oil in my car.* **2** a medical treatment: *A doctor performed a procedure for cleaning and closing a wound.* **3** rules of conduct of debates or formal meetings: *Parliamentary procedure requires speakers to go by the rules. -adj.* **procedural.**

pro·ceed /prə'sid, proʊ-/ *v.* **1** to continue, resume activity, esp. after a pause: *The plane stopped in Chicago, then proceeded to Los Angeles.* **2** to go forward, move ahead: *He proceeded to tell a funny story and we all laughed.*

pro·ceed·ing /prə'sidɪŋ/ *n.* [C] **1** a series of actions, esp. in a law court: *Legal proceedings often happen slowly.* **2** a record of formal actions: *We watched the proceedings of a United Nations' debate on television.*

pro·ceeds /'proʊ,sidz/ *n.pl.frml.* money from the sale of s.t.: *She used the proceeds from the sale of her old house to buy a new one.*

proc·ess /'prɑ,sɛs, 'proʊ-/ *v.* **1** to apply a procedure to s.t.: *A clerk processed my airline ticket and handed it to me.* **2** to change s.t. from one state to another: *That meatpacking plant processes beef into hamburger.* **3** to turn data into information by computer: *Early computers processed data very slowly.*
—*n.* [C;U] **1** general methods of doing s.t.: *The educational process requires that students attend school regularly.* **2** a procedure, specific method: *The process of filling out an application often requires time.* **3** changing s.t.: *The process of converting oil into gasoline involves distillation.* **4** (in law) a summons, demand to appear in court: *He was served a process to appear in court.*

pro·ces·sion /prə'sɛʃən/ *n.* **1** [C] a parade: *A procession of marchers and bands moved down Fifth Avenue.* **2** [U] groups of people, vehicles, etc.: *A procession of mourners walked by the casket. -n.* [U] *adj.* **processional.**

proc·es·sor /'prɑ,sɛsər/ *n.* **1** a person, device or business that processes things: *That company is a food processor.* **2** the central processing unit of a computer: *His computer has a powerful processor.*

P

pro·choice *adj.* supportive of a legal right to choose to have an abortion: *The pro-choice political candidate was yelled at by anti-abortionists.*

USAGE NOTE: People who are in favor of a woman's right to choose to have an abortion call themselves *pro-choice,* and call their opponents *anti-choice.* People who are opposed to abortion call themselves *pro-life,* and often call their opponents *pro-abortion.*

pro·claim /proʊ'kleɪm, prə-/ *v.* **1** to declare publicly, make a decree or law: *Congress proclaimed May 30 a national holiday.* **2** to announce a decision: *The 18-year-old girl proclaimed her independence and left her parents.*

proc·la·ma·tion /,prɑklə'meɪʃən/ *n.* a declaration of an event, esp. one made by an elected official: *The governor issued a proclamation that the last week in June will be "Protect Wildlife Week."*

pro·cliv·i·ty /proʊ'klɪvəti/ *n.frml.* a tendency: *She has a proclivity toward reading books for hours and hours.*

pro·cras·ti·nate /prə'kræstə,neɪt/ *v.* **-nated, -nating, -nates** to delay, put off s.t.: *He procrastinated in making an appointment to see his doctor.* *-n.* [U] **procrastination.**

pro·cre·ate /'proʊkri,eɪt/ *v.frml.* **-ated, -ating, -ates** to reproduce, have babies: *Biologists study how animals procreate.* *-n.* [U] **procreation** /,proʊkri'eɪʃən/.

pro·cure /prə'kyʊr/ *v.frml.* **-cured, -curing, -cures** **1** to obtain, purchase s.t.: *The army procures weapons from manufacturers* **2** to provide people for others' sexual satisfaction, (*syn.*) to pimp: *He procures women for male clients.* *-n.* [U] *adj.* **procurement.**

pro·cur·er /prə'kyʊrər/ *n.frml.pej.* a pimp.

prod /prɑd/ *n.* **1** a goad, such as a stick or rod-shaped electric device used to make animals or people move: *A farmer herded his cattle into the barn with a prod.* **2** *fig.* a reminder: *I gave my friend's memory a prod about returning my tennis racket.*
—v. **prodded, prodding, prods** to urge or goad, to remind: *I prodded my friend to return my tennis racket.* *-n.* **prodder.**

prod·i·gal /'prɑdəgəl/ *adj.n.frml.* wasteful and extravagant with money: *In the Bible, a prodigal son spent all his money and returned as a poor man to his father's house.*

pro·di·gious /prə'dɪdʒəs/ *adj.frml.* **1** huge in size or bulk: *Their dog consumes prodigious quantities of food every day.* **2** requiring great effort or skill: *Building the Panama Canal was a prodigious feat of engineering.* *-n.frml.* [U] **prodigiousness.**

prod·i·gy /'prɑdədʒi/ *n.* **-gies** a genius, s.o. of great ability: *She was a child prodigy on the violin.*

pro·duce /'proʊ,dus/ *n.* [U] food products, esp. vegetables: *Produce, esp. lettuce, is fresh at that market.*
—v. /prə'dus/ **-duced, -ducing, -duces** **1** to create, invent from the mind (write, compose, paint, etc.): *The artist produced a beautiful painting.* **2** to bring into being, give birth to: *Last year she also produced a baby boy.* **3** to show, bring into view: *A police officer stopped a speeding car and asked the driver to produce her driver's license.* **4** to manufacture, fabricate: *That factory produces shoes.* **5** to achieve results, make happen: *His doctor produced a cure for his illness.||A sales representative produced a sales increase.* **6** to organize financing for and present a film or play to the public: *That Italian director has produced a lovely movie.* **7** to cause a reaction, stir emotions: *His jokes produced laughter from the audience.*

pro·duc·er /prə'dusər/ *n.* **1** a manufacturer: *That company is a producer of television sets.* **2** a person or company that funds and presents entertainment: *She is a producer of sporting events (movies, theater, etc.).*

prod·uct /'prɑdəkt/ *n.* **1** anything produced with materials and labor, goods and services: *That store sells food products.* **2** the total sum resulting from multiplication: *The product of 2 x 2 is 4.* **3 product line:** a collection of related goods sold by a business

pro·duc·tion /prə'dʌkʃən/ *n.* **1** [U] the conversion of raw materials, manufacture or assembly of parts and products, into finished goods and services: *The production of electronic products is a complex assembly process.* **2** [C] a presentation of a theatrical performance: *The Metropolitan Opera's production of Romeo and Juliet was excellent.*

pro·duc·tive /prə'dʌktɪv/ *adj.* **1** producing good results, useful: *We had a productive meeting that solved some problems.* **2** producing profits: *Buying that house was a productive investment for him.*

pro·duc·tiv·i·ty /,proʊdʌk'tɪvəti, ,prɑ-/ *n.* [U] the relationship between how many quality products and services each worker or industry can produce in a given time: *Computers have greatly increased productivity in business offices.*

pro·fane /proʊ'feɪn/ *adj.n.v.frml.* **-faned, -faning, -fanes** disrespectful of God and religion, (*syns.*) blasphemous; vulgar: *That man uses* <*adj.*> *profane language.*

pro·fan·i·ty /proʊ'fænəti/ *n.* **-ties** [C;U] vulgar, coarse language: *She hurt her foot and yelled profanities.*

pro·fess /prə'fɛs/ *v.frml.* **1** to claim, say that s.t. is true, esp. when it is false: *He professes to be telling the truth, but he isn't.* **2** to state one's belief in a religion

pro·fes·sion /prə'fɛʃən/ *n.* **1** an occupation requiring an advanced degree, such as for a doctor or lawyer: *Her profession is accounting.* **2** a declaration, statement that s.t. is true: *The criminal's profession of innocence fooled no one.*

pro·fes·sion·al /prə'fɛʃənəl/ *adj.* **1** related to a profession: *Professional requirements to become a lawyer include going to law school and passing the bar examination.* **2** a person who makes his or her living as an artist or athlete: *Professional football players must train hard.* —*n.* **1** a person with proven ability in his or her occupation: *She is an excellent office manager; she is a real professional.* **2** a person engaged in a profession, such as law or medicine: *The class included college students, blue-collar workers, and professionals.*

pro·fes·sion·al·ism /prə'fɛʃənə,lɪzəm/ *n.* [U] the qualities of competence and integrity demonstrated by the best people in a field: *Professionalism among doctors requires them to learn about the newest medications available.* -*v.* **professionalize.**

pro·fes·sor /prə'fɛsər/ *n.* a teacher, esp. at the university level; the highest rank among instructors: *She is a professor of English at Cornell University.* See: teacher, USAGE NOTE.

pro·fi·cien·cy /prə'fɪʃənsi/ *n.frml.* [C;U] -**cies** ability to work with skill (*syn.*) expertise: *His proficiency as a surgeon is well known.*

pro·fi·cient /prə'fɪʃənt/ *adj.frml.* skillful, expert: *She is proficient at speaking French.*

pro·file /'prou,faɪl/ *n.v.* **1** the outline of the face viewed from the side: *The mountain's profile looks like a man's face.* **2** a group of characteristics, esp. of a person: *The teacher made a profile of the skills needed by a student to write, such as knowing how to write an outline and how to edit one's work.* —*v.* -**filed, -filing, -files** to make a profile: *The teacher profiled the student's needs.*

prof·it /'prɑfɪt/ *n.* **1** money remaining after business expenses are deducted: *That business made a $1 million profit last year.* **2** benefit, s.t. useful: *There is no profit in drinking too much alcohol.* —*v.* **1** to receive more money than one spends, gain money: *She profited from her investments in the stock market.* **2** to benefit from s.t., gain some advantage: *I profited from going to the library because I learned something new.*

pro·fit·a·ble /'prɑfətəbəl/ *adj.* **1** bringing in more money than is spent: *That business became profitable last year.* **2** beneficial, advantageous: *We had a profitable time at the*

conference because we made some new business contacts.

profit and loss statement or **P & L** *n.* a summary list of income and expenses for a business: *When a P & L is totaled, it shows either a profit or a loss.* /'piən'ɛl/.

prof·it·eer /,prɑfə'tɪr/ *n.v.* a person or business who tries to make excessive profit by selling s.t. that is in low supply at a high price: *A <n.> profiteer overcharged people for bottled water and ice after a hurricane polluted the water supply.||He <v.> profiteered from the shortage of pure water.*

profit sharing *n.* [U] an employee benefit of receiving a share of a company's profits: *Profit sharing is a process by which a company puts some of its own profits in an employee's account based on a percentage of the employee's salary and years of service.*

pro·found /prə'faund, prou-/ *adj.* **1** emotionally deep, heartfelt: *I give you my profound thanks for saving my life.* **2** intellectually deep, insightful: *A philosopher's profound insights into life inspire his readers. -n.frml.* [U] **profundity** /prə'fʌndəti, prou-/.

pro·fu·sion /prə'fyuʒən, prou-/ *n.* [U] a great amount of s.t., abundance: *A profusion of leaves bursts out on trees in the springtime. -adj.* **profuse** /prə'fyus, prou-/.

prog·e·ny /'prɑdʒəni/ *n.frml.* [U] **1** children: *My wife and I were blessed with progeny; we have three children.* **2** offspring (of animals or people): *That grandmother's progeny now include 50 children and grandchildren.*

prog·no·sis /prɑg'nousɪs/ *n.* -**ses** /-,siz/ **1** a prediction or forecast: *The prognosis for the economy is uncertain.* **2** (in medicine) a doctor's opinion of how a patient's disease will end: *The prognosis for the cancer patient is that he has six months to live.*

pro·gram /'prou,græm, -grəm/ *n.* **1** any organized plan to accomplish a goal: *Many government programs, such as mortgage interest deduction, help the wealthy.* **2** a television or radio show: *All the news programs include weather reports.* **3** a written schedule of events such as for a church, sports or theatrical event: *All the actors' names were listed in the program.* **4** a set of coded instructions telling a computer how to process information: *This program lets you make three-dimensional drawings on your computer.* —*v.* -**grammed, -gramming, -grams** **1** to make up a schedule, include s.t. in a program: *An organizer programmed meetings for a conference.* **2** to write a set of instructions for a computer: *She knows how to program in several computer languages.* **3** to give instructions to a computer: *I programmed my VCR to taperecord the football game.*

P

program director *n.* a person who selects and organizes programs for radio and television

pro·grammed /'proʊˌgræmd, -grəmd/ *adj.* coded with instructions on what to do: *That thermostat is programmed to keep the temperature at 70 degrees.*

pro·gram·mer /'proʊˌgræmər/ *n.* a person who programs computers: *Computer programmers must learn new programs as they appear on the market.*

pro·gram·ming /'proʊˌgræmɪŋ, -grə-/ *n.* [U] **1** selection and organization of shows for television and radio or other events: *She does the programming of children's shows for television.* **2** an act of writing instructions for a computer: *His programming experience is in FORTRAN and COBAL.* **3** the set of programs in a computer system: *The programming in that computer is old and obsolete.*

prog·ress /'prɑgˌrɛs, -rəs/ *n.* [U] advancement, movement toward a goal: *Progress is being made in building a new highway around the city.*
—*adj.* **in progress:** underway, happening now: *The meeting is in progress now.*
—*v.* **pro•gress** /prə'grɛs/ **1** to move ahead: *He is progressing nicely in his study of French.* **2** to develop: *Her disease has progressed more quickly than the doctors expected.*

pro·gres·sion /prə'grɛʃən/ *n.* [U] **1** a series of related events: *A progression of disagreements has lead to war between those nations.* **2** (in mathematics) an increase in a series of numbers or symbols: *Population is increasing in that country in a geometric progression.*

pro·gres·sive /prə'grɛsɪv/ *adj.* **1** related to making changes or reforming old ways, (*syn.*) alternative: *She attended a new, progressive school, where grades were optional.* **2** increasing in number: *Progressive economic sanctions against a government forced it to cooperate with other nations.* **3** moving forward
—*n.* a person who believes in reform of government, education, etc.: *She is a progressive in politics and a member of the Progressive Party.* See: Democratic Party, USAGE NOTE.

pro·hib·it /proʊ'hɪbɪt/ *v.* **1** to forbid, (*syn.*) to ban by order or law: *The law prohibits people from killing each other.* **2** to prevent from happening, block: *A severe storm prohibited people from going to work.* -*adj.* **prohibitive.**

pro·hi·bi·tion /ˌproʊə'bɪʃən/ *n.* **1** [C;U] a ban, a law against s.t.: *There is a prohibition against owning a pistol without a license.* **2** [C] the outlawing of manufacture and drinking of alcoholic beverages: *Prohibition was repealed in the USA in 1933.* -*n.* **Prohibitionist.**

pro·hib·i·tive·ly /proʊ'hɪbətəvli/ *adv.* making s.t. impossible: *Those medications are prohibitively expensive; no one can afford them.*

proj·ect /'prɑˌdʒɛkt, -dʒɪkt/ *n.* a specific task, piece of work: *His current project is to build a garage next to his house.*
—*v.* **pro·ject** /prə'dʒɛkt/ **1** to stretch out beyond a surface: *The balcony projects out beyond the wall of the house.* **2** to estimate s.t. in the future, predict: *The government projects that the defense budget will increase by 20%.* **3** to shine an image against a surface: *A movie projector projects a film onto a screen.* **4** *frml.* to move outward, (*syn.*) to propel: *The rocket projected the space vehicle into orbit.*

pro·jec·tile /prə'dʒɛktl, -ˌtaɪl/ *n.* an object thrown through space: *Spears, bullets, and rocks are types of projectiles.*

pro·jec·tion /prə'dʒɛkʃən/ *n.* **1** [C] anything that projects, extends out: *A balcony forms a projection beyond the wall of a house.* **2** [U] showing a film on a screen: *Projection of the movie began at 8:00 p.m.* **3** [U] *frml.* movement of s.t. through the air: *Projection of the satellite into space took place yesterday.* **4** [C] an estimate or prediction of future performance: *The staff discussed the projection for next year's sales.*

pro·jec·tor /prə'dʒɛktər/ *n.* a type of camera with a strong light used to shine films onto screens: *A movie projector can show a movie on a screen far away.*

pro·le·tar·i·at /proʊlə'tɛriət/ *n.* [U] **1** workers without property and with only labor to sell: *Members of the proletariat work in factories* **2** ordinary people: *Communist literature refers to the proletariat of society.* -*n.* **proletarian.**

pro·life *adj.* against legalizing abortion, (*syn.*) anti-abortion: *Pro-life demonstrators protested outside an abortion clinic.* -*n.* **pro-lifer.** See: pro-choice, USAGE NOTE.

pro·lif·er·ate /proʊ'lɪfəˌreɪt/ *v.* -**ated, -ating, -ates** **1** to increase in number rapidly, multiply: *Rabbits proliferate when they have plenty of food.* **2** to spread rapidly and widely: *Influenza proliferated throughout the country.* -*n.* [U] **proliferation.**

pro·lif·ic /prə'lɪfɪk/ *adj.frml.* **1** having many children: *Mice are prolific breeders.* **2** creating a lot of work, productive: *Some prolific authors write dozens of books.*

pro·logue /'proʊˌlɑg, -ˌlɔg/ *n.* a written or spoken introduction: *The book (play, poem) has a short prologue written by the author.*

pro·long /prə'lɔŋ/ *v.* **1** to make s.t. take longer, delay: *Two countries prolonged signing an agreement until details could be agreed on.* **2** to sustain, keep going: *The doctor prolonged his patient's life by many years by curing her cancer early.* -*n.* [C;U] **prolongation** /proʊlɔŋ'geɪʃən/.

prom /prɑm/ *n.* a dance usu. in formal dress at a high school: *He took his girlfriend to the senior prom.*

prom·e·nade /ˌprɑməˈneɪd, -ˈnad/ *n.* **1** a walkway, a special area for walking: *A wide promenade allows many people to walk at the same time.* **2** *frml.* a walk, stroll: *We took a promenade along the canal after Sunday dinner.*

prom·i·nence /ˈprɑmənəns/ *n.* [C;U] **1** being well known and respected, (*syn.*) renown: *The lawyer reached a position of prominence in her profession at an early age.* **2** *frml.* consequence, s.t. of importance: *An item of prominence on the conference agenda was infant health care.*

prom·i·nent /ˈprɑmənənt/ *adj.* **1** well-known and respected: *She is a prominent lawyer in Houston.* **2** important, s.t. that stands out: *A prominent point in the negotiations was agreeing on the selling price.*

pro·mis·cu·ous /prəˈmɪskyuəs/ *adj.* having sex with many people: *That man is promiscuous; he's with a different woman every night.* -*n.* [U] **promiscuity** /ˌprɑməˈskyuəti/.

prom·ise /ˈprɑmɪs/ *n.* [C;U] a commitment, (*syn.*) a pledge: *She made a promise to repay the loan in a week.* **2 to hold** or **have** [U] **promise:** to show signs or hope that s.t. good will result: *That new business holds promise of becoming a giant some day.*
—*v.* **-mised, -mising, -mises 1** to commit to s.t., (*syn.*) to pledge: *He promised to repay the loan next week.* **2** to indicate success in the future: *That new business promises to be big.*

prom·is·ing /ˈprɑməsɪŋ/ *adj.* presenting hope, success for the future: *That new business looks promising.*

prom·is·so·ry note /ˈprɑməˌsɔri/ *n.* an agreement to repay a loan: *I signed a promissory note from the bank to repay $1,000 in a year.*

pro·mo /ˈproʊmoʊ/ *n.infrml.* short for promotion, advertisement of products and services
—*adj.infrml.* short for promotional: *Our ad agency wrote promo copy for our newspaper ads.*

prom·on·to·ry /ˈprɑmənˌtɔri/ *n.* **-ries** a piece of land with a cliff extending into an ocean or lake: *That promontory overlooks the ocean below.*

pro·mote /prəˈmoʊt/ *v.* **-moted, -moting, -motes 1** to advance in rank, give s.o. a better job: *Her boss promoted her to supervisor in accounting.* **2** to make known to the public, advertise goods and services: *The marketing department promoted our new product in television commercials.* **3** to support, propose, esp. for the public good: *The mayor promoted the idea of building a new sports stadium in the city.* -*adj.* **promotable.**

pro·mot·er /prəˈmoʊtər/ *n.* a person who advertises and invests in promoting, such as in real estate, securities, and sporting events: *That fellow is a promoter of boxing events.*

pro·mo·tion /prəˈmoʊʃən/ *n.* **1** [C] movement to a new and better job: *He got a promotion to head of marketing.* **2** [U] making s.t. known to the public, advertising: *The promotion of our new product was done by an ad agency.*

pro·mo·tion·al /prəˈmoʊʃənəl/ *adj.* related to advertising: *Our staff produced promotional brochures.*

prompt /prɑmpt/ *adj.* **1** on time, punctual: *He was prompt; he arrived at noon, as planned.* **2** quick, done without delay: *I received a prompt response to my letter.* -*adv.* **promptly.**
—*v.* **1** to cause s.o. to do s.t., (*syn.*) to prod: *The forecast of rain prompted me to bring my umbrella.* **2** to provide an entertainer with forgotten lines: *The director prompted the actor when he forgot his lines.* -*n.* [U] **promptness.**

prompt·ing /ˈprɑmptɪŋ/ *n.* **1** a reminder, prod: *That student needs prompting to finish her homework.* **2** giving forgotten words to an entertainer: *That actor keeps forgetting his lines and needs prompting.*

prone /proʊn/ *adj.* **1** lying face down, (*syn.*) prostrate: *The police found him in a prone position with a knife in his back.* **2** lying flat: *He is lying prone on the ground.* **3** inclined toward, likely to do s.t.: *He is prone to forgetting his car keys.*

prong /prɑŋ, prɔŋ/ *n.v.* a thin rod, (*syn.*) a tine: *Forks have <n.> prongs for spearing food.*

pro·noun /ˈproʊˌnaʊn/ *n.* (in grammar) a word used in place of a noun: *"I, you, he, she, it, we," and "they" are personal pronouns.*

pro·nounce /prəˈnaʊns/ *v.* **-nounced, -nouncing, -nounces 1** to speak, utter words; to speak correctly: *She pronounces her words clearly.* **2** to declare, state s.t. as true: *A doctor pronounced the patient dead this morning.*

pro·nounced /prəˈnaʊnst/ *adj.* noticeable, large: *She speaks with a pronounced French accent.*

pro·nounce·ment /prəˈnaʊnsmənt/ *n.frml.* a public declaration, formal statement: *The mayor made a pronouncement that the city budget must be reduced.*

pron·to /ˈprɑntoʊ/ *adv.infrml.* fast, quickly: *You had better do your homework, pronto!*

pro·nun·ci·a·tion /prəˌnʌnsiˈeɪʃən/ *n.* [U] **1** the way in which a word should be spoken: *The pronunciation of words is listed in the dictionary.* **2** how correctly one pronounces words: *Her pronunciation is good, but she has a slight accent.*

proof /pruf/ *n.* **1** [U] evidence that s.t. is true, such as documentation or eyewitness accounts: *The lawyer presented proof to the jury of two eye witnesses who saw the accused commit the theft.* **2** [C] a sample, such as of

printed matter or a photograph made before the finished product: *The printer sent proofs of the brochure for correction.* **3** [U] the amount of alcohol in beer or liquor: *Eighty proof means that the liquor is 40% alcohol.* **4** [C] an uncirculated coin: *He bought some proof coins directly from the mint.*
—*v.* to examine a proof for errors: *He proofed the brochure for mistakes and sent it back to the printer.*

proof·read /'pruf,rid/ *v.* -read /-,rɛd/ , -reading, -reads to examine s.t. printed for mistakes, and correct it: *Proofreaders proofread the newspaper before it is printed. See:* edit.

prop /prɑp/ *n.* **1** a support, such as a pole or piece of wood, used to hold up s.t. else: *A worker put a prop against the wall of the tunnel to keep it from falling.* **2** a piece of scenery used in theatrical performances: *Workers changed the props between the acts of the play.* **3 prop** or **prop jet:** a small airplane: *She makes business trips in her company's prop jet.*
—*phrasal v. sep.* **propped, propping, props to prop s.t. up:** to support, keep s.t. from falling: *The government props up the prices of farm products to support farmers' incomes.‖It props them up.*

prop·a·gan·da /,prɑpə'gændə/ *n.* information made public, esp. by a government, to persuade people that s.t. is true and worthy of support: *During the war, the government published propaganda about victories of the troops when in fact they were losing battles. -v.* **propagandize.**

prop·a·gate /'prɑpə,geɪt/ *v.* -gated, -gating, -gates **1** to breed, reproduce and spread: *Plants have propagated near the pond and gradually covered it over.* **2** to transmit, make public: *The church propagates its religious message to the world. -n.* [U] **propagation.**

pro·pane /'prou,peɪn/ *n.adj.* [U] a gas used as a fuel: *He burns* <*n.*> *propane (or)* <*adj.*> *propane gas in his stove.*

pro·pel /prə'pɛl/ *v.* -pelled, -pelling, -pels to move s.t. with force, thrust: *A volcano erupted and propelled rocks high into the sky.*

pro·pel·lent /prə'pɛlənt/ *n.* [U] **1** a highly explosive fuel: *Rocket propellent can be dangerously explosive.* **2** a gas under pressure used to propel another chemical: *Some propellents used in spray cans are harmful to the atmosphere.*

pro·pel·ler /prə'pɛlər/ *n.* a rotor with curved blades used to propel a ship or aircraft: *The propellers of many airplanes have two, three, or four blades on each engine.*

pro·pen·si·ty /prə'pɛnsəti/ *n.frml.* -ties a tendency, habit: *He has a propensity for drinking too much alcohol. -v.frml.* **propend.**

prop·er /'prɑpər/ *adj.* **1** correct, right as to how to do s.t.: *The proper way to fix that engine is*

to overhaul it completely, not tinker with it.* **2** having good manners, correct behavior: *She is proper in the way she behaves.* **3** suitable, not inferior: *In this rainy climate, you have to have a proper raincoat and boots.* **4** in a specific area, not outside it: *She lives in Paris proper, not in the suburbs. -adv.* **properly.**

prop·er·ty /'prɑpərti/ *n.* [C;U] -ties **1** physical objects owned by s.o. (*syn.*) possessions. *His personal property consists of clothes, a wallet, and a watch.* **2** land and buildings, real estate: *She owns property in California.* **3** a characteristic, trait: *Chemicals have certain properties, like cleaners that dissolve grease.*

property tax *n.* a tax by a government on real estate and other possessions (boats, cars): *The property tax in rich neighborhoods is high.*

proph·e·cy /'prɑfəsi/ *n.* -cies a prediction, foretelling of the future: *A prophet made a prophecy that the kingdom would fall.*

proph·e·sy /'prɑfə,saɪ/ *v.* -sied, -sying, -sies to predict, foretell the future: *A wise man prophesied that I will be happy soon.*

proph·et /'prɑfɪt/ *n.* a religious person who predicts the future and provides religious teaching: *Daniel was one of the great Prophets in the Bible. -n.* **prophetess** /'prɑfɪtɪs/**.**

pro·phet·ic /prə'fɛtɪk/ *adj.* related to predicting the future, esp. by inspiration of God: *She made a prophetic prediction that a woman would soon become President.*

pro·phy·lac·tic /,proufə'læktɪk, ,prɑ-/ *n.* a barrier contraceptive, such as a condom: *He uses a prophylactic when he has sex so that his wife does not become pregnant.*

pro·pi·tious /prə'pɪʃəs/ *adj.* **1** favorable, likely to succeed: *He looked for a propitious moment to ask his girlfriend to marry him.* **2** lucky, fortunate: *My meeting that woman on the bus today was propitious since she offered me a job.*

pro·po·nent /prə'pounənt/ *n.frml.* a supporter, s.o. who favors s.t.: *That Senator is a proponent of lowering taxes.*

pro·por·tion /prə'pɔrʃən/ *n.* **1** [C;U] balance and harmony of s.t., the relationship of one part to another part in size and shape: *That artist draws people out of proportion, with big heads and little bodies.* **2** [U] a ratio, percentage of s.t.: *A large proportion of her salary goes to paying taxes.* **3** *fig.* **a sense of proportion:** common sense, being reasonable: *She takes her work seriously but has a sense of proportion and has fun, too.* **4 to blow s.t. out of proportion:** to exaggerate the importance of s.t.: *When she didn't want to see him yesterday, he blew it out of proportion and became angry. -adj.* **proportional.**

pro·por·tion·ate /prə'pɔrʃənət/ *adj.* in the correct proportion: *They are equal partners, so* *each receives a proportionate share -one half-of the company's profits.*

pro·pos·al /prə'pouzəl/ *n.* **1** an offer: *A competitor made a proposal to buy my business.* **2** an offer of marriage: *She accepted his (marriage) proposal.* **3** s.t. that is suggested as a possible plan

pro·pose /prə'pouz/ *v.* **-posed, -posing, -poses** **1** to suggest, recommend: *I propose that we go to the beach this weekend.* **2** to offer marriage: *He proposed that they get married.*

prop·o·si·tion /ˌprɑpə'zɪʃən/ *n.* **1** an offer, esp. in business: *She made a proposition to buy my company.* **2** an offer and request for sex: *He made her a proposition.*
—*v.* **1** to make a business offer: *They propositioned their competitors about merging with them.* **2** to request sex: *He propositioned her with promises of exotic vacations and beautiful clothes.*

pro·pri·e·tar·y /prə'praɪəˌtɛri/ *adj.* owned privately by a person or company: *Ownership of the restaurant name McDonald's™ is proprietary.*

pro·pri·e·tor /prə'praɪətər/ *n.frml.* the owner of a business, such as a shop or restaurant: *The proprietor of that shoe store waits on customers himself.*

pro·pri·e·ty /prə'praɪəti/ *n.* **-ties** [U] correct behavior, good manners: *The children observed the propriety of the church service and behaved themselves.*

pro·pul·sion /prə'pʌlʃən/ *n.* [U] a system used to start an object in motion and keep it moving: *Jet engines are the type of propulsion used on most commercial airplanes.*

pro rata /prou'reɪtə, -'ræ-, -'rɑ-/ *adj.* (Latin for) in proportion to s.t. else: *A pro rata tax refund to all real estate owners means each one receives an amount of money in proportion to the sum paid.*

pro·rate /'prou,reɪt/ *v.* **-rated, -rating, -rates** to divide or distribute (esp. expenses) proportionately: *I moved into the apartment on June 15, so the landlord prorated the month's rent and I paid him $400, instead of $800. -adj.* **proratable; -n.** [U] **proration.**

pro·sa·ic /prou'zeɪɪk/ *adj.frml.* dull, ordinary: *Cleaning the house and washing dishes are prosaic but necessary chores.*

proscribe /prou'skraɪb/ *v.* **-scribed, -scribing, -scribes** **1** to prohibit, forbid **2** to banish, legally force s.o. away: *The radical was proscribed by the government and forced to leave the country. -n.* [U] **proscription** /prou'skrɪpʃən/.

prose /prouz/ *n.* [U] written or spoken language that is not poetry: *Novels and essays are written in prose.*

pros·e·cute /'prɑsə,kyut/ *v.* **-cuted, -cuting, -cutes** to begin and carry through a lawsuit against s.o.: *The government prosecuted the criminal.*

pros·e·cu·tion /ˌprɑsə'kyuʃən/ *n.* [U] the person starting a lawsuit, (the plaintiff) and his or her lawyer(s): *The prosecution is pursuing a legal action against a company for polluting a river.*

pros·e·cu·tor /'prɑsə,kyutər/ *n.* the lawyer for the plaintiff: *A public prosecutor brings lawsuits on behalf of the citizens of the district.*

pros·e·ly·tize /'prɑsələ,taɪz/ *v.frml.* **-tized, -tizing, -tizes** to try to persuade s.o. to change (their religion, political party, etc.): *Political candidates proselytized among workers to vote for them. -n.* **proselyte** /'prɑsə,laɪt/.

pros·pect /'prɑs,pɛkt/ *v.* to explore, search: *Many people prospected for gold in California in the 1850s.*
—*n.* **1** [C] a possibility of success in the future, *(syn.)* an expectation: *She looks forward to the prospect of being accepted at her favorite college.* **2** [U] anticipation of a future event: *The prospect of having to attend a funeral is an unpleasant one.* **3** [C] a candidate for a purpose, such as becoming an employee or customer: *That company is a good prospect for buying our product.*
—*pl.* **good prospects:** a very good chance for a successful future: *With a law degree and a bright mind, she has good prospects for a fine career as a lawyer.*

pro·spec·tive /prə'spɛktɪv/ *adj.* **1** anticipated in the future, likely to happen: *His prospective employment with that company will be decided next week.* **2** being a candidate for s.t.: *The owner shows her house to prospective buyers.*

pros·pec·tor /'prɑs,pɛktər/ *n.* a person who searches for minerals, esp. gold and silver: *Prospectors dig for gold in the hills.*

USAGE NOTE: The most famous American *prospectors* were the Forty-niners, who went to California during the *Gold Rush* of 1849.

pro·spec·tus /prə'spɛktəs/ *n.* **-es** (in finance) a written, official statement that describes a security (stock, bond) or other commercial venture to prospective buyers: *That stock prospectus is so difficult to read that it is boring.*

pros·per /'prɑspər/ *v.* to grow in wealth, *(syn.)* to flourish: *Farmers prosper when good weather produces large crops.*

pros·per·i·ty /prɑ'spɛrəti/ *n.* [U] a good economic period: *After the war ended, a period of prosperity began.*

pros·per·ous /'prɑspərəs/ *adj.* successful in business, flourishing: *That family grew prosperous as its business grew.*

P

pros·the·sis /prɑs'θisəs/ *n.* **-ses** /-ˌsiz/(in medicine) an artificial limb (hand, arm, leg, etc.): *The doctor fitted the man with a prosthesis after his hand was chopped off.*

pros·ti·tute /'prɑstəˌtut/ *n.* a person who performs sexual acts for another person for pay: *Prostitutes walk the streets at night looking for customers.*
—*v.* **-tuted, -tuting, -tutes** **1** to perform sex for pay: *She prostituted herself to buy food for her children.* **2** *fig.* to use s.t. for a low purpose, (*syn.*) to debase: *He prostituted his talents as a lawyer by working for criminals.*

pros·ti·tu·tion /ˌprɑstə'tuʃən/ *n.* [U] performance of sexual acts for pay: *Prostitution is called the world's oldest profession.*

pros·trate /'prɑsˌtreɪt/ *adj.* **1** lying flat, face down in defeat, illness, or prayer: *The dog was prostrate on the ground.* **2** completely exhausted: *The runner was prostrate after racing in the heat.*
—*v.* **-trated, -trating, -trates** to lie face down: *He prostrated himself in fear before the king.* *-n.* [U] **prostration.**

pro·tag·o·nist /prou'tægənɪst/ *n.frml.* the leading character in a play or novel: *The protagonist is a wealthy woman whose children hurt her.*

pro·tect /prə'tɛkt/ *v.* to defend against harm or loss, (*syn.*) to shield: *She protected her face from the sun with a hat.*

pro·tec·tion /prə'tɛkʃən/ *n.* [C;U] **1** action taken against harm or loss, a defense: *He used a sunscreen as protection against the sun's rays.* **2** *slang* money paid to gangsters for not harming one's business: *The owner of that bar pays the mob thousands of dollars for protection.*

pro·tec·tive /prə'tɛktɪv/ *adj.* **1** having an attitude of defence: *He is very protective of his privacy and won't talk about himself.* **2** sheltering, concerned for the safety of s.o.: *She is so protective of her children that she won't allow them to play alone in the yard.*

pro·tec·tor /prə'tɛktər/ *n.* **1** a person who defends s.o. else: *A parent is a child's protector.* **2** a covering for sensitive body parts: *That hockey goalie wears a face protector.*

pro·tec·tor·ate /prə'tɛktərɪt/ *n.* a nation protected by a more powerful one: *That island kingdom is a protectorate of Great Britain.*

pro·té·gé /'proutəˌʒeɪ/ *n.* (French for) a person encouraged, taught, and protected by a more powerful one: *Her assistant is her protégé, whom she taught to speak English.*

pro·tein /'proutin/ *n.* [C;U] a substance, such as found in meat or fish, used by an animal's body: *Humans must eat foods that contain protein to stay healthy.*

pro·test /prə'tɛst, prou-, 'prouˌtɛst/ *v.* **1** to complain, object to s.t. as wrong, unfair, untrue, etc.: *She protested about not receiving a salary increase.* **2** to demonstrate in opposition to s.t.: *Workers protested against wage cuts at a rally.*
—*n.* /'prouˌtɛst/ a complaint, objection: *The workers' union lodged a protest with management over medical benefits.*

pro·to·col /'proutəˌkɔl/ *n.v.* acceptable practices in doing business, rules of behavior followed by diplomats: <*n.*> *Protocol demands that the Queen sit at the head of the table.*

pro·ton /'proutɑn/ *n.* a fundamental part of each atom's nucleus

pro·to·plasm /'proutəˌplæzəm/ *n.* [U] a sticky liquid present in all living things: *Protoplasm carries food into and waste out of human cells.*

pro·to·type /'proutəˌtaɪp/ *n.* a working model of a machine or other object used to test it before producing the final version: *A car manufacturer built a prototype of an electric car.*

pro·to·zo·a /ˌproutə'zouə/ *n.pl.* a tiny, single-celled organism: *Protozoa are among the simplest forms of life.* *-adj.* **protozoan** /ˌproutə'zouən/.

pro·tract·ed /prə'træktɪd, 'prouˌtræk-/ *adj.* spread out over time, lengthy, usu. unnecessarily so: *After protracted negotiations, the two governments signed a peace treaty.* *-v.* **protract;** *n.* [U] **protraction** /prə'trækʃən, prou-/.

protrude /prou'trud/ *v.frml.* **-truded, -truding, -trudes** to stick out, extend beyond s.t.: *His fat belly protruded over his belt.* *-n.* [C;U] **protrusion.**

proud /praud/ *adj.* **1** pleased, satisfied with an accomplishment: *She was proud that she had won the race.* **2** dignified, showing self-esteem: *That family is too proud to accept money from charity, even though they are very poor.* **3** arrogant, rude: *He is too proud to be a good friend to anyone. See:* **pride.**

prove /pruv/ *v.* **1** to show that s.t. is true or genuine, (*syn.*) to validate: *He proved how old he is by showing his driver's license.* **2** to result in: *His guess that it would rain today proved to be correct.*

proven /'pruvən/ *adj.* shown to be true or correct: *She has proven ability as a lawyer.*

proverb /'prɑvərb/ *n.v.* a short saying rich in meaning: *"Man's best friend is his dog" is a proverb.*

proverbial /prə'vɜrbial/ *adj.frml.* well known, widely accepted as true; like a proverb: *Like the proverbial "man's best friend," his dog saved him from dying in a fire.*

provide /prə'vaɪd/ *v.* **-vided, -viding, -vides** **1** to supply, furnish s.t.: *Parents provide their children with food, clothes, and shelter.* **2** to care for s.o.: *They provide for their child.* **3** to prepare for a present or future need: *She provides for her future by saving money each month.* **4** to require, esp. in a contract or by law: *That lease provides that the rent must be paid on the first of the month.*

—*conj.* **provided that** or **providing that**: if, on the condition that: *We will go to the beach today provided that it doesn't rain.*

prov·i·dence /'pravədəns/ *n.frml.* [U] the love given by God to the universe: (spelled with a capital "P") *He prayed for divine Providence to help him solve his problems.* -*adj.* **provident; providential** /,pravə'dɛnʃəl/.

prov·ince /'pravɪns/ *n.* **1** a governmental area, similar to states in the USA, into which many countries are divided: *Ontario and Quebec are two large provinces in Canada.* **2** the areas of a country away from the capital **3** *frml.* one's area of interest or responsibility: *Handling the family money is his wife's province.* -*adj.* **provincial** /prə'vɪnʃəl/.

proving ground *n.fig.* a place or job used to test the abilities of people: *Working in the sales department is a proving ground for promotion into management.*

pro·vi·sion /prə'vɪʒən/ *n.* **1** [C] a part of a contract, a clause: *A provision in that contract calls for half payment at the time of signing it.* **2** [U] *frml.* a preparation for the future: *She made provision for her retirement by saving money while she worked.*

—*pl.frml.* a supply of food: *A hunter bought provisions for the winter.* -*n.* **provisioner.**

pro·vi·sion·al /prə'vɪʒənəl/ *adj.* temporary, s.t. used until s.t. else can be done: *A provisional government runs the country until a permanent one can be formed.*

pro·vi·so /prə'vaɪzou/ *n.frml.* a provision, s.t. that must be done: *I agreed to buy the car with the proviso that the dealer provided the loan for it.*

prov·o·ca·tion /,pravə'keɪʃən/ *n.frml.* [C;U] an insult, a reason to protest or fight: *A provocation is when one calls someone a liar or a jerk.*

pro·voc·a·tive /prə'vakətɪv/ *adj.* **1** making s.o. angry: *Her provocative insults made him furious.* **2** arousing sexual desire: *He wore a sexy after-shave scent, which she found provocative.*

pro·voke /prə'vouk/ *v.* **-voked, -voking, -vokes 1** to make s.o. angry: *He provokes her by telling her that she is too fat.* **2** to cause a response, (*syn.*) to incite: *His remarks about her weight provoked her into telling him to shut up.*

pro·vo·lo·ne /,prouvə'louni/ *n.* [U] a mild, white cheese: *He ordered a pizza with provolone cheese.*

pro·vost /'prou,voust, -vəst/ *n.* the second in command below a college president: *The provost runs the college on a day-to-day basis.*

prow /prau/ *n.* the front part of a ship: *The prow splashed up and down in the high waves.*

prow·ess /'prauəs/ *n.* [U] fighting ability in battle, sports, etc.: *She showed her prowess on the basketball court by scoring 35 points for our team.*

prowl /praul/ *v.* to search secretively, hunt quietly: *Cats prowled for mice in the cellar.*

—*n.* **on the prowl:** to look secretively for a victim: *At night, criminals are on the prowl for people to rob.*

prowl·er /'praulər/ *n.* a person, esp. a criminal, looking for a victim: *A prowler walked through our backyard last night.*

prox·im·i·ty /prak'sɪməti/ *n.frml.* [U] nearness, closeness: *The hotel's proximity to the airport made it easy to catch our flight home.* -*adj.frml.* **proximate** /'praksəmɪt/.

prox·y /'praksi/ *n.* **1** [C;U] a document one person signs giving permission for s.o. else to vote on his or her behalf: *He had a proxy from his client to vote at the stockholders' meeting.* **2** [C] a person acting as a proxy: *My wife acted as my proxy at the vote at our church.*

prude /prud/ *n.* a person who is easily shocked, prissy, esp. at the bad behavior of others: *She acts like a prude when anyone tells a dirty joke.* -*adj.* **prudish.**

pru·dence /'prudns/ *n.* [U] care, planning to avoid a mistake: *She used prudence by not investing her savings in risky ventures.* -*adj.* **prudent.**

prune /prun/ *v.* **pruned, pruning, prunes 1** to cut off parts of plants, (*syn.*) to trim: *She prunes her rose bushes to make them produce more flowers.* **2** *fig.* to cut back, reduce: *That company pruned its expenses.*

—*n.* a dried plum: *He eats prunes with his cereal for breakfast.*

pru·ri·ent /'pruriənt/ *adj.* related to dirty thoughts and actions, esp. pornography: *Pornographic magazines excite his prurient interest.* -*n.* [U] **prurience.**

pry /praɪ/ *v.* **pried, prying, pries 1** to loosen or open s.t. with force: *He pried off the top of a paint can with a screwdriver.* **2** to be nosey, look into s.o. else's personal life closely: *He pried into his daughter's love life so closely that she stopped telling him anything.*

psalm /sam/ *n.v.* a sacred hymn or song: *The book of Psalms is in the Old Testament.* -*n.* **psalmist; Psalter** /'sɔltər/.

pseu·do- /'sudou/ *prefix* false, fake: *Advertisers use pseudo-scientific terms to sell products.*

pseu·do·nym /'sudn,ɪm/ *n.* a make-believe name that substitutes for one's real name: *The* author whose real name was Samuel Clemens wrote novels under the pseudonym of Mark Twain.

pso·ri·a·sis /sə'raɪəsɪs/ n. [U] a skin disease that forms itchy, red patches

psych /saɪk/ v.infrml. **1** to be enthusiastic, very excited about s.t.: *She is really psyched about her new job.* **2** phrasal v. sep. **to psych s.o. out:** to intimidate, defeat s.o. mentally: *That wrestler is so huge that he psyches out his opponents and they lose.||He psyches them out.* —n. short for psychology.

psy·che /'saɪki/ n. the human mind or spirit: *An actor tries to show us the psyche of the character he or she plays.*

psy·che·del·ic /ˌsaɪkə'dɛlɪk/ adj. related to drugs that produce hallucinations or to the culture of illegal drugs: *Her walls were covered with psychedelic posters.*

psy·chi·a·try /sə'kaɪətri, saɪ-/ n. [U] the branch of medicine that cures mental diseases: *That hospital has doctors who practice psychiatry.* -n. **psychiatrist.**

psy·chic /'saɪkɪk/ adj. **1** related to the mind: *The tragedy caused him great psychic distress.* **2** related to events that science cannot explain: *Psychic phenomena include finding lost people through mental telepathy.* —n. a person with psychic powers: *A psychic pictured woods in her mind and the police found the lost little girl there.*

psy·cho /'saɪkoʊ/ n.pej. short for psychopath

psy·cho·a·nal·y·sis /ˌsaɪkoʊə'næləsɪs/ n. [U] a method of curing mental problems -n. **psychoanalyst** /ˌsaɪkoʊ'ænəlɪst/; -v. **psychoanalyze.**

psy·chol·o·gy /saɪ'kɑlədʒi/ n. -gies [U] **1** study of human and animal behavior: *She is fascinated by the psychology of cats.* **2** the science of the mind: *She studied psychology in college.* **3** use of psychological principles in changing behavior: *She used psychology to get her boy to stop crying.* -n. **psychologist;** -adj. **psychological** /ˌsaɪkə'lɑdʒəkəl/.

psy·cho·path /'saɪkə,pæθ/ n. a person with mental illness and bad behavior toward others: *That psychopath yells at people on the street.* -adj. **psychopathic.**

psy·cho·sis /saɪ'koʊsɪs/ n. -choses a severe mental illness: *Paranoia is a psychosis in which a person thinks others are trying to hurt him when they are not.*

psy·cho·so·mat·ic /ˌsaɪkəsə'mætɪk, -koʊ-/ adj. of illness caused by a person's mind, not body: *He worries so much that a psychosomatic reaction makes his stomach ache.*

psy·cho·ther·a·pist /ˌsaɪkoʊ'θɛrəpɪst/ n. a person trained in psychology and treatment of mental disorders, but who is not a medical doc-

tor: *She visited her psychotherapist twice each week for two months.*

psy·cho·ther·a·py /ˌsaɪkoʊ'θɛrəpi/ n. -pies [U] a cure for emotional and other troubles by talking to a trained psychotherapist

psy·chot·ic /saɪ'kɑtɪk/ adj. related to psychosis, mental illness: *The man's psychotic behavior of shouting threats frightens people.* —n. a psychotic person

pter·o·dac·tyl /ˌtɛrə'dæktəl/ n. a type of ancient bird: *Pterodactyls flew in the sky millions of years ago. See:* dinosaur.

pto·maine poisoning /'toʊ,meɪn, toʊ'meɪn/ n. [U] severe illness caused by bacteria from bad food: *My brother had ptomaine poisoning and almost died.*

pub /pʌb/ n. a bar that often serves simple food: *She went to a pub for a hamburger and beer. See:* bar, USAGE NOTE.

pu·ber·ty /'pyubərti/ n. [U] sexual maturity, the stage of human growth when a girl can have a baby and a boy can father one: *Puberty usually occurs around the age of 13.*

pu·bes·cent /pyu'bɛsənt/ adj.frml. having reached sexual maturity: *Some youngsters develop pimples as they become pubescent.* -n.frml. [U] **pubescence.**

pu·bic /'pyubɪk/ adj. (in medicine) related to the pubes, lower abdomen: *Pubic hair starts to grow on the genitals around age 13.*

pub·lic /'pʌblɪk/ n. [U] **1** the people and area outside one's house, in the community: *He was sick and first appeared in public at the local food store.* **2** the citizens, the people of a local area, state, or country: *The President asked the public to support his tax cut program.* **3** admirers of a famous person: *The singer thanked her public for their applause.* —adj. **1** related to the community and people: *The government spends money on public building projects such as bridges and prisons.* **2** meant for use by the people: *People have fun walking and playing in public parks.* **3 to go public: a.** to reveal a secret, s.t. personal to the community: *A government employee went public by talking to reporters about theft of government property.* **b.** (in finance) to offer a stock to the public: *That company was privately owned, then went public by offering shares on the open market.* **4 to make s.t. public:** to tell s.t. to people: *A famous singer made public her plans to marry.*

public access n. a state of being open to the public: *Public access to the building was denied by the police because of a bomb threat.*

public address system loudspeakers: *I heard my name called over the public address system at the airport. n. abbr.* **P.A. system.**

public assistance n. welfare, government programs to give food, shelter, and medical care to poor people: *After he lost his job, he had to go on public assistance to get food for his children.*

pub·li·ca·tion /ˌpʌblə'keɪʃən/ *n.* **1** [C] a book, magazine, newspaper, etc.: *She reads all the publications in the field of medicine.* **2** [U] an act of publishing s.t.: *Publication of the novel will take place next month.*

public defender *n.* a lawyer hired by the state to defend poor people: *She was poor and needed a public defender to defend her in court.*

public domain *n.* [U] s.t. belonging to the public, out of copyright: *A publication, esp. a book, goes into the public domain when its copyright expires.*

pub·li·cist /'pʌbləsɪst/ *n.* a person who talks to the media for politicians, artists, etc. to make them famous: *She is a publicist who works for many musicians.*

pub·lic·i·ty /pʌb'lɪsəti/ *n.* [U] information given in the media (TV, newspapers, etc.) that creates public interest in a person or product: *A famous boxer received a lot of publicity when he was sent to jail.* *-v.* **publicize** /'pʌblə,saɪz/.

public relations *n.pl.* a field of work that creates good impressions of people, companies, and products with the public: *She works in public relations for the telephone company.*

public service *n.* [U] government employment: *People who work for the government work in public service.*

public television *n.* [U] nonprofit television that shows mainly educational programs, specialized entertainment, and news not found on commercial television: *Public television broadcasts wonderful nature programs.*

pub·lish /'pʌblɪʃ/ *v.* **-es** to print and distribute s.t. to the public: *That newspaper publishes daily and weekend editions.*

pub·lish·er /'pʌblɪʃər/ *n.* **1** a business that prints and sells newspapers, books, videos, etc., to the public: *He works for a textbook publisher in San Francisco.* **2** a person who runs a publication: *She is the publisher of a magazine for lawyers.*

puck·er /'pʌkər/ *v.n.* **1** to bring s.t. together so that folds or wrinkles are formed: *This cheap jacket <v.> puckers at the shoulders.* **2** *phrasal v.* **to pucker up:** to pucker one's lips and to kiss: *She told him to pucker up and give her a kiss.*

pud·ding /'pʊdɪŋ/ *n.* [C;U] a sweet, smooth, dessert made with eggs and milk: *We had chocolate pudding for dessert.*

pud·dle /'pʌdl/ *n.v.* **-dled, -dling, -dles** a small, temporary pool of water: *There were <n.> puddles of water on the street after it rained.*

pudg·y /'pʌdʒi/ *adj.infrml.* **-ier, -iest** chubby, fat: *That pudgy little boy eats too much ice cream.*

pueb·lo /'pwɛbloʊ/ *n.* **-los** **1** (Spanish for) a community, esp. in the American Southwest: *This pueblo in Arizona is known for making fine silver jewelry.* **2** the adobe buildings in a pueblo: *Some Native American pueblos were built hundreds of years ago.*

pu·er·ile /'pyuərəl, 'pyur-, -aɪl/ *adj.frml.* childish, foolish: *His puerile remarks annoyed everyone.*

puff /pʌf/ *v.* **1** to blow air, such as through the lips in short bursts: *She puffed and puffed after she ran up the hill* **2** *phrasal v. sep.* **to puff s.t. out:** to fill s.t. with air: *He puffed out his cheeks and made the kids laugh.* **3** *phrasal v. sep.* **to puff s.t. up:** to swell, grow large: *Her ankle puffed up after she fell and hurt it.* *—n.* **1** short bursts of air, smoke, clouds, etc.: *Puffs of smoke came out of the chimney.* **2** a slight breeze: *Light puffs of air cooled me on a hot afternoon.* *-adj.* **puffy.**

pu·gi·lis·tic /ˌpyudʒə'lɪstɪk/ *adj.frml.* related to fighting and boxing: *That boxer has excellent pugilistic skills.* *-n.frml.* [U] **pugilism** /'pyudʒə,lɪzəm/.

pug·na·cious /pʌg'neɪʃəs/ *adj.frml.* wanting to fight, (*syn.*) combative: *The pit bull is a nasty, pugnacious dog.* *-n.frml.* [U] **pugnacity** /pʌg'næsəti/.

puke /pyuk/ *v.n. slang* to throw up, vomit: *He had an upset stomach and <v.> puked all night.*

Pu·lit·zer Prize /'pʊlɪtsər, 'pyu-/ *n.* a yearly award in the USA for the best writing in newspapers, novels, poetry, etc.: *She won the Pulitzer Prize for best news reporting on a newspaper.*

pull /pʊl/ *v.* **1** to move s.t. toward one, (*syn.*) to tug: *A horse pulls a plow.||A fisherman pulled on the oars of a boat.* **2** to remove or tear: *A dentist pulled a man's tooth.||She pulled the electrical plug from the socket.* **3** to take s.o. away from an activity: *The coach pulled a player from the game.* **4** to show a weapon as a threat: *A robber pulled a gun on me and took my money.* **5** *infrml.fig.* **to pull a fast one:** to trick s.o., deceive: *He pulled a fast one on me by borrowing my tennis racket and never returning it.* **6** *phrasal v.* **to pull away:** to leave or go: *The boat pulled away from the dock.* **7** *phrasal v.* **to pull back:** to retreat, move back: *An army pulled back from the battle front.* **8** *phrasal v. insep.* **to pull for s.o.:** to show support, cheer: *I am pulling for you to pass your exam today.||Sports fans pull for their favorite team.* **9 to pull oneself together:** to stop crying, get control of one's emotions: *After his mother's funeral, he pulled himself together.* **10** *infrml.fig.* **to pull out all the stops:** to try

very hard, go to an extreme: *The bride's parents pulled out all the stops by giving a roast beef and champagne wedding party.* **11** *phrasal v. sep.* **to pull s.o. or s.t. in: a. s.o. or s.t.** to draw in, tug in: *A fisher pulled in fish caught in his net.* **b.** to arrive: *My train pulled in at 8:09 p.m.* **12** *phrasal v. sep.* **to pull s.t. off:** to succeed, esp. by doing s.t. difficult: *She pulled off a big deal by finding a new job at twice her old salary.* **13** *phrasal v. sep.* **to pull s.t. apart: a.** to take s.t. apart, *(syn.)* to disassemble: *A repairperson pulled the TV apart and fixed it.* **b.** to tear or rip apart: *A dog pulled apart an old shoe with his teeth.* **c.** *fig.* to look for mistakes, find fault with: *His boss pulled apart his report looking for mistakes.* **14** *phrasal v. sep.* **to pull s.t. down: a.** to tear down, demolish: *Workers pulled down an old building to make room for a new one.* **b.** *infrml.fig.* to earn money: *She pulls down a big salary as a lawyer.* **15** *phrasal v. sep.* **to pull s.t. out: a. s.t.:** to take out, use s.t.: *He pulled out a knife and opened the box with it.* **b.** to drive a vehicle on to the main road: *He pulled out of his driveway on to the street.* **c.** to recover, stop doing s.t.: *The economy pulled out of the recession and is better now.* **d.** to withdraw, stop participating: *He pulled out of a business deal.* **16** *phrasal v. sep.* **to pull s.t. over: a.** to put on clothes over one's head: *He pulled a sweater over his head.* **b.** to drive a car to the side of the road: *He pulled his car over and stopped for a rest.* **17** *phrasal v. sep.* **to pull s.t. up: a. s.t.:** to uproot, tear from s.t.: *We pulled up weeds from the garden.* **b.** to arrive somewhere: *We pulled up to the red traffic light and stopped the car.* **18** *phrasal v. insep.* **to pull through s.t.:** to survive an illness or crisis: *She had a heart attack, but pulled through in the hospital.* **19** *phrasal v.* **to pull together:** to work as a team: *We all pulled together to meet the deadline.*
—*n.* **1** a tug, a forceful movement: *A fisher gave his line a pull and hooked a fish.* **2** *infrml.fig.* **to have pull:** to have power, influence: *Some business leaders have pull with politicians who will do favors for them.*

pul·ley /'pʊli/ *n.* an apparatus used to lift or lower heavy objects: *A farmer used a pulley to pull bales of hay into his barn loft.*

pull·out /'pʊl,aʊt/ *n.* **1** a move away from s.t., withdrawal: *A pullout of troops from the city pleased the citizens.* **2** a foldout as in a book: *A map was printed on a pullout in the book.*

pull·over /'pʊl,oʊvər/ *n.* a type of sweater without buttons down the front: *He put a pullover on in the cold weather.*

pul·mo·nar·y /'pʊlmə,nɛri, 'pʌl-/ *adj.* (in medicine) related to the lungs: *The patient's pulmonary function is bad because she has pneumonia.*

pulp /pʌlp/ *n.* [U] **1** the soft inside of fruits and vegetables: *After you squeeze the juice from an orange, pulp is left over.* **2** any thick soup-like mass: *Paper is made from wood pulp.*
—*v.* to crush or mix into a mass: *Paper mills pulp wood to make paper.*

pul·pit /'pʊlpɪt, 'pʌl-/ *n.* a high stand or platform in a church: *A minister gave a sermon from the pulpit.*

pul·sar /'pʌl,sɑr/ *v.* a small star that sends out light rays in pulses: *The light rays from pulsars are regular like the ticking of a clock.*

pul·sate /'pʌl,seɪt/ *v.* **-sated, -sating, -sates** to act with a start-and-stop rhythm, *(syn.)* to throb: *Her head is pulsating with pain.* -*n.* [C;U] **pulsation** /pʌl'seɪʃən/.

pulse /pʌls/ *n.* **1** any burst of light, energy, waves, etc.: *This machine sends out pulses of sound to find objects underseas.* **2** the rhythm of blood pumped through the blood vessels: *The doctor put her fingers on my wrist to feel my pulse.* **3** *fig.* the rhythm of an activity: *The pulse of life in big cities is very fast.*
—*v.* **pulsed, pulsing, pulses** to beat rhythmically: *Blood pulses through the arteries.*

pul·ver·ize /'pʌlvə,raɪz/ *v.* **ized, -ising, -izes 1** to crush into dust, make powder: *A huge machine pulverized rock into powder.* **2** *fig.* to defeat s.o. badly: *Our basketball team pulverized the other team 105 to 55.* -*n.* [U] **pulverization.**

pu·ma /'pyumə, 'pu-/ *n.* a cougar, a large wild cat: *Cougars are native to the Americas.*

pum·ice /'pʌmɪs/ *n.* [U] a powder from volcanic rock: *Pumice is used to grind and polish things and to soften skin.*

pum·mel /'pʌməl/ *v.frml.* to punch rapidly, beat badly: *A boxer pummeled his opponent.*

pum·mel·ing /'pʌməlɪŋ/ *n.* a severe beating: *A boy gave another boy a pummeling with his fists.*

pump /pʌmp/ *n.* **1** a machine that forces gases or liquids from one place to another: *I used an air pump to fill up my bicycle tire with air.* **2** a type of woman's light shoe: *She wore a black dress and pumps to dinner.*
—*v.* **1** to use a pump: *A worker pumped water out of a flooded cellar.* **2** *fig.* to supply a lot of s.t.: *The government pumped money into building a big dam.* **3** *fig.* to ask questions, seek information: *His friend pumped him for information about what he had done on vacation.* **4** *phrasal v. sep.* **to pump s.o. up:** to make s.o. enthusiastic, excited: *The football coach pumped up the team before the game.||He pumped them up.||They got pumped up.*

pum·per·nick·el /'pʌmpər,nɪkəl/ *n.* [U] a dark rye bread: *She had a ham sandwich on pumpernickel.*

pump·kin /'pʌmpkɪn/ *n.* [C;U] a large orange-colored gourd with a hard outside shell and soft insides: *Pumpkins were part of the original Thanksgiving feasts of the American Pilgrims. See:* honey, USAGE NOTE.

USAGE NOTE: To celebrate *Halloween*, children in the USA make *jack-o'lanterns* by carving scary faces in pumpkins. The jack-o' lanterns are lit from inside with candles and put outside the house in the evening.

pun /pʌn/ *n.v.* **punned, punning, puns** a joke using words with similar sounds or two different meanings: *A pun is, for example: "I have a weak back that I hurt about a week back"; "weak" and "week" have the same sound but different meanings and "back" means "the human back" and in" the past."*

punch (1) /pʌntʃ/ *n.* **punches 1** [C] a blow with the fist: *One boxer gave the other one a punch in the stomach.* **2** [C] a tool used to make holes, such as in paper: *I used a punch to make three holes in my term paper to put it into a notebook.* **3** [U] liveliness, impact, force: *The music gives that TV commercial real punch.*
—*v.* **-es 1** to hit with the fist, strike: *The boxer punched his opponent in the nose.* **2** to make holes: *I punched holes in my term paper.* **3** *fig.*
to punch holes in s.t.: to show that s.t. is not reasonable, practical, true, etc.: *A lawyer punched holes in a witness' testimony by bringing witnesses who said what he said was not true.*
—*n.fig.* **to pull punches:** (usu. used in the negative) to hold back: *He says what he thinks and does not pull punches.*

punch (2) *n.* [C;U] a drink made by mixing fruit juices and other ingredients: *We made a fruit punch of orange and papaya juice with slices of orange and lemons.*

punching bag *n.* a heavy, round sack hung from the ceiling for boxers to practice punching: *A boxer pounded the punching bag with his fists.*

punch line *n.* the line that gives the meaning of a joke or pun: *In the pun, "Did you know that I hurt myself and have a weak back?" "No, when did it happen?" "Oh, about a week back!" the punch line is a "week back." See:* pun.

punch·y /'pʌntʃi/ *adj.infrml.fig.* **-ier, -iest** weak and confused as from being punched: *After staying up all night studying for exams, I felt punchy the next day.*

punc·til·i·ous /pəŋk'tɪliəs/ *adj.frml.* concerned about very fine points of behavior, (*syn.*) fastidious: *He is so punctilious that she never relaxes.*

punc·tu·al /'pʌŋktʃuəl/ *adj.* arriving or leaving on time, prompt: *He was punctual; he arrived at 9:00 on the dot.* -*n.* [U] **punctuality** /'pʌŋktʃu'æləti/.

punc·tu·ate /'pʌŋktʃu,eɪt/ *v.* **-ated, -ating, -ates 1** to put punctuation marks (commas, semicolons, periods, etc.) in sentences: *I punctuated this sentence with a period at the end.* **2** *fig.* to break a silence with noise: *Cries of an owl punctuated the silence of the night.*

punc·tu·a·tion /,pʌŋktʃu'eɪʃən/ *n.* [U] the use of specific marks to make ideas within writing clear: *Her writing is clear and her punctuation is accurate.*

punctuation mark *n.* any of a set of marks used in writing to make it clear: *Punctuation marks include the comma (,), semicolon (;), and period (.).*

punc·ture /'pʌŋktʃər/ *n.* a hole made by s.t. pointed: *There is a puncture in my car's front tire.*
—*v.* **1** to make a hole with a pointed object: *A nail has punctured the tire.* **2** to make s.t. go down in size, (*syn.*) to deflate: *A needle punctured the balloon.||The funny remark punctured the man's pride.*

pun·dit /'pʌndɪt/ *n.* an expert, esp. a person of high learning: *The pundits said that the economy would go down, but it went up.*

pun·gent /'pʌndʒənt/ *adj.* giving off a strong taste or smell: *The pungent smell of spices came from a stew cooking on the stove.* -*n.* [U] **pungency.**

pun·ish /'pʌnɪʃ/ *v.* **-es** to discipline, make s.o. pay for doing s.t. wrong: *The father punished his son by sending him to his room early at night.*

pun·ish·ment /'pʌnɪʃmənt/ *n.* [C;U] a payment for doing s.t. wrong, (*syn.*) a penalty: *The punishment for stealing is going to jail.*

pu·ni·tive /'pyunətɪv/ *adj.frml.* punishing s.o. for wrongdoing: *A boy would not stop talking in class, so the teacher took punitive action and sent him to the principal's office.*

punk /pʌŋk/ *n.* **1** a rough young person, esp. a young man, (*syn.*) a rowdy: *Some punks get into fist fights.* **2** a popular culture movement of young people with shocking dress and loud rock music as a protest against middle class life in Britain and the USA: *Their son dyed his hair green and played in a punk band.*
—*adj.* related to punk culture

punt (1) /pʌnt/ *n.v.* a small boat with square ends used in shallow waters: *A man fished from a <n.> punt.*

punt (2) *v.* to kick a football: *A football player punted the ball toward the opponent's goal.*

pu·ny /'pyuni/ *adj.* **nier, -niest** weak and small: *Puppies are puny and blind at birth.*

P

pup /pʌp/ *n. short for* puppy, a baby dog or seal: *Our dog gave birth to three pups today.*

pu·pil (1) /'pyupəl/ *n.* in USA, a student in elementary school, approx. ages 6–11: *Pupils sat in class with their hands folded.*

pupil (2) *n.* the dark, round opening in the center of the eye that controls the amount of light that enters it: *The pupil grows larger in darkness and smaller in sunlight.*

pup·pet /'pʌpɪt/ *n.* a type of doll moved by fingers, strings, or rods and used as actors in puppet shows: *Puppets move and talk in funny ways.*

pup·pet·eer /,pʌpə'tɪr/ *n.* an artist who makes puppets behave like actors: *Puppeteers make puppets move, talk, and sing.*

pup·py /'pʌpi/ *n.* **-pies** a young dog not fully grown: *Puppies love to play and eat. See:* pup.

puppy love *n.* a feeling of love, usu. between very young people, that does not last long,<syn> an infatuation: *That little boy has a puppy love for the girl next door.*

pur·chase /'pɜrtʃəs/ *v.* **-chased, -chasing, -chases** to buy s.t., to pay for goods and services: *She purchased a new car.*
—*n.* an act of buying: *The purchase of the car took several days of deciding which one to buy.* -*n.* **purchaser.**

pur·chas·ing /'pɜrtʃəsɪŋ/ *n.* **1** an act of buying: *Purchasing a book is one thing; reading it is another.* **2** a department in a business or institution that orders supplies: *Purchasing buys paper, pencils, and other office supplies.*

purchasing power *n.* the value of a country's money and how much it will buy: *The purchasing power of the US dollar is strong.*

pure /pyʊr/ *adj.* **purer, purest 1** clean, not dirty or polluted: *People must have pure water to drink.* **2** not mixed with other things: *The dress is made of pure cotton.* **3** total, complete: *It was pure luck that he found money lying on the street.* **4** free from badness, sin, or evil: *He thinks pure thoughts about blue skies and mountain lakes.* -*n.* [U] **purity.**

pu·rée /pyʊ'reɪ, 'pyʊreɪ/ *n.v.* (French for) a food made soft by forcing it through a strainer: *He puréed carrots for the baby to eat.* -*adj.* **puréed.**

pur·ga·tive /'pɜrgətɪv/ *n.adj.* a laxative: *He took a purgative to help him go to the bathroom.*

pur·ga·to·ry /'pɜrgə,tɔri/ *n.* **-ries** (in Roman Catholicism) a state of punishment after death before going to heaven: *Catholic children pray for the souls in purgatory.*

purge /pɜrdʒ/ *v.* **purged, purging, purges 1** to clean, make pure: *She had dirt in her eye and a nurse purged it with an eye wash.* **2** to remove people, esp. from a government or political party: *The party purged itself of its radical members.*
—*n.* cleansing, the removal of unwanted people: *That political party had a purge of members who no longer agreed with its beliefs.*

pu·ri·fi·er /'pyʊrə,faɪər/ *n.* a machine used to clean air, water, or other substances: *A water purifier removes dirt, salt, and other pollutants.*

pu·ri·fy /'pyʊrə,faɪ/ *v.* **-fied, -fying, -fies 1** to make s.t. clean, pure: *An air filter purifies the air of dirt and smoke.* **2** to cleanse of badness, sin, or guilt: *He asked God to purify his soul.* -*n.* [U] **purification** /,pyʊrəfə'keɪʃən/.

pur·ist /'pyʊrɪst/ *n.* a person who believes in doing things by strict rules: *The teacher is a purist who will speak only French to students, even beginners.*

pur·i·tan·i·cal /,pyʊrə'tænəkəl/ *adj.frml.* strict in religious matters and personal behavior: *Puritanical behavior includes not smoking, drinking, or dancing.*

pur·ple /'pɜrpəl/ *n.adj.* [U] **1** the color made by mixing red and blue: <n.> *Purple is an unusual color for a car.* **2** the color worn by royalty and some important clergy: *Noblemen in ancient Rome wore robes of* <n.> *purple.*

Purple Heart *n.* a military medal awarded to US soldiers wounded in action: *That soldier was wounded in the leg and got the Purple Heart.*

pur·port /pər'pɔrt/ *v.n.* to give an untrue impression: *He gave a story that he* <v.> *purports to be true about where he was when the crime was committed.*

pur·pose /'pɜrpəs/ *n.* **1** [C;U] a goal, reason: *The purpose of going to school is to learn.* **2 on purpose:** deliberately, often in a bad way: *She stepped on my foot on purpose, not by accident.* **3 with purpose:** with a strong desire for success: *That politician speaks with purpose about the need to take care of the poor.*

pur·pose·ful /'pɜrpəsfəl/ *adj.* with a goal in mind, dedicated, determined: *She studies in a purposeful way to earn her degree.*

purr /pɜr/ *n.* the soft, rhythmic hum made by a happy cat: *You can hear the purr of my kitten after she has eaten.*
—*v. fig.* to make a purring sound: *Since a mechanic fixed my car, it really purrs.*

purse /pɜrs/ *n.* **1** a woman's handbag: *She keeps her wallet, comb, and cosmetics in her purse.* **2** a wallet or small bag that holds money, credit cards, etc.: *He carries only a small coin purse and his keys.* **3** *frml.* a prize, sum of money to be won: *The purses in tennis and golf matches can be large amounts.* **4** *in-frml.* **the purse strings:** the money: *In that family, the mother controls the purse strings and gives money to her husband and children.*

—v. **pursed, pursing, purses** to gather together into folds or wrinkles, (*syn.*) to pucker: *He pursed his lips and gave her a kiss on the cheek.*

purs·er /'pɜrsər/ *n.* a ship's officer in charge of keeping money safe: *A passenger went to the purser's office to cash a check.*

pur·su·ant /pər'suənt/ *adj.frml.* in accordance with, following an agreement, contract, etc.: *Pursuant to our contract, the payment for the loan is due on the first of each month.*

pur·sue /pər'su/ *v.* **-sued, -suing, -sues** **1** to chase, go after s.o. to capture: *A police officer pursued the speeding car and stopped it.* **2** to work hard at s.t., strive for: *She is pursuing a college degree.*

pur·suit /pər'sut/ *n.* **1** a chase: *A police officer ran down the street in pursuit of the thief.* **2** a career, occupation: *Her current pursuit is a career in advertising.*

pur·vey·or /pər've ɪər/ *n.frml.* a business, esp. of food products: *That big store is a purveyor of foods imported from all over the world. -v.* **purvey.**

pus /pʌs/ *n.* [U] the white, sticky liquid that forms in an infected wound: *A nurse gently cleaned the pus from the injury on my hand.*

push /pʊʃ/ *v.* **-es** **1** to press against s.t. to move it: *He pushed the door open with his hands.‖I dialed a telephone number by pushing the buttons on the keypad.* **2** to shove, hit hard with the hands: *The boy pushed another child to the ground.* **3** to hurry, work extra hard: *We pushed to finish the job on time.* **4** to urge others to cooperate: *A politician pushed his party members for a new law against pollution.* **5** *infrml.fig.* to sell, esp. on a special sale: *The supermarket is pushing fresh tomatoes and melons this week.* **6** *phrasal v.* **to push off: a.** to leave, depart: *Well, it's getting late and I have to push off now.* **b.** to leave by boat: *Our ship pushes off at 8:00 a.m. tomorrow.* **7** *phrasal v. insep.* **to push on s.t.: a.** to continue a trip or task: *We arrived in New York this morning but pushed on to Boston, our destination.* **b.** to press against: *He pushed on the door and it opened.* **8** *phrasal v. sep.* **to push s.o. around:** to treat s.o. roughly or unfairly: *She tries to push the other committee members around.* **9** *phrasal v. sep.* **to push (s.t.) through: a.** to move through: *We pushed through the crowd and out of the sports stadium.* **b.** *s.t.:* to finish s.t. in a hurry: *The legislature pushed through a new law to lower taxes.‖They pushed it through.*

—n. **-es** **1** pressure or force against s.t.: *She gave the door a push to open it.* **2** a shove, an angry thrust of the hands: *A man gave another a push and they started to fight.* **3** hard work, a big effort: *Our company salespeople made a big push to sell a new product.* **4** **when push**

comes to shove: when it is an important time to act on a difficult decision: *When push comes to shove, I can depend on my friend to help me.*

push·cart /'pʊʃ,kɑrt/ *n.* a cart that is moved by pushing it by hand, not by a motor: *A shopping cart in supermarkets is a pushcart.*

push·er /'pʊʃər/ *n.slang* a seller of illegal drugs: *Police arrested drug pushers on the street.*

push·o·ver /'pʊʃ,ouvər/ *n.infrml.fig.* **1** (in sports) an opponent who is easily beaten: *Their team was a pushover and lost by two goals.* **2** s.t. that can be done easily: *That exam in math today was a pushover.* **3** s.o. who is very fond of s.o. or s.t.: *I'm a pushover for babies in blue blankets.*

push·up /'pʊʃ,ʌp/ *n.* an exercise done by lying on the floor and pushing the body up with the arms and hands: *Pushups make one's arms and shoulders strong.*

push·y /'pʊʃi/ *adj.* **-ier, -iest** aggressive, too demanding of the attention and cooperation of others: *He is so pushy that he interrupts other students when they are speaking with the teacher.*

pu·sil·lan·i·mous /,pyusə'lænəməs/ *adj.frml.* weak and afraid: *That pusillanimous jerk refused to help his neighbors when their house was on fire!*

puss /pʊs/ *n.infrml.* short for **1** pussycat: *See that nice yellow puss sitting in the window?* **2** *fig.* the human face

puss·y /'pʊsi/ or **puss·y·cat** /'pʊsi,kæt/ *n.infrml.* a house cat: *A little pussy cat rubbed against my ankle.*

puss·y·foot /'pʊsi,fʊt/ *v.infrml.* to act weakly, fearful of making a decision, (*syn.*) to hesitate: *He pussyfooted for weeks about where to go on vacation and his wife finally decided for him.*

put /pʊt/ *v.* **put, putting, puts** **1** to place, move s.t.: *I put the book on the shelf.‖She put her paycheck in the bank.* **2** to cause s.o. to experience s.t.: *The doctor put him under observation.* **3** to arrange, organize s.t.: *Before going on his trip, he put his affairs in order, like stopping delivery of the newspaper.* **4** to cause problems for others: *He put the typist to a lot of trouble by making many changes in a letter he wrote.* **5** to apply, use: *She put her knowledge of accounting to use in figuring out her taxes.* **6** to express, say: *To put it mildly, the rainy weather has been terrible lately.* **7** *phrasal v.* **to put about:** (with boats) to turn, esp. back: *We saw a bad storm ahead and we put about for our home port.* **8** *phrasal v. insep.* **to put in for s.t.:** to apply, request: *A soldier put in for a transfer to another army post.* **9** *infrml.* **to put one's best foot forward:** to make one's best effort or appearance:

P

You should dress nicely and put your best foot forward when you go to a job interview. **10 to put one's mind to:** to work hard at s.t.: *When she puts her mind to it, she is very helpful in solving problems.* **11** *phrasal v. sep.* **to put s.o. away:** to go to jail or a mental hospital: *His family put away my mentally-ill neighbor.* **12** *phrasal v. sep.* **to put s.o. or s.t. down:** to criticize, say bad things: *He puts down his coworkers by saying that they don't know what they are doing.* **13** *phrasal v. sep.* **to put s.t. forth** or **forward:** to offer for consideration, propose: *A politician put forth the idea that patriotism is important to the country.‖She put it forth.* **14** *phrasal v. sep.* **to put s.t. in:** to contribute, pay: *We each put in $10 to buy a gift for our friend who is leaving.‖We put it in.* **15 to put s.t. in perspective:** to be reasonable about s.t., understand and accept s.t.: *Hearing of her friend's tragedy helped her put her own problems in perspective.* **16** *phrasal v. sep.* **to put s.o. or s.t. off: a. s.o.:** to annoy or disgust: *His bad manners put off people and they avoid him.* **b.** s.o. or s.t.: to postpone, delay: *Our meeting for today was put off until tomorrow.‖We put it off.* **17** *phrasal v. sep.* **to put s.o. or s.t. on: a. s.o.:** to trick or tease s.o. by making believe s.t.: *He wasn't being serious; he was just putting her on.* **b.** s.t.: to dress: *She put on her coat and hat.‖She put them on.* **18** *phrasal v. sep.* **to put s.o. or s.t. out: a. s.o.:** to annoy, irritate: *He was really put out that she did not show up for their date.* **b.** s.t.: to take outside: *He put out the trash.* **c.** s.t.: to extinguish a fire: *Firefighters put out the fire with a water hose.* **19** *phrasal v. sep.* **to put s.t. over:** to trick, deceive: *He put one over on his neighbor by borrowing a hammer and never returning it.* **20** *phrasal v. sep.* **to put s.o. through s.t.:** to cause s.o. to suffer s.t.: *His boss put him through a difficult period.* **21 to put to the test:** to make s.t. or s.o. perform to see how well they do: *She claimed that she could speak Spanish, so the job interviewer put her to the test and started speaking Spanish with her.* **22** *phrasal v.* **to put through: a.** to approve, process s.t.: *The consulate put through my application for a visa to visit France.* **b.** to connect a telephone call **23** *phrasal v. sep.* **to put s.o. up:** to give s.o. hospitality: *They put me up for the weekend when I was in London.* **24** *infrml.* **to put up or shut up:** to be willing to support what one says with money or action: *You say that you can run faster than anyone else. Well, put up or shut up; let's race for money right now!* **25** *phrasal v. insep.* **to put up with s.o. or s.t.:** to tolerate, accept: *She puts up with the loud noise of living in the city because the city is so exciting.*
—*adj.* **1 put out:** annoyed, irritated with s.o.: *I*

am put out with my friend because he is late again. **2 put upon:** taken advantage of: *When her grown son keeps asking her for money, she feels put upon.* **3 to stay put:** not to move, stay still: *I told my friend to stay put while I went to the store to buy food.*

put-down *n.infrml.* an insult, a critical remark: *Calling him stupid was quite a put-down.*

put-on *n.infrml.* a friendly joke where one pretends s.t. is true: *His annoyance with her when she interrupted his conversation was just a put-on to tease her.*

put-put /'pʌt,pʌt/ *n.infrml.* the sound of a small gasoline engine: *I can hear the put-put of her motorboat coming this way.*
—*v.* to make such a sound: *A boat put-putted out in the lake.*

pu·trid /'pyutrɪd/ *adj.frml.* **1** rotten, badly spoiled: *Food left in the sun has turned putrid.* **2** no good, worthless

putt /pʌt/ *v.n.* to hit a golf ball a short distance: *When the ball is near the hole, you <v.> putt.*

putt·er /'pʌtər/ *v.* to do s.t. casually, waste time: *He puttered around in his garage moving tools from one place to another.*

put·ty /'pʌti/ *n.* **-ties** [U] a soft building material that hardens after it dries: *A worker used putty to put a plate of glass into a window frame.*
—*v.* **-tied, -tying, -ties** to fasten with putty: *She puttied a new window pane in place.*

puz·zle /'pʌzəl/ *n.* **1** a game in which a picture on cardboard that has been cut into pieces is put back together, (*syn.*) a jigsaw puzzle **2** a mystery, s.t. not understood: *What happened to the sunken treasure ship is still a puzzle.* **3** any game that involves solving a problem: *a crossword puzzle.*
—*v.* **-zled, -zling, -zles 1** to confuse, not understand: *Where the sunken treasure is puzzles explorers.* **2** *phrasal v. insep.* **to puzzle over s.t.:** to think hard: *They puzzled over where the treasure ship may have sunk.*

Pyg·my /'pɪgmi/ *n.* **-mies** a member of several African, Asian and Philippine peoples shorter than 59 inches or 1.5 meters: *Many Pygmies live in rain forests near the equator.*

py·lon /'paɪ,lɑn/ *n.* a metal tower that supports electrical transmission wires: *Pylons stretch for miles bringing electricity to factories and homes.*

pyr·a·mid /'pɪrəmɪd/ *n.* **1** a huge building used as a burial tomb for royalty in Egypt as well as tombs and ceremonial sites in Mexico **2** anything with sides shaped as triangles and a base like a square: *The acrobats stood on each other's backs to form a human pyramid.*

pyre /paɪr/ *n.* wood or other materials used esp. to burn a dead body in a burial ceremony:

In India, a son lit the funeral pyre of his dead father.

Py·rex /'paɪˌrɛks/ *n.adj.TM* a type of glass that can stand heat in an oven: *She heated soup in a <adj.> Pyrex dish in the microwave oven.*

py·ro·ma·niac /ˌpaɪroʊ'meɪniˌæk/ *n.* a mentally ill person with a strong desire to set fires: *A pyromaniac set fire to his own house.* *-n.* [U] **pyromania** /ˌpaɪroʊ'meɪniə/.

py·ro·tech·nics /ˌpaɪrə'tɛknɪks/ *n.pl. used with a sing.* or *pl. v.* the manufacture and display of fireworks: *Every July 4, people in the USA watch a display of pyrotechnics to celebrate the country's independence.*

py·thon /'paɪˌθɑn, -θən/ *n.* a large snake that wraps itself around its victims and suffocates them: *The python coiled itself around a pig and swallowed it.*

P

Q, q

Q, q /kyu/ *n.* **Q's, q's,** or **Qs, qs** the 17th letter of the English alphabet *See:* know, **5, to know one's p's and q's.**

Q & A /'kyuən'eɪ/ *n.adj.abbr. of* Question and Answer: *The politician held a Q & A session for the voters.*

q.t. /'kyu'ti/ *n.abbr. of* quiet **1** secrecy **2 to do s.t. on the q.t.:** to do s.t. in secret: *We made the plans for our friend's surprise party on the q.t.*

Q-tip /'kyu,tɪp/ *n.TM* a little rod with a small amount of soft cotton wrapped around both ends: *A Q-tip can be used to clean inside your ear.*

Q-tip

quack (1) /kwæk/ *n.v.* the sound made by a duck: *<n.> "Quack, quack!" said the duck.*

quack (2) *n.* a fake doctor: *The quack told him that the medicine would make him live forever.*

quack·er·y /'kwækəri/ *n.* [U] fake or fraudulent medicine: *The use of peach juice to cure cancer is quackery.*

quad /kwɑd/ *n.short for* quadrangle: *Universities often arrange buildings in quads.*

quad·ran·gle /kwɑd,ræŋgəl/ *n.* **1** a flat figure with four straight sides and four corners: *A parallelogram is a type of quadrangle.* **2** buildings arranged in a quadrangle: *My apartment building is part of a quadrangle that surrounds a pretty garden.*

quad·rant /'kwɑdrənt/ *n.* a quarter of a circle: *A circle has four quadrants.*

quad·ren·ni·al /kwɑd'rɛniəl/ *n.adj.* an event that happens once every four years: *The election of a President for the United States is a <adj.> quadrennial event.* *-adv.* **quadrennially.**

quad·ri·lat·er·al /,kwɑdrə'lætərəl/ *adj.* having four straight sides —*n.* a flat figure with four sides and four corners: *A square is a quadrilateral.*

quad·ru·ped /'kwɑdrə,pɛd/ *n.* an animal with four feet: *Horses, dogs, and cats are quadrupeds.*

quad·ru·ple /kwɑ'drupəl/ *n.sing.adj.* s.t. that has been multiplied by four: *He charges <n.> quadruple for coats when it is cold.* ‖*He charged <adj.> quadruple the normal price.*

—*v.* **-pled, -pling, -ples** to multiply by four: *He quadruples the price of coats every January.*

quad·ru·plet /kwɑ'druplɪt/ *n.* **1** one of four babies born to the same parents at the same time: *It is unusual for humans to have quadruplets.* **2** a group of four

quaff /kwɑf/ *n.v.frml.* to drink with energy: *She <v.> quaffs cold water on hot days.*

quag·mire /'kwæg,maɪr, 'kwɑg-/ *n.* **1** a soft, muddy area of land that is difficult to travel across: *My feet are sinking into the quagmire.* **2** *fig.* a difficult situation: *There is a quagmire of paperwork when you move to a new country.*

quail /kweɪl/ *n.* [C;U] a small bird with black and brown feathers that often hides: *Quail is a popular bird to eat.* —*v.* to become very afraid: *He quailed at the thought of fighting in the war.*

quail

quaint /kweɪnt/ *adj.* **-er, -est 1** attractive, often because of being old: *What a quaint old house!* **2** strange, unusual in a pleasing way: *She has a quaint way of speaking.*

quake /kweɪk/ *n.* a sudden, violent movement of the ground, *(syn.)* an earthquake: *Our house was destroyed during the quake.* —*v.* **quaked, quaking, quakes** to shake violently, tremble: *He quaked with fear.*

qual·i·fi·ca·tion /'kwɑləfɪ'keɪʃən/ *n.* **1** [C] an ability or characteristic that makes one fit to do s.t.: (ability) *That mechanic has the qualifications to fix your car.* ‖ (characteristic) *One qualification for receiving a California driver's license is that you must live in California.* **2** [C;U] s.t. that limits: *I have no qualifications* *to judge your plan to start a business, but I know you'll succeed!.*

USAGE NOTE: In job interviews in the USA, applicants describe their *qualifications,* including education, work experience, and relevant hobbies and interests: *He said he'd studied journalism in college, worked at summer jobs at his hometown newspaper, and that his hobby was photography, so the interviewer was impressed with his qualifications.*

qual·i·fi·er /'kwɑlə,faɪər/ *n.* **1** s.o. or s.t. that is fit to do s.t.: *She is a qualifier for the final race because she won her first three races.* **2** s.t. that must be done, *(syn.)* a requirement: *The qualifier that the bank put in our loan agreement said that we must pay for one quarter of the cost of the house now.* **3** *(in grammar)* a word that limits or adds to the meaning of another: *Adjectives and adverbs are qualifiers.*

qual·i·fy /'kwɑlə,faɪ/ *v.* **-fied, -fying, -fies 1** to pass tests to show one's fitness for s.t.: *He qualified for the teaching job.* **2** to put a limit on s.t. that one has said: *She qualified her approval of our plan by saying that we need to use our own money for it.*

qual·i·ta·tive /'kwɑlə,teɪtɪv/ *adj.* having to do with opinions, feelings, or judgments that are not based on facts: *Deciding the value of a friendship is a qualitative judgment.* **-adv. qualitatively.**

qual·i·ty /'kwɑləti/ *n.* **-ties 1** [U] the overall nature or general character of s.t.: *This product is excellent: it is of the highest quality.* **2** [C] s.t. that is typical of s.o.'s character and personality, *(syns.)* a trait, characteristic: *His best qualities are kindness, hard work, and intelligence.*
—*adj.* excellent: *Her company makes a quality product.*

quality assurance or **quality control** *n.* [C;U] the testing by a company of its own products for possible problems: *Businesses use quality control to make sure that their products look good and work well.*

qualm /kwɑm, kwɔm/ *n.* **1** *frml.* a sudden feeling of sickness in one's stomach **2** *fig.* **to have qualms:** to have doubts or suspicions: *I have some qualms about this person (deal, trip, etc.); s.t. seems wrong.*

quan·da·ry /'kwɑndəri, -dri/ *n.* **-ries 1** an uncertain, awkward situation, *(syn.)* a dilemma **2 to be in a quandary:** to be perplexed, uncertain: *I am in a quandary about going on vacation because it would be fun, but also costly.*

quan·ti·fy /'kwɑntə,faɪ/ *v.* **- fied, -fying, -fies** to state how many there is or how many there are of s.t.: *He was asked to quantify the number of phone calls he receives each day.*

quan·ti·fi·er /'kwɑntə,faɪər/ *n.* a word or phrase that refers to the amount, or quantity, of

s.t.: *Words like "less," "some," and many" are quantifiers often used in English.*

quan·ti·ta·tive /'kwɑntɪ,teɪtɪv/ *adj.* able to be measured: *Scientists use quantitative measures to do experiments.* **-adv. quantitatively.**

quan·ti·ty /'kwɑntɪti/ *n.* **1** [C;U] a general amount, a supply: *She bought a quantity of apples (computers, dresses, etc.).* **2** [C] an exact amount: *100 was the quantity ordered.* **3** [C] a value in a mathematical problem: *"a" is a quantity in* $a + b = c.$ **4 in quantity:** in a large amount at a lower price, in bulk: *Our company buys in quantity; we order thousands of pencils at one time.*

quan·tum /'kwɑntəm/ *n.* **quanta** /'kwɑntə/ (in physics) the smallest unit or amount of energy: *A quantum of energy cannot be broken down into smaller parts.*

quantum leap *n.* a very great change or advance in s.t.: *Our company had a quantum leap in profits last year.*

quar·an·tine /'kwɔrən,tin, 'kwɑr-/ *v.* **-tined, -tining, -tines** to keep a person or animal away from everyone else because that person or animal has a dangerous disease: *That man has smallpox and will be quarantined.*
—*n.* [C;U] the state of being quarantined: *They placed the dog in quarantine.*

quark /kwɔrk, kwɑrk/ *n.* (in physics) one of several types of very tiny pieces of matter: *The existence of quarks has not yet been proved.*

quar·rel /'kwɔrəl, kwɑr-/ *v.* **-reled** or **-relled, -reling** or **-relling, -rels** to argue very angrily: *He quarrels with his mother when she tells him he can't go out at night.*
—*n.* **1** a very angry argument **2** a feeling that s.o. is wronging you, *(syn.)* a complaint: *She has a quarrel with her company; they are not paying her enough.*

quar·rel·some /'kwɔrəlsəm, 'kwɑr-/ *adj.* always ready to fight about s.t., *(syn.)* argumentative: *Quarrelsome people are difficult to work with.* **-n.** [U] **quarrelsomeness.**

quar·ry /'kwɔri, 'kwɑri/ *n.* **-ries 1** [U] s.t. that is hunted, *(syn.)* prey: *Hunters kill deer (bears, rabbits, etc.) as quarry.* **2** [C] an open mining pit: *He works in a stone quarry.*
—*v.* **-ried, -rying, -ries** to cut stone from a quarry: *The workers quarried stone.*

quart /kwɔrt/ *n.* in USA, a liquid measure equal to 32 ounces or two pints: *I bought a quart of milk. See:* gallon, **USAGE NOTE.**

quar·ter /'kwɔrtər/ *n.* **1** one fourth of s.t.: *I need a quarter of a pound of butter.* **2** fifteen minutes: *It is quarter to five (o'clock).* **3** a U.S. or Canadian coin worth 25 cents, or a quarter of a dollar: *The pencil costs a quarter.* **4** a three- months period or a quarter of a year: *Many businesses report how much money they make each quarter.* **5** an area, esp. in a city:

Q

He lives in the old quarter of the city. **6** *pl.* **quarters** housing, esp. for the military: *She lives in the officers' quarters.* **7 close quarters:** without much space: *We live in close quarters on a small boat.*

—*v.* to cut s.t. in quarters: *He quartered the pie.*

quar·ter·back /'kwɔrtər,bæk/ *n.v.* **1** in USA and Canada, the football player who tells the others what to do and starts the team's action **2** *fig.* a leader, a person who directs the activities of others: *Our boss <v.> quarterbacks our sales effort himself.*

quar·ter·deck /'kwɔrtər,dɛk/ *n.* the deck on the top part of the back of a boat: *The captain is standing on the quarterdeck.*

quar·ter·fi·nal /'kwɔrtər,faɪnəl/ *n.adj.* one of four games in a sports competition: *The four winners of the quarterfinals at the U.S. Open play each other in two semifinal games; the two winners of these then play one final game.*

quarter hour *n.* 15 minutes: *That trip takes a quarter hour. See:* quarter, *n.,* **2.**

quar·ter·ly /'kwɔrtərli/*adv.adj.* during or at the end of a three-month period: *Many businesses report <adv.> quarterly on how much money they have made.* -*n.pl.* **quarterlies.**

quar·ter·mas·ter /'kwɔrtər,mæstər/ *n.* an army officer in charge of military supplies: *A quartermaster issues clothing, weapons, etc.*

quartz /kwɔrts/ *n.* [U] a hard, light-colored mineral or rock found worldwide, esp. in granite or sandstone: *Quartz looks pretty in the sunlight.*

quash /kwaʃ/ *v.* **quashes 1** to stop firmly, *(syn.)* to crush: *to quash a rumor (uprising, riot, etc.)* **2** (in law) to reject as not valid, *(syn.)* to nullify: *The judge quashed the accusation of murder because there was nothing to prove that Mr. Smith had killed Mr. Kim..*

quasi- /'kwazi/ *prefix* almost: *This is only a quasi-official report from the government; the official report comes next week.*

quat·rain /'kwɑ,treɪn/ *n.* (in poetry) a type of stanza (section of a poem) that has four lines: *That poem is written in quatrains.*

qua·ver /'kweɪvər/ *n.v.* to tremble: *His voice <v.> quavered with emotion when he spoke of his father's death.* -*adj.* **quavery.**

quay /ki, keɪ/ *n.* a place to unload and get off of ships, *(syn.)* a wharf: *Ships unload boxes on the quay.*

quea·sy /'kwizi/ *adj.* -**sier,** -**siest 1** feeling sick, *(syn.)* nauseated: *My stomach feels queasy.* **2** *fig.* uneasy, anxious: *She felt queasy as she waited to dive off of the cliff.* -*adv.* **queasily** -*n.* [U] **queasiness.**

queen /kwin/ *n.* **1** a female ruler or the wife of a king: *The queen sat on her throne.* **2** *fig.* a woman who is outstanding in a certain area

(singing, writing, etc.) or is the center of attention: *She is the queen of the art world.* **3** a playing card with a picture of a queen **4** an important piece in chess **5** *pej.* a homosexual man -*adv.* **queenly** -*n.* [U] **queenship.**

queen mother *n.* the mother of a currently ruling king or queen: *The queen mother of England is kind and generous.*

queen-size or **queen-sized** *adj.* having to do with a bed that is 60 inches wide by 80 inches long: *A queen-sized bed is bigger than a single bed, but smaller than a king-sized bed.*

queer /kwɪr/ *adj.* -**er,** -**est** different than normal, very strange: *He has been feeling queer lately; maybe he's sick.*

—*n.adj.pej.* a homosexual -*adv.* **queerly** -*n.* [U] **queerness.** *See:* gay, USAGE NOTE.

quell /kwɛl/ *v.frml.* to bring under control, quiet down: *The police quelled the riot.*

quench /kwɛnʧ/ *v.* -**es 1** to satisfy a strong thirst: *He quenched his thirst with water.* **2** to put out, *(syn.)* to extinguish: *The firefighters quenched the fire.* -*adj.* **quenchable.**

quer·u·lous /'kwɛrələs, 'kwɛryə-/ *adj.frml.* finding s.t. wrong with everything, *(syn.)* irritable: *Nothing pleased her; her querulous demands never stopped.* -*n.* [U] **querulousness.**

que·ry /'kwɪri/ *n.* -**ries** a question: *I have a query regarding your business plan for next year.*

—*v.* -**ried,** -**rying,** -**ries** to question s.t., esp. if you are not sure if it is correct: *He queried a customer about an unpaid bill.*

quest /kwɛst/ *n.v.frml.* a search for s.t., esp. over a long time period, *(syn.)* a crusade: *Scientists quest for the truth.*

ques·tion /'kwɛsʧən/ *v.* **1** to look for an answer to s.t. unknown or in doubt: *She questioned the teacher about a difficult problem.* **2** to try to get information from s.o., *(syn.)* to interrogate: *The police questioned the prisoner.* **3** to wonder if s.t. is just, good, or legal: *Some people question the legality of that government.*

—*n.* the act of seeking an answer: *I would like to ask you a question.* -*n.* **questioner.** *See:* ask, USAGE NOTE.

ques·tion·a·ble /'kwɛsʧənəbəl/ *adj.* **1** doubtful, uncertain: *It is questionable whether this report is true.* **2** odd, *(syn.)* suspicious: *He goes on many questionable trips in the middle of the night.* -*adv.* **questionably** -*n.* [U] **questionability** /,kwɛsʧənə'bɪləti/.

question mark *n.* **1** the symbol (?), showing that s.t. is a question: *What do you think?* **2** a mystery: *Why the money is missing is a question mark.*

ques·tion·naire /,kwɛsʧə'nɛr/ *n.* a list of questions related to a specific subject: *He answered a questionnaire about his health.*

queue /kyu/ *n.Brit.* a line: *There is a queue of*

people waiting to enter the theater.
—*v.* **queued, queuing, queues** to form a line: *We queued up and waited for the bank to open.*

USAGE NOTE: *Queue* is not used in American English. Instead, people use line. *"I waited in line for the bank to open."*

---

quib·ble /'kwɪbəl/ *n.v.* **-bled, -bling, -bles** to argue over small details, usu. avoiding the main point: *The buyer accepted the contract, but he had a <n.> quibble with me over the price of one item. -n.* **quibbler.**

quiche /kiʃ/ *n.* a pie made with eggs, cream, and cheese with no top crust: *We had some mushroom quiche for lunch.*

quick /kwɪk/ *adj.* **-er, -est 1** instant, *(syn.)* rapid: *He made a quick response to my call.* **2** short, *(syn.)* brief: *This is a quick meeting that will be over in ten minutes.* **3** able to understand ideas right away, intelligent: *She has a quick mind. -adv.* **quickly** *-n.* [U] **quickness.**

quick-and-dirty *adj.infrml.* fast and cheap, related to s.t. produced or done with haste and without concern for quality: *The workers boarded up the windows in a quick-and-dirty way to keep out thieves.*

quick assets *n.* cash, or things that can be sold quickly to get cash: *She needs money quickly; I hope she has some quick assets.*

quick·en /'kwɪkən/ *v.* to speed up: *As she watched the race, her heartbeat quickened.*

quick fix *n.infrml.* a quick, temporary repair to a problem: *He put some tape over the hole in the screen as a quick fix to keep the bugs out.*

quick·ie /'kwɪki/ *n.infrml.* s.t. done in a hurry: *She only had time to eat an apple for lunch; it was just a quickie.*

quick-freeze *v.* **-froze -frozen** /frouz frouzən/, to freeze food quickly to keep its freshness: *I am going to quick-freeze the fresh carrots. -adj. & past part.* **quick-frozen.**

quick·sand /'kwɪk,sænd/ *n.* **1** [C;U] soft, watery sand found in wet, muddy areas (swamps or bogs) in which people and animals can sink: *Struggling in quicksand makes you sink faster.* **2** [U] *fig.* a dangerous situation

quick·sil·ver /'kwɪk,sɪlvər/ *n.* [U] **1** mercury, a silvery metal that is liquid at room temperature **2** *fig.* s.t. that is undependable, like mercury's changeable nature: *Her plans are quicksilver; they are always changing.*

quick-tempered *adj.* quick to become angry, *(syn.)* irritable: *No one can give him any suggestions because he is so quick-tempered.*

quick time *n.* [U] a fast pace (from a quick drumbeat in military marches): *We are in a hurry; we need to work (walk, march, perform) in quick time.*

quick-witted *adj.* quick to understand, *(syn.)* alert: *The driver's quick-witted response saved us from having a car accident. -adv.*

quick-wittedly.

quid /kwɪd/ *n.infrml.Brit.* [C;U] a British pound sterling, the basic unit of British money: *This meal cost five quid.*

quid pro quo /'kwɪdprou'kwou/ *n.frml.* payment in some form other than money for goods or services: *The doctor fixed the farmer's broken leg, and later the farmer brought corn and potatoes to the doctor, as a quid pro quo.*

qui·es·cent /kwi'ɛsənt, kwaɪ-/ *adj.frml.* still, inactive: *There was no wind; all the trees and bushes lay quiescent under the winter snow. -n.* [U] **quiescence** *-adv.* **quiescently.**

qui·et /'kwaɪɪt/ *adj.* **-er, -est 1** without noise, silent: *The house was quiet because everyone was asleep.* **2** calm, peaceful. *(syn.)* serene: *I spent a quiet evening at home.* **3** inactive, slow: *Business is quiet now.*
—*n.* **1** the condition of being quiet: *We could hear the birds in the quiet of evening.* **2 peace and quiet:** silence, *(syn.)* calmness: *I like the peace and quiet in the old forest. -n.* [U] **quietude** /'kwaɪə,tud/.
—*v.* **1** to silence, *(syn.)* to hush: *He quieted the noisy crowd.* **2** to calm: *She quieted the child's fears.*

qui·et·ly /'kwaɪɪtli/*adv.* **to go quietly:** without noise or a fight: *The police caught the thief, and he agreed to go quietly to jail.*

quill /kwɪl/ *n.* **1** a large bird feather **2** a pen made from a bird feather: *People used to write with a quill* (or) *a quill pen.* **3** a sharp spine or spike: *The quills of a porcupine protect it.*

quilt /kwɪlt/ *n.* a bed covering made of pieces of material sewn together and filled with cotton, feathers, etc.: *Quilts are often sewn together to make patterns, such as stars or squares.*
—*v.* to make a quilt: *My grandmother likes to quilt. -n.* [U] **quilting.**

quilt

qui·nine /'kwaɪ,naɪn/ *n.* [U] a colorless, bitter powder: *Quinine can be used in medicines, esp. as a treatment for malaria.*

quin·tes·sence /kwɪn'tɛsəns/ *n.* the perfect example of s.t., the purest concentration or essence of s.t.: *That painting is the quintessence of beauty. -adj.* **quintessential** /,kwɪntə'sɛnʃəl/.

quin·tet /kwɪn'tɛt/ *n.* **1** a group of five singers or musicians **2** a musical piece written for five voices or instruments: *We heard a lovely quintet at the concert last night.*

quin·tu·ple /kwɪn'tʌpəl/ *v.adj.* **-pled, -pling, -ples** to multiply by five: *She <v.> quintupled her money in one year; she had $10,000 last year, and now she has $50,000!*

quin·tu·plet /kwɪn'tʌplɪt/ *n.* **1** one of five

Q

children born at the same time to the same parents: *Quintuplets are rare.* **2** a group of five

quip /kwɪp/ *n.* a short, funny remark: *He made a quip about the Queen's funny-looking hat.*
—*v.* **quipped, quipping, quips** to make a short, funny remark

quirk /kwɜrk/ *n.* **1** an unusual habit, *(syn.)* a peculiarity: *He always wears a hat indoors; it's a quirk of his.* **2** a sharp, sudden turn: *Be careful; there's a quirk in the road.* *-adj.* **quirky.**

quis·ling /'kwɪzlɪŋ/ *n.* s.o. who helps an enemy take over his or her own country, *(syn.)* a traitor: *The quisling told the enemy which parts of her country would be the easiest to capture.*

quit /kwɪt/ *v.* **quit, quitting, quits** **1** to leave, esp. a job: *He quit his job because he wasn't being paid enough.* **2** to stop doing s.t., *(syn.)* to cease: *She quit working for the day.* **3** to give up an activity, *(syn.)* abandon: *He quit smoking.*‖*She quit dancing when she broke her leg. See:* **quits.**

USAGE NOTE: When you *quit* a job, you leave it voluntarily; if your employer *lays you off* or *fires* you, he or she tells you that you must leave: *He told me he'd quit his job, but I think the company fired him.* It is usual to give notice or officially inform your employer that you plan to leave: *I gave my boss two weeks' notice today, because I want to move to California.* We use *resign* and *step down* when we speak of leaving a position formally: *The senator has resigned as head of the finance committee; he will step down at the end of this year.*

quite /kwaɪt/ *adv.* **1** completely, totally: *He is not quite done with his report.* **2** very, *(syn.)* extremely: *The weather is quite cold.* **3** really, *(syn.)* genuinely: *She is quite a scholar.*

quits /kwɪts/ *adj.* **1** to neither owe nor be owed (money, a favor, harm, etc.): *Here is the $100 I owed you, so now we are quits.* **2 to call it quits:** to stop doing s.t., to say s.t. is finished, over: *We've done enough work for today, so let's call it quits.*

quit·ter /'kwɪtər/ *n.* a person who stops doing s.t. as soon as it becomes difficult: *Quitters never finish what they start.*

quiv·er (1) /'kwɪvər/ *v.* to shake, *(syn.)* to tremble: *He quivered with fear.*‖*The dog was quivering in the cold.*
—*n.* the act or condition of quivering: *A quiver of fear ran through her.*

quiv·er (2) *n.* a holder for arrows: *Hunters keep the arrows for their bow in their quiver.*

quix·ot·ic /kwɪk'sɑtɪk/ *adj.frml.* too good and kind to be practical: *Bringing every homeless child in the city into your house is a quixotic act. -adv.* **quixotically.**

quiz /kwɪz/ *n.* **quizzes** a brief test, esp. on a single subject: *The teacher gave a math quiz to*

his students. *See:* test, USAGE NOTE.
—*v.* **quizzed, quizzing, quizzes** **1** to give a short test, such as those given by a teacher **2** to question s.o.: *Her mother quizzed her about where she was last night.*

quiz show *n.* a game played on television in which players win prizes for correctly answering questions: *He wants to be a contestant on that quiz show.*

quiz·zi·cal /'kwɪzɪkəl/ *adj.* confused, *(syn.)* puzzled: *She had a quizzical look on her face because she didn't understand the question. -adv.* **quizzically.**

quo·rum /'kwɔrəm/ *n.* the presence of enough members of a group to allow them to legally do business: *The Senate now has a quorum of its members present, so the vote can be taken.*

quo·ta /'kwoʊtə/ *n.* **1** an amount of s.t. that is required **2** (in business) a set amount or percentage that must be produced or sold in a certain period of time: *A salesperson must meet his or her monthly sales quota.* **2** a set amount of s.t., *(syn.)* an allotment: *That student receives a yearly quota of money from the government.* **3** a limit, a maximum amount: *The government put a quota on the number of foreign cars allowed to be sold in the USA.*

quo·ta·tion /kwoʊ'teɪʃən/ *n.* **1** [C] a small part quoted from s.t. longer (a book, play, speech, etc.): *She put a quotation from a novel in her speech.* **2** [C;U] a statement of prices for goods or services: *They called the store to get a quotation on the price of a new couch. -adj.* **quotable** /'kwoʊtəbəl/.

quotation marks *n.pl.* the symbols used to show that s.t. is quoted from another person's written or spoken words, shown as (" "): *"To be or not to be" is a line by Shakespeare that we often put quotation marks around.*

quote /kwoʊt/ *v.* **quoted, quoting, quotes** **1** to repeat s.t. that another has said or written: *In her speech, the mayor quoted a famous writer.* **2** to state the price of s.t.: *Before you fix my car, will you quote a price on the repairs for me?* **3** *infrml.* **quote . . . unquote:** to show, usu. while speaking, that one is using quotation marks to repeat s.o.'s words: *The mayor said, and I quote, "I won't raise taxes," unquote.*‖*The mayor said, quote unquote, "I won't raise taxes."*
—*n.infrml.* **1** a quotation: *That was a quote from the mayor's speech.* **2** a statement of a price: *She asked for a quote on the price of a gold ring.*

quo·ti·di·an /kwoʊ'tɪdiən/ *adj.frml.* s.t. that must be done every day, daily: *Feeding the dog is a quotidian chore.*

quo·tient /'kwoʊʃənt/ *n.* **1** the answer to a division problem: *When six is divided by three, the quotient is two.* **2** a set amount, a share: *You need your daily quotient of vitamins.*

R,r

R, r /ɑr/ *n.* **R's, r's** or **Rs, rs** **1** the 18th letter of the English alphabet: *Many Spanish speakers roll their R's.* **2 the three R's:** *short for* the three basic educational skills of reading, (w)riting, and (a)rithmetic: *School children must learn the three R's.* **3 R & R:** *infrml.short for* Rest and Relaxation, a vacation: *I worked hard all winter, and now it is time for two weeks of R & R in the country.*

rab·bi /ˈræbaɪ/ *n.* **1** a teacher: *The students who are studying Hebrew call their teacher rabbi.* **2** a spiritual leader and teacher of Jewish religion and law: *The rabbi leads the faithful in prayer in the synagogue. -adj.* **rabbinical** /rəˈbɪnəkəl/; *-n.* **rabbinate** / ˈræbənɪt, -neɪt/.

rab·bit /ˈræbɪt/ *n.* a small animal with long ears, a small fuzzy tail, and soft white, gray, or brown fur: *Rabbits are good jumpers and can run very quickly.*

rabbit

rab·ble /ˈræbəl/ *n.v.* **-bled, -bling, -bles** a crowd that is difficult to control, a mob: *A <n.> rabble gathered before the governor's mansion and shouted for food.*

rab·ble-rous·er /ˈræbəlˌraʊzər/ *n.* a person who excites a mob to protest and violence: *Rabble-rousers made angry speeches and got the mob to rush the gates of the state capitol.*

rab·id /ˈræbɪd/ *adj.* **1** having rabies: *Rabid animals are dangerous because they could bite other animals or people and make them sick.* **2** crazy, violent: *a rabid mob*

ra·bies /ˈreɪbiz/ *n.pl. used with a sing.v.* deadly disease that affects the brain and nervous system, usually passed on by animal bites: *If you think you've been bitten by an animal with rabies, it's important to get a tetanus shot.*

rac·coon /ræˈkun/ *n.* an animal with a gray furry body, a ringed fuzzy tail, and dark rings around its eyes: *It looks like the raccoon is wearing a mask over it's eyes.*

raccoon

race (1) /reɪs/ *n.* a contest to test who can go the fastest, such as in foot, auto, and sailing races, (*syn.*) a competition: *At a track meet, various races are run, such as the 100-meter and 1000-meter races.*

—v. **raced, racing, races** **1** to compete by going faster than s.o. else: *Bicycle riders race each year in Europe for big prizes.* **2** to go quickly: *It started to rain and we raced for cover inside.* **3 to race against the clock:** to try to do something faster each time it is tried or attempted: *The swimmer is racing against the clock to try to beat her best time.* **4 to race against time:** to try to finish an action before a certain time: *We are racing against time to get a surprise party ready for our mother by the time she gets home from work.* **5** *phrasal v. insep* **to race around:** to hurry to do many things at once: *Steve races around the house every morning getting ready for work so that he won't be late. See:* rat race.

race (2) *n.* **1** any of the groupings of human beings according to genes, blood types, color of skin, eyes, hair, etc.: *New York has many races among its population.* **2** people in general: *the human race*

race·horse /ˈreɪsˌhɔrs/ *n.* a horse used in races: *Racehorses are kept in stables at various racetracks.*

rac·er /ˈreɪsər/ *n.* an auto, boat, or animal (usu. a horse or dog) used in racing: *He loves boats and owns a racer with a powerful motor.*

race·track /ˈreɪsˌtræk/ *n.* a race course and the area around it used for racing between runners, cars, horses, dogs, etc.: *Joe's sister loves to go to the racetrack and bet on the horses.*

R

race·way /'reɪs,weɪ/ n. a racetrack: *We went to the stock car raceway on Saturday night.*

ra·cial /'reɪʃəl/ adj. related to race: *There are many different racial groups represented (white, Asian, etc.) in my neighborhood.*

rac·ing /'reɪsɪŋ/ n. the sport of competing in races: *Horse racing is called the "sport of kings."*

ra·cism /'reɪ,sɪzəm/ n. [U] prejudice or unfairness against people of a one race by those of another: *A black politician accused the white mayor of racism because of unfair hiring practices.*

rac·ist /'reɪsɪst/ n.adj. a person who believes that his or her race is better than other races: *A white person who believes that white people are better than black people is a <n.> racist.*

rack /ræk/ n. 1 a type of shelf: *Our library has racks of books.* 2 a torture instrument used long ago on which the human body was stretched to cause great pain
—v. 1 *phrasal v. infrml.fig.* **to rack one's brains:** to think very hard to remember s.t.: *I racked my brains but could not remember that man's name.* 2 *phrasal v. sep.* **to rack s.t. up:** to accumulate, gather lots of s.t.: *Our team racked up 20 points and beat the other team.||We racked them up.* 3 *phrasal v. insep.* **to rack s.t. with pain:** to feel great pain: *Cancer racked her body with pain.*

rack·et /'rækɪt/ n. 1 [C] a type of paddle used in sports: *I have two tennis rackets.* 2 [U] a noise, loud disturbance: *Construction workers are making a racket on the street with their machinery.* 3 [C] a business that takes advantage of people, esp. illegal gambling, extortion, prostitution, etc.: *The mafia runs the rackets in big cities.*

rack·et·eer /,rækə'tɪr/ n. a criminal who does illegal business in the rackets, such as illegal gambling, prostitution, etc.: *The police caught the racketeer and took him to jail.*

rac·y /'reɪsi/ adj. -ier, -iest related to sex and adventure: *She writes racy novels about rich men and beautiful women.*

ra·dar /'reɪ,dɑr/ n. [U] a system or device that sends radio waves to an object, which bounces them back to the device; this gives information about the object's location, speed, size, etc.: *Major airports use radar to control air traffic.*

ra·di·al /'reɪdiəl/ adj. having a pattern in which lines, rays, or spokes move outward from a central point: *A grapefruit has a radial pattern.*
—n. a radial tire: *I bought a new set of radials for my car.*

ra·di·ance /'reɪdiəns/ n. [U] 1 energy or heat: *The radiance of the sun is extremely hot.* 2 a bright shine, glow: *A full moon seems to shine with a white radiance.*

ra·di·ant /'reɪdiənt/ adj. 1 sending out energy or heat: *The sun sends out radiant energy.* 2 having a bright shine, glow: *The faces of the bride and groom were radiant at their wedding.*

ra·di·ate /'reɪdi,eɪt/ v. -ated, -ating, -ates to send s.t. out in every direction, such as light, heat, happiness, etc., (syn.) to emit: *The sun radiates light and heat.*

ra·di·a·tion /,reɪdi'eɪʃən/ n. [U] sending out waves (of light, heat, etc.), (syn.) emission: *Nuclear radiation can be very harmful.*

ra·di·a·tor /'reɪdi,eɪtər/ n. 1 a set of metal pipes with hot steam running through them, used to heat rooms and hallways: *My radiator warms my room in winter.* 2 part of the cooling system of an engine: *The radiator in my car boiled over last night.*

rad·i·cal /'rædəkəl/ n. a person with very strong nontraditional beliefs, esp. s.o. who wants change in politics or religion: *Radicals won several seats in Parliament this year.*
—adj. 1 having very strong nontraditional beliefs, ideas: *Radical students protested the President's visit to their college campus.* 2 very unusual, different from what is normal: *We noticed a radical difference in our son's behavior after he finished college and got a job.* -adv. **radically.**

ra·di·o /'reɪdiou/ n. an electronic device that gives out sound (voices, music): *She listens to the news on the radio each morning.*
—v. to communicate by radio: *A ship radioed to shore about its arrival time.*

ra·di·o·ac·tive /,reɪdiou'æktɪv/ adj. containing or giving off nuclear radiation: *Uranium is a radioactive element.* -n. **radioactivity.**

radio broadcast n. a program sent out to radio listeners: *A radio broadcast of the President's speech was heard throughout the nation.* -n. [U] **radio broadcasting.**

ra·di·o·cast /'reɪdiou,kæst/ v.n. to send by radio: *The President's speech was <v.> radiocast nationally.*

radio frequency n. -cies the AM or FM frequency used by a particular radio transmitter: *There are many newscasts on the AM radio frequencies.*

ra·di·ol·o·gy /,reɪdi'ɑlədʒi/ n. [U] the study of medicine that uses X-rays to analyze and treat illnesses: *She studied radiology at medical school.* -adj. **radiological** /,reɪdiə'lɑdʒəkəl/; -n. **radiologist.**

ra·di·o·tel·e·phone /'reɪdiou'tɛlə,foun/ n. a telephone whose messages are transmitted by radio: *Our ship has a radiotelephone to communicate with shore.*

ra·di·o·tel·e·scope /'reɪdiou'tɛlə,skoup/ n. [U] a dish-shaped antenna used to pick up weak radio wave signals from distant stars

ra·di·o·ther·a·py /ˌreɪdiouˈθɛrəpi/ *n.* [U] medical treatment with X-rays or other radiation, such as for cancer: *She is having radiotherapy for breast cancer.*

rad·ish /ˈrædɪʃ/ *n.* **-es** a small, hot-tasting, usu. round root, usu. red on the outside and white on the inside, eaten raw and in salads: *The reddish outside and white inside of radishes add color and taste to salads.*

ra·di·um /ˈreɪdiəm/ *n.* [U] a basic atomic element that is metallic and radioactive: *Radium is used in cancer treatments.*

ra·di·us /ˈreɪdiəs/ *n.* **-i** or **-uses** a measurement or line between the center and edge of a circle: *In geometry class, we learned how to measure the radius of a circle.*

ra·don /ˈreɪdɑn/ *n.* [U] a basic atomic element; it arises naturally from the ground as a gas and is believed to cause cancer in people: *Machines can discover radon in homes and help remove it.*

raf·fle /ˈræfəl/ *n.v.* **-fled, -fling, -fles** a game of chance in which people buy numbered tickets; a winning ticket is chosen randomly and the owner of that ticket wins a prize, *(syn.)* a lottery: *Our church held a <n.> raffle to raise money.‖They <v.> raffled off cakes and pies.*

raft /ræft/ *n.v.* a type of flat boat: *We floated in a <n.> raft down a river.‖We <v.> rafted for a week to see the scenery.*

raft·er /ˈræftər/ *n.* a piece of wood or metal used to hold up a roof: *Flat pieces of wood are nailed to rafters to make a roof.*

rag /ræg/ *n.* an old piece of cloth: *I use a rag to dust the wooden furniture.*
—*v.infrml.fig.* **ragged, ragging, rags** to kid, tease s.o.: *My friend ragged me about flunking an exam.*

rag·a·muf·fin /ˈrægəˌmʌfɪn/ *n.pej.* a dirty child wearing rags, *(syn.)* waif: *Ragamuffins begged for coins from tourists.*

rag doll *n.* a child's doll made of rags sewn together: *Her favorite toy is a rag doll with eyes made from buttons.*

rage /reɪdʒ/ *n.v.* **raged, raging, rages** [C;U] uncontrolled anger, *(syn.)* fury: *When he did not get what he wanted, he went into a <n.> rage.‖The hurricane <v.> raged for a full day.* *-adj.* **raging.**

rag·ged /ˈrægɪd/ *adj.* having a worn, uneven edge, *(syns.)* shabby, tattered: *His clothes are torn and ragged from living in the woods. -adj.* **raggedy.**

rag·out /ræˈgu/ *n.* [U] a spicy stew of meat and vegetables: *We had beef ragout for dinner.*

rag·tag /ˈrægˌtæg/ *adj.* wearing dirty or torn clothing, ragged, tattered: *Ragtag soldiers in dirty uniforms surrendered to the enemy soldiers.*

rag·time /ˈrægˌtaɪm/ *n.* [U] *adj.* a type of American jazz: *Scott Joplin made <n.> ragtime popular in 1893 and wrote <adj.> ragtime piano pieces.*

rag·weed /ˈrægˌwid/ *n.* [U] a plant, common in N. America, whose pollen causes watery eyes and sneezing in some people: *When ragweed makes people sneeze, we say those people have hay fever.*

rah-rah /ˈrɑˈrɑ/ *exclam. short for* hurrah, hurray, a loud sound of approval or general enthusiasm: *The audience at the football game cheered its team by chanting, "Rah-rah! Rah-rah!"*

raid /reɪd/ *n.* a sudden attack, such as one made by police on criminals: *Police conducted a raid on a drug dealer's house.*
—*v.* to attack s.o. suddenly: *Soldiers raided the enemy headquarters. -n.* **raider.**

rail /reɪl/ *n.* **1** a long, I-shaped piece of metal that trains run on: *Rails are made of welded steel for a smooth train ride.* **2** a bar beside stairs to help people go up and down safely, *(syn.)* a banister: *I hold on to the rail when I go down steep stairs.* **3** a long wooden crosspiece on a fence: *That fence for the horses is made of rails split from trees.* **4** related to trains: *My aunt prefers traveling by rail to traveling by air.*
—*v.* to attack with words, shout against with anger: *Radicals railed against the government.*

rail·ing /ˈreɪlɪŋ/ *n.* **1** a bar used as support beside stairs: *My elderly uncle holds onto the railing as he goes downstairs.* **2** a fence made of rails

rail·road /ˈreɪlˌroʊd/ *n.* **1** transportation for goods and passengers in trains on rails: *I prefer to ride the railroad to work.* **2** the system of rails, land they run on, and stations that trains use to stop at: *Children should be taught not to play on the railroad.*
—*v.* **1** to work for a railroad: *My father railroaded for 40 years.* **2** to punish s.o. unfairly for a crime that he or she did not commit **3** to hurry s.t. along so it is not closely examined: *Politicians railroaded a new tax bill through the legislature so fast that opponents had no time to stop it.*

rail·way /ˈreɪlˌweɪ/ *n.* a railroad

rai·ment /ˈreɪmənt/ *n.frml.* [U] clothes, costume: *The queen is dressed in beautiful raiment.*

rain /reɪn/ *n.* [U] **1** drops of water falling from clouds: *Rain fell on the city last night.* **2** *pl.* **the rains:** a rainy season, such as a monsoon season: *The rains come to northern California from November through May.* **3** *fig.* **right as rain:** in very good health: *My daughter felt sick this morning, but now she is right as rain.*
—*v.* **1** to fall from the sky as drops of water: *It rains in northern California 6 or 7 months of*

the year. **2** *phrasal v. sep.* **to rain s.t. out:** to stop or cancel an outdoor event because of rain: *The baseball game was rained out.* **3 to rain cats and dogs:** to rain very hard and fast: *Last night it rained cats and dogs, so I stayed inside to keep dry.* **4** *phrasal v. insep.* **to rain down on s.o. or s.t.:** to fall in a violent stream: *Criticism rains down on those who break the law.* **5 When it rains, it pours;** things tend to happen all at once: *I lost my job, my car needs a new engine, and the dog is sick. When it rains, it pours!*

rain·bow /ˈreɪnˌboʊ/ *n.* a curve (arc) of bright colors that sometimes forms in the sky after a rainstorm: *A rainbow with its red, blue, and yellow colors is a pretty sight.*

rain check *n.* **1** a replacement ticket for a sports or entertainment event that has been canceled because of rain: *The box office gave us all rain checks for tomorrow because the tennis match was postponed due to rain.* **2 to take a rain check:** to get a ticket, coupon, or invitation for another time: *When it started to rain at the baseball game, the ticket office asked us if we wanted to take a rain check for another game later on.*

USAGE NOTE: People also use the phrase, *take a raincheck* when they want to accept an invitation, but cannot. Saying *"I'll take a raincheck"* shows that you would like to be invited again later: *I'm sorry, I can't go to the movies with you today, but I'll take a raincheck.*

---

rain·coat /ˈreɪnˌkoʊt/ *n.* a coat resistant to rain: *I wear a raincoat when it rains.*

rain·drop /ˈreɪnˌdrɑp/ *n.* a drop of water from a cloud: *Raindrops fell on my window.*

rain·fall /ˈreɪnˌfɔl/ *n.* [C] **1** the rain that falls during a rainstorm: *Last night's rainfall should help the flowers to grow.* **2** [U] the measurement of the amount of rain that falls during a specified time: *The annual rainfall in the desert is only two inches.*

rain forest *n.* [C;U] a forest with a daily rainfall and very thick growth of trees and other plants: *Plants grow quickly in a rain forest.*

rain·mak·er /ˈreɪnˌmeɪkər/ *n.* **1** a person who is believed to be able to make rain fall during a dry period: *A rainmaker did a dance and it rained the next day.* **2** a business person who brings a lot of business to his or her company: *That lawyer is a rainmaker who brings many important clients to her firm every year. -n.* [U] **rainmaking.**

rain·storm /ˈreɪnˌstɔrm/ *n.* rain with strong winds: *We had a rainstorm that lasted an hour, and then the sky cleared.*

rain·wa·ter /ˈreɪnˌwɔtər, -ˌwɑt-/ *n.* [U] water that falls or has fallen as rain: *Rainwater formed puddles in the road.*

rain·y /ˈreɪni/ *adj.* **-ier, -iest** full of rain: *We have rainy weather this week.*

rainy day *n.fig.* a time of illness or other trouble: *The couple had saved money for a rainy day and were able to pay their lawyers' bills.*

raise /reɪz/ *v.* **raised, raising, raises** **1** to lift up, *(syn.)* to elevate: *A policeman raised his hand to stop traffic.* **2** to ask people for money: *Our church raises money to help the poor.* **3** to help a child to grow up: *My parents raised two sons.* **4** to give s.o. a higher salary: *My boss raised my salary by 5%.* **5** to grow plants or farm animals: *That farmer raises corn and cows.* **6** to bring up, suggest in conversation: *I raised a question at our meeting.* **7** *infrml.* **to raise Cain or hell or the roof:** to complain or criticize loudly: *When he was late for work again, his boss raised the roof.* **8 to raise one's voice:** to speak louder than usual: *If my father raises his voice, I know I am in trouble. See:* rear **(2)1.**

—*n.* an increase in salary: *My company gave me a raise last week.*

—*adj.* brought up as, reared as: *She was raised a Catholic, but became a Buddhist at age twenty-five.*

rai·sin /ˈreɪzən/ *n.* a dried grape: *He puts raisins on his cereal for breakfast.*

ra·jah /ˈrɑdʒə/ *n.* a Malay or Indian prince or ruler: *The rajah lives in a beautiful palace.*

rake /reɪk/ *n.* **1** a tool with metal or wooden teeth and a long handle, often used for collecting fallen leaves, small stones, etc.: *I used a rake to gather leaves from the lawn.* **2** *old usage* a man who drinks too much, is sexually immoral, and often cheats others

—*v.* **raked, raking, rakes** **1** to use a rake: *I raked up leaves fallen on the sidewalk.* **2** *phrasal v. sep.* **to rake s.t. in:** to earn a lot of money: *He rakes in a big salary on the cars that he sells.||He rakes it in.* **3** *phrasal v. sep.* **to rake s.t. up (about s.o.):** to search for and write in newspapers or say on TV bad things about s.o.: *The press raked up an old scandal about the new candidate for mayor.||They raked it up. See:* muckraker.

rak·ish /ˈreɪkɪʃ/ *adj.* **1** bold in style or action, *(syn.)* daring **2** very stylish, often in a sporty way. *-adv.* **rakishly;** *-n.* [U] **rakishness.**

ral·ly /ˈræli/ *n.* **-lies** a meeting of people to excite them about an idea, product, or sports event: *The football coach called a rally to build up the team's excitement for the next game.*

—*v.* **-lied, -lying, -lies** **1** to build excitement for s.t.: *The manager rallied her salespeople by giving them a powerful speech.* **2** to gain new strength, recover: *Doctors were afraid the* *child wouldn't live, but he rallied and lived.* **3** *phrasal v. insep.* **to rally around s.o.:** to support s.o. in times of trouble: *When the woman was sick, all of her relatives rallied around her to cheer her up and make her well again. See:* pep rally.

ram /ræm/ *n.* **1** a male sheep: *Rams butt heads during the mating season.* **2 RAM** *abbr. for* random-access memory: *My computer has 16 megabytes of RAM.* —*v.* **rammed, ramming, rams 1** to hit with great force: *A car went off the road and rammed into a tree.* **2** *infrml.fig.* to ram s.t. down s.o.'s throat: to force s.o. to do s.t.: *She did not want to fire some of her workers, but her boss rammed the order to fire them down her throat. See:* battering ram.

ram

USAGE NOTE: A computer's *RAM* is the memory the computer uses to hold programs. A computer with more RAM can run larger, more complicated programs. More RAM allows the use of detailed graphics, sound, and other powerful programs. Usually a computer with more RAM works faster, too. Having a lot of RAM is like having a large desk on which you can organize all of your information to use it easily.

ram·ble /ˈræmbəl/ *v.* **-bled, -bling, -bles 1** to talk or write without connections between ideas and without making sense: *When he talks about his youth, he rambles on and on.* **2** to walk or drive slowly for pleasure: *We rambled through the countryside on our bicycles.* -*n.* **rambler.**

ram·bunc·tious /ræmˈbʌŋkʃəs/ *adj.frml.* loud and full of energy, (*syns.*) rebellious, unruly: *Her rambunctious little boy is always chasing other children.*

ram·i·fi·ca·tion /ˌræməfəˈkeɪʃən/ *n.* a result, an effect of an action, (*syn.*) consequence: *After he lost his job, the financial ramification affected his daughter's birthday party.*

ramp /ræmp/ *n.* **1** a road that runs on and off a highway **2** a sloping walkway or metal plate between two levels of a building: *A woman rolled her wheelchair up the ramp to the doctor's door.*

ram·page /ˈræmˌpeɪdʒ/ *n.sing.v.* **-paged, -paging, -pages** violent behavior, such as yelling and knocking things over: *The crowd went on a <n.> rampage and broke into stores.*||*They <v.> rampaged through the streets.*

ram·pant /ˈræmpənt/ *adj.* uncontrollable and widespread: *Starvation was rampant in the country after the war.* -*n.* [U] **rampancy.**

ram·part /ˈræmˌpɑrt/ *n.* a barrier often made of raised earth around a fort to protect soldiers: *Soldiers stood behind the ramparts and shot at the enemy.*

ram·rod /ˈræmˌrɑd/ *n.* **1** a metal rod used to push powder and bullets down the barrels of old-fashioned guns or for cleaning a gun's barrel: *You need a ramrod to load an old gun.* **2** *infrml.fig.* a person who forces others to cooperate with him or her: *The sergeant is a ramrod who maintains strict discipline among his troops.* —*v.* **-rodded, -rodding, -rods** to force an idea or plan on others: *The Congresswoman ramrodded her proposal through the committee.*

ram·shack·le /ˈræmˌʃækəl/ *adj.* falling apart, needing to be fixed: *The doors won't close and the windows are broken in that ramshackle old house.*

ran /ræn/ *v. past tense of* run

ranch /ræntʃ/ *n.* **-es** a very large farm in the western USA and Canada: *My friend lives on a ranch and rides her horse every day.*

ranch·er /ˈræntʃər/ *n.* a person who owns a ranch: *Sheep ranchers don't like wolves because some kill their sheep.* -*n.* **ranchman.**

ranch house *n.* **1** a one-level house: *All the houses in our neighborhood are ranch houses.* **2** a house located on a ranch: *The rancher lives in the ranch house.*

ranch·ing /ˈræntʃɪŋ/ *n.* [U] farming, the raising of crops and animals on a ranch: *He likes ranching and being outdoors.*

ran·cid /ˈrænsɪd/ *adj.* spoiled or rotten food, esp. fats or oils: *The butter is rancid and tastes bad.*

ran·cor /ˈræŋkər/ *n.frml.* deep, long-lasting, and bitter hatred: *Both felt rancor toward each other long after their divorce.* -*adj.* **rancorous;** -*adv.* **rancorously.**

R & D /ˈɑrənˈdi/ *abbr. for* research and development: *The company put funds in its budget for R & D of new products.*

USAGE NOTE: Many companies have an *R & D* department that thinks of new products or services a company can offer and then tests them: *At that car company, the R & D department is testing a new design for wheels that will make cars safer and easier to drive.*

ran·dom /ˈrændəm/ *adj.* **1** happening at any time, unplanned, (*syn.*) haphazard: *Random rain showers will pass through our city today.* **2** (in statistics) having an equal chance of success: *Lotteries have random drawings of numbers to find a winner.* **3 at random:**

R

happening at any time, randomly: *Rainstorms occurred at random today.* -*v.* **randomize;** -*adv.* **randomly;** -*n.* [U] **randomness.**

random-access memory *n.* /ræm/ the working memory of a computer (not the hard disk) where any information in it can be accessed at random: *Computers require larger and larger random-access memories to handle more complicated programs. abbr.* **RAM**

R & R /'arən'ar/ *n.* [U] Rest and Relaxation, a vacation *See:* R, 3.

ran·dy /'rændi/ *adj.* **-dier, -diest** wanting to have sex, (*syn.*) lustful

range /reɪndʒ/ *v.* **ranged, ranging, ranges** **1** to cover a wide area of land, ideas, or products: *Cattle range over large pastures.||The professor's lecture ranged over 200 years of history.||That company's product line ranges from small televisions to ones with huge screens.* **2** to travel, move: *The cows range through the field eating grass.*
—*n.* [C] **1** an open field, large feeding area for cattle and sheep: *A rancher lets his cattle graze on the range near his ranch.* **2** *sing.* a variety of things, ideas, or products: *My friend and I talked about a wide range of topics: our families, our jobs, politics, and so on.* **3** [C] a stove for cooking: *I am boiling the potatoes on the range.* **4** *sing.* the distance that a car, truck, airplane, or missile can travel without running out of fuel: *My car has a range of 250 miles (approx. 400 km) before I have to stop for gasoline.* **5** [C] the low and high notes that a singer or musical instrument can produce: *A piano has a great range, from low to high notes.* **6** [C] a group of mountains: *The Rockies are a mountain range in the western USA.* **7** [C] a place to practice shooting: *My sister likes to shoot her gun at the shooting range.*

rang·er /'reɪndʒər/ *n.* an official who keeps order and watches out for danger: *A ranger in the national park watches out for fires.*

rang·y /'reɪndʒi/ *adj.* **-ier, -iest** being tall and thin with long legs and arms: *Basketball players look tall and rangy.*

rank /ræŋk/ *n.* one's position in the military or business: *She has the rank of general in the Air Force.*
—*v.* **1** to value, to think s.t. is important: *He ranks good food and good health as the most important things in his life.* **2** to have a certain place or position in an ordered group: *An admiral ranks above a captain in the navy.*
—*adj.* describes food that is spoiled and smelly: *The chicken meat looked good in the market, but it smells rank now.*

rank and file *n.* the workforce of average workers, not including managers: *The rank and file likes the new labor contract.* -*adj.* **rank-and-file:**

rank·ing /'ræŋkɪŋ/ *n.* [C;U] a place in an ordered system; a position of value, honor, or success: *That tennis player has the highest ranking in the world today; he's the best player.*

ran·kle /'ræŋkəl/ *v.* **-kled, -kling, -kles** to anger, annoy, (*syn.*) to irritate s.o.: *The noise that trucks and ambulances make in the avenue rankles him every day.*

ran·sack /'ræn,sæk/ *v.* to search thoroughly, esp. in looking for s.t. to steal: *The thief ransacked my apartment by emptying drawers on the floor looking for money.* -*n.* [U] **ransacking.**

ran·som /'rænsəm/ *n.* money paid for return of a person (or animal) taken by kidnappers: *The family paid a ransom of $100,000 for the return of their kidnapped daughter.*

rant /rænt/ *v.* **1** to shout with anger: *When he heard that taxes are going up, he ranted for an hour.* **2 rant and rave:** to shout and yell as if crazy: *My sister ranted and raved when I read the letters from her boyfriend.*

rap /ræp/ *n.* **1** [C] a knock, loud tap: *I heard a rap on the door, and I opened it.* **2** [C] *slang* the qualities or character (usu. negative) people believe s.o. to have, (*syn.*) reputation: *He has a bad rap as a thief, but actually he is honest.* **3** *slang* one's ability to talk well and at length: *She has a good rap once she starts talking.* **4** [U] a type of music in which the artist speaks to a strong rhythm: *Rap became popular in the 1980s.*
—*v.* **rapped, rapping, raps** **1** to knock, tap loudly: *My friend rapped on my door, and I let her in.* **2** *slang* to talk about s.t. a lot: *We rapped about going to college and decided to apply.* **3** *infrml.* **to take the rap:** to receive punishment for the wrongdoing of s.o. else: *The top mobster was responsible for the crime, but an underling took the rap and went to jail.*

USAGE NOTE: People who perform *rap* music are called *rap artists*, not rap musicians, because a rap performance combines dancing, talking, and singing in rhyme. Recently, some rap artists have been criticized for using violent words and ideas, but other artists use rap music to tell about life in American cities.

ra·pa·cious /rə'peɪʃəs/ *adj.frml.* **1** wanting and taking more than one needs, such as taking money or power by force, (*syn.*) grasping: *Long ago, some lords were rapacious in taking taxes from the peasants.* **2** living on food taken by force: *Jackals are rapacious in taking dead animals away from smaller ones.* -*adv.* **rapaciously;** -*n.* [U] **rapaciousness; rapacity** /rə'pæsəti/.

rape /reɪp/ *n.* [C;U] the crime of forcing a person to have sex when she or he does not want to: *A rape was committed in the park last night.* **2** [C] a type of plant grown and fed to sheep **3** [C] a type of plant whose seeds yield oil used as a lubricant: *rapeseed oil* **4** [U] grape skins, seeds, and stems left over after pressing

—*v.* **raped, raping, rapes** to force s.o. to have sex with you: *A man raped a woman in the park.* -*n.* **rapist.**

rap·id /'ræpɪd/ *adj.* very fast, quick: *His rapid speech is difficult to understand.* -*n.* [U] **ra·pidity;** /rə'pɪdəti/ -*adv.* **rapidly.**

rapid-fire *adj.* firing or shooting many bullets quickly: *Machine guns are rapid-fire weapons.*

rapid transit *n.* [U] a system, usu. of buses and subways, to move passengers quickly: *Rapid transit, such as express buses, allows people to get to work quickly.*

rap·ids /'ræpɪdz/ *n.pl.* a rocky place in a river where water moves very quickly: *The rapids can be dangerous for small boats.*

ra·pi·er /'reɪpiər/ *n.* a two-edged sword with a thin, round, pointed blade: *Two swordsmen fought with rapiers.*

rap·port /rə'pɔr/ *n.sing.* [U] a friendly, sympathetic relationship between people: *Our teacher has a good rapport with her students.*

rap·proche·ment /ˌræprouʃ'mãˌ/ *n.frml.* (in diplomacy) the beginning of friendly relations after a time of disagreement, esp. between two countries: *Two former enemies reached a rapprochement; they agreed not to fight again.*

rapt /ræpt/ *adj.* focused on only one thing with one's complete attention: *The audience listened with rapt attention to the excellent speaker.*

rap·ture /'ræptʃər/ *n.* [U] a very strong feeling of pleasure, (*syn.*) ecstasy: *Looking at a beautiful sunset gives me a feeling of rapture.* -*adj.* **rapturous;** -*adv.* **rapturously.**

rare /rɛr/ *adj.* **1** one of few in existence, (*syn.*) scarce: *He has a rare Roman coin.* **2** not often heard or seen, (*syn.*) infrequent: *The famous movie star made a rare public appearance.* **3** not completely cooked: *My father likes rare meat that is still a little pink inside.*

rar·e·fied /'rɛrəˌfaɪd/ *adj.fig.* **1** very special, unique: *She lives in the rarefied atmosphere of high society.* **2** thin: *Air is rarefied on a mountaintop.* -*v.* **rarefy** or **rarify.**

rare·ly /'rɛrli/ *adv.* not often, (*syn.*) seldom: *That famous old movie star is rarely seen in person these days.*

rar·ing /'rɛrɪŋ/ *adj.infrml.* full of energy, ready for action: *Now that vacation time is over, she is raring to go back to college.*

rar·i·ty /'rɛrəti/ *n.* **-ties** s.t. unusual, not often seen, *That painting is a valuable rarity; the painter seldom painted portraits.*

ras·cal /'ræskəl/ *n.* **1** a badly behaved child: *Her daughter is a little rascal, always causing mischief.* **2** a bad person, (*syn.*) scoundrel: *That rascal has stolen my car!*

rash /ræʃ/ *n.* **1** red spots on the skin, blotchy irritation: *That strong soap gives me a rash on my legs.* **2 to break out in a rash:** to start having a rash on the skin, often spreading: *We took our daughter to the doctor because she broke out in a rash.*

—*adj.* quick and foolish, without thinking, (*syn.*) reckless: *Charging an expensive vacation that he couldn't pay for on his credit card was a rash thing to do.* -*adv.* **rashly.**

rash·er /'ræʃər/ *n.* a serving or order of ham or bacon: *I ordered two fried eggs and a rasher of bacon for breakfast.*

rasp /ræsp/ *n.v.* **1** a type of tool, a rough file: *You should <v.> rasp this wood to make it smooth.* **2** a low, rough voice, hoarseness: *My father has a sore throat and speaks with a <n.> rasp.*

rasp·ber·ry /'ræzˌbɛri/ *n.adj.* **-ries 1** a thorny plant of the rose family and its red or black fruit: *I like to put <adj.> raspberry jam on my toast.* **2** *slang* a rude noise made with the lips, used to show a negative opinion: *The audience gave the bad singer the <n.> raspberry.*

rasp·y /'ræspi/ *adj.* **-ier, -iest** having a low, rough voice: *His voice is raspy from speaking for hours.*

rat /ræt/ *n.v.* **ratted, ratting, rats 1** a kind of rodent with a long hairless tail, a pointed nose, and very sharp teeth: *<n.> Rats look like mice, but are larger.* **2** *slang* to tell people in power about a person's illegal or unprofessional acts; a person who does this: *Don't be a <n.> rat and <v.> rat to the boss that I was late.* **3 to smell a rat:** to sense that s.t. is wrong: *The news reporter smelled a <n.> rat when the mayor refused to let her see the records of city office meetings.* See: rat race .

ratch·et /'rætʃɪt/ *n.* a wheel with V-shaped indentations on its edge. When turned, this wheel and a metal bar hold a spring tight. The wheel can move only in one direction: *Mechanical clocks and watches use ratchets to turn their hands.*

—*v.* **1** to turn s.t. little by little: *The doorknob was stuck, but I ratcheted it open and fixed it.* **2** to increase: *His salary ratcheted up each year.*

rate /reɪt/ *n.* **1** an amount of s.t.: *The rate of interest on bonds was 7%.* **2** the cost of s.t.: *The rate for a trip on that bus is $10 per person.* **3** a speed, velocity: *Jet airplanes travel at a great rate of speed.* **4** a rank, esp. in the US Navy: *She has a rate of seaman first-class.* **5 at any rate:** no matter what happens: *I may get a C in math, but at any rate I learned a lot.*

R

—v. **-rated, -rating, -rates 1** to be important enough to get or receive s.t., (*syns.*) to merit, deserve: *Her injury was serious and rated immediate attention from the doctors.* **2** *infrml.* to receive special attention, be privileged: *I saw the manager let you in the theater without paying; I guess you really rate.*

rate of exchange *n.* the amount that one country's money is worth in another country's money: *The rate of exchange between the US dollar and the British pound changes almost every day.*

rate of interest *n.* **1** the amount of interest that is paid for money at a savings bank, on a bond, etc.: *The rate of interest on that bond is 7%.* **2** the amount that one must pay for a loan: *The rate of interest on a car loan is 10%.*

rat fink *n.infrml. slang See:* rat 2.

rath·er /ˈræðər/ *adv.* **1** to like one thing more than another: *I would rather go shopping tomorrow than today.* **2** a little, somewhat, or very: *The weather is rather hot today.* **3** more exactly, really: *I got a B, or rather a B+, on the exam. See:* kind of, USAGE NOTE.

raths·kel·ler /ˈrɑt,skɛlər, ˈræt-, ˈræθ-/ *n.* a barroom that sells beer and has only a few kinds of food: *After studying, we went to the student rathskeller for a beer.*

rat·i·fi·ca·tion /ˌrætəfəˈkeɪʃən/ *n.* [U] formal approval, passage into law, (*syns.*) confirmation: *Ratification of the treaty took place in the Senate yesterday.*

rat·i·fy /ˈrætəˌfaɪ/ *v.* **-fied, -fying, -fies** to make into law, approve formally: *The US Senate ratified the treaty with Mexico.*

rat·ing /ˈreɪtɪŋ/ *n.* [C;U] a degree of excellence, a measure of good or bad quality, usu. in comparison with other like things: *The products of that company have the highest rating.*

ra·tio /ˈreɪʃou, -ʃiˌou/ *n.* a relationship between two numbers: *The ratio of women to men in our class is 3 to 1.*

ra·tion /ˈræʃən, ˈreɪ-/ *n.* a small, equal amount of food (gasoline, water, etc.) given to each person in a group: *Many food rations for soldiers come in cans.*

—v. to limit the amount of food and other items, esp. by governmental order: *During the war, the government rationed food supplies.*

ra·tion·al /ˈræʃənəl/ *adj.* **1** able to think clearly, clearheaded: *He hit his head when he fell and is not rational.* **2** showing logical thought, (*syns.*) reasonable, sensible: *The rational thing to do was to take the sick man to a doctor.*

ra·tion·ale /ˌræʃəˈnæl/ *n.* reason(s) to do s.t., the purpose for an action: *The rationale for buying a house instead of renting is to build personal riches.*

ra·tion·al·ism /ˈræʃənəˌlɪzəm/ *n.* [U] a belief that reason can explain all human behavior:

The author of this book believes in rationalism, and she says that all knowledge comes from reason. -n.adj. **rationalist.**

ra·tion·al·i·ty /ˌræʃəˈnælətɪ/ *n.* [U] ability to think clearly: *The patient has grown so confused that his nurses doubt his rationality now.*

ra·tion·al·ize /ˈræʃənəˌlaɪz/ *v.* **-ized, -izing, -izes 1** to think about and improve s.t. logically and systematically: *The school rationalized its schedule, and now students don't have to run to class.* **2** to give reasons for doing s.t. one knows is wrong or harmful: *He rationalized missing class by planning to do extra homework next week.*

rat race *n.infrml.fig.* rushed, daily routine where people work very hard to keep their jobs and be successful; unpleasant competition: *She gets away from the rat race at her office by going to the country on weekends.*

rat·tle /ˈrætl/ *n.* **1** a toy that makes short, quick noises when shaken: *Our baby likes to play with a rattle.* **2** the sound of a series of repeated noises, usu. heard when s.t. is moved: *I hear a rattle when I open my car door.*

—v. **-tled, -tling, -tles 1** to shake and sound like a rattle: *The tailpipe on my car is loose and rattles.* **2** *fig.* to frighten, upset s.o.: *He was nearly hit by a speeding car and that rattled him.* **3** *phrasal v. sep.* **to rattle s.t. off:** to say s.t. quickly, without thinking: *He rattled off his social security number.||He rattled it off.* **4** *phrasal v.* **to rattle on:** to speak quickly, without stopping: *She is a nice person but she just rattles on and on. -adj.n.* [U] **rattling.**

rat·tler /ˈrætlər/ *n.* short for rattlesnake: *I saw a rattler out in the desert yesterday.*

rat·tle·snake /ˈrætl,sneɪk/ *n.* a dangerous, poisonous snake that lives in N. and S. America and has hard skin at the end of its body which the snake rattles when preparing to bite

rat·trap /ˈræt,træp/ *n.* **1** a trap made to catch rats: *Rattraps in the subway catch hundreds of rats every day.* **2** an

rattlesnake

ugly old building where many rats often live: *That northern part of the city is loaded with rattraps.*

rat·ty /ˈrætɪ/ *adj.infrml.fig.* **-tier, -tiest** dirty, old, and ugly, (*syn.*) shabby: *The clothes on the poor homeless man were all ratty.*

rau·cous /ˈrɔkəs/ *adj.frml.* loud, wild: *Raucous laughter came from the people at the party. -adv.* **raucously.**

raun·chy /ˈrɔntʃi/ *adj.infrml.* **-chier, -chiest 1** dirty, smelly: *He went hunting deep in the woods for a week, and his clothes smelled raunchy when he returned.* **2** clearly displaying sex, (*syns.*) lustful, risqué: *Raunchy maga-*

zines are on sale at newsstands in many states.
-*n.* [U] **raunchiness.**

rav·age /'rævɪʤ/ *v.* **-aged, -aging, -ages** to enter violently and destroy: *Malaria and a high fever ravaged his body with sickness and pain.*

rave /reɪv/ *v.* **raved, raving, raves** **1** to speak or shout insanely or crazily: *That poor man is mentally ill and raves for hours.* **2** to praise greatly: *Critics raved about the new play.*
—*adj.* full of praise and high opinions: *The new play received rave reviews. See:* raving.

rav·el /'rævəl/ *v.* **1** to turn or twist around s.t.: *I raveled the thread around a spool.* **2** to undo, (*syn.*) to fray: *Threads in the old sweater raveled to make holes.*

ra·ven /'reɪvən/ *n.* a large black bird in the crow family, with shiny black feathers: *Ravens are found in Europe, the Americas, and Asia.*

rav·en·ous /'rævənəs/ *adj.* very much wanting or needing food, very hungry, (*syns.*) starving, voracious: *The lions have not eaten for three days and are ravenous.* -*adv.* **ravenously.**

ra·vine /rə'vin/ *n.* a low area in the earth with steep sides, deep gully, (*syn.*) gorge: *A fast river has cut out a ravine in the rock.*

rav·ing /'reɪvɪŋ/ *adj.n.* [U] speaking or shouting insanely, crazily: *A <adj.> raving man frightened those near him.||His <n.> raving scared everyone.*

ra·vi·o·li /ˌrævi'ouli, rɑ-/ *n.* [U] small pillow-shaped pasta filled usu. with meat or cheese: *Ravioli in tomato sauce is very tasty. See:* spaghetti, USAGE NOTE.

rav·ish /'rævɪʃ/ *v.frml.* to give great pleasure: *That beautiful painting simply ravishes me; the colors are breathtaking.*

rav·ish·ing /'rævɪʃɪŋ/ *adj.infrml.fig.* very beautiful, esp. about a woman, (*syns.*) dazzling, stunning: *She looks ravishing when she is all dressed up in beautiful clothes.* -*adv.* **ravishingly.**

raw /rɔ/ *adj.* **1** natural, uncooked: *Eating raw carrots is good for your eyesight.* **2** in a natural state, not yet manufactured: *Cotton and wool are raw materials from which cloth is made.* **3** very clearly or openly sexual, crude: *Pornographic magazines show raw sex.* **4** painful red areas where skin has been rubbed away: *The skin on my feet is raw because my shoes are too small.* **5** untrained, not yet tested: *In the army, all raw recruits must go to training camp first.* **6** being very cold and wet: *raw weather in the winter* **7** *infrml.* **in the raw:** in a natural state, unclothed, naked, nude: *Nudists spend a lot of their time in the raw.* **8** *infrml.* **raw deal:** an unfair exchange, a cruel trick: *They gave him a raw deal; they hired him to do a job and then didn't pay him for it.*

raw·hide /'rɔˌhaɪd/ *n.* [U] tough skin of cattle that has not been made into leather by tanning: *The shoelaces in his boots are made of rawhide.*

ray /reɪ/ *n.* **1** a thin line of light, energy, or heat: *Rays of light shine from a burning candle.* **2** a small amount of s.t.: *There is a ray of hope that he will be cured of cancer.*

ray·on /'reɪɑn/ *n.* [U] smooth, shiny cloth made from wood fibers, "artificial silk": *Clothing made of rayon is light and cool.*

raze /reɪz/ *v.* **razed, razing, razes** to knock down, destroy completely, (*syn.*) to demolish: *The government razed some old buildings and built new ones.* -*n.* **razing.**

ra·zor /'reɪzər/ *n.* a sharp cutting instrument: *Men use razors to shave their beards. See:* safety razor.

razor-sharp *adj.* **1** very sharp like a razor **2** very intelligent or able: *a razor-sharp mind*

raz·or·back /'reɪzərˌbæk/ *n.* **1** (chiefly in the southeastern USA a domestic pig that has become wild): *Razorbacks can be dangerous and bite people.* **2** a narrow ridge

razz /ræz/ *v.* **-es** to tease, make fun of s.o.: *My friends razzed me about failing an exam.*

raz·zle-daz·zle /'ræzəlˌdæzəl/ *n.infrml.* [U] showy behavior, flashiness for the purpose of confusing or impressing s.o.: *A football player did some razzle-dazzle with the ball and ran right around the other player.*

Rd. /roud/ *abbr. for* Road: *His address is 21 Fordham Rd. See:* street, USAGE NOTE.

re /ri, reɪ/ *prep.* regarding s.t., about s.t. (usu. used in business letters): *Re: our discussion, here is the information that you wanted.*
—*prefix* /ri/ **1** again: *to redo||to remake s.t.* **2** back: *to return*

reach /riʧ/ *v.* **-es** **1** to stretch out one's arm and hand: *He reached across the table to get the salt.* **2** to come to a point, go as far as: *We reached Nashville before our car needed gas.* **3** to make contact with s.o., get in touch with: *We couldn't reach you by telephone, so we are writing this letter.* **4** to be able to get to a necessary thing or place: *Can you reach the top shelf of books?* **5** to cover an area, go from one place to another: *Russia reaches across two continents.* **6** *phrasal v. sep.* **to reach out for s.t.:** to try to contact s.o. or s.t. physically or emotionally: *In his poetry, he seems to be reaching out for help.*
—*n.* **-es** [C;U] **1** the length an arm can be put or stretched out: *I don't have my notes within reach, so I can't answer your question.* **2** [C] a wide-open area of s.t., esp. water: *The reach of the ocean seems never-ending when you are in a small boat.* **3** [U] the possibility of getting or accomplishing s.t., (*syn.*) attainability: *An expensive car is beyond our reach because we*

R

don't have enough money. **4 your reach should exceed your grasp:** you should try to go farther than where you are now: *I probably don't have enough experience to get hired at this company, but I'll try; after all, your reach should exceed your grasp.*

re·ac·quaint /ˌriə'kweɪnt/ v. to learn about s.o. or s.t. again after not seeing it for some time: *He lived in California for 20 years then moved back home to New York and spent time reacquainting himself with his old town.*

re·act /ri'ækt/ v. **1** to speak or move when s.t. happens, (*syn.*) to respond: *When he heard the good news, he reacted with a smile.* **2** to act in a different way because of s.o. or s.t.: *The teacher reacted to the student's bad grades by giving him more homework.* **3** (in chemistry) to change because of contact with another chemical: *Oxygen and iron react together to form rust.*

re·ac·tion /ri'ækʃən/ n. [C;U] a response, an answer: *What was the teacher's reaction to your question?*

re·ac·tion·ar·y /ri'ækʃəˌnɛri/ n. **-ies** a person who doesn't want changes, esp. in government or business: *Reactionaries in parliament voted against a bill to cut government spending.*

re·ac·ti·vate /ri'æktəˌveɪt/ v. **-vated, -vating, -vates** to begin to use again: *His old military unit was reactivated and he had to leave his job.* **-n. reactivation.**

re·ac·tor /ri'æktər/ n. a power plant for nuclear energy: *Nuclear reactors supply most of the electricity in France.*

read /rid/ v. **read** /rɛd/, **reading, reads 1** to see and find meaning in written words and symbols: *She reads books already at age five.* **2** to say s.t. written out loud: *The professor read an important part of the textbook to the students.* **3** to find or show an exact amount from measuring equipment: *A man from the electric company reads the electric meter every month.* **4** to understand s.t. because of clues or hints: *She could read the feeling of happiness on his face.* **5 to read between the lines:** to find meaning although it is not stated clearly: *Even though she doesn't say so, I can read between the lines of her letter that she is homesick.* **6 to read s.o. his or her rights:** (in USA), police must tell a person they are taking to prison that person's legal rights: *The police officer read the man his rights, then she took him to prison.* **7 to read the signs:** to understand indirectly what is happening: *He never calls her or talks to her, and she can read the signs that he does not love her anymore.* **8 to take s.t. as read:** to believe s.t. is true without thinking much about it: *Since I cannot understand Spanish, I have to take your ability to speak Spanish as read.* **9** *phrasal v. insep.* **to read s.t. into s.t.:** to put meaning that may not be there into s.t.:

When she truthfully told him she was busy and couldn't go to dinner with him, he read into her words that she didn't like him. **10** *phrasal v. insep.* **to read up on s.t.:** to learn a lot about a subject by reading about it: *I'm reading up on the history of Greece before I go there on vacation.*

read·a·ble /'ridəbəl/ adj. easily read, clear: *That novel is full of action and quite readable.* **-n.** [U] **readability.**

read·er /'ridər/ n. **1** a person or people who read s.t. written, such as a novel or magazine: *Readers of that magazine are interested in sports.* **2** a collection of writings in book form: *We have a short story reader for our English class.*

read·er·ship /'ridərˌʃɪp/ n.sing. the people who read a certain newspaper, people who regularly buy a magazine: *The readership of the New Yorker is interested in art, literature, and theater.*

read·i·ly /'rɛdli/ adv. easily, without difficulty: *Good food is readily available anywhere in the country.*

read·i·ness /'rɛdinɪs/ n.sing. [U] ready to act, the ability to act quickly, (*syn.*) preparedness: *A fire truck is always in a state of readiness to go to a fire.*

read·ing /'ridɪŋ/ n. **1** [U] the process of seeing and understanding written material: *Schools teach reading in the first grade.* **2** [C] an exact amount shown by measuring equipment: *A reading of the gas meter in our house is done every month.* **3** [C] a spoken presentation of s.t. written: *The poet gave a reading of her poems to college students.* **4** [C] one's understanding of any situation or event using the information one has: *What is your reading on the chances for peace in that country?* **5** [U] written material to be read: *War and Peace by Tolstoy will be my summer reading.*

re·ad·just /ˌriə'dʒʌst/ v. [C;U] to learn to behave in certain ways again: *She left prison after five years and has now readjusted to living a normal life.*

re·ad·just·ment /ˌriə'dʒʌstmənt/ n. learning to behave in certain ways again: *Living at home again during summer college vacations is sometimes a difficult readjustment.*

read·y /'rɛdi/ adj. **-ier, -iest 1** prepared, set to do s.t.: *Our meal is ready, so let's eat.* **2** easily available: *ready answer, ready cash, ready money* **3 at the ready:** prepared to act quickly: *Soldiers held their rifles at the ready to shoot at the enemy.* **4 ready, willing, and able:** wanting to do s.t. promptly: *I don't know why you are waiting because I am ready, willing, and able to sign our agreement now.* **5 to make ready:** to prepare for use: *We made the food ready and then sat down to eat.*

R

ready-made *adj.* **1** prepared and set to be used without any changes needed: *My wife wanted to make her own furniture, but it was too much work; so we bought ready-made furniture instead.* **2** ordinary, common: *He always has simple, ready-made answers for any question.*

ready-to-wear *adj.n.* [U] clothes that are made in quantity to be worn by any buyer: *He buys <adj.> ready-to-wear suits from a store, rather than having the suits made especially for him. See:* off-the-rack.

re·af·firm /ˌriəˈfɜrm/ *v.frml.* to repeat one's belief in s.t., (*syns.*) to confirm, assure: *He reaffirms his love for her by telling her that he loves her every day.*

re·al /ˈriəl, ril/ *adj.* **1** true, not fake or imaginary, (*syn.*) genuine: *His real name is Bob Smith, not John Jones.* **2** *slang* **for real:** telling the truth, being honest, (*syn.*) genuine: *He said that he wants to buy my car, but I don't know if he is for real or not.*
—*adv. infrml.* very, extremely: *We had a real good time at the party last night.*

real estate *n.* [U] property that cannot be moved, such as land, houses, and office buildings: *She owns real estate in the country. -adj.* **real-estate.**

real-estate agent *n.* a person who sells real estate *See:* Realtor.

re·al·ism /ˈriəˌlɪzəm/ *n.* **1** a way of thinking in which only real facts and situations are believed, and imaginary, romantic, or idealistic ideas are not: *She is known for her realism and wisdom about life.* **2** art, such as literature, films, or painting that shows life as it is: *The lifelike paintings of that artist are good examples of realism.*

re·al·ist /ˈriəlɪst/ *n.* a person who believes only real facts and situations and does not believe or dream that everything is perfect and ideal: *The elderly man is a realist and does not try to look or act like a young man.*

re·al·is·tic /ˌriəˈlɪstɪk/ *adj.* having the quality of seeing and believing real facts and situations, rather than believing that everything is perfect: *She is realistic about the fact that with no education, she will have difficulty finding a high-paying job. -adv.* **realistically.**

re·al·i·ty /riˈæləti/ *n.* **-ties 1** [C;U] the real world of objects and living things as it is in fact and not a romantic or idealistic view of it: *People needed time to understand the reality of damage caused by the hurricane.* **2** [U] **in reality:** in fact: *In reality, the hurricane damage was much greater than anyone imagined.*

re·al·iz·a·ble /ˈriəˌlaɪzəbəl, ˌriəˈlaɪ-/ *adj.* able to be done, (*syns.*) doable, possible: *Her career goals are realizable because she is well educated and hardworking.*

re·al·i·za·tion /ˌriələˈzeɪʃən/ *n.sing.* [U] **1** understanding, belief that s.t. is true: *After looking for work, he came to the realization that he needs more education to find a job.* **2** [U] a hope or plan that has become reality: *The realization of our plan to build a house took many years and a lot of work.*

re·al·ize /ˈriəˌlaɪz/ *v.* **-ized, -izing, -izes 1** to understand, start to believe s.t. is true, (*syn.*) to recognize: *He realizes now that he needs to go back to college for more education.* **2** to gain, make money: *The woman realized a profit from the sale of her house.* **3** to make s.t. become true, (*syn.*) to accomplish: *This summer I will realize my dream of going to Italy.*

re·al·lo·cate /riˈæləˌkeɪt/ *v.* **-cated, -cating, -cates** to take s.t., such as money, away from one purpose and use it for another purpose: *The money we planned to use to build a new office building was reallocated to develop new products. -n.* [U] **reallocation.**

re·al·ly /ˈriəli, ˈrɪli/ *adv.* **1** in fact, truly, (*syns.*) genuinely, unquestionably: *Are you really happy, or are you just smiling to be nice to me?* **2** very: *I am really surprised to see you!*

realm /rɛlm/ *n.* **1** a general field, such as an area of knowledge: *In the realm of physics, Albert Einstein was a genius.* **2** a kingdom: *The queen rules her realm.*

real time *n.* [U] the broadcast of an event while it is happening, (*syn.*) live: *This football game is being broadcast in real time all over the world.*

Re·al·tor or **realtor** /ˈriəltər/ *n.TM* a member of the National Association of Realtors; a real-estate agent, a person who sells real estate: *She is a successful realtor with her own real-estate business.*

re·al·ty /ˈriəlti/ *n.* **-ties** [U] the business of buying, owning, and selling real estate: *He has a successful business in realty, especially developing land for commercial use.*

ream /rim/ *v.* **1** to make a hole in the center of s.t. by cutting: *Workers must ream holes in metal rods to make gun barrels.* **2** *fig.slang* **to get reamed:** to be severely criticized: *When my boss found out about the stupid mistake I made, I really got reamed.*
—*n.* a quantity of paper, usu. 500 sheets: *Our office uses 20 reams of paper each week.*

reap /rip/ *v.* to cut down and collect, (*syn.*) to harvest: *In the autumn, farmers reap their crops.*

reap·er /ˈripər/ *n.* **1** a person who harvests crops **2** a machine used to harvest crops: *The farmer drove his reaper to harvest the corn.* **3** **the Grim Reaper:** an image of Death as a skeleton dressed in a long, dark cloak and holding a tool used for reaping (a scythe): *The*

R

grim reaper took the old man last night; he died.

re·ap·pear /ˌriəˈpɪr/ v. to appear again, come back: *That couple left the neighborhood, then reappeared a year later.* -n. [U] **reappearance.**

re·ap·ply /ˌriəˈplaɪ/ v. **-plied, -plying, -plies** to apply again: *The first time he tried to get a job at that company, they hired another person, but they asked him to reapply later.*

re·ap·point /ˌriəˈpɔɪnt/ v. to renew s.o.'s employment: *The director of the tax department was reappointed by the new president.* -n. [C;U] **reappointment.**

re·ap·por·tion /ˌriəˈpɔrʃən/ v. **1** to give out again: *After the older child took all the toys, the mother reapportioned them so that each child had s.t. to play with.* **2** to change congressional districts according to new census figures: *The Congress reapportions districts all over the country every ten years.* -n. **reapportionment.** *See:* gerrymander.

re·ap·prais·al /ˌriəˈpreɪzəl/ n. thinking about the value of s.t. again, *(syn.)* reevaluation: *Congress is doing a reappraisal of the country's military system to try to make it smaller* -v. **reappraise.**

rear /rɪr/ **(1)** n.adj. **1** [U] the back area of s.t.: *He sat in the <n.> rear of the church.* **2** [C] *infrml.* the buttocks: *He fell on his <n.> rear* (or) *on his <adj.> rear end.* **3 to bring up the rear:** to be last in a parade or a line: *Clowns led the circus parade and elephants brought up the <n> rear.*

rear (2) v. **1** to help children or young animals to grow: *A mother rears her children to adulthood.* **2** to raise oneself up, lift onself up: *A horse reared up on its hind legs.*

re·arm /riˈɑrm/ v. to give weapons again to soldiers, sailors, etc., build up the military: *After a time of peace, that nation rearmed itself for war against its neighbor.* -n. **rearmament.**

re·ar·range /ˌriəˈreɪndʒ/ v. **-ranged, -ranging, -ranges** to put s.t. in a new order: *I've rearranged my work schedule; I no longer will work on weekends.* -n. [C;U] **rearrangement.**

rear·view /ˈrɪrˌvyu/ adj. looking to the back: *As she drives along, she looks in her rearview mirror to see cars behind her.*

rea·son /ˈrizən/ n. **1** [U] the ability to understand and think logically: *Scientists use reason to understand nature.* **2** [C] the purpose for doing s.t.: *His reason for going back to school is to learn new things.* **3** [C] the cause of s.t. happening: *The reason he bought a new TV is that his old TV is broken.* **4 to listen to reason:** to do what s.o. tells you to do because it is intelligent, right: *He listened to reason when his doctor told him that he must stop smoking cigarettes or he would die.* **5 with reason:** referring to doing s.t.

for a good reason, because: *She stopped talking to him with reason; he made her very angry.* **6 within reason:** at a level that one can agree to, because it is logical and reasonable: *Let's buy the house since the amount of money he wants is within reason.* **7 without rhyme or reason:** having no logical plan or purpose: *My boss makes decisions without rhyme or reason.*

—v. **1** to think logically, use reason: *He reasoned out the math problem and got the correct answer.* **2** *phrasal v. insep.* **to reason with s.o.:** to talk to s.o., trying to make him or her think logically and reasonably: *It is not possible to reason with a two-year-old child.* **3 to stand to reason:** to be right, correct: *It stands to reason that he wants to marry her because he loves her very much.*

rea·son·a·ble /ˈrizənəbəl/ adj. **1** referring to a logical and right thing to do, *(syns.)* acceptable, sensible: *That man works very hard, so it is reasonable for him to ask for more money.* **2** likely to be true, understandable, *(syn.)* conceivable: *It is reasonable to think that he will be unhappy if he doesn't get more money.* **3** not priced too high, *(syns.)* economical, inexpensive: *The price of the coat was very reasonable, so I bought it.* -n. [U] **reasonableness;** -adv. **reasonably.**

rea·son·ing /ˈrizənɪŋ/ n. [U] **1** an act of thinking: *Her reasoning is that she will marry a man who likes to cook because she never learned to cook.* **2** the ability to think logically: *His reasoning is very good about why he needs a new job.*

re·as·sert /ˌriəˈsɜrt/ v. to say again, repeat a strong belief: *In all of his speeches this week, the President reasserted the importance education has for the country.* -n. **reassertion.**

re·as·sess /ˌriəˈsɛs/ v. **-es** to think about s.t. again, *(syn.)* to reevaluate: *The owner reassessed the value of his land and changed its price.* -n. [C;U] **reassessment.**

re·as·sign /ˌriəˈsaɪn/ v. to put in a new position, give s.o. a new place or job: *After working in Japan for three years, the diplomat was reassigned to Washington, D.C.* -n. [C;U] **reassignment.**

re·as·sure /ˌriəˈʃʊr/ v. **-sured, -suring, -sures** to make s.o. believe that s.t. will be all right: *She reassured him that she still loves him.* -n. [C;U] **reassurance;** -adv. **reassuringly.**

re·a·wak·en /ˌriəˈweɪkən/ v. to wake up again: *The noise of trucks on the street reawakened him many times last night.*

re·bate /ˈriˌbeɪt/ n.v. **-bated, -bating, -bates** money given by a company to people who have bought a product: *The car manufacturer gave me a <n.> rebate of $1,000 on the price of my new car.‖They <v.> rebated that amount.*

USAGE NOTE: Compare *rebate* and *coupon*. A *rebate* is money returned to a buyer (often by mail) after the sale: *I sent in a form to get a $1.00 rebate on the shampoo I bought.* A *coupon* reduces the price of the item at the time of sale: *I used a coupon to buy cereal for 75 cents less than the regular price.* Some stores will double or triple the value of a coupon to increase their business.

---

reb·el /ˈrɛbəl/ *n.adj.* a person who fights against a person or group in power, esp. against a government: <*n.*> *Rebels (or)* <*adj.*> *rebel troops attacked an army outpost.* —*v.* /rəˈbɛl/ **-belled, -belling, -bels** to fight against a person or group in power: *He rebelled against his parents and left home.* -*adj.* **rebellious** /rəˈbɛlyəs/; -*n.* [U] **rebelliousness.**

re·bel·lion /rəˈbɛlyən/ *n.* [C;U] a fight against the people in power: *The young woman was put in jail because of her rebellion against the government.*

re·birth /riˈbɜrθ, ˈriˌbɜrθ/ *n.sing.fig.* **1** a new start, a feeling that one is born again, (*syn.*) renewal: *I changed jobs, and I've had a rebirth of energy and happiness with my work.* **2** a return to popularity or use, (*syn.*) revival: *The old movie had a rebirth of popularity this year.*

re·born /riˈbɔrn/ *adj.fig.* feeling as if one were born again, (*syn.*) renewed: *He moved to the country and feels reborn.*

re·bound /riˈbaʊnd/ *v.* to bounce back, return: *I threw the ball against the wall and it rebounded to me.* —*n.* /ˈriˌbaʊnd/ **1** a bounce back: *I caught the ball on the rebound.* **2 on the rebound:** a time of recovery, esp. after a love affair that has ended: *He fell in love with a new girlfriend on the rebound from a painful love affair that ended sadly.*

re·buff /rɪˈbʌf/ *n.v.* a quick and complete rejection, such as of an offer, proposal, (*syns.*) a refusal, turn down: *He wanted to kiss the woman, but he received a* <*n.*> *rebuff.*‖*She* <*v.*> *rebuffed him.*

re·build /riˈbɪld/ *v.* **-built** /bɪlt/ **-building, -builds** to build again, renew: *His house burned down and he rebuilt it.* -*n.* **rebuilding.**

re·buke /rɪˈbyuk/ *n.v.frml.* **-buked, -buking, -bukes** strong, angry words to tell s.o. he or she did s.t. wrong, (*syns.*) criticism, scolding: *He received a* <*n.*> *rebuke for his mistake.*‖*His supervisor* <*v.*> *rebuked him.*

re·but /rɪˈbʌt/ *v.frml.* **-butted, -butting, -buts** to speak against s.o. else's idea or opinion, to prove that it is wrong, (*syn.*) to refute: *Our lawyer saved our case when she rebutted the other lawyer's speech.* -*n.* [C;U] **rebuttal.**

re·cal·ci·trant /rɪˈkælsətrənt/ *adj.frml.* openly doing or saying things against people in power, (*syns.*) defiant, uncooperative: *Recalcitrant students are always in trouble with their teachers.* -*n.* [U] **recalcitrance.**

re·cal·cu·late /riˈkælkyəˌleɪt/ *v.* **-lated, -lating, -lates** to do math again, calculate again: *I made a mistake the first time, so I had to recalculate the numbers.* -*n.* [C;U] **recalculation.**

re·call /rɪˈkɔl/ *v.* **1** to remember s.t.: *I don't recall your name; I don't have a good memory for names.* **2** to ask that s.t. be returned: *The company recalled a product because it was not safe.* —*n.* /ˈrikɔl/ [U] **1** the ability to remember: *She has wonderful recall of people's names.* **2** a request for the return of unsafe goods by the company that made them

re·cant /rɪˈkænt/ *v.* to tell others formally that beliefs, statements, ideas, etc., that one said before are actually untrue: *The witness later recanted the things he said in court and said it was all not true.*

re·cap /ˈriˌkæp/ *n.v.infrml.* **-capped, -capping, -caps** *short for* recapitulation, a short summary of a situation, event, etc.: *Sports announcers give a* <*n.*> *recap of the day's sporting events each evening.*‖*They* <*v.*> *recapped the games.*

re·ca·pit·u·la·tion /ˌrikəˌpɪtʃəˈleɪʃən/ *n.* [C;U] a short summary of a situation, event, etc. that had already been explained once before: *Our professor gave a recapitulation of her previous lecture.* -*v.* **recapitulate.**

re·cap·ture /riˈkæptʃər/ *v.* **-tured, -turing, -tures** to capture s.o. that has escaped: *Police recaptured the prisoner who escaped from prison.*

re·cast /riˈkæst/ *v.* **-cast, -casting, -casts** to show s.t. in a different way, do s.t. again: *He wrote a report about a project's costs, then recast it to show the project's benefits.* -*n.* [U] **recasting.**

re·cede /rɪˈsid/ *v.* **-ceded, -ceding, -cedes** to move back, (*syn.*) to retreat: *Sea water recedes when the tide goes out.* -*adj.* **recessive** /rɪˈsɛsɪv/.

receding hairline *n.* usu. in men, a place on the front of a person's head where he is losing his hair: *My father is not bald, but he has a receding hairline.*

re·ceipt /rɪˈsit/ *n.* [U] a piece of paper showing that a bill is paid: *I bought a hat and the clerk gave me a receipt.* —*v.* to make a receipt for s.o.: *The clerk receipted the sale in case I need to return the coat.*

re·ceiv·a·ble /rɪˈsivəbəl/ *n.* an amount of money that one expects to receive, money due: *Our company has $10,000 in receivables due in this month.*

R

re·ceive /rɪ'siv/ v. **-ceived, -ceiving, -ceives 1** to get or take s.t. that is given or sent, accept, (*syn.*) to acquire: *I received a gift on my birthday.* **2** to formally greet s.o., meet s.o.: *The mayor received the delegation at City Hall.*

re·ceiv·er /rɪ'sivər/ n. **1** a device that receives signals, such as a radio receiver or a telephone receiver: *My telephone receiver is not working, so I can't hear what you say when you call me.* **2** in American football, the player who is supposed to catch the ball: *The receiver caught the ball and scored a touchdown.*

re·ceiv·er·ship /rɪ'sivər,ʃɪp/ n. [C;U] (in law) a legal state where an official person receives money and property for a person or company that is legally not able to pay its bills: *That company has filed for bankruptcy and is now in receivership.*

receiving line n. a line of hosts at a social occasion who meet the guests: *The ambassador and his wife greeted guests in the receiving line for the formal dinner.*

re·cent /'risənt/ adj. in the past, but not very long ago and still going on, such as yesterday, last week, last month: *I paid a recent visit to my parents, last month in fact.*

re·cent·ly /'risəntli/ adv. **1** not too long ago: *I saw my friend recently; we had dinner together last week.* **2** starting not too long ago and still going on, (*syn.*) currently: *Recently, he has been working on his master's degree at the university.*

re·cep·ta·cle /rə'sɛptəkəl/ n. s.t. in which to put or hold things, such as a box, can, or wastebasket: *I put some trash in the receptacle on the street corner.*

re·cep·tion /rə'sɛpʃən/ n. **1** [C] greeting, welcome: *I always receive a warm reception at my brother's house.* **2** [C] a type of party planned so people can meet a special guest and each other: *There was a reception after the wedding so everyone could meet the bride and groom.* **3** [C] the entrance of a business: *I met my friend at the reception of her office.* **4** [U] the quality of a TV or radio signal: *Cable TV gives good reception.*

re·cep·tion·ist /rə'sɛpʃənɪst/ n. a person who greets and directs people at a business entrance: *I gave the receptionist my name and waited for my appointment.*

re·cep·tive /rɪ'sɛptɪv/ adj. interested and wanting to listen to a plan, idea, etc.: *A person was receptive to what the sales clerk said about the TV and bought it. -adv.* **receptively.**

re·cep·tor /rə'sɛptər/ n. **1** (in biology) part of a nerve that receives information from the senses or from other nerves: *Nerve receptors receive information and send it to the brain.* **2** (in chemistry) part of a molecule that receives another chemical: *Molecules connect*
to receptors on other molecules and form new chemicals.

re·cess /'ri,sɛs, rɪ'sɛs/ n. **-es 1** [C;U] a short stop or break, such as in a meeting, school classes, or business: *The school children play in the schoolyard when they have recess outside.* **2** [C] a deep place as in a wall, (*syn.*) cavity: *There were small statues of gods and goddesses in the recesses of the temple wall.*
—v. to stop to relax, take a break in a meeting: *The court recessed at 4:00 P.M. today, and will reconvene at 9:00 A.M. tomorrow.*

re·ces·sion /rə'sɛʃən/ n. a time when economic activity is not strong, usu. defined as a decrease in a nation's GNP for six months: *In a recession, there are fewer jobs for workers, so people have less money.*

re·charge /ri'tʃɑrdʒ/ v. **-charged, -charging, -charges 1** to put energy back into s.t.: *My car battery was not working, so the mechanic recharged it for me.* **2** *infrml.* **to recharge one's batteries:** to take a vacation: *I was so tired that I went to the country for a week to recharge my batteries.*

rec·i·pe /'rɛsə,pi/ n. directions for cooking food: *She used her favorite recipe to make chocolate cake.*

re·cip·i·ent /rə'sɪpiənt/ n. a person who receives s.t. sent or given by another: *My grandmother was the recipient of 72 Christmas cards this year.||That man is a welfare recipient.*

re·cip·ro·cal /rə'sɪprəkəl/ adj. referring to an equal exchange, such as when several nations buy each other's goods, (*syn.*) mutual: *Our country has a reciprocal trade agreement with neighboring countries.*

re·cip·ro·cate /rə'sɪprə,keɪt/ v. **-cated, -cating, -cates** to give s.t. equal or similar to s.o. in exchange for what they have given you: *She invited me to a party, so I reciprocated and invited her to my party. -n.* [U] **reciprocation.**

rec·i·proc·i·ty /,rɛsə'prɑsəti/ n. **-ties** [C] a condition of equal exchange between two or more groups, such as nations trading each other's goods: *Our country has trading reciprocity with France whereby they import our cars and we import theirs.*

re·cit·al /rə'saɪtl/ n. a public musical show, usu. by a singer, musician, dancer, etc.: *The young violinist gave a recital at Symphony Hall.*

rec·i·ta·tion /,rɛsə'teɪʃən/ n. speaking a written part from a book, exam, etc., from memory in front of an audience: *The poet gave a recitation of her poems at the college.*

re·cite /rɪ'saɪt/ v. **-cited, -citing, -cites** to speak s.t. one knows from memory: *The child recited his prayers before going to bed.*

reck·less /'rɛklɪs/ adj. doing s.t. dangerous without thinking, (*syns.*) foolish, rash: *He is*

R

reckless when he drives his car too fast. -adv. **recklessly;** *-n.* [U] **recklessness.**

reck·on /ˈrɛkən/ *v.* **1** to do arithmetic, figure: *He reckoned the bill and handed it to me.* **2** *infrml.* to decide, think: *I reckon that the economy will improve.* **3 to be reckoned with:** (of a person or event) serious, not to be ignored: *He doesn't look very smart, but he is a businessperson to be reckoned with.* **4** *phrasal v. insep.* **to reckon with s.o. or s.t.:** to have to deal with: *If you try to hurt me, you'll have to reckon with my big brother.*

reck·on·ing /ˈrɛkənɪŋ/ *n.* **1** [C] the act of doing arithmetic, *(syn.)* calculation: *His reckonings show that he has enough money to buy a car.* **2** [U] a settlement of accounts: *After the final reckoning, we made money on the sale of our house.* **3** the figuring out of the position of an aircraft or ship **4 day of reckoning:** a day when a person must pay for his or her bad behavior: *He spent money without thinking, and the day of reckoning came when the bank took his car and his house to pay his bills.*

re·claim /riˈkleɪm/ *v.* **1** to take again: *The dictator returned to his country and reclaimed his power.* **2** to renew, improve buildings that need to be fixed or improved: *The city reclaimed its old empty buildings by fixing them up and selling them. -n.* [U] **reclamation** /ˌrɛkləˈmeɪʃən/.

re·clas·si·fy /riˈklæsəˌfaɪ/ *v.* **-fied, -fying, -fies** to put s.t. or s.o. in a new group or category: *She was reclassified from a part-time to a full-time student.*

re·cline /rɪˈklaɪn/ *v.* **-clined, -clining, -clines** **1** to lie back, lean: *He reclined against a wall and closed his eyes.* **2** to lie down, rest: *She reclined on her bed to take a nap.*

rec·luse /ˈrɛkˌlus, rɪˈklus/ *n.* a person who lives alone and avoids other people: *My neighbor is a recluse who never speaks to anyone in our apartment building.*

rec·og·ni·tion /ˌrɛkəgˈnɪʃən/ *n.* [U] **1** credit, praise for doing s.t. well: *An excellent employee was given recognition with an award for her good work.* **2** (in diplomacy) official agreement to another nation's right to national status, trade agreements, etc.: *Israel and the Palestinians gave recognition to each other's right to exist as a nation.* **3** signs that one remembers s.o. or s.t., *(syns.)* awareness, recall: *I saw an old friend, but he showed no recognition that he remembered me.*

rec·og·nize /ˈrɛkəgˌnaɪz/ *v.* **-nized, -nizing, -nizes** **1** to recall, remember s.o. or s.t. when one sees or hears that person or thing: *I recognized an old friend in a crowd and waved to her.* **2** in a formal meeting, to give s.o. a chance to speak: *The chairwoman recognized me and I told the committee my opinion. -adv.* **recognizably.**

rec·og·niz·a·ble /ˌrɛkəgˈnaɪzəbəl/ *adj.* familiar, possible to recognize: *He wore a costume and mask and was not recognizable.*

re·coil /rɪˈkɔɪl/ *v.* **1** to move back quickly from s.t., esp. in horror, fear, etc.: *The hunter recoiled when he saw a dangerous snake in front of him.* **2** to move backwards with force: *A rifle recoils against my shoulder when I shoot it.*

rec·ol·lect /ˌrɛkəˈlɛkt/ *v.* to remember, to recall: *He recollected what we had talked about yesterday and we came to an agreement.*

rec·ol·lec·tion /ˌrɛkəˈlɛkʃən/ *n.* [C;U] an ability or act of remembering, recall: *I have a clear recollection of what you said during our meeting.*

re·com·bine /ˌrikəmˈbaɪn/ *v.* **-bined, -bining, -bines** to put things together in a new way: *Three departments in that company were recombined into two.*

re·com·mence /ˌrikəˈmɛns/ *v.* **-menced, -mencing, -mences** to begin again, *(syn.)* to resume: *Rain interrupted the tennis match, but it recommenced after the rain stopped. -n.* [U] **recommencement.**

rec·om·mend /ˌrɛkəˈmɛnd/ *v.* **1** to tell others about s.t. one likes: *I recommend that restaurant to you because it has very good food.* **2** to advise s.o. to do s.t.: *My doctor recommends that I see a specialist for my skin condition.*

rec·om·men·da·tion /ˌrɛkəmənˈdeɪʃən/ *n.* [C;U] written or spoken praise about s.t. or s.o.'s good points, *(syn.)* approval: *He gave his friend a recommendation on a good movie to see.*‖*Her teacher gave her a good recommendation for college.*

rec·om·pense /ˈrɛkəmˌpɛns/ *n.* [U] payment, esp. for being hurt or for loss of property: *He was hurt in a car accident and finally received fair recompense from an insurance company.* —*v.* **-pensed, -pensing, -penses** to pay, *(syn.)* to compensate: *Insurance recompensed him for his injury.*

rec·on·cile /ˈrɛkənˌsaɪl/ *v.* **-ciled, -ciling, -ciles** **1** to bring together people or ideas that were separated, *(syn.)* to harmonize: *The husband and wife separated, then reconciled, and now live happily together.* **2** to get used to, adjust to s.t. difficult: *He has reconciled himself to the idea that he is getting old. -adj.* **reconcilable.**

rec·on·cil·i·a·tion /ˌrɛkənˌsɪliˈeɪʃən/ *n.* an agreement made after an argument or fight: *The two friends had a reconciliation after they disagreed, and now they are friends again.*

re·con·di·tion /ˌrikənˈdɪʃən/ *v.* to put s.t. back into good condition, *(syn.)* to refurbish: *She reconditioned her sailboat with a new coat of paint and a new engine. -n.* [U] **reconditioning.**

R

re·con·firm /ˌrikən'fɜrm/ v. to confirm again, establish more firmly: *I reconfirmed my airline reservations the day before my flight.* -n. [C;U] **reconfirmation** /ˌrikənfər'meɪʃən/.

re·con·nais·sance /rɪ'kɑnəsəns, -zəns/ n. [C;U] (in the military) to look over an area, check it out: *An air force plane made a reconnaissance over the area to track where the enemy is.*

re·con·sid·er /ˌrikən'sɪdər/ v. to rethink s.t. after deciding against it, to change one's mind: *She did not agree to marry him, but later she reconsidered and agreed to do so.*

re·con·sti·tute /ri'kɑnstɪˌtut/ v. **-tuted, -tuting, -tutes** to return s.t. to the way it was before, renew: *A mother reconstituted powdered milk by adding water to it for her child to drink.* -adj. **reconstituted;** -n. [U] **reconstitution.**

re·con·struct /ˌrikən'strʌkt/ v. **1** to rebuild, renew s.t. to its original state: *People reconstructed their homes after the hurricane destroyed them.* **2** to figure s.t. out piece by piece: *Police reconstructed how the murder happened by talking to people who saw it happen.* -n. [C;U] **reconstruction.**

re·con·vene /ˌrikən'vin/ v. **-vened, -vening, -venes** to convene again, begin a meeting again: *The court stopped for lunch and reconvened at 1:30 P.M.*

rec·ord /'rɛkərd/ n. **1** s.t. (usu. written) that proves that an event happened, including records of business transactions, scientific data, cultural, or other human activities: *The records of our business are kept in our computer and in printouts.* **2** the best time, distance, etc., in an athletic event: *She holds the world record for the 100-meter dash.* **3** a criminal's history of arrests and things he or she did wrong: *That thief has a long criminal record.* **4** a flat black disk onto which a sound recording, esp. music, has been pressed: *He has a collection of Elvis Presley, on records from the 1950s.* **5 break the record:** to make a new fastest time, distance, etc.: *A runner broke the world record for the 100-meter run yesterday.* **6 for the record:** indicating s.t. official for the public or for clarity: *The lawyer told the court, for the record, that the woman he represented would not officially speak in court.* **7 off the record:** referring to s.t. that should not be heard by the public, (syn.) unofficial: *The mayor called in reporters to talk to them off the record about the latest crime wave, and asked them not to publish what he said in their newspapers.* **8 on the record:** referring to s.t. that can be made public, (syn.) official: *The mayor then spoke on the record about what his plans are for fighting crime.*
—v. /rɪ'kɔrd/ **1** to make a written record of s.t.: *The cash register recorded the $10 purchase*

and printed a receipt. **2** to register s.t. officially: *After he bought the house, he recorded his ownership at City Hall.* **3** to make a sound or video recording of s.t., as on disk or tape: *The concert we went to was recorded for showing on TV.*

re·cord·er /rɪ'kɔrdər/ n. **1** a person who records things: *A recorder of births works at the City Hall.* **2** (music) a wind instrument **3** a device used to record sight or sound. *Most reporters have a tape recorder to use in interviews.*

re·cord·ing /rɪ'kɔrdɪŋ/ n. an electronic or magnetic copy of an audio or visual event: *Recordings of music are often sold as CD's.*

rec·ord player /'rɛkərd/ n. a device used to play records, (syn.) phonograph: *He has a record player to play 1950s records of pop music.*

re·count /rɪ'kaʊnt/ v. **1** to count s.t. again, refigure: *Workers recounted the ballots because the election was close, and they wanted to be sure of who won.* **2** to tell, describe (a story, situation): *She recounted stories about her youth in Indonesia.*
—n. /'ri,kaʊnt/ another count: *Workers did a recount of the ballots.*

re·coup /rɪ'kup/ v. to gain back s.t. after losing it, (syn.) to regain: *The price of our stocks fell, but we recouped our losses when prices rose again.*

re·course /'ri,kɔrs/ n.frml. a way, a method of fixing a bad situation: *The driver who hit my car refused to pay for fixing it, so I had no recourse but to go to court to get my money from him.*

re·cov·er /rɪ'kʌvər/ v. **1** to regain one's health: *He recovered from his illness and is well again.* **2** to get s.t. back, to get control again, (syn.) to retrieve: *Workers recovered a sunken boat from the lake.* **3** to make up for losses: *The race car driver recovered the time he lost at the start of the race and won.* **4** to put a new cover (new material) on s.t.: *to recover a sofa* -adj. **recoverable.** See: reupholster.

re·cov·er·y /rɪ'kʌvəri/ n. **-ies 1** return of one's good health: *She made a quick recovery after surgery.* **2** [U] regaining a loss: *The recovery of the missing painting took several years.*

recovery room n. a special room in a hospital where patients are taken and watched after surgery: *After the operation, the doctor watched his patient in the recovery room. See:* operating room.

re·cre·ate /ˌrikri'eɪt/ v. **-ated, -ating, -ates** to create again, piece together s.t. that was broken or lost: *A business lost some of its records in a fire and had to re-create them from the workers' memories.*

rec·re·a·tion /ˌrɛkri'eɪʃən/ n. [C;U] fun things to do, such as sports, hobbies, and amusements: *Her favorite recreation is playing tennis.*

re·cruit /rɪ'krut/ v. to interview and choose people to join an organization or cause: *She recruits people to become sales representatives for her company.*
—n. **1** a soldier who has just joined the military: *A sergeant shouted at the recruits to stand at attention.* **2** a new person in a group or cause: *New recruits join our club every summer.*

re·cruit·er /rɪ'krutər/ n. a person who recruits others: *A recruiter for our company visits college campuses to recruit students to work for us when they graduate. -n.* **recruiting.**

re·cruit·ment /rɪ'krutmənt/ n. [U] the process of interviewing and choosing people to do a job: *In the army, recruitment is done by sergeants.*

rec·tal /'rɛktəl/ adj. related to the rectum: *The mother took her baby's temperature with a rectal thermometer.*

rec·tan·gle /'rɛk,tæŋgəl/ n. any shape with four straight sides that make right angles: *My textbook is shaped like a rectangle. -adj.* **rectangular** /rɛk'tæŋgyələr/.

rec·ti·fi·a·ble /,rɛktə'faɪəbəl/ adj.frml. able to be made right, correctable: *There was a mistake made in the contract, but it is rectifiable.*

rec·ti·fy /'rɛktə,faɪ/ v.frml. **-fied, -fying, -fies** to correct, make right: *He rectified the mistake in the contract by changing its wording. -n.* [U] **rectification** /,rɛktəfə'keɪʃən/.

rec·ti·lin·e·ar /,rɛktə'lɪniər/ adj. having or forming straight lines

rec·ti·tude /'rɛktə,tud/ n. [U] strict honesty and/or strong morality in a person: *Her moral rectitude is much respected by her friends.*

rec·tor /'rɛktər/ n. **1** a minister, esp. an Episcopalian or Anglican priest, who is the head of an area served by a church: *The rector reports church business to other church officials.* **2** the head of some schools: *The rector scolded a rude student.*

rec·to·ry /'rɛktəri/ n. **-ries** the house that a church has for its minister to live in: *After the church service, the minister went to her rectory.*

rec·tum /'rɛktəm/ n. the lower part of the large intestine, which passes waste matter to the anus: *A doctor inserted a tube to examine the patient's rectum.*

re·cum·bent /rɪ'kʌmbənt/ adj. referring to s.o. or s.t. lying down, (syn.) reclining: *The Spanish artist Goya painted a famous picture of a recumbent woman.*

re·cu·per·ate /rɪ'kupə,reɪt/ v. **-ated, -ating, -ates** to feel better after illness or tiredness, (syn.) to heal: *He recuperated quickly after being in the hospital. -adj.* **recuperative**

/rɪ'kupə,reɪtɪv, -pərətɪv/; -n. [U] **recuperation** /rɪ,kupə'reɪʃən/.

re·cur /rɪ'kɜr/ v. **-curred, -curring, -curs** to happen again: *His sore throat recurs every winter. -n.* [C;U] **recurrence.**

re·cur·rent /rɪ'kɜrənt, -'kʌr-/ adj.frml. happening again and again or regularly: *His troubles with money are recurrent. -adv.* **recurrently.**

re·cy·cle /ri'saɪkəl/ v. **-cled, -cling, -cles** to process and reuse materials, esp. waste items: *New York City recycles newspapers, bottles, and other garbage, and makes them into new products. See:* biodegradable.

USAGE NOTE: *Recycling* has become common in North America, and there are special trash cans on the street where people can put glass and plastic bottles and aluminum cans to be recycled: *The store where we buy food collects plastic bags to be recycled.* At home, some people sort trash into paper, plastics, and metals and take them to a recycling center. In some communities special *recycling containers* and trucks pick up the recycling. Other communities have passed laws that require citizens to pay a fine if they do not recycle.

---

re·cy·cling /ri'saɪklɪŋ/ n. [U] the collection, processing, and reuse of waste items, such as used bottles and newspapers: *Recycling of aluminum cans saves energy because less energy is used in recycling aluminum than in making new aluminum.*

red /rɛd/ n.adj. **1** [C;U] a basic color like that of blood: *She likes to wear <n.> red and has several <adj.> red suits.* **2 to be in the red:** to be in debt: *Our company was making money, but now it's in the red. See:* in the black. **3 to see red:** to be very angry: *My father will see red when I tell him I wrecked his car.*

red alert n. a high state of being ready, esp. for a fight or war: *All men rushed to their guns when the ship went on red alert.*

red-blood·ed /'rɛd'blʌdɪd/ adj.fig. having qualities such as courage, energy, and love of country: *Like any red-blooded American, he is ready to fight for his country.*

red-carpet adj.fig. special, for important people: *When the new ambassador arrived, the embassy gave her a red-carpet welcome with a band and a big party.*
—n. **to roll out the red carpet:** to welcome s.o. with special honors, often including a red carpet for them to walk on

red cent n.infrml.fig. a very small amount of money, s.t. worthless: *That old car is not worth a red cent.*

Red Cross n. an international organization for relief of human pain and suffering and for im-

R

provement in public health: *The Red Cross is organized in over 100 countries to help provide better health care.*

red·den /'rɛdn/ v. to become red, (syn.) to blush: *When he is embarrassed, his face reddens.*

re·dec·o·rate /ri'dɛkə,reɪt/ v. **-rated, -rating, -rates** to decorate s.t. over again, (syn.) to refurbish: *After living in our house for ten years, we redecorated with new paint and furniture.*

re·dec·o·ra·tion /ri,dɛkə'reɪʃən/ n. [U] decoration of s.t. over again, esp. a home, office, or building: *The redecoration of our offices included a new carpet, fresh paint on the walls, and some new furniture.*

re·deem /rɪ'dim/ v. **1** to turn s.t. in, such as a coupon or shares in a mutual fund, for cash, a discount, or merchandise: *I redeemed coupons for cereal and mouthwash at the supermarket and saved $1.50.* **2** to put oneself back in good standing with s.o.: *He made a bad mistake but redeemed himself by fixing it before the problem became serious.* **3** (in religion) to save s.o. from sin: *His belief in God redeemed him.* **4** to pay for s.t. pawned, repay: *He redeemed his watch at the pawnbroker for $100.* -adj. **redeemable**; -n. **redeemer.** *See:* redemption.

re·de·fine /,ridə'faɪn/ v. **-fined, -fining, -fines** to describe s.t. differently, define anew: *The company redefined its plans for the future and hired more workers to complete the new plans.* -n. **redefinition** /,ridɛfə'nɪʃən/.

re·de·liv·er /,ridə'lɪvər/ v. to deliver again: *I was not home when the delivery person came with the package, so he redelivered it the next day.* -n. [C;U] **redelivery.**

re·demp·tion /rə'dɛmpʃən/ n. [U] **1** an act of redeeming, turning s.t. in, usu. for money: *I must return this rented VCR for redemption of my $100 deposit.* **2** (in religion) the state of being saved from sin: *Most Christians believe that redemption comes with belief in Jesus Christ. See:* redeem.

re·de·sign /,ridə'zaɪn/ v. to design or create s.t. differently: *Each year auto makers redesign their cars.*
—n. **1** the process of redesign: *The redesign of our plans will take several weeks.* **2** an example of redesign: *This year's Honda Civic™ is a redesign of last year's model.*

re·de·vel·op /,ridə'vɛləp/ v. to renew s.t., such as old buildings: *The city redeveloped its old waterfront into a new tourist attraction.* -n. [U] **redevelopment.**

red-eye adj. referring to late-night transportation when passengers are tired and have "red eyes": *I took the 11:00 P.M. red-eye flight from Los Angeles to New York and arrived at 8:00 A.M.*

red-hand·ed adj.fig. referring to s.o. caught in the act of doing s.t. bad: *Police caught the thief red-handed with the stolen money in his hand as he ran from the bank.*

red·head /'rɛd,hɛd/ n. a person with red hair, esp. a woman: *My sister is the redhead standing by the window. See:* blonde, brunette.

red herring n.fig. s.t. said or done to confuse s.o. about the true importance of s.t.: *He said I did not understand, but that was a red herring to avoid discussion of his mistake.*

red-hot adj. **1** very hot: *Iron looks red-hot when it is heated in a fire.* **2** s.t. very new and exciting: *That musical group just started selling a red-hot new recording.*

re·di·rect /,ridə'rɛkt/ v. to turn s.t. in a new direction: *The writer redirected her work from writing novels to writing poetry.* -n. [U] **redirection.**

re·dis·cov·er /,ridɪ'skʌvər/ v. to find s.t. again: *A famous painting was lost during the war, then s.o. rediscovered it at a small art store.* -n. **rediscovery.**

re·dis·trib·ute /,ridɪ'strɪbyut/ v. **-uted, -uting, -utes** to distribute again, give s.t. out in a different way: *Governments redistribute money by collecting taxes from everyone, and then giving welfare to those who need it.* -n. **redistribution** /,ridɪstrə'byuʃən/.

re·dis·trict /ri'dɪstrɪkt/ v. to draw new lines defining an area or a district: *Every ten years US states are redistricted so that representatives to Congress can be elected fairly.*

red-letter adj.fig. about good news: *It was a red-letter day for him when he won the contest.*

red-light district n. an area of a city or town with houses of prostitution: *Police patrol the red-light district to try to stop trouble.*

redneck /'rɛd,nɛk/ n.pej. (in USA) a stereotypical working-class Southern white man, seen as uneducated and disliking people not like himself: *Rednecks get the name from having sunburned necks from working outside.*

red·ness /'rɛdnɪs/ n. **1** [U] a red color: *The redness of the sun just before it set was beautiful.* **2** a condition of reddened skin that is a sign of swelling or itching: *Redness on the baby's bottom indicated he had a rash.*

re·do /ri'du/ **-did** /'dɪd/, **-done** /'dʌn/, **-doing, -does,** /'dʌz/ v. to do s.t. over again: *I redid my report to make it more complete.*

re·dou·ble /ri'dʌbəl/ v. **-bled, -bling, -bles** to try harder, work faster: *Firefighters redoubled their efforts to save the people in the burning building.* -n. [U] **redoubling.**

re·doubt·a·ble /ri'dautəbəl/ adj.frml. (often used humorously) getting or deserving respect because of one's ability or power, (syn.) awesome: *Champion boxers are redoubtable sportsmen.*

re·dress /rɪ'drɛs/ n. [U] a correction of s.t. wrong, (syns.) a compensation, a remedy: *He*

was hurt because his workplace was unsafe, so he went to court to try to find redress for his pain.
—*v.* to correct a wrong, (*syn.*) to remedy: *The court redressed her pain by making the company pay her $1 million.*

red tape *n.* [U] problems and delays caused by bureaucracy and official paperwork: *His visa application is tied up in red tape at the embassy.*

USAGE NOTE: The term *red tape* comes from the red tape used to tie up official documents to keep them together as they pass from one person to another.

---

re·duce /rɪ'dus/ *v.* **-duced, -ducing, -duces 1** to make s.t. smaller in size or weight: *He reduced his weight by 20 pounds by eating less and exercising.* **2** to lessen in severity, importance, etc.: *She stopped smoking cigarettes and reduced her risk of getting lung cancer.* **3** to make s.o. poor and unhappy: *The hurricane reduced many people to living without food or housing for days.*

re·duc·tion /rɪ'dʌkʃən/ *n.* [C;U] **1** a decrease, less of s.t.: *A reduction of 100 employees was made after the company was sold.* **2** a decrease in price: *This weekend there is a 30% reduction on all shoes at that store.*

re·dun·dant /rɪ'dʌndənt/ *adj.* **1** not necessary or needed, (*syns.*) repetitious, superfluous: *The teacher told him the ideas in his essay were redundant because he repeated the same idea three times.* **2** unneeded as an employee: *Her position at the company was declared redundant and she was told to find a new job. -n.* [C;U] **redundancy;** *-adv.* **redundantly.**

reed /rid/ *n.* **1** a long stem of certain water grasses used to make floor mats, roofs for houses, etc.: *People make baskets out of reeds.* **2** an instrument, such as a clarinet, bassoon, or oboe, that uses a reed to create sound

re·ed·u·cate /ri'edʒə,keɪt/ *v.* **-cated, -cating, -cates** to teach s.o. new ways of doing things: *Some countries have programs to reeducate farmers to use new ways of farming so they can grow more food. -n.* [U] **reeducation.**

reed·y /'ridi/ *adj.* **-ier, -iest 1** high-pitched: *That soprano has a reedy voice.* **2** full of reeds

reef /rif/ *n.* in the ocean, a long bar made of sand, coral, etc.: *A ship hit a coral reef and sank.*

reef·er /'rifər/ *n.slang* a marijuana cigarette: *He smoked a reefer and got in trouble with the police.*

reek /rik/ *v.* to have a very strong bad smell: *A drunkard reeks of alcohol.*

reel (1) /ril/ *n.* a fishing device on the handle of a fishing rod by which fish line is wound onto the rod: *He bought a new reel and*

stronger fish line, so he could catch bigger fish.
—*v.* **1** to wind or unwind fishing line: *The fisher reeled in a fish.* **2** *phrasal v. sep.* **to reel s.t. off:** to talk quickly: *He reeled off three reasons why he wanted to take a vacation. See:* rattle off.

reel (2) *n.* a type of dance in which people lock arms and turn around quickly to the music: *American folk dancers like to do the Virginia reel.*
—*v.* to move unsteadily, (*syn.*) to lurch: *A boxer reeled and fell when his opponent hit him in the head.*

re·e·lect /,riɪ'lɛkt/ *v.* to elect an official again: *The mayor was reelected for a third term in office. -n.* [C;U] **reelection.**

re·e·merge /,riɪ'mɜrdʒ/ *v.* **-merged, -merging, -merges** to come out again: *Hikers went into a cave and reemerged an hour later. -n.* [U] **reemergence.**

re·en·act /,riɪn'ækt/ *v.* to show how s.t. was done by acting it out: *Witnesses reenacted the crime for the police by showing them how the thieves held up the store. -n.* [C;U] **reenactment.**

re·en·force /,riən'fɔrs/ *v.* **-forced, -forcing, -forces 1** to strengthen, such as by adding more police officers or soldiers to others: *The general reenforced his men on the front line by sending 10,000 more troops there.* **2** to add additional meaning to s.t., (*syn.*) to emphasize: *Teachers reenforce their lectures by using visual aids.*

re·en·force·ment /,riən'fɔrsmənt/ *n.* [C;U] additional strength, such as more police officers or troops: *The department store clerk requested reinforcements when more customers showed up for the special sale.*

re·en·ter /ri'ɛntər/ *v.* to enter again: *He left college two years ago, then reentered this year.*

re·en·try /ri'ɛntri/ *n.* **-tries** [C;U] the act or process of entering again: *A space vehicle made a reentry into the earth's atmosphere after being in space for a week.*

re·e·val·u·ate /,riɪ'vælyu,eɪt/ *v.* **-ated, -ating, -ates** to evaluate again, rethink s.t.: *They didn't like the idea at first, but when they reevaluated it later, they decided that it would probably work. -n.* [C;U] **reevaluation.**

re·ex·am·ine /,riɪg'zæmɪn/ *v.* **-ined, -ining, -ines** to examine s.t. again, restudy: *A doctor reexamined her patient and found a problem she had not seen the first time.*

re·fash·ion /ri'fæʃən/ *v.* to remake s.t., redo: *I took my big old kitchen table to a wood worker; he refashioned it into a smaller table for my bedroom.*

re·fer /rɪ'fɜr/ *v.* **-ferred, -ferring, -fers 1** to direct one's attention to s.t. or s.o.: *A customer*

R

referred to an order that he had placed.||*My doctor referred me to a specialist.* **2** to send s.t. or s.o. for help: *The company referred me to their customer service department to solve my problem.*

ref·er·ee /ˌrɛfəˈri/ *n.* a type of official who makes players follow the rules of a sport: *The football referee blew his whistle to stop the game.*
—*v.* to act as a referee for a game or match: *My friend referees basketball games.*

ref·er·ence /ˈrɛfərəns, ˈrɛfrəns/ *n.* **1** [C;U] a source of information: *That student used an encyclopedia as a reference for his term paper.* **2** [C] a recommendation, esp. for employment: *My former boss said that I could use him as a reference.*
—*v.* to refer to s.t.: *The student referenced his term paper by quoting from several newspaper articles.*

ref·er·en·dum /ˌrɛfəˈrɛndəm/ *n.* **-dums** or **-da** /-də/ a direct popular vote taken nationally or regionally on an important question: *A national referendum was held to decide whether or not to pay off the national debt through increased taxes.*

re·fer·ral /rɪˈfɜrəl/ *n.* **1** [C;U] an act of referring one person to s.o. else: *My doctor gave me a referral to a skin specialist.* **2** [C] the person referred: *I came to the skin specialist as a referral from my general practitioner.*

re·fig·ure /riˈfɪgyər/ *v.* **-ured, -uring, -ures** to redo the arithmetic on s.t.: *My bill was incorrect, but the waiter refigured it and corrected the mistake.*

re·fill *n.* /ˈrifɪl/ **1** another serving or amount of s.t., esp. a drink: *He drank a cola and asked the waiter for a refill.* **2** a replacement: *During the essay exam, his favorite pen ran out of ink, so he inserted a refill to be able to continue writing with it.*
—*v.* /riˈfɪl/ to fill s.t. with more of whatever it had in it before: *I used all of my medicine, so the pharmacy refilled the prescription for me.*

re·fi·nance /ˌrifaɪˈnæns, riˈfaɪˌnæns/ *v.* **-nanced, -nancing, -nances** to finance s.t. again, such as taking out a new loan: *Interest rates went down by 1%, so I refinanced my loan at the lower rate.* *-n.* [U] **refinancing.**

re·fine /rɪˈfaɪn/ *v.* **-fined, -fining, -fines** **1** to change, process s.t. into a purer form that is ready to be used: *Oil companies refine crude oil into gasoline.* **2** to improve s.t., make it better: *My professor refined her lectures and used them to write a textbook.*

re·fined /rɪˈfaɪnd/ *adj.* **1** processed into a finer form: *Refined sugar is white.* **2** referring to a person or manner that is polite, educated, (*syn.*) polished: *She has refined manners; her behavior is always socially correct.*

re·fine·ment /rɪˈfaɪnmənt/ *n.* **1** [C;U] a polished form, a state of greater perfection of s.t., (*syn.*) elegance: *The kings and queens of France demanded refinement in dress and in manners.* **2** [U] the process of making s.t. pure: *the refinement of oil*

re·fin·er·y /rɪˈfaɪnəri/ *n.* **-ies** a place for refining raw materials into products for sale: *Sugar refineries refine sugar cane into syrup and sugar.* *-n.* **refining.**

re·fin·ish /riˈfɪnɪʃ/ *v.* **-es** to put a new finish or coating on s.t.: *I sanded the old paint off my table and refinished it with a new coat.*

re·fit /riˈfɪt/ *v.* **-fitted, -fitting, -fits** to fix s.t. so it looks new, esp. an old boat: *We refitted our boat with new sails and a new coat of paint.*

re·flect /rɪˈflɛkt/ *v.* **1** to give off a shine: *Sunlight reflected off the water.* **2** *phrasal v. insep.* **to reflect on: a. s.o. or s.t.:** to affect the quality or reputation of: *Students who do well on exams reflect well on their teachers.* **b. s.t.:** to think deeply about, (*syn.*) to ponder: *An old man reflected on what he had done in his lifetime.* **3** to show an image of s.t. in water, a mirror, etc.: *I like to watch clouds reflected in the water.* **4** to give a true image or idea about s.t.: *This writer's poetry reflects his love of nature. See:* reminisce.

re·flec·tion /rɪˈflɛkʃən/ *n.* **1** [C] an image created by reflected light: *He looked at his reflection in the mirror.* **2** [C;U] a shining: *The reflection of moonlight on the water is very romantic.* **3** [C;U] a deep thought, reference about s.t.: *This book has poems and the poet's reflections on what the poems mean.* **4** [U] the throwing back of light, sound, or heat: *This room is always warm because of the reflection of sunlight through the window.* **5** positive or negative credit s.t. gives to s.t. else: *A child's behavior is a reflection on her parents. -adj.* **reflective.**

re·flec·tor /rɪˈflɛktər/ *n.* an object that reflects s.t., esp. light: *Bicycles have yellow or red reflectors on the wheels to make them easier to see at night.*

re·flex /ˈriflɛks/ *n.* **-es** a quick reaction to s.t., usu. without thinking: *Because he has quick reflexes, he caught the glass before it broke on the floor.*

re·flex·ive /rɪˈflɛksɪv/ *adj.* (in grammar) a word that refers back to the subject or object in a sentence: *"Himself" is a reflexive pronoun in the sentence "He hurt himself when he fell."*

re·fo·cus /riˈfoukəs/ *v.* **-es** **1** to focus again after being focused on s.t. else: *I refocused my camera on the mountains far away.* **2** to change one's attention from one idea or job to another: *I work in an office during the day and refocus on my classes at night.*

re·form /rəˈfɔrm/ *v.* **1** to change s.t., improve s.t. that exists, esp. government: *A new presi-*

dent reformed the nation's health care system.
2 to correct bad behavior: *An alcoholic reformed his ways and never drank again.*

re·for·ma·tion /ˌrɛfər'meɪʃən/ n. [C;U] an improvement, reforming

re·for·ma·to·ry /rə'fɔrmə,tɔri/ n. **-ries** a type of prison for children and teenagers where they live and go to school, and attempts are made to improve their behavior: *A judge sentenced the 14-year-old boy to a year in a reformatory.*

re·formed /rə'fɔrmd/ adj. **1** changed for the better, corrected: *He is a reformed smoker; he hasn't had a cigarette in three years.* **2** changed, made new, (syn.) modernized: *She belongs to the reformed branch of an orthodox religion.*

re·for·mer /rə'fɔrmər/ n. a person who works for change and improvement, esp. in a system of government: *The mayor is a reformer who stopped dishonesty in city politics.*

reform school n.var. of reformatory.

re·for·mu·late /ri'fɔrmyə,leɪt/ v. **-lated, -lating, -lates** to rethink, redo s.t. in a new way: *The medicine was reformulated to make it taste better.* -n. [U] **reformulation.**

re·frac·tion /rɪ'frækʃən/ n. [U] the bending of light waves, such as through a prism: *Refraction of sunlight makes the sky seem blue by day and orange at sunset.* -n. **refractory;** -v. **refract.**

re·frain /rɪ'freɪn/ v. not to do s.t., to avoid doing s.t.: *Students refrain from smoking in the classroom.*
—n. a song, tune; lines repeated in a song or tune, (syn.) chorus: *We sang the refrain of the song many times.*

re·fresh /rɪ'frɛʃ/ v. **1** to make strong and clean again, (syn.) to revive: *Eight hours of sleep and a shower always refresh me.* **2 to refresh s.o.'s memory:** to remind s.o.: *I read the end of the book again to refresh my memory about the story.*

re·fresh·er course /rɪ'frɛʃər/ n. a course that gives students a review and some new information about a subject they studied before: *He took a refresher course in computers.*

re·fresh·ing /rɪ'frɛʃɪŋ/ adj. making s.o. feel strong and new again: *I took a refreshing bath after a hot day's work.* -adv. **refreshingly.**

re·fresh·ment /rɪ'frɛʃmənt/ n. [C;U] food and drink that refreshes: *He needed refreshment, so he drank a tall glass of cola.*

re·frig·er·a·tor /rɪ'frɪdʒə,reɪtər/ n. a storage box with cooling and usu. freezing sections for keeping food fresh: *We keep all our food in the refrigerator to keep it fresh.* -n. [U] **refrigeration;** -v. **refrigerate.**

re·fu·el /ri'fyuəl/ v. to put more fuel into the tanks of s.t., such as an airplane, car, or truck:

Our plane stopped in Chicago to refuel before flying on to New York.

ref·uge /'rɛfyudʒ/ n. [C;U] **to take** or **seek refuge:** a place of safety from danger and discomfort: *When it started to rain hard, I took refuge in the doorway of a building.*

ref·u·gee /ˌrɛfyu'dʒi/ n. a person trying to leave bad living conditions, such as oppression, war, hunger, etc.: *During the war, many refugees went to safer countries nearby to try to live better lives.*

re·fund /'ri,fʌnd/ n. an amount of money returned to the person who bought s.t.: *The new TV never worked well, so I brought it back to the store for a refund.*
—v. to give a refund: *They refunded my money when I returned it.*

re·fur·bish /ri'fɜrbɪʃ/ v.frml. **-es** to change a room, office, or home so that it looks newer, redecorate: *The new mayor refurbished his office.* -n. [U] **refurbishment.**

re·fur·nish /ri'fɜrnɪʃ/ v. **-es** to redecorate, redo the furnishings of a room, office, house, etc.: *After we lived in the house for ten years, we refurnished the living room with fresh wallpaper and new furniture.* -n. **refurnishing.**

re·fus·al /rə'fyuzəl/ n. [C;U] an act of rejecting s.t.: *Alice's refusal to marry Chandler made Chandler very sad.*

re·fuse (1) /rə'fyuz/ v. **-fused, -fusing, -fuses 1** to say no, (syn.) to decline: *He refused an invitation to a party.* **2** to reject, not agree to (do s.t.): *She refuses to drink alcohol or eat meat.*

ref·use (2) /'rɛfyus/ n. garbage, waste, things that should be thrown away: *Refuse is collected every Tuesday in our town.*

re·fute /rə'fyut/ v. **-futed, -futing, -futes** to prove s.t. is incorrect, disprove: *One witness refuted the statement of another by presenting new evidence.* -n. [C;U] **refutation.**

re·gain /ri'geɪn/ v. **1** to gain again, to get back, (syn.) to recover: *She regained the money that she lost.* **2** to add back on: *She regained the 15 pounds that she lost.*

re·gal /'rigəl/ adj. **1** related to kings and queens: *The regal crown is on the king's head.* **2** fig. great, good enough for a king or queen: *That lawyer makes a regal amount of money.* -adv. **regally.**

re·gale /rɪ'geɪl/ v.n.frml. **-galed, -galing, -gales** to entertain, (syn.) to amuse: *Our friend <v.> regaled us with stories of things he had done in Africa.*

re·ga·lia /rə'geɪlyə/ n. [U] the clothes and symbols used by people in ceremonies: *The queen's regalia consists of a crown, a scepter, and a long, beautiful robe.*

re·gard /rə'gɑrd/ v. **1** to think about the importance of s.t., (syn.) to value: *He regards his job as the most important thing in his life.* **2** to

view, look upon: *On our vacation, we regarded the mountains as we drove through them.* **3** to deal with a certain matter, (*syn.*) to concern: *This letter regards the payment for your new car.* **4** to show honor for, respect: *I regard teachers and doctors highly.*
—*n.sing.* [U] **1** respect, concern, or consideration for s.t. or s.o.: *I have high regard for mothers who take good care of their children.* **2** *n.pl.* **regards:** best wishes: *Give my regards to Joe when you see him.* **3 in** or **with regard to:** concerning: *In (or) With regard to our conversation yesterday, I am sending the book to you by mail.*

re·gard·ing /rə'gɑrdɪŋ/ *prep.* about, concerning, with regard to: *Regarding your order, we will ship it today.*

re·gard·less /rə'gɑrdlɪs/ *adv.* without thinking about the importance of s.t., disregarding no matter: *Regardless of what his parents think, he is going to leave home.*

re·gat·ta /rə'gɑtə, -'gæ-/ *n.* a boat race: *Small sailboats raced in a regatta on the river.*

re·gen·cy /'riʤənsi/ *n.* **-cies** [U] **1** a political head or group who rules a kingdom while the king or queen is too ill or too young to rule: *The priest ruled during the regency for the young king.* **2** the time of the rule of a regent

re·gen·er·ate /ri'ʤɛnə,reɪt/ *v.* **-ated, -ating, -ates 1** to make s.t. again, re-create: *Lobsters regenerate their claws when they lose them.* **2** to renew or cause to be reborn: *The election regenerated people's belief in government.* -*n.* **regeneration.**

re·gent /'riʤənt/ *n.* **1** a ruler who takes the place of a king or queen who is too young or too ill to rule: *The young king's aunt acted as his regent.* **2** a person who runs a university or other educational institution: *She is a member of the Board of Regents for New York State's educational system.*

reg·gae /'rɛgeɪ/ *n.* [U] a kind of music that began in the West Indies: *Bob Marley was one of the most famous reggae artists.*

reg·i·cide /'rɛʒə,saɪd/ *n.* [U] the killing of a king or queen: *Regicide has happened several times in British history.*

re·gime /reɪ'ʒim, rə-/ *n.* **1** a government, system of ruling: *A group of revolutionaries replaced the old regime of kings and queens.* **2** a diet to lose weight or any system of medical care or regular exercise, (*syn.*) regimen: *He follows a strict regime of eating only low-fat foods.*

reg·i·men /'rɛʤəmɪn/ *n.* **1** a diet, a way of eating: *She always follows a vegetarian regimen.* **2** a way of living: *His daily regimen always includes an hour of exercise.*

reg·i·ment *n.* /'rɛʤəmənt/ a group of soldiers made up of several battalions (approx. 400 sol-

diers): *He did his military service with the Third Training Regiment.*
—*v.* /'rɛʤə,mɛnt/ to control completely: *My chemistry teacher regiments our class very closely.* -*adj.* **regimental** /,rɛʤə'mɛntl/.

re·gion /'riʤən/ *n.* **1** a geographical area of a country: *The northeast region of the USA includes New York and the six New England states.* **2** part of the atmosphere: *Space vehicles enter the upper regions of the atmosphere as they return from outer space.* **3** an area of the body: *He has a pain in his abdominal region.* -*adv.* **regionally.** *See:* area.

re·gion·al /'riʤənəl/ *adj.* related to a region or geographical area: *I will be going to my company's regional meeting next week.*

re·gion·al·ism /'riʤənə,lɪzəm/ *n.* **1** [C] a phrase or saying common in a region of a nation: *"He squeals louder than a pig stuck under a fence" is a southern USA regionalism.* **2** [U] political, economic, and social interests special to a geographical area: *Regionalism in Canada has led to disagreement between eastern and western provinces of that country.* -*v.* **regionalize.**

reg·i·ster /'rɛʤɪstər/ *v.* **1** to write one's name on an official list, such as a voter list or a school's student list: *I registered to vote in the presidential election this year.* **2** *frml.* to include, indicate one's ideas, opinion, etc.: *At the town meeting, a citizen registered her opinion about new taxes.* **3** to show (of instruments or faces): *The scales registered 120 pounds.||His face registered anger.*
—*n.* **1** a list or other official record of people who register: *He wrote his name in the register of guests at the hotel.* **2** a range of sound made by a voice or instrument: *The lower register of her voice is very soft.* **3** a device for controlling air: *I sat by the heat register to stay warm.* *See:* cash register.

reg·is·tered /'rɛʤɪstərd/ *adj.* officially enrolled, such as a legal voter: *She is registered as a student at Fordham University.*

registered mail *n.* [U] a way to send important mail in which the post office uses registry numbers, safe storage, and signatures to deliver mail safely: *I sent an expensive watch to my friend in Seattle by registered mail.* *See:* certified mail.

registered nurse *n.* a nurse who has a degree and has passed a state examination for nurses: *She earns a good salary as a registered nurse.* -*abbr.* **RN.** *See:* physician's assistant.

USAGE NOTE: In the USA, different kinds of nurses have different amounts of education. A nurse who has finished two years of nursing school is called a *licensed practicing nurses (LPN).* A *registered nurse (RN)* has a university degree and practical training. *Nurse prac-*

titioners (NP) are *RNs* with additional training. They can give medical exams, prescribe some medicines, and do some jobs that doctors do. Not all states license *nurse practitioners*, but most do: *Steve passed the state exam to be a licensed practicing nurse, and he plans to go back to nursing school to become a registered nurse. Eventually he wants to become a nurse practitioner.*

reg·is·trant /ˈrɛʤɪstrənt/ *n.* a person who has registered, such as to vote: *A politician sent a letter to all registrants in his district.*

reg·is·trar /ˈrɛʤɪsˌtrɑr/ *n.* a person or office that keeps official records, usu. at a college or university: *I went to the registrar's office to get a copy of my grades.*

reg·is·tra·tion /ˌrɛʤɪsˈtreɪʃən/ *n.* **1** [U] an act of registering for s.t.: *I did my registration for classes on Monday.* **2** [C] a document that shows s.t. is registered: *Here is the registration for my boat.*

reg·is·try /ˈrɛʤɪstri/ *n.* **-tries** an office of official records: *He went to the registry of motor vehicles to get a new driver's license.*

re·gress /rɪˈgrɛs/ *v.* **-es** to go backwards, return, usu. to a worse condition: *His health has regressed to the point that he may die.* *-n.* [U] **regression** /rɪˈgrɛʃən/.

re·gres·sive /rɪˈgrɛsɪv/ *adj.* referring to a tax that costs poor people more of their income as the tax is raised: *Regressive taxes, like those on cigarettes and alcohol, fall most heavily on the poor.*

re·gret /rɪˈgrɛt/ *v.* **-gretted, -gretting, -grets 1** to feel sad because of s.t. that happened, feel compassion or sympathy: *I regret that your mother died and left you alone.* **2** to feel guilty about or sorry for s.t. one has done: *He regrets that he was angry with his son.*
—n. **1** an expression of sadness, sorrow: *She sent her regrets to her friend in a card when her friend's mother died.* **2** [C;U] a bad feeling about having done s.t. wrong, *(syn.)* remorse: *She has regrets about not being nice to her friend when she was ill.* *-adj.* **regretful; regrettable;** *-adv.* **regretfully.**

re·group /riˈgrup/ *v.* to come together again as a new group, *(syn.)* to reorganize: *When the police came, the angry group of people ran in many directions and regrouped on a different street.*

reg·u·lar /ˈrɛgyələr/ *adj.* **1** normal, usual: *The child's regular bedtime is 8:00 P.M.* **2** s.o. who is easy to like, *(syn.)* dependable, decent: *He is a regular guy with lots of friends.* **3** not unusual, average: *He has a regular build and an average weight.* **4** having normal bowel movements or menstrual periods: *He told his doctor that his bowels are regular and he uses the bathroom each morning.* **5** referring to s.t.

that happens many times with the same amount of time between each happening: *Healthy people have a regular heartbeat.*
—n. **1** a long-term, dependable member of a political party: *Democratic Party regulars give a lot of time and money at election time.* **2** a person or customer who comes to a store, restaurant, or meeting often: *My father is a regular in that restaurant, and all of the waiters know him.* *-v.* **regularize;** *-adv.* **regularly.**

reg·u·lar·i·ty /ˌrɛgyəˈlærəti/ *n.* **-ties** [C] **1** repetition of a happening or behavior: *The regularity of traffic lights keeps cars, trucks, and buses moving throughout the city.* **2** daily bowel movements and normal menstrual periods: *She has no problems with regularity.* *-v.* **regularize.**

reg·u·late /ˈrɛgyəˌleɪt/ *v.* **-lated, -lating, -lates 1** to control s.t., such as businesses, through governmental rules and regulations: *The government regulates the airlines by telling them what prices to charge customers.* **2** to change s.t., control it: *Temperature in this building is regulated by a device that raises the temperature in winter and lowers it in summer.*

reg·u·la·tion /ˌrɛgyəˈleɪʃən/ *n.* **1** [C] a rule, statement about what can be done and what cannot: *The state board of health makes many regulations about the food, water, and cleanliness in restaurants and food stores.* **2** [U] the general condition of controlling any part of human life: *Regulation of the banks is done by the federal government.*

reg·u·la·tor /ˈrɛgyəˌleɪtər/ *n.* **1** a person or agency that regulates, such as a governmental agency that regulates business: *The federal government is the main regulator of airlines.* **2** a device that controls the speed of a machine: *Cars owned by the state have regulators that hold their top speed at 55 MPH.*

re·gur·gi·tate /rɪˈgɜrʤəˌteɪt/ *v.* **-tated, -tating, -tates 1** to bring food up from the stomach to the mouth (syn.), vomit: *Birds regurgitate food to feed their young.* **2** to repeat s.t. without any critical thinking: *On tests, some students simply regurgitate what their textbooks say.* *-n.* [U] **regurgitation.**

re·ha·bil·i·tate /ˌrihəˈbɪləˌteɪt/ *v.* **-tated, -tating, -tates 1** to help s.o. or s.t. become better: *A hospital worker rehabilitated a man who had a broken leg so he could walk again.* **2** to fix up, put in good condition again, *(syn.)* to restore: *The city rehabilitated old empty buildings to make new housing.* *-n.* [U] **rehabilitation.**

re·hash *v.infrml.* /riˈhæʃ/ **-es** to repeat s.t., say s.t. again, usu. in an annoying way: *The committee rehashed the same disagreement it had at the last meeting.*

R

—n.infrml. /'ri,hæʃ/ a repetition: *Their arguments are a rehash of ones made many times before.*

re·hear /ri'hɪr/ *v.* **-heard** /'hɜrd/, **-hearing, -hears** (usu. in law) to hear s.t. again, reconsider: *The court reheard the testimony of the most important witness. -n.* **rehearing.**

re·hear·sal /rə'hɜrsəl/ *n.* [C;U] a practice session, esp. to prepare for an artistic performance: *She went to the rehearsal for the new musical. See:* dress rehearsal.

re·hearse /rə'hɜrs/ *v.* **-hearsed, -hearsing, -hearses** to practice, prepare for a performance: *She rehearsed the songs in the new show.*

re·heat /ri'hit/ *v.* to heat s.t. over again: *The soup was cold, so I reheated it in the microwave oven. -n.* [U] **reheating.**

re·hire /ri'haɪr/ *v.* **-hired, -hiring, -hires** to hire s.o. again, *(syn.)* to reemploy: *The factory rehired 500 workers six months after the workers had been laid off. -n.* [U] **rehiring.**

reign /reɪn/ *n.* the time period that a king or queen rules a country: *The reign of Louis XIV of France ended in 1715.*
—v. to rule a country: *Louis XIV reigned in France for over 70 years.*

re·ig·nite /,riɪg'naɪt/ *v.* **-nited, -niting, -nites** to light a fire again, *(syn.)* to rekindle: *The spacecraft reignited its engines so it could return to Earth. -n.* [U] **reignition** /,riɪg'nɪʃən/.

re·im·burse /,riɪm'bɜrs/ *v.* **-bursed, -bursing, -burses** to pay s.o. back for the money that they paid: *His company reimburses him for hotel, meal, and other travel expenses. -adj.* **reimbursable.**

re·im·burse·ment /,riɪm'bɜrsmənt/ *n.* [U] a payback of money spent by s.o.: *Reimbursement of his expenses takes three weeks.*

rein /reɪn/ *n. used in the pl.* long pieces of leather connected to an animal's head or mouth and used by the rider to control the animal: *A cowboy holds his horse's reins.*
—v. **1** *fig.* **to give s.o. free rein:** to allow s.o. control of s.t., give freedom to: *Our teacher gives us free rein to choose a topic to write about.* **2** *fig.* **to keep a tight rein on s.o. or s.t.:** to keep strong control, control closely: *Our boss keeps a tight rein on everything in our office.* **3** *phrasal v.* **to rein in:** to take freedom away from: *If those parents don't rein in their children a little, the children will never learn to behave.* **4** *fig.* **to take the reins:** to take control over s.t.: *The vice president of our club will take the reins while the president is ill.*

re·in·car·na·tion /,riɪnkɑr'neɪʃən/ *n.* [C;U] rebirth in a new person or form after death: *Many people believe in reincarnation either as new people or as animals. -v.adj.* **reincarnate.**

re·in·cor·po·rate /,riɪn'kɔrpə,reɪt/ *v.* **-rated, -rating, -rates 1** to incorporate again, include s.t. that had been taken out: *He reincorporated two paragraphs that had been taken out of a contract.* **2** to turn a business back into a corporation -n.* [C;U] **reincorporation.**

rein·deer /'reɪn,dɪr/ *n.* **-deer** or **-deers** a large, strong deer that lives in arctic areas, used for meat, milk, clothing, and transportation: *Reindeer can pull twice their own weight on a sled.*

re·in·force /,riɪn'fɔrs/ *v.* **-forced, -forcing, -forces** to add strength to s.t., make it stronger: *Steel rods reinforce concrete structures when they are placed inside the concrete.*

re·in·force·ments /,riɪn'fɔrsmənts/ *n.pl.* additional soldiers or more police: *A police officer saw three thieves robbing a bank and radioed for reinforcements to help him stop them.*

re·in·jure /ri'ɪndʒər/ *v.* **-jured, -juring, -jures** to injure or hurt s.t. again: *A runner reinjured her foot because she ran too soon after the first injury. -n.* [U] **reinjury.**

re·in·state /,riɪn'steɪt/ *v.* **-stated, -stating, -states** to put back to a previous position, *(syn.)* to restore: *A police officer who was asked to leave the police force for illegal behavior was reinstated when he was found not guilty. -n.* [C;U] **reinstatement.**

re·in·te·grate /ri'ɪntə,greɪt/ *v.* **-grated, -grating, -grates** to integrate s.t. again, make two or more things back into one: *After being a separate department for twenty years, the computer department was reintegrated into the electrical engineering department at the university. -n.* [U] **reintegration.**

re·in·ter·pret /,riɪn'tɜrprɪt/ *v.* to think about s.t. and get a new understanding of it, *(syn.)* to reanalyze, redefine: *Scientists reinterpreted facts about the death of the dinosaurs and decided the cause was a meteor and not disease as they thought before. -n.* [C;U] **reinterpretation.**

re·in·tro·duce /,riɪntrə'dus/ *v.* **-duced, -ducing, -duces** to introduce s.t. or s.o. again: *The new soap sold poorly until it was reintroduced in a new package.‖I don't remember your friend very well; could you reintroduce us? -n.* [U] **reintroduction** /,riɪntrə'dʌkʃən/.

re·in·vent /,riɪn'vɛnt/ *v.* **1** to take s.t. old and do or show it in a new way: *A director took an old opera and reinvented it by telling the same story with modern places and clothing.* **2** *infrml.fig.* **to reinvent the wheel:** to make unnecessary work by doing s.t. that has been done before, waste time and effort: *He told his boss that making a new system for sending bills to customers would be reinventing the wheel since the old system works very well. -n.* [U] **reinvention.**

re·in·vest /,riɪn'vɛst/ *v.* **1** to put money one makes (interest, dividends) back into stocks, bonds, or other investments: *He reinvests his dividends from General Electric into more of that company's stock.* **2** to invest money made by a company back into the company rather than paying it to stockholders: *That company reinvests its profits to expand the business.* -*n.* [U] **reinvestment.**

re·in·vig·o·rate /ˌriɪn'vɪgəˌreɪt/ *v.* -**rated, -rating, -rates** to make vigorous again: *Her vacation reinvigorated her, and she returned to work with new energy.*

re·is·sue /ri'ɪʃu/ *v.* -**sued, -suing, -sues** to make s.t. available again: *This book was out of print for ten years, but the publisher reissued it this year.*

re·it·er·ate /ri'ɪtəˌreɪt/ *v.frml.* -**ated, -ating, -ates** to say s.t. again, repeat s.t.: *The professor reiterated the main points in his lecture.* -*n.* [C;U] **reiteration.**

re·ject /rɪ'ʤɛkt/ *v.* to refuse, not accept: *He asked her to go to the movies four times, and each time she rejected him.*
—*n.* /'riˌʤɛkt/ s.t. refused, as not good enough, discarded: *Quality inspectors at factories make sure rejects are not sold as regular products.*

rejection /rɪ'ʤɛkʃən/ *n.* [C;U] s.t. that is not accepted, a refusal, rebuff: *Of the 10 college applications Erica submitted, she received seven acceptance letters and three rejections.*

re·joice /rɪ'ʤɔɪs/ *v.* -**joiced, -joicing, -joices** to feel great joy, (*syn.*) to celebrate: *When the war ended, the winners rejoiced.* -*n.* [U] **rejoicing.**

re·join /ri'ʤɔɪn/ *v.* **1** to put back together again, fix: *The doctor rejoined two broken bones in a patient's arm.* **2** to join, come together again: *I left my friends to make a telephone call, then rejoined them a few minutes later.*

re·join·der /rə'ʤɔɪndər/ *n.frml.* an answer, esp. a strong one: *A lawyer said the witness was lying, and the witness answered with an angry rejoinder, proving to the court that she was telling the truth.*

re·ju·ve·nate /rə'ʤuvəˌneɪt/ *v.frml.* -**nated, -nating, -nates** to make s.o. feel young again, refresh s.o.: *A long restful vacation will rejuvenate you.* -*n.frml.* [U] **rejuvenation.**

re·kin·dle /ri'kɪndl/ *v.* -**dled, -dling, -dles** to make a fire burn again, relight: *A hunter rekindled his campfire in the morning with fresh wood.*

re·lapse /'riˌlæps/ *n.* /rɪ'læps/ *v.* -**lapsed, -lapsing, -lapses** to become worse again after being better: *He was recovering from pneumonia, then he suffered a <n.> relapse.*

re·late /rə'leɪt/ *v.* -**lated, -lating, -lates 1** to be connected with, deal with s.t.: *Our teacher relates our class discussions to real life.* **2** to talk about s.t., tell a story, or inform: *When my neighbor returned from Asia, she related many stories about her trip.* **3** *phrasal v. insep.* **to relate to s.o. or s.t.: a.** s.o.: (usu. neg.) to have a good relationship with: *She doesn't relate well to her colleagues.* **b.** s.t.: to sympathize with s.t., understand: *I can relate to how bad it feels when a good friend dies.* **4** *phrasal v. insep.* **to relate s.t. to/with s.t.:** to connect two things: *He related his current troubles with the same problems from his unhappy childhood.*

re·lat·ed /rə'leɪtɪd/ *adj.* **1** connected by blood or marriage: *He is related to the governor; they are cousins.* **2** connected, dealing with: *My doctor says my headaches are related to stress.*

re·la·tion /rə'leɪʃən/ *n.* **1** [C] a relative by blood or marriage: *My mother, father, and brother are my closest relations.* **2** [U] a connection: *The relation between mathematics and physics is close.* **3 in relation to:** about, concerning: *I received the letter you wrote in relation to our meeting.*
—*n.pl.* **relations:** dealings, connections: *The two countries have close diplomatic relations.* -*adj.* **relational.**

re·la·tion·ship /rə'leɪʃənˌʃɪp/ *n.* **1** a connection between ideas, people, or things: *Those two people like each other and have a close (personal, working, friendly) relationship.* **2** connection by blood or marriage: *A family tree shows a person's relationship to all of his or her relatives.*

rel·a·tive /'rɛləˌtɪv/ *n.* a person connected by blood or marriage to s.o., relation: *My parents and brother are my only living relatives.*
—*adj.* comparative: *We discussed the relative advantages of buying a new or used car.‖The value of money is relative and not so important compared to health and happiness.* -*adv.* **relatively.**

rel·a·tiv·ism /'rɛlətəˌvɪzəm/ *n.* [U] a system of moral values that is not absolute but is relative to oneself and one's culture and time: *Relativism is one of many philosophies.*

rel·a·tiv·i·ty /ˌrɛlə'tɪvəti/ *n.* [U] **1** a condition where the importance of things is relative: *Our philosophy class discussed the relativity of happiness.* **2** a field of physics dealing with the relationship between time, mass, size, and speed: *Albert Einstein discovered special and general theories of relativity.*

re·lax /rə'læks/ *v.* -**es 1** to stop work and enjoy oneself: *She relaxes by riding her bicycle.* **2** to stop being nervous, tense, angry, etc.: *Why don't you stop being angry and relax for a while!* **3** to become or make weaker, looser, less strict: *Our dress code about what we should wear to work is relaxed in the summer.*

R

re·lax·ant /rə'læksənt/ n. a medicine or exercise that relaxes: *His back and neck hurt, so his doctor gave him a muscle relaxant.*

re·lax·a·tion /ˌrilæk'seɪʃən/ n. [U] a process of relaxing, such as stopping work and freeing the mind of worry: *For relaxation, he plays golf on the weekends.*

re·lay (1) /rə'leɪ, 'ri,leɪ/ v. **-layed, -laying, -lays** to pass on some information, communicate: *I relayed a message about a possible job from one friend to another.*
—n. /'ri,leɪ/ [C;U] a device that relays s.t., such as electricity, from one line to another: *A worker activated an electric relay, and the electricity came on in our house.*

relay (2) v. **-laid, -laying, -lays** to put s.t. down again after it was taken up: *Workers relaid the carpet after they fixed the floor.*

relay race /'ri,leɪ/ n. a race where each team member runs part of the race and passes a stick or baton to the next runner: *I ran relay races in high school.*

re·learn /ri'lɜrn/ v. **-learned** or **-learnt** /-'lɜrnt/, **-learning, -learns** to learn s.t. over again, esp. to correct one's learning: *My office bought new computers, and now I must relearn how to do my job using them.*

re·lease /ri'lis, rə-/ v. **-leased, -leasing, -leases** **1** to let s.t. go, set it free: *He releases his pet birds from their cage each day.* **2** to let s.t. be used publicly: *That movie was released last month and is appearing in neighborhood theaters.*
—n. **1** [C;U] permission to do s.t., freedom: *A prisoner got an early release from jail for good behavior.* **2** [C] a new movie or musical recording: *I bought two new releases at the music store.*

rel·e·gate /'rɛlə,geɪt/ v.frml. **-gated, -gating, -gates** to move s.t. to a lower position, throw away, (syns.) to dismiss, discard: *After his old car broke down five times, he relegated it to the junkyard.*

re·lent /rə'lɛnt/ v.frml. to stop doing s.t., to become weaker: *The hurricane caused damage for many hours, then slowly relented into a quiet rain.*

re·lent·less /rə'lɛntlɪs/ adj. **1** without stopping, (syn.) persistent: *The sound of the rain was relentless for hours on the roof.* **2** trying very hard to succeed, esp. to hurt s.o., (syn.) pitiless: *The politician suffered relentless criticism from the press after she was elected.*

rel·e·vance /'rɛləvəns/ or **rel·e·van·cy** /'rɛləvənsi/ n. [C;U] a close relationship to s.t. else, (syn.) appropriateness: *The actions that governments take to increase employment have a close relevance to a healthy economy.*

rel·e·vant /'rɛləvənt/ adj. closely connected, appropriate: *My classes about new kinds of*

computers are relevant to my plan to work in computer repair. *-adv.* **relevantly.**

re·li·a·bil·i·ty /rəˌlaɪə'bɪləti/ n. [U] **1** a degree to which s.o. or s.t. will do what is expected, (syn.) dependability: *I recommend this boy as a baby-sitter because of his reliability.* **2** ability to be trusted, (syn.) trustworthiness: *That bank has been in business for years and its reliability is the best.*

re·li·a·ble /rə'laɪəbəl/ adj. **1** regularly does what it should do, (syns.) dependable, sure: *The train service in this area is very reliable.* **2** can be trusted, (syn.) responsible: *He is a reliable worker who is always on time.*

re·li·ance /rə'laɪəns/ n. sing. [U] **1** a condition of needing s.t. or s.o. for support or help, (syn.) dependence: *His reliance on drugs is bad for his health.* **2** belief in the quality of s.t. or s.o., trust, (syn.) confidence: *You can have reliance in the quality of those clothes.*

re·li·ant /rə'laɪənt/ adj. a state of needing s.t. very much, (syns.) dependent on, indebted to: *Since he doesn't have a job, he is reliant on his parents to support him.*

rel·ic /'rɛlɪk/ n. an object from the past, esp. a souvenir of a time that no longer exists: *He collects relics of Native Americans, such as arrowheads and other tools made from stone.*

re·lief /rə'lif/ n. [U] **1** the taking away of or lessening of pain: *Two aspirin gave him relief from a headache.* **2** freedom from worry, the taking away of a concern: *When she learned that her daughter was safe, she felt great relief.* **3** help given in times of trouble, hunger, war, or natural disaster: *After the flood, we gave money for relief of the people who lost their homes.*
—adj. **in relief:** having a raised surface: *A relief map shows mountains and valleys in relief so that you can feel them with your fingers.*

re·lieve /rɪ'liv/ v. **-lieved, -lieving, -lieves 1** to lessen or take away s.t. unpleasant: *Aspirin relieves my pains.* **2** to free from worry, take away concern: *She was relieved when she learned that she doesn't have cancer.* **3** to take the place of s.o. who is working: *The guards relieve each other every four hours.* **4** **to relieve oneself:** to allow waste to leave the body, esp. urine, (syns.) to urinate, defecate: *He went to the bathroom and relieved himself.*

re·li·gion /rə'lɪdʒən/ n. **1** [C;U] a system of beliefs in a god or philosophy of life: *Buddhism and Hinduism are two of the world's major religions* **2** [C] any system that s.o. believes in strongly: *He loves to play golf so much it is like a religion for him.*

re·li·gious /rə'lɪdʒəs/ adj. **1** related to religion: *Her religious beliefs are very developed.* **2** having strong beliefs in religion: *He is very religious; he prays every day.* **3** to do s.t. carefully and regularly: *Her homework is always done with religious care.*

—*n.pl.* people who believe strongly in a religion: *The religious go to church regularly.* -*adv.* **religiously.**

re·line /ri'laɪn/ *v.* **-lined, -lining, -lines** to give s.t. a new lining: *The lining in my suit was worn, so I had it relined with silk.* -*n.* [U] **relining.**

re·lin·quish /rə'lɪŋkwɪʃ/ *v.frml.* **-es 1** to give up, hand over, (*syn.*) to surrender: *The thief relinquished his gun to the police.* **2** to stop doing s.t., (*syn.*) to give up: *He relinquished alcohol and fatty foods to go on a diet.*

rel·ish /'rɛlɪʃ/ *v.* **-es** to have a happy feeling about s.t., get delight from s.t.: *He relishes going on long winter vacations to warm places.*

—*n.* [U] a topping for food made of small pieces of pickle and tomatoes: *He puts relish on his hot dogs.*

re·live /ri'lɪv/ *v.* **-lived, -living, -lives** to repeat (usu. in one's mind) a past event: *The elderly lady relives her pleasant youth by telling stories to children.*

re·load /ri'loud/ *v.* to put more of s.t. in, such as bullets or batteries: *Soldiers reloaded their rifles and began shooting again.*

re·lo·cate /ri'lou,keɪt/ *v.* **-cated, -cating, -cates** to move to a new place: *My friend relocated from New York to Florida.* -*n.* [U] **relocation** /,rilou'keɪʃən/.

re·luc·tance /rɪ'lʌktəns/ *n.* [U] concern or fear about doing s.t., (*syn.*) hesitance: *I understand her reluctance about driving in a storm.*

re·luc·tant /rɪ'lʌktənt/ *adj.* concerned or afraid, (*syn.*) hesitant: *He is reluctant to spend much money because he thinks he may lose his job.* -*adv.* **reluctantly.**

re·ly /rə'laɪ/ *v.* **-lied, -lying, -lies** to depend on, count on: *I rely on the train to take me to and from work each day.||You can rely on me!*

REM /'ɑri'ɛm/ *short for* Rapid Eye Movement, a type of sleep whereby one dreams and the eyeball moves quickly: *Doctors believe that REM is very important for a good night's sleep.*

re·main /rə'meɪn/ *v.* **1** to stay after others are gone: *He remained to guard the camp while others went to look for food.* **2** to continue to be a certain way, (*syn.*) to endure: *That writer's books have remained popular for many years.* **3 to remain to be seen:** not to be certain yet: *His grades in school have gotten better, but it remains to be seen whether or not he will graduate.*

re·main·der /rə'meɪndər/ *n.* part of s.t. that still remains, the rest of s.t.: *It is 2:00 P.M. now, and I will spend the remainder of the afternoon studying chemistry.*

re·mains /rə'meɪnz/ *n.pl.* parts or things that are left: *We saw the remains of the old city.*

re·make /ri'meɪk/ *v.* **-made** /-'meɪd/, **-making, -makes** to make s.t. again: *She dropped the cake on the floor and had to remake it.*

—*n.* /'ri,meɪk/ s.t. done over again: *That song is a remake of a song from the 1970s.*

re·mand /rə'mænd/ *v.frml.* (in law) to send back (to court or to prison): *The lawsuit was remanded to another court.*

re·mark /rə'mɑrk/ *v.* **1** to say s.t., make a comment about s.t.: *He remarked that the flower garden looks beautiful.* **2** *phrasal v. insep.* **to remark on** or **upon s.t.:** to say or write about s.t.: *The press remarked upon the Senate's vote.*

—*n.* **1** a statement about s.t.: *She made a remark about his polished appearance.* **2** a negative statement, cutting criticism: *She made a remark that he behaves like a fool.*

re·mark·a·ble /rə'mɑrkəbəl/ *adj.* worthy of attention, noticeable, (*syns.*) extraordinary, outstanding: *The sick man was near death but made remarkable improvement and got well.* -*adv.* **remarkably.**

re·mar·ry /ri'mæri/ *v.* **-ried, -rying, -ries** to marry again: *After her husband died, she remarried.* -*n.* [C;U] **remarriage** /ri'mærɪdʒ/.

re·match /'ri,mæʧ, ri'mæʧ/ *n.v.* **-es** to play a game again with the same player(s): *Whenever I win a game against my brother, he demands a <n.> rematch.*

re·me·di·al /rə'midiəl/ *adj.* corrective, designed to improve s.t.: *She is doing well in remedial reading; she can read well now.* -*adj.* **remediable.**

re·me·di·a·tion /rə,midi'eɪʃən/ *n.frml.* [U] action taken to correct or improve s.t.: *The school system offers extra help to students and provides remediation in reading and writing.*

rem·e·dy /'rɛmədi/ *v.* **-died, -dying, -dies 1** to correct, fix s.t.: *The child behaved badly, so the school remedied the problem by making him leave school.* **2** to restore, return to normal: *He remedied his weak condition by exercising in a gym.*

—*n.* **-dies 1** a medication, s.t. that makes an illness better, (*syn.*) a cure: *She took a cold remedy to relieve her sneezing and headache.* **2** action to make s.t. better: *As a remedy for poor sales, the store ran a special sale.*

re·mem·ber /rɪ'mɛmbər/ *v.* **1** to recall, bring s.t. from the past to mind: *I still remember my first day at school as a little boy.* **2** to celebrate, observe, such as with a party, visit, flowers, etc.: *My friend remembered my birthday by giving me a surprise party.*

re·mem·brance /rɪ'mɛmbrəns/ *n.* an object that reminds you of a pleasant event, (*syns.*) a memento, souvenir: *I gave my boyfriend a ring as a remembrance of our love.*

R

re·mind /rə'maɪnd/ v. **1** to tell s.o. about doing s.t., cause s.o. to remember: *My wife reminded me to buy a present for our daughter's birthday.* **2** phrasal v. insep. **to remind s.o. of s.o. or s.t.:** to be like s.o. or s.t. in some way: *Her voice reminds me of my mother.*

re·mind·er /rə'maɪndər/ n. s.t. that helps s.o. to remember, telling s.o. not to forget s.t.: *My dentist sent me a reminder that I should have my teeth cleaned again.*

re·mind·ful /rə'maɪndful/ adj. to keep s.t. in one's memory, remember: *He is remindful that he owes his friend money.*

rem·i·nisce /,rɛmə'nɪs/ v. **-nisced, -niscing, -nisces** to think about past experiences, esp. pleasant ones, (syn.) to recollect: *An elderly lady reminisced about the good times of her youth. See:* reflect.

rem·i·nis·cence /,rɛmə'nɪsəns/ n. [C;U] memories, esp. pleasant ones of the past: *She told her daughter reminiscences of funny things she did as a child.*

rem·i·ni·scent /,rɛmə'nɪsənt/ adj. related to memories of the past, similar to s.t. past: *Cowboy stories are reminiscent of life in the American wild west.*

re·miss /rə'mɪs/ adj. careless about doing s.t., (syns.) neglectful, negligent: *It was remiss of me not to remember your birthday.*

re·mis·sion /rə'mɪʃən/ n. [C;U] a return to a normal state: *His cancer is in remission and he is feeling better now.*

re·mit /rə'mɪt/ v. **-mitted, -mitting, -mits 1** to return, send back: *When customers are billed, they remit payments by making a check.* **2** to forgive, to excuse s.o. from a sin or debt: *The woman prayed that her sins would be remitted.*

re·mit·tance /rə'mɪtns/ n. [C;U] s.t. returned, such as a payment or form: *People send their remittances for bills by check or money order.*

rem·nant /'rɛmnənt/ n. a leftover or s.t. that remains, esp. of cloth: *I made a colorful blanket from remnants of cloth.*

re·mod·el /ri'mɑdl/ v. to redo s.t., change s.t. by renewing it: *We remodeled our kitchen with new cabinets, a new stove, and a new refrigerator.* -n. [U] **remodeling.**

re·morse /rə'mɔrs/ n. [U] a very strong feeling of sadness or guilt about s.t.: *He was filled with remorse after he stole the watch, so he returned it to the owner.* -adj. **remorseful;** -adv. **remorsefully.**

re·morse·less /rə'mɔrslɪs/ adj. having no feelings of remorse or guilt, (syn.) merciless: *The remorseless teacher gave his students five hours of homework each night.*

remote /rə'mout/ adj. **1** referring to a far-away place or time, distant: *We traveled more than an hour to get to a beautiful, remote picnic area.* **2** not closely related: *There is only a re-*

mote connection between his training as a doctor and his training as a salesperson. **3** very little, (syn.) slight: *There is a remote possibility of rain today.* -adv. **remotely;** -n. [U] **remoteness.**

remote control n. **1** control of a device or machine from a distance, such as by radio waves: *The small toy plane is flown by remote control.* **2** a device that controls s.t. remotely: *I have three remote controls: one each for the TV, the stereo, and the VCR.*

re·mount /ri'maunt/ v. **1** to get onto s.t. again, such as a horse: *The little girl fell from her bike, but remounted without crying.* **2** to put s.t. onto a backing or frame again: *I remounted the photograph because it was not straight the first time I mounted it.*

re·mov·al /rə'muvəl/ n. [C;U] the act of taking s.t. away: *When we bought a new refrigerator, we had to pay for the removal of the old one.*

re·move /rə'muv/ v. **-moved, -moving, -moves 1** to move or take s.t. away: *You should remove all furniture from the room before you clean the carpet.* **2** to get rid of s.t. as in cleaning, (syn.) to eliminate: *We removed the dirt from the floor with soap and water.* **3** to make s.o. leave a job or office, (syn.) to dismiss: *She was removed from her job at the post office because she was stealing stamps.* -adj. **removable.**

re·mov·er /rə'muvər/ n. [C;U] a chemical that cleans s.t. that is usu. difficult to remove: *She used spot remover to clean the spot on the floor.*

re·mu·ner·a·tion /rə,myunə'reɪʃən/ n.frml. [U] the payment s.o. gets for work, a reward, (syn.) compensation: *The remuneration for the job is not very much, but the work is interesting.* -v. **remunerate;** -adj. **remunerative** /rə'myunərə,tɪv, -,reɪtɪv/.

ren·ais·sance /'rɛnə,sɑns, -,zɑns/ n. **1** a time of rebirth when s.t., such as a style of art or music, becomes very popular again, (syn.) revival: *Recently there has been a renaissance of interest in 1950s music and art in my town.* **2 Renaissance:** the 14th through 17th centuries in Europe, when classical art and ideas became popular again: *Michelangelo was a great painter and sculptor of the Italian Renaissance.*

re·nal /'rinəl/ adj. related to the kidneys: *My doctor thinks I have a renal problem and wants to do some tests.*

re·name /ri'neɪm/ v. **-named, -naming, -names** to change the name of s.t.: *A science building was renamed the "Einstein Building" in honor of the great physicist.* -n. **renaming.**

re·nas·cent /rə'næsənt, -'neɪ-/ adj.frml. being reborn or made new again: *The popular music of the 1960s is renascent with today's young people.* -n. [U] **renascence.**

R

rend /rɛnd/ v. **rent** /rɛnt/ or **rended, rending, rends** to tear, rip into pieces: *Lions rend meat with their teeth as they eat.* -n. adj. [U] **rending.**

ren·der /ˈrɛndər/ v. **1** to give s.t. or do s.t., (syn.) to provide: *That store renders good service to its customers.* **2** to give in return as payment: *He rendered thanks to God for his health and his family.* **3** to put into another language, translate: *It is difficult to render poetry into another language.* **4** to cause a change, make s.t. become true: *He was rendered speechless when his sister told him she was having a baby.||She was rendered helpless when she broke her leg.* **5** *frml.* to give an opinion or decision: *The judge will render his decision tomorrow.* **6** to draw s.t., to sketch: *I had an artist render a picture of my house to put in the paper since the house is for sale.*

ren·der·ing /ˈrɛndərɪŋ/ n. a drawing or interpretation of s.t.: *The artist showed us some of his renderings of our property.*

ren·dez·vous /ˈrɑndeɪˌvu, -də-/ n.v. **-vous** /ˌvuz/ **1** a meeting, esp. between lovers: *They had a <n.> rendezvous in the park this evening.* **2** a meeting place: *Soldiers <v.> rendezvoused at a secret place.||During the <n.> rendezvous, they planned their attack against the enemy.*

ren·di·tion /rɛnˈdɪʃən/ n. a version of s.t., esp. one's own way of singing a song: *A singer sang her own rendition of a popular song.*

ren·e·gade /ˈrɛnəˌgeɪd/ n.adj. an outlaw, s.o. who gives up or leaves lawful society: *<n.pl.> Renegades (or) a <adj.> renegade thief stole the farmer's cows.*

re·nege /rəˈnɛg, -ˈnɪg/ v. **-neged, -neging, -negs** n. to break a promise, not do what one said one would do: *He promised to buy my house, then reneged on the deal.*

re·ne·go·ti·ate /ˌrinəˈgoʊʃiˌeɪt/ v. **-ated, -ating, -ates** to change an earlier agreement: *We renegotiated our loan from an 11% interest rate down to a 7% interest rate.* -adj. **renegotiable** /ˌrinəˈgoʊʃəbəl, -ʃiə-/.

re·new /rɪˈnu/ v. **1** to agree to s.t. again, continue an agreement: *We renewed our magazine subscription.||The husband and wife renewed their marriage vows.* **2** to make s.o. or s.t. feel new, fresh, and better, (syns.) to refresh, rejuvenate: *She renewed her energy with a long vacation.* **3** to make s.o. or s.t. look new, (syns.) to remodel, refurbish: *Owners renew houses by renovating them.* **4** to add to a supply, get more of: *We must renew our paper supply in the office.*

re·new·a·ble /rɪˈnuəbəl/ adj. able to be renewed or continued: *My magazine subscriptions are renewable every year.*

re·new·al /rɪˈnuəl/ n. [C;U] **1** an act of making s.t. look new, (syns.) renovation, refurbishing: *Urban renewal means making old buildings in cities into good places to live.* **2** a feeling strong again, (syn.) rejuvenation: *She found renewal for her spirit in religion.*

re·nounce /rəˈnaʊns/ v. **-nounced, -nouncing, -nounces** to give s.t. up formally, to quit: *He renounced drinking alcohol by telling his friends that he had quit drinking.* -n. **renouncement.**

ren·o·vate /ˈrɛnəˌveɪt/ v. **-vated, -vating, -vates** to renew s.t., make s.t. (esp. a building) look like new, (syns.) to repair, restore: *He renovated an apartment building by cleaning it, painting it, putting in new windows, new kitchens, and a new elevator.*

ren·o·va·tion /ˌrɛnəˈveɪʃən/ n. [C;U] the process of renewing s.t.: *The renovation of our apartment took several months, but when it was finished the apartment looked like new.*

re·nown /rəˈnaʊn/ n. [U] fame, being well known for good things s.o. has done: *Her renown as a person who cares for the poor is worldwide.*

re·nowned /rəˈnaʊnd/ adj. famous, well known and liked or criticized, (syn.) celebrated: *Switzerland is renowned for its beautiful mountains.*

rent /rɛnt/ n. **1** [C;U] the amount of money paid for the use of a piece of property: *She pays a low rent on that apartment.* **2** for rent: able to be rented: *That house is for rent. See:* rent control.
—v. **1** to pay to use a piece of property, but not own it: *She has rented the apartment for many years.* **2** to pay to use s.t. (car, movie, etc.) for a short time: *Let's rent movies this weekend.*

rent-a-car n.adj. **1** a rented automobile: *I got a <n.> rent-a-car at the airport and drove it to a meeting.* **2** a business that rents cars, trucks, etc.: *I picked the car up at the <adj.> rent-a-car desk.*

rent·al /ˈrɛntl/ n. a piece of property that is rented out to others: *He does not own that fancy car; it's a rental.*
—adj. referring to s.t. rented, not owned: *He lives in a rental house owned by his neighbor.*

rent control n. [U] governmental laws made to control how fast rental prices get higher, esp. on apartments: *Rent control on apartments started many years ago in New York.*

rent·er /ˈrɛntər/ n. a person or business that rents things, such as apartments, from the owner(s): *He is a renter who does not want to own his apartment.*

re·num·ber /riˈnʌmbər/ v. to number s.t. again: *She added a page at the beginning of her report, and she had to renumber all the other pages.* -n. **renumbering.**

R

re·nun·ci·a·tion /rə,nʌnsi'eɪʃən/ *n.frml.* [C;U] giving up of s.t., refusal to use or do s.t., *(syn.)* rejection: *His renunciation of alcohol and of smoking cigarettes made him feel healthier.*

re·oc·cu·py /ri'ɑkyə,paɪ/ *v.* **-pied, -pying, -pies** to occupy or move into s.t. again: *Foreign soldiers left the country, then reoccupied it a month later.* *-n.* [U] **reoccupation.**

re·o·pen /ri'oʊpən/ *v.* to open again, start again: *Negotiations between the company and its workers stopped and then reopened again.* *-n.* **reopening.**

re·or·der /ri'ɔrdər/ *n.v.* a new order of the same thing: *She ordered new paper last year and placed a <n.> reorder for it today.‖She <v.> reordered it.*

re·or·gan·i·za·tion /ri,ɔrgənə'zeɪʃən/ *n.* [C;U] a change, new form for s.t.: *Our company planned a reorganization of its four sales teams into one large sales group.*

re·or·gan·ize /ri'ɔrgə,naɪz/ *v.* **-ized, -izing, -izes** to change s.t. into a new system: *We reorganized the furniture in our living room, and now the sofa faces the window.*

re·o·ri·ent /ri'ɔri,ɛnt/ *v.* to change the direction or nature of s.t.: *After her husband died, she had to reorient herself to being single.* *-n.* [U] **reorientation.**

rep /rɛp/ *n.infrml.* *short for* representative: *Sales reps visit our company to sell their products.*

re·pack·age /ri'pækɪdʒ/ *v.* **-aged, -aging, -ages** to put s.t. into a new covering: *The design of their product looked old-fashioned, so they repackaged it to look more modern.*

re·pair /rə'pɛr/ *v.* to fix s.t., make s.t. work again: *A mechanic repaired the motor in my car; it was overheating.*
—*n.* **1** state of being fixed: *The repairs on my car will be finished tomorrow.* **2 in a state of (good/bad) repair:** the condition s.t. is in: *My old car is in a state of good repair.* **3 to make repairs:** to fix s.t., *(syn.)* to overhaul: *I asked a handyman to make repairs on my house.* *-adj.* **repairable.**

re·pair·man /rə'pɛrmən/ *n.* **-men** /mən/ or **re·pair·person** a person who fixes things: *My refrigerator stopped running, so I called the repairman.*

rep·a·ra·tion /,rɛpə'reɪʃən/ *n.* payment to correct s.t. done wrong, *(syn.)* compensation: *After World War I, Germany had to make reparations to France and other countries for damages from the war.*

re·past /rə'pæst/ *n.v.* *frml.* a meal, food and drink: *The queen enjoyed her evening <n.> repast.*

re·pa·tri·ate /ri'peɪtri,eɪt/ *v.* **-ated, -ating, -ates** to return s.t. or s.o. to the country where s.t. or s.o. began: *Ancient artworks were repatriated from the USA to Greece.*

—*n.* a person who is repatriated: *Many repatriates came back to their country after the war.* *-n.* [U] **repatriation.**

re·pay /ri'peɪ/ *v.* to pay back (a loan, a favor, etc.): *I loaned my friend some money and he repaid me.* *-adj.* **repayable;** *-n.* [C;U] **repayment.**

re·peal /rə'pil/ *n.* (in government) the act of taking away the legal value of s.t., a cancellation of s.t.: *The new Congress' first act was a repeal of all of the old Congress's laws.*
—*v.* to cancel, make s.t. have no legal power: *They repealed the tax law.* *-adj.* **repealable.**

re·peat /rɪ'pit/ *v.* **1** to say or do s.t. over again: *He told me a story and then repeated it later to his wife.* **2** to say s.t. one has learned to remember: *The child repeated the poem she had memorized.*
—*n.* a repetition, s.t. said or done again: *That television program on nature is a repeat of a show I watched last month.*

re·peat·ed /rɪ'pitɪd/ *adj.* done many times, often, *(syn.)* frequent: *After repeated attempts, he finally passed the exam.* *-adv.* **repeatedly.**

re·peat·ing /rɪ'pitɪŋ/ *n.* [U] s.t. that is done or said again: *The repeating of that noise annoys me.*
—*adj.* s.t. that repeats: *He has a repeating parrot that will say anything he says to it.*

re·pel /rə'pɛl/ *v.* **-pelled, -pelling, -pels** to make s.o. or s.t. go away, force it to leave, *(syn.)* to repulse: *The smell of this candle repels insects so that they won't bother us while we're outside.*

re·pel·lent /rə'pɛlənt/ *n.* [C;U] s.t. that makes insects or animals go away: *He sprayed a repellent all over his body so mosquitoes wouldn't bite him.*
—*adj.* causing dislike, unpleasant: *The smell of her perfume is so bad it's repellent.*

re·pent /rə'pɛnt/ *v.* **1** to feel guilt and sorrow for one's actions: *He repented of his bad behavior and said he was sorry.* **2** (in religion) to confess bad things one has done wrong: *He repented and asked for forgiveness.*

re·pen·tance /rə'pɛntns/ *n.* [U] the state of feeling guilt and sorrow for one's actions: *His repentance of his sins brought him forgiveness.* *-adj.* **repentant;** *-adv.* **repentantly.**

re·per·cus·sion /,ripər'kʌʃən, ,rɛ-/ *n.* a reaction to s.t., esp. bad events: *When he yelled at his boss, the repercussion was that he was fired.* *-v.* **repercuss.**

rep·er·toire /'rɛpər,twɑr/ *n.* the group of musical pieces, jokes, etc., that an artist can play (sing, speak) readily: *There are a hundred popular songs in her repertoire; she can sing Broadway tunes, contemporary songs, and Big Band numbers from the 1940s.*

rep·e·ti·tion /,rɛpə'tɪʃən/ *n.* [C;U] the act of doing or saying s.t. again: *Repetition of the* *words in that song makes the song easy to remember.*

rep·e·ti·tious /ˌrɛpəˈtɪʃəs/ or **re·pet·i·tive** /rəˈpɛtətɪv/ *adj.* repeating the same thing over and over again: *His writing is repetitious and boring.‖Typing involves repetitive motions of the fingers and thumbs.*

re·phrase /riˈfreɪz/ *v.* **-phrased, -phrasing, -phrases** to say or write s.t. in a different way: *The class didn't understand what the teacher said, so she rephrased it.*

re·place /rəˈpleɪs/ *v.* **-placed, -placing, -places** **1** to get s.t. new to take the place of s.t. old, *(syn.)* to substitute: *I replaced my old car with a new one.* **2** to take the place of s.o. or s.t.: *Her boss retired and she replaced him.* **3** to put s.t. back into its proper position: *He played his violin and then replaced it in its case.* *-adj.* **replaceable.**

re·place·ment /rəˈpleɪsmənt/ *n.* **1** a person who takes the job of another: *A worker retired and his replacement started work today.* **2** s.t. that takes the place of another, *(syn.)* a substitute: *My TV broke and I bought a replacement.*

re·play /ˈriˌpleɪ/ *n.* [C;U] a second showing of an event, such as an exciting sports play on television: *On the evening TV news, I saw exciting replays from today's football game.*
—*v.* /riˈpleɪ/ to repeat s.t., play again: *I replayed the videotape on my VCR.*

re·plen·ish /rəˈplɛnɪʃ/ *v.frml.* **-es** to replace s.t. that was used, resupply: *The army replenished the supply of food for the soldiers.* *-n.* [U] **replenishment.**

re·plete /rəˈplit/ *adj.frml.* full of, having a lot of s.t. (usu. food), *(syn.)* plentiful: *The banquet for the ambassador was replete with good food and fine wine.* *-n.* [C;U] **repletion.**

rep·li·ca /ˈrɛplɪkə/ *n.* a copy of s.t., often made in a smaller size than the original: *While in New York, a tourist bought a small replica of the Statue of Liberty.*

rep·li·cate /ˈrɛplɪˌkeɪt/ *v.frml.* **-cated, -cating, -cates** to make a copy of s.t., *(syn.)* to reproduce: *An art student replicated a famous painting by painting a copy of it herself.* *-n.* [C;U] **replication.**

re·ply /rəˈplaɪ/ *v.* **-plied, -plying, -plies** to answer s.t., *(syn.)* to respond: *He replied to my letter that I sent last month.*
—*n.* **-plies** [C;U] an answer, response: *I received his reply yesterday.*

re·port /rəˈpɔrt/ *n.* **1** a written or spoken statement about s.t.: *He wrote a five-page report on the new computer system.* **2** a quick sound made by a shot or explosion: *I heard the report of the gunshot.*
—*v.* **1** to describe s.t., tell about s.t. (event, need, etc.): *The news program reported that an accident had occurred on Main Street.* **2** to

work for s.o.: *She reports directly to the company's president.* **3** to arrive to work: *He reported to work late this morning.* **4** *phrasal v. insep.* **to report on s.t.:** to give information about s.t.: *The committee reported on their investigation.* *-adv.* **reportedly.**

report card *n.* a summary of a student's grades or scores at a school: *She received straight A's on her report card from high school.*

USAGE NOTE: Compare *report card* and *grade report*. A report card is a summary of a child's school grades. A grade report shows a college or university student's grades.

---

re·port·er /rəˈpɔrtər/ *n.* a person who reports on events, such as for a newspaper, magazine, radio, or television station, *(syn.)* journalist: *She is a reporter who writes about city news for the local newspaper.*

re·pose /rəˈpouz/ *v.frml.* **-posed, -posing, -poses** to lie down to rest or sleep, *(syn.)* to recline: *She reposed on a sofa and fell asleep.*
—*n.* [U] a state of rest or sleep: *The artist painted a child in calm repose.*

re·po·si·tion /ˌripəˈzɪʃən/ *v.* **1** to put s.t. back in its place: *An astronaut repositioned his spacecraft back onto the correct path around Earth.* **2** to put s.t. in a new position: *If you reposition your chair, the sun won't hurt your eyes.*

re·pos·i·to·ry /rəˈpɑzəˌtɔri/ *n.* **-ries** **1** a place where things are kept safe: *At night, storekeepers put their money in a bank repository.* **2** *often fig.* a container or place where s.t. is kept, *(syn.)* a storehouse: *My grandfather is a repository of information about the town he lives in. See:* depository.

re·pos·sess /ˌripəˈzɛs/ *v.* **-es** to take property, esp. that on which a loan has not been paid on time: *The bank repossessed his car when he did not make monthly payments on it. -n.* [C;U] **repossession.**

rep·re·hen·si·ble /ˌrɛprəˈhɛnsəbəl/ *adj.frml.* shameful and deserving to be blamed or criticized: *Her bad behavior is reprehensible; no decent person would act like that!* *-v.* **reprehend;** *-adv.* **reprehensibly;** *-n.* [U] **reprehension.**

rep·re·sent /ˌrɛprəˈzɛnt/ *v.* **1** to show, give a picture or symbol of s.t.: *The Statue of Liberty represents the freedom immigrants wanted to find in America.* **2** to equal to, mean: *The damage from the fire represented a total loss for the store owner.* **3** to act in the place of, act on behalf of: *The U.S. Embassy represents the United States in other countries.* **4** to act like or say that you belong to a group: *He represents himself to others as a rich man, but he is*

R

not. **5** to be an example of: *This plant represents a rare kind of orchid.*

rep·re·sen·ta·tion /ˌrɛprəzɛn'teɪʃən/ *n.* **1** [C] s.t. that shows s.t., a picture, likeness, (*syn.*) illustration: *This book has many beautiful representations of Hindu gods.* **2** [C] *often pl.* statements of belief: *The woman's representations about her innocence were believable.* **3** [C;U] the act of officially taking s.o.'s place, a representing: *I need a lawyer to be my representation in court.*

rep·re·sen·ta·tive /ˌrɛprə'zɛntətɪv/ *n.* **1** a person who represents s.o. or s.t.: *She is a sales representative for a large company.* **2** a member of the U.S. House of Representatives: *We will elect a new representative in the next election.*
—*adj.* meaning, showing, or illustrating s.t., (*syn.*) typical: *Many of Renoir's paintings are representative of French Impressionism.*

re·press /rə'prɛs/ *v.* **-es** **1** to slow or stop s.t., (*syn.*) to oppress: *The police repressed a riot by arresting rioters.* **2** to keep s.t. secret: *The sick man repressed his fears about dying and stayed cheerful on the outside.* -*adj.* **repressed; repressive.**

re·pres·sion /rə'prɛʃən/ *n.* [U] the stopping of some action or feeling, (*syn.*) oppression: *Some people who disagreed with the government said they were living under repression and couldn't say what they thought. See:* repress.

re·prieve /rə'priv/ *n.v.* **-prieved, -prieving, -prieves** relief from difficulty or punishment for a short time: *The governor gave the criminal a <n.> reprieve from being put to death.||He <v.> reprieved the criminal.*

rep·ri·mand /'rɛprə,mænd/ *n.v.* an angry criticism for s.t. done wrong, (*syn.*) a rebuke: *A father <v.> reprimanded his daughter for driving too fast and getting a speeding ticket.||He gave her a <n.> reprimand.*

re·print *n.* /'ri'prɪnt/ *v.* /ri'prɪnt/ [C;U] to print s.t. again that had already been printed: *A publisher <v.> reprinted the best-selling book many times.||They made a <n.> reprint of it.*

re·print·ing /ri'prɪntɪŋ/ *n.* a reprint: *The new reprinting of the book is now in the bookstores.*

re·pri·sal /rə'praɪzəl/ *n.* [C;U] an act meant to pay back a physical or emotional hurt or injury, (*syn.*) revenge: *Many people believed the bomb in his car was a mafia reprisal because he gave information to the police.*

re·prise /rɪ'priz/ *n.v.frml.* **-prised, -prising, -prises** a beginning again, (*syn.*) resumption: *A <n.> reprise in the economy means there are more jobs.*

re·proach /rə'proʊtʃ/ *v.frml.* **-es** to criticize, make s.o. ashamed: *His teacher reproached him for not doing his homework.*

—*n.* [U] **1** criticism, disapproval of s.o.: *The teacher's reproach motivated him to do his work.* **2** **above** or **beyond reproach**: excellent, especially good: *Her reputation as a teacher is beyond reproach.* -*adj.* **reproachful;** -*adv.* **reproachfully.**

re·pro·bate /'rɛprə,beɪt/ *adj.n.* a morally bad person; (in religion) a person who will go to hell (often used humorously): *You old <n.> reprobate! You'll never stop telling lies!*

re·proc·ess /ri'prɑsɛs/ *v.* **-es** to treat s.t. so that it can be used again: *Aluminum cans and plastic bottles can be reprocessed into new ones.*

re·pro·duce /ˌriprə'dus/ *v.* **-duced, -ducing, -duces** **1** (in biology) to have babies: *Mice reproduce very quickly.* **2** to make copies of s.t.: *The teacher reproduced copies of an article for the class to read.* -*n.* **reproducer;** -*adj.* **reproducible.**

re·pro·duc·tion /ˌriprə'dʌkʃən/ *n.* **1** [C] a copy of s.t.: *That painting is a reproduction of one by Claude Monet.* **2** [U] (in biology) production of babies: *Reproduction is necessary to preserve each species.*

re·pro·duc·tive /ˌriprə'dʌktɪv/ *adj.* (in biology) related to having children or offspring: *Every animal has reproductive organs.*

re·pro·graph·ics /ˌriprə'græfɪks/ *n.pl.* used with a sing.v. the business of producing documents and visuals: *Reprographics uses copying machines to reproduce documents.*

re·proof /rɪ'pruf/ *n.frml.* [C;U] angry words of disapproval, (*syns.*) criticism, reproach: *The judge gave a reproof of the man's behavior in court.*

re·prove /rɪ'pruv/ *v.frml.* **-proved, -proving, -proves** to say angrily that one disapproves, (*syns.*) to criticize, reproach: *The judge reproved the lawyer for yelling in court.*

rep·tile /'rɛp,taɪl/ *n.* **1** a group of cold-blooded animals that have back bones, live on land, and usu. reproduce by laying eggs: *Snakes, lizards, turtles, and crocodiles are reptiles.* **2** *fig.* a bad or evil person: *That fellow is a reptile; don't trust him!* -*adj.* **reptilian** /rɛp'tɪliən/.

re·pub·lic /rə'pʌblɪk/ *n.* a form of government in which citizens vote for people to represent them and to make laws: *Long ago, the USA was a republic in which only men who owned property could vote.* -*adj.* **republican;** -*n.* [U] **republicanism.**

Re·pub·li·can /rə'pʌblɪkən/ *n.adj.* one of two major political parties in the USA: *Every four years, the <n.> Republicans (or) <adj.> Republican party choose a candidate to run for the presidency. See:* Democratic Party, USAGE NOTE.

USAGE NOTE: The US political system is basically a two-party system; most elected officials belong to either the *Republican* or *Democratic* party. Other parties are called *third parties*, but candidates from these parties are rarely elected. Sometimes the Republican party is referred to as the *GOP* which stands for the *Grand Old Party*. The symbol of the Republican party is an elephant, the Democrat's symbol is a donkey.

re·pub·li·ca·tion /ri,pʌblə'keɪʃən/ *n.* [C;U] publication or printing of s.t. again: *There was a republication of the important French news article in every major newspaper in Europe.* -*v.* **republish** /ri'pʌblɪʃ/. *See:* reprinting.

re·pu·di·ate /rɪ'pyudi,eɪt/ *v.* **-ated, -ating, -ates 1** to say s.t. is untrue, (*syn.*) to denounce: *A witness repudiated his earlier testimony and told the truth.* **2** not to pay a debt, esp. a government: *The state repudiated its bond and refused to pay the people.* -*n.* [U] **repudiation.**

re·pug·nant /rə'pʌgnənt/ *adj.frml.* causing dislike, unpleasant, (*syns.*) disgusting, offensive: *His bad behavior was repugnant to other guests at the party.* -*n.* [U] **repugnance.**

re·pulse /rə'pʌls/ *v.* **-pulsed, -pulsing, -pulses** to disgust, to make s.o. feel sick to his or her stomach: *Your bad breath, bad manners, and terrible insults repulse me. Get out of here! -n.* [U] **repulsion.**

re·pul·sive /rə'pʌlsɪv/ *adj.* making one want to look away, ugly, (*syn.*) disgusting: *Many people think that rats and snakes look repulsive.* -*adv.* **repulsively;** -*n.* [U] **repulsiveness.**

rep·u·ta·ble /'rɛpyətəbəl/ *adj.* having a good reputation, honest: *A reputable business will replace or repair any faulty products that it sells.* -*n.* **reputability;** -*adv.* **reputably.**

rep·u·ta·tion /,rɛpyə'teɪʃən/ *n.* [C;U] an opinion, about the quality of s.t., such as a person's character: *He has the reputation of being a smart businessperson.*

re·pute /rə'pyut/ *n.frml.* [U] reputation: *My sister is a doctor of good repute.*
—*v.frml.* **-puted, -puting, -putes** to think, believe: *The film is reputed to be excellent.*

re·put·ed /rə'pyutɪd/ *adj.* thought to be s.t., having a reputation of being, (*syn.*) alleged: *He is a reputed mobster.* -*adv.* **reputedly.**

re·quest /rə'kwɛst/ *v.* to ask for s.t., seek it: *Our teacher requested that the class be quiet.*
—*n.* an asking for s.t.: *The students couldn't hear the teacher's request because they were making too much noise.*

req·ui·em /'rɛkwiəm/ *n.adj.* a religious service to honor the dead or the music of such a service: *A <v.> requiem (or) <adj.> requiem service was held at the church for people who had died.*

re·quire /rə'kwaɪr/ *v.* **-quired, -quiring, -quires 1** to need: *This radio requires two batteries.* **2** *frml.* to ask for, desire: *He requires a quiet hotel room when he travels.*

re·quire·ment /rə'kwaɪrmənt/ *n.* **1** a necessity, s.t. needed, (*syn.*) an essential: *A college degree is a requirement for this job.* **2 to meet the requirements:** to have or do what is necessary: *She doesn't meet the requirements for graduation from high school.*

req·ui·site /'rɛkwəzɪt/ *n.frml.* [C;U] a requirement, necessity: *Ten years' experience is a requisite for the job. See:* prerequisite.

req·ui·si·tion /,rɛkwə'zɪʃən/ *n.* [C;U] a written order for s.t., a formal request: *Instructors must fill out a requisition to use a VCR in class.*

re·reg·is·ter /ri'rɛdʒɪstər/ *v.* to register again: *Although he didn't vote for many years, this year he reregistered to vote.* -*n.* [C;U] **reregistration.**

re·route /ri'rut, -'raut/ *v.* **-routed, -routing, -routes** to change the route of s.t.: *The police rerouted traffic around a car accident.*

re·run /'ri,rʌn/ *n.v.* repeat of a TV program: *Late at night, he watches <n.> reruns of old comedy shows.*
—*v.* /ri'rʌn/ **-ran** /-'ræn/, **-run, -running, -runs** to broadcast a TV or radio show again: *TV stations rerun popular old shows.*

re·sale /'ri,seɪl/ *n.* [C;U] a sale of s.t. again: *We made money on the resale of our house.*

re·sched·ule /ri'skɛdʒul/ *v.* **-uled, -uling, -ules** to schedule s.t. at a different time: *Our meeting for tomorrow was rescheduled for next Tuesday.*

re·scind /rɪ'sɪnd/ *v.* to take legal power away from s.t., (*syns.*) to revoke, cancel: *The Congress rescinded a tax law that people didn't like.*

res·cue /'rɛskyu/ *v.* **-cued, -cuing, -cues** to save s.o. or s.t. from danger, prison, etc.: *Firefighters rescued people from the burning building.*
—*n.* an act of saving s.o.: *The newspaper had a story about the rescue.* -*n.* **rescuer.**

re·search /rə'sɜrtʃ, 'ri,sɜrtʃ/ *v.* **-es** to study s.t. deeply, (*syn.*) to investigate: *He researched many books and magazines in the library for his term paper.*
—*n.* [U] a study of information about s.t., (*syn.*) an inquiry: *She did research in a chemical laboratory.* -*n.* **researcher.**

re·sell /ri'sɛl/ *v.* **-sold** /-'sould/, **-selling, -sells** to buy, then sell s.t.: *He buys things from the factory then resells them on the street to people.* -*n.* **reseller.**

re·sem·blance /rə'zɛmbləns/ *n.* [C;U] a likeness to s.o. or s.t., similarity: *The little girl bears a close resemblance to her mother.*

re·sem·ble /rə'zɛmbəl/ *v.* **-bled, -bling, -bles** to look like s.o. or s.t. else: *The boy resembles his father; they both have blond hair and blue eyes.*

R

re·send /ri'sɛnd/ v. -sent /'sɛnt/, -sending, -sends to send s.t. again: *The fax did not go through the first time, so I resent it.*

re·sent /rɪ'zɛnt/ v. to feel anger at s.t, feel hurt about s.t.: *I resent the unkind things he said about me.*

re·sent·ful /rɪ'zɛntfʊl/ adj. feeling anger, strong unhappiness toward s.o. or s.t., (syn.) bitter: *He is resentful about being asked to leave his job.* -adv. **resentfully.**

re·sent·ment /rɪ'zɛntmənt/ n. [U] a feeling of anger about s.t., unhappiness, (syn.) bitterness: *There was a feeling of resentment in the office after everyone's pay was lowered.*

re·ser·va·tion /ˌrɛzər'veɪʃən/ n. **1** [C] a place saved in a hotel, on an airplane ride, etc., (syn.) booking: *He has a reservation for three nights at the hotel.* **2** [C;U] a doubt about s.t., worry, or concern, (syn.) hesitation: *I have reservations about the new worker; she doesn't seem to be able to do the job.* **3** [C] special land in North America for tribes of Native Americans to live on: *We visited a Native American reservation in Arizona.* **4** [U] **without reservation:** having no doubt or concern: *I recommend her for the job without reservation.*

re·serve /rə'zɜrv/ v. **-served, -serving, -serves 1** to save a place in a hotel room, on an airplane, etc., (syn.) to book: *He reserved a room for three nights in the hotel.* **2** to hold or keep for oneself: *We are reserving these seats for my parents.||The producers reserve the right to cancel the outdoor concert if it rains.*
—n. **1** an amount of s.t. held back for later use: *She keeps a cash reserve in a savings account in case of emergencies.* **2** cool behavior, self-control in not reacting to things: *The man answered questions with a cool reserve and without smiling.* **3** special soldiers who are not part of the regular army, but who can be called into service: *He left the regular army and joined the reserves.* **4** land kept for a special purpose, (syn.) preserve: *You can sometimes see wild animals at that nature reserve.* **5 in reserve:** to keep s.t. for later use: *I keep a small radio in reserve, so I can listen to music if my stereo system breaks.*

reserve bank n. a central bank for other banks that is often part of a governmental system to regulate them: *Reserve banks lend money to other banks.*

re·served /rə'zɜrvd/ adj. **1** set aside for use by s.o.: *That seat in the theater is reserved for Mr. Jones.* **2** cool in one's behavior, not showing feelings, (syn.) restrained: *He is a very quiet and reserved person.* -adv. **reservedly** /rə'zɜrvɪdli/.

re·serv·ist /rə'zɜrvɪst/ n. a soldier not in the regular army but in the military reserves: *My father is a reservist.*

res·er·voir /'rɛzər,vwɑr, -,vwɔr/ n. **1** a body of water saved for use: *This lake is the reservoir for the city.* **2** any reserve supply of s.t.: *That corporation keeps a reservoir of cash available to buy other companies.*

re·set /ri'sɛt/ v. **-set, -setting, -sets** to set s.t. again: *I reset the alarm clock to ring later, so I could sleep more.*

re·shape /ri'ʃeɪp/ v. **-shaped, -shaping, -shapes** to shape s.t. differently, (syn.) to re-mold s.t.: *Designers reshaped new models of cars to make them look more sporty.*

re·ship /ri'ʃɪp/ v. **-shipped, -shipping, -ships** to send s.t. again: *My first order was lost, so the company reshipped it.*

re·shuf·fle /ri'ʃʌfəl/ v. **-fled, -fling, -fles** to mix again, organize differently, (syn.) to rearrange: *The Prime Minister reshuffled the duties of several members of her cabinet.*

re·side /rə'zaɪd/ v.frml. **-sided, -siding, -sides** to live someplace, (syn.) to inhabit: *She resides in Jacksonville, Florida.*

res·i·dence /'rɛzədəns, -dɛns/ n.frml. **1** [C] the place where one lives, such as a house, apartment, etc.: *His residence is a house in Hartford.* **2** [U] **in residence:** living or working in a place: *When the queen is in residence, visitors can't come to the palace.*

res·i·den·cy /'rɛzədənsi/ n. **-cies 1** [U] the condition of living somewhere: *He has residency in this country.* **2** [C] a final period of training for a doctor: *Her seven-year residency will end this year at New York Hospital.*

res·i·dent /'rɛzədənt/ n. **1** a person who lives in a certain area: *She is a resident of San Francisco.* **2** s.o. in a final training period to become a doctor

res·i·den·tial /ˌrɛzə'dɛnʃəl/ adj. related to houses, places where people live, and not to commercial business: *The north part of the city is nearly all residential.*

re·sid·u·al /rə'zɪdʒuəl/ adj.n. **1** related to a small amount of s.t. leftover: *After paying my bills and taxes, I put my <adj.> residual income (or) the <n.> residual into my savings.* **2** an amount paid to artists for repeat performances of their works: *She is a TV star who gets <n.> residuals for her reruns.*

res·i·due /'rɛzə,du/ n. s.t. left over after a process, (syn.) remainder: *My dishwasher is leaving soap residue on my glasses.*

re·sign /rə'zaɪn/ v. **1** to choose to leave one's job or post: *She resigned from her job because she wanted to travel.* **2** to accept s.t. reluctantly as true: *When he couldn't find a job with his college degree, he resigned himself to going to graduate school.* -adj. **resigned** See: quit, USAGE NOTE.

res·ig·na·tion /ˌrɛzɪg'neɪʃən/ n. **1** [C;U] an act of choosing to leave one's job or post: *He* handed in his resignation as ambassador to Japan. **2** [U] sad and unwilling acceptance of s.t.: *His resignation to the idea that he is now old took a long time.*

re·sil·ience /rə'zɪlyəns/ n. [U] **1** the ability of s.t. to return to its original shape: *Rubber has a lot of resilience.* **2** the ability to restore one's energy: *He works very hard, but his resilience keeps his strength up. -n.* [U] **resiliency.**

re·sil·ient /rə'zɪlyənt/ adj. **1** able to recover its original shape: *This resilient plastic won't break even under a lot of stress.* **2** able to restore one's energy, recover from difficulty: *The children are tired now, but they are resilient and will have more energy soon. -adv.* **resiliently.**

res·in /'rɛzɪn/ n. [U] a sticky substance found in some plants: *The resin that comes out when a rubber tree's bark is cut is used to make rubber. -adj.* **resinous.** *See:* rosin.

re·sist /rə'zɪst/ v. **1** not to allow s.t. to touch or hurt, (*syn.*) to fend off, withstand: *She resisted his kisses.||Stainless steel resists rust.* **2** to oppose, be against: *Conservative politicians resisted the reform plan.* **3** not to do s.t. that you want to, refrain from eating or drinking s.t., etc.: *He resisted eating the chocolate cake because it is too fattening. -adj.* **resistible.**

re·sis·tance /rə'zɪstəns/ n. [U] **1** refusal to do what s.o. wants, (*syn.*) rejection: *He met with resistance when he tried to kiss her.* **2** not to do s.t., to hold back: *He maintained his resistance against eating fattening foods.* **3** ability to fight against disease: *She has good resistance against sickness.* **4 Resistance:** a fighting force against an occupying army or power: *The French Resistance fought the Germans during World War II.* **5** the ability to slow or oppose electric current: *Electrical resistance is less in copper than in steel wire.*

re·sis·tant /rə'zɪstənt/ adj. **1** referring to s.t. that does not allow s.o. or s.t. to touch or hurt it: *That plastic is resistant to breakage and staining.* **2** immune to disease: *Her vaccinations make her resistant to many childhood diseases.* **3** not wanting to do s.t., not agreeable, (*syn.*) uncooperative: *He is resistant to the idea of seeing a doctor even though he doesn't feel well. -n.* **resister.**

re·sis·tor /rə'zɪstər/ n. (in electronics) a device in an electric circuit that controls current: *He put new resistors in the machine and fixed it.*

re·sole /ri'soʊl/ v. **-soled, -soling, -soles** to put a new sole on a shoe: *These are my favorite shoes, so I had the bottoms resoled instead of buying new shoes.*

res·o·lute /'rɛzə,lut/ adj. having a strong purpose, dedicated as to an idea, cause, etc.: *That religion has a large and resolute group of believers. -adv.* **resolutely;** *-n.* [U] **resoluteness.**

res·o·lu·tion /,rɛzə'luʃən/ n. **1** [C] a solution to a problem, result of an action: *Diplomats tried to find a resolution to the problems between their countries.* **2** [U] the quality of believing s.t. strongly and not changing one's mind: *Everyone admired his resolution when he quit smoking and never touched another cigarette.* **3** [C] **New Year's resolution:** a promise or plan to change s.t. about one's behavior or habits, a decision made on the first day of the new year: *I made New Year's resolutions to be nicer to my sister and to exercise each day.*

re·solve /rɪ'zalv/ n. [C;U] strong belief in an idea, cause, etc.: *The new president began to make changes with great resolve.*
—*v.* **-solved, -solving, -solves 1** to decide to do s.t.: *He resolved to reform the nation's laws.* **2** to solve s.t., find a solution to a problem: *He resolved a disagreement by giving each side s.t. to be happy about.*

res·o·nant /'rɛzənənt/ adj. having a deep and clear sound, (*syn.*) sonorous: *His resonant voice is pleasing to hear. -n.* [U] **resonance.**

res·o·nate /'rɛzə,neɪt/ v. **-nated, -nating, -nates** to sound clearly for a long time, (*syn.*) to resound: *The organ music resonated throughout the large church. -n.* **resonator.**

re·sorp·tion /ri'sɔrpʃən, -'zɔrp-/ n. [U] absorbing s.t. again, the process of taking s.t. into s.t. else: *After the heavy rain, the resorption of rain into the ground was slow, so the ground was very wet all week. -v.* **resorb.**

re·sort /rə'zɔrt/ n. **1** a hotel with recreation facilities (swimming pool, tennis courts, etc.) for rest and relaxation: *We went to a resort in Arizona for our vacation.* **2 as a last resort:** the last choice for a way of doing s.t.: *If I can't fly to Chicago, I can drive there as a last resort.*
—*phrasal v. insep.* **to resort to s.t.:** to do or use s.t. extreme, often dishonest: *He resorted to lying so his wife wouldn't know he wrecked their car.*

re·sound /rɪ'zaʊnd/ v. to sound loud and clear: *At war's end, church bells resounded throughout the land.*

re·sound·ing /rɪ'zaʊndɪŋ/ adj. clear, complete, (*syn.*) definite: *The new play was a resounding success. -adv.* **resoundingly.**

re·source /'ri,sɔrs, -,zɔrs, rɪ'sɔrs, -'zɔrs/ n. a useful way to find s.t., esp. information: *The college library is an important resource for learning.*
—*n.pl.* **1** money, funds: *She has the resources to buy a vacation home.* **2** useful things in general: *Our country is rich in natural resources, such as oil, gold, and farm land.*

re·source·ful /rɪ'sɔrsfəl, -'zɔrs-/ adj. able to solve problems in a creative way: *Resourceful people can think of more than one way to do*

R

something. *-adv.* **resourcefully;** *-n.* [U] **resourcefulness.**

re·spect /rə'spɛkt/ *n.* **1** [U] approval and honor for the qualities of a person or thing, (*syn.*) admiration: *I have respect for his high intelligence.* **2** [U] thoughtful concern about the importance of s.t.: *He has no respect for my rights!* **3** [C] a part of, detail, (*syn.*) aspect: *The company owner and the workers agree in most respects, but they have some small differences.* **4 to give one's respects:** a formal greeting: *Give my respects to your grandfather.* **5 to pay one's respects:** to honor s.o. who has died: *Many people came to the funeral to pay their respects.* **6 with respect to:** concerning, about, (*syn.*) regarding: *With respect to your job application, please come for an interview tomorrow.*
—*v.* to admire, have a high opinion of, (*syn.*) to appreciate: *I respect her hard work and good ideas.*

re·spect·a·bil·i·ty /rə,spɛktə'bɪləti/ *n.* [U] the state of being accepted by polite society: *That family thinks respectability is very important, so they are careful about what they do and say.*

re·spect·a·ble /rə'spɛktəbəl/ *adj.* **1** having a good place in society, (*syn.*) reputable: *They are respectable people who are liked and trusted in their town.* **2** clean and well-dressed, (*syn.*) presentable: *He shaved and put on clean clothes to look respectable for his guests. -adv.* **respectably.**

re·spect·ful /rə'spɛktfəl/ *adj.* having proper politeness toward s.o.: *Students and teachers should have a respectful attitude toward each other. -adv.* **respectfully.**

re·spect·ing /rə'spɛktɪŋ/ *prep.frml.* with regard to, in the matter of, about: *Respecting your taxes, they are due April 15.*

re·spect·ive·ly /rə'spɛktɪvli/ *adv.* in that order, (*syn.*) consecutively: *He likes coffee and tea, black and with cream, respectively. -adj.* **respective.**

res·pi·ra·tion /,rɛspə'reɪʃən/ *n.* [U] breathing, taking air in and out of the body: *Respiration is necessary for life. -v.* **respire** /rɪ'spaɪr/.

res·pi·ra·tor /'rɛspə,reɪtər/ *n.* a device used to help s.o. breathe: *Doctors put patients with breathing problems on respirators.*

res·pi·ra·to·ry /'rɛspərə,tɔri, rə'spaɪrə-/ *adj.* related to breathing: *Smoking cigarettes can cause respiratory problems.*

res·pite /'rɛspɪt/ *n.frml.* [C;U] relief, a pause or break from hard work or worry: *He took a short respite from work by going to another town for the weekend.*

re·splen·dent /rə'splɛndənt/ *adj.frml.* shining, brilliant: *The millionaire was resplendent in her gold and jewels. -adv.* **resplendently.**

re·spond /rɪ'spɑnd/ *v.* **1** *frml.* to answer, reply: *The company responded to my order by sending it quickly.* **2** to react, do s.t. because of s.t. else: *He responded to her farewell gift by kissing her hand.* **3** *phrasal v. insep.* **to respond to s.t.:** to change as a result of s.t.: *The plants have responded well to the fungicide you used.*

re·spon·dent /rɪ'spɑndənt/ *n.adj.frml.* **1** a person who answers or replies: *One hundred <n.> respondents answered our questionnaire.* **2** a defendant in a lawsuit: *He was a <n.> respondent in a court case.*

re·sponse /rɪ'spɑns/ *n.* **1** [C] an answer, reply: *My friend sent a response to my letter.* **2** [C;U] a reaction to s.t.: *He tried to kiss her, but her response was to slap his face.*

re·spon·si·bil·i·ty /rə,spɑnsə'bɪləti/ *n.* **-ties 1** [C;U] s.t. that s.o. must do because of moral or legal necessity, or because of a job, (*syns.*) a duty, obligation: *He has the responsibility of running the advertising department, and he also has responsibilities at home to his wife and two children.* **2** [C;U] a difficult job s.o. has to do, (*syn.*) burden: *Her father is ill, and she has the responsibility of caring for him.* **3** [C] a person or thing s.o. must take care of: *Until they are 18, children are the responsibility of their parents.*

re·spon·si·ble /rə'spɑnsəbəl/ *adj.* **1** required to do s.t., (*syn.*) accountable: *He is responsible for taking care of his younger brother while his parents are away.* **2** able to be relied on, (*syn.*) trustworthy: *She is very responsible and is always on time, so she should be here in five minutes.* **3** referring to s.o. who caused s.t. to happen, at fault, guilty: *He had to pay to repair both cars, because he was responsible for the accident. -adv.* **responsibly.**

re·spon·sive /rə'spɑnsɪv/ *adj.* willing to act, ready to help, (*syns.*) cooperative, receptive: *He was responsive to the idea of starting a new project. -n.* [U] **responsiveness.**

rest (1) /rɛst/ *v.* **1** to relax, stop work: *A worker stopped working and rested for five minutes.* **2** to take time to become healthy after an illness, (*syn.*) to convalesce: *She rested for two weeks after being in the hospital.* **3** to sleep: *I rested well last night.* **4** to place s.t. somewhere for support: *He was so tired that he couldn't stand up, so he rested his body against the wall.* **5** to stop movement or other action: *The ball rolled across the room and rested by the door.‖We will never agree, so we should let the argument rest.* **6 to rest assured:** to be sure: *You can rest assured that we will do the work right the first time.* **7 to rest a case:** (in law) to stop arguing a case and let the judge or jury make a decision: *The lawyer gave her final speech and said, "I rest my case."* **8** *phrasal v. insep.* **to rest on/upon s.o.** or **s.t.: a.** *fig.* to look at quietly: *While he thought about his family, his*

eyes rested on their photograph. **b.** to use for support: *Her beliefs rest upon the religion her parents taught her.* **9** *phrasal v. insep.* **to rest with s.o.:** to be s.o.'s responsibility: *The responsibility to pay a loan rests with the person who signed the official loan documents.*
—*n.* **1** [C] a pause from work: *The workers all get a rest at lunch time.* **2** [U] a time for recovering from an illness: *After his operation, he needed some rest in bed.* **3** [C;U] sleep: *She had a good night's rest.* **4** [C] a state of being without motion: *When the electricity went off, the clock's hands came to a rest.* **5** [C] (in music) a symbol for silence between notes: *Rests are an important part of a musical rhythm.* **6 to lay to rest:** to bury s.o. who has died: *Her grandfather was laid to rest last week and she is still very sad.* **7 to put one's mind at rest:** to stop s.o. from worrying: *My daughter put my mind at rest by calling to say she was going to be a little bit late tonight.*

rest (2) *n. sing.* the part of s.t. that remains, is left, (*syn.*) remainder: *It's noon now, and I am going to take the rest of the day off.*||*She had some cake and I ate the rest.*

re·start /ri'stɑrt/ *v.n.* to start s.t. again: *I <v.> restarted my car engine after it stalled in the cold weather.*

re·state /ri'steɪt/ *v.* **-stated, -stating, -states 1** to say s.t. again: *The judge restated the law a third time for the jury to realize its importance.* **2** to say s.t. in a different way: *The teacher restated the directions so the class could understand. -n.* [U] **restatement.**

res·tau·rant /'rɛstərənt, -tə,rɑnt, -,trɑnt/ *n.* a business that serves food: *It is expensive to eat at fine restaurants. See:* café, USAGE NOTE.

res·tau·ra·teur /,rɛstərə'tʊr/ *n.* a person who owns or runs a restaurant: *My uncle is a restaurateur, so sometimes he gives us free meals at his restaurant.*

rest·ful /'rɛstfəl/ *adj.* calm, making one feel peaceful, rested: *A vacation by a quiet lake is restful. -adv.* **restfully;** *-n.* [U] **restfulness.**

rest home *n.* a place where the elderly and very sick are cared for: *His aging parents live in a rest home.*

resting place *n.* a grave, a place s.o. is buried when they die: *He died yesterday and has been taken to his final resting place.*

res·ti·tu·tion /,rɛstə'tuʃən/ *n.frml.* [U] payment for a loss or damages, (*syn.*) reparation: *The man had to make restitution of $1,000 for the damage that he did.*

res·tive /'rɛstɪv/ *adj.frml.* not able to rest, (*syns.*) restless, agitated: *The angry people were restive and ready to riot.*

rest·less /'rɛstlɪs, 'rɛslɪs/ *adj.* wanting a change, s.t. new, (*syns.*) anxious, impatient: *She is restless in her present job and wants a*

new one.||*Children are restless and want to run and play.*

res·to·ra·tion /,rɛstə'reɪʃən/ *n.* **1** making s.t., esp. a building, look like it did when it was new, (*syn.*) renovation: *Restoration of the house means putting on a new roof, fixing broken windows, and painting it.* **2 Restoration:** the historical time in England (1660–1688) when King Charles II returned to power: *I enjoy reading plays written during the Restoration.*

res·tor·a·tive /rə'stɔrətɪv/ *adj.* having qualities that renew and refresh: *The restorative powers of good food and rest are well known.*

re·store /rə'stɔr/ *v.* **-stored, -storing, -stores 1** to return s.t., give back: *The police restored a stolen watch to its owner after they caught the thief.* **2** to renew, refresh: *A long stay at the hospital restored her health.* **3** to make s.t. look like it did when it was new: *We want to buy an old house and live there while we restore it. -n.* **restorer.**

re·strain /ri'streɪn/ *v.* to hold back, stop from doing s.t., control: *She restrains her dog by walking him on a leash.*

re·strained /ri'streɪnd/ *adj.* **1** stopped from moving freely as with a leash or handcuffs: *The prisoner is restrained in handcuffs.* **2** not talkative, quiet in manner: *He is restrained and shows it in the quiet way he talks.*

restraining order *n.* a court order telling one person to stay away from another: *She got a restraining order against her former husband so he wouldn't come near her.*

re·straint /ri'streɪnt/ *n.* **1** [C] s.t. that holds, restricts s.o.'s movements, such as a leash, handcuffs, etc.: *The prisoner's wrists were held in a restraint.* **2** [U] not acting with full force, control of emotions or power, (*syn.*) moderation: *Even though the mother was very angry, she acted with restraint and didn't yell at her child.*

re·strict /ri'strɪkt/ *v.* **1** to limit, (*syn.*) restrain: *Restaurants restrict the use of their toilets to customers only.* **2** to punish by limiting some freedom: *The soldier was restricted to his room because he didn't follow orders.*

re·strict·ed /ri'strɪktɪd/ *adj.* limited in use or availability: *She is on a restricted diet of no fat, salt, or alcohol.*

re·stric·tion /ri'strɪkʃən/ *n.* [C;U] a rule that limits s.t., (*syn.*) limitation: *Restrictions don't allow workers to use company cars for personal use. -adj.* **restrictive;** *-adv.* **restrictively.**

rest room *n.* a washroom, toilet, bathroom: *He went to the rest room at the store.*

USAGE NOTE: Compare *rest room* and *bathroom.* People commonly refer to a public toilet and washroom as a *rest room.* *Bathroom* refers to the room in a home where the toilet and bath are located.

re·struc·ture /riˈstrʌktʃər/ v. **-tured, -turing, -tures** to reorganize, often to make a work force smaller: *The corporation restructured from five divisions into two. -n.* **restructuring.**

re·sult /rəˈzʌlt/ n. **1** [C;U] an effect, a consequence of an action: *The results of the election surprised everyone.* **2 to get results:** to make good things happen: *The hard work he put into his job search got results, and he has a new, interesting job.*
—v. **1** to cause a result, happen: *When there are summer thunderstorms, tornadoes can result.* **2** *phrasal v. insep.* **to result in s.t.:** to have as a result, cause: *Her hard work resulted in a big bonus for her. -adj.* **resultant.**

re·sume /rɪˈzum/ v. **-sumed, -suming, -sumes 1** to begin again, restart: *The TV show will resume after this commercial.* **2** to take a place again: *After she had a baby, she resumed her job as manager.*

ré·su·mé /ˈrɛzəˌmeɪ, ˌrɛzʊˈmeɪ/ n. a short statement of one's work history and education used to get a new job, (syns.) curriculum vitae, summary: *He submitted a two-page résumé for a job interview.*

re·sump·tion /rɪˈzʌmpʃən/ n. [U] a restart, beginning again: *Resumption of growth in the economy resulted in more new jobs.*

re·sup·ply /ˌrisəˈplaɪ/ v. **-plied, -plying, -plies** to add more supplies: *Cargo ships resupplied the soldiers with fresh food and water.*

re·sur·face /riˈsɜrfɪs/ v. **-faced, -facing, -faces 1** to put a new surface on s.t.: *A carpenter resurfaced the table with fresh paint.* **2** to come up through the water to the air, show up again: *A submarine dove then resurfaced 10 miles (16 km) away. -n.* [U] **resurfacing.**

re·sur·gence /rɪˈsɜrdʒəns/ n. a rise or increase that happens after a time of no (or) slow movement, an upward trend: *A resurgence of growth in the economy is always good news. -v.* **resurge; -adj.** **resurgent.**

res·ur·rect /ˌrɛzəˈrɛkt/ v.frml. to bring back to life; to bring s.t. up again: *When a politician runs for office, the newspapers often resurrect old mistakes he or she made. -n.* [U] **resurrection.**

re·sus·ci·tate /rɪˈsʌsəˌteɪt/ v. **-tated, -tating, -tates** to bring back to consciousness, good health, etc., (syn.) to revive: *The doctors and nurses resuscitated an unconscious patient. -n.* [U] **resuscitation.**

re·sus·ci·ta·tor /rɪˈsʌsəˌteɪtər/ n. a device used to help s.o.'s heart start beating, help s.o. start breathing, etc.: *A nurse used a resuscitator to revive her patient.*

re·tail /ˈriteɪl/ v. to sell products or services directly to people and not to other stores: *That store retails computers and office supplies.*
—adj. related to retailing: *He works in retail clothing.*
—n. [U] **1** the selling of products or services to the public: *She works in retail.* **2 at retail:** at a price for all people, not at a wholesale price, which stores pay: *That table sells at retail for $100. -n.* **retailer.**

re·tain /rəˈteɪn/ v. **1** to keep s.t., maintain possession of s.t.: *The wife retained most of her dead husband's property, but some went to the children.* **2** to pay a professional for services: *When his neighbor drove a car into his house, he retained a lawyer. See:* retention.

re·tain·er /rəˈteɪnər/ n. a regular fee paid to so, such as a consultant or a lawyer: *He pays his accountant a monthly retainer.*

re·take /riˈteɪk/ v. **-took** /-ˈtʊk/, **-taken** /-ˈteɪkən/, **-taking, -takes** to take again, recapture: *Our soldiers retook a hill they had lost to the enemy.*
—n. /ˈriˌteɪk/ reshooting of a picture or acting scene: *Noise from an airplane spoiled the scene, so the actors did a retake.*

re·tal·i·ate /rəˈtæliˌeɪt/ v. **-ated, -ating, -ates** to do s.t. bad to s.o. because of what they did, to strike back, (syn.) to avenge: *When the boy broke her toy, the girl retaliated by hitting him. -n.* [U] **retaliation; -adj.** **retaliatory** /rəˈtælyəˌtɔri/.

re·tard v. /rəˈtard/ **1** to slow s.t., hold it back: *Lack of good food retarded the boy's growth.*
—n.pej. /ˈriˌtard/ a mentally handicapped person

ret·ardant /rəˈtardnt/ adj. able to hold s.t. back: *The rug and drapes are made of fire-retardant cloth.*
—n. s.t. that slows s.t. down, holds it back: *Poor education is a retardant to economic growth.*

re·tar·da·tion /ˌritarˈdeɪʃən/ n. [U] **1** a slowing down, holding back: *Retardation of economic growth is caused by poverty and poor education.* **2** a state of not having the same mental abilities as most people: *That poor baby was born with mental retardation.*

re·tard·ed /rəˈtardɪd/ adj. **1** held back, slowed down: *Retarded growth in the economy hurts everyone.* **2** not having the same mental development as most people: *Retarded children need special care.*

USAGE NOTE: Many people refer to *mentally retarded* people as *mentally challenged.*

retch /rɛtʃ/ v.n. **-es** to bring food up from the stomach or to make the motions of doing this, (syn.) to vomit: *He had a stomachache and <v.> retched all night.*

re·ten·tion /rɪˈtɛnʃən/ n. [U] ability to keep or retain s.t.: *Retention of students in that high* *school is low; only 50% of the students finish the 12th grade.*

re·ten·tive /rɪ'tɛntɪv/ *adj.* related to the ability to keep or retain s.t.: *She has a retentive memory; she never forgets. -n.* [U] **retentiveness.** *See:* retain.

re·think /ri'θɪŋk/ *v.* **-thought** /-'θɔt/, **-thinking, -thinks** to think about s.t. again, esp. in a different way, (*syn.*) to reconsider: *He rejected their offer as too little, so they rethought the offer and raised the amount.*

ret·i·cent /'rɛtəsənt/ *adj.frml.* not wanting to talk or act, (*syns.*) reserved, timid: *He is reticent about telling his girlfriend he loves her. -n.* [U] **reticence;** *-adv.* **reticently.**

ret·i·na /'rɛtnə/ *n.* the inner lining of the eye that contains many light-sensitive cells and sends messages about light and color to the brain: *The retina is a complex part of the eye. -adj.* **retinal.**

ret·i·nue /'rɛtn,u, -,yu/ *n.* a group of followers, (*syn.*) entourage: *The Queen has a retinue of 80 friends and servants who travel with her.*

re·tire /rə'taɪr/ *v.* **-tired, -tiring, -tires** **1** to leave the work force and stop working: *At age 70, he retired and moved to Florida.* **2** to go to sleep: *I retired at 11 o'clock last night.* **3** *frml.* to go away to a place with few or no people: *I was tired of the party, so I retired to my room.* **4** to stop using s.t.: *When the famous football player quit playing, his number was retired and never used by another player.*

re·tired /rə'taɪrd/ *adj. & past part.* of retire, having left the workforce, stopped working: *She is retired now and lives in Miami.*

re·tir·ee /rə,taɪr'i/ *n.* a person who has retired from work: *Many retirees live in Florida.*

re·tire·ment /rə'taɪrmənt/ *n.* [C;U] an act of leaving or time when one leaves the workforce and stops work: *He took early retirement and moved south.‖His retirement has been relaxing.*

re·tir·ing /rə'taɪrɪŋ/ *adj.* not very active or social, (*syns.*) timid, shy: *He is retiring and doesn't like to talk to people.*

re·tort /rə'tɔrt/ *n.v.frml.* a usu. quick or funny reply, answer: *He made a brief <n.> retort to his wife's question.*

re·touch /ri'tʌtʃ/ *v.* **-es** to change a negative or photograph to make it look better or different: *A photographer retouched the boy's picture to make his skin look clearer.*

re·trace /ri'treɪs/ *v.* **-traced, -tracing, -traces** to go over s.t. again, return: *He lost a glove and retraced his steps until he found it.*

re·tract /rɪ'trækt/ *v.* **1** to take s.t. back formally, withdraw s.t.: *A woman wanted to buy my car, but later she retracted her offer.* **2** to pull back in: *The turtle retracted its head into its shell. -adv.* **retractable.**

re·trac·tion /rɪ'trækʃən/ *n.* [C;U] a withdrawal of s.t., esp. a statement: *When newspapers make mistakes, they print a retraction of what they said wrong.*

re·train /ri'treɪn/ *v.* to train s.o. to do s.t. new, (*syn.*) to reeducate: *The steelworkers were retrained in repairing computers. -n.* [U] **retraining.**

re·tread /'ri,trɛd/ *n.* a worn tire whose tread has been replaced: *<n.> Retreads are much cheaper than new tires. -v.* **retread** /ri'trɛd/.

re·treat /rɪ'trit/ *v.* to move away from s.t., such as soldiers who move away from the enemy, (*syn.*) to withdraw: *The enemy was firing heavily, so the army had to retreat to safety.*
—n. a place of calm and safety, often where one goes to think, (*syn.*) a refuge: *Every summer, the priest goes to a retreat in the mountains.*

re·trench /ri'trɛntʃ/ *v.* **-es** to do less of s.t., cut back money or activity, (*syn.*) to economize: *The company retrenched by closing two factories and laying off 2,000 workers.*

re·trench·ment /ri'trɛntʃmənt/ *n.* [C;U] a cutback, reduction in funds or activity: *During bad economic times, businesses have to think about retrenchment, or laying people off.*

re·trial /'ri,traɪl/ *n.* a second trial of a legal case: *The man got a retrial because mistakes were made in his first trial.*

ret·ri·bu·tion /,rɛtrə'byuʃən/ *n.frml.* [U] punishment for or a demand for repayment for a wrong or harm: *When her husband left her, she demanded financial retribution. -adj.* **retributive** /rə'trɪbyətɪv/.

re·trieve /rə'triv/ *v.* **-trieved, -trieving, -trieves** **1** to bring s.t. back, (*syn.*) to fetch: *He throws a stick and his dog retrieves it.* **2** to get s.t. back, rescue it, (*syn.*) to reclaim: *His watch fell into the water, but he retrieved it with a fishing pole. -adj.* **retrievable;** *-n.* **retrieval.**

re·triev·er /rə'trivər/ *n.* a type of dog that retrieves or brings back animals that have been shot: *Our family pet is a golden retriever.*

ret·ro·ac·tive /,rɛtroʊ'æktɪv/ *adj.* becoming active or effective on a date that has already passed: *The tax increase is retroactive to January 1 of this year. -adv.* **retroactively.**

ret·ro·grade /'rɛtroʊ,greɪd/ *adj.* moving backwards: *The space shuttle is moving in a retrograde orbit now.*

ret·ro·gress /,rɛtrə'grɛs/ *v.* **-es** to move into a worse position or state: *The presidential election has retrogressed into ugly name-calling and fighting. -n.* [U] **retrogression;** *-adj.* **retrogressive.**

ret·ro·spec·tive /,rɛtrə'spɛktɪv/ *adj.* looking backward: *The former president wrote a retrospective book about his years in office.*

R

—*n.* a showing or report of s.t. that looks backward in time: *The magazine did a retrospective on women's fashion from today back to the 1920s.* -*n.* [U] **retrospection.**

re·turn /rɪ'tɜrn/ *v.* **1** to come back, as from a trip: *He returned to his office after lunch in a restaurant.* **2** to give s.t. back: *She returned an umbrella she had borrowed from a friend.* **3** to put s.t. back: *The friend returned the umbrella to a closet.* **4** to go back to s.t., as to an earlier thought: *The teacher returned to yesterday's lesson to explain it again.* **5** to repay, give s.t. in return: *She did him a favor, so he returned the favor by loaning her money.* **6** to pay, make money, or gain financially: *That investment returned 7% a year.* **7** *frml.* to report officially: *The committee returned a recommendation to the manager.* **8 to reach the point of no return:** to proceed to a point where one cannot stop or turn back: *He reached the point of no return; he has spent so much money on the project that he must finish it.*

—*n.* **1** [C;U] a coming or bringing back: *We were surprised by his sudden return from Iceland.* **2** [C] a payment, the amount of money gained as profit: *That savings account pays a 7% return.* **3** [C] a tax return, official government form for filing taxes: *His accountant filed his return for this year.* **4** [C] unsold merchandise sent back to a warehouse or other place for storage: *Our company received a small return of unsold hats from a store.*

—*n.pl.* **returns:** election results: *The election returns showed that the mayor was re-elected.*

—*adj.* **1** answered quickly: *He sent a response to my letter by return mail.* **2** related to a homeward journey: *He made the return trip back to New York last night using his return ticket.* **3** related to a repeat of an event in sports, theater, etc.: *The boxer's manager agreed to a return match in six months.*

re·turn·a·ble /rə'tɜrnəbəl/ *adj.* related to an item bought that a buyer may return to get money back or s.t. better: *That sweater is returnable if it doesn't fit you.*

re·type /ri'taɪp/ *v.* **-typed, -typing, -types** to type s.t. over again: *If you type on a computer, you don't have to retype everything if you want to make changes.*

re·u·ni·fy /ri'yunə,faɪ/ *v.* **-fied, -fying, -fies** to bring s.t. together again, put it back together: *Chancellor Helmut Kohl reunified East and West Germany.* -*n.* [U] **reunification.**

re·un·ion /ri'yunyən/ *n.* a time when people who have s.t. in common (college, family) get together again: *Our college class has a reunion at the college every five years.||My grandmother was the oldest person at the family reunion.*

re·u·nite /,riyu'naɪt/ *v.* **-nited, -niting, -nites** to put people or things back together again, unite again: *Their boat sank, but the couple was saved and reunited.*

re·up·hol·ster /,riə'poulstər/ *v.* to put new material on furniture, (*syn.*) to refurbish: *A worker reupholstered my sofa with new fabric.* -*n.* [U] **reupholstery.** *See:* recover.

re·us·a·ble /ri'yuzəbəl/ *adj.* able to be used again and again: *Microwave dishes are reusable.*

re·use /ri'yuz/ *v.* **-used, -using, -uses** to use s.t. again: *If we reuse our bottles and cans, there will be less garbage each week.* *See:* recycle, USAGE NOTE.
—*n.* /ri'yus/ [C;U] an instance of using s.t. over again: *I wash the microwave dish after each reuse.*

re·u·til·ize /ri'yutl,aɪz/ *v.frml.* **-ized, -izing, -izes** to reuse, use again

rev /rɛv/ *v.* **revved, revving, revs** to speed up an engine: *A race car driver revved his engine at the starting line.*

Rev. /'rɛvərənd, 'rɛvrənd/ *abbr. for* Reverend: *Rev. Allen is the minister at that church.*

re·val·ue /ri'vælyu/ *v.* **-ued, -uing, -ues** to place a new value on s.t., make a new estimate of how much s.t. should cost: *The painting was bought for $1,000 in 1920 and was revalued this year at $2 million.* -*n.* **revaluation.** *See:* devalue.

re·vamp /ri'væmp/ *v.* to redo, change s.t. completely: *The school revamped its curriculum to use computers to help teach many subjects.* -*n.* **revamping.**

re·veal /rə'vil/ *v.* to uncover s.t. hidden, (*syn.*) to disclose: *He revealed his secrets to his friend.*

re·veal·ing /rə'vilɪŋ/ *adj.* showing s.t. that was hidden: *A revealing story explained all about the lies a politician told about her life.* -*adv.* **revealingly.**

rev·eil·le /'rɛvəli/ *n.* [U] a musical sound or song used to wake military personnel in the morning: *A soldier sounded reveille on a bugle.*

re·vel /'rɛvəl/ *v.* **1** to have a good time, party: *They reveled all night going from party to party.* **2** *phrasal v. insep.* **to revel in s.t.:** to enjoy s.t. greatly, delight in s.t.: *She revels in her good grades at school.*
—*n.* a party: *We're having a party tonight, so if you want to join the revel, come at 10:00 P.M.*

rev·e·la·tion /,rɛvə'leɪʃən/ *n.* **1** [U] an uncovering of s.t. that was hidden, (*syn.*) a disclosure: *Revelation of the truth about the murder came out in court.* **2** [C] a surprise, shocking event: *It was a great revelation to him that people think he is unkind.*

rev·el·er /ˈrɛvələr/ *n.* a person who is enjoying a party, esp. loudly: *Noisy revelers kept me awake by singing and shouting all night.*

rev·el·ry /ˈrɛvəlri/ *n.frml.* [U] having fun at a party, (*syn.*) merrymaking: *On New Year's Eve, revelry lasts all night.*

re·venge /rəˈvɛndʒ/ *n.* [U] a desire or an act to insult or hurt s.o. in repayment for a wrong: *When his partner cheated him, he wanted revenge, so he had him put in jail.*
—*v.* **-venged, -venging, -venges** to commit an act of revenge, to get back at s.o. for s.t.: *In Shakespeare's play called "Hamlet," Hamlet revenges the murder of his father.* *-adj.* **revengeful;** *-adv.* **revengefully.**

rev·e·nue /ˈrɛvəˌnu, -ˌnyu/ *n.* [C;U] incoming monies, such as tax payments for the government: *The government has a huge need for tax revenue.*

revenue bond *n.* a bond sold by a government to raise money for a public project: *New Jersey issued revenue bonds to build a toll highway.*

rev·e·nu·er /ˈrɛvəˌnuər, -ˌnyu-/ *n.* a person, esp. a government employee, who collects taxes: *Revenuers try to find businesses that should but don't pay taxes.*

re·ver·ber·ate /rəˈvɜrbəˌreɪt/ *v.* **-ated, -ating, -ates** to echo, continue to sound: *His voice reverberated in the empty room.* *-n.* [C;U] **reverberation.**

re·vere /rəˈvɪr/ *v.* **-vered, -vering, -veres** to admire s.o. greatly: *Martin Luther King, Jr., was revered as a religious and social leader.*

rev·er·ence /ˈrɛvərəns/ *n.* **1** [U] great admiration: *The child looked up at his father with reverence.* **2** [U] respect for s.t. as sacred, holy, worthy to be worshiped: *Religious people have reverence for their church.* *-adj.* **reverent;** *-adv.* **reverently.**

Rev·er·end /ˈrɛvərənd, ˈrɛvrənd/ *n.* **1** a minister **2** a title of address for a minister: *Our minister is the Reverend Robert Smith.* *-abbr.* **Rev.**

rev·er·ie /ˈrɛvəri/ *n.* [C;U] a dream, esp. a daydream: *He sat after dinner in reverie about the beautiful day that he had had.*

re·ver·sal /rəˈvɜrsəl/ *n.* [C;U] a setback, defeat for s.o.: *After being successful for many years at work, he had a reversal of fortune and lost his job.*

re·verse /rəˈvɜrs/ *n.* **1** [U] a backwards direction: *He put the car in reverse and backed up.* **2** [C] a setback, defeat: *She had several reverses in her career, but is having better luck now.* **3 to reverse the charges:** to make a phone call and ask the person receiving the call to pay, to call collect: *When I call from a pay phone, I sometimes have to reverse the charges.*
—*adj.* **1** backwards, toward the rear: *He moved his car in a reverse direction.* **2** opposite, other: *The reverse side of a quarter has an eagle on it.* **3 in reverse order:** from the bottom to top or back to front: *Do the exercises in reverse order, starting with number ten.*

re·ver·si·ble /rəˈvɜrsəbəl/ *adj.* able to be reversed, turned inside out: *He wears a reversible jacket, which is orange for hunting and green for everyday wear.*

re·vert /rəˈvɜrt/ *v.* to return, go back to the state or condition s.t. was in before: *John gave his brother a house, and when his brother died, ownership reverted back to John.* *-n.* [U] **reversion** /rəˈvɜrʒən/.

re·view /rəˈvyu/ *v.* **1** to look s.t. over again, (*syns.*) peruse, reexamine: *I reviewed the information you gave me, and now I'd like to talk to you about it.* **2** to repeat s.t.: *Our teacher reviewed the last lesson before starting a new one.* **3** to write about the good and bad points of an artistic work, (*syns.*) to criticize, critique: *A critic reviewed the new Broadway play and wrote good things about it.*
—*n.* **1** [C] an article or speech about the good and bad points of an artistic work, (*syn.*) a critique: *A good review of the new play was in today's newspaper.* **2** [C;U] a repetition of s.t.: *Our teacher did a review of last week's lesson before we took the test.*

re·view·er /rəˈvyuər/ *n.* a person who writes about the good and bad points of s.t., s.o. who reviews, esp. artistic works: *A reviewer for the New York Times wrote a review saying the new movie was very bad.*

re·vile /rɪˈvaɪl/ *v.frml.* **-viled, -viling, -viles** to say negative, angry things about s.o., (*syn.*) abuse: *The newspaper reporter reviled the mayor for not keeping the promises she made to get elected.*

re·vise /rɪˈvaɪz/ *v.* **-vised, -vising, -vises 1** to read carefully to change and correct s.t., esp. a written work: *The author revised her book several times before publishing it.* **2** to change, choose s.t. new, esp. an opinion: *Many people who listened to the speaker revised their opinion about the new tax law.*

re·vi·sion /rɪˈvɪʒən/ *n.* **1** [C;U] the process of editing s.t.: *In English class, we talked about how revision can help us improve our writing.* **2** [C] a new copy of something written that has changes that were made by revising: *The writer handed in the revision of her new book.*

re·vi·tal·ize /riˈvaɪtlˌaɪz/ *v.* **-ized, -izing, -izes** to give new life or energy to s.t., (*syn.*) to energize: *Government action revitalized a weak economy.* *-n.* **revitalization.**

re·viv·al /rəˈvaɪvəl/ *n.* **1** [C;U] a reawakening, a new consciousness: *A religious revival swept the nation.* **2** [C] new performances of old artistic works: *Singers did a revival of songs*

R

from old musicals. **3** [C;U] a renewal of interest in or use of s.t.: *In the past 20 years, there has been a revival of interest in old trains and railroads.*

re·vive /rə'vaɪv/ *v.* **-vived, -viving, -vives** **1** to reawaken, return s.o. to consciousness: *A paramedic revived a man who had lost consciousness.* **2** to give new energy to s.t., (*syn.*) to revitalize: *Government programs rebuilding roads and bridges revived the country's economy.* **3** to begin to use or do s.t. again, make popular again: *Her trip to the museum revived her old interest in painting.*

re·voke /rə'vouk/ *v.* **-voked, -voking, -vokes** to take s.t. back such as a right or favor, (*syns.*) to cancel, void: *A judge revoked the driver's license of a man who caused four accidents.* **-adj. revocable; -n.** [C;U] **revocation** /ˌrɛvə'keɪʃən/.

re·volt /rə'voult/ *v.* **1** to fight against a government or other power, (*syn.*) to rebel: *The unemployed people revolted against the dictator.* **2** to make s.o. angry or sick, (*syn.*) to disgust: *His bad behavior and dirty clothes revolted everyone near him.*
—*n.* [C;U] a fight against authority, (*syn.*) rebellion: *Intellectuals lead a revolt against the rich and powerful.*

re·volt·ing /rə'voultɪŋ/ *adj.* referring to s.t. that makes one sick, unpleasant, (*syns.*) disgusting, nauseating: *His revolting behavior angered all of his friends.* **-adv. revoltingly.**

rev·o·lu·tion /ˌrɛvə'luʃən/ *n.* **1** [C;U] a big change, sometimes caused by force or war, esp. in a government, economy, or field of study: *The industrial revolution changed how people worked and lived.* **2** [C;U] a complete turn or circle made by s.t.: *The large hand on a clock makes one revolution each hour.*

rev·o·lu·tion·ar·y /ˌrɛvə'luʃəˌnɛri/ *n.* **-ies** a person who wants and works to cause a complete change, esp. in government: *Revolutionaries slowly caused the end of rule by kings and queens in France.*
—*adj.* wanting or causing a complete change, as in government, economy, or a field of study: *Revolutionary discoveries in medicine help people live longer, healthier lives.*

rev·o·lu·tion·ize /ˌrɛvə'luʃəˌnaɪz/ *v.* **-ized, -izing, -izes** to change completely, cause a new way of doing s.t.: *Discovery of electricity revolutionized the way people live.*

re·volve /rɪ'vɑlv/ *v.* **-volved, -volving, -volves** to turn around s.t., move in a circle, (*syn.*) to rotate: *The room began to revolve, then she fainted.* **2** *phrasal v. insep.* **to revolve around s.o.** or **s.t.:** to have as a focus: *His life revolves around his family.*

re·volv·er /rɪ'vɑlvər/ *n.* a gun, a type of pistol with a revolving cylinder to hold bullets: *A*

thief used a revolver to steal money from a store.

revolving door *n.* a type of door with three or four doors that rotate as people enter and leave buildings: *I'm always nervous going through a revolving door because if someone pushes too quickly, the door might hit me.*

re·vue /rə'vyu/ *n.* **1** a type of magazine that reviews a field or subject: *That magazine is a fashion revue.* **2** a type of theatrical show: *We went to a musical revue last night.*

re·vul·sion /rə'vʌlʃən/ *n.* [U] a strong reaction, feeling of sickness or disgust at s.t. sickening: *She had a feeling of revulsion when she saw the dog eating out of the garbage.*

re·ward /rə'wɔrd/ *n.* **1** an award, s.t. pleasant for s.t. well done: *She gave herself the reward of a winter vacation after working hard all autumn.* **2** money paid for the capture of a criminal: *A person who saw the crime committed got a $1,000 reward for information that helped police find the murderer.* **-adj. rewarding.**
—*v.* to give an award to s.o.: *I will reward $50 to the person who returns my lost dog.*

re·wed /ri'wɛd/ *v.* to remarry: *After her husband died, she rewed and married his best friend.*

re·wind /ri'waɪnd/ *v.* **-wound** /'waund/, **-winding, -winds** to wind again, esp. a mechanical clock: *Every Saturday, I rewind the big clock in the hallway.*

re·wire /ri'waɪr/ *v.* **-wired, -wiring, -wires** to put in new wiring: *A new owner rewired the old building with a modern telephone system.* **-n.** [U] **rewiring.**

re·word /ri'wɜrd/ *v.* to say s.t. in a different way, restate: *The mayor reworded his speech because his advisors told him to do so.*

re·work /ri'wɜrk/ *v.* to change s.t., redo it: *An artist reworked his painting to make it more colorful.*

re·write /ri'raɪt/ *v.* **-wrote** /-'rout/, **-writing, -writes** to change the wording of s.t., rework it: *A playwright rewrote his play using ideas his friends gave him.*
—*n.* an instance of rewriting: *His rewrite was a success.*

rhap·sod·ic /ræp'sɑdɪk/ *adj.* having or giving strong feelings, emotional, enthusiastic (said of musical and literary works): *The poet's rhapsodic writings gave many people feelings of great happiness.* **-adj. rhapsodical.**

rhap·so·dize /'ræpsəˌdaɪz/ *v.* **-dized, -dizing, -dizes** to write, compose or speak in an emotional, enthusiastic manner: *The speaker rhapsodized about the beauty of nature.*

rhap·so·dy /'ræpsədi/ *n.* **-dies** an emotional musical or literary work: *Composers have written many musical rhapsodies about Paris.*

R

rhet·o·ric /'rɛtərɪk/ *n.* [U] **1** the art of using words well: *She teaches rhetoric at a major university.* **2** empty words, meaningless speech: *The prime minister's speech was pure political rhetoric.* *-adj.* **rhetorical** /rə'tɔrəkəl/; *-adv.* **rhetorically.**

USAGE NOTE: College level writing and speech classes often focus on *rhetorical styles* (or *modes*). Each *rhetorical mode* is a way of using language in academic writing or speech for a specific purpose. Major rhetorical modes include narration, description, and persuasion: *In my speech class we are studying the rhetoric of formal persuasive speeches.*

rhetorical question *n.* a question to which no answer is expected: *The professor started with a rhetorical question, "And what shall we talk about today?" and she then began to lecture.*

rhet·o·ri·cian /ˌrɛtə'rɪʃən/ *n.* an expert in the use of words, such as a teacher of rhetoric: *He is a rhetorician at the University of Wisconsin.*

rheu·mat·ic fever /ru'mætɪk/ *n.* [U] a disease (usu. in children) of the joints and muscles that often causes heart damage: *Rheumatic fever is a major health problem in undeveloped countries.*

rheu·ma·tism /'rumə,tɪzəm/ *n.* [U] a popular name for rheumatoid arthritis, pain or swelling of the joints: *Her rheumatism is bothering her today.* *-adj.* **rheumatic** /ru'mætɪk/.

rheu·ma·toid arthritis /'rumə,tɔɪd/ *n.* [U] a painful disease of the joints: *He has rheumatoid arthritis in his hands, which makes it difficult for him to write.*

rhine·stone /'raɪn,stoʊn/ *n.* a glass stone made to look like a diamond: *Her necklace is made of rhinestones, not real diamonds.*

rhino /'raɪnoʊ/ *n.* short for rhinoceros

rhi·noc·er·os /raɪ'nɑsərəs/ *n.* **-os** or **-oses** a very large mammal of Africa, India, and SE Asia with one or two horns on its nose: *The rhinoceros is often hunted for its horns.*

Rhodes scholar /roʊdz/ *n.* a person given a scholarship to Oxford University in England funded by the deceased Cecil Rhodes: *To be a Rhodes scholar is a great honor.*

rho·do·den·dron /ˌroʊdə'dɛndrən/ *n.* a bushy plant that has groups of small flowers of white, pink, purple, or red: *Many people plant rhododendrons next to their houses.*

rhom·bus /'rɑmbəs/ *n.* a four-sided shape in which all sides are parallel and have equal length: *A square is a kind of rhombus.* *-adj.* **rhombic; rhomboid** /'rɑm,bɔɪd/.

rhu·barb /'ru,bɑrb/ *n.* [U] a plant with large green leaves on long green or reddish stems, shaped like celery: *Rhubarb tastes delicious when cooked with sugar.*

rhyme /raɪm/ *n.* **1** [C] words that sound alike: *"Rhyme" and "time" form a rhyme.* **2** [U] poetry, verse and other writings that rhyme: *Some poets write in rhyme.* **3 without rhyme or reason:** not making sense, without logic: *This map is drawn without rhyme or reason; we'll never find the right road.*
—v. **rhymed, rhyming, rhymes** to write or form rhymes: *"Sky" and "tie" rhyme.*

rhythm /'rɪðəm/ *n.* [C;U] a regular beat, esp. in music or movement: *A symphony conductor keeps the rhythm for the orchestra.*

rhythm and blues or **R & B** *n.pl. used with a sing.v.* a type of modern American music with a strong beat influenced by blues music: *He plays rhythm and blues on his guitar.*

rhyth·mic /'rɪðmɪk/ *adj.* having a regular beat, as in music: *Ocean waves make a rhythmic sound.* *-adj.* **rhythmical;** *-adv.* **rhythmically.**

rib /rɪb/ *n.* **1** any of the many horizontal curved bones in the front of the chest that form the rib cage: *He fell and broke a rib.* **2** anything similar in shape to a rib: *Cardboard with ribs bends easily in one direction, but is difficult to bend in the other direction.* **3** a piece of meat containing a rib: *We had beef ribs for dinner.*
—v.infrml.fig. **ribbed, ribbing, ribs** to laugh at s.o., kid, tease: *His friends ribbed him about his big feet.*

rib·ald /'rɪbəld, 'raɪ,bɔld/ *adj.frml.* offensive to most people, indecent, (*syns.*) lewd, vulgar: *He writes books full of ribald sex and drinking scenes.* *-n.* [U] **ribaldry.**

rib·bon /'rɪbən/ *n.* **1** [C;U] a thin, colorful strip of material often used to tie things up: *He tied the present for his wife with a bright red ribbon.* **2** [C] a piece of ribbon given as a prize or award: *The horse won a blue ribbon for first prize.*

rib cage *n.* the area of the upper body formed by the ribs: *Organs that are most important for life, such as the heart, lungs, and liver, are protected by the rib cage.*

rice /raɪs/ *n.* [U] a grain of the cereal grass family of ancient origin that is used for food and grows in watery areas: *Records show that people grew rice over 4,000 years ago in China.*

rich /rɪtʃ/ *adj.* **1** having a lot of money, property, etc., wealthy: *Rich people usually live in big houses.* **2** having a lot of ingredients considered tasty, esp. sugar and fat: *Eating too much rich food, like steaks and cake, can make you fat.* **3** (of colors and sounds) full or deep: *She bought a rich brown carpet for her bedroom.||The bass viol makes a rich sound.* **4** (of dirt or soil) able to grow many things: *The soil in my garden is very rich, so I get lots of vegetables.* *-n.* [U] **richness.**

R

—*n.pl.* **the rich:** rich people as a group: *The rich are often powerful because of their money.*

rich·es /'rɪtʃɪz/ *n.pl.* wealth, money, and property: *Kings had riches but were not all happy.*

richly /'rɪtʃli/ *adv.* **1** with riches: *He is paid richly for his work.* **2** greatly, much: *Because of her hard work, she richly deserves her promotion.*

rick·ets /'rɪkɪts/ *n.pl. used with a sing.v.* a disease of softening and weakening of the bones: *Rickets is caused by lack of vitamin D.*

rick·e·ty /'rɪkɪti/ *adj.* **-tier, -tiest** unstable, weak, and likely to fall: *I was worried that the rickety old chair would break when I sat on it.*

rick·shaw /'rɪkˌʃɔ/ *n.* a small 2-wheeled cart pulled by a person: *When I was in Taiwan, I rode in a rickshaw.*

ric·o·chet /'rɪkəˌʃeɪ/ *v.n.* **-cheted** /-ˌʃeɪd/, **-cheting** /-ˌʃeɪɪŋ/, **-chets** /-ˌʃeɪz/ to bounce off a surface and change direction: *A bullet <v.> ricocheted off a stone wall and hit a window.‖The <n.> ricochet broke the window.*

ri·cot·ta /rɪ'kɑtə/ *n.* an Italian type of soft, white, nutty-tasting cheese: *I like ricotta with pasta and tomato sauce.*

rid /rɪd/ *v.* **rid** or **ridded, ridding, rids** **1** to free, relieve: *She rid herself of bad habits, like smoking cigarettes.* **2 to be rid of:** to be free of, relieved of: *She was glad to be rid of both the bad habit and the expense of smoking.* **3 to get rid of s.t.** or **s.o.:** to free oneself of, throw away, (*syns.*) dispose of, eliminate: *She got rid of her old clothes by giving them to the poor.*

rid·dance /'rɪdns/ *n.* [U] the state of being rid of s.t., freedom from s.t. usu. used in the phrase "Good riddance!": *She said, "good riddance" when she finally got rid of her old car that was always breaking down.*

-rid·den /'rɪdn/ *adj.suffix* full of, controlled by s.t.: *That crime-ridden city is a dangerous place to live.*

rid·dle /'rɪdl/ *n.* a puzzle, question that requires cleverness to answer: *I have a riddle for you. "What is white and black and read all over? Answer? A newspaper!"*

—*v.* **-dled, -dling, -dles** *phrasal v. insep.* **to riddle s.t. with s.t.:** to fill with, usu. with bullets: *A soldier with a machine gun riddled an enemy soldier with bullets.*

ride /raɪd/ *v.* **rode** /roud/, **ridden** /'rɪdn/, **riding, rides** **1** to be carried in or on a vehicle such as a car, truck, bus, or bicycle: *He rides to work with a friend each day.* **2** to be carried by a horse or other animal: *She rides her horse on weekends.* **3** to give a certain feeling while being ridden: *Her horse rides smoothly.* **4** *infrml.fig.* to tease s.o., remind s.o. of a fault: *He rides his friend about his big nose.* **5** *infrml.fig.* **to let s.t. ride:** not to say anything about s.t. on purpose, let s.t. pass: *My friend*

has a loud voice, but I just let her loudness ride because I like her. **6** *infrml.fig.* **to ride one's hobby horse:** to repeat a favorite topic over and over again: *He rides his favorite hobby horse when he complains about the conservative political party.* **7** *phrasal v. sep.* **to ride s.t. out:** to wait for s.t. to end, stay safe until the end of a dangerous time: *We'll ride out the storm inside, and go swimming some other day.‖We'll ride it out.* **8 to ride shotgun:** *fig.* to go with s.o. in the front seat: *I'll ride shotgun on this trip in the front passenger seat and read the road map for you while you drive.* **9** *phrasal v.* **to ride up:** to move up, move out of place: *These pants are too small for me, and they ride up when I walk.*

—*n.* **1** a trip, such as in a vehicle or on a horse: *I take a ride to work with a friend each day.* **2** a vehicle or horse: *I meet my ride at the corner each morning.* **3** a journey, pleasure trip: *We went for a ride on the roller coaster at the amusement park.* **4 to take s.o. for a ride: a.** to drive s.o. around: *I took my guest for a ride to see the city.* **b.** *infrml.fig.* to deceive, cheat s.o.: *A swindler took me for a ride with a phony investment.*

rid·er /'raɪdər/ *n.* **1** a person who rides in a bus, car, etc., (*syn.*) passenger: *Riders on the subway have to stand sometimes.* **2** a person who rides on an animal: *Riders on horseback rode through the park.* **3** an additional rule or information added to a legal document: *The insurance company added a rider to my health insurance saying that I had to pay for my prescription medicine.*

ridge /rɪdʒ/ *n.* **1** any long, narrow, high piece of land: *You could see a deer standing on top of a ridge then disappear down the other side of the hill.* **2** any long raised narrow part of s.t.: *She has ridges in her fingernails.*

rid·i·cule /'rɪdəˌkyul/ *v.* **-culed, -culing, -cules** to laugh at or criticize s.o. or s.t., (*syns.*) to deride, mock: *An editorial in the newspaper ridiculed the mayor's speech.*

—*n.* [U] mockery, criticism: *The mayor received a lot of ridicule after he delivered an unpopular speech.*

ri·dic·u·lous /rɪ'dɪkyələs/ *adj.* stupid, foolish, (*syn.*) absurd: *He often has ridiculous ideas.* -*adv.* **ridiculously;** -*n.* [U] **ridiculousness.**

rid·ing /'raɪdɪŋ/ *adj. & pres. part. of* ride, sitting in or on s.t. moving: *He is riding in a car.* —*n.* [U] horsemanship: *She likes riding (or) riding horses.*

Ries·ling /'rɪslɪŋ, 'riz-/ *n.* a white wine made from the Riesling variety of grapes, often produced in the Rhine area of Germany: *A light Riesling wine tastes good with fish.*

rife /raɪf/ *adj.frml.* **rifer, rifest** full of s.t., much of it: *His report was rife with mistakes.*

rif·fle /ˈrɪfəl/ v. **-fled, -fling, -fles 1** to flip the pages of s.t. lightly and quickly: *He riffled through the pages of a magazine to see the pictures.* **2** to shuffle or mix playing cards: *I could tell by the way he riffled the cards that he had played many times.*

riff·raff /ˈrɪfˌræf/ n. [U] people who are unwanted or undesirable: *A doorman in front of the building keeps away the riffraff.*

ri·fle /ˈraɪfəl/ n. a type of gun with a long grooved barrel and stock held to the shoulder to fire it: *Soldiers carry rifles into battle.*
—v. **-fled, -fling, -fles 1** to make grooves in the barrel of a rifle: *The gunmaker rifled the barrel so the gun would shoot more accurately.* **2** to look through things in order to steal them, (*syn.*) to ransack: *A thief rifled through the trunk of the car and stole some things that were there.*

rift /rɪft/ n. **1** a crack, break, esp. in the earth's crust: *Earthquakes produce rifts in the ground.* **2** a break in relations between people: *After a fight, a rift developed between the two friends.*

rig /rɪg/ v. **rigged, rigging, rigs 1** to cheat, arrange events dishonestly to one's advantage: *A politician rigged the election by having votes of dead people counted for him so he would win.* **2** to put up rigging, put sails, ropes, etc., on a ship: *A captain rigged his ship with new sails.* **3** *infrml.fig.* to dress oneself: *He rigged himself for the party with his new shoes and a colorful shirt.* **4** *phrasal v. sep* **to rig s.t. up:** to put up s.t. in a way that is not permanent: *He rigged up an antenna for his radio by hanging a wire over a tree branch.*‖*He rigged it up.*
—n. a piece of equipment, esp. a large truck: *That truck driver bought a new rig.*

rig·a·ma·role /ˈrɪgəməˌroʊl/ n. [U] difficult rules that seem unimportant but are required to do s.t., (*syns.*) bureaucracy, red tape: *The customs official put me through a big rigamarole in order for me to bring my computer into the country.*

rig·ging /ˈrɪgɪŋ/ n. [U] the equipment, such as sails, ropes, and masts, on a boat: *The sailboat has new rigging.*

right /raɪt/ adj. **1** referring to the direction to the east when facing north: *I walked to the corner and made a right turn.* **2** correct, accurate, exact: *I made the right decision.*‖*He gave the right answer.* **3** politically conservative: *He voted for a candidate with a political view to the right.* **4 to be in one's right mind:** sane, not crazy, having normal mental abilities: *Was she in her right mind when she gave all of her money to a stranger? See:* right wing.
—n. **1** [C;U] permission to do s.t. guaranteed by law: *We have the right to free speech in this country.* **2** [C;U] a moral or legal power, just claim: *Because her house was insured against* *fire, she had a right to collect payment after it burned down.* **3** [U] morally correct behavior, good conduct: *He knows right from wrong.* **4** [C] ownership, an interest in s.t.: *Authors have rights in the sales of their works.* **5** [U] a conservative political party or wing: *He belongs to the political right.* **6** [U] the direction or side of the body which is to the east when facing north: *Her son stood on her right.* **7 in one's own right:** alone, without the help of others, by oneself: *She plays violin in an orchestra, but she is an excellent soloist in her own right.* **8 to be in the right:** to have legal or moral right on one's side: *She hit his car when it was standing still, so he is in the right to want her to pay for the damage.*
—adv. **1** correctly, in the proper way: *He did the job right the first time.* **2** in a direction to the right: *She drove to the corner and turned right.* **3 to go right: a.** to turn to the right: *Walk to the end of this street, then go right to the bank.* **b.** *fig.* to work properly, progress: *Things are not going right for him; he lost his job then broke his arm.* **4 right away:** without waiting, immediately, (*syn.*) promptly: *I will do the job right away.* **5** *infrml.* **right off** or **right off the bat:** immediately, without having to think: *I don't remember his name right off the bat, but it will come to me soon.*
—v. **1** to correct s.t., (*syn.*) to remedy: *He righted a wrong by telling his sister he was sorry for yelling at her.* **2** to turn upright: *I righted the lamp the cat had knocked down.*
—n.pl. **by rights:** in fairness, giving just or fair treatment, (*syn.*) equitably: *She did all the work, so by rights she should receive the credit for it.*

right angle n. a 90-degree angle: *A square has four right angles.*

right·eous /ˈraɪtʃəs/ adj. **1** faithful to one's religion, (*syns.*) devout, pious: *Many righteous people go to church regularly.* **2** morally good and pure, (*syn.*) virtuous: *She lives a righteous life and spends a lot of time helping others.* -adv. **righteously;** -n. [U] **righteousness.**

right·ful /ˈraɪtfʊl/ adj. having a fair or legal claim to s.t., lawful: *As his father's only relative, he has a rightful claim to his dead father's property.* -adv. **rightfully.**

right-hand adj. **1** located to the right: *A car made a right-hand turn at the corner.* **2** *infrml.fig.* (of a person) completely reliable, the best at helping: *He is the owner's right-hand man who does important things for the business.*

right-handed adj. using the right hand most of the time: *He is right-handed and uses right-handed scissors.*

right·ist /ˈraɪtɪst/ n. a person who agrees with or belongs to the political right, (*syn.*) a con-

R

servative: *My uncle is a rightist who believes the government should not control business.*

right·ly /'raɪtli/ *adv.* correctly or with reason, (*syns.*) justifiably, properly: *He is angry and rightly so because he was cheated.*

right-minded *adj.* having an attitude of doing the good or right thing: *Right-minded people help the poor.*

right of asylum *n.* (in law) the right of a person to be given a safe place in a foreign country: *The right of asylum is given to people leaving a country where they were politically oppressed.*

right of way *n.* **1** (in law) the right of one person to cross the property of another: *Railroad companies bought the rights of way from land owners to build railways across this country.* **2** the right of one person or vehicle (car, boat, airplane, etc.) to pass in front of another: *At a four-way stop sign, the car that arrives first or is on the right has the right of way.*

right-to-life *adj.* referring to s.o. or s.t. that is against abortion: *That right-to-life group has many members. See:* pro-choice, USAGE NOTE.

right-to-work law *n.* (in law) laws that allow a nonunion worker to work in a union shop; these laws limit the power of unions in a business or industry: *Some states have right-to-work laws that let workers choose not to join a union.*

right wing *adj.n.* [U] a politically conservative part of a political party: *The <n.> right wing of the Democratic party voted with members of the Republican party against raising taxes.*

USAGE NOTE: The term *right wing* describes those people in a group, such as a political party, with more conservative ideas; *Left wing* is used to describe the members of a group with more liberal ideas: *Members of the US Congress cannot agree on environmental laws. The right wing thinks the government should not interfere with businesses, but the left wing wants laws to stop businesses from polluting the environment.*

rig·id /'rɪdʒɪd/ *adj.* **1** stiff, firm, difficult to bend: *I need a rigid box that won't break when it is full of heavy books.* **2** strict, unbending: *The government has rigid laws about paying taxes. -n.* **rigidity** /rə'dʒɪdati/; *-adv.* **rigidly.**

rig·or /'rɪgər/ *n.* **1** [C] extreme living or weather conditions: *The rigors of an arctic winter include very cold temperatures and deep snow.* **2** [U] the following of high standards of behavior, actions, and rules: *Scientists do their experiments with rigor so that they get accurate data.*

rigor mortis /'mɔrtɪs/ *n.* [U] stiffening of a body after death: *The body has turned blue, and rigor mortis has set in.*

rig·o·rous /'rɪgərəs/ *adj.* **1** difficult, harsh: *Very strong winds and cold are some of the rigorous conditions people meet in the Arctic.* **2** having strict or high standards for behavior or action: *Students must finish rigorous programs of study to become doctors. -adv.* **rigorously.**

rile /raɪl/ *v.infrml.* **riled, riling, riles** to annoy or anger s.o., (*syns.*) to enrage, irritate: *Money problems rile the underpaid worker every day.*

rim /rɪm/ *n.* the outside edge or border of s.t. (usu. round): *A spoon rested against the rim of the bowl.*

—*v.* **rimmed, rimming, rims** (in basketball) to slide off and not enter the rim of s.t.: *The basketball rimmed the basket and fell to the floor.*

rimmed /rɪmd/ *adj.* having an edge or rim, bordered by s.t.: *He wears gold-rimmed eyeglasses.*

rind /raɪnd/ *n.* [C;U] the outer covering of sausages and fruits, such as oranges, lemons, watermelon, etc.: *I peeled off the rind and ate the orange.*

ring (1) /rɪŋ/ *v.* **rang** /ræŋ/, **rung** /rʌŋ/, **ringing, rings** **1** to make a sound like a bell: *Her phone rings all day long.* **2** to cause a bell to make a sound: *If you ring the bell, a clerk will come to help you.* **3 to ring a bell:** to cause s.o. to remember or recall s.t.: *John Smith? That name does not ring a bell with me.* **4 to ring true:** to seem true and sensible: *The witness' story rings true; I believe what she says!* **5** *phrasal v. insep.* **to ring out:** to make a loud sound: *On Sunday morning, church bells ring out loudly.* **6** *phrasal v. sep.* **to ring s.t. up:** to record, add up: *A cashier rings up the prices of the things you want to buy on a cash register.||He rings them up.*

—*n.* **1** [C] a sound like that of a bell: *The ring of the front doorbell startled me.* **2** *sing.* a telephone call: *I'll give you a ring this evening.*

ring (2) *n.* **1** a circular metal band to be worn on a finger, usu. made of expensive metal and often with gemstones: *She wears a diamond ring on her finger.* **2** any circular band of metal, plastic, or other material: *Doughnuts are shaped like rings.* **3** a circular group of s.t.: *A ring of people listened to a man play guitar in the park.* **4** a place with ropes on the side where boxers fight: *Two boxers are fighting in the ring.* **5** a group of criminals: *The police found out where five members of the drug ring live.* **6** a circle where circus acts are shown: *Three lions ran into the circus ring.* **7 to run rings around:** to do s.t. excellently, perform better than others: *She is such a good student that she runs rings around her classmates.*

—*v.* to make a ring around s.t., (*syn.*) to encircle: *People ringed around the speaker to listen to him.*

R

ring binder *n.* a type of notebook with rings inside that open and close to hold paper: *I keep my class notes in a ring binder.*

ringed /rɪŋd/ *adj.* having rings around it, (*syn.*) encircled: *Some birds, like pheasants, have necks ringed with circles of white and red.*

rin·ger /'rɪŋər/ *n.infrml.fig.* **1** a player in a game or sport who pretends to be a bad player but is really an expert: *That ringer played badly in the first game of cards, then in the second game he beat us.* **2** a person who rings a bell: *Bell-ringers make pleasant music.* **3** a **dead ringer for:** s.o. who looks just like s.o. else: *He is a dead ringer for Elvis Presley; he even sings like him.*

ringing /'rɪŋɪŋ/ *n.* [U] the sound of a bell: *The ringing of church bells can be heard on Sunday mornings.*

ring·lead·er /'rɪŋ,lidər/ *n.* a person who leads others, esp. in bad or illegal acts: *The ringleader of the gang planned the robbery himself.*

ring·let /'rɪŋlɪt/ *n.* a small curly piece of hair: *She gave her boyfriend a ringlet of her hair.*

ring·mas·ter /'rɪŋ,mæstər/ *n.* a person who introduces circus acts to the audience: *The ringmaster wears a black suit and has a loud voice.*

ring·side /'rɪŋ,saɪd/ *n.adj.* a place next to a boxing ring: *We sat at <n.> ringside because <adj.> ringside seats give the best view of the fight.*

ring·worm /'rɪŋ,wɜrm/ *n.* [U] a skin disease caused by a fungus that causes itchy red rings on the skin: *Ringworm looks as if a worm is under the skin.*

rink /rɪŋk/ *n.* a place for roller skating or ice skating that has a wall or fence around it: *We went to the hockey rink to watch the game.*

rin·ky-dink /'rɪŋki,dɪŋk/ *adj.slang* minor, not up to a high standard: *He has a rinky-dink little business that does not make much money.*

rinse /rɪns/ *v.* **rinsed, rinsing, rinses** to splash or soak with water to wash away soap or dirt: *I rinsed the dishes with cold water.*
—*n.* **1** [C] an act of splashing or soaking: *I gave the clothes a rinse in cool water.* **2** [C;U] chemical hair coloring: *She bought a rinse to change her hair color.*

rins·ing /'rɪnsɪŋ/ *n.* [C;U] an act of splashing or soaking with water: *I gave my car a rinsing in cold water after I washed it.*

ri·ot /'raɪət/ *v.* to act as part of a group in a violent or dangerous way, esp. against power, (*syns.*) to rebel, revolt: *People rioted and ran through the streets breaking windows.* *-n.* **ri·oter.**
—*n.* **1** [C] an act of rioting, violent behavior by a large group: *The riot caused a lot of dam-*

age *to the city's shopping area.* **2** *infrml.sing.fig.* a person or thing that is very funny: *That movie was a riot! I laughed a lot.*

riot act *n.* **1** (in law) a law against rioting: *The riot act makes rioting a crime.* **2** *infrml.fig.* **to read s.o. the riot act:** to criticize s.o. loudly and angrily: *His boss read him the riot act for being late to work all week.*

ri·ot·ing /'raɪtɪŋ/ *n.* [U] a riot, violence by a large group: *The rioting finally stopped after two days.*

riotous /'raɪətəs/ *adj.frml.* related to rioting: *Police arrested people for riotous behavior.* *-adv.* **riotously.**

rip /rɪp/ *v.* **ripped, ripping, rips** **1** to tear in pieces: *I ripped up a piece of paper and threw it in the wastebasket.* **2** *phrasal v. insep.* to speak against angrily, attack with words: *His wife really ripped into him for forgetting her birthday again.* **3** *phrasal v. sep.fig.slang* **to rip s.o. or s.t. off:** to cheat or steal from s.o. or s.t.: *A thief ripped off my car radio.||He ripped it off.* **4** *phrasal v. sep.* **to rip s.t. up:** to tear into very small pieces: *She ripped up his letter without reading it.*
—*n.* a tear, a place where s.t. has been pulled or cut in pieces: *A sharp tree branch made a rip in my jacket. See:* rip-off.

RIP /'raɪ'pi/ *abbr. for* rest in peace

rip cord *n.* a rope used to open a parachute: *After he jumped from the airplane, he pulled his rip cord to open his parachute.*

ripe /raɪp/ *adj.* **riper, ripest** at the best time to be used or eaten, full grown, (*syn.*) mature: *Fruit and cheese taste best when they are ripe.*

rip·en /'raɪpən/ *v.* to grow to full flavor, become ready to use or eat, (*syn.*) to mature: *Grapes ripen on the vine in autumn.*

rip-off *n.slang* an instance of being cheated or stolen from: *That advertisement for land in Florida was a rip-off because the land was under water.*

rip·ple /'rɪpəl/ *n.* a little wave: *There was a small ripple when I threw a stone into the water.*
—*v.* **-pled, -pling, -ples** to make little waves: *The water rippled when the fish jumped.*

rip-roaring *adj.infrml.* loud, very noisy, fun, and enjoyable: *We had a rip-roaring time at the football game.*

rise /raɪz/ *v.* **rose** /rouz/, **risen** /'rɪzən/, **rising, rises** **1** to move upwards: *The sun rises in the morning.* **2** to stretch or extend upwards from the ground toward the sky: *In New York City, the buildings rise from the sidewalks into the sky.* **3** to wake, get up: *I rise early every morning.* **4** to stand up from a seat: *The news reporters rose when the president walked into the room.* **5** to reach a higher level: *Prices are rising.||The temperature rises every afternoon.*

R

6 to become louder or stronger: *When mother's voice rises, we know we are in trouble.* **7** (of bread) to become larger as yeast works: *The bread must rise for one hour.* **8** *phrasal v. insep.* **to rise above s.t.: a.** to become higher than s.t. else: *The balloon rose above the trees and disappeared.* **b.** to do well even though one had problems or difficulties: *She rose above the difficulty of being deaf to become an excellent teacher.* **9 to rise to an occasion:** to do s.t. better than usual when faced with a difficult or important problem: *I am sure he will rise to the occasion.* **10** *phrasal v. insep.* **to rise up against s.o.** or **s.t.:** to fight against a government or other power, (*syns.*) to protest, rebel: *The workers rose up against unfair working hours.*
—*n.* **1** an elevation, raised piece of land: *We walked up on the rise, and we could see for many miles.* **2 to get a rise out of s.o.:** to try to anger s.o., say things to upset s.o.: *He bothers his wife about doing housework until he gets a rise out of her.* **3 to give rise to:** to cause, bring about: *Her strange behavior gave rise to rumors that she was crazy.*

riser /'raɪzər/ *n.* **1** the vertical part of a step: *These steps are unsafe because a riser has broken.* **2** a person who awakens: *I am an early riser every morning.*

ris·i·ble /'rɪzəbəl/ *adj.frml.* laughable, ridiculous: *His ideas are so grandiose that they are risible.*

risk /rɪsk/ *v.* **1** to put s.t. important in danger, chance s.t.: *If you put money into the stock market, you risk losing it.* **2** *infrml.fig.* **to risk one's neck:** to place one's life in danger: *When you were drowning in the ocean, a stranger risked his neck to save you.*
—*n.* **1** [C;U] a chance, danger of losing s.t. important: *When you buy land, you take the risk that it will lose value.* **2** [C] a person who may not do as good a job as one would like: *He is very smart, but he is a risk because he does not work very hard.* **3 at one's own risk:** agreeing that one is responsible for all problems or danger: *Swim at your own risk!* **4 run a risk:** to put oneself in danger: *If I ask a question, do I run the risk of looking stupid?*

risk capital *n.* money used (with the hope of making more money) to start up new businesses or improve businesses that aren't making money, (*syn.*) venture capital: *Many rich people like to allow a business to use their risk capital because they want to become richer.*

risk·y /'rɪski/ *adj.* **-ier, -iest 1** having the possibility of loss, dangerous: *Putting money in the stock market can be risky because you might lose all of that money.* **2** dangerous, harmful: *Driving a race car is risky because you can get killed.* -*adv.* **riskily.**

ris·qué /rɪs'keɪ/ *adj.frml.* clearly or close to being indecent, suggesting but not showing sex or scandal: *He writes risqué stories about young lovers.*

rite /raɪt/ *n.* an act with religious or ceremonial meaning, (*syns.*) ceremony, ritual: *As the man lay dying, a priest gave him his last rites before death.*

rite of passage *n.* a ceremonial event in a person's life that marks a change from one stage in life to another: *Graduation from high school is a rite of passage to becoming an educated adult.*

rit·u·al /'rɪtʃuəl/ *n.* **1** [C;U] a ceremony or rite done to mark a serious or sacred event or day: *A common ritual at a wedding is giving and receiving wedding rings.* **2** [C] an act or actions that one repeats often: *His morning ritual is to make coffee, take a shower, eat breakfast, and brush his teeth.* -*n.* [U] **ritualism;** -*v.* **ritualize.**

ritz·y /'rɪtsi/ *adj.infrml.* **-ier, -iest** (after the glamour of Ritz Hotels) special because of high class, good taste, and expense, (*syns.*) elegant, fashionable: *Fifth Avenue in New York is a very ritzy place to live.*

ri·val /'raɪvəl/ *n.* s.o. who wants to get s.t. and keep s.o. else from getting it, (*syn.*) a competitor: *Two men are rivals for the love of a beautiful woman.*‖*Two sports teams have been rivals for years.*
—*adj.* competing, wanting the same thing: *The rival sports teams play to see who is the best every year.*
—*v.* to be as good as, be similar to: *No city rivals Paris.* -*adj.frml.* **rivalrous.**

ri·val·ry /'raɪvəlri/ *n.* **-ries** [C;U] competition, a special desire to defeat an opponent: *Sibling rivalry is the competition between brothers and sisters for their parents' attention.*

riv·er /'rɪvər/ *n.* **1** a large body of water that moves in one direction between two river banks: *The Nile and the Mississippi are among the largest rivers in the world.* **2** *fig.* a great deal of some liquid: *The war caused a river of blood.*

riv·er·bank /'rɪvər,bæŋk/ *n.* the side of a river, esp. land holding water back from the area around the river: *When the Mississippi overflowed its riverbanks, many towns were flooded with water.*

riv·er·bed /'rɪvər,bɛd/ *n.* the low land on which a river flows: *When there is not a lot of rain, riverbeds often have no flowing water.*

riv·er·boat /'rɪvər,boʊt/ *n.* a boat used to move goods and people up and down a river: *Old riverboats had steam engines.*

riv·er·side /'rɪvər,saɪd/ *n.adj.* the edge of a river as seen from land: *We like to eat at a <adj.> riverside restaurant, located at the <n.> riverside.*

riv·et /ˈrɪvɪt/ *n.* a round, sturdy, metal plug with a cap, used to nail together metal beams and plates, or heavy fabric: *Rivets hold bridge beams together.*
—*v.* **1** to nail rivets into place: *He rivets beams together on the bridge.* **2** *fig.* to cause people to look and not look away, to hold s.o.'s attention: *When the leader was shot, everyone's eyes were riveted to the television.* -*n.* **riveter;** -*adv.* **riveting.**

riv·i·er·a /ˌrɪviˈɛrə/ *n.* a beautiful, sunny area near the sea noted for its rich lifestyle (after the French and Italian Riviera on the Mediterranean Sea): *The Laguna Beach area of southern California is the riviera of the USA.*

riv·u·let /ˈrɪvyələt/ *n.* a very small stream (often from rain): *Rivulets of rainwater ran down my window.*

R.N. /ˈɑrˈɛn/ *abbr.* for registered nurse: *My sister is an R.N.* See: registered nurse, USAGE NOTE.

roach /roʊtʃ/ *n.* -**es** a cockroach, any of over 1,000 kinds of a flat-bodied insect, a pest that lives in households: *It is disgusting to see roaches in your kitchen.*

road /roʊd/ *n.* **1** a place where cars, trucks, and buses can travel, esp. one narrower than a street or highway: *We live on a small but pleasant country road.* **2 to be on the road:** to be traveling: *The singer is on the road giving concerts on the east coast.* **3** *infrml.fig.* **to hit the road:** to leave, travel: *I have to hit the road and go home now.* **4 the road to:** the way to get s.t.: *Is money the road to happiness?* See: street, USAGE NOTE.
—*n.pl.* **roads:** roads, streets, and highways in general: *The roads have been cleared of snow.*
—*adj.* related to roads: *We have a good road system in this area.*

road·bed /ˈroʊdˌbɛd/ *n.* the earth and stones underneath a road: *The roadbeds made by the ancient Romans still exist today.*

road·block /ˈroʊdˌblɑk/ *n.* s.t. placed across a road to stop cars from moving: *Sometimes the police check cars at roadblocks.*

USAGE NOTE: The word *roadblock* refers to an event or a person that stops or slows down the progress of a plan: *My bad relationship with my boss has become a roadblock to getting a higher salary.*

road·house /ˈroʊdˌhaʊs/ *n.* a barroom often serving food located near a highway: *We stopped at a roadhouse for a sandwich and beer on our trip south.*

road map *n.* a map that shows the roads in an area: *We used a road map to plan our trip.*

USAGE NOTE: A *road map* can refer to a plan for a project: *When the project manager explained the road map for the project at our meeting last week, she showed us each step we will follow to get the work done.*

road runner *n.* a bird that runs very quickly and lives in deserts in the SW of N. America: *We saw road runners when we were in New Mexico.*

road show *n.* a traveling show, a kind of entertainment that gives performances in many places: *That popular singer has a road show that she takes from city to city.*

road·side /ˈroʊdˌsaɪd/ *adj.n.* located next to a road (street, highway): *We stopped at a <adj.> roadside restaurant and ordered lunch.*‖*We parked our car on the <n.> roadside.*

road test *n.v.* **1** a drive on a road in a car to see how one likes it: *I took a Mercedes for a road test and decided to buy it.* **2** a drive done by a car maker often under bad conditions to test the quality of a car, truck, etc.: *A professional driver does road tests of cars on bad roads to see how well they are made.* See: test-drive.

road·way /ˈroʊdˌweɪ/ *n.* the path made by a road, street, or highway: *The roadway in front of our house is always full of cars.*

road·wor·thy /ˈroʊdˌwɜrði/ *adj.* (said of vehicles) safe to drive: *He fixed his car engine and it is roadworthy now.*

roam /roʊm/ *v.* to go freely over a large area, (*syn.*) to wander: *We roamed through the woods after we had a picnic.* -*adj. n.* **roaming.**

roar /rɔr/ *v.* **1** to make a loud, scary sound: *Lions roar.* **2** to laugh loudly: *He roared when he heard the joke.*
—*n.* a loud, scary sound: *You could hear the roar of lions everywhere in the zoo.* -*n.* [U] **roaring.**

roast /roʊst/ *v.* **1** to cook at a high temperature, as in an oven: *We roasted a turkey for four hours in a 325-degree oven.* **2** *fig.* to make fun of s.o. at a dinner in their honor: *A famous actor was roasted by his friends at the Actors Club.* **3** to be or feel too hot: *We are roasting in the summer heat.*
—*n.* a piece of meat that is roasted, usu. beef or pork: *I have a roast in the oven.*
—*adj.* referring to s.t. roasted: *He likes roast beef for dinner.* -*n.* **roaster;** [U] **roasting.**

rob /rɑb/ *v.* **robbed, robbing, robs** to steal s.t. from s.o., take s.t. from s.o. illegally: *A thief robbed three houses on our street.*

rob·ber /ˈrɑbər/ *n.* a thief: *Robbers held up the bank.*

rob·ber·y /ˈrɑbəri/ *n.* -**ies** [C;U] an act of stealing s.t., (*syn.*) theft: *There was a bank robbery this morning.*

R

robe /roʊb/ *n.* **1** a type of long, dresslike outer clothing that covers a person from shoulder to foot: *Judges wear black robes over their suits.* **2** long clothing worn after taking a bath, bathrobe: *I wear a robe after my shower.*
—*v.* to wear a robe: *Students are robed in black when they graduate.*

rob·in /'rɑbɪn/ or **robin red•breast** /'rɛd,brɛst/ *n.* a songbird with red feathers in front and a black upper body: *In the northern USA, robins are called the first birds of spring.*

Robin Hood /'rɑbɪn,hʊd/ *n.* **1** the leader of a robber band, romanticized in English ballads and literature since the 15th century for stealing from the rich to help the poor **2** *fig.* any person who takes from the rich to help the poor: *The new president is a Robin Hood who raised taxes heavily on the rich.*

ro·bot /'roʊbɑt/ *n.* any of a variety of devices, some with humanlike characteristics, programmed to perform various chores: *Carmakers use robots to do unpleasant jobs, such as painting cars in hot conditions.* -*v.* **ro·botize** /'roʊbə,taɪz/.

ro·bot·ics /roʊ'bɑtɪks/ *n.* [U] the science of constructing robots to perform human chores: *Robotics is an advanced discipline that substitutes machines for workers.*

ro·bust /roʊ'bʌst/ *adj.* having physical vigor, energetic good health: *At age 60, he is robust and plays golf everyday.*

rock /rɑk/ *n.* **1** [C;U] stone, such as granite or limestone: *The shoreline is covered with rocks.* **2** [C] *infrml.fig.* a big gemstone, such as a diamond: *She wears a big rock on her finger.*
—*v.* to move s.t. back and forth gently: *A mother rocks her baby in her arms.*

rock and roll or **rock 'n' roll** /'rɑkən'roʊl/ *n.* [U] a type of modern American popular music: *Guitars and drums are the main instruments played in rock and roll.*

USAGE NOTE: Some people use the term *rock and roll* to refer to any popular music with drums and guitars; others use the term to describe the original rock and roll music of the 1950s. It is also very common to shorten the words rock and roll music to *rock* or *rock music*. In 1995 the *Rock and Roll Hall of Fame* was opened in Cleveland, Ohio. This museum shows photographs, instruments and other exhibitions about rock and roll music.

rock bottom *n.infrml.fig.* [U] the end of a descent, esp. into poverty or depravity: *He is a very sad man who hit rock bottom when he lost his job, his wife, and his health.*

rock·er /'rɑkər/ *n.* a piece of furniture, such as a baby's rocking crib or a rocking chair: *He enjoys sitting in his rocker on his front porch.*

rock·et /'rɑkɪt/ *n.* a cigar-shaped missile used to destroy military targets or to launch space vehicles: *A rocket lifted a communications satellite in orbit around the earth.*
—*v.* to speed like a rocket: *The spacecraft rocketed into the sky.* -*n.* [U] **rocketry.**

rocking chair *n.* a chair with wide, curved blades that moves back and forth: *She sits in her rocking chair and knits.*

rocking horse *n.* a child's plaything consisting of a wooden or plastic horse's body mounted on wide, curved blades: *A child rocks back and forth on her rocking horse.*

rock·y /'rɑki/ *adj.* **-ier, -iest** **1** having many rocks on or in the land's surface: *The rocky soil in New England makes farming difficult.* **2** *infrml.fig.* feeling faint, weak: *After surgery, he felt rocky.*

ro·co·co /rə'koʊkoʊ/ *adj.n.* [U] an 18th century French art and architectural style noted for its curving lines and fancy detail work: *<adj.> Rococo architecture is more human-sized than the big structures that came before it during the Baroque period.*

rod /rɑd/ *n.* a narrow, cylindrical piece of material (of metal, wood or plastic): *Long steel rods are used to reinforce concrete columns in new buildings.*

ro·dent /'roʊdnt/ *n.* a general class of animals that includes rats, mice, and squirrels: *Rodents carry diseases and are generally regarded as pests.*

ro·de·o /'roʊdi,oʊ, roʊ'deɪoʊ/ *n.* **-os** an entertainment event featuring horse riding and cattle roping: *Riding bulls and wild horses are always exciting events at a rodeo.*

roe /roʊ/ *n.* [U] **1** a type of deer: **2** fish eggs: *Salmon swim upstream to lay their roe each year.*

roger /'rɑdʒər/ *n.* a word used on radio to tell a speaker that one has heard and understood: *The policeman heard the message on the radio, said "roger," and drove to the scene of the crime.*

rogue /roʊg/ *n.adj.* **1** a wild, lone animal, such as an elephant: *<adj.> Rogue elephants can go crazy and cause a lot of damage.* **2** an evil, often dangerous man: *He is a <n.> rogue who fights and cheats people.* **3** a person who enjoys tricks and teasing: *Her little son is such a <n.> rogue! -n.* [U] **roguery.**

roil /rɔɪl/ *v.* to cause s.t. (esp. water) to move quickly, disturb: *Fish roil the water in a lake when they eat insects near the top of the water.* -*n.* [U] **roiling.**

role /roʊl/ *n.* **1** a part played by an actor or actress: *She plays the leading role in a television show.* **2** a part or job one takes in a group: *When he married, he had to get used to the role of husband.*

role model *n.* a person who is an example of success for young people to try to become like him or her: *Great athletes are popular role models for kids.*

roll /roʊl/ *n.* **1** a small round piece of bread: *He had a ham sandwich on a roll.* **2** an amount of s.t. in roll form: *a roll of carpet*‖*a roll of toilet paper*‖*She bought a roll of silk to make a dress.* **3** a move in gymnastics: *The gymnast did a forward roll on the floor.* **4** *slang* a lot of paper money: *That man always carries a big roll.* **5** a list of the names of people in a group: *There are 20 students on the roll in our class, but only 18 come every day.* **6** *infrml.fig.* **to be on a roll:** to have a series of good things happen, be very successful: *That man playing cards is on a roll; he has won every game!*
—*v.* **1** to turn over and over to move s.t.: *The ball rolled across the football field.* **2** to work in the correct way, (*syns.*) to function, operate: *Printing presses rolled and printed the newspaper.* **3** to make s.t. flat, press s.t. down: *Bakers roll dough to make pie crust.* **4** to move from side to side, (*syn.*) to undulate: *When the ship rolled, she felt sick.* **5** to curve up and down: *Flat land rolls into hills as you drive north.* **6** *infrml.fig.* to begin, get started: *Our sales plan got rolling this week with our first TV commercials.* **7** *infrml.fig.* to leave, depart: *I want to go home now; let's roll.* **8** to make into a ball or tube shape: *Please help me roll this paper.* **9 all rolled into one:** combined, all together: *Reading is a psychological act, a physical act, and a linguistic one all rolled into one.* **10** *phrasal v.* **to roll around: a.** to move back and forth: *He rolled around in pain on the floor.* **b.** *infrml.fig.* to arrive, appear: *As soon as the holiday season rolls around, I will be taking my vacation.* **11** *phrasal v. sep.* **to roll s.t. back:** to reduce prices etc.: *Ford has rolled back car prices.*‖*They rolled them back.* **12** *phrasal v.* **to roll by:** to arrive, then disappear: *As the years rolled by, he lost his hair.* **13** *phrasal v.* **to roll in:** to come regularly in large numbers: *Birthday cards rolled in all week.* **14** *phrasal v. insep.* **to roll in s.t.:** to have a lot of s.t.; *He's rolling in dough (money)!* **15** *infrml.fig.vulg.* **to roll in the hay:** to have sexual intercourse: *The man and woman enjoyed a roll in the hay.* **16** *phrasal v. insep.* **to roll off s.t.: a.** to fall, drop: *An egg rolled off the table.* **b.** to appear: *New cars roll off the assembly line.* **17** *phrasal v.* **to roll on:** to continue to move: *The wagon stopped then rolled on toward town.* **18 to roll one's r's:** to make an "r" with a tapping sound: *Speakers of Russian and Spanish roll their r's.* **19** *phrasal v. sep.* **to roll s.t. out:** to unroll, open s.t. that was rolled, to make s.t. flat, (*syns.*) to uncoil, unfurl: *The rug was rolled up, and a workman rolled it out on the*

floor. **20** *phrasal v. insep.* **to roll over: a.** to turn over: *He woke up then rolled over and went back to sleep.* **b.** to move on a surface: *The tractor rolled over the fields of corn.* **21** *phrasal v. sep.* **to roll s.t. up: a.** to arrive in a car, etc.: *We rolled up in a limousine.* **b.** to make s.t. flat into a long round shape, (*syn.*) to coil up: *She rolled up the window shade.*‖*She rolled it up.*

roll·back /'roʊlˌbæk/ *n.* a decrease, esp. making prices lower, (*syn.*) reduction: *The store had a price rollback so that people would buy more when they shopped there.*

roll call *n.* a check to see if anyone has not come: *A sergeant did a roll call; asking each soldier to say, "Here!" when his or her name was called.*

rol·ler /'roʊlər/ *n.* a long round piece of metal or other material: *Rollers on a printing press put images in ink on paper.*

roller bearing *n.* a round piece of metal used to allow movement, such as in wheels: *Cars' wheels have roller bearings that turn around so the wheels can move.*

roller coaster *n.* an amusement ride in which small cars travel very fast on a curving, hilly track to thrill riders: *Riders scream as the roller coaster speeds down hills and around curves.* See: Ferris wheel, USAGE NOTE.

roller coaster

Roller Derby *n.TM* a contest on roller skates between two teams where each team tries to have one team member go ahead of the other team by at least one time around the rink: *A Roller Derby is fun to watch as opponents knock each other down.*

roller skate *n.v.* wheels on boots or shoes that let a person move forward (skate) quickly: *She bought a pair of <n.> roller skates and goes rollerskating every day. -n.* **rollerskating**.

USAGE NOTE: Compare *roller skates* and *in-line skates.* Roller skates usually have wheels on the four corners of the shoe-like part of the skate, while in-line skates have wheels in a line down the center of the skate. One brand of in-line skates, Roller-blades ™, appeared in the USA in the late 1980s and became a popular way to get around in cities and towns. A skater using in-line skates can move around quickly and get exercise at the same time.

rol·lick·ing /'rɑləkɪŋ/ *adj.frml.* lively, happy: *We had a rollicking good time at the circus. -v.* **rollick.**

rolling pin *n.* a long, round wooden or metal kitchen tool used to make food (such as cookie dough) flat: *I need a rolling pin to make noodles.*

roll·o·ver /'roʊl,oʊvər/ *n.adj.* (in finance) money moved from one account to another: *You can use a <n.> rollover to transfer money from one bank to another.*

ro·ly-po·ly /,roʊli 'poʊli/ *adj.infrml.* referring to a person or animal that is round; short and fat: *He is a roly-poly man.*

Ro·man /'roʊmən/ *adj.* related to ancient or modern Rome, the Roman Empire, or its people: *The Roman Empire stretched for thousands of miles from Rome.*
—*n.pl.* **Romans:** the Roman people: *The Romans were proud of the roads and cities they built.*

ro·mance /roʊ'mæns, 'roʊ,mæns/ *n.* **1** [C;U] a love affair with excitement, adventure, and happiness: *Jane's and Paul's life together is full of romance.* **2** [C] an adventurous novel, poem, film, TV story, etc.: *She wrote a romance about an artist's life in Tokyo.*
—*v.* **manced, -mancing, -mances** to have a romantic love affair: *He romanced his girlfriend for a year before she would marry him.*

romance language any language that developed from Latin (the language of Rome): *Italian, French, and Rumanian are examples of romance languages.*

Roman numeral *n.* any of the symbols used by the Romans to indicate numbers: *In Roman numerals, M=1,000, D=500, C=100, L=50, X=10, V=5, and I=1.*

Ro·ma·no /rə'mɑnoʊ, roʊ-/ *n.* [U] a light-colored, strong-tasting hard cheese: *I like a slice of Romano with my apple pie.*

romantic /roʊ'mæntɪk/ *n.adj.* **1** an idealistic person who believes in the natural goodness of people: *Many young people are <n.> romantics.* **2 Romantic:** a member of the late 18th-century artistic movement of Romanticism: *P.B. Shelley was a <adj.> Romantic poet.* **3** related to love or romance: *They met at a very <adj.> romantic place and had a picnic.* -*adv.* **romantically;** -*v.* **romanticize** /roʊ'mæntə,saɪz/.

Ro·man·ti·cism /roʊ'mæntə,sɪzəm/ *n.* [U] an artistic movement of the late 18th century that was popular in Europe: *The beauty of nature and human feelings were important ideas in Romanticism.* -*n.* **romanticist.**

Ro·me·o /'roʊmi,oʊ/ **1** a character in Shakespeare's play *Romeo and Juliet: Romeo loved Juliet enough to die for her.* **2** *fig.* a man who is very popular with women: *He is a real Romeo, always surrounded by many women!*

romp /rɑmp/ *v.* to run, jump, play, and feel happy: *Children romped in the playground.*

—*n.* a happy, carefree time: *The child went for a romp in the forest.*

roof /ruf/ *n.* **1** the covering on top of a building: *The roof on that old house lets water in when it rains.* **2** the top of s.t.: *Chewing gum sticks to the roof of his mouth.* **3** *infrml.fig.* **to go through** or **hit the roof**: to become very angry: *He hit the roof when he heard the bad news.* **4** *infrml.fig.* **to have a roof over one's head:** to have a place to live: *He doesn't make much money, but he does have a roof over his head.* **5 all under one roof:** many different things that are together all in one place: *That large store has every kind of furniture for sale all under one roof.*

roof·ing /'rufɪŋ/ *n.* [U] materials, such as shingles of wood or metal, used to make a roof: *A big storm damaged some roofing on our house.*

roof top *n.* the top of a building: *We stood on the roof top and watched the parade on the street below.*

rook /rʊk/ *n.* **1** a chess piece that looks like a castle's tower: *The rook moves in straight lines on squares of the same color on a chess board.* **2** a type of blackbird: *We saw a rook sitting in a tree.*
—*v.infrml.* to cheat, trick s.o. in order to get their money dishonestly, (*syn.*) to swindle: *I sent money to a mail order company, and they rooked me out of my money by not sending the things I ordered.*

rook·ie /'rʊki/ *n.* a beginner, esp. an athlete in his first sports season or a soldier in his first year: *Even though he is a rookie, he scored lots of points for his team.*

room /rum/ *n.* **1** [C] a space with its own walls, door, ceiling, and floor: *That house has ten rooms.* **2** [U] space, area: *The elevator is so full of people that there is no room to move.*
—*v.* to live in a room as in a rooming house or dormitory: *I room in a dormitory at college.*

room and board *n.* [U] a place to live and food to eat: *Her parents pay the cost of her room and board at college.*

USAGE NOTE: College students in the USA usually pay three kinds of fees: *tuition* (fees for classes), *books and supplies* (required for the classes), and *room and board*. Room and board fees pay for the cost of living in a college dormitory and eating in a cafeteria: *He received a scholarship that paid for his room and board.*

room·er /'rumər/ *n.* a person who rents a room: *My mother has two roomers living in her house now.*

room·ful /'rumfʊl/ *n.* a quantity of s.t. that fills a room: *We had a roomful of guests over for a party.*

rooming house *n.* a house in which people rent rooms: *He stayed in a rooming house when he first came to town.*

room·mate /'rum,meɪt/ *n.* a person who lives with one in a room, apartment, or house: *My roommate has his own bedroom, and we share a kitchen and bath.*

USAGE NOTE: The word *roommate* describes any unrelated people who share a place to live. People who share a house but have separate bedrooms might call each other *roommates* or *housemates: I'm looking for a housemate who will share the rent for my house.* People who share an office at work usually use the word *officemate: Yuki, the new employee, will be your officemate.*

---

room service *n.* [U] hotel service that brings food or drink to a customer's room: *I'm too tired to go to a restaurant; let's order room service.*

room·y /'rumi/ *adj.* **-ier, -iest** having plenty of room: *Our house is old but roomy and comfortable.*

roost /rust/ *n.* **1** a place where birds sleep or rest, such as a chicken coop or roof on a building: *Pigeons use that tree as a roost at night.* **2** *infrml.fig.* **to rule the roost:** to have control over everyone in a place, (*syn.*) to dominate: *He rules the roost in that business, and everyone does what he says.*
—*v.* **1** to rest or sleep: *Chickens roost at night.* **2** *infrml.fig.* **one's chickens come home to roost:** to have bad things happen because of one's bad behavior or actions: *He drives too fast all the time, and his chickens came home to roost when the police caught him and put him in jail.*

roost·er /'rustər/ *n.* a male chicken: *Roosters usually have beautiful feathers and make a lot of noise early in the morning.*

root /rut/ *n.* **1** the part of a plant that grows downward into the soil and brings food and water into the plant: *The roots of trees grow*

rooster

deep into the earth. **2** the bottom part of s.t., such as a root that holds that thing in place: *He pulled a piece of his sister's hair out by the roots.* **3** the most important part or cause of s.t.: *Wanting to have more money is "the root of all evil."* **4** **to have roots:** important connections, such as having a family, job, and friends in a place: *He has roots in that town and does not want to leave it.* **5** (in grammar)

a word or part of a word that can be used to make other words: *"Spect" is the root of words like "spectacle" and "inspection."* **6** **square root:** (in mathematics) the number that, when multiplied by itself, equals a given number: *The square root of 9 is 3.*
—*v.* **1** to grow into the ground: *The tree rooted into good soil.* **2** to dig with one's nose: *Pigs root in the ground.* **3** *phrasal v.* **to root around:** to look for s.t. under other things or under the ground: *I rooted around in my big closet and found my old football.* **4** *phrasal v. insep.* **to root for:** to follow a player or team and want them to win: *We root for the local high school baseball team.* **5** *phrasal v. to* **root s.o.** or **s.t. out:** to completely eliminate s.o. or s.t. (usu. bad): *We rooted out the corruption.*||*We rooted it out.* **6** **to take root: a.** to grow strong roots: *Plants take root in the spring.* **b.** *fig.* to establish themselves (ideas, movements): *Democracy takes root in many countries.* -*adj.* **rootless.**

root beer *n.* [U] a nonalcoholic drink made from the roots of some trees: *Most root beer is now made with artificial flavoring.*

root·ed /'rutɪd/ *adj.* held in one place: *She was rooted to her seat because she was afraid to speak in front of a large group.*

rope /roʊp/ *n.* [C;U] **1** a thick cord used for tying or hanging things: *The boat was tied to a tree with a rope.*||*She hangs her wet clothes on a rope to dry.* **2** **to know the ropes:** to know one's job very well: *Al has worked here for 25 years, so he really knows the ropes.*

rope

—*v.* **-roped, -roping, -ropes 1** to catch cattle and horses with a rope: *Cowboys rope horses.* **2** **to give s.o. plenty of rope:** give s.o. freedom to do what that person thinks is best **3** *phrasal v. insep.* **to rope s.o. into doing s.t.:** to convince s.o. to do s.t.: *My friend roped me into helping him move his furniture to his new apartment.* **4** *phrasal v. sep.* **to rope s.t. off:** to block off an area: *Police roped off a crime scene.*||*They roped it off.*

Roque·fort /'roʊkfərt/ *n.* [U] a white French cheese with blue mold and a strong taste: *A little Roquefort tastes wonderful at the end of a meal.*

ro·sa·ry /'roʊzəri/ *n.* **-ries 1** a series of prayers: *She says the rosary each day.* **2** a string of beads used to count those prayers: *She says her prayers with her rosary in hand.*

rose /roʊz/ *n.* **1** [C] a bushy plant that has round, shiny leaves, thorns and large red, pink, white or yellow flowers with many petals and

R

a beautiful smell: *He gave his wife twelve dozen roses for her birthday.* **2** [U] a red or pink color: *My favorite color is rose.*

rose·bush /'rouz,bʌʃ/ *n.* **-es** the plant on which rose flowers grow: *We grow rosebushes in our backyard.*

rose-colored glasses *n.pl.fig.* a symbol for thinking life is always good and happy, optimism: *She looks at the world through rose-colored glasses and says things will always be easy, even when they aren't.*

rose·mar·y /'rouz,mɛri/ *n.* **-ies** [U] a plant with blue flowers and light-green leaves that is used in cooking and to make perfume: *I put some rosemary in the soup.*

ros·in /'rɑzɪn/ *n.* [U] a hard resin made by making the liquid from pine or fur trees pure: *Violin players put rosin on their bows before they play.*

ros·ter /'rɑstər/ *n.* list of people's names: *The teacher checked the roster to see when he would teach this year.*

ros·trum /'rɑstrəm/ *n.* a raised stage for speaking: *A speaker stood on the rostrum and spoke to her audience.*

ros·y /'rouzi/ *adj.* **-ier, -iest 1** having the pinkish-red color of a rose: *Rosy cheeks are a symbol of good health.* **2** full of cheerful optimism: *She always takes a rosy view of life.* **3** wonderful, excellent: *She got a new job and her life looks rosy.*

rot /rɑt/ *n.* [U] a state of decay, esp. caused by disease, or after death: *Rot in the tree trunk caused the tree to fall.*
—*v.* **rotted, rotting, rots** to break down into biochemical parts, usu. after death, (*syns.*) to decay, decompose: *Dead plants rot and become part of the soil again.*

ro·ta·ry /'routəri/ *n.* **-ries** a traffic circle: *When you come to a rotary, you should always drive to the right until you reach your turn.*
—*adj.* having a wheel-like motion, moving in a circle: *A rotary telephone has a wheel with holes for each number.*

ro·tate /'routeɪt/ *v.* **-tated, -tating, -tates 1** to move around s.t., esp. in a circle: *Planets rotate around the sun.* **2** to do s.t. by turns, one after another: *I had the tires on my car rotated so they would wear evenly.*

ro·ta·tion /rou'teɪʃən/ *n.* [C;U] a movement around s.t.: *The earth makes a complete rotation around the sun about every 365 days.*

ROTC /'arouti'si/ *n.* short for Reserve Officer's Training Corp., a program in which students receive training as army officers: *He earned some money for college in ROTC.*

rote /rout/ *n.* [U] learning s.t. by memory alone without thinking about it: *That young boy learned the alphabet by rote (or) rote memory.*

rot·gut /'rɑt,gʌt/ *n.infrml.fig.* [U] cheap wine or alcohol: *That guy drinks rotgut because the alcohol is more important to him than the taste.*

ro·tis·se·rie /rou'tɪsəri/ *n.* a cooking device that turns meat, such as a chicken, in a hot oven, so it will cook evenly: *That restaurant has a rotisserie for cooking chickens.*

ro·to·gra·vure /,routougrə'vyur/ *n.* [U] a high-quantity printing method

ro·tor /'routər/ *n.* the part of an engine or other machine that turns: *A rotor from the engine makes the wheels of the car turn.*

rot·ten /'rɑtn/ *adj.* **1** referring to s.t. that has gone bad, (*syns.*) decayed, spoiled: *Rotten logs decay slowly and make the earth rich for new plants.* **2** *fig.* bad, evil: *Stealing money from a friend is a rotten thing to do.* **3** to feel sick or ill: *I have a bad cold and feel rotten today.* **4** to feel guilty: *She feels rotten about telling her boyfriend that she doesn't love him anymore.* -*n.* [U] **rottenness.**

ro·tund /rou'tʌnd/ *adj.frml.* huge and round: *A fat man can also be called rotund.* -*n.* [U] **rotundity.**

ro·tun·da /rou'tʌndə/ *n.* a round room or building with a domed roof: *We could hear our voices echo in the large rotunda of the Capitol building in Washington, D.C.*

rouge /ruʒ/ *n.* [U] a powder or cream, usu. red or pink, used to color the cheeks: *Women put rouge on their cheeks to make their faces pretty.*

rough /rʌf/ *adj.* **1** not smooth, uneven, (*syn.*) coarse: *When wood is first cut, it feels rough.* **2** moving in a stormy or violent way: *Strong winds cause rough seas.* **3** impolite, having bad manners: *That fellow has a rough manner.* **4** not very high quality, done quickly, (*syns.*) crude, unpolished: *The artist did a rough drawing before doing a painting.* **5** close to correct but not exact, giving an idea of the final result, (*syn.*) approximate: *His drawing gives you a rough idea of what the final picture will look like.* **6** difficult and unfair: *It's rough being a single parent.*
—*v.* **1 to rough it:** to live without modern comforts: *We decided to go camping and rough it instead of getting a hotel.* **2** *phrasal v. sep.* **to rough s.t. out:** to give a general, crude idea: *She roughed out her plans before making them final.||She roughed them out.* **3** *phrasal v. sep.* **to rough s.o. up:** to treat s.o. badly, punch and shove s.o.: *The thief roughed up a man when he robbed him.||He roughed him up.*
—*n.* [U] part of a golf course where the grass is uncut: *He hit the ball into the rough.*

rough·age /'rʌfɪdʒ/ *n.* food, such as uncooked vegetables, that clear the digestive system, (*syn.*) dietary fiber: *He eats carrots and broccoli for roughage.*

rough-and-ready *adj.* rough, crude, but able to be used: *He is a rough-and-ready man who can do any kind of work around a house.*

rough-and-tumble *adj.fig.* related to a situation of people trying to be better than others in a rough or unkind way: *In the rough-and-tumble world of business, making money is most important.*

rough·en /'rʌfən/ *v.* to make s.t. rough, (*syn.*) to coarsen: *Working in the garden without wearing gloves roughens your hands.*

rough·house /'rʌf,haʊz/ or *v.* /'rʌf,haʊs/ *n. adj.* [U] to play in a rough way, such as hitting each other: *Some boys <v.> roughhoused in the schoolyard after school.*

rough·ly /'rʌfli/ *adv.* **1** with roughness, such as shoving and punching: *The police treated a criminal roughly because he tried to run away.* **2** about, but not exactly, (*syn.*) approximately: *The trip to Chicago takes roughly three hours by airplane.*

rough·ness /'rʌfnɪs/ *n.* [U] **1** the state of being rough, not smooth to touch: *In winter, she uses hand cream to smooth the roughness in her hands.* **2** cruelty or force, violence, (*syn.*) brutality: *Some people don't like boxing because of the roughness of the sport.*

rough·rid·er /'rʌf,raɪdər/ *n.* a rider who makes wild horses rideable: *Roughriders know how to make a wild horse wear a saddle.*

rough·shod /'rʌf,ʃad/ *adv.fig.* **to run rough-shod over s.o.:** to do s.t. without thinking about s.o.'s feelings, (*syn.*) callously: *He runs roughshod over his employees by yelling at them.*

rou·lette /ru'lɛt/ *n.* [U] a gambling game played by betting where a marble will stop on a spinning tray: *I lost $25 playing roulette in the casino. See:* Russian roulette.

round /raʊnd/ *adj.* **1** circular or curved in shape: *Balls are round.* **2** fat, plump: *He has a round belly.* **3** not exact, (*syn.*) approximate: *In round numbers, he paid $1000. (He paid about $1000.)*
—*v.* **1** to make s.t. round in shape: *A carpenter rounded the edges of a table top.* **2** *phrasal v. sep.* **to round s.t. down:** to lower a figure to the nearest whole number: *When you round decimals down, the number is easier to read.||$10.35 rounded down is $10.00.* **3** *phrasal v. sep.* **to round s.t. off** or **out:** to finish s.t., esp. in a pleasant way: *After going to the theater, we rounded out the evening with a nice dinner.||We rounded the evening out.* **4** *phrasal v. sep.* **to round s.t. up: a.** to collect, herd s.t. together: *Cowboys rounded up the cows.||They rounded them up.* **b.** to raise a number to the next highest one: *$10.55 rounded up is $11.*
—*adv.* **1** around: *He comes round to visit us every week.* **2 to come round:** to change one's

way of thinking: *Sooner or later, he will come round to your ideas.* **3 to go round-and-round:** to talk without coming to a decision: *We went round-and-round in our talks and we could not agree.* **4** *infrml.fig.* **to go round the bend:** to go crazy, become odd or strange: *When his wife left him, he went round the bend.*
—*prep.* around: *He lives round the corner from us.*
—*n.* **1** a group of things: *He bought a round of drinks for everyone.* **2** a period of time in a boxing match: *The boxers fought for 12 rounds.* **3** a series, such as discussions: *The economics ministers held a round of talks to discuss international trade.* **4** *usu.pl.* **rounds:** a series of stops or a regular walk, such as that taken by a security guard, police officer, or doctor: *Every hour, the guard makes his rounds of the office building.* **5** bullets for guns: *He fired 12 rounds at the target.* **6** a song in which three or four groups sing the same words and music at different times: *We sang "Row, Row, Row Your Boat" as a round.* **7** *pl.* **to make the round of:** to visit many places: *He made the round of his friends' New Year's parties.*

round·a·bout /'raʊndə,baʊt/ *adj.* indirect, taking a long time to say s.t. or way to go somewhere: *We took a roundabout way from Chicago to San Francisco by driving through Texas.*

round·ed /'raʊndɪd/ *adj.* having curved edges like part of a circle: *Corners on that table are rounded. See:* well-rounded.

round robin *n.* a game or competition in which all players play each other at least once: *Our tennis club plays a round robin each August.*

round table *n.* a discussion in which each person is equal, and the table is round so that no one has the most important seat: *Several experts had a round table discussion about the economy.*

round-the-clock *adv.adj.* all day and all night: *We work <adv.> round-the-clock to get the job done.||It was a <adj.> round-the-clock job.*

round trip or **round-trip** *adj.n.* a journey that starts and ends in the same place: *I bought a <adj.> round-trip ticket to San Diego and I'll make the <n.> round trip in four days.*

round·up /'raʊndʌp/ *n.* **1** a chasing together of cows, horses, etc., herding: *Cowboys do a roundup of cows.* **2** the arrest of many people the police think are doing s.t. illegal: *Police did a roundup of suspected drug sellers.*

rouse /raʊz/ *v.* **roused, rousing, rouses 1** to awaken and get up: *He rouses himself out of bed every morning at 6:30 A.M.* **2** to make s.o.

R

feel excited: *He roused a feeling of patriotism in me.*

rous·ing /ˈraʊzɪŋ/ *adj.fig.* happy and loud, exciting: *We had a rousing good time at the party.*

roust /raʊst/ *v.* to force out: *Sergeants roust soldiers out of bed each morning.*

roust·a·bout /ˈraʊstəˌbaʊt/ *n.* a worker, such as a person who works on ship docks or in oil fields: *He was a roustabout in a Texas oil field.*

rout /raʊt/ *v.* **1** to force s.o. to run away: *Our army routed the enemy into running for their lives.* **2** (in sports) to defeat another team badly: *Our team routed the competition.*
—*n.* **1** an instance of forcing s.o. to leave or run away: *We drove the enemy into a rout.* **2** (in sports) a strong or large defeat

route /raʊt, rut/ *n.* **1** a path along which one travels: *The airline route from Seattle to Tokyo goes over the North Pole.* **2** a series of stops made regularly as by s.o. who delivers things: *The newspaper delivery truck has a regular route for dropping off newspapers.*
—*v.* **routed, routing, routes** to tell s.o. to go a certain way: *Police routed cars onto a road away from an accident.*

rou·tine /ruˈtin/ *n.* [C;U] a series of things s.o. does regularly: *He has a different routine on Saturday and Sunday than he does on weekdays.*
—*adj.* normal, not unusual in any way: *My doctor wants to do some routine blood tests.* -*adv.* **routinely.**

rou·tin·ize /ruˈtiˌnaɪz, ˈrutnaɪz/ *v.* **-ized, -izing, -izes** to make s.t. into regular work that can be done without much thought: *Using a computer has become so routinized for her that she doesn't even look at the keyboard when she works.*

rove /roʊv/ *v.* **roved, roving, roves** to go from place to place, usu. without planning ahead, (*syns.*) to roam, wander: *He roved around the country doing odd jobs for several years.*

rov·er /ˈroʊvər/ *n.* **1** a person who roves, a wanderer: *I talked to a rover who told me stories about the interesting places he had seen.* **2** a person who leaves one mate for another: *He has married five times and is a real rover.* **3** a type of strong vehicle: *a land rover*

rov·ing /ˈroʊvɪŋ/ *adj.n.* **1** related to wandering, not staying in one place: *A <adj.> roving group of thieves made trouble all over the countryside.* **2 to have a roving eye:** to look for other women (or) men: *Even though he is married, he has a <adj.> roving eye (for other women).*

row (1) /roʊ/ *n.* **1** a line of things, people, pictures, etc., placed front to back or side by side: *A row of trees lines the street.* **2** a line of seating as in a theater: *We watched the play from the eighth row.*

row (2) /roʊ/ *v.* to move a boat in the water using oars: *He rowed his boat across the pond.*
—*n.* an act of rowing: *He went for a row this morning.*

row (3) /raʊ/ *n.* a loud argument or a fistfight, (*syn.*) a brawl: *Two men had a row outside a barroom.*‖*The two sisters had a loud row with lots of yelling.*

row·boat /ˈroʊˌboʊt/ *n.* a small boat moved by people pulling oars: *He uses a rowboat to go fishing on the lake.*

row·dy /ˈraʊdi/ *adj.* **-dier, -diest** loud, difficult to control or make quiet: *A rowdy group of boys ran through the streets.*
—*n.* a loud, uncontrollable person: *Those rowdies make a lot of noise.* -*adv.* **rowdily;** -*n.* [U] **rowdiness; rowdyism.**

row house /roʊ/ *n.* a line of houses that share walls: *They live in a row house on a quiet street.*

row·ing /ˈroʊɪŋ/ *n.* [U] an act of moving a boat by oars: *Rowing is hard work.*

roy·al /ˈrɔɪəl/ *adj.* **1** related to a king or queen: *The royal family lives in a large castle.* **2** *infrml.fig.* on a very large scale, huge, (*syn.*) tremendous: *He made a royal mess of the kitchen when he tried to bake a cake.* -*adv.* **royally.**
—*n.usu.pl.* **royals:** members of the ruling family and their relatives: *In England, the royals are loved.*

roy·al·ty /ˈrɔɪəlti/ *n.* **-ties 1** [U] a king or queen and family **2** [U] kings, queens, princes, and princesses, and nobility in general: *Royalty from all over the world came to see the princess become queen.* **3** [C] an amount of money, usu. a percentage of some larger amount, paid to s.o.: *Publishers pay a royalty to the authors who write their books.*

RSVP /ˈarɛsviˈpi/ *abbr.* (French for) please respond: *In the letter asking us to come to a party, she wrote, "RSVP by Monday."*

USAGE NOTE: *RSVP* appears on an invitation to a party, wedding, or other event when the host needs to know how many people will be coming: *You should RSVP by sending a letter or calling the person who sent you the invitation.* Another common abbreviation on invitations is *BYOB.* This stands for *Bring Your Own Bottle* and means that if you want to drink alcoholic drinks, you may bring them, but the host will not provide them. Both of these abbreviations are sometimes used like words: *When I RSVPed for her party, she told me it was BYOB.*

---

rub /rʌb/ *v.* **rubbed, rubbing, rubs 1** to touch s.t. while moving backwards and forwards: *A mother rubbed her child's back.* **2** to put s.t. on using a cloth and pressure: *I rubbed wax on the*

table so it would shine. **3** *phrasal v. sep.* **to rub s.t. away:** to push or brush aside: *A mother rubbed away the tears of her child when he hurt his knee.‖She rubbed them away.* **4** *phrasal v. sep.* **to rub s.o.** or **s.t. down:** to make smooth through rubbing: *Rub down the table with sandpaper.‖Rub it down.* **5** *infrml.fig.* **to rub elbows with s.o.:** to be in contact with people: *When you ride the subway in New York City, you rub elbows with people from all over the world.* **6** *phrasal v. sep.* **to rub s.t. in** or **into: a.** to apply liquid to a surface by rubbing: *The nurse rubbed lotion into my skin.* **b.** to remind s.o. of a mistake or other failing many times: *His father rubbed in his failure to pass exams nearly every day.‖He rubbed it in.* **7** *phrasal v. insep.* **to rub off on s.o.** or **s.t.: a.** *s.o.:* to make others feel the same way, *(syns.)* to affect, influence: *Her cheerfulness rubs off on everyone she meets and makes them happy.* **b.** *s.t.:* to come off on a surface after rubbing: *He rubbed some paint off on a rag.* **8** *phrasal v. sep.* **to rub s.o.** or **s.t. out:** *slang s.o.:* to kill, murder s.o.: *A gangster rubbed out a man who gave information to the police by shooting him.‖He rubbed him out.* **9** *infrml.fig.* **to rub s.o. the wrong way:** to make s.o. feel angry or uncomfortable, *(syns.)* to annoy, irritate: *His rude behavior rubs people the wrong way. See:* caress, USAGE NOTE.
—*n.* **1** an act of rubbing s.o. or s.t.: *After exercise, he gives his legs a rub with alcohol.* **2** *sing.infrml.fig.* a difficulty, problem: *The rub with computers is that people are scared to learn to use them.*

rub·ber /ˈrʌbər/ *n.* **1** [U] a natural elastic substance made either from a white liquid that comes from rubber trees or from chemicals (artificial rubber): *Tires for trucks, cars, and bicycles are made of rubber.* **2** [C] *infrml.* a condom -*adj.* **rubbery.** *See:* condom, USAGE NOTE.

rubber band *n.* a circular piece of rubber that can stretch and wrap around things to hold them together: *She put a rubber band around her pencils so they wouldn't get lost.*

rub·ber·neck /ˈrʌbərˌnɛk/ *v.infrml.fig.* to turn one's head to look at s.t. while driving or walking by: *Drivers slowed down and rubbernecked at the scene of a bad auto accident.*

rubber stamp *n.* a stamp with printing on it and made of rubber: *She stamps the company name on checks with a rubber stamp.*
—*v.fig.* **rubber-stamp** to agree to or approve s.t. automatically without asking any questions: *The boss rubber-stamps her ideas because she always gets good results.*

rub·bish /ˈrʌbɪʃ/ *n.* [U] **1** trash; unwanted, broken, or dirty things: *I put the rubbish in a plastic bag and threw it away.* **2** *fig.* stupid,

meaningless words, *(syns.)* nonsense, foolishness: *What he says is pure rubbish.*

rub·ble /ˈrʌbəl/ *n.* [U] parts of broken buildings, such as loose bricks and cracked walls: *After the earthquake, it took months to clean up the rubble.*

rub·down /ˈrʌbˌdaʊn/ *n.* rubbing of the body to make sore muscles feel better, *(syn.)* a massage: *A trainer gives an athlete a rubdown after a hard game.*

rube /rub/ *n.infrml.pej.* an uneducated person who never learned good manners, *(syn.)* a hick: *That rube spilled coffee all over me!*

ru·bel·la /ruˈbɛlə/ *n.* [U] a childhood disease also known as German measles: *The child is vaccinated against rubella.*

rub·out /ˈrʌbˌaʊt/ *n.slang* a murder, killing: *His death was a rubout done by the mafia.*

ru·bric /ˈrubrɪk/ *n.* a group or type of s.t., *(syns.)* category, variety: *Her novels fall under the rubric of science fiction.*

ru·by /ˈrubi/ *n.* **-bies** a precious red gemstone, a type of red gem or jewel: *She loves to wear rubies.*
—*adj.* a deep reddish color: *She has ruby lips.*

ruck·sack /ˈrʌkˌsæk, ˈrʊk-/ *n.* a backpack.

ruck·us /ˈrʌkəs/ *n.infrml.* a lot of noise and confusion, *(syns.)* a commotion, disturbance: *He made a ruckus at the meeting because he disagreed with the management.*

rud·der /ˈrʌdər/ *n.* s.t. flat and moveable used to steer a boat: *A sailor uses the rudder to make the ship go in the correct direction.*

rud·dy /ˈrʌdi/ *adj.* **-dier, -diest** reddish in color: *That hunter has a ruddy face because he is outdoors so much.* -*n.* [U] **ruddiness.**

rude /rud/ *adj.* **ruder, rudest 1** impolite, making people angry by one's bad behavior or unkind words: *It was rude to walk away while that customer was talking to you.* **2** rough, simple: *He ate a rude meal of bread, cheese, and water.* -*adv.* **rudely.**

rude·ness /ˈrudnɪs/ *n.* [U] impoliteness, an act of being nasty or unkind to s.o.: *He was asked to leave his job because of his rudeness to other workers.*

ru·di·ment /ˈrudəmənt/ *n.frml.* a basic part of s.t., *(syn.)* an essential: *The rudiments of reading are an understanding of the alphabet and knowledge of basic words.*

ru·di·men·ta·ry /ˌrudəˈmɛntəri/ *adj.frml.* simple, basic: *He has a rudimentary ability to read, but he can only read simple words.*

rue /ru/ *v.frml.* **rued, ruing, rues** to feel badly about s.t., *(syn.)* to regret: *He rued the day that he rode the motorcycle because he fell off and broke his leg.* -*adj.* **rueful.**

ruff /rʌf/ *n.* a collar, such as of hair, fur, feathers, or lace: *A lion's mane is a ruff of long hair.‖Men and women in Europe in the 16th* and *17th centuries wore ruffs around their necks.*

ruf·fian /ˈrʌfiən/ *n.frml.* a man who fights others for fun, (*syns.*) a hoodlum, thug: *Ruffians beat up an old man.*

ruf·fle /ˈrʌfəl/ *v.* **-fled, -fling, -fles 1** to spread and shake s.t., such as feathers or fur, and make them uneven, not smooth: *A duck shook itself and ruffled its feathers.* **2** *fig.* to annoy s.o., upset or anger, (*syn.*) to fluster: *His unkind words ruffled her self-confidence.* **3** *fig.* **to ruffle s.o.'s feathers:** to annoy s.o., cause s.o. to lose his or her calm: *His boss yelled at him and ruffled his feathers.*
—*n.* **1** a ruff, collar, ring, or border made of cloth, that is gathered or pleated on one edge: *Her blouse has a ruffle of lace around the neck.* **2** a slow drumbeat

rug /rʌg/ *n.* a heavy fabric floor covering: *They have a beautiful Oriental rug on their floor.*

rug·by /ˈrʌgbi/ *n.* [U] a type of football game played by two teams of 15 players each: *Rugby was first played at Rugby School in England.*

rug·ged /ˈrʌgɪd/ *adj.* **1** hilly, referring to land that is difficult to travel over: *The Rocky Mountains have rugged mountains and roads.* **2** strong, healthy, (*syn.*) vigorous: *Football players must be rugged.* -*n.* [U] **ruggedness.**

ru·in /ˈruɪn/ *v.* **1** to damage s.t., make s.t. no longer useful: *She spilled coffee on her white silk dress and ruined it.* **2** to spoil s.t., to take the fun or usefulness out of s.t., esp. an event: *His stupid behavior ruined our party.* **3** to destroy s.t., such as breaking, burning, or knocking s.t. down: *A fire ruined everything inside the museum.* **4** to cause s.o. to lose all of his or her money, (*syn.*) to bankrupt: *The stock market crash ruined him, so he has no money.*
—*n.* **1** [C;U] a state of destruction, anything unusable because of damage: *After the fire, the museum lay in ruins.* **2** broken parts of historical buildings that still exist after thousands of years: *We went to Greece to see the ruins of ancient temples.*

ru·in·a·tion /ˌruəˈneɪʃən/ *n.frml.* [U] a state of being ruined, destroyed, or bankrupted: *He spends so much money that he's headed for ruination.*

ru·in·ous /ˈruənəs/ *adj.* related to ruin: *Smoking cigarettes and drinking alcohol were ruinous to her health.*

rule /rul/ *n.* **1** [C] a statement about what must or should be done, (*syn.*) a regulation: *Our school has a rule that students must not eat or drink in class.* **2** [C] the straight line made by a ruler: *My writing paper has blue rules printed on each sheet.* **3** a general condition, the usual state of s.t.: *In democracies, decisions are made under rule of law, not by one person.*

—*v.* **ruled, ruling, rules 1** to make a society function, to govern, usu. as a king or dictator: *Tsars ruled in Russia until 1917.* **2** to decide officially, say what will be done: *The court ruled that the woman was guilty.* **3** to draw straight lines on s.t. as with a ruler: *Some writing paper is ruled with blue lines.* **4** *phrasal v. sep.* **to rule s.o.** or **s.t. out**: to decide s.t. is not possible: *Since we have ruled out the possibility of buying a new car, we must get the old one fixed.||We have ruled it out.*

rule of thumb *n.* an idea of how to do s.t. that can be used most of the time, (*syn.*) a guideline: *As a rule of thumb, you should spend no more than 1/4 of the money you make on renting an apartment.*

rul·er /ˈrulər/ *n.* **1** a person, such as a king or queen, that guides or controls a country: *The rulers of England governed for hundreds of years.* **2** a measuring stick: *I use a short ruler to draw straight lines.*

rul·ing /ˈrulɪŋ/ *n.* a decision, esp. one made by a court or an official agency: *The Environmental Protection Agency passed a new ruling about how cleanly cars and trucks must burn gasoline.*

rum /rʌm/ *n.* [U] a strong alcoholic drink made from sugar cane: *Puerto Rico is famous for its light and dark rum.*

rum·ble /ˈrʌmbəl/ *v.* **-bled, -bling, -bles** to make a low, powerful, rolling noise: *We could tell from the rumble of the thunder that rain was coming.*
—*n.* **1** a low, powerful, rolling noise: *You can hear the rumble of a railroad train as it goes through a tunnel.* **2** *slang* a riot, a big fight: *Two gangs had a rumble last night, and several boys were badly hurt.*

rum·bling /ˈrʌmblɪŋ/ *n.adj.* a low, powerful rolling noise: *You can hear the <n.> rumbling* (or) *a <adj.> rumbling noise of a train as it goes across a bridge.*

ru·mi·nant /ˈrumənənt/ *n.frml.* a grass-eating animal with several stomachs, such as cows and buffalo: *When ruminants chew their food a second time, we say they are chewing their cud.*

ru·mi·nate /ˈrumə,neɪt/ *v.fig.frml.* **-nated, -nating, -nates** to think about s.t. long and deeply, (*syn.*) to meditate, ponder: *She ruminated a long time before agreeing to marry him.*

rum·mage /ˈrʌmɪdʒ/ *v.n.* **-maged, -maging, -mages** [U] to look through many things, search: *I <v.> rummaged through my clothing, looking for a pair of winter socks.*

rummage sale *n.* a sale of many different kinds of things, esp. clothing, where customers look through piles of things to find what they want: *Rummage sales are sometimes held for charity, and sometimes stores have them to sell*

R

things that have been hard to sell. See: garage sale, USAGE NOTE.

rum·my /ˈrʌmi/ *n.* **-mies** *adj.* **-mier, -miest 1** [C] an alcoholic, such as a person who drinks rum regularly: *An old rummy is sleeping on a park bench.* **2** [U] a card game in which players try to collect cards of the same number or suit: *I beat my sister at rummy because I collected all the kings, queens, and aces.*

ru·mor /ˈrumər/ *n.* **1** [C;U] gossip, talk that comes from what other people say and not from true information or personal knowledge: *There is a false rumor going around that the water supply is unsafe.* **2 rumor has it:** people are saying: *Rumor has it that the franc will be devalued soon.*
—*v.* to spread a rumor: *It is rumored that the water supply is bad, but it's not true.*

ru·mor·mon·ger /ˈrumərˌmʌŋgər, -ˌmɑŋ-/ *n.* a person who likes to tell rumors to many people: *He is a rumormonger and cannot be believed.*

rump /rʌmp/ *n.adj.* the buttocks, hindquarters, esp. of animals: *She bought a <adj.> rump steak which she served with rice.*

rum·ple /ˈrʌmpəl/ *v.* **-pled, -pling, -ples** to make wrinkles in s.t., (*syn.*) to crease: *If you throw your clothes on the floor, they will rumple.*

run /rʌn/ *v.* **ran** /ræn/, **run, running, runs 1** to move the legs and feet quickly, one after the other, across the ground, faster than walking: *Every morning, he runs around the high school track.* **2** to race on foot: *The track star ran the 100 meters in record time.* **3** to finish or place in a race: *He ran second in the 1,000 meters.* **4** to get away from quickly on foot, (*syns.*) to escape, flee: *They heard the explosion and ran.* **5** to leave quickly: *I have to run now; I'm late for a meeting.* **6** to do some job or task: *She runs errands, like taking her daughter to dance class on Saturday morning.* **7** to try to get elected to political office: *She ran for the Senate and won.* **8** to look over s.t. quickly: *He ran his eyes over the instructions on how to put the toy together.* **9** to go in a certain direction: *That highway runs east and west.* **10** to come apart, (*syn.*) to unravel: *Her pantyhose ran and made a big hole.* **11** to drip, leak: *That faucet runs all the time.* **12** to pour: *I ran the hot water in the bathtub.* **13** to direct and make decisions about s.t., (*syns.*) to manage, supervise: *She runs her own business.* **14** to work or function in a certain way: *That engine runs smoothly.* **15** to make a machine work: *A farmer runs his tractor over the fields.* **16** to meet or experience, (*syn.*) to encounter: *We ran into trouble in the heavy traffic.* **17** to begin and end: *My fever ran its course for several days, then my temperature became normal again.* **18** to flow, move as water does:

Mountain streams run to the ocean. **19** to move as a group, (*syn.*) to migrate: *Fish run up rivers to lay eggs.* **20** to spread after becoming wet, (*syn.*) to smear: *Ink runs when the paper it is on gets wet.||My makeup ran in the rain.* **21** to cry: *His eyes ran with tears.* **22** to be very long, (*syn.*) to prolong: *When he talks, he runs on and on for hours.* **23** to bring s.t. into a place illegally, (*syn.*) to smuggle: *Smugglers run illegal guns into the country.* **24** to print in a newspaper or magazine, publish, advertise: *The Times ran an editorial about problems with the economy.||He ran an ad to hire a salesman.* **25** to pass by regularly, follow a regular path: *The bus runs past my house every hour.* **26** to be common in a family: *Blue eyes run in our family.* **27** *phrasal v. insep.* **to run across s.t.: a.** to go from one side to another quickly: *A dog ran across the road.* **b.** to find by accident: *I was going through some old papers, and I ran across a letter I thought was lost.* **28** *phrasal v. insep.* **to run after s.o.** or **s.t.: a.** *infrml. s.o.:* to try to get s.o.'s attention: *He's been running after her for years.* **b.** to chase, (*syn.*) to pursue: *She ran after the bus, yelling.* **29 to run aground:** (in shipping) to get stuck, be unable to move away from (usu. of boats): *A riverboat ran aground on a sandbar.* **30** *phrasal v.* **to run along:** (usu. as a command) to go away, leave: *Don't bother me while I'm working; run along now!* **31** *phrasal v.* **to run around: a.** to go to many places: *I had to run around today to do shopping.* **b.** to spend time with s.o.: *He's been running around with my cousin.* **32** *infrml.fig.* **to run around like a chicken with its head cut off:** to hurry in a confused, worried way: *He ran around like a chicken with its head cut off, looking for s.o. who could repair his computer.* **33** *phrasal v. insep.* **to run at s.o.** or **s.t.: a.** *s.o.:* to come toward quickly, charge at s.o., (*syn.*) to attack: *A crazy man with a knife ran at a policeman.* **b.** *s.t.:* to work at a certain speed, level, etc.: *That engine runs at a top speed of 120 miles (192 km) per hour.* **34** *phrasal v.* **to run away: a.** to leave home: *He ran away from home when he was a little boy.* **b.** to get away from quickly, (*syns.*) to escape, flee: *Deer run away from hunters.* **35** *phrasal v. insep.* **to run away** or **off with s.o.** or **s.t.: a.** *s.o.:* to escape with: *She ran away with her baby so that no one would take him.* **b.** *s.t.:* to take control of s.t. and do whatever one wants with it: *She put a young man in charge of a project for a short time, and he ran away with it and changed it completely.* **c.** *s.o.* or *s.t.:* to steal s.t.: *A thief ran away with a lady's purse.* **36** *phrasal v. sep.* **to run by s.o.** or **s.t.: a.** to make a quick visit: *I ran by my mother's house just to see whether she was OK.* **b.** to ask for s.o.'s opinion or ask s.o. to agree to s.t.: *I ran an idea by my boss to see if she liked it.* **37**

R

phrasal v. sep. **to run s.o.** or **s.t. down: a. s.o.:** to hit s.o. as with a car or truck: *A man was run down by a speeding car as he crossed the street.* **b. s.t.:** to look s.t. over quickly, (*syn.*) to scan: *I ran my eye down the page until I found the information that I wanted.* **c. s.o** or **s.t.:** to say bad things about s.o. or s.t., criticize: *He runs down life in the big city because of crime, pollution, and high costs.* **d. s.o.** or **s.t.:** to lose energy, stop functioning: *Taking care of those children ran him down.* **38 to run for cover** or **for it:** to get away from danger or discomfort, escape: *When it started to rain, we ran for cover in a small building* (or) *we ran for it.* **39 to run for office:** to try to get elected to public office: *She ran for the office of City Controller and won.* **40 to run for your life:** to get away from danger by running fast: *A flood is coming this way! Run for your life!* **41** *phrasal v. sep.* **to run s.o. in:** to arrest s.o.: *The FBI ran in the fugitive.||They ran her in.* **42** *phrasal v. insep.* **to run into s.o.** or **s.t.: a. s.o.:** to meet s.o. by chance: *I ran into an old friend at the airport in Seattle.* **b. s.t.:** to reach a total of: *Her college loans run into the thousands.* **c. s.o.** or **s.t.:** to hit s.o. or s.t.: *The two boys ran into each other when playing football.* **43 to run low:** to use almost all of s.t.: *My car is running low on gasoline.* **44** *phrasal v.* **to run off: a.** to chase s.o. away, make s.o. leave: *A farmer ran hunters off his land by yelling at them to leave.* **b.** to do s.t. without thinking about others, leave without having the right to do so: *A man ran off and left his wife and children.* **c.** to make copies of s.t.: *She ran off ten copies of the story she wrote.* **45** *phrasal v. insep.* **to run off with s.o.** or **s.t.:** *See:* to run away with s.o. or s.t. **46** *infrml.* **to run off at the mouth:** to talk too much, esp. making others angry or upset: *Because she ran off at the mouth about how much she hated her job, her boss fired her.* **47** *phrasal v. insep* **to run out of s.t.:** to use all of s.t., (*syns.*) to deplete, exhaust: *We have run out of paper for the photocopy machine.* **48** *phrasal v. sep.* **to run (s.o.** or **s.t.) over: a.** (of a liquid) to be too much for a container: *She wasn't paying attention, and so she didn't notice when the milk ran over.* **b.** to go beyond a time limit, deadline: *I was late because my meeting ran over.* **c. s.t.:** to read through or study s.t. quickly: *She ran over her notes before the test.* **d. s.o.** or **s.t.** to hit and crush under a vehicle: *A taxi ran over their dog and killed him.||It ran over him.* **49** *infrml.fig.* **to run scared:** to live in fear, esp. of losing one's job or life: *His boss warned him to improve his work, and he's running scared now.* **50** *infrml.fig.* **to run s.t. into the ground:** to ruin s.t., such as by not taking care of it, not repairing it, etc.: *He never changes the oil or spark plugs in his car; he is running it into the ground.* **51 to run short:** not to have enough

of s.t.: *The teacher ran short of class handouts, so two students didn't get one.* **52 to run the show:** *infrml.fig.* to take charge of a business, tell others what to do: *She is the big boss, and she likes to run the show.* **53** *phrasal v. insep.* **to run through s.t.: a.** to practice s.t.: *Actors run through their lines in rehearsal.* **b.** to read s.t. quickly: *I want to run through these notes.* **54** *phrasal v. insep.* **to run s.t. through s.t.:** to pass or draw s.t. directly through s.t. else: *She ran her fingers through her hair.* **55** *phrasal v. insep.* **to run to s.t.:** to add up to, amount to: *That book runs to 300 pages.* **56** *phrasal v. sep.* **to run together:** to blend or smear after becoming wet (usu. of colors): *The blue and yellow colors on the sign ran after they got wet.||They ran together.* **57** *phrasal v. sep.* **to run s.t. up:** to make s.t. become higher or greater: *He ran up a big bill at the bar.||He ran it up.* **58** *infrml.fig.* **to run up against a stone wall:** to meet a problem that will not move, be blocked: *When I talked with him, I ran up against a stone wall because he just will not agree to work together with us.*

—*n.* **1** an exercise period, like jogging: *She goes for a run in the park every morning.* **2** moving one's feet faster than a walk, the motions of running: *Our dog broke into a run as he came up to us.* **3** an area where animals can run: *We have a dog run with a fence behind our house.* **4** (in baseball) a point scored by a player hitting the ball and running around all four bases: *Our team got nine runs and the other team only got six.* **5** a rush by many people to take their money from a bank: *There was a run on the bank because people thought the bank was going to lose all of their money.* **6** a series of places one stops at, esp. while doing business: *The bakery truck makes its run (of stores) every morning.* **7** a place or course where sports are played: *There is a ski run on the side of that hill.* **8** a group of s.t. made at one time: *Our factory did a run of 1,000 pairs of shoes last week.* **9** a series of events or happenings: *She had a run of good luck in her business.* **10** a series of shows or performances: *The wonderful play had a two-year run in New York.* **11** life in general: *In the general run of things (general run of business, of life, etc.), he always makes time to play with his children.* **12** a hole or separation, as in pantyhose: *She has a run in her pantyhose.* **13** a movement of a large group of animals (usu. fish), (*syn.*) a migration: *A salmon run up a stream gives fresh fish to the bears.* **14 in the long run:** from now far into the future: *Losing weight now is difficult, but you will feel better in the long run if you lose it.* **15 in the short run:** from now into the near future: *In the short run, he can work two jobs and not get sick, but it will be bad for his health to do it for too long.* **16 to be on the run:** to hurry to get

R

away, escape, esp. from police: *That thief is on the run, so he is hiding in disguise.* **17 to give s.o. a run for his or her money:** to try very hard to win, to try to beat s.o.: *Our basketball team gave the champions a run for their money by beating them by two points.* **18 to go for a run:** to exercise by running: *He goes for a run around the park every morning.* **19 to have the run of the place:** to move about freely in s.o. else's house or property: *I gave my friend the run of my apartment while I am away.* **20 to make a run for it:** to go quickly to get to safety, flee danger: *The ceiling started to fall down in the old building, and the workers had to make a run for it. See:* walk, USAGE NOTE.
—*n.pl.* **the runs:** diarrhea, liquid bowel movement: *He has the runs and has to go to the bathroom often.*

run·a·round /'rʌnə,raʊnd/ *n.infrml.* [U] the act of not doing one's job, taking responsibility, or solving s.o.'s problem: *I tried to return a stereo that didn't work, but I just got the runaround: the store blamed the maker and the maker blamed the store, so no one returned my money.*

run·a·way /'rʌnə,weɪ/ *adj.* having lost control, moving wildly: *A runaway car rolled down a hill and crashed into ten cars.*
—*n.* a person, esp. a young person, who runs away from home: *Runaways come to this park and beg for money.*

run·down /'rʌn,daʊn/ *n.infrml.* a summary of important events or information: *I went to a computer conference, and then I gave my boss a rundown of what I learned there.*

run-down *adj.* in poor condition, needing to be fixed, (*syn.*) dilapidated: *That old house is run-down and needs repairs and painting.*

rung /rʌŋ/ *n.* **1** a step on a ladder: *To be safe, you should go up a ladder one rung at a time.* **2** a position or level of importance in a group or organization: *She has reached the highest rung of management and won't be promoted any more at work.*
—*v.past part. of* ring: *The telephone had rung three times when I picked it up.*

run-in *n.* an argument, angry fight with s.o.: *He is an angry person, and many people have had run-ins with him.*

run·ner /'rʌnər/ *n.* **1** a person who runs either for fun or competitively: *She is a long-distance runner, and she likes to run marathons.* **2** a strip of metal used to attach things to s.t., such as a wall or ceiling: *He put lights on a runner on his ceiling to light up the pictures on his walls.*

runner-up /,rʌnər'ʌp/ *n.* a person who places second, third, fourth, etc. in a competition or game: *In a Miss America contest, even the runners-up are talented young women.*

run·ning /'rʌnɪŋ/ *n.* [U] **1** an act of moving the legs and feet rapidly: *She likes running every morning.* **2 to be in/out of the running:** to have a possibility/no possibility to win: *These three contestants are still in the running and might win.‖He was out of the running early in the contest, so he went home.*
—*adj.* moving like water moves, (*syns.*) flowing, pouring: *That cabin in the woods has running water in the kitchen and the bathroom.*

running mate *n.* a person, esp. a politician, who tries to get elected to office with s.o. else: *The president and vice-president are running mates who are elected together.*

running start *n.fig.* a quick beginning of s.t., starting s.t. quickly and well: *He is off to a running start in his new job because he knows a lot about computers.*

run·ny /'rʌni/ *adj.* **-nier, -niest** more like a liquid than a solid, watery, (*syn.*) viscous: *That child's nose is runny because she has a cold.*

run·off /'rʌn,ɔf/ *n.adj.* **1** [C] a final contest between winners of earlier contests to choose the winner: *The two candidates had a <n.> runoff* (or) *<adj.> runoff election.* **2** [U] water that doesn't go into the ground, but runs from higher to lower ground, (*syn.*) drainage: *This pond collects runoff.*

run-of-the-mill *adj.fig.* regular, ordinary, average: *He is a run-of-the-mill student whose work is never perfect, but never very bad. See:* middle-of-the-road.

run-on *adj.* using a comma incorrectly to separate main clauses; lengthy, wordy: *Some students use commas incorrectly and thus make run-on sentences.*

runt /rʌnt/ *n.* **1** an animal that is smaller than others: *That dog is a runt who was smaller than his brothers and sisters.* **2** *pej.* a short person who is taller than a dwarf but shorter than normal: *He is a runt and he isn't strong physically, but he is very intelligent.*

run-through *n.* an informal performance of s.t., such as a rehearsal or review: *Actors did a first run-through of a new play.*

run-up *n.* an increase in s.t., esp. a large rise in a short time: *A run-up in the price of new cars caused people to drive older cars longer.*

run·way /'rʌn,weɪ/ *n.* **1** a place where airplanes take off and land: *A jetliner taxied down the runway and took off.* **2** a long stage where models walk, (*syn.*) catwalk: *Models moved down the runway, showing new clothing designs.*

rup·ture /'rʌptʃər/ *v.* **-tured, -turing, -tures** to burst or break open so that s.t. comes out of its closed container: *A water pipe ruptured and flooded the street.*
—*n.* [C;U] a break or split in s.t.: *There was a rupture in diplomatic relations between the*

R

two countries because of a disagreement about the countries' borders.

ru·ral /'rʊrəl/ *adj.* related to the countryside, not the city, (*syn.*) rustic: *They live on a farm in a rural area of Montana.*

ruse /ruz/ *n.* a trick, attempt to lie or cheat s.o.: *The children thought of a clever ruse to get their mother to leave the house so they could get ready for her surprise party.*

rush /rʌʃ/ *v.* **-es 1** to move about doing things quickly, hurry: *She rushed to get ready for an evening at the theater.* **2** to move quickly: *When she fell, a friend rushed to help her get up.* **3** *phrasal v. insep.* **to rush in/into s.t.: a.** to enter a place quickly, run into: *Firefighters rushed into the building to save people from the fire.* **b.** to make a decision too quickly, without thinking: *I don't think that you should rush into getting married so young.* **4** *phrasal v.* **to rush over:** to go someplace quickly: *When I saw that my friend was hurt, I rushed over to help her.*
—*n.* **1** [C;U] a hurry, the act of doing things quickly: *There is always a rush in the stores at holiday time.* **2 to be in a rush: a.** to hurry, do everything quickly: *She is always in a rush to go someplace.* **b.** to make a hasty and often unwise decision: *Don't be in a big rush to invest your money now; you might lose it.*

rush hour *n.* a time when traffic is very heavy, esp. when people are going to and from work: *Try not to drive between 4:00 and 6:00 P.M. because that's rush hour in this city.*

rus·set /'rʌsɪt/ *adj.* a reddish dark brown: *The leaves of oak trees turn to a russet color in the autumn.*

Rus·sian dressing /'rʌʃən/ *n.* [U] a salad dressing made of mayonnaise, ketchup, and often small pieces of pickles: *Russian dressing tastes good on a green salad.*

Russian roulette *n.* [U] a dangerous game in which one bullet is placed in a six-shooter revolver, the cylinder is spun around, the gun is pointed at one's head, and the trigger is pulled; if the bullet falls in line, the player kills himself: *In some James Bond™ movies, characters play Russian roulette.*

rust /rʌst/ *n.* [U] the reddish-brown material that forms on metal when oxygen reacts with

it: *Rust has made holes in the fenders of my car.*
—*adj.* a reddish-brown color: *The leaves of oak trees turn a rust color in the fall.*
—*v.* to form rust on metal: *My car's fenders have rusted.*

rus·tic /'rʌstɪk/ *adj.* related to the countryside, esp. with old, interesting buildings: *They live in a rustic fishing village.*

rus·tle /'rʌsəl/ *n.sing.* a soft sound, such as that made by a breeze moving through leaves: *You can hear the rustle of the leaves as the wind blows through them.*
—*v.* **-tled, -tling, -tles 1** to make a soft, brushing sound: *The wind blowing through the window rustled the papers on the table.* **2** to steal animals, such as cattle or horses: *We watched an old movie about two men who rustled horses.* **-n. rustler.**

rust·proof /'rʌst,pruf/ *adj.* not likely to rust: *Aluminum is a rustproof metal.*

rust·y /'rʌsti/ *adj.* **-ier, -iest 1** having rust, covered with rust: *My car is rusty and needs to be cleaned and painted.* **2** *fig.* (usu. of a skill) no longer as good as before: *His French is rusty because he hasn't spoken it for years.*

rut (1) /rʌt/ *n.* **1** a deep mark or long hole made by wheels in a road: *Ruts in the dirt road make it difficult to drive on.* **2 to get into a rut:** to do the same boring things over and over: *I need a new job because I feel like I've gotten into a rut.*
—*v.* **rutted, rutting, ruts** to form ruts: *When the ground is wet and muddy, vehicles rut the roads.*

rut (2) *n.* (with animals) the time when animals mate: *Deer go into rut in the autumn.*

ruth·less /'ruθlɪs/ *adj.* without pity, not thinking about the feelings or health of other people, (*syns.*) cold-blooded, merciless: *He is a ruthless businessman who thinks money is more important than people.* **-n.** [U] **ruthlessness.**

Rx /'ar'ɛks/ *n.abbr. for* prescription or remedy, medicine: *My doctor gave me an Rx for my high blood pressure.*

rye /raɪ/ *n.* [U] a cereal grain used to make flour and whiskey and to feed animals: *Rye is planted both in the autumn and in the spring.*

S,s

S,s /ɛs/ **S's, s's** or **Ss, ss** the 19th letter of the English alphabet

Sab·bath /'sæbəθ/ *n.* the last day of the week, the day of rest and worship: *Christians observe the Sabbath on Sunday.*

sab·bat·i·cal /sə'bætəkəl/ *n.adj.* a period of rest, usu. from a university, for travel and study, usu. with pay: *She isn't teaching this year because she's on <n.> sabbatical or on <adj.> sabbatical leave in Europe.*

USAGE NOTE: People take *sabbaticals* for both professional and personal development: *My physics professor is taking a sabbatical this year to finish writing a textbook for high school students.*

---

sa·ber /'seɪbər/ *n.* a heavy military sword with a curved blade: *His pirate costume includes a rusty saber.*

sab·o·tage /'sæbə,tɑʒ/ *n.v.* the deliberate damage of s.t.: *A worker <v.> sabotaged wires and cut off electricity to parts of the city.||It was an act of <n.> sabotage.*

sab·o·teur /,sæbə'tɜr/ *n.* a person who commits sabotage

sack /sæk/ *n.* **1** a bag made of cloth or paper: *The farmers put corn into the big, brown sacks.* **2** *slang* **to get the sack:** to be fired: *He got the sack and is now unemployed.* **3** *slang* **to hit the sack:** to go to bed: *I'm tired; I'm going to hit the sack.*
—*v.* **1** to place or pour into a sack: *They sacked the groceries at the supermarket.* **2** to rob or destroy: *to sack a city* **3** *infrml.* to end s.o.'s employment: *Her boss sacked her for missing too much work.* **4** *phrasal v.* **to sack out:** to go to bed, sleep: *After working all day, I like to sack out for an hour before dinner.*

sacrament /'sækrəmənt/ *n.* a religious act meant to have spiritual benefits: *To Christians, baptism is a sacrament in which people are welcomed into the Christian faith.*

sa·cred /'seɪkrɪd/ *adj.* **1** holy: *For religious people, a wedding ceremony is sacred.* **2** *fig.* **a sacred cow:** s.o. or s.t. that should not be harmed or destroyed: *Old-age pensions are a sacred cow; the government will always keep them.*

sac·ri·fice /'sækrə,faɪs/ *n.* [C;U] **1** loss, or giving up of s.t. valuable, for a specific purpose: *The parents made many sacrifices, such as wearing old clothes, to pay for their children's university education.* **2** an offering to a god: *Some religions think the sacrifice of an animal will bring wealth to their people.*
—*v.* **-ficed, -ficing, -fices** to suffer loss, pain, or injury to achieve a goal: *The father worked hard and made a lot of money, but he sacrificed his health. -adj.* **sacrificial** /,sækrə'fɪʃəl/.

sac·ri·le·gious /,sækrə'lɪdʒəs/ *adj.* s.t. wrong, going against religious rules: *My aunt thought it was sacrilegious when a construction company converted the church into apartments. -n.* [C;U] **sacrilege** /'sækrəlɪdʒ/.

sac·ro·sanct /'sækrou,sæŋkt/ *adj.* to be respected and never changed, holy: *Once that man makes a promise, it is sacrosanct; he will not break it.*

sad /sæd/ *adj.* **sadder, saddest 1** full of sorrow, unhappy, (*syn.*) sorrowful: *After her mother's death, she was sad for weeks.* **2** (s.t.) unfortunate, regrettable: *Being poor is a sad situation.* **3** bad, (*syn.*) lamentable: *The business lost lots of money; it's now in sad condition. -adv.* **sadly; -n.** **sadness.**

sad·den /'sædn/ *v.* to make unhappy: *I was saddened by my father's death.*

sad·dle /'sædl/ *n.* **1** the leather seat used for riding animals, usu. horses: *She put the saddle on her horse and then went riding.* **2** **back in the saddle:** working again: *He was sick for months, but got healthy and is back in the saddle again.*
—*v.* **-dled, -dling, -dles 1** to put a saddle (on a horse): *He saddled the horse quickly and rode away.* **2** to give s.o. too much work or responsibility: *The manager was saddled with so many problems that he could not work well.* **3** *phrasal v. sep.* **to saddle s.t. up:** to get on a horse, pony, etc.: *The calvary officer gave an order to saddle up at dawn.*

sa·dism /'seɪ,dɪzəm, 'sæ-/ *n.* [U] **1** pleasure (esp. sexual) from hurting others: *The word "sadism" comes from the Marquis de Sade, who hurt and tortured people for sexual pleasure.* **2** strong cruelty to others: *It was an act of sadism to tell the child her parents were dead, because they were alive. -n.* **sadist;** *-adj.* **sadistic** /sə'dɪstɪk/.

safe /seɪf/ *n.* a strong metal container, usu. with a lock, for protecting money and valuables: *She has a safe in her closet where she keeps her jewelry.*
—*adj.* **safer, safest 1** free from harm, protected: *She likes to feel safe, so she bought burglar alarm systems for her car and home.* **2 safe and sound:** unharmed, not hurt: *They arrived home safe and sound after driving in a storm.*

safe·guard /'seɪf,gɑrd/ *n.* [C] a guarantee against loss, harm, or injury: *A seat belt is a safeguard that must be in all new American cars.*
—*v.* to guarantee against loss, harm, or injury: *We have safeguarded the castle so that the enemy stays out.*

safe·keep·ing /'seɪf'kipɪŋ/ *n.* [U] care until s.t. is needed: *She put her money in a locked box for safekeeping.*

safe·ty /'seɪfti/ *n.* [U] **1** the condition of being free or protected from harm: *When the floods arrived, the farmers moved to high ground and safety.* **2 safety in numbers:** better protection because of being with others: *Fish seek safety in numbers by swimming in large groups.*

safety belt *n.* a long, thin piece of material that holds and protects a person in a car (truck, airplane, etc.): *I was wearing my safety belt, so I was not hurt when the car crashed. See:* seat belt, USAGE NOTE.

safety net *n.* **1** *lit.* a mesh of rope or wire to catch someone from above: *The circus performer walked on a rope in the air, fell, and landed in a safety net.* **2** *fig.* a situation, sometimes a government program, that makes sure people will have life's basic needs, such as food and shelter: *The state paid the poor family $500 a month as a safety net.*

safety pin *n.* a small piece of metal used to bring two pieces of cloth together: *Do you have a safety pin? The zipper on my pants is broken.*

safety pin

saf·fron /'sæfrən/ *n.* [U] a plant made into an expensive yellow-orange spice for cooking: *My Spanish grandfather uses saffron to flavor his rice.*

sag /sæg/ *n.* a low or loose area in s.t.: *All of the snow has caused a sag in the roof of our house. See:* dip.
—*v.* **1** to bend or sink downward from weight or pressure: *The tent sagged under the weight of the wet snow.* **2** to feel and look tired and depressed: *Business is so bad that the workers' spirits are sagging.*

sa·ga /'sɑgə/ *n.* a long, detailed story full of adventure: *The film was a three-hour saga of World War II.*

sage /seɪdʒ/ *n.* a very wise person: *The sage told the king to listen to his advisors.*
—*adj.* wise: *My mother gives me sage advice about my business, because she has owned her business for 30 years.*

said /sɛd/ **1** *past part. of* say: *He said that the meeting is today.* **2 when all is said and done:** in the final analysis: *When all is said and done, the meeting will only confirm the fact that everyone knows that the Director is resigning.*

sail /seɪl/ *n.* **1** [C] the strong cloth that helps a boat move with the wind: *The sails on the ship were not moving; there was no wind.* **2** *sing.* a trip by boat: *On Sunday afternoons, we like to go for a sail on the lake.*
—*v.* **1** to travel by boat: *We sailed across the lake and back.* **2** to begin a water trip: *The ship sails* (or) *sets sail tomorrow, good weather or bad.* **3** *fig.* to move easily, with no problems: *The happy woman sailed through her medical exam. -n.* [C;U] **sailing.**

sail·boat /'seɪl,boʊt/ *n.* a boat with one or more sails: *Our sailboat is small but moves fast on the pond.*

sail·or /'seɪlər/ *n.* **1** a person who works on a ship: *The sailors learned how to tie ropes and steer the ship.* **2** a person who knows how to use a sailboat: *My mother grew up on the coast and is a good sailor.*

saint /seɪnt/ *n.* **1** (in Christianity) a person chosen by God: *We prayed to the saints every Sunday in church.* **2** a very good and kind person: *You were a saint to give money to the hungry child. -n.* [U] **sainthood** /'seɪnt,hʊd/, **saintliness;** *-adj.* **saintly.**

sake /seɪk/ *n.* **1** peace of mind, good: *For your brother's sake, don't be late to his wedding.* **2** purpose: *For the sake of discussion, let's say the building will cost $1 million to build.* **3** *vulg.* **for Christ's** or **God's sake:** expression of annoyance: *Oh, for Christ's sake, will you shut up and get to work?*

sal·a·ble /'seɪləbəl/ *adj. See:* saleable.

sa·la·cious /sə'leɪʃəs/ *adj.frml.* related to sexual desire: *Don't let your ten-year-old read salacious books; she's too young to read about sex.*

sal·ad /'sæləd/ *n.* [C;U] **1** a mixture of vegetables, fruit, or other foods, usu. served cold with a dressing: *I made a salad of lettuce, tomatoes,*

S

and cucumbers, with a dressing of oil and vinegar. **2 chef's salad:** a large salad that includes meat and cheese **3 salad bar:** in a restaurant, a place to make one's own salad, with many choices of vegetables, meats, cheeses, and dressings

USAGE NOTE: *Salad bars* are common in restaurants in the USA. For a fixed price, customers can return to the salad bar as many times as they like. Some salad bars offer bread and soup as well as salad: *I didn't order a big meal at the restaurant last night; I just kept going back to the salad bar.*

salad days *n.fig.* days of one's youth, usu. full of different experiences and adventure: *During my salad days, I traveled around the country and fell in love many times.*

salad dressing *n.* a mixture of various liquid flavorings to pour over a salad, such as oil and vinegar or honey and mustard.

sa·la·mi /sə'lɑmi/ *n.* [C;U] a large, seasoned sausage: *I had a salami and cheese sandwich for lunch.*

sal·a·ry /'sæləri/ *n.* [C;U] **-ries** a regular payment from a business or organization for work done: *My salary increases 5 percent this year. See:* wage, USAGE NOTE.

sal·a·ried /'sælərid/ *adj.* related to receiving regular pay for work done: *Salaried employees get their checks once a week here.*

sale /seɪl/ *n.* **1** the exchange of s.t. for money: *the sale of a shirt (car, house, etc.)* **2** the selling of things at a lower price than usual: *The pet store is having a sale on dog food.* **3 for sale:** available for purchase: *We don't want our car anymore; it is for sale.* **4 on sale:** available for a lower price than usual: *I bought this coat on sale, for $20 less than the original price.* **5 to have a sale:** (for a seller) to offer things at a discount price: *The department store has a sale on shirts and ties.* **6 to make a sale:** (for a seller) to take money in exchange for s.t.: *The salesperson made a sale and earned a 5 percent commission.*

sale·a·ble /'seɪlëbël/ *adj.* in good condition for sale: *This bicycle is five years old, but it is still in saleable condition.*

sales clerk *n.* a person who helps customers and sells things, esp. in a store: *The sales clerk brought the pants to the dressing room for me to try on. See:* clerk.

sales·man /'seɪlzmən/ *n.* **-men** /-mən/ *See:* salesperson.

sales·man·ship /'seɪlzmən,ʃɪp/ *n.* [U] the ability to sell things and to convince people to buy things, (*syn.*) persuasiveness: *You showed great salesmanship in knowing all about these*

shoes, giving me a good price, and putting them in a box for me.

sales·per·son /'seɪlz,pərsən/ *n.* a man or woman whose job is to sell things: *My company gives a prize to the salesperson who sells the most.*

sales receipt *n.* a small piece of paper given to a buyer after a purchase, usu. showing the date, item(s) bought, and money spent: *When I returned the TV, the salesperson asked me for the sales receipt as proof of purchase.*

sales representative or **sales rep** *n.* s.o. whose job is to sell goods and services, a salesperson: *A sales representative called and tried to sell me some insurance.*

sales slip *n.* a sales receipt: *Did the clerk give you a sales slip when you bought those shoes?*

sales tax *n.* a percentage added to the price of s.t. and given to the local or state government: *In our state, we pay an 8 percent sales tax on all purchases except food.*

sales·wom·an /'seɪlz,wʊmən/ **-women** /-,wɪmən/ *n. See:* salesperson.

sa·li·ent /'seɪliənt, 'seɪlyənt/ *adj.* most obvious or noticeable: *I remembered only a few salient remarks from the long speech.*

sa·li·va /sə'laɪvə/ *n.* the liquid in the mouth that helps us chew and digest food -*v.* **salivate** /'sælə,veɪt/.

sal·low /'sælou/ *adj.* yellowish, sick-looking (skin): *The old lady in the hospital bed looked sallow and weak.*

salm·on /'sæmən/ *n.* a fish with reddish-pink flesh: *I like to eat grilled salmon with potatoes.* **2** *n.adj.* a reddish-pink color: *She wore a <adj.> salmon skirt with white shoes to the party.*

sa·lon /sə'lɑn, 'sæl,ɑn/ *n.* **1** a shop or place for business, usu. related to fashion or beauty: *I get my hair cut at Andre's Hair Salon.* **2** a formal living room: *After dinner we had coffee in the salon.*

sa·loon /sə'lun/ *n.* a place where alcoholic beverages are sold and drunk, esp. in the western USA many years ago: *In that old John Wayne movie, two men drink whiskey and play cards in a saloon. See:* bar.

sal·sa /'sɑlsə/ *n.* [U] **1** a mixture of tomatoes, onions, and peppers, usu. eaten with tortilla chips: *At my favorite Mexican restaurant, I always order chips with salsa.* **2** a lively style of Latin American music: *I listened to salsa when I lived in Central America. See:* enchilada, USAGE NOTE.

salt /sɔlt/ *n.* [U] **1** the chemical compound sodium chloride, used to flavor food: *Would you pass the salt, please?* **2 salt of the earth:** a good, helpful, friendly person: *He is the salt of the earth to lend me his car for a week.* **3 to**

S

be worth one's salt: to be good enough to deserve s.t., usu. money: *I need to work hard to be worth my salt.* **4 to rub salt in a wound:** to cause a bad or painful feeling to become worse: *The divorce made the child sad, and when her mother remarried, it rubbed salt in the wound.* **5 to take s.t. with a grain of salt:** to understand that s.t. may not be completely true: *You told me there were 300 people at the party; I'll take that with a grain of salt.*
—*v.* **1** to sprinkle salt on s.t.: *I salted the steak to make it taste better.*

salt·y /'sɔlti/ *adj.* **-ier, -iest 1** having the taste of salt: *This soup tastes too salty for me.* **2** *fig.* (of language) bad, (*syns.*) vulgar, colorful: *The old sailor told salty stories.*

sa·lu·bri·ous /sə'lubriəs/ *adj.frml.* good for the health: *After working so hard, I found my mountain vacation to be very salubrious.*

sal·u·ta·tion /ˌsælyə'teɪʃən/ *n.* [C;U] s.t. said or written at the beginning of a conversation or letter, (*syn.*) a greeting: *The salutation of the letter read "Dear Mom."*

sa·lute /sə'lut/ *n.* [C] **1** a hand, usu. the right one, raised to the forehead to recognize or honor s.o.: *Soldiers are trained to salute to greet other soldiers.* **2** a symbolic act of recognition: *The soldiers gave a 21-gun salute to honor the visit of the Korean president.*
—*v.* **1** to perform a symbolic act of recognition: *The president saluted the flag.* **2** to show respect or admiration: *I salute you for graduating with high honors from this great university.*

sal·vage /'sælvɪdʒ/ *n.* [U] the saving of s.t. damaged, esp. in a fire, wreck, etc.: *The ship is good for salvage because it can be raised from the bottom of the sea.*
—*v.* **-vaged, -vaging, -vages 1** to save s.t. that is damaged, esp. in a fire, wreck, etc.: *We will salvage the car parts from the accident.* **2** to save s.t. of value from an otherwise bad situation: *If you write Maria a note saying you're sorry, you can salvage your friendship with her.* -*adj.* **salvageable.**

sal·va·tion /sæl'veɪʃən/ *n.* [U] **1** the protection or saving of s.o. from difficulty or danger: *The job was her salvation, because she had no more money.* **2** the act of saving s.o. from sin: *The minister prayed for the evil woman's salvation.*

Sal·va·tion Army *n.* an international Christian organization that uses military titles and terms, known for helping the poor

salve /sæv, sav/ *n.* **1** a semi-solid medicine to rub on a cut or other discomfort on the skin: *He put salve on an itchy mosquito bite.* **2** s.t. that comforts or makes one feel better: *Her apology was a salve for my anger.*
—*v.* **salved, salving, salves** to make s.t. feel better, comfort, (*syn.*) to soothe: *Giving money to the local hospital salves my conscience.*

same /seɪm/ *adj.* identical, alike, equal: *He wore the same suit today as yesterday.*
—*adv.* **1** identically, equally: *She was sick yesterday, and she feels the same today.* **2 all the same** or **just the same:** in spite of: *I hate to lie in the sun, but I'm going to the beach all the same* (or) *just the same.*
—*n.* **1 all the same to me:** not making any difference: *Do you want to eat before or after the movie? It doesn't matter; it's all the same to me.* **2 same here:** an expression of agreement, (*syn.*) me too: *"I was born in July." "Same here!"*

same·ness /'seɪmnɪs/ *n.* [U] being alike, not changing, perhaps indicating boredom: *All those brick houses have a sameness to them.*

sam·ple /'sæmpəl/ *v.* **-pled, -pling, -ples** to try s.t.: *I sampled each dessert on the menu.||I sampled life in Hong Kong and loved it.*
—*n.* **1** a single thing that shows what a larger group is like: *The tailor showed us samples of silk, wool, and cotton.* **2** a small amount of s.t. to try: *The clerk gave me a sample of cheese to taste; it was so delicious that I bought a pound.* **3** a small part of a larger group, used to study the larger group: *The teacher asked a sample of students if the school should build a new library.*

san·a·tor·i·um /ˌsænə'tɔriəm/ *n.* a hospital for long-term care of people who are mentally or physically ill: *The family put their aging mother in a sanatorium. See:* sanitarium.

sanc·ti·fy /'sæŋktəˌfaɪ/ *v.* **-fied, -fying, -fies** to make holy: *The couple sanctified their wedding day by having a priest marry them in a church.*

sanc·ti·mo·ni·ous /ˌsæŋktə'moʊniəs/ *adj.* pretending to be better or more holy than one really is: *In a sanctimonious voice, you said I should go to church as often as you.*

sanc·tion /'sæŋkʃən/ *n.* **1** [U] approval, official permission (to do s.t.): *I need my parents' sanction to stay out late.* **2** [C] a law or rule that punishes or deprives s.o.: *Our government has sanctions against countries that ignore human rights.*
—*v.* to give formal approval of s.t.: *Dad sanctioned our use of the car on Saturday and Sunday.*

sanc·ti·ty /'sæŋktəti/ *n.* **-ties** sacredness, holiness: *Tourists should respect the sanctity of cathedrals they visit.*

sanc·tu·ar·y /'sæŋktʃuˌɛri/ *n.* **-ies 1** [C] a safe, protected place: *The little house gave us sanctuary from the wind and cold.* **2** [U] protection (from law or government), (*syn.*) asylum: *The escaped prisoner found sanctuary in a foreign embassy.* **3** [C] a holy place: *They built a sanctuary for the Virgin Mary high in the mountains.* **4** [C] the part of a Christian church where services or masses take place: *The nun*

S

sat in the sanctuary and listened to the choir above. **5** [C] a place where birds and animals may not be hunted: *We saw many interesting birds as we walked through the sanctuary.*

sand /sænd/ *n.* [U] tiny pieces of rock, millions of which form the surface of beaches and deserts: *At the beach, we like to dig for shells in the sand.* -*adj.* **sandy.** *See:* beach.
—*v.* to smooth the surface of s.t. with rough paper or a machine: *When you build a table, you should sand the wood before you paint it.* *See:* sandpaper.

san·dal /'sændl/ *n.* a shoe made of a sole with straps, allowing part of the foot to be seen: *I like to wear sandals in the summer; they feel very cool in the hot weather.*

sand·bag /'sænd,bæg/ *n.* a sack full of sand, used for weight or to hold water: *Thousands of sandbags kept the river from reaching the road.*
—*v.* **1** to lay sandbags for protection **2** *infrml.fig.* to force s.o., (*syn.*) to coerce: *I did not want to make the trip, but my boss sandbagged me into going.*

sand·blast /'sænd,blæst/ *v.n.* to clean brick, stone, or metal by shooting a mix of steam and sand onto it with great force: *They <v.> sandblasted the old brick building until it looked like new.*

sand·man /'sænd,mæn/ *n.fig.* an imaginary person who brings sleep, esp. to children: *At bedtime, the mother tells her little boy that the sandman will visit soon.*

sand·pa·per /'sænd,peɪpər/ *n.* [U] *v.* a strong paper with a layer of sand on one side to smooth wood or metal surfaces: *I used <n.> sandpaper to smooth the rough bookshelves.*

sand·stone /'sænd,stoʊn/ *n.* [U] a type of soft rock

sand·wich /'sændwɪʃ, 'sænwɪʧ/ *n.* two pieces of bread with other foods (such as cheese, meat, or vegetables) between them, eaten with the hands: *Would you put mustard on my ham sandwich, please?*
—*v.* to make time or room for s.t. between other events or objects: *My boss and I sandwiched a brief meeting between lunch and his appointment at 2:30.*

USAGE NOTE: Turkey and cheese with lettuce and tomato on wheat bread is a typical *sandwich.* Others are roast beef, ham and cheese, and bacon, lettuce, and tomato (called a "BLT"). When you order a *sandwich,* you say what *condiments* (mayonnaise, mustard, relish, etc.) you want on it as well as the kind of bread.

sane /seɪn/ *adj.* **1** mentally healthy: *Don't call me crazy; I am quite sane.* **2** sensible: *Going*

to bed early on Sunday night is the sane thing to do so you are ready for work on Monday.

san·i·tar·i·um /,sænə'tɛriəm/ *n.* a hospital for long-term care of people who are mentally or physically ill: *Their aunt had a bad alcohol problem, so she went to a sanitarium for treatment. See:* sanatorium.

san·i·tar·y /'sænə,tɛri/ *adj.* **1** free from dirt and germs: *The bathroom is sanitary now; I cleaned it with a germ killer.* **2** related to cleanliness and health: *We wash our hands before eating for sanitary reasons.*

sanitary napkin *n.* an absorbent pad worn in a woman's underpants during menstruation: *She bought sanitary napkins just before having her monthly period. See:* tampon.

san·i·ta·tion /,sænə'teɪʃən/ *n.* [U] **1** the act of keeping an area clean and germ-free: *Strict sanitation is used in businesses such as barber shops and restaurants.* **2** related to the collection of garbage: *The city's sanitation department collects garbage every Monday.*

san·i·tize /'sænə,taɪz/ *v.* **-tized, -tizing, -tizes** **1** to make very clean, (*syn.*) to disinfect: *Barbers sanitize scissors and combs by washing them with soap, then putting them in a germ-killing liquid.* **2** to make s.t. more acceptable to s.o. by removing parts of it (bad language, secret information, etc.): *Some movies with sex and strong language are sanitized for TV.*

san·i·ty /'sænəti/ *n.* [U] mental health: *He kept his sanity in prison by imagining a happy, free future.*

San·ta Claus /'sæntə,klɔz/ *n.* the imaginary old man with a white beard in a red suit who brings children presents at Christmas: *My little girl left milk and cookies for Santa Claus on Christmas Eve.*

sap /sæp/ *n.* **1** [U] the liquid that flows through plants to keep them alive and healthy: *We collect sap from maple trees to make syrup.* **2** [C] *infrml.* a rather stupid person who foolishly believes everything: *Don't be a sap; that guy is lying to you.*
—*v.* **sapped, sapping, saps** to remove (energy, strength, etc.): *He has cancer, and the disease saps his strength.* -*adj.* **sapped.**

sap·ling /'sæplɪŋ/ *n.* a young tree

sap·phire /'sæfaɪr/ *n.* [C;U] **1** a blue precious gemstone: *I have a sapphire in my ring.* **2** *n.adj.* a blue color: *Elizabeth Taylor has <adj.> sapphire eyes.*

sar·casm /'sar,kæzəm/ *n.* [U] an attitude or comments that hurt s.o.'s feelings, often by saying the opposite of what is meant: *She said with sarcasm, "Oh, sure, I'd love to spend all day listening to him gossip."*

S

sar·cas·tic /sar'kæstɪk/ *adj.* unkind, critical (comments, attitude): *Your sarcastic tone of voice shows that you don't respect your father.*

sar·dine /sar'din/ *n.* **1** a small fish, usu. sold packed tightly in cans **2 packed in like sardines:** very tightly together, with no space between: *At six o'clock, people pack into the subway like sardines.*

sar·don·ic /sar'danɪk/ *adj.* showing scorn, (*syns.*) sarcastic, cynical: *That journalist has a sardonic writing style; he criticizes everyone he writes about.*

sa·rong /sə'rɔŋ, -'raŋ/ *n.* a piece of cloth wrapped around the waist and hips as a skirt

sash /sæʃ/ *n.* **1** a long, thin strip of cloth used as a belt around the waist: *Will you tie the sash of my dress?* **2** the edge of a window

sass /sæs/ *v.n.* **-es** to speak to s.o. in a disrespectful way: *When the little boy <v.> sassed his parents, they sent him to his room.*

sas·sy /'sæsi/ *adj.* **-sier, -siest** quick and bold, often flirtatious: *The waitress loves to tease her customers with sassy jokes.*

Sa·tan /'seɪtn/ *n.* the Devil, the enemy of God and ruler of Hell **-n. satanism.**

sa·tan·ic /sə'tænɪk/ *adj.* evil, of Satan: *Satanic groups pray to the devil.*

satch·el /'sætʃəl/ *n.* a small bag worn over the shoulder, larger than a purse: *The woman left a satchel containing her gym clothes on the subway.*

sat·el·lite /'sætl,aɪt/ *n.* **1** a moon or other object in space that circles a larger object, such as a planet: *The moon we see at night is Earth's only satellite.* **2** a human-made object that circles a larger one in space: *The satellite had a camera that took pictures of Venus and Mars.* **3** an organization or a nation that is under the influence of a larger or more powerful one: *For many years, Eastern European countries were satellites of the Soviet Union.*

sat·in /'sætn/ *n.* [U] a fabric that is shiny and smooth on one side: *a dress made of satin* *—adj.* very smooth: *a table waxed to a satin finish* **-adv. satiny.**

sat·ire /'sætaɪr/ *n.* [C;U] an artistic style, often humorous, that makes people, society, or ideas seem foolish or ridiculous: *I read a satire that criticized the USA.* **-n.** [C] **satirist** /'sætərɪst/.

sa·tir·i·cal /sə'tɪrəkəl/ *adj.* critical by showing the foolishness of people, society, or ideas, often with humor: *The writer took a satirical look at rock music.*

sat·i·rize /'sætə,raɪz/ *v.* **-rized, -rizing, -rizes** to criticize by showing the foolishness of people, society, or ideas, often with humor: *A cartoon in the newspaper satirized the governor and his family.*

sat·is·fac·tion /,sætɪs'fækʃən/ *n.* **1** pleasure because of having enough, being content: *I get* satisfaction from exercising every day. **2** correction of s.t. wrong, payment of a debt: *The television that I bought was damaged, so the store gave me satisfaction by giving me a new one.*

sat·is·fac·to·ry /,sætɪs'fæktəri/ *adj.* **1** good enough, acceptable: *I would like to earn more, but my pay is satisfactory.* **2** not great, mediocre: *His homework is satisfactory, so I gave him a grade of C.*

sat·is·fy /'sætɪs,faɪ/ *v.* **-fied, -fying, -fies 1** to make happy: *She was satisfied with the new apartment.* **2** to meet wants or needs, get enough, (*syn.*) to fulfill: *She satisfied her hunger by eating a steak.||He satisfied his curiosity by asking lots of questions.* **-adj. satisfiable.**

sat·u·rate /'sætʃə,reɪt/ *v.* **-rated, -rating, -rates 1** to soak s.t. with a liquid until no more can be absorbed: *The rain is so heavy that it saturates the ground.* **2** *fig.* to be completely full of s.t.: *He was saturated with alcohol; he was so drunk he could not walk.||That book is saturated with incorrect facts.* **-n.** [U] **saturation.**

Sat·ur·day /'sætər,deɪ, -di/ *n.* the seventh day of the week, between Friday and Sunday

sa·tyr /'seɪtər, 'sæ-/ *n.* **1** (in mythology) a goatlike male with great sexual needs and powers **2** a man with strong sexual needs, (*syn.*) a lecher.

sauce /sɔs/ *n.* [C;U] **1** a flavored liquid poured over food: *I love to eat chocolate sauce on vanilla ice cream.||My father puts butter sauce on his fish.* **2** *infrml.fig.* **on the sauce:** drinking many alcoholic beverages: *He had four beers; he's on the sauce again.*

sau·cer /'sɔsər/ *n.* **1** a small plate, usu. with a circular mark for holding a cup **2 flying saucer:** a spaceship (esp. an imaginary one): *The little girl saw a movie about flying saucers from outer space.*

sauc·y /'sɔsi/ *adj.* **-ier, -iest** rude, (*syns.*) impertinent, insolent: *He's a saucy child who's always arguing with his parents.*

sate /seɪt/ *v.frml.* **sated, sating, sates** to get more than enough, fill: *He was sated after eating eggs, oatmeal, fruit, and coffee for breakfast.* **-adj. sated.**

sau·na /'sɔnə, 'saʊ-/ *n.* a type of bath in which water is poured on hot rocks to make steam

saun·ter /'sɔntər/ *v.* to walk without hurrying: *She had the whole afternoon to saunter around the neighborhood.*

sau·sage /'sɔsɪdʒ/ *n.* [C;U] a round section of seasoned meat: *We eat pork sausage for breakfast.*

sau·té /sɔ'teɪ/ *v.* **-téed, -téing, -tés** (French for) to fry food quickly in hot oil or fat: *I sautéed onions and garlic, then added a piece of chicken.* **-adj. sautéed.**

S

sav·age /'sævɪdʒ/ n. **1** a wild, fierce person, often from a primitive society: *The savages threw spears and killed their enemies.* **2** a person who acts wildly or badly: *The murderer is a savage who should to go jail.*
—*adj.* **1** wild, untamed: *Savage lions live in Africa.* **2** cruel, (*syn.*) ferocious: *The enemy planned a savage attack; many children were killed.*

save /seɪv/ v. **saved, saving, saves 1** not to spend or use, to keep s.t., esp. money, for the future: *I have saved all the photographs that I took when I was young.||I save a little money every month and put it in the bank.* **2** to spend less than usual on s.t.: *The shopper saved a lot of money by comparing prices.* **3** to make s.t. unnecessary: *You'll save a phone call later if you ask the question now.* **4** (in computers) to keep newly added information in a file by using a "save" command: *Please save the paragraph on your screen so it will not be lost.* **5** to prevent s.o. from being harmed: *The little boy was drowning in the lake; a woman jumped in and saved him.* **6 to save face:** to stay dignified, lessen embarrassment: *The poor student saved face with her rich classmates by always wearing nice, clean clothes.* **7** *phrasal v. insep.* **to save on s.t.:** to avoid wasting s.t.: *Installing solar panels saves on energy costs.* **8 to save one's breath:** to be quiet because talking is useless: *We are definitely not going to the beach; save your breath and stop asking! See:* penny; stitch. **9 to save one's skin** or **neck:** to escape injury: *His car crashed, but his seat belt saved his neck.* **10 to save s.t. for a rainy day:** to keep s.t. or to save money for difficult times: *The girl wanted to spend a dollar on candy, but her uncle told her to save it for a rainy day.*

sav·ings /'seɪvɪŋz/ n.pl. money saved: *I put my savings in the bank.*

savings account n. a bank account that receives small interest payments: *I put $600 in my savings account last year and earned 5 percent annual interest. See:* bank account, passbook.

savings and loan association n. a cooperative bank that takes in deposits as shares and makes mortgage loans on property

savings bank n. a bank where one can open savings accounts and get loans, esp. on mortgages

sav·ior /'seɪvyər/ n. **1** s.o. who saves s.o. else: *This mayor has created jobs and helped the poor; she is the city's savior.* **2** (in Christianity) Jesus Christ (usu. used with "the" or "our"): *The minister said, "Our Savior died on the cross."*

sa·voir faire /'sævwɑr'fɛr/ n. (French for "to know what to do") the ability to do the correct thing, to know how to act in various situations:

She showed her savoir faire by using the correct fork at a fancy dinner.

sa·vor /'seɪvər/ n. *usu.sing.*[C;U] a good taste or smell: *the savor of fine wine*
—*v.* **1** to taste and enjoy s.t.: *I savored dinner last night; we had roast beef and good red wine.* **2** to appreciate and enjoy an experience: *The baseball team savored their win.*

sa·vor·y /'seɪvəri/ adj. **1** having a good taste or smell: *We love the savory smell of Thanksgiving dinner.* **2** salty, not sweet: *The shop sells savory meat pies and sweet fruit pies.*

sav·vy /'sævi/ adj.infrml. **-vier, -viest** smart, knowledgeable: *Ask her to help you buy a camera; she's very savvy about photography.*
—*n.* know-how, knowledge: *That politician has a lot of savvy about how to talk to TV and newspaper reporters.*

saw /sɔ/ v.n. **1** a tool or machine with a sharp, rough edge and handle used for cutting wood or metal: *The woman <v.> sawed some wood for the fire.* **2 old saw:** an old, unoriginal idea: *Don't believe the old saw "an apple a day keeps the doctor away." See:* adage.

saw·dust /'sɔ,dʌst/ n. the small pieces of wood that fall off s.t. that is being sawed: *A little pile of sawdust formed under the log as the man sawed it in half.*

sax·o·phone /'sæksə,foʊn/ n. a musical horn, made of brass, with a reed in the mouthpiece, often U-shaped

say /seɪ/ v. **said** /sɛd/, **saying, says** /sɛz/ **1** to express in words from the mouth: *If you don't like me, then say it.* **2** to express thoughts in writing or another nonspoken way: *I said what I felt in a love letter.||Your eyes are saying you love me, too.*
—*n.* [C;U] an opinion to express, a vote: *I have a say in how much to spend; I think we should spend $90.*

saxophone

say·ing /'seɪɪŋ/ n. a wise thought, (*syns.*) a proverb, a maxim: *There is a saying that "you can't teach an old dog new tricks."*

say-so /'seɪ,soʊ/ n. power to decide, authority: *We want to hire a new salesperson, but we need the boss's say-so.*

scab /skæb/ n. **1** blood that dries and becomes hard on the skin: *I cut my knee when I fell, and now there's a scab.* **2** a person hired to replace striking union workers: *When the airline workers went on strike, the airline hired scabs to replace them. See:* picket line, USAGE NOTE.

scads /skædz/ n.pl.infrml. a lot of, many: *My brother works on Wall Street and makes scads of money.*

scaf·fold /'skæfəld, -,oʊld/ n. a temporary frame with a place where people can sit or stand while working on a building: *The* painters stood on a scaffold near the third-floor windows. -n. [U] **scaffolding.**

scald /skɔld/ v. to burn with hot liquid or steam: *The hot water in the shower scalded me.*

scald·ing /skɔldɪŋ/ adj. extremely hot: *scalding oil*

scale /skeɪl/ n. **1** an instrument for weighing things: *I weighed six apples on the scale.||According to the scale, I've lost four pounds.* **2** [C;U] a system of measurement or comparison: *On a scale of 1 to 10, I rate this film a 7, quite good.* **3** [C] on a map, a small chart that shows the actual distance: *The scale for this map is 1 inch equals 100 miles.* **4** [C] (in music) a set of notes with the same interval between each one: *She played a C-major scale on the piano.* **5** [C] a section of the skin on a fish or a reptile: *a fish scale* **6 on a large** or **small scale:** in a big (or) small way: *In a big city like New York, people think of life on a large scale.||The jeweler works on a small scale, with tiny tools.*

—v. **scaled, scaling, scales 1** to climb s.t.: *Monica scaled the ladder and painted her house.* **2** to remove the skin of fish **3** phrasal v.sep. **to scale s.t. down:** to reduce in size: *When business is bad, companies scale down the number of workers.||They scaled them down.*

scal·lop /ˈskæləp, ˈskɑ-/ n. an edible shellfish with a curved-edge shell: *Many people eat small bay scallops or large sea scallops in a butter sauce.*

—adj. a curved decorative edge: *That chair has a beautiful scalloped design.*

scalp /skælp/ n. the skin on the head, usu. covered with hair: *Some shampoos make your scalp itch.*

—v. to sell s.t. (esp. tickets) at a higher price than the original price: *We couldn't go to the basketball game, so we scalped our tickets.* -n. **scalper.**

scal·pel /ˈskælpəl/ n. a very sharp surgical knife: *With a scalpel, the doctor cut into the patient's leg.*

scal·y /ˈskeɪli/ adj. **-ier, -iest** full of scales (as an animal or fish) -n. [U] **scaliness.**

scam /skæm/ n. a plan to make money by deception or fraud, (syn.) a swindle: *They ran a scam where they burned cars and collected insurance money.*

scan /skæn/ n. , usu.sing. **1** a look at s.t. to see as much information as possible in a short time: *I gave the menu a quick scan and chose the chicken.* **2** an examination of the inside of the body with a special machine: *I have terrible headaches, so my doctor gave me a brain scan.*

—v. **scanned, scanning, scans 1** to look at s.t. and see as much as possible in a short time: *I*

scanned the newspaper. **2** (in medicine) to do an examination of an inside body part with a special machine: *The doctor scanned the patient's brain to look for damage after the accident.*

scan·dal /ˈskændl/ n. bad or embarrassing behavior (usu. of a famous person) and the reaction to it (publicity, etc.): *The politician did not pay his taxes, and there was a scandal that lasted for months.* -n. **scandalmonger** /ˈskændl,mɑŋgər, -,mʌŋ-/.

scan·dal·ize /ˈskændl,aɪz/ v. **-ized, -izing, -izes** to offend with shocking or bad behavior: *You scandalized your grandmother by wearing that little bathing suit.*

scan·dal·ous /ˈskændləs/ adj. causing shock or surprise, (syn.) outrageous: *The man got drunk at the party and pushed people into the pool; his behavior was scandalous!*

scant /skænt/ adj. not much, little: *He gave scant attention to directions, so he got lost.*

scape·goat /ˈskeɪp,goʊt/ n.v. s.o. blamed or punished for the mistakes of s.o. else: *The manager told people his secretary made an error that he made himself; the manager used his secretary as a <n.> scapegoat.* -n. [U] **scapegoating.**

scar /skɑr/ n. **1** a mark left by a cut or wound after it heals: *He had a scar on his cheek from a knife fight many years ago.* **2** a hurt left by emotional pain: *My mother and father divorced, and I still feel the scars.*

—v. **scarred, scarring, scars 1** to have or leave a scar: *She was scarred from the fire.* **2** left with emotional pain: *He was scarred by his sister's death.*

scarce /skɛrs/ adj. not available or plentiful: *Water is scarce in the desert.*

scarce·ly /ˈskɛrsli/ adv. almost not, hardly: *I can scarcely live on the money I earn.*

scar·ci·ty /ˈskɛrsəti/ n. [C;U] **-ties** a very small or limited amount of s.t.: *There is a scarcity of water in the desert.*

scare /skɛr/ n. a fear, a fright: *The little boy had a scare when his sister locked him in a closet.*

—v. to cause fear, to frighten: *The book about ghosts scared me.*

scare·crow /ˈskɛr,kroʊ/ n. an object that looks like a person, made of old clothes and straw and used to frighten birds away from a farm or garden: *Not many birds fly around our garden since we put up the scarecrow.*

scarf /skɑrf/ n. **scarves** /skɑrvz/ or **scarfs** a piece of cloth worn around the neck or on the head for warmth or decoration: *In winter, many people wear wool scarves.||She bought a silk scarf to match her blouse.*

scar·let /ˈskɑrlət/ n.adj. a bright red color: *We have yellow, white, and <adj.> scarlet roses in our garden.*

S

scar·y /'skɛri/ *adj.* **-ier, -iest** causing fear, frightful: *We were lost in the dark, and it was very scary.*

scath·ing /'skeɪðɪŋ/ *adj.* harsh, severe: *Try to be gentle; there is no need for scathing criticism.*

scat·ter /'skætər/ *v.* to go in all directions: *The newspapers scattered in the wind.* -n. [C] **scattering.**

scat·ter·brain /'skætər,breɪn/ *n.* a person who forgets things easily and can't focus on one idea: *That scatterbrain left her plane ticket and eyeglasses at home.* -adj. **scatterbrained.**

scav·enge /'skævəndʒ/ *v.* **-enged, -enging, -enges** to search for food or objects in s.t. dirty or thrown away: *A rat scavenged for food in the garbage.* -n. **scavenger.**

sce·nar·i·o /sə'nɛri,oʊ, -'nɑr-/ *n.* **1** a description of events that make up a general situation: *The scenario of the play has a man and a woman falling in love in Africa.* **2 worst case scenario:** the worst thing that can happen: *My aunt feels sick; in the worst case scenario she has cancer.*

scene /sin/ *n.* **1 a.** a piece of a film or play, usu. showing one situation: *There is a very exciting chase scene in that movie.* **b.** part of an act: *Let's rehearse Act III, Scene 2.* **2** anger or embarrassing behavior, often in public: *She made a scene at the party by drinking too much and falling into the swimming pool.* **3** a place where s.t. happens: *the crime scene* **4** a view of s.t. especially from a specific place: *She won a prize for her photo of a country scene.* **5 behind the scenes: a.** offstage: *The actor plays a nice man, but behind the scenes he is very cruel.* **b.** in a less obvious or secret place: *Not many people know what happens behind the scenes at the White House.* **6 to set the scene:** to make ready, prepare: *It is usually true that a happy childhood sets the scene for a happy future.*

scen·er·y /'sinəri/ *n.* [U] **1** nature, such as trees, mountains, sky, etc., seen by s.o.: *Each year, we vacation in the mountains and enjoy the scenery.* **2** the decorations on a theater stage: *For this play, the scenery included a park bench, a trash can, and some painted trees.*

sce·nic /'sinɪk/ *adj.* with a pleasing view of nature: *The country road is very scenic in the autumn when the leaves are colorful.*

scent /sɛnt/ *n.* **1** [C;U] a smell, usu. pleasant: *The scent of flowers relaxes me.* **2** [C] a smell left by an animal or human: *The dog followed the criminal's scent through the woods.*
—*v.* to fill with a smell, usu. pleasant: *The room was scented with roses.*

sched·ule /'skɛdʒul, -uəl/ *n.* a list of timed, planned activities or events: *On the airline schedule, I saw that there is a flight to Osaka at seven o'clock.*
—*v.* **-uled, -uling, -ules** to plan activities by date and time: *We scheduled meetings for each day of our business trip.*

sche·mat·ic /skɪ'mætɪk/ *n.adj.* a drawing or diagram of s.t., usu. in detail: *I did a <adj.> schematic drawing of the electrical wiring in the house.*

scheme /skim/ *n.* **1** an ordered arrangement, plan: *The color scheme in the room is blue and yellow.* **2** a secret or dishonest plan, (syn.) a plot: *I think he had a scheme to cheat the customer.* **3** a plan of action: *We have a scheme for finishing the job by Friday.*
—*v.* to plot, to plan s.t. secretly or dishonestly: *She schemed about how to escape through an open window.* -n. **schemer;** -adj. **scheming.**

schism /'skɪzəm, 'sɪ-/ *n.* [C;U] a division (of opinion), separation: *There is a schism in the company over where the new office should be built.*

schiz·o /'skɪtsoʊ/ *n.pej.* short for schizophrenic, a mentally ill person

schiz·o·phre·ni·a /,skɪtsə'friniə, -'frɛ-/ *n.* [U] a mental illness in which a person has trouble dealing with the real world and everyday life: *My sister takes drugs for her schizophrenia so that life is happier for her.* -n.adj. **schizophrenic** /,skɪtsə'frɛnɪk/.

schlepp or **schlep** /ʃlɛp/ *v.slang* (Yiddish for) **1** to carry s.t. in a tired way, (syns.) drag, haul: *Don't schlepp those bags all over town; leave them here.* **2** to move in a tired, unwilling way: *I have to schlepp all the way to the bus stop in the rain.*
—*n.* **1** a lazy, slow person: *You are such a schlepp; hurry up!* **2** a difficult or unwanted trip: *I hate the schlep from Dallas to Houston.*

schlock /ʃlɑk/ *n.* [U] *adj.slang* (Yiddish for) bad-quality items, cheap things: *That store sells schlock; everything breaks.*

schmaltz /ʃmɑlts/ *n.slang* [U] (Yiddish for) overly sentimental or sweet, esp. in music, literature, or art: *He loves schmaltz, where everything has a happy ending and no one has any problems.* -adj. **schmaltzy.**

schmooze /ʃmuz/ *v.slang* **schmoozed, schmoozing, schmoozes** (Yiddish for) to talk informally, (syn.) to chat: *The two women schmooze and drink coffee everyday before they start working.*

schmuck /ʃmʌk/ *n.slang* (Yiddish for) a stupid, unlikable person, a jerk: *He acted like a real schmuck on our date, so I won't go out with him again.*

S

schol·ar /'skɑlər/ n. **1** a person of great learning, usu. in a particular subject: *My teacher is a scholar of Shakespeare's writings.* **2** a student on a special scholarship: *My brother was a Rhodes scholar in England.*

schol·ar·ship /'skɑlərˌʃɪp/ n. **1** [U] study, learning, and knowledge: *The professor is very wise and famous for his scholarship.* **2** [C] a loan or grant that pays for study: *She got a $10,000 scholarship, so now she has enough money to go to college.*

scho·las·tic /skəˈlæstɪk/ adj. related to school or studying: *Her athletic performance is better than her scholastic performance; she gets low grades.* -adv. **scholastically**; -n. **scholastics**.

school /skul/ n. **1** [C;U] a place for teaching and learning: *I went to elementary school until I was 12.||His sister will get a car after she goes to driving school.||Her mother went back to school after the children were born.* **2** [C] a group of ideas: *He is a socialist; he belongs to that school of thought.* **3** [C] a group of fish: *a school of tuna*
—v. to teach s.o.: *He was schooled in the family business.*

school·ing /'skulɪŋ/ n. [U] education, learning: *He doesn't have much schooling, but he taught himself to read.*

school·teach·er /'skulˌtitʃər/ n. s.o. who teaches, usu. in a school for children: *I remember all of my schoolteachers' names, although I have not seen them in many years.*

sci·ence /'saɪəns/ n. **1** [U] facts and knowledge related to the natural world, such as biology, chemistry, or physics: *That TV show on science has programs on gravity, energy, and space travel.* **2** [C;U] facts and knowledge of a particular type: *social science||library science*

science fiction n. [U] a type of book or film about imaginary scientific events, such as space travel, the future, imaginary diseases, or strange animals: *The new movie about little green people is all science fiction. See:* sci-fi.

sci·en·tif·ic /ˌsaɪənˈtɪfɪk/ adj. **1** ordered, precise (thought, methods, etc.): *The new manager is scientific in his approach to solving problems.* **2** related to natural sciences: *Space travel is a scientific advancement of the 20th century.*

sci·en·tist /'saɪəntɪst/ n. a person who works in science: *I want to be a scientist because I like biology and chemistry.*

sci-fi /'saɪˈfaɪ/ n. short for science fiction

scin·til·late /'sɪntlˌeɪt/ v. **-ated, -ating, -ates** **1** to give off bits of fire, (syns.) to sparkle, shine **2** to be funny, brilliant, animated: *The party conversation scintillated as people told jokes and drank champagne.* -adj. **scintillating**.

scis·sors /'sɪzərz/ n. tool for cutting with two blades and a handle held with two fingers: *Hairdressers use scissors to cut people's hair.*

scissors

scoff /skɑf, skɔf/ v. to show negative opinions in a disrespectful way, (syn.) to disdain: *You scoffed at my ideas, but now you see I'm right.* -n. **scoffing**.

scold /skoʊld/ v. to find fault with s.o., to tell s.o., in an angry way, that he or she did s.t. wrong: *The teacher scolded the girl when she forgot her homework.* -n. [C;U] **scolding**.

scone /skoʊn, skɑn/ n. a pastry that is like an American biscuit, often with currants or raisins baked into it: *a blueberry scone.*

scoop /skup/ n. **1** a deep spoon used to hold an amount of s.t.: *The man in the food store uses a scoop to pour coffee beans into a bag.* **2** slang the newest information, the current situation: *What's the scoop? I heard that you have news for me.* **3** a news story that s.o. hears before anyone else: *The New York Times was the first to publish the story; it got the scoop.*
—v. to pick up s.t. with a scoop or scoop-like object: *At the beach I scooped up sand with my hand.*

scoot /skut/ v. **1** to move or leave quickly: *I have to scoot now, or I'll miss my plane.* **2** to move while sitting: *If you scoot over, I'll sit next to you.*

scoot·er /'skutər/ n. **1** a two-wheeled motor vehicle, smaller than a motorcycle: *I like to ride my scooter to work because I can park in a small space.* **2** a child's toy, with two wheels, a handle, and a surface on which to stand and push oneself along

scope /skoʊp/ n. [U] **1** a view, a way of seeing: *The company president thinks on a large scope; she thinks of everything.* **2** the limits or range of s.t.: *Calculus is outside the scope of my math knowledge.*

scorch /skɔrtʃ/ n. a brownish mark caused by a burn or heat: *The iron left a scorch on my dress.*
—v. to burn s.t. and cause a mark or damage: *The fire scorched the walls of the house.*

score /skɔr/ n. **1** a comparison of points between two people or teams: *The final score in the soccer game was 3 to 2.* **2** the number of points made in a contest or test: *The student has a score of 99 out of a possible 100.* **3** music on paper that shows all the instruments' parts: *The violin player bought the score to a Beethoven symphony.* **4** the music played in a film or play, (syn.) a soundtrack: *The score of the new movie uses a lot of jazz.* **5** a point made in a sport or game: *Our team made three*

scores and won the match. **6** *fig.* **on that score:** regarding that situation: *You ask if my husband helps clean the house; on that score, he is fine.* **7 to keep score:** to see and record the number of points made: *She kept score with the help of a pen and paper.* **8 to know the score:** to know what's happening, to be aware: *She's lived a long time; she knows the score.* **9 to settle the score:** to get even, seek revenge: *The gangster's partner was injured by the rival gang: now he's going to retaliate and settle the score.*
—*v.* **1** to make points in a sport or game: *Our hockey team scored in the last minute of the game.* **2** to make a line or holes in s.t. so it can be easily cut: *He scored the paper in the middle and tore it in half.* **3** *phrasal v. sep.* **to score s.t. out:** to draw a line through s.t. to show it should be ignored: *Please score out the incorrect answers.‖Score them out.* -*n.* [U] **scorekeeping.** *See:* cross out.

score·board /'skɔr,bɔrd/ *n.* a sign that shows the number of points each team has in a sporting event: *The scoreboard shows that our team is winning, 2 to 1.*

score·card /'skɔr,kɑrd/ *n.* a paper card with lines in which the scores of a sporting event are kept

scorn /skɔrn/ *n.* [U] a feeling of disrespect, expressed in a strong or angry way: *The scorn in your voice shows that you think I'm stupid.*
—*v.* to reject or ignore s.o. or s.t.: *She scorned my offer to help.*

scor·pi·on /'skɔrpiən/ *n.* a type of spider with poison in its long tail

scotch /skɑtʃ/ *v.* to put an end to, to stop: *to scotch a rumor (from spreading)*

Scotch /skɑtʃ/ *n.* a type of whiskey made in Scotland: *I drink Scotch and water with ice.*

scoun·drel /'skaʊndrəl/ *n.frml.* a bad and often dangerous person: *British novels of the 19th century often have a character who is a good hero and one who is a scoundrel.*

scour /skaʊr/ *v.* **1** to clean by rubbing with a brush or rough material: *to scour a pot* **2** to search a place thoroughly and in detail: *We scoured the woods for a lost child.*

scourge /skɜrdʒ/ *n.* a cause of pain and trouble: *The scourge of starvation hit the country when the crops failed.*

scout /skaʊt/ *n.* **1** a person sent to collect information about a place: *An army captain will send out scouts to see where the enemy is located.* **2** a person who looks for talented people: *Joe is a talent scout in Hollywood.* **3** a member of the Boy Scouts or Girl Scouts of America
—*v.* **1** to look for and collect information: *He scouts enemy armies.‖We scouted around for a*

new car. **2** to look for talented people -*n.* [U] **scouting.**

scowl /skaʊl/ *n.v.* an angry frown, usu. forming wrinkles on the forehead: *Her face went into a <n.> scowl when she saw the money was gone.‖The child <v.> scowled when his father asked him to share the cookie.*

scrab·ble /'skræbəl/ *v.* **-bled, -bling, -bles** to move quickly using fingers or claws, often when looking for s.t.: *A rat scrabbled for the cheese.*

scrag·gly /'skrægli/ *adj.* **-glier, -gliest** not neat or fully grown, (*syn.*) ragged: *The teenaged boy had a scraggly beard.*

scram /skræm/ *v.slang* to leave quickly: *This concert is boring; let's scram.‖The police are coming! Scram!*

scram·ble /'skræmbəl/ *v.* **-bled, -bling, -bles** **1** to move or climb quickly, esp. on the hands and knees: *The children scrambled up the hill quickly.* **2** to move toward s.t. one wants: *We scrambled for the head of the line.* **3** to mix s.t. together: *to scramble eggs* **4** to make an electronic message difficult to see or understand: *The television picture was scrambled.*
—*n.* a struggle or fight: *When the* Titanic *sank, there was a scramble to get on the lifeboats.*

scrambled eggs *n.pl.* eggs mixed with a fork and cooked in a frying pan

---

USAGE NOTE: A typical American breakfast might include *scrambled eggs,* bacon, toast, coffee, and orange juice. Other popular breakfast dishes are *cereal, oatmeal, pancakes,* and *waffles.* Some people have time to enjoy a big breakfast only on weekends, so on weekdays they often buy a small breakfast of coffee and a doughnut on their way to work or school.

---

scrap /skræp/ *n.* **1** [C] a small piece (of paper): *Write your phone number on this scrap of paper.* **2** [C] uneaten, leftover food: *We gave the dog the scraps from our plates.* **3** [U] *n.adj.* unwanted objects or parts that might be useful elsewhere: *a car sold as <n.> scrap‖ <adj.> scrap metal*
—*v.* **scrapped, scrapping, scraps** **1** to get rid of, (*syn.*) to abandon: *With the bad weather, we scrapped our plans for a vacation.* **2** to sell or get rid of an unwanted object: *Our truck is so old that we scrapped it in a junkyard.*

scrape /skreɪp/ *n.* **1** a mark on the surface of s.t. caused by rubbing against s.t. rough: *The girl got a scrape on her knee when she fell on the sidewalk.* **2** a difficult situation, a minor fight: *My little brother got a bloody nose in a scrape with an older boy.*
—*v.* **1** to rub against s.t. rough and receive a mark or injury: *I scraped my hand on the rusty doorknob.* **2** *phrasal v. sep.* **to scrape s.t. up** or **together:** to collect s.t., esp. money, with

S

difficulty: *He barely scraped together the rent money.‖He scraped it together.*

scrap·book /'skræp,bʊk/ *n.* a large book with empty pages on which one pastes photographs, newspaper stories, and other memories: *Dad has a scrapbook of his days in the navy.*

scrap·py /'skræpi/ *adj.* **-pier, -piest** liking to argue or fight, *(syn.)* quarrelsome: *She gets scrappy with people who don't agree with her politics.*

scratch /skrætʃ/ *n.* **-es** **1** a narrow mark in a surface, made by a sharp object: *I made a scratch in the wall with a nail.* **2** a light wound in the skin: *The little girl has a scratch on her hand from a pin.* **3 from scratch: a.** from the beginning: *He lost all his money; he had to start his life from scratch.* **b.** (in cooking) with fresh ingredients: *We like spaghetti sauce made from scratch, not from a jar.*
—*v.* **-es** **1** to stop an itch by rubbing it with the fingernails: *I scratched a mosquito bite.* **2** to make a mark or sound with fingernails or claws: *The dog scratched at the door.‖The cat scratched my cheek.* **3** erase or get rid of s.t.: *I scratched my name from the list.* **4 to scratch the surface:** to deal with only a small part of s.t.: *Scientists have barely scratched the surface in their understanding of cancer.*

scratch·y /'skrætʃi/ *adj.* **-ier, -iest** **1** with or able to cause scratches: *scratchy bark on a tree* **2** sore, hoarse: *I am sick; I have a headache, stomachache, and a scratchy throat.* -*n.* [U] **scratchiness.**

scratch paper *n.* [U] paper that has been printed on one side and may be reused: *My family saves scratch paper for writing telephone messages.*

scrawl /skrɔl/ *n.v.* handwriting done quickly or messily: *Your signature is a <n.> scrawl; I can't read it.‖He <v.> scrawled his ideas on paper and typed them neatly later.*

scraw·ny /'skrɔni/ *adj.* **-nier, -niest** extremely thin, with very little flesh on the bones, *(syn.)* skinny: *You are so scrawny; you look as if you haven't eaten in months.*

scream /skrim/ *n.* **1** a loud, high cry of strong feeling (pain, fear, anger, etc.): *She gave a scream when the man pulled out a knife.* **2** *fig.* s.t. very funny: *The new film comedy is a scream.*
—*v.* **1** to cry out with a high, loud voice in pain or fear: *He screamed for help.‖She screamed at him, "You stupid idiot!"* **2 to scream with laughter:** to laugh very loudly *See:* screech; shriek.

screech /skritʃ/ *n.* **-es** a loud, high sound from a voice or object: *Tires give out a screech when you press the brake too quickly.‖I let out a screech when I heard a noise in the night.*

—*v.* to cry out or make a loud, high sound: *A racing car screeched around the corner. See:* scream, shriek.

screen /skrin/ *n.* **1** a movable divider in a room, often painted with decorations: *I undressed behind a screen in the bedroom.* **2** a fine wire net in a window or door to let in air but keep out dirt, insects, etc.: *Our house is cooler with screens in the windows.* **3** an activity that hides another, usu. illegal, one: *The drug dealer uses that restaurant as a screen for selling cocaine.* **4** the surface on which a film or television show is seen: *a movie screen‖a TV screen* **5** the film business: *an actor on stage and screen*
—*v.* **1** to protect, divide, or hide an area: *The hat screened out the sun.* **2** to show a movie: *They are screening a new movie at the theater downtown.* **3** to look carefully at s.o.'s good and bad qualities and background to see if he or she is right for an activity or job: *The boss screened the new employee by calling her previous boss.* -*n.* [C;U] **screening.**

screen·play /'skrin,pleɪ/ *n.* the script for a movie; like a play but written for film: *A Hollywood producer asked the writer to put a car chase in the screenplay.*

screw /skru/ *n.* a small, nail-like object with spiral indents, put into wood or metal with a turning motion: *The carpenter uses screws to put the table parts together.*
—*v.* **1** to put a screw in s.t.: *She screwed a shelf onto the bookcase.* **2** *vulg.* to do wrong to s.o., esp. to cheat him or her: *He really screwed his wife by divorcing her and leaving her with no money.* **3** *phrasal v. slang* **to screw around:** to be playful, not serious, *(syn.)* to fool around: *My band isn't trying to be famous; we're just screwing around with guitars.* **4** *phrasal v. vulg.* **to screw off:** to be lazy, *(syns.)* to goof off, to hang out: *He has stopped looking for a job and screws off all the time.* **6** *phrasal v. sep. slang* **to screw s.t. up: a.** to make a mistake: *You really screwed up your life when you quit school.‖You screwed it up.* **b.** to twist or distort a part of the face: *The bitter medicine made him screw up his mouth.*
—*adj.* **1** *slang* **to be (all) screwed up:** to be in a state of confusion and difficulty: *She lost her job, and her boyfriend left her; her life is all screwed up.* **2** *infrml.* **to have one's head screwed on right:** to be sensible, not to be silly or stupid: *My sister will be a good mother because she really has her head screwed on right.* **3 to have a screw loose** or **a loose screw:** to act strangely, to be crazy: *He must have a screw loose, riding a bicycle in his underwear!*

screw·ball /'skru,bɔl/ *n.adj.slang* s.o. who acts strangely, a nut, crazy person: *She changed her hair color from blond to blue; what a <n.>*

S

screwball!‖*We watched a <adj.> screwball comedy from the 1930s.*

screw·driv·er /'skru,draɪvər/ *n.* **1** a tool for removing or putting in screws **2** a mixed drink of orange juice and vodka: *I'd like a screwdriver, and my friend would like a glass of white wine.*

screw-up *n.slang* **1** a mistake or misunderstanding: *He put the wrong addresses on 20 boxes; what a screw-up!* **2** *slang* a person who often makes mistakes *See:* screw.

screw·y /'skrui/ *adj.slang* **-ier, -iest 1** confusing: *These directions are screwy; I can't figure out where to go.* **2** crazy: *That guy is screwy, so we never listen to his advice.*

scrib·ble /'skrɪbəl/ *v.* **-bled, -bling, -bles 1** to write or draw meaningless things: *The little boy scribbled on the wall with a crayon.* **2** to write quickly and not neatly: *I scribbled "eggs, milk, cheese" on the list.*
—*n.* **1** [C] meaningless writing or drawing: *Save your scribbles; they may give you ideas later.* **2** [U] quick, messy handwriting: *Can you read this scribble? I was in a hurry when I wrote it.* -*n.* [U] **scribbling.**

scribe /skraɪb/ *n. old usage* a person who copies s.t. that is written, esp. before the invention of printing: *A scribe in ancient Israel copied religious texts.*

scrimp /skrɪmp/ *v.* **1** to keep or save money very carefully, to be frugal or stingy: *He scrimps by counting every penny.* **2 to scrimp and save:** to work very carefully, and sometimes for a long time, at saving money: *We scrimped and saved for years before we bought a house.*

scrim·shaw /'skrɪm,ʃɔ/ *n.* whalebone (ivory) with designs carved into it

script /skrɪpt/ *n.* **1** [C;U] the written words for a speaker or actor (in a film, play, etc.): *The actors memorized the script.* **2** [U] handwriting in which the letters are connected: *He wrote a thank-you note in fancy script. See:* printing.

Scrip·ture /'skrɪptʃər/ *n.* **1** [C;U] a part of the Bible: *I read the Scriptures every day.* **2 The Holy Scripture** or **The Holy Scriptures:** the Bible

scroll /skroʊl/ *n.* **1** paper rolled into a circular shape: *a valuable scroll of paper* **2** a curved design: *The wallpaper has dots and scrolls.*
—*v.* (in computers) to move quickly through a file: *Scroll to the end of a document to see what I wrote on page 5.*

scrooge /skrudʒ/ *n.* (from the character Ebenezer Scrooge in Charles Dickens's *A Christmas Carol*) a selfish person with money, (*syns.*) a miser, tightwad: *The boss is a scrooge; he pays his workers little and makes them work on weekends.*

scrounge /skraʊndʒ/ *n.* s.o. who finds s.t. of value in very little, (*syn.*) a scavenger: *The artist is a scrounge who finds old bits of paper, rock, and metal and makes beautiful things from them.*
—*v.* **scrounged, scrounging, scrounges** to look for s.t. of value from any available source: *He scrounged up money from his parents for a new computer.*‖*I scrounge around for interesting things in my neighbors' trash.*

scrub /skrʌb/ *n.* **1** [C] a thorough washing, esp. rubbing with soap and brush: *Once a week, I give my dog a scrub in the bathtub.* **2** *n.adj.* [U] small trees or bushes: *a <adj.> scrub pine*
—*v.* to wash by rubbing hard: *Before dinner, I scrub the dirt off my hands.* -*n.* [C;U] **scrubbing.**

scruff·y /'skrʌfi/ *adj.* **-ier, -iest** poorly dressed, perhaps dirty or needing a shave or haircut: *You look scruffy; use this razor and buy some new clothes.*

scru·ples /'skrupəlz/ *n.* [C;U] principles of personal conduct that stop you from doing s.t. wrong: *I have scruples about taking personal favors from suppliers to the company.*

scru·pu·lous /'skrupyələs/ *adj.* **1** attentive to detail and correctness: *Marta does her work with scrupulous efficiency.* **2** having scruples: *Manuel keeps the business records with scrupulous honesty.*

scru·ti·nize /'skrutn,aɪz/ *v.* **-nized, -nizing, -nized** to look at s.t. carefully and closely, examine: *We scrutinized the vase to see if there were cracks.*

scru·ti·ny /'skrutni/ *n.* [U] the act of looking closely and carefully, examining: *The woman gave the car close scrutiny before she decided to buy it.*

scuff /skʌf/ *n.v.* a rough mark on s.t., esp. a shoe: *I have a <n.> scuff or scuff mark on my shoe.*‖*<v.> scuffed my shoes on the sidewalk.*

scuf·fle /'skʌfəl/ *n.v.* **-fled, -fling, -fles** a brief fight without serious injury: *The two men got into a little scuffle outside the bar.*

sculp·tor /'skʌlptər/ *n.* an artist who makes non-flat art with stone, metal, and other substances: *A sculptor carved a statue of his lover in a piece of stone.* -*v.* **sculpt.**

sculp·ture /'skʌlptʃər/ *n.* [C;U] three-dimensional art made of stone, metal, or other objects: *I walked around that sculpture of a ballet dancer by Degas.*

scum /skʌm/ *n.* [U] **1** a very thin layer of s.t., usu. impure, on the surface of a liquid: *You can't see the bottom of the pond through the scum.* **2** *slang* a bad, evil person or group of people: *That man is scum; he lies to everyone.*

scur·ri·lous /'skɜrələs, 'skʌ-/ *adj.* using or containing very bad language: *The angry*

S

radio announcer said scurrilous things about unmarried teenage mothers.

scur·ry /'skɜri, 'skʌ-/ v. **-ried, -rying, -ries** to move quickly, often fearfully, (*syn.*) to scuttle: *When the child's father yelled, she scurried away.*

scut·tle /'skʌtl/ v. **-tled, -tling, -tles 1** to sink a ship by making holes in it: *The captain scuttled his enemy's ship off the coast, and divers found it years later.* **2** to move quickly, (*syn.*) to scurry: *A rat scuttled into the shadows.*

scuz·zy /'skʌzi/ adj. slang **-zier, -ziest** dirty, disgusting: *That guy never takes a bath; he's scuzzy.*

sea /si/ n. **1** [C] a body of salt water, smaller than an ocean: *The Caspian Sea is between Europe and Asia.* **2** [U] the part of the earth covered with water (opposite of *land*): *We traveled over land and sea.* **3** [C, usu. sing.] a large group of people or things: *We saw a sea of people in the square.* **4 to be at sea: a.** to be on a boat in open water: *The ship is at sea now; it left port two days ago.* **b.** *fig.* to be in doubt, emotionally lost: *The young man is at sea about what to do with his future.* **5 to be on the high seas:** open water: *The ship is in the mid-Atlantic on the high seas.*

sea·food /'si,fud/ n. [U] food (fish, lobster, seaweed, etc.) from the ocean or other body of water: *We learned to fish so we can catch our own seafood.*

seal /sil/ n. **1** part of a lid or opening that must be broken to reach inside a container: *We broke the seal on the new aspirin bottle.* **2** a tight, perfect closure: *The tube had a seal so air couldn't escape.* **3** symbols or words pressed into wax, clay, paper, etc. to show that s.t. is approved or official: *We have a letter with the prince's seal.* **4** a brown water animal with flippers that lives in cold areas: *They saw many seals off the Coast of Alaska.* **5 seal of approval:** permission or agreement of s.o.: *My parents gave their seal of approval to my living alone.*
—v. **1** to close s.t. firmly: *Please seal the envelope and mail it.* **2** to reach final agreement: *We sealed a plan to build five new houses.* **3** *phrasal v. sep.* **to seal s.o. or s.t. in:** to prevent from escaping: *The prison seals in inmates from 8 p.m. to 8 a.m.‖It seals them in.* **4** *phrasal v. sep.* **to seal s.t. off:** to keep an area secure and not let anyone in or out: *The police sealed off the area where the burglary happened.*

seam /sim/ n. the line where two pieces of cloth are sewed together: *There was a rip in the seam of his shirt.*

seam·less /'simlis/ adj.fig. without mistakes, completely logical: *Your plan of escape is seamless; you will get out with no problem.*

sea·port /'si,pɔrt/ n. an area with a harbor for ships and businesses, such as fishing and ship-building: *Boston, Hong Kong, and Santo Domingo are major seaports.*

sear /sɪr/ v. to cook the surface of s.t., esp. meat, over a hot fire: *She seared the beef for one minute, and then served it with rice.*

search /sɜrtʃ/ n. **-es** the action of looking for s.t.: *I made a search for my lost sock in the laundry room.*
—v. **-es 1** to look for s.t.: *They searched three towns for the boy who ran away.‖She searched the newspaper to find the weather report.* **2 Search me!:** I don't know: *Why is she leaving? Search me!*

search·ing /'sɜrtʃɪŋ/ adj. detailed and careful, (*syn.*) penetrating: *The police officer asked us many searching questions about the car accident. See:* soul-searching.

search·light /'sɜrtʃ,laɪt/ n. a strong, movable lamp used for seeing at a distance in the dark: *The searchlight on the police car sent a beam of light through the dark woods.*

search warrant n. written, legal permission for the police to search a place where a crime may have happened: *The police officer arrived with a search warrant, so we had to let her in.*

sea·shell /'si,ʃel/ n. the hard outer covering of water animals, such as clams and oysters: *The little children collected pretty seashells on the beach.*

sea·shore /'si,ʃɔr/ n. [U] the area of land next to the sea, usu. with a beach: *We enjoy going to the Florida seashore for vacation because we like sailing and swimming.*

sea·sick /'si,sɪk/ adj. dizzy with an upset stomach caused by the motion of a boat: *Half the passengers got seasick when it stormed.* **-n.** [U] **seasickness.**

sea·son /'sizən/ n. **1** a three-month period: *Summer and fall are her favorite seasons.* **2** a time for a certain activity: *In some states the hunting season begins September 1.*
—v. **1** to add spices or flavoring to food: *We season our vegetables with a little salt and garlic.* **2** to age s.t. properly: *to season wood for lumber*
—adj. **in season:** available because of the time of year: *Here, tomatoes are in season in August.*

sea·son·a·ble /'sizənəbəl/ adj. about normal (weather) for a season: *Cold temperatures are seasonable in winter.*

sea·son·al /'sizənəl/ adj. depending on the time of year: *In December, shops sell seasonal items like Christmas wreaths and tree decorations.*

sea·soned /'sizənd/ adj. **1** flavored with spices: *My friend cooks highly seasoned meals, full of pepper.* **2** aged, (*syn.*) matured: *His* *grandfather is a seasoned fisherman; he's been doing it all his life. See:* season.

sea·son·ing /'sizənɪŋ/ *n.* [U] spices and other flavoring added to food: *This spaghetti has no taste; add a little seasoning.*

seat /sit/ *n.* **1** a place to sit (a chair, sofa, bench, etc.): *We had great seats in the front row at the theater.‖Come on in and have a seat.* **2** the buttocks area: *the seat of his pants* —*v.* **1** to sit (s.o.) down: *The guests seated themselves at the table.* **2** to have places to sit: *The cathedral seats hundreds.*

seat·ing /'sitɪŋ/ *n.* [U] the availability and arrangement of seats (chairs, etc.): *The classroom has seating for hearing-impaired students in the first row.* —*adj.* having to do with where people sit: *The seating plan for the dinner is shown with name cards.*

seat belt *n.* a long, thin piece of material that holds a person in a car seat for safety: *I wear my seat belt in case I get in an accident. See:* safety belt.

USAGE NOTE: Many states in the USA have strict *seat belt* laws, and drivers and passengers who are caught not wearing their seat belts may be fined. Special car seats with seat belts are required for small children.

se·cede /sə'sid/ *v.* **-ceded, -ceding, -cedes** to remove oneself, withdraw, usu. by a legal act: *In the 1860s, Southern states wanted to secede from the unified nation.* -*n.* [U] **secession** /sə'sɛʃən/.

se·clud·ed /sə'kludɪd/ *adj.* hidden from sight, apart from others: *We drove to a secluded spot in the country and had a lovely picnic.* -*v.* **seclude.**

se·clu·sion /sə'kluʒən/ *n.* [U] privacy, withdrawal from human contact: *When his mother died, the artist went into total seclusion.*

sec·ond (1) /'sɛkənd/ *adj.* **1** a position after first: *You were in second place in a race.* **2 a second chance:** another opportunity to do s.t. right: *The student failed the test, but the teacher gave him a second chance to pass.* —*n.* number 2 in a series: *I am second in line.* —*v.* to show agreement with an idea before a vote: *If you second his nomination, we can see who wants to elect him.*

second (2) *n.* **1** a unit of time, 1/60 of a minute: *The rocket will take off in 20 seconds.* **2** a very short period of time, a moment: *I need to get my coat; I'll be out in a second.* **3** a used or imperfect item for sale in a store, often *pl.*: *It's cheaper to buy seconds than to pay full price in a fancy shop.*

sec·ond·ar·y /'sɛkən,dɛri/ *adj.* of lesser importance: *My job is of secondary importance* (or) *is secondary to my health.*

secondary school *n.* in the USA, a public or private high school, usu. grades 9-12: *Most students from my secondary school go on to college.*

USAGE NOTE: *Secondary school* begins in sixth or seventh grade. It includes two or three years of *junior high school* or *middle school,* followed by three or four years of *senior high school.* Compare *grade school.*

second class *n.* (in travel) a less expensive part of a train, plane, etc., (*syns.*) coach class, economy class: *We like to travel in second class and use our money for nice hotels.* —*adj.* less good, (*syns.*) inferior, mediocre: *The snobby waiter treated us like second-class citizens.*

second-guess *v.* to look back on an act and suggest a different way to do it, usu. in a critical way: *I sold our car for $5,000, and my wife second-guessed me by saying it was worth $7,000.*

second-hand *adj.* **1** used by s.o. else before: *We bought a second-hand car that had 25,000 miles on it.* **2** received from s.o. other than the original source: *This is second-hand information; you learned it from a friend of a friend.*

second-rate *adj.* less good, (*syns.*) inferior, mediocre: *The painter did a second-rate job on our apartment, so we had to hire a better painter.*

se·cre·cy /'sikrəsi/ *n.* [U] keeping information or knowledge private or hidden: *The plan was discussed quietly and in secrecy.*

se·cret /'sikrɪt/ *adj.n.* information or knowledge kept from others: *Your <n.> secret is safe; I won't tell anyone.‖I write my private thoughts in a <adj.> secret diary.*

sec·re·tar·y /'sɛkrə,tɛri/ *n.* **1** a person who works in an office, word-processing, filing, answering phones, and doing other jobs for a boss: *She asked her secretary to type a letter.* **2** the person in an organization whose job is to write down important information in meetings and write and send correspondence: *As the tennis club secretary, I send the results of our matches to the newspapers.* **3** the head of a government department: *The secretary of transportation wanted to build more highways.*

se·crete /sə'krit/ *v.* **-creted, -creting, -cretes** to come out of a living thing in liquid form: *The maple tree secreted sap.*

se·cre·tion /sə'kriʃən/ *n.* [C] a liquid that comes out of s.t., usu. a living thing: *The veterinarian cleaned the secretions from around the wound of the hurt animal.*

se·cre·tive /'sikrətɪv/ *adj.* acting in a way to keep information or knowledge hidden or pri-

S

vate, (*syn.*) clandestine: *The couple was secretive about their relationship at work.*

sect /sɛkt/ *n.* a group, usu. religious, that has separated from a larger, original organization: *There are many sects of Christianity.*

sec·tion /'sɛkʃən/ *n.* [C] a piece or part of s.t.: *They live in the section of town near the railroad station.||Would you like a section of this orange?||I read the sports section of the newspaper.*

sec·tor /'sɛktər/ *n.* **1** a division of land for a certain purpose: *a military sector* **2** a division of society: *Nhu Trin worked for five years in the government sector; now she works in the private (business) sector.*

sec·u·lar /'sɛkyələr/ *adj.* not religious: *They sent their child to Sunday school because they felt a secular education was not enough.*

se·cure /sə'kyʊr/ *adj.* **1** protected from danger, safe: *He feels secure in the locked apartment.* **2** not able to be opened or broken, closed tightly: *The jail was secure, with iron bars and a high fence.* **3** sure, confident: *She is secure in knowing that her parents love her.* —*v.frml.* **-cured, -curing, -cures 1** to get, obtain: *Chin-peng secured a job with a Taiwanese company in New York.* **2** to make a building or area safe: *He secured the office before leaving it for the night.*

se·cu·ri·ty /sə'kyʊrəti/ *n.* **1** [U] **-ties** protection from danger or loss: *The owner put two locks on every door for better security.||Job security is not part of an actor's life.* **2** [U] confidence in one's emotions and abilities: *Good physical and mental health gives her a strong sense of security.* **3** *pl.* part ownership, stocks and bonds: *Her company buys and sells securities.* **4** [U] people who help keep buildings and other areas safe, guards: *airport security*

security deposit *n.* a payment made to s.o., often a landlord, and returned if all conditions of the sale or lease are met: *We got back our security deposit because we didn't damage the apartment.*

se·dan /sə'dæn/ *n.* a car with two or four doors and a trunk: *My parents own a Ford sedan. See:* station wagon.

sed·a·tive /'sɛdətɪv/ *n.* a drug to make s.o. calmer or less nervous: *The doctor gave a sedative to the screaming, crying man.* -*n.* [U] **sedation** /sə'deɪʃən/.

sed·en·tar·y /'sɛdn,tɛri/ *adj.* related to sitting, not physical activity: *His sedentary lifestyle includes working at a desk all day and watching television at night. See:* couch potato.

se·der /'seɪdər/ *n.* **seders** or **sedarim** /sə'dɑrɪm/ a Jewish service and dinner on the first and sometimes second night of Passover

sed·i·ment /'sɛdəmənt/ *n.* [C, *usu. sing.*; U] tiny pieces of rock, sand, dirt, flood, etc. that

collect at the bottom of a liquid: *I washed the sediment out of my wine glass.*

se·duce /sə'dus/ *v.* **-duced, -ducing, -duces** to persuade or convince a person to do s.t., often sexual, against his or her wishes, using sexy behavior and false promises, (*syn.*) to lure: *She refused to kiss him, but he finally seduced her with candlelight dinners and an offer of marriage.* -*n.* **seducer.**

se·duc·tion /sə'dʌkʃən/ *n.* [C;U] the process and act of persuading or convincing s.o. to do s.t., often sexual, against his or her wishes: *The seduction of power makes some people want to be President.*

se·duc·tive /sə'dʌktɪv/ *adj.* tempting, (*syn.*) alluring: *That chocolate ice cream is very seductive, but I'm on a diet.||He has a seductive smile.*

see (1) /si/ *n.* the center of a bishop's power

see (2) /si/ *v.* saw /sɔ/, **seeing, sees 1** to sense with the eye, to look, to view: *I don't need glasses; I can see perfectly.* **2** to notice, identify s.t.: *Can you see the mountain in the distance?* **3** to understand: *The student sees what the professor is saying.* **4** to find out about s.t.: *Will you see what everyone wants to drink?* **5** to look at with interest, to examine: *Is that a new jazz CD? Let me see!* **6** to go somewhere with s.o., (*syn.*) to escort: *I will see you to the door.||Her boyfriend saw her home after their date.* **7** to meet professionally: *I will see the dentist about my toothache.* **8** to meet socially: *I'll see you at the restaurant at noon.* **9** (in saying good-bye) to meet later, in the future: *I'll see you later (soon, in a while, tomorrow, etc.).* **10** to make sure s.t. is done: *I will see that the children go to bed at 7:30.* **11** to be dating, to be romantically involved: *She and I have been seeing each other since Valentine's Day.* **12** *phrasal v. insep.* **to see about s.t.: a.** to find out about: *I'll go see about the car to see if the mechanic has fixed it.* **b.** to protest, object: *He says new tires will cost $600; we'll see about that!* **13 to see double:** to see more than one image because of a physical problem: *He bumped his head and saw double for a while.* **14 to see fit:** to decide to do s.t.: *She saw fit to stay late and help us wash the dishes.* **15 to see ourselves as others see us:** to be aware of our own faults: *If we could only see ourselves as others see us with all our strange habits, we would probably act differently.* **16** *phrasal v. sep.* **to see s.o. off:** to go or be with s.o. to say good-bye: *Our friends like to see off all their friends who are traveling.||They see us off.* **17** *phrasal v. sep.* **to see s.o. out:** to go with s.o. to an exit: *The hallways in this building are confusing; I will see you out.* **18** *phrasal v. sep.* **to see s.o. or s.t. through:** to stay until the end: *His scholarship will see him through next year.* **19 to see stars:** to be dizzy and confused, usu. from an injury: *He saw stars for a minute when he walked into a door.* **20 to see the light:** to understand some truth: *She used to sit and watch TV all the time, but then she saw the light and started exercising.* **21 to see the light at the end of the tunnel:** to see hope (or) the end of a long and difficult situation: *After 12 years in school, we now see the light at the end of the tunnel, graduation.* **22** *phrasal v. insep.* **to see through s.t.:** not to be fooled: *You can see through his lies.* **23 to see to s.t.:** to make sure s.t. is done: *We saw to it that the electric bill was paid.*

seed /sid/ *n.* **1** the part of a plant that is put into the ground and grows into another plant: *We bought grass seed for the lawn.||If you plant these seeds, they will grow into beans and corn.* **2** *frml.* beginning, origin: *My father planted the seed of an idea, and my sister started a business from that idea.* **3** a man's semen, sperm
—*v.* to sow or plant seed: *We seed our lawn in the early spring.*

seed money *n.* money used to start a business: *My parents and friends loaned me seed money to start a restaurant. See:* start-up.

seed·y /'sidi/ *adj.* **-ier, -iest** bad or dirty, (*syns.*) squalid, shabby: *The seedy bar was full of drunken, unwashed people.*

seek /sik/ *v.* **sought** /sɔt/, **seeking, seeks** **1** to look for s.t.: *The police are seeking a woman in a blond wig and a blue dress.* **2** to request: *We don't know what to do, so we will seek our father's advice.* **3** to try to get or win: *I am seeking love and happiness in my life.*

seem /sim/ *v.* to appear to be: *He seems like a successful businessman with his nice suit and big office.||She fell and hit her head, but she seems to be all right now.*

seem·ing /'simɪŋ/ *adj.* appearing obvious or true, but maybe not so: *His seeming reaction was happiness, but I think the smile hid tears.*

seep /sip/ *v.* (for a liquid) to flow slowly through s.t., to ooze: *Water is seeping through cracks in the ceiling.* -*n.* [U] **seepage.**

see·saw /'si,sɔ/ *n.* a children's plaything, a piece of wood balanced on a bar, where a person sits on each end to move up and down
—*v.* to be indecisive, not able to decide: *He seesawed between buying a car or a truck.*

seeth·ing /'siðɪŋ/ *adj.* extremely angry, trembling with rage: *The girl is seething with anger and will hit anyone who comes near.* -*v.* **seethe.**

see-through *adj.* able to be looked through (usu. clothing), (*syns.*) sheer, transparent: *That yellow scarf is see-through, making her blue blouse appear green.*

seg·ment /'sɛgmənt/ *n.* **1** a separate piece, a section of s.t.: *a line segment||a segment of a* grapefruit **2** a part of a radio, television, or musical work: *We listen to the radio news segment on every day from 5:00 to 5:10.*
—*v.* /sɛg'mɛnt/ to divide into segments -*adj.* **segmented.**

seg·re·gate /'sɛgrə,geɪt/ *v.* **-gated, -gating, -gates** **1** to separate, put apart: *I segregated the older children from the babies.* **2** to separate or isolate people according to race: *In my city in the 1950s, the law segregated whites and blacks.* -*n.* [U] **segregation.** *See:* apartheid, USAGE NOTE.

seis·mic waves /'saɪzmɪk/ *n.* shock waves caused by an earthquake

seize /siz/ *v.* **seized, seizing, seizes** **1** to take s.t. and hold it with force: *I seized his arm so he couldn't run away.* **2** to take by force or by law, (*syn.*) to confiscate: *The bank seized my house because I couldn't make the mortgage payments.*

sei·zure /'siʒər/ *n.* **1** [U] the act of taking s.t. by force or by law: *the seizure of property* **2** [C] a physical attack from a sickness or disease, such as heart failure or epilepsy: *The man had a seizure; he stopped breathing and started shaking.*

sel·dom /'sɛldəm/ *adv.* not often, infrequently: *I seldom go to the theater; I go two to three times a year.*

se·lect /sə'lɛkt/ *adj.* special, high quality: *The director chose a select group of dancers for the ballet.*
—*v.* to choose, to single out specific people or things: *The woman selected a pasta dish from the menu.*

se·lec·tion /sə'lɛkʃən/ *n.* **1** [C] a group of things from which to choose: *The candy store had a selection of chocolates and fruit drops.* **2** [C;U] a choice: *I looked at the various books in the library and made a selection of a mystery and a romance.*

se·lec·tive /sə'lɛktɪv/ *adj.* very careful when making a choice, (*syn.*) choosy: *The company is selective when hiring workers; they want the best people.*

self /sɛlf/ *n.* **selves** /sɛlvz/ **1** [C;U] an entire person having his or her own character: *You showed your best self in helping the old people.* **2** [C] part of a person's character: *I will return to my old self after I take my medicine.* **3 self-** *prefix* related to oneself *See:* self-absorbed, etc.

self-absorbed *adj.* interested only with one's own business and personal interests, not with other people: *Karen is so self-absorbed; she never asks me questions about my life. See:* self-centered.

self-abuse *n.* [U] behavior that is bad or harmful to one's body: *He smokes three packs of cigarettes a day; that's a lot of self-abuse.*

S

self-actualized *adj.* knowing what is right for oneself, sure of one's strengths and weaknesses: *That self-actualized woman has used all of her life experiences to make the best choices in work and love.*

self-analysis *n.* [U] a look inside one's own mind to learn about one's feelings and actions: *Self-analysis helped me understand why I am unhappy.*

self-appointed *adj.* put by oneself into a job or situation: *No one wanted the job of club president, so Mr. Park became its self-appointed president.*

self-assured *adj.* confident: *She studied math in college, so she is self-assured about teaching it.*

self-aware *adj.* knowing what one's feelings and actions mean: *He doesn't need a psychologist because he is very self-aware.*

self-centered *adj.* not interested in others, concerned with oneself: *He always talks about himself and never asks about me; he is self-centered.*

self-confident *adj.* sure that one's actions are good and right, (*syn.*) self-assured: *He has a self-confident way of speaking, with a strong voice and definite opinions. -n.* **self-confidence.**

self-conscious *adj.* uncomfortable in one's own body, awkward and shy: *The self-conscious boy tried to hide his bad teeth with his hand.*

self-contained *adj.* **1** (person) not showing strong emotions, calm, controlled: *She talks in a quiet, sure way; she is very self-contained.* **2** (thing) complete, able to work by itself: *The answering machine is self-contained in the telephone; you don't need to buy a separate answering machine.*

self-control *n.* [U] the ability to manage one's emotions and actions: *He drank too much and lost self-control; he started yelling and cursing.*

self-deception *n.* [U] the act of thinking the wrong thing about oneself, fooling oneself: *It was self-deception for the clumsy boy to think he was a good athlete.*

self-defeating *adj.* related to acting in an unwise way, against one's own best interests: *It is self-defeating to leave school now; you will need the education.*

self-defense *n.* [U] the act of protecting oneself from harm: *The police officer acted in self-defense when he shot the woman who tried to shoot him.*

self-denial *n.* [U] the act of limiting or not buying things one wants, showing willpower: *You showed great self-denial in not getting that beautiful shirt; I know you want it.*

self-destruct *v.* to destroy oneself or itself when in a harmful state or no longer useful: *Some rockets self-destruct when they go out of control.*

self-destructive *adj.* related to doing harmful things to oneself: *It is self-destructive to take drugs and drive a car.*

self-discipline *n.* [U] the ability to work hard without needing s.o. else to make it happen: *My parents don't have to tell me to practice my flute; with self-discipline, I practice every day. -adj.* **self-disciplined.**

self-doubt *n.* [U] a feeling of not being sure or confident about one's abilities: *After the runner lost several races, he was full of self-doubt about winning the next time.*

self-educated *adj.* taught by oneself without teachers: *He left school when he was 12, but he reads all the time and is self-educated.*

self-employed *adj.* related to working in a business owned by oneself: *She has been self-employed since she started that computer company years ago. -n.* [U] **self-employment.**

self-esteem *n.* [U] a feeling of liking oneself, a sense of self-worth: *When she got a better job, her self-esteem improved.*

self-evident *adj.* obvious: *It is self-evident from your loose clothes that you have lost weight.*

self-explanatory *adj.* needing nothing more to be understood, clear: *We do not need to ask her how to bake the cake; the recipe is self-explanatory.*

self-expression *n.* [U] showing one's own personality and beliefs, esp. in an artistic way: *She loves to paint as a form of self-expression.*

self-fulfilling prophecy *n.* s.t. that happens because s.o. thinks or predicts it will: *If you keep saying you will fail biology, it will become a self-fulfilling prophecy and you probably will fail.*

self-gratification *n.* [U] the act of pleasing oneself by buying or doing what one wants: *She worked very hard Monday through Friday, then slept late on weekends as self-gratification.*

self-help *adj.* of or about improving oneself with little or no outside aid: *I don't like going to psychologists, so I read self-help books when I have a problem.*

self-important *adj.* a feeling that one is very special and important, (*syn.*) arrogant: *The self-important king made everyone bow down to him.*

self-improvement *n.* [U] the process of making oneself better (through study, hard work, changing one's appearance, etc.): *Many seek self-improvement by learning a new sport or a new language.*

self-incriminating *adj.* related to words and actions that make oneself likely to receive punishment: *The thief dropped his driver's license at the scene of the robbery; it was self-incriminating evidence.* -*n.* [U] **self-incrimination.**

self-indulgent *adj.* buying or getting whatever one wants for oneself, (*syn.*) hedonistic: *That self-indulgent girl buys a new pair of shoes every week.* -*n.* [U] **self-indulgence.**

self-inflicted *adj.* caused by oneself: *self-inflicted pain*

self-interest *n.* [U] the attitude or act of doing what is best for oneself, sometimes without thinking of others: *He offered to buy the poor old lady's house to help her, but he acted in his own self-interest by offering her a small amount of money for it.*

self-involved *adj.* concerned more with one's own emotions, work, health, etc. than with other people's: *Don't be so self-involved; remember your friends have problems, too.*

self·ish /ˈsɛlfɪʃ/ *adj.* concerned with oneself more than others, not sharing, (*syn.*) possessive: *Your selfish brother took all the ice cream and left us none.* -*n.* [U] **selfishness.**

self-made *adj.* successful because of one's own effort, not because of money or help from others: *He is a self-made millionaire who grew up in a poor family.*

self-perpetuating *adj.* capable of continuing to exist by its or one's own power: *A forest is self-perpetuating; more trees grow every year on their own.*

self-pity *n.* [U] the sense of feeling sorry for oneself: *He was full of self-pity when he lost his job and couldn't find another one.*

self-portrait a picture or painting of an artist, done by that artist: *One impression of what Van Gogh looked like is from his many self-portraits.*

self-possessed *adj.* showing self-control, calm, (*syn.*) poised: *It is good to be with a self-possessed person when the house is on fire.*

self-preservation *n.* [U] the feeling or act of staying alive or keeping oneself out of danger: *Self-preservation made her jump out of the burning building.*||*I had to lie to keep my job; it was an act of self-preservation.*

self-proclaimed *adj.* said by oneself (to be s.t.): *Napoleon crowned himself emperor; he was the self-proclaimed ruler of much of Europe.*

self-protection *n.* [U] precautions taken to guard oneself against harm or loss: *We have special locks on our doors and an alarm system for self-protection against burglars.*||*Our company demands payment in advance for new customers as self-protection against unpaid bills.*

self-realization *n.* [U] the act of reaching one's potential, knowing oneself fully: *He had a sad childhood, but through self-realization, he became a normal adult.*

self-reflection *n.* [U] the act of thinking about oneself and one's life: *She did well in business, but through self-reflection, she decided she would like teaching better.* -*adj.* **self-reflective.**

self-regulating *adj.* related to controlling or governing itself or oneself, with little outside help: *Doctors make rules within their national society; they are a self-regulating professional group.* -*n.* [U] **self-regulation.**

self-reliant *adj.* able to take care of oneself without outside help: *She is elderly but quite self-reliant, as she does all of her own cleaning and shopping.* -*n.* [U] **self-reliance.**

self-respect *n.* [U] the act of having pride in oneself, knowing oneself to be a good person: *He had greater self-respect when he went back to school and earned a high school diploma.*

self-restraint *n.* [U] control over one's emotions and actions: *I was angry, but I showed self-restraint by not yelling.*

self-revealing *adj.* about showing itself or oneself, becoming obvious: *He tried to keep his drug habit secret, but it became self-revealing in his red eyes and shaking hands.*

self-righteous *adj.* overly sure that one is right, (*syns.*) moralizing, sanctimonious: *She sounds very self-righteous when she says, "You should listen to me; I know all the answers."* -*n.* [U] **self-righteousness.**

self-rule *n.* [U] self-government: *Russia is under self-rule now, no longer part of the USSR.*

self-sacrificing *adj.* related to ignoring one's own needs and pleasures so that others may have more: *The self-sacrificing mother never buys anything for herself; she gives everything to her children.* -*n.* [U] **self-sacrifice.**

self-satisfaction *n.* [U] a feeling of having done well at s.t., (*syn.*) smug: *That proud, rich man gets self-satisfaction out of his big house.*

self-satisfied *adj.* (perhaps overly) content with oneself, (*syn.*) smug: *You are so self-satisfied, but other people don't think your life is perfect.*

self-seeking *adj.* acting just for oneself, not for others, (*syns.*) selfish, greedy: *My self-seeking cousin calls me only when she needs money.*

self-service or **serve** *adj.* (of a store or other business) choosing s.t. oneself and paying for it at a cash register: *We buy gas for our car at a self-service gas station.*

USAGE NOTE: Many U.S. gas stations offer *self-service* and *full-service* pumps. You can

S

save money by going to the island marked "SELF" and pumping your own gas. See also USAGE NOTE for *filling station.*

self-serving *adj.* about acting just for oneself, not for others, (*syn.*) selfish: *The self-serving man seems nice, but he wants to be friends only if you can help him.*

self-starter *n.* s.o. who can do things by him- or herself and who can work without a boss, (*syn.*) self-motivated: *If you hire self-starters, you can leave them alone and do your own work.*

self-styled *adj.* created or described by oneself, often without the necessary background or skills, (*syn.*) self-appointed: *He is a self-styled lawyer, but no one knows if he really went to law school.*

self-sufficient *adj.* able to meet one's own needs without outside help, independent: *The old man is self-sufficient.‖He has his own apartment and knows how to cook. -n.* [U] **self-sufficiency.**

self-supporting *adj.* able to earn enough money, not needing outside help: *We have two grown children; they both have jobs and are self-supporting. -n.* [U] **self-support.**

self-sustaining *adj.* able to continue existing or (working) under its or one's own power without outside help: *Trees keep growing, so the forest is self-sustaining.*

self-taught *adj.* without formal schooling or lessons, self-instructed: *She is a self-taught pianist; she never had any lessons.*

self-will *n.* [U] the feeling that one must do whatever is necessary and not be influenced or affected by others: *The President's self-will makes helps him stand alone in difficult situations against his wife and the Vice President.*

sell /sɛl/ *v.* sold /soʊld/, selling, sells **1** to make a sale, to take money in exchange for a product or service: *I'll sell you my CD player for $150.‖The book sold well.* **2** to be for sale: *A pound of broccoli sells for $1.29.* **3 to sell one's soul to the devil:** to do s.t. (usu. bad) that creates a good or easy situation now, but that will cause pain or difficulty later: *She sold her soul to the devil when she married the cruel man only for his money.* **4 to sell oneself:** to talk about one's skills, to make oneself look good: *I really have to sell myself in this job interview.* **5 to sell s.o. on s.t.:** to make s.t. seem like a good idea or a smart choice: *We sold my mother on getting a dog because it can protect the house.* **6** *phrasal v. insep.* **to sell s.o. or s.t. out: a.** to have no more of s.t. to sell, to be all out: *The store sold out (or) is sold out of bread, but it still has muffins.* **b.** to do s.t. more for money than for one's own happiness: *The painter sold out when she got a job in an office.* **c. s.o.:** to betray: *The company*

sold out their employees by lowering saleries. **7 to sell s.o. short:** to think s.o. is not good, smart, etc. without giving him or her a chance: *Don't sell that man short; he is shy and quiet, but he has wonderful ideas.* **8** *phrasal v. sep.* **to sell s.t. off:** to get rid of s.t., usu. by offering it at a lower price: *He sold off his college texts after graduation.‖He sold them off.*

sell·er /ˈsɛlər/ *n.* **1** a person or business that takes money in exchange for s.t.: *The store is a seller of clothes.‖The seller wants $400, but the buyer wants to pay only $300.* **2 bestseller:** a product or service that sells very well: *Hemingway wrote many bestsellers.*

sell·ing /ˈsɛlɪŋ/ *n.* [U] **1** amount of sales taking place: *There is heavy selling in the real estate business now.* **2** the job or act of asking s.o. to buy s.t.: *Selling is his job with the company.*

selling point *n.* s.t. good about a product or service, used when making a sale or in advertisements: *The safety of this car is a selling point with couples who have children.*

sell·out /ˈsɛlˌaʊt/ *n.* **1** an event for which no more tickets are left: *The rock concert was a complete sellout on the day that tickets went on sale.* **2** an agreement to do s.t. against moral principle: *The owner agreed to sell the business to his employees, but sold it to a competitor instead, thereby putting them all out of work; it was a sellout.*

selt·zer /ˈsɛltsər/ *n.* [U] water to which carbonation (bubbles) has been added: *I drank a glass of seltzer with a slice of lime in it.*

se·man·tic /səˈmæntɪk/ *adj.* of or about meaning in language: *"Good-bye" and "See you later" have a small semantic difference.*

se·man·tics /səˈmæntɪks/ *n.pl. used with sing. verb* **1** the study of meanings of words: *Cheryl studied semantics to understand her own language better.* **2** the meaning of words: *Both lawyers are talking about the same thing in different words; it is a matter of semantics.*

sem·blance /ˈsɛmbləns/ *n. usu. sing.* an appearance (that may not be real or true): *I was sad, but my face had the semblance of a smile.*

se·men /ˈsimən/ *n.* [U] in a man's body, the thick, white liquid that carries sperm and comes out of the penis during sex: *A doctor tested the man's semen to see if he could become a father.*

se·mes·ter /səˈmɛstər/ *n.* half of the school year: *I took intermediate German in the fall semester and advanced German in the spring semester.*

USAGE NOTE: In the academic year, many colleges and universities have two *terms* called *semesters.* Some colleges operate on *quarters* or *trimesters* (three terms). *Semester* is often used interchangeably with the word *term.*

sem·i·cir·cle /'sɛmi,sɜrkəl/ n. **1** half a circle **2** people or things in an arc shape: *The children stood in a semicircle around their teacher.*

sem·i·co·lon /'sɛmi,koʊlən/ n. the punctuation mark " ; "

sem·i·con·duc·tor /'sɛmikən,dʌktər, 'sɛmaɪ -/ n. a silicon electronic device

sem·i·fi·nal /'sɛmi,faɪnəl, 'sɛmaɪ-/ n.adj. the next to final game or match in a sporting event: *The two winners of the <n.> semifinals will play against each other for the championship.*

sem·i·nal /'sɛmənəl/ adj. original, important for the future: *Thomas Jefferson's writings were seminal to the growth of democracy.*

sem·i·nar /'sɛmə,nɑr/ n. a meeting or short course on a specific topic: *I attended a two-day seminar on Native American art at the University of Arizona.*

sem·i·nar·y /'sɛmə,nɛri/ n. **-ies 1** a school for religious study: *A friend of mine went to a seminary to become a priest.* **2** a private school, often for girls: *My grandmother did not go to public school, but to a young ladies' seminary.*

sem·i·pre·cious /'sɛmi'prɛʃəs, 'sɛmaɪ-/ adj. of less value than a precious gem: *semiprecious stones*

sem·i·pri·vate /,sɛmi'praɪvɪt, ,sɛmaɪ-/ adj. occupied usu. by two people: *Would you like to pay for a private hospital room, or is a semi-private room OK?*

sem·i·re·tired /,sɛmirə'taɪrd, ,sɛmaɪ-/ adj. working less or part-time after retirement: *She is semiretired; she still works two days a week.*

Sem·ite /'sɛmaɪt/ n. a member or descendant of any of the Middle Eastern Semitic tribes or peoples

sem·i·year·ly /,sɛmi'yɪrli, ,sɛmaɪ-/ adj. twice a year: *a semiyearly dentist appointment See:* biannual.

sen·ate /'sɛnɪt/ n. a group of people in government, with the power to make laws: *The U.S. Senate meets in Washington, D.C.* -adj. **senatorial** /'sɛnə'tɔriəl/.

sen·a·tor /'sɛnətər/ n. an elected member of a senate: *Alma Perez is a senator from Oklahoma.*

send /sɛnd/ v. **sent** /sɛnt/, **sending, sends 1** to cause to go or move: *Each week, I send a letter to my parents in England.* **2** to cause s.o. to go somewhere: *I am sending my son to college.* **3** infrml.slang **to send s.o:** to cause happiness or pleasure: *Her beauty really sends me.* **4** phrasal v. insep. **to send away for s.t.:** to order by mail: *She sent away for flower seeds from a magazine.* **5** phrasal v. insep. **to send for s.o. or s.t.:** to ask for s.o. to come, (syn.) to summon: *My boss sent for me.||She sent for a taxi.* **6** phrasal v. sep. **to send s.o. away:** to

make s.o. leave: *A stranger who knocked at my door I sent away.||Send him away.* **7** phrasal v. sep. **to send s.o. or s.t. down:** to cause to fall, decline: *His mistake sent out company's profits down.||It sent them down.* **8** phrasal v. insep. **to send s.o. into s.t.:** to cause emotion: *The good news sent her into shouts of joy.||The sad news sent him into tears.* **9** phrasal v. sep. **to send s.t. out:** to distribute, usu. from a central location: *They sent out their fall catalogue.||They sent it out.* **10** phrasal v. sep. **to send s.o. or s.t. up: a.** slang **s.o.:** to send to prison **b. s.o.** or **s.t.:** to cause to rise: *The sinking ship sent up a flare.*

send-off n. a good-bye party: *Her friends gave her a good send-off before she left for South America.*

send-up n. a funny imitation of s.t. or s.o.: *The actors did a send-up of old movies from the 1920s.*

se·nile /'sinaɪl/ adj. mentally damaged from old age: *The old man cannot think clearly now because he is senile.*

se·nil·i·ty /sə'nɪləti/ n. [U] mental damage caused by old age: *Her senility makes it difficult to remember her grandchildren's names.*

se·nior /'sinyər/ n. **1** abbr. **Sr.:** the father of a son with exactly the same name: *John Page Borden, Sr., is the father, and John Page Borden, Jr., is the son.* **2** s.o. higher than another in rank or longer in length of service: *She is senior to the others in the company because she has worked here the longest.* **3** an older person: *His sister is eight years his senior.* **4** in USA, s.o. in the last (usu. fourth) year of high school or college: *Mr. Yamamoto's son is a senior in high school and about to graduate. See:* freshman, USAGE NOTE.

senior citizen n. an old person, s.o. usu. over 60 years old: *My great-aunt can get cheaper bus tickets because she is a senior citizen.*

sen·ior·i·ty /sin'yɔrəti, -'yɑr-/ n. [U] the state of being higher in rank or longer in length of service: *He has seniority because he has been with the company longer than the others have.*

sen·sa·tion /sɛn'seɪʃən/ n. **1** [C;U] a physical feeling: *I sat on my foot, and now I have no sensation in it.* **2** [C] a less definite feeling in the body: *When she watched the film, she had the sensation that she was in a moving car.* **3** [C] excitement, great interest: *The book on the politician's private life caused quite a sensation.*

sen·sa·tion·al /sɛn'seɪʃənəl/ adj. **1** very interesting or exciting: *The new play is sensational; you should see it!* **2** exciting in a negative way, often with wrong information: *I read a sensational story about a nine-year-old mother.*

S

sen·sa·tion·al·ism /sɛn'seɪʃənə,lɪzəm/ n. [U] real or imagined events that cause great excitement or interest: *The news item about the escaped prisoner was sensationalism; they caught him immediately, and there is no danger.*

sense /sɛns/ n. **1** [C] a meaning or significance: *I looked up the sense of a difficult word in The Newbury House Dictionary.* **2** [C] one of the five feelings of the body,—sight, hearing, taste, smell, and touch: *the five senses‖He smokes so many cigarettes that he has lost his sense of taste.* **3** [C, usu. sing.] a physical feeling: *She doesn't sleep enough, so she always has a sense of fatigue.* **4** a strong but unclear feeling: *a sense of danger, a sense of not belonging* **5** [U] intelligence, good judgment: *If you had any sense, you would get a better job.‖It shows good sense to save money.* **6** a talent or ability (usu. one that s.o. has naturally or from birth): *Roberta has a good sense for business; she invested $10,000 last year and now has $50,000.‖a sense of balance (humor, honor, etc.)* **7** [U] a general understanding: *The new boss has a sense of what is happening in the business.‖The student has a sense of what the professor is saying.* **8 common sense:** an ability to be sensible or act intelligently without special knowledge: *Show some common sense; stay home if you're sick.* **9 in a sense:** in a way, sort of: *I write many letters and keep a journal, so in a sense I'm a writer.* **10 in what sense?:** in what way, using which meaning?: *"This rice is hot!" "In what sense, heat or spices?"* **11 sixth sense:** a feeling without actual proof: *His sixth sense told him that something was wrong, and sure enough, his car had been stolen. See:* gut feeling. **12 to come to one's senses: a.** to get back one's physical senses: *She fell and fainted, but soon came to her senses.* **b.** to stop doing foolish things, become wiser: *Too much beer and wine was ruining his life; he finally came to his senses and stopped.* **13 to make sense: a.** to be understandable: *Talk slowly; you're not making sense!* **b.** to be wise, to do the right thing: *It makes sense to take the train; it's faster.* **14 to make sense of s.t.:** to understand s.t. with effort or time: *I can't make sense of this poem, but perhaps I will if I read it again.* **15 to take leave of one's senses:** to act in a crazy way: *Have you taken leave of your senses? Don't put your hand in the lion's cage!*
—v. **sensed, sensing, senses 1** to feel s.t. physically: *When the knife cut his finger, he sensed a sharp pain.* **2** to be aware of: *We sense the tension in the room.‖He sensed her love.* **3** to understand: *She senses the meaning of your words.*

sense·less /'sɛnslɪs/ adj. **1** unconscious: *The fighter hit the other man and knocked him senseless.* **2** without good reason, cruel, stu-

pid: *Stealing from small children is a senseless act.*

sen·si·bil·i·ty /,sɛnsə'bɪləti/ n. [U] **1** the ability to feel things physically: *A dog has great sensibility in its nose; it can smell things miles away.* **2** the ability to feel emotions and understand ideas well: *To be a counselor or psychiatrist requires great sensibility. See:* sensitivity.

sen·si·ble /'sɛnsəbəl/ adj. acting wisely, (syns.) reasonable, practical: *You were sensible to wear boots in the mud.*

sen·si·tive /'sɛnsətɪv/ adj. **1** sore or uncomfortable to the touch: *He hurt his ankle, and it is still sensitive.* **2** easily hurt or affected emotionally: *That sensitive child cries when someone frowns.* **3** able to sense or feel in a stronger than normal way: *His skin is sensitive to wool.‖This film is sensitive to light.* **4** needing care or tact, likely to cause strong emotion: *Abortion is a sensitive topic.*

sen·si·tiv·i·ty /,sɛnsə'tɪvəti/ n. [U] **1** soreness, physical discomfort: *My throat has sensitivity because I coughed all night.* **2** the state of being easily hurt or affected emotionally: *He has great sensitivity; he always cries at sad movies.* **3** the ability or state of feeling or sensing in a stronger than normal way: *My sensitivity to dust makes me sneeze.‖The radio's sensitivity lets me receive stations from far away.* **4** great care or tact, so as not to cause unpleasant emotion: *The politician showed sensitivity to people of other races.*

sen·sor /'sɛnsər/ n. a machine for sensing (heat, movement, light, etc.): *A motion sensor makes a light go on when people come to the door.*

sen·so·ry /'sɛnsəri/ adj. related to feeling or the senses: *heat as a sensory perception*

sen·su·al /'sɛnʃuəl/ adj. related to physical feeling, esp. sexual pleasure: *She thinks the feeling of silk on her skin is very sensual.*

sen·su·al·i·ty /,sɛnʃu'æləti/ n. [U] bodily pleasures, esp. sexual ones: *He is a man of strong sensuality who likes to give and receive back rubs.*

sen·su·ous /'sɛnʃuəs/ adj. related to pleasure as perceived by the senses: *sensuous music‖sensuous poetry*

sen·tence /'sɛntns/ n. **1** (in grammar) a thought expressed in words, usu. with a subject and verb, and, when written, beginning with a capital letter and ending with a period, exclamation point, or question mark **2** the punishment given by a court: *a prison sentence*
—v. **-tenced, -tencing, -tences** to give a punishment: *to sentence a criminal to 20 years in jail*

sen·tenc·ing /'sɛntnsɪŋ/ n. [U] the act of describing punishment by a judge: *The sentencing of the robber will take place in one month.*

sen·ti·ment /'sɛntəmənt/ *n.* **1** [C;U] an emotional feeling: *When our grandmother died, we remembered her life with strong sentiment.* **2** an opinion, usu. affected by some emotion: *What are your sentiments about having children?*

sen·ti·men·tal /ˌsɛntə'mɛntl/ *adj.* **1** emotional, not practical: *The ring is ugly, but it has sentimental value because my wife gave it to me.* **2** containing very great emotion, perhaps too much: *The novel has scenes full of love and loss; it is so sentimental!*

sen·ti·men·tal·i·ty /ˌsɛntəmɛn'tæləti/ *n.* [U] great feeling or emotionality, perhaps too much: *The music is full of sentimentality, with lots of sad violin music.*

sep·a·rate /'sɛpərɪt, 'sɛprɪt/ *adj.* **1** apart: *He and his wife sleep in separate beds.* **2** different from s.t. else: *The cost of making the product and the cost of selling it are two separate issues.*
—*v.* /'sɛpə,reɪt/ **-rated, -rating, -rates** to move s.t. apart or away from s.t. else: *We separated the salad forks from the dinner forks.||My wife and I separated a year ago.* *-adv.* **separately.**

sep·a·ra·tion /ˌsɛpə'reɪʃən/ *n.* [C;U] s.t. that divides or separates, the act of separating: *The fence makes a separation between the two yards.||The couple have a legal separation and live apart.*

sep·a·ra·tor /'sɛpə,reɪtər/ *n.* a divider: *We built a separator to close off the kitchen from the living room.*

Sep·tem·ber /sɛp'tɛmbər/ *n.* the ninth month of the year, between August and October

se·quel /'sikwəl/ *n.* **1** a novel, film, etc. that continues the story of a previous one: *The author's second novel is a sequel to her first one.* **2** another event in a series: *May flowers are the sequel to April showers.*

se·quence /'sikwəns/ *n.* **1** [C] a continuing and connected series of acts (events, steps, etc.): *There was a sequence of events leading up to the robbery.||You have to follow a sequence of commands to use a computer.* **2** [U] an order of things: *Please put your checks in sequence by number.*

se·quen·tial /sə'kwɛnʃəl/ *adj.* in order, one by one: *The steps for putting this toy together are sequential; you must do 1 before 2. -adv.* **sequentially.**

se·ques·ter /sə'kwɛstər/ *v.* **1** to put apart, (*syns.*) to segregate, isolate: *The judge sequestered himself in his office to think about the law.* **2** to keep from outside contact: *He sequestered the jury in the jury room and sent food in.*

ser·e·nade /ˌsɛrə'neɪd, 'sɛrə,neɪd/ *n.* a love song, played or sung outside at night: *My hus-*band sang me a serenade under a summer moon.*
—*v.* to sing love songs to s.o.: *The lover serenaded his lady beneath her window.*

ser·en·dip·i·ty /ˌsɛrən'dɪpəti/ *n.* [U] s.t. good that happens by chance, luck: *It was serendipity that I found a 10 dollar bill on the street.*

se·rene /sə'rin/ *adj.* **1** (of a place) very calm, peaceful: *The lakes in Maine are serene on hot summer mornings.* **2** (of a person) unworried, peaceful: *After she told him that she loves him, he became serene with relief and happiness.*

se·ren·i·ty /sə'rɛnəti/ *n.* [U] calmness, peace: *He is not afraid to die; he feels serenity at the end of his life.*

ser·geant /'sɑrdʒənt/ *n.* a low-level officer in the army, air force, or marines, or on a police force

se·ri·al /'sɪriəl/ *adj.* related to an ordered group of things or events: *The serial number on my car is H3963966.*
—*n.* part of a larger story: *TV soap operas are serials; the action continues the next day.*

se·ries /'sɪriz/ *n.* **1** a group of similar things or events: *We heard a series of gunshots: three in a row.* **2** a television show: *He acted in a TV series before he became a movie star.*

se·ri·ous /'sɪriəs/ *adj.* **1** thoughtful and quiet, humorless: *He is a serious man who works hard and doesn't smile.* **2** important, (*syn.*) grave: *I have a serious business matter to discuss with you.||AIDS is a serious illness.* **3** willing to act, sincere: *I am serious about getting married.*

ser·mon /'sɜrmən/ *n.* **1** a speech given by a religious leader: *The sermon last Sunday was about Moses and his teachings.* **2** a lecture, usu. critical: *My father gave me a sermon about saving money.*

ser·pent /'sɜrpənt/ *n.frml.* **1** a snake **2** the Devil (who appeared as a snake in the Garden of Eden) *-adj.* **serpentine** /'sɜrpən,tin, -,taɪn/.

se·rum /'sɪrəm/ *n.* [C;U] **-rums** or **-ra** the watery part of an animal's blood, often used in immunizations against disease: *serum for snake bites*

ser·vant /'sɜrvənt/ *n.* a person who is paid to do household jobs: *One servant polished the silver, and another prepared the tea.*

serve /sɜrv/ *v.* **served, serving, serves** **1** to act or function as: *This table can serve as a desk.* **2** to act as a servant, clerk, server, etc.: *The waitress served me coffee.* **3** to be in public office: *The mayor served four years.* **4** to put a ball into play: *to serve in tennis* **5** (in law) to give officially: *A sheriff served a summons on the woman to appear in court.* **6 to serve s.o. right:** to be the right punishment for s.t.: *The little boy hurt his hand when he hit his brother; it served him right.* **7** *phrasal v.*

S

sep.slang **to serve s.t. up:** to offer: *The cook served up some delicious pie.||He served it up.*
—*n.* the opening hit that puts a ball in play in court games (tennis, volleyball, etc.): *Her serve went over my head. See:* service; serving.

serv·er /'sɜrvər/ *n.* **1** a person who serves: *a food server* **2** the server in tennis **3** the part of a computer that stores and serves information on command

---

USAGE NOTE: A *server* or *waitperson* may be a man or a woman. More and more, these terms are used in place of *waiter* and *waitress.*

---

serv·ice /'sɜrvɪs/ *v.* **-iced, -icing, -ices** **1** to keep a machine in good working order: *The mechanic services our car every three months.* **2** to provide goods and services: *We service our customers with a smile and a "thank you."* **3** to make payments on a loan: *to service a debt*
—*n.* **1** [U] the care of a machine to keep it in good working order: *When our oven broke, we called a repairman for service.* **2** [U] general attention to customers' needs in a business (store, restaurant, etc.): *The service at our favorite restaurant is excellent; the waiters are quick and polite.* **3** [C;U] a specific service: *room service at a hotel* **4** [U] government work (when used with "the," meaning the armed forces): *Our nephew is in the service, the army.||His mother is in public service; she works for the U.S. Department of Education.* **5** [U] a service paid for with money: *bus service, electric service* **6** [C;U] a good deed, favor: *You did me a good service by driving me to work.* **7** [C] religious worship: *Our temple has a service on Friday night.* **8** [U] (in law): *a service of a summons* **9** [U] loan payments: *The debt service on our company's loan is very large each month.* **10** [C] (in tennis, volleyball, etc.) the act of putting a ball in play: *It's your service.* **11 at your service:** here to help you: *Let me finish my own work, and then I will be at your service.* **12 in service** or **out of service:** working or not working: *The elevator is out of service today; take the stairs. Tomorrow, it will be back in service. See:* other "service" words. **13 of service:** useful, helpful: *A dictionary is of service when you are learning a new language.||May I be of service and carry those bags?*

serv·ice·a·ble /'sɜrvəsəbəl/ *adj.* usable: *The lawn mower is serviceable since I filled it with gas.*

service charge *n.* an additional cost for s.o.'s help: *The tickets were $25, plus a service charge of $3.*

serv·ice·man /'sɜrvɪs,mæn, -mən/,

  serv·ice·wom·an /'sɜrvɪswumən/ *n.* /-mən, -,mɜn, -mən, -women, -,wɪmən/ **1** a person who fixes a machine that is broken: *The refrig-*

erator stopped working, and I called a service-man to come fix it. **2** a member of the military

service station *n.* a gas station, a car repair shop that sells gasoline and oil: *There are service stations located off the main highway.*

ser·vile /'sɜrvəl, -,vaɪl/ *adj.* acting like a servant, (*syns.*) subservient, humble: *He bowed and was servile to the prince.*

serv·ing /'sɜrvɪŋ/ *n.* a portion of food put on a plate: *a serving of meat*

ser·vi·tude /'sɜrvə,tud/ *n.* [U] a state of having no freedom, slavery: *Many black people lived in servitude until the end of the U.S. Civil War.*

ses·sion /'sɛʃən/ *n.* **1** a meeting or other activity within a specific time period: *a one-hour exercise session||the fall session (a semester in school)* **2 in session:** working, active: *The U.S. Congress is in session until the summer.*

set /sɛt/ *n.* [C] **1** a group of related objects: *a set of silverware||a set of golf clubs* **2** a group of similar people or friends: *We like her; she is in our set.* **3** a group of ideas: *a strong set of values* **4** a machine for watching or listening: *a TV set||a stereo set* **5** scenery in a theater: *a stage set* **6** (in tennis): *a set of games* **7** the position of a body part: *the set of her chin||the set of his shoulders. See:* jet set.
—*adj.* **1** hardened: *The glue is set on my toy airplane, so now I can fly it.* **2** agreed upon, decided: *We now have a set time for the meeting.* **3** ready, prepared: *Get set to leave now.* **4** not likely to change one's mind, determined: *She is set on studying physics in college.* **5 all set:** prepared: *We have our tickets and our bags are packed, so we are all set for our vacation.||All set? OK, let's begin.* **6 set in one's ways:** not easy to change, stubborn: *My mother won't learn how to use a computer; she's set in her ways.*
—*v.* **1** to put or place s.t.: *I have set the vase in the center of the table.* **2** to become firm or hardened: *The gelatin has set, so we can eat it now.* **3** to put a machine to a certain position, (*syn.*) to adjust: *Set the radio dial to 98.9 FM.||Set the clock for 5:30 a.m.* **4** to decide and agree upon s.t.: *We have set the price at $10.||She set a date for the picnic.* **5** to put in place, (*syn.*) to establish (a goal, a record, a fashion): *I have set a goal for myself to become an accountant.||Teenagers set the new fashion trend.* **6** to get s.t. ready: *set the table||set the stage* **7** to fix or hold with pressure or heat: *She set my hair with hair spray.||This stone is set in the necklace.* **8** to go below the horizon: *The sun set in the West.* **9** to cause s.t. to begin burning: *He set a match to dry sticks.||She set the house on fire.* **10 ready, set, go!** or **get ready, get set, go!:** phrase used to start a timed event, such as a race **11 to have one's mind** or **heart set on s.t.:** to want s.t. so much that nothing will prevent getting it (using "heart"

gives it a more emotional meaning): *He has his mind set on arriving on time.||She has her heart set on buying a new car.* **12** *phrasal v. insep.* **to set about s.t.:** to begin an action: *I set about planning the trip this morning.* **13 to set foot in:** to go in, enter: *I hate that restaurant; I will not set foot in the place!||I smelled onions cooking the minute I set foot in the house.* **14** *phrasal v. insep.* **to set forth s.t.: a.** *frml.* to express formally: *The judge set forth the law in a long speech.* **b.** *frml.* to begin: *The king set forth on a long journey.* **15 to set free:** to make free, let out, (*syn.*) to liberate: *We caught a butterfly in a net, but later we set it free.* **16** *phrasal v.* **to set in:** to move in: *She was not feeling well; then a high fever set in.||The fog had set in, so we could not see the road.* **17** *phrasal v. insep.* **to set off from s.o.:** to show s.o.'s difference: *She is the oldest woman, so that sets her off from the others.* **18 to set out:** to leave on a trip: *He then set out on a two-week trip.* **19 to set a precedent:** to do s.t. that can be used as an example in the future: *The owner refused to buy the sales manager a car, because that would set a precedent and others would then want one.* **20 to set sail:** to leave by ship: *We set sail tomorrow on a 10-day cruise.* **21** *phrasal v. insep.* **to set s.o.** or **s.t. against s.o. or s.t.: a. s.o.:** to cause two people to disagree: *An argument about their child set one parent against the other.* **b. s.t.:** to place s.t. against s.t.: *I've set the broom against the wall.* **22** *phrasal v. sep.* **to set s.o.** or **s.t. apart:** to cause to be different or distinct: *Her intelligence sets her apart from other workers.* **23 to set s.o.** or **s.t. back: a. s.o.:** to cost s.o. money: *That new car set him back $25,000.* **b. s.t.:** to move a date back, lose time: *The extra work set back the schedule a month.||It set it back.* **24** *phrasal v. sep.* **to set s.o.** or **s.t. off: a. s.o.:** to cause great anger: *Don't tell the boss the bad news; it will set her off.* **b. s.t.:** to cause to explode: *The boy set off a firecracker.* **25** *phrasal v. insep.* **to set s.o.** or **s.t. on s.o.** or **s.t.:** to cause to attack: *The woman set her dogs on the thief, and they chased him off.* **26 to set s.o.** or **s.t. straight:** to correct a wrong idea: *He thought he could get good grades without studying, but the teacher set him straight.* **27** *phrasal v. sep.* **to set s.t. aside: a.** to stop acting on s.t.: *He set aside the book until he had time to read it.||He set it aside.* **b.** to keep or save for later: *The parents set aside money each year for their children's education.* **28** *phrasal v. sep.* **to set s.t. down: a.** to put s.t. down: *He set down the bag.||He set it down.* **b.** to put in writing: *The writer set down her thoughts in a journal.* **29 to set store by:** to have confidence in: *You can set great store by what he says; he's honest.* **30 to set a trap:** to try to catch s.o. or s.t.: *The farmer sets traps to catch*

rabbits in his field. **31** *phrasal v. sep.* **to set up: a.** to get ready, arrange: *She set up chairs and tables for the party.* **b.** to fool, trick s.o.: *The police had an undercover agent invite the criminal to a hotel for a phony buy; they set him up.*

set·back /ˈsɛtˌbæk/ *n.* s.t. that causes a return to an earlier place or situation: *We had to turn back when the road ended; it was a setback in the trip.||Getting fired was a setback in his career.*

set·ting /ˈsɛtɪŋ/ *n.* **1** [C] a place for an event or a story: *The company chose a California hotel as a good setting for its yearly meeting.||The setting for the movie is a small town in Ohio.* **2** [C] the area or surroundings: *The beach is a peaceful setting.* **3** [C] the part of a piece of jewelry that holds a gem: *the setting for a ruby* **4** [C] silverware and plates arranged on a table: *five place settings for five dinner guests* **5.** [U] the action of setting: *We watched the setting of the full moon.*

set·tle /ˈsɛtl/ *v.* **-tled, -tling, -tles 1** to come to agreement: *We settled the details of the contract and signed it.* **2** to go to the bottom: *The sand settled at the bottom of the lake.* **3** to move in, to make a home: *Our family came from Russia and settled in New Jersey.* **4** to become comfortable: *I settled into my chair and picked up a book.* **5** *phrasal v. sep.* **to settle s.o.** or **s.t. down: a. s.o.:** to establish residence in a place: *Their family settled down in the Midwest and began farming.* **b. s.o.** or **s.t.:** to become calm: *The country was at war, but life there finally settled down.||Settle down, children; you're making too much noise!* **6** *phrasal v. insep.* **to settle for s.t.:** to accept s.t. (usu. less than what was wanted): *He wanted $2,000 for his car, but settled for $1,500.* **7** *phrasal v.* **to settle in:** to get used to a new place: *The kids settled in to their new school quickly.* **8** *phrasal v.* **to settle up:** to pay s.o. money owed, to make things even: *Let's settle up; I'll pay you for the drinks you bought.*

set·tle·ment /ˈsɛtlmənt/ *n.* a small, new town or area where a group of people has decided to live: *Many large midwestern cities started as settlements in the 1800s.*

set·tler /ˈsɛtlər/ *n.* a person who moves to and stays in a new, growing area: *The original settlers in the Midwest built towns and planted corn.*

set·up /ˈsɛtˌʌp/ *n.* [C, *usu. sing.*] **1** a situation meant to catch or trap s.o.: *You told me to meet my cousin at noon, but she wasn't there; it's a setup!* **2** the way a place or situation is arranged: *This is not the usual setup; they moved the table and chairs.*

sev·en /ˈsɛvən/ *n.* the cardinal number 7 —*adj.* 7 of something: *seven lemons*

S

sev·en·teen /ˌsɛvən'tin/ *n.* the cardinal number 17
—*adj.* 17 of something: *seventeen years old*

sev·en·ty /'sɛvənti/ *n.* the cardinal number 70
—*adj.* 70 of s.t.: *He is seventy years old.*

sev·er /'sɛvər/ *v.* **1** to cut apart: *He fell under a train, and it severed one of his legs.* **2** to cut off, to stop an activity: *The government severed relations with the other country, and it led to war.* -*n.* [U] **severance** /'sɛvərəns, 'sɛvrəns/.

sev·er·al /'sɛvərəl, 'sɛvrəl/ *adj.* a few, more than two: *Several people saw the accicent, not just you.||The hotel is several miles away, so let's drive.*

USAGE NOTE: *Several* describes a number greater than *two* but fewer than *many*. It is used for count nouns: *several books on the table||several friends.*

severance pay *n.* [U] money paid by a company to workers when they leave or are fired: *She received two months of severance pay, so she can take some time finding another job.*

se·vere /sə'vɪr/ *adj.* **1** very strong: *The severe storm blew down a tree.* **2** serious, dangerous: *She has a severe case of the flu.* **3** strict: *The owner gives a severe frown to anyone who is late.* -*adv.* **severely.**

se·ver·i·ty /sə'vɛrəti/ *n.* [U] **1** strength (of s.t. bad): *I couldn't walk because of the severity of the pain.* **2** seriousness: *The severity of the issue called for intense discussion.* **3** strictness: *The teacher treats her students with severity; they have homework every night and a quiz every week.*

sew /soʊ/ *v.* **sewed** or **sewn** /soʊn/, **sewing, sews** **1** to put together with a needle and thread: *I lost a button, and I sewed a new one on.||She sews her own dresses.* **2** *phrasal v. sep.* **to sew s.t. up: a.** to fix or mend a piece of clothing: *She sewed up a hole in her skirt.||She sewed it up.* **b.** *infrml.* to come to an agreement, to end: *We worked on the plan for months and sewed it up this morning.* **c.** to control completely, (*syn.*) to monopolize: *Our competitior has that market sewed up; we can't break in.*

sew·age /'suɪdʒ/ *n.* [U] waste and liquid that goes from toilets to pipes underground

sew·er /'suər/ *n.* the tunnels and pipes that carry sewage

sew·ing /'soʊɪŋ/ *n.* [U] **1** the act of sewing: *I like knitting better than sewing.* **2** things to be sewed: *She keeps her sewing in a basket.*

sewing machine *n.* an electrical machine that works by pressing one's foot on a pedal and that makes sewing faster

sex /sɛks/ *n.* **1** the state of being male or female, (*syn.*) gender: *What sex is the new baby?* **2 to have sex:** to have sexual intercourse

—*adj.* **1** related to being male or female: *sex differences* **2** related to sex: *sex education*

sex appeal *n.* [U] the sexual attractiveness of a person: *Most men think that beautiful actress has a lot of sex appeal.*

sex·less /'sɛkslɪs/ *adj.fig.* not giving off any sexual feeling: *That guy is totally sexless; I can't imagine him kissing any woman.*

sex·pot /'sɛks,pɑt/ *n.infrml.* a person who has a lot of sex or who gives off strong sexual feelings: *Look at that smile; what a sexpot!*

sex·u·al /'sɛkʃuəl/ *adj.* related to sexuality: *The couple has a strong sexual attraction for each other.*

sexual intercourse *n.* the act of having sex, (*syn.*) copulation

sex·u·al·i·ty /ˌsɛkʃu'æləti/ *n.* [U] **1** sexual life and experience: *The doctor studied human sexuality and learned about male and female attitudes toward love and sex.* **2** the quality of being sexual: *A person of strong sexuality can send messages with the eyes.*

sex·y /'sɛksi/ *adj.* **-ier, -iest** **1** causing desire, (*syns.*) erotic, seductive: *She thought he looked sexy in his bathing suit.* **2** attractive, interesting: *She drives a sexy new sports car.*

shab·by /'ʃæbi/ *adj.* **-bier, -biest** **1** worn, often not clean: *He looks shabby in his old clothes and dirty shoes.* **2** falling apart, dirty: *a shabby apartment building* **3** disrespectful, bad: *You were late and forgot to bring a gift to the party; what shabby behavior! -adv.* **shabbily.**

shack /ʃæk/ *n.* a small house or shed, usu. of wood and not well built: *The strange old lady lived in a tiny shack in the woods.*
—*phrasal v. slang* **to shack up:** to live together or have sex without being married: *They shacked up for a few months before the wedding, sharing her house.*

shack·le /'ʃækəl/ *n.* a metal chain and ring locked to s.o.'s hands and legs to prevent escape: *The prisoner was put in shackles and led slowly away.*
—*v.* **-led, -ling, -les** **1** to place s.o. in shackles: *She was shackled so she couldn't run.* **2** *fig.* to prevent s.o. from doing s.t.: *I cannot help you with your work; my boss has me shackled.*

shade /ʃeɪd/ *n.* **1** [U] an area that does not receive sunlight: *The sun is so hot; let's move into the shade under the tree.* **2** [C] a color that is only slightly different from a basic one: *Which shade of yellow do you like, lemon or gold?* **3** [C] a window for privacy and to lessen the amount of light: *I lowered all of the window shades so people couldn't see in.* **4** [C] a very small amount: *a shade of difference*
—*v.* to keep from light: *The big tree shades the house from the sun.*

shad·ing /ˈʃeɪdɪŋ/ *n.* [U] darkness that helps show depth in a picture: *The shading in the painting made the sea look very real.*

shad·ow /ˈʃædoʊ/ *n.* **1** the dark shape formed when s.o. or s.t. blocks the sun or other light: *The houses made long shadows in the late afternoon.‖At night, scary things hide in the shadows on city streets.* **2 afraid of one's own shadow:** easily frightened, very timid: *That nervous dog is afraid of his own shadow.* **3 to cast a long shadow:** to have great potential influence: *The power of the Arab states cast a long shadow over the oil business.*
—*v.* **1** (in art) to color in dark areas **2** *infrml.* to follow s.o.: *A police officer shadowed the suspect through the dark streets.* -*adj.* **shadowy.**

shad·y /ˈʃeɪdi/ *adj.* **-ier, -iest 1** out of the sunlight: *It's too hot in the sun; let's go under the tree where it is shady.* **2** bad or dishonest: *The stranger who offered me a ride from the airport looks like a shady character.*

shaft /ʃæft/ *n.* **1** a round metal bar that turns, giving power in a long section of machinery: *the drive shaft of a truck* **2** the stem of a plant: *a shaft of wheat* **3** a hollow tube or tunnel: *a mine shaft* **4** a ray of light: *a shaft of sunlight* **5** *n.v.vulg.* **to give s.o. the shaft:** to cheat or ignore s.o.: *You gave him the <n.> shaft when you promised to meet him at 10:00 and never showed up.‖His boss <v.> shafted him when she gave a raise to everyone but him.*

shag /ʃæg/ *n.* [U] **1** a loose, rough, messy texture in fabric or hair: *a shag rug‖a shag haircut* **2** a hopping dance
—*v.* **shagged, shagging, shags 1** (in baseball) to run after balls and throw them back into play **2** to catch fly balls in practice

shag·gy /ˈʃægi/ **-gier, -giest** *adj.* with rough, messy hair or fur: *a dog with a shaggy coat*

shake /ʃeɪk/ *v.* **shook** /ʃʊk/ **shaken** /ˈʃeɪkən/, **shaking, shakes 1** to make quick, repeated, back-and-forth movements: *I shook the sand out of the towel.‖An earthquake makes the ground shake.* **2** to make tiny, quick, repeated movements, usu. from fear or cold, (*syns.*) to tremble, quiver: *She was shaking until she put on a sweater.‖He is so frightened that he is shaking.* **3 to shake hands:** to join right hands with s.o. and move them up and down, in greeting or agreement **4** *phrasal v. insep.* **to shake on s.t.:** to show agreement, usu. with a handshake: *We both think the price is right, so let's shake on it.* **5** *phrasal v. sep.* **to shake (s.o.) down: a.** *s.o.:* to get money illegally: *The criminals tried to shake the store owner down by saying they would burn the place.* **b.** to get used to s.t. new: *I am shaking down well in my new job.* **6** *phrasal v. sep.*

to shake s.o. or **s.t. off: a.** *s.o.:* to get away from s.o.: *The bank robber shook off the police who tried to follow him.* **b.** *s.t.:* to ignore s.t.: *The football player was hurt, but he shook off the pain and continued playing.* **7** *phrasal v. sep.* **to shake s.o.** or **s.t. up: a.** *s.o.:* to make s.o. very scared or uncomfortable: *The pilot shook up the passengers when he said the plane was low on gas.‖He shook them up.* **b.** *s.t.:* to rearrange, disorganize: *The new boss decided to shake up the office.*
—*n.* **1** a quick motion: *He gave the blanket a shake.* **2** a handshake **3** a drink made of milk, flavored syrup, and ice cream, also called a milkshake **4 in two shakes (of a lamb's tail):** very soon: *I'm leaving now; I'll be at your house in two shakes.* **5** *infrml.* **no great shakes:** not very good, of little importance: *Don't see the movie; it's no great shakes.‖You are late for the appointment, but don't worry; it's no great shakes.* **6 the shakes: a.** fear: *He drives so badly that he gives me the shakes every time I ride with him.* **b.** uncontrollable movement of the body: *The addict got the shakes when they took away the drugs. See:* fair shake.

shake·down /ˈʃeɪkˌdaʊn/ *n.infrml.* **1** an illegal way of getting money: *In a shakedown, one robber pointed a gun while the other emptied the cash register.* **2** a trial run, a test to find weak spots or faults: *The tourist ship is new, so the crew is taking it on a shakedown to test it. See:* shake.

shake·out /ˈʃeɪkˌaʊt/ *n.* the reduction of the number of workers and companies during a period of economic difficulty: *Many small businesses in town are firing people and closing during a shakeout*

shak·er /ˈʃeɪkər/ *n.* a container for s.t. to be shaken, usu. salt or pepper

shake·up /ˈʃeɪkˌʌp/ *n.* a large reorganization, often of a business and its staff: *The new president fired half the managers and got rid of three departments; it was a big shakeup.*

shak·y /ˈʃeɪki/ *adj.* **-ier, -iest 1** characterized by shaking, trembling: *During an earthquake, the ground is shaky.* **2** *fig.* not firm or sure, doubtful: *The company is doing badly; its future is shaky.*

shall /ʃæl/ *v. aux. part. of* should **1** used in formal writing, esp. in law, to express a command: *The prisoner shall serve 20 years in jail.‖The amount shall be $1,000.* **2** used as part of a question when offering a suggestion: *Shall I go to the movies tonight?‖Shall we leave now? See:* will.

USAGE NOTE: In American English, the word *shall* is seldom used to express the simple fu-

S

ture, as in "I shall go tomorrow." Instead, the word *will* is used most commonly: *I will go (decide, arrive, etc.) tomorrow.*

shal·low /'ʃæloʊ/ *adj.* **1** not deep: *The pond is shallow; the water goes only up to my knees.* **2** not serious or complicated, (*syn.*) superficial: *A shallow person does not look beyond the obvious.* **3** weak: *shallow breaths*

sham /ʃæm/ *n.* **1** s.t. fake, s.t. false that pretends to be real: *His story is a sham; he was born in Nebraska, not Spain!* **2** a piece of cloth that covers a household item: *a pillow sham*

sha·man /'ʃɑmən, 'ʃeɪ-/ *n.* a wise man that is thought to have magic or spiritual powers: *The shaman said rain would soon come to the dry land.*

sham·bles /'ʃæmbəlz/ *n.pl.* **1** a messy or ruined place: *This bedroom is a shambles, with dirty clothes and toys everywhere.* **2 in shambles:** destroyed, in a mess: *After the flood, the house was in shambles.||The government was in shambles after many years of weak Presidents.*

shame /ʃeɪm/ *n.* [U] **1** a sad feeling because of knowing one has done wrong: *He stole money from the church and later felt great shame.* **2** a sad situation, a pity: *It's a shame you can't go shopping with us.* **3 shame on you:** you have done wrong and should feel badly: *Don't ever swear at me again; shame on you!*
—*v.* **shamed, shaming, shames** to cause s.o. to feel bad through guilt: *The minister shamed the thief by telling his name to the people.*

shame·ful /'ʃeɪmfəl/ *adj.* **1** very bad, (*syn.*) disgraceful: *It was a shameful lie to tell the old lady she had won a million dollars.* **2** sad, (*syns.*) regrettable, pitiful: *It is shameful that the police did not catch the thief.*

shame·less /'ʃeɪmlɪs/ *adj.* not caring about shame or guilt, bold: *She tells lies in a shameless way, looking me straight in the eye.* -*adv.* **shamelessly.**

sham·poo /ʃæm'pu/ *n.* **-poos 1** [C;U] a liquid soap for cleaning the hair: *I use gentle shampoo on my baby's hair.* **2** [C] the cleaning of the hair or other fibers: *The barber gives me a shampoo before a haircut.*
—*v.* to clean the hair with a liquid soap: *She shampoos her hair every time she takes a shower.*

sham·rock /'ʃæm,rɑk/ *n.* [C;U] a tiny green plant with three leaves, the symbol of Ireland

shang·hai /'ʃæŋ,haɪ, ʃæŋ'haɪ/ *v.* **1** to trick s.o. into working as a sailor against his or her wishes: *Long ago, men were hit over the head and dragged off to a ship; they were shanghaied.* **2** to trick s.o. into doing s.t.: *We shanghaied my mom into going to the action movie by telling her it was a love story.*

shank /ʃæŋk/ *n.* **1** the part of the human leg between knee and ankle **2** meat that comes from the leg of an animal: *lamb shank* **3** the long, narrow part of many objects, such as a nail, a (tobacco) pipe, or a drill.

shan·ty /'ʃænti/ *n.* **-ties** a small, badly built house, (*syn.*) a shack: *Homeless people built shanties in the park.*

shan·ty·town /'ʃænti,taʊn/ *n.* a poor section of a city or town with many shanties

shape /ʃeɪp/ *n.* **1** [C;U] the form or outline of s.t.: *The dollar bill is in the shape of a rectangle.||The sculptor worked the stone into a human shape.* **2** [C;U] the form of s.o.'s body: *She has a beautiful shape, with a small waist and curvy hips.* **3** [U] condition, readiness: *She exercises every day to stay in shape.||We're in good shape; we have everything planned and are about to begin.* **4 to take shape:** to develop: *As the writer worked on the novel, the characters took shape slowly.*
—*v.* **shaped, shaping, shapes 1** to make into a shape: *He shaped the meat into hamburgers.* **2** to have an effect, influence: *The struggle between countries shapes world events.* **3 shape up or ship out!:** behave better or leave: *the assistant was told "Shape up or ship out." when he arrived late to work three days in a row.* **4** *phrasal v. sep.* **to shape s.o.** or **s.t. up: a. s.o.:** to behave better: *Dad told the kids to shape up or they'd get no supper.* **b. s.t.:** to develop: *The way business is shaping up, it looks as though the company will make money this year.*

shape·ly /'ʃeɪpli/ *adj.* **-lier, -liest** with a curvy, pleasing body, usu. said of a woman: *Marilyn Monroe had a shapely figure.*

share /ʃer/ *n.* **1** one's own part or portion of s.t.: *I paid my share of the total cost.||She ate more than her share of potatoes.* **2** an equal portion of property or stock: *I own 12 shares in an oil company.*
—*v.* **shared, sharing, shares 1** to receive with others: *When we sold the business, my sister and I shared equally in the profits.* **2** to use or experience with others: *We shared a meal together.||The little girl shared her toys with her friend.* **3** to have s.t. in common: *He shares his father's blue eyes.* **4** to tell s.o. s.t. private: *I share my deepest thoughts with my wife.* **5 share and share alike:** an expression indicating mutual giving: *He gave me one of his sandwiches, and I gave him some of my candy; share and share alike.*

share·crop·per /'ʃer,krɑpər/ *n.* a person who does farm work for s.o. and receives a small part of the crops or money earned

share·hold·er /'ʃer,hoʊldər/ *n.* **1** the owner of shares in a stock: *The shareholders' meeting of our company will be in May.* **2** the owner of shares in a business: *My friend owns a big farm, and there are 16 family shareholders in it. See:* stockholder.

shark /ʃɑrk/ *n.* **1** meat-eating fish, usu. gray in color and with tough skin, sometimes dangerous **2** *fig.* a sly, cheating person: *That shark got his money from stealing credit cards.* **3** s.o. who is very good at an activity: *a card shark See:* loan.

shark

sharp /ʃɑrp/ *adj.* **-er, -est 1** with a fine point or edge that is able to go through a surface or cut with ease: *a sharp knife*\|*a sharp arrow* **2** (of feeling) strong, intense: *a sharp pain in my stomach* **3** *fig.* quick and intelligent: *She finds a lot of mistakes; she's sharp.* **4** angry, severe: *My aunt spoke to us with sharp words when we walked in her flowers.* **5** neat and stylish: *My brother shops at the best stores; he's a sharp dresser. -adv.* **sharply.**

sharp·en /ˈʃɑrpən/ *v.* **1** to make pointed or to give a cutting edge: *sharpen a razor*\|*sharpen a pencil* **2** to improve (skills, knowledge, etc.): *The pianist practices a lot to sharpen his playing.*

sharp·shoot·er /ˈʃɑrpˌʃutər/ *n.* **1** an expert with a gun **2** *fig.* s.o. highly critical of others and their actions

sharp-tongued *adj.* using slightly angry language, (*syns.*) sarcastic, critical: *When he doesn't agree with s.o., he becomes sharp-tongued.*

shave /ʃeɪv/ *v.* **shaved** or **shaven** /ˈʃeɪvən/, **shaving, shaves 1** to cut off thin layers: *The carpenter shaved pieces off the door so it will close properly.* **2** *fig.* to cut hair close to the skin with a razor: *My brother's chin is smooth after he shaves.*
—*n.* **1** the act of cutting hair close to the skin: *Your beard is growing too long; you need a shave.* **2 a close shave:** a bad or scary situation that one barely avoids: *The taxi just missed me as I stepped onto the street; that was a close shave! -n.* [C;U] **shaving.**

shav·er /ˈʃeɪvər/ *n.* a tool used to shave, a razor: *I left my shaver in the bathroom.*

shaving cream (gel, lotion) *n.* [U] a semi-liquid substance applied to the skin to make shaving easier: *My mother spreads shaving lotion on her legs before she shaves them.*

shawl /ʃɔl/ *n.* a large knit or woven piece of fabric worn around the head or shoulders: *She wore a shawl to keep warm in cold weather.*

she /ʃi/ *pron.* third person feminine singular: *She is a brilliant woman. See:* who, USAGE NOTE.

sheaf /ʃif/ *n.* **sheaves** /ʃivz/ **1** corn, wheat, or other grain tied together **2** a bundle of s.t.: *The lawyer took a sheaf of papers from his brief-case.*

shear /ʃir/ *v.* **sheared** or **shorn** /ʃɔrn/, **shearing, shears** to cut: *Farmers shear their sheep for their wool.*\|*The car door was shorn off in an accident.*
—*n.pl.* a large pair of scissors: *I used shears* (or) *a pair of shears to cut the thick paper.*

sheath /ʃiθ/ *n.* **sheaths** /ʃiθs, ʃiðz/ **1** an outer covering, often a holder: *The hunter put his knife back in its sheath.* **2** a simple, close-fitting dress
—*v.* **sheathe** /ʃið/, **sheathed, sheathing, sheathes** to put s.t. in a sheath: *to sheathe swords*

she·bang /ʃəˈbæŋ/ *n.slang* the whole shebang: all of something (objects, a situation, an event, etc.): *We packed all our files and equipment, and the movers took the whole shebang to our new offices.*\|*The wedding was expensive, but her parents paid for the whole shebang.*

shed /ʃɛd/ *n.* a small building, often used for storage: *We keep our gardening tools in a shed behind the house.*
—*v.* **shed, shedding, sheds 1** to lose hair or skin without cutting or pulling, (*syn.*) to molt: *In the spring, animals shed their winter coats.*\|*The snake shed its skin.* **2** to cause to flow: *In times of war, much blood is shed on battlefields.*\|*We shed tears at the funeral.* **3** to keep liquid from entering: *a waterproof coat that sheds rain* **4** to get rid of s.t. unwanted: *I have ten more pounds to shed.* **5 to shed some light on s.t.:** to make s.t. more understandable: *This book is very difficult. Could you shed some light on the author's meaning?*

she-devil *n.* an evil, wicked woman: *The she-devil who lives in that old house screams at children from her window.*

sheen /ʃin/ *n.* [C, usu. *sing.*; U] brightness or shine on s.t.: *silk that has a sheen*\|*the sheen of a cat's fur*

sheep /ʃip/ *n.* **sheep** an animal often seen on farms, kept for its wool and for meat: *The sheep looked like moving clouds as they ate grass in the field.*

sheep·ish /ˈʃipɪʃ/ *adj.* embarrassed and a bit shy: *The couple looked sheepish when we caught them kissing.*

sheep·skin /ˈʃipˌskɪn/ *n.* **1** the skin of a sheep, often used for leather **2** *fig.* a diploma

sheer /ʃɪr/ *adj.* **-er, -est 1** thin and able to be seen through: *We saw people moving behind the sheer curtains.* **2** absolute, complete: *The murderer killed a man in an act of sheer madness.*\|*I picked the right number and won by sheer luck.*

sheet /ʃit/ *n.* **1** a thin piece of cloth used as a bed covering **2** a thin surface or piece of s.t.: *a sheet of paper‖a cookie sheet for baking* **3** a surface: *The driveway was a sheet of ice.*

sheik /ʃik, ʃeɪk/ *n.* the head of an Arab nation, tribe, or village: *The sheiks met to discuss the price of oil.* **-n. sheikdom.**

shelf /ʃɛlf/ *n.* **shelves** /ʃɛlvz/ **1** a flat piece of wood, metal, etc. that is attached to a wall or other support and is used to hold objects: *My bookcase has six shelves.* **2 off the shelf:** on hand, ready to sell: *The store didn't need to order the stereo; I bought it off the shelf* (or) *it was an off-the-shelf item.* **3 on the shelf:** put away, inactive: *We worked hard on a new idea, but the boss put it on the shelf as too expensive.* —*v. See:* shelve.

shelf life *n.* the length of time that s.t. lasts or is available for sale before it goes bad or is not usable: *The shelf life for this milk is only one week.*

shell /ʃɛl/ *n.* **1** [C;U] the hard, protective outer covering of an animal, seed, or plant: *a turtle's shell‖the shell of a walnut* **2** [C] a bullet or other piece of ammunition: *shells from a gun* **3** [C] the outer structure of s.t.: *Workers removed the interior walls and floors of a building and left the shell standing.* **4** [C] the edible holder for a filling: *a pie shell* **5 to come out of one's shell:** to be less shy: *The quiet boy came out of his shell at the party.* **6 to go into one's shell:** to become quiet, to stop communicating: *When he is angry, he goes into his shell for a while and then comes back smiling.* —*v.* **1** to remove the shell or covering: *We shelled peanuts and put them in a bowl.* **2** to shoot at: *to shell the enemy* **3** *phrasal v. sep.* **to shell s.t. out:** to spend (money, often unwillingly): *I shelled out thousands of dollars to pay for a sailboat.‖I shelled them out.*

shell·fish /ˈʃɛlˌfɪʃ/ *n.* [C;U] **-fish** or **-fishes** any water animal with an outer shell (oyster, clam, mussel, lobster, crab, etc.)

shell-shocked /ˈʃɛlˌʃɑkt/ *adj.* **1** mentally ill because of the stress of war and battle **2** *fig.* not able to function because of a horrible experience: *He was shell-shocked when the boss fired him.*

shel·ter /ˈʃɛltər/ *n.* **1** [C;U] any building or covering (tree branches, a cave, etc.) that gives physical protection: *When it started to rain, we found shelter under a tree.* **2** [C] a place where homeless or abused people can sleep, eat, and be safe: *The woman moved to a shelter after her husband beat her.* **3** a protective arrangement: *We bought a second home as a tax shelter.* —*v.* to protect s.o. or s.t.: *The little house shelters us from the snow and cold.*

shelve /ʃɛlv/ *v.* **1** to place s.t. on a shelf: *to shelve books* **2** *fig.* to make s.t. inactive: *When*

our sister got sick, we shelved our vacation plans.

shelv·ing /ˈʃɛlvɪŋ/ *n.* [U] shelves: *The dining room has shelving for cups and plates.*

she·nan·i·gans /ʃəˈnænəgənz/ *n.pl.* **1** mischievous acts, tricks, (*syn.*) pranks: *The child's shenanigans included putting spiders in her sister's bed.* **2** wrong or illegal acts, trickery: *Now he is in jail, so there will be no more of his shenanigans.*

shep·herd /ˈʃɛpərd/ **shep·herd·ess** /ˈʃɛpərdɪs/ *n.* a person who takes care of sheep in the fields —*v.* **1** to keep sheep together **2** *fig.* to guide s.o. or s.t.: *The teacher shepherded the kids into the classroom.*

sher·bet /ˈʃɜrbɪt/ *n.* [U] a frozen dessert made of water, sugar, milk, and a fruit flavoring: *orange sherbet See:* sorbet.

sher·iff /ˈʃɛrəf/ *n.* a head or chief, usu. of a county's police department

sher·ry /ˈʃɛri/ *n.* [C;U] **-ries** a strong wine from Spain or made in the Spanish way, usually drunk before dinner: *We drank a bit of sherry, a gift from Spain.*

shield /ʃild/ *n.* **1** a piece of metal or other substance carried in one hand to protect oneself from flying objects: *The rocks bounced off the horseman's shield.* **2** a protective covering: *The electric saw has a shield over the blade.* **3** a policeman's badge —*v.* to protect s.t. with a physical or legal barrier: *I shielded my eyes from the sun.‖The business shielded its money against taxes.*

shift /ʃɪft/ *n.* **1** a change in position or location: *a shift of money from one bank to another* **2** a change of ideas: *a political shift from right to left* **3** a segment of work time: *The night shift begins at 11:00 p.m.* **4** a simple dress —*v.* **1** to change from one position to another: *The truck driver shifted gears.* **2** to change in general: *That singer is shifting from jazz to classical music.*

shift·less /ˈʃɪftlɪs/ *adj.* without plans or ambitions, lazy: *Stop being so shiftless; get out of bed and go to work!*

shift·y /ˈʃɪfti/ *adj.* **-ier, -iest** not to be trusted, (*syns.*) devious, crafty: *Don't loan your money to that shifty guy; you'll never see it again.*

shill /ʃɪl/ *n.* a person who works for a gambling business, salesperson, etc. who pretends to be a gambler or customer so as to attract others to spend money: *She acted like a tourist in Las Vegas, but she was a shill for the casino.*

shil·ling /ˈʃɪlɪŋ/ *n.* in the UK monetary system (until 1971), 1/20 of a pound

shil·ly-shal·ly /ˈʃɪliˌʃæli/ *v.n.adj.* to be indecisive: *I hate to shop with her because she <v.> shilly-shallies about every decision.*

S

shim·mer /'ʃɪmər/ *n.* [U] *v.* to give off gently moving light, (*syn.*) to sparkle: *The sun <v.> shimmers on the lake.*

shim·my /'ʃɪmi/ *n.v.* **-mied, -mying, -mies 1** a dance in which one shakes the body from the shoulders down: *The woman's dress made little waves as she <v.> shimmied.* **2** a shaking in a car's machinery: *My car has a <n.> shimmy in the front wheels; it must need new brakes.*

shin /ʃɪn/ *n.infrml.* the frontal part of the lower leg

shin·dig /'ʃɪn,dɪg/ *n.infrml.* a big party

shine /ʃaɪn/ *n. usu. sing.* **1** a brightness on s.t. because of smoothness or light: *He just polished the knives and forks to a brilliant shine.* **2** nice, sunny weather, usu. used in the expression *"rain or shine"* **3** a liking, a want: *She took a shine to that cute dog.*
—*v.* **shone** /ʃoʊn/ or **shined, shining, shines 1** to make s.t. bright and clean: *He shines his shoes every day.* **2** to do s.t. very well, (*syn.*) to excel: *Her violin performance shone because she had practiced a lot.* **3** to have a happy expression: *His face was shining after he won the game.*

shin·er /'ʃaɪnər/ *n.infrml.* a black eye: *He was in a fight and got a shiner on his right eye.*

shin·gle /'ʃɪŋgəl/ *n.* **1** a small, rectangular piece of wood or other material used in overlapping rows as the outer covering of a building's roof or walls: *Some shingles on the roof of our house blew off during a storm.* **2** *pl.* a viral disease that causes pain and later itchy blisters, usu. on one side of the body or on the face
—*v.* **-gled, -gling, -gles** to put shingles on: *We had the roof shingled so it wouldn't leak.*

shin·ny /'ʃɪni/ *v.* **-nied, -nying, -nies** to climb s.t. that has no branches or handles by pulling oneself up with the hands and feet: *The boy shinnied up the flagpole.*

ship /ʃɪp/ *n.* **1** a large boat: *The ship is bringing silk from Hong Kong.* **2** an airplane or rocket
—*v.* **shipped, shipping, ships 1** to send s.t. (by any method, not just by ship): *The mailorder company shipped my new boots by air.* **2** *phrasal v.* **to ship out:** to depart on a ship, usu. as part of the crew: *We ship out tomorrow for a six-month trip. See:* shape (up or ship out).

ship·load /'ʃɪp,loʊd/ *n.* the quantity of people or things that a ship can hold: *The cruise ship left with a shipload of passengers today.*

ship·ment /'ʃɪpmənt/ *n.* **1** [U] the act of shipping s.t.: *We sent the shipment of furniture by truck.* **2** [C] the contents of a shipment: *A shipment of books arrived at the library. -n.* [C] **shipper.**

ship·ping /'ʃɪpɪŋ/ *n.* [U] **1** the act of sending a shipment: *We have workers that do the shipping from our warehouse.* **2** the activities or business of ships: *Shipping in coastal towns was slowed by bad weather.*

ship·shape /'ʃɪp'ʃeɪp/ *adj.* very neat: *We cleaned the garage until it was shipshape.*

ship·wreck /'ʃɪp,rɛk/ *n.v.* the loss or destruction of a ship: *The terrible storm caused a <n.> shipwreck.*

shirk /ʃɜrk/ *v.* to avoid work and responsibility: *He arrives at the office on time, but he shirks his work. -n.* **shirker.**

shirt /ʃɜrt/ *n.* **1** a piece of clothing worn on the upper body, often with sleeves, a collar, and buttons: *He bought a tie to match his shirt.* **2** *slang* **to keep one's shirt on:** not to get too excited or angry, to keep one's temper: *Keep your shirt on; don't hit that guy.* **3** *slang* **to lose one's shirt:** to lose a lot of money: *They lost their shirt when they sold the stock. See:* blouse; sweat shirt; T-shirt.

shirt·less /'ʃɜrtlɪs/ *adj.* not wearing a shirt: *My husband goes shirtless when he mows the lawn in hot weather.*

shirt·sleeve /'ʃɜrt,sliv/ *n.* **1** the part of a shirt from shoulder to wrist **2** *pl.* not wearing a jacket: *We went to a casual meeting in our shirtsleeves.*
—*adj.fig.* informal and enthusiastic: *a shirtsleeve boss*

shiv·er /'ʃɪvər/ *v.* to shake in the body (from cold, fear, excitement, etc.), (*syns.*) to tremble, quiver: *She is shivering as she waits for a bus in the snow.*
—*n.* **1** a shake in the body: *a shiver of excitement* **2** **a shiver up one's spine:** a quick feeling or emotion (usu. fear or excitement): *Thoughts of her birthday party sent a shiver of delight up the little girl's spine.*

shoal /ʃoʊl/ *n.* **1** a strip of sand beneath shallow water: *The boat bottom hit a shoal.* **2** a large group of fish

shock /ʃɑk/ *n.* **1** [C;U] a sudden psychological blow: *She got a terrible shock when she learned that her son was in the hospital.* **2** [C;U] strong, quick impact: *The car hit a wall, and the shock threw the driver against the windshield.* **3** [C;U] a quick pain caused by electricity: *I got a shock when I plugged in the lamp.* **4 in shock:** in medical shock **5 to go into shock:** to lose blood pressure and other bodily processes from a medical crisis or injury: *Immediately after the accident, the driver went into shock.*
—*v.* **1** to cause strong emotion (usu. bad): *Her mother's sudden death shocked her.* **2** to surprise in a bad way, (*syn.*) to scandalize: *I was shocked when I saw the doctor's bill.*

S

shock·er /'ʃakər/ n. s.t. that causes surprise or strong emotion: *When I heard that you had twins, it was a shocker!*

shock·ing /'ʃakɪŋ/ adj. causing surprise or strong emotion, (syn.) scandalous: *The news of his leaving his high-paying job is shocking.*

shock waves n. **1** the movement through water, ground, or air caused by an explosion, earthquake, bomb, etc. **2** fig. great surprise, felt by many people: *The failure of many banks sent shock waves through the world in the 1930s.*

shod /ʃad/ adj. related to wearing shoes or other footwear: *The poor child was not even shod until a kind neighbor gave her some boots.||Horses are shod with horseshoes.*

shod·dy /'ʃadi/ adj. **-dier, -diest 1** poorly made: *Those are shoddy houses; they'll probably need new roofs in five years.* **2** careless and impolite: *The service was shoddy in the new restaurant; the waiters were slow and rude.* -adv. **shoddily.**

shoe /ʃu/ n. **1** a covering for the foot, usu. of leather and with a sole and heel: *My shoes have laces, and hers have high heels.* **2** a part of a vehicle's brake **3 if the shoe fits, wear it:** if the description is correct, accept it: *I know you don't like it when I say you're selfish, but if the shoe fits, wear it.* **4 in s.o.'s shoes:** to be in s.o.'s place: *I wish that I was in your shoes when you met that famous rock star. See:* boot; sandal; sneaker.

shoe·lace /'ʃu,leɪs/ n. the cloth or leather strings used to tie shoes

shoe·shine /'ʃu,ʃaɪn/ n. a cleaning and polishing of the shoes: *I paid a man for a shoeshine at the airport.*

shoe·string /'ʃu,strɪŋ/ n. **1** a shoelace **2 on a shoestring:** on a strict budget, (syn.) frugally: *That manager runs the company on a shoestring by not paying high salaries and renting inexpensive space.*

shoo /ʃu/ v. **1** to tell s.o. or s.t. to go away by using motions: *The cook shooed the flies away from the food with his hat.||The woman shoos dogs off her lawn.* **2** an expression meaning "go away": *Shoo! Go play outside!*

shoo-in n. a certain winner: *He is a shoo-in to win the tennis match because the other player has a weak arm.*

shook-up /ʃʊk'ʌp/ adj.frml. upset, (syns.) unnerved, rattled: *When his girlfriend told him that she had a new boyfriend, he was shook-up. See:* shake.

shoot /ʃut/ v. **shot** /ʃat/, **shooting, shoots 1** to use a gun: *to shoot a rifle* **2** to hit s.o. or s.t. with a bullet from a gun: *The robber shot a hole in the ceiling.||The hunter shot a deer.* **3** to hunt with guns: *We went out to shoot geese*

last weekend. **4** to cause to fly or move quickly: *He shot an arrow at a mark in the tree.* **5** to move quickly: *My arm shot out to catch the ball.||The frightened child shot across the room.* **6** to play some games: *to shoot marbles||to shoot pool* **7** to take pictures, use film: *I shot a roll of color film.||The director is shooting her new movie in Washington.* **8 shoot!:** a command meaning "go ahead, start talking": *Oh, do you have s.t. to say? Shoot!* **9 to shoot at:** to shoot a bullet at s.o. or s.t.: *Soldiers shoot at the enemy.* **10** phrasal v. insep. **to shoot around (by or past) s.o.:** to pass s.o. rapidly: *The football player shot around (by or past) the other man and scored a goal.* **11 to shoot baskets, to shoot hoops:** to throw a basketball through a hoop, to play basketball: *Let's go to the playground and shoot some hoops.* **12** phrasal v. sep. **to shoot for or at s.t.:** to try for, to have a goal: *The sales manager is shooting for a 20 percent sales increase this year.||He's shooting for it.* **13 to shoot from the hip:** to speak carelessly without thinking: *Try to work through the problem and find the best solution; don't just shoot from the hip.* **14** slang **to shoot off one's mouth:** to talk too much: *The more he shoots off his mouth, the less we listen.* **15 to shoot one's wad:** to use the last of s.t. (money, energy, etc.): *I shot my wad when I spent the morning in Las Vegas and could not buy a bus ticket home.* **16** phrasal v. sep. **to shoot (s.t.) out: a.** to (cause to) come out with force: *When she laughed, food shot out of her mouth.* **b. s.t.:** to decide by shooting: *They shot out their argument in the street.||They shot it out.* **17 to shoot over:** to go somewhere quickly: *I'll shoot over right now to return the shirt I borrowed.* **18** phrasal v. sep. **to shoot s.o. or s.t. down: a. s.o.:** fig. to say unkind things and make s.o. feel bad or ashamed: *Every time he tries to say something, his wife shoots down that man.||She shoots him down.* **b. s.t.:** to cause s.t. to fall down or out of the air by shooting: *Pilots shot down enemy airplanes in combat.* **19 to shoot the breeze:** to talk together in a relaxed way, (syn.) to chat: *I met two friends at a café, and we shot the breeze for a while.* **20** phrasal v. sep. **to shoot up: a.** to go upwards quickly: *After we watered our plants, they shot up.* **b.** slang to take drugs into the body with a needle: *She shoots up heroin and snorts cocaine; she's a drug addict.*

—n. **1** a party or gathering where there is a shooting contest: *a turkey shoot* **2** a small, young plant growth: *a shoot of grass* **3** a sudden, strong feeling: *a shoot of pain through my lower back* **4** the use of camera and film: *The model will wear different swimsuits for her shoot on the beach.*

—*interj.* used to express regret or annoyance, or to add emphasis to a response: *Shoot, I left my wallet at home!*||*Does your cat swim? Shoot, no!*

shoot-em-up /ˈʃutəm,ʌp/ *n.infrml.* a movie or TV show with a lot of gun action: *There's a shoot-'em-up about the Vietnam War on TV tonight.*

shooting star *n.* a meteor that makes a line of light as it moves through the night sky

shoot·out /ˈʃut,aut/ *n.* **1** a gunfight, esp. in movies about the old USA West: *The gunman in white and the gunman in black faced each other in a shootout.* **2** *fig.* a big fight: *Don't go into the boss's office; she's having a shootout with a vice president.*

shop /ʃap/ *n.* **1** a store, usu. small or with a limited number of items for sale: *I bought some candy and gum in that little shop on the corner.* **2** a place of business: *a print shop* **3** a place to work with one's hands: *My brother has a shop in the basement where he carves wood.*
—*v.* **shopped, shopping, shops** **1** to go to stores, usu. to buy: *We shop for food at the local supermarket.* **2 to set up shop:** to start a retail business, open a store: *As soon as I find a good location for my bicycle store, I can set up shop.* **3** *phrasal v.* **to shop around:** to search for a certain item or the best price: *I shopped around until I found a purple dress in size 8.* **4 to talk shop:** to talk about one's work: *Please don't talk shop while we're on vacation; I'm tired of work.*

USAGE NOTE: Compare *shop* and *store.* Americans use the term *shop* for a small, specialized establishment like a *barber shop, coffee shop,* or *dress shop,* or a place that offers pleasant but nonessential items, like a *flower shop* or *gift shop.* The term *store* is a more general one, used for both small *and* large establishments. Most *shopping malls* have one or two big *department stores* as well as several shoe stores, book stores, clothing stores, and specialty shops.

shop·keep·er /ˈʃap,kipər/ *n.* a shop owner or manager

shop·lift /ˈʃap,lɪft/ *v.* to steal things from a store: *When no one was looking, she shoplifted two lipsticks and put them in her purse.* -*n.* [C] **shoplifter;** [U] **shoplifting.**

shop·per /ˈʃapər/ *n.* a person who shops: *Shoppers fill the grocery stores on Saturday.*

shop·ping /ˈʃapɪŋ/ *n.* [U] the task of going to buy things in stores: *I did a little shopping during my lunch hour.*||*He goes shopping every day.*

shopping bag *n.* a large, strong bag, often with handles, used for carrying purchases: *I* asked for a shopping bag at the checkout counter.

shopping center *n.* a group of different types of stores and restaurants with a large parking lot: *Does that shopping center have a bakery and a bookstore?*

shopping mall *n.* a group of different types of stores and restaurants, all under one roof: *My teenage daughter likes to spend rainy days with her friends at the shopping mall.*

shop·talk /ˈʃap,tɔk/ *n.* [U] conversation about one's job or business: *When the lawyer meets another lawyer at a party, it's all shoptalk.*

shore /ʃɔr/ *n.* [C;U] **1** the sandy or rocky area of land next to a body of water: *She walked along the shore of Lake Michigan.* **2** a seaside area: *We like to spend our vacations at the Maryland shore.*
—*phrasal v. sep.* **to shore s.t. up:** to support s.t.: *The building was leaning, so a carpenter nailed on more pieces of wood to shore the walls up.*||*He shored it up.*

shore·line /ˈʃɔr,laɪn/ *n.* [U] the line made when a body of water meets the land: *We followed the island's shoreline on our bicycles. See:* coastline.

shorn /ʃɔrn/ *adj. & past part. of* shear **1** with all or most of one's hair or fur cut off: *The sheep were shorn of their wool.* **2** without s.t. because it has been taken away: *The former employee was shorn of his work responsibilities.*

short /ʃɔrt/ *adj.* **-er, -est** **1** not long, high, or tall: *The short man couldn't reach the top shelf.*||*Philadelphia is a short distance from New York.*||*These pants are too short.* **2** (in time) not long: *We had a short meeting.* **3** not having enough, limited: *I can't go to the movies; I'm short on money.* **4** a bit rude, (*syns.*) abrupt, curt: *I tried to ask my boss a question, but he was very short with me.* **5 in short order:** soon, quickly: *When we heard you were sick, we came in short order.*
—*v.* **1** (in business) to deliver fewer items than were ordered: *The customer ordered 12 chairs but received only ten; our warehouse shorted him two.* **2** a problem in electrical wiring: *Running the computer, the TV, and the VCR at the same time shorted the wiring.*
—*adv.* **1** suddenly, abruptly: *The bus stopped short, and some passengers fell off their seats.* **2** less than or before a certain distance or time: *She threw the ball three feet short of my baseball glove.*||*My daughter is nine, one year short of a decade.* **3 to sell s.o. short:** to think s.o. is not good (smart, talented, etc.) enough: *You thought he couldn't finish college in three years and he did; you sold him short. See:* sell; short run (under *run*); short circuit.

S

shor·tage /'ʃɔrtɪdʒ/ n. [C;U] a state of not having enough, a lack of s.t.: *A shortage of oil made gasoline more expensive.*

short·change /'ʃɔrt,tʃeɪndʒ/ v. **-changed, -changing, -changes** to give s.o. less than the correct amount: *I gave the waitress $10 to pay for a $5 lunch, and she gave me only $1 back; I was shortchanged $4.*

short circuit n. a problem in electrical wiring: *I had a short circuit in my apartment and had to call an electrician.*

short-circuit v. **1** *lit.* to cause a short circuit **2** *fig.* to make difficult, prevent: *We had our trip completely planned, but bad weather short-circuited the whole thing.*

short·com·ing /'ʃɔrt,kʌmɪŋ/ n. a fault, (*syns.*) a deficiency, inadequacy: *He is an excellent student in all subjects except for math, which is his shortcoming.‖She has many shortcomings, but her parents still love her.*

short·cut /'ʃɔrt,kʌt/ n. **1** a shorter way to a place than usual: *We take a shortcut through a field instead of following the road.* **2** a faster way to do s.t.: *I use spaghetti sauce in a jar instead of making it fresh, as a shortcut in preparing dinner.*

short·en /'ʃɔrtn/ v. to make shorter: *Her dress was too long, so she shortened it.‖His speech lasted two hours; he should have shortened it.*

short·en·ing /'ʃɔrtnɪŋ/ n. [U] **1** the act of making s.t. shorter: *Shortening the school year gave us a longer vacation.* **2** a semi-solid fat used in baking: *I added shortening to the pie crust ingredients.*

short·fall /'ʃɔrt,fɔl/ n. the amount lacking to make a total: *The factory made only 400 cars today, not the usual 500; there is a shortfall of 100 cars.*

short fuse n.fig. a tendency to become angry easily, a quick temper: *Usually, he is a nice guy, but he has a short fuse when he has to stand in line.*

short·hand /'ʃɔrt,hænd/ n. [U] **1** a writing system that uses symbols and can be done very quickly: *The secretary wrote a letter in shorthand and word-processed it later.* **2** a shorter way of expressing s.t.: *"OK" is shorthand for "all right."*

short·hand·ed /,ʃɔrt'hændɪd/ adj. lacking help, without the usual number of workers: *Both the office manager and secretary are sick today, so we are shorthanded.*

short·list /'ʃɔrt,lɪst/ n.v. a final list of people to consider (for a job, in a contest, etc.): *We interviewed 15 people, and three made the <n.> shortlist.*

short·lived /'ʃɔrt,laɪvd, -,lɪvd/ adj. not lasting a long time: *The play opened on Saturday and closed a week later; it was shortlived.*

short·ly /'ʃɔrtli/ adv. **1** soon: *We will be ready to leave shortly.* **2** a bit rudely or angrily: *She didn't like the man, so she answered his questions shortly.*

short·ness /'ʃɔrtnɪs/ n. [U] **1** the condition of being short: *the shortness of the schedule‖the little girl's shortness* **2 shortness of breath:** a difficulty in breathing: *After running, I felt a shortness of breath.*

short-order adj. **short-order cook:** a cook in a fast-food restaurant
—adv. **in short order:** soon, quickly: *The computer operator fixed the problem in short order.*

shorts /ʃɔrts/ n.pl. **1** pants that end at or above the knee: *In the summer, we like to wear shorts to stay cool.* **2** men's underpants, boxer shorts

USAGE NOTE: The word *shorts* is always used in the plural, like *pants: I'm wearing a T-shirt and shorts today because it's hot.*

short shrift n. [U] not enough care, attention, or pay: *The owner gives the workers short shrift when he doesn't say hello to them.‖The inventory clerk works hard for little money; she gets short shrift.*

short·sight·ed /'ʃɔrt,saɪtɪd/ adj.fig. not thinking about the future: *The computer company is shortsighted; it ignores new technology.*

short story n. a piece of fiction that is shorter and usu. less complicated in plot than a novel *See:* fiction, USAGE NOTE.

short-tempered adj. quick to anger: *My short-tempered father started yelling when he couldn't fit the key in the lock.*

short term n. [U] the near future: *During the next several months, that is, in the short term, the company will not hire new salespeople.*
—adj. immediate or not long: *My short-term plan is to finish school; then I will think about a career.*

short·wave /'ʃɔrt'weɪv/ adj. a radio wave or electronic wave having a length between 10 and 100 meters: *I like to listen to shortwave radio; I can hear news from Paris, London, Rio, and Bogota.*

shot /ʃɑt/ n. **1** the shooting of a gun: *In the fight, you could hear shots being fired.* **2** the bullet or ammunition used in a gun **3** a single use of a camera, (*syn.*) photograph: *We took some shots of the old castle.* **4** the view through a camera lens **5** a throw or stroke of s.t., trying to hit a certain spot: *Good shot! You hit the golf ball very close to the hole.* **6** a person trying to hit a certain spot: *She made seven goals in nine tries; she's a good shot.* **7** a heavy metal ball *See:* shot put. **8** the use of a needle to put medicine into a vein: *The doctor gave the little boy a shot in his right arm.* **9 a shot in the arm:** a positive event that gives

s.o. confidence, (*syns.*) a boost, thrill: *The magazine paid me a lot of money for my story; what a shot in the arm!* **10 a shot in the dark:** a guess, an attempt that is unlikely to succeed: *The scientific experiment may lead to a cure for cancer, but it's just a shot in the dark.* **11 big shot:** an important person, s.o. with power: *The big shot from Hollywood rode around in a fancy car.* **12** *slang* **like a shot:** very quickly, with great speed: *We ran out of the burning house like a shot.* **13 to give s.t. a shot** or **to take a shot at s.t.:** to try s.t.: *You've never swum? You should give it a shot* (or) *take a shot at it.*
—*v. past tense & past part. of* shoot

shot·gun /ˈʃɑtˌgʌn/ *n.* [U] a long gun (not a handgun) used mostly for hunting

shotgun marriage or **shotgun wedding** *n.old usage* a marriage forced by a pregnancy

shot put /ˈʃɑtˌpʊt/ *n.* a sport (in track and field competition) in which a large, heavy metal ball is thrown for distance

should /ʃʊd/ *aux.v.* **1** helps express duty or obligation: *I should visit my grandmother because she is sick.* **2** helps express s.t. expected: *We should arrive in 10 minutes if there is no traffic.* **3** helps express the possibility, but not certainty, of s.t.: *If I should succeed, so will my partners.* **4** used to make a statement or request nicer, more polite: *I should think the green dress would look better than the red one.* See: might, USAGE NOTE.

shoul·der /ˈʃoʊldər/ *n.* **1** the part of the body between the neck and upper arm: *The football player has big shoulders.* **2** the edge of a road, off the traveled part: *I drove onto the shoulder to avoid a bump.* **3 a shoulder to cry on:** a person who listens to s.o.'s troubles: *She needed a shoulder to cry on when her cat died.* **4 on one's shoulders:** one's own responsibility or problem: *Feeding the family was all on her shoulders.*
—*v.* **1** *lit.* to carry on the shoulder: *The workers shoulder a load of bricks.* **2** *fig.* to take on responsibility: *He shouldered the burden of caring for his brothers when his parents died.*

shoulder bag *n.* purse or bag that is carried on the shoulder by a strap

shout /ʃaʊt/ *n.* a loud cry, a yell: *A man gave a shout to call a taxi to the curb.*
—*v.* to yell: *He shouted, "Hey, over here!"*

shove /ʃʌv/ *n.* a hard push, usu. with the hands: *The angry man gave the other a shove.*
—*v.* **shoved, shoving, shoves 1** to push hard against s.t. or s.o.: *He shoved the heavy rock off the road.* **2** *phrasal v.* **to shove off: a.** to leave (esp. shore, in a boat): *We shove off at 9:00 a.m.* **b.** *infrml.* (in requests) to go away: *Shove off! We're working.* **3** *phrasal v. sep.* **to shove s.o. around:** See: to push around.

shovel /ˈʃʌvəl/ *n.v.* a curved metal or plastic surface with a handle used to pick up dirt, snow, etc.: *I bought a shovel to clear the sidewalk after the snowstorm.*
—*v.* **1** to use a shovel: *He shoveled a hole in the sand.* **2** to pick up or move s.t. with a shoveling motion: *She shoveled potatoes into her mouth.* **3 to shovel sand against the tide:** to try to do such a big task that it probably won't get finished: *Doing all the laundry for my family is like shoveling sand against the tide.*

shovel

show /ʃoʊ/ *n.* **1** [C] a play, movie, TV program, or other entertainment: *She plays a young wife in the new Broadway show.*‖*We watched a show about African animals on educational television.* **2** [C] a display or exhibition about a specific interest or product: *a horse show*‖*a boat show* **3** [C, *usu. sing.*] a way of behaving that may not be sincere: *She made a show of crying at her aunt's funeral, though she didn't like her aunt!* **4 to get the show on the road:** to start moving or start doing s.t., not to delay any longer: *We will be late if we don't get this show on the road!*
—*v.* **shown** /ʃoʊn/ or **showed, showing, shows 1** to cause s.o. to see, to point out: *Let me show you my new CD.* **2** to cause to be known, to indicate: *Your tears show that you're sad.* **3** to put before the public, display: *He showed a beagle at the dog show.*‖*The downtown cinema is showing movies from the 1950s.* **4** to teach, demonstrate (often used with "how"): *She showed him how to eat a lobster.* **5 it (all, just) goes to show:** it proves: *I started playing basketball and felt healthier; it just goes to show that exercise is good for you.* **6 to show for:** to have as a result: *I earned a lot of money and spent it all; I have nothing to show for all my work.* **7** *phrasal v. sep.* **to show (s.o. or s.t.) off: a.** to act in a way that calls attention to oneself: *The boy shows off by telling people his father is very rich.* **b.** s.o. or s.t.: to put s.o. or s.t. before people with pride: *She showed off her ruby ring when she met two friends for dinner.*‖*She showed it off.* **8 to show one's face:** to appear (often used in a negative way): *After getting so drunk at the last party, she was ashamed to show her face at the next one.* **9 to show one's hand: a.** (in a card game) to show one's cards to the other players **b.** *fig.* to let people know one's real thoughts or intentions: *He didn't seem interested in the house, but showed his hand by offering a lot of money for it.* **10** *phrasal v. sep.* **to show s.o. around:** to give a tour, to make a new place more familiar: *This is your new office; let me show you around.*

S

11 *phrasal v. sep.* **to show s.o. out:** to go to the door with a person who is leaving: *The maid brought my coat and showed me out.* **12 to show s.o. the door:** to indicate that s.o. should go, isn't welcome: *If you can't be more polite, I will show you the door.* **13** *phrasal v. sep.* **to show s.o.** or **s.t. up: a.** to arrive (sometimes unexpectedly or late): *They finally showed up at 11:30.* **b. s.o.:** to cause s.o. else to seem or look worse in some way: *He showed you up by wearing a handsomer suit.* **c. s.t.:** to make s.t. visible: *The strong light showed up the stains.*

show-and-tell *n.* [U] a school activity in which a child brings an object to class and talks about it

show·biz /'ʃoʊˌbɪz/ *n.* [U] *infrml. short for* show business

show·boat /'ʃoʊˌboʊt/ *n.* a boat with people who perform at various stops along the route (usu. a river)

show business *n.* [U] **1** the theater, film, TV, music, and other entertainment industries **2** *lit. and fig.* **that's show business** (or) **biz!:** that's what life is like in this business!: *Sales are down, but that's show biz!*

show·case /'ʃoʊˌkeɪs/ *n.* **1** a display case, usu. in a store: *The clerk led me to the showcase with the diamonds in it.* **2** a place to exhibit s.t. special: *The owner has a huge office with pictures of famous people as a showcase of his success.*
—*v.* **-cased, -casing, -cases** to display for examination and admiration: *At the annual meeting, the toy company showcased its new doll.*

show·down /'ʃoʊˌdaʊn/ *n.* a final and often public settling of a disagreement: *In the movie, the two families faced each other with guns in a showdown about land.*

show·er /'ʃaʊər/ *n.* **1** a brief rain (or snow): *After a shower in the morning, the sun came out at noon.* **2** the act of bathing under an overhead stream of water (or the place one does this): *I took a shower when I got home from running.||Our house has two bathrooms, but only one shower.* **3** a party for s.o. who is getting married or having a baby
—*v.* **1** to rain (or snow) for a short time: *It might shower this afternoon, so don't water the garden.* **2** to give a lot of s.t.: *He showers her with presents.||We showered praise on the good child.*

show·girl /'ʃoʊˌgɜrl/ *n.* a young woman who works as a dancer and singer

show·ing /'ʃoʊɪŋ/ *n.* **1** [C] a display of s.t.: *the showing of an artist's paintings* **2** [C, *usu. sing.*] a public performance: *Although he lost the tennis match, he made a good showing.*

show·man /'ʃoʊmən/ *n.* **-men** /-mən/ [C] **1** a man who works as an entertainer **2** a man who uses a strong personality, colorful clothes, drama, etc. to sell s.t. or call attention to himself: *The ice-cream man is a showman, dressing up as a clown and honking his truck horn.* -*n.* [U] **showmanship.**

show·off /'ʃoʊˌɔf, -ˌɑf/ *n.* a person who tries to impress others in a dramatic way: *She is a showoff who wears expensive-looking dresses every day.*

show·piece /'ʃoʊˌpis/ *n.* the best example of a group of things: *The vase in her living room is a showpiece among her other antiques.*

show·place /'ʃoʊˌpleɪs/ *n.* a beautiful piece of property: *The rich family has a showplace with 15 rooms, four garages, and a swimming pool.*

show·room /'ʃoʊˌrum/ *n.* a room for the display of things for sale: *an automobile showroom*

show·stop·per /'ʃoʊˌstɑpər/ *n.* **1** a performance that is so wonderful that the show stops while people clap: *At the spring fashion show, the young designer's new dress was a showstopper; people applauded for ten minutes.* **2** *fig.* anything wonderful that causes people to stop and admire: *Wow! That diamond necklace is a real showstopper!*

show·y /'ʃoʊi/ *adj.* **-ier, -iest** too dressed up or dramatic for the occasion, (*syns.*) ostentatious, gaudy: *The man wore a showy plaid tie to a business meeting.*

shrap·nel /'ʃræpnəl/ *n.* [U] pieces of metal or bullets left after a bomb blast or a battle: *On some French beaches, you can still find shrapnel from World War II.*

shred /ʃrɛd/ *v.* **shredded** or **shred, shredding, shreds** to cut or tear s.t. into small pieces: *He shredded the documents so no one could read them.*
—*n.* **1** a piece, (*syn.*) a fragment: *A shred of newspaper blew down the street.* **2** a tiny amount: *The police do not have a shred of a reason why he robbed your house.*

shrew /ʃru/ *n.* **1** the smallest mammal, which is active mostly at night and lives in holes in the ground **2** *fig.* a bad-tempered woman: *Your sister screams every time we step into her room; she is a shrew.*

shrewd /ʃrud/ *adj.* tending to make smart decisions, clever: *He is a shrewd businessman who always studies other companies.* -*n.* [U] **shrewdness.**

shriek /ʃrik/ *v.n.* a high-pitched, loud scream: *The teenage girls <v.> shrieked when the rock star appeared. See:* scream; screech.

shrill /ʃrɪl/ *adj.* **-er, -est** **1** high-pitched and piercing (sound, voice): *I could hear the shrill sound of an injured bird.* **2** annoying: *She is shrill in her demands for more money.*

shrimp /ʃrɪmp/ *n.* **1** a small, edible water animal with a soft shell **2** *pej.* a small person: *That little shrimp isn't strong enough to hurt you!*

shrine /ʃraɪn/ *n.* a religious place that honors a person or saint: *We lit a candle at the shrine to Saint Anthony.*

shrink /ʃrɪŋk/ *v.* **shrank** /ʃræŋk/ or **shrunk** /ʃrʌŋk/, **shrinking, shrinks** **1** to make or become smaller: *My wool sweater shrank when I washed it.* **2** *phrasal v. insep.* **to shrink (away) from s.t.:** to move away from (s.t. horrible or frightening): *He shrinks away from big barking dogs.*
—*n.slang* a psychiatrist or psychologist *See:* headshrinker.

shrink·age /ʃrɪŋkɪdʒ/ *n.* a lessening of s.t.'s size: *shrinkage in a skirt‖shrinkage in employment See:* shrink.

shrink·pack /ʃrɪŋkˌpæk/ or **shrink·pack·age** /ʃrɪŋkˌpækɪdʒ/ *n.* a transparent plastic wrapper molded around a product to protect it from wear and dust, yet allowing the product to be seen by customers: *Store personnel like the shrinkpacks because they are easy to handle.*

shrink·wrap /ʃrɪŋkˌræp/ *n.v.* **-wrapped, -wrapping, -wraps** a clear, tight plastic covering put on books and other products to keep them clean: *The student took his new chemistry book out of the <n.> shrinkwrap.*

shriv·el /ʃrɪvəl/ *n.* to become wrinkled and often smaller: *My skin has shriveled up from being in the water too long. -adj.* **shriveled.**

shroud /ʃraʊd/ *n.* a piece of cloth in which a dead person is wrapped for burial: *a funeral shroud*
—*v.* to make difficult to see, hide: *The house is shrouded by dark tree branches.*

shrub /ʃrʌb/ *n.* a plant with leaves, used esp. for decoration around buildings and in parks: *We cut the shrubs in front of our house every month.*
-*n.* [U] **shrubbery.** *See:* bush.

shrub

shrug /ʃrʌg/ *v.n.* **1** to lift the shoulders upward as a sign of not caring or not knowing: *She <v.> shrugged when we asked her what time it was.‖I laughed at the comedian, but my brother just gave a <n.> shrug.* **2** *phrasal v. sep.* **to shrug s.t. off:** to act as if s.t. isn't important: *The gambler lost a lot of money at cards, but he just shrugged off his loss.*

shuck /ʃʌk/ *v.* **1** to remove the outer covering of some foods: *to shuck clams‖to shuck corn* **2** *phrasal v. sep. infrml.* **to shuck s.t. off:** to throw s.t. off: *She shucked off her coat.‖She shucked it off.*

shucks /ʃʌks/ *exclam.* expresses modesty or slight annoyance: *Shucks, you are very nice to say I'm smart.‖Shucks! I forgot my watch.*

shud·der /ʃʌdər/ *v.n.* [C] to shake for a moment (from fear, disgust): *I <v.> shudder when I think how awful that food tasted.*

shuf·fle /ʃʌfəl/ *v.* **-fled, -fling, -fles** **1** to walk without lifting the feet: *The sad old man shuffled down the hall.* **2** to mix cards in a different order: *We started a new game, so I shuffled the cards. See:* walk, USAGE NOTE.

shun /ʃʌn/ *v.* **shunned, shunning, shuns** to stay away from, avoid: *I shun meat because I like vegetables more.*

shunt /ʃʌnt/ *v.* to move s.t. aside: *The company shunted an older worker aside for a younger man.*

shush /ʃʌʃ, ʃʊʃ/ *exclam.v.* be quiet: *<exclam.> Shush! I can't hear the TV!‖Her little boys were noisy, so she <v.> shushed them up.*

shut /ʃʌt/ *v.* **shut, shutting, shuts** **1** to move s.t. into a closed position: *to shut one's mouth‖to shut the door* **2** *phrasal v. sep.* **to shut s.o. away:** to keep s.o. completely isolated: *The king shut away the prisoner for ten years.‖He shut him away.* **3** *phrasal v. sep.* **to shut s.o. out:** to prevent s.o. from entering, to block out: *Management shut out the workers by locking the gates.‖It shut them out.* **4** *phrasal v. sep.* **to shut s.o. up: a. s.o.:** to (cause s.o.) stop making noise: *The angry wife shut up her husband with a look.‖She shut him up.* **b. s.t.:** to close securely, lock up: *We shut up the garage so no one would steal the car.‖We shut it up.* **5** *phrasal v. sep.* **to shut s.t. down:** to stop (business) activity, close: *The company has so little work that it shut down the factory.‖It shut it down.* **6** *phrasal v. sep.* **to shut s.t. or s.o. off: a. s.o.:** to prevent s.o. from drinking more: *The bartender shut the customer off after six beers.‖He shut her off.* **b. s.t.:** to make s.t. stop working, stop s.t. from moving or flowing: *I shut off the water in the sink.‖I shut it off.* **7 to shut the door on s.t.:** to refuse to think about s.t., ignore it: *She shut the door on her unhappy past.‖The boss shut the door on new product ideas.*
—*adj.* **1** closed: *The oven door is shut.* **2 shut in:** not able to get out or leave, often because of sickness: *His grandfather is shut in with a heart problem.*

USAGE NOTE: To say *shut up* to someone is considered very rude. It is more polite to ask, "Would you please be quiet?"

shut·down /ʃʌtˌdaʊn/ *n.* [C] a stopping of work or business: *A leak in a pipe caused a shutdown of the oil tank.‖Business is bad, so we are thinking about a shutdown of two factories.*

shut·eye /ʃʌtˌaɪ/ *n.infrml.* [U] sleep: *It is late; let's get some shuteye.*

S

shut-in *n.* a person who can't leave his or her home: *She has arthritis and is unable to walk; she is a shut-in.*

shut·off /'ʃʌt,ɔf, -,ɑf/ *n.* a stoppage: *a shutoff of electricity (water, heat, etc.)*

shut·ter /'ʃʌtər/ *n.* **1** a window covering or decoration that sometimes can be opened and closed: *A rainstorm began, and the woman closed the shutters.* **2** the part of a camera that lets in or shuts out light
—*v.* to close a window, shutter

shut·ter·bug /'ʃʌtər,bʌg/ *n.infrml.* a photographer, s.o. who loves to take pictures

shut·tle /'ʃʌtl/ *v.* **-tled, -tling, -tles** to travel back and forth: *Businesspeople shuttle between New York and Washington, D.C. every day.*
—*n.* **1** s.t. that weaves or holds thread **2** a vehicle (plane, bus, van, etc.) used for traveling back and forth: *The shuttles leave the hotel for the airport every hour.*

shy /ʃaɪ/ *adj.* **-er** or **-ier, -est** or **-iest 1** not liking to talk to people, esp. strangers, (*syns.*) bashful, timid: *The shy boy stood in a dark corner at the dance.* **2** short of, lacking: *I am shy $1 to pay for lunch. Can you lend it to me?*
-n. [U] **shyness.**
—*v.* **shied, shying, shies** to move away from s.t. with fear or disgust: *The nervous horse shied away when I tried to climb onto her.||He shies away from big parties.*

shy·ster /'ʃaɪstər/ *n.pej* a cheating or dishonest lawyer: *Find a better lawyer to write the will; that one's a shyster.*

Si·a·mese cat /,saɪə'miz, 'saɪə,miz/ *n.* a short-haired cat with blue eyes and light gray and black fur

Siamese twins *n.pl.* twins that are born joined together and at times share body parts

sib·ling /'sɪblɪŋ/ *n.* a person with the same parents as s.o. else, brother or sister: *I have two siblings: my brother and my sister.*

sibling rivalry *n.* competition between siblings: *The sibling rivalry is strong between my brother and me; we each try to make more money than the other.*

sic /sɪk/ *v.* **sicced, siccing, sics** to urge an animal to attack: *to sic dogs on a thief*

sick /sɪk/ *adj.* **1 a.** not well physically, ill, diseased: *He is sick with the flu.* **b.** nauseated, throwing up: *After eating too much he was sick into the toilet.* **2** not well mentally: *She killed herself because she was horribly sick.* **3** very unkind, in bad taste: *It was a sick joke to scare the little kids.* **4** very disappointed or upset: *I'm sick about missing the wedding.* **5 a.** not able to stand any more, tired: *After years of war, the whole nation was sick of battles and bloodshed.* **b. sick and tired:** *I'm sick and tired of the hot weather; let's move north.*

sick·en /'sɪkən/ *v.* **1** to make or become ill: *The AIDS patient slowly sickened.* **2** to make or to be upset emotionally: *Her family was sickened by her death.*

sick·en·ing /'sɪkənɪŋ/ *adj.* causing a sick feeling or disgust: *Nazis committed sickening crimes against Jews.*

sick·le /'sɪkəl/ *n.* a farm tool with a handle and sharp, curved blade used to cut long grass or crops

sickle-cell anemia *n.* a serious blood disease, usu. affecting black children and adults

sick leave *n.* **1** time away from work because of illness: *The secretary took two days' sick leave because she has a cold.* **2** a specified number of days given to workers for that purpose.

sick·ly /'sɪkli/ *adj.* **-lier, -liest 1** unhealthy, often ill: *He was a sickly child who missed a lot of school.* **2** weak: *Her sickly smile told me she was not really glad.*

sick·ness /'sɪknɪs/ *n.* [U] illness: *There is a lot of sickness in poor countries with few doctors.*

sick pay *n.* [U] salary or wages paid to workers who are sick: *He was out with a sore throat, but he got sick pay.*

side /saɪd/ *n.* **1** an edge or a surface of a shape or object: *the longest side of a triangle||A box has six sides.* **2** a surface that connects top and bottom: *A sign hung on the side of the building.* **3** a particular location: *the south side of the city||the shady side of a yard* **4** a part away from the main part: *We saw a fox on the side of the road.* **5** one of two surfaces of a flat object: *Which side of the paper should I write on?* **6** a group or team: *My side won the soccer game.||Which side are you on, the liberal or conservative side?* **7** the part of the body to the left or right of the chest and stomach area: *His side hurt from running too fast.* **8** part of one's personality: *He's serious, but he has a fun side.* **9** a section of a family (from one parent or another): *I get my green eyes from Mom's side.* **10 from (on) all sides (every side):** from or in every direction: *Teenagers crowded the famous singer from all sides.* **11 on the side: a.** not with or in the main part of the dish or meal: *salad with dressing on the side||a burger with french fries on the side* **b.** in addition to (regular activity): *It was a business trip, but we visited a museum on the side.* **12 on the (adjective) side:** somewhat, a small amount, rather: *It's on the cool side here at night.||She's on the thin side; she should eat more.* **13 side by side:** next to each other: *The students stood side by side for the class photo.* **14 to take sides:** to join one team or other, to share ideas with one group against another: *I don't want to take sides in the argument.* **15 (off) to one (the) side:** apart from: *The farm has two barns and a house off to one side.*

—v. to agree with s.o.: *He sided with me about whom to vote for.*

side·arm /'saɪd,ɑrm/ *adj.adv.* (in baseball or other throwing action) with the arm kept low, not over- or underhand: *She threw a <adj.> sidearm pitch.*

side·bar /'saɪd,bɑr/ *n.* in a newspaper or magazine, a short story that is related to a larger one, giving extra information about the main topic: *A sidebar to the story about poverty gave the details of the life of one little inner-city boy.*

side·sad·dle /'saɪd,sædl/ *n.adv.* a saddle for a woman, made so that she can sit with both legs to one side: *a new leather <n.> sidesaddle.||She rode <adv.> sidesaddle.*

side·burns /'saɪd,bɜrnz/ *n.pl.* hair that grows on the side of a man's face, just in front of the ears

USAGE NOTE: *Sideburns* go in and out of fashion. Other common styles for men's facial hair are the *beard*, hair that covers the lower part of the face; the *mustache*, hair that grows above the upper lip; and the *goatee*, a beard that is trimmed to cover only the chin.

side dish *n.* food that is separate from the main dish, often a vegetable or potato (sometimes shortened to "side," as in *a side of fries*): *We ordered a side dish of sauteed mushrooms. See:* side order.

side effect *n.* **1** an additional and possibly unexpected result of an action: *If we buy that company, the side effects will be a large bank loan and the need to fire many people.* **2** an effect of a medicine besides the expected effect: *The side effect of this pain pill was a dry mouth.*

side·kick /'saɪd,kɪk/ *n.infrml.* a close friend or helper, often younger or less powerful: *The plumber asked his sidekick to go to the hardware store.*

side·light /'saɪd,laɪt/ *n.* **1** *lit.* light coming from the side or from an indirect source **2** *fig.* a less important matter: *We were discussing the bad air-pollution problem, but as a sidelight, we should look at water pollution, too.*

side·line /'saɪd,laɪn/ *n.* a hobby or job in addition to one's main job: *He is a computer programmer during the day and sells real estate as a sideline on the weekends.*
—v. to be out of action, often from sports: *The football player hurt his knee and has been sidelined for a week.*

side·long /'saɪd,lɔŋ, -,lɑŋ/ *adj.* to the side, not direct: *a sidelong look*

side order *n. See:* side dish.

side·show /'saɪd,ʃoʊ/ *n.* a performance or show that is not the main attraction at a fair or circus: *We went to a small tent to see a sideshow of dancing monkeys.*

side·split·ting /'saɪd,splɪtɪŋ/ *adj.* very funny: *They laughed at a sidesplitting old movie.*

side·step /'saɪd,stɛp/ *v.* **-stepped, -stepping, -steps 1** to step aside or out of the way **2** *fig.* to avoid s.t.: *A reporter asked the politician a question, but he sidestepped it with a joke.*

side·tracked /'saɪd,trækt/ *adj.* with attention turned away from the main task: *I was reading, but then I got sidetracked when I heard my favorite song on the radio.*

side·walk /'saɪd,wɔk/ *n.* the path next to a street, meant for walkers: *A lady walked her dog along the sidewalk.*

side·ways /'saɪd,weɪz/ *adv.* from or toward the side: *I had to turn sideways to fit through the opening in the fence.||She looked sideways toward her left.*

sid·ing /'saɪdɪŋ/ *n.* [U] wood, metal, or vinyl used to cover the surface of a building: *That family is putting new blue siding on their old brown house.*

si·dle /'saɪdl/ *v.* **-dled, -dling, -dles** to walk rather slowly, usu. approaching s.o. in an indirect way: *She sidled up to the bar and ordered a beer.*

siege /sidʒ/ *n.* a military action in which forces surround an area and prevent supplies from entering: *During the siege, the army stopped all trains carrying food.*

si·es·ta /si'ɛstə/ *n.* (Spanish for) a nap, usu. after lunch: *I think I'll go to my room and take a siesta until about 3:00.*

sieve /sɪv/ *n.v.* **sieved, sieving, sieves 1** a tool with a container of tiny holes, used to separate (liquid from solid, large pieces from small, etc.): *We poured ocean water into the sieve, and shells and sand remained.* **2 a mind (brain, memory, etc.) like a sieve:** a forgetful mind, a bad memory: *Did I miss your birthday? I have a mind like a sieve!*

sift /sɪft/ *v.* **1** to put through a sieve: *I sifted flour and salt together for a cake.* **2** to look through s.t. carefully: *The tax worker sifted through the company's financial records.*

sigh /saɪ/ *v.n.* to let out air from the mouth from fatigue or emotion: *He <v.> sighed with relief.||She gave a <n.> sigh of disappointment.*

sight /saɪt/ *n.* **1** [U] the physical sense of seeing: *My sight is good; I don't need glasses.* **2** [C] s.t. or s.o. that is seen: *I like the sight of fresh snow in the winter.* **3** [C] a place to visit on a trip: *We saw the sights of Hong Kong by bus.* **4** [C] s.t. ugly or funny-looking: *Trash is everywhere; what a sight!* **5** [C] the part of a gun that helps s.o. aim: *He saw a duck through the sight and shot.* **6 a sight for sore eyes:** s.o. or s.t. that one is happy to see: *After a year in*

S

the desert, the ocean is a sight for sore eyes. **7 in (one's) sight:** within view: *The war started last year, and there is no end in sight.||The ship is in my sight.* **8 on sight:** when seen: *The soldiers will shoot you on sight if you go onto enemy land.* **9 out of one's sight:** no longer in view: *The airplane is out of sight behind a cloud.* **10 out of sight, out of mind:** forgotten when not present: *My girlfriend never calls me when I'm on a business trip: out of sight, out of mind.*

sight·ed /'saɪtɪd/ *adj.* able to see, not blind: *The blind woman asked her sighted sister to describe the action on the TV show.*

sight·less /'saɪtlɪs/ *adj.* not able to see, blind: *A sightless man crossed the street with a guide dog.*

sight·read /'saɪt,rid/ **-read** /-,rɛd/, **-reading, -reads** *v.* to play or sing music without prior practice: *He had never seen the music, but he sat down and sightread it.*

sight·see·ing /'saɪt,siɪŋ/ *n.v.* the act of visiting special places as a tourist: *We did some <n.> sightseeing at the Grand Canyon in Arizona.*

sign /saɪn/ *n.* **1** a board or poster with information on it: *The sign on our store says "The Clothes Boutique."||a stop sign* **2** an action or other nonspoken way of communicating: *The wave of her hand was a sign of greeting.||He sends her flowers as a sign of love.* **3** a symbol: *The (X) is a multiplication sign.*
—*v.* **1** to write one's name on s.t.: *He signed a check.* **2** to use finger motions to communicate with people who can't hear: *My hearing-impaired sister signed "good-bye" to me.* **3** *phrasal v. insep.* **to sign for s.t.:** to show that one has received s.t. by signing one's name: *My assistant signed for the package.* **4** *phrasal v. insep.* **to sign off on s.t.:** to give one's approval: *All committee members signed off on the new budget.* **5** *phrasal v.* **to sign on:** to join a group, (*syn.*) to enlist: *When they asked for help, she signed on.* **6** **to sign on the dotted line:** to show final agreement in a legal or official action: *After I signed on the dotted line, I owned a new house!* **7** *phrasal v. sep.* **to sign s.o. in:** to write down one's name to show one's presence at a meeting or other gathering, (*syn.*) to register: *We signed in our visitors.||We signed them in.* **8** *phrasal v. insep.* **to sign s.o. or s.t. out: a. s.o.:** to write one's name down to show one is leaving: *I signed out the salesman when he left this evening.||I signed him out.* **b. s.t.:** to take s.t. out, to borrow: *I signed out books at the university library.||I signed them out.* **9** *phrasal v. sep.* **to sign s.t. away:** to give up ownership or rights to s.t.: *The mother signed away her house to her children.||She signed it away.* **10** *phrasal v. sep.* **to sign s.t. over:** to change ownership: *The pres-*

ident signed over the company to the employees.||She signed it over.* **11** *phrasal v. sep.* **to sign (s.o.) up:** to join, agree to do s.t., (*syn.*) to enroll: *I signed up for swimming lessons.* -*n.* **signer.**
—*adj.phr.* **signed, sealed, and delivered:** successfully ended, agreed upon

sig·nal /'sɪgnəl/ *n.* **1** an action or thing that sends a message, often not using words: *A green light is a signal to go.* **2** an electronic picture or sound: *The TV is very clear; there must be a good signal.*
—*v.* to send a signal: *Ships signal their positions by radio.*

sig·na·to·ry /'sɪgnə,tɔri/ *n.* **-ries** a person who has signed a legal or official paper: *I am a signatory to the purchase agreement.*

sig·na·ture /'sɪgnətʃər/ *n.* one's name written by oneself: *My signature is on the birthday card.*

sig·nif·i·cance /sɪg'nɪfəkəns/ *n.* [U] **1** the importance of s.t.: *The end of the war was an event of great significance.* **2** the meaning of s.t.: *I don't understand the significance of your wearing black all the time; are you sad?*

sig·nif·i·cant /sɪg'nɪfəkənt/ *adj.* **1** important: *The two leaders' shaking hands is a significant step toward peace.* **2** worth noting, large, meaningful: *The company made a significant profit last year.*

sig·ni·fy /'sɪgnə,faɪ/ *v.* **-fied, -fying, -fies 1** to show, indicate: *The new neighbors sent us a cake to signify that they want to be friends.* **2** to mean: *An arrow will signify the correct direction.*

sign·ing /'saɪnɪŋ/ *n.* [U] the act of putting one's signature on s.t.: *We went to the lawyer's office for the signing.*

sign language *n.* [U] **1** a silent language for hearing-impaired people, using symbols formed with the hands and fingers: *They couldn't hear, so they used sign language to say "How are you?"* **2** any nonspoken hand language: *She used sign language to say hello from across the room.*

sign·post /'saɪn,poʊst/ *n.* **1** s.t. that holds up a sign **2** *fig.* anything that shows the way, a guide: *College is a signpost to a successful future.*

si·lence /'saɪləns/ *n.* [U] quiet, no noise: *There was absolute silence in the church as the people prayed.*
—*exclam.* Quiet!: *Silence! This is a library.*
—*v.* **-lenced, -lencing, -lences** to make quiet: *The teachers silenced the class before beginning to talk.*

si·lent /'saɪlənt/ *adj.* **1** quiet, noiseless: *The forest was silent; even the birds were quiet.* **2** not talking, not showing knowledge: *The criminal remained silent before the judge.*

silent partner *n.* an investor in a business who does not work in it: *Two silent partners own 10 percent of my business.*

silent treatment *n.* [U] not speaking with s.o. as a way to show dislike or as punishment: *He came home very late without a reason, and his wife gave him the silent treatment for two days.*

sil·hou·ette /ˌsɪluˈɛt/ *n.v.* **-etted, -etting, -ettes** an outline that is filled in with a dark color, against a light background: *A <n.> silhouette of the side view of the boy's face shows the shape of his nose.*

sil·i·con /ˈsɪlə,kɑn, -kən/ *n.* [U] a nonmetallic element found in the earth and used in glass, brick, and other materials

Silicon Valley *n.* [U] a part of California, near San Francisco and San Jose, with many high-technology and computer companies

USAGE NOTE: *Silicon Valley* was the first area in the USA to become known as a center of the computer industry. Today any place with a large computer industry may be compared to it: *Austin has become the Silicon Valley of Texas.*

silk /sɪlk/ *n.* [U] the material made by silkworms, the cloth made from the fiber: *She wears dresses made of silk.‖He bought four yards of silk.*

silk·en /ˈsɪlkən/ *adj.* **1** smooth, soft, and pleasing to the touch like silk, silky: *The lady has silken skin.* **2** made of silk: *a silken tablecloth*

silk·screen /ˈsɪlk,skrin/ *v.n.* to print s.t. onto cloth: *The man <v.> silkscreened a picture of the rock star onto a T-shirt. -adj.* **silkscreened.**

silk·y /ˈsɪlki/ *adj.* **-ier, -iest** smooth, soft: *silky hair. See:* silken.

sill /sɪl/ *n.* the bottom edge of a window that sticks out from the wall: *He placed a plant on the sill.*

sil·ly /ˈsɪli/ *adj.* **-lier, -liest** foolish, stupid: *When he drinks wine, he starts acting silly.*

si·lo /ˈsaɪloʊ/ *n.* **-los** a building on a farm, often round in shape, that holds grain or other plant food

silo

sil·ver /ˈsɪlvər/ *n.* [U] **1** a white, shiny, metallic element used for making jewelry, knives, forks, spoons, and other objects **2** the color of silver (metallic grayish white): *My grandfather has silver in his hair. -adj.* **silvery.**

silver anniversary *n.* a day honoring the 25th year of s.t., usu. marriage

silver plate *n.* metal with a thin covering of silver *-adj.* **silverplated.**

sil·ver·smith /ˈsɪlvər,smɪθ/ *n.* a person who makes silver jewelry or other objects

silver spoon *n.* **born with a silver spoon in his** or **her mouth:** born wealthy: *That rich boy was born with a silver spoon in his mouth.*

sil·ver·ware /ˈsɪlvər,wɛr/ *n.* [U] table tools made from silver (knives, forks, spoons, etc.): *Please put the plates and silverware on the table.*

sim·i·lar /ˈsɪmələr/ *adj.* almost alike, (*syn.*) resembling: *She has a blue dress similar to yours, but hers has a green collar.*

sim·i·lar·i·ty /ˌsɪməˈlærəti/ *n.* **-ties** the state of being almost alike, (*syn.*) resemblance: *There is a similarity between the two films, but one has more violence than the other.*

sim·mer /ˈsɪmər/ *v.n.* [U] **1** to cook at a temperature below the boiling point: *The cook let the stew <v.> simmer for a half hour.* **2** *phrasal v.* **to simmer down:** to become calm after being angry: *After their fight, they simmered down.*

simp /sɪmp/ *n.slang* a fool *See:* simpleton.

sim·per /ˈsɪmpər/ *v.n.* [C] to smile in a silly way: *Stop <v.> simpering and act serious!*

sim·ple /ˈsɪmpəl/ *adj.* **1** without many details, not complex: *I drew a simple map.‖Beef and potatoes is a simple meal.* **2** easy to do: *a simple math problem* **3** ordinary, pure: *the simple truth* **4** not able to think in a complicated way: *He's a bit simple, so don't ask him hard questions.*

simple interest *n.* [U] a percent of money paid on an original amount: *The simple interest on $1,000 at 7 percent is $70 a year, paid at $70 year after year. See:* compound interest.

sim·ple·mind·ed /ˈsɪmpəl,maɪndɪd/ *adj.* **1** not having full mental abilities: *The woman can't read because she is simpleminded.* **2** stupid, silly: *Riding a bike in the snow is a simpleminded idea.*

sim·plic·i·ty /sɪmˈplɪsəti/ *n.* [U] **1** a lack of complexity, plainness: *I would like to move to the country and lead a life of simplicity.* **2** ease of doing: *Changing a car's oil can be done with simplicity.*

sim·pli·fy /ˈsɪmplə,faɪ/ *v.* **-fied, -fying, -fies** to make less complex: *Let's simplify the job by dividing it into smaller tasks.*

sim·ply /ˈsɪmpli/ *adv.* **1** with ease: *The repair can be made simply with just a screwdriver.* **2** only, just: *Don't get angry; I was simply trying to help.* **3** very, absolutely: *I was simply amazed when he finished the job in an hour.*

sim·u·la·tion /ˌsɪmyəˈleɪʃən/ *n.* [C;U] an imitation of a real situation: *The pilots learned to fly airplanes by watching ground simulations. -v.* **simulate** *-n.* **simulator.**

si·mul·ta·ne·ous /ˌsaɪməlˈteɪniəs, ˌsɪ-/ *adj.* happening at the same time: *The final trumpet*

S

music was simultaneous with loud noise from the drums. -adv. **simultaneously.**

sin /sɪn/ *n.* **1** an act against religious beliefs: *The rabbi told the child that lying was a sin.* **2** any bad or wrong act: *It is a sin to waste food when others do not have enough to eat.*
—*v.* **sinned, sinning, sins** to do s.t. bad or wrong, *(syn.)* to commit a sin: *He sinned when he left his old and helpless parents alone.*

since /sɪns/ *conj.* **1** because: *The gas company turned your heat off, since you did not pay your bill.* **2** after a certain time: *I haven't seen any snow since I moved to Mississippi.*
—*adv.* **1** from that time or between that time and now: *I quit my job last year and have not worked since.* **2** before now: *She has long since stopped smoking.*
—*prep.* from a specific time: *The company has been in business since 1941.*

sin·cere /sɪnˈsɪr/ *adj.* honest in one's thought and action, true: *Her love for you is sincere; she will stay with you in bad times.*

sin·cere·ly /sɪnˈsɪrli/ *adv.* **1** honestly, truly: *Please believe me; I am sincerely interested in helping you.* **2** often used to close a letter: *See you soon. Sincerely, Joe Martin.*

sin·cer·i·ty /sɪnˈsɛrəti/ *n.* [U] honesty in thought and action: *I like her sincerity; she means what she says.*

sin·ew /ˈsɪnyu/ *n.* [C;U] **1** in the body, strong tissue connecting muscle to bone, a tendon **2** *fig.* strength: *Two sinews of the US government are voting rights and free speech. -adj.* **sinewy.**

sin·ful /ˈsɪnfəl/ *adj.* **1** against religious ideas of right: *Having sex outside of marriage is sinful in many religions.* **2** bad, wrong: *It was sinful to keep the dog in the hot car.*

sing /sɪŋ/ *v.* **sang** /sæŋ/ or **sung** /sʌŋ/, **singing, sings** **1** to make music with the voice: *She sings in a higher voice than her husband.* **2** to work as a singer: *She sang in nightclubs for many years.* **3** to be expressed in a beautiful and pleasing way: *That author writes so well that his words sing.* **4** *phrasal v.* **to sing out:** to sing, call out loudly: *If you need help, sing out!*

singe /sɪndʒ/ *v.* to burn the ends of or a small part of, *(syn.)* to scorch: *I singed some hair when I blew out the candle.*

sing·er /ˈsɪŋər/ *n.* a person who sings: *He is a singer in a jazz band.*

sin·gle /ˈsɪŋɡəl/ *adj.* **1** only one, *(syns.)* sole, lone: *You can start a fire with a single match.* **2** separate, individual: *Every single book in the library has a number.* **3** unmarried: *She is single because she doesn't want a husband.*
—*n.* **1** one person: *seat for a single* **2** an unmarried person: *The club had a party for singles.* **3** a one-dollar bill: *The magazine cost $2.95, so I paid for it with three singles.* **4** (in baseball) a hit in which the runner reaches first

base **5** *pl.* tennis with two players (not four): *The couple played singles against each other. See:* double.
—*v.* **-gled, -gling, -gles** **1** (in baseball) to reach first base with a hit **2** *phrasal v. sep.* **to single s.o. out:** to choose or indicate one person from a group: *The professor singled out the only person who answered the question correctly.||She singled him out.*

USAGE NOTE: In American culture, it is not considered polite to ask a person you do not know well if he or she is *single* or *married.*

single entry *n.* [U] (in accounting) a way of keeping financial records that shows only money owed and money due

single file *adv.* in a line, one person behind another: *The class lined up single file, in alphabetical order.*

sin·gle-hand·ed·ly /ˌsɪŋɡəlˈhændɪdli/ *adv.* by oneself, alone: *She built her company single-handedly, with no partners.*

sin·gle-mind·ed /ˈsɪŋɡəlˌmaɪndɪd/ *adj.* focused, fixed on one idea: *The salesman is single-minded in his work; making sales is all that is important.*

singles bar *n.* a bar or nightclub where people go to meet others and drink: *The man in the singles bar asked the woman for her telephone number.*

sin·gly /ˈsɪŋli/ *adv.* one by one, individually: *They sell eggs singly, not in dozens.*

sing·song /ˈsɪŋˌsɔŋ/ *adj.n.* a way of speaking in which the voice rises and falls with little variation: *He spoke to his baby in a <adj.> singsong voice to help the baby fall asleep.*

sin·gu·lar /ˈsɪŋɡyələr/ *adj.* **1** special, unusual: *She has the singular honor of winning the Nobel Prize in chemistry.* **2** unique, sole: *a singular sculpture from Roman times -adv.* **singularly.**
—*n.* [U] (in grammar) not the plural: *"I" is a singular pronoun.||"Box" is the singular of "boxes."*

sin·is·ter /ˈsɪnɪstər/ *adj.* seeming evil or harmful: *A sinister villain kidnapped the wealthy child.||The old house looked sinister in the dark.*

sink /sɪŋk/ *n.* the container for running water, often in a kitchen or bathroom: *He washed the dishes in the sink.*
—*v.* **sank** /sæŋk/ or **sunk** /sʌŋk/, **sinking, sinks** **1** to go or fall below the surface of water (mud, sand, etc.): *The boat had a hole, so it sank.* **2** to go into a worse or different physical state: *He took drugs and sank slowly into bad health.||When she is tired, she sinks into a deep sleep.* **3** to push s.t. into the ground: *The mining company sank a mine shaft into the hill.* **4** to cause to fail, ruin, or destroy: *The banks*

S

would not loan our company any more money, and this sank us; we went out of business. **5** to fall slowly: *She sank to her knees; she was so tired.* **6** (for s.t.) to become disappointed or sad: *His heart sank when he saw his girlfriend with another man.* **7** to spend money on s.t., (*syn.*) to invest: *I don't want to sink any more money into my old car.* **8** *slang* **to sink a basket:** to throw a basketball through a hoop **9** *phrasal v.* **to sink in:** to be slowly understood: *This algebra lesson is sinking in; I almost understand.* **10** *phrasal v. insep.* **to sink s.t. into s.t.:** to cause s.t. to penetrate s.t.: *I love to sink my toes into a soft rug.*

sin·ner /'sɪnər/ *n.* a person who acts against religious teaching: *The minister asked the church members to pray for sinners.*

sin·u·ous /'sɪnuəs/ *adj.* curvy, like a snake: *a sinuous dance*‖*a sinuous path through the woods*

si·nus·es /'saɪnəsɪz/ *n.pl.* in the nose and head, air-filled sections between the bones: *When I have a cold, my sinuses fill up.*

sip /sɪp/ *v.n.* **sipped, sipping, sips** to drink a small amount at a time: *He <v.> sipped his tea.*‖*He took a <n.> sip of tea.*

si·phon /'saɪfən/ *n.* a tube used to pull liquid from a container by gravity and suction: *He used a siphon to take gasoline from the car's tank.*
—*v.fig.* to take s.t. away from s.t.: *An employee siphoned off money from the company and put it in his own bank account.*

sir /sɜr/ *n.* **1 a.** a respectful word to use when talking to a man, often used instead of the man's name: *Would you like red or white wine, sir?* **b.** used to begin a formal letter to a man: *Dear Sir:* **2** a word used before a knight's or other titled man's name: *The queen made Laurence Olivier a knight, so then he was Sir Laurence Olivier.*

sire /saɪr/ *n.* **1** a male parent, often a horse **2** a word used when talking to a king: *Shall I bring your crown, Sire?*
—*v.* **sired, siring, sires** to father children or animals: *a stallion that sired many fine racehorses*

si·ren /'saɪrən/ *n.* **1** on a fire truck, ambulance, police car, etc., a loud, high-pitched alarm: *The fire engine's siren warned drivers to move out of the way.* **2** a beautiful woman who attracts men, (*syn.*) a temptress: *She is dressed like a siren tonight; many guys will ask her to dance.*

sir·loin /'sɜr,lɔɪn/ *n.* [C;U] a very good cut of beef from the cow's back: *a sirloin steak*

sis·sy /'sɪsi/ *n.infrml.* **1** a sister **2** *pej.* a cowardly, weak boy or man: *Don't be a sissy; jump into the cold water!*

sis·ter /'sɪstər/ *n.* **1** a daughter with the same parents as another daughter or son: *My parents thought my brother needed a sister, so they were happy when I was a girl.* **2 Sister:** a nun, what one calls a nun: *The Sister got down on her knees and prayed.*‖*Sister, will you help me understand this Bible story?* **3** a woman who one feels close to (often used by another woman): *Though she was born in Africa and is much older, we are sisters.* -*adj.* **sisterly.**

sis·ter·hood /'sɪstər,hʊd/ *n.* [U] **1** the state of being sisters **2** the feeling or state of being close or united with other women: *The women in my group are a sisterhood, fighting against domestic violence.*

sister-in-law *n.* **sisters-in-law** the sister of a husband or wife, or the wife of a brother

sit /sɪt/ *v.* **sat** /sæt/, **sitting, sits 1** to bend one's knees and rest on one's buttocks: *He sat on a chair.* **2** to be located: *The skier's hotel sits in a valley.*‖*A computer sat on the desk.* **3** to pose: *to sit for a painting or photograph* **4** *short for* to babysit: *I sit for my little brother every Saturday night.* **5** to be happening, in session: *The Congress is sitting.* **6 to be sitting pretty:** to be in a good position: *Since he married the rich woman, he is sitting pretty.* **7 to just sit there:** to do nothing, to not act: *Don't just sit there; help me move the table!* **8** *phrasal v.* **to sit around s.t.:** to be lazy, to not do much: *The workmen are sitting around with nothing to do.* **9** *phrasal v.* **to sit back:** to wait in a comfortable position: *I sat back and enjoyed the movie.* **10 to sit down:** to seat oneself: *I sat down on a bench in the park.* **11** *phrasal v. insep.* **to sit in for** or **on: a. for:** to substitute for: *She is sitting in for the boss.* **b. on:** to attend, be there: *I sat in on the professor's lecture.* **12 to sit on one's hands:** to not act, (*syn.*) to stall: *The secretary asked her boss for a decision, but the boss sat on his hands for months.* **13** *phrasal v. sep.* **to sit (s.t.) out:** to not participate: *His ankle hurt, so he sat the game out.* **14 to sit through:** to stay during (often not wanting to): *We sat through the long, boring opera.* **15 to sit tight:** to be patient: *I'll have the information for you tomorrow; just sit tight.* **16** *phrasal v.* **to sit up: a.** to raise oneself up: *The patient sat up in bed; he feels better.* **b.** to wait for s.o.: *His mother was angry he was late; she sat up until 12:00.* **17 to sit up and take notice:** to see and be affected: *He played a good game of tennis, and his friends sat up and took notice.* **18 to sit well with:** to feel good or be agreeable to s.o.: *The plan to move to the city does not sit well with him.*

sit·com /'sɪt,kɑm/ *n.short for* situation comedy

sit-down *n.adj.* **1** a work stoppage in which people won't leave a workplace until a problem is settled: *The unhappy auto workers* *started a <n.> sit-down and stayed overnight until the bosses listened.* **2** done while sitting: *a <adj.> sit-down dinner*

site /saɪt/ *n.* an area or place: *the site of the crime∥a building site*
—*v.* **sited, siting, sites** to put s.t. in a particular place: *to site a skyscraper on a corner*

sit-in *n.* a protest in which people sit in one place and refuse to leave until they are physically moved or until their problem is solved: *The neighborhood people had a sit-in against racial discrimination.*

sit·ter /'sɪtər/ *n.short for* babysitter: *We'll need a sitter tonight so we can go to the theater.*

sit·ting /'sɪtɪŋ/ *n.* time spent seated and doing one thing, *(syn.)* a session: *a sitting for a painting∥She read the book in one sitting.*

sitting duck *adj.* an easy target or victim: *I was alone in the unlocked house; I was a sitting duck for the thieves.*

sit·u·ate /'sɪtʃu,eɪt/ *v.* **-ated, -ating, -ates** to put or build, locate: *We situated our house near the beach.*

sit·u·at·ed /'sɪtʃu,eɪtɪd/ *adj.* in a certain place, located: *The flagpole is situated in the center of the park.*

sit·u·a·tion /,sɪtʃu'eɪʃən/ *n.* **1** the way things are at a certain time, the state of what's happening: *The child was in a bad situation, with no food or water.∥The leaders are meeting to talk about the situation in the Middle East.* **2** *frml.* a job: *She no longer cleans house for us; she is looking for a different situation.* **3** a location, the way s.t. stands in its surroundings: *Our house's situation lets us look west over the desert.*

situation comedy *n.* a funny 30-minute weekly television program, using the same characters but with different stories each week

sit-up *n.* an exercise to make the stomach area stronger and flatter, in which one lies back and then sits up repeatedly

six /sɪks/ *n.* **-es 1** the cardinal number 6 **2 at sixes and sevens:** confused, in a mess: *I am at sixes and sevens with my difficult daughter.* **3 six of one, a half-dozen of the other:** with little difference between two things: *I don't care if we go on Sunday or Monday; it's six of one, a half-dozen of the other.*
—*adj.* 6 of s.t.: *six cans of beer*

six-pack *n.* 6 cans or bottles of a beverage, bought together: *a six-pack of beer∥a six-pack of ginger ale*

six·teen /sɪks'tin/ *adj.n.* the cardinal number 16: *<adj.> sixteen candles on the cake*

sixth sense /sɪksθ/ *n.* [U] the ability to feel things (danger, s.o.'s thoughts, the future, etc.) beyond the five senses of sight, smell, hearing, taste, and touch: *I have a sixth sense that my mother will phone tonight.*

USAGE NOTE: A *sixth sense* may also be called a *gut feeling*, a *funny feeling*, or a *hunch*: *My gut feeling is that I should take the job.∥I have a funny feeling that I forgot to turn off the gas stove at home.∥It's just a hunch, but I think the test will be pretty easy.*

six·ty /'sɪksti/ *adj.n.* the cardinal number 60: *60 pages in the history lesson*

siz·a·ble or **size·a·ble** /'saɪzəbəl/ *adj.* large: *a sizable amount of money∥a sizable town*

size /saɪz/ *n.* **1** [C;U] the physical measure of s.o. or s.t. (bigness, smallness, etc.): *Look at the size of that baby; she's huge!∥I would like the smaller size coffee, please.∥The two boys are the same size.* **2** [C] a number that tells how big or small clothing items or shoes are: *After she lost weight, she went from a size 16 to a size 12.∥His boots are a size 11.* **3** [U] the way things are: *Right is right and wrong is wrong; that's the size of it.*
—*v.* **sized, sizing, sizes 1** to measure s.t.: *We sized the living room to see if we had space for a couch:* **2** *phrasal v. sep.* **to size s.o. or s.t. up:** to form an opinion of s.o.: *She sized up her new teacher and decided he was strict but fair.∥She sized him up.*
—*suffix* **-sized** /-,saɪzd/ or **-size** /-,saɪz/ related to the size (small, large, etc.) of s.t.: *a medium-sized meal∥a king-size bed∥a child-sized chair*

siz·zle /'sɪzəl/ *v.* **-zled, -zling, -zles 1** to make the sound of s.t. cooking in hot fat: *I can hear the steaks sizzling on the grill.* **2** *fig.* to be exciting and brilliant: *That commercial sizzles; people are buying the product heavily.* **-adj. sizzling.**

skate /skeɪt/ *n.* [C] *v.* **skated, skating, skates 1** a boot with wheels or a blade attached, worn to slide along **2** *short for* ice skate, rollerskate: *I <v.> skate in the park each morning.* **3** [C;U] a type of fish **-n.** [U] **skating.**

skate·board /'skeɪt,bɔrd/ *n.* a board with four wheels on which one stands and rolls along a surface

skein /skeɪn/ *n.* a long section of thread or wool, gathered in a smaller roll

skel·e·ton /'skɛlətn/ *n.* **1** a body's bones: *We studied the skeleton in biology class.* **2** the basic or beginning structure: *The skeleton of the house is built, but there are no walls.* **3** an incomplete

skateboard

thing: *the skeleton of an idea* **4 to have a skeleton in one's closet:** to hide s.t. embarrassing: *He has a skeleton in his closet; he spent a year in jail when he was young.*

skep·tic /'skɛptɪk/ *n.* a person who doubts or doesn't believe: *She is a skeptic about the future of this planet, because there are so many difficult problems.* **-adj. skeptical; -n.** [U] **skepticism** /'skɛptə,sɪzəm/.

sketch /skɛtʃ/ *n.* **-es 1** a drawing done quickly and without many details: *The artist drew a sketch of the woman's face in two minutes.* **2** a short piece of writing that gives the main ideas, (*syn.*) an outline: *The editor read a sketch of my book idea and asked to see a complete chapter.*
—v. **-es 1** to draw quickly, without details: *I sketched a picture of our new house.* **2** to write the main ideas, (*syn.*) to outline: *to sketch out an idea on paper*

sketch·y /'skɛtʃi/ *adj.* **-ier, -iest** without many details, vague, incomplete: *He has a sketchy idea of what cities he wants to visit, but those are his only plans.*

skew /skyu/ *v.* **1** to make information different, (*syn.*) to distort: *The newspaper skewed the facts; the story is untrue.* **2** to turn to the side: *If you skew the desk, the chair will fit better.* **-adj. skewed.**

skew·er /'skyuər/ *n.* a long, thin piece of metal used to hold pieces of meat or vegetables for cooking

ski /ski/ *n.v.* **skied, skiing, skis 1** a long, narrow piece of wood, fiberglass, or plastic, attached to special boots and used for moving on snow **2** a waterski *See:* cross-country ski; waterski.

ski·ing /'skiɪŋ/ *n.* the sport of sliding down or across snowy surfaces on skis

skid /skɪd/ *v.* **skidded, skidding, skids** to move across a surface, often sideways, with a bumpy or sliding motion: *The truck skidded to a stop just before the fence.*
—n. **1** the motion of skidding: *She put on the brakes too hard and went into a skid.* **2** a flat surface of wood put under heavy items, such as cartons, to move them **3 to be on the skids:** to be going toward failure: *He drinks too much and is on the skids.*

skid row *n.* a state of poverty, bad luck, drunkenness, etc. (originally from the name of a street in New York City): *He was a famous singer, but he took drugs and now is on skid row.*

ski lift *n.* one of several types of machines that move skiers to the top of a hill or mountain

skill /skɪl/ *n.* [C;U] **1** an ability to do s.t. well because of practice, talent, or special training: *She has excellent musical skills.* **2** a trade: *Plumbing is his skill.*

skilled /skɪld/ *adj.* **1** having an ability: *She is very skilled at typing.* **2** good at one's job: *He is a skilled carpenter.*

skill·ful /'skɪlfəl/ *adj.* able to do s.t. well, (*syn.*) adept: *She is skillful at managing a large staff.||He is skillful at building furniture.*

skim /skɪm/ *v.* **skimmed, skimming, skims 1** to read or look through quickly: *I skimmed the magazine for the interesting articles.* **2** to remove the thin, top layer of s.t.: *The cook skimmed the fat off the chicken soup with a spoon.* **3** to throw or move across the surface of s.t.: *The fast boat skimmed across the lake.* **4** to remove money illegally from a business: *to skim the profits* **5 to skim the surface:** to look at or think about only the easy or obvious part of s.t.: *The problem of poverty is very difficult; we have just skimmed the surface in trying to solve it.*
—n. illegal removal of money from a business: *the skim from the cash register -n.* [U] **skimming.**

skim milk *n.* milk with its cream (fat) removed

USAGE NOTE: Milk is sold in four forms, according to its fat content: (1) *skim* or nonfat, (2) one percent fat content, (3) two percent fat content, and (4) whole milk (four percent fat): *When you go to the store, would you get me a quart of two percent milk?*

---

skimp /skɪmp/ *v.* **1** to use low-quality materials: *The tailor skimped on the cloth for the suit, so it fell apart.* **2** to try hard to save money: *I don't get paid until next week, so I must skimp until then.*

skimp·y /'skɪmpi/ *adj.* **-ier, -iest** not enough, too small: *a skimpy bathing suit||a skimpy breakfast*

skin /skɪn/ *n.* **1** [U] the outer covering of a body: *His skin is very light, but it turns pink when he goes out in the sun.* **2** [C;U] the outer covering of a fruit or vegetable: *a potato skin||the skin of an onion* **3** [C] the outer covering of an animal from which leather is made: *seal skin||the skin of a deer* **4 by the skin of one's teeth:** just barely, by the smallest amount or distance: *Two men ran after the boy, but he was able to get away from them by the skin of his teeth.* **5 to get under one's skin:** to have an effect on, to anger or bother: *That movie got under my skin; I've been thinking about it all day.||Loud music really gets under my dad's skin.* **6 to have a thick skin:** not to be upset or bothered by unkindness or criticism: *She has a thick skin, so she doesn't mind when the teacher corrects her grammar.* **7 to have a thin skin:** to be easily upset, dislike criticism: *I hate it when my mother yells at me; I have very thin skin.* **8 to make one's skin**

S

crawl: to cause a feeling of fear, disgust, or dislike: *He felt someone was following him in the dark, and it made his skin crawl.*
—*v.* **skinned, skinning, skins 1** to remove the skin: *The hunter skinned the dead bear.* **2** to cut the skin so that it barely bleeds, (*syn.*) to scrape: *to skin a knee* **3 there is more than one way to skin a cat:** There is more than one way to do s.t., to solve a problem: *If you can't reach your brother by phone, write a letter; there's more than one way to skin a cat.*

skin-deep *adj.* **1** shallow, not deep: *The cut is only skin-deep, so I don't need a doctor.* **2** *fig.* not important or lasting: *Our fight was skin-deep; we weren't too angry.* **3 beauty is only skin-deep:** being a good person is more important than looking good: *My aunt is not pretty, but she is kind and generous; beauty is only skin-deep.*

skin-dive *v.* **-dived, -diving, -dives** to swim underwater with a face mask and some kind of breathing equipment -*n.* [U] **skin-diving.** *See:* SCUBA.

skin-flint /'skɪn,flɪnt/ *n.* a person who hates to spend money, (*syns.*) a cheapskate, miser: *Buy your wife a birthday present, or she will think you're a skinflint.*

skin-head /'skɪn,hɛd/ *n.* s.o. who shaves his or her head, often as a sign of membership in one of several groups of young people who go to rock concerts and sometimes show hatred of blacks, Jews, and others: *A skinhead tried to tell my son that Hitler was a hero.*

-skinned /-ˌskɪnd/ *suffix* related to skin: *a fair-skinned person*

skin-ny /'skɪni/ *adj.* **-nier, -niest** very thin: *The skinny boy went through a small hole in the fence. See:* trim, USAGE NOTE.

skinny-dipping *n.slang* swimming naked: *We took off our bathing suits and went skinny-dipping in the pond.*

skin-tight /'skɪn,taɪt/ *adj.* very tight, fitting closely: *skintight jeans*

skip /skɪp/ *v.* **skipped, skipping, skips 1** to run in a hopping way: *The little girl skipped happily to her friend's house.* **2** to use a jump rope: *to skip rope* **3** not to do s.t. that one usu. does, to miss: *to skip a meal‖to skip school for a day* **4** to pass over: *I read Chapters 2 and 4, but skipped Chapter 3.*

skip-per /'skɪpər/ *n.v.* the captain of a ship: *a <n.> skipper in the navy*

skir-mish /'skɜrmɪʃ/ *n.v.* (in the military) a small fight or battle

skirt (1) /skɜrt/ *n.* a piece of women's clothing that covers the waist, hips, and part of the legs and has no leg dividers: *My mother wore pants, but my sister wore a skirt and blouse.*

skirt (2) *v.* to go around, to avoid: *to skirt a bad problem‖We took a road that skirted the city.*

skit /skɪt/ *n.* a short, often funny scene that is part of a larger show or event: *At the picnic, the cousins put on a short skit about their grandparents.*

skit-tish /'skɪtɪʃ/ *adj.* easily frightened, nervous: *I am skittish about going to the doctor.‖The young horse was very skittish, so I couldn't put her saddle on.*

skull /skʌl/ *n.* the bone part of the head: *The scientists used the dead animal's skull to estimate its age.*

skull-cap /'skʌl,kæp/ *n.* a small, round cloth hat worn by men and boys, usu. as a sign of religious devotion *See:* yarmulke.

skull-dug-ger-y /skʌl'dʌgəri/ *n.frml.* [U] evil acts, (*syns.*) cheating, deception: *The gang burned houses and performed other acts of skullduggery.*

skunk /skʌŋk/ *n.* **1** a small animal with black fur and white stripes that gives off a bad-smelling liquid when frightened or attacked **2** *slang* a bad or mean person: *That man left his family for another woman; he's a skunk.*

skunk

sky /skaɪ/ *n.* [C;U] **skies 1** the air we see above the earth: *The sky is blue today, though it was cloudy yesterday.‖He saw a plane fly through the sky.* **2** *pl.* **the skies:** (same meaning): *The skies above our town looked dark before the rain.*

sky-cap /'skaɪ,kæp/ *n.* a person who works at an airport, carrying luggage, (*syn.*) porter: *A skycap helped bring my suitcase inside.*

sky-div-ing /'skaɪ,daɪvɪŋ/ *n.* [U] the sport of jumping out of a plane and floating to the ground with the help of a parachute -*n.* [C] **skydiver.**

sky-high *adj.* very high: *My son hit the baseball sky-high.‖The price of oil has gone sky-high.*

sky-jack /'skaɪ,dʒæk/ *v.* to make the pilot of an airplane fly to a place it isn't supposed to go: *Our plane was skyjacked by a man and a woman with guns. See:* hijack.

sky-light /'skaɪ,laɪt/ *n.* a window, often in a roof, that lets light in from above

sky-line /'skaɪ,laɪn/ *n.* **1** the line where the sky seems to meet the earth, (*syn.*) the horizon **2** the view of buildings, hills, mountains, etc., against the sky: *We saw the Eiffel Tower as part of the Paris skyline.*

sky-rock-et /'skaɪ,rɑkɪt/ *v.* to go up high and quickly: *The price of our house skyrocketed from $100,000 to $200,000 in two years.*

sky-scrap-er /'skaɪ,skreɪpər/ *n.* a very tall building: *The Empire State Building is a famous skyscraper.*

slab /slæb/ n. a thick, flat slice of s.t.: *The cook cut off a slab of beef and put it on my plate.*

slack /slæk/ n. [U] **1** lack of tightness, looseness in s.t., such as a string, fish line, or rope: *There is some slack in this rope, so you can pull it tighter.* **2** *infrml.* **to cut** or **give s.o. some slack:** to give s.o. the right to be wrong, to give s.o. more of a chance: *You're too strict with your son; cut him some slack.* -n. [U] **slackness.**
—*adj.* **1** not tight or firm: *a slack wire* **2** not working hard, not busy, lazy: *The boss told the slack worker to take fewer coffee breaks.*
—*v.* **to slack off:** to be less active, slow down: *The rain is slacking off; let's go outside.*||*This job is almost done; let's slack off for a while.* See: slacken.

slack·en /'slækən/ v. to be less active, slow down: *We're not selling as much; business has slackened.*||*We skated fast, then slackened our pace.*

slacks /slæks/ n. [U] pants, trousers: *Don't wear blue jeans to the wedding; put on slacks instead.*

slain /sleɪn/ past part. of slay
—*adj.* killed, murdered: *He was slain by a man with a knife.*
—*n.* people who have been killed (no "s" for plural form): *After the battle, the slain lay silent in a field.*

slake /sleɪk/ v. to satisfy s.t., esp. thirst: *A tall glass of lemonade slaked his thirst.*

slam /slæm/ v. **slammed, slamming, slams** **1** to hit s.t. hard: *The angry man slammed his fist on the desk.* **2** to close hard: *She slammed the door shut.*
—*n.* [C, *usu. sing.*] **1** a hard hit: *The car drove into the fence with a slam.* **2** a forceful closing: *We heard the slam of the window in the wind.*

slam·mer /'slæmər/ n.slang prison, jail: *He went to the slammer for 15 years for robbery.*

slan·der /'slændər/ v. to say bad or untrue things about s.o., to hurt s.o.'s reputation: *The radio program slandered the politician by saying he took drugs.*
—*n.* [C;U] the act of saying bad or untrue things about s.o.: *It was slander to say I don't pay my taxes; I do pay them.*

slang /slæŋ/ n. [U] informal language and expressions that are considered unacceptable in formal speech and writing, (syns.) argot, street language: *When we moved, I quickly learned the slang of the local teenagers.*

slant /slænt/ v. **1** to be put or to be at an angle, not to be straight up-and-down: *The flagpole is slanting; soon it will fall.* **2** to allow one's opinion to show when telling a story: *The angry wife slanted the story of her divorce.*
—*n.* **1** [C, *usu. sing.*] the angle of s.t.: *the slant of a roof* **2** [C] s.t.'s attitude or particular opinion: *my slant on the news item*

slap /slæp/ v. **slapped, slapping, slaps** to hit with a flat surface, esp. with the hand: *The girl slapped her brother, and he started to cry.*
—*n.* **1** a hit with a flat surface: *I gave the fly a slap.* **2 a slap in the face:** a bad surprise or insult: *I worked hard on the paper, so it was a slap in the face to get a bad grade.*

slap·dash /'slæp,dæʃ/ adj. done quickly and not well, (syns.) careless, hasty: *They made a slapdash attempt at repairing the roof, but it still leaked.*

slap·hap·py /'slæp,hæpi/ adj. having no worries, silly: *The man was slaphappy after too much beer and not enough sleep.*

slap·stick /'slæp,stɪk/ n. [U] adj. a type of acting that uses physical movement for comic effect: *In a funny piece of <n.> slapstick, a woman threw a pie in her husband's face.*

slash /slæʃ/ v. **1** to make a long cut with s.t. sharp: *The knife slashed through the sack of flour.* **2** to lessen, (syn.) to reduce (prices, cost): *At the end of the summer, the store slashed prices on bathing suits.*
—*n.* **1** a long cut made by s.t. sharp: *I opened the box with a slash of a razor blade.* **2** a great lessening, (syn.) a reduction: *He bought many T-shirts because there was a slash in their usual price.*

slat /slæt/ n. a flat, narrow piece of wood, metal, or plastic, usu. spaced evenly with other slats: *The new bed had slats to hold up the mattress.*

slate /sleɪt/ n. **1** [U] a gray rock cut into smooth, flat pieces, often used as roof shingles or for a ground or floor covering: *A slate path led to the porch.* **2** [C] a list of available people or things: *Do you like the slate of candidates running for the Senate?* **3 a clean slate:** a new, fresh beginning: *When he got out of jail, he decided to start over with a clean slate.*
—*v.* planned: *The meeting is slated for next Tuesday.*

slath·er /'slæðər/ v. to use a lot of s.t.: *I slathered on sunblock before playing volleyball on the beach.*

slaugh·ter /'slɔtər/ v. **1** to kill in a violent and bloody way, often in large numbers: *The army slaughtered the enemy with guns and knives.* **2** to kill animals for food: *The farmer had cows slaughtered for beef.* **3** *slang* (in sports) to win, to beat by a large amount: *Our soccer team slaughtered the other team by a score of 15 to 2.*
—*n.* [U] **1** the act of killing violently, often in large numbers: *The slaughter of hundreds of soldiers weakened the army.* **2** the act of killing animals for food: *the slaughter of sheep*

S

slave /sleɪv/ v. **slaved, slaving, slaves** **1** to work very hard for little or no money: *His parents slaved for years to save enough money for a house.* **2** to live and work as a slave: *During the Civil War, many people slaved for plantation owners.*
—n. a person who is owned by s.o. else and who works for no money: *My grandmother's grandfather was a slave who was owned by a rich cotton farmer.*

slave driver n.*infrml.* a person who makes people work very hard, often unfairly, (*syn.*) a taskmaster: *The boss told us to work late on a holiday; he's a slavedriver.*

slav·er·y /'sleɪvəri/ n. [U] the state of being owned by another person and working for money: *Until slavery was ended in the United States, many African-American people were not free.*

slav·ish /'sleɪvɪʃ/ adj. [U] about acting as if one is worth less than s.o. else, like a slave, (*syn.*) servile: *The secretary is slavish toward the boss; he yells at her, and she just keeps working quietly.*

slay /sleɪ/ v. **slew** /slu/ or **slayed** or **slain** /sleɪn/, **slaying, slays** **1** to kill on purpose: *The hunter slew the deer.* **2** *fig.* to make s.o. laugh a lot, amuse: *The funny movie slayed him.*

slea·zy /'slizi/ adj.*infrml.* **-zier, -ziest** dishonest, dirty, perhaps obviously sexual: *Drunks and cocaine dealers live in that sleazy neighborhood.* -n. [U] **sleaze; sleaziness.**

sled /slɛd/ n. **1** a vehicle that slides on runners over the snow, and that is pulled by animals: *In Alaska, we saw dogs pulling a sled.* **2** a child's toy for sliding down snowy hills: *Two kids sat on the sled and went down the hill.*
—v. **sledded, sledding, sleds** to travel by sled

sled·ding /'slɛdɪŋ/ n. **1** [U] the activity of using a sled: *The children got wet when they went sledding.* **2 tough** or **rough sledding:** difficult times: *Starting a small business is rough sledding at first.*

sledge /slɛdʒ/ n. a sled pulled by an animal

sledge·ham·mer /'slɛdʒ,hæmər/ n.v. a heavy piece of metal on a handle, used for breaking hard things or pounding things: *With a <n.> sledgehammer, he drove a piece of wood into the ground.*

sleek /slik/ adj. **-er, -est** **1** healthy-looking, well-dressed: *The rich man had a sleek appearance.* **2** smooth, shiny: *The cat had a sleek coat after giving himself a bath.*

sleep /slip/ v. **slept** /slɛpt/, **sleeping, sleeps** **1** to rest in an unconscious state, not to be awake: *I have not slept all night, so I am very tired.* **2** to have places to sleep: *A double bed sleeps two.* **3** *phrasal v.* **to sleep around:** to have sex with many people: *If he sleeps around, he might get AIDS.* **4** *phrasal v.* **to**

sleep in: to sleep later than usual: *When I'm on vacation, I like to sleep in.* **5 to sleep like a log:** to sleep well and deeply **6** *phrasal v. insep.* **to sleep on s.t.:** not to decide on or deal with s.t. until after a night's rest: *He'll answer your question after he's slept on it.* **7** *phrasal v. sep.* **to sleep s.t. off:** to get rid of a bad feeling or effect by sleeping: *She slept off five glasses of wine.‖She slept them off.* **8** *phrasal v. insep.* **to sleep through s.t.:** *She slept through church.* **9** *phrasal v. insep.* **to sleep together** or **with s.o.:** to have sex with s.o.:
—n. [C, *usu.* sing; U] the state of resting unconsciously: *Sleep is important for good health.*

sleep·er /'slipər/ n. **1** a person who is sleeping **2** *fig.* an unexpected, gradual success: *No one thought this movie would be popular, but it has gained respect from millions of people, despite its little commercial success; it's a sleeper.*

sleeping bag n. a large, quilt-like bag with a zipper in which s.o. can sleep outside in cold weather

sleeping pill n. a pill that contains medicine to help people sleep

sleep·less /'sliplɪs/ adj. **1** without sleep: *The bed was uncomfortable, so she had a sleepless night.* **2** not resting, always paying attention: *The guard kept a sleepless eye on the prisoner.*

sleep·y /'slipi/ adj. **-ier, -iest** needing sleep, tired, (*syn.*) drowsy: *I feel sleepy; I'm going to lie down.*

sleep·y·head /'slipi,hɛd/ n. s.o. who is tired (*usu.* used to refer to small children or a loved one): *Wake up, sleepyhead, it's time to go to school!*

sleet /slit/ v.n. [U] frozen rain, a mixture of snow and rain: *If it gets colder, the <n.> sleet may turn to snow.*

sleeve /sliv/ n. **1** the part of a piece of clothing that covers all or part of the arm: *In the summer, she likes blouses with short sleeves.* **2** any envelope or covering: *a sleeve for a record album‖a protective metal sleeve over a pipe* **3 to be in one's shirtsleeves:** to be without a suit jacket or sport jacket: *The businessmen had a casual lunch in their shirtsleeves, then put on jackets for a meeting.* **4 to have** or **keep s.t. up one's sleeve:** to have a secret or information one plans to use later: *You two were whispering when I came in. What do you have up your sleeve?* **5 to wear one's heart on one's sleeve:** to show one's feelings: *It's easy to see how much he loves her, since he wears his heart on his sleeve.*

sleigh /sleɪ/ n. a vehicle that holds people and that is pulled over snow by a horse

sleigh

sleight-of-hand /ˈsleɪtəvˈhænd/ *n*. [U] tricks that look like magic, because the performer's hands move so quickly and skillfully: *The man seemed to make two balls appear in the air, in an act of sleight-of-hand.*

slen·der /ˈslɛndər/ *adj*. **1** thin, slim: *She is very slender, so she can wear her teenaged daughter's clothes.* **2** narrow: *a slender stem on a flower* **3** small, not much or enough: *We hope the sick man will live through the summer, but it is a slender hope.*

sleuth /sluθ/ *n.v.frml*. a person who tries to solve mysteries, (*syn*.) a detective: *The woman hired a <n.> sleuth to find out who stole her jewelry.*

slew /slu/ *n*. [U] a lot, a large amount of s.t.: *A slew of ants crawled over the candy bar.*

slice /slaɪs/ *v*. **sliced, slicing, slices 1** to cut into thin, flat pieces: *My father sliced the roast turkey for the family dinner.* **2** (in golf or tennis) to hit the ball so it goes off to the right or left, not straight

—*n*. **1** a thin, flat piece of s.t.: *a slice of bread* **2** (in golf or tennis): a hit so the ball goes off to the right or left, not straight **3 slice-of-life:** a play or other performance that is realistic, that shows life without any great plot: *The show was a slice-of-life; we saw a typical day in the life of an Iowa farmer.*

slick /slɪk/ *n*. a slippery layer: *The leak in the boat caused an oil slick on the water.*

—*adj*. **1** smooth and slippery: *Don't fall on the ice; it's slick.* **2** seeming smart and honest, but not so really: *That slick guy had a nice smile, but he never paid me back my money.* -*n*. [U] **slickness.**

—*v*. to make smooth: *I wet my hand and slicked back my hair.*

slide /slaɪd/ *v*. **slid** /slɪd/, **sliding, slides 1** to move s.t. across a surface: *Workers slid boxes across the floor.* **2** to move easily and quietly: *We arrived late and slid into our seats.* **3** to go downward or to a worse state or place: *He has been sliding into depression since his wife died.* **4 to let s.t. or things slide:** to ignore s.t., to not take care of it: *We let fixing the house slide, and now it needs a lot of repairs.* **5** *phrasal v*. **to slide by: a.** to pass by with little space: *There is room enough; you can slide by me.* **b.** to work as little as possible: *He goes to college, but he just slides by with low grades.* **6** *phrasal v*. **to slide over:** to move over: *Slide over so I can join you on the bench.*

—*n*. **1** on a children's playground, a wooden or metal slope where one climbs up a ladder to the top, sits, and moves down quickly **2** the act of sliding: *a slide down a hill in the snow* **3** a lessening, (*syn*.) a decline: *a slide in prices* **4** a photograph shown against a screen: *We gathered in the living room and watched slides of my trip to Greece.* **5** on a microscope, the

glass that holds the thing being seen: *a slide of a fly's wing*

sliding scale *n*. a situation in which one amount changes when s.t. else changes: *My doctor works on a sliding scale; rich people pay more than poor for the same services.*

slight /slaɪt/ *adj*. **-er, -est 1** small: *a slight difference between a lemon and a lime* **2** thin and small: *My four-year-old is so slight that she looks only two.* -*n*. [U] **slightness.**

—*v. n*. to not pay much attention to, ignore: *Her friends <v.> slighted her by not inviting her to the baseball game.*

slim /slɪm/ *adj*. **slimmer, slimmest 1** thin, slender: *He is slim because he eats no meat and runs five kilometers a day.* **2** unlikely, (*syn*.) remote: *a slim chance of success* -*adj*. **slimming.**

—*v*. **slimmed, slimming, slims** *phrasal v*. **to slim down:** to get thinner: *She lost 40 pounds; she has slimmed down a lot.* See: trim, USAGE NOTE.

slime /slaɪm/ *n*. [U] any wet, sticky, dirty substance: *We cleaned the slime out of the old garbage can.* -*adj*. **slimy.**

sling /slɪŋ/ *v*. **slung** /slʌŋ/, **slinging, slings 1** to throw with a wide motion, (*syn*.) to hurl: *She slung her heavy suitcase into the back of the truck.* **2** to move with a sling

—*n*. **1** See: slingshot. **2** a cloth or leather support (as for a broken arm): *He broke his wrist, and it is in a sling.*

sling·shot /ˈslɪŋˌʃɑt/ *n*. a Y-shaped toy with a rubber band used to project stones or other objects

slink /slɪŋk/ *v*. **slunk** /slʌŋk/ or **slinked, slinking, slinks** to walk as if one is afraid or guilty: *He slinks around the house as though he shouldn't be there.*

slink·y /ˈslɪŋki/ *adj*. **1** acting afraid or guilty **2** smooth and sexy: *She wears slinky dresses when she goes dancing.*

slip /slɪp/ *n*. **1** a small piece of s.t.: *a slip of paper* **2** a small person: *That slip of a boy can't lift the heavy box.* **3** a piece of women's underclothes that looks like a dress or skirt: *a silk slip under her dress* **4** a mistake: *a slip in arithmetic* **5** a mistake in speaking: *a slip of the tongue* **6** a movement or fall caused by s.t. slippery: *a slip on a banana peel* **7** a space to keep a boat: *a slip for my sailboat in the harbor* **8 to give s.o. the slip:** to get away from s.o. who is following: *A policewoman followed a thief, but he gave her the slip in the dark.*

—*v*. **slipped, slipping, slips 1** to fall or almost fall because of s.t. slippery: *She slipped on the wet grass.* **2** to lessen: *The price of coffee has slipped.* **3** to become worse or do less well: *Her English is slipping with no practice.* **4** to move easily and quickly: *The cat slipped out* the open door. **5 to let s.t. slip:** to tell a secret: *Don't let news of the party slip; it's a surprise.* **6** *phrasal v. insep.* **to slip into s.t.:** to put on clothes: *She slipped into her nightgown.* **7 to slip one or s.t. by** or **over on s.o.:** to do s.t. tricky, to keep s.t. hidden: *She slipped one over on the hotel manager when she brought her cat in.* **8 to slip one's mind:** to be forgotten: *The date of the picnic slipped my mind, so I looked for it on the calendar.* **9 to slip through one's fingers:** to be unable to be held or kept: *I let the chance at a new job slip through my fingers.* **10** *phrasal v.* **to slip up:** to do s.t. wrong, make a mistake: *I added the numbers, but the total was wrong; I slipped up because I forgot to add tax. See:* Freudian slip; pink slip.

slip·page /'slɪpɪdʒ/ n. [U] a small movement in s.t.: *slippage between rocks in a wall*

slipped disk n. a bone that has moved in one's spine, causing pain

slip·per·y /'slɪpəri/ adj. **1** causing people or things to fall or slide, (syn.) slick: *The roads are very slippery with ice.* **2** not to be trusted, (syn.) evasive: *You cannot loan that slippery guy your car; he'll steal it.*

slip·shod /'slɪpˌʃad/ adj. made or done badly, (syn.) shoddy: *This paper shows slipshod work; you need to learn to write better.*

slip-up n. a mistake, usu. a small one: *The letter did not arrive because there was a slip-up on the address.*

slit /slɪt/ v. **slit, slitting, slits** to make a narrow cut: *The murderer slit his victim's throat with a razor.*
—n. a narrow cut or opening: *You can see through a slit in the door.*

slith·er /'slɪðər/ v. to move by sliding and making a lot of turns: *A snake slithered along the ground.*

sliv·er /'slɪvər/ v. to cut or break into thin or small pieces: *The cook slivered onions with a knife.*
—n. a thin or small piece of s.t.: *I stepped on a sliver of glass and cut my foot.*

slob /slab/ n. a dirty, messy person, often with bad manners: *He eats with his fingers, drops food, and never bathes; what a big slob.*

slob·ber /'slabər/ v.n. [U] **1** to drop saliva, liquid, or food from the mouth: *The baby <v.> slobbered milk all over the table.* **2** feelings shown in too open a way, embarrassing sentiment: *His love letters are filled with <n.> slobber; I hate to read them.*

slog /slag/ v. **slogged, slogging, slogs 1** to walk with difficulty (as in deep snow or mud): *We slogged through deep puddles in the driveway.* **2** to work with difficulty: *The new accountant slogs through a pile of old financial records.*

slo·gan /'slougən/ n. a saying or phrase that expresses a group's or a company's main message: *"We bring good things to life" is the slogan of the General Electric Company. -n.* **sloganeer.**

sloop /slup/ n. a small sailboat

slop /slap/ n. [U] **1** a wet mixture of old food, water, etc. fed to pigs **2** any bad or disgusting food: *I won't eat this slop; it's been in the refrigerator for months!*
—v. **slopped, slopping, slops 1** to spill over: *Water slopped over the sides of the bucket.* **2** to serve food in a careless way: *She slopped the mashed potatoes into a dish.*

slope /sloup/ n. a surface at an angle, esp. of a hill or roof, (syn.) an incline: *The slope is gentle, so children can ski down it.*
—v. **sloped, sloping, slopes** to incline at an angle: *The ground slopes down from the house to the street.*

slop·py /'slapi/ adj. **-pier, -piest 1** dirty and wet: *We put on boots to walk through the sloppy mud.* **2** messy, careless, (syn.) slipshod: *She can't read your sloppy handwriting.||The living room was sloppy, with magazines all over the floor. -adv.* **sloppily.**

slosh /slaʃ/ v. **-es** to move liquid, or s.t. in liquid, so that the liquid splashes: *I washed my shirt by sloshing it around in hot, soapy water.*

sloshed /slaʃt/ adj.infrml. drunk: *He drank beer all evening, and now he is sloshed.*

slot /slat/ n. **1** a small opening, usu. rectangular: *The mailman puts the mail through a slot in the door.* **2** a time or place for s.t.: *Fifty people wanted to run in the race, but there were slots for only 20.*
—v. **slotted, slotting, slots** to schedule s.t. for a time or place: *She needs to slot time for visiting her great-aunt.*

sloth /slɔθ, slouθ, slaθ/ n. **1** [U] laziness, lack of ambition: *The rich young woman won't work; she prefers to live in sloth.* **2** [C] a slow-moving animal that lives in trees in Central and South America -adj. **slothful.**

slouch /slauʧ/ v. **-es** to let one's shoulders fall, to be bent over, (syns.) to droop, slump: *Stop slouching and sit up straight, please!*
—n. a lazy person: *She's no slouch; she finished college in three years.*

slov·en·ly /'slʌvənli/ adj. **1** messy, dirty (of one's body): *He would look less slovenly if he took a shower and put on clean clothes.* **2** careless: *The dishes were done in a slovenly manner; there's still food on them.*

slow /slou/ adj. **-er, -est 1** not fast, moving at a low speed: *The traffic is very slow today.* **2** not smart, (syns.) dim-witted, dull: *Repeat the directions; he is a bit slow.* **3** not busy or active, quiet: *During the summer season, sales are slow for us.* **4** behind the correct time: *My watch is slow; it says 3:00, but the time is 3:15.*

—v. **1** to go less quickly, lessen speed: *Work has slowed this week, so we can go home earlier.* **2** *phrasal v. sep.* **to slow s.t. down:** to lessen the speed of s.t., to go less fast: *I put on the brakes and slowed the car down.||I slowed it down.* -*adv.* **slowly** -*n.* **slowness.**

slow·down /'sloʊˌdaʊn/ *n.* a lessening of the normal pace of an activity, often done by workers as a protest: *The factory has produced half as much since the workers started their slowdown.*

slow motion *n.* [U] (in film) action looking slower than real-life action

slow·poke /'sloʊˌpoʊk/ *n.* s.o. who works or acts slowly (usu. said in a friendly way): *Stop smelling the flowers and hurry up, slowpoke!*

slow-witted *adj.* stupid, not quick to understand: *The slow-witted student could not do the simple arithmetic problem.*

sludge /slʌdʒ/ *n.* [U] thick, oily dirt or mud: *the sludge in the old car engine*

slug /slʌg/ *n.* **1** a round bullet for a gun **2** a fake coin: *She put a slug in a public telephone, but it didn't work.* **3** a small, snail-like animal without a shell **4** *infrml.* a hard hit: *One guy gave the other a slug in the face.* **5** a single, quick swallow: *a slug of lemonade*
—*v.infrml.* **1** to hit hard: *We called the police when we saw a neighbor slug her child.* **2** to drink quickly, in big swallows: *She slugged beer and was soon drunk.*

slug·gish /'slʌgɪʃ/ *adj.* **1** slow, not active: *business that is sluggish* **2** lacking energy, not completely awake or conscious: *She felt sluggish after only four hours of sleep.*

sluice /slus/ *n.* **1** a machine that controls the flow of water into or out of a lake, river, etc. **2** the flow itself
—*v.* **sluiced, sluicing, sluices** to send a flow of water: *I washed the soap off as the water sluiced over my body.*

slum /slʌm/ *n.* part of a city where poor people live in bad housing, often with lots of crime (singular for a building, plural for a larger area): *She saved money and moved away from the slums so her kids could have a better life.*

slum·ber /'slʌmbər/ *n.frml.* [U] sleep: *I went into a deep slumber that lasted all night.*
—*v.* to sleep, to be inactive

slumber party *n.* a party in which (usu.) girls spend the night at one girl's house

slum·lord /'slʌmˌlɔrd/ *n.* an owner of an old, dirty building who often doesn't treat his tenants well: *The slumlord would not fix the broken windows or clean the stairway.*

slump /slʌmp/ *n.* **1** a time of slow economic activity: *The market for coffee beans has been in a slump for months.* **2** a sinking down, (*syn.*) collapse: *to fall over in a slump*

—*v.* **1** to fall, sink: *prices that slump* **2** to lose an upright position by bending or falling suddenly, (*syns.*) to slouch, collapse: *The poor man slumped over from a heart attack.*

slur /slɜr/ *n.* an expression in which s.o. says unkind things, often about another racial or religious group: *The woman made an ethnic slur toward the black man.*
—*v.* **1** to say an unkind thing **2** to speak in an unclear way: *She took too much medicine and started to slur her words.*

slurp /slɜrp/ *n.v.* the sucking sound of food or liquid in the mouth: *The mother asked her little boy not to <v.> slurp his soup.*

slush /slʌʃ/ *n.* [U] **1** soft, melting snow mixed with dirt: *The slush on the sidewalk made our shoes wet.* **2** a frozen dessert made with juice or syrup

slush fund *n.* money saved for various reasons: *The group has a slush fund that it uses to give money to politicians.*

slut /slʌt/ *n.pej.* a woman who has sex with many different people, (*syn.*) a whore

sly /slaɪ/ *adj.* **-er, -est 1** of or about doing things secretly, (*syns.*) devious, cunning: *The sly child quietly took a cookie when her mother wasn't looking.* **2** playful, teasing: *His sly remark made her turn red and giggle.* **3 on the sly:** secretly: *The couple was meeting on the sly so their parents would not know.* -*adv.* **slyly;** -*n.* [U] **slyness.**

smack /smæk/ *n.* **1** a hit, usu. with the hand: *to give s.o. a smack in the face* **2** *slang* a light, quick kiss: *He gave his wife a loving smack on the cheek and went to work.* **3** *slang* the drug heroin
—*v.* **1** to hit s.t. with force: *The car smacked into a wall.* **2** *phrasal v. insep.* **to smack of s.t.:** to seem, to indicate: *The plan smacks of something illegal.*
—*adv.* directly, exactly: *I jumped smack into the middle of the pool.*

smack-dab /'smæk'dæb/ *adv.infrml.* directly, sometimes unexpectedly: *He walked around the corner and ran smack-dab into an old friend.*

smack·er /'smækər/ *n.slang* **1** a kiss **2** a dollar

small /smɔl/ *adj.* **-er, -est 1** physically little, not big: *a small child||a small car with two seats* **2** not important, insignificant: *It's a small problem; don't worry.* **3** low in quantity or amount: *a small salary||a small amount of butter* **4** not as large or important: *We studied the small playwrights, not the big ones like Shakespeare.*
—*adv.* **1 to feel small:** to feel bad or stupid, to feel humiliated: *Her boss said her work was not good; he made her feel small.* **2 to think small:** to keep one's ideas possible, to think in

a modest manner: *All he wants is an apartment, a dog, and a regular job; he thinks small.*

small change *n.* [U] **1** a small number of coins: *I have only small change, a few nickels and dimes.* **2** insignificance, unimportance: *The cost of engine oil is small change in comparison to the cost of the engine itself.*

small-claims court *n.* in the USA, a court where a judge helps settle minor financial disagreements: *That man owes me $500, and I am going to take him to small-claims court to get it.*

small fry *n.fig.* [U] **1** child or children: *I am taking the small fry to the zoo today.* **2** people of little importance: *In her mind, the small town is full of small fry and the city is more interesting.*

small-minded *adj.* not thinking of others, concerned with unimportant or limited ideas: *The small-minded woman should read more to learn about the world's problems.*

small potatoes *n.fig.* [U] s.t. unimportant or of little value: *This business is really small potatoes; I'd rather work on Wall Street.*

small·pox /'smɔl,pɑks/ *n.* [U] a very serious disease marked by fever, vomiting, and pimples that leave scars, no longer common in richer countries because of an effective vaccine

small-scale *adj.* limited, little in size or amount: *He runs a small-scale operation; he owns three corner grocery stores.* -*n.* **small scale.**

small talk *n.* [U] light conversation about everyday topics like the weather: *We made a bit of small talk about our children.*

small-time *adj.* not important, insignificant: *He is a small-time thief who steals wallets and purses instead of robbing banks.*

smart /smɑrt/ *adj.* **-er, -est 1** able to think well, intelligent: *His son is a very smart boy; he is first in his class.* **2** somewhat rude, (*syn.*) impertinent: *The child made a smart remark to her father, so she was sent to bed without dinner.* **3** fashionable and neat: *He wore a smart suit with new shoes.*
—*v.* **1** to be physically painful, to hurt: *Putting alcohol on a cut smarts, but it cleans the dirt out.* **2** to be emotionally painful: *Yesterday you said I was too fat, and the remark still smarts.*

smart a·leck /'ælɪk/ *n.* a person who thinks that he knows everything and tries to show it: *That smart aleck tried to tell me how to live my life, but I didn't listen.*

smart·ly /'smɑrtli/ *adv.* well, fashionably: *a smartly dressed woman*

smart bomb *n.* a bomb or missile that can be directed to hit a target by guiding it with radio waves or a laser

smar·ty·pants /'smɑrti,pænts/ *n.slang* [U] a smart aleck, often used when speaking to a naughty child

smash /smæʃ/ *v.* **-es 1** to break into pieces with force: *The vase fell on the floor and smashed into little bits.* **2** to hit against s.t., to crash: *The bicycle smashed into a fence, and the rider flew off.* **3** *phrasal v. sep.* **to smash s.t. up:** to break or ruin: *He smashed up his car in an accident.*||*He smashed it up.*
—*n.* **1** the sound or act of smashing **2** *fig.* a very successful piece of entertainment, (*syn.*) a hit: *The new comedy is a smash.*

smashed /smæʃt/ *past part. of* smash
—*adj.* **1** broken into pieces: *a smashed window* **2** *slang* drunk: *He was so smashed that he could hardly walk.*

smat·ter·ing /'smætərɪŋ/ *n.* [C, *usu. sing.*] a small amount, a bit here and there: *I know a smattering of Russian, enough to ask simple questions.*||*The open land had only a smattering of houses.*

smear /smɪr/ *n.* **1** a mark or spot made by spreading or quickly wiping: *There was a smear on the glass from the child's dirty hands.*||*I cleaned a smear of honey off the tabletop.* **2** an attempt to make people believe s.t. bad about s.o.: *Your lies were a smear on my reputation.* **3** s.t. on a microscope slide
—*v.* **1** to spread or quickly wipe with a substance: *The clown smeared makeup on his face.* **2** to make people believe s.t. bad about s.o.: *The paper smeared the mayor, and very few people voted for him again.*

smell /smɛl/ *n.* **1** [U] the sense for which the nose is used: *My dog's sense of smell is excellent.* **2** [C] the feeling sensed through the nose, (*syns.*) odor, scent, aroma: *The smell of soup cooking on the stove made me hungry.* **3** [C, *usu. sing.*] a feeling or quality about s.t.: *This fancy neighborhood has the smell of money.*
—*v.* **1** to sense an odor: *I smell the roses in the garden.* **2** to have an odor: *This place smells like pine trees.* **3** to have a bad odor: *Something smells in the refrigerator.* **4** to sense s.t.: *I smell danger around that dark corner.* **5 to smell a rat:** to sense that s.o. or s.t. is wrong, bad, or not to be trusted: *She borrowed $100 and left town; I smell a rat.* **6** *phrasal v. insep.* **to smell of s.t.:** to seem like, to be related to: *My grandmother's house smells of happier days.*

USAGE NOTE: Something can smell *good* or *bad*, but if s.t. simply smells (with no adverb or simile following), the assumption is "it smells bad:" *This bathroom smells!*

---

smell·y /'smɛli/ *adj.* **-ier, -iest** having a bad or strong smell, stinky: *smelly cheese*

smid·gen *or* **smid·geon** *or* **smid·gin**

S

/'smɪʤən/ *n.* [C] a tiny amount: *I'd like only a smidgen of cake; I'm trying to lose weight.*

smile /smaɪl/ *v.* **smiled, smiling, smiles** to turn the lips up at their corners, usu. to show good feelings, such as amusement or happiness: *She smiles when she watches her kids play.*
—*n.* the expression of smiling: *He gave her the good news with a smile.*

USAGE NOTE: Compare *smile, grin, smirk,* and *laugh.* A grin is a smile that shows the teeth: *The proud new father was holding his baby and grinning from ear to ear.* A smirk is a smile of triumph, conceit, or stupidity: *She's smirking because she thinks she's the only one who knows the answer.* A *chuckle* is a low, soft sound of amusement: *He chuckled to himself as he read his friend's letter.* A *laugh* is a louder sound of amusement, made with the mouth open and often written as the word *ha-ha: The movie was so funny that we couldn't stop laughing.*

smirk /smɜrk/ *n.* a smile that shows somewhat unkind amusement or a feeling that one is a bit smarter or better: *He could not find his glasses, and his wife smirked at him; they were on top of his head. See:* smile, USAGE NOTE.

smith /smɪθ/ *n.* a person who works with metal, usu. used as a suffix: *silversmith‖goldsmith*

smith·er·eens /ˌsmɪðə'rinz/ *n.pl.* tiny pieces, (*syn.*) fragments: *The wine bottle smashed into smithereens when the waiter dropped it.*

smit·ten /'smɪtn/ *adj.* **1** affected by s.t. bad: *My whole family has been smitten by a disease.* **2** very attracted or in love: *He was smitten with his girlfriend from the day they met.*

smock /smɑk/ *n.* a piece of clothing worn over other clothing to protect it: *The artist spilled some paint on his smock.*

smog /smɔg, smɑg/ *n.* [U] a mixture of smoke and fog, air pollution: *The heavy smog in Los Angeles looks like a gray-yellow blanket over the city. -adj.* **smoggy.**

smoke /smoʊk/ *v.* **smoked, smoking, smokes 1** to use cigarettes, cigars, pipes, etc.: *I smoke cigarettes, but I'm trying to quit.* **2** to give off small pieces of burned material and gas into the air: *The fire is smoking.*
—*n.* [U] **1** the blackish-gray, gaseous substance from s.t. that is burning: *Smoke comes from that chimney.* **2 to go up in smoke: a.** to be completely burned: *Our house went up in smoke when the oil tank blew up.* **b.** to leave nothing behind, to become useless: *Our vacation plans went up in smoke, because we had to use the money for taxes.* **3 where there's smoke, there's fire:** if it seems like there's trouble, there probably is

smok·er /'smoʊkər/ *n.* **1** s.o. who smokes: *Smokers have a separate section in this restaurant.* **2** a party where people try different cigars, often for men only

smoke screen *n.fig.* s.t. that is used to hide the truth: *His big house is just a smoke screen; he has no money.*

smoke·stack /'smoʊk,stæk/ *n.* a tall chimney in a factory: *the smokestacks of the steel mill*

smok·ing /'smoʊkɪŋ/ *n.* [U] the use of tobacco: *Smoking is not permitted on many airline flights.*

smoking gun *n.fig.* definite proof of who committed a crime: *The police found a knife with a woman's fingerprints on it; that was the smoking gun they needed to arrest her.*

smok·y /'smoʊki/ *adj.* **-ier, -iest 1** filled with smoke: *The kitchen is smoky from the stove.* **2** tasting of smoke: *smoky bacon*

smol·der /'smoʊldər/ *v.* **1** to burn slowly with no flame: *The fire burned brightly, then smoldered quietly.* **2** *fig.* to be angry but not show it in an obvious way: *I smoldered with hidden rage.*

smooch /smutʃ/ *n.v.slang* **-es** a kiss: *I love you; give me a <n.> smooch.‖He <v.> smooched me.*

smooth /smuð/ *adj.* **-er, -est 1** without roughness or bumps, flat, even: *The new road is smooth.‖the smooth silk of her dress* **2** without trouble or difficulty: *a smooth flight* **3** seeming calm and pleasant, but maybe not: *The smooth salesman may talk you into buying a bad car. -n.* [C] **smoothie;** [U] **smoothness.**
—*v.* **1** to make flat, even, without bumps: *A carpenter smoothes the top of the table with sandpaper.* **2** *phrasal v. sep.* **to smooth s.t. over:** to remove difficulties or obstacles: *Their presidents promised to smooth the way.* **3** to make better, calm: *to smooth relations between two countries‖They smoothed them over.*

smor·gas·bord /'smɔrgəs,bɔrd/ *n.* tables spread with a variety of food, usu. both warm and cold, to which people help themselves

smoth·er /'smʌðər/ *v.* **1** to take away a person's oxygen: *The killer smothered the man by putting a pillow over his face.* **2** to put out a fire by covering it or taking away its oxygen **3** to cover s.t.: *She smothered her hot dog with ketchup.‖The boy smothers his kitten with love.*

smudge /smʌʤ/ *n.* a mark made by dirt, oil, food, etc., (*syns.*) a blotch, smear: *a smudge of lipstick on his cheek*
—*v.* **smudged, smudging, smudges** to make a small, irregular mark by rubbing: *My pen's eraser smudged the letter.*

S

smug /smʌg/ *adj.* **-smugger, -smuggest** sure that one is right, self-satisfied: *Don't be so smug; you may have the wrong answer.*

smug·gle /ˈsmʌgəl/ *v.* **-gled, -gling, -gles** to bring things into or out of another country or area illegally: *Dealers in cocaine smuggle the drug into the USA.* *-n.* **smuggler.**

smut /smʌt/ *n.* [U] s.t. (such as a film or book) that is highly sexual and not of good quality, (*syn.*) pornography: *He reads smut that is full of pictures of naked people.* *-adj.* **smutty.**

snack /snæk/ *n.* a small amount of food, usu. eaten between meals: *My favorite snack is potato chips.*
—*v.* to eat a small amount, (*syn.*) to nibble: *We snacked on crackers and cheese.*

snack bar *n. See:* bar, USAGE NOTE.

sna·fu /snæˈfu/ *n.slang* a very confused situation: *We sent back the shirt because it was the wrong color. Then the company sent us the right color but the wrong size. What a snafu!*

snag /snæg/ *n.* **1** a break or tear in a piece of cloth: *Her stocking got a snag on a sharp corner.* **2** a temporary problem in a process: *We hit a snag when typing the addresses; the computer stopped working.*
—*v.* **snagged, snagging, snags 1** to catch on s.t.: *He snagged his fish line on a log in the river.* **2** *infrml.* to catch or get s.t.: *We never thought he would snag such a great job.*

snail /sneɪl/ *n.* **1** a small, soft animal with a hard shell, noted for its slowness **2 at a snail's pace:** very slowly: *The rush-hour traffic moved at a snail's pace.*

snake /sneɪk/ *n.* **1** a long, slender reptile with no legs that moves with a curvy, winding motion **2** a bad, dishonest person: *That snake never paid me the money he owed me.*
—*v.* **snaked, snaking, snakes 1** to move in a winding way: *The river snakes through the forest to the ocean.* **2** to move s.t. long and thin through a small space: *He snaked the electrical wire through the radio.*

snake·bite /ˈsneɪkˌbaɪt/ *n.* the bite, often poisonous, from a snake

snake pit *n.* **1** a hole or cave where snakes gather **2** *fig.* a dangerous place full of anger and emotion: *That office is a snake pit, with everyone fighting with each other.*

snap /snæp/ *n.* **1** a sudden sound or action like a crack or a pop: *the snap of two fingers ||to close the notebook with a snap||the snap of a twig breaking off a tree* **2** a closure for s.t., with one piece locking into another: *The baby's pants have snaps.* **3** an easy job or activity: *Sailing a boat is a snap in nice weather.* **4** a period of cold weather: *During the cold snap, we wore thick sweaters.*
—*v.* **snapped, snapping, snaps 1** to break suddenly and with a sharp sound: *The pencil snapped in half.* **2** to have a mental break-

down: *The pressure of her job was too much, and she snapped.* **3** *phrasal v. insep.* **to snap at s.t.: a.** to grab, to reach for: *I snapped at the chance to take ballet lessons.* **b.** to speak in an angry or impatient way: *I'm sorry I snapped at you; I was tired and hungry.* **c.** to show one's teeth and try to get s.t. with one's mouth: *The dog snapped at the piece of meat.* **4** *phrasal v. sep.* **to snap s.t. up:** to take s.t. quickly: *We snapped up their offer to help us.||We snapped it up.*
—*adj.* quick, without much thought: *a snap decision*

snap·py /ˈsnæpi/ *adj.infrml.* **1** lively, energetic: *a snappy song* **2** stylish and bright: *He is a snappy dresser.* **3 make it snappy:** hurry up: *Bring me a cup of coffee and make it snappy!*

snap·shot /ˈsnæpˌʃɑt/ *n.* an informal photograph: *She took a snapshot of her kids around the picnic table.*

snare /snɛr/ *n.* **1** a trap: *a snare for catching rabbits* **2** a hidden danger, trap: *The letter is a snare to have you come; don't do it!*
—*v.* **snared, snaring, snares** to get, catch: *to snare a raccoon||to snare a good job*

snarl /snɑrl/ *v.* **1** to make an angry sound while showing one's teeth: *The dog snarled at a cat.* **2** to speak angrily: *The boss snarled at a salesman.* **3** to become tangled: *The traffic is all snarled up.||The wind snarled my hair.*
—*n.* **1** an angry sound while showing one's teeth: *a lion's snarl* **2** a show of anger: *Her snarl warned me to stay away.* **3** a tangle: *a snarl in the wires* **4** confusion: *Because of a snarl in the plans, no one knew what to do.*

snatch /snætʃ/ *v.* **-es 1** to take s.t. quickly, grab, seize: *The boy snatched a piece of cake and ate it hungrily.* **2** to steal: *to snatch a purse (wallet, watch, etc.)* **3** *phrasal v. insep.* **to snatch at s.t.:** to try to get s.t.: *It annoys me when you snatch at my arm.*
—*n.* **-es 1** a quick grab **2** a small amount: *We could hear snatches of noise from the neighbor's TV.* **3** a short period of time: *He worked a lot and rested in snatches.*

snaz·zy /ˈsnæzi/ *adj.slang* new and stylish, often colorful or bright: *a snazzy car||a snazzy suit*

sneak /snik/ *v.* **sneaked** or **snuck** /snʌk/, **sneaking, sneaks** to go quietly, to try not to be seen: *The boy sneaks into the movie without paying.||She sneaked cookies from the jar.*
—*n.* a coward, a dishonest person: *You sneak! You tried to run away without telling me!*
—*adj.* **sneaking suspicion:** an uncomfortable feeling about s.t. bad happening: *She*

has a sneaking suspicion that she failed the biology test.

USAGE NOTE: The standard past tense form is *sneaked,* but in many dialects people say *snuck.* Use *sneaked* in school and business situations: *Late again, I sneaked in quietly.*

sneak·er /'snikər/ *n.* a soft canvas or leather shoe, usu. worn for sports or casual activities: *My daughter put on her sneakers and ran outside to play.*

USAGE NOTE: *Sneaker* is a general term for an athletic shoe, which can also be called *a tennis shoe, basketball shoe, running shoe,* etc., depending on its specific function.

sneak·y /'sniki/ *adj.* done in a secret or dishonest way, *(syns.)* devious, furtive: *You were sneaky to climb out of your bedroom window without your parents seeing. -n.* [U] **sneakiness.**

sneer /snɪr/ *v.* to show contempt by raising one side of the mouth: *He sneered at the offer and said it was too low.*
—*n.* an expression of sneering or showing contempt: *The rich kids looked at my old clothes with a sneer.*

sneeze /sniz/ *v.n.* [C] **sneezed, sneezing, sneezes** **1** to send air forcefully through the nose and mouth because of an irritation, cold, allergy, etc.: *She <v.> sneezes every time that she smells pepper.* **2 nothing to sneeze at:** worthy of admiration, good enough: *My raise in pay was not huge, but it was nothing to sneeze at, either.*

snick·er /'snikər/ *v.n.* [C] to laugh unkindly or to show disbelief: *He says that he is the strongest guy around, and everyone just <v.> snickers.*

snide /snaɪd/ *adj.* **snider, snidest** acting superior, *(syns.)* sarcastic, cutting: *The boss made a snide comment about his secretary's lack of intelligence.*

sniff /snɪf/ *v.n.* **1** to breathe in air with the nose in a way that can be heard, to smell: *She <v.> sniffed the perfume, then bought it.||One <n.> sniff told me the milk was bad.* **2** to show one thinks s.o. or s.t. is bad or inferior: *The poor man asked the lady for money, but she just sniffed and walked on.* **3** *phrasal v. insep.* **to sniff at s.t.:** to refuse s.t. out of pride: *He sniffed at our invitation to dinner.*

snif·fle /'snɪfəl/ *v.n.* **-fled, -fling, -fles** **1** to breathe with difficulty because of a mucous-filled nose: *I had a cold and was <v.> sniffling all day.* **2** to cry quietly: *People <v.> sniffled at the funeral.* **3** *n.pl.* a slight cold: *The little boy stayed home from school with the sniffles.*

snig·ger /'snɪgər/ *v.* to snicker

snip /snɪp/ *v.* **snipped, snipping, snips** to cut s.t. with a short, quick motion: *The gardener snipped off dead leaves from plants with scissors.*
—*n.* a cut or a small piece of s.t. that has been cut: *I put a snip in the cloth.||He saved a snip of his baby's hair.*

snipe /snaɪp/ *v.* **sniped, sniping, snipes** **1** to shoot from a hidden place: *to snipe at enemy soldiers from behind a tree* **2** to say unkind, critical things: *I heard the neighbors sniping about my mother's clothes.*

snip·er /'snaɪpər/ *n.* a person who shoots people from a hidden place: *A sniper shot three men from a rooftop.*

snip·py /'snɪpi/ *adj.* **-pier, -piest** rude, *(syn.)* impertinent: *The boy was snippy, so his father made him apologize.*

snit /snɪt/ *n.* **in a snit:** irritated, angry: *He was in a snit because he did not get any mail.*

snitch /snɪtʃ/ *v.* **-es** **1** to steal s.t.: *The boy snitched a candy bar from the store.* **2** to tell about s.o.'s illegal activity: *She saw a man get on the train without a ticket, so she snitched on him.*
—*n.* **1** a thief **2** a person who tells about s.o.'s illegal activity, *(syn.)* an informer: *The snitch told the police who had sold him the drugs.*

sniv·el /'snɪvəl/ *v.* to cry or complain in a weak, whining manner: *"I want to go home! I hate it here!" the child sniveled.*

snob /snab/ *n.* a person who thinks he or she is better than others in intelligence, social class, taste, etc.: *They are snobs who drink only expensive French wine and won't listen to rock 'n' roll. -n.* [U] **snobbery.**

snob·by /'snabi/ *adj.* **-bier, -biest** thinking of oneself as better than others (in intelligence, social class, taste, etc.): *He is snobby toward anyone who wasn't born in the northeastern USA. -adj.* **snobbish.**

snoop /snup/ *v.* to look around secretly in a place one doesn't belong: *He got caught snooping in his boss's desk drawer.*
—*n.* s.o. who looks around secretly in a place where he or she doesn't belong

snoot·y /'snuti/ *adj.infrml.* **-ier, -iest** **1** acting as if others are not worthy of one's attention, *(syns.)* snobby, haughty: *I tried to join the tennis club and found the people there a bit snooty with me.* **2** upper-class, *(syn.)* exclusive: *The yacht club is very snooty; they accept only rich men who went to Harvard or Yale.*

snooze /snuz/ *n.infrml.* a nap: *I'm going to lie down and take a snooze.*
—*v.* **snoozed, snoozing, snoozes** to take a nap, sleep, *(syn.)* to doze: *You've snoozed for an hour; it's time to wake up!*

snore /snɔr/ *v.* **snored, snoring, snores** to make sounds from one's nose and mouth while

S

sleeping: *He snores loudly, so his wife can't sleep.*
—*n.* the sound of snoring: *Her snores are so loud you can hear them downstairs.*

snor·kel /'snɔrkəl/ *n.* (in skin diving) a tube for breathing underwater, one end of which fits in the mouth and the other of which sticks above the surface of the water -*n.* [U] **snorkeling.**

snort /snɔrt/ *v.* **1** to make a loud sound from the throat or nose: *The horses snorted and pawed the ground.||She snorts when she laughs.* **2** to show contempt or disbelief: *"You do not have a Rolls Royce!" he snorted.*
—*n.* **1** the sound or act of snorting **2** *slang* a drink of liquor: *Let's go into this bar and have a snort.*

snot /snɑt/ *n.vulg.* **1** [U] the wet material in the nose, (*syn.*) mucous **2** [C] *slang* a snobby or bad person -*adj.* **snotty.**

snout /snaʊt/ *n.* an animal's nose and other facial parts that stick out: *a pig's snout*

snow /snoʊ/ *n.* [U] **1** the white flakes formed by frozen water that falls from the sky in cold weather: *mountains covered with snow* **2** the whiteness on a TV screen that shows bad reception **3** *slang* the drug cocaine
—*v.* **1** to fall from the sky in the form of snow: *It snowed all night and now the ground is covered.* **2** *phrasal v.* **to be snowed in:** to be unable to leave a place because of deep snow: *We were snowed in; the car was buried.* **3** *slang* **to snow s.o.:** to tell s.o. a big false story: *He really snowed her when he said he was the company president; he's only a salesman. See:* snow job. **4** *phrasal v. insep.* **to be snowed under s.t.:** to have a huge amount of work: *I have four books to read this week; I am snowed under.*

snow·ball /'snoʊ,bɔl/ *n.* **1** a ball of snow formed with the hands: *Children love to make and throw snowballs.* **2** *infrml.fig.* **a snowball's chance in hell:** no possibility of success: *A new tax increase does not have a snowball's chance in hell of passing into law.*
—*v.fig.* to grow in size quickly and uncontrollably: *The problem of poverty is snowballing with each new teenage pregnancy.*

snow·bound /'snoʊ,baʊnd/ *adj.* unable to leave because of snow *See:* snow, *v.,* 2.

snow·fall /'snoʊ,fɔl/ *n.* **1** [C;U] an amount of fallen snow: *We had a heavy snowfall that covered our car.||Alaska's yearly snowfall is much higher than Arizona's.* **2** [U] falling of snow: *We may have some snowfall this afternoon.*

snow·flake /'snoʊ,fleɪk/ *n.* a single piece of snow: *I could see separate snowflakes on my mittens.*

snow job *n.slang* a big false story: *The guy gave his girlfriend a snow job about how he knows lots of famous actors.*

s n o w · p l o w /'snoʊ,plaʊ/ *n.* a truck with a large, curved piece of metal attached to it for pushing snow off streets: *Snowplows started clearing our road as soon as the snowstorm began.*

snowplow

snow·storm /'snoʊ,stɔrm/ *n.* a heavy, serious fall of snow, usu. with high winds: *We are having a snowstorm now, so there will be no school.*

snow·y /'snoʊi/ *adj.* **-ier, -iest** full of snow: *snowy weather||wet, snowy gloves* -*n.* [U] **snowiness.**

snub /snʌb/ *v.* **snubbed, snubbing, snubs** **1** to ignore s.o. in a cold or impolite way: *His ex-wife snubbed him at the party by turning her back.* **2** to reject s.o.: *She sent a love letter, but he snubbed her by not answering it.*
—*n.* the act of snubbing s.o.: *I thought it was a snub when he said he was "too busy" to come to my party.*

snuck *v. See:* sneak, USAGE NOTE.

snuff /snʌf/ *n.* [U] **1** a powder of tobacco that is breathed through the nose **2 up to snuff: a.** in good health: *I left work because I wasn't feeling up to snuff.* **b.** good enough: *This paper is not up to snuff; please rewrite it.*

snug /snʌg/ *adj.* **1** in a small, comfortable place, (*syn.*) cozy: *The baby is snug in its mother's arms.* **2** tight: *This dress is a bit snug since I've gained weight.* **3** small but cozy: *a snug bedroom*

snug·gle /'snʌgəl/ *v.* **-gled, -gling, -gles** to lie or sit close to s.o. and touch in a loving way, (*syn.*) to cuddle: *On cold winter nights, they like to snuggle in bed.||The baby snuggled against its mother.*

so /soʊ/ *adv.* **1** to the degree or extent that: *He is so strong that he can bend a metal pipe.* **2** to a great extent, very: *That elephant is so big!* **3** in that way, (*syn.*) thus: *Why are you running so?* **4** because, for that reason: *I was thirsty, so I drank.* **5** also, in the same way: *She loves animals, and so does her husband.* **6** indeed, truly (used to emphasize): *"You are not 40 years old." "I am so!"* **7 or so:** about, nearly: *Meet us at 4:00 or so.||That ticket costs $20 or so.* **8 so be it:** that's the way things are (shows reluctant acceptance): *If our friendship is over, well, then so be it.* **9 and so forth and so on:** and other things, (*syn.*) et cetera: *We talked for hours about our kids, our jobs, and so forth and so on.* **10** <*adv.*> **So what?: a.** I don't care; who cares?: *You don't like what I say? So what?* **b.** what's the next step; now what?: *You've got a high school education; so what?*

—adj. true, real: *She is getting married; I know it's so because I saw her ring.*

—conj. with a result that: *She is unemployed, so she is looking for a job.*

—interj. indicating surprise or disapproval: *So! You just got back from Italy!||So, there you are, late again!*

soak /soʊk/ *v.* **1** to put or be in water for a long time: *I soaked in the tub with bubble bath.* **2** to make very wet: *The rain soaked the vegetable garden.* **3** *infrml.fig.* to change s.o. too much money: *My car broke down, and the garage soaked me to fix it.* **4** *phrasal v. sep.* **to soak s.t. in** or **up**: to take in, *(syn.)* to absorb: *The soft ground soaked up* (or) *in the rain as it fell.||It soaked it up.*

—n. a time spent in water: *The dishes had a good soak in the sink.*

soak·ing /'soʊkɪŋ/ *n.usu. sing.* [C] **1** wetness, *(syn.)* a drenching: *I was caught in a rainstorm without an umbrella and got a good soaking.* **2** too much money paid: *The expensive meal was a real soaking.*

—adj. adv. very wet: *We came out of the pool <adv.> soaking wet.||She is soaking.*

so-and-so *n.infrml.* **1** a person one doesn't like: *That so-and-so was very rude to me!* **2** an unnamed person: *Oh, I can't think of his name—you know, so-and-so who works at the bank.*

soap /soʊp/ *n.* **1** [U] a liquid or solid cleaning substance: *I washed my face with soap.* **2 no soap:** I don't agree, no: *"I want to go to the movies tonight." "No soap, you stay home and watch TV."* **3 the soaps:** soap operas

—v. to use soap: *The boy stood under the shower and soaped himself all over.*

soap opera *n.* **1** a television show, usu. shown in the afternoon, with complicated love stories, high emotion, and unrealistic drama: *In that soap opera, two sisters died, came back to life, and married brothers.* **2** a highly dramatic real-life situation: *Her life is a soap opera; her father drinks too much, her sister is in jail, and she's getting a divorce.*

soap·y /'soʊpi/ *adj.* **-ier, -iest** full of soap: *soapy water*

soar /sɔr/ *v.* **1** to fly high through the air with no difficulty: *The birds soared above us.* **2** to become happy, reach a higher level than usual: *Her spirits soared when she learned that she was pregnant.||The beautiful music soared.*

soar·ing /'sɔrɪŋ/ *n.* [U] the sport of gliding on wind currents without engine power in an airplane or hang glider: *I went soaring in a glider over the mountains.*

sob /sɑb/ *v.n.* **sobbed, sobbing, sobs** to cry loudly with the body shaking: *She <v.> sobbed and screamed when she learned of her son's death.*

S.O.B. /'ɛsoʊ'bi/ *n.vulg.abbr. for* son of a bitch, an unkind, bad person, usu. a man: *That S.O.B. hit my car and drove away.*

so·ber /'soʊbər/ *adj.* **1** not drunk or affected by drugs: *He is sober enough to drive.* **2** no longer using alcohol: *She drank too much in her twenties, but she is sober now.* **3** not colorful or bright, plain: *a nun's sober black clothing* **4** rational and sensible: *a serious, sober decision*

—v.phrasal v. sep. **to sober up: a.** to become free of the effects of alcohol: *He has sobered up after a night of drinking.* **b.** to think more clearly: *The owner has to sober up to the fact that we need to borrow money.* *-n.* [U] **sobriety** /sə'braɪəti/.

sob story *n.* a sad story that is probably exaggerated or untrue, meant to cause pity or guilt: *She gave me a sob story about her horrible marriage so that I would not become friendly with her husband.*

so-called *adj.* **1** usually known as: *This is a so-called economy car because of its cheap price.* **2** incorrectly known as: *a so-called nice guy who is really a thief*

soc·cer /'sɑkər/ *n.* [U] a sport of two teams of 11 players each, who kick a ball into nets at either end of a rectangular field (called "football" outside the USA)

so·cia·ble /'soʊʃəbəl/ *adj.* friendly, liking to be with other people: *Our friends are very sociable; they go to lots of parties.* *-n.* [U] **sociability.**

so·cial /'soʊʃəl/ *adj.* **1** of or about people and society: *social problems such as homelessness and unemployment* **2** friendly, liking to be with others: *My wife likes social activities, such as tennis and golf.* **3** living in a group: *social animals, like cattle and monkeys*

—n.old usage a gathering of people, a type of party: *a Saturday night social at the church*

social climber *n.* a person who tries to rise in social class, *(syn.)* an arriviste: *He is a social climber; he goes to wine tastings and tries to meet wealthy people.*

social disease *n.* an illness caught from an infected person through sexual contact, *(syns.)* a venereal disease, sexually transmitted disease

so·cial·ism /'soʊʃəˌlɪzəm/ *n.* [U] a political belief or philosophy that says the government should own and run factories, hospitals, schools, etc., with the people sharing in work and products: *Under socialism, the government pays for most education.*

so·cial·ist /'soʊʃəlɪst/ *adj.* related to socialism

—n. a person who believes in socialism

so·cial·ite /'soʊʃəˌlaɪt/ *n.* a person who is well known among fashionable, rich people: *She is a socialite who goes to many big parties.*

S

so·cial·ize /'souʃə,laɪz/ v. **-ized, -izing, -izes 1** to be with other people in a friendly way, for talking, dining, etc.: *We socialize with two other couples almost every weekend.* **2** to turn a government or business to a socialist form of ownership: *In the USA, some senators want to socialize medicine so the government pays more health-care costs.*

social science n. [C] one of many areas of study, such as sociology, history, psychology, and economics, that examine people's relationships with each other and with the world

Social Security n. [U] in USA, a governmental program that pays a monthly amount of money to older, nonworking people and others who can't work: *My grandmother buys groceries and clothing with her check from Social Security. See:* unemployment insurance.

USAGE NOTE: *Social Security* tax, federal tax, and state tax are deducted from most Americans' paychecks. Many retired people depend on their monthly Social Security checks to pay for many of their needs.

social studies n.pl. a subject in elementary or high school, combining history, geography, government, and other social sciences

social worker n. a person who works with poor or troubled people in order to improve their lives: *A social worker visited us every week after our parents died to make sure we had enough to eat.* -n. **social work.**

so·ci·e·tal /sə'saɪətl/ adj.frml. of or about society: *The societal problems of cities include homelessness and crime.*

so·ci·e·ty /sə'saɪəti/ n. **-ties 1** a wide, non-specific group of people who share some of the same background and culture: *American society* **2** the lives and activities of rich, fashionable people: *When she was 16, she entered society and met her future husband.* **3** a club or organization: *a musical society* **4** company: *We like the society of our friends when we play golf.*

so·ci·o·ec·o·nom·ic /,sousiou,ɛkə'namɪk, -,ikə-/ adj. of or about a mix of human and financial factors: *Poverty is a socioeconomic problem.*

so·ci·ol·o·gy /,sousi'aləʤi, -ʃi-/ n. [U] the study of human relationships and the way these relationships affect their world: *In a sociology class, we learned about population growth in big cities.* -adj. **sociological** /,sousiə'laʤəkəl, -ʃi-/; -n. **sociologist.**

so·ci·o·path /'sousiə,pæθ, -ʃi-/ n. a mentally ill person who has trouble being with others: *She is a sociopath who is angry with the world and talks to no one.*

sock /sak/ n. a piece of cloth worn over the foot and under a shoe, and reaching partway up the leg
—v.infrml. **1** to hit s.o.: *He socked me in the nose and I bled.* **2** phrasal v. sep. **to sock s.t. away:** to put aside, hide away for future use: *She socked away money to pay for Christmas presents.*||*She socked it away. See:* ankle sock; knee sock; stockings.

sock·et /'sakɪt/ n. **1** a place in a wall to plug in an electrical wire: *We put the lamp on a table and plugged it into a socket.* **2** the eye holes in a skull

sod /sad/ n. [U] v. a section of dirt with grass, used to cover a piece of ground without having to plant seed: *We put <n.> sod in the backyard.*||*We <v.> sodded it.*

so·da /'soudə/ n. **1** [U] bubbly water, carbonated water, drunk alone or mixed with another beverage: *whiskey and soda* **2** a flavored, bubbly drink, (syn.) a carbonated beverage: *We bought two types of soda: ginger ale and root beer.* **3** [C] a special drink made from soda water or a flavored soda, flavoring, and ice cream: *I bought my girlfriend a chocolate soda.*

USAGE NOTE: *Soda* is also called *soda pop, pop, and tonic,* in different parts of the USA. It's considered a *soft drink* because it contains no alcohol.

sod·den /'sadn/ adj. completely wet, soaked: *His sodden pants were put into the clothes dryer.*

so·di·um /'soudiəm/ n. [U] a white-silver metallic element that is always combined with other elements

sodium chloride /'klɔraɪd/ n. [U] chemical name for table salt

sod·om·y /'sadəmi/ n. [U] anal intercourse or intercourse with an animal -n. **sodomite.**

so·fa /'soufə/ n. a long, soft seat covered with cloth or leather with a back, arms, and room for two or more people, (syn.) a couch: *We like to sit on the sofa and watch television.*

soft /sɔft/ adj. **1** not hard; easy to bend, cut, or make holes in: *a soft pillow*||*soft wood* **2** nice to touch, smooth: *a kitten's soft fur*||*soft leather* **3** not sharp or bright, (syn.) subdued: *a soft shade of blue* **4** not loud or strong, gentle: *soft flute music*||*a soft breeze through the trees* **5** pej. not smart or not completely sane: *Don't be soft and go out in the storm.*||*He's a bit soft in the head from a serious fall.* **6** in love: *She's soft on the cute guy in biology class.* **7** not strong or strict: *You are too soft on your child; she needs to be punished.* **8** (of consonants) making a less sharp or hard sound: *the "c" in "city" is soft, while the "c" in "cook" is hard.* **9** to have a soft spot for s.o. or s.t.: to like,

S

often because of a happy memory: *My husband and I have a soft spot in our hearts for the little Vermont town.*

soft·ball /'sɔft,bɔl/ *n.* [U] a sport much like baseball, but using a larger, softer ball; a smaller playing field; and an underhand pitch

soft-boiled *adj.* (of an egg) cooked for a short time in water so the inside stays soft

soft·bound /'sɔft,baʊnd/ *adj.* (of a book) with a strong but bendable paper cover: *I'm buying a softbound book because it's easier to carry.* *See:* paperback.

soft currency *n.* the money of some countries that is not accepted in exchange for the currencies of richer nations *See:* hard currency.

soft drink *n.* a flavored, bubbly drink with no alcohol, such as cola or orange soda

soft·en /'sɔfən/ *v.* **1** to make less hard: *He softened stale bread by dipping it in milk.* **2** to make a bad feeling less serious: *She softened his anger by saying "I'm sorry."*

soft goods *n.pl.* cloth products, such as clothing, sheets, etc. *See:* dry goods.

soft·head·ed /'sɔft,hɛdɪd/ *adj.* foolish, stupid: *That softheaded guy is taking pictures at night with no light.*

soft·heart·ed /'sɔft,hartɪd/ *adj.* kind, generous: *A softhearted woman picked up the hurt puppy and brought him home.*

soft-pedal *v.* to make s.t. seem less bad or serious, (*syn.*) to downplay s.t.: *He soft-pedaled the fact that sales are weak and talked about how good profits are.*

soft rock *n.* [U] rock music that uses fewer electronic instruments and is less loud than hard rock: *Many radio stations play soft rock for adults who don't like their kids' music.*

soft sell *n.* [U] *adj.* a way of selling s.t. that is gentle and convincing: *The salesman used a soft sell; he told us about the different stereos and let us decide.*

soft-spoken *adj.* having a gentle, quiet voice: *The soft-spoken man told the children a bedtime story.*

soft touch *n.* **1** a gentle and usu. expert way of touching: *to play the piano with a soft touch* **2** a generous person who is easy to convince or persuade: *He is such a soft touch; he will give his kids any toys they ask for.*

soft·ware /'sɔft,wɛr/ *n.* [U] in a computer, a set of instructions that lets a person perform certain tasks, such as word processing, adding numbers, or reading information on the Internet; software is not part of the machine itself: *I use communications software to exchange knowledge with other computer users.*

soft·y /'sɔfti/ *n.infrml.* a person who is not strict; a generous, kind-hearted person: *He pretends to be a tough guy, but underneath he's a softy.*

sog·gy /'sagi, 'sɔ-/ *adj.* **-gier, -giest** wet and soft, mushy: *The grass is soggy from the rain.*‖*a soggy beach towel*

soil /sɔɪl/ *n.* [U] **1** a particular kind of earth or dirt: *The soil near the beach is sandy and rocky.* **2** the top layers of earth in which plants grow: *The soil in Minnesota and Iowa is good for farming.* **3** a country, land: *It was good to be back on US soil after our trip to Australia.* —*v.* to make dirty: *to soil one's hands with grease*

so·journ /'sou,dʒɜrn, sou'dʒɜrn/ *v.n.frml.* to visit temporarily, to live somewhere for a short time: *They <v.> sojourn in England and France for a few months each year.*

sol·ace /'salɪs/ *n.* [C;U] relief, comfort (from grief, hurt, etc.): *When he is sad or worried, he takes solace in his religion.*

so·lar /'soulər/ *adj.* related to the sun: *solar energy*

solar-powered *adj.* getting energy from sunlight: *a solar-powered calculator*

solar system *n.* the Sun, Earth, eight other planets, moons, comets, etc., that move around the sun: *Exploration of the solar system fascinates everyone.*

sold /sould/ *adj.& past part.* of sell *adj.* **1** given in exchange for money: *If that house is not sold, I will buy it.* **2 to be sold on:** to be sure, convinced of s.t.: *The owner is sold on the idea that we need more space.* **3 to be sold out:** to have no more left: *All the tickets for this show are sold out.*

sol·der /'sadər/ *v.n.* [U] to join together or fix metal by melting it and then allowing it to cool: *He <v.> soldered a new exhaust pipe onto the car.*

sol·dier /'souldʒər/ *n.* a member of the military, esp. in an army: *A soldier from the Vietnam War marched in the parade.* —*phrasal v.* **to soldier on:** to keep doing in a brave way: *In spite of the heavy snow, we soldiered on to the top of the mountain.*

sole (1) /soul/ *n.* **1** the bottom of the foot: *The hot sidewalk burned the sole of my bare foot.* **2** the bottom of a shoe: *The soles of my shoes have holes in them from walking a lot.*

sole (2) *n.* **sole** or **soles** a type of edible white fish similar to a flounder

sole (3) *adj.* referring to one of s.t., (*syns.*) only, single, lone: *I don't have enough money; that's the sole reason I don't have a car.*‖*One sole person stood off from the crowd.*

sole·ly /'souli/ *adv.* **1** alone, singly: *It was solely my fault that the cat ran out the door.* **2** entirely, (*syn.*) exclusively: *He went to the circus solely for the fun of it.*

sol·emn /'saləm/ *adj.* **1** serious, (*syn.*) somber: *She had a solemn expression on her face as she gave the bad news.* **2** religious, (*syn.*)

S

holy: *A marriage ceremony is a solemn occasion.* **-v. solemnify** /sə'lɛmnə,faɪ/; **-n.** [U] **solemnity** /sə'lɛmnəti/.

so·li·cit /sə'lɪsɪt/ *v.* **1** to ask for, to seek out: *A person called on the phone to solicit votes for the politician.* **2** to offer to have sex with s.o., (*syn.*) to proposition: *A prostitute solicited a man who sat parked in a car.* **-n. solicitor.**

so·lic·i·tous /sə'lɪsətəs/ *adj.frml.* eager to help, concerned: *He was solicitous of his grandmother as he helped her sit down.*

sol·id /'salɪd/ *adj.* **1** hard and difficult to break: *solid rock* **2** not liquid or gas: *solid food* **3** without holes or breaks, the same throughout: *The statue is solid marble.* **4** trustworthy, reliable: *a solid reputation for honesty* —*n.* s.t. that is not liquid or gas: *The baby drinks breast milk and eats some solids, like bananas.* **-n.** [U] **solidity** /sə'lɪdəti/.

so·li·dar·i·ty /,salə'dærəti/ *n.* [U] a feeling or state of togetherness or having the same opinions as others in a group: *The political party showed solidarity when everyone voted for the same woman.*

so·lid·i·fy /sə'lɪdə,faɪ/ *v.* **-fied, -fying, -fies 1** to make hard, become a solid: *The cold water solidified into ice.* **2** to make s.t. definite, to jell: *to solidify one's plans*

so·lil·o·quy /sə'lɪləkwi/ *n.* **-quies** a speech, usu. in a play, in which a person shows his or her thoughts by speaking alone and out loud: *One actor stood on stage and gave a soliloquy about the meaning of death.*

sol·i·taire /'salə,tɛr/ *n.* **1** [U] a card game played by one person **2** [C] a gem or stone set by itself: *Her engagement ring was a diamond solitaire.*

sol·i·tar·y /'salə,tɛri/ *adj.* **1** lone, single: *A solitary house stood in an open field.* **2** alone: *My aunt lives alone and likes her solitary life.*

solitary confinement *n.* in a prison, a serious punishment in which s.o. is put in a small room with no communication with the outside world

sol·i·tude /'salə,tud/ *n.* [U] the state of being alone: *He found solitude in a quiet forest.*

so·lo /'soʊloʊ/ *adv.* by oneself, alone: *I didn't want to go swimming, so my husband went solo.* —*adj.* alone: *a solo performance* —*n.* a piece of music written for one voice or instrument: *to sing a solo||a violin solo* **-n. soloist.**

so long *interj.infrml.* good-bye: *"So long for now; I'll see you later."*

sol·u·ble /'salyəbəl/ *adj.* **1** able to be dissolved in a liquid: *Sugar is soluble in water.* **2** able to be solved, (*syn.*) solvable: *Is this math problem soluble? It seems too hard.*

so·lu·tion /sə'luʃən/ *n.* **1** [C] an answer to a problem, a way of solving it: *The police found the solution to the mystery.* **2** [C;U] a mixture of a solid and a liquid, in which the solid dissolves (one can no longer see the solid): *a solution of salt and water*

solv·a·ble /'salvəbəl/ *adj.* able to be solved, (*syn.*) soluble: *a solvable problem*

solve /salv/ *v.* **solved, solving, solves** to find an answer or solution for s.t.: *We solved the problem by reading the directions.*

sol·vent /'salvənt, 'sɔl-/ *n.* [C;U] a liquid that can dissolve or soften s.t. else: *We used a solvent to remove old paint from a table.*

so many *adj.* **1** a limited number: *I tried to finish the job, but there are only so many hours in a day.* **2** in such a way as: *We ate dinner like so many hungry lions.*

som·ber /'sambər/ *adj.* **1** dark: *No sun came into the somber room.* **2** serious and sad: *A newspaper story about a fire put us in a somber mood.*

some /sʌm, səm/ *adj.* **1** an unknown amount, probably not a lot: *some bread||some money* **2** unnamed, unknown: *Some neighbor left a cake on our front porch.* **3** *fig.* incredible, impressive: *He got three goals; he is some hockey player!* —*pron.* part of s.t. mentioned before: *We have yogurt. Would you like some?* —*adv.* about, approximately: *The necklace cost some $400.*

some·bod·y /'sʌm,badi, -,bʌdi/ *pron.* **1** an unknown person: *Somebody telephoned but didn't give his name.* **2** an important person: *He just got a big new job, and now he thinks he's somebody. See:* someone.

some·day /'sʌm,deɪ/ *adv.* at a time in the future, maybe not known now: *Someday you will be famous. See:* sometime.

some·how /'sʌm,haʊ/ *adv.* in a way not known or understood: *Somehow, we will find water in the desert.*

some·one /'sʌm,wʌn/ *pron.* an unknown person: *Someone should ask the policeman how to get to the park.*

USAGE NOTE: *Somebody* and *someone* both mean an unidentified person. Both can be used in speech or writing.

some·place /'sʌm,pleɪs/ *adv.* (at) an unknown place: *She left her purse someplace. See:* somewhere.

som·er·sault /'sʌmər,sɔlt/ *v.n.* **1** to roll one's body over headfirst and land on the feet **2 to turn somersaults for s.o.:** to make a great effort: *My boss is turning somersaults for me, trying to get me a raise in pay.*

some·thing /'sʌm,θɪŋ/ *pron.* **1** an unknown thing: *Something in his eyes makes me think of my father.* **2** *fig.* s.o. or s.t. wonderful: *What a beautiful dress; it's really something!*

—*adj.* **something else:** remarkable, extraordinary: *Your CD collection is something else; you have thousands!*

some·time /'sʌm,taɪm/ *adv.* at an unknown time: *We can't stay forever; we have to go sometime. See:* someday.

some·times /'sʌm,taɪmz/ *adv.* not always, now and then: *Sometimes we go to the beach, but usually we go to the mountains.*

some·way /'sʌm,weɪ/ *adv. See:* somehow.

some·what /'sʌm,wɑt, -,wʌt/ *adv.* to a small degree, a bit, rather: *Wear a sweater; it's somewhat cool.*

some·where /'sʌm,wɛr/ *adv.* **1** (at) an unknown place: *I can't find my glasses; I put them somewhere.* **2 to get somewhere:** to make progress: *We agree on a few things, so now we are getting somewhere. See:* someplace.

so much *n.* (of an amount) unknown: *Chicken costs so much a pound.*

—*adv.* **so much the better:** then things will be even better than before: *If the rain stops, so much the better.*

—*adj.* like some kind of: *His ideas are so much nonsense.*

son /sʌn/ *n.* **1** a male child: *They have two sons, so they want a daughter.* **2** a boy or man who is associated with a place or event: *The statue is for the sons of France who died in World War I.* **3** name for a boy instead of his proper name: *Do you want some milk, son?*

so·na·ta /sə'nɑtə/ *n.* a piece of music for an instrument, often the piano, with three or four separate sections (movements)

song /sɔŋ, sɑŋ/ *n.* **1** a piece of music that is sung: *a love song‖a bird's song* **2 for a song:** for very little money: *He bought that car for a song — only $50.*

song and dance *n.* **1** a performance that combines singing and dancing **2** *fig.* a complicated, often untrue excuse or explanation: *He was late for work again, and gave his boss a big song and dance about how his car broke down.*

song·writ·er /'sɔŋ,raɪtər, 'sɑŋ-/ *n.* a person who writes music and/or words for songs

son·ic boom /'sɑnɪk/ *n.* a very loud noise caused by an aircraft going faster than the speed of sound: *That loud sound when the fighter jet went by was the sonic boom.*

son-in-law *n.* **sons-in-law** the husband of one's daughter

son·net /'sɑnɪt/ *n.* a poem with 14 lines and a specific pattern and rhythm: *a Shakespearean sonnet*

son·ny /'sʌni/ *n.* s.t. one calls a boy: *Sonny, would you help me carry these groceries?*

son of a gun *exclam.* showing surprise or hurt: *Are you really 40 years old? Son of a*

gun!‖Son of a gun! I hit my finger with a hammer!

—*n.* a difficult or somewhat bad man: *That son of a gun is never on time.*

soon /sun/ *adv.* **1** in the near future, not long from now: *We've been traveling all day and will arrive soon.* **2** quickly, without delay: *She needs to get to the hospital as soon as possible.* **3 just as soon:** preferably, willingly: *I would just as soon leave now, before trouble starts.* **4 no sooner (did s.t. happen) than:** at the same time, as soon as: *No sooner did we sit down to dinner than the phone rang.*

soot /sʊt/ *n.* [U] the powdery black dirt created by burning s.t.: *The man cleaned the chimney, and he is covered with soot.* -*adj.* **sooty.**

soothe /suð/ *v.* **soothed, soothing, soothes 1** to ease mental or physical pain: *After playing tennis, she soothed her aching muscles by taking a warm bath.* **2** to calm and relax: *She soothed the barking dog with a low, soft voice.* -*adj.* **soothing.**

sop /sɑp/ *v.* **sopped, sopping, sops** to take up liquid by absorbing and wiping it, (*syn.*) to blot: *to sop up milk with a sponge*

—*n.fig.* s.t. given to make s.o. feel better: *They did not make him president of the company, but they gave him a new title as a sop.*

SOP /'ɛsoʊ'pi/ *n.abbr.* of standard operating procedure, a usual way of doing s.t.: *Everybody must be searched by guards before entering the building; the search is SOP.*

so·phis·ti·cat·ed /sə'fɪstə,keɪtɪd/ *adj.* **1** with high-class tastes and understanding, (*syn.*) worldly: *My cousins are very sophisticated, since they have lived in Paris and Rome.* **2** intricate, complex: *sophisticated computer equipment* -*n.* **sophisticate** /sə'fɪstəkɪt/; [U] **sophistication** /sə,fɪstə'keɪʃən/.

soph·o·more /'safə,mɔr, 'saf,mɔr/ *n.* **1** a student in his or her second year of high school or college **2** a person in his or her second year of a job or activity **3 sophomore slump:** the tendency to do worse after a good first year or good beginning: *The baseball player is having sophomore slump; last year he got many more hits.*

soph·o·mor·ic /,safə'mɔrɪk, saf'mɔr-/ *adv.* silly, immature: *My kids like movies with sophomoric comedy.*

sop·o·rif·ic /,sapə'rɪfɪk/ *n.adj.* a drug to help s.o. sleep: *He took a <n.> soporific and rested well that night.*

sop·ping /'sapɪŋ/ *adj.* completely wet, (*syns.*) dripping, soaking: *I shook water out of the sopping towel.*

so·pra·no /sə'prænoʊ, -'prɑ-/ *n.* **1** a woman or boy who sings in the highest voice range: *She and her sister are sopranos in the church choir.* **2** the high range itself: *The young boy* *sings in soprano, but soon his voice will change.*

sor·bet /sɔrˈbeɪ, ˈsɔrbɪt/ *n.* [U] a frozen dessert, usu. fruit-flavored and with little or no fat

sor·cer·y /ˈsɔrsəri/ *n.* [U] the practice of (usu. evil) magic, witchcraft: *In the story, a witch used sorcery to turn a man into a mouse.* **-n. sorcerer; sorceress.**

sor·did /ˈsɔrdɪd/ *adj.* dirty, shameful: *The newspapers printed all the sordid details of the scandal.*

sore /sɔr/ *adj.* **1** painful: *sore muscles* **2** *infrml.* angry, irritated: *He is sore about the fact that he did not get a raise.* **-n.** [U] **soreness.**

sore·ly /ˈsɔrli/ *adv.* a great deal, usu. with emotional pain: *My brother died and I miss him sorely.*

sore throat *n.* a general feeling of pain in the throat, caused by a cold, infection, talking too much, etc.: *She coughed a lot, so she has a sore throat. See:* headache, USAGE NOTE.

so·ror·i·ty /səˈrɔrəti, -ˈrɑr-/ *n.* **-ties** a women's social club or group, esp. in a college or university: *Her sorority had a party to celebrate the tennis team's win.*

sor·row /ˈsɑroʊ, ˈsɔ-/ *n.* [C;U] deep sadness, *(syn.)* melancholy: *We were full of sorrow when we learned our favorite uncle had died.* **-adj. sorrowful.**

sor·ry /ˈsɑri, ˈsɔ-/ *adj.* **1** regretful, apologetic: *I'm sorry! I didn't mean to hurt you.* **2** no good, bad: *She gave me a weak, sorry excuse about a sick grandmother.* **3** causing sympathy, pitiful: *a sorry sight of poor people without food*

sort /sɔrt/ *n.* **1** a type, kind: *What sort of ice cream do you want?* **2** a kind or type of person: *Invite that guy; he's a good sort.* **3** a separation of various items: *a computer sort of our different accounts* **4 out of sorts:** feeling bad or angry: *Don't pet the dog; he's feeling a little out of sorts.* **5 sort of:** a little, somewhat: *I was sort of hungry, so I ate a banana.*
-v. 1 to separate things into groups: *Would you sort these names alphabetically, please?* **2** *phrasal v. sep.* **to sort s.t. out: a.** to separate: *He sorted out the white laundry from the colored.||He sorted it out.* **b.** to make sense of s.t.: *We have to sort out this mess and try to understand it.* **3** *phrasal v. insep.* **to sort through s.t.:** to look through, to search: *He sorted through his papers and found the correct one.*

sort·ing /ˈsɔrtɪŋ/ *n.* [U] the process of sorting: *The computer is doing the sorting now and will print soon.*

SOS /ˈɛsoʊˈɛs/ *abbr. for* save our ship, a call for help: *The sinking ship sent an SOS over the radio.||The company is failing, so they sent an SOS to investors.*

so-so *adj.* not wonderful, fair, mediocre: *During the recession, we had a so-so sales year.*
-adv. not very well, but not very poorly: *"Do you feel better?" — "Oh, just so-so."*

sot /sɑt/ *n.* a person who drinks too much liquor

souf·flé /suˈfleɪ/ *n.* a light, air-filled dish made with egg whites and other foods, and cooked until it increases in size: *a cheese soufflé||a chocolate soufflé*

sought /sɔt/ *past tense and past part. of* seek

sought-after *adj.* desired, wanted: *The Nobel Prize is a much sought-after award; many scholars and artists want it.*

soul /soʊl/ *n.* [C] **1** the part of a person that is not the body; that is, the spirit, thoughts, emotions, etc., that some people think live on after death: *She believes the soul of her dead husband is in heaven.||I will be happy someday; I feel it in my soul.* **2** [C] a person: *There were 20 souls living on that island.* **3** [C] the most important part of s.t.: *The owner is the soul of this company.* **4** [U] *infrml.* in African-American life, a feeling of togetherness and emotion, often expressed in music *See:* soul food, soul music. **5 body and soul:** (with) all of oneself: *She gave body and soul to her job; she worked 18 hours a day.||I love you body and soul.*

soul food *n.* [U] traditional food of African-American people from the southern US, such as collard greens and black-eyed peas

soul-searching *n.* [U] the act of looking inside oneself, examining one's feelings to find an answer: *Her career is going nowhere, and she is doing a lot of soul-searching about what to do.*

sound (1) /saʊnd/ *n.* **1** s.t. that can be heard, a noise: *Stand still and don't make a sound.||I heard the sound of music.* **2** the way s.t. seems, *(syn.)* the implication: *By the sound of your letter, it seems you're very happy.*
-adj. 1 in good condition: *The company is sound; sales are good and employees are happy.* **2** learned or known from study and experience: *a sound decision||The scientific paper has a sound background in research.* **3** unbroken, uninterrupted: *sound sleep* **4** (in law) mentally healthy, *(syn.)* rational: *to be of sound mind.*
-v. 1 to make a sound: *The bell sounds at noon.* **2** to appear: *You sound sad.||That idea sounds good to me.* **3** *phrasal v. insep.* **to sound off on** or **about s.t.:** to make one's thoughts known in a loud or unpleasant way: *She keeps sounding off about the homeless, but never does anything to help.* **4** *phrasal v. sep.* **to sound s.o. out:** to talk with s.o. about his or her opinion: *I'll sound out my boss on the idea*

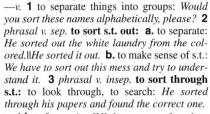

for the new building downtown.||I'll sound him out.

sound (2) a long, wide body of water that connects larger bodies of water: *We sailed our boat in Long Island Sound.*

sound barrier *n.usu. sing.* the point at which aircraft begin moving faster than the speed of sound: *When airplanes break the sound barrier, there is a loud noise.*

sound effects *n.pl.* in a play, movie, or radio show, the noises made offstage to seem like real sounds: *The play included sound effects of a door slamming and a toilet flushing.*

sounding board *n.fig.* a helpful and trusted person who listens to one's ideas: *The manager uses his wife as a sounding board for changes that he wants to make.*

sound·proof /'saʊnd,pruf/ *adj.* able to keep out sounds: *soundproof walls* -*n.* [U] **soundproofing.**

sound·track /'saʊnd,træk/ *n.* the music for a film: *I bought the soundtrack of the new movie on compact disc.*

soup /sup/ *n.* **1** [C;U] liquid food cooked, then served hot or cold, made from meat or vegetable juice, often with pieces of solid food: *chicken-noodle soup||tomato soup* **2** [U] *infrml.fig.* **in the soup:** in trouble or difficulty: *The student failed his final tests and now he's in the soup; he can't graduate. -adj.* **soupy.** —*phrasal v.* **to soup s.t. up:** to increase the power of s.t., usu. a vehicle: *He souped up his car by putting a stronger engine in it.||He souped it up.* —*adj.* **souped-up:** improved or with more power: *The marketing plan is a souped-up version of last year's plan.*

soup spoon *n.* a spoon that is slightly larger than a teaspoon, used for eating soup

sour /saʊr/ *adj.* **1** acidic to the taste (*syns.*) sharp, tangy: *sour lemon||sour milk* **2** bad-tempered, unhappy: *a sour attitude that everything is wrong* **3 to go sour: a.** to become bitter, spoil: *The wine has gone sour.* **b.** to get worse, go wrong: *The company was doing quite well, then things went sour and people left.* —*v.* **1** to make or become sour: *Don't drink the orange juice; it's old and has soured.* **2** to get worse, become bad: *Our moods soured in the continuing rain.*

source /sɔrs/ *n.* **1** beginning origin: *The source of our difficulties is not having enough money.* **2** a place where information is obtained: *This history book is my source for accurate dates.* **3** (of a river) the start, beginning: *A mountain lake is the source of this river.*

—*v.slang.* to look for and find people and companies to provide what is needed: *to source suppliers for medical supplies*

sour cream or **soured cream** *n.* [U] a thick, white, semisolid food made from milk or cream, used in cooking, esp. in soups, sauces, and on baked potatoes

sour·dough /'saʊr,doʊ/ *n.* [U] a type of bread dough with a sharp taste, very popular in northern California

sour·puss /'saʊr,pʊs/ *n.infrml.* s.o. who is usu. unhappy or gloomy: *She is a sourpuss, always complaining.*

souse /saʊs/ *v.* **soused, sousing, souses 1** to make very wet: *She soused the dog with water and gave him a bath.* **2** to cover with liquid: *He soused the cucumbers in vinegar to make pickles.* **3** to make drunk -*adj.* **soused.** —*n.infrml.* a drunken person, s.o. who drinks a lot of liquor

south /saʊθ/ *n.* **1** the "down" direction on a compass and most maps, the direction to the left when facing a sunset: *Go toward the south to get to Mexico from Texas.* **2** the southern part of a country: *People in the north like to go south for vacation.* **3 the South:** in USA the southeastern part of the country, usu. thought to include the states that fought against the North in the Civil War —*adv.* toward a southerly direction: *The birds flew south for the winter.* —*adj.* **1** located to the south: *the south side of the city* **2** coming from the south: *a south wind* -*adj.* **southerly.**

south·bound /'saʊθ,baʊnd/ *adj.* going toward the south: *The southbound train goes from Chicago to St. Louis.*

south·east /saʊθ'ist/ *n.adj.adv.* **1** the direction on a compass or map that goes diagonally down to the right **2 the Southeast:** the part of the USA east of Texas and south of Pennsylvania, Ohio, Indiana, and Illinois; sometimes called "the South"

south·ern /'sʌðərn/ *adj.* located in or about the south: *southern food||a southern accent||southern literature*

south·ern·er /'sʌðərnər/ *n.* a person living in or from the southern part of a country

south·paw /'saʊθ,pɔ/ *n.infrml.fig.* a left-handed person: *The baseball player is a southpaw.*

South Pole *n.* the southernmost part of the earth's north-south axis

south·west /saʊθ'wɛst/ *n.adj.adv.* **1** the direction on a compass or map that goes diagonally down to the left **2 the Southwest:** the part of the USA that includes Utah, Colorado, Arizona, New Mexico, and sections of California and Texas

S

sou·ve·nir /ˌsuvəˈnɪr/ *n.* an object bought in order to remember a place, (*syn.*) a memento: *I bought a little Statue of Liberty as a souvenir of New York City.*

sov·er·eign /ˈsavərɪn, ˈsavrɪn/ *n.* a king or queen: *The sovereign of England during World War II was King George VI.*
—*adj.* **1** most powerful, (*syn.*) supreme: *a sovereign ruler* **2** self-governing: *a sovereign nation* -*n.* **sovereignty.**

so·vi·et /ˈsouviɪt, -ˌɛt, ˈsa-/ *n.* **1** an elected group of lawmakers in the former Soviet Union, the most powerful having been the Supreme Soviet **2 the Soviets:** the people of the former Soviet Union
—*adj.* **Soviet:** of or about the Soviets

sow (1) /sou/ *v.* **sowed, sown** /soun/or **sowed, sowing, sows 1** to plant seeds: *The farmer sowed his corn in the spring.* **2** *fig.* to cause s.t. to spread: *She sowed the rumor that the company is losing money; it's not true.* **3 as you sow, so shall you reap:** you will get what you deserve based on the way you live your life

sow (2) /sau/ *n.* an adult female pig

sox /saks/ *n.pl.infrml. var. of* socks

soy·bean /ˈsɔɪˌbin/ *n.* a plant native to Asia, used for foods such as tofu, soy sauce, etc.

spa /spa/ *n.* **1** a natural fountain of pure water from the ground, (*syn.*) a mineral spring **2** a place with mineral springs, often visited by people who want to improve their health: *In the 1800s, rich people went to European spas to help cure muscle pain.* **3** a vacation area or resort where people eat healthy meals, exercise, and relax for good health: *He lost five pounds at a spa in California.*

space /speɪs/ *n.* **1** [U] the area beyond earth in which planets, stars, moons, etc., exist: *My son pretends he is a traveler in space in the year 2020.∥The USA sent a research satellite into space.* **2** [U] a blank or empty area: *the space between the couch and the TV* **3** [C;U] a place used for s.t., an available place, (*syns.*) room, a spot: *My car is parked in a handicapped space.∥Is there enough space for three in your truck?* **4** *fig.* [U] time away from others, used to think, plan, live life one's own way, etc.: *My boyfriend said he didn't want to live with me because he needed more space.*
—*v.* **spaced, spacing, spaces** to put objects in order with empty areas in between: *I spaced the bottles neatly on the kitchen counter.*

space cadet *n.fig.* a person who forgets easily and is impractical: *That space cadet forgot to pay rent three months in a row.*

space capsule *n.* the area of a spaceship where people live and work

space·craft /ˈspeɪsˌkræft/ *n.* a vehicle that flies in space

spaced out *adj.slang* without the full use of one's mind due to tiredness or drugs, (*syns.*) out of it, groggy: *I'm spaced out from the medicine I took for my cold. See:* spacy.

space·ship /ˈspeɪsˌʃɪp/ *n.* a spacecraft: *I read a book about a spaceship that landed on Mars.*

space shuttle *n.* a vehicle that carries astronauts into space in order to do research and gather information

spac·ing /ˈspeɪsɪŋ/ *n.* [U] the distance or area between objects: *the spacing between lines in a book* -*n.* **spaciness.**

spa·cious /ˈspeɪʃəs/ *adv.* large, with plenty of room: *a big, spacious room*

spac·y or **spac·ey** /ˈspeɪsi/ *adj.slang.* **-ier, -iest** forgetful, impractical: *He's spacy; he left his car keys and wallet in the restaurant.*

spade /speɪd/ *n.* **1** a shovel for digging earth: *I made a hole with a spade and planted a rose bush.* **2** a black, pointed symbol found on playing cards of a particular suit **3 to call a spade a spade:** to speak truthfully: *Let's call a spade a spade; that hat is ugly and we all know it.*

spa·ghet·ti /spəˈgɛti/ *n.* [U] long, thin pasta, usu. eaten by winding it around a fork

USAGE NOTE: *Pasta* is made from flour, water, and sometimes eggs or other flavorings such as spinach. In the USA, *spaghetti* is probably the most popular form of pasta, which comes in a variety of shapes (*macaroni, penne, fettucine, linguine, ziti*). All types of pasta basically taste the same.

span /spæn/ *v.* **spanned, spanning, spans 1** to connect two points with s.t.: *to span a river with a bridge* **2** to last through time: *Love is a human need that spans the centuries.* **3** to measure or circle with the hands: *I spanned my dog's neck so I could buy the right size collar.*
—*n.* **1** the measure of space across, from one point to another: *The span of the roof from front to back is 20 meters.* **2** s.t. that joins two points, usu. across open air: *A tree branch was used as a span across the stream.* **3** an amount of time: *the long life span of an elephant*

span·gle /ˈspæŋgəl/ *n.* a small, shiny piece of metal or plastic, used as a decoration for a costume: *red, white, and blue spangles on her dance costume*

span·iel /ˈspænyəl/ *n.* a medium-sized dog with long, silky fur and long ears that hang *See:* cocker spaniel; springer spaniel.

Spanish onion *n.* a common onion with yellow skin

spank /spæŋk/ *v.* to slap the buttocks with the hand as punishment: *The mother spanked her naughty child.* -*n.* [C] **spanking.**

spar /spar/ *v.* **sparred, sparring, spars 1** to move about in a small area and lightly punch with one's hands, (*syn.*) to box, esp. for practice: *He sparred with his trainer before the big fight.* **2** *fig.* to argue: *The two workers sparred with each other about who should have the larger office.*

spare /sper/ *v.* **spared, sparing, spares 1** to save or prevent s.o. from harm: *The enemy soldier didn't shoot me; he spared me* (or) *he spared my life.* **2** to keep s.o. from having to do s.t.: *If you pick up the kids at school, you'll spare me the trouble.* **3** to have enough to give or share, (*syn.*) to afford: *Can you spare a few dollars to lend her?* **4 s.t. to spare:** more, left over: *We have enough hamburgers for everyone, and two to spare.*
—*adj.* **sparer, sparest 1** unused, extra: *a spare room for a guest* **2** thin, lean: *a spare man who doesn't eat much*
—*n.* (in bowling) the act of causing all the pins to fall with two rolls of the ball

spare·ribs /'sper,rɪbs/ *n.pl.* bones from a pig with a small amount of pork meat attached, usu. cooked with barbecue sauce and eaten with the fingers

spark /spark/ *n.* **1** a hot flash or bit of light caused by hard surfaces scraping together or from fire: *The train came to a quick stop and sparks flew from the wheels.* **2** *fig.* the beginning of a good idea: *The artist saw a beautiful sunset, and that was the spark he needed to start a new painting.*
—*v.* **1** to produce sparks: *The electrical wires sparked.* **2** *fig.* to cause an action: *The funny clown sparked a smile from the child.*

spar·kle /'sparkəl/ *v.* **-kled, -kling, -kles 1** to give off flashes or bits of light: *diamonds that sparkle* **2** to be fun to watch or listen to, to show great personality or talent: *The dancer's performance sparkled.*
—*n.* [C;U] the act of sparkling: *the sparkle of white snow in the sun* -*adj.* **sparkling.**

spar·kler /'sparklər/ *n.* a stick, often used on the US Independence Day, that sends out sparks when lit

spark plug *n.* a small piece of metal that causes an engine to start by firing a mixture of gasoline and air

spar·row /'spærou/ *n.* a small grayish-brown bird

sparse /spars/ *adj.* **sparser, sparsest** without a lot of, with much space between: *sparse desert*||*a man with sparse hair*||*Food for birds is often sparse in the winter.*

spar·tan /'spartn/ *n.adj.* **1** *fig.* with few possessions and strict discipline: *She lives a spartan life in a one-bedroom apartment with no TV or radio.* **2 Spartan:** related to the ancient city-state of Sparta or its inhabitants

spasm /'spæzəm/ *n.* **1** a quick, often painful movement in a muscle **2** sudden emotion or

activity: *a spasm of joy*||*a housecleaning spasm* -*adj.* **spasmodic** /spæz'madɪk/.

spas·tic /'spæstɪk/ *adj.* having sudden, quick motions
—*n.* a person who has spasms because of disease

spat /spæt/ *n.* a short argument: *The couple had a spat over money, but they worked out their problem.*

spate /speɪt/ *n.* a sudden rush or flood: *a spate of work before a rest*

spa·tial /'speɪʃəl/ *adj.* of or about space or area: *She has good spatial skills; she knows how to build a house from plans on paper.*

spat·ter /'spætər/ *v.* to fly out in drops, (*syn.*) to splatter: *Hot fat spattered from the frying pan.*

spat·u·la /'spætʃələ/ *n.* a cooking tool with a broad, flat end, used to turn food in a pan or to scrape soft food from a bowl

spawn /spɔn/ *v.* **1** (of water creatures) to lay eggs: *Fish spawn in rivers.* **2** to have children or offspring: *My grandparents spawned a family of doctors.* **3** *fig.* to cause, give life to: *to spawn a revolution*
—*n.* [U] **1** eggs of a water creature **2** children or offspring: *Their spawn all have red hair.* **3** the result of s.t.: *the spawn of a brilliant mind*

speak /spik/ *v.* **spoke** /spouk/, **spoken** /'spoukən/, **speaking, speaks 1** to say words, to talk: *I spoke with my friend on the telephone.* **2** to give a speech: *He will speak at his high school graduation.* **3** to be friendly with (usu. used in the negative): *They had a fight and are not speaking.* **4** to know a language: *to speak Portuguese* **5 so to speak:** in a way: *I've known him for years; he is my friend, so to speak.* **6 speaking of:** with regard to s.t. or s.o. just mentioned: *Speaking of him, does he like his job?* **7** *phrasal v.* **to speak at:** to give a speech at: *The president will speak at a meeting of governors.* **8** *phrasal v. insep.* **to speak down to s.o.:** to talk to s.o. as if he or she were not smart: *Don't speak down to me; I can understand complex things.* **9 to speak for oneself** or **itself: a.** to be obvious: *You cannot trust him; his lying speaks for itself.* **b.** don't think that others share one's opinion: *"Spinach is delicious." "Speak for yourself; I hate it."* **10** *phrasal v. insep.* **a. to speak for s.o.** or **s.t.:** to give an opinion: *She speaks for protecting wildlife.* **b.** to get the right to s.t.: *I wanted to buy that chair, but it was spoken for.* **11 to speak of:** worth mentioning, talking about: *She didn't go to high school; she has no education to speak of.*||*We've had no rain to speak of.* **12 to speak one's mind:** to say exactly what one thinks: *The boss spoke his mind about the future of the company.* **13** *phrasal v.* **to speak out:** to protest: *He speaks out about problems in government.* **14** *phrasal v.* **to**

S

speak up: a. to talk louder: *Will you speak up? I can't hear you.* **b.** to express one's interests strongly: *He tried to force me to pay for a bad meal, but I spoke up and told him I would not.* **15** *phrasal v. insep.* **to speak with s.o.:** to talk with s.o. about a problem: *I must speak with my son about his cigarette smoking.*

speak·er /'spikər/ *n.* s.o. who talks to an audience: *The speaker talked about health care in China.*

spear /spɪr/ *n.* **1** a long, thin pole with a sharp point, used in hunting and warfare: *Men in India killed a tiger with a spear.* **2** a long piece of s.t.: *a spear of asparagus*
—*v.* the act of piercing or hitting s.t. with a spear

spear·mint /'spɪr,mɪnt/ *n.* [U] a type of mint: *spearmint chewing gum*

spe·cial /'spɛʃəl/ *adj.* **1** important, meaningful: *A birthday party is a special occasion.* **2** careful, greater than usual: *We gave the sick boy special attention.* **3** respected, admired, loved: *My brother is a special person in my life.*
—*n.* **1** a discount or unusual sale: *The grocery store is having a special on canned tuna.* **2** a television show that is not part of the usual schedule: *We all watched a Christmas special.*

special delivery *n.* [U] a mailing or shipment of s.t. that needs hand delivery or particular care: *We have sent your check by special delivery.*

special effects *n.pl.* (in film, radio, TV, etc.) sights and sounds created by people to seem real, such as things disappearing, strange monsters walking around etc.: *You should see the dinosaurs and other special effects in that new movie!*

spe·cial·ist /'spɛʃəlɪst/ *n.* **1** a doctor who works in one particular area of medicine: *His family physician sent him to see a heart specialist.* **2** a person with highly specific skills: *a specialist in computer design*

spe·ci·al·i·ty /,spɛʃi'æləti/ *n.* **-ties** specialty; fine food: *Excellent steaks are a speciality of this restaurant.*

spe·cial·i·za·tion /,spɛʃələ'zeɪʃən/ *n.* **1** [C] a topic or subject about which s.o. knows a lot: *a specialization in Asian history* **2** [U] the process of specializing: *Medicine is moving toward specialization, with more specific study of diseases.*

spe·cial·ize /'spɛʃə,laɪz/ *v.* **-ized, -izing, -izes** to study and work in a specific subject: *She specializes in AIDS research.*

spe·cial·ty /'spɛʃəlti/ *n.* **-ties** a job or subject about which one knows a lot: *As a manager, her specialty is starting new factories.||Surgery is that doctor's specialty.*

spe·cies /'spiʃiz, -siz/ *n.* **-cies 1** a grouping of living things: *the human species* **2** a type, category, kind of s.t.: *a different species of insect*

spe·cif·ic /spə'sɪfɪk/ *adj.* **1** exact, definite, clear: *The bank knows the specific amount of money in your account.* **2** unlike any other, special, unique: *I am not talking about all books; I am talking about one specific novel.*
—*n.pl.* **the specifics:** the particular qualities, the details: *Let's get down to the specifics of our vacation, like plane reservations and how much money to take.*

spec·i·fi·ca·tion /,spɛsəfə'keɪʃən/ *n.usu.pl.* [C] the exact details (of a product or service), usu. in writing or drawn plans: *Automobiles are built to exact specifications.* **2** [U] the act of specifying

spec·i·fy /'spɛsə,faɪ/ *v.* **-fied, -fying, -fies** to say or communicate exactly what one wants or needs: *I specified that I wanted 100 pads of paper, not 1,000.*

spec·i·men /'spɛsəmən/ *n.* **1** an item that is an example of a larger group: *a fine specimen of a dog* **2** fluid or tissue from the body, taken for medical testing, a sample: *a blood specimen*

spe·cious /'spiʃəs/ *adj.* seeming true but actually false: *a specious argument*

speck /spɛk/ *n.* a tiny piece: *a speck of dust||The airplane looks like a speck in the clouds.*

speck·led /'spɛkəld/ *adj.* covered with dots or little spots of a different color: *speckled eggs*

specs /spɛks/ *n.infrml.* **1** *short for* specifications: *Could you please give me the specs for the new computer?* **2** *short for* spectacles, eyeglasses: *I lost my specs; I can't see well enough to drive.*

spec·ta·cle /'spɛktəkəl/ *n.* **1** a strange or amazing sight: *We climbed the mountain and looked out at the beautiful spectacle of valley and sky.* **2** a public celebration or performance: *The Independence Day parade was a wonderful spectacle.* **3 to make a spectacle of oneself:** to be loud or behave badly in public: *He made a spectacle of himself by getting drunk and falling in the pool.*

spec·ta·cles /'spɛktəkəlz/ *n.pl.old usage* eyeglasses.

spec·tac·u·lar /spɛk'tækyələr/ *adj.* wonderful, exciting: *We had a spectacular time at the party.*

spec·ta·tor /'spɛk,teɪtər/ *n.* an observer of an event: *The football stadium is full of screaming spectators.*
—*adj.* (of a sport) watched by many: *Baseball is a popular spectator sport.*

spec·ter /'spɛktər/ *n.* **1** a ghost, (*syn.*) a phantom: *She told a Halloween story about a specter that visited in the night.* **2** a bad, frightening possibility: *The specter of war hung over the nation.*

spec·trum /'spɛktrəm/ *n.* **-tra** or **-trums 1** the distribution of radiation across frequencies, esp. of light across its colors: *the color spectrum* **2** a wide range: *We have a whole spectrum of problems to solve.*

spec·u·late /'spɛkyə,leɪt/ *v.* **-lated, -lating, -lates** to guess about: *She is so quiet; we can only speculate about what she is thinking.* **2** to take business or financial risks: *to speculate in real estate (the stock market, etc.)* *-n.*[C;U] **speculation.**

spec·u·la·tive /'spɛkyələtɪv, -,leɪ-/ *adj.* risky: *We are uncertain if the new business will succeed; it's speculative.*

spec·u·la·tor /'spɛkyə,leɪtər/ *n.* a person who takes large business risks: *He is a big speculator in Texas oil wells.*

speech /spitʃ/ *n.* **-es 1** [C] a talk about a subject to an audience: *The politician gave a speech to his supporters.* **2** [U] the expression of thoughts with spoken words: *We can say what we want; we have freedom of speech.*

speech·less /'spitʃlɪs/ *adj.* **1** not able to speak, silent **2** so surprised that one can barely speak, (*syn.*) dumbfounded: *I was speechless at the sight of the huge mountains.* *-adv.* **speechlessly.**

speed /spid/ *n.* **1** [C] the rate at which s.t. moves: *Traffic today is moving at a slow speed.* **2** [C] a gear in a vehicle: *With the car in a low speed, it is easier to climb hills.* **3** [U] fast movement: *His speed on skis is amazing.* **4** *slang* a drug that makes s.o. feel more awake or nervous, (*syn.*) amphetamine
—*v.* **sped** /spɛd/ or **speeded, speeding, speeds 1** to move quickly: *Ambulances speed sick people to the hospital.* **2** to drive faster than the legal limit: *He was speeding at 75 mph (120 km), so the police stopped him.* **3** *phrasal v.* **to speed by:** to pass rapidly: *This summer is speeding by.*‖*The police car sped by us.* **4** *phrasal v. sep.* **to speed s.t. up:** to go faster, (*syn.*) to accelerate: *The boss told his men to speed up their work.*‖*They sped it up.* *-n.* **speeder.**

speed·boat /'spid,boʊt/ *n.* a powerful boat that can go very fast: *In our speedboat, we went from one end of the lake to the other in minutes.*

speed·ing /'spidɪŋ/ *n.* [U] driving faster than the legal speed limit: *The driver was caught for speeding.*

speed limit *n.* the legal maximum speed, posted on signs along roads and highways: *The speed limit in many states is 55 miles per hour.*

speed·om·e·ter /spɪ'dɑmətər/ *n.* a gauge on a vehicle that shows a driver how fast he or she

is going: *Your speedometer reads 80 kilometers per hour.*

speed-reading *n.* [U] a very fast way of reading in which one takes in several words at a time and gets a general, not detailed, sense of what is written

speed·up /'spid,ʌp/ *n.* a faster rate of progress, (*syn.*) an acceleration: *a speedup in factory production*

speed·y /'spidi/ *adj.* **-ier, -iest 1** fast, quick: *That runner is speedy; he wins every race.* **2** happening soon, (*syn.*) imminent: *We want a speedy end to the project.*

spell /spɛl/ *n.* **1** words or actions that cause a magic effect: *The witch's spell turned a frog into a prince.* **2** *infrml.* a period of time: *You must have patience; you should wait a spell before doing anything.* **3** a period of weather: *a cold spell* **4** a period of illness or discomfort: *a dizzy spell* **5 to cast a spell: a.** to make magic happen **b.** to affect greatly: *She is so beautiful that she casts a spell over men.* **6 under s.o.'s spell:** very affected by s.o.: *The teacher has the students under her spell.*
—*v.* **spelled** or **spelt** /spɛlt/, **spelling, spells 1** to say or write the letters of a word in order: *"Dictionary" is spelled D-I-C-T-I-O-N-A-R-Y.* **2** to be the letters of a word: *Y-E-S spells "yes."* **3** to mean, seem like: *If it rains, that will spell trouble for the picnic.* **4** to let s.o. rest by doing that person's job for a while: *I've been digging this hole for hours; can you spell me?* **5** *phrasal v. sep.* **to spell s.t. out: a.** to give the exact letters in order: *She spelled out her name over the phone.*‖*She spelled it out.* **b.** to explain in detail: *He does not understand the process; you will have to spell it out for him.*

spell·bind·ing /'spɛl,baɪndɪŋ/ *adj.* extremely interesting, fascinating: *The old man told a spellbinding story about hiding from the Nazis.* *-v.* **spellbind.**

spell·bound /'spɛl,baʊnd/ *adj.* extremely interested, fascinated: *The speaker held his audience spellbound with his descriptions of Africa.*

spel·ling /'spɛlɪŋ/ *n.* **1** [U] the ability to write words correctly letter by letter: *Her spelling is excellent; she knows many difficult words.* **2** [C] how a word is spelled: *Can you tell me the spelling of "prestidigitation"?*

spend /spɛnd/ *v.* **spent** /spɛnt/, **spending, spends 1** to pay money for s.t.: *Governments spend taxpayers' money.*‖*He spent $400 to fix his car.* **2** to use time and effort: *He spends a lot of time with his girlfriend.*‖*We spent a lot of energy playing tennis.*

spend·ing /'spɛndɪŋ/ *n.* [U] the act of paying money: *Your spending is too high; you must try to save more money.*

S

spend·thrift /ˈspɛndˌθrɪft/ *n.* a person who wastes or spends too much money: *Every week, my husband spends his entire paycheck on silly things; what a spendthrift!*

spent /spɛnt/ *adj.& past part.* of spend **1** paid out: *spent capital* **2** very tired because of exercise or activity, (*syn.*) exhausted: *She was spent after running seven miles.*

sperm /spɜrm/ *n.* **1** [U] the fluid from a man's penis that comes out during sexual intercourse, (*syn.*) semen **2** [C] a round male cell with a tail that can join with a female egg and cause pregnancy; part of a male's semen

spew /spyu/ *v.* to come out or push out with force: *Bad words spewed from his mouth when he hit his thumb with a hammer.*‖*Water spewed out of the faucet.*

sphere /sfɪr/ *n.* **1** a round object: *a globe shaped like a sphere* **2** the sky that one can see: *the heavenly sphere* **3** an area, the extent of one's experience: *Within his social sphere, there are many rich people.*

spher·i·cal /ˈsfɪrəkəl, ˈsfɛr-/ *adj.* round: *A ball is spherical.*

sphinx /sfɪŋks/ *n.* **1** in Egyptian mythology, a being with the head of a man and the body of a lion **2** the Sphinx: a famous Egyptian statue visited by many tourists **3** a person who does not speak much, a mysterious person: *When you try to talk to him about his personal life, that man is a sphinx.*

spice /spaɪs/ *n.* [C;U] **1** a flavoring for foods, such as pepper, cinnamon, or clove, often bought in small jars in powdered form **2** *usu.sing. fig.* special enjoyment, excitement: *Add spice to your life by taking a trip to a place you've never been.*

spick-and-span /ˈspɪkənˈspæn/ *adj.* clean and neat: *The bathroom is spick-and-span after being cleaned.*

spic·y /ˈspaɪsi/ *adj.* **-ier, -iest** **1** tasting of spices, (*syn.*) hot: *spicy tomato sauce* **2** sexy, (*syn.*) scandalous: *I read a spicy story about a film star and his many love affairs.*

spi·der /ˈspaɪdər/ *n.* a small, eight-legged animal that traps insects in silken webs

spiel /spil, ʃpil/ *n.infrml.* a story, usu. told to sell s.t. or convince s.o.: *The refrigerator salesman went into a spiel about how great his product is.*

spif·fy /ˈspɪfi/ *adj.* **-fier, -fiest** with a neat appearance, well-dressed: *You look very spiffy in your new suit and tie.*

spike /spaɪk/ *n.* **1** a long, sharp piece of metal, like a large nail: *He pounded spikes into the railroad tracks to hold them in place.* **2** metal points on the bottom of athletic shoes; the shoes themselves **3** (in sports) the motion of quickly pushing a ball downward *-adj.* **spiky.**

—*v.* **spiked, spiking, spikes** **1** to put a spike (*n.* 1) in s.t. **2** to add liquor to a drink: *She spiked the fruit punch with rum.* **3** (in sports) to force a ball downward with a quick push or throw: *He spiked the volleyball, so the other player couldn't hit it.*

spill /spɪl/ *v.* **spilled** or **spilt** /spɪlt/, **spilling, spills** **1** to cause or allow a liquid to fall from its container: *I spilled my coffee as I carried it to the table.* **2** to drop or fall out of a container: *Juice spilled from the carton.* **3** to rush out all at once: *We spilled out onto the dance floor when the band started playing.* **4** *fig.* **it's no use crying over spilled** or **spilt milk:** it doesn't help to be sad about something that happened in the past: *I'm sorry that I never went to college, but it's no use crying over spilled milk.* **5** *phrasal v.* **to spill over: a.** to overflow: *The water is spilling over the bathtub onto the floor.* **b.** to affect other matters: *The bad luck of this computer company has spilled over and made the entire computer industry look bad.* **6** *fig.* **to spill the beans:** to tell a secret: *Don't spill the beans about how much money I make; I don't want him to know.*

—*n.* **1** an act of spilling a liquid: *an oil spill from a ship* **2** a fall: *a spill from a horse*

spin /spɪn/ *v.* **spun** /spʌn/, **spinning, spins** **1** to twist a substance (wool, cotton, etc.) into thread: *to spin yarn* **2** to turn around in a small circle or cause to do so, (*syn.*) to rotate: *to spin a top*‖*He said, "Look behind you!" and I spun around.* **3** *fig.* to tell a story: *to spin a tale* (or) *a yarn* **4** **to make one's head spin:** to cause confusion: *All the choices are making my head spin.* **5** *phrasal v. sep.* **to spin s.t. off:** to make or become s.t. new by separating from an original thing or group: *The company spun off its sales department and that became a new business.*‖*They spun it off. See:* spin-off. **6** *phrasal v. sep.* **to spin s.t. out:** to make s.t. longer: *The author spun out her idea into a play.*‖*She spun it out.* **7** *fig.* **to spin one's wheels:** to work hard with few results: *He works 18 hours a day in real estate, but doesn't sell anything; he is just spinning his wheels.*

—*n.* **1** [C;U] a fast turning or spinning motion: *Give the wheel a spin.* **2** *infrml.fig.* [C] a short ride in a car: *Let's go for a spin.* **3** [U] a particular opinion about s.t., (*syn.*) an interpretation: *The newspaper put its own spin on the election story.*

spin·ach /ˈspɪnɪtʃ/ *n.* [U] a dark green, leafy vegetable, usu. eaten boiled or steamed

spi·nal cord /ˈspaɪnəl/ *n.* a thick nerve that runs through the bones (spine) in the back

spin·dly /ˈspɪndli/ *adj.* **-dlier, -dliest** very thin, often weak: *the spindly legs of a small table*

spine /spaɪn/ *n.* **1** [C] the connected bones in the back, backbone **2** [C] a sharp, pointed needle on living things: *the spines of a porcupine*

S

3 [C] the part of a book that is bound; the part seen on a bookcase: *Please read the spine and tell me the title.* **4** *fig.* [U] courage, (*syn.*) fortitude: *He has the spine to make the difficult decisions.* See: backbone.

spine·less /'spaɪnlɪs/ *adj.fig.* weak, cowardly: *He was spineless to leave his wife without saying good-bye.*

spin·et /'spɪnɪt/ *n.* a small piano

spin·na·ker /'spɪnəkər/ *n.* a type of sail on a boat

spin-off *n.* **1** s.t. created from a larger thing (company, product, etc.): *This doll is a spin-off of another popular doll.* **2** a television show whose main character was a minor character on another show

spin·ster /'spɪnstər/ *n.* an older woman who has never married

spin·y /'spaɪni/ *adj.* **-ier, -iest** **1** covered with hard or sharp skin: *a spiny plant* **2** *fig.* difficult, dangerous: *a spiny problem*

spi·ral /'spaɪrəl/ *n.adj.* s.t. that curves in a circular way around a center point, and sometimes up and down, like a screw or a winding staircase, (*syn.*) coiled
—*v.* **1** to twist up or down: *The staircase spirals to the second floor.* **2** to go up or down quickly and steadily: *to spiral out of control*

spire /spaɪr/ *n.* (in architecture) the sharply pointed top of a church: *He could see the church spire above the trees.*

spir·it /'spɪrɪt/ *n.* **1** [C;U] the nonphysical part of a person, made up of thoughts, emotions, etc., the soul: *My aunt feels the spirit of my uncle, even many years after his death.* **2** [C] a being who is not of this world, a ghost: *People think that old house is full of spirits that come out at night.* **3** [U] a feeling or mood: *The spirit of the Civil War lives on in many southern states.* **4** *pl.* **spirits:** alcoholic beverages, liquor: *The corner store sells both soft drinks and spirits.* **5 the Holy Spirit:** (in Christianity) the third part of the Trinity, along with the Father (God) and Son (Jesus Christ); also called Holy Ghost **6 in (good, bad, etc.) spirits:** in a (good, bad, etc.) mood: *Thoughts of summer put me in high spirits.*
—*phrasal v. sep.* **to spirit s.o. away:** to take s.o. away, often unexpectedly or in a mysterious way: *She spirited away her boyfriend to a Caribbean island.‖She spirited him away.*

spir·it·less /'spɪrɪtlɪs/ *adj.* with no energy or enthusiasm: *I'm feeling spiritless since my best friend moved away.*

spir·i·tu·al /'spɪrɪtʃuəl/ *n.* of or about the spirit, religious: *We got married in a church because we wanted the wedding to be a spiritual experience.*

—*n.* a religious song that was first sung by African Americans: *He sang a spiritual about freedom.* -*n.* [U] **spirituality** /ˌspɪrɪtʃu'æləti/**.**

spit /spɪt/ *v.* **spat** /spæt/ **, spit, spitting, spits** **1** to send forth saliva or s.t. else from the mouth, (*syn.*) to expectorate: *The little boy spit a baby tooth into my hand.* **2** to talk angrily in short, hissing phrases: *"Get out of here right now!" she spat.* **3** to rain lightly: *Go back and get the umbrella; it's spitting a bit.* **4** *phrasal v. sep.* **to spit s.t. out: a.** to send from the mouth: *She spit out the bad-tasting food.‖She spit it out.* **b.** to reveal with hesitation: *He finally spit out the truth.* **5** *phrasal v. sep.* **to spit s.t. up:** to vomit: *The baby became sick and spit up her dinner.*
—*n.* **1** [U] saliva, (*syn.*) spittle **2** [C] a long, thin piece of metal on which meat is cooked over a fire

spite /spaɪt/ *n.* [U] **1** a feeling of wanting to hurt others, (*syn.*) malice: *That man broke our car window out of spite.* **2 in spite of:** against what might be logical, (*syns.*) regardless of, despite: *I write letters in spite of the fact that most people call.*
—*v.* to irritate, annoy: *She spites people by telling their secrets.*

spite·ful /'spaɪtfəl/ *adj.* malicious, resentful: *to have a spiteful attitude*

spit·fire /'spɪt,faɪr/ *n.fig.* a person with quick, changeable emotions: *She threw a glass at a man in a bar; what a spitfire!*

spitting image *n.fig.* a person who looks just like s.o. else: *The little girl is the spitting image of her mother.*

spittle /'spɪtl/ *n.* [U] saliva

splash /splæʃ/ *n.* **-es** **1** the movement and sound of a liquid as it falls or is hit: *I can hear the splash of water in the sink.* **2** a mark of s.t.: *a splash of green in the brown desert* **3** brief excitement and publicity: *The singing star made a splash in a new musical.*
—*v.* (of a liquid) **1** to fly into the air: *Water splashed down a waterfall.* **2** to throw liquid, to cause a splash: *I gently splashed water over the baby's legs.*

splash·y /'splæʃi/ *adj.* **-ier, -iest** colorful, exciting, (*syn.*) gaudy: *The opening of the new opera house was a splashy occasion.*

splat /splæt/ *n.* the noise of s.t. soft hitting s.t. hard: *The eggs fell on the floor with a splat.*

splat·ter /'splætər/ *v.n.* (of a liquid) **1** to fly off in drops: *Oil <v.> splattered from the frying pan onto the stove.* **2** to cause to fly off in drops: *She <v.> splattered him with her iced tea.*

splay /spleɪ/ *v.* to spread out: *I sat on my beach towel, splaying my legs.* -*adj.* **splayed.**

spleen /splin/ *n.* **1** an internal body part on the left, near the stomach, that filters and restores

S

blood **2 to vent one's spleen:** to say what one means in an angry way: *He vented his spleen for an hour about all his ex-wife's faults.*

splen·did /'splɛndɪd/ *adj.* **1** excellent, wonderful: *We had a splendid time on our vacation.* **2** grand and formal, *(syn.)* magnificent: *a splendid cathedral*

splen·dor /'splɛndər/ *n.* [U] great beauty, *(syns.)* magnificence, grandeur: *the splendor of the Grand Canyon*

splint /splɪnt/ *n.v.* a thin piece of wood or other material used to prevent a broken bone from moving: *The doctor put a splint on the boy's broken arm to hold it in place.*

splin·ter /'splɪntər/ *n.* **1** a small piece of wood or metal that breaks off a larger piece: *I got a splinter in my foot from the old wooden floor.* **2** a group broken off from another one: *a political splinter group*
—*v.* to break into little pieces: *The chair splintered when it fell from the truck.*

split /splɪt/ *v.* **split, splitting, splits 1** to divide s.t. by cutting or breaking: *to split wood with an axe* **2** to divide among people: *We split a large sandwich.‖They split $100: $50 each.* **3** *slang* to leave: *The game's over; let's split.* **4** *fig.* **to split hairs:** to talk about unimportant details: *Arguing about Grandfather's age is splitting hairs; the important thing is that he's alive.*
—*n.* **1** a rip, break or division in s.t.: *My old jeans have a split in the seam.‖The split in that political party was caused by disagreement among the old members.* **2** an action in which one's legs are completely spread in opposite directions, side to side or front to back: *The dancer did a split on the stage to finish her act. See:* banana split.

split second *n.* a tiny period of time, less than a second: *The lights went off, and a split second later he screamed.*

split·ting /'splɪtɪŋ/ *n.* a division: *the splitting of wood (political parties, the atom, etc.)*

splurge /splɜrdʒ/ *v.n.* **splurged, splurging, splurges** to spend money freely, with little thought for prices: *We went to Paris and <v.> splurged on expensive meals in restaurants.*

spoil /spɔɪl/ *v.* **spoiled** or **spoilt** /spɔɪlt/, **spoiling, spoils 1** (of food) to become bad or rotten: *The meat has spoiled; let's throw it out.* **2** to make imperfect or bad, ruin: *You spoiled the paint by touching it when it was wet.* **3** to give s.o. everything he or she wants, *(syn.)* to pamper: *They spoil their child by buying him a toy every time they go shopping.* *-adj.* **spoiled.**
—*n.pl.frml.* **the spoils:** the booty, plunder: *the spoils of war*

spoil·age /'spɔɪlɪdʒ/ *n.* [U] **1** the process of going bad: *Spoilage is heavy in the grocery business because vegetables rot.* **2** s.t. rotten or spoiled

spoil·er /'spɔɪlər/ *n.* a troublemaker, a person who spoils the fun or business dealing of others: *He plays the spoiler in every deal that we try to make.*

spoil·sport /'spɔɪl,spɔrt/ *n.* a person who tries to ruin others' pleasure or fun: *Instead of playing the game with us, he was a spoilsport and said the game was stupid.*

spokes·man /'spoʊksmən/ *n.* **-men** /-mən/ a male spokesperson

spokes·per·son /'spoʊks,pɜrsən/ *n.* a person who communicates the ideas and opinions of another person, group, or company: *A spokesperson for the car company said that the new station wagons were the safest cars available.*

spokes·wom·an /'spoʊks,wʊmən/ *n.* **-women** /-,wɪmɪn/ a female spokesperson

sponge /spʌndʒ/ *n.* **1** [C] a water animal with many holes in its skeleton and bodily tissues **2** [C;U] such an animal after it has died, or a similar-looking piece of cellulose, used to take up liquid or for cleaning: *Get a sponge; I spilled some juice.* **3** [C] a person who rarely pays, who always takes money from others: *Their son won't get a job and pay rent; he's nothing but a sponge.*
—*v.* **sponged, sponging, sponges 1** to wipe or clean with a sponge: *He sponged up spilled water.‖She sponged the dirty bathtub.* **2** to get s.t. for free from s.o.: *She never pays for cigarettes; she just sponges them from her friends.*

sponge cake *n.* [C;U] a very light cake, full of tiny air holes

spon·sor /'spɑnsər/ *n.* a person, business, or group that helps pay for s.t. (cultural or sporting event, TV show, etc.): *The sports equipment store is the sponsor of the local baseball team; it pays for uniforms and transportation.*
—*v.* to act as a sponsor: *A beer company sponsored the baseball game by paying for television advertising.*

spon·ta·ne·i·ty /,spɑnte'neɪəti, -'ni-/ *n.* [U] action that happens without much thought or planning: *We admired the spontaneity of her reading a book about Mexico, and then just flying there the next day.*

spon·ta·ne·ous /spɑn'teɪniəs/ *adj.* **1** not planned, full of feeling: *spontaneous laughter at a clown* **2** happening in a natural way, not practiced or rehearsed: *the spontaneous flow of jazz music* **3** happening without being caused by s.t. outside: *a spontaneous fire -adv.* **spontaneously.**

spoof /spuf/ *n.v.* comic performance that makes fun of a more serious topic, *(syns.)* parody, satire: *The comedian did a <n.> spoof of the situation in the White House.*

spook /spuk/ *n.infrml.* a ghost: *My sister thinks there are spooks in the attic.*

—v. to make s.o. or an animal feel nervous, to frighten: *The horses were spooked by a loud gunshot. -adj.* **spooky.**

spool /spul/ *n.* a rounded object (cylinder) used for wrapping thread, rope, wire, etc.: *a spool of thread*
—v. **1** to wind on a spool **2** (in computers) to store information temporarily while the computer is working

spoon /spun/ *n.* an eating tool shaped like a small, shallow bowl with a handle: *He ate his cereal with a spoon.*
—v. to eat or move with a spoon: *to spoon soup into a dish*

spoo·ner·ism /'spunə,rızəm/ *n.* a reversal of sounds in words: *flower pot/power flot*

spoon-feed *v.fig.* to make s.t. very easy for s.o. by giving more than is necessary, *(syn.)* to coddle: *She will never learn anything if you spoon-feed all the answers to her.*

spoon·ful /'spunfʊl/ *n.* the amount that a spoon holds: *a spoonful of medicine*

spo·rad·ic /spə'rædɪk/ *adj.* **1** happening in an irregular way: *sporadic waves‖sporadic payments on a bill* **2** not often or steady: *sporadic rain*

sport /spɔrt/ *n.* **1** [C;U] a game that involves physical exercise (football, baseball, tennis, etc.): *He uses his running and throwing skills in many sports.* **2** [C] a person who loses or fails with a certain attitude (used with "good," "bad," or "poor"): *His girlfriend beat him at tennis, but he was a good sport about it.‖What a poor sport; she didn't even congratulate the winner.* **3 to make sport of:** to make fun of in an unkind way, *(syn.)* to mock: *The kids made sport of the little boy who had to wear eyeglasses.*
—v. to wear or show s.t. in an obvious way: *to sport a new suit (beard, hat, etc.)*
—adj. **1** worn for athletics: *sport socks* **2** casual, not dressy: *a sport shirt with no tie*

sport·ing /'spɔrtɪŋ/ *adj.* having a good, fair attitude: *It was very sporting of you to shake hands with the woman who beat you in chess.*

sporting chance *n.* a fair opportunity to win or do well: *I have lost money in the stock market, but I have a sporting chance to get it back if I'm smart.*

sports car *n.* an automobile that is similar to a race car, with a powerful engine and good handling on curvy roads

sports·cast /'spɔrts,kæst/ *n.* a game that one can see or hear on TV or radio

sports·man·ship /'spɔrtsmən,ʃɪp/ *n.* [U] the way an athlete behaves (good or bad): *She lost the match, yet she showed good sportsmanship by thanking her opponent for a good game. See:* gamemanship.

sports·wear /'spɔrts,wɛr/ *n.* [U] clothing worn for sports or casual activities: *My soccer team buys its sportswear from Italy.‖He can't dress in sportswear at the office.*

sport·y /'spɔrti/ *adj.* colorful and casual: *He is wearing a sporty blue jacket with white trousers.*

spot /spɑt/ *n.* **1** a mark that looks different from its background, *(syns.)* a blot, stain: *She has a spot of lipstick on her dress.‖The sick baby is covered with spots.* **2** a bad part of s.o.'s experience: *He has a spot on his record because he spent time in jail.* **3** *usu.sing.* a slightly difficult situation: *I'm in a bit of a spot; will you help me?* **4** a place, location: *We found a cool spot in the shade.‖We stayed at a nice spot, a hotel near a lake.* **5 to hit the spot:** (of food and drink) to be just right, taste very good: *That ice cream hit the spot!* **6 on the spot:** right away: *We bought our tickets and left on the spot.*
—v. **spotted, spotting, spots 1** to stain s.t.: *to spot a dress with wine* **2** to find with the eye, to see: *I spotted a friend in a crowd and stopped to talk.*

spot check *n.* a quick, incomplete look: *I gave the pages a final spot check to make sure all the illustrations were there. -v.* **spot-check.**

spot·less /'spɑtlɪs/ *adj.* **1** very clean: *The washed dishes are spotless.* **2** without any bad parts, *(syn.)* unblemished: *a spotless reputation -n.* [U] **spotlessness.**

spot·light /'spɑt,laɪt/ *n.* a powerful light that shines directly on s.o. or s.t.: *A spotlight on our pool allows us to swim at night.*
—v. **1** to shine a spotlight on s.o.: *to spotlight the actor on the stage* **2** to focus attention on: *The press spotlighted the election with daily headlines.*

spot·ted /'spɑtɪd/ *adj.& past part. of* spot, *adj.* covered with spots: *a spotted leopard*

spot·ty /'spɑti/ *adj.* **1** covered with stains or spots: *a spotty tablecloth* **2** not steady or consistent, containing some bad parts, *(syn.)* erratic: *He has done some good things in his career, but overall his past is spotty.*

spouse /spaʊs/ *n.* a husband or wife: *My spouse and I have been married for seven years.*

spout /spaʊt/ *n.* a tube through which liquid passes: *a water spout, the spout on a teapot*
—v. **1** to pass through a spout: *to spout water* **2** to speak loudly and long, usu. to express one's opinions: *He spouts (or) spouts off about politics all the time.*

sprain /spreɪn/ *v.* to hurt a body part by twisting or putting too much pressure on it: *to sprain an ankle*
—n. the act or condition of a sprain: *I lifted a heavy box and have a sprain in my arm.*

S

sprang /spræŋ/ *past part. of* spring

sprawl /sprɔl/ *v.* to spread out widely in different directions: *My son came into the room and sprawled on the sofa.*‖*New York City sprawls out for many miles.*
—*n.* [U] **urban sprawl:** growth away from the center of a city

spray /spreɪ/ *v.* to send s.t. out so that it spreads over an area: *In summer, the kids spray each other with the water hose.*‖*The soldier sprayed the woods with bullets.*
—*n.* [C;U] **1** liquid that spreads in drops over an area: *a spray of ocean water from a wave*‖*a spray of perfume* **2** a small plant arrangement: *a spray of flowers*

spread /sprɛd/ *v.* **spread, spreading, spreads** **1** to cover a surface by pushing s.t. toward the edges of the surface: *to spread butter on bread* **2** to cause to go or travel a distance or to many people: *to spread the news*‖*to spread disease* **3** to lay out smoothly and flat: *to spread a tablecloth (napkin, towel, map, etc.)* **4** to make space between: *to spread your fingers* **5** to set a table with dishes, knives, forks, etc. **6 to spread oneself too thin:** to be doing too many things: *She goes to college, takes care of children and works nights, too; she has spread herself too thin.* **7** *phrasal v. sep.* **to spread s.t. or s.o. apart:** to increase the distance between: *Two men were fighting and the police spread them apart.*‖*The man spread his legs far apart.* **8** *phrasal v. sep.* **to spread s.t. around: a.** to cause s.t. to cover a wider area: *The flu has spread around the company.* **b.** to use in different ways, (*syn.*) to distribute: *Politicians spread around money in the government budget among various projects.*‖*They spread it around.* **9** *phrasal v. sep.* **to spread s.t. open:** to extend: *The bird spread its wings open.* **10** *phrasal v. sep.* **to spread (s.t.) out: a.** to stretch out: *He was tired, so he spread out on the sofa to rest.* **b.** to become wider or bigger, (*syn.*) to expand: *The city has spread out into the suburbs.*
—*n.usu. sing.* [C] **1** a food that can be pressed on bread, crackers, etc. with a knife: *a cheese spread* **2** a bed covering that goes above sheets and blankets: *a bedspread* **3** the difference between two amounts: *the difference between the cost and the selling price* **4** *infrml.* a farm or ranch: *a large spread in Texas* **5** movement over an area: *the spread of good news* **6** an arrangement of s.t. over a larger area: *the spread of her hair on the pillow* **7** *infrml.* a lot of different foods available at a meal: *They had a big spread of fish, meat, vegetables, bread, and cake.* **8** a story in a newspaper or magazine that covers two facing pages: *a spread about the World Cup soccer tournament*

spree /spri/ *n.* a time of careless or wild activity: *I spent my entire paycheck on a shopping spree.*

sprig /sprɪg/ *n.* a small twig from a plant or a tiny bunch of flowers: *a sprig of pine*‖*a sprig of violets and daisies*

spring /sprɪŋ/ *n.* [C] **1** a piece of metal wire, wound in a coil, that stretches and goes back to its original shape: *My couch has springs, so it doesn't feel hard when I sit down.* **2** a jump or leap: *the spring of a kangaroo* **3** a place where water comes naturally out of the ground: *We drank from a spring in the mountains.* **4** the season between winter and autumn: *In the spring, we plant flowers and watch the days grow longer.*
—*v.* **sprang** /spræŋ/, **sprung** /sprʌŋ/, **springing, springs** **1** to jump with strength by bending and then straightening the knees, (*syn.*) to leap: *A ballet dancer sprang into the other dancer's arms.*‖*The deer springs across the field.* **2** *phrasal v. insep.* **to spring at s.o.:** to jump toward, (*syn.*) to attack: *The dog growled and sprang at the robber.* **3 to spring at the chance:** to happily take the opportunity: *When the boss offered her a business trip, she sprang at the chance to go.* **4 to spring a trap:** to trick s.o.: *Government agents lured the criminal to a hotel and gave him a bribe; then they sprang a trap on him and arrested him.* **5 to spring a leak:** to get a hole and let air or water through: *The little boat sprang a leak and sank.* **6 to spring into action:** to begin to act quickly: *When the general gives the order, his army springs into action against the enemy.* **7** *phrasal v.* **to spring open or shut:** to open or shut with a quick, sudden motion **8 to spring to life:** to become more active and lively: *The crocodile appeared to be asleep, then he sprang to life and captured a fish.* **9** *phrasal v. insep.* **to spring s.t. on s.o.:** to surprise s.o. with s.t.: *We sprang the news that we were having a baby on our parents.* **10 to spring to s.o.'s defense:** to protect s.o. strongly: *When people say unkind things about her husband, she springs to his defense.* **11** *phrasal v.* **to spring up:** to appear suddenly: *We had a great chance spring up to buy a new company.*

spring·board /ˈsprɪŋˌbɔrd/ *n.* **1** a flexible piece of wood or other material used for diving into a pool or (in gymnastics) jumping onto a piece of equipment **2** *fig.* s.t that leads to another action: *He used our discussion about education as a springboard to taking night classes.*

spring chicken *n.infrml.fig.* **no spring chicken:** not a young person: *She is much older than she looks; she is no spring chicken.*

spring·er spaniel /ˈsprɪŋər/ *n.* a medium-sized dog with silky brown and white or black and white fur and long ears

spring fever *n.* [U] a good feeling of new beginnings and energy caused by warm weather in the springtime: *She has spring fever; she has been cleaning her house and buying new clothes all week.*

spring·time /'sprɪŋ,taɪm/ *n.* [U] the season between winter and summer: *We enjoy fishing in the springtime.*

spring·y /'sprɪŋi/ *adj.* **-ier, -iest** bouncing back to an original position, stretchy: *a springy mattress on a bed*

sprin·kle /'sprɪŋkəl/ *n.* **1** a brief, light rainfall **2** drops of liquid or tiny pieces of s.t. falling or scattering: *a sprinkle of plant food on a plant* —*v.* **-kled, -kling, -kles 1** to rain lightly: *Oh, it's sprinkling; I'll get my hat.* **2** to cause to fall in drops or tiny pieces: *to sprinkle salt on meat‖I sprinkled water on the lawn.* -*n.* **sprinkler; sprinkling.**

sprint /sprɪnt/ *v.n.* to run very fast for a short distance, often in a race -*n.* **sprinter.**

sprout /spraʊt/ *v.* to start to grow: *Trees sprout leaves in the spring.* —*n.* **1** new growth on a plant, (*syn.*) a shoot **2 brussels sprouts:** part of a type of cabbage

spruce (1) /sprus/ *n.* [C;U] a type of tall pine tree

spruce (2) /sprus/ *v.* **spruced, sprucing, spruces** to dress up: *I took a shower and spruced up for the party.*

sprung /sprʌŋ/ *past part. of* spring

spry /spraɪ/ *adj.* active, alert (usu. said of healthy old people): *My spry grandfather walks his dog twice a day.*

spud /spʌd/ *n.infrml.* a potato

spunk·y /'spʌŋki/ *adj.* **-ier, -iest** having energy, courage, and a good attitude about the future: *My little girl broke her arm, but she's very spunky and says it doesn't hurt.*

spur /spɜr/ *n.* **1** a piece of metal worn on boot heels and pressed into the side of a horse to make it run faster **2 on the spur of the moment:** quickly and without much thought, (*syn.*) on impulse: *The boss called his workers together on the spur of the moment.* —*v.* **spurred, spurring, spurs 1** to make a horse run faster **2** to cause action: *The dark clouds spurred us to work faster before the rain started.*

spu·ri·ous /'spyʊriəs/ *adj.* not to be believed, (*syn.*) false: *The movie star told spurious lies about his ex-wife.‖I think this is a spurious painting, not a valuable work of Leonardo da Vinci as the museum says.*

spurn /spɜrn/ *v.n.* to reject in an unkind way: *He called his girlfriend, and she spurned him by not returning his call.*

spurt /spɜrt/ *v.* **1** to move out or forward with great force, (*syn.*) to gush forth: *The water spurted from the fountain.* **2** to move ahead with a sudden burst of energy: *The runner spurted past the others.* —*n.* **1** a sudden burst of liquid: *a spurt of blood from a vein* **2** a sudden burst of energy: *a spurt of effort to finish a job*

sput·ter /'spʌtər/ *v.n.* **1** to make irregular sounds: *an engine that sputters* **2** to show anger or frustration by talking in an unclear way, along with spitting or throat noises: *You s-s-say you're s-s-sorry right n-n-now!" he <v.> sputtered.*

spy /spaɪ/ *n.* **spies** a person who collects secret information and reports back to his or her government: *A spy dressed as a woman listened to a conversation while pretending to drink a glass of wine.* —*v.* **spied, spying, spies 1** to look for, listen to, or collect information secretly: *He followed his wife to the movies and spied on her from another seat.* **2** to see after looking around a bit, (*syn.*) to spot: *to spy a friend in a crowd*

squab·ble /'skwɑbəl/ *v.n.* **-bled, -bling, -bles** to fight or argue, often about unimportant things: *They <v.> squabbled about whether to leave at 2:00 or 3:00.*

squad /skwɑd/ *n.* a small, organized group of people: *a squad of soldiers‖a football squad*

squal·id /'skwɑlɪd/ *adj.* very dirty, (*syns.*) filthy, wretched: *The poor family lived in a squalid apartment full of rats.*

squall /skwɔl/ *n.v.* **1** a sudden windstorm, followed by wind or snow **2** a loud cry: *the <n.> squall of a hungry baby*

squal·or /'skwɑlər/ *n.* [U] a place or situation of dirt and poverty: *The neighborhood people helped turn the park from squalor to a clean, happy place.*

squan·der /'skwɑndər/ *v.* to spend too much, (*syn.*) to waste: *He squandered his savings on a new boat.‖We must not squander our forests and rivers by not managing them properly.*

square /skwɛr/ *n.* **1** a shape with four equal sides: *The side of this box is a square.* **2** (in math) the result of multiplying a number by itself: *The square of 3 is 9.* **3** a place in a town where several streets meet and form a business area: *There's a sandwich shop in the square.* **4** *infrml.fig.* a person with two bad habits, little humor, and no sense of adventure: *He goes to bed at 10:00 P.M. on weekends and never goes out; he is a real square.* —*adj.* **squarer, squarest 1** having four equal sides: *a square mirror* **2** a measurement for an area: *square meters* **3** fitting exactly against s.t. else: *The carpenter made the window square with the window frame.* **4** even, settled: *Here is the $5 I owe you, so now we are square.* **5** honest: *If you ask her for the truth, she'll be square with you.* —*v.* **squared, squaring, squares 1** (in math) to multiply s.t. by itself: *I squared 4 and got*

S

16. **2** to fit s.t. properly: *to square a door so it hangs straight* **3** to make even, settle: *Last night you paid for dinner and tonight I will; we'll square the matter* (or) *square up.* **4** *phrasal v. sep.* **to square s.t. away:** to get ready, put in order: *Let me get my purse and turn off the lights — I like to square away the office before I leave.||I want to square it away.* **5** *phrasal v.* **to square off:** to face each other and get ready to fight

square dance *n.* a type of group dance in which couples form a square and step to spoken directions and lively music

USAGE NOTE: *Square dancing* began in rural areas of the USA and is often danced in barns and church halls to country or folk music.

squash (1) /skwɑʃ, skwɔʃ/ *v.* **1** to make flat by pressing strongly, *(syn.)* to crush: *I squashed an insect with my foot.* **2** to stop by force or strength: *The king squashed a revolution.*

squash (2) *n.* **1** [C;U] any of a variety of vegetables with a hard or firm rind (skin) and seeds inside: *zucchini squash||butternut squash* **2** [U] a racquet game played in a four-walled indoor court

squat /skwɑt/ *v.* **squatted, squatting, squats** to bend the knees and sit on the heels: *He squatted behind a chair so he wouldn't be seen.* —*adj.* **-er, -est 1** close to the ground, thick: *a fat man with a squat body*

squawk /skwɔk/ *n.v.* **1** a loud, harsh bird cry: *the <n.> squawk of a chicken* **2** a cry or complaint: *He let out a squawk when I stepped on his toe.*

squeak /skwik/ *n.* a sharp, high-pitched sound that is not very loud: *a squeak in a door||the squeak of a frightened child* —*v.* **1** to make a squeaking sound: *We could hear a mouse squeak in a hole in the wall.* **2** *phrasal v.* **to squeak by:** to succeed, but just barely: *The student passed the examination by one point; she just squeaked by.* -*adj.* **squeaky.**

squeal /skwil/ *n.* a high-pitched scream: *the squeal of a pig* —*v.* **1** to let out a high-pitched scream: *The little girl squealed when she opened the birthday present.* **2** *infrml.fig.* to tell on s.o.: *He saw you steal the candy, and he's going to squeal to the police.*

squea·mish /ˈskwimɪʃ/ *adj.* tending to feel sick to one's stomach, usu. because of blood or s.t. unpleasant: *He can't go to war movies; they make him squeamish.*

squeeze /skwiz/ *v.* **squeezed, squeezing, squeezes** to press from two or more sides: *He put his arms around his girlfriend and squeezed her.||I squeezed lemon juice into my iced tea.*

—*n.* **1** the act of pressing from two or more sides: *She gave the beach ball a squeeze to let the air out.* **2** a tight fit into s.t.: *My car has room for four; five is a squeeze.* **3 to put the squeeze on s.o.:** to force s.o. to do s.t. by giving limited options: *The manager told the salesman to move from New York to Chicago or to leave the company; he put the squeeze on him to move.*

squelch /skwɛltʃ/ *v.n.* to force silence or stop action: *The speaker squelched her listener's argument with several examples and facts.*

squid /skwɪd/ *n.* [C] **squid** or **squids** an edible water animal with 10 legs

squint /skwɪnt/ *v.n.* to look with partly-opened eyes: *I <v.> squinted in the bright sunlight.||He <v.> squints at the page; he needs glasses.*

squire /skwaɪr/ *n. old usage* a country gentleman, a large landowner in a village —*v.old usage* to take (a woman) to a social event, *(syn.)* to escort: *He squired a lady to a ball.*

squirm /skwɜrm/ *v.* **1** to move one's body by twisting like a snake, *(syn.)* to wriggle: *I squirmed under the sink to reach the leaky pipe.* **2** to feel embarrassed and show it in one's body: *He squirmed when his boss told him to dress better in front of the other workers.*

squir·rel /ˈskwɜrəl, ˈskwʌ-/ *n.* a small, gray animal with a long fluffy tail —*phrasal v. sep.* **to squirrel s.t. away:** to save: *Each week, he squirrels away $50 from his paycheck.||He squirrels it away.*

squirrel

squirt /skwɜrt/ *v.* (of liquid) to send or come out in a thin line: *I squirted dishwashing soap onto the plate.||Water squirted out of the hose.* —*n.* **1** a thin stream of liquid: *a squirt of window cleaner* **2** *pej.* a small or unimportant person: *You little squirt, you can't talk to me like that!*

stab /stæb/ *v.* **stabbed, stabbing, stabs 1** to pierce with s.t. sharp: *to stab s.o. with a knife* **2** *fig.* **to stab s.o. in the back:** to treat s.o. badly, often while acting nice: *You stabbed her in the back when you smiled and laughed with her, and then told everyone not to go to her party.* —*n.* **1** the motion of piercing with s.t. sharp: *He gave the meat a stab with his fork.* **2** *fig.* **to give s.t. a stab** or **to make a stab at s.t.** or **to take a stab at s.t.:** to try: *I can't get the top off this jar; will you give it a stab?||The car broke*

down and I took a stab at repairing it myself.
-*n.* **stabber; stabbing.**

sta·bil·i·ty /stə'bɪləti/ *n.* [U] **-ties 1** firmness, strength, reliability: *Put a nail here to improve the stability of this chair.* **2** a state of very little change or upset: *There is political stability in the country, now that the war is over.*

sta·bi·lize /'steɪbə,laɪz/ *v.* **-lized, -lizing, -lizes 1** to make firmer or stronger: *We need to stabilize the old barn because it is leaning to one side.* **2** to reach a calm, undisturbed state: *Her health stabilizes when she takes her medicine.*

sta·ble (1) /'steɪbəl/ *adj.* **1** strong, steady: *a stable table with four thick legs* **2** a calm, undisturbed state: *My life is more stable since I found a job and moved to the country.* **3** without emotional difficulties, *(syn.)* dependable: *a stable home life for a child*

stable (2) *n.* a building like a small barn for keeping horses, cows, etc.

stack /stæk/ *v.* **1** to place one object upon another: *to stack boxes* **2 to stack the deck:** to cheat by creating a situation that is good for oneself and bad for s.o. else: *She stacked the deck against you by giving you the wrong pages to study for the test.* **3** *phrasal v.* **to stack up:** to seem (next to s.t. else), to compare to: *He's smarter and handsomer; I'll never stack up.*
—*n.* **1** a group of objects placed one upon the other: *a stack of newspapers* **2** a chimney or other hollow tube through which smoke passes *See:* smokestack. **3** (in computers) a section of memory for information
—*adj.vulg.* **stacked:** with large breasts, *(syn.)* buxom

sta·di·um /'steɪdiəm/ *n.* **-diums** or **-dia** /-diə/ a playing area surrounded by seats, for sports, concerts, and other events: *We went to the football stadium on Saturday to watch the game.*

staff /stæf/ *n.* [C] **1** a group of workers: *the secretarial staff||the sales staff* **2** all the workers in a place: *The staff signed a birthday card for me.* **3** *old usage* a stick, rod or pole: *He used a staff to make it easier to walk up the hill.||The cruel teacher hit the boy with her staff.* **4** (in music) the five lines and four spaces on which (or above and below which) notes are written
—*v.* to interview and hire workers for specific jobs: *to staff a new office*

staf·fer /'stæfər/ *n.* a non-management worker, a support person

staf·fing /'stæfɪŋ/ *n.* [U] the act of hiring workers: *The staffing of the new office is now complete; we hired 20 people.*

stag /stæg/ *n.* **1** a male deer: *a stag elk*
—*adj.* for or with only men: *a stag party*

—*adv.* alone, without a woman: *He didn't have a date, so he went stag to the dance.*

stage /steɪʤ/ *v.* **staged, staging, stages 1** to put on entertainment for the public: *to stage a play (show, rock concert, etc.)* **2** to fake a situation: *to stage an accident to collect insurance*
—*n.* **1** in a theater or auditorium, a floor that is higher than the audience's seats, used for performers and speakers: *This huge stage is for ballets and other dance performances.* **2** the job of acting: *She has spent her life on the stage, on Broadway and traveling the country.* **3 on stage:** on a stage, performing: *The star is on stage and singing beautifully.* **4 center stage:** the focus of attention: *The woman running for president is on center stage now in all the newscasts.* **5** a period of time in a process: *We are at the roofing stage in building our house.* **6** a particular level or place: *The river water is at a very high stage and will soon overflow onto farmland.* **7** short for stagecoach

stage·coach /'steɪʤ,koʊʧ/ *n.* **-es** in the old USA, a four-wheeled vehicle pulled by horses, used to carry mail and people from place to place

stage fright *n.* [U] fear of performing or public speaking

stag·fla·tion /stæg'fleɪʃən/ *n.* [U] (in economics) slow growth and high inflation

stag·ger /'stægər/ *v.* **1** to walk or run with unsteady movements: *The drunk woman staggered out of the bar.||I staggered to the refrigerator with four grocery bags.* **2** to surprise greatly, *(syn.)* to astonish: *The child's mathematical ability staggered her teachers.*
-*adj.* **staggering.**
—*n.* an unsteady walk or run

stag·ing /'steɪʤɪŋ/ *n.* [C;U] **1** the process of putting a performance on stage: *the staging of a new opera*

stag·nant /'stægnənt/ *adj.* **1** (of liquid) not moving, often with a bad smell: *We could not drink the water in the stagnant pond.* **2** with little growth or activity: *a stagnant economy* -*v.* **stagnate** /'stægneɪt/; -*n.* [U] **stagnation.**

staid /steɪd/ *adj.* serious and a bit boring, *(syns.)* prim, reserved: *My aunt leads a staid life; she works 9:00 to 5:00, reads most of the evening, and goes to bed at 9:30.*

stain /steɪn/ *v.* **1** to get a spot of color (on s.t.), *(syns.)* to soil, spot: *He stained his shirt with red wine.* **2** to make one's good reputation or character bad by saying or doing s.t. bad or wrong: *Getting arrested for drunk driving stained his reputation.* **3** to paint with a stain: *to stain wood with a brush*
—*n.* [C;U] **1** a spot of color (dirt, liquid, etc.): *a grass stain on pants* **2** damage, *(syn.)* a blemish: *Her one grade of C was a stain on*

S

her good school record. **3** a type of thin paint through which wood is still visible

stain·less /'steɪnlɪs/ *adj.* **1** without soil or damage, perfect: *a stainless reputation* **2** resistant to rust: *stainless steel knives and forks*

stair /stɛr/ *n.* **1** a step in a flight of steps: *The girl stood on a stair and said goodnight before going upstairs.* **2** *pl.* **stairs:** several steps going up, a staircase: *I took the stairs to the second floor.*

stair·case /'stɛr,keɪs/ *n.* a set of steps going up, (*syn.*) a stairway, flight of stairs: *the staircase to the attic*

stair·way /'stɛr,weɪ/ *n. See:* staircase.

stake /steɪk/ *v.* **staked, staking, stakes 1** to offer to give in exchange, to risk: *I'm telling the truth; I stake my life on it.* **2** to provide money for: *The company staked that new factory from last year's profits.* **3 to stake a claim:** to declare s.t. for oneself: *The new boss has staked a claim (or) staked out a claim to that empty office.* **4** *phrasal v. sep.* **to stake s.t. out:** to hide in order to spy on s.o.: *The police have staked out a criminal's house to see what time he usually leaves. ‖They staked it out. -n.* **stakeout.**

—*n.* **1** a narrow, pointed piece of wood or metal used as a marker: *A stake in the ground shows where our yard ends.* **2** an interest in s.t. (often a financial one): *I have a stake in the restaurant's success, since my money helped start it.*

stale /steɪl/ *adj.* not fresh or new: *stale bread‖stale old war stories*

stale·mate /'steɪl,meɪt/ *n.v.* a situation in which two people or groups can take no more action, (*syn.*) a deadlock: *The president and the Congress are at a stalemate; neither side can agree.*

stalk (1) /stɔk/ *v.* **1** to follow s.o., usu. waiting for a chance to attack: *a hunter who stalks deer in the woods* **2** to walk in an angry way: *I tried to tell her I was sorry, but she just stalked away.*

stalk (2) *n.* a stem of a plant: *a bean stalk*

stall /stɔl/ *v.* **1** to keep s.t. from happening, (*syn.*) to delay: *We're late meeting our friend; I think you're stalling by trying on all those clothes.* **2** (of an engine) to stop working: *My car stalled and I couldn't get it started again.*

—*n.* **1** the act of stalling **2** in a barn, a walled-in area for an animal: *He led the horse out of the stall.* **3** a section of a public bathroom, with a door that closes for privacy

stal·lion /'stælyən/ *n.* a male horse that still has its testicles.

stal·wart /'stɔlwərt/ *n.* a strong supporter of a cause or idea: *a Republican party stalwart*
—*adj.* morally and physically strong: *The stalwart soldiers fought bravely for freedom.*

stam·i·na /'stæmənə/ *n.* [U] the ability to exercise or work for long periods of time: *I don't have much stamina; I need to rest between tennis games.*

stam·mer /'stæmər/ *v.* to speak with many pauses and repeated words or syllables: *The shy boy stammered when he asked the pretty girl to the movies.*
—*n.* a way of speaking with pauses and repeated words or syllables *See:* stutter.

stamp /stæmp/ *v.* **1** to force a foot down to the floor or ground: *The child stamped her foot and said, "I won't eat these carrots!"* **2** to walk with a heavy step: *They stamped into the apartment building and snow flew off their boots.* **3** to print or make a raised mark with s.t.: *The lawyer stamped the paper to show it was legal.* **4** *phrasal v. sep.* **to stamp s.t. out:** to get rid of completely, (*syn.*) to eradicate: *A new police chief stamped out crime in the city.‖He stamped it out.*

—*n.* **1** a tiny rectangle of paper with a picture and amount of money printed on it, used on letters and other things to be mailed; a postage stamp: *I put a stamp on a postcard and mailed it.* **2** s.t. that prints or causes a raised mark (on paper, etc.): *She has a rubber stamp of a flower.* **3** the mark made by a stamp: *This leather purse has a stamp of the maker's name.*

stam·pede /stæm'pid/ *v.* **-peded, -peding, -pedes** to rush forward as a group: *The gates opened and the people stampeded in to the rock concert.*
—*n.* a rush forward as a group: *a cattle stampede*

stance /stæns/ *n.* **1** a still position taken just before an action, esp. in sports: *The baseball player took his stance and waited for the pitch.* **2** an attitude or opinion about s.t.: *The governor's stance is against new taxes.*

stanch /stɔntʃ, stæntʃ, stɑntʃ/ *adj. var. of* staunch.

stand /stænd/ *n.* **1** a piece of furniture that holds or displays s.t.: *a plant stand‖The little table was used as a lamp stand.* **2** a small area, often just a table, for selling things: *The children set up a lemonade stand for people walking by.* **3** an opinion that one expresses firmly: *The mayor took a stand for the building of a new high school.* **4** *pl.* **stands:** the seats for spectators at a sports arena or stadium: *The hockey player hit the puck into the stands.* **5** in a courtroom, the seat and area where the people being questioned sit: *the witness stand*

—*v.* **stood** /stʊd/, **standing, stands 1** to rise (from sitting or lying) to an upright position on one's feet: *She got out of bed and stood.* **2** to be on one's feet: *I'm tired of standing;*

let's find some chairs. **3** to measure a certain height: *a man who stands six feet tall* **4** to remain unchanged or as before: *We made the rules last year and they still stand.* **5** to hold or keep a certain idea: *I stand on my previous opinion.* **6** to be still, unmoving: *standing water* **7** *infrml.* to like (often used in the negative): *I never want to see her again; I can't stand her.* **8** *infrml.* to like enough, *(syns.)* to tolerate, endure: *The ocean water is cold, but I can stand it enough to go swimming.*||*He can't stand the pressure of his job.* **9** *fig.* **(to do s.t.) standing on one's head:** (to do s.t.) very easily: *I could sail a boat standing on my head.* **10 to know where one stands (with s.o.):** to know one's poition (in the opinion of others): *I believe in equality for women; that's where I stand*||*Tell me how long you want me to stay, so I know where I stand with you.* **11 to stand a chance:** to have a possibility to succeed: *We have no good players, so our team does not stand a chance of winning this season.* **12** *phrasal v. insep.* **to stand against s.t.: a.** to lean against: *They stood the boards against the wall.* **b.** to be located next to: *The dresser stands against the wall.* **c.** to be against, *(syn.)* to oppose: *The politician stands against higher taxes.* **13** *phrasal v.* **to stand around:** not to be doing much: *People stand around until the employment office opens.* **14 to stand at attention:** (in the military) to stand stiff and still, often waiting for orders: *Soldiers stand at attention when commanded to do so.* **15** *phrasal v.* **to stand by:** at an airport, to wait to find out if there is space on a flight: *The ticket seller said we should stand by, and we did get on the flight. See:* standby, 2. **16** *phrasal v. insep.* **to stand by s.t.** or **s.o.:** to not change, to stay faithful to: *She won't change her mind; she's standing by her opinion.*||*I will always stand by you and be your friend.* **17** *phrasal v. insep.* **to stand for s.t.: a.** to have or represent an idea: *This country stands for life, liberty, and the pursuit of happiness.* **b.** to mean: *X in that math equation stands for an unknown amount.* **18** *phrasal v. insep.* **to stand in for s.o.:** to take the place of, *(syn.)* to substitute for: *When the star is sick, another actor stands in for him. See:* understudy. **19 to stand in s.o.'s way:** to prevent (s.o.) from doing: *I will not stand in your way; you may go to graduate school.*||*Don't let the cost stand in your way; she'll pay for it.* **20** *phrasal v. sep.* **to stand off:** to prevent an attack: *The enemy attacked the fort, but the citizens stood the enemy off.* **21 to stand one's ground:** to remain sure, firm about s.t.: *She asked for a raise and the boss said no, but she stood her ground and finally received it.* **22 to stand on one's own two feet:** not

to need any help, to be self-supporting: *He can stand on his own two feet, without money from his parents.* **23** *phrasal v.* **to stand out:** to be easily seen, *(syns.)* to be noticeable, conspicuous: *His excellent work stands out.* **24 to stand pat:** not to change, to hold one's position: *The owner wants $10 million for his company; he will stand pat and not lower the price.* **25 to stand to reason:** to make sense, be logical: *If he does not like his job, it stands to reason that he should find another one.* **26 to stand trial:** to be accused of a crime and defended in court: *She stood trial for helping to rob a bank.* **27** *phrasal v.* **to stand up: a.** to get on one's feet: *He was sitting, then he stood up.* **b.** to remain true: *His argument stands up, even after looking at the facts.* **28** *phrasal v. insep.* **to stand up to s.o.:** to argue or fight with s.o. (often s.o. stronger): *The woman stood up to her boss and charged him with sexual harassment.*

stand-alone *n.adj.* a piece of furniture or equipment that can do its function by itself: *We have five <n.> stand-alones in our computer section; they are not connected.*

stan·dard /'stændərd/ *n.* **1** s.t. against which other things or ideas are measured: *All new cars must meet the standard far air pollution control.*||*That singer sets the standard for a beautiful voice.* **2** *pl.* **standards:** needs or expectations: *She has high standards; she dates only handsome, rich men.* **3** a flag, often for a military group
—*adj.* **1** commonly accepted as normal, usual: *B+ is my standard grade in history.* **2** always part of s.t.: *Seat belts are now standard on all new cars.*

standard-bearer *n.* **1** a person who carries the flag of a certain group, esp. a military unit **2** a person who represents a group and what it stands for: *The president is the standard-bearer of his party.*

stan·dard·ize /'stændər,daɪz/ *v.* **-ized, -zing, -izes** to make s.t. fit to a certain measure, often to match s.t. else: *We have to standardize the rules of the game, so people from all different countries will be able to play. -n.* [U] **standardization.**

standard of living *n.* the way people live in terms of the quality of housing, food, buying power, leisure opportunities, etc., in a nation, region, or local area: *The standard of living in the poor country got better when more people became educated and found jobs.*

standard operating procedure *n.* the accepted set of steps to be followed for a situation, whether that situation is routine or an emergency: *It is standard operating procedure for the person who answers the phone to ask the name of the caller. See:* SOP.

S

stand·by /'stænd,baɪ/ *n.* **1** s.o. or s.t. that is always ready and available: *I have a new sports car, but this truck is my old standby.* **2 on standby: a.** ready to work if needed: *The doctor is on standby in case of an emergency.* **b.** at an airport, ready to go if space becomes available: *We could not get a reservation on the flight that we wanted, so we were on standby.*

stand-in *n.* s.o. who takes the place of, (*syn.*) a substitute: *The mayor was sick, so his wife served as a stand-in at the celebration.*

stand·ing /'stændɪŋ/ *n.* [U] one's situation and place among others: *to be an employee in good standing*
—*adj.* related to standing: *Almost all the tickets are sold; standing room is all that is available at this performance.*

stand·off /'stænd,ɔf, -,ɑf/ *n.* **1** an inability to agree: *a standoff in an argument* **2** an equal score, a tie: *to play a game to a standoff*

stand·out /'stænd,aʊt/ *n.* clearly different or better, excellent: *She is a standout on the sales staff.*

stand·point /'stænd,pɔɪnt/ *n.* a situation from which s.t. is seen, (*syn.*) a viewpoint: *From my standpoint as a parent, the local school is not difficult enough.*

stand·still /'stænd,stɪl/ *n.usu.sing.* [C] a stopping of action, a halt: *Traffic came to a standstill in the deep snow.*

sta·ple (1) /'steɪpəl/ *n.* a tiny piece of metal whose ends bend to hold papers together or to attach s.t. to s.t. else
—*v.* **-pled, -pling, -ples** to attach or put together with staples and a stapler: *She stapled a picture of her baby to the card.*

staple (2) *n.* a common or important item: *Olive oil is a staple of the Greek diet.*

sta·pler /'steɪplər/ *n.* an office tool that holds staples (1) and presses them through paper, wood, etc.

stapler

star /stɑr/ *n.* **1** a bright, hot ball of gas in the sky, the closest one being our sun, and the others seen at night as dots of light **2** a shape, usu. with five or six points going in different directions from a central point **3** *pl.fig.* **stars:** s.t. that decides the future, often thought to be more powerful than anything: *Whether I have a girl or boy baby is not my decision; it's in the stars.* **4 a.** very famous performer: *a movie star* **b.** an actor with a large or impor-tant part: *The star took a bow at the end of the play.*
—*v.* **starred, starring, stars** to have a large, important part as an actor: *He stars in a new film.*

star·board /'stɑrbərd/ *n.* [U] *adj.adv.* the right-hand side of a ship or plane: *The captain looked <adv.> starboard and saw an island.* See: port.

starch /stɑrtʃ/ *n.* **-es 1** [U] a sticky liquid sprayed or put on clothes to stiffen them: *Dad asked the cleaner to put starch in his shirts.* **2** [C;U] a part of many foods, including bread, potatoes, and rice, necessary in the human diet along with fat and protein: *There is a lot of starch in this meal, with baked potatoes and corn.* See: carbohydrate.
—*v.* **-es** to put starch on clothes: *I starched my linen dress.* -*adj.* **starchy.**

star·dom /'stɑrdəm/ *n.* [U] the condition of being a famous performer: *The actress's goal is to achieve Hollywood stardom.*

stare /stɛr/ *v.* **stared, staring, stares 1** to look at s.o. or s.t. steadily with wide-opened eyes: *I told my son to stop staring at the fat woman; it wasn't nice.* **2** *phrasal v. sep.* **to stare s.o. down:** to make a person or animal look away by staring: *He stared down the attacking dog.‖He stared it down.*
—*n.* a wide-eyed look at s.o. or s.t.: *I saw my fearful stare in the mirror.*

star·fish /'stɑr,fɪʃ/ *n.* **-fish** or **-fishes** a star-shaped water animal with five arms

stark /stɑrk/ *adj.* **1** not cheerful, empty: *a stark hillside with no plants* **2** complete, utter: *stark fear*
—*adv.* completely: *stark naked*

star·ry-eyed /'stɑri,aɪd/ *adj.* seeing only the fame of s.o., awed, naive: *a starry-eyed admirer of a rock star*

Stars and Stripes *n.pl.* used with *sing.* or *pl. v.* the flag of the USA: *The Stars and Stripes was raised on the fourth of July.*

USAGE NOTE: The American flag has 50 stars, for the number of states in the union, and 13 stripes, for the original 13 colonies. The number of stars has changed over history as more states have joined the union.

Star-Spangled Banner *n.* the national song (anthem) of the USA

start /stɑrt/ *v.* **1** to begin: *I started a letter to my aunt.‖He started to cry.* **2** to set up, (*syn.*) to found: *to start a business* **3** to cause to begin an action: *She started everyone wearing plaid skirts.* **4** (in sports) to be among the first group of players at the beginning of a game: *The best goalie will start, and the other will play in the second half.* **5** to move one's body quickly and suddenly in surprise: *She started when the door slammed.* **6** *phrasal v.* **to start off:** to begin, commence: *The speaker started off by describing her background.* **7** *phrasal v.* **to start out: a.** to begin: *The movie started out* *well, but got very boring.* **b.** to leave, depart: *We are taking a trip and will start out at 2:00 P.M. tomorrow.* **8 to start (all) over:** to begin again: *The artist didn't like the painting and decided to start over.* **9 to start s.t.:** to create trouble: *Calm down! Are you trying to start something?* **10** *phrasal v. sep.* **to start s.t. up: a.** to begin s.t., *(syn.)* to found: *He started up his company in 1990.‖He started it up.* **b.** to turn on an engine: *The driver started her car up and drove away.* **11** *phrasal v. insep.* **to start with s.t.:** to begin, commence: *Let's start with fresh shrimp as an appetizer.‖To start with, let's talk about how much money we need.*

—*n.* **1** a beginning: *to make a start on a difficult journey* **2** a quick movement, a surprised reaction: *The man appeared in the dark and gave me a start.* **3 to give s.o. a start:** to help s.o. to begin: *The manager hired me when I had no experience; he gave me a start.* **4 to make a (brand-)new start:** to begin again: *He failed in a retail business but moved to another town and made a new start.*

start·er /'stɑrtər/ *n.* **1** a person or animal that begins a game or race: *That horse is a starter in the first race.* **2** a person who signals that a race is beginning: *The starter will wave a black-and-white flag and the runners will begin.* **3** in a car, s.t. that causes an engine to begin working **4** *infrml.* **for starters:** to begin with (used at the beginning of a list or explanation): *Why don't I like the city? Well for starters, there's too much noise.*

star·tle /'stɑrtl/ *v.* **-tled, -tling, -tles** **1** to surprise, sometimes causing s.o. to jump: *I was studying when the phone rang and startled me.* **-*adj.* startled; startling.**

start·up /'stɑrt,ʌp/ *n.adj.* new, just begun: *That computer company is a <n.> startup; all it has are a few employees and a good idea.*

star·va·tion /stɑr'veɪʃən/ *n.* [U] the state of having no food, being extremely hungry: *In 19th-century Ireland, people died of starvation when the potato crop failed.*

starve /stɑrv/ *v.* **starved, starving, starves** **1** to feel pain or to die from lack of food: *The travelers got lost in the mountains and starved to death.* **2** *fig.* to be very hungry: *I'm starving; let's have a big dinner.* **3** to suffer a lack of s.t.: *Many children starve for love. -*adj.* starved; starving.**

stash /stæʃ/ *v.* **-es** to keep in a secret place: *He stashed money under his mattress.*
—*n.* s.t. hidden, *(syn.)* a cache: *a stash of candy in a desk drawer*

state /steɪt/ *n.* **1** [C;U] a nation, country: *the State of Israel* **2** [C] a part of a country that has its own government and laws in addition to those of the country: *Rhode Island is the smallest state in the USA.* **3** [C] a situation or

position, physical, mental, or emotional: *She has cancer, so the state of her health is bad.‖The move to a sunnier climate has put him in a happier state.* **4** [C] the condition or situation of s.t.: *We hope the state of the economy improves.*
—*v.* **stated, stating, states** to say, often in a formal way, *(syn.)* to declare: *The law states that you cannot smoke on short airline flights.*

state·ly /'steɪtli/ *adj.* very grand and serious, *(syn.)* formal: *The queen walked toward the throne dressed in stately robes.*

state·ment /'steɪtmənt/ *n.* **1** the act of saying (or writing) s.t., *(syn.)* a declaration: *People asked the mayor to make a statement about crime in the city.* **2** a symbolic show of one's values and beliefs: *She does not wear fur, to make a statement about the killing of animals.*

state-of-the-art *adj.n.* the latest and most advanced methods and technology available: *Our company uses <adj.> state-of-the-art computers.*

state·room /'steɪt,rum/ *n.* on a ship or train, a private compartment with places to sit and sleep: *I returned to my stateroom to wash up for dinner.*

states·man /'steɪtsmən/ *n.* **-men** /-mən/ **1** a government leader, usu. one who does good things: *Winston Churchill was a great statesman for England during World War II.* **2** a person known in his profession: *an elder statesman in the banking business. -*adj.* statesmanlike; -*n.* [U] statesmanship.**

stat·ic /'stætɪk/ *adj.* not moving or changing, *(syns.)* motionless, immobile: *Business was static in the summer but improved in the fall.*
—*n.* [U] **1** the crackling noise on the radio or TV caused by electrical problems or interference: *I can't hear the ball game through the static.* **2** *infrml.fig.* **to give s.o. static:** angry words, criticism: *My boss is giving me some static because sales are too low.*

sta·tion /'steɪʃən/ *n.* **1** a place or building for the arrival and departure of transportation: *a railroad (bus, taxi, etc.) station* **2** a place or building from which a service is provided: *a television station‖a police station* **3** a social position or rank: *When he married the rich woman, people said he married above his station.*
—*v.* to place at a location: *to station a soldier at a training camp*

sta·tion·ar·y /'steɪʃə,nɛri/ *adj.* not moving or able to be moved: *The teacher asked us to remain stationary in our seats.‖The gate opens, but the fence is stationary.*

sta·tion·er /'steɪʃənər/ *n.* a person or store that sells office supplies, such as paper, paper clips, rulers, scissors, etc.

S

sta·tion·ery /'steɪʃə,nɛri/ n. [U] envelopes and paper for writing letters: *Her stationery is decorated with roses.*

station wagon n. a long car with a covered back section: *We have a big family, but we can all fit in a station wagon.*

station wagon

sta·tis·tic /stə'tɪstɪk/ n. a number that represents s.t.: *His death in an auto accident became just another statistic in the annual death rate.* -adj. **statistical;** -n. **statistician** /stætə'stɪʃən/.

sta·tis·tics /stə'tɪstɪks/ n.pl. **1** used with a sing. v. the collection and study of numerical information: *Statistics is an easy subject for s.o. who is good at math.* **2** used with a pl.v. a collection of numerical information: *The statistics on AIDS deaths are frightening.*

stat·ue /'stætʃu/ n. the form of a person, animal, or thing, usu. made from stone, wood, or metal: *a statue of George Washington* -n. [U] **statuary** /'stætʃu,ɛri/.

Statue of Liberty n. the huge statue of a woman holding a torch, standing on an island near the southern tip of Manhattan in New York City; a very famous symbol of freedom in the USA, and a popular tourist spot

stat·u·esque /,stætʃu'ɛsk/ adj. graceful, often tall, making one think of a statue: *That statuesque blonde would make a good fashion model.*

stat·ure /'stætʃər/ n. [U] **1** one's height: *Most professional basketball players are tall in stature.* **2** level of respect, reputation: *He is a man of great stature in the government.*

stat·us /'stætəs, 'steɪ-/ n. [C;U] **1** the situation of s.t. at a particular time: *What is the status of our request for a loan with the bank?* **2** one's position in society in terms of power and importance: *Doctors have more status than mechanics in US society.* **3** a legal condition: *to have the status (or) legal status of a US citizen*

status quo /'kwoʊ/ n. the way things are now: *The people voted for the same president to stay in power because they wanted to keep the status quo.*

status symbol n. an item that shows off one's wealth or place in society: *The couple doesn't need a big car, but they have one as a status symbol.*

stat·ute /'stætʃut/ n. a law made by a state or national government: *the statutes that control business corporations* -adj. **statutory.**

statute of limitations n. the time period after which legal action cannot be taken: *The murder happened 20 years ago, but they can still have a trial because there is no statute of limitations on murder cases.*

stat·u·to·ry rape /'stætʃə,tɔri/ n. sexual intercourse with a person who is not over the age of consent: *In that state, a person must be over 18 years of age to have sex; otherwise to do so is statutory rape.*

staunch or **stanch** /stɔntʃ, stæntʃ/ adj. firm, dedicated: *a staunch supporter of the political party*
—v. to stop or slow bleeding: *We staunched the flow of blood with a shirt until we could get to the hospital.*

stave /steɪv/ phrasal v. sep. **staved** or **stove** /stoʊv/, **staving, staves to stave s.t. off:** to prevent, (syn.) to ward off: *She staves off a cold with vitamin C.*
—n. **1** a piece of wood **2** (in music) a staff **3** a verse in a song or poem, (syn.) a stanza

stay /steɪ/ v. **1** to remain or continue to be in one place: *I can't stay long; I have to leave soon.||She stayed at the office and worked late.||He stayed on the corner while his friend bought a newspaper.* **2** (in law) to stop for a time, (syns.) to postpone, delay: *to stay a court order to pay a debt* **3** phrasal v. **to stay at: a.** to visit, esp. as a guest: *We stay at the same hotel when we go on vacation each year.* **b.** to remain at the same level: *The temperature has stayed at zero for days this winter.* **4** phrasal v. **to stay behind:** to remain while others leave: *I stayed behind to help wash dishes after the party.* **5** phrasal v. **to stay down:** to remain hidden in a low place: *They are shooting at us; stay down!* **6** phrasal v. **to stay in: a.** not to go out socially: *Sometimes I stay in on Saturday nights.* **b.** not to go outside: *He stays in when it's cold.* **7** phrasal v. **to stay out: a.** to remain outside: *She stays out for hours when the sun shines.* **b.** not to come home: *My parents don't like it when I stay out late with my friends.* **8 to stay put:** to remain in one place, usu. waiting for s.t.: *The mother told her kids to stay put in the car while she ran into the store.* **9 to stay the course:** to keep doing the same thing in the same way: *He got good grades in high school, and if he stays the course, he will do well in college.* **10** phrasal v. **to stay up:** to keep awake: *The student stayed up all night to study.*
—n. **1** [C] a visit: *a stay in the country* **2** [C] a support, (syn.) a brace: *a stay in a tunnel structure||a stay in a man's shirt collar* **3** [C;U] (in law) a delay, (syn.) a postponement: *to obtain a stay of execution of a murderer*

staying power n. [U] the strength to keep doing s.t. for a long period of time, esp. under difficult conditions: *In good economic times and bad, our company has done well; it has staying power.*

stead /stɛd/ n. **1** frml. **in s.o.'s stead:** in place of s.o.: *The prince could not attend the cere-*

mony, so the princess went in his stead. **2 to stand s.o. in good stead:** to be a positive or wise thing for s.o.: *Learning Portuguese will stand you in good stead if you go to Brazil.*

stead·fast /'stɛd,fæst/ *adj.* **1** firm, unchanging: *Our farm has been a steadfast source of food for our family.* **2** always available, loyal: *He has been a steadfast friend since we were eight.*

stead·y /'stɛdi/ *v.* **-ied, -ying, -ies 1** to make firm, (*syn.*) to stabilize: *He felt dizzy and steadied himself by sitting down.*‖*He held the ladder to steady it.* **2** to make calm: *to steady one's nerves*
—*adj.* **-ier, -iest 1** firm, stable: *The chair is steady since I fixed it.* **2** without interruption, continuous: *a steady rainfall*‖*a steady diet of good food* **3** calm, (*syn.*) dependable: *She is a steady person who thinks before she acts.* **4** *infrml.* (of a girlfriend or boyfriend) regular or exclusive: *my steady girlfriend* **5 to go steady:** to date (without dating anyone else), usu. said of teenagers, not adults: *The boy and girl have been going steady all through the school year.*
—*n.* a boyfriend or girlfriend with whom one goes steady

steak /steɪk/ *n.* [C;U] a piece of meat or fish, usu. about an inch thick: *Today, I'll have a broiled swordfish steak.*

steal /stil/ *v.* **stole** /stoʊl/, **stolen** /'stoʊlən/, **stealing, steals 1** to take s.t. that belongs to s.o. else without permission: *A thief stole my car.* **2** to move quietly and secretly: *She away while the lights were off.*
—*n.usu. sing.* [C] s.t. valuable that can be purchased for a very low price, (*syn.*) a bargain: *I bought a used bike in excellent condition for $50; what a steal!*

stealth /stɛlθ/ *n.* [U] secrecy, esp. with a plan to harm: *The robber approached the house with stealth.* *-adv.* **stealthily;** *-adj.* **stealthy.**

steam /stim/ *n.* [U] **1** gas in the air made by heated water under pressure: *Steam came out of the teakettle.* **2** *infrml.fig.* power or energy: *I've been swimming for an hour and I'm out of steam.* **3 to let off steam:** to show anger instead of holding it in: *He shouted and threw things to let off steam.*
—*adj.* using steam: *a steam iron*‖*a steam engine*
—*v.* to give off steam: *a broken pipe that steams*

steam heat *n.* [U] a way of warming buildings by forcing hot steam through pipes and radiators

steam·ing /'stimɪŋ/ *adj.* **1** hot and humid like steam: *the steaming jungle* **2** *adj.adv.* angry, (*syn.*) fuming: *to be <adv.> steaming mad*

steam iron *n.* an electrical instrument with a steam capacity for ironing clothes

steam·roll /'stim,roʊl/ *v.* **1** to make flat with a steamroller **2** *fig.* to force oneself at or through s.t.: *He is not very smart or kind, but he usually succeeds by steamrolling his way through life.*

steam·rol·ler /'stim,roʊlər/ *n.* a type of vehicle used for flattening soft tar or asphalt on roads

steam·y /'stimi/ *adj.* **-ier, -iest 1** hot and humid: *a steamy summer's day* **2** sexy: *a steamy novel*

steel /stil/ *n.* [U] **1** a much-used, hard metal made of carbon and iron: *a ship made of wood and steel* **2** *fig.* great strength or bravery: *a pilot who has nerves of steel*
—*v.* to be prepared for s.t. bad: *The man with cancer steeled himself against the pain of chemotherapy.*

steel wool *n.* [U] a tangled bunch of fine steel wires, used for cleaning or polishing

steep /stip/ *adj.* **-er, -est 1** at an angle at which s.t. or s.o. could easily fall: *a steep mountain road* **2** rising or falling quickly and to a large extent: *a steep increase in business activity* **3** *infrml.* expensive: *These ticket prices are pretty steep. -v.* **steepen.**
—*v.* **1** to put in liquid for a period of time: *The tea is steeping.* **2** *fig.* to get very involved in: *to steep oneself in learning new computer software*

stee·ple /'stipəl/ *n.* the top, pointed section of a church, (*syn.*) a spire

steer (1) /stɪr/ *v.* **1** to control the direction of a vehicle: *I steered my car into a parking space.* **2** to guide s.o. by gently pushing or leading: *My dad steered me into his office and sat me down.* **3 to steer s.o. in the right direction:** to guide: *Parents try to steer their children in the right direction by teaching them good manners.*

steeple

steer (2) *n.* a young ox that is raised for beef *See:* bovine; bull; ox.

steer·age /'stɪrɪdʒ/ *n.* [U] the least expensive passenger section on a ship: *Many immigrants traveled in steerage to America.*

steer·ing /'stɪrɪŋ/ *n.* [U] the act or function of controlling a vehicle's direction: *I can't turn right; I must have a mechanic look at the steering in my truck.*

steering wheel *n.* in a vehicle, the circular object held and turned by a driver to control direction: *The driver turned the steering wheel to the left and the car went left.*

stel·lar /'stɛlər/ *adj.* **1** related to stars: *a stellar formation in the sky* **2** outstanding, brilliant: *a stellar piano concert*

stem /stɛm/ *n.* **1** the long, thin part of a plant from which a flower grows: *the thorny stem of*

S

a rose **2** a long part of s.t.: *the stem of a wine glass*

—*v.* **stemmed, stemming, stems** **1** to come from, originate from: *Many English words stem from Latin.* **2** to stop or hold back: *The nurse stemmed the flow of blood with a clean cloth.*

stench /stɛntʃ/ *n.* **-es** a bad smell, *(syn.)* a stink: *the stench of rotting garbage*

sten·cil /'stɛnsəl/ *n.* a flat, stiff piece of paper, plastic, metal, etc., with simple picture or words cut out of it so that ink or paint will appear on a surface below in the form of those pictures or words: *We bought some leaf stencils to decorate our walls.*

—*v.* to mark with a stencil: *The factory stencils our company name on all our boxes.*

sten·o /'stɛnoʊ/ *n.* **-os** *short for* stenographer *or* stenography

ste·nog·ra·pher /stə'nɑgrəfər/ *n.* a person who understands and writes shorthand (a type of fast writing that uses symbols, not letters)

ste·nog·ra·phy /stə'nɑgrəfi/ *See:* shorthand.

step /stɛp/ *n.* **1** a walking movement, the act of lifting the foot, moving it forward, and putting it down: *The baby took her first step today!* **2** the distance of this movement: *The shopping area is a few steps from the parking lot.* **3** one surface in a set of stairs, *(syn.)* a stair: *She came partway downstairs, stopping on the bottom step.* **4** *n.pl.* **steps:** a set of stairs, staircase: *We put flowerpots on the front steps of the house.* **5** one action toward a goal: *the first step in our plan* **6** (in music) one tone up or down in a scale **7 in step with** or **out of step with: a.** moving at the same (or) different pace or rhythm as others: *The soldier was in step with the others in the parade.* **b.** understanding and doing (or) not understanding and not doing as others do: *My grandmother is out of step with today's music.* **8 to keep step with: a.** to match or walk in exactly the same way as others: *The little boy kept step with his mother, although her legs were longer.* **b.** to stay aware of what's going on: *He keeps step with the computer business by reading lots of magazines.* **9 step by step:** one section or part at a time: *She learned how to change a tire step by step.* **10 step up:** a higher or better position: *Moving from secretary to salesman was a step up for him.* **11 step-up:** an increase: *a step-up in factory production since last year* **12 to take steps:** to take necessary actions in order to get s.t. done: *The hospital is taking steps to give better care by hiring more nurses.* **13 to watch one's step: a.** to be careful walking: *Watch your step; there's a bump in the sidewalk.* **b.** to be careful: *Tell the girl to watch her step with matches or she'll start a fire.*

—*v.* **stepped, stepping, steps** **1** to walk: *to step quickly along the road* **2** to place the foot: *to step on the sidewalk*||*to step on an insect* **3** *phrasal v.* **to step down: a.** to go lower, *(syn.)* to descend: *The worker stepped down from the ladder.* **b.** to end one's time as a witness in court: *The woman stepped down from the witness chair.* **c.** to leave a job, *(syn.)* to resign: *The manager stepped down.* **4** *phrasal v.* **to step forward:** to present oneself: *The chairwoman asked for people to help, and I stepped forward.* **5** *phrasal v.* **to step in:** to go near or enter in order to give advice, *(syn.)* to intercede: *Two friends were arguing and I stepped in to calm them.* **6 to step on it** or **the gas:** go faster, *(syn.)* to accelerate: *We are late; step on the gas!*||*You walk too slowly, let's step on it and get there on time.* **7** *fig.* **to step on s.o.'s toes:** to take action in s.o. else's area: *She stepped on the tailor's toes when she told him how to mend the dress.* **8** *phrasal v.* **to step out: a.** to leave for a moment: *He is not in his office; he stepped out but will be back shortly.* **b.** *old usage* to go out socially (to a party, dance, etc.): *My grandmother talks about stepping out with my grandfather in the 1930s.* **9** *phrasal v. sep.* **to step s.t. up:** to increase: *The company received a large order and we stepped up production to fill it.*||*We stepped it up.*

step·broth·er /'stɛp,brʌðər/ *n.* the son of a parent's spouse who does not share a parent with oneself

step·child /'stɛp,tʃaɪld/ *n.* **-children** /-,tʃɪldrən/ a son or daughter of one's spouse that is not one's own natural-born child

step·daugh·ter /'stɛp,dɔtər/ *n.* a daughter of one's spouse that is not one's own natural-born child

step·fa·ther /'stɛp,fɑðər/ *n.* the husband of a child's mother who is not one's own father

step·lad·der /'stɛp,lædər/ *n.* a ladder with a support section that is put into a locked position, usu. with a platform at the top to hold paint or tools

step·moth·er /'stɛp,mʌðər/ *n.* the wife of a child's father who is not the child's own mother

step·par·ent /'stɛp,pɛrənt, -,pær-/ *n.* a stepfather or stepmother

stepped-up /'stɛpt,ʌp/ *adj.* increased: *stepped-up activity in the stock market*

stepladder

step·ping-stone /'stɛpɪŋ,stoʊn/ *n.* **1** one in a series of stones used to go across water **2** *fig.* one in a series of steps in a process: *The owner used his small company as a stepping-stone to buy others and expand into a large business.*

step·sis·ter /'stɛp,sɪstər/ *n.* the daughter of a parent's spouse that is not one's own natural-born sister

step·son /'stɛp,sʌn/ *n.* a son of one's spouse that is not one's own natural-born son

ster·e·o /'stɛri,oʊ, 'stɪr-/ *n. short for* stereophonic **1** a sound system (radio, CD player, etc.) that uses two speakers **2 in stereo:** using two or more channels

ster·e·o·type /'stɛriə,taɪp, 'stɪr-/ *n.* **1** a person who is typical of a group: *The stereotype of a Wall Street banker carries a briefcase.* **2** a too-simple and often mistaken idea about a particular group: *It is a stereotype that all women cry easily.*
—*v.* **-typed, -typing, -types** to think of a group in a too-simple way by not considering individual differences: *She stereotypes Indians when she says they all eat spicy food.*

ster·ile /'stɛrəl/ *adj.* **1** completely clean, with no germs or bacteria: *A hospital's operating room is a sterile area.* **2** with no excitement or creative energy: *I found my job as a tax collector to be very sterile.* **3** unable to have children, (*syns.*) infertile, impotent: *The couple adopted a baby because the father is sterile.*

ster·il·ize /'stɛrə,laɪz/ *v.* **-ized, -izing, -izes** **1** to make completely free of dirt and bacteria: *to sterilize a needle with a match* **2** to make unable to have children: *An X-ray can sterilize a human being if a protective cloth is not worn.* -*n.*[C;U] **sterilization.**

ster·ling /'stɛrlɪŋ/ *n.* **1** a metal that is more than 92 percent pure silver **2** British money: *the pound sterling*
—*adj.* **1** made of sterling silver: *a sterling bracelet* **2** of the best quality (usu. said of one's behavior): *sterling character*

stern (1) /stɛrn/ *n.* the rear section of a ship

stern (2) *adj.* **1** unsmiling, very serious: *The judge's face was stern when she said, "Guilty!"* **2** not flexible, severe: *His stern mother makes him do all his homework before dinner.* -*n.* [U] **sternness.**

ster·oid /'stɛrɔɪd, 'stɪr-/ *n.* a drug sometimes taken by athletes to become stronger or more muscular, usu. illegal or not permitted

steth·o·scope /'stɛθə,skoʊp/ *n.* an instrument used by medical professionals to listen to sounds within the body, such as a heartbeat

stethoscope

stew /stu/ *n.* [C;U] **1** a thick soup, usu. a mixture of meat and vegetables: *beef stew* **2** *infrml.* a state of worry: *She is in a stew about going to the huge university.*

—*v.* **1** to cook for a long time to soften and thicken food **2** *fig.* to worry: *He stews over big decisions.*

stew·ard /'stuərd/ *n.* **1** a man who helps passengers and serves meals on an airplane or ship **2** a type of manager in a club, hotel, or union *See:* flight attendant. -*n.* [U] **stewardship.**
—*v.* to manage s.o.'s money

stew·ard·ess /'stuərdɪs/ *n.* a woman who helps passengers on an airplane and serves meals *See:* flight attendant.

stick /stɪk/ *v.* **stuck** /stʌk/, **sticking, sticks** **1** to attach or put in place with a pointed object: *He stuck a nail in the wood to mark the spot.* **2** to attach or put in place with glue or tape: *The student stuck a poster on the wall with masking tape.* **3** to make a hole or indent with a thin or pointed object: *She accidentally stuck a finger in her eye.* **4** to put s.t. firmly in place, (*syns.*) to poke, thrust: *He stuck a cassette in the tape recorder.* **5** to cause to move outward or forward, to be outward or forward, (*syn.*) to protrude: *The little girl stuck her tongue out.* **6** to be close or together: *The mother told the boy to stick with her in the grocery store.* **7** not to move, even when pushed or pulled: *The top drawer sticks; I can't open it.* **8** *phrasal v.* **to stick around:** to stay, wait: *I think that we should stick around until we get an answer.* **9** *phrasal v. insep.* **to stick by s.o.** or **s.t.:** to remain faithful to s.o. or s.t.: *He stuck by his story about the accident.* **10 to stick it to s.o.:** to treat s.o. badly, to take advantage of s.o.: *My car broke down on the highway and the garage really stuck it to me on the cost of repairs.* **11 to stick one's neck out:** to take a chance without being sure of any return: *I stuck my neck out for my cousin when I loaned him money.* **12** *phrasal v.* **to stick out** (or **to stick out like a sore thumb**): to be very obvious, (*syn.*) to be conspicuous: *The redhead sticks out in a room full of blondes.*||*I was the only one with a dresscoat on, so I stuck out like a sore thumb.* **13** *phrasal v. sep.* **to stick s.t. out:** to be located outside of, beyond: *She stuck out her swollen foot so I could see it.*||*She stuck it out.* **14** *phrasal v. sep.* **to stick s.o.** or **s.t. up:** to rob with a gun or knife: *The thief stuck up a grocery store and stole $3,000.*||*She stuck it up.* **15** *phrasal v.* **to stick together:** to stay close or loyal to others, (*syn.*) to unite: *That family sticks together and helps each other.* **16** *fig.* **to stick to one's guns:** to keep one's opinions or beliefs even when others think differently: *Most people don't agree with him, but he sticks to his guns.* **17 to stick to one's ribs:** (of food) to be filling and satisfying: *The warm beef stew really sticks to my ribs.* **18 to stick to one's word:** to keep one's promise despite difficulty in doing so: *He lost his job, but he stuck to his word and repaid the*

S

loan. **19** *phrasal v. insep.* **to stick to s.t.:** to be patient, *(syn.)* to persevere: *She has many, many problems with her business; but she sticks to it and makes it run.* **20** *phrasal v. insep.* **to stick with s.t.:** to continue doing s.t., *(syn.)* to persevere: *At first, he had trouble with his job, but he stuck with it and is now doing well.*

—n. **1** a small tree branch, esp. one that has fallen off the tree: *to burn sticks in the fireplace* **2** a long, thin piece of s.t.: *a stick of wood*||*a stick of dynamite* **3** *n.pl.* **the sticks:** the country, a rural area without much activity or entertainment: *Our cousins live on a farm in the sticks.*

stick·er /'stɪkər/ *n.* **1** a label or small decoration with a type of glue on the back: *She put a sticker on the envelope to mark it "Airmail."*||*The little girl put stickers of Mickey Mouse on her bedroom door.* **2** a sharp part of a plant: *I got cut with stickers as I walked through the woods.*

stick-in-the-mud *n.infrml.* dull person: *That stick-in-the-mud never goes out on weekends.*

stick·ler /'stɪklər/ *n.* a person who thinks about small details, *(syn.)* a perfectionist: *The violin player practices every day because he is a stickler for getting it right.*

stick·up /'stɪk,ʌp/ *n.slang* a robbery, esp. by s.o. with a gun, *(syn.)* a holdup: *There was a stickup at the bank this morning.*

stick·y /'stɪki/ *adj.* **-ier, -iest** **1** tending to attach because of a glue-like surface, *(syns.)* adhesive, gummy: *sticky wet paint* **2** humid, hot, and uncomfortable: *sticky summer weather* **3** sensitive, difficult: *Meeting an old girlfriend on the street is a sticky situation.*

stiff /stɪf/ *adj.* **-er, -est** **1** difficult to bend, *(syn.)* rigid: *a stiff piece of wood* **2** not easily moved: *a stiff neck* **3** severe, serious: *a stiff fine for drunk driving* **4** very formal and uncomfortable: *I felt stiff at the tea party, in my new suit and tight shoes.* **5** (of liquor) strong: *a stiff drink of rum* **6** strong in movement: *a stiff wind* -n. [U] **stiffness.**

—n.slang **1** an ordinary person: *a working stiff* **2** a dead person, *(syn.)* a corpse

—v.slang not to pay a debt: *We let him in the restaurant, but he never paid the bill; he stiffed us.*

—adv. completely, totally: *scared stiff*

stiff·en /'stɪfən/ *v.* to grow hard or rigid, not easily moved: *a hip that has stiffened with age*

sti·fle /'staɪfəl/ *v.* **-fled, -fling, -fles** **1** to prevent s.o. from breathing or getting air, often killing s.o., *(syn.)* to suffocate: *The murderer stifled the man with a bed pillow.* **2** *fig.* to prevent or keep from doing s.t., *(syns.)* to oppress, discourage: *The management in that company stifles their workers' opinions.* **3** to keep

down, *(syns.)* to suppress, restrict: *to stifle criticism* -adj. **stifling.**

stig·ma /'stɪgmə/ *n.* **-mas** or **-mata** a mark of shame or disgrace: *His father was a criminal and that has been a stigma all his life.* -v. **stigmatize;** -adj. **stigmatized.**

sti·let·to /stə'lɛtoʊ/ *n.* **-tos** or **-toes** a type of knife with a small, sharp blade

stiletto heel *n.* a very tall, thin heel on a woman's shoe (the shoes are called "stilettos")

still /stɪl/ *v.* **1** to make quiet: *The teacher stilled the voices of the children.* **2** to calm: *to still someone's fears*

—adv. **1** motionless: *to stand still* **2** until a certain time, yet: *She was still asleep when I went to work.* **3** all the same, nevertheless: *I don't eat much; still, I like to go to restaurants.* **4** more, further: *to need still more time*

—adj. **-er, -est** **1** not moving, calm, *(syn.)* tranquil: *a still lake* **2** silent, quiet: *The woods were still, with no wind in the trees.* **3** (of wine) not bubbly: *a still white Burgundy* -n. [U] **stillness.**

—n. **1** a piece of equipment for making liquor, *(syn.)* a distillery: *a still for making whiskey* **2** a photograph from or publicizing a film: *a still of the movie star on a poster*

still·born /'stɪl,bɔrn/ *adj.* dead at birth *-n.* **still-birth** /'stɪl,bɜrθ/.

still life *n.* [C;U] (in art) the painting or photography of unmoving objects, such as fruit or flowers: *a still life of a bowl of pears*

stilt·ed /'stɪltɪd/ *adj.* formal, *(syns.)* artificial, pretentious: *I like to learn slang so that I sound less stilted.*

stilts /stɪlts/ *n.pl.* a pair of long poles, held with the hands and with places for the feet to rest, allowing a person to be taller: *At the circus, a man on stilts was taller than the giraffe.*

stim·u·lant /'stɪmyələnt/ *n.* **1** s.t. that increases energy or activity: *I drink coffee as a stimulant in the morning.* **2** s.t. that causes an action or response: *Lower interest rates are a stimulant to the economy.*

stim·u·late /'stɪmyə,leɪt/ *v.* **-lated, -lating, -lates** to increase energy or activity: *Her love for him stimulates his creativity.*||*Cold air stimulates me.* -n. **stimulation.**

stim·u·lus /'stɪmyələs/ *n.* [C] **-li** /-,laɪ/ s.t. that causes an action or response: *The desire for a good education was the stimulus for my studying hard.*

sting /stɪŋ/ *v.* **stung** /stʌŋ/, **stinging, stings** **1** to pierce the skin, usu. with poison: *This summer, I was stung by a bee.* **2** to feel or cause a sharp pain: *It stung when you slapped me.* **3** to feel emotional pain: *Your rude behavior stung your aunt.* **4** to charge too much money, cheat: *I paid $5 for this bad chocolate; I got stung.*

—*n.* **1** the act or result of stinging: *a bee sting* **2** the painful sensation of a sting: *the sting of alcohol on a cut* **3** a complicated plan to catch criminals while they are doing s.t. illegal: *The policeman, dressed as a drug dealer, brought a man to a hotel, where the man took drugs and got arrested; it was a sting.*

stin·gy /'stɪndʒi/ *adj.* **-gier, -giest** unwilling to share or spend, *(syns.)* miserly, penny-pinching: *Don't be stingy; give me a bite of your sandwich.||That stingy lady won't spend money on heating her apartment.* *-n.* [U] **stinginess.**

stink /stɪŋk/ *v.* **stank** /stæŋk/, **stunk** /stʌŋk/, **stinking, stinks 1** to smell bad: *a dirty refrigerator that stinks* **2** to have a bad quality: *This story stinks of dishonesty.* **3** to be very bad, of poor quality: *Don't read this book; it stinks.*
—*n.* **1** a bad smell, a stench: *the stink from rotting vegetables* **2** an angry and loud reaction to s.t.: *She made a big stink about paying too much at a store.*

stink·er /'stɪŋkər/ *n.fig.* a bad, unkind person

stink·ing /'stɪŋkɪŋ/ *adj.* **1** bad-smelling: *The dog made a stinking mess on the carpet.* **2** bad, offensive: *Her attitude is stinking; she should be nicer.* **3** very drunk

stint /stɪnt/ *n.* a job for a limited time: *to do a six-month stint in the army*
—*v.* not to spend much, *(syn.)* to be frugal: *to stint on food and clothing*

sti·pend /'staɪˌpɛnd, -pənd/ *n.* a sum of money paid for work: *The professor receives a stipend from the university.*

stip·u·late /'stɪpyəˌleɪt/ *v.* **-lated, -lating, -lates** to require by a legal paper, *(syn.)* to specify: *The lease stipulates that the rent must be paid on the first of each month.||Her will stipulates that her children will receive her house after she dies.*

stip·u·la·tion /ˌstɪpyə'leɪʃən/ *n.* a specific requirement, a necessary condition: *One stipulation of living in our house is that you must share in the chores.*

stir /stɜr/ *v.* **stirred, stirring, stirs 1** to move s.t. (such as a spoon) in a circular motion through a liquid or mixture: *He stirred sugar into the tea.* **2** to move slightly: *to stir in one's sleep* **3** to make active, *(syn.)* to motivate: *The weather was hot, but we stirred our friends into taking a trip to the beach.* **4** *phrasal v. sep.* **to stir s.t. up:** to cause, difficulties etc., *(syn.)* to incite: *He likes to stir up trouble by causing arguments.||He stirs it up.*
—*n.* **1** a circular movement with s.t. (such as a spoon): *to give the soup a stir* **2** *usu. sing.* excitement: *The movie star created a stir when he came to our town.*

stir crazy *n.infrml.* an uncomfortable, restless feeling caused by staying in one place for a long time: *She lives and works in a small apartment and is going stir crazy.*

stir-fry *v.* **-fried, -frying, -fries** to cook food quickly in oil over high heat while moving the food around with a kitchen tool (fork, chopsticks, etc.); a common cooking method in parts of Asia: *I love chicken stir-fry.*

stir·rup /'stɜrəp, 'stɪr-/ *n.* **1** on a horse's saddle, a ring of metal with a flat bottom for the rider's foot **2** a small bone in the ear, *(syn.)* stapes

stitch /stɪtʃ/ *v.* **-es 1** to sew together with thread: *I stitched a sleeve onto a dress with a sewing machine.* **2** to join skin with medical thread in order to close a cut or wound: *The doctor stitched the deep cut in my forehead.*
—*n.* **-es 1** one movement of a needle with thread attached, in and then out of cloth or (in medicine) skin: *Her mother taught her to sew with tiny, neat stitches.||He cut his hand with a knife and needed eight stitches.* **2** (in knitting) one loop of yarn around a needle: *He made a mistake and had to redo a row of stitches in the sweater.* **3** a sudden pain in the side of one's body, near the stomach: *When I began running for exercise, I always got a stitch in my side in the first kilometer.* **4** *infrml.* a piece of clothing (usu. used in the negative): *He was naked, not wearing one stitch, when he went swimming.* **5** a tiny amount: *She went out with her friends and didn't do a stitch of homework.* **6 a stitch in time saves nine.** *s.t.* done now will save more work later: *He noticed a leaky pipe and fixed it immediately so it wouldn't cause a flood; a stitch in time saves nine.* **7 in stitches:** laughing hard: *The comedian had his audience in stitches with his jokes.* *-n.* [U] **stitching.**

stock /stɑk/ *v.* **1** to keep or have for sale: *The auto parts store stocks headlights.||Does the drugstore stock pink bath soap?* **2** *phrasal v. insep.* **to stock up on** or **with s.t.:** to collect or gather a large amount of s.t.: *Mom stocks up on light bulbs when the store has a sale.*
—*n.* **1** [U] the items available for sale in a store: *Some stock is on the shelves; the rest is in a back room.* **2** [C] a supply collected for the future: *We have a stock of candles in case the lights go out during a storm.* **3** [U] animals on a farm: *All the stock are in the barn for the night.* See: livestock. **4** [C;U] a piece of a business, bought in the form of shares: *She bought stock in a toy company.* See: share. **5** [U] one's parents, grandparents, and other older or past relatives, sometimes including an entire race: *My great-grandparents were of Swedish fishermen's stock.* **6** [U] the liquid from boiled meat, fish, or vegetables: *He made a stew with beef stock, potatoes, and carrots.* **7** [U] theatrical activity, usu. during the summer in a vacation area: *She played a nun in*

S

The Sound of Music *in summer stock.* **8** [U] the opinion others have of s.o., (*syn.*) a reputation: *That author's stock with me went up when I read his last book.* **9** [C] the handle of a gun: *a rifle's stock* **10** *pl.old usage* **stocks:** a place for punishing criminals, made of wood and metal, with holes for the head, wrists, or ankles **11 in stock:** available for sale: *We have the paint that you need in stock.* **12 out of stock:** not available for sale (sold out or no longer carried): *I'm sorry, but the dress that you want is out of stock.* **13 stock in trade:** a usual or typical response or action from s.o.: *He is always telling stories and making jokes; that's his stock in trade.* **14 to take stock:** to look at a situation seriously in order to make a good decision: *His wife said she would leave him because he was never home; that made him take stock of his behavior and stay home more.*

stock·ade /stɑˈkeɪd/ *n.v.* **-aded, -ading, -ades** **1** an area with high walls used to keep in prisoners **2** the high walls themselves

stock·bro·ker /ˈstɑkˌbroʊkər/ *n.* a person who gives advice and helps people buy and sell securities: *My stockbroker told me to sell quickly and make a lot of money.* *-n.* **stockbrokerage;** [U] **stockbrokering.**

stock certificate *n.* an official piece of paper that tells how much stock (shares) s.o. owns in a company

stock company *n.* **1** a business whose money is represented by shares of stock **2** a group of actors and others who work for a theater and perform the same plays for a period of time

stock exchange *n.* a place where securities (part-ownerships of companies) are bought and sold by traders according to rules and laws: *He works as a computer operator at the New York Stock Exchange.*

stock·hold·er /ˈstɑkˌhoʊldər/ *n.* a person who owns part of a company because of having bought stocks or shares

stock·ing /ˈstɑkɪŋ/ *n.* **1** a covering for the foot and leg: *The woman bought nylon stockings. See:* nylons; pantyhose.

stock market *n.* **1** the place for or business of buying and selling securities **2** the prices of securities: *The London stock market is rising.*

stock·pile /ˈstɑkˌpaɪl/ *v.n.* **-piled, -piling, -piles** to collect a lot of items for future use: *The electricity companies have <v.> stockpiled coal and barrels of oil for future use.||They have huge <n.> stockpiles of coal.*

stock·room /ˈstɑkˌrum/ *n.* an area where extra items are kept and gotten as needed: *We keep our office supplies in a stockroom.*

stock·y /ˈstɑki/ *adj.* **-ier, -iest** **1** strongly built: *a stocky hockey player* **2** fat, plump: *stocky legs*

stock·yard /ˈstɑkˌyɑrd/ *n.* a place where animals are kept before they are killed for food: *Chicago was once famous for its huge stockyards of cattle.*

stodg·y /ˈstɑdʒi/ *adj.* **-ier, -iest** **1** dull, boring, (*syn.*) stuffy: *The man sat in a stodgy, windowless library reading an old, dusty book.* **2** without humor, (*syn.*) pompous: *The stodgy lady told the children to be quiet.* *-n.* [U] **stodginess.**

sto·ic /ˈstoʊɪk/ *adj.* n. seeming unaffected by pain or s.t. bad, indifferent: *Many city-dwellers accept the high crime rate with a <adj.> stoic attitude.||The doctor can look at blood with the face of a <n.> stoic.* *-adj.* **stoical;** *-n.* [U] **stoicism.**

stoke /stoʊk/ *v.* **stoked, stoking, stokes** to add fuel to a fire or furnace: *Please cut more wood; we need to stoke the fire.*

stole /stoʊl/ *n.* a long piece of cloth or fur worn over the shoulders

sto·len /ˈstoʊlən/ *adj. & past part. of* steal, taken illegally: *The police followed a woman driving a stolen car.*

stol·id /ˈstɑlɪd/ *adj.* showing little feeling or emotion: *She didn't smile or laugh: she kept her usual stolid face.* *-adv.* **stolidly;** *-n.* [U] **stolidness.**

stomach /ˈstʌmək/ *n.* **1** [C] the internal body part where food goes after being swallowed: *My stomach feels full after eating the ice cream.* **2** [C;U] the general area of the stomach, (*syn.*) the belly: *He punched me in the stomach.* **3** [U] liking or strength, the ability to bear s.t.: *He has no stomach for people who tell lies.*
—v. to be able to bear s.t.: *I can't stomach the thought of a long train trip.*

stom·ach·ache /ˈstʌmək.eɪk/ *n.* [C;U] pain in the belly or abdomen *See:* headache, USAGE NOTE.

stomp /stɑmp, stɔmp/ *v.n.* to step down strongly with the foot: *He <v.> stomped on a snake. See:* stamp, **1,2.**

stone /stoʊn/ *n.* **1** [U] rock: *a house made of stone||a stone wall* **2** [C] a small piece of rock: *The little girl threw stones into the pond.* **3** [C] a jewel or gem: *How many stones are in your diamond ring?* **4** *Brit.* a measure of weight, 14 pounds **5** [C] the hard single seed inside some fruits, such as peaches, cherries, etc.
—v. **stoned, stoning, stones** to kill or hurt by throwing stones: *to stone a sinner to death*

Stone Age *n.* the very beginning of human life and culture, millions of years ago

stoned /stoʊnd/ *adj. & past part. of* stone, **1** drunk **2** affected by drugs

stone·wall /ˈstoʊnˌwɔl/ *v.* to refuse to cooperate, to remain silent: *The criminal stonewalled the lawyer and refused to open his mouth.*

ston·y or **ston·ey** /'stoʊni/ *adj.* **-ier, -iest 1** full of rocks or stones: *a stony field* **2** with no emotion, *(syns.)* hard, rigid: *His sister cried at the funeral, but he sat with a stony face. -adj.* **stonyhearted** /'stoʊni,hɑrtɪd/; *-adv.* **stonily.**

stooge /studʒ/ *n.v.* **stooged, stooging, stooges 1** a person who acts like the stupid one with another comedian, *(syn.)* a straight man: *One man put a banana peel on the floor, and his stooge slipped on it.* **2** anyone who allows others to use him or her to their own advantage: *That guy is a stooge for his boss by agreeing to do anything for him.*

stool /stul/ *n.* **1** a three- or four-legged seat without a back: *She sat on a stool and ordered a beer.‖He stood on a stool to reach the high shelf.* **2** *frml.* solid bodily waste, a bowel movement: *The doctor tested a stool sample.*

stool pigeon *n.slang* s.o. who tells about another's wrongdoing, *(syn.)* a squealer: *That stool pigeon told the teacher we were passing notes in class.*

stoop /stup/ *v.* **1** to bend forward at the waist: *The farmer stooped over to pick up his baby.* **2** to walk or stand with the head and shoulders bent forward: *The old lady stoops.* **3** *phrasal v. insep.* **to stoop to s.t.:** to lower oneself to bad behavior, *(syn.)* to condescend: *The king will not stoop to apologize to the farmer.*
—n. **1** the act of bending forward with the head lowered: *to walk with a stoop* **2** the stairs or small porch in front of a house or building: *Our neighbors sit on the stoop in the evening.*

stop /stɑp/ *v.* **stopped, stopping, stops 1** to end a movement, halt: *I put on the brakes and the car stopped.* **2** to end an activity: *Stop eating; you've had enough.‖The bank stopped payment on a check.* **3** to fill in an opening, *(syn.)* to plug up: *to stop a leak in a pipe‖to stop up a hole* **4 to stop at nothing:** to do anything to reach a goal: *He wants to be president of the company and will stop at nothing to succeed.* **5** *phrasal v. insep.* **to stop at s.t.:** to pause in a trip: *The bus stops at the corner.* **6** *phrasal v. insep.* **to stop by s.t.:** to make a short, sometimes unannounced visit: *If you're in town, you should stop by our house for dinner.* **7 to stop (dead) in one's tracks:** to come to a halt and not move: *When the cop shouted, "Freeze!" I stopped dead in my tracks.* **8** *phrasal v.* **to stop in:** to visit for a short time: *Our friend was passing by and stopped in to say hi.* **9** *phrasal v. insep.* **to stop off** or **over in a place:** to interrupt a trip: *We were on our way to Hong Kong and stopped off in Hawaii for a few days.*
—n. **1** an end to motion, halt: *The train came to a stop.* **2** an end to activity: *There was a stop in work when lunchtime came.* **3** a place for stopping: *a bus stop* **4** a pause along a trip, a visit: *The truck makes stops at many*

stores.‖a stop at my cousin's apartment **5** a bank order not to pay a check **6** on a musical instrument, a hole one can cover **7** on an organ, a knob to pull to make a new or different sound **8 to put a stop to:** to end s.t.: *I put a stop to his nap when I woke him up.*

stop·gap /'stɑp,gæp/ *n.* a less-than-good solution to a problem, used until a better one can be found: *The loan is just a stopgap until I start earning money.*

stop·light /'stɑp,laɪt/ *n.* a traffic light: *Stop the car when the stoplight turns red.*

stop order *n.* an order to a stockbroker to buy or sell a security when a certain price is reached: *I bought 100 shares at $100 per share and put a stop order on the shares at $95.*

stop·o·ver /'stɑp,oʊvər/ *n.* a short visit in a longer journey: *to fly to Moscow with an overnight stopover in London*

stop·page /'stɑpɪdʒ/ *n.* a halt in an activity: *a work stoppage*

stop·per /'stɑpər/ *n.* a piece of plastic, metal, cork, or wood used to seal a container, *(syn.)* a plug: *She put a stopper in a perfume bottle.*

stop·watch /'stɑp,wɑtʃ/ *n.* a watch that can be stopped and started by pushing a button, used to time events: *A stopwatch timed the speed of the race horses.*

sto·rage /'stɔrɪdʒ/ *n.* [U] **1** a place (closet, warehouse, etc.) for keeping items until they are needed: *Our business puts old financial records in storage until tax time.* **2** the placement of these items: *My books are dusty from storage.*

store /stɔr/ *n.* **1** a place where things are bought and sold, a shop: *My friend worked in a grocery store in the fruit section.* **2** a supply, stock of s.t.: *Dad has a store of batteries in a drawer.* **3** *pl.* **stores:** supplies, esp. of food, clothing and weapons: *military stores* **4 in store:** about to happen (whether planned or not): *There is a big surprise in store for you.‖We do not know what the future has in store for us.* **5 to set store by:** to trust: *My friend is honest; you can set store by his promise. See:* shop, USAGE NOTE.
—v. **1** to keep somewhere for future use: *We store meat in a freezer downstairs.* **2** *phrasal v. insep.* **to store up on s.t.:** to collect a large amount: *We are storing up on oil for the winter. -n.* **storing.**

store·house /'stɔr,haʊs/ *n.* **1** a building where items are kept for future use, *(syn.)* a warehouse **2** *fig.* a great supply: *That professor is a storehouse of information about history.*

store·keep·er /'stɔr,kipər/ *n.* an owner of a store who also works there, a shopkeeper

store·room /'stɔr,rum/ *n.* a room where items are kept for present and future use: *The science*

S

department keeps its laboratory supplies in a storeroom.

storey *var. of.* story (2)

stor·ied /'stɔrid/ *adj.* well known, famous: *He has had a storied life with many adventures.*

stork /stɔrk/ *n.* a large bird with a long bill and long legs that likes to walk in or near water

storm /stɔrm/ *v.* **1** to rain or snow heavily, with strong winds: *We could not see across the street; it was storming so hard.* **2** to move in an angry way: *She stormed out of the office, shouting, "I quit!"* —*n.* heavy rain or snow with high winds: *The storm lasted all night and now the river is flooded.*

storm·y /'stɔrmi/ *adj.* **-ier, -iest** **1** related to a storm: *stormy weather* **2** angry, very emotional: *a stormy relationship between two people*

sto·ry (1) /'stɔri/ *n.* **-ries** **1** a piece of fiction (made up in one's mind; not true or real) written or told out loud, (*syn.*) a tale: *He read the child a story about a rabbit who talks.* **2** an actual event, written or told out loud: *My aunt told the story of her childhood in Mexico.||He read a newspaper story about a South African election.* **3** a written tale, usu. for adults *See:* short story. **4** a lie: *The boy says he lives in a big house with a swimming pool, but I think he's telling stories.* **5 that's the story of my life:** that's what always happens to me (a statement of self-pity): *Someone hit my car in a parking lot and drove away; that's the story of my life!* **6 to make a long story short:** to give a short description of a complicated event **7 what's the story?:** What is the situation now?: *You have been discussing the problem; what's the story? Do you have a solution?*

story or **storey (2)** *n.* a level of a building, (*syn.*) a floor: *Our house has three bedrooms on the second story.*

sto·ry·book /'stɔri,bʊk/ *n.* a fiction book for young children, usu. with lots of pictures and meant to be read aloud

sto·ry·tell·er /'stɔri,tɛlər/ *n.* a person who recites or acts out stories aloud

stout /staʊt/ *adj.* **1** slightly fat, (*syns.*) portly, plump: *The stout man filled the whole chair.* **2** strong, brave: *a stout traveler* **3** a very dark, thick beer: *Many Irish pubs serve stout.*

stove /stoʊv/ *n.* **1** a piece of kitchen equipment, with electric or gas burners, usu. containing an oven, used to cook food: *Please turn down the heat on the stove or the soup will burn.* **2** a place to burn wood, coal, or gas for warmth *See:* oven.

stow /stoʊ/ *v.* to put s.t. away: *She stowed her books in her locker.*

stow·a·way /'stoʊə,weɪ/ *n.* a person who hides on a ship, train, etc. to get a free ride (usu. on a long trip)

strad·dle /'strædl/ *v.* **-dled, -dling, -dles** **1** to put one's leg on either side of s.t.: *to straddle a horse when riding it* **2 to straddle the fence:** to see both sides of a problem, to have trouble making a decision: *He cannot make up his mind whether or not to buy the new computer; he is straddling the fence.*

strag·gle /'strægəl/ *v.* **-gled, -gling, -gles** to move a bit slower and in a more disorganized way than the rest of a group: *The new soldiers straggled behind the neat lines.* *-n.* **straggler.**

straight /streɪt/ *adj.* **-er, -est** **1** going in the form of a line without bending or curving: *a straight ruler* **2** direct, clear: *a straight answer to a question* **3** continuous, without interruption: *The storm lasted for three straight days.* **4** obeying rules and laws, not wild or risk-taking: *The straight woman has never been in debt.* **5** not homosexual, (*syn.*) heterosexual **6** not taking or under the effects of drugs or alcohol **7** without water added (to a drink of liquor): *straight gin* **8** honest, truthtelling: *Be straight with me; do you like this haircut?* **9 with a straight face:** without showing expression or emotion: *He can't keep a straight face when he hears a funny joke.* —*adv.* **1** with no water added: *to drink vodka straight* **2** not bending, (*syns.*) erect, upright: *to stand straight* **3** without stopping: *I went straight to the bank when I got paid.* **4** honestly: *Tell me straight.* —*n.* **1** (in cards) five cards in numerical order **2 to walk the straight and narrow:** to follow and respect rules and laws: *The judge warned the criminal to walk the straight and narrow from now on.*

straight·en /'streɪtn/ *v.* **1** to make straight, even: *The worker straightened a bent wire.||He was leaning over, then he straightened.* **2** to make neat and orderly: *She straightened her messy closet.* **3** *phrasal v. sep.* **to straighten s.o.** or **s.t. out:** **a. s.o.:** to help s.o. become a better-behaved person: *When he was young, he drank too much, but his wife has straightened him out.* **b. s.t.:** to solve problems, come to understand: *We are straightening the details out.||We are straightening them out.* **4** *phrasal v.* **to straighten up:** **a.** to behave better: *You kids straighten up or we won't go out for ice cream.* **b.** to make neat and orderly: *The place was a mess after the party, so I straightened up.*

straight·for·ward /streɪt'fɔrwərd/ *adj.* **1** clear, direct, without complications: *Your directions for changing a tire were straightforward; it was easy!* **2** direct, honest: *A straightforward person is easy to do business with.*

S

straight·jacket /'streɪt,dʒækɪt/ *n. var. of* straitjacket

strain /streɪn/ *v.* **1** to use great effort: *I strained to lift a heavy box.*||*The singer strained to hit a high note.* **2** to cause tension and disagreement: *She married s.o. of a different religion, and that strained her relationship with her parents.* **3** to stretch a part of one's body until there is pain or damage: *I strained a muscle in my back playing baseball.* **4** to separate s.t. from s.t. else by passing or pouring it through holes: *She strained ocean water and was left with sand and shells. n.*
—*n.* **1** [C;U] difficulty, pressure: *It was a strain on her finances to buy a new TV.* **2** [C] anger, tension: *There is a strain in my relationship with my brother.* **3** [C] injury: *a strain in my neck* **4** [C] species, type: *a new strain of disease -adj.* **strained.**

strain·er /'streɪnər/ *n.* a tool, usu. in a kitchen, used to separate liquids and solids: *He put the tomatoes through a strainer to remove the skin and seeds.*

strait /streɪt/ *n.* **1** a narrow area of water joining two larger areas of water: *the Straits of Hormuz between the Persian Gulf and the Gulf of Oman* **2** *fig.* **in dire straits:** in great trouble, with many problems: *Both he and his wife are ill and have lost their jobs: they are in dire straits.*

strait·jack·et or **straight·jack·et** /'streɪt ,dʒækɪt/ *n.* a type of jacket with long sleeves that can be attached to the body in order to keep the person wearing it from becoming violent

strait·laced /'streɪt,leɪst/ *adj.* never doing anything wrong, (*syns.*) conventional, prim: *My straightlaced daughter does all her homework and goes to bed early.*

strand /strænd/ *v.* to leave s.o. helpless, often without transportation: *The bus broke down on a country road and we were left stranded there for three hours.*||*When the man stole her purse, she was stranded in London with no money.*
—*n.* **1** long, thin piece of s.t.: *a strand of hair*||*a strand of woolen yarn* **2** land next to a body of water, (*syn.*) a beach: *From our boat, the strand was a brown line in the distance.*

strange /streɪndʒ/ *adj.* **-er, -est** **1** unusual, out of the ordinary: *The girl picked a strange and beautiful flower.* **2** difficult to understand, (*syns.*) odd, peculiar: *We find it strange that your child doesn't like toys.* **3** unfamiliar, unknown: *His accent is strange to me; where is he from?* -*n.* [U] **strangeness.**

strang·er /'streɪndʒər/ *n.* **1** an unfamiliar person, s.o. new to a place: *A stranger on the street asked for directions to the highway.* **2** a person who doesn't know, is not familiar with s.t.: *My friend from Florida is a stranger to life in cold climates.*

stran·gle /'stræŋgəl/ *v.* **-gled, -gling, -gles** to kill or harm by squeezing the throat, so no air can get through, (*syn.*) to choke, throttle: *The murderer strangled the man by pressing his throat with his hands.* -*v.* **strangulate** /'stræŋ gyə,leɪt/; -*n.* [U] **strangulation.**

stran·gle·hold /'stræŋgəl,hould/ *n.* **1** a death grip, a grip of hands about the throat: *The fighter had a stranglehold on his opponent.* **2** *fig.* a force or power that prevents freedom or movement: *The queen had a stranglehold on the country's land; she owned it all.*

strap /stræp/ *n.* **1** a long, narrow piece of material, such as leather or cloth: *She tied the horse to the fence with a strap.* **2** a loop: *Standing on the bus, he stood and held a strap so he wouldn't fall.*
—*v.* to attach or hold s.o. or s.t.: *She strapped herself into the car with a seat belt.*

strap·less /'stræplɪs/ *adj.* (of women's clothing) with no sleeves or straps, leaving the shoulders bare: *a strapless dress (slip, bra)*

strapped /stræpt/ *adj.infrml.* with little or no money: *Can you lend me a few bucks? I'm really strapped tonight.*

strap·ping /'stræpɪŋ/ *adj.* tall and strong: *Our little boy grew into a strapping, athletic teenager.*

stra·ta /'streɪtə, 'stræ-/ *n.pl.* of stratum

stra·te·gy /'strætədʒi/ *n.* **1** [U] (in the military) planning actions in preparation for war or battle: *The navy's strategy was to move their ships into open sea during the night.* **2** [C;U] planning in order to achieve a goal: *Our company's strategy is to make good products while keeping prices lower than the competition.* -*adj.* **strategic;** /strə'tidʒɪk/ -*n.* **strategist.**

strat·i·fi·ca·tion /,strætəfə'keɪʃən/ *n.* [U] an instance of geologic or social stratifying See: stratify.

strat·i·fy /'strætə,faɪ/ *v.* **-fied, -fying, -fies** **1** to form in layers: *The different-colored rocks have stratified over millions of years.* **2** to go into or form different levels (based on money, education, etc.): *That city is stratified into rich and poor neighborhoods.*

strat·o·sphere /'strætə,sfɪr/ *n.* [U] the layer of the sky approx. 5.5 (9 km) to 20 miles (32 km) above the earth

stra·tum /'streɪtəm, 'stræ-/ *n.* [C] **-ta** a layer or level: *Our science class looked at the strata of different-colored rock on the side of the mountain.*||*My parents want me to marry someone from a wealthier stratum of society.*

straw /strɔ/ *n.* **1** [U] dried grain stems without the grain, used for animal beds and for weaving mats, hats, and baskets: *We put clean straw in the pigpen.*||*She bought a straw hat from an island woman.* **2** [C] a thin tube of plastic or strong paper, used to draw a drink into the

S

mouth: *She took a sip of cola through a straw.*
3 *fig.* **the last straw** or **the straw that broke the camel's back:** the final event, the last difficulty one can bear: *My husband's affair with another woman was the last straw, so I divorced him.* **4** *fig.* **to grasp at straws:** to base one's hopes on only vague possibilities: *She is grasping at straws by applying for a teaching job; she needs much more education.*

straw·ber·ry /'strɔ,bɛri/ *n.* **-ries** a small, red, sweet fruit with tiny seeds, high in vitamin C

strawberries

stray /streɪ/ *v.* **1** to go beyond the limits of an area: *Our dog strayed into a neighbor's yard.* **2** to do bad or illegal things, to follow the wrong path in life: *Their daughter has strayed: she left school and started using drugs.*
—*n.* a lost, tame animal: *a stray cat*
—*adj.* not with a larger group of s.t., separate: *A few stray hairs blew into her face in the wind.*

streak /strik/ *v.* **1** to move or run very fast: *The speedboat streaked by and was across the lake in seconds.* **2** to make marks or stains in the form of lines, (*syns.*) to smear, blur: *The windshield is so streaked with dirt that I can't see the road.*
—*n.* **1** a mark or stain in the form of a line, (*syns.*) a smear, blur: *Let the ink dry, or it will make streaks when you touch it.* **2** a period of time in which s.t. continues to happen: *I'm on a lucky streak: I found $5 on the street, got no bills in the mail, and won a free pizza!* **3** a part of one's personality, (*syn.*) a trait: *She seems nice, but when you know her longer, you'll see her mean streak.* -*n.* [U] **streaking;** -*adj.* **streaky.**

stream /strim/ *n.* **1** a flowing body of water, smaller than a river: *They had a picnic near a stream that ran down the mountain.* **2** liquid moving steadily, without separating: *a stream of water from the garden hose* **3** a lot of s.t., coming one right after another: *A stream of angry words came from Mom's mouth.*
—*v.* to flow like a stream: *People streamed into the train station.*

stream·line /'strim,laɪn/ *v.* **-lined, -lining, -lines** **1** to make s.t. smooth and without rough edges: *The auto maker streamlined the cars by rounding the corners and curving flat surfaces.* **2** to make s.t. simpler and more efficient: *We cut out five steps in our billing process; we streamlined it.* -*adj.* **streamlined.**

street /strit/ *n.* **1** a road for cars and trucks, often with sidewalks for walkers: *The car turned right on Washington Street.‖He walked down the street. See:* avenue, boulevard, road.

2 *pl.fig.* **streets:** a term for big-city dangers, such as crime: *Unfortunately, the young boy understands the life of the streets.‖She will be out on the streets if she doesn't find a job by next week.*

USAGE NOTE: We usu. speak of *streets* in the city and *roads* in both the country and city: *The streets were crowded with shoppers.‖My car almost hit a dog that was crossing the road.* A *lane* is a narrow way, often between houses, walls, or fences. A *court* is a short street. A *cul-de-sac* is a road closed at one end, often with houses built around a small circle of pavement. An *avenue* is a wide street, often but not always lined with trees: *Fifth Avenue is one of New York City's most famous streets.* A *boulevard* is a broad, tree-lined avenue, which may have a central island dividing the lanes of traffic: *Hollywood Boulevard is lined with palm trees.* These terms are sometimes used incorrectly in naming streets, often because s.o. simply likes the way they sound.

street·car /'strit,kar/ *n.* a piece of public transportation like a subway, but traveling aboveground, (*syn.*) a trolley car; *We rode the streetcars while we were in San Francisco.*

street·light /'strit,laɪt/ *n.* a light on a tall pole to make a section of a street less dark at night

street·walk·er /'strit,wɔkər/ *n.* a person who sells sex for money, finding business on the street, (*syn.*) a prostitute

strength /strɛŋkθ, strɛnθ/ *n.* **1** [U] muscle power: *I don't have the strength to move that table alone.* **2** [U] mental or emotional toughness, (*syns.*) fortitude, courage: *She has the strength to help us with our problems.* **3** [U] not able to be gone through or broken, power, toughness: *the strength of a heavy wooden door* **4** [C;U] an activity at which one is skilled or talented: *Art is not one of her strengths.* **5** [U] the quality of not being weakened with water or another substance, (*syn.*) potency: *the strength of one aspirin‖the strength of vodka with no ice* **6 on the strength of:** by the force of: *She is remaining quiet on the strength of your suggestion. See:* strong.

strengthen /'strɛŋkθən, 'strɛnθ-/ *v.* to make or become stronger: *The company has strengthened its position with new advertisements.‖Exercising every day strengthens the heart.*

stren·u·ous /'strɛnyuəs/ *adj.* needing great effort: *Running fast is strenuous exercise.*

strep throat /strɛp/ *n.* a sore throat caused by the streptococcus virus

stress /strɛs/ *n.* [C;U] **-es** **1** mental or physical strain or difficulty caused by pressure: *She is full of stress because her boss gives her too*

much work. **2** strength given or put on s.t., (*syn.*) emphasis: *In our family, the stress is on a good education.*
—*v.* **-es 1** to give strength to, (*syn.*) to emphasize: *Her husband stressed the idea that she should change jobs and relax more.* **2** to cause pressure: *Lifting these boxes has stressed my back.*

stressed or **stressed out** /strɛst/ *adj.infrml.* tired and worried: *I'm stressed out by my sister's drinking problem.*

stress·ful /ˈstrɛsfəl/ *adj.* causing worry and tension: *He is a policeman in a dangerous area; he leads a very stressful life.*

stretch /strɛtʃ/ *v.* **-es 1** to make wider, longer, or larger by pushing outward or pulling: *If I wear my new shoes for a while, the leather will stretch.* **2** to make a body part longer by reaching out or (*syn.*) extending that part: *The cat stretched after her nap.‖The man stretched his leg muscles by touching his toes.* **3** to go off for a long way, (*syn.*) to extend: *The highway stretches for many miles to the west.* **4** to make s.t. larger, to fill available space or time: *I didn't have much meat, so I stretched the soup with vegetables.* **5** to go beyond the limits of, to bend: *You're stretching the truth when you say your sister knows lots of movie stars.*
—*n.* **-es 1** [C] the act of pushing outward or pulling to make larger: *the stretch of a telephone cord* **2** [C] an unbroken area, (*syn.*) an expanse: *After a long, dry stretch of land, we reached a small lake.* **3** [U] the ability to get larger or wider: *socks with a lot of stretch* **4** *infrml.* s.t. that is difficult to do or believe: *They may believe that you are 21, but it will be a stretch, since you're 30.* -*n.* [U] **stretching.**

stretch·er /ˈstrɛtʃər/ *n.* a piece of hospital equipment used to carry patients who are lying down: *He had a heart attack and was carried to the ambulance in a stretcher.*

strew /stru/ *v.* **strewed, strewn, strewing, strews** to throw or place things about in a messy way, (*syn.*) to scatter: *He is strewing dirty clothes all over his bedroom floor.* -*adj.* **strewn** /strun/.

strick·en /ˈstrɪkən/ *adj.& past part. of* strike, **1** ill or troubled by s.t.: *The poor lady was stricken with cancer.* **2** taken out, (*syn.*) eliminated: *A witness's comment was stricken from the court record.*

strict /strɪkt/ *adj.* **-er, -est 1** expecting rules to be followed, requiring obedience, (*syns.*) stern, severe: *The strict teacher makes us stay after school if we don't do our homework.* **2** unchanging, exact: *There is no one strict way to play the piano; different people have different methods.* -*adv.* **strictly;** -*n.* [U] **strictness.**

stride /straɪd/ *v.* **strode** /stroʊd/, **stridden** /strɪdn/, **striding, strides** to walk strongly

with long steps: *The president strode across the White House lawn to the helicopter.*
—*n.* **1** a long step **2** the walking or running motion of a person or animal: *The horse's stride was smooth and graceful.* **3 to make strides:** to go forward, make progress: *The company has made great strides in recent years, with increased sales and excellent profits.* **4 to take s.t. in one's stride:** to accept s.t. easily, to not be upset or bothered by: *My daughter hates to go to the dentist, but my son takes it in stride.*

stri·dent /ˈstraɪdnt/ *adj.* loud and unpleasant, (*syns.*) harsh, shrill: *I could hear her angry, strident voice from next door.*

strife /straɪf/ *n.* [U] angry disagreement, (*syn.*) conflict: *There was bitter strife between the warring nations.*

strike /straɪk/ *v.* **struck** /strʌk/, **struck** or **stricken** /ˈstrɪkən/, **striking, strikes 1** to hit hard: *She struck her brother and gave him a bloody nose.‖The hammer struck the nail.* **2** to run into, (*syn.*) to collide with: *The car rolled down the hill and struck a tree.* **3** to attack: *The army struck by surprise at night.* **4** to happen or appear suddenly: *A good idea struck me as I was reading the newspaper.* **5** to have an effect on, to affect: *The power of her words struck me.* **6** to find suddenly, discover: *The workers will strike oil if they dig deep enough.* **7** to take away, (*syns.*) to erase, eliminate: *Strike the second paragraph, but leave the first and third.* **8** to stop working because of disagreements with management: *The bus drivers are striking until the owners give them more vacation time.* **9** to make fire or light by hitting or rubbing: *to strike a match* **10** to make a note or sound: *He struck a C-sharp on the piano.‖The clock is striking midnight.* **11 to strike a balance:** (for two different or opposite things) to reach a comfortable, satisfactory agreement or position: *The painter struck a balance between bright, sharp colors and soft, blurred lines.* **12 to strike a bargain** or **deal:** to reach an agreement that is acceptable to both sides: *Let's strike a deal: I'll let you borrow my bike if you wash my car.* **13 to strike a pose:** to go into a position and be still (for an artist, photographer, etc.): *The little girl struck a pose and her dad took a picture.* **14** *phrasal v. sep.* **to strike s.t. down:** (in law) to make no longer effective: *The Supreme Court struck down an earlier decision in a rape case.‖They struck it down.* **15 to strike gold** or **it rich:** to get a lot of money quickly or unexpectedly: *The writer struck it rich with her first successful novel.‖You may strike gold if you play the lottery.* **16** *phrasal v. sep.* **to strike s.o. off:** to remove s.o.'s name from a list or official panel, group, etc.: *The steering committee struck off three members.‖They struck them*

S

off. **17** *phrasal v. sep.* **to strike s.t. out: a.** to cross out, (*syn.*) to erase: *Please strike out the second line and type a new one.* **b.** to begin a trip or journey: *We will strike out on our walk at 6:00 A.M.* **c. to strike out (on one's own):** to begin to do s.t. alone: *After working for a big shoe company for years, he is striking out on his own and opening a shoe store.* **d.** (in baseball) not to get on base, either by swinging and missing, fouling, or choosing not to swing at good pitches **18 to strike s.o. as:** to seem to s.o.: *He strikes me as really stupid.*‖*I'm surprised she left; she struck me as a person who would stay.* **19** *phrasal v. sep.* **to strike up s.t.: a.** to begin playing music: *The band struck up a lively dance tune.* **b.** to begin (speaking): *The old friends struck up a conversation about high school.* **20** *fig.* **to strike while the iron is hot:** to act quickly while the situation is good: *Dad is happy and relaxed and just got paid; let's strike while the iron is hot and ask if we can use the car. See:* struck.
—*n.* **1** a hard hit: *the strike of metal on metal* **2** a discovery of s.t. valuable: *a gold strike* **3** a work stoppage because of disagreements with management: *During the strike, workers carried signs that read, "Better pay, shorter day!"* **4** (in baseball) a swing with the bat that misses the ball, a good pitch at which the batter doesn't swing, or the first two foul balls hit **5** (in bowling) knocking over all 10 pins with the first roll of the ball **6 to have two strikes against s.o.:** (from baseball): to be at a disadvantage, with few solutions or choices left: *The baby started life with two strikes against her; her mother is a poor drug addict and her father is unknown.*

striker /ˈstraɪkər/ *n.* a worker who won't work because of disagreements with the employer: *Strikers walked in a circle near the factory gate.*

striking /ˈstraɪkɪŋ/ *adj.* immediately noticeable, usu. in a positive or good sense: *She is a striking woman, quite beautiful.*‖*There is a striking difference between this year's cool, dry summer and last year's warm, wet summer.*

string /strɪŋ/ *n.* **1** [C;U] a rope-like cord: *We wrapped the box and tied a string around it.* **2** [C] a series of related or similar events: *a string of successes in business* **3** [C] a line of objects with a string pulled through them: *a string of pearls (seashells, beads, etc.)* **4** [C] (in sports) a group within a team that have similar skills: *He is not the best player; he is on the second string.* **5** [C] (in music) on certain instruments, such as guitars and violins, one thin cord that is pulled (plucked) or rubbed (bowed) to make a sound **6** *pl.* **strings:** (in music) the instruments in the violin family (violin, viola, cello, bass fiddle, etc.) **7** (a gift with) **no strings attached:** without needing to pay back or do s.t. for the giver of a gift,

able to use a gift however one chooses: *My uncle gave me $500 with no strings attached, so I am saving half and spending half on new clothes.* **8** *fig.* **to pull strings:** to use influence: *The senator pulled strings to get his son a job in the government.* **9** *fig.* **to pull the strings:** to be in control, (*syn.*) to dominate: *In that company, it's the president who pulls the strings.*
—*v.* **strung** /strʌŋ/, **stringing, strings 1** to put a string or strings on a musical instrument: *to string a banjo* **2** to thread (put a string through): *I strung some red and black beads for a necklace.* **3** to attach s.t. at two ends: *to string wires from pole to pole* **4** *phrasal v. sep.* **to string s.t. out:** to delay s.t. on purpose: *The lawyer says to do one thing, we do it; then he says to do it over again; he has strung out the situation for months.*‖*He has strung it out.* **5** *phrasal v. sep.* **to string s.o. along:** to delay and mislead s.o.: *She strings her boyfriend along; she says that she'll marry him, but never will.* **6** *phrasal v. sep.* **to string s.o. up:** to hang s.o. by the neck: *In the old movie, cattle ranchers strung the three men up for stealing cows.*‖*They strung them up.*

string bean *n.* **1** a long, green bean **2** *infrml.fig.* a tall, thin person

strin·gent /ˈstrɪndʒənt/ *adj.* without much freedom of flexibility, (*syns.*) severe, strict: *The company is losing money and must have a stringent financial plan to survive.* -*n.* [U] **stringency.**

string beans.

string·er /ˈstrɪŋər/ *n.* a part-time or freelance worker: *The sales department hires only stringers and has no full-time salespeople.*

strip /strɪp/ *n.* a thin, narrow piece of s.t.: *a strip of bacon (cloth, leather, tape, etc.)*
—*v.* **stripped** or **stript, stripping, strips 1** to remove an outer layer: *to strip wallpaper off the wall* **2** to take away (power, rank, things, etc.): *He stripped leaves off a tree branch.*‖*The king was stripped of his power and became an ordinary citizen.* **3** to take off one's clothes: *The boys stripped off their shirts and jumped into the pool.*

stripe /straɪp/ *n.v.* **striped, striping, stripes 1** a band of color against a background of a different color: *a pink <n.> stripe on a white blouse* **2** a V-shaped decoration on the uniform of a soldier to show rank **3** type, sort, kind: *My second husband is of a different <n.> stripe than my first.*

strip·ed /straɪpt, ˈstraɪpɪd/ *adj.* having stripes: *a striped tablecloth*

strip·per /ˈstrɪpər/ *n.* a person who takes off his or her clothes as a performance, with music playing and people watching

strip·tease /'strɪp,tiz/ n. [C;U] **-teased, -teasing, -teases** the dance or performance of a stripper

strive /straɪv/ v. **strove** /strouv/, **striven** /'strɪvən/ or **strived, striving, strives** to work hard for s.t.: *to strive for perfection* -n. **striver.**

stroke /strouk/ v. **stroked, stroking, strokes** to pass the hand lightly over s.t., (*syns.*) to rub, caress: *He stroked the cat's back.*||*I like to stroke a baby's soft cheek.*
—n. [C] **1** a light rubbing motion: *one stroke of my hand* **2** a motion of a body part from one position to another, done in a sport to move or hit s.t.: *The people in the boat used smooth strokes, saying "One, two" as they rowed.*||*The golf teacher said his stroke was strong.* **3** the hitting or sound of a bell, gong, or clock: *At the stroke of two, begin writing.* **4** one mark with a writing tool: *She used four strokes of a pen to make an E.* **5** a sudden, immediate event: *By a stroke of luck, you appeared just when my car broke down.* **6** a blocked or broken blood vessel in the brain that causes a lack of muscle control, difficulty speaking, and sometimes death, (*syn.*) apoplexy

stroll /stroul/ n.v. a relaxed, unhurried walk: *After dinner, we went for a <n.> stroll on the beach. See:* walk, USAGE NOTE.

stroll·er /'stroulər/ n. **1** a person who walks in a slow, relaxed manner **2** a chair with four wheels used to hold and push a baby: *The boy's mother pushed his stroller into the mall.*

strong /strɔŋ/ adj. **1** having physical strength: *A strong man helped me push the car up the hill.* **2** with mental or moral strength, (*syn.*) unwavering: *She has stayed strong through much sadness in her life.* **3** in good health: *If you take your medicine, you will become stronger.* **4** having force, intensity, or strength: *She has a strong belief in God.* **5** able to be easily sensed, (*syn.*) potent: *the strong smell of onions and garlic* **6** with a lot of alcohol: *There's too much gin in this drink; it's too strong.* -adv. **strongly.**

strong-arm v.adj. to use physical force or threats to make s.o. do s.t., (*syn.*) to coerce: *If she doesn't pay him the money soon, he will <v.> strong-arm her into paying it.*||*The policeman used <adj.> strong-arm tactics with the man.*

strong·box /'strɔŋ,bɑks/ n. **-es** a locked, secure box for valuable items, (*syn.*) a safety deposit box: *I keep my grandmother's ring in a strongbox in the bank.*

strong·hold /'strɔŋ,hould/ n. an area where a group has a lot of strength: *The US South is a stronghold for the Baptist religion.*

strong-minded adj. firm and sure in one's ideas, (*syn.*) willful: *She knows what she wants and is strong-minded about getting it.*

struck /strʌk/ adj. & past part. of strike, hit by: *struck by lightning*||*struck by an idea See:* stricken.

struc·ture /'strʌktʃər/ n. **1** [C] a building of any kind: *A new structure is being built on the corner.* **2** [C] any architectural object of any kind: *The Eiffel Tower is a famous Parisian structure.* **3** [U] the way parts are put together or organized: *the structure of a song*||*a business's structure*
—v. **-tured, -turing, -tures** to put together or organize parts of s.t.: *We are structuring a plan to hire new teachers.* -adj. **structural.**

struc·tured /'strʌktʃərd/ adj. organized, logical: *My child has a structured day: he goes to day care, we pick him up, we have dinner and play, and he goes to bed.*

strug·gle /'strʌgəl/ n. **1** a difficult time or task using much effort and energy: *He has had a struggle all his life with bad health.* **2** a conflict or war: *a struggle between Croats and Serbs* **3** a fight: *Two men got into a struggle outside a bar.* **4** a use of physical force or energy to try to do s.t.: *It is a struggle to zip up these tight jeans.*
—v. **-gled, -gling, -gles** to use much physical or mental effort and energy to do s.t.: *I struggled to reach the seat belt behind me.*

strum /strʌm/ v. **strummed, strumming, strums** to play a stringed musical instrument by moving one's fingertips over the strings: *He strummed the guitar.*

strung out /strʌŋ/ adj. **1** lasting for too long: *The planning has strung out for months; now it is time to act.* **2** slang badly affected by drug use: *He is too strung out to work; he can barely walk.*

strut /strʌt/ v. **strutted, strutting, struts** to walk in a proud or self-important way: *The boy strutted around town with the pretty girl holding his arm.*
—n. **1** the movement or act of walking proudly: *The rooster had a proud strut.* **2** a wood or metal support against a structure: *the struts that held up a crumbling wall*

stub /stʌb/ n. **1** the part of a ticket kept as proof of purchase: *The man at the show tore my ticket in two and handed me the stub.* **2** a short piece of s.t. broken or used: *This eraser is worn down to a stub.*
—v. **stubbed, stubbing, stubs** to hit one's foot on s.t.: *I stubbed my toes on the stairs.*

stub·ble /'stʌbəl/ n. [U] **1** the short pieces of grain (corn, wheat, etc.) in a field after the grain has been cut **2** a short growth of hair, (*syn.*) whiskers: *He has not shaved today and his face is covered with stubble.*

stub·born /'stʌbərn/ adj. **1** unwilling to change one's mind, (*syns.*) obstinate, willful: *My stubborn little boy would not put his coat on; he held his arms to his sides and said,*

S

"No, no." **2** continuing to do s.t. even if it is difficult, *(syn.)* persistent: *My sister won't ever stop trying to sell her paintings; she is very stubborn.*

stuck /stʌk/ *adj. & past part. of* stick, *infrml.* **1** unable to continue: *I am stuck on this problem; I can't figure it out.* **2 to be stuck on s.o.:** in love with or having romantic feelings for: *My brother is really stuck on that girl; he's asked her out for coffee three times.* **3 to be stuck with s.o.** or **s.t.:** to have s.o. or s.t. one doesn't really want: *I bought a used car that does not run very well, and now I'm stuck with it.*

stuck-up *adj.* thinking one is better than others, *(syn.)* conceited: *The stuck-up boy won't date poor girls.*

stud /stʌd/ *n.* **1** a male animal, esp. a horse that is used to father other fine horses **2** *slang* a very masculine, sexy man **3** a piece of wood in a vertical (up-and-down) position that is used to support a wall: *He nailed a piece of wallboard to the stud.* **4** a decorative button on a tuxedo shirt **5** a small earring made for a pierced ear that doesn't hang below the earlobe

stud·ded /ˈstʌdɪd/ *adj.* **1** decorated with studs (stones, gems, etc.): *Her new earrings are studded with pearls.* **2 star-studded:** with many famous people (usu. actors and singers) present: *My cousin went to a star-studded Hollywood party.*

stu·dent /ˈstudnt/ *n.* **1** a person who learns from teachers or professors at any school, college, or university: *She is a high-school student and will start college next fall.* **2** a person who studies s.t. seriously, in or out of school: *a student of football*

stud·ied /ˈstʌdid/ *adj.* well thought out, *(syns.)* informed, prepared: *He is good at discussing films because he has a very studied way of watching them.*

stu·di·o /ˈstudioʊ/ *n.* **1** a place where an artist works: *We take lessons at a ballet studio.‖He develops black-and-white pictures in his photo studio.* **2** a one-room apartment: *My studio is too small; I'm moving to a one-bedroom.*

stu·di·ous /ˈstudiəs/ *adj.* liking or tending to study: *I see a studious young woman in the library every day.*

stud·y /ˈstʌdi/ *n.* **-ies** **1** a room in a living space for reading, writing, and other quiet activities: *Her study is filled with books.* **2** the act of learning: *the study of foreign languages* **3** a report on a specific topic: *a governmental study on poverty* **4 a fast** or **quick study:** a person who learns s.t. easily in a short time: *The actor is a quick study; he knew all his lines in one week.*
—*v.* **-ied, -ying, -ies** **1** to work to learn, by practicing, reading, and listening: *She studied*

for the math test.‖*He studies African history.* **2** to look at carefully, *(syn.)* to examine: *I study the chessboard carefully before I make a move.*

stuff /stʌf/ *v.* **1** to fill, usu. tightly or completely, by pushing s.t. into s.t. else: *She stuffed her notebooks into a desk drawer.‖I am going to stuff this toy doll with cotton.* **2** to eat too much: *He stuffed himself with bread and cheese.*
—*n.* [U] **1** a general word for unnamed or unknown things: *There's some old, smelly stuff in the back of the refrigerator.‖What's that stuff you're rubbing on your hands?* **2** *infrml.* a group of objects: *She's moving to a smaller house, so she's giving away some of her stuff.* **3** what s.o. or s.t. is made of, *(syns.)* character, ability: *You are showing the right stuff: kindness and patience.* **4** unwanted talk or actions: *Stop yelling at me; I don't need that stuff from you.*

stuffed shirt *n.* a person who is very formal, with too-proper manners: *What a stuffed shirt; he spent the whole dinner telling us what fork to use!*

stuff·ing /ˈstʌfɪŋ/ *n.* [U] s.t. used to fill s.t. tightly: *the foam stuffing in a cushion‖the bread stuffing in a turkey*

stuff·y /ˈstʌfi/ *adj.* **-ier, -iest** **1** without fresh air: *The windows are closed and everyone is smoking cigarettes; the air is stuffy.* **2** formal, *(syn.)* pompous: *He is too stuffy to enjoy the clowns at the circus. -n.* [U] **stuffiness.**

stum·ble /ˈstʌmbəl/ *v.* **-bled, -bling, -bles** **1** to trip or have trouble walking: *The man was hurt and stumbled into the police station for help.‖She is stumbling because she drank too much beer.* **2** to have trouble speaking, *(syn.)* to falter: *The shy boy is stumbling over his words.* **3** *phrasal v. insep.* **to stumble across** or **upon s.t.:** to find or reach accidentally or by surprise: *She stumbled upon the book she lost last week.*
—*n.* the act of walking or speaking with difficulty

stum·bling block /ˈstʌmblɪŋ/ *n.* s.t. in the way, *(syn.)* an obstacle: *He wants to take a vacation, but lack of money is a stumbling block.*

stump /stʌmp/ *n.* **1** the part of a tree left after it has fallen or been cut: *She sat on a stump in the woods to rest.* **2** a body part, most of which has been cut off or worn down: *He had bone cancer in his arm, so the doctors removed his arm, leaving a stump.‖the stump of a tooth*
—*v.* **1** to travel and try to get votes: *The president's wife is stumping for him throughout the western states.* **2** to cause s.o. to be without an answer, *(syn.)* to baffle: *The student was stumped by the difficult question.*

stun /stʌn/ *v.* **stunned, stunning, stuns** **1** to make unconscious or senseless, *(syn.)* to daze: *When I hit my head, the bump <v.> stunned me* *and I fell to the floor.* **2** to surprise or shock, to make speechless: *The news of your friend's death <v.> stunned me.*

stun·ning /'stʌnɪŋ/ *adj.* **1** very beautiful: *a stunning dress* **2** very surprising: *a stunning loss*

stung /stʌŋ/ *past tense & past part. of* sting

stunt /stʌnt/ *n.* **1** a difficult or dangerous action: *The man did a stunt where he rode a motorcycle up a ramp and over 20 parked cars.* **2 to pull a stunt:** to do s.t. foolish, often to attract attention: *The young man took his father's car and drove it into a lake; he often pulls stunts like that!*
—*v.* to stop or slow the growth of s.t.: *These small ears of corn were stunted because no rain fell for weeks.*

stunt·man /'stʌnt,mæn/ or **stunt·wom·an** /'stʌnt,wʊmən/ *n.* **-men** /-,mɛn/, **-women** /-,wɪmən/ in the movie business, a person who does dangerous or difficult acts, such as falling off a horse or jumping from a moving car

stu·pe·fy /'stupə,faɪ/ *v.* **-fied, -fying, -fies** **1** to make s.o. senseless: *drugs that stupefy the mind* **2** *fig.* to surprise, (*syns.*) to shock, astound: *He was stupefied by the changes in her face after many years.* -*adj.* **stupefied.**

stu·pen·dous /stu'pɛndəs/ *adj.* **1** very big, huge, (*syn.*) tremendous: *We saw stupendous, snow-covered mountains in Switzerland.* **2** amazing, awesome: *The new dinosaur movie is a stupendous success.* -*adv.* **stupendously.**

stu·pid /'stupɪd/ *adj.* **1** not smart, (*syns.*) dumb, dull: *He makes the same mistakes over and over; he is so stupid!* **2** not using one's brain or logic, foolish: *It was a stupid thing for her to leave her car keys in the car; it was stolen!* **3** worthless: *This book is so stupid, I don't want to finish it.* -*n.* [U] **stupidity.**

stu·por /'stupər/ *n.* [U] a state of senselessness, a complete lack of mental power: *The drunken man fell to the floor in a stupor.*

stur·dy /'stɜrdi/ *adj.* **-dier, -diest** **1** strong, well-built: *He can walk for miles on his sturdy legs.* **2** strong, lasting, (*syn.*) durable: *I bought this sturdy pair of shoes many years ago.*

stut·ter /'stʌtər/ *n.* a problem with speaking in which the person repeats words or pauses, and has difficulty getting thoughts into spoken words -*n.* **stutterer.**
—*v.* to speak with a stutter *See:* stammer.

style /staɪl/ *n.* **1** [C;U] the particular way that s.t. is done: *Her writing style is very simple and clear.* **2** [C;U] sort, kind, type: *What style of food does the restaurant serve?* **3** [U] good, special, often unusual behavior: *She is kind, generous, and enjoys doing new things; we like her style.* **4** [U] a comfortable way of living, often with plenty of money and nice things: *We had to stop living in style when my*

wife lost her high-paying job. **5** [C;U] fashion, the way of dressing or appearing: *I like the styles of the 1940s, with longer skirts and wide shoulders.* **6 a. in style:** popular at that time: *My mom's old clothes are in style again!* **b. out of style:** not popular at that time: *Big band music is out of style, but I still enjoy it.* **7** [C] the way one uses punctuation and words in writing or printing: *The publishing company's style is to use very few commas.*
—*v.* **styled, styling, styles** **1** to make or create s.t. in a special way: *to style men's clothes||to style a woman's hair* **2** *phrasal v. insep.* **to style s.t. after s.t.** or **s.o.:** to form or create s.t. in the same way as s.o. or s.t. else: *She styles her life after her mother.* -*n.* **stylist;** -*v.* **stylize** /'staɪlaɪz/.

styl·ish /'staɪlɪʃ/ *adj.* fashionable, attractive: *The lady wears colorful, stylish dresses.*

sty·mie /'staɪmi/ *v.* **-mied, -mieing** or **-mying, -mies** to stop or block s.o. or s.t., (*syn.*) to thwart: *Our company needs to buy new computers, but we are stymied because we don't know much about them.*

suave /swɑv/ *adj.* with attractive, effortless charm and social skills (used to describe men more often than women): *That guy is so suave, offering chairs to the women and telling them he's happy they're here.*

sub·com·mit·tee /'sʌbkə,mɪti/ *n.* part of a larger group, formed to look at a more specific topic: *The education committee formed a subcommittee to study high-school safety. See:* committee.

sub·con·tract /'sʌb,kɑntrækt, -kən'trækt/ *v.* to sign a legal agreement and then buy various goods and services from others to fulfill parts of it: *The airplane maker agreed to provide a finished aircraft, but subcontracted the engines and tires to other companies.* -*n.* **subcontract; subcontractor.**

sub·cul·ture /'sʌb,kʌltʃər/ *n.* a specific group and lifestyle within a larger one: *New York City has many subcultures with their own ways of living: theater people, Wall Street workers, and homeless people are only three of them.*

sub·di·vide /'sʌbdə,vaɪd/ *v.* **-vided, -viding, -vides** to separate (usu. land) into smaller pieces: *A real estate company bought a large, wooded area and subdivided it into four groups of housing.*

sub·di·vi·sion /'sʌbdə,vɪʒən/ *n.* [C;U] a section of a town, usu. in a suburb.

sub·due /səb'du/ *v.* **-dued, -duing, -dues** **1** to beat, (*syn.*) to conquer: *The army subdued the enemy.* **2** to make calmer or quieter: *He subdued the screaming baby with soft music.*

sub·dued /səb'dud/ *adj.* quiet, sometimes a little sad: *You seem a little subdued today, is anything wrong?*

S

sub·freez·ing /'sʌb,frizɪŋ/ *adj.* a temperature below 32 degrees Fahrenheit or 0 degrees Celsius: *Last winter, we had subfreezing weather for weeks.*

sub·group /'sʌb,grup/ *n.* a group within a group: *Rap and country are subgroups of popular music.*

sub·ject /'sʌbdʒɪkt/ *n.* **1** an idea being thought, talked, or read about, a topic: *The subject of this book is teenage smoking.* **2** s.t. studied in school: *English is her favorite subject.* **3** a person ruled by s.o.: *a subject of the queen* **4** a person that is looked at or examined (as in a medical study): *For his paper on AIDS, he studied four different subjects.* **5** (in grammar) the noun that does the action in a sentence; *cat* is the subject of the sentence *The cat came home.*
—*v.* /sɘb'dʒɛkt/ to cause s.o. to receive some action: *The boss is an unkind man and he subjects his workers to his anger every day.*
—*adj.* /'sʌbdʒɪkt/ **1** under a legal power: *Rich and poor, we are all subject to the laws of this country.* **2** likely to receive: *If you don't wear a hat, you make yourself subject to catching a cold.* **3** likely to happen only if s.t. else is done, (*syns.*) contingent, dependent: *The agreement is subject to your signature; only then will it be legal.*

sub·jec·tive /sɘb'dʒɛktɪv/ *adj.* related to personal feeling and opinion, rather than facts: *He must be subjective about the difficult girl; she's his daughter and he loves her. See:* objective.
-*adv.* **subjectively;** -*n.* [U] **subjectivity** /,sʌbdʒɛk'tɪvɘti/.

subject matter /'sʌbdʒɪkt/ *n.* the topic being read about or discussed: *The subject matter of this class is international banking*

sub·ju·gate /'sʌbdʒɘ,geɪt/ *v.* **-gated, -gating, -gates** to bring under control: *The parents subjugated the child's bank account.‖Ancient Rome subjugated many nations and brought them into its empire.*

sub·lease /sʌb'lis, 'sʌb,lis/ *v.n.* **-leased, -leasing, -leases** to rent from so who is the original renter: *We found an apartment and <v.> subleased it from the woman who lives there now.‖We signed a <n.> sublease yesterday.*

sub·let /'sʌb,lɛt/ *v.n.* **-let, -letting, -lets** to sublease: *Yesterday, the tenant <v.> sublet an apartment to us.*

sub·lime /sɘ'blaɪm/ *adj.* the very best, wonderful, heavenly: *We spent a sublime vacation in Hawaii.*

sub·lim·i·nal /sɘ'blɪmɘnɘl/ *adj.* sensed (heard, felt, or seen) without being aware of it, related to the subconscious mind: *Under the music that I could hear were subliminal voices telling me I was a good person.*

sub·marine /'sʌbmɘ,rin, ,sʌbmɘ'rin/ *n.* a tube-shaped ship that can travel underwater

sub·merge /sɘb'mɝdʒ/ *v.* **-merged, -merging, -merges** to go or put beneath the surface of water: *The girl was submerged in the shallow end of the pool.‖I submerged my hands in the sink to wash dishes.* -*n.* [U] **submersion.**

sub·mis·sion /sɘb'mɪʃɘn/ *n.* **1** [U] a giving up, (*syn.*) a surrender: *The enemy was beaten into submission.* **2** [U] weak agreement, (*syn.*) compliance: *her husband's submission to her wishes* **3** [C;U] s.t. passed in or given to s.o., esp. a piece of writing or artistic work: *The artists' submission of their work to the art gallery takes place today.*

sub·mis·sive /sɘb'mɪsɪv/ *adj.* tending to agree or go along with an action, (*syns.*) compliant, cooperative: *She does everything that he asks of her; she is quite submissive to him.*

sub·mit /sɘb'mɪt/ *v.* **-mitted, -mitting, -mits 1** to give up to a greater power, (*syn.*) to surrender: *The British forces submitted to American soldiers during the Revolutionary War.* **2** to agree, (*syn.*) to comply: *You know more, so I submit to your decision.* **3** to pass in or give s.t., esp. a piece of writing or artistic work, to s.o.: *When I finish this short story, I'll submit it to a magazine.* **4** to introduce or propose s.t.: *We submitted our ideas about a new city park to the mayor.*

sub·or·di·nate /sɘ'bɔrdnɪt/ *n.v.* **-nated, -nating, -nates** a person of lower rank: *The general spoke to his <n.> subordinates.*
—*adj.* /sɘ'bɔrdnɪt/ not as important, secondary: *I want to take a vacation but that is subordinate to finding a new job.* -*n.* [U] **subordination.**

sub·plot /'sʌb,plɑt/ *n.* in a story, a situation that is less important than the main situation: *The novel is about a murder, with a love story as a subplot.*

sub·poe·na /sɘ'pinɘ/ *v.n.* (in law) to give s.o. a legal paper requiring him or her to appear in court: *Judges <v.> subpoenaed many people for jury duty last month.‖The court delivered a <n.> subpoena to a woman who saw the robbery.*

sub·scribe /sɘb'skraɪb/ *v.* **-scribed, -scribing, -scribes 1** to pay money for a certain number of issues of a magazine or newspaper: *I subscribe to a monthly magazine about skiing.* **2** to sign one's name to s.t. to show agreement or as a witness: *to subscribe a will* **3** to share an opinion, agree: *I do not subscribe to his religious ideas.*

sub·scrip·tion /sɘb'skrɪpʃɘn/ *n.* **1** an agreement to buy a certain number of magazines or newspapers: *My subscription to that computer magazine runs out next month.* **2** the signing of one's name on a legal document

sub·se·quent /'sʌbsɘkwɘnt/ *adj.* happening later, (*syn.*) succeeding: *In the first letter she* *said she loved me, but in subsequent letters she changed her mind. -adv.* **subsequently.**

sub·ser·vi·ent /səb'sɜrviənt/ *adj.* acting like a servant, obedient: *He is subservient to his wife because he's afraid of her. -n.* [U] **subservience.**

sub·set /'sʌbˌsɛt/ *n.* a set contained within a set: *The company's financial problems are a subset of its mismanagement in general.*

sub·side /səb'saɪd/ *v.* **-sided, -siding, -sides** to become less strong or intense, to lessen: *Her high fever has subsided.*

sub·sid·i·ar·y /səb'sɪdiˌɛri/ *adj.* less important, secondary: *Unfortunately, in our company, the happiness of the workers is subsidiary to yearly profits.*
—*n.* **-ies** a company that is controlled by another company: *My brother works for a smaller subsidiary of a big car company.*

sub·si·dize /'sʌbsɪˌdaɪz/ *v.* **-dized, -dizing, -dizes** to give money to a person, group, or business that is not self-supporting: *The City Opera is subsidized by individual and corporate donations. -n.* [U] **subsidization.**

sub·si·dy /'sʌbsədi/ *n.* **-dies** money paid to a person, group, or business to support it or them: *As long as my parents give my brother a subsidy every month, he will never get a job.*

sub·sist /səb'sɪst/ *v.* to exist, to live at basic or minimal level: *The old lady subsists on a little bit of money her dead husband left her.*

sub·sis·tence /səb'sɪstəns/ *n.* [U] a basic level of living or existence
—*adj.* with just enough and no more: *He lives on subsistence wages; he has no money left over.*

sub·stance /'sʌbstəns/ *n.* **1** [U] anything one can touch, material, matter: *This face cream is a white, sticky substance.*‖*Tires are made of rubber and other substances.* **2** *usu. sing.* [C;U] meaning, truth: *What she says has substance because of her knowledge and experience.* **3** [U] wealth, possessions: *The family owns a successful business; they are people of substance.*

sub·stan·dard /sʌb'stændərd/ *adj.* not good enough: *Unfortunately, there is a lot of substandard housing in the poor section of town.*

sub·stan·tial /səb'stænʃəl/ *adj.* **1** large, (*syn.*) considerable: *He earns a substantial income.*‖*The politician won the election by a substantial number of votes.* **2** strong, durable: *substantial furniture* **3** satisfying, filling: *to eat a substantial meal*

sub·stan·ti·ate /səb'stænʃiˌeɪt/ *v.* **-ated, -ating, -ates** to support or prove s.t. with facts: *He can't substantiate her story; he wasn't there. -n.* [U] **substantiation.**

sub·stan·tive /'sʌbstəntɪv/ *adj.* real, solid, (*syn.*) substantial: *In a murder case, fingerprints are substantive evidence.*
—*n.* (in grammar) a noun

sub·sti·tute /'sʌbstɪˌtut/ *v.* **-tuted, -tuting, -tutes** to replace: *I substitute olive oil for butter in cooking.*‖*The new player substituted for the injured star.*
—*n.* a person or thing that works or acts in place of s.o. or s.t. else, a replacement: *Our teacher is having a baby, so we have a substitute. -n.* [U] **substitution.**

sub·ter·fuge /'sʌbtərˌfyudʒ/ *n.* [C;U] a plan in which the whole truth is not told or s.t. is hidden, (*syns.*) a ruse, scheme: *The company used the name of a more famous company as subterfuge to trick people into buying from them.*

sub·ter·ra·ne·an /ˌsʌbtə'reɪniən/ *adj.* below the surface of the earth, underground: *Little subterranean animals live under our garden.*

sub·ti·tles /'sʌbˌtaɪtlz/ *n.pl.* in a foreign-language film, the words at the bottom of the screen that translate what the actors are saying

sub·tle /'sʌtl/ *adj.* **1** not easy to sense, not obvious: *The violin is very subtle in this piece of music.* **2** indirect: *Turning off all the lights is a subtle way of saying, "Don't waste electricity."* **3** small, refined: *The lawyer is smart; he sees subtle, but important, distinctions in the law. -n.* [C;U] **subtlety.**

sub·to·tal /'sʌbˌtoʊtl/ *n.v.* the sum of some, but not all, numbers being added: *I added up a subtotal of the items before adding the cost of the tax.*

sub·tract /səb'trækt/ *v.* to take away a number (amount) from another: *1 subtracted from 4 equals 3.*‖*If you subtract the cost of the speakers, I can buy the stereo.*

sub·trac·tion /səb'trækʃən/ *n.* [U] the act of subtracting: *The children learned subtraction before multiplication.*

sub·urb /'sʌbˌɜrb/ *n.* **1** a small city or town outside a large city, usu. with more housing than business places, but including some shopping or service areas: *We moved to a house with a yard in a suburb of Dallas.* **2** *pl.* **the suburbs:** the general term for an area outside a big city: *He moved to the suburbs, so he needs to buy a car. -adj.* **suburban** /sə'bɜrbən/; *-n.* [U] **suburbia.**

sub·ven·tion /səb'vɛnʃən/ *n.* [C] a subsidy: *a foundation that provides subventions to artists*

sub·ver·sive /səb'vɜrsɪv/ *adj.* done to ruin, destroy, or overpower a person or government, sometimes with secret or harsh methods: *Spying was a subversive way to learn about the nation's nuclear weapons and plans to use them. -n.* [U] **subversion; -v.** **subvert.**

sub·way /'sʌbˌweɪ/ *n.* a public transportation system with trains that run underground: *In*

S

Boston, thousands of people take the subway to work every day.

suc·ceed /sək'sid/ *v.* **1** to accomplish a task or reach a goal: *She tried to quit smoking, and she succeeded.* **2** to do well in life: *She has succeeded in business and is now a millionaire.* **3** to come after s.o. or s.t.: *a king succeeded by his son*

suc·cess /sək'sɛs/ *n.* **-es** **1** [C] accomplishment of a task, the reaching of a goal: *The meeting was a success; we agreed on everything.* **2** [C;U] a good event, an achievement: *She had success in medical school and became a fine doctor.* **3** [U] wealth, good luck in life: *The man has had a lot of financial success and has no money worries.*

suc·cess·ful /sək'sɛsfəl/ *adj.* with success: *No one likes the new movie; it's not successful.*‖*A sucessful result brings happiness.*

suc·ces·sion /sək'sɛʃən/ *n.* **1** [U] the act of coming after or following another: *We sat in alphabetical order and the teacher asked us to give our names in succession.* **2** [U] the act of land, a title, or other honor passing from one person to another (usu. a child or other relative): *In England, the oldest son is always first in the line of succession to the throne.* **3** [C] a group of people or things following in order, (*syn.*) a sequence: *A succession of peace talks could not prevent the two countries from going to war.* *-adj.* **successive.**

suc·ces·sor /sək'sɛsər/ *n.* a person who follows another in a position: *The company president has named his daughter as his successor.*

suc·cinct /sək'sɪŋkt/ *adj.* brief and clear: *Her succinct letter was one page long and stayed on one topic.*

suc·cor /'sʌkər/ *n.frml.* [U] help or relief when in trouble or pain: *My family gave succor to a lost little boy we saw in the park.*

suc·cu·lent /'sʌkyələnt/ *adj.* tasting good, usu. juicy: *a succulent peach*‖*succulent beef stew*
—*n.* a type of plant, including the cactus family, that holds water in thick leaves

suc·cumb /sə'kʌm/ *v.* **1** to show weakness or give up to a greater strength or desire: *I'm trying to lose weight, but I always succumb to chocolate ice cream!* **2** to die: *to succumb to an illness*

such /sʌtʃ/ *adv.* to a large degree, very: *I have such great news!*‖*She was in such a terrible accident!*
—*adj.* **1** of a certain kind: *I have never seen such children in my life.* **2** used to refer to s.t. being discussed: *You say you want to understand those people, but such people can never be understood.*
—*pron.* **1** a person or thing in general: *His girlfriend left him; such are the risks of ro-*

mance. **2** for example: *He collects musical instruments, such as trumpets and guitars.*

such and such *adj.* an expression used in place of s.o. not known: *They live on such and such street — I don't know the street's name.*

suck /sʌk/ *v.* **1** to take liquid into the mouth by putting the lips around s.t. and pulling with the mouth muscles: *She sucked lemonade through a straw.*‖*The baby sucks milk at his mother's breast.* **2** to pull s.t. in by removing air (creating a vacuum): *The pump sucked water from the well.* **3** to dissolve s.t. slowly by moving it around in the mouth: *to suck on a candy* **4** *infrml.* **to be sucked in:** to think wrongly s.t. might be good, to be taken advantage of: *I was sucked in by the woman; she seemed nice, but then she left town with my wallet!* **5** *phrasal v. insep.* **to suck up to s.o.:** to treat s.o. well only for personal gain, (*syns.*) to flatter, to fawn over: *He sucks up to his boss in the hope of getting more money.*
—*n.* **1** the act of sucking *-v.* **suckle.**

suck·er /'sʌkər/ *n.* **1** s.o. who is easily fooled, a gullible person: *I bought a watch from a man on the street and it broke the next day; what a sucker I was to buy it.* **2** hard candy kept in the mouth until it is gone, a lollipop: *The little boy's tongue was red from a cherry sucker.*

su·crose /'su,krous/ *n.* [U] a natural sweetener found in sugar cane and other plants

suc·tion /'sʌkʃən/ *n.* [U] *v.* a lack of air created to pull s.t. in or cause s.t. to stick: *The pencil sharpener stayed on the table with* <n.> *suction from its rubber bottom.*‖*He* <v.> *suctioned gas from a tank.*

sud·den /'sʌdn/ *adj.* **1** quick and unexpected: *We all jumped at the sudden loud noise.* **2** without warning, (*syn.*) abrupt: *He was surprised at the sudden death of his aunt; she did not seem sick.* **3** **all of a sudden:** quickly, without warning, (*syn.*) all at once: *It was sunny; then all of a sudden it started to rain.* *-adv.* **suddenly.**

suds /sʌdz/ *n.pl.* **1** a mass of tiny bubbles created by soap, (*syns.*) lather, foam: *He squirted dish soap under the running water to make suds.* **2** *infrml.* beer

sue /su/ *v.* **sued, suing, sues** **1** to file a lawsuit, to make a claim in court that one's legal rights have been violated by others, that they should be protected or restored, and that the others should pay for one's suffering and damages: *She sued the company because it was unfair to women and racial minorities.* **2** *frml.* to plea for special attention, favors, or love: *He sang beautiful songs that sued for her love.*

suede /sweɪd/ *n.* [U] a soft leather with one side that is smooth and another with a fuzzy texture, like a bath towel: *Suede is nice to touch, but it shows marks easily.*

suf·fer /'sʌfər/ *v.* **1** to experience pain, loss, hardship, etc.: *His wife suffered when her mother died.* **2** to experience a painful or unpleasant event: *The bank suffered losses from bad real estate loans.* **3** to put up with, endure: *He was willing to suffer her constant complaints.* **4** *phrasal v. insep.* **to suffer from s.t.:** to be ill with s.t., usu. over a long period of time: *She suffers from arthritis.*

suf·fer·er /'sʌfərər/ *n.* [U] a person who suffers: *Sufferers from hay fever are often miserable in the spring.*

suf·fer·ing /'sʌfərɪŋ, 'sʌfrɪŋ/ *n.* a feeling of pain in body or mind: *Hunger and disease cause great suffering in the world.*

suf·fice /sə'faɪs/ *v.* **-ficed, -ficing, -fices 1** to be enough: *I told him 10 gallons of gas would suffice to get me home.* **2** to meet the basic needs of: *His salary will not suffice for a family of four.*

suf·fi·cien·cy /sə'fɪʃənsi/ *n. usu. sing.* **-cies** [C;U] a satisfactory level, supply, or amount: *the company has produced a sufficiency of inventory to meet future sales.*

suf·fi·cient /sə'fɪʃənt/ *adj.* **1** adequate, satisfactory: *We have a sufficient supply of goods on hand now.* **2** ample, enough: *Our money was sufficient for a two-week vacation.*

suf·fo·cate /'sʌfə,keɪt/ *v.* **-cated, -cating, -cates 1** to cause or have difficulty in breathing: *The smoky fire was suffocating us.*‖*We were suffocating from the intense heat.* **2** to cause to die from lack of air; to kill by choking or smothering: *In the spy novel, the hero suffocated the murderer under a pillow.* *-n.* [U] **suffocation.**

sug·ar /'ʃugər/ *n.* [C;U] a sweet substance, usu. in the form of fine white crystals, obtained from plants, added to or used in cooking and preparing foods and drinks: *She put a teaspoon of sugar in her coffee.*
—v. to add sugar to: *He sugared his cereal and then poured milk over it.* *-adj.* **sugary.**

sug·ar·coat /'ʃugər,koʊt/ *v.* **1** to cover with a layer of sugar: *Children like to sugarcoat all of their food.* **2** to make s.t., such as bad news, appear more pleasant than it is: *She is afraid of the truth, so she sugarcoats everything she says.*

sug·ar·y /'ʃugəri/ *adj.* **1** containing or tasting of sugar: *sugary water* **2** too sweet: *This lemonade is refreshing, but very sugary.*

sug·gest /səg'dʒɛst/ *v.* **1** to propose s.t. to do or to offer an idea for consideration: *He suggested that we have lunch at the hotel.* **2** to bring (an idea) to mind, to indicate: *This picture suggests an ancient battle scene.*‖*The results of the test suggested that I was ill.*

sug·gest·i·ble /səg'dʒɛstəbəl/ *adj.* easily swayed or influenced: *He was new to this country and very suggestible.*

sug·ges·tion /səg'dʒɛstʃən/ *n.* **1** [U] the act of suggesting: *At my suggestion we traveled first class.* **2** [C] s.t. suggested (an idea, proposal, plan, etc.): *They rejected my suggestion because it was too expensive.* **3** [C] a slight hint or indication: *There was a suggestion of evil in his motives.*

sug·ges·tive /səg'dʒɛstɪv/ *adj.* **1** interesting, (*syn.*) provocative: *He made several suggestive remarks about how to save money at the planning meeting.* **2** leading to sexual proposals, (*syn.*) seductive: *She made very suggestive looks at him over dinner.*

su·i·cid·al /,suə'saɪdl/ *adj.* **1** having a tendency to commit suicide: *She has severe depressions and could become suicidal.* **2** very dangerous and likely to lead to death: *Driving too fast is suicidal.*

su·i·cide /'suə,saɪd/ *n.* [U] **1** the taking of one's own life: *to commit suicide* **2** action destructive of one's own interests or welfare: *He is committing academic suicide by never studying and not writing his papers.*

suit /sut/ *n.* **1** a set of pieces of clothing, such as a coat and pants or a coat and skirt, made of the same material and meant to be worn together, usu. for business or formal occasions: *Everyone wore his or her best suit to the company's annual meeting.* **2** a lawsuit: *His suit against the phone company is not likely to succeed.* **3** a plea, argument, or other attempt to persuade s.o. in a position of authority or respect to give favors or special rights: *His suit for her love is doomed to fail.* **4** one of the four sets of cards used in games: *He arranged his cards by suits.* **5 to follow suit:** to behave as s.o. else has: *She dove into the lake and I followed suit.*
—v. **1** to satisfy or please; to meet the needs of or be convenient for: *Your proposal suits my schedule.*‖*Fresh air and good food would suit you well.* **2** to look good or well-matched with other things: *That big dress does not suit her slim figure.* **3 to be suited (to/for):** to have the right qualities (skills, attitudes, etc.) for: *He is not suited to that job.* **4 to suit oneself:** to do what one likes or thinks is best; to decide for one's self: *I cannot tell you what to do, so suit yourself.* **5** *phrasal v.* **to suit up:** to put on a uniform or other clothing designed for a specific activity: *The team suited up for the big match.*

suit·a·ble /'sutəbəl/ *adj.* **1** convenient: *Please set a suitable time to meet.* **2** appropriate: *You should wear clothes suitable for the occasion.* *-adv.* **suitably.**

suit·case /'sut,keɪs/ *n.* a ﬂat, sturdy box with a top and bottom, usu. attached by hinges on

S

one side and held closed by latches, and with a handle for carrying; made to carry suits and other clothes when travelling: *I carry one suitcase and a briefcase on business trips.*

suite /swit/ *n.* **1** a set of connected rooms in a hotel or office building: *The lawyers' offices are in the suite on the second floor.* **2** a set of matching pieces of furniture: *a bedroom suite||a living-room suite* **3** any loose collection of similar or related items: *a suite of new products||a musical suite*

suit·or /'sutər/ *n.* a man who seeks to marry a woman: *That woman has many suitors.*

sul·fur /'sʌlfər/ *n.* [U] a yellow non-metallic element found widely in nature as a powder and used in industry and medicine: *Eggs contain sulfur in the yolks.* *-adj.* **sulfurous** /'sʌlfərəs, səl'fyurəs/; **sulfuric** /səl'fyurık/.

sulk /sʌlk/ *v.* to act as if hurt and angry by being silent, childish, and resentful: *When his girlfriend will not see him, he sulks for days.* *-adv.* **sulkily;** *-adj.* **sulky.**

sul·len /'sʌlən/ *adj.* **1** showing irritation or resentment by being silent and withdrawn: *When the group voted against his plan, he became sullen.* **2** dark and gloomy: *a sullen sky*

sul·phur /'sʌlfər/ *n.var. of* sulfur

sul·tan /'sʌltən/ *n.* a hereditary ruler of a Muslim country: *the Sultan of Morocco -n.* **sultanate.**

sul·try /'sʌltri/ *adj.* **-trier, -triest 1** (of the weather) hot and humid: *sultry weather* **2** (of persons) erotic, sexy: *a sultry woman*

sum /sʌm/ *n.* **1** the total reached by adding together numbers, things, or amounts: *The sum of our revenues is greater than the sum of our expenses.* **2** an amount of money: *They spent quite a sum for that house.* **3 the sum and total:** the totality of s.t.: *The company has put the sum and total of all of its efforts into this new program.*
—*v.* **summed, summing, sums 1** to give the total of: *He summed the last row of numbers and then quit for the day.* **2** *phrasal v. sep.* **to sum s.t. up:** to summarize, to finish esp. a speech: *I would like to sum up my presentation by saying that we need to cut costs and increase sales.||I'd like to sum it up.*

sum·ma·rize /'sʌmə,raɪz/ *v.* **-rized, -rizing, -rizes 1** to give a summary, to condense: *He summarized a long report by giving its main ideas.* **2** to finish, conclude: *a speaker who summarizes her talk by reviewing its main points*

sum·ma·ry /'sʌməri/ *n.* **-ries** a brief statement of the most important features (ideas, facts, actions, etc.) of an event or a work: *He wrote a summary of his book to send to a publisher.*
—*adj.* **1** brief, quick: *She gave a summary report on her findings.* **2** hasty, rushed, and with-

out proper care: *He was given only summary justice.*

sum·ma·tion /sə'meɪʃən/ *n.frml.* **1** a conclusion: *the summation of a speech* **2** a summary: *a summation of the main points*

sum·mer /'sʌmər/ *n.* [C;U] the warm season between spring and autumn: *The gardens are beautiful in the summer.*
—*v.* to locate during the summer months: *Our family summers in New England. -adj.* **summery.**

sum·mer·house /'sʌmər,haʊs/ *n.* a vacation home used mainly in the summertime: *Our friends have a summerhouse by the seashore.*

sum·mer·time /'sʌmər,taɪm/ *n.* [U] the warm months of June, July, and August in the northern hemisphere: *Schoolchildren enjoy the summertime.*

sum·mit /'sʌmɪt/ *n.* **1** the top of a mountain: *When they reached the mountain summit, they planted a flag in the snow.* **2** the highest point or part, (*syns.*) peak, pinnacle: *She has reached the summit of her career.* **3 summit conference:** a meeting of heads of state: *Next year, the summit conference will be held in Vienna.*

sum·mit·ry /'sʌmɪtri/ *n.* [U] the art of managing international relations through high-level (summit) conferences: *The president's assistant was a master of summitry.*

sum·mon /'sʌmən/ *v.* **1** to call or send for: *My partner summoned me over to talk with him.* **2** to issue an official order to appear somewhere or to perform an act: *The king summoned the nobles to Versailles.* **3** *phrasal v. sep.* **to summon (s.t.) up:** to gather or call forth from one's character: *She had to summon up all her courage before talking to her boss.||She summoned it up.*

sum·mons /'sʌmənz/ *n.* **-es** an order to appear in a court of law: *We received a summons to appear in court on Monday.*

sump·tu·ous /'sʌmptʃuəs/ *adj.* expensive, luxurious: *a sumptuous party (meal, social affair, etc.)*

sun /sʌn/ *n.* **1** [C] the star around which the Earth and other planets revolve and draw light, heat, and energy: *The sun rises every morning and sets every evening.* **2** [U] the heat and light of the sun: *Have fun at the beach, but don't get too much sun.*
—*v.* **sunned, sunning, suns** to bathe in the sunlight: *She loved to sun herself on the beach.*

sun·bathe /'sʌn,beɪð/ *v.* **-bathed, -bathing, -bathes** to expose oneself to the sun's rays: *On vacation, we sunbathe on the beach. -n.* [U] **sunbathing.**

Sun·belt /'sʌn,bɛlt/ *n.* [U] the southern and southwestern United States, from California to Florida, where warm weather is prevalent: *Our parents retired to the Sunbelt in San Diego.*

sun·burn /'sʌn,bɜrn/ *n.* the painful, reddened, sometimes blistering condition of the skin caused by overexposure to the sun: *She fell asleep on the beach and had a bad case of sunburn. -adj.* **sunburned; sunburnt.**

sun·dae /'sʌn,deɪ, -di/ *n.* a dish of ice cream topped with syrup and delicacies, such as chopped nuts and cherries: *I'll have a hot fudge sundae with vanilla ice cream, please.*

Sun·day /'sʌn,deɪ, -di/ *n.* **1** the first day of the week, between Saturday and Monday, regarded by most Christians as the Sabbath, the day of worship and rest: *We spend Sundays in the park.* **2** [C;U] **Sunday school:** religious teaching for children, usu. held while their parents attend church service

sun·down /'sʌn,daʊn/ *n.* sunset: *After sundown, there is still about a half hour of light left when the sky is clear.*

sun·dry /'sʌndri/ *adj.n.* **-dries** various, miscellaneous: *The store carries <adj.> sundry items from souvenirs, caps, and scarves to pens and postcards.*

sun·flower /'sʌn,flaʊər/ *n.* a long-stemmed plant with large flowers of golden petals surrounding dark brown edible seeds noted as well for their oil: *Our sunflowers grew taller than the corn.*

sunflower

sun·glass·es /'sʌn,glæsɪz/ *n.pl.* eyeglasses with colored lenses designed to shield the eyes from harmful rays of the sun: *In California, nearly everyone wears sunglasses.*

sunk /sʌŋk/ *adj.infrml. & past part. of* sink, in big trouble, beyond help, a failure: *The company is bankrupt and has fired everyone; it is sunk.‖I forgot my car keys and now I'm sunk.*

sunk·en /'sʌŋkən/ *adj. & past part. of* sink, submerged: *a search for sunken treasure*

sun·light /'sʌn,laɪt/ *n.* [U] the natural light of the sun: *The sunlight lasts about 12 hours in September.‖Let's move out of the shade and into the sunlight where it's warm.*

sun·lit /'sʌn,lɪt/ *adj.* filled with sunlight: *Her kitchen is a lovely, sunlit room.*

sun·ny /'sʌni/ *adj.* **-nier, -niest** **1** brightly lit with sunlight: *She showed me to the sunny greenhouse.‖a sunny room in the house* **2** cheerful: *a person with a sunny disposition*

sun·rise /'sʌn,raɪz/ *n.* [C;U] sunup, the moment when the sun appears in the east: *The sunrise glows in a bright orange color on clear days.*

sun·screen /'sʌn,skrin/ *n.* [U] a skin cream that blocks the harmful rays of the sun: *Many* people use sunscreen to protect themselves from skin cancer.

sun·set /'sʌn,sɛt/ *n.* [C;U] sundown, the moment when the sun disappears in the west: *At day's end, we watched the many colors of the sunset.*

sun·shine /'sʌn,ʃaɪn/ *n.* [U] sunlight: *Most plants like plenty of sunshine.*

sun·tan /'sʌn,tæn/ *n.* [U] the browning (or darkening) of the skin due to exposure to sunlight: *She went to the beach to get a suntan.*

sun·up /'sʌn,ʌp/ *n.* [U] sunrise, the moment when the sun rises in the east: *We love to travel and get going each day at sunup.*

su·per (1) /'supər/ *n.* short for superintendent, the head maintenance man in an apartment building

super (2) *adj.infrml.* outstanding, excellent: *We had a super time on our vacation.*

su·perb /su'pɜrb/ *adj.* wonderful, first-class: *The designer did a superb job on the artwork for that project.*

Super Bowl *n.* (in USA) the national football championship: *The Super Bowl is the most important football game of the year.*

USAGE NOTE: The *Super Bowl* is played on a Sunday in January and is the most popular sporting event of the year, with millions of people watching the game on television and holding Super Bowl parties in their homes.

su·per·cil·i·ous /,supər'sɪliəs/ *adj.* acting as if superior to others, snobbish, (*syn.*) arrogant: *He thought himself a genius and had a supercilious smile. -adv.* **superciliously.**

su·per·fi·cial /,supər'fɪʃəl/ *adj.* **1** on the surface only; not deep: *He gave us a superficial overview of the project.* **2** lacking in serious thought, limited in understanding: *Her knowledge of the subject is very superficial.*

su·per·flu·ous /sə'pɜrfluəs/ *adj.* more than is needed or wanted: *He worked so well that my help was superfluous.*

su·per·high·way /,supər'haɪ,weɪ/ *n.* (in the USA) a wide, divided highway with two or more lanes in either direction, usu. leading from one region or state to another: *You can drive fast on a superhighway.*

su·per·hu·man /,supər'hyumən/ *adj.* extraordinary, beyond the strength or ability of ordinary people: *He had a superhuman ability to work long hours.*

su·per·in·tend /,supərɪn'tɛnd/ *v.* to watch over, manage, direct: *They asked her to superintend the ceremony.*

su·per·in·ten·dent /,supərɪn'tɛndənt/ *n.* **1** person who manages or directs a large project or public service organization: *the superinten-*

S

dent of schools/public works **2** the person in charge of a large (esp. apartment) building: *I lost my key, so the superintendent opened the building for me.*

su·pe·ri·or /su'pɪriər/ *n.* a person who is higher in rank or importance: *My superiors in the company have requested that I cut costs.* —*adj.* **1** better (than); above average; of high quality: *Our product is superior to our competitor's.‖That is superior work.* **2** of higher rank or position: *her superior officer* **3** giving the impression that one is better than others: *She acts superior because she is proud and rich.*

superior court *n.* (in the USA) a court of law of general jurisdiction, superior to the lower courts, yet below the courts of appeal: *Our company filed a lawsuit in superior court against patent infringement.*

su·pe·ri·or·i·ty /su,pɪri'ɔrəti, -'ar-/ *n.* [U] a superior position; the state of being better than others: *Our product (team, position, legal case, etc.) has superiority over our competitor's.*

su·per·la·tive /su'pɜrlətɪv/ *n.* **1** (in grammar) the highest degree of comparison of an adjective or adverb: *"Best" is the superlative of "good."* **2** a descriptive word in the superlative form: *The critic used superlatives to describe the new movie.* —*adj.* of the highest quality: *He said that the set designer did a superlative job.* See: comparative.

Superman *n.* the fictional cartoon character of great powers: *Superman wears a red cape and a large "S" on his chest.*

su·per·mar·ket /'supər,markət/ *n.* a large self-service store offering food and general household items: *We go shopping at the supermarket every Thursday.*

su·per·nat·u·ral /,supər'næʧərəl/ *adj.* beyond nature; spiritual; not explained by science or natural laws: *Ghosts are supernatural.* —*n.* **the supernatural:** the world of spirits or events beyond our knowledge of the natural world: *He believes that the supernatural is visible to some people.*

su·per·pow·er /'supər,pauər/ *n.adj.* a country with great military and economic power: *The superpowers held a meeting to promote cooperation.*

su·per·sede /,supər'sid/ *v.* **-seded, -seding, -sedes** to replace an old or existing version or model of s.t. with a new or better one: *This fancy new washing machine supersedes that old one.*

su·per·son·ic /,supər'sanɪk/ *adj.* faster than the speed of sound: *a supersonic airplane*

su·per·star /'supər,star/ *n.* a performer, such as a movie star, singer, or athlete, who is very fa-

mous: *There were lots of superstars at the rock concert.*

su·per·sti·tion /,supər'stɪʃən/ *n.* **1** [U] the belief in magical or supernatural beings and events: *His mind is filled with superstition.* **2** [C] a story that relies on such a belief: *There is a superstition in that village that the house is haunted by ghosts.*

su·per·sti·tious /,supər'stɪʃəs/ *adj.* believing in, influenced by, or caused by superstitions: *a superstitious tale (old man/fear)*

su·per·struc·ture /'supər,strʌkʧər/ *n.* s.t. built on top of s.t. else: *The storm blew off the superstructure of the lighthouse tower.*

su·per·vise /'supər,vaɪz/ *v.* **-vised, -vising, -vises** to watch over the activity of others to maintain order and discipline: *She supervises a bookkeeping department of 20 employees.‖He supervised the children at the playground.*

su·per·vi·sion /,supər'vɪʒən/ *n.* [U] the activity of supervising: *She is responsible for the supervision of new employees.*

su·per·vi·sor /'supər,vaɪzər/ *n.* a person who supervises others and their work: *a supervisor of a manufacturing operation*

su·per·vi·so·ry /,supər'vaɪzəri/ *adj.* related to supervision: *supervisory duties*

sup·per /'sʌpər/ *n.* [C;U] the evening meal: *At our house, we have supper at 7:00 P.M.*

sup·plant /sə'plænt/ *v.* to take the place of, to replace s.o., often as if by force or deception: *After the election, all the department heads were supplanted by their political enemies.*

sup·ple /'sʌpəl/ *adj.* pliant, easily bent: *Dancers have supple limbs and their costumes are made of supple material.*

sup·ple·ment /'sʌpləmənt/ *n.* **1** something added to an existing thing to complete or improve it: *One year after we made our report, we had to add a supplement to cover new events.* **2** an extra part of s.t.: *a newspaper supplement* —*v.* /'sʌplə,mɛnt/ to make an addition or additions to: *He supplemented his income by taking a night job.*

sup·ple·men·tal /,sʌplə'mɛntl/ *adj.* additional: *She has a supplemental income from interest on savings.*

sup·ple·men·ta·ry /,sʌplə'mɛntəri, -tri/ *adj.* **1** additional, extra **2** temporary, provisional: *The government had to take supplementary action to avoid a budget crisis.*

sup·pli·er /sə'plaɪər/ *n.* a business that supplies goods or services to a purchaser: *Our company has many suppliers who provide (sell) everything from office supplies, furniture, to cleaning services.*

sup·ply /sə'plaɪ/ *v.* **-plied, -plying, -plies** to give or provide s.t. needed: *They supplied guns to the revolutionaries.*

S

—n.[C;U] **1** a quantity of goods: *We need a supply of pens because we are out of them.* **2** a system for supplying or delivering goods or services: *Their water supply is old and filled with leaks.*

—n.pl. **supplies:** a quantity of goods of a specific kind necessary for an operation: *That farm buys its supplies of feed and grain from the local feed store.*

supply and demand *n.* [U] (in economics) the relation between the amount of products and services available at certain prices and the demand for them: *The supply of diamonds is limited and the demand for them is high, so by the law of supply and demand, their prices are high.*

sup·port /sə'pɔrt/ *v.* **1** to hold up or bear the weight of: *a beam that supports a ceiling* **2** to provide the money for necessities of life: *She supports her family by working two jobs.* **3** to contribute to; to encourage and assist by giving money to or working for: *We support our local hospital by giving blood regularly.* **4** to agree with, advocate, or express loyalty to: *He supports our efforts to end hunger in the world.* **5** to count in favor of: *The new findings support your theory.* **6** to work with: *This software supports all kinds of computers.*

—n. **1** [C] s.t. that holds up or bears the weight of s.t. else: *If you take away the supports, the wall will fall down.*‖(*fig.*) *She is his sole support in life.* **2** [U] the act of supporting s.t.: *Can we have your support at the next meeting?* **3** [U] money to buy the necessities of life: *When he lost his job, he was suddenly without support.* **4** [U] moral, emotional, or financial assistance: *Her family always gave her lots of support.*

sup·port·er /sə'pɔrtər/ *n.* a person or group that provides support: *The politician's supporters held a dinner in his honor.*

sup·por·tive /sə'pɔrtɪv/ *adj.* helpful to another person, sympathetic: *a person with a supportive spouse*

sup·pose /sə'pouz/ *v.* **-posed, -posing, -poses** **1** to assume or imagine as if true; to consider possible: *Do you suppose he left late and got caught in traffic?*‖*Let's suppose that our plan fails—then what shall we do?* **2** to believe, conclude, or think (often with uncertainty): *She supposed she should go visit her mother.* **3 be supposed to: a.** expected or required by custom, law, duty, or personal obligation: *We are supposed to meet her at the train station.*‖*You are supposed to pay income taxes.* **b.** (in the negative) not allowed to: *You are not supposed to drive on the left side of the road.*

sup·pos·ed·ly /sə'pouzɪdli/ *adv.* as it seems, so it is assumed: *They will supposedly arrive in time for dinner.*

sup·pos·ing /sə'pouzɪŋ/ *conj.* if, assuming that: *Supposing we do buy the house, how much will our monthly payments be?*

sup·po·si·tion /ˌsʌpə'zɪʃən/ *n.* **1** [U] an imaginary proposition or speculation, (*syn.*) hypothesis: *Just as a supposition, let's assume that he agrees to the deal; how do we proceed?* **2** [C] a guess: *He may agree, but that is only a supposition on your part.*

sup·press /sə'prɛs/ *v.* **-es** **1** to use force to hold down, defeat, or eliminate another force, activity, or thought: *The army suppressed the rebel peasants.* **2** to conceal or keep from being seen or heard: *She suppressed the police report to save his reputation.* *-n.* [U] **suppression.**

su·prem·a·cy /su'prɛməsi/ *n.* [U] **1** dominance: *a corporation that seeks supremacy in its marketplace* **2** sovereignty: *the supremacy of law in governing society* **3** preeminence: *the supremacy of reason in guiding action*

su·preme /su'prim/ *adj.* **1** highest in rank, authority, or power: *the Supreme Court*‖*a Supreme Being* **2** of the highest quality: *This is a supreme work of art.* **3** greatest or most extreme: *She made a supreme effort to be polite.*

Supreme Court *n.* the highest court in the USA system of justice, located in Washington, DC

sur·charge /'sɜrˌtʃɑrdʒ/ *n.* an amount added to the regular cost of a product or service to cover special conditions: *I had to pay a surcharge on my plane ticket because my baggage weighed too much.*

—v. **-charged, -charging, -charges** to add a surcharge

sure /ʃʊr, ʃɜr/ *adj.* **1** (of persons) without doubt, confident, positive: *I'm perfectly sure that he will be here for dinner.*‖*She isn't sure what to do about the leak in her roof.* **2** (of events) certain, bound to be: *The re-election of the president is by no means a sure thing.*‖*It is sure to be hot in July.* **3** reliable, dependable: *I think you have found the sure solution to our problems.*‖*Before I walk on it, is this bridge sure?*‖*All the data in this report are absolutely sure.* **4** okay, fine, yes: *"Would you like coffee?" "Sure".* **5 be sure to:** don't forget or fail to: *Be sure to lock the door before you leave.* **6 make sure (of/that): a.** to confirm or find out for certain (as by checking the facts): *You'd better make sure of those statements you're making.* **b.** to make definite (as by settling the details) as in a plan: *I had my secretary make sure that all our papers are in order.* **7 sure of oneself:** confident in one's abilities: *To succeed in business, you must be sure of yourself.* **8 sure thing:** certain to be successful: *This new software program is a sure thing.* **9 to be sure:** indeed, of course: *To*

S

be sure, this project will require a lot of patience and hard work.

—*adv.* **1** certainly: *This sure is a great dinner.*||*Sure you can!* **2 for sure:** definitely, you can bet on it: *This is going to be a great party, for sure.* **3 sure enough:** as expected: *Sure enough, everything turned out okay.*

sure·fire /'ʃur,faɪr/ *adj.infrml.* sure to work as expected; certain, definite: *That product will be a surefire success.*

sure·ly /'ʃurli/ *adv.* **1** certainly, without doubt: *Surely, you don't believe that nonsense.* ||*We will surely be glad to see you.* **2 slowly but surely:** steadily, dependably, with definite progress: *Slowly but surely, we are improving our services (product, performance, standard of living, etc.).*

surf /sɜrf/ *n.* [U] ocean waves as they approach and break on a shore creating rolling banks of water topped by white form and spray: *At the beach, children played in the surf.*

—*v.* to ride the ocean's waves as they break in approaching the shore, esp. while standing on a narrow board (surfboard): *She went to California to surf.* -*n.* [U] **surfing; surfer.**

sur·face /'sɜrfəs/ *n.* [C] **1** the outside layer of an object: *Rocks found on the beach usually have a smooth surface.* **2** the flat top level of s.t.: *the surface of a table (a pond, a mirror)* **3** outward appearance: *On the surface, that looks like a good car, but the engine is bad.* **4 to skim the surface:** to treat superficially: *The solution that you propose only skims the surface of the problem.*

—*v.* **-faced, -facing, -faces 1** to rise to the surface: *We saw two whales surface and then dive back into the ocean.* **2** to appear: *That problem surfaced when our mechanic examined the car.* **3** to cover a road with asphalt or paving material: *They surfaced the new road last week.*

surf·board /'sɜrf,bɔrd/ *n.* a long, narrow board used for the sport of surfing

sur·feit /'sɜrfɪt/ *n.frml.usu. sing.* **1** too much of s.t., esp. food or drink: *a surfeit of ice cream*||*pleasure* **2** a feeling of disgust from taking or having too much: *He felt a surfeit that made him ill.*

surfboard

surge /sɜrdʒ/ *n.* [C] **1** a strong forward or upward movement, like a wave: *The boat was rocked by the surge of the sea.* **2** a sudden, powerful increase of energy, motion, or emotion: *She felt a surge of pleasure when she saw him coming.*

—*v.* **surged, surging, surges 1** to push forward in strong waves: *A crowd of people surged toward the train platform.*||*The ship* surged in the ocean waves. **2** to rise suddenly or strongly: *Trading activity surged in the stock market.*

sur·geon /'sɜrdʒən/ *n.* a doctor who performs surgery: *The surgeon operated on my broken leg last week.*

sur·ger·y /'sɜrdʒəri/ *n.* [C;U] **-ies** the medical practice of treating injuries and disease by operating on the body: *My friend went into surgery today to have a growth on his arm removed.*

sur·gi·cal /'sɜrdʒɪkəl/ *adj.* related to surgery: *The nurse placed the doctor's surgical tools by the operating table.*

sur·ly /'sɜrli/ *adj.* **-lier, -liest** rude and hostile in manner or attitude: *Surly young men gathered on the street corner, looking for trouble.*

sur·mise /sər'maɪz/ *n.* a reasonable guess: *Her surmise about the weather turned out wrong.*

—*v.* **-mised, -mising, -mises** to make a reasonable guess: *After seeing that the room was empty, he surmised that the party was over.*

sur·mount /sər'maʊnt/ *v.* to overcome: *The company has surmounted some difficult problems and is now doing well.*

sur·pass /sər'pæs/ *v.* **-es 1** to exceed or go beyond: *Profits surpassed those of last year.* **2** to do better than: *The runner surpassed his old record by 10 seconds.*

sur·plus /'sɜr,plʌs, -pləs/ *n.* **-es** [C] an amount more than what is needed or used: *When the party was over, we had a surplus of beer and wine.*

—*adj.* extra, too much: *the farmer's surplus wheat had to be sold at a loss.*

sur·prise /sər'praɪz, sə-/ *n.* [C;U] **1** an unexpected event that causes a mild feeling of wonder or shock: *The court's decision was a surprise to us.* **2** the mild feeling of wonder or shock caused by an unexpected event: *I felt a surprise when I heard he was gone.*

—*adj.* unexpected or unannounced: *a surprise birthday party*

—*v.* **-prised, -prising, -prises 1** to cause or create a surprise: *He surprised us by saying that he was leaving the company.* **2** to feel a sense of surprise: *She was surprised to find him at home.* **3** to encounter unexpectedly: *Last night he surprised a burglar in the office.*

sur·re·al /sə'riəl/ *adj.* strange, dreamlike, unreal: *The movie had a surreal segment in which all the characters wore strange masks.* -*adj.* **surrealistic.**

sur·re·al·ism /sə'riə,lɪzəm/ *n.* [U] a modern style of art based on the logic and experience of dreams

sur·ren·der /sə'rɛndər/ *v.* **1** to concede defeat: *an army that surrenders to its enemy* **2** to yield: *an army that surrendered its arms*||*a person who surrenders to another's demands*

3 to yeild to an enemy or opposing force: *The town surrendered to the invading army.* **4** to give up possesion: *She surrendered the money she was hiding.*
—*n.* [U] the act of surrendering: *The terrorist's surrender was a relief to everyone.*

sur·rep·ti·tious /ˌsɜrəp'tɪʃəs/ *adj.frml.* done secretly to avoid discovery: *He made a surreptitious attempt to leave town.*

sur·ro·gate /'sɜrəgɪt, -ˌgeɪt, 'sʌr-/ *n.* a person who acts in place of another, a substitute: *When the little girl's mother died, her aunt became a surrogate for her mother. -adj.* **surrogate.**

sur·round /sə'raʊnd/ *v.* to extend all around, to encircle: *The stone wall surrounds our house.‖The ski resort is surrounded by mountains.*

sur·round·ing /sə'raʊndɪŋ/ *adj.* extending around, nearby: *The surrounding countryside is very pretty.*

sur·round·ings /sə'raʊndɪŋz/ *n.pl.* everything around or about the place or area in which one is located: *She lives in a pleasant neighborhood and enjoys her surroundings.*

sur·tax /'sɜrˌtæks/ *n.* **-es** an extra tax added to a tax, usu. as a percentage: *The city imposed a surtax to pay for the new school.*

sur·veil·lance /sər'veɪləns/ *n.* [U] a close watch kept on s.o. suspected of doing wrong: *The police have a suspected criminal under surveillance.*

sur·vey /sər'veɪ, 'sɜrˌveɪ/ *v.* **1** to take a wide view of an entire area: *She surveyed the room, looking for s.o. she knew.* **2** to examine the condition of s.t. (a situation, building, project): *He surveyed his finances before buying a new car.* **3** to make a precise map of an area: *Engineers surveyed the land before starting to build the highway.* **4** to examine the opinions of a group of people by asking them a question or set of questions and recording their answers: *The news agency surveyed voters about the proposed taxes.*
—*n.* **1** the act of surveying **2** a general view or examination of a place or condition: *Our survey of the company showed that it was in trouble.* **3** the act of mapping an area, or the map itself: *He had a survey of the land done before he bought it.* **4** a set of questions designed to measure the opinions of a group of people: *She prepared a survey about immigration.*

sur·vi·val /sər'vaɪvəl/ *n.* **1** [U] the ability to continue to exist or live: *The poor man's survival depends on the help of others.‖They prayed for the survival of the sailors.* **2** [C] s.t. that has continued to live or exist beyond its original conditions: *These books are survivals of earlier centuries.* **3 survival of the fittest:** the idea that those living things best able to

adapt to changes in the world are those most likely to survive

sur·vive /sər'vaɪv/ *v.* **-vived, -viving, -vives 1** to continue to live or exist, esp. for a long time or under hard conditions, to endure: *This tree has survived for many years.* **2** to outlast adversity or a threat to existence: *She was lucky to survive the plane crash.*

sur·vi·vor /sər'vaɪvər/ *n.* **1** a person who survives a life-threatening event: *a survivor of a car crash* **2** a person who is able to live through hard times: *Don't worry about him— he's a survivor!*

sus·cep·ti·ble /sə'septəbəl/ *adj.* **1 susceptible to: a.** easily influenced or affected by: *a child who is susceptible to disease* **b.** easily moved by the feelings of others, sensitive: *Children are very susceptible to their parents.* **2 susceptible of:** capable of being treated in a certain way or producing a certain result: *This metal is susceptible of a high polish.‖These calculations are susceptible of error.*

sus·pect /sə'spekt/ *v.* **1** to have an uncertain belief or expectation about the likelihood of s.t.: *I suspect that rain is going to spoil our picnic.* **2** to think that s.o. is guilty of s.t.: *I suspect him of stealing the money.* **3** to have doubts about the truth or value of s.t.: *They suspected his testimony because he had lied before.*
—*adj.* /'sʌsˌpekt, sə'spekt/ doubtful, questionable: *His story is suspect because it contains many factual errors.*
—*n.* /'sʌsˌpekt/ a person suspected of guilt: *That man is the prime suspect in a murder.*

sus·pend /sə'spend/ *v.* **1** to hang from a point so as to allow free movement: *In the museum hallway, many large banners were suspended from the ceiling.* **2** to stop or delay for a period of time; to interrupt, postpone, or withhold: *They suspended the game because of the rain.* **3** to take away s.o.'s right to belong to or participate in a group, or to enjoy certain rights and privileges, esp. because of misbehavior, failure to pay dues, violation of rules, etc.: *He was suspended from school for smoking.‖My driver's license was suspended for speeding.*

sus·pend·ers /sə'spendərz/ *n.pl.* straps worn over the shoulders to hold up men's pants, used instead of a belt: *Many men wear suspenders because they are more comfortable than belts.*

sus·pense /sə'spens/ *n.* [U] a state or feeling of anxiety and tension caused by uncertain expectations: *That action movie created a lot of suspense.‖He was in suspense about the birth of his first child. -adj.* **suspenseful.**

sus·pen·sion /sə'spenʃən/ *n.* **1** [U] an act of suspending or state of being suspended: *She said her suspension from school was unfair.* **2** [C;U] a support system in automobiles that ab-

S

sorbs shocks from the road: *Your car is uncomfortable because the suspension is old.* **3 suspension bridge:** a bridge that is supported by cables suspended from high towers

sus·pi·cion /sə'spɪʃən/ *n.* **1** [U] **a.** the act or condition of suspecting: *He treated her with suspicion after he learned about her past.* **b.** the state of being suspected: *She is under suspicion of having lied to the police.* **2** [U] feelings of doubt and distrust: *His odd behavior fills me with suspicion.* **3** [C] an uncertain feeling of belief or disbelief based on limited evidence: *I have a suspicion that he will be the best employee we ever hired.*

sus·pi·cious /sə'spɪʃəs/ *adj.* **1** having suspicions, distrustful of others: *He is suspicious of everyone who disagrees with him.* **2** causing suspicions, appearing as if guilty or worthy of distrust: *She was very bothered by her husband's suspicious behavior.*

sus·tain /sə'steɪn/ *v.* **1** to keep in existence by providing support, strength, or necessities: *This poor diet is not enough to sustain the population in this country.* **2** to keep up or maintain an activity: *Do you think we can sustain our commitment to delivering the papers on time?* **3** to suffer or endure: *The passengers sustained severe wounds from the train crash.*

sus·te·nance /'sʌstənəns/ *n.frml.* [U] anything that gives support, endurance, or strength, including food: *His daily walk by the ocean gave him a great deal of sustenance to live.*

swab /swɑb/ *n.* **1** a mop used to clean floors, decks, walls, etc.: *She made a swab with a towel and a stick to clean the bathroom.* **2** a piece of absorbent material used to clean, apply medicine to, or take specimens from the body: *The nurse cleaned my wound with a swab.*
—*v.* **swabbed, swabbing, swabs** to wipe or clean with a swab: *She swabbed my arm before inserting the needle.*

swag·ger /'swægər/ *v.* to walk in a self-important manner, (*syn.*) to strut: *After their team won the game, all the boys swaggered like movie stars.*

swal·low (1) /'swɑloʊ/ *v.* **1** to take food or drink into the throat from the mouth **2** *fig.* to consume: *The business swallowed up all my savings.* **3** *fig.* to accept without objection: *He didn't like his assignment, but he swallowed it and went ahead.*
—*n.* the act of swallowing: *He took big swallows of beer.*

swallow (2) *n.* a small bird with black top, white breast, brownish orange markings, and a double-pointed tail, noted for its rapid, swooping flight

swamp /swɑmp, swɔmp/ *n.* soft wet land with dense vegetation: *Swamps are filled with natural wild life.* -*adj.* **swampy.**

—*v.* **1** to flood with water: *The storm caused high tides that swamped our boat.* **2** *fig.*to overwhelm: *Our new product was so popular that we were swamped with work.*

swan /swɑn/ *n.* a large water bird, usu. all white or all black, with a long, graceful neck: *Children love to feed the swans in the pond near the park.*

swank·y /'swæŋki/ *adj.* **-ier, -iest** expensively stylish: *He dined only in swanky restaurants.*

swan song *n.infrml.fig.* a person's last (and sometimes finest) act or performance before retirement or death: *Just before the rock musician died, he gave one last concert as his swan song.*

swap /swɑp/ *v.* **swapped, swapping, swaps** to trade one thing for another, to exchange: *I swapped my bicycle for a guitar with a friend.*
—*n.* an instance of swapping: *The bicycle and the guitar both cost the same; so it was an even swap.*

swarm /swɔrm/ *n.* **1** a large number of insects or birds flying in a shapeless mass: *A swarm of bees passed over the field like a cloud.* **2** *fig.* a crowd of people: *A swarm of football fans filled the street.*
—*v.* **1** to move in a crowd: *Students swarmed into the auditorium.* **2** to be crowded: *The station was swarming with commuters running for trains.*

swarth·y /'swɔrði/ *adj.* **-ier, -iest** having a dark skin: *Many people from that country have swarthy complexions.*

swat /swɑt/ *v.* **swatted, swatting, swats** to strike with a flat object or the hand: *She swatted the flies with an old newspaper.*
—*n.* an act of swatting: *He gave his dog a swat to keep it from barking.*

swatch /swɑtʃ/ *n.* a sample of material, usu. of cloth: *The designer had swatches of drapery to choose from.*

swathe /swɑð, swɔð, sweɪð/ *v.* **swathed, swathing, swathes** to wrap in bandages or blankets: *She gave her baby a bath and swathed it in soft linen.*

sway /sweɪ/ *v.* **1** to move back and forth, to rock: *The trees swayed in the strong breeze.* **2** to influence, persuade: *He tried to sway my opinion in favor of new immigration laws.*
—*n.* [U] **1** a swaying movement: *the sway of the boat tipped me over.* **2** authority, power: *A dangerous tyrant holds sway in the country.*

swear /swɛr/ *v.* **swore** /swɔr/, **sworn** /swɔrn/, **swearing, swears 1** to curse, use offensive language: *He swears when he is angry.* **2** to say strongly: *She swore she would never go out with him again.* **3** to declare or promise when taking an oath: *We swore to be loyal forever.* **4** *phrasal v. insep.* **to swear by s.t.:** to believe in, trust: *She swears by eating raw garlic to stay healthy.* **5** *phrasal v. sep.* **to swear s.o. in:** to take an oath before beginning an elected position: *The judge swore in new governor.||He swore her in.*

sweat /swɛt/ *n.* **1** [U] a salty moisture produced by the body through the skin when it is overheated, (*syn.*) perspiration: *The runner's sweat soaked through his shirt.* **2** [C] the condition of being covered in sweat from exertion or effort: *She worked up a sweat in the gym.||He broke into a sweat from pushing his car.* **3** *usu.sing.* [C] a state of worry or anxiety: *We were in a sweat because we were late for the plane.* **4** *slang* **no sweat:** without worry or difficulty: *I told him that his job would be done on time, no sweat.*
—*v.* **1** to produce sweat from heat, exertion, or hard work: *She was sweating from working in her garden.* **2** to work hard: *He sweat for long hours writing that report.* **3 to make s.o. sweat:** to make s.o. wait anxiously for an opinion or judgment: *She made him sweat before she gave him an answer to his question.* **4** *phrasal v. sep.* **to sweat s.t. out:** to wait anxiously for s.t. to happen: *While his wife was in the hospital, he sweated out her illness at home.||He sweated it out.*

sweat·er /'swɛtər/ *n.* a garment with or without sleeves worn over the upper body and made of wool, cotton, or other fabric: *In winter, he wears a wool sweater over his shirt.*

sweat shirt *n.* a loose-fitting cotton garment with long sleeves, worn over the upper body for sports and leisure: *He dresses casually in a sweat shirt and jeans.*

sweat shirt

sweat shop *n.* a factory or shop where laborers work hard for long hours and low wages

sweat suit *n.* sportswear covering the torso and legs: *She wears a sweat suit when she jogs.*

sweep /swip/ *v.* **swept** /swɛpt/, **sweeping, sweeps 1** to clear a surface (such as a floor or wall) of dirt, dust, or other matter using a broom or brush: *She was sweeping the kitchen floor.||He swept the dust off his desk.* **2** to move forcefully or quickly over or through: *The wind swept through the trees.||The waves swept over the beach.* **3** to extend in a curve over a broad area: *The road sweeps along the coastline.* **4** to pass over as if in search of s.t.: *The beacon light swept the night sky.* **5** to move through an area with grace or power: *The president swept into the room where we were waiting.* **6** (in sports) to win completely (each contest in a series, or all places in a

race): *Our team swept the championship games.||Their team swept the mile run.* **7** *phrasal v. sep.* **to sweep s.t. up:** to clean, collect s.t. by sweeping: *Please sweep up the sand on the floor.||Please sweep it up.*
—*n.* **1** an act of sweeping: *This street needs a good sweep.* **2** a long, smooth movement of the hand or arm: *He pushed away the books with one broad sweep.* **3** a long, curving stretch of land: *The sweep of mountains extended for miles.* **4** a search: *The police made a sweep of the neighborhood.* **5 (to make) a clean sweep: a.** to clear away everything to allow for a new start: *After the election, they made a clean sweep of the government offices.* **b.** to win everything: *He made a clean sweep of his tennis matches.*

sweep·er /'swipər/ *n.* a person or thing that sweeps: *a chimney sweeper||a street sweeper*

sweep·ing /'swipiŋ/ *adj.* **1** broad, extensive, far-reaching: *The citizens voted for sweeping reforms.* **2** overreaching, too general: *His sweeping remarks offended many people.*

sweep·stakes /'swip,steɪks/ *n.pl.* a race or contest in which the entire prize goes to the winner: *He won the sweepstakes and became very rich.*

sweet /swit/ *adj.* **-er, -est 1** having a taste like sugar or honey: *This ice cream is very sweet.* **2** pleasing, delightful: *She gave me a sweet smile when I arrived.* **3** fresh, clean: *These flowers have a sweet smell.* **4** charming, attractive: *She fell in love with a sweet guy.* **5 to be sweet on s.o.:** to be fond of: *He is sweet on her.*
—*n.* a piece or portion of something sweet to eat, such as candy or chocolates: *Would you like a sweet for dessert?||No, thank you, I don't eat sweets.*

sweet·en /'switn/ *v.* **1** to make or become sweet: *I sweeten my cereal with honey.* **2** to make a business deal or offer more attractive by adding more money or benefits: *She sweetened the deal by offering him a bonus.*

sweet·en·er /'switnər/ *n.* **1** [C;U] a sweet substance, such as sugar or syrup for making food or drink taste sweet: *They say this sweetener is better for your health than sugar.* **2** [C] additional money or advantages in a business arrangement: *to add a sweetener to the deal*

sweet·heart /'swit,hɑrt/ *n.* **1** s.o. who is loved with tender affection and feels the same: *They have been sweethearts for many years.* **2** a person who is kind and cheerful to everyone: *She's a sweetheart and has no enemies.* **3** a term of endearment

sweet·ie /'switi/ *n.infrml.* (a term of endearment) sweetheart *See:* honey, **USAGE NOTE.**

sweet talk *n.* [U] **1** affectionate talk between lovers: *His phone calls to his girlfriend are full*

S

of sweet talk. **2** smooth, but empty persuasion: *Don't let him fool you with sweet talk.*
—*v.* **1** to speak in sweet talk: *He sweet-talks her all the time.* **2** to flatter, persuade: *She sweet-talked him into buying her a diamond ring.*

swell /swɛl/ *v.* **swelled, swollen** /ˈswoʊlən/, **swelling, swells 1** to enlarge or expand in size, usu. from absorbing fluids: *I twisted my ankle and it swelled up.*‖*The wet weather caused the window frames to swell.* **2** to fill out into a rounded shape: *the sheets on the clothesline swelled in the wind.* **3** *fig.* to fill up with: *He swelled with pride at his daughter's wedding.*
—*n.* **1** a long, unbroken wave on the ocean: *The ocean swells gently rocked the boat.* **2** a gradual increase in the loudness of sound: *The noise of the crowd swelled as the star came on stage.*
—*adj.exclam.* excellent!, wonderful!: *What a swell day to go to the beach!*

swell·ing /ˈswɛlɪŋ/ *n.* [U] enlargement usu. caused by injury or disease: *The swelling in my sprained ankle has gone down.*

swel·ter·ing /ˈswɛltərɪŋ/ *adj.* very hot and humid (weather, climate, etc.): *She loves the sweltering heat of the tropics.*

swerve /swɜrv/ *v.n.* **swerved, swerving, swerves** to turn suddenly and rapidly: *I <v.> swerved to avoid a child that ran in front of my car.*

swift /swɪft/ *adj.* **-er, -est** quick, rapid: *The artist drew my portrait with a few swift movements of his pencil.* -*adv.* **swiftly.**

swim /swɪm/ *v.* **swam** /swæm/, **swum** /swʌm/, **swimming, swims 1** to move through water by moving parts of the body (legs, arms, fins, tails): *He swam across the river and back again.* **2** to go a certain distance or across a body of water by swimming: *She swam a mile yesterday.* **3** to be covered with or floating in a liquid: *The scallops were swimming in a white wine sauce.* **4** to feel confused, off balance, dizzy: *He had too much to drink, and his head was swimming.* **5 to sink or swim:** to do what is necessary to survive: *This company must stop losing money or go out of business; it's sink or swim.* **6 to swim against the tide** or **current:** to go against the common trends: *People who want more leisure time are swimming against the tide; we're all working more.*
—*n.* the act of swimming: *Let's go for a swim.*

swim·ming /ˈswɪmɪŋ/ *n.* [U] the act, recreation, and water sport of those who swim: *We like to go swimming in the summer.*

swim·suit /ˈswɪmˌsut/ *n.* a bathing suit: *She put her swimsuit in the suitcase to go on vacation.*

swin·dle /ˈswɪndl/ *v.* **-dled, -dling, -dles** to cheat s.o. out of money or property: *He swindled the old couple out of their life's savings.*

—*n.* **1** an act of swindling **2** a false promise that deceives: *That insurance policy is a swindle because the company did not pay for my car repair.* -*n.* **swindler.**

swine /swaɪn/ *n.* **swine 1** a pig **2** *fig.* an ill-mannered and unethical person: *Only a swine would steal from children.*

swing /swɪŋ/ *v.* **swang** /swæŋ/, **swung** /swʌŋ/, **swinging, swings 1** to move forward and backward in an arc, or around in a circle, while attached to a fixed point: *The boy loved to swing from tree branches.*‖*The policeman was swinging his keys on a keychain.* ‖*When the wind blew, the door swung shut.* **2** to turn around quickly: *She swung around when he called her name.*‖*I swung the car around and headed north.* **3** (of music) to play with a lively rhythm: *This music really swings.* **4** to ride on a swing: *Children love to swing as high as they can go.* **5** to try to hit s.t. with an extended, arching movement of the arm, a stick, a baseball bat, etc.: *He swung at the ball and knocked it over the fence.*
—*n.* **1** [C;U] a swinging movement: *She has a slight swing in her walk.*‖*He took a swing at his father, but he missed.* **2** [C] a seat suspended on ropes or chains that hang from a framework, tree branch, etc. and allow the seat to sway forward and backward: *Children play on the swings in the park.* **3** [C] a passing movement through an area: *Let's take a swing through town to see if anything is going on.* **4** [C] a large shift in mood, atmosphere, opinion, etc.: *She goes through these mood swings when her husband is out of town.* **5 in full swing:** in full operation, at peak activity: *The party didn't get into full swing until after midnight.*

swing·ing /ˈswɪŋɪŋ/ *adj.* **1** socially active and exciting: *We had a swinging time in town last night.* **2** free-spirited and casual, esp. regarding sex -*n.* **swinger.**

swipe /swaɪp/ *n.* a broad, swinging stroke with the arm in an attempt to hit s.t.: *He took a swipe at the apples hanging from a tree.*
—*v.* **swiped, swiping, swipes 1** (to try) to hit with a broad stroke: *He swiped at the ball with all his strength.* **2** to steal: *The children swiped all the candy from the jar.*

swirl /swɜrl/ *v.* to move in a twisting and turning motion: *The dancers swirled across the ballroom floor.*
—*n.* **1** a swirling movement: *The swirl of water around her feet made the little girl laugh.* **2** a twisting or turning shape: *swirls of hair*‖*swirls of smoke*

swish /swɪʃ/ *v.* **-es 1** to move through air or water swiftly, creating the sound of blowing wind or streaming water: *The taxis swished by us in the rain.* **2** to move back and forth with a brushing or sweeping motion: *The horse swished its tail to get rid of the flies.*

—*n.* a hissing or rustling sound: *The swish of a lady's silk gown broke the silence of the library.*

switch /swɪtʃ/ *n.* **-es** **1** a device for turning on (or off) the electrical current that runs an appliance or machine, such as a light, computer, television, etc.: *Can you show me where the switch is on the TV?*||*This switch turns on the hall lights.* **2** a device that directs trains from one track to another: *If the switch is closed, the train cannot go on the other track.* **3** a shift or change: *There was a switch in the schedule, so we met in the morning instead of the afternoon.* **4** a thin, flexible stick used to drive horses or cattle: *The boy made a switch from the branch of a cherry tree.*

—*v.* **-es** **1** to use a switch: *She switched on the light.* **2** to change or exchange: *He switched trains in Chicago.*||*Between acts, the actress switched costumes.* **3 to pull a switch:** to surprise or deceive by making a sudden or secret change: *I expected to find him in the office, but he pulled a switch on me and wasn't there.* **4** *phrasal v. sep.* **to switch s.t. off: a.** to turn off a machine, etc: *Switch off the lights when you leave.*||*Switch them off.* **b.** to ignore: *She switched off the loud conversation at the next table.* **5** *phrasal v. sep.* **to switch s.t. on:** to turn on a machine, etc.: *I forgot to switch on the oven, dinner is going to be late.*||*I didn't switch it on.* **6** *phrasal v.* **to switch over: a.** to change allegiance from one group to another: *She switched over to the opposition party.* **b.** to change channels on a TV, etc.: *I want to switch over to the ball game; give me the remote control!*

switch·board /'swɪtʃ,bɔrd/ *n.* **1** a central telephone device where incoming calls are taken and routed to the individual **2 switchboard operator:** a person who operates a switchboard: *I called the XYZ Company and the switchboard operator put me through to Mr. Jones.*

swol·len /'swoʊlən/ *past part of* swell

swoon /swun/ *v.* to faint from shock or too much emotion: *She swooned when he proposed marriage to her.*

swoop /swup/ *v.* to descend rapidly on s.t., esp. in attack: *The hawk swooped down on the rabbit and killed it.*

—*n.* **1** a swooping movement: *The planes made a swoop over the city.* **2 in one fell swoop:** all at once: *She did all her food shopping in one fell swoop at the supermarket.*

sword /sɔrd/ *n.* a weapon with a handle and long steel blade: *Swords are not used in modern warfare.*

sword·fish /'sɔrd,fɪʃ/ *n.* [C;U] an edible, salt-water game fish with a sword-like upper jaw: *It takes strength and skill to catch a swordfish.*

syc·o·phant /'sɪkəfənt, 'saɪ-/ *n.* a person who seeks personal advantages and favors by praising and pleasing those who are richer and more powerful: *The king was surrounded by sycophants who told him what he wanted to hear.* -*adj.* **sycophantic** /,sɪkə'fæntɪk, ,saɪ-/.

syl·la·ble /'sɪləbəl/ *n.* **1** a part of a word as determined by vowel sounds and rhythm: *"Cat" is a word of one syllable; "hotel" has two syllables.* **2 to speak in words of one syllable:** to say s.t as plainly as possible: *In words of one syllable: "Just say no!"*

syl·la·bus /'sɪləbəs/ *n.* **-es** or **-bi** /-,baɪ/ an outline of topics for a course of study: *The syllabus for our course in American history included the colonial period, the Revolution, and the Constitution.*

sym·bol /'sɪmbəl/ *n.* **1** a sign, mark, picture, other object, or event taken or understood to be the representation of s.t. else, esp. s.t. important or meaningful: *The symbol of our country is displayed on our flag.*||*The road signs use symbols to give information and warnings.* **2** a written character that is part of a special language or sign system: *The book contains symbols that I cannot read.* **3** signs used in mathematics, chemistry, or other sciences (such as, $\div$, $\int$, CO_2)

sym·bol·ic /sɪm'bɑlɪk/ *adj.* **1** of, used as, or using a symbol: *Algebra is a symbolic language.* **2** not real, only for show: *The president threatened to use military force, but it was only a symbolic gesture.*

sym·bol·ism /'sɪmbə,lɪzəm/ *n.* [U] the use of symbols to represent meaning in literature and the arts: *Artists use symbolism to express deep feelings.*

sym·bol·ize /'sɪmbə,laɪz/ *v.* **-ized, -izing, -izes** to represent, to be a symbol of: *This flag symbolizes the unity of our country.*

sym·met·ri·cal /sə'mɛtrəkəl/ *adj.* having symmetry, balanced, and in proportion, with two parts that are mirror images of each other: *The symmetrical design of this church makes it very beautiful.*

sym·me·try /'sɪmətri/ *n.* [U] **-tries** the quality of balance and proportion in objects with two sides that correspond like mirror images in size, form, and arrangement of parts: *The human body has a symmetry that is basic to our sense of beauty.*||*The dancers danced in perfect symmetry.*

S

sym·pa·thet·ic /ˌsɪmpəˈθɛtɪk/ *adj.* **1** having, feeling, or showing sympathy: *Sending flowers was a sympathetic thing to do.*||*I am sympathetic to the cause of political prisoners.* **2** (of persons) kind and considerate: *She's very sympathetic to injured animals.*

sym·pa·thize /ˈsɪmpəˌθaɪz/ *v.* **-thized, -thizing, -thizes** to express or feel sympathy on behalf of: *The boy's mother sympathized with him when his dog died.*

sym·pa·thy /ˈsɪmpəθi/ *n.* [U] **-thies 1** a feeling of pity and compassion for the suffering of others: *I have no sympathy for criminals.*||*She felt sympathy for the war victims.* **2** the ability to share the feelings of others: *He has great sympathy for people of different cultures.* **3** agreement in feeling or opinion: *I am in sympathy with the striking teacher's union.*

sym·pho·ny /ˈsɪmfəni/ *n.* **-nies 1** a long and complex musical composition to be performed by an orchestra, usu. in four parts: *We went to the concert hall to hear a romantic symphony.* **2** an orchestra that plays symphonies: *We went to hear the symphony with other classical music lovers.*

sym·po·si·um /sɪmˈpouziəm/ *n.* **-siums** or **-sia** /-ziə/ a conference for the presentation of scientific or scholarly research papers: *The symposium on AIDS research lasted two days.*

symp·tom /ˈsɪmptəm/ *n.* **1** a change in the condition or appearance of the body that is a sign of disease: *A fever and muscular aches and pains are symptoms of the flu.* **2** a small change in appearance or behavior that indicates a larger development or problem: *Juvenile crime is a symptom of the failure of our schools.*

syn·a·gogue /ˈsɪnəˌgɑg, -ˌgɔg/ *n.* a place of religious study and worship for Jewish people: *They celebrated the Jewish new year at their synagogue.*

sync /sɪŋk/ *n. short for* synchronization

syn·chro·nize /ˈsɪŋkrəˌnaɪz/ *v.* **-nized, -nizing, -nizes 1** to adjust a number of clocks to show the same time: *Before departing, we synchronized our watches so we would return at the same time.* **2** to coordinate the schedule or timing of one or more activities: *A choreographer synchronizes dancers.*

syn·di·cate /ˈsɪndəkɪt/ *n.* **1** a group of individuals or companies combined to carry out projects requiring large resources or cooperative agreements: *Many Japanese companies form syndicates to reduce costs and improve efficiency.* **2** a business that sells the work of artists and writers to publishers
—*v.* /ˈsɪndəˌkeɪt/ **-cated, -cating, -cates** to sell and distribute the work of artists and writ-

ers to publishers: *The company syndicates cartoons to newspapers across the country.* -*n.* [U] **syndication.**

syn·drome /ˈsɪnˌdroum/ *n.* **1** a number of symptoms that belong to a specific disease: *The spots on his throat are part of a syndrome.* **2** a number of characteristics that typify a condition: *the poverty syndrome*

syn·er·gy /ˈsɪnərdʒi/ *n.* [C;U] **-gies** the extra energy, power, or capability produced by combining two or more agents, operations, or processes: *I think that if we join our efforts we will benefit from a new synergy.*

syn·od /ˈsɪnəd/ *n.* a meeting of church leaders to determine church policy: *He went before the synod to argue against racial discrimination.*

syn·o·nym /ˈsɪnəˌnɪm/ *n.* a word that means the same as another word: *"Sympathy" and "compassion" are synonyms. See:* antonym.

syn·op·sis /səˈnɑpsɪs/ *n.* **-ses** /-ˌsiz/ a brief summary of a book, movie, article, etc.: *I had no time to read that report, so I read a synopsis of it.*

syn·tax /ˈsɪnˌtæks/ *n.* [U] **-es 1** the order and relationship of phrases in a sentence **2** the grammatical rules that describe that order: *Syntax is an important part of style and meaning in language.*

syn·the·sis /ˈsɪnθəsɪs/ *n.* [C;U] **-ses** /-ˌsiz/ **1** a blend of various elements into a whole: *The corporate planning department made a synthesis of all their studies for the future.* **2** in chemistry, the formation of complex compounds from simpler ones

syn·the·size /ˈsɪnθəˌsaɪz/ *v.* **-sized, -sizing, -sizes 1** to make s.t. new and whole out of different parts or elements: *I think we can synthesize our efforts by creating one company.* **2** to imitate a natural substance by man-made processes: *The researchers synthesized insulin for a new medicine.*

syn·the·tic /sɪnˈθɛtɪk/ *adj.* artificial, manmade: *Synthetic drugs are increasingly important for public health.*
—*n.* [C] s.t. artificial: *Nylon is a synthetic; it is not from nature.*

syph·i·lis /ˈsɪfələs/ *n.* [U] an infectious venereal disease -*n.adj.* **syphilitic** /ˌsɪfəˈlɪtɪk/

sy·ringe /səˈrɪndʒ/ *n.* a hollow tube with a plunger, usu. attached to a needle through which it draws or injects fluids out of or into the body: *The nurse took a sample of my blood in a syringe.*

syr·up /ˈsɪrəp, ˈsɜr-/ *n.* [C;U] **1** a thick, sweet liquid made from sugar cane, maple sugar, or other natural sugars: *He poured syrup on his pancakes.* **2** a medicine in the form of a sweet liquid: *cough syrup*

sys·tem /'sɪstəm/ *n.* **1** [C] a group of related parts that function together for a purpose: *The air conditioning system in this building does not work very well.* **2** [C] an ordered, logical set of ideas: *He has a system for everything.* **3** [U] a philosophy: *According to his system, a wise person must learn to control her emotions.* **4** [C;U] a method or procedure with a set series of steps: *You must follow this system of rules if you want to work here.* **5** **the system:** the way things are done, esp. when controlled by an invisible authority: *She said that if you go against the system, you will get into trouble.*

sys·tem·at·ic /ˌsɪstə'mætɪk/ *adj.* based on a system; regular, orderly, methodical: *The scientist took a very systematic approach to solving problems.*

sys·tem·a·tize /'sɪstəmə,taɪz/ *v.* **-tized, -tizing, -tizes** to arrange into a system or in an orderly manner: *We must systematize our thinking if we want to produce reliable results.*

sys·tem·ic /sɪ'stɛmɪk/ *adj.* related to a system: *Hardening of the arteries is a systemic disorder of the circulatory system.*

S

T, t

T, t /ti/ *n.* **T's, t's** or **Ts, ts 1** the 20th letter of the English alphabet **2 to suit s.o. to a T:** to complement s.o.'s personality or interests perfectly: *As s.o. who likes teenagers, John finds that teaching high school suits him to a T.*

tab /tæb/ *n.* **1** an identifying marker, such as a colored metal clip: *The doctor's files have a different colored tab for each letter of the alphabet.* **2** the part of a strip that sticks out: *You pull a tab to open envelopes and packages.* **3** a bill, such as in a restaurant or bar: *I took my friend to lunch and paid the tab.* **4 to keep tabs on s.o.** or **s.t.:** to notice what s.o. is doing, *(syn.)* to monitor: *John keeps tabs on his younger brother to keep him out of trouble.* **5 to run a tab:** to have an ongoing bill: *Jane eats lunch at the same restaurant every day and runs a tab that she pays weekly.*
—*v.* to mark with a tab: *The doctor's assistant tabbed the files.*

tab·by /'tæbi/ *n.adj.* **-bies** a house cat with stripes: *We have a brown <n.> tabby* (or) *<adj.> tabby cat.*

tab·er·na·cle /'tæbər,nækəl/ *n.* a temple or church: *The Mormon Tabernacle Choir is a world-famous singing group.*

ta·ble (1) /'teɪbəl/ *n.* [C] **1** a piece of furniture with a flat top on legs: *Our dining room table is large enough for six people.* **2** the group of people sitting at a table: *Our table laughed at the waiter's jokes.* **3 at the table:** during a meal: *My father always said, "No singing at the table; it's impolite."* **4 to bring s.t. to the table:** to offer s.t. in negotiations: *The chemist brought knowledge of a new product to the table while the bankers brought financial information.* **5** *infrml.fig.* **to drink s.o. under the table:** to stay more sober while others drink a lot of alcohol: *She is small but can drink any man under the table.* **6 to lay one's cards on the table:** to be honest, tell one's thoughts: *After much talk, he finally laid his cards on the table and told the truth.* **7 to set the table:** to put out dishes, silverware, etc. on a dining table: *I set the dinner table while my husband cooked the meal.* **8 to turn the tables**

on s.o.: to change a bad situation to one's advantage: *A man was annoying a woman and she turned the tables on him by calling the police.* **9 under the table:** about s.t. illegal done secretly: *She works at the restaurant and is paid under the table, so she doesn't have to pay taxes.*
—*v.* **-bled, -bling, -bles** to postpone action on s.t.: *The tax committee tabled a motion by its chairperson to vote on a new tax bill.*

table (2) *n.* a display of numbers or other information: *That report has two tables showing people's incomes in the country. See:* tabular, timetable.

ta·ble·cloth /'teɪbəl,klɔθ/ *n.* a covering of linen, cotton, etc. placed over a table: *That restaurant has pink tablecloths.*

ta·ble·spoon /'teɪbəl,spun/ *n.* a large spoon used for measuring and eating food: *I use a tablespoon to measure ingredients in food that I cook. -n.* **tablespoonful.** *See:* teaspoon.

tab·let /'tæblɪt/ *n.* **1** pieces of paper glued at the top edge into a block: *Schoolchildren use tablets of writing paper.* **2** medication or other chemicals pressed usu. into a flat, round shape, a pill: *I take two aspirin tablets to stop a headache.* **3** a large, flat block of stone with writing, decoration, images, etc.: *Ancient peoples wrote on tablets made of clay.*

table tennis *n.* [U] a game two or four people play on a tabletop using wooden paddles and a small ball, also called Ping-Pong™: *Table tennis is a very fast game.*

ta·ble·ware /'teɪbəl,wɛr/ *n.* [U] silverware, glasses, and dishes used for eating: *Department stores sell ordinary tableware in their kitchen departments.*

table wine *n.* [U] ordinary red, pink, or white wine drunk with meals: *We ordered a bottle of red table wine to have with our roast beef dinner last night.*

tab·loid /'tæb,lɔɪd/ *n.* a newspaper with many pictures and articles about scandals, news, sports, and other everyday topics: *The tabloids try to get your attention by telling you personal information about famous people.*

ta·boo /tæˈbu/ *n.* [C;U] a forbidden act, esp. one that goes against social customs or religious practices: *Drinking alcohol is <adj.> taboo* (or) *a <n.> taboo in some cultures.*

tab·u·lar /ˈtæbyələr/ *adj.* shown in columns or lists in a table: *Bus schedules are listed in tabular form on timetables.* -*v.* **tabularize.**

tab·u·late /ˈtæbyəˌleɪt/ *v.* **-lated, -lating, -lates** to organize, usu. statistical information: *News reporters tabulated and announced the latest national election results.* -*n.* [U] **tabulation; tabulator.**

tac·it /ˈtæsɪt/ *adj.* unspoken, implied: *Management gave tacit approval to a marketing plan by asking to be told about its progress.* -*adv.* **tacitly.**

tac·i·turn /ˈtæsəˌtɜrn/ *adj.* very quiet, sour, (*syn.*) grim: *The old man has a taciturn expression on his face.*

tack /tæk/ *n.* **1** [C] a small, sharp nail: *Workers nail carpets to floors with tacks.* **2** [C;U] (in sailing) a controlled change of direction depending on the wind **3** *fig.* **to take a different tack:** to use a different approach: *We tried marketing the product by brochure, then we took a different tack by selling it through distributors. See:* thumbtack.
—*v.* **1** to nail s.t. with tacks: *Workers tacked the carpet to the floor.* **2** to change the direction of a sailboat according to the wind **3** *phrasal v.* **to tack on:** to add s.t.: *She tacked another page on to her report.*

tack·i·ness /ˈtækinɪs/ *n.* **1** stickiness: *The paint has not dried and you can feel its tackiness.* **2** cheapness, (*syn.*) shoddiness **3** poor taste

tack·le /ˈtækəl/ *n.* **1** [U] equipment used in a sport: *We take fishing tackle on camping trips.* **2** [C] (in USA football) knocking a player carrying the ball to the ground
—*v.* **-led, -ling, -les 1** (in USA football) to knock a ball carrier down: *A guard tackled the ball carrier.* **2** *fig.* to begin a job with a lot of energy: *I tackled the problem of lowering the company's costs.*

tack·y /ˈtæki/ *adj.* **-ier, -iest 1** sticky, not dried: *The paint is still tacky on the wood.* **2** *infrml.* cheap, not well-made, (*syn.*) shoddy: *That neighborhood is run-down and tacky.* **3** *infrml.* poor taste, rude: *He made tacky comments to guests at the party.*

ta·co /ˈtɑkoʊ/ *n.* **-cos** a thin, flat pancake made of flour or cornmeal, filled with meat, vegetables, etc.: *I like a cheese taco for lunch once in a while. See:* enchilada, USAGE NOTE.

tact /tækt/ *n.* [U] consideration, care in dealing with others, esp. not to offend or shock: *She is a psychologist who uses tact in her relationships with her patients.* -*adj.* **tactful;** -*adv.* **tactfully.**

tac·tic /ˈtæktɪk/ *n.* [C] **1** a military plan: *Napoleon was an expert in military tactics who usually won his battles.* **2** a way, method of doing s.t.: *He uses power as a tactic in making others do what he wants.* -*adj.* **tactical;** -*adv.* **tactically.**

tac·ti·cian /tækˈtɪʃən/ *n.* a person skilled usu. in military strategy

tac·tics /ˈtæktɪks/ *n.used with a pl.verb* **1** the combination of military plans to achieve a strategy: *Generals use tactics of attacks by artillery, tanks, and foot soldiers to reach their objectives.* **2** controlling plans or approaches, (*syn.*) maneuverings: *She uses psychological tactics in her advertising plans.* **3 strong-arm tactics:** pushiness, force: *Thugs used strong-arm tactics to break up a labor strike.*

tac·tile /ˈtæktəl, -ˌtaɪl/ *adj.* capable of being felt by touch, (*syn.*) tangible: *A doctor's tactile ability is important in examining patients.* -*n.* **tactility** /tækˈtɪləti/.

tact·less /ˈtæktlɪs/ *adj.* rude, inconsiderate, (*syn.*) uncouth: *It was tactless of him to ask why she wasn't married.* -*adv.* **tactlessly;** -*n.* [U] **tactlessness.**

tad /tæd/ *n.* a small amount: *He put a tad more butter on his toast.*

tad·pole /ˈtædˌpoʊl/ *n.* the young of frogs and toads: *Tadpoles are born in the pond each spring.*

taf·fe·ta /ˈtæfətə/ *n.* [U] *adj.* a smooth, often shiny material used in women's clothes: *She wore a <adj.> taffeta dress to the dance.*

taf·fy /ˈtæfi/ *n.* **-fies** [C;U] a soft, chewy candy made of boiled sugar or molasses and butter: *Taffy is pulled until it is firm.*

tag /tæg/ *n.* **1** a marker, such as a sticker or label: *A clerk put red tags on items on sale in the store.* **2** a vehicle's license plate(s): *He bought a new car and put new tags on it.* **3 to play tag:** a game where one child chases the others until one is touched or tagged as "it": *Children love to play tag.*
—*v.* **tagged, tagging, tags 1** to put tags on things: *Workers tagged clothes in the store.* **2** to touch another player in a game of tag: *The child who was "it" chased the others and tagged her friend.* **3** *phrasal v.* **to tag along:** to go with others: *My friends decided to go to a movie and I tagged along.*

tag·a·long /ˈtægəˌlɔŋ/ *n.* a person who follows others: *A little boy is a tagalong with his older brother and his friends.*

tag sale *n.* **1** a sale where merchandise is marked with a special tag showing reduced price: *The local men's store has a tag sale on Saturday.* **2** a garage or yard sale: *We had a tag sale of all our old stuff. See:* garage sale, USAGE NOTE.

T

tail /teɪl/ *n.* **1** a movable extension of the spine of many animals: *Dogs wag their tails in greeting.* **2** *slang* the buttocks: *I fell down and hurt my tail* (or) *tailbone.* **3** *infrml.fig.* a secret observer following s.o.: *The police put a tail on the mobster to see where he went.*
—*adj.* related to the end of s.t.: *She was late and arrived only at the tail end of the meeting.*
—*v.* **1** *slang* to follow and observe s.o. secretly: *A strange man has tailed us since we left the movie theater.* **2** *phrasal v.* **to tail off** or **away:** to blend into and disappear, (*syn.*) to diminish: *The fog tailed* (or) *tailed off into the evening darkness.*

tail·gate /ˈteɪlˌgeɪt/ *n.* **1** the back section of a truck that can be moved up or down to load or take off cargo: *After loading his pickup truck, the farmer put up the tailgate and locked it.* **2** an outdoor, informal party at a sports event: *We had sandwiches and coffee at the tailgate before the football game.*
—*v.infrml.* **-gating, -gated, -gates** to drive very closely to another vehicle: *On the highway, a farmer tailgated another one for a moment, then passed him.*

tail·light /ˈteɪlˌlaɪt/ *n.* the red, rear lights on vehicles: *When you step on the brakes, the taillights go on.*

tai·lor /ˈteɪlər/ *v.* **1** to cut, sew, alter, and repair clothes: *He tailors women's clothes in a fine Fifth Avenue shop.* **2** to make s.t. to specific requirements, customize: *That accountant tailors her services to meet clients' needs.* -*adj.* **tailored.**
—*n.* a person who makes, sews, or repairs clothes

tai·lor·ing /ˈteɪlərɪŋ/ *n.* [U] **1** the art and craft of making clothes: *That men's store offers tailoring of fine suits.* **2** the cut and finish of a garment made by a tailor: *They offer custom tailoring as well as alterations.*

tailor-made *adj.* **1** custom-made, cut, and finished by a tailor **2** suitable, just right: *That job is tailor-made for her personality and skills.*

tail pipe *n.* a tube through which a car's exhaust gases are released: *Smoke comes out the tail pipe of that old car.*

tail·spin /ˈteɪlˌspɪn/ *n.* **1** a downward spin of an airplane out of control: *The plane's engines stopped working and it went into a tailspin.* **2** *fig.* **to go into a tailspin:** an emotional crisis: *When his wife died, he went into a tailspin and only his friends helped him get through it.*

taint /teɪnt/ *n.* [C;U] **1** a sign of decay or contamination: *The bread has a taint of green mold on it.* **2** a trace of scandal or corruption: *Your plan to embarass your boss has a taint of evil about it.*
—*v.* **1** to spoil, (*syn.*) to contaminate s.t.: *The food has spoiled and is tainted with mold.* **2** to spoil, (*syns.*) to stigmatize, blemish: *His in-*volvement in the scandal tainted the politician's reputation. -*adj.* **tainted.**

take /teɪk/ *v.* **took** /tʊk/ or **taken** /ˈteɪkən/, **taking, takes 1** to grasp, (*syn.*) to clench: *He took the baby from his wife's hands.* **2** to remove, obtain: *I took some money from my wallet.* **3** to do, perform: *We take a vacation every August.* **4** to happen, occur: *The meeting took place yesterday.* **5** to consume, (*syn.*) to ingest: *He took some tea (water, pills, dessert, etc.) with his lunch.* **6** to experience: *He took some air (some sun, a walk, etc.).* **7** to understand, (*syn.*) to presume: *I take it from what you say that you don't feel well today.* **8** to invite s.o. somewhere: *She took her daughter to lunch.* **9** to record: *She took her child's temperature.* **10** to move, transport: *That road (bus, train, etc.) takes you to the city.* **11** to become part of: *The idea of a four-day work week took hold in the company.* **12** to require, need: *That car takes hi-octane gasoline to run well.*‖*It takes years of practice to become a great musician.* **13** to capture: *Soldiers take prisoners.* **14** to defeat, (*syn.*) to vanquish: *The boxer took his opponent in five rounds.* **15** *vulg.* (for a man) to have sex with a woman **16** to acknowledge, accept criticism, disagreement, etc.: *Your suggestion is well taken, thank you.* **17** to disagree: *He took exception to what you said.* **18** to control, manage: *She took charge of the situation.* **19** to subtract: *Take 90 from 100 and you have 10.* **20** *infrml.* **to be** or **get taken:** to be swindled, cheated: *I was overcharged and really got taken at that store.* **21 to have what it takes:** to be competent, ambitious: *He has what it takes to succeed in a hard business.* **22** *phrasal v. insep.* **to take account of s.t.:** to consider, note: *The judge took account of the fact that the guy had not been arrested before and only gave him a small fine.* **23** *phrasal v. insep.* **to take advantage of s.o.** or **s.t.: a. s.o.:** to cheat, abuse s.o.: *Cheats take advantage of tourists by charging them too much for things.* **b. s.t.:** to use an opportunity: *We took advantage of the beautiful sunshine and took a long walk.* **24** *phrasal v. insep.* **to take after s.o.:** to look like, imitate: *She takes after her mother in looks and attitudes.* **25** *phrasal v. sep.* **to take away: a.** to remove: *The waiter took away the dirty dishes.* **b.** to withdraw, (*syn.*) to revoke: *A manager took away my parking space.* **c.** to subtract: *Five take away two equals three.* **26** *phrasal v. sep.* **to take s.t. back: a.** to repossess s.t.: *He took back the tools that he loaned me.* **b.** to apologize for saying s.t., (*syn.*) to retract: *He called me a bad name then took back what he had said.* **27** *phrasal v. sep.* **to take down s.o.** or **s.t.: a. s.o.:** to remove from office, destroy, etc.: *The scandal took down the Prime Minister.*‖*It took* *her down.* **b. s.t.:** *phrasal v. sep.* to remove (from above): *She took down the decorations after the party.* **c. s.t.:** *phrasal v.* to write, note: *Students take down what professors say.* **28 to take effect:** to become valid, go into effect: *The new law takes effect next month.* **29 to take five** or **ten** (minutes' break) or **a breather:** to stop work and relax briefly: *We worked for three hours straight then took ten* (or) *a breather.* **30 to take for granted: a.** not to notice or feel grateful for s.o. or s.t.: *He takes his wife for granted.* **b.** to assume, (*syn.*) to presume to be true: *She took it for granted that the invitation addressed to her included her husband, too.* **31 take ill** or **sick:** to become sick **32** *phrasal v. sep.* **to take s.o.** or **s.t. in: a. s.o.:** to deceive, (*syn.*) to trick: *The sales representative took in her clients on product prices.||She took them in.* **b.** to give shelter, care for: *She takes in stray cats who have no home.* **c. s.t.:** to bring indoors: *He took in the laundry from the clothesline.* **33 to take into account:** to consider s.t. in making a judgment: *The boss takes into account how much experience a person has in deciding whether to hire him or her.* **34 to take it:** to survive pain, criticism, etc.: *The doctor told me that the operation would be painful, but I told her that I can take it.* **35 to take it easy: a.** to relax, not work too hard: *When the weather is hot, I try to take it easy.* **b.** not to treat s.o. too harshly: *When you criticize her, take it easy because she's very sensitive.* **36 to take it for what it's worth:** to provide a limited but useful amount of information or an opinion: *You can take it for what it's worth but I think that stock is too risky.* **37 to take it from me:** believe me: *Take it from me, it will rain tomorrow.* **38 to take it hard:** to suffer, react badly to s.t.: *When he was fired from his job, he took it hard.* **39** *infrml.fig.* **to take it lying down:** to accept bad treatment without complaint, usu. used with *not: He told false stories about her and she didn't take it lying down; she told him to stop immediately.* **40 to take it or leave it: a.** having no choice: *You accept what I give you or you will get nothing; take it or leave it.* **b.** to be indifferent, not to care: *I don't like coffee that much; I can take it or leave it.* **41** *phrasal v. insep.* **to take s.t. out on s.o.:** to express one's frustrations on s.o., be angry with s.o. wrongly: *When his boss yelled at him, he took it out on his wife by yelling at her when he got home.* **42 to take it upon oneself:** to act independently: *He took it upon himself to buy his wife a new car without telling her first.* **43** *phrasal v. sep.* **to take (s.t.) off: a.** to remove clothes, disrobe: *He took his clothes off and put on pajamas.* **b.** to lose weight: *He took off 20 pounds.* **c.** to go up into the air, (*syn.*) to ascend: *The airplane took off from the airport.* **d.** *fig.* to increase

quickly: *Sales of the new product have taken off.* **e.** to leave quickly, flee: *When the police arrived, the thief took off.* **44** *phrasal v. sep.* **to take s.o.** or **s.t. on: a.** to accept responsibility, manage: *He takes on a lot both at work and in civic affairs.* **b. s.t.:** to load up with s.t.: *The ship took on water in the storm.* **c. s.o.** or **s.t.:** to challenge s.o. or s.t.: *The boy took on the school bully in a fight.* **45 to take one's time:** to act slowly: *My grandfather has to take his time walking home.* **46** *phrasal v. sep.* **to take s.t. out: a.** to remove physically: *I take out the trash each morning.* **b.** to subtract, extract: *The government takes taxes out of my paycheck.* **47** *phrasal v. sep.* **to take one's frustrations out:** to act in anger against s.o. wrongly: *He takes his frustrations from his job out on his family.* **48** *phrasal v. sep.* **to take s.t. over: a.** to carry, transport: *A driver took supplies over to a customer's warehouse.* **b.** to take command: *A new leader took over the government.* **49 to take part:** to participate, join in: *We took part in the conference.* **50** *infrml.fig.* **to take pot shots** or **cheap shots at s.o.:** to criticize, (*syn.*) to snipe at: *Politicians take pot shots at each other during election campaigns.* **51 to take shape:** to form, develop: *Our vacation plans are taking shape and will be final soon.* **52 to take some doing:** to require a lot of effort: *To become a doctor takes some doing, first years of study and then an internship.* **53** *infrml.fig.* **to take s.o. down a peg** (or) **a notch:** to reduce s.o.'s high opinion of himself or herself: *He was a high school basketball champion but was badly beaten in his first college game and that took him down a peg.* **54 to take s.o. for all he or she is worth:** to ruin s.o. financially: *She injured s.o. in an accident and that person took her for all that she is worth in a lawsuit.* **55** *phrasal v. insep.* **to take to s.o.** or **s.t.: a.** to become addicted to s.t.: *He took to drink later in life.* **b. s.t.:** to go, retreat: *The old lady took to her bed and stayed for days.* **c. s.o.** or **s.t.:** to like: *She took to him the moment that she met him.* **56** *phrasal v. sep.* **to take s.t. up: a.** to shorten: *She took up the hem on her skirt. ||She took it up.* **b.** to do s.t.: *He took up tennis for the first time last week.* **57** *phrasal v. insep.* **to take up with s.o.:** to start a relationship: *She took up with her new boyfriend last month.*

—*n.* **1** a photographic session: *The actors got the scene right on the second take.* **2** *infrml.fig.* **on the take:** taking money illegally (bribes, kickbacks, graft, etc.): *His job is to give out permits and he is always on the take.* **3 to do a double take:** to look twice in surprise: *I had not seen my old friend in years and I did a double take when we met by accident.*

take-home pay *n.* [U] the amount of money in one's paycheck after taxes and deductions are taken out: *Her take-home pay is enough to give her a comfortable lifestyle.*

tak·en /'teɪkən/ *past part. & adj. of* take **1** captivated, charmed: *John met Jane for the first time and was taken with her.* **2** *slang* cheated, deceived: *That deal sounded good, but I got taken for a lot of money.* **3 to be taken by** or **with:** charmed, delighted by: *From the moment he met her, he was taken by* (or) *with her.* **4 to be taken in:** cheated, deceived: *He was taken in by the swindler's promise of great profits. See:* take.

take·off /'teɪk,ɔf/ *n.* a rise or ascent, as of an aircraft from the runway: *The takeoff of the jet went very smoothly. See:* landing.

take·out /'teɪk,aʊt/ *n.* [U] *adj.* related to food ordered from a restaurant to be eaten elsewhere: *He owns a Chinese food <n.> takeout where customers come in and order <adj.> takeout food.*

take·o·ver /'teɪk,oʊvər/ *n.* **1** a forced replacement of old leaders with new ones: *The takeover of the government in a military coup was quick and bloodless.* **2** (in business) getting control of a corporation: *A takeover can be friendly or hostile.*

tak·er /'teɪkər/ *n.* **1** person who accepts or buys s.t.: *She offered her house for sale and there was one taker.* **2** a person who takes money, favors, etc. from others but gives nothing back: *There are givers and takers in life.*

tak·ing /'teɪkɪŋ/ *n.* **1** [U] **for the taking:** available: *You can pick wild raspberries by the roadside because they are there simply for the taking.* **2** [U] *pl.* the earnings or receipts of a store: *On the day of the sale, the shoe store's takings were large.*

talc /tælk/ *n.* [U] a soft silicate mineral: *Talc is refined and made into talcum powder.*

tale /teɪl/ *n.* **1** a story, narrative: *That novel is a tale about the Old South.* **2 to tell tall tales:** to exaggerate, lie: *He tells tall tales about catching huge fish.* **3 to tell tales: a.** to lie **b.** to gossip, tell confidential information: *He tells tales about people in town. See:* tattletale.

tal·ent /'tælənt/ *n.* [C;U] **1** an ability to do s.t. well: *She has a talent for singing.* **2** people with ability: *New York is full of artistic talent.* *-adj.* **talented.**

talent scout *n.* a person who searches for talented performers and athletes: *He is a talent scout for a baseball team.*

tal·is·man /'tælɪsmən, -ɪz-/ *n.* **-mans** a magic object, (*syn.*) a charm: *The tribal chief wears a talisman on a chain around his neck.*

talk /tɔk/ *n.* **1** [C] an act of speaking, esp. with s.o.: *Two friends had a good talk over coffee.* **2** [C] a speech to an audience: *The professor gave a talk on her new book at a conference.* **3** [U] gossip, scandal: *Talk around town says that the local factory is going to close.* **4 big talk:** exaggerated claims of wealth, power, etc.: *He's full of big talk about how much money he makes.* **5 to have a talk: a.** to chat, converse: *My friend and I went to lunch and had a good talk.* **b.** to have a serious, often critical, discussion: *He has made a serious mistake and I will have a talk with him about it.* **6 to make small talk:** to chat about unimportant things, such as the weather, clothes, etc.: *She is such a serious woman that she does not know how to make small talk.*

—v. **1** to speak: *My friend and I talked about the future.* **2** to reveal confidences, (*syn.*) to tattle: *A criminal talked to the police about his partner.* **3** *phrasal v. insep.* **to talk around s.t.:** to avoid discussing the main point: *The politician talked around the matter of a tax increase without saying that he wanted one.* **4 to talk away the hours:** to chat, speak of many things: *Two old friends met and talked away the hours about the past.* **5** *phrasal v. insep.* **to talk back to s.o.:** to speak back rudely, (*syn.*) to sass: *A student talked back to the teacher and said she is wrong and mean.* **6** *infrml.* **to talk big:** to make exaggerated statements about one's power, wealth, etc.: *He talks big about how much money he has and what great things he's done.* **7** *phrasal v. insep.* **to talk down to s.o.:** to talk to s.o. as though he or she is stupid and unimportant, (*syns.*) to condescend, to patronize: *He talked down to me about how stupid I was to invest in the stock market without doing a lot of research.* **8** *phrasal v. insep.* **to talk s.o. into doing s.t.:** to persuade, convince: *I talked her into applying for the job, even though she didn't think she would get it.* **9** *infrml.fig.* **to talk one's ear off:** to speak at great length and not allow the listener to speak: *She was so nervous that she talked my ear off for two hours.* **10** *infrml.fig.* **to talk oneself blue in the face:** to try very hard to convince s.o.: *I talked myself blue in the face trying to persuade her to save money for retirement, but she won't.* **11** *infrml.fig.* **to talk out of both sides of one's mouth:** to contradict oneself: *The manager promised to lower costs then said costs must go up, so he was talking out of both sides of his mouth at the same time.* **12 to talk one's way out of:** to avoid punishment by talking: *He talked his way out of getting a speeding ticket.* **13** *phrasal v. sep.* **to talk s.t. out:** to discuss a topic until it is completely understood: *We thought of buying a second home, but we talked out costs and accessibility before doing anything.* ‖*We talked it out.* **14** *phrasal v. insep.* **to talk s.o. out of doing s.t.:** to discourage s.o. from doing s.t., (*syn.*) to dissuade: *A doctor talked the insane man out of jumping off*

the bridge. **15** *phrasal v. sep.* **to talk s.t. over:** to discuss a matter, esp. to reach an understanding: *We talked our budget over and decided to make an offer on a new house.* ||*We talked it over.* **16** *phrasal v. sep.* **to talk s.t. up:** to promote, create interest: *Salespeople talk up their products to customers.* ||*They talked them up. See:* doubletalk.

talk·a·tive /'tɔkətɪv/ *adj.* liking to talk, (*syn.*) garrulous: *He is a happy, talkative man.*

talk·er /'tɔkər/ *n.* **1** a person who likes to talk **2** a gossip, s.o. who reveals secrets: *Watch out what you say to him; he's a talker.*

talking-to *n.* **-tos** a scolding, (*syn.*) a reprimand: *When the little boy would not behave politely, his father gave him a talking-to.*

talk show *n.* a radio or television show where guests are interviewed by a host and listeners call in with questions

tall /tɔl/ *adj.* **1** referring to height: *That fellow is six feet tall.* **2** characterized by above average height: *Manhattan is full of tall buildings.* **3 a tall order:** a large, usu. unreasonable request: *My boss wants this project finished a week early; that's a tall order!* —*adv.* erect, proudly: *Soldiers stand tall for inspection.* -*n.* [U] **tallness.** *See:* tale.

tal·low /'tælou/ *n.* [U] animal fat used for making candles, soap, etc.

tal·ly /'tæli/ *v.* **-lied, -lying, lies 1** to count up: *Accountants tallied columns of numbers.* **2** to equal, agree with: *Her tax figures don't tally with the accountants.* —*n.* **-lies** a total of s.t., score: *A warehouse worker calculated the tally of goods received today.*

tal·on /'tælən/ *n.* a bird's claw, esp. of predators: *The eagle put its talons into the fish and lifted it from the water.*

ta·ma·le /tə'mali/ *n.* [C] a Mexican dish of cooked seasoned meat and peppers rolled in corn meal and steamed in corn husks

tam·bou·rine /ˌtæmbə'rin/ *n.* a musical instrument like a drum with bells in its rim: *A gypsy sang and played the tambourine with her hands.*

tame /teɪm/ *adj.* **tamer, tamest 1** domesticated, (*syn.*) docile: *Dogs and house cats are tame animals.* **2** harmless, (*syn.*) innocuous: *The party was noisy but actually quite tame.* -*adv.* **tamely;** -*n.* **tameness.** —*v.* **tamed, taming, tames 1** to domesticate, train: *She tamed a stray cat she found on the street.* **2** to control, (*syn.*) to repress: *He tamed his bad temper to keep his customer's business.*

tam·per /'tæmpər/ *phrasal v. insep.* **to tamper with s.o.** or **s.t.:** to damage s.t., influence improperly (*syn.*) to interfere: *A burglar tampered with the locks on the door.*

tam·pon /'tæm,pɑn/ *n.* a cotton plug used to stop blood, esp. menstrual flow

tan /tæn/ *n.adj.* a light brownish color: *She drives a <adj.> tan car. See:* suntan. —*v.* **tanned, tanning, tans 1** to get a tan: *She tans easily.* **2** to preserve or cure leather: *Tanners tan hides to make leather shoes.*

tan·dem /'tændəm/ *n.adj.* **in tandem:** two together one before the other: *The couple arrived in <n.> tandem, the husband behind the wife.*||*They ride a <adj.> tandem bicycle.*

tang /tæŋ/ *n.* a distinct, strong taste or odor: *Garlic has a special tang. -adj.* **tangy.**

tan·gent /'tændʒənt/ *n.* **1** a line, curve or surface that touches but does not intersect s.t.: *The spokes of a wheel are tangents from the hub.* **2** *infrml.* **to go off on a tangent:** to leave the main point, (*syn.*) to digress: *Once he starts talking, he is likely to go off on a tangent. -n.* **tangency.**

tan·gen·tial /tæn'dʒɛnʃəl/ *adj.* **1** in the position of a tangent: *One line is tangential to another.* **2** beside the point, minor: *The negotiator lost the main point and spoke of tangential issues.*

tan·ger·ine /ˌtændʒə'rin/ *n.* a small, sweet orange —*adj.* a dark orange color: *She wore a <adj.> tangerine sweater.*

tan·gi·ble /'tændʒəbəl/ *adj.* **1** touchable, real: *Tangible assets include cash, real estate, and machinery.* **2** able to be felt, (*syns.*) perceptible, palpable: *Her love for him is so intense that it is tangible–you can really feel it. See:* intangible.

tan·gle /'tæŋgəl/ *n.* a snarl, knot: *She combed a tangle out of her hair. -adj.* **tangled.** —*v.* **-gled, -gling, -gles 1** to snarl, knot up: *Ropes on ships tangle.* **2** *phrasal v. sep.* **to tangle s.t. up:** to become confused and complex: *Red tape tangled up my visa application.*||*It tangled it up.* **3** *phrasal v. insep.* **to tangle with s.o.:** to fight or have bad contact with: *He drove over the speed limit and tangled with the police. -n.* [U] *frml.* **tanglement.** *See:* entanglement; untangle.

tan·gled /'tæŋgəld/ *adj.* snarled, knotted up: *Traffic is all tangled up at the bridge.*

tan·go /'tæŋgou/ *n.* **-gos** [C;U] *v.* **-goed, -going, -gos** a Latin American dance: *The <n.> tango is a dance of passion and love.*

tank /tæŋk/ *n.* **1** a closed container, such as for oil, gasoline, or water: *The oil tank in our basement holds 800 gallons of heating oil.* **2** a heavily armored combat vehicle *-adj.* **tanked.** — *phrasal v. insep.* **to tank up (on s.t.): a.** to fill up: *We drove into a gas station and tanked up on gasoline.* **b.** *infrml.fig.* to drink excessively: *Every Saturday night, he tanks up on beer.*

T

tank·ard /'tæŋkərd/ *n.* a large mug made of pewter or ceramic, often with a cover and handle

tank·er /'tæŋkər/ *n.adj.* a large boat or truck used to transport liquid: *Oil <n.> tankers sail from the Middle East to Japan.*

tanned /tænd/ *adj.* of skin darkened by the sun: *She came back from her vacation tanned and rested.*

tan·ner /'tænər/ *n.* a person or business who tans leather hides: *A tanner's work is often smelly. See:* tan.

tan·ner·y /'tænəri/ *n.* **-ies** a business where hides are tanned: *He moved his tannery from the USA to the tropics where costs are lower.*

tan·nin /'tænɪn/ *n.* [U] tannic acid, a chemical from plants used in tanning hides, wine making, and as an astringent

tan·ning /'tænɪŋ/ *n.* [U] **1** the process of preparing hides and leather: *Tanning is a chemical process.* **2** darkening of the skin: *Tanning happens when one sits in the sun.*

tan·ta·lize /'tæntə,laɪz/ *v.* **-lized, -lizing, -lizes** to offer but not satisfy, *(syn.)* to tempt: *The chocolates in the store window tantalized me, but I did not buy any. -adj.* **tantalizing.**

tan·ta·mount /'tæntə,maʊnt/ *adj.* equal to, similar to: *Driving on that icy road is tantamount to suicide.*

tan·trum /'tæntrəm/ *n.* a fit of anger, bad temper: *The baby had a temper tantrum and screamed for an hour.*

tap /tæp/ *v.* **tapped, tapping, taps 1** to hit lightly as with the fingers: *A stranger tapped me on the shoulder and asked directions.* **2** to use, *(syn.)* to draw upon: *The company tapped the financial resources of its banks by taking out loans.* **3** to insert a tap and take from: *The bartender tapped a keg of beer.* **4** to listen secretly using a wiretap on a phone line
—*n.* **1** a light knock: *He gave me a tap on the shoulder to get my attention.* **2** a faucet: *He drew some water from the tap and drank.* **3** an apparatus used to remove liquids: *A bartender put a tap in a keg of beer.* **4** an electronic listening device, a bug: *The FBI put taps in the cars of suspected Mafia members.* **5 on tap: a.** ready to pour, such as beer from a keg: *That bar keeps several kinds of beer on tap.* **b.** ready for use: *We keep some money on tap in case we need it for an emergency.*

tap dancing *n.* [U] a style of dancing, usu. to jazz music, wearing shoes that make a tapping sound as they touch the floor

tape /teɪp/ *n.* [C;U] **1** strips of adhesive material: *An electrician uses rubberized tape to cover wires.* **2** recording material for sound and images: *I have the television program on tape.*
—*v.* **taped, taping, tapes 1** to wrap or attach with adhesive tape: *I taped the wire to the wall.* **2** to record on tape: *He tapes television programs on his videocassette recorder. -n.* **taping.** *See:* red tape.

tape deck *n.* a tape player and recorder, part of a larger sound system

tape measure *n.* a flexible ruler made in a cloth or metal strip: *A tailor uses a tape measure to measure your waist.*

tape measure

tape player *n.* a machine for playing sounds: *I listen to music on a tape player when I drive to work.*

tap·er /'teɪpər/ *v.* **1** to narrow gradually in width: *His body tapers from the chest to his waist.* **2** *phrasal v.* **to taper off:** to lessen, *(syn.)* to diminish: *The rain (stock market activity, criticism, etc.) is tapering off now and may stop soon.*
—*n.frml.* a candle

tape-re·cord /'teɪprɪ,kɔrd/ *v.* to record s.t. on tape: *I tape-recorded the professor's lecture.*

tape recorder *n.* a machine for recording and playing sounds: *I use a tape recorder to give dictation. -n.* **tape recording.**

tap·es·try /'tæpɪstri/ *n.* **-tries** an artwork made of cloth that is woven of thread in decorative designs or images, used often as a wall hanging: *They have a lovely gold and blue tapestry hanging on their living room wall.*

tape worm *n.* a long, flat parasite in people and animals

taps /tæps/ *n.* [U] **1** a bugle call to turn lights out: *A soldier blows taps to tell the troops that it's bedtime.* **2** a funeral farewell: *A bugler blew taps over the grave of a soldier.* **3** *old usage* the end: *It was taps for her when the boss caught her making fun of him.*

tar /tar/ *n.* [U] a black, sticky mass made of decomposed organic matter: *Tar is used to cover roads and roofs.*
—*v.* **tarred, tarring, tars 1** to cover with tar: *Workers tarred the roof to waterproof it.* **2 to tar and feather: a:** to cover with tar and feathers as punishment: *In colonial times, criminals were tarred and feathered and sent out of town.* **b.** *fig.* to persecute, punish

ta·ran·tu·la /tə'ræntʃələ/ *n.* [C] a large, hairy, poisonous spider that lives in the Americas

tar·dy /'tardi/ **-dier, -diest** *adj.* late, overdue: *Students who are tardy to school are given a warning. -adv.* **tardily;** *-n.* [U] **tardiness.**

tar·get /'targɪt/ *n.adj.* **1** an object, animal, or person aimed at with a bullet, arrow, rock, etc.:

T

Paper <*n.*> *targets have bull's-eyes printed on them.* **2** a person chosen for investigation, punishment, or jokes: *The tall boy became the* <*n.*> *target of students' jokes.* **3** a person or group chosen for analysis or action: *Marketing people refer to certain age groups as* <*n.*> *targets or* <*adj.*> *target populations.* **4** a goal or objective: *Our* <*adj.*> *target date for moving is January 1.*
—*v.* **1** to aim at: *Gunners targeted enemy aircraft.* **2** to choose for investigation: *The government targets people to review their tax forms.*
—*adj.* **on target: a.** to be accurate with a weapon: *The bombs landed on target and destroyed the bridge.* **b.** to be correct, accurate in judgment: *His recommendations for improvement are right on target.*

target market *n.* a group of consumers for whom a business has designed a product and marketing strategy

tar·iff /'tærəf/ *n.* a tax on imported goods: *A tariff protects the importing nation's industries from foreign competition.*

tar·mac /'tɑr,mæk/ *n.* a surface covered with tar, such as an airport runway

tar·nish /'tɑrnɪʃ/ *v.* **-es 1** to make dull (with a film coating): *Silver tarnishes when it is exposed to air.* **2** *fig.* to stain or discredit: *Scandal tarnished his reputation.*
—*n.* **-es** [U] a dull coating: *Polish takes tarnish off silver.*

tar·ot /'tærou, tə'rou/ *n.* [C] 78 playing cards used in telling fortunes: *Fortune-tellers read your future in the tarot.*

tar·pau·lin /'tɑrpəlɪn/ or **tarp** /tɑrp/ *n.* [C] a heavy sheet of cloth or plastic that is waterproof

tar·ra·gon /'tærəgən, -,gɑn/ *n.* [U] an herb used to flavor foods: *A local chef uses tarragon to cook chicken.*

tar·ry /'tæri/ **-ried, -rying, -ries** *v.frml.* to stay, (*syn.*) to linger: *The view of the ocean was so beautiful that we tarried a while before continuing our trip.*

tart /tɑrt/ *adj.* sour: *Lemons taste tart.*
—*n.* **1** a pastry with a sweet filling, a pie: *I had an apple tart for dessert.* **2** *slang* a prostitute or immoral woman

tar·tan /'tɑrtn/ *n.* [C;U] a Scottish woolen cloth made in a plaid pattern, sometimes used to identify a clan (family group)

tar·tar /'tɑrtər/ *n.* [U] a brownish calcium deposit on the teeth made by saliva

tar·tar sauce /'tɑrtər/ *n.* [U] a mixture of mayonnaise, pickles, and olives, often served with fish

task /tæsk/ *n.* **1** an assignment, job to be performed: *His boss gives him specific tasks to do each week.* **2 to take s.o. to task:** to repri-

mand, criticize: *When he doesn't work hard, his boss takes him to task.*

task force *n.* **1** a group of police or military working together to perform a mission: *A task force made up of Marines, the Navy, and Air Force attacked the enemy coastal defenses.* **2** *fig.* a small group in charge of solving a particular problem: *She was put on the task force to develop a policy on smoking at work.*

task·mas·ter /'tæsk,mæstər/ *n.* a difficult person who demands hard work from others: *He is a strict taskmaster with his employees.* -*n.* **taskmistress** /'tæsk,mɪstrəs/.

tas·sel /'tæsəl/ *n.* a decoration made of woven threads: *Tassels hung from the velvet curtains in the living room.*

taste /teɪst/ *n.* **1** [C;U] the sense of flavor that comes from experiencing foods and liquids on the tongue: *I like the taste of bananas.* **2** [C] a small amount of s.t.: *She had a taste of my chocolate cake.* **3** [C] a sense of style and quality in manners, clothes, the arts, etc.: *She has good taste in clothes.* -*adj.* **tasteful;** -*adv.* **tastefully.**
—*v.* **tasted, tasting, tastes 1** to sense the flavor of food and liquids: *The food in that restaurant tastes good.* **2** to experience: *She tasted life in Mexico during a long vacation there.*

taste bud *n.* cells on the tongue that sense sweetness, sourness, bitterness, or saltiness: *Smoking cigarettes makes the taste buds less sensitive.*

taste·less /'teɪstlɪs/ *adj.* **1** without taste, (*syn.*) insipid: *That oatmeal is so bland that it is tasteless.* **2** in poor taste, rude, ill-mannered: *He makes tasteless remarks about his co-workers.*

tast·er /'teɪstər/ *n.* a person who judges the quality of food, wine, and other products: *He works as a taster for a coffee merchant.*

tast·y /'teɪsti/ *adj.* **-ier, -iest** flavorful, (*syn.*) savory: *That cook makes tasty food, rich in spices and seasonings.*

tat /tæt/ *v.* **tatted, tatting, tats** to make lace using bobbins: *She tatted placemats for her dining room table.* See: **tit for tat.**

tat·ter /'tætər/ *v.* to tear into pieces, shred: *He fell down a rough hillside and tattered his shirt and pants.*
—*n.pl.* **in tatters:** in shreds, strips: *His shirt was torn in tatters.* -*adj.* **tattered.**

tat·tle /'tætl/ *v.* **-tled, -tling, -tles** to tell, reveal, esp. s.o.'s wrongdoing: *The little boy stole some candy and his sister tattled on him to their mother.* -*n.* **tattler.**

tat·tle·tale /'tætl,teɪl/ *n.* a gossip, s.o. who tells the secrets of others: *Both brother and sister are tattletales on other children.*

T

tattoo *n.* a staining of the skin with decorations: *He wears a tattoo that says "Mom" on his chest.*
—*v.* to decorate the skin with tattoos: *He had a heart tattooed on his arm.* -*n.* **tatooist;** [U] **tattooing.**

taunt /tɔnt/ *v.* to tease with unkind remarks, (*syn.*) to mock: *Older boys taunted a little one, "Hey, Shorty, when are you going to grow up?"*
—*n.* a cruel remark: *They yelled taunts at him.*

taupe /toup/ *n.* [U] a gray color mixed with yellow or brown

Tau·rus /'tɔrəs/ *n.* a constellation of stars called "the Bull"; the second sign of the zodiac: *The constellation Taurus is located in the Northern Hemisphere.*

taut /tɔt/ *adj.* firm, tight: *The clothesline hangs taut between two poles.* -*adv.* **tautly;** -*n.* [U] **tautness.**

tav·ern /'tævərn/ *n.* a pub, barroom that also serves meals *See:* bar, USAGE NOTE.

taw·dry /'tɔdri/ *adj.* **-drier, -driest** showy in a bright-colored, cheap way, (*syn.*) gaudy: *He wears tawdry clothes to parties.*

taw·ny /'tɔni/ **-nier, -niest** *adj.* dark yellow: *African lions have tawny-colored fur.*

tax /tæks/ *n.* **-es 1** a necessary payment on incomes, sales, etc., to the government: *The income tax was raised again last year.* **2** *fig.* **a tax on:** a strain, (*syn.*) a burden: *His child's constant questions put a tax on his patience.* -*adj.* **taxable.**
—*v.* **-es 1** to impose a tax: *Sales of all items except food are taxed by the city at 8.25 percent.* **2** to tire, burden, annoy: *The old man climbed the hill and it taxed his strength.*

tax·a·tion /tæk'seɪʃən/ *n.* [U] an act of imposing taxes: *Congress passed new taxation on the people.*

tax cut *n.* governmental policy to reduce taxes: *Congress gave everyone a 10 percent income tax cut.*

tax-de·duct·i·ble *adj.* referring to legitimate deductions from income that are taxed: *Gifts to charity are tax-deductible.* -*n.* **tax deduction.**

tax evasion *n.* illegal avoidance of taxes by refusing to pay taxes or buying smuggled goods: *The accountant was found guilty of tax evasion and sent to jail.*

tax-ex·empt *adj.* referring to items on which all or certain taxes are not required: *Tax-exempt bonds can be free of federal, state, and local income taxes.*

tax·i /'tæksi/ *n.* a taxicab or cab: *We take taxis to get to our business meetings.*

taxi

—*v.* **-ied, -iing, -ies 1** to travel a short distance on the ground or water: *Airplanes taxied onto the runway before taking off.* **2** to travel by taxi: *I taxied a package to a client's office.*

tax·i·cab /'tæksi,kæb/ *n.* a car with driver for hire: *Taxicabs fill the streets of the big city.*

tax·i·der·my /'tæksə,dɜrmi/ *n.* [U] the stuffing of dead animals to preserve and display them: *Taxidermy is used to preserve animals killed in hunting.* -*n.* **taxidermist.**

tax·ing /'tæksɪŋ/ *n.* [U] taxation: *Some think taxing the poor is unfair.*
—*adj.* difficult, burdensome: *He finds walking up stairs taxing on his strength.*

taxi stand *n.* a place where taxis can be found or called for a pickup: *Taxis take passengers to their homes and return to the taxi stand to pick up others.*

tax·on·o·my /tæk'sɑnəmi/ *n.* [U] the systematic classification of plants and animals

tax·pay·er /'tæks,peɪər/ *n.* a person or business that pays taxes: *Individual taxpayers formed a political lobby to get their taxes lowered.* -*adj.* **taxpaying.**

tax return *n.* a form used to report a taxpayer's income to state and federal governments: *April 15 is the deadline for sending in our annual tax returns.*

tax shelter *n.* an investment in which taxes are reduced because of expense deductions or laws: *In the USA, Individual Retirement Accounts are a tax shelter in which no taxes are paid until a person starts taking out the money.*

tax write-off *n.* a reduction in income taxes due to a business loss: *The small firm was not able to make a profit last year, so it claimed its business losses as a tax write-off.*

TB /'ti'bi/ *abbr. of* tuberculosis

T bill /'ti,bɪl/ *n. short for* Treasury bill: *T bills are a very safe investment.*

tea /ti/ *n.* [C;U] a shrub with fragrant flowers and leaves that are dried, shredded, and brewed into a drink: *There are teas both with and without caffeine. See:* cup (of tea).

tea bag *n.* a small, thin, paper sac of tea leaves that is put in hot water to make the drink, tea

teach /titʃ/ *v.* **taught** /tɔt/, **-ing, -es 1** to instruct, educate: *She teaches mathematics to college students.* **2 to teach s.o. a lesson:** to hurt or punish s.o.: *He drove too fast and crashed his car and that taught him a costly lesson. See:* to learn.

teach·a·ble /'titʃəbəl/ *adj.* capable of being easily understood: *That textbook is so badly written that it is not teachable* -*n.* [U] **teachability.**

teach·er /'titʃər/ *n.* a person, such as a professor, whose job is to instruct others: *My music teacher has a lot of students.*

USAGE NOTE: *Teachers* work in schools up through twelfth grade (secondary school). At the post-secondary level (university), teachers are often called *lecturers* or *instructors* if they do not have a doctorate (PhD). Teachers with PhDs are usu. called *professors.*

---

teacher's pet *n.* usu. *pej.* a teacher's favorite student: *He is the smartest in the class and is also the teacher's pet.*

teach-in *n.* a political protest with lectures, discussions, etc. about social issues: *Teach-ins happened at many universities as a protest against the war.*

teach·ing /ˈtiʧɪŋ/ *n.* **1** [U] the profession of instructing students: *Teaching requires time and patience.* **2** *n.pl.* the wisdom, views, ideas, etc., of s.o. often famous: *The teachings of Confucius have influenced millions of people for centuries.*

tea·cup /ˈti,kʌp/ *n.* a cup, usu. small and decorated, used for tea drinking

teak /tik/ *n.* [U] the dark brown hard wood of the teak tree of East India used to make furniture, ships, etc.: *The chairs and tables are made of teak.*

tea·ket·tle /ˈti,kɛtl/ *n.* a metal pot used to boil water: *I heated the teakettle until it whistled. See:* teapot.

team /tim/ *n.* two or more people working together, esp. in sports: *Our high school football team won the state championship.*
—*phrasal v. insep.* **to team up (with s.o.):** to join together in a team: *Our company in Miami teamed up with one in Chicago to develop a joint project.*

team·mate /ˈtim,meɪt/ *n.* another player on one's team: *One of my teammates on the tennis team will be national champion this year.*

team player *n.* a person who works well with others and does not look for personal glory

team·ster /ˈtimstər/ *n.* a truck driver: *Many truckers belong to a teamsters' union.*

team·work /ˈtim,wɜrk/ *n.* a cooperative effort with each person working to reach a common goal: *Football requires complex teamwork with each player doing a specific function.*

tea·pot /ˈti,pɑt/ *n.* a ceramic (clay, porcelain) pot with a cover and spout to make and keep tea hot: *She put the teapot on a table, so all could help themselves. See:* tempest.

tear (1) /tɛr/ *v.* **tore** /tɔr/ or **torn** /tɔrn/, **tearing, tears** **1** to pull apart: *Lions tear at the zebra's flesh.* **2** to move quickly: *We tore out of the building when the fire alarm went off.* **3** *phrasal v. insep.* **to tear around s.t.:** to hurry to different places: *He tears around town in a fast car.* **4** *phrasal v. insep.* **to tear at s.t.:** to

rip violently, claw: *Lions tear at a deer with their claws and teeth.* **5** *phrasal v. sep.* **to tear s.o.** or **s.t. down: a. s.o.:** to criticize, (*syns.*) to denigrate, malign: *He keeps tearing down others by criticizing them.‖He tears them down.* **b. s.t.:** to destroy, demolish: *A work crew tore down the old building.* **6** *phrasal v. insep.* **to tear into s.o.** or **s.t.: a. s.o.:** to attack sharply with words: *In the debate, the presidential candidates tore into each other.* **b. s.t.:** to begin eating with energy: *The children tore into their dinner.* **7** *phrasal v. insep.* **to tear (s.t.) off: a.** to take off quickly: *His clothes caught on fire and he tore them off.* **b.** to leave in a hurry: *He took his coat and tore off to a meeting.* **8** *infrml.fig.* **to tear oneself away:** to leave with difficulty: *He loves her and hates to tear himself away when he must leave her.* **9** *phrasal v. sep.* **to tear s.t. up:** to rip into pieces: *She tore up a sheet of paper.*
—*n.* **1** a rip, (*syn.*) a gash: *He has a tear in his shirt after it caught on a nail.* **2 into a tear:** anger, frustration: *When her computer broke down, she went into a tear.*

tear (2) /tɪr/ *n.* [C;U] a drop of salty liquid from the eye: *Tears ran down her cheeks as she watched a sad movie; she was in tears.*
—*v.* to form tears: *His eyes teared in the cold wind. -adj.* **teary.**

tear·drop /ˈtɪr,drɑp/ *n.* a drop of liquid from the eye: *Teardrops ran down his face at the funeral.*
—*adj.* a shape: *She wears a teardrop diamond engagement ring.*

tear·ful /ˈtɪrfəl/ *adj.* sad and crying: *They said goodbye in a tearful farewell at the airport.* *-adv.* **tearfully.**

tear·gas /ˈtɪr,gæs/ *n.* [U] gas used to break up crowds or disable soldiers: *Police threw tear-gas at rioters.*

tear·jerk·er /ˈtɪr,ʤɜrkər/ *n.infrml.* a sentimental movie, story, play, etc., that can make one cry: *The movie Love Story is a tearjerker.*

tea·room /ˈti,rum/ *n.* a restaurant that serves mainly tea, cookies, and cake: *After class, we stopped by a tearoom for refreshment.*

tease /tiz/ *v.* **teased, teasing, teases** **1** to kid, mock playfully: *The boys teased Jane about the braces on her teeth.* **2** to use a comb to make s.o.'s hair look bigger or fuller: *The hairdresser teased Ana's hair.*
—*n.* **1** a person who teases others: *He's a tease, always joking with others.* **2** s.t. that is desirable, but not available: *The offer of free merchandise at that store is just a tease to get you to come in and buy.*

tea·spoon /ˈti,spun/ *n.* a spoon holding approx. 1/3 of a tablespoon or 1/4 fluid ounce: *People use teaspoons to stir coffee and tea.*

teat /tit, tɪt/ *n.* a nipple usu. of an animal: *Cows are milked by squeezing their teats.*

T

tech·ni·cal /'tɛknəkəl/ *adj.* **1** related to a specialized field of science or technology: *The technical procedures needed to fix that computer can be done only by a qualified technician.* **2** specialized, (*syn.*) esoteric: *The banker made some technical points about the economy in her speech.* *-adv.* **technically.**

tech·ni·cal·i·ty /ˌtɛknə'kæləti/ *n.* **-ties** a small, specialized rule or point: *The criminal was freed on a technicality in the law.*

tech·ni·cian /tɛk'nɪʃən/ *n.* a worker trained in a specific area of technology: *She is a computer technician who knows how to fix computer equipment.*

tech·nique /tɛk'nik/ *n.* [C;U] **1** a method, procedure by which s.t. is performed: *Surgical techniques have developed, so that only small cuts are needed for many operations.* **2** skill, ability to do s.t. complex: *Her technique in ice skating is superb.*

tech·no·crat /'tɛknə,kræt/ *n.* a person trained in technical analysis and its applications to industry and government; *-n.* [U] **technocracy** /tɛk'nakrəsi/ *-adj.* **technocratic.**

tech·nol·o·gy /tɛk'naləʤi/ *n.* [C;U] **-gies 1** science and theoretical engineering used in practical applications: *That college offers courses in medical technology.* **2** all kinds of technology in general: *Advances in technology have improved the standard of living. -n.* **technologist;** *-v.* **technologize;** *-adj.* **technological.**

tec·ton·ic /tɛk'tanɪk/ *adj.* related to the formation of the earth's crust: *The movement of tectonic plates can cause earthquakes. -n.pl.* **tectonics.**

ted·dy bear /'tɛdi/ *n.* a stuffed toy bear: *My four-year-old has a brown teddy bear that he takes everywhere he goes.*

te·di·ous /'tidiəs/ *adj.* boring, long and dull: *She has a tedious job as a file clerk. -n.* [U] **tedium.**

tee /ti/ *v.* **teed, teeing, tees 1** *phrasal v.* **to tee off:** (in golf) to take the first shot on each of 18 holes **2** *infrml.fig.* **to be teed off:** to be angry, annoyed: *My wife was teed off at me for being late to pick her up.*
—*n.* **1** (in golf) an area for teeing off **2** a peg or stand on which a ball is placed to tee off

teem /tim/ *v.* to be full, (*syns.*) to abound, brim: *The forest is teeming with rabbits and other wildlife.*

teen /tin/ *n.* a teenager

teen·a·ger /'tin,eɪʤər/ *n.* a person between the ages of 13 and 19: *Teenagers love to go to shopping malls on weekends. -adj.* **teenage.**

teen·sy·ween·sy /'tinsi'winsi/ *infrml. See:* teeny-weeny.

teen·y·bop·per /'tini,bapər/ *n. slang* a teenager fascinated by the latest fads in music,
clothes, and speech: *Most of the fans at the rock concert were teenyboppers.*

teen·y·ween·y /'tini'wini/ *adj.infrml. fig.* tiny, very small: *When she was a teeny-weeny baby, she wore teeny-weeny shoes.*

tee·pee /'tipi/ *var. of* **tepee**

tee shirt or **T-shirt** /'ti,ʃərt/ *n.* a lightweight knit cotton, short-sleeved garment: *He wears a white tee shirt as an undershirt.*

tee·ter /'titər/ *v.* **1** to walk unsteadily: *She teeters when she walks in high-heeled shoes.* **2** to rock back and forth dangerously: *He teetered on the edge of the cliff before getting his balance back.* **3** to seesaw

tee·ter-tot·ter /'titər,tatər/ *n.* a seesaw: *Children rock on a teeter-totter.*
—*v.* to walk unsteadily: *He felt dizzy and teeter-tottered.*

teeth /tiθ/ *n.pl.* of **tooth: 1** dental structures in the mouth: *His teeth are white and shiny.* **2** **armed to the teeth:** having many weapons **3** **to bare one's teeth:** to show anger, rage: *The dog growled and bared its teeth at the stranger.* **4** *fig.* **to show one's teeth:** to demonstrate readiness to argue, fight, etc. **5** *infrml.fig.* **to sink** or **get one's teeth into:** to get very involved in s.t.: *She really sank her teeth into the problem and solved it.*

teethe /tið/ *v.* **teethed, teething, teethes** to grow teeth: *Babies teethe until they have a full set.*

tee·to·tal·er /'ti,toutlər/ *n.* a person who does not drink alcoholic beverages: *He is a teetotaler, but he does not mind others drinking. -v.* **teetotal.**

Tef·lon /'tɛf,lan/ *n.* [U] *TM* a non-stick coating mainly for frying pans and industrial uses: *You can fry an egg without fat in a Teflon-coated pan and it will not stick.*

tel·e·cast /'tɛlə,kæst/ *v.* to send, broadcast by television: *Television stations telecast the Olympics all over the world.*

tel·e·com·mu·ni·ca·tion /ˌtɛləkə,myunə'keɪʃən/ *n.* [C;U] *n.pl.* transmission of messages and images by radio, television, cable, satellite, computer, etc.: *Telecommunications is a complex and growing field.*

tel·e·com·mut·er /'tɛləkə,myutər/ *n.* a person who works at home and is connected to the office by telecommunications equipment: *Nancy Jordan is a telecommuter who works at home with two telephone lines, a computer with a modem, and a fax machine. -v.* **telecommute.** *See:* office, USAGE NOTE.

tel·e·con·fer·ence /'tɛlə,kanfrəns/ *v.* **-enced, -encing, -ences** to hold a discussion with people in different places by connecting them electronically with computers and video
—*n.* an electronic discussion using computers and video

tel·e·gram /'tɛlə,græm/ n. [C;U] a brief written message sent by wire
—v. **-grammed, -gramming, -grams** to send a message by wire or telephone: *I telegrammed my congratulations to the senator on her winning re-election.*

tel·e·graph /'tɛlə,græf/ v. **1** to send messages by wire or telephone, formerly by Morse Code: *People telegraphed messages long before the telephone was commonly used.* **2** to make known in advance: *Some boxers telegraph their punches by making an identifying move before punching.*
—n. [U] a telegraph installation: *The telegraph was the first means of long-distance electronic communication.*

tel·e·ki·ne·sis /,tɛləkə'nisɪs, -kaɪ-/ n. [U] the power to move or transform objects by force of mind: *A performer demonstrated telekinesis by bending keys without touching them.* -adj. **telekinetic** /,tɛləkə'nɛtɪk, -kaɪ-/.

te·lep·a·thy /tə'lɛpəθi/ n. [U] mental communication without speech, vision, or touch: *People who know the old lady swear that she uses telepathy to contact them.* -adj. **telepathic** /,tɛlə'pæθɪk/; -adv. **telepathically.**

tel·e·phone /'tɛlə,foʊn/ n. an electronic device used for the communication of voice or electronic data: *He has a telephone in several rooms at home.* -adj. **telephonic** /,tɛlə'fɑnɪk/.
—v. **-phoned, -phoning, -phones** to communicate by telephone: *I telephoned my parents to find out how they were.*

telephone booth n. a tall box with a telephone, (syn.) phone booth: *I close the door of the telephone booth to keep out noise.*

telephone directory n. a book that has the names, addresses, and telephone numbers of people, businesses, etc., in an area: *See:* Yellow Pages.

tel·e·pho·to /'tɛlə,foʊtoʊ/ adj. capable of magnifying distant objects: *That photographer uses a telephoto lens to film sports events.*

tel·e·proc·ess·ing /,tɛlə'prɑ,sɛsɪŋ/ n. [U] the use of remote terminals to communicate with a computer

tel·e·scope /'tɛlə,skoʊp/ n. an optical instrument used to make distant objects seem larger: *Observatories use giant telescopes to look at the sky.*
—v. **-scoped, -scoping, -scopes** to compress, make compact as with the parts of some telescopes:

telescope

The company telescoped development of a new product into several months, instead

of years. -adj. **telescopic** /,tɛlə'skɑpɪk/.

tel·e·thon /'tɛlə,θɑn/ n. a long television program that raises money for charity: *Several celebrities give their time to host telethons.*

tel·e·vise /'tɛlə,vaɪz/ v. **-vised, -vising, -vises** to send by television: *All major TV networks televised the Presidential elections.*

tel·e·vi·sion /'tɛlə,vɪʒən/ or **TV** /'ti'vi/ n. **1** [U] the sending of images and sound via the airwaves or cable to a television set: *Most major sports events are shown on television.* **2** [C] a box-like device that receives and displays pictures and sound: *My favorite show is on television tonight.* **3** the industry that creates programs to show on television *See:* boob tube.

tel·ex /'tɛlɛks/ n. [U] v. **-es** a system of teletypewriters connected by telephone wires that sends messages internationally: *I dialed our London office and sent a telex there.*

tell /tɛl/ v. **told** /toʊld/, **telling, tells 1** to say in words, (syn.) to narrate: *She tells a story to her child each night.* **2** to instruct, direct: *The boss tells the employees what to do.* **3** to identify, distinguish: *I can't tell where we are in the dark night.* **4** phrasal v. insep. **to tell about s.o.** or **s.t.:** to characterize, describe: *Our friends told us about their experiences on their vacation.* **5** phrasal v. sep. **to tell s.o.** or **s.t. apart:** to distinguish, identify: *It's hard to tell the sisters apart.* **6 to tell it like it is:** to describe reality honestly: *His work is no good, so when you see him, tell it like it is.* **7** phrasal v. sep. **to tell s.o. off:** to get angry at s.o., (syn.) to scold: *The guy was rude and a woman told him off.* **7** phrasal v. insep. **to tell on s.o.:** to reveal, (syn.) to tattle: *A student stole some pencils and another told on him.* **8 to tell the difference:** to distinguish, (syn.) to discern: *The real and fake diamonds look alike; I can't tell the difference between them. See:* all told; telling.

tell·er /'tɛlər/ n. **1** a person who takes in and pays out money at a bank: *I gave the teller my deposit and she gave me a receipt.* **2** a storyteller

tell·ing /'tɛlɪŋ/ adj. **1** having a strong impact, very important: *The lawyer made a telling point and the judge dismissed the lawsuit.* **2** **there's no telling:** it's difficult to know: *There's no telling what time she'll come back.* -adv. **tellingly.**

tell·tale /'tɛl,teɪl/ adj. an identifying sign: *The criminal's footprints in the mud were a telltale sign that he was at the crime scene.*

tem·blor /'tɛmblər/ n. an earthquake: *Los Angeles experienced another temblor.*

te·mer·i·ty /tə'mɛrəti/ n. [U] boldness, (syn.) impetuosity: *He had the temerity to tell his boss what he thought of her.*

T

temp /tɛmp/ *n.infrml. short for* temporary worker: *We hire temps to work for us when our employees are on vacation.*

tem·per /'tɛmpər/ *n.* **1** [C;U] one's emotional nature, often of anger: *He has a bad temper and is easily angered.* **2** [C] mood or characteristics: *the temper of the times* **3** [U] the strength of metal **4 to keep** or **lose one's temper:** to keep or lose control of one's anger: *She's very patient; she never loses her temper.* —*v.* to moderate, lessen in intensity: *Old age tempered his impatience with weaknesses in other people.*

tem·per·a·ment /'tɛmprəmənt/ *n.* [C;U] general nature, mental disposition: *That horse has a good temperament.*

tem·per·a·men·tal /,tɛmprə'mɛntl/ *adj.* easily upset, difficult: *The opera singer is very temperamental.* -*adv.* **temperamentally.**

tem·per·ance /'tɛmpərəns, 'tɛmprəns/ *n.* [U] **1** moderation, self-control, usu. in eating, drinking, and sex **2** not drinking alcohol: *Some religions preach total temperance.*

tem·per·ate /'tɛmpərɪt, 'tɛmprɪt/ *adj.* **1** moderate in temperature: *The USA is in the temperate zone.* **2** using self-control: *That family is temperate in its consumption of alcohol.*

tem·per·a·ture /'tɛmpərətʃər, 'tɛmprə-/ *n.* **1** [C;U] the degree of heat or cold: *The temperature outside is chilly today.* **2** [C, used in sing.] a fever: *My son has a cold and a temperature.* **3 to take s.o.'s temperature:** to measure the body's temperature using a thermometer *See:* headache, USAGE NOTE.

tem·pered /'tɛmpərd/ *adj.* **1** moderated, restrained: *His hurry to get things done is tempered by having a weak heart.* **2** treated as by putting hot metal in water: *That knife is made of tempered steel.*

tem·pest /'tɛmpɪst/ *n.frml.* **1** a storm **2** *fig.* **a tempest in a teapot:** upset about s.t. unimportant: *He felt rejected because he was not invited, but it was just a tempest in a teapot.*

tem·pes·tu·ous /tɛm'pɛstʃuəs/ *adj.frml.* emotionally charged, (*syn.*) turbulent: *That couple has a tempestuous relationship.* -*adv.* **tempestuously.**

tem·plate /'tɛmplɪt/ *n.* **1** a guide with codes, symbols, etc.: *Templates with computer commands fit on your keyboard as a convenient reference.* **2** a plate with holes cut in it as symbols representing objects, measurements, devices, etc.

tem·ple /'tɛmpəl/ *n.* **1** a building for worship: *We entered the temple to worship.* **2** a flat part of the face to the side and behind the eyes: *He gets tension headaches in his temples.*

tem·po /'tɛmpoʊ/ *n.* **1** rate of speed of a piece of music: *That song has a fast tempo.* **2** pace of activity: *The tempo of life downtown on a Sunday is pretty slow.*

tem·po·ral /'tɛmpərəl, 'tɛmprəl/ *adj.* related to matters on earth as opposed to religious ones: *The clergy concerns itself less with temporal matters than spiritual ones.*

tem·po·rar·y /'tɛmpə,rɛri/ *adj.* passing, impermanent: *The detour is temporary until the main road is fixed.* -*adv.* **temporarily**

temporary employee or **worker** *n.* a worker hired only for a brief period *See:* temp.

tempt /tɛmpt/ *v.* **1** to attract, (*syn.*) to entice: *Every time he sees chocolates in shop windows, they tempt him.* **2** to attract, seduce, esp. into doing s.t. wrong: *He tempted her with promises of fame, yet she resisted.* **3 to tempt (the) fate(s):** to risk harm or ruin: *The storm is very bad, so let's not tempt the fates by going out in it now.* -*adj.* **tempting.**

temp·ta·tion /tɛmp'teɪʃən/ *n.* [C;U] **1** a desire for s.t., (*syn.*) an enticement: *He gives in to temptation when he sees a nice tie and buys it.* **2** an attraction, esp. to s.t. wrong, harmful, or evil: *A reformed alcoholic gives in to temptation by taking another drink.*

temp·ting /'tɛmptɪŋ/ *adj.* attractive, (*syns.*) enticing, tantalizing: *Sweet desserts are tempting to her, but she resists.*

ten /tɛn/ *n.* the cardinal number 10 —*adj.* 10 of s.t.: *I have ten dollars.*

ten·a·ble /'tɛnəbəl/ *adj.* capable of being held, defended, or supported: *Their negotiating position (military plan, scientific paper, etc.) is not tenable; it is too weak.* -*n.* **tenability.**

te·na·cious /tə'neɪʃəs/ *adj.* determined, persistent: *The reporter is tenacious in speaking to every witness of the crime.*

te·nac·i·ty /tə'næsəti/ *n.* [U] determination, resolve: *She works on her project with tenacity.*

ten·an·cy /'tɛnənsi/ *n.* **-cies** [U] living in or possession of property: *His tenancy in that apartment has lasted 25 years.*

ten·ant /'tɛnənt/ *n.* a person who pays rent for the use of an apartment office, etc.

USAGE NOTE: *Tenant* usually refers to a person who rents an apartment or house from a *landlord,* or owner of the property. In many states, tenants' rights are protected by the law.

tend /tɛnd/ *v.* **1** to lean, incline toward in attitude, preference, action, etc.: *She tends to come to work early on Mondays.* **2** to watch over, care for: *Shepherds tend sheep.*

ten·den·cy /'tɛndənsi/ *n.* **-cies** an inclination, leaning in attitude or behavior: *When he talks, he has a tendency to get lost in details.*

ten·der /'tɛndər/ *adj.* **1** soft, gentle: *The father caressed his child's cheek with tender strokes.* **2** kind, caring: *They have tender feelings for each other.* **3** sore, painful when touched: *The bruise on the girl's knee is tender to the touch.*

4 (of food) soft and chewable: *That steak was tender and tasty.* **5** young and innocent: *He left home at the tender age of 15.* **6** needing careful handling, sensitive: *The negotiators reached a tender moment where their talks might end.* -*v.* **tenderize;** -*adv.* **tenderly.**

—*n.* **1** an offer of a price to buy s.t., as the offer of one company to buy another's stock **2** **legal tender:** money that can be taken as payment: *The US dollar is legal tender.*

—*v.* to offer, such as to resign or to buy stock: *An official tendered his resignation to the mayor.*

ten·der·foot /ˈtɛndərˌfʊt/ *n.infrml. fig.* a person not used to life in the outdoors: *After several months of hard work in a national park, she was no longer a tenderfoot.*

ten·der·heart·ed /ˈtɛndərˌhɑrtɪd/ *adj.* kind, caring: *She is tenderhearted and takes in stray animals.*

ten·der·loin /ˈtɛndərˌlɔɪn/ *n.* a cut of beef near the backbone

ten·der·ness /ˈtɛndərnɪs/ *n.* [U] **1** gentleness, kindness: *She showed tenderness toward the hurt animal and cared for it.* **2** soreness to the touch: *After he hurt his ankle, the tenderness lasted for a week.*

ten·di·ni·tis /ˌtɛndəˈnaɪtɪs/ *n.* [U] inflammation of a tendon: *I have tendinitis in my right elbow.*

ten·don /ˈtɛndən/ *n.* sinews, tough fibrous tissue connecting muscles to bones or to other muscles

ten·dril /ˈtɛndrəl/ *n.* **1** a thin, thread-like part of a vine or climbing plant **2** *fig.* s.t. vine-like, such as a lock of hair

ten·e·ment /ˈtɛnəmənt/ *n.* a crowded, low-quality house or apartment building: *City officials try to tear down tenements and build modern housing.*

USAGE NOTE: *Tenement* describes old apartment buildings that are in bad condition, which can be found in poor areas of a city.

---

ten·et /ˈtɛnɪt/ *n.* a principle, axiom in a set of beliefs: *The tenets of capitalism, such as private ownership of business, are the basis of the American economy.*

ten·nis /ˈtɛnɪs/ *n.* [U] a game played on a court with two or four players who use rackets to hit the ball over a net, so that the opponent(s) cannot hit it back

tennis

ten·or /ˈtɛnər/ *n.adj.* **1** in males, the high-

est natural singing voice: *He is a <n.> tenor with the City Opera.||He has a <adj.> tenor voice (part, range, etc.).* **2** nature, (*syn.*) ambiance: *The tenor of the times is one of conservatism in public spending.*

tense /tɛns/ *adj.* **tenser, tensest** **1** nervous, jumpy, (*syn.*) jittery: *He is very tense and irritable from too much work.* **2** nerve-wracking, strained: *Opposing countries are threatening war in a tense situation.*

—*n.* the part of a verb that shows the past, present, and future time: *Many English verbs like "go" and "do" are irregular in the past tense.*

—*v.* **tensed, tensing, tenses** to tighten up physically, become nervous (irritated, ready to fight, etc.): *As the argument became hotter, each person tensed up.* -*adv.* **tensely**

ten·sion /ˈtɛnʃən/ *n.* **1** [C;U] a state of stress, nervousness: *The tension in a hospital emergency room can be very high.* **2** tautness, rigidity: *The tension in steel bridge cables is measured after they are installed.*

tent /tɛnt/ *n.* a portable shelter made of canvas, nylon, etc.: *The Red Cross put up tents to house the refugees temporarily.*

tent

ten·ta·cle /ˈtɛntəkəl/ *n.* a flexible "arm" of ocean creatures, such as the octopus or squid: *An octopus wraps its tentacles around the food it catches.*

ten·ta·tive /ˈtɛntətɪv/ *adj.* **1** indefinite, provisional: *We have a tentative appointment next week, but we need to confirm it.* **2** hesitant, doubtful: *She has a tentative feeling about going ahead with the project.*

ten·ter·hook /ˈtɛntərˌhʊk/ *n.* **1** a hook used to hold cloth on a frame **2** *fig.* **on tenterhooks:** anxious, tense: *We are on tenterhooks while we see if he recovers from surgery.*

ten·u·ous /ˈtɛnyuəs/ *adj.* **1** thin, delicate: *the tenuous threads of a piece of lace* **2** weak, unimportant: *His arguments in support of the project are so tenuous that management decided not to do it.*

ten·ure /ˈtɛnyər/ *n.* **1** a period in which s.o. holds a position (job, post, responsibility, etc.): *During the mayor's tenure in office, she made many improvements.* **2** permanent employment, esp. in a teaching position: *The assistant professor was promoted and given tenure.* -*adj.* **tenured.**

te·pee /ˈtipi/ *n. var. of* teepee, a triangular tent used originally by Native Americans: *Tepees were often made from animal skins.*

tep·id /ˈtɛpɪd/ *adj.* lukewarm: *Babies are bathed in tepid water, not too hot. See:* warm, USAGE NOTE.

T

te·qui·la /təˈkilə/ *n.* a strong liquor made from the agave plant

term /tɜrm/ *n.* **1** a word or expression that describes s.t.: *He used the terms "casual" and "relaxed" to describe his attitude.* **2** a condition, requirement as in a contract: *The terms of the agreement are clear and complete.* **3** a time period, such as in elected office or education: *The senator is serving his last six-year term in office.* **4 in terms of:** about, concerning: *In terms of financing, our bank has agreed to provide it.* **5 in no uncertain terms:** clearly, strongly: *The boss told him in no uncertain terms to finish the project today.* **6** *n.pl.* **on (good, bad, etc.) terms:** the condition of the relationship between people: *John and I are on good (or bad) terms with each other.‖Jane and John are angry with each other and are not on speaking terms.* **7 to bring to term:** to complete a pregnancy: *She brought her baby to term and gave birth last week.* **8 to come to terms:** to agree on or accept s.t.: *We came to terms on the contract and signed it.‖He came to terms with his father's death.*
—*v.* to label, describe: *I term the way he acted as rude!*

ter·mi·nal /ˈtɜrmənəl/ *n.* **1** a station, depot (rail, bus, airline): *The bus terminal is on the city's west side.* **2** the last stop on a transportation line **3** an electrical post: *The terminals on the car battery are old and dirty.* **4** a machine that works by being connected to another computer and that has no CPU of its own (also called a dumb terminal)
—*adj.* going to die, fatal: *He has terminal cancer; he's going to die.* -*adv.* **terminally.**

ter·mi·nate /ˈtɜrməˌneɪt/ *v.* **-nated, -nating, -nates** **1** to end, stop: *Our company's management terminated negotiations on a new union contract.* **2** to finish, end: *The railroad line terminates at Central Station.* **3** *fig.* to fire from employment: *My friend was terminated from her job yesterday.* -*adj.* **terminable;** -*n.* [U] **termination.**

ter·mi·nol·o·gy /ˌtɜrməˈnɑlədʒi/ *n.* [C;U] the technical vocabulary of a field: *The terminology in science has exact meanings.*

ter·mi·nus /ˈtɜrmənəs/ *n.* **-nuses** or **-ni** /-ˌnaɪ/ the end, finish: *The terminus of our airline flight is Athens, Greece.*

ter·mite /ˈtɜrˌmaɪt/ *n.* an ant-like insect that eats through wood: *Some kinds of termites build huge hills of dirt to house their colonies.*

term paper *n.* a long essay or research study on a course topic: *I have five courses and have to do term papers for each one.*

terms /tɜrmz/ *n.* items in a contract or agreement: *She did not agree to all the terms in the contract.*

tern /tɜrn/ *n.* sea birds that are smaller than gulls: *Terns have long slender wings and dive for small fish.*

ter·race /ˈtɛrəs/ *n.* a raised, flat piece of land: *The house has a grassy terrace behind it.*
—*v.* **-raced, -racing, -races** to form in terraces: *Asians terrace hillsides with rice paddies.*

ter·ra cot·ta /ˈtɛrəˈkɑtə/ *n.* [U] pottery and building materials made from red clay: *Our kitchen floor is covered with terra cotta tiles.*

ter·rain /təˈreɪn/ *n.* land, landscape: *The trucks must travel over rough terrain to reach the town.*

ter·res·tri·al /təˈrɛstriəl/ *adj.* related to earth: *Terrestrial weather is different from that on Mars.*
—*n.* a person from earth, (*syn.*) earthling: *Science fiction tells of terrestrials visiting other planets. See:* extraterrestrial.

ter·ri·ble /ˈtɛrəbəl/ *adj.* **1** horrible, dreadful, (*syn.*) ghastly: *There was a terrible car accident.* **2** ugly, (*syn.*) hideous: *A terrible monster came out of a cave.* **3** very bad, severe: *She has a terrible case of the flu.* **4** poor quality, badly done: *That movie is absolutely terrible.* -*adv.* **terribly.**

ter·ri·er /ˈtɛriər/ *n.* any of approx. 20 breeds of small, furry dogs used to dig things out of the ground

ter·rif·ic /təˈrɪfɪk/ *adj.* **1** *fig.* wonderful, superior: *He did a terrific job in remodeling the kitchen.* **2** powerful, tremendous: *The storm had terrific winds of 100 MPH (160 km).* **3** very bad, awful: *We are having terrific difficulty with our telephone system.*

ter·ri·fy /ˈtɛrəˌfaɪ/ *v.* **-fied, -fying, -fies** to horrify, put strong fear in s.o.: *An ugly man terrified a small child for a moment.* -*adj.* **terrifying;** -*adv.* **terrifyingly.**

ter·ri·tor·i·al /ˌtɛrəˈtɔriəl/ *adj.* **1** related to a territory: *Cats are territorial animals that fight over their area.* **2** related to an area of sovereignty: *The territorial waters of each country reach a certain number of miles offshore.*

ter·ri·to·ry /ˈtɛrəˌtɔri/ *n.* **-ries** **1** [C;U] an area or region of land: *The territory to the north of here is mountainous.* **2** an area of land not totally self-governing or considered a state or province by a central government: *The island of Guam is a territory of the USA.* **3** an area marked for a specific purpose, such as for a salesperson: *Her sales territory includes the six New England states.* **4** *infrml.fig.* **to come with the territory:** s.t. included, usu. in a negative sense: *The President gets constant criticism from the press; it comes with the territory (the Presidency).*

ter·ror /ˈtɛrər/ *n.* **1** [C;U] extreme fear, panic: *A burglar at the window put terror into my heart.* **2** *fig.* an irritating person, usu. a child

ter·ror·ism /ˈtɛrəˌrɪzəm/ *n.* the use of murder, arson, kidnapping, etc., to reach political objectives: *Governments work together to stop terrorism.*

ter·ror·ist /ˈtɛrərɪst/ *n.adj.* a person who uses terrorism: *<n.> Terrorists shot tourists in the airport.||The killing was a <adj.> terrorist act.*

ter·ror·ize /ˈtɛrəˌraɪz/ *v.* **-ized, -izing, -izes 1** to put extreme fear in s.o., terrify: *Bandits terrorized people by robbing them.* **2** to intimidate, harass: *Soldiers terrorized the civilian population into doing what they asked.*

terse /tɜrs/ *adj.* **terser, tersest** brief, and often abrupt, (*syn.*) curt: *She asked her boss a question and received a terse reply.* *-adv.* **tersely;** *-n.* [U] **terseness.**

ter·ti·ar·y /ˈtɜrʃiˌɛri/ *adj.* third in place or order: *The tertiary layer of soil is solid rock covered by layers of gravel and sand.*

test /tɛst/ *n.* **1** an examination, quiz to measure knowledge or ability: *Our teacher gave us a spelling test.* **2** an experiment, probe: *The laboratory reported the results of my blood test.*
—v. **1** to examine, quiz s.o.: *The state tests people who want to get a driver's license.* **2** to try out, (*syn.*) to verify: *After his operation, he tested his strength by walking a few steps.* **3** *infrml.fig.* **to test the waters:** to experiment carefully: *She tested the waters of graduate school by taking one course part-time before enrolling full-time. -n.* [U] *adj.* **testing.**

USAGE NOTE: In school, a *test* is larger and more important than a *quiz,* but not as comprehensive as an *examination.*

tes·ta·ment /ˈtɛstəmənt/ *n.* **1** a statement of belief: *The Old and New Testaments form the two parts of the Christian Bible.* **2** a person's will, instructions for giving away property after death: *A lawyer read the dead man's last will and testament.*

tes·tate /ˈtɛsˌteɪt/ *adj.* having a will when one dies *See:* intestate.

test ban *n.* an agreement to stop weapons testing, esp. nuclear weapons

test case *n.* a lawsuit whose decision will have general importance: *The test case against affirmative action could change government policy on discrimination.*

test-drive /ˈtɛstˈdraɪv/ *n.* a drive in a vehicle to see if one likes it: *I took a new Mercedes for a test-drive.*

tes·tes /ˈtɛstiz/ *n.pl.* the male reproductive gland, which occur in pairs: *The testes are in the scrotum in human males.*

test-fly *v.* to fly an airplane experimentally

tes·ti·cle /ˈtɛstəkəl/ *n.* the human male reproductive gland: *Each male has two testicles that have sperm.*

tes·ti·fy /ˈtɛstəˌfaɪ/ *v.* **-fied, -fying, -fies 1** to tell what one knows, esp. under oath in a court of law, (*syn.*) to bear witness: *Two witnesses testified against the defendant.* **2** *fig.* to demonstrate s.t.: *Her success testifies to much hard work.*

tes·ti·mo·ni·al /ˌtɛstəˈmouniəl/ *n.adj.* **1** a formal recognition of value or merit: *The foreign minister gave a <n.> testimonial in honor of a retiring ambassador.||He gave a <adj.> testimonial dinner in her honor.* **2** a formal statement of fact sworn under oath to be true: *A witness from another country sent a <n.> testimonial of evidence to the court.*

tes·ti·mo·ny /ˈtɛstəˌmouni/ *n.* **-nies 1** [U] formal, sworn evidence given in court **2** proof, clear indication: *A man returned $100 that he found on the street; that act is testimony to his honesty.*

test·ing /ˈtɛstɪŋ/ *n.* [U] the act of examination: *Testing for job applicants will begin tomorrow morning.*
—adj. related to examining and measuring: *The military has a testing ground located in the desert.*

test market *n.v.* an area in which a new product is sold to learn how well it would sell nationally: *Our company used Dallas and Boston as <n.> test markets for our new products.*

tes·tos·ter·one /tɛsˈtɑstəˌroun/ *n.* [U] the major male hormone: *The amount of testosterone in a man's body is said to affect how aggressive he is.*

test tube *n.adj.* a hollow cylinder made of glass or plastic used for experiments: *Medical laboratories use large numbers of <n.> test tubes.*

tes·ty /ˈtɛsti/ *adj.* **-tier, -tiest** touchy, easily angered: *When you talk about the money he lost in gambling, the man becomes testy.*

test tube

tet·a·nus /ˈtɛtnəs/ *n.* [U] a viral infection that can cause death; lockjaw: *She stepped on a rusty piece of metal and immediately got a vaccine for tetanus.*

tête-à-tête /ˌtɛtəˈtɛt, ˌteɪtəˈteɪt/ *n.adv.* (French for) a private, personal conversation: *Two close friends are having a tête-à-tête over coffee.*

teth·er /ˈtɛðər/ *n.v.* **1** a restraint, such as a rope or leash: *She keeps her dog on a <n.> tether in the backyard.* **2** *fig.* **at the end of one's tether** or **rope:** out of patience, (*syn.*) exasperated

text /tɛkst/ *n.* [C;U] **1** written material: *The writer corrected the text of his letter.* **2** a textbook: *The teacher told the students to look on page 10 of the text.*

T

text·book /'tɛkst,bʊk/ n. a book written on a particular subject and used for study in courses: *Students study biology textbooks, listen to lectures, and do laboratory experiments.*

tex·tile /'tɛks,taɪl, -təl/ n. [U] cloth, fabric made by weaving: *Textiles are woven on power looms in textile factories.*

tex·tu·al /'tɛkstʃuəl/ adj. related to text: *Photographs illustrate the textual material in the book.*

tex·ture /'tɛkstʃər/ n. [C;U] **1** the visual pattern and degree of smoothness or roughness of touch produced by a material, such as the placement of fibers in fabric: *Wool flannel has a smooth, soft texture.* **2** *fig.* the pattern and feel (of a painting, daily life, etc.): *The texture of life in Buenos Aires is one of charm and sophistication.*

thal·a·mus /'θæləməs/ n. **-mi** /-,maɪ/ the brain's center for sensing pain, temperature, and touch, and maintaining consciousness: *The thalamus is located in the lower part of the brain.*

than /θən, *strong form* ðæn/ conj. used after adjectives and adverbs to show comparison: *The weather is hotter (colder, better, worse, etc.) than it was last year.*

thank /θæŋk/ v. **1** to express gratitude: *I thanked my friend for taking me to dinner.* **2** to give credit: *He thanks his parents for teaching him to be sensitive to others.*
—n.pl. **1** gratitude, (syn.) appreciation: *He gives thanks to his professors for their patience.* **2 thanks to:** because of: *Thanks to his being late, we missed the train.*

thank·ful /'θæŋkfəl/ adj. grateful, (syn.) appreciative: *She is thankful to her doctor for saving her life.* -n. [U] **thankfulness.**

thank·less /'θæŋklɪs/ adj. difficult, necessary but unpopular: *Cleaning bathrooms is a thankless job.* -adv. **thanklessly.**

Thanksgiving Day n. a national holiday of celebration giving thanks for all good things [observed in the USA on the fourth Thursday of November and in Canada on the second Monday of October]: *We had a turkey and pumpkin pie for dinner on Thanksgiving Day. See:* pilgrim, USAGE NOTE.

thank-you n. an expression of gratitude: *She offered her thank-yous to the people who helped her.*

that /ðæt/ pron. **1** referring to s.t. specific (but not nearby): *That person needs help.* **2 after that:** then **3 all that:** referring to all the rest, the remaining items: *I took care of the chores, washing the dishes, doing the laundry, and all that.* **4 at that: a.** referring to the limits of a situation: *I apologized for making a mistake and my boss and I agreed to leave the matter at that.* **b.** moreover, in addition: *Our business trip was interrupted by a storm, and cost us extra at that!* **5 that is:** in other words **6 that's that:** the end of the matter; it's settled: *We're going home now, and that's that. See:* this.
—adv. so; as much as: *I'm not that hungry; I'll eat later.*
—conj.: *The book that you wanted is out of the library right now.*

USAGE NOTE: *That* is used in clauses or phrases (as in this sentence) that define the subject or action and are therefore necessary to understand the sentence. *Which* is used where the clause or phrase is not required, as in "My car, which is green, runs well."

thatch /θætʃ/ n. [U] v.adj. **-es** reeds, straw, or leaves used to make a roof: *The Pacific Islanders put <n.> thatch on their huts to keep out rain and sun.* -n. (person) **thatcher;** (act) [U] **thatching.**

thaw /θɔ/ n. [C, *usu. sing.*] v. **1** a slow melting of ice: *During the spring <n.> thaw, ice melts on rivers and lakes.* **2** *fig.* an improvement in tense, cold relationships, esp. between governments: *A limited trade agreement created a <n.> thaw in relations between the two nations.*

the /ðə *before consonant;* ði *before a vowel*/ definite art. **1** referring to a specific singular or plural noun: *I closed the door and opened the windows.* **2** used before a sing n. to form a group n.: *The poor need government help but the politicians disagree on how to give it.*

the·a·ter /'θiətər/ n. **1** the industry of writing and performing live musicals and dramas (not movie theaters): *Many people enjoy going to the theater.* **2** a building, such as for movies, or outdoor shell with seats for the audience and a stage for performers: *Many theaters in New York are on or near Broadway.*

theater

the·at·ri·cal /θi'ætrəkəl/ adj. **1** related to the theater: *Our college puts on theatrical productions twice a year.* **2** of exaggerated behavior, dramatic: *When she gives presentations to clients, she is very theatrical as she talks in a loud voice, laughs, and walks around a lot.* -adv. **theatrically.**

the·at·rics /θi'ætrɪks/ n.pl. exaggerated behavior: *Her theatrics annoy everyone; they are tired of her selfish behavior.*

theft /θɛft/ n. [C;U] the act of stealing: *The theft of the queen's jewels was a scandal.*

their /ðɛr/ pron. possessive form of *they*: *Their apartment is on the second floor.*

theirs /ðɛrz/ *pron.* possessive collective form of *they: The corner apartment on the second floor is theirs.||That child is one of theirs.*

them /ðəm; *strong form* ðɛm/ *pron.* objective form of *they: The corner apartment belongs to them.||She sent them a wedding gift.*

theme /θim/ *n.* a central idea or main pattern, such as in daily life, an artistic work, or another area: *The theme in that novel is one of adventure in exploring the Arctic. -adj.* **thematic;** /θɪ'mætɪk/ *-adv.* **thematically.**

them·selves /ðəm'sɛlvz, ðɛm-/ *pron.* **1** reflexive objective form of *they* and *them: Farmers do a lot of the farm work themselves.* **2** for emphasis: *They fixed their car (by) themselves.*

then /ðɛn/ *adv.conj.* **1** at that time: *I wasn't alive <adv.> then.* **2** an order of events: *I went to the pharmacy, <conj.> then to the supermarket, <conj.> then home.* **3** in addition, also: *We have to write the report, and <conj.> then there's editing and printing too.* **4** therefore, in that case: *If you don't feel well, then go home early.* **5 and then some:** in addition, in excess of: *The champion won the race by a wide margin and <conj.> then some.* **6 then and there:** at that moment, esp. referring to a quick, decisive action: *The police moved in and stopped the riot <adv.> then and there as it began.*
—*adv.* former: *The then-president of the company has since retired.*

the·o·lo·gian /ˌθiə'loʊdʒən/ *n.* a scholar of religion: *Famous theologians have been both controversial and influential.*

the·ol·o·gy /θi'ɑlədʒi/ *n.* [U] the study of God and religion: *The minister studied theology at college. -adj.* **theological** /ˌθiə'lɑdʒəkəl/.

the·o·ret·i·cal /ˌθiə'rɛtəkəl/ *adj.* **1** conceptual, speculative but unproven: *His ideas are only theoretical and have not been tested.* **2** related to the ideas behind s.t. practical: *The theoretical concepts of economics are very different from the reality. -adv.* **theoretically.** *See:* applied.

the·o·rize /'θiə,raɪz/ *v.* **-rized, -rizing, -rizes** to form or propose a theory: *Albert Einstein theorized about relativity.*

the·o·ry /'θiəri, 'θɪri/ *n.* **-ries 1** [C] an idea, argument that s.t. is true, (*syn.*) a speculation: *Darwin's theory of evolution is based on the survival of the fittest creatures.* **2** [C;U] a body of beliefs used as guiding principles: *Social theory contains many ideas about governing. -n.* **theorist; theoretician** /ˌθiərə'tɪʃən, ˌθɪrə-/. *See:* hypothesis.

ther·a·peu·tic /ˌθɛrə'pyutɪk/ *adj.* healing, (*syn.*) curative: *The mineral waters of the spa have a therapeutic effect on people with arthritis.*

ther·a·peu·tics /ˌθɛrə'pyutɪks/ *n.pl. used with sing. v.* the art and science of healing

ther·a·pist /'θɛrəpɪst/ *n.* **1** a person skilled in the healing of disease or disorders: *He is a physical therapist who works with the disabled.* **2** a psychiatrist or psychologist who counsels patients for mental health: *She visits her therapist once a week to fight depression.*

ther·a·py /'θɛrəpi/ *n.* [U] treatment of mental and physical illnesses and disorders, usu. without surgery, such as speech therapy, physical therapy, etc.: *She began therapy to overcome her fear of crowds.*

there /ðɛr/ *adv.* **1** at or to a specific place: *The meeting is at the church and I promised to be there.* **2** about a certain matter: *I understand what you mean there in your essay.*
—*adj.* here, present: **1 here and there:** in various places: *The clothes in his room were scattered here and there.* **2** to emphasize: *That desk there needs repair.* **3** *fig.* **not all there:** mentally deficient, retarded, stupid, tired, etc.: *The boy is not all there.*
—*pron.* to begin a statement: *There <sing.> is still time to finish the project and there <pl.> are many tasks to be done.*
—*interj.* **1 so there: a.** to express relief: *So there, I'm glad that tooth extraction is over.* **b.** to express anger or triumph: *So there! You made a mistake again!* **2 there, there:** to express sympathy, compassion: *The girl fell down and her mother said to her, "There, there, you'll be all right."*

there·a·bout(s) /'ðɛrə,baʊt(s)/ *adv.* near that place, time, amount, etc.: *You will find the stadium on the edge of town or thereabouts.||The coat costs $200 or thereabouts.*

there·af·ter /ðɛr'æftər/ *adv.frml.* afterwards, after that

there·by /'ðɛr,baɪ/ *adv.frml.* by this means, (*syn.*) in consequence of: *You receive interest on your savings account, thereby your money grows faster.*

there·fore /'ðɛr,fɔr/ *adv.* consequently, for that reason: *He practices the piano every day and therefore plays well.*

there·in /'ðɛrɪn, ðɛr'ɪn/ *adv.conj.frml.* within, found within: *An investigation showed theft of city funds and <conj.> therein lies the truth. See:* herein.

there·of /ðɛr'ʌv/ *adv.frml.* related to, (*syn.*) regarding: *The lawsuit deals with an accident and the damages thereof.*

there·up·on /'ðɛrə,pɑn, -,pɔn/ *adv.conj.frml.* as a consequence of, immediately following: *We discovered the problem; <conj.> thereupon we fixed it.*

ther·mal /'θɜrməl/ n. updraft, current of air heading upward: *Birds soar on the thermals above valleys.*
—*adj.* related to heat: *In winter, we wear thermal underwear to keep warm.*

ther·mo·dy·nam·ics /,θɜrmoudaɪ'næmɪks/ n.pl. used with a sing. v. the science of heat, heat flow, and mechanical forms of energy

ther·mom·e·ter /θər'mɑmətər/ n. a device used to measure and show temperature: *We placed a thermometer outside our window.*

ther·mo·nu·cle·ar /,θɜrmoʊ'nukliər/ adj. referring to reactions caused by the fusion of nuclei at high temperatures, as in the sun

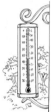
thermometer

ther·mo·stat /'θɜrmə,stæt/ n. a device that controls temperature inside a building: *It's cold in here; turn up the thermostat!*

the·sau·rus /θə'sɔrəs/ n. **-ri, -ruses** /-,raɪ/ a dictionary of synonyms: *When you look up the word "big" in a thesaurus, you learn that "large" is a synonym for "big."*

these /ðiz/ pron.pl. of this, referring to nearby things: *I am taking these flowers to my sick neighbor. See:* this.

the·sis /'θisɪs/ n. **-ses 1** an argument or theory: *The writer's thesis states that all human problems can be solved by logic.* **2** a study made and written by a student as part of getting an academic degree

they /ðeɪ/ pron. **1** third person plural: *John and Jane have just married and they are on their honeymoon.* **2** people in general: *They say that the economy will improve soon.*

thick /θɪk/ adj. **1** having bulk, width, or depth: *The walls of the library are thick.* **2** specifying width or measurement: *That steak is two inches thick.* **3** dense, closely packed: *He has a thick head of hair.* **4** obscure, *(syn.)* impenetrable: *The ground is covered with thick fog (smoke, snow).* **5** stupid, *(syn.)* dull-witted: *She loves her son, but realizes that he's a bit thick.* **6 thick with:** having a close relationship: *The company owner and his consultant are thick with each other.* **7 to lay it on thick:** to exaggerate, dramatize, flatter: *He lays it on thick when he tells about how he escaped from a mugger. -adv.* **thickly.**
—*n.fig.* [U] **1** the most intense part of s.t.: *The soldiers fought through the thick of battle.* **2 through thick and thin:** dedicated, loyal through difficult times: *Their marriage has had difficulties, but they have stayed together through thick and thin.*

thick·en /'θɪkən/ v. **1** to make thicker (wider, deeper, etc.): *Workers thickened the walls around the fort by adding more dirt to them.* **2** to enrich, *(syn.)* to fortify: *The cook thickened the gravy by adding more butter and flour.* **3** to become more complex: *The novel's plot thickened as more characters appeared. -n.* [C] **thickener.**

thick·et /'θɪkɪt/ n. an area of dense growth, usu. of bushes or hedges: *Rabbits hide in a thicket.*

thick·head·ed /'θɪk,hedɪd/ adj. stupid and stubborn: *He acts thickheaded at times and won't listen to anyone.*

thick·ness /'θɪknɪs/ n. the width or depth of s.t.: *In the thickness of the fog, we could not see the road well.*

thick-skinned adj. not easily angered, insensitive to criticism: *Politicians must be thick-skinned or they will suffer from the news media's criticisms. See:* thin-skinned.

thief /θif/ n. **thieves** /θivz/ a robber, person who steals: *A thief stole my luggage at the airport.*

thieve /θiv/ v. **thieved, thieving, thieves** to steal: *She called him a lying, useless guy, who was always thieving.*

thiev·er·y /'θivəri/ n. **-ies** [U] an act of theft, stealing: *Thievery of gold chains from people's necks is a problem in the subway.*

thigh /θaɪ/ n. the part of the leg between the hip and knee: *She biked all day and her thighs hurt.*

thim·ble /'θɪmbəl/ n. a hard metal or plastic cap that protects the fingertip while sewing: *The tailor wears a thimble on his index finger.*

thim·ble·ful /'θɪmbəl,fʊl/ n. a small amount

thin /θɪn/ adj. **thinner, thinnest 1** slender, slim: *She is tall and thin.* **2** not thick, wide, or deep: *A thin layer of dirt covers the rock below.* **3** sparse, not dense: *The plant cover is thin on sandy soil.* **4** light, not thick: *In summer, we wear thin clothing.* **5** weak, high-pitched: *a thin voice -adv.* **thinly.**
—*v.* **thinned, thinning, thins 1** to become sparse: *His hair is thinning.* **2** to make less dense: *I thinned the plants in my garden.* **3** phrasal v. **to thin down:** to lose weight: *He went on a diet and thinned down.*

thing /θɪŋ/ n. **1** a term for an unspecified material object, person, or animal: *We found a strange thing on the road.* **2** a concern, worry: *I don't have a thing on my mind.* **3** matter, task: *I don't have a thing to do right now.* **4 the** or **a thing:** the concern, matter: *The thing that is wrong with his plan is it costs too much.* **5 first thing:** early, at the beginning **6 it's a good thing:** it's lucky: *It's a good thing I made extra copies of the report as there were a lot of people at the meeting.* **7 to have a thing for** or **about: a.** *infrml.fig.* to be concerned, annoyed, etc.: *He has a thing about noise; he*

can't stand it. **b.** to like s.o. romantically: *She has a thing for her neighbor.* **8 the thing to do:** a proper, correct action: *The thing to do is to apologize right away.* **9 to do one's thing** or **one's own thing:** to act on one's special interest(s), usu. in a creative way: *He used to be a big executive, but now he's doing his own thing as a writer.* **10 to make a (big) thing about s.t.:** to have an argument, make a fuss: *Let's not make a big thing about him being late again.*
—n.pl. **1** one's possessions: *When we moved, we took all of our things with us in a truck.* **2** matters in general: *Things are bad now, but things will change soon.* **3 to hear** or **see things:** to imagine sounds or sights: *The child sees things in the night that are not there.*

thing·a·ma·bob /'θɪŋəmə,bɑb/ or **thing·a·ma·jig** / 'θɪŋəmə,dʒɪg/ *n.infrml.* s.t. whose name has been forgotten, (*syn.*) a whatchamacallit: *That thingamabob over there, what did you call it?*

think /θɪŋk/ *v.* **thought** /θɔt/, **thinking, thinks**
1 to reason, to use the brain: *She thinks of solutions to mathematical problems.* **2** to remember, recall: *He thinks that he sent the check to his landlord last week.* **3** to believe, desire: *I think that I should go now.* **4** to consider, have an opinion: *They thought that he acted like a jerk.* **5** *phrasal v. insep.* **to think about** or **of s.o.** or **s.t.:** to hold s.o. or s.t. in one's thoughts: *He thinks of his girlfriend all the time.* **6 to think aloud** or **out loud:** to speak as one is thinking without worrying about if it makes sense: *I'm just thinking out loud when I say that we should invest a lot of money in new equipment.* **7 to think better of:** to change one's mind: *He decided to buy a new car, then thought better of it and kept his old one.* **8 to think that:** to express amazement, relief: *To think that s.t. bad could have happened when we became lost in the mountains!* **9 to think nothing of:** to consider s.t. normal, routine: *He thinks nothing of flying from New York to London and back for a long weekend.* **10** *phrasal v. sep.* **to think s.t. out** or **through:** to plan carefully: *He thought out each detail of his presentation.||He thought them over.* **11** *phrasal v. sep.* **to think s.t. over:** to reflect, (*syn.*) to ponder before deciding: *She thought over his marriage proposal for several weeks before accepting.||She thought it over.* **12 to think twice about:** to be careful, cautious: *I would think twice about investing in stocks; they are too risky.* **13** *phrasal v. sep.* **to think s.t. up:** to invent, (*syn.*) to devise: *He thinks up excuses for being late.* *-adj.* **thinkable;** *-n.* **thinker.** *See:* unthinkable.

thinking cap *n. fig.* **to put on one's thinking cap:** to think hard: *We have a difficult problem*

and I must put on my thinking cap and find a solution.

think tank *n.fig.* a research institution or group that produces studies, often of a theoretical nature: *She works for an economics think tank in Washington, D.C.*

thin·ner /'θɪnər/ *n.* [U] a liquid used to thin other liquids: *I used turpentine as a paint thinner.*
—adj. comp. of thin

thin-skinned *adj.infrml. fig.* touchy, sensitive to criticism: *He is so thin-skinned that you have to be careful what you say to him. See:* thick-skinned.

third /θɜrd/ *adj.n.* **1** the ordinal number 3: *She is the <adj.> third child* (or) *the <n.> third in a group of four.* **2** one of three equal parts: *one <n.> third, two <n.> thirds*

third class *n.adj.* **1** a cheaper level of travel accomodations, esp. on a ship: *The refugees left Europe and traveled by <n.> third class to New York.* **2** in the USA, a postage rate for printed material, except for newspapers and magazines, weighing less than 16 ounces: *The books were shipped <n.> third class* (or) *by <adj.> third class mail.*

third degree *n.infrml.* **to give s.o. the third degree:** *infrml.fig.* to question or criticize severely, including the use of torture: *When she came home late, her parents gave her the third degree about where she had been.*

third-degree burn *n.* a severe burn that destroys the skin: *Surgeons graft (transfer) skin from unharmed places on the body to repair third-degree burns.*

third dimension *n.* depth, thickness (in addition to width and height)

third party *n.* **1** s.o. not directly related to a business transaction between two parties: *I received a check from ABC Corp., but the bank would not let me sign it over to a third party, XYZ, Inc.* **2** a political party different from two main parties: *Candidates of a third party take votes away from candidates of the main parties in an election.*

third person *n.* (in grammar) a person or thing in the singular as *he, she,* or *it* and in the plural as *they:* In learning English, students often forget to add an "s" to the third person singular form of verbs in the present tense.

third rate *adj.* of very bad quality

third world *n.* developing countries, usu. not industrialized: *Countries of the third world work at developing their basic resources.*

USAGE NOTE: Many people use the term *developing* nation instead of *third world* nation to avoid ranking the countries of the world. *Developing* suggests that a country's economy and industry are getting stronger.

thirst /θɜrst/ *n.* [U] **1** the need to drink liquid: *I slake* (or) *quench my thirst by drinking lots of water.* **2** *fig.* a desire for s.t.: *She has a thirst for knowledge.*
—*v.* **1** to want to drink liquids: *Travelers in the desert thirsted for water.* **2** *fig.* to desire s.t.: *He thirsts for an opportunity to prove himself.* -*adv.* **thirstily;** -*adj.* **thirsty.**

thir·teen /θər'tin/ *n.* [C] the cardinal number 13: *Thirteen is considered an unlucky number in many cultures.*

thir·ty /'θɜrti/ *n.* [C] the cardinal number 30: *She is thirty years old today.*

this /ðɪs/ *pron.* **1** referring to s.t. nearby: *You should read this book. This book is better than that one.* **2** (in stories) a certain, particular: *Then this stranger asked me the time.* **3 this and that:** one thing or another, different things: *My friend and I talked about this and that. See:* that.

this·tle /'θɪsəl/ *n.* any of a variety of spiny weeds, often with showy flowers: *Thistles have seeds that are a favorite food of birds.*

thong /θɑŋ, θɔŋ/ *n.* a narrow strip of leather used esp in shoes and clothes for tying: *Thong sandals have a small piece of plastic or leather between the big toe and the other toes.*

thor·ax /'θɔræks/ *n.* **-raxes 1** in humans, the chest area between the throat and abdomen: *Doctors examine the thorax for signs of disease.* **2** in insects, the middle section

thorn /θɔrn/ *n.* sharp, pointed parts of the stems in some plants: *Roses are beautiful, but have thorns.* -*n.* **thornbush** /'θɔrn,bʊʃ/.

thorn·y /'θɔrni/ *adj.* **-ier, -iest 1** having thorns **2** *fig.* difficult, complex, esp. causing pain: *Raising taxes is always a thorny issue.* **3** *fig.* **a thorn in one's side:** an ongoing problem, cause of irritation

thor·ough /'θɜrou, 'θʌ-/ *adj.* complete, (*syn.*) exhaustive: *A team of doctors made a thorough examination of the patient, then suggested a treatment.* -*adv.* **thoroughly;** -*n.* [U] **thoroughness.**

thor·ough·bred /'θɜrou,brɛd, 'θɜrə-, 'θʌ-/ *n.adj.* **1** a horse, esp. a race horse of pure stock: <*n.*> *Thoroughbreds* (or) <*adj.*> *Thoroughbred race horses are known for their spirit, beauty, speed and power.* **2** *fig.* referring to a well-bred person: *That person is very well-educated a real* <*n.*> *thoroughbred.*

thor·ough·fare /'θɜrou,fɛr, θɜrə-'θʌ-/ *n.* a main road that goes through a town: *Fifth Avenue is one of the main thoroughfares in New York City.*

those /ðouz/ *pron.pl. of* that, referring to specific people or things not close by: *Those people need help.*

though /ðou/ *conj.* although, even though: *I*

enjoy playing tennis, though it is tiring.
—*adv.* **1** despite the fact that, nevertheless: *Tennis is fun, though its also tiring.* **2 as though:** as if: *He acts as though it's also he's stupid, but he's not.*

thought /θɔt/ *n.* **1** [C] a mental picture, image: *The thought of the beautiful sunset filled his mind.* **2** [C] an idea, (*syn.*) impulse: *The thought of going out in the rain and fog discouraged him.* **3** [U] the process of reasoning, (*syn.*) evaluation: *He gave a lot of thought to moving to the country before doing so. See:* penny. **4** [C] an intention, plan: *I had thoughts of leaving work early today.* **5 second thought(s):** reconsidering s.t., (*syn.*) misgivings: *I said it would rain today, but on second thought, I think it won't.*

thought·ful /'θɔtfəl/ *adj.* **1** considerate, kind: *Her children were thoughtful and always took care of their elderly mother.* **2** reflective: *She doesn't say the first thing she thinks; she's very thoughtful.* -*adv.* **thoughtfully;** -*n.* [U] **thoughtfulness.**

thought·less /'θɔtlɪs/ *adj.* **1** insensitive, crude: *At the funeral, he made thoughtless remarks about the dead woman.* **2** unthinking, unconcerned: *The children played in the park, thoughtless of the time.* -*adv.* **thoughtlessly;** -*n.* [U] **thoughtlessness.**

thought·out *adj.* well-planned, paying attention to detail: *Their construction plan was well thought-out and made the best use of the land.*

thou·sand /'θauzənd/ *n.adj.* the cardinal number 1,000: *A* <*adj.*> *thousand people attended the lecture.*

thrash /θræʃ/ *v.* **-es 1** to beat severely, whip: *A mugger thrashed his victim with a club.* **2** *fig.* to win by a large amount: *Our team thrashed our opponents in football.* **3** to shake convulsively, (*syn.*) to writhe: *The dying animal thrashed on the ground.* **4** *phrasal v. sep.* **to thrash s.t. out:** to discuss for a long time before making a decision: *We thrashed out the details of the contract, then signed it.* -*n.* [U] **thrashing.**

thread /θrɛd/ *n.* **1** [C;U] a twisted fiber, such as cotton, wool, etc.: *A seamstress sewed a hole with a needle and thread.* **2** [C] a chain or line of events in a story: *She lost the thread of her story when the phone rang.* **3** [C] in a screw, the raised ridge that forms a spiral around it
—*v.* **1** to put thread through the eye of a needle **2** *fig.* to move carefully around obstacles: *He threaded his way through the crowd of people to the exit.*

thread

thread·bare /'θrɛd,bɛr/ *adj.* badly worn, (*syn.*) tattered: *The poor man wore threadbare clothes.*

threat /θrɛt/ *n.* **1** [C] a warning of harm: *They had to leave the building because of a bomb threat.* **2** [U] a danger, (*syn.*) menace: *An epidemic of the flu is a threat to public health.*

threat·en /'θrɛtn/ *v.* **1** to make threats: *A manager threatens to fire an employee unless her work improves.* **2** to make hostile motions toward s.o., (*syn.*) to menace: *One country threatened another by moving an army to the border.* **3** to warn: *The sky is threatening to snow.* *-adv.* **threateningly.**

three /θri/ *adj.n.* the cardinal number 3: *The couple has <adj.> three sons.*

three-dimensional or **3-D** /'θri'dɪ/ *adj.* having height, width, and depth: *A stone wall is three-dimensional.*

three R's /'θri'ɑrz/ *n.pl.* *short for* (r)eading, w(r)iting and a(r)ithmetic as the basic skills taught in school: *Every school child must learn the three R's.*

thresh /θrɛʃ/ *v.* **-es** to beat grain stalks to separate grain: *Farmers thresh grain with threshing machines.* *-n.* **thresher.**

thresh·old /'θrɛʃ,oʊld, -,hoʊld/ *n.* **1** the piece of stone (wood, etc.) under a door: *A wedding custom is for husbands to carry their wives over the threshold into the house.* **2** *fig.* **on the threshold:** at the beginning, on the point of: *Scientists are on the threshold of a major breakthrough in cancer research.*

thrift /θrɪft/ *n.* spending money carefully, (*syn.*) frugality: *New Englanders are noted for their thrift.* *-adj.* **thrifty.**

thrift shop *n.* a store that resells second-hand items, esp. clothes: *Thrift shops for used children's clothes are everywhere.*

thrill /θrɪl/ *n.* a feeling of strong excitement, fear, or pleasure: *Riding a roller coaster gives you a thrill.*
—*v.* to excite intensely: *Watching professional basketball games thrills the audience.* *-adj.* **thrilling;** *-adv.* **thrillingly.**

thril·ler /'θrɪlər/ *n.* **1** a mystery or adventure story, such as a novel or movie **2** *fig.* an exciting event: *The World Series baseball game was a thriller; the final score was 12-11.*

thrive /θraɪv/ *v.* **thrived** or **throve** /θroʊv/ or **thrived** or **thriven** /'θrɪvən/, **thriving, thrives** **1** to grow strong and healthy: *Our children thrived on life in the country.* **2** to be motivated, energized by: *Athletes thrive on competition.* *-adj.* **thriving.**

throat /θroʊt/ *n.* **1** the front of the neck between chin and chest; inside the mouth to the esophagus: *She has a sore throat and a cold.* **2** *fig.* **to cut** or **slit one's own throat:** to make oneself fail at s.t.: *She cut her own throat by*

volunteering to do an extra project when she already had too much work. **3 to ram, force, push s.t. down s.o.'s throat:** to make s.o. accept s.t. (ideas, etc.), usu. unwillingly

throat·y /'θroʊti/ *adj.* **-ier, -iest** of a sound, low and rough, harsh: *Smokers often have throaty voices.*

throb /θrɑb/ *n.* a beating, pulsating sensation, usu. inside the body
—*v.* **throbbed, throbbing, throbs** to beat strongly, usu. from pain, (*syn.*) to pulsate: *His head throbs from a fever.*

throne /θroʊn/ *n.* a decorated chair used esp. by royalty in ceremonies as a symbol of power and position

throng /θrɑŋ, θrɔŋ/ *n.frml.* a mob, large group of people: *A throng of people gathered to hear the political candidate.*
—*v.* to form into a group: *Fans thronged around the celebrity.*

throt·tle /'θrɑtl/ *n.* on a machine, the valve that controls fuel, air, etc.
—*v.* **-tled, -tling, -tles** **1** *fig.* to choke, strangle: *A murderer throttled his victim.* **2** to adjust a machine's throttle

through /θru/ *prep.* in one side and out the other: *The boy walked through the backyard.*
—*adv.* **1** making a connection: *I got through to Moscow by telephone.* **2** completely, from beginning to end: *He read through the magazine.* **3 through and through:** completely, (*syn.*) to the core: *She is a liar through and through. See:* **thru,** USAGE NOTE.
—*adj.* **1** finished, done: *The maid is through cleaning the room now.* **2** referring to the end of a job, career, or other relationship: *His boss told him that he was through at that company.*

through·out /θru'aʊt/ *prep.* everywhere: *The rumor spread throughout the city.*

through·way /'θru,weɪ/ *n.* a major highway, esp. with few exits, expressway: *The throughway runs across the state into the city.*

throw /θroʊ/ *v.* **threw** /θru/ or **thrown** /θroʊn/, **throwing, throws** **1** to send s.t. through the air, (*syn.*) to toss: *One player throws the ball to the other.* **2** to send with force or anger, (*syn.*) to hurl: *One wrestler threw the other to the mat.* **3** to put on quickly: *She took off her jeans and threw on a dress for the funeral.||He threw up some decorations for the party.* **4** to punch: *One fighter threw a punch at the other.* **5** to make fall off: *My horse threw me and I hit the ground.* **6 a.** *infrml.* to add casually, toss: *She threw some more wood on the fire.* **b.** *fig.* to add casually, (*syn.*) to augment: *He threw in a few extra rewards in the deal to sweeten it.* **7** to move s.t. on a machine: *to throw a switch* **8** *phrasal v. sep.* **to throw s.t. around:** to scatter s.t.: *She was throwing around a lot of money last year.||She was throwing it around.* **9** *phrasal v. sep.* **to throw s.t. away: a.** to dis-

card, get rid of: *He threw away the old newspapers.* **b.** *fig.* not to take advantage of s.t.: *She threw away her chances for a promotion by yelling at her boss.‖She threw them away.* **10** *phrasal v. sep.* **to throw s.t. back:** to return, put back in: *He threw back the small fish he caught in the river.‖He threw it back.* **11** *phrasal v. sep.* **to throw s.t. in:** to enter: *She threw in her name as a candidate for mayor.‖She threw it in.* **12** *phrasal v. sep.* **to throw s.t. off: a.** to remove, uncover: *The child threw off her blankets while she was sleeping.‖She threw them off.* **b.** to trick, deceive: *The criminal threw the police off his trail by hiding in the woods.* **13** *phrasal v. sep.* **to throw s.t. out: a.** to discard **b.** to put out for consideration: *He threw out the idea of ordering a pizza for dinner.‖He threw it out.* **c.** to kick out, (*syn.*) to eject: *She threw her husband out of the house.* **14** *phrasal v. sep.* **to throw s.o.** or **s.t. over: a. s.o.:** to leave, abandon: *She threw over her old job for a new one.* **b. s.t.:** to cover: *He threw a sheet over the sleeping baby.* **15** *phrasal v. sep.* **to throw s.t. together:** to put together quickly: *I can throw together a salad for lunch.‖I can throw it together.* **16** *phrasal v. sep.* **to throw s.t. up: a.** to vomit: *He threw up his dinner because he had food poisoning.‖He threw up.* **b.** to build quickly, (*syn.*) to erect: *We threw up our tent at the campground.*
—*n.* **1** the act of throwing **2** the distance s.t. is thrown: *a 50-foot (15.3m) throw*

throw-away *adj.* discarding things after use, being wasteful: *The USA is called a throwaway society where old or broken things are discarded instead of being fixed or reused.*

throw·back /ˈθroʊˌbæk/ *n.* s.o. or s.t. that is similar to an earlier type or time: *She looks like a 19th century British lady, a throwback to an earlier century. See:* anachronism.

thru /θru/ *infrml. prep. short for* through:

USAGE NOTE: *Thru* is not used in formal writing; rather, use *through.*

---

thrush /θrʌʃ/ *n.* a spotted brown and gray songbird: *Thrushes fill meadows and marshes with their beautiful song.*

thrust /θrʌst/ *n.* a quick forward motion as with the arm or feet, a lunge: *Fencers lunge at each other with sword thrusts.*
—*v.* **thrust, thrusting, thrusts 1** to move one's arm or foot forward quickly: *She thrusted the knife into the watermelon.* **2** *fig.* to be forced suddenly into a situation: *An employee was thrust into a new job without any training.*

thud /θʌd/ *n.* the sound that a falling heavy object makes when it hits the ground: *The big textbook fell on the floor with a thud.*

—*v.* **thudded, thudding, thuds** to fall with a thud: *The big book thudded onto the floor.*

thug /θʌg/ *n.* a criminal, a tough guy

thumb /θʌm/ *n.* **1** on the hand, the digit opposite the index finger: *The thumb allows humans to hold things.* **2** *fig.* **under one's thumb:** dominated, controlled, esp. by fear: *The owner likes to have employees under his thumb.‖She's under the thumb of her grandfather.* **3** *pl.* **thumbs down:** a sign of disapproval: *Movie reviewers give a thumbs down if they don't like a film.* **4** *pl.* **thumbs up:** a sign of approval, support, or victory: *The executive committee gave thumbs up to a research proposal.* **5** *pl.* **all thumbs:** awkward, clumsy: *I am dropping things and seem to be all thumbs today.* **6 a rule of thumb:** a guideline, rule **7** *infrml.* **to stick out like a sore thumb:** to seem different, out of place: *His expensive new car sticks out like a sore thumb in this poor neighborhood.*
—*v. infrml.* **1 to thumb a ride:** to stand on the road with one's thumb extended, (*syn.*) to hitchhike: *As a college student, he thumbed a ride home on weekends.* **2** *phrasal v. insep.* **to thumb through s.t.:** to look or search through quickly: *A clerk thumbed through the files looking for a letter.*

thumb·nail /ˈθʌmˌneɪl/ *n.* the nail of the thumb
—*adj.* small, unfinished, brief: *We draw thumbnail sketches before doing a finished drawing.*

thumb·tack /ˈθʌmˌtæk/ *n.* a small pin or tack used to attach things to a wall or board

thump /θʌmp/ *v.* to hit with a heavy sound, (*syn.*) to thud: *A child thumped on a drum with her hands.*
—*n.* a thud: *The ball hit the wall with a thump.*
-*n.* **thumper;** -*n.* [U] *adj.* **thumping.**

thun·der /ˈθʌndər/ *n.* [U] **1** the loud, strong noise that follows lightning: *Thunder frightens some animals and people.* **2 to steal s.o.'s thunder:** to stop s.o. from impressing others by speaking first
—*v.* **1** to create thunder **2** *fig.* to sound like thunder: *A herd of cattle thundered by.* **3** to yell, shout loudly -*n.* [U] *adj.* **thundering;** -*adj.* **thunderous;** -*adv.* **thunderously.**

thun·der·bolt /ˈθʌndərˌboʊlt/ *n.* **1** a flash of lightning with thunder **2** *fig.* a hard, unexpected blow: *The news of his wife's sudden death struck him like a thunderbolt.*

thun·der·storm /ˈθʌndərˌstɔrm/ *n.* a storm with heavy rain, thunder, and lightning

thun·der·struck /ˈθʌndərˌstrʌk/ *adj. fig.* extremely surprised, (*syn.*) amazed

Thurs·day /ˈθɜrzˌdeɪ/ *n.* the fifth day of the week, coming between Wednesday and Friday: *On Thursdays, she takes a course after work.*

thus /ðʌs/ *adv.conj.* **1** for that reason, therefore: *He does not watch television, <conj.> thus he does not own a television set.* **2** in this way **3 thus far:** so far, until now

thwart /θwɔrt/ *v.* to block s.o. from doing s.t., (*syn.*) to obstruct: *A detective thwarted a crime by catching the robber trying to escape.*

thyme /taɪm/ *n.* [U] an herb used to flavor food: *One of my favorite meals is chicken in a creamy sauce flavored with thyme.*

thy·roid /ˈθaɪˌrɔɪd/ *n.adj.* the gland that controls the energy and growth in the body and is located in the neck: *The <n.> thyroid* (or) *<adj.> thyroid gland can get too big and need an operation.*

ti·a·ra /tiˈærə, -ˈɑrə/ *n.* a small crown with jewels that women wear on formal occasions: *The princess wore a tiara to the winter ball.*

tib·i·a /ˈtɪbiə/ *n.* **-ias** or **-iae** /-i,i/ the larger leg bone between the knee and to the ankle: *She broke her tibia in a skiing accident.*

tic /tɪk/ *n.* a nervous spasm or twitch of a muscle: *He has an eye tic that makes him look like he is winking.*

tick /tɪk/ *n.* **1** the sound of a clock in motion: *The grandfather clock in our front hall has a loud tick.* **2** a small, bloodsucking insect that attaches itself to larger animals: *Dog owners remove ticks from their pets.* **3** (in finance) the increments in the price of a security: *Stocks are traded in eighths; each eighth up or down is a tick.*
—*v.* **1** to make the sound of a clock: *Old clocks tick away with the sound, "tick-tock tick-tock."* **2 to make s.o.** or **s.t. tick:** to make s.o. act a certain way, (*syn.*) to motivate s.o.: *I don't understand what makes him tick; he doesn't seem to have any goals or pleasures.* **3** *phrasal v. sep.* **to tick s.o. off:** to make angry: *It's not a good idea to tick off people you have to work with.||Don't tick them off.* **4** *Brit.* to make a check mark: *She ticked off the items on her grocery list.*
—*adj.infrml. fig.* **ticked off:** angry, annoyed: *She is ticked off because she didn't get a raise this year.*

tick·er /ˈtɪkər/ *n.* **1** *short for* an old-fashioned telegraphic machine that gives stock prices: *The prices came over the ticker for buyers to see.* **2 ticker tape:** paper from a ticker machine, now thrown as confetti: *After the war, there was a ticker tape parade on Wall Street.* **3** *slang for* heart: *My father says his ticker's not as strong as it used to be.*

tick·et /ˈtɪkɪt/ *n.* **1** a printed piece of paper bought for transportation or entertainment events: *I have two tickets to the theater tonight.* **2** a written legal notice: *A traffic officer gave me a ticket for parking in an illegal spot.* **3** *infrml.fig.* **that's just the ticket:** an

expression of approval: *I suggested to my friend that we go to the beach, and he said, "That's just the ticket!"*

ticket

—*v.* **1** to create and sell tickets: *Travel agents ticket passengers for an ocean cruise.* **2** to write notices, such as traffic tickets: *A police officer ticketed a driver for speeding.*

ticket agency *n.* a person or business that sells tickets for entertainment or travel: *I bought two concert tickets from the agent at the ticket agency.* **-n. ticket agent.**

ticket or **box office** *n.* a place, such as in a theater, that sells tickets: *The ticket office at the theater opens one hour before the performance begins.*

tick·ing /ˈtɪkɪŋ/ *n.* [U] a strong fabric covering a pillow or mattress: *The ticking on mattresses is often blue-and-white stripes.*

tick·le /ˈtɪkəl/ *v.* **-led, -ling, -les 1** to touch lightly the sensitive parts of the body so as to cause laughter: *The baby's father tickled its foot with his fingers.* **2** *fig.* to please, delight: *She is really tickled with her new car.* **3** *infrml.fig.* **to tickle one's fancy:** to please, amuse: *Does the idea of a walk in the moonlight tickle your fancy?* **4 tickled pink** or **to death:** very pleased, excited: *They were tickled pink when their first grandchild was born.* **-n. tickler.**

tick·lish /ˈtɪklɪʃ/ *adj.* **1** sensitive to being tickled: *She is ticklish and can't stand being tickled.* **2** *fig.* delicate, difficult: *Arranging marriages between people is a ticklish occupation.*

tick·tack·toe or **tic·tac·toe** /ˈtɪktækˈtoʊ/ *n.* [U] a game for two players where the object is to mark three X's or 0's in a row and block the other player

tid·al /ˈtaɪdl/ *adj.* referring to the actions of tides: *When the tide goes down, it leaves tidal pools in the rocks and sand.*

tidal wave *n.* a gigantic wave that floods the coastline: *After the earthquakes a tidal wave hit the coast and washed many houses out to sea.*

tid·bit /ˈtɪdˌbɪt/ *n.* **1** a small amount of food: *He ate some tidbits of cheese and fruit.* **2** a small, often unrelated amount of s.t.: *She had tidbits of information about her company's competitors.*

tid·dly·winks /ˈtɪdliˌwɪŋks/ *n.* a game played with thin disks snapped at a cup: *The winner of tiddlywinks is the player who puts the most disks into the cup.*

tide /taɪd/ *n.* [C;U] the change in levels of sea and ocean water caused mainly by the moon's

T

force of gravity: *Boats go out to sea on the high tide.*

—*v.* **tided, tiding, tides** *phrasal v.sep.* **to tide s.o. over:** to carry s.o. through a period of need: *He is staying with friends to tide him over until he finds an apartment of his own.*

tide·wa·ter /'taɪd,wɔtər, -,wɑ-/ *n.* [U] *adj.* the water from tides that flows into inlets: <*n.*> *Tidewater is salty and mixes with fresh water from rivers.*||*The* <*adj.*> *tidewater marshes around Chesapeake Bay are home to much wildlife.*

tid·ing /'taɪdɪŋ/ *n.frml. old usage* news, a message: *Christmastime brings tidings of joy.*

ti·dy /'taɪdi/ *adj.* **-dier, -diest** neat, orderly: *The boy's room is never tidy.*

tie /taɪ/ *v.* **tied, tying, ties** **1** to fasten together, (*syn.*) to bind: *He tied his shoelaces.* **2** to equal s.o. in a competition, have a draw: *The tennis match is tied 2-2 in the 2ⁿᵈ set.* **3** *phrasal v. sep.* **to tie s.o.** or **s.t. down: a. s.o.:** to keep in one place, (*syn.*) to restrict: *She takes care of her elderly parents, so she is tied down.* **b. s.t.:** to bind, (*syn.*) to lash down: *We tied our suitcases down on the car's luggage rack.* **4** *phrasal v. sep.* **to tie s.t. in (with s.t.):** to connect, blend together: *We tied in television commercials for our products with radio and newspaper advertising.*||*We tied them in.* **5** *phrasal v. sep.* **to tie s.t. up: a.** to bind, fasten together: *I tied up old newspapers and put them outside for recycling.* ||*I tied them up.* **b.** to block, (*syn.*) to hinder: *We were tied up in traffic.* **6 tied up:** busy, occupied: *The manager can't talk to you now as she's tied up in a meeting.*

—*n.* **1** a necktie **2** a bond, link: *He still has ties to his old neighborhood.* **3** a draw, equality in competition: *The two teams had a 2-2 tie.* **4** the pieces of wood, metal, etc., that connect the rails on a railroad track

tie breaker *n.* in sports, a point made by a team or player to break an equal score: *A tennis player scored a tie breaker and won the match.*

tier /tɪr/ *n.* **1** a group of rows of seats: *The highest tier in the stadium is the fifth tier.* **2** a row of s.t., usu. rising higher than the one before it: *Boxes are stacked in tiers in the warehouse.* **3** a ranking or rating: *Her grades were not very good, so she could only get into a third tier of a small school.*

tie-up *n.* a delay, (*syn.*) blockage: *A traffic tie-up made us late. See:* tie, **5b.**

tiff /tɪf/ *n.* a minor argument, (*syn.*) a spat: *The two neighbors had a tiff, but are friends again.*

ti·ger /'taɪgər/ *n.* large, fierce, wild yellow cat that lives in Asia: *Indian tigers have been hunted almost to extinction.*

tight /taɪt/ *adj.* **1** stretched firmly, (*syn.*) taut: *The belt is tight around his waist.* **2** not allow-

ing s.t., such as water or air to pass through: *The seal on the jar is tight.*||*Cans of food are air-tight.* **3** not wanting to spend money: *He is tight with his money.* **4** not available, in short supply: *Loan money is tight now.* **5** rigid, firm: *The government keeps tight control over the news media.* **6** *infrml.fig.* drunk: *She drank too much and is tight.* **7** *infrml.fig.* good friends, close to s.o.: *Those two people are tight* (or) *tight with each other.* **8** close: *She held her baby tight.* **9 in a tight spot:** in difficulty or danger of harm: *She is in a tight spot at work because her company is laying people off.* **10 sit tight:** stay where you are, wait -*adv.* **tightly;** -*n.* [U] **tightness.**

tight·en /'taɪtn/ *v.* **1** to fasten firmly, make taut: *He tightens his belt before he takes a walk.* **2** to restrict: *Border police tightened controls on tourists. See:* loosen.

tight·fist·ed /'taɪt,fɪstɪd/ *adj.infrml.* reluctant to spend money, cheap: *Even though she is wealthy, everyone knows she's tightfisted.*

tight-lipped /'taɪt,lɪpt/ *adj.* quiet, unwilling to give information: *Witnesses to the crime are tight-lipped from fear.*

tight·rope /'taɪt,roʊp/ *n.* **1** a rope between two high points: *Circus performers cross a tightrope to thrill crowds.* **2** *fig.* **to walk a tightrope:** to be in a dangerous, tricky situation: *The President must walk a tightrope between conservatives on one side and liberals on the other.*

tights /taɪts/ *n.pl.* close-fitting hosiery, stockings: *Ballet dancers wear tights to cover their legs.*

tight·wad /'taɪt,wɑd/ *n.* a tightfisted person, (*syn.*) cheapskate: *He is such an old tightwad that he still has the first dollar he earned.*

'til or **till** /tɪl/ *infrml. prep. short for* until: *We'll wait 'til six o'clock, then leave.*

tile /taɪl/ *n. v.* **tiled, tiling, tiles** thin plates of ceramic, metal, etc., put down to cover a floor or wall: *A worker* <*v.*> *tiled the bathroom with new* <*n.*> *tiles.*

till /tɪl/ *v.* to work the land; plow, plant, and harvest: *Farmers till the soil in the springtime.*

—*n.* **1** the drawer of a cash register: *A cashier puts money in the till.* **2** pieces of clay and small rocks from a glacier: *Water drains down the glacial till.* -*adj.* **tillable.**

till·er /'tɪlər/ *n.* **1** a person who works the soil: *A farmer is a tiller of the land.* **2** a lever used to move a ship's rudder: *The captain turned the tiller to head the ship to sea.*

tilt /tɪlt/ *n.* **1** an inclination in an angle, (*syn.*) a slope: *A rocket takes off vertically, then has a tilt in its path.* **2 at full tilt:** at top speed: *The motorboat sped away at full tilt.*

—*v.* to lean away from the vertical: *A computer operator tilts the screen into a comfortable position.*

T

tim·ber /'tɪmbər/ *n.* **1** [U] wood for construction, lumber: *Loggers cut timber and take it away on logging trucks.* **2** a wooden beam or support **3** a shout to watch out for a falling tree: *As a logger cuts down a tree, he shouts, "Timmmm---berrr!" -n.* [U] **timberland** /'tɪmbər,lænd/.

time /taɪm/ *n.* **1** [U] the duration of existence, esp. as measured in days, months, years, etc., or by clocks, watches, etc.: *There is a saying that "time and tide wait for no man."* **2** [C, usu. sing.; U] the exact hour, minute, or second in a day: *The time is now 8:00 A.M.* **3** [U] a duration, period: *We have time to have lunch before the meeting.* **4** [U] a moment, (*syn.*) opportunity: *Now is the time to make an offer on the house we want.* **5** [C] an experience: *We had a good (bad, high, etc.) time at the party.* **6 against time:** to meet a deadline, often in an emergency: *Rescue workers worked against time to free the trapped boy before the water covered his head.* **7 ahead of one's time:** having a vision, modern **8 ahead of time:** early, done before a certain time: *She plans events ahead of time and is well organized.* **9 all in good time:** not to be hurried, slow(ly): *The administration will take care of the matter all in good time.* **10 all the time:** always, often: *She goes to the movies all the time.* **11 at one time: a.** before, a long time ago: *At one time, the railroad used to pass through this town, but no longer.* **b.** together, at the same time: *He organized his debts all at one time by putting them into one loan.* **12 at the same time: a.** together: *We all left at the same time.* **b.** on the one hand, considered together with: *I like this suit; at the same time, it is too warm to wear except in winter.* **13 at times:** sometimes, (*syn.*) periodically: *At times, she feels discouraged and at other times, optimistic.* **14 behind the times: a.** outdated, unaware of recent developments: *He is behind the times and quite old-fashioned.* **b.** outmoded, (*syn.*) obsolete: *Their machinery is behind the times and inefficient.* **15 for the time being:** for now, temporarily **16 from time to time:** periodically, every so often: *He writes to his parents from time to time.* **17 in one's own time:** not to be hurried: *He gets things done slowly in his own time.* **18 in no time (flat):** quickly, fast: *I asked her to do s.t. and she did it in no time flat!* **19 in the nick of time:** just in time, usu. to avoid harm, trouble, etc.: *The firefighters came in the nick of time and saved people from the burning building.* **20 in time: a.** over a period of time: *In time, she will feel less sad about her mother's death.* **b.** on time, at the right time: *He arrived in time to get a good seat at the show.* **21 just in time: a.** in time to avoid difficulty, harm, etc.: *She arrived just in time to catch the bus.* **b.** (in business) a type of

inventory management where new stock arrives as the old is sold: *We use just-in-time inventory management in our company.* **22 one at a time:** in order, individually: *Please speak one at a time, not all at once.* **23 once upon a time:** long ago, many years past: *Fairy tales often begin, "Once upon a time, etc."* **24 on one's own time:** after working hours: *On her own time she likes to paint and draw.* **25 on time:** punctual, (*syn.*) precise: *The train left on time.* **26** *infrml.fig.* **small time:** *infrml.fig.* unimportant, not big in size, power, prestige, etc.: *He is a small-time thief who steals cars.* **27** *infrml.fig.* **the big time:** the top of any profession or activity: *She is a Hollywood star who made it to the big time.* **28 time after time:** repeatedly, constantly: *I told him time after time not to go near the water and now he fell in and almost drowned.* **29 time and again:** repeatedly, constantly **30 Time heals all wounds:** with the passing of time, anger between people goes away: *Two nations that were enemies are now friends as time heals all wounds.* **31 time off:** vacation, time not working: *He took time off and went to Mexico for a week.* **32 Time out!:** Stop play! (in sports): *The basketball referee shouted, "Time out!"* **33 to bide one's time:** to wait for opportunity: *I'm going to bide my time until those shoes I want go on sale.* **34** *slang* **to do time:** to serve time in prison: *She has done time for burglary.* **35 to have the time: a.** to know what time it is: *"Excuse me, do you have the time?"—"Yes, it's two o'clock."* **b.** to have time to do s.t.: *I have time to talk with you now.* **36 to have the time of one's life:** to enjoy oneself a lot **37 to keep time: a.** (in music) to keep the tempo: *The conductor keeps time for the orchestra.* **b.** to measure time in sports: *Two officials keep time in championship games.* **38** *infrml.fig.* **to kill time:** to do little while waiting, (*syn.*) to idle: *We killed time by talking and joking, until our airplane took off.* **39 to lose time:** to be slowed down, get behind schedule: *A traffic jam made us lose time on our trip.* **40 to make time:** to travel fast, on or ahead of schedule: *There was no traffic, so we really made time on our drive.* **41 to make up time:** to work extra because of time taken off from work: *She was out with a flat tire for a day, so she made up the time by working on Saturday.* **42 to pass the time (of day):** to idle, do nothing special: *On vacation, we passed the time reading, watching TV, and sleeping.* **43 to take time out: a.** (in sports) *The team took time out to rest.* **b.** to stop what one is doing to do s.t. else: *The father took time out to be with his children.* **44 to tell time:** to read the hands of a clock to know the time: *She learned to tell time at the age of five.*

T

time /taɪm/ v. **timed, timing, times 1** to measure the amount of time needed to complete s.t.: *We timed our trip to Boston; it took three hours.* **2** to select the correct time to do s.t.: *They timed their visit so they could be with her for the fair.* **3** to adjust, regulate machinery: *The VCR is timed to record every day at 2:00.*

time and a half n. [U] pay at the regular hourly rate plus 50%, such as $20 per hour = $30: *She gets time and a half for overtime work. See:* comp time, USAGE NOTE.

time bomb n. **1** an explosive that has a timer: *A time bomb was set to go off in an hour.* **2** *fig.* s.o. or a situation that may explode into a bigger problem: *Her anger at working every weekend makes her a real time bomb.*

time card or **sheet** n. a card on which a worker's hours at work are noted: *He puts his time card in a time clock when he gets to and leaves work.*

time-consuming adj. needing a lot of time, lengthy: *Making bread is very time-consuming.*

timed /taɪmd/ adj. measured by the amount of time needed to do s.t.: *Each time horses race, they are timed.*

time-honored adj. done for many years, traditional: *Giving presents on birthdays is a time-honored tradition.*

time·keep·er /ˈtaɪmˌkipər/ n. a person who keeps time, esp. of sporting events: *The time-keeper at basketball games stops the clock whenever the officials signal to do so.*

time·less /ˈtaɪmlɪs/ adj. lasting forever, (syn.) eternal: *The timeless beauty of a great painting always delights people. -n.* [U] **timelessness.**

time limit n. a set period of time for doing s.t.: *The time limit for the exam is two hours.*

time·ly /ˈtaɪmli/ adj. **-lier, -liest 1** fortunate, (syn.) opportune: *The arrival of help was timely because it saved everyone from starvation.* **2** in time: *The package was sent overnight on a timely basis for the meeting today.*

time-out n. a brief stopping of activity, esp. in a sporting event: *The basketball team called a time-out and rested.*

tim·er /ˈtaɪmər/ n. a clock or person who times events, usu. to the minute or second: *She uses an egg timer in the kitchen to boil eggs.*

times /taɪmz/ prep. multiplied by: *Ten times 10 equals 100.*

—n.pl. **1 the times:** modern life, now: *These are conservative times.* **2 behind the times:** outdated, outmoded **3 for old times' sake:** because of good memories: *She went out with her old boyfriend once more for old times' sake.*

time-share n. a form of joint ownership of a vacation home that gives each owner a certain number of weeks use each year: *I have a two-*

week time-share in a ski house in Vermont. -n. [U] **time-sharing.**

time sheet n. a record of hours an employee has worked: *The office manager keeps a time sheet on each employee for payroll purposes.*

times sign n. the sign (x), which is used to indicate multiplication: *10 x 15 = 150.*

time·ta·ble /ˈtaɪmˌteɪbəl/ n. **1** a printed chart or display of transportation departure and arrival times: *I carry a commuter train timetable, so I can check when my train leaves.* **2** a plan, schedule: *We have a timetable for testing and marketing a new product.*

time zone n. one of 24 15-degree longitudinal divisions of the earth as measured from Greenwich, England: *When it is 11:00 A.M. in New York, it is 8:00 A.M. in the Pacific time zone.*

tim·id /ˈtɪmɪd/ adj. **1** easily frightened, (syn.) skittish: *Many birds are timid and fly away as you come near them.* **2** shy, (syn.) hesitant: *The boy is timid about asking girls for dates. -n.* [U] **timidity** /tɪˈmɪdəti/; -adv. **timidly.**

tim·ing /ˈtaɪmɪŋ/ n. [U] **1** the time that an event occurs: *The timing of your visit is excellent, as we need to talk to you.* **2** (in sports) an athlete's ability to act at the right moment: *The tennis player's timing is off and she is not reaching her opponent's shots.*

tim·or·ous /ˈtɪmərəs/ adj.frml. fearful, timid: *Wild creatures are timorous of humans.*

tin /tɪn/ n. **1** [U] a grayish, flexible, metallic element used as a protective coating and as an alloy with other metals: *Aluminum now functions in many old uses for tin.* **2** [C] *Brit.* a can

tinc·ture /ˈtɪŋktʃər/ n. [U] an alcohol solution of a medication: *She uses tincture of iodine to clean wounds.*

tin·der /ˈtɪndər/ n. [U] kindling, or anything that burns easily, used to start fires

tin·der·box /ˈtɪndərˌbɑks/ n. **1** a box used to hold tinder **2** *fig.* a locale or situation that could easily catch fire or become violent: *The forest is so dry this summer that it is a tinder-box.‖Those old houses are dangerous tinder-boxes.*

tin ear n. the inability to appreciate s.t., not interested, usu. in music: *He has a tin ear for classical music.*

tin foil n. [U] a thin sheet of aluminum used as a covering, esp. for food

tinge /tɪndʒ/ n. a slight amount of color, a hint of s.t.: *His voice was tinged with sadness.*

—v. **tinged, tingeing, tinges** to add a little color, tint: *Age has tinged his hair with gray.*

tin·gle /ˈtɪŋgəl/ v. **-gled, -gling, -gles** to have a prickly feeling: *Her fingers tingle from the cold.*

—n. a prickly feeling: *She can feel the tingle in her toes from the cold. -n.* [U] adj. **tingling.**

tin·ker /'tɪŋkər/ n. a person who goes from place to place fixing metal utensils and implements: *Tinkers go from house to house offering to sharpen knives and fix pots and pans.*
—v. **1** to work as a tinker **2** *fig.* to work with s.t. casually, (*syn.*) to putter: *He tinkered with his car to see if he could make it work.*

tin·kle /'tɪŋkəl/ v. **-kled, -kling, -kles 1** to make light metallic sounds: *Small bells tinkle.* **2** *infrml.fig.vulg.* to urinate (baby talk): *The little boy had to tinkle.*
—n. a metallic sound: *You can hear the tinkle of the wind chimes on the porch.*

tin·ny /'tɪni/ adj. **-nier, -niest** having an unpleasant, thin sound: *That old piano sounds tinny.*

tin·sel /'tɪnsəl/ n. [U] thin strips of shiny, silvery metal used for decoration, esp. on Christmas trees: *The tinsel on the tree makes it look covered with ice and snow.*
—adj. showy, bright but cheap: *Hollywood is called "Tinsel Town."*

tint /tɪnt/ n. a color with white added, a light shade of a color: *White added to black produces a tint of gray.*
—v. to color: *She tints her hair to cover the gray.*

ti·ny /'taɪni/ adj. **-nier, -niest** very small, (*syn.*) minute: *Cells are too tiny to see with the bare eye; one needs a microscope to see them.*

tip /tɪp/ n. **1** the point of s.t.: *The tip of a needle is very sharp.* **2** advice, helpful information: *The coach gave a player a tip on how to improve her tennis stroke.‖A friend gave me a tip on the stock market.* **3** money given to s.o. for doing s.t., (*syn.*) a gratuity: *I left the waiter a generous tip.*
—v. **tipped, tipping, tips 1** to leave a little money: *I tipped the waiter and left.* **2** to lean, incline: *She tipped the bucket and poured water out of it.* **3** to spill, knock over: *The child tipped over a glass of water.*

tip-off n.v.infrml. a hint, telling secret information: *An informer gave the police a <n.> tip-off that a gang planned to rob a bank.‖He <v.> tipped them off.*

tip·per /'tɪpər/ n. s.o. who gives money as a gratuity, esp. to a server at a restaurant: *That woman is a good tipper.*

tip·sy /'tɪpsi/ adj. **-sier, -siest** a little bit drunk: *He drank too much and is a little tipsy.*

tip·toe /'tɪp,toʊ/ v. **-toed, -toeing, -toes 1** to walk quietly on one's toes: *She tiptoed up the stairs, so as not to wake up her sleeping parents.* **2** *fig.* to talk carefully around s.t.: *She tiptoed around the question of a raise with her boss.*

tip-top /'tɪp,tɑp/ adj. excellent, first rate: *She exercises every day and is in tip-top condition.*

ti·rade /'taɪ,reɪd/ n. a long, complaining speech or criticism: *The boss gave a long tirade about how we had to meet the deadline.*

tire /taɪr/ v. **tired, tiring, tires 1** to weaken, become fatigued: *He tires when he walks a long distance.* **2** to bore, irritate: *Listening to long speeches tires the audience.*
—n. the outer covering of a vehicle's wheel where air is put: *My bicycle got a flat tire this morning on my way to work.* -adj. **tiring.**

tired /taɪrd/ adj. **1** exhausted, fatigued: *She is tired after working all day.* **2** *fig.* annoyed, wearied: *I am tired of listening to your problems.* -adv. **tiredly.**

tire·less /'taɪrlɪs/ adj. dedicated, (*syn.*) unflagging: *Her efforts for her clients are tireless.* -n. [U] **tirelessness.**

tire·some /'taɪrsəm/ adj. annoying, wearying: *His complaints are tiresome.*

tis·sue /'tɪʃu/ n. **1** [U] a group of animal or plant cells that together makes up an organ that performs a certain function, such as nerve tissue or muscle tissue: *Human liver tissue can grow again if it is injured.* **2** [C] paper products, such as toilet tissue or paper handkerchiefs: *After I sneezed, I wiped my nose with a tissue.* See: Kleenex.

tit /tɪt/ n. **1** a small bird **2** the nipple on a breast: *The baby sucked milk from a tit.* **3** *vulg.* a woman's breast **4** **tit for tat:** an act of doing the same thing to s.o. who has hurt or annoyed you, (*syn.*) retaliation: *The U.S. government caught a foreign spy, and the spy's government seized an American in a tit for tat.*

ti·tan·ic /taɪ'tænɪk/ adj. gigantic, of great size, strength, importance, etc.: *Sumo wrestlers have titanic strength.* -n. **titan** /'taɪtn/.

tithe /taɪð/ n. 10% of one's income given to a church or charity: *The family gives a tithe to their church.*
—v. **tithed, tithing, tithes** to give or receive a percentage, usu. 1/10th of an income: *The church tithed its members.*

tit·il·late /'tɪtl,eɪt/ v. **-lated, -lating, -lates** to excite briefly, (*syn.*) to entice: *The sexual adventures of TV soap opera characters titillate large audiences.* -n. [U] **titillation.**

ti·tle /'taɪtl/ n. **1** [C] the name of a book, musical piece, painting, etc.: *The title of that great novel is* War and Peace. **2** [C;U] legal proof, such as a document, of ownership of property: *I have title to two automobiles.* **3** [C] the name of a rank of nobility, academic degree, or office: *Dr. Jones has the title of Doctor of Medical Dentistry.*
—v. **-tled, -tling, -tles** to give a name or title to s.t.: *The songwriter titled the song "Happy Days."* -adj. **titled.**

ti·tle·hold·er /'taɪtl,hoʊldər/ n. **1** (in law) one who has title to property: *The titleholder to* *that land is an elderly woman.* **2** (in sports) a record holder

title role *n.* the main character in a play, for whom it is named

tit·mouse /'tɪt,maʊs/ *n.* **-mice** /-,maɪs/ a family of small, energetic birds, such as the chickadee, with long tails: *Titmice fly quickly from tree to tree in search of food.*

tit·ter /'tɪtər/ *v.* to laugh nervously and quietly: *The schoolchildren tittered when the teacher lost his glasses.* -*n.* [U] **tittering.**

tit·u·lar /'tɪtʃələr/ *adj.* referring to s.o. who holds a title, but not its power: *The president is the titular head of the company, but the owner is really in charge.*

tiz·zy /'tɪzi/ *n.infrml.* **-zies** confusion, (*syn.*) a whirl: *He is in a tizzy because he can't find his car keys and has to leave.*

TLC /'tiɛl'si/ *n.infrml.abbr. of* tender loving care: *Patients in hospitals need lots of TLC.*

TNT /'tiɛn'ti/ *n.* [U] *abbr. of* trinitrotoluene, an explosive: *Workers used TNT to make holes in rock.*

to /tə, *strong form* tu/ *particle* **1** used to begin an infinitive of a verb, as in "to go" and "to know": *We have to go home now.‖I want you to know that you are right.* **2** used in place of an infinitive: *He needs to fix his car but doesn't know how to.* **3** used to indicate an indirect object: *The sales clerk sold the dress to her.* **4** used with many verbs to show motion: *A police officer came to help us.*

—*adv.* in the direction of, such as up and down or from side to side: *The pendulum on the clock swings to and fro.*

—*prep.* **1** toward, in the direction of: *That highway leads to Florida.* **2** part of, making up: *There are four quarts to a gallon.* **3** headed toward a state (status, condition, etc.): *The country is moving to the left politically.* **4** extending to, reaching as far as: *That path leads to the woods.* **5** regarding pleasure or lack of it: *Those roses are to her liking.‖I prefer golf to tennis.* **6** regarding the senses (smell, touch, sight, etc.): *That cloth feels like silk to the touch.‖To my eye, that color looks green, not blue.* **7** including, between certain times, spaces, etc.: *He works from morning to evening (from 9 to 5).‖She read the book from beginning to end.* **8** regarding time, scores, and ratios: *It is 10 to noon.‖Our team won 10 to 6.‖That building will take 3 to 4 years to complete.* **9** relating, belonging to, fitting s.o. or s.t.: *That is the key to the door.‖She is the assistant to the manager.*

toad /toʊd/ *n.* a frog-like amphibian with warty skin: *Toads spend more time on land than frogs do.*

toad·stool /'toʊd,stul/ *n.* a large mushroom-like plant, usu. poisonous

to-and-fro /'tuən'froʊ/ *adj.adv.phr.* back and forth, side to side: *Children swing <adv.> to-and-fro in the playground.*

—*n.* [U] back-and-forth movement: *Commuters get used to the to-and-fro of traveling to and from work.*

toast /toʊst/ *v.* **1** to make bread or other foods brown with heat: *I toasted some white bread for sandwiches.* **2** to call for s.o.'s good health or honor s.o., esp. with a drink: *We toasted the guest of honor with a glass of wine.*

—*n.* **1** [U] pieces of bread that have been heated until they are brown: *I had toast for breakfast.* **2** [C] a gesture to honor s.o.: *The host proposed a toast to the bride and groom.*

toast·er /'toʊstər/ *n.* an electrical device that browns food

toast·y /'toʊsti/ *adj.fig.* **-ier, -iest** warm and cozy: *The mountain cabin was warm and toasty.*

to·bac·co /tə'bækoʊ/ *n.* [U] a variety of leafy plants dried and cut for smoking or chewing: *Nicotine is the active narcotic in tobacco.*

to·bac·co·nist /tə'bækənɪst/ *n.* a person or business that sells tobacco products

to·bog·gan /tə'bagən/ *n.v.* a large flat sled with a curved front used to slide down snowy hills: *Our <n.> toboggan will seat three, and we <v.> tobogganed down a nearby hill in it this winter.*

toboggan

to·day /tə'deɪ/ *adv.* **1** now, this present day: *Today, I'm going to work.* **2** these times: *Today, our government needs to do s.t. about the economy.*

—*n.* in this time, age, etc.: *In today's world, one cannot plan on having the same employer for 25 years.*

tod·dle /'tadl/ *v.* **-dled, -dling, -dles** to walk with short, unsteady steps: *Little children toddle when they learn to walk.*

tod·dler /'tadlər/ *n.* a small child: *Parents hold the hands of toddlers when they learn to walk.*

to-do /tə'du/ *n.infrml.* a confusion, (*syn.*) a fuss: *He makes a big to-do about paying his taxes.*

toe /toʊ/ *n.* **1** each of five digits on the foot: *Her big toe hurts.* **2** *fig.* **on one's toes:** alert, ready to move or act: *The boss keeps everyone on their toes by checking their work.* **3** *fig.* **to step** or **tread on s.o.'s toes:** to annoy s.o., esp. by taking over their plans or authority: *He stepped on his daughter's toes by interfering in her wedding plans. See:* finger.

—*v.* **toed, toeing, toes 1** to touch or move with the toe: *He toed the curbstone as he talked.* **2 to toe the line:** to stick to strict rules of behavior: *After his release from jail, the authorities made him toe the line.*

toe·hold /'toʊ,hoʊld/ *n.* **1** a space large enough only for one's toes: *A rock climber finds toeholds as she climbs a cliff.* **2** *infrml.* **to gain a toehold:** to make a small beginning: *Our company gained a toehold in the foreign market through a distributor in Hong Kong.*

toe·nail /'toʊ,neɪl/ *n.* the nail on each toe of the foot: *Toenails grow more slowly than fingernails.*

tof·fee or **tof·fy** /'tɔfi, 'tɑ-/ *n.* [C;U] a hard candy made of sugar and butter boiled together

to·fu /'toʊfu/ *n.* [U] a cheeselike curd made from soybeans: *Tofu is a very healthy source of protein.*

to·ga /'toʊgə/ *n.* a loosely draped outer garment worn by the Romans

to·geth·er /tə'gɛðɛr/ *adv.* **1** as a group: *We went together to the party.* **2** (to join) in a group: *We joined together into a trade association.* **3** (to join) as a unit or assembly, etc.: *Carpenters nail pieces of wood together.* **4** in unison: *The senators in each party voted together along party lines.* **5** *infrml.fig.* **to get it** or **one's act together:** to organize oneself to act effectively: *He finally got his act together and graduated from college.* **6** *infrml.fig.* **to have it together:** to be well organized, effective (a person): *He has it together and is doing well in business.* -*n.* [U] **togetherness.**

tog·gle /'tɑgəl/ *n.* a pin or bar that keeps s.t. together: *He wears a wool coat that fastens with toggles.*
—*v.* to alternate between two or more electronic configurations, esp. when using a computer: *On my computer, I can toggle between two software programs very easily.*

togs /tɑgz/ *n.pl. infrml.* an outfit, clothes, esp. for sports: *He wears tennis togs on the court.*

toil /tɔɪl/ *v.* to work hard, labor with little reward or relief: *He toils in the fields under a hot sun.*
—*n.* [U] hard work with little reward, (*syn.*) drudgery: *The toil in farming is unending.*

toi·let /'tɔɪlɪt/ *n.* **1** a bathroom fixture, usu. ceramic, with a water tank, bowl, and drain pipe, used to flush away bodily waste: *The toilet is stopped up.* **2** a bathroom, the room with a sink, toilet, bathtub, or shower: *He excused himself to go to the toilet.*

toilet paper *n.* [U] paper tissue used for hygienic purposes: *Toilet paper comes in rolls.*

toi·let·ries /'tɔɪlɪtriz/ *n.pl.* items used for personal care, such as soap, shampoo, lotions, etc.: *Drugstores and grocery stores sell toiletries.*

to·ken /'toʊkən/ *n.* **1** a substitute coin: *The local subways and buses take tokens as well as*

coins. **2** *fig.* a sign, indication of s.t.: *He gives her roses as a token of his affection for her.*

to·ken·ism /'toʊkə,nɪzəm/ *n.* [U] (in race relations) hiring few minority workers: *A company with two employees was accused of tokenism because it has one black worker, one Asian worker, one gay worker, and one Hispanic worker.*

USAGE NOTE: *Tokenism* is a fairly serious statement to make about a company or organization, because it implies that a company really doesn't want to hire women and minority workers.

tol·er·a·ble /'tɑlərəbəl/ *adj.* **1** bearable, (*syn.*) endurable: *The heat in this area is tolerable during the summer.* **2** not very good but acceptable, somewhat satisfactory: *The food in that cafeteria is tolerable.* -*n.* [U] **tolerability.** *See:* intolerable.

tol·er·ance /'tɑlərəns/ *n.* **1** [U] the ability to suffer or endure s.t.: *She has a high tolerance for pain.* **2** [U] acceptance, esp. of beliefs and behavior different from the dominant culture: *That city is famous for its tolerance of crime.* **3** [C] (in machinery) small differences from standard: *Precision tools must be machined to close tolerances. See:* intolerance.

tol·er·ant /'tɑlərənt/ *adj.* accepting of different beliefs and behavior: *The boy's parents are tolerant of his naughty behavior. See:* intolerant.

tol·er·ate /'tɑlə,reɪt/ *v.* -ated, -ating, -ates **1** to allow, put up with s.t.: *She cannot tolerate anyone who does not act as she does.* **2** to endure, suffer: *I cannot tolerate hot, spicy foods.* **3** to accept, receive: *Most people in that country will tolerate people from other nations as neighbors.* -*n.* [U] **toleration.**

toll /toʊl/ *n.* [C] **1** a fee charged for passage: *Authorities charge a toll to use certain bridges and roads.* **2** [usu. sing.] the slow regular sound as of a bell: *You can hear the toll of church bells on Sunday.* **3** [usu. sing.] wear and tear: *Working many long days took its toll on her health.*
—*v.* to ring, sound slowly: *The grandfather clock tolled 12 midnight.*

toll·booth /'toʊl,buθ/ *n.* a small structure from which tolls are collected: *We stopped at the tollbooth and paid the toll.*

toll call *n.* a call requiring an extra payment in addition to a base rate: *I get some free calls each month; the rest are toll calls.*

toll·gate /'toʊl,geɪt/ *n.* **1** a gate that goes up when one pays a toll **2** the area of tollbooths and gates on a highway: *We stopped at the tollgates and paid.*

toll road *n.* a road, thruway, etc., that requires payment of tolls for passage

T

tom·a·hawk /'tɑməˌhɔk/ *n.* a small hatchet used by Native Americans: *Tomahawks were used in war to kill enemies.*

to·ma·to /tə'meɪtoʊ/ *n.* **-toes** a South American plant with large red fruit eaten as a vegetable: *Tomatoes have a lot of vitamin C.*

tomb /tum/ *n.* a burial room or grave with a monument over it: *Egyptian pyramids are tombs and monuments to dead rulers.*

tom·boy /'tɑmˌbɔɪ/ *n.* a girl who behaves like a boy, esp. in sports and choice of clothes: *She is a tomboy who is better at football and tennis than most boys are.* **-adj. tomboyish.**

tomb·stone /'tumˌstoʊn/ *n.* a grave marker: *His tombstone is carved with the words, "Rest in Peace."*

tom·cat /'tɑmˌkæt/ *n.* a mature male domestic cat

Tom, Dick, and Har·ry /'tɑm'dɪkən'hæri/ *n.* [U] an expression meaning everybody, ordinary men: *She is a snob and won't speak to just any Tom, Dick, and Harry.*

tome /toʊm/ *n.frml.* a large, heavy book: *One-volume encyclopedias are tomes.*

tom·fool·er·y /tɑm'fuləri/ *n.* [U] senseless behavior, silliness: *Teachers will not allow tomfoolery in the classroom.*

to·mor·row /tə'mɔroʊ, -'mɑ-/ *n.adv.* the day after today: *<n.> Tomorrow is Saturday and I have to work <adv.> tomorrow.*

ton /tʌn/ *n.* **1** a unit of measurement of weight, in the USA, 2,000 lbs.; in the British Commonwealth, 2,240 lbs. **2** a metric ton: weight of 1,000 kilos **3** a displacement ton of ships equal to 35 cubic feet of seawater: *Large ocean-going ships weigh thousands of tons.* **4** *infrml.* general expression of heaviness or large amount of s.t.: *That bookcase is too heavy for me to carry; it weighs a ton.‖I have a ton of work to do today.*

to·nal·i·ty /toʊ'næləti/ *n.* **-ties 1** (in music) relationships of tones based on keys **2** the relationship of colors and tone of a painting: *The tonality of her painting is based on the use of primary colors.* **-adj. tonal** /'toʊnəl/.

tone /toʊn/ *n.* **1** the loudness or character of a voice: *He speaks to his baby in soft tones.* **2** the mood in a voice or gathering: *Our meeting had a pleasant (unfriendly, serious, etc.) tone.* **3** an electronic sound, such as the dial tone (the sound of a telephone when picked up) or another signal: *On the radio one hears, "At the sound of the tone, it will be 10:00 o'clock."* **4** (in music) a full interval on a diatonic scale: *The interval goes up a whole tone.* **5** (in art) the characteristic of a color or shade: *Her watercolor paintings have a light tone.* **6** the firmness and flexibility of skin or muscles: *An athlete has good muscle tone.*

—v. toned, toning, tones 1 to increase firmness or vitality: *He tones his muscles by exercising.* **2** *phrasal v. sep.* **to tone s.t. down:** to lessen the intensity of s.t.: *The critic toned down her attacks on the government.‖She toned them down.* **3** *phrasal v. sep.* **to tone s.t. up: a.** to make s.t. stronger, firmer: *He toned up his muscles by exercising.‖He toned them up.* **b.** to improve s.t.: *She toned up her apartment by having it painted.*

tone-deaf *adj.* unable to hear differences in musical notes

tone·less /'toʊnlɪs/ *adj.* flat, lacking spirit, lifeless: *She gave a toneless answer to his question.* **-adv. tonelessly.**

tongs /tɔŋz, tɑŋz/ *n.pl.* **a pair of tongs:** a V-shaped tool used to hold and lift things: *I took some lettuce from a bowl with a pair of tongs and put it on my plate.*

tongue /tʌŋ/ *n.* **1** the movable organ in the mouth used for tasting and producing speech: *He drank hot tea and burned his tongue.* **2** a language: *He speaks in a foreign tongue.* **3** a type or tone of speech: *That boy has a sharp tongue.* **4 on the tip of one's tongue:** about to be recalled: *Oh, I have the man's name right on the tip of my tongue; yes, it's George Smith!* **5 to have a silver tongue:** to speak well, (*syn.*) to be eloquent: *He was a great orator who spoke with a silver tongue.* **6 to hold one's tongue:** not to speak even though one wants to: *He wanted to yell at the rude man, but held his tongue.* **7 to speak with a forked tongue:** to lie: *He's a liar who speaks with a forked tongue.* **8 to stick or pull out one's tongue:** to show contempt for s.o.: *The girl stuck out her tongue at a boy who annoyed her.* **9 tongue-in-cheek:** jokingly, (*syn.*) ironically: *She spoke with tongue-in-cheek when she asked her friend to loan her a million dollars.*

—v. tongued, tonguing, tongues to use the tongue to form separate notes on a musical instrument: *The musician tongued notes on the oboe.*

tongue-lashing *n.fig.* severe criticism: *The boss gave the worker a tongue-lashing for coming to work late.*

tongue-tied *adj.fig.* unable to speak because of nervousness: *A guy met a very pretty woman and was tongue-tied.*

tongue-twister *n.* words that are difficult to pronounce: *"Peter Piper picked a peck of pickled peppers" is a tongue-twister.*

ton·ic /'tɑnɪk/ *n.adj.* **1** a medicinal liquid that gives energy: *He made a <n.> tonic of herbal tea and honey.* **2** a stimulant: *The cool autumn air is a <n.> tonic; it has a <adj.> tonic effect.* **3 tonic water:** water with gas bubbles and quinine: *I'll have a glass of tonic water, please. See:* soda, USAGE NOTE.

to·night /tə'naɪt/ *adv.* the hours of darkness following this day: *The concert takes place tonight.*

USAGE NOTE: *Tonight* includes both *evening* and *night* of a given day: *Tonight at 7 p.m. (–this evening), I'm having dinner with friends. Tonight at midnight (–late at night), I'm meeting a friend at a nightclub.*

ton·nage /'tʌnɪdʒ/ *n.* [U] **1** the weight in tons of freight or ships' cargo: *Ships carry a huge tonnage of wheat from the Great Lakes' ports.* **2** the total shipping capacity of a nation: *The country of Panama registers a great tonnage of ships every year.*

ton·sil /'tɑnsəl/ *n.* one of two oval-shaped organs located back in the human throat: *The boy's tonsils are inflamed and must be removed.*

ton·sil·li·tis /,tɑnsə'laɪtɪs/ *n.* [U] inflammation of the tonsils

ton·y /'touni/ *adj.infrml.* **-ier, -iest** classy, fashionable: *My rich friends live in a tony neighborhood.*

too /tu/ *adv.* **1** in addition, as well, also: *She went to the movie, and I decided to go, too.* **2** excessively, unreasonably: *That investment is too risky for us.* **3** *infrml.* extreme, *(syn.)* intolerable (often used humorously): *George, you are just too much.*

took /tʊk/ *past tense of* take

tool /tul/ *n.* **1** an implement, such as a pair of pliers, screwdriver, hammer, or saw, used to make or repair things: *He keeps his tools in the cellar.* **2** person manipulated by others, *(syn.)* a dupe: *She drove the getaway car in the bank robbery, but was only a tool of those who planned it.* **3** *slang:* s.o. who studies a lot, a grind: *That tool is always in the library!*
—*v.* **1** to decorate, make designs in s.t.: *She tooled the leather belt with geometric designs.* **2** *phrasal v.* **to tool along:** to drive fast and calmly: *I tooled along on the highway until I reached Atlanta and a lot of traffic.* **3** *phrasal v.* **to tool up:** to design and make manufacturing tools used to make products: *Each year, automakers tool up for next year's new car models.*

toolbox /'tul,bɑks/ *n.* a steel, wooden, etc. case in which tools are kept and carried: *The carpenter takes a toolbox to work.*

toot /tut/ *v.n.* **1** to beep or blow a horn: *A driver <v.> tooted (the horn) to warn people crossing the road.* **2** *infrml.* to play a brass instrument: *A musician <v.> tooted a trumpet.* **3** *slang:* cocaine **4** *infrml.fig.* **to toot one's own horn:** to boast, brag: *Oh, you should listen to him <v.> toot his own horn!*

tooth /tuθ/ *n.* **teeth** /tiθ/ **1** one of a set forming a dental structure in the mouth used for biting and chewing: *A dentist examines one tooth at* a time. **2** pointed parts of s.t., such as teeth on a saw, rake, comb, etc. **3 long in the tooth:** old *See:* sweet tooth. **4** *fig.* **to fight tooth and nail:** to fight with all one's power: *She fought tooth and nail to keep her job.*

toothache /'tuθ,eɪk/ *n.* [C, *usu. sing.*] a pain in a tooth or teeth

tooth·brush /'tuθ,brʌʃ/ *n.* **-brushes** a brush with a handle used to clean teeth

tooth·less /'tuθlɪs/ *adj.* without teeth, weak

tooth·paste /'tuθ,peɪst/ *n.* [U] sweetened, gritty paste used to clean teeth: *Baking soda and water can be used as toothpaste.*

tooth·pick /'tuθ,pɪk/ *n.* a slender piece of wood, plastic, etc. used to remove food pieces from between the teeth

top /tɑp/ *n.* **1** the highest or uppermost part (level, layer, etc.) of s.t.: *He touched the top of his head.* **2** a lid, covering, cap: *The top of the jar is made of metal.* **3** a shirt, a piece of clothing for the upper body: *She bought a new top to go with her skirt.* **4** the best, first: *He is at the top of his class.* **5** a toy that spins: *Children play with tops.* **6 in top form:** at the best of one's ability: *That skier is in top racing form today.* **7 off the top of my head:** quickly, without research or thought: *Off the top of my head, I don't know the answer, but I will find out.* **8 on top: a.** in a stronger position, *(syn.)* dominant: *Labor is on top in the negotiations with management.* **b.** the top person: *She was promoted to general manager and is on top now.* **9 on top of: a.** totally aware and in control of a situation: *He is on top of all that is going on in his department.* **b.** in addition to: *I have a lot of work to do; on top of that my babysitter is sick.* **10** *fig.* **on top of the world:** to feel happy, thrilled: *She told him that she loves him, and he is now on top of the world.* **11 over the top:** exceeding goals, doing s.t. very well: *Our sales volume this month has already gone over the top.* **12 to blow one's top: a.** to explode the top off s.t.: *The volcano shook, then blew its top.* **b.** *infrml.fig.* to explode in anger or rage: *He blew his top when his proposal was refused.* **13 top of the line:** the best of a group: *That special model Mercedes is the top of the line in automobiles.*
—*n.pl.* **1** the uppermost parts: *The tops of the trees move in the wind.* **2** *fig.* excellent, terrific: *He (She, It, etc.) is tops, just terrific!* **3** *fig.* first, *(syn.)* foremost: *He (She, etc.) is tops in the country in his field.*
—*v.* **topped, topping, tops 1 to top it (all) off:** in addition, usu. s.t. especially good or very bad: *We had a wonderful party and to top it all off we were driven home in a limousine.* **2** *phrasal v.* **to top out:** to level off, flatten: *Sales volume on that product is topping out and beginning to decline.* **3** *phrasal v. sep.* **to top s.t. off: a.** to add a last remaining amount

T

to s.t.: *The worker carefully topped off the oil tank with a few drops more.*‖*She topped it off.* **b.** to add more to s.o.'s drink, to freshen: *Can I top off your glass of wine?*

to·paz /'toupæz/ *n.* [C;U] a semi-precious gemstone in pink, brown, blue, yellow: *She wears a large yellow topaz set in a gold ring.*

top brass *n.pl.* the most important, highest ranking people: *The top brass from the military visited the troops.*

top-down *adj.adv.* in descending order of importance: *The guests are listed <adv.> top-down with the guest of honor heading the list.*

top hat *n.* a high, black, flat-topped hat: *On very formal occasions, men wore top hats and formal suits.*

top-heavy *adj.* having a heavier, fuller top than bottom: *That organization is top-heavy with managers and assistants.*

to·pi·ar·y /'toupi,ɛri/ *n.* **-ries** a garden of trees, hedges, etc., that are cut in artistic shapes

top·ic /'tapɪk/ *n.* a subject of attention, writing, conversation; a field: *Today's topic in class was linear algebra.*

top·i·cal /'tapəkəl/ *adj.* **1** related to a topic, subject, field, etc.: *The professor made topical remarks about the subject of today's lecture.* **2** local, not general: *This medicinal lotion is for topical use only.* *-adv.* **topically.**

topic sentence *n.* a sentence that gives the main subject of concern: *The topic sentence began the first paragraph of her term paper.*

top·less /'taplɪs/ *adv.adj.* without a shirt, (*syn.*) bare-breasted: *Men go <adv.> topless on the beach.*

top-level *adj.* at the highest level, esp. of an organization: *The Presidents and Prime Ministers held a top-level meeting on economic cooperation.*

top-notch *adj.* first rate, excellent: *She did a top-notch job on her report.*

to·pog·ra·phy /tə'pagrəfi/ *n.* [U] **1** the physical landscape: *The topography of the Balkans is mountainous.* **2** maps of the physical features of an area: *The US government makes maps showing the topography of the USA.* *-n.* [C] **topographer.**

top·ping /'tapɪŋ/ *n.* [C;U] sweets, sauces, garnishes, etc., put on top of foods: *The dessert has a topping of whipped cream and a cherry.*

top·ple /'tapəl/ *v.* **-pled, -pling, -ples 1** to knock down: *Workers toppled statues of old leaders.* **2** *fig.* to overturn, bring down: *Revolutionaries topple governments by making coups.*

top secret *adj.* the highest level of secrecy, esp. in the military: *Military plans are kept top secret for security reasons.*

top·soil /'tap,sɔɪl/ *n.* [U] the first level of soil: *Topsoil on hillsides can be washed away by heavy rains.*

top·sy-tur·vy /,tapsi'tɜrvi/ *adj.infrml.* upside down, confused: *After the storm, the whole area was topsy-turvy.*

torch /tɔrtʃ/ *n.* **-es 1** a lighting device with a flame atop a handle: *The Olympic torch is used to light the flame to begin the games.* **2 to carry a torch for s.o.:** to be in love with s.o. who usu. does not love one in return: *She always carried a torch for her old boyfriend.*
—*v.* **-es** to set afire: *Vandals torched buildings in the city.*

tor·e·a·dor /'tɔriə,dɔr/ *n.* a bullfighter: *A toreador must be very brave and skillful.*

tor·ment /'tɔr,mɛnt/ *n.* [U] great mental or physical pain, (*syn.*) agony: *During the war, he suffered torment as a prisoner.*
—*v.* /*also* tɔr'mɛnt/ to make miserable, inflict torment: *The little boy tormented insects by pulling off their legs.* *-adj.* **tormented;** *-n.* [C] **tormentor.**

tor·na·do /tɔr'neɪdou/ *n.* **-does** a twister; violent, swirling, fast-moving winds: *Tornadoes can lift houses and trees and put them down miles away.*

tor·pe·do /tɔr'pidou/ *n.* **-does** a naval weapon driven by its own motor in the water that explodes when it hits a vessel: *Torpedoes can damage a ship and sink it.*
—*v.* **-doed, -doing, -does 1** to hit with a torpedo: *Submarines torpedoed many ships during World War II.* **2** *fig.* to ruin, (*syn.*) to sabotage: *An opponent torpedoed proposed legislation by having it voted down in Congress.*

tor·por /'tɔrpər/ *n.frml.* [U] inactivity because of lack of energy, ambition, etc., (*syn.*) lethargy: *The noonday heat in some areas causes torpor among people.* *-adj.* **torpid** /'tɔrpɪd/.

torque /tɔrk/ *n.* [U] the movement and usu. measurement of a mechanical system that causes rotation: *Racing cars develop high torque as their engines reach full speed.*

tor·rent /'tɔrənt, 'tar-/ *n.* **1** a violent flood, esp. of water: *A torrent of water rushed down the canyon.* **2** *fig.* a rush: *A torrent of criticism followed the proposed tax increases.* *-adj.* **torrential.**

tor·rid /'tɔrɪd, 'tar-/ *adj.* **1** extremely hot: *The fire was so torrid that firefighters could not get near it.* **2** intensely passionate, hot: *The couple had a torrid love affair.* *-adv.* **torridly.**

tor·so /'tɔrsou/ *n.* the area of the human body from the hips to the neck, the trunk: *Many Greek statues are of the torso only.*

tort /tɔrt/ *n.* (in law) a private or civil wrongful act that causes another person harm or damage and entitles him or her to compensation: *A guy ran into my car, which is a tort.*

tor·tel·li·ni /ˌtɔrtl'ini/ *n.* [U] small, round pasta filled with meat, cheese, etc.

tor·til·la /tɔr'tiə/ *n.* a Mexican bread of corn meal made in a thin layer and cooked on a grill

tor·toise /'tɔrtəs/ *n.* a land turtle noted for its high humped shell and slow motion

tor·tu·ous /'tɔrtʃuəs/ *adj.* **1** winding, bending: *The road through the mountains is tortuous and narrow.* **2** *fig.* complex, involved: *Wage and benefit negotiations can be tortuous.* -*adv.* **tortuously.**

tor·ture /'tɔrtʃər/ *n.* **1** [C;U] physical abuse that causes great pain and mental anguish: *Prisoners are subjected to torture by some military groups.* **2** [U] strong emotional pain
—*v.* **-tured, -turing, -tures** to abuse, harm: *Prison workers tortured captured soldiers during the war.*

toss /tɔs/ *v.* **-es 1** to throw, pitch: *The baseball player tossed the ball to the catcher.* **2** to mix lightly: *I tossed a salad for dinner.* **3** to throw away: *She tosses old memos in the wastebasket.* **4** to jerk, nod: *A horse tosses its head.* **5** to flip: *The referee tossed a coin to see who kicks off.* **6** *phrasal v. sep.* **to toss s.t. around:** to discuss s.t. informally: *I tossed around the idea of going to the beach with my friends and they liked it.‖I tossed it around.* **7** *phrasal v. sep.* **to toss s.t. away:** to discard, dispose of s.t.: *He tosses away the paper after reading it.‖He tosses it away.* **8** *phrasal v. sep.* **to toss s.t. off:** to do s.t. quickly: *She tossed off a letter to her sister.*
—*n.* **1** a heave, hard throw: *Fifty yards is a long toss in football.* **2** a lob, easy throw: *I gave the ball a toss to my daughter.* **3** a flip: *The referee gave the coin a toss.*

toss-up *n.* [U] a guess that anything could happen, an even likelihood: *Both teams are so good that it is a toss-up as to who will win.*

tot /tat/ *n.* a small child: *The mother carried her tiny tot.*

to·tal /'toʊtl/ *n.* a sum, final adding up of numbers, things, etc.: *The total of this month's sales is up 20%.*
—*adj.* **1** complete, entire: *That amount represents the total cost of the project.* **2** absolute, (*syn.*) utter: *The house destroyed in the storm is a total loss.*
—*v.* **1** to add up, reach a final figure: *The clerk totaled the bill.* **2** *infrml.fig.* to destroy, esp. a car: *He drove too fast and totaled his car.* -*adv.* **totally.**

to·tal·i·tar·i·an /toʊˌtælə'tɛriən/ *adj.* dictatorship by an individual or a group over a nation's people: *Totalitarian regimes never last forever.* -*n.* [U] **totalitarianism.**

to·tal·i·ty /toʊ'tæləti/ *n.* **-ties** [U] everything included, the whole: *The totality of human life on this planet numbers in the billions.*

total quality management or **TQM** /'tikyu-'ɛm/ *n.* a concept that focuses on cooperation and employee training in order to ensure continual quality improvement

tote /toʊt/ *v.* **toted, toting, totes** to carry, lug: *A porter toted my luggage up to my hotel room.*
—*n.* a light, cloth bag: *I carry my computer in a small tote.*

to·tem /'toʊtəm/ *n.* the image of a bird, animal, or other living thing used as an object of worship or respect: *Some Native American tribes honor the bear as a totem.*

totem pole *n.* a tree carved and usu. painted with totems and displayed in the open: *Some tribes place a totem pole before their communal house.*

tot·ter /'tatər/ *v.* to move unsteadily: *The economy tottered on the edge of depression.‖The child tottered as she learned to walk.* -*n.* [C] **totterer;** -*adj. n.* [U] **tottering.**

tou·can /'tu,kæn, tu'kæn/ *n.* a brightly colored tropical South American bird with a large beak

touch /tʌtʃ/ *v.* **-es 1** to feel with the skin, esp. with the hand: *The doctor touched the patient's stomach to feel for problems.* **2** to make contact: *The bookcase is touching the wall.‖Two passengers touched as they entered the train.* **3** to evoke emotion, move s.o. to tears, laughter, sorrow, etc.: *The sad music touched me and made me feel blue.* **4** to use, act on: *to touch one's food, alcohol, etc.* **5** to match, compare with: *Nothing touches our school's basketball team.* **6 to touch base:** to communicate informally with s.o., esp. about a project or concern of mutual interest: *(on the telephone) Hi Ramón, I'm calling to touch base with you on the sales report due next week.* **7** *phrasal v.* **to touch down:** to land an aircraft: *Our plane touched down at San Francisco airport in a smooth landing.* **8** *phrasal v. insep.* **to touch on s.t.:** to speak about briefly: *In our discussion, we touched on the subject of price.* **9** *phrasal v. sep.* **to touch s.t. off: a.** to start, (*syn.*) to instigate: *Food shortages touched off rioting.* **b.** to start, (*syn.*) to initiate: *A spark touched off an explosion of a gas leak.* **10** *phrasal v. sep.* **to touch s.t. up:** to make minor improvements: *A worker touched up bare spots on the wall with paint.*
—*n.* **-es 1** [U] skin sensation: *The patient felt the touch of the doctor's hand.* **2** [C] physical contact: *The touch of her hand calmed him down.* **3** [C] a small amount: *Put a touch of salt in the soup.* **4** [C] skillfulness, (*syn.*) dexterity: *That nurse has a good touch with inserting a needle.* **5 in touch:** communication between people: *She stays in touch with her*

T

parents by telephoning them every week. **6** [C] **the finishing touch:** a detail, last preparation **7** *infrml.fig.* **to be a soft touch:** soft-hearted, responsive to the troubles of others, esp. in giving money: *He is such a soft touch that he cannot pass a beggar on the street without giving some money.* **8 to have the touch:** to have finesse, skillfulness: *She has the touch for making money.||He has the touch for making good bread.*

touch-and-go *adj.* uncertain, (*syn.*) unstable: *The patient is being operated on, and it is touch-and-go as to whether she'll recover.*

touch·down /'tʌʧ,daʊn/ *n.* **1** the moment of an aircraft's landing: *Touchdown of the space vehicle is expected in ten minutes.* **2** (in USA football) a six-point score: *A runner carried the ball over the goal line for a touchdown.*

tou·ché /tu'ʃeɪ/ *exclam.* (from fencing) (French for) admiration for a comment s.o. makes: *I said, "Touché!" when he pointed out my mistake.*

touched /tʌʧt/ *adj.infrml.* **1** emotionally affected by s.t.: *I was touched by her sweet love letter to me.* **2** mentally unbalanced, such as senile: *The old man is touched in the head these days.*

touch·ing /'tʌʧɪŋ/ *adj.* evoking emotion, (*syn.*) poignant: *Watching people say goodbye can be touching.*

touch·stone /'tʌʧ,stoʊn/ *n.fig.* a standard by which s.t. is measured: *Trust between bank and customer is the touchstone of quality in banking.*

touch-up *n.* a slight improvement, repair: *She did a touch-up of her makeup.*

touch·y /'tʌʧi/ *adj.* **-ier, -iest** irritable, too sensitive: *He is touchy about being bald, so don't mention it to him.*

tough /tʌf/ *adj.* **-er, -est** **1** difficult, demanding: *Training to be a doctor is tough.* **2** rubbery, difficult to chew, penetrate, etc.: *The meat for dinner was tough.* **3** mean, (*syn.*) hostile: *Street gangs act tough.* **4** strong, (*syn.*) durable: *Cowhide boots are tough.* **5 a tough call:** a difficult decision to make: *It is a tough call to raise taxes on old people in order to cut the government's debt.*
—*n.infrml.* a thug, criminal: *Many street toughs join gangs.*
—*v.* **to tough it out** or **through: a.** to keep going despite difficulties: *She suffered when she started a business, but toughed it out and succeeded.* **b.** to act tough in a bluff: *Thugs threatened him, but he toughed it through and left unharmed. -n.* [U] **toughness.**

tough·en /'tʌfən/ *v.* **1** to harden, make stronger: *Exercise toughened her muscles.* **2** *fig.* to resist, (*syn.*) to dig in one's heels: *Labor's position toughens when management demands wage reductions.*

tough·ie /'tʌfi/ *n.infrml.* a difficult situation or problem: *That problem in trigonometry is a toughie.*

tou·pee /tu'peɪ/ *n.* a hairpiece, wig for men: *He wears a toupee that looks natural.*

tour /tʊr/ *n.* **1** a series of stops as on a vacation or official trip: *The Secretary of State made a tour of four capitals in the Middle East.* **2** a series of sports competitions: *Players can make a lot of money on the professional tennis (golf, etc.) tour.*
—*v.* to make a tour: *We toured several countries in Europe on our vacation.*

tour·ism /'tʊr,ɪzəm/ *n.* [U] the tourist industry: *Tourism has increased between Europe and America.*

tour·ist /'tʊrɪst/ *n.* a visitor who travels for pleasure, vacationer: *Tourists go to beach and mountain resorts in August.*
—*adj.* related to tourism: *The consulate gave us a tourist visa.*

tour·na·ment /'tʊrnəmənt, 'tɜr-/ or **tourney** /'tʊrni, 'tɜr-/ *n.* competition in a series of events leading to a winner or winners, as in tennis, chess, and golf

tour·ni·quet /'tʊrnəkɪt, 'tɜr-/ *n.* a band or bandage that stops the flow of blood: *A paramedic tied a tourniquet on an accident victim's leg.*

tou·sle /'taʊzəl/ *v.* **-sled, -sling, -sles** to make messy, (*syns.*) to muss, dishevel: *Wind tousled the child's hair.*

tout /taʊt/ *v.n.* to sell with too much praise: *Sidewalk vendors <v.> touted their goods.*

tow /toʊ/ *v.* to pull a vehicle (boat, object, etc.) behind another by a rope, chain, or metal bar: *My car broke down, and a truck towed it to the garage.*
—*n.* **1** an act of towing: *A tugboat gives big ships a tow into the harbor.* **2 in tow:** accompanying, brought with: *The teenager came home with six friends in tow.*

to·ward /tɔrd, tə'wɔrd/ or **towards** /tɔrdz, tə'wɔrdz/ *prep.* **1** in the direction of, to: *The captain headed the boat toward home.* **2** concerning, regarding: *His feelings towards his wife have stayed the same for 25 years.* **3** soon before: *Toward the end of the play, my father fell asleep.* **4** paying or saving for s.t.: *She saves $25 each week toward a new car.*

tow·a·way /'toʊə,weɪ/ *adj.n.* regarding removal, esp. of an illegally parked vehicle: *The truck was parked in a <adj.> towaway zone and got a parking ticket.*

tow·el /'taʊəl/ *n.* **1** a piece of cloth or paper used to dry s.t.: *People use a towel to dry the dishes.* **2** *infrml.fig.* **to throw in the towel:** to give up, quit, such as in a boxing match: *Arguing with him is too hard, so I threw in the towel and shut up.*

—*v.* to use a towel: *After a bath, she toweled herself dry.*

tow·er /'tauər/ *n.* a tall, cylindrical structure: *The castle has towers at each of its four corners.*

—*v.* to rise over in size, (*syn.*) to loom: *The tall man towers over his friends.* -*adj.* **towering.**

tow·line /'tou,laɪn/ *n.* s.t., such as a cable, chain, or rope, used to connect a towing vehicle or boat: *The towlines between the tugboat and the barges are very strong.*

town /taun/ *n.* **1** a settlement smaller than a city: *He comes from a small town in the Middle West.* **2** the residents of a town as a group: *The town is against more businesses being built near their houses.* **3 on the town:** to go to a restaurant, nightclub, theater, etc. and have a good time: *We went out for a night on the town.* **4** *infrml.fig.* **to go to town:** to do a lot very energetically: *The salesperson went to town and sold a lot of a new product.* **5 to paint the town red:** to spend a lot of money on entertainment: *The couple celebrated New Year's Eve by painting the town red. See:* city; village.

town hall *n.* a town's local government office building for the town clerk, police, fire department, and meeting hall, etc.: *The old wooden town hall was replaced with modern brick buildings.*

town·house /'taun,haus/ *n.* one of a series of houses attached to each other in a row or communal building: *Washington, D.C., has streets with old brick townhouses.*

town·ship /'taun,ʃɪp/ *n.* a political and territorial subdivision of a county that has local governmental powers

tow truck *n.* a truck used to tow other vehicles: *The tow truck lifted up the front of my car and towed it to a garage.*

tox·ic /'taksɪk/ *adj.* **1** poisonous, deadly: *Rat poison is also toxic to rabbits and other small animals.* **2** harmful, (*syn.*) injurious: *Dumping chemicals in rivers is toxic to the environment.* -*n.* [U] **toxicity** /tak'sɪsəti/.

tox·i·col·o·gy /,taksə'kalədʒi/ *n.* [U] the science of poisons: *Doctors study toxicology in their training.* -*n.* [C] **toxicologist.**

tox·in /'taksɪn/ *n.* a poison made by organisms: *Certain bacteria produce toxins that make humans ill.*

toy /tɔɪ/ *n.* a plaything: *Children like to play with toys, such as little cars and dolls.*

—*adj.* small, miniature: *a toy poodle*

—*v.* to treat s.o. or s.t. lightly, (*syn.*) to trifle with: *For a day or two, I toyed with the idea of going to Korea for vacation, then realized it would be too expensive.*

TQM *n. abbr. of* total quality management

trace /treɪs/ *n.adj.* **1** a very small amount: *Chemists found <n.> traces of poison in the food.*||*They found <adj.> trace evidence.* **2** a hint of evidence, faint track: *<n.> Traces of footprints were found in the mud. See:* tracing, copy.

—*v.* **traced, tracing, traces 1** to follow s.t. to its origin, track down: *Agents traced the illegal funds from New York to London to the Middle East.* **2** to copy onto thin paper from an image underneath: *Children trace letters of the alphabet to learn how to make them.*

—*adj.* referring to s.t. that can be traced: *Radiologists use a trace element, such as barium sulfate, to show the insides of a body on an X-ray.*

trac·er /'treɪsər/ *n.* a request to search for a lost package, letter, etc.: *My package has not arrived and I asked the post office to put a tracer on it.*

trac·ing /'treɪsɪŋ/ *n.* a rubbing, copy of an image underneath tracing paper: *We made tracings of images on old gravestones in the cemetery.*

tracing paper *n.* [U] a thin, semitransparent paper used to copy images below it: *I used tracing paper to make a copy of a map.*

track /træk/ *n.* **1** an oval-shaped path used for running: *Competitors raced each other around the track.* **2** metal rails or concrete paths for railroad, subway trains, etc.: *Railroad trains roll along steel tracks as they travel.* **3** signs of movement of s.t., such as footprints, paw marks, or tire marks: *Hunters followed the lion's tracks.* **4 to cover one's tracks:** to make sure that one's actions are defensible or kept secret: *He covers his tracks by never putting anything in writing, so that later he can deny that he made any commitments.* **5 to keep or lose track of s.t.:** to pay sharp attention to s.t., remain aware: *He keeps track of his expenses by writing them in a notebook.*||*I lost track of my old friend after he moved away.* **6** *infrml.fig.* **to make tracks:** to move quickly toward s.t.: *When I heard of the sale, I made tracks for the store immediately.* **7 to stop in one's tracks:** to stop quickly, often in fear or shock: *The dog barked and charged, but the owner stopped it in its tracks.*

—*v.* **1** to go after, (*syn.*) to pursue: *Hunters track deer.* **2** to follow the movement of s.t.: *Technicians tracked the satellite through its orbits.* **3** to make a mess with one's shoes (boots, etc.): *Workers tracked mud into the house on their boots.* **4** *phrasal v. sep.* **to track s.t. down:** to hunt down, search for: *I tracked down that book in the library.*||*I tracked it down.*

—*adj.fig.* **1 off track:** stopped, derailed: *The project got knocked off track by a delay in a shipment of parts.* **2 on track:** on schedule,

T

performing well: *The project is on track and moving along nicely.*

track-and-field *n.* sporting events, such as foot races, long jumping, and pole vaulting: *In college, she tried out for track-and-field and made the team.*

track record *n.fig.* one's past performance, esp. in business: *Her track record as a sales representative is excellent.*

tract /trækt/ *n.* **1** an area of land: *She owns a large tract of land north of town.* **2** a short article, often on a religious subject
—*adj.* referring to a tract of land, esp. houses that are all designed the same way: *She has built tract housing on part of her land.*

trac·ta·ble /'træktəbəl/ *adj.* capable of being controlled or persuaded, (*syn.*) malleable: *He is tractable on the matter of negotiating price.||That dog is tractable and pays attention to her owner.*

trac·tion /'trækʃən/ *n.* [U] the ability of s.t. to stay on a road surface: *Radial tires have excellent traction.||I can't get any traction on the icy sidewalk.*

trac·tor /'træktər/ *n.* a piece of farm machinery used for plowing and hauling: *The farmer uses a tractor for spring plowing.*

tractor

trade /treɪd/ *n.* **1** [U] commerce in general: *Trade between the two countries is active.* **2** [C] an exchange: *She made a trade of her bicycle to a friend for a CD player.* **3** [C] a business transaction: *Brokers make trades on the stock exchange.* **4** [C] a type of work, skill: *Her trade is as a carpenter (plumber, electrician, etc.).* **5** [U] the customers of a business: *The trade at that fancy store is rich.* **6 stock in trade:** one's occupation or behavior: *His stock in trade is inventing new electronic products.*
—*v.* **traded, trading, trades 1** to exchange, (*syn.*) barter: *I traded a computer for a bicycle.* **2** to transact: *Brokers trade on stock (commodity, currency, etc.) exchanges.* **3** to engage in business: *She trades in farm equipment.* **4** *phrasal v. insep.* **to trade on s.t.:** to rely on, make good use of: *She trades on her honesty, and her customers trust her for it.* **5** *phrasal v. sep.* **to trade s.t. in:** to use property as partial payment: *He traded in his old car while buying a new one.||He traded it in.* **6** *phrasal v.* **to trade up:** to buy s.t. better than one had before, such as a car or house: *He traded up by selling his house and buying a bigger, more expensive new one.*

trade deficit *n.* condition in which there are more goods imported than exported

trade discount *n.* a reduction on the retail price given to members of the same trade: *She works in the book business and receives a trade discount of 10% on books from other publishers.*

trade-in *n.* property, esp. a car, used as partial payment on a new purchase: *He used his old car as a trade-in on a new one.*

trade journal *n.* a magazine that reports on a trade or industry, usu. not sold in stores: *The Journal of Home Design is a trade journal for interior designers.*

trade·mark /'treɪd,mɑrk/ *n.* a name, motto, or symbol, such as ™, used to indicate exclusive legal ownership of a product by a firm: *Band-Aid™ is a trademark of the Johnson & Johnson company.*
—*v.* to place s.t. under a trademark: *Many companies trademark their products so no one else can use their name.*

trade name or **brand name** *n.* the name a person, business, or product uses commercially: *The trade name for George Smith's product is Sterofertilizers, but it is sold under other names to the public.*

trade-off *n.* an advantage that is reduced by a disadvantage: *In the stock market, the trade-off for making high profits is taking on a higher risk of losing money.*

trad·er /'treɪdər/ *n.* **1** a person who buys and sells stocks, bonds, etc.: *George is a trader of securities for his own account.* **2** a person or firm that buys and sells goods or services for other goods: *He is a silk trader who barters silk for spices and gold.*

trade route *n.* a sea lane usu. traveled by cargo ships or a route of roads and towns along which traders buy and sell goods: *The ancient trade route for silk stretched from China to the Mediterranean, to Rome, and back.*

trade school *n.* in the USA, an educational institution for occupational skills, such as for auto mechanics, computer technicians, secretaries, or hairdressers: *She went to a trade school to learn how to be a computer technician.*

trade secret *n.* secret business information, such as a product formula or manufacturing process: *The formula for Coca-Cola™ is a closely guarded trade secret.*

trades·man /'treɪdzmən/ *n.frml.* **-men** /-mən/ or **trades·person** anyone working in a retail trade, esp. shopkeepers

trade wind *n.* northeasterly winds in the Northern Hemisphere and southeasterly winds in the Southern that help ships, esp. sailing ships: *Cargo ships followed the trade winds across the Atlantic.*

trading post *n.* a store in an area far from towns or cities, esp. one that trades goods for natural products, such as furs: *Trading posts in northern Canada were also the source of news and supplies.*

tra·di·tion /trə'dɪʃən/ *n.* **1** [U] the passing of customs and beliefs from one generation to another: *The New Year's Eve tradition of watching the "Big Apple" fall is renewed every year in Times Square, New York.* **2** [C] a custom, a traditional way of celebrating a religious and cultural event and belief: *Thanksgiving dinner is an old tradition in North America.* -*adj.* **traditional** -*adv.* **traditionally.**

tra·di·tion·al·ist /trə'dɪʃənəlɪst/ *n.* a person devoted to tradition, esp. in religion: *Traditionalists respect all the religious holy days.*

traf·fic /'træfɪk/ *n.* [U] **1** the movement of vehicles, people, aircraft, etc. in a certain area: *Boat traffic on the river is heavy in summer.* **2** *infrml.* **stuck in traffic:** delayed: *An accident blocked the road, and I got stuck in traffic for an hour.*
—*phrasal v. insep.* **to traffic in s.t.:** to deal, trade in, esp. illegally: *That gang traffics in stolen goods.*

traffic jam *n.* vehicles blocking each other, causing congestion and delay: *After baseball games, traffic jams occur as everyone leaves the stadium at once.*

traffic light or **signal** *n.* a post with lights that control the flow of traffic: *We stopped at the red traffic light and waited for it to change to green.*

traffic light

trag·e·dy /'trædʒədi/ *n.* **-dies** [C;U] **1** a drama in which s.o. suffers because of a personal flaw or hostile outside forces or events: *Shakespeare's play* Othello *is considered a great tragedy.* **2** a sad event, disaster: *The accidental death of their child is a tragedy.* -*adj.* **tragic** /'trædʒɪk/ -*adv.* **tragically.**

trag·i·com·e·dy /ˌtrædʒə'kɑmədi/ *n.* **-dies** a drama that mixes comedy and tragedy: *Tragicomedies are found even on television.*

trail /treɪl/ *n.* **1** a path, such as for hiking or horseback riding: *The Appalachian Trail goes for 2,050 miles (3,280 km) from Maine to Georgia.* **2** traces, tracks, such as footprints or pieces of information: *The criminal left a trail of evidence.*||*Jets leave trails of frozen condensation in the sky.*
—*v.* **1** to follow, track: *Detectives trailed the criminal to his hideout.* **2** to grow along the

ground **3** *phrasal v. insep.* **to trail behind s.o. or s.t.:** to follow slowly: *Children trailed behind their parents on the way to the store.*

trail·blaz·er /'treɪlˌbleɪzər/ *n.* **1** a person who opens a trail for others to follow: *Native guides act as trailblazers for explorers.* **2** *fig.* an innovator: *The President's wife is a trailblazer in working for children's rights.*

trail·er /'treɪlər/ *n.* **1** a vehicle or metal house on wheels pulled by a motorized vehicle: *We pulled a trailer across the state to a campground.* **2** a preview advertisement for a movie

train (1) /treɪn/ *v.* **1** to educate, instruct: *Trade schools train students in occupational skills.* **2** to make obedient: *People train their dogs to sit and stay.* **3** to drill, exercise: *Coaches train athletes for competition.* **4** to aim s.t. at s.o. **5** to make a plant grow in a certain direction

train (2) *n.* **1** a line of vehicles, such as railroad cars pulled by a locomotive, subway cars, etc.: *Passengers took the train from Los Angeles to San Francisco.* **2** an extension of a dress or cape: *Her wedding dress has a long train.*

train·ee /treɪ'ni/ *n.* a person in training, beginner: *She is a trainee at a bank.*

train·ing /'treɪnɪŋ/ *n.* [U] **1** a process of education, instruction: *He had training on how to use a computer.* **2** **in training:** preparing for an event or competition

train·load /'treɪnˌloʊd/ *n.* amount of cargo that would fill a train: *A trainload of passengers got off at Grand Central Station.*

traipse /treɪps/ *v.* **traipsed, traipsing, traipses** to walk without direction, (*syn.*) to trudge: *A tired little boy traipsed along behind his older brother.*

trait /treɪt/ *n.* a characteristic, (*syn.*) attribute: *Intelligence and good humor are among her personality traits.*

trai·tor /'treɪtər/ *n.* one who betrays one's country or other loyalty: *A traitor sold military secrets to an enemy country.* -*adj.* **traitorous.** *See:* treachery, quisling.

tra·jec·to·ry /trə'dʒɛktəri/ *n.* **-ries** the curved path of an object in the air, such as a bullet or space vehicle: *Rifle fire follows a low trajectory almost level with the ground.*

tram /træm/ *n.Brit.* a street car, trolley: *People take the tram to work.*

tramp /træmp/ *n.* **1** a homeless person, (*syn.*) vagabond: *Tramps often wander from place to place.* **2** *pej.* a promiscuous woman: *She is a tramp who'll go with anyone.*
—*adj.* a vessel: *A tramp steamer runs up and down the river.*
—*v.* to walk with heavy feet, (*syn.*) to trudge: *We tramped through the snow to a cabin.*

T

tram·ple /'træmpəl/ *v.* **-pled, -pling, -ples 1** to crush with the feet: *At harvest time, workers trample grapes.* **2** *fig.* to oppress, treat harshly: *He trampled on the feelings of his assistant when she made a mistake.*

tram·po·line /'træmpə,lin/ *n.* an apparatus made of a sheet of springy material on a metal frame that gymnasts jump on

trance /træns/ *n.* a dream-like state: *Hypnotists put others into a trance.*

tran·quil /'træŋkwəl, 'træn-/ *adj.* calm, peaceful: *The lake was tranquil in the morning.* -*n.* [U] **tranquility** /træŋ'kwɪləti, træn-/ -*adv.* **tranquilly.**

tran·quil·ize /'træŋkwə,laɪz, 'træn-/ *v.* **-ized, -izing, -izes** to sedate, inject with a sedative drug: *Zookeepers tranquilize animals to prevent them from attacking.*

tran·quil·iz·er /'træŋkwə,laɪzər, 'træn-/ *n.* a drug used to calm or sedate: *A doctor injected a tranquilizer to calm an upset patient.*

trans·act /træn'sækt, -'zækt/ *v.* to do business, (*syn.*) to negotiate s.t.: *We met with the banker and transacted a mortgage contract.*

trans·ac·tion /træn'sækʃən, -'zæk-/ *n.* [C;U] an act of doing business, (*syns.*) a deal, negotiation: *Transactions of shares on the stock exchange were up today.*

trans·at·lan·tic /,trænsət'læntɪk, ,trænz-/ *adj.* across the Atlantic Ocean: *Transatlantic telephone calls are carried by underwater cable.*

tran·scend /træn'sɛnd/ *v.* **1** to go beyond or above a measure or standard, (*syn.*) to surpass: *His concern about his business transcends money; he thinks of the benefits to his customers.* **2** to reach beyond human understanding: *The nature of God transcends human comprehension.* -*n.* [U] **transcendence; -**adj.* **transcendent.**

tran·scen·den·tal·ism /,trænsɛn'dɛntl,ɪzəm/ *n.* [U] (in philosophy) a concept that understanding goes beyond human reason to the intuitive: *Transcendentalism is found in several religions as the way to understand God.* -*adj.* **transcendental.**

trans·con·ti·nen·tal /,trænskɑntə'nɛntl/ *adj.* going across a continent: *The transcontinental railroad united the USA in the nineteenth century.*

tran·scribe /træn'skraɪb/ *v.* **-scribed, -scribing, -scribes** to transfer information from one form to another: *Secretaries transcribed tapes of a meeting into typed documents.*

tran·script /'træn,skrɪpt/ *n.* a written or typed copy, esp. of an oral meeting: *Lawyers got transcripts of the witness's testimony.||Students receive transcripts of their grades.*

tran·scrip·tion /træn'skrɪpʃən/ *n.* [U] an act of transcribing s.t.: *Transcription of the testimony took a day.*

tran·sect /træn'sɛkt/ *v.frml.* to cross and pass through, cut across: *Vertical columns in a building transect its horizontal floors.* -*n.* [U] **transection.**

trans·fer /træns'fɜr, 'trænsfər/ *v.* **-ferred, -ferring, -fers 1** to move from one place, vehicle, etc. to another: *We transferred our bags from the bus to the car.* **2** to change ownership, as in a legal document: *After purchase, the deed to a house transfers it to new owners.*
—*n.* /'trænsfər/ **1** [C] a move: *The transfer of my suitcases between planes was quick.* **2** [C;U] legal change, (*syn.*) conveyance: *Transfer of ownership of the stocks is done in a week.* **3** [C] a ticket allowing one to change transportation lines; doing such a move: *The bus driver gave me a transfer, and I made the transfer at Fifth Avenue.* -*n.* [U] **transference.**

trans·fer·al /træns'fɜrəl/ *n.frml.* [U] a transfer of things or legal entities: *Transferal of the property deed and other documents went quickly.*

trans·fig·ure /træns'fɪgyər/ *v.* **-ured, -uring, -ures** to change the way s.t. looks because of fascination, emotion, etc.: *His face was transfigured with happiness when he saw his baby being born.* -*n.* [U] **transfiguration.**

trans·fix /træns'fɪks/ *v.* **-es 1** to run through, (*syn.*) to impale: *A worker fell and was transfixed on a steel rod.* **2** to stun, paralyze with fear or amazement: *The mother was transfixed when she finally met her long-lost child.*

trans·form /træns'fɔrm/ *v.* to change from one shape or appearance to another: *Remodeling transformed an old, dark house into a cheerful one.* -*n.* [U] **transformation** /,trænsfər'meɪʃən/.

trans·form·er /træns'fɔrmər/ *n.* a device that converts electrical current from one circuit to another and changes its voltage: *A transformer blew up and shut off the neighborhood's electricity until it was fixed.*

trans·fuse /træns'fyuz/ *v.* **-fused, -fusing, -fuses 1** to inject into veins **2** to flood: *Sunlight transfused our living room at dawn.*

trans·fu·sion /træns'fyuʒən/ *n.* [C;U] injection of blood: *The accident victim was given a blood transfusion.*

trans·gress /træns'grɛs, trænz-/ *v.* **-es** to violate, (*syn.*) to infringe: *Dictators transgress on the people's rights.* -*n.* **transgressor.**

trans·gres·sion /træns'grɛʃən, trænz-/ *n.* [C;U] **1** bad behavior, going beyond limits: *The son lied and cheated, but his mother forgave his transgressions.* **2** crime, violation: *She robbed a bank and the law punished her transgression.*

tran·sient /'trænʃənt, -ʒənt, -ziənt/ *adj.* passing, temporary: *His stomach pains were transient, lasting only a day.*

—*n.* a person, esp. a guest who stays temporarily: *Hotels serve transient guests.*

tran·sis·tor /træn'zɪstər/ *n.adj.* an electronic part that controls the flow of electricity in a machine (computer, TV, etc.): *My computer has hundreds of <n.> transistors inside on small boards.||I have a <adj.> transistor radio.*

tran·sit /'trænsɪt, -zɪt/ *n.* **1** [C] a telescopic device that measures angles: *Road builders use transits to measure angles for constructing roads.* **2** [U] an orbit: *Transit of the moon around the earth occurs at varied angles.* **3** [U] **in transit:** on a journey, in passage, en route: *The goods are in transit from the warehouse to the customer.*
—*v.* to cross, pass by: *Meteors transit the earth's orbit occasionally.*

tran·si·tion /træn'zɪʃən/ *n.* [C;U] a change from one condition to another: *The transition from high school to college can be difficult for students.* -*adj.* **transitional;** -*adv.* **transitionally.**

tran·si·tive /'trænsətɪv, -zə-/ *n.adj.* related to a verb that has an object: *The verb "to drop" is <adj.> transitive because it takes an object: John dropped his pencil. See:* intransitive.

tran·si·to·ry /'trænsə,tɔri, -zə-/ *adj.* temporary, short-lived: *His arthritis attack was transitory.*

trans·late /'trænsl, eɪt, 'trænz-, træns'leɪt, trænz-/ *v.* **-lated, -lating, -lates 1** to change, interpret as from one language to another: *He translated a letter from French into English.* **2** to change into, (*syn.*) to convert: *A ten percent interest rate translated into a payment of $200 a month.* -*n.* **translation.** *See:* interpret.

trans·lu·cent /træns'lusənt, trænz-/ *adj.* clear enough to allow light but not images to pass through: *The frosted glass in the bathroom window is translucent.* -*n.* [U] **translucence.**

trans·mis·si·ble /træns'mɪsəbəl, trænz-/ *adj.frml.* capable of being passed around, esp. disease: *Cold viruses are transmissible by physical contact and by air.*

trans·mis·sion /træns'mɪʃən, trænz-/ *n.* **1** [U] passage from one thing to another, such as the spread of disease: *The transmission of germs can occur by contact, breathing, and eating.* **2** [C] the assembly that changes the gears of an engine: *Her car has a four-speed transmission.* **3** [U] a broadcast: *The television transmission is sent from a tall tower.*

trans·mit /træns'mɪt, trænz-/ *v.* **-mitted, -mitting, -mits 1** to pass from one to another, send: *He transmitted the package by courier.* **2** to broadcast: *That radio station transmits programs 24 hours a day.* **3** to spread disease: *The flu is transmitted from person to person.*

trans·mit·tal /træns'mɪtl, trænz-/ *n.* [U] **1** an act of transfer, (*syn.*) a conveyance **2** a document of transfer: *The transmittal was a letter with accompanying documents.*

trans·mit·ter /træns'mɪtər, trænz-, 'træns-,mɪt-, 'trænz-/ *n.* an electronic device that sends out signals: *A shortwave radio transmitter can send signals for thousands of miles.*

trans·na·tion·al /træns'næʃənəl, trænz-/ *adj.* going beyond national boundaries: *Help for earthquake victims came from transnational sources.*

trans·o·ce·an·ic /,trænsouʃi'ænɪk, ,trænz-/ *adj.* from one side of an ocean to the other: *Transoceanic telephone calls are made by underwater cable and satellite.*

tran·som /'trænsəm/ *n.* a panel above a door that can be opened for air to enter: *Older buildings have transoms over the doors.*

trans·par·en·cy /træns'pɛrənsi, -'pæ-/ *n.* **-cies 1** [U] clearness, the quality of allowing light to pass through so images can be seen: *Old window glass often has a wavy transparency.* **2** [C] a visual aid with text and images placed on a projector: *The teacher lectured from transparencies that showed graphs of numbers.*

trans·par·ent /træns'pɛrənt, -'pæ-/ *adj.* **1** allowing light to pass through so images can be clearly seen, clear: *Window glass is transparent.* **2** *fig.* obvious, (*syn.*) blatant: *His lies are transparent.* -*adv.* **transparently.**

tran·spire /træn'spaɪr/ *v.* **-spired, -spiring, -spires 1** to happen, occur: *She gave a report on what transpired at the meeting.* **2** (in plants) to breathe, give off gases: *Plants transpire through pores in their leaves.*

trans·plant /træns'plænt/ *v.* **1** to uproot carefully and replant somewhere else: *A gardener transplanted small trees from a nursery to a garden.* **2** to move an organ (heart, lungs, etc.) from one person to another
—*n.fig.* /'træns,plænt/ *s.t.* transplanted: *He lives in Chicago, but is a transplant from Boston.*

trans·port /træns'pɔrt/ *v.* **1** to move, (*syn.*) to convey: *Trucks transport most of our goods to our customers.* **2** to move emotionally: *Beautiful music transports listeners into a pleasant dream world.*
—*n.* /'træns,pɔrt/ [U] transportation: *Transport in some countries is slow and unsafe.*

trans·por·ta·tion /,trænspər'teɪʃən/ *n.* [U] ways to move from one place to another: *Transportation by air, rail, and road is readily available in the USA.* -*n.* [C] **transporter.**

trans·pose /træns'pouz/ *v.* **-posed, -posing, -poses** to move from one position to another: *He mistakenly transposed letters in the word "the" as "hte."* -*n.* [C;U] **transposition** /,trænspə'zɪʃən/.

trans·sex·u·al /træn'sɛkʃuəl/ *n.adj.* a person who has an operation to take on the characteristics of the opposite sex: *See:* transvestite.

trans·verse /træns'vɜrs, trænz-, 'træns,vɜrs, 'trænz-/ *adj.n.* a cross beam: *The <n.pl.> transverses (or) <adj.> transverse beams in that building are made of steel. -adv.* **transversely.**

trans·ves·tite /træns'vɛstaɪt, trænz-/ *n.adj.* a cross-dresser, esp. a man who wears women's clothing: *He is a <n.> transvestite who wears dresses and makeup. See:* transsexual.

trap /træp/ *n.* **1** a mechanical device with jaws that close, used to catch animals: *Hunters use traps to capture beavers.* **2** a surprise situation planned to discomfort, harm, or kill s.o.: *Soldiers entered a cave and fell into a trap as their enemy blasted the entrance shut.* **3** *fig.slang* **to keep one's trap shut:** to say nothing, keep one's mouth closed: *A boy witnessed a crime, and the criminal told him to keep his trap shut.*
—*v.* **trapped, trapping, traps** **1** to hunt animals with traps **2** to catch or harm s.o. in a trap: *The dogcatcher trapped a stray dog.*

trap door *n.* a hidden panel that opens when s.o. steps on it: *A trap door released, and a soldier fell into a hole in the cellar.*

tra·peze /trə'piz/ *n.* a swing in a group of them hung from a circus tent top: *Circus performers swing from trapeze to trapeze.*

trap·e·zoid /'træpə,zɔɪd/ *n.* a geometric figure with four sides, two of which are parallel: *A modern painter grouped bright-colored trapezoids on a canvas. -adj.* **trapezoidal.**

trapezoid

trap·per /'træpər/ *n.* a person who hunts with traps, esp. for animals with valuable fur

trap·pings /'træpɪŋz/ *n.pl.* clothes, surroundings, and possessions that give an impression: *She owns a Mercedes, a big house, and beautiful clothes, all the trappings of a rich woman.*

trash /træʃ/ *n.* **-es** **1** waste, *(syn.)* rubbish: *Once a week, we put out the trash for collection.* **2** *s.t.* of poor quality or indecency, such as pornography: *A lot of the magazines sold in the store are trash.*
—*v.* **-es** **1** to destroy, *(syn.)* to vandalize: *Rioters trashed and looted stores.* **2** to criticize severely, *(syn.)* to condemn: *Critics trashed the new play. -adj.* **trashy.**

trau·ma /'traumə, 'trɔ-/ *n.[C;U]* **1** psychological shock and pain: *The mother's trauma of losing her child haunts her.* **2** (in medicine) an injury: *He suffered trauma to his head in the accident. -n.[U]* **traumatization; -v.** **traumatize.**

trau·mat·ic /trau'mætɪk, trɔ-/ *adj.* shocking, harmful -adv. **traumatically.**

tra·vail /trə'veɪl/ *n.* [U] *v.frml.* hard, often agonizing experience or work, ordeal: *After much <n.> travail and suffering, he survived cancer.*

trav·el /'trævəl/ *v.* **1** to go, journey: *We traveled from Atlanta to New Orleans by bus.* **2** to maintain, remain in good condition: *Some wines do not travel well when they are shipped long distances.* **3** to carry a long way: *The goalkeeper kicked the ball and it really traveled.* **4 to travel light:** to take little with one when traveling
—*n.* **1** [U] traffic, amount of traveling: *Travel along the busy highway is high.* **2** [C, *usu. pl.*] touring, vacation: *During our travels to Europe, we enjoyed France most of all.*

travel agency *n.* a business that organizes travel accommodations for a fee: *Our company reserves all of our business travel through a travel agency. -n.* **travel agent.**

trav·el·er /'trævələr, 'trævlər/ *n.* a person going somewhere: *Travelers rush through the train station during vacation time.*

traveler's check *n.* a substitute form of money that can be replaced if stolen or lost: *We bought traveler's checks instead of taking a lot of cash on our trip.*

trav·el·ogue /'trævə,lɑg, -,lɔg/ *n.* a book, film, or slide show that describes a place and its tourist attractions

tra·verse /trə'vɜrs, 'trævɜrs/ *v.frml.* **-versed, -versing, -verses** to cross, travel over: *Explorers traversed the ice cap to the North Pole.*
—*n.* **1** [U] a crossing: *The traverse across the snow was difficult.* **2** [C] a crossbeam: *Traverses in the tall building are made of steel.*

trav·es·ty /'trævəsti/ *n.* **-ties** a joke, *(syns.)* mockery, parody: *The false testimony at the trial made it a travesty of justice.*

trawl /trɔl/ *n.* a large sac-shaped fishing net that is pulled on the bottom of the ocean
—*v.* to fish with a trawl: *The fishing boat trawled several miles offshore. See:* troll.

trawl·er /'trɔlər/ *n.* a fishing boat equipped to trawl: *Shrimp trawlers leave the harbor just before dawn.*

tray /treɪ/ *n.* a flat item with a raised edge for carrying food, displaying items, etc.: *Waiters bring food on trays.*

treach·er·ous /'trɛtʃərəs/ *adj.* **1** dangerous, harmful: *The road down the mountain is treacherous in the snow.* **2** deceitful, *(syn.)* traitorous: *He is a treacherous man who pretends friendship, then harms people.*

treach·er·y /'trɛtʃəri/ *n.* [U] betrayal, disloyalty: *It was treachery when the spy led others into a trap.*

tread /trɛd/ *v.frml.* **trod** /trad/, **trodden** /'tradn/, **treaded, trodding, treads** **1** to walk, step: *"Don't tread on me" was the motto of the*

Colonists. **2** to mat down, trample: *People tread on the grass.* **3 to tread softly, lightly, carefully: a.** to walk quietly: *In church, everyone treads softly.* **b.** *fig.* to be careful, cautious: *That neighborhood is dangerous, so tread carefully there.* **4 to tread water: a.** to move one's feet and hands slowly in water while staying in one place: *She swam a long distance, then treaded water to rest.* **b.** *fig.* to give the impression of activity without really doing much: *His job is not satisfying and he won't get a promotion; he is only treading water there.*
—*n.* **1** a step, pace: *You could hear the tread of feet on the path.* **2** a step in a staircase **3** that part of a tire that touches the road: *The tread on that car's tires is worn.*

tread·mill /'trɛd,mɪl/ *n.* **1** machine, such as a wheel with treads that moves while one walks or runs in the same place: *She uses a treadmill at the gym when it is too cold to go jogging outside.* **2** *fig.* a meaningless, boring activity: *Her job is a treadmill of typing forms all day.*

trea·son /'trizən/ *n.* [U] the crime of active disloyalty to one's government: *Treason in time of war can be punishable by death.* -*adj.* **treasonable; treasonous.**

treas·ure /'trɛʒər/ *n.* **1** [C;U] riches, such as gold and jewels: *Pirates stole treasure taken from ships.* **2** [C] valuable objects
—*v.* **-ured, -uring, -ures** to value greatly, (*syn.*) to cherish: *She treasures memories of her childhood.*

treasure hunt *n.* a search for lost riches: *Ships with special equipment go on treasure hunts in the Caribbean.*

treas·ur·er /'trɛʒərər/ *n.* the person in charge of an organization's finances: *Our company's treasurer deals mainly with our banks and outside accountants.*

treas·ur·y /'trɛʒəri/ *n.* **-ries 1** the amount of money in a government's or business's accounts: *The state's treasury is almost bankrupt.* **2** the government office that controls public money: *The USA's treasury is located in Washington, D.C.*

Treasury bill or **T-bill** *n.* US government's short-term securities of 91 and 182 days offered by the US Treasury: *Treasury bill interest rates vary from day to day.*

Treasury bond *n.* US government's long-term securities of ten years or more issued in minimum denominations of $1,000

Treasury note *n.* US government's intermediate-term securities of one to ten years: *Some dealers prefer Treasury notes because they mature sooner than bonds, but carry a higher rate than bills.*

treat /trit/ *v.* **1** to act or behave toward: *She treats her children with loving care.* **2** to han-

dle, take care of: *The computer department treated the computer breakdown by switching quickly to another system.* **3** to doctor, give medical attention to: *The physician treats her patients in her office.* **4** to apply chemicals or other agents to s.t.: *The wooden floors are treated with a special paint.* **5** to entertain, do s.t. special for s.o.: *My friend treated me to a birthday dinner.*
—*n.* s.t. special, such as a gift or pleasant occasion: *Seeing the opera star perform was a real treat.*

treat·a·ble /'tritəbəl/ *adj.* (in medicine) capable of being cured: *She has a treatable illness.*

trea·tise /'tritɪs/ *n.* a serious, long written work: *The professor wrote a treatise on 17th century literature.*

treat·ment /'tritmənt/ *n.* **1** [U] behavior toward s.o.: *His treatment of his friends is very kind and warm.* **2** [C;U] medical attention, cure: *She went into the hospital for treatment.*

trea·ty /'triti/ *n.* **-ties** a formal agreement between nations, accord: *European countries signed a treaty on economic cooperation.*

treb·le /'trɛbəl/ *adj.n.* **1** (in music) the highest voice or instrument parts **2** (in musical notation) the treble clef for higher notes: *The notes of the <adj.> treble clef are played mainly with the right hand on a piano.* **3** *frml.* triple, threefold: *The judge awarded the defendant <adj.> treble damages.*
—*v.frml.* **-bled, -bling, -bles** to triple: *The judge trebled the amount of damages.*

tree /tri/ *n.* **1** a tall, woody evergreen or deciduous plant with a trunk, branches, and leaves: *Trees line the avenues and make them pretty in autumn.* **2** *infrml.* **to bark up the wrong tree:** to complain to the wrong person: *You are barking up the wrong tree as I don't have anything to do with your problem and I can't help.*
—*v.* **treed, treeing, trees** (of an animal) to trap s.t. in a tree: *The dog treed a cat and wouldn't let it come down.*

tree·top /'tri,tɑp/ *n.* the uppermost parts of trees

trek /trɛk/ *n.* a long, difficult journey: *The long trek between the seacoast and the interior took the explorers months.*
—*v.* **trekked, trekking, treks** to travel with difficulty: *Pioneers trekked across the plains on foot.* -*n.* **trekker.**

trel·lis /'trɛlɪs/ *n.* **-lises** a structure of wood, etc. used to support climbing plants, (*syn.*) a lattice: *A trellis of ivy and roses frames the entrance to the garden.*

trem·ble /'trɛmbəl/ *v.* **-bled, -bling, -bles** to shake as with fear or fever, shiver: *The boy trembled in fear when he saw a lion.*
—*n.* a shaking motion: *An earthquake hit with a jolt and a tremble.*

T

tre·men·dous /trəˈmɛndəs/ *adj.* **1** huge, (*syn.*) vast: *A landslide left a tremendous pile of rocks on the road.* **2** *infrml.fig.* wonderful, excellent: *We had a tremendous time on our vacation.* -*adv.* **tremendously.**

trem·or /ˈtrɛmər/ *n.frml.* a shaking motion: *Earthquakes produce tremors in the earth's crust.*

trem·u·lous /ˈtrɛmyələs/ *adj.frml.* shaking, fearful: *Peasants were tremulous in front of the king.* -*adv.* **tremulously.**

trench /trɛntʃ/ *n.* **-es 1** a long ditch in the ground: *In World War I, soldiers lived in the trenches.* **2 in the trenches:** where daily, basic activity (conflict, competition) takes place: *Salespeople compete in the trenches every day with other companies' representatives.*

trench·ant /ˈtrɛntʃənt/ *adj.* intelligent and brief, (*syn.*) cogent: *The consultant provided trenchant advice to her client.*

trench coat *n.* a belted topcoat in a World War I military style: *Trench coats with a wool lining are worn by many people in northern regions.*

trend /trɛnd/ *n.* **1** a fashion, current style: *Short skirts are the trend for summer this year.* **2** a general curve or pattern: *The current trend of interest rates is down.*
—*v.* to form a trend: *Rates are trending down now.*

trend·y /ˈtrɛndi/ *adj.* **-ier, -iest** fashionable, stylish: *Her clothes are very trendy.*

trep·i·da·tion /ˌtrɛpəˈdeɪʃən/ *n.frml.* [U] fear, anxiety: *She has trepidation about going out alone at night.*

tres·pass /ˈtrɛsˌpæs, -pəs/ *v.* **-es 1** to go illegally on private property: *Hunters trespassed onto the farmer's fields.* **2** *fig.* to do wrong to or take advantage of others
—*n.* [U] an act of trespassing: *Their trespass on city property after hours brought the police.* -*n.* [C] **trespasser.**

tres·tle /ˈtrɛsəl/ *n.* **1** a type of railroad bridge made of horizontal beams **2** a wooden support, as for a table

tri·ad /ˈtraɪˌæd/ *n.* objects with three legs, ideas with three parts: *A stool for milking cows has a triad of three legs in a round seat.*

tri·age /ˈtriˌɑʒ, triˈɑʒ/ *adj.n.* [U] a system of giving emergency medical care to people, depending on their degree of illness and chance of living: *The <adj.> triage nurse gave priority to patients with heart attacks and gunshot wounds.*

tri·al /ˈtraɪəl, traɪl/ *n.* **1** a legal proceeding before a judge or judge and jury to establish facts and decide guilt or innocence: *The murder trial caused a sensation.* **2** a competition to reduce the number of competitors: *The field trials for hunting dogs eliminated half the contestants.*

3 *fig.* a stressful ordeal: *A major operation was a time of trial for him.* **4** an experiment, test: *He gave the sports car a trial around the track.* **5 on trial: a.** to be a defendant in a court proceeding: *The state put the criminal on trial for theft.* **b.** to do s.t. temporarily at first: *She was on trial for three months, then became a permanent employee.* **6 by trial and error:** trying different ideas, methods to see if they work: *We tried one thing after another, and by trial and error we got the computer program to work.* **7 trials and tribulations:** difficulties and hardships: *She went through the trials and tribulations of divorce and survived.*

trial lawyer *n.* a lawyer who can try a legal case before a judge and jury, (*syn.*) a litigator: *Trial lawyers have to be good actors as well as attorneys.*

trial run *n.* a test before a final decision: *We gave the new computer system a trial run before turning off the old one.*

tri·an·gle /ˈtraɪˌæŋgəl/ *n.* **1** a flat, three-sided geometric figure: *The sculpture is shaped in the form of a triangle.* **2** a romantic situation involving three people: *A woman and two men were involved in a love triangle.* -*adj.* **triangular** /traɪˈæŋgyələr/.

trib·al /ˈtraɪbəl/ *adj.* related to a tribe: *Tribal customs are passed from one generation to another.*

tribe /traɪb/ *n.* **1** a group of people from a hunting-gathering or nomadic culture with common customs and ancestry, usu. led by a chief: *Native American tribes once lived all over North America.* **2** *infrml.fig.* a large family: *When our tribe gets together for Thanksgiving, we fill the whole house.* -*n.* [U] **tribalism.** *See:* race.

trib·u·la·tion /ˌtrɪbyəˈleɪʃən/ *n.frml.* [C;U] distress, suffering: *The tribulations of major surgery bothered him for weeks. See:* trials.

tri·bu·nal /traɪˈbyunəl/ *n.frml.* a court or other body with power to examine and judge: *The government set up a tribunal to investigate corruption.*

trib·une /ˈtrɪbˌyun, trɪˈbyun/ *n.old usage* a spokesperson for ordinary people's rights

trib·u·tar·y /ˈtrɪbyəˌtɛri/ *n.* **-ies** a smaller stream flowing into a river: *In springtime, tributaries flood the river.*

trib·ute /ˈtrɪbyut/ *n.* [C;U] **1** *fig.* praise, honor, admiration: *Soldiers gathered to pay tribute to their fallen comrades.* **2** a payment, such as money, paid by a defeated people to a conqueror

tri·ceps /ˈtraɪˌsɛps/ *n.* [U] the muscle on the back of the upper arm: *He does pushups to strengthen his triceps. See:* biceps.

trick /trɪk/ *n.* **1** a deception, (*syn.*) ruse: *An undercover detective bought illegal drugs in a*

trick to arrest a drug dealer. **2** magic: *Magicians do magic tricks.* **3** actions an animal is trained to do: *Mary taught her dog to roll over and do other tricks.* **4** a special solution or technique: *The trick to using computers successfully is having different ways of doing things if one way does not work.* **5** *infrml.* **How's tricks?:** How are things?: *Hi, Jane, good to see you, how's tricks?* **6** *infrml.* **to do the trick:** to manage, accomplish s.t.: *My door lock was stuck, and some oil did the trick (to loosen it).* **7 to play tricks** or **a trick on s.o.:** a practical joke: *Friends played a trick on John by having a stranger call him to say that he had won a million dollars.*
—*v.* to deceive, fool: *A swindler tricked a victim into thinking that the real estate offer was genuine.*

trick·er·y /'trɪkəri/ *n.* **-ies** [U] using deception, ruses: *A con man used trickery to swindle an old woman.*

trick·le /'trɪkəl/ *v.* **-led, -ling, -les 1** to run in a thin stream, drip: *Water trickled from the trees during the rain.* **2** *phrasal v.* **to trickle down: a.** to drip down: *Water trickled down the wall from a leak.* **b.** *fig.* to go from a higher to a lower economic class: *Wealth trickled down from the rich to the poor.*
—*n.* **1** a drip, thin stream: *Water came from the pump in only a trickle.* **2 to slow to a trickle:** to lessen to almost nothing: *Sales are bad; they have slowed to a trickle.*

trick or treat *n.* [U] a custom of children at Halloween where if they do not receive candy from s.o., the children play a trick: *Children came to our door and shouted, "Trick or treat!" See:* Halloween, USAGE NOTE.

trick·ster /'trɪkstər/ *n.* **1** s.o. who plays practical jokes **2** a person who deceives others: *Swindlers are tricksters.*

trick·y /'trɪki/ *adj.* **-ier, -iest 1** deceitful, sly: *He is a tricky guy who can't be trusted.* **2** needing special care or technique in doing s.t., difficult: *Trying to repair an old wristwatch is tricky.* -*n.* **trickiness.**

tri·col·or /'traɪˌkʌlər/ *adj.* having three colors: *We have a tricolor dog, a basset hound.*

tri·cy·cle /'traɪsəkəl, -ˌsɪ-/ *n.* a cycle with three wheels: *Children ride tricycles before they learn how to ride a bicycle.*

tri·dent /'traɪdnt/ *n.frml.* a three-pronged spear, symbolic of the sea: *The god Poseidon carries a trident.*

tried /traɪd/ *adj. & past part. of* try **1** tested, proven **2 tried and true:** proven and dependable: *These methods are tried and true; we've used them for years and they have always worked for us.*

tri·en·ni·al /traɪˈɛniəl/ *n.* a third anniversary

—*adj.* every three years: *The Language Society has a triennial conference.* -*n.* **triennium.**

tri·fle /'traɪfəl/ *v.* **-fled, -fling, -fles** *phrasal v. insep.* **to trifle with s.o.:** to toy with, treat lightly: *He trifled with his girlfriend, then broke up with her. What a jerk!*
—*n.* **1** an unimportant thing, such as a small amount or cheap item: *Carrying your groceries was a mere trifle; I was glad to do it.* **2 a trifle:** a small amount, little bit: *Those pants are a trifle tight on me.*

tri·fling /'traɪflɪŋ/ *adj.* unimportant, (*syn.*) piddling: *One person offered a trifling amount to purchase our used television set.*

trig /trɪg/ *n.* [U] *short for* trigonometry

trig·ger /'trɪgər/ *n.* **1** a lever used to fire a gun: *He pulled the gun's trigger and shot at the target.* **2** any device used to set s.t. off
—*v.* **1** to start an explosion: *The terrorist triggered the bomb.* **2** to start a reaction: *The tax increase triggered a protest by homeowners.*

trigger-happy *adj.infrml.fig.* ready and willing to start a shooting conflict: *People fear a trigger-happy leader who might start a war.*

tri·glyc·er·ide /traɪˈglɪsəˌraɪd/ *n.* one of the main fatty substances (along with cholesterol) in the blood that can clog the arteries

trig·o·nom·e·try /ˌtrɪgəˈɑmətri/ *n.* [U] a branch of mathematics dealing with the measurement of triangles: *Trigonometry is important in science, surveying, and navigation.*

trill /trɪl/ *n.* a quick repetition of sound, (*syn.*) a tremolo: *A bird's trill calls a mate.*
—*v.* to make a trilling sound: *Many Spanish-speaking people trill their r's.*

tril·lion /'trɪlyən/ *n.* [C] a thousand billions and written as 1,000,000,000,000: *The government spending deficit went into the trillions of dollars. See:* zillion, USAGE NOTE.

tril·o·gy /'trɪlədʒi/ *n.* **-gies** a work on a subject in three parts, esp. three books: *A scholar wrote a trilogy on the Civil War about its origins, the war itself, and the events afterwards.*

trim /trɪm/ *adj.* slender, in good physical condition: *She exercises regularly and stays trim.*
—*n.* **1** good physical condition: *She is in good trim from jogging every day.* **2** decoration: *Wooden frames around windows are called trims.* **3** a haircut that cuts only the ends of the hair
—*v.* **trimmed, trimming, trims 1** to cut off, esp. the outer section of s.t.: *The butcher trims fat from the meat.* **2** to make neat: *The barber trimmed the boy's hair with scissors.* **3** to tighten, adjust: *Sailors trimmed the ship's sails.* **4** to decorate: *We trimmed the Christmas tree with ornaments.* -*n.* [U] **trimness.**

T

USAGE NOTE: *Trim* or *slim* can describe someone in good physical shape, without a lot of fat. *Skinny* describes someone who is too thin and looks unhealthy.

---

tri·mes·ter /'traɪ,mɛstər/ *n.* **1** one of three terms in an academic year: *Our college is on the trimester system.* **2** one of three stages of human pregnancy: *She is in her third trimester now; she is eight months' pregnant.*

trim·mer /'trɪmər/ *n.* a device that cuts edges off things: *I use an electric trimmer to clip the bushes.*

trim·mings /'trɪmɪŋz/ *n.pl.* **1** decorations, adornments: *The Christmas tree trimmings include ornaments, lights, and tinsel.* **2** special extras: *We had a turkey for Thanksgiving dinner with all the trimmings.*

trin·ket /'trɪŋkɪt/ *n.* small decorative items, esp. jewelry of little value: *The child keeps trinkets in a box.*

tri·o /'trioʊ/ *n.* a group of three, esp. singers and musicians: *A trio sang old favorite songs.*

trip /trɪp/ *n.* **1** a journey, travel: *We took a trip north to see our cousin.* **2** *slang* **bad trip:** unhappy situation (originally from a bad drug experience): *After the fight, the police arrested us; it was a bad trip.*
—*v.* **tripped, tripping, trips** **1** to lose one's balance by stepping badly on s.t., (*syn.*) to stumble: *I tripped over the loose rug and fell.* **2** to make a mistake: *He tripped over his words and had to repeat his sentence.* **3** to move lightly: *The children tripped down the street, singing songs.*

tri·par·tite /traɪ'pɑrtaɪt/ *adj.* in three parts (sections, parties, etc.): *Three nations made a tripartite treaty.*

tripe /traɪp/ *n.* [U] the lining of a cow's stomach: *Some people like to eat tripe.*

tri·ple /'trɪpəl/ *adj.* threefold, three times: *Inflation ran into triple digits, that is, more than 100% last year.*
—*n.* (in baseball) a three-base hit: *The batter hit a triple.*
—*v.* **-pled, -pling, -ples** to increase by three times: *The value of her investments tripled.*

trip·let /'trɪplɪt/ *n.* **1** three of a similar kind, such as children: *The woman gave birth to triplets.* **2** a group of three lines of poetry: *The poets wrote a poem in triplets.*

trip·li·cate /'trɪpləkɪt/ *adj.v.* **-cated, -cating, -cates** in three copies or parts: *I gave <adj.> triplicate copies of the report to my boss.*

tri·pod /'traɪ,pɑd/ *n.* a three-legged support, such as for a camera: *The photographer set up a tripod and camera.*

trite /traɪt/ *adj.* common, overused, boring: *A politician excused the problem of high taxes with some trite phrases and left.* *-adv.* **tritely;** *-n.* [U] **triteness.** *See:* hackneyed.

tri·umph /'traɪəmf/ *n.* **1** [C] great success, victory: *His winning the tennis tournament was a triumph for him.* **2** [U] glory, (*syn.*) exultation: *He has a feeling of triumph from winning.*
—*v.* **1** to win, succeed greatly: *As an unknown player, he triumphed over the champion.* **2 to triumph over adversity:** to succeed despite obstacles: *She triumphed over adversity as she came from a poor family, but became a successful businessperson.* *-adj.* **triumphant** /traɪ'ʌmfənt/; *-adv.* **triumphantly.**

tri·um·vi·rate /traɪ'ʌmvərɪt/ *n.* a group of three, esp. rulers in politics or business: *The country is ruled by a triumvirate of three leaders.*

triv·i·a /'trɪviə/ *n.pl.* unimportant details, things: *He pays attention to trivia while he ignores important matters.*

triv·i·al /'trɪviəl/ *adj.* unimportant, (*syn.*) inconsequential: *Trivial matters, such as typing the contract clearly, are less important than what it says.* *-adv.* **trivially;** *-n.* [U] **triviality** /,trɪvi'æləti/.

triv·i·al·ize /'trɪviə,laɪz/ *v.* **-ized, -izing, -izes** to make small, reduce to the unimportant: *That newspaper trivializes events by focusing on their sensational aspects.*

trod·den /'trɑdn/ *adj. & past part.* of tread walked upon, flattened: *Many hikers follow well-trodden trails.*

troi·ka /'trɔɪkə/ *n.* (Russian for) a triumvirate, three important people or ideas: *For years, the former Soviet Union was run by a troika.*

troll /troʊl/ *n.* an imaginary human-like creature, either a giant or dwarf, that lives in forests: *Trolls do mischief, according to folk legend in some countries.*
—*v.* to fish by pulling baited lines behind a boat: *My friend trolled for fish while I rowed the boat. See:* trawl.

trol·ley /'trɑli/ *adj.n.* **-leys** **1** a streetcar: *<adj.> Trolley cars run down the middle of the street on metal rails.* **2** a wheeled bin used to move things: *Mines use <n.> trolleys to bring metal ore to the surface.*

trol·lop /'trɑləp/ *n.pej.* a messy woman with a bad reputation: *She is a trollop who frequents sleazy bars.*

trom·bone /trɑm'boʊn, trəm-, 'trɑm,boʊn/ *n.* a brass horn with a slide, also called a slide trombone: *Trombones make a mellow sound.* *-n.* **trombonist.**

tromp /trɑmp/ *v.* **1** to step on hard, (*syns.*) to stomp, trample: *A farmer tromped on a snake and killed it.* **2** *fig.* to defeat decisively: *Our team tromped our rival.*

troop /trup/ *n.* **1** a group of animals or people: *Troops of baboons look for food in the grass.‖A troop of soldiers went into the canteen.‖a Boy or Girl Scout troop* **2** *pl.* military personnel, esp. soldiers: *The President sent in troops to guard our citizens.*

—*v.fig.* to move in a group: *Our whole family trooped off to church on Sunday.*

troop·er /'trupər/ *n.* a state police officer: *A state trooper stopped a speeding driver.* See: trouper.

tro·phy /'troufi/ *n.* **-phies 1** a prize, such as a silver cup or bowl: *The race car driver held the trophy up high after he won the race.* **2** an animal that has been hunted and stuffed

tropics /'trapɪks/ *n.pl.* the hot region (Torrid Zone) of the earth lying between approx. 23 degrees north and 23 degrees south of the equator: *The afternoon heat in the tropics can be almost intolerable.* *-adj.* **tropical.**

tro·po·sphere /'troupə,sfɪr, 'trap-/ *n.* [U] layer of the atmosphere extending six to 12 miles immediately above the earth: *The earth's weather occurs in the troposphere.*

trot /trat/ *n.* **1** a fast walk, esp. for horses: *Horses moved in a trot around a racetrack.* **2** *pl.* **the trots:** diarrhea: *Every time I visit Europe, I get the trots.*

—*v.* **trotted, trotting, trots 1** to move at a trot: *As the woman jogged, her dog trotted beside her.* **2** *phrasal v. sep.* **to trot s.o. or s.t. out:** to bring out for display: *After her party guests had arrived, the hostess trotted out her children to show everyone.*‖*She trotted them out.*

trou·ba·dour /'trubə,dɔr, -,dʊr/ *n.frml.* a wandering singer and poet in olden times

trou·ble /'trʌbəl/ *n.* **1** [C;U] a civil disturbance, crisis (riot, criminal act, etc.): *There is trouble at the American embassy.* **2** [C] a person or other source of annoyance, inconvenience: *Oh, oh, there's George; here comes trouble!* **3** [C;U] difficulty, distress, esp. by accident: *Our friends are having car trouble.* **4** [C;U] mental anguish, anxiety: *He has trouble working and functioning after his wife's death.* **5** [C;U] physical pain or ailment: *He has heart trouble.* **6 to be** or **get in trouble:** to do illegal acts, unlawful behavior: *That thief is always in trouble with the law.* **7 to make** or **cause trouble:** to create difficulty, annoyance: *The boy makes trouble for his parents by misbehaving.*

—*adj.* **1** worried, anxious, often mentally ill: *He is a troubled man.* **2** physically ill: *She is troubled by a bad back.*

—*v.* **-bled, -bling, -bles 1** to annoy, bother: *The street noise troubled him, so he couldn't sleep.* **2** to ask for s.t. politely: *May I trouble you to tell me what time it is (to pass the sugar, go to the store, etc.)?*

trou·ble·mak·er /'trʌbəl,meɪkər/ *n.* a person who often creates problems: *He is a thief, a troublemaker, always breaking the law.*

trou·ble·shoot /'trʌbəl,ʃut/ *v.* **-shot** /-,ʃat/, **-shooting, -shoots** to investigate a problem and offer solutions: *He is a consultant who troubleshoots for companies in financial trouble.* *-n.* **troubleshooter.**

trou·ble·some /'trʌbəlsəm/ *adj.* causing difficulty, annoyance, inconvenience: *A divorce is usually troublesome for all concerned.*

trough /trɔf, traf/ *n.* **1** a long, often U-shaped container, such as for holding animal feed: *The farmer puts feed into the pig trough.* **2** (in finance) a depression, (*syn.*) a slump: *The bond market (economy, company earnings, etc.) is in a trough.*

trounce /trauns/ *v.* **trounced, trouncing, trounces 1** to beat up, (*syn.*) to batter: *A police officer trounced a street thug.* **2** *fig.* to win decisively, beat easily: *The national champions trounced a challenger.*

troupe /trup/ *n.* a group of entertainers, such as actors: *A troupe of singers gave a concert last evening.*

troup·er /'trupər/ *n.* **1** a show business person who entertains despite problems: *That singer is a real trouper because she put on her show even though the microphone didn't work.* **2** a reliable, competent person: *You can always depend on him; he is a real trouper.*

trou·sers /'trauzərz/ *n.pl.* men's pants: *He had a pair of trousers cleaned and pressed.*

trout /traut/ *n.* **trout** a freshwater game fish related to but smaller than the salmon: *Trout have a nutty, sweet taste when cooked properly.*

trove /trouv/ *n.* a group of valuable items: *Relatives found a treasure trove of valuable antiques in their aunt's attic.*

trow·el /'trauəl/ *n.* a flat, metal, triangular-shaped tool with a handle used for gardening and laying down cement: *A bricklayer uses a trowel to lay bricks.*

troy /trɔɪ/ *adj.* (from *n.* [U] **troy weight**) a system of measuring gems and precious metals where one lb. equals 12 ounces and one ounce equals 20 pennyweights, each equaling approx. 480 grains: *Gold coins are sold in gram weights, or troy ounces or fractions thereof.*

tru·ant /'truənt/ *adj.n.* a pupil who doesn't go to school, (*syn.*) a chronic absentee: *School authorities send <adj.> truant officers to find <n.> truants.* *-n.* [U] **truancy.** See: hooky.

truce /trus/ *n.* a temporary stopping of hostilities, usu. while peace is being made: *Each side in the war agreed to a truce while diplomats discussed a peace plan.*

truck /trʌk/ *n.* a vehicle larger than a car used to carry things: *A dump truck carries gravel and sand.*

—*v.* **1** to ship by truck: *Our company trucks large orders to customers.* **2** *phrasal v. sep.* **to**

truck s.t. in: to deliver s.t.: *After the storm, the National Guard trucked in food and water.||They trucked it in. -adj.n.* [U] **trucking.**

truck·er /ˈtrʌkər/ *n.* **1** a person who drives a truck: *Truckers stop at truck stops for food and fuel.* **2** a trucking business: *We called a trucker to move a large shipment.*

truck·load /ˈtrʌk,loʊd/ *n.* the amount that a truck can hold: *We shipped a truckload of furniture to our store.*

truc·u·lence /ˈtrʌkyələns/ *n.* [U] rude disobedience, (*syn.*) belligerence: *The boy's truculence led to his being expelled from school. -adj.* **truculent.**

trudge /trʌdʒ/ *v.n.* **trudged, trudging, trudges** to walk with difficulty, (*syn.*) to tramp wearily: *We <v.> trudged through deep snow to a cabin.*

true /tru/ *adj.* **truer, truest 1** accurate, correct: *Reporters dig for the true facts in a story, not rumor.* **2** proven, (*syn.*) verified: *What she says is true because witnesses testified to it.* **3** faithful, loyal: *He is true to his wife and does not fool around.* **4** sincere, dedicated: *Our teacher has a true interest in her students.* **5** genuine, legal: *The safe deposit box contained a true copy of my father's will.* **6** correctly positioned, level, square, etc.: *That brick wall is level and true.* **7 to come true:** to happen as one desires or predicts: *All of his warnings came true when the stock market crashed.||When she won the national tennis contest, her childhood dreams came true.*
—*n.* **in true:** correctly positioned: *Those beams are in true.*
—*v.* **trued, truing, trues** to position correctly: *A carpenter trued the beams. See:* tried and true.

true-blue *adj.* loyal, devoted: *She is a true-blue friend who helped me when I really needed it.*

true-false test *n.* an examination in which one marks each answer either true or false

true love *n.* **1** deep and lasting love: *After years of loneliness, he finally found true love.* **2** the person one deeply loves: *He met his true love in a physics class.*

truf·fle /ˈtrʌfəl/ *n.* **1** an edible mushroom-like fungus **2** a soft candy, often made with chocolate

tru·ism /ˈtru,ɪzəm/ *n.* a saying that is obviously true: *"Crime is evil" is a truism. See:* cliché.

tru·ly /ˈtruli/ *adv.* **1** with truth, accurately: *She spoke truly.* **2** genuinely, really: *That is truly gold, not fake.* **3** sincerely: *Many people close their letters with "Yours truly" or "Truly yours."*

trump /trʌmp/ *n.* a suit of cards that is higher in rank than the others in a game: *We played a hand of bridge in which clubs were trump.*

—*v.* **1 to play a trump card: a.** to play the winning hand **b.** *infrml.fig.* to use an advantage to win: *He played his trump card when he offered investors a risk-free, guaranteed profit.* **2** *phrasal v. sep.* **to trump s.t. up:** to make false accusations: *His political opponents trumped up false charges against their opponent.||They trumped them up.*

trumped-up *adj.* falsified, (*syn.*) fabricated: *She was jailed on trumped-up charges.*

trum·pet /ˈtrʌmpət/ *n.* **1** a brass wind musical instrument with a high-pitched sound **2** the loud cry of some animals, such as elephants -*n.* **trumpeter.**

trun·cate /ˈtrʌŋ,keɪt/ *v.frml.* **-cated, -cating, -cates** to shorten, reduce in length: *The speaker truncated her speech so*

trumpet

as not to bore the audience. -adj. **truncated;** -*n.* [U] **truncation.**

trun·cheon /ˈtrʌntʃən/ *n.* a club, esp. one used by police: *Police clubbed rioters with rubber truncheons.*

trun·dle /ˈtrʌndl/ *n.adj.* a roller, small wheel: *Under my bed there is a <adj.> trundle bed that I pull out when I have a guest.*
—*v.* **-dled, -dling, -dles** to roll along: *Wagons trundle goods to market.*

trunk /trʌŋk/ *n.* **1** a large, rectangular, box-like piece of luggage: *I put my books and other objects in a trunk for shipment to my new house.* **2** an elephant's nose: *An elephant put out its trunk and picked up a peanut.* **3** the storage space in the back of a car: *She carries a blanket and boots in her trunk in case of emergencies.* **4** the main stem of a tree **5** the central part of the body, without the head, arms, or legs **6** *pl.* men's shorts, esp. a bathing suit: *I put on my swim trunks and headed for the beach.*

truss /trʌs/ *n.* **-es 1** a physical support, a brace: *The athlete wore a truss until his bad back could be operated on.* **2** (in building, mines, etc.) a support beam or group of supports used to hold up a tunnel: *Trusses were installed to prevent the tunnel from falling in.*
—*v.* **-es 1** to support an injury with a truss: *A medic trussed up a soldier with a broken leg.* **2** to install beams, etc.: *Workers truss unstable walls of tunnels.* **3** to tie up tightly: *to truss a turkey*

trust /trʌst/ *n.* **1** [U] confidence in the honesty and reliability of s.o. or s.t.: *I have complete trust in his ability to keep a secret.* **2** [U] responsibility for s.o. or s.t.: *She left her car in my trust while she went on vacation.* **3** [C] a legal contract where property owned by one person or group is held and managed for s.o.

else: *When the rich man died, his estate went into a trust managed by a bank for his children.*
—*v.* **1** to have faith in s.o.: *I trust my friend completely.* **2** to hope with confidence: *I trust that help will be here soon.* **3** *phrasal v. sep.* **to trust s.o. to:** to have confidence in s.o.: *I trust you to do as I say and not argue.*
—*adj.* **1 In trust:** referring to property held in a legal arrangement with a trustee: *His fortune is held in trust for his children by a bank.* **2 to put** or **place in trust:** to place property in a trust: *The rich widow placed her money in trust for her children.*

trust company *n.* a bank that manages trusts and makes loans: *She manages the trusts of wealthy people at a trust company.*

trus·tee /trʌˈsti/ *n.* **1** a person who oversees a university, church, or other institution: *George is a member of the board of trustees of Williams College.* **2** a person, bank, brokerage firm, etc. that manages trusts: *The U.S. Bank is trustee for his father's estate.*

trust·ful /ˈtrʌstfəl/ or **trusting** /ˈtrʌstɪŋ/ *adj.* believing in the honesty and reliability of s.o.: *He is very trustful of his older brother.*

trust fund *n.* property, monies, etc. that produce income held in trust for s.o.: *Money from a trust fund will start going to my grandson on his 21st birthday.*

trust·wor·thy /ˈtrʌstˌwɜrði/ *adj.* capable of being trusted; honest and reliable: *That guy looks strange, but he is very trustworthy.* -*n.* [U] **trustworthiness.**

truth /truθ/ *n.* **truths** /truðs, truθs/ **1** [U] accuracy, correctness: *She always speaks the truth.* **2** [C] s.t. factual, proven: *Cross examination by attorneys brought out the truth about the crime.* **3 the truth will out:** the truth will eventually be known

truth·ful /ˈtruθfəl/ *adj.* **1** accurate, factual: *His version of the event is truthful.* **2** habitually honest and accurate: *He is a truthful person.* -*adv.* **truthfully;** -*n.* [U] **truthfulness.**

truth serum *n.* [U] a chemical, such as Phenobarbital™, used to make people give information: *Authorities used truth serum on the spy to get the truth from him.*

try /traɪ/ *v.* **tried, trying, tries 1** to attempt, (*syn.*) to endeavor: *He tried to solve the math problem, but couldn't.* **2** to test, experiment: *She tried eating octopus, but didn't like it.* **3** (in law) to have a legal proceeding: *The state tried the criminal for theft.* **4 to try one's hand at:** to attempt s.t.: *He tried his hand at playing golf, but found it too difficult and slow.* **5 to try s.o.** or **s.o.'s patience:** to annoy, fatigue: *That child is so noisy that he tries my patience.* **6** *phrasal v. sep.* **to try s.t. on:** to put on an item of clothing to see if it fits: *He tried*

on the slippers I gave him.‖He tried them on. **7** *phrasal v. sep.* **to try (s.t.) out: a.** to perform and look for acceptance, such as for a team or a theatrical part: *She tried out for a singing part in the play and got it.* **b.** s.t.: to test, experiment: *I tried out camping in the mountains and really liked it.*
—*n.* **tries 1** attempt, (*syn.*) endeavor: *His attempt to climb Mt. Everest failed, but it was a good try.* **2 to give s.t. a try:** test, experiment: *She gave eating squid a try, but didn't like it.*

try·ing /ˈtraɪɪŋ/ *adj.* difficult, (*syn.*) harrowing: *Being lost in a bad snowstorm was a trying experience.*

try·out /ˈtraɪˌaʊt/ *n.* a test, audition, such as for a role or place on a team: *Tryouts for the football team (school play, debating society, etc.) are scheduled for next week.*

tryst /trɪst/ *n.* a meeting, usu. secret, as between lovers: *The two go away to the country for weekend trysts.*

tsar or **czar** /zɑr, tsɑr/ *n.* formerly emperor of Russia: *The rule of the tsars came to a tragic end.* -*n.* **tsarina** /zɑˈrinə, tsɑ-/.

T-shirt or **tee-shirt** /ˈtiˌʃɜrt/ *n.* a lightweight, short-sleeved garment worn over the upper body: *T-shirts are cool and comfortable.*

tub /tʌb/ *n.* **1** a large container with slanting sides used to hold food, etc.: *I bought a small tub of butter at the store.* **2** a bathtub: *After working in the garden, she had a bath in the tub.* **3** *infrml.pej.* a fat person: *He eats so much that he has become a tub. See:* tubby.

tu·ba /ˈtubə/ *n.* a low-pitched brass instrument usu. used for rhythm: *He plays the tuba in the college band.*

tub·by /ˈtʌbi/ *adj.pej.infrml.* **-bier, -biest** fat, (*syn.*) roly-poly: *That little boy eats so much that he is tubby.*

tube /tub/ *n.* **1** a hollow, flexible container: *I bought a tube of toothpaste this morning.* **2** *infrml.* **to go down the tubes:** to disappear, esp. s.t. valuable going to ruin: *The stock market crashed, and his life's savings went down the tubes.*

tu·ber·cu·lo·sis /təˌbɜrkyəˈloʊsɪs, tʊ-/ *n.* [U] a contagious lung disease: *People used to go to special health spas to recover from tuberculosis.* -*adj.* **tubercular.**

tub·ing /ˈtubɪŋ/ *n.* [U] tubes in general: *The tubing used for plumbing in the building is made of plastic.*

tub·u·lar /ˈtubyələr/ *adj.* having a round or slightly flat shape: *The shape of a toothpaste tube is tubular.*

tuck /tʌk/ *n.* **1** a fold sewn for better fit or decoration in clothes, draperies, etc.: *She sewed tucks in the waist of her skirt.* **2** a tight fold: *Military beds are made with tucks.* **3** a type of

cosmetic surgery: *He had a tummy tuck to make himself thinner.*
—*v.* **1** to put inside s.t else: *She tucked her shirt into her skirt.* **2** to fold, esp. bedclothes **3** *phrasal v. sep.* **to tuck s.o. in:** to put sheets, blankets, etc. around s.o. tightly: *She tucks in her children before they go to sleep.* ‖*She tucks them in.*

Tues·day /'tuz,deɪ, -di/ *n.* the second day of the week, between Monday and Wednesday

tuft /tʌft/ *n.* a bunch, patch that sticks out: *Many bird species have a tuft of feathers sticking up from their heads.*
—*adj.* **tufted** to have a tuft: *The tufted titmouse is a small bird.*

tug /tʌg/ *n.* a hard pull, (*syn.*) a yank: *I gave the rope a tug to be sure it was tied tightly.*
—*v.* **tugged, tugging, tugs** to pull hard: *A farmer tugged on the horse's bridle to get it to move.*

tug·boat /'tʌg,boʊt/ *n.* a powerful, strong boat used to pull or push other vessels, esp. in and out of harbors and docks: *Two tugboats guided the ocean liner into its dock.*

tug-of-war *n.* **1** a game in which two teams pull on opposite ends of a rope to pull the other team over a line between them **2** *fig.* a struggle between opposing forces: *The President and the Congress are in a tug-of-war over the new budget.*

tu·i·tion /tu'ɪʃən/ *n.* [U] **1** the cost of going to an educational institution: *In the USA, the cost of tuition at private colleges is very high.* **2** teaching, instruction *See:* room and board, USAGE NOTE.

tu·lip /'tulɪp/ *n.* a bulb-rooted plant with bright bell-shaped flowers: *Red tulips are beautiful in the springtime.*

tum·ble /'tʌmbəl/ *v.* **-bled, -bling, -bles** **1** to roll, esp. end over end: *Children tumble over each other in play.* **2** to do acrobatics: *At school, we tumbled today in gym.* **3** to fall suddenly: *His toe caught, and he tumbled down the stairs.*
—*n.* a fall: *He took a tumble down the stairs.*

tum·ble·down /'tʌmbəl,daʊn/ *adj.* old, falling apart, (*syn.*) dilapidated: *The tumbledown house on the corner should be torn down.*

tum·bler /'tʌmblər/ *n.* **1** a large drinking glass: *Tumblers are often thick, so they don't break easily.* **2** an acrobat: *Tumblers did somersaults in the circus.* **3** an inner part of a lock: *Tumblers must fit a key or combination for a lock to turn.*

tum·my /'tʌmi/ *n.infrml.* **-mies** the stomach: *I ate a big Thanksgiving dinner, and now my tummy hurts.*

tu·mor /'tumər/ *n.* a growth of diseased tissue: *A surgeon removed a benign tumor from the patient's stomach.*

tu·mult /'tu,mʊlt/ *n.* [U] **1** the noise made by an excited crowd: *The tumult from the angry mob was frightening.* **2** a commotion, including confusion of the mind: *He was threatened with death, and it caused a tumult in his head. -adj.* **tumultuous** /tə'mʌltʃuəs, tu-/.

tu·na /'tunə/ *adj.n.* [C;U] a large food and game fish: *I had a <adj.> tuna sandwich for lunch.*

tun·dra /'tʌndrə/ *n.* [U] treeless flat land found mostly in the Arctic Circle: *The tundra has permanently frozen soil.*

tune /tun/ *n.* **1** a song: *He played a tune on the piano.* **2 to carry a tune:** to sing on key: *His voice sounds funny, but he can carry a tune.* **3 to change one's tune:** to change one's opinion: *At first he didn't want to come to the movies, then he changed his tune and came.*
—*v.* **tuned, tuning, tunes** **1** to adjust a musical instrument to the correct pitch: *A piano tuner tuned my piano.* **2** to set a piece of audio equipment to receive a signal: *I tuned my radio to my favorite station.* **3** *phrasal v. insep.* **to tune in to s.t.:** to listen: *I tuned in on the basketball game.* **4** *phrasal v. sep.* **to tune s.o. or s.t. out: a.** *s.o.:* to ignore, esp. what s.o. says: *He complains all the time, so I just tune his comments out.*‖*I tune them out.* **b.** *s.t.:* to adjust a radio dial to avoid static **5** *phrasal v. sep.* **to tune s.t. up:** to clean and adjust a motor: *I tuned up my car myself.*‖*I tuned it up.*
—*adj.* **1 in tune:** in proper musical pitch: *The first violinist put the orchestra in tune.* **2** *infrml.fig.* **in tune with:** in agreement, cooperation with: *Everyone is in tune with your recommendations.* **3 out of tune: a.** not having proper musical pitch: *My piano is old and out of tune.* **b.** *infrml.fig.* not in agreement with, uncooperative: *He is out of tune with his colleagues.* **4 to stay tuned:** to remain tuned to the same radio or TV station: *The announcer said, "Stay tuned; we'll be right back after this commercial message."*

tuned in *adj.* **1** listening to a radio or TV program: *The TV is tuned in to the station that broadcasts the news.* **2** *infrml.fig.* informed, aware: *She is tuned in to what is going on in the company.*

tune·ful /'tunfəl/ *adj.frml.* pleasing to the ear, (*syn.*) melodious: *The band plays tuneful music. -adv.* **tunefully.**

tune·less /'tunlɪs/ *adj.* unmelodious, unpleasant to listen to *See:* tone-deaf.

tuner /'tunər/ *n.* **1** a radio receiver: *My tuner is on the right station.* **2** a person who tunes musical instruments: *a piano tuner*

tune-up *n.* a cleaning and adjustment of a motor: *I took my car in for a tune-up.*

tung·sten /'tʌŋstən/ *n.* [U] a gray-white metallic element used in lighting and cutting tools:

Lamps with filaments of tungsten shine very brightly.

tu·nic /'tunɪk/ *n.* **1** a loose, sack-like garment tied at the waist: *Tunics are fashionable even after thousands of years.* **2** a short jacket that is part of a uniform

tun·nel /'tʌnəl/ *n.* **1** a passage under the ground: *Construction teams dig tunnels for roads to go through hills and mountains.* **2** *infrml.* **to see light at the end of the tunnel:** to get near the end of a long, difficult task: *We have experimented for years and now see light at the end of the tunnel for a new wonder drug.*

tunnel

3 tunnel vision: narrow-mindedness: *He has tunnel vision and considers only a few things.* —*v.* to make a tunnel: *Workers tunneled into a hill, then under a river.*

tur·ban /'tɜrbən/ *n.* a long piece of cloth wrapped around the head: *Indian men wear bright-colored turbans.*

tur·bid /'tɜrbɪd/ *adj.frml.* muddy, cloudy: *The lake's water is turbid.* -*n.* [U] **turbidity.**

tur·bine /'tɜrbɪn, -,baɪn/ *n.* a machine that produces power by turning blades with steam, water, or gas, esp. to create electricity: *Huge steam turbines can produce electricity for an entire city.*

tur·bo·charg·er /'tɜrboʊ,ʧɑrʤər/ *n.* a device on an engine that increases its power: *That heavy truck has a turbocharger on its engine.*

tur·bot /'tɜrbət/ *n.* [U] a large edible flatfish: *Some like to broil turbot.*

tur·bu·lence /'tɜrbyələns/ *n.* [U] **1** hard or violent movement, such as in air flow or water: *Our airplane went through heavy turbulence in a thunderstorm.* **2** *fig.* emotional or physical upset: *The turbulence in his life has come from accidents and illness.* -*adj.* **turbulent.**

tu·reen /tʊ'rin/ *n.* a deep, covered serving dish: *The waiter put a tureen of hot soup on our table.*

turf /tɜrf/ *n.* [C;U] **1** sod, grass with roots and earth: *The turf on golf courses is fertilized and watered.* **2** *infrml.fig.* one's territory, area of authority: *The dog does not like anyone to come into his turf.*

tur·gid /'tɜrʤɪd/ *adj.* **1** swollen, (*syn.*) bloated **2** *fig.* heavy, complex, and boring (said of prose): *His writing is so turgid that it puts people to sleep.* -*adv.* **turgidly;** -*n.* [U] **turgidity.**

tur·key /'tɜrki/ *n.* [C;U] **1** a large game and poultry bird in North America: *Traditionally, many North Americans have a roast turkey for Thanksgiving dinner.* **2** [C] *infrml.fig.* a bad movie, play, show, etc.: *That movie I saw last*

night was a real turkey. **3** [C] a jerk: *That guy is a turkey; stay away from him.* **4 to go cold turkey:** stopping use of drugs, etc. all at once: *When I stopped smoking cigarettes, I went cold turkey.* **5** *infrml.fig.* **to talk turkey:** to discuss business: *Let's talk turkey about how much the product will cost and when you can deliver it.*

turkey

tur·moil /'tɜr,mɔɪl/ *n.* [C] disruption, chaos, often with mental suffering: *An accident caused turmoil in his life.*

turn /tɜrn/ *v.* **1** to move in a different direction: *The truck turned right onto a side street.* **2** to change, transform: *The weather turned stormy today.*‖*An architect turned an old barn into a cute house.* **3** to rotate, adjust: *I turned the knob on the radio to another station.* **4** to go around, spin: *The earth turns on its axis.* **5** to point, aim: *The astronomer turned her telescope on a distant star.* **6** to reverse: *A cook turned the hamburgers on the grill.*‖*A seamstress turned the collar on my shirt.* **7** (in farming) to plow: *The farmer turned the soil with his plow.* **8** to nauseate, injure: *That horror film turned my stomach.*‖*I tripped and turned my ankle.* **9** to carve as on a lathe: *A worker turns table legs on a wood lathe.* **10** *infrml.fig.* **to turn a blind eye:** to ignore, overlook: *The father turned a blind eye to his son's laziness and left him the family business.* **11** *infrml.fig.* **to turn a deaf ear:** to ignore, avoid: *He turned a deaf ear to his wife's advice.* **12 to turn a profit:** to make a profit: *His business is new and does not turn a profit.* **13** *phrasal v.* **to turn about:** to turn in the opposite direction: *She forgot her eyeglasses and turned about to get them.* **14 to turn blue:** to show signs of cold and lack of oxygen: *His hands turned blue from the cold.* **15** *infrml.fig.* **turn cartwheels:** to jump for joy: *When he heard the good news, he felt like turning cartwheels.* **16 to turn green: a.** to become ill: *He ate some bad food and turned green with nausea.* **b.** to become envious or jealous: *When he saw his neighbor's new car, he turned green with envy.* **17** *phrasal v. insep.* **to turn into s.o. or s.t.:** to change into, become: *The nice boy turned into a bad man.* **18 to turn loose:** to set free: *Zookeepers turned some birds raised in captivity loose in the wild.* **19** *infrml.* **to turn on a dime:** to change direction quickly: *That football star can turn on a dime and speed off in another direction.* **20 to turn one's back on:** to reject, (*syn.*) to repudiate: *He turned his back on his father and never spoke to him again.* **21 to turn over a new**

leaf: to change, esp. to correct one's bad behavior: *Managers who ignored their workers turned over a new leaf and worked closely with them.* **22** *infrml.fig.* **to turn over in one's grave:** an expression of disapproval (disgust, horror): *Beethoven would turn over in his grave if he could hear today's popular music.* **23 to turn red:** to blush, flush: *Her face turned red with embarrassment.* **24** *phrasal v. insep.* **to turn s.o. against s.o. or s.t.:** to become hostile, oppose: *The public turned against the leader and voted him out of office.* **25** *phrasal v. sep.* **to turn s.o. or s.t. around: a.** to reverse direction: *He turned his car around and headed home.* **b.** to change a bad business situation: *The company was losing money and hired a new president to turn it around.* **26** *phrasal v. sep.* **to turn (s.o.) away: a.** to avoid looking, (*syn.*) to avert the eyes: *When he saw the dead body, he turned away in horror.* **b.** *s.o.:* to change, such as to stop doing bad things: *He turned away from drinking alcohol and gambling.* **c.** *s.o.:* to keep s.o. from entering: *The security guard turned away people who didn't have invitations to the party.||She turned them away.* **27** *phrasal v. sep.* **to turn s.o. back:** to reverse direction, such as stop a journey: *The bad snowstorm made me turn back and stay at home.* **28** *phrasal v. sep.* **to turn s.o. or s.t. down: a.** *s.t.:* to fold over: *The maid turned down the bedsheet and blanket for hotel guests each evening.* **b.** *s.o. or s.t.:* to refuse, disapprove: *His manager turned down his proposal for a new project.* **29** *phrasal v. sep.* **to turn (s.o. or s.t.) in: a.** to go to bed, sleep: *I turned in at 11:00 P.M. last night.* **b.** *s.o.:* to surrender s.o. to the police: *A young girl turned in her parents for using drugs.||She turned them in.* **c.** *s.t.:* to hand in, give s.t. to s.o.: *Students turned in their test papers when the period was over.* **d.** *s.t.:* to exchange as a down payment, esp. cars: *He turned in his old car for a new one.* **30** *phrasal v. sep.* **to turn s.o. or s.t. off: a.** *s.o.:* *slang* to disgust, offend: *His unfriendly attitude turns off most people.||It turns them off.* **b.** *s.t.:* to shut off: *I turned off the light and went to sleep.* **31** *phrasal v. sep.* **to turn s.o. or s.t. on: a.** *s.o.:* to excite, cause enjoyment: *Playing tennis turns her on; she loves it!* **b.** *s.o.:* to excite sexually, arouse: *He turns her on with his good looks and curly hair.* **c.** *s.t.:* to switch on, operate: *I turned on the lights in a dark room.* **d.** *s.t.:* to attack physically or verbally: *The dog turned on his owner and bit her. ||It turned on her.* **32** *phrasal v. sep.* **to turn s.o. or s.t. out: a.** to develop into, become: *The young woman turned out well as the manager of a magazine.* **b.** *s.o.:* to expel, reject: *The mean man turned his son out into the cold night.||He turned him out.* **c.** *s.o.:* to cause people to assemble: *The announcement of a*

public debate turned out a large crowd. **d.** *s.t.:* to produce s.t.: *Her company turns out beautiful shoes and accessories.* **e.** *s.t.:* to put out, extinguish (a light) **33 to turn s.o.'s head:** to attract, (*syn.*) to beguile: *She is so tall that she turns lots of heads when she walks down the street.* **34** *phrasal v. sep.* **to turn s.t. over: a.** to reverse sides, flip over: *He turned over and slept on his stomach.* **b.** to give. *The manager turned over her responsibilities to a new person.||She turned them over.* **35** *phrasal v. sep.* **to turn (s.t.) up: a.** to arrive: *She turned up at the meeting late.* **b.** to occur, happen, esp. unexpectedly: *Something wonderful turned up. I won a prize!* **c.** *s.t.:* to lift up: *He turned up the brim of his hat.* **d.** *s.t.:* to increase the volume: *Turn up the radio so we can hear the music better.* **e.** *s.t.:* to produce results, uncover: *The scientist experimented for months and finally turned up a new substance.||She turned it up.* **36** *infrml.* **to turn tail:** to reverse direction, esp. in a hurried and often cowardly fashion: *When the criminal saw the police arrive, she turned tail and ran.* **37** *fig.* **to turn the other cheek:** to ignore criticism (rejection, harm, etc.): *If a person hurts you, some people urge you to turn the other cheek.* **38** *infrml.fig.* **to turn the tables:** to change weakness into strength, esp. in the same way: *I turned the tables on a person who threatened to sue me by having my lawyer sue her first.* **39** *fig.* **to turn the tide:** to change, reverse a situation: *The entrance of their allies into the war turned the tide against their enemies.* **40** *phrasal v. insep.* **to turn to (s.o. or s.t.): a.** to apply oneself, work hard: *In a financial crisis, the whole family turned to and paid off the debt.* **b.** to look at cerain pages in a book **c.** *s.o. or s.t.:* to find comfort in: *After her divorce, she turned to her friends.* **41 to turn to one's advantage:** to change a difficult situation into a good one: *He turned losing his job to his advantage by starting his own business.* **42 to turn up one's nose:** to reject, esp. in a snobbish fashion: *My cat turns up his nose at ordinary cat food.*

—*n.* **1** a bend, curve: *The road makes a turn to the left at the intersection.* **2** a change of direction: *We took a turn at the river.* **3** a rotation: *The windmill turned in the breeze.* **4** a time for a person to act: *It was my turn to wash the dishes (serve the tennis ball, speak in class, etc.).* **5** *fig.* **at every turn:** at every moment, on every occasion: *At every turn, he likes to discuss politics.* **6 in turn:** in sequence, in addition: *She smiled at him, and he in turn smiled back.* **7 out of turn: a.** not in sequence: *She should have hit the golf ball last; when she hit first, she played out of turn.* **b.** wrongly, rudely: *He spoke out of turn when he criticized her unfairly.* **8 to do a good turn:** to do s.t. good, help s.o.: *He did a good turn for a stranded motorist by stopping and fixing her*

tire. **9 to take a turn for the better** or **worse:** to improve or worsen: *The hospital patient took a turn for the better.* **10 turn of events:** a change, esp. by chance: *In a sudden turn of events, the Prime Minister resigned.*
—*pl.* **1 by turns:** alternately, (*syn.*) sequentially: *Each table of guests went to the buffet by turns.* **2 to take turns:** to act in sequence: *He and his wife take turns washing the dishes.*
—*adj. n.* **turn of the century:** a period just before, during, and after a century and its characteristics in life, culture, art, etc.: *The <n.> turn of the nineteenth century in France was called the Belle Epoque.*

turn·a·bout /ˈtɜrnəˌbaʊt/ *n.* **1** a reversal, such as of power, chance, or opinion: *A turnabout in public opinion helped the political candidate.* **2 turnabout is fair play:** to do to s.o. what they do to you is fair: *A little boy hurt by a bully made the bully cry by punching him in the nose; turnabout is fair play.*

turn·a·round /ˈtɜrnəˌraʊnd/ *adj.n.* **1** a turnabout area **2** the time needed to restart an action, such as to clean and refuel an airplane: *The <n.> turnaround for that airplane is one hour.* **3** related to completing an action: *The <adj.> turnaround time on reprinting that book is a month.* **4** related to improving a business: *Lisa is a consultant for a turnaround firm; she helps other companies recover from financial troubles.*

turn·coat /ˈtɜrnˌkoʊt/ *n.* s.o. who changes to the other side, a traitor: *Turncoats in wartime are shot if they are caught.*

turned-on *adj.infrml.fig.* excited, enthusiastic: *She is really turned on by rock music.*

tur·nip /ˈtɜrnɪp/ *n.* a white or yellow root vegetable whose tops are often cooked like spinach: *Some cooks can make turnips tasty.*

turn·key /ˈtɜrnˌki/ *adj.* referring to s.t. that is prepared and ready to operate: *The company provides turnkey computer systems for doctors' offices.*

turn-off *n.infrml.fig.* s.t. disturbing, (*syn.*) repulsive: *His bad behavior at the party was a turn-off for his girlfriend.*

turn-on *n.infrml.fig.* s.t. exciting, pleasant: *Driving very fast is a turn-on for Ned.*

turn·out /ˈtɜrnˌaʊt/ *n.* [C;U] the number of people at an event: *The turnout for the basketball game was good.*

turn·o·ver /ˈtɜrnˌoʊvər/ *n.* **1** [U] the rate at which employees leave a job or company: *The turnover at the business is very high.* **2** [U] an act of handing s.t. over, such as a change of ownership: *The turnover of the deed for the house is tomorrow.* **3** [U] the amount of annual business: *That company has a $5 million a year turnover.* **4** [C] a small pastry filled

with fruit: *She likes an apple turnover with coffee for breakfast.*

turn·pike /ˈtɜrnˌpaɪk/ *n.* a main highway, usu. with tolls: *The turnpike from New York to Boston has frequent stops for tolls.*

turn·stile /ˈtɜrnˌstaɪl/ *n.* a gate with rotating arms: *He put his subway fare in the turnstile and walked through it.*

turn·ta·ble /ˈtɜrnˌteɪbəl/ *n.* in audio equipment, a rotating part that holds a record: *The turntable on that old stereo is broken.*

turned-up *adj.* pointing in an upward direction: *She has a cute turned-up nose.*

tur·pen·tine /ˈtɜrpənˌtaɪn/ *n.* [U] a liquid made from pine resin used as a paint thinner and drying agent: *Some old paint was too thick, so I thinned it with turpentine.*

tur·pi·tude /ˈtɜrpɪˌtud/ *n.frml.* [U] baseness: *The criminal is guilty of moral turpitude.*

tur·quoise /ˈtɜrˌkwɔɪz, -ˌkɔɪz/ *n.* [U] a light blue to blue-green semi-precious gemstone: *She loves to wear turquoise necklaces and silver rings.*

tur·ret /ˈtɜrɪt, ˈtʌr-/ *n.* **1** a rotating enclosure from which guns are fired, such as on battleships and tanks: *The turret on the tank turned, and a gunner fired the cannon.* **2** a small architectural structure mounted on a larger one: *Turrets on the castle walls allow guards to watch for an attack.* -*adj.* **turreted.**

tur·tle /ˈtɜrtl/ *n.* a reptile with a hard shell and strong beak: *People keep small turtles as pets.* See: tortoise.

tur·tle·neck /ˈtɜrtlˌnɛk/ *n.adj.* a pullover or sweater with a high, close-fitting neck: *He wears <n.> turtlenecks in the winter to keep warm.*

turtle

tush /tʊʃ/ *n.infrml.* the buttocks: *The child fell down and hurt her tush.*

tusk /tʌsk/ *n.* a long, thick front tooth, such as of elephants, warthogs, etc.: *A walrus has two long tusks.*

tus·sle /ˈtʌsəl/ *v.n.* -**sled, -sling, -sles** to wrestle, struggle: *Two boys <v.> tussled in the schoolyard.*

tut /*a sucked in sound similar to a t,* tʌt/ *exclam.* of disapproval or impatience: *Tut, tut, don't use dirty language around me.*

tu·tel·age /ˈtutlɪdʒ/ *n.frml.* [U] instruction, teaching: *She learned to sing under the tutelage of a famous voice coach.*

tu·tor /ˈtutər/ *n.* a teacher who helps students individually with other courses: *She is a tutor who helps foreign students improve their English.*

T

—*v.* to act as a tutor: *She tutors students in English.* -*n.* [U] **tutorship.**

tu·tor·i·al /tu'tɔriəl/ *adj.n.* an educational process where a teacher gives classes to individual students: *I have a writing <n.> tutorial every Friday with my teacher.*

tut·ti-frut·ti /'tuti'fruti/ *n.* [U] ice cream with chopped fruits: *A tutti-frutti is refreshing on a hot day.*

tu·tu /'tutu/ *n.* a short, classical dance costume extending out from the waist: *Ballerinas dancing in their tutus are a pretty sight.*

tux /tʌks/ *n.short for* tuxedo

tux·e·do /tʌk'sidoʊ/ *n.* a black suit worn to formal occasions: *The invitation called for tuxedos and white ties as proper attire.*

TV /ti'vi/ *infrml.abbr. for* television: *We watch the evening news on TV.*

TV dinner *n.* a frozen, packaged meal that is heated and eaten

twang /twæŋ/ *n.* a nasal accent in the USA that is different from a standard accent: *She speaks with a southern twang.*

tweak /twik/ *v.n.* to pinch, squeeze hard: *One little boy <v.> tweaked another's nose and ran away.||He gave it a <n.> tweak.*

tweed /twid/ *n.* [C;U] a strong, thick, woolen fabric for coats and suits: *He wears jackets that are made of tweed.* -*adj.* **tweedy.**

tweet /twit/ *v.n.* to make a squeaky, high-pitched sound, as some birds do: *Songbirds <v.> tweeted in the trees.*

tweet·er /'twitər/ *n.* the speaker in an audio system that produces high-pitched sounds: *The tweeter in my speaker picks up high notes beautifully. See:* woofer.

tweeze /twiz/ *v.* **tweezed, tweezing, tweezes** to remove with a tweezer: *She tweezes her eyebrows.*

tweez·ers /'twizərz/ *n.pl.* a small tool with two arms that are pushed together to remove s.t.: *I used tweezers to remove a splinter from my foot.*

twelve /twɛlv/ *n.* the cardinal number 12 -*adj.* 12 of s.t., *(syn.)* a dozen: *There are 12 eggs in a carton.* -*n.adj.* **twelfth** /twɛlfθ/. *See:* dozen.

twen·ti·eth /'twɛntiəθ/ *adj.n.* the ordinal number 20: *Tomorrow is her <adj.> twentieth birthday; it is her <n.> twentieth.*

twen·ty /'twɛnti/ *n.* the cardinal number 20 -*adj.* 20 of s.t.: *Twenty children lined up for lunch.*

twenty-one *n.* the cardinal number 21 -*adj.* **1** 21 of s.t.: *He is 21 years old today.* **2** the age of majority, which gives the right to vote and drink alcohol: *Congress changed the voting age from 21 to 18.* -*n.adj.* **twenty-first.**

USAGE NOTE: At age *21*, Americans are allowed to buy alcohol and drink in a public establishment such as a restaurant or bar.

twenty-twenty *n.adj.* **1** a designation for normal, good eyesight: *He has <adj.> twenty-twenty (or) 20-20 vision.* **2 twenty-twenty hindsight:** the ability to see things in the past clearly: *With the benefit of <adj.> 20-20 hindsight, he knows that he should have driven more carefully to avoid the accident.*

twerp /twɜrp/ *n.infrml.* a jerk, an offensive person: *That twerp tries to act important.*

twice /twaɪs/ *adv.* two times: *She rang the doorbell twice.*

twid·dle /'twɪdl/ *v.* **-dled, -dling, -dles 1** to rotate, spin **2** *infrml.* **to twiddle one's thumbs:** to wait impatiently, doing nothing: *My doctor is always late, so I have to twiddle my thumbs until he's ready for me.*

twig /twɪg/ *n.* a small branch: *A hiker picked up twigs to build a campfire.* -*adj.* **twiggy.**

twi·light /'twaɪˌlaɪt/ *n.* **1** the period between sunset and darkness: *The street lights come on at twilight.* **2** *fig.* a time of decline: *He is old now, in the twilight of his life. See:* dusk.

twin /twɪn/ *n.* one of two children born of the same mother at the same time: *The sisters are twins; both are blonde, and tall, and twenty years old.*
—*adj.* referring to exact copies of s.t.: *He flies a twin-engine airplane.*

twin bed *n.* one of two single beds: *My brother and I sleep in twin beds.*

twine /twaɪn/ *n.* [U] strong, coarse string: *We wrapped the packages with twine.*

twinge /twɪndʒ/ *n.* a brief, sharp pain or emotion: *After jogging, he had a twinge in his thigh muscle.*
—*v.* **twinged, twinging, twinges** to produce a twinge: *His thigh muscle twinged then relaxed.*

twin·kle /'twɪŋkəl/ *v.* **-kled, -kling, -kles** to shine, gleam off and on: *Stars twinkle in the night sky.*
—*n.* **1** a gleam **2** a sign of wit, laughter, high spirits: *He told a joke with a twinkle in his eye.*

twin·kling /'twɪŋklɪŋ/ *n.* [U] **1** gleaming, shining: *The twinkling of stars is a pretty sight.* **2** a sign of wit, etc.: *You could see the twinkling in her eyes as she laughed with her children.* **3** a short moment: *I'll finish this in a twinkling.*

twin-size *adj.* related to twin beds: *She bought twin-size sheets for the beds.*

twirl /twɜrl/ *v.* to spin, rotate: *The girl twirled a rope over her head.*

twist /twɪst/ *v.* **1** to turn, rotate: *I twisted the door knob, but the door wouldn't open.* **2** to wrap, bend around each other: *I twisted two pieces of thread on a needle to sew a hole in my coat.* **3** to turn and break, *(syn.)* to wrench off: *Workers twisted dead branches off trees.* **4**

to twist s.o.'s arm: a. to bend s.o.'s arm: *One wrestler twisted his opponent's arm into an armlock.* **b.** *fig.* to pressure s.o. into doing s.t. that they may not want to do: *His boss twisted an employee's arm into taking a new job by threatening to fire him unless he took it.*
—*n.* **1** a turn, rotation: *I gave the doorknob a twist and opened the door.* **2 a new twist:** an unusual development, a new version: *The police came up with a new twist in the crime story; that it was done by a different person.*

twist·ed /'twɪstɪd/ *adj.* **1** wrapped, rotated: *The dog's leash was twisted around a tree, and he couldn't move.* **2** mentally ill, (*syns.*) deranged, perverted: *That madman has a twisted mind.*

twist·er /'twɪstər/ *n.infrml.* a tornado: *Twisters cause severe damage to houses and trees.*

twit /twɪt/ *n.* a silly person, jerk, (*syn.*) twerp: *That twit is totally incompetent.*

twitch /twɪtʃ/ *v.* **-es** to shake briefly or uncontrollably, (*syn.*) to quiver: *A nerve twitched in the man's cheek.*
—*n.* **-es** a nervous reaction, such as a tic: *He has a twitch in his cheek.*

twit·ter /'twɪtər/ *v.* to call or chirp rapidly like birds: *Birds twittered in the trees.*
—*n.* **1** a rapid chirp **2** a state of nervous agitation: *I could hear the twitter of sparrows gathered in their favorite bush. See:* atwitter.

two /tu/ *n.* the cardinal number 2
—*adj.* **1** 2 of s.t.: *People have two eyes.* **2 two's company:** a couple enjoys each other's company, but doesn't want a third person: *I told my friend that I have a date tonight and two's company, three's a crowd. See:* second.

two bits *n.pl.* 25 cents, a quarter (of a dollar): *Can you loan me two bits?*

two cents' worth *n.infrml.* **to put in one's two cents' worth:** to give one's opinion, but not care if s.o. disagrees with it: *Two of my friends were having a political argument, and I finally put in my two cents' worth about what I thought.*

two-dimensional *adj.* **1** having vertical and horizontal planes (height and width): *A painting is two-dimensional.* **2** *fig.* shallow, weak: *That essay is two-dimensional and overlooks too many ideas.*

two-faced *adj.fig.* insincere, (*syn.*) hypocritical: *She is two-faced, friendly at first; then she says bad things about you behind your back.*

two·fer /'tufər/ *n.infrml.* referring to paying for one thing and receiving two (or) "two for" the price of one: *I bought a pair of shoes and got a twofer, another pair for free.*

two-fisted *adj.* **1** using both hands: *She's a two-fisted beer drinker.* **2** *fig.* strong, decisive: *He is a tough-minded, two-fisted manager.*

two·fold /'tu,fould/ *adj.* two times: *That company has a twofold increase in sales (personnel, costs, etc.).*

two-party *adj.* referring to a system of two political parties: *There is usually a two-party race for President—a Democratic candidate running against a Republican.*

two-piece *adj.* having two parts: *He wears two-piece suits, a coat with trousers.*

two-sided *adj.* **1** having two aspects: *The issue of raising taxes is two-sided.* **2** covered on both sides: *The printing on that brochure is two-sided, both back and front.*

two-timer *n.infrml.fig.* an adulterer, a person who commits to one person while seeing another: *That guy is a two-timer who cheats on his wife.*

two-tone *adj.* having two colors: *He wears two-tone shoes in the summer, white with black trim.*

two-way street *n.fig.* a situation that affects both parties or requires mutual cooperation: *Business is a two-way street where both the buyer and seller must feel satisfied.*

ty·coon /taɪ'kun/ *n.* a businessperson of great wealth and power: *He is a tycoon who owns steel mills, a shipyard, and other businesses.*

tyke /taɪk/ *n.infrml.* a small child: *Little tykes play in kindergarten.*

tym·pa·num /'tɪmpənəm/ *n.frml.* **-nums, -na** the eardrum: *The tympanum of his right ear was pierced in an accident.*

type /taɪp/ *v.* **typed, typing, types** **1** to write on a typewriter, computer keyboard, etc.: *She types letters and memos on a computer.* **2** to characterize by category: *Zoologists typed that animal as a mammal.* **3** to typecast
—*n.* **1** [C] a category, characterization: *That type of steel is very strong.* **2** [U] a typeface: *That manuscript is now set in type.* **3** [C] personality: *He is the strong, silent type.*

type·cast /'taɪp,kæst/ *v.* **-cast, -casting, -casts** (in films, plays, etc.) to give an actor or actress roles according to their appearance and personality: *The actor with the mean look was typecast as a gangster.*

type·face /'taɪp,feɪs/ *n.* [C] the style of a group of characters of the alphabet and other symbols: *Times Roman is a commonly used typeface.*

type·set /'taɪp,sɛt/ *v.* **-set, -setting, -sets** to put written material into type, to input into a typesetting machine: *He typesets his own material on a desktop publishing computer.*
—*adj.* set in type: *His manuscript is now being typeset by the publisher.*

type·writ·er /'taɪp,raɪtər/ *n.* a manual or electric machine used to print words in type: *Since he bought a computer, his old typewriter sits in the closet.*

T

ty·phoid /ˈtaɪˌfɔɪd/ or **typhoid fever** *n.* [U] a highly infectious disease with high fever, intestinal inflammation, and rash caused by food or water contaminated with bacteria: *Typhoid fever is still a great health threat.*

ty·phoon /taɪˈfun/ *n.* a hurricane or cyclone in Asia: *Typhoons are so powerful that they sink ships.*

typ·i·cal /ˈtɪpɪkəl/ *adj.* characteristic, representative: *The high quality of that machine is typical of all of that company's products.‖Behaving like a jerk is typical of my horrible brother-in-law.* -*adv.* **typically.**

typ·i·fy /ˈtɪpəˌfaɪ/ *v.* **-fied, -fying, -fies** to characterize, represent: *The speed of that computer typifies that of others like it.*

typ·ist /ˈtaɪpɪst/ *n.* a person who types: *He works part-time as a typist in a computer office.*

ty·po /ˈtaɪpoʊ/ *n.* **-pos** *short for* a typographical error: *The word "teh" has a typo in it as it should be "the."*

ty·pog·ra·pher /taɪˈpɑgrəfər/ *n.* **1** a person who sets type: *He is a typographer who inputs manuscript.* **2** a designer of type: *Most typographers are also artists.*

ty·pog·ra·phy /taɪˈpɑgrəfi/ *n.* [U] the art and craft of designing type: *Typography has evolved into nine general families of type.*

ty·pol·o·gy /taɪˈpɑlədʒi/ *n.* [U] the science of types or categories: *Social workers use typology to classify their clients' needs.*

tyr·an·ny /ˈtɪrəni/ *n.* **-nies** [C;U] **1** a dictatorship enforced by power and terror: *Tyranny ended in that country with the assassination of its tyrant.* **2** a condition or act of tyranny: *It was an act of tyranny when the dictator canceled free elections.* -*v.* **tyrannize.**

ty·rant /ˈtaɪrənt/ *n.* a dictator who uses terror and a police state to enforce a regime: *The tyrant and his wife were shot after a short trial by revolutionaries.* -*adj.* **tyrannical** /təˈrænəkəl, taɪ-/.

tzar /zɑr, tsɑr/ *n.* *var. of* tsar

T

U,u

U, u /yu/ *n*. **U's, u's** or **Us, us** **1** the 21st letter of the English alphabet **2** s.t. shaped like a *U* See: U-turn.

u·biq·ui·tous /yu'bɪkwətəs/ *adj.frml.* everywhere, found all over: *Pine trees are ubiquitous in North America; they grow everywhere.* *-n.* [U] **ubiquity.**

ud·der /'ʌdər/ *n*. the milk-producing organ of a cow: *A milk cow has a large udder.*

UFO /,yuɛf'oʊ/ *n*. **UFO's** *abbr. for* Unidentified Flying Object, a space vehicle from another planet: *People often mistake shooting stars for UFO's.*

ugh /ʌg, ʊx/ *exclam.* used to express disgust: *Ugh! This room is a mess!*

ug·ly /'ʌgli/ *adj*. **-lier, -liest 1** offensive to see, *(syn.)* repulsive: *His face was burned in a fire, and the scars are ugly.* **2** unpleasant, upsetting: *Two men shouted at each other and made an ugly scene. -n.* [U] **ugliness.**

uh-huh /ə'hʌ/ *adv. slang* yes, indeed: *I asked if she would like to go to dinner, and she said, "Uh-huh!" See:* yes, USAGE NOTE.

u·ku·le·le /,yukə'leɪli/ *n*. a four-stringed musical instrument that looks like a small guitar: *A singer plays his ukulele while singing Hawaiian songs.*

ul·cer /'ʌlsər/ *n*. a break in the skin or inside the body that may bleed and hurt, a sore: *Spicy food hurt his stomach ulcer. -adj.* **ulcerous.**

ul·cer·ate /'ʌlsə,reɪt/ *v*. **-ated, -ating, -ates** to form an ulcer: *His stomach has ulcerated. -n.* **ulceration** /,ʌlsə'reɪʃən/.

ul·te·ri·or /ʌl'tɪriər/ *adj*. hidden for a reason: *She has an ulterior motive for visiting her parents: she wants to move back in with them.*

ul·ti·mate /'ʌltəmɪt/ *adj*. **1** last, highest: *The ultimate responsibility for this project belongs to the boss.* **2** most basic, fundamental: *The ultimate proof of his guilt was that s.o. actually saw him steal the money.* **3** greatest, most costly: *The soldier made the ultimate sacrifice by dying for her country.*

—n. an extreme of any kind (best, worst, etc.): *A Rolls Royce is the ultimate in expensive cars.*

ul·ti·mate·ly /'ʌltəmɪtli/ *adv*. in the end: *Ultimately, the war had to end; it cost too much in both lives and dollars.*

ul·ti·ma·tum /,ʌltə'meɪtəm/ *n*. [C] a final demand that s.t. be done (usu. made with a threat of punishment): *She gave an ultimatum that either he stop drinking or she would leave.*

ultra- /'ʌltrə/ *prefix* **1** beyond the normal or usual: *That special telephone wire is ultrathin.* **2** very much, exceedingly (used esp. in politics): *Political extremists can be ultraconservative or ultraliberal.*

ul·tra·con·ser·va·tive /,ʌltrəkən'sɜrvətɪv/ *adj*. describing a person's beliefs as on the far right politically or as orthodox in religion *—n*. a person who is ultraconservative: *The Senator's promise to run government like a business made her popular with ultraconservatives.*

ul·tra·lib·er·al /,ʌltrə'lɪbərəl, -'lɪbrəl/ *adj*. describing a person's beliefs as on the far left politically or as reform-minded in religion *—n*. a person who is ultraliberal: *The elders of the church thought the young preacher was an ultraliberal.*

ul·tra·son·ic /,ʌltrə'sanɪk/ *adj*. related to sound beyond the range of human hearing; i.e., above 16 to 20 kilohertz: *She used an ultrasonic whistle to call her dog.*

ul·tra·sound /'ʌltrə,saund/ *n*. (in medicine) a procedure involving a machine that uses waves to show internal body organs: *The doctor did an ultrasound to see if the woman's heart was OK.*

um·bil·i·cal cord /ʌm'bɪlɪkəl/ *n*. the tube connecting an unborn baby to its mother: *Unborn babies are fed through the umbilical cord.*

um·brel·la /ʌm'brɛlə/ *n*. a foldable covering made of fabric on a han-

umbrella

dle used for protection above the head against rain and bright sunlight: *She opens her umbrella when it rains.*

um·pire /'ʌmˌpaɪr/ *n.* a sports referee, judge: *An umpire stands behind the catcher in baseball. See:* referee.

ump·teen /'ʌmpˌtin/ *adj.infrml.* very many of s.t., countless: *We have umpteen thousand of those useless products in our warehouses, and we've had umpteen for years.*

U.N. /ˌyuˈɛn/ *n.abbr.* the United Nations: *The U.N. funds many projects for peace throughout the world.*

un·a·bashed /ˌʌnəˈbæʃt/ *adj.frml.* **1** unintimidated, calm in the face of embarrassment or defeat: *The dancer tripped but appeared unabashed.* **2** obvious, undisguised: *To his unabashed delight, his competitor went bankrupt.* -*adv.* **unabashedly** /ˌʌnəˈbæʃɪdli/.

un·a·bat·ed /ˌʌnəˈbeɪtɪd/ *adj.* without stop: *Despite difficulties, the work continues unabated; we must finish by Tuesday.*

un·a·ble /ʌnˈeɪbəl/ *adj.* **1** not able, incapable: *He is unable to walk because of a bad ankle.* **2** not skilled, incompetent: *He is unable to do the job for lack of experience.*

un·a·bridged /ˌʌnəˈbrɪdʒd/ *adj.* not made shorter, complete: *Unabridged dictionaries are very large.*

un·ac·cept·a·ble /ˌʌnɪkˈsɛptəbəl/ *adj.* **1** not acceptable because s.t. is offensive or bad: *That student's bad behavior in class is unacceptable.* **2** not acceptable because s.t. is incorrect or wrong: *That report is unacceptable because it has mistakes in it.* -*adv.* **unacceptably.**

un·ac·com·pa·nied /ˌʌnəˈkʌmpənɪd, -ˈkʌmpnɪd/ *adj.* alone, without s.o. else: *He went to a party unaccompanied.*

un·ac·com·plished /ˌʌnəˈkɑmplɪʃt/ *adj.* without proven success: *He is an unaccomplished writer with nothing published.*

un·ac·count·a·ble /ˌʌnəˈkaʊntəbəl/ *adj.* **1** not responsible, esp. for one's actions: *He is a troublemaker who believes that he is unaccountable to others.* **2** not accounted for: *There were unaccountable losses of money during the weeks she worked at the cash register.* -*adv.* **unaccountably.**

un·ac·cus·tomed /ˌʌnəˈkʌstəmd/ *adj.* not used to: *People from the tropics are unaccustomed to cold winters.*

un·a·dorned /ˌʌnəˈdɔrnd/ *adj.frml.* **1** plain, without decoration: *That room unadorned with pictures or curtains looks bare.* **2** simple, plain: *The unadorned truth is sometimes difficult to hear.*

un·a·dul·ter·at·ed /ˌʌnəˈdʌltəˌreɪtɪd/ *adj.frml.* not containing unwanted substances, pure: *That hamburger is made of 100% delicious, government-inspected, unadulterated beef.*

un·af·fect·ed /ˌʌnəˈfɛktɪd/ *adj.* **1** not influenced by s.t., intact: *The economy is unaffected by recent bank failures.* **2** natural, without fancy manners: *Although he is an important person, he has an unaffected way of behaving.*

un·af·ford·a·ble /ˌʌnəˈfɔrdəbəl/ *adj.* too expensive: *Houses in that fancy neighborhood are unaffordable for most people.*

un·a·fraid /ˌʌnəˈfreɪd/ *adj.* not afraid, fearless: *She is a skier who is unafraid of danger.*

un·al·ien·a·ble /ʌnˈeɪlyənəbəl, -ˈeɪliənə-/ *adj.* not capable of being taken away, permanent: *In America, people have unalienable rights under the Constitution, such as freedom of speech.*

un·al·ter·a·ble /ʌnˈɔltərəbəl/ *adj.* not capable of being changed, (*syn.*) inalterable: *Once a contract is signed, it becomes unalterable.* -*adv.* **unalterably.**

un·am·big·u·ous /ˌʌnæmˈbɪgyuəs/ *adj.* clear, without doubt: *The law is unambiguous: if you steal, you go to jail.* -*adv.* **unambiguously.**

un-A·mer·i·can /ˌʌnəˈmɛrɪkən/ *adj.* against or offensive to ideals held in the USA: *In the USA, people are sometimes seen as unAmerican if they burn the American flag.*

u·na·nim·i·ty /ˌyunəˈnɪməti/ *n.* [U] complete agreement, unity: *Since members of the committee always argue and disagree, there is never a unanimity of opinion.*

u·nan·i·mous /yuˈnænəməs/ *adj.* completely in agreement: *Everyone on the committee agreed in a unanimous decision.* -*adv.* **unanimously.**

un·an·swer·a·ble /ʌnˈænsərəbəl/ *adj.* not capable of being answered: *How the man died is unanswerable; no one saw him die.*

un·an·tic·i·pat·ed /ˌʌnænˈtɪsəˌpeɪtɪd/ *adj.* not expected, (*syn.*) unforeseen: *Unanticipated expenses can occur when you travel.*

un·ap·peal·ing /ˌʌnəˈpilɪŋ/ *adj.* **1** not attractive, uninteresting: *Dull movies are unappealing.* **2** unpleasant, distasteful: *Worn furniture (bad behavior, dirty surroundings, etc.) is unappealing.* -*adv.* **unappealingly.**

un·ap·pe·tiz·ing /ʌnˈæpəˌtaɪzɪŋ/ *adj.* not appealing to taste, (*syn.*) unsavory: *Burned toast and greasy eggs are unappetizing.*

un·ap·proach·a·ble /ˌʌnəˈproʊtʃəbəl/ *adj.* unfriendly, (*syn.*) intimidating: *That strict professor's unapproachable; his students are afraid to ask him questions.*

un·ap·pro·pri·at·ed /ˌʌnəˈproʊpriˌeɪtɪd/ *adj.* not yet made available: *Funds are as yet unappropriated for the government project; there is no money for it yet.*

un·armed /ʌnˈɑrmd/ *adj.* without a weapon: *Unarmed civilians were helpless in the war.*

un·as·sist·ed /ˌʌnəˈsɪstɪd/ *adj.* alone, without help: *He was hurt but able to go to the hospital unassisted.*

un·as·sum·ing /ˌʌnəˈsumɪŋ/ *adj.* quiet, modest, (*syn.*) unpretentious: *She is an unassuming person with a soft voice.* -*adv.* **unassumingly.**

un·at·tached /ˌʌnəˈtæʧt/ *adj.* **1** single, not married or engaged: *He is unattached now but was married before.* **2** not fastened or connected: *We could not hear the stereo because the speakers were unattached.*

un·a·vail·ing /ˌʌnəˈveɪlɪŋ/ *adj.frml.* without success, (*syn.*) futile: *My requests for information were unanswered, and unavailing.*

un·a·void·a·ble /ˌʌnəˈvɔɪdəbəl/ *adj.* that which cannot be avoided, (*syns.*) inescapable, inevitable: *Pain is unavoidable when you are having surgery.* -*adv.* **unavoidably.**

un·a·ware /ˌʌnəˈwɛr/ *adj.* **1** uninformed, not notified: *He was unaware that the meeting was this morning; no one told him.* **2** not to see or know s.t., (*syn.*) oblivious: *He is unaware of what is happening right in front of him.*

un·a·wares /ˌʌnəˈwɛrz/ *adv.* without warning, by surprise: *She was caught unawares (by a sudden event).*

un·bal·anced /ʌnˈbælənst/ *adj.* **1** unstable, unsteady: *An object or person becomes unbalanced and falls.* **2** crazy or eccentric: *She is unbalanced and does strange things.*

un·bear·a·ble /ʌnˈbɛrəbəl/ *adj.* not bearable, intolerable: *The ocean water is so cold that it is unbearable for swimming now.* -*adv.* **unbearably.**

un·beat·a·ble /ʌnˈbitəbəl/ *adj.* **1** not capable of being beaten or overcome, (*syn.*) invincible: *He is an unbeatable opponent.* **2** excellent, beyond compare: *We got an unbeatable bargain (opportunity, offer, etc.) in buying a new TV on sale.*

un·beat·en /ʌnˈbitn/ *adj.* without a loss: *Our school has an unbeaten football team.*

un·be·com·ing /ˌʌnbiˈkʌmɪŋ/ *adj.* unsuitable, not flattering: *She is wearing an unbecoming dress.* -*adv.* **unbecomingly.**

un·be·liev·a·ble /ˌʌnbiˈlivəbəl/ *adj.* **1** false, not worthy of belief, (*syn.*) incredible: *That story (explanation, statement, etc.) is unbelievable.* **2** *fig.* fantastic, wonderful: *We had an unbelievable opportunity to go on a vacation to Rio.* -*adv.* **unbelievably.**

un·bend /ʌnˈbɛnd/ *v.* **-bent** /ˈbɛnt/ , **-bending, -bends** **1** to straighten: *A branch unbends when the heavy snow melts from it.* **2** to relax, to become less formal: *He has learned to unbend a little in dealing with others and is more friendly.* See: unbending.

un·bend·ing /ʌnˈbɛndɪŋ/ *adj.* stubborn, unwilling to change one's mind: *She has an unbending attitude and will not stop drinking.*

un·bi·ased /ʌnˈbaɪəst/ *adj.* not biased or prejudiced, neutral: *His unbiased attitude toward all people made him a fair judge.*

un·born /ʌnˈbɔrn/ *adj.* not yet in existence, still inside the mother: *Unborn children are fed through the umbilical cord.*

un·bound /ʌnˈbaʊnd/ *adj.* **1** without ropes, chains, etc.: *Prisoners were tied with ropes, then released unbound.* **2** *frml.* not obligated, not required: *He was unbound by the contract to work on weekends.*

un·bound·ed /ʌnˈbaʊndɪd/ *adj.* without limit, extensive: *She had an unbounded ability to make money.*

un·bri·dled /ʌnˈbraɪdld/ *adj.* without limit, uncontrolled: *He has unbridled greed (lust, anger, etc.).*

un·buck·le /ʌnˈbʌkəl/ *v.* **-led, -ling, -les** to unfasten a buckle: *He unbuckled his seat belt when the plane landed.*

un·bur·den /ʌnˈbɜrdn/ *v.* **1** to remove a burden, unload: *He unburdened a camel of its load.* **2** to release emotions: *She unburdened herself by telling her troubles to a friend.*

un·but·ton /ʌnˈbʌtn/ *v.* to undo buttons: *He unbuttoned his shirt and took it off.*

un·called-for /ʌnˈkɔld,fɔr/ *adj.* offensive, not polite: *At a party, a man made some rude remarks that were uncalled-for.*

un·can·ny /ʌnˈkæni/ *adj.* extraordinary, remarkable: *She has an uncanny ability to remember the exact dates when things happen.* -*adv.* **uncannily.**

un·cared-for /ʌnˈkɛrd,fɔr/ *adj.* not cared for, (*syn.*) neglected: *Some children are uncared-for and left hungry.*

un·car·ing /ʌnˈkɛrɪŋ/ *adj.* not interested, insensitive: *The uncaring son did not visit his sick mother.*

un·ceas·ing /ʌnˈsisɪŋ/ *adj.* without stop, continuous: *She makes an unceasing effort to help others.* -*adv.* **unceasingly.**

un·cer·e·mo·ni·ous·ly /ˌʌnsɛrəˈmoʊniəsli/ *adv.* rudely, abruptly: *The homeless man was thrown out of a restaurant unceremoniously.*

un·cer·tain /ʌnˈsɜrtn/ *adj.* doubtful, unsure: *He has been out of work for a year; his future is uncertain.* -*adv.* **uncertainly;** -*n.* [C;U] **uncertainty.**

U

un·chang·ing /ʌnˈʧeɪndʒɪŋ/ *adj.* constant, without change: *It rains every morning; the weather seems unchanging here.*

un·char·i·ta·ble /ʌnˈʧærətəbəl/ *adj.* unkind, critical: *He made uncharitable remarks about the ball player's ability.* -*adv.* **uncharitably.**

un·chart·ed /ʌnˈʧɑrtɪd/ *adj.* unknown, not mapped: *In the 1500s, the explorer Vasco da Gama sailed in uncharted seas.*

un·checked /ʌnˈtʃɛkt/ *adj.* not stopped, (*syn.*) unrestrained: *Stealing from the store went unchecked until they hired a guard.*

un·civ·i·lized /ʌnˈsɪvəˌlaɪzd/ *adj.* **1** without comforts, (*syn.*) primitive: *They lived in an uncivilized place without electricity or plumbing.* **2** lacking in good manners, wild: *The uncivilized guest chewed with his mouth open.*

un·clasp /ʌnˈklæsp/ *v.* to unfasten a clasp: *She unclasped the metal bracelet on her wrist.*

un·clas·si·fied /ʌnˈklæsəˌfaɪd/ *adj.* not confidential or secret: *The military gave unclassified information to the newspapers.*

un·cle /ˈʌŋkəl/ *n.* **1** one's mother's or father's brother: *My uncle John came over to visit.* **2 to say "uncle":** to surrender: *Two boys wrestled until one of them gave up and said "uncle."*

un·clean /ʌnˈklin/ *adj.* **1** dirty, soiled: *The floors (clothes, people, etc.) are unclean; they haven't been washed.* **2** morally impure: *The young man confessed to having unclean thoughts.*

un·clear /ʌnˈklɪr/ *adj.* **1** poorly said or written, not clear: *Unclear writing is difficult to understand.* **2** doubtful, uncertain: *It is unclear whether the economy will get better.*

Uncle Sam /sæm/ *n.* a nickname for the U.S. government: *We pay our taxes every year to Uncle Sam.*

Uncle Sam

un·clut·tered /ʌnˈklʌtərd/ *adj.* neat, clear: *Her uncluttered desk made her look organized.*

un·com·fort·a·ble /ʌnˈkʌmftəbəl, -fərtəbəl/ *adj.* **1** feeling pain or discomfort: *She feels uncomfortable sitting on a hard chair in a hot room.* **2** causing pain or discomfort: *That hard chair is uncomfortable.* **3** bothered, worried: *He feels uncomfortable spending so much money for a vacation.* -*adv.* **uncomfortably.**

un·com·mit·ted /ˌʌnkəˈmɪtɪd/ *adj.* **1** undecided, related to people who have not made up their minds: *The politician's vote on that law is still uncommitted.* **2** not willing to say yes, wavering: *The young man is uncommitted to marrying his girlfriend.*

un·com·mon /ʌnˈkɑmən/ *adj.* **1** unusual, not commonly found or experienced: *Those birds are uncommon in this area.* **2** extraordinary, excellent: *That is uncommon coffee; it tastes great!* -*adv.* **uncommonly.**

un·com·mu·ni·ca·tive /ˌʌnkəˈmyunɪkətɪv, -ˌkeɪtɪv/ *adj.* silent, unresponsive: *I asked him many times for an answer, but he is uncommunicative.*

un·com·pli·cat·ed /ʌnˈkɑmplɪˌkeɪtɪd/ *adj.* not difficult, simple: *That job application is uncomplicated, just one page of short questions.*

un·com·pli·men·ta·ry /ˌʌnkɑmpləˈmɛntəri, -tri/ *adj.* unflattering, nasty: *He made uncomplimentary remarks about her dress being out of style.*

un·com·pro·mis·ing /ʌnˈkɑmprəˌmaɪzɪŋ/ *adj.* not willing to cooperate, unbending, (*syn.*) stubborn: *He is uncompromising in his business dealings.* -*adv.* **uncompromisingly.**

un·con·cerned /ˌʌnkənˈsɜrnd/ *adj.* **1** unbothered, uninterested, (*syn.*) indifferent: *He is unconcerned about his losses.* **2** uncaring, (*syn.*) apathetic: *She is unconcerned for the poor.* **3** not a party to s.t., uninvolved: *He was an unconcerned party, so both sides trusted him.* -*n.* [U] **unconcern;** -*adv.* **unconcernedly** /ˌʌnkənˈsɜrnɪdli/.

un·con·di·tion·al /ˌʌnkənˈdɪʃənəl/ *adj.* without conditions or terms: *The general demanded unconditional surrender from the defeated enemy.* -*adv.* **unconditionally.**

unconditional guarantee *n.* a promise made by a business to its customers of complete satisfaction with its product or service: *Our company gives an unconditional guarantee of satisfaction with our products or we will replace the item at no charge.*

un·con·for·mi·ty /ˌʌnkənˈfɔrməti/ *n.* [U] **1** not fitting a normal requirement, such as one's behavior or lifestyle within ordinary society: *The unconformity of her lifestyle gave her the appearance of being a rebel.* **2** lack of conformity to standards or regulations: *His unconformity in dressing caused him to be fired by the law firm.*

un·con·nect·ed /ˌʌnkəˈnɛktɪd/ *adj.* **1** not connected, not attached: *The electric plug was unconnected, so the machine did not run.* **2** not related: *Although they seemed similar, the two crimes were unconnected.*

un·con·quer·a·ble /ʌnˈkɑŋkərəbəl/ *adj.* invincible, not capable of being overcome or depleted: *Howard decided to see a psychologist because he felt that some of his psychological concerns were unconquerable on his own.*

un·con·scion·a·ble /ʌnˈkɑnʃənəbəl/ *adj.frml.* immoral, unethical and therefore shocking, (*syn.*) indefensible: *Murder is an unconscionable act.* -*adv.* **unconscionably.**

un·con·scious /ʌnˈkɑnʃəs/ *adj.* **1** senseless, knocked out: *He was knocked unconscious by a blow on the head.* **2** unaware, not conscious of some event: *He was unconscious of the fact the bill was not paid because the check was lost.* **3** unthinking, without conscious thought, (*syn.*) involuntary: *He hurt his attacker in an unconscious act of self-defense.* -*adv.* **unconsciously;** -*n.* [U] **unconsciousness.**

un·con·sid·ered /ˌʌnkənˈsɪdərd/ *adj.* **1** not thought about, (*syn.*) offhand: *In my unconsid-*

ered opinion, that is the wrong thing to do. **2** ill-considered, reckless: *His remarks were un-considered—stupid, in fact.*

un·con·sti·tu·tion·al /ˌʌnkɑnstɪ'tuʃənəl, -ʃnəl/ *adj.* (in law) found to be against the Constitution (of the United States, any organization with a constitution): *The Supreme Court decided that the law is unconstitutional.* -*n.* |U| **unconstitutionality;** -*adv.* **unconstitutionally.**

un·con·trol·la·ble /ˌʌnkən'troʊləbəl/ *adj.* not capable of being controlled, out of control: *The budget for the city is uncontrollable because there are too many unknown expenses.* -*adv.* **uncontrollably.**

un·con·trolled /ˌʌnkən'troʊld/ *adj.* **1** not controlled, (*syn.*) unchecked: *Their heavy spending was uncontrolled.* **2** unregulated, not stopped, such as by the government: *Uncontrolled practices in the banking industry (securities business, real estate industries, etc.) lead to bankruptcies.*

un·con·ven·tion·al /ˌʌnkən'vɛnʃənəl/ *adj.* **1** outside common practice or behavior, (*syns.*) peculiar, eccentric: *Her unconventional behavior shocks people.* **2** original, not thought before: *She found an unconventional but excellent solution to the problem.* -*n.* [U] **unconventionality;** -*adv.* **unconventionally.**

un·cool /ʌn'kul/ *adj.slang* **1** unacceptable and usu. embarrassing: *He poured beer over everyone, which was an uncool thing to do.* **2** socially awkward: *His inability to talk to women made him appear uncool.*

un·cork /ʌn'kɔrk/ *v.* to remove the cork: *She uncorked a bottle of wine.*

un·count·ed /ʌn'kaʊntɪd/ *adj.* **1** not counted: *Today's money from the store is still uncounted; please count it for me now.* **2** limitless, uncountable: *There are uncounted millions of people who can vote but don't.*

un·cou·ple /ʌn'kʌpəl/ *v.* **-pled, -pling, -ples** to pull apart, to unlock, separate: *A worker uncoupled two railroad cars and one rolled away.*

un·couth /ʌn'kuθ/ *adj.* ill-mannered, foul-mouthed, (*syn.*) crude: *That uncouth man uses dirty language all the time.* -*adv.* **uncouthly.**

un·cov·ered /ʌn'kʌvərd/ *adj.* **1** without a covering: *She became uncovered while asleep.* **2** without having money available: *Their loan (bet, proposition, etc.) is uncovered.* **3** discovered, removed from hiding: *The swindler uncovered by the detective was put in jail.*

unc·tu·ous /'ʌŋktʃuəs/ *adj.* **1** *frml.* oily **2** *fig.* speaking smoothly, esp. showing interest but not really meaning it: *The unctuous employee tried to gain favor by asking to see his boss's vacation pictures.* -*n.* [U] **unction, unctuousness;** -*adv.* **unctuously.**

un·cut /ʌn'kʌt/ *adj.* **1** whole, without being sliced: *I bought an uncut loaf of bread, then sliced it.* **2** unedited, unabridged: *The uncut version of that novel (film, literary work, etc.) was too long and boring.*

un·daunt·ed /ʌn'dɔntɪd/ *adj.* determined, not frightened: *He moved ahead undaunted by obstacles.* -*adv.* **undauntedly.**

un·de·cid·ed /ˌʌndɪ'saɪdɪd/ *adj.* not decided, still under consideration: *She is undecided as to where she wants to go on vacation.*

un·de·mon·stra·tive /ˌʌndɪ'mɑnstrətɪv/ *adj.* unresponsive, not showing emotion: *I thought he didn't like me, but he is just undemonstrative; he has trouble showing affection.*

un·de·ni·a·ble /ˌʌndɪ'naɪəbəl/ *adj.* not capable of being disputed, absolute: *When you have no money, it is an undeniable truth that you can't buy things.* -*adv.* **undeniably.**

un·der /'ʌndər/ *prep.* **1** beneath, below: *Roots are under the soil.* **2** directed by: *Those employees are under her management (control, direction).* **3** less than: *He is under the legal age (to drink alcohol, to vote, etc.).* **4 under consideration:** being evaluated: *The buyer has the proposal under consideration and will decide tomorrow.* **5 under control:** in control, being managed: *The fire is under control now and is not spreading.* **6 under cultivation:** planted with food crops: *He is a wheat farmer who has large fields under cultivation.* **7 under discussion:** being discussed and evaluated: *The new project is under discussion now.* **8** *fam.fig.* **under s.o.'s thumb:** under s.o.'s complete control: *He is a bossy manager who has his employees under his thumb.* **9 under present circumstances:** considering the present situation: *Under present circumstances, namely that our sales are strong, we should expand our sales force.* **10 under the cover of darkness:** during the night: *The enemy force advanced under the cover of darkness.* **11** *infrml.fig.* **under the gun:** related to s.o. who is experiencing pressure, usu. involving a time deadline: *He is under the gun to finish the report or possibly be punished.* **12 under the heading of:** categorized as: *That statement comes under the heading of "The Latest News" (pure nonsense, biology, etc.).* **13 under the influence of:** controlled by s.t., such as a drug or another person: *She was caught driving under the influence of alcohol.* **14 under the name of:** to be known by or as: *That company goes under the name of Imperial Computers, Ltd.* **15 under the threat of:** in danger of: *He is under the threat of deportation if found guilty of a crime.* **16** *infrml.fig.* **under your hat:** secret: *Keep this under your hat—the business is about to be sold.*
—*adv. See:* go under.

U

un·der·a·chiev·er /ˌʌndərə'tʃivər/ *n.* a person who does not try his or her best: *The child is quite intelligent but receives poor grades in school; he is an underachiever.*

un·der·age /ˌʌndər'eɪdʒ/ *adj.* describing a person who is below the legal age for some purpose: *Anyone below the age of 21 is underage and cannot drink alcohol in this state.*

un·der·arm /'ʌndər,ɑrm/ *n.adj.* the armpit: *He uses an <adj.> underarm deodorant so that his armpits don't smell.*

un·der·bel·ly /'ʌndər,bɛli/ *n.* **-lies** the lower part of the stomach: *The underbelly of a reptile is soft and not protected.*

un·der·bid /ˌʌndər'bɪd/ *v.* **-bid, -bidding, -bids** to offer s.t. at a cost lower than others: *Our company underbid other companies and won the contract for printing.*

un·der·brush /'ʌndər,brʌʃ/ *n.* [U] plant growth close to the ground: *The thick underbrush in a forest makes walking difficult.*

un·der·car·riage /'ʌndər,kærɪdʒ/ *n.* the beams of steel located under a vehicle: *That car has an undercarriage in the shape of an "H."*

un·der·class /'ʌndər,klæs/ *n.* **-classes** the lowest class of people in a society: *The poor are an underclass who cannot escape poverty.*

USAGE NOTE: American society does not have clear social class distinctions; most people consider themselves to be *working, middle,* or *upper-middle class.* The *underclass* are people below the working class, who for many reasons have trouble finding work and who often rely on help from the government to survive.

---

un·der·class·man /'ʌndər,klæsmən/ *n.* **-men** /-mən/ a male or female student in freshman or sophomore year of high school or college: *Those underclassmen will graduate in a few years.*

un·der·coat /'ʌndər,koʊt/ *n.* [U] a first layer of paint: *He applied an undercoat on the walls, then painted a topcoat over it.*

un·der·coat·ing /'ʌndər,koʊtɪŋ/ *n.* [U] a layer of paint applied to the underside of a car to prevent rust: *She always buys cars with undercoating.*

un·der·cov·er /ˌʌndər'kʌvər/ *adj.* disguised, referring to a spy or police dressed as an ordinary person: *Two undercover police officers, dressed in jeans, arrested a drug dealer.*

un·der·cur·rent /'ʌndər,kərənt, -,kʌr-/ *n.* [U] **1** a flow of water beneath the surface: *The river has a strong undercurrent.* **2** a wave of hidden emotion: *An undercurrent of fear ran among the employees when they heard the business might close.*

un·der·cut /ˌʌndər'kʌt/ *v.* **-cut, -cutting, -cuts** to offer goods at a lower price than s.o. else: *That drugstore undercuts its competitors by*

selling at 20 percent cheaper than its competitors do.

un·der·de·vel·oped /ˌʌndərdɪ'vɛləpt/ *adj.* **1** not fully matured: *He has an underdeveloped sense of right and wrong; he has no conscience.* **2** not developed economically: *Two underdeveloped countries worked together to improve their economies.* -n. [U] **underdevelopment.** *See.* developing.

USAGE NOTE: Instead of using *underdeveloped* to describe poorer nations, many people use the term *developing.* A *developing nation* is a country that is becoming economically stronger and more competitive on the world market.

---

un·der·dog /'ʌndər,dɔg/ *n.* a person or team with little chance of winning, esp. in sports competition; the weaker competitor: *Our team was the underdog in the basketball game, but we won.*

un·der·done /ˌʌndər'dʌn/ *adj.* not cooked enough: *The steak was underdone and was very red. See:* rare.

un·der·em·ployed /ˌʌndərɪm'plɔɪd/ *adj.* related to people who are forced to work below their abilities: *She is a former schoolteacher who works as a sales clerk and is underemployed.*

un·der·es·ti·mate /ˌʌndər'ɛstə,meɪt/ *v.* **-mated, -mating, -mates 1** to guess too low at the cost of s.t.: *He underestimated the cost of a vacation (product, construction job, etc.) and ran out of money.* **2** to guess wrong about a person's abilities: *Don't underestimate him, for he is determined to succeed.* -n. [U] **underestimation.**

un·der·foot /ˌʌndər'fʊt/ *adv.* **1** under one's feet: *It snowed, so it is slippery underfoot.* **2** in the way: *The children's toys are always underfoot.*

un·der·gar·ment /'ʌndər,gɑrmənt/ *n.frml.* [C] an item of underwear (undershorts, panties): *They wear undergarments beneath their clothes.*

un·der·go /ˌʌndər'goʊ/ *v.* **-went** /-'wɛnt/ , **-gone** /-'gɔn, -'gɑn/ , **-going, -goes 1** to experience: *He will undergo an operation to remove his appendix.* **2** to suffer, bear: *In order to get the job, she had to undergo five tests and an interview.*

un·der·grad·u·ate /ˌʌndər'grædʒuɪt/ *n.* a student in any of the first four years of college: *She is an undergraduate at the state university.* —*adj.* related to that level of college education: *She is taking undergraduate courses in English.*

un·der·ground /'ʌndər,graʊnd/ *adj.* [U] **1** located below the earth's surface: *We drove our car into an underground parking garage.* **2** re-

lating to a secret or hidden organization: *They had an underground plot to assassinate the president.*
—*adv.* /ˌʌndər'graʊnd/ below the surface of the earth
—*n.* /'ʌndər,graʊnd/ a secret, hidden organization: *Members of the underground want to change the government.*

un·der·growth /'ʌndər,groʊθ/ *n.* [U] short plants growing under trees: *The undergrowth in that forest is very thick.*

un·der·hand /'ʌndər,hænd/ *adj.* relating to an upward swinging motion of the arm: *In softball, the pitcher throws underhand pitches.*

un·der·hand·ed /ˌʌndər'hændɪd/ *adj.* tricky, cheating esp. in a secret way: *He has an underhanded scheme to cheat her out of her savings.* -*adv.* **underhandedly.**

un·der·lie /ˌʌndər'laɪ/ *v.* -**lay** /-'leɪ/ , -**lain** /-'leɪn/ , -**lying, -lies** to be beneath the surface, esp. in reasoning: *Many reasons, including low pay, underlie her thinking about finding a new job.*

un·der·line /'ʌndər,laɪn, ˌʌndər'laɪn/ *v.* -**lined, -lining, -lines** **1** to draw a line under s.t.: *He underlined words in his book with a pen.* **2** *fig.*to emphasize, to show the importance of s.t.: *The boss underlined the necessity to cut costs.*

un·der·ling /'ʌndərlɪŋ/ *n. pej.* an unimportant person, esp. working for an important one, (*syn.*) subordinate: *The king arrived with all of his underlings.*

un·der·ly·ing /'ʌndər,laɪ ɪŋ, ˌʌndər'laɪ ɪŋ/ *adj.* **1** supporting: *A need for money was underlying her decision to look for a new job.* **2** located beneath: *The ground underlying the building is too soft.*

un·der·mine /ˌʌndər'maɪn, 'ʌndər,maɪn/ *v.* -**mined, -mining, -mines** to ruin the efforts of s.o., (*syn.*) to sabotage: *She undermined her health by smoking cigarettes.*

un·der·neath /ˌʌndər'niθ/ *prep.* below: *That cave is underneath the ground.*

un·der·nour·ished /ˌʌndər'nɜrɪʃt, -'nʌr-/ *adj.* starved, fed with inferior food: *Undernourished children do not grow properly. -n.* [U] **undernourishment.**

un·der·pants /'ʌndər,pænts/ *n.pl.* men's undershorts or women's panties: *He wears cotton underpants. See:* boxer shorts.

un·der·pass /'ʌndər,pæs/ *n.* -**passes** a roadway that passes under another road or structure: *An underpass runs under the highway.*

un·der·pin·ning /'ʌndər,pɪnɪŋ/ *n.* **1** an architectural support of a structure: *The underpinnings of the bridge are tall beams.* **2** related to the base of s.t.: *The underpinnings of your argument are all wrong.*

un·der·priv·i·leged /ˌʌndər'prɪvəlɪdʒd, -'prɪvlɪdʒd/ *adj.n.pl.* not receiving the benefits others do from society, (*syn.*) impoverished: *The <n.pl.> underprivileged receive money from charity.*

un·der·rate /ˌʌndər'reɪt/ *v.* -**rated, -rating, -rates** to give s.o. less credit (respect, praise, esteem) than is due: *She is underrated as a tennis player, and she will win the championship.*

un·der·score /'ʌndər,skɔr, ˌʌndər'skɔr/ *v.* -**scored, -scoring, -scores** **1** to underline: *He underscored an important idea in the report with a pen.* **2** to emphasize, tell how important s.t. is: *She underscored her desire to cooperate with the police by going with them.*

un·der·sea /'ʌndər,si/ *adj.* beneath the sea: *A diver found an undersea treasure.*

un·der·shirt /'ʌndər,ʃɜrt/ *n.* a T-shirt or sleeveless shirt worn under other clothing: *He wears an undershirt under his dress shirt.*

un·der·shorts /'ʌndər,ʃɔrts/ *n.pl.* underpants: *His undershorts are white. See:* boxer shorts.

un·der·side /'ʌndər,saɪd/ *n.* the side beneath: *The underside of the carpet is against the floor.*

un·der·sign /'ʌndər,saɪn/ *v.* [U] to sign one's signature, usu. at the end of a document (letter, contract, etc.), to make the document official: *Both parties have undersigned the contract.*

un·der·signed /'ʌndər,saɪnd/ *n.* the person(s) or business(es) that has signed a contract: *The undersigned is responsible for payment.*

un·der·staffed /ˌʌndər'stæft/ *adj.* lacking enough workers to get the work done well or fast: *The accounting department is understaffed and cannot process all the bills quickly.*

un·der·stand /ˌʌndər'stænd/ *v.* -**stood** /-'stʊd/, -**standing, -stands** **1** to comprehend, to get the meaning of: *I understand exactly what you want.* **2** to know: *She understands Spanish because she lived in Spain for a year.* **3** to be informed, made aware: *I understand that you will leave tomorrow. Is that true?* **4** to appreciate, value: *She understands the value of a good education.* **5** to sympathize with, to sense another's feelings: *He understood how she felt when she lost her cat.*

un·der·stand·ing /ˌʌndər'stændɪŋ/ *n.* **1** [U] a comprehension of, ability to get the meaning of: *I have a good understanding of the problem.* **2** [U] an appreciation of: *She has an understanding of modern art.* **3** [U] sympathy for: *Since your mother is dead, you have an understanding of how people feel when their parents die.* **4 to have an** [C] **understanding:** to have an agreement: *My brother and I have an understanding; he does the dishes and I do the laundry.*

U

un·der·state /ˌʌndər'steɪt/ v. -stated, -stating, -states 1 to make s.t. seem less important than it is, downplay: *He understated the importance of a big problem.* 2 to not give accurate figures, (syn.) to underestimate: *The profits are understated in the report.* -n. **understatement** /'ʌndər,steɪtmənt/.

understood /ˌʌndər'stʊd/ agreed upon: *It is understood that the customer will pay half now and the other half on delivery.*

un·der·stud·y /'ʌndər,stʌdi/ n. -ies a replacement for another person, esp. a performer: *The opera singer was ill, so her understudy sang in her place.*

un·der·take /ˌʌndər'teɪk/ v. -took /-'tʊk/ , -taken /-'teɪkən/ -taking, -takes 1 to accept and begin work on s.t. usu. large and serious: *The government will undertake the building of a large courthouse.* 2 to try, (syn.) to endeavor: *He undertook the job of trying to have the government pass a law against polluters.*

un·der·tak·er /'ʌndər,teɪkər/ n. a person or business that arranges funerals and burials for the dead, (syn.) a mortician: *The local undertaker is a serious man.*

un·der·tak·ing /'ʌndər,teɪkɪŋ/ n. [C;U] endeavor, a big task, job, etc.: *To build a dam across the river is a large undertaking.*

under-the-counter adv. fig. related to s.t. illegal that is sold secretly: *That store sells fake ID cards under-the-counter.*

under-the-table adv. fig. related to a secret, illegal transaction, such as the passing of a bribe: *He gave a bribe under-the-table.*

un·der·tone /'ʌndər,toʊn/ n. [C] 1 an implied meaning, undercurrent: *There was an undertone of emotion in the statement she made in court.* 2 a soft tone of voice: *He said in an undertone, "This party is boring; let's leave."*

un·der·tow /'ʌndər,toʊ/ n. [U] a strong, often dangerous current of ocean water made from the pull of a wave beneath the surface after it has crested: *A swimmer caught in the undertow may drown.*

un·der·val·ued /ˌʌndər'vælyud/ adj. low priced, not valued for its true worth: *Because that house needs to be painted, it is undervalued.*

un·der·wa·ter /ˌʌndər'wɔtər, -'wɑ-/ adj.adv. beneath the surface of water: *His hobby is underwater <adj.> photography.‖He swims <adv.> underwater.*
—adj. sunken, submerged: *My boat is underwater after the bad storm.*

under way adv. 1 in motion: *The ship has left the dock and is under way.* 2 in progress, happening: *The politician's election campaign is under way now as she gives speeches on TV.*

un·der·wear /'ʌndər,wɛr/ n.adj. [U] clothing, such as underpants, T-shirts, and slips, worn

under other clothing and not usu. seen by other people, (syn.) underclothes: *He bought boxer shorts in the store's <adj.> underwear department.*

un·der·weight /'ʌndər,weɪt, ˌʌndər'weɪt/ adj. below normal weight for one's age, size, or occupation: *That child is too thin and is underweight.*

un·der·world /'ʌndər,wɜrld/ n. the world of criminals
—adj. criminal, of bad reputation: *John Smith, an underworld figure, is on trial for murder.*

un·der·write /'ʌndər,raɪt/ v. -wrote /-,roʊt/ , -written /,rɪtn/ , -writing, -writes (in business) to approve, support, and usu. to provide money for s.t.: *The manager underwrote the project with a big budget.* -n. **underwriter**.

un·de·served /ˌʌndɪ'zɜrvd/ adj. not earned, (syn.) unwarranted: *He received an undeserved promotion because he was the boss's son.* -adv. **undeservedly** /ˌʌndɪ'zɜrvɪdli/.

un·de·sir·a·ble /ˌʌndɪ'zaɪrəbəl/ adj. 1 unwanted, disagreeable: *Having pimples is the undesirable result of being stressed-out.* 2 inappropriate, unsuitable: *The price that she offered was undesirable; it was too low.* 3 unpleasant: *undesirable behavior*
—n. [C] a person who is regarded as disgusting: *Police removed the undesirables from the train station because they were causing trouble.*

un·de·ter·mined /ˌʌndɪ'tɜrmɪnd/ adj. not known: *The cost of the new building is still undetermined; we are estimating the cost now.*

un·de·vel·oped /ˌʌndɪ'vɛləpt/ adj. not developed, in a natural state: *That woodland is undeveloped; no houses are built on it.*

un·dies /'ʌndiz/ n.infrml. underwear

un·dig·ni·fied /ʌn'dɪgnə,faɪd/ adj. not formal: *He arrived dressed in jeans for the wedding; his dress was undignified.*

un·dip·lo·mat·ic /ˌʌndɪplə'mætɪk/ adj. not polite, rude, (syn.) tactless: *He was undiplomatic when he criticized his wife in front of other people.* -adv. **undiplomatically.**

un·dis·crim·i·nat·ing /ˌʌndɪ'skrɪmə,neɪtɪŋ/ adj. related to s.o. who lacks knowledge or good taste: *She is undiscriminating in her choice of clothes; she will wear anything.*

un·dis·tin·guished /ˌʌndɪ'stɪŋgwɪʃt/ adj. lacking distinction or excellence, (syn.) mediocre: *The pianist's performance was undistinguished; we were not favorably impressed.*

un·dis·turbed /ˌʌndɪ'stɜrbd/ adj. not disturbed by s.o., natural: *That forest is wilderness undisturbed by man.*

un·do /ʌn'du/ v. -did /-'dɪd/ , -done /-'dʌn/ , -doing, -does /-'dʌz/ 1 to unfasten: *He undid* *the buttons on his shirt.* **2** to reverse s.t., cancel: *to undo an agreement See:* undone.

un·do·ing /ʌn'duɪŋ/ *n.* [U] downfall, defeat: *He spent too much money, which was his undoing.*

un·done /ʌn'dʌn/ *adj.* **1** unfinished, incomplete: *His work was left undone.* **2** distraught, in a bad emotional condition: *She was completely undone by the death of her husband.*

un·doubt·ed /ʌn'daʊtɪd/ *adj.* certain, unquestioned: *He is an employee of undoubted loyalty.* **-adv. undoubtedly.**

un·dress /ʌn'drɛs/ *v.* **-dresses** to remove one's clothing: *Her mother told her to undress and put on pajamas before bedtime.*

un·dressed /ʌn'drɛst/ *adj.* without clothes, nude: *He was undressed when the doorbell rang, so he had to put his clothes on quickly.*

un·due /ʌn'du/ *adj.* excessive, too much: *She suffered undue hardship when her husband left her.*

un·du·late /'ʌndʒə,leɪt, -dʒə-/ *v.* **-lated, -lating, -lates** to move in a waving motion: *The ground undulates from an earthquake.* **-adj. undulant; -n.** [U] **undulation** /,ʌndʒə'leɪʃən, -dʒə-/.

un·du·ly /ʌn'duli/ *adv.* **1** excessively, too much: *He was not unduly surprised by the announcement.* **2** incorrectly, improperly: *He was unduly delayed because he was searched by customs without reason.*

un·dy·ing /ʌn'daɪɪŋ/ *adj.* eternal, lasting forever: *You have my undying thanks (loyalty, attention, etc.) for loaning me money when I needed it.*

un·earned /ʌn'ɜrnd/ *adj.* **1** not earned through work: *He has unearned income from interest on his savings.* **2** not deserved: *He received unearned praise for the song that his friend wrote.*

un·earth /ʌn'ɜrθ/ *v.* to dig up, discover: *She unearthed a skeleton from the field.*

un·earth·ly /ʌn'ɜrθli/ *adj.* not of this world, abnormal, weird: *She heard an unearthly scream.*

un·eas·y /ʌn'izi/ **-ier, -iest** *adj.* nervous, worried: *He feels uneasy about taking the test today.* **-adv. uneasily.**

un·ed·u·cat·ed /ʌn'ɛdʒə,keɪtɪd/ *adj.* without education, illiterate: *She is an uneducated person who cannot read.*

un·e·mo·tion·al /,ʌni'moʊʃənəl, -'moʊʃnəl/ *adj.* calm, (syns.) self-possessed, stoic: *He suffered a large loss, but was unemotional about it.* **-adv. unemotionally.**

un·em·ploy·a·ble /,ʌnɪm'plɔɪəbəl/ *adj.* not capable of having a job usu. because of bad health or not enough education or skills: *Her husband was unemployable after an accident disabled him.*

un·em·ploy·ed /,ʌnɪm'plɔɪd/ *adj.* without a job, idle: *He was unemployed for three months.*

—n.pl. the unemployed: the group of people who are without work: *The bad economy forced the government to take care of the unemployed.*

un·em·ploy·ment /,ʌnɪm'plɔɪmənt/ *n.* [U] **1** the general condition of being without work: *The rate of unemployment now is 5 percent nationally.* **2** *infrml.* unemployment compensation: *He went on unemployment until he could find another job.*

unemployment compensation *n.* [U] in the USA, regular payments made for a limited time by a state to qualified, unemployed workers until they find another job: *He is drawing unemployment compensation, but it runs out in six months.*

un·e·qual /ʌn'ikwəl/ *adj.* **1** not equal, different (in amount, quantity, size, time, etc.): *The sleeves on that jacket are of unequal length.* **2** unfair, unjust: *The government gives unequal justice (treatment, education, etc.) to some citizens.* **-adv. unequally.**

un·e·qualed /ʌn'ikwəld/ *adj.* outstanding, not equaled by s.t. else: *She has an unequaled opportunity to win (buy s.t., go to college, etc.).*

un·e·quiv·o·cal /,ʌnɪ'kwɪvəkəl/ *adj.* definite, clear, (syn.) unambiguous: *She gave him an unequivocal answer: "No, absolutely not!"* **-adv. unequivocally.**

un·err·ing /ʌn'ɜrɪŋ, -'ɛr-/ *adj.frml.* without error, correct: *She has an unerring sense for the right thing to do.* **-adv. unerringly.**

un·e·ven /ʌn'ivən/ *adj.* **1** not equal in ability, intelligence, strength, etc.: *We watched an uneven competition where one team was much better than the other.* **2** rough, unsmooth, irregular: *an uneven surface, an uneven performance* **3** not of the same height, length, size, width, etc.: *There are two pieces of wood of uneven length.* **-adv. unevenly.**

un·e·vent·ful /,ʌnɪ'vɛntfəl/ *adj.* without anything special happening, routine: *The day (meeting, weekend, etc.) was uneventful; nothing unusual happened.* **-adv. uneventfully.**

un·ex·cep·tion·al /,ʌnɪk'sɛpʃənəl/ *adj.* ordinary, (syn.) mediocre: *The singer gave an unexceptional performance; we were disappointed.* **-adv. unexceptionally.**

un·ex·pect·ed /,ʌnɪk'spɛktɪd/ *adj.* surprising, unanticipated: *An unexpected visitor (storm, surprise, etc.) arrived.* **-adv. unexpectedly.**

un·ex·ploit·ed /,ʌnɪk'splɔɪtɪd/ *adj.* unused, not taken advantage of: *That country has unexploited natural resources in gold, iron, and trees.*

un·fail·ing /ʌn'feɪlɪŋ/ *adj.* without failure, highly dependable: *He made unfailing efforts*

U

to help his friend get well, and she did get better. -adv. **unfailingly.**

un·fair /ʌnˈfɛɪr/ adj. not fair or just to those concerned: *He was unfair in giving higher raises to his favorite employees.* -adv. **unfairly.**

un·faith·ful /ʌnˈfeɪθfəl/ adj. not loyal to one's wife, husband, or lover, (syn.) adulterous: *He was unfaithful by having a sexual affair with his secretary.*

un·fa·mil·iar /ˌʌnfəˈmɪlyər/ adj. **1** strange, new: *He got lost in an unfamiliar neighborhood.* **2** ignorant, uninformed: *He was totally unfamiliar with the course content when he took the exam, so he failed.*

un·fash·ion·a·ble /ʌnˈfæʃənəbəl, -ˈfæʃnə-/ adj. **1** out of fashion, not currently admired: *It is unfashionable to wear fur now.* **2** lower-class, run-down: *They live in an unfashionable neighborhood.* -adv. **unfashionably.**

un·fas·ten /ʌnˈfæsən/ v. to undo: *He unfastened the buttons on his shirt (the buckle on his belt).*

un·fath·om·a·ble /ʌnˈfæðəməbəl/ adj. **1** bottomless: *the unfathomable depths of the ocean* **2** fig. beyond understanding: *That problem is unfathomable for anyone but a genius.* -adv. **unfathomably.**

un·fa·vor·a·ble /ʌnˈfeɪvərəbəl, -ˈfeɪvrə-/ adj. **1** bad: *Unfavorable weather prevented the game from being played.* **2** negative, disapproving: *She received an unfavorable decision on her job application; they said "no."* -adv. **unfavorably.**

un·feel·ing /ʌnˈfilɪŋ/ adj. insensitive, having no feeling or sympathy: *The unfeeling manager fired her secretary just before the holidays.* -adv. **unfeelingly.**

un·fet·ter /ʌnˈfɛtər/ v. to free, unchain: *He unfettered an animal and let it go free.*

un·fin·ished /ʌnˈfɪnɪʃt/ adj. **1** uncompleted, undone: *When he died, the author left several unfinished works.* **2** without a finish, such as a coat of paint: *The unfinished cabinet looked bare in the room.*

un·fit /ʌnˈfɪt/ adj. **1** not in good condition: *That airplane is unfit to fly because one engine is broken.* **2** lacking in good personal qualities: *Dishonest politicians are unfit to serve in office.*

un·flap·pa·ble /ʌnˈflæpəbəl/ adj. calm under pressure, (syn.) imperturbable: *A general must be unflappable when fighting the enemy.* -adv. **unflappably.**

un·flat·ter·ing /ʌnˈflætərɪŋ/ adj. **1** unbecoming, esp. referring to clothing or makeup that makes s.o. look bad: *That purple dress is unflattering on that woman.* **2** critical, unfriendly: *Her husband made some unflattering remarks about the dress.*

un·flinch·ing /ʌnˈflɪntʃɪŋ/ adj. cool under pressure, (syn.) unwavering: *Her goals are unpopular, but she is unflinching in staying with them.* -adv. **unflinchingly.**

un·fold /ʌnˈfoʊld/ v. **1** to open up: *He unfolded the napkin and put it on his lap.* **2** to happen, become clear: *The story about the explosion unfolded quickly in the newspaper.*

un·fore·seen /ˌʌnfɔrˈsin/ adj. unexpected, happening by accident: *Due to unforeseen circumstances (because of catching the flu), he could not go to the office.*

un·for·get·ta·ble /ˌʌnfərˈgɛtəbəl/ adj. memorable, wonderful: *We had an unforgettable vacation; it was wonderful!* -adv. **unforgettably.**

un·for·tu·nate /ʌnˈfɔrtʃənɪt/ adj. **1** not lucky: *It is unfortunate that you just missed her.* **2** sad: *How unfortunate that his wife died.* —n.frml. **the unfortunate:** the poor: *The family is very poor; they are among the unfortunate.* -adv. **unfortunately.**

un·found·ed /ˌʌnˈfaʊndɪd/ adj. false, not factual: *The bad stories told about her are unfounded.*

un·friend·ly /ʌnˈfrɛndli/ adj. **1** cool toward s.o., distant, (syn.) inhospitable: *The unfriendly waiter made our meal unpleasant.* **2** hostile, rude: *That fellow made unfriendly remarks to me; he's looking for a fight.*

un·furl /ʌnˈfɜrl/ v. to unroll, open up: *That flag unfurled and waved in the breeze.*

un·gain·ly /ʌnˈgeɪnli/ adj. awkward: *He is ungainly when he walks, but graceful when he dances.*

un·glued /ʌnˈglud/ adj. & past part. of unglue **1** to become detached, loose: *The arm of the wooden chair has come unglued.* **2** infrml.fig. upset, distressed: *He came unglued when he found that his wallet was missing.*

un·god·ly /ʌnˈgɑdli/ adj.fig. awful, terrible: *It's 2:00 A.M.; why do you call me at this ungodly hour?!*

un·gov·ern·a·ble /ʌnˈgʌvərnəbəl/ adj. unruly, related usu. to a society that cannot be ruled by law and other governmental functions: *The people there fight with each other so much that the country is ungovernable.*

un·gram·mat·i·cal /ˌʌngrəˈmætɪkəl/ adj. related to speech or writing that does not follow the accepted rules of grammar: *Her ungrammatical speech made her seem unintelligent.* -adv. **ungrammatically.**

un·grate·ful /ʌnˈgreɪtfəl/ adj. unappreciative, not thankful: *The ungrateful child did not write a "thank you" note for her gift.* -adv. **ungratefully.**

un·hap·py /ʌnˈhæpi/ adj. **-pier, -piest 1** sad, sorrowful: *His lack of friends makes him unhappy and lonely.* **2** not satisfied: *She is un-*

happy with her job because of her low salary.
-adv. **unhappily.**

un·health·y /ʌn'hɛlθi/ *adj.* **-ier, -iest** **1** sick, diseased: *He is an unhealthy person with a bad heart.* **2** harmful, causing injury: *He eats unhealthy foods full of fat.* **3** harmful to one's best interests: *She has an unhealthy attitude toward work; she thinks it's more important than her family. -adv.* **unhealthily.**

un·heard-of /ʌn'hɜrd,ʌv, -,ɑv/ *adj.* **1** extraordinary, unusual: *An unheard-of number of people attended the concert; it was mobbed.* **2** ridiculous: *He is making these unheard-of demands, wanting a $10,000 raise.*

un·hinge /ʌn'hɪndʒ/ *v.* **-hinged, -hinging, -hinges** **1** to take off the hinges: *A workman unhinged a door to repair it.* **2** *fig.* to make crazy, unable to act normally: *After he lost his job and his wife, he became unhinged.*

un·ho·ly /ʌn'houli/ *adj.* **-lier, -liest** **1** not holy, unrighteous: *Stealing is an unholy act.* **2** *fig.* awful, offensive: *He made an unholy mess of his life by having an affair and then losing his job.*

un·hook /ʌn'huk/ *v.* **1** to remove, detach: *He unhooked a wire from a gadget.* **2** to remove a hook: *She unhooked the fish from the fishline.*

u·ni·corn /'yunə,kɔrn/ *n.* an unreal white horse with a horn on its forehead: *The magic unicorn is in stories of love and adventure.*

un·i·den·ti·fied flying object /,ʌnaɪ'dɛntə,faɪd, ,ʌnə-/ *n.abbr. as* **UFO** aircraft from outer space: *There are numerous sightings of unidentified flying objects each year.*

u·ni·form /'yunə,fɔrm/ *n.* a special type of clothing worn by members of certain organizations (soldiers, police officers, airline personnel): *Soldiers wear uniforms. -adj.* the same all through s.t.: *The recipe says to mix the sauce well, so the flavor will be uniform. -n.* [U] **uniformity** /,yunə'fɔrməti/; *-adv.* **uniformly.**

u·ni·fy /'yunə,faɪ/ *v.* **-fied, -fying, -fies** **1** to unite **2** to bring together as a whole, *(syn.)* to integrate: *to unify separate ideas into one -n.* [U] **unification** /,yunəfə'keɪʃən/.

u·ni·lat·er·al /,yunə'lætərəl/ *adj.* one-sided, done without the approval of others: *The workers protested but the owner made a unilateral decision to shut down the factory. -adv.* **unilaterally.**

un·im·por·tant /,ʌnɪm'pɔrtnt/ *adj.* not important, *(syn.)* insignificant: *He left a comma out of the sentence, but that is an unimportant detail.*

un·in·form·a·tive /,ʌnɪn'fɔrmətɪv/ *adj.* lacking in information, not revealing: *The politician held a press conference, but it was uninformative; he had nothing new to say.*

un·in·formed /,ʌnɪn'fɔrmd/ *adj.* not having information, *(syn.)* ignorant: *She has not read the newspaper, so she can offer only uninformed opinions.*

un·in·hab·it·a·ble /,ʌnɪn'hæbɪtəbəl/ *adj.* not fit to be lived in: *The board of health said the crumbling building was uninhabitable.*

un·in·hab·it·ed /,ʌnɪn'hæbɪtɪd/ *adj.* unpopulated, without people: *That uninhabited island has no people and no drinking water.*

un·in·hib·it·ed /,ʌnɪn'hɪbɪtɪd/ *adj.* uncontrolled, wild, without restraint: *He is an uninhibited person who says anything that comes into his mind. -adv.* **uninhibitedly.**

un·in·spired /,ʌnɪn'spaɪrd/ *adj.* lackluster, dull: *The singer's uninspired performance put us to sleep.*

un·in·ter·est·ed /ʌn'ɪntrəstɪd, -'ɪntə,rɛstɪd/ *adj.* not interested: *He is uninterested in buying our product; he doesn't need it.*

un·ion /'yunyən/ *n.* **1** [C] an organization of workers: *She joined a carpenter's union.* **2** [C;U] a marriage: *The union of two people in marriage is a wonderful thing.* **3** [C;U] a joining of forces: *A union of nations brings peace to the world.* **4** [C;U] a biological joining: *A union of two cells occurred after we increased the temperature by five degrees in the lab.*

un·ion·ize /'yunyə,naɪz/ *v.* **-ized, -izing, -izes** to organize a group of workers into joining in a union: *A representative from a labor union unionized the workers in our company. -n.* [U] **unionization** /,yunyənə'zeɪʃən/.

Union Jack *n.* the British flag: *A ship flies the Union Jack to show that it is from England.*

u·nique /yu'nik/ *adj.* singular, one of a kind: *Each person in the world has a unique personality. -adv.* **uniquely**

USAGE NOTE: The term *unique* is often misused when people are trying to say *special.* Unique means one of a kind, without equal: *A snowflake has a unique shape.* BUT *Hans and Lisa have a special relationship.*

u·ni·sex /'yunə,sɛks/ *adj.* suitable to both men and women: *The unisex hair salon attracts an equal number of men and women.*

u·ni·son /'yunəsən, -zən/ *n.* **in unison:** done all together at the same time as a cooperative act or performance: *A group of companies acted in unison to give money to charity.||Members of a church choir sing in unison.*

u·nit /'yunɪt/ *n.* **1** a part or section of s.t.: *a unit of information||a unit in a lesson||a unit of currency* **2** a standard of measurement: *An inch (foot, meter, mile, etc.) is a unit of measurement.* **3** a bookcase or other piece of furniture: *That wall unit holds stereo equipment.* **4** a department or other group of workers (soldiers,

U

people, etc.): *Andy Martin oversees a sales unit within the company.*
—*adj.* related to a unit: *a unit cost*||*unit price* -*adj.* **unitary** /'yunɪˌtɛri/; -*v.* **unitize** /'yunɪˌtaɪz/.

u·nite /yu'naɪt/ *v.* **united, uniting, unites 1** to come together for a reason or purpose: *The nation united against its enemy.* **2** to consolidate, to bring together for a purpose: *The leader united his followers.* **3** to join in marriage: *A pastor united a couple in marriage.* **4** to combine, join: *The two sections of a new bridge were united over the river.*

United Nations *n.pl.* used with a sing. *v.* an international organization founded and headquartered in New York City in 1945: *The United Nations promotes cooperation and peace among nations.* See: UN.

u·ni·ty /'yunəti/ *n.* -**ties** [C;U] **1** a condition of oneness in belief (action, purpose), (*syn.*) unanimity: *Those two countries have a unity of purpose in wanting peace.* **2** two or more things made into one: *Playing a sport requires a unity of body and mind.*

u·ni·ver·sal /ˌyunə'vɜrsəl/ *adj.* found or practiced everywhere, (*syn.*) ubiquitous: *Poverty is a universal problem all over the world.* -*n.* [U] **universality** /ˌyunəvər'sæləti/; -*adv.* **universally.**

u·ni·verse /'yunəˌvɜrs/ *n.* the stars, planets, other heavenly bodies, and space taken together: *She explores the universe by telescope.*

u·ni·ver·si·ty /ˌyunə'vɜrsəti/ *n.* -**ties** a place of higher education that gives advanced degrees: *She got her Ph.D. in astronomy at a well-known university.*

USAGE NOTE: In the American educational system, after high school (secondary school) students can go to *college, university,* or a *technical institute.* The university is the largest of these institutions, and offers graduate degree programs in addition to undergraduate degrees. Most American students will say they go to college, rather than university, no matter which type of institution they attend.

---

un·just /ʌn'dʒʌst/ *adj.* lacking justice, unfair: *He was denied a job because of his race, and this is unjust.* -*adv.* **unjustly.**

un·jus·ti·fied /ʌn'dʒʌstəˌfaɪd/ *adj.* **1** against common sense, good practice, or rules: *He wasted money by making an unjustified payment.* **2** incorrect, unproven, without reason: *She has unjustified criticism about nearly everyone.*

un·kempt /ʌn'kɛmpt/ *adj.* messy: *His hair is unkempt because he never combs it.*

un·kind /ʌn'kaɪnd/ *adj.* **1** thoughtless, uncaring: *He was unkind to leave his wife alone when she was ill.* **2** mean, vicious: *The woman*

made unkind remarks about the man's weight and looks. -*adv.* **unkindly;** -*n.*[C;U] **unkindness.**

un·know·ing /ʌn'noʊɪŋ/ *adj.* lacking knowledge of s.t., uninformed: *He was unknowing about the surprise party his friends were planning.* -*adv.* **unknowingly.**

un·known /ʌn'noʊn/ *adj.* not known: *The location of his home is unknown.*
—*n.* **1** [C;U] s.t. that is not known: *His location is an unknown.* **2** [C] (in math) a quantity that is not known: *Solve for the unknown in the equation.*

un·law·ful /ʌn'lɔfəl/ *adj.* illegal, against the law: *It is unlawful to steal.* -*adv.* **unlawfully.**

un·lead·ed /ʌn'lɛdɪd/ *adj.* without the metal lead as an ingredient: *He uses unleaded gasoline in his car.*

un·leash /ʌn'liʃ/ *v.* -**leashes 1** to remove a leash: *He unleashed his dog, so it could run.* **2** *fig.*to release a force: *A newspaper reporter unleashed criticism against the mayor.*

un·leav·ened /ʌn'lɛvənd/ *adj.* baked without yeast: *Unleavened bread is flatter than regular bread.*

un·less /ʌn'lɛs, ən-/ *conj.* except that, on the condition that: *Unless he agrees, we have no contract.*

un·li·censed /ʌn'laɪsənst/ *adj.* operating without a license, illegal, (*syn.*) uncertified: *The person who caused the accident was an unlicensed driver.*

un·like /ʌn'laɪk/ *prep.* **1** different from, dissimilar to: *That odd situation is unlike any I've seen before.* **2** not typical of: *It is unlike him to complain; he is usually quiet.*
—*adj.* different, dissimilar: *The two boys are completely unlike; you wouldn't think they were brothers.*

un·like·ly /ˌʌn'laɪkli/ *adj.* doubtful, not probable: *It is unlikely that it will rain today; the clouds are breaking.*

un·lim·it·ed /ʌn'lɪmɪtɪd/ *adj.* without limits, without end: *The wealthy seem to have unlimited amounts of money to spend.*

un·list·ed /ʌn'lɪstɪd/ *adj.* not in public records: *He has an unlisted telephone number, so I can't call him.*

un·load /ʌn'loʊd/ *v.* **1** to remove s.t. (from a vehicle): *A worker unloaded the supplies off the truck.* **2** to take ammunition, such as bullets, from a gun: *A soldier unloaded his rifle.* **3** *infrml.fig.* to express freely: *When the worker was late again, the foreman unloaded his anger on him.*

un·lock /ʌn'lɑk/ *v.* **1** to open: *She unlocked a door with a key.* **2** *fig.* to remove obstacles, to make s.t. possible: *The government unlocked opportunities for the poor by giving them jobs.*

un·luck·y /ʌnˈlʌki/ *adj.* **-ier, -iest 1** having bad things happen to s.o. by chance: *She was unlucky and did not win the bet.* **2** having bad luck that harms s.o., such as having accidents: *He is unlucky: last week he broke his leg, and yesterday his car was stolen.*

un·man·ly /ʌnˈmænli/ *adj.* not what is expected of a man in cowardly or irresponsible behavior: *He ran when he saw a spider, and his friends regarded that as unmanly.*

un·manned /ʌnˈmænd/ *adj.* without an operator or pilot: *An unmanned space vehicle was sent to Mars.*

un·marked /ʌnˈmɑrkt/ *adj.* **1** without identification, disguised: *An unmarked police car is looking for speeders.* **2** unharmed, unbruised: *He had a fistfight but is unmarked.*

un·mar·ried /ʌnˈmærid/ *adj.* not married, single: *I have two brothers, one is married and the other is unmarried.*

un·mask /ʌnˈmæsk/ *v.* **1** to remove a mask: *The costumed party-goers unmasked at midnight.* **2** *fig.* to expose, uncover: *A police officer unmasked a swindler (thief, a crime, etc.).*

un·meant /ʌnˈmɛnt/ *adj.* not meant, not intended in the way s.t. appeared: *She made up the guest list from memory; any omissions were unmeant.*

un·mer·ci·ful /ʌnˈmɜrsɪfəl/ *adj.* savage, without pity, (*syns.*) merciless, ruthless: *The soldiers made an unmerciful attack (assault, etc.) on the enemy, killing them all. -adv.* **unmercifully.**

un·mis·tak·a·ble /ˌʌnmɪˈsteɪkəbəl/ *adj.* **1** that which cannot be questioned: *It is an unmistakable truth that the sky is blue.* **2** obvious, clear: *The child has an unmistakable likeness to her mother. -adv.* **unmistakably.**

un·mit·i·gat·ed /ʌnˈmɪtɪˌɡeɪtɪd/ *adj.frml.* **1** not lessened or softened: *He is suffering unmitigated pain from cancer.* **2** total, without exception: *She is an unmitigated liar who cannot be trusted.*

un·nat·u·ral /ʌnˈnætʃərəl, -ˈnætʃrəl/ *adj.* **1** not from nature, artificial: *Those artificial eggs are made from unnatural chemicals.* **2** against nature, not normal, atypical: *It is unnatural for trees to grow in the desert.* **3** against accepted norms, (*syn.*) perverse: *Taking pleasure in s.o.'s pain is unnatural behavior. -adv.* **unnaturally.**

un·nec·es·sar·y /ʌnˈnɛsəˌsɛri/ *adj.* **1** needless, wasteful: *The salesperson got me to buy a lot of unnecessary things.* **2** unwanted, not justified (often hurtful): *He made some critical comments that were unnecessary.||He made unnecessary remarks. -adv.* **unnecessarily** /ˌʌnnɛsəˈsɛrəli/.

un·nerve /ʌnˈnɜrv/ *v.* **-nerved, -nerving, -nerves** to upset s.o., to cause s.o. to lose his or her calm: *She unnerved me when she said the company planned to fire me. -adj.* **unnerving.**

un·no·tice·a·ble /ʌnˈnoʊtɪsəbəl/ *adj.* not noticeable or obvious, (*syn.*) insignificant: *That tiny spot on your sleeve is practically unnoticeable.*

un·no·ticed /ʌnˈnoʊtɪst/ *adj.adv.* not noticed, unobserved: *His presence at the party was* <*adj.*> *unnoticed; he went* <*adv.*> *unnoticed.*

un·ob·tru·sive /ˌʌnəbˈtrusɪv/ *adj.* not easily noticed or seen: *That is a small, unobtrusive building; no wonder I couldn't find it. -adv.* **unobtrusively.**

un·oc·cu·pied /ʌnˈɑkyəˌpaɪd/ *adj.* **1** empty, with no people: *The unoccupied building was falling apart.* **2** unemployed, without work or other meaningful activity: *He is unoccupied now and very bored.*

un·of·fi·cial /ˌʌnəˈfɪʃəl/ *adj.* informal, without official approval: *An unofficial announcement was made that the company might be closing soon. -adv.* **unofficially.**

un·or·ga·nized /ʌnˈɔrɡəˌnaɪzd/ *adj.* **1** not in order, without a system: *She has lots of papers on her desk that are unorganized.* **2** not belonging to a labor union: *The unorganized workers were not well-paid.*

un·or·tho·dox /ʌnˈɔrθəˌdɑks/ *adj.* **1** unusual: *He has an unorthodox way of playing football, but he's a good player.* **2** not accepted or approved by an established religious body: *Eating pork is an unorthodox practice for some religions.*

un·pack /ʌnˈpæk/ *v.* to remove articles from a container: *He unpacked his suitcase.*

un·paid /ʌnˈpeɪd/ *adj.* not paid as yet: *He has many unpaid bills.*

un·pal·at·a·ble /ʌnˈpælətəbəl/ *adj.* **1** not good to eat, distasteful: *That burned food is unpalatable.* **2** *fig.frml.* unpleasant, disagreeable: *She finds having dinner with her ex-husband unpalatable.*

un·par·al·leled /ʌnˈpærəˌlɛld/ *adj.* **1** unequalled, extraordinary: *We have an unparalleled opportunity to increase our business.* **2** unusual, peculiar

un·pleas·ant /ʌnˈplɛzənt/ *adj.* **1** irritating, uncomfortable: *We had an unpleasant vacation because it rained all the time.* **2** rude, offensive: *That bully was very unpleasant to me. -adv.* **unpleasantly;** *-n.* [U] **unpleasantness.**

un·plug /ʌnˈplʌɡ/ *v.* **-plugged, -plugging, -plugs 1** to detach (a plug) usu. from an electrical supply: *The room went dark when he unplugged the lamp.* **2** to clear, unstop: *The plumber unplugged a stopped-up sink.*

un·pop·u·lar /ʌnˈpɑpyələr/ *adj.* **1** not liked by many people: *The new tax on food is very unpopular.*

U

un·prec·e·dent·ed /ʌn'prɛsə,dɛntɪd/ *adj.* unusual, not having happened before: *The governor was elected for an unprecedented fourth time. -adv.* **unprecedentedly.**

un·pre·dict·a·ble /,ʌnprɪ'dɪktəbəl/ *adj.* uncertain, cannot be predicted: *The weather here is unpredictable; we don't know if it will be rainy or sunny. -n.* [U] **unpredictability; -adv.** **unpredictably.**

un·prej·u·diced /ʌn'prɛʤədɪst/ *adj.* **1** without racial bias: *The police chief should be an unprejudiced person.* **2** balanced, not favoring one side over another: *An expert gave her an unprejudiced opinion that the painting is fake.*

un·pre·pared /,ʌnprɪ'pɛrd/ *adj.* **1** unqualified, unskilled: *He is unprepared to take the job; he needs experience.* **2** not ready, not yet done: *Dinner is unprepared, but will be ready in an hour.*

un·pre·ten·tious /,ʌnprɪ'tɛnʃəs/ *adj.frml.* modest, not showy or flashy: *They are rich but live in a simple, unpretentious house.*

un·prin·ci·pled /ʌn'prɪnsəpəld/ *adj.* dishonest, (*syn.*) unscrupulous: *That cheat is unprincipled in his dealings with others.*

un·print·a·ble /ʌn'prɪntəbəl/ *adj.* related to language or information that is too vulgar or bloody to be printed in newspapers or magazines: *The man used so much dirty language that what he said is unprintable.*

un·pro·duc·tive /,ʌnprə'dʌktɪv/ *adj.* useless, not resulting in s.t. useful: *We had an unproductive meeting where nothing was decided. -adv.* **unproductively.**

un·pro·fes·sion·al /,ʌnprə'fɛʃənəl, -'fɛʃnəl/ *adj.* below the quality expected from a professional person or business, (*syn.*) amateurish: *The repair shop refused to fix the bad work that they did; both the work and the management were unprofessional. -n.* [U] **unprofessionality** /,ʌnprə,fɛʃə'næləti/; -adv. **unprofessionally.**

un·prof·it·a·ble /ʌn'prɑfɪtəbəl/ *adj.* **1** not making a profit, losing money: *That is an unprofitable company; it's almost bankrupt.* **2** unproductive, not useful: *We had an unprofitable discussion in which no business was done. -adv.* **unprofitably.**

un·pro·voked /,ʌnprə'voʊkt/ *adj.* uninvited, not caused by the victim: *One country invaded its neighbor in an unprovoked attack.*

un·qual·i·fied /ʌn'kwɑlə,faɪd/ *adj.* **1** unskilled, untrained: *He is unqualified for the job because of his lack of the proper skills.* **2** unconditional, without exceptions: *The play (person, venture, etc.) is an unqualified success.*

un·ques·tion·a·ble /ʌn'kwɛsʧənəbəl/ *adj.* certain, without doubt: *The meeting was an unquestionable success; much was decided. -adv.* **unquestionably.**

un·ques·tioned /ʌn'kwɛsʧənd/ *adj.* not challenged, unexamined: *The strange statement went unquestioned by anyone.*

un·rav·el /ʌn'rævəl/ *v.* **1** to become undone, to loosen: *Threads of wool unravel from an old sweater.* **2** to solve, to understand in a slow, painstaking way: *In books, detectives unravel mysteries step by step.*

un·real /ʌn'riəl, -'ril/ *adj.* **1** imaginary: *Her pains are unreal because they are in her imagination.* **2** *infrml.fig.* incredible, astonishing: *The salary that she makes is unreal, tremendous!*

un·rea·son·a·ble /ʌn'rizənəbəl, -'riznəbəl/ *adj.* **1** not rational, not sensible: *The old man makes unreasonable demands on his son to visit him every day.* **2** too high, uneconomical: *The price of that new car is unreasonable. -n.* [U] **unreasonableness; -adv.** **unreasonably.**

un·re·hearsed /,ʌnrɪ'hɜrst/ *adj.* spontaneous, not practiced in advance, (*syn.*) extemporaneous: *A comedian sometimes makes unrehearsed jokes part of her act.*

un·re·lent·ing /,ʌnrɪ'lɛntɪŋ/ *adj.* persistent, without stopping: *Her unrelenting efforts made the project a success. -adv.* **unrelentingly.**

un·re·li·a·ble /,ʌnrɪ'laɪəbəl/ *adj.* **1** not to be trusted, irresponsible: *You can't believe his promises because he's unreliable.* **2** undependable, not working well: *The bus system in this area is unreliable; the buses do not run on time. -n.* [U] **unreliability** /,ʌnrɪ,laɪə'bɪləti/; -adv. **unreliably.**

un·re·served /,ʌnrɪ'zɜrvd/ *adj.* **1** not assigned in advance, open to whomever arrives first: *There is some unreserved seating available at the football game.* **2** outgoing, loud: *She is very unreserved; she'll talk to anyone. -adv.* **unreservedly** /,ʌnrɪ'zɜrvɪdli/.

un·re·spon·sive /,ʌnrɪ'spɑnsɪv/ *adj.* **1** not reacting, silent, (*syn.*) uncommunicative: *I sent a letter to the company, but they were unresponsive.* **2** cold, unsympathetic: *He tried to kiss her, but she was unresponsive. -n.* [U] **unresponsiveness; -adv.** **unresponsively.**

un·rest /ʌn'rɛst/ *n.* [U] **1** discontent, uneasiness: *There was unrest in the crowd when the singer suddenly cancelled the show.* **2** demonstrations, rioting: *After the president was killed, there was widespread unrest in the streets.*

un·re·strained /,ʌnrɪ'streɪnd/ *adj.* spontaneous, flowing freely (emotions), (*syn.*) unreserved: *Unrestrained applause (jeers, laughter, etc.) came from the audience.*

un·ripe /ʌn'raɪp/ *adj.* immature, not ready for harvest or eating: *If you eat unripe fruit, you can get sick.*

un·ri·valed /ʌn'raɪvəld/ *adj.* unequaled, the best, (*syn.*) unparalleled: *He has an unrivaled ability to speak English.*

un·roll /ʌn'roʊl/ *v.* to open, spread out: *A worker unrolled the carpet onto the wood floor.*

un·ruf·fled /ʌn'rʌfəld/ *adj.* calm, not upset emotionally: *She fell down but was unruffled.*

un·ru·ly /ʌn'ruli/ *adj.* disobedient, loud, and wild: *A group of unruly children ran through the hallway.* -*n.* [U] **unruliness.**

un·safe /ʌn'seɪf/ *adj.* in bad condition, in disrepair, dangerous: *That old, rotting building is unsafe to live in.*‖*That street is unsafe to walk in after dark; you might be robbed.* -*adv.* **unsafely.**

un·san·i·tar·y /ʌn'sænə,tɛri/ *adj.* full of germs, not clean, not healthy: *There are unsanitary conditions in that bathroom; it needs cleaning.*

un·sat·is·fac·to·ry /,ʌnsætɪs'fæktəri, -tri/ *adj.* unacceptable, not meeting standards: *We received an unsatisfactory offer for the property, so we didn't sell it.* -*adv.* **unsatisfactorily.**

un·sa·vor·y /ʌn'seɪvəri, -'seɪvri/ *adj.* **1** bland, tasteless: *unsavory food* **2** *fig.* morally offensive, disagreeable: *That crime was committed by two unsavory criminals.*

un·scathed /ʌn'skeɪðd/ *adj.* uninjured, not hurt: *He came through the accident unscathed.*

un·sci·en·tif·ic /,ʌnsaɪən'tɪfɪk/ *adj.* not following accepted ways of doing things in science: *His research proved to be unscientific and was rejected by the academy.* -*adv.* **unscientifically.**

un·screw /ʌn'skru/ *v.* **1** to loosen or remove a screw or a bolt **2** to turn or twist open: *He unscrewed (the top of) a jar of mustard.*

un·scru·pu·lous /ʌn'skrupyələs/ *adj.* unprincipled, dishonest: *She tries to cheat everyone in her dealings; she's unscrupulous.* -*adv.* **unscrupulously;** -*n.* [U] **unscrupulousness.**

un·sea·son·a·ble /ʌn'sizənəbəl, -'siznəbəl/ *adj.* not normal weather for a particular season: *The warm periods this winter are unseasonable.* -*adv.* **unseasonably.**

un·seat /ʌn'sit/ *v.* to defeat s.o. in power: *She unseated her opponent in the election.*

un·seem·ly /ʌn'simli/ *adj.frml.* undignified, offensive: *He behaved in an unseemly manner when he argued with the host at the party.* -*n.* [U] **unseemliness.**

un·seen /ʌn'sin/ *adj.* not seen or observed, invisible: *The politician snuck out of the building unseen by reporters. See:* sight.

un·seg·re·gat·ed /ʌn'sɛgrə,geɪtɪd/ *adj.* racially mixed, (*syn.*) integrated: *That is an unsegregated neighborhood where people of all races live together.*

un·self·ish /ʌn'sɛlfɪʃ/ *adj.* generous, giving: *She is an unselfish person who gives to the poor.* -*adv.* **unselfishly;** -*n.* [U] **unselfishness.**

un·set·tled /ʌn'sɛtld/ *adj. & past part. of* unsettle **1** upset, emotionally distressed: *She was unsettled after the robbery.* **2** unresolved, not decided or finished: *The lawsuit (situation, agreement, etc.) is still unsettled; nothing has been decided.*

un·shak·a·ble /ʌn'ʃeɪkəbəl/ *adj.* not changeable, (*syn.*) steadfast: *She has an unshakable loyalty to her family.* -*adv.* **unshakably.**

un·sight·ly /ʌn'saɪtli/ *adj.* unpleasant to look at, ugly: *He has an unsightly wound covered with blood.*

un·skilled /ʌn'skɪld/ *adj.* without special skills or education: *Cutting the grass or sweeping the sidewalks requires unskilled workers only.*

un·snap /ʌn'snæp/ *v.* **-snapped, -snapping, -snaps** to open a snap: *He unsnapped his jacket and took it off.*

un·so·cia·ble /ʌn'soʊʃəbəl/ *adj.* pertaining to s.o. who avoids the company of others, unfriendly: *He likes to be by himself; he is unsociable.* -*adv.* **unsociably.**

un·so·phis·ti·cat·ed /,ʌnsə'fɪstə,keɪtɪd/ *adj.* **1** unworldly, simple: *He is an unsophisticated country boy who doesn't know the ways of big city life.* **2** simple-minded: *She has an unsophisticated approach to solving difficult problems.*

un·sound /ʌn'saʊnd/ *adj.* **1** in disrepair, likely to fall down: *The floors in that old building are unsound.* **2** not logical, faulty: *The young lawyer lost the case because his arguments were unsound.* **3** not to be trusted, unwise: *The manager made an unsound decision to cut back on safety.* -*adv.* **unsoundly.**

un·spar·ing /ʌn'spɛrɪŋ/ *adj.* generous, unstinting: *He was unsparing in his efforts to help us.* -*adv.* **unsparingly.**

un·speak·a·ble /ʌn'spikəbəl/ *adj.* so bad or shocking as to prevent speaking about it: *There are unspeakable truths about his bad behavior.* -*adv.* **unspeakably.**

un·spo·ken /ʌn'spoʊkən/ *adj. past part. of* unspeak: not said, not discussed: *Everyone knew she was lying, but the thought was unspoken.*

un·sports·man·like /ʌn'spɔrtsmən,laɪk/ *adj.* not fair, unethical: *After he swore at the umpire, the baseball player was kicked out of the game for unsportsmanlike conduct.*

un·sta·ble /ʌn'steɪbəl/ *adj.* **1** irrational, not behaving or thinking normally: *He is an unstable person who cries often at work.* **2** shaky, unsteady, liable to fall into ruin: *an unstable company (bridge, situation, etc.)* **3** volatile, subject to explosion or fire: *Gas is an*

U

unstable substance that can easily explode near fire. -adv. **unstably.**

un·stead·y /ʌn'stɛdi/ adj. **1** wobbly, subject to tipping or falling: *He is drunk and unsteady on his feet.* **2** erratic, not working all the time, (syn.) inconsistent: *That city has an unsteady supply of electricity (money, water, etc.).* -adv. **unsteadily;** -n. [U] **unsteadiness.**

un·stop·pa·ble /ʌn'stɑpəbəl/ adj. impossible to stop, (syn.) relentless: *An unstoppable wind blew when the hurricane hit.*

un·strap /ʌn'stræp/ v. **-strapped, -strapping, -straps** to remove or untie the straps from s.t.: *He unstrapped his boots (the cinch on a saddle, a backpack, etc.).*

un·strung /ʌn'strʌŋ/ adj. **1** having loosened strings: *a violin that has come unstrung* **2** fig. upset, distressed: *He became unstrung when he lost his wallet in a foreign city and couldn't find a police officer.*

un·stuck /ʌn'stʌk/ adj. & past part. of unstick: unglued, loosened: *The postage stamp became unstuck from the envelope.*

un·suc·cess·ful /ˌʌnsək'sɛsfəl/ adj. failed, disappointing: *He made an unsuccessful attempt to start his own business; it failed.* -adv. **unsuccessfully.**

un·suit·a·ble /ʌn'sutəbəl/ adj. **1** unacceptable, not what is wanted: *We received an unsuitable offer for our house; it was too low.* **2** inappropriate, not suitable for s.t.: *The property is unsuitable for building; it's too small.* -n. [U] **unsuitability** /ʌnˌsutə'bɪləti/; -adv. **unsuitably.**

un·sung /ʌn'sʌŋ/ adj. fig. unpraised, not seen as important, overlooked: *The player who helped win the game was an unsung hero; no one praised him.*

un·sus·pect·ing /ˌʌnsə'spɛktɪŋ/ adj. unprepared for trouble, trusting, (syn.) naive: *The unsuspecting clerk accepted the man's check, but it was no good.* -adv. **unsuspectingly.**

un·sym·met·ri·cal /ˌʌnsɪ'mɛtrɪkəl/ adj. irregular, lacking a balanced design, (syn.) asymmetrical: *The human foot has an unsymmetrical shape.* -adv. **unsymmetrically.**

un·tan·gle /ʌn'tæŋgəl/ v. **-gled, -gling, -gles** to unravel, unknot: *She untangled a knot in a piece of string.*

un·ten·a·ble /ʌn'tɛnəbəl/ adj.frml. describing s.t. (an opinion, lawsuit, etc.) which cannot be defended, (syn.) indefensible: *The army is located in an untenable place and must retreat or be killed.*

un·think·a·ble /ʌn'θɪŋkəbəl/ adj. so bad that one cannot think about it: *For me to commit murder is unthinkable.*

un·think·ing /ʌn'θɪŋkɪŋ/ adj. **1** done without thinking or conscious planning: *In unthinking bravery, she ran into the burning building to* save the child.||*He lives day by day in an unthinking way.* **2** done without care, reckless: *Unthinking, he gambled away all his money at cards.* -adv. **unthinkingly.**

un·ti·dy /ʌn'taɪdi/ adj. **-dier, -diest** messy, cluttered: *Her untidy room has clothes all over the floor.* -n. [U] **untidiness.**

un·tie /ʌn'taɪ/ v. **-tied, -tying, -ties** to undo (a necktie, knot, etc.): *He untied his shoes and took them off.*

un·til /ʌn'tɪl, ən-/ prep. **1** up to a particular time: *We worked until noon, and then had lunch.* **2** before a particular time: *We can't work again until Monday.*
—conj. up to the time that, before: *We will not be able to leave until our work is finished.*

USAGE NOTE: Many people drop the first syllable, "un" from the word *until,* when they pronounce it. This form is written as *till,* or contracted as *'til,* but in formal writing the complete word *until* is preferred.

un·time·ly /ʌn'taɪmli/ adj. **1** premature, happening too soon: *a young man's untimely death* **2** awkward, happening at the wrong time: *The loss of his job was untimely because he had just bought a new house.*

un·tir·ing /ʌn'taɪrɪŋ/ adj. dedicated, done without resting, (syn.) indefatigable: *Her untiring efforts made the business grow.* -adv. **untiringly.**

un·to /'ʌntu/ prep.frml. to: *And the Lord said unto Moses. . . .*

un·told /ʌn'toʊld/ adj. **1** not said: *an untold story* **2** infinite, so great as to be uncountable: *That factory cost untold millions of dollars to build.*

un·touch·a·ble /ʌn'tʌtʃəbəl/ adj. related to a person who is beyond the power of others to control: *He is so powerful that he is untouchable by the law.*

un·to·ward /ʌn'tɔrd/ adj.frml. **1** critical, unfriendly: *He makes untoward and often offensive comments about others.* **2** difficult, bad: *to find oneself in an untoward situation, such as having no money*

un·tried /ʌn'traɪd/ adj. **1** unattempted: *Swimming across the Atlantic Ocean is an untried feat that would be difficult to accomplish.* **2** fig. unproven, not tested: *That powerful new telescope is as yet untried by the scientist.*

un·true /ʌn'tru/ adj. **1** false, incorrect: *What he said is untrue; he's lying.* **2** unfaithful: *He is a husband who is untrue to his wife.*

un·truth /ʌn'truθ/ n. **-truths** /-'truðz, -'truθs/ a lie, falsehood: *She tells untruths.*

un·truth·ful /ʌn'truθfəl/ adj. lying, saying s.t. that is false: *The reporter wrote untruthful reports to get attention.* -adv. **untruthfully.**

un·used /ʌn'yuzd/ *adj.* **1** not used, sitting idle: *He has unused equipment sitting in his backyard.* **2** new, not worn yet: *She has unused clothes in her closet; they still have price tags.*

un·u·su·al /ʌn'yuʒuəl/ *adj.* **1** peculiar, not normal: *His unusual behavior shocks others.* **2** special, exceptional: *She has an unusual talent for playing the piano.*

un·u·su·al·ly /ʌn'yuʒuəli, -ʒəli/ *adv.* very, exceptionally: *We are having unusually good weather for this time of year.*

un·veil /ʌn'veɪl/ *v.* to reveal or uncover often in a formal way: *The mayor pulled back the curtain and unveiled a statue of the local hero.*

un·war·rant·ed /ʌn'wɔrəntɪd, -'wɑr-/ *adj.* **1** unjustified, needless: *The expense of taking a taxi when we could easily walk home is unwarranted.* **2** uncalled-for, offensive: *He made rude and unwarranted remarks about someone.*

un·war·y /ʌn'wɛri/ *adj.n.pl.* unsuspecting, not watching for danger: *A cheat can steal from an <adj.> unwary person or <n.pl.> the unwary.* *-n.* [U] **unwariness.**

un·well /ʌn'wɛl/ *adj.* ill, sick: *The rotten food made her unwell.*

un·whole·some /ʌn'hoʊlsəm/ *adj.* unhealthy, not pure, bad: *He eats unwholesome food with a lot of salt and fat in it.* *-adv.* **unwholesomely;** *-n.* [U] **unwholesomeness.**

un·wield·y /ʌn'wildi/ *adj.* awkward, bulky: *The sofa was unwieldy and hard to move up the stairs.* *-n.* [U] **unwieldiness.**

un·will·ing /ʌn'wɪlɪŋ/ *adj.* **1** against, (*syn.*) averse: *She is unwilling to take a cut in pay.* **2** forced, coerced: *She was an unwilling guest at the wedding; she did not want to go.* *-adv.* **unwillingly;** *-n.* [U] **unwillingness.**

un·wind /ʌn'waɪnd/ *v.* **-wound** /-'waʊnd/ , **-winding, -winds** **1** to unravel: *She unwinds thread from a spool.* **2** *fig.* to relax: *She likes to lie down and unwind at home after a hard day's work.*

un·wise /ʌn'waɪz/ *adj.* **1** stupid, dumb: *He was unwise to quit school.* **2** inadvisable, not sensible: *It is unwise to invest in real estate at this unstable time.* *-adv.* **unwisely.**

un·wit·ting·ly /ʌn'wɪtɪŋli/ *adv.* unintentionally, accidentally: *A shopper unwittingly walked into a grocery store while a robbery was taking place.*

un·wor·thy /ʌn'wɜrði/ *adj.* undeserving, not good enough for s.t.: *That corrupt man is unworthy of praise.* *-n.* [U] **unworthiness.**

un·wrap /ʌn'ræp/ *v.* **-wrapped, -wrapping, -wraps** to uncover, to take the wrapping off s.t.: *He unwrapped a package.||Children love to unwrap presents.*

un·writ·ten /ʌn'rɪtn/ *adj.* **1** not done in writing: *That report is still unwritten.* **2 unwritten**

law: a rule that is understood through word of mouth: *It is an unwritten law in the college library that nobody has long, loud conversations.*

un·yield·ing /ʌn'yildɪŋ/ *adj.* unwilling to change, (*syns.*) uncompromising, stubborn: *He is unyielding in his demand that costs must be cut.*

un·zip /ʌn'zɪp/ *v.* **-zipped, -zipping, -zips** to undo the zipper on s.t.: *She unzipped her jacket (skirt, pants, purse, etc.).*

up /ʌp/ *adv.* **1** in or to a higher direction, upward: *He looked up at the sky and then walked up the hill.* **2** at or to a higher level, more: *Prices are up.||The temperature is up another 10 degrees.* **3** finished, ended: *Your time (visit, test, contract, etc.) is up.* **4** built, installed: *The building is up and ready for people to move in.||The new computer system is up and running.||The curtains are up in our new house.* **5** out of bed, arisen: *I was up at 7:00 o'clock this morning.||The sun was up at 6:32 A.M.* **6** able to do: *Do you think he is up to the task (up to going to graduate school, up to finding a job, etc.)?* **7** dependent on, responsible for: *It's up to you to decide.||It's up to me to finish the job.* **8** doing, occupied with: *What is he up to now?||He is up to something.* **9** as far as, until: *Up to now, he's done a lot of work.* **10 to come up: a.** to visit: *Come up and visit us soon.* **b.** to interfere, prevent s.t.: *Something has come up, and I cannot visit now.* **c.** to occur in the future: *What's coming up next week at the movies?* **11 to have it up to here:** frustrated, angered: *This job is driving me crazy—I've had it up to here!* **12 to hold up:** to delay: *The post office is on strike, and that is holding up our mail.* **13 to hold s.o. up:** to rob at gun or knifepoint: *A robber held me up with a gun.* **14 to be on one's way up: a.** to go up, ascend: *He rang the doorbell downstairs and is on his way up to visit.* **b.** to have a promising career, progress: *He is young, but he is on his way up in banking.* **15 to be on the up and up:** to be legitimate, honest: *He seems like an honest man and his offer is on the up and up.* **16 to pay up:** to settle a debt: *My credit card account is all paid up.* **17 to play up:** to emphasize: *To get the job, she really played up the fact that she knows computers.* **18 to play up to:** to flatter, seek to please a lot: *He plays up to his boss all the time with compliments.* **19 to be stuck up:** snobbish, thinking you are better than others: *She's so stuck up, she thinks that she's smarter than everyone else.* **20 to be up against:** to face a difficulty: *Our company is up against hard competition.* **21 to be up against it:** to suffer in a difficult situation: *They are poor and he lost his job, so they are up against it.* **22** *infrml.fig.* **to be up a tree:** to be angry: *He*

U

is really angry; he's up a tree. **23 to be up all night:** to be awake all night: *She stayed up all night to finish the project.* **24 to be up from:** to visit from: *He's up from Florida to visit Boston.* **25 to be up in the air:** to be undecided, indefinite: *We have no plans; everything is up in the air.* **26** *infrml.fig.* **to have s.t. up one's sleeve:** to deceive, have a hidden purpose: *He agreed to sell his business for a low price but wants me to give him my house in part payment; he always has s.t. up his sleeve.* **27 to be** or **keep up on what is happening:** to be current, informed: *I listen to the news to keep up on what is happening.* **28 to up the ante:** to increase the risk or cost of doing s.t.: *At first, he wanted a small down payment, and now he wants double that, so he's upped the ante.* **29** *infrml.fig.* **to be up the creek without a paddle:** to be in a bad situation: *The government stopped providing money to build a new airplane, so the workers will be up the creek without a paddle (have no jobs).* **30 What's up?:** what is happening: *What's up? I bought a new stereo; otherwise, nothing's up.*
—*n.* **to have ups and downs:** successes and disappointments: *The company has had its ups and downs, good years and bad years.*
—*adj.* moving up: *Take the up elevator to the furniture department.*
—*v.* **upped, upping, ups** *infrml.* to act suddenly: *He upped and punched the man in the nose.||Then he upped and left.*
—*prep.* to a higher place on: *(to be) up a tree, (to climb) up the stairs*

up-and-coming *adj.* making good progress, promising: *She is an up-and-coming young lawyer.*

up·beat /'ʌp,bit/ *adj.* enthusiastic, positive: *That energetic teacher has an upbeat attitude toward his students.*

up·bring·ing /'ʌp,brɪŋɪŋ/ *n.* [U] rearing, how parents, teachers and others give a good or bad education and manners to a young person growing up: *Her good manners show she had an excellent upbringing.*

up·chuck /'ʌp,tʃʌk/ *v. slang* to throw up, vomit: *He ate too much and upchucked in the bathroom.*

up·com·ing /'ʌp,kʌmɪŋ/ *adj.* forthcoming, happening soon: *We shall be attending the upcoming concert.*

up·date /,ʌp'deɪt, 'ʌp,deɪt/ *v.* **-dated, -dating, -dates** to make s.t. current, up-to-date: *The TV updated a news story on the bad storm coming to our area.*
—*n.* /'ʌp,deɪt/ [C] an act of updating s.t., a report: *Our daughter at college calls to give us an update on what she's doing every weekend.*

up·end /ʌp'ɛnd/ *v.* to turn s.t. up on its end: *The car upended and rolled over.*

up-front /,ʌp'frʌnt/ *adj.* **1** frank, honest: *I was upfront with him; I told him I needed money.* **2** in advance, prepaid, done: *Before the company would ship the goods, they demanded an upfront payment.*
—*adv.* **up front:** in the forward area: *When I'm a passenger in a car, I always like to sit up front.*

up·grade /'ʌp,greɪd/ *n.* [C] **1** land that heads upwards, (*syn.*) an incline: *Freight trains travel slowly on upgrades into the hills.* **2** s.t. better, an improvement: *He got an upgrade from tourist to first class on the airplane.*
—*v.* /'ʌp,greɪd, ,ʌp'greɪd/ **-graded, -grading, -grades** to improve s.t.: *The company upgraded its computer system by buying new software.*

up·heav·al /ʌp'hivəl/ *n.* [C;U] disorder, change that disturbs daily life: *That country is in upheaval with earthquakes and little food.* **-v. upheave.**

up·hill /,ʌp'hɪl/ *adv.* in an upward direction on land: *She had to walk her bicycle uphill.*
—*adj. fig.* /'ʌp,hɪl/ difficult, (*syn.*) arduous: *He has an uphill battle (fight, struggle) against illness.*

up·hold /ʌp'hoʊld/ *v.* **-held** /-'hɛld/ , **-holding, -holds** to sustain, to make sure s.t. is done correctly: *Police officers uphold the law by arresting people who break it.*

up·hol·ster /ə'poʊlstər, ʌp'hoʊl-/ *v.* to stuff furniture and cover it with cloth, leather, etc.: *We upholstered our sofa in a gold fabric.* **-n. upholsterer.** *See:* recover.

up·hol·ster·y /ə'poʊlstəri, ʌp'hoʊl-/ *n.* [U] cloth, leather, or other covering on furniture: *The upholstery on that chair is worn.*

up·keep /'ʌp,kip/ *n.* [U] the cost and work needed to keep property and machines repaired and working well: *Old houses are inexpensive to buy, but the cost of upkeep can be tremendous.*

up·lift /,ʌp'lɪft/ *v.* **1** to raise upward: *The earth uplifted in an earthquake.* **2** to cheer, to make s.o. feel well: *A good vacation uplifted him.*

up·on /ə'pɑn, ə'pɔn/ *prep.frml.* **1** on: *She sat upon the sofa.* **2** at the time of: *Upon seeing her, I smiled and ran toward her.*

up·per /'ʌpər/ *adj.* located in a higher area or region: *His upper body hurts in the neck and chest.*
—*n.* the upper part of s.t.: *The upper of his shoe (part above the sole) has come loose from the sole.*

up·per·case /,ʌpər'keɪs/ *adj.* written or printed in capital letters: *This name is written in uppercase: JOEL DEUTSER.*

upper class *n.pl.adj.* **classes 1** the highest social class: *They belong to the <n.> upper class and have <adj.> upper-class tastes.* **2**

students in the last two years of high school or college: *Only the <n.> upper classes were allowed to have proms.*

USAGE NOTE: Although American society is often called "classless," there is a small group of wealthy and powerful Americans who comprise the *upper class* of society. Rich Americans whose families have been in the USA for a long time are often called *blue bloods.*

up·per·class·man /ˌʌpərˈklæsmən/ *n.* **-men** /-mən/ a student in the last two years of high school or college: *The upperclassmen at the University of Michigan include women and men who are juniors and seniors.*

upper crust *adj.n.fig.* related to the highest class in society: *She belongs to the <n.> upper crust and has <adj.> upper crust friends.* See: upper class.

upper hand *n.* [U] **to have the upper hand:** dominance, control in a situation: *She is more intelligent than her brother, and she always has the upper hand with him.*

up·per·most /ˈʌpərˌmoʊst/ *adj.* highest: *After hiking all day we finally reached the uppermost part of the mountain.*
—*adv.* most important: *Uppermost in his mind is the need for safety.*

up·pi·ty /ˈʌpɪti/ *adj.adv.* having an attitude that one is better than others, (*syn.*) haughty: *She acts <adv.> uppity with everyone who serves her.*

up·right /ˈʌpˌraɪt/ *adv.* standing up: *People walk upright, but cats don't.*
—*adj.* **1** in a vertical position: *The cabinet is standing in an upright position.* **2** law-abiding, honest: *He is an upright citizen who obeys the law.*

up·ris·ing /ˈʌpˌraɪzɪŋ/ *n.* [C] a rebellion, revolt: *An uprising of the people happened when there was no food available.*

up·roar /ˈʌpˌrɔr/ *n.* [U] clamor, people complaining or shouting: *There was an uproar by the people over a tax increase.*

up·roar·i·ous /ʌpˈrɔriəs/ *adj.frml.* extremely funny, (*syn.*) hilarious: *That movie is an uproarious comedy.* **-adv. uproariously.**

ups and downs *n.* pleasant and unpleasant events: *Life has its ups and downs.*

up·set /ʌpˈsɛt/ *adj.* **1** troubled, distressed: *He was upset by the bad news.* **2** ill, esp. nauseated: *She suffers from an upset stomach.*
—*v.* /ʌpˈsɛt/ **-set, -setting, -sets 1** to knock s.t. over: *to upset a lamp* **2** to distress or trouble s.o.: *to upset one's neighbors with loud noise* **3** to defeat completely, (*syn.*) to vanquish: *to upset an opponent in a surprise victory*
—*n.* /ˈʌpˌsɛt/ **1** a complete, total defeat: *His*

win was an upset. **2** an illness, esp. an upset stomach: *The child had an upset last night.*

up·shot /ˈʌpˌʃɑt/ *n.* [C, usu. *sing.*] result, conclusion: *The upshot of the court case was the criminal was found guilty.*

up·side down /ˈʌpˌsaɪdˈdaʊn/ *adv.* turned with the bottom part at the top: *The clown stood upside down on her hands.* **-adj. upside-down.**

up·stage /ˌʌpˈsteɪdʒ/ *adv.* toward the back of a theater's stage: *The actor moved upstage away from the audience.*
—*v.* **-staged, -staging, -stages** to take attention away from s.o., (*syn.*) to show up: *He tried to upstage his boss at the meeting.*

up·stairs /ˌʌpˈstɛrz/ *adv.* in the direction of the level above: *He climbed the steps to go upstairs.*
—*adj.* located on the level above: *the upstairs bedroom*

up·stand·ing /ˌʌpˈstændɪŋ/ *adj.* law-abiding, honest: *She is an upstanding citizen.*

up·start /ˈʌpˌstɑrt/ *n.* an arrogant person, esp. one who was poor but becomes rich: *He is an upstart who inherited sudden wealth.*

up·state /ˈʌpˌsteɪt/ *adj.* of the northern area of a state: *Syracuse and Rochester are in upstate New York.*
—*adv.* /ˌʌpˈsteɪt/ in the direction of the northern area of a state: *We will drive upstate this weekend.*

up·stream /ˌʌpˈstrim/ *adv.* toward the beginning of a river (stream, brook, etc.): *We swim upstream against the current.*

up·surge /ˈʌpˌsɜrdʒ/ *n.* [C] a sudden rush, increase: *Our company had an upsurge in sales this month.*

up·swing /ˈʌpˌswɪŋ/ *n.* [C] an upward movement, usu. sudden: *The upswing in stock prices helped the economy.*

up·take /ˈʌpˌteɪk/ *n.* **to be quick on the uptake:** to understand rapidly: *He was quick on the uptake so he didn't need a lot of instruction.*

up·tight /ˌʌpˈtaɪt/ *adj.infrml.* **1** temporarily tense or nervous: *She is very uptight about public speaking.* **2** worried, a person who is overly self-conscious: *He is too uptight to enjoy life.*

up·time /ˈʌpˌtaɪm/ *n.* [U] the amount of time that a machine or facility is performing its function: *The uptime of a power plant producing electricity averages 11 months a year.*

up·to·date /ˌʌptəˈdeɪt/ *adj.* **1** current, not behind: *All my work is up-to-date.* **2** modern, state of the art: *Our business has the most up-to-date equipment.*

up·to·the·minute /ˌʌptəðəˈmɪnɪt/ *adj.* most current, what is happening right now: *I saw an up-to-the-minute news report on TV.*

U

up·town /'ʌp,taʊn/ *adv.adj.* in or toward the upper part of a city: *I'm going <adv.> uptown now, or to the <adj.> uptown section of Manhattan.*

up·turn /'ʌp,tɜrn/ *n.* [C] an increase: *The economy had an upturn last month that made more jobs.*

up·ward /'ʌpwərd/ or **upwards** /'ʌpwərdz/ *adv.* **1** up, rising: *He looked upward at the sky.*‖*Sales are headed upward* (or) *upwards.* **2** equal to or more than: *We have upwards of ten copies of the report available.*

u·ra·ni·um /yʊ'reɪniəm/ *n.* [U] a heavy metallic chemical that is radioactive and used in fuel for nuclear power plants and in nuclear warheads: *The government keeps close control of uranium.*

U·ra·nus /yʊ'reɪnəs, 'yʊrənəs/ *n.* the seventh planet from the sun: *Uranus is quite far from the sun.*

ur·ban /'ɜrbən/ *adj.* related to a city: *Many people move to urban areas to have the excitement of city life.* -*n.* [U] **urbanization.**

ur·bane /ər'beɪn/ *adj.* well-mannered and worldly: *Our host's urbane manner put us at ease.* -*n.* [U] **urbanity** /ər'bænəti/; -*adv.* **urbanely.**

urban renewal *n.* [U] the tearing down of old city buildings to replace them with modern ones: *The government supports urban renewal to replace the old buildings with new houses.*

urban sprawl *n.* [U] the spread of the city to the suburbs: *Los Angeles and other big cities suffer from urban sprawl.*

ur·chin /'ɜrtʃɪn/ *n.* a child, esp. a boy, who plays tricks on people and runs wild

urge /ɜrdʒ/ *v.* **urged, urging, urges** to pressure, to advise s.o. to do s.t. in a serious way: *I urge you to finish your schooling.*
—*n.* [C] a desire, (*syns.*) a craving, yearning: *I have an urge to eat some chocolates.*

ur·gen·cy /'ɜrdʒənsi/ *n.* [U] a strong need, an emergency: *He has a sense of urgency to act now and not wait.*

ur·gent /'ɜrdʒənt/ *adj.* pressing, demanding immediate action: *We have an urgent need for help; we are running out of food.* -*adv.* **urgently.**

u·rine /'yʊrɪn/ *n.* [U] liquid waste from the body: *Urine is flushed away in the bathroom toilet.* -*v.* **urinate** /'yʊrə,neɪt/.

urn /ɜrn/ *n.* **1** a large, closed container to hold and pour liquids: *There is a coffee urn in the cafeteria.* **2** a type of vase or vase-like vessel used to decorate or store things, can be used to store ashes of a dead person: *After the woman's body was cremated, her ashes were placed in a black urn and she was buried.*

us /ʌs; *weak form* əs/ *pron.* a group of two or more that includes myself: *Let's keep the secret between us.*

us·a·ble or **useable** /'yuzəbəl/ *adj.* serviceable, capable of being used: *The machine is usable now after repair.*

us·age /'yusɪdʒ, -zɪdʒ/ *n.adj.* **1** [U] utilization, use: *The <n.> usage of heating oil increased during the cold winter.* **2** [C;U] the manner in which language is actually or correctly used: *It is important to learn the <adj.> usage rules of a language.*

use /yuz/ *v.* **used, using, uses 1** to utilize, employ: *She used her intelligence to solve a problem.* **2** /yus/ to feel s.t. is normal, to grow accustomed to s.t.: *As an Inuit from Alaska, he is used to cold weather.* **3** to consume: *He uses underarm deodorant every day.* **4** to manipulate others, to get others to do what one wants: *He uses others to do his dirty work for him.* **5** *phrasal v. sep.* **to use s.t. up:** to use s.t. completely, (*syn.*) to exhaust: *She won the lottery last year, and used up the money in six months.*‖*She used it up.*
—*n.* /yus/ **1** [C;U] a purpose, (*syn.*) utilization: *The computer is of use to her in her work.* **2** [U] a right given by another: *She has the use of the office computer when she needs it.* **3** [U] the ability to use s.t. again, the regaining of control: *He hurt his hand, but he has the use of it again now.* **4 in use:** being used: *That computer is in use every day.*

used /yuzd/ *adj.* **1** /yuzd/ not new, already in use, pre-owned: *a used car* **2** /yust/ accustomed to: *He is used to hard work (hot weather, difficult times, etc.).* **3** /yuzd/ **to be** or **feel ill-used by s.o.:** to be treated badly: *I worked hard on that report but my boss took the credit; I feel ill-used by him.*

use·ful /'yusfəl/ *adj.* **1** helpful, handy: *Tools, such as a hammer and screwdriver, are useful when you want to fix something.* **2** valuable, worthwhile: *Her language skills make her a useful addition to our team.* -*adv.* **usefully;** -*n.* [U] **usefulness.**

use·less /'yuslɪs/ *adj.* **1** worthless: *His old telephone number is useless now.* **2** not worth trying, in vain, (*syn.*) futile: *It is useless to try; the telephone doesn't work.* -*adv.* **uselessly;** -*n.* [U] **uselessness.**

us·er /'yuzər/ *n.* a person or group that uses s.t.: *The user of that computer simply turns it on and starts typing.*

user-friendly *adj.* easy to understand or use, esp. a friendly computer system: *Our company bought a user-friendly computer system to save on training time.*

ush·er /'ʌʃər/ *n.* a person who shows customers to their seats, esp. in a theater
—*v.* **1** to act as an usher **2** *fig.* to make, bring into being: *Two countries ushered in a new era*

of peace by agreeing to stop fighting with each other.

u·su·al /'yuʒuəl/ *adj.* normal, customary: *Arguing is not his usual behavior.||As usual, she is on time. -adv.* **usually** /'yudʒuəli, -dʒəli/.

u·sur·pa·tion /,yusər'peɪʃən, -zər-/ *n.* [U] the seizure of control of the rights, property, or role of another: *The usurpation of power by the dictator was done with the help of the army. -v.* **usurp** /,yu'sɜrp, -'zɜrp/.

u·su·ry /'yuʒəri/ *n.* [U] the practice of lending money, often at a high rate of interest: *The Mafia practices usury, and punishes anyone who can't pay the high interest rates. -n.* **usurer;** *-adj.* **usurious** /yu'ʒuriəs/.

u·ten·sil /yu'tɛnsəl/ *n.* a tool or implement, esp. for eating food: *Utensils for eating include knives, forks, and spoons.*

u·ter·us /'yutərəs/ *n.* **uteri** /'yutə,raɪ/ or **uteruses** the female organ where a baby develops, the womb: *The uterus is located inside a woman's abdomen. -adj.* **uterine** /'yutərɪn, -,raɪn/.

u·til·i·tar·i·an /yu,tɪlə'tɛriən/ *adj.frml.* useful, (*syn.*) functional: *That old car is of little utilitarian value. -n.* [U] **utilitarianism.**

u·til·i·ty /yu'tɪləti/ *n.* **-ties 1** any basic necessity or service, such as running water, electricity, or gas: *Our utilities are shut off for repair, so we can't bathe.* **2** a business or facility that supplies water, electricity, etc.: *The local electric company is a utility.* **3** [U] usefulness: *a procedure (building, machine, etc.) that is of little utility*

u·ti·li·za·tion /,yutlə'zeɪʃən/ *n.frml.* [U] use of s.t.: *The utilization of drugs to cure illnesses is necessary.*

u·ti·lize /'yutl,aɪz/ *v.* **-lized, -lizing, -lizes** to use, to bring into use: *We utilized an old building to store our business files.*

ut·most /'ʌt,moust/ *n.* [U] the greatest, without holding back: *She tries her utmost to do a good job.*

u·to·pi·a /yu'toupiə/ *n.* a place of ideal peace, cooperation, and good living: *Many people have dreamed and written about living in a utopia. -adj.* **utopian.**

ut·ter /'ʌtər/ *adj.* complete, total: *He suffered from utter exhaustion after playing tennis.||That new play is an utter success (or failure).*

—*v.* to speak: *We waited for the prophet to utter words of wisdom. -n.* **utterance.**

ut·ter·ly /'ʌtərli/ *adv.* completely, totally: *She was utterly exhausted (surprised, delighted, etc.).*

U-turn /'yu,tɜrn/ *n.* a 180° turn: *He was heading north and then made a U-turn and headed south.*

U

V,v

V,v /vi/ *n.* **V's, v's** or **Vs, vs, 1** the 22nd letter of the English alphabet **2** the Roman numeral for five
—*adj.* shaped like a "V": *He raised two fingers in the air and made the V sign for victory.*

va·can·cy /ˈveɪkənsi/ *n.* [C;U] **-cies 1** an empty room or building, such as a hotel room: *That office building has some vacancies on the first floor.* **2** emptiness. *See:* vacant.

va·cant /ˈveɪkənt/ *adj.* without a guest or resident, empty, unoccupied: *There are two vacant apartments in that building.*

va·cate /ˈveɪˌkeɪt/ *v.* **-cated, -cating, -cates** to move out of, leave: *Our company vacated its offices and moved to a new building.*

va·ca·tion /veɪˈkeɪʃən, və-/ *n.* a time period away from work or one's regular activities, a holiday: *We took a vacation in the mountains.*
—*v.* to take time off for pleasure: *We vacationed in Italy.*

USAGE NOTE: Most American workers get two weeks of *vacation,* often called "two week's paid vacation." *The benefits at my new job are insurance and two week's paid vacation.* Nine out of ten Americans take a vacation in the summer time when the weather is good and children are not in school.

---

vac·ci·nate /ˈvæksəˌneɪt/ *v.* **-nated, -nating, -nates** to give medication to prevent a disease by injection with a needle: *The nurse vaccinated the child against the flu. -n.* **vaccination** /ˌvæksəˈneɪʃən/ [C;U].

vac·cine /vækˈsin/ *n.* [C;U] a medication taken to prevent against many diseases, such as measles and cholera: *She takes a vaccine against influenza every fall. See:* serum.

vac·il·late /ˈvæsəˌleɪt/ *v.frml.* **-lated, -lating, -lates** to waver, hesitate: *He vacillated between going away on vacation or staying home -n.* [U] **vacillation.**

vac·u·ous /ˈvækyuəs/ *adj.frml.* empty, without substance: *He has a vacuous mind -adv.* **vacuously; -n.** [U] **vacuity** /væˈkyuəti/

vac·u·um /ˈvækˌyum, -ˌyuəm/ *n.* **1** a totally empty and airless space, such as in a bottle without air **2** a state of being alone, usu. without useful information or others to help: *When I work alone at home, I feel like I work in a vacuum.* **3** a vacuum cleaner: *He cleaned the rug with a vacuum cleaner.*
—*v.* to clean with a vacuum cleaner: *He vacuumed the carpet.*

vacuum cleaner *n.* a machine that picks up dust and dirt in a strong current of air: *He used a vacuum cleaner to clean the rug. See:* vacuum.

vacuum-packed *adj.* related to food and other objects put in a container with no air in order to keep them fresh: *Coffee comes in vacuum-packed cans.*

vacuum cleaner

vag·a·bond /ˈvægəˌbɑnd/ *n.* **1** *old usage* a wanderer, (*syn.*) a drifter: *The vagabond turned west and headed for California.* **2** a vacationer without a fixed schedule or itinerary *See:* vagrant.

va·ga·ry /ˈveɪɡəri/ *n.frml.* **-ries** a strange happening, whim: *Economists don't understand all the vagaries of the stock market.*

va·gi·na /vəˈdʒaɪnə/ *n.* a woman's sex organ: *The vagina opens into the uterus. -adj.* **vaginal** /ˈvædʒənəl/; *-adv.* **vaginally.**

va·grant /ˈveɪɡrənt/ *n.* a homeless person with no job: *He is a vagrant who sits in the park all day.*
—*adj.* homeless, wandering: *The vagrant couple walked about the city. -n.* [U] **vagrancy.**

vague /veɪɡ/ *adj.* **vaguer, vaguest** unclear, (*syn.*) inexplicit: *He has some vague ideas about what to do, but nothing specific. -n.* [U] **vagueness; -adv.** **vaguely.**

vain /veɪn/ *adj.* **vainer, vainest 1** overly concerned with one's own looks, (*syn.*) conceited: *He is always looking at himself in the mirror; he's so vain!* **2** useless, unsuccessful: *He made a vain attempt to fix his car.* **3 in vain:** for nothing, without success: *His proposal* *was denied, so he did all the work in vain.*

val·e·dic·to·ri·an /ˌvælədɪkˈtɔriən/ *n.* the top student in a graduating class: *She was an excellent student who was the valedictorian of her class. -adj.* **valedictory** /ˌvæləˈdɪktəri/.

val·en·tine /ˈvælənˌtaɪn/ *n.* a love letter or greeting card given to a person to show affection or love on Saint Valentine's Day (February 14): *I sent my sweetheart a valentine for Valentine's Day.*

val·et /væˈleɪ, ˈvæleɪ, ˈvælɪt/ *n.* a person who performs small jobs for others: *A valet at the hotel parked my car.*

USAGE NOTE: *Valet parking* is a service where a worker (called a valet) parks your car when you arrive at a place such as a hotel or restaurant, and then brings the car back to you when you leave. You pay for parking and give a tip to the valet. Valet parking is most common at expensive restaurants and hotels: *On his business trip he stayed at a nice hotel with valet parking.*

---

val·iant /ˈvælyənt/ *adj.frml.* brave, bold: *The firefighter made a valiant effort to save the child from the burning house.*

val·id /ˈvælɪd/ *adj.* **1** having a good reason for s.t., convincing: *He has a valid reason for being late; his car broke down.* **2** legally usable for a set time period: *She has a passport that's valid for five years. -n.* [U] **validity** /vəˈlɪdəti/.

val·i·date /ˈvæləˌdeɪt/ *v.* **-dated, -dating, -dates 1** to confirm, learn whether s.t. is true or not: *The police officer validated the man's story that he had been robbed.* **2** to show officially that s.t. is valid: *The consulate validated her passport by putting the country's stamp on it. -n.* [C;U] **validation.**

va·lise /vəˈlis/ *n. old usage* a small suitcase: *He packed a valise for an overnight trip.*

val·ley /ˈvæli/ *n.* a low area of land between hills and mountains: *Farmers plant crops in valleys.*

val·or /ˈvælər/ *n.* [U] bravery, courage, esp. in combat: *The soldier was decorated for valor in battle. -adj.* **valorous.**

val·ua·ble /ˈvælyuəbəl, -yəbəl/ *adj.* **1** having worth, value: *Gold coins are valuable.* **2** useful, helpful: *a valuable piece of information —n.pl.* personal objects, such as jewelry or art: *She keeps her valuables in a safe.*

val·u·a·tion /ˌvælyuˈeɪʃən/ *n.* [C;U] the value placed on s.t.: *The valuation of property is done by experts. -v.* **valuate.**

val·ue /ˈvælyu/ *v.* **-ued, -uing, -ues 1** to appreciate, think s.t. is important: *I value my best friend's advice.* **2** to put a price on s.t., (*syn.*) appraise: *An expert valued the painting at $1 million.*

—n. **1** [U] worth: *Mr. Perez is a rich man who owns many pieces of art of great value.||The value of this home has doubled since we bought it.* **2** [C;U] quality: *This book is a ten-dollar value that is now on sale for five dollars.* **3** [U] liking, (*syn.*) esteem: *She places great value on her friendships with others.* **4** *pl.* ideals, standards of a society: *We have tried to teach our children solid values.*

val·ued /ˈvælyud/ *adj.* **1** priced or estimated at: *That house is valued at $100,000.* **2** appreciated: *Her advice is highly valued by her friends.*

val·ue·less /ˈvælyulɪs/ *adj.* worthless: *That bracelet is a cheap, valueless piece of jewelry.*

valve /vælv/ *n.* a device that opens and closes to stop or allow liquid or air to pass: *The heart has valves to let blood flow in and out of it.*

vam·pire /ˈvæmˌpaɪr/ *n.* **1** any of a variety of blood-sucking bats **2** a monster in human form that lives on blood: *Dracula was the first of the vampire movies.*

van /væn/ *n.* a box-like truck used for carrying large, bulky items: *People use moving vans to move their furniture to a new house.*

van·dal /ˈvændl/ *n.* a person who destroys property for fun: *The vandals destroyed some benches and set fires in the park. -n.* [U] **vandalism; -v.** **vandalize.**

vane /veɪn/ *n.* an arrow-like pointer that turns on a metal pole: *Farmers often have a weather vane on their barns to show which way the wind is blowing.*

van·guard /ˈvænˌgɑrd/ *n.* **1** [C] soldiers in the front of a military movement **2** [U] people in the front of any area of human activity: *That writer is in the vanguard of those who want political change.*

va·nil·la /vəˈnɪlə/ *n.* [U] *adj.* a flavoring used in foods: *He likes vanilla ice cream.*

van·ish /ˈvænɪʃ/ *v.* **-es** to disappear: *The man vanished from sight. -adj.* **vanishing.**

van·i·ty /ˈvænəti/ *n.* [U] conceit, too much concern with one's looks or importance: *His vanity about his appearance is ridiculous; he is always looking at himself in the mirror.*

van·quish /ˈvæŋkwɪʃ/ *v.* **-es** to defeat: *The soldiers vanquished the enemy.*

van·tage /ˈvæntɪdʒ/ *adj.* a superior position: *We stood on a vantage point that overlooked a valley.*

vap·id /ˈvæpɪd, ˈveɪ-/ *adj.frml.* dull, empty: *He has a vapid personality.*

va·por /ˈveɪpər/ *n.* **1** [U] a gas, usu. one that cannot be seen: *Boiling water turns into vapor in the air.* **2** [C;U] a mist, haze, or smog that is barely visible *-adj.* **vaporous.**

va·por·ize /ˈveɪpəˌraɪz/ *v.* **-ized, -izing, -izes** to change one substance into another that usu.

cannot be seen: *When water boils, it vaporizes into the air.*

va·por·iz·er /'veɪpə,raɪzər/ *n.* a machine that heats water to produce steam, such as for medical purposes: *He used a vaporizer to relieve his bad cold.*

var·i·a·ble /'vɛriəbəl, 'vær-/ *adj.* **1** changing, alternating: *The forecast is that we will have variable weather, with rain and sunshine today.* **2** changeable: *a variable interest rate* —*n.* (in math) a factor, usu. an unknown, in an equation or situation: *In the equation "3x=6"x is a variable.* -*n.* [U] **variability.**

var·i·ance /'vɛriəns, 'vær-/ *n.* **1** [C] an exception to a rule or standard **2** [U] not in agreement with s.o. or s.t.: *The builder's plans were at variance with the limit on building heights because her building was too tall.*

var·i·ant /'vɛriənt, 'vær-/ *n.* a different spelling of a word: *A variant of "color" is "colour."*

var·i·a·tion /,vɛri'eɪʃən, ,vær-/ *n.* [C;U] **1** a change: *The variation in the weather was from sunshine to rain.* **2** a small difference: *A variation in the electrical current made the lights dim.*

var·i·cose /'væri,koʊs/ *n.pl.* swollen, blue: *Many people suffer from varicose veins when they grow older.*

var·ied /'vɛrid, 'vær-/ *adj. & past part. of* vary, of different kinds: *That store offers a varied selection of candies.*

var·i·e·ty /və'raɪəti/ *n.* -**ties** **1** [U] different types of experiences: *He added variety to his life by taking a wonderful vacation.* **2** [U] different types of things: *That store carries a wide variety of merchandise, from clothes to furniture.* **3** [C] (in biology) a type of plant: *He grows six varieties of roses.*

var·i·ous /'vɛriəs, 'vær-/ *adj.* **1** a general number of people or things: *Various people attended the meeting.* **2** assorted, diverse: *The store carries various items, such as clothes and furniture.* -*adv.* **variously.**

var·nish /'vɑrnɪʃ/ *n.* -**es** [C;U] an oil-based liquid painted on wood to give it a shiny finish, (*syn.*) shellac: *He put a coat of varnish on the bookcase.* —*v.* to apply varnish: *He varnished the table.*

var·si·ty /'vɑrsəti/ *n.* -**ties** the school team playing at the highest level (not the junior varsity or JV)

var·y /'vɛri, 'væri/ *v.* -**ied, -ying, -ies** **1** to change or modify: *The bank varies the interest rates every month.* **2** to differ: *Air fares vary from one airline to another.* **3** to depart from the usual, (*syn.*) to deviate: *The stock market varied from its upward trend and went down.*

vase /veɪs, vaz, veɪz/ *n.* a decorative glass or clay jar usu. used to hold flowers: *The vase on the table has roses in it.*

va·sec·to·my /væ'sɛktəmi, və-/ *n.* [C;U] -**mies** surgery on a man's genitals to keep him from having children: *After fathering two children, he had a vasectomy.*

vast /væst/ *adj.* **1** wide in area, (*syn.*) immense: *Mr. Rockefeller owns a vast piece of land with two lakes and four houses.* **2** important, great: *A good rainfall makes a vast difference in growing food crops.* -*n.* [U] **vastness;** -*adv.* **vastly.**

vat /væt/ *n.* a large, round container: *Chemicals are mixed in vats.*

Vat·i·can /'vætəkən/ *n.* the governmental seat of the Roman Catholic Church and the residence of the Pope in Rome: *Millions of tourists visit the Vatican each year.*

vault /vɔlt/ *v.* **1** to leap over s.t. *He vaulted the fence.* **2** *fig.* to appear suddenly: *She vaulted into prominence as a new politician running for mayor.* —*n.* a large safe used to keep money, documents, and other valuables: *a bank vault*

vault·ed /'vɔltɪd/ *adj.* built with arches: *That church has a vaulted ceiling*

VCR /'visi'ɑr/ *n. See:* videocassette recorder.

VD /vi'di/ *abbr. for* venereal disease: *He's got VD.*

veal /vil/ *n.* [U] calf meat: *She ate veal with a wine sauce.*

veer /vɪr/ *v.* to turn sharply: *The airplane (car, tank, etc.) veered sharply to avoid danger.*

veg·e·ta·ble /'vɛdʒtəbəl/ *n.* various plants raised as food: *Lettuce, carrots, and string beans are my favorite vegetables.*

veg·e·tar·i·an /,vɛdʒə'tɛriən/ *n.adj.* a person who eats only plant foods: *She is a <n.> vegetarian; she eats only <adj.> vegetarian foods.* -*n.* [U] **vegetarianism.**

USAGE NOTE: There are several types of *vegetarians,* depending on the kinds of foods they eat. A *lacto-ovo vegetarian* eats plant products, milk products, and eggs. There are also *lacto-vegetarians* who eat plant products and milk products, but no eggs. *Ovo-vegetarians* eat plant products and eggs, but not milk products. Finally, people who eat only plant products are called *vegans.* Vegans do not eat any animal products.

veg·e·tate /'vɛdʒə,teɪt/ *v.* -**tated, -tating, -tates** to do nothing useful or interesting, to idle: *He is a person who vegetates by watching television all day.* -*adj.* **vegetative.**

veg·e·ta·tion /,vɛdʒə'teɪʃən/ *n.* [U] the plant covering in an area: *Jungle vegetation is very thick.*

veg·gies /'vɛdʒiz/ *n.pl. infrml.* short for vegetables: *Mothers tell children to eat their veggies.*

ve·he·ment /'viəmənt/ *adj.* fierce, very angry: *He made a vehement denial of his guilt.* -*n.* [U] **vehemence; -***adv.* **vehemently.**

ve·hi·cle /'viɪkəl/ *n.* a machine, such as a car or truck, that travels to transport people or goods: *We took our vehicle to the mechanic for its yearly safety inspection.* -*adj.* **vehicular** /vɪ'hɪkyələr/.

veil /veɪl/ *n.v.* a light, cloth covering worn over the face by women: *She wore a <n.> veil made of a light silk to the wedding.||Her face was <v.> veiled.*

veil

vein /veɪn/ *n.* **1** any of many blood vessels that bring blood to the heart and lungs: *You can see the blue veins on the back of his hand.* **2** an area in the ground that contains valuable minerals, such as coal or gold

ve·loc·i·ty /və'lɑsəti/ *n.* **-ties** [C;U] speed, such as that measured in miles per hour or feet per second: *A bullet travels at a high velocity.*

ve·lour /və'lʊr/ *n.* [C;U] a velvety type of cloth used in making clothing and furniture: *That sofa is covered in green velour.*

vel·vet /'vɛlvɪt/ *n.* [C;U] a soft, thick cloth made of cotton, silk, etc.: *She wore a jacket made of blue velvet.* -*adj.* **velvety.**

ve·nal /'vinəl/ *adj.frml.* corrupt, dishonest: *He is a venal politician who takes money illegally from important people.* -*adv.* **venally; -***n.* [U] **venality** /vi'næləti/.

vend /vɛnd/ *v.* to offer for sale, sell: *Machines vend candy in the lunch room. See:* vending machine.

vend·er or **ven·dor** /'vɛndər/ *n.* **1** a person who sells s.t.: *a hot dog vender on the street corner* **2** a general term for a business or agent who supplies goods and services to other companies: *Our company works with 20 vendors.*

vending machine *n.* a machine that gives packaged food, soft drinks, or other items after coins are placed in it: *He often buys soft drinks from the vending machine.*

ve·neer /və'nɪr/ *n.* **1** [C;U] a thin covering of decorative wood or plastic over a cheaper material: *The veneer on the wooden coffee table is wearing off.* **2** [C, *usu. sing.*] *fig.* a false appearance: *He has a veneer of friendliness over a very nasty personality.*

ven·er·a·ble /'vɛnərəbəl/ *adj.* respected, admired because of old age, dignity, etc.: *He is a venerable old man.* -*v.* **venerate; -***n.* [U] **veneration** /,vɛnə'reɪʃən/.

ve·ne·re·al disease /və'nɪriəl/ *n.* [C;U] any of a variety of contagious sex organ diseases, such as gonorrhea or syphilis: *Venereal disease is caught during sexual acts.*

ve·ne·tian blind /və'niʃən/ *n.* a window shade with thin plastic or metal blades: *I closed the venetian blinds to keep the bright sunlight out.*

venetian blind

ven·geance /'vɛndʒəns/ *n.* [U] bitter retaliation, a harmful act against s.o. who has done s.t. wrong to you: *He is seeking vengeance for the murder of his brother.*

venge·ful /'vɛndʒful/ *adj.* wanting to harm s.o. who wronged you, (*syn.*) spiteful: *He has a vengeful attitude and wants to kill his brother's murderer.*

ven·i·son /'vɛnəsən/ *n.* [U] deer meat: *In the autumn hunting season, we eat venison.*

ven·om /'vɛnəm/ *n.* [U] **1** the poison in some snakes and insects: *snake venom* **2** *fig.* hatred: *He is full of venom toward his enemies.* -*adj.* **venomous.** *See:* anger.

vent /vɛnt/ *v.* **1** to make air or fumes escape: *to vent a room of smoke* **2** to let go with force: *He vented his anger by screaming at his dog.*
—*n.* an opening used to let air or fumes escape: *There is a vent from my kitchen stove to the outside of the house.*

ven·ti·late /'vɛntl,eɪt/ *v.* **-lated, -lating, -lates** to change the air in an enclosed space: *She ventilated the room by opening a window.*

ven·ti·la·tion /,vɛntl'eɪʃən/ *n.* [U] a system, such as air openings and blowers, used to change the air in a room or building: *The poor ventilation in my hotel room makes me feel sick.* -*n.* [C] **ventilator.**

ven·tri·cle /'vɛntrəkəl/ *n.* a chamber: *The left ventricle is the biggest of four chambers in the heart.*

ven·tril·o·quist /vɛn'trɪləkwɪst/ *n.* a person who entertains others by appearing to be silent while making a type of doll (dummy) talk: *Ventriloquists are very funny because their lips don't seem to move while their dummy talks.* -*n.* [U] **ventriloquism.**

ven·ture /'vɛntʃər/ *v.* **-tured, -turing, -tures** to act with some risk of harm or money: *I told my wife not to venture to the edge of the cliff.*
—*n.* an act, esp. a business deal with risk: *Two companies made a joint venture to send a rocket to the moon.* -*adj.* **venturesome.** *See:* joint venture.

ven·ue /'vɛnyu/ *n.* [C;U] (in law) the location of an event: *The lawyer asked the judge for a change in venue.*

Ve·nus /'vinəs/ *n.* the second planet from the sun: *Venus is between Mercury and Mars.*

ve·rac·i·ty /və'ræsəti/ *n.frml.* [U] truthfulness: *I do not doubt his veracity.*

V

ve·ran·da /vəˈrændə/ *n.* a porch: *We often sit on the veranda on hot evenings.*

veranda

verb /vɜrb/ *n.* an action word a predicate: *"Be," "do," and "go" are verbs.*

ver·bal /ˈvɜrbəl/ *adj.* **1** related to written or spoken words: *She has good verbal skills; she speaks and writes well.* **2** *infrml.* spoken words versus written ones: *We had only a verbal agreement, with nothing in writing.* *-v.* **verbalize;** *-adv.* **verbally.**

ver·ba·tim /vərˈbeɪtəm/ *adj.adv.* word-for-word, related to using s.o.'s exact words: *I quoted <adv.> verbatim what the professor said; I made a <adj.> verbatim quote.*

ver·bi·age /ˈvɜrbiɪdʒ/ *n.* [U] words, esp. too many of them: *She cut all the verbiage from the report and made it clear and simple.*

ver·bose /vərˈboʊs/ *adj.* wordy, long-winded: *That long report is a verbose piece of writing.* *-adv.* **verbosely;** *-n.* [U] **verbosity** /vərˈbasəti/.

ver·dict /ˈvɜrdɪkt/ *n.* a decision of guilty or not guilty: *The jury arrived at a verdict of "not guilty" for the defendant.*

verge /vɜrdʒ/ *n.* the edge or border of s.t.: *She is on the verge of making a decision.*
—*v.* **verged, verging, verges** to border on, approach: *That singer has a career that verges on greatness.*

ver·i·fi·a·ble /ˌvɛrəˈfaɪəbəl/ *adj.* capable of being verified or proven: *The police got a verifiable account of the accident from witnesses.*

ver·i·fy /ˈvɛrəˌfaɪ/ *v.* **-fied, -fying, -fies** to prove s.t. is true, confirm: *I verified the store's address by calling to check it.* *-n.* [U] **verification** /ˌvɛrəfəˈkeɪʃən/.

ver·i·ta·ble /ˈvɛrətəbəl/ *adj.* true, real: *His mind is a veritable encyclopedia of information.*

ver·i·ty /ˈvɛrəti/ *n.frml.* **-ties** truth: *Beauty, love, and honor are eternal verities.*

ver·min /ˈvɜrmɪn/ *n.* [U] small animals that are considered pests, such as mice, rats, and cockroaches: *He got rid of the vermin in his apartment by putting some traps on the floor.*

ver·mouth /vərˈmuθ/ *n.* [U] in USA, a wine used mainly as a mixer in cocktails: *We use dry vermouth in martinis and sweet vermouth in Manhattans.*

ver·nac·u·lar /vərˈnækyələr/ *n.* [U] language in everyday use in a country or region: *The local vernacular in some areas is very different from the English that is taught in schools.*

ver·sa·tile /ˈvɜrsətl, -ˌtaɪl/ *adj.* **1** capable in many ways, talented: *She is a versatile musician who can play many instruments.* **2** useful in many ways, multipurpose: *A screwdriver or adjustable wrench is a versatile tool.* *-n.* [U]

versatility /ˌvɜrsəˈtɪləti/.

verse /vɜrs/ *n.* **1** [U] poetry: *Poets write in verse.* **2** [C] a section of poetry or of the Bible —*v.* **versed, versing, verses** to learn, (*syn.*) to school: *He versed himself in history.*

ver·sion /ˈvɜrʒən/ *n.* **1** an account of s.t.: *He told his own version of the funny story.* **2** a translation or edition: *I own the King James Version of the Bible.*

ver·sus /ˈvɜrsəs, -səz/ *prep.* in opposition to, against: *It was Argentina versus West Germany in the World Cup soccer match.*

ver·te·bra /ˈvɜrtəbrə/ *n.* **-brae** /-brei, -bri/ a section of the spine: *He broke two vertebrae in a fall.*

ver·te·brate /ˈvɜrtəbrɪt, -ˌbreɪt/ *adj.* having a spine: *vertebrate animals*
—*n.* an animal with a spine: *The vertebrates include lions and elephants.*

ver·ti·cal /ˈvɜrtɪkəl/ *adj.* upright, at 90 degrees to the horizontal: *The hospital patient is sitting in the vertical position, upright in bed.* *-adv.* **vertically.**

ver·ti·go /ˈvɜrtɪˌgoʊ/ *n.* [U] dizziness, feeling of weakness: *He suffers from vertigo when he looks down from a great height.*

verve /vɜrv/ *n.* [U] enthusiasm, energy: *She does things with a lot of verve.*

ver·y /ˈvɛri/ *adv.* absolutely, extremely: *He was very pleased to see his friend.*
—*adj.* absolute: *She is at the very beginning of a long project.*

ves·sel /ˈvɛsəl/ *n.* **1** a tube that carries fluid: *the blood vessels* **2** a container, such as a cup: *a vessel used in religious services* **3** a ship: *Cargo vessels sail the Atlantic.*

vest /vɛst/ *n.* a sleeveless garment worn on the upper body: *He often wears a vest as part of a three-piece suit.*
—*v.* **1** *frml.* to wear, put on: *The priest vested himself in the robes of his office.* **2** *fig.* give power to, (*syn.*) to entrust: *to vest an official with the right to spend money* **3** to become the property of s.o.: *The pension fund vests assets to its members' accounts after five years.*

ves·ti·bule /ˈvɛstəˌbyul/ *n.* a small entrance hall in a house or other building: *The doorman at that apartment building usually stands in the vestibule when it rains.*

ves·tige /ˈvɛstɪdʒ/ *n.frml.* a small part or amount of s.t., remains: *Vestiges of their clothes were found after the fire in the house.*

vest·ment /ˈvɛstmənt/ *n.* ceremonial clothes: *The priest is dressed in holy vestments.*

vet /vɛt/ *n.* short for **1** veteran: *My father is a war vet.* **2** veterinarian: *to take the cat to the vet*
—*v.frml.* **vetted, vetting, vets** to examine s.t. carefully: *Government experts vetted information about the new drug to make sure that it was safe.*

V

vet·er·an /'vɛtərən, 'vɛtrən/ *n.* any person honorably discharged from the military: *She is a veteran of military service in Africa.*
—*adj.* anyone with a lot of experience in a job, profession, or art: *He is a veteran newspaper reporter.*

Veterans Day *n.* a holiday honoring the war veterans in the USA on November 11: *We watched the Veterans Day parade.*

vet·er·i·nar·i·an /,vɛtərə'nɛriən, ,vɛtrə-/ *n.* a doctor for animals: *The veterinarian came to see our sick horse. -adj.* **veterinary.** *See;* vet.

ve·to /'vitoʊ/ *v.* **-toed, -toing, -toes** to cancel or block the passage of a law: *The President vetoed the budget bill sent to him by Congress.*
—*n.* [C;U] the act of vetoing legislation

USAGE NOTE: In the USA, the President can *veto* any law that Congress passes. However, if on a second vote, two thirds of the members of Congress vote for the law, Congress can override the President's veto. Veto can be used by anyone who has the power to change a decision: *Dad said we could go to the movie, but Mom vetoed the decision.||Our boss vetoed our group's plan.*

vex /vɛks/ *v.* **vexed, vexing, vexes** to irritate, make s.o. angry: *His demands for money vexed his wife. -adj.* **vexatious** /vɛk'seɪʃəs/; *-n.* [C;U] **vexation.**

vi·a /'viə, 'vaɪə/ *prep.* **1** by way of: *We flew to Paris via London.* **2** through means of: *I sent a package via messenger.*

vi·a·ble /'vaɪəbəl/ *adj.* workable, capable of succeeding: *He found a viable solution to the problem. -n.* [U] **viability.**

vi·a·duct /'vaɪə,dʌkt/ *n.* a bridge across a valley: *A viaduct carries railroad tracks from one mountain to the next.*

vi·al /'vaɪəl/ *n.* a small, round container made of glass or plastic: *There is a vial of medicine (perfume, illegal drugs, etc.) on the shelf.*

vibes /vaɪbz/ *n.pl.slang* short for vibrations: the unspoken good or bad feelings given off by a person or event: *I get good vibes from my new friend.*

vi·brant /'vaɪbrənt/ *adj.* **1** full of life, spirited: *She has a vibrant personality.* **2** intense, colorful: *That painting has vibrant colors of red and yellow in it.*

vi·brate /'vaɪ,breɪt/ *v.* **-brated, -brating, -brates 1** to quiver, shake: *A violin string vibrates.* **2** to resonate, shake: *His stereo was so loud that it made the room vibrate.*

vi·bra·tion /vaɪ'breɪʃən/ *n.* **1** [C;U] quivering, shaking: *I felt the vibration caused by a passing train.* **2** *pl.infrml.* the feelings given off by a person or event: *We had good vibrations from the successful business meeting.*

vi·bra·tor /'vaɪbreɪtər/ *n.* a device used for massage or sexual stimulation: *He uses a vibrator to massage his sore legs.*

vic·ar /'vɪkər/ *n.* **1** a clergyman **2** a parish priest: *The vicar gave a sermon on the evils of alcohol.*

vic·ar·age /'vɪkərɪdʒ/ *n.* a vicar's house: *We visited the vicarage next to the church.*

vi·car·i·ous /vaɪ'kɛriəs, -'kær-/ *adj.* felt and understood through the experience of another, indirect: *I got vicarious pleasure from hearing about their trip. -adv.* **vicariously.**

vice /vaɪs/ *n.* [C;U] sin or crime, including illegal drugs and prostitution: *There is a lot of vice in big cities.*

Vice President /vaɪs/ *n.* **1** the second in line to the President of the US government: *The Vice President represents the government at many official events.* **2** (without capital letters) a title in other business organizations given to executives and officers below the rank of president: *Large corporations often have many vice presidents. -n.* **the Vice Presidency; a vice presidency.**

USAGE NOTE: The *Vice President* is an advisor to both the President of the USA and the president of the Senate. In the USA, the Vice President and President run for office and are elected together.

vice squad *n.* police responsible for stopping crime: *The vice squad often works at night to arrest prostitutes and drug dealers.*

vi·ce ver·sa /'vaɪsə'vɜrsə, 'vaɪs/ *adv.* the same in reverse order: *What may be too expensive for you may seem reasonable to me or vice versa.||He loves her and vice versa.*

vi·cin·i·ty /və'sɪnəti/ *n.* **-ties** [U] the local area, places nearby: *Our house is located in this vicinity; it's three blocks away, in fact.*

vi·cious /'vɪʃəs/ *adj.* **1** cruel, mean: *His vicious comments are cruel and hurtful.* **2** ferocious, savage: *That vicious dog attacks and bites people. -n.* [U] **viciousness;** *-adv.* **viciously.**

vicious circle *n.* [U] a chain of events in which one difficulty leads to another, often of the same kind: *Poor people don't have enough money for a good education, which keeps their children poor as well; poverty is a vicious circle.*

vic·tim /'vɪktəm/ *n.* s.o. or s.t. that suffers from an accident, crime, illness, or bad luck: *The accident victim was helped by ambulance attendants.*

vic·tim·ize /'vɪktə,maɪz/ *v.* **-ized, -izing, -izes** to deceive and exploit another person: *The dishonest man victimized an old lady by cheating her.*

V

vic·tor /'vɪktər/ *n.* the winner in a contest or battle: *The victor in the competition won a prize.*

vic·to·ri·ous /vɪk'tɔriəs/ *adj.* related to winning a competition or battle, (*syn.*) triumphant: *Our nation emerged victorious in the battle.* -*adv.* **victoriously.**

vic·to·ry /'vɪktəri/ *n.* -**ries 1** [C;U] triumph, conquest: *She led her basketball team to victory by scoring the winning point.* **2** [C] success, achievement: *He finally stopped smoking, and doing that was a big victory for him.*

vid·e·o /'vɪdiou/ *adj.* related to television images: *The video part of the television broadcast was clear, but the sound was poor.* —*n.* [C;U] television or videotape pictures: *We saw the movie on video.*

video camera *n.* a camera used to record the pictures and sounds of events, using videotape: *Many families own a video camera today.*

vid·e·o·cas·sette /ˌvɪdioukə'sɛt/ *n.* videotape in a plastic cassette suitable for playing in a videocassette recorder attached to a television set: *We often watch old movies on videocassette.*

videocassette recorder *n.* usu. called a **VCR**: an electronic machine that both records television programs on videotape for later viewing and is used to play videotapes: *He watched a movie on our new VCR.*

vid·e·o·disc /'vɪdiouˌdɪsk/ *n.* a a flat, circular object containing video and audio recording played on a disk player attached to a television screen: *We watch movies on videodisc.*

video game *n.* an electronic game played on a television set or arcade machine: *Video games are fun to play.*

vid·e·o·tape /'vɪdiouˌteɪp/ *n.* [C;U] video recording tape —*v.* -**taped, -taping, -tapes** to record on videotape: *We videotaped a sporting event.*

vie /vaɪ/ *v.* **vied, vying, vies** to attempt to win s.t., to compete: *Two athletes vied for first place in the competition.*

view /vyu/ *v.* **1** to look at: *We viewed the mountain scenery.* **2** to hold the opinion that, (*syn.*) to regard: *She views marriage as a serious matter.* **3** to inspect, examine: *I viewed a collection of paintings.*
—*n.* **1** a scene, (*syn.*) vista: *Our house has a view of the park.* **2** opinion, belief: *Many people have views on how to fix the economy.* **3 in my (her, our, etc.) view:** in one's opinion, belief: *In my view, the economy is in trouble.* **4 to come into view:** to appear: *A ship came into view on the horizon.* **5 in view:** seeable, present: *That ship is now in view. Can you see it, too?* **6 in view of:** because of, with regard to: *In view of our difficulties with money, let's not*

go on vacation. **7 on view:** displayed, available to see: *The Van Gogh paintings are on view in the Metropolitan Museum of Art this week.* **8 to have** or **hold views:** to believe, to be a spokesperson for ideas: *She has unusual views on politics and is criticized for them.*

view·er /'vyuər/ *n.* **1** a person who watches television programs: *The viewers sit at home in their living rooms.* **2** a video device used for display: *Put the slide in the viewer so that we can see it.*

view·ing /'vyuɪŋ/ *n.* [C;U] a type of exhibition, a showing of s.t.: *The movie producer held a private viewing of her new film for the press.*

view·point /'vyuˌpɔɪnt/ *n.* an opinion, (*syn.*) perspective: *Her viewpoint is that she wants to get married, but not at this time.*

vig·il /'vɪdʒəl/ *n.* **1** a gathering of people who wait in silence for a reason: *The crowd held a candlelight vigil for peace.* **2** a period of waiting: *She keeps an all-night vigil for her sick child.*

vig·i·lance /'vɪdʒələns/ *n.* [U] alertness to danger, watchfulness: *Very young children need an adult's constant vigilance.* -*adj.* **vigilant**

vig·i·lan·te /ˌvɪdʒə'lænti/ *n.* a person who takes the law into his or her own hands by punishing a suspected criminal: *Vigilantes killed the suspected murderer.*

vig·or·ous /'vɪgərəs/ *adj.* energetic, strong: *She does vigorous exercises every morning.* -*adv.* **vigorously.**

vile /vaɪl/ *adj.* **viler, vilest 1** evil, wicked: *Murder is a vile act.* **2** dirty, foul: *He uses vile language.*

vil·i·fy /'vɪləˌfaɪ/ *v.frml.* -**fied, -fying, -fies** to criticize harshly, to defame or slander: *The politician was vilified in the newspapers as a criminal.*

vil·la /'vɪlə/ *n.* a country house: *They have a villa in the Swiss Alps.*

vil·lage /'vɪlɪdʒ/ *n.* a group of houses forming a settlement smaller than a town or city: *They live in a country village.*

vil·lag·er /'vɪlədʒər/ *n.* a person who lives in a village: *The villagers do their shopping at the general store.*

vil·lain /'vɪlən/ *n.* a bad person, esp. a criminal: *Villains commit crimes.* -*adj.* **villainous;** -*n.* [U] **villainy.**

vim /vɪm/ *n.* [U] vitality, energy: *She has a lot of vim and vigor.*

vin·ai·grette /ˌvɪnə'grɛt/ *n.* [U] a salad dressing of olive oil and vinegar usu. with spices: *I poured vinaigrette on my salad.*

vin·di·cate /'vɪndəˌkeɪt/ *v.* -**cated, -cating, -cates 1** to support one's actions in the face of opposition, (*syn.*) to justify: *History vindicates the wise who offer peace, not war.* **2** to prove,

V

(*syn.*) to substantiate: *She vindicated her claim to the land by producing legal documents showing that she owns it.* *-n.* [U] **vindication.**

vin·dic·tive /vɪnˈdɪktɪv/ *adj.* seeking to harm another, (*syns.*) vengeful, spiteful: *She has a vindictive attitude toward her ex-husband.* *-adv.* **vindictively.**

vine /vaɪn/ *n.* a climbing plant, such as ivy or grape: *Vines cover the hills in wine country.*

vin·e·gar /ˈvɪnəgər/ *n.* [U] an acid-tasting liquid made from wine, malt, etc.: *She poured vinegar and oil on her salad.* *-adj.* **vinegary.**

vine·yard /ˈvɪnyərd/ *n.* an area with grapevines: *Many vineyards are located near San Francisco.*

vin·tage /ˈvɪntɪdʒ/ *n.* a wine harvest, esp. the year: *They drank a French wine of a 1986 vintage.*
—adj. **1** indicating good quality and old age: *a vintage wine (car, year, etc.).* **2** from an earlier time, but often still fashionable or desirable: *I got a great sweater from the 1960's at the vintage clothing store.*

vint·ner /ˈvɪntnər/ *n.frml.* **1** a winemaker: *The vintners of Napa Valley produce good wine.* **2** a wine merchant: *He is the vintner who has a shop on the corner.*

vi·nyl /ˈvaɪnəl/ *n.* a tough plastic used to make clothes and upholstery: *The seat covering in my car is made of vinyl.*

vi·o·late /ˈvaɪəˌleɪt/ *v.* **-lated, -lating, -lates** **1** to break, (*syn.*) breach: *He violated the law (a contract, s.o.'s rights, etc.).* **2** to rape: *It is a very serious crime to violate s.o.*

vi·o·la·tion /ˌvaɪəˈleɪʃən/ *n.* [C;U] an act of breaking a law, contract, rule, etc., (*syn.*) a breach: *A violation of a law can bring punishment.* *-adj.* **violable** /ˈvaɪələbəl/.

vi·o·lence /ˈvaɪələns/ *n.* [U] **1** injury or damage, brutality: *The criminal committed violence in stabbing his victim.* **2** fury, strong force, such as wind: *The violence of the hurricane caused great damage.* *-adj.* **violent;** *-adv.* **violently.**

vi·o·let /ˈvaɪələt/ *n.* a plant with bluish-purple flowers: *an African violet*
—adj. a bluish-purple color: *She wore a violet dress.*

vi·o·lin /ˌvaɪəˈlɪn/ *n.* a stringed musical instrument played with a bow: *The violin is a great solo instrument.*

VIP /ˈviaɪˈpi/ *n.abbr. for* very important person: *She is a VIP in the government who works closely with the President.*

vi·per /ˈvaɪpər/ *n.* **1** a small, poisonous snake **2** *fig.* a dangerous, deceitful person: *She seems sweet, but she is really a viper out to do harm.*

vi·ral /ˈvaɪrəl/ *adj.* related to viruses: *He has a viral infection, that is, viral pneumonia.*

vir·gin /ˈvɜrdʒən/ *n.* a person who has not had sexual intercourse: *She was a virgin when she married, and so was her husband.*
—adj. untouched, in its original state: *There is a lot of virgin land in Alaska.*

vir·gin·i·ty /vərˈdʒɪnəti/ *n.* [U] the condition of never having had sex: *Many teenagers value their virginity.* *-adj.* **virginal** /ˈvɜrdʒənəl/.

vir·ile /ˈvɪrəl, -ˌaɪl/ *adj.* strong, manly: *A virile man has strong sexual powers.* *-n.* [U] **virility** /vəˈrɪləti/.

vir·tu·al /ˈvɜrtʃuəl/ *adj.* nearly, almost but not quite: *He is nearly deaf; he has suffered the virtual loss of his hearing.* *-adv.* **virtually.**

virtual reality *n.* [U] experiencing events that seem like real life by putting on special eyeglasses, hearing devices, and gloves attached to a computer: *Virtual reality can make you feel like you are an actor moving around in a movie you are watching.* See: cyberspace.

USAGE NOTE: *Virtual reality* technology is often used to make lifelike computer games, but it may also be used, for example, to practice skills such as driving or flying an airplane without danger. *Virtual reality* works by using (1) sound, (2) computer pictures that move with a user's eyes, and (3) machines that help you experience the sense of touch: *Virtual reality requires extremely fast computers and complicated software.*

vir·tue /ˈvɜrtʃu/ *n.* **1** [U] moral goodness, such as honesty or clean living: *He is a man of great virtue.* **2** [C] advantage, special quality: *That new medicine has the virtue of being inexpensive.* **3 by virtue of:** because of: *By virtue of the fact that the medicine is inexpensive, it has a big market.*

vir·tu·o·so /ˌvɜrtʃuˈousou/ *n.* **-sos** a musician or singer who is a star: *A piano virtuoso often performs alone.*

vir·tu·ous /ˈvɜrtʃuəs/ *adj.* **1** moral, upright: *A virtuous person does not tell lies.* **2** virginal: *a virtuous young person* *-adv.* **virtuously.**

vir·u·lent /ˈvɪryələnt, ˈvɪrə-/ *adj.* **1** related to disease, bacteria, and viruses that spread fast and are very harmful: *Cholera and smallpox are virulent diseases.* **2** extremely harsh, biting: *Jon was fired after receiving a report from his boss with virulent criticism* *-n.* [U] **virulence;** *-adv.* **virulently.**

vi·rus /ˈvaɪrəs/ *n.* any microorganism smaller than bacteria that causes such diseases as the common cold, influenza, measles, and HIV: *He caught a virus and was sick for a week.*

vi·sa /ˈvizə, -sə/ *n.* a foreign travel authorization: *The American consulate granted me a six-month visa and stamped my passport.*

V

Vi·sa /'vizə, -sə/ *n.TM* the name of a popular credit card: *When she travels, she charges her expenses on her Visa.*

vis·age /'vɪzɪʤ/ *n.frml.* the human face: *Her visage is marked by worry and care.*

vis-à-vis /'vizə'vi/ *prep.* in relation to, compared with: *Vis-à-vis the competition, our company is doing well.*

vis·cer·al /'vɪsərəl/ *adj.* **1** related to the intestines **2** characterized by a feeling in the abdomen: *When he saw the lion, he had a visceral feeling of fear.* *-n.pl.* **viscera;** *-adv.* **viscerally.**

vis·cos·i·ty /vɪs'kasəti/ *n.* [U] the thickness of a fluid: *A motor oil with a low viscosity is used in cold weather so engine parts can move easily.* *-adj.* **viscous** /'vɪs'kəs/.

vise /vais/ *n.* a two-pronged tool with a screw handle that tightens against an object to hold the object so that it can be worked on: *I put the piece of metal in the vise and cut it.*

vis·i·bil·i·ty /,vɪzə'bɪləti/ *n.* [U] clearness of the air and sky: *The visibility is good today, with no clouds or fog.*

vis·i·ble /'vɪzəbəl/ *adj.* **1** seeable, (*syn.*) perceptible: *The coastline became visible through the fog.* **2** apparent, obvious: *Her health made a visible improvement.* *-adv.* **visibly.**

vi·sion /'vɪʤən/ *n.* **1** [U] eyesight: *She has good (poor, clear, etc.) vision.* **2** [C] a fantasy, an imaginary event: *to have a vision in a dream* **3** [U] foresight, ability to imagine the future: *There are men (women, leaders) of vision in every industry.* *-n.* [C] **visionary.**

visit /'vɪzɪt/ *v.* **1** to go to a place and stay for a time: *We visited relatives in the next town for two days.* **2 to pay s.o. a visit:** to make a usu. brief visit: *His friend is ill, so he pays a visit to him every day.* **3** *phrasal v.sep.* **to visit s.t. on s.o.:** *frml.* to direct anger, punishment, etc., against s.o.; *Our boss visited her wrath on the whole department.*
—n. a stay with s.o. or at a place: *We had a nice visit with our cousins in Ohio.*

vis·it·a·tion /,vɪzə'teɪʃən/ *n.* [C] *adj.frml.* a visit usu. arranged through an institution: *Friends and family members of prisoners receive <adj.> visitation rights once a week.*

visiting hours *n.pl.* the time period allowed, esp. by a hospital, for family and friends to visit patients: *The hospital visiting hours are from 2:00 to 4:00 P.M.*

visiting nurse *n.* a nurse who travels from house to house and town to town to help sick patients: *In many areas, a visiting nurse is the only medical care some poor people have.*

vis·i·tor /'vɪzətər/ *n.* **1** a person who visits others: *Our company had some visitors yesterday from another business.* **2** tourists, vacationers: *New York has many visitors from overseas.*

vi·sor /'vaɪzər/ *n.* the front of a hat or helmet that sticks out over the eyes: *A baseball cap has a long visor.*

visor

vis·ta /'vɪstə/ *n.* a view, esp. a panoramic one: *We looked at a beautiful vista of the valley below.*

vi·su·al /'vɪʤuəl/ *adj.* **1** related to being seen: *A picture is a visual object.* **2** seeable, (*syn.*) discernible: *The sailor made a visual sighting of a distant ship.* *-adv.* **visually.**

vi·su·al·ize /'vɪʤuə,laɪz/ *v.* **-ized, -izing, -izes** to picture s.t. in the mind, imagine: *When it snows, I like to visualize a vacation on a warm, sunny beach.*

vi·tal /'vaɪtl/ *adj.* **1** most important, absolutely necessary: *Water is vital to life.* **2** energetic, lively: *She has a vital personality.*
—n.pl. **vitals** important organs, such as the heart, lungs, and digestive system: *His vitals are in bad condition.* *-adv.* **vitally.**

vital statistics *n.pl.* information collected by governments about people, such as their age, race, and birth, death, and marriage dates: *The Census Bureau collects and compiles vital statistics on the population every ten years.*

vi·tal·i·ty /vaɪ'tæləti/ *n.* [U] strength and health, mental and physical energy level: *She has great vitality and is always doing s.t.*

vi·tal·ize /'vaɪtl,aɪz/ *v.* **-ized, -izing, -izes** to fill with energy: *She vitalizes her family with confidence and good health.* *-n.* [U] **vitalization** /,vaɪtlə'zeɪʃən/.

vi·ta·min /,vaɪtəmɪn/ *n.* any of many chemical substances necessary for good health: *Vitamin C is found in fruits, potatoes, etc.*

vit·tles /'vɪtlz/ *n.pl. slang* **1** food in general **2** a meal: *Cowboys like to eat vittles.*

vi·tu·per·a·tive /vaɪ'tupərətɪv, -pə,reɪ-/ *adj.frml.* harshly critical: *He made vituperative remarks to s.o.* *-v.* **vituperate;** *-n.* [U] **vituperation.**

vi·va·cious /vaɪ'veɪʃəs, və'veɪ-/ *adj.* lively, cheerful: *She is a vivacious girl, always happy and smiling.* *-adv.* **vivaciously;** *-n.* [U] **vivacity** /və'væsəti, vaɪ-/.

viv·id /'vɪvɪd/ *adj.* easy to see or imagine, clear, intense: *The reporter wrote a vivid story about the disaster.* *-n.* [U] **vividness;** *-adv.* **vividly.**

viv·i·sec·tion /,vɪvə'sɛkʃən, 'vɪvə,sɛk-/ *n.* [C;U] an operation performed on an animal for medical research purposes: *The doctor performed vivisections on cows to see how well artificial hearts work.* *-v.* **vivisect.**

V-neck /'vi,nɛk/ *n.adj.* a sweater, pullover, or other garment with the neckline shaped downward in a "V": *In winter, he wears a <adj.> V-neck sweater and a warm coat.*

V

vo·cab·u·lar·y /vouˈkæbyəˌlɛri/ n. -ies [C;U]
1 a group of words that forms a language,
(syn.) a lexicon: *She learns some French vocabulary every day.* **2** the words used in a particular kind of work: *The vocabulary of
computers is called "computerese."*

vo·cal /ˈvoukəl/ adj. **1** related to speaking and
the voice: *His vocal chords hurt from talking
too much.* **2** loud, complaining: *A vocal group
of protesters complained about air pollution.*
-adv. **vocally.**

vo·cal·ist /ˈvoukəlɪst/ n. a singer: *That vocalist sings with a local band.*

vo·cal·ize /ˈvoukəˌlaɪz/ v. -ized, -izing, -izes
to speak: *At our weekly meetings, my boss encourages me to vocalize my thoughts on important issues.*

vo·ca·tion /vouˈkeɪʃən/ n. **1** [C] one's livelihood, work: *His writing is not a vocation, just
a hobby.* **2** [C, usu. sing.] a call to serve God:
He felt a vocation for the religious life.

vo·ca·tion·al /vouˈkeɪʃənəl/ adj. related to
work: *She is taking vocational training to
learn to be a hairdresser.*

vocational school n. a trade school where
job skills are taught, such as auto mechanics,
computer repair, or secretarial skills: *He goes
to a vocational school and is learning carpentry.*

USAGE NOTE: Some students go to a *vocational
school* for the last few years of high school if
they want to start working after high school instead of going to college: *She entered a vocational school in the tenth grade to become a
health care worker.* Most vocational schools
also have programs for adults who want to
learn job skills: *He's taking wordprocessing
classes at a vocational school.*

---

vo·cif·er·ous /vouˈsɪfərəs/ adj.frml. loud and
demanding, noisy, (syn.) clamorous: *He was
very vociferous about getting a refund for the
bad merchandise he had purchased.* -v. **vociferate;** -adv. **vociferously.**

vod·ka /ˈvɑdkə/ n. [C;U] a colorless alcoholic
drink made from grain or potatoes: *A Bloody
Mary is made with vodka and tomato juice.*

vogue /voug/ n. [C, usu. sing.] fashion, trend:
*The clothes that are in vogue this season will
change next year.* -adj. **voguish.**

voice /vɔɪs/ v. **voiced, voicing, voices** to
speak, utter: *He voiced his opinions about politics.*
—n. **1** [C] the ability to speak: *She speaks in a
clear voice.* **2** [U] the quality of a singing
voice: *a singer who is in good voice* **3** [C] a
spokesperson: *She is a voice of support for the
poor.* **4** [C] any of several parts in singing: *She
sings the soprano voice.* **5 to speak with one
voice:** to be united in opinion or action: *The*
committee spoke with one voice; they all
agreed on what should be done.

voice mail n. [U] a telephone answering system on which spoken messages are left by one
person for another: *John was not at his desk,
but I left a message for him on his voice mail.*

void /vɔɪd/ v. **1** to cancel, (syn.) to nullify: *I
voided the check by writing "Void" over my
signature.* **2** frml. (in medicine) to empty: *to
void one's bowels*
—n. a dark, empty place, (syn.) an abyss: *After
her lover's death, she fell into a void of sadness.*
—adj. empty, barren: *The moon is void of all
life.*

void·ed /ˈvɔɪdɪd/ adj. canceled, made useless:
A voided check cannot be cashed.

vol·a·tile /ˈvɑlətl, -ˌtaɪl/ adj. **1** explosive:
*Gasoline is a volatile chemical and can catch
fire easily.* **2** fig. unstable, likely to produce
change or harm: *The situation is very volatile;
rioters may try to overthrow the government.*
-n. [U] **volatility** /ˌvɑləˈtɪləti/.

vol·ca·no /vɑlˈkeɪnou/ n. -nos or -noes a hill
or mountain formed by hot, melted rock escaping from beneath the earth: *Mt. Vesuvius in
Italy is an active volcano.* -adj. **volcanic**
/vɑlˈkænɪk/.

vo·li·tion /vəˈlɪʃən/ n. [U] s.o.'s free will: *Of
his own volition, the rich man gave up everything he owned and became a priest.*

vol·ley /ˈvɑli/ v. (in sports) a hitting of the ball
back and forth between opponents: *The tennis
players volleyed for ten minutes.*
—n. **1** a series of bullets, arrows, etc., shot at
the same time: *a volley of gunfire* **2** an act of
volleying as in tennis

vol·ley·ball /ˈvɑliˌbɔl/ n. **1** [U] a sport played
with six players on each side of a net who
score a point by grounding the ball on the opponent's side: *Volleyball is an Olympic sport.*
2 the ball used in that sport

volt /voult/ n. a unit of measurement in electricity: *The electricity in our home is 120 volts
of alternating current.* -n. [C;U] **voltage.**

vol·ume /ˈvɑlˌyum/ n. **1** [C] a book or one of a
series of books: *The dictionary is the largest
volume on that shelf.* **2** [U] intensity of sound,
loudness: *Turn up the volume on the radio.* **3**
[U] space: *The volume of that tank is 50 cubic
yards.* **4** [C;U] amount of activity: *There is a
large volume of traffic on the highways, this
summer.*

vo·lu·mi·nous /vəˈlumənəs/ adj. **1** containing
many pages, bulky **2** containing many books:
That professor's library is big and voluminous.
-n. [U] **voluminousness.**

vol·un·tar·y /ˈvɑlənˌtɛri/ adj. done of one's
own will without being forced or paid: *She
gives money to the church on a voluntary*

V

basis, not because she has to. -*adv.* **voluntar-ily.**

vol·un·teer /ˌvalənˈtɪr/ *v.* to agree to do s.t. of one's own free will rather than by necessity: *He volunteers his time at the church.*
—*n.* a person who volunteers: *The USA has a military made up of volunteers.* -*n.* [U] **volunteerism.**

vo·lup·tu·ous /vəˈlʌpʧuəs/ *adj.* sensual, sexy: *She is a woman with a voluptuous figure* -*adv.* **voluptuously;** -*n.* **voluptuary** /vəˈlʌpʧu,ɛri/.

vom·it /ˈvamɪt/ *v.* to expel (food, liquid from the stomach) through the mouth, (*syn.*) to throw up: *The child vomited when he had the flu.*
—*n.* [U] stomach contents that have been vomited

voo·doo /ˈvudu/ *n.* [U] religious beliefs of African origin, practiced in Africa and in parts of Latin America and the Caribbean -*n.* [U] **voodooism.**

vo·ra·cious /vəˈreɪʃəs, vɔ-/ *adj.* very hungry, (*syn.*) ravenous: *Teenagers often have voracious appetites.* -*n.* [U] **voraciousness;** [U] **voracity** /vɔˈræsəti/; -*adv.* **voraciously.**

vor·tex /ˈvɔrtɛks/ *n.* -**texes** or -**tices** /-təˌsiz/ a swirling force, esp. a whirlpool: *A flooded river can form a vortex as the water rushes to the sea.*

vote /voʊt/ *v.* **voted, voting, votes** **1** to cast a ballot or a vote for or against: *He voted for a Presidential candidate.* **2** *phrasal v. sep.* **to vote s.t. down:** to refuse, deny s.t.: *The people in our state voted down money for a new highway.||They voted it down.* **3** *phrasal v. sep.* **to vote s.o. out:** to force s.o. from office: *The politician was so disliked that the voters voted him out.*
—*n.* **1** the act of voting for your favorite candidate: *She has my vote for governor.* **2 a vote of confidence** or **of thanks:** an act of support or appreciation: *A group of people can give a person a vote of confidence* (or) *thanks.*

vote get·ter /ˈgɛtər/ *n.* a person or an issue that attracts votes: *He is handsome and well-spoken; he is a big vote getter.*

vot·er /ˈvoʊtər/ *n.* **1** a person who votes **2** a person of legal age to vote **3 the voters:** the electorate, those people registered and eligible to vote: *The voters turned down a referendum to raise taxes.*

voting booth *n.* an enclosed space for casting votes in privacy: *Voting booths are located in polling places.*

vouch /vaʊʧ/ *v.* -**es** to confirm, say s.t. is true: *I vouched for his innocence; he did not steal anything.*

vouch·er /ˈvaʊʧər/ *n.* **1** an official piece of paper used in place of money: *I have a travel voucher good for $500 on any airline.* **2** (in law) a document showing that money has been paid or goods received

vow /vaʊ/ *v.* **1** to swear, solemnly promise: *He vowed to repay the debt (correct his behavior, murder s.o., etc.).* **2** to swear, (*syn.*) to attest: *When I married her, I vowed to love her forever.*
—*n.* **1** a solemn promise: *She made a vow to go to church regularly.* **2 to take the vows:** to commit oneself by solemn promise: *He took the vows of priesthood.*

vow·el /ˈvaʊəl/ *n.* in English, the letters a, e, i, o, u, and sometimes y.

voy·age /ˈvɔɪɪʤ/ *v.frml.* -**aged, -aging, -ages** to travel over long distances, (*syn.*) to journey: *He voyaged around the world in a small boat.*
—*n.* a long journey: *She took a voyage by boat from London to India.* -*n.* **voyager.**

voy·eur /vɔɪˈɜr/ *n.* a person who gets pleasure, esp. sexual thrills, from secretly watching others who are nude or making love: *He is a voyeur who uses binoculars to spy on others.* -*n.* [U] **voyeurism.**

V-shaped /ˈviˌʃeɪpt/ *adj.* shaped in the form of a "V": *A dress with a V-shaped neckline.*

V sign *n.* a victory sign, usu. given by extending the index and second fingers of the hand skyward: *The winner gave a V sign as she left the sports stadium.*

vul·gar /ˈvʌlgər/ *adj.* unsuitable for polite company, (*syns.*) offensive, crude: *He uses vulgar language and dirty expressions.* -*v.* **vulgarize;** -*n.* [U] **vulgarity** /vəlˈgærəti/.

vul·ner·able /ˈvʌlnərəbəl/ *adj.* **1** exposed, unprotected: *The soldiers were in a position vulnerable to attack by the enemy.* **2** likely to be hurt or made to feel bad: *She has been feeling very vulnerable since her husband died.* -*n.* [U] **vulnerability** /ˌvʌlnərəˈbɪləti/.

vul·ture /ˈvʌlʧər/ *n.* **1** a type of bird that eats dead animals **2** *fig.* a person who takes advantage of another's misfortune: *The company had to be closed, and the vultures tried to buy its equipment for nothing.*

V

W, w

W, w /ˈdʌbəlyu, -yə/ **W's, w's** or **Ws, ws** the 23rd letter of the English alphabet

wack·y /ˈwæki/ *adj.infrml.* **-ier, -iest 1** crazy, foolish: *He always has these wacky ideas for strange inventions.* **2** funny, (*syn.*) zany: *That comedian makes wacky movies.* -*n.* [U] **wackiness.**

wad /wɑd/ *n.* **1** a rolled-up ball of s.t.: *She was not happy with her writing, so she crumpled the paper into a wad.* **2** a handful of money: *He always carries a wad of cash in his pocket.* —*v.* **wadded, wadding, wads** to compress s.t. into a wad: *He wadded paper into a ball and threw it into the wastebasket.* -*n.* [U] **wadding.**

wad·dle /ˈwɑdl/ *v.* **-dled, -dling, -dles** to walk with short, awkward, side-to-side steps: *Ducks waddle into the water.* —*n.* a side-to-side walk: *The fat person walked with a waddle.*

wade /weɪd/ *v.* **waded, wading, wades 1** to walk by forcing the legs through water or snow: *The hunter waded across the shallow river.* **2** *phrasal v. insep.* **to wade through s.t.:** to finish s.t. long or difficult after much effort: *She waded through the paperwork.*

wad·er /ˈweɪdər/ *n.* **1** a type of water bird **2** *pl.* waterproof hip boots

wa·fer /ˈweɪfər/ *n.* a thin, crisp cake or cookie: *We each ate a chocolate wafer after dinner.*

waf·fle /ˈwɑfəl/ *n.* a breakfast cake with a pattern of square holes, baked in a special pan called a waffle iron: *We sometimes have waffles with syrup for breakfast.* —*v.infrml.* **-fled, -fling, -fles** to change one's opinion back and forth, (*syn.*) to vacillate: *He keeps waffling about changing jobs.*

waft /wɑft, wæft/ *v.n.* to move slowly in the air: *The smell of brewing coffee <v.> wafted through the house.*

wag /wæg/ *v.* **wagged, wagging, wags** to shake back and forth: *A happy dog wags its tail.* —*n.* **1** a swinging back and forth: *Our dog greeted us with a wag of its tail.* **2** a person who likes to make jokes

wage /weɪdʒ/ *n. usu. sing.* [C] money paid for work done, usu. by the hour: *That company pays a good wage to its workers.* —*v.* **waged, waging, wages** to begin and continue (a war or military operation), (*syn.*) to engage in: *Armies waged war often in the 20th century.*

USAGE NOTE: A *wage* is money paid to an hourly worker, who by law has the right to overtime pay for extra hours worked beyond 40 hours per week. A *salary* is a fixed annual amount paid to a worker in a higher position, who does not get compensation for extra hours worked. A salary can be paid weekly, bimonthly, or monthly, and often includes paid sick and vacation time.

wage earner *n.* a worker who earns wages: *Wage earners are usually paid by the hour.*

wage level *n.* the general or common amount of money paid in a company or area: *The wage level in farming areas is quite low.*

wa·ger /ˈweɪdʒər/ *v.* to bet money, (*syn.*) to gamble: *She is very lucky, because when she wagers in a card game, she often wins.* —*n.* [C] a bet, gamble: *He places wagers on the horseraces.*

wage scale *n.* the various levels of hourly wages paid by a company or industry: *The wage scale in automaking is very high; even a beginning-level job pays a good wage.*

wag·on /ˈwægən/ *n.* **1** a four-wheeled vehicle usu. pulled by horses or oxen: *Before we had trucks, large shipments were sent in wagons.* **2** a child's cart pulled by a handle: *We saw a very small girl pulling a red wagon full of toys.* **3 to be on the wagon:** to stop drinking alcoholic beverages, usu. temporarily: *I haven't had a beer in weeks because I'm on the wagon.* See: station wagon. -*n.* **wagoner.**

wagon train *n.* a group of wagons traveling together, usu. in a line: *In the 1800s, many Americans moved west in wagon trains.*

waif /weɪf/ n. [C] a homeless, lonely child or animal: *The poor waif had no family to care for her.*

wail /weɪl/ v. to cry out in sadness: *The children wailed at the grave of their mother.* —n. [C] a wailing sound: *When she saw her dead son, the woman let out a wail.*||*the wail of a police siren* -n. [U] adj. **wailing.**

wain·scot·ing or **wainscotting** /'weɪn,skɑtɪŋ, -skə-, -,skoʊ-/ n. [U] a layer of wood put over a wall or the lower half of a wall in a room: *The wainscoting is made of oak.* -v. **wainscot** /'weɪnskət, -,skɑt, -,skoʊt/.

waist /'weɪst/ n. **1** the middle section of a person's body: *She must have a small waist; look how tiny her belt is!* **2** the part of a piece of clothing around the waist area: *The waist on that skirt is too big for the woman.*

waist·band /weɪst,bænd/ n. the part of a skirt or pants that fits around the waist: *My waistband is too big, so I wear a belt.*

waist·line /'weɪst,laɪn/ n. the line around the narrowest part of a person's waist: *His waistline measures 36 inches (approx. 70 cm).*

wait /weɪt/ v. **1** to stay in one place until s.t. happens: *He waited in line to buy a theater ticket.* **2** to delay action: *I am waiting to see who does the best work before hiring anyone.* **3** to serve food and drinks, to work as a waiter: *He waits (on) tables in a restaurant.* **4** *infrml.* **can't wait:** be very eager: *I can't wait for my vacation to start!* **5 to wait in vain:** to wait for s.t. that, in the end, doesn't happen: *I waited in vain for a bus to come and ended up walking instead.* **6** *phrasal v. insep.* **to wait on s.o.:** to serve s.o.'s needs as a servant would: *He waits on her because she is sick and cannot do things for herself.* **7 to wait on s.o. hand and foot:** to serve faithfully in every way possible: *She waits on him hand and foot, but he never lifts a finger to help her.* **8** *phrasal v. sep.* **to wait s.t. out:** to delay until the end of s.t.: *They waited out the rain by staying inside and drinking tea.*||*They waited it out.* **9** *phrasal v. insep.* **to wait up (for s.o.):** to delay going to bed: *He gets home so late; I am too tired to wait up for him.* —n. [U] **1** the time spent waiting: *They had a long wait in the doctor's office.* **2 to lie in wait:** to watch secretly for the chance to attack: *The cat was eagerly lying in wait for the mouse.*

wait·er /'weɪtər/ n. a person who serves food and drinks to earn money: *He works as a waiter in a fancy restaurant.*

waiting list n. a list of people waiting for an opening, as in public housing, a club, a university, etc.: *We put our names on a waiting list for a table at the crowded restaurant.*

waiting room n. a room where people can sit while waiting (for a doctor, train, etc.): *The waiting room in the train station was chilly and crowded.*

wait·ress /'weɪtrɪs/ n. **-resses** a woman who serves food and drinks to earn money: *She works as a cocktail waitress in a bar.*

waive /weɪv/ v. **waived, waiving, waives 1** to give up (rights, privileges, etc.): *She wanted to defend herself, so she waived her right to a lawyer.* **2** to make unnecessary, (syn.) to dispense with: *He excelled in the course so the teacher waived his final exam.*

waiv·er /'weɪvər/ n. **1** a giving up of a right or claim, (syn.) a relinquishment: *She will never agree to a waiver of her legal rights.* **2** freedom from s.t. that is usu. required, (syns.) an exemption, exclusion: *The planning board gave a waiver for an environmental study before building the project.* **3** a document showing that s.o. has given up a right or privilege: *I signed a waiver saying that I would not sue the doctor if the operation was a failure.*

wake /weɪk/ v. **woke** /woʊk/ or **waked or woken** /'woʊkən/ or **waked, waking, wakes 1** to stop sleeping, to awaken: *I woke (up) this morning at six o'clock.*||*Please don't wake the baby.* **2** *phrasal v. insep.* **to wake up to s.t.:** to realize the importance of s.t.: *He finally woke up to the fact that he could easily be fired from his job.*

wake (1) n. [C] a time to visit a dead person's body before burial

wake (2) n. [C] **1** waves made by boats moving through the water: *The ship left a huge wake behind it.* **2 in the wake of:** directly following, as a result of: *In the wake of the hurricane, buildings lay in ruins.*

wak·en /'weɪkən/ v. to wake, awaken: *He wakens early each morning.*

walk /wɔk/ v. **1** to move forward by putting one foot in front of the other: *I walk to work each morning.* **2** to go with, (syn.) to accompany: *The nurse walked her patient to the bathroom.* **3 to walk all over s.o.:** to take advantage of s.o., treat s.o. badly or without respect: *He walks all over her and never lets her talk.* **4** *phrasal v. insep.* **to walk around s.t.:** to explore, wander around: *We walked around while we waited for the stores to open.* **5** *phrasal v. insep.* **to walk away from s.t.:** to stop doing s.t., to have nothing more to do with it: *The football player was hurt so many times that he finally walked away from the sport.* **6** *phrasal v.* **to walk off:** to leave in anger: *We started to argue and he simply walked off.* **7 to walk off the job:** to stop working in protest of s.t.: *The wage demands were not met, so workers walked off the job.* **8** *phrasal v. insep.* **to walk off** or **away with s.t.: a.** to steal: *Somebody walked off with my coat.* **b.** to win easily: *The girl walked away with first prize in the cooking contest.* **9 to walk on air:** to feel wonderful:

W

After she won the contest, she was walking on air. **10 to walk on water:** to perform miracles, to be a very special person: *She thinks he is so great; to her, he walks on water.* **11** *phrasal v. insep.* **to walk out (of s.t.): a.** to leave, usu. suddenly: *She became so angry that she simply walked out.* **b.** to stop working in protest: *Workers walked out when their pay was cut.* **12** *phrasal v. insep.* **to walk out on s.o.:** to leave suddenly, (*syn.*) to abandon: *The husband walked out on his family one day and never returned.* **13** *phrasal v. insep.* **to walk over s.o.: a.** to defeat easily: *Our team walked over their team with a score of 10–0.* **b.** to treat s.o. badly: *That little girl walks all over her parents.*

—*n.* **1** a stroll, exercise by walking: *I go for a walk (or) take a walk each morning.* **2** a path, sidewalk: *The walk leading to the garden is covered with small stones.* **3 all walks of life:** different positions in society: *People from all walks of life, the poor and rich alike, come to church.*

USAGE NOTE: When one *walks* at a slow pace, one *ambles* or *strolls*. When one walks without lifting the feet very far off the ground, one *shuffles*. At a faster pace, one *marches*, as in a military style. At the fastest pace, one *runs*.

walk·er /ˈwɔkər/ *n.* **1** a person who walks: *He loves to exercise and is a long-distance walker.* **2** a metal support used to help in walking: *After her leg operation, she used a walker to go from one place to another.*

walk·ie-talk·ie /ˌwɔkiˈtɔki/ *n.* a two-way radio small enough to carry by hand: *Some police officers use walkie-talkies to speak to each other from a distance.*

walk-in /ˈwɔkˌɪn/ *adj.* **1** large enough to walk into: *We have a large walk-in closet in our bedroom.* **2** not requiring an appointment: *A doctor at a walk-in medical clinic gave me a pregnancy test.*

walk·ing /ˈwɔkɪŋ/ *n.* [U] (the act of) moving forward on foot: *Walking is good exercise.*

walking papers *n.pl.infrml.* written notice that one no longer has a job, (*syn.*) a dismissal notice: *The manager handed two employees their walking papers and they left.*

walk·out /ˈwɔkˌaʊt/ *n.* a work stoppage, (*syn.*) a strike: *Union workers held a walkout to protest low wages.*

walk-up /ˈwɔkˌʌp/ *n.* an apartment building without an elevator: *We live in a four-story walk-up in Brooklyn.*

wall /wɔl/ *n.* **1** the side of a room or building: *I have many pictures on my bedroom walls.* **2** a barrier between two areas, usu. of stone or brick, used to protect, divide, or enclose: *She built a stone wall around her garden.* **3** a

block, barrier: *The government met a wall of opposition.*||*A wall of fire ran up the mountainside.* **4** *infrml.* **off the wall:** strange, (*syns.*) weird, bizarre: *She's a little off the wall sometimes and does crazy things.* **5** *infrml.* **to beat one's head against the wall:** to work hard but make no progress: *I can't finish this project; it feels like I am beating my head against the wall.* **6** *infrml.* **to climb the walls:** to be nervous, (*syn.*) to be frustrated: *I have been studying so hard for exams that I'm climbing the walls waiting for them to be over.* **7** *infrml.* **to drive s.o. up the (a) wall:** to annoy s.o. very much: *He keeps complaining about little things and is driving me up the wall.* **8** *infrml.* **to have one's back up against** or **to the wall:** to be in a hopeless situation, to be trapped: *He has his back to the wall because he has bills to pay and no money.* **9** *infrml.* **to run into a brick wall:** to be blocked, to face strong opposition: *I have run into a brick wall because my boss won't agree to my plan.* **10** *infrml.* **to see the handwriting on the wall:** *See:* handwriting. *See:* hole-in-the-wall.

wall·board /ˈwɔlˌbɔrd/ *n.* [U] large pieces of building material (such as plywood or Sheetrock™) used to make walls: *Carpenters put up more wallboard to make another room.*

wal·let /ˈwɑlɪt, ˈwɔ-/ *n.* a type of purse that can be folded and put in one's pocket, (*syn.*) a billfold: *He carries cash and credit cards in his wallet.*

wall·flow·er /ˈwɔlˌflaʊər/ *n.fig.* a shy or unpopular person: *She is a wallflower who does not talk with anyone at a party.*

wal·lop /ˈwɑləp/ *v.n.* to hit hard: *The fighter <v.> walloped the other guy.* -*n.* [U], *adj.* **walloping.**

wal·low /ˈwɑloʊ/ *n.* a muddy or dusty place: *Pigs cool off by rolling in a wallow.*

—*v.* to roll or lie about in a lazy, comfortable way: *They were wallowing in money (luxury, self-pity, etc.).*

wall·pa·per /ˈwɔlˌpeɪpər/ *n.* [U] *v.* paper for covering and decorating the walls of a room: *We hung new <n.> wallpaper in our dining room.*

Wall Street *n.* **1** a street in New York's financial district: *The New York Stock Exchange is located on Wall Street.* **2** *fig.* a symbol of money, power, and influence in the USA: *When things go wrong on Wall Street, the whole nation suffers.*

wall-to-wall *adj.* going from one edge of a room to the other: *We have wall-to-wall carpeting in our living room.*

wal·nut /ˈwɔlˌnʌt, -nət/ *n.* **1** [C] an edible nut: *I love chocolate-covered walnuts.* **2** [C;U] the wood from a walnut tree: *Walnut is a popular hardwood for making furniture.*

W

wal·rus /'wɔlrəs, 'wɑl-/ n. **-ruses** or **-rus** a large sea animal, like a seal, with long teeth called tusks: *Walruses pull shellfish off rocks with their long tusks.*

waltz /wɔlts, wɔls/ n. **waltzes** **1** a ballroom dance with a one-two-three beat: *Very few people know how to dance a graceful waltz anymore.* **2** music with a one-two-three beat, to which people can dance a waltz: *The band played a waltz.*
—v. **waltzes 1** to dance the waltz: *We waltzed to German music all evening.* **2** *fig.* to do s.t. very easily and with grace: *She waltzed through the interview and got the job.*

wam·pum /'wɑmpəm, 'wɔm-/ n. [U] strings of shells used in the past by Native Americans as money: *She wore a beautiful necklace made of wampum.*

wan /wɑn/ adj. pale, tired-looking, (syn.) pallid: *After his stay in the hospital, he looked wan, without color.*

wand /wɑnd/ n. a narrow stick, esp. one used to make magic: *The fairy used a magic wand to make the boy fly.*

wan·der /'wɑndər/ v. **1** to go from place to place without a fixed plan or goal, (syn.) to roam: *The travelers wandered from country to country.* **2** to move away from a subject, clear idea, or fixed course: *He is old, and his mind wanders at times.* -n. **wanderer.**

wan·der·lust /'wɑndər,lʌst/ n. [U] a strong desire to travel: *He had wanderlust, so he traveled around the country for six months.*

wane /weɪn/ n. [U] **on the wane:** lessening in size: *The fishing industry is on the wane in this area, and soon will vanish.*
—v. **waned, waning, wanes** to weaken, get smaller, (syn.) to diminish: *Each month the moon waxes and wanes.*

wan·na /'wɑnə, 'wɔ-, 'wʌ-/ v.slang short for want to

wan·na·be /'wɑnə,bi, 'wɔ-/ n.adj.slang from "want to be," a person who wants to be s.o. or s.t. other than what he or she really is: *He is a <n.> wannabe in the music business, but he hasn't written any hit songs.*

want /wɑnt, wɔnt/ v. **1** to desire: *I want to buy some groceries this morning.‖The baby wants his mother.* **2** *phrasal v. insep.* **to want for s.t.:** to need, (syn.) to lack: *The king never wanted for anything during his childhood.* **3 wanted:** looked for by the police: *The police aren't planning to arrest him, but he is wanted for questioning.*
—n. **1** [C;U] a desire: *He has more wants than he can afford.* **2** [U] a need, (syn.) a lack: *She is poor and in want of basic things.*

USAGE NOTE: *Would like* is used to ask politely for s.t. that one *wants: I would like to go home now; I'm very tired.*

want ad n. an advertisement for jobs or things for sale: *He reads the want ads, looking for a job, but finds only things he wants to buy.*

want·ing /'wɑntɪŋ, 'wɔn-/ adj. not good enough, less than expected, (syn.) deficient: *His job performance was found wanting.*

wan·ton /'wɑntən, 'wɔn-/ adj. **1** sexually immoral, (syns.) lewd, lascivious: *He was put in jail for wanton behavior.* **2** out of control, (syn.) excessive: *He has no more money because of his wanton spending habits.*
—n. an immoral or out-of-control person: *She is a wanton who spends all her time in bars.* -adv. **wantonly;** -n. **wantonness.**

war /wɔr/ n. [C;U] fighting with guns and other weapons between groups, armies, nations, etc.: *The civil war in that country lasted five years.*
—v. **warred, warring, wars** to take part or engage in war: *The two sides warred for years and never reached an agreement.* -adj. **warring.**

war·ble /'wɔrbəl/ n.v. usu. sing. [C] **-bled, -bling, -bles** a shaking sound in the voice when singing, (syn.) a trill: *Birds <v.> warbled in the trees.* -n. **warbler.**

war bride n. a woman who marries a soldier during wartime: *She was a war bride who married an American soldier in France.*

war crime n. any crime committed against humanity during a war: *The murder of millions of Jews was a terrible war crime in World War II.*

ward /wɔrd/ n. **1** a section or district of a city: *She is a city councilor from the 12th ward.* **2** a section of a hospital: *She is in the maternity ward because she just had a baby.* **3** s.o. protected by a court or older person: *Her parents died, so now she is a ward of the court.*
—phrasal v. sep. **to ward s.t. off:** to prevent, (syn.) to fend off: *I warded off a cold by staying in bed.‖I warded it off.*
—suffix **-ward** /wɔrd/ in the direction of: *Look upward at the clouds.*

war·den /'wɔrdn/ n. the director of a jail: *The prison guards do not like their boss, the warden.*

ward·robe /'wɔr,droʊb/ n. **1** a collection of clothing: *The rich lady has a large wardrobe.* **2** (in theater or film) the costume department: *The actor returned his costume to wardrobe.* **3** a piece of furniture that acts as a movable closet: *We didn't have enough built-in closets, so we bought a wardrobe.*

ware /wɛr/ n.suffix things of the same general kind: *Dishes, pots, and utensils make up kitchenware.*

ware·house /'wɛr,haʊs/ n. **-houses** /-,haʊzɪz/ a building where goods are received, stored, and shipped: *Our warehouse has more auto parts in it than we can sell.*

W

war·fare /'wɔr,fɛr/ n. [U] the way a war is fought: *The general knows everything about tank warfare (germ warfare, guerrilla warfare, etc.).*

war game n. a practice battle, (syn.) maneuvers: *The army practiced war games in the desert.*

war·head /'wɔr,hɛd/ n. the explosive part of a bomb or missile: *The most powerful missiles have more than one warhead.*

warily /'wɛrəli/ adv. See: wary.

war·like /'wɔr,laɪk/ adj. related to war, (syn.) threatening: *Military planes flew over the country in a warlike action.*

war·lock /'wɔr,lɑk/ n. a male witch, a man who does magical things, (syn.) a sorcerer: *In the fairy tale, a warlock turned a man into a horse.*

war·lord /'wɔr,lɔrd/ n. a leader of a fighting group: *Warlords of city gangs make the laws of the streets.*

warm /wɔrm/ **1** to heat, increase the temperature of: *We warmed ourselves by sitting near the fireplace.* **2** *phrasal v. insep.* **to warm up s.o. or s.t.: a.** to heat up: *He warmed up the coffee from earlier that day.* **b.** to get ready for action: *She won the tennis match because she had warmed up before it started.* **3** *phrasal v. insep.* **to warm up to s.o. or s.t.:** to grow to like s.o. or s.t.: *We are warming up to our son-in-law; he's not so bad after all.*
—adj. **1** having heat, but not hot: *I like warm summer days.* **2** friendly, having compassion: *Her friends love her for her warm personality.* See: hot.

USAGE NOTE: In a range of temperatures, *warm* is between *hot* and *cold*. *Lukewarm* means mildly warm; *tepid* is a little bit cooler.

warm-blood·ed /'wɔrm,blʌdɪd/ adj. with constant high body heat in any temperature: *Humans are warm-blooded, unlike reptiles and insects.*

warmed-o·ver /'wɔrmd,oʊvər/ adj. **1** reheated: *We ate last night's warmed-over turkey.* **2** repeating old ideas, (syn.) rehashed: *Those ideas are just warmed-over political thoughts from the last election.*

warm front n. (in weather) a mass of warm air that moves into an area: *A warm front from the Caribbean is arriving on the East Coast this weekend.*

warm-heart·ed /'wɔrm'hɑrtɪd/ adj. friendly, generous: *She is a warm-hearted woman, loved by all.* -n. [U] **warmheartedness.**

warm·ly /'wɔrmli/ adv. with warmth, in a friendly way: *The man giving the party received his guests warmly with welcoming handshakes.*

war·mon·ger /'wɔr,mʌŋgər, -,mɑŋ-/ n. [C] a person who likes to make war: *The President was called a warmonger for sending our army to fight in another country.* -n. [U] **warmongering.**

warmth /wɔrmθ/ n. [U] **1** the state of being warm, a heated condition: *The warmth of the blanket helped her relax.* **2** friendliness, (syn.) compassion: *Her warmth gives comfort and good feeling to others.*

warm-up /'wɔr,mʌp/ n.adj. exercise done to prepare muscles for physical activity: *I do a short <n.> warm-up or <adj.> warm-up exercises before running.*

warn /wɔrn/ v. to tell that danger or trouble is near, (syn.) to caution: *A sign warned us that the road was closed.||The lawyer warned her client not to say anything in public.*

warn·ing /'wɔrnɪŋ/ n. [C;U] **1** a danger sign, (syn.) an omen: *The pain in his chest was a warning about a possible heart attack.* **2** a statement that s.t. bad might happen, (syn.) a caution: *The boss gave his workers a warning about being late.*

warp /wɔrp/ v. to bend out of shape: *Wood left out in the rain will warp.*
—n. [C] **1** deviation from what is straight or true: *There's a serious warp in this chair leg.* **2** the threads that run vertically through a piece of fabric: *He set up the warp on the loom.*

warp·ed /wɔrpt/ adj. **1** bent out of shape: *a warped door* **2** crazy, (syn.) abnormal: *His cruel acts come from a warped mind.*

war·path /'wɔr,pæθ/ n. [U] *infrml.* **on the warpath:** in an angry mood: *The boss is on the warpath today about unfinished work.*

warp speed n. [U] the high speed at which futuristic spaceships may travel: *Spaceships in movies can travel at warp speed, which is much faster than the speed of light.*

war·rant /'wɔrənt, 'wɑr-/ n. (in law) a written order permitting legal action, such as an arrest, search, or seizure: *The policeman has a warrant for your arrest.*
—v. **1** to give enough reason for doing s.t.: *That dangerous situation warrants immediate action.* **2** to guarantee, esp. facts about property, money, etc.: *The bank warranted that the property was free of debt or damage.*

war·ran·ty /'wɔrənti, 'wɑr-/ n. **-ties** [C;U] **1** a guarantee of quality: *The manufacturer gives a one-year warranty against any problems with its products.* **2** a guarantee that facts are true about property, money, etc.: *He signed a warranty on his application that the information he gave was true.*

war·ren /'wɔrən, 'wɑr-/ n. **1** an underground tunnel where rabbits live, (syn.) a burrow: *An area near our garden is a rabbit warren.* **2** a

W

small wooden house for raising rabbits, *(syn.)* a hutch: *The farmer kept his rabbits in a warren.* **3** *fig.* a crowded housing area: *That apartment house is a warren of small apartments and hallways.*

war·ri·or /'wɔriər, 'war-/ *n.* a fighter, soldier: *The chief sent his best warriors to fight against the enemy.*

wart /wɔrt/ *n.* a small, raised spot on the skin caused by a virus: *The doctor removed the warts on the patient's hands.*

war·time /'wɔr,taɪm/ *n.* [U] a period of war: *During wartime, many soldiers and civilians suffer.*

war·y /'wɛri/ *adj.* **-ier, -iest** concerned about danger, *(syn.)* cautious: *He is very wary of driving his car late at night.* -*adv.* **warily;** -*n.* **wariness.**

war zone *n.* an area where war is happening: *The war zone between the two nations was full of soldiers.*

was /wʌz, waz; *weak form* wəz/ *v.* past tense of be

wash /waʃ, wɔʃ/ *v.* **washes** **1** to clean, usu. with soap and water: *I washed the dishes (laundry, car, etc.) this morning.* **2** to pour over, spread: *Ocean waves washed over the rocks.*‖*Tears washed down his face.* **3** *infrml.* to be believed: *His excuses never wash with his teacher.* **4** *phrasal v. sep.* **to wash s.t. down: a.** to spray clean, usu. with water, *(syn.)* to hose down: *The man washed down the sidewalk with a hose.* **b.** to drink after eating s.t.: *He washed down a doughnut with a cup of coffee.* **5 to wash in on the tide:** to come onto the beach with the waves: *A dead body washed in on the tide.* **6** *fig.* **to wash one's hands of s.o. or s.t.:** to refuse further responsibility for s.o. or s.t., *(syn.)* to abandon: *This business is becoming illegal, and I wash my hands of it.* **7 to wash out: a.** to remove or be removed by washing: *Will this ink stain wash out?* **b.** to carry or be carried away by moving water: *The mountain road washed out in the storm.* **c.** *infrml.* to fail and be forced out of a program: *He is a <adj.> washed-out cadet from the military school.* **8 to wash up: a** to clean oneself: *I am going to the bathroom to wash up.* **b.** to come onto shore: *The storm washed up seaweed and driftwood on the beach.* —*n.* [U] **1** things to be cleaned, *(syn.)* the laundry: *I do the wash every Saturday morning.* **2** the liquid with which s.t. is washed: *She rinsed her mouth with a wash of salt and water.* **3 to come out in the wash:** to become clear, *(syn.)* to resolve itself: *The policemen are investigating the scandal, so the truth will soon come out in the wash.*

wash·a·ble /'waʃəbəl, 'wɔ-/ *adj.* able to be washed by usual methods: *That dress is washable and doesn't need dry cleaning.*

wash·ba·sin /'waʃ,beɪsən, 'wɔʃ-/ *n.* in a bathroom, a bowl for washing, *(syn.)* a sink: *I filled the washbasin with warm water and washed my hands.*

wash·cloth /'waʃ,klɔθ, 'wɔʃ-/ *n.* **-cloths** /-,klɔðz, -,klaθs/ a small cloth used for cleaning the body: *She uses a washcloth to clean her children.*

washed-out /,waʃt'aut, ,wɔʃt-/ *adj.* pale, weak-looking: *She looked washed-out after her surgery.*

washed-up /,waʃt'ʌp, ,wɔʃt-/ *adj.fig.* finished in one's career, undesirable as an employee: *He is too old to play and is all washed-up as a football player.*

wash·er /'waʃər, 'wɔ-/ *n.* **1** a machine for cleaning clothes, *(syn.)* a washing machine: *I put my dirty clothes in the washer.* **2** a flat round piece of metal or rubber with a hole: *We use washers to keep screws tight.*

wash·ing /'waʃɪŋ, 'wɔ-/ *n.* [U] dirty clothes to be washed, the laundry: *I do the washing once a week.*

washing machine *n.* a machine for cleaning clothes: *I poured soap into the washing machine.*

wash·out /'waʃ,aut, 'wɔʃ-/ *n.* [C] **1** destruction caused by water from a flood: *The area is a washout from the river flood.* **2** *infrml.* s.o. who has done badly, *(syn.)* a failure: *He is a washout from the military academy.*

wash·room /'waʃ,rum, 'wɔʃ-/ *n.* a bathroom: *I am going to the washroom to clean my hands.*

wasp /wasp, wɔsp/ *n.* any of a group of flying insects, including hornets and yellow jackets, with a narrow body and, in the females, a painful sting. *See:* bee; hornet.

WASP or **Wasp** /wasp, wɔsp/ *n.infrml.* (often *pej.*) *abbr. for* white Anglo-Saxon Protestant: *That club used to allow only WASPs to become members.*

wast·age /'weɪstɪdʒ/ *n.* [U] an amount wasted, esp. in an industrial process: *The wastage in making flour from wheat is little.*

waste /weɪst/ *n.* [U] **1** a poor use (of effort, time, resources): *He's too difficult, so dealing with him is a waste of time.* **2** loss of s.t. through improper use: *I had to throw away the extra spaghetti. What a waste of good food!* **3** things that are not wanted and get thrown away, garbage, *(syn.)* refuse: *Garbage collectors in large trucks pick up household waste.* **4** liquids or solids not used by the body, *(syn.)* excrement: *Waste goes from toilets into the sewer system.* **5 to go to waste:** (of s.t. good and useful) to not be used: *We ordered too much food for the party, and some of it will go to waste.* **6 to lay waste:** to destroy, *(syn.)* to devastate: *The army laid waste to the city.*

—*v.* **wasted, wasting, wastes 1** to make poor use of s.t. valuable, (*syn.*) to squander: *The builder wasted wood by ordering too much.* **2** *slang* to kill **3** *phrasal v.* **to waste away:** to die slowly, (*syn.*) to wither: *She has cancer and is slowly wasting away.* *-adj.* **waste.**

waste·bas·ket /'weɪst,bæskɪt/ *n.* a container (barrel, bucket, basket, etc.) for trash: *I throw old papers in the wastebasket.*

waste·ful /'weɪstfəl/ *adj.* using s.t. unwisely, leaving waste: *Spending money on things you don't need is wasteful.* *-adv.* [U] **wastefully; -***n.* [U] **wastefulness.**

waste·land /'weɪst,lænd/ *n.* [C] **1** a place where nothing will grow or with no useful purpose: *The desert outside the village is wasteland.* **2** *fig.* an empty and useless place: *Many people say that television is an intellectual wasteland.*

waste·pa·per /'weɪst,peɪpər/ *n.* [U] old or useless paper: *Offices have a lot of wastepaper from people's computer printers.*

watch /wɑʧ/ *v.* **watches 1** to look at, (*syn.*) to observe: *The mother watched her children play.* **2** to guard, observe closely: *A guard watches prisoners.* **3 to watch for:** to expect and look for: *The man watched for his bus to arrive.* **4** *infrml.* **to watch it:** to be careful not to go beyond certain limits: *That guy tried to kiss her, and she told him to watch it.* **5** *phrasal v.* (*insep.*) **to watch out (for s.o.** or **s.t.):** to be aware of danger, be careful: *I told my son to watch out for ice on the road ahead.* **6** *phrasal v. insep.* **to watch over s.o.:** to protect, guard: *A father watches over his child.*

—*n.* **watches 1** [C] a small clock worn on the wrist, (*syn.*) a timepiece: *I looked at my watch to see if I was late.* **2** [C;U] a state of continuous attention or close observation, (*syn.*) surveillance: *The police kept a watch on the house.*

watch·dog /'wɑʧ,dɔg/ *n.* **1** a guard dog: *Two watchdogs guard the store at night.* **2** *fig.* a guardian, observer for any wrongdoing: *The police are watchdogs over the small town.*

watch·ful /'wɑʧfəl/ *adj.* always watching or looking, (*syn.*) vigilant: *The boy's mother keeps a watchful eye on him as he plays.* *-adv.* **watchfully;** *-n.* [U] **watchfulness.**

watch·mak·er /'wɑʧ,meɪkər/ *n.* a person who makes, sells, and repairs watches or clocks: *My watch is broken, so I took it to the watchmaker.*

watch·man /'wɑʧmən/ *n.* **-men** /-mən/ a guard: *The night watchman checks on the building every hour.*

watch·word /'wɑʧ,wɜrd/ *n.* **1** a secret word or phrase that means that it's all right to allow s.o. in, (*syn.*) a password: *When she gave the right watchword, the guard let her through the*

gates. **2** a word or idea shared by a group, (*syn.*) a rallying cry: *These days, the company watchword is to cut costs.*

wa·ter /'wɔtər, 'wɑ-/ *n.* [C;U] **1** a colorless liquid made of hydrogen and oxygen that is necessary for life: *Most of the earth's surface is covered with water.* **2** any body of water, such as a stream, lake or ocean: *We like to vacation at the water.* **3** *pl.* the sea near a country: *We fished in Canadian waters.* **4** *infrml.* **in hot water:** in trouble: *He's in hot water with the boss.* **5 to hold water:** to seem true or plausible: *His story is so unbelievable that it does not hold water.*

—*v.* **1** to pour water on: *She waters the plants every day.* **2** to give drinking water to: *Farmers water their cows.* **3** to provide water to, (*syn.*) to irrigate: *Farmers water their crops, too.* **4** *phrasal v. sep.* **to water s.t. down: a.** to spray with water: *City workers water down the sidewalks in summer.*‖*They water it down.* **b.** to weaken, usu. by adding water, (*syn.*) to dilute: *They water down the beer to save money.* **c.** *fig.* to weaken the value of: *Companies water down their stock by selling more without adding value.* *-adj.* **watered-down.**

water bed *n.* a bed whose mattress is filled with water: *Water beds move as your body moves, and they are very comfortable.*

water boy *n.* a boy who brings water to workers or people playing sports

water buffalo *n.* **-loes** or **-lo** a large Asian animal with horns, often used to pull farm equipment

wa·ter·col·or /'wɔtər,kʌlər, 'wɑ-/ *n.* [C;U] **1** a method of painting using watered-down paint to produce soft, light colors: *Watercolor is my daughter's favorite way to paint pictures.* **2** the watercolor artwork itself: *She has several framed watercolors on her wall.*

wa·ter·cress /'wɔtər,krɛs, 'wɑ-/ *n.* a small plant with dark green leaves having a peppery taste, used esp. in salads

wa·ter·fall /'wɔtər,fɔl, 'wɑ-/ *n.* water falling from a high place, (*syn.*) a cascade: *Niagara Falls is a huge waterfall between New York and Canada.*

wa·ter·fowl /'wɔtər,faʊl, 'wɑ-/ *n.* **-fowl** [U] water birds, such as ducks and geese: *Waterfowl are everywhere along the Mississippi River.*

wa·ter·front /'wɔtər,frʌnt, 'wɑ-/ *n.* land that borders a body of water (sometimes with warehouses and docks): *The ships unloaded fish on the waterfront.*

W

water heater *n.* a tank in which water is heated for bathing, dishwashing, etc.: *Our water heater works so well that we never run out of hot water.*

water hole *n.* a place similar to a small pond, esp. where animals find water to drink: *In Africa, lions, elephants, and small animals drink at water holes.*

watering hole *n.* **1** a water hole: *The thirsty horse ran straight for the watering hole.* **2** *fig.* a bar or nightclub: *Our neighborhood watering hole is an Irish pub.*

water level *n.* the height that a body of water rises or falls to: *The water level in the lake is high this spring.*

water lily *n.* **-ies** a water plant with white or pink flowers and large, floating leaves: *Water lilies covered the surface of the pond.*

water lily

wa·ter·logged /ˈwɔtərˌlɔgd, -ˌlɑgd, ˈwɑ-/ *adj.* completely full of water, *(syn.)* saturated: *The piece of wood was so waterlogged that it fell to the lake bottom.*

water main *n.* a large underground pipe carrying drinking water: *The water main broke, and we lost our water supply.*

wa·ter·mark /ˈwɔtərˌmɑrk, ˈwɑ-/ *n.* **1** a design pressed into paper that one can see when it is held up to light: *You can see the watermark in this stationery says "Miracle Bond."* **2** a stain left by a rising water level: *You can see the high watermark made by the flood on the brick wall.*

wa·ter·mel·on /ˈwɔtərˌmɛlən, ˈwɑ-/ *n.* [C;U] a large, green, oval-shaped fruit with a sweet, juicy, pink interior: *At the cookout, we had hamburgers and hotdogs, then watermelon for dessert.*

watermelon

water meter *n.* a machine for measuring the amount of water used: *A city worker reads our water meter once a month to see how much we use.*

water pistol *n.* a toy gun that shoots water: *Children love to shoot at each other with water pistols.*

water polo *n.* a ball game played by two teams in a pool: *People who play water polo must be strong swimmers.*

wa·ter·proof /ˈwɔtərˌpruf, ˈwɑ-/ *v.* to make or seal s.t. to prevent water from entering it: *Shoemakers waterproof boots to keep your feet dry.*
—*adj.* made so that water cannot pass through: *I can wear my watch when I swim because it is waterproof.* *-n.* [U] **waterproofing.**

water-repellent *adj.* almost waterproof; water-resistant: *My raincoat is water-repellent,*

so light rain rolls off it without wetting through.

water-resistant *adj.* nearly waterproof, made so water cannot easily pass through: *My watch is water-resistant down to 200 feet below sea level.*

wa·ter·shed /ˈwɔtərˌʃɛd, ˈwɑ-/ *n.* **1** a high place where water drains downward on either side: *The Rocky Mountains are a great watershed.* **2** the area of land that drains into a river or other body of water: *No building is allowed on the reservoir watershed.* **3** *fig.* a time of important change: *The fall of Communism was a great watershed in human history.*

water ski *v.* **skied, skiing, skis** to ski on water while being pulled by a boat: *We water ski on a lake in the summer.*
—*n.* a flat board with a raised tip, attached to the foot, used to keep a person above water when being pulled by a boat *-n.* [C] **water-skier;** [U] **water-skiing.**

wa·ter·spout /ˈwɔtərˌspaʊt, ˈwɑ-/ *n.* **1** a tube through which water pours: *Cool water ran through the waterspout on my watering can onto the flowers.* **2** a type of metal tube on the side of a house, *(syn.)* a downspout: *Water drains off the roof, through the gutters, and into waterspouts.*

water supply *n.* **-plies** a central system that provides water, esp. to homes, towns, and cities: *The city water supply comes from special ponds called "reservoirs," out in the country.*

water table *n.* the water level in the ground in any given area: *The water table is near the surface of the land in areas near the sea.*

wa·ter·tight /ˈwɔtərˌtaɪt, ˈwɑ-/ *adj.* made so that water cannot pass through, *(syn.)* impervious: *The wooden boat was made watertight with special sealants.*

wa·ter·way /ˈwɔtərˌweɪ, ˈwɑ-/ *n.* [C] a canal, river, or other water passage: *The Mississippi River is a major waterway, dividing the eastern USA from the West.*

wa·ter·wheel /ˈwɔtərˌwil, ˈwɑ-/ *n.* a large wheel turned by flowing water: *Mills located beside rivers got their power from waterwheels.*

wa·ter·works /ˈwɔtərˌwɜrks, ˈwɑ-/ *n.pl.* (*used with a sing. or pl. verb*) the public system for providing water to the people in a city or town: *The town's waterworks cleans and pumps water to each house.*

wa·ter·y /ˈwɔtəri, ˈwɑ-/ *adj.* **1** having or containing a lot of water: *Don't plant corn in that field; it's too watery.* **2** made weak with water, *(syn.)* diluted: *The soup is watery and tasteless.*

watt /wɑt/ *n.* a measuring unit of electrical or mechanical power: *My desk lamp uses a 60-watt light bulb.* *-n.* [U] **wattage** /ˈwɑtɪdʒ/.

wave /weɪv/ *v.* **waved, waving, waves 1** to move softly back and forth, (*syn.*) to undulate: *Flags waved in the breeze.* **2** to communicate with s.o. by raising and moving the hand: *She waved good-bye to her husband.* **3** to curl: *The hairdresser waved the woman's hair.* **4** *phrasal v. sep.* **to wave s.t. aside:** to push away and not pay attention to: *She waved aside my ideas for increasing sales.||She waved them aside.*

—*n.* **1** a sign of greeting made by raising and moving the hand: *He gave me a wave of hello.* **2** a long raised mass of water moving across the surface of the sea: *The waves on the ocean are high today.* **3** an electronic, light, or sound movement of energy: *Radio waves bring us music and news.* **4** a sudden increase in an activity or a condition: *a crime wave||a heat wave* **5 wave of the future:** s.t. sure to be popular later, (*syn.*) a trend: *In the 1960s concern for the environment was the wave of the future. -n.* **waver.**

wave·length /'weɪv,lɛŋkθ, -lɛŋθ/ *n.* [C] **1** the distance from one point to the same point on the next sound or electromagnetic wave **2 to be on the same wavelength:** to understand and communicate easily with s.o.: *My friend and I are on the same wavelength; we never argue.*

wa·ver /'weɪvər/ *v.* to move back and forth, not know what to do, (*syn.*) to vacillate: *He wavered between buying stock and keeping his money in the bank. -n.* [C] **waverer;** *-n.* [U] *adj.* **wavering.**

wav·y /'weɪvi/ *adj.* **-ier, -iest** having waves: *She has wavy hair. -n.* [U] **waviness.**

wax /wæks/ *n.* [U] **1** a soft, flexible, slightly greasy substance used in candles, furniture and car polish, etc.: *Some wax comes from bees.* **2** an increase (said of the moon): *The moon is on the wax now.*

—*v.* **waxes 1** to apply wax or polish to: *I waxed the table this morning.* **2** to grow, (*syn.*) to increase: *We see more of the moon as it waxes.*

wax bean *n.* in USA, a yellow string bean with a light waxy coating: *We had wax beans with meat and potatoes for dinner.*

wax paper or **waxed paper** /wækst/ *n.* [U] paper with a thin coating of wax, used for wrapping food: *The butcher wraps meat in waxed paper.*

wax·y /'wæksi/ *adj.* **-ier, -iest 1** covered with wax: *After polishing the car, my hands were waxy.* **2** looking shiny and smooth and feeling slightly greasy: *Candles feel waxy when touched. -n.* [U] **waxiness.**

way /weɪ/ *n.* **1** [C] a method, manner, style: *One way to travel is by air.||She speaks to people in a friendly way.* **2** [C] a direction: *Go that way, then to the right, and you will see the*

store. **3** [U] a distance: *That store is a long way from here.* **4** [C] a path or road: *The way through the garden is covered with small stones.||He lives on Hamilton Way.* **5** [U] the space or opening for a course of action: *The way is clear for our two companies to join together.||He sees no way out of his money problems except to sell his house.* **6** [C] a manner or condition of living: *He is poor and in a bad way.* **7** [C] everyday habits, (*syn.*) customs: *We travel to other countries to learn the ways of other peoples.||our way of life* **8** *pl.* [C] a ramp used to slide a ship into the water **9 by the way:** an expression used to change the subject in a conversation, (*syn.*) incidentally: *Oh, by the way, do you have my new address?* **10 by way of: a.** from the direction of, (*syn.*) via: *We flew from New York to St. Louis by way of Chicago.* **b.** as a form or means of: *He nodded his head by way of showing he approved.* **11 in a way:** to some degree, partly: *In a way, you are right, but I still have doubts.* **12 in** or **out of the way:** in or out of a position that blocks traffic or keeps people from passing: *The men stood in the way and would not let us enter the building.* **13** *infrml.* **no way:** an expression of strong disagreement or disapproval: *"Are you going out in this rain?" "No way."||No way am I going to lend him money.* **14 on one's** or **the way: a.** traveling, (*syn.*) en route: *Our friends are on their way here now.* **b.** on one's planned route of travel: *I can easily bring the papers to your office because it is on my way home.* **c.** *fig.* making progress: *She is on the way to becoming a great doctor.||That bright young man is on his way up in the company.* **d.** (of a baby) soon to be born: *She has two children and a third on the way.* **15** *infrml.* **on the way out:** in the process of being fired or pushed out of a job: *No one likes the president, so he is on the way out.* **16 out-of-the-way:** quiet and uncrowded, remote: *We visited a little out-of-the-way town in the mountains.* **17 to come one's way:** to come to s.o. by luck: *A good job just came his way one day when a friend told him about it.* **18 to get** or **have one's (own) way:** to have others agree to what one wants, (*syn.*) to prevail: *He is stubborn and insists on having his way all the time.* **19 to give way to s.o.** or **s.t.:** to allow s.o. or s.t. to win or take control: *At the funeral, family members gave way to their emotions and cried openly.* **20** *infrml.* **to go all the way:** to have sex: *The girl refused to go all the way with her boyfriend.* **21 to go one's own way:** to be different from others, to do what one wants independently: *He had several business partners, but he left the company and went his own way.* **22 to go out of one's way: a.** to travel an extra distance for s.o. or s.t.: *My friend goes out of his way to pick me up to play golf.* **b.** *fig.* to give extra effort: *She goes out*

of her way to help others. **23 to have a way with:** to have a special talent or gift for (people, animals, words, etc.): *She will be a good teacher because she has a way with children.* **24 to have it both ways:** to get s.t. good out of two opposing actions or situations: *She wants to go on vacation, but she doesn't want to spend money; she can't have it both ways!* **25 to make way:** to move aside or create a space: *He made way so others could pass.||Trees were cut down to make way for the new road.* **26 to pay one's own way:** to pay one's expenses instead of depending on others: *My friend and I went on vacation, and we each paid our own way.* **27 to see one's way clear to do s.t.:** to agree to do s.t., often after much delay: *The owner finally saw his way clear to hiring more help for his busy store.* **28 under way:** in progress: *The concert got under way at seven o'clock.*

—*suffix* **1** direction: *a one-way street* **2** participant: *We made it a three-way partnership.*

—*adv.infrml.* very, a lot: *We could see the birds in the sky way up high.||He is way off in his totals and needs to check his arithmetic.*

way·lay /'weɪ,leɪ/ v. **-laid** /-,leɪd/, **-laying, -lays** **1** to wait for and then stop a person: *The movie star was waylaid by television reporters.* **2** to stop and rob: *Thieves sometimes waylay travelers on dark, lonely roads.*

way-out /,weɪ'aʊt/ adj.slang strange, (syns.) eccentric, abnormal: *He has way-out ideas on politics.*

ways and means n.pl. methods and money to do s.t.: *The committee on ways and means voted to support the new laws.*

way·side /'weɪ,saɪd/ n. [C, usu. sing.] **1** the side of the road, (syn.) the roadside: *The poor little cat was left by the wayside.* **2 to fall by the wayside:** to lose strength or popularity: *That company's products slowly fell by the wayside as their sales went down.*

way station n. a resting place between main stops, usu. for getting gas or food: *The Boston-to-New York bus pulled into a way station in Connecticut for gas.*

way·ward /'weɪwərd/ adj. not following the rules, (syns.) misbehaving, deviant: *Their wayward son was arrested by the police many times last year.*

we /wi/ pron. first person pl. used by a speaker or writer to refer to himself or herself and one or more others: *We eat dinner together every evening.*

weak /wik/ adj. **1** not physically strong, (syn.) feeble: *The patient is losing blood and becoming weak.* **2** not strong in character: *A weak leader doesn't have control of the situation.* **3** containing too much water, (syn.) diluted: *This soup is weak; it has little flavor.* **4** lacking the force to persuade, (syn.) unconvincing: *a weak*

argument **5** (in business) losing financial strength, (syn.) declining: *The market for those goods is weak.* **-adv. weakly.**

weak·en /'wikən/ v. **1** to make or become less strong, (syn.) to debilitate: *The sick lady weakens each day.||Heavy traffic has weakened the bridge.* **2** to make or become lower, (syn.) to decline: *Prices of foreign goods are weakening.*

weak-kneed /'wik,nid/ adj.fig. afraid, (syn.) cowardly: *He is weak-kneed about asking his boss for a raise.*

weak·ling /'wiklɪŋ/ n. a person who is not very strong: *The boy who is smaller than the other kids in his class is a weakling.*

weak-mind·ed /'wik'maɪndɪd/ adj. **1** not smart, (syn.) feebleminded: *He is weak-minded, so he can never have a real job.* **2** not able to make a firm decision, (syn.) indecisive, spineless: *The weak-minded worker never uses independent ideas, and instead follows others.*

weak·ness /'wiknɪs/ n. **-nesses** **1** [U] lack of strength: *The patient is suffering from weakness after the operation.* **2** [U] a physical problem, (syn.) dysfunction: *He has a weakness in his blood circulation.* **3** [C;U] a desire or fondness for s.t.: *She has a weakness for chocolate.||He has a weakness for redheaded women.*

wealth /wɛlθ/ n. **1** [U] a large amount of money and property: *They are a family of great wealth.* **2** a large number amount: *a wealth of information*

wealth·y /'wɛlθi/ adj. **-ier, -iest** having lots of money, rich: *Wealthy people often eat in expensive restaurants.* **-n.** [U] **wealthiness.**

wean /win/ v. **1** to change diet after drinking only mother's milk: *Farmers wean baby cows by feeding them light grain.* **2** to stop former habits: *He weaned himself away from smoking cigarettes by eating candy instead.*

weap·on /'wɛpən/ n. a tool used to harm or kill: *Knives and guns are dangerous weapons.* **-n.** [U] **weaponry** /'wɛpənri/.

wear /wɛr/ v. **wore** /wɔr/ or **worn** /wɔrn/, **wearing, wears** **1** to have on one's body, such as clothes, glasses, or jewelry: *He wears suits to work.* **2** to get smaller or lose quality through use: *Heels of shoes wear down.* **3** to last a long time, (syn.) to endure: *My heavy winter coat has worn well for five years.* **4** to have as an expression on the face: *My father wore a smile when we arrived.* **5** phrasal v. **to wear off: a.** to lose effect: *The pain medication wore off after surgery.* **b.** to lose color, shine, etc. by rubbing, time, etc.: *Her lipstick wore off by noon.* **6** phrasal v. sep. **to wear s.o. or s.t. out: a.** s.o.: to tire, (syns.) to exhaust, fatigue: *He wore out his family with his complaining.||He wore them out.* **b.** s.t.: to make useless through use, to use up: *I wear out a*

W

pair of shoes every six months. **7** phrasal v. sep. **to wear s.t. away:** to cause to lose shine, smoothness, paint, etc.: *The dog scratched at the door and wore away the paint.‖He wore it away.* **8** phrasal v. sep. **to wear s.t. down: a.** to weaken in structure, (syn.) to deteriorate: *The bad roads have worn down the tires on my car.‖They have worn them down.* **b.** to make tired, (syns.) to fatigue, exhaust: *The long argument wore me down, so I went to bed.* **9 to wear the pants in one's family:** to have the most power in a family: *My mother wore the pants in my family as I grew up.* **10 to wear thin:** to grow tiring or boring: *After hearing him tell the same joke five times, hearing it again wears thin.* -adj. **wearable.**

wear and tear /tɛr/ n. [U] use that causes damage, (syn.) deterioration: *Office furniture becomes old and scratched through daily wear and tear.*

wear·ing /ˈwɛrɪŋ/ adj. tiring, (syn.) wearying: *The long car trip was wearing.*

wea·ri·some /ˈwɪrɪsəm/ adj. annoying, tiresome, (syn.) oppressive: *His nonstop complaining is wearisome.*

wea·ry /ˈwɪri/ adj. **-rier, -riest 1** tired, (syn.) fatigued: *She is weary from so much work.* **2** having little patience for, bored: *He is weary of arguing with you all the time.* -adv. **wearily;** -n. [U] **weariness.**

wea·sel /ˈwizəl/ n. **1** a small, brown and white meat-eating animal: *Weasels sometimes eat chickens on farms.* **2** infrml. a person who is not to be trusted: *Don't hire that weasel; he'll steal from you.*
—v.infrml. **to weasel out of s.t.:** to avoid doing s.t. in a sneaky or lying way: *He weaseled out of paying by leaving the restaurant while I was in the bathroom.*

weath·er /ˈwɛðər/ n. [U] **1** the conditions of the sky and air relating to rain, snow, heat, cold, etc.: *In good weather, we go outside.* **2** **under the weather:** not feeling well, sick, ill: *This morning she felt under the weather, so she didn't go to work.*
—v. **1** to pass through safely: *The ship weathered the storm in the harbor.* **2** fig. to last through a difficult situation, (syn.) to endure: *My grandfather weathered World Wars I and II.* **3** to change or be changed by the weather: *The sun weathered the wooden house.* -adj. **weathered.**

weather-beaten adj. damaged or marked by the wind, rain, sun, etc.: *Our garden furniture is weather-beaten.*

weather bureau n. a government office that studies and reports weather conditions: *I called the weather bureau to find out if a storm was coming.*

weather forecast n. a description of expected weather conditions: *She listens to the*

weather forecast on the radio each morning. -n. **weather forecaster.**

weather vane n. [C] a pointer on the top of a building, usu. a barn, that shows wind direction: *Our weather vane is in the shape of a bird.*

weather vane

weave (1) /wiv/ v. **wove** /wouv/ or **woven** /ˈwouvən/, **weaving, weaves** to make fabric by crossing threads or other material over and under one another: *My grandmother wove rugs from old pieces of cloth.*
—n. the pattern formed by the way a fabric is woven: *That cloth is made of a fine weave.* -n. [C] **weaver;** [U] **weaving.** See: woven.

weave (2) v. **weaved, weaving, weaves 1** to move along by passing around things and changing direction often: *We weaved through traffic to find our way here.* **2** to move unsteadily: *The drunk woman is weaving as she walks.*

web /wɛb/ n. **1** a net of thin threads formed by an insect or a spider: *We could see a fly caught in the spider web.* **2** a detailed and complicated arrangement of things: *a web of lies See:* cobweb.
—v. **webbed, webbing, webs** to form a web: *Roads webbed across the city.* -n. [U] **webbing.**

web-foot·ed /ˈwɛbˌfutɪd/ adj. having toes connected by thick skin: *Ducks and frogs are web-footed.*

we'd /wid/ contr of we had or we would

wed /wɛd/ v.frml. **wedded** or **wed, wedding, weds 1** to marry: *We wed and became husband and wife.* **2** to bring together, join, (syn.) to unite: *Management wedded sales and marketing into one single department.*

wed·ding /ˈwɛdɪŋ/ n. a marriage ceremony: *The wedding took place in a church.*

wedding ring n. a marriage ring, band: *The man placed the wedding ring on the woman's finger during the marriage ceremony.*

wedge /wɛdʒ/ n. **1** a V-shaped piece of metal, wood, etc. used to separate two parts: *The worker cut the log by driving a wedge into it.* **2** s.t. in a triangular shape: *a wedge of cheese*
—v. **wedged, wedging, wedges 1** to open or split apart with a wedge: *Workmen wedged a locked door open with their tools.* **2** phrasal v. insep. **to wedge in:** to put or go tightly between other people or things: *I wedged in between other passengers in the subway car.*

wed·lock /ˈwɛdˌlɑk/ n.frml. [U] **1** a state of being legally married **2 out of wedlock:** not legally married: *The child was born to a couple out of wedlock.*

Wednes·day /'wɛnzdeɪ, -di/ *n.* the day of the week between Tuesday and Thursday

wee /wi/ *adj.* **1** tiny, very small: *He is a wee young boy.* **2** early: *We stayed out until the wee hours of the morning.*

weed /wid/ *n.* [C] a wild plant that is not wanted in a yard or garden: *My garden has more weeds than flowers.*
—*v.* **1** to pull out weeds from: *I weeded our lawn yesterday, and it looks much nicer.* **2** *phrasal v. sep.* **to weed s.t. out:** to remove s.t. that is not wanted or needed: *The student weeded out the old books he didn't need for school. -adj.* **weedy.**

week /wik/ *n.* **1** the seven-day period, from Sunday through Saturday: *There are 52 weeks in the year.* **2** seven days: *I'll see you one week from today.*

week·day /'wik,deɪ/ *n.* Monday, Tuesday, Wednesday, Thursday, or Friday: *The park is not crowded on weekdays because the children are in school.*

week·end /'wik,ɛnd/ *n.* Saturday and Sunday: *I spent this past weekend in the country.*

week·ly /'wikli/ *adj.* happening once a week or every week: *This is a weekly newspaper.*
—*adv.* once a week or every week: *She visits her grandmother weekly.*
—*n.* [C] a magazine or newspaper that appears once a week: *The village newspaper is a weekly; I buy it every Thursday.*

week·night /'wik,naɪt/ *n.* any night but Saturday or Sunday: *I stay home on weeknights and then go out on Saturday night.*

weep /wip/ *v.frml.* **wept** /wɛpt/, **weeping, weeps** to cry: *The wife wept at her husband's funeral. -adj.* **weepy.**

weft /wɛft/ *n.* threads woven horizontally through a fabric: *The weft in that fabric is red. See:* warp.

weigh /weɪ/ *v.* **1** to measure how heavy s.t. is: *I weighed myself on the scale this morning.* **2** to have a certain weight: *The apples weighed one pound.* **3** to think about carefully before choosing, (*syns.*) to evaluate, consider: *The student weighed his choices as to which university to attend.* **4** *phrasal v.* **to weigh in:** (said of wrestlers, jockeys, etc.) to have a certain official weight before a competition: *The heavyweight boxers weighed in at 215 lbs. each before the fight.* **5** *phrasal v. insep.* **to weight on s.o.** or **s.t.:** to cause s.o. or s.t. to worry: *Her illness weighed on her family.* **6** to **weigh one's words:** to speak carefully: *The judge weighed his words when he spoke to the jury about the trial.* **7** *phrasal v. sep.* **to weigh s.o.** or **s.t. down: a.** to make heavy: *Many books weighed down the student's bag.* **b.** to worry, (*syn.*) to burden: *Thoughts about his*

bad health weighed down my neighbor.||*They weighed him down.* **8** *phrasal v. sep.* **to weigh s.t. out:** to measure s.t. by weight: *The clerk weighed out three pounds of beans.||She weighed them out.*

weight /weɪt/ *n.* **1** [U] the measure of how heavy s.t. or s.o. is: *His weight is 200 lbs.* **2** [C] a heavy object: *The fisherman attached a weight to his line.||Some people lift weights for exercise.* **3** *fig.* [U] a responsibility that causes worry: *His mother's sickness has been a weight on his mind.* **4** **to carry weight:** to have importance: *His opinion carries a lot of weight with the city leaders.* **5** **to give weight:** to add value, show the importance of: *The new book gives weight to the author's ideas.* **6** **to pull one's own weight:** to do one's share of the work: *She pulls her own weight in this company; she does more than anyone.* **7** **to put on** or **lose weight:** to become heavier or thinner: *I have been putting on weight and need to lose 10 lbs.* **8** *infrml.* **to throw one's weight around:** to use one's influence forcefully: *The president throws his weight around and makes all the big decisions.*
—*v.* **1** to make heavier by adding weights: *She weighted my fishing net before throwing it into the sea.* **2** *phrasal v. sep.* **to weight s.o.** or **s.t. down:** to make or cause to feel heavy: *The heavy load of boxes weighted down the truck.||It weighted it down.*

weight lifter *n.* [C] a person who lifts heavy pieces of iron for exercise: *She is a weight lifter who can hold 100 lbs. over her head. -n.* [U] **weightlifting.**

weight·y /'weɪti/ *adj.fig.* **-ier, -iest** having importance, serious: *Nuclear power is a weighty subject for every country. -n.* [U] **weightiness.**

weird /wɪrd/ *adj.* strange, (*syns.*) odd, bizarre: *Sometimes we hear weird noises that sound like crying in the night. -adv.* **weirdly;** *-n.* [U] **weirdness.**

weird·o /'wɪrdoʊ/ *n.infrml.* **-os** a person who seems very strange, (*syns.*) a kook, an eccentric: *He is a weirdo who believes creatures from the moon visit us on Earth.*

wel·come /'wɛlkəm/ *v.* **-comed, -coming, -comes** **1** to greet in a friendly way when s.o. arrives: *The woman giving the party welcomed her friends at the door.* **2** to accept happily or gratefully: *He welcomed the idea of taking a vacation.*
—*n.* [C] **1** a friendly greeting: *My friend shouted a welcome to me as I approached his house.* **2** **to wear out one's welcome:** to be no longer wanted or tolerated: *Our guest stayed too long and wore out his welcome.*
—*adj.* **1** easily accepted, liked: *This book is a welcome addition to the library.* **2** a polite response to "thank you": *"Thank you for the loan." "You're welcome."*

W

weld /wɛld/ *v.* to join metal things by melting them slightly and putting them together: *A worker welded steel pieces together for the new building.*
—*n.* [C] a place where two pieces of metal are welded together -*n.* [C] **welder;** [U] **welding.**

wel·fare /'wɛl,fɛr/ *n.* **1** one's general condition, (*syn.*) well-being: *The mother is concerned about her son's welfare.* **2** money from the government for food, housing, health services, etc.: *He lost his job and is now on welfare.* -*n.* [U] **welfarism.**

USAGE NOTE: *Welfare* is an American governmental system that includes services such as unemployment compensation, food stamps, and housing assistance to the poor.

welfare state *n.* a government that provides money and services to improve the living conditions of people who are without work: *The welfare state has different ways to help the poor.*

well /wɛl/ *adv.* **better** /'bɛtər/, **best** /bɛst/ **1** in a good way, (*syns.*) skillfully, competently: *She performs well as an actress.‖He plays the piano very well.* **2** very much: *He finished the exam well before the exam period ended.* **3** as **well as:** in addition to: *She has a dog as well as two cats as pets.* **4** to leave well enough alone:** to keep quiet or stop doing s.t. so as not to cause trouble: *You can't win, so leave well enough alone and stop arguing.* **5** well done:** I approve, congratulations: *You won the race. Well done! See:* well-done.
—*adj.* in good health: *I hope you are well.*
—*n.* a hole made in the ground (for water, oil, etc.): *Please fill this bucket from the water well.*
—*phrasal v.* **to well up:** to rise: *Protests welled up into riots.‖Tears welled up in his eyes as he said good-bye to his family.*
—*interj.* an expression to show surprise, doubt, hesitation, etc.: *Well! That's an interesting idea!*

well-advised *adj.* **1** given good suggestions on how to do s.t.: *He was well-advised by a good lawyer.* **2** showing good judgment, sensible: *You would be well-advised to see a doctor about the pains in your chest.*

well-being *n.* [U] one's mental and physical condition: *He telephones his ailing mother daily because he is worried about her well-being.*

well-bred *adj.* having good manners and education, (*syn.*) well brought up: *That couple's children are well-bred; they behave nicely in restaurants.*

well-defined *adj.* **1** written in a way that is easily understood: *The instructions in that letter are clear and well-defined.* **2** having clear lines: *Her facial features are well-defined, with a sharp chin and long nose.*

well-disposed *adj.* agreeable to s.t., (*syn.*) amenable: *The boss is well-disposed toward accepting your plan.*

well-done *adj.* **1** skillfully accomplished, excellent, (*syn.*) successful: *His test was well-done, so he received a good grade.* **2** cooked thoroughly: *She likes her meat well-done.*

well-founded *adj.* based on good reasons (information, facts, etc.): *After listening to the weather report, I knew my worries about bad weather were well-founded.*

well-groomed *adj.* neat and clean in the way s.o. looks and dresses: *Her hair, makeup, and clothes are always perfect; she is well-groomed.*

well-heeled *adj.fig.* rich, (*syns.*) prosperous, affluent: *A well-heeled group of people eats at that expensive restaurant.*

well-in·ten·tioned *adj.* done with the hope of success: *His help was well-intentioned, though not very useful.*

well-known *adj.* **1** famous, (*syn.*) renowned: *He is a well-known television actor.* **2** part of common knowledge, widely known: *It is a well-known fact that there are many homeless people in our cities. See:* infamous.

well-meaning *adj.* having good hopes or intentions, (*syn.*) well-intentioned: *Your calls are well-meaning, but you call too often.*

well·ness concept /'wɛlnɪs/ *n.* [U] in USA, a health-care idea that supports good health habits among workers to prevent sickness and cut the cost of a company's medical insurance: *Many companies pay for their workers' health club memberships to encourage the wellness concept.*

well-off *adj.* rich, (*syns.*) prosperous, affluent: *He owns his own business and is well-off, so he doesn't worry about money.*

well-read *adj.* having read many books and other things, educated: *She is a well-read English teacher.*

well-rounded *adj.* having many abilities, both intellectual and physical: *He is a well-rounded student who plays football, sings, and speaks German.*

well-spoken *adj.* able to speak clearly and correctly: *We chose her to talk for us because she is well-spoken.*

well-thought-of *adj.* having a good reputation, respected: *He is very well-thought-of by other doctors.*

well-to-do *adj.* rich, (*syns.*) prosperous, affluent: *That well-to-do family lives in a big house with a swimming pool.*

welsh /wɛlʃ, wɛlʧ/ *v.* **welshes** to agree to do s.t. and then not do it: *He welshed on me by promising to pay half but then leaving town.*

W

welt /wɛlt/ *n.* a raised mark on the skin: *I have a welt on my face from the tree branch that hit me.*

wel·ter /'wɛltər/ *n.* a confused mix, (*syn.*) a clutter: *His office is covered with a welter of old papers.*

wend /wɛnd/ *v.* to move in a slow, indirect way: *The river wends toward the ocean.||She wended her way to school.*

wept /wɛpt/ *past tense & past part. of* weep

were /wɜr; *weak form* wər/ *v.pl. past tense of* be

we're /wɪr/ *contr. of* we are

were·wolf /'wɛr,wʊlf, 'wɪr-/ *n.* **-wolves** /-,wʊlvz/ an imaginary person who sometimes changes from a man into a wolflike animal: *In the horror movie, a werewolf howled at the moon.*

west /wɛst/ *n.* [U] **1** the direction in which the sun sets **2** the western part of a country: *California is in the west of the USA.* **3 the West:** the western part of the world, esp. Western Europe, the USA, and Canada **4 out West:** the western part of the U.S., including California, Oregon, and Washington: *Beatrix lives out West, in Portland, Oregon.* **5 the Wild West:** the western part of the USA during the 19th century: *In the Wild West, there was little law and order.*
—*adv.* moving toward the west: *We are driving west on the main highway.||Have you ever been out west?*
—*adj.* **1** located in the west: *We live on the west side of the park.* **2** coming from the west: *a west wind*

west·bound /'wɛst,baʊnd/ *adj.* headed toward the west: *Westbound traffic on the highway is stopped because of an accident.*

west·er·ly /'wɛstərli/ *adj.* coming from or headed toward the west: *Westerly winds brought warm air.*

West·ern /'wɛstərn/ *adj.* of or belonging to the west: *Western clothes include cowboy hats and boots.*
—*n.* a story, movie, etc. about cowboys, Native Americans, etc. in the western USA: *The old Westerns are still popular movies today.*

West·ern·er /'wɛstərnər/ *n.* s.o. from or living in the western part of a country: *He is a Westerner who now lives in Miami.*

Western hemisphere *n.* the half of the earth that includes North and South America

west·ern·ize or **West·ern·ize** /'wɛstər,naɪz/ *v.* **-ized, -izing, -izes** to cause to have ideas, behavior, etc. typical of the West (western Europe, the USA, and Canada) -*n.* [U] **westernization** /,wɛstərnə'zeɪʃən/.

west·ward /'wɛstwərd/ *adj.adv.* toward the west, in a westerly direction: *The ship sailed <adv.> westward toward the sunset.*

wet /wɛt/ *adj.* **wetter, wettest 1** covered with or full of water or another liquid, (*syns.*) soaked, drenched: *The ground is wet from today's rain.* **2 to be all wet:** to be wrong, mistaken: *He's all wet; he doesn't know what he's talking about.* **3 to be (still) wet behind the ears:** to be young and lacking experience: *The cowboys laughed at the newcomer and said he was wet behind the ears.*
—*v.* **wet** or **wetted, wetting, wets** to cover or fill with water, (*syns.*) to soak, drench: *We wet the dry ground with a hose. -n.* [U] **wetness.**

wet·back /'wɛt,bæk/ *n.pej.* a Mexican worker who crosses the U.S. border illegally

wet blanket *n.* a person who spoils the fun of others: *He is always angry, a wet blanket at any party.*

wet·land /'wɛt,lænd/ or **wet·lands** /'wɛt,lændz/ *n.* or *n.pl.* a watery area, such as a swamp: *Wetlands near the ocean were made into a park to protect the birds.*

wet nurse *n.* a woman who breastfeeds the child of another: *A wet nurse breastfed me when I was a baby, because my mother couldn't.*

wet suit *n.* a thick, waterproof body suit worn by swimmers and divers to keep warm in the water: *We put on wet suits and dove into the cold ocean.*

we've /wiv/ *contr. of* we have

whack /wæk/ *v.* to hit hard: *The fisherman whacked the fish on the head to kill it.*
—*n.* **1** a sharp blow: *The fisherman gave the fish a whack on the head.* **2** *infrml.* a try: *He didn't cook often, but he took a whack at making dinner for everyone.* **3 out of whack: a.** not agreeing with or matching: *He has ideas that are out of whack with the other people in his company.* **b.** not working properly, broken, (*syn.*) out of order: *The refrigerator is out of whack.*

whack·y /'wæki/ **-ier, -iest** *See:* wacky.

whale /weɪl/ *n.* **1** a very large mammal shaped like a fish and found in the ocean: *The blue whale may reach 100 feet in length and weigh 150 tons.* **2** *infrml.* **a whale of a s.t.:** an extremely good s.t.: *We had a whale of a time at the beach.*

whal·ing /'weɪlɪŋ/ *n.* [U] the business of hunting and killing whales for their oil, whalebone, and other materials: *Whaling is still done in some countries.*

whal·er /'weɪlər/ *n.* **1** a ship used in hunting whales **2** a person who hunts whales

wham /wæm/ *n.v.exclam.* the sound of a hard hit: *The race car crashed into the wall with a <n.> "wham!"*

wham·my /ˈwæmi/ *n.infrml.* a strong, bad force, (*syns.*) a jinx, curse: *The rain put a whammy on our picnic.*

wharf /wɔrf/ **wharves** /wɔrvz/ or **wharfs** *n.* a long platform built over the water, where ships can pull up to load or unload, (*syns.*) a pier, dock: *Boats sailed up to the wharf, and the passengers got off.*

what /wʌt, wɑt; *weak form* wət/ *pron.* **1** (used in a question to get information about s.t.): *What did you say?‖What is your name?* **2** (used to show surprise, alarm): *What a terrible thing to have happen!* **3** the thing or things that: *The teacher told the students what to do.* **4** *infrml.* **and what have you:** and so on, and other things like that: *The flood destroyed the house, the car, and what have you.* **5 and what not:** and so on, and other things: *We brought food, camping equipment, fishing rods, and what not.* **6 What do you do?:** What is your job, profession, etc.? **7 What .. . for?:** why, for what reason: *What did you do that for?‖"I'm going home." "What for?"* **8 What if?:** What will happen if, supposing that: *What if we are wrong?* **9 what's in it for s.o.:** what good thing or benefit is likely or can be expected for s.o.: *The new project sounds interesting, but I want to know what's in it for me.* **10 what it takes:** the necessary ability: *He has what it takes to succeed in business.* **11 what with:** because of: *She has been depressed, what with losing her job and having to move.* **12** *infrml.* **What's up?:** What are you doing, what is happening? **13 what's what:** what is correct, how s.t. should be done: *She explained the different rules of the game to me so I would know what's what.* **14** *infrml.* **what's with s.o.** or **s.t.:** what is the matter with s.o. or s.t.: *What's with him? He seems angry.*
—*adj.* a word used in a question to get information about s.t.: *What color is your car?*
—*interj.* a word used to show surprise, alarm: *"He broke his leg." "What!"*

USAGE NOTE: If you did not hear s.o. or would like to have s.t. repeated, it is polite to say "Pardon me," "Excuse me," or "Would you please repeat what you said?" rather than just "*What?*"

---

what·cha·ma·call·it /ˈwʌtʃəməˌkɔlɪt, ˈwɑ-/ *n.infrml.* a word used for s.t. when its name has been forgotten: *Where is the whatchamacallit I was using to open this wine bottle?*

what·ev·er /wətˈɛvər, wɑt-/ *pron.* **1** no matter what: *Whatever you decide, we need to leave soon.* **2** anything, whatsoever: *I'll buy you whatever you want for your birthday.* **3** what (shows surprise in a question): *Whatever made you say a thing like that?*

—*adj.* **1** of any kind, at all, whatsoever: *I have no plans whatever; I am free all day.* **2** no matter what: *All movies, whatever the subject, interest me.*

what·not /ˈwʌtˌnɑt, ˈwɑt-/ *n.* small decorative objects, (*syn.*) bric-a-brac: *She has whatnots on a bookshelf.*
—*pron.* and other similar things: *I bought toothpaste, shampoo, soap, and whatnot.*

what·so·ever /ˌwʌtsoʊˈɛvər, ˌwɑt-/ *adj.* (anything) at all: *I've eaten no food whatsoever since yesterday. See:* whatever.

wheat /wit/ *n.* [U] a cereal plant or grain usu. ground into flour and used to make bread, cake, pasta, etc.: *Wheat is a major food source, grown throughout the world for 7,000 years.*

whee /wi/ *exclam.* an expression of happiness, pleasure: *Children shouted "Whee!" as they played on the swings.*

wheel /wil/ *n.* **1** a circular piece of metal, rubber, wood, etc. allowing s.t. to turn and roll: *Cars have four wheels; bicycles have two.* **2** *infrml.* **a big wheel:** an important person: *He's a big wheel in city government.* **3** *slang* **(set of) wheels:** a car or other vehicle: *I have no wheels today because my car is being repaired.* **4 at** or **behind the wheel:** driving a car or other vehicle: *She is behind the wheel while her husband is a passenger.* **5 to put the wheels in motion:** to start s.t., begin work: *I put the wheels in motion on the project by ordering materials for the new building.*
—*v.* **1** to push s.t. on wheels: *A nurse wheeled the patient into the operating room.* **2** to turn suddenly, (*syn.*) to rotate: *Surprised, the man wheeled around and greeted his old friend.* **3** *infrml.* **to wheel and deal:** to make money in a quick, often dishonest, way: *He wheels and deals in selling used cars. -n.* **wheeler-dealer.**

wheel·bar·row /ˈwilˌbæroʊ/ *n.* a small cart with one wheel and handles for pushing, used for moving small loads: *Gardeners put dirt into a wheelbarrow to move it across the garden.*

wheel·chair /ˈwilˌtʃɛr/ *n.* a chair with wheels, used by a person who cannot walk: *The nurse pushed the sick child in a wheelchair.*

wheeze /wiz/ *v.* **wheezed, wheezing, wheezes** to breathe with difficulty while making a whistling sound: *He has a bad chest cold and wheezes a lot. -adj.* **wheezy.**

whelk /ˌwɛlk/ *n.* a sea animal that lives in a shell like a snail, and is sometimes used as food

when /wɛn; *weak form* wən/ *adv.* at what time: *When do you think that he will arrive?*
—*conj.* **1** at the time that: *It started to rain when we left the house.* **2** considering that, although: *Why does he smoke when he knows it*

W

is so unhealthy? **3** immediately after, as soon as: *Please call us when you arrive.*
—*pron.* what time: *Since when has she been managing the store?*

USAGE NOTE: The expression *since when* is an informal way to express surprise or dislike for s.t. that one has just heard: *The bank closes at 3 P.M. now? Since when?*

---

when·ev·er /wɛˈnɛvər, wə-/ *adv.conj.* at whatever time: *The roof leaks <conj.> whenever it rains.*

where /wɛr; *weak form* wər/ *adv.* **1** at which place: *Where have you been for the last week?* **2** to what place: *Where did you go after school?* **3** from what person, place, or source: *Where did you hear the bad news?*
—*pron.* what place: *Where do they come from?||She lives only a mile from where she was born.*
—*conj.* **1** in or at which place: *He spent the weekend in Dallas, where his parents live.* **2** to which place: *I don't like the restaurant where we're going.*

where·a·bouts /ˈwɛrəˌbaʊts/ *n.pl.* used with a sing. or pl. verb location: *No one knows his whereabouts; he's lost.*

where·as /wɛrˈæz/ *conj.frml.* but, in fact, (*syns.*) by contrast, on the contrary: *He says that he paid me, whereas I have not received money from him.*

where·by /wɛrˈbaɪ/ *adv.frml.* by means of which, through which: *That school gives money whereby students can study music for free.*

where·in /wɛrˈɪn/ *adv.frml.* in which: *This contract has a requirement wherein payment must be made each month.*

where·up·on /ˌwɛrəˈpɑn, -ˈpɔn, ˈwɛrəˌpɑn, -ˌpɔn/ *adv.* and then, after which: *The soldier refused to surrender, whereupon the army captured him.*

wher·ev·er /wɛrˈɛvər, wər-/ *adv.conj.* at or to any place: *We can eat <adv.> wherever you would like to.||<adv.> Wherever did you get that idea?*

where·with·al /ˈwɛrwɪˌðɔl, -ˌθɔl/ *n.* [U] the ability to afford something, (*syns.*) funds, means: *He has the wherewithal to live wherever he wants to.*

whet /wɛt/ *v.frml.* **whetted, whetting, whets 1** to sharpen, (*syn.*) to hone: *Before he cuts, he whets his knife on a stone.* **2 to whet s.o.'s appetite:** to make s.o. want something, to create a desire in s.o. (for food, money, pleasure, etc.): *Cold weather and hard work whetted my appetite for a big, hot dinner.*

wheth·er /ˈwɛðər/ *conj.* **1** if (shows choice): *Please tell me whether (or not) you want to go to the party.* **2** no matter if (shows it is not im-

portant what one chooses or decides): *Whether you stay at home or come with me, I'm going to the party.*

whew /hwyu, hwu, hyu/ *exclam.* **1** an expression of being tired, hot, etc.: *Whew! It's very hot and humid today.* **2** an expression of relief: *Whew! I'm glad that math test is over.*

which /wɪʧ/ *adj.* **1** (used in questions) what one or ones in a group of people or things: *Which day is better for us to meet, Monday or Tuesday?||Which children in the class were absent?* **2** mentioned earlier: *I will see you tomorrow, at which time we can discuss our plans.*
—*pron.* **1** (used in questions) what one or ones in a group of people or things: *Which of the movies did you like best?* **2** (used to show the object or objects one is referring to): *This is the car (which or that) I want to buy.* **3** (used to give more information about an object, objects, or the first part of the sentence): *This pin, which my brother gave me, is made of gold.||The politician said he had always paid his taxes, which was true.*

USAGE NOTE: As a pronoun, *which* is used to introduce a part of the sentence that includes information that is not necessary to the meaning of the sentence. *The sweater, which my grandmother made for me, is too small for me now.* When the information is necessary to understanding the sentence, *that* is usually used instead. *The sweater that my grandmother made for me is my favorite one.*

---

which·ev·er /wɪˈʧevər/ *adj.pron.* **1** one or the other, either: *Buy <pron.> whichever you want.* **2** no matter what: *<adj.> Whichever way you want to do it is fine with me. See:* whatever.

whiff /wɪf/ *n.v.* a slight smell, (*syn.*) scent: *I got a whiff of garlic as I walked by the restaurant.*

while /waɪl/ *conj.* **1** at that time, during: *While you were away, the weather was terrible.* **2** although: *While I do not agree with what you say, I understand your reasons for saying it.*
—*n.* **1** a short amount of time: *Let's stay for a while, then go home.* **2 worth one's while:** deserving of s.o.'s time and trouble, valuable financially: *If you drive me to the airport, I will make it worth your while by buying you dinner.*
—*phrasal v. sep.* **whiled, whiling, whiles: to while s.t. away:** to spend time in a pleasant, lazy way: *She whiles away her time watching television.||She whiles it away.*

whim /wɪm/ *n.* **1** a sudden desire, esp. an unreasonable one: *She felt a whim for a new hat.* **2 on a whim:** done without thinking, (*syn.*) impulsively: *He bought a gift for his girlfriend on a whim.*

whim·per /'wɪmpər/ v.n. to give a soft cry of sadness or pain: *The hungry dog <v.> whimpered for food.*‖*The baby gave a <n.> whimper when his mother walked away.*

whim·si·cal /'wɪmzɪkəl/ adj. **1** having the sudden desire to do s.t. playful without thinking, (syn.) impulsive: *I have a whimsical idea: let's rent a car and drive to the beach right now!* **2** unpredictable and fun, (syn.) fanciful: *Her room is decorated with whimsical balloons and flowers.* -adv. **whimsically.**

whine /waɪn/ v. **whined, whining, whines 1** to give a long, soft, high cry: *The dog whined from pain.* **2** to complain, act irritably: *The child whined for more candy after her mother took it away.*
—n. the act of whining: *I heard the whine of a car climbing the hill.* -n. [C] **whiner;** [U] **whining.**

whin·ny /'wɪni/ v. **-nied, -nying, -nies** n. **-nies** to make a high, shaking sound, like a horse, (syn.) to neigh: *My horse <v.> whinnied as I approached her.*

whip /wɪp/ n. a long piece of rope or leather held in the hand, used to hit an animal or person: *Horseback riders use whips to make their horses run faster.*
—v. **whipped, whipping, whips 1** to hit with a whip: *The ship's captain whipped the slaves.* **2** (in cooking) to mix together or beat until stiff: *I whipped some fresh cream and put it on strawberries.* **3** to (cause to) move quickly: *I whipped my money out of my wallet.*‖*I drive an old car, so new ones whip by me on the highway.* **4** to defeat badly or by a large amount: *Our team whipped our opponent by a score of 56 to 0.* **5** infrml. **to whip into shape:** to organize quickly and well: *The new manager whipped the workers into shape, so they work well as a team.* **6** phrasal v. sep. **to whip s.t. up: a.** to start, (syns.) to incite, arouse: *The baseball players whipped up excitement for winning the game.*‖*They whipped it up.* **b.** to make quickly: *The chef whipped up a delicious dinner in one hour.*

whip·lash /'wɪp,læʃ/ n. **-lashes 1** [C] a hit with a whip: *The slave wore the marks of whiplashes on his back.* **2** [U] a neck injury that is caused by sudden forward and backward movements: *A car crashed into mine and gave me whiplash.*

whipped /wɪpt/ adj.infrml.fig. very tired, (syn.) exhausted: *I am whipped after working all day and all night.*

whip·per·snap·per /'wɪpər,snæpər/ n. a young person who doesn't show the respect due older people: *That little whippersnapper thinks he runs the business, but he doesn't.*

whip·ping /'wɪpɪŋ/ n. **1** a series of hits with a whip: *Whipping was used as a punishment for many years.* **2** a beating, as in a fistfight, (syn.) a thrashing: *The older boy gave the younger boy a whipping.*

whip·poor·will /'wɪpər,wɪl, ,wɪpər'wɪl/ n. a dark-colored bird active at night with a repeated call that sounds like its name

whir /wɜr/ n. [C, usu. sing.] v. **whirred, whirring, whirs** a sound of s.t. spinning around very quickly: *You could hear the <n.> whir of the helicopter blades.*

whirl /wɜrl/ n. a fast turning motion, (syn.) a spin: *The whirl of the airplane propeller is extremely fast.*
—v. to turn or rotate very quickly, (syn.) to spin: *Dancers whirled on the stage.*

whirl·pool /'wɜrl,pul/ n. water moving quickly in a circle, (syn.) a vortex: *Water forms a whirlpool as it runs down the drain of a sink.*

whirl·wind /'wɜrl,wɪnd/ n. **1** air moving very quickly in a circle, often causing a storm: *We saw a little whirlwind of dust in the desert.* **2** a rushed or hurried activity: *The job was finished with a whirlwind of late-night writing and typing.*

whisk /wɪsk/ v. **1** to brush off: *The waiter whisked crumbs of food off the table.* **2** to remove s.o. or s.t. quickly: *She ran from the building, and a taxi whisked her to the airport.*
—n.v. a kitchen tool used to quickly mix or beat liquid (eggs, cream, etc.): *The cook beat the eggs with a wire <n.> whisk.*

whisk·broom /'wɪsk,brum/ n. a small stiff brush held in the hand, used to push dirt, dust, etc.: *I used a whiskbroom to clean up broken glass from the floor.*

whisk·er /'wɪskər/ n. **1** a long protecting hair that grows near the mouth of some animals: *The cat had white whiskers.* **2** fig. a tiny amount (of distance, space, etc.): *The bullet missed the soldier by a whisker.* **3** pl. short hair on a man's face: *He shaves his whiskers every morning.*

whis·key /'wɪski/ n. **-keys** or **-kies** [C;U] an alcoholic drink made from fermented grain, such as barley or rye: *I ordered beer, and she ordered whiskey.*

whis·per /'wɪspər/ n. soft, quiet talking: *She didn't want the others to hear, so she spoke in a whisper.*
—v. **1** to speak in a soft, quiet voice: *She whispered secrets in his ear.* **2** to make a soft sound: *Wind whispered through the pine trees.*

whis·tle /'wɪsəl/ n. **1** a musical sound made by blowing air through the lips: *We could hear the man's happy whistle.* **2** a high-pitched sound: *a train whistle* **3** a small pipe or instrument that makes a whistle **4** infrml. **to blow the whistle on:** to tell about s.o.'s wrong or illegal activity and so stop it: *People were stealing from the company store until s.o. blew the whistle on them.* **5** infrml. **to wet one's whis-**

W

tle: to drink: *He wet his whistle with a cold beer on a hot day.*
—*v.* **-tled, -tling, -tles** to make a whistling sound: *The boy whistled a song as he walked to school.* -*n.* **whistler.**

whit /wɪt/ *n.* (usu. used in the negative) a tiny amount: *He does not care one whit about making a lot of money.*

white /waɪt/ *n.* **1** the complete lack of color, or the lightest of all colors: *White is the color of snow and milk.* **2** a person of a pale-skinned race: *There has often been trouble between whites and blacks in the USA.* **3** the part of an egg that is white when cooked, albumen: *The cook separated the egg yolks from the whites.*
—*adj.* **whiter, whitest 1** having a white color: *He wears white shirts to work.* **2** of a pale-skinned race **3 white as a sheet:** without much color in the face, usu. from sickness or fear, pale: *She went white as a sheet when I said there had been an accident.*

white-collar *adj.* professional or working in an office: *I got a white-collar job as a computer programmer. See:* blue-collar, USAGE NOTE.

white elephant *n.fig.* s.t. no one wants: *The old car is a white elephant that they can't sell.*

white flag *n.* **1** a sign of giving up or surrender: *Enemy soldiers waved a white flag to show they would fight no more.* **2** a sign of peace: *The trucks carrying leaders of the fighting countries carried white flags to show their peaceful intentions.*

white-head /'waɪt,hɛd/ *n.* a raised mark on the skin caused by oil *See:* blackhead; pimple.

White House *n.* **1** in the USA, the President's house in Washington, D.C. **2** a symbol of the U.S. government and its President: *The White House announced its choice for Secretary of State.*

white lie *n.* an untrue statement, usu. about s.t. that is not important, told to keep from hurting s.o.: *She told a white lie when she said, "I can't go to the party. I'm not feeling well."*

white meat *n.* the part of cooked meat (chicken, turkey, etc.) that is lighter than the leg meat: *I like the white meat of turkey breasts.*

whiten /'waɪtn/ *v.* to color white, (*syn.*) to bleach: *He whitened his shirts by cleaning them with soap and bleach.*

white-out /'waɪt,aʊt/ *n.* a serious weather condition, such as snow, or sunshine on snow that makes it difficult to see: *A whiteout made it impossible to drive, so we waited until the storm was over.*

white sale *n.* in a store, a sale of bed linen and towels at low prices: *We bought new sheets at a white sale over the weekend.*

white trash *n.pej.* [U] poor white people, usu. from the country

whitewash /'waɪt,waʃ, -,wɔʃ/ *n.* [U] **1** a type of white paint: *A boy spread whitewash on the fence to make it look new.* **2** *fig.* an attempt to hide s.t. wrong or illegal, (*syn.*) a cover-up: *The newspaper helped in the whitewash of the mayor's troubled life by printing only good things about him.*
—*v.* **washes 1** to cover with whitewash: *The girl whitewashed the new wooden garden furniture.* **2** *fig.* to cover up (a scandal, wrongdoing, etc.): *Officials tried to whitewash their mistakes with lies.*

white water *n.* [U] river water flowing very fast, making it appear white and foamy: *Tourists go boating on white water for a fun adventure.*

whith·er /'wɪðər/ *adv.frml.old usage* where, in which direction

whit·ish /'waɪtɪʃ/ *adj.* almost white in color: *The wall paint is whitish; he thinks it looks gray.*

whit·tle /'wɪtl/ *v.* **-tled, -tling, -tles 1** to cut off small pieces (of wood) with a knife, (*syn.*) to carve: *For his birthday, he often whittles small toys for his son.* **2** *phrasal v. sep.* **to whittle s.t. away:** to reduce or weaken by taking away a little at a time: *The owner whittled away at my authority by giving me less and less to do.*‖*She whittled it away.* -*n.* [C] **whittler;** [U] **whittling.**

whiz or **whizz** /wɪz/ *v.* **whizzed, whizzing, whizzes** to pass by very quickly: *A baseball whizzed by the player's head.*
—*n.* **whizzes 1** a whizzing sound **2** a very smart and capable person: *She is a whiz in math.* -*adj.* **whizzing.**

whiz kid *n.* a young, very smart person: *He was a whiz kid in high school, with the best grades in his class.*

who /hu/ *pron.* **1** what or which person: *Who are you?*‖*Who was that black-haired man?* **2** the person or persons that: *I am the woman who just telephoned you.* **3** (used to give more information about a person or persons): *My sisters, who live in Denver, are coming to visit next week.*

USAGE NOTE: *Who* replaces *he, she, it,* or *they* in a sentence or question. *Who* agrees with the subject in number: *Who is that guy? Who are your friends? Whom* replaces the object of an action in a sentence or question: *I gave the book to her. To whom did you give the book? That is the woman to whom I gave the book.*

whoa /wou, hou/ *exclam.* (used to stop a horse): *The rider pulled on the reins and said, "Whoa!"*

W

who·dun·it /hu'dʌnɪt/ *n.infrml.* a mystery or detective story: *I like to read whodunits about people who solve crimes.*

who·ev·er /hu'ɛvər/ *pron.* any person that, no matter who: *Whoever arrives first should unlock the door.*

whole /hoʊl/ *adj.* **1** complete, entire: *We ate the whole pie for dessert.* **2** in good health, with nothing wrong: *She is feeling whole again after her accident.*
—*n.* [C, usu. *sing.*] **1** a complete thing or amount, (*syn.*) an entity: *She wants to sell the living-room furniture as a whole and not piece by piece.* **2 on the whole:** in general, all things considered: *There are some problems there, but on the whole, Florida is a nice place to live.* **3 taken as a whole:** thought of as a set or one large group: *Taken as a whole, their products are very good.*

whole·heart·ed /,hoʊl'hartɪd/ *adj.* with no doubts, complete: *You have our wholehearted support for your new project.*

whole·sale /'hoʊl,seɪl/ *n.* [U] *adj.* **1** related to selling things in large amounts, and usu. at lower prices, to stores and businesses: *Our company buys its office supplies at <n.> wholesale.* **2** large in number or amount, extensive: *The strong winds of the hurricane caused <adj.> wholesale damage to the beaches.*

whole·some /'hoʊlsəm/ *adj.* **1** good, with no bad habits or influences: *They lead a wholesome life away from the city's crime and pollution.* **2** good for one's health, healthy, (*syn.*) nourishing: *Our family eats wholesome food, such as fresh fruits and vegetables. -n.* [U] **wholesomeness.**

whole-wheat *adj.* made with the complete wheat grain: *I like to eat whole-wheat bread.*

who'll /hul/ *contr. of* who will

whol·ly /'hoʊli, 'hoʊlli/ *adv.* completely: *We wholly agree with your argument.*

whom /hum/ *pron.frml.* a form of *who* used as the object of a verb or preposition: *She is the person to whom I have sent the letter.*‖*He is a man whom we like. See:* USAGE NOTE *at who.*

whom·ev·er /hu'mɛvər/ *pron.frml.* form of *whoever* used as the object of a verb or preposition: *You may send the invitation to whomever you wish to invite.*

whom·so·ever /,humsoʊ'ɛvər/ *pron. See:* whomever.

whoop /hup, wup/ *n.* a shout (of joy, surprise, etc.): *He let out a whoop when he won the prize.*
—*v.* **1** to let out a whoop: *She whooped for joy.* **2 to whoop it up:** to have fun and make a lot of noise: *We had a party and whooped it up all night.*

whoop·ee /,wʊ'pi, ,wu-, 'wʊpi, 'wu-/ *exclam.* used to show joy, surprise, delight: *Whoopee! We won the game!*

whoop·ing cough /'hupɪŋ, 'wu-, 'hʊ-/ *n.* [U] a disease of the lungs, often affecting children: *Children get immunization shots to protect them from whooping cough.*

whoops /wʊps, wups/ *exclam.* a word showing unpleasant surprise, mild alarm: *Whoops, I broke a dish!*

whoosh /wʊʃ, wuʃ/ *n.v.* **wooshes** to move fast with the sound of rushing air: *Cars raced by us with a <n.> "whoosh!"‖They <v.> whooshed by us.*

whop·per /'wɑpər/ *n.infrml.* **1** s.t. big: *The huge fish that I caught was a whopper.* **2** a big lie: *He tells whoppers about his childhood, but we don't believe him. -adj.* **whopping.**

whore /hɔr/ *n.pej.* a woman who takes money for sex, (*syn.*) a prostitute

who's /huz/ *contr.* **1** who is **2** who has

whose /huz/ *pron.adj.* possessive form of *who,* of which person: *<adj.> Whose coat is that?‖<pron.> Whose are these shoes?*

who·so·ever /,husoʊ'ɛvər/ *pron.frml. See:* whoever.

Who's Who *n.* a list of important people in a profession, country, or other area: *She is in the Who's Who of national political leaders.*

why /waɪ/ *adv.conj.* for what reason (need, cause, purpose, etc.): *<adv.> Why are you crying?‖I don't know <conj.> why he is not here.*

wick /wɪk/ *n.* [C;U] a string used in candles and lamps that burns when it is lighted: *I lit the wick with a match, and the candle made the room lighter.*

wick·ed /'wɪkɪd/ *adj.* **1** very bad, evil: *A wicked man took the child from his parents.* **2** *fig.* severe, (*syn.*) formidable: *I have a wicked pain in my back.* **3** *adj.adv.slang* very: *The concert last night was <adv.> wicked good. -adv.* **wickedly;** *-n.* [U] **wickedness.**

wick·er /'wɪkər/ *n.* [U] **1** small pieces of trees (twigs) used to make furniture and other objects: *That chair is made of wicker.* **2** objects, usu. furniture, made of woven twigs: *We have white porch furniture made of wicker.*

wick·et /'wɪkɪt/ *n.* **1** (in croquet) a wire arch or hoop through which a ball is hit **2** (in cricket) a set of sticks at which the ball is thrown **3** *infrml.fig.* **a sticky wicket:** a difficult problem: *The tax issue has become a sticky wicket for the Republican Party.*

wide /waɪd/ *adj.* **wider, widest 1** related to the distance from side to side: *That table is three feet wide.* **2** with a great distance from side to side: *A long bridge crossed the wide river.* **3** large, (*syn.*) extensive: *She can play a wide range of musical instruments: the piano, guitar, and trumpet.*

—adv. **1** completely, fully: *wide-open‖wide-awake* **2 wide of the mark: a.** away from the target: *The arrow missed the center; it was wide of the mark.* **b.** *fig.* wrong, incorrect: *His answer to the question was wide of the mark.*

—suffix-wide extending over or all through an area: *The position of governor is a state-wide elective office. -adv.* **widely;** *-n.* **wideness.**

wide-eyed /'waɪd,aɪd/ *adj.* surprised, *(syns.)* astonished, bewildered: *The children were wide-eyed when they entered the toy store.*

wid·en /'waɪdn/ *v.* **1** to make wider, *(syn.)* to broaden: *Workers widened the road so more cars could pass.* **2** to make greater, *(syn.)* to enhance: *He widened his knowledge of the company by visiting all its offices.*

wide-open *adj.* **1** completely open: *We came home to find the garage door wide-open and our bicycles stolen!* **2** *fig.* **with one's eyes wide open:** to be fully aware of realities, dangers: *You should study the stock market first so you have your eyes wide open when you start buying stock.*

wide·spread /,waɪd'sprɛd, 'waɪd,sprɛd/ *adj.* covering a large area, *(syn.)* ubiquitous: *The forest fires were widespread through the mountains.*

wid·ow /'wɪdoʊ/ *n.* a wife whose husband has died: *The widow married again a year after her first husband's death. -n.* [U] **widowhood** /'wɪdoʊ,hʊd/.

wid·owed /'wɪdoʊd/ *adj.* left after the death of one's husband or wife

wid·ow·er /'wɪdoʊər/ *n.* a husband whose wife has died: *He has been a widower since his wife died of cancer.*

width /wɪdθ, wɪtθ/ *n.* [U] the distance across, *(syn.)* breadth: *The width of the floor is 12 feet.*

wield /wild/ *v.* **1** to use, exercise: *He wields great power as President.* **2** to swing or use as a tool: *The woodsman wielded an ax to chop down a tree.*

wie·ner /'winər/ *n.* a sausage made of meat and other fillings, *(syns.)* a frankfurter, hot dog: *I like boiled wieners with mustard.*

wife /waɪf/ *n.* **wives** /waɪvz/ a woman who is married: *His wife is very busy; she has a job and helps him raise two children. -adj.* **wifely.**

wig /wɪg/ *n.* a head covering made of false or human hair: *The actor wore a gray wig to look like an older man in the play.*

wig·gle /'wɪgəl/ *n.* a quick twisting and turning movement, usu. from side to side: *The key was stuck, so he gave it a wiggle and it came out.*

—v. **-gled, -gling, -gles** to move with a wiggle: *Her hips wiggled when she walked.*

wig·wam /'wɪgwɑm, -,wɔm/ *n.* a kind of tent made of wood and covered with natural materials, used by Native Americans

wigwam

wild /waɪld/ *adj.* **1** related to living in nature, not grown or cared for by humans: *Wild strawberries grow in the field behind my house.* **2** not tamed by humans, *(syn.)* uncivilized: *That island has many wild ponies that run free.* **3** exciting, unruly: *The college students had a wild time at the New Year's party.* **4** violent, *(syns.)* savage, ferocious: *Lions attack smaller animals in a wild fury.* **5** without control, *(syns.)* reckless, brash: *He was a wild skier who went too fast down the mountain.* **6** misbehaving, *(syn.)* unruly: *Her children are wild; they scream and run around all the time.* **7** *infrml.* **to be wild about:** to like very much: *She is wild about chocolate cake.*

—adv. **1 to go wild:** to act roughly or savagely: *On hearing the news about losing his job, he went wild and broke all the furniture.* **2 to grow wild:** to live in nature, *(syns.)* to be uncultivated, undomesticated: *Blueberries and roses grow wild in the woods near our house.* **3 to run wild: a.** to live freely and untamed in nature: *Horses run wild in the plains of Wyoming.* **b.** to be out of control and cause damage: *Rioters ran wild, robbing shops and setting fires.*

—n. or *n.pl.* area away from people, towns, and cities, *(syn.)* the wilderness: *I went on a jungle trip in the wilds of Africa. -adv.* **wildly;** *-n.* **wildness.**

wild·cat /'waɪld,kæt/ *n.* **1** a small or medium-sized wild cat, such as the bobcat or lynx **2** an angry, quick-tempered person who is ready to fight: *When she gets mad, she is a wildcat.*

—adj. **wildcat strike:** a work stoppage not approved by a union: *Workers started a wildcat strike to show they wanted higher pay.*

wild·er·ness /'wɪldərnɪs/ *n.* [U] **1** land in its natural state, esp. a large area unspoiled by humans: *Wilderness is protected in many of our national parks.* **2** *fig.* a large, unknown place: *We are still exploring the wilderness of outer space.*

wild·fire /'waɪld,faɪr/ *n.* **1** a fire that spreads very quickly and in an uncontrolled way: *A wildfire moved up the mountainside in minutes.* **2 like wildfire:** very quickly: *Bad news always spreads like wildfire.*

wild·flower /'waɪld,flaʊər/ *n.* a flower that grows without being cared for by humans: *In the spring, we pick wildflowers and put them in a basket on the table.*

W

wild goose chase *n.fig.* an attempt to find s.t. that cannot be found, a wasted effort: *Someone sent us on a wild goose chase, looking for a store that wasn't open anymore.*

wild·life /'waɪld,laɪf/ *n.* [U] animals living in their natural setting: *There is much wildlife in the forests of Maine.*

wiles /waɪlz/ *n.pl.* clever tricks used to fool s.o.: *I used my wiles to get the man to buy my old car.*

will (1) /wɪl; *weak form* wəl, əl, l/*aux.v.* **1** (used to show future action): *I will see you at noon tomorrow.||Will the plane arrive on time?* **2** (used to ask s.o. to do s.t.) would, could: *Will you please pass the bread?* **3** (to be) willing or ready to: *Please come in; the doctor will see you now.||The cleaning woman won't wash windows.* **4** (used to state what is probable in the future): *You will be sorry later if you quit school now.* **5** (used to show what s.t. can do): *This cake will serve 16 people.*

will (2) /wɪl/ *v.* **1** to influence or control by the power of one's mind: *We didn't want rain, so we tried to will the clouds away.* **2** to give (money or property) in one's will: *She willed her house and all she owned to her son.*
—*n.* **1** [C;U] the strength of the mind to control one's actions, (*syn.*) determination: *He has a very strong will; when he decides to do something, nothing can stop him.* **2** [C, usu. sing.] power to decide, (*syn.*) volition: *It is the will of the congress (the king, the majority) that taxes be raised.* **3** [C] a legal document that tells who will receive s.o.'s money and property when that person dies: *My mother left me a gold necklace in her will.* **4 at will:** whenever one wants: *He eats candy at will throughout the day.* **5 ill will:** bad feeling, (*syn.*) bitterness: *There was much ill will between the man and woman who were divorcing.* **6 where there's a will, there's a way:** if s.o. wants s.t. enough, it can be done somehow: *She doesn't have much money, but she is still going to college; where there's a will, there's a way.* **7 willpower:** inner strength (to do s.t.): *It takes willpower to stop smoking.*
-willed /wɪld/ *suffix* related to a person's desires or strengths: *He is a strong-willed man; he never changes his mind.*

will·ful or **wil·ful** /'wɪlfəl/ *adj.* **1** always wanting to have one's way, (*syns.*) stubborn, obstinate: *He is a willful man who won't let anyone help him drive.* **2** done on purpose, (*syns.*) calculated, deliberate: *That building is in bad shape because of willful neglect by the owner.* -*adv.* **willfully;** -*n.* **willfulness.**

wil·lies /'wɪliz/ *n.pl.infrml.* fear, (*syn.*) the creeps: *That old, empty house gives me the willies every time I pass it at night.*

will·ing /'wɪlɪŋ/ *adj.* ready (to do s.t.), (*syn.*) agreeable: *He is willing to help us paint the kitchen.* -*adv.* **willingly;** -*n.* **willingness.**

will-o'-the-wisp /,wɪləðə'wɪsp/ *n.fig.* a false hope, (*syn.*) a delusion: *His dream of being a Hollywood star was only a will-o'-the-wisp.*

wil·low /'wɪloʊ/ *n.* a tree with narrow leaves

wil·low·y /'wɪloʊi/ *adj.fig.* graceful and slim: *The ballet dancer has a willowy figure.*

wilt /wɪlt/ *v.* **1** to become less fresh and start to bend down, (*syn.*) to droop: *The plant wilted because it needed water.* **2** to grow very tired: *We wilted in the summer heat and had to lie down.*

wil·y /'waɪli/ *adj.* **-ier, -iest** with lots of tricks, (*syns.*) cunning, shrewd: *He is a wily old man who likes to take advantage of people.*

wimp /wɪmp/ *n.pej.* a weak person: *That wimp can't even run 50 meters!*

win /wɪn/ *v.* **won** /wʌn/, **winning, wins 1** to score more points than another person or team, beat: *We won our tennis match today.* **2** to get, (*syns.*) to acquire, gain: *Our company won a contract to build offices for the government.* **3** *phrasal v.* **to win out:** to succeed after a struggle: *He fought for his right to be heard and won out in the end by getting the chance to speak in public.* **4** *phrasal v. sep.* **to win s.o. over:** to change s.o.'s mind, (*syns.*) to persuade, convince: *At first her husband didn't want to buy the suit, but she won him over by showing him the low price.*

wince /wɪns/ *v.* **winced, wincing, winces** *n.* to make a facial expression of pain, (*syn.*) to flinch: *He <v.> winced when the door shut on his thumb.*

winch /wɪntʃ/ *n.v.* **winches** a machine used to lift heavy objects: *The car mechanic used a <n.> winch to lift the engine out of the car.*

wind (1) /wɪnd/ *n.* **1** [C;U] the natural movement of air outdoors: *The wind is strong, so the leaves are falling quickly.* **2** [U] breath, the power of breathing: *She had the wind knocked out of her when she fell.* **3** *infrml.fig.* [U] talk that has no meaning: *What that guy says is just wind; don't listen to him.* **4** *pl.fig.* force or influence in a new direction: *The winds of independence were blowing through many small colonial countries.* **5** *pl.* musical instruments that require blowing air to play them, such as the flute, oboe, and clarinet **6 in the wind:** about to happen: *With the new President now in power, big changes are in the wind.* **7 second wind:** a burst of new energy: *The runner got tired in the middle of the race, then got his second wind and felt strong again.* **8 the way** or **how the wind blows:** the way things will probably be: *The company will likely fail because it lost its big account, and that is the way (or) how the wind blows.* **9 to be down-**

wind (or) **upwind of s.t.:** to be in a position so that the wind carries the smell of s.t. to or away from one: *The bear is upwind of the hunters, so he can't smell them.* **10** *vulg.* **to break wind:** to let out anal gas **11 to catch wind of** or **to get wind of:** to learn about s.t. by chance: *My mother got wind of a sale at that store and bought some inexpensive shoes.* **12** *infrml.fig.* **to take the wind out of one's sails:** to make s.o. lose excitement, to discourage s.o., (*syn.*) to dishearten: *The boss criticized the young man in front of everyone and really took the wind out of his sails.*

wind (2) /waɪnd/ *v.* **wound** /waʊnd/, **winding, winds 1** to wrap s.t. around: *I wind yarn into a ball before I start to knit a sweater.* **2** to turn and tighten: *You can wind a clock or a watch.* **3** to curve, twist, (*syn.*) to meander: *Roads wound through the hills.* **4 to be (all) wound up:** to be nervous, tense: *She is all wound up from traveling all night.* **5** *phrasal v.* **to wind down:** to get slower, (*syns.*) to decrease, diminish: *That company is going out of business and is winding down its activity.* **6 to wind s.o. around one's little finger:** to have s.o. do anything one wants: *She winds her boyfriend around her little finger; he follows her everywhere.* **7** *phrasal v. sep.* **to wind s.t. up: a. s.t.:** to turn and tighten, (*syn.*) to crank: *I wind up the grandfather clock once a week.* **b.** *fig.* to finally arrive: *We started in Japan and wound up in China.||We got lost and wound up being two hours late.* *-adj.* **winding.**

wind·bag /ˈwɪnd,bæg, ˈwɪn-/ *n.infrml.fig.* a person who talks a lot but does not say anything meaningful: *He is just a windbag, so nobody listens to him.*

wind·blown /ˈwɪnd,bloʊn, ˈwɪn-/ *adj.* messed up by the wind: *After being outside, her hair is windblown and all over her face.*

Wind·break·er /ˈwɪnd,breɪkər, ˈwɪn-/ *n.TM* a light jacket: *It's a cool day, so I'll wear my Windbreaker.*

wind·burn /ˈwɪnd,bɜrn, ˈwɪn-/ *n.* [U] dry, red skin caused by lots of wind: *I have a windburn on my face after skiing all day.* *-adj.* **windburned.**

wind-chill factor /ˈwɪnd,tʃɪl/ *n.* [U] in cold weather, the temperature combined with wind speed: *The temperature is at the freezing point, but the wind-chill factor makes it feel much colder because of a strong wind.*

wind·ed /ˈwɪndɪd/ *adj.* out of breath, exhausted: *The runners were winded after a long race.*

wind·fall /ˈwɪnd,fɔl, ˈwɪn-/ *n.fig.* sudden good luck, esp. unexpected money: *I had just bought the stock when I received a windfall of an extra dividend.*

wind·mill /ˈwɪnd,mɪl, ˈwɪn-/ *n.* a machine or building that gets its power from the wind turning its blades *See:* mill.

win·dow /ˈwɪndoʊ/ *n.* **1** an opening in a building, usu. covered with glass: *Windows allow sunlight and air into buildings.* **2** a rectangle on a computer screen where information is shown: *Some computers can have several windows open at the same time.* **3** a limited period of time when s.t. can be done: *We must start building now to finish before winter; this is our window of opportunity.*

windmill

window dressing *n.* [U] **1** decorations for store windows: *The window dressing during the holiday season is always the most beautiful.* **2** *fig.* the act of making s.t. look more attractive than it really is: *The new advertising plan is just window dressing to cover up the company's difficulties.*

window envelope *n.* a mailing envelope with a clear rectangle through which the receiver's address shows: *The electric bill came in a window envelope.*

window pane *n.* a single piece of glass in a window: *Older houses usually have many small window panes in a window.*

window shade *n.* any of a variety of window coverings, such as a curtain or Venetian blind: *I pull down the window shades to keep out the afternoon sun.*

window-shop *v.* **-shopped, -shopping, -shops** to look at things in store windows without buying: *He likes to window-shop on that street of expensive stores.* *-n.* [U] **window-shopper.**

window sill *n.* the small surface at the bottom of a window: *We put flower boxes on the window sills in summer.*

wind·pipe /ˈwɪnd,paɪp, ˈwɪn-/ *n.* in the throat, the tube that allows air to pass in and out of the lungs: *A man at the restaurant had a piece of food stuck in his windpipe, but he is OK now.*

wind·shield /ˈwɪnd,ʃild/ *n.* the glass across the front of a car that protects the driver and passengers from the wind: *The windshield on my car needs to be cleaned.*

windshield wiper *n.* a thin rubber blade on a metal rod that clears a vehicle's windshield of rain, snow, and dirt

wind·storm /ˈwɪnd,stɔrm, ˈwɪn-/ *n.* a storm of high winds and usu. little rain: *We had a windstorm last night with winds that damaged trees.*

wind·swept /ˈwɪnd,swɛpt, ˈwɪn-/ *adj.* made flat or messy from the wind: *The trees and* grass near the shore were windswept in the storm.

wind-up /'waɪn,dʌp/ *adj.* having a spring that can be turned and tightened: *My son's favorite toys are his wind-up cars that race around the floor.*

wind·ward /'wɪndwərd, 'wɪn-/ *adv.* from the direction that the wind is blowing *See:* lee; leeward.

wind·y /'wɪndi/ *adj.* **-ier, -iest 1** with a lot of wind, (*syns.*) gusty, breezy: *It is windy today, so hold on to your hat.* **2** long (as a talk), (*syn.*) verbose: *He gives long, windy speeches.* *-n.* [U] **windiness.**

wine /waɪn/ *n.* [C;U] an alcoholic drink made from fermented fruit, esp. grapes: *We drink red wine with dinner every evening.*
—*v.* **wined, wining, wines to wine and dine:** to provide with a good meal, (*syn.*) to entertain: *Businesspeople wine and dine their customers.*

wine cellar *n.* a cool place, usu. in a basement, where wine is stored: *Please go down to the wine cellar and get a bottle of white.*

wineglass /'waɪn,glæs/ *n.* **glasses** a glass with a thin stem, used for serving wine: *Red wine is often served in a large, round wineglass.*

winegrower /'waɪn,groʊər/ *n.* s.o. who grows grapes and makes wine, (*syn.*) a vintner: *Many winegrowers live in California's Napa Valley.* *-n.* **winemaker.**

win·er·y /'waɪnəri/ *n.* **-ies** a place where wine is made: *We enjoyed taking a tour of Spanish wineries.*

wing /wɪŋ/ *n.* **1** the part of a bird, insect, or airplane that helps it fly: *The bird had a broken wing and couldn't fly.* **2** a section of a building: *Offices are located in the west wing of the classroom building.* **3** *pl.* side sections of a stage that cannot be seen from the audience: *Actors waited in the wings until it was their turn to go on stage.* **4** *infrml.* **to earn one's wings:** to work hard and earn the right to s.t.: *The young doctor earned his wings by studying hard and always being prepared.* **5 to spread one's wings:** to grow more independent: *She went to college away from home to spread her wings and learn to live alone.* **6 to take s.o. under one's wing:** to help or protect s.o., (*syn.*) to mentor: *The ballet teacher takes young ballerinas under her wing.* **7 to wait in the wings:** (from the theater) to wait one's turn while s.o. else is more important or visible: *He had to wait in the wings for several years until the older man who ran the department finally retired.*
—*v.* **1** to fly with wings: *Birds winged across the blue sky.* **2** *infrml.* **to wing s.t.:** to speak or act without preparation, (*syn.*) to improvise: *The salesman had no time to prepare his pre-*

sentation, so he just winged it to a group of possible buyers.

winged /wɪŋd/ *adj.* having wings: *Bats are winged animals.*

wing·span /'wɪŋ,spæn/ *n.* the distance between the ends of the wings: *That airplane's wingspan is 80 feet (24.4 m).*

wing tip or **wing·tip** /'wɪŋ,tɪp/ *n.* **1** the end of a wing **2** *pl.* a type of men's dress shoe with a pointed toe and a pattern that looks like a wing on it: *The bankers wear wing tips.*

wink /wɪŋk/ *v.* **1** to close and open one eye quickly, usu. in a joking or flirting way: *She winked and smiled at a guy she liked.* **2** (of a light) to turn on and off: *The car lights winked as a signal.* **3** *infrml.* **to wink at:** to excuse, (*syn.*) to condone: *The boy's mother winks at his bad habits; she doesn't punish him.*
—*n.* a winking movement: *She gave him a wink as a signal.*

win·ner /'wɪnər/ *n.* **1** a person or team who gets more points or beats another: *She is the winner of the tennis match.* **2** a good, fun, or successful thing: *That new TV show is a real winner.*

win·ning /'wɪnɪŋ/ *n.* **1** [U] an act of beating or outscoring s.o.: *That baseball coach cares only about winning.* **2** *pl.* money that was won: *He spent his winnings on a party to celebrate his victory.*
—*adj.* **1** pleasing, charming: *a winning smile* **2 winning ways:** appealing and charming behavior: *She is bright and enthusiastic, full of winning ways.*

win·o /'waɪnoʊ/*infrml.* **-os** an alcoholic who drinks too much wine: *We sometimes see winos sleeping on park benches.*

win·some /'wɪnsəm/ *adj.* charming often in a shy way: *Our little girl has a winsome smile.*

win·ter /'wɪntər/ *n.* the cold season between autumn and spring: *The winters in Wyoming are very cold.*

wintergreen /'wɪntər,grin/ *n.adj.* a small evergreen shrub with leaves that yield an oil having a sharp, cool taste: *This chewing gum has a refreshing <adj.> wintergreen flavor.*

win·ter·ize /'wɪntə,raɪz/ *v.* **-ized, -izing, -izes** to make ready for winter: *I winterized my house by putting in storm windows.*

win·ter·time /'wɪntər,taɪm/ *n.* the winter season: *We burn wood in the fireplace during the wintertime.*

win·try /'wɪntri/ or **wintery** /'wɪntəri/ *adj.* cold, snowy: *We are having wintry weather this week with snow and cold winds.*

wipe /waɪp/ *v.* **wiped, wiping, wipes 1** to rub away (unwanted dirt, water, tears, etc.): *A waiter wiped the table clean with a damp cloth.* **2 to wipe out: a.** to destroy, ruin: *The crash of the stock market wiped out many peo-*

ple's fortunes. **b.** *infrml.* to beat badly: *We wiped out the other basketball team, 85 to 50.* **c.** *infrml.* to exhaust: *The long walk wiped me out.*
—*n.* **1** an act of wiping: *He gave the table a wipe.* **2** a type of cloth used to wipe s.t.: *She used a wipe to clean her hands.*

wipe·out /'waɪpˌaʊt/ *n.* complete destruction, (*syn.*) devastation: *The flood caused a wipeout of all roads and electricity.*

wlp·er /'waɪpər/ *n. s.t.* used to wipe, esp. a device for wiping a vehicle's windshield: *I always use the wipers when it rains.*

wire /waɪr/ *n.* [C;U] **1** metal in the form of a thin string or of several strings twisted together: *Most metal fences are made of wire.* **2** insulated strands of metal used to conduct electricity: *A wire in my stereo is broken.* **3 by wire:** sent via a wire, such as a telephone line or cable: *I sent her money by wire.* **4 down to the wire:** until the last possible minute: *We had a noon deadline to finish the job, and we worked right down to the wire to get it done.* **5 under the wire:** at the last moment before the deadline: *We got our application in just under the wire.*
—*v.* **wired, wiring, wires 1** to install wire: *Electricians wired the house for electricity.* **2** to send by means of a telephone or cable: *I wired money to my daughter in San Francisco.* See: **wired.**

wired /waɪrd/ *adj.* **1** set up with wiring for electricity: *The office is wired for computers.* **2** tied or secured with wire: *The gates are wired shut.* **3** *slang* high on drugs: *He was wired when the police arrested him.* **4** *infrml.* very nervous or tense: *She was so angry that she was wired for hours.*

wire·tap /'waɪrˌtæp/ *n.* a listening tool placed secretly on a telephone: *The wiretap was placed inside each telephone in the house.*
—*v.* **-tapped, -tapping, -taps** to set up a wiretap: *Detectives wiretapped his telephone.*

wir·ing /'waɪrɪŋ/ *n.* a system of wires, usu. for electricity: *The wiring in that old building needs to be changed.*

wir·y /'waɪri/ *adj.* **-ier, -iest** (of a person) thin yet strong: *Jockeys are usually short and wiry.*

wis·dom /'wɪzdəm/ *n.* **1** good sense learned from experience: *He is an old man of great wisdom.* **2** knowledge, understanding: *There is much wisdom in old religious writings.*

wisdom tooth *n.* **teeth** one of four large teeth at the very back of the mouth, the last teeth to grow in: *She had her wisdom teeth removed.*

wise /waɪz/ *adj.* **wiser, wisest 1** showing good judgment based on experience, (*syn.*) prudent: *Taking care of your health is the wise thing to do.* **2** having good judgment, (*syns.*) discerning, knowledgeable: *She is a wise old woman, so others seek her advice.*

—*phrasal v.* **wised, wising, wises to wise up:** to learn the right information: *The new student had to wise up to a new set of rules in his new school. -adv.* **wisely.**

wise·crack /'waɪzˌkræk/ *n.v.infrml.* a joking or insulting remark: *He made a <n.> wisecrack about his manager's long speech.*

wise guy *n.infrml.* a troublemaker who thinks he or she knows everything: *That wise guy always blames his mistakes on others; then he doesn't get in trouble.*

wish /wɪʃ/ *v.* **-es 1** to desire, want: *He wished that his girlfriend would marry him.* **2** to express hope for s.t.: *I wish you a happy birthday (good luck, success, etc.).*
—*n.* **wishes 1** [C] a desire, a want: *Her marrying him is his fondest wish.* **2** [U] **wish fulfillment:** getting what one wants, esp. in the imagination: *Successes seen in dreams are wish fulfillment. -adj.* **wishful.**

wish·bone /'wɪʃˌboʊn/ *n.* a Y-shaped breastbone, esp. of a chicken or turkey, on which a wish is made: *My father gave me the turkey's wishbone and told me to make a wish for the family.*

wishful thinking *n.* [U] the unrealistic belief that s.t. wished for will happen: *He is poor, so his plan to buy a new car is just wishful thinking.*

wish·y-wash·y /'wɪʃiˌwɑʃi, -ˌwɔ-/ *adj.infrml.pej.* unable to make decisions, (*syn.*) vacillating: *He is wishy-washy about his studies and will probably fail.*

wisp /wɪsp/ *n.* a small thin amount, such as a puff of smoke or a few strands of hair: *A wisp of cloud floated across the sky. -adj.* **wispy.**

wist·ful /'wɪstfəl/ *adj.* thinking sadly about s.t. one cannot have now, such as past happiness, (*syns.*) yearning, pensive: *He has wistful desires for happier days. -adv.* **wistfully;** *-n.* [U] **wistfulness.**

wit /wɪt/ *n.* **1** [C;U] intelligence, (*syn.*) acumen: *She has a keen wit and understands quickly.* **2** [U] an intelligent sense of humor: *He has a quick wit and makes funny comments on things.* **3** [C] an intelligent and amusing person: *She is a wit who writes funny plays.* **4 to be at one's wit's end:** to be frustrated or in despair: *Her son keeps getting into trouble, and she is at her wit's end about what to do.* **5 to keep** or **have one's wits about one:** to think quickly in a difficult situation: *She kept her wits about her when her bag was stolen, and she screamed for a policeman nearby.* See: dimwit; quick-witted.

witch /wɪtʃ/ *n.* **witches** a woman who practices magic, (*syn.*) a sorceress: *Many people do not believe in witches and their magical powers.*

witch·craft /'wɪtʃˌkræft/ *n.* [U] the practice of using magic or supernatural powers: *Many people do not trust witchcraft and fear its evil.*

W

witch doctor *n.* a person in some tribes who works to heal sick people by using magic or supernatural powers

witch hunt *n.* a search for people whose political beliefs and activities are claimed to be dangerous: *Politicians' staffs may go on witch hunts in order to make another politician look bad.*

with /wɪð, wɪθ/ *prep.* **1** in the company of: *I will go with you to the zoo.* **2** having, showing: *He wants a car with four doors.* **3** by means of, using: *He ate the cake with a fork.* **4** in support of: *Are you with us or against us?* **5** in the same direction: *The car went with the traffic.* **6** concerning: *My boss is very patient with me.* **7** in spite of, despite: *With all his success, he was still not happy.* **8** as a result of: *shaking with laughter‖eyes wet with tears* **9 with it:** aware, up-to-date: *For an 80-year-old woman, she is really with it.*

with·draw /wɪð'drɔ, wɪθ-/ *v.* **-drew** /-'dru/ or **-drawn** /-'drɔn/, **-drawing, -draws** **1** to move back, (*syn.*) to retreat: *Enemy forces withdrew from the city.* **2** to take out: *I withdrew some money from my checking account.* **3** to take back, (*syn.*) to retract: *The buyer withdrew his offer when the price became too high.*

with·draw·al /wɪð'drɔəl, -'drɔl, wɪθ-/ *n.* **1** [U] a retreat: *The withdrawal of the soldiers happened at the end of the war.* **2** [C] a removal, a taking out: *I made a withdrawal of $100 from my savings account.* **3** [U] a retraction, a taking back: *If the politician makes one more mistake, he'll see a withdrawal of his party's support.* **4 to go through withdrawal:** to suffer effects from no longer using drugs: *The drug addict went through withdrawal in the hospital.*

with·drawn /wɪð'drɔn, wɪθ-/ *past part. of* withdraw
—adj.fig. quiet, shy, not communicative: *As a child, he was withdrawn and didn't speak to other children.*

with·er /'wɪðər/ *v.* **1** to dry up and die, (*syn.*) to shrivel: *Plants wither from lack of water.* **2** to lose freshness, esp. because of age: *The old woman's thin, withered face looked sad.* **3 to wither** or **die on the vine:** to fail before being put into action: *They made plans to expand the business that withered on the vine when the economy worsened.*

with·hold /wɪθ'hoʊld, wɪð-/ *v.* **-held** /-'hɛld/, **-holding, -holds** **1** to deny, not give: *She withheld approval of the plan until she understood it completely.* **2** to subtract (taxes from a worker's pay), (*syn.*) to retain: *The company withholds taxes from your paycheck. -n.* [U] **withholding.**

withholding tax *n.* **taxes** a part of an employee's pay taken from a paycheck for the federal, state, or local government:

Withholding taxes take a large part of our paychecks.

with·in /wɪ'ðɪn, wɪ'θɪn/ *prep.* inside (a person, container, time period, etc.): *He keeps his feelings within himself.‖The bill is due within 30 days.*

with·out /wɪ'ðaʊt, wɪ'θaʊt/ *prep.* **1** not in the company of, (*syn.*) absent: *I went shopping without my husband.* **2** not having, lacking: *a day without sunshine*
—adv. **1** *frml.* outside: *The world without can be cold and cruel.* **2 to do** or **go without:** to not have or to be deprived of (comforts, luxuries, etc.): *My parents did without so they could pay for me to go to college.*

with·stand /wɪθ'stænd, wɪð-/ *v.* **-stood** /-'stʊd/, **-standing, -stands** to last in spite of, (*syns.*) to endure, to tolerate: *She is strong and can withstand pain.*

wit·less /'wɪtlɪs/ *adj.* stupid, foolish: *He lost all his money in witless investments and unsuccessful businesses.*

wit·ness /'wɪtnɪs/ *v.* **-nesses** **1** to see, observe an incident: *He witnessed the auto accident and wrote a report.* **2** to sign a document as a witness: *They asked me to witness their contract.*
—n. **1** a person who saw s.t. and can tell about it, (*syn.*) an observer: *I was a witness to the accident.* **2** a person who attests or certifies that s.t. is real or genuine: *I signed as a witness to the authenticity of the will.*

witness stand *n.* **1** the place next to the judge in a court of law where a witness sits when questioned **2 to take the witness stand:** to answer questions as a witness in court: *The lawyer for the defense had several witnesses take the witness stand.*

wit·ty /'wɪti/ *adj.* humorous in a clever way: *She is very witty and bright. -n.* **witticism.**

wives /waɪvz/ *n.pl. of* wife

wiz /wɪz/ *n.infrml.short for* wizard, a very talented or gifted person: *She is a wiz with computers.*

wiz·ard /'wɪzərd/ *n.* [C] **1** a man who has magic powers, (*syn.*) a sorcerer: *In medieval times, wizards did magic tricks.* **2** a very capable or gifted person: *He is a financial wizard. -n.* [U] **wizardry** /'wɪzərdri/.

wiz·ened /'wɪzənd/ *adj.* dried up with age, withered: *The child stared at the lines in the face of the wizened old man.*

wob·ble /'wɑbəl/ *v.* **-bled, -bling, -bles** to move in an unbalanced way from one side to another: *The table wobbled because one of its legs was too short.*
—n. an unsteady motion from side to side: *The drunk man walked with a wobble. -adj.* **wobbly.**

woe /wou/ *n.old usage* **1** problems, hardships, (*syn.*) adversity: *With bad health and no money, his life is full of woe.* **2** sadness, grief: *His wife told us his tale of woe.* *-adj.* **woeful.**

woe·be·gone /'woubɪ,gɔn, -,gɑn/ *adj.* looking very sad, miserable, (*syn.*) forlorn: *He lost everything in a house fire and is woebegone.*

wok /wɑk/ *n.* a deep, round, metal pan: *Chinese food is cooked in a wok.*

woke /wouk/ *v.* past tense of wake

wo·ken /'woukən/ *v. past part. of* wake

wolf /wʊlf/ *n.* **wolves** /wʊlvz/ **1** a wild, dog-like animal that travels in groups: *Wolves hunt deer.* **2** *infrml.* an aggressive man intent on having sex with women: *He is a wolf who spends his evenings chasing after women.* **3** *infrml.* **a**

wolf

wolf in sheep's clothing: an evil person who pretends to be good: *He smiles and shakes everybody's hand, but he's a wolf in sheep's clothing.* **4** *infrml.* **to cry wolf:** to pretend there is danger or trouble when there is not: *He's an alarmist who cries wolf all the time.*
—*v.* to eat very fast: *When he is very hungry, he wolfs his food.*

wol·ver·ine /,wʊlvə'rin, 'wʊlvə,rin/ *n.* a small weasel-like animal living in the northern USA and Canada: *Wolverines are famous for their aggressive behavior.*

wom·an /'wʊmən/ *n.* **women** /'wɪmən/ a mature female human: *A girl grows up to be a woman.* *-adj.* **womanish; womanly.**

wom·an·kind /'wʊmən,kaɪnd/ *n.* [U] women as a group

wom·an·hood /'wʊmən,hʊd/ *n.* [U] the state of being a woman: *Girls reach womanhood after their teen years.*

womb /wum/ *n.* the part of a woman's body where a baby can grow, the uterus: *She has a healthy baby girl in her womb.*

women /'wɪmən/ *n.pl. of* woman

women's rights *n.pl.* economic, social, and legal rights for women equal to those of men: *Women's rights include equal pay for equal work.*

won /wʌn/ *past tense & past part. of* win

won·der /'wʌndər/ *v.* **1** to express an interest in knowing, (*syn.*) to speculate: *I wonder whether it will rain today.* **2** to feel surprise: *I wonder that he hasn't called yet.* **3** to admire: *Many people wonder at the beauty of nature around them.*
—*n.* **1** a spectacular thing: *The Rocky Mountains are a wonder to see.* **2** a surprise: *It is a wonder that he is still alive after such a bad accident.*

won·der·ful /'wʌndərfəl/ *adj.* excellent, very pleasing: *We had a wonderful time on our vacation.* *-adv.* **wonderfully.**

won·der·land /'wʌndər,lænd/ *n.* a beautiful place: *The state of Maine is a wonderland for vacations and recreation.*

won·drous /'wʌndrəs/ *adj.* causing surprise and admiration, impressive: *The portable computer is a wondrous example of modern technology.* *-adv.* **wondrously.**

wonk /wɑŋk/ *n.infrml.* a student who does little else besides study, a grind: *That engineering school is full of wonks.* *-adj.infrml.* **wonky.**

wont /wount, wɔnt, wɑnt, wʌnt/ *adj.frml.* inclined: *He is wont to make long speeches about the world today.*
—*n.frml.* a habit or custom: *He brought me another lovely gift, as is his wont.*

won't /wount/ *contr. of* will not

woo /wu/ *v.* to pay special attention to s.o. for love, (*syn.*) to romance: *The young man wooed the girl by calling her every day.*

wood /wʊd/ *n.* [C;U] **1** the hard material below the bark of trees: *The wood in that old oak tree is rotten.* **2** the material from trees used to make furniture, fuel, paper, etc.: *We used wood from our own land to build our house.* See: woods.

wood alcohol *n.* [U] a poisonous alcoholic liquid made from wood: *People must not drink wood alcohol.*

wood·carv·ing /'wʊd,kɑrvɪŋ/ *n.* [U] the art and craft of cutting and shaping wood: *There are many sharp tools used in woodcarving.* *-n.* [C] **woodcarver.**

wood·cut /'wʊd,kʌt/ *n.* (in art) a print made from an image cut in wood: *We have woodcuts on our walls for decorations.*

wood·ed /'wʊdɪd/ *adj.* covered with trees: *There is a wooded hill behind the house.*

wood·en /'wʊdn/ *adj.* **1** made of wood: *The house is full of wooden furniture.* **2** stiff, does not bend easily: *The baby made wooden movements when he started to walk.* **3** *fig.* dull, without feeling, (*syn.*) uninspired: *He writes boring, wooden letters.* *-adv.* **woodenly.**

wood·land /'wʊdlənd, -,lænd/ *n.* a forested area: *The small town is surrounded by woodlands.*

wood·peck·er /'wʊd,pɛkər/ *n.* a type of bird with a long, pointed beak used to knock holes in trees to find insects to eat and to make nests

wood·pile /'wʊd,paɪl/ *n.* a stack of wood: *The farmer keeps a woodpile near the house for firewood in winter.*

woods /wʊdz/ *n.pl.* **1** a small forest: *We like to go for a walk in the woods.* **2 to be out of the woods:** to be out of danger: *He is recovering from a serious illness, but he is not out of the woods as yet.* *-adj.* **woodsy.**

wood·shed /ˈwʊdˌʃɛd/ *n.* a small building used to store wood: *Each week the farmer cuts wood and stores it in his woodshed.*

woods·man /ˈwʊdzmən/ *n.* **1** a person who cuts wood, a woodcutter: *Woodsmen cut down trees for building houses.* **2** a person who works or lives in the woods: *He is a woodsman living in a log cabin.*

wood·wind /ˈwʊdˌwɪnd/ *n.* any of the instruments in an orchestra that are played by blowing into them, such as the clarinet, bassoon, and oboe

wood·work /ˈwʊdˌwɜrk/ *n.* [U] **1** floors, doors, furniture, and walls made from wood: *The woodwork in the library is made of oak and walnut.* **2 out of the woodwork: a.** from a hidden place: *Bugs appeared out of the woodwork.* **b.** *fig.* unexpectedly, by surprise: *Important papers that had been lost suddenly appeared out of the woodwork.*

wood·work·ing /ˈwʊdˌwɜrkɪŋ/ *n.* [U] the art and craft of making things from wood, esp. furniture: *Woodworking is a popular class in many high schools.*

wood·y /ˈwʊdi/ *adj.* **-ier, -iest** like wood in taste, texture, or feel: *Red wine often has a woody taste.*

woof /wʊf, wuf/ *n.* **1** [U] a fabric's texture, weft: *Fixed threads form the warp, and those woven between them are the woof.* **2** [C] *infrml.* a word used to describe the sound (bark) of a dog

woof·er /ˈwʊfər/ *n.* (in music) a sound system's speaker that makes low tones: *The woofer in my stereo has trouble making the lowest tones. See:* tweeter.

wool /wʊl/ *n.* [U] **1** sheep's hair: *It is hard work to take the wool from sheep.* **2** the thick threads or fabric made from wool: *My sweater is made of wool.* **3 to pull the wool over s.o.'s eyes:** to trick, deceive s.o.: *A salesman tried to pull the wool over my eyes by selling me an old computer at a higher price.*

wool·en /ˈwʊlən/ *adj.* made of wool: *She wears woolen skirts in the winter.*

wool·ens /ˈwʊlənz/ *n.pl.* clothes made from wool, such as sweaters and mittens: *In the winter, we wear our woolens every day.*

wool·gath·er·ing /ˈwʊlˌgæðərɪŋ/ *n.fig.* [U] daydreaming, loafing: *He spends too much time in woolgathering on the job. -n.* [C] **woolgatherer.**

wool·ly /ˈwʊli/ *adj.* **-ier, -iest 1** having a fuzzy, woolen texture: *That rug's surface is very woolly.* **2** (of thoughts) not clear in the mind: *Her ideas are usually woolly.*

woo·zy /ˈwuzi/ *adj.* **-zier, -ziest** feeling faint, dizzy: *The summer heat made me feel woozy. -adv.* **woozily;** *-n.* **wooziness.**

word /wɜrd/ *n.* **1** a written or spoken unit of language having one or more meanings, usu. the smallest unit of meaning that can be used alone: *There are many words to describe the feeling of happiness.* **2** speech in general, in written or spoken form: *The author put her thoughts into words.* **3** a brief discussion: *I had a word with my secretary about her being late today.*||*I gave her a word of advice.* **4** a promise, a pledge: *I gave my word to my friend that I would help him.*||*You can trust her to keep her word.* **5** message, news: *They sent word that they would be late.*||*We just got word of your new job!* **6 in a word:** to summarize: *In a word, the party's over.* **7 in one's own words:** without repeating what s.o. else said: *Tell the court what happened in your own words.* **8 to be a man** or **woman of his/her word:** to keep one's promise, to be honorable: *She is a woman of her word because she repaid the loan exactly when she said she would.* **9 to break one's word** or **go back on one's word:** not to do what one has promised: *He went back on his word and did not repay the loan.* **10** *infrml.* **to eat one's words:** to take back s.t. one said after being proven wrong: *He kept saying that he would win the tennis championship, but he lost and now he has to eat his words.* **11 to have a good word:** to be cheerful, supportive: *He is a pleasure to work with because he always has a good word for everyone.* **12 to have words with s.o.:** to argue with or shout at s.o.: *His behavior made me mad, so I had words with him.* **13 to mince words:** to speak quietly and indirectly, usu. used negatively: *That man does not mince words; he tells you the truth immediately.* **14 to put in a good word for s.o.:** to recommend s.o.: *I am looking for a new job, and my friend said she would put in a good word for me at her company.* **15 to take s.o.'s word for it** or **to take s.o. at his/her word:** to believe what s.o. says without proof: *He says he did not do anything wrong, and he is honest, so I take his word for it* (or) *I take him at his word.* **16 word for word:** spoken, read, or copied exactly from s.o. else's words: *She told me exactly what he said, word for word.* **17 word play:** cleverness of expression, puns: *The word play in his writing is very witty.*
—v. to express in words: *He worded his introduction carefully.*

word·ing /ˈwɜrdɪŋ/ *n.* [U] the way words are arranged, (*syn.*) phrasing: *The wording of the contract is not quite right.*

word processing *n.* [U] **1** the input, editing, and output of words and numbers on computer: *Word processing has taken the place of typing in most businesses.* **2** the occupation (used with *to do*): *She does word processing at a bank.*

W

word processor *n.* a small computer used for word processing: *The author wrote his book on a word processor.*

word·y /'wɜrdi/ *adj.* **-ier, -iest** using lots of words, (*syn.*) verbose: *His writing is very wordy and needs editing.* *-n.* [U] **wordiness.**

wore /wɔr/ *past tense of* wear

work /wɜrk/ *v.* **1** to be employed: *He works in a hospital.*‖*He works as a machinist.* **2** to labor, exert force: *The mechanic worked on the car all day.* **3** to operate, cause to function: *He works on a computer all day.*‖*Do you know how to work this camera?* **4** to function well, to operate: *The clock was broken, but it works now.* **5** to make productive: *A farmer works the land.* **6** to change, process, transform: *She works clay into bowls and plates.* **7** to force others to work: *The owner works her employees hard.* **8** to produce results: *That medicine works well in relieving pain.* **9** to move in a series of small movements: *The movers worked a large refrigerator into a small kitchen space.* **10** *infrml.* **to be (all) worked up:** to be tense, upset: *The student was all worked up about finishing her term paper on time.* **11** *phrasal v. insep.* **to work against s.o. or s.t.: a.** s.o. to not help, (*syn.*) to hinder: *His lack of education works against him when he looks for a job.* **b.** s.t. to fight, battle: *Our political party worked against the opposing candidates.* **12 to work against the clock:** to work very fast to meet a deadline: *The television team worked against the clock to produce the show on time.* **13** *phrasal v. insep.* **to work around s.t.:** to manage in spite of s.t. that blocks the way: *We worked around the staffing problem by hiring some temporary workers.* **14 to work around the clock** or **work night and day:** to labor without stopping: *We worked around the clock until the report was finished.* **15** *phrasal v. insep.* **to work at s.t.:** to make great efforts, apply oneself, (*syn.*) to persevere: *He works at his studies and makes good grades.* **16** *phrasal v.* **to work away:** to labor very hard, (*syn.*) to persevere: *The cobbler works away tirelessly at fixing shoes all day.* **17** *infrml.* **to work like a charm:** to succeed, perform well: *The repairman put a new part in our old television, and now it works like a charm.* **18** *infrml.* **to work like a dog** or **a mule:** to work very hard **19** *phrasal v. sep.* **to work on s.t.:** to continue working: *Some firefighters worked on, while others rested.* **20** *infrml.* **to work one's fingers to the bone:** to work very hard: *The mother of five children worked her fingers to the bone to send them all through college.* **21 to work one's way:** to move slowly: *Rust has worked its way into the car's body and destroyed it.*‖*We worked our way through the crowd.* **22** *phrasal v.* **to work out: a.** to end in success: *The company's financial trouble* worked out, so they can hire new people now. **b.** to develop, (*syn.*) to formulate: *The president worked out a solution to the company's problems.* **c.** to exercise: *She works out at the local health club.* **23** *phrasal v. insep.* **to work s.o. or s.t. in (to): a.** s.t.: to push or rub: *He worked the shoe polish into the leather.* **b.** s.o. or s.t.: to arrange, fit into an activity: *I was afraid the doctor wouldn't have time to see me, but he worked me in.* **24** *phrasal v. sep.* **to work s.o. over:** to beat s.o. badly: *After the thieves robbed the store, they worked over the owner.*‖*They worked him over.* **25** *phrasal v. sep.* **to work s.o or s.t. up:** to excite the feelings of: *The team captain was able to work up enthusiasm in his team members.*‖*He worked them up.* **26** *phrasal v. sep.* **to work s.t. off:** to reduce, diminish: *He worked off his extra weight by exercising.* **27 to work things through:** to solve problems: *The computer broke down, but we were able to work things through and finish our reports.* **28 to work wonders** or **miracles:** to do extraordinary things, to accomplish much: *The teacher worked wonders with his slowest students.*
—*n.* **1** [U] employment: *Students will be looking for work after they finish college.* **2** [U] the change of energy into force: *Machines do the heavy work in our society.* **3** [U] an occupation, job type: *She has work as a store manager.* **4** [C] a creation, esp. an artistic work: *The museum is showing the works of Van Gogh.* **5** *pl.* a factory or industrial plant: *Workers drive to the company electronic works every day.* **6** the moving parts of an object, esp. a watch **7 out of work:** lacking a job, unemployed **8** *slang* **the works:** everything extra: *I would like a hot dog with the works (mustard, onions, and ketchup).* **9 to be all in a day's work:** to be routine, even if difficult: *The policeman chased a thief, caught him, then put him in jail, but it was simply all in a day's work.*

work·a·ble /'wɜrkəbəl/ *adj.* practical, capable of being done: *We made a workable agreement with another company to build a house together.*

work·a·hol·ic /ˌwɜrkə'hɔlɪk, -'hɑ-/ *n.* a person who works all the time: *He is a workaholic who works seven days a week with no vacations.*

work·bench /'wɜrkˌbɛntʃ/ *n.* **-benches** a hard, flat surface of wood or metal on which work is done: *The carpenter has a wooden workbench in his garage.*

work·book /'wɜrkˌbʊk/ *n.* a book with exercises: *Students in the science class do exercises in the workbook that goes along with their textbook.*

work·day /'wɜrkˌdeɪ/ or **working day** *n.* **1** work hours: *Our workday is eight hours long.*

2 a day that is not a holiday: *Monday is a workday.*

work·er /'wɜrkər/ *n.* a person who works: *Steel workers are highly paid for their hard work.*

workers' compensation *n.* [U] in the USA, payments made by employers or their insurance company to cover injuries or sicknesses resulting from work: *Workers' compensation in this state now provides for injured or sick workers to receive more than half of their pay.*

work ethic *n.* [U] the belief that work is morally good: *The boy learned the work ethic from his father, who worked in the same company for 45 years.*

work·fare /'wɜrk,fɛr/ *n.* [U] a form of public assistance for food, housing, health services, etc. that requires people to do public work: *He is on workfare, so he sweeps floors in the city hall in return for a welfare check. See:* welfare.

work·force /'wɜrk,fɔrs/ *n.* [U] all workers employed nationally, regionally, or in an individual business: *The workforce in this area is well-educated and very reliable.*

work·horse /'wɜrk,hɔrs/ *n.* **1** a horse that performs heavy work: *That farmer keeps several workhorses to do the plowing.* **2** *fig.* a person or machine that works very hard: *That central computer is the workhorse that does most of the company's accounting.*

working capital *n.* [U] the money invested (in cash, inventory, and accounts receivable): *Our business borrows its working capital from a bank.*

working class *n.* [U] *adj.* the part of society that does work for wages, esp. work with the hands, such as blue collar and clerical workers, (*syn.*) the proletariat: *Many people in the <n.> working class do not have a college education. See:* blue collar, USAGE NOTE.

working knowledge *n.* [U] enough practical knowledge to do s.t.: *He has a working knowledge of cars, so he fixes his own.*

working papers *n.pl.* **1** a written document stating that a young person is old enough to work: *In some states, young people must have working papers to get their first job.* **2** in the USA, a green card and Social Security number: *She is a legal immigrant and has working papers.*

work·ings /'wɜrkɪŋz/ *n.pl.* the way s.t. works: *I don't understand the workings of a car.*

work·load /'wɜrk,loʊd/ *n.* [U] the amount of work to be done: *The workload in the accounting department is very heavy.*

work·man·like /'wɜrkmən,laɪk/ *adj.* showing qualities of a good worker, (*syn.*) skillful: *Our carpenter did a careful, workmanlike job.*

work·man·ship /'wɜrkmən,ʃɪp/ *n.* [U] the quality of work as seen in products: *The workmanship in my new car is excellent.*

workmen's compensation *n. See:* workers' compensation.

work·out /'wɜrk,aʊt/ *n.* a session of physical exercise: *He goes to a gym for a daily workout.*

work permit *n.* written permission given by a government to a foreigner to work in the country: *When a work permit expires, the immigrant often returns to his or her homeland.*

work release *n.* [U] an arrangement for a prisoner to work outside the prison: *The prisoner is on work release at a farm and works there every day.*

work·shop /'wɜrk,ʃɑp/ *n.* **1** a building or area with machinery and tools: *We make machine parts in our workshop.* **2** a small group of students or professionals who study together: *My English workshop met this morning to discuss a new book.*

work·sta·tion /'wɜrk,steɪʃən/ *n.* **1** a place within a workshop where a specific task is performed: *At my workstation, we make electrical switches.* **2** a computer on a network: *This network has 12 workstations that share the same printer.*

work·up /'wɜrk,ʌp/ *n.* a series of medical tests to help a doctor tell what sickness a person may have: *The doctor worried about cancer and ordered a complete workup for her patient.*

work·week /'wɜrk,wik/ *n.* the number of days and hours of a business or an employee: *Most U.S. companies have a five-day workweek.*

world /wɜrld/ *n.* **1** the earth: *It is possible to fly around the world in an airplane.* **2** the state of affairs of humans and the planet in general: *What a wonderful (crazy, sad, etc.) world we live in.* **3** a group of living things: *People are curious to know about the plant (animal, scientific, etc.) world.* **4** a part of human activity: *He knows everything about the world of baseball.* **5** all people, everyone: *He emptied his garage for the world to see.* **6 on top of the world:** feeling very happy, wonderful, terrific: *On my wedding day, I was on top of the world.* **7 out of this world:** wonderful, terrific: *The food at that restaurant is out of this world.* **8 to think the world of s.o.:** to have a very high opinion of s.o.: *She's a wonderful neighbor; I think the world of her.* **9 What (Why, Who, etc.) in the world:** (an expression of angry questioning): *What in the world do you think you are doing taking money from my wallet?*

W

world-class *adj.* referring to the best in the world of s.t., esp. in sports: *She is a world-class runner in the Olympics.*

world·ly /ˈwɜrldli/ *adj.* related to real life rather than spiritual existence: *He is devoted to worldly pleasures with no thought for religion.* *-n.* [U] **worldliness.**

world power *n.* a nation with global influence, esp. in finance and military strength: *The USA is a world power.*

World Series *n.* **Series** [U] the North American baseball championship: *The World Series winner must win four of the seven games in the series.*

World War I /wʌn/ *n.* the great war (1914-1918) between the Allies (USA, Canada, Great Britain, France, Japan, et al.) and Germany, Austria, Hungary, et al.

World War II /tu/ *n.* the great war (1939-1945) between the Allies (USA, Canada, Great Britain, France, et al.) and the Axis (Germany, Japan, et al.)

world·wide /ˌwɜrldˈwaɪd/ *adj.adv.* all over the world: *Interest in the computer business is now <adj.> worldwide.*

World Wide Web *n.* a network of the places you can visit on the Internet to view, listen to, and save text, graphics, sound, or video: *I upgraded my computer so that I could access the World Wide Web. See:* information superhighway USAGE NOTE.

worm /wɜrm/ *n.* **1** a small, crawling animal with a long, soft body and no legs: *Earthworms help the soil by digging holes in it.* **2** *fig.* a bad person: *That little worm of a man can't be trusted.* **3** *infrml.* **can of worms:** a complicated problem: *When the company bought a new computer system, it opened a can of worms that created many new problems.*
—*v.* **1** to remove parasitic worms: *We had our dog wormed by the veterinarian.* **2** to move like a worm, crawling and twisting: *The soldier wormed his way through the woods.* **3 to worm s.t. out of s.o.:** to get (information) by continued questioning: *I tried to keep our secret, but she wormed it out of me.*

worn /wɔrn/ *past part. of* wear
—*adj.* used, (*syn.*) threadbare: *The knees of my pants are worn.*

worn-out *adj.* **1** very tired, exhausted: *I am all worn-out from working too hard.* **2** no longer usable from wear: *The bottoms of my shoes are worn-out.*

wor·ri·some /ˈwɜrisəm, ˈwʌr-/ *adj.* causing worry: *Her poor health is a worrisome situation.*

wor·ry /ˈwɜri, ˈwʌri/ *n.* [C;U] fear that s.t. bad or worse may happen, anxiety: *He has worries about his health and his job.*
—*v.* **-ried, -rying, -ries** to feel troubled or anxious: *She worries about the safety of her children at school.* *-adj.* **worried;** *-n.* [C] **worrier.**

wor·ry·wart /ˈwɜri,wɔrt, ˈwʌr-/ *n.infrml.* a person who worries all the time, often without a

reason: *He is such a worrywart that he stays inside his house all day.*

worse /wɜrs/ *adj.comp. of* bad **1** lower in quality: *The weather was bad yesterday, but today it is even worse.* **2** more harmful, more serious: *His health is getting worse every day.* **3 a change for the worse:** a very bad change: *After one night in the hospital, she took a change for the worse.* **4 no worse for wear:** all right physically after an incident: *He had an accident but is OK, no worse for wear.*
—*adv.* in a worse way: *The child behaved badly by day and acted worse at night.*

wors·en /ˈwɜrsən/ *v.* **1** to become worse, decline: *His health worsens daily.* **2** to make worse: *The bad weather worsens our mood.*

wor·ship /ˈwɜrʃɪp/ *v.* **-shiped** or **-shipped, -shiping** or **-shipping, -ships 1** to show great respect for, (*syn.*) to revere: *Many people worship God.* **2** to love very much, (*syns.*) to adore, cherish: *He worshipped his girlfriend.*
—*n.* [U] (the act of showing) great respect, reverence: *The worship of God is common among the faithful. -n.* **worshiper;** *-adj.* **worshipful** /ˈwɜrʃɪpfəl/.

worst /wɜrst/ *adj.superlative of* bad **1** lowest in quality: *The movie was bad; it was the worst one I have ever seen!* **2** most harmful, gravest: *This winter's weather is the worst in years.* **3** *infrml.* **in the worst way:** very much: *He needs a new car in the worst way.*
—*adv.* most badly: *She played tennis the worst that she has all summer.*
—*n.* **1** that which is worst: *There have been bad storms this winter, but this one is the worst.* **2 if (the) worst comes to (the) worst:** if the worst possible thing happens: *If worst comes to worst and I fail the course, I'll take it again next year.*

wor·sted /ˈwʊrstɪd, ˈwɜrstɪd/ *n.* [U] cloth tightly woven for long wear: *He buys suits made of wool worsted.*

worth /wɜrθ/ *n.* [U] **1** value, cost: *That painting is an art object of great worth.* **2** excellence, merit: *The professor's ideas have great worth.* **3** quantity of s.t.: *I would like $10 worth of gas, please. See:* net worth.
—*adj.* **1** equal in value to: *That dress is worth $100.* **2** having wealth equal to: *She is worth a million dollars.* **3** good enough for, deserving: *That book is worth reading.*

worth·less /ˈwɜrθlɪs/ *adj.* without value, excellence, or wealth: *That ring is a worthless imitation. -n.* [U] **worthlessness.**

worth·while /ˌwɜrθˈwaɪl/ *adj.* worth doing, worth the trouble: *Seeing that art exhibit is worthwhile.‖She is alone in her big house now, and that makes it worthwhile for her to rent out rooms.*

wor·thy /ˈwɜrði/ *adj.* **-thier, -thiest 1** deserving, due: *That new play is worthy of praise.* **2**

deserving special consideration: *She is a worthy young lady deserving of a scholarship.* *-adv.* **worthily; -*n.*** [C] **worthiness.**

would /wʊd; *weak form* wəd, əd, d/ *aux. verb* **1** (used as past tense of *will*): *He said he would be here.* **2** was (or) were willing to: *I asked her to change her mind, but she wouldn't.* **3** (used to ask s.o. to do s.t.) will, could: *Would you please help me move this table?* **4** (used to show a past custom or habit) used to: *When I was a child, I would spend Sundays with my grandparents.*

would-be /ˈwʊd,bi/ *adj.* referring to s.o. or s.t. that wants to be, but is not: *He is the would-be replacement for the president, but he won't get the job.*

wouldn't /ˈwʊdnt/ *contr. of* would not

wound (1) /wund/ *n.* a cut, puncture, or other hurt cutting into the body: *The police officer has a knife wound in his arm.*
—v. **1** to cause a wound: *The bullet wounded the soldier.* **2** to hurt emotionally: *She left her boyfriend, and that wounded him.* **3 to wound s.o.'s pride:** to hurt s.o.'s self-esteem: *He was the champion but was beaten by an unknown, and that wounded his pride.*

wound (2) /waʊnd/ *past tense & past part. of* wind

wound-up /ˌwaʊndˈʌp/ *adj.* nervous, high-strung: *I am all wound-up today; I can't stop moving.*

wove /woʊv/ *past tense of* weave

woven /ˈwoʊvən/ *past part. of* weave
—adj. put together by weaving: *That cloth is finely woven.*

wow /waʊ/ *exclam.* (used to show surprise, delight): *Wow! What a pretty girl!*
—v.infrml. to excite, impress: *The musicians wowed the audience with their talent.*

wran·gle /ˈræŋgəl/ *v.* **-gled, -gling, -gles** to argue noisily, quarrel: *The boss told the two employees to stop wrangling with each other.*

wran·gler /ˈræŋglər/ *n.* a cowboy, esp. one who tends horses: *My grandfather was a wrangler on a ranch in Texas.*

wrap /ræp/ *v.* **wrapped, wrapping, wraps 1** to cover (with material that surrounds s.t.): *The butcher wrapped the meat in waxed paper.‖I wrapped the gift with colorful paper.* **2** *phrasal v. sep.* **to wrap s.t. up:** to finish: *We wrapped up the class with a review of the lessons.‖We wrapped it up.* **3** *phrasal v.* **to wrap up:** to wear warm clothes: *We should wrap up well in the winter.*
—adj. **wrapped up in:** giving complete attention to: *She is so wrapped up in her boyfriend that she has no time for her other friends.*
—n. (clothing) an outer covering: *She wears a shawl as an evening wrap.*

wrap·a·round /ˈræpə,raʊnd/ *n.adj.* s.t. that folds around: *She is wearing a <adj.> wrap-around skirt.*

wrap·per /ˈræpər/ *n.* a cover: *Candy bars have colorful wrappers.*

wrap·ping /ˈræpɪŋ/ *n.* [C;U] material used to wrap s.t.: *Christmas presents come with colorful wrapping.*

wrap-up *n.infrml.* a summary, final review: *Sports announcers gave a wrap-up of the game's score and highlights on the news.*

wrath /ræθ/ *n.frml.* [U] anger, hostility: *He feared his father's wrath.* *-adj.* **wrathful** /ˈræθfəl/.

wreak /rik/ *v.frml.* **to wreak havoc:** to do violence (destruction, punishment, etc.): *The hurricane wreaked havoc on the coastal area.*

wreath /riθ/ *n.* **wreaths** /riðz, riθs/ a round arrangement of flowers or leaves used for decoration: *Many people hang wreaths of pine branches on their doors at Christmastime.* *-v.* **wreathe** /rið/.

wreath

wreck /rɛk/ *v.* **1** to ruin, destroy: *He wrecked his car in an accident.* **2** to destroy, tear down, (*syn.*) to demolish: *Workers wrecked an old house to make way for a new one.*
—n. **1** [C] s.t. or s.o. ruined: *After the accident, his car was a wreck.‖He is a wreck after drinking for so many years.* **2** [C] a ship lost at sea: *Some divers like to dive for wrecks in the ocean.* **3** [U] destruction, ruin **4 a nervous wreck:** a person who is so nervous that he or she has trouble functioning: *Those children are so bad that they make a nervous wreck out of their mother.*

wreck·age /ˈrɛkɪdʒ/ *n.* [U] the remains of s.t. that has been destroyed: *The wreckage of houses and cars after the storm was everywhere.*

wreck·er /ˈrɛkər/ *n.* **1** s.o. or s.t. that wrecks: *That hurricane was a wrecker.* **2** a tow truck: *A wrecker towed his car away after the accident.*

wren /rɛn/ *n.* a small brown bird: *I hear the wrens singing in the tree outside my window.*

wrench /rɛntʃ/ *n.* **wrenches 1** a metal tool that adjusts to tighten or loosen things: *He used a wrench to tighten the water pipes.* **2** a sudden twisting movement: *With one wrench, he loosened the cap off the jar.*
—v. **wrenches 1** to twist badly, hurt: *I fell and wrenched my back.* **2** to pull with a hard, twisting movement: *She had to wrench the door handle to open it.*

wrest /rɛst/ *v.* to remove by force: *A thief wrested my briefcase from my hands.*

W

wres·tle /'rɛsəl/ v. -tled, -tling, -tles **1** to fight with s.o. using the force of the body: *A police officer wrestled a criminal to the ground.* **2** to engage in the sport of wrestling: *One wrestler managed to wrestle the other to the mat.* **3** to struggle: *We wrestled with the problem and finally solved it.* -n. **wrestler.**

wres·tling /'rɛslɪŋ/ n. [U] the sport of fighting with an opponent and trying to pin him to the ground: *Professional wrestling is entertainment as well as a sport.*

wretch /rɛtʃ/ n. **wretches** a person living in miserable conditions: *The wretches living on the streets ask for money.*

wretch·ed /'rɛtʃɪd/ adj. **1** dirty, poor, and very unhappy, (syn.) miserable: *Life in those old buildings must be wretched.* **2** hateful, (syns.) despicable, contemptible: *Abandoning his children is a wretched thing for him to do.* -adv. **wretchedly;** -n. [C] **wretchedness.**

wrig·gle /'rɪgəl/ v. -gled, -gling, -gles to move back and forth rapidly, wiggle: *A worm wriggles on a fish hook.*

wring /rɪŋ/ v. **wrung** /rʌŋ/, **wringing, wrings 1** to twist or squeeze forcefully, esp. with hands: *He wrung the water from the clothes he had just washed.* **2** infrml. **to wring s.o.'s neck:** to punish s.o.: *I am so angry at him that I could wring his neck.* **3 wringing wet:** very wet, (syn.) drenched: *He fell into the river and came out wringing wet.*

wring·er /'rɪŋər/ n. **1** small machine with two rollers that turn to press water from clothes **2 to put s.o. through the wringer:** to give s.o. a trying, difficult situation: *The airport officials put me through the wringer by questioning me for hours and searching in my bags.*

wring·ing /'rɪŋɪŋ/ adj. **wringing wet:** very wet: *He fell into the water and came out with his clothes wringing wet.*

wrin·kle /'rɪŋkəl/ v. -kled, -kling, -kles to put lines or folds in s.t.: *The back of her skirt was wrinkled from her sitting on it.*
—n. **1** a line or fold in s.t., (syn.) a crease: *The old lady has wrinkles in her face.* **2** a small problem: *The more they study the plan for the sports center, the more new wrinkles they find.* **3 to iron out the wrinkles:** to solve any remaining problems: *The basic financial plan was approved, but the accountants met to iron out the wrinkles that remained.*

wrist /rɪst/ n. the flexible joint attaching the human hand to the forearm: *I always wear my watch on my left wrist.*

wrist·watch /'rɪst,wɑtʃ/ n. **-watches** a watch worn on the wrist: *My wristwatch is run by a small battery.*

writ /rɪt/ n. (in law) a legal document issued by a court: *The judge issued a writ ordering the woman to pay a fine for putting garbage in the street.*

write /raɪt/ v. **wrote** /roʊt/ or **written** /'rɪtn/, **writing, writes 1** to present ideas in words, such as on paper or electronically: *He has to write a term paper for his history class.* **2** to create literary works: *She writes novels for a living.* **3** to communicate with s.o. in writing: *I wrote (a letter) to my brother about my new job.* **4** phrasal v. insep. **to write in** or **away for s.t.:** to request s.t. by letter or mail: *He wrote in for concert tickets.* **5** phrasal v. sep. **to write s.o. or s.t. off:** to pay no attention to, ignore, dismiss: *I write off his comments as stupid.‖I write them off. See:* write-off. **6** phrasal v. sep. **to write s.t. down: a.** to write on paper: *I wrote down my friend's new address.‖I wrote it down.* **b.** (in business) to make s.t. less valuable, (syn.) to devalue an asset: *We wrote down old inventory. See:* write-down. **7** phrasal v. insep. **to write s.t. out:** to copy completely: *She wrote out her recipe for lemon cake.‖She wrote it out.* **8** phrasal v. sep. **to write s.t. up:** to describe, esp. in a newspaper: *A reporter wrote up our baseball team's win in the newspaper.‖He wrote it up.*

write-down n. (in accounting) a lowering of the price or cost of goods, (syn.) devaluation: *Each year we take a write-down of what we did not sell.*

write-in adj. referring to voting for a candidate who is not listed on the ballot by writing in his or her name there: *He was a write-in candidate for President and got many votes.*

write-off n. **1** s.t. that is ruined: *After the fire, their house was a write-off.* **2** (in business) a subtraction of s.t.'s value from income: *The interest payments on a house loan can be a write-off when figuring out income taxes.*

writ·er /'raɪtər/ n. **1** s.o. who writes: *The writer of the letter expresses herself well.* **2** a person who makes a living by writing: *He is a writer of fiction.*

write-up n. a description, article (in a newspaper, magazine, etc.): *There was a write-up on the New Year's Eve party in today's newspaper.*

writhe /raɪð/ v. **writhed, writhing, writhes** to twist and turn in great pain: *After being run over by a car, the snake writhed on the road.*

writ·ing /'raɪtɪŋ/ n. [U] **1** the act of expressing ideas in words: *The writing of the U.S. Constitution took many months.* **2** the occupation or activity of a writer: *The author of this book moved from medicine to writing as a career.* **3** handwriting: *Can you read her messy writing?*

writ·ten /'rɪtn/ past part. of write

wrong /rɔŋ/ adj. **1** incorrect, mistaken: *The price marked on those shoes is wrong.* **2** related to bad behavior, not right: *It was wrong of him to cheat you.*
—n. **1** a mistake or bad action: *The boy broke his sister's toy because she broke his, but two*

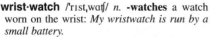

wrongs don't make a right. **2 to right a wrong:** to correct s.t. unjust or morally bad: *Politicians promise to right the wrongs of society.*

—*adv.* **1** in a wrong way, incorrectly: *I wrote down the address wrong, so I could not find your house.* **2 to go wrong:** to make a mistake: *The boy is in trouble with the law, and his parents wonder where they went wrong in raising him.* **3 to go wrong with:** to stop working: *Nothing went wrong with the car today. -adv.* **wrongly.**

wrong·do·ing /ˈrɔŋˌduɪŋ, ˌrɔŋˈduɪŋ/ *n.* [U] an act of breaking the law: *The police try to prevent people from too much wrongdoing. -n.* [C] **wrongdoer.**

wrong·head·ed /ˌrɔŋˈhɛdɪd, ˈrɔŋˌhɛdɪd/ *adj.* holding on to mistaken ideas: *He is a wrongheaded boy who insists on taking drugs.*

wrote /roʊt/ *past tense of* write

wrought /rɔt/ *adj.* **1** made, esp. by hammering: *We have a wrought iron gate in front of our house.* **2 wrought up:** upset, disturbed: *He became wrought up when he heard the bad news.*

wrought iron *n.* [U] iron hammered into shapes when still hot: *The wrought iron gate in front of our house is painted black.*

wrung /rʌŋ/ *past tense & past part. of* wring: **wrung out:** very tired, (*syns.*) exhausted, fatigued: *We were wrung out after a day in the hot sun.*

wry /raɪ/ *adj.* **wrier, wriest** humorous, esp. in an ironic, dry manner: *He has a wry sense of humor. -adv.* **wryly;** *-n.* [U] **wryness.**

wurst /wɜrst, wʊrst/ *n.* [U] a kind of sausage often used in combination with another word: *knockwurst, liverwurst*

W

X,x

X, x /ɛks/ *n.* **X's, x's** or **Xs, xs, 1** the 24th letter of the English alphabet **2** a substitute for a signature: *People who can't write will often mark an X on a document in place of their names.* **3** a mark for a location: *X marks the spot on the map where I live.* **4** the Roman numeral for ten
—*v.* to cross out with an X: *She X'd out a paragraph in the letter. See:* ex, X-rated.

Xe·rox /'zɪrɑks/ *n.TM* **-es 1** a process for photocopying **2** a photocopy: *I made a Xerox of my report.*
—*v.* **-es** to photocopy s.t.: *I Xeroxed my report.*

USAGE NOTE: Though *Xerox*™ is a registered trademark, it is often used to mean photocopy: *My boss asked me to Xerox*™ *a few pages from the sales report.* //*She sent me a Xerox*™ *of the article she wrote.*

XL /'ɛks'ɛl/ *abbr. for* extra large size: *The label of that coat says its size is XL.*

X·mas /'krɪsməs/ *n.infrml.abbr. for* Christmas: *This year I will spend the Xmas holidays with my family.*

USAGE NOTE: *Xmas* is used in informal writing but is not used in speaking.

X-rat·ed /'ɛks,reɪtɪd/ *adj.* in the USA, a rating for films that have nude sex scenes and often obscene language: *Children under the age of 17 cannot buy tickets for X-rated films.*

x-ray /'ɛksreɪ/ *n.* **1** a type of strong light that passes through the body and makes a picture of bones and other body parts **2** a photograph taken with x-rays
—*v.* to photograph using x-rays: *A doctor x-rayed my broken ankle.*

x-ray therapy *n.* [C;U] the use of x-rays in treating disease: *X-ray therapy can stop the growth of cancer. See:* chemotherapy.

xy·lo·phone /'zaɪlə,foʊn/ *n.* a musical instrument made of two rows of bars, each sounding a different note when hit with light wooden hammers

XXL /'ɛksɛks'ɛl/ *abbr. for* extra, extra large size: *Clothing with an XXL label is for very big people.*

xylophone

Y,y

Y, y /waɪ/ **Y's, y's,** or **Ys, ys** **1** the 25th letter of the English alphabet **2 the Y:** *n. abbr. for* YMCA, the Young Men's Christian Association, or YWCA, the Young Women's Christian Association: *He lives in a room at the Y.*

yacht /yɑt/ *n.* an expensive boat used for pleasure or racing
—*v.* to sail in a yacht: *They yacht in the summer.*

yacht

yachts·man /'yɑtsmən/ *n.* **-men** /-mən/ a man who loves to sail, esp. in a yacht

yack /yæk/ *v.slang* to talk about everyday life, *(syn.)* to chitchat: *They yack on the phone every day.*

yack·e·ty-yack /'yækəti'yæk/ *v.slang* to talk or chat a lot: *They yackety-yack for hours without getting tired.*

ya·hoo /'yɑ,hu/ *n.infrml.* a stupid person: *That yahoo nearly hit me with his car!*
—*exclam. of* excitement: *yahoo! I win the prize!*

yak /yæk/ *n.* a long-haired wild ox

y'all /yɔl/ *pron.infrml.contr. of* you all

USAGE NOTE: *Y'all* is used to mean "you all" by many people in the southern part of the USA (South Carolina, Georgia, Alabama, etc.). In other parts of the USA, people are more likely to say *you all, you guys,* or *all of you* to refer to two or more people.

---

yam /yæm/ *n.* a plant with a root, *(syn.)* sweet potato: *Some people eat yams with their turkey for Thanksgiving dinner.*

yam·mer /'yæmər/ *v.* **1** to chatter, talk loudly **2** to complain, *(syn.)* to whine: *That person yammers about how difficult life is. -n.* [U] **yammering.**

yank /yæŋk/ *v.* to give a strong, sharp pull on s.t.: *He yanked a fish from the water.*

—*n.* **1** a strong pull: *He gave his fishing line a yank.* **2** *infrml.* **Yank** short for Yankee, a person from the USA, esp. a soldier from one of the two world wars: *The Yanks invaded France in World War II.*

Yank·ee /'yæŋki/ *n.* **1** an American as called by some foreigners: *My wife is from England and I am American. She calls me a Yankee.* **2** a northerner in the U.S. Civil War: *the Yankees invaded the South* **3** a member of one of New York's professional baseball teams

yap /yæp/ *n.slang* the mouth: *He is a loudmouth who has his yap open all the time.*
—*v.* **yapped, yapping, yaps** to make loud talk or noise: *That little dog yaps all night. -n.* [U] **yapping.**

yard /yɑrd/ *n.* **1** a length of three feet or 36 inches (0.91 meter): *a yard of cloth* **2** an area usu. behind or in front of a house: *The children went outside to play in the yard.* *See* inch.

yard·age /'yɑrdɪʤ/ *n.* [U] a general measure of length and width: *We measured the yardage of rug needed to cover the office floor.*

yard sale *n.* the sale of unwanted household items, such as old lamps and tables, in a person's yard: *We bought a beautiful old table at a yard sale for $10!*

yard·stick /'yɑrd,stɪk/ *n.* **1** a ruler 36 inches (0.91 meter) long **2** *fig.* any measure of performance or results: *A 10% profit after taxes is widely seen as a yardstick for making money in a business.*

yar·mul·ke /'yɑrməlkə, 'yɑməl-/ *n.* a small cap worn by religious Jews: *I wear a yarmulke on top of my head when I go to the synagogue.*

yarn /'yɑrn/ *n.* [C;U] **1** threads of wool or other material wound into thicker thread: *Wool yarn is used to make socks.* **2** *infrml,fig.* a long story: *The old soldier was spinning yarns about his wartime experiences.*

yaw /yɔ/ *v.* (said of boats and spacecraft) to lean to one side: *The ship yawed before changing direction.*

yawn /yɔn/ *v.* to open the mouth to show that one is tired or bored: *She yawned at midnight because she was very tired.*

Y

yea /yeɪ/ *exclam.* wonderful, *(syn.)* hooray: *Yea! We won the game!*
—*adv.* yes: *to vote yea*

yeah /'yɛə/ *adv.slang* yes, indeed *See:* yes, USAGE NOTE.

year /yɪr/ *n.* **1** a time period of 12 months or 365 days: *He worked in Japan for a year.* **2** an annual date: *the year 2001, 1939, or 1995*
—*adv.* **years:** a long time: *That big project will take years to complete.*

year·book /'yɪr,bʊk/ *n.* usu. a book for high school students that records important events: *A high school yearbook has pictures of graduating students.*

year·ling /'yɪrlɪŋ/ *n.* a cow or horse that is one but not two years old: *The farmer puts her yearlings in the barn.*

year·long /'yɪr,lɔŋ/ *adj.* continuing through a year: *In the state of Washington, rain is a yearlong happening.*

year·ly /'yɪrli/ *adv.* during or at the end of a 12-month period: *Americans must file their taxes yearly.*

yearn /yɜrn/ *v.* to feel a strong desire or need for s.t. or s.o., *(syn.)* to long for: *He yearns for a better life.‖She yearns for affection (a loved one, a pet dog, etc.).* -*n.* [C;U] **yearning.**

year-round *adj.* yearlong, continuing throughout the year: *Tennis, swimming, and golf are year-round activities in Florida.*

yeast /yist/ *n.* [U] part of a plant (a fungus) that causes chemical change (fermentation) with many uses, such as in making cheeses, wine, beer, and some breads: *The best yeast for making sourdough bread is found in San Francisco.* -*adj.* **yeasty.**

yeh /'yɛə/ *adv.slang* yes, indeed *See:* yes, USAGE NOTE.

yell /yɛl/ *v.* **1** to shout: *He yelled to a friend across the street.* **2** to cheer, *(syn.)* to root for: *We yell when our team scores a goal.* **3** to complain: *to yell about a high repair bill* **4** to express anger, *(syn.)* to bellow: *The mother yelled at her child to behave.*
—*n.* a shout of recognition, applause, complaint, anger, or disapproval -*n.* [U] **yelling.**

yel·low /'yɛloʊ/ *n.* [U] a primary color, such as the yellow of a lemon
—*adj.infrml.pej.* afraid, *(syn.)* cowardly: *He is yellow and won't fight for his rights.*

yel·low·bel·ly /'yɛloʊ,bɛli/ *n.infrml.fig.* -**lies** a coward: *He's a yellowbelly who runs away from a fight.*

yellow fever *n.* [U] a disease of the tropics carried by mosquitoes and causing a yellowing of the skin, fever, and vomiting: *Medicine has helped stop yellow fever in many countries.*

Yellow Pages *n.* in the USA, a book that lists the telephone numbers and addresses of businesses and professionals arranged by their

goods or services: *If you need to find a doctor, look under "Physicians" in the Yellow Pages.*

yelp /yɛlp/ *v.n.* to make a sharp cry, to yip: *A dog <v.> yelps in pain* (or) *lets out a <n.> yelp.*

yen /yɛn/ *n.* **1** [U] a desire, longing: *He has a yen for the girl next door.* **2** [U] a strong desire, *(syn.)* a craving: *I have a yen for a hamburger and a soda.* **3** [C] the currency of Japan

yeo·man /'yoʊmən/ *n.* -**men** /-mən/ **1** originally, an English farmer who owned and worked his own land, *(syn.)* a freeholder **2** a naval petty officer **3** a good, dependable worker **4 to do yeoman's duty** or **service:** to work dependably and well: *When the hurricane damaged our roof, our neighbor did yeoman's duty and helped me repair it.*

yeow /yaʊ/ **1** *exclam.* of pain: *Yeow! I burned my finger.* **2** *exclam.* of joy or surprise: *Yeow! I've found the answer!*

yep /yɛp/ *adv.slang* yes, indeed *See:* yes, USAGE NOTE.

yes /yɛs/ *adv.* **1** (used to express agreement) affirmatively: *Would you like to go? Yes, I would.* **2** very much so, indeed: *Would you like to drive my new car? Oh, yes, I would!*

USAGE NOTE: The use of *yes, yes, sir,* and *yes, ma'am* is formal. *Yeah, uh-huh, mm-hmm, yep,* and *yup* are informal, and commonly used in everyday conversation: *"Do you know Ann?" "Uh-huh." "Have you seen her today?" "Mm-hmm." "Will she be at the meeting?" "Yup."* The body language for yes is a small, forward nod of the head.

yes man *n.* **men** a person who agrees with everything his or her boss says: *The owner doesn't like yes men; he wants people to say what they think.*

yes·ter·day /'yɛstər,deɪ/ *adv.* the day before today: *It happened yesterday.*
—*n.* recently, in the recent past: *It seems like only yesterday* (or) *just yesterday that we talked, but it was a month ago.*

yes·ter·year /'yɛstər,yɪr/ *n.* in years past: *Some people like to talk about the good old days of yesteryear.*

yet /yɛt/ *adv.* **1** now, presently: *Don't go yet.* **2** up to now, up to the present time: *The mail has not arrived yet* (or) *as yet.* **3** in the future, still: *The mail may yet arrive before we leave.*
—*conj.* nonetheless, still: *He said that he would pay, yet he didn't.*

Yid·dish /'yɪdɪʃ/ *n.* [U] a language based on German and spoken throughout the world by some Jewish people: *The jeweler on 47th Street in New York City speaks Yiddish and five other languages.*

yield /yild/ *v.* **1** to produce s.t. of value: *Her work yielded results.‖Our farm yields 20*

arn money,
at savings
tc.) yields
d to s.o.'s
to yield
y, army,

nds: an
ings of

(syn.)
'ts out

...ciam. of pain or sur-
...pe: *I hurt my foot!*

yip·pee /'yıpi/ *exclam.* of triumph or happiness: *Yippee, I just won the lottery!*

YMCA /'waıemsi'eı/ *n.abbr. for* Young Men's Christian Association. *See:* Y.

YWCA /'waı,dʌbəlyusi'eı/ *n.abbr. for* Young Women's Christian Association: *She has a room at the YWCA.*

yo·del /'youdl/ *v.* to sing in a high voice from the back of the throat: *The cowboy yodels for fun.*

yo·ga /'yougə/ *n.* [U] exercises done to perfect the body and mind: *She learned yoga in order to relax.*

yo·gurt /'yougərt/ *n.* [U] a thick, creamy food made from milk and available plain or fruit flavored: *People eat yogurt for meals or as a dessert or snack.*

yoke /youk/ *n.* **1** a piece of wood fit around the necks of cattle to pull wagons and farm equipment (plows, etc.) **2** *fig.* a sign of slavery: *to live under the yoke of slavery*
—*v.* **yoked, yoking, yokes 1** to fit with a yoke: *the farmer yoked oxen to a plow.* **2** *fig.* to be joined very closely with s.o. or s.t.: *I'm so busy at work that I feel yoked to my desk.*

yo·kel /'youkəl/ *n.pej.* an ordinary country person, *(syn.)* a country bumpkin: *That guy is a yokel; he is not good enough for her.*

yolk /youk/ *n.* [C;U] the yellow part of an egg: *The yolk in a chicken's egg is bright yellow.*

Yom Kip·pur /'yɔm'kıpər, -ki'pur/ *n.* the Day of Atonement: *Yom Kippur is the holiest of Jewish holidays.*

yon·der /'yandər/ *adj.old usage* over there, in the distance: *Cowboys talk about stolen horses in yonder canyon.*
—*n.* the distance, the heavens: *Pilots talk about flying in the wild, blue yonder.*

yore /yɔr/ *n.frml.* old usage the past: *In the days of yore, kings and queens ruled many lands.*

York·shire pudding /'yɔrkʃər/ *n.* a traditional pastry made with milk, flour, and eggs: *Yorkshire pudding is browned on the*

outside *and* served with roast beef.

you /yu/ *pron.* the person or persons being spoken to: *Do you like my new hat?*||*What do you in the audience think of the speaker's talk?*

you all /yɔl/ *pron.infrml.* both of you or all of you: *I'm so glad to see you all. See:* y'all.

you'd /yud/ *contr. of* **1** you would: *You'd be better off going tomorrow.* **2** you had: *You'd better go now before it rains.*

you'll /yul/ *contr. of* **1** you will: *You'll receive it tomorrow.* **2** you shall: *You'll report that robbery to the police!*

young /yʌŋ/ *n.* **-er, -est 1** youth in general: *The young in Europe love American music.* **2** children, offspring, usu. of animals: *Most animals take care of their young for only a short time.*
—*adj.* **1** not old, of few years: *young children* **2** youthful, spirited: *to look (feel, act) young* **3** inexperienced, immature: *That child is too young to understand right from wrong.*

young adult *n.adj.* a person approx. 12–18 years old, *(syn.)* a youth: *Many young adults in our town work after school and on weekends. See:* juvenile, teenager, youth, **1.**

young·ster /'yʌŋstər/ *n.* a young girl or boy older than a baby and younger than a teenager: *That couple has two youngsters, ages eight and ten.*

your /yər; *strong form* yur, yɔr/ *poss.pron.* belonging to the person being spoken to: *Is this your hat (car, project, son, etc.)?*

you're /yur, yɔr/ *contr. of* you are: *You're going with me, aren't you?*

your·self /yər'sɛlf, yur-, yɔr-/ *reflexive pron.* **-selves** related to the person(s) being spoken to: *Are you doing the work yourself (or) yourselves, or having others do it?*

yours /yurz, yɔrz/ *poss.pron.*possessed by the person or persons being spoken to: *Is that car yours?*

yours truly 1 an expression used to end a letter and placed above the signature: *Yours truly, Nancy Mann* **2** *fig.infrml.* me or I: *We were all at the party, including yours truly.*||*Yours truly was there.*

youth /yuθ/ *n.* **1** [U] young people: *The youth of today are worried about jobs.* **2** [C] a young man: *a youth involved in a crime*

youth·ful /'yuθfʊl/ *adj.* typical of the young: *He has youthful good looks.*

you've /yuv/ *contr. of* you have: *You've made me feel better.*

yow /yaʊ/ *exclam.var. of* yeow, expressing joy, surprise, or pain: *Yow! I hurt my foot!*

yowl /yaʊl/ *v.n.* to cry out, *(syn.)* to howl: *That dog <v.> yowls at night; it let out a <n.> yowl at 4:00 a.m.*

Y

o-yo /'you,you/ *n.* **1** a toy that spins up and down on a string moved by the hand **2** *slang* a jerk, an ineffectual person: *My boss is a real yo-yo!*
—*v.fig.infrml.* to move up and down: *The price of oil yo-yoed for months.*

yuck·y /'yʌki/ *adj.slang* **-ier, -iest 1** offensive, disgusting: *That food tastes yucky.* **2** dirty: *Shoes covered with mud look yucky.*

yuk /yʌk/ *v.slang* **yukked, yukking, yuks** to laugh: *Those kids yuk it up all the time.*

Yule·tide /'yul,taɪd/ *n.frml.* [U] Christmas time: *People go to parties during the Yuletide season.*

yum·my /'yʌmi/ *adj.slang* **-mier, -miest** good

tasting: *This chocol*

yum-yum /'yʌm'yʌm*
ful: *Yum-yum! This food*

yup /yʌp/ *adv.slang* yes,
USAGE NOTE.

yup·pie /'yʌpi/ *n.infrml. short for*
professional, a city person who ma
money: *My son is a yuppie who work*
Street, owns a beautiful home, and d
BMW.

USAGE NOTE: *Yuppie* couples without childr
are sometimes called DINKS, which stands for
double-income, no kids.

Y

Z,z

Z, z /zi/ **Z's, z's,** or **Zs, zs** **1** the 26th letter of the English alphabet **2** *pl.fig.infrml.* a sign for sleep: *I am tired; I am going to bed now to get some Z's.*

za·ny /'zeɪni/ *adj.* **-nier, -niest** funny in behavior, like a clown: *That actor does zany things, such as making funny faces.*

zap /zæp/ *v.slang* **zapped, zapping, zaps** **1** to kill with heavy gunfire **2** to criticize severely: *The newspapers zapped that movie; they said it was really bad.* **3** to stop the sound on a TV: *I zap the sound when the commercials come on TV. -n.* **zapper.**

zeal /zil/ *n.* [U] a strong desire and hard work, esp. in a political or religious movement, *(syn.)* great enthusiasm: *Her zeal to help poor people has made their lives better.*

zeal·ous /'zɛləs/ *adj.* having a strong desire to do s.t., *(syn.)* enthusiastic: *He is zealous about going to church everyday. -adv.* **zealously.**

ze·bra /'zibrə/ *n.* **-bras** or **-bra** a horse-like animal with broad white and black stripes: *Lions like to eat zebras.*

zebra

ze·nith /'ziniθ/ *n.* **1** the highest point in a curve or orbit: *The sun is at its zenith around noontime.* **2** the highest point of s.t.: *She is a top lawyer, and her career is at its zenith now.*

zeph·yr /'zɛfər/ *n.frml. litr.* a light, pleasant breeze: *A cooling zephyr feels good on a hot day.*

zep·pel·in /'zɛpəlɪn/ *n.* a large airship, *(syn.)* blimp: *Zeppelins carried passengers in the 1920s.*

ze·ro /'zɪroʊ/ *n.* **-ros** or **-roes** **1** the mathematical symbol (0) that means "nothing" **2** 32 degrees below the freezing p ͮ ͜on the Fahrenheit temperature scale, or ͜ͅe freezing point on the Celsius temperature scale **3** nothing, the lack of s.t.: *All our work came to zero when our computers stopped working.*
—*adj.* characterized by a total lack of s.t.: *zero growth in sales*
—*phrasal v. insep.* **to zero in on s.t.:** to find out s.t. exactly, *(syn.)* to pinpoint: *The electrician (bookkeeper, doctor, etc.) zeroed in on the exact cause of the problem.*

zest /zɛst/ *n.* [U] a feeling of enthusiasm, *(syn.)* gusto: *She has a zest for life. -adj.* **zestful.**

zig·zag /'zɪg,zæg/ *n.v.* **-zagged, -zagging, -zags** to run (move, fly) to the left then right in a generally forward direction: *A soldier <v.> zigzagged to escape from enemy fire.*

zilch /zɪltʃ/ *n.slang* **1** [U] nothing, zero: *a product whose profit is zilch* **2** [C] a dull person who does nothing: *That guy is a zilch; he never works.*

zil·lion /'zɪlyən/ *n.slang* an amount too high to count: *I told you a zillion times not to do that!*

USAGE NOTE: Some people say *jillion* to mean the same thing: He's got about a jillion cookbooks.

zinc /zɪŋk/ *n.* [U] a basic metal with many practical uses, esp. as an alloy: *The abbreviation for zinc is Zn.*

zing /zɪŋ/ *n.infrml.* [U] liveliness, enthusiasm, *(syn.)* vitality: *She's a dancer with a lot of zing.*
—*v.* **1** to travel at high speed: *The baseball zinged past his head.* **2** to criticize: *He zinged me by saying I was stupid. -adj.* **zingy.**

zing·er /'zɪŋər/ *n.slang* a biting remark or criticism: *The sales manager shoots zingers at his sales representatives for not selling enough.*

zip /zɪp/ *v.* **zipped, zipping, zips** **1** to open, close, or fasten with a zipper: *She zipped up her jacket.* **2** to travel or move rapidly: *Cars zipped by on the highway.*
—*n.* **1** *abbr.* for Zip Code **2** *infrml.fig.* enthusiasm, *(syn.)* vigor: *My mother has a lot of zip. -adj.* **zippy.**

Zip Code *n.* in the USA, five numbers or nine numbers added to addresses on letters and other items that indicate their location for postal delivery: *The Zip Code of our office in New York is 10019 or 10019-6845.*

Z

zip·per /'zɪpər/ n. a metal or plastic fastener with teeth, used to open and close clothes, bags, etc.: *Jeans have zippers in the front.*

zit /zɪt/ n.slang a red sore spot on the skin, esp. a large one, *(syn.)* a pimple: *He gets zits on his face from eating too much junk food.*

zo·di·ac /'zoʊdi,æk/ n. a circular picture divided into 12 equal periods with names and signs related to the placement of stars and planets, often used in astrology to tell what a person's life will be like: *The zodiac shows that a person born between November 22 and December 21 is called a Sagittarius.*

zom·bie /'zɑmbi/ n. **1** an imaginary person who turns into a monster and rises from the dead with great strength and the desire to do evil: *Horror movies feature zombies and other monsters.* **2** infrml.fig. a person who acts like a walking dead person, esp. from being very tired: *He stayed up all night at a party, and the next day he was a zombie.*

zone /zoʊn/ n. an area of land or sky marked by a government, business, or person for a special purpose: *The city passed a law to create a business zone on some empty land.*
—v. **zoned, zoning, zones** to say that an area is a zone: *The city zoned the land for business.* -adj. **zonal.**

zonked /zɔŋkt, zɑŋkt/ adj.slang **1** very tired, nearly asleep from alcohol, drugs, or overwork **2 to be zonked out:** *He is zonked out from drinking and lack of sleep.*

zoo /zu/ n. **1** a place where animals are displayed in cages, *(syn.)* a zoological garden **2** infrml.fig. a place of confusion and often bad behavior: *The sale in the department store was a zoo, with people pushing each other to get cheap clothing.*

zo·o·log·i·cal garden /,zoʊə'lɑdʒəkəl/ n.frml. a park where people can see animals in cages and fenced off areas: *The New York Zoological Garden is a delight, esp. for city children.* See: zoo, **1.**

zo·ol·o·gy /zoʊ'ɑlədʒi/ n. [U] **1** the science of animals **2** a course or courses in the study of animal life: *He studied zoology in college before he became a veterinarian.* -n. **zoologist** -adj. **zoological** /,zoʊə'lɑdʒəkəl/.

zoom /zum/ v. **1** to move quickly (fly an airplane, drive a car): *A plane zooms into the air on takeoff.* **2** to dive down, *(syn.)* to swoop: *A jet fighter zoomed down on the enemy.* **3 to zoom in on s.t.:** to move a camera picture in closely: *A cameraman zoomed in on the fire with a zoom lens.*
—n. quick movement the sound made by a speeding object

zuc·chi·ni /zu'kini/ n. **-ni** or **-nis** a long round green-skinned vegetable related to the squash: *He ate meat with potatoes and zucchini as the vegetables.*

zucchini

APPENDIXES

American and Contemporary Cultural Terms

aerobics
African American
AIDS
American Dream
antiperspirant
associate degree
ATM
B.A.
bag lady
Band-Aid™
barbecue or BBQ
baseball
basketball
bebop
bed and breakfast
bicameral
Bill of Rights
biodegradable
bluegrass
cheerleader
cable TV
chuck
CIA
citizens band
civil rights
club sandwich
compact disc
convenience store
cost-of-living index
counterculture
country music or country and
    western
county
cowboy
cowgirl
cracker
cranberry
cruiser
Day-Glo
dean's list
delicatessen
Democrat
Democratic Party
denim
depression
desegregation
disabled

discount rate
district attorney or D.A.
district court
Dixie
Dixieland jazz
DJ
doggie bag or doggy bag
dollar sign
down-home
drive-in
drive-up window
dungarees
dysfunction
Electoral College
elevatedtrain or railway
Emmy
Equal Rights Amendment or
    ERA
fanny pack
fast food
Father's Day
FDA
Fed
Federal Bureau of
    Investigation, FBI
Federal Reserve System
Ferris wheel
Fifth Amendment
filibuster
filling station
first base
first lady or First Lady
First World War
folk music
founding father
Fourth of July
fraternity
french dressing
frontier
frontiersman
garage sale
GED
Generation X
glass ceiling
GOP
green card
greenhouse effect

grits
groovy
grunge
Hall of Fame
Halloween
hamburger
hearing-impaired
HMO
homecoming
hot dog
housewarming
information superhighway
in-line skates
jack-o'lantern
jazz
Jell-O
jerkwater
John Doe or Jane Doe
Joint Chiefs of Staff
junior college
junior high school
junk mail
latchkey child
law
left field
lending library
Little League
living room
lobster
loop
LPN
lunch counter
Marine Corps
Master's Degree (M.A.)
Mayflower
Medal of Honor
melting pot
Memorial Day
mom-and-pop store
MPH
Ms.
NAACP
NASA
national park
NOW
nuke
Oscar

American and Contemporary Cultural Terms, continued:

package store
Peace Corps
peanut butter
picket line
politically correct
primary
prohibition
primary school
pro-choice
rap
Republican
rock and roll or rock-n-roll
Roller Derby
self-service or serve
service charge
service station
sexism
shopping mall
shrink wrap
Silicon Valley
singles bar
sitcom or situation comedy
skateboard
skinhead
sneaker
sneaker
soap opera
social security
soft drink
soft rock
software
sorority
soul food
space shuttle
spare ribs
square dance
Star Spangled Banner
Stars and Stripes
Statue of Liberty
Sunbelt
sundae
Super Bowl
Superman
supermarket
Supreme Court
teddy bear
teenybopper
tepee
telecommuter
ten-gallon hat
Thanksgiving Day
third class
third world

tokenism
tom-tom
ton
tongue
totem
totem pole
touchdown
trade school
Treasury bill or T-bill
Treasury bond
Treasury note
trick or treat
trillion
triple
trooper
twang
veep
vegetarian
vocational school
Wall Street
Washington's Birthday
wax bean
wellness concept
west
Western
White House
wigwam
workers' compensation
workfare
World Series
Xerox
X-mas
y'all

Business Terms

account executive
acquisition
administer
administration
administrative
administrator
agenda
agent
allowance
analysis
analyst
annuity
antitrust
applicant
application
apply
appointment
appraisal

appraise
appreciable
appreciate
appreciation
arrears
assess
assessment
asset
assignable
attaché case
audit
auditor
balance of payments or trade
balance sheet
bank
bank account
bankbook
banker
bankroll
bankrupt
bankruptcy
belt
bills
blue-collar
board
bond
bookkeeper
borrowing(s)
bottom line
branch
brand
brand name
broker
brokerage
budget
business card
businesslike
businessman
businesswoman
buyer
cancel
canned
capacity
capital
capital asset
capital gain
capitalization
capitalize
cash
cash flow
certificate of deposit or CD
certified check
chamber of commerce

Business Terms, continued:

charge
chargeable
charge account
charge card
Chief Financial Officer
clear
clearinghouse
clerical
clerk
client
clientele
clock
close
close-out
COBOL
C.O.D. or COD
collection agency
collective
collective bargaining
commercial bank
commission
Common Market
common stock
comp time
company
competition
competitor
complaint
comp time
comptroller
conference
conference call
conglomerate
consumer
consumer credit
consumer goods
consumer price index
contract
contractor
controller
cooperative
copyright
corporate
corporation
cosign
cost
cost-effective
cost of living
cost-of-living adjustment
cost-of-living index
count
counteroffer
countersign
coupon

cover
coverage
cover letter
coworker
CPA
crash
credentials
credit
credit card
credit line
credit limit
credit memo or credit slip
creditor
credit rating
current
custodian
custom
customer
customize
custom-made
cutback
database
data entry
data processing
deadline
deal
dealer
dealership
dealings
debit
debt
debtor
declaration
deductible
deed
deficit
deficit financing
deficit spending
delinquent
demand-pull inflation
demote
depreciate
depreciation
depressed
depression
deregulate
desktop computer
devaluate
differential
dilute
diminishing returns
directorate
directorship
disbursal

discount
discount rate
disinflation
disinvestment
disposable
distributing
distribution
distributor
diversification
divest
divestiture
dividend
division
documentation
dog-eat-dog
dollar
dollar diplomacy
dollar sign
domino effect
double-dip
double entry
doughnut or donut
Dow Jones Average
down payment
downscale
downsize
downtime
downtrend
downturn
dump
European Union
face value
Fed
Federal Reserve System
file clerk
finance
finance charge
financial
financial institution
financial markets
financial statement
financial year
financier
financing
fire
firm
fiscal
flat
float
flow chart
fold
Food and Drug
   Administration
foreclose

1009

Business Terms, continued:

foreign exchange	insurance policy	livelihood
forfeit	insure	loading dock
forfeiture	insured	loaner
forgery	insurer	loan shark
formulation	intangible	lobby
forwarder	interest	lockout
401(k) plan	Internal Revenue Service	logo
fourth estate	inventory	loss
franc	invest	lot
franchise	investor	lucrative
franchisee	invoice	marketplace
franchiser	itemize	market research
fraudulent	Jaycees	marketshare
free enterprise	jingle	money
free-floating	job	money-order
free market	job action	monopolize
fringe benefit	joint venture	odd lot
front office	journal	offer
fungible	journeyman	office
game plan	kickback	off-line
gilt-edged	labor	offshore
glass ceiling	Labor Day	off-site
glut	laborer	open
GMAT	labor-saving	opening
GNP	labor union	open-market
grace period	laissez-faire	operating expense
gross	landlady, landlord	option
gross domestic product	larceny	order
gross national product (GNP)	launder	organization
growth	Laundromat	outbid
growth fund	lawsuit	outgo
growth rate	lawyer	outlay
guarantee	ledger	outlet
guarantor	legal holiday	out-of-pocket
hardball	lend	outplacement
hedge	lessor	output
help	let	outside
higher-up	letterhead	outsourcing
high roller	letter of credit	overage
hockshop	levy	overcharge
holding	liability	overestimate
holding company	liaison	overextended
honorarium	licensee	overhead
hostile takeover	lien	overqualified
hot line	lieu	oversee
house	life insurance	oversell
housecleaning	line	overspend
household word	line of credit	over-the-counter
human resources or HR	liquid	overtime
incentive	liquidate	partner
indemnify	list	partnership
inflation	listing	part-time
infrastructure	litigant	pay
insurance	litigate	payback

Business Terms, continued:

paycheck
payday
payee
payer
payout
payroll
personnel
plow
point
policy
portfolio
position
pretax
price
price index
price war
prime rate
principal
private enterprise
procure
product
productivity
profit
profitable
profit and loss or P & L
profiteer
profit sharing
promote
promotion
proprietary
prospectus
public
purchasing power
savings account
stagflation
standard of living
standard operating procedure
  or SOP
table
tackle
take-home pay
takeover
tally
target market
tariff
taskmaster
tax
taxation
tax credit
tax cut
tax-deductible
tax deduction
tax evasion
tax-exempt

taxing
taxpayer
tax return
tax shelter
tax write-off
teamster
technician
technocrat
Teflon
telecommunication
telecommuter
teleconference
telex
temp
temporary employee or worker
tenant farmer
tender
terms
test-drive
test market
third party
ticker
time
time and a half
time card or sheet
time-share
time sheet
timetable
title
titleholder
titular
tokenism
toll
toll call
total quality management,
  TQM
track record
trade
trade deficit
trade discount
trade-in
trade journal
trademark
trade name, brand name
trade-off
trader
trade route
trade school
trade secret
tradesman or -person
trading post
traffic
trainee
transaction

transfer
transferal
travel agency
travel agent
traveler's check
traveling representative or
  salesperson
treasurer
treasury
Treasury bill, T-bill
Treasury bond
Treasury note
trust
trust company
trust department
trustee
trusteeship
trust fund
turnover
tycoon
underbid
undercut
underdeveloped
underemployed
underestimate
understaffed
underwrite
unemployable
unemployed
unemployment
unemployment compensation
union
unionize
unprofessional
unprofitable
wage
wage earner
wage level
wage scale
walking papers
walkout
Wall Street
welfare
white-collar
white sale
wholesale
wildcat
window-shop
workday or working day
worker
workers' compensation
work ethic
workfare
workforce

Business Terms, continued:

working capital
working class
working papers
working visa
workload
workmanlike
workmanship
workmen's compensation
work permit
work release
work stoppage
workweek
write
write-down
write-off
yield

Technology Terms

bug
byte
CD-ROM
COBOL
compatible
compiler
computer
computerize
computer language
crash
cyberspace
data
database
data entry
data processing
debug
dedicated
depress
desktop computer
digitize
disk
disk drive
diskette
document
documentation
down
download
drive
dump
electronic mail or E-mail
feedback
file
file name
flame
floppy
floppy disk

floppy disk or diskette
fluorocarbon
flow chart
font
FORTRAN
gateway
gigabyte
gopher
grayscale
GUI
hacker
hard copy
hardware
hertz
icon
import
incomparable
information superhighway
input
interface
italic
Internet
k or K
keyboard
kilobyte
language
laptop
laserdisc
line
log
lurk
mainframe
megabyte
megahertz
modem
mouse
multimedia
multimedia player
multitasking
multiplex
network
off-line
online
online or on-line
operating system
output
PC
peripheral
personal computer
photocopy
port
print
printer
printout

process
processor
program
programmer
programming
RAM
server
technician
technocrat
technology
telecommuter
teleconference
telemetry
telephone
teleprocessing
telex
template
terminal
toggle
transistor
type
typeset
upgrade
user-friendly
virtual reality
VCR, videocassette recorder
window
word processing
word processor
word wrap
workstation
World Wide Web

2. GRAMMAR AND PUNCTUATION TERMS THAT ARE DICTIONARY ENTRIES

The following terms are defined and explained in *The Newbury House Dictionary of American English*. In many cases, the notation "(in grammar)" is used to help one find the grammatical meaning of a given word.

adjective
adverb
be (verb chart)
clause
colon
comma
comparative (form of adjectives)
conjunction
contraction
do (auxiliary verb)
exclamation point
feminine (gender of nouns)
have (auxiliary verb)
imperative
indefinite article
indicative
indirect object
infinitive
intransitive (verb)
masculine (gender of nouns)
modal auxiliary
modifier
mood (e.g., conditional)
neuter (gender of nouns)
nominative
nonrestrictive (e.g., clause)
noun
object
parentheses
part of speech
participle

passive
past participle
past tense
period
perfect
personal pronoun
phrasal verb
phrase
pluperfect
preposition
present participle
present perfect
present tense
pronoun
punctuation
punctuation mark
qualifier
quantifier
question mark
quotation marks
reflexive (pronoun)
run-on
semi-colon
sentence
spelling
subject
subjunctive
superlative (form of adjectives)
tense
transitive (verb)
verb

3. COUNTRIES/NATIONALITIES/LANGUAGES

Country	Nationality	Language(s)
Afghanistan	Afghan(s)	Pashtu, Afghan Persian
Albania	Albanian(s)	Albanian, Greek
Algeria	Algerian(s)	Arabic, French
American Samoa	American Samoan(s)	Samoan, English
Andorra	Andorran(s)	Catalan, French
Angola	Angolan(s)	Portuguese
Anguilla	Anguillan(s)	English
Antigua and Barbuda	Antiguan(s), Barbudan(s)	English
Argentina	Argentine(s)	Spanish, English, Italian
Armenia	Armenian(s)	Armenian, Russian
Aruba	Aruban(s)	Dutch, Papiamento
Australia	Australian(s)	English
Austria	Austrian(s)	German
Azerbaijan	Azerbaijani(s)	Azeri, Russian, Armenian
The Bahamas	Bahamian(s)	English, Creole
Bahrain	Bahraini(s)	Arabic, English, Farsi
Bangladesh	Bangladeshi(s)	Bangla, English
Barbados	Barbadian(s)	English
Belarus	Belarusian(s)	Byelorussian, Russian
Belgium	Belgian(s)	Flemish, French
Belize	Belizean(s)	English, Spanish, Maya
Benin	Beninese	French, Fon, Yoruba
Bermuda	Bermudian(s)	English
Bhutan	Bhutanese	Dzongkha
Bolivia	Bolivian(s)	Spanish, Quechua, Aymara
Bosnia and Herzegovina	Bosnian(s), Herzegovinian(s)	Serbo-Croatian
Botswana	Motswana (*sing.*), Batswana (*pl.*)	English, Setswana
Brazil	Brazilian(s)	Portuguese, Spanish, English
British Virgin Islands	British Virgin Islander(s)	English
Brunei	Bruneian(s)	Malay, English, Chinese
Bulgaria	Bulgarian(s)	Bulgarian
Burma	Burmese	Burmese
Burundi	Burundian(s)	Kirundi, French, Swahili
Cambodia	Cambodian(s)	Khmer, French
Cameroon	Cameroonian(s)	English, French
Canada	Canadian(s)	English, French
Cape Verde	Cape Verdean(s)	Portuguese, Crioulo
Cayman Islands	Caymanian(s)	English
Central African Rep.	Central African(s)	French
Chad	Chadian	French, Arabic

Country	Nationality	Language(s)
China	Chinese	Standard Chinese or Mandarin
Colombia	Colombian(s)	Spanish
Congo	Congolese	French, African languages
Costa Rica	Costa Rican(s)	Spanish, English
Croatia	Croat(s)	Serbo-Croation
Cuba	Cuban(s)	Spanish
Cyprus	Cypriot(s)	Greek, Turkish, English
Czech Republic	Czech(s)	Czech, Slovak
Denmark	Dane(s)	Danish, Faroese
Djibouti	Djiboutian(s)	French, Arabic
Dominican Republic	Dominican(s)	Spanish
Ecuador	Ecuadorian(s)	Spanish
Egypt	Egyptian(s)	Arabic, English, French
El Salvador	Salvadoran(s)	Spanish
Eritrea	Eritrean(s)	Tigre and Kunama
Estonia	Estonian(s)	Estonian, Latvian, Lithuanian
Ethiopia	Ethiopian(s)	Amharic
Finland	Finn(s)	Finnish, Swedish
France	Frenchman, Frenchwoman	French
Georgia	Georgian(s)	Georgian, Armenian, Azerbaijani
Germany	German(s)	German
Ghana	Ghanaian(s)	English, African languages
Greece	Greek(s)	Greek, English, French
Haiti	Haitian(s)	French, Creole
Honduras	Honduran(s)	Spanish
Hong Kong	Chinese	Chinese, English
Hungary	Hungarian(s)	Hungarian
Iceland	Icelander(s)	Icelandic
India	Indian(s)	English, Hindi, Bengali, Telugu, Marathi, Tamil, Urdu, Gujarati, Malayalam, Kannada, Oriya, Punjabi, Assamese, Kashmiri, Sindhi, Sanskrit
Indonesia	Indonesian(s)	Bahasa Indonesia, English, Dutch
Iran	Iranian(s)	Persian, Turkic, Kurdish
Iraq	Iraqi(s)	Arabic, Kurdish, Assyrian
Ireland	Irishman, Irishwoman, Irish	Irish (Gaelic), English
Israel	Israeli(s)	Hebrew, Arabic, English
Italy	Italian(s)	Italian, German
Ivory Coast	Ivorian(s)	French
Jamaica	Jamaican(s)	English, Creole
Japan	Japanese	Japanese
Jordan	Jordanian(s)	Arabic
Kazakhstan	Kazakhstani(s)	Kazakh, Russian

Country	Nationality	Language(s)
Kenya	Kenyan(s)	English, Swahili
North Korea	Korean(s)	Korean
South Korea	Korean(s)	Korean
Kuwait	Kuwaiti(s)	Arabic
Kyrgyzstan	Kirghiz(s)	Kirghiz, Russian
Laos	Lao(s) or Laotian(s)	Lao, French, English
Latvia	Latvian(s)	Latvian, Lithuanian, Russian
Lebanon	Lebanese	Arabic, French
Lesotho	Mosotho(singular), Basotho(plural)	Sesotho, English
Liberia	Liberian(s)	English
Libya	Libyan(s)	Arabic, Italian, English
Liechtenstein	Liechtensteiner(s)	German
Lithuania	Lithuanian(s)	Lithuanian, Polish, Russian
Luxembourg	Luxembourger(s)	Luxembourgisch, German, French
Macedonia	Macedonian(s)	Macedonian, Albanian
Madagascar	Malagasy	French, Malagasy
Malawi	Malawian(s)	English, Chichewa
Malaysia	Malaysian(s)	Malay, English, Chinese
Malta	Maltese	Maltese, English
Martinique	Martiniquais	French, Creole patois
Mauritania	Mauritanian(s)	Hasaniya Arabic, Wolof
Mauritius	Mauritian(s)	English, Creole, French
Mexico	Mexican(s)	Spanish
Micronesia	Micronesian(s)	English, Trukese
Moldova	Moldovan(s)	Moldovan, Russian
Monaco	Monacan(s) or Monegasque(s)	French, English, Italian
Mongolia	Mongolian(s)	Khalkha Mongol, Turkic
Morocco	Moroccan(s)	Arabic, Berber, French
Mozambique	Mozambican(s)	Portuguese
Namibia	Namibian(s)	English, Afrikaans, German
Nepal	Nepalese	Nepali
Netherlands	Dutchman, Dutchwoman	Dutch
New Zealand	New Zealander(s)	English, Maori
Nicaragua	Nicaraguan(s)	Spanish, English
Niger	Nigerien(s)	French, Hausa
Nigeria	Nigerian(s)	English, Hausa
Norway	Norwegian(s)	Norwegian
Oman	Omani(s)	Arabic, English
Pakistan	Pakistani(s)	Urdu, English
Panama	Panamanian(s)	Spanish, English
Papua New Guinea	Papua New Guinean(s)	English
Paraguay	Paraguayan(s)	Spanish, Guarani
Peru	Peruvian(s)	Spanish, Quechua
Philippines	Filipino(s)	Pilipino, English
Poland	Pole(s)	Polish
Portugal	Portuguese	Portuguese
Puerto Rico	Puerto Rican(s)	Spanish, English

Country	Nationality	Language(s)
Qatar	Qatari(s)	Arabic, English
Romania	Romanian(s)	Romanian, Hungarian, German
Russia	Russian(s)	Russian
Rwanda	Rwandan(s)	Kinyarwanda, French
Saudi Arabia	Saudi(s)	Arabic
Senegal	Senegalese	French, Wolof
Serbia and Montenegro	Serb(s) and Montenegrin(s)	Serbo-Croatian, Albanian
Sierra Leone	Sierra Leonean	English, Mende, Temne
Singapore	Singaporean(s)	Chinese, Malay, Tamil, English
Slovakia	Slovak(s)	Slovak, Hungarian
Slovenia	Slovene(s)	Slovenian, Serbo-Croatian
Somalia	Somali(s)	Somali, Arabic, Italian
South Africa	South African(s)	Afrikaans, English, Zulu
Spain	Spaniard(s)	Castilian Spanish, Catalan
Sri Lanka	Sri Lankan(s)	Sinhala, Tamil
Sudan	Sudanese	Arabic, Nubian
Swaziland	Swazi(s)	English, Swati
Sweden	Swede(s)	Swedish
Switzerland	Swiss	German, French, Italian, Romansch
Syria	Syrian(s)	Arabic, Kurdish
Taiwan	Chinese	Madarin Chinese, Taiwanese
Tajikistan	Tajik(s)	Tajik
Tanzania	Tanzanian(s)	Swahili, English
Thailand	Thai	Thai, English
Togo	Togolese	French, Ewe
Trinidad and Tobago	Trinidadian(s), Tobagian(s)	English, Hindi
Tunisia	Tunisian(s)	Arabic, French
Turkey	Turk(s)	Turkish, Kurdish, Arabic
Turkmenistan	Turkmen(s)	Turkmen, Russian
Uganda	Ugandan(s)	English, Luganda
Ukraine	Ukrainian(s)	Ukrainian, Russian, Romanian, Polish
United Arab Emirates	Emirian(s)	Arabic, Persian
United Kingdom	Briton(s), British	English, Welsh, Scottish form of Gaelic
United States of America	American(s)	English, Spanish
Uruguay	Uruguayan(s)	Spanish
Uzbekistan	Uzbek(s)	Uzbek, Russian
Venezuela	Venezuelan(s)	Spanish
Vietnam	Vietnamese	Vietnamese, French, Chinese
Western Sahara	Sahrawi(s), Sahraoui(s)	Hassaniya Arabic
Western Samoa	Western Samoan(s)	Samoan, English
Yemen	Yemeni(s)	Arabic
Zaire	Zairian(s)	French, Lingala
Zambia	Zambian(s)	English
Zimbabwe	Zimbabwean(s)	English, Shona

4. IRREGULAR VERBS

Simple Form	Past	Past Participle
be	was, were	been
become	became	become
beat	beat	beaten
bend	bent	bent
begin	begin	begin
bite	bite	bite
blow	blow	blow
break	broke	broken
bring	brought	brought
build	built	built
buy	bought	bought
catch	caught	caught
choose	chose	chosen
come	came	come
cost	cost	cost
cut	cut	cut
do	did	done
draw	drew	drawn
drink	drank	drunk
drive	drove	driven
eat	ate	eaten
fall	fell	fallen
feel	felt	felt
fight	fought	fought
find	found	found
fit	fit	fit
fly	flew	flown
forget	forgot	forgotten
forgive	forgave	forgiven
freeze	froze	frozen
get	got	gotten
give	gave	given
go	went	gone
grow	grew	grown
hang	hung	hanged/hung
have	had	had
hear	heard	heard
hide	hid	hidden

Simple Form	Past Form	Past Participle Form
hit	hit	hit
hold	held	held
hurt	hurt	hurt
keep	kept	kept
know	knew	known
lay	laid	laid
lead	led	led
leave	left	left
lend	lent	lent
let	let	let
light	lit	lit
lie (down)	lay	lain
lie (untruth)	lied	lied
lose	lost	lost
make	made	made
mean	meant	meant
meet	met	met
pay	paid	paid
put	put	put
quit	quit	quit
read	read	read
ride	rode	ridden
ring	rang	rung
rise	rose	risen
run	ran	run
say	said	said
see	saw	seen
sell	sold	sold
send	sent	sent
set	set	set
shake	shook	shaken
shine	shone	shone
shoot	shot	shot
shut	shut	shut
sing	sang	sung
sit	sat	sat
sleep	slept	slept
slide	slid	slid
speak	spoke	spoken
spend	spent	spent
split	split	split
spread	spread	spread
stand	stood	stood
steal	stole	stolen

Simple Form	Past Form	Past Participle Form
stick	stuck	stuck
sting	stung	stung
sweep	swept	swept
swim	swam	swum
swing	swung	swung
take	took	taken
teach	taught	taught
tear	tore	torn
tell	told	told
think	thought	thought
throw	threw	thrown
understand	understood	understood
wake	woke	woken
wear	wore	worn
win	won	won
write	wrote	written

5. Major World Religions

Religion	Believer	Deity
Buddhism	Buddhist	Siddhartha Gautama, the Buddha
Hinduism	Hindu	multitude of Gods
Islam	Moslem/Muslim	Allah
Judaism	Jew, Jewish	God the coming Messiah
Christianity	Christian	God (Creator, Father) Jesus Christ (Redeemer, Son) Holy Spirit (Sustainer)

Major Christian Denominations:

Baptist

Christian Science

Church of England/Anglicanism

The Church of Jesus Christ of Latter-Day Saints

Congregationalism

Coptic Church

The Episcopal Church (The Church of England
   as established in the USA)

Jehovah's Witness

Lutheran Church

Methodist

Orthodox Church

Protestantism

Quaker

(Roman) Catholicism

Seventh Day Advent

6. GEOGRAPHICAL FEATURES: CONTINENTS, MOUNTAINS, AND MAJOR BODIES OF WATER

The Continents

Name	Area in sq. miles
Asia	17,128,500
Africa	11,707,000
North America	9,363,000
South America	6,875,000
Antarctica	5,500,000
Europe	4,057,000
Australia	2,966,136

Oceans and Major Seas

Name	Area in sq. miles
Pacific Ocean	64,186,000
Atlantic Ocean	31,862,000
Indian Ocean	28,350,000
Arctic Ocean	5,427,000
Caribbean Sea	970,000
Mediterranean Sea	969,000
South China Sea	895,000
Bering Sea	875,000
Gulf of Mexico	600,000
Sea of Okhotsk	590,000

Principal Mountains

Name	Country	Height in feet
Mt. Everest	China/Nepal	29,028
K-2	China/Pakistan	28,250
Communism Peak	Tajikistan	24,590
Aconcagua	Argentina	22,831
Mt. McKinley	USA	20,320
Mt. Logan	Canada	19,524
Citlaltépetl	Mexico	18,701
Damavand	Iran	18,606
Mt. Elbrus	Russia	18,510
Jaya Peak	Indonesia	16,503

Longest Rivers

Name	Continent/Country	Length in miles
Nile	Egypt	4,145
Amazon	Brazil	4,000
Yangtze	China	3,915
Mississippi/Missouri	USA	3,740
Ob/Irtysh	Russia/Kazakhstan	3,362
Huang	China	2,877
Congo	Zaire	2,900
Paraná	Brazil	2,796
Lena	Russia	2,734
Mekong	Vietnam	2,600

Principal Natural Lakes

Name	Country	Area in square miles
Caspian Sea	Asia	143,243
Lake Superior	USA/Canada	31,820
Lake Victoria	Africa	26,724
Lake Huron	USA/Canada	23,010
Lake Michigan	USA	22,400
Aral Sea	Kazakhstan/Uzbekistan	15,830
Lake Tanganyika	Africa	12,650
Lake Baykal	Russia	12,162
Great Bear Lake	Canada	12,096
Lake Nyasa	Africa	11,555

THE WORLD

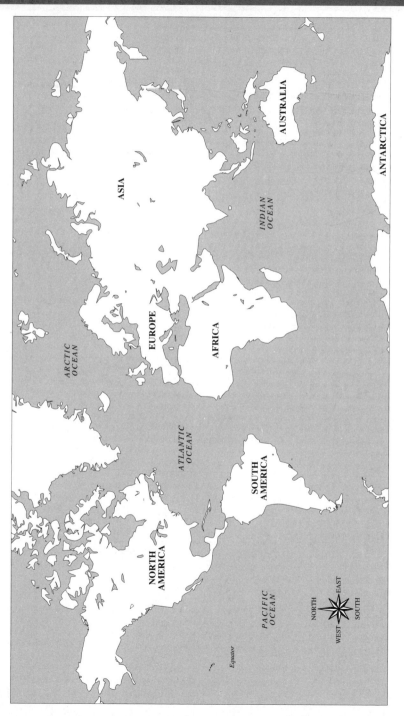

BAHAMAS

GUATEMALA

CUBA

DOMINICAN REPUBLIC

JAMAICA

BELIZE

PUERTO RICO

HONDURAS

HAITI

VIRGIN ISLANDS

DOMINICA

MARTINIQUE

NICARAGUA

ST. LUCIA

BARBADOS

EL
SALVADOR

GRENADA

TRINIDAD & TOBAGO

COSTA
RICA

VENEZUELA

PANAMA

FRENCH GUIANA

COLOMBIA

GUYANA

ECUADOR

SURINAME

PERU

BRAZIL

PACIFIC
OCEAN

BOLIVIA

CHILE

PARAGUAY

URUGUAY

ATLANTIC
OCEAN

ARGENTINA

NORTH

WEST

EAST

SOUTH

Europe, Africa, Asia, and Australia

ARCTIC OCEAN

GREENLAND

Alaska (U.S.)

Baffin Bay

Yukon Territory

Northwest Territories

Hudson Bay

Newfoundland

British Columbia

Alberta

C A N A D A

Manitoba

Saskatchewan

Ontario

Quebec

Prince Edward Island

New Hampshire

New Brunswick

Washington

Montana

North Dakota

Minnesota

Vermont

Maine

Nova Scotia

Oregon

Idaho

South Dakota

Wisconsin

Massachusetts

Wyoming

Michigan

New York

Rhode Island

Connecticut

Nevada

Utah

Nebraska

Iowa

Ohio

Pennsylvania

New Jersey

California

Colorado

Kansas

Illinois

Indiana

West Virginia

Maryland

Delaware

U N I T E D   S T A T E S

Missouri

Kentucky

Virginia

Washington, D.C.

Arizona

New Mexico

Oklahoma

Arkansas

Tennessee

North Carolina

South Carolina

Mississippi

Alabama

Georgia

ATLANTIC OCEAN

Texas

Louisiana

PACIFIC OCEAN

Florida

Hawaii

MEXICO

Gulf of Mexico

PUERTO RICO

NORTH

WEST   EAST

SOUTH

8. ADDRESSES OF ORGANIZATIONS AND SELECTED EMBASSIES

The following is a listing of some organizations and selected embassies that can provide information on studying English either in the United States or elsewhere. It is only a partial listing and is not meant to be comprehensive.

Department of Education,
Div. of Community Colleges
325 West Gaines St. Rm 1314 FEC
Talahasse, FL 32399-0400
(904) 488- 0555

International Institute of Learning
110 E. 59th St., 6th Floor
New York, NY 10022
(212) 758- 0177

NAFSA Association of International
Educators
1875 Connecticut Ave., N.W.
Suite 1000
Washington, D.C. 20009-5728
(202) 462-4811

Teachers of English to Speakers of Other
Languages (TESOL)
1600 Cameron Street, Suite 300
Alexandria, VA 22314-2751
(703) 836-0774

Texas Education Agency
Bilingual Education
1701 North Congress St.
Austin, TX 78701
(512) 475- 3555

Truman College
1145 West Wilson St.
Chicago, IL 60640
(312) 878- 1700

United States Information Agency
301 4th St. Southwest
Washington DC 20547
(202) 619-4700

University of California
Office of the President
Academic Advancement
300 Lakeside Dr. 18th Floor
Oakland, CA 94612- 3550
(510) 987- 9479

World Learning
PO Box 676
Brattleboro, VT 05302
(802) 257-7751

US Embassies

Brazil:
SES, Av. das Nacoes, Lote 3,
70403 Brasilia, DF
tel# (55) 61 321-7272

Colombia:
Calle 38, No 8- 61,
Apdo Aereo 3831
Santa Fe de Bogota DC
tel# (57) 1 320-1300

Japan:
1-10-5 Akasaka,
Mianato-ku
Tokyo 107
tel# (81) 3 3224-5000

Mexico:
Paseo de la Reforma 305,
Col. Cuauhtemoc
06500 Mexico DF
tel# (52) 5 211-0042

Republic of Korea:
82 Sejong-no, Chongno-ku
Seoul
tel# (82) 2 397-4114

9. Days of the Week, Months of the Year, Ordinal and Cardinal Numbers, Weights and Measures, Temperature Chart

Numbers

Cardinal		Ordinal
1	one	first
2	two	second
3	three	third
4	four	fourth
5	five	fifth
6	six	sixth
7	seven	seventh
8	eight	eighth
9	nine	ninth
10	ten	tenth
11	eleven	
12	twelve	
13	thirteen	
14	fourteen	
15	fifteen	
16	sixteen	
17	seventeen	
18	eighteen	
19	nineteen	
20	twenty	
21	twenty-one	
22	twenty-two	
23	twenty-three	
30	thirty	
40	fourty	
50	fifty	
60	sixty	
70	seventy	
80	eighty	
90	ninety	
100	one hundred	
200	two hundred	
1000	one thousand	
10,000	ten thousand	
100,000	one hundred thousand	
1,000,000	one million	

Days of the Week

Sunday
Monday
Tuesday
Wednesday
Thursday
Friday
Saturday

Months of the Year

January	July
February	August
March	September
April	October
May	November
June	December

Standard Weights and Measurements

1 pound (lb.) = 453.6 grams (g.)
16 ounces (oz.) = 1 pound (lb.)
2,000 pounds (lb.) = 1 ton

1 inch (in., or ") = 2.54 centimeters (cm)
1 foot (ft., or ') = 0.3048 meters (m)
1 mile (mi.) = 1.609 kilometers (km)
12 inches = 1 foot (1') (12")
3 feet = 1 yard (yd.) (3')
1 mile = 5,280 feet (5,280')

Temperature chart: Celsius and Fahrenheit

degrees (°) Celsius (C) = 5/9(degrees Fahrenheit −32)
degrees (°) Fahrenheit (F) = (9/5 degrees Celsius) +32

C:	100°	30°	25°	20°	15°
F:	212°	86°	77°	68°	59°

C:	10°	5°	0°	-5°
F:	50°	41°	32°	23°

10. PARTS OF THE BODY

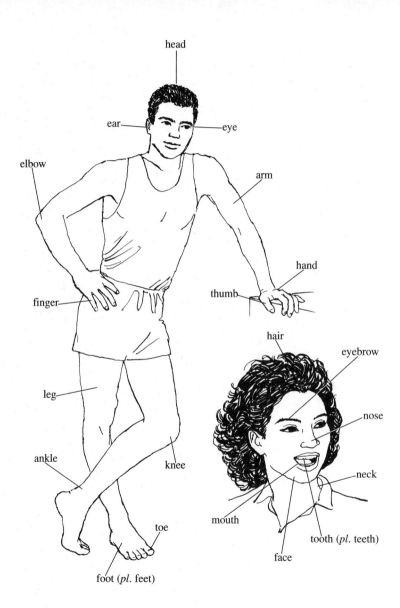

head

ear — — eye

elbow

arm

hand

thumb

finger

hair

eyebrow

nose

leg

ankle

knee

neck

mouth

tooth (*pl.* teeth)

toe

face

foot (*pl.* feet)

II. US STATES, CAPITALS, AND POSTAL ABBREVIATIONS

State	Capital	P.A.	State	Capital	P.A.
Alabama	Montgomery	AL	Montana	Helena	MT
Alaska	Juneau	AK	Nebraska	Lincoln	NE
Arizona	Phoenix	AZ	Nevada	Carson City	NV
Arkansas	Little Rock	AR	New Hampshire	Concord	NH
California	Sacramento	CA	New Jersey	Trenton	NJ
Colorado	Denver	CO	New Mexico	Santa Fe	NM
Connecticut	Hartford	CT	New York	Albany	NY
Delaware	Dover	DE	North Carolina	Raleigh	NC
Florida	Tallahassee	FL	North Dakota	Bismarck	ND
Georgia	Atlanta	GA	Ohio	Columbus	OH
Hawaii	Honolulu	HI	Oklahoma	Oklahoma City	OK
Idaho	Boise	ID	Oregon	Salem	OR
Illinois	Springfield	IL	Pennsylvania	Harrisburg	PA
Indiana	Indianapolis	IN	Rhode Island	Providence	RI
Iowa	Des Moines	IA	South Carolina	Columbia	SC
Kansas	Topeka	KS	South Dakota	Pierre	SD
Kentucky	Frankfort	KY	Tennessee	Nashville	TN
Louisiana	Baton Rouge	LA	Texas	Austin	TX
Maine	Augusta	ME	Utah	Salt Lake City	UT
Maryland	Annapolis	MD	Vermont	Montpelier	VT
Massachusetts	Boston	MA	Virginia	Richmond	VA
Michigan	Lansing	MI	Washington	Olympia	WA
Minnesota	St. Paul	MN	West Virginia	Charleston	WV
Mississippi	Jackson	MS	Wisconsin	Madison	WI
Missouri	Jefferson City	MO	Wyoming	Cheyenne	WY

Capital of the USA
District of Columbia, Washington   DC
(commonly abbreviated: Washington, DC)

12. Guide to Pronunciation Symbols

Vowels

Symbol	Key Word	Pronunciation
/ɑ/	hot	/hɑt/
	far	/fɑr/
/æ/	cat	/kæt/
/aɪ/	fine	/faɪn/
/aʊ/	house	/haʊs/
/ɛ/	bed	/bɛd/
/eɪ/	name	/neɪm/
/i/	need	/nid/
/ɪ/	sit	/sɪt/
/oʊ/	go	/goʊ/
/ʊ/	book	/bʊk/
/u/	boot	/but/
/ɔ/	dog	/dɔg/
	four	/fɔr/
/ɔɪ/	toy	/tɔɪ/
/ʌ/	cup	/kʌp/
/ɚr/	bird	/bɚrd/
/ə/	about	/əˈbaʊt/
	after	/ˈæftər/
/ð/	they	/ðeɪ/
/θ/	think	/θɪŋk/
/ʃ/	shoe	/ʃu/
/ʒ/	vision	/ˈvɪʒən/

Consonants

Symbol	Key Word	Pronunciation
/b/	boy	/bɔɪ/
/d/	day	/deɪ/
/dʒ/	just	/dʒʌst/
/f/	face	/feɪs/
/g/	get	/gɛt/
/h/	hat	/hæt/
/k/	car	/kɑr/
/l/	light	/laɪt/
/m/	my	/maɪ/
/n/	nine	/naɪn/
/ŋ/	sing	/sɪŋ/
/p/	pen	/pɛn/
/r/	right	/raɪt/
/s/	see	/si/
/t/	tea	/ti/
/tʃ/	cheap	/tʃip/
/v/	vote	/voʊt/
/w/	west	/wɛst/
/y/	yes	/yɛs/
/z/	zoo	/zu/

Stress

/ˈ/ city /ˈsɪti/
used before a syllable to show primary (main) stress
/ˌ/ dictionary /ˈdɪkʃəˌnɛri/
used before a syllable to show secondary stress

abbr.	abbreviation
adj. & past.part. of	adjective and past participle of
adj.	adjective
adv.	adverb
&	and
auxiliary verb	auxillary verb
Brit.	Brit.
comp. of	comparative of
[C]	countable noun
conj.	conjunction
contr.	contraction
contr. of	contraction of
esp.	especially
exclam.	exclamation
fig.	figurative
frml.	formal
indef. article	indefinite article
infrml.	informal
interj.	interjection
lit.	literally
litr.	literary use
n.	noun
n.pl.	plural noun
n.pl. used with a sing.v.	plural noun used with a singular verb
old usage	old usage
past tense of	past tense of
past part. of	past participle of
pej.	pejorative
phr.	phrase, as in n.phr., or v.phr.
phrasal v.	phrasal verb
phrasal v.insep.	inseparable phrasal verb
phrasal v.sep.	separable phrasal verb
pl.	plural
poss.	possessive
prefix	prefix
prep.	preposition
pron.	pronoun
reflexive pron.	reflexive pronoun
See:	cross reference
sing.	singular
slang	slang
s.o.	someone
s.t.	something
superlative of	(best, worst)
suffix	suffix
(syn.) or (syns.)	challenge synonym(s)
TM	trademark
[U]	uncountable noun
⎡A	United States of America
ith a pl.v.	used with a plural verb
⌐ sing.v.	used with a singular verb
⌐ng. or pl. v.	used with a singular or plural verb
	usually
	verb
	variation of
	vulgar